PHILIP'S

WORLD ATLAS

Philip's are grateful to the following for acting as specialist geography consultants on 'The World in Focus' front section:

Professor D. Brunsden, Kings College, University of London, UK
Dr C. Clarke, Oxford University, UK
Dr I. S. Evans, Durham University, UK
Professor P. Haggett, University of Bristol, UK
Professor K. McLachlan, University of London, UK
Professor M. Monmonier, Syracuse University, New York, USA
Professor M-L. Hsu, University of Minnesota, Minnesota, USA
Professor M. J. Tooley, University of St Andrews, UK
Dr T. Unwin, Royal Holloway, University of London, UK

THE WORLD IN FOCUS
Cartography by Philip's

Picture Acknowledgements
NASA/GSFC page 14

Illustrations: Stefan Chabluk

WORLD CITIES
Cartography by Philip's

Page 10, Dublin: The town plan of Dublin is based on Ordnance Survey Ireland by permission of the Government Permit Number 8097. © Ordnance Survey Ireland and Government of Ireland.

Page 11, Edinburgh, and page 15, London:
This product includes mapping data licensed from Ordnance Survey® with the permission of the Controller of Her Majesty's Stationery Office. © Crown copyright 2006. All rights reserved. Licence number 100011710.

Vector data courtesy of Gräfe and Unser Verlag GmbH, München, Germany
(city-centre maps of Bangkok, Beijing, Cape Town, Jerusalem, Mexico City, Moscow, Singapore, Sydney, Tokyo and Washington D.C.)
The following city maps utilize base data supplied courtesy of MapQuest.com, Inc. (© MapQuest)
(Las Vegas, New Orleans, Orlando)

All satellite images in this section courtesy of NPA Group, Edenbridge, Kent (www.satmaps.com)

Published in Great Britain in 2006
by Philip's,
a division of Octopus Publishing Group Limited,
2–4 Heron Quays, London E14 4JP

Copyright © 2006 Philip's

Cartography by Philip's

ISBN-13 978–0–540–08898–0
ISBN-10 0–540–08898–6

A CIP catalogue record for this book is available from the British Library.

Printed in Hong Kong

Details of other Philip's titles and services can be found on our website at: www.philips-maps.co.uk

Philip's World Atlases are published in association with The Royal Geographical Society (with The Institute of British Geographers).

The Society was founded in 1830 and given a Royal Charter in 1859 for 'the advancement of geographical science'. It holds historical collections of national and international importance, many of which relate to the Society's association with and support for scientific exploration and research from the 19th century onwards. It was pivotal in establishing geography as a teaching and research discipline in British universities close to the turn of the century, and has played a key role in geographical and environmental education ever since.

Today the Society is a leading world centre for geographical learning – supporting education, teaching, research and expeditions, and promoting public understanding of the subject.

The Society welcomes those interested in geography as members. For further information, please visit the website at: www.rgs.org

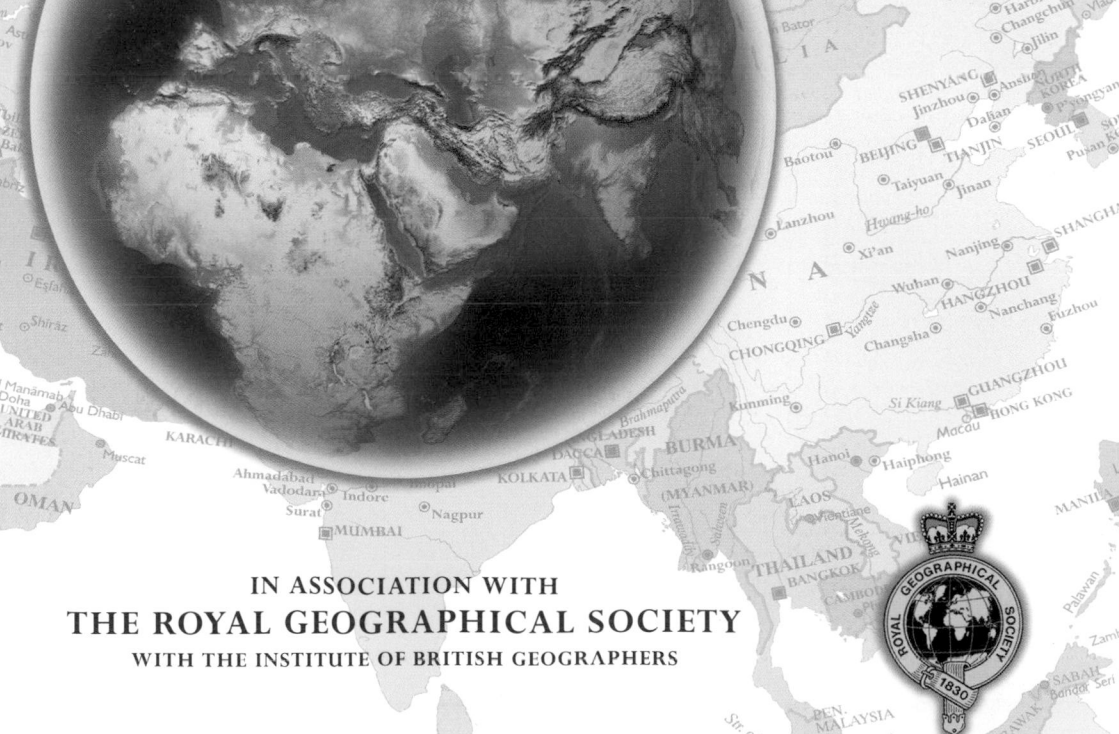

PHILIP'S

WORLD ATLAS

PAPERBACK EDITION

IN ASSOCIATION WITH
THE ROYAL GEOGRAPHICAL SOCIETY
WITH THE INSTITUTE OF BRITISH GEOGRAPHERS

Contents

World Maps

Europe

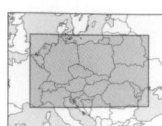

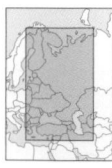

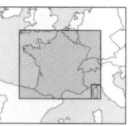

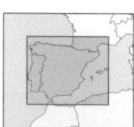

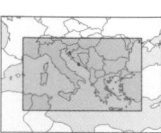

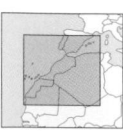

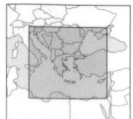

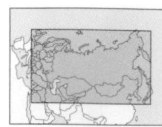

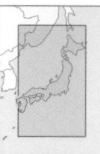

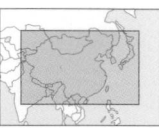

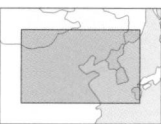

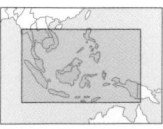

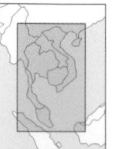

Asia

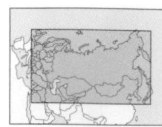

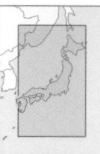

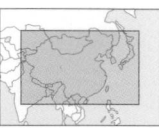

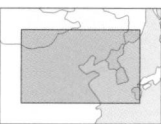

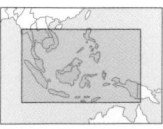

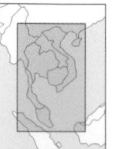

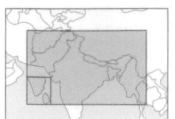

Northern India, Pakistan and Nepal
1:6 000 000
Jammu and Kashmir 1:6 000 000

42–43

The Middle East
1:7 000 000

44–45

The Near East 1:2 500 000

46

Arabia and the Horn of Africa 1:15 000 000

47

Africa

Africa: Physical
1:42 000 000   **48**

Africa: Political
1:42 000 000   **49**

Northern Africa
1:15 000 000
Azores 1:15 000 000
Cape Verde Islands 1:10 000 000

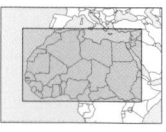

50–51

Central and Southern Africa
1:15 000 000
Seychelles 1:2 500 000
Réunion 1:2 500 000
Mauritius 1:2 500 000
Comoros 1:8 000 000

52–53

East Africa 1:8 000 000

54–55

Southern Africa
1:8 000 000
Madagascar 1:8 000 000

56–57

Australia and Oceania

Australia and Oceania: Physical and Political
1:50 000 000   **58**

New Zealand 1:6 000 000
Samoan Islands 1:6 000 000
Fiji 1:6 000 000
Tonga 1:6 000 000
Tahiti and Moorea 1:1 000 000

59

Western Australia
1:8 000 000

60–61

Eastern Australia
1:8 000 000
Whitsunday Islands 1:2 500 000
Tasmania 1:8 000 000

62–63

Pacific Ocean
1:54 000 000   **64–65**

North America

North America: Physical
1:35 000 000   **66**

North America: Political
1:35 000 000   **67**

Canada 1:15 000 000

68–69

Western Canada 1:7 000 000

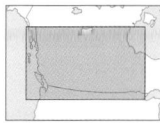

70–71

Eastern Canada 1:7 000 000

72–73

United States 1:12 000 000
Hawai'i 1:10 000 000
Alaska 1:30 000 000

74–75

United States – West
1:6 700 000

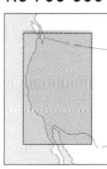

76–77

Central and Southern California and Western Washington
1:2 500 000

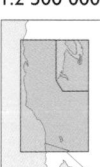

78–79

United States – Midwest and North-east
1:6 700 000

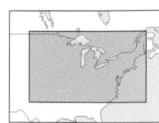

80–81

North-eastern United States
1:2 500 000

82–83

United States – South
1:6 700 000

84–85

Mexico 1:8 000 000

86–87

Central America and the West Indies 1:8 000 000
Jamaica 1:3 000 000
Guadeloupe 1:2 000 000
Martinique 1:2 000 000
Puerto Rico 1:3 000 000
Virgin Islands 1:2 000 000
St Lucia 1:2 000 000
Barbados 1:2 000 000

88–89

South America

South America: Physical
1:35 000 000   **90**

South America: Political
1:35 000 000   **91**

South America – North
1:16 000 000
Trinidad and Tobago 1:2 500 000

92–93

Central South America
1:8 000 000

94–95

South America – South
1:16 000 000

96

Index to World Maps

97–176

World Statistics: Countries

This alphabetical list includes the principal countries and territories of the world. If a territory is not completely independent, the country it is associated with is named. The area figures give the total area of land, inland water and ice. The population figures are 2005 estimates where available. The annual income is the Gross Domestic Product per capita in US dollars. The figures are the latest available, usually 2005 estimates.

Country/Territory	Area km² *Thousands*	Area miles² *Thousands*	Population *Thousands*	Capital	Annual Income US $
Afghanistan	652	252	29,929	Kabul	800
Albania	28.7	11.1	3,563	Tirana	4,900
Algeria	2,382	920	32,532	Algiers	7,300
American Samoa (US)	0.20	0.08	58	Pago Pago	8,000
Andorra	0.47	0.18	71	Andorra La Vella	26,800
Angola	1,247	481	11,191	Luanda	2,500
Anguilla (UK)	0.10	0.04	13	The Valley	7,500
Antigua & Barbuda	0.44	0.17	69	St John's	11,000
Argentina	2,780	1,074	39,538	Buenos Aires	13,600
Armenia	29.8	11.5	2,983	Yerevan	5,100
Aruba (Netherlands)	0.19	0.07	72	Oranjestad	28,000
Australia	7,741	2,989	20,090	Canberra	32,000
Austria	83.9	32.4	8,185	Vienna	32,900
Azerbaijan	86.6	33.4	7,912	Baku	4,600
Azores (Portugal)	2.2	0.86	236	Ponta Delgada	15,000
Bahamas	13.9	5.4	302	Nassau	18,800
Bahrain	0.69	0.27	688	Manama	20,500
Bangladesh	144	55.6	144,320	Dhaka	2,100
Barbados	0.43	0.17	279	Bridgetown	17,300
Belarus	208	80.2	10,300	Minsk	7,600
Belgium	30.5	11.8	10,364	Brussels	31,800
Belize	23.0	8.9	279	Belmopan	6,800
Benin	113	43.5	7,460	Porto-Novo	1,200
Bermuda (UK)	0.05	0.02	65	Hamilton	36,000
Bhutan	47.0	18.1	2,232	Thimphu	1,400
Bolivia	1,099	424	8,858	La Paz/Sucre	2,700
Bosnia-Herzegovina	51.2	19.8	4,025	Sarajevo	6,800
Botswana	582	225	1,640	Gaborone	10,100
Brazil	8,514	3,287	186,113	Brasília	8,500
Brunei	5.8	2.2	372	Bandar Seri Begawan	23,600
Bulgaria	111	42.8	7,450	Sofia	9,000
Burkina Faso	274	106	13,925	Ouagadougou	1,200
Burma (Myanmar)	677	261	42,909	Rangoon/Pyinmana	1,800
Burundi	27.8	10.7	6,371	Bujumbura	700
Cambodia	181	69.9	13,607	Phnom Penh	2,100
Cameroon	475	184	16,380	Yaoundé	2,000
Canada	9,971	3,850	32,805	Ottawa	32,800
Canary Is. (Spain)	7.2	2.8	1,682	Las Palmas/Santa Cruz	19,900
Cape Verde Is.	4.0	1.6	418	Praia	6,200
Cayman Is. (UK)	0.26	0.10	44	George Town	32,300
Central African Republic	623	241	3,800	Bangui	1,200
Chad	1,284	496	9,826	Ndjaména	1,900
Chile	757	292	15,981	Santiago	11,300
China	9,597	3,705	1,306,314	Beijing	6,200
Colombia	1,139	440	42,954	Bogotá	7,100
Comoros	2.2	0.86	671	Moroni	600
Congo	342	132	3,039	Brazzaville	800
Congo (Dem. Rep. of the)	2,345	905	60,086	Kinshasa	800
Cook Is. (NZ)	0.24	0.09	21	Avarua	5,000
Costa Rica	51.1	19.7	4,016	San José	10,000
Croatia	56.5	21.8	4,496	Zagreb	11,600
Cuba	111	42.8	11,347	Havana	3,300
Cyprus	9.3	3.6	780	Nicosia	21,600
Czech Republic	78.9	30.5	10,241	Prague	18,100
Denmark	43.1	16.6	5,432	Copenhagen	33,500
Djibouti	23.2	9.0	477	Djibouti	1,300
Dominica	0.75	0.29	69	Roseau	5,500
Dominican Republic	48.5	18.7	8,950	Santo Domingo	6,500
East Timor	14.9	5.7	1,041	Dili	400
Ecuador	284	109	13,364	Quito	3,900
Egypt	1,001	387	77,506	Cairo	4,400
El Salvador	21.0	8.1	6,705	San Salvador	5,100
Equatorial Guinea	28.1	10.8	536	Malabo	2,700
Eritrea	118	45.4	4,562	Asmara	1,000
Estonia	45.1	17.4	1,333	Tallinn	16,400
Ethiopia	1,104	426	73,053	Addis Ababa	800
Faroe Is. (Denmark)	1.4	0.54	47	Tórshavn	22,000
Fiji	18.3	7.1	893	Suva	6,000
Finland	338	131	5,223	Helsinki	30,300
France	552	213	60,656	Paris	29,900
French Guiana (France)	90.0	34.7	196	Cayenne	8,300
French Polynesia (France)	4.0	1.5	270	Papeete	17,500
Gabon	268	103	1,389	Libreville	5,800
Gambia, The	11.3	4.4	1,593	Banjul	1,900
Gaza Strip	0.36	0.14	1,376	–	600
Georgia	69.7	26.9	4,677	Tbilisi	3,400
Germany	357	138	82,431	Berlin	29,700
Ghana	239	92.1	21,030	Accra	2,500
Gibraltar (UK)	0.006	0.002	28	Gibraltar Town	27,900
Greece	132	50.9	10,668	Athens	22,800
Greenland (Denmark)	2,176	840	56	Nuuk	20,000
Grenada	0.34	0.13	90	St George's	5,000
Guadeloupe (France)	1.7	0.66	449	Basse-Terre	7,900
Guam (US)	0.55	0.21	169	Agana	21,000
Guatemala	109	42.0	14,655	Guatemala City	4,300
Guinea	246	94.9	9,468	Conakry	2,200
Guinea-Bissau	36.1	13.9	1,416	Bissau	800
Guyana	215	83.0	765	Georgetown	3,900
Haiti	27.8	10.7	8,122	Port-au-Prince	1,600
Honduras	112	43.3	6,975	Tegucigalpa	2,900
Hungary	93.0	35.9	10,007	Budapest	15,900
Iceland	103	39.8	297	Reykjavik	34,600
India	3,287	1,269	1,080,264	New Delhi	3,400
Indonesia	1,905	735	241,974	Jakarta	3,700
Iran	1,648	636	68,018	Tehran	8,100
Iraq	438	169	26,075	Baghdad	3,400
Ireland	70.3	27.1	4,016	Dublin	34,100
Israel	20.6	8.0	6,277	Jerusalem	22,200
Italy	301	116	58,103	Rome	28,300
Ivory Coast (Côte d'Ivoire)	322	125	17,298	Yamoussoukro	1,400
Jamaica	11.0	4.2	2,732	Kingston	4,300
Japan	378	146	127,417	Tokyo	30,400
Jordan	89.3	34.5	5,760	Amman	4,800
Kazakhstan	2,725	1,052	15,186	Astana	8,700
Kenya	580	224	33,830	Nairobi	1,200
Kiribati	0.73	0.28	103	Tarawa	800
Korea, North	121	46.5	22,912	Pyŏngyang	1,800
Korea, South	99.3	38.3	48,423	Seoul	20,300
Kuwait	17.8	6.9	2,336	Kuwait City	22,100
Kyrgyzstan	200	77.2	5,146	Bishkek	1,800
Laos	237	91.4	6,217	Vientiane	1,900
Latvia	64.6	24.9	2,290	Riga	12,800

Country/Territory	Area km² *Thousands*	Area miles² *Thousands*	Population *Thousands*	Capital	Annual Income US $
Lebanon	10.4	4.0	3,826	Beirut	5,100
Lesotho	30.4	11.7	1,867	Maseru	3,300
Liberia	111	43.0	3,482	Monrovia	700
Libya	1,760	679	5,766	Tripoli	8,400
Liechtenstein	0.16	0.06	34	Vaduz	25,000
Lithuania	65.2	25.2	3,597	Vilnius	13,700
Luxembourg	2.6	1.0	469	Luxembourg	62,700
Macedonia (FYROM)	25.7	9.9	2,045	Skopje	7,400
Madagascar	587	227	18,040	Antananarivo	900
Madeira (Portugal)	0.78	0.30	241	Funchal	22,700
Malawi	118	45.7	12,159	Lilongwe	600
Malaysia	330	127	23,953	Kuala Lumpur/Putrajaya	10,400
Maldives	0.30	0.12	349	Malé	3,900
Mali	1,240	479	12,292	Bamako	1,000
Malta	0.32	0.12	399	Valletta	18,800
Marshall Is.	0.18	0.07	59	Majuro	1,600
Martinique (France)	1.1	0.43	433	Fort-de-France	14,400
Mauritania	1,026	396	3,087	Nouakchott	2,000
Mauritius	2.0	0.79	1,231	Port Louis	13,300
Mayotte (France)	0.37	0.14	194	Mamoundzou	2,600
Mexico	1,958	756	106,203	Mexico City	10,000
Micronesia, Fed. States of	0.70	0.27	108	Palikir	2,000
Moldova	33.9	13.1	4,455	Chişinău	2,100
Monaco	0.001	0.0004	32	Monaco	27,000
Mongolia	1,567	605	2,791	Ulan Bator	2,200
Montserrat (UK)	0.10	0.04	9	Plymouth	3,400
Morocco	447	172	32,726	Rabat	4,300
Mozambique	802	309	19,407	Maputo	1,300
Namibia	824	318	2,031	Windhoek	7,800
Nauru	0.02	0.008	13	Yaren District	5,000
Nepal	147	56.8	27,677	Katmandu	1,500
Netherlands	41.5	16.0	16,407	Amsterdam/The Hague	30,500
Netherlands Antilles (Neths)	0.80	0.31	220	Willemstad	11,400
New Caledonia (France)	18.6	7.2	216	Nouméa	15,000
New Zealand	271	104	4,035	Wellington	24,100
Nicaragua	130	50.2	5,465	Managua	2,800
Niger	1,267	489	11,665	Niamey	900
Nigeria	924	357	128,772	Abuja	1,000
Northern Mariana Is. (US)	0.46	0.18	80	Saipan	12,500
Norway	324	125	4,593	Oslo	42,400
Oman	310	119	3,002	Muscat	13,400
Pakistan	796	307	162,420	Islamabad	2,400
Palau	0.46	0.18	20	Koror	9,000
Panama	75.5	29.2	3,039	Panamá	7,300
Papua New Guinea	463	179	5,545	Port Moresby	2,400
Paraguay	407	157	6,348	Asunción	4,900
Peru	1,285	496	27,926	Lima	6,000
Philippines	300	116	87,857	Manila	5,100
Poland	323	125	38,635	Warsaw	12,700
Portugal	88.8	34.3	10,566	Lisbon	18,400
Puerto Rico (US)	8.9	3.4	3,917	San Juan	18,500
Qatar	11.0	4.2	863	Doha	26,000
Réunion (France)	2.5	0.97	777	St-Denis	6,200
Romania	238	92.0	22,330	Bucharest	8,300
Russia	17,075	6,593	143,420	Moscow	10,700
Rwanda	26.3	10.2	8,441	Kigali	1,300
St Kitts & Nevis	0.26	0.10	39	Basseterre	8,800
St Lucia	0.54	0.21	166	Castries	5,400
St Vincent & Grenadines	0.39	0.15	118	Kingstown	2,900
Samoa	2.8	1.1	177	Apia	5,600
San Marino	0.06	0.02	29	San Marino	34,600
São Tomé & Príncipe	0.96	0.37	187	São Tomé	1,200
Saudi Arabia	2,150	830	26,418	Riyadh	12,900
Senegal	197	76.0	11,127	Dakar	1,800
Serbia & Montenegro†	102	39.4	10,829	Belgrade	2,600
Seychelles	0.46	0.18	81	Victoria	7,800
Sierra Leone	71.7	27.7	6,018	Freetown	800
Singapore	0.68	0.26	4,426	Singapore City	29,700
Slovak Republic	49.0	18.9	5,431	Bratislava	15,700
Slovenia	20.3	7.8	2,011	Ljubljana	20,900
Solomon Is.	28.9	11.2	538	Honiara	1,700
Somalia	638	246	8,592	Mogadishu	600
South Africa	1,221	471	44,344	Cape Town/Pretoria	11,900
Spain	498	192	40,341	Madrid	25,100
Sri Lanka	65.6	25.3	20,065	Colombo	4,300
Sudan	2,506	967	40,187	Khartoum	2,100
Suriname	163	63.0	438	Paramaribo	4,700
Swaziland	17.4	6.7	1,174	Mbabane	5,300
Sweden	450	174	9,002	Stockholm	29,600
Switzerland	41.3	15.9	7,489	Bern	35,000
Syria	185	71.5	18,449	Damascus	3,500
Taiwan	36.0	13.9	22,894	Taipei	26,700
Tajikistan	143	55.3	7,164	Dushanbe	1,200
Tanzania	945	365	36,766	Dodoma	700
Thailand	513	198	65,444	Bangkok	8,300
Togo	56.8	21.9	5,682	Lomé	1,600
Tonga	0.65	0.25	112	Nuku'alofa	2,300
Trinidad & Tobago	5.1	2.0	1,089	Port of Spain	12,700
Tunisia	164	63.2	10,075	Tunis	7,600
Turkey	775	299	69,661	Ankara	7,900
Turkmenistan	488	188	4,952	Ashkhabad	5,900
Turks & Caicos Is. (UK)	0.43	0.17	21	Cockburn Town	11,500
Tuvalu	0.03	0.01	12	Fongafale	1,100
Uganda	241	93.1	27,269	Kampala	1,700
Ukraine	604	233	47,425	Kiev	6,800
United Arab Emirates	83.6	32.3	2,563	Abu Dhabi	29,100
United Kingdom	242	93.4	60,441	London	30,900
United States of America	9,629	3,718	295,734	Washington, DC	41,800
Uruguay	175	67.6	3,416	Montevideo	10,000
Uzbekistan	447	173	26,851	Tashkent	1,900
Vanuatu	12.2	4.7	206	Port-Vila	2,900
Vatican City	0.0004	0.0002	1	Vatican City	N/A
Venezuela	912	352	25,375	Caracas	6,400
Vietnam	332	128	83,536	Hanoi	3,000
Virgin Is. (UK)	0.15	0.06	23	Road Town	38,500
Virgin Is. (US)	0.35	0.13	109	Charlotte Amalie	17,200
Wallis & Futuna Is. (France)	0.20	0.08	16	Mata-Utu	3,800
West Bank (OPT)*	5.9	2.3	2,386	–	1,100
Western Sahara	266	103	273	El Aaiún	N/A
Yemen	528	204	20,727	Sana'	800
Zambia	753	291	11,262	Lusaka	900
Zimbabwe	391	151	12,747	Harare	1,900

*OPT = Occupied Palestinian Territory N/A = Not available

† In June 2006, Serbia and Montenegro formally declared their independence and are now separate sovereign states.

World Statistics: Physical Dimensions

Each topic list is divided into continents and within a continent the items are listed in order of size. The bottom part of many of the lists is selective in order to give examples from as many different countries as possible. The order of the continents is the same as in the atlas, beginning with Europe and ending with South America. The figures are rounded as appropriate.

World, Continents, Oceans

	km²	miles²	%
The World	509,450,000	196,672,000	–
Land	149,450,000	57,688,000	29.3
Water	360,000,000	138,984,000	70.7
Asia	44,500,000	17,177,000	29.8
Africa	30,302,000	11,697,000	20.3
North America	24,241,000	9,357,000	16.2
South America	17,793,000	6,868,000	11.9
Antarctica	14,100,000	5,443,000	9.4
Europe	9,957,000	3,843,000	6.7
Australia & Oceania	8,557,000	3,303,000	5.7
Pacific Ocean	155,557,000	60,061,000	46.4
Atlantic Ocean	76,762,000	29,638,000	22.9
Indian Ocean	68,556,000	26,470,000	20.4
Southern Ocean	20,327,000	7,848,000	6.1
Arctic Ocean	14,056,000	5,427,000	4.2

Ocean Depths

Atlantic Ocean		m	ft
Puerto Rico (Milwaukee) Deep		9,220	30,249
Cayman Trench		7,680	25,197
Gulf of Mexico		5,203	17,070
Mediterranean Sea		5,121	16,801
Black Sea		2,211	7,254
North Sea		660	2,165
Indian Ocean		m	ft
Java Trench		7,450	24,442
Red Sea		2,635	8,454
Pacific Ocean		m	ft
Mariana Trench		11,022	36,161
Tonga Trench		10,882	35,702
Japan Trench		10,554	34,626
Kuril Trench		10,542	34,587
Arctic Ocean		m	ft
Molloy Deep		5,608	18,399
Southern Ocean		m	ft
South Sandwich Trench		7,235	23,737

Mountains

Europe		m	ft
Elbrus	Russia	5,642	18,510
Mont Blanc	France/Italy	4,807	15,771
Monte Rosa	Italy/Switzerland	4,634	15,203
Dom	Switzerland	4,545	14,911
Liskamm	Switzerland	4,527	14,852
Weisshorn	Switzerland	4,505	14,780
Taschorn	Switzerland	4,490	14,730
Matterhorn/Cervino	Italy/Switzerland	4,478	14,691
Mont Maudit	France/Italy	4,465	14,649
Dent Blanche	Switzerland	4,356	14,291
Nadelhorn	Switzerland	4,327	14,196
Grandes Jorasses	France/Italy	4,208	13,806
Jungfrau	Switzerland	4,158	13,642
Grossglockner	Austria	3,797	12,457
Mulhacén	Spain	3,478	11,411
Zugspitze	Germany	2,962	9,718
Olympus	Greece	2,917	9,570
Triglav	Slovenia	2,863	9,393
Gerlachovka	Slovak Republic	2,655	8,711
Galdhøpiggen	Norway	2,469	8,100
Ben Nevis	UK	1,342	4,403

Asia		m	ft
Everest	China/Nepal	8,850	29,035
K2 (Godwin Austen)	China/Kashmir	8,611	28,251
Kanchenjunga	India/Nepal	8,598	28,208
Lhotse	China/Nepal	8,516	27,939
Makalu	China/Nepal	8,481	27,824
Cho Oyu	China/Nepal	8,201	26,906
Dhaulagiri	Nepal	8,167	26,795
Manaslu	Nepal	8,156	26,758
Nanga Parbat	Kashmir	8,126	26,660
Annapurna	Nepal	8,078	26,502
Gasherbrum	China/Kashmir	8,068	26,469
Broad Peak	China/Kashmir	8,051	26,414
Xixabangma	China	8,012	26,286
Kangbachen	Nepal	7,858	25,781
Trivor	Pakistan	7,720	25,328
Pik Imeni Ismail Samani	Tajikistan	7,495	24,590
Demavend	Iran	5,604	18,386
Ararat	Turkey	5,165	16,945
Gunong Kinabalu	Malaysia (Borneo)	4,101	13,455
Fuji-San	Japan	3,776	12,388

Africa		m	ft
Kilimanjaro	Tanzania	5,895	19,340
Mt Kenya	Kenya	5,199	17,057
Ruwenzori (Margherita)	Ug./Congo (D.R.)	5,109	16,762
Ras Dashen	Ethiopia	4,620	15,157
Meru	Tanzania	4,565	14,977
Karisimbi	Rwanda/Congo (D.R.)	4,507	14,787
Mt Elgon	Kenya/Uganda	4,321	14,176
Batu	Ethiopia	4,307	14,130
Toubkal	Morocco	4,165	13,665
Mt Cameroun	Cameroon	4,070	13,353

Oceania		m	ft
Puncak Jaya	Indonesia	5,029	16,499
Puncak Trikora	Indonesia	4,730	15,518
Puncak Mandala	Indonesia	4,702	15,427
Mt Wilhelm	Papua New Guinea	4,508	14,790
Mauna Kea	USA (Hawai'i)	4,205	13,796
Mauna Loa	USA (Hawai'i)	4,169	13,681
Aoraki Mt Cook	New Zealand	3,753	12,313
Mt Kosciuszko	Australia	2,230	7,316

North America		m	ft
Mt McKinley (Denali)	USA (Alaska)	6,194	20,321
Mt Logan	Canada	5,959	19,551
Pico de Orizaba	Mexico	5,610	18,405
Mt St Elias	USA/Canada	5,489	18,008
Popocatépetl	Mexico	5,452	17,887
Mt Foraker	USA (Alaska)	5,304	17,401
Iztaccihuatl	Mexico	5,286	17,343
Lucania	Canada	5,226	17,146
Mt Steele	Canada	5,073	16,644
Mt Bona	USA (Alaska)	5,005	16,420
Mt Whitney	USA	4,418	14,495
Tajumulco	Guatemala	4,220	13,845
Chirripó Grande	Costa Rica	3,837	12,589
Pico Duarte	Dominican Rep.	3,175	10,417

South America		m	ft
Aconcagua	Argentina	6,962	22,841
Bonete	Argentina	6,872	22,546
Ojos del Salado	Argentina/Chile	6,863	22,516
Pissis	Argentina	6,779	22,241
Mercedario	Argentina/Chile	6,770	22,211
Huascarán	Peru	6,768	22,204
Llullaillaco	Argentina/Chile	6,723	22,057
Nudo de Cachi	Argentina	6,720	22,047
Yerupaja	Peru	6,632	21,758
Sajama	Bolivia	6,520	21,391
Chimborazo	Ecuador	6,267	20,561
Pico Cristóbal Colón	Colombia	5,800	19,029
Pico Bolivar	Venezuela	5,007	16,427

Antarctica		m	ft
Vinson Massif		4,897	16,066
Mt Kirkpatrick		4,528	14,855

Rivers

Europe		km	miles
Volga	Caspian Sea	3,700	2,300
Danube	Black Sea	2,850	1,770
Ural	Caspian Sea	2,535	1,575
Dnepr (Dnipro)	Black Sea	2,285	1,420
Kama	Volga	2,030	1,260
Don	Black Sea	1,990	1,240
Petchora	Arctic Ocean	1,790	1,110
Oka	Volga	1,480	920
Dnister (Dniester)	Black Sea	1,400	870
Vyatka	Kama	1,370	850
Rhine	North Sea	1,320	820
N. Dvina	Arctic Ocean	1,290	800
Elbe	North Sea	1,145	710

Asia		km	miles
Yangtze	Pacific Ocean	6,380	3,960
Yenisey–Angara	Arctic Ocean	5,550	3,445
Huang He	Pacific Ocean	5,464	3,395
Ob–Irtysh	Arctic Ocean	5,410	3,360
Mekong	Pacific Ocean	4,500	2,795
Amur	Pacific Ocean	4,442	2,760
Lena	Arctic Ocean	4,402	2,735
Irtysh	Ob	4,250	2,640
Yenisey	Arctic Ocean	4,090	2,540
Ob	Arctic Ocean	3,680	2,285
Indus	Indian Ocean	3,100	1,925
Brahmaputra	Indian Ocean	2,900	1,800
Syrdarya	Aral Sea	2,860	1,775
Salween	Indian Ocean	2,800	1,740
Euphrates	Indian Ocean	2,700	1,675
Amudarya	Aral Sea	2,540	1,575

Africa		km	miles
Nile	Mediterranean	6,670	4,140
Congo	Atlantic Ocean	4,670	2,900
Niger	Atlantic Ocean	4,180	2,595
Zambezi	Indian Ocean	3,540	2,200
Oubangi/Uele	Congo (D.R.)	2,250	1,400
Kasai	Congo (D.R.)	1,950	1,210
Shaballe	Indian Ocean	1,930	1,200
Orange	Atlantic Ocean	1,860	1,155
Cubango	Okavango Delta	1,800	1,120
Limpopo	Indian Ocean	1,770	1,100
Senegal	Atlantic Ocean	1,640	1,020

Australia		km	miles
Murray–Darling	Southern Ocean	3,750	2,330
Darling	Murray	3,070	1,905
Murray	Southern Ocean	2,575	1,600
Murrumbidgee	Murray	1,690	1,050

North America		km	miles
Mississippi–Missouri	Gulf of Mexico	5,971	3,710
Mackenzie	Arctic Ocean	4,240	2,630
Missouri	Mississippi	4,088	2,540
Mississippi	Gulf of Mexico	3,782	2,350
Yukon	Pacific Ocean	3,185	1,980
Rio Grande	Gulf of Mexico	3,030	1,880
Arkansas	Mississippi	2,340	1,450
Colorado	Pacific Ocean	2,330	1,445
Red	Mississippi	2,040	1,270
Columbia	Pacific Ocean	1,950	1,210
Saskatchewan	Lake Winnipeg	1,940	1,205

South America		km	miles
Amazon	Atlantic Ocean	6,450	4,010
Paraná–Plate	Atlantic Ocean	4,500	2,800
Purus	Amazon	3,350	2,080
Madeira	Amazon	3,200	1,990
São Francisco	Atlantic Ocean	2,900	1,800
Paraná	Plate	2,800	1,740
Tocantins	Atlantic Ocean	2,750	1,710
Orinoco	Atlantic Ocean	2,740	1,700
Paraguay	Paraná	2,550	1,580
Pilcomayo	Paraná	2,500	1,550
Araguaia	Tocantins	2,250	1,400

Lakes

Europe		km²	miles²
Lake Ladoga	Russia	17,700	6,800
Lake Onega	Russia	9,700	3,700
Saimaa system	Finland	8,000	3,100
Vänern	Sweden	5,500	2,100
Asia		km²	miles²
Caspian Sea	Asia	371,000	143,000
Lake Baikal	Russia	30,500	11,780
Tonlé Sap	Cambodia	20,000	7,700
Lake Balqash	Kazakhstan	18,500	7,100
Aral Sea	Kazakhstan/Uzbekistan	17,160	6,625
Africa		km²	miles²
Lake Victoria	East Africa	68,000	26,300
Lake Tanganyika	Central Africa	33,000	13,000
Lake Malawi/Nyasa	East Africa	29,600	11,430
Lake Chad	Central Africa	25,000	9,700
Lake Turkana	Ethiopia/Kenya	8,500	3,290
Lake Volta	Ghana	8,480	3,270
Australia		km²	miles²
Lake Eyre	Australia	8,900	3,400
Lake Torrens	Australia	5,800	2,200
Lake Gairdner	Australia	4,800	1,900
North America		km²	miles²
Lake Superior	Canada/USA	82,350	31,800
Lake Huron	Canada/USA	59,600	23,010
Lake Michigan	USA	58,000	22,400
Great Bear Lake	Canada	31,800	12,280
Great Slave Lake	Canada	28,500	11,000
Lake Erie	Canada/USA	25,700	9,900
Lake Winnipeg	Canada	24,400	9,400
Lake Ontario	Canada/USA	19,500	7,500
Lake Nicaragua	Nicaragua	8,200	3,200
South America		km²	miles²
Lake Titicaca	Bolivia/Peru	8,300	3,200
Lake Poopo	Bolivia	2,800	1,100

Islands

Europe		km²	miles²
Great Britain	UK	229,880	88,700
Iceland	Atlantic Ocean	103,000	39,800
Ireland	Ireland/UK	84,400	32,600
Novaya Zemlya (N.)	Russia	48,200	18,600
Sicily	Italy	25,500	9,800
Corsica	France	8,700	3,400
Asia		km²	miles²
Borneo	South-east Asia	744,360	287,400
Sumatra	Indonesia	473,600	182,860
Honshu	Japan	230,500	88,980
Sulawesi (Celebes)	Indonesia	189,000	73,000
Java	Indonesia	126,700	48,900
Luzon	Philippines	104,700	40,400
Hokkaido	Japan	78,400	30,300
Africa		km²	miles²
Madagascar	Indian Ocean	587,040	226,660
Socotra	Indian Ocean	3,600	1,400
Réunion	Indian Ocean	2,500	965
Oceania		km²	miles²
New Guinea	Indonesia/Papua NG	821,030	317,000
New Zealand (S.)	Pacific Ocean	150,500	58,100
New Zealand (N.)	Pacific Ocean	114,700	44,300
Tasmania	Australia	67,800	26,200
Hawai'i	Pacific Ocean	10,450	4,000
North America		km²	miles²
Greenland	Atlantic Ocean	2,175,600	839,800
Baffin Is.	Canada	508,000	196,100
Victoria Is.	Canada	212,200	81,900
Ellesmere Is.	Canada	212,000	81,800
Cuba	Caribbean Sea	110,860	42,800
Hispaniola	Dominican Rep./Haiti	76,200	29,400
Jamaica	Caribbean Sea	11,400	4,400
Puerto Rico	Atlantic Ocean	8,900	3,400
South America		km²	miles²
Tierra del Fuego	Argentina/Chile	47,000	18,100
Falkland Is. (E.)	Atlantic Ocean	6,800	2,600

User Guide

The reference maps which form the main body of this atlas have been prepared in accordance with the highest standards of international cartography to provide an accurate and detailed representation of the Earth. The scales and projections used have been carefully chosen to give balanced coverage of the world, while emphasizing the most densely populated and economically significant regions. A hallmark of Philip's mapping is the use of hill shading and relief colouring to create a graphic impression of landforms: this makes the maps exceptionally easy to read. However, knowledge of the key features employed in the construction and presentation of the maps will enable the reader to derive the fullest benefit from the atlas.

Map sequence

The atlas covers the Earth continent by continent: first Europe; then its land neighbour Asia (mapped north before south, in a clockwise sequence), then Africa, Australia and Oceania, North America and South America. This is the classic arrangement adopted by most cartographers since the 16th century. For each continent, there are maps at a variety of scales. First, physical relief and political maps of the whole continent; then a series of larger-scale maps of the regions within the continent, each followed, where required, by still larger-scale maps of the most important or densely populated areas. The governing principle is that by turning the pages of the atlas, the reader moves steadily from north to south through each continent, with each map overlapping its neighbours.

Map presentation

With very few exceptions (for example, for the Arctic and Antarctica), the maps are drawn with north at the top, regardless of whether they are presented upright or sideways on the page. In the borders will be found the map title; a locator diagram showing the area covered; continuation arrows showing the page numbers for maps of adjacent areas; the scale; the projection used; the degrees of latitude and longitude; and the letters and figures used in the index for locating place names and geographical features. Physical relief maps also have a height reference panel identifying the colours used for each layer of contouring.

Map symbols

Each map contains a vast amount of detail which can only be conveyed clearly and accurately by the use of symbols. Points and circles of varying sizes locate and identify the relative importance of towns and cities; different styles of type are employed for administrative, geographical and regional place names. A variety of pictorial symbols denote features such as glaciers and marshes, as well as man-made structures including roads, railways, airports and canals.

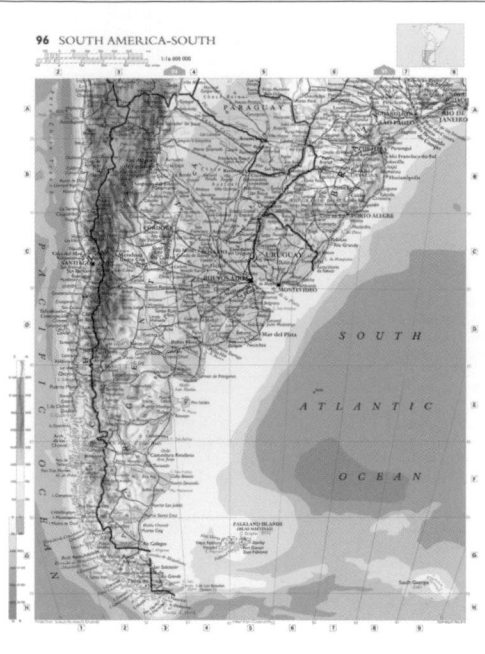

International borders are shown by red lines. Where neighbouring countries are in dispute, for example in the Middle East, the maps show the *de facto* boundary between nations, regardless of the legal or historical situation. The symbols are explained on the first page of the World Maps section of the atlas.

Map scales

The scale of each map is given in the numerical form known as the 'representative fraction'. The first figure is always one, signifying one unit of distance on the map; the second figure, usually in millions, is the number by which the map unit must be multiplied to give the equivalent distance on the Earth's surface. Calculations can easily be made in centimetres and kilometres, by dividing the Earth units figure by 100 000 (i.e. deleting the last five 0s). Thus 1:1 000 000 means 1 cm = 10 km. The calculation for inches and miles is more laborious, but 1 000 000 divided by 63 360 (the number of inches in a mile) shows that the ratio 1:1 000 000 means approximately 1 inch = 16 miles. The table below provides distance equivalents for scales down to 1:50 000 000.

LARGE SCALE		
1:1 000 000	1 cm = 10 km	1 inch = 16 miles
1:2 500 000	1 cm = 25 km	1 inch = 39.5 miles
1:5 000 000	1 cm = 50 km	1 inch = 79 miles
1:6 000 000	1 cm = 60 km	1 inch = 95 miles
1:8 000 000	1 cm = 80 km	1 inch = 126 miles
1:10 000 000	1 cm = 100 km	1 inch = 158 miles
1:15 000 000	1 cm = 150 km	1 inch = 237 miles
1:20 000 000	1 cm = 200 km	1 inch = 316 miles
1:50 000 000	1 cm = 500 km	1 inch = 790 miles
SMALL SCALE		

Measuring distances

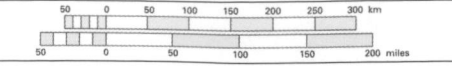

Although each map is accompanied by a scale bar, distances cannot always be measured with confidence because of the distortions involved in portraying the curved surface of the Earth on a flat page. As a general rule, the larger the map scale (i.e. the lower the number of Earth units in the representative fraction), the more accurate and reliable will be the distance measured. On small-scale maps such as those of the world and of entire continents, measurement may only be accurate along the 'standard parallels', or central axes, and should not be attempted without considering the map projection.

Latitude and longitude

Accurate positioning of individual points on the Earth's surface is made possible by reference to the geometrical system of latitude and longitude. Latitude *parallels* are drawn west–east around the Earth and numbered by degrees north and south of the Equator, which is designated 0° of latitude. Longitude *meridians* are drawn north–south and numbered by degrees east and west of the *prime meridian*, 0° of longitude, which passes through Greenwich in England. By referring to these co-ordinates and their subdivisions of minutes (¹⁄60th of a degree) and seconds (¹⁄60th of a minute), any place on Earth can be located to within a few hundred metres. Latitude and longitude are indicated by blue lines on the maps; they are straight or curved according to the projection employed. Reference to these lines is the easiest way of determining the relative positions of places on different maps, and for plotting compass directions.

Name forms

For ease of reference, both English and local name forms appear in the atlas. Oceans, seas and countries are shown in English throughout the atlas; country names may be abbreviated to their commonly accepted form (for example, Germany, not The Federal Republic of Germany). Conventional English forms are also used for place names on the smaller-scale maps of the continents. However, local name forms are used on all large-scale and regional maps, with the English form given in brackets only for important cities – the large-scale map of Russia and Central Asia thus shows Moskva (Moscow). For countries which do not use a Roman script, place names have been transcribed according to the systems adopted by the British and US Geographic Names Authorities. For China, the Pin Yin system has been used, with some more widely known forms appearing in brackets, as with Beijing (Peking). Both English and local names appear in the index, the English form being cross-referenced to the local form.

THE
WORLD
IN FOCUS

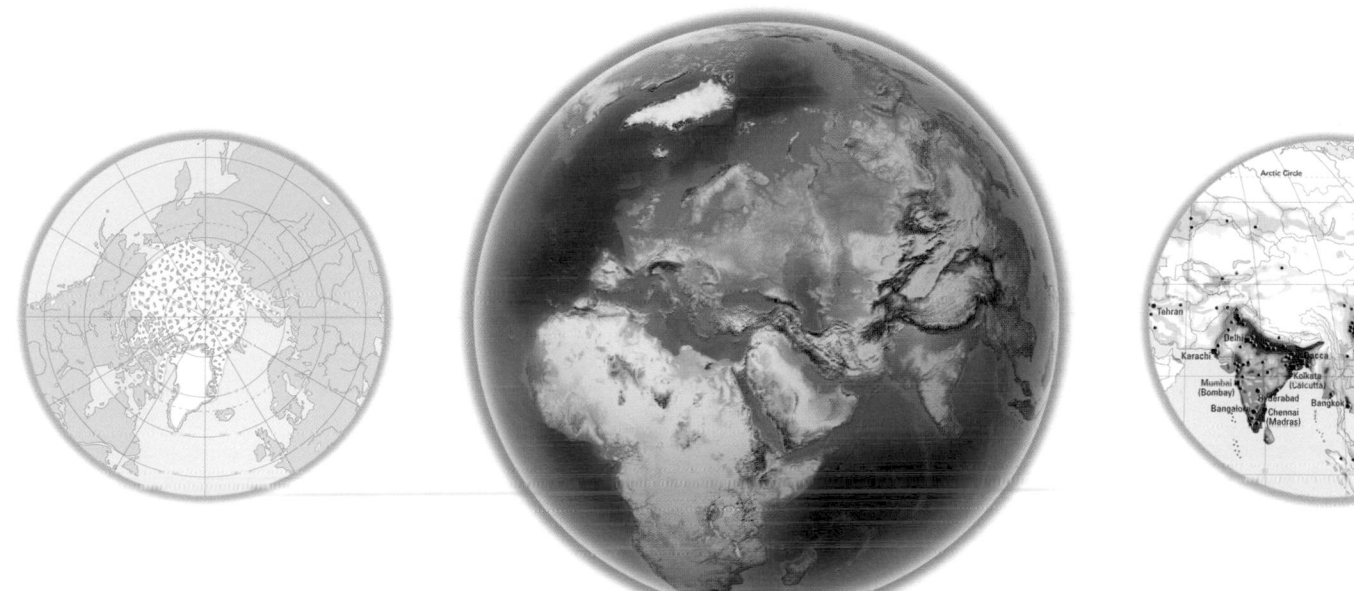

Planet Earth	2	Water & Vegetation	12	Quality of Life	22
Restless Earth	4	Environment	14	Energy	24
Landforms	6	Population	16	Production	26
Oceans	8	The Human Family	18	Trade	28
Climate	10	Wealth	20	Travel & Tourism	30

Planet Earth

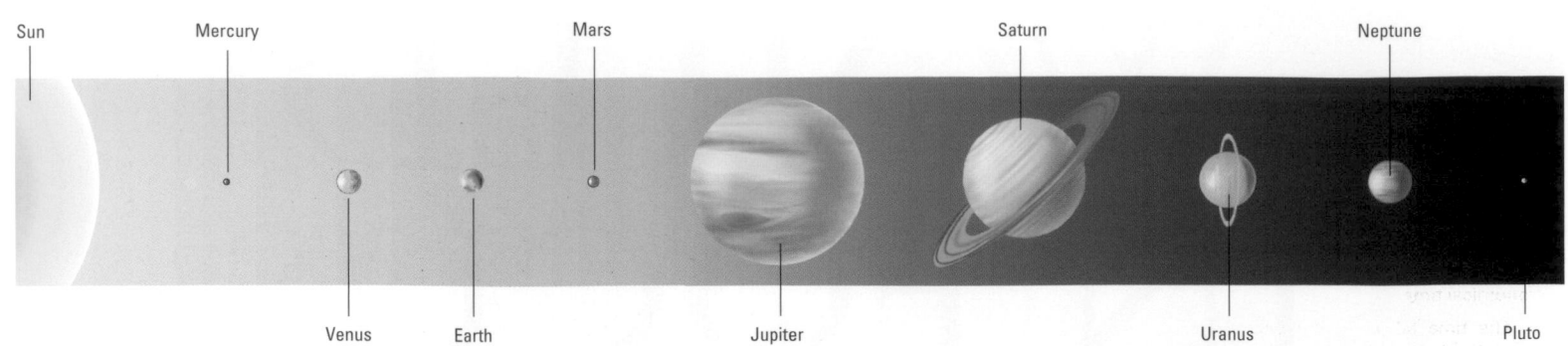

Sun · Mercury · Mars · Saturn · Neptune · Venus · Earth · Jupiter · Uranus · Pluto

The Solar System

A minute part of one of the billions of galaxies (collections of stars) that populate the Universe, the Solar System lies about 26,000 light-years from the centre of our own galaxy, the 'Milky Way'. Thought to be about 5 billion years old, it consists of a central Sun with nine planets and their moons revolving around it, attracted by its gravitational pull. The planets orbit the Sun in the same direction – anti-clockwise when viewed from above the Sun's north pole – and almost in the same plane. Their orbital distances, however, vary enormously.

The Sun's diameter is 109 times that of the Earth, and the temperature at its core – caused by continuous thermonuclear fusions of hydrogen into helium – is estimated to be 15 million degrees Celsius. It is the Solar System's only source of light and heat.

Profile of the Planets

	Mean distance from Sun (million km)	Mass (Earth = 1)	Period of orbit (Earth days/years)	Period of rotation (Earth days)	Equatorial diameter (km)	Number of known satellites*
Mercury	57.9	0.06	87.97 days	58.65	4,879	0
Venus	108.2	0.82	224.7 days	243.02	12,104	0
Earth	149.6	1.00	365.3 days	1.00	12,756	1
Mars	227.9	0.11	687.0 days	1.029	6,792	2
Jupiter	778	317.8	11.86 years	0.411	142,984	63
Saturn	1,427	95.2	29.45 years	0.428	120,536	47
Uranus	2,871	14.5	84.02 years	0.720	51,118	27
Neptune	4,498	17.2	164.8 years	0.673	49,528	13
Pluto	5,906	0.002	247.9 years	6.39	2,390	3

* Number of known satellites at mid-2006

All planetary orbits are elliptical in form, but only Pluto and Mercury follow paths that deviate noticeably from a circular one. Near perihelion – its closest approach to the Sun – Pluto actually passes inside the orbit of Neptune, an event that last occurred in 1979. Pluto did not regain its station as outermost planet until February 1999.

The Seasons

Seasons occur because the Earth's axis is tilted at an angle of approximately 23½°. When the northern hemisphere is tilted to a maximum extent towards the Sun, on 21 June, the Sun is overhead at the Tropic of Cancer (latitude 23½° North). This is midsummer, or the summer solstice, in the northern hemisphere.

On 22 or 23 September, the Sun is overhead at the equator, and day and night are of equal length throughout the world. This is the autumnal equinox in the northern hemisphere. On 21 or 22 December, the Sun is overhead at the Tropic of Capricorn (23½° South), the winter solstice in the northern hemisphere. The overhead Sun then tracks north until, on 21 March, it is overhead at the equator. This is the spring (vernal) equinox in the northern hemisphere.

In the southern hemisphere, the seasons are the reverse of those in the north.

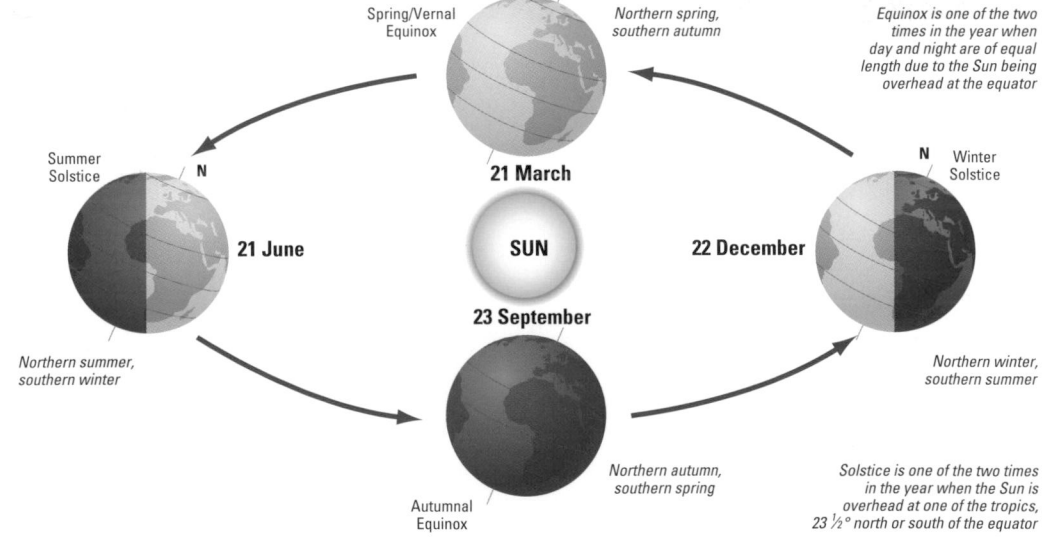

Spring/Vernal Equinox · Northern spring, southern autumn · Equinox is one of the two times in the year when day and night are of equal length due to the Sun being overhead at the equator

Summer Solstice · N · 21 March · N · Winter Solstice

21 June · SUN · 22 December

23 September

Northern summer, southern winter · Northern winter, southern summer

Northern autumn, southern spring · Solstice is one of the two times in the year when the Sun is overhead at one of the tropics, 23½° north or south of the equator

Autumnal Equinox

Day and Night

The Sun appears to rise in the east, reach its highest point at noon, and then set in the west, to be followed by night. In reality, it is not the Sun that is moving but the Earth rotating from west to east. The moment when the Sun's upper limb first appears above the horizon is termed sunrise; the moment when the Sun's upper limb disappears below the horizon is sunset.

At the summer solstice in the northern hemisphere (21 June), the Arctic has total daylight and the Antarctic total darkness. The opposite occurs at the winter solstice (21 or 22 December). At the equator, the length of day and night are almost equal all year.

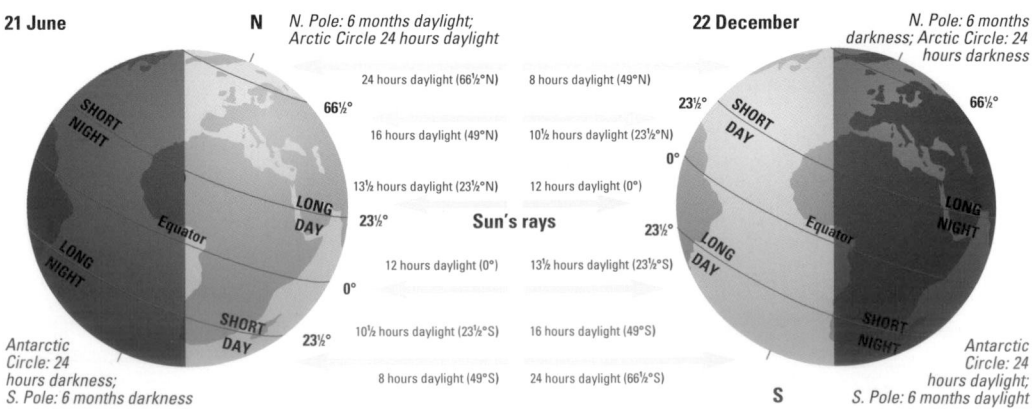

21 June · N · N. Pole: 6 months daylight; Arctic Circle 24 hours daylight

66½° · 24 hours daylight (66½°N) · 8 hours daylight (49°N) · 23½°
16 hours daylight (49°N) · 10½ hours daylight (23½°N)
LONG DAY · 0°
13½ hours daylight (23½°N) · 12 hours daylight (0°)
Equator · 23½° · Sun's rays · 23½°
LONG NIGHT · 12 hours daylight (0°) · 13½ hours daylight (23½°S)
0°
SHORT DAY · 23½° · 10½ hours daylight (23½°S) · 16 hours daylight (49°S)

Antarctic Circle: 24 hours darkness; S. Pole: 6 months darkness · 8 hours daylight (49°S) · 24 hours daylight (66½°S)

22 December · N. Pole: 6 months darkness; Arctic Circle: 24 hours darkness

23½° · SHORT DAY · 66½°

LONG NIGHT

Equator

LONG DAY

SHORT NIGHT · Antarctic Circle: 24 hours daylight; S. Pole: 6 months daylight

S

Time

Year: The time taken by the Earth to revolve around the Sun, or 365.24 days.

Leap Year: A calendar year of 366 days, 29 February being the additional day. It offsets the difference between the calendar and the solar year.

Month: The 12 calendar months of the year are approximately equal in length to a lunar month.

Week: An artificial period of 7 days, not based on astronomical time.

Day: The time taken by the Earth to complete one rotation on its axis.

Hour: 24 hours make one day. The day is divided into hours a.m. (ante meridiem or before noon) and p.m. (post meridiem or after noon), although most timetables now use the 24-hour system, from midnight to midnight.

Sunrise

Sunset

The Moon

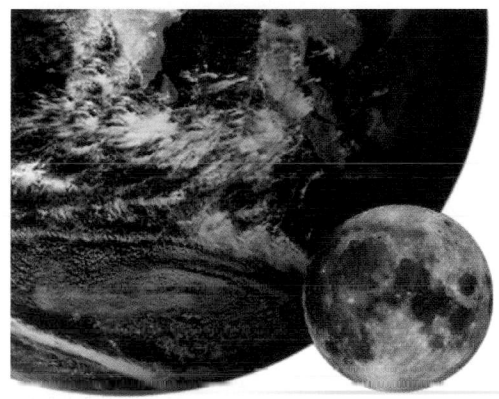

Phases of the Moon

Mean distance from Earth: 384,401 km; Mean diameter: 3,475 km;
Mass: approximately 1/80 that of Earth; Surface gravity: one-sixth of Earth's;
Daily range of temperature at lunar equator: 280°C; Average orbital speed: 3,681 km/h

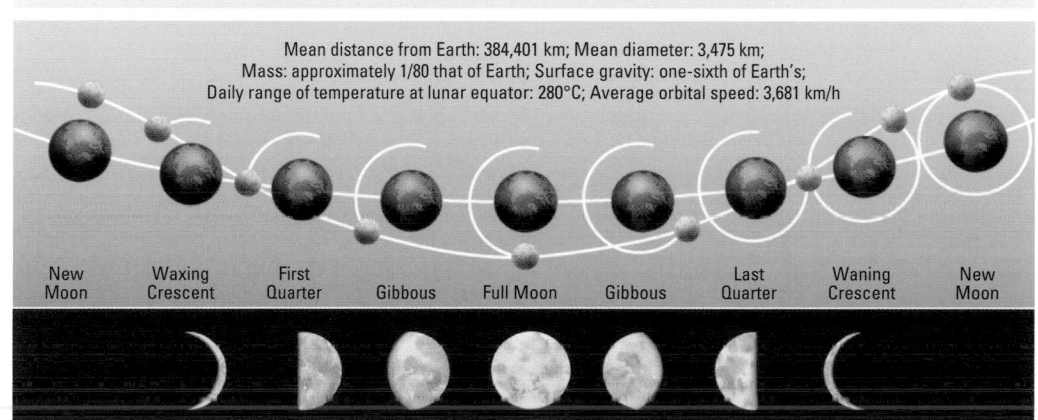

| New Moon | Waxing Crescent | First Quarter | Gibbous | Full Moon | Gibbous | Last Quarter | Waning Crescent | New Moon |

The Moon rotates more slowly than the Earth, taking just over 27 days to make one complete rotation on its axis. Since this corresponds to the Moon's orbital period around the Earth, the Moon always presents the same hemisphere towards us, and we never see the far side. The interval between one New Moon and the next is 29½ days – this is called a lunation, or lunar month. The Moon shines only by reflected sunlight, and emits no light of its own. During each lunation the Moon displays a complete cycle of phases, caused by the changing angle of illumination from the Sun.

Eclipses

When the Moon passes between the Sun and the Earth, the Sun becomes partially eclipsed (1). A partial eclipse can become a total eclipse if the Moon covers the Sun completely (2) and the dark central part of the lunar shadow touches the Earth. The broad geographical zone covered by the Moon's outer shadow (P) has only a very small central area (often less than 100 km wide) that experiences totality. Totality can never last for more than 7½ minutes, and it is usually briefer than this. Lunar eclipses take place when the Moon moves through the shadow of the Earth, and can also be partial or total. Any single location on Earth can experience a maximum of four solar and three lunar eclipses in any single year, while a total solar eclipse occurs an average of once every 360 years for any given location.

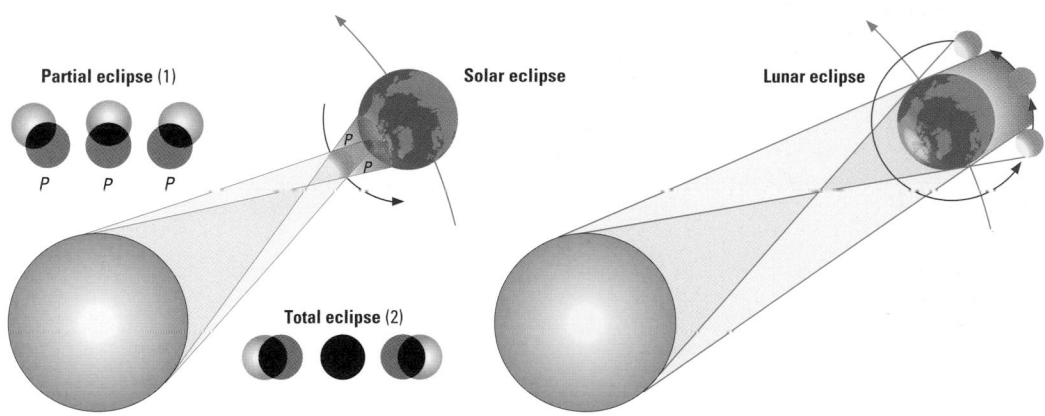

Tides

The daily rise and fall of the ocean's tides are the result of the gravitational pull of the Moon and that of the Sun, though the effect of the latter is not as strong as that of the Moon. This effect is greatest on the hemisphere facing the Moon and causes a tidal 'bulge'.

When the Sun, Earth and Moon are in line, spring tides occur: high tide reaches the highest values, and low tide falls to low levels. When lunar and solar forces are least coincidental with the Sun and Moon at an angle (near the Moon's first and third quarters), neap tides occur, which have a small tidal range.

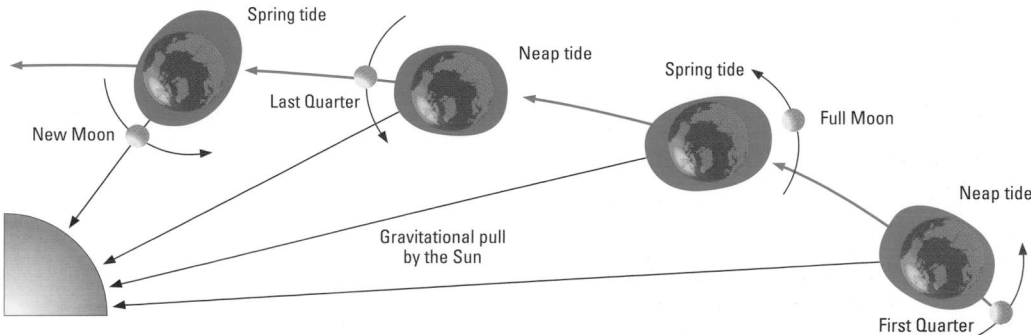

Restless Earth

The Earth's Structure

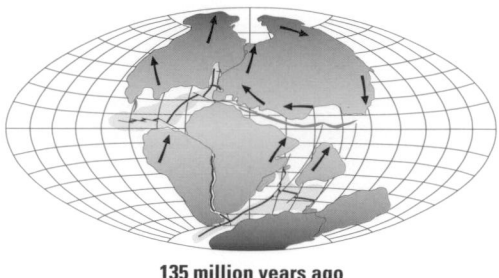

- Upper mantle (c. 370 km)
- Crust (average 5–50 km)
- Transitional zone (600 km)
- Outer core (2,100 km)
- Lower mantle (1,700 km)
- Inner core (1,350 km)

Continental Drift

About 200 million years ago the original Pangaea landmass began to split into two continental groups, which further separated over time to produce the present-day configuration.

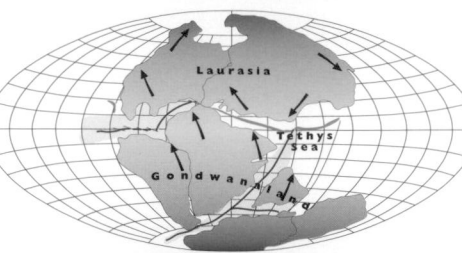

180 million years ago

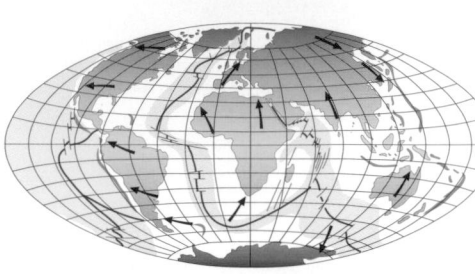

135 million years ago

Present day

- Trench
- Rift
- New ocean floor
- Zones of slippage

Notable Earthquakes Since 1900

Year	Location	Richter Scale	Deaths
1906	San Francisco, USA	8.3	3,000
1906	Valparaiso, Chile	8.6	22,000
1908	Messina, Italy	7.5	83,000
1915	Avezzano, Italy	7.5	30,000
1920	Gansu (Kansu), China	8.6	180,000
1923	Yokohama, Japan	8.3	143,000
1927	Nan Shan, China	8.3	200,000
1932	Gansu (Kansu), China	7.6	70,000
1933	Sanriku, Japan	8.9	2,990
1934	Bihar, India/Nepal	8.4	10,700
1935	Quetta, India (now Pakistan)	7.5	60,000
1939	Chillan, Chile	8.3	28,000
1939	Erzincan, Turkey	7.9	30,000
1960	S. W. Chile	9.5	2,200
1960	Agadir, Morocco	5.8	12,000
1962	Khorasan, Iran	7.1	12,230
1964	Anchorage, USA	9.2	125
1968	N. E. Iran	7.4	12,000
1970	N. Peru	7.8	70,000
1972	Managua, Nicaragua	6.2	5,000
1974	N. Pakistan	6.3	5,200
1976	Guatemala	7.5	22,500
1976	Tangshan, China	8.2	255,000
1978	Tabas, Iran	7.7	25,000
1980	El Asnam, Algeria	7.3	20,000
1980	S. Italy	7.2	4,800
1985	Mexico City, Mexico	8.1	4,200
1988	N.W. Armenia	6.8	55,000
1990	N. Iran	7.7	36,000
1992	Flores, Indonesia	6.8	1,895
1993	Maharashtra, India	6.4	30,000
1994	Los Angeles, USA	6.6	51
1995	Kobe, Japan	7.2	5,000
1995	Sakhalin Is., Russia	7.5	2,000
1996	Yunnan, China	7.0	240
1997	N. E. Iran	7.1	2,400
1998	Takhar, Afghanistan	6.1	4,200
1998	Rostag, Afghanistan	7.0	5,000
1999	Izmit, Turkey	7.4	15,000
1999	Taipei, Taiwan	7.6	1,700
2001	Gujarat, India	7.7	14,000
2002	Baghlan, Afghanistan	6.1	1,000
2003	Boumerdes, Algeria	6.8	2,200
2003	Bam, Iran	6.6	30,000
2004	Sumatra, Indonesia	9.0	250,000
2005	N. Pakistan	7.6	74,000
2006	Java, Indonesia	6.4	6,200

Earthquakes

Earthquake magnitude is usually rated according to either the Richter or the Modified Mercalli scale, both devised by seismologists in the 1930s. The Richter scale measures absolute earthquake power with mathematical precision: each step upwards represents a tenfold increase in shockwave amplitude. Theoretically, there is no upper limit, but most of the largest earthquakes measured have been rated at between 8.8 and 8.9. The 12–point Mercalli scale, based on observed effects, is often more meaningful, ranging from I (earthquakes noticed only by seismographs) to XII (total destruction); intermediate points include V (people awakened at night; unstable objects overturned), VII (collapse of ordinary buildings; chimneys and monuments fall), and IX (conspicuous cracks in ground; serious damage to reservoirs).

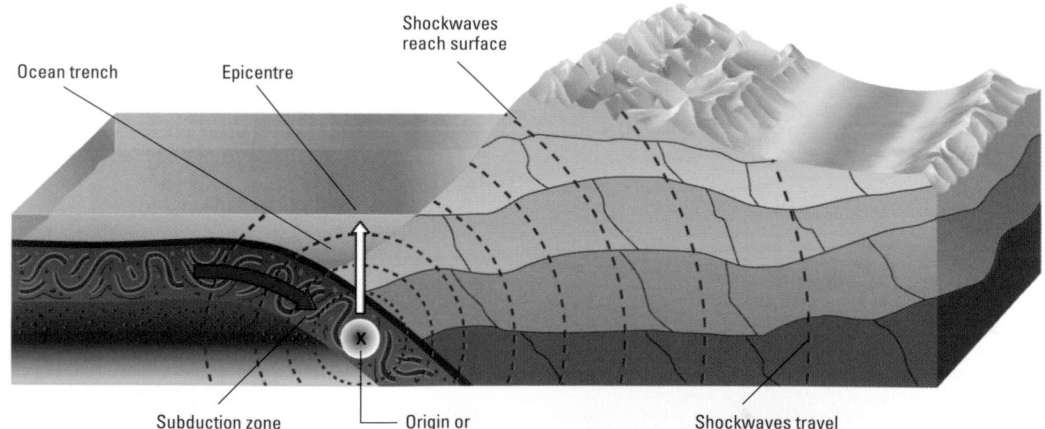

- Ocean trench
- Epicentre
- Shockwaves reach surface
- Subduction zone
- Origin or focus
- Shockwaves travel away from focus

Structure and Earthquakes

- Mobile land areas
- Submarine zones of mobile land areas
- Stable land platforms
- Submarine extensions of stable land platforms
- Mid-oceanic volcanic ridges
- Oceanic platforms

1976○ Principal earthquakes and dates (since 1900)

Earthquakes are a series of rapid vibrations originating from the slipping or faulting of parts of the Earth's crust when stresses within build up to breaking point. They usually happen at depths varying from 8 km to 30 km. Severe earthquakes cause extensive damage when they take place in populated areas, destroying structures and severing communications. Most initial loss of life occurs due to secondary causes such as falling masonry, fires and flooding.

Projection: Interrupted Mollweide

Plate Tectonics

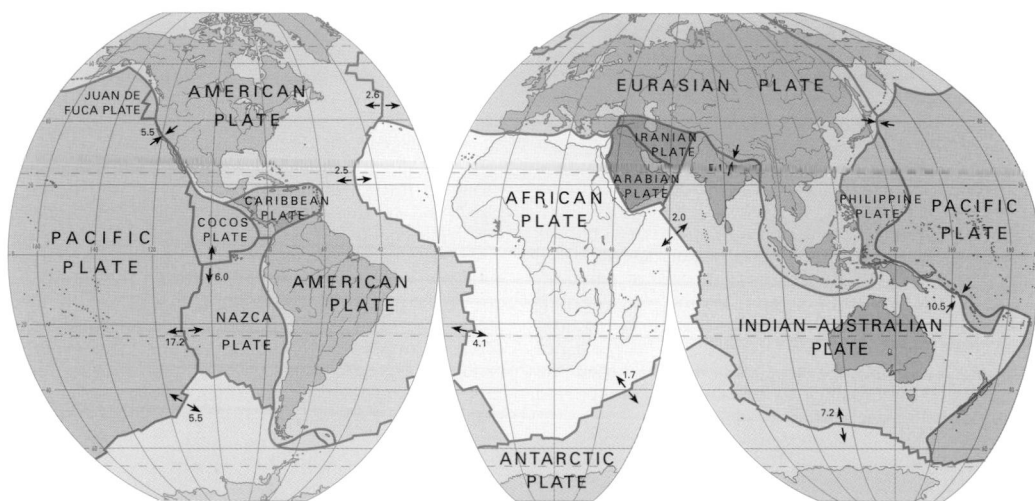

—— Plate boundaries   PACIFIC   Major plates

——➤ Direction of plate movements and rate of movement (cm/year)

The drifting of the continents is a feature that is unique to Planet Earth. The complementary, almost jigsaw-puzzle fit of the coastlines on each side of the Atlantic Ocean inspired Alfred Wegener's theory of continental drift in 1915. The theory suggested that the ancient super-continent, which Wegener named Pangaea, incorporated all of the Earth's landmasses and gradually split up to form today's continents.

The original debate about continental drift was a prelude to a more radical idea: plate tectonics. The basic theory is that the Earth's crust is made up of a series of rigid plates which float on a soft layer of the mantle and are moved about by continental convection currents within the Earth's interior. These plates diverge and converge along margins marked by seismic activity. Plates diverge from mid-ocean ridges where molten lava pushes upwards and forces the plates apart at rates of up to 40 mm [1.6 in] a year.

The three diagrams, left, give some examples of plate boundaries from around the world. Diagram (a) shows sea-floor spreading at the Mid-Atlantic Ridge as the American and African plates slowly diverge. The same thing is happening in (b) where sea-floor spreading at the Mid-Indian Ocean Ridge is forcing the Indian–Australian plate to collide into the Eurasian plate. In (c) oceanic crust (sima) is being subducted beneath lighter continental crust (sial).

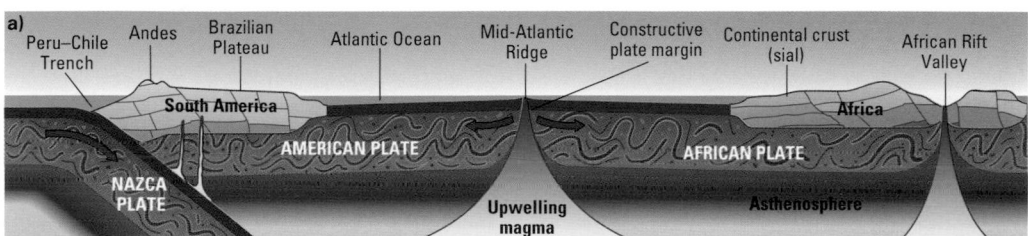

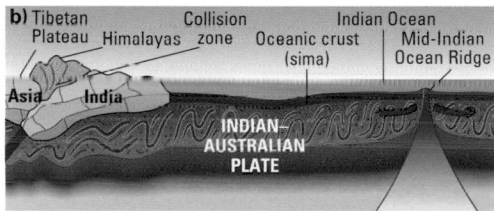

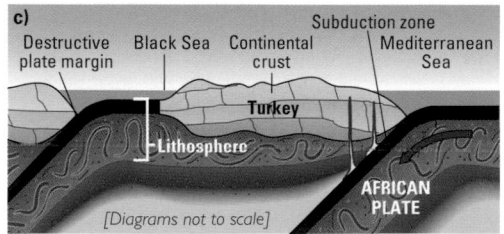

Volcanoes

Volcanoes occur when hot liquefied rock beneath the Earth's crust is pushed up by pressure to the surface as molten lava. Some volcanoes erupt in an explosive way, throwing out rocks and ash, whilst others are effusive and lava flows out of the vent. There are volcanoes which are both, such as Mount Fuji. An accumulation of lava and cinders creates cones of variable size and shape. As a result of many eruptions over centuries, Mount Etna in Sicily has a circumference of more than 120 km [75 miles].

Climatologists believe that volcanic ash, if ejected high into the atmosphere, can influence temperature and weather for several years afterwards. The 1991 eruption of Mount Pinatubo in the Philippines ejected more than 20 million tonnes of dust and ash 32 km [20 miles] into the atmosphere and is believed to have accelerated ozone depletion over a large part of the globe.

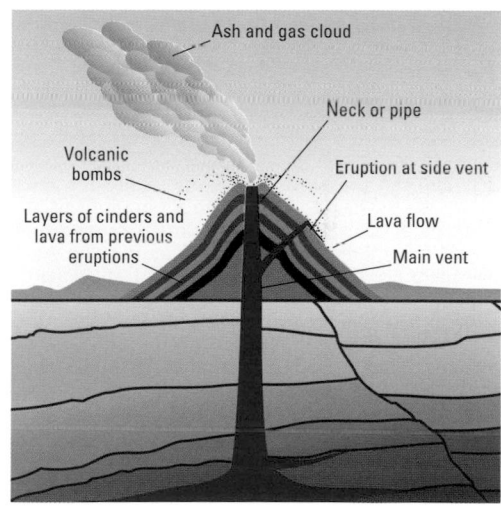

Distribution of Volcanoes

Volcanoes today may be the subject of considerable scientific study but they remain both dramatic and unpredictable: in 1991 Mount Pinatubo, 100 km [62 miles] north of the Philippines capital Manila, suddenly burst into life after lying dormant for more than six centuries. Most of the world's active volcanoes occur in a belt around the Pacific Ocean, on the edge of the Pacific plate, called the 'ring of fire'. Indonesia has the greatest concentration with 90 volcanoes, 12 of which are active. The most famous, Krakatoa, erupted in 1883 with such force that the resulting tidal wave killed 36,000 people and tremors were felt as far away as Australia.

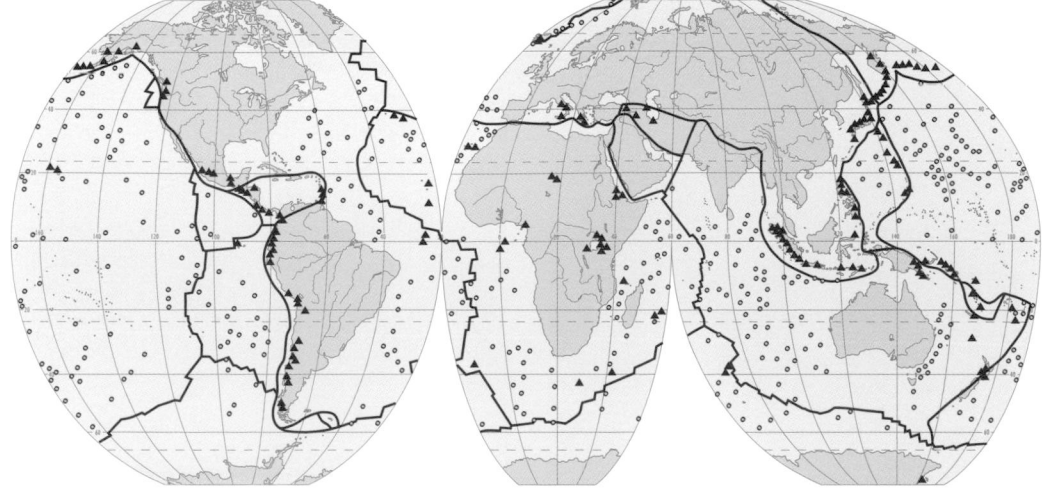

○ Submarine volcanoes

▲ Land volcanoes active since 1700

—— Boundaries of tectonic plates

Landforms

The Rock Cycle

James Hutton first proposed the rock cycle in the late 1700s after he observed the slow but steady effects of erosion.

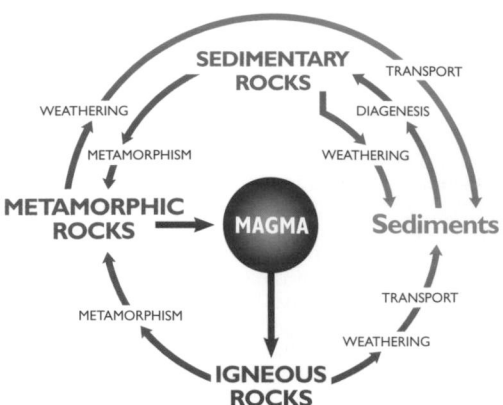

Above and below the surface of the oceans, the features of the Earth's crust are constantly changing. The phenomenal forces generated by convection currents in the molten core of our planet carry the vast segments or 'plates' of the crust across the globe in an endless cycle of creation and destruction. A continent may travel little more than 25 mm [1 in] per year, yet in the vast span of geological time this process throws up giant mountain ranges and creates new land.

Destruction of the landscape, however, begins as soon as it is formed. Wind, water, ice and sea, the main agents of erosion, mount a constant assault that even the most resistant rocks cannot withstand. Mountain peaks may dwindle by as little as a few millimetres each year, but if they are not uplifted by further movements of the crust they will eventually be reduced to rubble and transported away.

Water is the most powerful agent of erosion – it has been estimated that 100 billion tonnes of sediment are washed into the oceans every year. Three

Asian rivers account for 20% of this total, the Huang He, in China, and the Brahmaputra and Ganges in Bangladesh.

Rivers and glaciers, like the sea itself, generate much of their effect through abrasion – pounding the land with the debris they carry with them. But as well as destroying they also create new landforms, many of them spectacular: vast deltas like those of the Mississippi and the Nile, or the deep fjords cut by glaciers in British Columbia, Norway and New Zealand.

Geologists once considered that landscapes evolved from 'young', newly uplifted mountainous areas, through a 'mature' hilly stage, to an 'old age' stage when the land was reduced to an almost flat plain, or peneplain. This theory, called the 'cycle of erosion', fell into disuse when it became evident that so many factors, including the effects of plate tectonics and climatic change, constantly interrupt the cycle, which takes no account of the highly complex interactions that shape the surface of our planet.

Mountain Building

Mountains are formed when pressures on the Earth's crust caused by continental drift become so intense that the surface buckles or cracks. This happens where oceanic crust is subducted by continental crust or, more dramatically, where two tectonic plates collide: the Rockies, Andes, Alps, Urals and Himalayas resulted from such impacts. These are all known as fold mountains because they were formed by the compression of the rocks, forcing the surface to bend and fold like a crumpled rug. The Himalayas are formed from the folded former sediments of the Tethys Sea which was trapped in the collision zone between the Indian and Eurasian plates.

The other main mountain-building process occurs when the crust fractures to create faults, allowing rock to be forced upwards in large blocks; or when the pressure of magma within the crust forces the surface to bulge into a dome, or erupts to form a volcano. Large mountain ranges may reveal a combination of those features; the Alps, for example, have been compressed so violently that the folds are fragmented by numerous faults and intrusions of molten igneous rock.

Over millions of years, even the greatest mountain ranges can be reduced by the agents of erosion (most notably rivers) to a low rugged landscape known as a peneplain.

Types of faults: Faults occur where the crust is being stretched or compressed so violently that the rock strata break in a horizontal or vertical movement. They are classified by the direction in which the blocks of rock have moved. A normal fault results when a vertical movement causes the surface to break apart; compression causes a reverse fault. Horizontal movement causes shearing, known as a strike-slip fault. When the rock breaks in two places, the central block may be pushed up in a horst fault, or sink (creating a rift valley) in a graben fault.

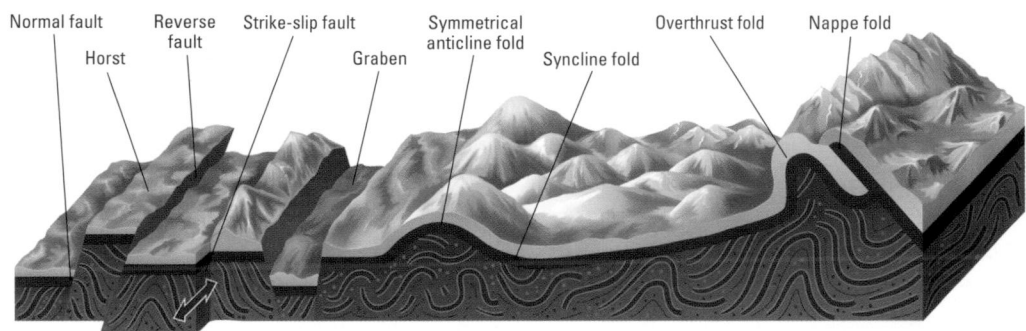

Types of fold: Folds occur when rock strata are squeezed and compressed. They are common, therefore, at destructive plate margins and where plates have collided, forcing the rocks to buckle into mountain ranges. Geographers give different names to the degrees of fold that result from continuing pressure on the rock. A simple fold may be symmetric, with even slopes on either side, but as the pressure builds up, one slope becomes steeper and the fold becomes asymmetric. Later, the ridge or 'anticline' at the top of the fold may slide over the lower ground or 'syncline' to form a recumbent fold. Eventually, the rock strata may break under the pressure to form an overthrust and finally a nappe fold.

Continental Glaciation

Ice sheets were at their greatest extent about 200,000 years ago. The maximum advance of the last Ice Age was about 18,000 years ago, when ice covered virtually all of Canada and reached as far south as the Bristol Channel in Britain.

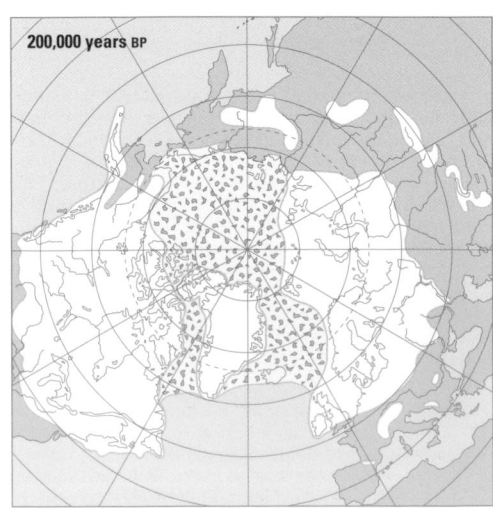

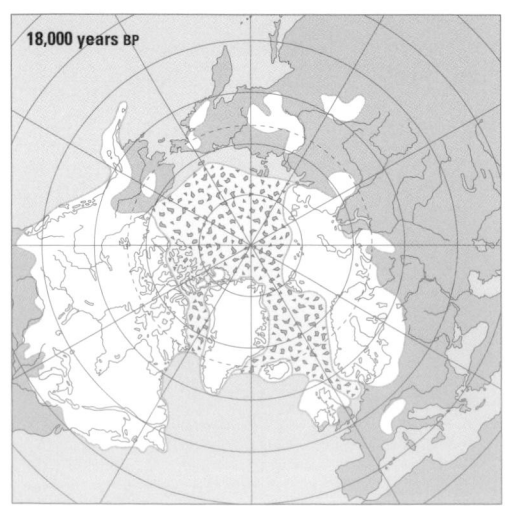

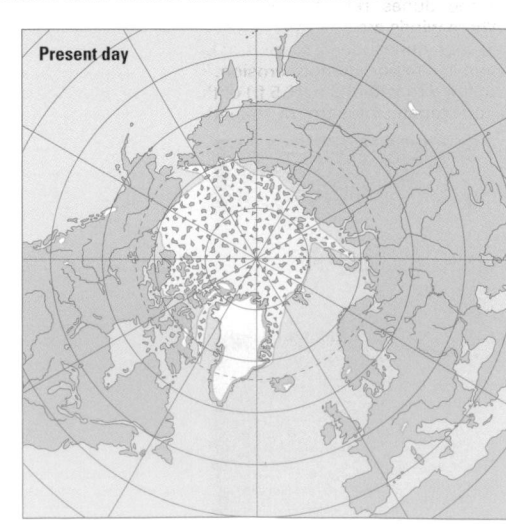

Natural Landforms

A stylized diagram to show a selection of landforms found in the mid-latitudes.

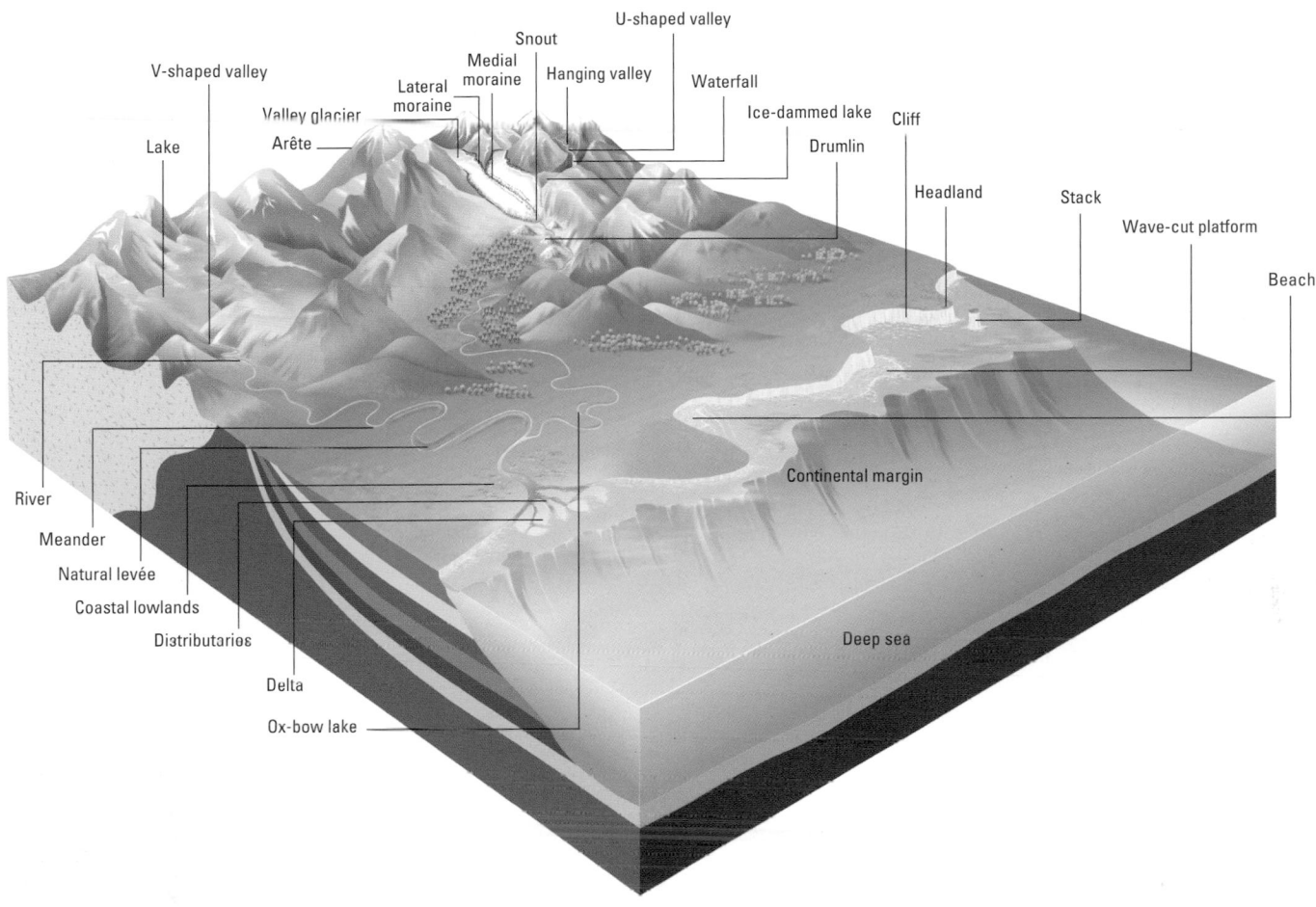

Desert Landscapes

The popular image that deserts are all huge expanses of sand is wrong. Despite harsh conditions, deserts contain some of the most varied and interesting landscapes in the world. They are also one of the most extensive environments – the hot and cold deserts together cover almost 40% of the Earth's surface.

The three types of hot desert are known by their Arabic names: sand desert, called *erg*, covers only about one-fifth of the world's desert; the rest is divided between *hammada* (areas of bare rock) and *reg* (broad plains covered by loose gravel or pebbles).

In areas of *erg*, such as the Namib Desert, the shape of the dunes reflects the character of local winds. Where winds are constant in direction, crescent-shaped *barchan* dunes form. In areas of bare rock, wind-blown sand is a major agent of erosion. The erosion is mainly confined to within 2 m [6.5 ft] of the surface, producing characteristic, mushroom-shaped rocks.

Surface Processes

Catastrophic changes to natural landforms are periodically caused by such phenomena as avalanches, landslides and volcanic eruptions, but most of the processes that shape the Earth's surface operate extremely slowly in human terms. One estimate, based on a study in the United States, suggested that 1 m [3 ft] of land was removed from the entire surface of the country, on average, every 29,500 years. However, the time-scale varies from 1,300 years to 154,200 years depending on the terrain and climate.

In hot, dry climates, mechanical weathering, a result of rapid temperature changes, causes the outer layers of rock to peel away, while in cold mountainous regions, boulders are prised apart when water freezes in cracks in rocks. Chemical weathering, at its greatest in warm, humid regions, is responsible for hollowing out limestone caves and decomposing granites.

The erosion of soil and rock is greatest on sloping land and the steeper the slope, the greater the tendency for mass wasting – the movement of soil and rock downhill under the influence of gravity. The mechanisms of mass wasting (ranging from very slow to very rapid) vary with the type of material, but the presence of water as a lubricant is usually an important factor.

Running water is the world's leading agent of erosion and transportation. The energy of a river depends on several factors, including its velocity and volume, and its erosive power is at its peak when it is in full flood. Sea waves also exert tremendous erosive power during storms when they hurl pebbles against the shore, undercutting cliffs and hollowing out caves.

Glacier ice forms in mountain hollows and spills out to form valley glaciers, which transport rocks shattered by frost action. As glaciers move, rocks embedded into the ice erode steep-sided, U-shaped valleys. Evidence of glaciation in mountain regions includes cirques, knife-edged ridges, or arêtes, and pyramidal peaks.

Oceans

The Great Oceans

Relative sizes of the world's oceans

- Pacific
- Atlantic
- Indian
- Southern
- Arctic

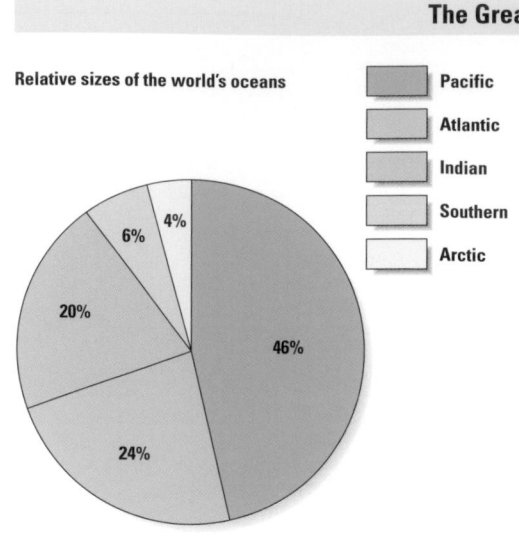

46%
24%
20%
6%
4%

From ancient times to about the 15th century, the legendary 'Seven Seas' comprised the Red Sea, Mediterranean Sea, Persian Gulf, Black Sea, Adriatic Sea, Caspian Sea and Indian Sea.

The Earth is a watery planet: more than 70% of its surface – over 360,000,000 sq km [140,000,000 sq miles] – is covered by the oceans and seas. The mighty Pacific alone accounts for nearly 36% of the total, and more than 46% of the sea area. Gravity holds in around 1,400 million cu. km [320 million cu. miles] of water, of which over 97% is saline.

The vast underwater world starts in the shallows of the seaside and plunges to depths of more than 11,000 m [36,000 ft]. The continental shelf, part of the landmass, drops gently to around 200 m [650 ft]; here the seabed falls away suddenly at an angle of 3° to 6° – the continental slope. The third stage, called the continental rise, is more gradual with gradients varying from 1 in 100 to 1 in 700. At an average depth of 5,000 m [16,500 ft] there begins the aptly-named abyssal plain – massive submarine depths where sunlight fails to penetrate and few creatures can survive.

From these plains rise volcanoes which, taken from base to top, rival and even surpass the tallest continental mountains in height. Mauna Kea, on Hawai'i, reaches a total of 10,203 m [33,400 ft], some 1,355 m [4,500 ft] more than Mount Everest, though scarcely 40% is visible above sea level.

In addition, there are underwater mountain chains up to 1,000 km [600 miles] across, whose peaks sometimes appear above sea level as islands, such as Iceland and Tristan da Cunha.

The Ocean Depths

Average and maximum depths of the world's great oceans, in metres

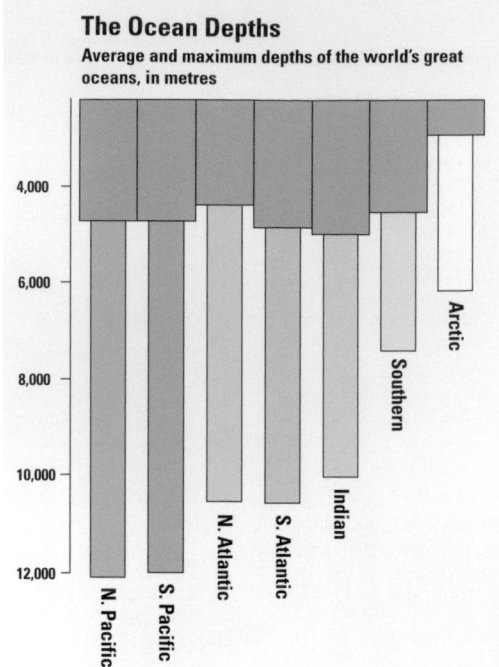

Ocean Currents

January ocean currents

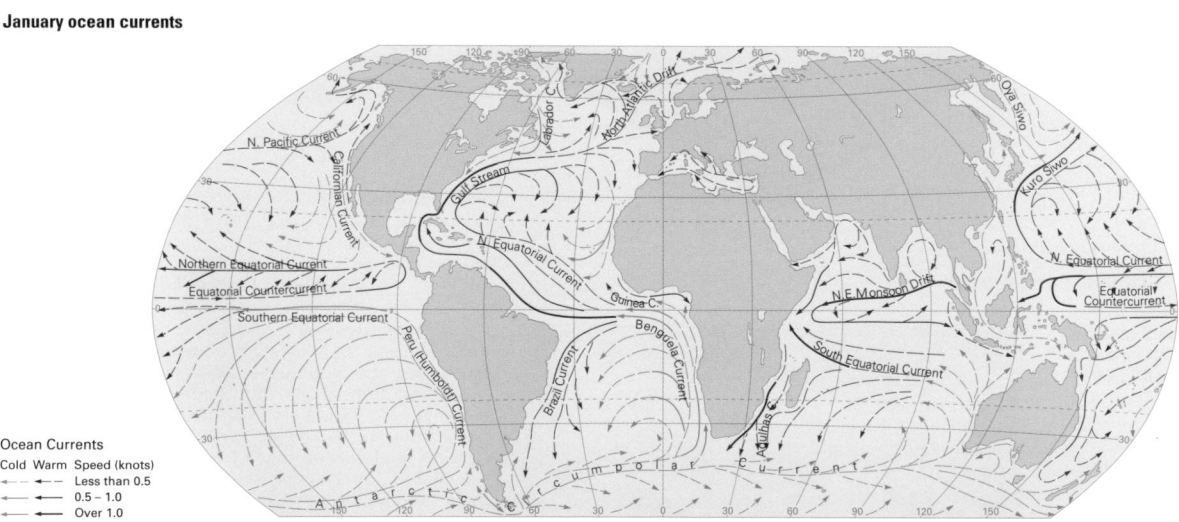

Ocean Currents
Cold Warm Speed (knots)
- Less than 0.5
- 0.5 – 1.0
- Over 1.0

July ocean currents

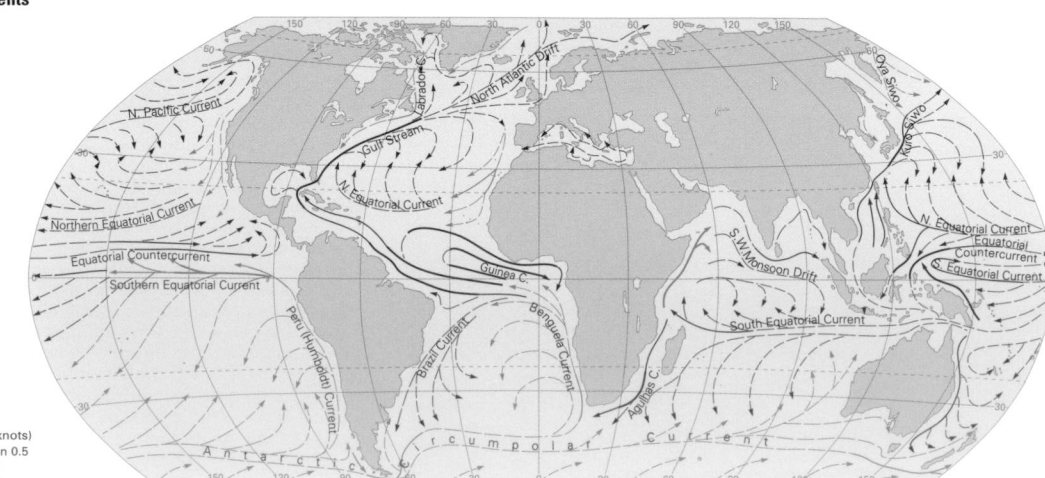

Ocean Currents
Cold Warm Speed (knots)
- Less than 0.5
- 0.5 – 1.0
- Over 1.0

Moving immense quantities of energy as well as billions of tonnes of water every hour, the ocean currents are a vital part of the great heat engine that drives the Earth's climate. They themselves are produced by a twofold mechanism. At the surface, winds push huge masses of water before them; in the deep ocean, below an abrupt temperature gradient that separates the churning surface waters from the still depths, density variations cause slow vertical movements.

The pattern of circulation of the great surface currents is determined by the displacement known as the Coriolis effect. As the Earth turns beneath a moving object – whether it is a tennis ball or a vast mass of water – it appears to be deflected to one side. The deflection is most obvious near the Equator, where the Earth's surface is spinning eastwards at 1,700 km/h [1,050 mph]; currents moving polewards are curved clockwise in the northern hemisphere and anti-clockwise in the southern.

The result is a system of spinning circles known as gyres. The Coriolis effect piles up water on the left of each gyre, creating a narrow, fast-moving stream that is matched by a slower, broader returning current on the right. North and south of the Equator, the fastest currents are located in the west and in the east respectively. In each case, warm water moves from the Equator and cold water returns to it. Cold currents often bring an upwelling of nutrients with them, supporting the world's most economically important fisheries.

Depending on the prevailing winds, some currents on or near the Equator may reverse their direction in the course of the year – a seasonal variation on which Asian monsoon rains depend, and whose occasional failure can bring disaster to millions.

World Fishing Areas

Main commercial fishing areas (numbered FAO regions)

Catch by top marine fishing areas, million tonnes (2002)

1.	Pacific, NW	[61]	21.4	25.3%
2.	Pacific, SE	[87]	13.8	16.3%
3.	Atlantic, NE	[27]	11.0	13.0%
4.	Pacific, WC	[71]	10.5	12.4%
5.	Indian, E	[57]	5.1	6.0%
6.	Indian, W	[51]	4.2	5.0%
7.	Atlantic, EC	[34]	3.4	4.0%
8.	Pacific, NE	[67]	2.7	3.2%
9.	Atlantic, NW	[21]	2.2	2.6%
10.	Atlantic, WC	[31]	2.1	2.5%

◻ Principal fishing areas

Leading fishing nations

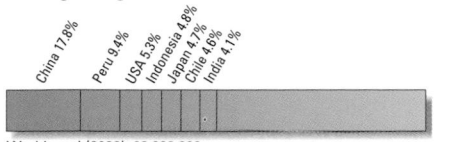

China 17.8% Peru 9.4% USA 5.3% Indonesia 4.8% Japan 4.7% Chile 4.6% India 4.1%

World total (2002): 93,200,000 tonnes
(Marine catch 90.7% Inland catch 9.3%)

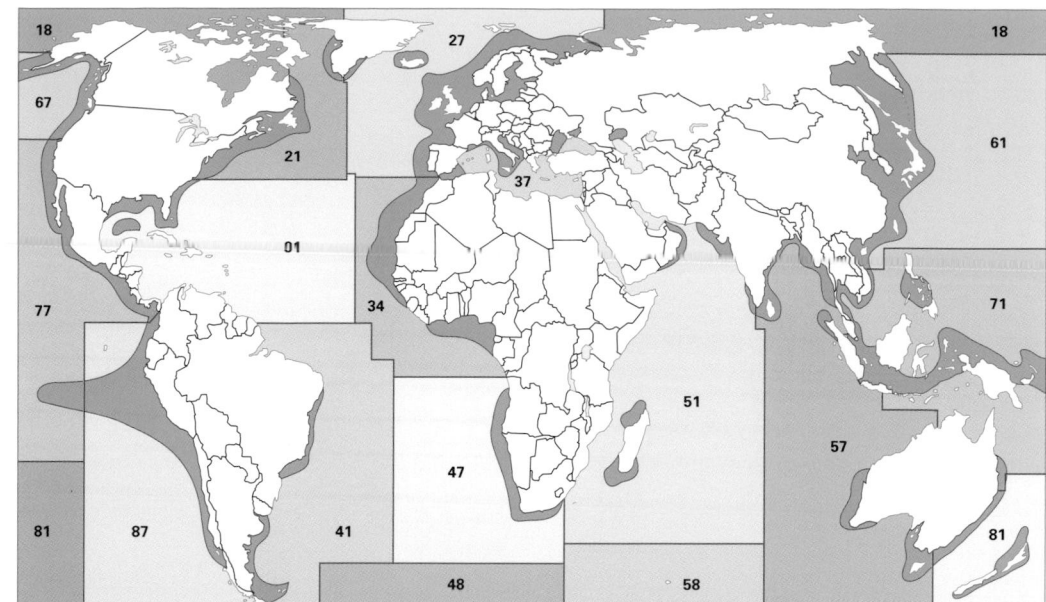

Marine Pollution

Sources of marine oil pollution

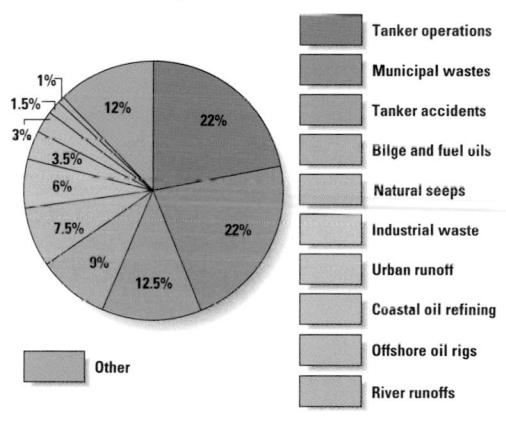

1%, 1.5%, 3%, 3.5%, 6%, 7.5%, 9%, 12.5%, 22%, 22%, 12%

- ◼ Tanker operations
- ◼ Municipal wastes
- ◼ Tanker accidents
- ◼ Bilge and fuel oils
- ◼ Natural seeps
- ◼ Industrial waste
- ◼ Urban runoff
- ◼ Coastal oil refining
- ◼ Offshore oil rigs
- ◼ River runoffs

◻ Other

Oil Spills

Major oil spills from tankers and combined carriers

Year	Vessel	Location	Spill (barrels) *	Cause
1979	Atlantic Empress	West Indies	1,890,000	collision
1983	Castillo De Bellver	South Africa	1,760,000	fire
1978	Amoco Cadiz	France	1,628,000	grounding
1991	Haven	Italy	1,029,000	explosion
1988	Odyssey	Canada	1,000,000	fire
1967	Torrey Canyon	UK	909,000	grounding
1972	Sea Star	Gulf of Oman	902,250	collision
1977	Hawaiian Patriot	Hawaiian Is.	742,500	fire
1979	Independenta	Turkey	696,350	collision
1993	Braer	UK	625,000	grounding
1996	Sea Empress	UK	515,000	grounding
2002	Prestige	Spain	463,250	storm

Other sources of major oil spills

1983	Nowruz oilfield	Persian Gulf	4,250,000[†]	war
1979	Ixtoc 1 oilwell	Gulf of Mexico	4,200,000	blow-out
1991	Kuwait	Persian Gulf	2,500,000[†]	war

* 1 barrel = 0.136 tonnes/159 lit./35 Imperial gal./42 US gal. [†] estimated

River Pollution

Sources of river pollution, USA

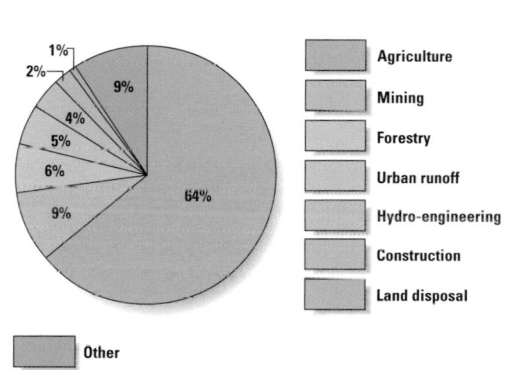

1%, 2%, 4%, 5%, 6%, 9%, 9%, 64%

- ◼ Agriculture
- ◼ Mining
- ◼ Forestry
- ◼ Urban runoff
- ◼ Hydro-engineering
- ◼ Construction
- ◼ Land disposal

◻ Other

Water Pollution

- ◼ Severely polluted sea areas and lakes
- ◼ Polluted sea areas and lakes
- ◼ Areas of frequent oil pollution by shipping

- ◤ Major oil tanker spills
- ▲ Major oil rig blow-outs
- ▼ Offshore dumpsites for industrial and municipal waste
- — Severely polluted rivers and estuaries

The most notorious tanker spillage of the 1980s occurred when the *Exxon Valdez* ran aground in Prince William Sound, Alaska, in 1989, spilling 267,000 barrels of crude oil close to shore in a sensitive ecological area. This rates as the world's 28th worst spill in terms of volume.

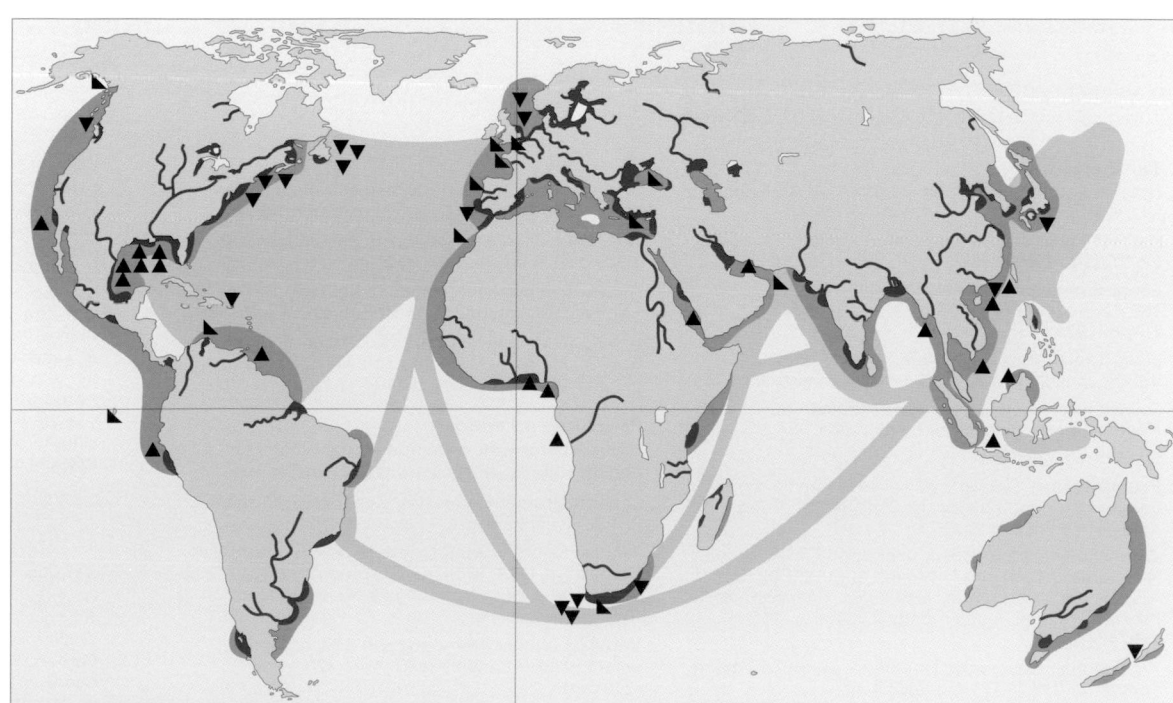

Climate

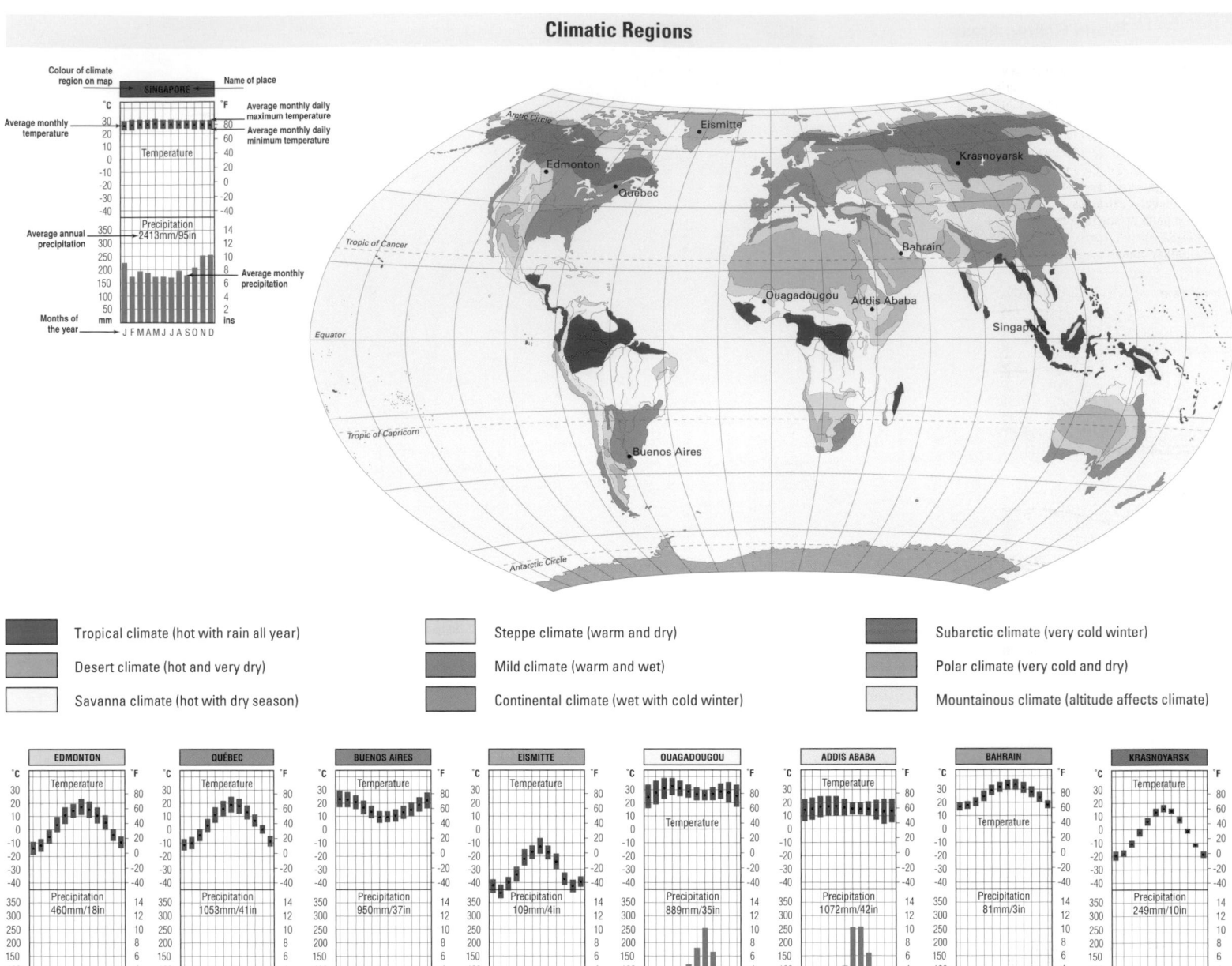

Legend:

- Tropical climate (hot with rain all year)
- Desert climate (hot and very dry)
- Savanna climate (hot with dry season)
- Steppe climate (warm and dry)
- Mild climate (warm and wet)
- Continental climate (wet with cold winter)
- Subarctic climate (very cold winter)
- Polar climate (very cold and dry)
- Mountainous climate (altitude affects climate)

Climate Records

Temperature

Highest recorded shade temperature: Al Aziziyah, Libya, 58°C [136.4°F], 13 September 1922.

Highest mean annual temperature: Dallol, Ethiopia, 34.4°C [94°F], 1960–66.

Longest heatwave: Marble Bar, W. Australia, 162 days over 38°C [100°F], 23 October 1923 to 7 April 1924.

Lowest recorded temperature (outside poles): Verkhoyansk, Siberia, –68°C [–90°F], 6 February 1933.

Lowest mean annual temperature: Polus Nedostupnosti, Pole of Cold, Antarctica, –57.8°C [–72°F].

Precipitation

Longest drought: Calama, N. Chile, no recorded rainfall in 400 years to 1971.

Wettest place (12 months): Cherrapunji, Meghalaya, N. E. India, 26,470 mm [1,040 in], August 1860 to August 1861. Cherrapunji also holds the record for the most rainfall in one month: 2,930 mm [115 in], July 1861.

Wettest place (average): Tututendo, Colombia, mean annual rainfall 11,770 mm [463.4 in].

Wettest place (24 hours): Cilaos, Réunion, Indian Ocean, 1,870 mm [73.6 in], 15–16 March 1952.

Heaviest hailstones: Gopalganj, Bangladesh, up to 1.02 kg [2.25 lb], 14 April 1986 (killed 92 people).

Heaviest snowfall (continuous): Bessans, Savoie, France, 1,730 mm [68 in] in 19 hours, 5–6 April 1969.

Heaviest snowfall (season/year): Paradise Ranger Station, Mt Rainier, Washington, USA, 31,102 mm [1,224.5 in], 19 February 1971 to 18 February 1972.

Pressure and winds

Highest barometric pressure: Agata, Siberia (at 262 m [862 ft] altitude), 1,083.8 mb, 31 December 1968.

Lowest barometric pressure: Typhoon Tip, Guam, Pacific Ocean, 870 mb, 12 October 1979.

Highest recorded wind speed: Mt Washington, New Hampshire, USA, 371 km/h [231 mph], 12 April 1934. This is three times as strong as hurricane force on the Beaufort Scale.

Windiest place: Commonwealth Bay, Antarctica, where gales frequently reach over 320 km/h [200 mph].

Climate

Climate is weather in the long term: the seasonal pattern of hot and cold, wet and dry, averaged over time (usually 30 years). At the simplest level, it is caused by the uneven heating of the Earth. Surplus heat at the Equator passes towards the poles, levelling out the energy differential. Its passage is marked by a ceaseless churning of the atmosphere and the oceans, further agitated by the Earth's diurnal spin and the motion it imparts to moving air and water. The heat's means of transport – by winds and ocean currents, by the continual evaporation and recondensation of water molecules – is the weather itself. There are four basic types of climate, each of which can be further subdivided: tropical, desert (dry), temperate and polar.

Composition of Dry Air

Nitrogen	78.09%	Sulphur dioxide	trace
Oxygen	20.95%	Nitrogen oxide	trace
Argon	0.93%	Methane	trace
Water vapour	0.2–4.0%	Dust	trace
Carbon dioxide	0.03%	Helium	trace
Ozone	0.00006%	Neon	trace

El Niño

In a normal year, south-easterly trade winds drive surface waters westwards off the coast of South America, drawing cold, nutrient-rich water up from below. In an El Niño year (which occurs every 2–7 years), warm water from the west Pacific suppresses upwelling in the east, depriving the region of nutrients. The water is warmed by as much as 7°C [12°F], disturbing the tropical atmospheric circulation. During an intense El Niño, the south-east trade winds change direction and become equatorial westerlies, resulting in climatic extremes in many regions of the world, such as drought in parts of Australia and India, and heavy rainfall in south-eastern USA. An intense El Niño occurred in 1997–8, with resultant freak weather conditions across the entire Pacific region.

Normal year

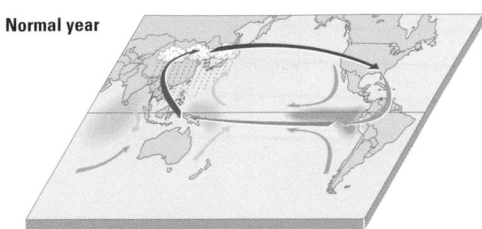

El Niño event

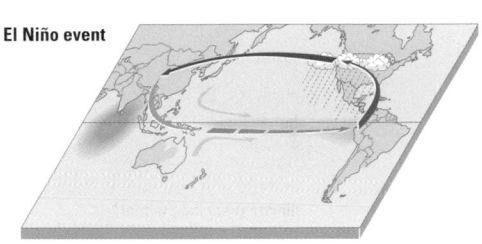

Beaufort Wind Scale

Named after the 19th-century British naval officer who devised it, the Beaufort Scale assesses wind speed according to its effects. It was originally designed as an aid for sailors, but has since been adapted for use on the land.

Scale	Wind speed km/h	mph	Effect
0	0–1	0–1	**Calm** Smoke rises vertically
1	1–5	1–3	**Light air** Wind direction shown only by smoke drift
2	6–11	4–7	**Light breeze** Wind felt on face; leaves rustle; vanes moved by wind
3	12–19	8–12	**Gentle breeze** Leaves and small twigs in constant motion; wind extends small flag
4	20–28	13–18	**Moderate** Raises dust and loose paper; small branches move
5	29–38	19–24	**Fresh** Small trees in leaf sway; wavelets on inland waters
6	39–49	25–31	**Strong** Large branches move; difficult to use umbrellas
7	50–61	32–38	**Near gale** Whole trees in motion; difficult to walk against wind
8	62–74	39–46	**Gale** Twigs break from trees; walking very difficult
9	75–88	47–54	**Strong gale** Slight structural damage
10	89–102	55–63	**Storm** Trees uprooted; serious structural damage
11	103–117	64–72	**Violent storm** Widespread damage
12	118+	73+	**Hurricane**

Conversions

°C = (°F − 32) × 5/9; °F = (°C × 9/5) + 32; 0°C = 32°F
1 in = 25.4 mm; 1 mm = 0.0394 in; 100 mm = 3.94 in

Temperature

Average temperature in January

Temperature

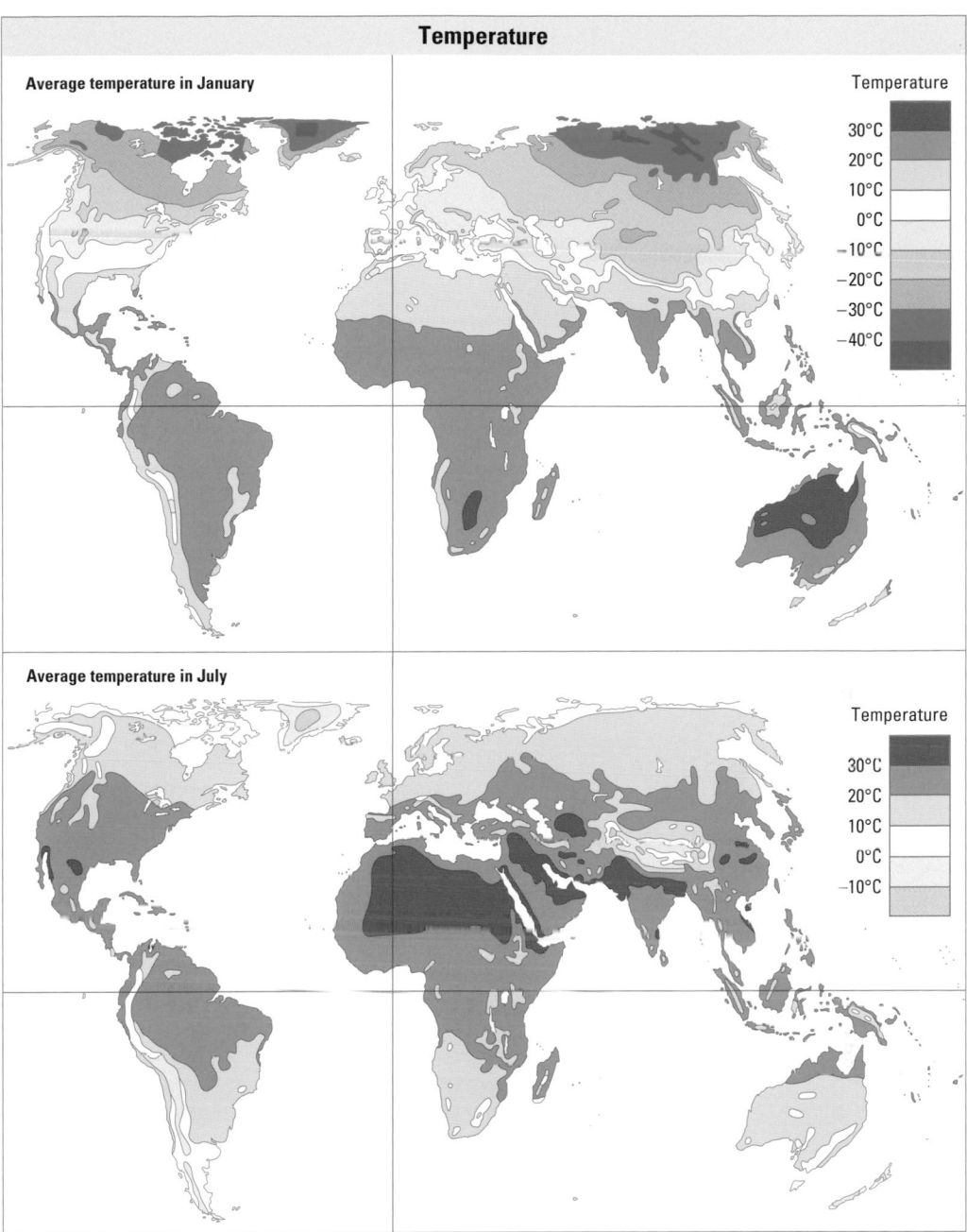

Average temperature in July

Temperature

Precipitation

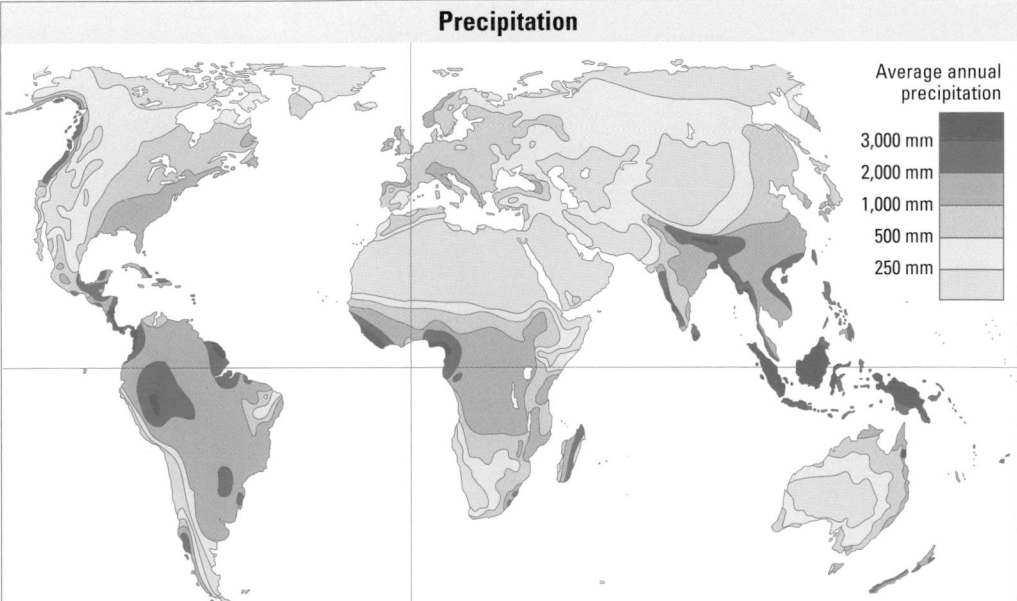

Average annual precipitation

11

Water and Vegetation

The Hydrological Cycle

The world's water balance is regulated by the constant recycling of water between the oceans, atmosphere and land. The movement of water between these three reservoirs is known as the hydrological cycle. The oceans play a vital role in the hydrological cycle: 74% of the total precipitation falls over the oceans and 84% of the total evaporation comes from the oceans.

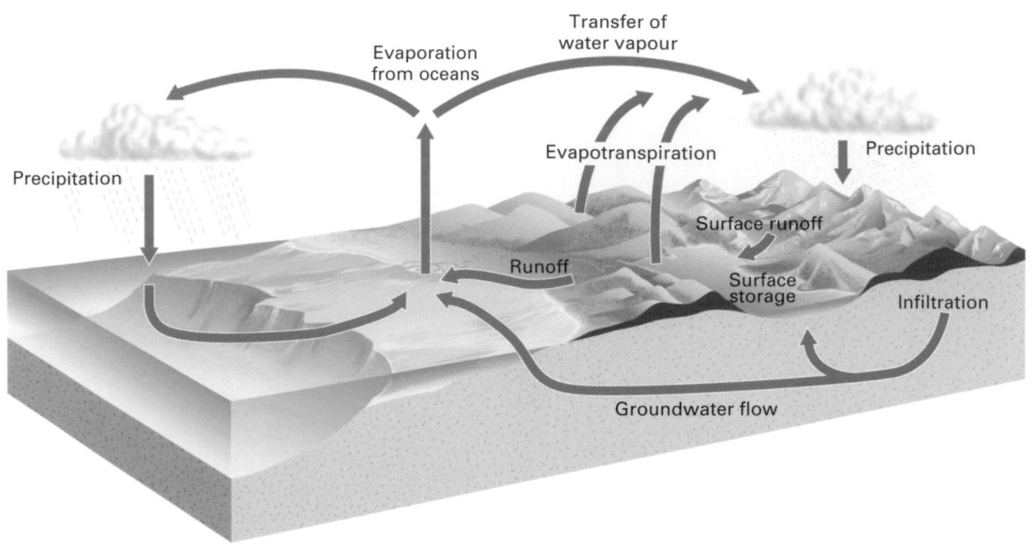

Water Distribution

The distribution of planetary water, by percentage. Oceans and ice caps together account for more than 99% of the total; the breakdown of the remainder is estimated.

All water
- Oceans 97.4%
- Fresh water 2.6%

Fresh water
- Ice caps and glaciers 76.6%
- Groundwater 22.7%
- Active water 0.5%

Active water
- Lakes 52%
- Soil moisture 36%
- Atmosphere 7.1%
- Rivers 1.4%
- Living things 3.5%

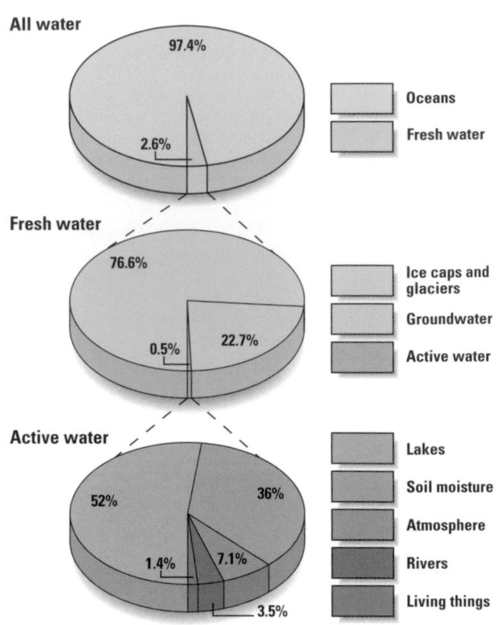

Water Utilization

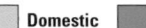

Domestic · Industrial · Agriculture

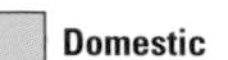

The percentage breakdown of water usage by sector, selected countries (2000)

Algeria, Australia, Egypt, France, Ghana, India, Mexico, Poland, Russia, Saudi Arabia, UK, USA

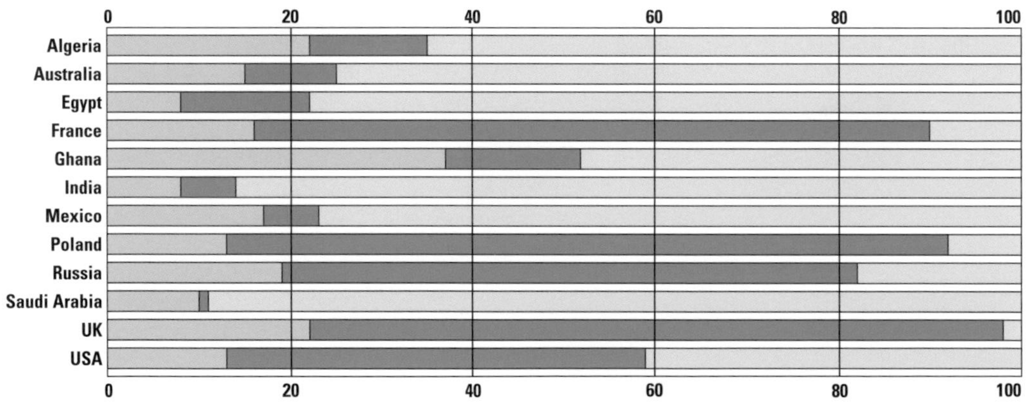

Water Usage

Almost all the world's water is 3,000 million years old, and all of it cycles endlessly through the hydrosphere, though at different rates. Water vapour circulates over days, even hours, deep ocean water circulates over millennia, and ice-cap water remains solid for millions of years.

Fresh water is essential to all terrestrial life. Humans cannot survive more than a few days without it, and even the hardiest desert plants and animals could not exist without some water. Agriculture requires huge quantities of fresh water: without large-scale irrigation most of the world's people would starve. In the USA, agriculture uses 41% and industry 46% of all water withdrawals.

According to the latest figures, the average North American uses 1.3 million litres per year. This is more than six times the average African, who uses just 186,000 litres of water each year. Europeans and Australians use 694,000 litres per year.

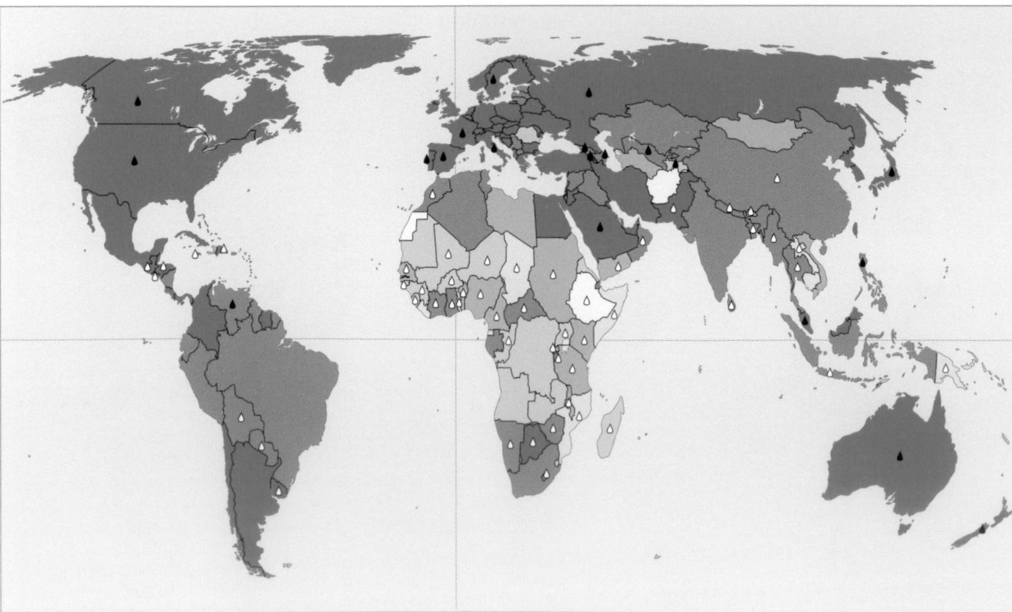

Water Supply

Percentage of total population with access to safe drinking water (2002)

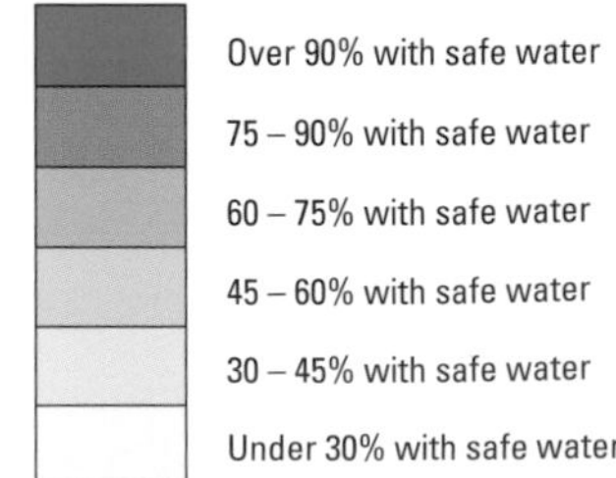

- Over 90% with safe water
- 75 – 90% with safe water
- 60 – 75% with safe water
- 45 – 60% with safe water
- 30 – 45% with safe water
- Under 30% with safe water
- ◊ Under 80 litres per person per day domestic water consumption
- ◆ Over 320 litres per person per day domestic water consumption

NB: 80 litres of water a day is considered necessary for a reasonable quality of life.

Least well-provided countries

Country	%	Country	%
Afghanistan	13%	Cambodia	34%
Ethiopia	22%	Papua New Guinea	39%
Chad	34%	Mozambique	42%

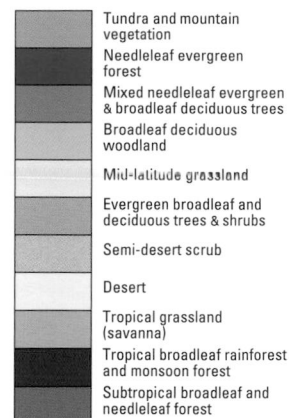

Natural Vegetation

Regional variation in vegetation

- Tundra and mountain vegetation
- Needleleaf evergreen forest
- Mixed needleleaf evergreen & broadleaf deciduous trees
- Broadleaf deciduous woodland
- Mid-latitude grassland
- Evergreen broadleaf and deciduous trees & shrubs
- Semi-desert scrub
- Desert
- Tropical grassland (savanna)
- Tropical broadleaf rainforest and monsoon forest
- Subtropical broadleaf and needleleaf forest

The map shows the natural 'climax vegetation' of regions, as dictated by climate and topography. In most cases, however, agricultural activity has drastically altered the vegetation pattern. Western Europe, for example, lost most of its broadleaf forest many centuries ago, while irrigation has turned some natural semi-desert into productive land.

Land Use by Continent (2003)

- Forest
- Permanent pasture
- Permanent crops
- Arable
- Other

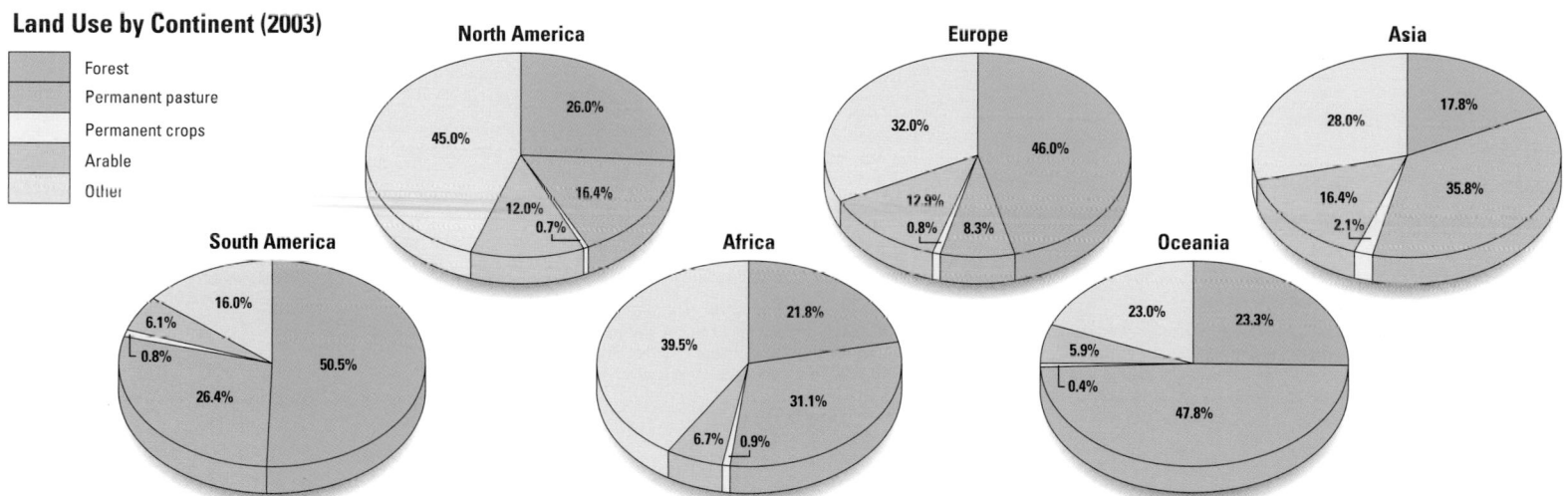

North America: 26.0%, 16.4%, 0.7%, 12.0%, 45.0%

Europe: 46.0%, 8.3%, 0.8%, 12.9%, 32.0%

Asia: 17.8%, 35.8%, 2.1%, 16.4%, 28.0%

South America: 50.5%, 26.4%, 0.8%, 6.1%, 16.0%

Africa: 21.8%, 31.1%, 0.9%, 6.7%, 39.5%

Oceania: 23.3%, 47.8%, 0.4%, 5.9%, 23.0%

Forestry: Production

Forest and woodland (million hectares)	Annual production (2004, million cubic metres) Fuelwood	Industrial roundwood*
World	*1,772.0*	*1654.7*
3,869.5		
Europe 1,039.3	116.7	510.9
S. America 885.6	192.2	163.5
Africa 649.9	549.7	70.2
N. & C. America 549.3	130.2	623.6
Asia 547.8	774.2	229.3
Oceania 197.6	9.0	48.1

Paper and Board

Top producers (2004)**		Top exporters (2004)**	
USA	83,611	Canada	15,352
China	53,463	Finland	12,708
Japan	29,253	Germany	11,525
Canada	20,578	Sweden	10,211
Germany	20,392	USA	8,934

* roundwood is timber as it is felled

** in thousand tonnes

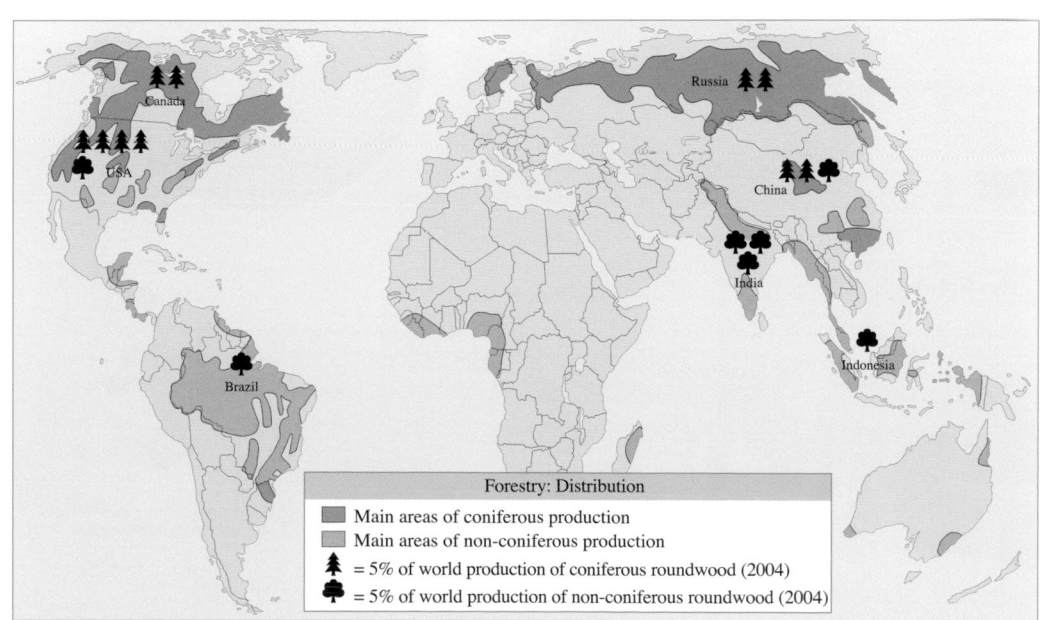

Forestry: Distribution

- Main areas of coniferous production
- Main areas of non-coniferous production
- 🌲 = 5% of world production of coniferous roundwood (2004)
- ♣ = 5% of world production of non-coniferous roundwood (2004)

Environment

Humans have always had a dramatic effect on their environment, at least since the development of agriculture almost 10,000 years ago. Generally, the Earth has accepted human interference without obvious ill effects: the complex systems that regulate the global environment have been able to absorb substantial damage while maintaining a stable and comfortable home for the planet's trillions of lifeforms. But advancing human technology and the rapidly-expanding populations it supports are now threatening to overwhelm the Earth's ability to compensate.

Industrial wastes, acid rainfall, desertification and large-scale deforestation all combine to create environmental change at a rate far faster than the great slow cycles of planetary evolution can accommodate. As a result of overcultivation, overgrazing and overcutting of groundcover for firewood, desertification is affecting as much as 60% of the world's croplands. In addition, with fire and chain-saws, humans are destroying more forest in a day than their ancestors could have done in a century, upsetting the balance between plant and animal, carbon dioxide and oxygen, on which all life ultimately depends.

The fossil fuels that power industrial civilization have pumped enough carbon dioxide and other so-called greenhouse gases into the atmosphere to make climatic change a near-certainty. As a result of the combination of these factors, the Earth's average temperature has risen by approximately 0.5°C [1°F] since the beginning of the 20th century, and it is still rising.

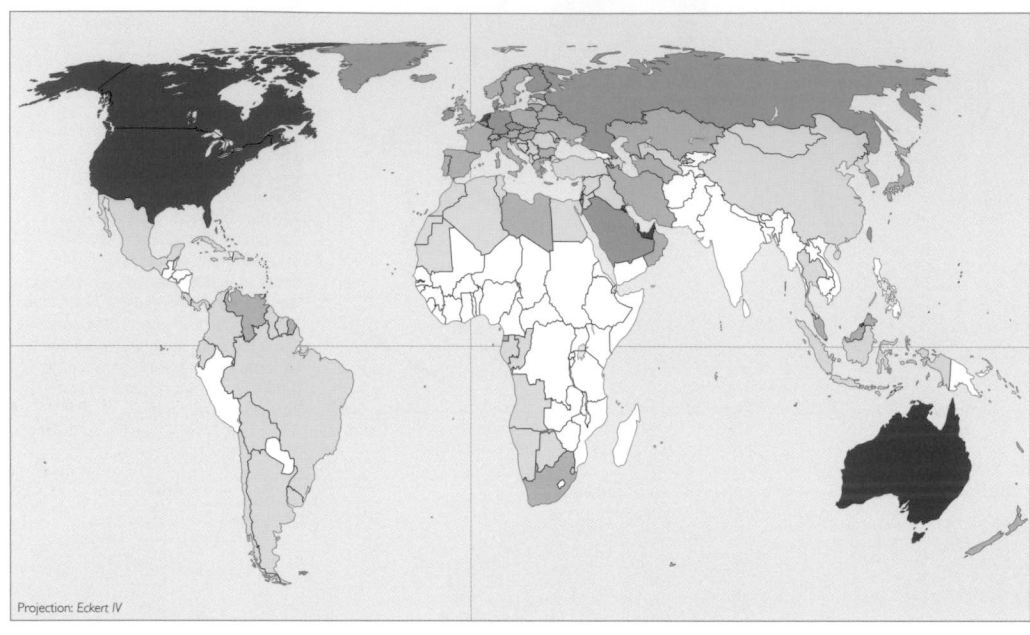

Projection: Eckert IV

Global Warming

Carbon dioxide emissions in tonnes per capita (2003)

■	Over 15
■	10 – 15
■	5 – 10
■	1 – 5
□	Under 1

High atmospheric concentrations of heat-absorbing gases appear to be causing a rise in average temperatures worldwide – up to 1.5°C [3°F] by the year 2020, according to some estimates. Global warming is likely to bring about a rise in sea levels that may flood some of the world's densely populated coastal areas.

Greenhouse Power

Relative contributions to the Greenhouse Effect by the major heat-absorbing gases in the atmosphere.

The chart combines greenhouse potency and volume. Carbon dioxide has a greenhouse potential of only 1, but its concentration of 350 parts per million makes it predominate. CFC 12, with 25,000 times the absorption capacity of CO_2, is present only as 0.00044 ppm.

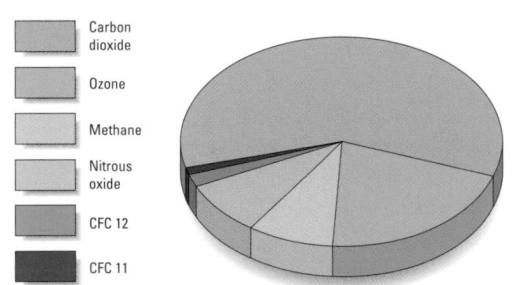

■	Carbon dioxide
■	Ozone
■	Methane
■	Nitrous oxide
■	CFC 12
■	CFC 11

Ozone Layer

The ozone 'hole' over the northern hemisphere in March 2000.

The colours represent Dobson Units (DU). The ozone 'hole' is seen as the dark blue and purple patch in the centre, where ozone values are around 120 DU or lower. Normal levels are around 280 DU. The ozone 'hole' over Antarctica is much larger.

Carbon Dioxide

Estimated percentage share of total world CO_2 emissions (2003)

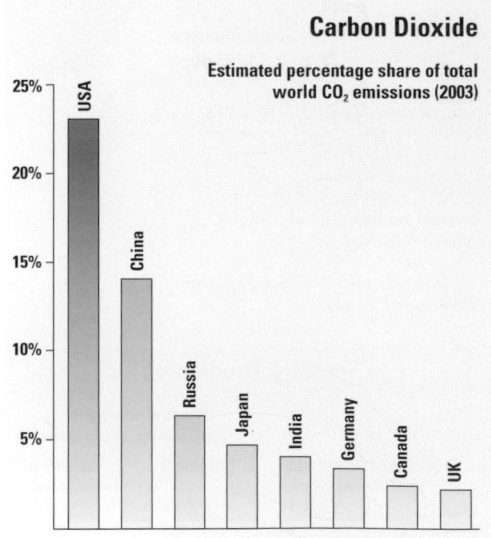

The Greenhouse Effect

Carbon dioxide is increased by burning fossil fuels and cutting forests

Carbon Dioxide

Rising temperatures would melt snow and ice causing oceans to rise

Carbon dioxide and other greenhouse gases trap the heat being reflected from the Earth, although some heat is lost

The warming increases water vapour in the air, leading to even greater absorption of heat

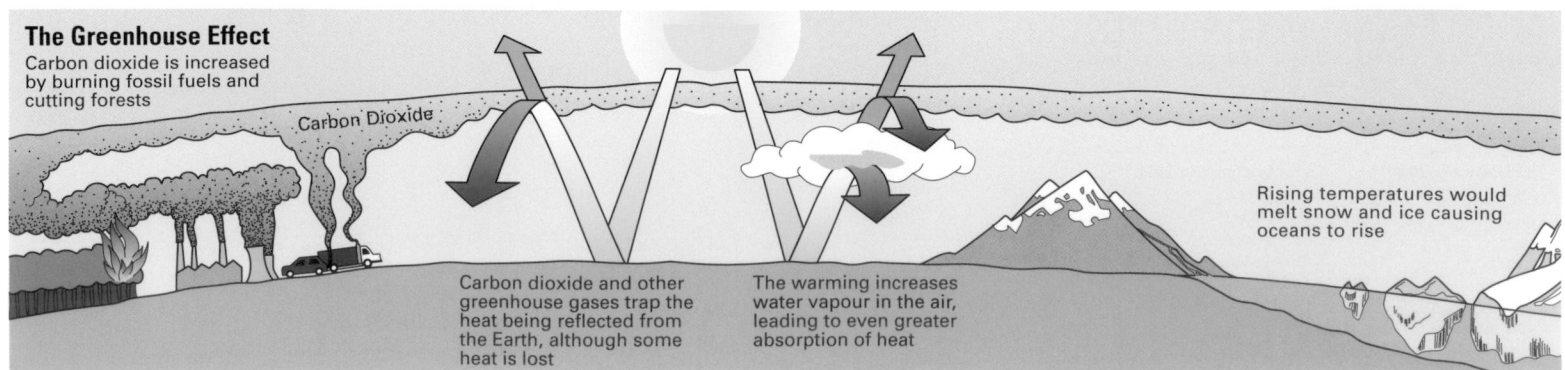

Desertification

	Existing deserts
	Areas with a high risk of desertification
	Areas with a moderate risk of desertification
	Former areas of rainforest
	Existing rainforest

Forest Clearance

Thousands of hectares of forest cleared annually, tropical countries surveyed 1980–85, 1990–95 and 2000–05. Loss as a percentage of remaining stocks is shown in figures on each column. Gain is indicated as a minus figure.

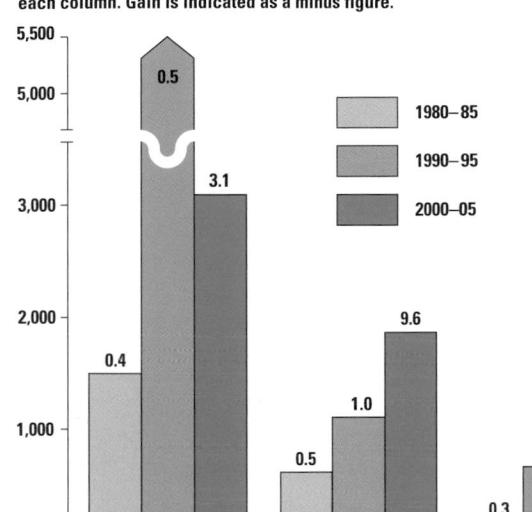

Legend:
- 1980–85
- 1990–95
- 2000–05

Brazil: 0.4, 0.5, 3.1
Indonesia: 0.5, 1.0, 9.6
India: 0.3, 0.0, 0.7
Burma: 0.3, 1.4, 4.7
Thailand: 2.4, 2.6, 2.0
Vietnam: 0.7, 1.4, -12.2
Philippines: 1.0, 3.5, 4.2
Costa Rica: 4.0, 3.0, -0.6

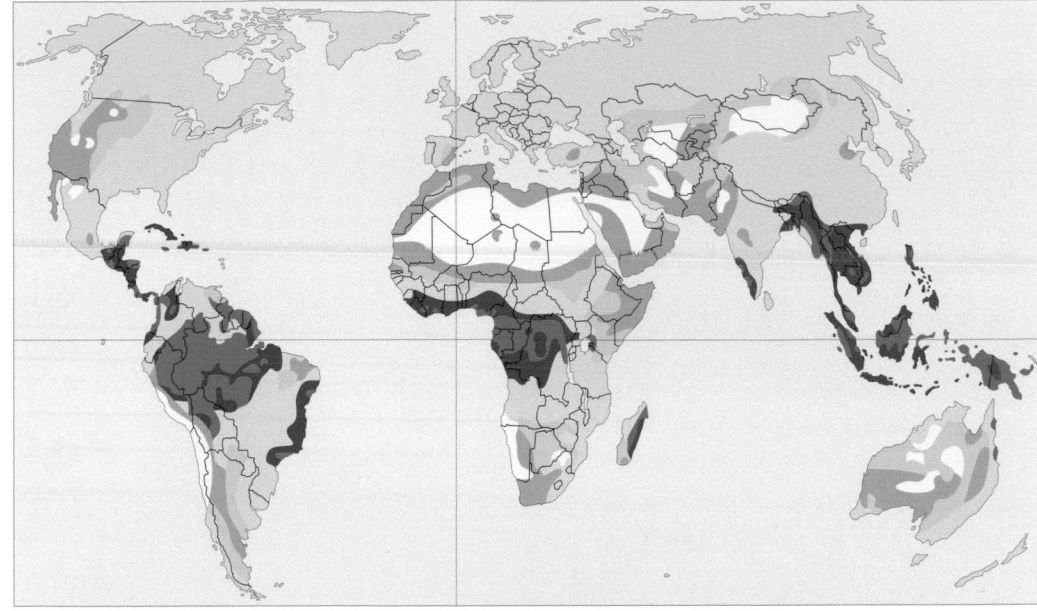

Deforestation

The Earth's remaining forests are under attack from three directions: expanding agriculture, logging, and growing consumption of fuelwood, often in combination. Sometimes deforestation is the direct result of government policy, as in the efforts made to resettle the urban poor in some parts of Brazil; just as often, it comes about despite state attempts at conservation. Loggers, licensed or unlicensed, blaze a trail into virgin forest, often destroying twice as many trees as they harvest. Landless farmers follow, burning away most of what remains to plant their crops, completing the destruction. Some countries such as Vietnam and Costa Rica have successfully implemented reafforestation programmes.

Ozone Depletion

The ozone layer, 25–30 km [15–18 miles] above sea level, acts as a barrier to most of the Sun's harmful ultra-violet radiation, protecting us from the ionizing radiation that can cause skin cancer and cataracts. In recent years, however, two holes in the ozone layer have been observed during winter: one over the Arctic and the other, the size of the USA, over Antarctica. By 1996, ozone had been reduced to around a half of its 1970 amount. The ozone (O_3) is broken down by chlorine released into the atmosphere as CFCs (chlorofluorocarbons) – chemicals used in refrigerators, packaging and aerosols.

Air Pollution

Sulphur dioxide is the main pollutant associated with industrial cities. According to the World Health Organization, at least 600 million people live in urban areas where sulphur dioxide concentrations regularly reach damaging levels. One of the world's most dangerously polluted urban areas is Mexico City, due to a combination of its enclosed valley location, 3 million cars and 60,000 factories. In May 1998, this lethal cocktail was added to by nearby forest fires and the resultant air pollution led to over 20% of the population (3 million people) complaining of respiratory problems.

Acid Rain

Killing trees, poisoning lakes, and rivers and eating away buildings, acid rain is mostly produced by sulphur dioxide emissions from industry and volcanic eruptions. By the mid 1990s, acid rain had sterilized 4,000 or more of Sweden's lakes and left 45% of Switzerland's alpine conifers dead or dying, while the monuments of Greece were dissolving in Athens' smog. Prevailing wind patterns mean that the acids often fall many hundred kilometres from where the original pollutants were discharged. In parts of Europe acid deposition has slightly decreased, following reductions in emissions, but not by enough.

World Pollution

Acid rain and sources of acidic emissions (latest available year)

Acid rain is caused by high levels of sulphur and nitrogen in the atmosphere. They combine with water vapour and oxygen to form acids (H_2SO_4 and HNO_3) which fall as precipitation.

- Regions where sulphur and nitrogen oxides are released in high concentrations, mainly from fossil fuel combustion
- Major cities with high levels of air pollution (including nitrogen and sulphur emissions)

Areas of heavy acid deposition

pH numbers indicate acidity, decreasing from a neutral 7. Normal rain, slightly acid from dissolved carbon dioxide, never exceeds a pH of 5.6.

- pH less than 4.0 (most acidic)
- pH 4.0 to 4.5
- pH 4.5 to 5.0
- Areas where acid rain is a potential problem

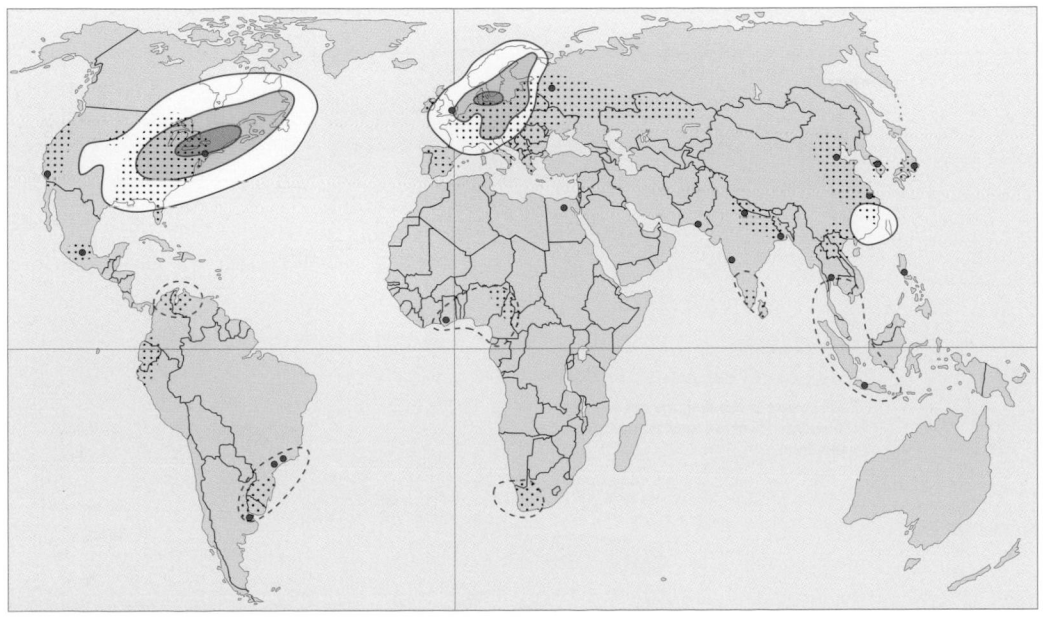

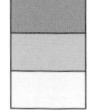

Population

Demographic Profiles

Developed nations such as the UK have populations evenly spread across the age groups and, usually, a growing proportion of elderly people. The great majority of the people in developing nations, however, are in the younger age groups, about to enter their most fertile years. In time, these population profiles should resemble the world profile (even Nigeria has made recent progress with reducing its birth rate), but the transition will come about only after a few more generations of rapid population growth.

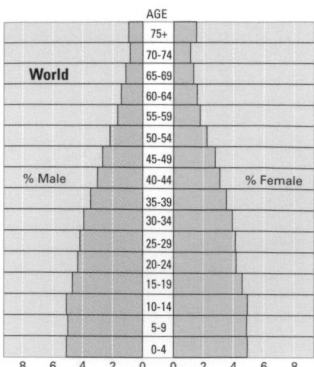

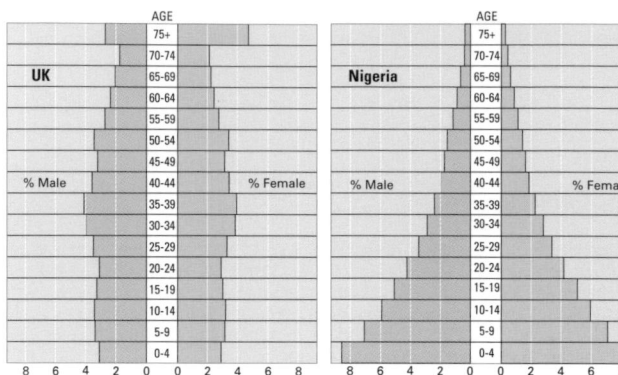

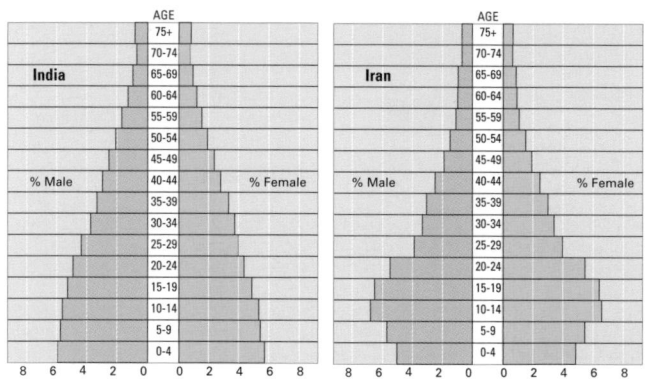

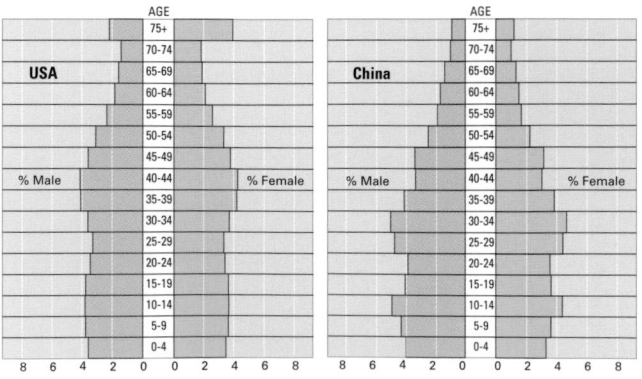

Most Populous Nations, in millions (2005 estimates)

1.	China	1,306	9. Nigeria	129	17. Turkey	70
2.	India	1,080	10. Japan	127	18. Iran	68
3.	USA	296	11. Mexico	106	19. Thailand	65
4.	Indonesia	242	12. Philippines	88	20. France	61
5.	Brazil	186	13. Vietnam	84	21. UK	60
6.	Pakistan	162	14. Germany	82	22. Congo (Dem. Rep.)	60
7.	Bangladesh	144	15. Egypt	78	23. Italy	58
8.	Russia	143	16. Ethiopia	73	24. South Korea	48

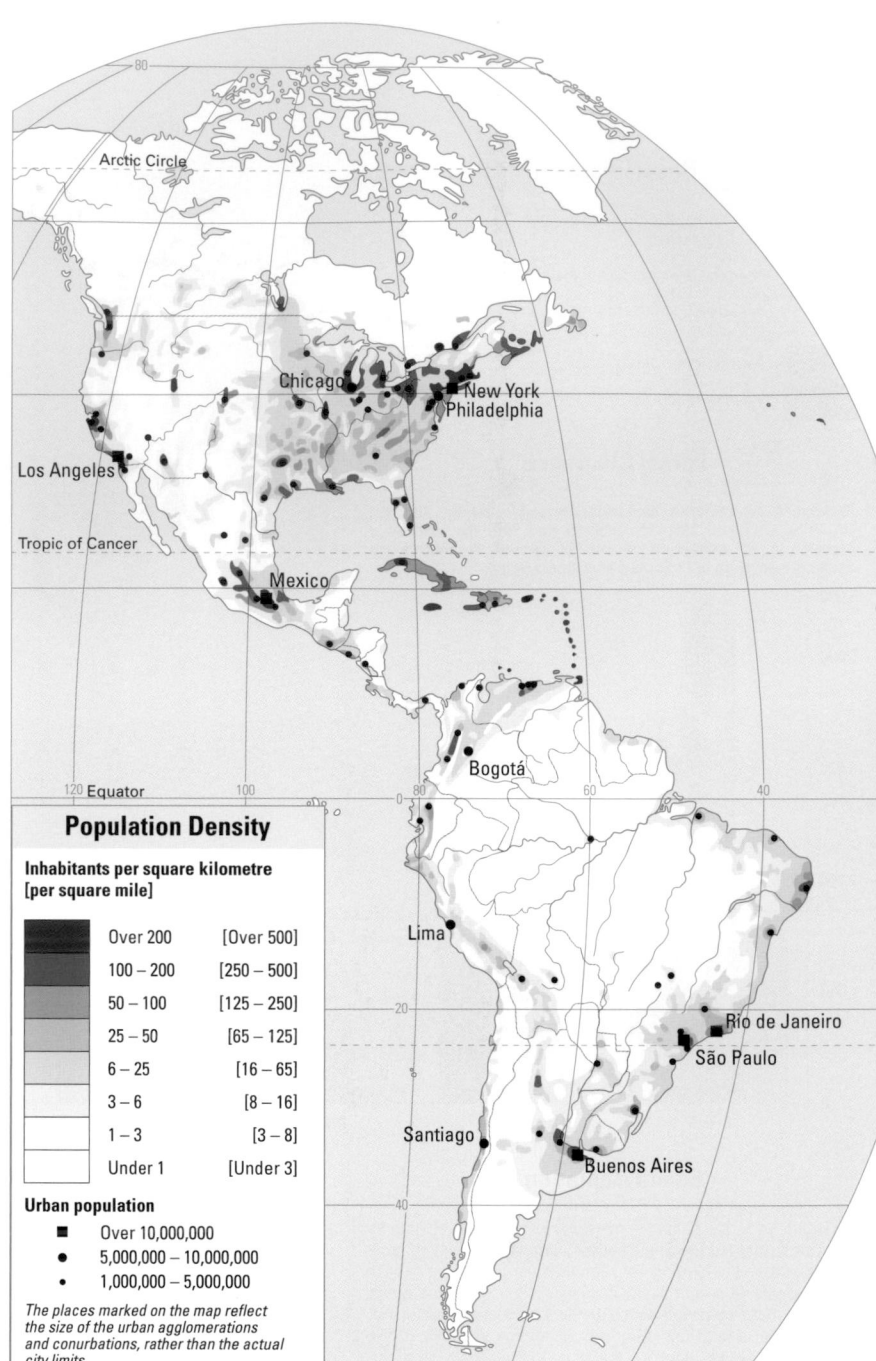

Population Density

Inhabitants per square kilometre [per square mile]

Over 200	[Over 500]
100 – 200	[250 – 500]
50 – 100	[125 – 250]
25 – 50	[65 – 125]
6 – 25	[16 – 65]
3 – 6	[8 – 16]
1 – 3	[3 – 8]
Under 1	[Under 3]

Urban population

- ■ Over 10,000,000
- ● 5,000,000 – 10,000,000
- • 1,000,000 – 5,000,000

The places marked on the map reflect the size of the urban agglomerations and conurbations, rather than the actual city limits.

Continental Comparisons

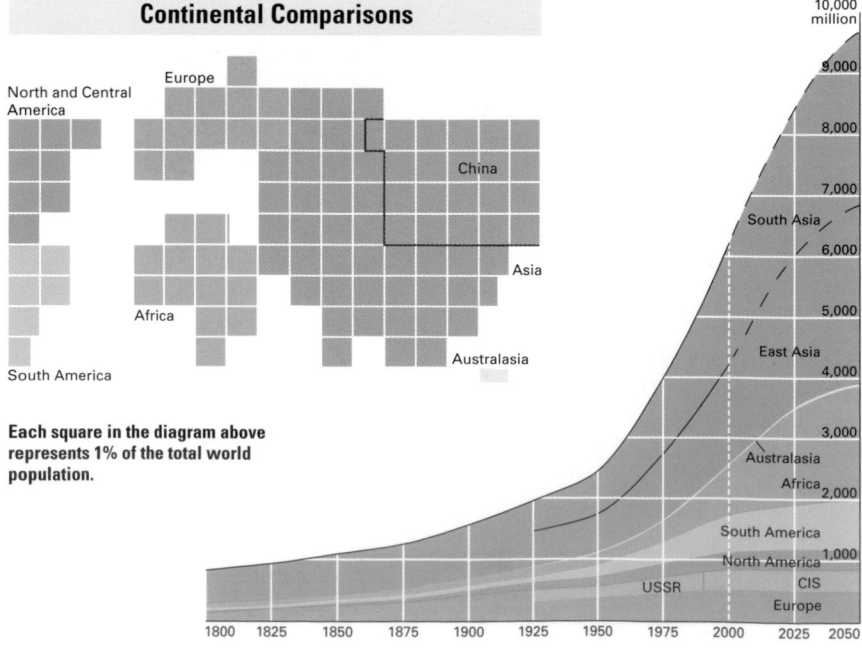

Each square in the diagram above represents 1% of the total world population.

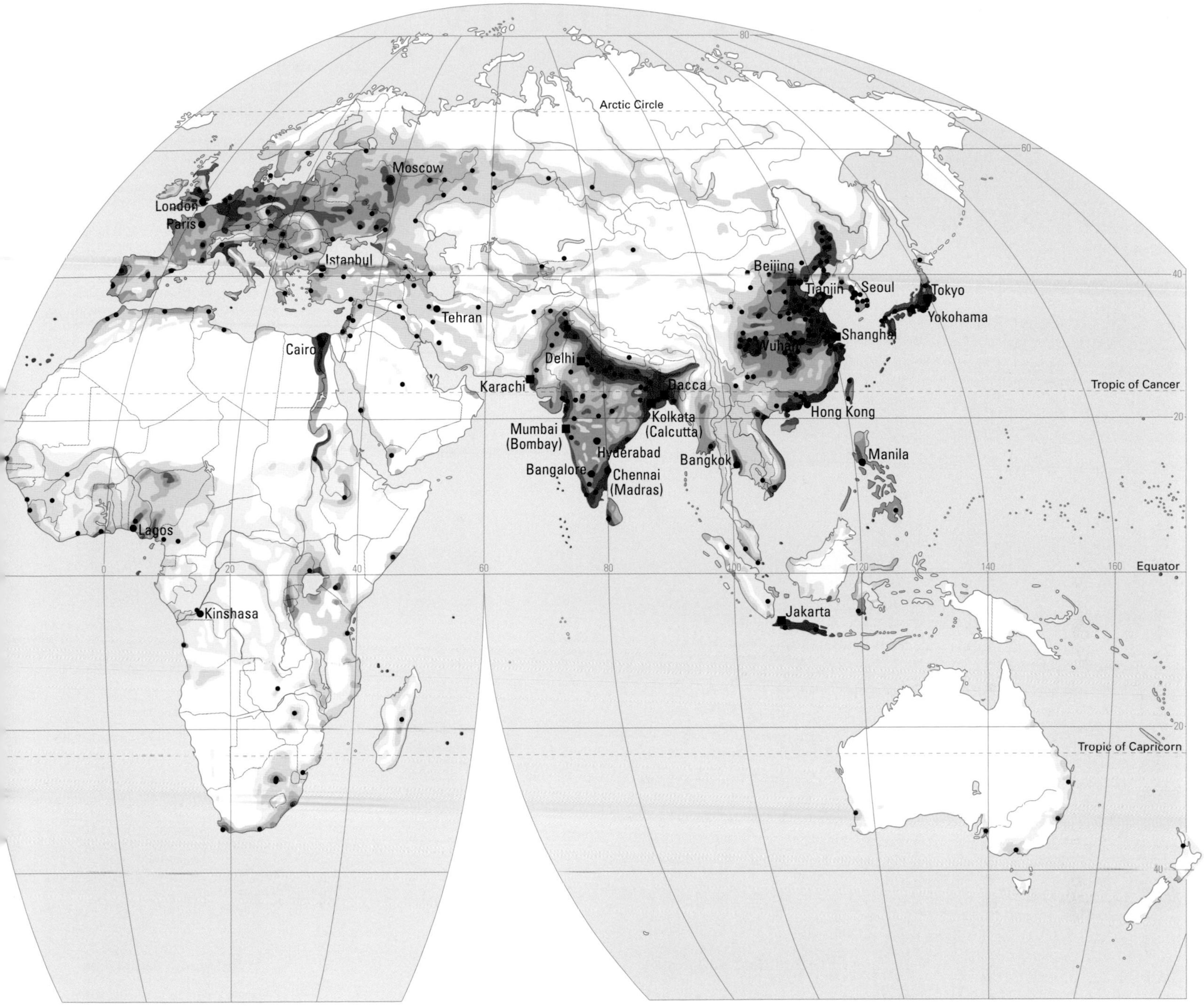

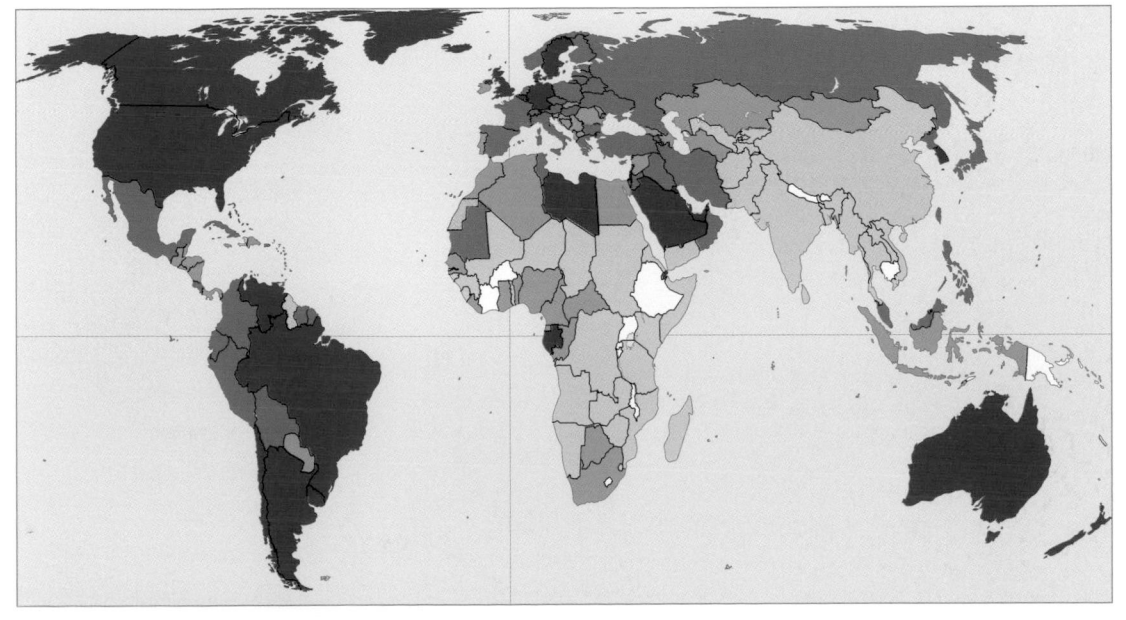

Arctic Circle

Moscow

London
Paris

Istanbul

Tehran

Cairo

Beijing

Tianjin   Seoul   Tokyo

Yokohama

Wuhan   Shanghai

Delhi

Tropic of Cancer

Karachi   Dacca

Hong Kong

Mumbai   Kolkata
(Bombay)   (Calcutta)

Hyderabad   Manila

Bangalore   Bangkok

Chennai
(Madras)

Lagos

Equator

Jakarta

Kinshasa

Tropic of Capricorn

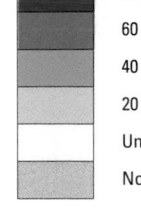

Urban Population

**Percentage of total population living in towns and
cities (2003)**

■	Over 80%
■	60 – 80%
■	40 – 60%
■	20 – 40%
☐	Under 20%
	No data available

Most urbanized

Singapore 100%
Belgium 97%
Kuwait 96%
Iceland 93%
Uruguay 92%

Least urbanized

East Timor 8%
Bhutan 8%
Burundi 10%
Uganda 12%
Papua New Guinea .13%

The Human Family

Predominant Languages

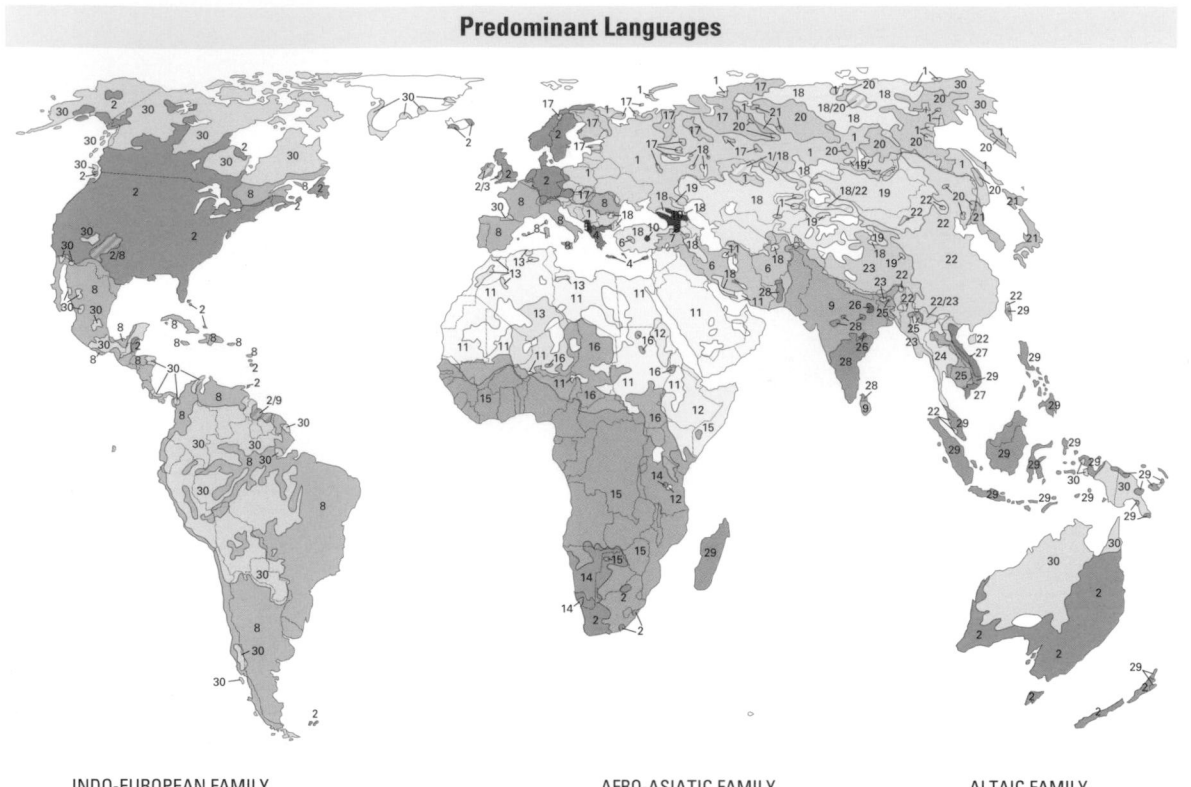

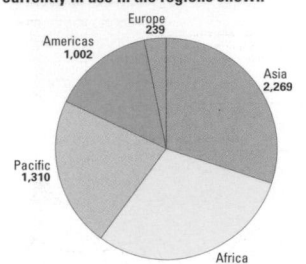
INDO-EUROPEAN FAMILY

1 Balto-Slavic group (incl. Russian, Ukrainian)
2 Germanic group (incl. English, German)
3 Celtic group
4 Greek
5 Albanian
6 Iranian group
7 Armenian
8 Romance group (incl. Spanish, Portuguese, French, Italian)
9 Indo-Aryan group (incl. Hindi, Bengali, Urdu, Punjabi, Marathi)
10 CAUCASIAN FAMILY

AFRO-ASIATIC FAMILY

11 Semitic group (incl. Arabic)
12 Kushitic group
13 Berber group

14 KHOISAN FAMILY

15 NIGER-CONGO FAMILY

16 NILO-SAHARAN FAMILY

17 URALIC FAMILY

ALTAIC FAMILY

18 Turkic group (incl. Turkish)
19 Mongolian group
20 Tungus-Manchu group
21 Japanese and Korean

SINO-TIBETAN FAMILY

22 Sinitic (Chinese) languages (incl. Mandarin, Wu, Yue)
23 Tibetic-Burmic languages

24 TAI FAMILY

AUSTRO-ASIATIC FAMILY

25 Mon-Khmer group
26 Munda group
27 Vietnamese

28 DRAVIDIAN FAMILY (incl. Telugu, Tamil)

29 AUSTRONESIAN FAMILY (incl. Malay-Indonesian, Javanese)

30 OTHER LANGUAGES

Predominant Religions

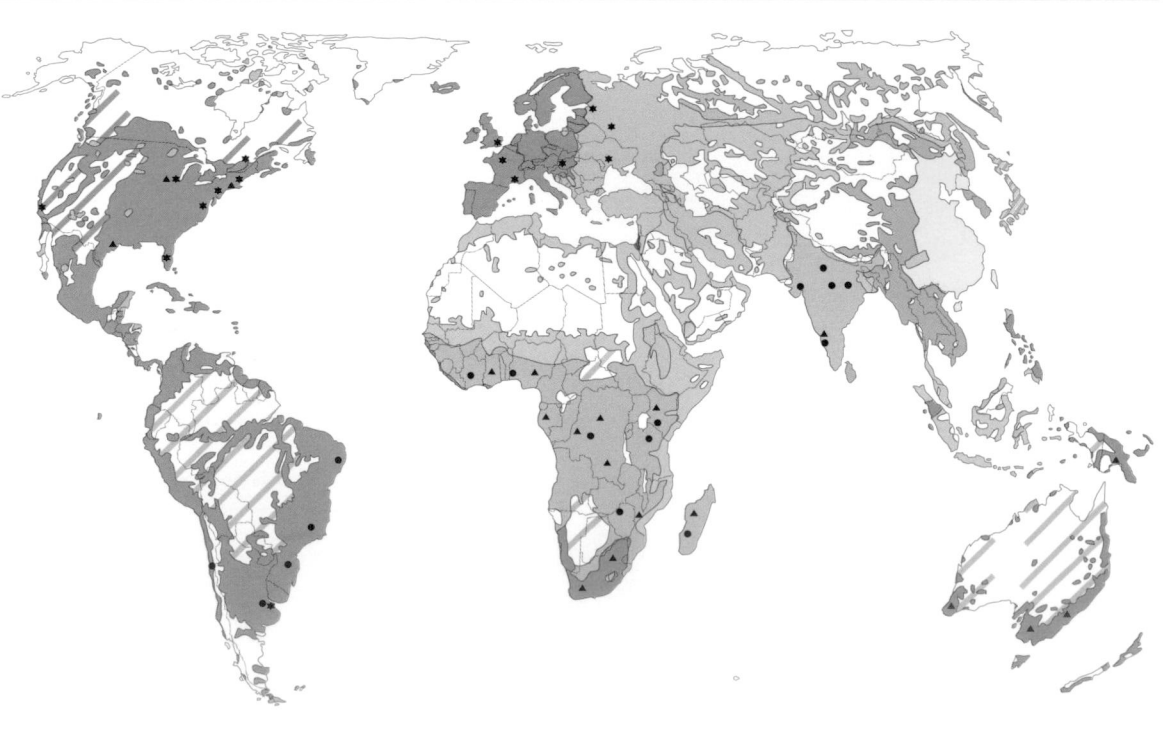

Religious Adherents

Religious adherents in millions (2005)

Christianity	2,100	Hindu	832
Roman Catholic	*1,050*	Chinese folk	394
Protestant	*396*	Buddhism	329
Orthodox	*240*	Ethnic religions	300
Anglican	*73*	New religions	103
Others	*341*	Sikhism	23
Islam	1,070	Judaism	15
Sunni	*940*	Spiritism	12
Shi'ite	*120*	Baha'i	6
Others	*10*	Confucianism	6
Non-religious/		Jainism	5
Agnostic/Atheist	1,100	Shintoism	3

- Roman Catholicism
- Orthodox and other Eastern Churches
- Protestantism
- Sunni Islam
- Shi'ite Islam
- Buddhism
- Hinduism
- Confucianism
- Judaism
- Shintoism
- Tribal Religions

United Nations

Created in 1945 to promote peace and co-operation and based in New York, the United Nations is the world's largest international organization, with 191 members and an annual budget of US $1.8 billion (2005). Each member of the General Assembly has one vote, while the five permanent members of the 15-nation Security Council – China, France, Russia, UK and USA – hold a veto. The Secretariat is the UN's principal administrative arm. The 54 members of the Economic and Social Council are responsible for economic, social, cultural, educational, health and related matters. The UN has 16 specialized agencies – based in Canada, France, Switzerland and Italy, as well as the USA – which help members in fields such as education (UNESCO), agriculture (FAO), medicine (WHO) and finance (IFC). By the end of 1994, all the original 11 trust territories of the Trusteeship Council had become independent.

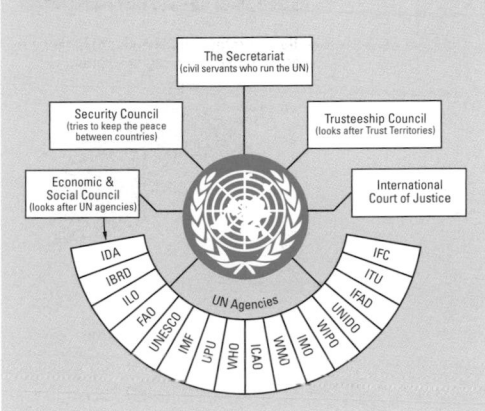

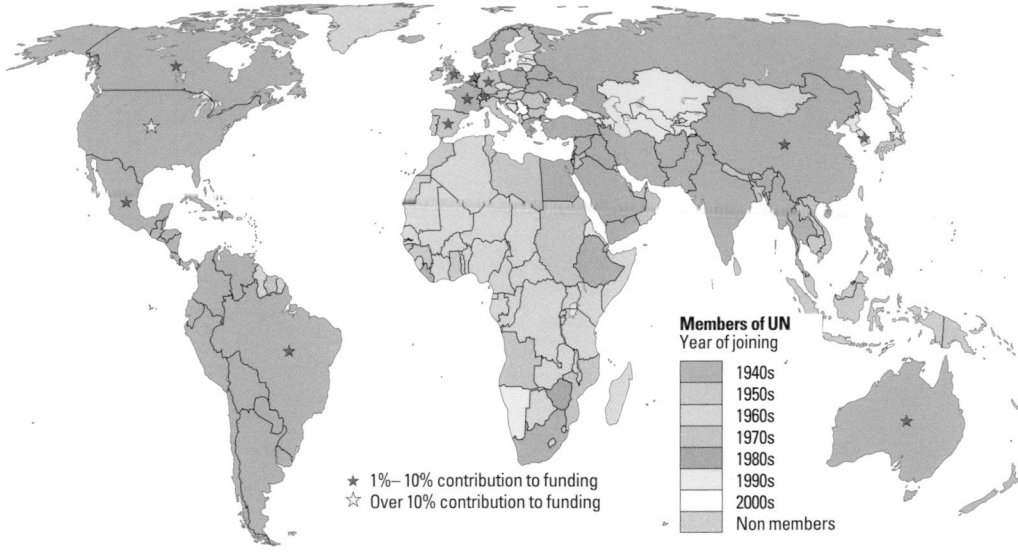

Members of UN
Year of joining
- 1940s
- 1950s
- 1960s
- 1970s
- 1980s
- 1990s
- 2000s

★ 1%– 10% contribution to funding
☆ Over 10% contribution to funding

☆ Non members

MEMBERSHIP OF THE UN In 1945 there were 51 members; by the end of 2002 membership had increased to 191 following the admission of East Timor and Switzerland. There are 2 independent states which are not members of the UN – Taiwan and the Vatican City. All the successor states of the former USSR had joined by the end of 1992. The official languages of the UN are Chinese, English, French, Russian, Spanish and Arabic.

FUNDING The UN regular budget for 2005 was US $1.8 billion. Contributions are assessed by the members' ability to pay, with the maximum 22% of the total (USA's share), the minimum 0.01%. The European Union pays over 37% of the budget.

PEACEKEEPING The UN has been involved in 54 peacekeeping operations worldwide since 1948.

International Organizations

ACP African-Caribbean-Pacific (formed in 1963). Members have economic ties with the EU.

APEC Asia-Pacific Economic Co-operation (formed in 1989). It aims to enhance economic growth and prosperity for the region and to strengthen the Asia-Pacific community. APEC is the only intergovernmental grouping in the world operating on the basis of non-binding commitments, open dialogue, and equal respect for the views of all participants. There are 21 member economies.

ARAB LEAGUE (formed in 1945). The League's aim is to promote economic, social, political and military co-operation. There are 22 member nations.

ASEAN Association of South-east Asian Nations (formed in 1967). Cambodia joined in 1999.

AU The African Union replaced the Organization of African Unity (formed in 1963) in 2002. Its 53 members represent over 94% of Africa's population. Arabic, French, Portuguese and English are recognized as working languages.

COLOMBO PLAN (formed in 1951). Its 25 members aim to promote economic and social development in Asia and the Pacific.

COMMONWEALTH The Commonwealth of Nations evolved from the British Empire. Pakistan was suspended in 1999, and Zimbabwe in 2002. In response to its continued suspension, Zimbabwe left the Commonwealth in December 2003. It now comprises 16 Queen's realms, 31 republics and 6 indigenous monarchies, giving a total of 53 member states.

EU European Union (evolved from the European Community in 1993). Cyprus, the Czech Republic, Estonia, Hungary, Latvia, Lithuania, Malta, Poland, the Slovak Republic and Slovenia joined the EU in May 2004. The other members are Austria, Belgium, Denmark, Finland, France, Germany, Greece, Ireland, Italy, Luxembourg, Netherlands, Portugal, Spain, Sweden and the UK – together these 25 countries aim to integrate economies, co-ordinate social developments and bring about political union. Bulgaria and Romania are expected to join in 2007.

LAIA Latin American Integration Association (1980). Its aim is to promote freer regional trade.

NATO North Atlantic Treaty Organization (formed in 1949). It continues after 1991 despite the winding up of the Warsaw Pact. Bulgaria, Estonia, Latvia, Lithuania, Romania, the Slovak Republic and Slovenia became members in 2004.

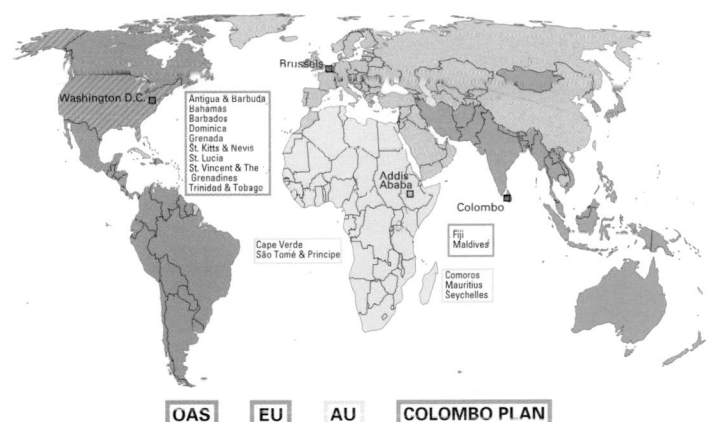

OAS EU AU COLOMBO PLAN

OAS Organization of American States (formed in 1948). It aims to promote social and economic co-operation between developed countries of North America and developing nations of Latin America.

OECD Organization for Economic Co-operation and Development (formed in 1961). It comprises 30 major free-market economies. Poland, Hungary and South Korea joined in 1996, and the Slovak Republic in 2000. 'G8' is its 'inner group' of leading industrial nations, comprising Canada, France, Germany, Italy, Japan, Russia, UK and USA.

OPEC Organization of Petroleum Exporting Countries (formed in 1960). It controls about three-quarters of the world's oil supply. Gabon left the organization in 1996.

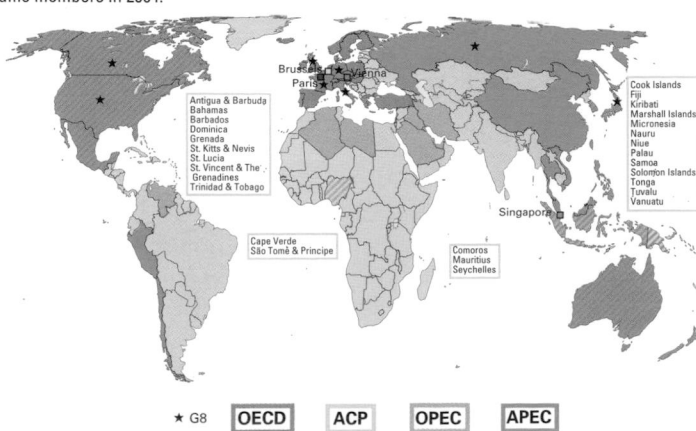

★ G8 OECD ACP OPEC APEC

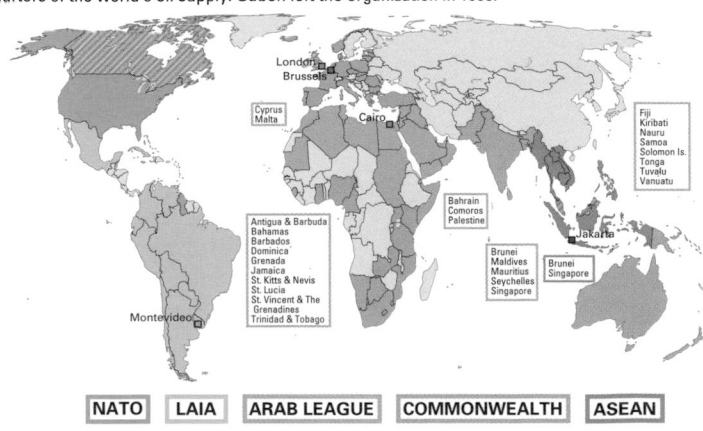

NATO LAIA ARAB LEAGUE COMMONWEALTH ASEAN

Wealth

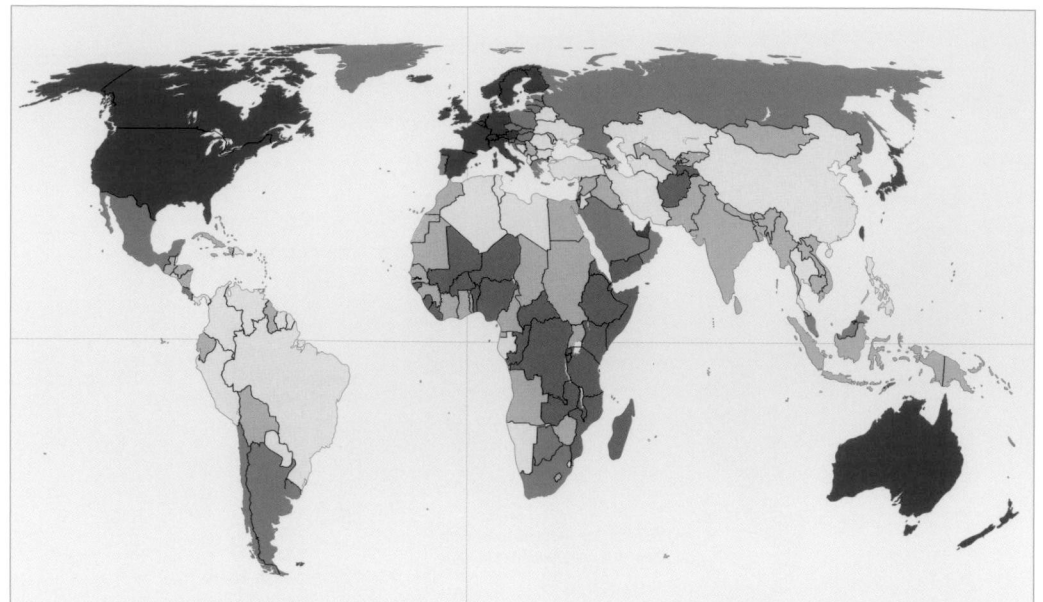

Levels of Income

Gross Domestic Product per capita: the annual value of goods and services divided by the population, using purchasing power parity (PPP) (2005)

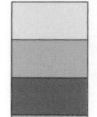

- Over 250% of world average
- 100% – 250% of world average

[World average per person US $9,300]

- 50% – 100% of world average
- 15% – 50% of world average
- Under 15% of world average
- No data available

Wealth Creation

The Gross Domestic Product (GDP) of the world's largest economies, US $ million (2005)

1.	USA	12,370,000	23. Netherlands	500,000
2.	China	8,158,000	24. Poland	489,000
3.	Japan	3,867,000	25. Philippines	451,000
4.	India	3,678,000	26. Pakistan	385,000
5.	Germany	2,446,000	27. Saudi Arabia	341,000
6.	UK	1,867,000	28. Egypt	338,000
7.	France	1,816,000	29. Belgium	329,000
8.	Italy	1,645,000	30. Ukraine	321,000
9.	Brazil	1,580,000	31. Colombia	303,000
10.	Russia	1,535,000	32. Bangladesh	300,000
11.	Canada	1,077,000	33. Austria	269,000
12.	Mexico	1,066,000	34. Sweden	267,000
13.	Spain	1,014,000	35. Switzerland	262,000
14.	South Korea	983,000	36. Hong Kong	254,000
15.	Indonesia	899,000	37. Vietnam	252,000
16.	Australia	643,000	38. Malaysia	248,000
17.	Taiwan	611,000	39. Greece	243,000
18.	Turkey	552,000	40. Algeria	237,000
19.	Iran	552,000	41. Portugal	195,000
20.	Thailand	546,000	42. Norway	195,000
21.	Argentina	537,000	43. Romania	186,000
22.	South Africa	527,000	44. Czech Republic	185,000

The Wealth Gap

The world's richest and poorest countries, by Gross Domestic Product per capita in US $ (2005)

1.	Luxembourg	62,700	1. East Timor	400
2.	Norway	42,400	2. Comoros	600
3.	USA	41,800	3. Gaza Strip	600
4.	Hong Kong (China)	36,800	4. Malawi	600
5.	Switzerland	35,000	5. Somalia	600
6.	Iceland	34,600	6. Burundi	700
7.	San Marino	34,600	7. Liberia	700
8.	Ireland	34,100	8. Tanzania	700
9.	Denmark	33,500	9. Afghanistan	800
10.	Austria	32,900	10. Congo	800
11.	Canada	32,800	11. Congo (Dem. Rep.)	800
12.	Australia	32,000	12. Ethiopia	800
13.	Belgium	31,800	13. Guinea-Bissau	800
14.	UK	30,900	14. Kiribati	800
15.	Netherlands	30,500	15. Sierra Leone	800
16.	Japan	30,400	16. Yemen	800
17.	Finland	30,300	17. Madagascar	900
18.	France	29,900	18. Niger	900
19.	Germany	29,700	19. Zambia	900
20.	Singapore	29,700	20. Eritrea	1,100

GDP per capita is calculated by dividing a country's Gross Domestic Product by its total population.

Continental Shares

Shares of population and of wealth (GNI) by continent

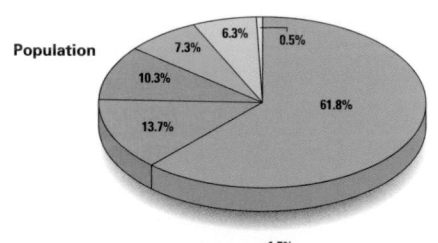
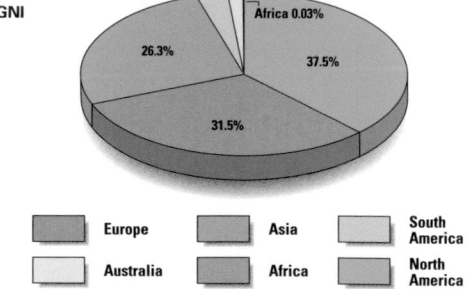

- Europe
- Asia
- South America
- Australia
- Africa
- North America

Inflation

Average annual rate of inflation (2005)

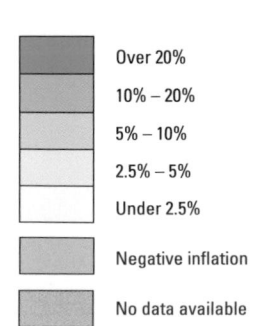

- Over 20%
- 10% – 20%
- 5% – 10%
- 2.5% – 5%
- Under 2.5%
- Negative inflation
- No data available

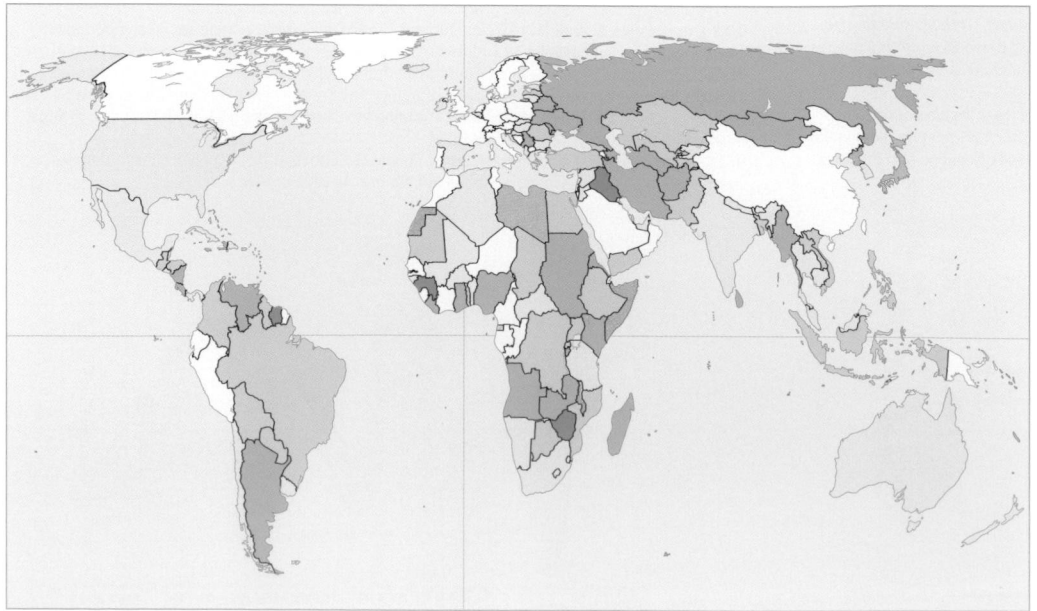

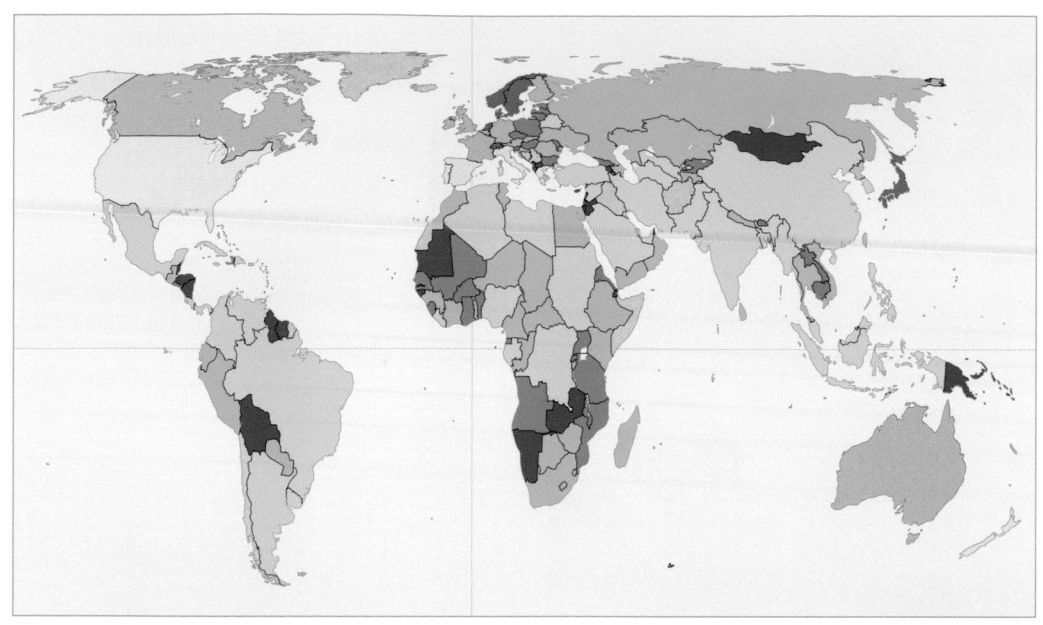

Official Development Assistance (ODA) provided and received, per capita (2002)

- Over $100 per person
- $50 – $100 per person
- $20 – $50 per person

Providers

- Under $10 per person
- $10 – $25 per person
- $25 – $50 per person
- Over $50 per person

Receivers

- No data available

Debt and Aid

International debtors and the aid they receive

Although aid grants make a vital contribution to many of the world's poorer countries, they are usually dwarfed by the burden of debt that the developing economies are expected to repay. It is estimated that the total debt burden of developing countries is US $523 billion.

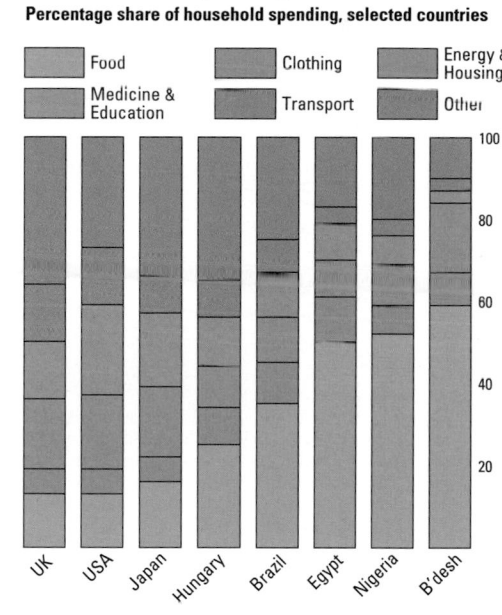

- Debt, US $ per capita (2002)
- Aid, US $ per capita (2002)

Distribution of Spending

Percentage share of household spending, selected countries

- Food
- Clothing
- Energy & Housing
- Medicine & Education
- Transport
- Other

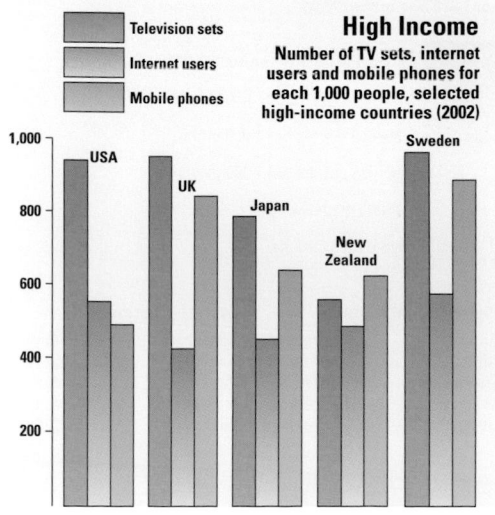

High Income

- Television sets
- Internet users
- Mobile phones

Number of TV sets, internet users and mobile phones for each 1,000 people, selected high-income countries (2002)

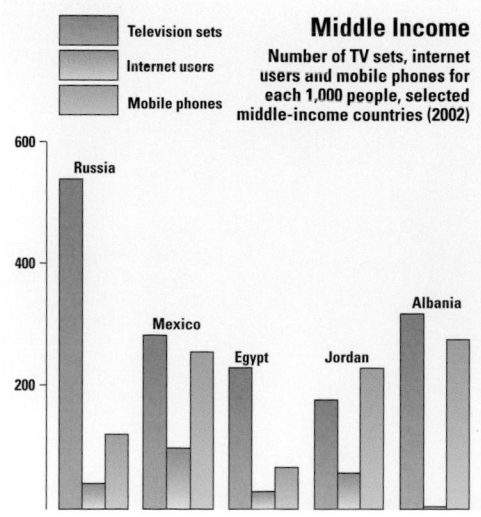

Middle Income

- Television sets
- Internet users
- Mobile phones

Number of TV sets, internet users and mobile phones for each 1,000 people, selected middle-income countries (2002)

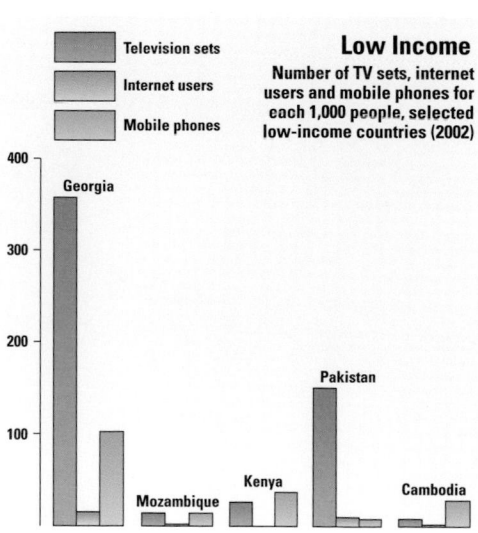

Low Income

- Television sets
- Internet users
- Mobile phones

Number of TV sets, internet users and mobile phones for each 1,000 people, selected low-income countries (2002)

Quality of Life

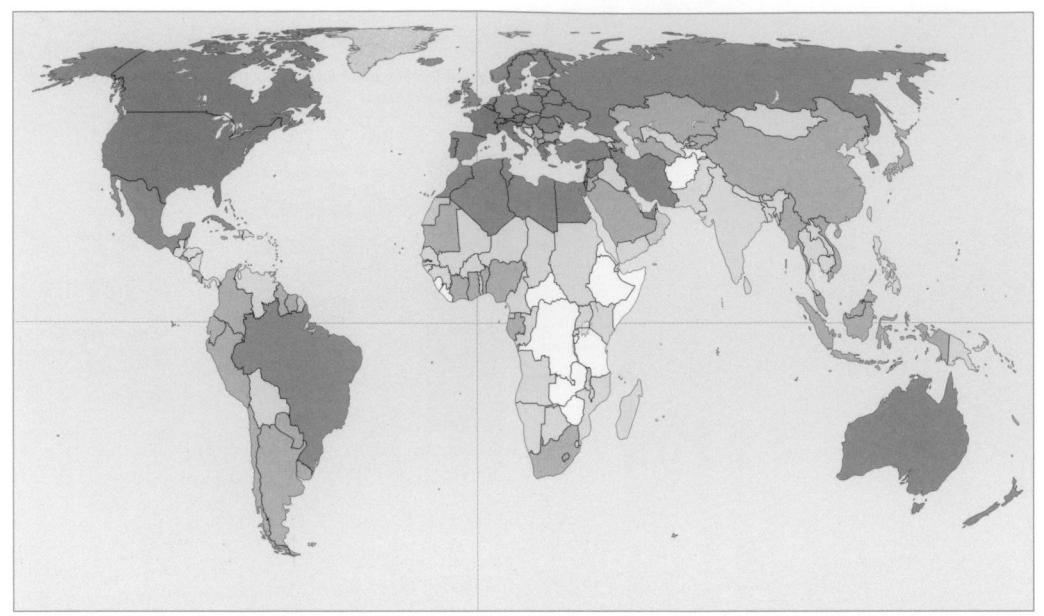

Daily Food Consumption

Average daily food intake in calories per person (2003)

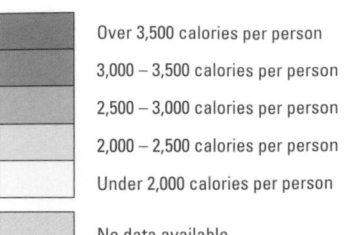

Over 3,500 calories per person

3,000 – 3,500 calories per person

2,500 – 3,000 calories per person

2,000 – 2,500 calories per person

Under 2,000 calories per person

No data available

Hospital Capacity

Hospital beds available for each 1,000 people (2003)

Highest capacity		Lowest capacity	
Monaco	19.6	Nepal	0.2
Japan	14.7	Bangladesh	0.3
North Korea	13.6	Somalia	0.4
Niue	13.0	Afghanistan	0.4
Belarus	11.3	Guatemala	0.5
Russia	10.5	Cambodia	0.5
Germany	8.9	Yemen	0.6
Ukraine	8.8	Burma (Myanmar)	0.6
Lithuania	8.7	Sudan	0.7
Czech Republic	8.6	Pakistan	0.7

Although the ratio of people to hospital beds gives a good approximation of a country's health provision, it is not an absolute indicator. Raw numbers may mask inefficiency and other weaknesses: the high availability of beds in Belarus, for example, has not prevented infant mortality rates over three times as high as in the United Kingdom and the United States.

Life Expectancy

Years of life expectancy at birth, selected countries (2005)

The chart shows combined data for both sexes. On average, women live longer than men worldwide, even in developing countries with high maternal mortality rates. Overall, life expectancy is steadily rising, though the difference between rich and poor nations remains dramatic.

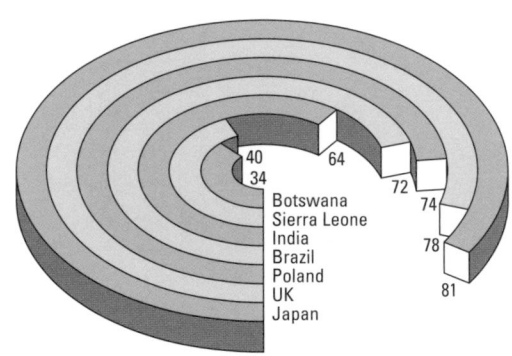

40	64
34	72
	74
Botswana	78
Sierra Leone	81
India	
Brazil	
Poland	
UK	
Japan	

Causes of Death

Causes of death for selected countries by percentage

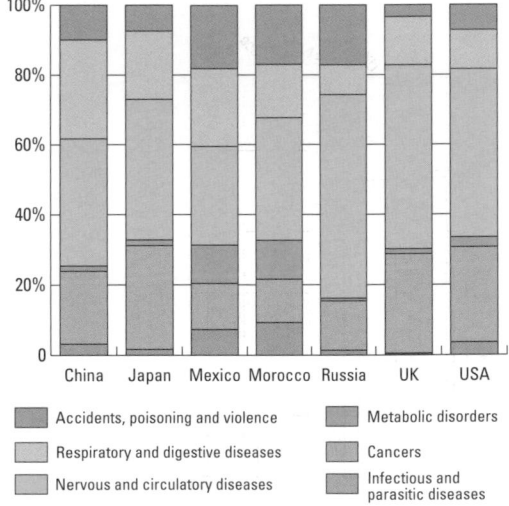

China   Japan   Mexico   Morocco   Russia   UK   USA

Accidents, poisoning and violence   Metabolic disorders

Respiratory and digestive diseases   Cancers

Nervous and circulatory diseases   Infectious and parasitic diseases

Infant Mortality

Number of babies who died under the age of one, per 1,000 live births (2004)

Over 100 deaths per 1,000 births

50 – 100 deaths per 1,000 births

25 – 50 deaths per 1,000 births

10 – 25 deaths per 1,000 births

Under 10 deaths per 1,000 births

No data available

Highest infant mortality		Lowest infant mortality	
Angola	193 deaths	Singapore	2 deaths
Afghanistan	166 deaths	Sweden	3 deaths
Sierra Leone	145 deaths	Japan	3 deaths
Mozambique	137 deaths	Iceland	3 deaths
Liberia	131 deaths	Finland	4 deaths

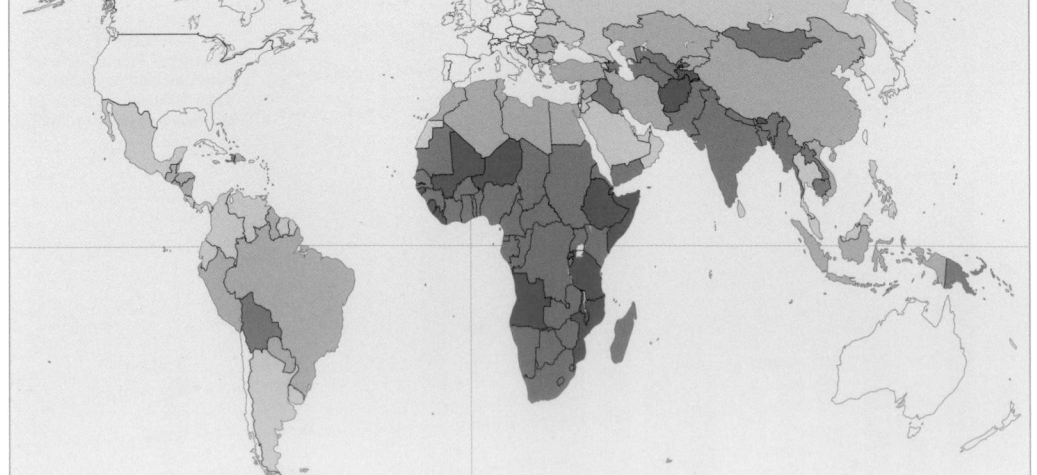

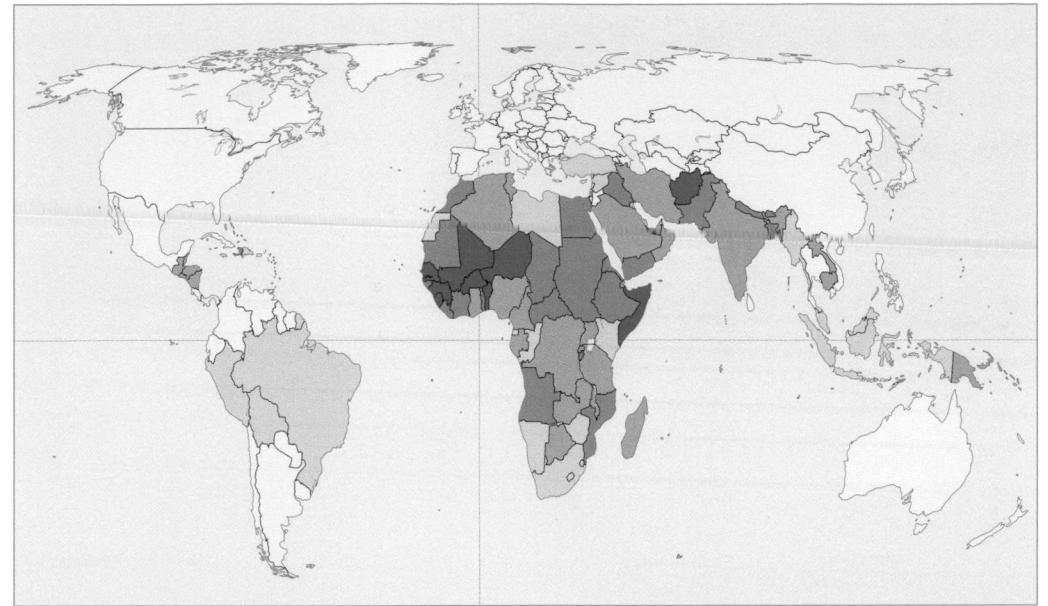

Percentage of the total adult population unable to read or write (2004)

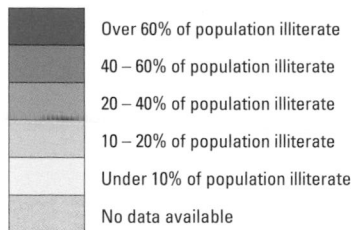

Over 60% of population illiterate

40 – 60% of population illiterate

20 – 40% of population illiterate

10 – 20% of population illiterate

Under 10% of population illiterate

No data available

Countries with the highest and lowest illiteracy rates

Highest		Lowest	
Burkina Faso	87	Australia	0
Niger	83	Denmark	0
Mali	81	Finland	0
Sierra Leone	69	Liechtenstein	0
Guinea	64	Luxembourg	0

Fertility and Education

Fertility rates compared with female education, selected countries (2000–2005)

Percentage of females aged 12–17 in secondary education

Fertility rate: average number of children borne per woman

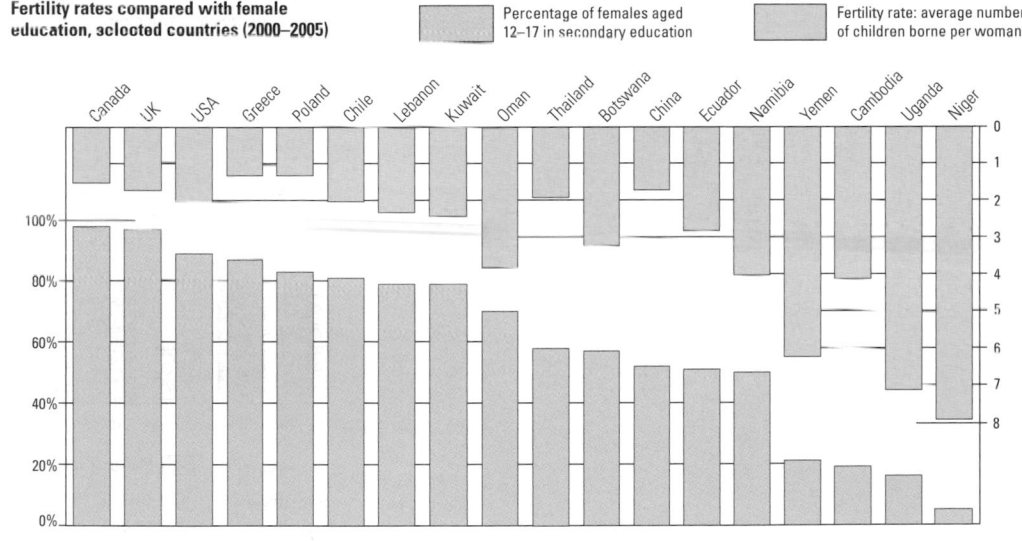

Living Standards

At first sight, most international contrasts in living standards are swamped by differences in wealth. The rich not only have more money, they have more of everything, including years of life. Those with only a little money are obliged to spend most of it on food and clothing, the basic maintenance costs of their existence; air travel and tourism are unlikely to feature on their expenditure lists. However, poverty and wealth are both relative: slum dwellers living on social security payments in an affluent industrial country have far more resources at their disposal than an average African peasant, but feel their own poverty nonetheless. A middle-class Indian lawyer cannot command a fraction of the earnings of a counterpart living in New York, London or Rome; nevertheless, he rightly sees himself as prosperous.

The rich not only live longer, on average, than the poor, they also die from different causes. Infectious and parasitic diseases, all but eliminated in the developed world, remain a scourge in the developing nations. On the other hand, more than two-thirds of the populations of OECD nations eventually succumb to cancer or circulatory disease.

Human Development Index

The Human Development Index (HDI), calculated by the UN Development Programme, gives a value to countries using indicators of life expectancy, education and standards of living in 2003. Higher values show more developed countries.

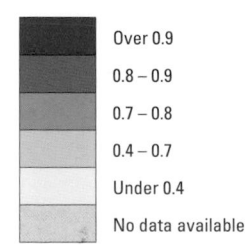

Over 0.9

0.8 – 0.9

0.7 – 0.8

0.4 – 0.7

Under 0.4

No data available

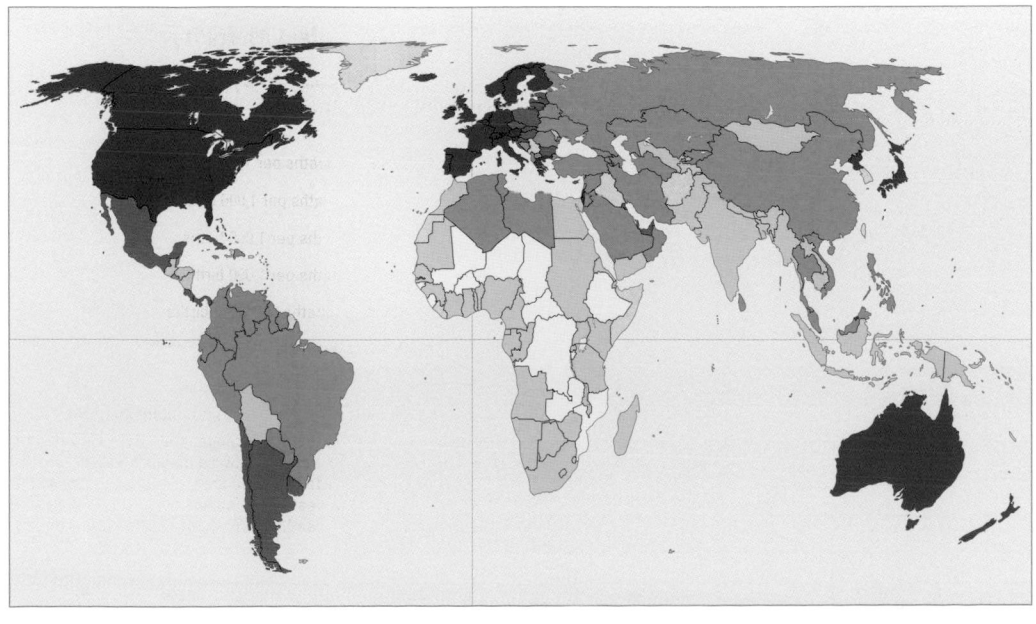

Highest values		Lowest values	
Norway	0.963	Niger	0.281
Iceland	0.956	Sierra Leone	0.298
Australia	0.955	Burkina Faso	0.317
Canada	0.949	Mali	0.333
Luxembourg	0.949	Chad	0.341

Energy

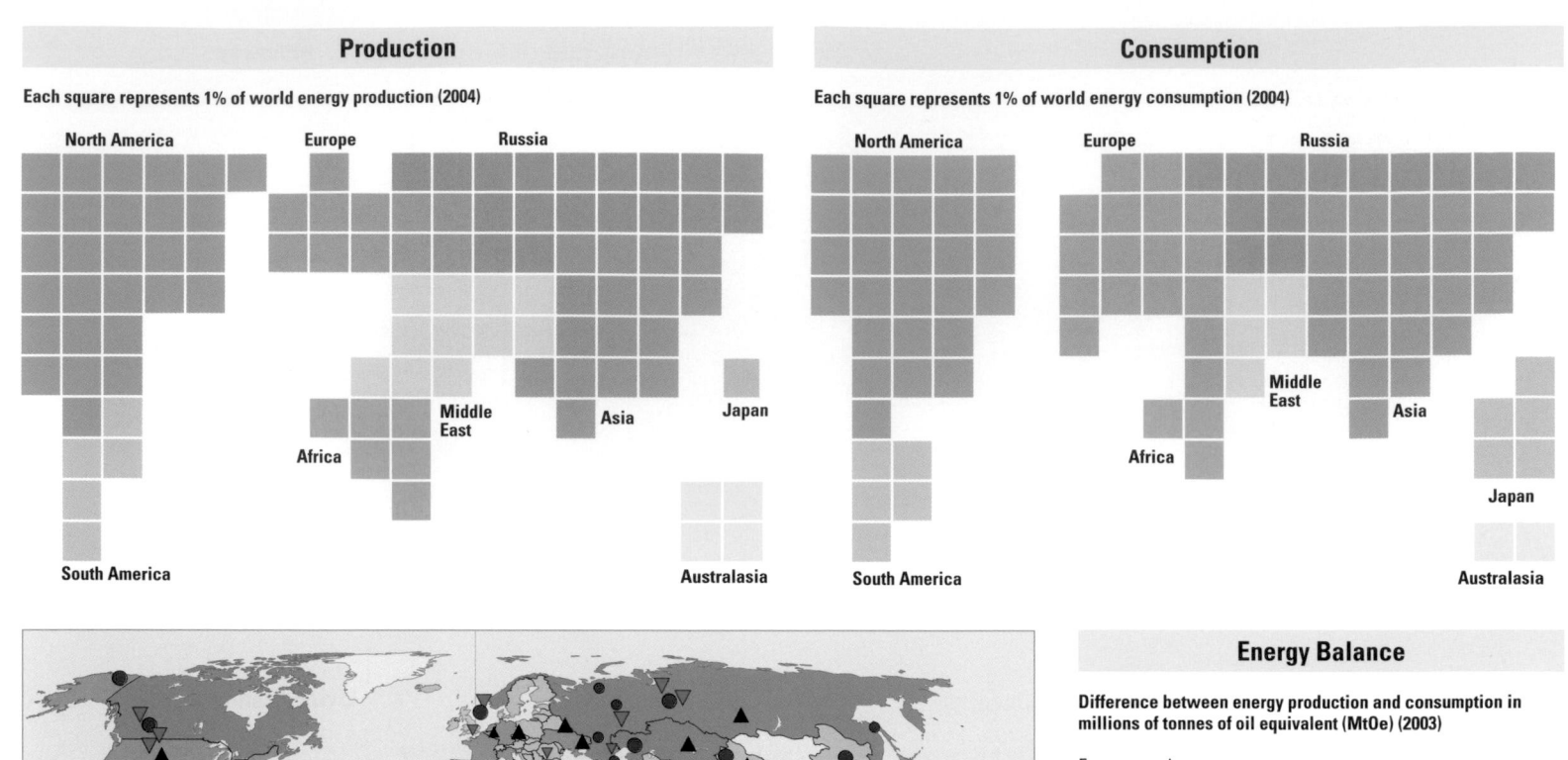

Production

Each square represents 1% of world energy production (2004)

North America · Europe · Russia · Middle East · Africa · Asia · Japan · South America · Australasia

Consumption

Each square represents 1% of world energy consumption (2004)

North America · Europe · Russia · Middle East · Africa · Asia · Japan · South America · Australasia

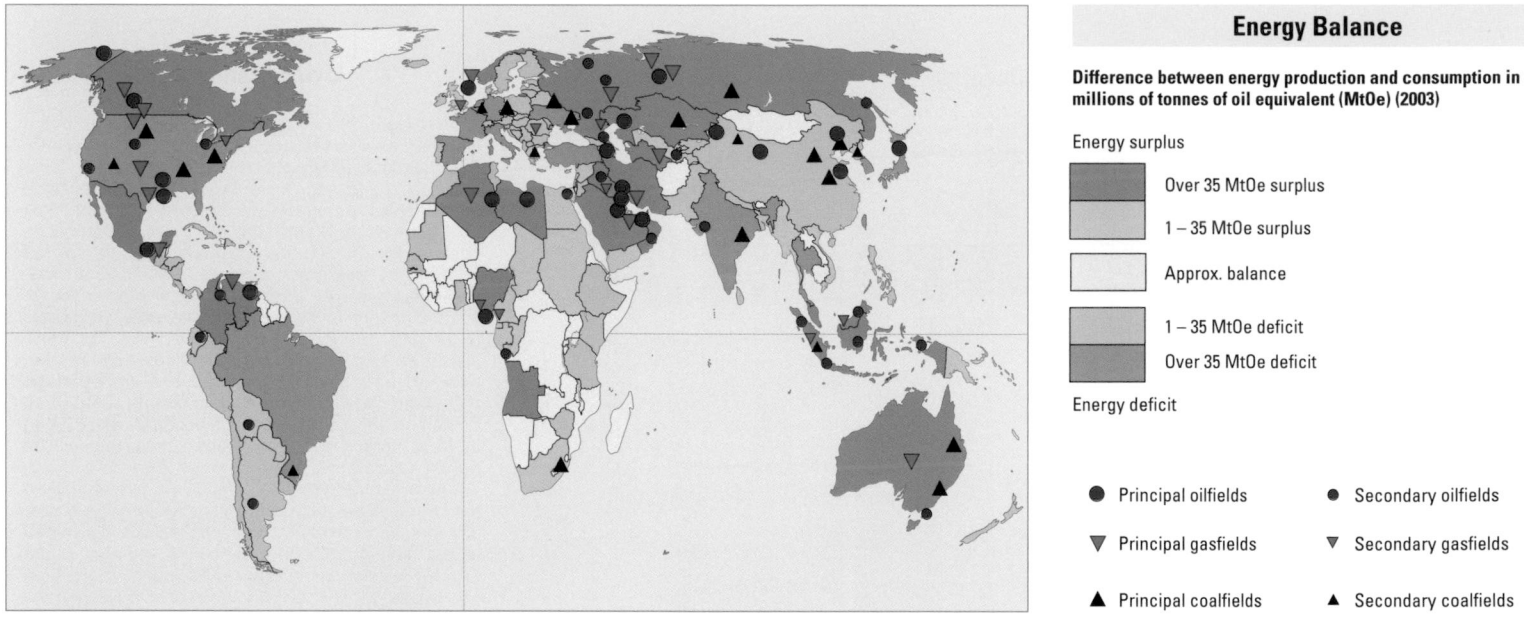

Energy Balance

Difference between energy production and consumption in millions of tonnes of oil equivalent (MtOe) (2003)

Energy surplus

	Over 35 MtOe surplus
	1 – 35 MtOe surplus
	Approx. balance
	1 – 35 MtOe deficit
	Over 35 MtOe deficit

Energy deficit

● Principal oilfields   ● Secondary oilfields

▼ Principal gasfields   ▼ Secondary gasfields

▲ Principal coalfields   ▲ Secondary coalfields

World Energy Consumption

Energy consumed by world regions, measured in million tonnes of oil equivalent in 2004. Total world consumption was 10,224 MtOe. Only energy from oil, gas, coal, nuclear and hydroelectric sources are included. Excluded are fuels such as wood, peat, animal waste, wind, solar and geothermal which, though important in some countries, are unreliably documented in terms of consumption statistics.

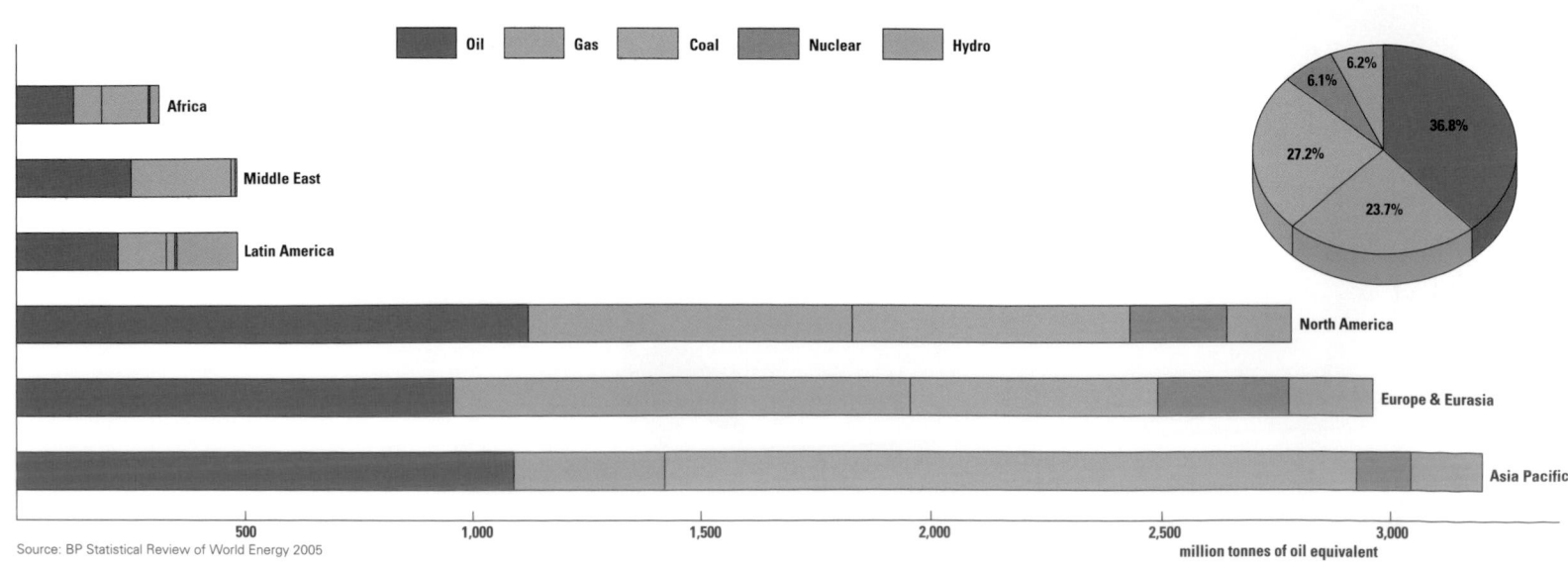

■ Oil   ■ Gas   ■ Coal   ■ Nuclear   ■ Hydro

Africa · Middle East · Latin America · North America · Europe & Eurasia · Asia Pacific

500 · 1,000 · 1,500 · 2,000 · 2,500 · 3,000

million tonnes of oil equivalent

36.8% · 23.7% · 27.2% · 6.1% · 6.2%

Source: BP Statistical Review of World Energy 2005

Energy

Energy is used to keep us warm or cool, fuel our industries and our transport systems, and even feed us; high-intensity agriculture, with its use of fertilizers, pesticides and machinery, is heavily energy-dependent. Although we live in a high-energy society, there are vast discrepancies between rich and poor; for example, a North American consumes 13 times as much energy as a Chinese person. But even developing nations have more power at their disposal than was imaginable a century ago.

The distribution of energy supplies, most importantly fossil fuels (coal, oil and natural gas), is very uneven. In addition, the diagrams and map opposite show that the largest producers of energy are not necessarily the largest consumers. The movement of energy supplies around the world is therefore an important component of international trade. In 2004, total world movements in oil amounted to 2,381 million tonnes.

As the finite reserves of fossil fuels are depleted, renewable energy sources, such as solar, hydro-thermal, wind, tidal and biomass, will become increasingly important around the world.

Nuclear Power

Major producers by percentage of world total and by percentage of domestic electricity generation (2003)

Country	% of world total production	Country	% of nuclear as proportion of domestic electricity
1. USA	30.4%	1. Lithuania	79.9%
2. France	16.7%	2. France	77.7%
3. Japan	8.7%	3. Slovak Rep.	57.4%
4. Germany	8.2%	4. Belgium	55.5%
5. Russia	5.7%	5. Sweden	50.0%
6. South Korea	4.9%	6. Ukraine	45.9%
7. UK	3.4%	7. Slovenia	40.4%
8. Ukraine	3.1%	8. South Korea	40.0%
9. Canada	2.8%	9. Switzerland	39.7%
= Sweden	2.6%	10. Bulgaria	37.7%

Although the 1980s were a bad time for the nuclear power industry (major projects ran over budget and fears of long-term environmental damage were heavily reinforced by the 1986 disaster at Chernobyl), the industry picked up in the early 1990s. Whilst the number of reactors is still increasing, however, orders for new plants have shrunk. Sixteen countries currently rely on nuclear power to supply over 25% of their electricity requirements.

Hydroelectricity

Major producers by percentage of world total and by percentage of domestic electricity generation (2003)

Country	% of world total production	Country	% of hydroelectric as proportion of domestic electricity
1. Brazil	11.6%	1. Bhutan	99.9%
2. Canada	11.5%	2. Paraguay	99.8%
3. China	10.8%	= Zambia	99.8%
4. USA	10.2%	4. Norway	99.1%
5. Russia	8.0%	5. Ethiopia	98.1%
6. Norway	4.0%	6. Congo (Rep. Dem.)	97.9%
7. Japan	3.8%	7. Tajikistan	97.8%
8. India	2.6%	8. Cameroon	97.3%
9. France	2.5%	9. Albania	97.2%
10. Venezuela	2.3%	= Laos	97.2%

Countries heavily reliant on hydroelectricity are usually small and non-industrial: a high proportion of hydroelectric power more often reflects a modest energy budget than vast hydroelectric resources. The USA, for instance, produces only 2.6% of its power requirements from hydroelectricity; yet that 2.6% amounts to more than three times the hydropower generated by most of Africa.

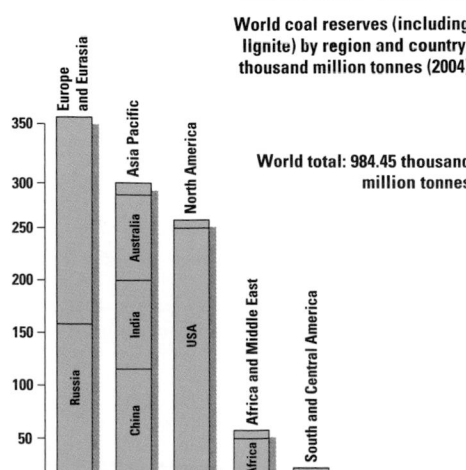

Measurements

For historical reasons, oil is traded in 'barrels'. The weight and volume equivalents (shown right) are all based on average-density 'Arabian light' crude oil.

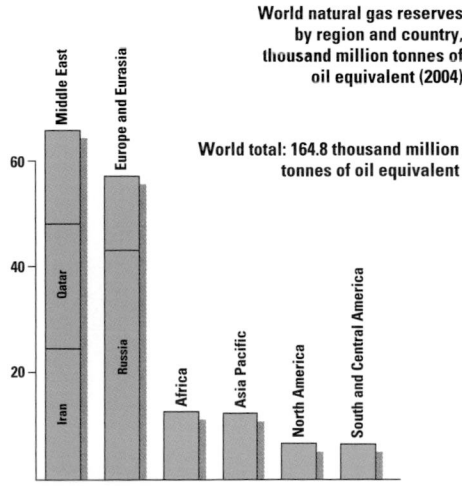

The energy equivalents given for a tonne of oil are also somewhat imprecise: oil and coal of different qualities will have varying energy contents, a fact usually reflected in their price on world markets.

Fuel Exports

Fuels as a percentage of total value of exports (2004)

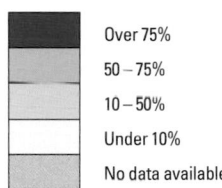

- Over 75%
- 50 – 75%
- 10 – 50%
- Under 10%
- No data available

In the 1970s, oil exports became a political issue when OPEC sought to increase the influence of developing countries in world affairs by raising oil prices and restricting production. But its power was short-lived, following a fall in demand for oil in the 1980s, due to an increase in energy efficiency and development of alternative resources. However, with the heavy energy demands of the Asian economies early in the 21st century, both oil and gas prices have risen sharply.

Conversion Rates

1 barrel = 0.136 tonnes or 159 litres or 35 Imperial gallons or 42 US gallons

1 tonne = 7.33 barrels or 1,185 litres or 256 Imperial gallons or 261 US gallons

1 tonne oil = 1.5 tonnes hard coal or 3.0 tonnes lignite or 12,000 kWh

1 Imperial gallon = 1.201 US gallons or 4.546 litres or 277.4 cubic inches

World Coal Reserves

World coal reserves (including lignite) by region and country, thousand million tonnes (2004)

World total: 984.45 thousand million tonnes

World Gas Reserves

World natural gas reserves by region and country, thousand million tonnes of oil equivalent (2004)

World total: 164.8 thousand million tonnes of oil equivalent

World Oil Reserves

World oil reserves by region and country, thousand million tonnes (2004)

World total: 156.7 thousand million tonnes

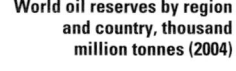
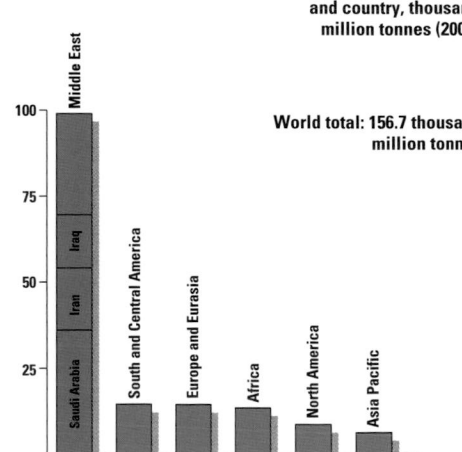

Production

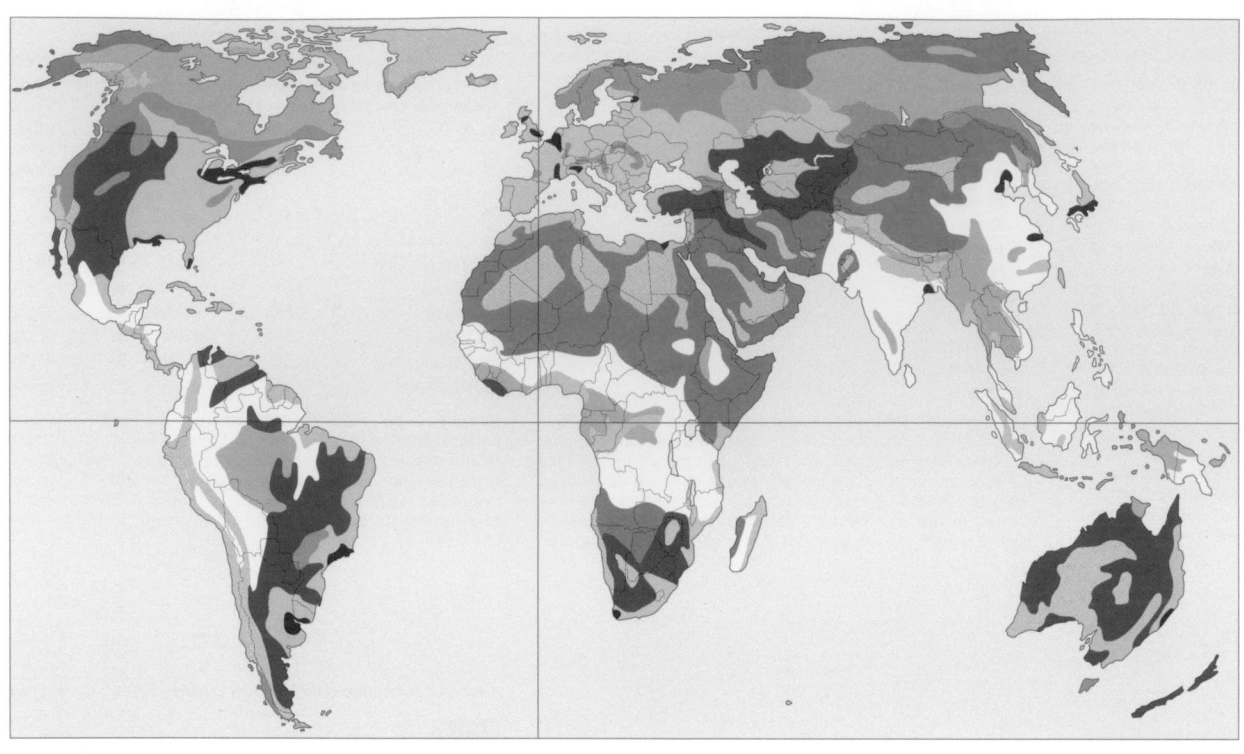

Agriculture

Predominant type of farming or land use.

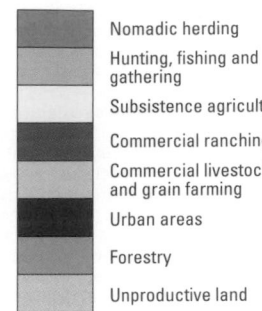

- Nomadic herding
- Hunting, fishing and gathering
- Subsistence agriculture
- Commercial ranching
- Commercial livestock and grain farming
- Urban areas
- Forestry
- Unproductive land

The development of agriculture has transformed human existence more than any other. The whole business of farming is constantly developing: due mainly to the new varieties of rice and wheat, world grain production has increased by over 70% since 1965. New machinery and modern agricultural techniques enable relatively few farmers to produce enough food for the world's 6 billion or so people.

Staple Crops

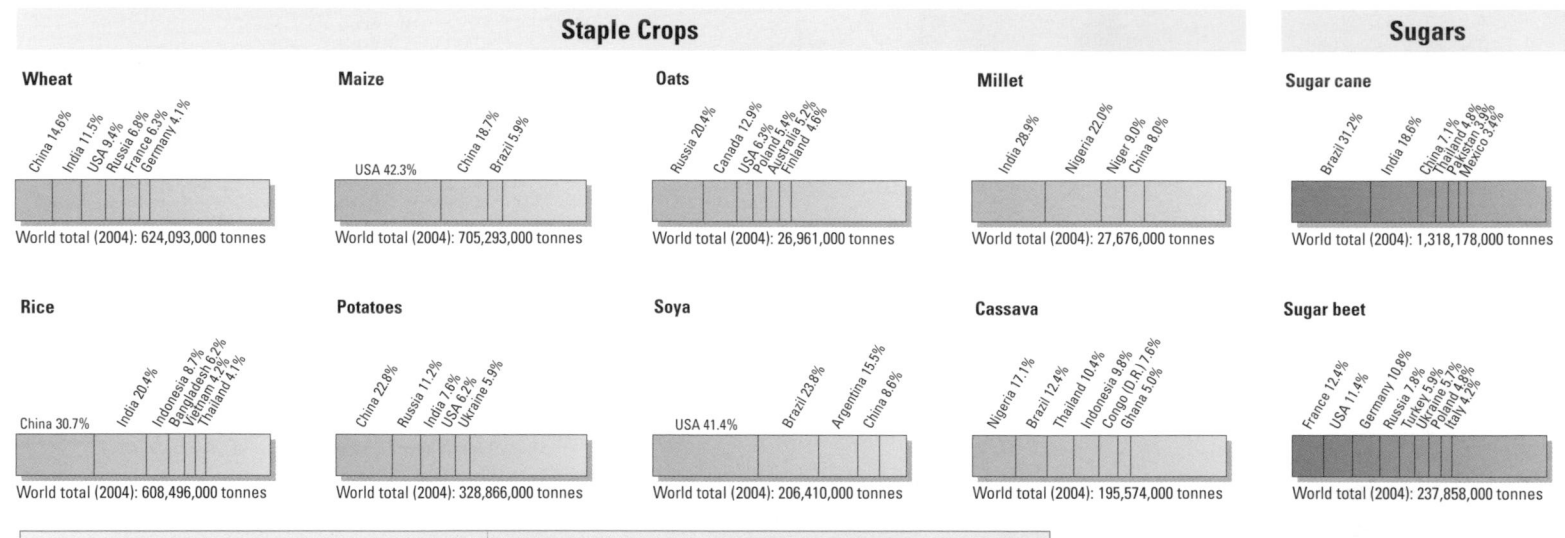

Wheat
China 14.6% | India 11.5% | USA 9.4% | Russia 6.9% | France 6.3% | Germany 4.1%
World total (2004): 624,093,000 tonnes

Maize
USA 42.3% | China 18.7% | Brazil 5.9%
World total (2004): 705,293,000 tonnes

Oats
Russia 20.4% | Canada 12.9% | USA 6.3% | Poland 5.4% | Australia 5.2% | Finland 4.5%
World total (2004): 26,961,000 tonnes

Millet
India 28.9% | Nigeria 22.0% | Niger 9.0% | China 8.0%
World total (2004): 27,676,000 tonnes

Rice
China 30.7% | India 20.4% | Indonesia 8.7% | Bangladesh 6.2% | Vietnam 4.2% | Thailand 4.1%
World total (2004): 608,496,000 tonnes

Potatoes
China 22.8% | Russia 11.2% | India 7.6% | USA 6.2% | Ukraine 5.9%
World total (2004): 328,866,000 tonnes

Soya
USA 41.4% | Brazil 23.8% | Argentina 15.5% | China 8.6%
World total (2004): 206,410,000 tonnes

Cassava
Nigeria 17.1% | Brazil 12.4% | Thailand 10.4% | Indonesia 9.8% | Congo (D.R.) 7.6% | Ghana 5.0%
World total (2004): 195,574,000 tonnes

Sugars

Sugar cane
Brazil 31.2% | India 18.6% | China 7.1% | Thailand 4.6% | Pakistan 3.9% | Mexico 3.4%
World total (2004): 1,318,178,000 tonnes

Sugar beet
France 12.4% | USA 11.4% | Germany 10.8% | Russia 7.8% | Turkey 5.9% | Ukraine 5.1% | Poland 4.8% | Italy 4.2%
World total (2004): 237,858,000 tonnes

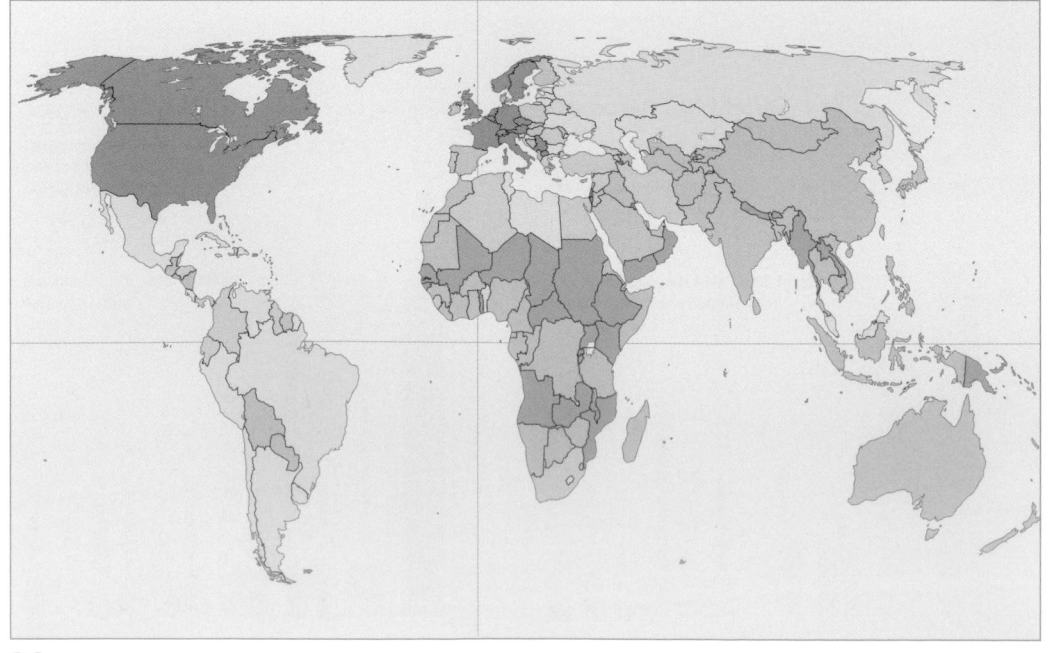

Employment

The number of workers employed in manufacturing for every 100 workers engaged in agriculture (2003)

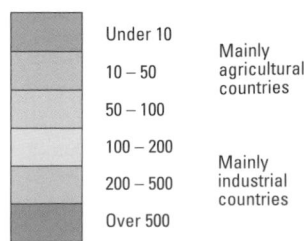

- Under 10 — Mainly agricultural countries
- 10 – 50
- 50 – 100
- 100 – 200 — Mainly industrial countries
- 200 – 500
- Over 500

Countries with the highest and lowest number of workers employed in manufacturing per 100 workers engaged in agriculture (2003)

Highest		Lowest	
Bahrain	3,900	Bhutan	2.2
Liechtenstein	3,646	Burundi	2.5
USA	3,242	Nepal	3.7
UK	2,500	Yemen	5.0
Andorra	2,100	Malawi	5.0

Energy

Energy is used to keep us warm or cool, fuel our industries and our transport systems, and even feed us; high-intensity agriculture, with its use of fertilizers, pesticides and machinery, is heavily energy-dependent. Although we live in a high-energy society, there are vast discrepancies between rich and poor; for example, a North American consumes 13 times as much energy as a Chinese person. But even developing nations have more power at their disposal than was imaginable a century ago.

The distribution of energy supplies, most importantly fossil fuels (coal, oil and natural gas), is very uneven. In addition, the diagrams and map opposite show that the largest producers of energy are not necessarily the largest consumers. The movement of energy supplies around the world is therefore an important component of international trade. In 2004, total world movements in oil amounted to 2,381 million tonnes.

As the finite reserves of fossil fuels are depleted, renewable energy sources, such as solar, hydro-thermal, wind, tidal and biomass, will become increasingly important around the world.

Nuclear Power

Major producers by percentage of world total and by percentage of domestic electricity generation (2003)

Country	% of world total production	Country	% of nuclear as proportion of domestic electricity
1. USA	30.4%	1. Lithuania	79.9%
2. France	16.7%	2. France	77.7%
3. Japan	8.7%	3. Slovak Rep.	57.4%
4. Germany	6.2%	4. Belgium	55.5%
5. Russia	5.7%	5. Sweden	50.0%
6. South Korea	4.9%	6. Ukraine	45.9%
7. UK	3.4%	7. Slovenia	40.4%
8. Ukraine	3.1%	8. South Korea	40.0%
9. Canada	2.8%	9. Switzerland	39.7%
= Sweden	2.6%	10. Bulgaria	37.7%

Although the 1980s were a bad time for the nuclear power industry (major projects ran over budget and fears of long-term environmental damage were heavily reinforced by the 1986 disaster at Chernobyl), the industry picked up in the early 1990s. Whilst the number of reactors is still increasing, however, orders for new plants have shrunk. Sixteen countries currently rely on nuclear power to supply over 25% of their electricity requirements.

Hydroelectricity

Major producers by percentage of world total and by percentage of domestic electricity generation (2003)

Country	% of world total production	Country	% of hydroelectric as proportion of domestic electricity
1. Brazil	11.6%	1. Bhutan	99.9%
2. Canada	11.5%	2. Paraguay	99.8%
3. China	10.8%	= Zambia	99.8%
4. USA	10.2%	4. Norway	99.1%
5. Russia	6.0%	5. Ethiopia	98.1%
6. Norway	4.0%	6. Congo (Rep. Dem.)	97.9%
7. Japan	3.8%	7. Tajikistan	97.8%
8. India	2.6%	8. Cameroon	97.3%
9. France	2.5%	9. Albania	97.2%
10. Venezuela	2.3%	= Laos	97.2%

Countries heavily reliant on hydroelectricity are usually small and non-industrial: a high proportion of hydroelectric power more often reflects a modest energy budget than vast hydroelectric resources. The USA, for instance, produces only 2.6% of its power requirements from hydroelectricity; yet that 2.6% amounts to more than three times the hydropower generated by most of Africa.

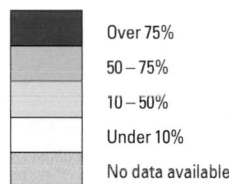

Fuel Exports

Fuels as a percentage of total value of exports (2004)

- Over 75%
- 50 – 75%
- 10 – 50%
- Under 10%
- No data available

In the 1970s, oil exports became a political issue when OPEC sought to increase the influence of developing countries in world affairs by raising oil prices and restricting production. But its power was short-lived, following a fall in demand for oil in the 1980s, due to an increase in energy efficiency and development of alternative resources. However, with the heavy energy demands of the Asian economies early in the 21st century, both oil and gas prices have risen sharply.

Conversion Rates

1 barrel = 0.136 tonnes or 159 litres or 35 Imperial gallons or 42 US gallons

1 tonne = 7.33 barrels or 1,185 litres or 256 Imperial gallons or 261 US gallons

1 tonne oil = 1.5 tonnes hard coal or 3.0 tonnes lignite or 12,000 kWh

1 Imperial gallon = 1.201 US gallons or 4.546 litres or 277.4 cubic inches

Measurements

For historical reasons, oil is traded in 'barrels'. The weight and volume equivalents (shown right) are all based on average-density 'Arabian light' crude oil.

The energy equivalents given for a tonne of oil are also somewhat imprecise: oil and coal of different qualities will have varying energy contents, a fact usually reflected in their price on world markets.

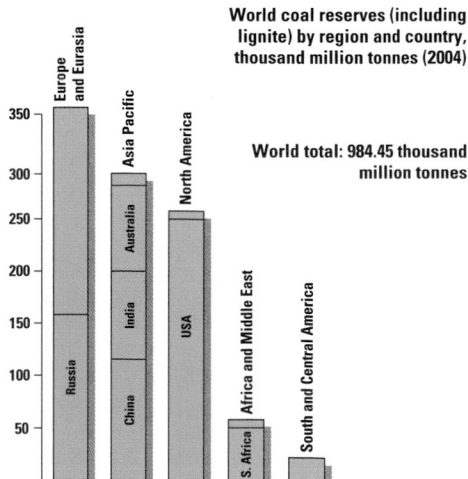

World Coal Reserves

World coal reserves (including lignite) by region and country, thousand million tonnes (2004)

World total: 984.45 thousand million tonnes

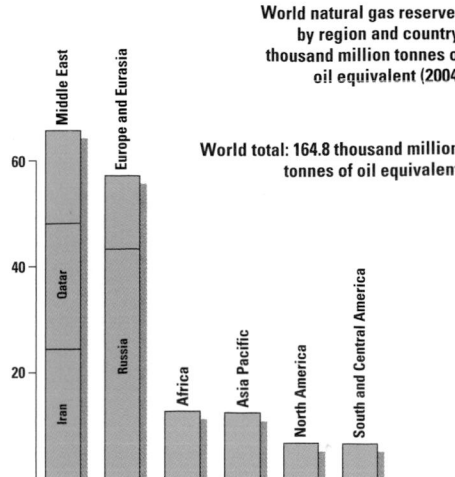

World Gas Reserves

World natural gas reserves by region and country, thousand million tonnes of oil equivalent (2004)

World total: 164.8 thousand million tonnes of oil equivalent

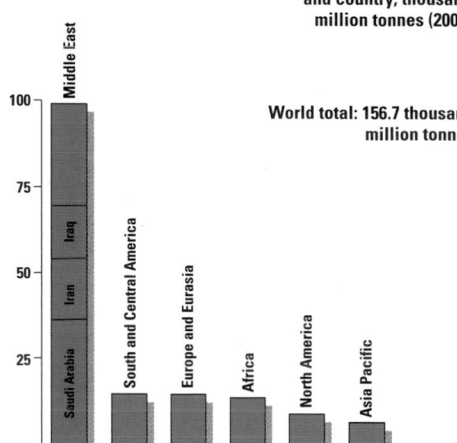

World Oil Reserves

World oil reserves by region and country, thousand million tonnes (2004)

World total: 156.7 thousand million tonnes

Production

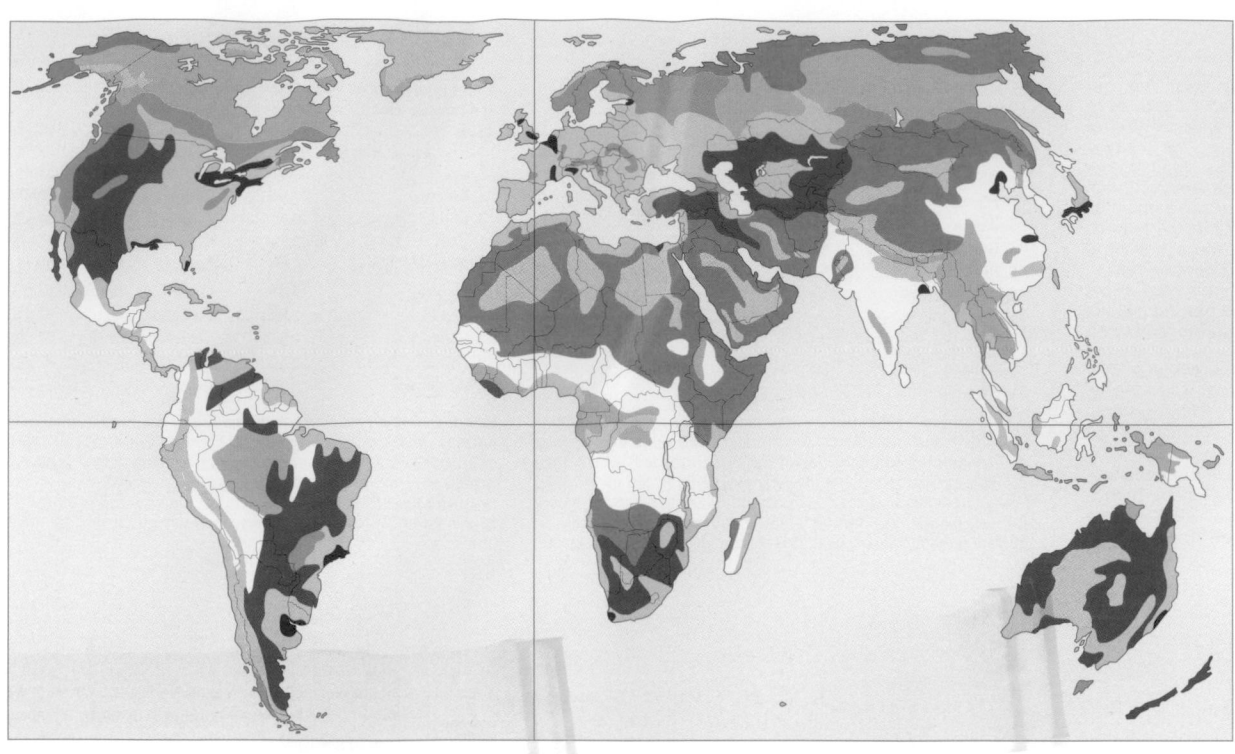

The development of agriculture has transformed human existence more than any other. The whole business of farming is constantly developing: due mainly to the new varieties of rice and wheat, world grain production has increased by over 70% since 1965. New machinery and modern agricultural techniques enable relatively few farmers to produce enough food for the world's 6 billion or so people.

Staple Crops

Wheat
China 14.6% | India 11.5% | USA 9.4% | Russia 6.8% | France 6.3% | Germany 4.1%

World total (2004): 624,093,000 tonnes

Maize
USA 42.3% | China 18.7% | Brazil 5.9%

World total (2004): 705,293,000 tonnes

Oats
Russia 20.4% | Canada 12.9% | USA 6.3% | Poland 5.4% | Australia 5.2% | Finland 4.6%

World total (2004): 26,961,000 tonnes

Millet
India 28.9% | Nigeria 22.0% | Niger 9.0% | China 8.0%

World total (2004): 27,676,000 tonnes

Rice
China 30.7% | India 20.4% | Indonesia 8.7% | Bangladesh 6.2% | Vietnam 4.2% | Thailand 4.1%

World total (2004): 608,496,000 tonnes

Potatoes
China 22.8% | Russia 11.2% | India 7.6% | USA 6.2% | Ukraine 5.9%

World total (2004): 328,866,000 tonnes

Soya
USA 41.4% | Brazil 23.8% | Argentina 15.5% | China 8.6%

World total (2004): 206,410,000 tonnes

Cassava
Nigeria 17.1% | Brazil 12.4% | Thailand 10.4% | Indonesia 9.8% | Congo (D.R.) 7.6% | Ghana 5.1%

World total (2004): 195,574,000 tonnes

Sugars

Sugar cane
Brazil 37.2% | India 18.6% | China 7.1% | Thailand 4.8% | Pakistan 3.9% | Mexico 3.4%

World total (2004): 1,318,178,000 tonnes

Sugar beet
France 12.4% | USA 11.4% | Germany 10.8% | Russia 7.8% | Turkey 5.9% | Poland 5.1% | Italy 4.2%

World total (2004): 237,858,000 tonnes

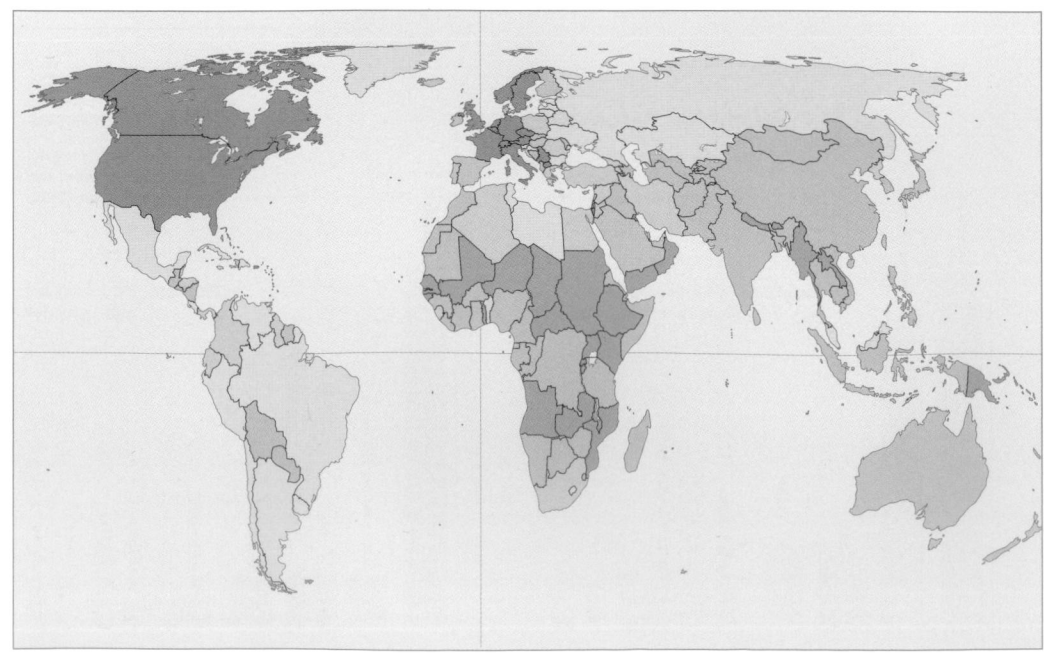

Employment

The number of workers employed in manufacturing for every 100 workers engaged in agriculture (2003)

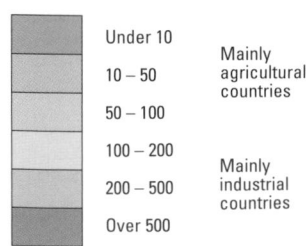

- Under 10 — Mainly agricultural countries
- 10 – 50
- 50 – 100
- 100 – 200 — Mainly industrial countries
- 200 – 500
- Over 500

Countries with the highest and lowest number of workers employed in manufacturing per 100 workers engaged in agriculture (2003)

Highest		Lowest	
Bahrain	3,900	Bhutan	2.2
Liechtenstein	3,646	Burundi	2.5
USA	3,242	Nepal	3.7
UK	2,500	Yemen	5.0
Andorra	2,100	Malawi	5.0

Mineral Production

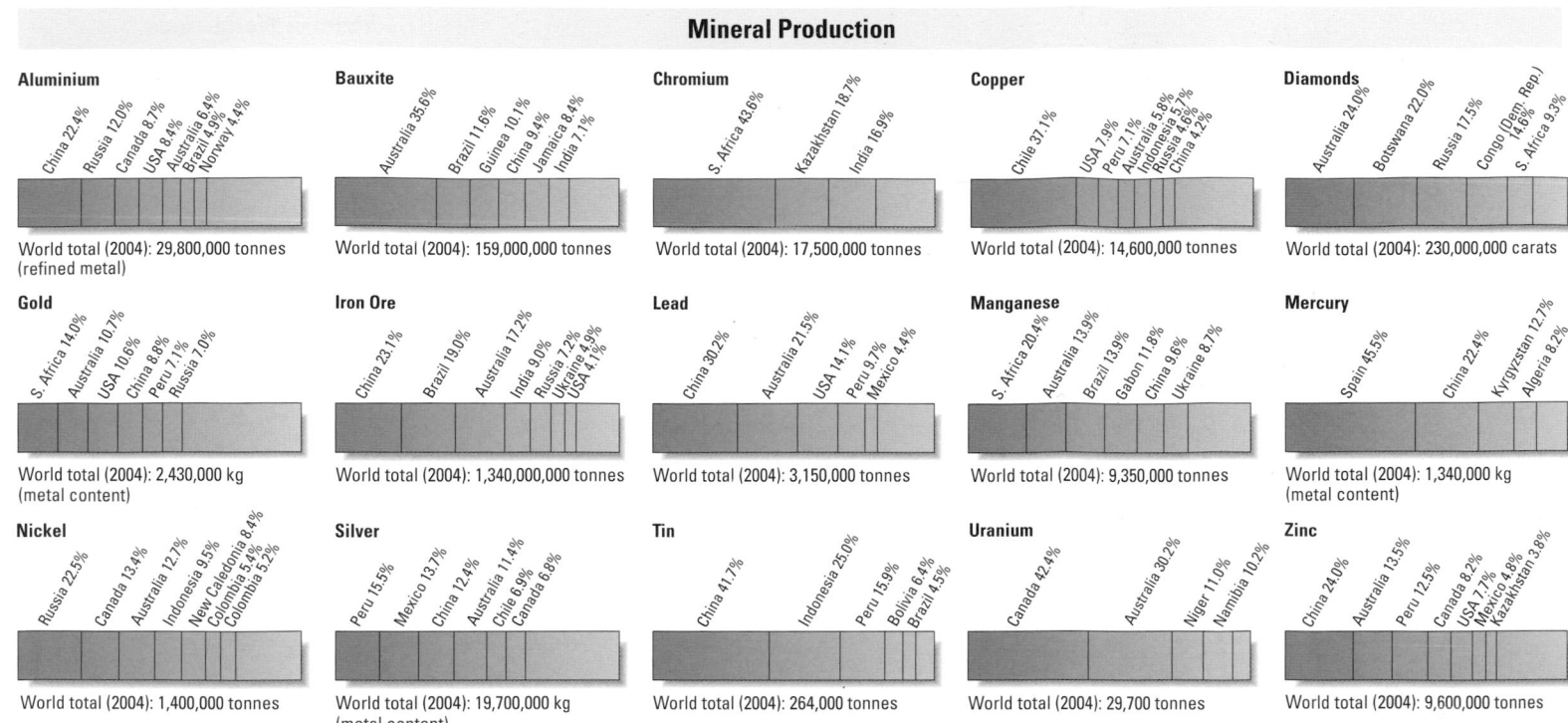

Aluminium
China 22.4% · Russia 12.0% · Canada 8.7% · USA 8.4% · Australia 6.4% · Brazil 4.9% · Norway 4.4%
World total (2004): 29,800,000 tonnes (refined metal)

Bauxite
Australia 35.6% · Brazil 11.6% · Guinea 10.1% · China 9.4% · Jamaica 8.4% · India 7.1%
World total (2004): 159,000,000 tonnes

Chromium
S. Africa 43.6% · Kazakhstan 18.7% · India 16.9%
World total (2004): 17,500,000 tonnes

Copper
Chile 37.1% · USA 7.9% · Peru 7.1% · Australia 5.8% · Indonesia 5.7% · Russia 4.6% · China 4.2%
World total (2004): 14,600,000 tonnes

Diamonds
Australia 24.0% · Botswana 22.0% · Russia 17.5% · Congo (Dem. Rep.) 14.6% · S. Africa 9.3%
World total (2004): 230,000,000 carats

Gold
S. Africa 14.0% · Australia 10.7% · USA 10.6% · China 8.8% · Peru 7.1% · Russia 7.0%
World total (2004): 2,430,000 kg (metal content)

Iron Ore
China 23.1% · Brazil 19.0% · Australia 17.2% · India 9.0% · Russia 7.2% · Ukraine 4.9% · USA 4.1%
World total (2004): 1,340,000,000 tonnes

Lead
China 30.2% · Australia 21.5% · USA 14.1% · Peru 9.7% · Mexico 4.4%
World total (2004): 3,150,000 tonnes

Manganese
S. Africa 20.4% · Australia 13.9% · Brazil 13.9% · Gabon 11.8% · China 9.6% · Ukraine 8.7%
World total (2004): 9,350,000 tonnes

Mercury
Spain 45.5% · China 22.4% · Kyrgyzstan 12.7% · Algeria 8.2%
World total (2004): 1,340,000 kg (metal content)

Nickel
Russia 22.5% · Canada 13.4% · Australia 12.7% · Indonesia 9.5% · New Caledonia 8.4% · Colombia 5.4% · Colombia 5.2%
World total (2004): 1,400,000 tonnes

Silver
Peru 15.5% · Mexico 13.7% · China 12.4% · Australia 11.4% · Chile 6.9% · Canada 6.6%
World total (2004): 19,700,000 kg (metal content)

Tin
China 41.7% · Indonesia 25.0% · Peru 15.9% · Bolivia 6.4% · Brazil 4.3%
World total (2004): 264,000 tonnes

Uranium
Canada 42.4% · Australia 30.2% · Niger 11.0% · Namibia 10.2%
World total (2004): 29,700 tonnes

Zinc
China 24.0% · Australia 13.5% · Peru 12.5% · Canada 8.2% · USA 7.7% · Mexico 4.6% · Kazakhstan 3.8%
World total (2004): 9,600,000 tonnes

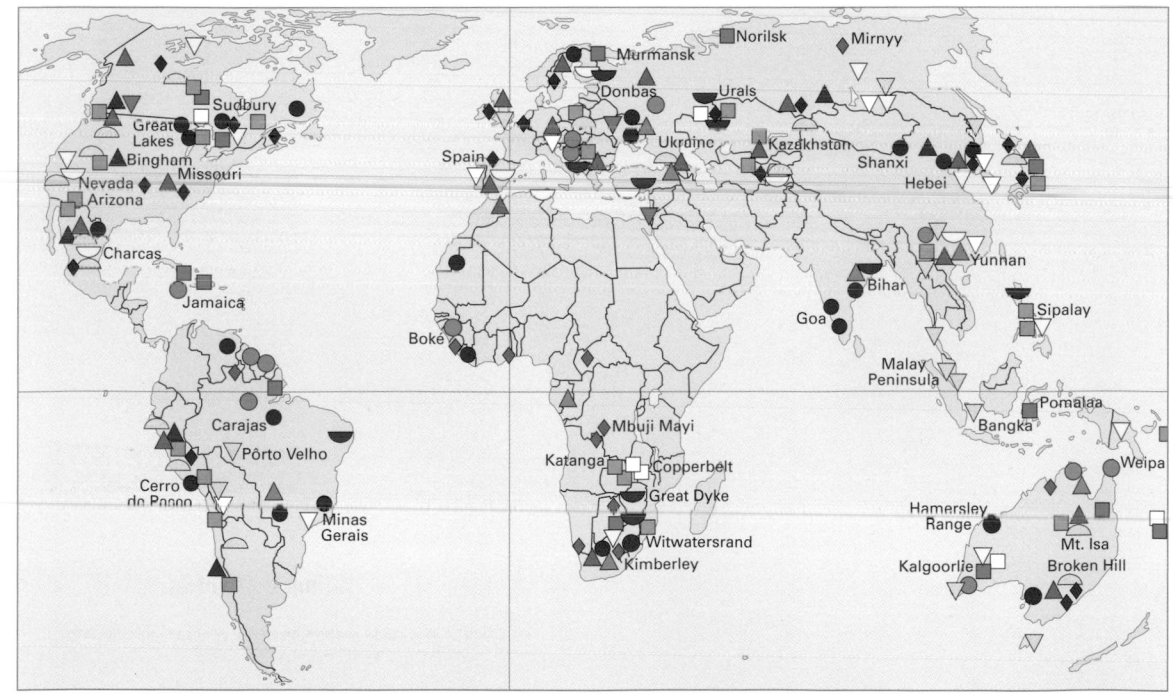

Mineral Distribution

The map shows the richest sources of the most important minerals. Major mineral locations are named.

- ● Bauxite
- ◗ Chromium
- □ Cobalt
- ▪ Copper
- ◆ Diamonds
- ▽ Gold
- ● Iron ore
- ▲ Lead
- ▲ Manganese
- ▽ Mercury
- ▲ Molybdenum
- ▪ Nickel
- ▼ Potash
- ◖ Silver
- ▽ Tin
- ▽ Tungsten
- ◆ Zinc

The map does not show undersea deposits, most of which are considered inaccessible.

Named locations: Norilsk, Mirnyy, Murmansk, Donbas, Urals, Ukraine, Kazakhstan, Shanxi, Hebei, Spain, Yunnan, Bihar, Goa, Sipalay, Malay Peninsula, Bangka, Pomalaa, Hamersley Range, Weipa, Mt. Isa, Broken Hill, Kalgoorlie, Kimberley, Witwatersrand, Great Dyke, Copperbelt, Katanga, Mbuji Mayi, Boké, Sudbury, Great Lakes, Bingham, Missouri, Nevada, Arizona, Charcas, Jamaica, Carajas, Pôrto Velho, Cerro de Pasco, Minas Gerais

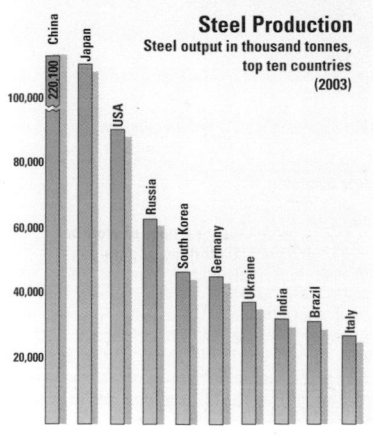

Steel Production
Steel output in thousand tonnes, top ten countries (2003)
China 220,100 · Japan · USA · Russia · South Korea · Germany · Ukraine · India · Brazil · Italy

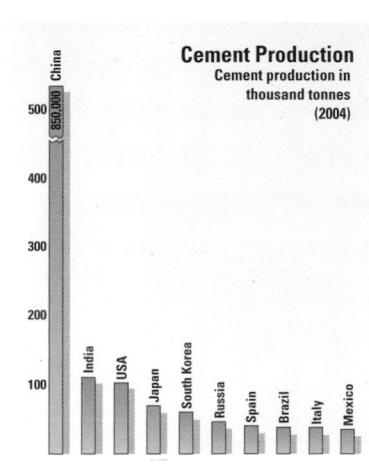

Cement Production
Cement production in thousand tonnes (2004)
China 850,000 · India · USA · Japan · South Korea · Russia · Spain · Brazil · Italy · Mexico

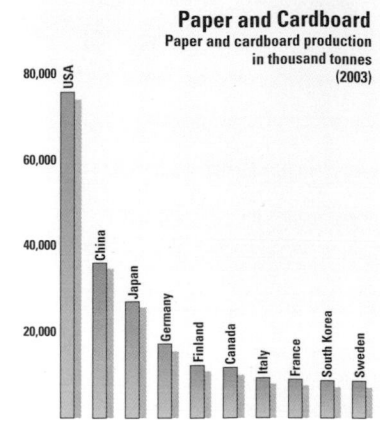

Paper and Cardboard
Paper and cardboard production in thousand tonnes (2003)
USA · China · Japan · Germany · Finland · Canada · Italy · France · South Korea · Sweden

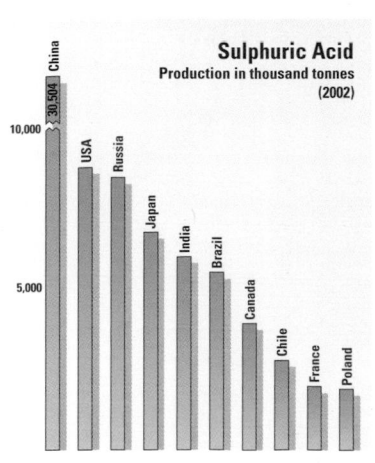

Sulphuric Acid
Production in thousand tonnes (2002)
China 30,500 · USA · Russia · Japan · India · Brazil · Canada · Chile · France · Poland

Trade

Share of World Trade

Percentage share of total world exports by value (2005)

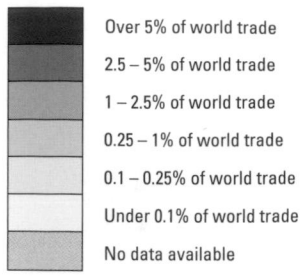

- Over 5% of world trade
- 2.5 – 5% of world trade
- 1 – 2.5% of world trade
- 0.25 – 1% of world trade
- 0.1 – 0.25% of world trade
- Under 0.1% of world trade
- No data available

International trade is dominated by a handful of powerful maritime nations. The members of 'G8', the inner circle of OECD (see page 19), and the top seven countries listed in the diagram below, account for more than half the total. The majority of nations – including all but four in Africa – contribute less than one quarter of 1% to the worldwide total of exports; the EU countries account for 35%, the Pacific Rim nations over 50%.

The Main Trading Nations

The imports and exports of the top ten trading nations as a percentage of world trade (2004). Each country's trade in manufactured goods is shown in dark blue.

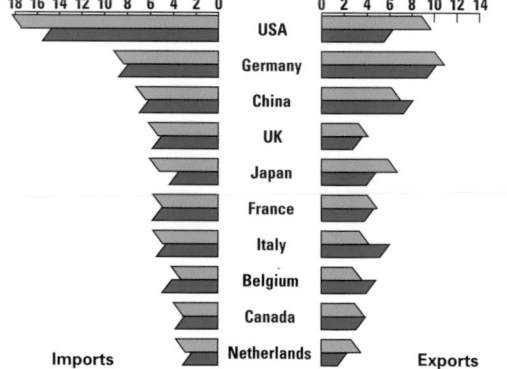

18 16 14 12 10 8 6 4 2 0 | 0 2 4 6 8 10 12 14

USA
Germany
China
UK
Japan
France
Italy
Belgium
Canada
Netherlands

Imports   Exports

Major exports

Leading manufactured items and their exporters (2004)

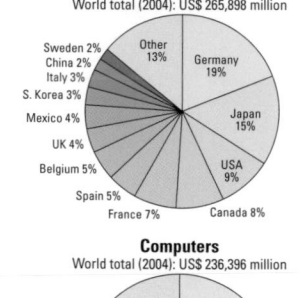

Motor Vehicles
World total (2004): US$ 265,898 million

Other 13%, Germany 19%, Japan 15%, USA 9%, Canada 8%, France 7%, Spain 5%, Belgium 5%, UK 4%, Mexico 4%, S. Korea 3%, Italy 3%, China 2%, Sweden 2%

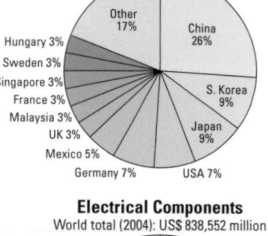

Telecommunications Gear
World total (2004): US$ 405,989 million

Other 17%, China 26%, S. Korea 9%, Japan 9%, USA 7%, Germany 7%, Mexico 5%, UK 3%, Malaysia 3%, France 3%, Singapore 3%, Sweden 3%, Hungary 3%

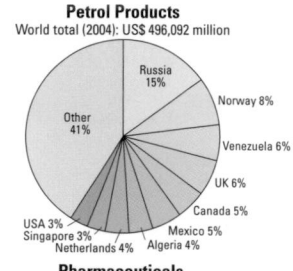

Petrol Products
World total (2004): US$ 496,092 million

Other 41%, Russia 15%, Norway 8%, Venezuela 6%, UK 6%, Canada 5%, Mexico 5%, Algeria 4%, Netherlands 4%, Singapore 3%, USA 3%

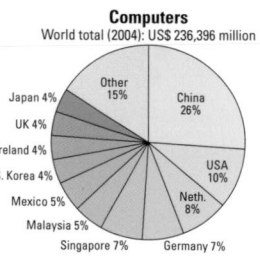

Computers
World total (2004): US$ 236,396 million

Other 15%, China 26%, USA 10%, Neth. 8%, Germany 7%, Singapore 7%, Malaysia 5%, Mexico 5%, S. Korea 4%, Ireland 4%, UK 4%, Japan 4%

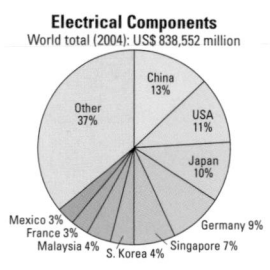

Electrical Components
World total (2004): US$ 838,552 million

Other 37%, China 13%, USA 11%, Japan 10%, Germany 9%, Singapore 7%, S. Korea 4%, Malaysia 4%, France 3%, Mexico 3%

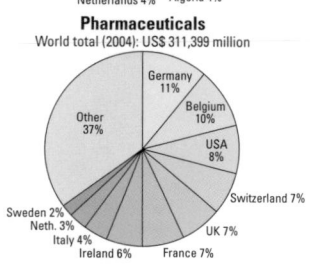

Pharmaceuticals
World total (2004): US$ 311,399 million

Other 37%, Germany 11%, Belgium 10%, USA 8%, Switzerland 7%, UK 7%, France 7%, Ireland 6%, Italy 4%, Neth. 3%, Sweden 2%

Balance of Trade

Value of exports in proportion to the value of imports (2005)

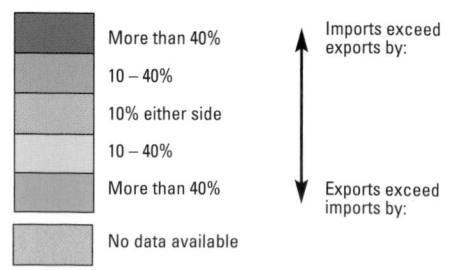

- More than 40%
- 10 – 40%
- 10% either side
- 10 – 40%
- More than 40%
- No data available

Imports exceed exports by:

Exports exceed imports by:

The total world trade balance should amount to zero, since exports must equal imports on a global scale. In practice, at least $100 billion in exports go unrecorded, leaving the world with an apparent deficit and many countries in a better position than public accounting reveals. However, a favourable trade balance is not necessarily a sign of prosperity: many poorer countries must maintain a high surplus in order to service debts, and do so by restricting imports below the levels needed to sustain successful economies.

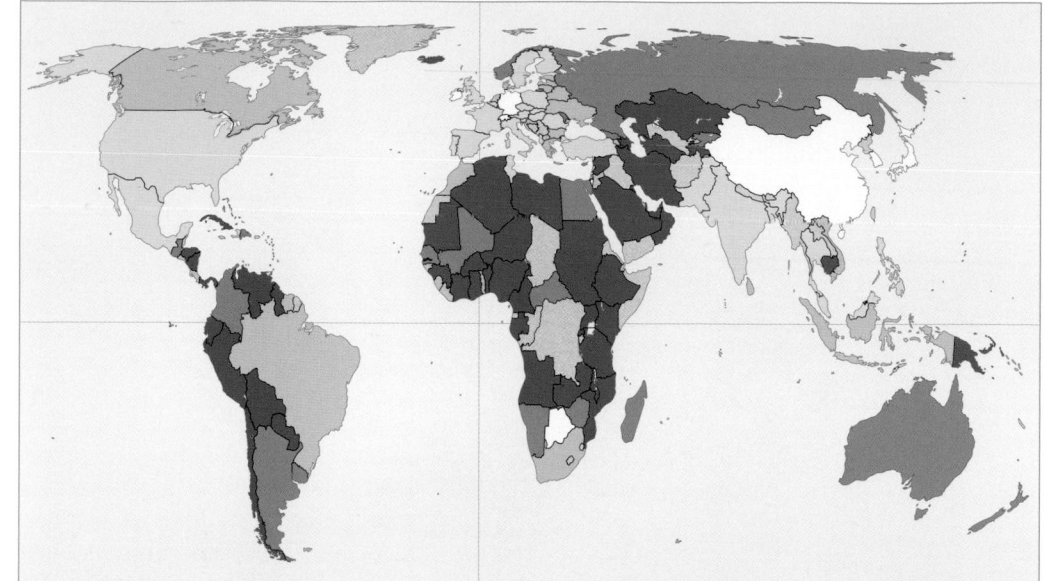

Trade in Primary Exports

Primary exports as a percentage of total export value (2003)

- Over 75%
- 50 – 75%
- 25 – 50%
- 10 – 25%
- Under 10%
- No data available

Primary exports are raw materials or partly processed products that form the basis for manufacturing. They are the necessary requirements of industries and include agricultural products, minerals, fuels and timber, as well as many semi-manufactured goods such as cotton, which has been spun but not woven, wood pulp or flour. Many developed countries have few natural resources and rely on imports for the majority of their primary products. The countries of South-east Asia export hardwoods to the rest of the world, while many South American countries are heavily dependent on coffee exports.

Merchant Fleets

Merchant fleets in thousand gross registered tonnage (2004). Although a large number of vessels are registered in Liberia and Panama, they are not part of the national fleet

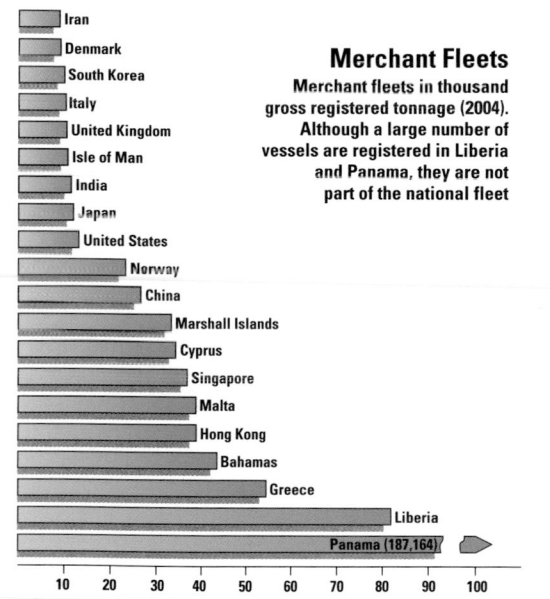

Iran
Denmark
South Korea
Italy
United Kingdom
Isle of Man
India
Japan
United States
Norway
China
Marshall Islands
Cyprus
Singapore
Malta
Hong Kong
Bahamas
Greece
Liberia
Panama (187,164)

10 20 30 40 50 60 70 80 90 100

Top Ten Ports

Total container traffic, in million TEU (2003) ('TEU'stands for Twenty-foot Equivalent Unit, the equivalent of a standard container)

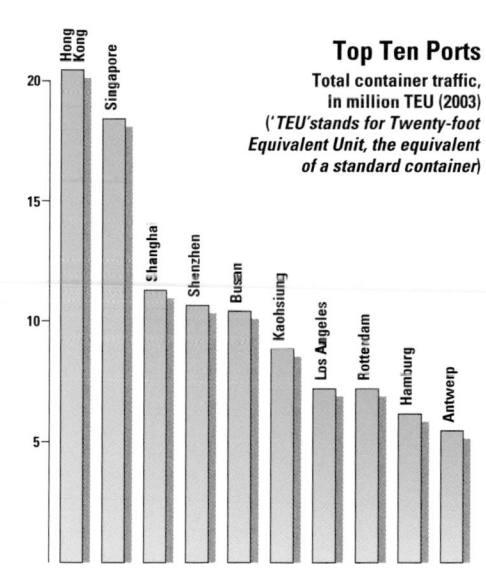

Hong Kong
Singapore
Shanghai
Shenzhen
Busan
Kaohsiung
Los Angeles
Rotterdam
Hamburg
Antwerp

Types of Vessels

World merchant fleet by type of vessel and deadweight tonnage (2003)

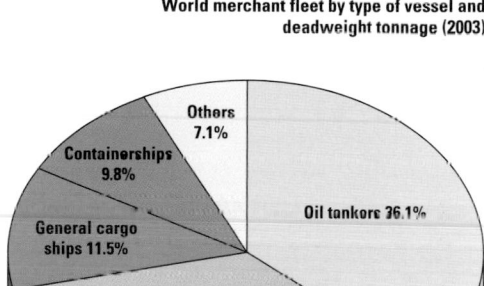

Others 7.1%
Containerships 9.8%
General cargo ships 11.5%
Oil tankers 36.1%
Bulk carriers 35.5%

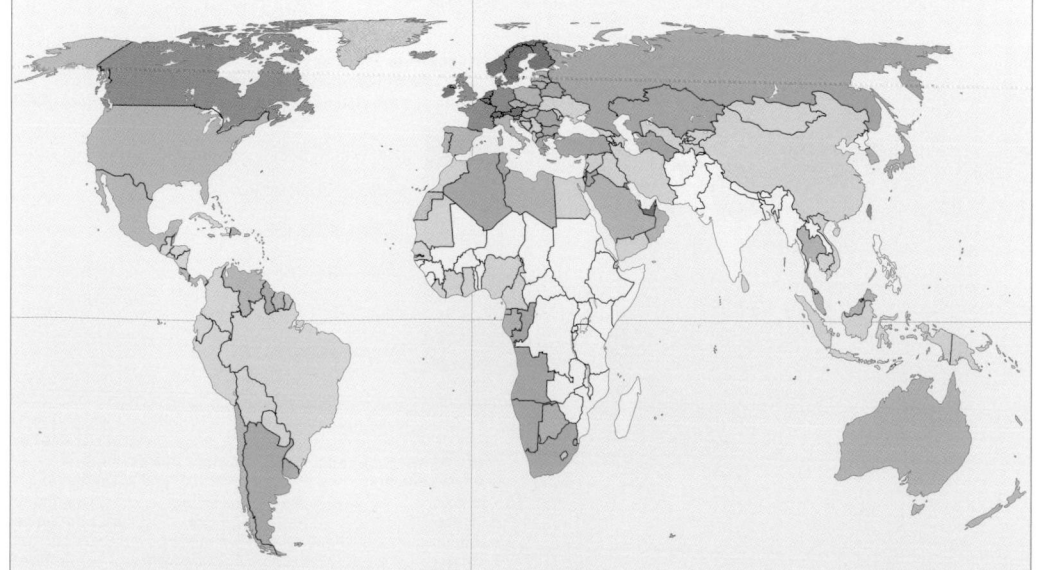

Exports Per Capita

Value of exports in US $, divided by total population (2003)

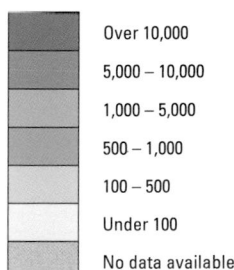

- Over 10,000
- 5,000 – 10,000
- 1,000 – 5,000
- 500 – 1,000
- 100 – 500
- Under 100
- No data available

Highest per capita

Singapore	32,364
Ireland	24,578
United Arab Emirates	22,692
Belgium	17,757
Luxembourg	17,142
Netherlands	15,534

Travel and Tourism

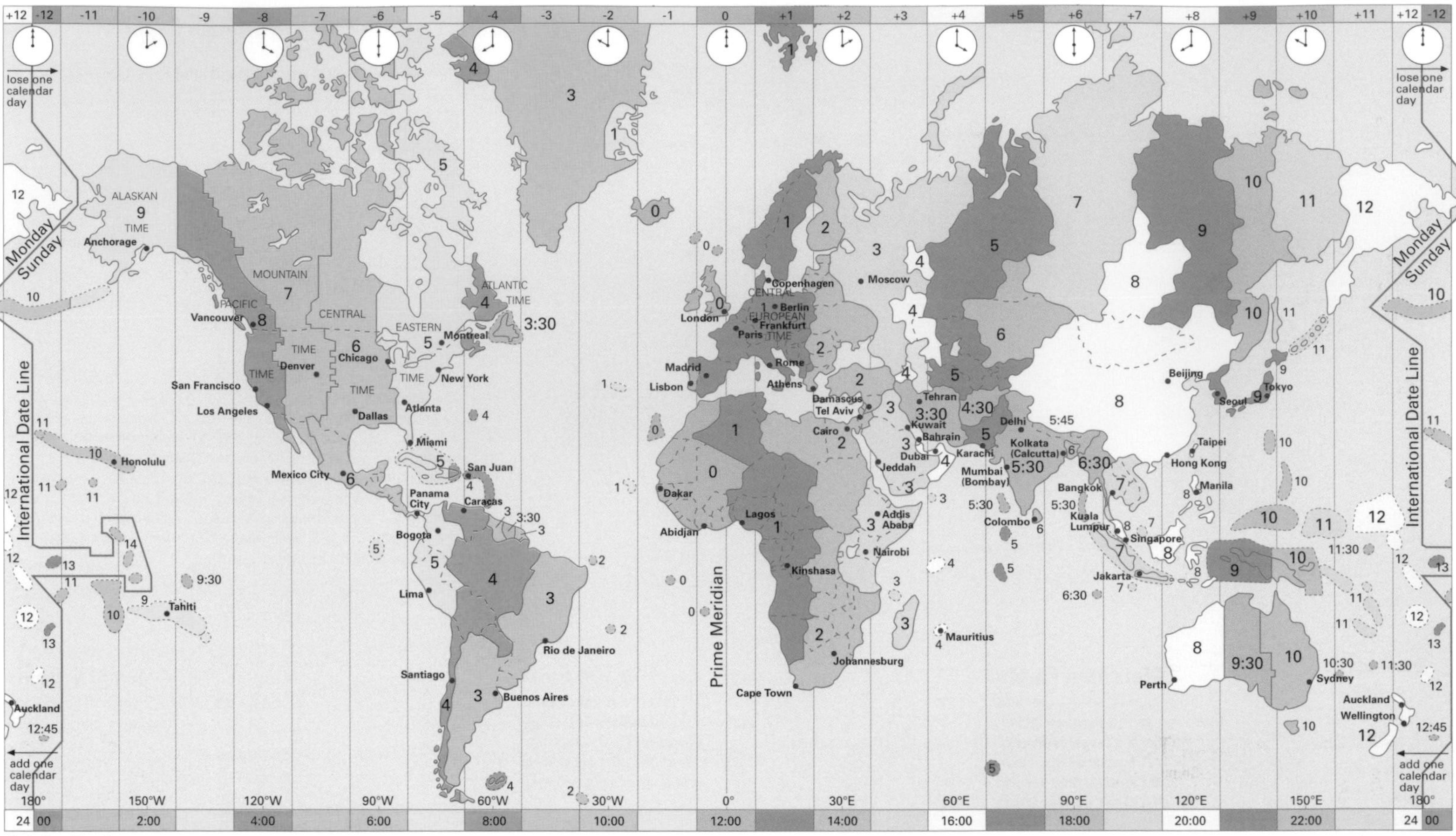

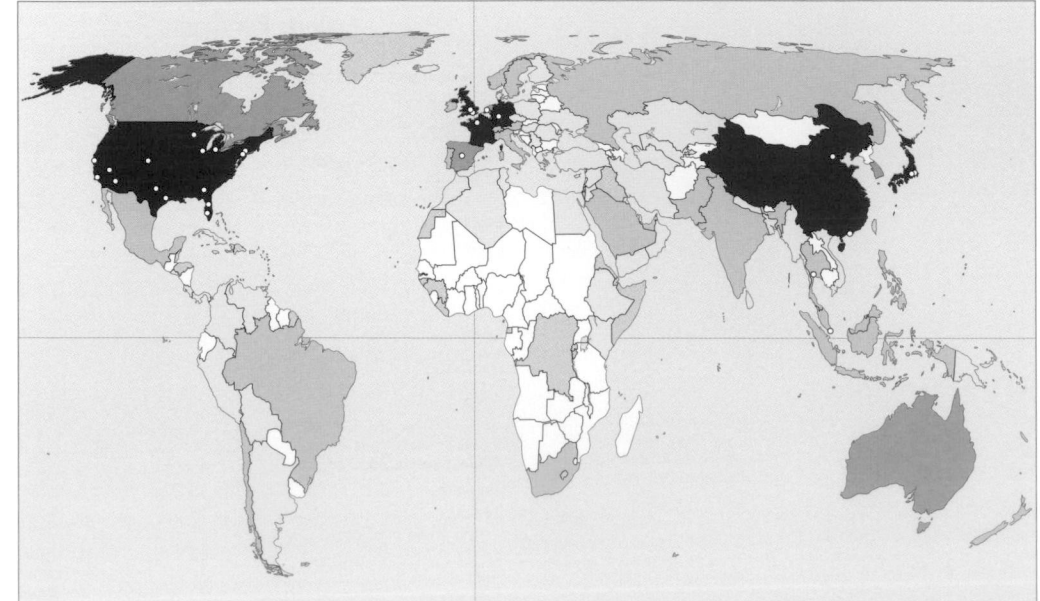

Projection: Mercator

Time Zones

Zones using UT (GMT)	Zones ahead of UT (GMT)	Certain time zones are affected by the incidence of daylight saving time in countries where it is adopted.
Zones behind UT (GMT)	Half-hour zones	
----- International boundaries	Time-zone boundaries	Actual solar time, when it is noon at Greenwich, is shown along the top of the map.
10 Hours fast or slow of UT or Co-ordinated Universal Time	International Date Line	

The world is divided into 24 time zones, each centred on meridians at 15° intervals, which is the longitudinal distance the sun travels every hour. The meridian running through Greenwich, London, passes through the middle of the first zone.

Rail and Road: The Leading Nations

Total rail network ('000 km)		Passenger km per head per year		Total road network ('000 km)		Vehicle km per head per year		Number of vehicles per km of roads	
1. USA	233.8	Japan	1,891	USA	6,378.3	USA	12,505	Hong Kong	287
2. Russia	85.5	Switzerland	1,751	India	3,319.6	Luxembourg	7,989	Qatar	284
3. Canada	73.2	Belarus	1,334	China	1,765.2	Kuwait	7,251	UAE	232
4. India	63.1	France	1,203	Brazil	1,724.9	France	7,142	Germany	195
5. China	60.5	Ukraine	1,100	Canada	1,408.8	Sweden	6,991	Lebanon	191
6. Germany	36.1	Russia	1,080	Japan	1,171.4	Germany	6,806	Macau	172
7. Argentina	34.2	Austria	1,008	France	893.1	Denmark	6,764	Singapore	167
8. France	29.3	Denmark	999	Australia	811.6	Austria	6,518	South Korea	160
9. Mexico	26.5	Netherlands	855	Spain	664.9	Netherlands	5,984	Kuwait	156
10. South Africa	22.7	Germany	842	Russia	537.3	UK	5,738	Taiwan	150
11. Brazil	22.1	Italy	811	Italy	479.7	Canada	5,493	Israel	111
12. Ukraine	22.1	Belgium	795	UK	371.9	Italy	4,852	Malta	110

Air Travel

Passenger kilometres flown on scheduled flights (the number of passengers in thousands – international and domestic – multiplied by the distance flown from the airport of origin) (2002)

	Over 100,000 million
	50,000 – 100,000 million
	10,000 – 50,000 million
	1,000 – 10,000 million
	Under 1,000 million
	No data available
○	Major airports (handling over 30 million passengers)

World's busiest airports (total passengers)		World's busiest airports (international passengers)	
1. Atlanta	(Hartsfield)	1. London	(Heathrow)
2. Chicago	(O'Hare)	2. Paris	(Charles de Gaulle)
3. London	(Heathrow)	3. Frankfurt	(International)
4. Tokyo	(Haneda)	4. Amsterdam	(Schipol)
5. Los Angeles	(International)	5. Hong Kong	(International)

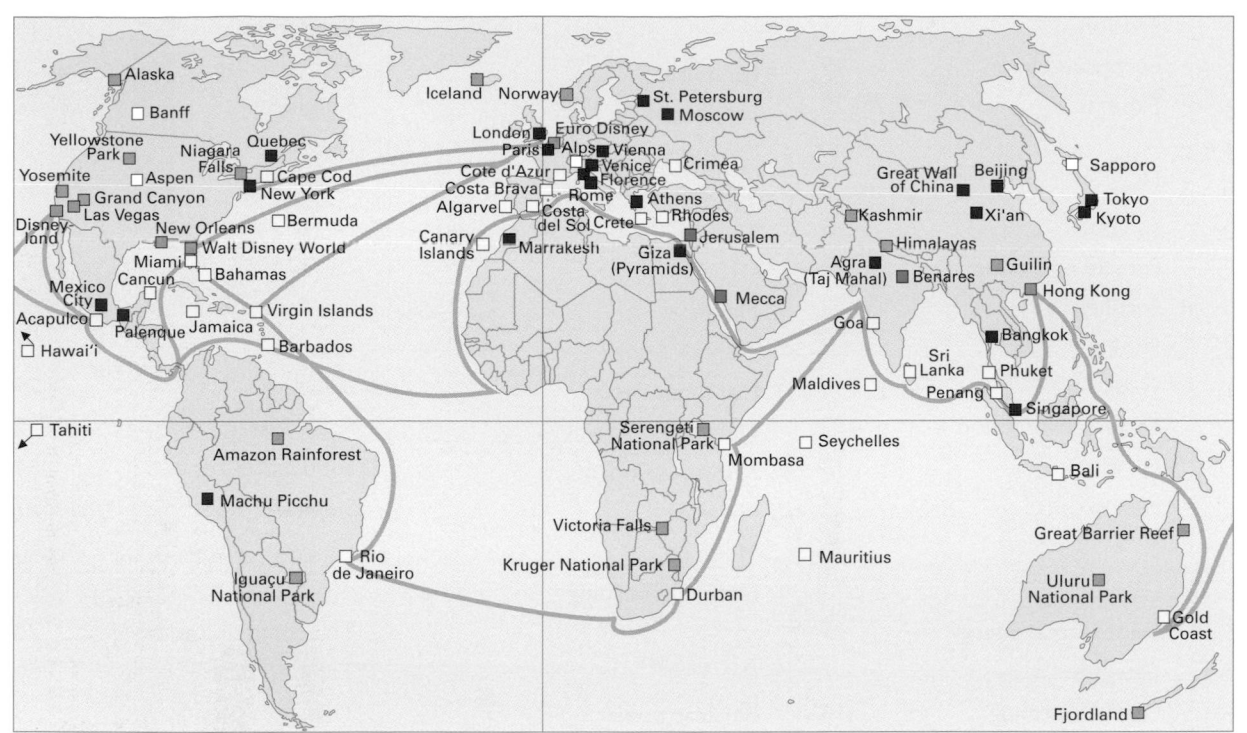

Destinations

- ■ Cultural and historical centres
- □ Coastal resorts
- □ Ski resorts
- ■ Centres of entertainment
- ■ Places of pilgrimage
- ■ Places of great natural beauty
- —— Popular holiday cruise routes

Visitors to the USA

Overseas arrivals to the USA, in thousands (2004)

1.	Canada	13,849
2.	UK	4,302
3.	Mexico	3,993
4.	Japan	3,748
5.	Germany	1,319
6.	France	775
7.	South Korea	627
8.	Australia	520
9.	Italy	470
10.	Netherlands	424

Tourist Spending

Countries spending the most on overseas tourism, US$ million (2003)

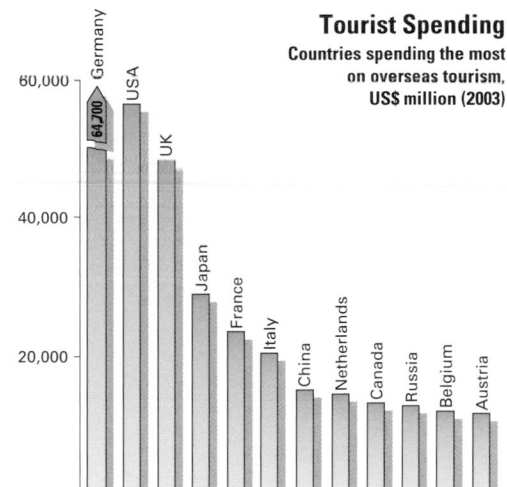

Importance of Tourism

		Arrivals from abroad (2004)	% of world total (2004)
1	France	75,121,000	9.9%
2	Spain	53,599,000	7.1%
3	USA	46,077,000	6.1%
4	China	41,761,000	5.5%
5	Italy	37,071,000	4.9%
6	UK	27,755,000	3.7%
7	Hong Kong	21,811,000	2.9%
8	Mexico	20,618,000	2.7%
9	Germany	20,137,000	2.7%
10	Austria	19,373,000	2.6%
11	Canada	19,150,000	2.5%
12	Turkey	16,826,000	2.2%

After 3 years of stagnant growth, international tourist arrivals reached an all-time record of 763 million in 2004, almost 11% more than in 2003. Growth was common to all regions, but particularly strong in Asia and the Pacific, and in the Middle East.

Tourist Earnings

Countries receiving the most from overseas tourism, US$ million (2003)

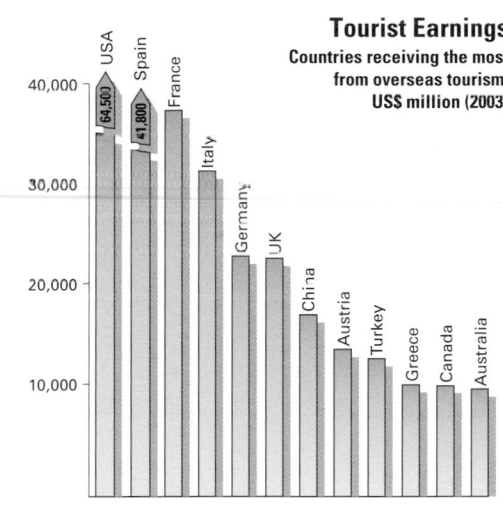

Tourism

Tourism receipts as a percentage of Gross National Income (2004)

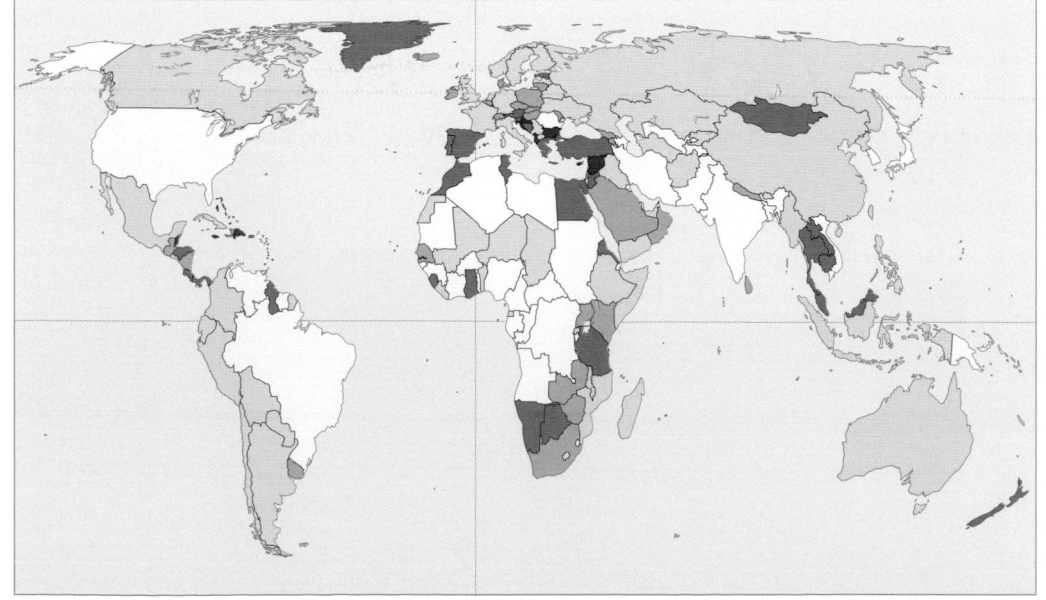

- Over 10%
- 5 – 10%
- 2.5 – 5%
- 1 – 2.5%
- Under 1%
- No data available

Percentage change in tourist arrivals from 2003 to 2004 (top six countries in total number of arrivals)

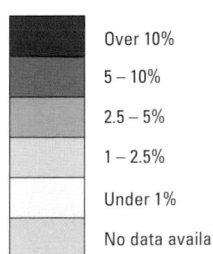

China	+26.7%	(increase)
UK	+12.3%	
USA	+11.8%	
Spain	+3.4%	
France	+0.1%	
Italy	–6.4%	(decrease)

The World In Focus: Index

A

Acid rain 15
Agriculture 26
Aid 21
Airports 30
Air travel 30

B

Balance of trade 28
Beaufort Wind Scale 11

C

Carbon dioxide 10, 14
Cement production 27
Climate regions 10
Coal 25
Continental drift 4
Crops 26
Crust 4–5
Currents 8

D

Day and night 2
Debt 21
Deforestation 15
Desertification 15

E

Earth's structure 4
Earthquakes 4
Eclipses 3
Education 23
El Niño 11
Employment 26
Energy balance 24
Epicentre 4
Equinox 2–3

Erosion 7
European Union 19
Exports 28–29

F

Faults 6
Female education 23
Fertility 23
Fishing 9
Folds 6
Food consumption 22
Forestry 13
Fuel exports 25

G

Geothermal energy 25
Glaciers 7
Global warming 14
Greenhouse effect 14
Gross Domestic Product 20
Gross National Income 20

H

Holiday destinations 31
Hospital beds 22
Household spending 21
Human Development Index 23
Hydroelectricity 25
Hydrological cycle 12

I

Illiteracy 23
Imports 28
Infant mortality 22
Infectious diseases 22
Inflation 20
International organizations 19

L

Land use 13
Landforms 7
Language 18
Life expectancy 22

M

Mantle 4–5
Mercalli Scale 4
Merchant fleets 29
Metals 27
Mid-ocean ridge 5
Minerals 27
Moon 3
Mountain building 6

N

Nuclear power 25

O

Oceans 8
OECD 19, 28
Oil 24–25
Oil spills 9
Ozone 14–15

P

Paper and cardboard 27
Planets 2
Plate tectonics 5
Pollution 9
Population density 16–17
Ports 29
Precipitation 10–12

R

Railways 30

Rainforest 13, 15
Richter Scale 4
Religions 18
Rivers 7
Roads 30

S

Sea-floor spreading 5
Seasons 2
Shipping 29
Solar System 2
Subduction zone 6
Sulphuric acid 27

T

Telecommunications gear 28
Temperature 11
Tides 3
Time 3
Time zones 30
Tourism 31
Trading nations 28
Transport networks 30

U

United Nations 19
Urban population 17

V

Vegetation 13
Vehicles 28, 30
Volcanoes 5

W

Water 12
Wealth gap 20
Wind power 25

WORLD CITIES

Amsterdam	2	Hong Kong	12	Mumbai	20	Tehran	31
Athens	2	Istanbul	12	Munich	21	Toronto	31
Atlanta	3	Jakarta	12	New Orleans	21	Vienna	32
Baghdad	3	Jerusalem	13	New York	22	Warsaw	32
Bangkok	3	Johannesburg	13	Orlando	23	Washington	33
Barcelona	4	Karachi	13	Osaka	23	Wellington	33
Beijing	4	Kolkata	14	Oslo	23		
Berlin	5	Lagos	14	Paris	24	Index	34–39
Boston	6	Las Vegas	14	Prague	25		
Brussels	6	Lima	14	Rio de Janeiro	25		
Budapest	7	London	15	Rome	26	WORLD CITIES	
Buenos Aires	7	Los Angeles	16	San Francisco	26	SATELLITE IMAGES	
Cairo	7	Lisbon	16	St Petersburg	27	Cape Town	40
Cape Town	8	Madrid	17	Santiago	27	Chicago	41
Copenhagen	8	Manila	17	São Paulo	27	Karachi	42
Chicago	9	Melbourne	18	Seoul	27	London	43
Delhi	10	Mexico City	18	Shanghai	28	New York	44
Dublin	10	Miami	18	Singapore	28	San Francisco	45
Edinburgh	11	Milan	19	Stockholm	29	Santiago	46
Guangzhou	11	Moscow	19	Sydney	29	Sydney	47
Helsinki	11	Montréal	20	Tokyo	30	Tokyo	48

CITY MAPS

Motorway, freeway, expressway with toll – with road number — A10	**Primary road** – with road number dual carriageway — 14 single carriageway — 14	**Principal station** Estación del Norte
Motorway, freeway, expressway – with European road number — E51	**Secondary road** – with road number dual carriageway — 96 single carriageway — 96	**Height above sea level** (m) 705 ▲
		Airport ✈
		Airfield ✈
Road junction	**Other road**	**Central area coverage**
Under construction = = =	**Ferry**	
		Urban area
Tunnel	**Railroad**	**Woodlands and parks**

CENTRAL AREA MAPS

Motorway, freeway, expressway	**Limited access/ pedestrian road**	**Abbey, cathedral** ✝
Through route	**Parking** (Europe only) Ⓟ	**Church of interest** †
Secondary road	**Railroad**	**Synagogue** ✡
		Shrine, temple
Dual carriageway	**Rail/bus station**	**Mosque**
Other road	**Underground, metro station**	**Public building**
	Funicular	**Tourist information** ⓘ
Tunnel	**Cable car**	**Place of interest** Palace

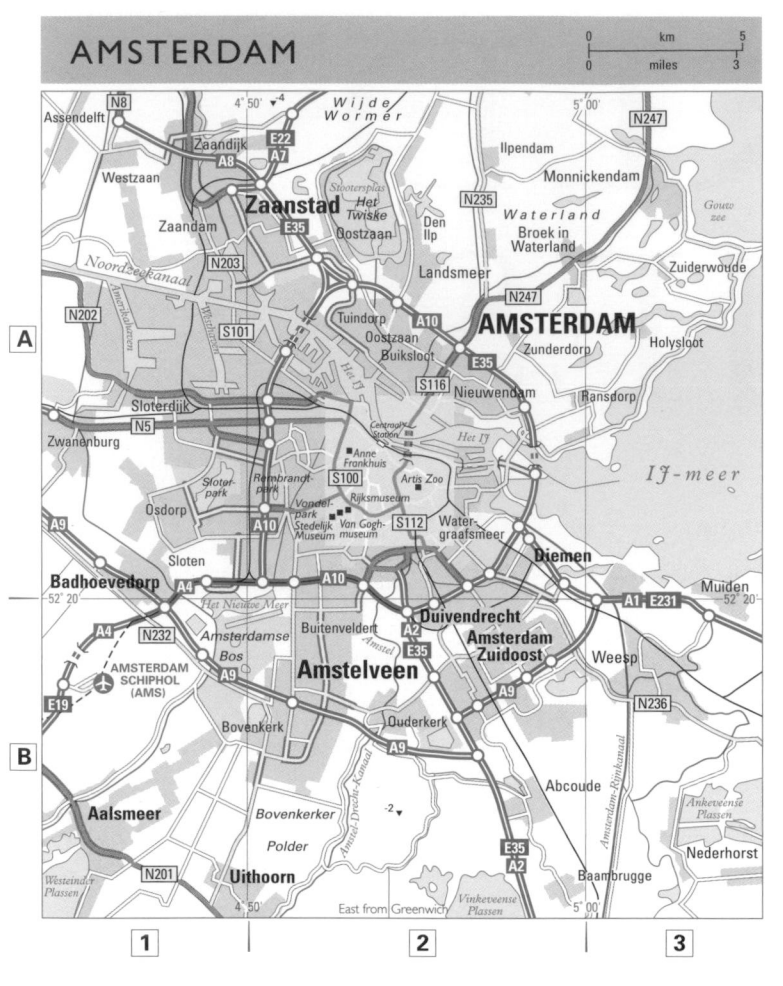

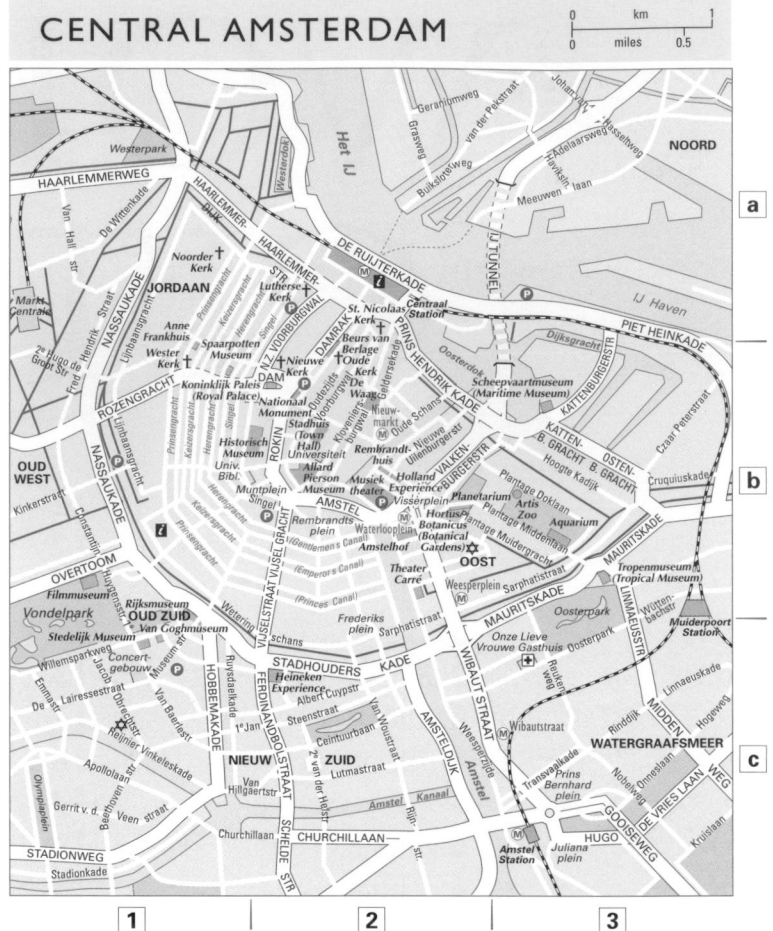

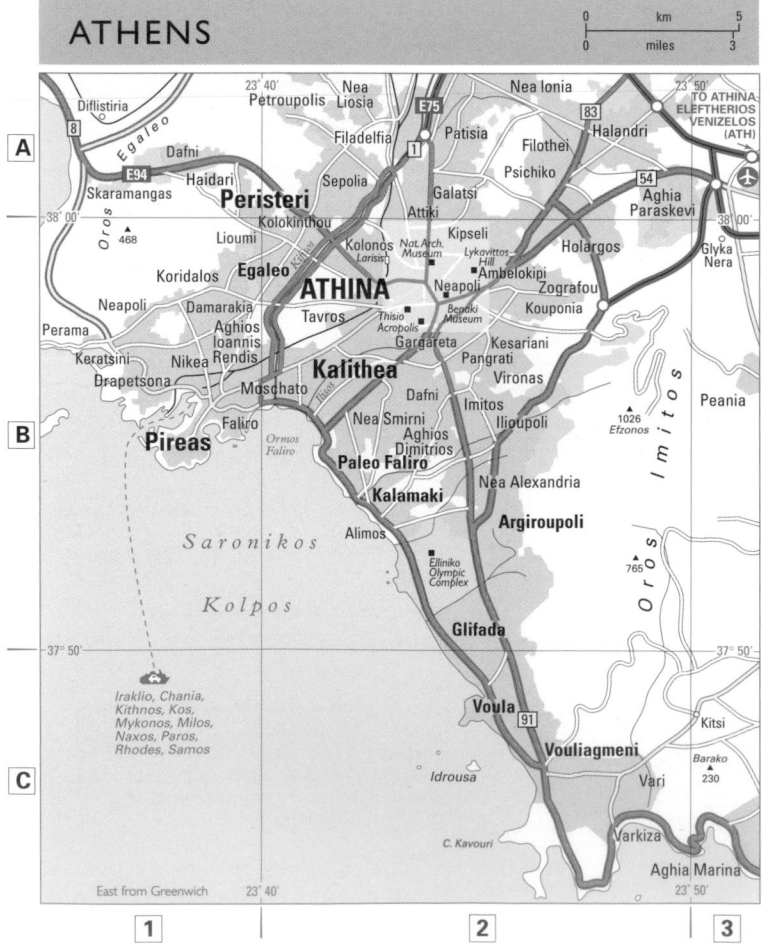

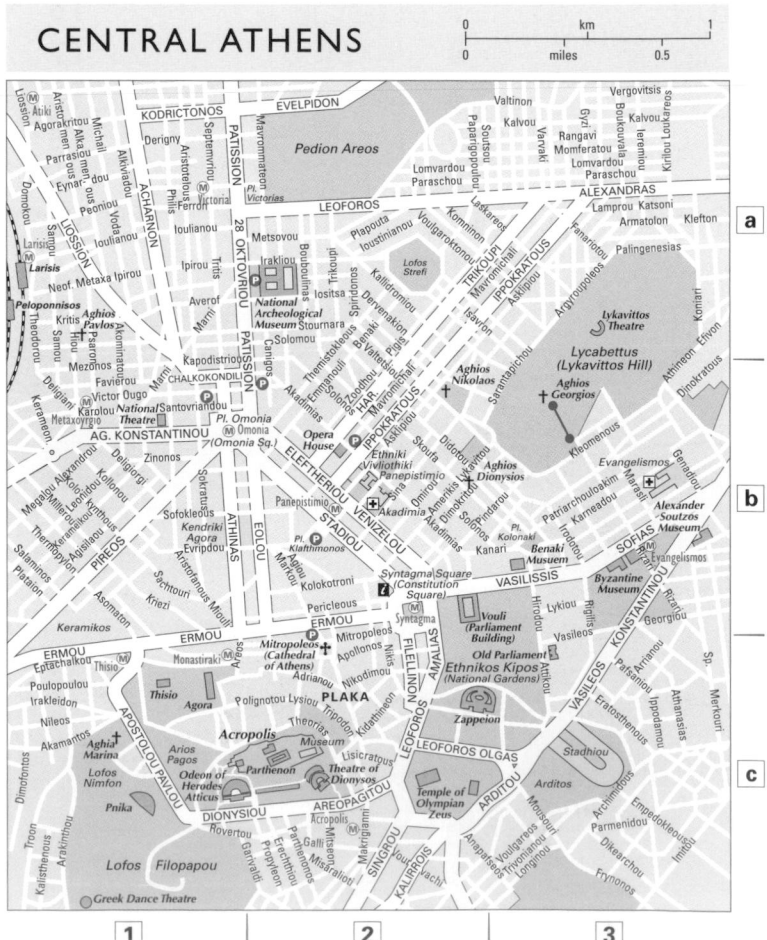

ATLANTA

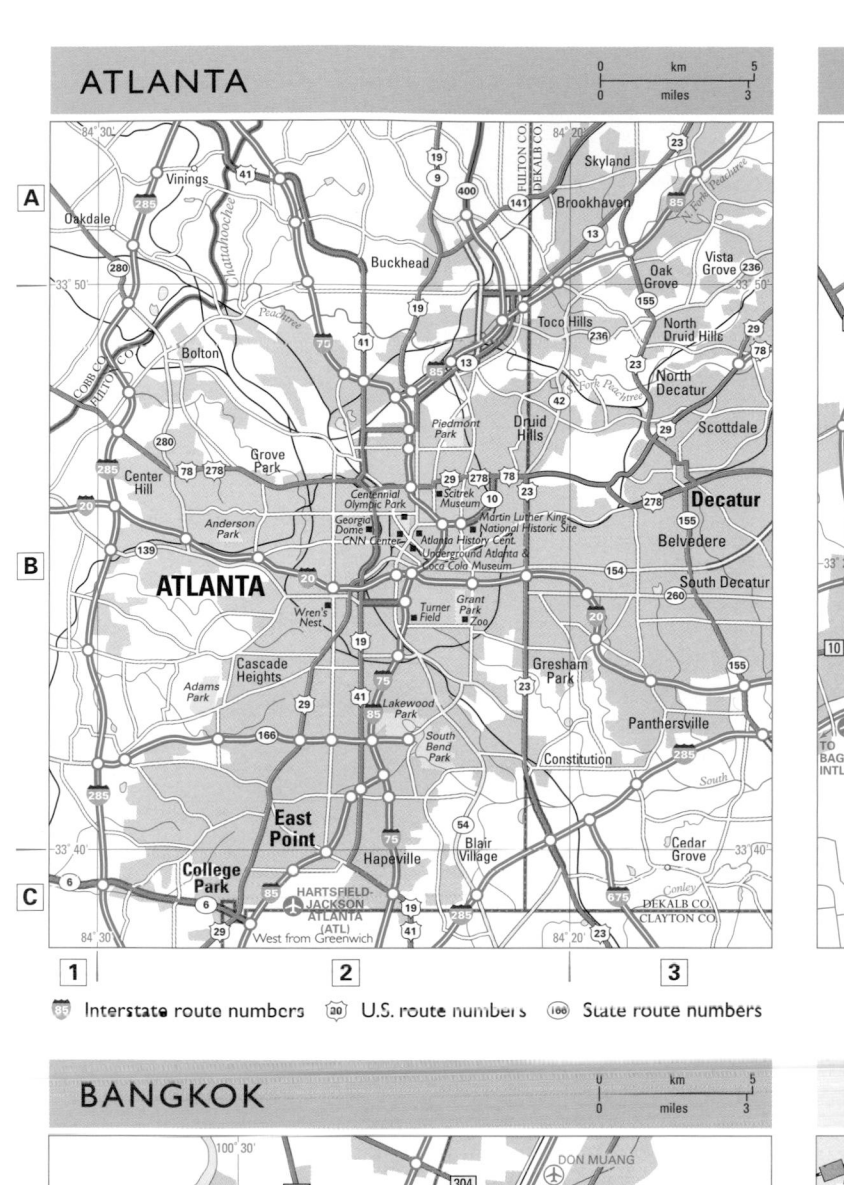

Interstate route numbers · U.S. route numbers · State route numbers

BAGHDAD

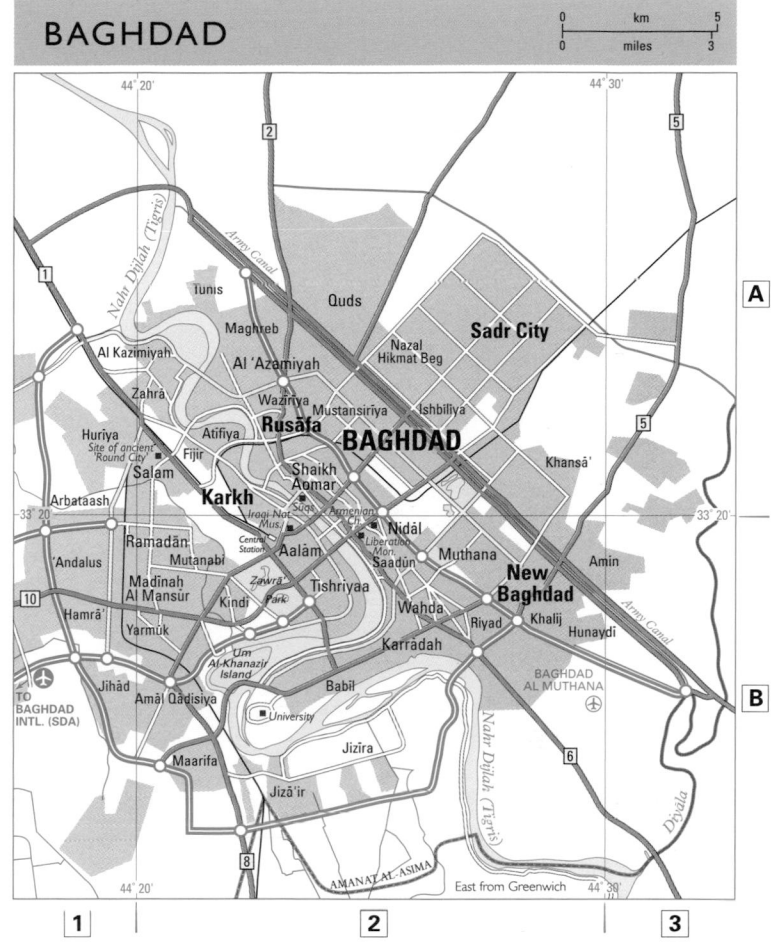

BANGKOK

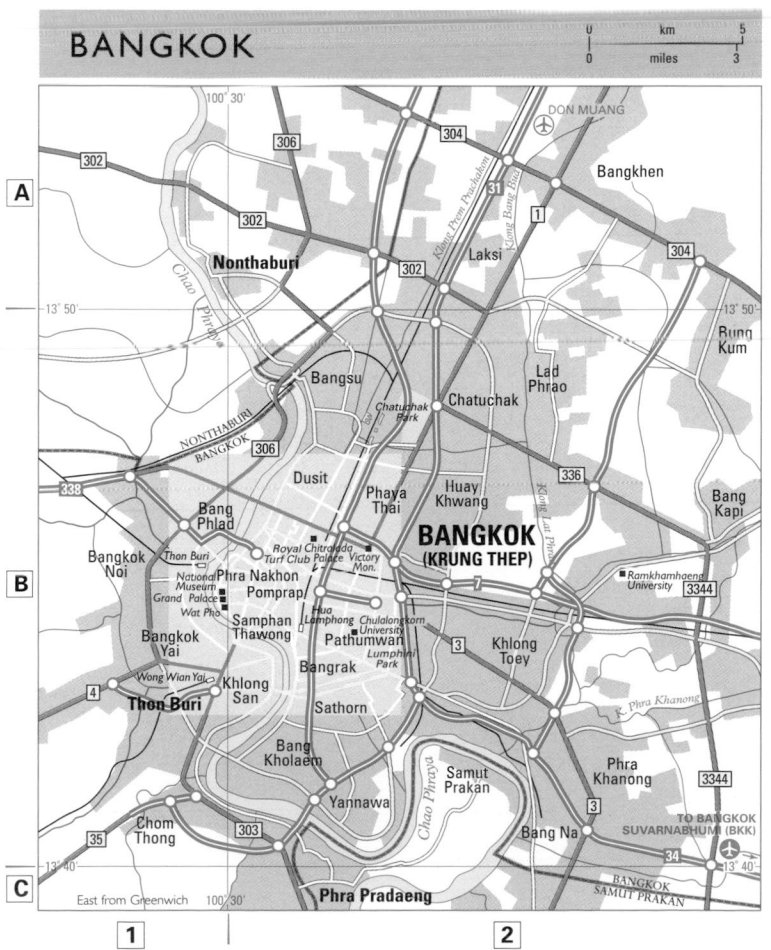

CENTRAL BANGKOK

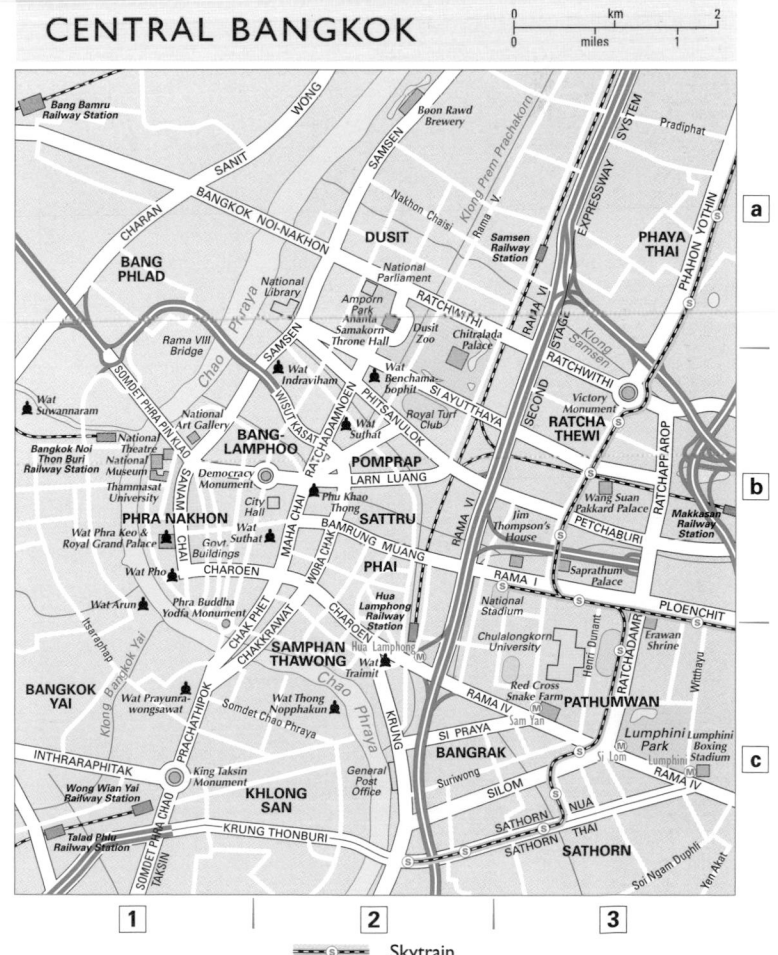

Skytrain

COPYRIGHT PHILIP'S

BARCELONA

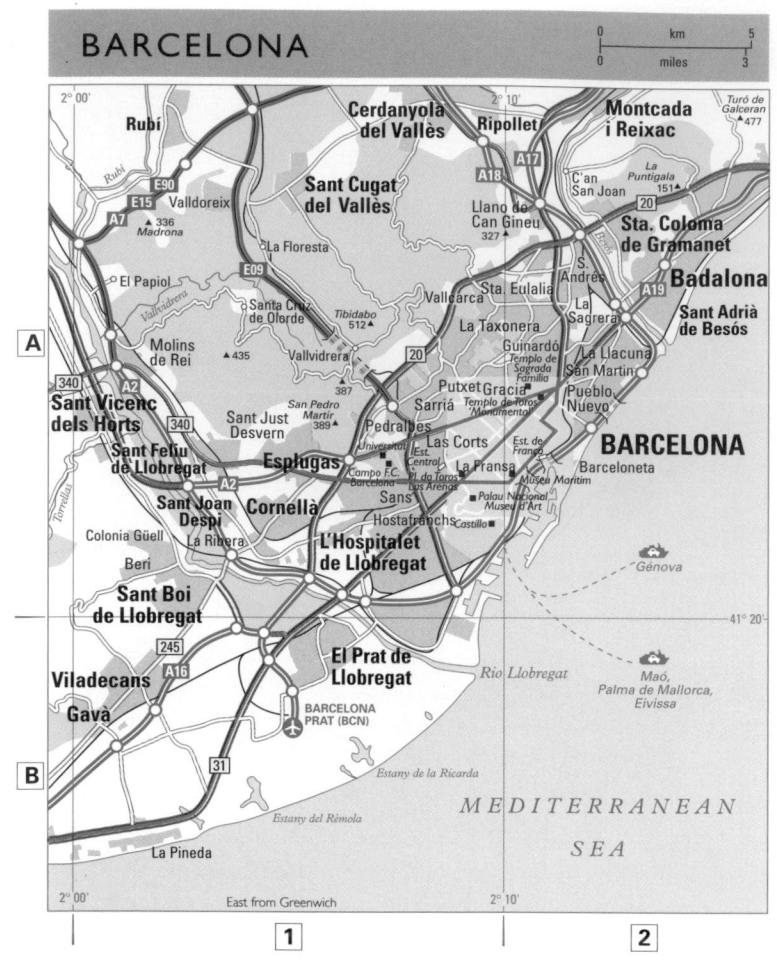

CENTRAL BARCELONA

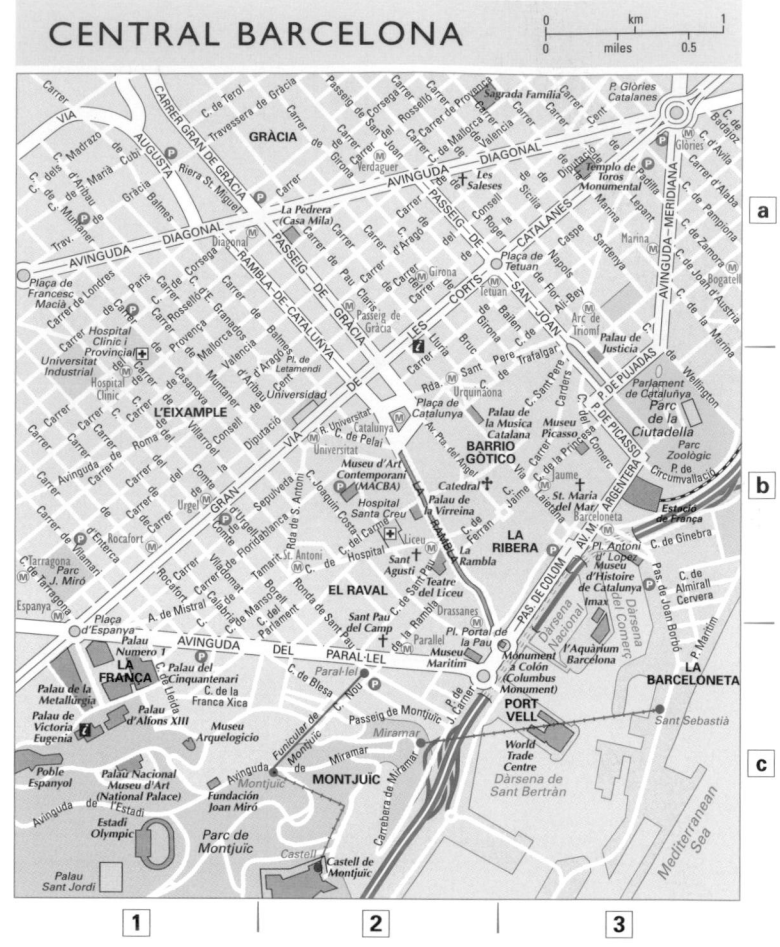

BEIJING

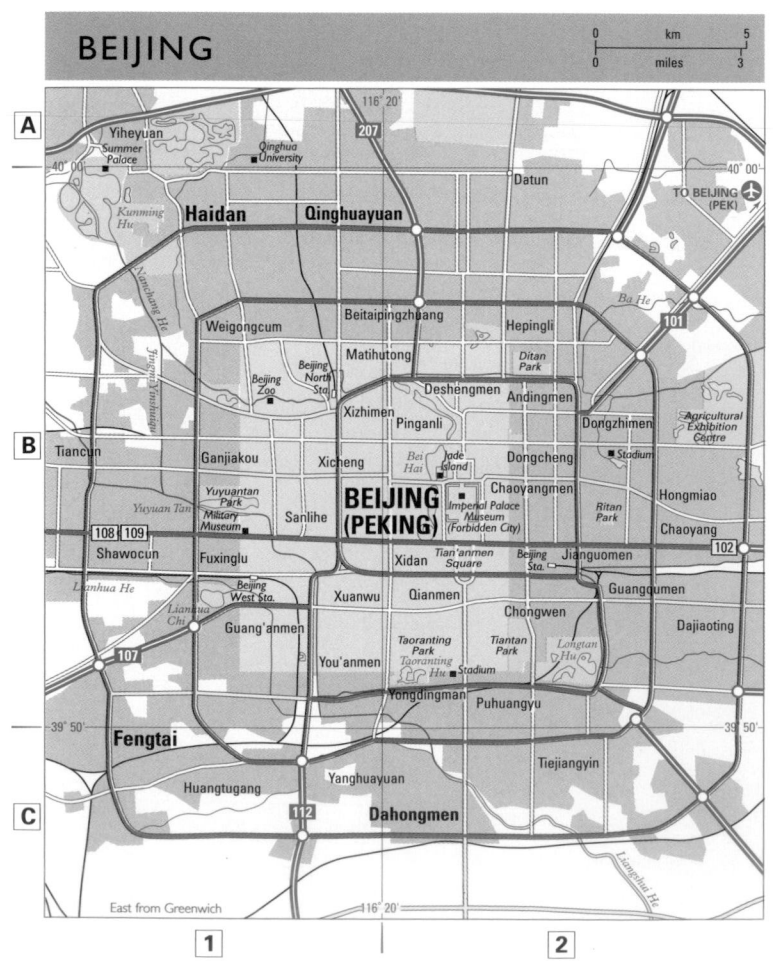

CENTRAL BEIJING

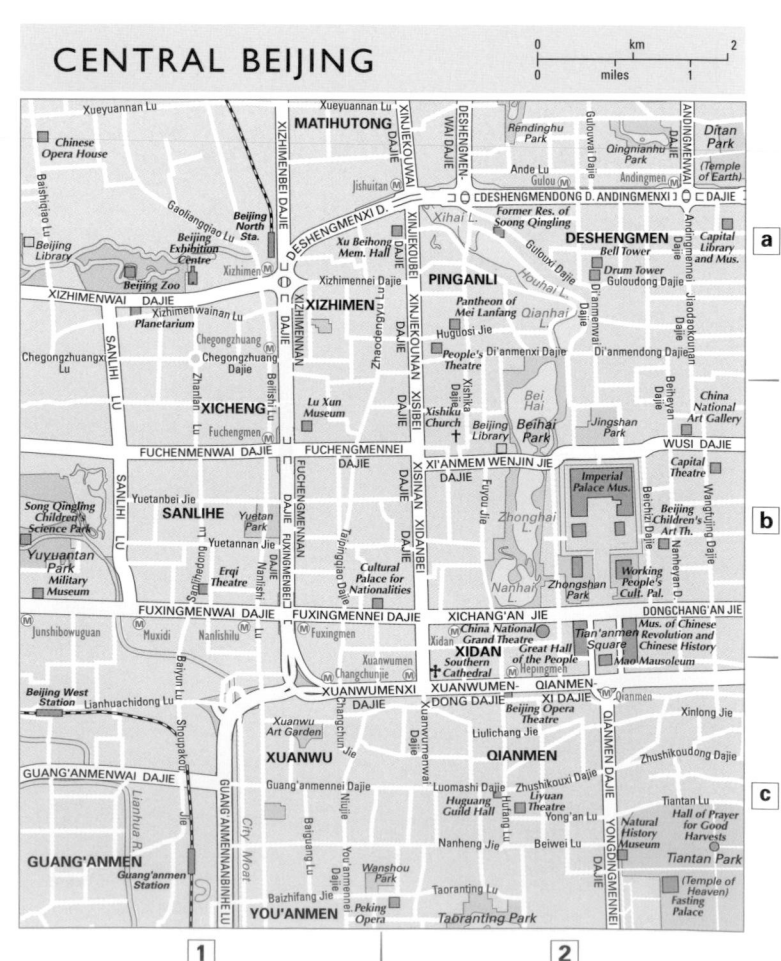

BERLIN

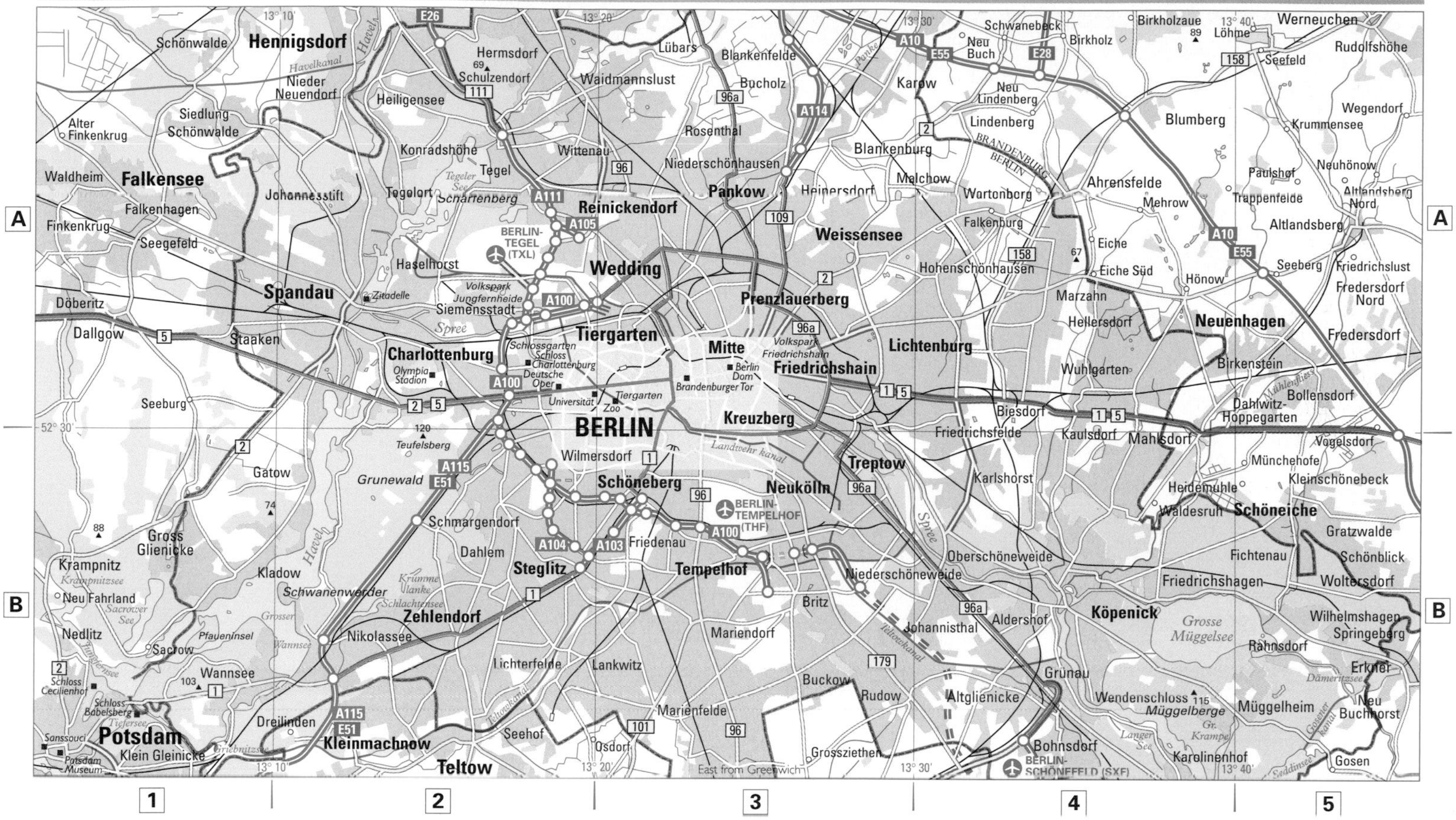

km 0 — 5
miles 0 — 3

Schönwalde · Hennigsdorf · Lübars · Blankenfelde · Birkholzaue · Werneuchen
Hermsdorf · Schulzendorf · Waidmannslust · Bucholz · Neu Buch · Schwanebeck · Birkholz · Löhme · Rudolfshöhe
Nieder Neuendorf · Heiligensee · Karow · Neu Lindenberg · Seefeld · Rudolfshöhe
Alter Finkenkrug · Siedlung Schönwalde · Konradshöhe · Tegel · Niederschönhausen · Rosenthal · Blankenburg · Blumberg · Krummensee · Wegendorf
Waldheim · **Falkensee** · Falkenhagen · Johannisstift · Tegelort · Scharfenberg · Reinickendorf · **Pankow** · Heinersdorf · Malchow · Wartenberg · Ahrensfelde · Mehrow · Neuhönow · Wegendorf
Finkenkrug · Seegefeld · **BERLIN-TEGEL (TXL)** · **Wedding** · **Weissensee** · Hohenschönhausen · Marzahn · Hellersdorf · **Neuenhagen** · Fredersdorf
A Döberitz · Dallgow · **Spandau** · Haselhorst · Siemensstadt · **Tiergarten** · **Mitte** · **Prenzlauerberg** · Eiche · Eiche Süd · Hönow · Seeberg · Friedrichslust · Fredersdorf Nord · **A**
Staaken · Volkspark Jungfernheide · Schlossgarten Charlottenburg · Volkspark Friedrichshain · **Lichtenburg** · Wuhlgarten · Birkenstein
Seeburg · **Charlottenburg** · Olympia Stadion · Deutsche Oper · Universität · **Friedrichshain** · Biesdorf · Kaulsdorf · Mahlsdorf · Dahlwitz-Hoppegarten · Münchehofe
BERLIN · Zoo · Brandenburger Tor · Berlin Dom · **Kreuzberg** · Friedrichsfelde · Kleinschönebeck
Teufelsberg · Wilmersdorf · **Treptow** · Karlshorst · **Schöneiche** · Gratzwalde
Grunewald · **Schöneberg** · **Neukölln** · Oberschöneweide · Heidemühle · Fichtenau · Schönblick
B Krampnitz · Gross Glienicke · Schmargendorf · Dahlem · **BERLIN-TEMPELHOF (THF)** · Friedenau · **Tempelhof** · Niederschöneweide · Waldesruh · Woltersdorf · **B**
Neu Fahrland · Kladow · **Steglitz** · Britz · Johannisthal · Aldershof · **Köpenick** · Rahnsdorf · Wilhelmshagen · Springberg
Nedlitz · Sacrow · Nikolassee · **Zehlendorf** · Lichterfelde · Mariendorf · Grunau · Grosse Müggelsee · Erkner
Wannsee · Lankwitz · Buckow · Wendenschloss · Müggelberge · Müggelheim · Neu Buchhorst
Potsdam · Klein Gleinicke · Dreilinden · **Kleinmachnow** · Seehof · Marienfelde · Rudow · Altglienicke · Bohnsdorf · Karolinenhof · Gosen
Sanssouci · Potsdam Museum · **Teltow** · Osdorf · Grossziethen · **BERLIN-SCHÖNEFELD (SXF)**

East from Greenwich

1 · 2 · 3 · 4 · 5

CENTRAL BERLIN

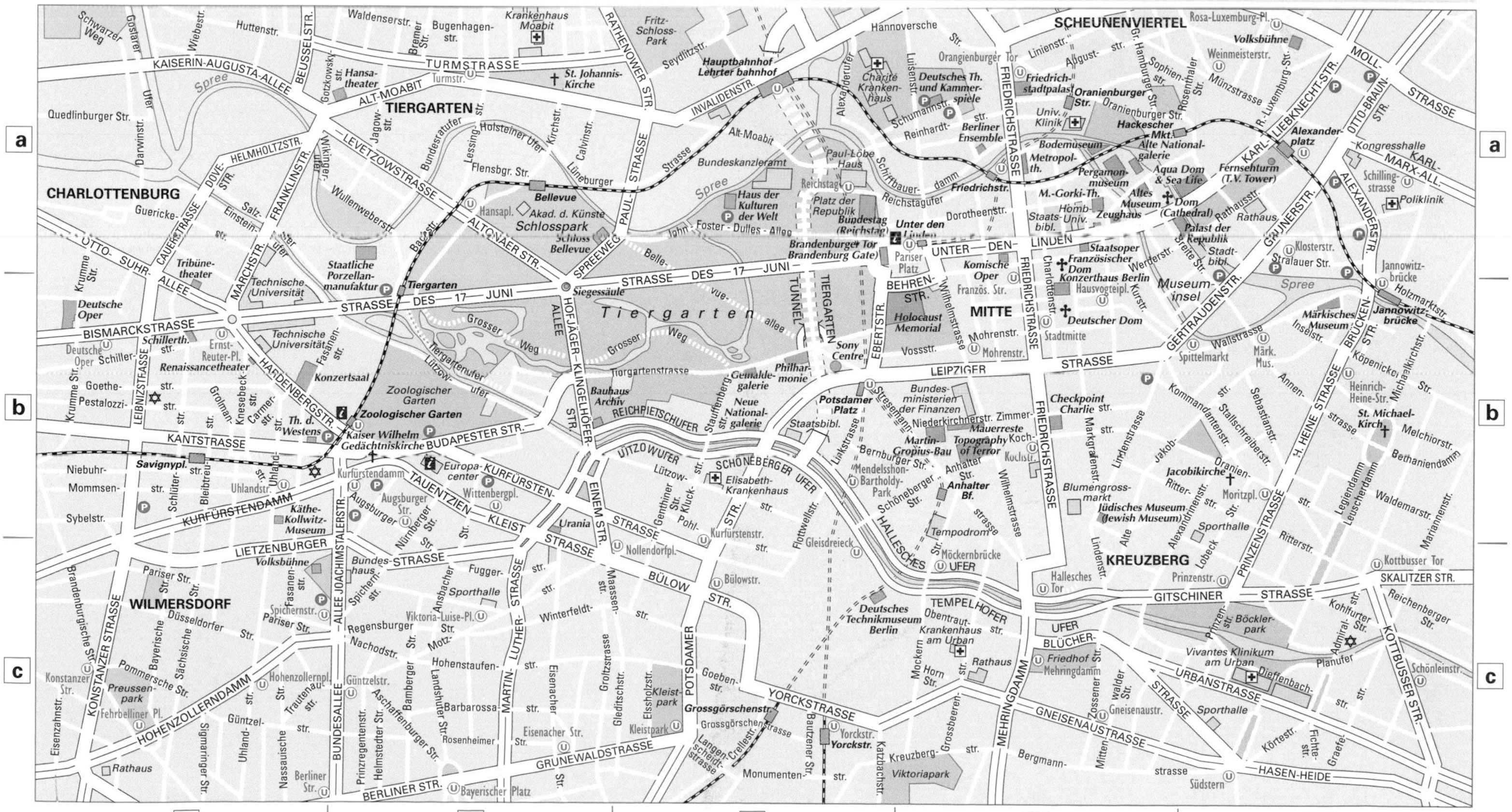

km 0 — 1
miles 0 — 0.5

SCHEUNENVIERTEL · Rosa-Luxemburg-Pl.
Hauptbahnhof Lehrter bahnhof · Friedrichstadtpalast · Oranienburger Tor
TIERGARTEN · Deutsche Th. und Kammerspiele · Hackesche · **KARL LIEBKNECHT STR.** · Alexanderplatz · Kongresshalle
a **CHARLOTTENBURG** · Bellevue · Schlosspark · Schloss Bellevue · Haus der Kulturen der Welt · Bundeskanzleramt · Reichstag · Platz der Republik · Bodemuseum · Pergamonmuseum · Alte Nationalgalerie · Aqua Dom & Sea Life · Fernsehturm (T.V. Tower) · **a**
Tiergarten · Siegessäule · STRASSE DES 17 JUNI · Brandenburger Tor (Brandenburg Gate) · Pariser Platz · UNTER-DEN-LINDEN · Staatsoper · Dom (Cathedral) · Palast der Republik · Rathaus
Deutsche Oper · Technische Universität · Konzertsaal · Holocaust Memorial · **MITTE** · Komische Oper · Konzerthaus Berlin · Deutscher Dom · Museuminsel · Spree
b Zoologischer Garten · Kaiser Wilhelm Gedächtniskirche · Europa-Center · Bauhaus Archiv · Gemäldegalerie · Neue Nationalgalerie · Philharmonie · Sony Centre · Potsdamer Platz · Bundesministerium der Finanzen · Martin-Gropius-Bau · Topography of Terror · Checkpoint Charlie · Märkisches Museum · **b**
WILMERSDORF · KURFÜRSTENDAMM · Volksbühne · Käthe-Kollwitz-Museum · Urania · Anhalter Bf. · Jüdisches Museum (Jewish Museum) · **KREUZBERG**
c Rathaus · Deutsches Technikmuseum Berlin · Tempodrom · Friedhof Mehringdamm · Vivantes Klinikum am Urban · **c**
Grossgörschenstr. · Yorckstr. · Kreuzberg · Viktoriapark

1 · 2 · 3 · 4 · 5

BOSTON

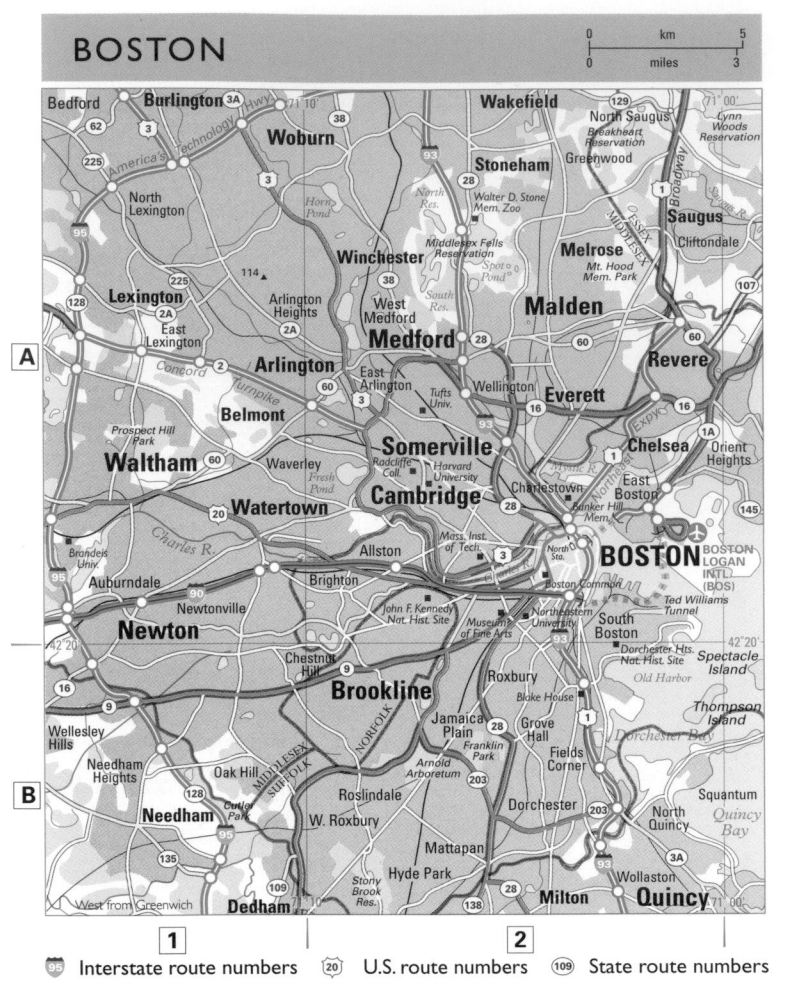

Interstate route numbers ⬤ U.S. route numbers ⬤ State route numbers

CENTRAL BOSTON

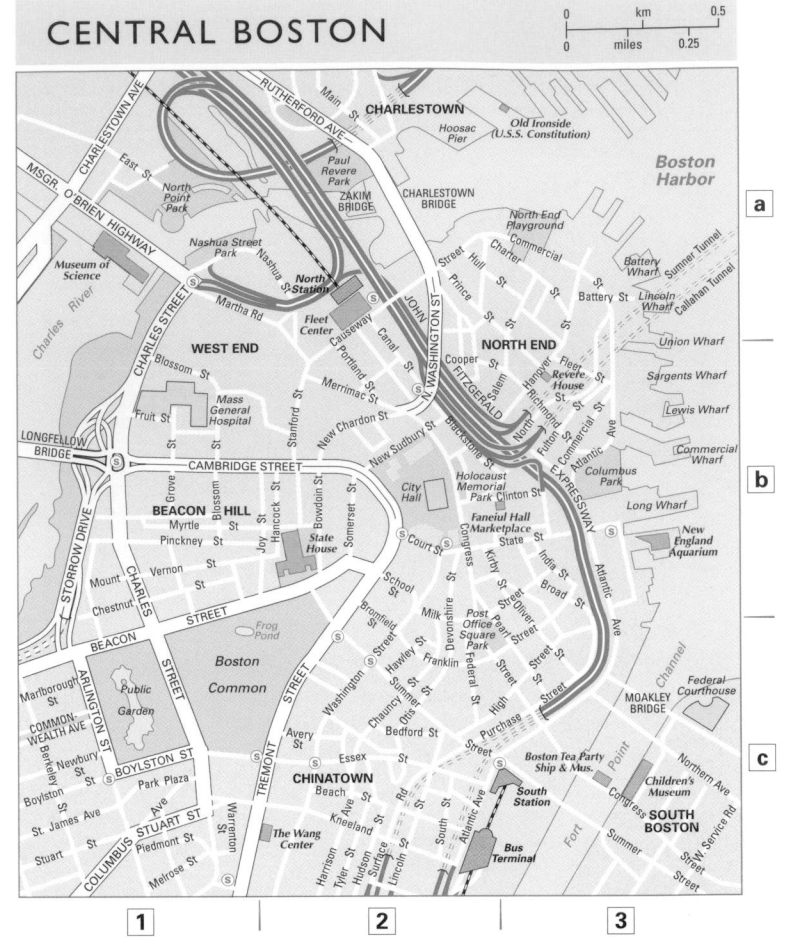

BRUSSELS

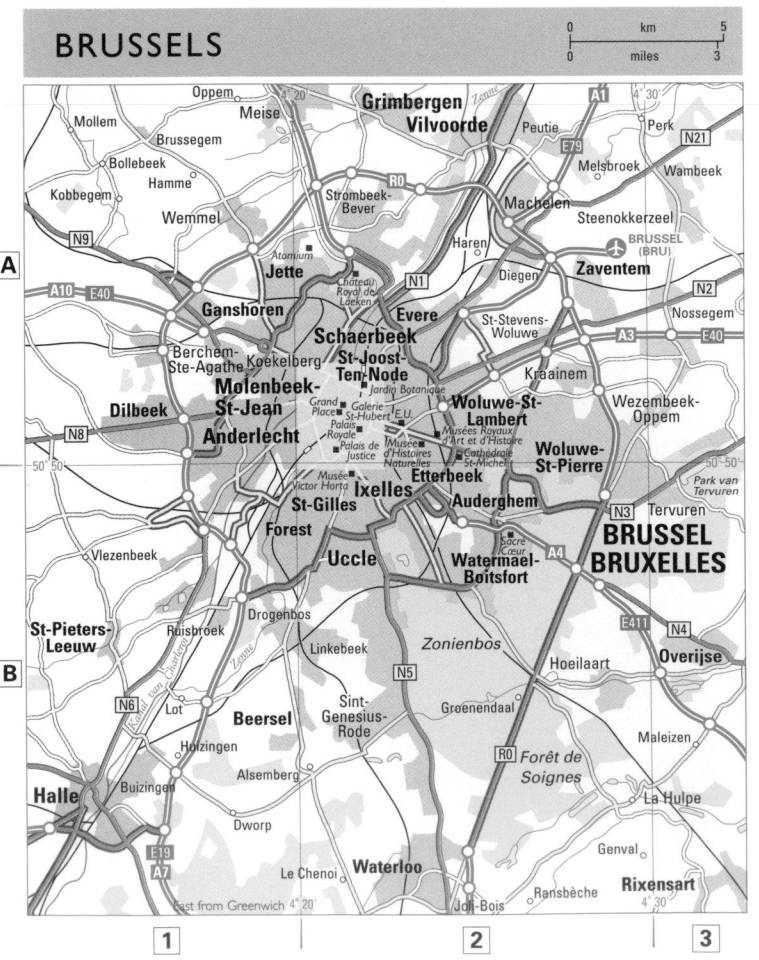

CENTRAL BRUSSELS

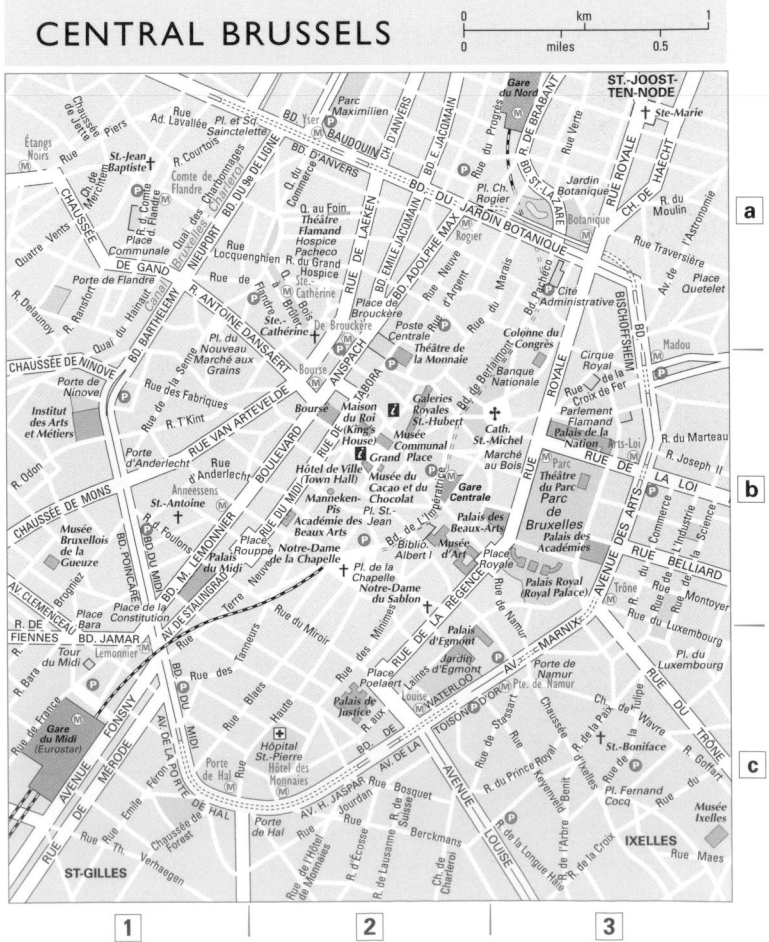

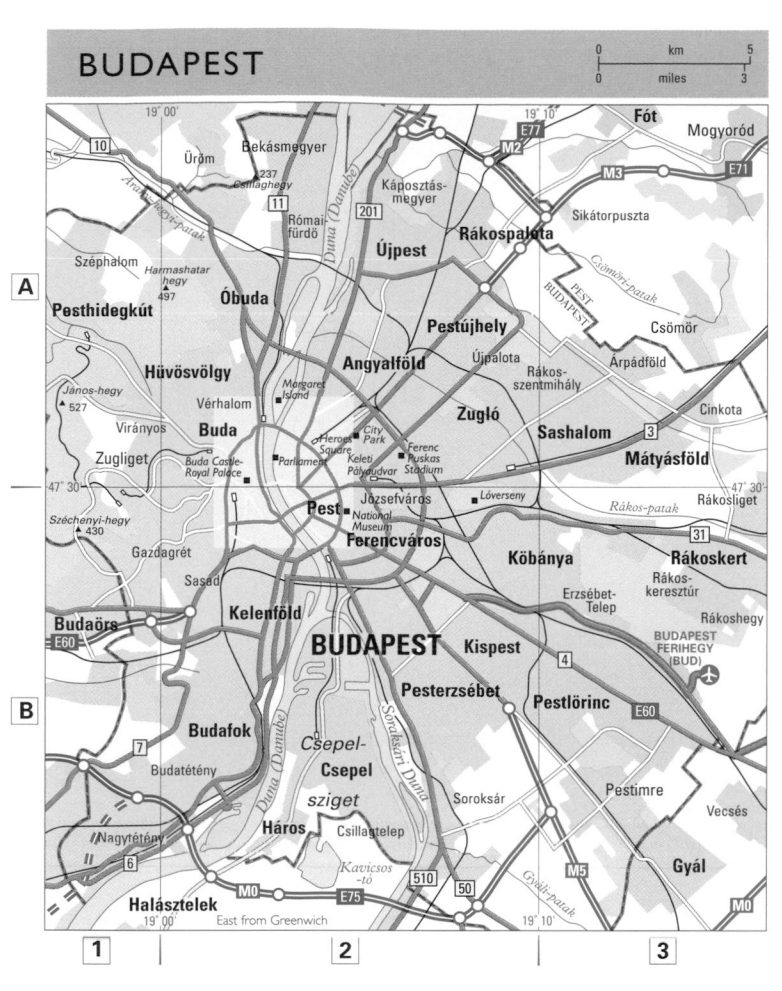
BUDAPEST
0 km 5
0 miles 3
Fót
Mogyoród
Üröm
Békásmegyer
Káposztás-megyer
Sikátorpuszta
Római-fürdő
Újpest
Rákospalota
Széphalom
Hármashatár hegy 497
Óbuda
Pesthidegkút
Pestújhely
Csömör
Hűvösvölgy
Angyalföld
Újpalota
Árpádföld
Rákos-szentmihály
Vérhalom
Cinkota
János-hegy 527
Virányos
Buda
Zugló
Sashalom
Zugliget
Mátyásföld
Buda Castle-Royal Palace
Parliament
Heroes' Square
City Park
Ferenc Puskás Stadium
Keleti Pályaudvar
Józsefváros
Lóverseny
Rákosliget
Széchenyi-hegy 430
Pest
National Museum
Rákos-patak
Gazdagrét
Ferencváros
Kőbánya
Rákoskert
Sasad
Rákos-keresztúr
Erzsébet-Telep
Rákoshegy
Budaörs
Kelenföld
BUDAPEST
Kispest
BUDAPEST FERIHEGY (BUD)
Pesterzsébet
Pestlőrinc
Budafok
Budatétény
Csepel-
Csepel
sziget
Soroksári Duna
Soroksár
Pestimre
Vecsés
Nagytétény
Háros
Csillagtelep
Gyál
Kavicsos -tó
Halásztelek
Gyáli-patak
19° 00'
19° 10'
47° 30'
East from Greenwich
Duna (Danube)
A
B
1
2
3

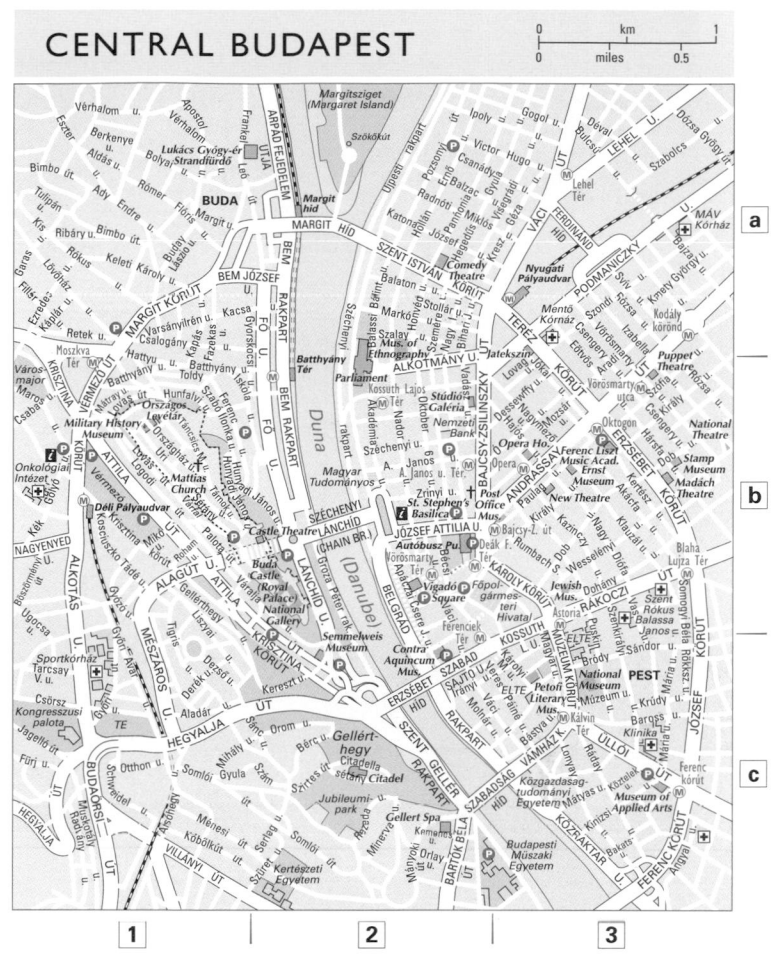
CENTRAL BUDAPEST
0 km 1
0 miles 0.5
Margitsziget (Margaret Island)
Szökőkút
Lukács Gyógy-ér Strandfürdő
BUDA
MARGIT HÍD
Margit híd
Nyugati Pályaudvar
MÁV Kórház
Comedy Theatre
Batthyány Tér
Parliament
Ethnography Mus. of
Puppet Theatre
Military History Museum
Országos Levéltár
Stúdió Galéria
Nemzeti Bank
Opera
Opera Ho.
Ferenc Liszt Music Acad.
Ernst Museum
National Theatre
Stamp Museum
Madách Theatre
New Theatre
Mattias Church
Onkológiai Intézet
Déli Pályaudvar
Castle Theatre
SZÉCHENYI LÁNCHÍD (CHAIN BR.)
St. Stephen's Basilica
Post Office Mus.
Buda Castle (Royal Palace)
National Gallery
Autóbusz Pu.
Deák F. Tér
Vigadó
Jewish Mus.
Semmelweis Museum
Contra Aquincum Mus.
Astoria
Szent Rókus
Sportkórház
National Museum
Petőfi Literary Mus.
Kálvin Tér
Gellért-hegy
Citadella
Citadel
Jubileumi-park
Gellert Spa
Budapesti Műszaki Egyetem
Közgazdaság-tudományi Egyetem
Museum of Applied Arts
Kertészeti Egyetem
Duna
(Danube)
a
b
c
1
2
3

BUENOS AIRES
0 km 5
0 miles 3
58° 30'
Acassuso
Juan Anchorena
Martinez
58° 20'
34° 30'
La Lucila
Olivos
Ruta Panamericana
Villa Adelina
Vicente Lopez
Carapachay
Munro
Florida
Ciudad Universitaria
Rio de la Plata
Núñez
Saavedra
Estadio Monumental
Villa Ballester
JORGE NEWBERY
Parque Pres. Sarmiento
Belgrano
BUENOS AIRES
Hipódromo Argentino
Parque 3 de Febrero
Villa Urquiza
Colegiales
General San Martin
Chacarita
Palermo
Puerto Retiro
Museo Nacional de Bellas Artes
Villa Bosch
Estación Lacroze
Recoleta
Retiro
Estación Retiro
Villa Lynch
La Paternal
Parque Natural Reserva Ecologica Costanera Sur
Estación Once
Teatro Colón
San Nicolás
Plaza de Mayo
Almagro
Villa Sáenz Pena
Villa Devota
Monserrat
San Telmo
Balvanera
Floresta
Puerto Madero
Caballito
Villa Ciudadela
Versailles
Constitución
Estación Constitución
Boedo
San Cristobal
Parque Avellaneda
Flores
Parque Chacabuco
Parque Patricios
La Boca
Ramos Mejía
Liniers
Riachuelo
Nueva Pompeya
Barracas
Mataderos
Avellaneda
34° 40'
San Justo
DISTRITO FEDERAL BUENOS AIRES
Almirante G. Brown
Villa Diamante
Sarandi
Villa Dominico
Tablada
Villa Madero
Villa Lugano
Gerli
Autódromo Oscar A. Gálvez
Caraza
Villa C. Colón
Fiorito
Tapiales
Ciudad General Belgrano
Aldo Bonzi
Lanús
Villa Barilari
TO BUENOS AIRES EZEIZA (EZE)
Salada
Remedios de Escalada
Monte Chingolo
West from Greenwich
A
B
C
1
2
3

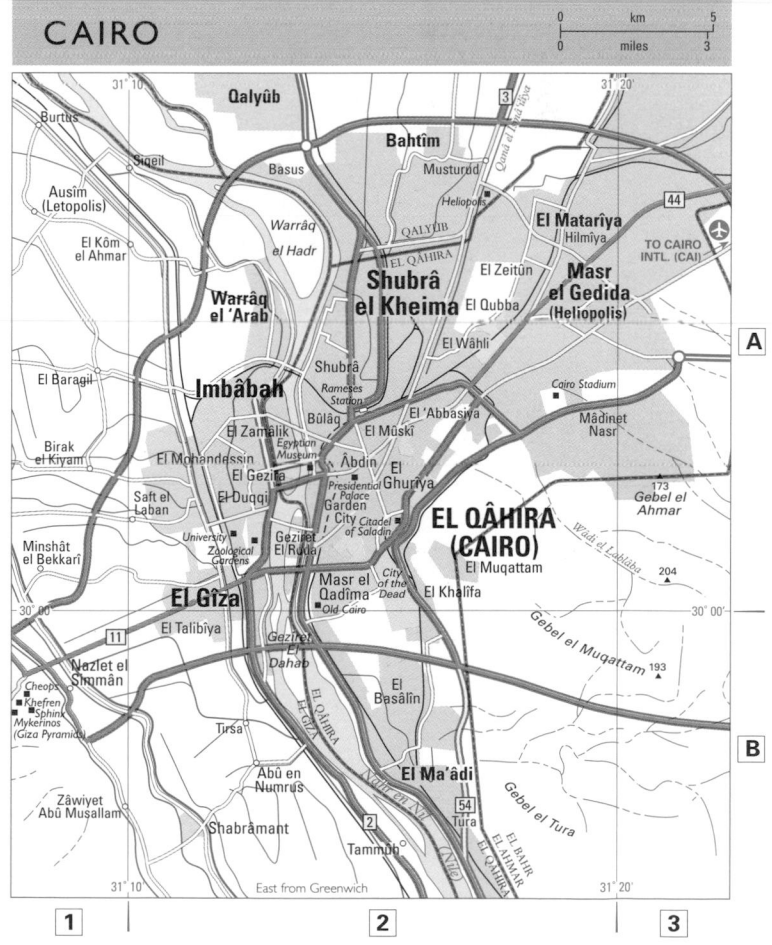
CAIRO
0 km 5
0 miles 3
31° 10'
31° 20'
Qalyûb
Burtus
Bahtîm
Sigeil
Basus
Mustur
Heliopolis
Ausîm (Letopolis)
El Matarîya
Warrâq el Hadr
Hilmîya
El Kôm el Ahmar
TO CAIRO INTL. (CAI)
Shubrâ el Kheima
El Zeitûn
Masr el Gedida (Heliopolis)
Warrâq el 'Arab
El Qubba
El Wâhli
Shubrâ
Imbâbah
El Baragil
Rameses Station
Cairo Stadium
Bûlâq
El 'Abbasîya
Mâdînet Nasr
El Zamâlik
El Mûski
Egyptian Museum
Birak el Kiyam
El Mohandessin
'Âbdin
Presidential Palace
El Gezîra
El Ghurîya
173 Gebel el Ahmar
Saft el Laban
El Duqqi
Garden City
Citadel of Saladin
EL QÂHIRA (CAIRO)
University
Zoological Gardens
Gezîret El Rôda
El Muqattam
Minshât el Bekkarî
City of the Dead
204
Masr el Qadîma
Old Cairo
El Khalîfa
El Gîza
30° 00'
El Talibîya
Gebel el Muqattam
193
Gezîret El Dahab
Nazlet el Simmân
El Basâtîn
Cheops
Khefren
Sphinx
Mykerinos (Giza Pyramids)
Tirsa
Abû en Numrus
El Ma'âdi
Gebel el Tura
Zâwiyet Abû Musallam
Shabrâmant
Tura
Tammûh
Nahr en Nîl (Nile)
East from Greenwich
A
B
1
2
3

CAPE TOWN

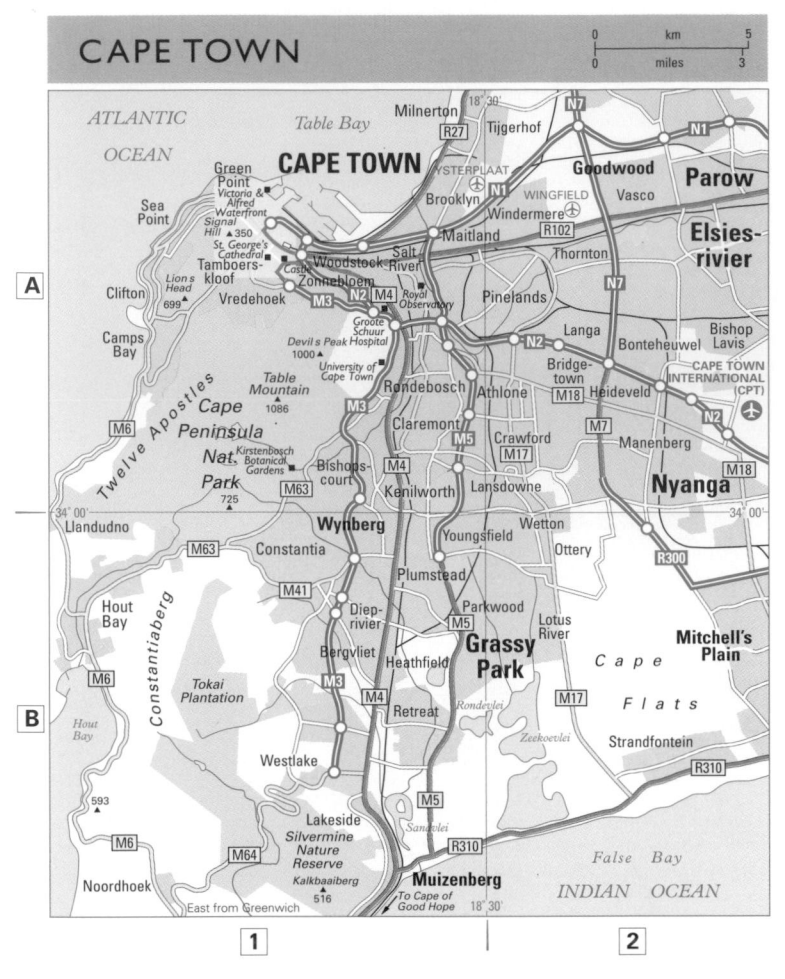

CENTRAL CAPE TOWN

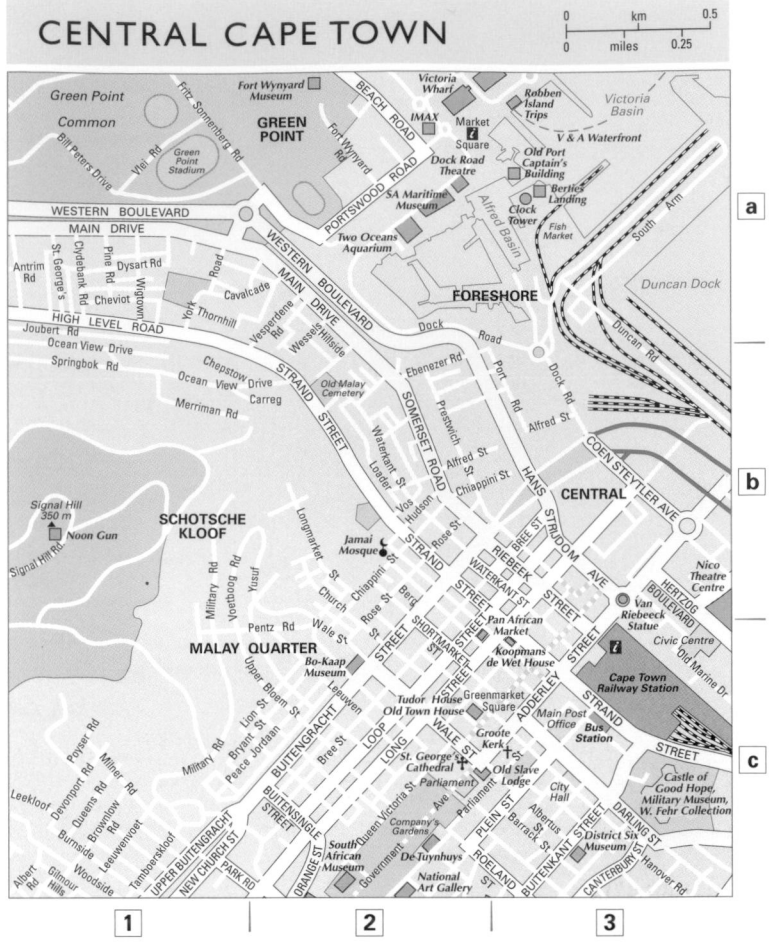

COPENHAGEN

CENTRAL COPENHAGEN

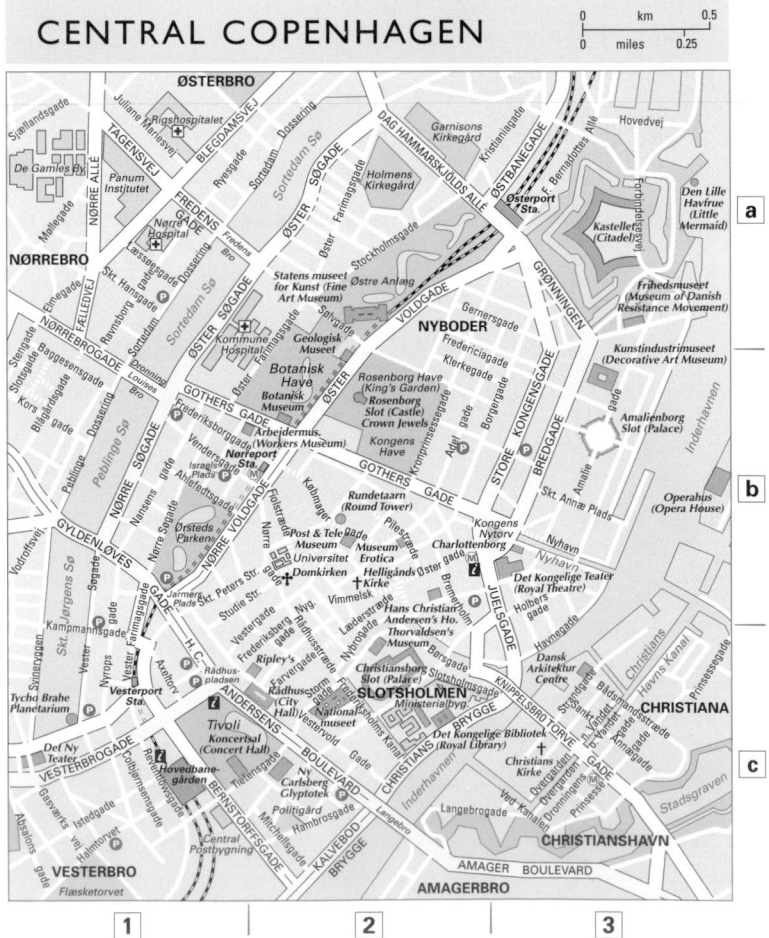

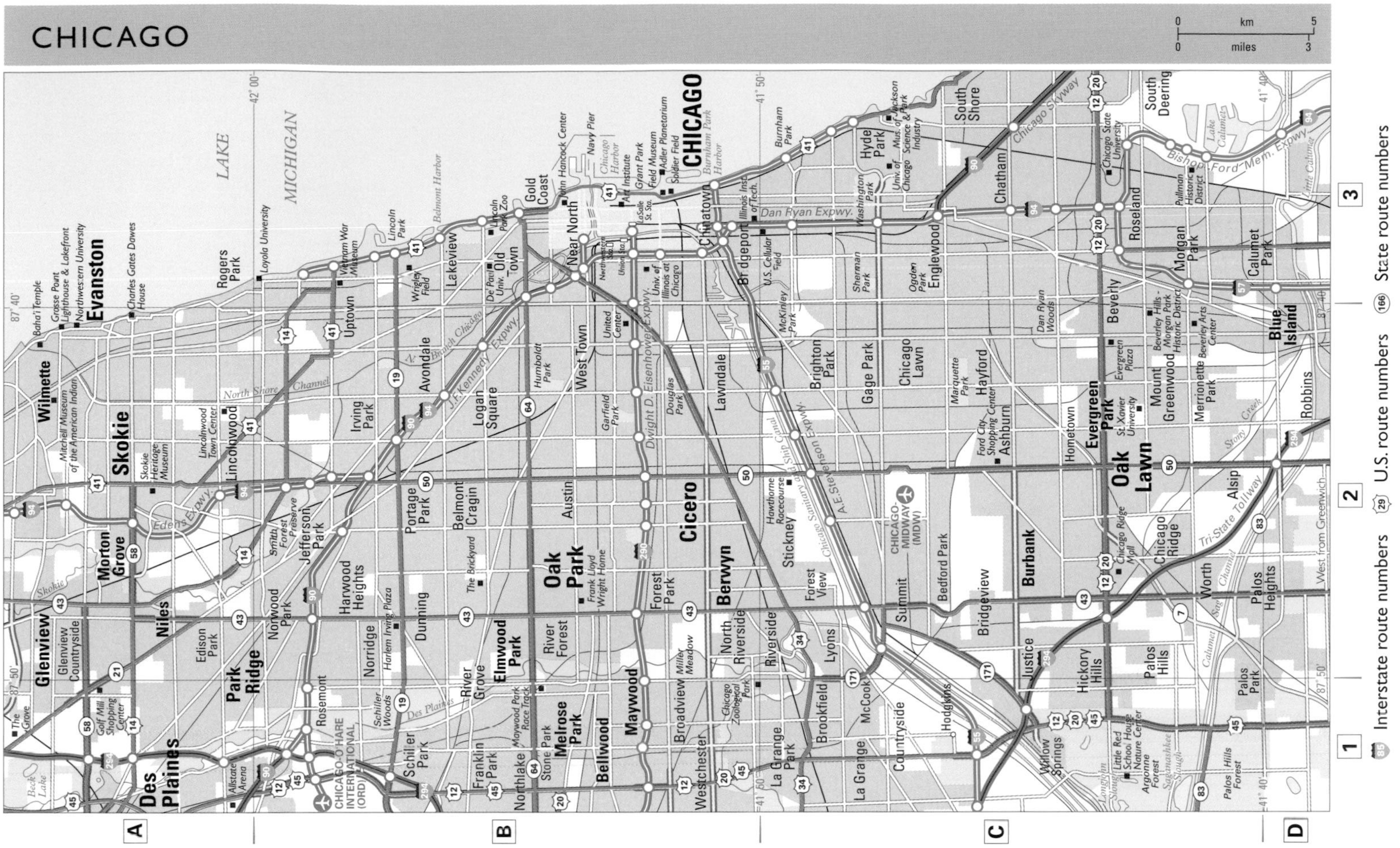

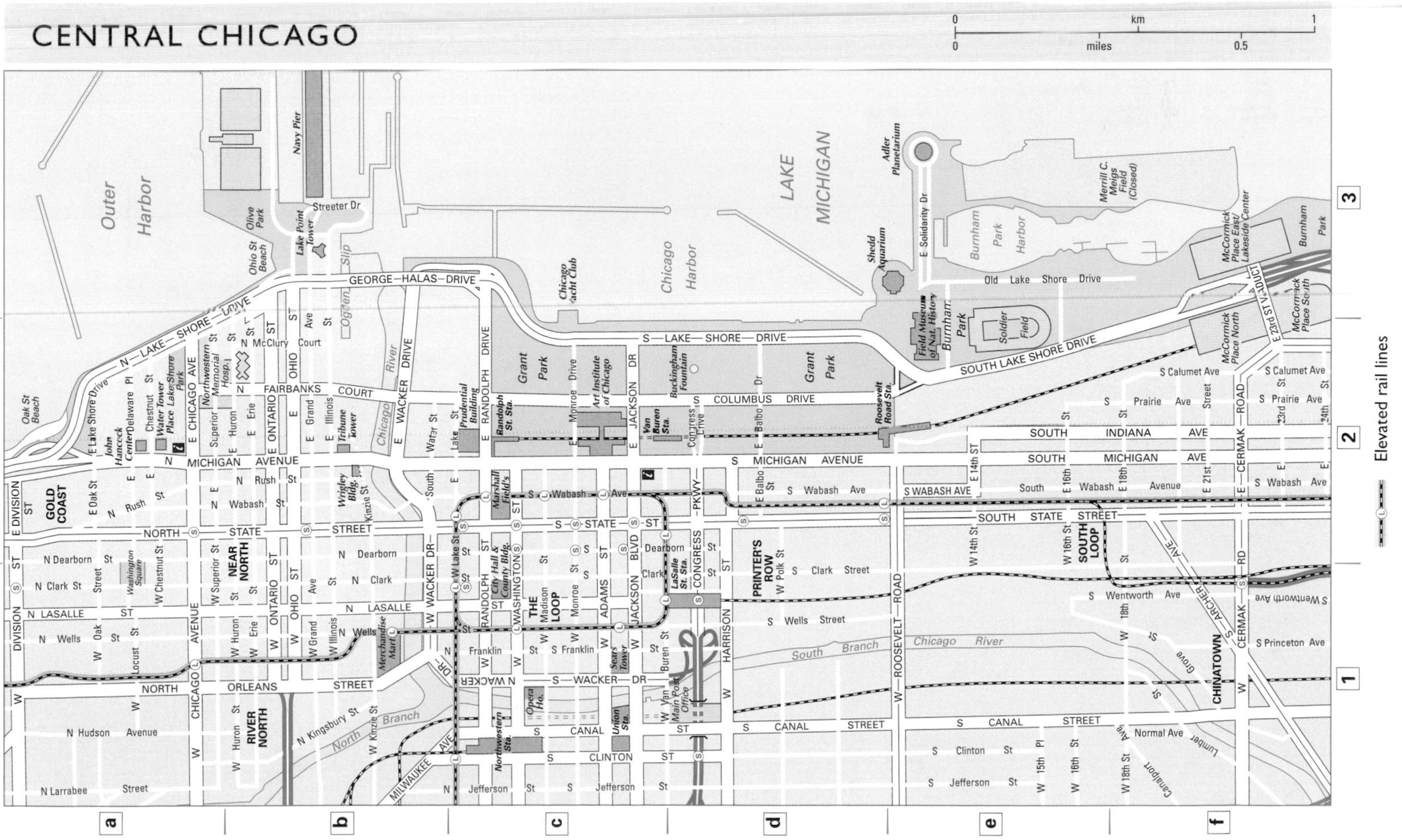

CHICAGO

km 0 — 5
miles 0 — 3

LAKE MICHIGAN

Evanston · Wilmette · Skokie · Morton Grove · Niles · Glenview · Glenview Countryside · Park Ridge · Des Plaines · Rosemont · Norridge · Harwood Heights · Schiller Park · Franklin Park · Northlake · Melrose Park · Bellwood · Maywood · Broadview · Westchester · La Grange Park · La Grange · Brookfield · Riverside · North Riverside · Forest Park · River Forest · Oak Park · Elmwood Park · River Grove · Dunning · Belmont Cragin · Portage Park · Irving Park · Avondale · Logan Square · Humboldt Park · West Town · Austin · Cicero · Berwyn · Stickney · Forest View · Lyons · McCook · Hodgkins · Countryside · Summit · Bridgeview · Bedford Park · Burbank · Chicago Ridge · Oak Lawn · Evergreen Park · Hometown · Ashburn · Chicago Lawn · Gage Park · Brighton Park · Bridgeport · Englewood · Chatham · Hyde Park · South Shore · South Deering · Roseland · Morgan Park · Beverly · Blue Island · Robbins · Alsip · Worth · Palos Hills · Palos Park · Palos Heights · Hickory Hills · Justice · Willow Springs

Lincolnwood · Lincoln Park · Lakeview · Uptown · Rogers Park · Loyola University · Northwestern University

CHICAGO · Gold Coast · Near North · Old Town · Navy Pier · Lincoln Park Zoo · Field Museum · Adler Planetarium · Soldier Field · Grant Park · Burnham Park · Museum of Science & Industry

CHICAGO O'HARE INTERNATIONAL (ORD) · CHICAGO MIDWAY (MDW)

Dan Ryan Expwy. · J.F.Kennedy Expwy. · Eisenhower Expwy. · A.E.Stevenson Expwy. · Dwight D. · Tri-State Tollway · Chicago Skyway · Bishop Ford Mem. Expwy.

Univ. of Illinois at Chicago · Univ. of Chicago · Illinois Inst. of Tech. · U.S. Cellular Field · United Center · Wrigley Field

CENTRAL CHICAGO

km 0 — 1
miles 0 — 0.5

Outer Harbor · LAKE MICHIGAN · Chicago Harbor · Burnham Park Harbor

Navy Pier · Olive Park · Ohio St. Beach · Lake Point Tower · Streeter Dr · George Halas Drive · Chicago Yacht Club · Shedd Aquarium · Adler Planetarium · E. Solidarity Dr · Merrill C. Meigs Field (Closed) · Field Museum of Nat. History · Soldier Field · Burnham Park · McCormick Place East · McCormick Place North · McCormick Place South · Lakeside Center

N LAKE SHORE DRIVE · S LAKE SHORE DRIVE · SOUTH LAKE SHORE DRIVE · Old Lake Shore Drive

GOLD COAST · NEAR NORTH · RIVER NORTH · THE LOOP · PRINTER'S ROW · SOUTH LOOP · CHINATOWN

Oak St Beach · Water Tower · John Hancock Center · Wrigley Bldg. · Tribune Tower · Prudential Building · Art Institute of Chicago · Grant Park · Buckingham Fountain · Merchandise Mart · City Hall · County Bldg. · Sears Tower · Opera Ho. · Main Post Office

MICHIGAN AVENUE · SOUTH MICHIGAN AVENUE · STATE STREET · SOUTH STATE STREET · COLUMBUS DRIVE · N WACKER DR · S WACKER DR · ROOSEVELT ROAD · W ROOSEVELT ROAD · CONGRESS PKWY · RANDOLPH · WASHINGTON · MADISON · MONROE · ADAMS · JACKSON · VAN BUREN · CONGRESS · HARRISON · POLK · CERMAK ROAD · ARCHER AVE · WENTWORTH AVE

Chicago River · North Branch · South Branch

COPYRIGHT PHILIP'S

DELHI

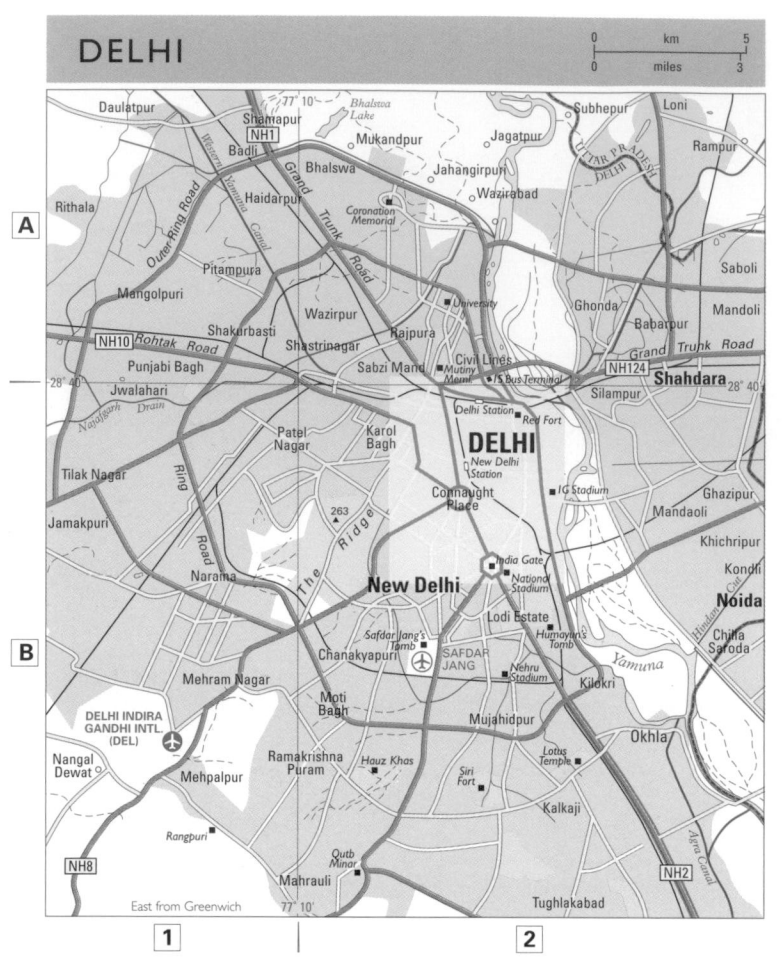

CENTRAL DELHI

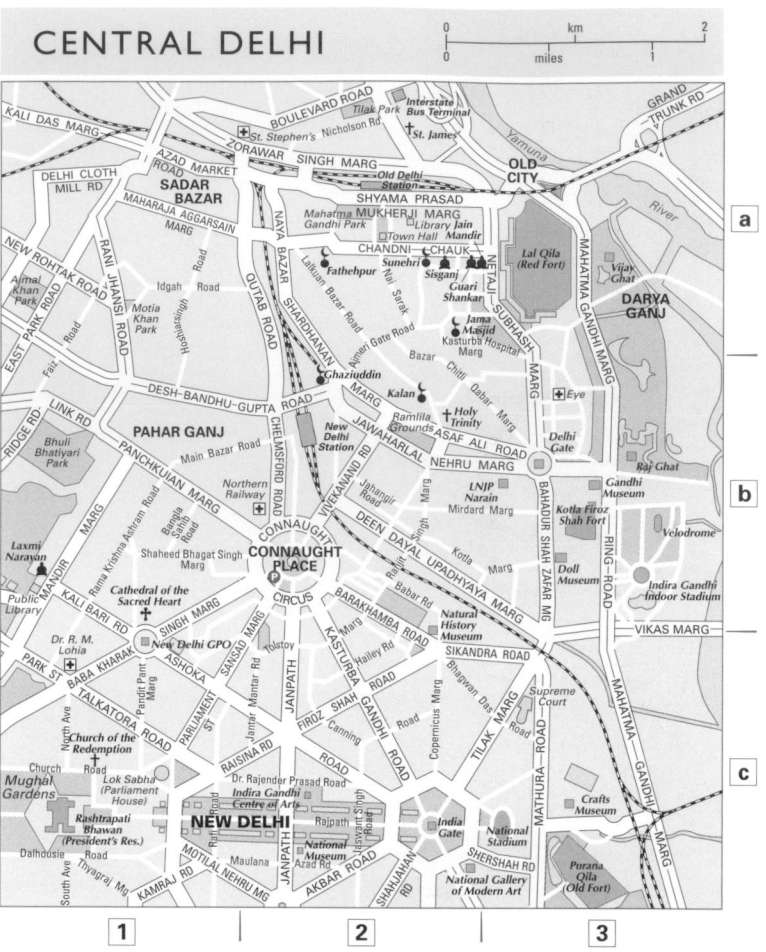

DUBLIN

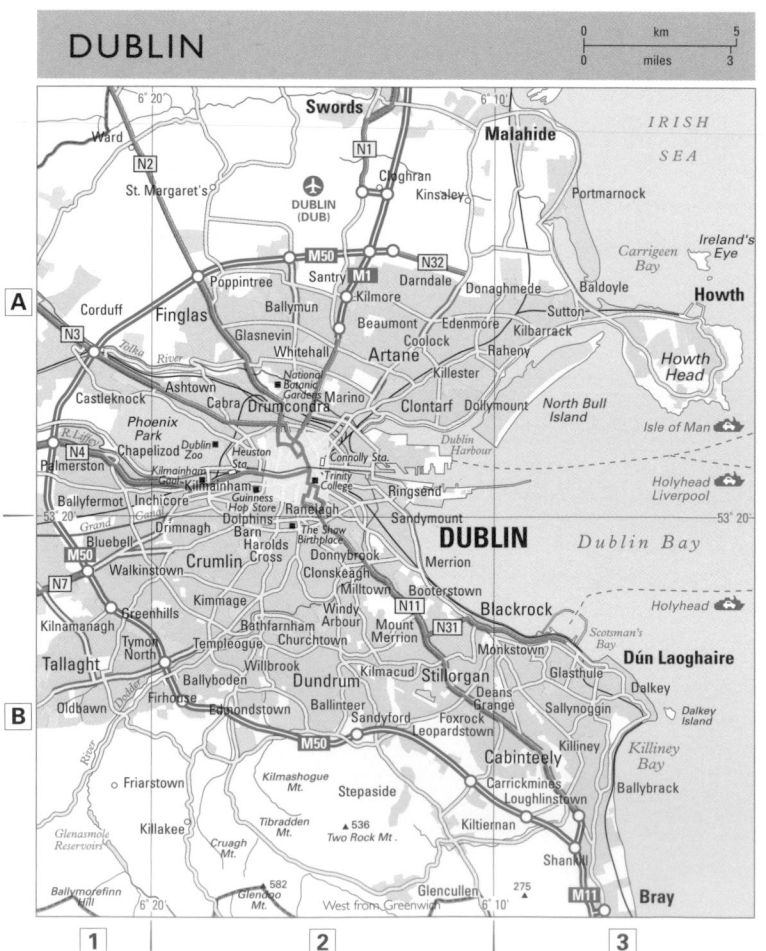

CENTRAL DUBLIN

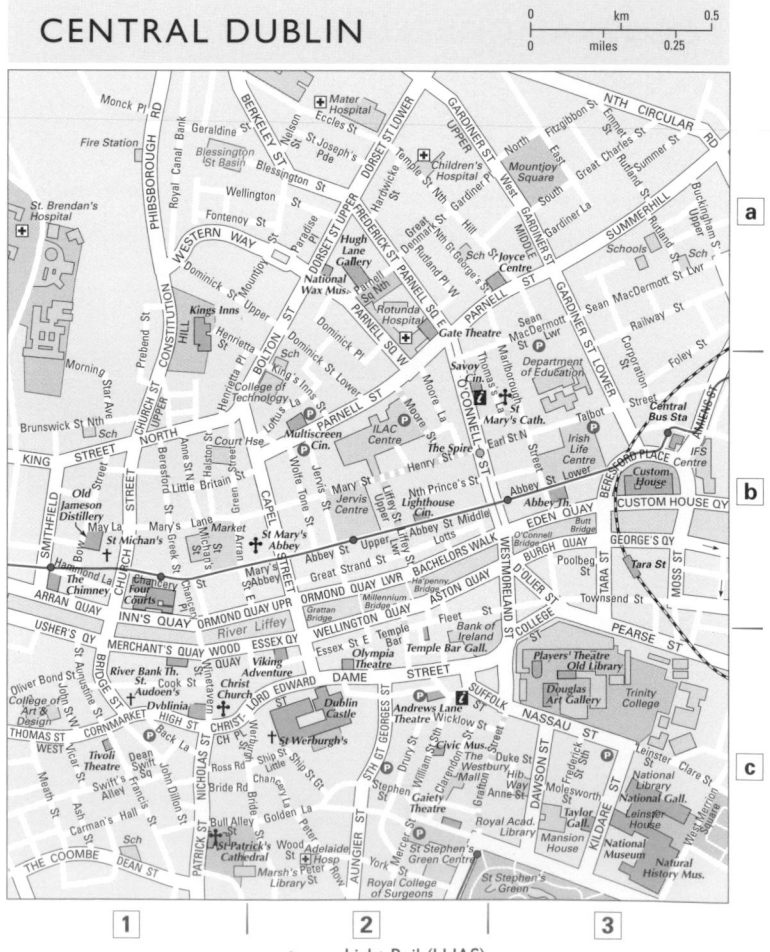

●—— Light Rail (LUAS)

EDINBURGH

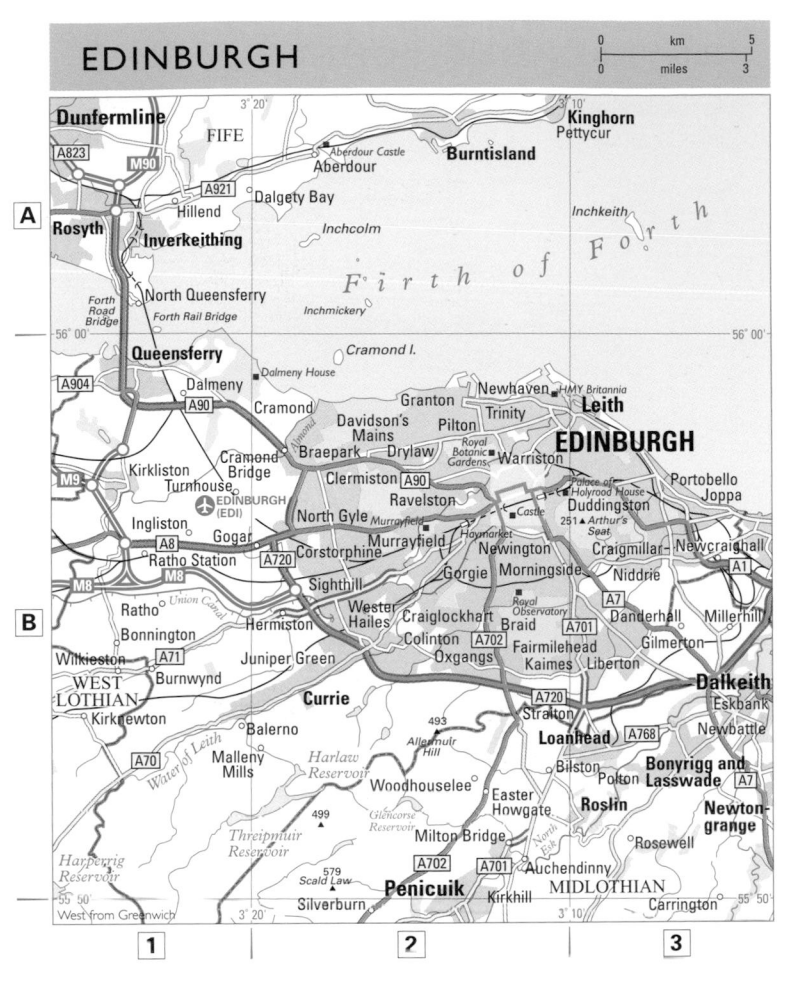

CENTRAL EDINBURGH

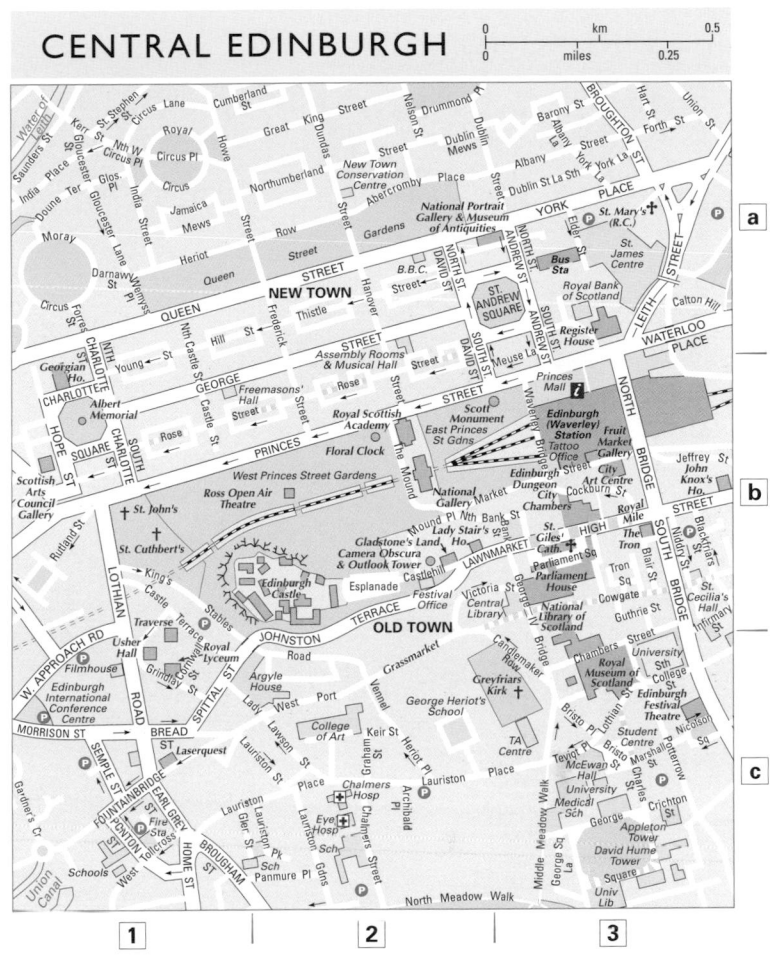

GUANGZHOU

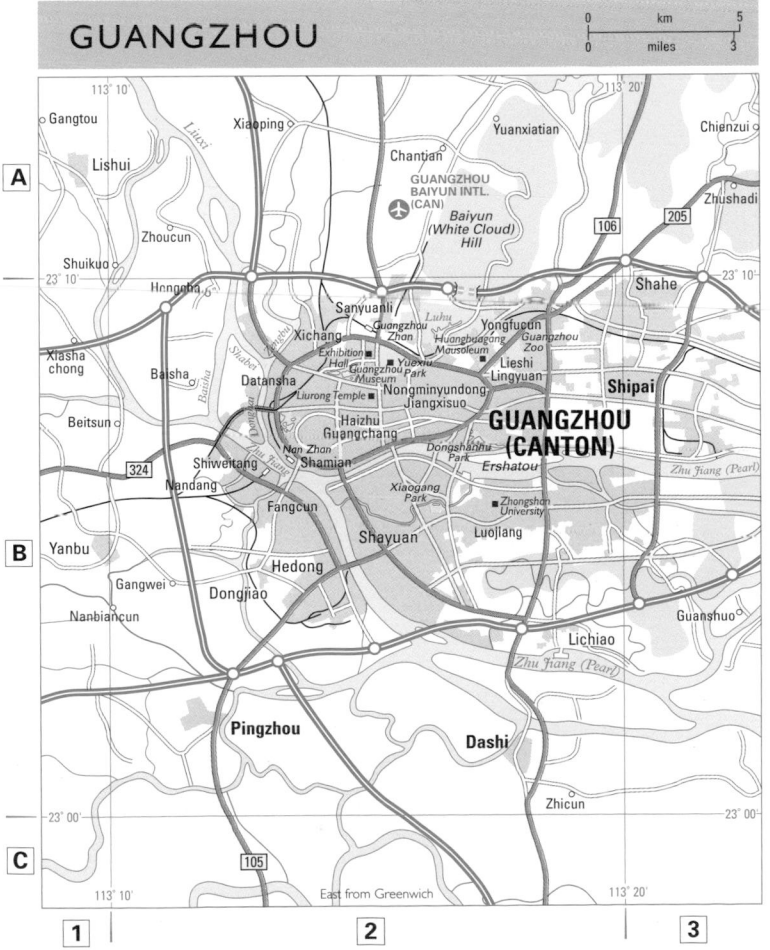

HELSINKI

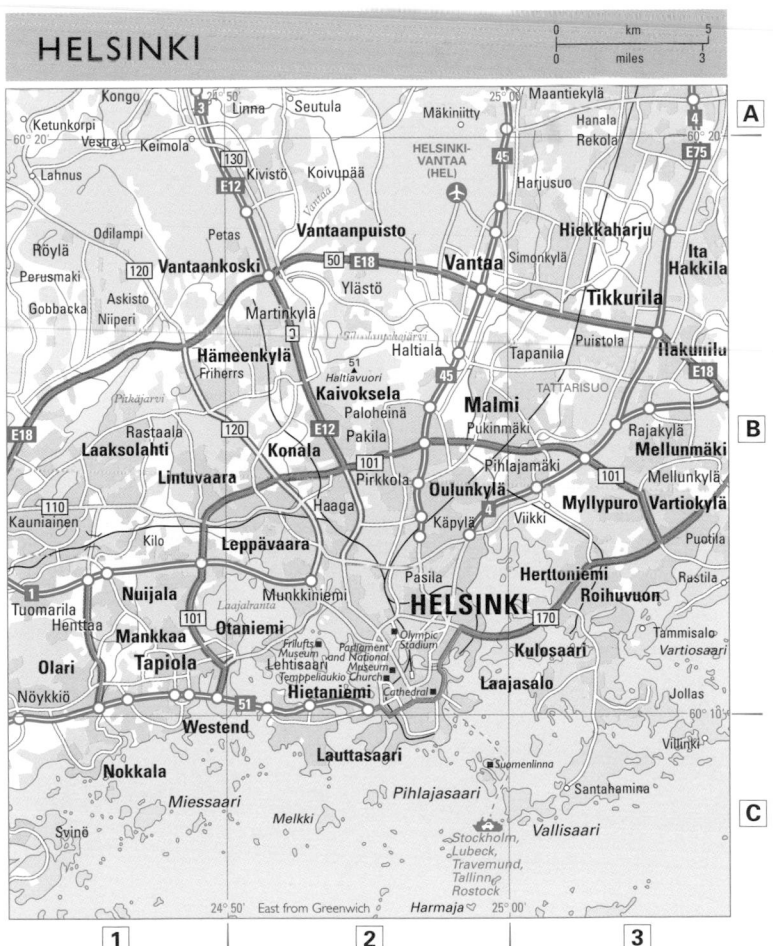

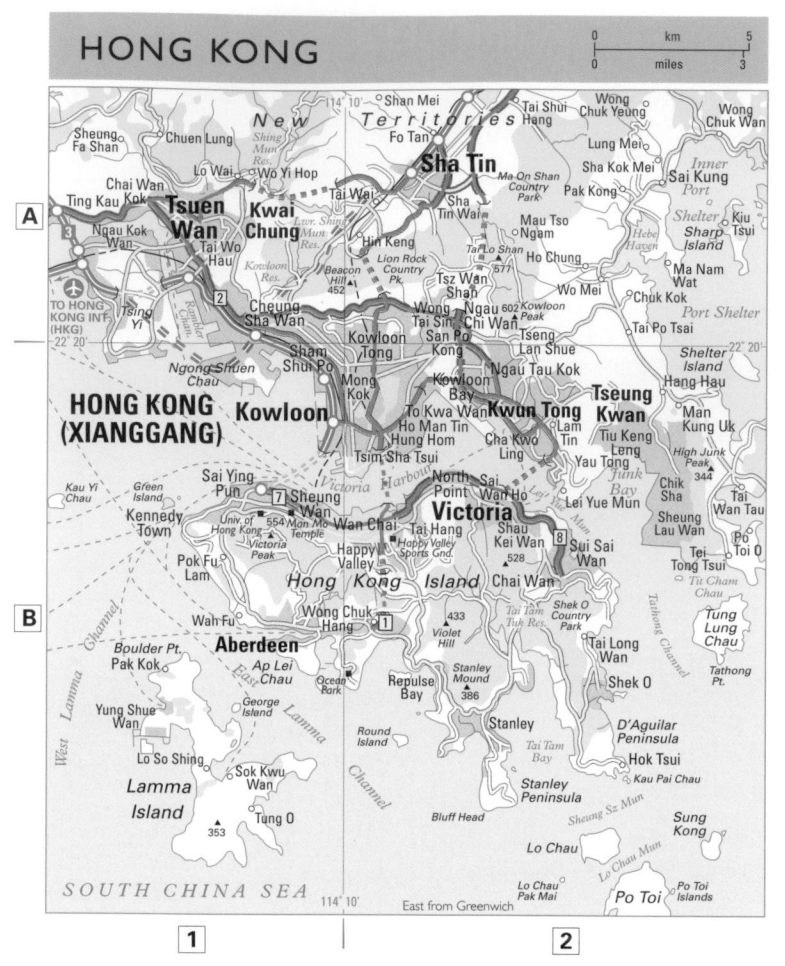
HONG KONG
0 km 5
0 miles 3
New Territories
Sha Tin
Tsuen Wan
Kwai Chung
HONG KONG (XIANGGANG)
Kowloon
Kwun Tong
Tseung Kwan
Victoria
Hong Kong Island
Aberdeen
Lamma Island
Lamma Channel
East Lamma Channel
West Lamma Channel
Victoria Harbour
Tai Wo Hau
Cheung Sha Wan
Sham Shui Po
Mong Kok
Kowloon Tong
Tsim Sha Tsui
Wong Tai Sin
San Po Kong
Ngau Tau Kok
Sai Kung
Port Shelter
Tolo Harbour
Junk Bay
Stanley
Stanley Peninsula
D'Aguilar Peninsula
Repulse Bay
Pok Fu Lam
Kennedy Town
Happy Valley
Wan Chai
Chai Wan
Shau Kei Wan
Tai Tam Bay
Ap Lei Chau
Po Toi Islands
Lo Chau
Lo So Shing
Sok Kwu Wan
Yung Shue Wan
Boulder Pt.
Pak Kok
Tathong Channel
Tathong Pt.
Tung Lung Chau
Kau Yi Chau
Green Island
Ngong Shuen Chau
Tsing Yi
TO HONG KONG INT. (HKG)
SOUTH CHINA SEA
114° 10'
22° 20'
East from Greenwich
A
B
1
2

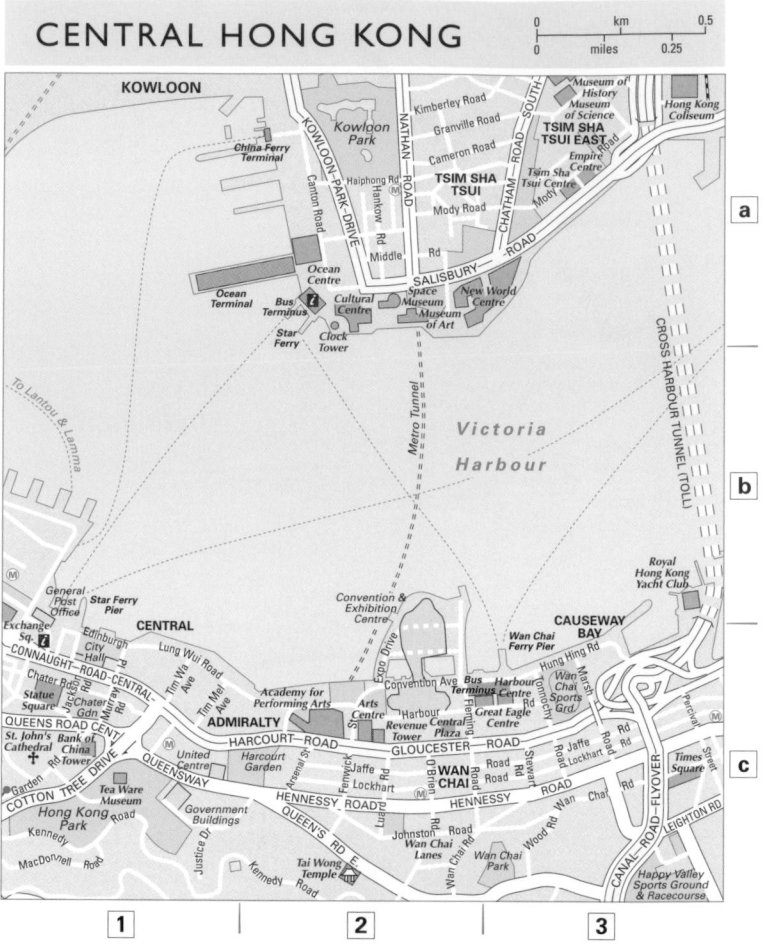
CENTRAL HONG KONG
0 km 0.5
0 miles 0.25
KOWLOON
Kowloon Park
TSIM SHA TSUI
TSIM SHA TSUI EAST
Victoria Harbour
CENTRAL
ADMIRALTY
WAN CHAI
CAUSEWAY BAY
China Ferry Terminal
Ocean Terminal
Ocean Centre
Star Ferry
Clock Tower
Cultural Centre
Space Museum
Museum of Art
Museum of History
Museum of Science
Hong Kong Coliseum
New World Centre
Empire Centre
Metro Tunnel
CROSS HARBOUR TUNNEL (TOLL)
Royal Hong Kong Yacht Club
Convention & Exhibition Centre
Academy for Performing Arts
Hong Kong Park
Happy Valley Sports Ground & Racecourse
Times Square
Government Buildings
St. John's Cathedral
Tai Wong Temple
NATHAN ROAD
SALISBURY ROAD
CHATHAM ROAD SOUTH
KOWLOON PARK DRIVE
CONNAUGHT ROAD CENTRAL
QUEENS ROAD CENTRAL
HARCOURT ROAD
GLOUCESTER ROAD
HENNESSY ROAD
QUEENSWAY
COTTON TREE DRIVE
QUEEN'S RD E.
CANAL ROAD FLYOVER
To Lantau & Lamma
a
b
c
1
2
3

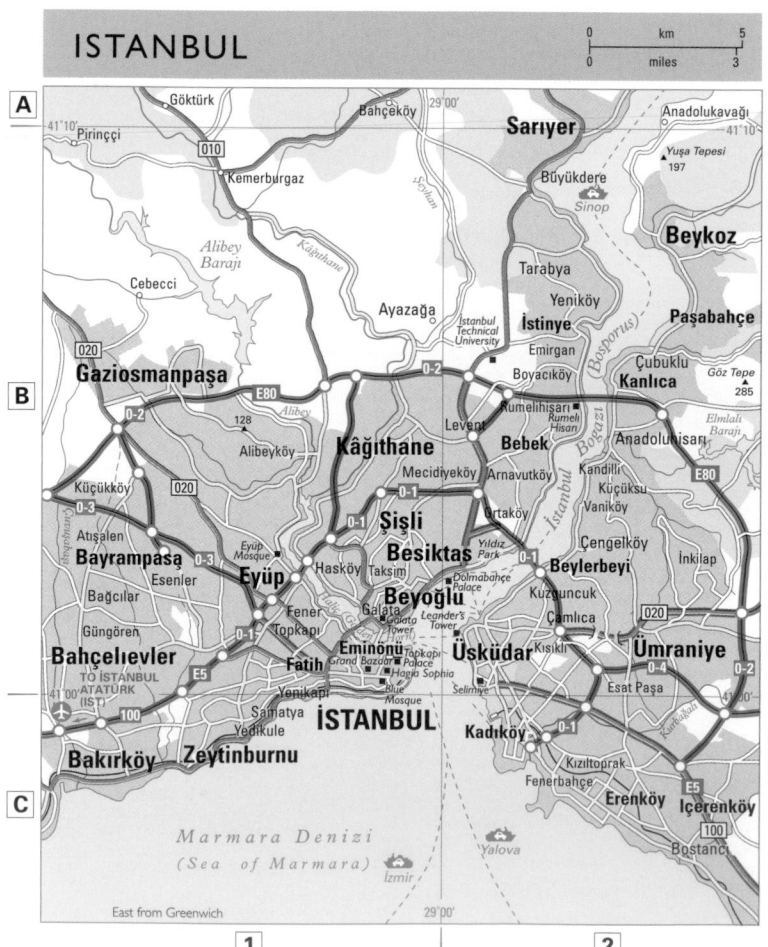
ISTANBUL
0 km 5
0 miles 3
Sarıyer
Beykoz
Paşabahçe
İstinye
Kanlıca
Gaziosmanpaşa
Kâğıthane
Şişli
Besiktas
Beyoğlu
Eyüp
Bayrampaşa
Bahçelievler
Bakırköy
Zeytinburnu
İSTANBUL
Üsküdar
Ümraniye
Kadıköy
Erenköy
Içerenköy
Bostancı
Beylerbeyi
Bebek
Levent
Fatih
Eminönü
Göktürk
Bahçeköy
Kemerburgaz
Büyükdere
Tarabya
Yeniköy
Alibey Barajı
Cebecci
Ayazağa
Alibeyköy
Küçükköy
Esenler
Bağcılar
Güngören
Topkapı
Yenikapı
Samatya
Yedikule
Kızıltoprak
Fenerbahçe
TO İSTANBUL ATATÜRK (IST)
Marmara Denizi (Sea of Marmara)
İstanbul Boğazı (Bosporus)
Anadoluhisarı
Anadolukavağı
Çengelköy
Kandilli
Kuzguncuk
Çamlıca
Esat Paşa
İnkilap
East from Greenwich
29°00'
41°10'
41°00'
A
B
C
1
2

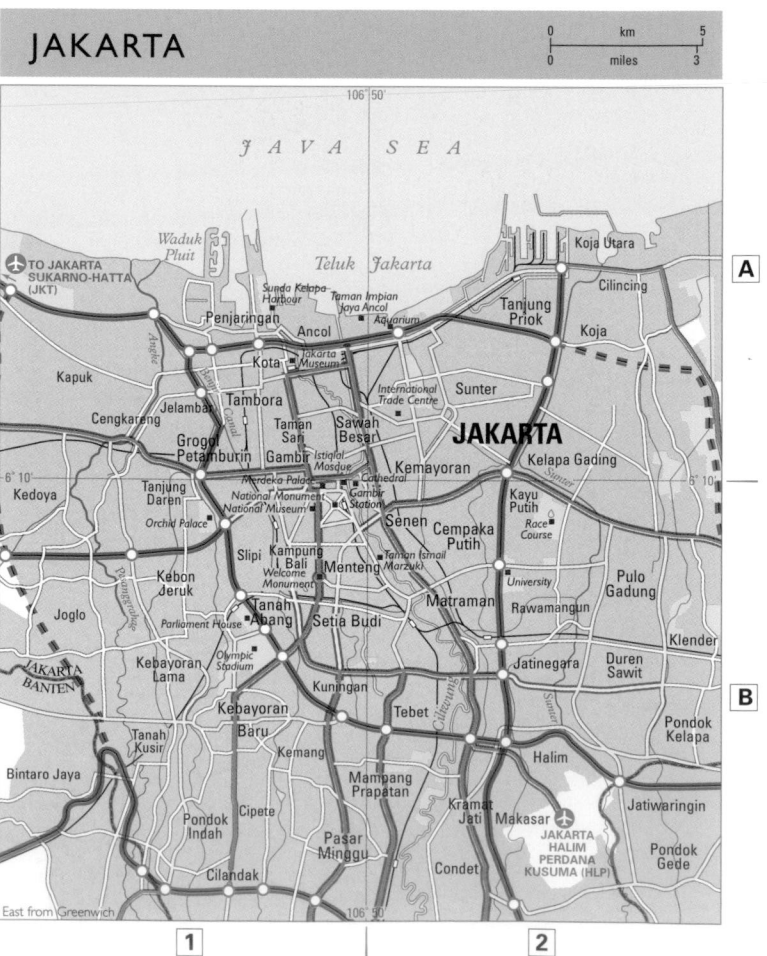
JAKARTA
0 km 5
0 miles 3
JAVA SEA
Teluk Jakarta
JAKARTA
TO JAKARTA SUKARNO-HATTA (JKT)
Tanjung Priok
Koja Utara
Cilincing
Koja
Penjaringan
Ancol
Kota
Kapuk
Cengkareng
Jelambar
Tambora
Taman Sari
Sawah Besar
Sunter
Grogol Petamburin
Gambir
Kemayoran
Kelapa Gading
Kedoya
Tanjung Duren
Senen
Cempaka Putih
Kayu Putih
Pulo Gadung
Kebon Jeruk
Slipi
Menteng
Joglo
Tanah Abang
Setia Budi
Matraman
Rawamangun
Klender
Kebayoran Lama
Kuningan
Jatinegara
Duren Sawit
Kebayoran Baru
Tebet
Kemang
Mampang Prapatan
Tanah Kusir
Bintaro Jaya
Pondok Indah
Cipete
Pasar Minggu
Kramat Jati
Makasar
Halim
Pondok Kelapa
Jatiwaringin
Pondok Gede
Condet
Cilandak
JAKARTA HALIM PERDANA KUSUMA (HLP)
JAKARTA BANTEN
East from Greenwich
106°50'
6°10'
A
B
1
2

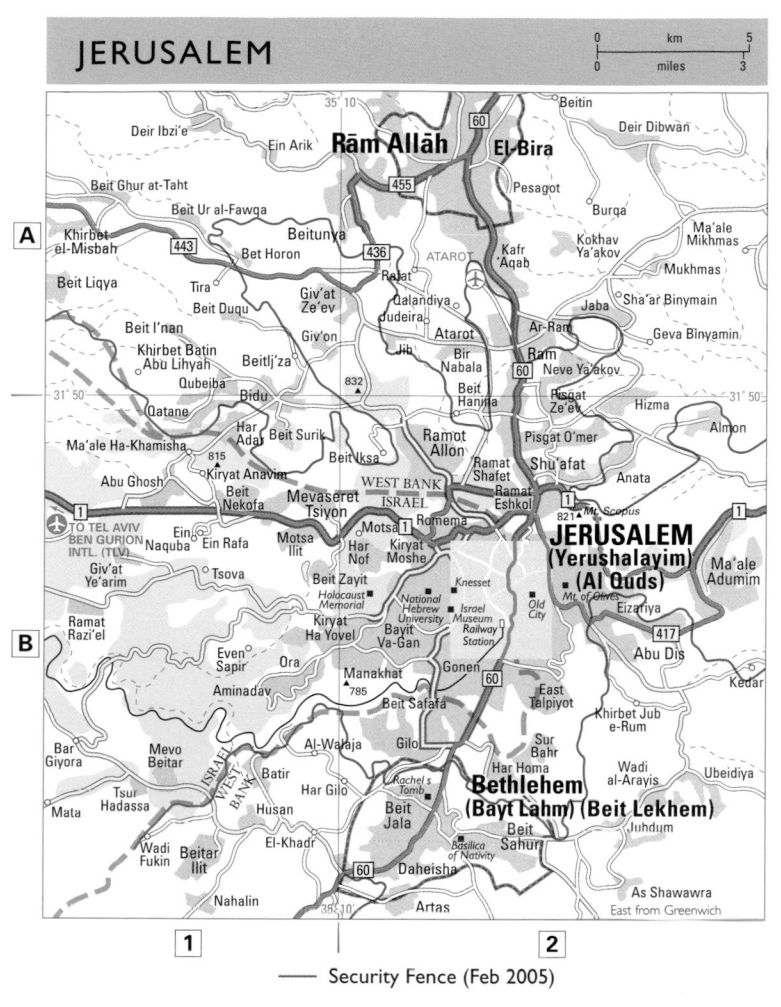

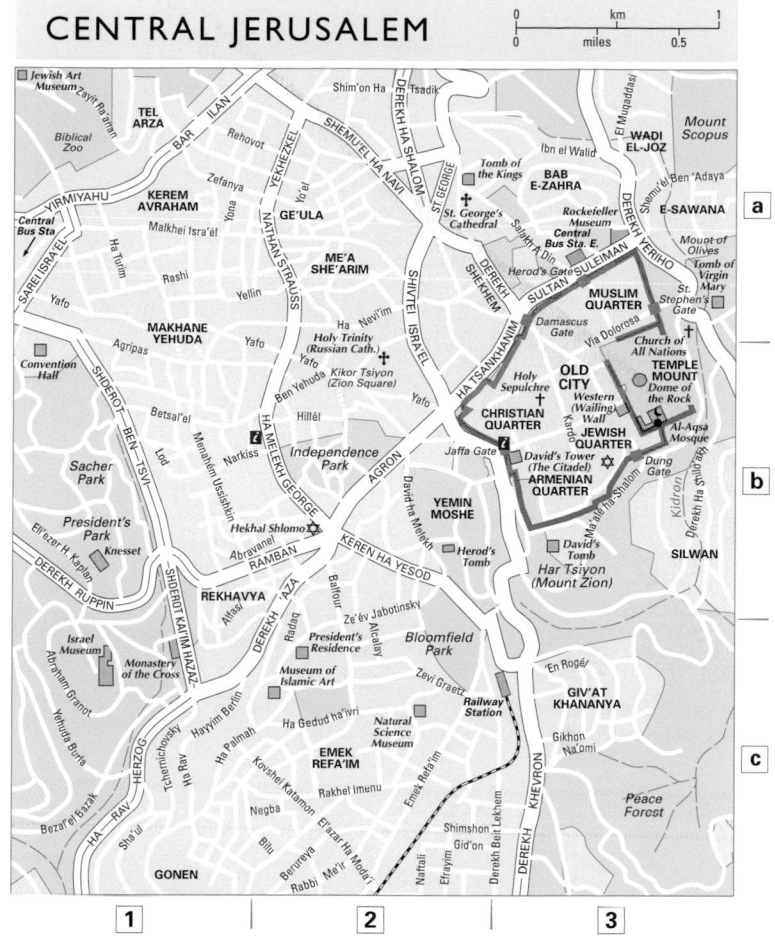

— Security Fence (Feb 2005)

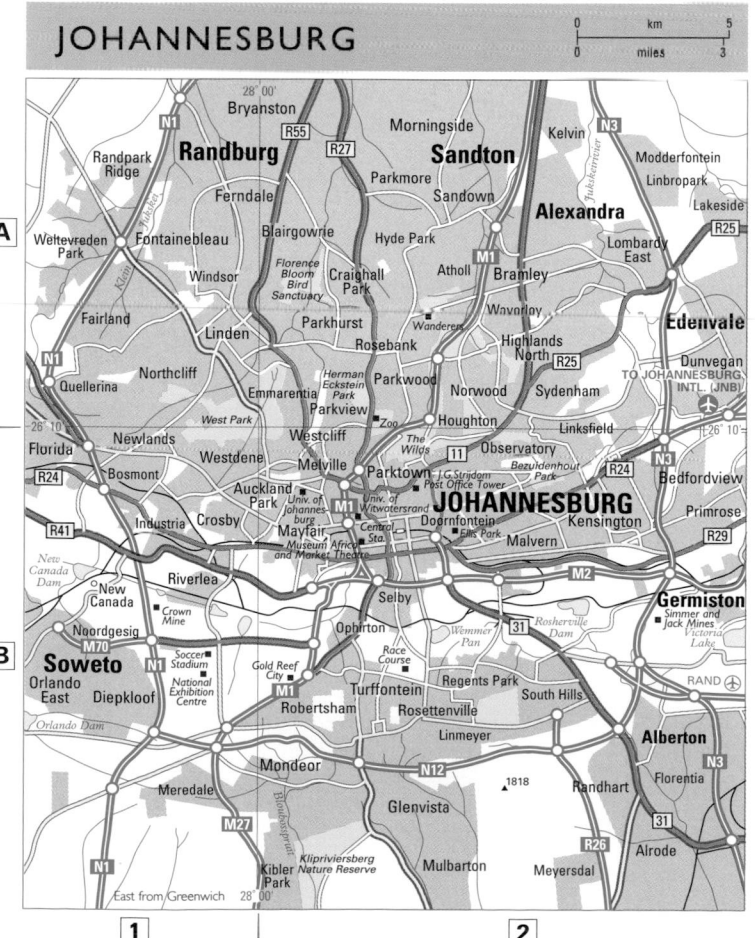

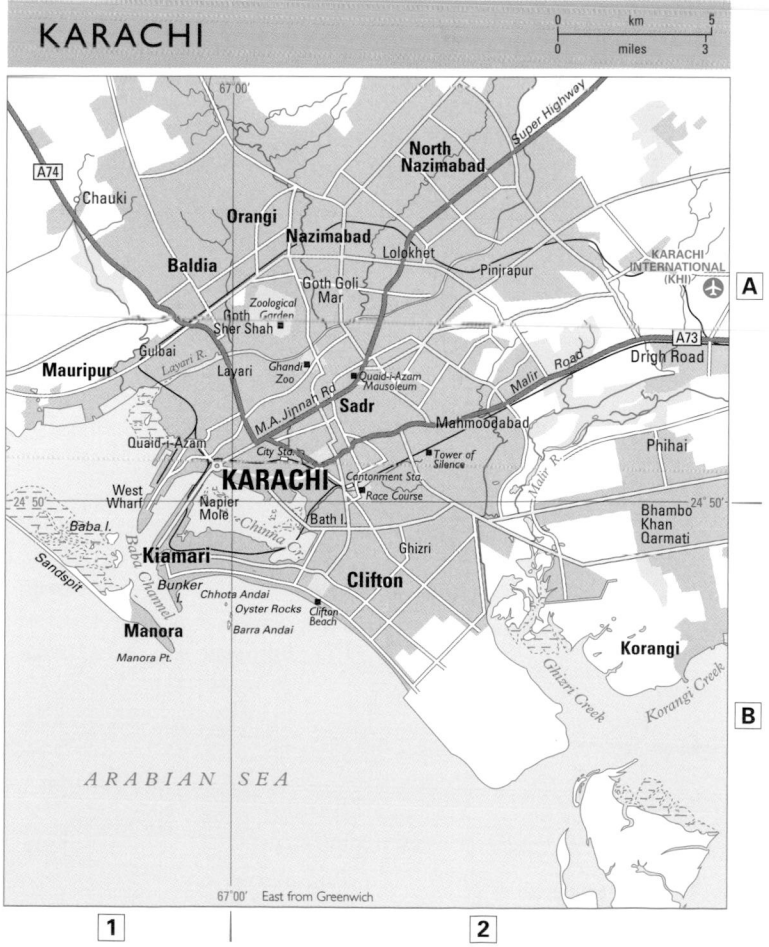

COPYRIGHT PHILIP'S

KOLKATA

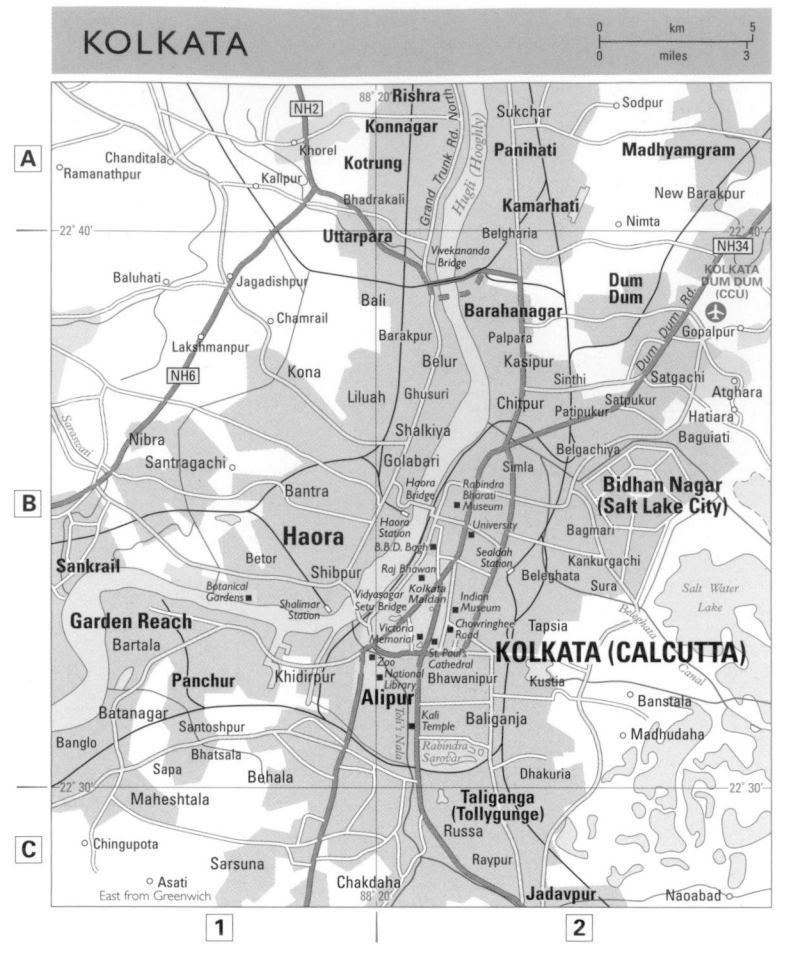

LAGOS

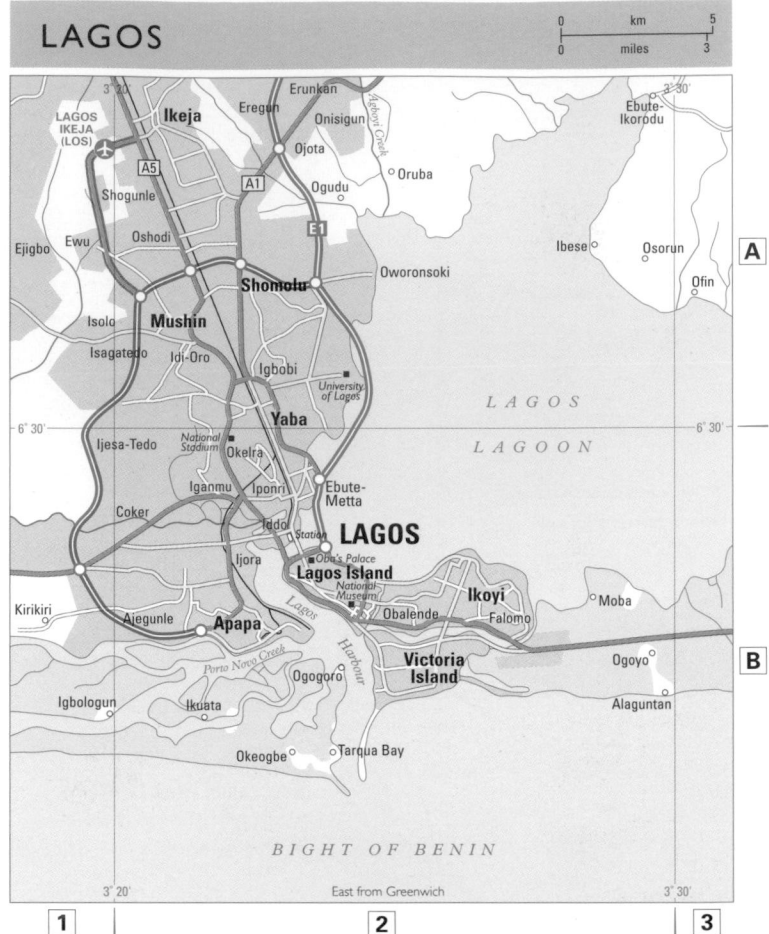

LAS VEGAS

LIMA

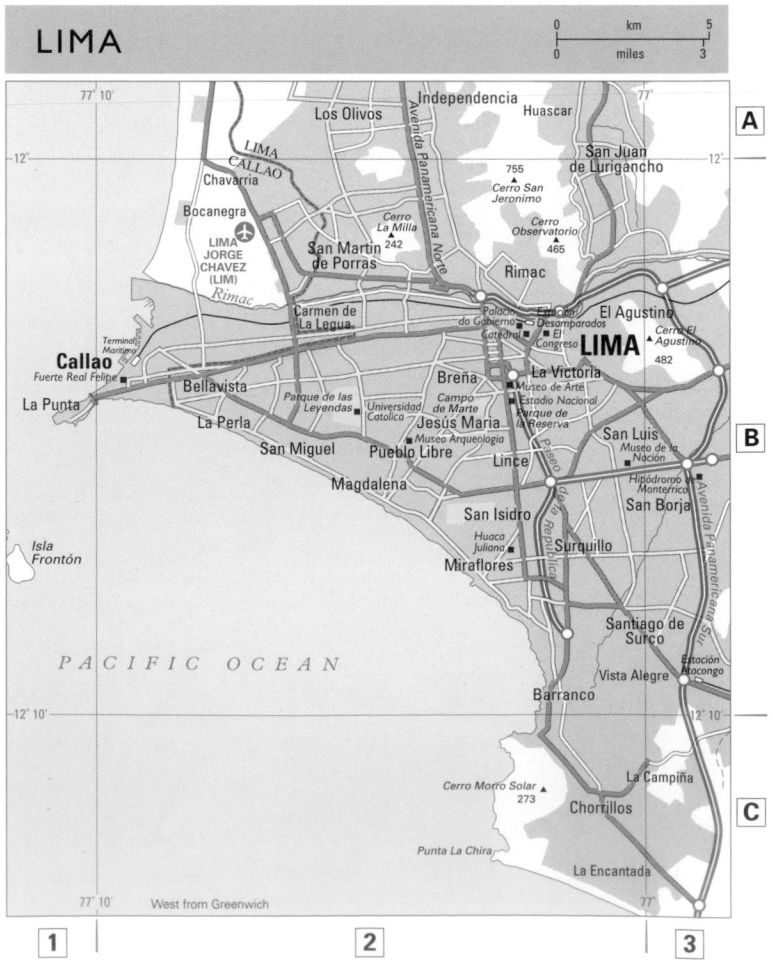

🛡15 Interstate route numbers   95 U.S. route numbers   147 State route numbers

LONDON

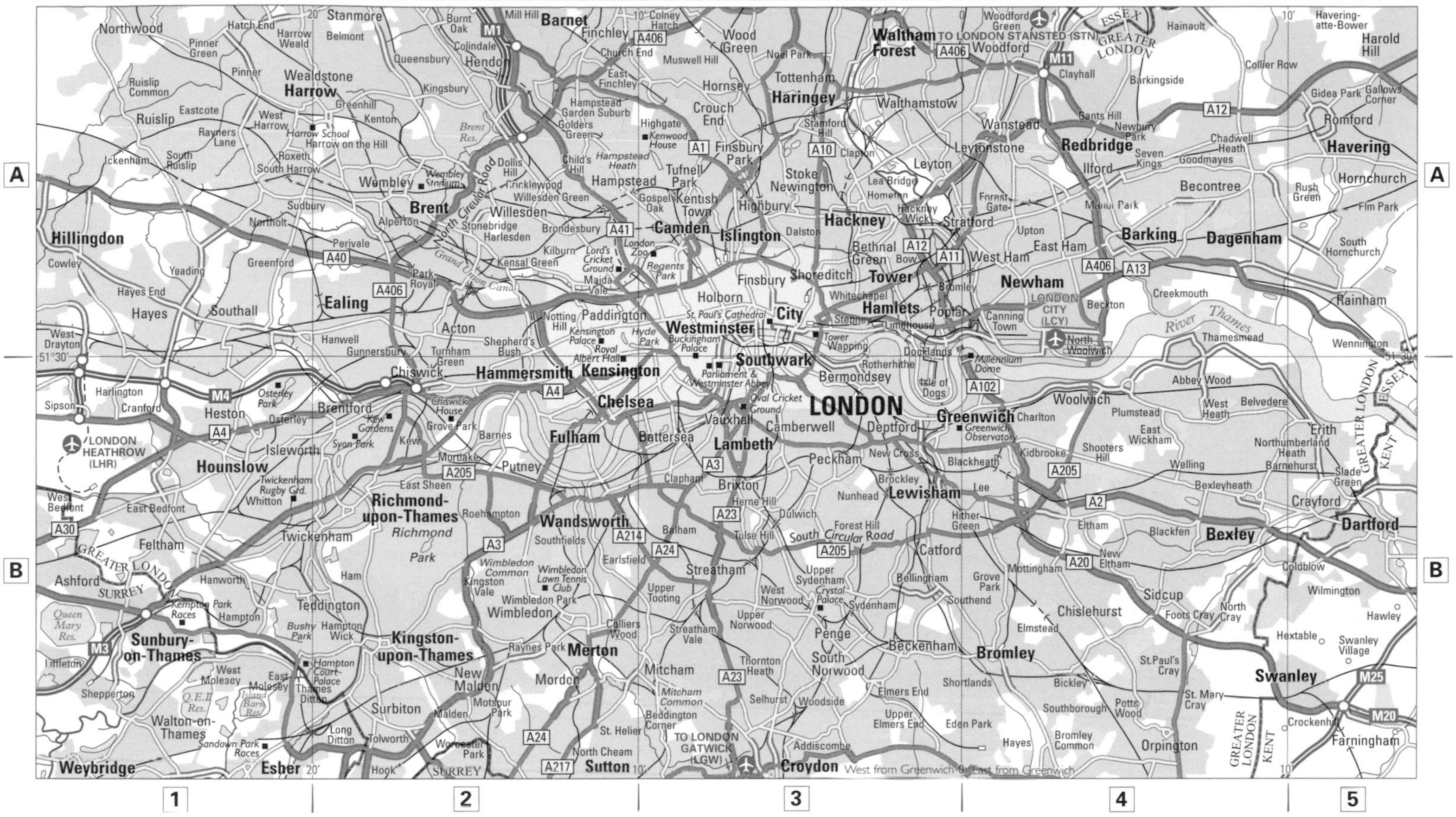

km 5
miles 3

A
Northwood · Stanmore · Belmont · Mill Hill · Barnet · Finchley · Colney Hatch · Wood Green · Waltham Forest · Woodford · GREATER LONDON · Hainault · Havering-atte-Bower · Harold Hill
Pinner Green · Hatch End · Harrow Weald · Burnt Oak · Hendon · Church End · Muswell Hill · Hornsey · Tottenham · Woodford Green · Collier Row · Gidea Park · Gallows Corner
Ruislip Common · Pinner · Wealdstone · Queensbury · Colindale · East Finchley · Highgate · Crouch End · Finsbury Park · Walthamstow · Wanstead · Leytonstone · Sants Hill · Romford · Harold Wood
HARROW · Greenhill · Kingsbury · Hampstead Garden Suburb · Golders Green · Kenwood Hse · Hampstead Heath · Stoke Newington · Leyton · Forest Gate · Becontree · Chadwell Heath · Goodmayes
Eastcote · West Harrow · Harrow School · Harrow on the Hill · Roxeth · Dollis Hill · Childs Hill · Tufnell Hill · Kentish Town · Highbury · Hackney Wick · Stratford · Redbridge · Ilford · Heath
Hillingdon · Rayners Lane · South Harrow · Northolt · Wembley · Willesden Green · Cricklewood · Brondesbury · Kilburn · Lord's Cricket Ground · Camden · Islington · Dalston · Bethnal Green · West Ham · Upton · East Ham · Barking · Dagenham · South Hornchurch · Hornchurch
Cowley · Yeading · Perivale · Alperton · Harlesden · Kensal Green · Maida Vale · Regents Park · Finsbury · Shoreditch · Tower Hamlets · Bromley · Poplar · Newham · LONDON CITY (LCY) · Rainham
Ickenham

LONDON

M4 · Heston · Osterley · Brentford · Chiswick · Hammersmith · Kensington · Westminster · City · Southwark · Bermondsey · Greenwich · Woolwich · Plumstead · Belvedere · Erith
LONDON HEATHROW (LHR) · Hounslow · Isleworth · Kew Gardens · Chelsea · Fulham · Battersea · Vauxhall · Lambeth · Camberwell · Deptford · Greenwich Observatory · East Wickham · Welling · Bexleyheath · Crayford
Cranford · Twickenham · Richmond-upon-Thames · Richmond Park · Barnes · Putney · Wandsworth · Clapham · Brixton · Herne Hill · Dulwich · Peckham · New Cross · Lewisham · Eltham · Blackfen · Bexley · Dartford
B
Feltham · Teddington · Ham · Roehampton · Southfields · Earlsfield · Balham · Streatham · Upper Sydenham · Crystal Palace · Catford · Hither Green · Mottingham · Sidcup · Foots Cray · North Cray · Hawley
Ashford · Hampton · Kingston-upon-Thames · Wimbledon Common · Kingston Vale · Wimbledon Park · Upper Tooting · West Norwood · Sydenham · Penge · Beckenham · Chislehurst · Swanley Village · Wilmington
Queen Mary Res. · Sunbury-on-Thames · Hampton Wick · New Malden · Morden · Mitcham · Thornton Heath · South Norwood · Bromley · Bickley · St Paul's Cray · St Mary Cray · Hextable
Littleton · M3 · West Molesey · Thames Ditton · Surbiton · Tolworth · Motspur Park · Mitcham Common · Beddington Corner · Elmers End · Shortlands · Southborough · Petts Wood · Orpington · Swanley · M25
Shepperton · Walton-on-Thames · Long Ditton · Worcester Park · St Helier · Carshalton · Selhurst · Woodside · Eden Park · Hayes · Bromley Common · Crockenhill · Farningham · M20
Weybridge · Esher · Hook · Chessington · North Cheam · Sutton · Croydon · Addiscombe · Elmers End

West from Greenwich 0° East from Greenwich

1 2 3 4 5

CENTRAL LONDON

km 2
miles 1

a
QUEEN'S PARK · WEST KILBURN · ST JOHN'S WOOD · Regent's Park · London Zoo · King's Cross · HOXTON · SHOREDITCH
MAIDA VALE · WESTBOURNE GREEN · PADDINGTON · Madame Tussaud's · Euston · St Pancras · BLOOMSBURY · CLERKENWELL · Wesley's Chapel
NOTTING HILL · BAYSWATER · Wallace Collection · SOHO · British Museum · HOLBORN · Barbican · Museum of London · Liverpool St · Whitechapel Art Gall.
b
Holland Park · Kensington Gardens · Hyde Park · MAYFAIR · The Serpentine · ST JAMES'S · Trafalgar Sq · Temple Ch · St Paul's · Monument · Tower of London · Tower Bridge
KENSINGTON · Kensington Palace · Serpentine Gallery · Apsley House & Wellington Mus. · Green Park · Buckingham Palace · Downing Street · SOUTHWARK · London Dungeon · London Bridge · City Hall
Olympia · Royal Albert Hall · KNIGHTSBRIDGE · BELGRAVIA · Houses of Parliament · Westminster Abbey · Lambeth Palace · Tate Modern · The Design Museum
c
WEST KENSINGTON · BROMPTON · SOUTH KENSINGTON · Nat. History & Geological Mus. · Victoria Coach Sta · PIMLICO · Tate Britain · LAMBETH · NEWINGTON · BERMONDSEY
Earl's Court Exhibition Hall · CHELSEA · National Army Mus. · Chelsea Embankment · River Thames · KENNINGTON · The Oval Cricket Gd. · WALWORTH · Burgess Park

1 2 3 4 5

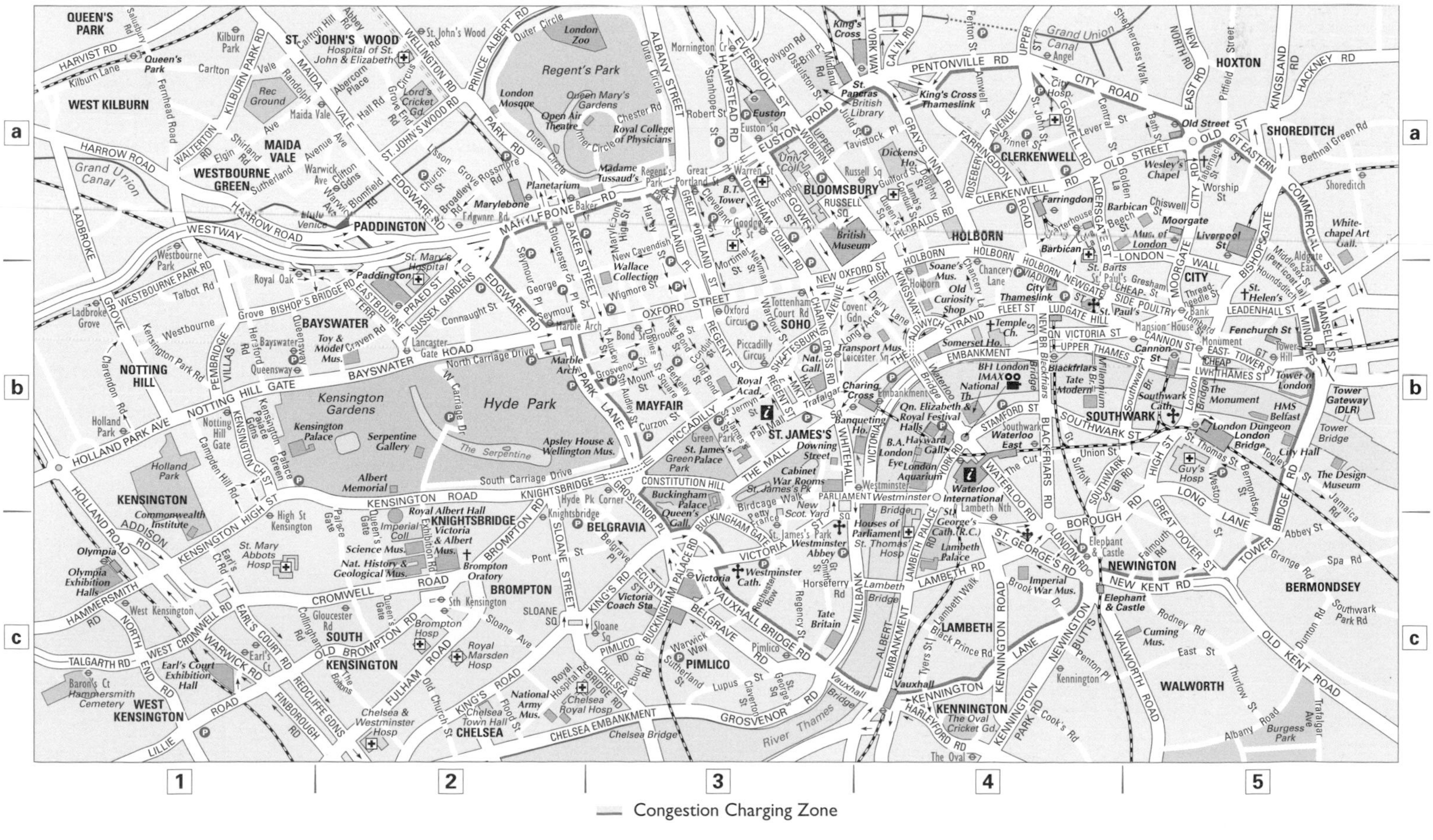

— Congestion Charging Zone

COPYRIGHT PHILIP'S

LISBON

km 0 — 5
miles 0 — 3

Almargem do Bispo, Botica Sete, São Julião do Tojal, Santo Antão do Tojal, Sta. Iria da Azóia, Montemor 357, Tapada, Piedade, Camaroes, Loures, Unhos, Apelação, Sabugo, Venda Seca, Ada Beja, Amoreira, Póvoa de Santo Adrião, Camarate, Sacavém, Rio de Mouro, Odivelas, Charneca, Ponte Vasco da Gama, Moscavide, Parque das Nações (Park of Nations), Amadora, Lumiar, Pontinha, Carnide, Campo Grando, University, Olivais, Matinha, Queluz, Damaia, Benfica, Campo Pequeno, Alto do Pina, Beato, Xabregas, Barcarena, Parque Florestal de Monsanto, Rato, Campolide, Bairro Lopes, LISBOA, Carnaxide, Linda-a-Pastora, Ajuda, Alcântara, Estação do Rossio, Estação Santa Apolónia, Terrugem, Caxias, Algés, Santo Amaro, Basílica da Estrela, Estação Cais do Sodré, Praça do Comércio, Mosteiro dos Jerónimos Monastery, Belém, Torre de Belém (Tower of Belém), Porto Brandão, Banática, Cacilhas, Almada, Oeiras, Paço de Arcos, Padrão dos Descobrimentos (Discoveries Monument), Trafaria, Raposo, Caparica, Cova de Piedade, Lavradio, Bugio, Barreiro, Coina, Quinta de Santo António, Costa da Caparica, Capuchos, Sobreda, Corroios, Seixal, Santo André, Amora, Cruz de Pau, Arrentela, Palhais, Charneca

ATLANTIC OCEAN
West from Greenwich

A9, A8, A1, E80, E01, IC2, IC22, IC17, IC19, IC16, A5, IP1, IC20, A2, E90, E01, IC21

A / B — 1 / 2

CENTRAL LISBON

km 0 — 1
miles 0 — 0.5

Palácio da Penitenciária, Palacio de Justiça, Praça Duque Saldanha, Instituto Superior Técnico, Praça de Chile, Cemitério Alto s. João, Parque Eduardo VII, Pavilhão dos Desportos, ESTEFÂNIA, PENHA FRANÇA, AMOREIROS, ANJOS, Hospital de Santa Marta, Hospital dos Capuchos, BAIRRO LOPES, RATO, Academia das Ciências, Jardim Botánico, GRAÇA, Instituto de Medicina Legal, Palácio de Assembleia Nacional, Igreja de Graça, BAIRRO ALTO, Theatro Nac. de Dona Maria II, Estação do Rossio, Praça Rossio, Museu de Arqueologia, Castelo de São Jorge (St. George's Castle), Elevador de Santa Justa, Museu de Arte Decorativas, ALFAMA, Theatro Nac. de São Carlos, Biblioteca Nacional, Museu de Chiado, Praça do Comércio, Museu Antoniano (St. Anthony Mus.), Sé Catedral, Military Museum, Estação Santa Apolónia, AV. VINTE E QUATRO DE JULHO, BAIXA, RUA DO ARSENAL, Dom José I, R. DA ALFÂNDEGA, INFANTE DOM HENRIQUE, Estação Cais do Sodré, AV. RIBEIRA DAS NAUS, Estação Fluvial, Rio Tejo (Tagus)

a / b / c — 1 / 2 / 3

LOS ANGELES

km 0 — 5
miles 0 — 3

Tarzana, Sepulveda Dam Rec. Area, Van Nuys, San Fernando Valley, Verdugo Mts., Burbank, Altadena, San Gabriel Mts., Eaton Canyon Park, Encino, North Hollywood, N.B.C. Studios, Disney Studios, Pasadena, Sierra Madre, Colorado Fwy., Sherman Oaks, Studio City, C.B.S. Fox Studios, Warner Brothers Studios, Zoo, Glendale, California Institute of Technology, Monrovia, Santa Anita Park, Encino Reservoir, Topanga State Park, Cahuenga Peak, Universal Studios, Griffith Park, Lake Hollywood, Glendale Galleria, Eagle Rock, South Pasadena, Arcadia, Santa Monica Mts. Rec. Area, Griffith Observatory, Highland Park, Garvanza, San Marino, Temple City, Beverly Glen, Hollywood, Hollywood Bowl, Southwest Museum, El Sereno, The Getty Center, Bel Air, Franklin Reservoir, Mann's Chinese Theatre, Sunset Blvd., Silver Lake Reservoir, Alhambra, San Gabriel, Beverly Hills, West Hollywood, Santa Monica Blvd., Paramount Studios, Elysian Park Dodger Stadium, Rosemead, University of California Los Angeles, Westwood Village, Los Angeles County Art Museum, Wilshire Blvd., MacArthur Park, Lincoln Heights, California State University, Monterey Park, South San Gabriel, El Monte, South El Monte, Will Rogers State Historical Park, Brentwood Park, LOS ANGELES, Civic Center, Union Sta., Boyle Heights, Whittier Narrows, Flood Control Basin, Pacific Palisades, Santa Monica, Museum of Art, Santa Monica Fwy., Convention Center, University of Southern California, California Space & Science Center, Memorial Coliseum, Exposition Park, East Los Angeles, Montebello, Commerce, Puente Hills, Santa Monica Pier, California Heritage Museum, SANTA MONICA, Sony Picture Studio, Baldwin Hills Reservoir, Culver City, View Park, Vernon, Pico Rivera, Pio Pico State Historic Park, Venice, Venice Boardwalk, Windsor Hills, Maywood, Bell, Bell Gardens, Montebello Town Center, Bicentennial Park, Whittier, PACIFIC OCEAN, Marina del Rey, Ladera Heights, Huntington Park, Florence, Walnut Park, Cudahy, Los Nietos, Westchester, University of West Los Angeles, Great Western Forum, Inglewood, South Gate, Downey, Santa Fe Springs, LOS ANGELES INTERNATIONAL (LAX), Lennox, West from Greenwich

A / B / C — 1 / 2 / 3 / 4

⑧⑤ Interstate route numbers   ⑯⑥ State route numbers

MADRID

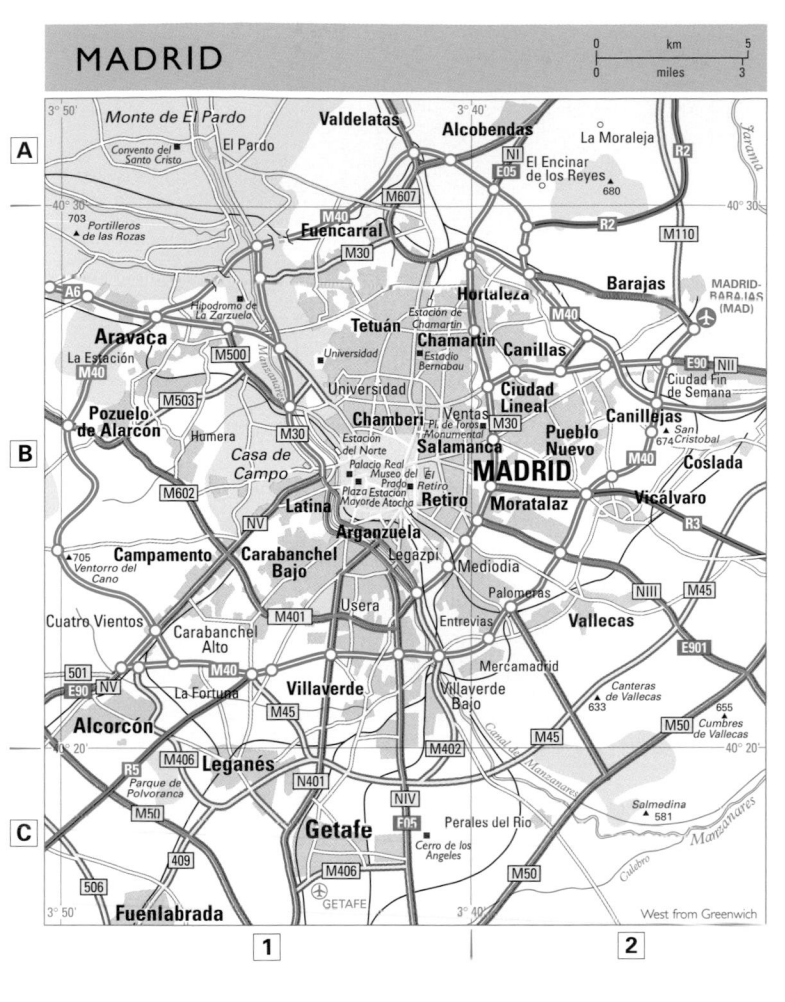

CENTRAL MADRID

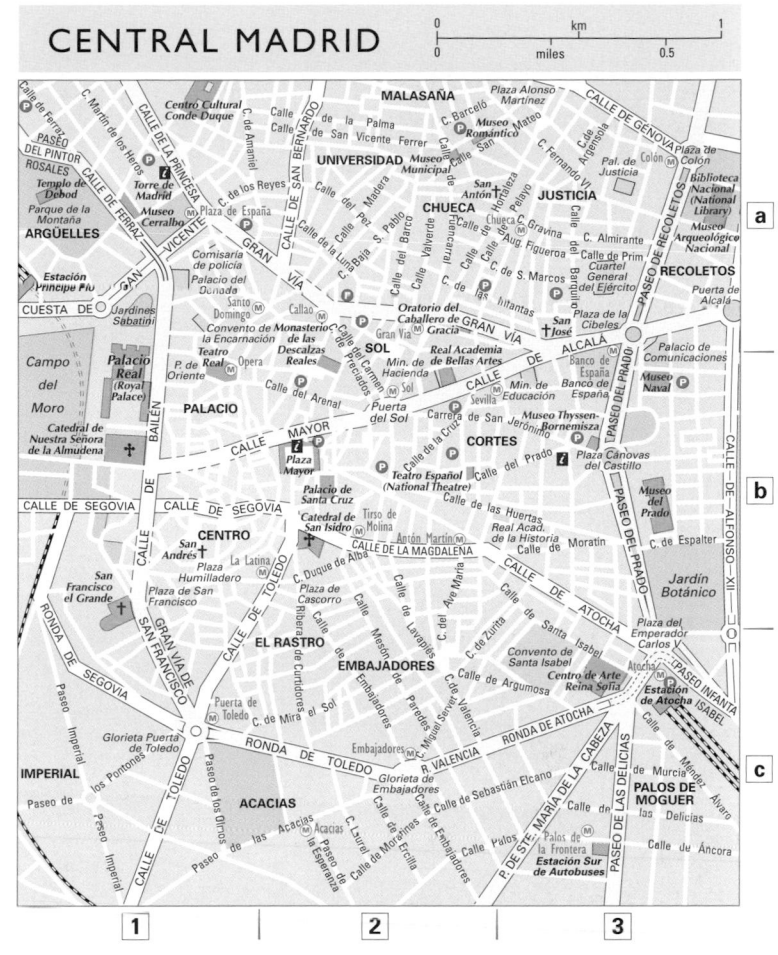

CENTRAL LOS ANGELES

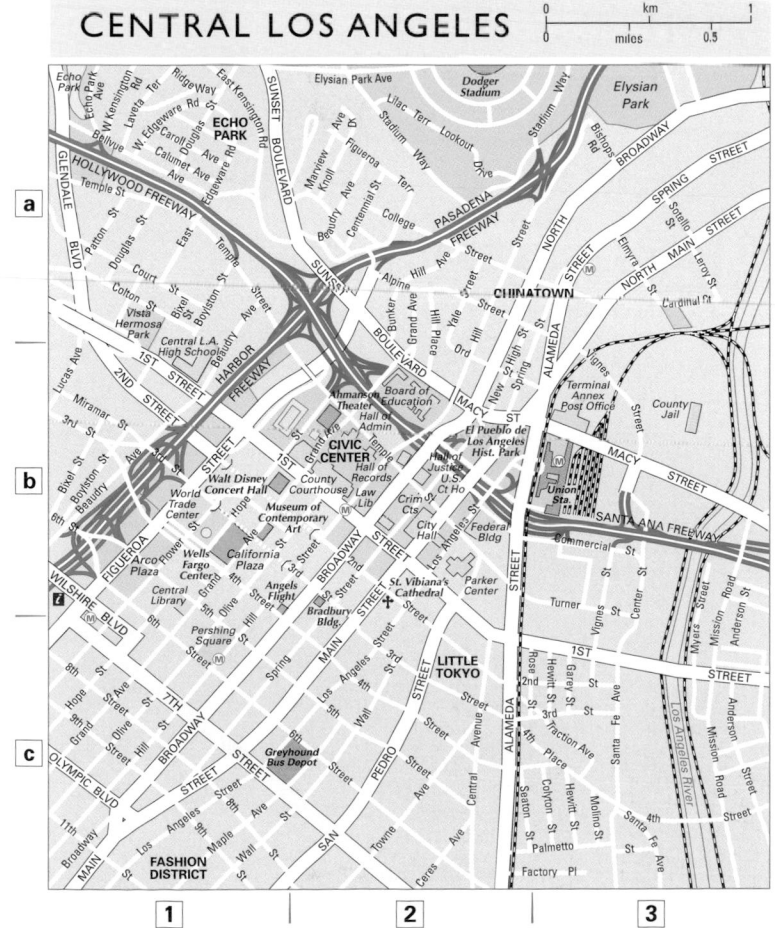

MANILA

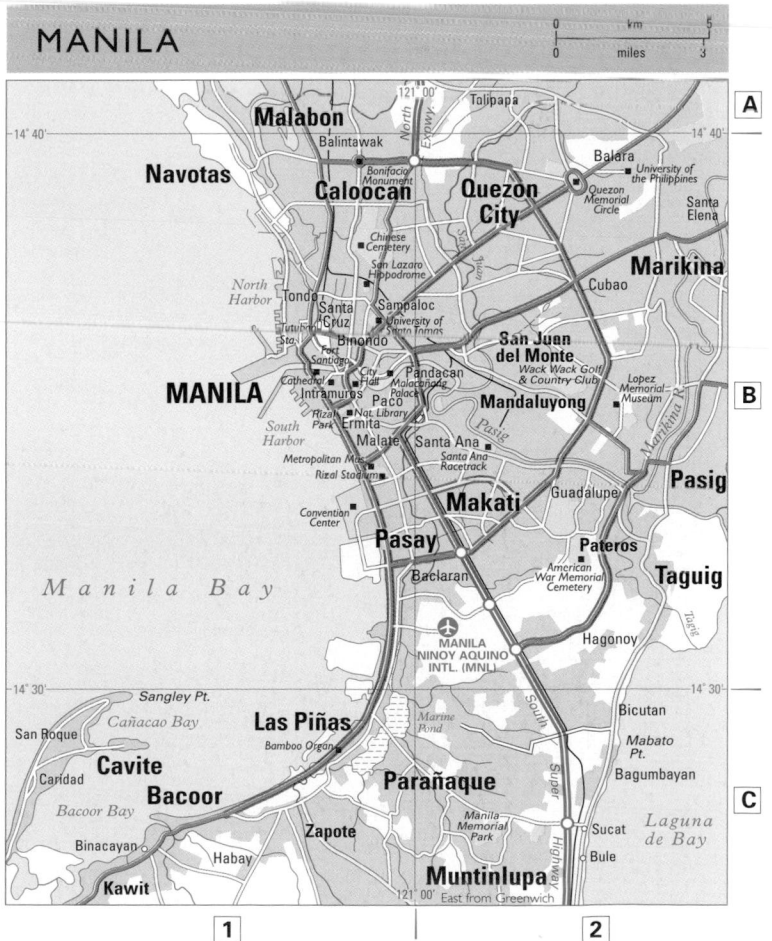

MEXICO CITY

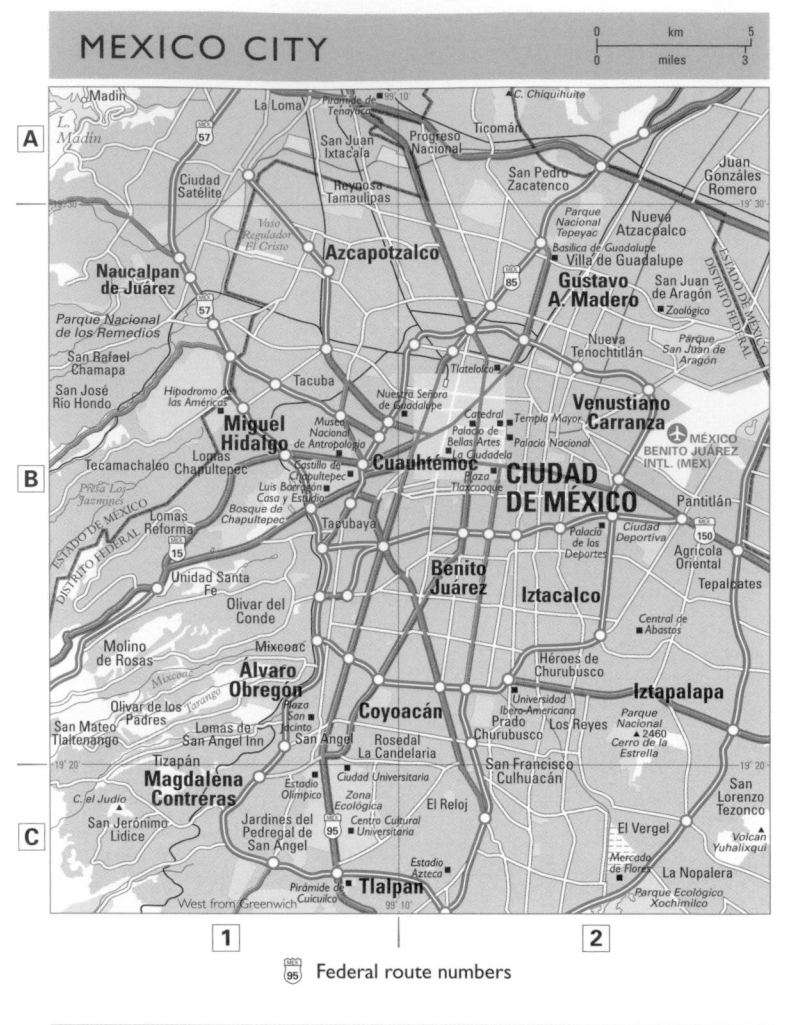

km 0 — 5
miles 0 — 3

Federal route numbers

CENTRAL MEXICO CITY

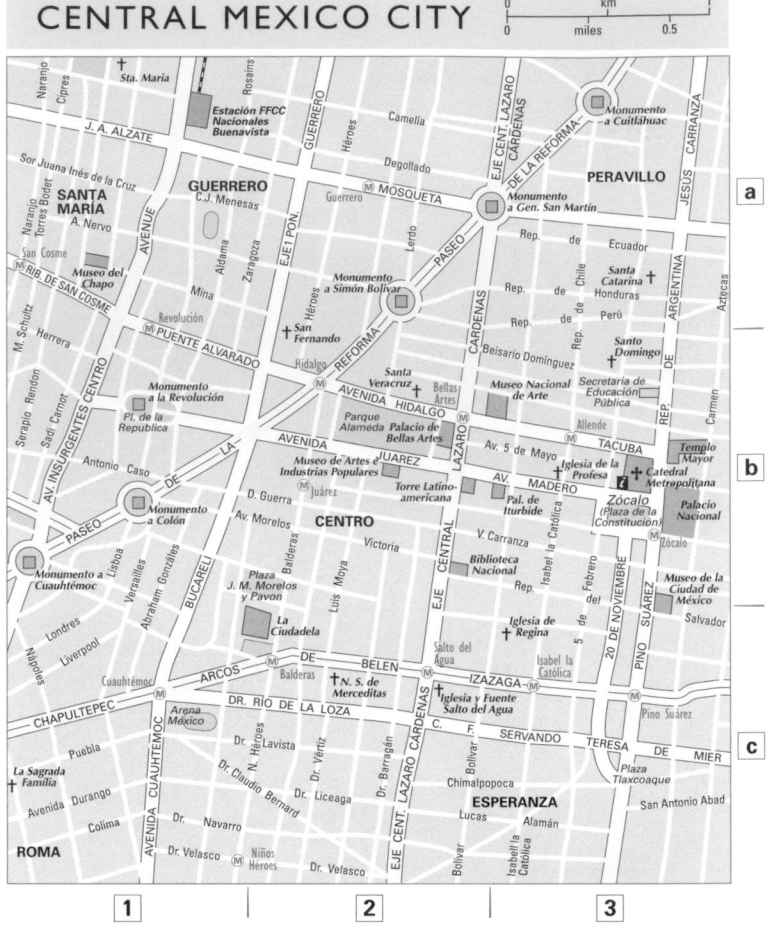

km 0 — 0.5
miles

MELBOURNE

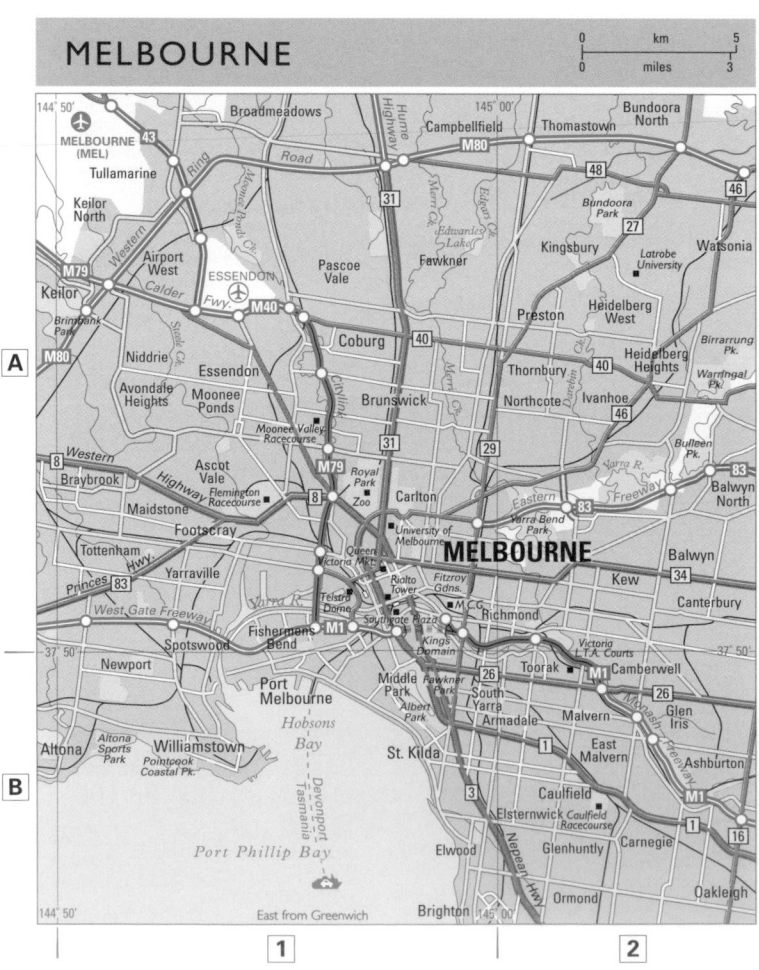

km 0 — 5
miles 0 — 3

MIAMI

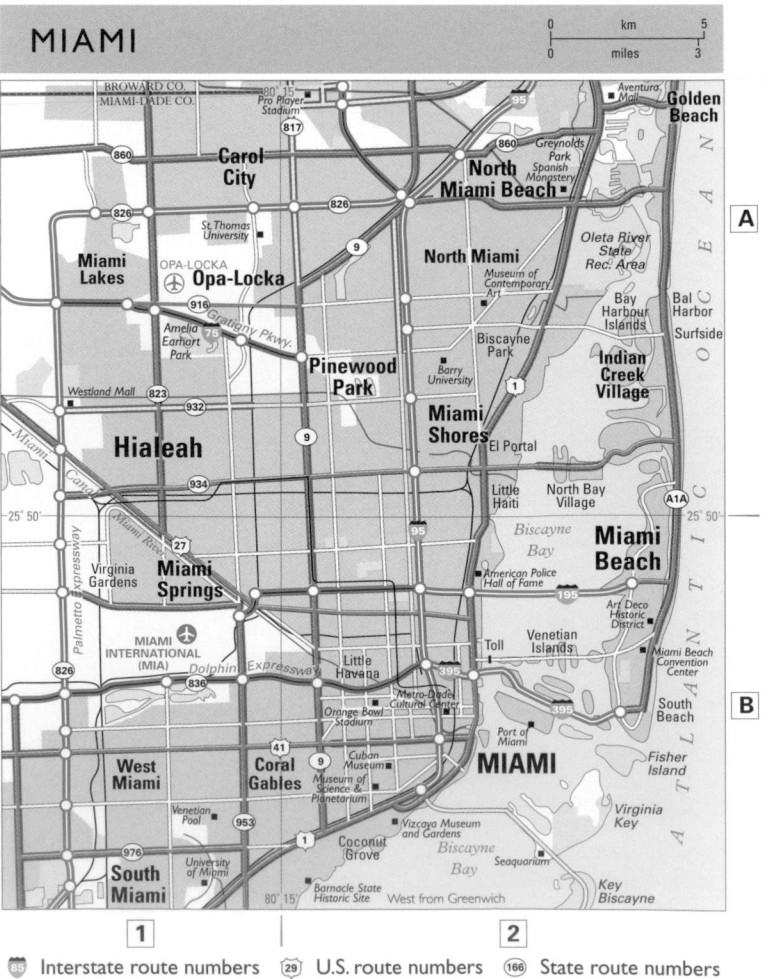

km 0 — 5
miles 0 — 3

Interstate route numbers   U.S. route numbers   State route numbers

MILAN

km 0 5
miles 0 3

Coronno · Cesate · Limbiate · Varedo · Muggiò · Concorezzo
Pertusella · Autodromo
Garbagnate Milanese · Palazzolo Milanese · Nova Milanese · Monza
Senago · Amata · Cassina Nuova · Paderno · Dugnano · 527
Lainate · Valera · San Fruttuoso · E66 · A4
Arese · Cusano Milanino · Cinisello Balsamo · Brughério
Passirana · Terrazzano · Ospiate · Cormano · A51
Rho · Bollate · Bruzzano · Bresso · San Maurizio al Lambro
Cornaredo · Àffori · Cologno Monzese
Vighignolo · Figino · Pero · Musocco · Precotto · Vimodrone
Séttimo Milanese · Trenno · Boldinasco · Greco · Crescenzago · Pioltello
Cornaredo · San Siro · Bovisa · Loreto · Milano Due
Quinto Romano · Fiera Camp. · MILANO · Lambrate · Segrate
Bággio · Quinto de' Stampi · Città degli Studi · Ortica
Cesano Boscone · San Cristóforo · Morivione · San Felice
Córsico · Vigentino · San Bóvio
Quartiere Zingone · Romano Banco · Mezzate · Peschiera Borromeo
Trezzano sul Naviglio · Assago · Chiaravalle Milanese · Triulzo · 415
Gaggiano · Buccinasco · Gratosóglio · San Donato Milanese
San Novo · Quinto de' Stampi · Poasco · San Giuliano Milanese
Barate · Gudo Gamb. · Mirasole · Mediglia
San Pietro Cúsico · Pontesesto · Ópera · Zivido · San Brera
Noviglio · Tainate · Rozzano · Fizzonasco · Mezzano
Zibido San Giacomo · Mairano · Tolcinasco · Locate di Triulzi · Zúnico

km 0 1
miles 0 0.5

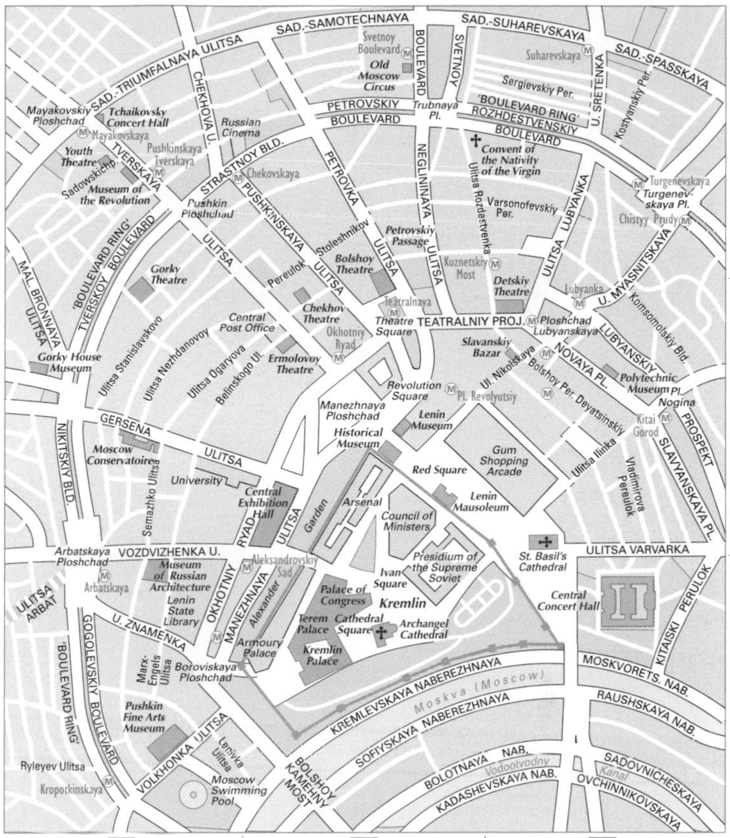

SAD.-SAMOTECHNAYA · SAD.-SUHAREVSKAYA · SAD.-SPASSKAYA
Svetnoy Boulevard · Old Moscow Circus
Mayakovskaya · TRIUMFALNAYA ULITSA · CHEKHOVA U. · Russian Cinema
Mayakovskiy Ploshchad · Tchaikovsky Concert Hall · Convent of the Nativity of the Virgin
Youth Theatre · PETROVSKIY · Trubnaya Pl. · BOULEVARD RING · ROZHDESTVENSKY BOULEVARD
Museum of the Revolution · Pushkinskaya · TVERSKAYA · PETROVKA · U. SRETENKA
BOULEVARD BOULEVARD · Pushkin Ploshchad · ULITSA · Turgenevskaya Pl. · Chistyy Prudy U.
Gorky Theatre · Stoleshnikov · Bolshoy Theatre · Kuznetskiy Most · Lubyanka
Central Post Office · Chekhov Theatre · Teatralnaya · Slavyanskiy Bazar · NOVAYA PL.
Gorky House Museum · Ermolovoy Theatre · Ókhotny Ryad · TEATRALNIY PROJ. · Polytechnic Museum
University · Ulitsa Nezhdanovoy · Ulitsa Ogaryova · Revolution Square · Gum Shopping Arcade · Kitai Gorod
Moscow Conservatoire · Manezhnaya Ploshchad · Pl. Revolyutsiy · Red Square · Lenin Mausoleum
GERSENA ULITSA · Historical Museum · Lenin Museum
NIKITSKIY BLD. · Central Exhibition Hall · Arsenal · ULITSA VARVARKA
Arbatskaya Ploshchad · VOZDVIZHENKA U. · Council of Ministers · St. Basil's Cathedral
Museum of Russian Architecture · Aleksandrovsky Sad · Presidium of the Supreme Soviet · Central Concert Hall
ULITSA ARBAT · Lenin State Library · Palace of Congress · Kremlin · Ivan Square
GOGOLEVSKIY BOULEVARD · Armoury Palace · Terem Palace · Cathedral Square · Archangel Cathedral
BOULEVARD RING · Kremlin Palace · Boroviskaya Ploshchad
Pushkin Fine Arts Museum · KREMLEVSKAYA NABEREZHNAYA · Moskva (Moscow)
Ryleyev Ulitsa · VOLKHONKA ULITSA · Moscow Swimming Pool · SOFIYSKAYA NABEREZHNAYA · MOSKVORETS. NAB. · RAUSHSKAYA NAB.
Kropotkinskaya · BOLOTNAYA · NAB. · KADASHEVSKAYA NAB. · OVCHINNIKOVSKAYA

MOSCOW

km 0 5
miles 0 3

Putilkovo · Degunino · Vladykino · Medvezhiy Ozyora
Novonikolskoye · Mitino · TO MOSCOW SHEREMETYEVO INTL. (SVO) · Babushkin · Pekhra-Pokrovskoye · Almazova
Chernyovo · Penyagino · Tushino · Nikolskiy · Petrovsko-Razumovskoye · Losiny Ostrov National Park
Krasnogorsk · Pavshino · Strogino · Timiryazev Park · Ostankino · Bogorodskoye · Galyanovo · Vostochnyy · Balashikha
Gnlyevo · Myakinino · Pokrovsko-Sresnevo · Petrovsky Park · Abramtsevo · Novaya
Arkhangelskoye · Troitse-Lykovo · Khorosovo · Sokolniki · Izmaylovo · Pekhra-Yakovievskaya
Zakharkovo · Rublovo · Tatarovo · Frunze · Dzerzhinskiy · Vishnyaki · Nikolskoye
Razdory · Cherepkovo · Mnevniki · MOSKVA · Sverdlov · Izmaylovskiy Park · Leportovo · Saltykovka
Barvikha · Krylatskoye · Krasno-Presnenskaya · Bolshoy Theatre · Bauman · Novogireyevo · Reutov
Romashkovo · Kuntsevo · Fili-Mazilovo · Kremlin · Red Square · Kuskovo · Perovo · Serebryanka · Zheleznodorozhnyy
Poduskino · Nemchinovka · Davydkovo · Kiev Station · Tretyakov Art Gallery · Zhdanov · Plyushchevo · Veshnyaki · Fenino
Novoivanovskoye · Novodevichy Convent · Gorky Park · Pavelet Station · Vykhino · Kosino · Kozhukhovo
Lochino · Aminyevo · Luzhniki Sports Centre, Lenin Stadium · Moskvoretskiy · Kuzyminki · Zhulebino · Mikhelysona
Odintsovo · Mamonovo · Bakovka · Ochakovo · Lomonosov Moscow State University · Leninskiye Gory · Moscow Circus · Lyublino · Lyubertsy · Nekrasovka
Meshcherskiy · Zarechye · Ramenki · Oktyabrskiy · Nogatino · Tomilino · Koreneво
Nikulino · Yugo-Zarad · Cheryomushki · Dyakovo · Maryino · Kotelniki · Malakhovka
Troparevo · Zyuzino · Volkhonka-Zil · Kúryanovo · Kamotnya · Kraskovo
Choboty · Solntsevo · Belyayevo Bogorodskoye · Bittsevsky Forest Park · Lenino · Brateyevo · Dzerzhinskiy · Chkalova
Peredelkino · Orlovo · Chertanovo · Borisovo · Tokarevo
Vnukovo · Rasskazovka · Rumyantsevo · Chertanovo

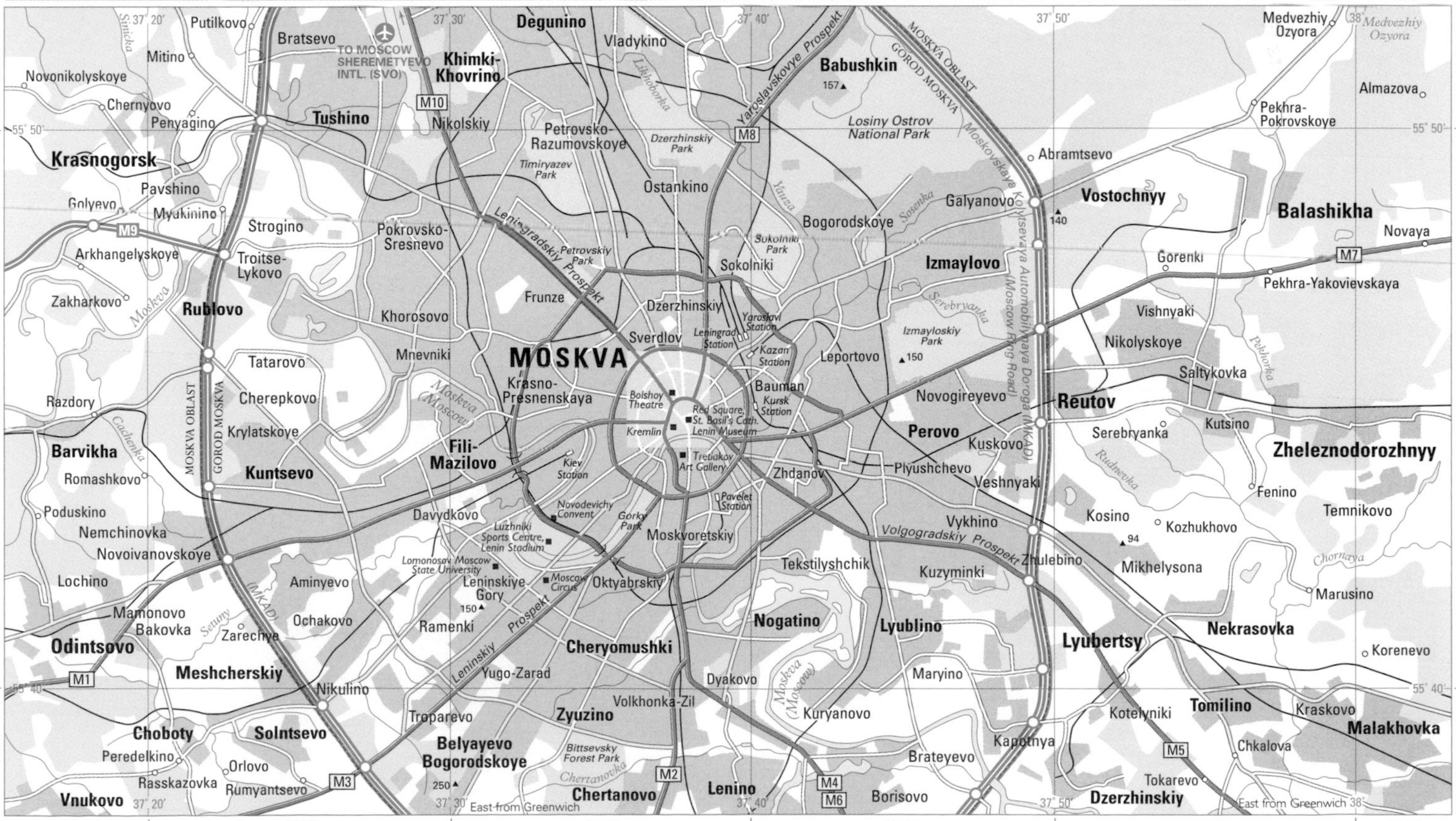

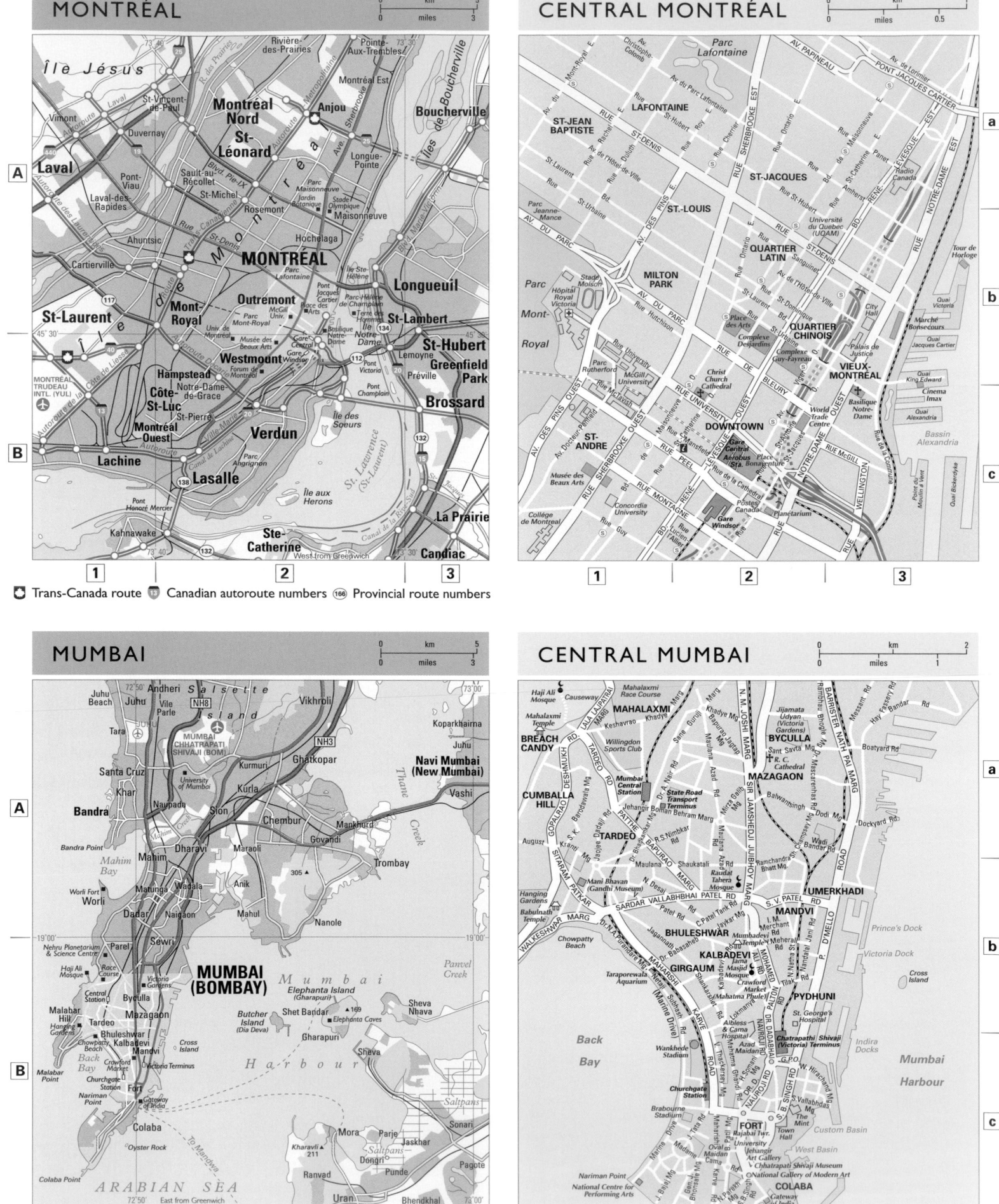

MONTRÉAL

km 5 / miles 3

Île Jésus
Rivière-des-Prairies
Pointe-Aux-Trembles
Montréal Est
Anjou
Boucherville
Îles de Boucherville
Montréal Nord
St-Léonard
Vimont
Laval
Duvernay
St-Vincent-de-Paul
Laval-des-Rapides
Pont-Viau
Sault-au-Récollet
St-Michel
Rosemont
Jardin Botanique
Parc Maisonneuve
Maisonneuve
Longue-Pointe
Ahuntsic
Cartierville
Hochelaga
MONTRÉAL
Île Ste-Hélène
Longueuil
St-Laurent
Mont-Royal
Outremont
Parc Mont-Royal
Univ. de Montréal
Parc Jean-Drapeau
Parc Jacques Cartier
Terre des Hommes
Île Notre-Dame
St-Lambert
MONTRÉAL TRUDEAU INTL. (YUL)
Westmount
Musée des Beaux Arts
Gare Centrale
Gare Windsor
Basilique Notre-Dame
Lemoyne
Préville
St-Hubert
Greenfield Park
Hampstead
Notre-Dame-de-Grâce
Forum de Montréal
Pont Victoria
Côte-St-Luc
St-Pierre
Brossard
Montréal Ouest
Verdun
Île des Soeurs
Lachine
Parc Angrignon
Canal de Lachine
Pont Champlain
La Prairie
Lasalle
Île aux Herons
St-Laurent (St-Laurent)
Pont Honoré Mercier
Kahnawake
Ste-Catherine
Candiac
West from Greenwich

🛡 Trans-Canada route   🔟 Canadian autoroute numbers   ⑯⑥ Provincial route numbers

CENTRAL MONTRÉAL

km 1 / miles 0.5

Parc Lafontaine
AV. PAPINEAU
PONT JACQUES CARTIER
Av. de Lormier
ST-JEAN BAPTISTE
LAFONTAINE
RUE SHERBROOKE EST
ST-JACQUES
Radio Canada
ST-LOUIS
Université du Quebec (UQAM)
Tour de Horloge
QUARTIER LATIN
ST-DENIS
AV. DU PARC
MILTON PARK
Parc Jeanne-Mance
Quai Victoria
Marché Bonsecours
Parc Mont-Royal
Hôpital Royal Victoria
Place des Arts
Complexe Desjardins
QUARTIER CHINOIS
Quai Jacques Cartier
McGill University
Parc Rutherford
Complexe Guy-Favreau
Palais de Justice
VIEUX-MONTRÉAL
Quai King Edward
Cinema Imax
Christ Church Cathedral
RUE UNIVERSITY
DOWNTOWN
World Trade Centre
Basilique Notre-Dame
Quai Alexandria
Bassin Alexandria
ST-ANDRE
Gare Central Aerobus Sta.
Place Bonaventure
NOTRE-DAME
RUE McGILL
WELLINGTON
Point du Moulin à Vent
Quai Bickerdyke
Musée des Beaux Arts
Concordia University
Postes Canada
Collège de Montréal
Gare Windsor
Planétarium

MUMBAI

km 5 / miles 3

Salsette Island
Andheri
Vikhroli
NH8
Juhu Beach
Juhu
Vile Parle
Koparkhairna
Tara
Santa Cruz
MUMBAI CHHATRAPATI (SHIVAJI) (BOM)
NH3
Juhu
Ghatkopar
Navi Mumbai (New Mumbai)
Khar
Kurmuri
Vashi
University of Mumbai
Kurla
Bandra
Naupada
Sion
Chembur
Thane Creek
Bandra Point
Mahim
Dharavi
Maraoli
Govandi
Mankhurd
Mahim Bay
Matunga
Wadala
Anik
Trombay
305 ▲
Worli Fort
Worli
Dadar
Naigaon
Mahul
Nanole
Nehru Planetarium & Science Centre
Parel
Sewri
Panvel Creek
Haji Ali Mosque
Race Course
MUMBAI (BOMBAY)
Mumbai Elephanta Island (Gharapuri)
Central Station
Byculla
Mazagaon
Elephanta Caves (Dia Deva)
Sheva Nhava
Malabar Hill
Tardeo
Butcher Island
Shet Bandar
Hanging Gardens
Bhuleshwar
Chowpatty
Kalbadevi
Mandvi
Victoria Terminus
Cross Island
Gharapuri
Sheva
Malabar Point
Churchgate Station
Crawford Market
Harbour
Fort
Nariman Point
Gateway of India
Mora
Parje
Jaskhar
Colaba
Oyster Rock
Kharavli 211 ▲
Dongri
Punde
Pagote
Colaba Point
Saltpans
Sonari
ARABIAN SEA
East from Greenwich
Ranvad
Uran
Bhendkhal

CENTRAL MUMBAI

km 2 / miles 1

Haji Ali Mosque
Mahalaxmi Race Course
N. M. JOSHI MARG
BARRISTER NATH PAI MARG
MAHALAXMI
Mahalaxmi Temple
Jijamata Udyan (Victoria Gardens)
BREACH CANDY
Willingdon Sports Club
BYCULLA
Boatyard Rd
MAZAGAON
R. C. Cathedral
CUMBALLA HILL
Mumbai Central Station
State Road Transport Terminus
Dockyard Rd
TARDEO
Jehangir Boman Behram Marg
Wadi Bandar Rd
UMERKHADI
Mani Bhavan (Gandhi Museum)
Raudat Tahera Mosque
MANDVI
Hanging Gardens
SARDAR VALLABHBHAI PATEL RD
S. V. PATEL RD
Babulnath Temple
BHULESHWAR
Mumbadevi Temple
Chowpatty Beach
Jagannath
KALBADEVI
Jama Masjid
PYDHUNI
GIRGAUM
Taraporewala Aquarium
Crawford Market (Mahatma Phule)
St. George's Hospital
Marine Drive
Albless & Cama Hospital
Prince's Dock
Azad Maidan
Victoria Dock
Back Bay
Wankhede Stadium
Chatrapati Shivaji (Victoria Terminus)
Cross Island
G.P.O.
Indira Docks
Churchgate Station
Mumbai Harbour
Brabourne Stadium
The Mint
Custom Basin
FORT
Rajabai Twr.
Town Hall
University
West Basin
Jehangir Art Gallery
Chhatrapati Shivaji Museum
Oval Maidan
National Gallery of Modern Art
Nariman Point
National Centre for Performing Arts
COLABA
Gateway of India

MUNICH

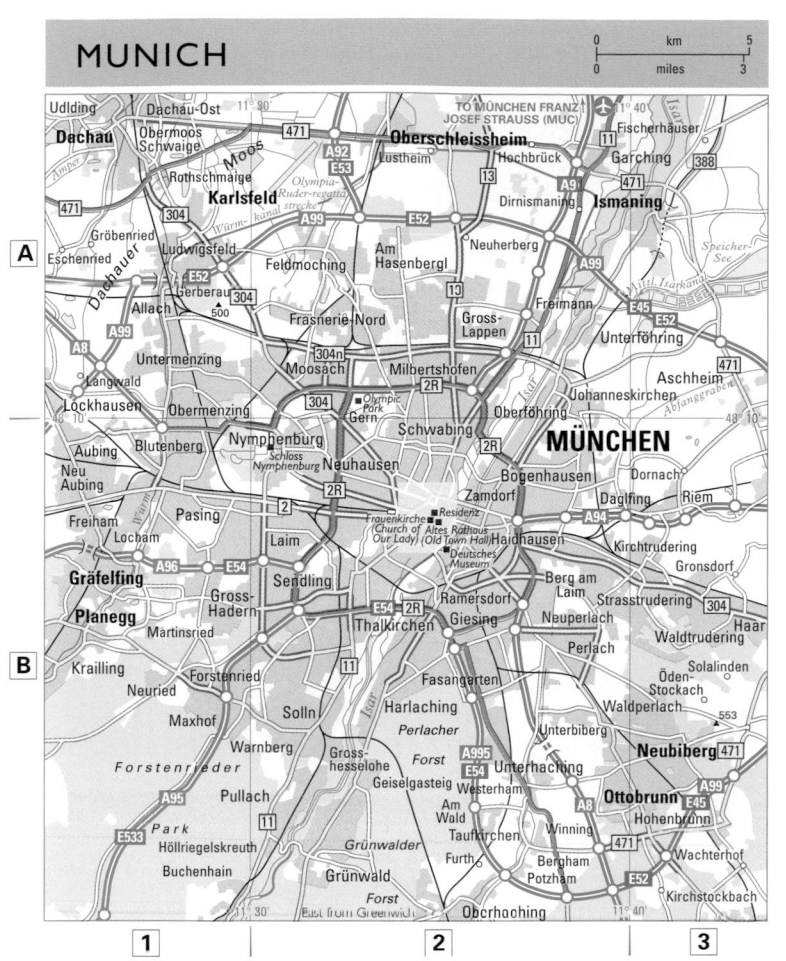

CENTRAL MUNICH

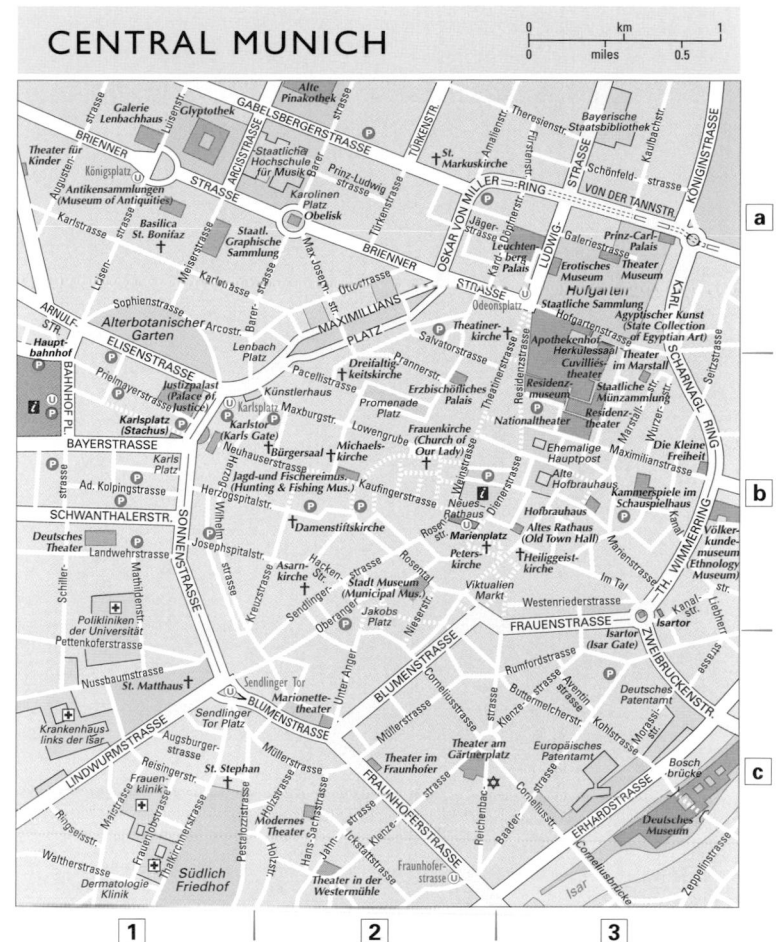

NEW ORLEANS

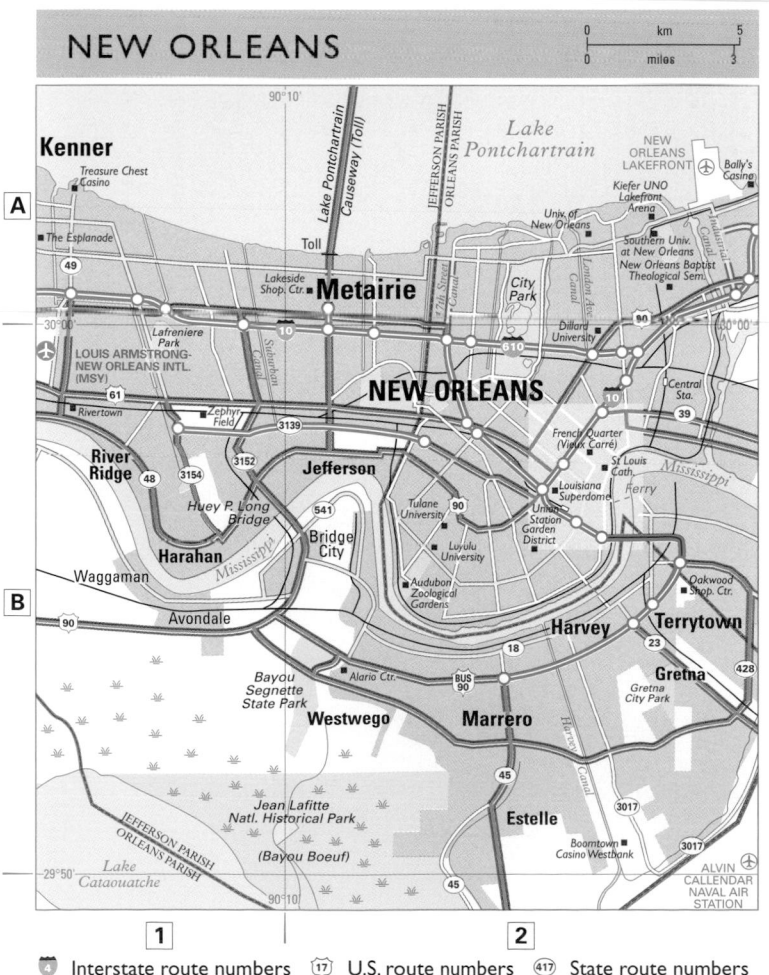

CENTRAL NEW ORLEANS

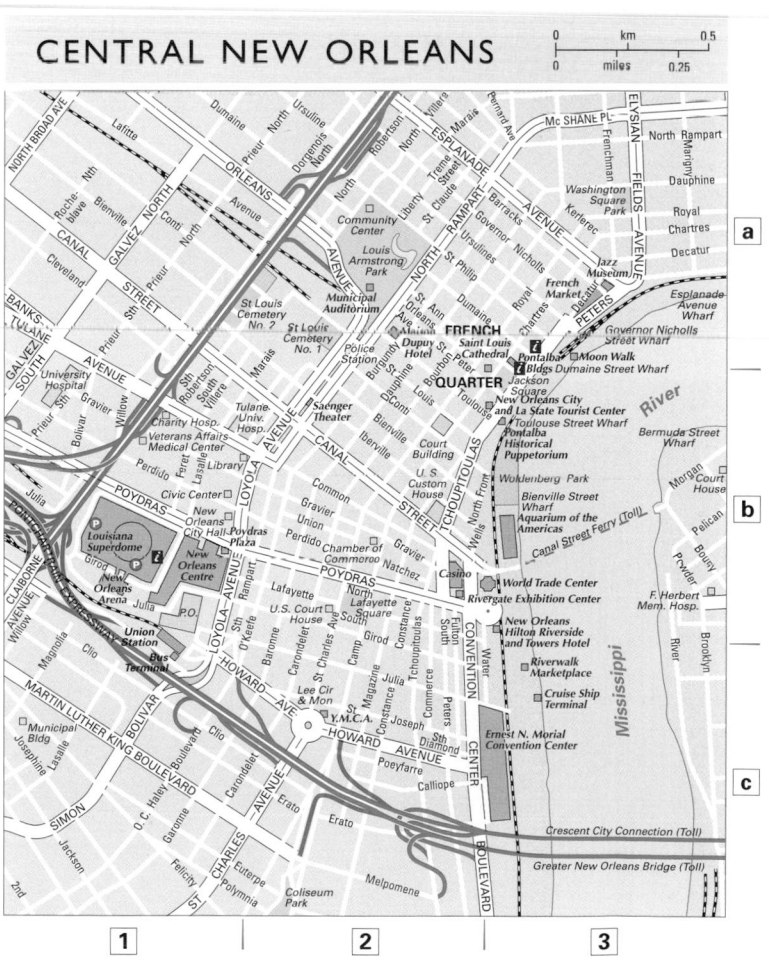

Interstate route numbers   U.S. route numbers   State route numbers

NEW YORK

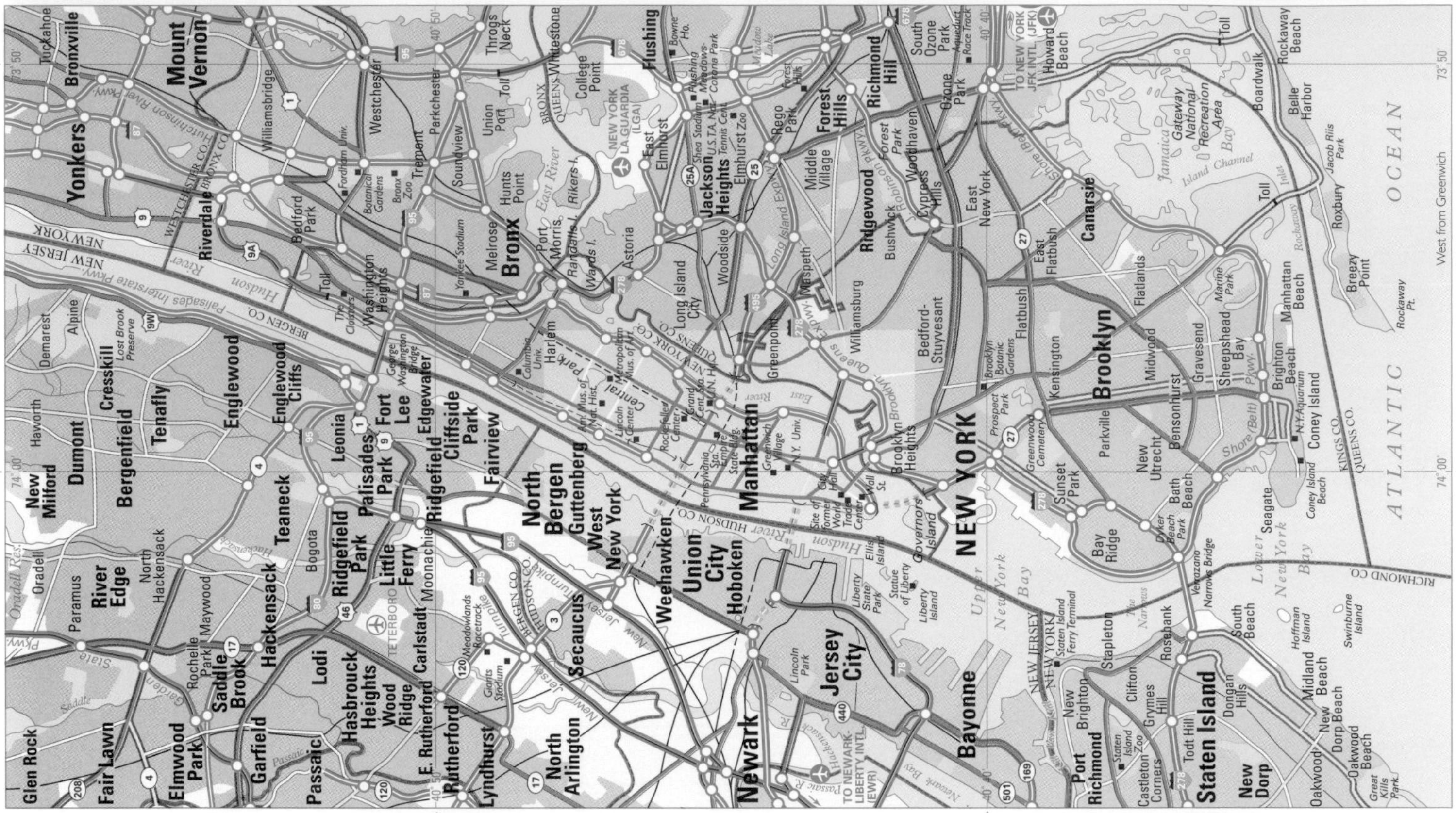

km 5
miles 3

Interstate route numbers
U.S. route numbers
State route numbers

Tuckahoe · Bronxville · Mount Vernon · Yonkers · Riverdale · Westchester · Williamsbridge · Throgs Neck · Whitestone · Flushing · Queens · South Ozone Park · Rockaway Beach

Demarest · Alpine · Cresskill · Tenafly · Englewood · Englewood Cliffs · Bronx · College Point · East Elmhurst · Richmond Hill · Howard Beach · Belle Harbor · Boardwalk

New Milford · Dumont · Bergenfield · Teaneck · Leonia · Fort Lee · Edgewater · Harlem · Astoria · Jackson Heights · Rego Park · Forest Hills · Woodhaven · Ridgewood · Bushwick · Cypress Hills · East New York · Canarsie

Glen Rock · Fair Lawn · Elmwood Park · Garfield · Passaic · Paramus · Rochelle Park · Saddle Brook · Lodi · Hasbrouck Heights · Wood Ridge · Carlstadt · E. Rutherford · Rutherford · Lyndhurst · North Arlington · Newark · Bayonne

River Edge · Hackensack · Maywood · Little Ferry · Moonachie · Secaucus · Weehawken · Union City · Hoboken · Jersey City

Ridgefield Park · Palisades Park · Ridgefield · Cliffside Park · Fairview · North Bergen · Guttenberg · West New York

Manhattan · Greenpoint · Williamsburg · Bedford-Stuyvesant · Flatbush · Brooklyn · Midwood · Gravesend · Bensonhurst · Bath Beach · Coney Island · Brighton Beach · Manhattan Beach · Breezy Point

NEW YORK · Sunset Park · Bay Ridge · New Utrecht · Parkville · Sheepshead Bay

Port Richmond · New Brighton · Clifton · Stapleton · Rosebank · South Beach · Dongan Hills · Grymes Hill · Todt Hill · Staten Island · New Dorp · Oakwood

ATLANTIC OCEAN

Hudson River · East River · Long Island City · Upper New York Bay · Lower New York Bay

A B C

CENTRAL NEW YORK

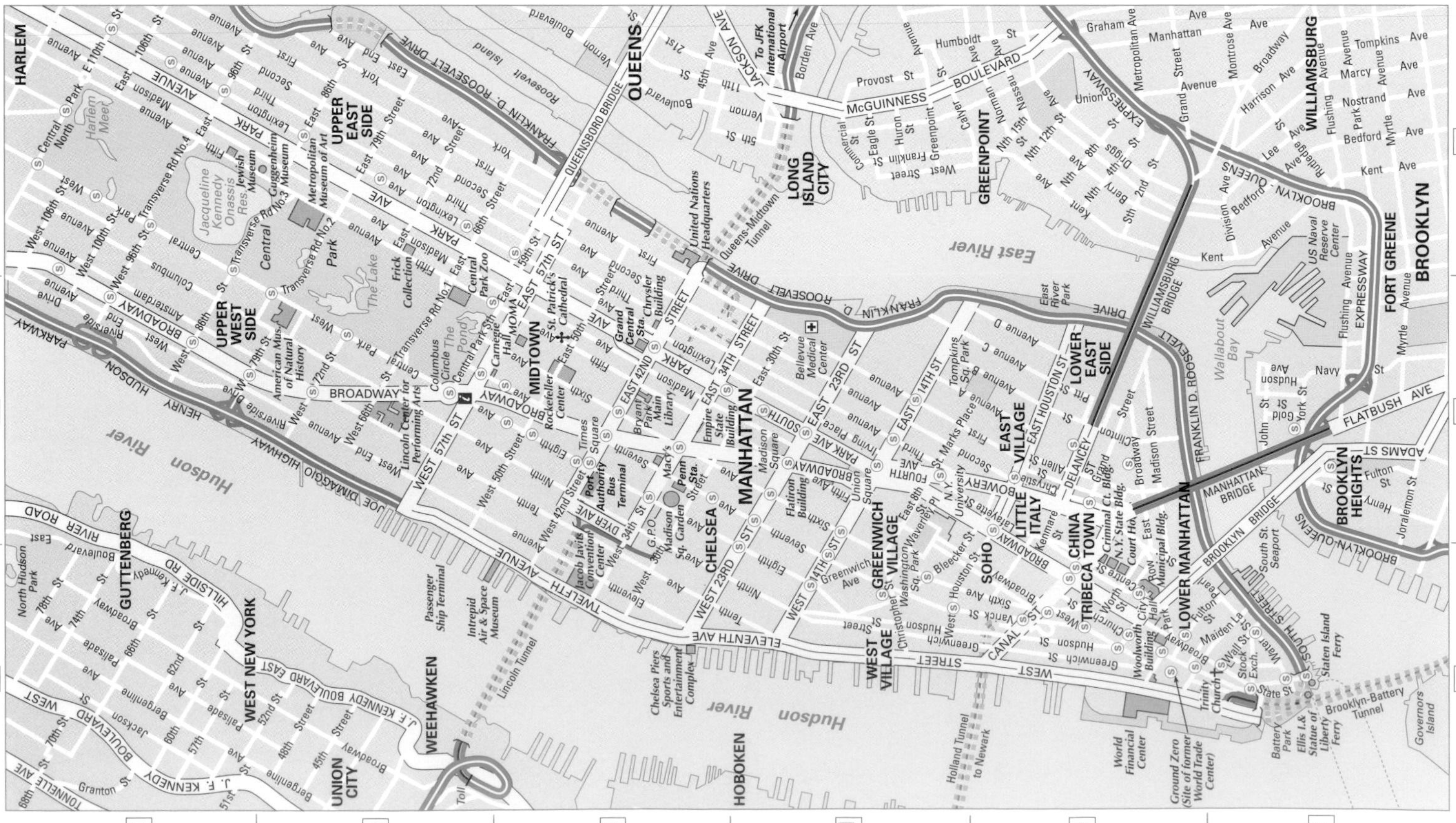

km 2
miles 1

HARLEM · QUEENS · WILLIAMSBURG · BROOKLYN

UPPER EAST SIDE · UPPER WEST SIDE · LONG ISLAND CITY · GREENPOINT · FORT GREENE

MIDTOWN · MANHATTAN · LOWER EAST SIDE · EAST VILLAGE · GREENWICH VILLAGE · CHELSEA · WEST VILLAGE · SOHO · LITTLE ITALY · CHINA TOWN · TRIBECA · LOWER MANHATTAN · BROOKLYN HEIGHTS

GUTTENBERG · WEST NEW YORK · WEEHAWKEN · UNION CITY · HOBOKEN

Hudson River · East River

Central Park · Metropolitan Museum · American Mus. of Natural History · Lincoln Center for Performing Arts · Times Square · Penn Sta. · Empire State Building · Grand Central Sta. · United Nations Headquarters · Chrysler Building · Port Authority Bus Terminal · Madison Sq. Garden · Ground Zero · World Financial Center · Statue of Liberty

a b c d e f

ORLANDO

km 0 — 5
miles 0 — 3

A

B

1 2 3

🛡️ Interstate route numbers ⑰ U.S. route numbers ④¹⁷ State route numbers

OSAKA

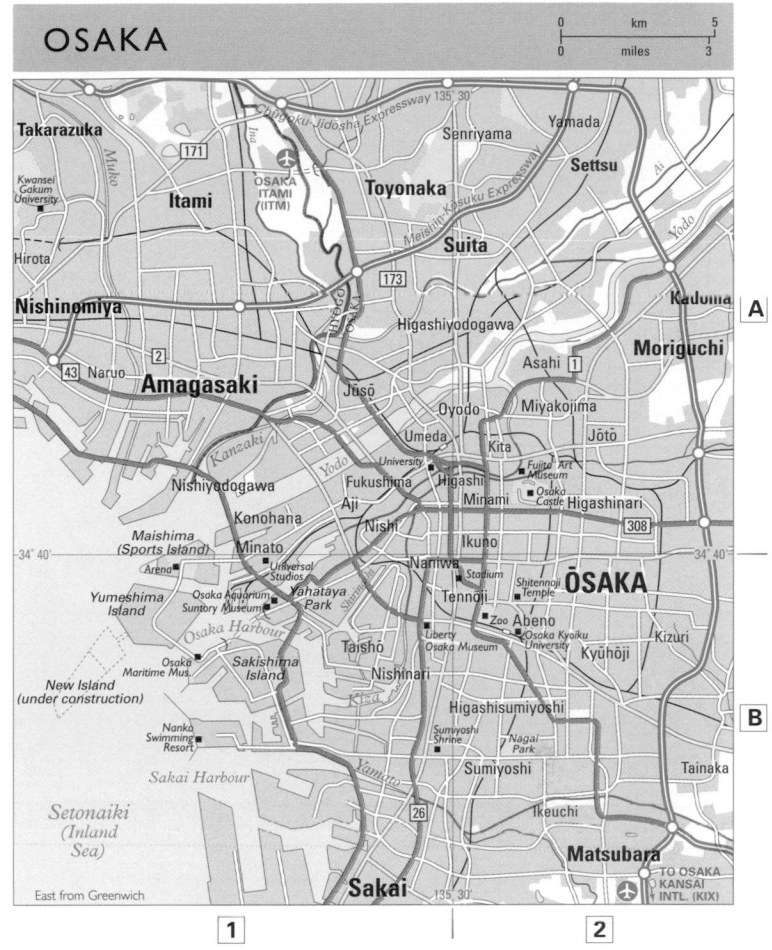

km 0 — 5
miles 0 — 3

A

B

1 2

OSLO

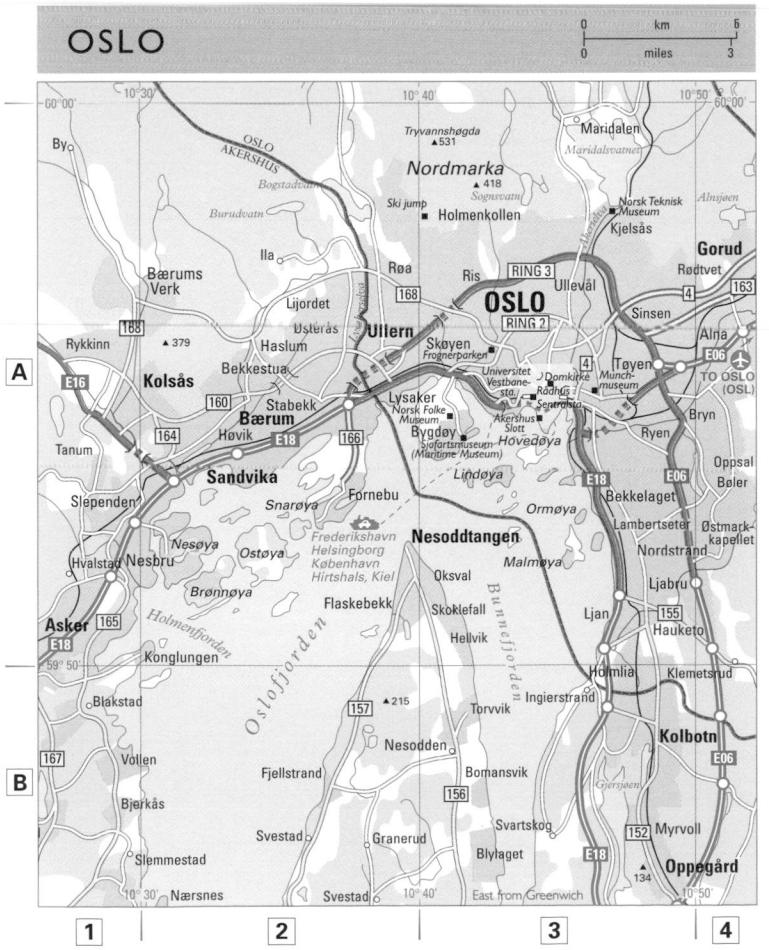

km 0 — 6
miles 0 — 3

A

B

1 2 3 4

CENTRAL OSLO

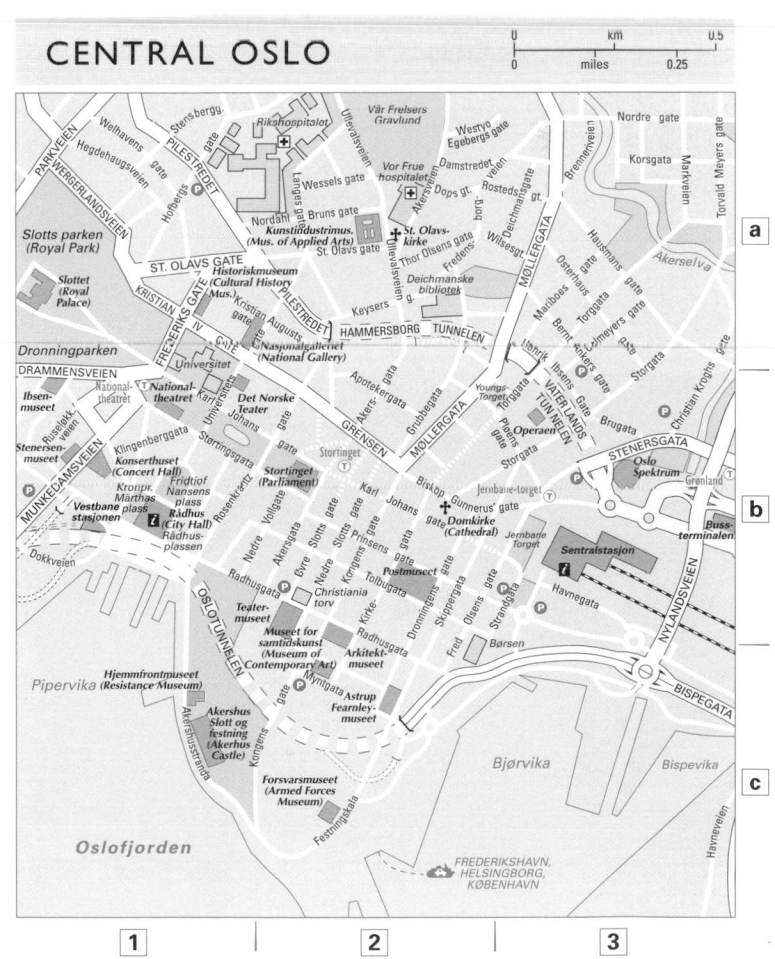

km 0 — 0.5
miles 0 — 0.25

a

b

c

1 2 3

COPYRIGHT PHILIP'S

PARIS

0 km 5
0 miles 3

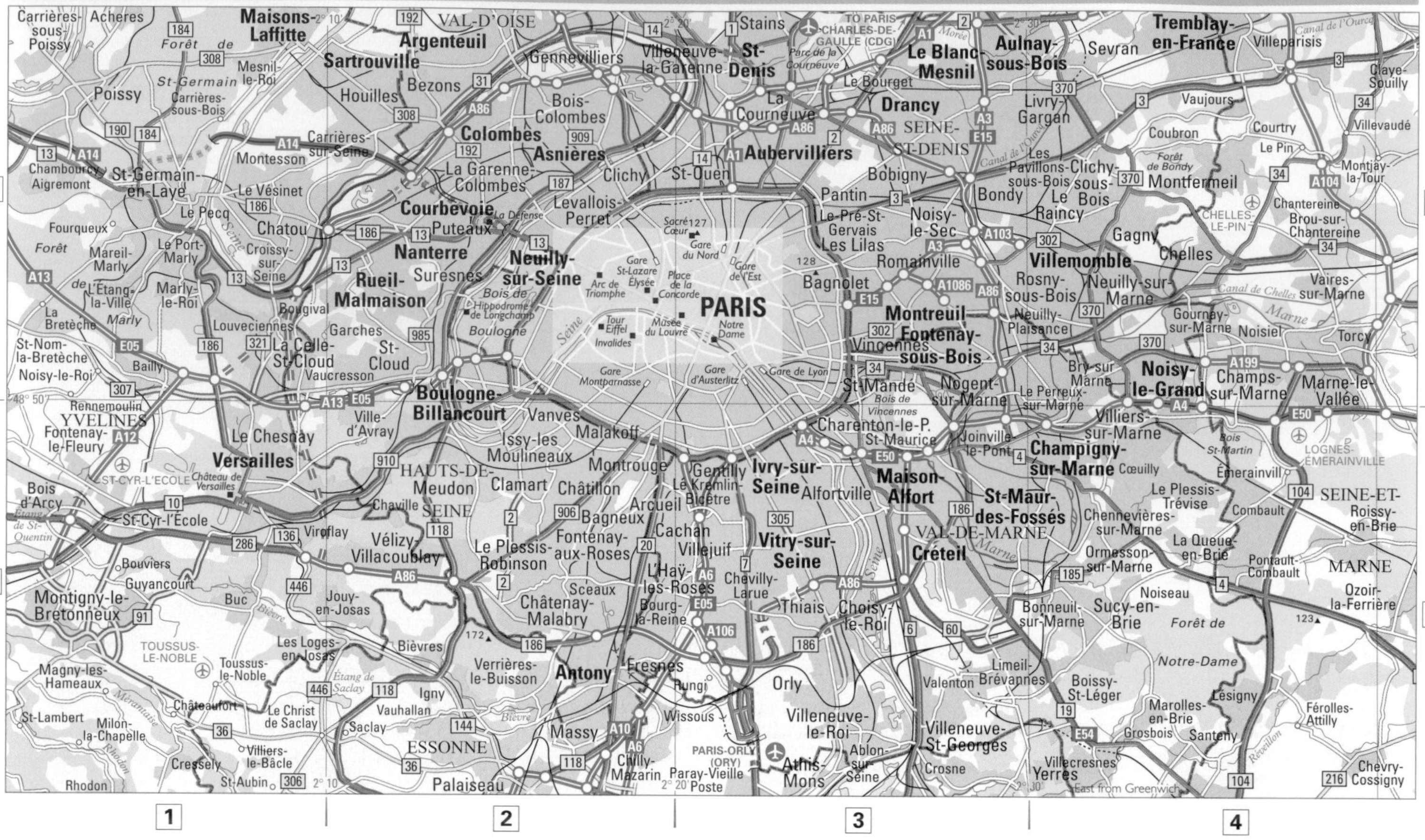

Carrières-sous-Poissy
Achères
Maisons-Laffitte
Argenteuil
VAL-D'OISE
Stains
St-Denis
TO PARIS-CHARLES-DE-GAULLE (CDG)
Le Blanc-Mesnil
Aulnay-sous-Bois
Sevran
Tremblay-en-France
Villeparisis
Sartrouville
Gennevilliers
Villeneuve-la-Garenne
Drancy
Poissy
Houilles
Bezons
La Courneuve
Le Bourget
Livry-Gargan
Colombes
Asnières
Aubervilliers
SEINE-ST-DENIS
Bois-Colombes
Coubron
Courtry
Montesson
St-Germain-en-Laye
La Garenne-Colombes
Clichy
St-Ouen
Bobigny
Les Pavillons-sous-Bois
Clichy-sous-Bois
Montfermeil
Le Vésinet
Le Pecq
Chatou
Courbevoie
Levallois-Perret
Pantin
Noisy-le-Sec
Bondy
Le Raincy
Gagny
Chelles
Nanterre
Puteaux
Neuilly-sur-Seine
Le Pré-St-Gervais
Les Lilas
Romainville
Rueil-Malmaison
Suresnes
Bagnolet
Villemomble
Rosny-sous-Bois
Neuilly-sur-Marne
PARIS
Montreuil
Fontenay-sous-Bois
Vincennes
St-Mandé
Bougival
Louveciennes
La Celle-St-Cloud
Garches
St-Cloud
Vaucresson
Boulogne-Billancourt
Noisy-le-Grand
Champs-sur-Marne
Marne-la-Vallée
Torcy
Noisiel
YVELINES
Le Chesnay
Versailles
Ville-d'Avray
Issy-les-Moulineaux
Vanves
Malakoff
Charenton-le-P.
St-Maurice
Nogent-sur-Marne
Joinville-le-Pont
Champigny-sur-Marne
Villiers-sur-Marne
HAUTS-DE-SEINE
Meudon
Clamart
Châtillon
Montrouge
Gentilly
Le Kremlin-Bicêtre
Ivry-sur-Seine
Alfortville
Maison-Alfort
St-Maur-des-Fossés
Chennevières-sur-Marne
SEINE-ET-MARNE
St-Cyr-l'École
Viroflay
Vélizy-Villacoublay
Bagneux
Arcueil
Cachan
Villejuif
Vitry-sur-Seine
Créteil
VAL-DE-MARNE
Le Plessis-Robinson
Fontenay-aux-Roses
L'Haÿ-les-Roses
Chevilly-Larue
Thiais
Choisy-le-Roi
Sucy-en-Brie
Montigny-le-Bretonneux
Guyancourt
Buc
Jouy-en-Josas
Sceaux
Châtenay-Malabry
Bourg-la-Reine
Bièvres
Verrières-le-Buisson
Antony
Fresnes
Orly
Villeneuve-le-Roi
Valenton
Limeil-Brévannes
Boissy-St-Léger
Forêt de Notre-Dame
Magny-les-Hameaux
Châteaufort
Le Christ de Saclay
Igny
Vauhallan
Saclay
Massy
Wissous
PARIS-ORLY (ORY)
Athis-Mons
Villeneuve-St-Georges
ESSONNE
Chilly-Mazarin
Paray-Vieille Poste
Ablon-sur-Seine
Crosne
Yerres
Villecresnes
Marolles-en-Brie
Santeny
Lésigny
Férolles-Attilly
Chevry-Cossigny
Palaiseau
Rhodon
St-Aubin
East from Greenwich
A
B
1
2
3
4

CENTRAL PARIS

0 km 1
0 miles 0.5

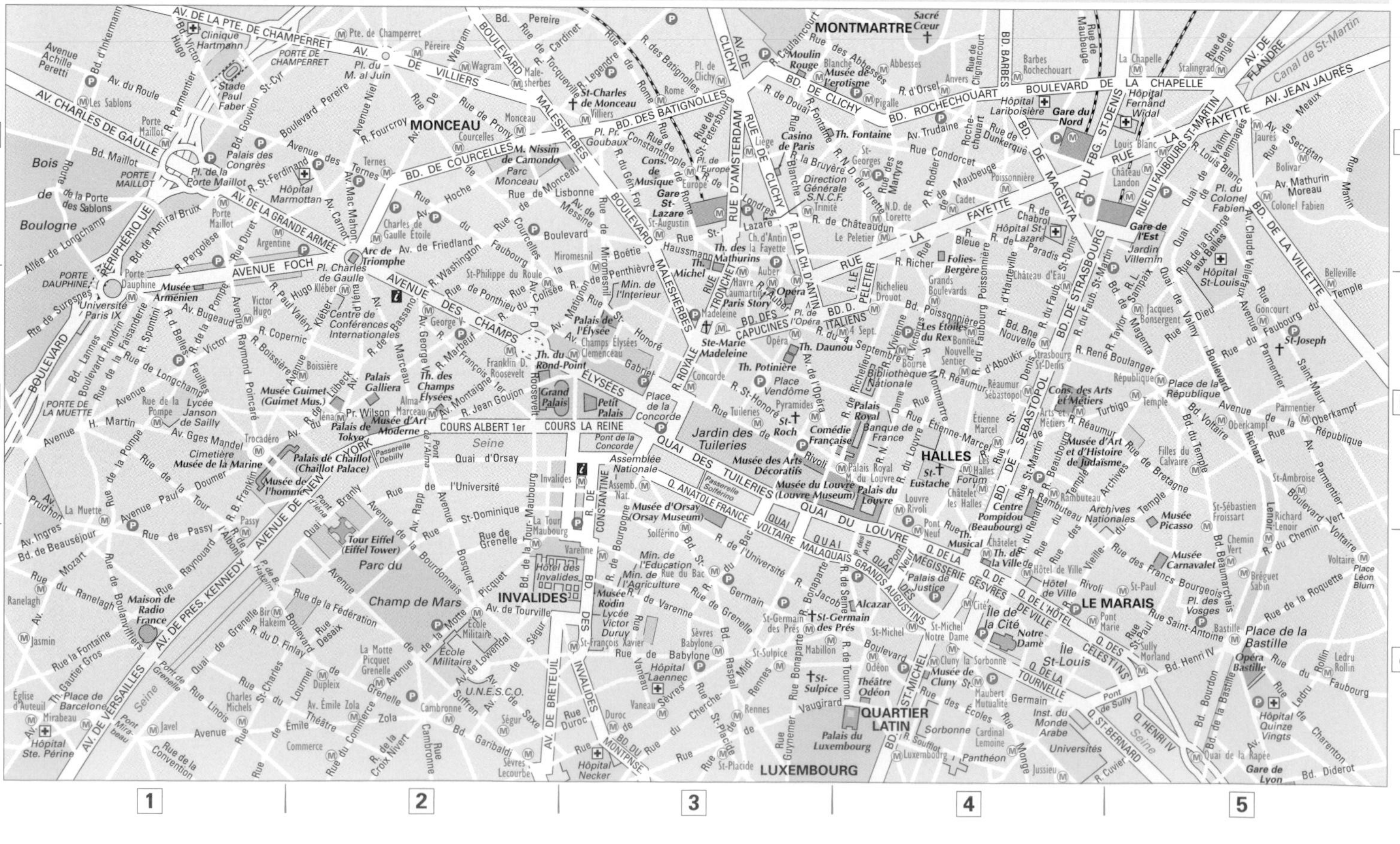

MONTMARTRE
Sacré Cœur
MONCEAU
Bois de Boulogne
Arc de Triomphe
AVENUE FOCH
AV. DE LA GRANDE ARMÉE
AV. CHARLES DE GAULLE
Gare St-Lazare
Gare du Nord
Gare de l'Est
Opéra
Palais de l'Élysée
AVENUE DES CHAMPS ÉLYSÉES
Place de la Concorde
Jardin des Tuileries
Musée du Louvre (Louvre Museum)
HALLES
Centre Pompidou (Beaubourg)
LE MARAIS
Place de la République
Palais de Chaillot (Chaillot Palace)
Tour Eiffel (Eiffel Tower)
Champ de Mars
INVALIDES
Hôtel des Invalides
Musée d'Orsay (Orsay Museum)
Seine
Île de la Cité
Notre Dame
Île St-Louis
QUARTIER LATIN
Panthéon
Palais du Luxembourg
LUXEMBOURG
Place de la Bastille
Opéra Bastille
Gare de Lyon
Maison de Radio France
a
b
c
1
2
3
4
5

PRAGUE

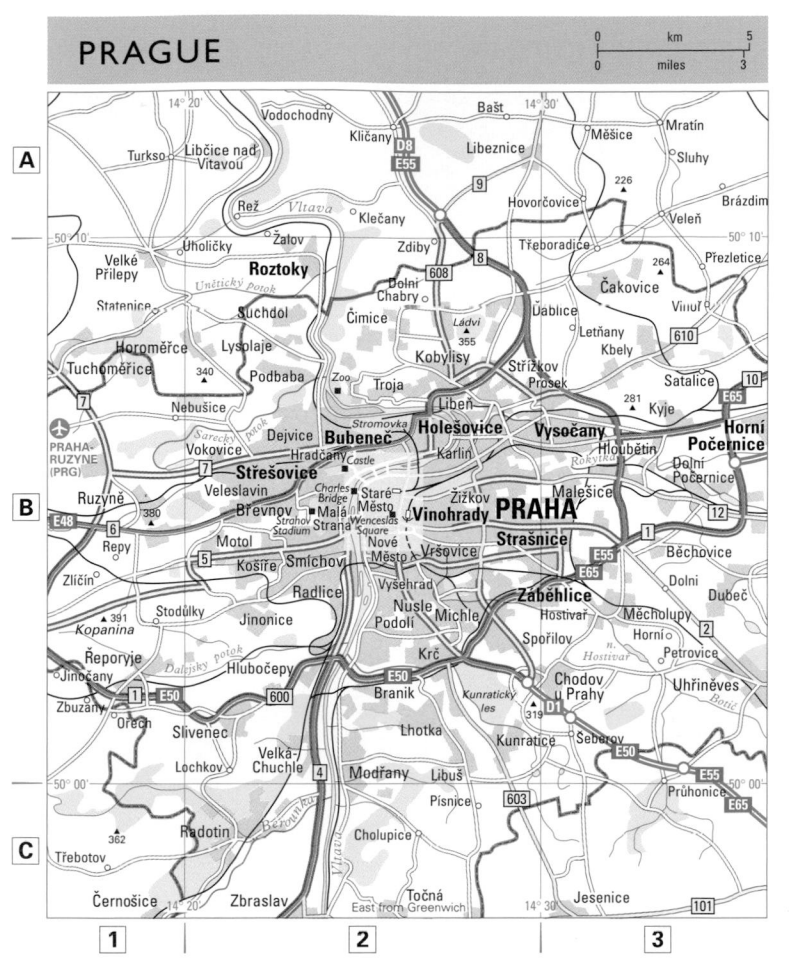

CENTRAL PRAGUE

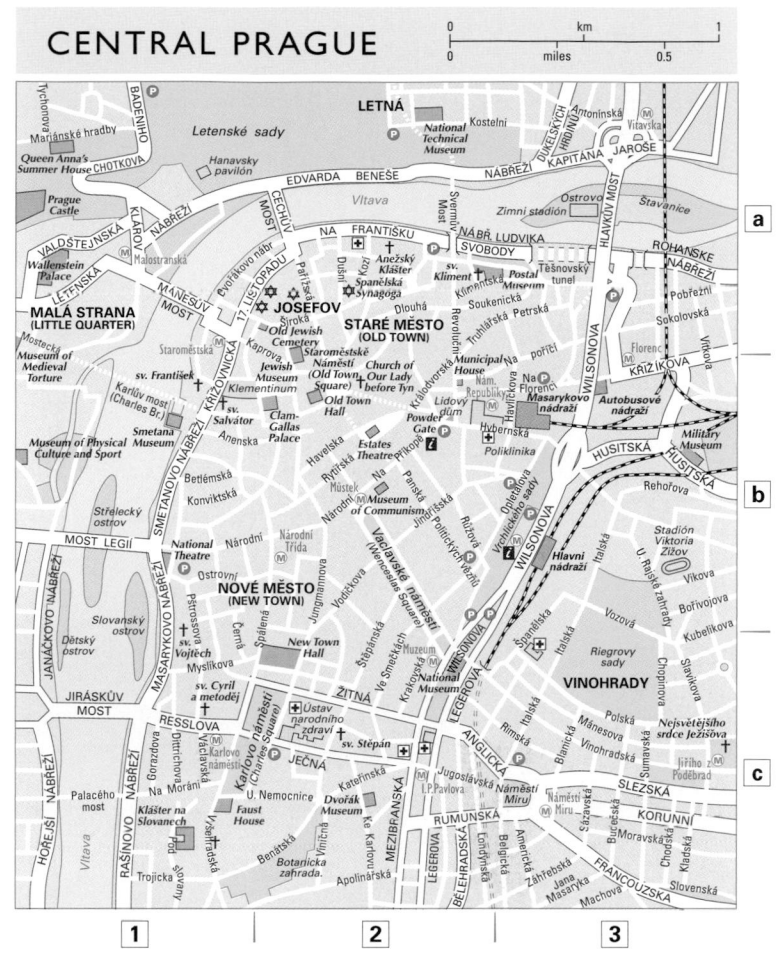

RIO DE JANEIRO

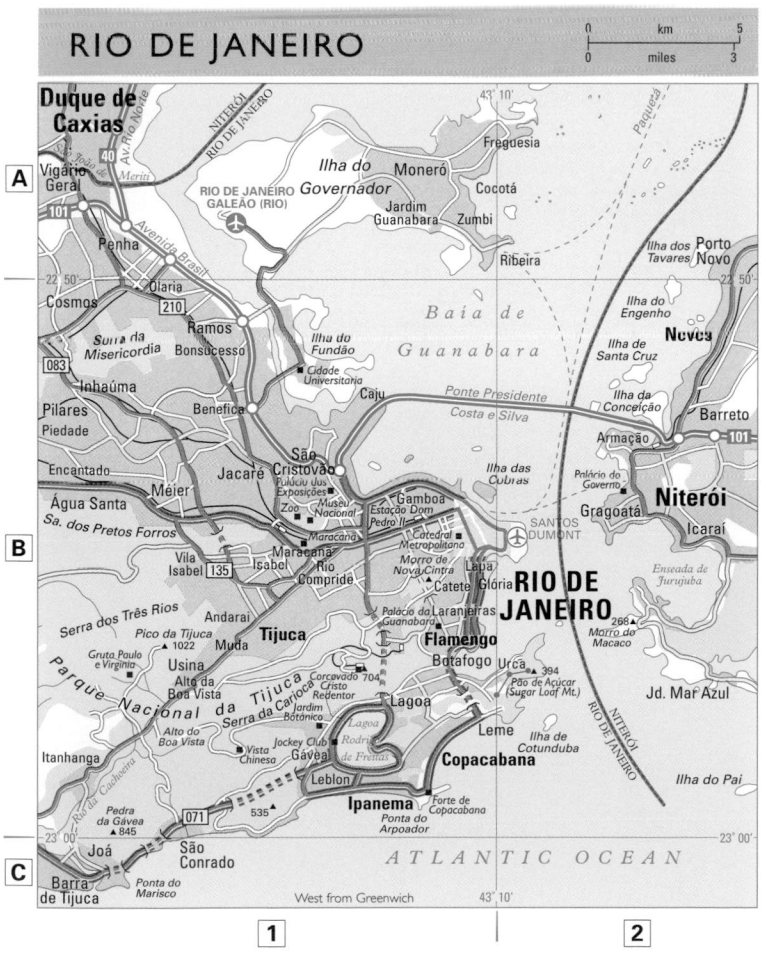

CENTRAL RIO DE JANEIRO

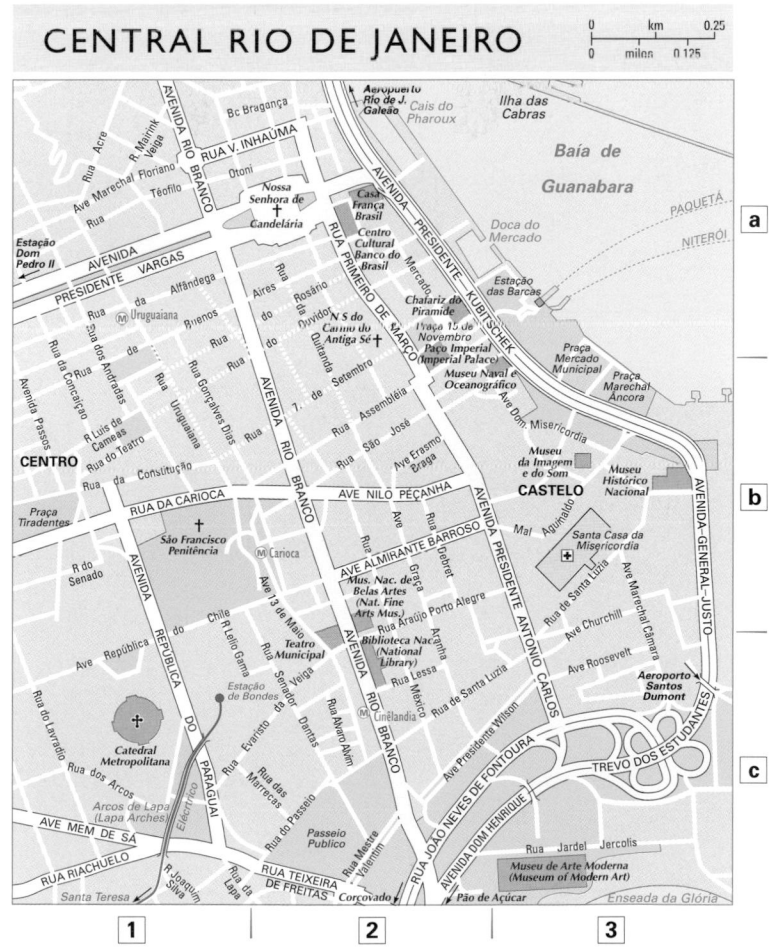

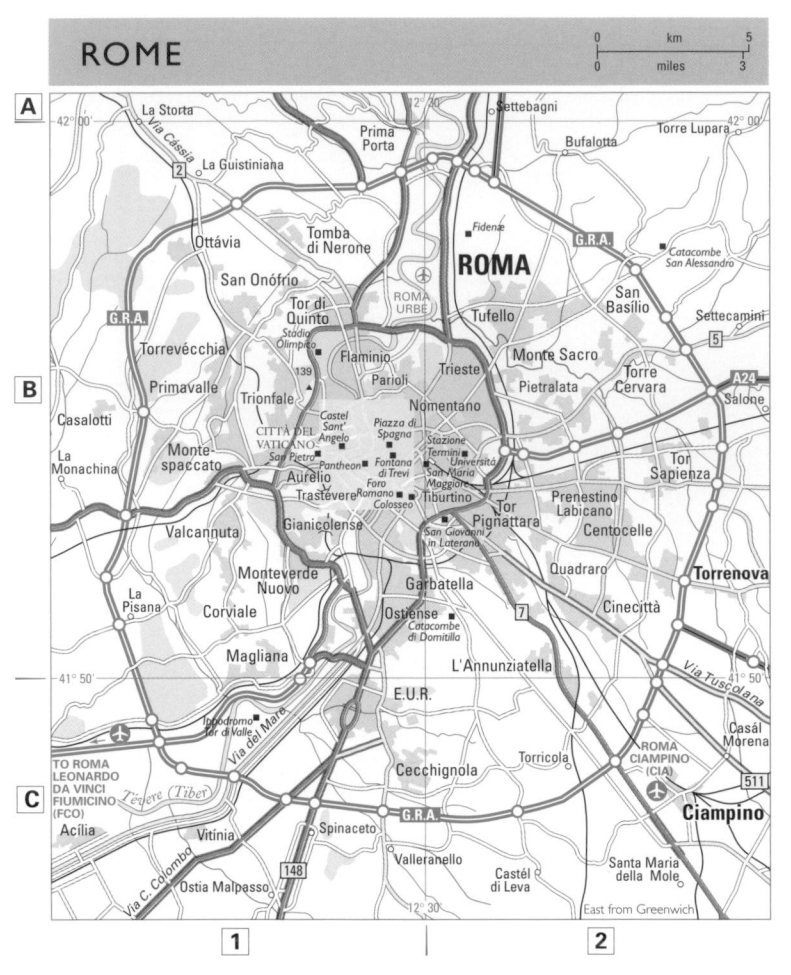

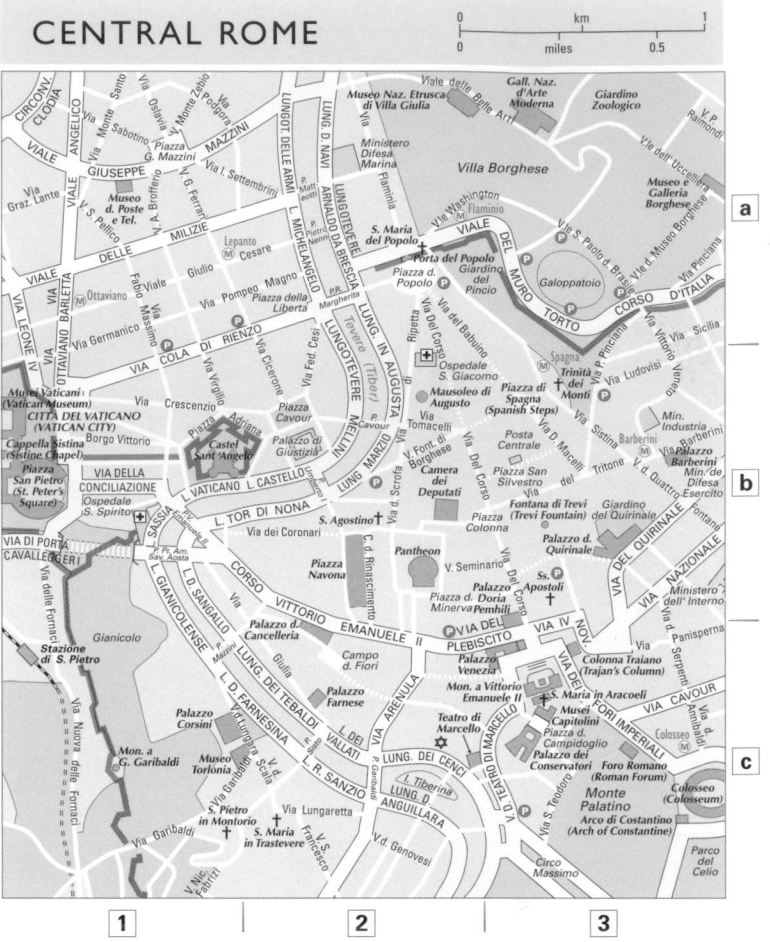

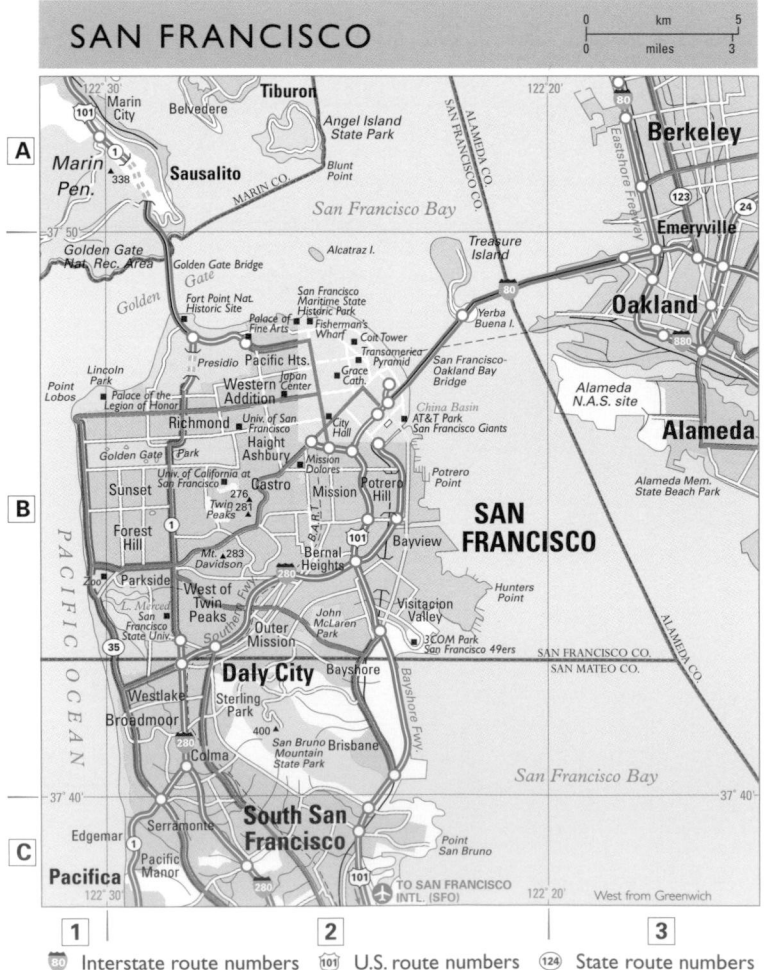

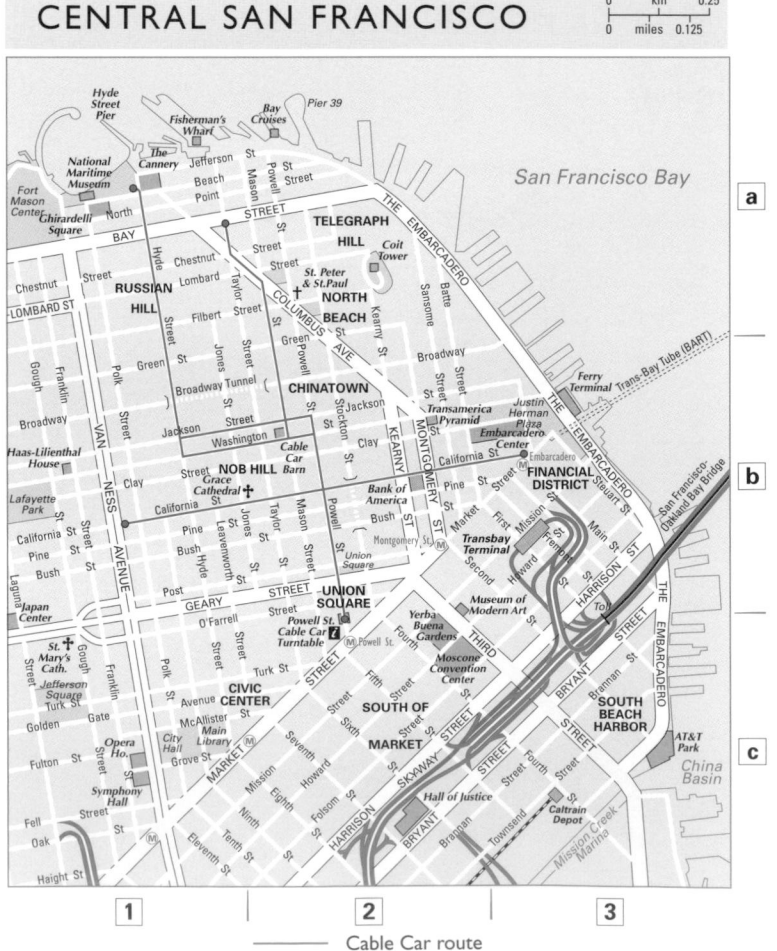

80 Interstate route numbers   101 U.S. route numbers   124 State route numbers

Cable Car route

COPYRIGHT PHILIP'S

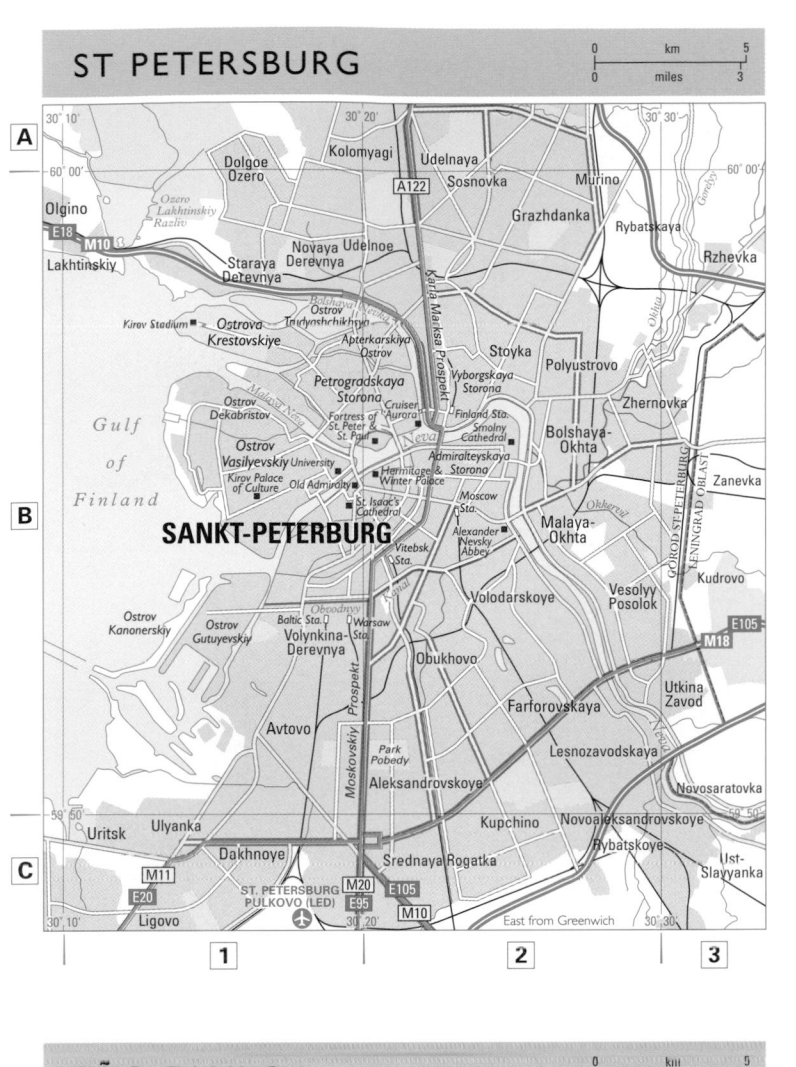
ST PETERSBURG
0 km 5
0 miles 3
A
B
C
1
2
3
30° 10'
30° 20'
30° 30'
60° 00'
59° 50'
East from Greenwich
Kolomyagi
Dolgoe Ozero
Udelnaya
Sosnovka
Murino
Olgino
Ozero Lakhtinskiy Razliv
Lakhtinskiy
Grazhdanka
Rybatskaya
Novaya Derevnya
Udelnoe
Staraya Derevnya
Rzhevka
Karla Marksa Prospekt
Kirov Stadium
Ostrova Krestovskiye
Apterkarskiy Ostrov
Stoyka
Polyustrovo
Petrogradskaya Storona
Vyborgskaya Storona
Zhernovka
Gulf of Finland
Ostrov Dekabristov
Cruiser Aurora
Fortress of St. Peter & St. Paul
Finland Sta.
Smolny Cathedral
Bolshaya-Okhta
Neva
Ostrov Vasilyevskiy
University
Admiralteyskaya Storona
Kirov Palace of Culture
Hermitage & Winter Palace
Old Admiralty
St. Isaac's Cathedral
Moscow Sta.
Zanevka
SANKT-PETERBURG
Alexander Nevsky Abbey
Malaya-Okhta
Vitebsk Sta.
Okkervil
GOROD ST PETERBURG
LENINGRAD OBLAST
Kudrovo
Ostrov Kanonerskiy
Ostrov Gutuyevskiy
Baltic Sta.
Warsaw Sta.
Volynkina-Derevnya
Volodarskoye
Vesolyy Posolok
Obukhovo
Utkina Zavod
Moskovskiy Prospekt
Farforovskaya
Avtovo
Park Pobedy
Lesnozavodskaya
Aleksandrovskoye
Novosaratovka
Uritsk
Ulyanka
Kupchino
Novoaleksandrovskoye
Dakhnoye
Srednaya Rogatka
Rybatskoye
Ust-Slavyanka
ST. PETERSBURG PULKOVO (LED)
Ligovo
E18
M10
A122
M18
E105
M11
E20
M20
E95

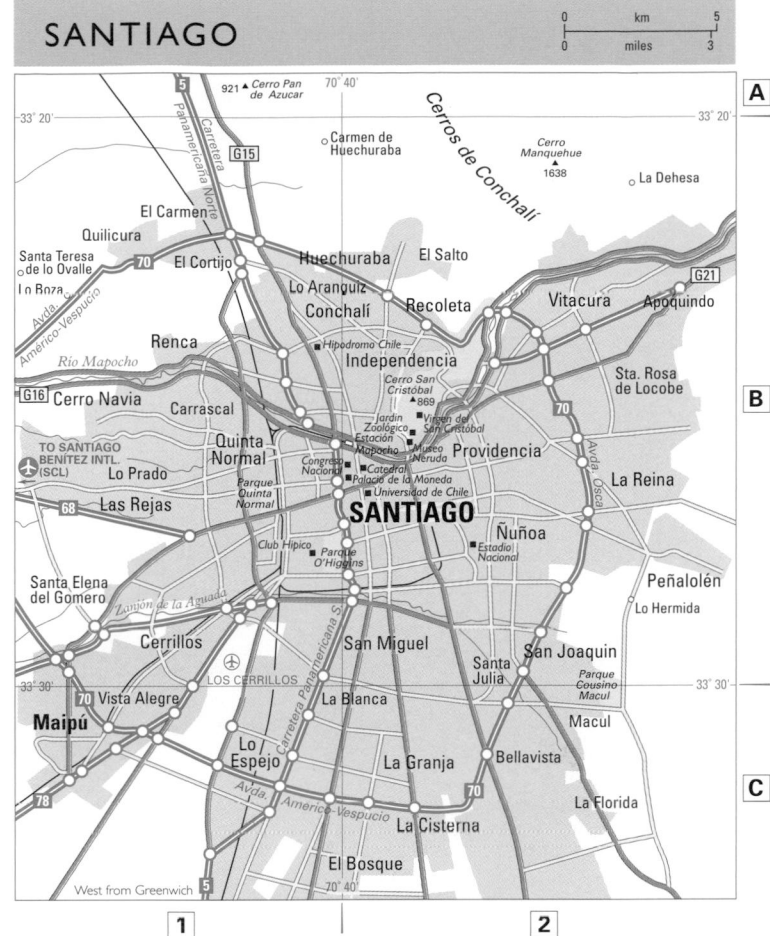
SANTIAGO
0 km 5
0 miles 3
A
B
C
1
2
33° 20'
33° 30'
70° 40'
West from Greenwich
921 Cerro Pan de Azucar
Carretera Panamericana Norte
Cerros de Conchalí
Carmen de Huechuraba
Cerro Manquehue 1638
La Dehesa
El Carmen
Quilicura
Santa Teresa de lo Ovalle
El Cortijo
Huechuraba
El Salto
Lo Boza
Lo Aranguiz
Conchalí
Recoleta
Vitacura
Apoquindo
Avda. Américo Vespucio
Renca
Hipódromo Chile
Independencia
Río Mapocho
Cerro Navia
Carrascal
Cerro San Cristóbal 869
Sta. Rosa de Locobe
Jardín Zoológico
Virgen del San Cristóbal
Quinta Normal
Estación Mapocho
Providencia
TO SANTIAGO BENITEZ INTL. (SCL)
Lo Prado
Congreso Nacional
Catedral
Palacio de la Moneda
Museo Neruda
Universidad de Chile
La Reina
Las Rejas
Parque Quinta Normal
SANTIAGO
Ñuñoa
Club Hípico
Parque O'Higgins
Estadio Nacional
Peñalolén
Santa Elena del Gomero
Zanjón de la Aguada
Lo Hermida
Cerrillos
San Miguel
Santa Julia
San Joaquín
LOS CERRILLOS
Parque Cousino Macul
Vista Alegre
La Blanca
Maipú
Macul
Lo Espejo
La Granja
Bellavista
La Florida
La Cisterna
El Bosque
G15
G16
G21
68
70
78

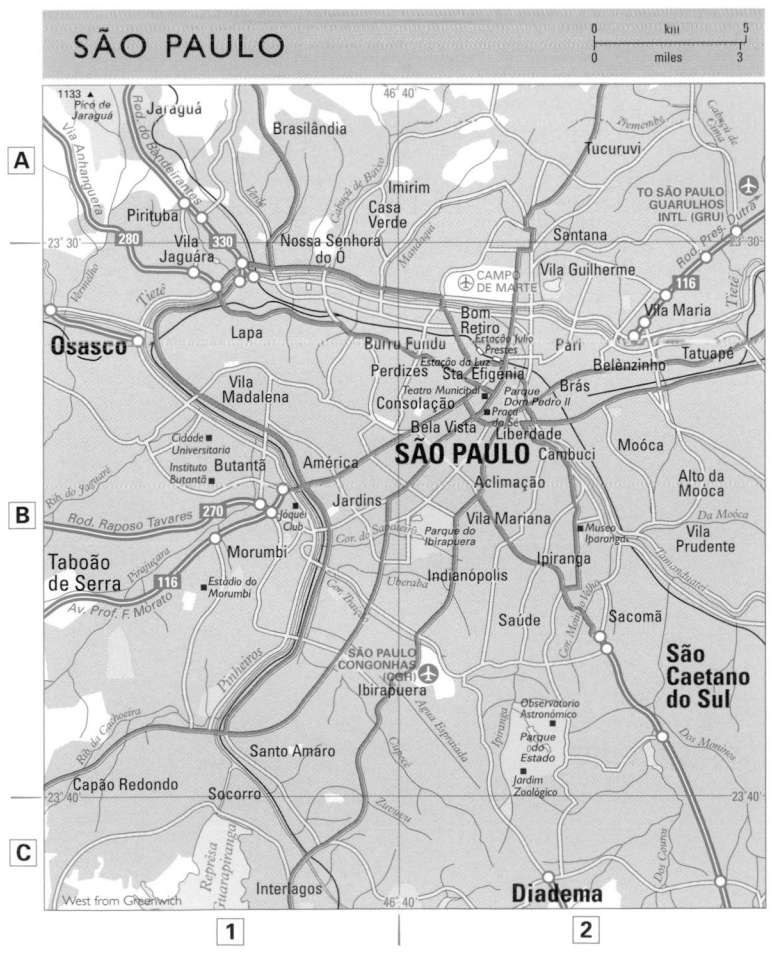
SÃO PAULO
0 km 5
0 miles 3
A
B
C
1
2
23° 30'
23° 40'
46° 40'
West from Greenwich
1133 Pico de Jaraguá
Jaraguá
Brasilândia
Tucuruvi
Via Anhanguera
Rod. dos Bandeirantes
Imirim
TO SÃO PAULO GUARULHOS INTL. (GRU)
Pirituba
Casa Verde
Santana
Vila Jaguára
Nossa Senhora do Ó
Rod. Pres. Dutra
CAMPO DE MARTE
Vila Guilherme
Tietê
Vila Maria
Lapa
Bom Retiro
Osasco
Barra Funda
Estação Júlio Prestes
Pari
Tatuapé
Estação da Luz
Belènzinho
Perdizes
Sta. Efigênia
Teatro Municipal
Brás
Vila Madalena
Consolação
Parque Dom Pedro II
Praça da Sé
Bela Vista
Liberdade
Cidade Universitaria
Mooca
Instituto Butantã
Butantã
América
SÃO PAULO
Cambuci
Alto da Mooca
Aclimação
Jardins
Jóquei Club
Rod. Raposo Tavares
Vila Mariana
Museu Ipiranga
Vila Prudente
Parque do Ibirapuera
Taboão de Serra
Morumbi
Ipiranga
Estádio do Morumbi
Indianópolis
Av. Prof. F. Morato
Sacomã
Saúde
São Caetano do Sul
SÃO PAULO CONGONHAS (CGH)
Ibirapuera
Observatório Astronômico
Parque do Estado
Jardim Zoológico
Santo Amaro
Capão Redondo
Socorro
Represa Guarapiranga
Interlagos
Diadema
270
280
330
116

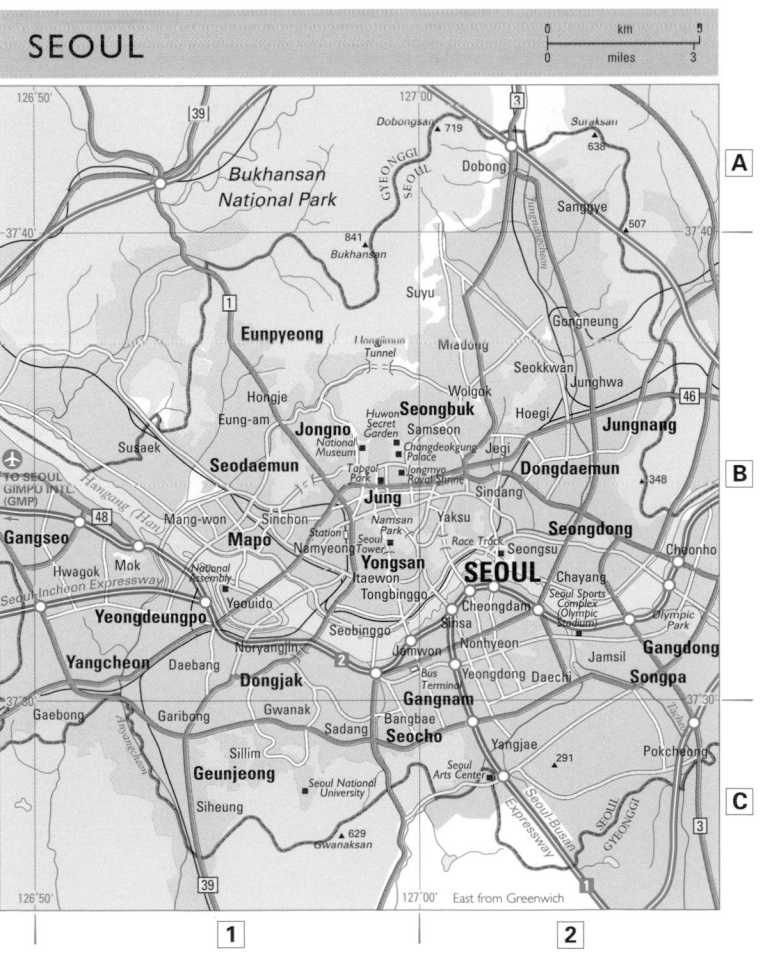
SEOUL
0 km 5
0 miles 3
A
B
C
1
2
126°50'
127°00'
37°40'
37°30'
East from Greenwich
Dobongsan 719
Suraksan 638
Bukhansan National Park
GYEONGGI
SEOUL
Dobong
Sanggye
507
841 Bukhansan
Suyu
Gongneung
Eunpyeong
Hongjimun Tunnel
Miadong
Seokkwan
Junghwa
Wolgok
Hongje
Seongbuk
Hoegi
Jungnang
Huwon Secret Garden
Eung-am
Jongno
Samseon
National Museum
Changdeokgung Palace
Susaek
Jegi
Seodaemun
Tapgol Park
Dongdaemun
Jongmyo Royal Shrine
348
TO SEOUL GIMPO INTL. (GMP)
Jung
Sindang
Mang-won
Sinchon
Hangang (Han)
Namsan Park
Yaksu
Seongdong
Gangseo
Mapo
Station
Seoul Tower
Race Track
Seongsu
Mok
Namyeong
Yongsan
Chyonho
Hwagok
National Assembly
Itaewon
SEOUL
Chayang
Seoul Incheon Expressway
Tongbinggo
Seoul Sports Complex (Olympic Stadium)
Yeouido
Yeongdeungpo
Cheongdam
Olympic Park
Sinsa
Noryangjin
Seobinggo
Nonhyeon
Gangdong
Jamwon
Yangcheon
Daebang
Yeongdong
Daechi
Jamsil
Bus Terminal
Dongjak
Songpa
Gangnam
Gaebong
Garibong
Gwanak
Bangbae
Sadang
Seocho
Yangjae
Pokcheong
291
Sillim
Seoul Arts Center
Geunjeong
Seoul National University
Seoul-Busan Expressway
Siheung
629 Gwanaksan
1
2
3
39
46
48

SHANGHAI

km 0 — 5
miles 0 — 3

Liuhang · Yangjiazhuang · Wusong · Baoshan · Chang J. (Yangtze) · Gaoqiao · Tangqiao · Yinhangzhen · Jiangwan · Wujiaochang · DACHANG · Beijiao · Donggou · Zhenru · Lu Xun Park · Heping Park · Yangpu · Fuxing Dao · Dachang · Tomb of Lu Xun · Hongkou Stadium · Hongkou · Qingningsi · Zhabei · Shanghai University · Tilanqiao · Yangshupu · Zhoujiazhen · Shanghai West · Putuo · Jade Buddha Temple · Nanjing Road · Huangpu Park · The Bund · Pudong Dadao · 312 · Jingan · People's Square · Lujiazui · Yangjing · Beixing Jing Park · Jiaodong University · Changfeng Park · Xi Zhan · People's Park · Shanghai Museum · Yuyuan Garden · Huangpu · SHANGHAI · Changning · Zhongshan Park · Former Residence · Fuxing Park · Puxi · Pudong New Area · Science & Technology Museum · Century Park · 318 · Sun Yat Sen's Former Residence · Luwan · Nanshi · Shanghai International Expo Centre · Shanghai Zoo · Xujiahui Zhan · Xuhui · Nanpu · Nanpu Bridge · Beicai · TO SHANGHAI HONGQIAO (SHA) · Hongqiao · Shanghai Stadium · Zhoujiadu · Nanshi · TO SHANGHAI PUDONG (PVG) · Caoheijing · Longhua Park · Longhua Pagoda · Sanlintang · Chuanyang · LONGHUA · Botanical Gardens · Shanghai South · 320 · Gangkou · East from Greenwich 121°30'

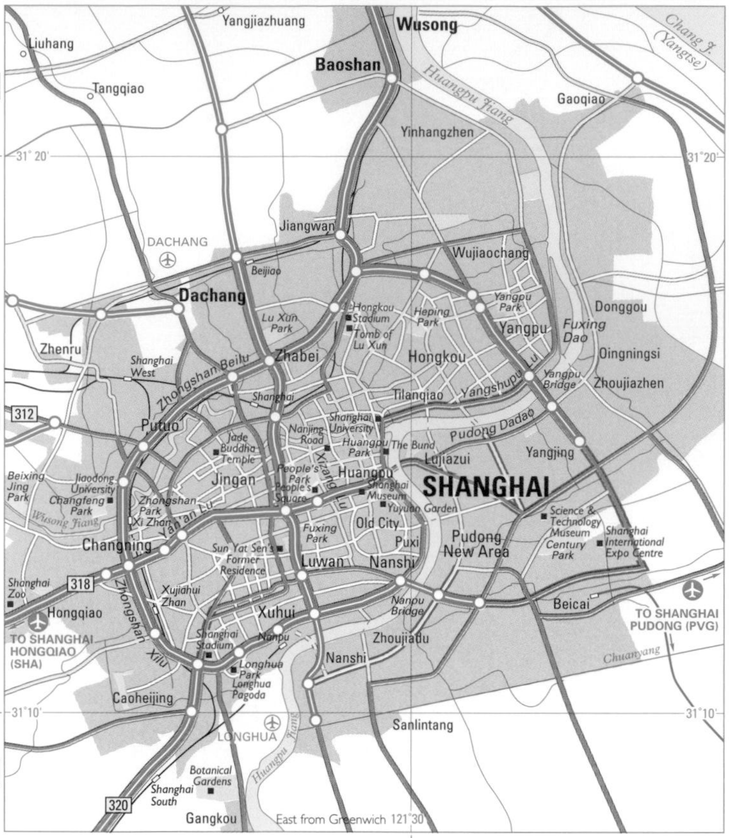

— Magnetic Levitation (Maglev) Railway

CENTRAL SINGAPORE

km 0 — 1
miles 0 — 0.5

CAIRNHILL ROAD · CLEMENCEAU AVE · Istana (President's Residence) · Kandang Kerbau Hospital · Cuff Rd · Upper Weld Rd · Central Park · Edinburgh · Sophia Road · Mount · Emily · Mackenzie Road · Bukit Timah Rd · Zhujiao Centre · Dunlop · Clive · Abdul Gaffoor Mosque · Jalan Besar · Sim Lim Tower · BIDEFORD RD · Thong Sia Building · Emerald Hill · Sri Temasek · White Road · Emily Park · Sophia · SHORT STREET · Sim Lim Square · ROCHOR CANAL RD · ORCHARD ROAD · Cuppage Centre · Centre point · Cuppage Road · Orchard Plaza · Orchard Point · ORCHARD ROAD · Handy Road · SELEGIE ROAD · MIDDLE ROAD · E1 Bugis · Bus Station · Blanco Court · Faber House · N2 · Somerset · U N1 Dhoby Ghaut · Bencoolen Mosque · BENCOOLEN · Singapore Art Museum · St Joseph's Church · COLONIAL DISTRICT · VICTORIA · Saah St · Beach Rd · KILLINEY · Lloyd Rd · OXLEY ROAD · EBER ROAD · PENANG ROAD · FORT CANNING ROAD · Singapore Hist. Mus. · BRAS BASAH · Cath. of the Good Shepherd · Raffles Hotel · Chesed-El Synagogue · Sacred Heart Church · Fort Canning Park · CITY CENTRE · Fort Canning Reservoir · Asian Civ. Mus. · C2 City Hall · Raffles City · RIVER VALLEY ROAD · Sri Thandayuthapani Temple · TANK ROAD · Van Kleef Aquarium · Singapore Philatelic Mus. · Funan Centre · HILL STREET · NORTH BRIDGE ROAD · St. Andrew's Cathedral · War Memorial Park · Hong San See Temple · Sultan · Clarke Quay · North Boat Quay · South Boat Quay · City Hall · Padang · Singapore Cricket Club · CONNAUGHT DR · Esplanade-Theatres on the Bay · CLEMENCEAU · Singapore River · HAVELOCK ROAD · MERCHANT ROAD · Supreme Court · Parliament Hse. · Raffles Landing Site · Victoria Concert Hall & Theatre · Empress Pl. Museum · FULLERTON RD · Merlion Park · Marina Bay · Melaka Mosque · NORTH CANAL ROAD · PICKERING ST · Boat Quay · Clifford Pier · SENTOSA · CENTRAL EXPRESSWAY · Pearl's Hill City Park · UPPER CROSS STREET · Chin Swee Road · Outram Park · SOUTH BRIDGE ROAD · Bus Station · Wak Hai Cheng Bio Temple · CHULIA ST · OUB Centre · C1 Raffles Place · RAFFLES QUAY · Pearl's Hill Reservoir · People's Park Complex · NEW BRIDGE ROAD · Pagoda St · Smith · Jamae Mosque · CHINATOWN · Sri Mariamman Temple · Fuk Tak Ch'i Temple · Oriental Theatre

SINGAPORE

km 0 — 5
miles 0 — 3

103°40'E · 103°50'E · 104°00'E · Johor Bahru · Senoko Ind. Est. · Sembawang · Selat Johor · Causeway · Sungei Buloh Nature Park · Kranji Ind. Est. · Woodlands · Chong Pang · Pulau Seletar · MALAYSIA SINGAPORE · Lim Chu Kang · Seletar Expy · Yishun · Sarimbun Res. · Sungai Kadut Ind. Est. · Singapore Turf Club · Dam · Sungai Seletar Reservoir · SELETAR · Punggol Point · Pulau Tekong Kechil · Pulau Tekong · Sarimbun 85 · Ama Keng · Zoological Gardens · Seletar Reservoir · Nee Soon · Jalan Kayu · Seletar Golf Course · Punggol · Pulau Serangoon · Pulau Ubin · Tg. Ladang · Choa Chu Kang · Bukit Timah Expy · Central Catchment Nature Reserve · Pulau Ketam · Sengkang · Serangoon Harbour · Pasir Ris · Loyang Ind. Est. · Changi · Mandai Expy · Choa Chu Kang · Bukit Panjang · Upper Peirce Reservoir · Yio Chu Kang · Ang Mo Kio · Chia Keng · Hougang · Pasir Ris · SINGAPORE CHANGI (SIN) · 132 · Bt. Panjang · Bukit Timah Nature Reserve · MacRitchie Reservoir · Serangoon · Bishan · Bedok Reservoir · Tampines · Yan Kit · Changi Prison Museum · Reclaimed Land · 106 · 162 · Bukit Batok Nature Parks · Pan-Island Expy · Paya Lebar · Tai Seng · Simei · Singapore Expo · South Env. Res. · Tanah Merah Golf Course · Nanyang University · Choa Chu Kang 88 · Air View Park · Raffles Park · Toa Payoh · Dunearn · Kg Landang · Jurong West · Chinese & Japanese Gardens · Jurong East · Geylang Serai · Chai Chee · Bedok · Boon Lay · Singapore Discovery Centre · Dynasty Museum · Clementi · Maryland · Victoria Park · University of Singapore Botanic Gardens · Frankel · Katong · East Coast Park · Raffles Golf Course & Country Club · Ayer Rajah Expy · Pandan Res. · Holland Village · Queenstown · National Stadium · Kallang Park · Tuas · Jurong Industrial Estate · Jurong · Jurong Bird Park · National University of Singapore · Pasir Panjang · Teluk Blangah · St Andrew's Cathedral · City Hall · National Museum · SINGAPORE · Tuas Second Link · Poyan Res. · Kg Tanjong Penjuru · Buona Vista Park · Mt. 105 Faber · Thian Hock Keng Temple · East Coast Pkwy · Tengeh Res. · Selat Jurong · Pulau Jurong · Seraya · Pasir Panjang Terminal · World Trade Centre · P. Brani · Pulau Ubin · Reclaimed Land · Sakra · Underwater World · Cable Car · Sentosa Gardens · Tanjong Golf Course · Straits of Singapore · Reclaimed Land · Selat Pandan · Pulau Busing · Pulau Bukum · Sentosa · 1°20'N

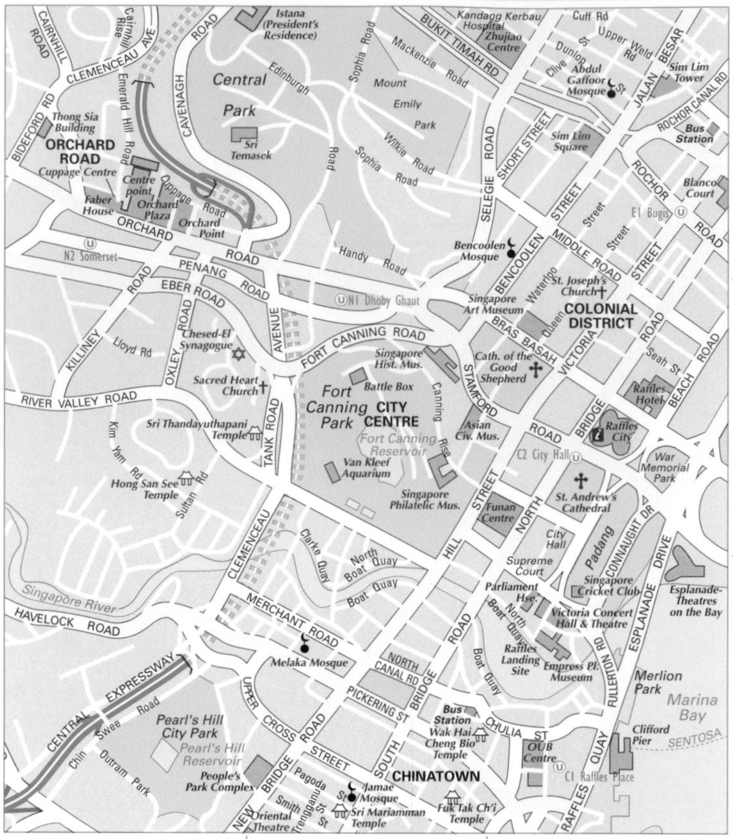

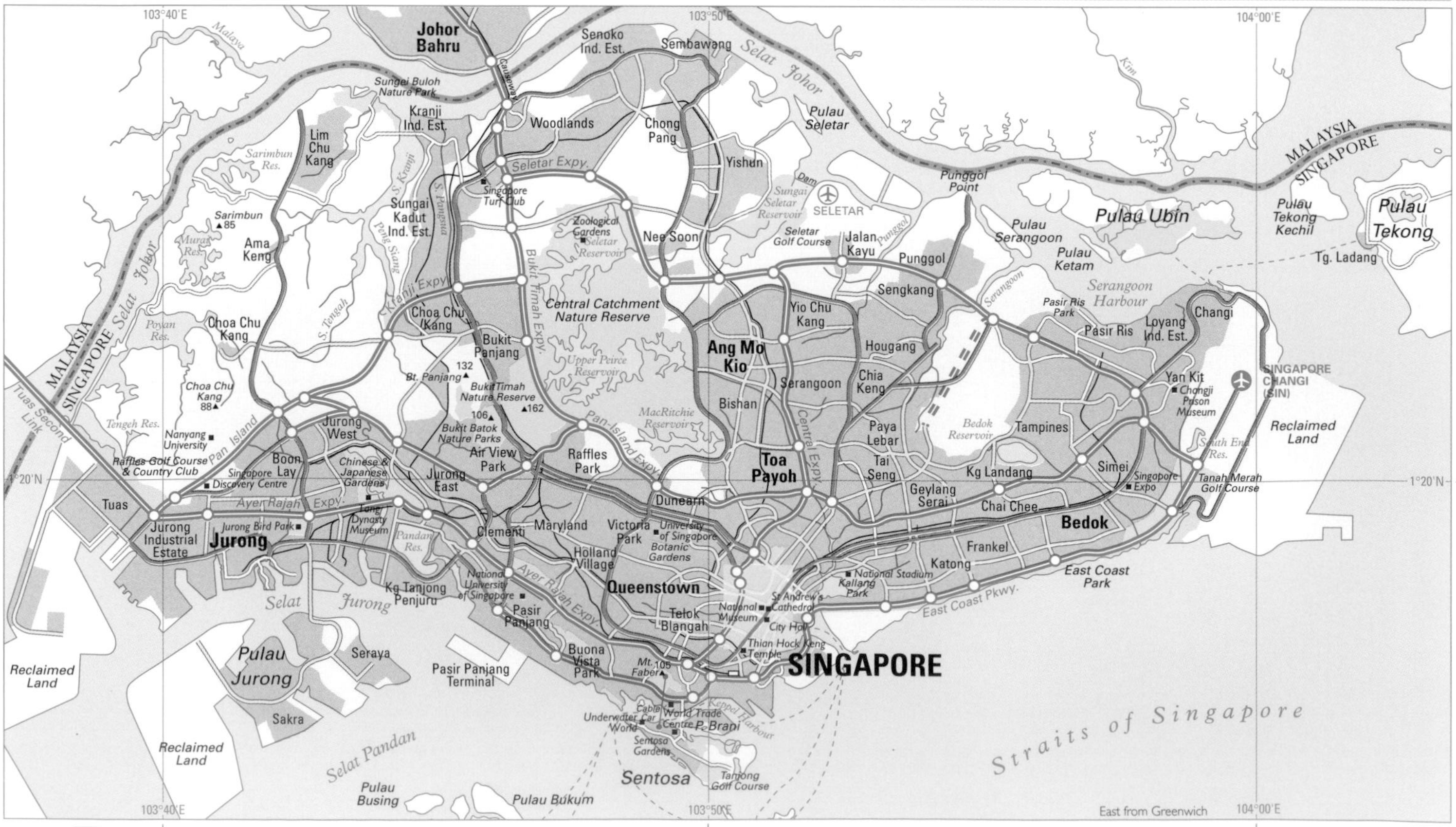

STOCKHOLM

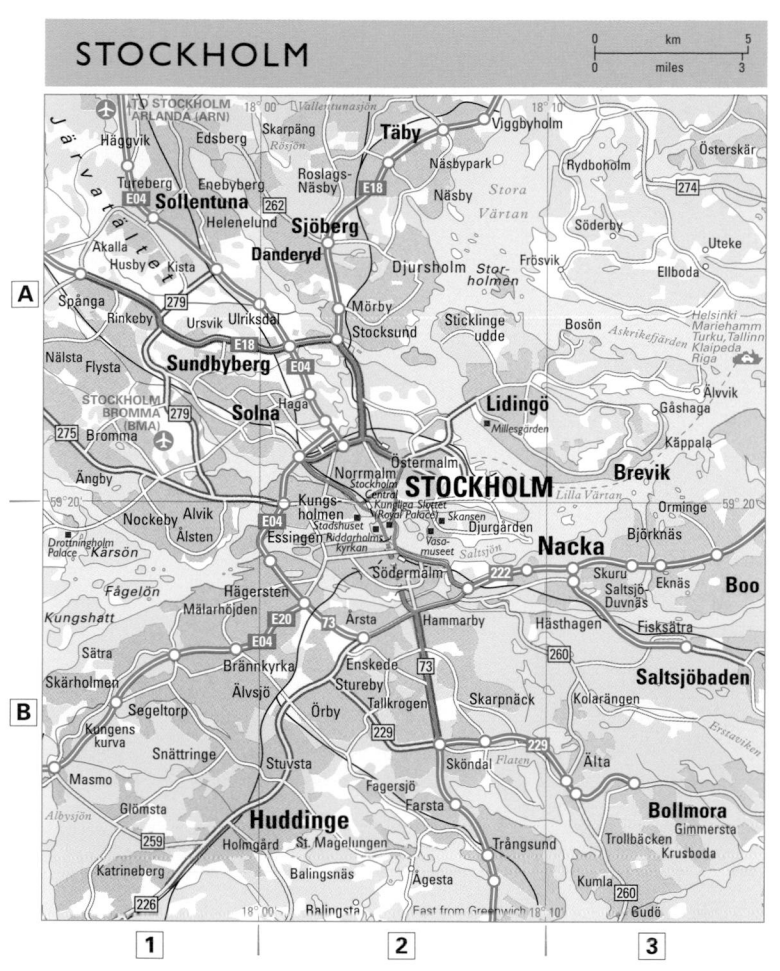

CENTRAL STOCKHOLM

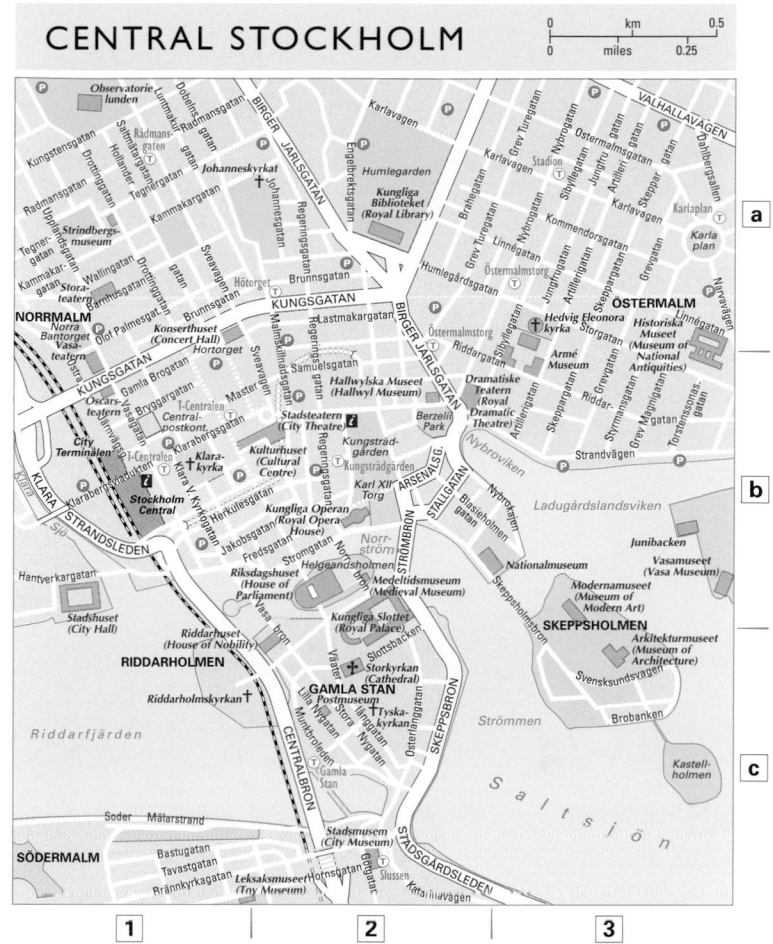

SYDNEY

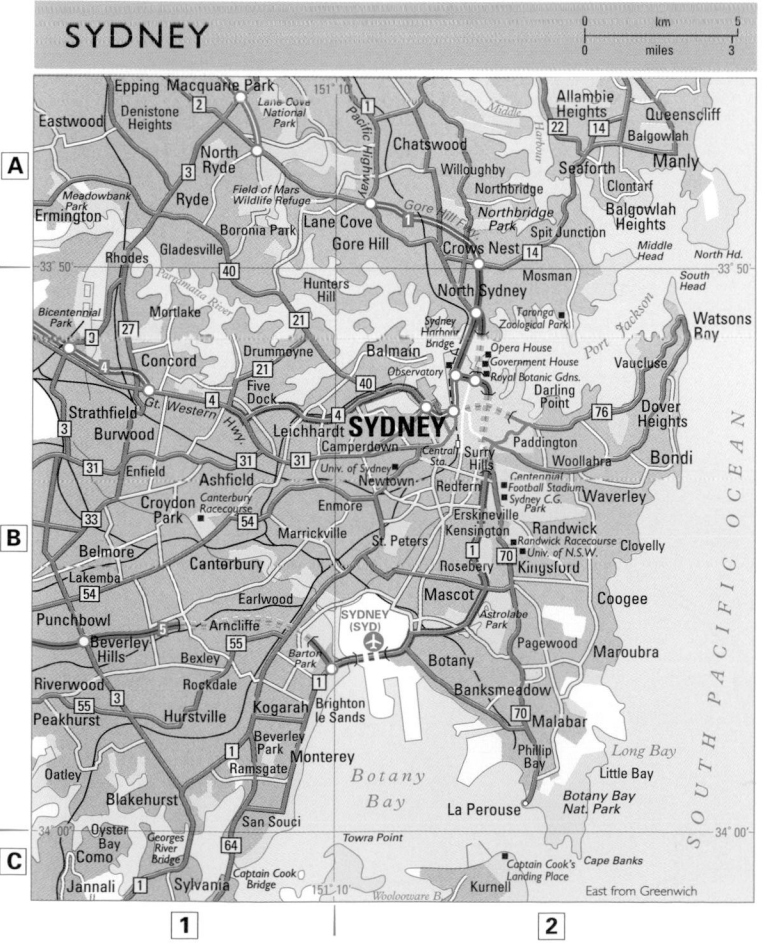

CENTRAL SYDNEY

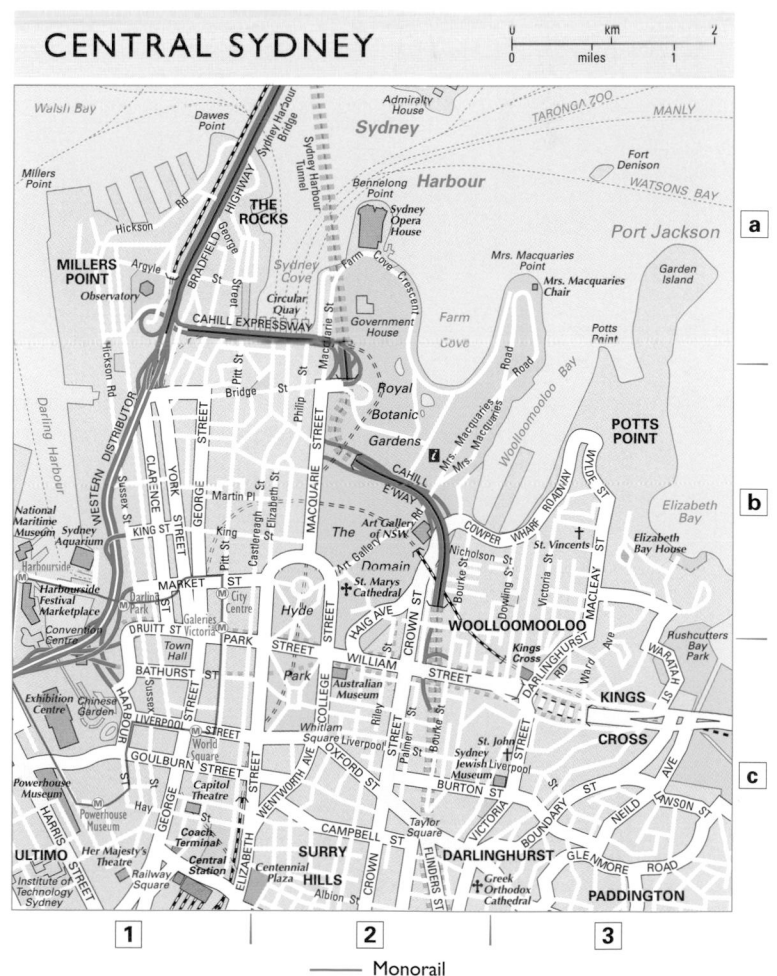

— Monorail

CENTRAL TOKYO

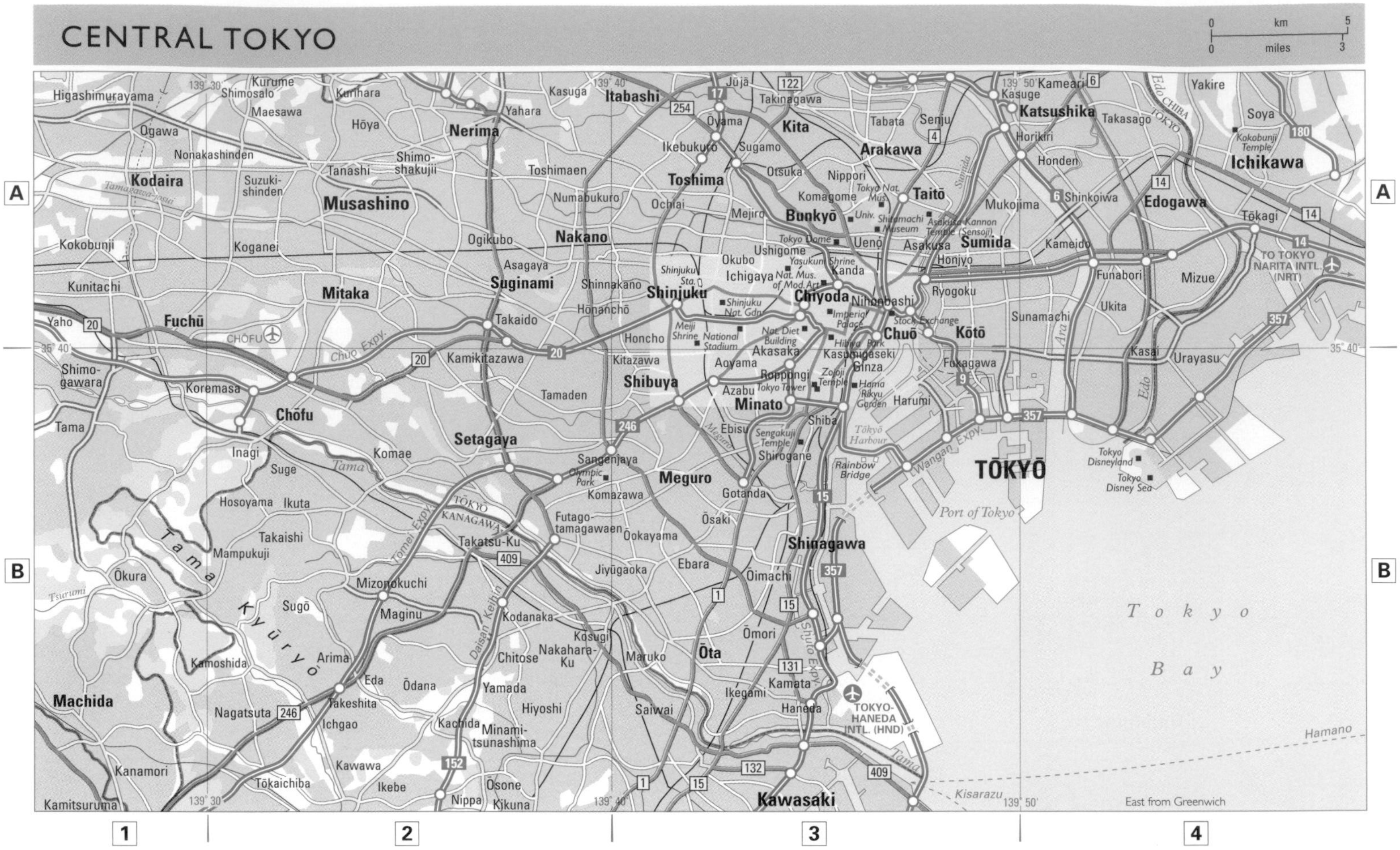

km 5
miles 3

CENTRAL TOKYO

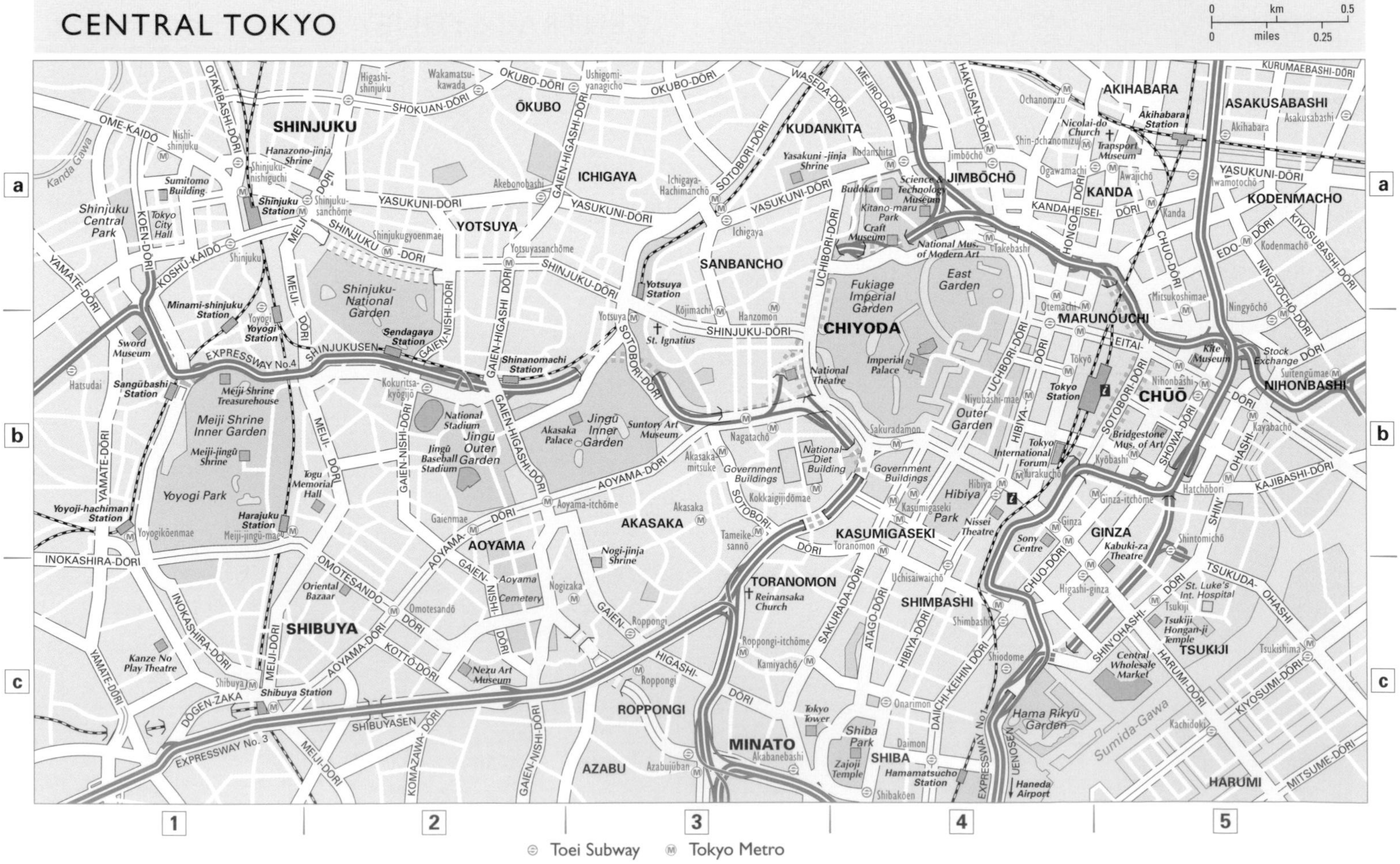

km 0.5
miles 0.25

Ⓣ Toei Subway   Ⓜ Tokyo Metro

TEHRAN

0 km 5
0 miles 3

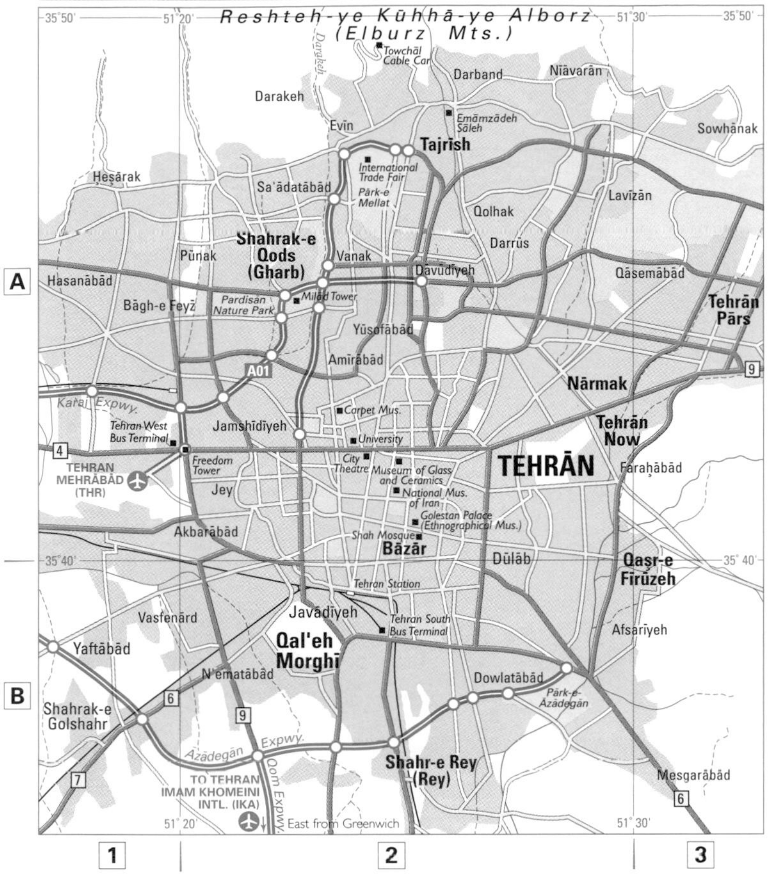

Reshteh-ye Kūhhā-ye Alborz
(Elburz Mts.)
Towchāl Cable Car
Darband
Nīāvarān
Darakeh
Emāmzādeh Sāleh
Evīn
Tajrīsh
Sowhānak
International Trade Fair
Hesārak
Sa'ādatābād
Pārk-e Mellat
Lavīzān
Qolhak
Darrūs
Pūnak
Shahrak-e Qods (Gharb)
Vanak
Dāvūdīyeh
Hasanābād
Qāsemābād
Bāgh-e Feyz
Pardisān Nature Park
Mīlād Tower
Tehrān Pārs
Yūsofābād
Amīrābād
A01
Nārmak
Karaj Expwy.
Carpet Mus.
Tehran West Bus Terminal
Jamshīdīyeh
University
Tehrān Now
Freedom Tower
City Theatre
Museum of Glass and Ceramics
TEHRĀN
Farahābād
TEHRAN MEHRĀBĀD (THR)
Jey
National Mus. of Iran
Golestan Palace (Ethnographical Mus.)
Akbarābād
Shah Mosque
Bāzār
Dūlāb
Qasr-e Fīrūzeh
Tehran Station
Javādīyeh
Vasfenārd
Tehran South Bus Terminal
Afsarīyeh
Yaftābād
Qal'eh Morghī
N'ematābād
Dowlatābād
Pārk-e Āzādegān
Shahrak-e Golshahr
Āzādegān Expwy.
TO TEHRAN IMAM KHOMEINI INTL. (IKA)
Qom Expwy.
Shahr-e Rey (Rey)
Mesgarābād
East from Greenwich
35°50'
35°40'
51°20'
51°30'
A
B
1
2
3

CENTRAL TORONTO

0 km 0.5
0 miles 0.25

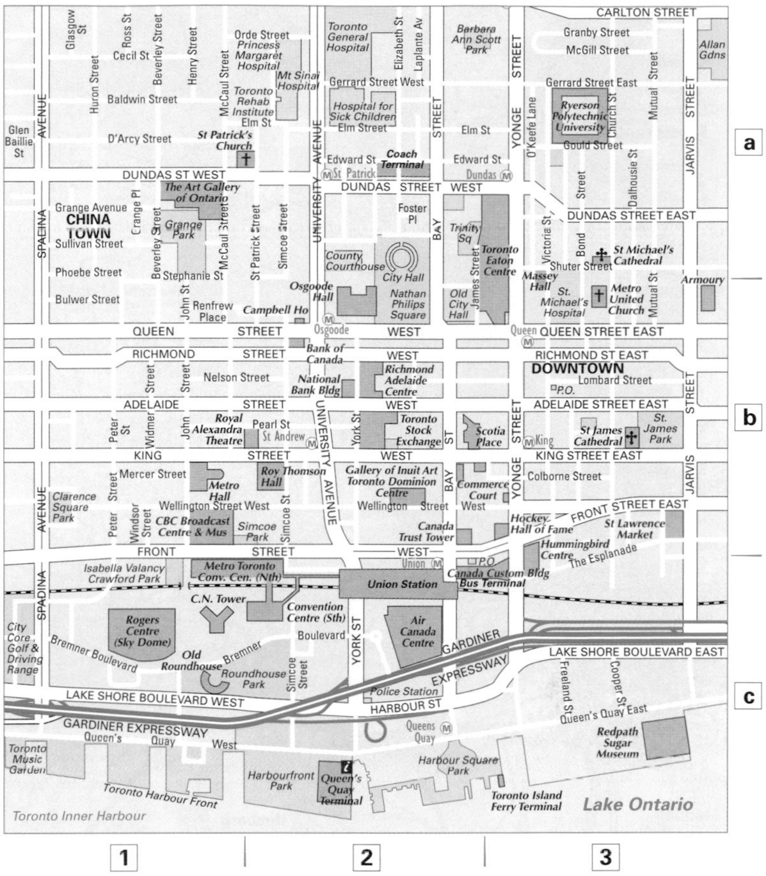

CARLTON STREET
Toronto General Hospital
Barbara Ann Scott Park
Granby Street
McGill Street
Allan Gdns
Orde Street
Princess Margaret Hospital
Mt Sinai Hospital
Gerrard Street West
Gerrard Street East
Ryerson Polytechnic University
Baldwin Street
Toronto Rehab Institute
Hospital for Sick Children
Elm Street
Elm St
D'Arcy Street
St Patrick's Church
Edward St
Coach Terminal
Gould Street
Glen Baillie St
DUNDAS ST WEST
DUNDAS STREET WEST
The Art Gallery of Ontario
Grange Avenue
CHINA TOWN
Grange Park
Foster Pl
Trinity Sq
DUNDAS STREET EAST
Sullivan Street
County Courthouse
Toronto Eaton Centre
St Michael's Cathedral
Phoebe Street
Stephanie St
City Hall
Shuter Street
Massey Hall
Armoury
Osgoode Hall
Nathan Philips Square
Old City Hall
St. Michael's Hospital
Metro United Church
Bulwer Street
Renfrew Place
Campbell Ho
QUEEN STREET WEST
QUEEN STREET EAST
Bank of Canada
RICHMOND STREET WEST
Richmond Adelaide Centre
RICHMOND ST EAST
DOWNTOWN
Nelson Street
National Bank Bldg
P.O.
Lombard Street
ADELAIDE STREET WEST
ADELAIDE STREET EAST
Royal Alexandra Theatre
Pearl St
Toronto Stock Exchange
Scotia Place
St James Cathedral
St. James Park
KING STREET WEST
KING STREET EAST
Mercer Street
Roy Thomson Hall
Gallery of Inuit Art
Toronto Dominion Centre
Commerce Court
Colborne Street
Clarence Square Park
Metro Hall
Wellington Street West
CBC Broadcast Centre & Mus
Simcoe Park
Canada Trust Tower
Hockey Hall of Fame
FRONT STREET EAST
St Lawrence Market
Hummingbird Centre
The Esplanade
FRONT STREET WEST
Isabella Valancy Crawford Park
Metro Toronto Comv. Cen. (Nth)
Union Station
Canada Custom Bldg
Bus Terminal
C.N. Tower
Convention Centre (Sth)
City Core Golf & Driving Range
Rogers Centre (Sky Dome)
Bremner Boulevard
Old Roundhouse
Roundhouse Park
Air Canada Centre
GARDINER EXPRESSWAY
LAKE SHORE BOULEVARD EAST
LAKE SHORE BOULEVARD WEST
Police Station
HARBOUR ST
Queen's Quay East
Queen's Quay West
Redpath Sugar Museum
Toronto Music Garden
Harbourfront Park
Queen's Quay Terminal
Harbour Square Park
Toronto Island Ferry Terminal
Lake Ontario
Toronto Harbour Front
Toronto Inner Harbour
SPADINA AVENUE
UNIVERSITY AVENUE
BAY STREET
YONGE STREET
JARVIS STREET
YORK ST
a
b
c
1
2
3

TORONTO

0 km 5
0 miles 3

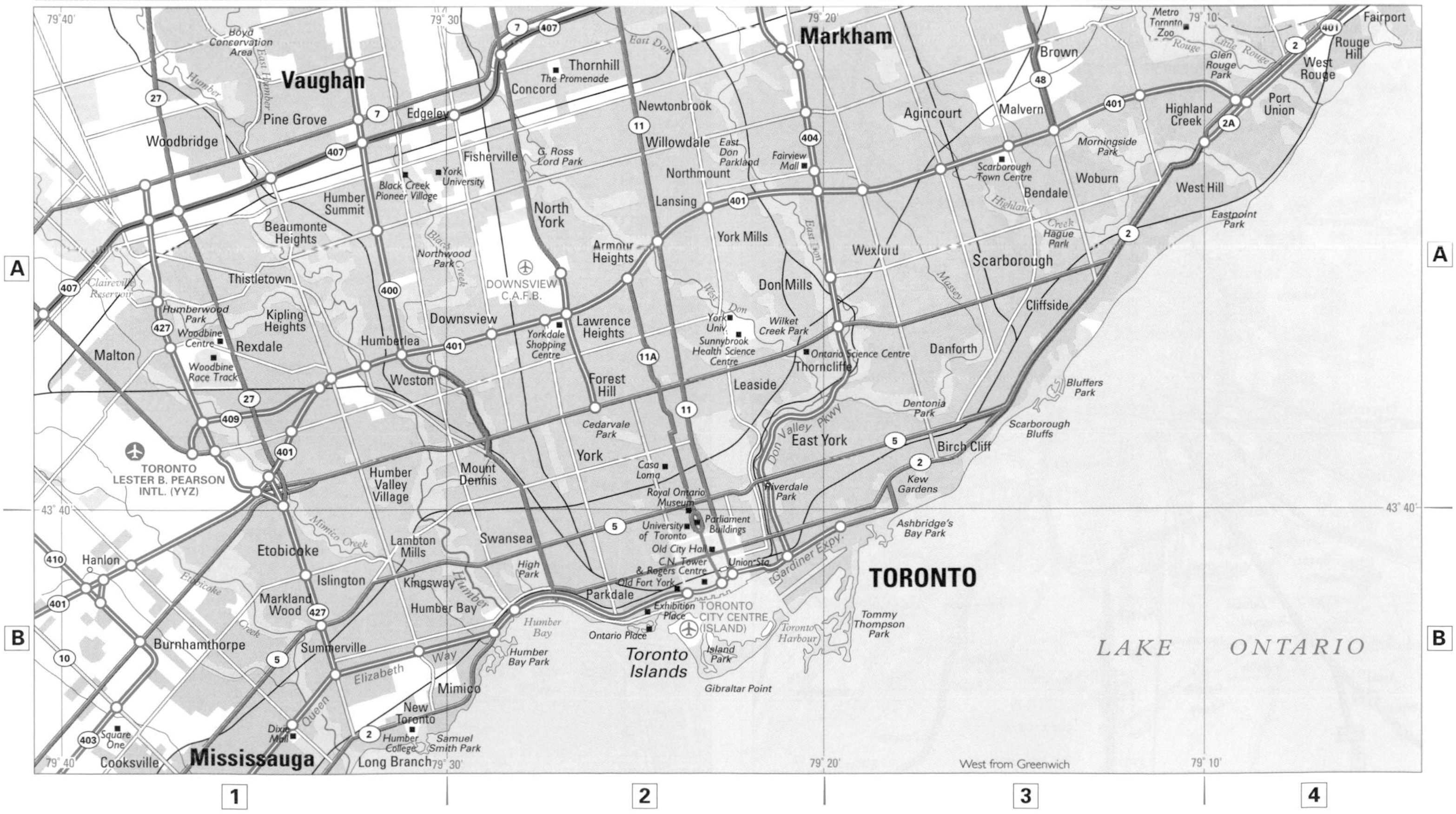

Boyd Conservation Area
Vaughan
Thornhill
The Promenade
Concord
Markham
Metro Toronto Zoo
Brown
Fairport
Rouge Hill
West Rouge
Glen Rouge Park
Port Union
Pine Grove
Edgeley
Newtonbrook
Woodbridge
Fisherville
G. Ross Lord Park
Willowdale
East Don Parkland
Fairview Mall
Agincourt
Malvern
Highland Creek
Morningside Park
Woburn
Humber Summit
Black Creek Pioneer Village
York University
Northmount
Scarborough Town Centre
Bendale
West Hill
Lansing
North York
Beaumonte Heights
Armour Heights
York Mills
Wexford
Hague Park
Eastpoint Park
Scarborough
Thistletown
Northwood Park
Claireville Reservoir
Don Mills
DOWNSVIEW C.F.B.
Cliffside
Humberwood Park
Kipling Heights
Woodbine Centre
Rexdale
Downsview
Lawrence Heights
York Univ.
Wilket Creek Park
Malton
Humberlea
Yorkdale Shopping Centre
Sunnybrook Health Science Centre
Ontario Science Centre
Danforth
Woodbine Race Track
Weston
Thorncliffe
Forest Hill
Leaside
Bluffers Park
Dentonia Park
Cedarvale Park
Scarborough Bluffs
TORONTO LESTER B. PEARSON INTL. (YYZ)
York
East York
Don Valley Pkwy
Birch Cliff
Humber Valley Village
Mount Dennis
Casa Loma
Kew Gardens
Royal Ontario Museum
Riverdale Park
Parliament Buildings
University of Toronto
Old City Hall
Ashbridge's Bay Park
Hanlon
Etobicoke
Lambton Mills
Swansea
C.N. Tower & Rogers Centre
Union Sta.
Gardiner Expy.
High Park
Old Fort York
TORONTO
Islington
Kingsway
Parkdale
Markland Wood
Humber Bay
Exhibition Place
TORONTO CITY CENTRE (ISLAND)
Tommy Thompson Park
Humber Bay
Ontario Place
Toronto Harbour
Burnhamthorpe
Summerville
Humber Bay Park
Toronto Islands
Island Park
LAKE ONTARIO
Elizabeth Way
Mimico
Gibraltar Point
New Toronto
Dixie Mall
Square One
Humber College
Samuel Smith Park
Cooksville
Mississauga
Long Branch
West from Greenwich
79°40'
79°30'
79°20'
79°10'
43°40'
A
B
1
2
3
4

(427) Provincial route numbers

COPYRIGHT PHILIP'S

INDEX TO CITY MAPS

The index contains the names of all the principal places and features shown on the City Maps. Each name is followed by an additional entry in italics giving the name of the City Map within which it is located.

The number in bold type which follows each name refers to the number of the City Map page where that feature or place will be found.

The letter and figure which are immediately after the page number give the grid square on the map within which the feature or place is situated.

The letter represents the latitude and the figure the longitude. The full geographic reference is provided in the border of the City Maps.

The location given is the centre of the city, suburb or feature and is not necessarily the name. Rivers, canals and roads are indexed to their name. Rivers carry the symbol → after their name.

An explanation of the alphabetical order rules and a list of the abbreviations used are to be found at the beginning of the World Map Index.

A

Aalām Baghdad 3 B2
Abbey Wood London 15 B4
Abcoude Amsterdam 2 B2
Ābdin Cairo 7 A2
Abeno Osaka 23 B2
Aberdeen Hong Kong 12 B1
Aberdour Edinburgh 11 A2
Aberdour Castle Edinburgh 11 A2
Abfanggraben → Munich 21 A3
Ablon-sur-Seine Paris 24 B3
Abramtsevo Moscow 19 B3
Abu Dis Jerusalem 13 B2
Abû en Numrus Cairo 7 B2
Abu Ghosh Jerusalem 13 B1
Acassuso Buenos Aires 7 A1
Accotink, L. Washington 33 C2
Accotink Cr. → Washington 33 B2
Achères Paris 24 A1
Acilia Rome 26 C1
Aclimação São Paulo 27 B2
Acropolis Athens 2 B2
Acton London 15 A2
Açúcar, Pão de Rio de Janeiro 25 B2
Ada Beja Lisbon 16 A1
Adams Park Atlanta 3 B2
Addiscombe London 15 B3
Adelphi Washington 33 A4
Aderklaa Vienna 32 A3
Adler Planetarium Chicago 9 B3
Admiralteyskaya Storona St. Petersburg 27 B2
Affori Milan 19 A2
Aflandshage Copenhagen 8 B3
Afsarīyeh Tehran 31 B2
Agboyi Cr. → Lagos 14 A2
Ågerup Copenhagen 8 A1
Ägesta Stockholm 29 B2
Aghia Marina Athens 2 C3
Aghia Paraskevi Athens 2 A2
Aghios Dimitrios Athens 2 B2
Aghios Ioannis Rendis Athens 2 B1
Agincourt Toronto 31 A3
Agra Canal Delhi 10 B2
Agricola Oriental Mexico City 18 B2
Agua Espraiada → São Paulo 27 B2
Agualva-Cacem Lisbon 16 A1
Agustino, Cerro El Lima 14 B3
Ahrensfelde Berlin 5 A4
Ahuntsic Montreal 20 A1
Ai → Osaka 23 A2
Aigremont Paris 24 A1
Air View Park Singapore 28 A2
Airport West Melbourne 18 A1
Ajegunle Lagos 14 B2
Aji Osaka 23 A1
Ajuda Lisbon 16 A1
Akalla Stockholm 29 A1
Akasaka Tokyo 30 A3
Akbarābād Tehran 31 A2
Akershus Castle = Akershus Slott Oslo 23 A3
Akershus Slott Oslo 23 A3
Al 'Azamīyah Baghdad 3 A2
Al Quds = Jerusalem Jerusalem 13 B2
Al-Walaja Jerusalem 13 B1
Alaguntan Lagos 14 B2
Alameda San Francisco 26 B3
Alameda Memorial State Beach Park San Francisco 26 B3
Albern Vienna 32 B2
Albert Park Melbourne 18 B1
Alberton Johannesburg 13 B2
Albertslund Copenhagen 8 B2
Albysjön Stockholm 29 B1
Alcantara Lisbon 16 A1
Alcatraz I. San Francisco 26 B2
Alcobendas Madrid 17 A2
Alcorcón Madrid 17 B1
Aldershof Berlin 5 B4
Aldo Bonzi Buenos Aires 7 C1
Aleksandrovskoye St. Petersburg 27 B2
Alexander Nevsky Abbey St. Petersburg 27 B2
Alexandra Johannesburg 13 A2
Alexandra Singapore 28 B2
Alexandria Washington 33 C3
Alfortville Paris 24 B3
Algés Lisbon 16 A1
Alhambra Los Angeles 16 B4
Alibey → Istanbul 12 B1
Alibey Barajı Istanbul 12 B1
Alibeyköy Istanbul 12 B1
Alimos Athens 2 B2
Alipur Calcutta 14 B1
Allach Munich 21 A1
Allambie Heights Sydney 29 A2
Allermuir Hill Edinburgh 11 B2
Allstate Arena Chicago 9 A1
Allston Boston 6 A2
Almada Lisbon 16 A2
Almagro Buenos Aires 7 B2
Almargem do Bispo Lisbon 16 A1
Almirante G. Brown, Parque Buenos Aires 7 C2
Almon Jerusalem 13 B2
Almond → Edinburgh 11 B2
Alna Oslo 23 A4
Alnsjøen Oslo 23 A4
Alperton London 15 A2
Alpine New York 22 A2
Alrode Johannesburg 13 B2
Alsemberg Brussels 6 B1
Alsergrund Vienna 32 A2
Alsip Chicago 9 C2
Älsten Stockholm 29 B1
Älta Stockholm 29 B3
Altadena Los Angeles 16 A4
Alte-Donau → Vienna 32 A2
Alter Finkenkrug Berlin 5 A1
Altes Rathaus Munich 21 B2
Altglienicke Berlin 5 B4
Altlandsberg Berlin 5 A5
Altlandsberg Nord Berlin 5 A5
Altmannsdorf Vienna 32 B1
Alto da Boa Vista Rio de Janeiro 25 B1
Alto da Moóca São Paulo 27 B2
Alto do Pina Lisbon 16 A2
Altona Melbourne 18 B1
Alvik Stockholm 29 B1
Älvsjo Stockholm 29 B2
Älvvik Stockholm 29 A3
Am Hasenbergl Munich 21 A2
Am Steinhof Vienna 32 A1
Am Wald Munich 21 B2
Ama Keng Singapore 28 A2
Amadora Lisbon 16 A1
Amagasaki Osaka 23 A1
Amager Copenhagen 8 B3
Amāl Qādisiya Baghdad 3 B2
Amalienborg Slot Copenhagen 8 A3
Amata Milan 19 A1
Ambelokipi Athens 2 B2
Ameixoeira Lisbon 16 A2
América São Paulo 27 B1
American Police Hall of Fame Miami 18 B2
American University Washington 33 B3
Amin Baghdad 3 B2
Aminadav Jerusalem 13 B1
Amīrābād Tehran 31 A2
Amora Lisbon 16 B2
Amoreira Lisbon 16 A1
Amper → Munich 21 A1
Amstel-Drecht-Kanaal Amsterdam 2 B2
Amstelveen Amsterdam 2 B2
Amsterdam Amsterdam 2 A2
Amsterdam ✕ (AMS) Amsterdam 2 B1
Amsterdam-Rijnkanaal Amsterdam 2 B3
Amsterdam Zuidoost Amsterdam 2 B2
Amsterdamse Bos Amsterdam 2 B1
Anacosta → Washington 33 B4
Anacostia Washington 33 B4
Anadoluhisarı Istanbul 12 B2
Anadolukavağı Istanbul 12 A2
Anata Jerusalem 13 B2
Ancol Jakarta 12 A1
'Andalus Baghdad 3 B1
Andaraí Rio de Janeiro 25 B1
Anderlecht Brussels 6 A1
Anderson Park Atlanta 3 B2
Andingmen Beijing 4 B2
Ang Mo Kio Singapore 28 A3
Ängby Stockholm 29 A1
Angel I. San Francisco 26 A2
Angel Island State Park △ San Francisco 26 A2
Angke, Kali → Jakarta 12 A1
Angyalföld Budapest 7 A2
Anik Mumbai 20 A2
Anin Warsaw 32 B2
Anjou Montreal 20 A2
Annalee Heights Washington 33 B2
Annandale Washington 33 C2
Anne Frankhuis Amsterdam 2 A2
Antony Paris 24 B2
Aoyama Tokyo 30 B3
Ap Lei Chau Hong Kong 12 B1
Apapa Lagos 14 B2
Apelacão Lisbon 16 A2
Apopka, L. Orlando 23 A1
Apoquindo Santiago 27 B2
Apterkarskiy Ostrov St. Petersburg 27 B2
Ar Kazimiyah Baghdad 3 B1
Ar Ram Jerusalem 13 A2
Ara → Tokyo 30 A4
Arakawa Tokyo 30 A3
Arany-hegyi-patak → Budapest 7 A2
Aravaca Madrid 17 B1
Arbataash Baghdad 3 A1
Arc de Triomphe Paris 24 A2
Arcadia Los Angeles 16 B4
Arcueil Paris 24 B2
Arese Milan 19 A1
Arganzuela Madrid 17 B1
Argenteuil Paris 24 A2
Argiroupoli Athens 2 B2
Argonne Forest Chicago 9 C1
Arima Tokyo 30 B2
Arlanda ✕ (ARN) Stockholm 29 A1
Arlington Boston 6 A1
Arlington Washington 33 B3
Arlington Heights Boston 6 A1
Arlington Nat. Cemetery Washington 33 B3
Armação Rio de Janeiro 25 B2
Armadale Melbourne 18 B2
Armour Heights Toronto 31 A2
Arncliffe Sydney 29 B1
Arnold Arboretum Boston 6 B2
Árpádföld Budapest 7 A3
Arrentela Lisbon 16 B2
Arroyo Seco Park Los Angeles 16 B3
Årsta Stockholm 29 B2
Art Institute Chicago 9 B3
Artane Dublin 10 A2
Artas Jerusalem 13 B2
Arthur's Seat Edinburgh 11 B3
Arts, Place des Montreal 20 A2
As Shawawra Jerusalem 13 B2
Asagaya Tokyo 30 A2
Asahi Osaka 23 A2
Asakusa Tokyo 30 A3
Asati Calcutta 14 C1
Aschheim Munich 21 A3
Ascot Vale Melbourne 18 A1
Ashbridge's Bay Park Toronto 31 B3
Ashburn Chicago 9 C2
Ashburton Melbourne 18 B2
Ashfield Sydney 29 B1
Ashford London 15 B1
Ashtown Dublin 10 A2
Askisto Helsinki 11 B1
Askrikefjärden Stockholm 29 A3
Asnières Paris 24 A2
Aspern Vienna 32 A2
Aspern ✕ Vienna 32 A3
Assago Milan 19 B1
Assendelft Amsterdam 2 A1
Assiano Milan 19 B1
Astoria New York 22 B2
Astrolabe Park Sydney 29 B2
Atarot Jerusalem 13 A2
Atarot ✕ Jerusalem 13 A2
Atghara Calcutta 14 B2
Athens = Athina Athens 2 B2
Athina Athens 2 B2
Athina ✕ (ATH) Athens 2 A3
Athínai = Athina Athens 2 B2
Athis-Mons Paris 24 B3
Athlone Cape Town 8 A2
Atholl Johannesburg 13 A2
Atifiya Baghdad 3 A2
Atişalen Istanbul 12 B1
Atlanta Atlanta 3 B2
Atlanta Hartsfield Int. ✕ (ATL) Atlanta 3 C2
Atlanta Zoo Atlanta 3 B2
Atomium Brussels 6 A2
Attiki Athens 2 A2
Atzgersdorf Vienna 32 B1
Aubervilliers Paris 24 A3
Aubing Munich 21 B1
Auburndale Boston 6 A1
Auchendinny Edinburgh 11 B2
Auckland Park Johannesburg 13 B2
Auderghem Brussels 6 B2
Augustówka Warsaw 32 B2
Aulnay-sous-Bois Paris 24 A3
Aurelio Rome 26 B1
Ausīm Cairo 7 A1
Austerlitz, Gare d' Paris 24 A3
Austin Chicago 9 B2
Avalon Wellington 33 B2
Avedøre Copenhagen 8 B2
Avellaneda Buenos Aires 7 C2
Avenel Washington 33 B4
Avondale Chicago 9 B2
Avondale Heights Melbourne 18 A1
Avtovo St. Petersburg 27 B1
Ayazağa Istanbul 12 B1
Ayer Chawan, Pulau Singapore 28 B2
Ayer Merbau, Pulau Singapore 28 B2
Azabu Tokyo 30 B3
Azcapotzalco Mexico City 18 B1
Azteca, Estadia Mexico City 18 C2
Azucar, Cerro Pan de Santiago 27 A1

B

Baambrugge Amsterdam 2 B2
Baba Ch. Karachi 13 B1
Baba I. Karachi 13 B1
Babarpur Delhi 10 A2
Babushkin Moscow 19 A3
Back B. Mumbai 20 B1
Baclaran Manila 17 B2
Bacoor Manila 17 C1
Bacoor B. Manila 17 C1
Badalona Barcelona 4 A2
Badhoevedorp Amsterdam 2 A1
Badli Delhi 10 A1
Bærum Oslo 23 A2
Bağcılar Istanbul 12 B1
Bàggio Milan 19 B1
Bāgh-e-Feyz Tehran 31 A1
Baghdād Baghdad 3 A2
Baghdad al Muthana ✕ Baghdad 3 B2
Baghdad Int. ✕ (SDA) Baghdad 3 B1
Bagmari Calcutta 14 B2
Bagneux Paris 24 B2
Bagnolet Paris 24 A3
Bagsværd Copenhagen 8 A2
Bagsværd Sø Copenhagen 8 A2
Baguiati Calcutta 14 B2
Bagumbayan Manila 17 C2
Baha'i Temple Chicago 9 A2
Bahçeköy Istanbul 12 A1
Bahçelievler Istanbul 12 B1
Bahtim Cairo 7 A2
Baile Atha Cliath = Dublin Dublin 10 A2
Baileys Crossroads Washington 33 B3
Bailly Paris 24 A1
Bairro Lopes Lisbon 16 A2
Baisha Canton 11 B2
Baiyun Hill Canton 11 B2
Baiyun Int. ✕ (CAN) Canton 11 A2
Bakırköy Istanbul 12 C1
Bal Harbor Miami 18 A2
Balara Manila 17 B2
Baldia Karachi 13 A1
Baldoyle Dublin 10 A3
Baldwin, L. Orlando 23 A3
Baldwin Hills Los Angeles 16 B2
Baldwin Hills Res. Los Angeles 16 B2
Balgowlah Sydney 29 A2
Balgowlah Heights Sydney 29 A2
Balham London 15 B3
Bali Calcutta 14 B1
Baliganja Calcutta 14 B2
Balingsnäs Stockholm 29 B2
Balingsta Stockholm 29 B2
Balintawak Manila 17 B1
Ballerup Copenhagen 8 A2
Ballinteer Dublin 10 B2
Ballyboden Dublin 10 B2
Ballybrack Dublin 10 B3
Ballyfermot Dublin 10 A1
Ballymorefinn Hill Dublin 10 B1
Ballymun Dublin 10 A2
Balmain Sydney 29 B2
Balta Calcutta 14 B1
Balvanera Buenos Aires 7 B2
Balwyn Melbourne 18 A2
Balwyn North Melbourne 18 A2
Banática Lisbon 16 A1
Bandra Mumbai 20 A1
Bandra Pt. Mumbai 20 A1
Bang Kapi Bangkok 3 B2
Bang Na Bangkok 3 B2
Bangbae Seoul 27 C1
Bangkhen Bangkok 3 A2
Bangkok Bangkok 3 B2
Bangkok Noi Bangkok 3 B1
Bangkok Yai Bangkok 3 B1
Banglo Calcutta 14 B1
Bangrak Bangkok 3 B2
Bangsu Bangkok 3 B2
Banks, C. Sydney 29 C2
Banksmeadow Sydney 29 B2
Banstala Calcutta 14 B2
Bantra Calcutta 14 B1
Baoshan Shanghai 28 A1
Bar Giyora Jerusalem 13 B1
Barahanagar Calcutta 14 B2
Barajas Madrid 17 B2
Barajas, Madrid ✕ (MAD) Madrid 17 B2
Barakpur Calcutta 14 A2
Barcarena Lisbon 16 A1
Barcarena, Rib. de → Lisbon 16 A1
Barcelona Barcelona 4 A2
Barcelona-Prat ✕ (BCN) Barcelona 4 B1
Barceloneta Barcelona 4 A2
Barcroft, L. Washington 33 B3
Barking London 15 A4
Barkingside London 15 A4
Barnes London 15 B2
Barnet London 15 A2
Barra Andai Karachi 13 B2
Barra Funda São Paulo 27 B2
Barracas Buenos Aires 7 B2
Barrackpur = Barakpur Calcutta 14 A2
Barranco Lima 14 B2
Barreiro Lisbon 16 B2
Barreto Rio de Janeiro 25 B2
Bartala Calcutta 14 B1
Barton Park Sydney 29 B1
Bartyki Warsaw 32 C2
Basus Cairo 7 A2
Batanagar Calcutta 14 B1
Bath Beach New York 22 C1
Bath I. Karachi 13 B2
Batir Jerusalem 13 B1
Batok, Bukit Singapore 28 A2
Battersea London 15 B3
Bauman Moscow 19 B3
Baumgarten Vienna 32 A1
Bay, L. Orlando 23 A2
Bay Harbour Islands Miami 18 A2
Bay Hill Orlando 23 B1
Bay Ridge New York 22 C1
Bayit Va-Gan Jerusalem 13 B2
Bayonne New York 22 B1
Bayrampaşa Istanbul 12 B1
Bayshore San Francisco 26 B2
Bayt Lahm Jerusalem 13 B2
Bayview San Francisco 26 B2
Bāzār Tehran 31 A2
Beacon Hill Hong Kong 12 A2
Beato Lisbon 16 A2
Beaumont Dublin 10 A2
Beaumonte Heights Toronto 31 A1
Bebek Istanbul 12 B2
Běchovice Prague 25 B3
Beck L. Chicago 9 A1
Beckenham London 15 B3
Beckton London 15 A4
Becontree London 15 A4
Beddington Corner London 15 B3
Bedford Boston 6 A1
Bedford Park Chicago 9 C2
Bedford Park New York 22 A2
Bedford Stuyvesant New York 22 B2
Bedford View Johannesburg 13 B2
Bedok Singapore 28 B3
Bedok, Res. Singapore 28 A3
Beersel Brussels 6 B1
Behala Calcutta 14 B1
Bei Hai Beijing 4 B2
Beicai Shanghai 28 B2
Beijing Beijing 4 B1
Beit Duqu Jerusalem 13 A1
Beit Ghur at-Tahta Jerusalem 13 A1
Beit Ghur el-Fawqa Jerusalem 13 A1
Beit Hanina Jerusalem 13 B2
Beit Ij'za Jerusalem 13 A1
Beit Iksa Jerusalem 13 B2
Beit I'nan Jerusalem 13 A1
Beit Jala Jerusalem 13 B2
Beit Lekhem = Bayt Lahm Jerusalem 13 B2
Beit Liqya Jerusalem 13 A1
Beit Nekofa Jerusalem 13 B1
Beit Sahur Jerusalem 13 B2
Beit Sofafa Jerusalem 13 B2
Beit Surik Jerusalem 13 B1
Beit Ur al-Fawqa Jerusalem 13 A1
Beit Zayit Jerusalem 13 B1
Beitaipingzhuan Beijing 4 B1
Beitar Illit Jerusalem 13 B1
Beitin Jerusalem 13 A2
Beitsun Canton 11 B2
Beitunya Jerusalem 13 A2
Beixing Jing Park Shanghai 28 B1
Békásmegyer Budapest 7 A2
Bekkelaget Oslo 23 A3
Bekkestua Oslo 23 A2
Bel Air Los Angeles 16 B2
Bela Vista São Paulo 27 B2
Bélanger Montreal 20 A1
Belas Lisbon 16 A1
Beleghata Calcutta 14 B2
Belém Lisbon 16 A1
Belém, Torre de Lisbon 16 A1
Belènzinho São Paulo 27 B2
Belgachiya Calcutta 14 B2
Belgharia Calcutta 14 B2
Belgrano Buenos Aires 7 B2
Bell Los Angeles 16 C3
Bell Gardens Los Angeles 16 C4
Bellavista Lima 14 B2
Bellavista Santiago 27 C2
Belle Harbor New York 22 C2
Belle Isle Orlando 23 B2
Belle View Washington 33 B2
Bellingham London 15 B3
Bellwood Chicago 9 B1
Belmont Boston 6 A1
Belmont London 15 A2
Belmont, Mt. Wellington 33 B2
Belmont Cragin Chicago 9 B2
Belmont Harbor Chicago 9 B3
Belmore Sydney 29 B1
Belur Calcutta 14 B2
Belvedere Atlanta 3 B3
Belvedere London 15 B4
Belvedere San Francisco 26 A2
Belyayevo Bogorodskoye Moscow 19 C2
Bemowo Warsaw 32 B1
Benaki Museum Athens 2 B2
Bendale Toronto 31 A3
Benefica Rio de Janeiro 25 B1
Benfica Lisbon 16 A1
Benito Juárez Mexico City 18 B2
Benito Juárez, Int. ✕ (MEX) Mexico City 18 B2
Bensonhurst New York 22 C2
Berchem-Ste-Agathe Brussels 6 A1
Berg am Laim Munich 21 B2
Bergenfield New York 22 A2
Bergham Munich 21 B2
Bergvliet Cape Town 8 B1
Beri Barcelona 4 A1
Berkeley San Francisco 26 A3
Berlin Berlin 5 A3
Berlin Dom Berlin 5 A3
Berlin Tegel ✕ (TXL) Berlin 5 A2
Berlin Tempelhof ✕ (THF) Berlin 5 B3
Bermondsey London 15 B3
Bernabeu, Estadio Madrid 17 B1
Bernal Heights San Francisco 26 B2
Berwyn Chicago 9 B2
Berwyn Heights Washington 33 B4
Besiktas Istanbul 12 B2
Besós → Barcelona 4 A2
Bessie, L. Orlando 23 B1
Bet Horon Jerusalem 13 A1
Bethesda Washington 33 B3
Bethlehem = Bayt Lahm Jerusalem 13 B2
Bethnal Green London 15 A3
Betor Calcutta 14 B1
Beulah Orlando 23 A1
Beulah, L. Orlando 23 A1
Beverley Hills Sydney 29 B1
Beverley Park Sydney 29 B1
Beverly Chicago 9 C3
Beverly Arts Center Chicago 9 C2
Beverly Glen Los Angeles 16 B2
Beverly Hills Los Angeles 16 B2
Beverly Hills -Morgan Park Historic District Chicago 9 C2
Bexley Sydney 29 B1
Bexley □ London 15 B4
Bexleyheath London 15 B4
Beykoz Istanbul 12 B2
Beylerbeyi Istanbul 12 B2
Beyoğlu Istanbul 12 B1
Bezons Paris 24 A2
Bezuidenhout Park Johannesburg 13 B2
Bhadrakali Calcutta 14 A2
Bhalswa Delhi 10 A2
Bhambo Khan Qarmati Karachi 13 B2
Bhatsala Calcutta 14 B1
Bhawanipur Calcutta 14 B2
Bhendkhal Mumbai 20 B2
Bhuleshwar Mumbai 20 B1
Bialoleka Dworska Warsaw 32 B2
Bicentennial Park Los Angeles 16 B4
Bicentennial Park Sydney 29 B1
Bickley London 15 B4
Bicutan Manila 17 C2
Bidhan Nagar Calcutta 14 B2
Bidu Jerusalem 13 B1
Bielany Warsaw 32 B1
Bielawa Warsaw 32 C2
Biesdorf Berlin 5 A4
Bièvre → Paris 24 B1
Bièvres Paris 24 B2
Big Sand Lake Orlando 23 B2
Bilston Edinburgh 11 B2
Binacayan Manila 17 C1
Binondo Manila 17 B1
Bintaro Jaya Jakarta 12 B1
Bir Nabala Jerusalem 13 A2
Birak el Kiyam Cairo 7 A1
Birch Cliff Toronto 31 A3
Birkenstein Berlin 5 A5
Birkholz Berlin 5 A4
Birkholzaue Berlin 5 A4
Birrarrung Park Melbourne 18 A2
Biscayne Park Miami 18 A2
Bishop Lavis Cape Town 8 A2
Bishopscourt Cape Town 8 A1
Bispebjerg Copenhagen 8 A3
Bittsevsky Forest Park Moscow 19 C2
Björknas Stockholm 29 B3
Black Cr. → Toronto 31 A2
Black Creek Pioneer Village Toronto 31 A1
Blackfen London 15 B4
Blackheath London 15 B4
Blackrock Dublin 10 B2
Bladensburg Washington 33 B4
Blair Village Atlanta 3 C2
Blairgowrie Johannesburg 13 A2
Blake House Boston 6 B2
Blakehurst Sydney 29 B1
Blakstad Oslo 23 B1
Blanche, L. Orlando 23 B1
Blankenburg Berlin 5 A3
Blankenfelde Berlin 5 A3
Bliźne Warsaw 32 B1
Błota Warsaw 32 C3
Blue Island Chicago 9 D2
Blue Mosque = Sultanahme Camil Istanbul 12 B1
Bluebell Dublin 10 B1
Bluff Hd. Hong Kong 12 B2
Bluffers Park Toronto 31 A3
Blumberg Berlin 5 A4
Blunt Pt. San Francisco 26 A2
Blutenberg Munich 21 B1
Blylaget Oslo 23 B3
Boa Vista, Alto da Rio de Janeiro 25 B1
Boardwalk New York 22 C3
Boavista Lisbon 16 A2
Bobigny Paris 24 A3
Bocanegra Lima 14 B2
Boedo Buenos Aires 7 B2
Bogenhausen Munich 21 B2
Boggy Creek Swamp Orlando 23 B2
Bogorodskoye Moscow 19 B3
Bogota New York 22 A1
Bogstadvatnet Oslo 23 A2
Bohnsdorf Berlin 5 B4
Bois-Colombes Paris 24 A2
Bois-d'Arcy Paris 24 B1
Boissy-St-Léger Paris 24 B4
Boldinasco Milan 19 B1
Bøler Oslo 23 A4
Bollate Milan 19 A1
Bollebeek Brussels 6 A1
Bollensdorf Berlin 5 A5
Bollmora Stockholm 29 B3
Bolshaya Okhta St. Petersburg 27 B2
Bolton Atlanta 3 B2
Bom Retiro São Paulo 27 B2
Bombay = Mumbai Mumbai 20 B2
Bondi Sydney 29 B2
Bondy Paris 24 A3
Bondy, Forêt de Paris 24 A4
Bonifacio Monument Manila 17 B1
Bonneuil-sur-Marne Paris 24 B4
Bonnington Edinburgh 11 B1
Bonnyrigg and Lasswade Edinburgh 11 B3
Bonsucesso Rio de Janeiro 25 B1
Bonteheuwel Cape Town 8 A2
Boo Stockholm 29 A3
Booterstown Dublin 10 B2
Borisovo Moscow 19 C3
Borle Mumbai 20 A2
Boronia Park Sydney 29 A1
Bosmont Johannesburg 13 B1
Bosön Stockholm 29 A3
Bosporus = İstanbul Boğazı Istanbul 12 B2
Bostancı Istanbul 12 C2
Boston Boston 6 A2
Boston Common Boston 6 A2
Boston Logan Int. ✕ (BOS) Boston 6 A2
Botafogo Rio de Janeiro 25 B1
Botany Sydney 29 B2
Botany B. Sydney 29 B2
Botany Bay Nat. Park △ Sydney 29 B2
Botič → Prague 25 B3
Botica Sete Lisbon 16 A1
Boucherville Montreal 20 A3
Boucherville, Is. de Montreal 20 A3
Bougival Paris 24 A1
Boulder Pt. Hong Kong 12 B1
Boulogne, Bois de Paris 24 A2
Boulogne-Billancourt Paris 24 A2
Bourg-la-Reine Paris 24 B2
Bouviers Paris 24 B1
Bovenkerk Amsterdam 2 B2
Bovenkerker Polder Amsterdam 2 B2
Bovisa Milan 19 A2
Bow London 15 A3
Boyacıköy Istanbul 12 B2
Boyd Conservation Area Toronto 31 A1
Boyle Heights Los Angeles 16 B3
Braepark Edinburgh 11 B2
Braid Edinburgh 11 B2
Bramley Johannesburg 13 A2
Brandeis University Boston 6 A1
Brandenburger Tor Berlin 5 A3
Brani, Pulau Singapore 28 B3
Branik Prague 25 B2
Brännkyrka Stockholm 29 B2
Brás São Paulo 27 B2
Brasilândia São Paulo 27 A1
Brateyevo Moscow 19 C3
Braybrook Melbourne 18 A1
Brázdim Prague 25 A3
Breakheart Reservation Boston 6 A2
Brede Copenhagen 8 A3
Breezy Point New York 22 C2
Breitenlee Vienna 32 A3
Breña Lima 14 B2
Brent □ London 15 A2
Brent Res. London 15 A2
Brentford London 15 B2
Brentwood Park Los Angeles 16 B2
Brera Milan 19 B2
Bresso Milan 19 A2
Brevik Stockholm 29 A3
Břevnov Prague 25 B2
Brickyard, The Chicago 9 B2
Bridgeport Chicago 9 B3
Bridgetown Cape Town 8 A2
Bridgeview Chicago 9 C2
Brighton Boston 6 A2
Brighton Melbourne 18 B1
Brighton Beach New York 22 C2
Brighton le Sands Sydney 29 B1
Brighton Park Chicago 9 C2
Brightwood Washington 33 B3
Brigittenau Vienna 32 A2
Brimbank Park Melbourne 18 A1
Brisbane San Francisco 26 B2
Britz Berlin 5 B3
Brixton London 15 B3
Broadmeadows Melbourne 18 A1
Broadmoor San Francisco 26 B2
Broadview Chicago 9 B1
Brockley London 15 B3
Brödno Warsaw 32 B2
Bródnowski, Kanal Warsaw 32 B2
Broek Amsterdam 2 A2
Bromley □ London 15 B4
Bromley Common London 15 B4
Bromma Stockholm 29 A1
Bromma ✕ Stockholm 29 A1
Brøndby Strand Copenhagen 8 B2
Brøndbyøster Copenhagen 8 B2
Brøndbyvester Copenhagen 8 B2
Brondesbury London 15 A2
Brønnøya Oslo 23 A2
Brønshøj Copenhagen 8 A2
Bronxville New York 22 A3
Brookfield Chicago 9 C1
Brookhaven Atlanta 3 A2
Brookline Boston 6 B2
Brooklyn Cape Town 8 A1
Brooklyn New York 22 C2
Brooklyn Wellington 33 B1
Brooklyn Heights New York 22 B2
Brookmont Washington 33 B3
Brossard Montreal 20 B3
Brou-sur-Chantereine Paris 24 A4
Brown Toronto 31 A3
Broyhill Park Washington 33 B2
Brughério Milan 19 A2
Brunswick Melbourne 18 A1
Brussegem Brussels 6 A1
Brussel Brussels 6 A2
Brussel ✕ (BRU) Brussels 6 A2
Brussels = Brussel Brussels 6 A2
Bruxelles = Brussel Brussels 6 A2
Bruzzano Milan 19 A2
Bry-sur-Marne Paris 24 A4
Bryan, L. Orlando 23 B2
Bryanston Johannesburg 13 A1
Bryn Oslo 23 A1
Brzeziny Warsaw 32 B2
Bubeneč Prague 25 B2
Buc Paris 24 B1
Buchenhain Munich 21 B1
Buchholz Berlin 5 A3
Buckhead Atlanta 3 A2
Buckingham Palace London 15 A3
Buckow Berlin 5 B3
Buda Budapest 7 A2
Buda Castle = Budavárpalota Budapest 7 A2
Budafok Budapest 7 B2
Budaörs Budapest 7 B1
Budapest Budapest 7 B2
Budapest ✕ (BUD) Budapest 7 B3
Budatétény Budapest 7 B2
Budavárpalota Budapest 7 A2
Buddinge Copenhagen 8 A3
Buena Ventura Lakes Orlando 23 B2
Buena Vista San Francisco 26 B2
Buenos Aires Buenos Aires 7 B2
Bufalotta Rome 26 B2
Bugio Lisbon 16 B1
Buiksloot Amsterdam 2 A2
Buitenveldert Amsterdam 2 B2
Buizingen Brussels 6 B1
Bukhansan Seoul 27 B1
Bukit Panjang Nature Reserve Singapore 28 A2
Bukit Timah Nature Reserve Singapore 28 A2
Bukum, Pulau Singapore 28 B2
Bûlâq Cairo 7 A2
Bule Manila 17 C2
Bulim Singapore 28 A2
Bullen Park Melbourne 18 A2
Bund, The Shanghai 28 B1
Bundoora North Melbourne 18 A2
Bundoora Park Melbourne 18 A2
Bunker Hill Memorial Boston 6 A2
Bunker I. Karachi 13 B1
Bunkyō Tokyo 30 A3
Bunnefjorden Oslo 23 A3
Buona Vista Park Singapore 28 B2
Burbank Chicago 9 C2
Burbank Los Angeles 16 A3
Burden, L. Orlando 23 B1
Burlington Boston 6 A1
Burnham Park Chicago 9 C3
Burnham Park Harbor Chicago 9 B3
Burnhamthorpe Toronto 31 B1
Burnt Oak London 15 A2
Burntisland Edinburgh 11 A2
Burnwynd Edinburgh 11 B1
Burqa Jerusalem 13 A2
Burtus Cairo 7 A1
Burudvatn Oslo 23 A2
Burwood Sydney 29 B1
Bushwick New York 22 B2
Bushy Park London 15 B1
Butantã São Paulo 27 B1
Butcher I. Mumbai 20 B2
Butler, L. Orlando 23 B1
Butts Corner Washington 33 C2
Büyükdere Istanbul 12 B2
Byculla Mumbai 20 B2
Bygdøy Oslo 23 A3

C

C.B.S. Fox Studios Los Angeles 16 B2
C.N.N. Center Atlanta 3 B2
C.N. Tower Toronto 31 B2
Caballito Buenos Aires 7 B2
Cabin John Washington 33 B2
Cabin John Regional Park → Washington 33 A2
Cabinteely Dublin 10 B3
Cabra Dublin 10 A2
Cabuçú de Baixo → São Paulo 27 A1
Cabuçú de Cima → São Paulo 27 A2
Cachan Paris 24 B2
Cachoeira, Rib. da → São Paulo 27 B1
Cacilhas Lisbon 16 A2
Cahuenga Park Los Angeles 16 B3
Cain, L. Orlando 23 B2
Cairo = El Qâhira Cairo 7 A2
Cairo Int. ✕ (CAI) Cairo 7 A3
Caju Rio de Janeiro 25 B1
Čakovice Prague 25 B3
Calcutta = Kolkata Calcutta 14 B2
California Inst. of Tech. Los Angeles 16 B4
California Los Angeles, University of Los Angeles 16 B2
California State University Los Angeles 16 B3
Callao Lima 14 B2
Caloocan Manila 17 B1
Calumet L. Chicago 9 C3
Calumet Park Chicago 9 C3

Calumet Sag Channel → Chicago 9 C2
Calvairate Milan 19 B2
Camarate Lisbon 16 A2
Camaroes Lisbon 16 A1
Camberwell London 15 B3
Camberwell Melbourne 18 B2
Cambridge Boston 6 A2
Cambuci São Paulo 27 B2
Camden □ London 15 A3
Cameron, Mt. Wellington 33 B2
Çamlıca Istanbul 12 B2
Camp Springs Washington 33 C4
Campamento Madrid 17 B1
Campbellfield Melbourne 18 A1
Camperdown Sydney 29 B2
Campo, Casa de Madrid 17 B1
Campo F.C. Barcelona Barcelona 4 A1
Campo Grando Lisbon 16 A2
Campo Pequeño Lisbon 16 A2
Campolide Lisbon 16 A2
Camps Bay Cape Town 8 A1
C'an San Joan Barcelona 4 A2
Cañacao B. Manila 17 C1
Canarsie New York 22 C2
Candiac Montreal 20 B3
Caneças Lisbon 16 A1
Canillas Madrid 17 B2
Canillejas Madrid 17 B2
Canning Town London 15 A4
Canteras de Vallecas Madrid 17 B2
Canterbury Melbourne 18 A2
Canterbury Sydney 29 B1
Canton = Guangzhou Canton 11 B2
Caoheijing Shanghai 28 B1
Capão Redondo São Paulo 27 B1
Caparica Lisbon 16 A2
Caparica, Costa da Lisbon 16 B1
Cape Flats Cape Town 8 B2
Cape Peninsula △ Cape Town 8 A1
Cape Town Cape Town 8 A1
Cape Town Int. ✈ (CPT) Cape Town 8 A2
Capitol Heights Washington 33 B4
Captain Cook Bridge Sydney 29 C1
Captain Cook Landing Place Park Sydney 29 C2
Capuchos Lisbon 16 B1
Carabanchel Alto Madrid 17 B1
Carabanchel Bajo Madrid 17 B1
Carapachay Buenos Aires 7 B1
Caraza Buenos Aires 7 C2
Caridad Manila 17 C1
Carioca, Sa. da Rio de Janeiro 25 B1
Carlstadt New York 22 A1
Carlton Melbourne 18 A1
Carmen de Huechuraba Santiago 27 B1
Carmen de la Legua Lima 14 B2
Carnaxide Lisbon 16 A1
Carnegie Melbourne 18 B2
Carnide Lisbon 16 A1
Carol City Miami 18 A1
Carrascal Santiago 27 B1
Carrickmines Dublin 10 B3
Carrières-sous-Bois Paris 24 A1
Carrières-sous-Poissy Paris 24 A1
Carrières-sur-Seine Paris 24 A2
Carrigeen B. Dublin 10 A3
Cartierville Montreal 20 A1
Casa Loma Toronto 31 A2
Casa Verde São Paulo 27 A1
Casál Morena Rome 26 C2
Casalotti Rome 26 B1
Cascade Heights Atlanta 3 B2
Castèl di Leva Rome 26 C2
Castèl Sant'Angelo Rome 26 B1
Castleknock Dublin 10 A1
Castleton Corners New York 22 C1
Catete Rio de Janeiro 25 B1
Catford London 15 B3
Catherine, L. Orlando 23 B2
Caulfield Melbourne 18 B2
Cavite Manila 17 C1
Caxias Lisbon 16 A1
Cebecci Istanbul 12 B1
Cecchignola Rome 26 C2
Cecilienhof, Schloss Berlin 5 B1
Cedar Grove Atlanta 3 C3
Cedarvale Park Toronto 31 A2
Cempaka Putih Jakarta 12 B2
Çengelköy Istanbul 12 B2
Cengkareng Jakarta 12 A1
Centennial Olympic Park Atlanta 3 B2
Centennial Park Sydney 29 B2
Center Hill Atlanta 3 B2
Centocelle Rome 26 B2
Central, Gare Montreal 20 B2
Central Park New York 22 B2
Cerdanyola del Vallès Barcelona 4 A1
Cerillos Santiago 27 B1
Cerro de la Estrella, Parque Nacional △ Mexico City 18 B2
Cerro de los Angeles Madrid 17 C1
Cerro Navia Santiago 27 B1
Cesano Boscone Milan 19 B1
Cesate Milan 19 A1
Cha Kwo Ling Hong Kong 12 B2
Chacarrita Buenos Aires 7 B2
Chadwell Heath London 15 A4
Chai Chee Singapore 28 B3
Chai Wan Hong Kong 12 B2
Chai Wan Kok Hong Kong 12 A1
Chakdaha Calcutta 14 C1
Chamartín Madrid 17 B1
Chamberí Madrid 17 B1
Chambourcy Paris 24 A1
Champigny-sur-Marne Paris 24 B4
Champlain, Pont Montreal 20 B2
Champs-sur-Marne Paris 24 A4
Chamrail Calcutta 14 B1
Chanakyapuri Delhi 10 B2
Chanditala Calcutta 14 A1
Changfeng Park Shanghai 28 B1
Changhai = Shanghai Shanghai 28 B2
Changi Singapore 28 A3
Changi, Singapore ✈ (SIN) Singapore 28 A3
Changning Shanghai 28 B1
Chantereine Paris 24 A4
Chantian Canton 11 A2
Chaoyang Beijing 4 B2
Chaoyangmen Beijing 4 B2
Chapelizod Dublin 10 A1
Chapultepec, Bosque de Mexico City 18 B1
Chapultepec, Castillo de Mexico City 18 B1
Charenton-le-Pont Paris 24 B3
Charleroi, Kanal de → Brussels 6 B1
Charles Bridge = Karlův most Prague 25 B2
Charles Gates Dawes House Chicago 9 A2
Charlestown Boston 6 A2
Charlottenburg Berlin 5 A2
Charlottenburg, Schloss Berlin 5 A2
Charlottenlund Copenhagen 8 A3
Charlton London 15 B4
Charneca Lisbon 16 A2
Chase, L. Orlando 23 B1
Châteaufort Paris 24 B1
Châtenay-Malabry Paris 24 B2
Chatham Chicago 9 C3
Chatillon Paris 24 B2
Chatou Paris 24 A1
Chatpur Calcutta 14 B2
Chatswood Sydney 29 A2
Chatuchak Bangkok 3 B2
Chatuchak Park Bangkok 3 B2
Chauki Karachi 13 A1
Chavarria Lima 14 B2
Chaville Paris 24 B2
Chayang Seoul 27 B2
Chelles Paris 24 A4
Chelles, Canal de Paris 24 A4
Chells-le-Pin ✈ Paris 24 A4
Chelsea Boston 6 A2
Chelsea London 15 B2
Chembur Mumbai 20 A2
Chennevières-sur-Marne Paris 24 B4
Cheongdam Seoul 27 B2
Cheonho Seoul 27 B2
Cheops Cairo 7 B1
Chertanovka → Moscow 19 C2
Chertanovo Moscow 19 C2
Cheryomushki Moscow 19 B2
Chestnut Hill Boston 6 B1
Cheung Sha Wan Hong Kong 12 A1
Cheverly Washington 33 B4
Chevilly-Larue Paris 24 B3
Chevry-Cossigny Paris 24 B4
Chevy Chase Washington 33 B3
Chhatrapati Shivaji, Mumbai ✈ (BOM) Mumbai 20 A2
Chia Keng Singapore 28 A3
Chiaravalle Milanese Milan 19 B2
Chicago Chicago 9 B3
Chicago, University of Chicago 9 C3
Chicago Harbor Chicago 9 B3
Chicago Lawn Chicago 9 C2
Chicago-Midway ✈ (MDW) Chicago 9 C2
Chicago O'Hare Int. ✈ (ORD) Chicago 9 B1
Chicago Ridge Chicago 9 C2
Chicago River, North Branch → Chicago 9 B2
Chicago Sanitary and Ship Canal Chicago 9 C2
Chicago State University Chicago 9 C3
Chicago Zoo Chicago 9 B1
Chienzui Canton 11 A3
Chik Sha Hong Kong 12 B2
Child's Hill London 15 A2
Chilla Saroda Delhi 10 B2
Chillum Washington 33 B4
Chilly-Mazarin Paris 24 B2
China Basin San Francisco 26 B2
Chingupota Calcutta 14 C1
Chinna Cr. → Karachi 13 B2
Chiquihuite, Cerro Mexico City 18 A2
Chislehurst London 15 B4
Chiswick London 15 B2
Chiswick House London 15 B2
Chitose Tokyo 30 B2
Chitralada Palace Bangkok 3 B2
Chiyoda Tokyo 30 A3
Choa Chu Kang Singapore 28 A2
Chodov u Prahy Prague 25 B3
Chōfu Tokyo 30 B2
Choisy-le-Roi Paris 24 B3
Cholupice Prague 25 C2
Chom Thong Bangkok 3 B1
Chong Pang Singapore 28 A2
Chongwen Beijing 4 B2
Chorrillos Lima 14 C2
Chowpatty Beach Mumbai 20 B1
Christianshavn Copenhagen 8 A3
Chrzanów Warsaw 32 B1
Chuen Lung Hong Kong 12 A1
Chuk Kok Hong Kong 12 A2
Chulalongkorn Univ. Bangkok 3 B2
Chuō Tokyo 30 A3
Church End London 15 A2
Churchtown Dublin 10 B2
Ciampino Rome 26 C2
Ciampino ✈ Rome 26 C2
Cicero Chicago 9 B2
Cilandak Jakarta 12 B1
Cilincing Jakarta 12 A2
Ciliwung → Jakarta 12 B2
Čimice Prague 25 B2
Cinecittà Rome 26 B2
Cinisello Bálsamo Milan 19 A2
Cinkota Budapest 7 A3
Cipete Jakarta 12 B1
Citta degli Studi Milan 19 B2
Città del Vaticano = Vatican City ■ Rome 26 B1
City, The London 15 A3
City of the Dead Cairo 7 A2
Ciudad de México Mexico City 18 B2
Ciudad Deportiva Mexico City 18 B2
Ciudad Fin de Semana Madrid 17 B2
Ciudad General Belgrano Buenos Aires 7 C1
Ciudad Lineál Madrid 17 B2
Ciudad Satélite Mexico City 18 A1
Ciudad Universitaria Buenos Aires 7 B2
Ciudad Universitaria Mexico City 18 C1
Claireville Res. Toronto 31 A1
Clamart Paris 24 B2
Clapham London 15 B3
Clapton London 15 A3
Claremont Cape Town 8 A1
Clayhall London 15 A4
Clear, L. Orlando 23 A2
Clermiston Edinburgh 11 B2
Clichy Paris 24 A2
Clichy-sous-Bois Paris 24 A4
Cliffside Toronto 31 A3
Cliffside Park New York 22 B2
Clifton Cape Town 8 A1
Clifton Karachi 13 B2
Clifton New York 22 C1
Clifton Beach Karachi 13 B2
Cliftondale Boston 6 A2
Cloghran Dublin 10 A2
Clonskeagh Dublin 10 B2
Clontarf Dublin 10 A2
Clontarf Sydney 29 A2
Clovelly Sydney 29 B2
Cobras, I. das Rio de Janeiro 25 B2
Coburg Melbourne 18 A1
Cocotá Rio de Janeiro 25 A1
Cœuilly Paris 24 B4
Coina Lisbon 16 B2
Coker Lagos 14 B2
Colaba Mumbai 20 B1
Colaba Pt. Mumbai 20 B1
Colegiales Buenos Aires 7 B2
Colindale London 15 A2
Colinton Edinburgh 11 B2
College Park Atlanta 3 C2
College Park Washington 33 B4
College Point New York 22 B2
Collégien Paris 24 A4
Collier Row London 15 A4
Colliers Wood London 15 B2
Colma San Francisco 26 B2
Colney Hatch London 15 A3
Cologno Monzese Milan 19 A2
Colombes Paris 24 A2
Colonia Güell Barcelona 4 A1
Colonial Knob Wellington 33 A1
Colosseo Rome 26 B1
Colosseum = Colosseo Rome 26 B1
Combault Paris 24 B4
Comércio, Praça do Lisbon 16 A2
Commerce Los Angeles 16 B4
Como Sydney 29 C1
Conceição, I. da Rio de Janeiro 25 B2
Conchali Santiago 27 B2
Concord Sydney 29 B1
Concord Toronto 31 A2
Concorde, Place de la Paris 24 A2
Concorezzo Milan 19 A2
Condet Jakarta 12 A2
Coney Island New York 22 C2
Congonhas São Paulo ✈ (CGH) São Paulo 27 B2
Conley → Atlanta 3 C3
Connaught Place Delhi 10 B2
Consolação São Paulo 27 B2
Constantia Cape Town 8 A1
Constitución Buenos Aires 7 B2
Constitution Atlanta 3 B2
Convention Center Los Angeles 16 B3
Conway Orlando 23 B2
Conway, L. Orlando 23 B2
Coogee Sydney 29 B2
Cooksville Toronto 31 B1
Coolock Dublin 10 A2
Copacabana Rio de Janeiro 25 B1
Copenhagen = København Copenhagen 8 A2
Coral Gables Miami 18 B2
Coral Hills Washington 33 B4
Corcovado, Cristo Redentor Rio de Janeiro 25 B1
Corduff Dublin 10 A1
Cormano Milan 19 A2
Cornaredo Milan 19 A1
Córsico Milan 19 B1
Corstorphine Edinburgh 11 B2
Corviale Rome 26 B1
Coslada Madrid 17 B2
Cossigny Paris 24 B4
Cotao Lisbon 16 A1
Côte-St-Luc Montreal 20 B2
Cotunduba, I. de Rio de Janeiro 25 B2
Coubron Paris 24 A4
Countryside Chicago 9 C1
County Art Museum Los Angeles 16 B2
Courbevoie Paris 24 A2
Courtry Paris 24 A4
Cowley London 15 A1
Coyoacán Mexico City 18 B2
Craighall Park Johannesburg 13 A2
Craiglockhart Edinburgh 11 B2
Craigmillar Edinburgh 11 B3
Cramond Edinburgh 11 B2
Cramond Bridge Edinburgh 11 B1
Cramond I. Edinburgh 11 B2
Cranford London 15 B1
Crawford Cape Town 8 A2
Crayford London 15 B5
Creekmouth London 15 A4
Crescent, L. Orlando 23 B2
Crescenzago Milan 19 A2
Cressely Paris 24 B1
Cresskill New York 22 A2
Créteil Paris 24 B3
Cricklewood London 15 A2
Cristo Redentor, Estatua do Rio de Janeiro 25 B1
Crockenhill London 15 B4
Croissy-Beaubourg Paris 24 B4
Croissy-sur-Seine Paris 24 A1
Crosby Johannesburg 13 B1
Crosne Paris 24 B3
Cross I. Mumbai 20 B2
Crouch End London 15 A3
Crown Mine Johannesburg 13 B1
Crows Nest Sydney 29 A2
Croydon London 15 B3
Croydon Park Sydney 29 B1
Cruagh Mt. Dublin 10 B2
Crumlin Dublin 10 B2
Cruz de Pau Lisbon 16 B2
Crystal Palace London 15 B3
Csepel Budapest 7 B2
Csepelsziget Budapest 7 B2
Csillaghegy Budapest 7 A2
Csillagtelep Budapest 7 B2
Csömör Budapest 7 A3
Csömöri-patak → Budapest 7 A3
Cuatro Vientos Madrid 17 B1
Cuauhtémoc Mexico City 18 B2
Cuban Museum Miami 18 B2
Cubao Manila 17 B2
Çubuklu Istanbul 12 B2
Cudahy Los Angeles 16 C3
Cuicuilco, Pirámido de Mexico City 18 C1
Culmore Washington 33 B3
Culver City Los Angeles 16 B2
Cumbres de Vallecas Madrid 17 B2
Cupecé São Paulo 27 B1
Currie Edinburgh 11 B2
Cusago Milan 19 B1
Cusano Milanino Milan 19 A2
Cutler Park Boston 6 B1
Çuvuşabaşi → Istanbul 12 B1
Cypress Hills New York 22 B2
Czerniaków Warsaw 32 B2
Czyste Warsaw 32 B1

D

Da Moóca → São Paulo 27 B2
Ďáblice Prague 25 B2
Dąbrowa Warsaw 32 B1
Dachang Shanghai 28 B1
Dachang ✈ Shanghai 28 B1
Dachau Munich 21 A1
Dachau-Ost Munich 21 A1
Dachauer Moos Munich 21 A1
Dadar Mumbai 20 A1
Daebang Seoul 27 B1
Daechi Seoul 27 B2
Dafni Athens 2 B2
Dagenham London 15 A4
Dagfling Munich 21 B2
Dahab, Gezîret el Cairo 7 B2
Daheisha Jerusalem 13 B2
Dahlem Berlin 5 B2
Dahlwitz-Hoppegarten Berlin 5 A5
Dahongmen Beijing 4 C2
Dajiaoting Beijing 4 B2
Dakhnoye St. Petersburg 27 C1
Dalejsky potok → Prague 25 B2
Dalgety Bay Edinburgh 11 A1
Dalkeith Edinburgh 11 B3
Dalkey Dublin 10 B3
Dalkey I. Dublin 10 B3
Dallgow Berlin 5 A1
Dalmeny Edinburgh 11 B1
Dalston London 15 A3
Daly City San Francisco 26 B2
Damaia Lisbon 16 A1
Damarakia Athens 2 B1
Dämeritzsee Berlin 5 B5
Dan Ryan Woods Chicago 9 C2
Danderhall Edinburgh 11 B3
Danderyd Stockholm 29 A2
Danforth Toronto 31 A3
Darakeh Tehran 31 A2
Darband Tehran 31 A2
Darling Point Sydney 29 B2
Darndale Dublin 10 A2
Darrūs Tehran 31 A2
Dartford London 15 B5
Dashi Canton 11 B2
Datansha Canton 11 B2
Datun Beijing 4 A2
Daulatpur Delhi 10 A1
Davidson, Mt. San Francisco 26 B2
Davidson's Mains Edinburgh 11 B2
Dāvūdiyeh Tehran 31 A2
Davydkovo Moscow 19 B1
Dawidy Warsaw 32 C1
Days Bay Wellington 33 B2
Decatur Atlanta 3 B3
Dedham Boston 6 B1
Degunino Moscow 19 A2
Deir Dibwan Jerusalem 13 A2
Deir Ibzi'e Jerusalem 13 A1
Dejvice Prague 25 B2
Dekabristov, Ostrov St. Petersburg 27 B1
Delhi Delhi 10 B2
Demarest New York 22 A2
Den Ilp Amsterdam 2 A2
Denistone Heights Sydney 29 A1
Dentonia Park Toronto 31 A3
DePaul University Chicago 9 B3
Deptford London 15 B3
Des Plaines Chicago 9 A1
Deshengmen Beijing 4 B2
Deutsch-Wagram Vienna 32 A3
Deutsche Oper Berlin 5 A2
Deutscher Museum Munich 21 B2
Devil's Peak Cape Town 8 A1
Dhakuria Calcutta 14 B2
Dharavi Mumbai 20 A2
Diadema São Paulo 27 C2
Diegen Brussels 6 A2
Diemen Amsterdam 2 A2
Diepkloof Johannesburg 13 B1
Dieprivier Cape Town 8 B1
Difficult Run → Washington 33 B2
Dilbeek Brussels 6 A1
Dilli = Delhi Delhi 10 B2
Dirnismaning Munich 21 A2
Disney-M.G.M. Studios Orlando 23 B1
Disney Studios Los Angeles 16 B3
District Heights Washington 33 B4
Djakarta = Jakarta Jakarta 12 A2
Djursholm Stockholm 29 A2
Döberitz Berlin 5 A1
Döbling Vienna 32 A2
Dobong Seoul 27 B2
Dobongsan Seoul 27 A2
Docklands London 15 A3
Doctor Phillips Orlando 23 B2
Dodder → Dublin 10 B1
Dodger Stadium Los Angeles 16 B3
Dogs, Isle of London 15 B3
Dolgoe Ozero St. Petersburg 27 A1
Dollis Hill London 15 A2
Dollymount Dublin 10 A2
Dolni Prague 25 B3
Dolni Chabry Prague 25 B2
Dolni Počernice Prague 25 B3
Dolphins Barn Dublin 10 B2
Dom Pedro II, Parque São Paulo 27 B2
Don Mills Toronto 31 A2
Don Muang Int. ✈ (BKK) Bangkok 3 A2
Donaghmede Dublin 10 A2
Donau-Oder Kanal Vienna 32 A3
Donaufeld Vienna 32 A2
Donaupark Vienna 32 A2
Donaustadt Vienna 32 A2
Dongan Hills New York 22 C1
Dongcheng Beijing 4 B2
Dongdaemung Seoul 27 B2
Donggou Shanghai 28 B2
Dongjak Seoul 27 B1
Dongjiao Canton 11 B2
Dongri Mumbai 20 B2
Dongshanhu Park Canton 11 B2
Dongzhimen Beijing 4 B2
Donnybrook Dublin 10 B2
Doornfontein Johannesburg 13 B2
Dorchester Boston 6 B2
Dorchester B. Boston 6 B2
Dorchester Heights Nat. Historical Site ⌂ Boston 6 B2
Dornach Munich 21 B3
Dorval Int., Montréal ✈ (YUL) Montreal 20 B1
Dos Couros → São Paulo 27 C2
Dos Moninos → São Paulo 27 C2
Douglas Park Chicago 9 B2
Dover Heights Sydney 29 B2
Dowlatābād Tehran 31 B2
Down, L. Orlando 23 A1
Downey Los Angeles 16 C4
Downsview Toronto 31 A1
Downsview C.A.F.B. ✈ Toronto 31 A2
Dragør Copenhagen 8 B3
Drancy Paris 24 A3
Dranesville Washington 33 A1
Drapetsona Athens 2 B1
Dreilinden Berlin 5 B2
Drewnica Warsaw 32 B2
Drigh Road Karachi 13 A2
Drimnagh Dublin 10 B2
Drogenbos Brussels 6 B1
Druid Hills Atlanta 3 B2
Drumcondra Dublin 10 A2
Drummoyne Sydney 29 B1
Drylaw Edinburgh 11 B2
Dubeč Prague 25 B3
Dublin Dublin 10 A2
Dublin ✈ (DUB) Dublin 10 A2
Dublin B. Dublin 10 B2
Dublin Harbour Dublin 10 A2
Duddingston Edinburgh 11 B3
Dugnano Milan 19 A2
Duivendrecht Amsterdam 2 B2
Dūlāb Tehran 31 B2
Dulwich London 15 B3
Dum Dum Calcutta 14 B2
Dum Dum Int. ✈ (CCU) Calcutta 14 B2
Dumont New York 22 A2
Dún Laoghaire Dublin 10 B3
Dundrum Dublin 10 B2
Dunearn Singapore 28 B2
Dúnleary = Dún Laoghaire Dublin 10 B3
Dunn Loring Washington 33 B2
Dunning Chicago 9 B2
Dunvegan Johannesburg 13 A2
Duomo Milan 19 B2
Duque de Caxias Rio de Janeiro 25 A1
Duren Sawit Jakarta 12 A2
Dusit Bangkok 3 B2
Dworp Brussels 6 B1
Dyakovo Moscow 19 B2
Dyker Beach Park New York 22 C1
Dzerzhinskiy Moscow 19 B2
Dzerzhinskiy Park Moscow 19 B2

E

E.U.R. = Esposizione Universale di Roma Rome 26 C1
Eagle Rock Los Angeles 16 B3
Ealing □ London 15 A2
Earlsfield London 15 B2
Earlwood Sydney 29 B1
East Arlington Boston 6 A2
East Arlington Washington 33 B3
East Bedfont London 15 B1
East Boston Boston 6 A2
East Don → Toronto 31 A2
East Don Parkland Toronto 31 A2
East Elmhurst New York 22 B2
East Finchley London 15 A2
East Flatbush New York 22 C2
East Ham London 15 A4
East Humber → Toronto 31 A1
East Lamma Channel Hong Kong 12 B1
East Lexington Boston 6 A1
East Los Angeles Los Angeles 16 B3
East Molesey London 15 B1
East New York New York 22 B2
East Pines Washington 33 B4
East Point Atlanta 3 B2
East Potomac Park Washington 33 B3
East River → New York 22 B2
East Rutherford New York 22 A1
East Sheen London 15 B2
East Talpiyot Jerusalem 13 B2
East Wickham London 15 B4
East York Toronto 31 A2
Eastbourne Wellington 33 B2
Eastcote London 15 A1
Easter Howgate Edinburgh 11 B2
Eastpoint Park Toronto 31 A4
Eastwood Sydney 29 A1
Eaton Canyon Park Los Angeles 16 A4
Ebara Tokyo 30 B3
Ebisu Tokyo 30 B3
Ebute-Ikorodu Lagos 14 A2
Ebute-Metta Lagos 14 B2
Eda Tokyo 30 B2
Edendale Johannesburg 13 A2
Edenmore Dublin 10 A2
Edgars Cr. → Melbourne 18 A1
Edgeley Toronto 31 A1
Edgemar San Francisco 26 C2
Edgewater New York 22 B2
Edgewood Orlando 23 B2
Edinburgh Edinburgh 11 B2
Edinburgh ✈ (EDI) Edinburgh 11 B1
Edinburgh Castle Edinburgh 11 B2
Edison Park Chicago 9 A2
Edmondston Washington 33 B4
Edmondstown Dublin 10 B2
Edo → Tokyo 30 B4
Edogawa Tokyo 30 A4
Edsberg Stockholm 29 A1
Edwards L. Melbourne 18 A1
Efzonos Athens 2 B2
Egaleo Athens 2 B1
Egaleo, Oros Athens 2 B1
Eiche Berlin 5 A4
Eiche Sud Berlin 5 A4
Eiffel, Tour Paris 24 A2
Ein Arik Jerusalem 13 A1
Ein Naquba Jerusalem 13 B1
Ein Rafa Jerusalem 13 B1
Eizariya Jerusalem 13 B2
Ejby Copenhagen 8 A2
Ejigbo Lagos 14 A1
Ekeberg Oslo 23 A3
Eknäs Stockholm 29 B3
El 'Abbasiya Cairo 7 A2
El Agustino Lima 14 B2
El Baragil Cairo 7 A1
El Basâtîn Cairo 7 B2
El Bira Jerusalem 13 A2
El Bosque Santiago 27 C2
El Carmen Santiago 27 B1
El Cortijo Santiago 27 B1
El Cristo, Vaso Regulador Mexico City 18 B1
El Duqqi Cairo 7 A2
El Encinar de los Reyes Madrid 17 A2
El Gezîra Cairo 7 A2
El Ghurîya Cairo 7 A2
El Gîza Cairo 7 A2
El Khadr Jerusalem 13 B1
El Khalîfa Cairo 7 A2
El Kôm el Ahmar Cairo 7 A2
El Ma'âdi Cairo 7 B2
El Matarîya Cairo 7 A2
El Mohandessin Cairo 7 A2
El Monte Los Angeles 16 B4
El Muqattam Cairo 7 A2
El Mûskî Cairo 7 A2
El Pardo Madrid 17 A1
El Portal Miami 18 A2
El Prat de Llobregat Barcelona 4 B1
El Qâhira Cairo 7 A2
El Qubba Cairo 7 A2
El Reloj Mexico City 18 C2
El Retiro Madrid 17 B1
El Salto Santiago 27 B2
El Sereno Los Angeles 16 B3
El Talibîya Cairo 7 B2
El Vergel Mexico City 18 C2
El Wâhli Cairo 7 A2
El Zamâlik Cairo 7 A2
El Zeitûn Cairo 7 A2
Elephanta Caves Mumbai 20 B2
Elephanta I. Mumbai 20 B2
Ellboda Stockholm 29 A3
Ellenor, L. Orlando 23 B2
Elliniko Olympic Complex Athens 2 B2
Ellis I. New York 22 B1
Elm Park London 15 A5
Elmers End London 15 B3
Elmhurst New York 22 B2
Elmstead London 15 B4
Elmwood Park Chicago 9 B2
Elmwood Park New York 22 A1
Elsdon Wellington 33 A1
Elsiesrivier Cape Town 8 A2
Elsternwick Melbourne 18 B2
Eltham London 15 B4
Elwood Melbourne 18 B1
Élysée Paris 24 A2
Elysian Park Los Angeles 16 B3
Emāmzādeh Sāleh Tehran 31 A2
Émerainville Paris 24 B4
Emeryville San Francisco 26 A3
Eminönü Istanbul 12 B1
Emirgan Istanbul 12 B2
Emmarentia Johannesburg 13 A2
Empire State Building New York 22 B2
Encantado Rio de Janeiro 25 B1
Encino Los Angeles 16 B2
Encino Res. Los Angeles 16 B1
Enebyberg Stockholm 29 A1
Enfield Sydney 29 B1
Engenho, I. do Rio de Janeiro 25 B2
Englewood Chicago 9 C3
Englewood New York 22 A2
Englewood Cliffs New York 22 A2
Enmore Sydney 29 B2
Enskede Stockholm 29 B2
Entrevias Madrid 17 B1
Epcot Orlando 23 B1
Epping Sydney 29 A1
Eregun Lagos 14 A2
Erenköy Istanbul 12 C2
Erith London 15 B5
Erlaa Vienna 32 B1
Ermington Sydney 29 A1
Ermita Manila 17 B1
Ershatou Canton 11 B2
Erskineville Sydney 29 B2
Erunkan Lagos 14 A2
Erzsébet Telep Budapest 7 B2
Eschenried Munich 21 A1
Esenler Istanbul 12 B1
Esher London 15 B1
Eskbank Edinburgh 11 B3
Esplugas Barcelona 4 A1
Esposizione Universale di Roma Rome 26 C1
Essendon Melbourne 18 A1
Essendon ✈ (MEB) Melbourne 18 A1
Essingen Stockholm 29 B1
Essling Vienna 32 A3
Est, Gare de l' Paris 24 A3
Estado, Parque do São Paulo 27 B2
Estrela, Basilica da Lisbon 16 A2
Etobicoke Toronto 31 B1
Etobicoke Cr. → Toronto 31 B1
Etterbeek Brussels 6 B2
Eung-am Seoul 27 B1
Eunpyeong Seoul 27 B1
Evanston Chicago 9 A2
Even Sapir Jerusalem 13 B1
Evere Brussels 6 A2
Everett Boston 6 A2
Evergreen Park Chicago 9 C2
Evin Tehran 31 A2
Ewu Lagos 14 A1
Exhibition Place Toronto 31 B2
Exposições, Palácio das Rio de Janeiro 25 B1
Eyüp Istanbul 12 B1
Ezeiza ✈ (EZE) Buenos Aires 7 B2

F

Fabour, Mt. Singapore 28 B2
Fælledparken Copenhagen 8 A3
Fågelön Stockholm 29 B1
Fagersjö Stockholm 29 B2
Fair Lawn New York 22 A1
Fairfax Washington 33 B2
Fairfax Station Washington 33 C2
Fairland Johannesburg 13 A1
Fairmilehead Edinburgh 11 B2
Fairmount Heights Washington 33 B4
Fairport Toronto 31 A4
Fairview New York 22 B2
Fairview, L. Orlando 23 A2
Falenty Warsaw 32 C1
Faliro Athens 2 B1
Faliro, Ormos Athens 2 B2
Falkenburg Berlin 5 A4
Falkenhagen Berlin 5 A1
Falkensee Berlin 5 A1
Falls Church Washington 33 B2
Falomo Lagos 14 B2
False Bay Cape Town 8 B2
Fangcun Canton 11 B2
Farahābād Tehran 31 A2
Farforovskaya St. Petersburg 27 B2
Farningham London 15 B5
Farsta Stockholm 29 B2
Fasanerie-Nord Munich 21 A2
Fasangarten Munich 21 B2
Fatih Istanbul 12 B1
Favoriten Vienna 32 B2
Fawkner Melbourne 18 A1
Fawkner Park Melbourne 18 B1
FedEx Stadium Washington 33 B4
Feijó Lisbon 16 B2
Feldkirchen Munich 21 B3
Feldmoching Munich 21 A2
Feltham London 15 B1
Fener Istanbul 12 B1
Fenerbahçe Istanbul 12 C2
Fengtai Beijing 4 C1
Ferencváros Budapest 7 B2
Ferihegy, Budapest ✈ (BUD) Budapest 7 B3
Ferndale Johannesburg 13 A2
Férolles-Attilly Paris 24 B4
Fichtenau Berlin 5 B5
Field Museum of Natural History Chicago 9 B3
Fields Corner Boston 6 B2
Fiera Camp Milan 19 B1
Figino Milan 19 B1
Fijir Baghdad 3 A2
Filadelfia Athens 2 A2
Fili-Mazilovo Moscow 19 B1
Filothei Athens 2 A2
Finchley London 15 A2
Fine Arts, Museum of Boston 6 A2
Finglas Dublin 10 A2
Finsbury London 15 A3
Finsbury Park London 15 A3
Fiorito Buenos Aires 7 C2
Firhouse Dublin 10 B2
Fischerhäuser Munich 21 A3
Fisher Island Miami 18 B2
Fishermans Bend Melbourne 18 A1
Fisherville Toronto 31 A2
Fisksätra Stockholm 29 B3
Fitzroy Gardens Melbourne 18 A1
Five Dock Sydney 29 B1
Fjellstrand Oslo 23 B2
Flamengo Rio de Janeiro 25 B1
Flamingo Orlando 23 B2
Flaminio Rome 26 B1
Flaskebekk Oslo 23 A2
Flatbush New York 22 C2
Flaten Stockholm 29 B2
Flatlands New York 22 C2
Flemington Racecourse Melbourne 18 A1
Flint Pk. Los Angeles 16 B3
Florence Los Angeles 16 C3
Florence Bloom Bird Sanctuary ⌂ Johannesburg 13 A2
Florentia Johannesburg 13 B2
Flores Buenos Aires 7 B2
Flores, Mercado de Mexico City 18 C2
Floresta Buenos Aires 7 B2
Florida Buenos Aires 7 B2
Florida Johannesburg 13 B1
Floridsdorf Vienna 32 A2
Flushing New York 22 B3
Flushing Meadows Corona Park New York 22 B2
Flysta Stockholm 29 A1
Fo Tan Hong Kong 12 A2
Föhrenhain Vienna 32 A2
Fontainebleau Johannesburg 13 A1
Fontenay-aux-Roses Paris 24 B2
Fontenay-le-Fleury Paris 24 B1
Fontenay-sous-Bois Paris 24 A3
Foots Cray London 15 B4
Footscray Melbourne 18 A1
Forbidden City = Imperial Palace Museum Beijing 4 B2
Forest Brussels 6 B1
Forest Gate London 15 A4
Forest Heights Washington 33 C3
Forest Hill London 15 B3
Forest Hill Toronto 31 A2
Forest Hills New York 22 C3
Forest Park Chicago 9 B2
Forest Park New York 22 B2
Forest View Chicago 9 C2
Forestville Washington 33 B4
Fornebu Oslo 23 A2
Foro Romano Rome 26 B1
Forstenried Munich 21 B1
Forstenrieder Park Munich 21 B1
Fort Mumbai 20 B1
Fort Dupont Park Washington 33 B4
Fort Foote Village Washington 33 C3
Fort Lee New York 22 A2
Forth, Firth of Edinburgh 11 A2
Forth Rail Bridge Edinburgh 11 A1
Forth Road Bridge Edinburgh 11 A1
Fót Budapest 7 A3
Fourqueux Paris 24 A1
Foxrock Dublin 10 B2
Franconia Washington 33 C3
Frank Lloyd Wright Home Chicago 9 B2
Frankel Singapore 28 B3
Franklin Park Boston 6 B2
Franklin Park Chicago 9 B1
Franklin Park Washington 33 B3
Franklin Res. Los Angeles 16 B2
Frauenkirche Munich 21 B2
Frederiksberg Copenhagen 8 A3
Frederiksdal Copenhagen 8 A2
Fredersdorf Berlin 5 A5
Freguesia Rio de Janeiro 25 A1
Friedrichshain, Volkspark Berlin 5 A3
Freiham Munich 21 B1
Freimann Munich 21 A2
French Quarter New Orleans 21 B2
Fresh Pond Boston 6 A2
Fresnes Paris 24 B2
Freudenau Vienna 32 A2
Friarstown Dublin 10 B1
Friedenau Berlin 5 B3
Friedrichsfelde Berlin 5 B4
Friedrichshagen Berlin 5 B4
Friedrichshain Berlin 5 A3
Friedrichslust Berlin 5 A5
Friherrs Helsinki 11 B1
Frilufts Museum Helsinki 11 B2
Frontón, I. Lima 14 B1
Frunze Moscow 19 B2
Fūchū Tokyo 30 A1
Fuencarral Madrid 17 B1
Fuenlabrada Madrid 17 C1
Fukagawa Tokyo 30 B3
Fukushima Osaka 23 A1
Fulham London 15 B2
Funabori Tokyo 30 A4
Fundão, I. do Rio de Janeiro 25 B1
Fünfhaus Vienna 32 A2
Furesø Copenhagen 8 A2
Fürth Munich 21 B2
Futago-tamagawaen Tokyo 30 B2
Fuxing Dao Shanghai 28 B2
Fuxing Park Shanghai 28 B2
Fuxinglu Beijing 4 B1

G

G. Ross Lord Park Toronto 31 A2
Gaebong Seoul 27 C1
Gage Park Chicago 9 C2
Gagny Paris 24 A4
Galata Istanbul 12 B1
Galata Tower Istanbul 12 B1
Galatsi Athens 2 A2
Galeão, Int. de ✈ (GIG) Rio de Janeiro 25 A1
Galyanovo Moscow 19 B3
Gambir Jakarta 12 A1
Gamboa Rio de Janeiro 25 B1
Gambolóita Milan 19 B2
Gamlebyen Oslo 23 A3
Gangdong Seoul 27 B2
Gangnam Seoul 27 B1
Gangseo Seoul 27 B1
Gangtou Canton 11 A1
Gangwei Canton 11 B2
Ganjiakou Beijing 4 B1
Ganshoren Brussels 6 A1
Gants Hill London 15 A4
Gaoqiao Shanghai 28 A2
Garbagnate Milanese Milan 19 A1
Garbatella Rome 26 B2
Garches Paris 24 A2
Garching Munich 21 A3
Garden City Cairo 7 A2
Garden Reach Calcutta 14 B1
Garder Oslo 23 B2
Garfield New York 22 A1
Garfield Park Chicago 9 B2
Gargareta Athens 2 B2
Garibong Seoul 27 C1
Garvanza Los Angeles 16 B3
Gåshaga Stockholm 29 A3
Gateway ⌂ New York 22 C2
Gateway of India Mumbai 20 B2
Gatow Berlin 5 B1
Gavà Barcelona 4 B1
Gávea Rio de Janeiro 25 B1
Gávea, Pedra da Rio de Janeiro 25 B1
Gazdagrét Budapest 7 B1
Gaziosmanpaşa Istanbul 12 B1
Gebel el Ahmar Cairo 7 A3
Gebel el Muqattam Cairo 7 A2
Gebel el Tura Cairo 7 B2
Geiselgasteig Munich 21 B2
General San Martín Buenos Aires 7 B1
Gennevilliers Paris 24 A2
Gentilly Paris 24 B3
Gentofte Copenhagen 8 A3
Genval Brussels 6 B2
George I. Hong Kong 12 B1
Georges River Bridge Sydney 29 C1
Georgetown Washington 33 B3
Georgia Dome Atlanta 3 B2
Gerasdorf bei Wien Vienna 32 A2
Gerberau Munich 21 A1
Gerli Buenos Aires 7 C2
Germiston Johannesburg 13 B2
Gern Munich 21 B2
Getafe Madrid 17 C1
Getty Center, The Los Angeles 16 B2
Geunjeong Seoul 27 C1
Geva Binyamin Jerusalem 13 A2
Geylang Serai Singapore 28 B3
Gharapuri Mumbai 20 B2
Gharb = Shahrak-e Qods Tehran 31 A2
Ghatkopar Mumbai 20 A2
Ghazipur Delhi 10 B2
Ghizri Karachi 13 B2
Ghizri Cr. → Karachi 13 B2
Ghonda Delhi 10 A2
Ghusuri Calcutta 14 B2
Gianicolense Rome 26 B1
Giant Wheel = Riesenrad Vienna 32 A2
Gibraltar Pt. Toronto 31 B2
Gidea Park London 15 A5
Giesing Munich 21 B2
Gilmerton Edinburgh 11 B3
Gilo Jerusalem 13 B2
Gimmersta Stockholm 29 B3
Ginza Tokyo 30 B3
Giv'at Ram Jerusalem 13 B2
Giv'at Ye'arim Jerusalem 13 B1
Giv'at Ze'ev Jerusalem 13 A2
Giv'on Jerusalem 13 A1
Giza = El Gîza Cairo 7 A2
Giza Pyramids Cairo 7 B1
Gjersjøen Oslo 23 B3
Gladesville Sydney 29 B1
Gladsakse Copenhagen 8 A2
Glasnevin Dublin 10 A2
Glassmanor Washington 33 C4
Glasthule Dublin 10 B3
Glen Iris Melbourne 18 B2
Glen Mar Park Washington 33 B3
Glen Rock New York 22 A1
Glen Rouge Park Toronto 31 A4
Glenarden Washington 33 B4
Glenasmole Reservoirs Dublin 10 B1
Glencorse Res. Edinburgh 11 B2
Glencullen Dublin 10 B3
Glendale Los Angeles 16 B3
Glendoo Mt. Dublin 10 B2
Glenhuntly Melbourne 18 B2
Glenside Wellington 33 B1
Glenview Chicago 9 A2
Glenview Countryside Chicago 9 A2
Glenvista Johannesburg 13 B2
Glifada Athens 2 B2
Glömsta Stockholm 29 B1
Glostrup Copenhagen 8 B2
Gogar Edinburgh 11 B2
Göktürk Istanbul 12 A1
Golabari Calcutta 14 B2
Golabki Warsaw 32 B1
Gold Coast Chicago 9 B3
Golden Gate San Francisco 26 B2
Golden Gate ⌂ San Francisco 26 A2
Golden Gate Bridge San Francisco 26 B2
Golden Gate Park San Francisco 26 B2
Golden Horn = Haliç Istanbul 12 B1
Golders Green London 15 A2
Golestan Palace Tehran 31 A2
Gollans Stream → Wellington 33 B2
Gonen Jerusalem 13 B2
Gongneung Seoul 27 B2
Goodmayes London 15 A4
Goodwood Cape Town 8 A2
Gopalpur Calcutta 14 B2
Gorce Wielkie Warsaw 32 B1
Gore Hill Sydney 29 A2

Gorelyy → St. Petersburg 27 A3
Gorgie Edinburgh 11 B2
Gorky Park Moscow 19 B2
Gosen Berlin 5 B5
Gosener kanal Berlin 5 B5
Gospel Oak London 15 A3
Gotanda Tokyo 30 B3
Goth Goli Mar Karachi 13 A2
Goth Sher Shah Karachi 13 A1
Gotha Orlando 23 A1
Gournay-sur-Marne Paris 24 A4
Governador, I. do Rio de Janeiro 25 A1
Governors I. New York 22 B1
Grabów Warsaw 32 C1
Grace, Mt. Wellington 33 B2
Gracefield Wellington 33 B2
Gracia Barcelona 4 A2
Gräfelfing Munich 21 B1
Gragoatá Rio de Janeiro 25 B2
Grand Bazaar = Kapali Carsi Istanbul 12 B1
Grand Central Station New York 22 B2
Grand Palace Bangkok 3 B1
Grande Place Brussels 6 A2
Grankulla = Kauniainen Helsinki 11 B1
Grant Park Chicago 9 B3
Granton Edinburgh 11 B2
Grassy Park Cape Town 8 B2
Gratosóglio Milan 19 B2
Gratzwalde Berlin 5 B5
Gravesend New York 22 C2
Grazhdanka St. Petersburg 27 B2
Great Falls Washington 33 B2
Great Falls Park Washington 33 B2
Great Western Forum Los Angeles 16 C2
Greco Milan 19 A2
Green I. Hong Kong 12 B1
Green Point Cape Town 8 A1
Greenbelt Washington 33 A4
Greenbelt Park Washington 33 B4
Greenfield Park Montreal 20 B3
Greenford London 15 A1
Greenhill London 15 A2
Greenhills Dublin 10 B1
Greenpoint New York 22 B2
Greenwich □ London 15 B3
Greenwich Observatory London 15 B3
Greenwich Village New York 22 B2
Greenwood Boston 6 A2
Grefsen Oslo 23 A3
Gresham Park Atlanta 3 B2
Greve Strand Copenhagen 8 B1
Griebnitzsee Berlin 5 B1
Griffith Park Los Angeles 16 B3
Grimbergen Brussels 6 A2
Grinzing Vienna 32 A2
Gröbenried Munich 21 A1
Grochów Warsaw 32 B2
Grodzisk Warsaw 32 B2
Groenendaal Brussels 6 B2
Grogol Petamburin Jakarta 12 A1
Gronsdorf Munich 21 B3
Grorud Oslo 23 A4
Gross-Glienicke Berlin 5 B1
Gross-Hadern Munich 21 B1
Gross-Lappen Munich 21 A2
Grosse Krampe Berlin 5 B5
Grosse Müggelsee Berlin 5 B4
Grosse Point Lighthouse Chicago 9 A2
Grossenzersdorf Vienna 32 A3
Grossenzersdorfer Arm → Vienna 32 A3
Grosser Biberhaufen Vienna 32 A2
Grosser Wannsee Berlin 5 B2
Grossfeld-Siedlung Vienna 32 A2
Grosshesselohe Munich 21 B2
Grossjedlersdorf Vienna 32 A2
Grossziethen Berlin 5 B3
Ground Zero New York 22 B1
Grove, The Chicago 9 A1
Grove Hall Boston 6 B2
Grove Park Atlanta 3 B2
Grove Park Hounslow, London 15 B2
Grove Park Lewisham, London 15 B4
Groveton Washington 33 C3
Grünau Berlin 5 B4
Grunewald Berlin 5 B2
Grünwald Munich 21 B2
Grünwalder Forst Munich 21 B2
Grymes Hill New York 22 C1
Guadalupe Manila 17 B2
Guadalupe, Basilica de Mexico City 18 B2
Guanabara, B. de Rio de Janeiro 25 B1
Guanabara, Jardim Rio de Janeiro 25 A1
Guanabara, Palácio da Rio de Janeiro 25 B1
Guang'anmen Beijing 4 B1
Guangqumen Beijing 4 B2
Guangzhou Canton 11 B2
Guanshuo Canton 11 B3
Gudö Stockholm 29 B3
Güell, Parque de Barcelona 4 A2
Guinardó Barcelona 4 A2
Gulbai Karachi 13 A1
Güngören Istanbul 12 B1
Gunnersbury London 15 B2
Gustavo A. Madero Mexico City 18 B2
Guttenberg New York 22 B1
Gutuyevskiy, Ostrov St. Petersburg 27 B1
Guyancourt Paris 24 B1
Gwanak Seoul 27 C1
Gwanaksan Seoul 27 C1
Gyál Budapest 7 B3
Gyáli-patak → Budapest 7 B2

H

Haaga Helsinki 11 B2
Haar Munich 21 B3
Habay Manila 17 C1
Hackbridge London 15 B3
Hackensack New York 22 A1
Hackensack → New York 22 B1
Hackney □ London 15 A3
Hackney Wick London 15 A3
Hadr, Wârrâq el Cairo 7 A2
Haga Stockholm 29 A2
Hagenbrunn Vienna 32 A2
Hägersten Stockholm 29 B1
Häggvik Stockholm 29 A1
Hagonoy Manila 17 B2
Hague Park Toronto 31 A3
Haidan Beijing 4 B1
Haidari Athens 2 A1
Haidarpur Delhi 10 A1
Haidhausen Munich 21 B2
Haight-Ashbury San Francisco 26 B2
Hainault London 15 A4
Haizhu Guangchang Canton 11 B2
Hakunila Helsinki 11 B3
Halandri Athens 2 A2
Halásztelek Budapest 7 B1
Haliç Istanbul 12 B1
Halim Perdana Kusuma Int. ✈ (HLP) Jakarta 12 B2
Halle Brussels 6 B1
Haltiala Helsinki 11 B2
Haltiavuori Helsinki 11 B2
Ham London 15 B2
Hämeenkylä Helsinki 11 B1
Hammarby Stockholm 29 B2
Hamme Brussels 6 A1
Hammersmith London 15 B2
Hampstead London 15 A2
Hampstead Montreal 20 B2
Hampstead Garden Suburb London 15 A2
Hampstead Heath London 15 A2
Hampton London 15 B1
Hampton Court Palace London 15 B1
Hampton Wick London 15 B2
Hamrā' Baghdad 3 B1
Hanala Helsinki 11 A3
Haneda Tokyo 30 B3
Haneda, Tōkyō ✈ (HND) Tokyo 30 B3
Hang Hau Hong Kong 12 B2
Hanging Gardens Mumbai 20 B1
Hanlon Toronto 31 B1
Hanwell London 15 A1
Hanworth London 15 B1
Haora Calcutta 14 B1
Hapeville Atlanta 3 C2
Happy Valley Hong Kong 12 B2
Har Adar Jerusalem 13 B1
Har Gilo Jerusalem 13 B2
Har Homa Jerusalem 13 B2
Har Nof Jerusalem 13 B2
Haren Brussels 6 A2
Hareskovby Copenhagen 8 A2
Haringey □ London 15 A3
Harjusuo Helsinki 11 B3
Harlaching Munich 21 B2
Harlaw Res. Edinburgh 11 B2
Harlem New York 22 B2
Harlesden London 15 A2
Harlington London 15 B1
Harmaja Helsinki 11 C2
Harmashatar hegy Budapest 7 A2
Harolds Cross Dublin 10 B2
Háros Budapest 7 B2
Harperrig Res. Edinburgh 11 B1
Harrow □ London 15 A1
Harrow on the Hill London 15 A1
Harrow School London 15 A1
Harrow Weald London 15 A1
Hartsfield-Atlanta Int. ✈ (ATL) Atlanta 3 C2
Harumi Tokyo 30 B3
Harvard University Boston 6 A2
Harwood Heights Chicago 9 B2
Ḩasanābād Tehran 31 A1
Hasbrouck Heights New York 22 A1
Haselhorst Berlin 5 A2
Hasköy Istanbul 12 B1
Hasle Oslo 23 B2
Haslum Oslo 23 A2
Hästhagen Stockholm 29 B2
Hataitai Wellington 33 B1
Hatch End London 15 A1
Hatiara Calcutta 14 B2
Hauketo Oslo 23 B3
Hauz Khas Delhi 10 B2
Havel → Berlin 5 A2
Havelkanal Berlin 5 A2
Havering □ London 15 A5
Havering-atte-Bower London 15 A5
Haworth New York 22 A2
Hawthorne Racecourse Chicago 9 C2
Hayes Bromley, London 15 B4
Hayes Hillingdon, London 15 A1
Hayes End London 15 A1
Hayford Chicago 9 C2
Haywards Wellington 33 A2
Heathfield Cape Town 8 B1
Heathrow, London ✈ (LHR) London 15 B1
Hebe Haven Hong Kong 12 A2
Hedong Canton 11 B2
Heidelberg Heights Melbourne 18 A2
Heidelberg West Melbourne 18 A2
Heidemühle Berlin 5 B5
Heideveld Cape Town 8 A2
Heiligensee Berlin 5 A2
Heiligenstadt Vienna 32 A2
Heinersdorf Berlin 5 A3
Hélène de Champlain, Parc ⌂ Montreal 20 A2
Helenelund Stockholm 29 A1
Heliopolis = Masr el Gedida Cairo 7 A2
Hellersdorf Berlin 5 A4
Hellerup Copenhagen 8 A3
Helmahof Vienna 32 A3
Helsingfors = Helsinki Helsinki 11 B2
Helsinki Helsinki 11 B2
Helsinki-Vantaa ✈ (HEL) Helsinki 11 B2
Hendon London 15 A2
Hengsha Canton 11 A2
Hennigsdorf Berlin 5 A2
Henryków Warsaw 32 B1
Henson Cr. → Washington 33 C4
Henttaa Helsinki 11 B1
Heping Park Shanghai 28 B2
Hepingli Beijing 4 B2
Herlev Copenhagen 8 A2
Herman Eckstein Park Johannesburg 13 A2
Hermannskogel Vienna 32 A1
Hermiston Edinburgh 11 B2
Hermitage and Winter Palace St. Petersburg 27 B1
Hermsdorf Berlin 5 A2
Hernals Vienna 32 A2
Herne Hill London 15 B3
Héroes de Churubusco Mexico City 18 B2
Herons, Î. aux Montreal 20 B2
Herstedøster Copenhagen 8 A2
Herttoniemi Helsinki 11 B3
Ḩeşārak Tehran 31 A1
Heston London 15 B1
Hetzendorf Vienna 32 B1
Hextable London 15 B5
Hialeah Miami 18 A1
Hiawassa, L. Orlando 23 A2
Hickory Hills Chicago 9 C2
Hiekkaharju Helsinki 11 B3
Hietaniemi Helsinki 11 B2
Hietzing Vienna 32 A1
Higashi Osaka 23 A2
Higashimurayama Tokyo 30 A1
Higashinari Osaka 23 A2
Higashisumiyoshi Osaka 23 B2
Higashiyodogawa Osaka 23 A1
High Park Toronto 31 B2
Highbury London 15 A3
Highgate London 15 A3
Highland Cr. → Toronto 31 A3
Highland Creek Toronto 31 A3
Highland Park Los Angeles 16 B3
Highlands North Johannesburg 13 A2
Hillcrest Heights Washington 33 C4
Hillend Edinburgh 11 A1
Hillingdon □ London 15 A1
Hillwood Washington 33 B3
Hilmîya Cairo 7 A2
Hin Keng Hong Kong 12 A2
Hirota Osaka 23 A1
Hirschstetten Vienna 32 A2
History Center Atlanta 3 B2
Hither Green London 15 B3
Hiyoshi Tokyo 30 B2
Hizma Jerusalem 13 B2
Hjortekær Copenhagen 8 A3
Hjortespring Copenhagen 8 A2
Hlubočepy Prague 25 B2
Ho Chung Hong Kong 12 A2
Ho Man Tin Hong Kong 12 B2
Hoboken New York 22 B1
Hobsons B. Melbourne 18 B1
Hochbrück Munich 21 A2
Hochelaga Montreal 20 A2
Hodgkins Chicago 9 C1
Hoegi Seoul 27 B2
Hoeilaart Brussels 6 B2
Hofburg Vienna 32 A2
Hoffman I. New York 22 C1
Hohenbrunn Munich 21 B3
Hohenschönhausen Berlin 5 A4
Holargos Athens 2 B2
Holborn London 15 A3
Holden, L. Orlando 23 B2
Holešovice Prague 25 B2
Holland Village Singapore 28 B2
Höllriegelskreuth Munich 21 B1
Hollywood Los Angeles 16 B3
Hollywood Bowl Los Angeles 16 B2
Holmenkollen Oslo 23 A3
Holmes Run Acres Washington 33 B2
Holmgård Stockholm 29 B1
Holmlia Oslo 23 B3
Holocaust Memorial Jerusalem 13 B2
Holyrood House, Palace of Edinburgh 11 B3
Holysloot Amsterdam 2 A3
Homerton London 15 A3
Hometown Chicago 9 C2
Hōnanchō Tokyo 30 A2
Honcho Tokyo 30 A3
Honden Tokyo 30 A4
Hondo, Rio → Los Angeles 16 B4
Hong Kong Hong Kong 12 B1
Hong Kong, Univ. of Hong Kong 12 B1
Hong Kong I. Hong Kong 12 B2
Hongje Seoul 27 B1
Hongjimun Tunnel Seoul 27 B1
Hongkou Shanghai 28 B1
Hongmiao Beijing 4 B2
Hongqiao Shanghai 28 B1
Honjyo Tokyo 30 A3
Honoré Mercier, Pont Montreal 20 B1
Hönow Berlin 5 A4
Hook London 15 B2
Horikiri Tokyo 30 A4
Horn Pond Boston 6 A1
Hornchurch London 15 A5
Horní Prague 25 B3
Horní Počernice Prague 25 B3
Hornsey London 15 A3
Horoměřice Prague 25 B1
Hortaleza Madrid 17 B2
Hosoyama Tokyo 30 B2
Hostafranchs Barcelona 4 A1
Hostivař Prague 25 B3
Houbětin Prague 25 B3
Houghton Johannesburg 13 B2
Houilles Paris 24 A2
Hounslow □ London 15 B1
Hout Bay Cape Town 8 B1
Hove Å → Copenhagen 8 A1
Hovedøya Oslo 23 A3
Høvik Oslo 23 A2
Hovorčovice Prague 25 A3
Howard Beach New York 22 C2
Howrah = Haora Calcutta 14 B1
Howth Dublin 10 A3
Howth Hd. Dublin 10 A3
Hōya Tokyo 30 A2
Hradčany Prague 25 B2
Huanghuagang Mausoleum Canton 11 B2
Huangpu Shanghai 28 B2
Huangpu Jiang → Shanghai 28 B1
Huangpu Park Shanghai 28 B1
Huangtugang Beijing 4 C1
Huascar Lima 14 A2
Huay Khwang Bangkok 3 B2
Huddinge Stockholm 29 B2
Huechuraba Santiago 27 B1
Huertas de San Beltran Barcelona 4 A1
Huizingen Brussels 6 B1
Humayun's Tomb Delhi 10 B2
Humber → Toronto 31 A1
Humber B. Toronto 31 B2
Humber Bay Toronto 31 B2
Humber Bay Park Toronto 31 B2
Humber College Toronto 31 B1
Humber Summit Toronto 31 A1
Humber Valley Village Toronto 31 A1
Humberlea Toronto 31 A1
Humberwood Park Toronto 31 A1
Humboldt Park Chicago 9 B2
Humera Madrid 17 B1
Hunayḑī Baghdad 3 B2
Hundige Copenhagen 8 B1
Hundige Strand Copenhagen 8 B2
Hung Hom Hong Kong 12 B2
Hunters Hill Sydney 29 B1
Hunters Pt. San Francisco 26 B2
Hunters Valley Washington 33 B2
Huntington Washington 33 C3
Huntington Park Los Angeles 16 C3
Hurīya Baghdad 3 A1
Hurstville Sydney 29 B1
Husan Jerusalem 13 B1
Husby Stockholm 29 A1
Husum Copenhagen 8 A2
Hutt → Wellington 33 B2
Hütteldorf Vienna 32 A1
Hüvösvölgy Budapest 7 A2
Huwon Secret Garden Seoul 27 B1
Hvalstad Oslo 23 A1
Hvalstrand Oslo 23 A2
Hvidovre Copenhagen 8 B2
Hwagok Seoul 27 B1
Hyattsville Washington 33 B4
Hyde Park Boston 6 B2
Hyde Park Chicago 9 C3
Hyde Park Johannesburg 13 A2
Hyde Park London 15 A2
Hyde Park Sydney 29 B2

I

Ibese Lagos 14 A2
Ibirapuera São Paulo 27 B1
Ibirapuera, Parque do São Paulo 27 B2
Icarai Rio de Janeiro 25 B2
Içerenköy Istanbul 12 C2
Ichgao Tokyo 30 B2
Ichigaya Tokyo 30 A3
Ichikawa Tokyo 30 A4
Ickenham London 15 A1
Iddo Lagos 14 B2
Idi-Oro Lagos 14 A2
Iganmu Lagos 14 B2
Igbobi Lagos 14 A2
Igbologun Lagos 14 B1
Igny Paris 24 B2
IJ, Het → Amsterdam 2 A2
IJ-meer Amsterdam 2 A3
Ijesa-Tedo Lagos 14 B1
Ijora Lagos 14 B2
Ikebe Tokyo 30 B2
Ikebukuro Tokyo 30 A3
Ikegami Tokyo 30 B3
Ikeja Lagos 14 A2
Ikeuchi Osaka 23 B2
Ikoyi Lagos 14 B2
Ikuata Lagos 14 B2
Ikuno Osaka 23 A2
Ikuta Tokyo 30 B2
Ila Oslo 23 A3
Ilford London 15 A4
Ilioupoli Athens 2 B2
Illinois at Chicago, University of Chicago 9 B3
Illinois Institute of Technology Chicago 9 B3
Ilpendam Amsterdam 2 A2
Ilsos → Athens 2 B2
Imbâbah Cairo 7 A2
Imielin Warsaw 32 C2
Imirim São Paulo 27 A2
Imitos Athens 2 B2
Imitos, Oros Athens 2 B2
Imperial Palace Museum Beijing 4 B2
Inagi Tokyo 30 B2
Inchcolm Edinburgh 11 A2
Inchicore Dublin 10 A1
Inchkeith Edinburgh 11 A3
Inchmickery Edinburgh 11 A2
Incirano Milan 19 A1
Independencia Lima 14 A2
Independencia Santiago 27 B2
India Gate Delhi 10 B2
Indian Creek Village Miami 18 A2
Indianópolis São Paulo 27 B2
Indira Gandhi Int. ✈ (DEL) Delhi 10 B1
Industria Johannesburg 13 B1
Ingierstrand Oslo 23 B3
Inglewood Los Angeles 16 C3
Ingliston Edinburgh 11 B1
Inhaúma Rio de Janeiro 25 B1
Inner Port Shelter Hong Kong 12 A2
Interlagos São Paulo 27 C1
Intramuros Manila 17 B1
Invalides Paris 24 A2
Inverkeithing Edinburgh 11 A1
Inzersdorf Vienna 32 B2
Ipanema Rio de Janeiro 25 B1
Ipiranga São Paulo 27 B2
Ipiranga → São Paulo 27 B2
Iponri Lagos 14 B2
Ireland's Eye Dublin 10 A3
Irving Park Chicago 9 B2
Isabel Rio de Janeiro 25 B1
Isagatedo Lagos 14 A1
Isar → Munich 21 A3
Ishbiliya Baghdad 3 A2
Ishøj Strand Copenhagen 8 B2
Island Bay Wellington 33 B1
Island Park Toronto 31 B2
Islev Copenhagen 8 A2
Isleworth London 15 B2
Islington Toronto 31 B1
Islington □ London 15 A3
Ismaning Munich 21 A3
Ismayloskiy Park Moscow 19 B3
Isolo Lagos 14 A1
Issy-les-Moulineaux Paris 24 B2
İstanbul Istanbul 12 C1
İstanbul Boğazı Istanbul 12 B2
Istinye Istanbul 12 B2
Itä Hakkila Helsinki 11 B3
Itaewon Seoul 27 B1
Itami Osaka 23 A1
Itanhanga Rio de Janeiro 25 B1
Ivanhoe Melbourne 18 A2
Ivry-sur-Seine Paris 24 B3
Ixelles Brussels 6 B2
Izmaylovo Moscow 19 B3
Iztacalco Mexico City 18 B2
Iztapalapa Mexico City 18 B2

J

Jaba Jerusalem 13 A2
Jacaré Rio de Janeiro 25 B1
Jackson Heights New York 22 B2
Jackson Park Chicago 9 C3
Jacques-Cartier Montreal 20 A3
Jacques-Cartier, Pont Montreal 20 A2
Jadavpur Calcutta 14 C2
Jade Buddha Temple Shanghai 28 B1
Jægersborg Copenhagen 8 A3
Jægersborg Dyrehave Copenhagen 8 A3
Jagadishpur Calcutta 14 B1
Jagatpur Delhi 10 A2
Jaguaré, Rib. do → São Paulo 27 B1
Jahangirpur Delhi 10 A2
Jakarta Jakarta 12 A2
Jakarta, Teluk Jakarta 12 A1
Jalan Kayu Singapore 28 A3
Jamaica B. New York 22 C3
Jamaica Plain Boston 6 B2
Jamakpuri Delhi 10 B1
Jamshīdīyeh Tehran 31 A2
Jamsil Seoul 27 B2
Jamwon Seoul 27 B2
Janki Warsaw 32 C1
Jannali Sydney 29 C1
Jaraguá São Paulo 27 A1
Jaraguá, Pico de São Paulo 27 A1
Jardim Paulista São Paulo 27 B1
Järvatältet Stockholm 29 A1
Jaskhar Mumbai 20 B2
Jatinegara Jakarta 12 B2
Javādīyeh Tehran 31 B2
Jaworowa Warsaw 32 C1
Jedlesee Vienna 32 A2
Jefferson Memorial Washington 33 B3
Jefferson Park Chicago 9 B2
Jegi Seoul 27 B2
Jelambar Jakarta 12 A1
Jelonki Warsaw 32 B1
Jerónimos, Mosteiro dos Lisbon 16 A1
Jersey City New York 22 B1
Jerusalem Jerusalem 13 B2
Jessamine, L. Orlando 23 B2
Jésus, Î. Montreal 20 A1
Jesús María Lima 14 B2
Jette Brussels 6 A1
Jey Tehran 31 B2
Jianguomen Beijing 4 B2
Jiangwan Shanghai 28 B1
Jib Jerusalem 13 A2
Jīhād Baghdad 3 B1
Jingan Shanghai 28 B1
Jinočany Prague 25 B1
Jinonice Prague 25 B2
Jiulong = Kowloon Hong Kong 12 B1
Jiyūgaoka Tokyo 30 B3
Jizā'ir Baghdad 3 B2
Jizīra Baghdad 3 B2
Joglo Jakarta 12 B1
Johannesburg Johannesburg 13 B2
Johannesburg, Univ. of Johannesburg 13 B2
Johannesburg Int. ✈ (GCJ) Johannesburg 13 A2
Johanneskirchen Munich 21 A2
Johannestift Berlin 5 A2
Johannisthal Berlin 5 B4
John F. Kennedy Nat. Historic Site ⌂ Boston 6 A2
John McLaren Park San Francisco 26 B2
Johnsonville Wellington 33 B1
Joinville-le-Pont Paris 24 B3
Joli-Bois Brussels 6 B2
Jollas Helsinki 11 B3
Jongmyo Royal Shrine Seoul 27 B1
Jongno Seoul 27 B1
Jonstrup Copenhagen 8 A2
Joppa Edinburgh 11 B3
Jorge Chavez, Int. ✈ (LIM) Lima 14 B2
Jorge Newbery ✈ Buenos Aires 7 B2
Józefa Pilsudskiego Park Warsaw 32 B1
Jōtō Osaka 23 A2
Jouy-en-Josas Paris 24 B2
Juan Anchorena Buenos Aires 7 A2
Juan González Romero Mexico City 18 A2
Juárez Int. ✈ (MEX) Mexico City 18 B2
Judeira Jerusalem 13 A2
Juhdum Jerusalem 13 B2
Juhu Mumbai 20 A2
Jūjā Tokyo 30 A3
Jukskeirivier → Johannesburg 13 A2
Julianów Warsaw 32 B2
Jung Seoul 27 B1
Jungfernheide, Volkspark Berlin 5 A2
Jungfernsee Berlin 5 B1
Junghwa Seoul 27 B2
Jungnang Seoul 27 B2
Jungnangcheon → Seoul 27 B1
Juniper Green Edinburgh 11 B2
Junk B. Hong Kong 12 B2
Jurong Singapore 28 B2
Jurong, Selat Singapore 28 B2
Jurong Industrial Estate Singapore 28 B1
Jurujuba, Enseada de Rio de Janeiro 25 B2
Jūsō Osaka 23 A1
Justice Chicago 9 C2
Jwalahari Delhi 10 B1

K

Kaapstad = Cape Town Cape Town 8 A1
Kabaty Warsaw 32 C2
Kadıköy Istanbul 12 C2
Kadoma Osaka 23 A2
Kafr 'Aqab Jerusalem 13 A2
Kâğıthane Istanbul 12 B1
Kâğıthane → Istanbul 12 B1
Kagran Vienna 32 A2
Kahnawake Montreal 20 B1
Kaimes Edinburgh 11 B2
Kaiserebersdorf Vienna 32 B2
Kaivoksela Helsinki 11 B2
Kalamaki Athens 2 B2
Kalbadevi Mumbai 20 B1
Kalipur Calcutta 14 A1
Kalithea Athens 2 B2
Kalkaji Delhi 10 B2
Kalvebod Fælled Copenhagen 8 B3
Kalveboderne Copenhagen 8 B3
Kamarhati Calcutta 14 A2
Kamata Tokyo 30 B3
Kameari Tokyo 30 A4
Kameido Tokyo 30 A4
Kami-Itabashi Tokyo 30 A3
Kamikitazawa Tokyo 30 B3
Kamitsuruma Tokyo 30 B1
Kamoshida Tokyo 30 B2
Kampong Landang Singapore 28 A3
Kampong Tanjong Penjuru Singapore 28 B2
Kampung Bali Jakarta 12 B1
Kanamori Tokyo 30 B1
Kanda Tokyo 30 A3
Kandilli Istanbul 12 B2
Kankurgachi Calcutta 14 B2
Kanlıca Istanbul 12 B2
Kanonerskiy, Ostrov St. Petersburg 27 B1
Kanzaki → Osaka 23 A1
Kapali Carsi Istanbul 12 B1
Kapellerfeld Vienna 32 A2
Káposztásmegyer Budapest 7 A2
Kapotnya Moscow 19 C3
Käppala Stockholm 29 A3
Kapuk Jakarta 12 A1
Käpylä Helsinki 11 B2
Karachi Karachi 13 A2
Karachi Int. ✈ (KHI) Karachi 13 A2
Karkh Baghdad 3 A2
Karlin Prague 25 B2
Karlsfeld Munich 21 A1
Karlshorst Berlin 5 B4
Karlův most Prague 25 B2
Karol Bagh Delhi 10 B2
Karolinenhof Berlin 5 B4
Karori Wellington 33 B1
Karow Berlin 5 A3
Karrādah Baghdad 3 B2
Kärsön Stockholm 29 B1
Kasai Tokyo 30 B4
Kasipur Calcutta 14 B2
Kastrup Copenhagen 8 B3
Kastrup, København ✈ (CPH) Copenhagen 8 B3
Kasuga Tokyo 30 A2
Kasuge Tokyo 30 A3
Kasumigaseki Tokyo 30 B3
Katong Singapore 28 B3
Katrineberg Stockholm 29 B1
Katsushika Tokyo 30 A4
Kau Pai Chau Hong Kong 12 B2
Kau Yi Chau Hong Kong 12 B1
Kaulsdorf Berlin 5 B4
Kauniainen Helsinki 11 B1
Kawasaki Tokyo 30 B3
Kawawa Tokyo 30 B2
Kawęczyn Warsaw 32 B2
Kayu Putih Jakarta 12 B2
Kbely Prague 25 B3
Kebayoran Baru Jakarta 12 B1
Kebayoran Lama Jakarta 12 B1
Kebon Jeruk Jakarta 12 B1
Kedar Jerusalem 13 B2
Kedoya Jakarta 12 B1
Keilor Melbourne 18 A1
Keilor North Melbourne 18 A1
Keimola Helsinki 11 A1
Kelapa Gading Jakarta 12 A2
Kelenföld Budapest 7 B2
Kelvin Johannesburg 13 A2
Kemang Jakarta 12 B1
Kemayoran Jakarta 12 B2
Kemerburgaz Istanbul 12 B1
Kempton Park Races London 15 B1
Kenilworth Cape Town 8 A1
Kennedy Town Hong Kong 12 B1
Kensal Green London 15 A2
Kensington Johannesburg 13 B2
Kensington London 15 A2
Kensington New York 22 C2
Kensington Sydney 29 B2
Kensington Palace London 15 A2
Kent Village Washington 33 B4
Kentish Town London 15 A3
Kenton London 15 A2
Kenwood House London 15 A3
Kepa Warsaw 32 B2
Keppel Harbour Singapore 28 B2
Kesariani Athens 2 B2
Kettering Washington 33 B5
Kew London 15 B2
Kew Melbourne 18 A2
Kew Gardens London 15 B2
Kew Gardens Toronto 31 B3
Key Biscayne Miami 18 B2
Khalīj Baghdad 3 B2
Khandallah Wellington 33 B1
Khansā' Baghdad 3 A2
Kharavli Mumbai 20 B2
Khefren Cairo 7 B1
Khichripur Delhi 10 B2
Khidirpur Calcutta 14 B1
Khimki-Khovrino Moscow 19 A2
Khirbet Batin Abu Lihyah Jerusalem 13 A1
Khirbet el-Misbah Jerusalem 13 A1
Khirbet Jub e-Rum Jerusalem 13 B2
Khlong San Bangkok 3 B2
Khlong Toey Bangkok 3 B2
Khorel Calcutta 14 A1
Khorosovo Moscow 19 B1
Kiamari Karachi 13 B1
Kierling Vienna 32 A1
Kierlingbach → Vienna 32 A1
Kifisos → Athens 2 B2
Kikuna Tokyo 30 B2
Kilbarrack Dublin 10 A3
Kilbirnie Wellington 33 B1
Kilburn London 15 A2
Killakee Dublin 10 B2
Killester Dublin 10 A2
Killiney Dublin 10 B3
Killiney B. Dublin 10 B3
Kilmacud Dublin 10 B2
Kilmainham Dublin 10 A2
Kilmainham Gaol Dublin 10 A2
Kilmashogue Mt. Dublin 10 B2
Kilmore Dublin 10 A2
Kilnamanagh Dublin 10 B1
Kilo Helsinki 11 B1
Kilokri Delhi 10 B2
Kiltiernan Dublin 10 B2
Kimmage Dublin 10 B2
Kindi Baghdad 3 B2
Kinghorn Edinburgh 11 A2
Kings Domain Melbourne 18 A1
Kings Forest = Kongelunden Copenhagen 8 B3
Kings Park Washington 33 C2
Kings Park West Washington 33 C2
Kingsbury London 15 A2
Kingsbury Melbourne 18 A2
Kingsford Sydney 29 B2
Kingsford Smith, Sydney ✈ (SYD) Sydney 29 B2
Kingston-upon-Thames □ London 15 B2
Kingston Vale London 15 B2
Kingsway Toronto 31 B1
Kinsaley Dublin 10 A2
Kipling Heights Toronto 31 A1
Kipseli Athens 2 B2
Kirchstockbach Munich 21 B3
Kirchtrudering Munich 21 B3
Kirikiri Lagos 14 B1
Kirke Værløse Copenhagen 8 A1
Kirkhill Edinburgh 11 B2
Kirkliston Edinburgh 11 B1
Kirknewton Edinburgh 11 B1
Kirov Palace of Culture St. Petersburg 27 B1
Kiryat Anavim Jerusalem 13 B1
Kiryat Ha Yovel Jerusalem 13 B1
Kısıklı Istanbul 12 B2
Kispest Budapest 7 B2
Kista Stockholm 29 A1
Kita Osaka 23 A2
Kita Tokyo 30 A3
Kitazawa Tokyo 30 B3
Kiu Tsiu Hong Kong 12 A2
Kivistö Helsinki 11 B2
Kızıltoprak Istanbul 12 C2
Kizuri Osaka 23 B2
Kjelsås Oslo 23 A3
Kladow Berlin 5 B1
Klampenborg Copenhagen 8 A3
Klaudyń Warsaw 32 B1
Klečany Prague 25 A2
Kledering Vienna 32 B2
Klein Jukskei → Johannesburg 13 A1
Kleinmachnow Berlin 5 B2
Kleinschönebeck Berlin 5 B5
Klemetsrud Oslo 23 A4
Klender Jakarta 12 A2
Klíčany Prague 25 A2
Klipriviersberg Nature Reserve Johannesburg 13 B2
Klosterneuburg Vienna 32 A1
Kőbánya Budapest 7 B2
Kobbegem Brussels 6 A1
København Copenhagen 8 A2
København ✈ (CPH) Copenhagen 8 B3
Kobylisy Prague 25 B2
Kobyłka Warsaw 32 A3
Kodaira Tokyo 30 A1
Kodanaka Tokyo 30 B2
Koekelberg Brussels 6 A1
Koganei Tokyo 30 A2
Kogarah Sydney 29 B1
Koivupää Helsinki 11 B2
Koja Jakarta 12 A2
Koja Utara Jakarta 12 A2
Kokhav Ya'akov Jerusalem 13 A2
Kokobunji Tokyo 30 A1
Kokobunji-Temple Tokyo 30 A4
Kolarängen Stockholm 29 B3
Kolbotn Oslo 23 B3
Kolkata Calcutta 14 B2
Kolkata Dum Dum Int. ✈ (CCU) Calcutta 14 B2
Kolkata Maidan Calcutta 14 B1
Koło Warsaw 32 B1
Kolokinthou Athens 2 B2
Kolomyagi St. Petersburg 27 A1
Kolonos Athens 2 B2
Kolsås Oslo 23 A2
Komae Tokyo 30 B2
Komagome Tokyo 30 A3
Komazawa Tokyo 30 B3
Kona Calcutta 14 B1
Konala Helsinki 11 B2
Kondli Delhi 10 B2
Kongelunden Copenhagen 8 B3
Kongens Lyngby Copenhagen 8 A3
Kongo Helsinki 11 A1
Konnagar Calcutta 14 A2
Konohana Osaka 23 A1
Konradshöhe Berlin 5 A2
Kopanina Prague 25 B1
Koparkhairna Mumbai 20 A2
Köpenick Berlin 5 B4
Korangi Karachi 13 B2
Koremasa Tokyo 30 B1
Koridalos Athens 2 B1
Korokoro Wellington 33 B2
Korokoro Stream → Wellington 33 B2
Kosino Moscow 19 B4
Kosugi Tokyo 30 B2
Kota Jakarta 12 A1
Kōtō Tokyo 30 A3
Kotrung Calcutta 14 A2
Kouponia Athens 2 B2
Kowloon Hong Kong 12 B1
Kowloon Peak Hong Kong 12 A2
Kowloon Res. Hong Kong 12 A1
Kowloon Tong Hong Kong 12 A2
Kraainem Brussels 6 A2
Krailling Munich 21 B1
Krampnitz Berlin 5 B1
Krampnitzsee Berlin 5 B1
Kranji, Sungei → Singapore 28 A2
Kranji Industrial Estate Singapore 28 A2
Krasno-Presnenskaya Moscow 19 B2
Krč Prague 25 B2
Kremlin Moscow 19 B2
Krestovskiye, Ostrov St. Petersburg 27 B1
Kreuzberg Berlin 5 A3
Kritzendorf Vienna 32 A1
Krumme Lanke Berlin 5 B2
Krummensee Berlin 5 A5
Krung Thep = Bangkok Bangkok 3 B2
Krusboda Stockholm 29 B3
Kuangchou = Guangzhou Canton 11 B2
Küçükköy Istanbul 12 B1
Küçüksu Istanbul 12 B2
Kudrovo St. Petersburg 27 B3
Kulosaari Helsinki 11 B3
Kumla Stockholm 29 B3
Kungens kurva Stockholm 29 B1
Kungliga Slottet Stockholm 29 B2
Kungshatt Stockholm 29 B1
Kungsholmen Stockholm 29 A2
Kuningan Jakarta 12 B1
Kunitachi Tokyo 30 A1
Kunming Hu Beijing 4 B1
Kunratice Prague 25 B2
Kupchino St. Petersburg 27 B2
Kurbağalı → Istanbul 12 C2
Kurihara Tokyo 30 A2
Kurla Mumbai 20 A2
Kurmuri Mumbai 20 A2
Kurume Tokyo 30 A2
Kuryanovo Moscow 19 C3
Kuskovo Moscow 19 B3
Kustia Calcutta 14 B2
Kuzguncuk Istanbul 12 B2
Kuzyminki Moscow 19 B3
Kwai Chung Hong Kong 12 A1
Kwangchow = Guangzhou Canton 11 B2
Kwun Tong Hong Kong 12 B2
Kyje Prague 25 B3
Kyūhōji Osaka 23 B2

L

La Blanca Santiago 27 C2
La Boca Buenos Aires 7 B2
La Bretèche Paris 24 A1
La Campiña Lima 14 C2
La Celle-St-Cloud Paris 24 A1
La Cisterna Santiago 27 C2
La Courneuve Paris 24 A3
La Dehesa Santiago 27 B2
La Encantada Lima 14 C2
La Estación Madrid 17 B1
La Floresta Barcelona 4 A1
La Florida Santiago 27 C2
La Fortuna Madrid 17 B1
La Fransa Barcelona 4 A1
La Garenne-Colombes Paris 24 A2
La Giustiniana Rome 26 B1
La Grange Chicago 9 C1
La Grange Park Chicago 9 C1
La Granja Santiago 27 C2
La Guardia, New York ✈ (LGA) New York 22 B2
La Hulpe Brussels 6 B2
La Llacuna Barcelona 4 A2
La Loma Mexico City 18 A1
La Lucila Buenos Aires 7 B2
La Maladrerie Paris 24 A1
La Milla, Cerro Lima 14 B2
La Monachina Rome 26 B1
La Moraleja Madrid 17 A2
La Nopalera Mexico City 18 C2
La Paternal Buenos Aires 7 B2
La Perla Lima 14 B2
La Perouse Sydney 29 B2
La Pineda Barcelona 4 B1
La Pisana Rome 26 B1
La Prairie Montreal 20 B3
La Punta Lima 14 B1
La Puntigala Barcelona 4 A2
La Queue-en-Brie Paris 24 B4
La Reina Santiago 27 B2
La Ribera Barcelona 4 A1
La Sagrera Barcelona 4 A2
La Salada Buenos Aires 7 C2
La Scala Milan 19 B2
La Storta Rome 26 A1
La Taxonera Barcelona 4 A2
La Victoria Lima 14 B2
Laajalahti Helsinki 11 B1
Laajasalo Helsinki 11 B3
Laaksolahti Helsinki 11 B1
Lablâba, W. el → Cairo 7 A2
Lachine Montreal 20 B1
Lachine, Canal de Montreal 20 B2
Lad Phrao Bangkok 3 B2
Ladera Heights Los Angeles 16 C2
Ládví Prague 25 B2
Łady Warsaw 32 C1
Lafontaine, Parc Montreal 20 A2
Lagoa Rio de Janeiro 25 B1
Lagos Lagos 14 B2
Lagos Harbour Lagos 14 B2
Lagos-Ikeja ✈ (LOS) Lagos 14 A1
Lagos Island Lagos 14 B2
Lagos Lagoon Lagos 14 B2
Laguna de B. Manila 17 C2
Laim Munich 21 B2
Lainate Milan 19 A1
Lainz Vienna 32 B1
Lake Buena Vista Orlando 23 B1
Lake Cain Hills Orlando 23 B2
Lake Fairfax Park Washington 33 B2
Lakemba Sydney 29 B1
Lakeside Cape Town 8 B1
Lakeside Johannesburg 13 A2
Lakeview Chicago 9 B3
Lakewood Park Atlanta 3 B2
Lakhtinskiy St. Petersburg 27 B1
Lakhtinskiy Razliv, Oz. St. Petersburg 27 B1
Lakshmanpur Calcutta 14 B1
Laksi Bangkok 3 A2
Lal Qila Delhi 10 B2
Lam Tin Hong Kong 12 B2
Lambert Oslo 23 A3
Lambeth □ London 15 B3
Lambrate Milan 19 B2
Lambro, Parco Milan 19 B2
Lambton Mills Toronto 31 B1
Lamma I. Hong Kong 12 B1
Landover Hills Washington 33 B4
Landsmeer Amsterdam 2 A2
Landstrasse Vienna 32 A2
Landwehr kanal Berlin 5 B3
Lane Cove Sydney 29 A1
Lane Cove National Park △ Sydney 29 A1
Langa Cape Town 8 A2
Langenzersdorf Vienna 32 A2
Langer See Berlin 5 B4
Langley Washington 33 B2
Langley Park Washington 33 B4
Langwald Munich 21 A1
Lanham Washington 33 B4
Lankwitz Berlin 5 B3
L'Annunziatella Rome 26 C2
Lansdowne Cape Town 8 A2
Lansing Toronto 31 A2
Lanus Buenos Aires 7 C2
Lapa Rio de Janeiro 25 B1
Laranjeiras Rio de Janeiro 25 B1
Las Warsaw 32 B2
Las Corts Barcelona 4 A1
Las Kabacki Warsaw 32 C2
Las Pinas Manila 17 C1
Las Rejas Santiago 27 B1
Lasalle Montreal 20 B2
LaSalle Street Station Chicago 9 B3
Lasek Bielański Warsaw 32 B1
Lasek Na Kole Warsaw 32 B1
Laski Warsaw 32 B1
Latina Madrid 17 B1
Lauttasaari Helsinki 11 C2
Laval-des-Rapides Montreal 20 A1
Lavīzān Tehran 31 A2
Lavradio Lisbon 16 A2
Lawndale Chicago 9 B2
Lawne L. Orlando 23 A2
Lawrence Heights Toronto 31 A2
Layari Karachi 13 A2
Layari → Karachi 13 A1
Łazienkowski Park Warsaw 32 B2
Le Blanc-Mesnil Paris 24 A3
Le Bourget Paris 24 A3
Le Chenoi Brussels 6 B2
Le Chesnay Paris 24 B1
Le Christ de Saclay Paris 24 B2
Le Kremlin-Bicêtre Paris 24 B3
Le Mesnil-le-Roi Paris 24 A1
Le Pecq Paris 24 A1
Le Perreux Paris 24 A3
Le Pin Paris 24 A4
Le Plessis-Robinson Paris 24 B2
Le Plessis-Trévise Paris 24 B4
Le Port-Marly Paris 24 A1
Le Pré-St-Gervais Paris 24 A3
Le Raincy Paris 24 A4
Le Vésinet Paris 24 A1
Lea Bridge London 15 A3
Leaside Toronto 31 A2
Leblon Rio de Janeiro 25 B1
Lee London 15 B4
Leganés Madrid 17 C1
Legazpi Madrid 17 B1

Lehtisaari Helsinki 11 B2
Lei Yue Mun Hong Kong 12 B2
Leião Lisbon 16 A1
Leichhardt Sydney 29 B1
Leith Edinburgh 11 B3
Leme Rio de Janeiro 25 B1
Lemoyne Montreal 20 B3
Lenin Moscow 19 B2
Lenino Moscow 19 C2
Leninskiye Gory Moscow 19 B2
Lennox Los Angeles 16 C2
Leonia New York 22 A2
Leopardstown Dublin 10 B2
Leopoldau Vienna 32 A2
Leopoldsdorf Vienna 32 B2
Leopoldstadt Vienna 32 A2
Leportovo Moscow 19 B3
Leppävaara Helsinki 11 B1
Les Lilas Paris 24 A3
Les Loges-en-Josas Paris 24 B1
Les Pavillons-sous-Bois Paris 24 A4
Lésigny Paris 24 B4
Lesnozavodskaya St. Petersburg 27 B2
Lester B. Pearson Int., Toronto ✕ (YYZ) Toronto 31 A1
L'Étang-la-Ville Paris 24 A1
Letňany Prague 25 B3
Letopolis = Ausîm Cairo 7 A1
Levallois-Perret Paris 24 A2
Levent Istanbul 12 B2
Lewisdale Washington 33 B4
Lewisham □ London 15 B3
Lexington Boston 6 A1
Leyton London 15 A3
Leytonstone London 15 A4
L'Haÿ-les-Roses Paris 24 B3
L'Hospitalet de Llobregat Barcelona 4 A1
Lhotka Prague 25 B2
Liangshui He → Beijing 4 C2
Lianhua Chi Beijing 4 B1
Lianhua He → Beijing 4 B1
Libčice nad Vltavou Prague 25 A2
Libeň Prague 25 B2
Liberdade São Paulo 27 B2
Liberton Edinburgh 11 B3
Liberty I. New York 22 B1
Liberty Osaka Museum Osaka 23 B1
Liberty State Park ⌂ New York 22 B1
Libeznice Prague 25 A2
Libuš Prague 25 B2
Lichiao Canton 11 B2
Lichtenburg Berlin 5 A4
Lichterfelde Berlin 5 B2
Lidingö Stockholm 29 A2
Lieshi Lingyuan Canton 11 B2
Liesing Vienna 32 B1
Liesing → Vienna 32 B2
Ligovo St. Petersburg 27 C1
Lijordet Oslo 23 A2
Likhoborka → Moscow 19 A2
Lilla Värtan Stockholm 29 A3
Lille Værløse Copenhagen 8 A2
Liluah Calcutta 14 B1
Lim Chu Kang Singapore 28 A2
Lima Lima 14 B2
Limbiate Milan 19 A1
Limehouse London 15 A3
Limeil-Brévannes Paris 24 B3
Linate, Milano ✕ (LIN) Milan 19 B2
Linbropark Johannesburg 13 A2
Lincoln Center for Performing Arts New York 22 B2
Lincoln Heights Los Angeles 16 B3
Lincoln Memorial Washington 33 B3
Lincoln Park Chicago 9 B3
Lincoln Park New York 22 B1
Lincoln Park San Francisco 26 B1
Lincoln Park Zoo Chicago 9 B3
Lincolnwood Chicago 9 A2
Linda-a-Pastora Lisbon 16 A1
Linden Johannesburg 13 A2
Linden Wellington 33 A1
Lindenberg Berlin 5 A4
Lindøya Oslo 23 A3
Liniers Buenos Aires 7 B1
Linkebeek Brussels 6 B2
Linksfield Johannesburg 13 A2
Linmeyer Johannesburg 13 B2
Linna Helsinki 11 A2
Lintuvaara Helsinki 11 B1
Lion Rock Country Park ⌂ Hong Kong 12 A2
Lion's Head Cape Town 8 A1
Lioumi Athens 2 B2
Lisboa Lisbon 16 A2
Lisboa ✕ (LIS) Lisbon 16 A2
Lisbon = Lisboa Lisbon 16 A2
Lishui Canton 11 A1
Little B. Sydney 29 B2
Little Calumet → Chicago 9 D3
Little Ferry New York 22 A1
Little Lake Conway Orlando 23 B2
Little Red School House Nature Center Chicago 9 C1
Little Rouge → Toronto 31 A4
Liuhang Shanghai 28 A1
Liurong Temple Canton 11 B2
Livry-Gargan Paris 24 A4
Ljan Oslo 23 A3
Llano de Can Gineu Barcelona 4 A2
Lo Aranguiz Santiago 27 B2
Lo Boza Santiago 27 B1
Lo Chau Hong Kong 12 B2
Lo Chau Pak Mai Hong Kong 12 B2
Lo Espejo Santiago 27 C1
Lo Hermida Santiago 27 B2
Lo Prado Santiago 27 B1
Lo So Shing Hong Kong 12 B1
Lo Wai Hong Kong 12 A1
Loanhead Edinburgh 11 B3
Lobau Vienna 32 A3
Lobos, Pt. San Francisco 26 B1
Locham Munich 21 B1
Lochkov Prague 25 B2
Lockhausen Munich 21 A1
Lodi New York 22 A1
Lodi Estate Delhi 10 B2
Logan Int., Boston ✕ (BOS) Boston 6 A2
Logan Square Chicago 9 B2
Lognes-Émerainville ✕ Paris 24 B4
Löhme Berlin 5 A5
Lolokhet Karachi 13 A2
Lomas Chapultepec Mexico City 18 B1
Lomas de San Angel Inn Mexico City 18 B1
Lombardy East Johannesburg 13 A2
Lomianki Warsaw 32 A1
Lomus Reforma Mexico City 18 B1
London London 15 B3
London City ✕ (LCY) London 15 A4
London Heathrow ✕ (LHR) London 15 B1
London Zoo London 15 A3
Long B. Sydney 29 B2
Long Branch Toronto 31 B1
Long Brook → Washington 33 C2
Long Ditton London 15 B2
Long Island City New York 22 B2
Longchamp, Hippodrome de Paris 24 A2
Longhua Pagoda Shanghai 28 B1
Longhua Park Shanghai 28 B1
Longjohn Slough Chicago 9 C1
Longtan Hu → Beijing 4 B2
Longue-Pointe Montreal 20 A2
Longueuil Montreal 20 A3
Longueuil-St-Hubert = St-Hubert Montreal 20 B3
Loni Delhi 10 A2
Loop, The Chicago 9 B3
Lord's Cricket Ground London 15 A2
Loreto Milan 19 B2
Los Angeles Los Angeles 16 B3
Los Angeles Int. ✕ (LAX) Los Angeles 16 C2
Los Cerrillos ✕ (ULC) Santiago 27 B1
Los Nietos Los Angeles 16 C4
Los Olivos Lima 14 A2
Los Reyes Mexico City 18 B2
Losiny Ostrov △ Moscow 19 A3
Lot Brussels 6 B1
Lotus River Cape Town 8 B2
Lotus Temple Delhi 10 B2
Loughlinstown Dublin 10 B3
Louise, L. Orlando 23 B1
Louisiana Superdome New Orleans 21 B2
Loures Lisbon 16 A1
Louveciennes Paris 24 A1
Louvre, Musée du Paris 24 A3
Lower B. New York 22 C1
Lower Hutt Wellington 33 B2
Lower New York B. = Lower B. New York 22 C1
Lower Shing Mun Res. Hong Kong 12 A1
Lowry Bay Wellington 33 B2
Loyola University Chicago 9 B3
Lu Xun, Tomb of Shanghai 28 B1
Lu Xun Park Shanghai 28 B1
Lübars Berlin 5 A3
Lucy, L. Orlando 23 A2
Ludwigsfeld Munich 21 A1
Luhu Canton 11 B2
Lumiar Lisbon 16 A2
Lundtofte Copenhagen 8 A3
Lung Mei Hong Kong 12 A2
Luojiang Canton 11 B2
Lustheim Munich 21 A2
Luwan Shanghai 28 B1
Luzhniki Sports Centre Moscow 19 B2
Lyndhurst New York 22 B1
Lynn Woods Res. Boston 6 A2
Lyon, Gare de Paris 24 A3
Lyons Chicago 9 C2
Lysaker Oslo 23 A2
Lysakerselva → Oslo 23 A2
Lysolaje Prague 25 B2
Lyublino Moscow 19 B3

M

Ma Nam Wat Hong Kong 12 A2
Ma On Shan Country Park ⌂ Hong Kong 12 A2
Ma'ale Adumim Jerusalem 13 B2
Ma'ale Ha Khamisha Jerusalem 13 B1
Ma'ale Mikhmas Jerusalem 13 A2
Maantiekylä Helsinki 11 A3
Maarifa Baghdad 3 B2
Mabato Pt. Manila 17 C2
Mabel, L. Orlando 23 B1
Macaco, Morro do Rio de Janeiro 25 B2
McCook Chicago 9 C2
McGill University Montreal 20 A2
Machelen Brussels 6 A2
Machida Tokyo 30 B1
Maciolki Warsaw 32 B2
McKerrow, Mt. Wellington 33 B2
McKinley Park Chicago 9 C2
McLean Washington 33 B2
Macopocho → Santiago 27 B1
MacRitchie Res. Singapore 28 A2
Macul Santiago 27 C2
Madhudaha Calcutta 14 B2
Madhyamgram Calcutta 14 A2
Madín Mexico City 18 A1
Madín, L. Mexico City 18 A1
Madinah Al Mansūr Baghdad 3 B2
Mādinet Nasr Cairo 7 A2
Madrid Madrid 17 B1
Madrid Barajas ✕ (MAD) Madrid 17 B2
Madrona Barcelona 4 A1
Maesawa Tokyo 30 A2
Magdalena Lima 14 B2
Magdalena Contreras Mexico City 18 C1
Maghreb Baghdad 3 A2
Maginu Tokyo 30 B2
Magliana Rome 26 B1
Magny-les-Hameaux Paris 24 B1
Maheshtala Calcutta 14 C1
Mahim Mumbai 20 A2
Mahim B. Mumbai 20 A1
Mahlsdorf Berlin 5 A4
Mahmoodabad Karachi 13 A2
Mahrauli Delhi 10 B2
Mahul Mumbai 20 A2
Maida Vale London 15 A2
Maidstone Melbourne 18 A1
Maipú Santiago 27 B1
Maisonneuve, Parc Montreal 20 A2
Maisons-Alfort Paris 24 B3
Maisons-Laffitte Paris 24 A1
Maissoneuve Montreal 20 A2
Maitland Cape Town 8 A1
Makasar Jakarta 12 A2
Makati Manila 17 B2
Mäkiniitty Helsinki 11 A2
Malá Strana Prague 25 B2
Malabar Sydney 29 B2
Malabar Hill Mumbai 20 B1
Malabar Pt. Mumbai 20 B1
Malabon Manila 17 B1
Malacañang Palace Manila 17 B1
Malahide Dublin 10 A3
Malakoff Paris 24 B2
Mälarhöjden Stockholm 29 B1
Malate Manila 17 B1
Malaya Neva St. Petersburg 27 B1
Malaya Okhta St. Petersburg 27 B2
Malchow Berlin 5 A3
Malden Boston 6 A2
Malden London 15 B2
Maleizen Brussels 6 B3
Malešice Prague 25 B3
Malir → Karachi 13 B2
Malleny Mills Edinburgh 11 B2
Malmi Helsinki 11 B2
Malmøya Oslo 23 A3
Målöv Copenhagen 8 A2
Malton Toronto 31 A1
Malvern Johannesburg 13 B2
Malvern Melbourne 18 B2
Malvern Toronto 31 A3
Mampang Prapatan Jakarta 12 B1
Mampukuji Tokyo 30 B2
Man Budrukh Mumbai 20 A2
Man Khurd Mumbai 20 A2
Manakhat Jerusalem 13 B2
Mandaluyong Manila 17 B2
Mandaoli Delhi 10 B2
Mandaqui → São Paulo 27 A2
Mandoli Delhi 10 A2
Mandvi Mumbai 20 B2
Manenberg Cape Town 8 A2
Mang Kung Uk Hong Kong 12 B2
Mang-won Seoul 27 B1
Mangolpuri Delhi 10 A1
Manguinhos ✕ Rio de Janeiro 25 B1
Manhattan New York 22 B2
Manhattan Beach New York 22 C2
Manila Manila 17 B1
Manila Ninoy Aquino Int. ✕ (MNL) Manila 17 B2
Mankkaa Helsinki 11 B1
Manly Sydney 29 A2
Mann, L. Orlando 23 A2
Mann's Chinese Theatre Los Angeles 16 B2
Mannswörth Vienna 32 B3
Manor Park London 15 A4
Manor Park Wellington 33 A2
Manora Karachi 13 B1
Manora Pt. Karachi 13 B1
Manquehue, Cerro Santiago 27 B2
Manzanares, Canal de Madrid 17 C2
Mapo Seoul 27 B1
Maracanã Rio de Janeiro 25 B1
Maraoli Mumbai 20 A2
Marcelin Warsaw 32 B1
Mareil-Marly Paris 24 A1
Margareten Vienna 32 A2
Maria Vienna 32 A2
Maridalen Oslo 23 A3
Maridalsvatnet Oslo 23 A3
Mariendorf Berlin 5 B3
Marienfelde Berlin 5 B3
Marikina Manila 17 B2
Marikina → Manila 17 B2
Marin City San Francisco 26 A1
Marin Pen. San Francisco 26 A1
Marina del Rey Los Angeles 16 C2
Marino Dublin 10 A2
Marisco, Ponta do Rio de Janeiro 25 C1
Markham Toronto 31 A2
Marki Warsaw 32 B2
Markland Wood Toronto 31 B1
Marly, Forêt de Paris 24 A1
Marly-le-Roi Paris 24 A1
Marne-la-Vallée Paris 24 A4
Marolles-en-Brie Paris 24 B4
Maroubra Sydney 29 B2
Marquette Park Chicago 9 C2
Marrickville Sydney 29 B1
Marsfield Sydney 29 A1
Marsha, L. Orlando 23 B2
Marte, Campo de São Paulo 27 B2
Martesana, Naviglio della Milan 19 A2
Martin Luther King Nat. Historic Site ⌂ Atlanta 3 B2
Martinez Buenos Aires 7 A1
Martinkylä Helsinki 11 B2
Martinsried Munich 21 B1
Maruko Tokyo 30 B3
Maryino Moscow 19 B3
Maryland Singapore 28 B2
Marymont Warsaw 32 B1
Marysin Wawerski Warsaw 32 B2
Marzahn Berlin 5 A4
Mascot Sydney 29 B2
Masmo Stockholm 29 B1
Maspeth New York 22 B2
Masr el Gedida Cairo 7 A2
Masr el Qadima Cairo 7 A2
Massachusetts Inst. of Tech. Boston 6 A2
Massamá Lisbon 16 A1
Massey → Toronto 31 A3
Massy Paris 24 B2
Mata Jerusalem 13 B1
Matihutong Beijing 4 B1
Matinha Lisbon 16 A2
Matramam Jakarta 12 B2
Matsubara Osaka 23 B2
Mattapan Boston 6 B2
Mátyásföld Budapest 7 A3
Mau Tso Ngam Hong Kong 12 A2
Mauer Vienna 32 B1
Mauripur Karachi 13 A1
Maxhof Munich 21 B1
Mayfair Johannesburg 13 B2
Mayor, Plaza Madrid 17 B1
Maywood Chicago 9 B1
Maywood Los Angeles 16 C3
Maywood New York 22 A1
Maywood Park Race Track Chicago 9 B1
Mazagaon Mumbai 20 B2
Meadowbank Park Sydney 29 A1
Měcholupy Prague 25 B3
Měčice Prague 25 A3
Mecidiyeköy Istanbul 12 B2
Medford Boston 6 A2
Mediodia Madrid 17 B2
Meguro Tokyo 30 B3
Meguro → Tokyo 30 B3
Mehpalpur Delhi 10 B1
Mehrābād ✕ (THR) Tehran 31 A1
Mehram Nagar Delhi 10 B1
Mehrow Berlin 5 A4
Meidling Vienna 32 A2
Méier Rio de Janeiro 25 B1
Meiji Shrine Tokyo 30 A3
Meise Brussels 6 A1
Mejiro Tokyo 30 A3
Melbourne Melbourne 18 A1
Melbourne ✕ (MEL) Melbourne 18 A1
Melkki Helsinki 11 C2
Mellunkylä Helsinki 11 B3
Mellunmäki Helsinki 11 B3
Melrose Boston 6 A2
Melrose New York 22 B2
Melrose Park Chicago 9 B1
Melsbroek Brussels 6 A2
Melville Johannesburg 13 B2
Menteng Jakarta 12 B1
Mérantaise → Paris 24 B1
Mercamadrid Madrid 17 B2
Merced, L. San Francisco 26 B2
Meredale Johannesburg 13 B1
Merlimau, Pulau Singapore 28 B2
Merri Cr. → Melbourne 18 A1
Merrion Dublin 10 B2
Merrionette Park Chicago 9 C2
Merton □ London 15 B2
Mesgarābād Tehran 31 B3
Messe Vienna 32 A2
Metanópoli Milan 19 B2
Metro-Dade Cultural Centre Miami 18 B2
Metro Toronto Zoo Toronto 31 A3
Metropolitan Museum of Art New York 22 B2
Meudon Paris 24 B2
Mevaseret Tsiyon Jerusalem 13 B1
Mevo Beitar Jerusalem 13 B1
México Mexico City 18 B2
México, Ciudad de Mexico City 18 B2
Mexico City Int. ✕ (MEX) Mexico City 18 B2
Meyersdal Johannesburg 13 B2
Mezzate Milan 19 B2
Miadong Seoul 27 B2
Miami Miami 18 B2
Miami Beach Miami 18 B2
Miami Canal Miami 18 A1
Miami Int. ✕ (MIA) Miami 18 B1
Miami Shores Miami 18 A2
Miami Springs Miami 18 B1
Miasto Warsaw 32 B2
Michalowice Warsaw 32 B1
Michle Prague 25 B2
Middle Harbour Sydney 29 A2
Middle Hd. Sydney 29 A2
Middle Park Melbourne 18 B1
Middle Village New York 22 B2
Middlesex Fells Reservation Boston 6 A2
Midland Beach New York 22 C1
Midwood New York 22 C2
Miedzeszyn Warsaw 32 B3
Międzylesie Warsaw 32 B3
Miessaari Helsinki 11 C1
Miguel Hidalgo Mexico City 18 B1
Milan = Milano Milan 19 B1
Milanese, Parco Regionale ⌂ Milan 19 A1
Milano Milan 19 B1
Milano Due Milan 19 B2
Milano Linate ✕ (LIN) Milan 19 B2
Milano San Felice Milan 19 B2
Milbertshofen Munich 21 A2
Mill Hill London 15 A2
Millennium Dome London 15 A4
Miller Meadow Chicago 9 B2
Millerhill Edinburgh 11 B3
Milltown Dublin 10 B2
Millwood Washington 33 B4
Milnerton Cape Town 8 A1
Milon-la-Chapelle Paris 24 B1
Milton Boston 6 B2
Milton Bridge Edinburgh 11 B2
Mimico Toronto 31 B2
Mimico Creek → Toronto 31 B1
Minami Osaka 23 A2
Minamitsunashima Tokyo 30 B2
Minato Osaka 23 B1
Minato Tokyo 30 B3
Minshât el Bekkârî Cairo 7 A1
Miraflores Lima 14 B2
Miramar Wellington 33 B1
Misericordia, Sa. da Rio de Janeiro 25 B1
Mission San Francisco 26 B2
Mississauga Toronto 31 B1
Mitaka Tokyo 30 A2
Mitcham London 15 B2
Mitcham Common London 15 B3
Mitchell Museum of the American Indian Chicago 9 A2
Mitchell's Plain Cape Town 8 B2
Mitte Berlin 5 A3
Mittel Isarkanal → Munich 21 A3
Mixcoac Mexico City 18 B1
Miyakojima Osaka 23 A2
Mizonokuchi Tokyo 30 B2
Mizue Tokyo 30 A4
Mlocinski Park Warsaw 32 B1
Mlociny Warsaw 32 B1
Mnevniki Moscow 19 B1
Moba Lagos 14 B2
Moczydlo Warsaw 32 C2
Modderfontein Johannesburg 13 A2
Modřany Prague 25 B2
Mogyoród Budapest 7 A3
Moinho Velho, Cor. → São Paulo 27 B2
Mok Seoul 27 B1
Mokotów Warsaw 32 B2
Molenbeek-St-Jean Brussels 6 A1
Molino de Rosas Mexico City 18 B1
Mollem Brussels 6 A1
Mollins de Rey Barcelona 4 A1
Mondeor Johannesburg 13 B2
Moneda, Palacio de la Santiago 27 B2
Monerό Rio de Janeiro 25 A1
Mong Kok Hong Kong 12 B2
Monkstown Dublin 10 B3
Monnickendam Amsterdam 2 A3
Monrovia Los Angeles 16 B4
Monsanto Lisbon 16 A1
Monsanto, Parque Florestal de Lisbon 16 A1
Mont-Royal Montreal 20 A2
Mont-Royal, Parc Montreal 20 A2
Montana de Montjuich Barcelona 4 A1
Montcada i Reixac Barcelona 4 A2
Monte Chingolo Buenos Aires 7 C2
Montebello Los Angeles 16 B4
Montemor Lisbon 16 A1
Monterey Park Los Angeles 16 B4
Montespaccato Rome 26 B1
Montesson Paris 24 A1
Monteverde Nuovo Rome 26 B1
Montfermeil Paris 24 A4
Montigny-le-Bretonneux Paris 24 B1
Montjay-la-Tour Paris 24 A4
Montparnasse, Gare Paris 24 A2
Montréal Montreal 20 A2
Montréal, Î. de Montreal 20 A2
Montréal, Université de Montreal 20 B2
Montréal Est Montreal 20 A2
Montréal-Nord Montreal 20 A2
Montréal-Ouest Montreal 20 B1
Montréal Trudeau Int. ✕ (YUL) Montreal 20 B1
Montreuil Paris 24 A3
Montrouge Paris 24 B2
Montserrat Buenos Aires 7 B2
Monza Milan 19 A2
Monzoro Milan 19 B1
Moóca São Paulo 27 B2
Moonachie New York 22 B1
Moonee Ponds Melbourne 18 A1
Moonee Valley Racecourse Melbourne 18 A1
Moosach Munich 21 A2
Mora Mumbai 20 B2
Moratalaz Madrid 17 B2
Mörby Stockholm 29 A2
Morden London 15 B2
Morée → Paris 24 A3
Morgan Park Chicago 9 C3
Moriguchi Osaka 23 A2
Morivione Milan 19 B2
Morningside Edinburgh 11 B2
Morningside Johannesburg 13 A2
Morningside Washington 33 C4
Morningside Park Orlando 23 B2
Morningside Park Toronto 31 A3
Morro Solar, Cerro Lima 14 C2
Mortlake London 15 B2
Mortlake Sydney 29 B1
Morton Grove Chicago 9 A2
Morumbi São Paulo 27 B1
Moscavide Lisbon 16 A2
Moschato Athens 2 B2
Moscow = Moskva Moscow 19 B2
Moskva Moscow 19 B2
Moskvoretskiy Moscow 19 B2
Mosman Sydney 29 A2
Móstoles Madrid 17 C1
Moti Bagh Delhi 10 B2
Motol Prague 25 B1
Motsa Jerusalem 13 B2
Motsa Ilit Jerusalem 13 B1
Motspur Park London 15 B2
Mottingham London 15 B4
Mount Dennis Toronto 31 A2
Mount Greenwood Chicago 9 C2
Mount Hood Memorial Park ⌂ Boston 6 A2
Mount Merrion Dublin 10 B2
Mount Rainier Washington 33 B4
Mount Vernon New York 22 A3
Müggelberge Berlin 5 B4
Müggelheim Berlin 5 B5
Muggiò Milan 19 A2
Mühleiten Vienna 32 A3
Mühlenfliess → Berlin 5 A5
Muiden Amsterdam 2 A3
Muizenberg Cape Town 8 B1
Mujahidpur Delhi 10 B2
Mukandpur Delhi 10 A2
Mukhmas Jerusalem 13 A2
Muko → Osaka 23 A1
Mukojima Tokyo 30 A3
Mulbarton Johannesburg 13 B2
Mumbai Mumbai 20 B2
Mumbai Chhatrapati Shivaji Int. ✕ (BOM) Mumbai 20 A2
Mumbai Harbour Mumbai 20 B2
Munch Museum Oslo 23 A3
Münchehofe Berlin 5 B5
München Munich 21 B2
München Franz Josef Strauss ✕ (MUC) Munich 21 A2
Munich = München Munich 21 B2
Munkkiniemi Helsinki 11 B2
Munro Buenos Aires 7 B1
Muntinlupa Manila 17 C2
Murai Res. Singapore 28 A2
Muranów Warsaw 32 B1
Murino St. Petersburg 27 B2
Murrayfield Edinburgh 11 B2
Musashino Tokyo 30 A2
Museu Nacional Rio de Janeiro 25 B1
Mushin Lagos 14 A2
Musocco Milan 19 B1
Mustansiriya Baghdad 3 A2
Musturud Cairo 7 A2
Muswell Hill London 15 A3
Mutanabi Baghdad 3 B2
Muthana Baghdad 3 B2
Mykerinos Cairo 7 B1
Myllypuro Helsinki 11 B3
Mystic → Boston 6 A2

N

Nacka Stockholm 29 B3
Naenae Wellington 33 B2
Næsnes Oslo 23 B1
Nagatsuta Tokyo 30 B2
Nagytétény Budapest 7 B1
Nahalin Jerusalem 13 B1
Najafgarh Drain → Delhi 10 B1
Nakahara Tokyo 30 B2
Nakano Tokyo 30 A2
Namsan Park Seoul 27 B1
Namyeong Seoul 27 B1
Nanbiancun Canton 11 B1
Nanchang He → Beijing 4 B1
Nandang Canton 11 B2
Nangal Dewat Delhi 10 B1
Naniwa Osaka 23 B1
Nanole Mumbai 20 A2
Nanpu Bridge Shanghai 28 B2
Nanshi Shanghai 28 B1
Nanterre Paris 24 A2
Naoabad Calcutta 14 C2
Napier Mole Karachi 13 B1
Naraina Delhi 10 B1
Nariman Point Mumbai 20 B1
Nariman Pt. Mumbai 20 B1
Nārmak Tehran 31 A2
Naruo Osaka 23 A1
Näsby Stockholm 29 A2
Näsbypark Stockholm 29 A2
National Arboretum Washington 33 B3
National Zoological Park Washington 33 B3
Nativity, Basilica of Jerusalem 13 B2
Natolin Warsaw 32 C2
Naucalpan de Juárez Mexico City 18 B1
Naupada Mumbai 20 A2
Navi Mumbai Mumbai 20 A2
Naviglio di Pavia Milan 19 B1
Naviglio Grande Milan 19 B1
Navotas Manila 17 B1
Navy Pier Chicago 9 B3
Nazal Hikmat Beg Baghdad 3 A2
Nazimabad Karachi 13 A2
Nazlet el Simmân Cairo 7 B1
Nea Alexandria Athens 2 B2
Nea Ionia Athens 2 A2
Nea Liosia Athens 2 A2
Nea Smirni Athens 2 B2
Neapoli Athens 2 B2
Near North Chicago 9 B3
Nebušice Prague 25 B2
Nederhorst Amsterdam 2 B3
Nedlitz Berlin 5 B1
Nee Soon Singapore 28 A2
Needham Boston 6 B1
Needham Heights Boston 6 B1
N'emātābād Tehran 31 B2
Nerima Tokyo 30 A3
Nesodden Oslo 23 B3
Nesoddtangen Oslo 23 A3
Nesøya Oslo 23 A2
Neu Aubing Munich 21 B1
Neu Buch Berlin 5 A4
Neu Buchhorst Berlin 5 B5
Neu Fahrland Berlin 5 B1
Neu Lindenberg Berlin 5 A4
Neubiberg Munich 21 B3
Neuenhagen Berlin 5 A4
Neuessling Vienna 32 A3
Neuhausen Munich 21 B2
Neuherberg Munich 21 A2
Neuhönow Berlin 5 A5
Neuilly-Plaisance Paris 24 A4
Neuilly-sur-Marne Paris 24 A4
Neuilly-sur-Seine Paris 24 A2
Neukagran Vienna 32 A2
Neukettenhof Vienna 32 B2
Neukölln Berlin 5 B3
Neuperlach Munich 21 B2
Neuried Munich 21 B1
Neustift am Walde Vienna 32 A1
Neusüssenbrunn Vienna 32 A2
Neuwaldegg Vienna 32 A1
Neve Ya'akov Jerusalem 13 A2
Neves Rio de Janeiro 25 B2
New Baghdād Baghdad 3 B2
New Barakpur Calcutta 14 A2
New Brighton New York 22 C1
New Canada Johannesburg 13 B1
New Canada Dam Johannesburg 13 B1
New Carrollton Washington 33 B4
New Cross London 15 B3
New Delhi Delhi 10 B2
New Dorp New York 22 C1
New Dorp Beach New York 22 C1
New Malden London 15 B2
New Milford New York 22 A1
New Mumbai = Navi Mumbai Mumbai 20 A2
New Territories Hong Kong 12 A1
New Toronto Toronto 31 B1
New Utrecht New York 22 C2
New York New York 22 B3
New York La Guardia ✕ (LGA) New York 22 B2
Newark B. New York 22 B1
Newbattle Edinburgh 11 B3
Newbury Park London 15 A4
Newcraighall Edinburgh 11 B3
Newham □ London 15 A4
Newhaven Edinburgh 11 B2
Newington Edinburgh 11 B2
Newlands Johannesburg 13 B1
Newlands Wellington 33 B1
Newport Melbourne 18 B1
Newton Boston 6 B1
Newtonbrook Toronto 31 A2
Newtongrange Edinburgh 11 B3
Newtonville Boston 6 A1
Newtown Sydney 29 B2
Ngaio Wellington 33 B1
Ngau Chi Wan Hong Kong 12 A2
Ngau Tau Kok Hong Kong 12 B2
Ngauranga Wellington 33 B1
Ngong Shuen Chau Hong Kong 12 B1
Ngua Kok Wan Hong Kong 12 A1
Niāvarān Tehran 31 A2
Nibra Calcutta 14 B1
Nidāl Baghdad 3 B2
Niddrie Edinburgh 11 B3
Niddrie Melbourne 18 A1
Nieder Neuendorf Berlin 5 A2
Niederschöneweide Berlin 5 B3
Niederschönhausen Berlin 5 A3
Niemeyer Rio de Janeiro 25 B1
Nieuwendam Amsterdam 2 A2
Nihonbashi Tokyo 30 A3
Niipperi Helsinki 11 B1
Nikea Athens 2 B1
Nikolassee Berlin 5 B2
Nikolskiy Moscow 19 B1
Niles Chicago 9 A2
Nimta Calcutta 14 A2
Ninoy Aquino Int. ✕ (MNL) Manila 17 B2
Nippa Tokyo 30 B2
Nippori Tokyo 30 A3
Nishi Osaka 23 A1
Nishinari Osaka 23 B1
Nishinomiya Osaka 23 A1
Nishiyodogawa Osaka 23 A1
Niterói Rio de Janeiro 25 B2
Nockeby Stockholm 29 B1
Noel Park London 15 A3
Nogatino Moscow 19 B3
Nogent-sur-Marne Paris 24 A3
Noida Delhi 10 B2
Noiseau Paris 24 B4
Noisiel Paris 24 A4
Noisy-le-Grand Paris 24 A4
Noisy-le-Roi Paris 24 A1
Noisy-le-Sec Paris 24 A3
Nokkala Helsinki 11 C1
Nomentano Rome 26 B2
Nonakashinden Tokyo 30 A2
Nongminyundong Jiangxisuo Canton 11 B2
Nonhyeon Seoul 27 B2
Nonthaburi Bangkok 3 A1
Noordgesig Johannesburg 13 B1
Noordzeekanaal Amsterdam 2 A1
Nord, Gare du Paris 24 A3
Nordmarka Oslo 23 A3
Nordrand-Siedlung Vienna 32 A2
Nordstrand Oslo 23 A3
Normandale Wellington 33 B2
Norridge Chicago 9 B2
Norrmalm Stockholm 29 A2
North Arlington New York 22 B1
North Bay Village Miami 18 A2
North Bergen New York 22 B1
North Bull I. Dublin 10 A3
North Cheam London 15 B2
North Cray London 15 B4
North Decatur Atlanta 3 B3
North Druid Hills Atlanta 3 B3
North Esk → Edinburgh 11 B2
North Gyle Edinburgh 11 B2
North Hackensack New York 22 A1
North Harbor Manila 17 B1
North Hd. Sydney 29 A2
North Hollywood Los Angeles 16 B2
North Lexington Boston 6 A1
North Miami Miami 18 A2
North Miami Beach Miami 18 A2
North Nazimabad Karachi 13 A2
North Pt. Hong Kong 12 B2
North Queensferry Edinburgh 11 A1
North Quincy Boston 6 B2
North Res. Boston 6 A2
North Riverside Chicago 9 B2
North Saugus Boston 6 A2
North Shore Channel → Chicago 9 B2
North Springfield Washington 33 C2
North Station Boston 6 A2
North Sydney Sydney 29 B2
North Woolwich London 15 A4
North York Toronto 31 A2
Northbridge Sydney 29 A2
Northbridge Park Sydney 29 A2
Northcliff Johannesburg 13 A1
Northcote Melbourne 18 A2
Northeastern University Boston 6 A2
Northern Virginia Regional Park ⌂ Washington 33 B3
Northlake Chicago 9 B1
Northmount Toronto 31 A2
Northolt London 15 A1
Northumberland Heath London 15 B5
Northwestern Station Chicago 9 B3
Northwestern University Chicago 9 A2
Northwood London 15 A1
Northwood Park Toronto 31 A1
Norwood Johannesburg 13 A2
Norwood Park Chicago 9 B2
Noryangjin Seoul 27 B1
Nossa Senhora do Ó São Paulo 27 B1
Nossegem Brussels 6 A3
Notre-Dame Paris 24 A3
Notre-Dame, Basilique Montreal 20 B2
Notre-Dame, Bois Paris 24 B4
Notre-Dame-de-Grace Montreal 20 B2
Notting Hill London 15 A2
Nova Milanese Milan 19 A2
Novate Milanese Milan 19 A1
Novaya Derevnya St. Petersburg 27 A1
Nové Město Prague 25 B2
Novoaleksandrovskoye St. Petersburg 27 B2
Novodevichy Convent Moscow 19 B2
Novogireyevo Moscow 19 B3
Novosaratovka St. Petersburg 27 B3
Nowe-Babice Warsaw 32 B1
Nowe Miasto Warsaw 32 B2
Nöykkiö Helsinki 11 D1
Nueva Atzacoalco Mexico City 18 B2
Nueva Pompeya Buenos Aires 7 C2
Nueva Tenochtitlán Mexico City 18 B2
Nuijala Helsinki 11 B1
Numabukuro Tokyo 30 A2
Nuñez Buenos Aires 7 B2
Nunhead London 15 B3
Ñuñoa Santiago 27 B2
Nusle Prague 25 B2
Nussdorf Vienna 32 A2
Nyanga Cape Town 8 A2
Nymphenburg Munich 21 B2
Nymphenburg, Schloss Munich 21 B2

O

Oak Grove Atlanta 3 A3
Oak Hill Boston 6 B1
Oak Lawn Chicago 9 C2
Oak Park Chicago 9 B2
Oak View Washington 33 A4
Oakdale Atlanta 3 A2
Oakland San Francisco 26 B3
Oakland Washington 33 B4
Oaklawn Washington 33 C4
Oakleigh Melbourne 18 B2
Oakton Washington 33 B2
Oakwood Beach New York 22 C1
Oatley Sydney 29 B1
Obalende Lagos 14 B2
Oba's Palace Lagos 14 B2
Oberföhring Munich 21 B2
Oberhaching Munich 21 B2
Oberlaa Vienna 32 B2
Oberlisse Vienna 32 A2
Obermenzing Munich 21 A1
Obermoos Schwaige Munich 21 A1
Oberschleissheim Munich 21 A2
Oberschöneweide Berlin 5 B4
Observatory Johannesburg 13 B2
Óbuda Budapest 7 A2
Obukhovo St. Petersburg 27 B2
Obvodnyy Kanal St. Petersburg 27 B1
Ocean Park Hong Kong 12 B2
Ochota Warsaw 32 B1
Ocoee Orlando 23 A1
Ōdana Tokyo 30 B2
Öden-Stockach Munich 21 B3
Odilampi Helsinki 11 B1
Odivelas Lisbon 16 A1
Odolany Warsaw 32 B1
Oeiras Lisbon 16 A1
Ofin Lagos 14 A3
Ogawa Tokyo 30 A1
Ogden Park Chicago 9 C2
Ogikubo Tokyo 30 A2
Ogogoro Lagos 14 B2
Ogoyo Lagos 14 B2
Ogudu Lagos 14 A2
O'Hare Int., Chicago ✕ (ORD) Chicago 9 B1
Ohariu Stream → Wellington 33 B1
O'Higgins, Parque Santiago 27 B2
Ōimachi Tokyo 30 B3
Ojota Lagos 14 A2
Okęcie Warsaw 32 B1
Okęcie, Warszawa ✕ (WAW) Warsaw 32 B1
Okelra Lagos 14 B2
Okeogbe Lagos 14 B2
Okhla Delhi 10 B2
Okhta → St. Petersburg 27 B2
Okkervil → St. Petersburg 27 B2
Okrzeszyn Warsaw 32 C2
Oksval Oslo 23 A3
Oktyabrskiy Moscow 19 B2
Okubo Tokyo 30 A3
Ōkura Tokyo 30 B1
Olari Helsinki 11 B1
Olaria Rio de Janeiro 25 B1
Old Admiralty St. Petersburg 27 B1
Old City Jerusalem 13 B2
Old City Shanghai 28 B1
Old City Hall Toronto 31 B2
Old Fort York Toronto 31 B2
Old Harbor Boston 6 B2
Old Town Chicago 9 B3
Old Town Hall = Altes Rathaus Munich 21 B2
Oldbawn Dublin 10 B1
Olgino St. Petersburg 27 A1
Olimpico, Estadio Mexico City 18 C1
Olivais Lisbon 16 A2
Olivar de los Padres Mexico City 18 B1
Olivar del Conde Mexico City 18 B1
Olives, Mt. of Jerusalem 13 B2
Olivia, L. Orlando 23 A1
Olivos Buenos Aires 7 B2
Olona → Milan 19 B1
Olympia, L. Orlando 23 A1
Olympic Stadium = Turner Field Atlanta 3 B2
Olympic Stadium Helsinki 11 B2
Olympique, Stade Montreal 20 A2
Ōmori Tokyo 30 B3
Onisigun Lagos 14 A2
Ontario Science Centre Toronto 31 A2
Ōokayama Tokyo 30 B3
Oostzaan Amsterdam 2 A2
Opa-Locka Miami 18 A1
Opa-Locka ✕ (OPF) Miami 18 A1
Opacz Warsaw 32 B1
Ophirton Johannesburg 13 B2
Oppegård Oslo 23 B3
Oppem Brussels 6 A1
Oppsal Oslo 23 A4
Ora Jerusalem 13 B1
Oradell New York 22 A1
Oradell Res. New York 22 A1
Orange Bowl Stadium Miami 18 B2
Orangi Karachi 13 A2
Ordrup Copenhagen 8 A3
Orech Prague 25 B1
Orient Heights Boston 6 A3
Orlando Orlando 23 A2
Orlando Dam Johannesburg 13 B1
Orlando East Johannesburg 13 B1
Orlando Executive ✕ Orlando 23 A2
Orlando Int. ✕ (MCO) Orlando 23 B3
Orlovista Orlando 23 A2
Orly Paris 24 B3
Orly, Paris ✕ (ORY) Paris 24 B3
Ormesson-sur-Marne Paris 24 B4
Ormond Melbourne 18 B2
Ormøya Oslo 23 A3
Orpington London 15 B4
Ortaköy Istanbul 12 B2
Ortica Milan 19 B2
Oruba Lagos 14 A2
Ōsaka Osaka 23 B2
Ōsaka Castle Osaka 23 A2
Ōsaka Harbour Osaka 23 B1
Ōsaka Itami Int. ✕ (ITM) Osaka 23 A1
Ōsaka Kansai ✕ (KIX) Osaka 23 B2
Ōsaki Tokyo 30 B3
Osasco São Paulo 27 B1
Osdorf Berlin 5 B3
Osdorp Amsterdam 2 A1
Oshodi Lagos 14 A2
Oslo Oslo 23 A3
Oslo ✕ (OSL) Oslo 23 A4
Osone Tokyo 30 B2
Osorun Lagos 14 A2
Ospiate Milan 19 A1
Ostankino Moscow 19 B2
Osterley London 15 B1
Osterley Park London 15 B1
Östermalm Stockholm 29 A2
Österskär Stockholm 29 A3
Ostia Malpasso Rome 26 C1
Ostiense Rome 26 B1
Østmarkkapellet Oslo 23 A4
Østøya Oslo 23 A2
Østre Aker Oslo 23 A3
Ōta Tokyo 30 B3
Otaniemi Helsinki 11 B1
Otari Open Air Museum Wellington 33 B1
Otsuka Tokyo 30 A3
Ottakring Vienna 32 A1
Ottàvia Rome 26 B1
Ottery Cape Town 8 B2
Ottobrunn Munich 21 B3
Ouderkerk Amsterdam 2 B2
Oulunkylä Helsinki 11 B2
Ourcq, Canal de l' Paris 24 A3
Outer Mission San Francisco 26 B2
Outremont Montreal 20 A2
Overijse Brussels 6 B3
Owhiro Bay Wellington 33 C1
Oworonsoki Lagos 14 A2
Oxgangs Edinburgh 11 B2
Oxon Hill Washington 33 C4
Oyodo Osaka 23 A1
Oyster B. Sydney 29 C1
Oyster Rock Mumbai 20 B1
Oyster Rocks Karachi 13 B2
Ozoir-la-Ferrière Paris 24 B4
Ozone Park New York 22 B2

P

Pacific Heights San Francisco 26 B2
Pacific Manor San Francisco 26 C2
Pacific Palisades Los Angeles 16 B1
Pacifica San Francisco 26 C2
Paco Manila 17 B1
Paco de Arcos Lisbon 16 A1
Paddington London 15 A2

Paddington Sydney 29 B2
Paderno Milan 19 A1
Pagewood Sydney 29 B2
Pagote Mumbai 20 B2
Pai, I. do Rio de Janeiro 25 B2
Pak Kok Hong Kong 12 B1
Pak Kong Hong Kong 12 A2
Pakila Helsinki 11 B2
Palacio Real Madrid 17 B1
Palaiseau Paris 24 B2
Palazzolo Milan 19 A1
Paleo Faliro Athens 2 B2
Palermo Buenos Aires 7 B2
Palhais Lisbon 16 B2
Palisades Park New York 22 A1
Palmer Park Washington 33 B4
Palmerston Dublin 10 A1
Paloheinä Helsinki 11 B2
Palomeras Madrid 17 B2
Palos Heights Chicago 9 D2
Palos Hills Chicago 9 C2
Palos Hills Forest Chicago 9 C1
Palos Park Chicago 9 C1
Palpara Calcutta 14 B2
Panchur Calcutta 14 B1
Pandacan Manila 17 B2
Pandan, Selat Singapore 28 B2
Pandan Res. Singapore 28 B2
Pangrati Athens 2 B2
Pangsua, Sungei → Singapore 28 A2
Panihati Calcutta 14 A2
Panjang, Bukit Singapore 28 A2
Panke → Berlin 5 A3
Pankow Berlin 5 A3
Pantheon Rome 26 B1
Panthersville Atlanta 3 B3
Pantin Paris 24 A3
Pantitlán Mexico City 18 B2
Panvel Cr. → Mumbai 20 B2
Paparangi Wellington 33 B1
Papiol Barcelona 4 A1
Paramount Studios Los Angeles 16 B3
Paramus New York 22 A1
Paranaque Manila 17 B1
Paray-Vieille-Poste Paris 24 B3
Pardisān Nature Park Tehran 31 A2
Parel Mumbai 20 B1
Pari São Paulo 27 B2
Parioli Rome 26 B1
Paris Paris 24 A3
Paris Orly ✈ (ORY) Paris 24 B3
Parje Mumbai 20 B2
Pārk-e Āzādegān Tehran 31 B2
Pārk-e Mellat Tehran 31 A2
Park Ridge Chicago 9 A1
Park Royal London 15 A2
Parkchester New York 22 B2
Parkdale Toronto 31 B2
Parkhurst Johannesburg 13 A2
Parklawn Washington 33 B3
Parkmore Johannesburg 13 A2
Parkside San Francisco 26 B2
Parktown Johannesburg 13 B2
Parkview Johannesburg 13 A2
Parkville New York 22 C2
Parkwood Cape Town 8 B1
Parkwood Johannesburg 13 A2
Parow Cape Town 8 A2
Parque Chacabuco Buenos Aires 7 B2
Parque Patricios Buenos Aires 7 B2
Parramatta → Sydney 29 A1
Paşabahçe Istanbul 12 B2
Pasadena Los Angeles 16 B4
Pasar Minggu Jakarta 12 B1
Pasay Manila 17 B1
Pascoe Vale Melbourne 18 A1
Pasig Manila 17 B2
Pasig → Manila 17 B2
Pasila Helsinki 11 B2
Pasing Munich 21 B1
Pasir Panjang Singapore 28 B2
Pasir Ris Singapore 28 A3
Passaic New York 22 A1
Passaic → New York 22 B1
Passirana Milan 19 A1
Patel Nagar Delhi 10 B1
Pateros Manila 17 B2
Pathumwan Bangkok 3 B2
Patipukur Calcutta 14 B2
Patisia Athens 2 A2
Paulo E. Virginia, Gruta Rio de Janeiro 25 B1
Paulshof Berlin 5 A5
Paya Lebar Singapore 28 A3
Peakhurst Sydney 29 B1
Peania Athens 2 B3
Pearson Int. Toronto ✈ (YYZ) Toronto 31 A1
Peckham London 15 B3
Pederstrup Copenhagen 8 A2
Pedralbes Barcelona 4 A1
Pedregal de San Angel, Jardines del Mexico City 18 C1
Peip'ing = Beijing Beijing 4 B1
Peking = Beijing Beijing 4 B1
Pelcowizna Warsaw 32 B2
Peñalolén Santiago 27 B2
Pencarrow Hd. Wellington 33 C2
Peng Siang → Singapore 28 A2
Penge London 15 B3
Penha Rio de Janeiro 25 A1
Penicuik Edinburgh 11 B2
Penjaringan Jakarta 12 A1
Pentagon Washington 33 B3
Penzing Vienna 32 A1
People's Park Shanghai 28 B1
People's Square Shanghai 28 B1
Perales del Rio Madrid 17 C2
Perchtoldsdorf Vienna 32 B1
Perdizes São Paulo 27 B2
Peristeri Athens 2 A2
Perivale London 15 A2
Perk Brussels 6 A2
Perlach Munich 21 B2
Perlacher Forst Munich 21 B2
Pero Milan 19 A1
Peropok, Bukit Singapore 28 B2
Perovo Moscow 19 B3
Pertusella Milan 19 A1
Pesagot Jerusalem 13 A2
Pesanggrahag, Kali → Jakarta 12 B1
Peschiera Borromeo Milan 19 B2
Pesek, Pulau Singapore 28 B2
Pest Budapest 7 B2
Pesterzsébet Budapest 7 B2
Pesthidegkút Budapest 7 A1
Pestimre Budapest 7 B3
Pestlőrinc Budapest 7 B3
Pestújhely Budapest 7 A2
Petas Helsinki 11 B2
Petone Wellington 33 B2
Petrogradskaya Storona St. Petersburg 27 B2
Petroupoli Athens 2 A2
Petrovice Prague 25 B3
Petrovskiy Park Moscow 19 B2
Petrovsko-Razumovskoye Moscow 19 B2
Pettycur Edinburgh 11 A2
Peutie Brussels 6 A2
Pfaueninsel Berlin 5 B1
Phaya Thai Bangkok 3 B2
Phihai Karachi 13 A2
Phillip B. Sydney 29 B2
Phoenix Park Dublin 10 A2
Phra Khanong Bangkok 3 B2
Phra Nakhon Bangkok 3 B2
Phra Pradaeng Bangkok 3 C2
Phranakhon Bangkok 3 B1
Pico Rivera Los Angeles 16 C4
Piedade Lisbon 16 A1
Piedade Rio de Janeiro 25 B1
Piedade, Cova da Lisbon 16 A2
Piedmont Park Atlanta 3 B2
Pierre Elliott Trudeau ✈ (YUL) Montreal 20 B1
Pietralata Rome 26 B2
Pihlajamäki Helsinki 11 B2
Pihlajasaari Helsinki 11 C2
Pilares Rio de Janeiro 25 B1
Pilton Edinburgh 11 B2
Pimmit Hills Washington 33 B2
Pine Castle Orlando 23 B2
Pine Grove Toronto 31 A1
Pine Hills Orlando 23 A2
Pinewood Park Miami 18 A2
Piney Run → Washington 33 B2
Pinganli Beijing 4 B2
Pingzhou Canton 11 B2
Pinheiros → São Paulo 27 B1
Pinjrapur Karachi 13 A2
Pinner London 15 A1
Pinner Green London 15 A1
Pioltello Milan 19 A2
Pipinui Pt. Wellington 33 A1
Piræus = Pireas Athens 2 B1
Piraiévs = Pireas Athens 2 B1
Pirajuçara → São Paulo 27 B1
Pireas Athens 2 B1
Pirinççi Istanbul 12 B1
Pirituba São Paulo 27 A1
Pirkkola Helsinki 11 B2
Pisgat O'mer Jerusalem 13 B2
Pisgat Ze'ev Jerusalem 13 B2
Pisnice Prague 25 C2
Pitampura Delhi 10 A1
Pitkäjärvi Helsinki 11 B1
Planegg Munich 21 B1
Pleasure Island Orlando 23 B1
Plumstead Cape Town 8 B1
Plumstead London 15 B4
Plyushchevo Moscow 19 B3
Po Toi Hong Kong 12 B2
Po Toi O Hong Kong 12 B2
Poasco Milan 19 B2
Podbaba Prague 25 B2
Podoli Prague 25 B2
Pohick Creek → Washington 33 C2
Pointe-Aux-Trembles Montreal 20 A2
Poissy Paris 24 A1
Pok Fu Lam Hong Kong 12 B1
Pokcheong Seoul 27 C2
Pokrovsko-Sresnevo Moscow 19 B1
Polton Edinburgh 11 B3
Polvoranca, Parque de Madrid 17 C1
Polyustrovo St. Petersburg 27 B2
Pomprap Bangkok 3 B2
Pondok Gede Jakarta 12 A2
Pondok Indah Jakarta 12 B1
Pont-Viau Montreal 20 A1
Pontault-Combault Paris 24 B4
Pontinha Lisbon 16 A1
Poplar London 15 A3
Poppintree Dublin 10 A2
Porirua Wellington 33 A2
Porirua East Wellington 33 A2
Port Melbourne Melbourne 18 B1
Port Nicholson Wellington 33 B2
Port Richmond New York 22 C1
Port Shelter Hong Kong 12 A2
Port Union Toronto 31 A4
Portage Park Chicago 9 B2
Portela, Lisboa ✈ (LIS) Lisbon 16 A2
Porter, L. Orlando 23 A3
Portmarnock Dublin 10 A3
Porto Brandão Lisbon 16 A1
Pôrto Novo Rio de Janeiro 25 A2
Porto Novo Cr. → Lagos 14 B2
Portobello Edinburgh 11 B3
Portrero San Francisco 26 B3
Potomac Washington 33 A2
Potrero Pt. San Francisco 26 B2
Potsdam Berlin 5 B1
Potzham Munich 21 B2
Pötzleinsdorf Vienna 32 A1
Povoa de Santo Adriao Lisbon 16 A2
Powązki Warsaw 32 B1
Powiśle Warsaw 32 B2
Powsin Warsaw 32 C2
Powsinek Warsaw 32 C2
Poyan Res. Singapore 28 A2
Pozuelo de Alarcón Madrid 17 B1
Prado, Museo del Madrid 17 B1
Prado Churubusco Mexico City 18 B2
Praga Warsaw 32 B2
Prague = Praha Prague 25 B2
Praha Prague 25 B2
Praha ✈ (PRG) Prague 25 B1
Praires, R. des → Montreal 20 A2
Prater Vienna 32 A2
Precotto Milan 19 A2
Prenestino Labicano Rome 26 B2
Prenzlauerberg Berlin 5 A3
Preston Melbourne 18 A1
Pretos Forros, Sa. dos Rio de Janeiro 25 B1
Préville Montreal 20 B3
Přezletice Prague 25 B3
Prima Porta Rome 26 B1
Primavalle Rome 26 B1
Primrose Johannesburg 13 B2
Progreso Nacional Mexico City 18 A2
Prosek Prague 25 B3
Prospect Hill Park Boston 6 A1
Providencia Santiago 27 B2
Průhonice Prague 25 C3
Psichiko Athens 2 A2
Pudong New Area Shanghai 28 B2
Pueblo Libre Lima 14 B2
Pueblo Nuevo Barcelona 4 A2
Pueblo Nuevo Madrid 17 B2
Puerto Madero Buenos Aires 7 B2
Puhuangyu Beijing 4 B2
Puistola Helsinki 11 B3
Pukinmäki Helsinki 11 B2
Pulkovo Int. ✈ (LED) St. Petersburg 27 C1
Pullach Munich 21 B1
Pullman Historic District Chicago 9 C3
Pulo Gadung Jakarta 12 B2
Pūnak Tehran 31 A2
Punchbowl Sydney 29 B1
Punde Mumbai 20 B2
Punggol Singapore 28 A3
Punggol, Sungei → Singapore 28 A3
Punggol Pt. Singapore 28 A3
Punjabi Bagh Delhi 10 A1
Puotila Helsinki 11 B3
Puteaux Paris 24 A2
Putney London 15 B2
Putuo Shanghai 28 B1
Putxet Barcelona 4 A1
Puxi Shanghai 28 B1
Pyramids Cairo 7 B1
Pyry Warsaw 32 C1

Q

Qalandiya Jerusalem 13 A2
Qal'eh Morghi Tehran 31 B2
Qanâ el Ismâ'iliya Cairo 7 A2
Qāsemābād Tehran 31 A3
Qasr-e Firūzeh Tehran 31 B3
Qatane Jerusalem 13 B1
Qianmen Beijing 4 B2
Qinghuayuan Beijing 4 B1
Qingningsi Shanghai 28 B2
Qolhak Tehran 31 A2
Quadraro Rome 26 B2
Quaid-i-Azam Karachi 13 A1
Quartiere Zingone Milan 19 B1
Qubeiba Jerusalem 13 A1
Quds Baghdad 3 A2
Queen Mary Res. London 15 B1
Queen Victoria Market Melbourne 18 A1
Queensbury London 15 A2
Queenscliffe Sydney 29 A2
Queensferry Edinburgh 11 B1
Queenstown Singapore 28 B2
Quellerina Johannesburg 13 A1
Queluz Lisbon 16 A1
Quezon City Manila 17 B2
Quilicura Santiago 27 B1
Quincy Boston 6 B2
Quincy B. Boston 6 B3
Quinta Normal Santiago 27 B1
Quinto de Stampi Milan 19 B2
Quinto Romano Milan 19 B1
Quirinale Rome 26 B1

R

R.F.K. Memorial Stadium Washington 33 B4
Raasdorf Vienna 32 A3
Radcliffe College Boston 6 A2
Rådhus Oslo 23 A3
Radlice Prague 25 B2
Radość Warsaw 32 B3
Radotin Prague 25 C2
Rafat Jerusalem 13 A2
Raffles Park Singapore 28 B2
Raheny Dublin 10 A3
Rahnsdorf Berlin 5 B5
Rainham London 15 A5
Rajakylä Helsinki 11 B3
Rajpura Delhi 10 A2
Rákos-patak → Budapest 7 B3
Rákoshegy Budapest 7 B3
Rákoskeresztúr Budapest 7 B3
Rákoskert Budapest 7 B3
Rákosliget Budapest 7 B3
Rákospalota Budapest 7 A2
Rákosszentmihály Budapest 7 A2
Raków Warsaw 32 B1
Ram Jerusalem 13 A2
Rām Allāh Jerusalem 13 A2
Ramadān Baghdad 3 B2
Ramakrishna Puram Delhi 10 B1
Rāmallāh = Rām Allāh Jerusalem 13 A2
Ramanathpur Calcutta 14 A1
Ramat Allon Jerusalem 13 B2
Ramat Eshkol Jerusalem 13 B2
Ramat Razi'el Jerusalem 13 B1
Ramat Shafet Jerusalem 13 B2
Rambler Channel Hong Kong 12 A1
Ramenki Moscow 19 B1
Ramersdorf Munich 21 B2
Rameses Station Cairo 7 A2
Ramos Rio de Janeiro 25 B1
Ramos Mejía Buenos Aires 7 B1
Ramot Jerusalem 13 B2
Rampur Delhi 10 A2
Ramsgate Sydney 29 B1
Rand ✈ (QRA) Johannesburg 13 B2
Randalls I. New York 22 B2
Randburg Johannesburg 13 A1
Randhart Johannesburg 13 B2
Randpark Ridge Johannesburg 13 A1
Randwick Sydney 29 B2
Ranelagh Dublin 10 A2
Rangpuri Delhi 10 B1
Rannersdorf Vienna 32 B2
Ransbèche Brussels 6 B2
Ransdorp Amsterdam 2 A2
Ranvad Mumbai 20 B2
Raposo Lisbon 16 A1
Rastaala Helsinki 11 B1
Rastila Helsinki 11 B3
Raszyn Warsaw 32 C1
Rathfarnham Dublin 10 B2
Ratho Edinburgh 11 B1
Ratho Station Edinburgh 11 B1
Rato Lisbon 16 A2
Ravelston Edinburgh 11 B2
Rawamangun Jakarta 12 B2
Rayners Lane London 15 A1
Raynes Park London 15 B2
Raypur Calcutta 14 C2
Real Felipe, Fuerte Lima 14 B2
Reams, L. Orlando 23 B1
Recoleta Buenos Aires 7 B2
Recoleta Santiago 27 B2
Red Fort = Lal Qila Delhi 10 B2
Red Square Moscow 19 B2
Redbridge ☐ London 15 A4
Redfern Sydney 29 B2
Redwood Wellington 33 B1
Refshaleøen Copenhagen 8 A3
Regents Park Johannesburg 13 B2
Regent's Park London 15 A3
Rego Park New York 22 B2
Reinickendorf Berlin 5 A3
Rekola Helsinki 11 B3
Rembertów Warsaw 32 B2
Rembrandtpark Amsterdam 2 A2
Remedios, Parque Nacional de los △ Mexico City 18 B1
Remedios de Escalada Buenos Aires 7 C2
Rémola, Estany del Barcelona 4 B1
Renca Santiago 27 B1
Rennemoulin Paris 24 A1
Řeporyje Prague 25 B1
Repulse Bay Hong Kong 12 B2
Repy Prague 25 B1
Residenz Munich 21 B2
Reston Washington 33 B2
Retiro Buenos Aires 7 B2
Retiro Madrid 17 B1
Retiro, Puerto Buenos Aires 7 B2
Retreat Cape Town 8 B1
Reutov Moscow 19 B4
Réveillon → Paris 24 B4
Revere Boston 6 A2
Rexdale Toronto 31 A1
Reynosa Tamaulipas Mexico City 18 A1
Rho Milan 19 A1
Rhodes Sydney 29 A1
Rhodon Paris 24 B1
Rhodon → Paris 24 B1
Rialto Towers Melbourne 18 A1
Ribeira Rio de Janeiro 25 A1
Ricarda, Estany de la Barcelona 4 B1
Richmond Melbourne 18 A2
Richmond San Francisco 26 B2
Richmond Hill New York 22 B2
Richmond Park London 15 B2
Richmond-upon-Thames ☐ London 15 B2
Ridge, The Delhi 10 B2
Ridgefield New York 22 B1
Ridgefield Park New York 22 A1
Ridgewood New York 22 B2
Riem Munich 21 B3
Riesenrad Vienna 32 A2
Rijksmuseum Amsterdam 2 A2
Rikers I. New York 22 B2
Rimac Lima 14 B2
Ringsend Dublin 10 A2
Rinkeby Stockholm 29 A1
Rio Compride Rio de Janeiro 25 B1
Rio de Janeiro Rio de Janeiro 25 B1
Rio de Janeiro Galeão ✈ (GIG) Rio de Janeiro 25 A1
Rio de Mouro Lisbon 16 A1
Ripollet Barcelona 4 A1
Ris Oslo 23 A3
Risby Copenhagen 8 A1
Rishra Calcutta 14 A2
Ritchie Washington 33 B4
Rithala Delhi 10 A1
Rive Sud, Canal de la Montreal 20 B2
River Edge New York 22 A1
River Forest Chicago 9 B2
River Grove Chicago 9 B1
Riverdale New York 22 A2
Riverdale Washington 33 B4
Riverdale Park Toronto 31 A2
Riverlea Johannesburg 13 B1
Riverside Chicago 9 C2
Riverwood Sydney 29 B1
Rivière-des-Praires Montreal 20 A2
Rixensart Brussels 6 B3
Riyad Baghdad 3 B2
Rizal Park Manila 17 B1
Rizal Stadium Manila 17 B1
Røa Oslo 23 A2
Robbins Chicago 9 D2
Robertsham Johannesburg 13 B2
Rochelle Park New York 22 A1
Rock Cr. → Washington 33 B3
Rock Creek Park Washington 33 B3
Rock Pt. Wellington 33 A1
Rockaway Beach New York 22 C3
Rockaway Pt. New York 22 C2
Rockdale Sydney 29 B1
Rockefeller Center New York 22 B2
Rocky Run → Washington 33 B2
Roda, Gezîret el Cairo 7 A2
Roda I. = Roda, Gezîret el Cairo 7 A2
Rodaon Vienna 32 B1
Rødovre Copenhagen 8 A2
Rodrigo de Freitas, L. Rio de Janeiro 25 B1
Roehampton London 15 B2
Rogers Park Chicago 9 A3
Roihuvuori Helsinki 11 B3
Roissy-en-Brie Paris 24 B4
Rokytka → Prague 25 B3
Roma Rome 26 B1
Roma Urbe ✈ Rome 26 B2
Római-Fürdö Budapest 7 A2
Romainville Paris 24 A3
Roman Forum = Foro Romano Rome 26 B1
Romano Banco Milan 19 B1
Rome = Roma Rome 26 B1
Romema Jerusalem 13 B2
Romford London 15 A5
Ronald Reagan National, Washington ✈ (DCA) Washington 33 B3
Rondebosch Cape Town 8 A1
Roppongi Tokyo 30 B3
Rose, L. Orlando 23 A1
Rose Hill Washington 33 C3
Rosebank Johannesburg 13 A2
Rosebank New York 22 C1
Rosebery Sydney 29 B2
Rosedal La Candelaria Mexico City 18 B2
Roseland Chicago 9 C3
Rosemead Los Angeles 16 B4
Rosemont Chicago 9 B1
Rosemont Montreal 20 A2
Rosenborg Slot Copenhagen 8 A3
Rosenthal Berlin 5 A3
Rosettenville Johannesburg 13 B2
Rosewell Edinburgh 11 B3
Rosherville Dam Johannesburg 13 B2
Rösjön Stockholm 29 A2
Roslags-Näsby Stockholm 29 A2
Roslin Edinburgh 11 B3
Roslindale Boston 6 B2
Rosny-sous-Bois Paris 24 A4
Rosslyn Washington 33 B3
Rosyth Edinburgh 11 A1
Rotherhithe London 15 B3
Rothneusiedl Vienna 32 B2
Rothschmaige Munich 21 A1
Rouge Hill Toronto 31 A4
Round I. Hong Kong 12 B2
Roxbury Boston 6 B2
Roxeth London 15 A1
Royal Botanic Gardens Edinburgh 11 B2
Royal Observatory Edinburgh 11 B2
Royal Palace = Kungliga Slottet Stockholm 29 B2
Royal Park Melbourne 18 A1
Röylä Helsinki 11 B1
Rozas, Portilleros de las Madrid 17 B1
Roztoky Prague 25 B2
Rozzano Milan 19 B1
Rubí → Barcelona 4 A1
Rudolfsheim Vienna 32 A2
Rudolfshöhe Berlin 5 A5
Rudow Berlin 5 B3
Rueil-Malmaison Paris 24 A2
Ruisbroek Brussels 6 B1
Ruislip London 15 A1
Rumelihisarı Istanbul 12 B2
Rungis Paris 24 B3
Rusāfa Baghdad 3 A2
Rush Green London 15 A5
Russa Calcutta 14 C2
Rutherford New York 22 B1
Ruzyně Prague 25 B1
Ruzyne, Praha ✈ (PRG) Prague 25 B1
Rybatskaya St. Petersburg 27 B2
Rydboholm Stockholm 29 A3
Ryde Sydney 29 A1
Ryogoku Tokyo 30 A3
Rzhevka St. Petersburg 27 B3

S

Sa'ādatābād Tehran 31 A2
Saadūn Baghdad 3 B2
Saavedra Buenos Aires 7 B2
Saboli Delhi 10 A2
Sabugo Lisbon 16 A1
Sabzi Mand Delhi 10 A2
Sacavém Lisbon 16 A2
Saclay Paris 24 B2
Saclay, Étang de Paris 24 B1
Sacomã São Paulo 27 B2
Sacré Cœur Paris 24 A3
Sacrow Berlin 5 B1
Sacrower See Berlin 5 B1
Sadang Seoul 27 C1
Saddle → New York 22 A1
Saddle Brook New York 22 A1
Sadr Karachi 13 A2
Sadr City Baghdad 3 A2
Sadyba Warsaw 32 B2
Safdar Jang's Tomb Delhi 10 B2
Saft el Laban Cairo 7 A2
Saganashkee Slough Chicago 9 C1
Sagene Oslo 23 A3
Sagrada Família, Templo de Barcelona 4 A2
Sahar, Mumbai ✈ (BOM) Mumbai 20 A2
Sai Kung Hong Kong 12 A2
Sai Wan Ho Hong Kong 12 B2
Sai Ying Pun Hong Kong 12 B1
St-Aubin Paris 24 B1
St-Cloud Paris 24 A2
St-Cyr-l'École Paris 24 B1
St-Cyr-l'École ✈ Paris 24 B1
St-Denis Paris 24 A3
St-Germain, Forêt de Paris 24 A1
St-Germain-en-Laye Paris 24 A1
St-Gilles Brussels 6 B2
St. Helier London 15 B2
St-Hubert Montreal 20 B3
St. Hubert, Galeries Royales Brussels 6 A2
St. Isaac's Cathedral St. Petersburg 27 B1
St-Jacques → Montreal 20 B3
St-Joost-Ten-Node Brussels 6 A2
St. Kilda Melbourne 18 B1
St-Lambert Montreal 20 A3
St-Lambert Paris 24 B1
St-Laurent Montreal 20 A1
St-Léonard Montreal 20 A2
St. Magelungen Stockholm 29 B2
St-Mandé Paris 24 A3
St. Margaret's Dublin 10 A2
St-Martin, Bois Paris 24 B4
St. Mary Cray London 15 B4
St-Maur-des-Fossés Paris 24 B3
St-Maurice Paris 24 B3
St-Michel Montreal 20 A2
St. Nikolaus-Kirken Prague 25 B2
St-Ouen Paris 24 A3
St. Paul's Cray London 15 B4
St. Peters Sydney 29 B2
St. Petersburg = Sankt-Peterburg St. Petersburg 27 B1
St-Pierre Montreal 20 B2
St-Pieters Leew Brussels 6 B1
St-Quentin, Étang de Paris 24 B1
St-Stevens-Woluwe Brussels 6 A2
St-Vincent-de-Paul Montreal 20 A2
St. Xavier University Chicago 9 C2
Ste-Catherine Montreal 20 B2
Ste-Hélène, Î. Montreal 20 A2
Saiwai Tokyo 30 B3
Sakai Osaka 23 B1
Sakai Harbour Osaka 23 B1
Sakra, Pulau Singapore 28 B2
Salam Baghdad 3 A2
Salamanca Madrid 17 B1
Sallynoggin Dublin 10 B3
Salmannsdorf Vienna 32 A1
Salmedina Madrid 17 C2
Salomea Warsaw 32 B1
Salsette I. Mumbai 20 A2
Salt Lake City = Bidhan Nagar Calcutta 14 B2
Salt River Cape Town 8 A1
Salt Water L. Calcutta 14 B2
Saltsjö-Duvnäs Stockholm 29 B3
Samatya Istanbul 12 C1
Sampaloc Manila 17 B1
Samphan Thawong Bangkok 3 B2
Samseon Seoul 27 B2
Samuel Smith Park Toronto 31 B1
Samut Prakan Bangkok 3 B2
San Andrés Barcelona 4 A2
San Angel Mexico City 18 B1
San Basilio Rome 26 B2
San Borja Lima 14 B3
San Bóvio Milan 19 B2
San Bruno, Pt. San Francisco 26 C2
San Bruno Mountain State Park ⌂ San Francisco 26 B2
San Cristobal Buenos Aires 7 B2
San Cristobal Madrid 17 B2
San Cristóbal, Cerro Santiago 27 B2
San Cristoforo Milan 19 B1
San Donato Milanese Milan 19 B2
San Francisco San Francisco 26 B2
San Francisco B. San Francisco 26 B3
San Francisco Culhuacán Mexico City 18 C2
San Fruttuoso Milan 19 A2
San Gabriel Los Angeles 16 B4
San Gabriel → Los Angeles 16 C4
San Giuliano Milanese Milan 19 B2
San Isidro Lima 14 B2
San Jerónimo Lídice Mexico City 18 C1
San Joaquin Santiago 27 B2
San José Rio Hondo Mexico City 18 B1
San Juan → Manila 17 B2
San Juan de Aragón Mexico City 18 B2
San Juan de Aragón, Parque Mexico City 18 B2
San Juan de Lurigancho Lima 14 A2
San Juan del Monte Manila 17 B2
San Juan Ixtacala Mexico City 18 B1
San Just Desvern Barcelona 4 A1
San Justo Buenos Aires 7 C1
San Lorenzo Tezonco Mexico City 18 C2
San Luis Lima 14 B2
San Marino Los Angeles 16 B4
San Martin Barcelona 4 A2
San Martin de Porras Lima 14 B2
San Mateo Tlaltenango Mexico City 18 B1
San Miguel Lima 14 B2
San Miguel Santiago 27 B2
San Nicolás Buenos Aires 7 B2
San Onófrio Rome 26 B1
San Pedro Martir Barcelona 4 A1
San Pedro Zacatenco Mexico City 18 A2
San Pietro, Piazza Rome 26 B1
San Po Kong Hong Kong 12 A2
San Rafael Chamapa Mexico City 18 B1
San Rafael Hills Los Angeles 16 A3
San Roque Manila 17 B2
San Siro Milan 19 B1
San Souci Sydney 29 B1
San Telmo Buenos Aires 7 B2
San Vicenc dels Horts Barcelona 4 A1
Sandown Johannesburg 13 A2
Sandown Park Races London 15 B1
Sandton Johannesburg 13 A2
Sandvika Oslo 23 A2
Sandyford Dublin 10 B2
Sandymount Dublin 10 B2
Sangenjaya Tokyo 30 B2
Sanggye Seoul 27 B2
Sangley Pt. Manila 17 C1
Sankrail Calcutta 14 B1
Sankt-Peterburg St. Petersburg 27 B2
Sankt Veit Vienna 32 A1
Sanlihe Beijing 4 B1
Sanlintang Shanghai 28 C1
Sans Barcelona 4 A1
Sanssouci Berlin 5 B1
Sant Ambrogio, Basilica di Milan 19 B2
Sant Boi de Llobregat Barcelona 4 A1
Sant Cugat Barcelona 4 A1
Sant Feliu de Llobregat Barcelona 4 A1
Sant Joan Despi Barcelona 4 A1
Santa Ana Manila 17 B2
Santa Anita Park Los Angeles 16 B4
Santa Coloma de Gramenet Barcelona 4 A2
Santa Cruz Manila 17 B1
Santa Cruz Mumbai 20 A1
Santa Cruz, I. de Rio de Janeiro 25 B2
Santa Cruz de Olorde Barcelona 4 A1
Santa Efigênia São Paulo 27 B2
Santa Elena Manila 17 B2
Santa Elena del Gomero Santiago 27 B1
Santa Eulalia Barcelona 4 A2
Santa Fe Springs Los Angeles 16 C4
Santa Iria da Azóia Lisbon 16 A2
Santa Julia Santiago 27 C2
Santa Monica Los Angeles 16 B2
Santa Monica Mts. Los Angeles 16 B2
Santa Rosa de Locobe Santiago 27 B2
Santa Teresa de la Ovalle Santiago 27 B1
Santahamina Helsinki 11 C3
Santana São Paulo 27 A2
Santeny Paris 24 B4
Santiago Santiago 27 B2
Santiago Benitez ✈ (SCL) Santiago 27 B1
Santiago de Surco Lima 14 B2
Santo Amaro Lisbon 16 A1
Santo Amaro São Paulo 27 B1
Santo Andre Lisbon 16 B2
Santo Antão do Tojal Lisbon 16 A2
Santo António, Qta. de Lisbon 16 B1
Santo Tomas, Univ. of Manila 17 B1
Santos Dumont ✈ (SDU) Rio de Janeiro 25 B2
Santoshpur Calcutta 14 B1
Santragachi Calcutta 14 B1
Santry Dublin 10 A2
Sanyuanli Canton 11 B2
São Caetano do Sul São Paulo 27 B2
São Conrado Rio de Janeiro 25 C1
São Cristóvão Rio de Janeiro 25 B1
São Jorge, Castelo de Lisbon 16 A2
São Julião do Tojal Lisbon 16 A2
São Paulo São Paulo 27 B2
São Paulo Congonhas ✈ (CGH) São Paulo 27 B2
Sapa Calcutta 14 B1
Sapateiro, Cor. do → São Paulo 27 B1
Sarandi Buenos Aires 7 C2
Saraswati → Calcutta 14 A1
Sarecky potok → Prague 25 B2
Sarimbun Singapore 28 A2
Sarimbun Res. Singapore 28 A2
Sarıyer Istanbul 12 A2
Sarrià Barcelona 4 A1
Sarsuna Calcutta 14 C1
Sartrouville Paris 24 A2
Sasad Budapest 7 B2
Sashalom Budapest 7 A3
Saska Warsaw 32 B2
Satalice Prague 25 B3
Satgachi Calcutta 14 B2
Satpukur Calcutta 14 B2
Sätra Stockholm 29 B1
Saúde São Paulo 27 B2
Saugus Boston 6 A2
Saugus → Boston 6 A2
Sault-au-Récollet Montreal 20 A2
Sausalito San Francisco 26 A2
Sawah Besar Jakarta 12 A1
Scald Law Edinburgh 11 B2
Scarborough Toronto 31 A3
Scarborough Bluffs Toronto 31 A3
Sceaux Paris 24 B2
Schaerbeek Brussels 6 A2
Scharfenberg Berlin 5 A2
Schiller Park Chicago 9 B1
Schiller Woods Chicago 9 B1
Schiphol, Amsterdam ✈ (AMS) Amsterdam 2 B1
Schlachtensee Berlin 5 B2
Schlossgarten Berlin 5 A2
Schmargendorf Berlin 5 B2
Schönblick Berlin 5 B5
Schönbrunn Vienna 32 A1
Schöneberg Berlin 5 B3
Schönefeld Berlin 5 B4
Schöneiche Berlin 5 B5
Schönwalde Berlin 5 A1
Schulzendorf Berlin 5 A2
Schwabing Munich 21 B2
Schwanebeck Berlin 5 A4
Schwanenwerder Berlin 5 B2
Schwarzlackenau Vienna 32 A2
Schwechat Vienna 32 B2
Schwechat, Wien ✈ (VIE) Vienna 32 B3
Science and Industry, Museum of Chicago 9 C3
Scitrek Museum Atlanta 3 B2
Scopus, Mt. Jerusalem 13 B2
Scottdale Atlanta 3 B3
Scutari = Üsküdar Istanbul 12 B2
Sea Point Cape Town 8 A1
Seabrook Washington 33 B5
Seacliff San Francisco 26 B2
Seaforth Sydney 29 A2
Seagate New York 22 C1
Seat Pleasant Washington 33 B4
Seaview Wellington 33 B2
SeaWorld Orlando 23 B2
Šeberov Prague 25 B3
Secaucus New York 22 B1
Seddinsee Berlin 5 B5
Seeberg Berlin 5 A5
Seeburg Berlin 5 A1
Seefeld Berlin 5 A5
Seegefeld Berlin 5 A1
Seehof Berlin 5 B2
Segeltorp Stockholm 29 B1
Segrate Milan 19 B2
Seguro Milan 19 B1
Seixal Lisbon 16 B2
Selby Johannesburg 13 B2
Seletar, Pulau Singapore 28 A3
Seletar Hills Singapore 28 A3
Seletar Res. Singapore 28 A2
Selhurst London 15 B3
Sembawang Singapore 28 A2
Senago Milan 19 A1
Sendling Munich 21 B2
Senju Tokyo 30 A3
Senriyama Osaka 23 A2
Sentosa Singapore 28 B2
Seobinggo Seoul 27 B1
Seocho Seoul 27 C1
Seodaemun Seoul 27 B1
Seokkwan Seoul 27 B2
Seongbuk Seoul 27 B2
Seongdong Seoul 27 B2
Seongsu Seoul 27 B2
Seoul Seoul 27 B2
Seoul National University Seoul 27 C1
Seoul Tower Seoul 27 B1
Sepolia Athens 2 A2
Sepulveda Dam Rec. Area ⌂ Los Angeles 16 A2
Serangoon Singapore 28 A3
Serangoon, Pulau Singapore 28 A3
Serangoon, Sungei → Singapore 28 A3
Serangoon Harbour Singapore 28 A3
Seraya, Pulau Singapore 28 B2
Serebryanka → Moscow 19 B3
Serramonte San Francisco 26 C2
Sesto San Giovanni Milan 19 A2
Sesto Ulteriano Milan 19 B2
Setagaya Tokyo 30 B2
Seter Oslo 23 A3
Setia Budi Jakarta 12 B1
Settebagni Rome 26 A2
Settecamini Rome 26 B2
Séttimo Milanese Milan 19 B1
Settsu Osaka 23 A2
Seutula Helsinki 11 A2
Seven Corners Washington 33 B3
Seven Kings London 15 A4
Sévesco → Milan 19 A1
Sevran Paris 24 A4
Sewri Mumbai 20 B2
Sforzesso, Castello Milan 19 B2
Sha Kok Mei Hong Kong 12 A2
Sha Tin Hong Kong 12 A2
Sha Tin Wai Hong Kong 12 A2
Sha'ar Binyamin Jerusalem 13 A2
Shabramant Cairo 7 B2
Shah Mosque Tehran 31 A2
Shahdara Delhi 10 A2
Shahe Canton 11 B2
Shahr-e Rey Tehran 31 B2
Shahrak-e Golshahr Tehran 31 B1
Shahrak-e Qods Tehran 31 A2
Shaikh Aomar Baghdad 3 A2
Shakurbasti Delhi 10 A1
Shalkiya Calcutta 14 B2
Sham Shui Po Hong Kong 12 B1
Shamapur Delhi 10 A1
Shamian Canton 11 B2
Shan Mei Hong Kong 12 A2
Shanghai Shanghai 28 B1
Shanghai Hongqiao ✈ (SHA) Shanghai 28 B1
Shanghai Pudong ✈ (PVG) Shanghai 28 B2
Shankill Dublin 10 B3
Sharp I. Hong Kong 12 A2
Shastrinagar Delhi 10 A2
Shau Kei Wan Hong Kong 12 B2
Shawocun Beijing 4 B1
Shayuan Canton 11 B2
Sheen, L. Orlando 23 B1
Sheepshead Bay New York 22 C2
Shek O Hong Kong 12 B2
Shelter I. Hong Kong 12 B2
Shepherds Bush London 15 A2
Shepperton London 15 B1
Sheremetyevo ✈ (SVO) Moscow 19 A2
Sherman Oaks Los Angeles 16 B2
Sherman Park Chicago 9 C2
Sherwood, L. Orlando 23 A2
Shet Bandar Mumbai 20 B2
Sheung Fa Shan Hong Kong 12 A1
Sheung Lau Wan Hong Kong 12 B2
Sheung Wan Hong Kong 12 B1
Sheva Mumbai 20 B2
Sheva Nhava Mumbai 20 B2
Shiba Tokyo 30 B3
Shibpur Calcutta 14 B1
Shibuya Tokyo 30 B3
Shimogawara Tokyo 30 B1
Shimosalo Tokyo 30 A2
Shimoshakujii Tokyo 30 A2
Shinagawa Tokyo 30 B3
Shing Mun Res. Hong Kong 12 A1
Shinjuku Tokyo 30 A3
Shinjuku National Garden Tokyo 30 A3
Shinkoiwa Tokyo 30 A4
Shinnakano Tokyo 30 A3
Shipai Canton 11 B3
Shirinashi → Osaka 23 B1
Shirogane Tokyo 30 B3
Shitennoji Temple Osaka 23 B2
Shiweitang Canton 11 B2
Shogunle Lagos 14 A2
Shomolu Lagos 14 A2
Shooters Hill London 15 B4
Shoreditch London 15 A3
Shortlands London 15 B4
Shu'afat Jerusalem 13 B2
Shubrâ Cairo 7 A2
Shubrâ el Kheima Cairo 7 A2
Shuikou Canton 11 A2
Sidcup London 15 B4
Siebenhirten Vienna 32 B1
Siedlung Berlin 5 A1
Siekierki Warsaw 32 B2
Sielce Warsaw 32 B2
Siemensstadt Berlin 5 A2
Sierra Madre Los Angeles 16 B4
Sievering Vienna 32 A2
Sighthill Edinburgh 11 B2
Signal Hill Cape Town 8 A1
Siheung Seoul 27 C1
Sikátorpuszta Budapest 7 A3
Silampur Delhi 10 B2
Sillim Seoul 27 C1
Silver, L. Orlando 23 A2
Silver Hill Washington 33 C4
Silver Spring Washington 33 A3
Silvermine Nature Reserve Cape Town 8 B1
Silvolantekojärvi Helsinki 11 B2
Simei Singapore 28 A3
Simla Calcutta 14 B2
Simmering Vienna 32 A2
Simmeringer Heide Vienna 32 A2
Simonkylä Helsinki 11 B3
Sinchon Seoul 27 B1
Sindang Seoul 27 B2
Singapore ■ Singapore 28 B3
Singapore, Univ. of Singapore 28 B2
Singapore Changi ✈ (SIN) Singapore 28 A3
Sinki, Selat Singapore 28 B2
Sinsa Seoul 27 B2
Sint-Genesius-Rode Brussels 6 B2
Sion Mumbai 20 A2
Sipson London 15 B1
Siqeil Cairo 7 A1
Şişli Istanbul 12 B1
Site of Former World Trade Center = Ground Zero New York 22 B1
Skansen Stockholm 29 B2
Skärholmen Stockholm 29 B1
Skarpäng Stockholm 29 A2
Skarpnäck Stockholm 29 B2
Skaryszewski, Park Warsaw 32 B2
Skokie Chicago 9 A2
Skokie → Chicago 9 A2
Skokie Heritage Museum Chicago 9 A2
Skoklefall Oslo 23 A3
Sköndal Stockholm 29 B2
Skovlunde Copenhagen 8 A2
Skovshoved Copenhagen 8 A3
Skuru Stockholm 29 B3
Sky Lake Orlando 23 B2
Skyland Atlanta 3 A3
Slade Green London 15 B5
Slemmestad Oslo 23 B1
Slependen Oslo 23 A2
Slipi Jakarta 12 B1
Slivenec Prague 25 B2
Sloten Amsterdam 2 A1
Sloterdijk Amsterdam 2 A1
Sloterpark Amsterdam 2 A1
Sluhy Prague 25 A3
Służew Warsaw 32 B2
Służewiec Warsaw 32 B2
Smíchov Prague 25 B2
Smith Forest Preserve Chicago 9 B2
Smolny St. Petersburg 27 B2
Smolny Cathedral St. Petersburg 27 B2
Snake Creek Canal Miami 18 A2
Snakeden Branch → Washington 33 B1
Snarøya Oslo 23 A2
Snättringe Stockholm 29 B1
Søborg Copenhagen 8 A2
Sobreda Lisbon 16 B1
Söderby Stockholm 29 A3
Södermalm Stockholm 29 B2
Sodpur Calcutta 14 A2
Soeurs, Î. des Montreal 20 B2
Sognsvatn Oslo 23 A3
Soignes, Forêt de Brussels 6 B2
Sok Kwu Wan Hong Kong 12 B1
Sokolniki Moscow 19 B3
Sokolniki Park Moscow 19 B3
Sokolów Warsaw 32 C1
Solalinden Munich 21 B3
Sollentuna Stockholm 29 A1
Solln Munich 21 B2
Solna Stockholm 29 A1
Somerset Washington 33 B3
Somerville Boston 6 A2
Somes I. Wellington 33 B2
Sonari Mumbai 20 B2
Sønderso Copenhagen 8 A2
Songpa Seoul 27 B2
Sony Picture Studio Los Angeles 16 B2

Soroksár *Budapest* **7** B2
Soroksári Duna → *Budapest* **7** B2
Sosenka → *Moscow* **19** B3
Sosnovka *St. Petersburg* **27** B2
Sŏul = Seoul *Seoul* **27** B2
Soundview *New York* **22** B2
South Beach *New York* **22** C1
South Bend Park *Atlanta* **3** B2
South Boston *Boston* **6** A2
South Decatur *Atlanta* **3** B3
South Deering *Chicago* **9** C3
South El Monte *Los Angeles* **16** B4
South Gate *Los Angeles* **16** C3
South Harbor *Manila* **17** B1
South Harrow *London* **15** A1
South Hd. *Sydney* **29** B2
South Hills *Johannesburg* **13** B2
South Hornchurch *London* **15** A5
South Lawn *Washington* **33** C3
South Miami *Miami* **18** B1
South Norwood *London* **15** B3
South of Market *San Francisco* **26** B2
South Ozone Park *New York* **22** B3
South Pasadena *Los Angeles* **16** B4
South Res. *Boston* **6** A2
South Ruislip *London* **15** A1
South San Francisco *San Francisco* **26** C2
South San Gabriel *Los Angeles* **16** B4
South Shore *Chicago* **9** C3
Southall *London* **15** A1
Southborough *London* **15** B4
Southend *London* **15** B3
Southern California, University of *Los Angeles* **16** B3
Southfields *London* **15** B2
Southwark ☐ *London* **15** B3
Southwest Museum *Los Angeles* **16** B3
Søvang *Copenhagen* **8** B3
Soweto *Johannesburg* **13** B1
Sowhānak *Tehran* **31** A3
Soya *Tokyo* **30** A4
Spandau *Berlin* **5** A1
Spånga *Stockholm* **29** A1
Spanish Monastery *Miami* **18** A2
Spectacle I. *Boston* **6** A3
Speicher-See *Munich* **21** A3
Speising *Vienna* **32** B1
Sphinx *Cairo* **7** B1
Spinaceto *Rome* **26** C1
Spit Junction *Sydney* **29** A2
Spořilov *Prague* **25** B3
Spot Pond *Boston* **6** A2
Spotswood *Melbourne* **18** B1
Springeberg *Berlin* **5** B5
Springfield *Washington* **33** C2
Squantum *Boston* **6** B2
Srednaya Rogatka *St. Petersburg* **27** C2
Śródmieście *Warsaw* **32** B2
Staaken *Berlin* **5** A1
Stabekk *Oslo* **23** A2
Stadlau *Vienna* **32** A2
Stadshuset *Stockholm* **29** B2
Stains *Paris* **24** A3
Stamford Hill *London* **15** A3
Stammersdorf *Vienna* **32** A2
Stanley *Hong Kong* **12** B2
Stanley Pen. *Hong Kong* **12** B2
Stanmore *London* **15** A2
Stapleton *New York* **22** C1
Staraya Derevnya *St. Petersburg* **27** B1
Staré Město *Prague* **25** B2
Stare Miasto *Warsaw* **32** B2
Starke, L. *Orlando* **23** A1
Staten Island Zoo *New York* **22** C1
Staten Islands Ferry Terminal *New York* **22** C1
Statenice *Prague* **25** B1
Stedelijk Museum *Amsterdam* **2** A2
Steele Creek *Melbourne* **18** A1
Steenokkerzeel *Brussels* **6** A2
Steer, L. *Orlando* **23** A2
Steglitz *Berlin* **5** B2
Stepaside *Dublin* **10** B2
Stephansdom *Vienna* **32** A2
Stepney *London* **15** A3
Sterling Park *San Francisco* **26** B2
Sticklinge udde *Stockholm* **29** A2
Stickney *Chicago* **9** C2
Stillorgan *Dublin* **10** B2
Stockholm *Stockholm* **29** B2
Stocksund *Stockholm* **29** A2
Stodůlky *Prague* **25** B1
Stoke Newington *London* **15** A3
Stokes Valley *Wellington* **33** B2
Stone Canyon Res. *Los Angeles* **16** B2
Stone Park *Chicago* **9** B1
Stonebridge *London* **15** A2
Stoneham *Boston* **6** A2
Stony Brook Res. *Boston* **6** B2
Stony Creek → *Chicago* **9** C2
Stora Värtan *Stockholm* **29** A2
Store Hareskov *Copenhagen* **8** A2
Store Magleby *Copenhagen* **8** B3
Storholmen *Stockholm* **29** A2
Stoyka *St. Petersburg* **27** B2
Straiton *Edinburgh* **11** B3
Strandfontein *Cape Town* **8** B2
Strašnice *Prague* **25** B2
Strasstrudering *Munich* **21** B3
Stratford *London* **15** A4
Strathfield *Sydney* **29** B1
Streatham *London* **15** B3
Streatham Vale *London* **15** B3
Strebersdorf *Vienna* **32** A2
Střešovice *Prague* **25** B2
Střížkov *Prague* **25** B2
Strombeek-Bever *Brussels* **6** A2
Stromovka *Prague* **25** B2
Studio City *Los Angeles* **16** B2
Stureby *Stockholm* **29** B2
Stuvsta *Stockholm* **29** B2
Subhepur *Delhi* **10** A2
Sucat *Manila* **17** C2
Suchdol *Prague* **25** B2
Sucy-en-Brie *Paris* **24** B4
Sue, L. *Orlando* **23** A2
Sugamo *Tokyo* **30** A3
Sugar Loaf Mt. = Açúcar, Pão de *Rio de Janeiro* **25** B2
Suge *Tokyo* **30** B2
Suginami *Tokyo* **30** A2
Sugō *Tokyo* **30** B2
Sui Sai Wan *Hong Kong* **12** B1
Suita *Osaka* **23** A2
Suitland *Washington* **33** B4
Sukchar *Calcutta* **14** A2
Sultanahme Camil *Istanbul* **12** B1
Sumida *Tokyo* **30** A3
Sumida → *Tokyo* **30** A3
Sumiyoshi *Osaka* **23** B2
Sumiyoshi Shrine *Osaka* **23** B1
Summerville *Toronto* **31** B1
Summit *Chicago* **9** C2
Sunamachi *Tokyo* **30** A4
Sunbury-on-Thames *London* **15** B1
Sundbyberg *Stockholm* **29** A1
Sundbyerne *Copenhagen* **8** B3
Sung Kong *Hong Kong* **12** B2
Sungei Kadut Industrial Estate *Singapore* **28** A2
Sungei Selatar Res. *Singapore* **28** A3
Sunset Park *New York* **22** C2
Sunter *Jakarta* **12** A2
Sunter, Kali → *Jakarta* **12** B2
Suomenlinna *Helsinki* **11** C2
Sur Bahr *Jerusalem* **13** B2
Sura *Calcutta* **14** B2
Suraksan *Seoul* **27** A2
Surbiton *London* **15** B2
Suresnes *Paris* **24** A2
Surfside *Miami* **18** A2
Surquillo *Lima* **14** B2
Surrey Hills *Sydney* **29** B2
Susaek *Seoul* **27** B1
Süssenbrunn *Vienna* **32** A2
Sutton *Dublin* **10** A3
Sutton *London* **15** B2
Suyu *Seoul* **27** B2
Suzukishinden *Tokyo* **30** A2
Svanemøllen *Copenhagen* **8** A3
Sveaborg = Suomenlinna *Helsinki* **11** C2
Sverdlov *Moscow* **19** B2
Svestad *Oslo* **23** B2
Svinö *Helsinki* **11** C1
Swanley *London* **15** B4
Swansea *Toronto* **31** B2
Swinburne I. *New York* **22** C1
Swords *Dublin* **10** A2
Sydenham *Johannesburg* **13** A2
Sydney *Sydney* **29** B2
Sydney, Univ. of *Sydney* **29** B2
Sydney Harbour Bridge *Sydney* **29** B2
Sydney Kingsford Smith ✈ (SYD) *Sydney* **29** B2
Sydstranden *Copenhagen* **8** B3
Sylvania *Sydney* **29** C1
Syon Park *London* **15** B2
Szczęśliwice *Warsaw* **32** B1
Széchnenyi-hegy *Budapest* **7** B1
Széphalom *Budapest* **7** A1

T

Taastrup *Copenhagen* **8** B1
Tabata *Tokyo* **30** A3
Tablada *Buenos Aires* **7** C1
Table B. *Cape Town* **8** A1
Table Mt. *Cape Town* **8** A1
Taboão da Serra *São Paulo* **27** B1
Täby *Stockholm* **29** A2
Tacuba *Mexico City* **18** B1
Tacubaya *Mexico City* **18** B1
Tafelbaai = Table B. *Cape Town* **8** A1
Taft *Orlando* **23** B2
Tagig → *Manila* **17** B2
Taguig *Manila* **17** B2
Tai Hang *Hong Kong* **12** B2
Tai Lo Shan *Hong Kong* **12** A2
Tai Po Tsai *Hong Kong* **12** A2
Tai Seng *Singapore* **28** A3
Tai Shui Hang *Hong Kong* **12** A2
Tai Tam B. *Hong Kong* **12** B2
Tai Tam Tuk Res. *Hong Kong* **12** B2
Tai Wai *Hong Kong* **12** A2
Tai Wan Tau *Hong Kong* **12** B2
Tai Wo Hau *Hong Kong* **12** A1
Tainaka *Osaka* **23** B2
Taishō *Osaka* **23** B1
Taita *Wellington* **33** B2
Tajrīsh *Tehran* **31** A2
Takaido *Tokyo* **30** A2
Takaishi *Tokyo* **30** B2
Takarazuka *Osaka* **23** A1
Takasago *Tokyo* **30** A4
Takatsu *Tokyo* **30** B2
Takeshita *Tokyo* **30** B2
Takinegawa *Tokyo* **30** A3
Takoma Park *Washington* **33** B3
Taksim *Istanbul* **12** B1
Talaide *Lisbon* **16** A1
Taliganga *Calcutta* **14** B2
Talipapa *Manila* **17** A2
Tallaght *Dublin* **10** B1
Tallkrogen *Stockholm* **29** B2
Tama *Tokyo* **30** B1
Tama → *Tokyo* **30** B2
Tama Kyūryō *Tokyo* **30** B2
Tamaden *Tokyo* **30** B2
Tamagawa-josui → *Tokyo* **30** A1
Taman Sari *Jakarta* **12** A1
Tamanduateí → *São Paulo* **27** B2
Tamboerskloof *Cape Town* **8** A1
Tambora *Jakarta* **12** A1
Tammisalo *Helsinki* **11** B3
Tammûh *Cairo* **7** B2
Tampines *Singapore* **28** A3
Tanah Abang *Jakarta* **12** A1
Tanah Kusir *Jakarta* **12** B1
Tangelo Park *Orlando* **23** B2
Tanjung Duren *Jakarta* **12** B1
Tanjung Priok *Jakarta* **12** A2
Tanum *Oslo* **23** A1
Tapada *Lisbon* **16** A1
Tapanila *Helsinki* **11** B3
Tapiales *Buenos Aires* **7** C1
Tapiola *Helsinki* **11** B1
Tapsia *Calcutta* **14** B2
Tara *Mumbai* **20** A1
Tarabya *Istanbul* **12** B2
Tårbæk *Copenhagen* **8** A3
Tarchomin *Warsaw* **32** B1
Tardeo *Mumbai* **20** B1
Targówek *Warsaw* **32** B2
Tårnby *Copenhagen* **8** B3
Tarqua Bay *Lagos* **14** B2
Tathong Channel *Hong Kong* **12** B2
Tathong Pt. *Hong Kong* **12** B2
Tatuapé *São Paulo* **27** B2
Taufkirchen *Munich* **21** B2
Tavares, I. dos *Rio de Janeiro* **25** A2
Tavros *Athens* **2** B2
Tawa *Wellington* **33** A1
Te Papa Museum *Wellington* **33** B1
Teaneck *New York* **22** A1
Tebet *Jakarta* **12** B2
Tecamachalco *Mexico City* **18** B1
Ted Williams Tunnel *Boston* **6** A2
Teddington *London* **15** B1
Tegel *Berlin* **5** A2
Tegel, Berlin ✈ (TXL) *Berlin* **5** A2
Tegeler See *Berlin* **5** A2
Tegelort *Berlin* **5** A2
Teheran = Tehrān *Tehran* **31** A2
Tehrān *Tehran* **31** A2
Tehrān Pārs *Tehran* **31** A3
Tei Tong Tsui *Hong Kong* **12** B2
Tejo, Rio → *Lisbon* **16** A2
Tekstilyshchik *Moscow* **19** B3
Telhal *Lisbon* **16** A1
Telok Blangah *Singapore* **28** B2
Teltow *Berlin* **5** B2
Teltow kanal *Berlin* **5** B3
Tempelhof *Berlin* **5** B3
Tempelhof, Berlin ✈ (THF) *Berlin* **5** B3
Temple City *Los Angeles* **16** B4
Temple Hills *Washington* **33** C4
Templeogue *Dublin* **10** B2
Temppeliaukio Church *Helsinki* **11** B2
Tenafly *New York* **22** A2
Tenayuca, Piramide de *Mexico City* **18** A1
Tengah → *Singapore* **28** A2
Tennoji *Osaka* **23** B2
Tepalcates *Mexico City* **18** B2
Tepeyac, Parque Nacional △ *Mexico City* **18** B2
Terrazzano *Milan* **19** A1
Terre des Hommes *Montreal* **20** A2
Terrugem *Lisbon* **16** A1
Tervuren *Brussels* **6** B2
Tervuren, Park van *Brussels* **6** B3
Tetuán *Madrid* **17** B1
Teufelsberg *Berlin* **5** B2
Thalkirchen *Munich* **21** B2
Thames Ditton *London* **15** B1
Thamesmead *London* **15** A4
Thana Cr. → *Mumbai* **20** A2
Thiais *Paris* **24** B3
Thisio *Athens* **2** B2
Thistletown *Toronto* **31** A1
Thomastown *Melbourne* **18** A2
Thompson I. *Boston* **6** B3
Thon Buri *Bangkok* **3** B1
Thornbury *Melbourne* **18** A2
Thorncliffe *Toronto* **31** A2
Thornhill *Toronto* **31** A2
Thornton *Cape Town* **8** A2
Thornton Heath *London* **15** B3
Threipmuir Res. *Edinburgh* **11** B2
Throgs Neck *New York* **22** B2
Tian'anmen Square *Beijing* **4** B2
Tiancun *Beijing* **4** B1
Tibet, L. *Orlando* **23** B1
Tibidabo *Barcelona* **4** A1
Tibradden Mt. *Dublin* **10** B2
Tiburon *San Francisco* **26** A2
Tiburtino *Rome* **26** B2
Ticomán *Mexico City* **18** A2
Tiefersee *Berlin* **5** B1
Tiejiangyin *Beijing* **4** C2
Tiergarten *Berlin* **5** A3
Tijgerhof *Cape Town* **8** A2
Tijuca *Rio de Janeiro* **25** B1
Tijuca, Pico da *Rio de Janeiro* **25** B1
Tijuca △ *Rio de Janeiro* **25** B1
Tikkurila *Helsinki* **11** B3
Tilak Nagar *Delhi* **10** B1
Tilanqiao *Shanghai* **28** B1
Timah, Bukit *Singapore* **28** A2
Timiryazev Park *Moscow* **19** B2
Ting Kau *Hong Kong* **12** A1
Tira *Jerusalem* **13** A1
Tirsa *Cairo* **7** B2
Tishrīyaa *Baghdad* **3** B2
Tiu Keng Leng *Hong Kong* **12** B2
Tizapán *Mexico City* **18** C1
Tlalnepantla → *Mexico City* **18** A1
Tlalpan *Mexico City* **18** C2
To Kwai Wan *Hong Kong* **12** B2
Toa Payoh *Singapore* **28** A3
Točná *Prague* **25** C2
Toco Hills *Atlanta* **3** B2
Todt Hill *New York* **22** C1
Tōkagi *Tokyo* **30** A4
Tokai Plantation *Cape Town* **8** B1
Tōkaichiba *Tokyo* **30** B2
Tōkyō *Tokyo* **30** B3
Tōkyō B. = Tōkyō-Wan *Tokyo* **30** B4
Tōkyō Disneyland *Tokyo* **30** B4
Tōkyō Haneda ✈ (HND) *Tokyo* **30** B3
Tōkyō Harbour *Tokyo* **30** B3
Tōkyō-Wan *Tokyo* **30** B4
Tolka → *Dublin* **10** A1
Tollygunge = Taliganga *Calcutta* **14** B2
Tolworth *London* **15** B2
Tomba di Nerone *Rome* **26** B1
Tommy Thompson Park *Toronto* **31** B3
Tondo *Manila* **17** B1
Tongbinggo *Seoul* **27** B1
Tongqiao *Shanghai* **28** A1
Toorak *Melbourne* **18** B2
Topanga State Park ⌂ *Los Angeles* **16** B1
Topkapı *Istanbul* **12** B1
Topkapı Palaca *Istanbul* **12** B1
Tor di Quinto *Rome* **26** B1
Tor Pignattara *Rome* **26** B2
Tor Sapienza *Rome* **26** B2
Torcy *Paris* **24** A4
Toronto *Toronto* **31** B2
Toronto, Univ. of *Toronto* **31** B2
Toronto City Centre ✈ (YTZ) *Toronto* **31** B2
Toronto Harbour *Toronto* **31** B2
Toronto I. *Toronto* **31** B2
Toronto Lester B. Pearson Int. ✈ (YYZ) *Toronto* **31** A1
Torre Lupara *Rome* **26** B2
Torre Nova *Rome* **26** B2
Torrellas → *Barcelona* **4** A1
Torrevécchia *Rome* **26** B1
Toshima *Tokyo* **30** A3
Toshimaen *Tokyo* **30** A2
Tottenham *London* **15** A3
Tottenham *Melbourne* **18** A1
Toussus-le-Noble *Paris* **24** B1
Toussus-le-Noble ✈ *Paris* **24** B1
Towchāl Cable Car *Tehran* **31** A2
Tower Hamlets ☐ *London* **15** A3
Tower of London *London* **15** A3
Towra Pt. *Sydney* **29** C2
Tøyen *Oslo* **23** A3
Toyonaka *Osaka* **23** A1
Trafaria *Lisbon* **16** A1
Traição, Cor. → *São Paulo* **27** B2
Tranegilde *Copenhagen* **8** B2
Trångsund *Stockholm* **29** B2
Trappenfelde *Berlin* **5** A4
Trastévere *Rome* **26** B1
Treasure I. *San Francisco* **26** B2
Třeboradice *Prague* **25** B3
Třebotov *Prague* **25** C1
Tremblay-en-France *Paris* **24** A4
Tremembe → *São Paulo* **27** A2
Tremont *New York* **22** A2
Trenno *Milan* **19** B1
Treptow *Berlin* **5** B3
Três Rios, Sa. dos *Rio de Janeiro* **25** B1
Trevi, Fontana di *Rome* **26** B1
Trezzano sul Naviglio *Milan* **19** B1
Trieste *Rome* **26** B2
Trinidad *Washington* **33** B4
Trinity *Edinburgh* **11** B2
Trinity College *Dublin* **10** A2
Trionfale *Rome* **26** B1
Triulzo *Milan* **19** B2
Troja *Prague* **25** B2
Trollbäcken *Stockholm* **29** B3
Trombay *Mumbai* **20** A2
Troparevo *Moscow* **19** C1
Trudeau, Montréal ✈ (YUL) *Montreal* **20** B1
Trudyashchikhsya, Ostrov *St. Petersburg* **27** B1
Tryvasshøgda *Oslo* **23** A3
Tseng Lan Shue *Hong Kong* **12** A2
Tseung Kwan *Hong Kong* **12** B2
Tsim Sha Tsui *Hong Kong* **12** B2
Tsing Yi *Hong Kong* **12** A1
Tsova *Jerusalem* **13** B1
Tsuen Wan *Hong Kong* **12** A1
Tsur Hadassa *Jerusalem* **13** B1
Tsurumi → *Tokyo* **30** B3
Tsz Wan Shan *Hong Kong* **12** A2
Tuas *Singapore* **28** B1
Tuchoměřice *Prague* **25** B1
Tuckahoe *New York* **22** A3
Tucuruvi *São Paulo* **27** A2
Tufello *Rome* **26** B2
Tufnell Park *London* **15** A3
Tufts University *Boston* **6** A2
Tughlakabad *Delhi* **10** B2
Tuindorp *Amsterdam* **2** A2
Tullamarine *Melbourne* **18** A1
Tulse Hill *London* **15** B3
Tung Lung Chau *Hong Kong* **12** B2
Tung O *Hong Kong* **12** B1
Tunis *Baghdad* **3** A2
Tuomarila *Helsinki* **11** B1
Tureberg *Stockholm* **29** A1
Turffontein *Johannesburg* **13** B2
Turkey L. *Orlando* **23** A2
Turkey Lake Park *Orlando* **23** A2
Turner Field *Atlanta* **3** B2
Turnham Green *London* **15** B2
Turnhouse *Edinburgh* **11** B1
Tuscolana, Via *Rome* **26** B2
Twelve Apostles *Cape Town* **8** A1
Twickenham *London* **15** B1
Twickenham Rugby Ground *London* **15** B1
Twin Peaks *San Francisco* **26** B2
Two Rock Mt. *Dublin* **10** B2
Tymon North *Dublin* **10** B1
Tysons Corner *Washington* **33** B2

U

U.S. Capitol *Washington* **33** B3
U.S. Cellular Field *Chicago* **9** C3
Ubeidiya *Jerusalem* **13** B2
Uberaba → *São Paulo* **27** B2
Ubin, Pulau *Singapore* **28** A3
Uccle *Brussels* **6** B2
Udelnaya *St. Petersburg* **27** A2
Udelnoe *St. Petersburg* **27** B1
Udlding *Munich* **21** A1
Ueno *Tokyo* **30** A3
Úholičky *Prague* **25** B1
Uhříněves *Prague* **25** B3
Uithoorn *Amsterdam* **2** B1
Ujazdów *Warsaw* **32** B2
Újpalota *Budapest* **7** A2
Újpest *Budapest* **7** A2
Ukita *Tokyo* **30** A4
Ullerup *Copenhagen* **8** B3
Ullevål *Oslo* **23** A3
Ulriksdal *Stockholm* **29** A1
Ulyanka *St. Petersburg* **27** B1
Um Al-Khanazir Island *Baghdad* **3** B2
Umeda *Osaka* **23** A1
Ümraniye *Istanbul* **12** B2
Underground Atlanta *Atlanta* **3** B2
Underhill, L. *Orlando* **23** A3
Unětický potok → *Prague* **25** B2
Unhos *Lisbon* **16** A2
Unidad Santa Fe *Mexico City* **18** B1
Union City *New York* **22** B1
Union Port *New York* **22** B2
Union Station *Toronto* **31** B2
United Center *Chicago* **9** B2
United Nations Headquarters *New York* **22** B2
Universal Studios *Los Angeles* **16** B2
Universal Studios *Orlando* **23** B2
Universidad *Madrid* **17** B1
Universidad de Chile *Santiago* **27** B2
University Park *Washington* **33** B4
Unterbiberg *Munich* **21** B2
Unterföhring *Munich* **21** A3
Unterhaching *Munich* **21** B2
Unterlaa *Vienna* **32** B2
Untermenzing *Munich* **21** A1
Upper B. *New York* **22** C1
Upper Elmers End *London* **15** B3
Upper New York B. = Upper B. *New York* **22** C1
Upper Norwood *London* **15** B3
Upper Peirce Res. *Singapore* **28** A2
Upper Sydenham *London* **15** B3
Upper Tooting *London* **15** B3
Upton *London* **15** A4
Uptown *Chicago* **9** B2
Uran *Mumbai* **20** B2
Urayasu *Tokyo* **30** B4
Urbe ✈ *Rome* **26** B2
Urca *Rio de Janeiro* **25** B2
Uritsk *St. Petersburg* **27** C1
Úrōm *Budapest* **7** A2
Ursus *Warsaw* **32** B1
Ursvik *Stockholm* **29** A1
Usera *Madrid* **17** B1
Ushigome *Tokyo* **30** A3
Usina *Rio de Janeiro* **25** B1
Üsküdar *Istanbul* **12** B2
Ust-Slavyanka *St. Petersburg* **27** C3
Uteke *Stockholm* **29** A3
Utrata *Warsaw* **32** B2
Uttarpara *Calcutta* **14** B1
Utterslev Mose *Copenhagen* **8** A2

V

Vaclavské náměstí *Prague* **25** B2
Vadaul *Mumbai* **20** A2
Vaires-sur-Marne *Paris* **24** A4
Valby *Copenhagen* **8** B2
Valcannuta *Rome* **26** B1
Valdelatas *Madrid* **17** A1
Vale *Washington* **33** B1
Valenton *Paris* **24** B3
Valera *Milan* **19** A1
Vallcarca *Barcelona* **4** A1
Valldoreix *Barcelona* **4** A1
Vallecas *Madrid* **17** B2
Vallensbæk *Copenhagen* **8** B2
Vallensbæk Strand *Copenhagen* **8** B2
Vallentunasjön *Stockholm* **29** A2
Valleranello *Rome* **26** C1
Vallisaari *Helsinki* **11** C3
Vallvidrera *Barcelona* **4** A1
Valvidrera → *Barcelona* **4** A1
Van Gogh-museum *Amsterdam* **2** A2
Vanak *Tehran* **31** A2
Vanda = Vantaa *Helsinki* **11** B2
Vangede *Copenhagen* **8** A3
Vaniköy *Istanbul* **12** B2
Vanløse *Copenhagen* **8** A2
Vantaa *Helsinki* **11** B2
Vantaankoski *Helsinki* **11** B2
Vantaanpuisto *Helsinki* **11** B2
Vanves *Paris* **24** B2
Varedo *Milan* **19** A1
Varkiza *Athens* **2** C2
Vartiokylä *Helsinki* **11** B3
Vartiosaari *Helsinki* **11** B3
Vasamuseet *Stockholm* **29** B2
Vasco *Cape Town* **8** A2
Vasfanārd *Tehran* **31** B2
Vashi *Mumbai* **20** A2
Vasilyevskiy, Ostrov *St. Petersburg* **27** B1
Vatican City ■ *Rome* **26** B1
Vaucluse *Sydney* **29** B2
Vaucresson *Paris* **24** A1
Vaughan *Toronto* **31** A1
Vauhallan *Paris* **24** B2
Vaujours *Paris* **24** A4
Vauxhall *London* **15** B3
Vecsés *Budapest* **7** B3
Veleň *Prague* **25** A3
Veleslavin *Prague* **25** B2
Vélizy-Villacoublay *Paris* **24** B2
Velka-Chuchle *Prague* **25** B2
Velké Přílepy *Prague* **25** B1
Venda Seca *Lisbon* **16** A1
Venetian Islands *Miami* **18** B2
Venice *Los Angeles* **16** C2
Ventas *Madrid* **17** B1
Ventorro del Cano *Madrid* **17** B1
Venustiano Carranza *Mexico City* **18** B2
Verde → *São Paulo* **27** A1
Verdi *Athens* **2** A2
Verdugo Mts. *Los Angeles* **16** A2
Verdun *Montreal* **20** B2
Vérhalom *Budapest* **7** A2
Vermelho → *São Paulo* **27** B1
Vernon *Los Angeles* **16** B3
Verrières-le-Buisson *Paris* **24** B2
Versailles *Buenos Aires* **7** B1
Versailles *Paris* **24** B1
Veshnyaki *Moscow* **19** B3
Vesolyy Posolok *St. Petersburg* **27** B2
Vestra *Helsinki* **11** B1
Vestskoven *Copenhagen* **8** A2
Vicálvaro *Madrid* **17** B2
Vicente Lopez *Buenos Aires* **7** B2
Victoria *Hong Kong* **12** B2
Victoria, Mt. *Wellington* **33** B1
Victoria, Pont *Montreal* **20** B2
Victoria and Alfred Waterfront *Cape Town* **8** A1
Victoria Gardens *Mumbai* **20** B2
Victoria Harbour *Hong Kong* **12** B1
Victoria Island *Lagos* **14** B2
Victoria L. *Johannesburg* **13** B2
Victoria Lawn Tennis Courts *Melbourne* **18** B2
Victoria Park *Singapore* **28** B2
Victoria Peak *Hong Kong* **12** B1
Vienna = Wien *Vienna* **32** A2
Vienna *Washington* **33** B2
Vietnam Veterans Memorial *Washington* **33** B3
Vietnam War Museum *Chicago* **9** B3
View Park *Los Angeles* **16** B3
Vigário Geral *Rio de Janeiro* **25** A1
Vigentino *Milan* **19** B2
Viggbyholm *Stockholm* **29** A2
Vighignolo *Milan* **19** B1
Viikki *Helsinki* **11** B3
Vikhroli *Mumbai* **20** A2
Vila Guilherme *São Paulo* **27** B2
Vila Isabel *Rio de Janeiro* **25** B1
Vila Jaguára *São Paulo* **27** B1
Vila Madalena *São Paulo* **27** B1
Vila Maria *São Paulo* **27** B2
Vila Mariana *São Paulo* **27** B2
Vila Prudente *São Paulo* **27** B2
Viladecans *Barcelona* **4** B1
Vile Parle *Mumbai* **20** A2
Villa Adelina *Buenos Aires* **7** B1
Villa Ballester *Buenos Aires* **7** B1
Villa Barilari *Buenos Aires* **7** C2
Villa Bosch *Buenos Aires* **7** B1
Villa C. Colon *Buenos Aires* **7** C2
Villa Ciudadela *Buenos Aires* **7** B1
Villa de Guadalupe *Mexico City* **18** B2
Villa Devoto *Buenos Aires* **7** B1
Villa Diamante *Buenos Aires* **7** C2
Villa Dominico *Buenos Aires* **7** C3
Villa Lugano *Buenos Aires* **7** C2
Villa Lynch *Buenos Aires* **7** B1
Villa Madero *Buenos Aires* **7** C1
Villa Sáenz Pena *Buenos Aires* **7** B1
Villa Urquiza *Buenos Aires* **7** B2
Villaverde *Madrid* **17** B1
Villaverde Bajo *Madrid* **17** B1
Ville-d'Avray *Paris* **24** B2
Villecresnes *Paris* **24** B4
Villejuif *Paris* **24** B3
Villemomble *Paris* **24** A4
Villeneuve-la-Garenne *Paris* **24** A2
Villeneuve-le-Roi *Paris* **24** B3
Villeneuve-St-Georges *Paris* **24** B3
Villeparisis *Paris* **24** A4
Villevaudé *Paris* **24** A4
Villiers-le-Bâcle *Paris* **24** B1
Villiers-sur-Marne *Paris* **24** B4
Villinki *Helsinki* **11** C3
Villoresi, Canale *Milan* **19** A1
Vilvoorde *Brussels* **6** A2
Vimodrone *Milan* **19** A2
Vimont *Montreal* **20** A1
Vincennes *Paris* **24** A3
Vincennes, Bois de *Paris* **24** B3
Vineland *Orlando* **23** B1
Vinings *Atlanta* **3** A2
Vinohrady *Prague* **25** B2
Vinoř *Prague* **25** B3
Violet Hill *Hong Kong* **12** B2
Virányos *Budapest* **7** A1
Virgen del San Cristóbal *Santiago* **27** B2
Virginia, L. *Orlando* **23** A2
Virginia Gardens *Miami* **18** B1
Virginia Key *Miami* **18** B2
Viroflay *Paris* **24** B2
Vironas *Athens* **2** B2
Virum *Copenhagen* **8** A2
Visitacion Valley *San Francisco* **26** B2
Vista Alegre *Lima* **14** B3
Vista Alegre *Santiago* **27** C1
Vista Grove *Atlanta* **3** A3
Vitacura *Santiago* **27** B2
Vitínia *Rome* **26** C1
Vitry-sur-Seine *Paris* **24** B3
Vizcaya Museum and Gardens *Miami* **18** B2
Vladykino *Moscow* **19** A2
Vlezenbeek *Brussels* **6** B1
Vokovice *Prague* **25** B2
Volgelsdorf *Berlin* **5** B5
Volkhonka-Zil *Moscow* **19** C2
Vollen *Oslo* **23** B1
Volodarskoye *St. Petersburg* **27** B2
Volynkina-Derevnya *St. Petersburg* **27** B1
Vondelpark *Amsterdam* **2** A2
Vösendorf *Vienna* **32** B2
Voula *Athens* **2** C2
Vouliagmeni *Athens* **2** C2
Vredehoek *Cape Town* **8** A1
Vršovice *Prague* **25** B2
Vyborgskaya Storona *St. Petersburg* **27** B2
Vykhino *Moscow* **19** B3
Vyšehrad *Prague* **25** B2

W

Wachterhof *Munich* **21** B3
Wadala *Mumbai* **20** A2
Wadestown *Wellington* **33** B1
Wadi al-Arayis *Jerusalem* **13** B2
Wadi Fukin *Jerusalem* **13** B1
Waduk Pluit *Jakarta* **12** A1
Wah Fu *Hong Kong* **12** B1
Wahda *Baghdad* **3** B2
Währing *Vienna* **32** A2
Waidmannslust *Berlin* **5** A3
Wainuiomata *Wellington* **33** B2
Wainuiomata → *Wellington* **33** B2
Wakefield *Boston* **6** A2
Waldesruh *Berlin* **5** B4
Waldperlach *Munich* **21** B3
Waldtrudering *Munich* **21** B3
Walkinstown *Dublin* **10** B1
Wall Street *New York* **22** B1
Walt Disney World *Orlando* **23** B1
Walter D. Stone Memorial Zoo *Boston* **6** A2
Waltham *Boston* **6** A1
Waltham Forest ☐ *London* **15** A3
Walthamstow *London* **15** A3
Walton-on-Thames *London* **15** B1
Wambeek *Brussels* **6** A3
Wan Chai *Hong Kong* **12** B2
Wandsworth ☐ *London* **15** B2
Wannsee *Berlin* **5** B1
Wansdorf *Berlin* **5** A1
Wanstead *London* **15** A4
Wapping *London* **15** A3
Ward *Dublin* **10** A1
Ward I. *Wellington* **33** B2
Wards I. *New York* **22** B2
Warnberg *Munich* **21** B2
Warner Brothers Studios *Los Angeles* **16** B2
Warrâq el 'Arab *Cairo* **7** A2
Warringal Park *Melbourne* **18** A2
Warriston *Edinburgh* **11** B2
Warsaw = Warszawa *Warsaw* **32** B2
Warszawa *Warsaw* **32** B2
Warszawa ✈ (WAW) *Warsaw* **32** B1
Wartenberg *Berlin* **5** A4
Washington *Washington* **33** B3
Washington Heights *New York* **22** A2
Washington Park *Chicago* **9** C3
Washington Ronald Reagan National ✈ (DCA) *Washington* **33** B3
Wat Pho *Bangkok* **3** B1
Water of Leith → *Edinburgh* **11** B1
Watergraafsmeer *Amsterdam* **2** A2
Waterland *Amsterdam* **2** A2
Waterloo *Brussels* **6** B2
Waterloo *Wellington* **33** B2
Watermeal-Boitsfort *Brussels* **6** B2
Watertown *Boston* **6** A1
Watsonia *Melbourne* **18** A2
Waverley *Boston* **6** A1
Waverley *Johannesburg* **13** A2
Waverley *Sydney* **29** B2
Wawer *Warsaw* **32** B2
Wawrzyszew *Warsaw* **32** B1
Wazirabad *Delhi* **10** A2
Wazīrīya *Baghdad* **3** A2
Wazirpur *Delhi* **10** A2
Wealdstone *London* **15** A1
Wedding *Berlin* **5** A3
Weehawken *New York* **22** B1
Weesp *Amsterdam* **2** B3
Weidling *Vienna* **32** A1
Weidlingbach *Vienna* **32** A1
Weigongcun *Beijing* **4** B1
Weissensee *Berlin* **5** A3
Wellesley Hills *Boston* **6** B1
Welling *London* **15** B4
Wellington *Boston* **6** A2
Wellington *Wellington* **33** B1
Wellington Int. ✈ (WLE) *Wellington* **33** B1
Weltevreden Park *Johannesburg* **13** A1
Wembley *London* **15** A2
Wemmel *Brussels* **6** A1
Wemmer Pan *Johannesburg* **13** B2
Wenceslas Square = Vaclavské náměstí *Prague* **25** B2
Wendenschloss *Berlin* **5** B4
Wennington *London* **15** A5
Werneuchen *Berlin* **5** A5
West Don → *Toronto* **31** A2
West Drayton *London* **15** A1
West Ham *London* **15** A4
West Harrow *London* **15** A1
West Heath *London* **15** B4
West Hill *Toronto* **31** A3
West Hollywood *Los Angeles* **16** B2
West Lamma Channel *Hong Kong* **12** B1
West Los Angeles, University of *Los Angeles* **16** C2
West Medford *Boston* **6** A2
West Miami *Miami* **18** B1
West Molesey *London* **15** B1
West New York *New York* **22** B1
West of Twin Peaks *San Francisco* **26** B2
West Park *Johannesburg* **13** A1
West Rouge *Toronto* **31** A4
West Roxbury *Boston* **6** B2
West Springfield *Washington* **33** C2
West Town *Chicago* **9** B2
West Wharf *Karachi* **13** B1
Westchester *Chicago* **9** B1
Westchester *Los Angeles* **16** C2
Westchester *New York* **22** A2
Westcliff *Johannesburg* **13** B2
Westdene *Johannesburg* **13** B1
Westend *Helsinki* **11** C1
Wester Hailes *Edinburgh* **11** B2
Westerham *Munich* **21** B2
Western Addition *San Francisco* **26** B2
Westgate *Washington* **33** B3
Westlake *Cape Town* **8** B1
Westlake *San Francisco* **26** B2
Westminster *London* **15** A3
Westmount *Montreal* **20** B2
Weston *Toronto* **31** A1
Westwood Village *Los Angeles* **16** B2
Westzaan *Amsterdam* **2** A1
Wetton *Cape Town* **8** B2
Wexford *Toronto* **31** A3
Weybridge *London* **15** B1
Wezembeek-Oppem *Brussels* **6** A2
White Cloud Hill = Baiyun Hill *Canton* **11** B2
White House, The *Washington* **33** B3
Whitechapel *London* **15** A3
Whitehall *Dublin* **10** A2
Whittier *Los Angeles* **16** C4
Whitton *London* **15** B1
Wieden *Vienna* **32** A2
Wien *Vienna* **32** A2
Wien-Schwechat ✈ (VIE) *Vienna* **32** B3
Wienerberg *Vienna* **32** B2
Wierzbno *Warsaw* **32** B2
Wijde Wormer *Amsterdam* **2** A2
Wilanów *Warsaw* **32** B2
Wilanówka → *Warsaw* **32** C2
Wilds, The *Johannesburg* **13** B2
Wilhelmshagen *Berlin* **5** B5
Wilket Creek Park *Toronto* **31** A2
Wilkieston *Edinburgh* **11** B1
Will Rogers State Historical Park ⌂ *Los Angeles* **16** B1
Willbrook *Dublin* **10** B2
Willesden *London* **15** A2
Willesden Green *London* **15** A2
Williamsbridge *New York* **22** A2
Williamsburg *New York* **22** B2
Williamsburg *Orlando* **23** B2
Williamstown *Melbourne* **18** B1
Willis, L. *Orlando* **23** B2
Willoughby *Sydney* **29** A2
Willow Springs *Chicago* **9** C1
Willowdale *Toronto* **31** A2
Wilmersdorf *Berlin* **5** B2
Wilmette *Chicago* **9** A2
Wilmington *London* **15** B5
Wimbledon *London* **15** B2
Wimbledon Common *London* **15** B2
Wimbledon Park *London* **15** B2
Wimbledon Tennis Ground *London* **15** B2
Winchester *Boston* **6** A2
Windermere *Cape Town* **8** A2
Windermere *Orlando* **23** B1
Windsor *Johannesburg* **13** A1
Windsor, Gare *Montreal* **20** B2
Windsor Hills *Los Angeles* **16** C2
Windy Arbour *Dublin* **10** B2
Winning *Munich* **21** B2
Wissous *Paris* **24** B2
Wittenau *Berlin* **5** A2
Witwatersrand, Univ. of *Johannesburg* **13** B2
Włochy *Warsaw* **32** B1
Wo Mei *Hong Kong* **12** A2
Wo Yi Hop *Hong Kong* **12** A1
Woburn *Boston* **6** A2
Woburn *Toronto* **31** A3
Wola *Warsaw* **32** B1
Wolf Trap Farm Park *Washington* **33** B2
Wolgok *Seoul* **27** B2
Wolica *Warsaw* **32** C2
Wólka Węglowa *Warsaw* **32** B1
Wollaston *Boston* **6** B2
Woltersdorf *Berlin* **5** B6
Woluwe-St-Lambert *Brussels* **6** A2
Woluwe-St-Pierre *Brussels* **6** A2
Wong Chuk Hang *Hong Kong* **12** B2
Wong Chuk Wan *Hong Kong* **12** A2
Wong Chuk Yeung *Hong Kong* **12** A2
Wong Tai Sin *Hong Kong* **12** A2
Wood Green *London* **15** A3
Wood Ridge *New York* **22** A1
Woodbine Race Track *Toronto* **31** A1
Woodbridge *Toronto* **31** A1
Woodford *London* **15** A4
Woodford Bridge *London* **15** A4
Woodford Green *London* **15** A4
Woodhaven *New York* **22** B2
Woodhouselee *Edinburgh* **11** B2
Woodlands *Singapore* **28** A2
Woodmont *Washington* **33** B3
Woodside *London* **15** B3
Woodside *New York* **22** B2
Woodstock *Cape Town* **8** A1
Woollahra *Sydney* **29** B2
Woolooware B. *Sydney* **29** C1
Woolwich *London* **15** B4
World Trade Center, site of former *New York* **22** B1
Worli *Mumbai* **20** A1
Worth *Chicago* **9** C2
Wren's Nest *Atlanta* **3** B2
Wrigley Field *Chicago* **9** B3
Wuhlgarten *Berlin* **5** A4
Wujiaochang *Shanghai* **28** B2
Würm → *Munich* **21** B1
Würm-kanal *Munich* **21** A1
Wusong *Shanghai* **28** A1
Wyczółki *Warsaw* **32** C1
Wygoda *Warsaw* **32** B2
Wynberg *Cape Town* **8** B1

X

Xabregas *Lisbon* **16** A2
Xianggang = Hong Kong *Hong Kong* **12** B1
Xiaoguang Park *Canton* **11** B2
Xiaoping *Canton* **11** A2
Xiasha chong *Canton* **11** B1
Xichang *Canton* **11** B2
Xicheng *Beijing* **4** B1
Xidan *Beijing* **4** B2
Xizhimen *Beijing* **4** B1
Xochimilco, Parque Ecológico *Mexico City* **18** C2
Xuanwu *Beijing* **4** B1
Xuhui *Shanghai* **28** B1

Y

Yaba *Lagos* **14** A2
Yaftābād *Tehran* **31** B1
Yahara *Tokyo* **30** A2
Yaho *Tokyo* **30** A1
Yakire *Tokyo* **30** A4
Yaksu *Seoul* **27** B2
Yamada *Osaka* **23** A2
Yamada *Tokyo* **30** B2
Yamato → *Osaka* **23** B1
Yan Kit *Singapore* **28** A3
Yanbu *Canton* **11** B1
Yangcheon *Seoul* **27** B1
Yanghuayuan *Beijing* **4** C1
Yangjae *Seoul* **27** C2
Yangjiazhuang *Shanghai* **28** A1
Yangjing *Shanghai* **28** B2
Yangpu *Shanghai* **28** B2
Yangpu Park *Shanghai* **28** B2
Yannawa *Bangkok* **3** B2
Yarmūk *Baghdad* **3** B1
Yarra Bend Park *Melbourne* **18** A2
Yarraville *Melbourne* **18** A1
Yau Tong *Hong Kong* **12** B2
Yauza → *Moscow* **19** A3
Yeading *London* **15** A1
Yedikule *Istanbul* **12** C1
Yenikapı *Istanbul* **12** B1
Yeniköy *Istanbul* **12** B2
Yeongdeungpo *Seoul* **27** B1
Yeongdong *Seoul* **27** B2
Yeouido *Seoul* **27** B1
Yerba Buena I. *San Francisco* **26** B2
Yerres *Paris* **24** B4
Yerushalayim = Jerusalem *Jerusalem* **13** B2
Yiheyuan *Beijing* **4** A1
Yıldız Park *Istanbul* **12** B2
Yinhangzhen *Shanghai* **28** A2
Yishun *Singapore* **28** A3
Ylästö *Helsinki* **11** B2
Yodo → *Osaka* **23** A2
Yongdingmen *Beijing* **4** B2
Yongfucun *Canton* **11** B2
Yongsan *Seoul* **27** B1
Yonkers *New York* **22** A2
York *Toronto* **31** A2
York Mills *Toronto* **31** A2
York University *Toronto* **31** A1
You'anmen *Beijing* **4** B1
Youngsfield *Cape Town* **8** B1
Yuanxiatian *Canton* **11** A2
Yuexiu Park *Canton* **11** B2
Yugo-Zarad *Moscow* **19** B2
Yuhalixqui, Volcan *Mexico City* **18** C2
Yung Shue Wan *Hong Kong* **12** B1
Yūsofābād *Tehran* **31** A2

Z

Zaandam *Amsterdam* **2** A1
Zaandijk *Amsterdam* **2** A1
Zaanstad *Amsterdam* **2** A1
Záběhlice *Prague* **25** B2
Zabki *Warsaw* **32** B2
Żacisze *Warsaw* **32** B2
Zahrā *Baghdad* **3** A1
Žalov *Prague* **25** A2
Załuski *Warsaw* **32** C1
Zamdorf *Munich* **21** B2
Zanevka *St. Petersburg* **27** B3
Zapote *Manila* **17** C1
Zaventem *Brussels* **6** A2
Zawady *Warsaw* **32** B2
Zāwiyet Abû Musallam *Cairo* **7** B1
Zawrā' Park *Baghdad* **3** B2
Zbraslav *Prague* **25** C2
Zbuzany *Prague* **25** B1
Zdiby *Prague* **25** B2
Zeekoevlei *Cape Town* **8** B2
Zehlendorf *Berlin* **5** B2
Zenne → *Brussels* **6** B1
Żerań *Warsaw* **32** B2
Zerzeń *Warsaw* **32** B2
Zeytinburnu *Istanbul* **12** C1
Zhabei *Shanghai* **28** B1
Zhdanov *Moscow* **19** B3
Zhenru *Shanghai* **28** B1
Zhernovka *St. Petersburg* **27** B2
Zhicun *Canton* **11** B2
Zhongshan Park *Shanghai* **28** B1
Zhoucun *Canton* **11** B2
Zhoujiadu *Shanghai* **28** B1
Zhoujiazhen *Shanghai* **28** B2
Zhulebino *Moscow* **19** B4
Zhushadi *Canton* **11** A3
Zielona *Warsaw* **32** B3
Zielonka *Warsaw* **32** B2
Žižkov *Prague* **25** B2
Zličín *Prague* **25** B1
Zografou *Athens* **2** B2
Żoliborz *Warsaw* **32** B1
Zonnebloem *Cape Town* **8** A1
Zugliget *Budapest* **7** B1
Zuglō *Budapest* **7** A2
Zuiderwoude *Amsterdam* **2** A3
Zumbi *Rio de Janeiro* **25** A1
Zunderdorp *Amsterdam* **2** A2
Zuvuvu → *São Paulo* **27** C2
Zwanenburg *Amsterdam* **2** A1
Zwölfaxing *Vienna* **32** B2

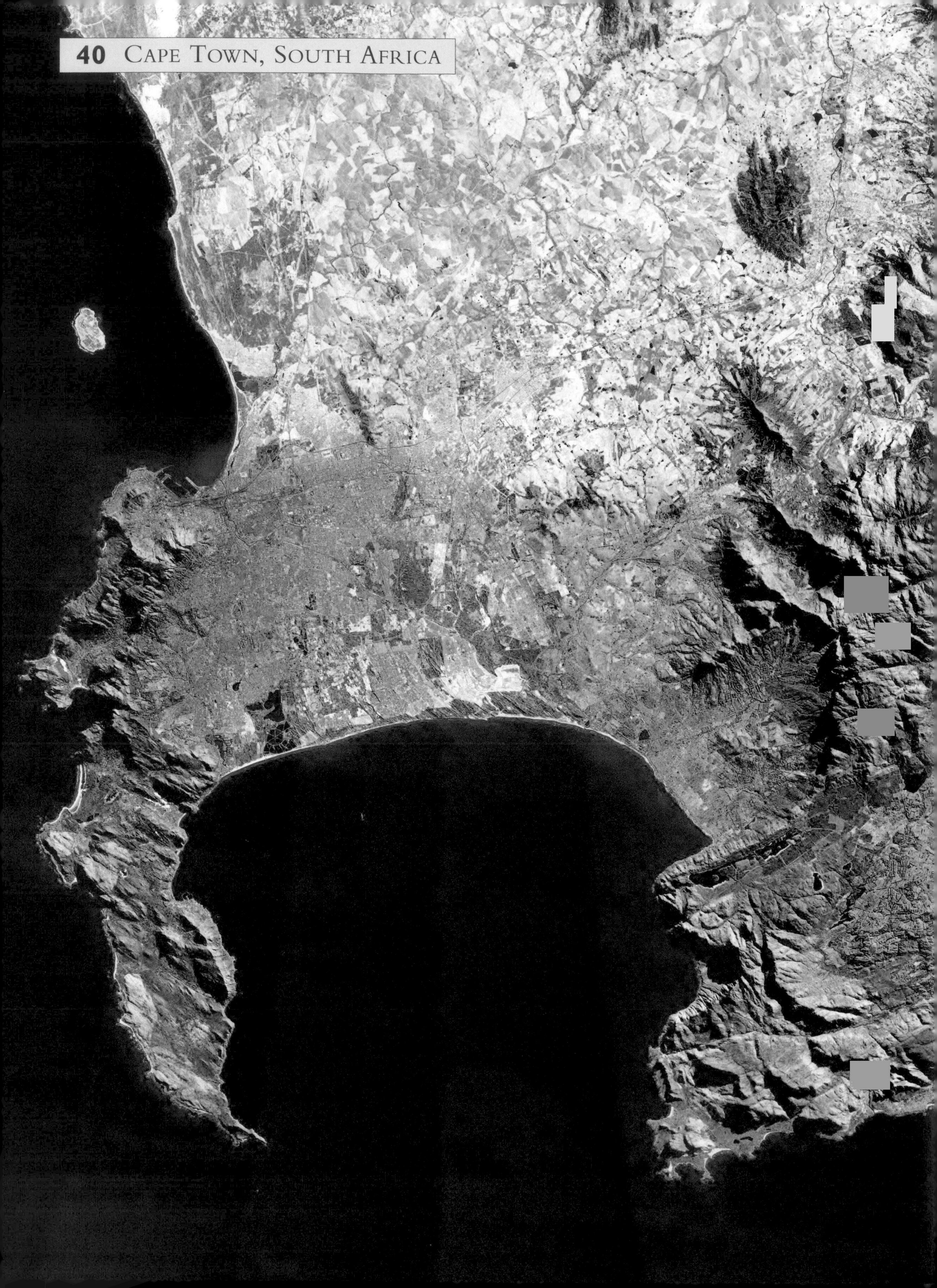

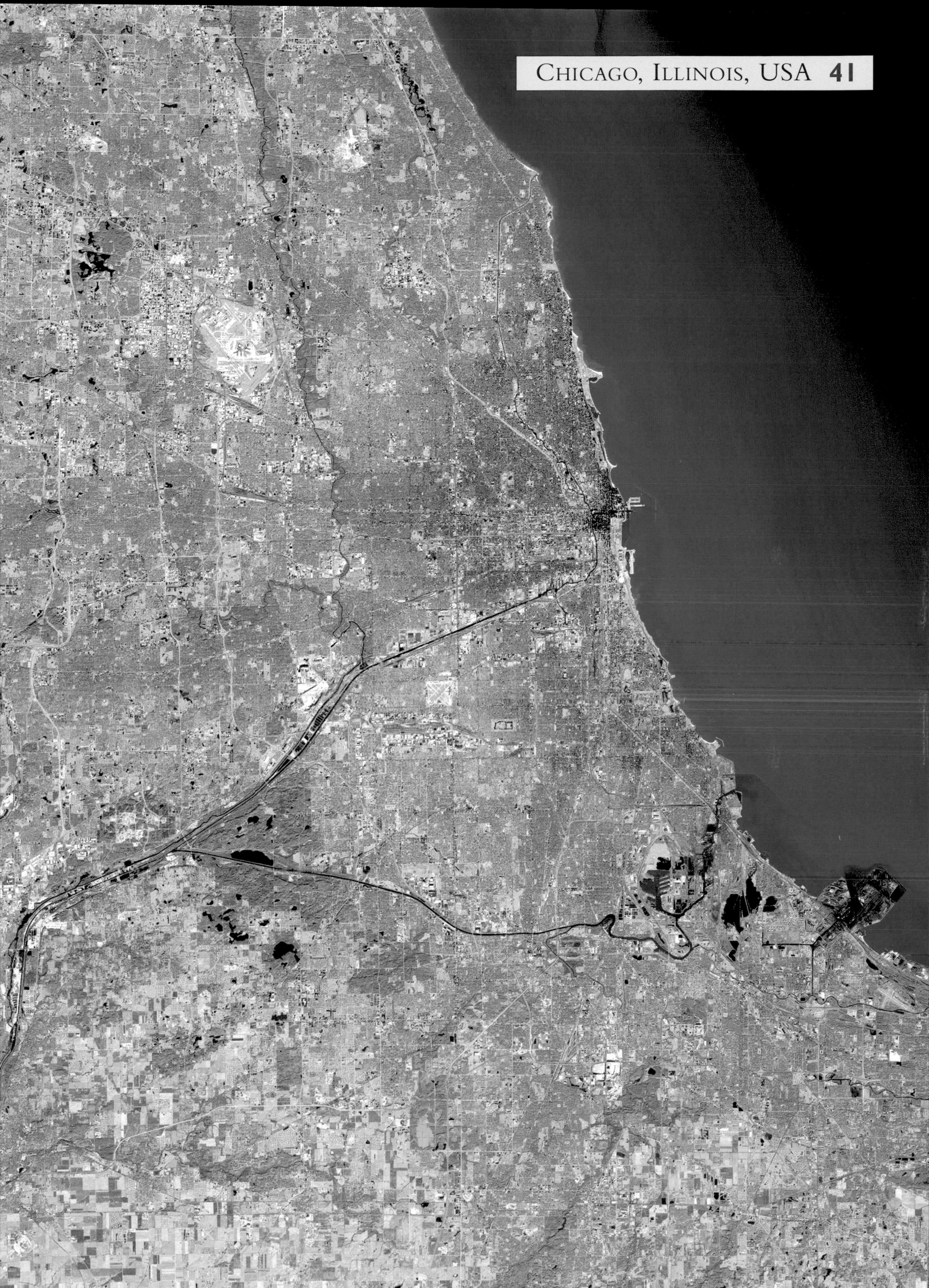

42 Karachi, Pakistan

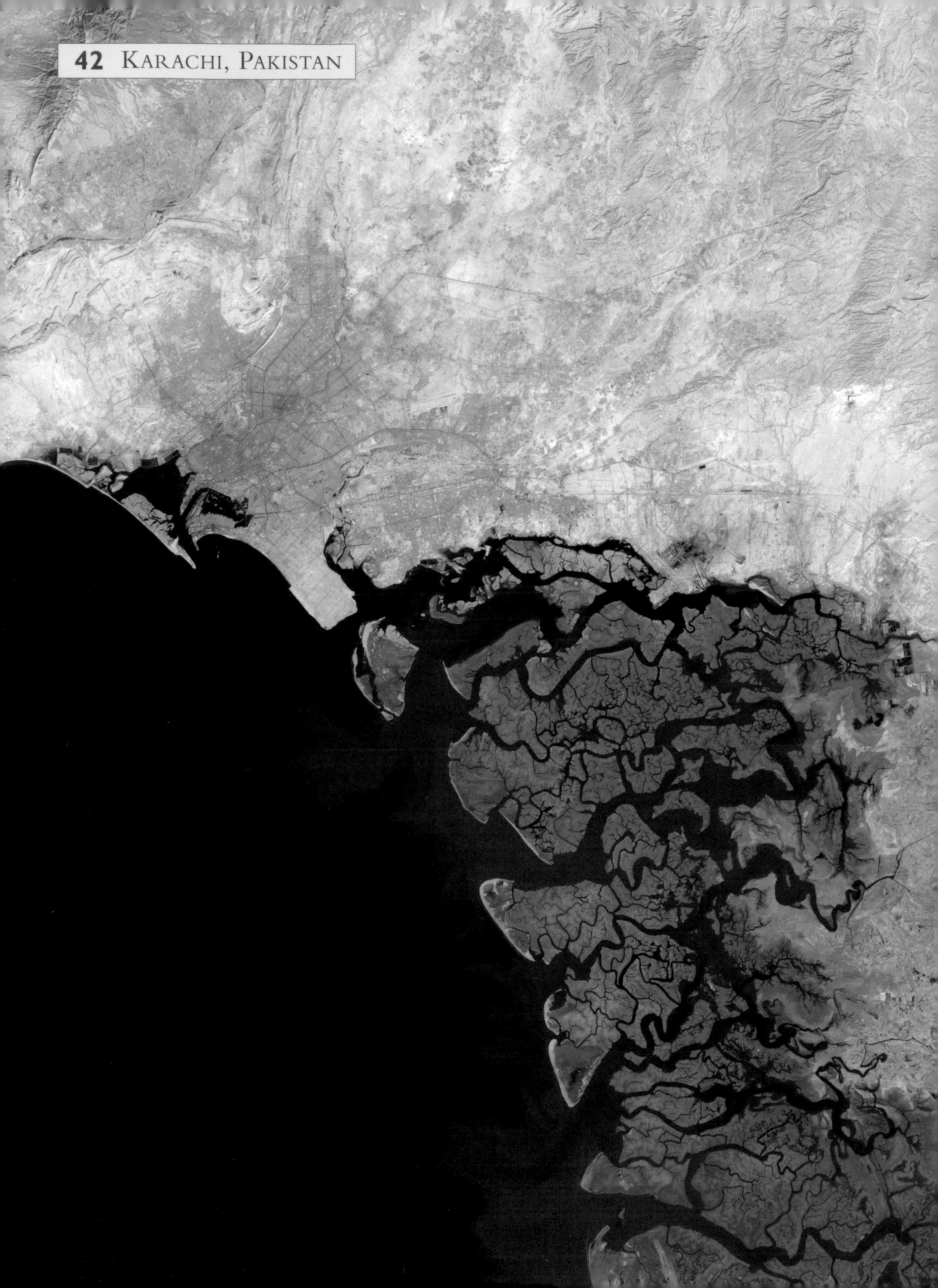

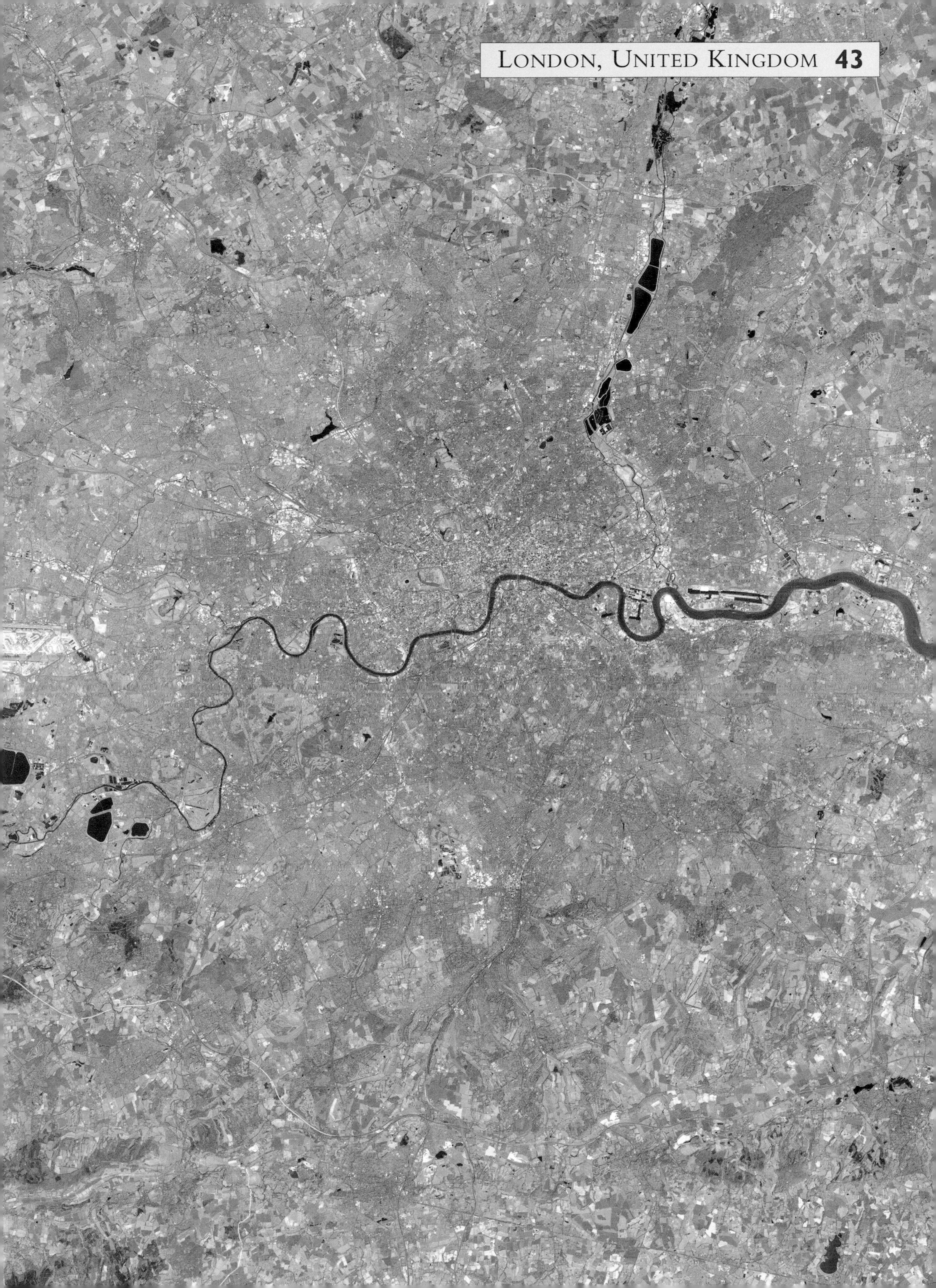

44 New York, NY, USA

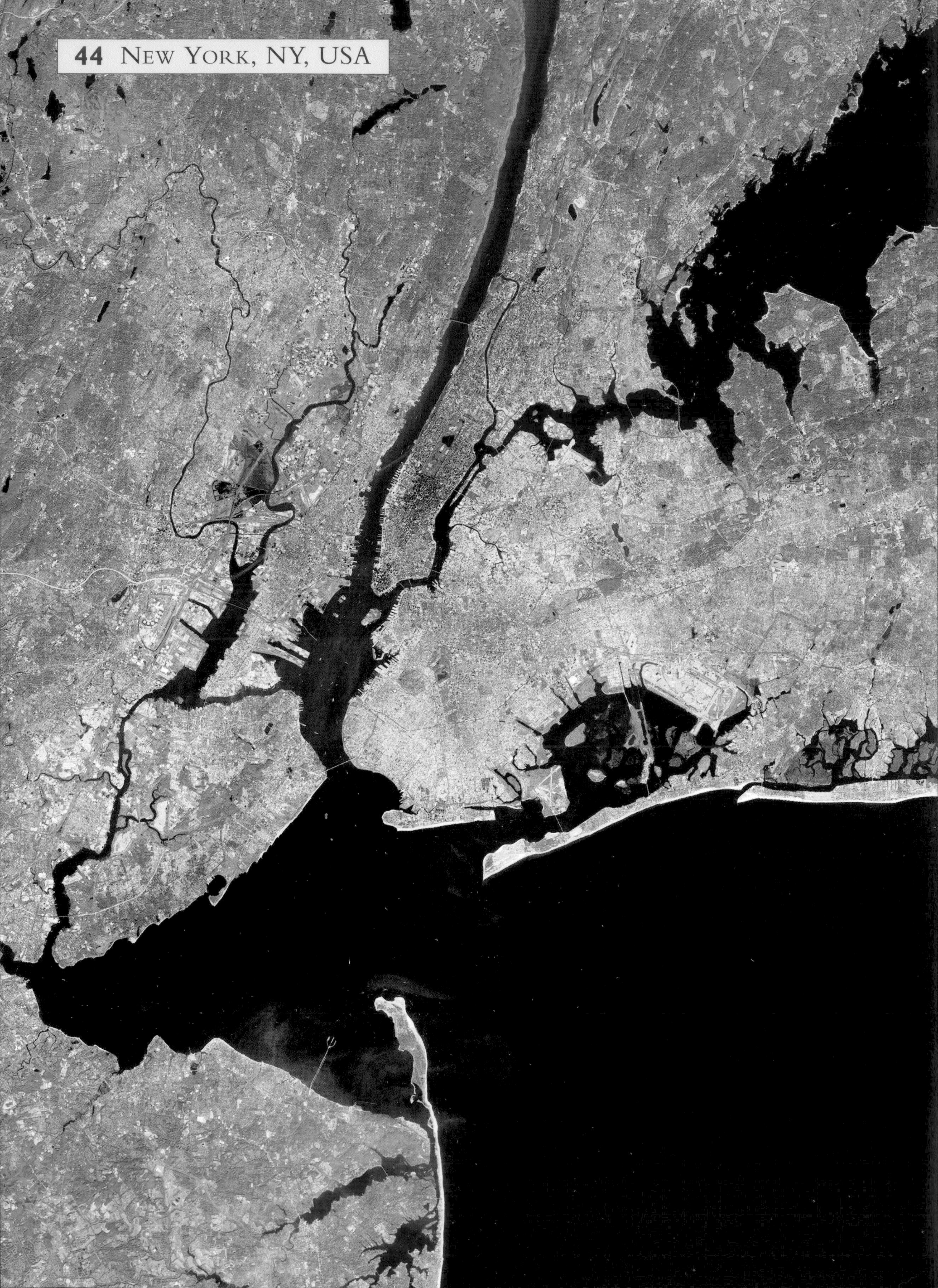

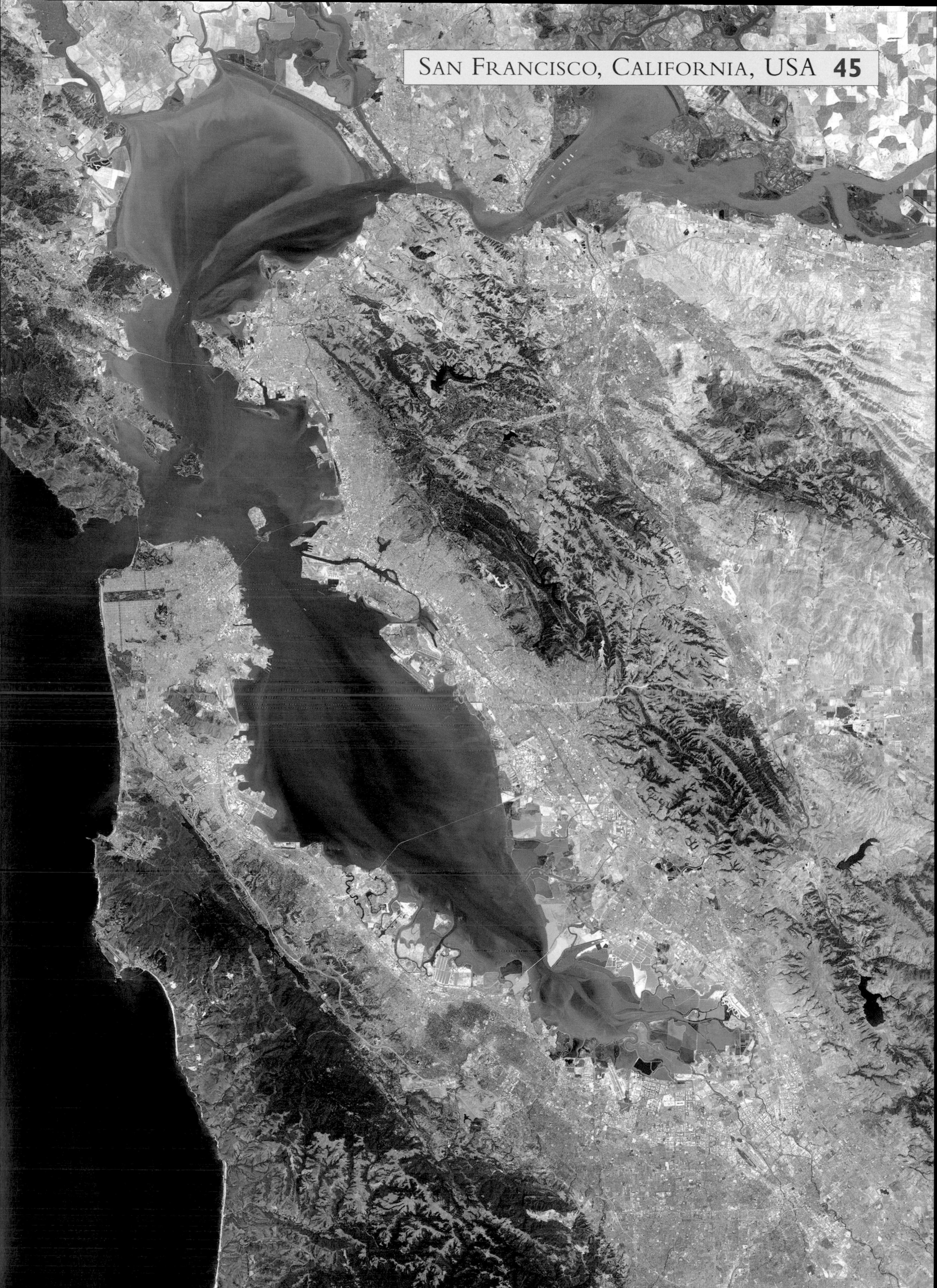

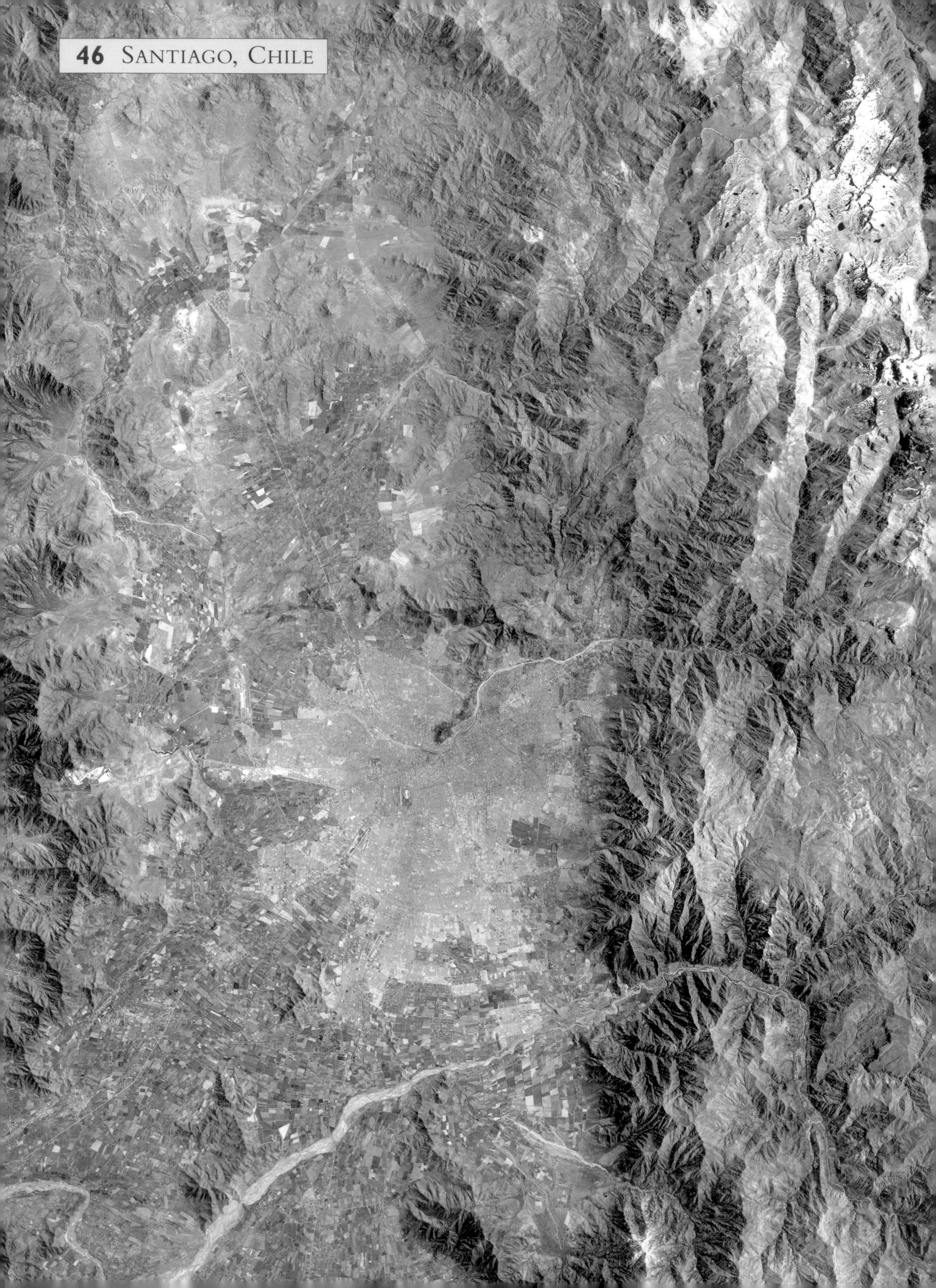
46 SANTIAGO, CHILE

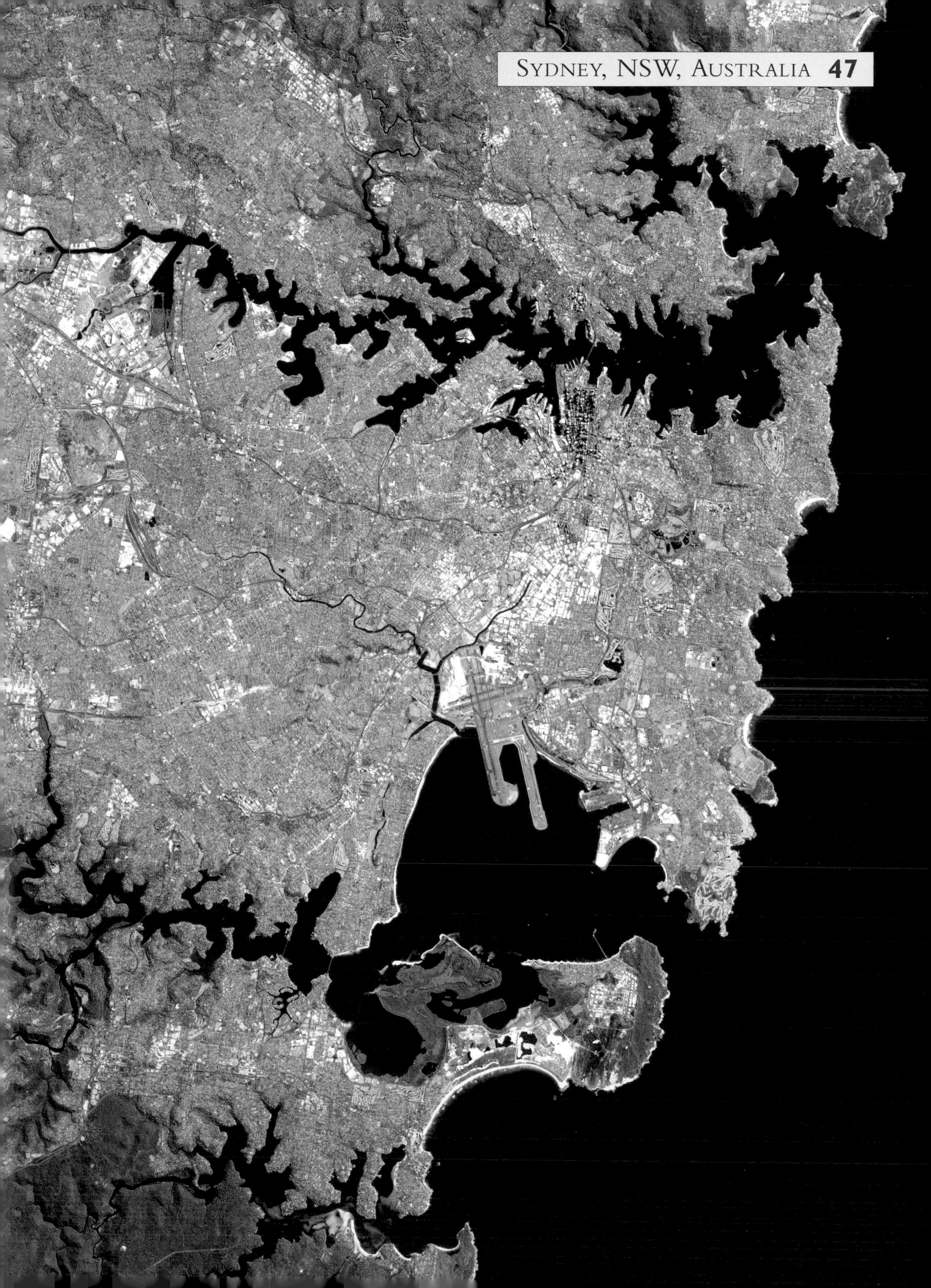

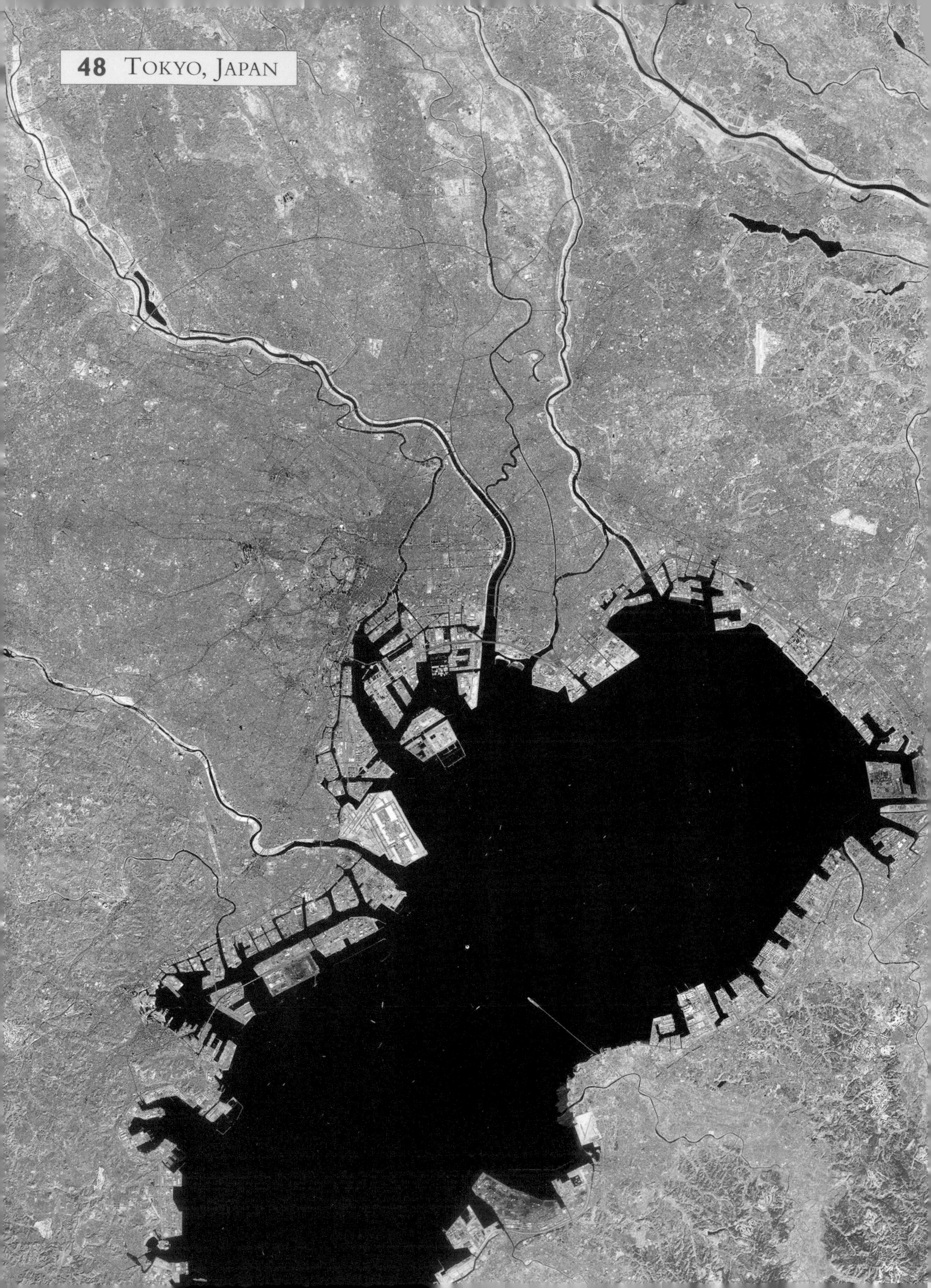
48 TOKYO, JAPAN

WORLD
MAPS

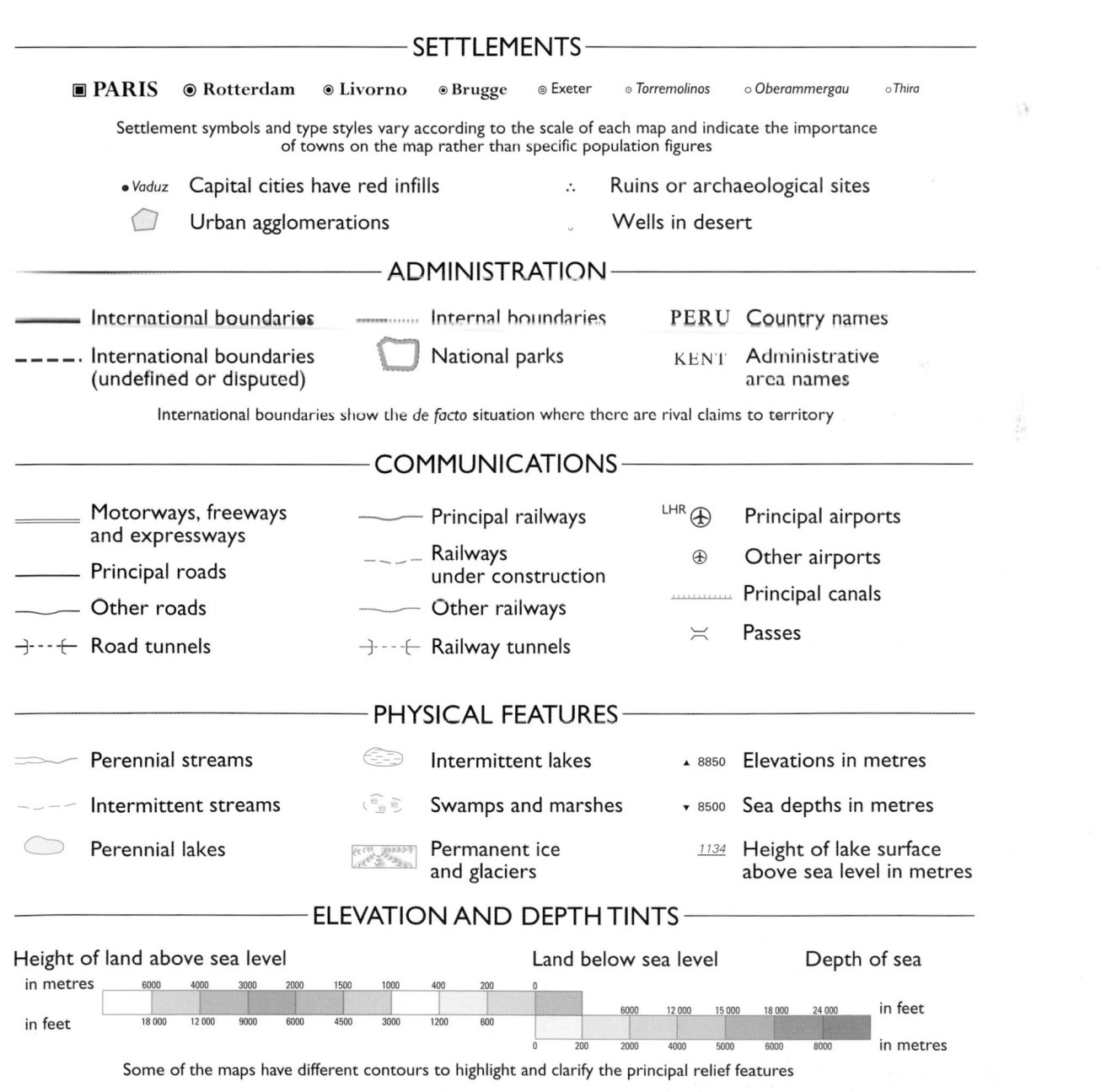

SETTLEMENTS

■ **PARIS**   ◉ **Rotterdam**   ◉ **Livorno**   ◉ Brugge   ◎ Exeter   ◦ *Torremolinos*   ◦ *Oberammergau*   ◦ *Thira*

Settlement symbols and type styles vary according to the scale of each map and indicate the importance
of towns on the map rather than specific population figures

● *Vaduz*   Capital cities have red infills   ∴   Ruins or archaeological sites

⬠   Urban agglomerations   ⌄   Wells in desert

ADMINISTRATION

───── International boundaries   ┄┄┄┄ Internal boundaries   **PERU** Country names

─ ─ ─ ─ International boundaries
(undefined or disputed)   ⬡ National parks   KENT Administrative
area names

International boundaries show the *de facto* situation where there are rival claims to territory

COMMUNICATIONS

═══ Motorways, freeways
and expressways

─── Principal roads

─── Other roads

+---+ Road tunnels

─── Principal railways

─ ─ ─ Railways
under construction

─── Other railways

+---+ Railway tunnels

ᴸᴴᴿ ✈ Principal airports

✈ Other airports

┈┈┈┈ Principal canals

≍ Passes

PHYSICAL FEATURES

∿ Perennial streams

─ ─ ─ Intermittent streams

◯ Perennial lakes

⬭ Intermittent lakes

Swamps and marshes

Permanent ice
and glaciers

▲ 8850 Elevations in metres

▼ 8500 Sea depths in metres

1134 Height of lake surface
above sea level in metres

ELEVATION AND DEPTH TINTS

Height of land above sea level   Land below sea level   Depth of sea

in metres 6000 4000 3000 2000 1500 1000 400 200 0

6000 12 000 15 000 18 000 24 000 in feet

in feet 18 000 12 000 9000 6000 4500 3000 1200 600

0 200 2000 4000 5000 6000 8000 in metres

Some of the maps have different contours to highlight and clarify the principal relief features

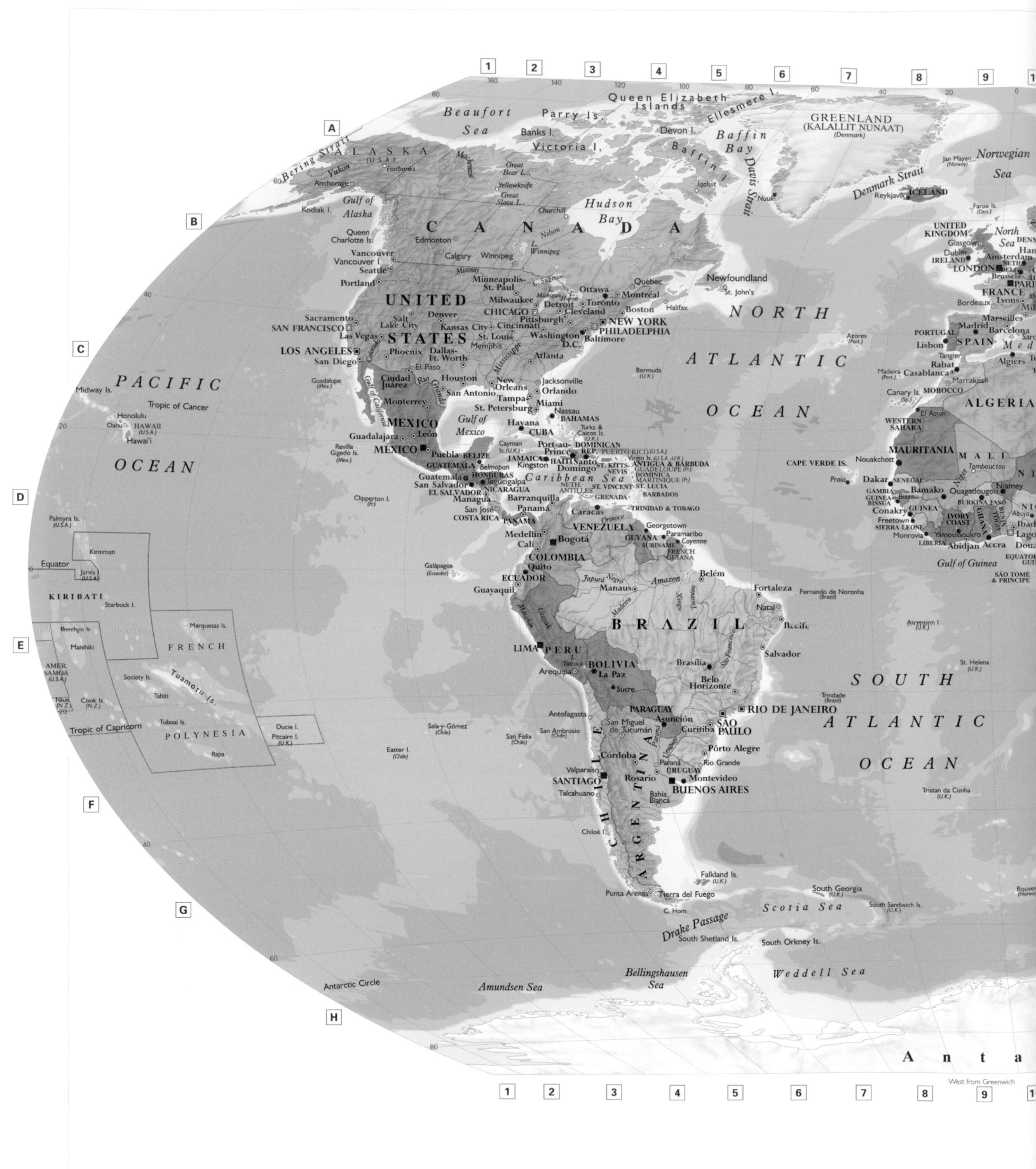

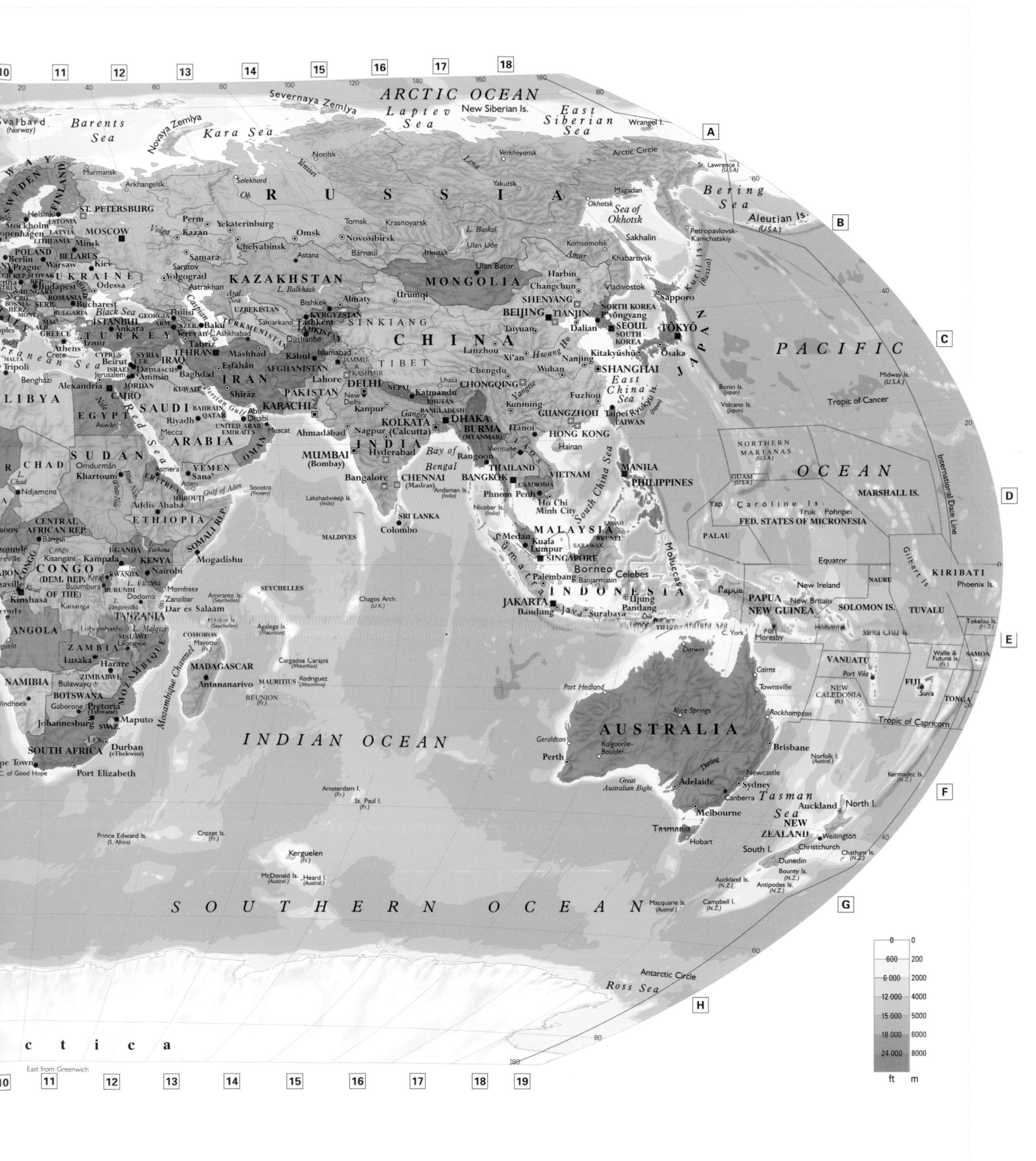
ARCTIC OCEAN
Severnaya Zemlya
Laptev Sea
New Siberian Is.
East Siberian Sea
Wrangel I.
Barents Sea
Kara Sea
Novaya Zemlya
Svalbard (Norway)
Arctic Circle
Bering Sea
Aleutian Is. (U.S.A.)
Sea of Okhotsk
Sakhalin
R U S S I A
Murmansk
Arkhangelsk
ST. PETERSBURG
MOSCOW
Perm
Yekaterinburg
Kazan
Omsk
Tomsk
Krasnoyarsk
Novosibirsk
Chelyabinsk
Samara
Saratov
Volgograd
Astrakhan
Astana
Barnaul
Irkutsk
L. Baikal
Ulan Ude
Norilsk
Yakutsk
Verkhoyansk
Magadan
Okhotsk
Petropavlovsk-Kamchatskiy
Komsomolsk
Khabarovsk
Vladivostok
Harbin
Changchun
SHENYANG
KAZAKHSTAN
L. Balkhash
MONGOLIA
Ulan Bator
Ürümqi
Almaty
Bishkek
KYRGYZSTAN
UZBEKISTAN
Tashkent
Samarkand
TAJIKISTAN
Dushanbe
Ashkhabad
TURKMENISTAN
SINKIANG
C H I N A
TIBET
BEIJING
TIANJIN
Dalian
Taiyuan
Lanzhou
Xi'an
Nanjing
Wuhan
Chengdu
CHONGQING
SHANGHAI
Kunming
Fuzhou
GUANGZHOU
HONG KONG
Hainan
Taipei
TAIWAN
NORTH KOREA
P'yŏngyang
SEOUL
SOUTH KOREA
Kitakyūshū
Ōsaka
TŌKYŌ
Sapporo
JAPAN
Kuril Is. (Russia)
East China Sea
Ryukyu Is. (Japan)
PACIFIC OCEAN
Midway Is. (U.S.A.)
Bonin Is. (Japan)
Volcano Is. (Japan)
Tropic of Cancer
NORTHERN MARIANAS (U.S.A.)
GUAM (U.S.A.)
MARSHALL IS.
Caroline Is.
Yap
Truk
Pohnpei
FED. STATES OF MICRONESIA
PALAU
International Date Line
Equator
KIRIBATI
Gilbert Is.
Phoenix Is.
NAURU
TUVALU
Tokelau Is.
SAMOA
Wallis & Futuna Is. (Fr.)
FIJI
Suva
TONGA
VANUATU
Port Vila
NEW CALEDONIA (Fr.)
SOLOMON IS.
Santa Cruz Is.
PAPUA NEW GUINEA
New Ireland
New Britain
Port Moresby
Tropic of Capricorn
HELSINKI
Stockholm
Copenhagen
ESTONIA
LATVIA
LITHUANIA
Minsk
BELARUS
POLAND
Berlin
Prague
Warsaw
Kiev
UKRAINE
Odessa
Budapest
Bucharest
ROMANIA
BULGARIA
Black Sea
GEORGIA
Tbilisi
ARM.
AZER.
Baku
Yerevan
Caspian Sea
ISTANBUL
Ankara
TURKEY
Izmir
Athens
GREECE
Tabriz
Crete
CYPRUS
SYRIA
Beirut
LEB.
ISRAEL
Damascus
Jerusalem
Amman
JORDAN
IRAQ
Baghdad
TEHRAN
Mashhad
Esfahān
IRAN
Shīrāz
KUWAIT
Persian Gulf
BAHRAIN
QATAR
Abu Dhabi
UNITED ARAB EMIRATES
Muscat
OMAN
Riyadh
SAUDI ARABIA
Mecca
Red Sea
AFGHANISTAN
Kābul
Islamabad
JAMMU & KASHMIR
Lahore
PAKISTAN
KARACHI
DELHI
New Delhi
Kanpur
NEPAL
Katmandu
Lhasa
BHUTAN
BANGLADESH
DHAKA
KOLKATA (Calcutta)
Nagpur
Ahmadabad
INDIA
MUMBAI (Bombay)
Hyderabad
Bangalore
CHENNAI (Madras)
Bay of Bengal
BURMA (MYANMAR)
Rangoon
Hanoi
LAOS
Vientiane
THAILAND
BANGKOK
VIETNAM
CAMBODIA
Phnom Penh
Ho Chi Minh City
South China Sea
MANILA
PHILIPPINES
SRI LANKA
Colombo
MALDIVES
Lakshadweep Is. (India)
Andaman Is. (India)
Nicobar Is. (India)
MALAYSIA
SABAH
SARAWAK
BRUNEI
Medan
Kuala Lumpur
SINGAPORE
Sumatra
Borneo
Celebes
Moluccas
Palembang
Banjarmasin
INDONESIA
Ujung Pandang
JAKARTA
Bandung
Java
Surabaya
Papua
Arafura Sea
Timor
C. York
Darwin
Cairns
Townsville
Port Hedland
Alice Springs
Rockhampton
AUSTRALIA
Geraldton
Kalgoorlie-Boulder
Perth
Brisbane
Great Australian Bight
Darling
Adelaide
Newcastle
Sydney
Canberra
Melbourne
Tasmania
Hobart
Tasman Sea
Norfolk I. (Austral.)
Kermadec Is. (N.Z.)
NEW ZEALAND
North I.
Auckland
Wellington
South I.
Christchurch
Dunedin
Chatham Is. (N.Z.)
Bounty Is. (N.Z.)
Antipodes Is. (N.Z.)
Auckland Is. (N.Z.)
Campbell I. (N.Z.)
Macquarie Is. (Austral.)
Tripoli
Benghazi
LIBYA
Alexandria
CAIRO
Nile
EGYPT
Aswân
SUDAN
CHAD
L. Chad
Ndjamena
Omdurmân
Khartoum
Blue Nile
White Nile
Asmera
ERITREA
YEMEN
Sana'
Aden
Gulf of Aden
DJIBOUTI
Socotra (Yemen)
Addis Ababa
ETHIOPIA
SOMALI REP.
Mogadishu
CENTRAL AFRICAN REP.
Bangui
Kisangani
UGANDA
Kampala
L. Turkana
KENYA
Nairobi
CONGO (DEM. REP. OF THE)
Kigali
RWANDA
BURUNDI
Bujumbura
L. Victoria
Mombasa
Kinshasa
Dodoma
Zanzibar
Dar es Salaam
TANZANIA
L. Tanganyika
L. Malawi
MALAWI
Lilongwe
ANGOLA
ZAMBIA
Lusaka
Harare
ZIMBABWE
Bulawayo
MOZAMBIQUE
Mozambique Channel
NAMIBIA
BOTSWANA
Gaborone
Pretoria (Tshwane)
Maputo
Johannesburg
SWZ.
LES.
Durban (eThekwini)
SOUTH AFRICA
Cape Town
C. of Good Hope
Port Elizabeth
COMOROS
Mayotte (Fr.)
MADAGASCAR
Antananarivo
MAURITIUS
RÉUNION (Fr.)
Rodriguez (Mauritius)
Cargados Carajos (Mauritius)
SEYCHELLES
Amirante Is. (Seychelles)
Agalega Is. (Mauritius)
Chagos Arch. (U.K.)
INDIAN OCEAN
Amsterdam I. (Fr.)
St. Paul I. (Fr.)
Prince Edward Is. (S. Africa)
Crozet Is. (Fr.)
Kerguelen (Fr.)
McDonald Is. (Austral.)
Heard I. (Austral.)
SOUTHERN OCEAN
Antarctic Circle
Ross Sea
Antarctica
East from Greenwich
ft m
0 0
600 200
6 000 2000
12 000 4000
15 000 5000
18 000 6000
24 000 8000

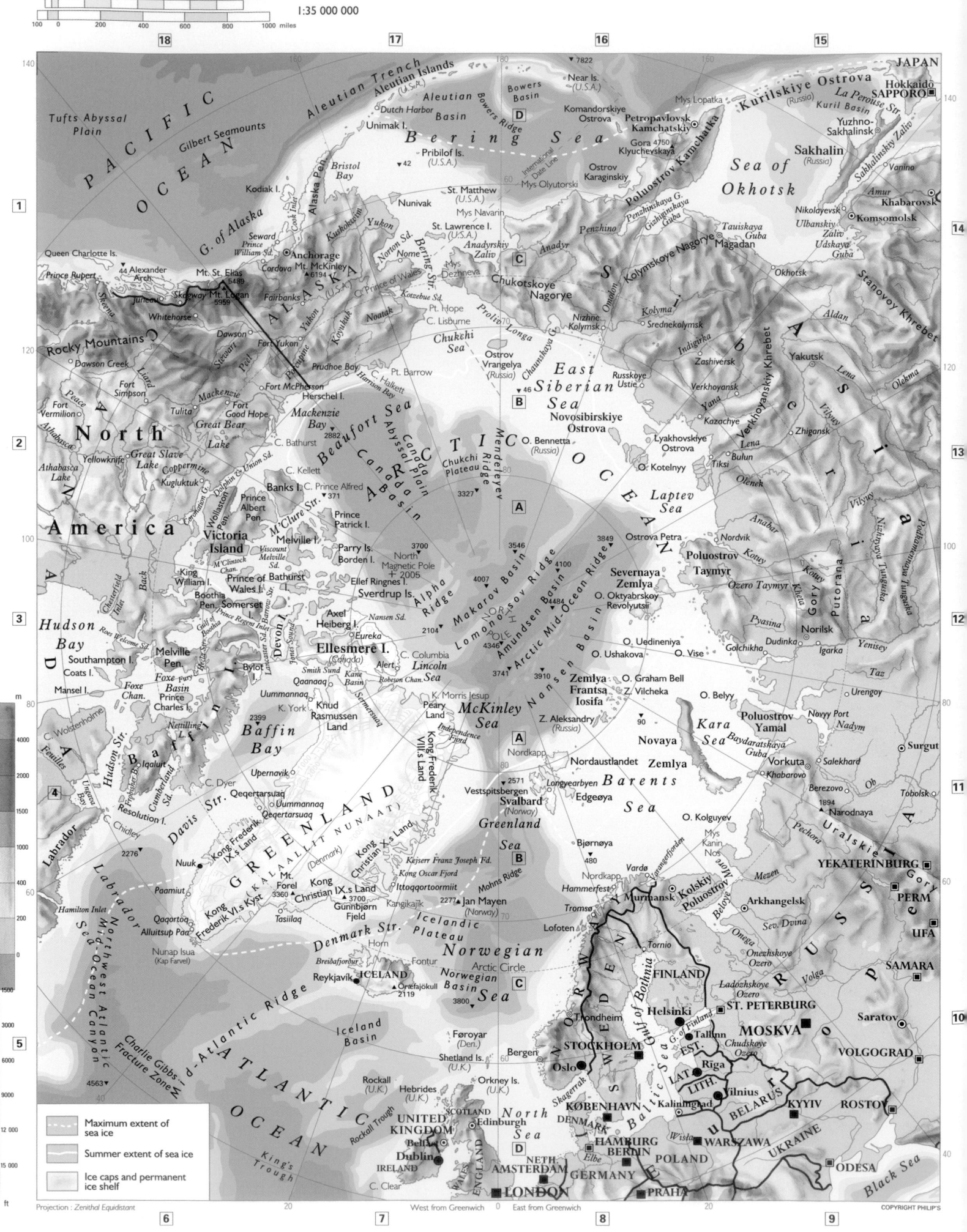

100 0 200 400 600 800 1000 1200 1400 km
100 0 200 400 600 800 1000 miles

1:35 000 000

Projection : Zenithal Equidistant

West from Greenwich   East from Greenwich

COPYRIGHT PHILIP'S

ft   m
12 000 4000
6000   2000
4500   1500
3000   1000
1200   400
600   200
0   0
        500   1500
        1000   3000
        2000   6000
        3000   9000
        4000   12 000
        5000   15 000
m   ft

Maximum extent of
sea ice

Summer extent of sea ice

Ice caps and permanent
ice shelf

PACIFIC OCEAN

Tufts Abyssal Plain

Gilbert Seamounts

Aleutian Trench
Aleutian Islands (U.S.A.)
Dutch Harbor
Unimak I.
Bristol Bay
Kodiak I.
Bering Basin
Bowers Ridge
Bowers Basin
Near Is. (U.S.A.)
7822

Bering Sea

Komandorskiye Ostrova
Petropavlovsk-Kamchatskiy
Gora 4750 Klyuchevskaya
Poluostrov Kamchatka

JAPAN
Hokkaido SAPPORO
Kurilskiye Ostrova (Russia)
Kuril Basin
La Perouse Str.
Yuzhno-Sakhalinsk

Sea of Okhotsk

Sakhalin (Russia)
Sakhalinskiy Zaliv
Vanino
Amur
Nikolayevsk
Ulbanskiy Zaliv
Udskaya Guba
Khabarovsk
Komsomolsk

Pribilof Is. (U.S.A.)
42
St. Matthew (U.S.A.)
Nunivak
St. Lawrence I. (U.S.A.)
Mys Navarin
Anadyrskiy Zaliv
International Date Line
Mys Olyutorski
Ostrov Karaginskiy
Penzhino
Penzhinskaya G.
Gizhiginskaya Guba
Tauiskaya Guba
Magadan

Seward
Prince William Sd.
Anchorage
Cordova Mt. McKinley 6194
Mt. St. Elias 5489
Mt. Logan 5959
Skagway
Juneau
Whitehorse

Nome
Bering Str.
Pt. of Wales
Mys Dezhneva
Chukotskoye Nagorye
Anadyr

Okhotsk
Kolymskoye Nagorye
Stanovoy Khrebet
Aldan

ALASKA (U.S.A.)
Fairbanks
Yukon
Kuskokwim
Kotzebue Sd.
Noatak
Pt. Hope
C. Lisburne
Proliv Longa

Nizhne-Kolymsk
Srednekolymsk
Kolyma
Indigirka
Zashiversk
Verkhoyanskiy Khrebet
Yakutsk
Lena
Olekma

Queen Charlotte Is.
Prince Rupert
44 Alexander Arch.
5489
Skeena

Rocky Mountains
Dawson Creek
Fort Nelson
Fort Liard
Peace
Fort Simpson
Fort Vermilion
Athabasca

North America

CANADA

Great Bear Lake
Coppermine
Yellowknife
Great Slave Lake
Athabasca Lake

Prudhoe Bay
Fort McPherson
Herschel I.
C. Halkett
Harrison Bay
Pt. Barrow

Chukchi Sea
Ostrov Vrangelya (Russia)
46
Chaunskaya

East Siberian Sea
Russkoye Ustie
Novosibirskiye Ostrova
Lyakhovskiye Ostrova
Kazachye
Zhigansk

ARCTIC OCEAN

Verkhoyansk
Yana
Bulun
Tiksi
Olenek

Mackenzie
Tulita
Fort Good Hope
Mackenzie Bay
2882
C. Bathurst
C. Kellett

Beaufort Sea

Canada Abyssal Plain
Canada Basin

Chukchi Plateau
Mendeleyev Ridge
Makarov Basin
3546
3849
Ostrova Petra
Nordvik
Kotuy
Ozero Taymyr
Khatanga
Pyasina

Laptev Sea
Olenek
Anabar
Vilyuy

Banks I. C. Prince Alfred
371
Prince Albert Pen.
M'Clure Str.
Melville I.
Prince Patrick I.
Borden I.
Ellef Ringnes I.
Sverdrup Is.

Victoria Island
Wollaston Pen.
M'Clintock Chan.
King William I.
Prince of Bathurst I.
Parry Is.
North Magnetic Pole + 2005
3700

Alpha Ridge
4007
Lomonosov Ridge
NORTH POLE H
2104
4346
3741
3910
4484 Amundsen Basin
4100
Arctic Mid-Ocean Ridge
Nansen Basin

Severnaya Zemlya
O. Oktyabrskoy Revolyutsii
Poluostrov Taymyr
Norilsk
Dudinka
Igarka
Yenisey
Putorana
Gory

Boothia Pen.
Somerset
Prince Regent Inlet
Axel Heiberg I.
Nansen Sd.
Devon I.

Chesterfield Inlet
Back
Gulf of Boothia
Eureka

Hudson Bay
Southampton I.
Coats I.
Mansel I.
Roes Welcome Sd.
Melville Pen.
Foxe Basin
Prince Charles I.
Foxe Chan.

Bylot I.
Jones Sd.
Smith Sd.
Kane Basin
Robeson Chan.
Barrow Str.

Ellesmere I. (Canada)
Alert
C. Columbia
Lincoln Sea
Kong Frederik VIII's Land

McKinley Sea
Nansen Basin
3747
Zemlya Frantsa Iosifa
O. Graham Bell
Z. Vilcheka
O. Belyy
90

Kara Sea
Poluostrov Yamal
Baydaratskaya Guba
Novyy Port
Nadym
Urengoy

C. Wolstenholme
Nettilling L.
2399
Qaanaaq
K. York
Knud Rasmussen Land
Peary Land
Independence Fjord
Kong Frederik VIII's Land

Z. Aleksandry (Russia)
Nordkapp
Nordaustlandet
Novaya Zemlya

Surgut
Ob
Salekhard
Vorkuta
Khabarovo
Berezovo
Narodnaya
1894
Tobolsk

Baffin Bay
Baffin Island
Melville B.
Upernavik
Uummannaq
K. Dyer
Qeqertarsuaq
Uummannaq
Qeqertarsuaq

Vestspitsbergen
2571
Longyearbyen
Svalbard (Norway)
Edgeøya

Barents Sea
O. Kolguyev
Mys Kanin Nos

Hudson Str.
Iqaluit
Frobisher B.
Resolution I.
C. Chidley
2276

GREENLAND
(KALAALLIT NUNAAT)
(Denmark)
Nuuk
Kong Frederik IX's Land

Greenland Sea
Bjørnøya
480
Vardø
Stangerfjorden

Poluostrov Kanin
Mezen
Pechora
Uralskie

RUSSIA
YEKATERINBURG
PERM
UFA

Labrador
Hamilton Inlet
Northwest Atlantic Mid-Ocean Canyon

Paamiut
Kong Frederik VI's Kyst
Mt. Forel 3360
Kong Christian IX's Land
Gunnbjørn Fjeld 3700
Kong Oscar Fjord
Kejserr Franz Joseph Fd.
Ittoqqortoormiit
Kangikajik

Jan Mayen (Norway)
2277
Mohns Ridge
Nordkapp
Hammerfest
Tromsø
Lofoten

Murmansk
Kolskiy Poluostrov
Onega
Arkhangelsk
Sev. Dvina
Onezhskoye Ozero

Qaqortoq
Alluitsup Paa
Tasiilaq
Nunap Isua (Kap Farvel)
Breiðafjörður
Horn

Denmark Str.
Icelandic Plateau
Fontur
Norwegian Basin

Mid-Atlantic Ridge

Reykjavík
ICELAND
Öræfajökull 2119

Iceland Basin

Charlie Gibbs Fracture Zone
4563

ATLANTIC OCEAN
King's Trough

Rockall (U.K.)
Rockall Trough
Hebrides (U.K.)
C. Clear
IRELAND
Dublin
ENGLAND
LONDON

Norwegian Sea
3800
Arctic Circle

NORWAY
Trondheim
SWEDEN
Oslo
Bergen
STOCKHOLM

FINLAND
Helsinki
Gulf of Bothnia
Tallinn
EST.
Gulf of Finland
ST. PETERBURG
Ladozhskoye Ozero
Chudskoye Ozero
Onega

MOSKVA
Volga
Saratov
SAMARA
VOLGOGRAD

North Sea
Shetland Is. (U.K.)
Orkney Is. (U.K.)
SCOTLAND
Edinburgh
Belfast
UNITED KINGDOM

Skagerrak
DENMARK
KØBENHAVN
HAMBURG
BERLIN
NETH.
AMSTERDAM
GERMANY
PRAHA
POLAND
WARSZAWA

Føroyar (Den.)

Baltic Sea
Riga
LAT.
LITH.
Vilnius
Kaliningrad
BELARUS
KYYIV
UKRAINE
ROSTOV
ODESA
Black Sea
Elbe
Wisła

1 : 35 000 000

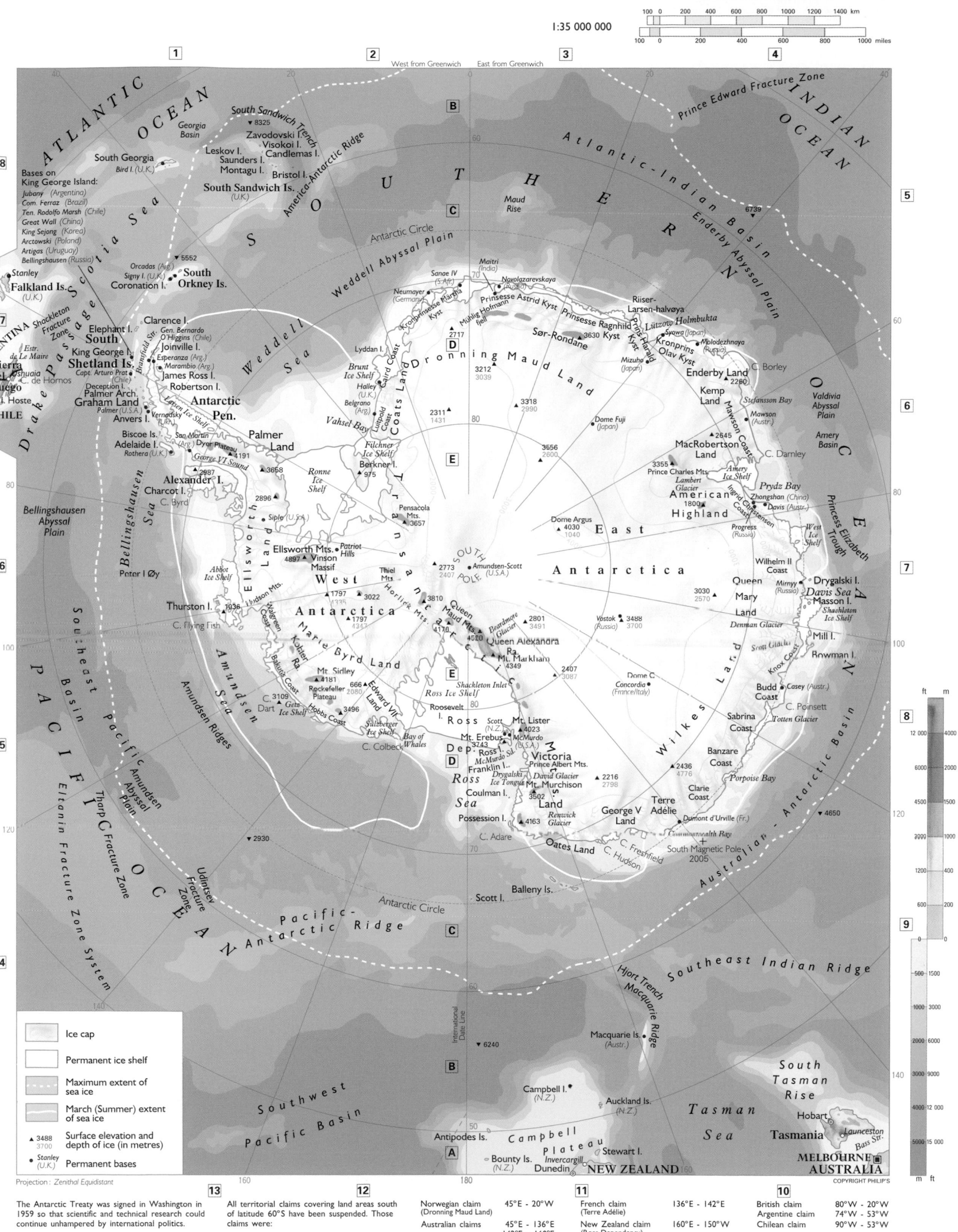

Projection : Zenithal Equidistant

Legend

- Ice cap
- Permanent ice shelf
- Maximum extent of sea ice
- March (Summer) extent of sea ice
- ▲ 3488 / 3700 — Surface elevation and depth of ice (in metres)
- • Stanley (U.K.) — Permanent bases

The Antarctic Treaty was signed in Washington in 1959 so that scientific and technical research could continue unhampered by international politics.

All territorial claims covering land areas south of latitude 60°S have been suspended. Those claims were:

Norwegian claim (Dronning Maud Land)	45°E – 20°W
Australian claims	45°E – 136°E
	142°E – 160°E
French claim (Terre Adélie)	136°E – 142°E
New Zealand claim (Ross Dependency)	160°E – 150°W
British claim	80°W – 20°W
Argentine claim	74°W – 53°W
Chilean claim	90°W – 53°W

COPYRIGHT PHILIP'S

Elevation / Depth Scale

ft	m
12 000	4000
6000	2000
4500	1500
3000	1000
1200	400
600	200
—	0
1500	500
3000	1000
6000	2000
9000	3000
12 000	4000
15 000	5000

Bases on King George Island:
Jubany (Argentina)
Com. Ferraz (Brazil)
Ten. Rodolfo Marsh (Chile)
Great Wall (China)
King Sejong (Korea)
Arctowski (Poland)
Artigas (Uruguay)
Bellingshausen (Russia)

6 EUROPE : Physical

1:20 000 000

100 0 100 200 300 400 500 600 700 800 km
100 0 100 200 300 400 500 miles

Projection: Bonne   West from Greenwich 0 East from Greenwich

ROCKALL Sea areas named in weather forecasts

ATLANTIC OCEAN

Norwegian Sea

North Sea

Baltic Sea

Mediterranean Sea

Black Sea

Caspian Sea

Adriatic Sea

Tyrrhenian Sea

Ligurian Sea

Ionian Sea

Aegean Sea

Sea of Azov

White Sea

Gulf of Bothnia

G. of Finland

Gulf of Gdansk

Kattegat

Skagerrak

Bay of Biscay

English Channel

Irish Sea

Celtic Sea

North Channel

Str. of Gibraltar

Str. of Messina

Str. of Otranto

Str. of Bonifacio

Sea of Crete

Sea of Marmara

Dardanelles

Bosporus

Land regions and features

Iceland   Hvítárvatn   Hofsjökull   Hekla 1491   Vatnajökull   Öraefajökull 2119   Breidafjördur   Faxaflói   Reykjanes   SOUTH EAST ICELAND

British Isles   Great Britain   Ireland   Hebrides   Shetland   Orkney   Fair Isle   Faeroes   Pennines   Grampian Mts.   Ben Nevis 1343   Snowdon 1085   Lough Neagh   Lough Corrib   Lundy   Wight I.   Thames   Trent   Severn   Shannon

Scandinavia   Lapland   Norway   Vesterålen   Lofoten   Vestfjorden   Galdhøpiggen 2469   Jotunheimen   Sognefjorden   Trondheimsfjorden   Hardangervidda   Kebnekaise 2117   North Cape   Nordkinn   Kanin Pen.   Kola Pen.   Kola

Finland   Åland   Gotland   Öland   Bornholm   Zealand   Fyn   Jutland   Lolland   Helgoland   Zuiderzee   Zeeland

Russian Plain   Central Russian Uplands   Valdai Hills   Timan Ridge   Northern Urals   Ural Mountains   West Siberian Lowlands   Ob Lowlands   Obshchi Syrt   Kirgiziya Steppe   Caspian Depression   Volga Hts.

Ukraine   Wallachia   Plain of Hungary   Carpathians   Tatra 2655   Transylvanian Alps   Sudeten   Moravian Hts.   Bohemian Forest   Black Forest   Erzgebirge   Harz   Vosges   Jura   Alps   Mont Blanc 4808   Monte Rosa   Matterhorn   Grossglockner 3797   Gran Sasso 2914   Dolomites   Apennines   Dinaric Alps   Balkans   Rhodope   Pindus   Olympus 2917   Peloponnese   Cyclades   Dodecanese   Northern Sporades   Euboea   Lesbos   Crete

Massif Central   Pyrenees   Pico de Aneto 3404   Picos de Europa   Old Castile   New Castile   Iberian Peninsula   Cantabrian Mts.   Sierra Morena   Sierra Nevada   Mulhacén 3478   Andalusia   Guadalquivir   Tagus   Douro   Ebro   Duero   Guadiana   Garonne   Loire   Seine   Rhône   Rhine   Elbe   Oder   Danube   Vistula   Po   Tiber

Balearic Is.   Majorca   Minorca   Ibiza   Corsica   Sardinia   Sicily   Etna 3340   Elba   Malta   Pantelleria   Calabria   Vesuvius 1277   Brittany   C. Finisterre   C. da Roca   C. St. Vincent   C. de Gata   C. Trafalgar   C. Matapan

Africa   Atlas Mts.   Plateau of the Shotts   C. Bon   Gulf of Antalya   Cyprus   Rhodes   Euphrates   Tigris   Mesopotamia   Kurdistan   Anatolia (Asia Minor)   Taurus Mts.   Pontine Mts.   Caucasus   Transcaucasia   Armenia   Elbrus 5642   Ararat 5122   Agri Dagi

Rivers and lakes

Volga   Kama   Ural   Don   Donets   Dnieper   Dniester   Desna   Bug   Vistula   Niemen   W. Dvina   N. Dvina   Pechora   Mezen   Vychegda   Sukhona   Oka   Sura   Vyatka   Belaya   Pelym   Tobol   Pripet   Prut   Siret   Olt   Mures   Tisza   Drava   Sava   Morava   Vardar   Struma   Maritsa   Axios   Drin

L. Ladoga   L. Onega   L. Ilmen   L. Peipus   L. Chudskoye   Rybinsk Res.   Kuibyshev Res.   Volgograd Res.   Kama Res.   Tsimlyansk Res.   Kakhovka Res.   Kremenchuk Res.   Kiev Res.   Vänern   Vättern   Mälaren   Siljan   Saimaa   Päijänne   L. Inari   L. Oulu   L. Constance   L. Geneva   L. Garda   L. Como   L. Maggiore   L. Neusiedl   L. Balaton   L. Ohrid   L. Scutari

1:20 000 000

100 0 100 200 300 400 500 600 700 800 km
100 0 100 200 300 400 500 miles

COPYRIGHT PHILIP'S

Projection: Bonne

■ LONDON Capital Cities

BARENTS SEA

RUSSIA

KARELIA

FINLAND

LAPLAND

Murmansk

Rybachiy Poluostrov

Maanselkä

Varanger-halvøya

Rovaniemi

Kemi

Tornio

Haparanda

Oulu

Luleå

Kiruna

Gällivare

Boden

Piteå

Skellefteå

Umeå

Örnsköldsvik

Härnösand

Sundsvall

Kajaani

Kuopio

Jyväskylä

Tampere

Pori

Vaasa

Kokkola

Narvik

Tromsø

Harstad

Bodø

Mo i Rana

Mosjøen

Östersund

Trondheim

Steinkjer

Namsos

Levanger

Hamar

Lillehammer

Ålesund

Molde

Kristiansund

GULF OF BOTHNIA

Jämtland

Härjedalen

Trøndelag

Dalarna

Hälsingland

Ångermanland

Västerbotten

Norrbotten

Helgeland

Nordland

Dovrefjell

Gudbrandsdalen

Österdalen

Rondane

Jotunheimen

ATLANTIC OCEAN

NORWEGIAN SEA

Vesterålen

Lofoten

Senja

Andøya

Hinnøya

Austvågøya

Vestvågøya

Moskenesøya

Røst

Værøy

Sørøya

Magerøya

Kvaløya

Ringvassøya

ICELAND on same scale

Reykjavík

Akranes

Keflavík

Vatnajökull

Akureyri

Ísafjörður

Faxaflói

Breiðafjörður

Hvalfjörður

FAEROE ISLANDS on same scale

Tórshavn

Streymoy

Eysturoy

Vágar

Sandoy

Suðuroy

Føroyar (Faeroe Is.) (Den.)

West from Greenwich

Arctic Circle

1:6 000

50 0 25 50 75 100 125 150 175 km

50 0 25 50 75 100 125 miles

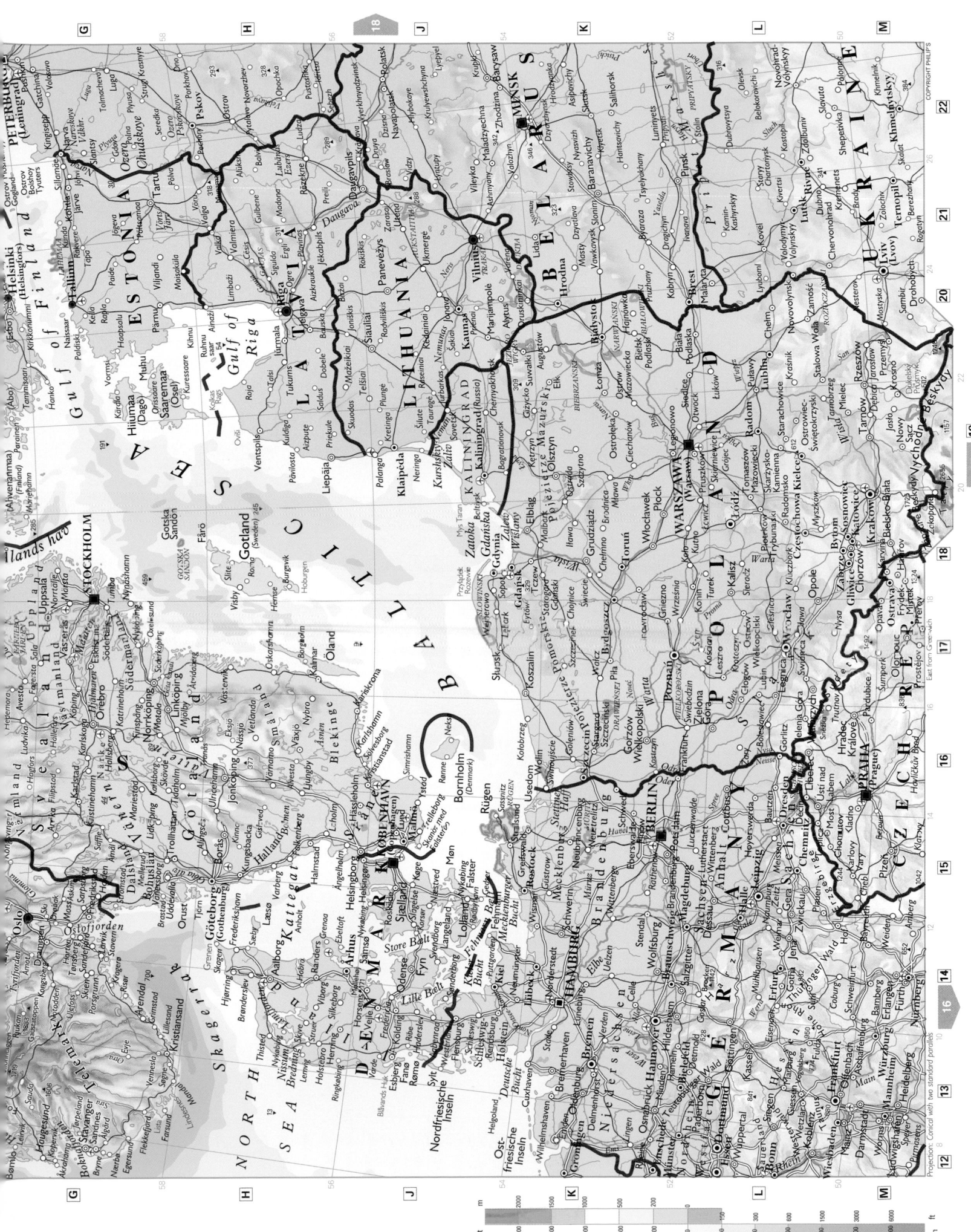

Projection: Conical with two standard parallels

1:2 000 000

10 0 10 20 30 40 50 60 70 80 km
10 0 10 20 30 40 50 miles

11 1 10 2 9 3 8 4 7 5 6 5

ATLANTIC OCEAN

NORTH CHANNEL

IRISH SEA

CELTIC SEA

St. George's Channel

Firth of Clyde

Brodick
Arran
Campbeltown
Ailsa Craig
Kintyre
Mull of Kintyre
Cairnryan
Stranraer
Mull of Oa
Giants Causeway
Rathlin I.
Fair Hd.
Mts. of Antrim
Ballycastle
Cushendall
Carncastle
Larne
Portpatrick
269

Malin Hd.
Inishtrahull
Trawbreaga B.
Malin
Malin Pen.
Glengad Hd.
Carndonagh
Moville
Inishowen Pen.
Buncrana
Portstewart
Portrush
Coleraine
Limavady
Ballymoney
554 Trostan
GLENARIFF
Bloody Foreland
Tory I.
Horn Hd.
Sheep Haven
Dunfanaghy
Rathmelton
L. Foyle
Londonderry
LONDONDERRY
Ballymena
Randalstown
Ballyclare
Carrickfergus
Belfast
Bangor
Donaghadee
Newtownards

Inishfree B.
Gweedore
Errigal 752
Derryveagh Mts.
GLENVEAGH
Letterkenny
DONEGAL
Lifford
Strabane
Sion Mills
Newtownstewart
Sawel Mt. 683
Sperrin Mts.
Cookstown
Moneymore
Magherafelt
Lough Neagh
Antrim
NORTHERN
Newtownabbey
Lisburn
Comber
Strangford L.
DOWN
Ards Pen.
Saintfield
Ballynahinch
Portaferry
Ballyquintin Pt.

Aran I.
The Rosses
Dungloe
683
Crohy Hd.
Gweebarra B.
Dawros Hd.
601 Slieve League
Killybegs
St. John's Pt.
Ardara
Lavagh More 676
Glenties
Ballybofey
Omagh
TYRONE
Dromore
Dungannon
Coalisland
Armagh
Craigavon
Lurgan
Lagan
Portadown
Banbridge
Dromore
Dundrum
Newcastle
Slieve Donard
Dundrum B.
St. John's Pt.
Ardglass
Downpatrick

Glencolumbkille
Rossan Pt.
Donegal
Ballyshannon
Bundoran
Belleek
Lower L. Erne
Enniskillen
FERMANAGH
Upper Erne
Clones
MONAGHAN
Monaghan
Castleblaney
Crossmaglen
577 Slieve Gullion
Newry
Warrenpoint
Mourne Mts.
Kilkeel
Greenore
Carlingford L.

Loughros More B.
Donegal Bay
Inishmurray I.
Manorhamilton
Lackagh Hills
L. Allen
LEITRIM
L. Oughter
Cavan
CAVAN
Carrickmacross
Dundalk
LOUTH
Dundalk Bay
Clogher Hd.

Downpatrick Hd.
Portacloy
Broad Haven
Erris Hd.
Belmullet
Mullet Pen.
Inishkea North
Inishkea South
Blacksod Bay
Achill Hd.
Achill I.
Clare I.
Inishturk
Inishbofin
Inishshark
Slyne Hd.

Lenadoon Pt.
Killala B.
Killala
Ballina
Crossmolina
Nephin Beg Range
806 Nephin
L. Conn
544
Foxford
Swinford
Charlestown
Knock
Ballyhaunis
ROSCOMMON
Strokestown
LONGFORD
Longford
Granard
L. Sheelin
Oldcastle
Ceanannus Mor (Kells)
Blackwater
MEATH
Navan
Trim
Kingscourt
Ardee
Dunleer
Drogheda
Balbriggan
Rush
Lambay I.

Sligo Bay
Sligo
Dromore West
Collooney
SLIGO
Ballymote
L. Arrow
L. Key
Boyle
Carrick-on-Shannon
L. Gara
Ballaghaderreen
Castlerea
Roscommon
Strokestown
Ballymahon
Mullingar
WESTMEATH
Royal Canal
Kilbeggan
Moate
Edenderry
KILDARE
Maynooth
Clane
Naas
DUBLIN
Dublin
Howth Hd.
Dun Laoghaire
Killiney
Bray
Greystones
123

Erris Hd.
Mayo
MAYO
Castlebar
Newport
Westport
Clew Bay
Croagh Patrick 765
Louisburgh
Mweelrea 819
Killary Harbour
Partry Mts.
683
Lough Mask
Ballinrobe
Claremorris
Knock
CONNACHT
L. Carra
Glennamaddy
Castlerea
Roscommon
L. Ree
Athlone
Ballinasloe
Shannon
Banagher
Clara
Tullamore
OFFALY
Bog of Allen
Grand Canal
Portarlington
Mountmellick
Port Laoise
Monasterevin
Kildare
Athy
Droichead Nua
Newbridge
Rathangan
Poulaphouca Res.
WICKLOW
Wicklow Mts.
Lugnaquilla 926
Wicklow Hd.
Rathdrum
Avoca
Arklow

Connemara
CONNEMARA
Clifden
Roundstone
Bertraghboy B.
Slyne Hd.
Kilkieran B.
Galway Bay
Aran Is.
Inishmore
Inishmaan
Inisheer
Black Hd.
Cliffs of Moher
Hags Hd.
Liscannor Bay
Mal Bay
Mutton I.
Loop Hd.

Oughterard
Tuam
Mount Bellew Bridge
Lough Corrib
GALWAY
Galway
Athenry
Loughrea
Aughrim
Portumna
Slieve Aughty
368
Gort
345
Lisdoonvarna
BURREN
Ennistimon
Crusheen
Feakle
Tulla
CLARE
Ennis
Kilrush
Shannon Airport
Limerick
LIMERICK
Silvermine Mts. 694
Keeper Hill
Nenagh
Borrisokane
Roscrea
Shannonbridge
Birr
Mountmellick
Slieve Bloom Mts. 528
Arderin
Mountrath
Durrow
LAOIS
Abbeyleix
Carlow
CARLOW
Muine Bheag
Tullow
Shillelagh
Gorey
Ballycanew
Cahore Pt.

Spiddle
Kinvarra
Aughrim

Kilrush
Kilkee
Tarbert
Foynes
Glin
Mouth of the Shannon
Kerry Hd.
Ballybunion
Ballyheige
Ardfert
Tralee
Tralee Bay
Brandon B.
Smerwick Harbour
Brandon Mt. 953
Dingle
Dingle Bay
Slieve Mish 853
Castlemaine
Newcastle West
Abbeyfeale
Listowel
Rathkeale
Golden Vale
Rath Luirc (Charleville)
519
Mitchelstown
Kilfinnane
Galtymore 920
Galty Mts.
TIPPERARY
Tipperary
Cashel
Thurles
Templemore
Johnstown
Urlingford
KILKENNY
Kilkenny
Callan
Thomastown
Knocktopher
New Ross
WEXFORD
Enniscorthy
Wexford
Wexford Harbour
Rosslare
Rosslare Harbour
Greenore Pt.

Slievenamon 722
Clonmel
Carrick-on-Suir
Comeragh Mts. 792
Dungarvan
Dungarvan Harbour
WATERFORD
Waterford
Passage East
Dunmore East
Waterford Harbour
Hook Hd.
Saltee Is.
Carnsore Pt.
Tramore
Tramore B.

Great Blasket I.
Inishvickillane
Dunmore Hd.
Dingle Bay
Valencia I.
Puffin I.
Great Skellig
Ballinskelligs B.
Dursey I.
Crow Hd.
Bantry Bay
Dunmanus B.
Mizen Hd.
C. Clear
Clear I.
Fastnet Rock

KERRY
Killorglin
Carrauntoohil 1041
Macgillycuddy's Reeks
KILLARNEY
Killarney
Milltown
Millstreet
L. Leane
Glenbeigh
Caherciveen
Kenmare
Sneem
707
Caha Mts.
Glengarriff
646
Kenmare River
Whiddy I.
Bear I.
Castletown Bearhaven
Sheriff I.
Baltimore
Sherkin I.
Skibbereen
Clonakilty
Clonakilty B.
Galley Hd.

Macroom
Blarney
Boggeragh Mts. 646
Nagles Mts. 429
Kanturk
Mallow
Buttevant
Newmarket
CORK
Cork
Cork Harbour
Cobh
Crosshaven
Midleton
Youghal
Youghal B.
Old Head of Kinsale
Kinsale
Bandon
Timoleague
Dunmanway
Bantry
Ballydehob
Skull
Long I.

MUNSTER
Fermoy
Nagles Mts.
Blackwater
WATERFORD
Lismore
Tallow
Mitchelstown
Knockmealdown Mts. 795

582
Silvermine Mts.
Killaloe
Lough Derg
Sixmilebridge
Feakle

ft m
1500
1000
600
300
0
50
100
200
500
1000
2000

m ft
500
200
100
0
150
300
600
1500
3000
6000

Projection: Lambert's Conformal Conic
West from Greenwich
COPYRIGHT PHILIP'S

National Parks

1:2 000 000

ORKNEY IS.
on same scale

ORKNEY

SHETLAND IS.
on same scale

SHETLAND

Key to Scottish unitary
authorities on map

1 CITY OF ABERDEEN
2 DUNDEE CITY
3 WEST DUNBARTONSHIRE
4 EAST DUNBARTONSHIRE
5 CITY OF GLASGOW
6 INVERCLYDE
7 RENFREWSHIRE
8 EAST RENFREWSHIRE
9 NORTH LANARKSHIRE
10 FALKIRK
11 CLACKMANNANSHIRE
12 WEST LOTHIAN
13 CITY OF EDINBURGH
14 MIDLOTHIAN

Projection : Lambert's Conformal Conic

National Parks and Forest Parks in Scotland

COPYRIGHT PHILIP'S

10 0 10 20 30 40 50 60 70 80 km
10 0 10 20 30 40 50 miles

1:2 000 000

Key to English unitary authorities on map

25 HARTLEPOOL
26 DARLINGTON
27 STOCKTON-ON-TEES
28 MIDDLESBROUGH
29 REDCAR AND CLEVELAND
30 BLACKPOOL
31 BLACKBURN WITH DARWEN
32 HALTON
33 WARRINGTON
34 KINGSTON UPON HULL
35 NORTH EAST LINCOLNSHIRE
36 NORTH LINCOLNSHIRE
37 STOKE-ON-TRENT
38 TELFORD AND WREKIN
39 DERBY CITY
40 CITY OF NOTTINGHAM
41 LEICESTER CITY
42 RUTLAND
43 PETERBOROUGH
44 MILTON KEYNES
45 LUTON
46 NORTH SOMERSET
47 CITY OF BRISTOL
48 BATH AND NORTH EAST SOMERSET
49 SWINDON
50 READING
51 WOKINGHAM
52 WINDSOR AND MAIDENHEAD
53 SLOUGH
54 BRACKNELL FOREST
55 THURROCK
56 SOUTHEND-ON-SEA
57 MEDWAY
58 PLYMOUTH
59 TORBAY
60 POOLE
61 BOURNEMOUTH
62 SOUTHAMPTON
63 PORTSMOUTH
64 BRIGHTON AND HOVE

Key to Welsh unitary authorities on map

15 SWANSEA
16 NEATH PORT TALBOT
17 BRIDGEND
18 RHONDDA CYNON TAFF
19 MERTHYR TYDFIL
20 BLAENAU GWENT
21 CAERPHILLY
22 TORFAEN
23 CARDIFF
24 NEWPORT

NORTH SEA

IRISH SEA

North Channel

NORTHERN IRELAND

SCOTLAND

ENGLAND

WALES

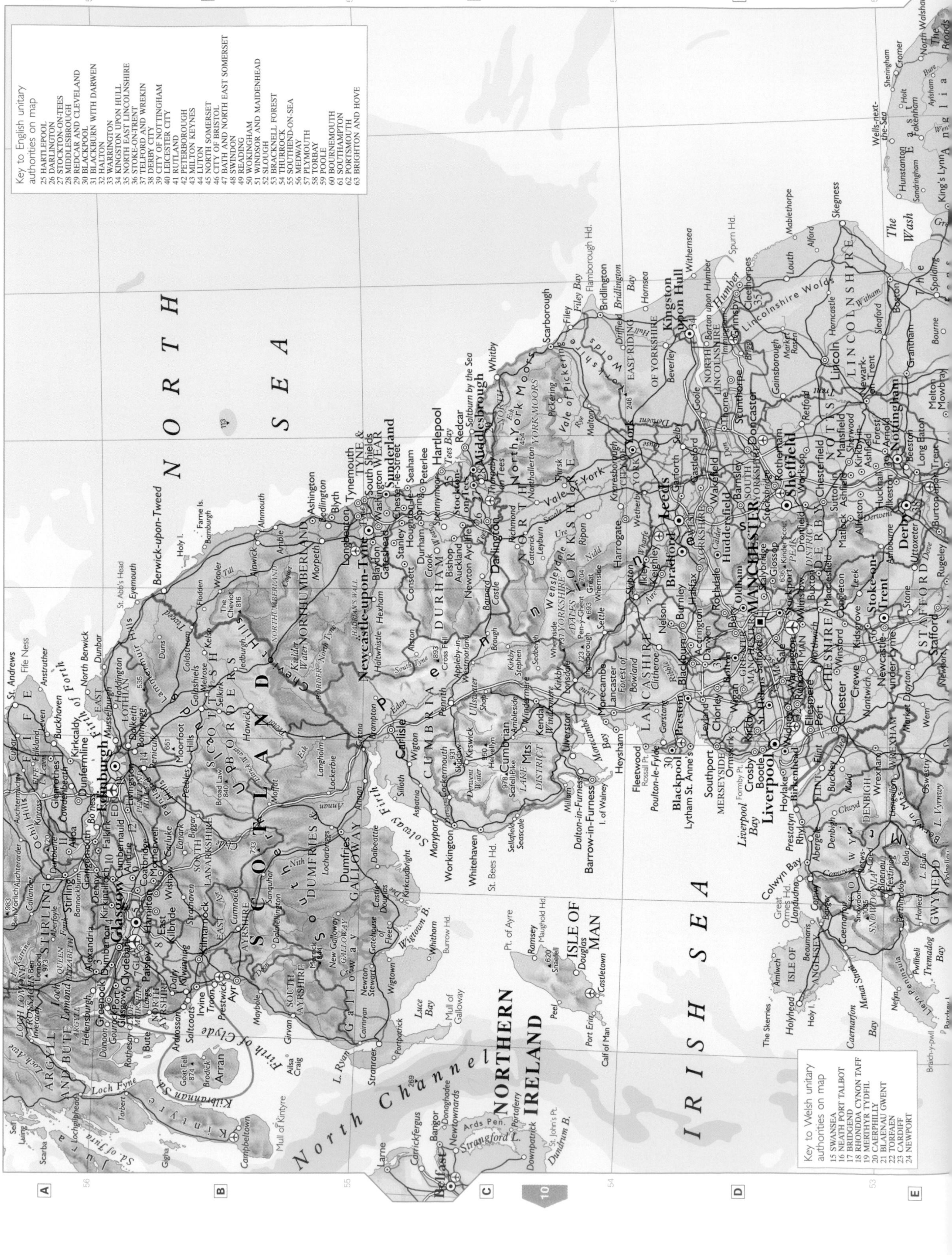

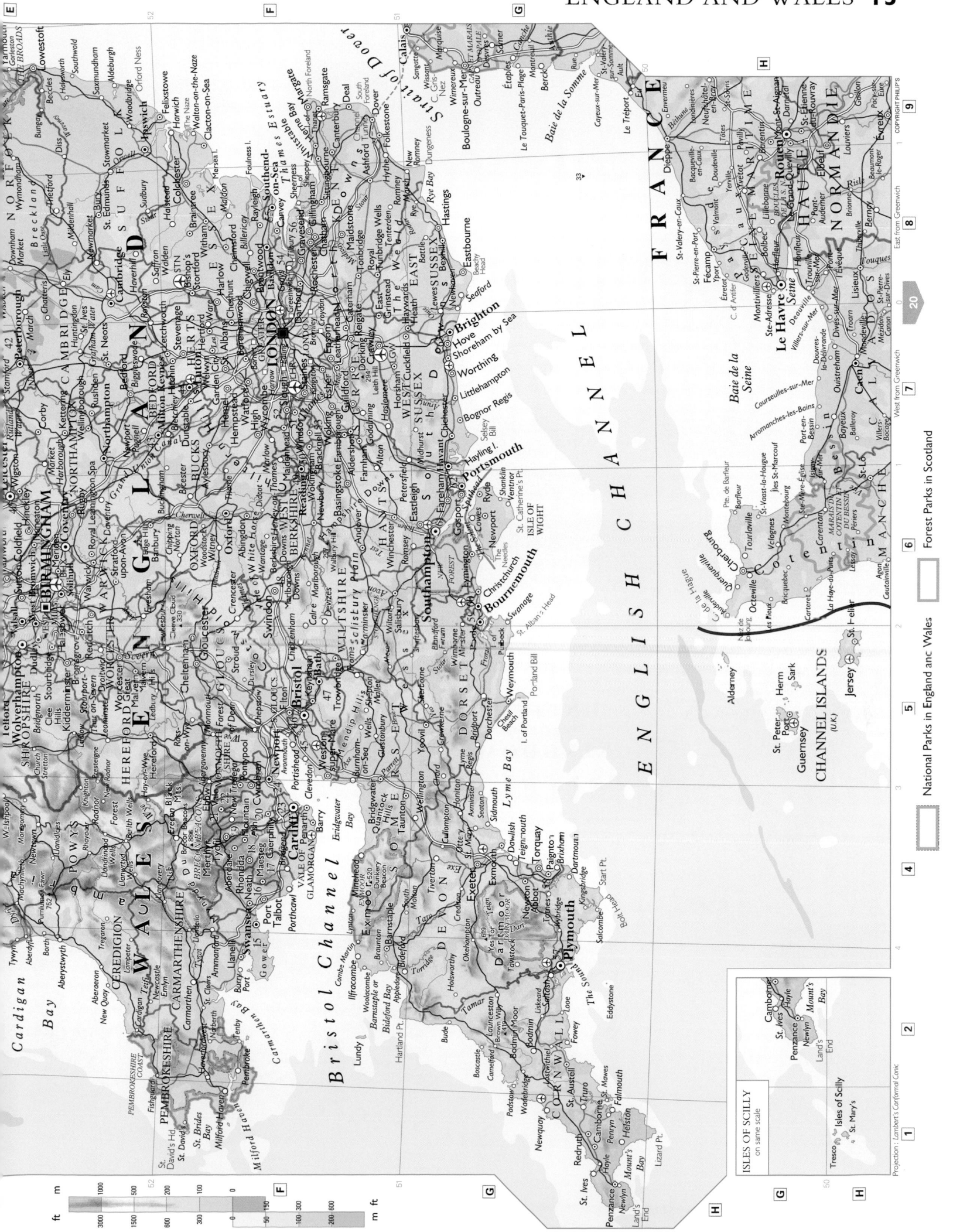

East from Greenwich

West from Greenwich

20

Projection: Lambert's Conformal Conic

National Parks in England and Wales

Forest Parks in Scotland

ISLES OF SCILLY
on same scale

Tresco   Isles of Scilly
          St. Mary's

50   0   25   50   75   100   125   150   175 km
50   0   25   50   75   100   125 miles

1:5 000 000

Projection: Conical with two standard parallels

East from Greenwich
COPYRIGHT PHILIP'S

West from Greenwich

ATLANTIC OCEAN

Shetland Is.

Yell
Fetlar
Unst

Foula

Mainland
Lerwick

Fair Isle

Orkney Is.

Westray
Sanday
Stronsay

Mainland
Kirkwall
Hoy
South
Ronaldsay

C. Wrath

Pentland Firth

Thurso
Wick

Helmsdale

Lewis
Stornoway

North Minch

Harris

Laing
Golspie
Tain
Helmsdale

St. Kilda

North
Uist
Benbecula

South Uist

Ullapool

North West Highlands

Moray Firth
Buckie
Banff
Fraserburgh
Elgin
Nairn
Inverness
Huntly
Peterhead
Inverurie

SCOTLAND
Glen Moe
L. Ness
Aviemore
CAIRNGORMS
Don
Aberdeen
Stonehaven

Skye

Portree

Mallaig
Rhum
Eigg

1182

Ben Nevis
Fort William
1344

Grampian Mts.

1311
Ballater
Dee

Coll

Tobermory

Mull

Oban

Tiree

1214

Dundee
St. Andrews

NORTH

SEA

238

Colonsay

L. Awe
L. Lomond
Perth
Stirling
Glenrothes
Kirkcaldy
Dunfermline
Dunbar

973

Jura

Islay

Dumbarton
Greenock
Paisley
Glasgow
Motherwell
Hamilton
East Kilbride
Irvine
Kilmarnock

Edinburgh
Berwick-upon-Tweed

Campbeltown
Arran
Ayr

Southern Uplands
Galashiels
840
Jedburgh
Hawick
816
Cheviot Hills
Alnwick

Malin Hd.

Buncrana
Letterkenny
Coleraine
Ballymena
Larne

Aran I.
Lifford
NORTHERN IRELAND
Antrim
Bangor
Belfast

Stranraer
Kirkcudbright
Dumfries
Carlisle
Hexham
NORTHUMBERLAND
Newcastle-upon-Tyne
South Shields
Sunderland
Gateshead
Durham
Hartlepool
Redcar

Donegal
GLENVEAGH
Omagh
L. Neagh
Lurgan
Lisburn
Portadown
Armagh
Newry

Workington
Whitehaven
Cumbrian Mts.
893
Darlington
Middlesbrough
Stockton-
on-Tees
Scarborough
N. YORK MOORS

Bundoran
Lower L.
Erne
Enniskillen
Clones
Castleblayney

978
**LAKE
DISTRICT**

Mull of Galloway

UNITED

Douglas
I. of Man

Barrow-
in-Furness
Lancaster
Harrogate
**YORKSHIRE
DALES**
Bridlington

Ballina
Sligo
Leitrim
Cavan

KINGDOM

Beverley
Kingston upon Hull

Achill I.
Castlebar
Westport

Roscommon
Longford
Athlone
Mullingar

Ceanannus Mor
Drogheda
Boyne

Blackpool
Preston
Blackburn
Burnley
Keighley
Halifax
Bradford
Huddersfield
Oldham

Leeds
York
Wakefield
Barnsley
Doncaster
Grimsby
Scunthorpe

Louth

IRISH

SEA

Lough
Mask
Lough
Corrib

Galway B.
Galway
Aran Is.
Ballinasloe

Roscommon
Longford
Lough
Ree

Tullamore
Dublin
Dun Laoghaire
Bray

Holyhead
Anglesey
Bangor
Colwyn Bay
Chester
MANCHESTER
Liverpool
Warrington
Stockport
636
Sheffield
Chesterfield
Mansfield
Lincoln

SEA

Ennis
Limerick

Nenagh
Thurles
Tipperary

Carrick-on-Suir

Athy
Carlow
Kilkenny

Wexford
Rosslare

IRELAND

Connemara

953

Dingle
Tralee
Listowel

Killarney
Mallow

Macgillycuddy's Reeks
1041

Valencia I.

Bantry
Bandon
Kinsale

Cork
Cobh
Youghal

Dungarvan
Waterford

Clonmel

Blackwater

C. Clear

St. George's Channel

Fishguard
Haverfordwest
Milford Haven
Pembroke
**PEMBROKESHIRE
COAST**

99

Cardigan
Bay
Aberystwyth

Cambrian Mts.

Pwllheli
SNOWDONIA
Snowdon
1085
Wrexham
Crewe
**Stoke-
on-Trent**
Stafford
Derby
Nottingham
Granthan

ENGLAND
Telford
Shrewsbury
Welshpool

Carmarthen
**BRECON
BEACONS**
886
Brecon
WALES
Merthyr Tydfil
Neath
Llanelli
Rhondda
Cwmbran
Swansea
Port Talbot
Barry
Cardiff

Hereford
Worcester
Redditch
Royal
Leamington Spa
BIRMINGHAM
Coventry
Rugby
Corby
Leicester
Peterborough
Nuneaton
Northampton
Milton Keynes
Bedford
Cambridge

The Wash
King's Lynn
**THE
BROADS**
Norwich
Great Yarmouth
Lowestoft

Cheltenham
Gloucester
Cotswold Hills
Oxford
Banbury
Newbury
Bury St. Edmunds
Ipswich
Harwich
Colchester
Felixstowe
Chelmsford

Bristol Channel

Weston-super-
Mare

Barnstaple
Exmoor
Bude
Taunton

618
DARTMOOR
Exeter
Exmouth

Newquay
Truro
Plymouth
Torbay
St. Austell
Penzance
Falmouth

Land's End

Isles of Scilly

CELTIC

SEA

Bath
Bristol
Swindon
High Wycombe
Slough
LONDON
Watford
Basildon
Southend-on-Sea
Reading
Thames
Maidstone
Chatham
Margate
Canterbury
Crawley
Hastings

Salisbury
Yeovil
Southampton
Fareham
**NEW
FOREST**
Bournemouth
Poole
Weymouth
Newport
Isle of
Wight
Portsmouth
Worthing
Brighton
Eastbourne

Basingstoke
Guildford
Ashford
Folkestone

St. of Dover

English Channel

C. de la
Hague
Alderney
Pte. de
Barfleur

Guernsey
St. Peter
Port
Sark

Channel Is.
(U.K.)
St. Helier
Jersey

Cherbourg
Valognes
Cotentin

Le Havre
Trouville-sur-Mer
Bayeux
Caen
Lisieux

FRANCE

Fécamp
Bolbec
Rouen
Seine
Elbeuf

Dieppe
Pays de
Caux

St. Valery
Abbeville

Le Tréport

Amiens

Picardie

St. Quentin
Laon

Gris-
Nez
Boulogne-
sur-Mer
Le Touquet-
Paris-Plage

Calais
St-Omer
Dunkerque
Ostende
Zeebrugge

Lille
Tourcoing
Roubaix
Tournai
Béthune
Bruay-la-
Buissière
Lens
Douai
Valenciennes
Cambrai

BELGIUM
BRUSSEL
(Bruxelles)
Gent
Mechelen
Brugge
Antwerpen

NETHERLANDS
's-Gravenhage
(Den Haag)
Hoek van Holland
ROTTERDAM
Dordrecht

Vlissingen
Zeebrugge

Haarlem

Alkmaar
Den Helder
Texel

NORWAY
Bergen
Askøyna
Osøyro
Stord
Bømlo
Leirvik
Boknafjo
Haugesund
Kopervik
Åkrahamn
Stavanger
Sandnes
Bryne
Nærbø

38
Ascension

ft   m
3000   1000
1500   500
600   200
300   100
150   0
0   0
        150
        200   600
        500 1500
        1000 3000
        2000 6000
m   ft

1:2 500 000

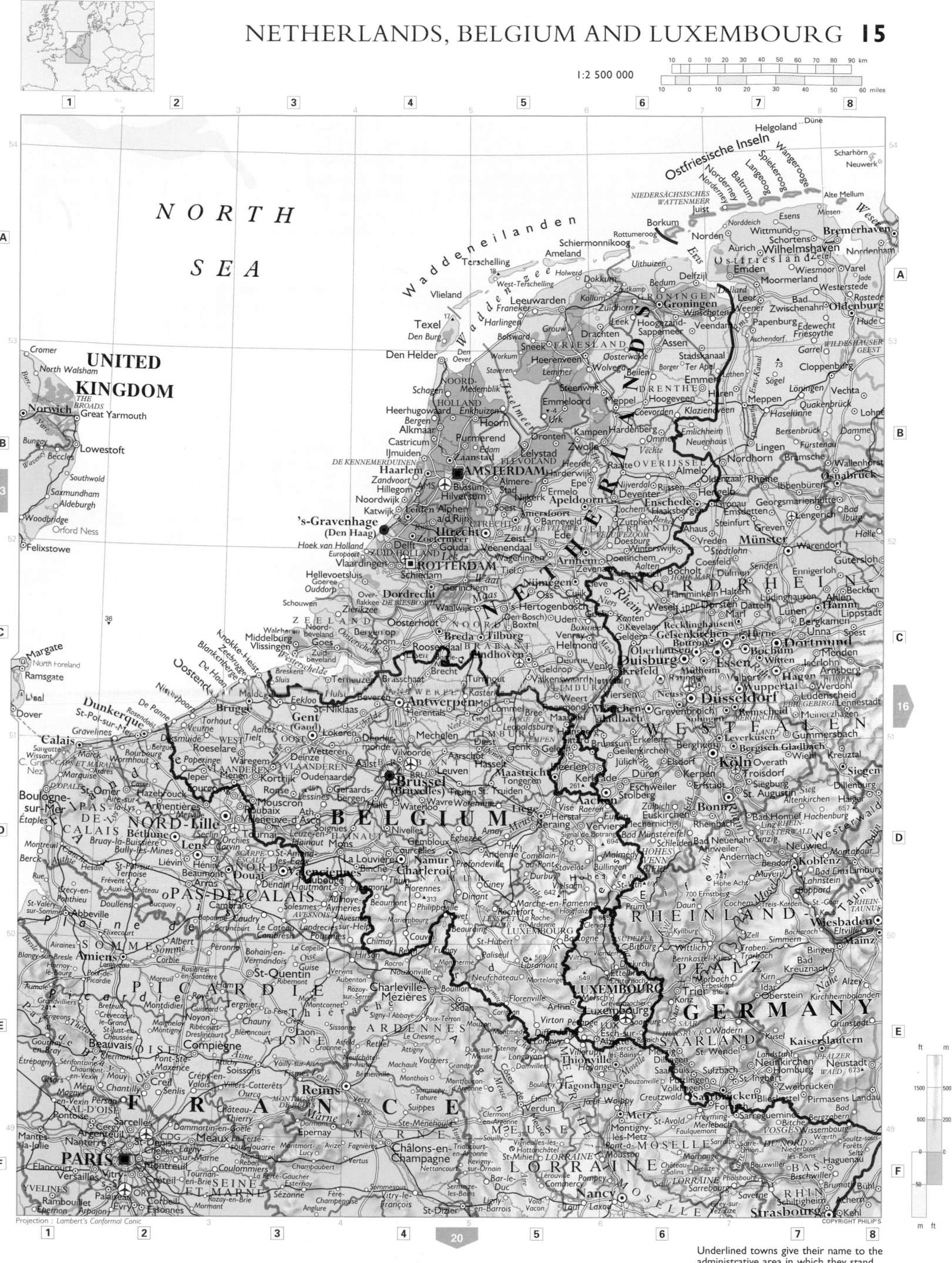

Underlined towns give their name to the administrative area in which they stand.

Projection : Lambert's Conformal Conic

COPYRIGHT PHILIP'S

1:5 000 000

Projection: Conical with two standard parallels

LITHUANIA
BELARUS
POLAND
UKRAINE
SLOVAK REP.
HUNGARY
ROMANIA
MOLDOVA
SERBIA
BOSNIA-HERZEGOVINA
BULGARIA
Vilnius
Kaliningrad (Russia)
Zatoka Gdańska
Gdańsk
Gdynia
Elbląg
Olsztyn
Hrodna
Białystok
Bydgoszcz
Toruń
Włocławek
Płock
Poznań
WARSZAWA (Warsaw)
Łódź
Radom
Lublin
Kielce
Częstochowa
Wrocław
Opole
Katowice
Kraków
Tarnów
Rzeszów
Brest
MINSK
Mahilyow
Babruysk
Homyel
Baranavichy
Pinsk
Mazyr
Lida
Pripet Marshes
Kovel
Lutsk
Rivne
Zhytomyr
KYYIV (Kiev)
Lviv (Lvov)
Ternopil
Khmelnytskyy
Vinnytsya
Chernivtsi
Uzhhorod
Košice
Prešov
Žilina
Bratislava
Budapest
Miskolc
Debrecen
Szeged
Pécs
Győr
Balaton
Nyíregyháza
Satu Mare
Baia Mare
Oradea
Cluj-Napoca
Arad
Timişoara
Sibiu
Braşov
Iaşi
Suceava
Bacău
Bălţi
Chişinău (Kishinev)
Tiraspol
Galaţi
Brăila
Constanţa
Ploieşti
BUCUREŞTI (Bucharest)
Craiova
Piteşti
Ruse
Varna
Osijek
Novi Sad
BEOGRAD (Belgrade)
Sarajevo
Tuzla
Transilvania
Carpaţii Meridionali
Moldova
Podilska Vysochyna
Dunărea (Danube)
Dnister
East from Greenwich
COPYRIGHT PHILIP'S

1:10 000 000

BARENTS SEA
Ostrov Kolguyev
Pechorskaya Guba
Poluostrov Kanin
Cheshskaya Guba
Kolskiy Poluostrov
Beloye More (White Sea)
Murmansk
Arkhangelsk
Severodvinsk
KOMI
SEVERO-ZAPADNYY
URALSKIY
Uralskiye Gory
Timanskiy Kryazh
Severnyye Uvaly
KARELIA
Onezhskoye Ozero
Ladozhskoye Ozero
SANKT-PETERBURG
RUSSIA
MOSKVA (Moscow)
TSENTRALNYY
PRIVOLZHSKIY
UDMURTIA
TATARSTAN
BASHKORTOSTAN
CHUVASHIA
MARI EL
MORDVINIA
NIZHNIY NOVGOROD
SAMARA
KAZAN
PERM
UFA
MINSK
BELARUS
LATVIA
LITHUANIA
ESTONIA
POLAND
WARSZAWA (Warsaw)
FINLAND
SWEDEN
NORWAY
Lappland
Helsinki
Tallinn
Riga
Vilnius
Gulf of Finland
Gulf of Bothnia
Gulf of Riga
BALTIC SEA
Kaliningrad (Russia)
Volga
Kama
Pechora
Arctic Circle

BLACK SEA

CASPIAN SEA

Sea of Azov

MEDITERRANEAN SEA

KAZAKHSTAN

UKRAINE

MOLDOVA

ROMANIA

BULGARIA

TURKEY

GEORGIA

ARMENIA

AZERBAIJAN

TURKMENISTAN

IRAN

IRAQ

SYRIA

LEBANON

CYPRUS

CRIMEA

Projection: Conical with two standard parallels

East from Greenwich

m	ft
4000	12 000
3000	9000
2000	6000
1500	4500
1000	3000
500	1500
200	600
0	0
50	150
100	300
200	600
500	1500
1000	3000
3000	9000
4000	12000

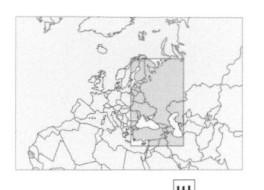

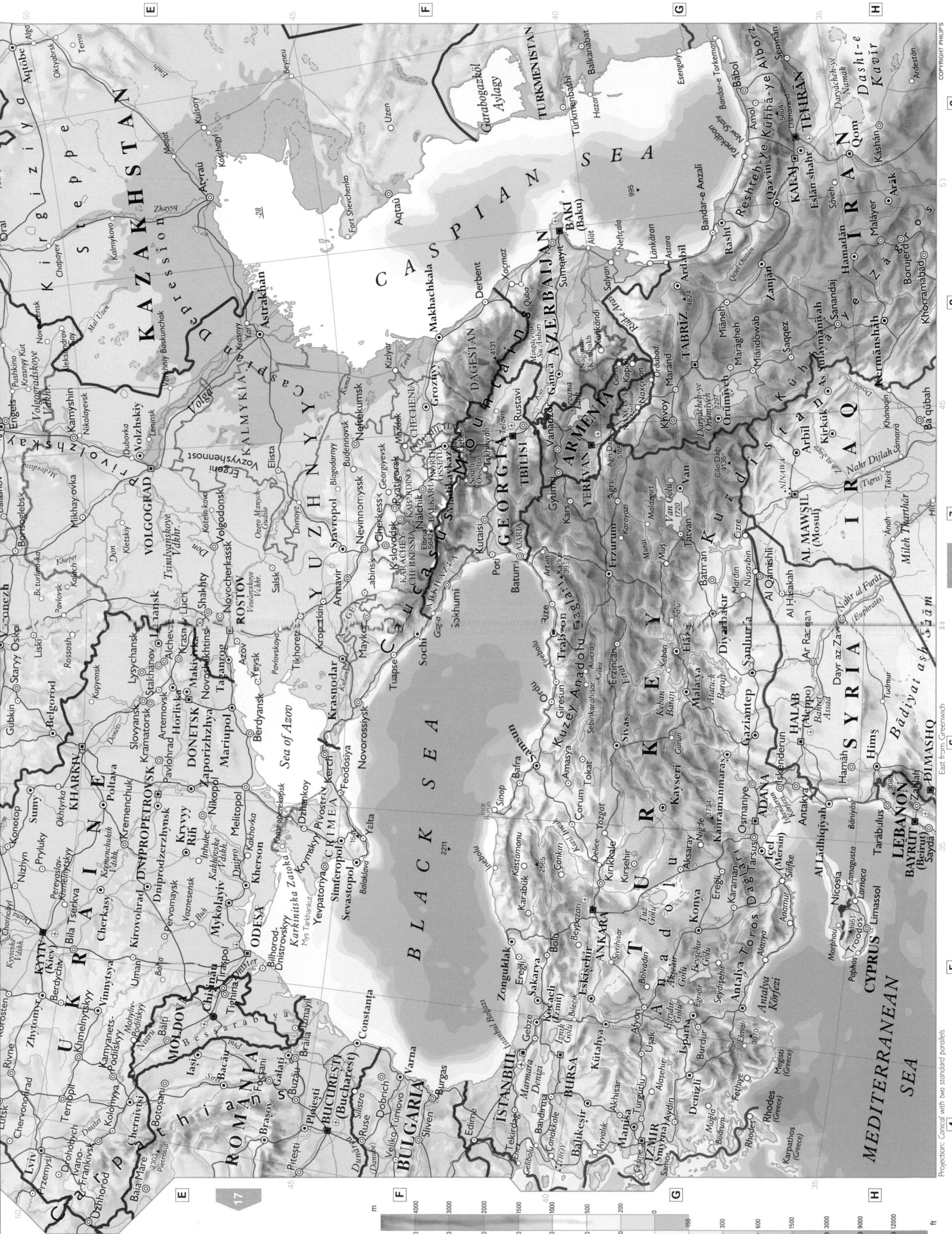

1:5 000 000

Projection: Conical with two standard parallels

Corse (Corsica)

COPYRIGHT PHILIP'S

1:5 000 000

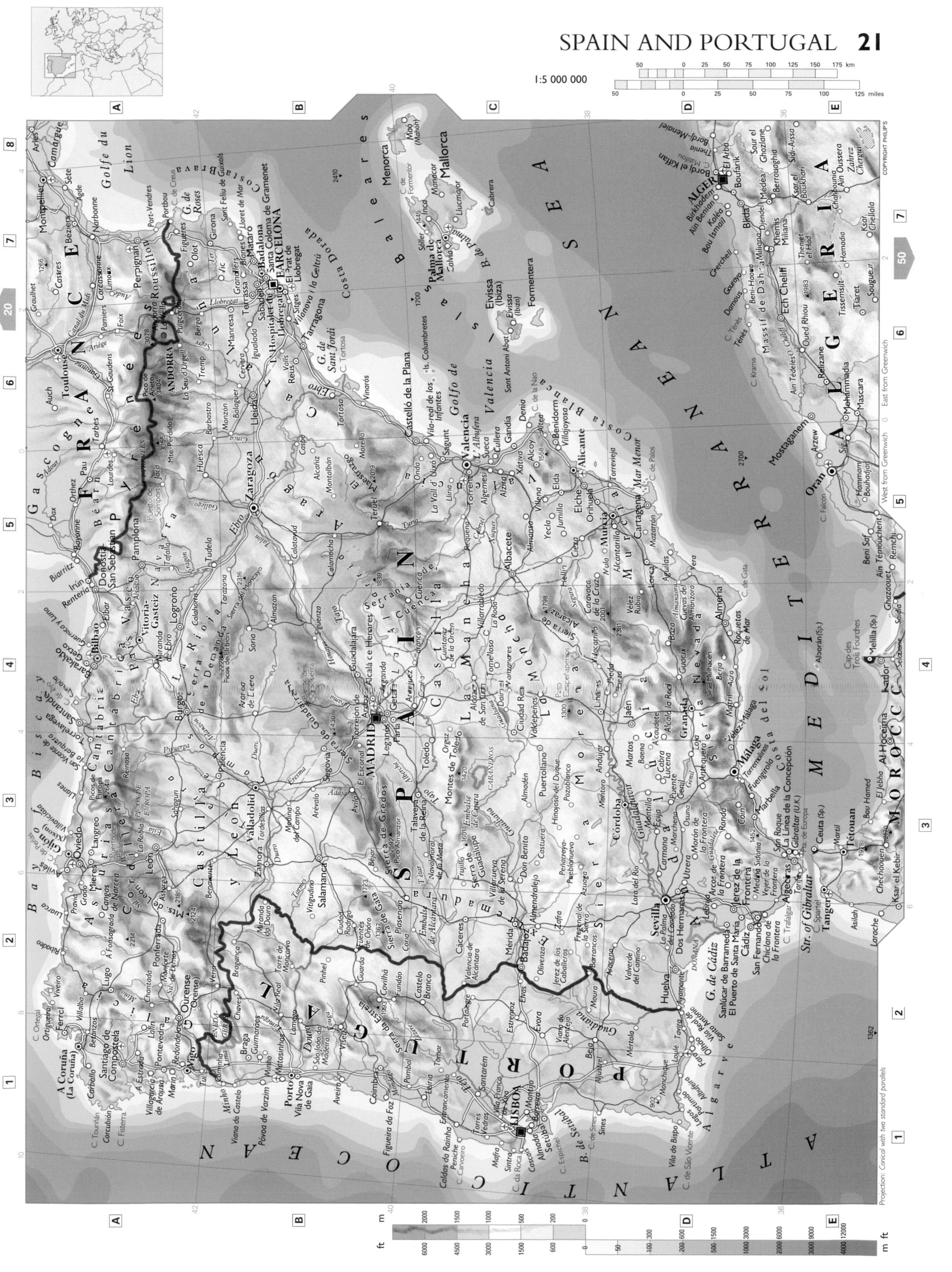
SPAIN
PORTUGAL
FRANCE
ANDORRA
MOROCCO
ALGERIA
MEDITERRANEAN SEA
ATLANTIC OCEAN
Bay of Biscay
Golfe du Lion
Islas Baleares
MADRID
LISBOA
BARCELONA
Valencia
Sevilla
Zaragoza
Málaga
Porto
Bilbao
Str. of Gibraltar
Projection: Conical with two standard parallels
COPYRIGHT PHILIP'S
West from Greenwich
East from Greenwich

SWITZERLAND
AUSTRIA
SLOVENIA
CROATIA
FRANCE
ALGERIA
TUNISIA
MALTA
LIGURIAN SEA
TYRRHENIAN SEA
ADRIATIC SEA
MEDITER
Str. of Sicily
Golfo di Génova
Golfo di Venézia
Golfo di Táranto
Golfe de Tunis
Golfe de Hammamet
Bouches de Bonifacio
Corse (Corsica)
Sardegna (Sardinia)
Sicilia
Ísole Eólie
Ísole Égadi
Ísole Pelagie (Italy)
Ísole Ponziane
Pantelleria (Italy)
Ústica (Italy)
LYON
MARSEILLE
MONACO
MILANO
Torino (Turin)
Génova
Venézia (Venice)
Bologna
Firenze (Florence)
SAN MARINO
ROMA
VATICAN CITY
Nápoli
Bari
Palermo
Catánia
Messina
Cágliari
Sassari
Ajaccio
Bastia
TUNIS
Constantine
Annaba
Ljubljana
ZAGREB
Trieste
Rijeka
Split
Ancona
Pescara
Pérugia
Livorno
Verona
Pádova
Brescia
Bérgamo
Parma
Módena
Ravenna
Rímini
Fóggia
Salerno
Cosenza
Catanzaro
Réggio di Calábria
Siracusa
Valletta
Gozo
Lampedusa
Linosa
Sousse
Kairouan
Bizerte
Grenoble
Avignon
Nice
Toulon
Massif du Pelvoux
Lake di Como
Lago di Garda
L. Trasimeno
Dolomiti
Alpi
Appennini
Piemonte
Liguria
Lombardia
Toscana
Lazio
Calábria
Puglia
Dalmacija
Projection: Conical with two standard parallels
ft m
12000 4000
9000 3000
6000 2000
4500 1500
3000 1000
1500 500
600 200
0 0
50 150
100 300
200 600
500 1500
1000 3000
2000 6000
3000 9000
4000 12000
m ft

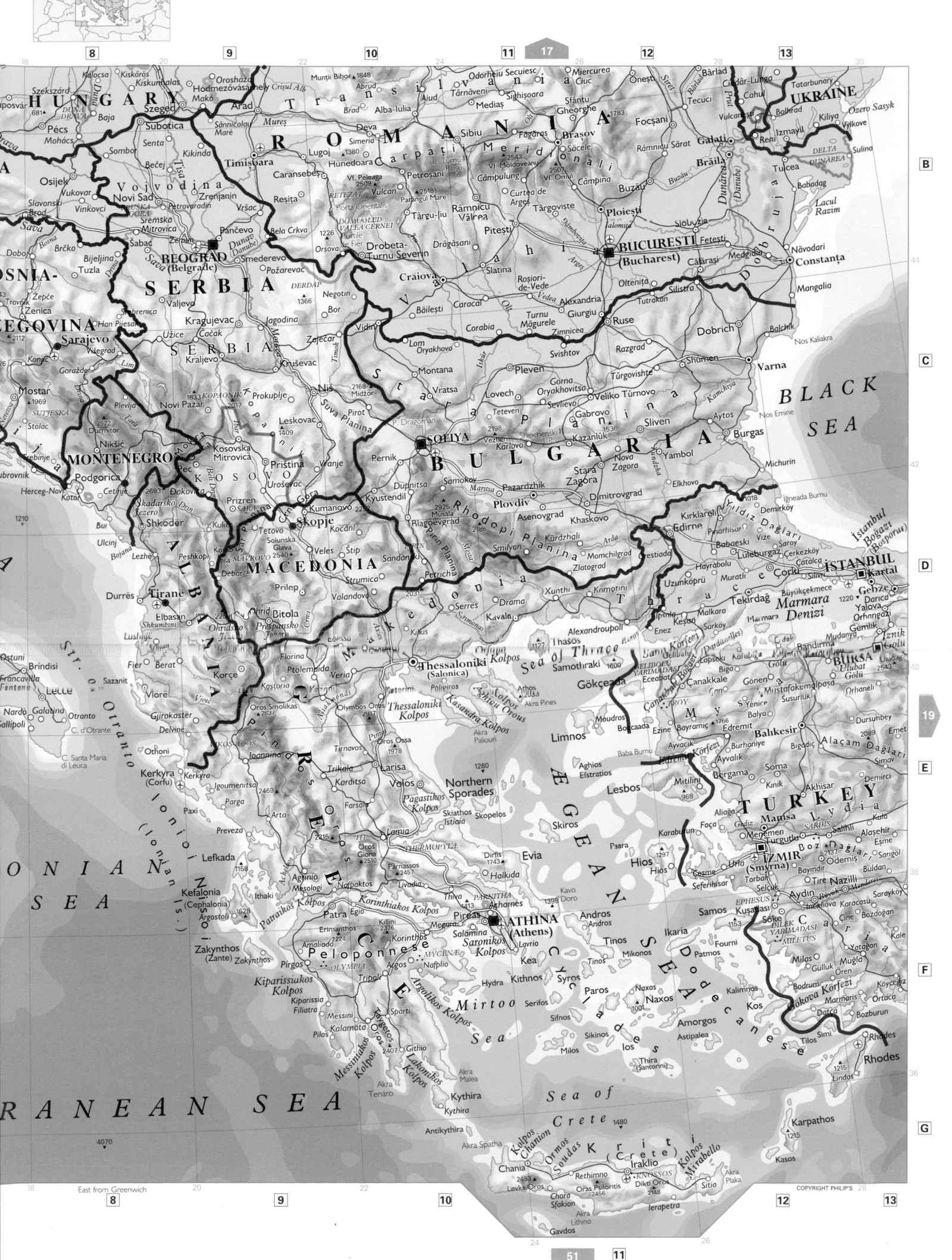
HUNGARY
ROMANIA
UKRAINE
SERBIA
MONTENEGRO
KOSOVO
ALBANIA
MACEDONIA
BULGARIA
GREECE
TURKEY
BLACK SEA
MARMARA DENIZI
AEGEAN SEA
IONIAN SEA
MEDITERRANEAN SEA
Sea of Crete
Str. of Otranto
BEOGRAD (Belgrade)
BUCUREŞTI (Bucharest)
SOFIYA
ATHINA (Athens)
ISTANBUL
Tiranë
Skopje
Sarajevo
Podgorica
Thessaloniki (Salonica)
İZMIR (Smyrna)
BURSA
Constanţa
Varna
Burgas
Plovdiv
Edirne
Kerkyra (Corfu)
Kefalonia (Cephalonia)
Zakynthos (Zante)
Peloponnese
Lesbos
Hios
Samos
Rhodes
Kriti (Crete)
Iraklio
Chania
Karpathos
Limnos
Thasos
Samothraki
Gökçeada
Evia
Andros
Tinos
Naxos
Paros
Milos
Kythira
Cyclades
Dodecanese
Northern Sporades
East from Greenwich
COPYRIGHT PHILIP'S

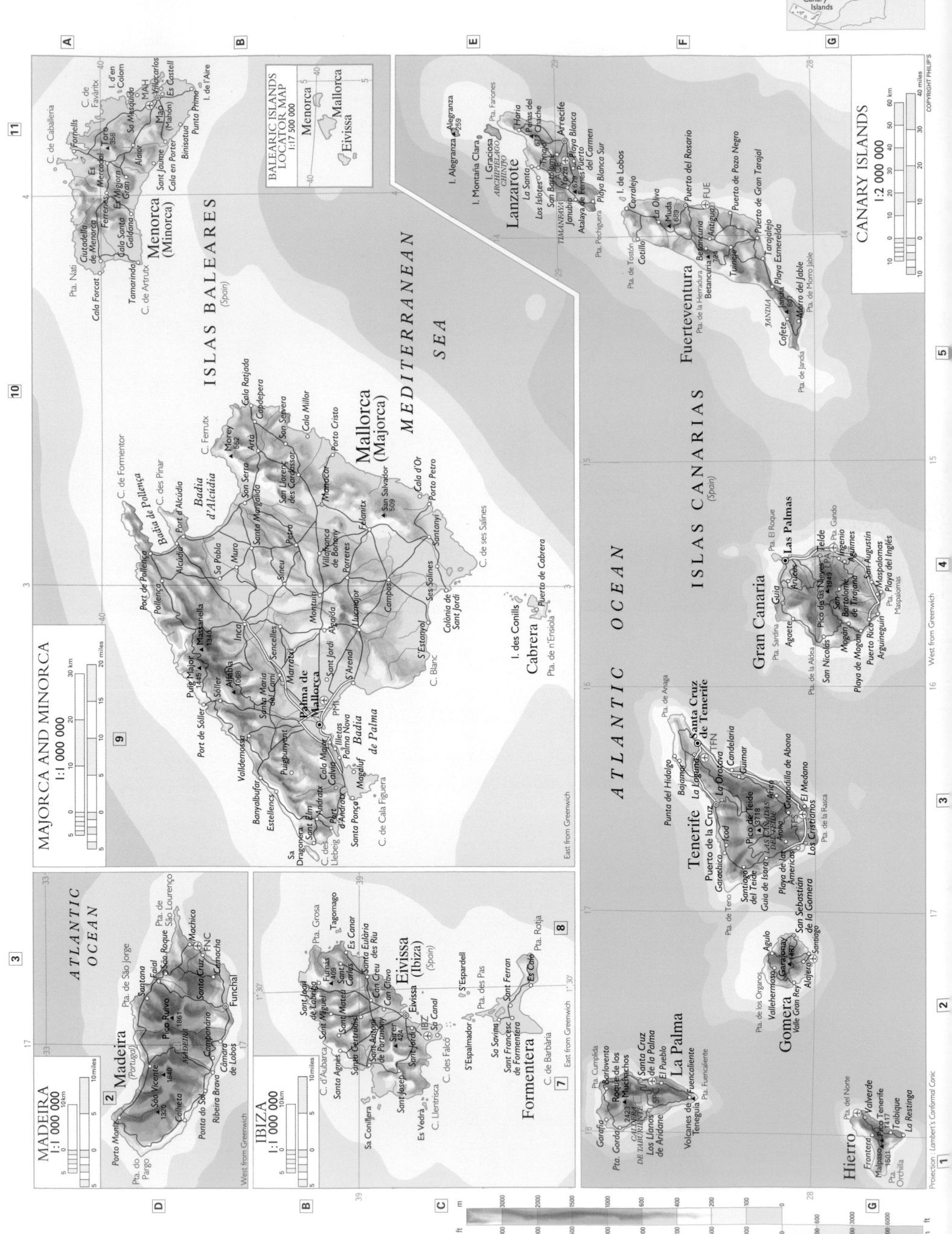

ISLAS BALEARES (Spain)

Menorca (Minorca)

MEDITERRANEAN SEA

Mallorca (Majorca)

Cabrera

BALEARIC ISLANDS LOCATOR MAP
1:17 500 000

Menorca
Mallorca
Eivissa

MAJORCA AND MINORCA
1:1 000 000

MADEIRA 1:1 000 000

ATLANTIC OCEAN

Madeira (Portugal)

IBIZA 1:1 000 000

Eivissa (Ibiza) (Spain)

Formentera

ISLAS CANARIAS (Spain)

ATLANTIC OCEAN

Lanzarote

Fuerteventura

Gran Canaria

Tenerife

Gomera

La Palma

Hierro

CANARY ISLANDS
1:2 000 000

COPYRIGHT PHILIP'S

Projection: Lambert's Conformal Conic

East from Greenwich

West from Greenwich

m / ft elevation scale

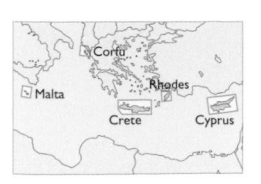

CRETE
1:1 300 000

40 km
25 miles

SEA OF CRETE

Akra Sideros
Akra Plaka
Vai
Akra Agrios Ioannis
Dionisades
Spinalonga
Elounda
Kolpos Mirabellu
Psira
Sitia
Skopi
Mouliana
Zakros
Zíros
Koufonisi
Akra Goudouras
Gaidouronisi

LASITHI
Neapoli
Agios Nikolaos
Kritsa
Kato Chorio
Ierapetra
Makrigialos

Milatos
Malia
Chersonisou
Limenas
Kolpos
Mochos
Lasithi
Díkti Óros 2148
 Víanos
Arvi

IRAKLIO
Iraklio
HER (KNOSSOS)
Kastelli
Archanes
Agia Varvara
Charakas
Asterousia
Pirgos

RETHIMNO
Rethimno
Perama
Spili
Amari
Psiloritis Óros 2456
Timbaki
Vori
Míres
GORTIS
PHESTOS
Pombia
Lentas
Matala
Akra Litinou

Chania
CHANIA
Léfka Óros 2453
Omalos
Samaria
Aghia Roumeli
Chora Sfakion
Gavdos 368
Gavdopoula

Akra Spatha
Kolpos Kissamos
Kasteli
Rodopos
Kolpos Chanion
Akra Vouxa
Platanos
Stomio
Akra Krios
Akra Drepano
Ormos Soudas
Souda
Akrotiri
Chersonisos
Akra D'repano
Georgioupoli
Episkopi
Argiroupoli
Selia

Kriti (Crete) (Greece)

MALTA
1:1 000 000

GOZO
San Dimitri Pt.
Victoria (Rabat)
Xlendi
Nadur
Marsalforn
Qala Pt.
Comino

Mellieha
Bugibba
Mosta
Rabat
Zebbug
Sliema
Valletta
Paola's Pt.
Zejtun
Birzebbuga
Filfla

MEDITERRANEAN SEA

CORFU
1:1 000 000

KERKYRA
Kerkyra (Corfu) (Greece)

ALBANIA
GREECE
Sarandë (Santi-Quaranta)
Akra Aghia Ekaterinis
Sagiada
Igoumenitsa
Xarrë
Kavos
Akra Asprokavos
Sivota
Lefkimi

Kassiopi
Roda
Sidari
Karousades
Erikoussa
Mathraki
Pandokratoras 906
Ipsos
Gouvia
CFU
Kerkyra
Anolipsis
Perama
Benitses
Moraitika
Messongi
Sinarades
Aghios Matheos
Korakiana

IONIAN SEA

RHODES
1:1 000 000

Rhodes
Akra Milon
RHO
Triand
Paradisi
Kremasti
Koskinou
Faliraki
Afandou
Arhangelos
Kalathos
Akra Lindos
Lindos
Ormos Lindos
Lardos
Gennadi
Lahania
Akra Viglas
Holokas
Apolakia
Ormos Apolakia
Kattavia
Akra Praso
Monolithos
Profitis Ilias 1215
Embonas
Aghios Isidoros
Alimia
Kamiros
Soroni

AEGEAN SEA
MEDITERRANEAN SEA

Rhodes (Greece)

CYPRUS
1:1 300 000

40 km
25 miles

MEDITERRANEAN SEA

Kleides
C. Apostolos Andreas
Rizokarpaso
Galinoporni
Komi Kebir
Komnou
Yialou
Ayios Theodhoros
C. Elea
Ayios Elea
Trikomo
Famagusta Bay
Famagusta (Ammochostos)
SALAMIS
Ayios Seryios
Dherinia
Paralimni
Ayia Napa
C. Greco
Xylophagou

Akanthou
Olymbos
Kythrea
Mesaoria
Vatili
Athna
DHEKELIA SOVEREIGN BASE AREA
Larnaca Bay
Larnaca
Liopetri
C. Pyla
C. Kiti

Kyrenia
Lapithos
Under Turkish Administration
Nicosia (Lefkosia)
Dheftera
Athalassa
Aradhippou

Morphou
Morphou Bay
Lefka
Troodos Óros 1951
Kakopetria
Pedhoulas
Mílikouri
Mandria
Kato Pyrgos
Kokkina
Pomos
C. Pomos
C. Kormakiti

Khrysokhou Bay
Polis
Stavros
Paphos
PFO
Kissonerga
C. Drepanum
C. Arnauti

Limassol
Akrotiri
AKROTIRI SOVEREIGN BASE
Akrotiri Bay
C. Gata
Kolossi
Episkopi
Episkopi Bay

CYPRUS

Projection: Lambert's Conformal Conic
East from Greenwich
COPYRIGHT PHILIP'S

m / ft elevation scale: 2000 1500 1000 600 400 200 100 0 200 4000 6000

1:47 000 000

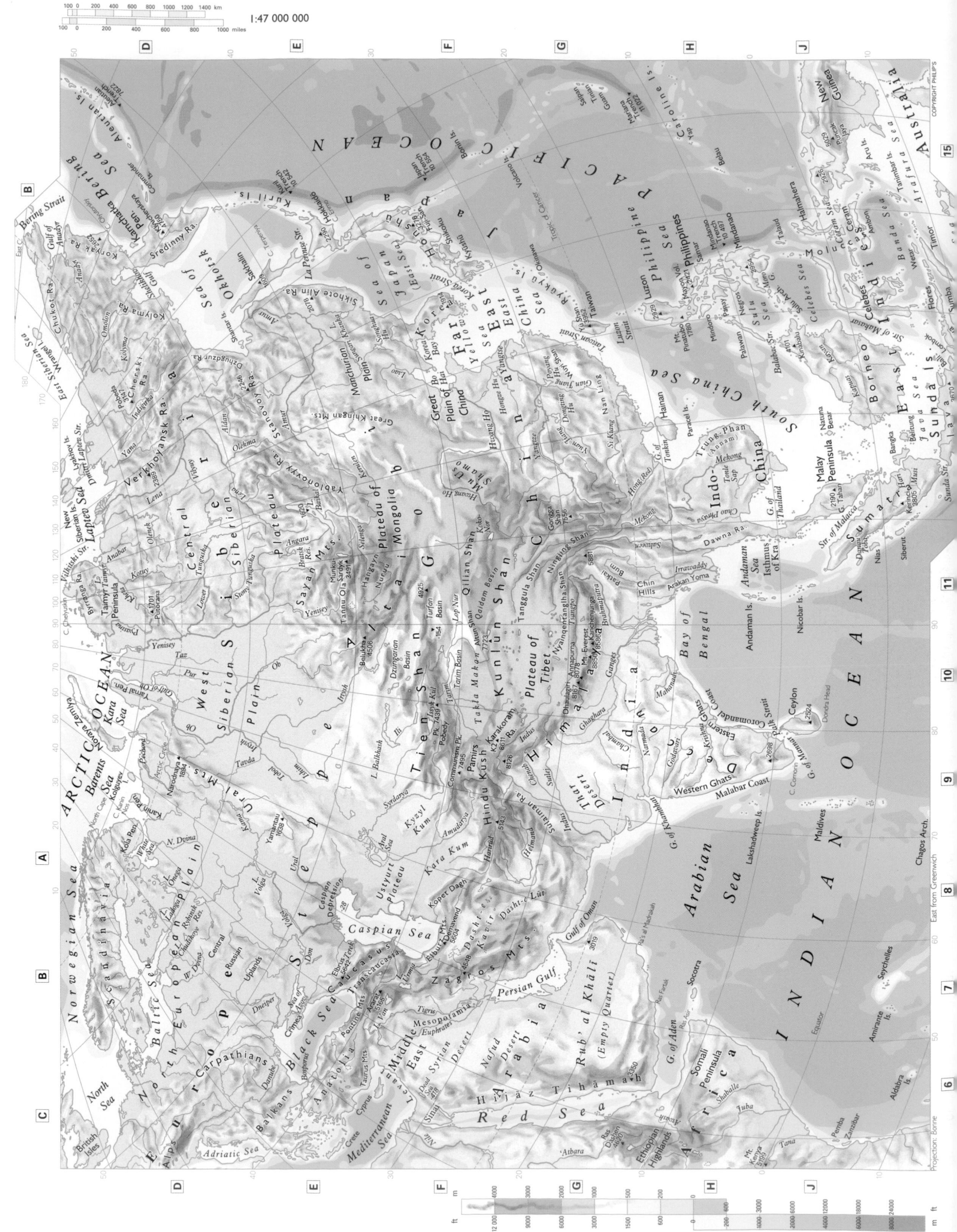

ARCTIC OCEAN
PACIFIC OCEAN
INDIAN OCEAN
Norwegian Sea
Barents Sea
Kara Sea
Laptev Sea
East Siberian Sea
Bering Sea
Sea of Okhotsk
Sea of Japan (East Sea)
Yellow Sea
East China Sea
South China Sea
Philippine Sea
Arabian Sea
Bay of Bengal
Andaman Sea
Caspian Sea
Black Sea
Baltic Sea
North Sea
Mediterranean Sea
Red Sea
Persian Gulf
Gulf of Oman
G. of Aden
Scandinavia
North European Plain
Central Russian Uplands
Europe
Ural Mts.
West Siberian Plain
Siberia
Central Siberian Plateau
Verkhoyansk Ra.
Steppe
Tien Shan
Altai
Plateau of Mongolia
Gobi
Kunlun Shan
Plateau of Tibet
Himalaya
Hindu Kush
Pamirs
Karakoram Ra.
Takla Makan
Tarim Basin
Dzungarian Basin
Great Plain of China
Manchurian Plain
Far East
China
India
Deccan
Thar Desert
Arabia
Rub' al Khālī (Empty Quarter)
Nafud Desert
Syrian Desert
Middle East
Anatolia
Caucasus
Zagros Mts.
Indo-China
Malay Peninsula
Sumatra
Borneo
Java
Philippines
East Indies
Sunda Is.
Japan
Korea
Taiwan
Hainan
Ceylon
Maldives
Africa
Somali Peninsula
Ethiopian Highlands
Australia
New Guinea
Mt. Everest 8850
Kanchenjunga 8586
Annapurna 8078
Dhaulagiri 8167
K2 8611
Communism Pk. 7495
Pk. Pobedy 7439
Elbrus 5642
Demavend 5604
Ararat 5165
Lena
Yenisey
Ob
Amur
Yangtze
Hwang Ho
Mekong
Ganges
Indus
Brahmaputra
Euphrates
Tigris
Volga
Arctic Circle
Tropic of Cancer
Equator
Projection: Bonne
East from Greenwich
COPYRIGHT PHILIP'S

1:47 000 000

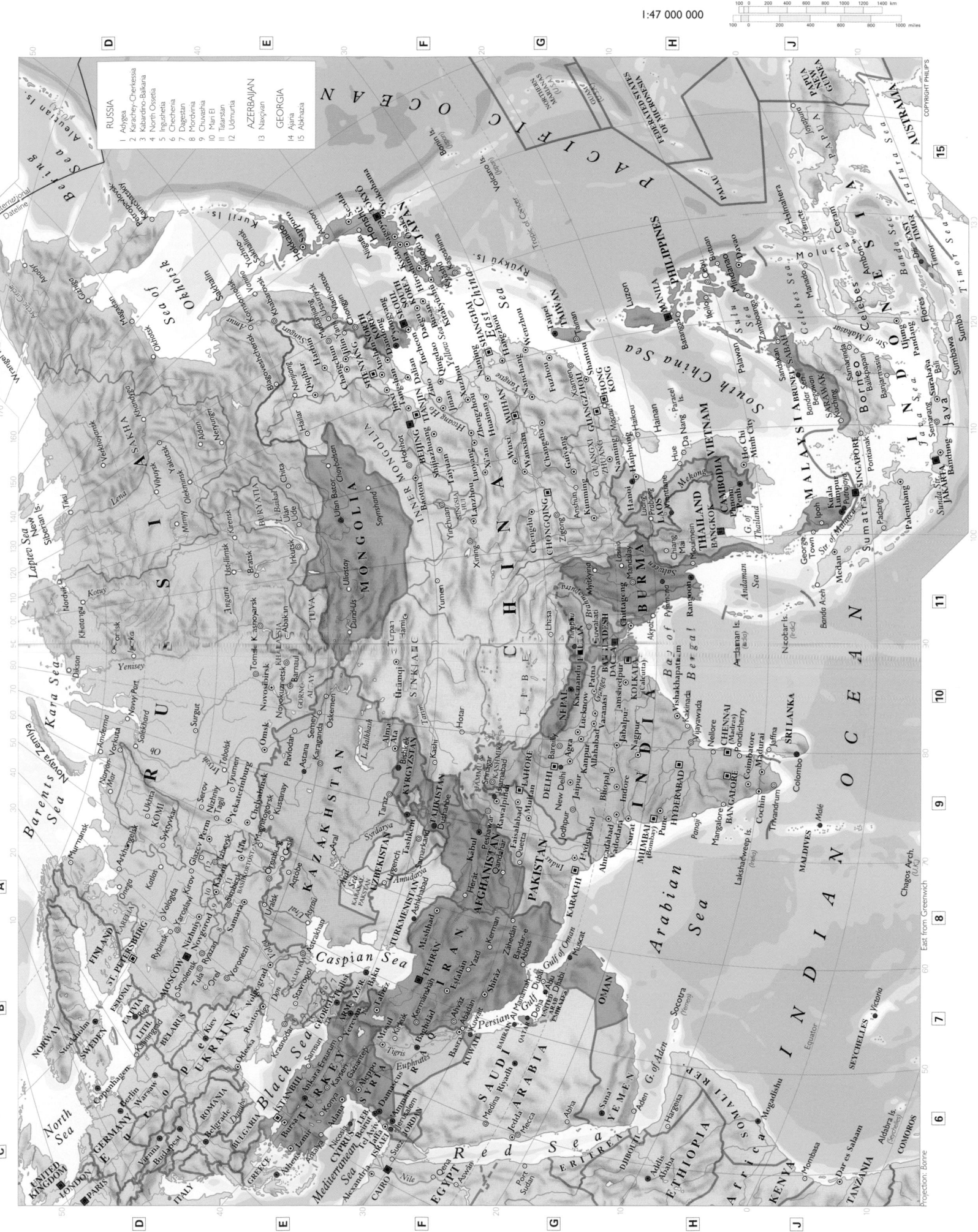
RUSSIA
1 Adygea
2 Karachey-Cherkessia
3 Kabardino-Balkaria
4 North Ossetia
5 Ingushetia
6 Chechenia
7 Dagestan
8 Mordvinia
9 Chuvashia
10 Mari El
11 Tatarstan
12 Udmurtia
AZERBAIJAN
13 Naxçivan
GEORGIA
14 Ajaria
15 Abkhazia
R U S S I A
K A Z A K H S T A N
MONGOLIA
C H I N A
I N D I A
PAKISTAN
AFGHANISTAN
I R A N
SAUDI ARABIA
TURKEY
BURMA
THAILAND
CAMBODIA
VIETNAM
MALAYSIA
PHILIPPINES
JAPAN
I N D O N E S I A
SRI LANKA
NEPAL
P A C I F I C O C E A N
I N D I A N O C E A N
Arabian Sea
Bay of Bengal
South China Sea
East China Sea
Sea of Okhotsk
Caspian Sea
Black Sea
Red Sea
Mediterranean Sea
Barents Sea
Kara Sea
Laptev Sea
Bering Sea
North Sea
Tropic of Cancer
Equator
East from Greenwich
Projection: Bonne

1:20 000 000

RUSSIA
1 Adygea
2 Karachey-Cherkessia
3 Kabardino-Balkaria
4 North Ossetia
5 Ingushetia
6 Chechenia
7 Dagestan
8 Mordvinia
9 Chuvashia
10 Mari El
11 Tatarstan
12 Udmurtia
13 Khakassia
AZERBAIJAN
14 Naxçivan
GEORGIA   UKRAINE
15 Ajaria   17 Crimea
16 Abkhazia

Projection: Conical Orthomorphic with two standard parallels

East from Greenwich

Mys Dezhneva (East C.)
Chukchi Sea
St. Lawrence I. (U.S.A.)
Bering Sea
East Siberian Sea
Laptev Sea
OCEAN
Ostrov Vrangelya
Novosibirskiye Ostrova
Severnaya Zemlya
Poluostrov Taymyr
Gory Byrranga
Chukotskoye Nagorye
Koryakskoye Nagorye
Kolymskoye Nagorye
Khrebet Cherskogo
Verkhoyanskiy Khrebet
DALNEVOSTOCHNY
Poluostrov Kamchatka
Sea of Okhotsk
Sakhalin
Kurilskiye Ostrova
Stanovoy Khrebet
Yablonovyy Khrebet
Khrebet Dzhugdzur
Sikhote Alin
Vostochnyy Sayan
RUSSIA
MONGOLIA
Gobi
CHINA
Hangayn Nuruu
Hentiyn Nuruu
Da Hinggan Ling
Dongbei (Manchuria)
Sea of Japan (East Sea)
Hokkaidō
Honshū
JAPAN
NORTH KOREA
SOUTH KOREA
Yakutsk
Magadan
Petropavlovsk-Kamchatskiy
Khabarovsk
Vladivostok
Irkutsk
Krasnoyarsk
Bratsk
Chita
Ulan Ude
Ulaanbaatar
BEIJING
HARBIN
CHANGCHUN
SHENYANG
P'YONGYANG
SEOUL
SAPPORO
Arctic Circle
Lena
Amur
Kolyma
Indigirka
Yana
Aldan
Vilyuy
Olenek
Ozero Baykal
Yuzhno-Sakhalinsk
Tatarskiy Proliv
La Perouse Str.
Proliv Vilkitskogo
Proliv Dmitriya Lapteva

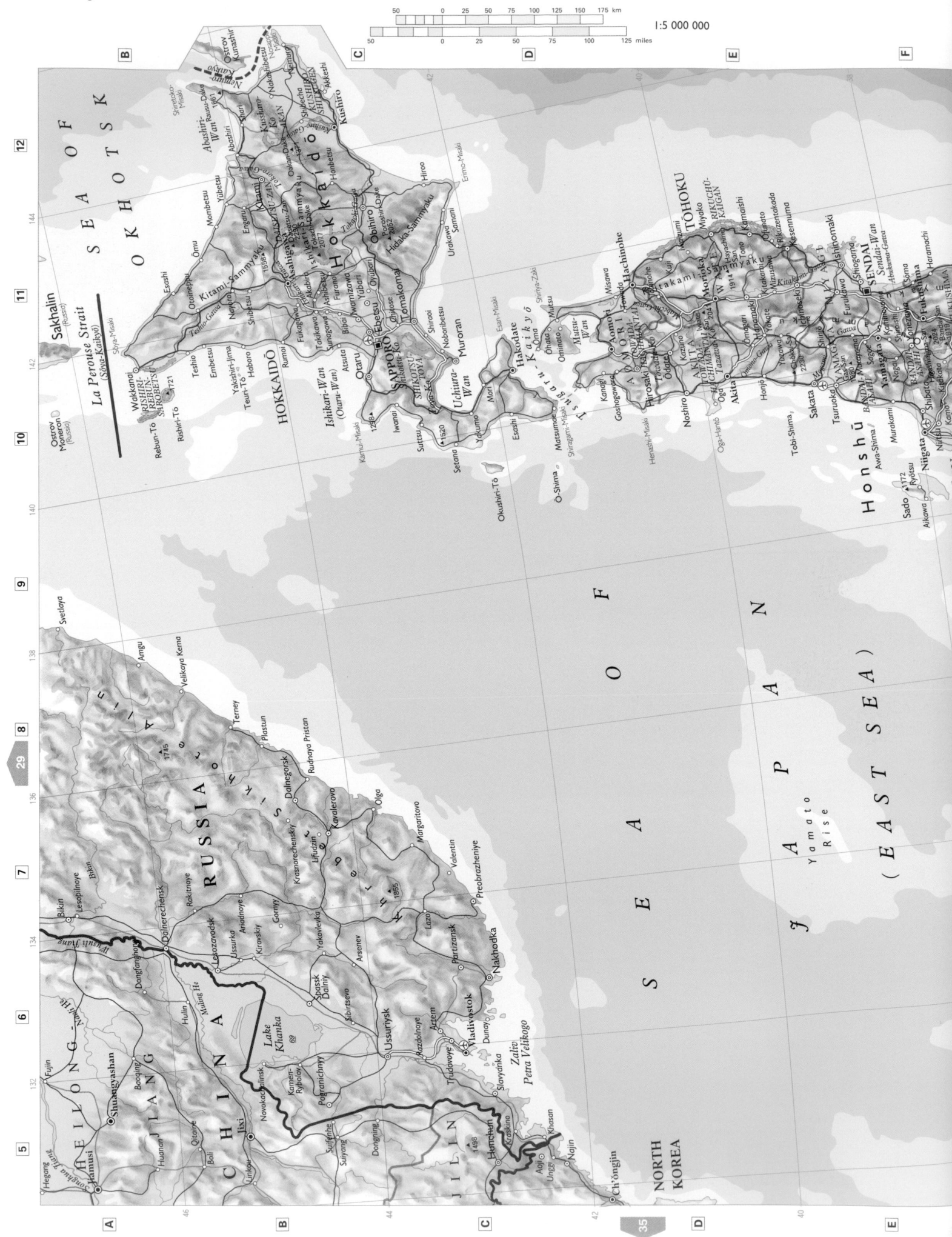

50 0 25 50 75 100 125 150 175 km
50 0   25   50   75   100 125 miles

1:5 000 000

SEA OF OKHOTSK

Sakhalin

La Perouse Strait
(Sōya-Kaikyō)

Ostrov Moneron
(Russia)

HOKKAIDŌ

SAPPORO

HOKKAIDŌ

Ishikari-Wan
(Otaru-Wan)

Uchiura-Wan

Tsugaru-Kaikyō

Hakodate

TOHOKU

RIKUCHŪ-KAIGAN

AOMORI

MORIOKA

SENDAI

Honshū

Sado

RUSSIA

CHINA

HEILONGJIANG

JILIN

Lake Khanka

Vladivostok

Zaliv Petra Velikogo

NORTH KOREA

SEA OF JAPAN (EAST SEA)

Yamato Rise

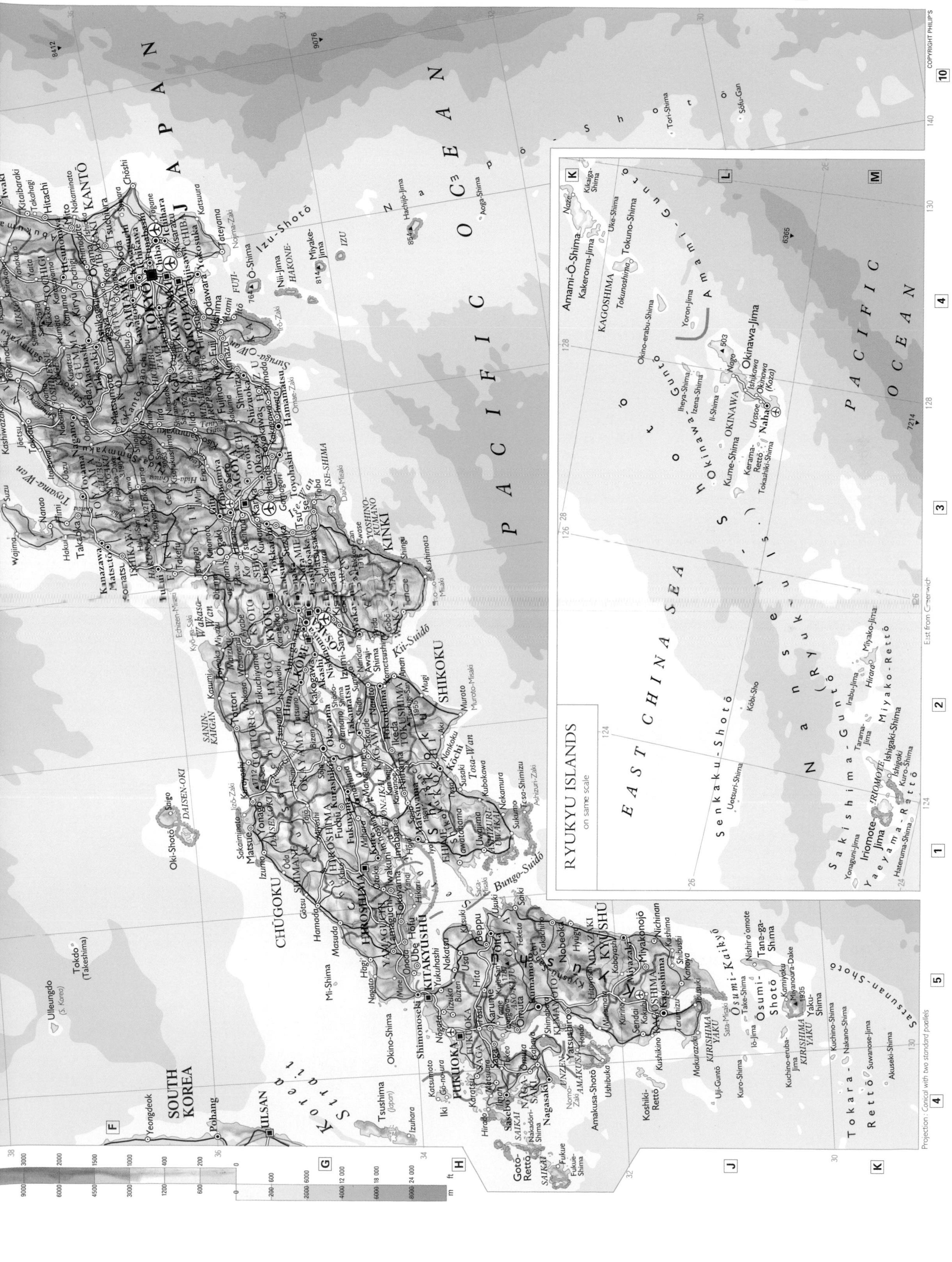

RYUKYU ISLANDS
on same scale

Projection: Conical with two standard parallels

1:15 000 000

Projection: Bonne

East from Greenwich

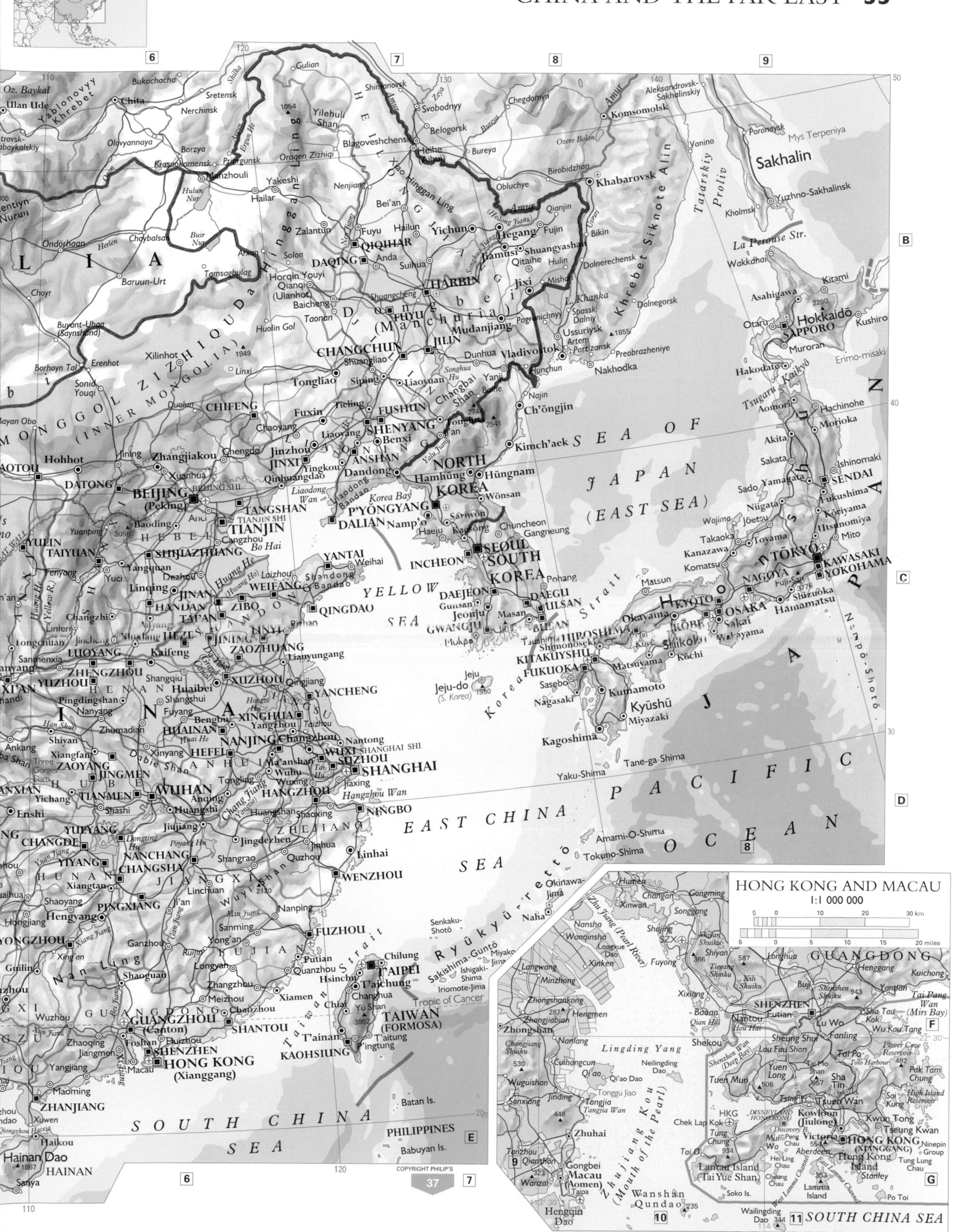

HONG KONG AND MACAU

1:1 000 000

5   0   10   20   30 km

5   0   5   10   15   20 miles

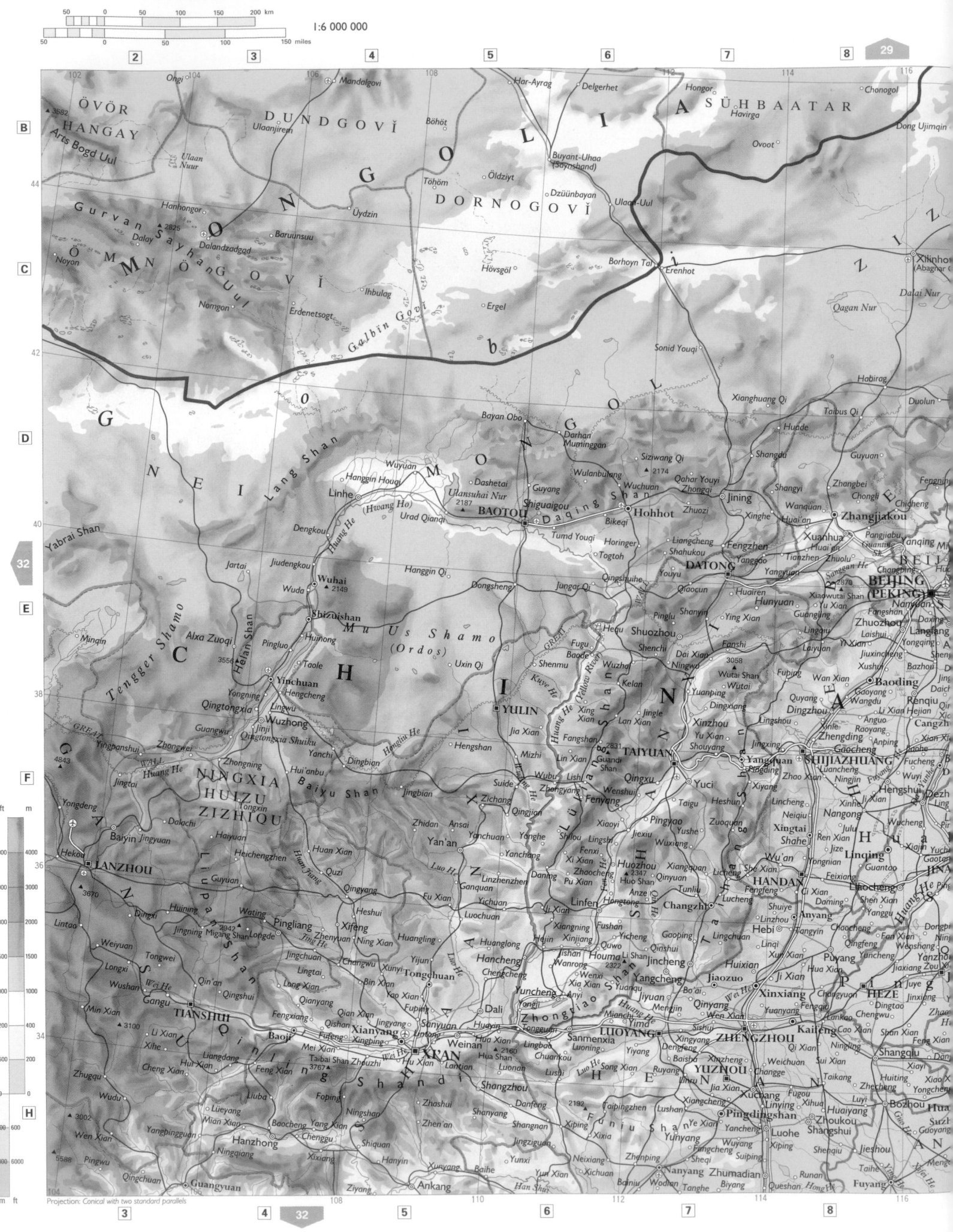

1:6 000 000

Projection: Conical with two standard parallels

HARBIN
Harbin
Qiqihar
Daqing
Heilongjiang
Jilin
CHANGCHUN
JILIN
SHENYANG
FUSHUN
ANSHAN
DALIAN
(Lüda)
Dandong
CHIFENG
Fuxin
Jinzhou
Yingkou
Huludao
Qinhuangdao
TIANJIN
Bo Hai
Liaodong Wan
Korea Bay
YANTAI
Weihai
WEIFANG
ZIBO
QINGDAO
LINYI
XINTAI
ZAOZHUANG
Lianyungang
HUAI'AN
YANCHENG
XINGHUA
SUQIAN
YELLOW SEA
(Huang Hai)
NORTH KOREA
P'YŎNGYANG
Hamhŭng
Ch'ŏngjin
Kimch'aek
Sinŭiju
Wŏnsan
Kaesŏng
Nampo
Haeju
SOUTH KOREA
SEOUL
INCHEON
SUWON
SEONGNAM
Chuncheon
Gangneung
Cheongju
DAEJEON
DAEGU
Jeonju
GWANGJU
ULSAN
BUSAN
Pohang
Mokpo
Jeju
Jeju-do (S. Korea)
Korea Strait
SEA OF JAPAN
(EAST SEA)
RUSSIA
Vladivostok
Ussuriysk
Mudanjiang
Yanji
Tumen
JAPAN
Tsushima (Japan)
Iki
Sasebo
Nagasaki
Chengshan Jiao
Shandong Bandao
Laizhou Wan
Miaodao Qundao
Changbai Shan
Paektu-san
Yalu Jiang
Songhua Jiang
Liao He
East from Greenwich
COPYRIGHT PHILIP'S
9 10 11 12 13 14 15 16
B C D E F G H
30
31
33

1:12 500 000

Projection: Mercator

East from Greenwich

33

A

JAVA AND MADURA
1:7 500 000

50   0   50   100   150   200   250   300 km
50   0   50   100   150   200 miles

BALI
1:2 000 000

10   0   10   20   30 km
10   0   10   20 miles

Java and Madura

Selat Sunda Pulau Rakata Panaitan Labuhan Pelabuhanratu Teluk Pelabuhan Ratu Tanjung Guhakolak Merak Anyer Rangkasbitung Pandeglang BANTEN **JAKARTA** Tangerang Bogor Pamanukan Karawang Kandanghaur Indramayu **Bandung** 3078 Cianjur Sumedang Purwakarta Subang Jatibarang Cirebon Kuningan Cremai Brebes Tegal Pemalang Pekalongan Kendal Kudus Demak **Semarang** Jepara Rembang Kragan Tuban Madura Bangkalan Sumenep Pamekasan Tambuku Sampang **SURABAYA** Sidoarjo Selat Madura Gresik Jombang Mojokerto Pasuruan Probolinggo Situbondo Bondowoso Jember **Malang** Banyuwangi Bali

JAWA BARAT JAWA TENGAH JAWA TIMUR Genteng Sindangbarang Pengalengan Garut Tasikmalaya Cijulang Pamanukan Banyumas Purwokerto Cilacap Nusa Kambangan Kebumen Wonosobo 3428 Magelang Boyolali **Surakarta** Madiun Ponorogo Kediri **Yogyakarta** Wonosari Pacitan Tulungagung Blitar Trenggalek Nusa Barung

Bali

Gunung 3332 Banyuwangi Ketapang Tanjung Batugondang Pulau Menjangan Gilimanuk Singaraja Kubutambahan BALI SEA Tejakula Jambewangi Cekik Gerokgak Seririt Lovina Bayun Tianyar Kubu Melaya Merbuk 1385 Busungbiu Kintamani Batur Songan Gunung Gulik Beluki Rogojampi Negara Pupuan Baturiti 2276 Danau Batur Amed Tirtagangga Genteng Srono Mendoyo Yehbuah Tatuluwih Rendang Saren Karangasem (Amlapura) Tegalsari Muncar Perancak Belimbing Pasar Bajera Sembung Blahkiuh Bangli Manggis Candi Dasa **Lombok** Bajatrejo Pekutatan **Bali** Tabanan Muncari Ubud Klungkung Kusamba Montongbuwon Grajagan Gianyar Sukawati Ampenan **Mataram** **Jawa** Tanjung Kucur **Denpasar** Sanur Badung Sampalan Lembar Gerung Tanjung Purwo Semenanjung Blambangan Teluk Jimbaran Kuta Toyapakeh 530 Suwana Teluk Terang Uluwatu DPS Nusa Dua Nusa Penida Tanjung Abah Blongas Tanjung Mebulu Bukit Badung **INDIAN OCEAN** Tanjung Pamenang Tanjung Pangga Tanjung Tampa

Philippines and Luzon

Claveria Babuyan Chan. C. Engaño Bacarra Laoag Batac 2048 Aparri Tuguegarao Bangued Vigan Bontoc Solano Ilagan Palanan Pt. Palanan San Fernando Baguio Bayombong Casiguran Lingayen 2929 Solano Bolinao Lingayen G. Dagupan San Ildefonso Tarlac San Jose Mt. Pinatubo 1759 Cabanatuan **Angeles** San Fernando Polillo Is. Olongapo Mololos **Quezon City** Lamon Bay Bataan **MANILA** Cavite Santa Cruz Daet Yog Pt. Manila B. Batangas Lucena Calauag Catanduanes Lipa 2188 Lucena Naga Virac Calapan Marinduque Legazpi Mayon Volcano 2462 Sorsogon Mindoro Halcon 2586 Romblon Tablas Burias Masbate San Bernardino Str. Laoang Mindoro Str. San Jose Sibuyan Sea Masbate Catarman Samar 5245 Semirara Is. Sibuyan Calbayog Oras Taft Busuanga Pandan Panay 2117 Roxas Capiz Kalibo Visayan Sea Borongan General MacArthur Cuyo Is. **Iloilo** Pototan Ormoc Leyte Baybay Guiuan San Jose de Buenavista Guimaras **Bacolod** **Cebu** Mandaue Talibon Maasin Dinagat Dumaran Negros Tanjay Binalbagan 2585 Panay G. Tagbilaran Bohol Siquijor Siargao Puerto Princesa Dipolog Dumaguete Camiguin Tandag 2012 L. Mainit **Cagayan de Oro** Butuan Lianga Sindangan 2425 Iligan Malaybalay Cateel Bislig Kabasalan Ozamiz 2938 **Mindanao** Tagum 2804 Bislig Zamboanga Pagadian Parang Cotabato Datu Piang Mt. 2854 **DAVAO** Mati Isabela Basilan Lebak Koronadal Digos C. San Agustin General Santos 2083 Kiamba Malita Parang Jolo Samales Group Kiamba 5824 Sarangani Pt. Tinaca Pt. Pangutaran Group Siasi Tapul Group Sarangani B. Balimbing Tawi-Tawi Sibutu Sibutu Passage

Sulawesi and eastern islands

CELEBES SEA Pulau Kawio Kepulauan Nanusa Karakelong Kepulauan Talaud Miangas (Palmas) Tahulandang Biaro Siau Kepulauan Sangihe Doi Sopi Morotai Berebere Bunaken 2022 Bangka Galela Tobelo Akelamo **Manado** Kema Tandano Ibu 1325 Jailolo **Halmahera** Toli-Toli Buol Paleleh Sumalata Kuandang Kotamobagu MALUKU UTARA Ternate Teluk Buli Kepulauan Asia Tanjung Mangkalihat Tomini 2490 **GORONTALO** Gorontalo Tanjung Flesko Tidore Weda Teluk Weda Kepulauan Mapia Teluk Tomini SULAWESI UTARA Kayoa Wosi Umera Waigeo Kepulauan Ayu Donggala Toboli SULAWESI TENGAH Tojo Poh Peleng Obilatu Gebe Dampier Sorong 2452 Kwoka Manokwari Numfoor Biak Palu 2355 Luwuk Banggai Kasiruta 4970 Gani 2111 Bisa Kawasi Seget Kofiau Salawati Klamono 2926 Ransiki Yapen Serui Poso 2630 Kolonodale Teluk Tolo Kepulauan Banggai Mangole Sanana Misool **IRIAN JAYA BARAT** Inanwatan Wendesi Saberania Gehyem Sentani Jayapura Kolaka Teluk Towuti Danau Towuti Taliabu Todeli Kepulauan Sula Adua Lenmalu Teminabuan Bintuni Teluk Berau Wasior Pegunungan Van Rees Krau Makale 3440 Malili Masamba Mondeodo Manui Namlea Buru 2736 Seram (Ceram) Sawai Wahai Kokas Babo Nabire Waghete Enarotali 6029 Puncak Jaya Puncak Trikora Wamena Parepare Singkang Kendari Monse Wowoni Piru Amahai 3019 Tehoru Bula Fakfak Wenut Kwatisore Uta Enarotali 4730 Pegunungan Sudirman Tembagapura Oksibil Watampone Buapinang Buton Raha Lawele **Ambon** Saparua Geser Weri Ibonma Kaimana **PAPUA** Pegunungan Maoke 4702 Jayawijaya Mandala Sinjai Pising Muna Wangiwangi Kepulauan Tukangbesi Kepulauan Gorong Manggawitu Adi Amamapare Yapera Trikora Sumba Bulukumba Kabaena Baubau Benteng Batuata **BANDA SEA** Kepulauan Banda Bandanaira Kepulauan Watubela Pulau Dolak Agats Mindiptana Salayar Lompobatang 2871 Tanahjampea Kepulauan Bonerate Kalaotoa 5888 Gunungapi 7440 Nila Serua Hari Kai Besar Kola Gumzai Wokam Sewer Kepulauan Aru Rebi Wangal Kaba Gomogomo Pirimapun Tanahmerah Kepi Bade Muting Bonerate Damar Teun Molu Tafermaar Trangan Okaba Merauke Sumbawa 5123 Flores Komodo 2350 Ruteng Aimere Ende Maumere Larantuka Adonara Lomblen Pantar Alor Ataoro Baucau Tutuala Leti Wetar Wesiri Romang Barat Tepa Wuliaru Alusi Kepulauan Tanimbar Yamdena Saumlaki Tanjung Ngabordamlu Tanjung Vals Pulau Komoran Pulau Kimaam Sawu Waingapu Melolo NUSA TENGGARA TIMUR Kupang Dili **EAST TIMOR** Viqueque Kefamenanu Nikiniki Macassar Pante Makassar (E.Timor) Roti Baa Raijua Dana **ARAFURA SEA** Eliase Selaru Adaut Masela Sermata

SULU SEA SULU ARCHIPELAGO Jolo Moro G. Illana B.

PACIFIC OCEAN Tobi (Palau) Helen Atoll (Palau) Merir (Palau) 5798 Equator Kepulauan Raja Ampat

PAPUA NEW GUINEA

INDIAN OCEAN

KO PHUKET
1:1 000 000
KO SAMUI
1:1 000 000
Gulf of Thailand
PINANG
1:1 000 000
SINGAPORE
1:1 000 000
1:1 000 000
Gulf of Thailand
SOUTH CHINA SEA
ANDAMAN SEA
Straits of Malacca
Straits of Singapore
MALAYSIA
PENINSULAR MALAYSIA
INDONESIA
PHNOM PENH
THANH PHO HO CHI MINH (SAIGON)
KUALA LUMPUR
SINGAPORE
MEDAN
Kho Khot Kra (Isthmus of Kra)
Myeik Kyunzu (Mergui Archipelago)
Projection: Conical with two standard parallels
East from Greenwich
COPYRIGHT PHILIP'S

50 0 100 200 300 400 km
50 0 50 100 150 200 250 miles
1:10 000 000

Projection: Conical with two standard parallels

ft m (elevation scale)
18 000 / 6000
12 000 / 4000
9000 / 3000
6000 / 2000
4500 / 1500
3000 / 1000
1200 / 400
600 / 200
0 / 0
200 / 600
m ft

TURKMENISTAN

A F G H A N I S T A N
Herat · Kabul · Kandahar · Ghazni
HERAT · GHOWR · DAY KUNDI · GHAZNI · PAKTIA · PAKTIKA
FARAH · NIMRUZ · HELMAND · ORUZGAN
Hindu Kush · PANJSHER · BADAKHSHAN · NURISTAN
BAGHLAN · PARVAN · KAPISA · LAGHMAN · NANGARHAR · LOWGAR · WARDAK

I R A N
Zahedan · Birjand

P A K I S T A N
B A L U C H I S T A N
Quetta · Kalat · Turbat · Gwadar · Pasni · Ormara
Makran Coast Range · Central Makran Range · Siahan Range
N.W.F.P · Peshawar · RAWALPINDI · Islamabad
NORTH WEST FRONTIER
Kabul · Khyber Pass
PUNJAB · FAISALABAD · LAHORE · MULTAN · GUJRANWALA
Jhang · Sahiwal · Bahawalpur
SIND · KARACHI · HYDERABAD · Sukkur · Larkana · Nawabshah · Mirpur Khas
Indus · Kirthar Range

J A M M U & K A S H M I R
Srinagar · Jammu · Leh · K2 · Nanga Parbat · Aksai Chin
Karakoram Range · Northern Areas · Gilgit

I N D I A
DELHI · New Delhi · FARIDABAD · MEERUT · AGRA · KANPUR · Gwalior
PUNJAB · Amritsar · LUDHIANA · Chandigarh · Jullundur
HARYANA · HIMACHAL PRADESH · Simla
UTTARANCHAL · Dehra Dun
RAJASTHAN · JAIPUR · Jodhpur · Bikaner · Udaipur · Kota · Ajmer · Alwar
Thar Desert · Indian Desert
GUJARAT · AHMADABAD · VADODARA (Baroda) · SURAT · Rajkot · Jamnagar · Bhavnagar
Gulf of Kachchh · Gulf of Khambhat · Rann of Kachchh · Diu
MADHYA PRADESH · BHOPAL · INDORE · JABALPUR · Ujjain · Ratlam · Satpura Range
MAHARASHTRA · MUMBAI (BOMBAY) · PUNE (Poona) · NAGPUR · NASIK · Amravati · Solapur · Aurangabad · Kolhapur
ANDHRA PRADESH · HYDERABAD · Secunderabad · Gulbarga · Nalgonda
KARNATAKA · BANGALORE · Hubli · Dharwad · Belgaum · Mangalore · Mysore · Bellary
Narmada · Tapti

Malabar Coast
KERALA · COCHIN (Kochi) · Trivandrum (Thiruvananthapuram) · Calicut (Kozhikode) · Quilon (Kollam) · Ernakulam · C. Comorin
TAMIL NADU · CHENNAI (Madras) · COIMBATORE · MADURAI · Salem · Tiruchchirappalli · Tirunelveli · Vellore · Pondicherry · Tuticorin · Nagercoil
Coromandel Coast · Palk Strait · Gulf of Mannar · Adam's Bridge
GOA · Panaji · Marmagao

SRI LANKA
Colombo · Kandy · Jaffna · Trincomalee · Batticaloa · Negombo · Moratuwa · Galle · Dondra Head · Adam's Peak

ARABIAN SEA
INDIAN OCEAN
Tropic of Cancer

Continuation Southwards on same scale

XIZANG ZIZHIQU (TIBET)

CHINA

QINGHAI

Hoh Xil Shan

Bayan Har Shan

Tanggula (Dangla) Shan

Nyainqentanglha Shan

Gangdisê Shan

NEPAL

Lhasa

KATMANDU

SIKKIM

BHUTAN

Thimphu

ARUNACHAL PRADESH

ASSAM

Guwahati

MEGHALAYA

NAGALAND

MANIPUR

Imphal

MIZORAM

TRIPURA

Agartala

BIHAR

PATNA

JHARKHAND

WEST BENGAL

KOLKATA (CALCUTTA)

BANGLADESH

DHAKA

RAJSHAHI

KHULNA

CHITTAGONG

CHHATTISGARH

ORISSA

Bhubaneshwar

Cuttack

VISHAKHAPATNAM

BAY OF BENGAL

INDIAN OCEAN

Mouths of the Ganges

BURMA (MYANMAR)

KACHIN

SAGAING

CHIN

MAGWE

MANDALAY

SHAN

KAYAH

ARAKAN

PEGU

RANGOON

IRRAWADDY

MON

G. of Martaban

Mouths of the Irrawaddy

YUNNAN

SICHUAN

THAILAND

East from Greenwich

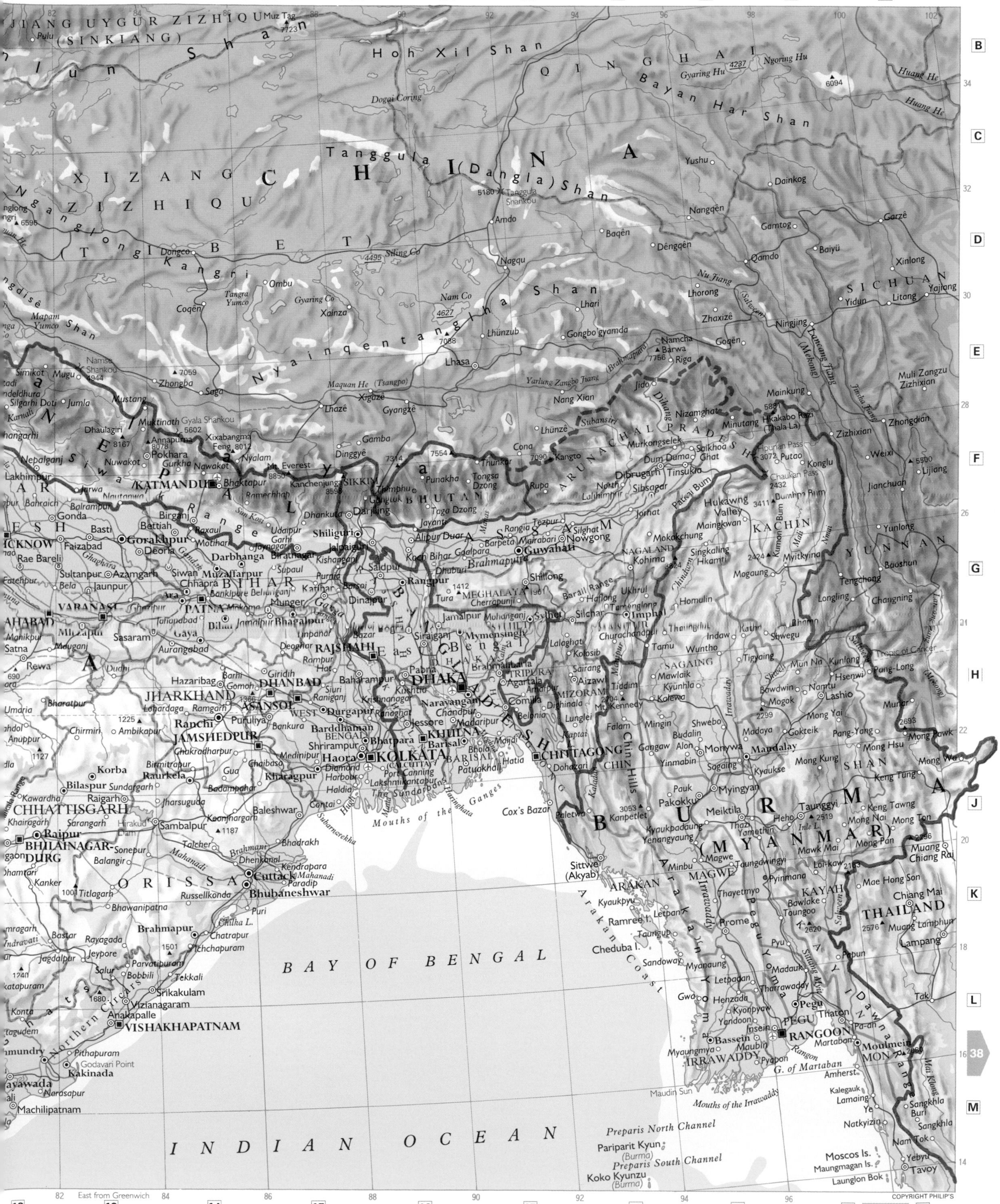

1:6 000 000

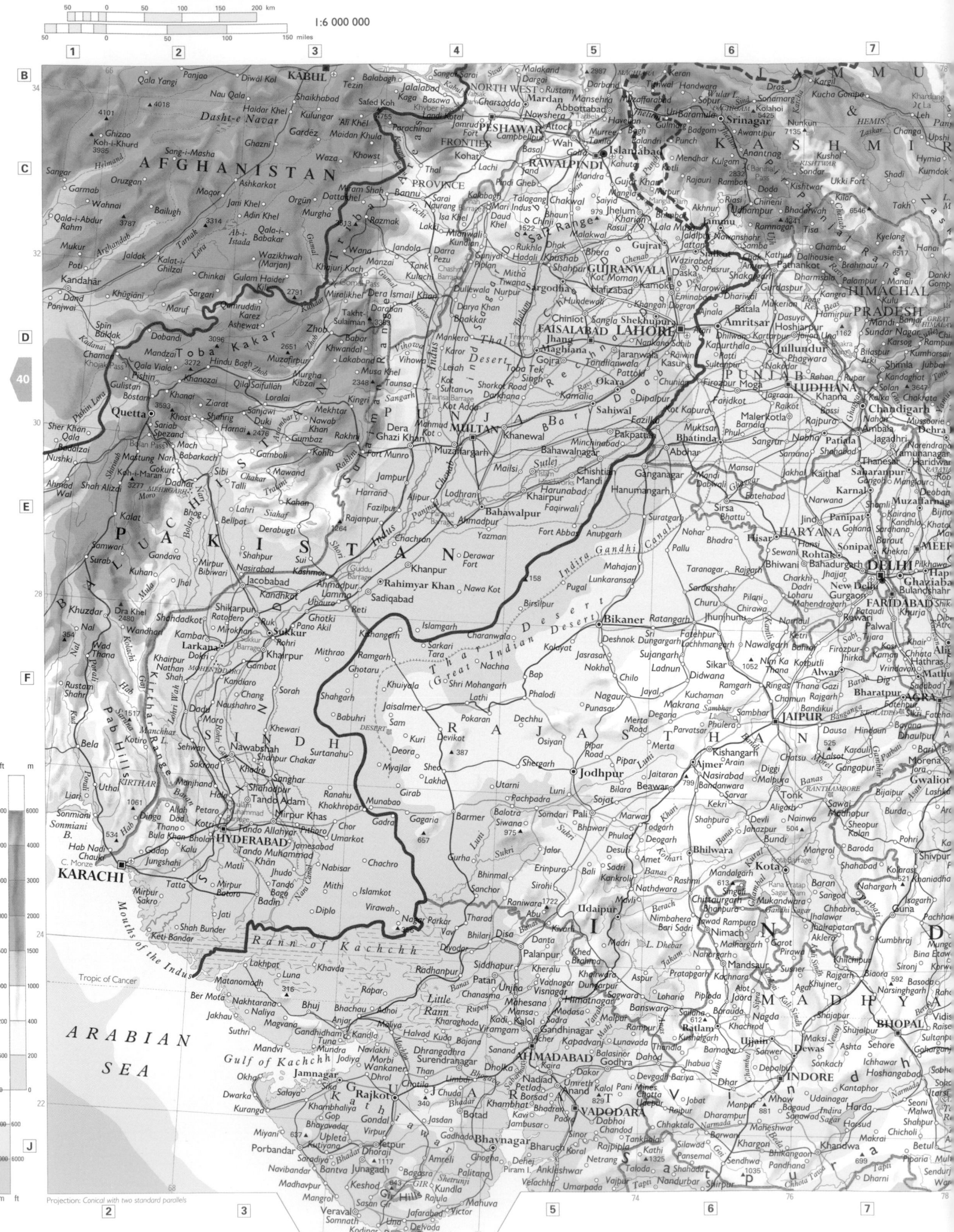

JAMMU AND KASHMIR
on same scale

COPYRIGHT PHILIP'S

50 0 50 100 150 200 250 300 km

1:7 000 000

50 0 50 100 150 200 miles

Underlined towns in Iraq give their name
to the administrative area in which they stand

6 7 8 28 9 10

TURKMENISTAN

Garagum (Kara Kum)

Kopet Dagh

CASPIAN SEA

Ashgabat

Mary

Türkmenbashi

Balkanabat (Nebitdag)

BAKI (Baku)

Reshteh-ye Kūhhā-ye Alborz (Elburz Mts.)

TEHRĀN

KARAJ

Qom

Qazvīn

Rasht

MASHHAD

Neyshābūr

Sabzevār

Dasht-e Kavīr (Great Salt Desert)

IRAN

Eşfahān

Kāshān

Yazd

Dasht-e Lūt (Great Sand Desert)

Kermān

SHĪRĀZ

Zāgros

Ahvāz

Ābādān

Bandar-e Abbās

Zāhedān

HERĀT

AFGHANISTAN

Dasht-e Mārgow

Dasht-e Khāsh

PAKISTAN

PERSIAN GULF

Gulf of Oman

Str. of Hormuz

Al Kuwayt (Kuwait)

Ad Dammām

Al Manāmah

BAHRAIN

QATAR

Ad Dawhah (Doha)

Abū Zāby (Abu Dhabi)

Dubayy (Dubai)

Ash Shāriqah (Sharjah)

UNITED ARAB EMIRATES

OMAN

Musandam (Oman)

Chāh Bahār

Tropic of Cancer

B C D E F

40

East from Greenwich

6 8 9

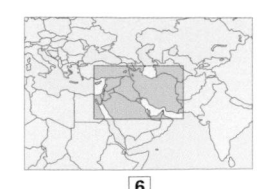

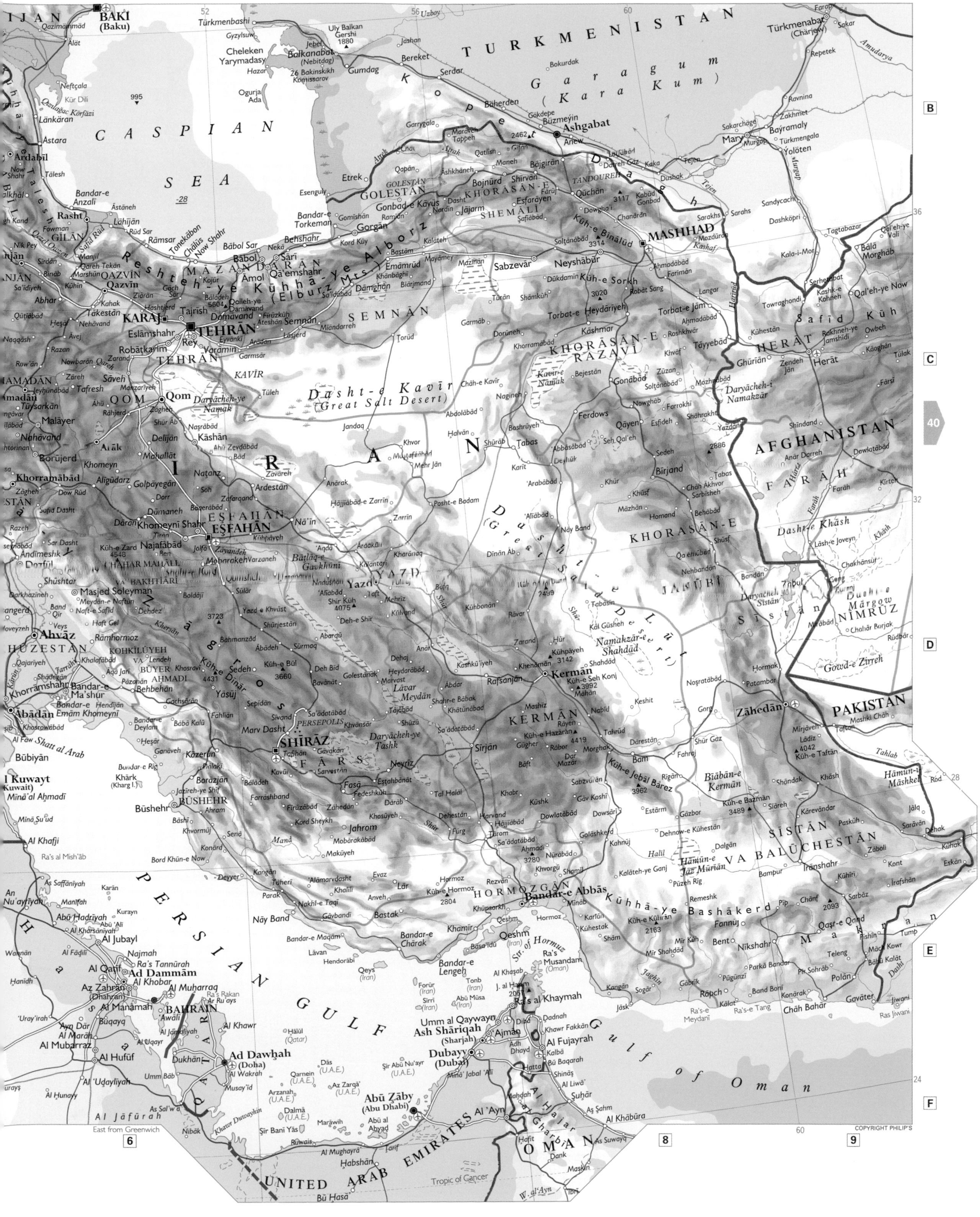

1:2 500 000

10 0 10 20 30 40 50 60 70 80 100 km
10 0 10 20 30 40 50 60 miles

1 **2** **3** **4** 44 **5** **6**

CYPRUS
Paphos
Kividnes
Zyi
Episkopi
Limassol
Akrotiri
Episkopi Bay
Bay
C. Gata

M E D I T E R R A N E A N

S E A

2775

2089

Al Hamidiyah
Ḥimṣ (Ḥuṃṣ)
Shinshār
Furqlus
Kalakh
Halbā
ASH
SHAMĀL
Al Ḥirmil
HIMS
Tarābulus (Tripoli)
Al Minā
Zgharta
Qurnat as Sawdá
3088
Al Qusayr
Al Qaryatayn
Al Batrūn
Bsharri
Al Buryj
2464
Jubayl
Qartabā
Al Labwah
An Nabk
Bi'r Ghadir
Ibrāhim
2616
Jūniyah
Ba'labakk
Yabrūd
BAYRŪT (Beirut)
Bikfayyā
2628
J. Sannin
Zaḥlah
Al Quṭayfah
SYRIA
Ash Shuwayfāt
'Alayh
Ḥawsh
Mussa
Dumayr
Khān Abū Shāmat
Ad Dāmūr
JABAL LUBNĀN
1942
Az Zabadāni
Baradá
LEBANON
al Bārak
DIMASHQ
Saydā (Sidon)
Jazzīn
Qaṭana
Dūma
DAM.
DIMASHQ (Damascus)
An Nabatiyah at Tahta
Marj 'Uyūn
Ṣarayyā
Jaramānah
Al Ḥājānah
AL
Ash Shayh
Mt. Hermon
Al Kiswah
2814
JANŪB
Al Khiyām
Sūr (Tyre)
Qiryat Shemona
Al Qunaytirah
Jayrūd
Burāq
Ar Rafid
As Sanamayn
Ṣafa
Naharriyya
Me'ona
1208
Ḥagalil
HAZAFON
Zefat
Yesud
Ya'qui
Shaykh Miskin
DAR'Ā
Izra
Shahbā
'Akko (Acre)
Qiryat
Karmi'el
Kinneret (Sea of Galilee)
Fiq
Saham al Jowlān
As Suwaydā
Mifraẓ Hefa
HEFA
Teverya (Tiberias)
-210
Darā
Ṣalah
1800
Ad Durūz
Hefa (Haifa)
Qiryat Ata
Nazerat (Nazareth)
Afula
Taibe
IRBID
Buṣrá ash Sham
Salkhad
Malah
Daliyat el Karmel
HEFA
KARMEL
Yarmūk
'AJLŪN
At Ramthā
Umm al Qittayn
TEL MEGIDDO
Bet She'an
'Ajlūn
'Irbid
Umm ad Darai
Jarash
CAESAREA
Umm el Fahm
Jenin
JARASH
Al Mafraq
AL MAFRAQ
Hadera
Ḥanna
Karkur
Shomṛon
Tūbās
SAMARIA
Az Zarqā
ISRAEL
Netanya
Talkarm
Nābulus
AL BALQĀ
Herzliyya
HAMERKAZ
Ra'ananna
Kafar Sava
SHILO
AMMĀN
Benē Beraq
Petah Tiqwa
As Salt
'AMMĀN
TEL AVIV-YAFO
Ramat Gan
Wādi as Sir
Az Zarqā
Bat Yam
TLV
WEST
Karama
AMM
Azraq ash Shīshān
Holon
Lod
BANK
289
AZ ZARQĀ
Rishon le Ziyyon
Ramla
Rām Allāh
El Arihā (Jericho)
Na'ūr
Yavne
Rehovot
Ma'daba
At Tunayb
Ashdod
Jerusalem (Yerushalayim) (Al Quds)
Qiryat Mal'akhi
Bet Shemesh
Bayt Lahm (Bethlehem)
MA'DABA
Ashqelon
Qiryat Gat
TEL LAKHISH
Al Khalil (Hebron)
Ma Da ba
MA'DABA
Gaza
N. Shiqma
Dhibān
Al Ḥadithah
GAZA STRIP
Sederot
Az Zāhiriyya
418
W. al Ḥaydān
Khān Yūnis
ESHKOL
'En Gedi
Rafah
W. Beŝor
Be'er Sheva (Beersheba)
MASADA
Bûr Sa'îd (Port Said)
Bûr Fu'ad
Rås Burûn
Arad
Al Karak
BÛR SA'ÎD
Khalîg el Tîna
Sabkhat el Bardawil
El Daheir
Bor Mashash
Sedom
1305
AL KARAK
Al Mazar
Ramâni
Bîr el 'Abd
Dimona
W. al Ḥasā
W. Ba'ir
El 'Arîsh
HADAROM
333
W. al Ghadaf
Al Qaṭrānah
El Qantara
Bîr el Garârât
Bîr Lahfân
W. 'Arîsh
W. el Bruk
Qezi'ot
Sedé Boqér
At Tafilah
JORDAN
El Qantara
Bîr Qaṭia
Bîr el Duweidar
Bîr Kaseiba
AT TAFILAH
Bâ'ir
Isma'iliya
Bîr el Jafir
Abu Aweigîla
-121
J. ash Shawmari
Talâta
Bîr Madkûr
Muweilih
El Quseima
1072
ISMA'ILÎYA
892
N. Paran
Khamsa
El Buheirat el Murrat el Kubra (Great Bitter L.)
SHAMÂL SÎNÎ
Birein
Mizpe Ramon
Nijil
Mahattat 'Unayzah
G. Yi 'Allaq
1094
Bîr Hasana
Hanegev (Negev Desert)
Rujm Talat
al Jamā'ah
1736
Gineifa
PETRA
El Jafr
Qa'el Jafr
Wâhid
El 'Agrûd
N. Hiyyon
Wādi Mūsa
El Suweis (Suez)
Mamarr Mitla
W. el Bârûd
El Agrûd
Ma'ān
MA'ĀN
Bûr Taufîq
Adabiya
E G Y P T
Es Sînâ' (Sinai)
Bîr el Thamâda
El Kuntilla
Bîr al Mârî
Uyûn Mûsa
Gebel Hisn
948
W. el Aqaba
Yotvata
Ra's an Naqb
1435
SAUDI
Sudr
G. el Kabrit
W. Mahashim
En 'Avrona
Ra's an Naqb
Mahattat ash Shīdiyah
Abu Ruqaba
Gebel el Tih
El Thamad
1592
Rum
1754
WADI RUM
ARABIA
El Wabeira
JANÛB SÎNÎ
W. Abu Ga'da
Ela
Al 'Aqabah
Rum
Batn al Ghûl
Ghubbet el Bûs
1272
Bîr el Biarat
Gulf of Aqaba
At Tubayq
Abu Sandug
Rås Matarma
Bîr el Heisi
W. an Mudha
Al Mudawwarah
EL SUWEIS
1165
Haql

Projection: Polyconic   East from Greenwich   COPYRIGHT PHILIP'S

1 33 **2** 51 **3** 34 **4** 35 **5** 36 **6** 37

━ ━ ━ 1974 Cease Fire Lines

1:15 000 000

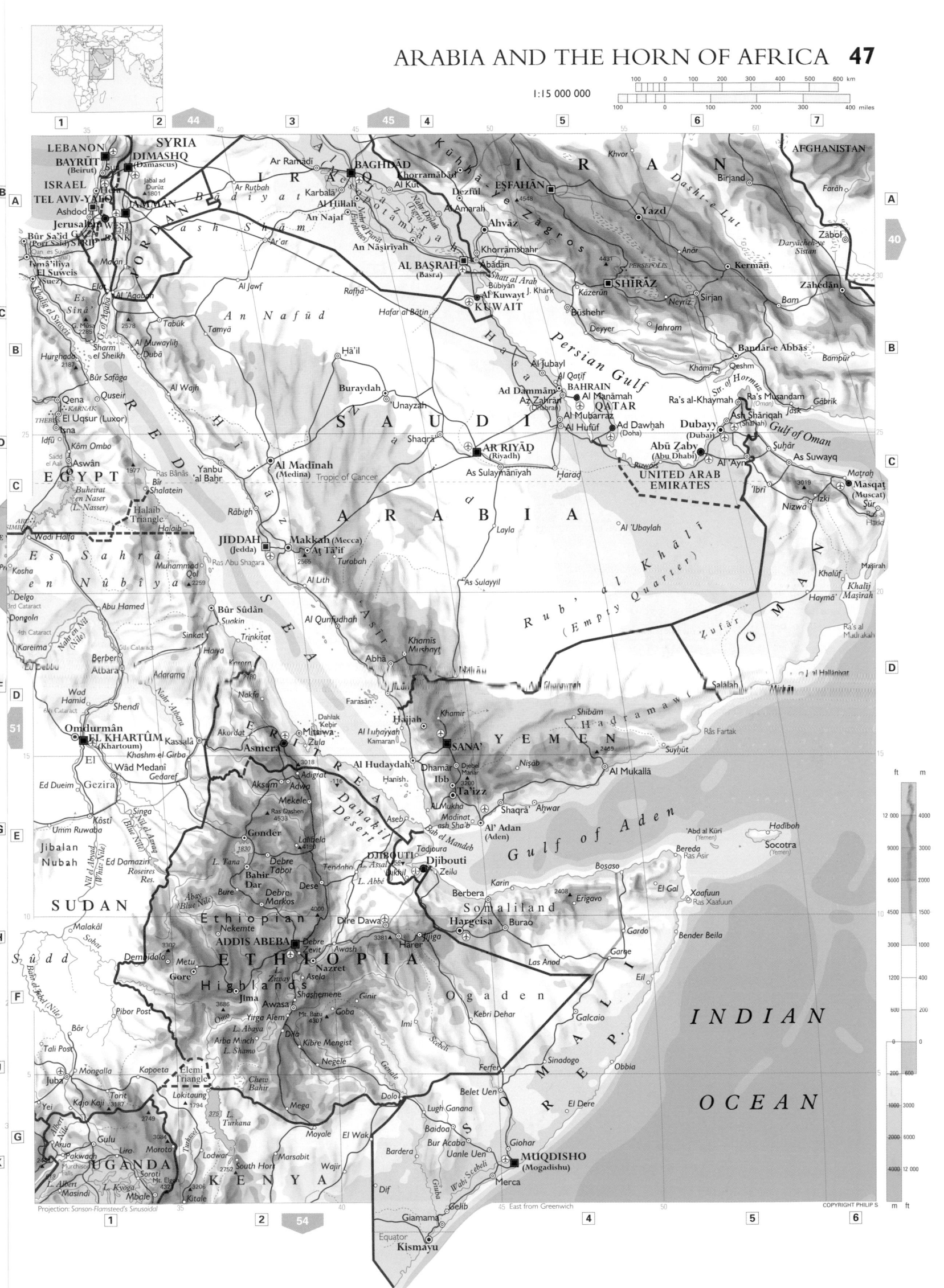

Projection: Sanson-Flamsteed's Sinusoidal

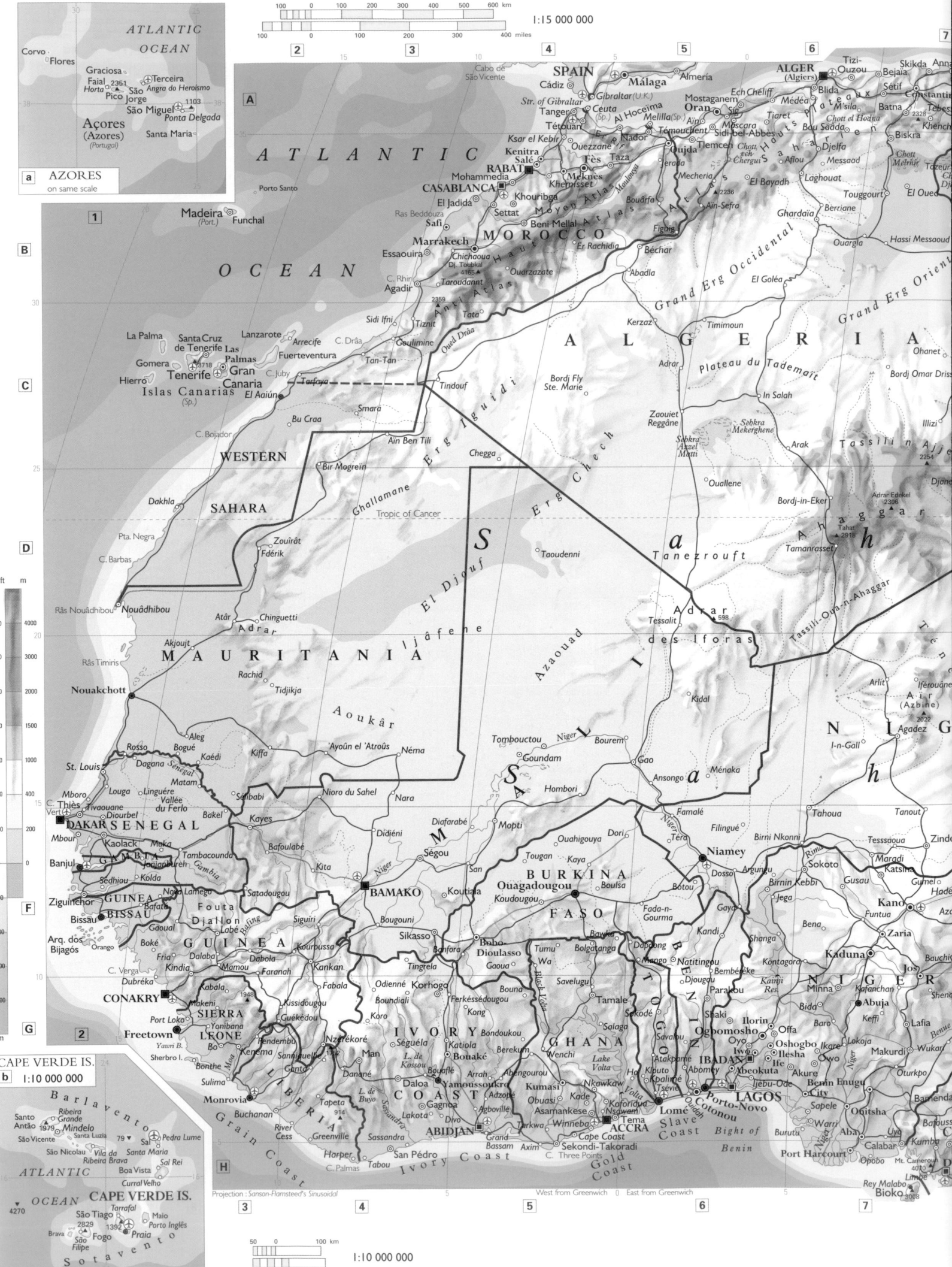

ATLANTIC OCEAN

Corvo · Flores

Graciosa
Faial · 2351 · Terceira
Horta · São · Angra do Heroísmo
Pico Jorge
São Miguel · 1103
Ponta Delgada
Santa Maria

Açores
(Azores)
(Portugal)

a AZORES
on same scale

1:15 000 000

100 0 100 200 300 400 500 600 km
100 0 100 200 300 400 miles

CAPE VERDE IS.
b 1:10 000 000

Barlavento

Santo
Antão · Ribeira · Grande
São · Mindelo · Santa Luzia · 79
Vicente · São Nicolau · Vila da · Santa Maria
Ribeira Brava · Sal Rei
ATLANTIC · Boa Vista
OCEAN · Curral Velho
4270 **CAPE VERDE IS.**
Tarrafal
São Tiago · 2829 · Maio
Brava · 1392 · Porto Inglês
São · Fogo · Praia
Filipe

Sotavento

50 0 100 km
50 0 50 miles
1:10 000 000

Projection : Sanson-Flamsteed's Sinusoidal

ATLANTIC OCEAN

SPAIN
Cabo de São Vicente
Cádiz · Málaga · Almería
Str. of Gibraltar
Tanger · Gibraltar (U.K.)
Ceuta (Sp.) · Al Hoceima · Melilla (Sp.)
Tétouan · Nador
Ksar el Kebir · Oujda
Salé · **RABAT** · Fès · Taza
Mohammedia · Meknès
CASABLANCA · Khouribga
El Jadida · Settat
Safi · Beni Mellal
Ras Beddouza
Marrakech · **MOROCCO**
Essaouira · Chichaoua
Agadir · Taroudannt
C. Rhir · Dj. Toubkal
Sidi Ifni · Tiznit · Tata
Tan-Tan
C. Draa · Goulimine
Tarfaya · Tindouf

ALGER (Algiers) · Tizi-Ouzou · Skikda
Blida · Béjaïa · Sétif
Mostaganem · Constantine
Oran · Médéa · M'sila · Batna
Mascara · Tiaret · Bou Saâda · Biskra
Tlemcen · Aflou · Djelfa
El Bayadh · Laghouat · Touggourt
Aïn-Sefra · Ghardaïa · Berriane · El Oued
Béchar · El Goléa · Ouargla · Hassi Messaoud
Abadla

ALGERIA
Grand Erg Occidental
Grand Erg Oriental
Kerzaz · Timimoun · In Salah
Adrar · Plateau du Tademaït
Reggâne · Arak
Bordj-in-Eker
Ahaggar · Tamanrasset
Tahat 2918

WESTERN SAHARA
Dakhla
Pta. Negra
C. Barbas
Bir Mogreïn
Zouîrat · Fdérik
Chegga
Taoudenni

Tropic of Cancer

MAURITANIA
Râs Nouâdhibou · Nouâdhibou
Atâr · Chinguetti · Adrar
Akjoujt
Râs Timiris
Nouakchott
Rachid · Tidjikja
Aoukâr
'Ayoûn el 'Atroûs · Néma
Kiffa
Aleg · Bogué · Kaédi
Rosso
St. Louis · Dagana · Matam
Louga · Linguère · Vallée du Ferlo
Mboro · Sélibabi
C. Vert · Diourbel · Bakel
DAKAR · **SENEGAL** · Kayes
Mbour · Kaolack · Kita
Banjul · Tambacounda
GAMBIA
Ziguinchor · **GUINEA**
Bissau · **BISSAU**
Gaoual · Boké
Arq. dos Bijagós
C. Verga · Fria · Kindia
Dubréka
CONAKRY
Makeni · Port Loko
SIERRA
Freetown **LEONE**
Sherbro I.

Tombouctou · Bourem
Goundam · Gao
Ansongo
MALI · Ménaka
Mopti · Hombori
Diafarabé
Ségou · San
BAMAKO
Koutiala
Sikasso
Bobo-Dioulasso
Ouagadougou
BURKINA FASO
Koudougou
Fada-n-Gourma
Banfora
Tamale

NIGER
Arlit
Aïr (Azbine)
Agadez
In-Gall
Tahoua
Niamey
Birni Nkonni · Tessaoua
Dosso · Sokoto · Maradi · Katsina
Gusau · Zaria
Kaduna
Abuja
Minna · Bida
NIGER
Kano · Funtua

GHANA
IVORY COAST
Daloa · Yamoussoukro
ABIDJAN · **ACCRA**
Kumasi · Tamale
Sekondi-Takoradi
Cape Coast

TOGO · **BENIN**
Lomé · Porto-Novo
Cotonou
LAGOS · **IBADAN**
Abeokuta
Benin City
Enugu

LIBERIA
Monrovia · Buchanan
Greenville
C. Palmas
Grain Coast
Ivory Coast
Gold Coast
Slave Coast
Bight of Benin

MEDITERRANEAN SEA
TUNIS
Sicilia
ITALY
MALTA
Valletta
GREECE
Kriti
TURKEY
Antalya
ADANA
HALAB (Aleppo)
SYRIA
CYPRUS
Nicosia
LEBANON
BAYRŪT (Beirut)
DIMASHQ (Damascus)
IRAQ
ISRAEL
TEL AVIV-YAFO
Jerusalem
'AMMĀN
JORDAN
TARĀBULUS (Tripoli)
Al Khums
Misrātah
Banghāzī
Tripolitania
Cyrenaica
Khalīj Surt
EL ISKANDARĪYA (Alexandria)
EL QÂHIRA (Cairo)
El Gîza
Es Sinâ'
SAUDI ARABIA
LIBYA
EGYPT
Sahrâ' Lîbîya
Sabhā
Fezzan
Aswân
El Uqsur (Luxor)
RED SEA
Sahara
Tibesti
Aozou Strip
Borkou
Ennedi
Es Sahrâ en Nûbîya
CHAD
Ndjamena
Lac Tchad
SUDAN
EL KHARTÛM (Khartoum)
Omdurmân
ERITREA
ETHIOPIA
Darfur
Kordofân
El Obeid
CENTRAL AFRICAN REPUBLIC
Bangui
CAMEROON
YAOUNDÉ
Juba
Bahr el Ghazâl
Sudd
Halaib Triangle
Elemi Triangle
COPYRIGHT PHILIPS

1:15 000 000

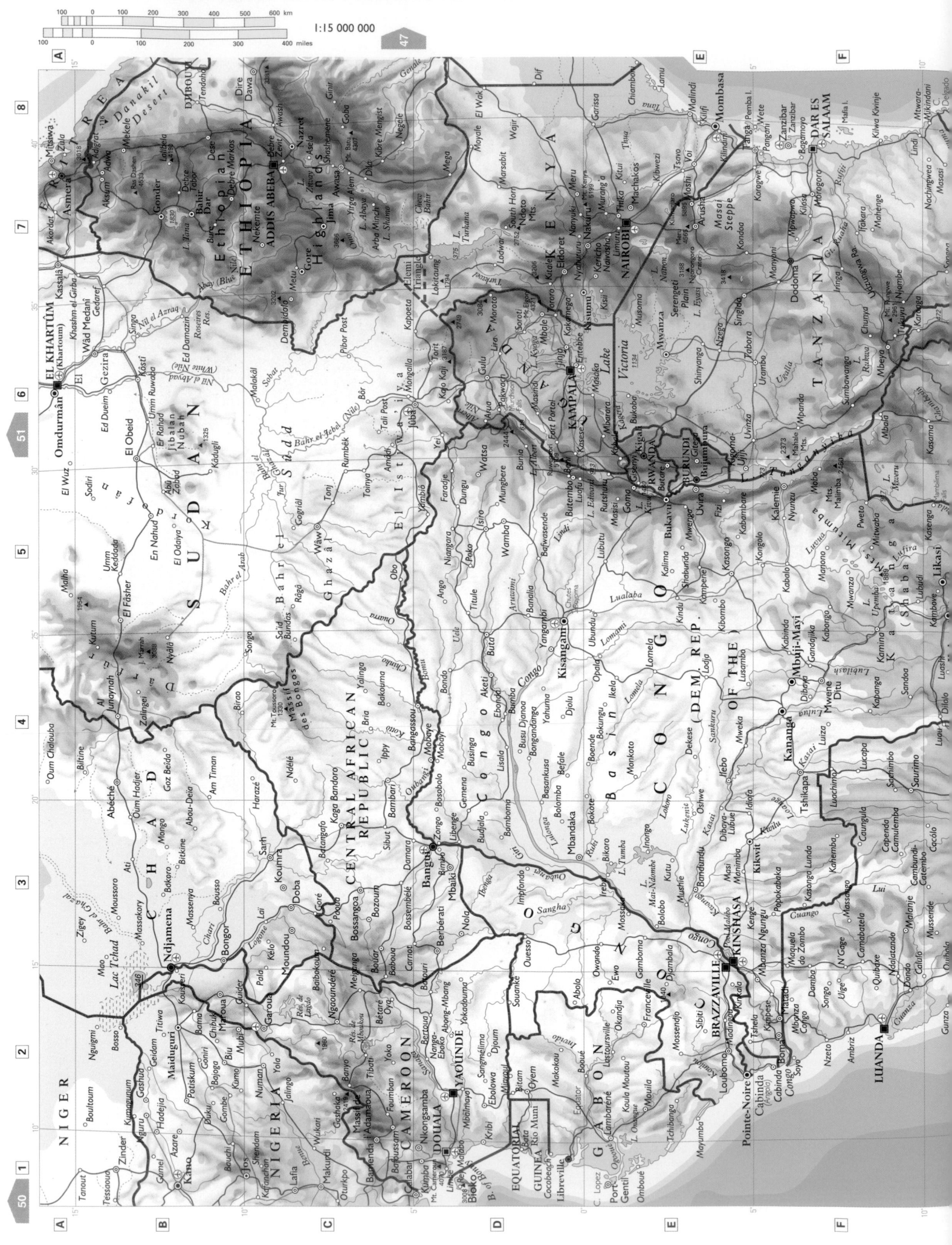

100 0 100 200 300 400 500 600 km
100 0 100 200 300 400 miles
50
51
47
NIGER
CHAD
Lac Tchad
Ndjamena
NIGERIA
Kano
Maiduguri
CAMEROON
YAOUNDÉ
DOUALA
EQUATORIAL GUINEA
Rio Muni
Libreville
GABON
CONGO
BRAZZAVILLE
Pointe-Noire
Cabinda
LUANDA
KINSHASA
CENTRAL AFRICAN REPUBLIC
Bangui
SUDAN
EL KHARTÛM
(Khartoum)
Omdurmân
Bahr el Ghazâl
Sudd
Jubâ
CONGO (DEM. REP. OF THE)
Congo Basin
Kisangani
Mbuji-Mayi
Kananga
Likasi
UGANDA
KAMPALA
Lake Victoria
RWANDA
Kigali
BURUNDI
Bujumbura
KENYA
NAIROBI
Mombasa
TANZANIA
DAR ES SALAAM
Dodoma
Zanzibar
Masai Steppe
ETHIOPIA
ADDIS ABEBA
Ethiopian Highlands
ERITREA
Asmera
DJIBOUTI
Elemi Triangle

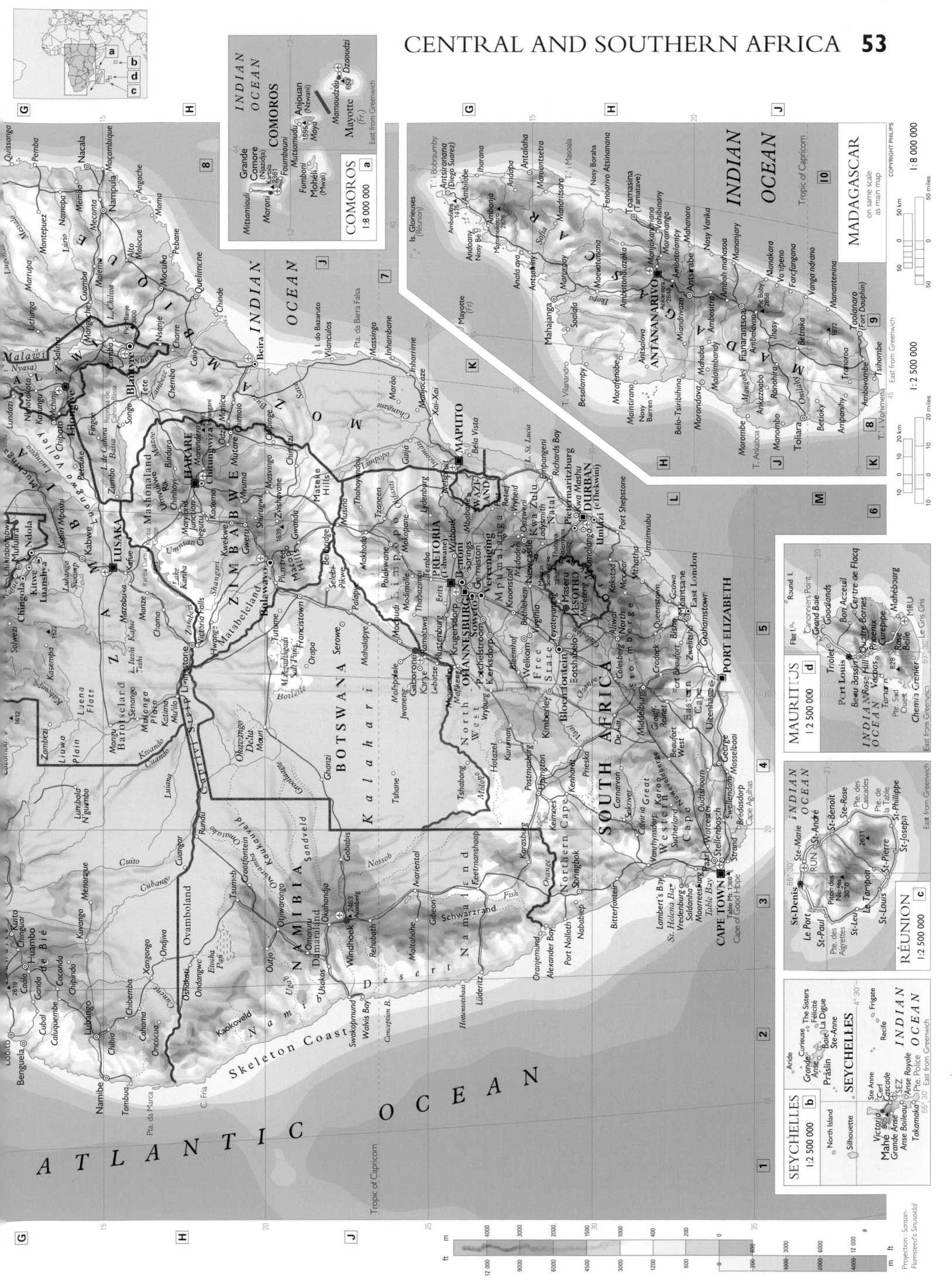

INDIAN OCEAN

COMOROS

Grande Comore (Njazidja)
2361
Mitsamiouli
Moroni
Foumbouni
Mutsamudu
Fomboni
Mohéli (Mwali)
Anjouan (Nzwani)
1595
Moya
Mamoudzou 662 Dzaoudzi
Mayotte (Fr.)

COMOROS
1:8 000 000 **a**

East from Greenwich

MOZAMBIQUE

Quissanga
Pemba
Nacala
Mecontá
Nampula
Angoche
Moma
Mocuba
Quelimane
Chinde
Mocimboa
Montepuez
Lúrio
Namapa
Meconta
Alto Molócue
Marrupa
Cuamba
Mangoche
L. Chilwa
Nsanje
Charre
Caia
Beira
Pta. da Barra Falsa
I. do Bazaruto
I. Vilanculos
Massinga
Inhambane
Homoine
Pta. da Barra
Maxixe
Massinga
Marão

INDIAN OCEAN

MADAGASCAR

on same scale as main map
1:8 000 000

COPYRIGHT PHILIPS

Tropic of Capricorn

INDIAN OCEAN

Antananarivo
Mahajanga
Toliara
Toamasina
Fianarantsoa
Antsiranana (Diego Suarez)
Nosy Be
Ambilobe

1:2 500 000

ATLANTIC OCEAN

NAMIBIA
BOTSWANA
ZAMBIA
ZIMBABWE
SOUTH AFRICA
LESOTHO
SWAZILAND
Kalahari
Namib Desert

Windhoek
Gaborone
Pretoria (Tshwane)
JOHANNESBURG
Maputo
Harare
Lusaka
Bulawayo
Blantyre
Lilongwe
CAPE TOWN
DURBAN
PORT ELIZABETH
Bloemfontein
Kimberley
Maseru

Victoria Falls

Cape of Good Hope
Cape Agulhas
Skeleton Coast
Tropic of Capricorn

SEYCHELLES
1:2 500 000 **b**

North Island
Silhouette
Victoria 905
Mahé
Grande Anse
Praslin
La Digue

Aride
Curieuse
Cerf
Anse Boileau
Anse Royale
Takamaka

The Sisters
Félicité
Frégate
Recife

INDIAN OCEAN

RÉUNION
1:2 500 000 **c**

St-Denis
Ste-Marie
St-André
St-Benoît
Le Port
St-Paul
St-Leu
St-Louis
St-Pierre
St-Joseph
St-Philippe
2631

INDIAN OCEAN

MAURITIUS
1:2 500 000 **d**

Port Louis
Beau Bassin
Curepipe
Mahébourg
828

INDIAN OCEAN

East from Greenwich

Projection: Sanson-Flamsteed's Sinusoidal

1:8 000 000

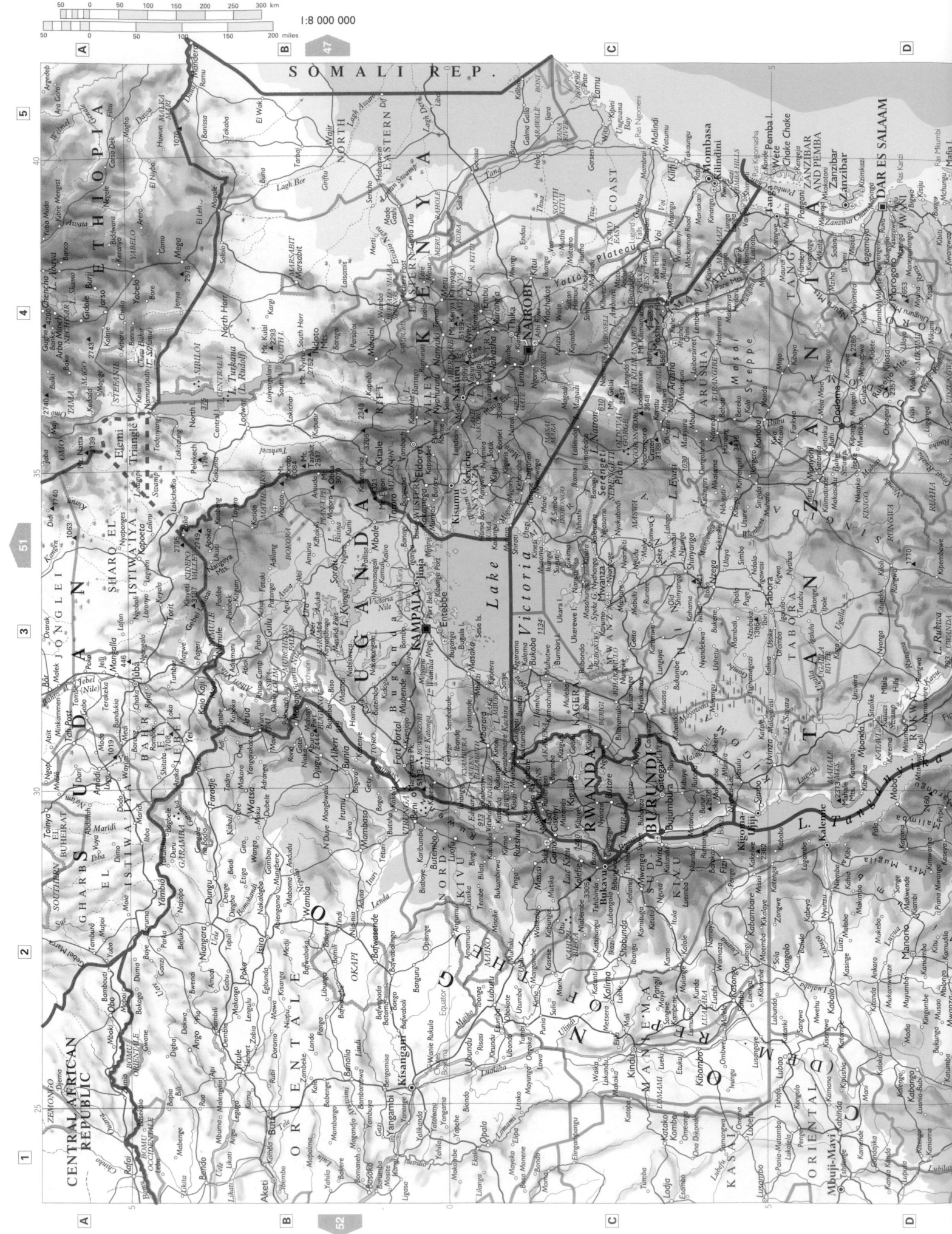

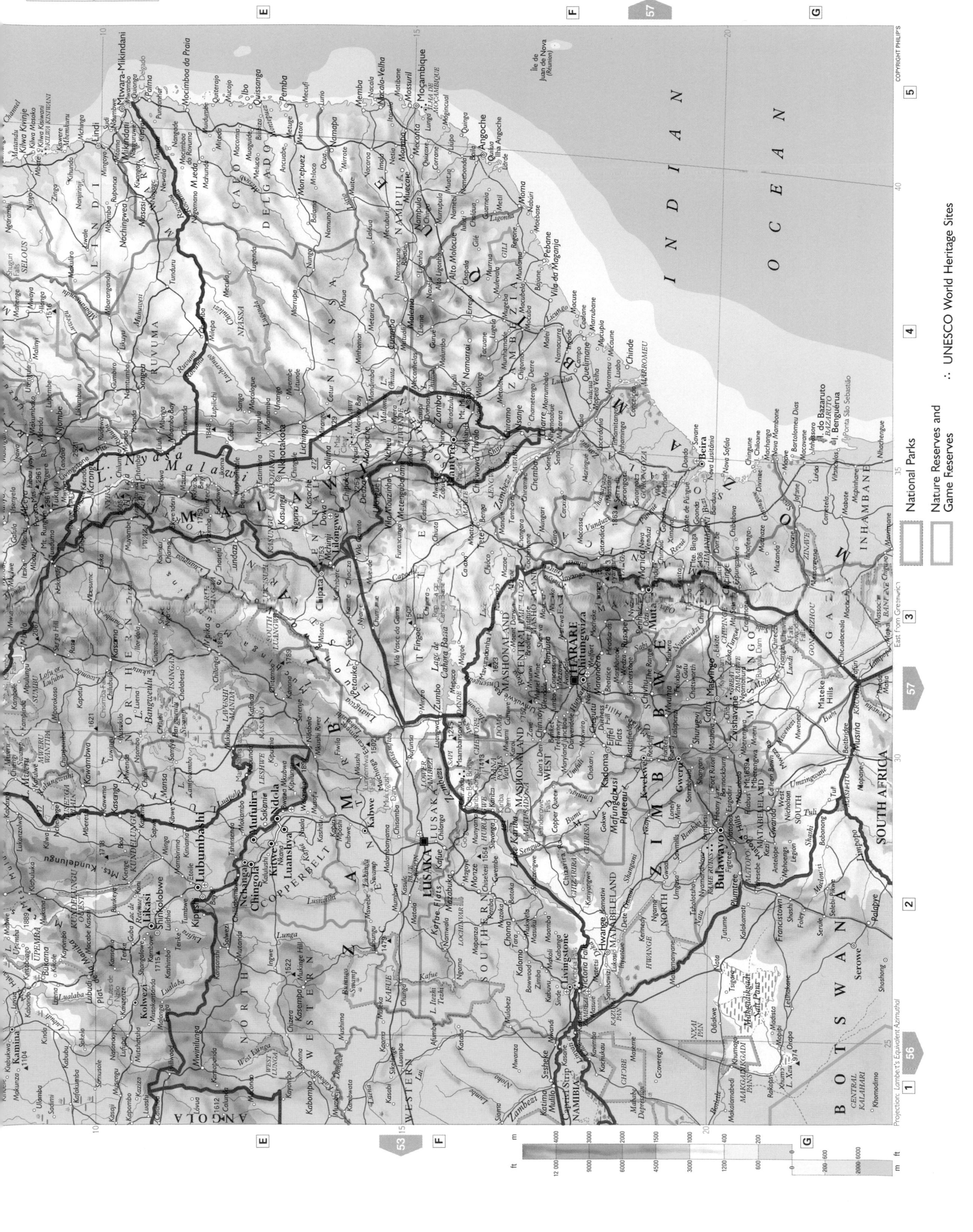

50 0   50 100 150 200 250 300 km
50 0   50   100   150   200 miles

1:8 000 000

Projection: Lambert's Equivalent Azimuthal

5
55
6
7

B

ZAMBEZIA

Angoche

Î. Angoche

Î. de
Juan de Nova
(Fr.)

MALAWI

TETE

HARARE
Chitungwiza

MASHONALAND
WEST

MASHONALAND
CENTRAL

MASHONALAND
EAST

ZIMBABWE

Mutare

MOZAMBIQUE

Beira

A

Îs. Glorieuses
(Fr.)

Antsiranana
(Diego Suarez)

MONTAGNE
D'AMBRE

Nosy Mitsio

Nosy Bé

Iharana

ANTSIR-
ANANA

Bulawayo

MATABELELAND
SOUTH

MASVINGO

GONAREZHOU

I. do Bazaruto
BAZARUTO
I. Benguérua

Mahajanga

MAROJEJY

MASOALA

Marantsetra

Nosy Boraha
(Île Ste-Marie)

15

LIMPOPO

KRUGER

Inhambane

Toliara

MOZAMBIQUE CHANNEL

MADAGASCAR

Maintirano

Morondava

Belo-Tsiribihina

ANTANANARIVO

Antsirabe

Toamasina
(Tamatave)

B

PRETORIA

JOHANNESBURG
MPUMALANGA

MAPUTO

SWAZILAND

Vereeniging

KWAZULU
NATAL

GREATER
ST LUCIA
WETLANDS

Morombe

FIANARANTSOA

Manakara

C

Pietermaritzburg

DURBAN (eThekwini)
Umlazi

EASTERN
CAPE

Toliara

Benenitra

ANDRINGITRA
2658

ISALO

Vangaindrano

Tropic of Capricorn

INDIAN

OCEAN

Mthatha

ANDOHAHELA
1972

Taolanaro
(Fort Dauphin)

Tanjon' i Vohimena

MADAGASCAR

on same scale

D

30
East from Greenwich
5
7
45
8
9

COPYRIGHT PHILIP'S

National Parks

Nature Reserves and
Game Reserves

∴ UNESCO World Heritage Sites

1:50 000 000

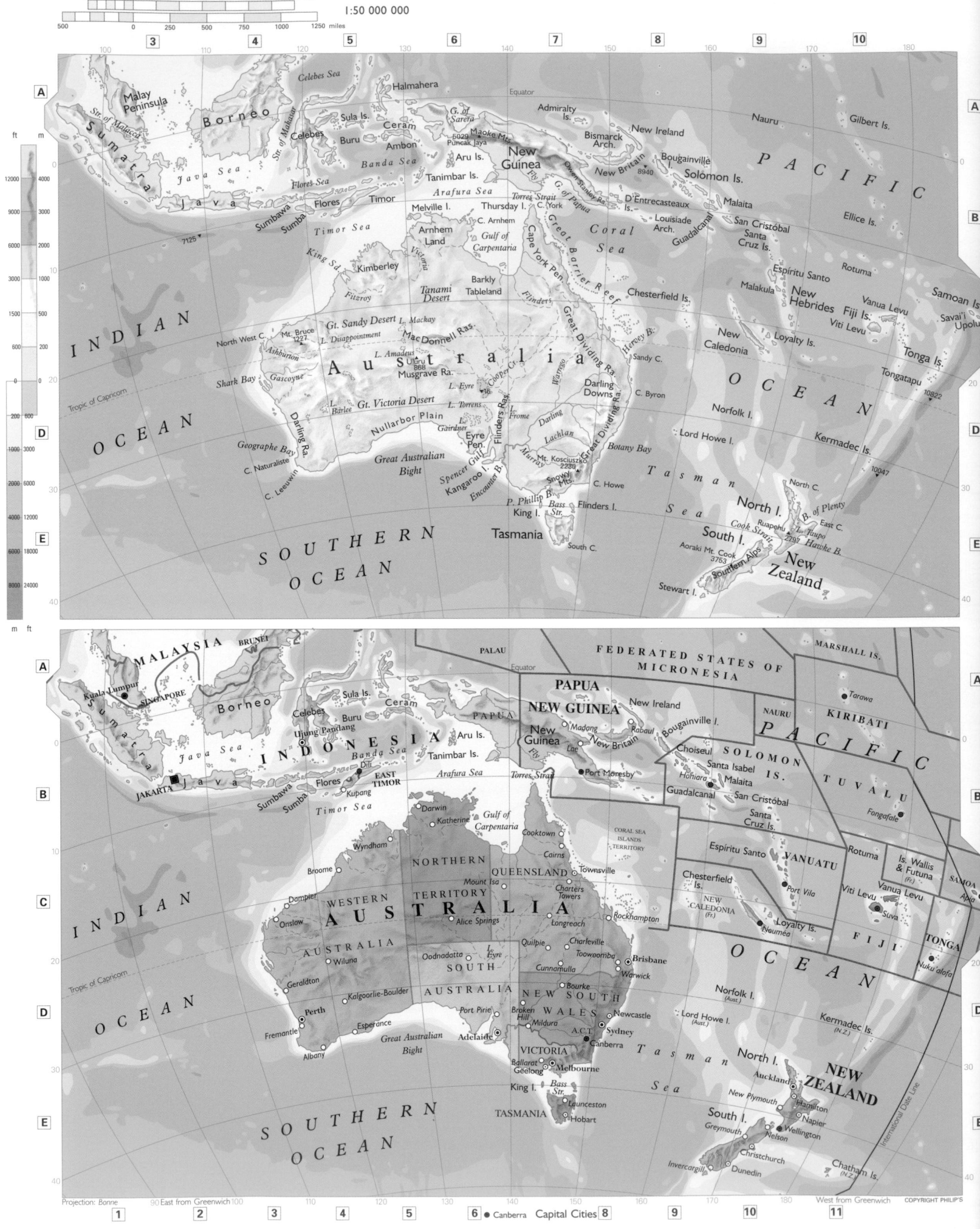

Physical map (top):

INDIAN OCEAN

SOUTHERN OCEAN

PACIFIC OCEAN

Australia

Malay Peninsula, Str. of Malacca, Sumatra, Borneo, Celebes Sea, Halmahera, Admiralty Is., Nauru, Gilbert Is., Java Sea, Str. of Macassar, Celebes, Buru, Ceram, G. of Sarera, Maoke Mts., Puncak Jaya 5029, New Ireland, Bismarck Arch., New Britain 8940, Bougainville, Solomon Is., Malaita, Ellice Is., Java, Sumbawa, Sumba, Flores Sea, Flores, Timor, Banda Sea, Ambon, Aru Is., New Guinea, Fly, G. of Papua, Owen Stanley Ra., D'Entrecasteaux, San Cristóbal, Santa Cruz Is., Espiritu Santo, Rotuma, Samoan Is., Savai'i, Upolu

Timor Sea, Melville I., Thursday I., Torres Strait, C. York, Coral Sea, Louisiade Arch., Guadalcanal, Malakula, New Hebrides, Fiji Is., Vanua Levu, Tanimbar Is., Arafura Sea, Arnhem Land, Gulf of Carpentaria, Cape York Pen., Great Barrier Reef, Chesterfield Is., New Caledonia, Loyalty Is., Viti Levu, Tonga Is.

7125, King Sd., Kimberley, Fitzroy, Barkly Tableland, Flinders, Hervey B., Sandy C., North West C., Mt. Bruce 1227, Gt. Sandy Desert, L. Mackay, MacDonnell Ras., Great Dividing Ra., Ashburton, L. Disappointment, Tanami Desert, L. Amadeus, Uluru 868, Musgrave Ra., Darling Downs, C. Byron, Norfolk I., Gascoyne, Shark Bay, Gt. Victoria Desert, L. Eyre, Cooper Ck., Warrego, Darling, L. Barlee, Nullarbor Plain, L. Torrens, Flinders Ras., L. Frome, Lachlan, Geographe Bay, C. Naturaliste, C. Leeuwin, Great Australian Bight, Gairdner, Eyre Pen., Spencer Gulf, Kangaroo I., Encounter B., Murray, Mt. Kosciuszko 2230, Snowy Mts., Botany Bay, Lord Howe I., Kermadec Is., 10047

P. Phillip B., Bass Str., Flinders I., King I., C. Howe, Tasman Sea, North I., North C., B. of Plenty, East C., Ruapehu, Taupo 2797, Hawke B., South I., Cook Strait, Aoraki Mt. Cook 3753, Southern Alps, New Zealand, Stewart I., Tasmania, South C., Tonga Is., Tongatapu 10822

Political map (bottom):

MALAYSIA, BRUNEI, Kuala Lumpur, SINGAPORE, Sumatra, Borneo, INDONESIA, PALAU, FEDERATED STATES OF MICRONESIA, MARSHALL IS., Equator

Celebes, Buru, Ceram, Sula Is., PAPUA, NAURU, Tarawa, KIRIBATI, PACIFIC OCEAN

Ujung Pandang, PAPUA NEW GUINEA, New Ireland, Madang, Rabaul, Bougainville I., New Guinea, New Britain, Lae, Choiseul, SOLOMON IS., TUVALU

Java Sea, Banda Sea, Aru Is., Tanimbar Is., Santa Isabel, Hohiara, Malaita

JAKARTA, Java, Dili, EAST TIMOR, Kupang, Flores, Sumbawa, Sumba, Timor Sea, Arafura Sea, Port Moresby, Torres Strait, Guadalcanal, San Cristóbal, Santa Cruz Is., Fongafale

INDIAN OCEAN

Darwin, Katherine, Gulf of Carpentaria, Espiritu Santo, Rotuma, Is. Wallis & Futuna (Fr.), SAMOA, Apia

Broome, Wyndham, NORTHERN TERRITORY, Cooktown, Cairns, CORAL SEA ISLANDS TERRITORY, Chesterfield Is., VANUATU, Port Vila, Vanua Levu

Dampier, WESTERN AUSTRALIA, Mount Isa, QUEENSLAND, Townsville, Charters Towers, NEW CALEDONIA (Fr.), Viti Levu, Suva

Onslow, Alice Springs, Longreach, Rockhampton, Loyalty Is., Nouméa, FIJI, TONGA

AUSTRALIA, Wiluna, SOUTH AUSTRALIA, Oodnadatta, L. Eyre, Quilpie, Charleville, Toowoomba, Cunnamulla, Bourke, Warwick, Brisbane, Norfolk I. (Aust.), Nuku'alofa

Geraldton, Kalgoorlie-Boulder, Port Pirie, NEW SOUTH WALES, Broken Hill, Mildura, Newcastle, Lord Howe I. (Aust.), Kermadec Is. (N.Z.)

Perth, Fremantle, Esperance, Albany, Adelaide, A.C.T., Sydney, Canberra, VICTORIA, Ballarat, Geelong, Melbourne, Tasman Sea, North I.

Great Australian Bight, King I., Bass Str., Launceston, TASMANIA, Hobart, South I., Greymouth, Nelson, NEW ZEALAND, Auckland, New Plymouth, Hamilton, Napier, Wellington, Chatham Is. (N.Z.)

SOUTHERN OCEAN, Invercargill, Dunedin, Christchurch, PACIFIC OCEAN

1:6 000 000

50   0   50   100   150   200 km
50   0   50   100   150 miles

FIJI a
on same scale

PACIFIC OCEAN

Great Sea Reef   Kia   Udu Pt.   Ringgold Is.
Yaqaga   Labasa   Natewa Bay   Rabi
Yasawa Group   Yadua   Buca   Qamea   Naitaba
Nacula   **Vanua Levu** ▲1031   SOMOSOMO   Taveuni
Yasawa   Nabouwalu   Savusavu   Namenalala   Kanacea   Vanua Balavu
Viwa   Naviti   Nasau   Koro   Vacata   Lomaloma
Waya   Makogai   Northern
Vomo   Tavua   Levuka   Vatu   Lau
Mba   **Tomanivi** ▲1323   **Ovalau**   Vara   Mago   Group
Lautoka   KOROYANITU   Nairai   Cicia   Tuvuca
Malolo   Yunidawa   Nayau   Tubou
Nadi   Keiyasi   Lakeba Passage   Lakeba
SIGATOKA   Korolevu   **Viti Levu**   Batiki   Oneata
Sigatoka   Yanuca   Novugu   Sawaleke   Vanua Vatu   Moce
Vatulele   **Suva**   Beqa   Namuka-i-Lau
Kadavu Passage   **FIJI**   Yagasa Cluster
Tavuki   Ono   Totoya   Fulaga
Kadavu   Yunisea   Matuku   Moala   Ogea Levu   Ogea Driki

KORO SEA

18 S   178 E   180   East from Greenwich   170 W   West from Greenwich

SAMOA
Asau   Safune   Falelima   Pu'apu'a   Saleilolga
Savai'i ▲1858   Mulifanua   Falefa   Apia
Taga   Satupa'itea   Manono   Amaile
Falelatai   'Upolu
OLE PUPU PUE   Salani
Safata B.

PACIFIC OCEAN

AMERICAN SAMOA (U.S.A.)
AMERICAN SAMOA   Ofu   Olosega   Ta'u
Tutuila   Pago Pago   Luma   AMERICAN SAMOA
Leone   Vaitogi   Manu'a Is.

14 S   172 W   West from Greenwich

SAMOAN ISLANDS b
on same scale

TONGA c
on same scale

PACIFIC OCEAN

Fonualei   Toku
Vava'u   Neiafu
Late   Vava'u Group
Home Reef
Disney Reef
Ofolanga   Ha'ano
Tofua   Foa   Lifuka
Kao   Uiha   Ha'apai Group
Kotu Group
Fonuafo'ou   Nomuka   Mango
Nomuka Group   Oto Tolu Group
Hunga Ha'apai   Tonumea

TONGA
Nuku'alofa   Tongatapu
Tongatapu Group   Eua

18 S   174 W
20 S

West from Greenwich

North Island

C. Reinga   North C.
C. Maria van Diemen   Houhora Heads
Ahipara B.   Manganui   Whangaroa Harb.
Kaitaia   Okaihau   B. of Islands
Tauroa Pt.   Waitangi   C. Brett
Rawene   Opua
Hokianga Harbour   Kaikohe   **Hikurangi**
Waipoua Forest   Waipu   **Whangarei**
Dargaville   Whangarei Harb.
Bream B.
Little Barrier I.
Great Barrier I.
Warkworth   C. Rodney   C. Colville   Cuvier I.
Kaipara Harbour   Helensville   Hauraki Gulf   Coromandel   Whitianga
Takapuna   **AUCKLAND**   Thames   Mayor I.
Manukau   Papakura   Whangamata   Tauranga Harb.
Waiuku   Pukekohe   Waihi   Whakaari (White I.)   Runaway
Mercer   Paeroa   Mount Maunganui   Bay of Plenty   East C.
Te Aroha   **Tauranga**
Hamilton   Morrinsville   Te Puke   Opotiki   Hikurangi ▲1753
Raglan   Huntly   Cambridge   Whakatane   Raukumara Ra.   Waipiro
Kawhia Harbour   Matamata   Kawerau   Motu   Tolaga Bay
Kawhia   Otorohanga   Rotorua   L. Tarawera   UREWERA   Ormond
Waitomo Caves   Te Kuiti   Mokai   **Rotorua**   Murupara   Waikaremoana   **Gisborne**
North Taranaki Bight   Mokau   Mangakino   Wairakei   Poverty Bay
Waitara   Ongarue   Taupo   Kaingaroa   Nuhaka   Wairoa
New Plymouth   Taumarunui   Turangi   Taharua   Mahia Pen.
Mt. Taranaki or Mt. Egmont   Inglewood   **WHANGANUI**   Whangamomona   Ruapehu ▲2797   Hawke Bay
▲2518   Stratford   **TONGARIRO**   Waiouru   **Napier**
Opunake   Eltham   Raetihi   **Hastings**
Hawera   Waverley   Ohakune   Waipawa
South Taranaki Bight   Patea   Raetihi   Waipukurau
Wanganui   Marton   Halcombe   Dannevirke
Bulls   Feilding   Woodville
Palmerston North   Pahiatua
Foxton   Shannon   Eketahuna
Levin   Otaki   Masterton
Paraparaumu   Kapiti I.   Carterton
Upper Hutt   Featherston   Martinborough
Lower Hutt   Greytown
Wellington   C. Palliser

Cook Strait

South Island

C. Farewell   Golden B.   ABEL TASMAN   D'Urville I.
Collingwood   Tasman B.   Motueka
KAHURANGI   **Tasman Mts.**   Motueka   Picton
Karamea   Takaka   **Nelson**   Havelock
Karamea Bight   Matiri Ra.   NELSON LAKES   Blenheim
Seddonville   Tadmor   Richmond   Wakefield   Seddon
Granity   Lyell   Murchison   Ward
Westport   Inangahua   Rotoiti   Kaikoura   Clarence
PAPAROA   L. Rotoroa   ▲2885 Tapuae-o-Uenuku
Punakaiki   Reefton   Spenser Mts.   Hanmer   Kaikoura
Blackball   Springs
Runanga   Kumara   Waiau
Greymouth   L. Brunner   Culverden
Hokitika   Jacksons   ARTHUR'S PASS   Waikari   Amberley
Ross   Waipara
Abut Hd.   Oxford   Rangiora
Christchurch   Pegasus Bay
WESTLAND   Aoraki Mt. Cook   Methven   New Brighton
▲3753   Staveley   Riccarton   Lyttelton
Mount Cook   Fairlie   Rakaia   Banks Pen.
MT COOK (Aoraki/Mt Cook)   Tekapo   Little River
Southern Alps (Tiritiri o te Moana)   Ashburton   Akaroa
MOUNT ASPIRING   Mt. Aspiring ▲3027   Temuka   L. Ellesmere
Mt. Earnslaw ▲2818   Pukaki   **Timaru**
Milford Sd.   Ohau   Waimate   Canterbury Bight
Sutherland Falls   Wanaka   St. Andrews
Bligh Sound   Arrowtown   Kurow   Oamaru
George Sound   Cromwell   Tokarahi   Maheno
Secretary I.   Clyde   Naseby   Hampden
Doubtful Sd.   **Queenstown**   Alexandra   Danback   Palmerston
FIORDLAND   Wakatipu   Ranfurly   Port Chalmers
Resolution I.   Manapouri   Roxburgh   Waikouaiti   Otago Harbour
Dusky Sd.   Garvie Mts.   C. Saunders
Breaksea Sd.   Mossburn   Milton   **Dunedin**
SOUTHLAND   Ohai   Kelso   Lawrence   Nugget Pt.
Chalky Inlet   Lumsden   Clifden   Tapanui   Balclutha
Preservation Inlet   Nightcaps   Clinton   Kaitangata
Solander I.   Winton   Gore   Wyndham   Owaka
Te Waewae B.   Orepuki   Mataura   Takakopa
Riverton   Edendale
Orepuki   Hedgehope   Woodlands
Invercargill   South Invercargill
Bluff   Ruapuke I.
Foveaux Strait
Stewart I. (Rakiura)
Halfmoon Bay
RAKIURA   Port Pegasus
South West C.

TASMAN SEA

PACIFIC OCEAN

TAHITI & MOOREA d   1:1 000 000

B. de Matavai   Pte. Vénus
Papetoai   Papao   Pte. Aroa   Mahina
Mt. Tohiea ▲1207   Afareaitu   Arue   Papenoo   Tiarei
Haapiti   Papeete   Pirae   Papeari
Faaa   Hitiaa
Moorea (France)   Mt. Aorai ▲2060   Mt. Orohena ▲2241
Punaauia   Mt. Tetufera ▲1799   Faaone   **Tahiti** (France)
Paea   Lac Vaihiria   Taravao   Isthme de Taravao
Marda   Papara   Tautira   Afaahiti
Atimaono   Mataiea   Vairao   Pte. Tatatua
Mt. Rooniu ▲1332   Tautira
Teahupoo   **Presqu'île de Taiarapu**

17°30'S   17°45'S
149°30'W   149°15'W   West from Greenwich

ft   m
9000   3000
6000   2000
3000   1000
1200   400
600   200
0   0
200   600
2000   6000
4000   12 000
6000   18 000
m   ft

Projection : Conical with two standard parallels   East from Greenwich   COPYRIGHT PHILIP'S

10   0   10 km
10   0   10 miles
1:1 000 000

1:8 000 000

50   0   100   150   200   250   300 km
50   0   50   100   150   200 miles

INDONESIA

TIMOR SEA

INDIAN

OCEAN

INDIAN OCEAN

Timor

Kupang

Sumba

Waingapu

Sumbawa

Lombok

Bali

NORTHERN TERRITORY

Darwin
Palmerston

Melville

Bathurst I.

Tanami Desert

Great Sandy Desert

Gibson Desert

Little Sandy Desert

King Leopold Ranges

Kimberley Plateau

Bonaparte Archipelago

Joseph Bonaparte Gulf

Broome

Port Hedland

Karratha

Exmouth Gulf

Ningaloo Marine

Hamersley Range

Rudall River

Eighty Mile Beach

Tropic of Capricorn

WESTERN AUSTRALIA

SOUTH AUSTRALIA

Great Victoria Desert

Nullarbor Plain

Hampton Tableland

NULLARBOR

Great Australian Bight

SOUTHERN OCEAN

INDIAN OCEAN

Kata Tjuta (The Olgas) 1069
Uluru KATA TJUTA
Uluru (Ayers Rock)
Petermann Ranges
Everard Ranges
L. Maramangye
L. Meramangye
Wilkinson
Mt. Woodroffe 1440
Amata
Morris 1288
Mt. Musgrave Ranges
L. Maurice
L. Dey-Dey
Serpentine Lakes
Mt. Aloysius 1058
Tomkinson Ra.
Blackstone Ra.
1058
Oodea
Maralinga
L. Ilma
Cook
Reid
Forrest
Loongana
Watson
Mundrabilla
Eucla
Wilson Bluff
Low Pt.
Red Rocks Pt.
Madura
Pt. Dover
Cocklebiddy
Pt. Culver
Balladonia
Mt. Ragged 585
CAPE ARID
C. Arid
Sandy Bight
Eastern Group
Pt. Malcolm
Middle I.
South East Is.
Archipelago of the Recherche
Esperance
Cape Le Grand
PEAK CHARLES
Mt. Ridley
Salmon Gums
Grass Patch
Scaddan
Gibson
Norseman
Dundas
Widgiemooltha
Kambalda West
Coolgardie
Kalgoorlie-Boulder
Broad Arrow
Menzies GOONGARRIE
Kookynie
Malcolm
Leonora
Mt. Leinster
Mt. Redcliffe 576
Wiluna
Bar Smith Ra.
Agnew
Barr Smith Ra.
L. Nabberu
L. Carnegie
Mt. Essendon 914
Carnarvon Ra.
Robinson Ra.
Peak Hill
Mt. Fraser 799
COLLIER RANGE
Kumarina Roadhouse
Collier Ra.
Mt. Augustus 1106
Waldburg Ra.
Mt. Eureka 499
L. Way
L. Carnegie
L. Wells
L. Minigwal
L. Rason
L. Throssell
L. Gillen
L. Carey
L. Darlot
Mt. Ballard 654
Mt. Burges
BOORABBIN
Southern Cross
L. Seabrook
L. Deborah
L. Cronin
Koolyanobbing
Merredin
Bullfinch
L. Moore
WUBIN
Paynes Find
Mount Magnet
Cue
Meekatharra
L. Austin
Sandstone
Wemen 543
L. Annean
Nannine
Montague Ra.
Tuckanarra
Lawlers
L. Gregory
L. Nabberu
Gascoyne Junction
Kennedy Range
KENNEDY RANGE
Gascoyne R.
Minilya Roadhouse
Minilya
Wooramel Roadhouse
Wooramel
Hamelin Pool
Denham
SHARK BAY
Dirk Hartog I.
Steep Pt.
Dorre I.
Bernier I.
C. Cuvier
C. Ronsard
C. St. Cricq
Carnarvon
Gascoyne Channel
FRANCIS PRON
Monkey Mia
Nanga
Useless Loop
PENINSULA
Zuytdorp Cliffs
Murchison R.
Kalbarri
KALBARRI
Bluff Pt.
Gantheaume B.
Northampton
Geraldton
Greenough
Houtman Abrolhos
Dongara
Mingenew
Three Springs
Carnamah
Morawa
Perenjori
Mullewa
Yalgoo
Paynes Find
Wubin
Dalwallinu
Latham
Kalannie
Koorda
Wongan Hills
New Norcia
Moora
Watheroo
Dandaragan
Eneabba
Leeman
Green Head
Jurien
Cervantes
LESUEUR
NAMBUNG
BADGINGARRA
Lancelin
Gingin
Bindoon
Toodyay
Northam
York
Quairading
Kellerberrin
Bruce Rock
Merredin
Nungarin
Mukinbudin
Bencubbin
Beacon
Koorda
Wyalkatchem
Goomalling
Dowerin
Mukinbudin
Wongan Hills
Cunderdin
Kellerberrin
Tammin
Meckering
MOORE RIVER
Wanneroo
PERTH
Midland
Fremantle
Kwinana
Rockingham
Mandurah
Armadale
Kelmscott
Pinjarra
Waroona
Harvey
Brunswick Junction
Australind
Bunbury
Busselton
Dunsborough
Yallingup
C. Naturaliste
Margaret River
Augusta
C. Leeuwin
LEEUWIN-NATURALISTE
D'ENTRECASTEAUX
Pt. D'Entrecasteaux
Nannup
Bridgetown
Greenbushes
Boyup Brook
Collie
Darkan
Williams
Wagin
Narrogin
Pingelly
Brookton
Beverley
Wickepin
Kulin
Corrigin
Narembeen
Hyden
Lake King
Newdegate
Lake Grace
Dumbleyung
Katanning
Kojonup
Cranbrook
Mt. Barker
Tambellup
Gnowangerup
Ongerup
Jerramungup
Bremer Bay
Ravensthorpe
Hopetoun
FRANK HANN
STOKES
Munglinup
Fitzgerald R.
PORONGURUP
STIRLING RANGE
MT. FRANKLAND
WALPOLE-NORNALUP
Walpole
Nornalup
Denmark
Albany
King George Sound
Vancouver Pen.
Bald I.
Cheyne B.
C. Riche
Eclipse I.
Torndirrup
Cape Howe
Boddington
Dwellingup
Wandering
Pingelly
Quairading
Bruce Rock
Merredin
Southern Cross
Bullabulling
Bonnie Rock
Mount Walker
Karlgarin
Babakin
Kondinin
Kulin
Dudinin
Lake Varley
Ravensthorpe
WESTERN AUSTRALIA

Projection: Bonne
East from Greenwich
COPYRIGHT PHILIP'S

Scale bar:
m: 3000 1200 600 400 200 0
ft: 12 000 6000 2000 1000 600 200 0
ft / m
4000 2000

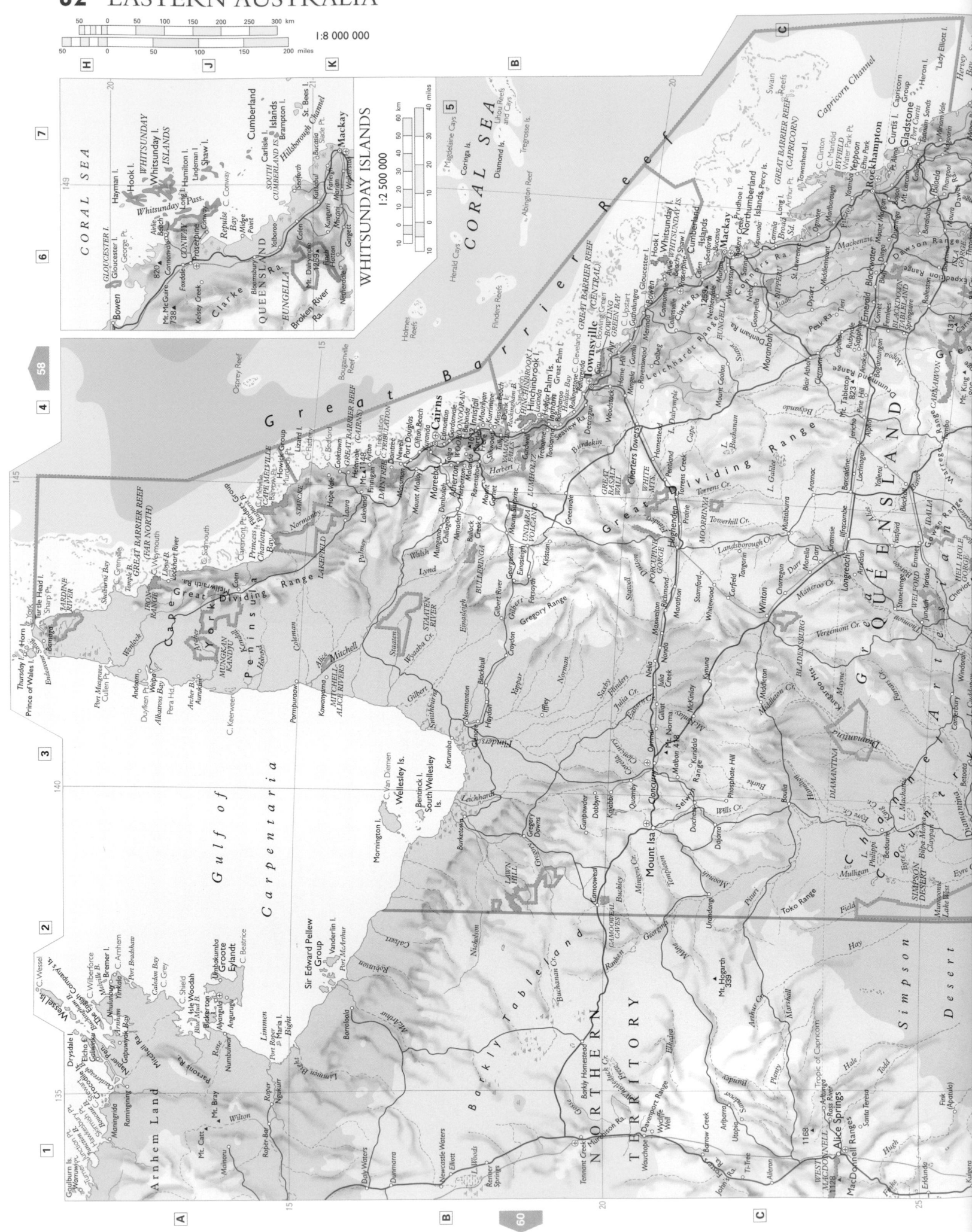

1:8 000 000

50   0   50   100   150   200   250   300 km
50   0   50   100   150   200 miles

WHITSUNDAY ISLANDS
1:2 500 000

10   0   10   20   30   40   50   60 km
10   0   10   20   30   40 miles

CORAL SEA

Gulf of Carpentaria

QUEENSLAND

NORTHERN TERRITORY

Arnhem Land

Great Dividing Range

Cape York Peninsula

Great Barrier Reef

Townsville

Cairns

Mackay

Rockhampton

Gladstone

Mount Isa

Alice Springs

Simpson Desert

TASMAN SEA

COPYRIGHT, GEORGE PHILIP LTD.

NEW SOUTH WALES

SOUTH AUSTRALIA

QUEENSLAND

VICTORIA

TASMANIA

BRISBANE
Gold Coast
Sunshine Coast
Toowoomba
Ipswich
SYDNEY
Newcastle
Gosford
Wollongong
Campbelltown
Nowra
Canberra
Queanbeyan
Goulburn
Bathurst
Orange
Dubbo
Tamworth
Armidale
Port Macquarie
Coffs Harbour
ADELAIDE
Port Augusta
Whyalla
Port Lincoln
Broken Hill
Mildura
Wagga Wagga
Albury
MELBOURNE
Geelong
Ballarat
Bendigo
Shepparton
Sale
Bairnsdale
Warrnambool
Mount Gambier
Horsham
Hobart
Launceston
Devonport

Lake Eyre
Lake Torrens
Lake Gairdner
Lake Frome
Darling R.
Murray R.
Murrumbidgee R.
Great Dividing Range
Flinders Ranges
Barrier Range
Grampians
Gippsland
Bass Strait
Flinders Island
King Island
Furneaux Group
Kangaroo I.
Spencer Gulf
Gulf St. Vincent
Eyre Peninsula
Yorke Peninsula

Projection Bonne

East from Greenwich

on same scale

6 7 8 9 10

1 2 3 4 5

B

Moskva
Volga
Yekaterinburg
Astana (Aqmola)
Semey
R U S S I A
Tomsk
Novosibirsk
Ob'
Lena
Irkutsk
Oz. Baykal
Chita
Blagoveshchensk
Amur
Khabarovsk
Okhotsk
Sea of Okhotsk
Poluostrov Kamchatka
Shirshov Ridge
Komandorskiye Ostrova (Russia)
Near Is. (U.S.A.)
Andreanof Is. (U.S.A.)
Aleutian Basin
Beri... Sea
Aleutia...

C
KAZAKHSTAN
Aral Sea
Balqash Köl
MONGOLIA
Ulaanbaatar
Altai
Sakhalin
Petropavlovsk-Kamchatskiy
La Perouse Str.
Kurilskiye Ostrova (Russia)
Kuril-Kamchatka Trench
10,542
Northwest
Chinook Tro...
Emperor Seamount Chain
Almaty
Ürümqi
Toshkent
KYRGYZSTAN
Changchun
Shenyang
Vladivostok
Hakodate
Sapporo
Sea of Japan

D
TAJIKISTAN
Kabul
AFGHANISTAN
Srinagar
PAKISTAN
Lahore
Delhi
C H I N A
Kunlun Shan
XIZANG
Lanzhou
Beijing
Tianjin
Taiyuan
Huang He
Dalian
NORTH KOREA
SOUTH KOREA
Seoul
Qingdao
Nagoya
Kyoto
Osaka
Kitakyushu
Kyūshū
Yellow Sea
Sendai
Tōkyō
Yokohama
JAPAN
Fuji-San 3776
Japan Trench
10,554
Shatsky Rise
Pacific
Midway Is. (U.S.A.)

E
Kanpur
Himalaya
Everest 8848
NEPAL
Lhasa
Xi'an
Nanjing
Chongqing
Wuhan
Hangzhou
Shanghai
East China Sea
Okinawa
Ryūkyū-retto (Japan)
Iwo-Jima (Japan)
Ogasawara Gunto (Japan)
Minami-Tori-Shima (Japan)
Lisianski I. (U.S.A.)
Ganga
Brahmaputra
Kolkata (Calcutta)
Dhaka
BANGLADESH
Mandalay
Irrawaddy
Changsha
Fuzhou
Taipei
Kunming
Guangzhou
TAIWAN
Kazan-Rettō (Japan)
Ho...

F
INDIA
Hyderabad
Chennai (Madras)
Bay of Bengal
Rangoon
BURMA
Salween
Mekong
LAOS
Hanoi
Macau
Hong Kong
Hainan
Luzon
Paracel Is.
Manila
C. Engano
Philippine Sea
Philippine Basin
West Mariana Basin
NORTHERN MARIANAS (U.S.A.)
Tinian
Saipan
East Mariana Basin
MARSHALL IS.
Bikini Atoll
Enewetak Atoll
Wake I. (U.S.A.)
P
P A
Kyushu-Palau Ridge
Nampo Shoto
Mid-Pacific Mou...
International Date Line
THAILAND
Bangkok
CAMBODIA
Phnom Penh
Andaman Is. (India)

G
SRI LANKA
Colombo
Nicobar Is. (India)
G. of Thailand
South China Sea
Thanh Pho Ho Chi Minh
VIETNAM
Palawan
Mindoro
Samar
10,497
PHILIPPINES
Sulu Sea
Mindanao
Davao
Mindanao Trench
Celebes Sea
Yap
Koror
PALAU
West Caroline Basin
Eauripik Rise
Caroline Is.
Truk
FED. STATES OF MICRONESIA
East Caroline Basin
Pohnpei
Palikir
Jaluit
Majuro
Micro...
Challenger 11,022 Deep
Mariana Trench
Micronesia
Kwajalein
Ralik Chain
Ratak Chain

H
MALAYSIA
Kuala Lumpur
PEN. MALAYSIA
Singapore
Sumatera
Sunda Ridge
Ninetyeast Ridge
Borneo
BRUNEI
SABAH
SARAWAK
Sulawesi
Halmahera
Buru
Seram
Maluku
Banda Sea
Admiralty Is.
Puncak Jaya 5029
PAPUA
New Guinea
Bismarck Arch.
New Ireland
Rabaul 8940
New Britain
Bougainville
PAPUA NEW GUINEA
NAURU
Butaritari
Tarawa
Gilbert Is.
Banaba
Melanesian Basin
Solomon Rise
SOLOMON IS.
Phoenix Is.
Abariringa
Enderbury
K I...
P O...
Mel...
Melanesia
Fongafale
TUVALU
Tokelau (N.Z.)
Howland I. (U.S.A.)
Baker I. (U.S.A.)

INDONESIA
Ujung Pandang
Palembang
Java Sea
Jakarta
Jawa
Surabaya
Bali
Sumbawa
Flores Sea
Flores
Sumba
7440
Dili
EAST TIMOR
Timor
Arafura Sea
Torres Strait
C. York
Port Moresby
Lae
Honiara
Guadalcanal
Santa Cruz Is. 9165
Espiritu Santo
Rotuma
Is. Wallis & Futuna (Fr.)
SAMOA
Apia

L
Christmas I. (Austral.)
Cocos Is. (Austral.)
Wharton Basin
North Australian Basin
Exmouth Plateau
Broome
C. Arnhem
Darwin
North West C.
Gulf of Carpentaria
Cairns
Townsville
Rockhampton
Louisiade Arch.
Great Barrier Reef
Coral Sea Basin
Coral Sea
Is. Chesterfield
VANUATU
Port Vila
West Fiji Basin
Vanua Levu
Viti Levu
FIJI
Suva
7670
Nuku'alofa
TON...

M
INDIAN
Mount Isa
AUSTRALIA
Alice Springs
L. Eyre
Broken Ridge
Perth Basin
Perth
Geraldton
Naturaliste Plateau
Albany
Great Australian Bight
Adelaide
Murray
Canberra
Mt. Kosciuszko 2230
Melbourne
Sydney
Brisbane
New Caledonia Trough
NEW CALEDONIA (Fr.)
Nouméa
Is. Loyauté
Lord Howe Rise
Norfolk I. (Austral.)
South Fiji Basin
Middleton Basin
Lord Howe I. (Austral.)
Kermadec Is. (N.Z.)
Kermadec Trench 10,047
Tonga Trench 10,822
Norfolk Ridge
New Caledonia Ridge
Darling
Tasman Sea
NEW ZEALAND
Auckland

OCEAN
South Australian Basin
Bass Str.
Tasmania
Hobart
East Tasman Plateau
Tasman Basin
Cook Strait
Wellington
Christchurch
Chatham Rise
Chatham... (N.Z.)
Aoraki Mt. Cook 3753
Dunedin
Bounty Trough
Bounty Is. (N.Z.)

N
Nouvelle Amsterdam (Fr.)
I. St. Paul (Fr.)
Mid-Indian Ridge
S O U T H E R N   O C E A N
Is. Crozet (Fr.)
Kerguelen (Fr.)
Heard I. (Austral.)
Invercargill
Antipodes Is. (N.Z.)
Auckland Is. (N.Z.)
Campbell I. (N.Z.)
Campbell Plateau
Macquarie Is. (Austral.)

ft m
12 000 4000
9000 3000
6000 2000
3000 1000
1500 500
600 200
0 0
200 600
1000 3000
2000 6000
4000 12 000
6000 18 000
8000 24 000
m ft

Arctic Circle

ALASKA
(U.S.A.)
Anchorage
Bristol Bay
Gulf of Alaska
5959
Juneau

S. (U.S.A.)

Prince of Wales I.
(U.S.A.) Prince Rupert
Queen Charlotte Is.
(Canada)
Tufts
Abyssal
Plain

ROCKY

CANADA

Edmonton
L. Winnipeg
Calgary
Vancouver
Vancouver I. Victoria
Seattle
Portland
Boise
Regina
Winnipeg
L. Superior
Snake
Missouri

Newfoundland

NORTH

St. Lawrence
Québec
Montréal Ottawa
L. Huron
L. Michigan Toronto
Ontario Detroit Buffalo Boston
L. Erie
Pittsburgh New York
Philadelphia
Baltimore
Washington D.C.

St. John's

50

B

C

Northeast
Mendocino Fracture Zone C. Mendocino
6741
Murray Fracture Zone
4418

Minneapolis
Salt Lake
City
Denver
Sacramento
San Francisco
Kansas City
St. Louis
Chicago
Cincinnati
UNITED STATES
Oklahoma City Memphis
Atlanta

ATLANTIC

40

D

Pacific

Los Angeles
San Diego
Ciudad
Juárez
Phoenix
Dallas
Houston
San Antonio
New
Orleans
Mississippi
Appalachian Mts.
C. Hatteras
Jacksonville

Bermuda
(U.K.)

Sargasso Sea

30

Guadalupe
(Mex.)
Molokai Fracture Zone
Tropic of Cancer
Baja California
Gulf of Mexico
Monterrey
Tampa
Miami
BAHAMAS
OCEAN

E

Basin
C. San Lucas
Gallo de California

La Habana
CUBA
West Indies
Florida Str.

20

Honolulu
Kauai Maui
Oahu HAWAIIAN IS.
4205 (U.S.A.)
Hilo Hawaii
nston I.
.A.)
Clarion Fracture Zone Is. Revilla Gigedo
(Mex.)
Guadalajara
Acapulco
Mexico
5610
Puebla
MEXICO
Mérida
7680
9200
Canal de Yucatán
BELIZE
JAMAICA HAITI DOMINICAN REP.
Kingston PUERTO
RICO
(U.S.A.)
Leeward
Is.

F

C I F I C

n West Christmas Ridge

Middle America Trench
GUATEMALA HONDURAS
6662 Guatemala
San Salvador NICARAGUA
EL SALVADOR Managua
Guatemala
Basin
Caribbean Sea
Barranquilla
Windward Is.
BARBADOS
Maracaibo
Caracas
Orinoco

10

Palmyra Is.
(U.S.A.)
Teraina
Tabuaeran
Kiritimati
I. Clipperton
(Fr.)
Clipperton Fracture Zone
COSTA
RICA San José
Colón Panamá
PANAMA
I. del Coco
(Costa Rica)
Coco Ridge
Panama
Basin
Medellín
Bogotá
Cali
VENEZUELA
COLOMBIA

G

sin
Jarvis I.
(U.S.A.)
B A T I
A N
E A N
Malden I.
Starbuck I.
Equator
Galápagos Fracture Zone
I. de Malpelo
(Colombia)
Galápagos
(Ecuador)
Carnegie Ridge
Quito
ECUADOR
0

Penrhyn
(Tongareva)
Manihiki
Pukapuka Manihiki
Plateau
Suwarrow Is.
Line Islands
Nuku Hiva
Îs. Marquises
Hiva Oa
Vostok I. Caroline I.
(Millennium I.)
Flint I.
Marquesas Fracture Zone
Yupanqui
Basin
Mendaña
Fracture Zone
Guayaquil
Îqiítós
Palinas
Trujillo
6369
Amazonas
BRAZIL

H

Îs. de la
Société
Bora Bora
Huahine Rangiroa
Raiatéa Tahiti
Papeete Îs. Tuamotu
PERU
Lima
Cuzco
East Pacific Ridge
Peru Basin
6866
Peru-
10

A
Seamount Chain
FRENCH POLYNESIA
Aitutaki
Cook Is.
(N.Z.)
Îs. Gambier
Mururoa
Nazca Ridge
L. Titicaca
Arequipa
Nevada Ancohuma
6550
La Paz
BOLIVIA
Arica

J

Rarotonga
Atiu
Mangaia
Îs. Tubuai
Tropic of Capricorn
Iquique
Chile
Antofagasta
PARAGUAY
20

Oeno I.
Henderson I.
Pitcairn I. Ducie I.
(U.K.)
Easter Fracture Zone
Sala-y-Gómez
(Chile)
I. de Pascua
(Chile)
Sala y Gómez Ridge
San Felix
(Chile) San Ambrosio
(Chile)
8050
Trench
San Miguel
de Tucumán
Asunción
PARAGUAY

K

Rapa

Roggeveen
Basin
Arch. de
Juan Fernández
(Chile)
Córdoba
Aconcagua
6962
Rosario
URUGUAY
Pôrto
Alegre

30

Southwest

Valparaíso
Santiago
Buenos
Aires
Montevideo
Río de la Plata

L

Pacific
Challenger Fracture Zone
Chile Rise
Concepción
ARGENTINA
40

Basin
Menard Fracture Zone
SOUTH

M

Pacific-Antarctic Ridge
East Pacific
Ridge
Patagonia
6212
ATLANTIC
OCEAN

50

Ridge

Southeast
Pacific Basin
Punta Arenas
Est. de Magallanes
C. de Hornos Tierra del Fuego
Drake Passage
Falkland Is.
(U.K.)
South Georgia
(U.K.)

N

1:35 000 000

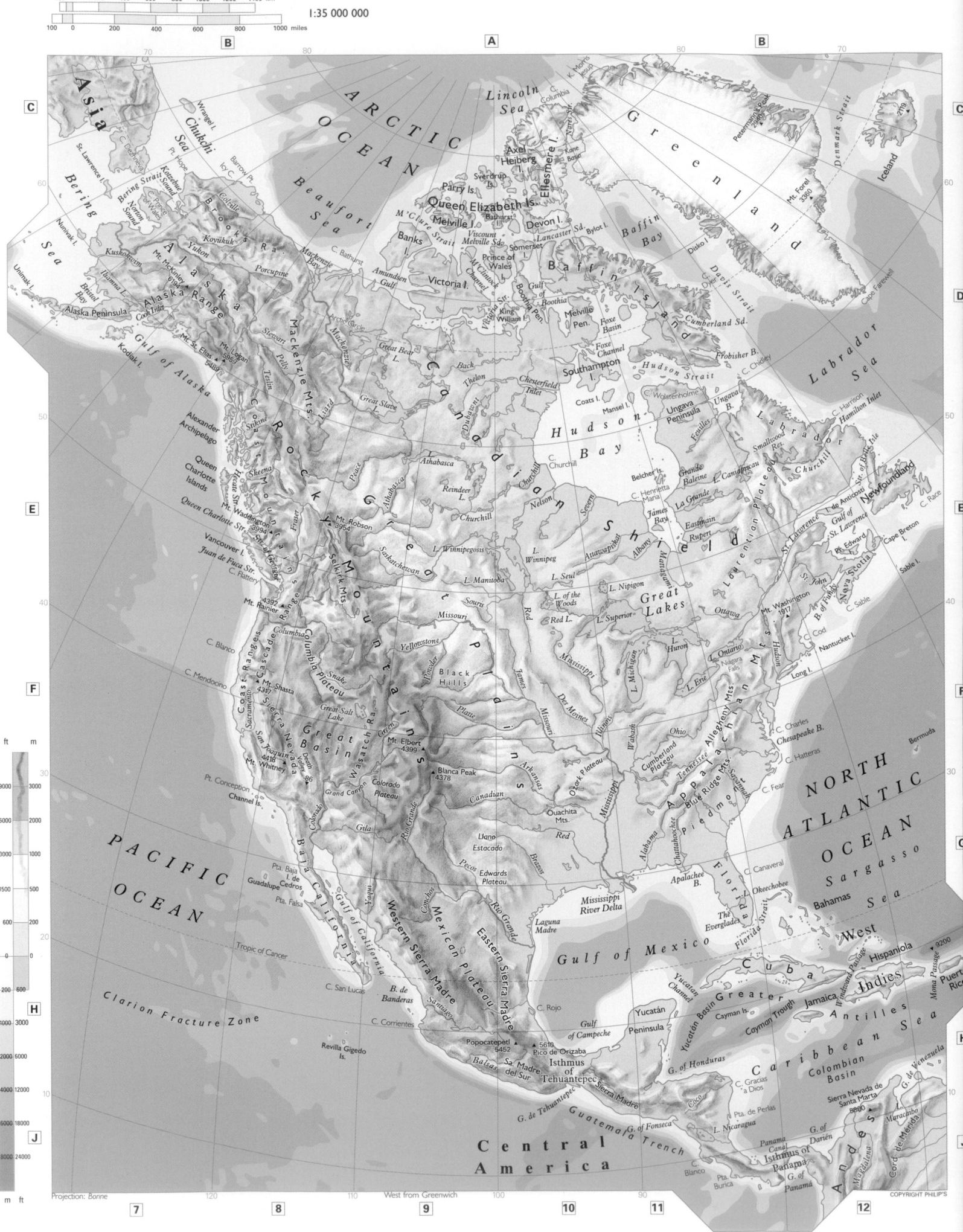

Projection: Bonne

West from Greenwich

COPYRIGHT PHILIP'S

1:35 000 000

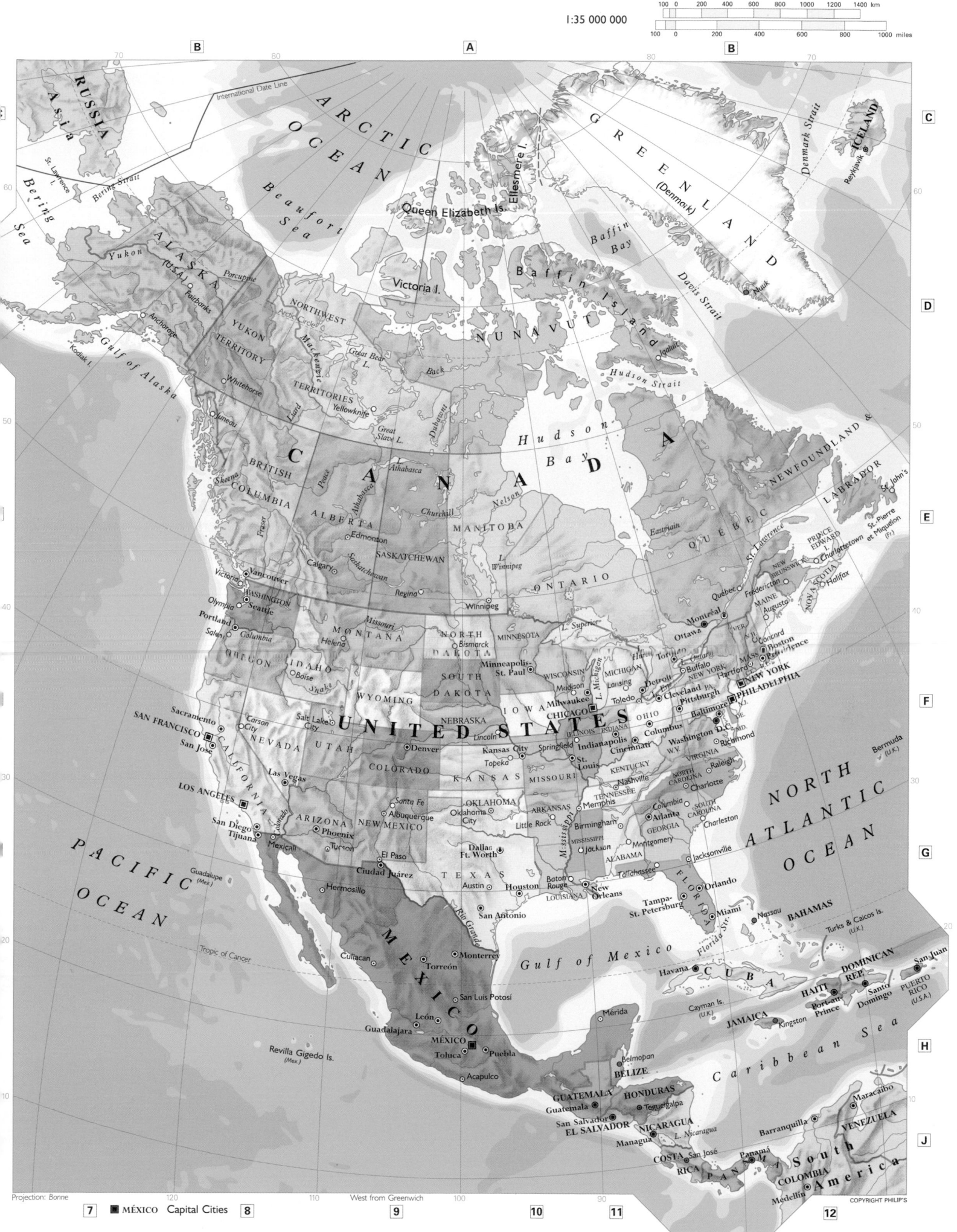

Projection: Bonne

7 ■ MÉXICO Capital Cities 8 9 10 11 12

West from Greenwich

1:15 000 000

Projection : Bonne

NORTHERN CANADA
continuation northwards on same
scale as main map

ARCTIC OCEAN

Northern Canada inset:

North Magnetic Pole
Sverdrup Islands
Meighen I.
Borden I.
Brock I.
Mackenzie King I.
Lougheed I.
Amund Ringnes
Ellef Ringnes
Prince Patrick I.
Eglinton I.
Cornwall
Belcher Chan.
Queen Elizabeth Is.
Melville I.
Norwegian Bay
Grise Fiord
Jones Sound
Ellesmere Island
Greenland (Denmark)
C. Columbia
Alert
2616
Axel Heiberg
Eureka
Arctic Bay
Hans I.
Smith Sound
Prince Alfred
Banks Island
M'Clure Strait
Viscount Melville Sound
Bathurst
Cornwallis
Resolute
Wellington Chan.
Devon Island
Lancaster Sound
747
Holman
Victoria Island
Prince Albert Pen.
M'Clintock Channel
Prince of Wales Island
Somerset Island
Arctic Bay
Nanisivik
Bylot I.
1951
Pond Inlet
Brodeur Peninsula
Baffin Island
NUNAVUT
NORTHWEST TERRITORIES

Main map:

Baffin Bay
Devon I.
Lancaster Sound
Arctic Bay
Nanisivik
Bylot I.
1951
Pond Inlet
Borden Pen.
2136
C. Adair
Clyde River
C. Raper
Home I.
Qikiqtarjuaq
Baffin Island
Fury and Hecla Str.
Igloolik
Hall Beach
Melville Peninsula
Foxe Basin
Prince Charles I.
Cumberland Peninsula
Pangnirtung
Hoare B.
C. Mercy
Cumberland Sd.
Dyer
Committee B.
Repulse Bay
Rae Isthmus
NUNAVUT
C. Dorchester
Amadjuak L.
Foxe Pen.
Cape Dorset
Meta Incognita Peninsula
Kimmirut
Iqaluit
Hall Peninsula
Frobisher Bay
Resolution I.
Salisbury I.
Nottingham I.
Hudson Strait
Coats I.
Mansel I.
Southampton I.
Coral Harbour
Bell Pen.
Roes Welcome Sd.
Chesterfield Inlet
Ivujivik
Salluit
Quaqtaq
Akpatok I.
C. Chidley
Kangiqsujuaq
Kangirsuk
Ungava Bay
Puvirnituq
Péninsule d'Ungava
Arnaud
L. Payne
Feuilles
Kangiqsualujjuaq
Hebron
1652
Nain
Hudson Bay
257
Ottawa Is.
Inukjuak
L. Minto
Mélèze
Koksoak
Kuujjuaq
George
Caniapiscau
Baleine
Labrador Sea
3809
Sleeper Is.
King George Is.
Sanikiluaq
Belcher Is.
Kuujjuarapik
Grande r. de la Baleine
Pte. Louis XIV
Chisasibi
L. à l'Eau Claire
La Grande
Kanaaupscow
L. Bienville
L. Caniapiscau
Kawawachikamach (Schefferville)
Petitsikapau L.
Esker
Labrador City
Fermont
Ashuanipi L.
Gagnon
Churchill Falls
Churchill
North West River
Happy Valley-Goose Bay
Harrison
Cartwright
Rigolet
Hopedale
Makkovic
C. Harrison
St-Augustin
Natashquan
Belle Isle
St. Anthony
Baie Verte
Grand Falls-Windsor
Gander
Bonavista
Carbonear
St. John's
Placentia
C. Race
Deer Lake
Corner Brook
Stephenville
Newfoundland
Marystown
Channel-Port aux Basques
Cabot Str.
ST-PIERRE et MIQUELON
Gulf of St. Lawrence
Î. d'Anticosti
Havre-St-Pierre
Sept-Îles
Port-Cartier
Manicouagan
Baie-Comeau
Manicouagan Rés.
1135
QUÉBEC
L. Mistassini
Chibougamau
Matagami
L. Albanel
Rupert
Eastmain
Waskaganish
James Bay
Akimiski I.
Wemindji
Fort Albany
Attawapiskat
Peawanuck
Winisk
Big Trout L.
Attawapiskat
Moosonee
Albany
Charlton
ONTARIO
Henrietta Maria
Hearst
Kapuskasing
Oba
Cochrane
Timmins
Kirkland Lake
New Liskeard
Rouyn-Noranda
Amos
Val-d'Or
Res. Gouin
La Tuque
Dolbeau-Mistassini
St-Jean
Roberval
Jonquière
Chicoutimi
1190
Tadoussac
Rimouski
Matane
Pén. de la Gaspésie
Gaspé
Campbellton
Bathurst
Miramichi
NEW BRUNSWICK
Moncton
Amherst
PR. EDWARD I.
Summerside
Charlottetown
Northumberland Str.
Cape Breton I.
Sydney
Glace Bay
New Glasgow
Port Hawkesbury
Antigonish
Truro
NOVA SCOTIA
Dartmouth
Halifax
Bridgewater
Liverpool
Yarmouth
C. Sable
B. of Fundy
Digby
Kentville
Saint John
Fredericton
Woodstock
Edmundston
MAINE
Bangor
Augusta
Lewiston
Portland
Grand Falls
Lévis
Thetford Mines
Québec
Trois-Rivières
Shawinigan
Mont-Laurier
Rés. Cabonga
Joliette
St-Hyacinthe
Sherbrooke
Granby
MONTRÉAL
Hull
OTTAWA
Cornwall
L. Champlain
Montpelier
VERMONT
NEW HAMPSHIRE
Concord
Manchester
MASS.
Springfield
BOSTON
C. Cod
PROVIDENCE
R.I.
Hartford
CONN.
New Haven
NEW YORK
Bridgeport
Newark
N.J.
Allentown
Trenton
Scranton
Binghamton
Elmira
Albany
Syracuse
Rochester
Buffalo
Niagara Falls
Jamestown
Erie
PENNSYLVANIA
OHIO
CLEVELAND
Toledo
South Bend
Gary
INDIANA
CHICAGO
DETROIT
Windsor
Sarnia
London
Kitchener
Hamilton
TORONTO
Oshawa
Belleville
Kingston
Peterborough
Barrie
Owen Sound
Orillia
Parry Sound
Huntsville
North Bay
Sudbury
Elliot Lake
Sault Ste. Marie
Wawa
Chapleau
Marathon
Greenstone
Thunder Bay
Lake Superior
183
Houghton
Marquette
Escanaba
Menominee
Green Bay
Sheboygan
MILWAUKEE
Racine
Kenosha
WISCONSIN
Madison
Lansing
Flint
Saginaw
Cadillac
Traverse City
Petoskey
Manistique
MICHIGAN
Lake Michigan
Lake Huron
Manitoulin I.
Georgian Bay
Grand Rapids
L. Nipissing
Pembroke
Kirkland
174
L. Erie
Lake St. Clair
6309
ATLANTIC OCEAN
Labrador Sea
West from Greenwich

COPYRIGHT PHILIP'S

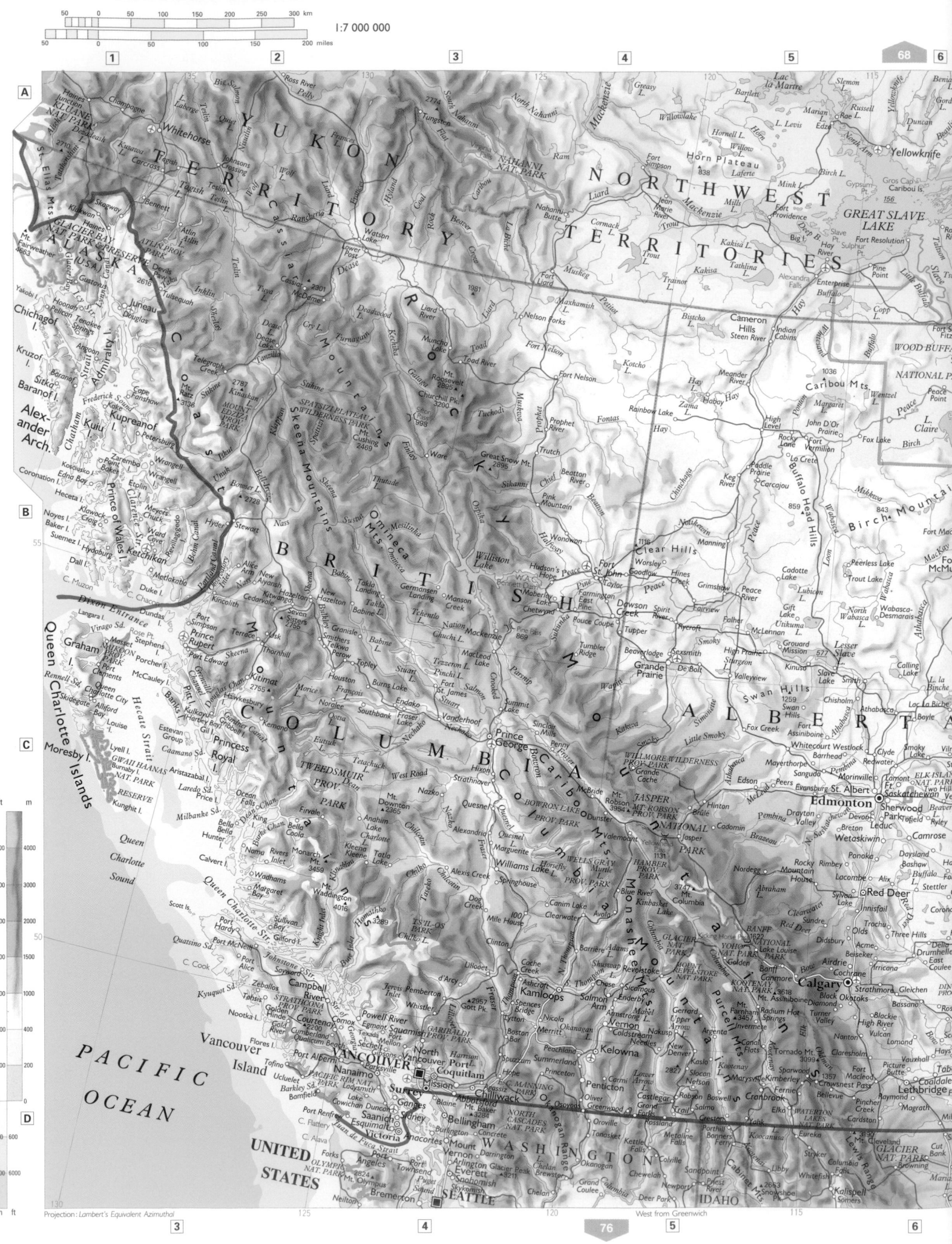

Projection : Lambert's Equivalent Azimuthal

West from Greenwich

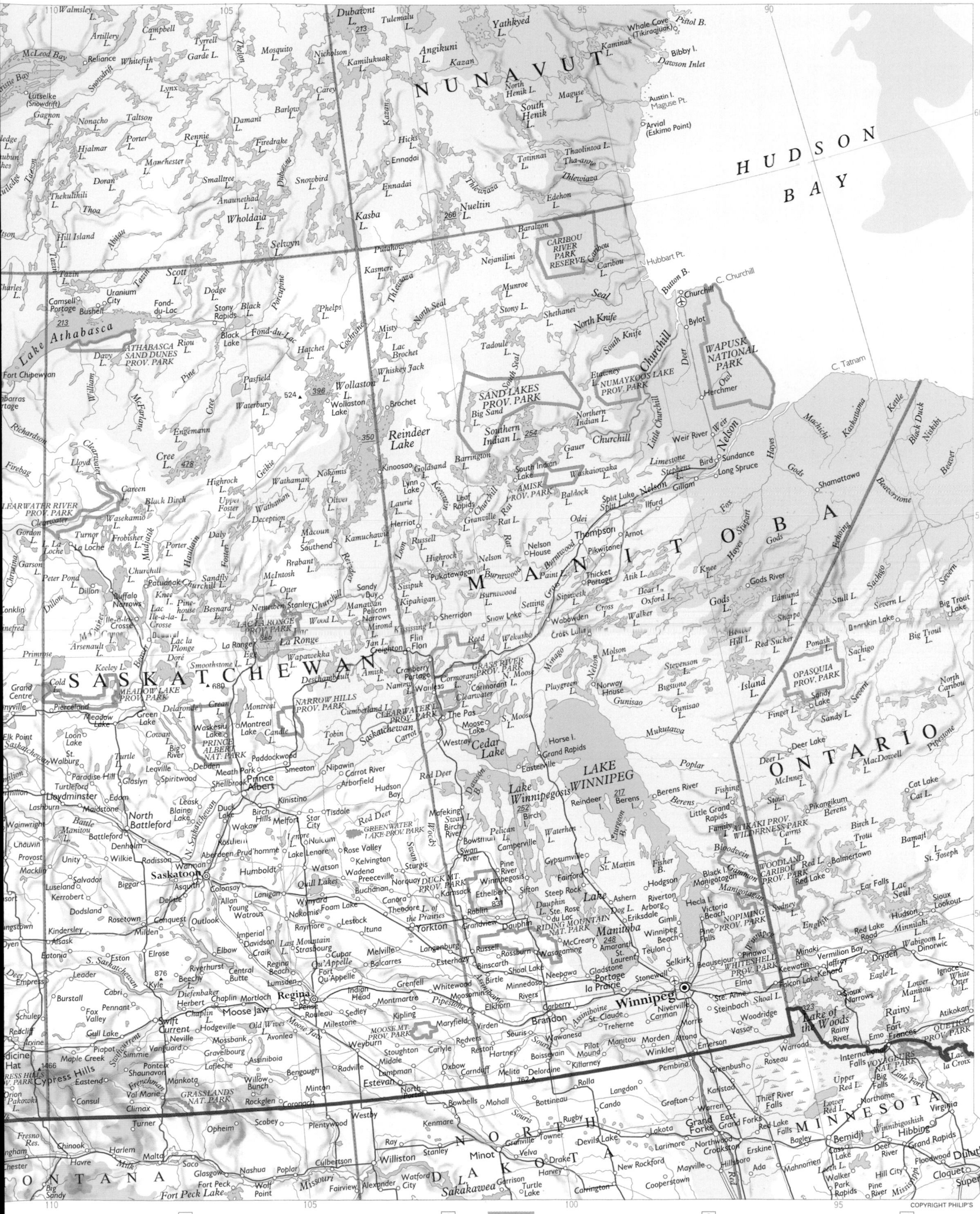

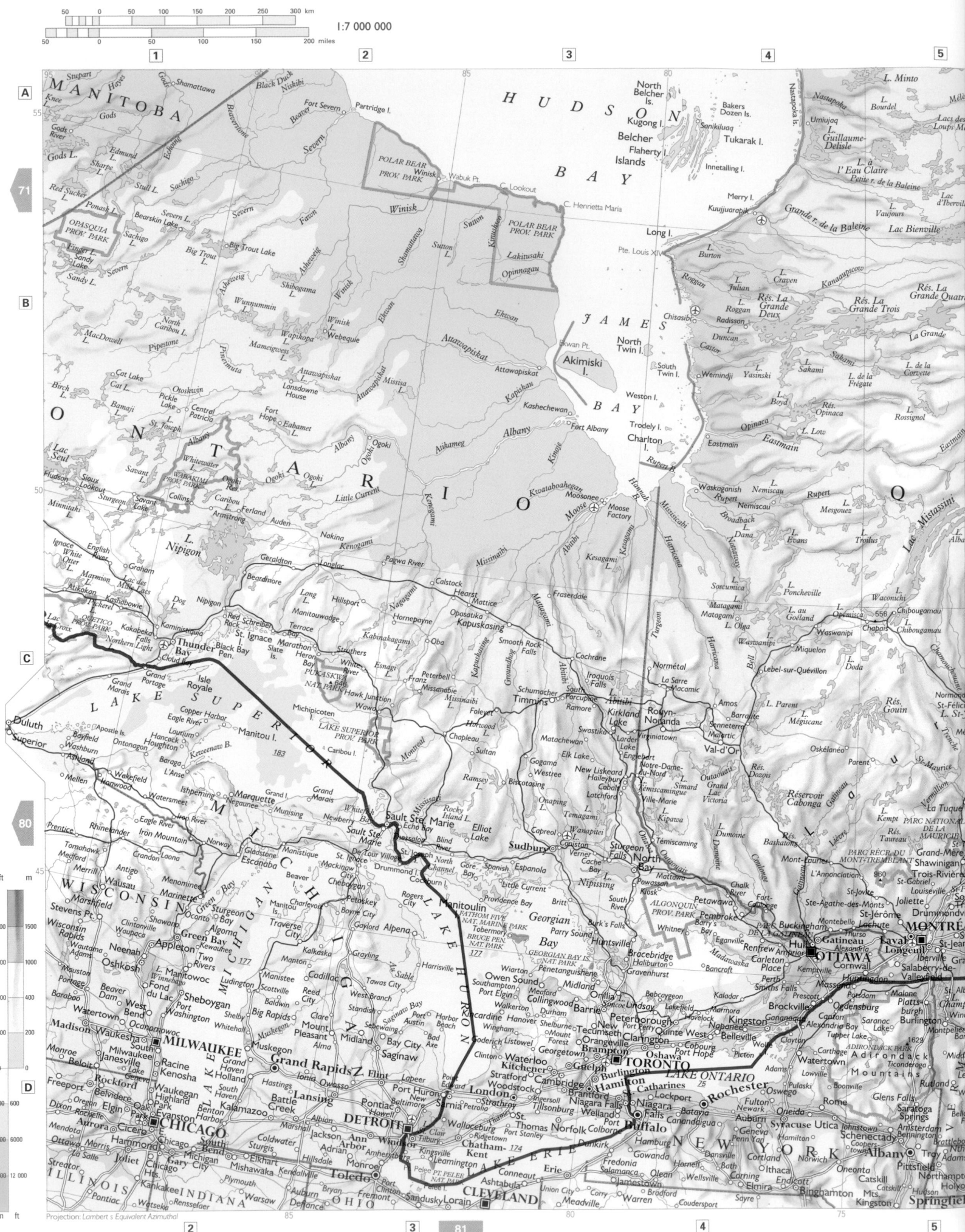

1:7 000 000

Projection: Lambert's Equivalent Azimuthal

A

LABRADOR

SEA

B

NEWFOUNDLAND &

Labrador

QUÉBEC

LABRADOR

Newfoundland

50

C

GULF OF

ST. LAWRENCE

I. d'Anticosti

Cabot Strait

ST-PIERRE
et MIQUELON
(France)

NEW

BRUNSWICK

PRINCE EDWARD
ISLAND

Cape Breton
Island

45

MAINE

NOVA SCOTIA

Bay of Fundy

ATLANTIC

Sable I.
(Nova Scotia)

D

NEW HAMPSHIRE

OCEAN

UNITED STATES

BOSTON

1:12 000 000

Projection: Albers' Equal Area with two standard parallels

ALASKA
1:30 000 000

HAWAI'I
1:10 000 000

West from Greenwich

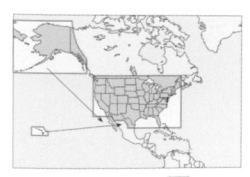

Tallahassee ✶ State capitals

COPYRIGHT PHILIP'S

1:6 700 000

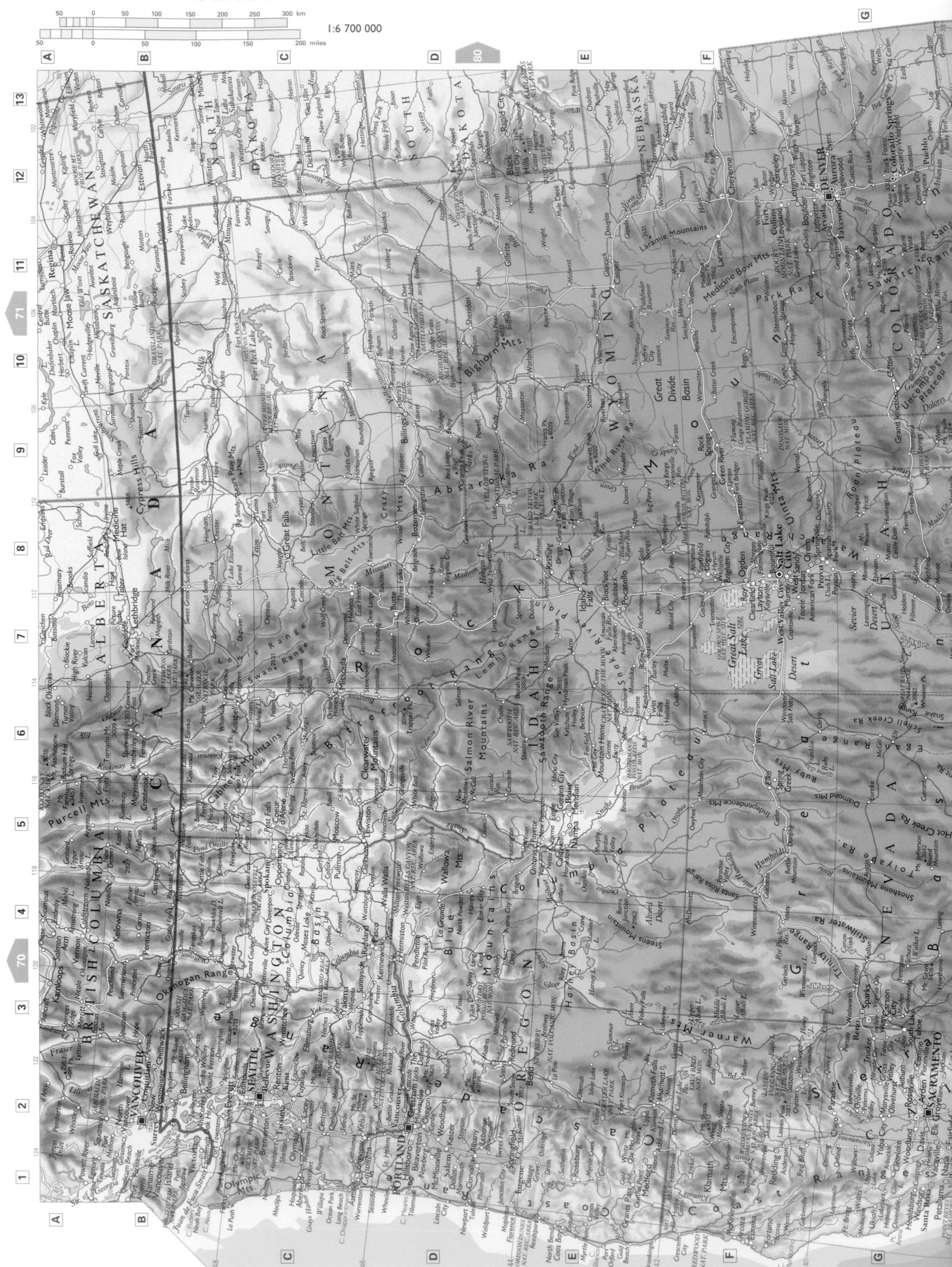

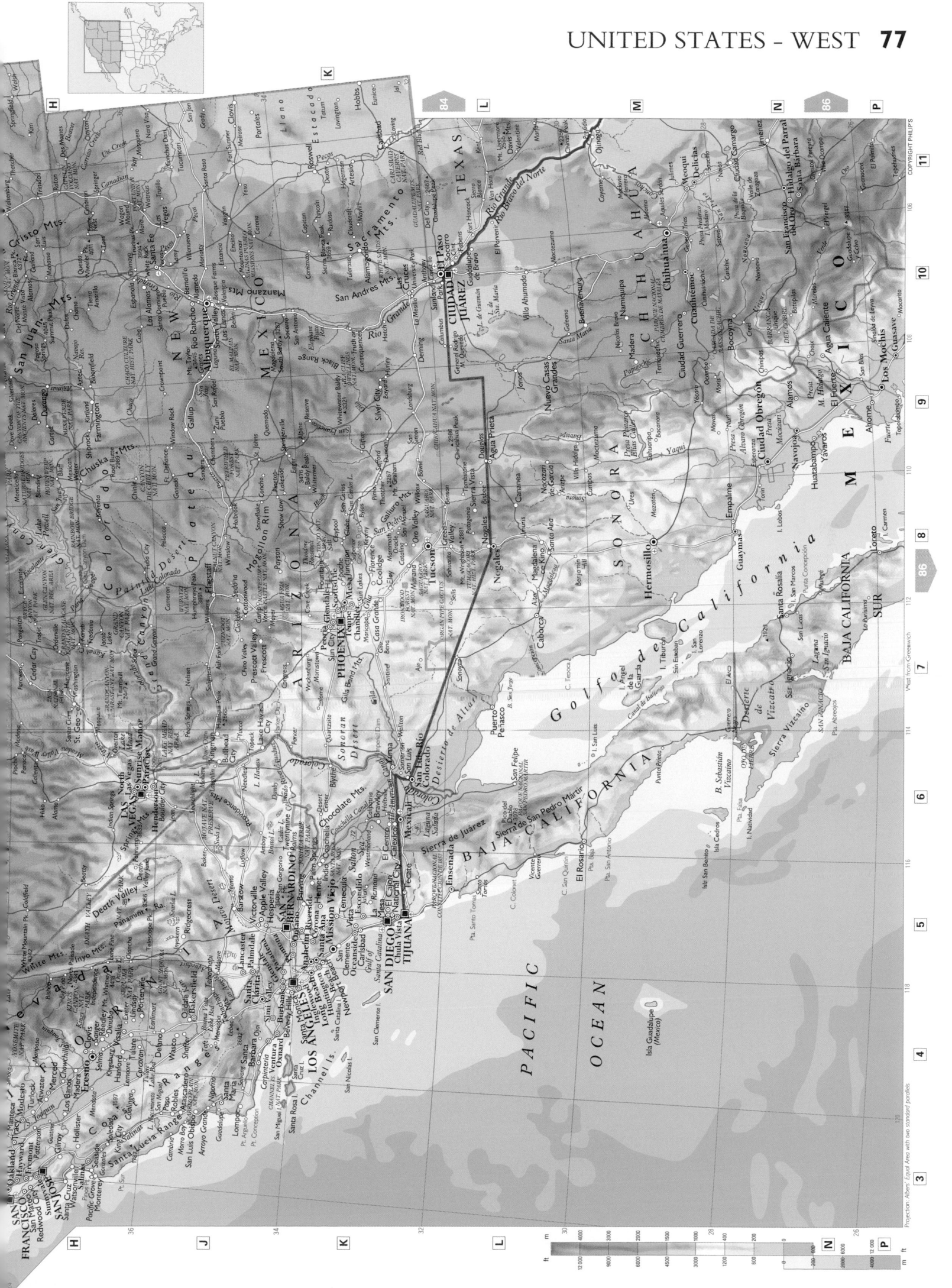
PACIFIC
OCEAN
ARIZONA
NEW MEXICO
TEXAS
SONORA
CHIHUAHUA
MEXICO
BAJA CALIFORNIA
BAJA CALIFORNIA SUR
Golfo de California
Colorado Plateau
Sonoran Desert
Mogollon Rim
Grand Canyon
Painted Desert
Death Valley
Mojave Desert
Sacramento Mts.
San Andres Mts.
Channel Is.
Isla Guadalupe (Mexico)
LOS ANGELES
SAN DIEGO
TIJUANA
PHOENIX
Tucson
Albuquerque
Santa Fe
El Paso
CIUDAD JUÁREZ
Chihuahua
Hermosillo
LAS VEGAS
SAN FRANCISCO
SAN JOSE
Fresno
Bakersfield
SAN BERNARDINO
Mexicali
Flagstaff
Ensenada
Guaymas
Ciudad Obregón
Los Mochis
Rio Grande
COPYRIGHT PHILIP'S
Projection: Albers' Equal Area with two standard parallels
West from Greenwich
H
J
K
L
M
N
P
3
4
5
6
7
8
9
10
11
84
86
m
ft

1:2 500 000

WESTERN WASHINGTON REGION
on same scale

PACIFIC OCEAN

BRITISH COLUMBIA
Vancouver Island

Strait of Georgia
Strait of Juan de Fuca

OLYMPIC NATIONAL PARK
Olympic Mountains
Mt Olympus

WASHINGTON

VANCOUVER

SEATTLE

Puget Sound

OREGON

PORTLAND

MT RAINIER NAT PARK

MT ST HELENS NATIONAL VOLCANIC MONUMENT
Mt St Helens 2550

Mt Adams 3742

White Mts.

Inyo Mts.

Reno
Sparks

Carson City

Lake Tahoe 1899

South Lake Tahoe

YOSEMITE NATIONAL PARK

KINGS CANYON NATIONAL PARK

SEQUOIA NATIONAL PARK
Mt Whitney 4418

Mono Lake

SACRAMENTO

Sacramento Valley

CALIFORNIA

Stockton
Modesto

San Joaquin Valley

Fresno
Clovis
Visalia

SAN FRANCISCO
Oakland
San Jose
Santa Clara Valley

Monterey Bay
Monterey

Salinas Valley
Santa Lucia Range

Santa Cruz

m ft 4000 12 000 3000 9000 2000 6000 1500 4500 1000 3000 400 1200 200 600 0 0 200 600 2000 6000 m ft

1:6 700 000

Projection: Albers' Equal Area with two standard parallels   West from Greenwich

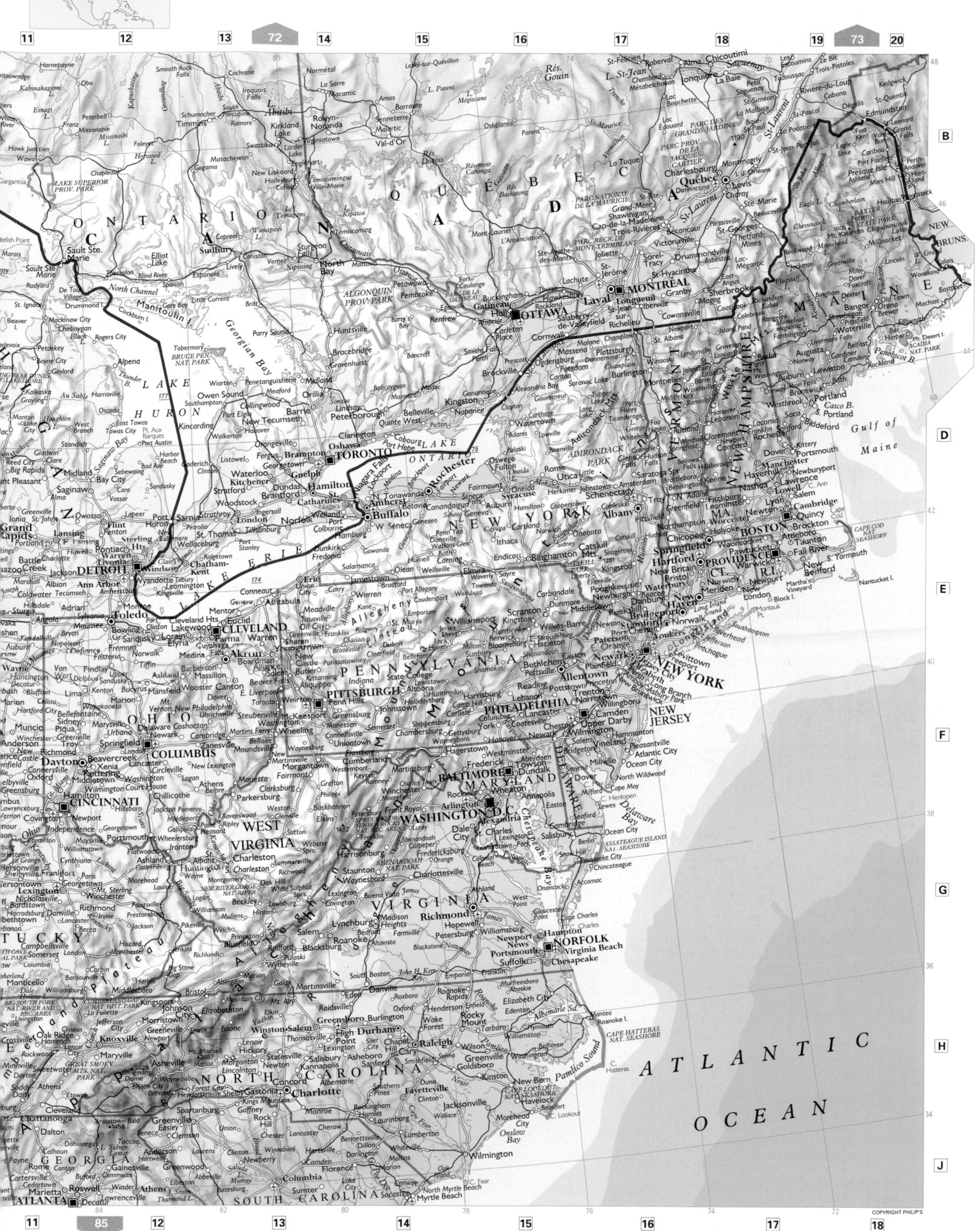

11 12 13 14 15 16 17 18 19 20

B D E F G H J

COPYRIGHT PHILIP'S

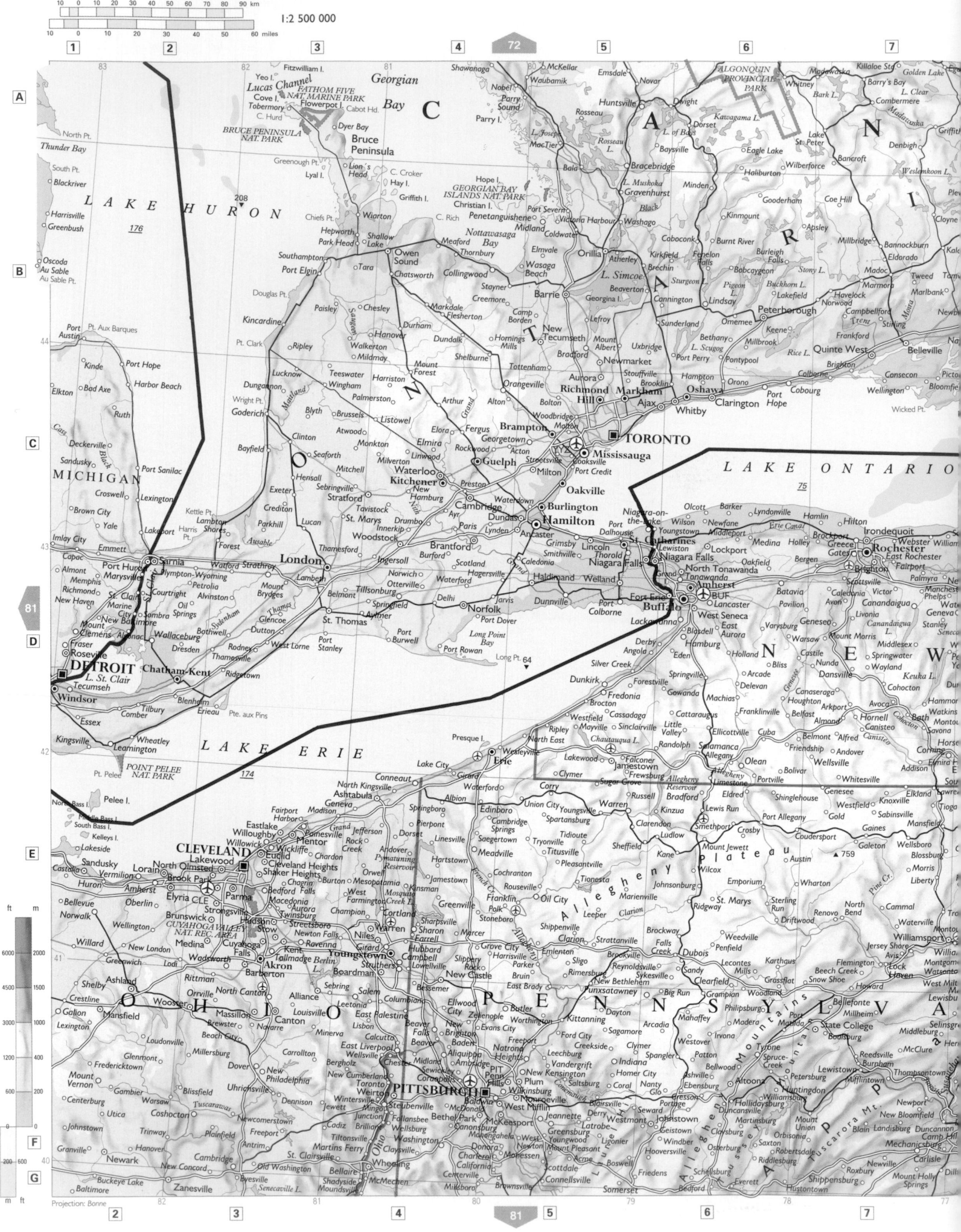
10 0 10 20 30 40 50 60 70 80 90 km
10 0 10 20 30 40 50 60 miles
1:2 500 000
72
81
A
B
C
D
E
F
G
1 2 3 4 5 6 7
Georgian Bay
Bruce Peninsula
BRUCE PENINSULA NAT. PARK
FATHOM FIVE NAT. MARINE PARK
GEORGIAN BAY ISLANDS NAT. PARK
ALGONQUIN PROVINCIAL PARK
ONTARIO
LAKE HURON
LAKE ONTARIO
LAKE ERIE
MICHIGAN
OHIO
PENNSYLVANIA
NEW YORK
Allegheny Plateau
Allegheny Mountains
Tuscarora Mt.
L. Simcoe
L. St. Clair
POINT PELEE NAT. PARK
CUYAHOGA VALLEY NAT. REC. AREA
TORONTO
Mississauga
Hamilton
Burlington
Oakville
Brampton
Richmond Hill
Markham
Oshawa
Kitchener
Waterloo
Guelph
Cambridge
Brantford
London
St. Catharines
Niagara Falls
Barrie
Orillia
Peterborough
Belleville
Owen Sound
Sarnia
Port Huron
DETROIT
Windsor
Chatham-Kent
Buffalo
Amherst
Rochester
Erie
CLEVELAND
Lakewood
Parma
Akron
Canton
Youngstown
Warren
PITTSBURGH
State College
Altoona
Johnstown
Projection: Bonne
ft m
6000 2000
4500 1500
3000 1000
1200 400
600 200
0 0
200 600
m ft

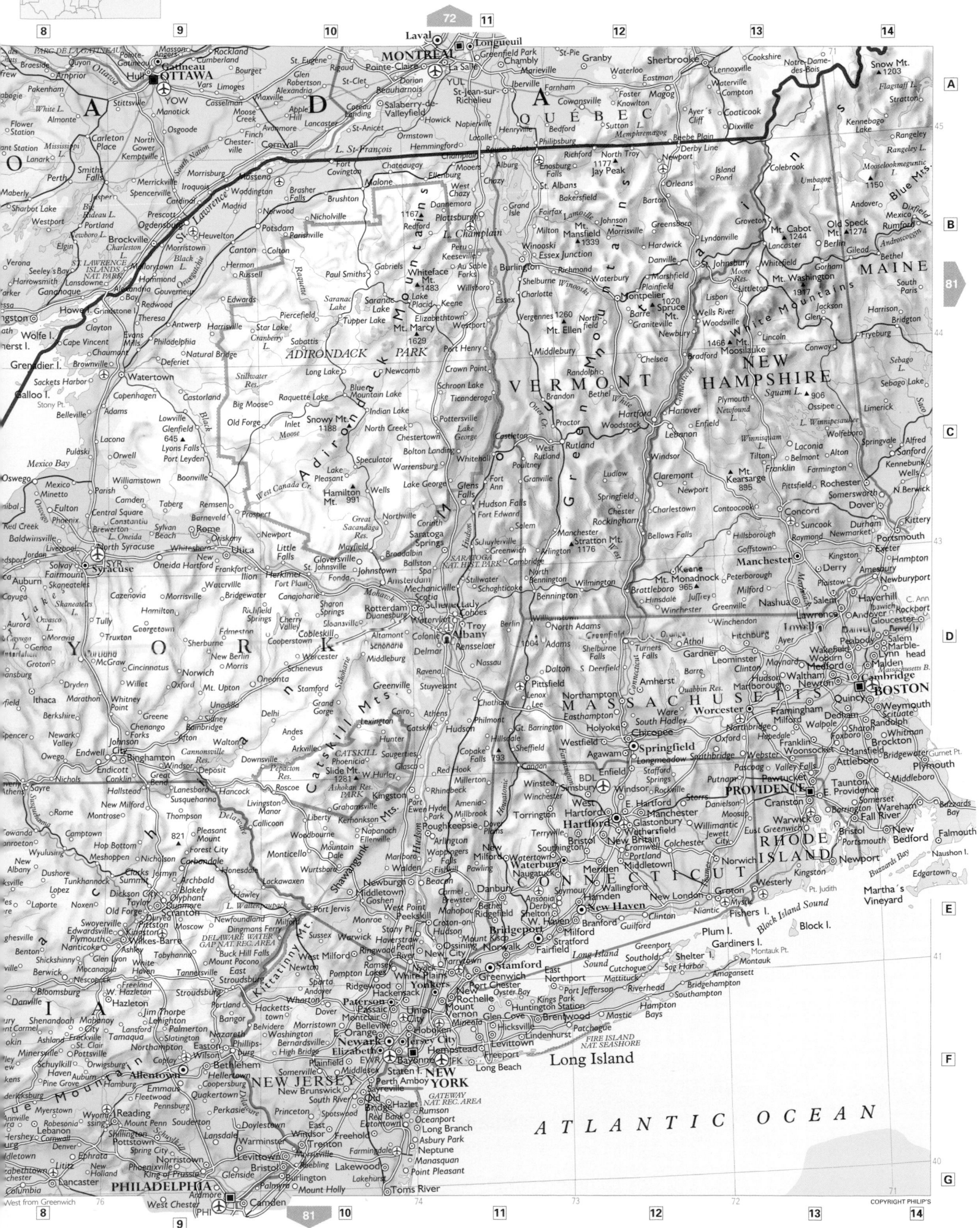

72
81
8
9
10
11
12
13
14
A
B
C
D
E
F
G
MONTREAL
OTTAWA
QUÉBEC
Sherbrooke
Laval
Longueuil
L. St-François
L. Champlain
Plattsburgh
Burlington
Montpelier
Barre
St. Johnsbury
Lancaster
Berlin
Mt. Washington
1917
White Mountains
Mt. Marcy
1629
ADIRONDACK PARK
Adirondack Mountains
Green Mountains
VERMONT
NEW HAMPSHIRE
MAINE
Watertown
Ogdensburg
Syracuse
Utica
Rome
Oneida L.
Saratoga Springs
Schenectady
Albany
Troy
Rutland
Concord
Manchester
Nashua
Portsmouth
Lowell
Lawrence
Gloucester
BOSTON
Cambridge
Worcester
MASSACHUSETTS
Springfield
Hartford
New Haven
Bridgeport
Stamford
CONNECTICUT
PROVIDENCE
RHODE ISLAND
Newport
New Bedford
Fall River
Martha´s Vineyard
Nantucket
Block Island Sound
Block I.
Long Island Sound
Long Island
FIRE ISLAND NAT. SEASHORE
YONKERS
NEW YORK
Jersey City
Newark
Elizabeth
Paterson
NEW JERSEY
Trenton
Allentown
Bethlehem
Reading
Scranton
Wilkes-Barre
Binghamton
Catskill Mts.
CATSKILL PARK
Slide Mt. 1281
Kittatinny Mt.
Shawangunk Mts.
DELAWARE WATER GAP NAT. REC. AREA
GATEWAY NAT. REC. AREA
PHILADELPHIA
Camden
ATLANTIC OCEAN
Mt. Mansfield 1339
Whiteface Mt. 1483
Snowy Mt. 1188
Mt. Monadnock 965
Stratton Mt. 1176
Mt. Cabot 1244
Mt. Moosilauke 1466
Snow Mt. 1203
West from Greenwich
COPYRIGHT PHILIP'S

1:6 700 000
km
miles
80
77
86
NEBRASKA
IOWA
KANSAS
MISSOURI
COLORADO
OKLAHOMA
ARKANSAS
NEW MEXICO
TEXAS
LOUISIANA
MEXICO
COAHUILA
CHIHUAHUA
NUEVO LEON
GULF
Rocky Mts.
Sangre de Cristo Mts.
San Juan Mts.
Sawatch Range
Smoky Hills
Llano Estacado
Edwards Plateau
Stockton Plateau
Balcones Escarpment
Ozark Plateau
Ouachita Mts.
Boston Mts.
Bolsón de Mapimí
Sacramento Mts.
Davis Mts.
Rio Grande
Rio Bravo del Norte
Red
Arkansas
Canadian
Pecos
Colorado
Brazos
Trinity
Sabine
Nueces
Cimarron
Missouri
DENVER
Boulder
Aurora
Lakewood
Colorado Springs
Pueblo
Trinidad
Raton
Santa Fe
Los Alamos
Albuquerque
Rio Rancho
Roswell
Clovis
Alamogordo
Carlsbad
Hobbs
El Paso
Lincoln
Topeka
KANSAS CITY
Independence
St. Joseph
Wichita
Hutchinson
Dodge City
Liberal
Garden City
Salina
Springfield
Joplin
Jefferson City
Columbia
Oklahoma City
Norman
Tulsa
Broken Arrow
Lawton
Enid
Muskogee
Fort Smith
Little Rock
North Little Rock
Hot Springs
Fayetteville
Amarillo
Lubbock
Midland
Odessa
Abilene
Wichita Falls
San Angelo
DALLAS
Fort Worth
Arlington
Garland
Irving
Grand Prairie
Plano
Denton
Tyler
Longview
Texarkana
Shreveport
Monroe
Alexandria
Lake Charles
Lafayette
Baton Rouge
Waco
Killeen
Temple
Austin
SAN ANTONIO
HOUSTON
Pasadena
Galveston
Beaumont
Port Arthur
Corpus Christi
Victoria
Laredo
Nuevo Laredo
McAllen
Brownsville
Matamoros
Reynosa
Harlingen
Del Rio
Ciudad Acuña
Eagle Pass
Piedras Negras
Monclova
Saltillo
MONTERREY
Torreón
Gómez Palacio
Ciudad Lerdo
Ojinaga
Big Bend Nat. Park
Padre I.
Matagorda I.
Projection: Albers' Equal Area with two standard parallels
West from Greenwich

9
10
11
12
81
13
14
15
16
17
B
C
D
E
F
G
H
J
ILLINOIS
INDIANA
OHIO
PENNSYLVANIA
MARYLAND
DELAWARE
WEST VIRGINIA
VIRGINIA
KENTUCKY
TENNESSEE
NORTH CAROLINA
SOUTH CAROLINA
GEORGIA
ALABAMA
MISSISSIPPI
FLORIDA
BAHAMAS
ATLANTIC
OCEAN
OF MEXICO
Appalachian Mts.
Cumberland Plateau
Blue Ridge
PITTSBURGH
PHILADELPHIA
BALTIMORE
WASHINGTON D.C.
COLUMBUS
CINCINNATI
INDIANAPOLIS
Louisville
Lexington
Nashville
Memphis
Knoxville
Chattanooga
Charlotte
Raleigh
Greensboro
Richmond
NORFOLK
Virginia Beach
Wilmington
Columbia
Charleston
Savannah
ATLANTA
Birmingham
Montgomery
Huntsville
Mobile
NEW ORLEANS
Jackson
Jacksonville
Tallahassee
Orlando
TAMPA
St. Petersburg
Sarasota
West Palm Beach
Fort Lauderdale
MIAMI
Key West
Florida Keys
Str. of Florida
Florida Bay
Dry Tortugas
Nassau
New Providence
Grand Bahama
Freeport
Andros I.
Great Abaco
Mississippi River Delta
10
11
12
15
88
16
COPYRIGHT PHILIP'S

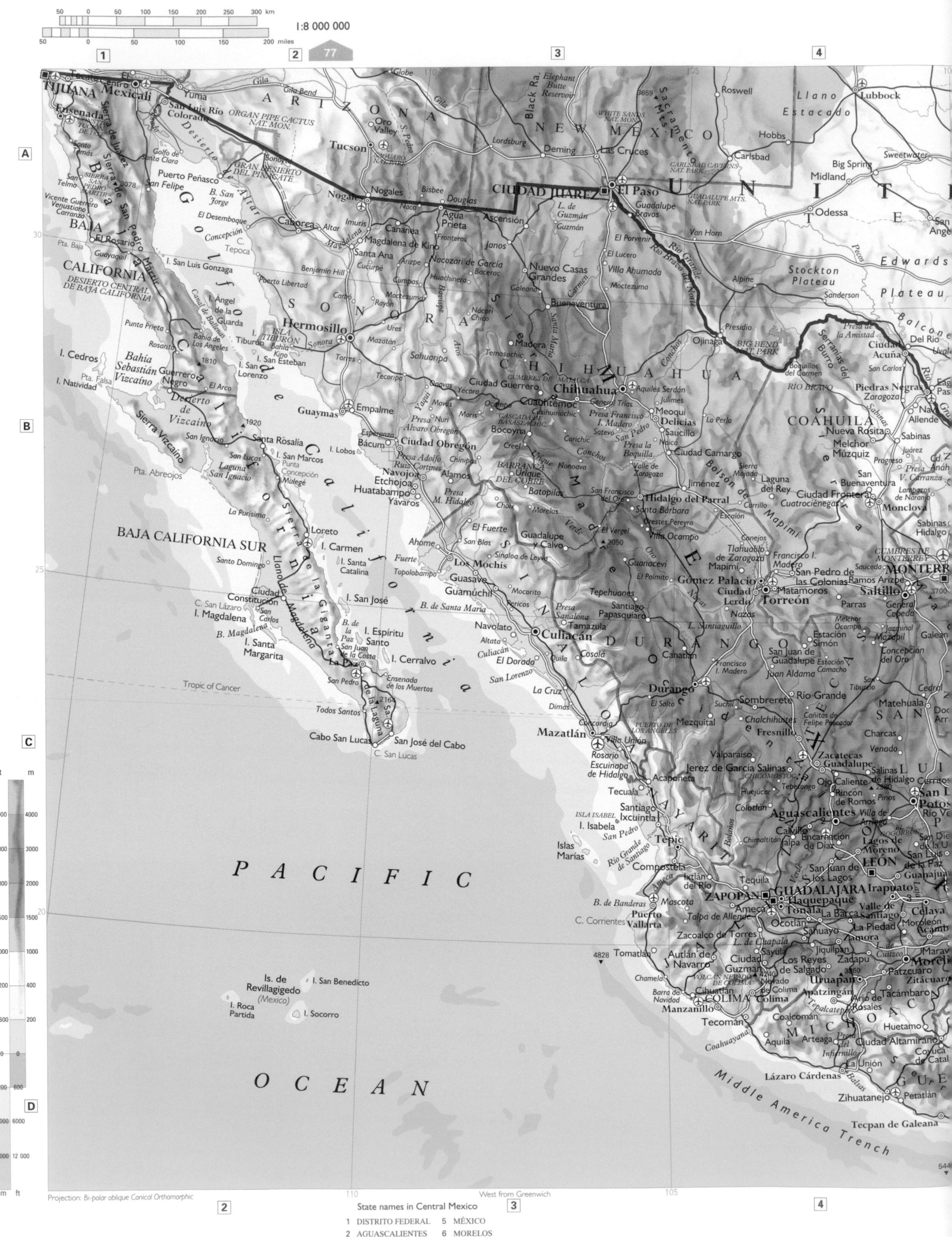

50 0 50 100 150 200 250 300 km
1:8 000 000
50 0 50 100 150 200 miles

Projection: Bi-polar oblique Conical Orthomorphic

West from Greenwich

State names in Central Mexico

1 DISTRITO FEDERAL   5 MÉXICO
2 AGUASCALIENTES   6 MORELOS
3 GUANAJUATO   7 QUERÉTARO
4 HIDALGO   8 TLAXCALA

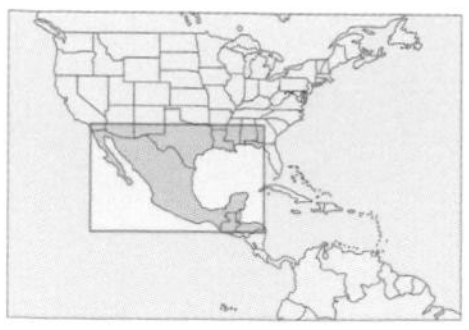

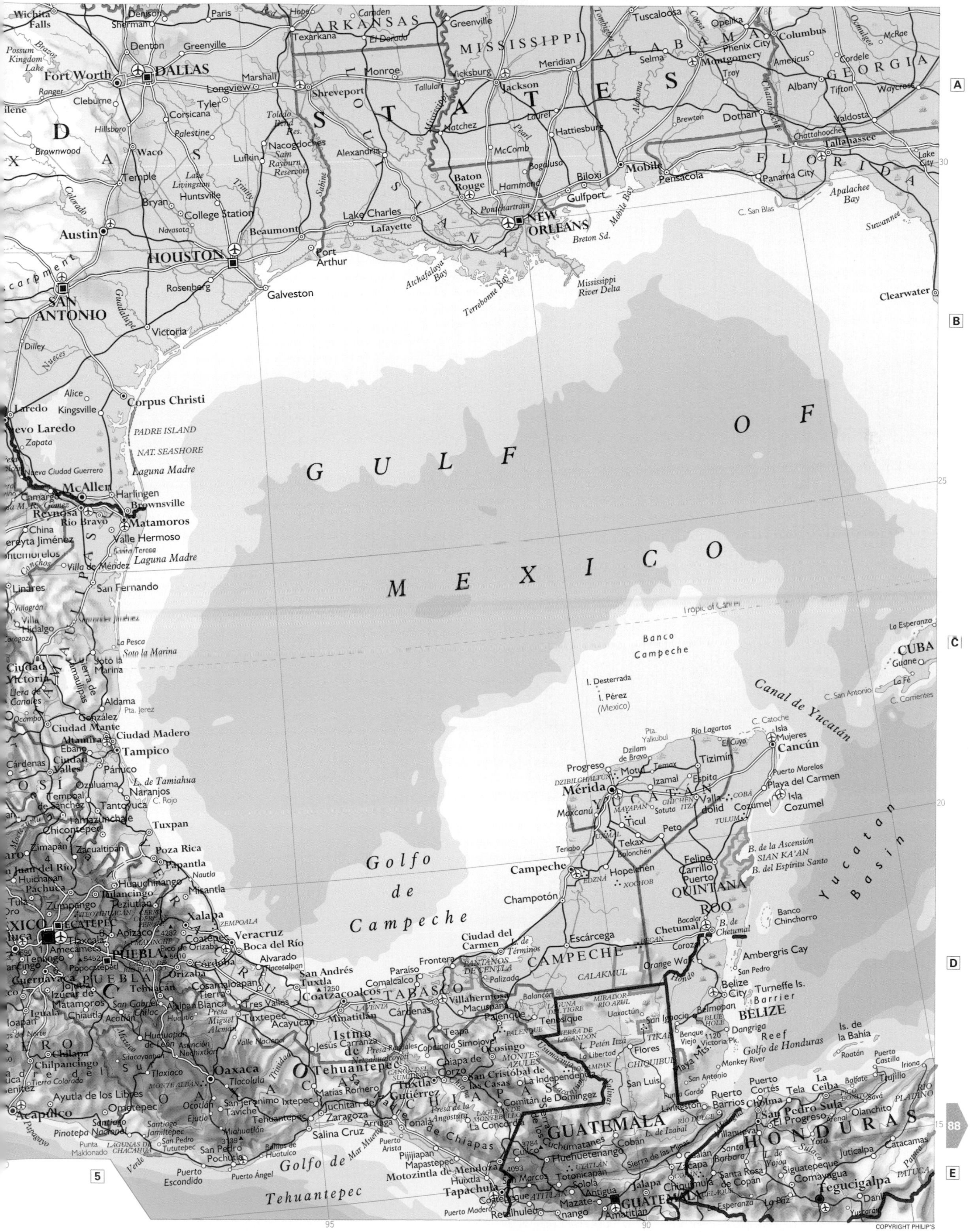

GULF OF MEXICO

UNITED STATES

TEXAS
Fort Worth
DALLAS
Denton
Greenville
Sherman
Paris
Denison
Wichita Falls
Possum Kingdom Lake
Ranger
Cleburne
Hillsboro
Brownwood
Waco
Temple
Bryan
Austin
Navasota
College Station
Huntsville
Lufkin
Nacogdoches
Tyler
Longview
Marshall
Palestine
Corsicana
San Antonio
Dilley
Victoria
Rosenberg
HOUSTON
Beaumont
Port Arthur
Galveston

ARKANSAS
Texarkana
El Dorado
Camden
Greenville
Monroe
Tallulah
Vicksburg
Natchez
MISSISSIPPI
Jackson
Meridian
Laurel
Hattiesburg
McComb
Bogalusa
Baton Rouge
Hammond
NEW ORLEANS
Lafayette
Lake Charles
Alexandria
Shreveport

ALABAMA
Tuscaloosa
Selma
Montgomery
Troy
Brewton
Dothan
Mobile
Biloxi
Gulfport
Pensacola

GEORGIA
Opelika
Phenix City
Columbus
McRae
Americus
Cordele
Albany
Tifton
Waycross
Valdosta
Tallahassee
FLORIDA
Panama City
Apalachee Bay
Lake City
Clearwater
Suwannee

Mississippi River Delta
Breton Sd.
Mobile Bay
Atchafalaya Bay
Terrebonne Bay
C. San Blas

Laredo
Nuevo Laredo
Zapata
McAllen
Reynosa
Rio Bravo
Matamoros
Harlingen
Brownsville
Valle Hermoso
Corpus Christi
Kingsville
Alice
PADRE ISLAND
NAT. SEASHORE
Laguna Madre
San Fernando
Linares
Ciudad Victoria
Soto la Marina
La Pesca
Ciudad Mante
Altamira
Tampico
Ciudad Madero
Ebano
Pánuco
Naranjos
Tuxpan
Poza Rica
Papantla
Nautla
Misantla
Veracruz
Boca del Río
Alvarado
MEXICO
PUEBLA
Orizaba
Córdoba
Coatzacoalcos
Minatitlán
Acayucan
Tres Valles
San Andrés Tuxtla
Comalcalco
Paraíso
Frontera
Ciudad del Carmen
Villahermosa
TABASCO
Cárdenas
Macuspana
Palenque
Teapa
CAMPECHE
Escárcega
Champotón
Campeche
Hopelchén
QUINTANA ROO
Chetumal
B. de Chetumal
BELIZE
Belize City
Dangriga
GUATEMALA
HONDURAS
Tegucigalpa

GULF OF MEXICO
Banco Campeche
I. Desterrada
I. Pérez (Mexico)
Tropic of Cancer
CUBA
Guane
La Fé
C. San Antonio
C. Corrientes
Canal de Yucatán
C. Catoche
Isla Mujeres
Cancún
Puerto Morelos
Playa del Carmen
Cozumel
Isla Cozumel
Progreso
Mérida
YUCATÁN
Valladolid
Tizimín
Motul
Izamal
Espita
Tulum
Felipe Carrillo Puerto
B. de la Ascensión
SIAN KA'AN
B. del Espíritu Santo
Yucatan Basin
Banco Chinchorro
Ambergris Cay
San Pedro
Turneffe Is.
Barrier Reef
Golfo de Honduras
Is. de la Bahía
Roatán
Puerto Castilla
Trujillo

Golfo de Campeche
Golfo de Tehuantepec

OAXACA
Oaxaca
CHIAPAS
Tehuantepec
Salina Cruz
Tapachula
Puerto Madero

COPYRIGHT PHILIP'S

CENTRAL AMERICA AND THE WEST INDIES

1:8 000 000

50 0 50 100 150 200 250 300 km
50 0 50 100 150 200 miles

JAMAICA
1:3 000 000

10 0 10 20 30 40 50 km
10 0 10 20 30 miles

CARIBBEAN SEA

Montego Bay, Falmouth, Runaway Bay, St. Ann's Bay, Galina Point, Port Maria, Annotto Bay, Port Antonio, Lucea, Wakefield, Ocho Rios, Dry Harbour Mountains, Moneague, Negril, Cambridge, The Cockpit Country, Mount Denham 985▲, Linstead, Spanish Town, The Blue Mountains, Blue Mountain Peak 2256▲, John Crow Mtns, Port Morant, Morant Point, South Negril Pt., Savanna-la-Mar, Black River, Maggotty, Don Figuero Mts., Mandeville, Santa Cruz Mts., May Pen, Portmore, KINGSTON, Great Pedro Bluff, Alligator Pond, Portland Bight, Portland Point, Morant Bay

GULF OF MEXICO

MEXICO · YUCATÁN · CAMPECHE · QUINTANA ROO

BELIZE · GUATEMALA · HONDURAS · EL SALVADOR · NICARAGUA · COSTA RICA · PANAMÁ

U.S.A. · MIAMI · LA HABANA (Havana) · CUBA

Cayman Islands (U.K.)

PACIFIC OCEAN

CARIBBEAN

GUADELOUPE
(Fr.)

MARTINIQUE
(Fr.)

GUADELOUPE AND MARTINIQUE
1:2 000 000

10 0 10 20 30 40 50 60 km
10 0 10 20 30 40 miles

Projection: Bi-polar oblique Conical Orthomorphic

ATLANTIC OCEAN

MAS

PUERTO RICO d
1:3 000 000

ATLANTIC OCEAN

PUERTO RICO (U.S.A.)

Pta. Aguijereada
Aguadilla
Isabela
Barceloneta
Arecibo
Manati
Vega
Baja
Bayamón
SAN JUAN
SJU
Rio Grande
Carolina
Fajardo
Dewey
Utuado
Caguas
Humacao
Naguabo
Culebra
Sierra de
Luquillo
San Sebastian
Mayagüez
Adjuntas
Cordillera Central
Cerro
1338 de Punta
Cayey
Coamo
San German
Uroyan Mts.
Yauco
Ponce
Guayama
Yabucoa
Esperanza
Vieques
Pta. Aguila
Guanica
I. Caja de Muertos

VIRGIN ISLANDS e
1:2 000 000

Rufling Pt.
The Settlement
Anegada
East Pt.

Virgin Islands (U.K.)
Great Camanoe
Virgin Is. (U.S.A.)
Jost Van Dyke
Hans Lollik I.
Guana I. 521
Beef I.
Virgin Gorda
Tortola
Road Town
Spanish Town
Cruz Bay
Charlotte Amalie
VIRGIN IS.
St. Thomas I.
St. John I.
Peter I.

ST. LUCIA f
1:2 000 000

Cap Point
Pte. Hardy
Gros Islet
Esperance Bay
Castries
Marquis
L'Anse la Raye
Canaries
Millet
Dennery
Soufrière
Mt. Gimie
950
Trou Gras Pt.
Soufrière Bay
Petit Piton 750
Micoud
Gros Piton Pt.
Grds Piton 798
Vierge Pt.
Choiseul
Laborie
Vieux Fort
ST. LUCIA
C. Moule à Chique

BARBADOS
Crabhill
North Point
Fustic
Spring Hall
Portland
Boscobelle
Speightstown
245
Belleplaine
Westmoreland
Bathsheba
BARBADOS
Alleynes Bay
Mt. Hillaby
Hillcrest
Holetown
340
Martin's Bay
Jackson
Bridgefield
Massiah Street
Black Rock
Ellerton
Six Cross Roads
Ragged Pt.
Bridgetown
Ivy
Edey
The Crane
Carlisle Bay
Distins
St. Martins
Worthing
BGI
Chancery Lane
Oistins Bay
South Point

BARBADOS g
1:2 000 000

ATLANTIC OCEAN

arthur's Town
The Bight
Cat I.
San Salvador I.
Conception I.
Rum Cay
Long I.
Clarence Town
Samana Cay
Crooked I. Passage
Albert Town
Plana Cays
Snug Corner
Mayaguana I.
Acklins I.
Mira por vos Cay
Cay Verde
Hogsty Reef
Little Inagua I.
Turks & Caicos (U.K.)
Lake Rose
INAGUA
Caicos Is.
Cockburn Town
Matthew Town
Great Inagua I.
Turks Is.
Caicos Passage
Turks Island Passage

Baracoa
Pta. de Maisí
Moa
Monte Cristi
LA ISABELA
Santiago de los Caballeros
GUANTANAMO
BAY (U.S.A.)
Cap-Haïtien
Puerto Plata
San Francisco de Macorís
Milwaukee Deep 9200
Puerto Rico Trench
Jean Rabel
Port-de-Paix
La Vega
Nagua
Samana
Virgin Gorda
Anegada
Virgin Is.
Cap-à-Foux
Fort Liberté
Cord.
3175
Sanchez
Bayamón SAN JUAN
Sombrero (U.K.)
St-Marc
Hinche
Central
Sabana de la Mar
Arecibo
Carolina
St. Thomas
Road Town
Anguilla (U.K.)
HAITI
ARMANDO
Pico Duarte
Hato Mayor
SAN JUAN
Virgin Is. (U.S.A.)
St-Martin (Fr.)
Jérémie
DOMINICAN REP.
C. Engaño
Aguadilla
Charlotte Amalie
St-Barthélemy (Fr.)
PORT
AU-PRINCE
San Juan
de Macorís
Higüey
Mayagüez
Ponce
Christiansted
St. Maarten (Neth.)
Saba (Neth.)
Dame Marie
Massif de la Hotte
2680
SIERRA DE
SANTO DOMINGO
B. de Yuma
PUERTO RICO (U.S.A.)
Frederiksted
St. Croix
St. Eustatius (Neth.)
Barbuda
Les Cayes
Aquin
Petit Goâve
Jacmel
San Cristóbal
Isla Mona (U.S.A.)
ST. KITTS & NEVIS
ANTIGUA & BARBUDA
Pédernales
Barahona
Basseterre
St. John's
Î. à Vache
Compostela
Nevis
Antigua
Pointe-à-Gravois
I. Beata
C. Beata
Redonda (U.K.)
Montserrat
Hispaniola
Antilles
GUADELOUPE (Fr.)
Le Moule
1467
La Désirade
Ste-Rose
Pointe-à-Pitre (Fr.)
Basse-Terre
Marie-Galante (Fr.)
I. des Saintes (Fr.)
Grand-Bourg
Dominica Passage
Portsmouth
144
DOMINICA
Roseau
MORNE TROIS PITONS
I. de Aves (Venezuela)
Martinique Passage
Mt. Pelée
Ste-Marie
1397
Le François
Fort-de-France
Rivière-Pilote
MARTINIQUE
St. Lucia Channel (Fr.)
Castries
950
ST. LUCIA
Soufrière
St. Vincent Passage
Soufrière 1234
St. Vincent
Speightstown
Kingstown
BARBADOS
Bridgetown
Lesser Antilles
Leeward Islands
Windward Islands
Hillsborough
Grenadines
ST. VINCENT & THE GRENADINES
St. George's
GRENADA

BEAN SEA
(CARIBBEAN SEA)

Lesser Antilles

Tobago
Scarborough
Galera Point
Port of Spain
TRINIDAD & TOBAGO
Arima
San Fernando
Serpent's Mouth

Pta. Gallinas
MACUIRA
Oranjestad
Aruba (Neth.)
Curaçao
Bonaire
Is. Las Aves (Ven.)
I. La Blanquilla (Ven.)
Is. Los Hermanos (Ven.)
Is. Los Testigos (Ven.)
C. San Román
Willemstad
NETH. ANTILLES
ARC. LOS ROQUES
Is. Los Roques (Ven.)
I. Orchila (Ven.)
NUEVA ESPARTA
I. de Margarita
Pen. de Paraguaná
Pta. Espada
Pen. de la Guajira
Punto Fijo
La Asunción
Porlamar
Dragon's Mouth
GUAJIRA
MÉDANOS DE CORO
Puerto Cumarebo
I. La Tortuga (Ven.)
LAGUNA DE LA RESTINGA
Riohacha
Golfo de Venezuela
La Vela de Coro
CERRO EL COPEY
Carupano
Santa Marta
Uribia
Punta Cardón
CUEVA DE LA QUEBRADA DEL TORO
MARACAY
Maiquetía
Pen. de Paria
TAYRONA
SA. DE SAN LUIS
FALCÓN
CARACAS
La Guaira
Cumaná
Guira
ISLA DE SALAMANCA
Mene de Mauroa
Tucacas
VARGAS
MOCHIMA
RRAN-UILLA
Ciénaga
Altagracia
Puerto Cabello
Los Teques
Río Chico
Cariaco
TURUÉPANO
TRINIDAD
Soledad
Sierra Nevada de Sta. Marta
San Rafael
Barquea
HENRI PITTIER
Higuerote
Puerto La Cruz
SUCRE
& TOBAGO
Sabanalarga
COLOMBIA
Mene Grande
San Felipe
CARABOBO
Ocumare del Tuy
Barcelona
Caripito
Baranoa
Fundación
La Concepción
Baragua
Yaracuy
VALENCIA
Villa de Cura
Maturín
MARIUSA DELTA
Calamar
Agustín Codazzi
Villa del Rosario
Santa Rita
Carora
LARA
San Juan de los Morros
Aragua de Barcelona
MONAGAS
Tucupita
MAGDALEN
Plato
MARACAIBO
Ciudad Ojeda
CERRO SARISARIÑAMA
San Carlos
Altagracia de Orituco
Santa María de Ipire
AMACURO
Zambrano
CÉSAR
Machiques
Lago de Maracaibo
Cabimas
El Tocuyo
El Guache
Acarigua
Valle de la Pascua
Anaco
Los Barrancos
ZULIA
TRUJILLO
PORTUGUESA
COJEDES
Cantaura
El Tigre
Ciudad Guayana
El Pao
Mompós
Magangue
PERIJÁ
Betijoque
Trujillo
GUÁRICO
ANZOÁTEGUI
Sierra Imataca
Simití
Valera
El Baúl
Guanare
Calabozo
Soledad
CATATUMBO-BARI
MÉRIDA
Barinas
 sice
Majagual
El Banco
San Carlos del Zulia
San Fernando de Apure
Ciudad Bolívar
Caucasia
Santa Bárbara
MÉRIDA
BARINAS
Libertad
Embalse de Guri
Ayapel
Cúcuta
SANTANDER
Cord.
5800
TÁCHIRA
Bruzual
Puerto de Nutrias
San Fernando
de Apure
Calcara
El Callao
Tumeremo
VENEZUELA
Achaguas
Apure
Guasipati
Orinoco
Mapire

West from Greenwich

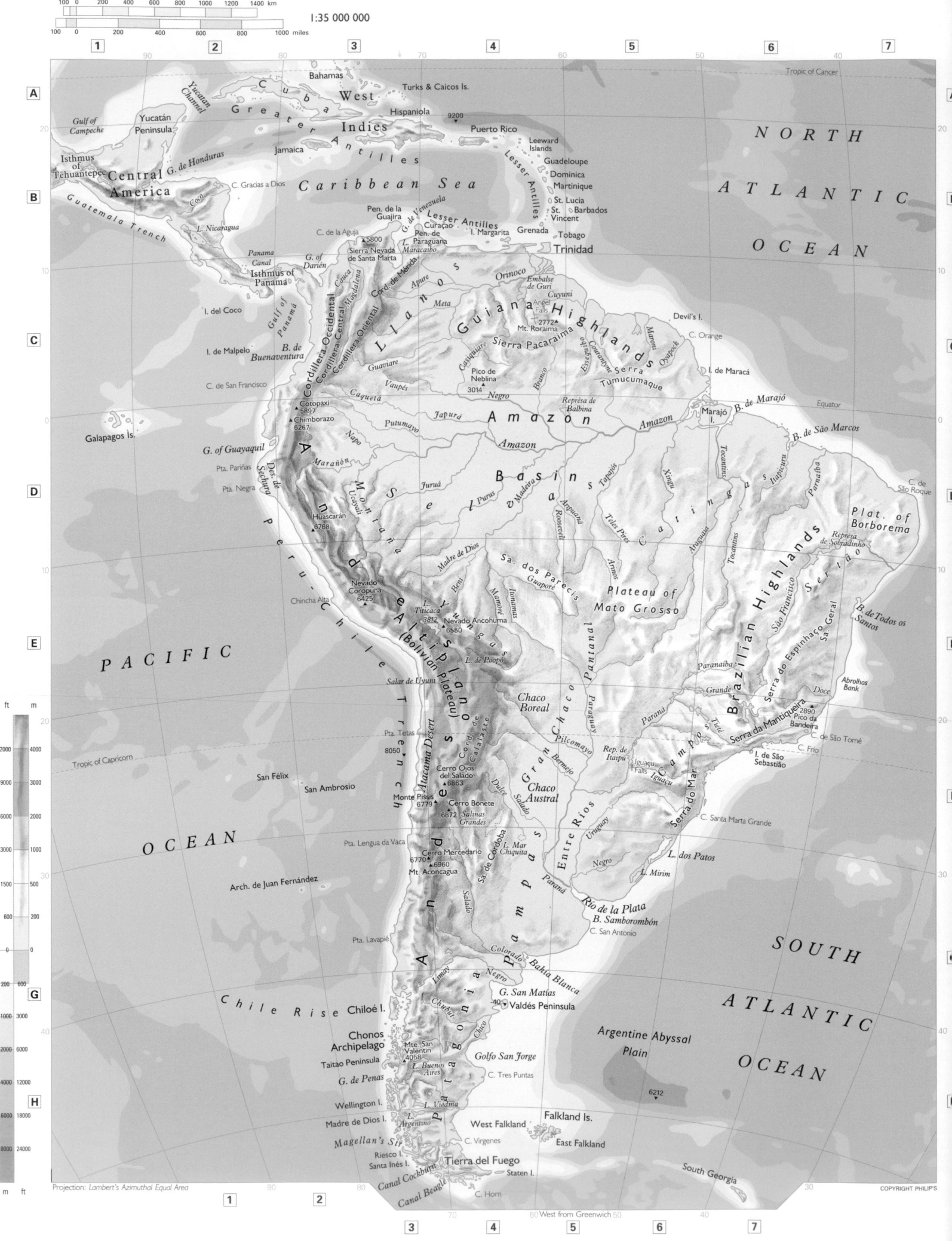

Projection: Lambert's Azimuthal Equal Area

COPYRIGHT PHILIP'S

1:35 000 000

100   0   200   400   600   800   1000   1200   1400 km

100   0   200   400   600   800   1000 miles

North Atlantic Ocean

Tropic of Cancer

Havana   BAHAMAS   Turks & Caicos Is.
CUBA   (U.K.)

Cayman Is.   HAITI   DOMINICAN
(U.K.)   REP.   San Juan   Virgin Is. (U.S.A. - U.K.)
JAMAICA   Port-au-   Santo   PUERTO   Anguilla (U.K.)
Kingston   Prince   Domingo   RICO   St. Martin (Fr. - Neth.)
                            (U.S.A.)   ANTIGUA &
MEXICO   BARBUDA
BELIZE   Basse-Terre   GUADELOUPE
GUATEMALA   DOMINICA   (Fr.)
HONDURAS   Fort-de-France   MARTINIQUE
Guatemala   Tegucigalpa   Castries   (Fr.)
San Salvador   ST. VINCENT   ST. LUCIA
EL SALVADOR   NICARAGUA   Kingstown   BARBADOS
Managua   GRENADA   Bridgetown
COSTA   San José   Aruba   St. George's
RICA   San José   (Neth.)   NETH.   Port of   TRINIDAD &
PANAMA   G. of   Oranjestad ANTILLES Spain   TOBAGO
Darién   Willemstad
Caribbean Sea   C. de
I. del Coco   Barranquilla   la Aguja   Maracaibo   Caracas
(Costa Rica)   Cartagena   Barquisimeto   Valencia
Gulf of Panama   Cúcuta   San Cristóbal
I. de Malpelo   Medellín   San   VENEZUELA   Ciudad Guayana   Georgetown
(Colombia)   Bucaramanga   GUYANA   Paramaribo
        BOGOTÁ   SURINAME   Cayenne
        Cali   RORAIMA   FRENCH   C. Orange
        COLOMBIA   GUIANA
Galapagos Is.   Quito   AMAPÁ   Equator
(Ecuador)   ECUADOR   Marajó I.   Belém
    Guayaquil   Iquitos   Amazon   Manaus   Santarém   São Luís   Fortaleza
G. of Guayaquil   AMAZONAS   PARÁ   C. de
    Chiclayo   Amazon   MARANHÃO   Teresina   São Roque
    Trujillo   CEARÁ   Natal
    Chimbote   ACRE   Pôrto Velho   PIAUÍ
    PERU   RONDÔNIA   PERNAMBUCO   Recife
    Callao   LIMA   BRAZIL   TOCANTINS   BAHÍA   Maceió
                MATO GROSSO   Aracaju
            Cuzco   GOIÁS   São Francisco
            BOLIVIA   Cuiabá   DIS. FED.   Brasília   Salvador
        Arequipa   La Paz   Cochabamba   Goiânia   MINAS GERAIS
                Santa Cruz   Belo
            Sucre   Horizonte
    Iquique   MATO GROSSO   Ribeirão   Juiz   ESPÍRITO
                        DO SUL   Prêto   de Fora   SANTO
    Antofagasta   PARAGUAY   SÃO PAULO   Campinas   Vitória
                        Pilcomayo   PARANÁ   SÃO   Campos
        Salta   Asunción   PAULO   RIO DE
    San Miguel   Curitiba   Santos   JANEIRO
    de Tucumán   Resistencia   Corrientes   SANTA CATARINA   Niterói
    San Félix   ARGENTINA   Uruguay
    (Chile)   Córdoba   Santa Fe   RIO GRANDE   Pôrto Alegre
    San Ambrosio   San Juan   Paraná   DO SUL
    (Chile)   Viña del Mar   Rosario   URUGUAY   Pelotas
Arch. de Juan Fernández   Valparaíso   Mendoza
    (Chile)   SANTIAGO   BUENOS AIRES   Montevideo
        Talca   La Plata   Rio de la Plata
    Concepción   Bahía   Mar del Plata
        Valdivia   Colorado   Blanca
    Puerto Montt   Negro   Viedma

Tropic of Capricorn

PACIFIC OCEAN

Comodoro Rivadavia
Gulf of San Jorge

Gulf of Penas   SOUTH
ATLANTIC
OCEAN
    West Falkland   FALKLAND IS.
        (U.K.)
    Magellan's Str.   Stanley
            East Falkland
    Punta Arenas
    Tierra del Fuego
        South Georgia
        (U.K.)
    C. Horn

Projection: Lambert's Azimuthal Equal Area   West from Greenwich   COPYRIGHT PHILIP'S

■ LIMA   Capital Cities

1:16 000 000

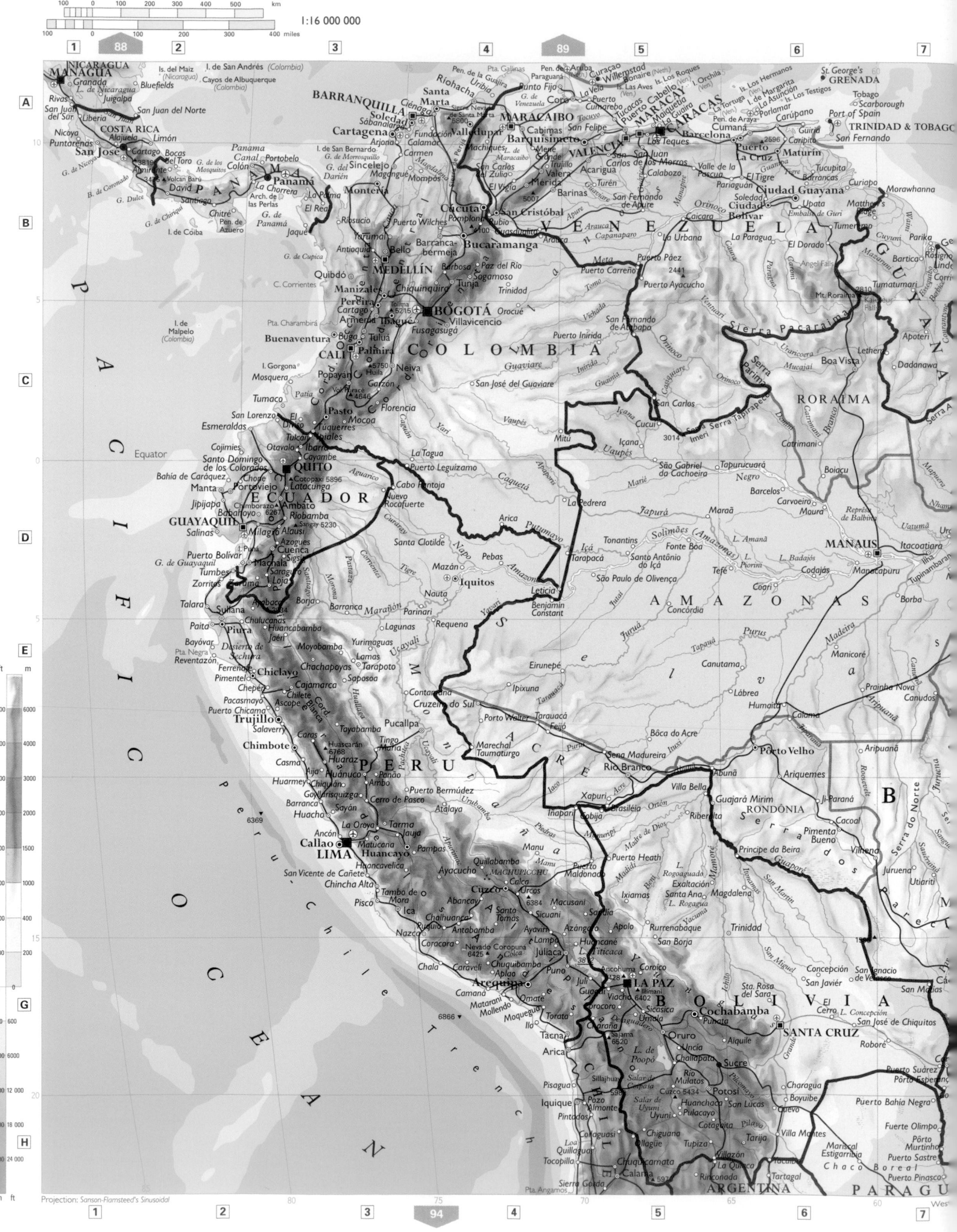

Projection: Sanson-Flamsteed's Sinusoidal

ATLANTIC

OCEAN

TRINIDAD AND TOBAGO
1:2 500 000

10   0   10   20   30   40   50 km

10   0   10   20   30 miles

Tobago
Charlotteville   North Pt.
Castara   565 ▲   Little
Plymouth   Main Ridge   Tobago
Bucco Reef   Roxborough
Crown Pt.   Scarborough
Rocky Bay

North Pt.

VENEZUELA
Pen. de
Paria   Macuro
Güiria

Corozal
Monos   Maraval
Dragon's Mouths   Chupara Pt.   Blanchisseuse   Sans Souci
La Vache Pt.   Matelot   Toco
Village   Northern Range   Redhead
936 ▲ Mt. Aripo   Salybia
Port of Spain   Tunapuna   Valencia   Galera Pt.
San Juan   Arima   Gugico   Matura
Chaguanas   Carenage   Sangre Grande   Bay
Couva   Talparo   Upper Manzanilla
Point Lisas   Cocos
Otaheite Bay   Gasparillo   Narival   Bay
San Fernando   Brighton   Rio Claro   Swamp   Guataro Pt.
Guapo Bay   La Brea   Pitch   Pierreville
Point Fortin   Lake   Princes Town   Mayaro Bay
Cedros Bay   Penal   Basse Terre   Guayaguayare
Bonasse   Palo Seco   Siparia   304 ▲   Galeota Pt.
Icacos Pt.   La Lune   Moruga   Trinity Hills

ATLANTIC
OCEAN
Trinidad

Golfo de Paria

Serpent's Mouth
VENEZUELA   Pta. Bombedor

West from Greenwich

São Pedro &
São Paulo
(Braz.)

Equator

● Fernando de Noronha
(Braz.)

Rocas

6059 ▼

27

Trindade
(Braz.)

1:8 000 000

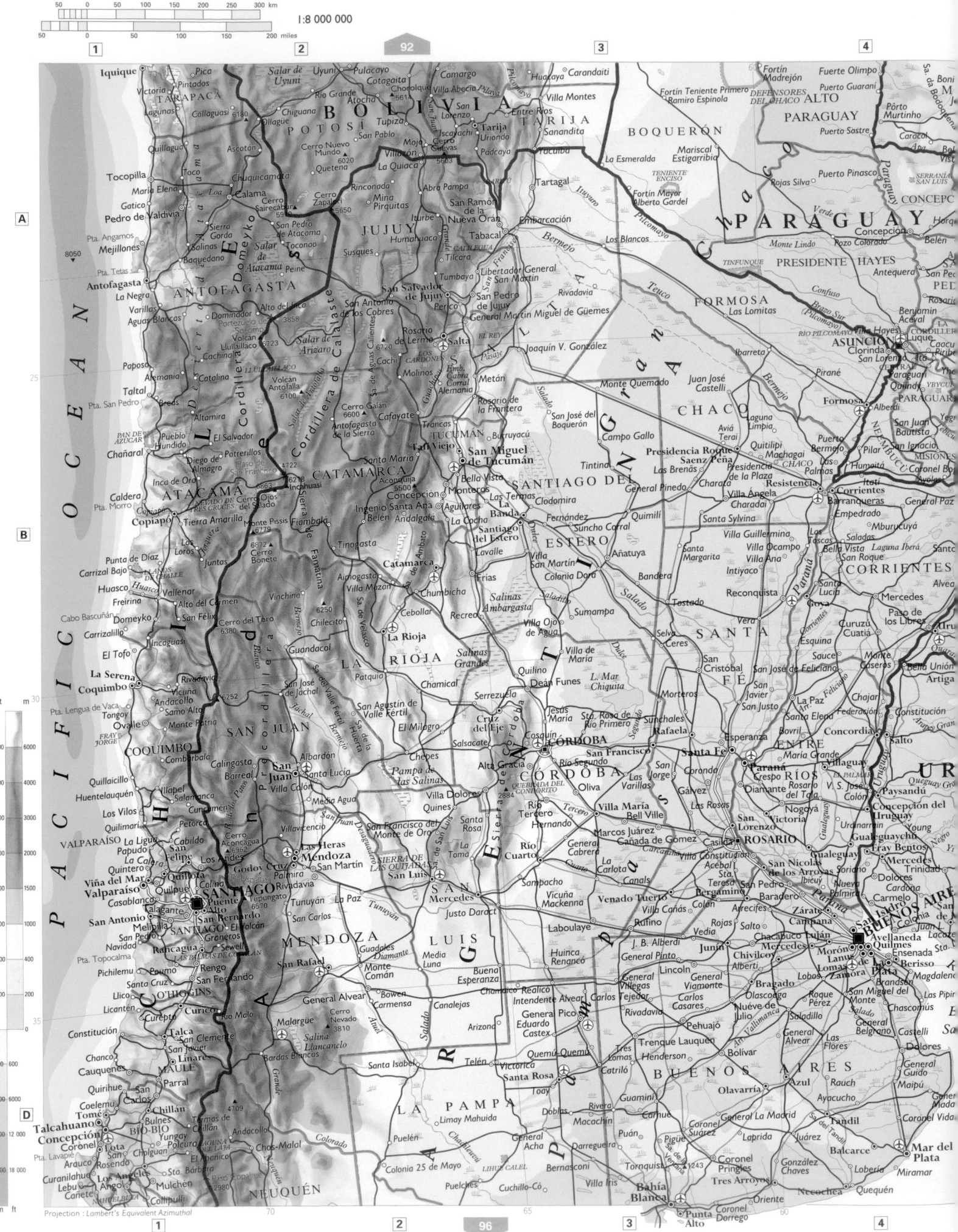

Projection : Lambert's Equivalent Azimuthal

93
5
6
7
A
B
C
D
BELO HORIZONTE
Nova Lima
Itabirito
Vitória
Vila Velha
Guarapari
Cachoeiro de Itapemirim
Campos
Cabo de São Tomé
Três Lagoas
Andradina
Araçatuba
Birigui
Presidente Prudente
Marília
Bauru
Jaú
Rio Claro
Limeira
CAMPINAS
Jundiaí
Sorocaba
SÃO PAULO
Guarulhos
Santo André
SANTOS
Moji das Cruzes
Taubaté
São José dos Campos
Ribeirão Prêto
Juiz de Fora
Volta Redonda
Barra Mansa
Petrópolis
Nova Iguaçu
Duque de Caxias
São Gonçalo
Niterói
RIO DE JANEIRO
Cabo Frio
Angra dos Reis
Ilha Grande
Tropic of Capricorn
Ilha de São Sebastião
Guarujá
Itanhaém
Registro
Iguape
Ilha Comprida
Ilha do Cardoso
Londrina
Maringá
Apucarana
Arapongas
Umuarama
Cascavel
Guarapuava
Ponta Grossa
CURITIBA
Paranaguá
Joinville
São Francisco do Sul
Itajaí
Blumenau
Brusque
Florianópolis
Ilha de Santa Catarina
Lajes
Laguna
Tubarão
Criciúma
Araranguá
Cabo Santa Marta Grande
Torres
Caxias do Sul
Nôvo Hamburgo
São Leopoldo
PORTO ALEGRE
Passo Fundo
Santa Maria
Pelotas
Rio Grande
São José do Norte
Lagoa dos Patos
Lagoa Mirim
Lagoa Mangueira
Bagé
Jaguarão
Santa Vitória do Palmar
Chuy
Rocha
Maldonado
San Carlos
MONTEVIDEO
Foz do Iguaçu
Ciudad del Este
Encarnación
Posadas
Pedro Juan Caballero
Dourados
BRAZIL
PARANÁ
SANTA CATARINA
RIO GRANDE DO SUL
SÃO PAULO
MISIONES
URUGUAY
ATLANTIC OCEAN
5304
55
50
45
40
West from Greenwich
25
30
35

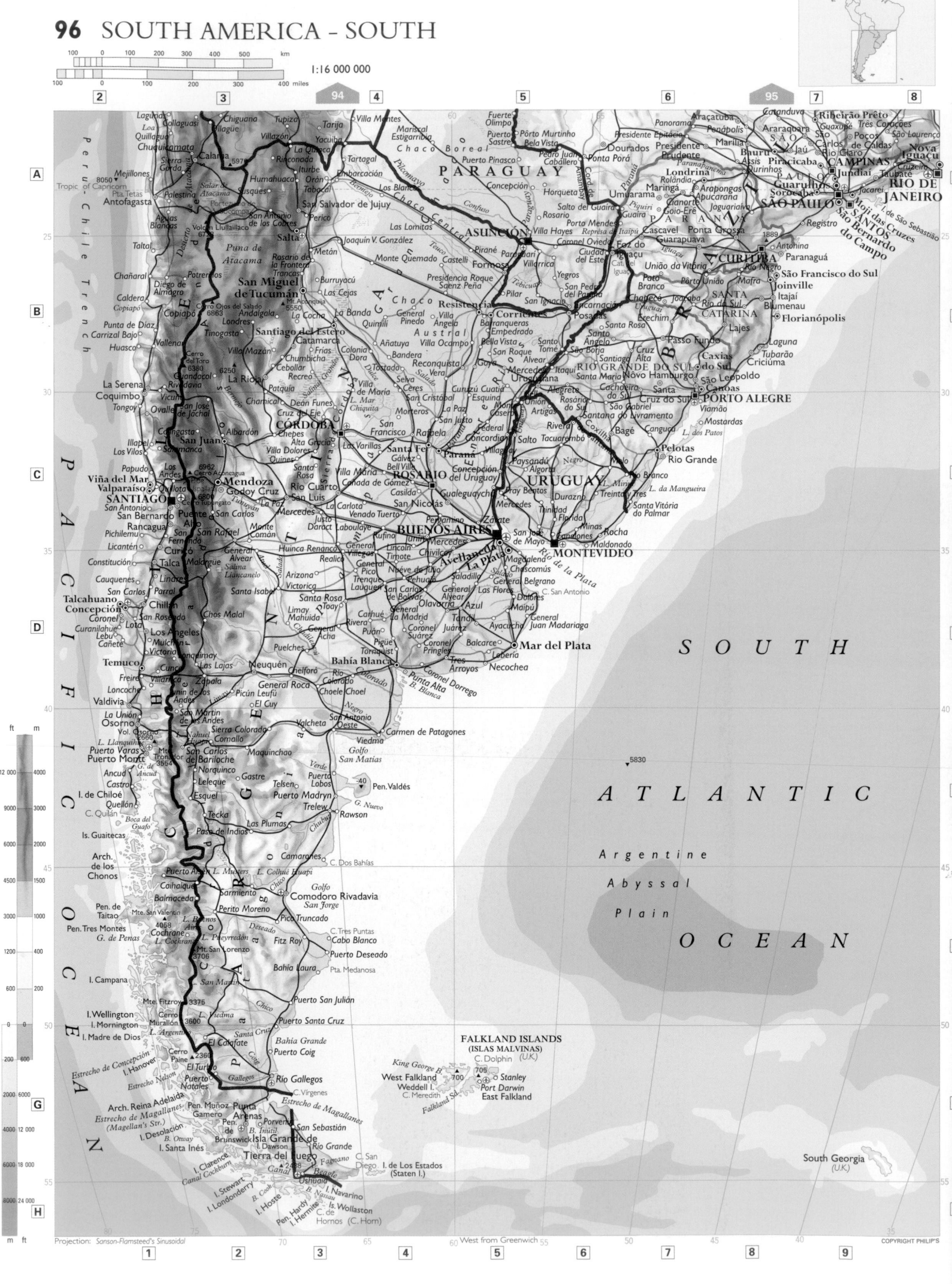

1:16 000 000

SOUTH

ATLANTIC

Argentine

Abyssal

Plain

OCEAN

PACIFIC OCEAN

PARAGUAY

PARANÁ

SÃO PAULO

RIO GRANDE DO SUL

SANTA CATARINA

URUGUAY

FALKLAND ISLANDS
(ISLAS MALVINAS)
(U.K.)

West Falkland
East Falkland
Stanley
Port Darwin

South Georgia
(U.K.)

Projection: Sanson-Flamsteed's Sinusoidal

West from Greenwich

COPYRIGHT PHILIP'S

INDEX TO WORLD MAPS

The index contains the names of all the principal places and features shown on the World Maps. Each name is followed by an additional entry in italics giving the country or region within which it is located. The alphabetical order of names composed of two or more words is governed primarily by the first word, then by the second, and then by the country or region name that follows. This is an example of the rule:

Mīr Kūh *Iran*	26°22N 58°55E	**45** E8
Mīr Shahdād *Iran*	26°15N 58°29E	**45** E8
Mira *Italy*	45°26N 12°8E	**22** B5
Mira por vos Cay *Bahamas*	22°9N 74°30W	**89** B5

Physical features composed of a proper name (Erie) and a description (Lake) are positioned alphabetically by the proper name. The description is positioned after the proper name and is usually abbreviated:

Erie, L. *N. Amer.*	42°15N 81°0W	**82** D4

Where a description forms part of a settlement or administrative name, however, it is always written in full and put in its true alphabetical position:

Mount Morris *U.S.A.*	42°44N 77°52W	**82** D7

Names beginning with M' and Mc are indexed as if they were spelled Mac. Names beginning St. are alphabetized under Saint, but Sankt, Sint, Sant', Santa and San are all spelt in full and are alphabetized accordingly. If the same place name occurs two or more times in the index and all are in the same country, each is followed by the name of the administrative subdivision in which it is located.

The geographical co-ordinates which follow each name in the index give the latitude and longitude of each place. The first co-ordinate indicates latitude – the distance north or south of the Equator. The second co-ordinate indicates longitude – the distance east or west of the Greenwich Meridian. Both latitude and longitude are measured in degrees and minutes (there are 60 minutes in a degree).

The latitude is followed by N(orth) or S(outh) and the longitude by E(ast) or W(est).

The number in bold type which follows the geographical co-ordinates refers to the number of the map page where that feature or place will be found. This is usually the largest scale at which the place or feature appears.

The letter and figure that are immediately after the page number give the grid square on the map page, within which the feature is situated. The letter represents the latitude and the figure the longitude. A lower-case letter immediately after the page number refers to an inset map on that page.

In some cases the feature itself may fall within the specified square, while the name is outside. This is usually the case only with features that are larger than a grid square.

Rivers are indexed to their mouths or confluences, and carry the symbol ➤ after their names. The following symbols are also used in the index: ■ country, ☑ overseas territory or dependency, □ first-order administrative area, △ national park, ⌂ other park (provincial park, nature reserve or game reserve), ✈ (LHR) principal airport (and location identifier).

Abbreviations used in the index

A.C.T. – Australian Capital Territory
A.R. – Autonomous Region
Afghan – Afghanistan
Afr. – Africa
Ala. – Alabama
Alta. – Alberta
Amer. – America(n)
Ant. – Antilles
Arch. – Archipelago
Ariz. – Arizona
Ark. – Arkansas
Atl. Oc. – Atlantic Ocean
B. – Baie, Bahía, Bay, Bucht, Bugt
B.C. – British Columbia
Bangla. – Bangladesh
Barr. – Barrage
Bos.-H. – Bosnia-Herzegovina
C. – Cabo, Cap, Cape, Coast
C.A.R. – Central African Republic
C. Prov. – Cape Province
Calif. – California
Cat. – Catarata
Cent. – Central
Chan. – Channel
Colo. – Colorado
Conn. – Connecticut
Cord. – Cordillera
Cr. – Creek
Czech. – Czech Republic
D.C. – District of Columbia
Del. – Delaware
Dem. – Democratic
Dep. – Dependency
Des. – Desert
Dét. – Détroit
Dist. – District
Dj. – Djebel
Dom. Rep. – Dominican Republic

E. – East
El Salv. – El Salvador
Eq. Guin. – Equatorial Guinea
Est. – Estrecho
Falk. Is. – Falkland Is.
Fd. – Fjord
Fla. – Florida
Fr. – French
G. – Golfe, Golfo, Gulf, Guba, Gebel
Ga. – Georgia
Gt. – Great, Greater
Guinea-Biss. – Guinea-Bissau
H.K. – Hong Kong
H.P. – Himachal Pradesh
Hants. – Hampshire
Harb. – Harbor, Harbour
Hd. – Head
Hts. – Heights
I.(s). – Île, Ilha, Insel, Isla, Island, Isle
Ill. – Illinois
Ind. – Indiana
Ind. Oc. – Indian Ocean
Ivory C. – Ivory Coast
J. – Jabal, Jebel
Jaz. – Jazīrah
Junc. – Junction
K. – Kap, Kapp
Kans. – Kansas
Kep. – Kepulauan
Ky. – Kentucky
L. – Lac, Lacul, Lago, Lagoa, Lake, Limni, Loch, Lough
La. – Louisiana
Ld. – Land
Liech. – Liechtenstein
Lux. – Luxembourg
Mad. P. – Madhya Pradesh
Madag. – Madagascar
Man. – Manitoba
Mass. – Massachusetts

Md. – Maryland
Me. – Maine
Medit. S. – Mediterranean Sea
Mich. – Michigan
Minn. – Minnesota
Miss. – Mississippi
Mo. – Missouri
Mont. – Montana
Mozam. – Mozambique
Mt.(s) – Mont, Montaña, Mountain
Mte. – Monte
Mti. – Monti
N. – Nord, Norte, North, Northern, Nouveau, Nahal, Nahr
N.B. – New Brunswick
N.C. – North Carolina
N. Cal. – New Caledonia
N. Dak. – North Dakota
N.H. – New Hampshire
N.I. – North Island
N.J. – New Jersey
N. Mex. – New Mexico
N.S. – Nova Scotia
N.S.W. – New South Wales
N.W.T. – North West Territory
N.Y. – New York
N.Z. – New Zealand
Nac. – Nacional
Nat. – National
Nebr. – Nebraska
Neths. – Netherlands
Nev. – Nevada
Nfld & L. – Newfoundland and Labrador
Nic. – Nicaragua
O. – Oued, Ouadi
Occ. – Occidentale
Okla. – Oklahoma
Ont. – Ontario
Or. – Orientale

Oreg. – Oregon
Os. – Ostrov
Oz. – Ozero
P. – Pass, Passo, Pasul, Pulau
P.E.I. – Prince Edward Island
Pa. – Pennsylvania
Pac. Oc. – Pacific Ocean
Papua N.G. – Papua New Guinea
Pass. – Passage
Peg. – Pegunungan
Pen. – Peninsula, Péninsule
Phil. – Philippines
Pk. – Peak
Plat. – Plateau
Prov. – Province, Provincial
Pt. – Point
Pta. – Ponta, Punta
Pte. – Pointe
Qué. – Québec
Queens. – Queensland
R. – Rio, River
R.I. – Rhode Island
Ra. – Range
Raj. – Rajasthan
Recr. – Recreational, Récréatif
Reg. – Region
Rep. – Republic
Res. – Reserve, Reservoir
Rhld-Pfz. – Rheinland-Pfalz
S. – South, Southern, Sur
Si. Arabia – Saudi Arabia
S.C. – South Carolina
S. Dak. – South Dakota
S.I. – South Island
S. Leone – Sierra Leone
Sa. – Serra, Sierra
Sask. – Saskatchewan
Scot. – Scotland
Sd. – Sound
Sev. – Severnaya
Sib. – Siberia

Sprs. – Springs
St. – Saint
Sta. – Santa
Ste. – Sainte
Sto. – Santo
Str. – Strait, Stretto
Switz. – Switzerland
Tas. – Tasmania
Tenn. – Tennessee
Terr. – Territory, Territoire
Tex. – Texas
Tg. – Tanjung
Trin. & Tob. – Trinidad & Tobago
U.A.E. – United Arab Emirates
U.K. – United Kingdom
U.S.A. – United States of America
Ut. P. – Uttar Pradesh
Va. – Virginia
Vdkhr. – Vodokhranilishche
Vdskh. – Vodoskhovyshche
Vf. – Vírful
Vic. – Victoria
Vol. – Volcano
Vt. – Vermont
W. – Wadi, West
W. Va. – West Virginia
Wall. & F. Is. – Wallis and Futuna Is.
Wash. – Washington
Wis. – Wisconsin
Wlkp. – Wielkopolski
Wyo. – Wyoming
Yorks. – Yorkshire

A

A Coruña *Spain* 43°20N 8°25W **21** A1
A Estrada *Spain* 42°43N 8°27W **21** A1
A Fonsagrada *Spain* 43°8N 7°4W **21** A2
Aabenraa *Denmark* 55°3N 9°25E **9** J13
Aachen *Germany* 50°45N 6°6E **16** C4
Aalborg *Denmark* 57°2N 9°54E **9** H13
Aalen *Germany* 48°51N 10°6E **16** D6
Aalst *Belgium* 50°56N 4°2E **15** D4
Aalten *Neths.* 51°56N 6°35E **15** C6
Aalter *Belgium* 51°5N 3°28E **15** C3
Äänekoski *Finland* 62°36N 25°44E **8** E21
Aarau *Switz.* 47°23N 8°4E **20** C8
Aare → *Switz.* 47°33N 8°14E **20** C8
Aarhus = Århus *Denmark* 56°8N 10°11E **9** H14
Aarschot *Belgium* 50°59N 4°49E **15** D4
Aba *Dem. Rep. of the Congo* 3°58N 30°17E **54** B3
Aba *Nigeria* 5°10N 7°19E **50** G7
Abaco I. *Bahamas* 26°25N 77°10W **88** A4
Ābādān *Iran* 30°22N 48°20E **45** D6
Ābādeh *Iran* 31°8N 52°40E **45** D7
Abadla *Algeria* 31°2N 2°45W **50** B5
Abaetetuba *Brazil* 1°40S 48°50W **93** D9
Abagnar Qi *China* 43°52N 116°2E **34** C9
Abah, Tanjung *Indonesia* 8°46S 115°38E **37** K18
Abai *Paraguay* 25°58S 55°54W **95** B4
Abakan *Russia* 53°40N 91°10E **29** D10
Abancay *Peru* 13°35S 72°55W **92** F4
Abariringa *Kiribati* 2°50S 171°40W **64** H10
Abarqū *Iran* 31°10N 53°20E **45** D7
Abashiri *Japan* 44°0N 144°15E **30** B12
Abashiri-Wan *Japan* 44°0N 144°30E **30** C12
Ābay = Nîl el Azraq → *Sudan* 15°38N 32°31E **51** E12
Abay *Kazakhstan* 49°38N 72°53E **28** E8
Abaya, L. *Ethiopia* 6°30N 37°50E **47** F2
Abaza *Russia* 52°39N 90°6E **28** D9
'Abbāsābād *Iran* 33°34N 58°23E **45** C8
Abbay = Nîl el Azraq → *Sudan* 15°38N 32°31E **51** E12
Abbaye, Pt. *U.S.A.* 46°58N 88°8W **80** B9
Abbé, L. *Ethiopia* 11°8N 41°47E **47** E3
Abbeville *France* 50°6N 1°49E **20** A4
Abbeville *Ala., U.S.A.* 31°34N 85°15W **85** F12
Abbeville *La., U.S.A.* 29°58N 92°8W **84** G8
Abbeville *S.C., U.S.A.* 34°11N 82°23W **85** D13
Abbeyfeale *Ireland* 52°23N 9°18W **10** D2
Abbot Ice Shelf *Antarctica* 73°0S 92°0W **5** D16
Abbotsford *Canada* 49°5N 122°20W **70** D4
Abbottabad *Pakistan* 34°10N 73°15E **42** B5
ABC Islands = Netherlands Antilles ☒ *W. Indies* 12°15N 69°0W **92** A5
Abd al Kūrī *Yemen* 12°5N 52°20E **47** E5
Ābdar *Iran* 30°16N 55°19E **45** D7
'Abdolābād *Iran* 34°12N 56°30E **45** C8
Abdulpur *Bangla.* 24°15N 88°59E **43** G13
Abéché *Chad* 13°50N 20°35E **51** F10
Abel Tasman △ *N.Z.* 40°59S 173°3E **59** D4
Abengourou *Ivory C.* 6°42N 3°27W **50** G5
Åbenrå = Aabenraa *Denmark* 55°3N 9°25E **9** J13
Abeokuta *Nigeria* 7°3N 3°19E **50** G6
Aber *Uganda* 2°12N 32°25E **54** B3
Aberaeron *U.K.* 52°15N 4°15W **13** E3
Aberayron = Aberaeron *U.K.* 52°15N 4°15W **13** E3
Aberchirder *U.K.* 57°34N 2°37W **11** D6
Abercorn *Australia* 25°12S 151°5E **63** D5
Aberdare *U.K.* 51°43N 3°27W **13** F4
Aberdare △ *Kenya* 0°22S 36°44E **54** C4
Aberdare Ra. *Kenya* 0°15S 36°50E **54** C4
Aberdeen *Australia* 32°9S 150°56E **63** E5
Aberdeen *Canada* 52°20N 106°8W **71** C7
Aberdeen *China* 22°14N 114°8E **33** G11
Aberdeen *S. Africa* 32°28S 24°2E **56** E3
Aberdeen *U.K.* 57°9N 2°5W **11** D6
Aberdeen *Ala., U.S.A.* 33°49N 88°33W **85** E10
Aberdeen *Idaho, U.S.A.* 42°57N 112°50W **76** E7
Aberdeen *Md., U.S.A.* 39°31N 76°10W **81** F15
Aberdeen *S. Dak., U.S.A.* 45°28N 98°29W **80** C4
Aberdeen *Wash., U.S.A.* 46°59N 123°50W **78** D3
Aberdeen, City of □ *U.K.* 57°10N 2°10W **11** D6
Aberdeenshire □ *U.K.* 57°17N 2°36W **11** D6
Aberdovey = Aberdyfi *U.K.* 52°33N 4°3W **13** E3
Aberdyfi *U.K.* 52°33N 4°3W **13** E3
Aberfeldy *U.K.* 56°37N 3°51W **11** E5
Aberfoyle *U.K.* 56°11N 4°23W **11** E4
Abergavenny *U.K.* 51°49N 3°1W **13** F4
Abergele *U.K.* 53°17N 3°35W **12** D4
Abernathy *U.S.A.* 33°50N 101°51W **84** E4
Abert, L. *U.S.A.* 42°38N 120°14W **76** E3
Aberystwyth *U.K.* 52°25N 4°5W **13** E3
Abhā *Si. Arabia* 18°0N 42°34E **47** D3
Abhar *Iran* 36°9N 49°13E **45** B6
Abhayapuri *India* 26°24N 90°38E **43** F14
Abidjan *Ivory C.* 5°26N 3°58W **50** G5
Abilene *Kans., U.S.A.* 38°55N 97°13W **80** F5
Abilene *Tex., U.S.A.* 32°28N 99°43W **84** E5
Abingdon *U.K.* 51°40N 1°17W **13** F6
Abingdon *U.S.A.* 36°43N 81°59W **81** G13
Abington Reef *Australia* 18°0S 149°35E **62** B4
Abitau → *Canada* 59°53N 109°3W **71** B7
Abitibi → *Canada* 51°3N 80°55W **72** B3
Abitibi, L. *Canada* 48°40N 79°40W **72** C4
Abkhaz Republic = Abkhazia □ *Georgia* 43°12N 41°5E **19** F7
Abkhazia □ *Georgia* 43°12N 41°5E **19** F7
Abminga *Australia* 26°8S 134°51E **63** D1
Åbo = Turku *Finland* 60°30N 22°19E **9** F20
Abohar *India* 30°10N 74°10E **42** D6
Abomey *Benin* 7°10N 2°5E **50** G6
Abong-Mbang *Cameroon* 4°0N 13°8E **52** D2
Abou-Deïa *Chad* 11°20N 19°20E **51** F9
Aboyne *U.K.* 57°4N 2°47W **11** D6
Abra Pampa *Argentina* 22°43S 65°42W **94** A2
Abraham L. *Canada* 52°15N 116°35W **70** C5
Abreojos, Pta. *Mexico* 26°50N 113°40W **86** B2
Abrolhos, Banco *Brazil* 18°0S 38°0W **93** F11
Abrud *Romania* 46°19N 23°5E **17** E12
Absaroka Range *U.S.A.* 44°45N 109°50W **76** D9
Abu *India* 24°41N 72°50E **42** G5
Abū al Abyad *U.A.E.* 24°11N 53°50E **45** E7
Abū al Khaşīb *Iraq* 30°25N 48°0E **45** D6
Abū 'Alī *Si. Arabia* 27°20N 49°27E **45** E6
Abū 'Alī → *Lebanon* 34°25N 35°50E **46** A4
Abu Dhabi = Abū Ẓāby *U.A.E.* 24°28N 54°22E **45** E7
Abū Du'ān *Syria* 36°25N 38°15E **44** B3
Abu el Gaīn, W. → *Egypt* 29°35N 33°30E **46** F2
Abu Ga'da, W. → *Egypt* 29°15N 32°53E **46** F1
Abū Ḩadrīyah *Si. Arabia* 27°20N 48°58E **45** E6
Abu Hamed *Sudan* 19°32N 33°13E **51** E12
Abū Kamāl *Syria* 34°30N 41°0E **44** C4
Abū Madd, Ra's *Si. Arabia* 24°50N 37°7E **44** E3
Abū Mūsā *U.A.E.* 25°52N 55°3E **45** E7
Abū Qaşr *Si. Arabia* 30°21N 38°34E **44** D3
Abu Shagara, Ras *Sudan* 21°4N 37°19E **51** D13
Abu Simbel *Egypt* 22°18N 31°40E **51** D12
Abū Şukhayr *Iraq* 31°54N 44°30E **44** D5
Abu Zabad *Sudan* 12°25N 29°10E **51** F11
Abū Ẓāby *U.A.E.* 24°28N 54°22E **45** E7
Abū Zeydābād *Iran* 33°54N 51°45E **45** C6
Abuja *Nigeria* 9°5N 7°32E **50** G7
Abukuma-Gawa → *Japan* 38°6N 140°52E **30** E10
Abukuma-Sammyaku *Japan* 37°30N 140°45E **30** F10
Abunã *Brazil* 9°40S 65°20W **92** E5
Abunã → *Brazil* 9°41S 65°20W **92** E5
Aburo *Dem. Rep. of the Congo* 2°4N 30°53E **54** B3
Abut Hd. *N.Z.* 43°7S 170°15E **59** E3
Acadia △ *U.S.A.* 44°20N 68°13W **81** C19
Açailândia *Brazil* 4°57S 47°0W **93** D9
Acajutla *El Salv.* 13°36N 89°50W **88** D2
Acámbaro *Mexico* 20°2N 100°44W **86** D4
Acaponeta *Mexico* 22°30N 105°22W **86** C3
Acapulco *Mexico* 16°51N 99°55W **87** D5
Acarai, Serra *Brazil* 1°50N 57°50W **92** C7
Acarigua *Venezuela* 9°33N 69°12W **92** B5
Acatlán *Mexico* 18°12N 98°3W **87** D5
Acayucán *Mexico* 17°57N 94°55W **87** D6
Accomac *U.S.A.* 37°43N 75°40W **81** G16
Accra *Ghana* 5°35N 0°6W **50** G5
Accrington *U.K.* 53°45N 2°22W **12** D5
Acebal *Argentina* 33°20S 60°50W **94** C3
Aceh □ *Indonesia* 4°15N 97°30E **36** D1
Achalpur *India* 21°22N 77°32E **40** J10
Acharnes *Greece* 38°5N 23°44E **23** E10
Acheloos → *Greece* 38°19N 21°7E **23** E9
Acheng *China* 45°30N 126°58E **35** B14
Acher *India* 23°10N 72°32E **42** H5
Achill Hd. *Ireland* 53°58N 10°15W **10** C1
Achill I. *Ireland* 53°58N 10°1W **10** C1
Achinsk *Russia* 56°20N 90°20E **29** D10
Acireale *Italy* 37°37N 15°10E **22** F6
Ackerman *U.S.A.* 33°19N 89°11W **85** E10
Acklins I. *Bahamas* 22°30N 74°0W **89** B5
Acme *Canada* 51°33N 113°30W **70** C6
Acme *U.S.A.* 40°8N 79°26W **82** F5
Aconcagua, Cerro *Argentina* 32°39S 70°0W **94** C2
Aconquija, Mt. *Argentina* 27°0S 66°0W **94** B2
Açores, Is. dos *Atl. Oc.* 38°0N 27°0W **50** a
Acornhoek *S. Africa* 24°37S 31°2E **57** C5
Acraman, L. *Australia* 32°2S 135°23E **63** E2
Acre = 'Akko *Israel* 32°55N 35°4E **46** C4
Acre □ *Brazil* 9°1S 71°0W **92** E4
Acre → *Brazil* 8°45S 67°22W **92** E5
Acton *Canada* 43°38N 80°3W **82** C4
Ad Dammām *Si. Arabia* 26°20N 50°5E **45** E6
Ad Dāmūr *Lebanon* 33°43N 35°27E **46** B4
Ad Dawādimī *Si. Arabia* 24°35N 44°15E **44** E5
Ad Dawḩah *Qatar* 25°15N 51°35E **45** E6
Ad Dawr *Iraq* 34°27N 43°47E **44** C4
Ad Dir'īyah *Si. Arabia* 24°44N 46°35E **44** E5
Ad Dīwānīyah *Iraq* 32°0N 45°0E **44** D5
Ad Dujayl *Iraq* 33°51N 44°14E **44** C5
Ad Duwayd *Si. Arabia* 30°15N 42°17E **44** D4
Ada *Minn., U.S.A.* 47°18N 96°31W **80** B5
Ada *Okla., U.S.A.* 34°46N 96°41W **84** D6
Adabiya *Egypt* 29°53N 32°28E **46** F1
Adair, C. *Canada* 71°30N 71°34W **69** B12
Adaja → *Spain* 41°32N 4°52W **21** B3
Adak I. *U.S.A.* 51°45N 176°45W **74** a
Adamaoua, Massif de l' *Cameroon* 7°20N 12°20E **51** G8
Adamawa Highlands = Adamaoua, Massif de l' *Cameroon* 7°20N 12°20E **51** G8
Adamello, Mte. *Italy* 46°9N 10°30E **20** C9
Adaminaby *Australia* 36°0S 148°45E **63** F4
Adams *Mass., U.S.A.* 42°38N 73°7W **83** D11
Adams *N.Y., U.S.A.* 43°49N 76°1W **83** C8
Adams *Wis., U.S.A.* 43°57N 89°49W **80** D9
Adams, Mt. *U.S.A.* 46°12N 121°30W **78** D5
Adam's Bridge *Sri Lanka* 9°15N 79°40E **40** Q11
Adams L. *Canada* 51°10N 119°40W **70** C5
Adam's Peak *Sri Lanka* 6°48N 80°30E **40** R12
Adana *Turkey* 37°0N 35°16E **44** B2
Adapazarı = Sakarya *Turkey* 40°48N 30°25E **19** F5
Adarama *Sudan* 17°10N 34°52E **51** E12
Adare, C. *Antarctica* 71°0S 171°0E **5** D11
Adaut *Indonesia* 8°8S 131°7E **37** F8
Adavale *Australia* 25°52S 144°32E **63** D3
Adda → *Italy* 45°8N 9°53E **20** D8
Addis Ababa = Addis Abeba *Ethiopia* 9°2N 38°42E **47** F2
Addis Abeba *Ethiopia* 9°2N 38°42E **47** F2
Addison *U.S.A.* 42°1N 77°14W **82** D7
Addo *S. Africa* 33°32S 25°45E **56** E4
Addo △ *S. Africa* 33°30S 25°50E **56** E4
Ādeh *Iran* 37°42N 45°11E **44** B5
Adel *U.S.A.* 31°8N 83°25W **85** F13
Adelaide *Australia* 34°52S 138°30E **63** E2
Adelaide *S. Africa* 32°42S 26°20E **56** E4
Adelaide I. *Antarctica* 67°15S 68°30W **5** C17
Adelaide Pen. *Canada* 68°15N 97°30W **68** C10
Adelaide River *Australia* 13°15S 131°7E **60** B5
Adelaide Village *Bahamas* 25°0N 77°31W **88** A4
Adelanto *U.S.A.* 34°35N 117°22W **79** L9
Adele I. *Australia* 15°32S 123°9E **60** C3
Adélie, Terre *Antarctica* 68°0S 140°0E **5** C10
Adelie Land = Adélie, Terre *Antarctica* 68°0S 140°0E **5** C10
Aden = Al 'Adan *Yemen* 12°45N 45°0E **47** E4
Aden, G. of *Asia* 12°30N 47°30E **47** E4
Adendorp *S. Africa* 32°15S 24°30E **56** E3
Adh Dhayd *U.A.E.* 25°17N 55°53E **45** E7
Adhoi *India* 23°26N 70°32E **42** H4
Adi *Indonesia* 4°15S 133°30E **37** E8
Adieu, C. *Australia* 32°0S 132°10E **61** F5
Adieu Pt. *Australia* 15°14S 124°35E **60** C3
Adige → *Italy* 45°9N 12°20E **22** B5
Adigrat *Ethiopia* 14°20N 39°26E **47** E2
Adilabad *India* 19°33N 78°20E **40** K11
Adirondack ⌂ *U.S.A.* 44°0N 74°20W **83** C10
Adirondack Mts. *U.S.A.* 44°0N 74°0W **83** C10
Adis Abeba = Addis Abeba *Ethiopia* 9°2N 38°42E **47** F2
Adjumani *Uganda* 3°20N 31°50E **54** B3
Adjuntas *Puerto Rico* 18°10N 66°43W **89** d
Adlavik Is. *Canada* 55°0N 58°40W **73** B8
Admiralty G. *Australia* 14°20S 125°55E **60** B4
Admiralty I. *U.S.A.* 57°30N 134°30W **70** B2
Admiralty Is. *Papua N. G.* 2°0S 147°0E **58** B7
Adolfo Ruiz Cortines, Presa *Mexico* 27°15N 109°6W **86** B3
Adonara *Indonesia* 8°15S 123°5E **37** F6
Adoni *India* 15°33N 77°18E **40** M10
Adour → *France* 43°32N 1°32W **20** E3
Adra *India* 23°30N 86°42E **43** H12
Adra *Spain* 36°43N 3°3W **21** D4
Adrano *Italy* 37°40N 14°50E **22** F6
Adrar *Algeria* 27°51N 0°11E **50** C6
Adrar *Mauritania* 20°30N 7°30W **50** D3
Adrar des Iforas *Africa* 19°40N 1°40E **50** E6
Adrian *Mich., U.S.A.* 41°54N 84°2W **81** E11
Adrian *Tex., U.S.A.* 35°16N 102°40W **84** D3
Adriatic Sea *Medit. S.* 43°0N 16°0E **22** C6
Adua *Indonesia* 1°45S 129°50E **37** E7
Adwa *Ethiopia* 14°15N 38°52E **47** E2
Adygea □ *Russia* 45°0N 40°0E **19** F7
Adzhar Republic = Ajaria □ *Georgia* 41°30N 42°0E **19** F7
Adzopé *Ivory C.* 6°7N 3°49W **50** G5
Ægean Sea *Medit. S.* 38°30N 25°0E **23** E11
Aerhtai Shan *Mongolia* 46°40N 92°45E **32** B4
Afaahiti *Tahiti* 17°45S 149°17W **59** d
'Afak *Iraq* 32°4N 45°15E **44** C5
Afandou *Greece* 36°18N 28°12E **25** C10
Afareaitu *Moorea* 17°33S 149°47W **59** d
Afghanistan ■ *Asia* 33°0N 65°0E **40** C4
Aflou *Algeria* 34°7N 2°3E **50** B6
Africa 10°0N 20°0E **48** E6
'Afrīn *Syria* 36°32N 36°50E **44** B3
Afton *N.Y., U.S.A.* 42°14N 75°32W **83** D9
Afton *Wyo., U.S.A.* 42°44N 110°56W **76** E8
Afuá *Brazil* 0°15S 50°20W **93** D8
'Afula *Israel* 32°37N 35°17E **46** C4
Afyon *Turkey* 38°45N 30°33E **19** G5
Afyonkarahisar = Afyon *Turkey* 38°45N 30°33E **19** G5
Agadès = Agadez *Niger* 16°58N 7°59E **50** E7
Agadez *Niger* 16°58N 7°59E **50** E7
Agadir *Morocco* 30°28N 9°55W **50** B4
Agaete *Canary Is.* 28°6N 15°43W **24** F4
Agalega Is. *Mauritius* 11°0S 57°0E **3** E12
Agar *India* 23°40N 76°2E **42** H7
Agartala *India* 23°50N 91°23E **41** H17
Agassiz *Canada* 49°14N 121°46W **70** D4
Agats *Indonesia* 5°33S 138°0E **37** F9
Agawam *U.S.A.* 42°5N 72°37W **83** D12
Agboville *Ivory C.* 5°55N 4°15W **50** G5
Ağdam *Azerbaijan* 40°0N 46°58E **44** B5
Agde *France* 43°19N 3°28E **20** E5
Agen *France* 44°12N 0°38E **20** D4
Āgh Kand *Iran* 37°15N 48°4E **45** B6
Aghia Deka *Greece* 35°3N 24°58E **25** D6
Aghia Ekaterinis, Akra *Greece* 39°50N 19°50E **25** A3
Aghia Galini *Greece* 35°6N 24°41E **25** D6
Aghia Varvara *Greece* 35°8N 25°1E **25** D7
Aghios Efstratios *Greece* 39°34N 24°58E **23** E11
Aghios Ioannis, Akra *Greece* 35°20N 25°40E **25** D7
Aghios Isidoros *Greece* 36°9N 27°51E **25** C9
Aghios Matheos *Greece* 39°30N 19°47E **25** B3
Aghios Nikolaos *Greece* 35°11N 25°41E **25** D7
Aghiou Orous, Kolpos *Greece* 40°6N 24°0E **23** D11
Aginskoye *Russia* 51°6N 114°32E **29** D12
Agnew *Australia* 28°1S 120°31E **61** E3
Agori *India* 24°33N 82°57E **43** G10
Agra *India* 27°17N 77°58E **42** F7
Agri *Turkey* 39°44N 43°3E **19** G7
Agri → *Italy* 40°13N 16°44E **22** D7
Ağrı Dağı *Turkey* 39°50N 44°15E **44** B5
Ağri Karakose = Ağri *Turkey* 39°44N 43°3E **19** G7
Agrigento *Italy* 37°19N 13°34E **22** F5
Agrinio *Greece* 38°37N 21°27E **23** E9
Agua Caliente *Mexico* 32°29N 116°59W **79** N10
Agua Caliente Springs *U.S.A.* 32°56N 116°19W **79** N10
Água Clara *Brazil* 20°25S 52°45W **93** H8
Agua Fria ⌂ *U.S.A.* 34°14N 112°0W **77** J8
Agua Hechicera *Mexico* 32°28N 116°15W **79** N10
Agua Prieta *Mexico* 31°18N 109°34W **86** A3
Aguadilla *Puerto Rico* 18°26N 67°10W **89** d
Aguadulce *Panama* 8°15N 80°32W **88** E3
Aguanga *U.S.A.* 33°27N 116°51W **79** M10
Aguanish *Canada* 50°14N 62°2W **73** B7
Aguanus → *Canada* 50°13N 62°5W **73** B7
Aguapey → *Argentina* 29°7S 56°36W **94** B4
Aguaray Guazú → *Paraguay* 24°47S 57°19W **94** A4
Aguarico → *Ecuador* 0°59S 75°11W **92** D3
Aguaro-Guariquito △ *Venezuela* 8°20N 66°35W **89** E6
Aguas Blancas *Chile* 24°15S 69°55W **94** A2
Aguas Calientes, Sierra de *Argentina* 25°26S 66°40W **94** B2
Aguascalientes *Mexico* 21°53N 102°18W **86** C4
Aguascalientes □ *Mexico* 22°0N 102°20W **86** C4
Aguila, Punta *Puerto Rico* 17°57N 67°13W **89** d
Aguilares *Argentina* 27°26S 65°35W **94** B2
Aguilas *Spain* 37°23N 1°35W **21** D5
Agüimes *Canary Is.* 27°58N 15°27W **24** G4
Aguja, C. de la *Colombia* 11°18N 74°12W **90** B3
Agujereada, Pta. *Puerto Rico* 18°30N 67°8W **89** d
Agulhas, C. *S. Africa* 34°52S 20°0E **56** E3
Agulo *Canary Is.* 28°11N 17°12W **24** F2
Agung, Gunung *Indonesia* 8°20S 115°28E **36** F5
Agur *Uganda* 2°28N 32°55E **54** B3
Agusan → *Phil.* 9°0N 125°30E **37** C7
Aha Mts. *Botswana* 19°45S 21°0E **56** B3
Ahaggar *Algeria* 23°0N 6°30E **50** D7
Ahar *Iran* 38°35N 47°0E **44** B5
Ahipara B. *N.Z.* 35°5S 173°5E **59** A4
Ahiri *India* 19°30N 80°0E **40** K12
Ahmad Wal *Pakistan* 29°18N 65°58E **42** E1
Ahmadabad *India* 23°0N 72°40E **42** H5
Aḩmadābād *Khorāsān, Iran* 35°3N 60°50E **45** C9
Aḩmadābād *Khorāsān, Iran* 35°49N 59°42E **45** C8
Aḩmadī *Iran* 27°56N 56°42E **45** E8
Ahmadnagar *India* 19°7N 74°46E **40** K9
Ahmadpur *Pakistan* 29°12N 71°10E **42** E4
Ahmadpur Lamma *Pakistan* 28°19N 70°3E **42** E4
Ahmedabad = Ahmadabad *India* 23°0N 72°40E **42** H5
Ahmednagar = Ahmadnagar *India* 19°7N 74°46E **40** K9
Ahome *Mexico* 25°55N 109°11W **86** B3
Ahoskie *U.S.A.* 36°17N 76°59W **85** C16
Ahram *Iran* 28°52N 51°16E **45** D6
Ahrax Pt. *Malta* 36°0N 14°22E **25** D1
Āhū *Iran* 34°33N 50°2E **45** C6
Ahuachapán *El Salv.* 13°54N 89°52W **88** D2
Ahvāz *Iran* 31°20N 48°40E **45** D6
Ahvenanmaa = Åland *Finland* 60°15N 20°0E **9** F19
Aḩwar *Yemen* 13°30N 46°40E **47** E4
Ai → *India* 26°26N 90°44E **43** F14
Ai-Ais *Namibia* 27°54S 17°59E **56** D2
Ai-Ais and Fish River Canyon △ *Namibia* 24°45S 17°15E **56** C2
Aichi □ *Japan* 35°0N 137°15E **31** G8
Aigrettes, Pte. des *Réunion* 21°3S 55°13E **53** c
Aigua *Uruguay* 34°13S 54°46W **95** C5
Aigues-Mortes *France* 43°35N 4°12E **20** E6
Aihui *China* 50°10N 127°30E **33** A7
Aija *Peru* 9°50S 77°45W **92** E3
Aikawa *Japan* 38°2N 138°15E **30** E9
Aiken *U.S.A.* 33°34N 81°43W **85** E14
Aileron *Australia* 22°39S 133°20E **62** C1
Aillik *Canada* 55°11N 59°18W **73** A8
Ailsa Craig *U.K.* 55°15N 5°6W **11** F3
Aim *Russia* 59°0N 133°55E **29** D14
Aimere *Indonesia* 8°45S 121°3E **37** F6
Aimogasta *Argentina* 28°33S 66°50W **94** B2
Aïn Ben Tili *Mauritania* 25°59N 9°27W **50** C4
Aïn Sefra *Algeria* 32°47N 0°37W **50** B5
Ain Sudr *Egypt* 29°50N 33°6E **46** F2
Aïn Témouchent *Algeria* 35°16N 1°8W **50** A5
Ainaži *Latvia* 57°50N 24°24E **9** H21
Ainsworth *U.S.A.* 42°33N 99°52W **80** D4
Aiquile *Bolivia* 18°10S 65°10W **92** G5
Aïr *Niger* 18°30N 8°0E **50** E7
Air Force I. *Canada* 67°58N 74°5W **69** C12
Air Hitam *Malaysia* 1°55N 103°11E **39** M4
Airdrie *Canada* 51°18N 114°2W **70** C6
Airdrie *U.K.* 55°52N 3°57W **11** F5
Aire → *U.K.* 53°43N 0°55W **12** D7
Aire, I. de l' *Spain* 39°48N 4°16E **24** B11
Airlie Beach *Australia* 20°16S 148°43E **62** J6
Aisne → *France* 49°26N 2°50E **20** B5
Ait *India* 25°54N 79°14E **43** G8
Aitkin *U.S.A.* 46°32N 93°42W **80** B7
Aitutaki *Cook Is.* 18°52S 159°45W **65** J12
Aiud *Romania* 46°19N 23°44E **17** E12
Aix-en-Provence *France* 43°32N 5°27E **20** E6
Aix-la-Chapelle = Aachen *Germany* 50°45N 6°6E **16** C4
Aix-les-Bains *France* 45°41N 5°53E **20** D6
Aizawl *India* 23°40N 92°44E **41** H18
Aizkraukle *Latvia* 56°36N 25°11E **9** H21
Aizpute *Latvia* 56°43N 21°40E **9** H19
Aizuwakamatsu *Japan* 37°30N 139°56E **30** F9
Ajaccio *France* 41°55N 8°40E **20** F8
Ajai ⌂ *Uganda* 2°52N 31°16E **54** B3
Ajaigarh *India* 24°52N 80°16E **43** G9
Ajalpan *Mexico* 18°22N 97°15W **87** D5
Ajanta Ra. *India* 20°28N 75°50E **40** J9
Ajari Rep. = Ajaria □ *Georgia* 41°30N 42°0E **19** F7
Ajaria □ *Georgia* 41°30N 42°0E **19** F7
Ajax *Canada* 43°50N 79°1W **82** C5
Ajdābiyā *Libya* 30°54N 20°4E **51** B10
Ajka *Hungary* 47°4N 17°31E **17** E9
'Ajlūn *Jordan* 32°18N 35°47E **46** C4
'Ajlūn □ *Jordan* 32°18N 35°47E **46** C4
'Ajmān *U.A.E.* 25°25N 55°30E **45** E7
Ajmer *India* 26°28N 74°37E **42** F6
Ajnala *India* 31°50N 74°48E **42** D6
Ajo *U.S.A.* 32°22N 112°52W **77** K7
Ajo, C. de *Spain* 43°31N 3°35W **21** A4
Akabira *Japan* 43°33N 142°5E **30** C11
Akagera △ *Rwanda* 1°31S 30°33E **54** C3
Akamas *Cyprus* 35°3N 32°18E **25** D11
Akan △ *Japan* 43°20N 144°20E **30** C12
Akanthou *Cyprus* 35°22N 33°45E **25** D12
Akaroa *N.Z.* 43°49S 172°59E **59** E4
Akashi *Japan* 34°45N 134°58E **31** G7
Akbarpur *Bihar, India* 24°39N 83°58E **43** G10
Akbarpur *Ut. P., India* 26°25N 82°32E **43** F10
Akelamo *Indonesia* 1°35N 129°40E **37** D7
Aketi *Dem. Rep. of the Congo* 2°38N 23°47E **52** D4
Akhisar *Turkey* 38°56N 27°48E **23** E12
Akhnur *India* 32°52N 74°45E **43** C6
Akhtyrka = Okhtyrka *Ukraine* 50°25N 35°0E **19** D5
Aki *Japan* 33°30N 133°54E **31** H6
Akimiski I. *Canada* 52°50N 81°30W **72** B3
Akita *Japan* 39°45N 140°7E **30** E10
Akita □ *Japan* 39°40N 140°30E **30** E10
Akjoujt *Mauritania* 19°45N 14°15W **50** E3
Akkeshi *Japan* 43°2N 144°51E **30** C12
'Akko *Israel* 32°55N 35°4E **46** C4
Aklavik *Canada* 68°12N 135°0W **68** C6
Aklera *India* 24°26N 76°32E **42** G7
Akō *Japan* 34°45N 134°24E **31** G7
Akola *India* 20°42N 77°2E **40** J10
Akordat *Eritrea* 15°30N 37°40E **47** D2
Akpatok I. *Canada* 60°25N 68°8W **69** C13
Åkrahamn *Norway* 59°15N 5°10E **9** G11
Akranes *Iceland* 64°19N 22°5W **8** D2
Akron *Colo., U.S.A.* 40°10N 103°13W **76** F12
Akron *Ohio, U.S.A.* 41°5N 81°31W **82** E3
Akrotiri *Cyprus* 34°36N 32°57E **25** E11
Akrotiri Bay *Cyprus* 34°35N 33°10E **25** E12
Aksai Chin *China* 35°15N 79°55E **43** B8
Aksaray *Turkey* 38°25N 34°2E **44** B2
Aksay = Aqsay *Kazakhstan* 51°11N 53°0E **19** D9
Akşehir *Turkey* 38°18N 31°30E **44** B1
Akşehir Gölü *Turkey* 38°30N 31°25E **19** G5
Aksu *China* 41°5N 80°10E **32** B3
Aksum *Ethiopia* 14°5N 38°40E **47** E2
Aktsyabrski *Belarus* 52°38N 28°53E **17** B15
Aktyubinsk = Aqtöbe *Kazakhstan* 50°17N 57°10E **19** D10
Akure *Nigeria* 7°15N 5°5E **50** G7
Akureyri *Iceland* 65°40N 18°6W **8** D4
Akuseki-Shima *Japan* 29°27N 129°37E **31** K4
Akyab = Sittwe *Burma* 20°18N 92°45E **41** J18
Al 'Adan *Yemen* 12°45N 45°0E **47** E4
Al Aḩsā = Hasa *Si. Arabia* 25°50N 49°0E **45** E6
Al Ajfar *Si. Arabia* 27°26N 43°0E **44** E4
Al Amādīyah *Iraq* 37°5N 43°30E **44** B4
Al 'Amārah *Iraq* 31°55N 47°15E **44** D5
Al Anbār □ *Iraq* 33°25N 42°0E **44** C4
Al 'Aqabah *Jordan* 29°31N 35°0E **46** F4
Al 'Aqabah □ *Jordan* 29°30N 35°0E **46** F4
Al Arak *Syria* 34°38N 38°35E **44** C3
Al 'Aramah *Si. Arabia* 25°30N 46°0E **44** E5
Al 'Arţāwīyah *Si. Arabia* 26°31N 45°20E **44** E5
Al 'Āşimah = 'Ammān □ *Jordan* 31°40N 36°30E **46** D5
Al 'Assāfīyah *Si. Arabia* 28°17N 38°59E **44** D3
Al 'Ayn *Si. Arabia* 25°4N 38°6E **44** E3
Al 'Ayn *U.A.E.* 24°15N 55°45E **45** E7
Al 'Azīzīyah *Iraq* 32°54N 45°4E **44** C5
Al Bāb *Syria* 36°23N 37°29E **44** B3
Al Bad' *Si. Arabia* 28°28N 35°1E **44** D2
Al Bādī *Iraq* 35°56N 41°32E **44** C4
Al Baḩrah *Kuwait* 29°40N 47°52E **44** D5
Al Baḩral Mayyit = Dead Sea *Asia* 31°30N 35°30E **46** D4
Al Balqā' □ *Jordan* 32°5N 35°45E **46** C4
Al Bārūk, J. *Lebanon* 33°39N 35°40E **46** B4
Al Başrah *Iraq* 30°30N 47°50E **44** D5
Al Baṭḩā *Iraq* 31°6N 45°53E **44** D5
Al Batrūn *Lebanon* 34°15N 35°40E **46** A4
Al Bayḑā *Libya* 32°50N 21°44E **51** B10
Al Biqā *Lebanon* 34°10N 36°10E **46** A5
Al Bi'r *Si. Arabia* 28°51N 36°16E **44** D3
Al Bukayrīyah *Si. Arabia* 26°9N 43°40E **44** E4
Al Burayj *Syria* 34°15N 36°46E **46** A5
Al Faḑilī *Si. Arabia* 26°58N 49°10E **45** E6
Al Fallūjah *Iraq* 33°20N 43°55E **44** C4
Al Fāw *Iraq* 30°0N 48°30E **45** D6
Al Fujayrah *U.A.E.* 25°7N 56°18E **45** E8
Al Ghadaf, W. → *Jordan* 31°26N 36°43E **46** D5
Al Ghammās *Iraq* 31°45N 44°37E **44** D5
Al Ghazālah *Si. Arabia* 26°48N 41°19E **44** E4
Al Ḩadīthah *Iraq* 34°0N 41°13E **44** C4
Al Ḩadīthah *Si. Arabia* 31°28N 37°8E **46** D6
Al Ḩaḑr *Iraq* 35°35N 42°44E **44** C4
Al Ḩājānah *Syria* 33°20N 36°33E **46** B5
Al Ḩajar al Gharbī *Oman* 24°10N 56°15E **45** E8

Al Ḩamād Si. Arabia 31°30N 39°30E 44 D3
Al Ḩamdānīyah Syria 35°25N 36°50E 44 C3
Al Ḩamīdīyah Syria 34°42N 35°57E 46 A4
Al Ḩammār Iraq 30°57N 46°51E 44 D5
Al Ḩamrā' Si. Arabia 24°2N 38°55E 44 E3
Al Ḩamzah Iraq 31°43N 44°58E 44 D5
Al Ḩanākīyah Si. Arabia 24°51N 40°31E 44 E4
Al Harūj al Aswad Libya 27°0N 17°10E 51 C9
Al Ḩasakah Syria 36°35N 40°45E 44 B4
Al Ḩayy Iraq 32°5N 46°5E 44 C5
Al Ḩijarah Asia 30°0N 44°0E 44 D4
Al Ḩillah Iraq 32°30N 44°25E 44 C5
Al Ḩillah Si. Arabia 23°35N 46°50E 47 B4
Al Hindīyah Iraq 32°30N 44°10E 44 C5
Al Hirmil Lebanon 34°26N 36°24E 46 A5
Al Hoceïma Morocco 35°8N 3°58W 50 A5
Al Ḩudaydah Yemen 14°50N 43°0E 47 E3
Al Ḩudūd ash Shamālīyah □ Si. Arabia 29°10N 42°30E 44 D4
Al Hufūf Si. Arabia 25°25N 49°45E 45 E6
Al Ḩumayḑah Si. Arabia 29°14N 34°56E 44 D2
Al Ḩunayy Si. Arabia 25°58N 48°45E 45 E6
Al Īsāwīyah Si. Arabia 30°43N 37°59E 44 D3
Al Jafr Jordan 30°18N 36°14E 46 E5
Al Jāfūrah Si. Arabia 25°0N 50°15E 45 E7
Al Jaghbūb Libya 29°42N 24°38E 51 C10
Al Jahrah Kuwait 29°25N 47°40E 44 D5
Al Jalāmīd Si. Arabia 31°20N 40°6E 44 D3
Al Jamalīyah Qatar 25°37N 51°5E 45 E6
Al Janūb □ Lebanon 33°20N 35°20E 46 B4
Al Jawf Libya 24°10N 23°24E 51 D10
Al Jawf Si. Arabia 29°55N 39°40E 44 D3
Al Jawf □ Si. Arabia 29°30N 39°30E 44 D3
Al Jazair = Algeria ■ Africa 28°30N 2°0E 50 C6
Al Jazirah Iraq 33°30N 44°0E 44 C5
Al Jithāmīyah Si. Arabia 27°41N 41°43E 44 E4
Al Jubayl Si. Arabia 27°0N 49°50E 45 E6
Al Jubaylah Si. Arabia 24°55N 46°25E 44 E5
Al Jubb Si. Arabia 27°11N 42°17E 44 E4
Al Junaynah Sudan 13°27N 22°45E 51 F10
Al Kabā'ish Iraq 30°58N 47°0E 44 D5
Al Karak Jordan 31°11N 35°42E 46 D4
Al Karak □ Jordan 31°0N 36°0E 46 E5
Al Kāzimīyah Iraq 33°22N 44°18E 44 C5
Al Khābūra Oman 23°57N 57°5E 45 F8
Al Khafjī Si. Arabia 28°24N 48°29E 45 E6
Al Khalīl West Bank 31°32N 35°6E 46 D4
Al Khāliş Iraq 33°49N 44°32E 44 C5
Al Kharsānīyah Si. Arabia 27°13N 49°18E 45 E6
Al Khaşab Oman 26°14N 56°15E 45 E8
Al Khawr Qatar 25°41N 51°30E 45 E6
Al Khiḑr Iraq 31°12N 45°33E 44 D5
Al Khiyām Lebanon 33°20N 35°36E 46 B4
Al Khobar Si. Arabia 26°17N 50°12E 45 E6
Al Khums Libya 32°40N 14°17E 51 B8
Al Kiswah Syria 33°23N 36°14E 46 B5
Al Kūfah Iraq 32°2N 44°24E 44 C5
Al Kufrah Libya 24°17N 23°15E 51 D10
Al Kuhayfīyah Si. Arabia 27°12N 43°3E 44 E4
Al Kūt Iraq 32°30N 46°0E 44 C5
Al Kuwayt Kuwait 29°30N 48°0E 44 D5
Al Labwah Lebanon 34°11N 36°20E 46 A5
Al Lādhiqīyah Syria 35°30N 35°45E 44 C2
Al Līth Si. Arabia 20°9N 40°15E 47 C3
Al Liwā' Oman 24°31N 56°36E 45 E8
Al Luḩayyah Yemen 15°45N 42°40E 47 D3
Al Madīnah Iraq 30°57N 47°16E 44 D5
Al Madīnah Si. Arabia 24°35N 39°52E 44 E3
Al Mafraq Jordan 32°17N 36°14E 46 C5
Al Mafraq □ Jordan 32°17N 36°15E 46 C5
Al Maghreb = Morocco ■ N. Afr. 32°0N 5°50W 50 B4
Al Maḩmūdīyah Iraq 33°3N 44°21E 44 C5
Al Majma'ah Si. Arabia 25°57N 45°22E 44 E5
Al Makhruq, W. → Jordan 31°28N 37°0E 46 D6
Al Makḩūl Si. Arabia 26°37N 42°39E 44 E4
Al Manāmah Bahrain 26°10N 50°30E 45 E6
Al Maqwa' Kuwait 29°10N 47°59E 44 D5
Al Murūḩ Si. Arabia 25°35N 49°35E 45 E6
Al Marj Libya 32°25N 20°30E 51 B10
Al Maţlā Kuwait 29°24N 47°40E 44 D5
Al Mawşil Iraq 36°15N 43°5E 44 B4
Al Mayādin Syria 35°1N 40°27E 44 C4
Al Mazār Jordan 31°4N 35°41E 46 D4
Al Midhnab Si. Arabia 25°50N 44°18E 44 E5
Al Minā' Lebanon 34°24N 35°49E 46 A4
Al Miqdādīyah Iraq 34°0N 45°0E 44 C5
Al Mubarraz Si. Arabia 25°30N 49°40E 45 E6
Al Mudawwarah Jordan 29°19N 36°0E 46 F5
Al Mughayrā' U.A.E. 24°5N 53°32E 45 E7
Al Muḩarraq Bahrain 26°15N 50°40E 45 E6
Al Mukallā Yemen 14°33N 49°2E 47 E4
Al Mukhā Yemen 13°18N 43°15E 47 E3
Al Musayjīd Si. Arabia 24°5N 39°5E 44 E3
Al Musayyib Iraq 32°49N 44°20E 44 C5
Al Muthanná □ Iraq 30°30N 45°15E 44 D5
Al Muwayliḩ Si. Arabia 27°40N 35°30E 44 E2
Al Qādisīyah □ Iraq 32°0N 45°0E 44 D5
Al Qā'im Iraq 34°21N 41°7E 44 C4
Al Qalībah Si. Arabia 28°24N 37°42E 44 D3
Al Qāmishlī Syria 37°2N 41°14E 44 B4
Al Qaryatayn Syria 34°12N 37°13E 46 A6
Al Qaşīm □ Si. Arabia 26°0N 43°0E 44 E4
Al Qaţ'ā Syria 34°40N 40°48E 44 C4
Al Qaţīf Si. Arabia 26°35N 50°0E 45 E6
Al Qatrānah Jordan 31°12N 36°6E 46 D5
Al Qaţrūn Libya 24°56N 15°3E 51 D9
Al Qayşūmah Si. Arabia 28°20N 46°7E 44 D5
Al Quds = Jerusalem Israel/West Bank 31°47N 35°10E 46 D4
Al Qunayţirah Syria 32°55N 35°45E 46 C4
Al Qunfudhah Si. Arabia 19°3N 41°4E 47 D3
Al Qurnah Iraq 31°1N 47°25E 44 D5
Al Quşayr Iraq 30°39N 45°50E 44 D5
Al Quşayr Syria 34°31N 36°34E 46 A5
Al Quţayfah Syria 33°44N 36°36E 46 B5
Al 'Ubaylah Si. Arabia 21°59N 50°57E 47 C5
Al 'Uḑaylīyah Si. Arabia 25°8N 49°18E 45 E6
Al 'Ulā Si. Arabia 26°35N 38°0E 44 E3
Al 'Uqayr Si. Arabia 25°40N 50°15E 45 E6
Al 'Uwaynid Si. Arabia 24°50N 46°0E 44 E5
Al 'Uwayqīlah Si. Arabia 30°30N 42°10E 44 D4
Al 'Uyūn Ḩijāz, Si. Arabia 24°33N 39°35E 44 E3
Al 'Uyūn Najd, Si. Arabia 26°30N 43°50E 44 E4
Al 'Uzayr Iraq 31°19N 47°25E 44 D5
Al Wajh Si. Arabia 26°10N 36°30E 44 E3
Al Wakrah Qatar 25°10N 51°40E 45 E6
Al Waqbah Si. Arabia 28°48N 45°33E 44 D5
Al Wari'āh Si. Arabia 27°51N 47°25E 44 E5
Al Yaman = Yemen ■ Asia 15°0N 44°0E 47 E3
Ala Dağ Turkey 37°44N 35°9E 44 B2
Ala Tau Shankou = Dzungarian Gate Asia 45°10N 82°0E 32 B3
Alabama □ U.S.A. 33°0N 87°0W 85 E11
Alabama → U.S.A. 31°8N 87°57W 85 F11
Alabaster U.S.A. 33°15N 86°49W 85 E11
Alaçam Dağları Turkey 39°18N 28°49E 23 E13
Alacant = Alicante Spain 38°23N 0°30W 21 C5
Alachua U.S.A. 29°47N 82°30W 85 G13
Alagoa Grande Brazil 7°3S 35°35W 93 E11
Alagoas □ Brazil 9°0S 36°0W 93 E11
Alagoinhas Brazil 12°7S 38°20W 93 F11
Alaior Spain 39°57N 4°8E 24 B11
Alajero Canary Is. 28°3N 17°13W 24 F2
Alajuela Costa Rica 10°2N 84°8W 88 D3
Alakamisy Madag. 21°19S 47°14E 57 C8
Alaknanda → India 30°8N 78°36E 43 D8
Alakurtti Russia 66°58N 30°25E 8 C24
Alamarvdasht Iran 27°37N 52°59E 45 E7
Alameda Calif., U.S.A. 37°46N 122°15W 78 H4
Alameda N. Mex., U.S.A. 35°11N 106°37W 77 J10
Alamo U.S.A. 37°22N 115°10W 79 H11
Alamogordo U.S.A. 32°54N 105°57W 77 K11
Alamos Mexico 27°1N 108°56W 86 B3
Alamosa U.S.A. 37°28N 105°52W 77 H11
Åland Finland 60°15N 20°0E 9 F19
Ålands hav Europe 60°0N 19°30E 9 G18
Alania = North Ossetia □ Russia 43°30N 44°30E 19 F7
Alanya Turkey 36°38N 32°0E 44 B1
Alaotra, Farihin' Madag. 17°30S 48°30E 57 B8
Alapayevsk Russia 57°52N 61°42E 28 D7
Alappuzha = Alleppey India 9°30N 76°28E 40 Q10
Alarobia-Vohiposa Madag. 20°59S 47°9E 57 C8
Alaşehir Turkey 38°23N 28°30E 23 E13
Alaska □ U.S.A. 64°0N 154°0W 74 a
Alaska, G. of Pac. Oc. 58°0N 145°0W 74 a
Alaska Peninsula U.S.A. 56°0N 159°0W 74 a
Alaska Range U.S.A. 62°50N 151°0W 74 a
Älät Azerbaijan 39°58N 49°25E 45 B6
Alatyr Russia 54°55N 46°35E 18 D8
Alausi Ecuador 2°0S 78°50W 92 D3
Alava, C. U.S.A. 48°10N 124°44W 78 B1
Alavo = Alavus Finland 62°35N 23°36E 8 E20
Alavus Finland 62°35N 23°36E 8 E20
Alawoona Australia 34°45S 140°30E 63 E3
'Alayh Lebanon 33°46N 35°33E 46 B4
Alba Italy 44°42N 8°2E 20 D8
Alba-Iulia Romania 46°8N 23°39E 17 E12
Albacete Spain 39°0N 1°50W 21 C5
Albacutya, L. Australia 35°45S 141°58E 63 F3
Albanel, L. Canada 50°55N 73°12W 72 B5
Albania ■ Europe 41°0N 20°0E 23 D9
Albany Australia 35°1S 117°58E 61 G2
Albany Ga., U.S.A. 31°35N 84°10W 85 F12
Albany N.Y., U.S.A. 42°39N 73°45W 83 D11
Albany Oreg., U.S.A. 44°38N 123°6W 76 D2
Albany Tex., U.S.A. 32°44N 99°18W 84 E5
Albany → Canada 52°17N 81°31W 72 B3
Albardón Argentina 31°20S 68°30W 94 C2
Albatross B. Australia 12°45S 141°30E 62 A3
Albemarle U.S.A. 35°21N 80°12W 85 D14
Albemarle Sd. U.S.A. 36°5N 76°0W 85 C16
Alberche → Spain 39°58N 4°46W 21 C3
Alberdi Paraguay 26°14S 58°20W 94 B4
Alberga → Australia 27°6S 135°33E 63 D2
Albert, L. Africa 1°30N 31°0E 54 B3
Albert, L. Australia 35°30S 139°10E 63 F2
Albert Edward Ra. Australia 18°17S 127°57E 60 C4
Albert Lea U.S.A. 43°39N 93°22W 80 D7
Albert Nile → Uganda 3°36N 32°2E 54 B3
Albert Town Bahamas 22°37N 74°33W 89 B5
Alberta □ Canada 54°40N 115°0W 70 C6
Alberti Argentina 35°1S 60°16W 94 D3
Albertinia S. Africa 34°11S 21°34E 56 E3
Alberton Canada 46°50N 64°0W 73 C7
Albertville France 45°40N 6°22E 20 D7
Albertville U.S.A. 34°16N 86°13W 85 D11
Albi France 43°56N 2°9E 20 E5
Albia U.S.A. 41°2N 92°48W 80 E7
Albina Suriname 5°37N 54°15W 93 B8
Albina, Ponta Angola 15°52S 11°44E 56 B1
Albion Mich., U.S.A. 42°15N 84°45W 81 D11
Albion Nebr., U.S.A. 41°42N 98°0W 80 E4
Albion Pa., U.S.A. 41°53N 80°22W 82 E4
Alborán Medit. S. 35°57N 3°0W 21 E4
Ålborg = Aalborg Denmark 57°2N 9°54E 9 H13
Alborz, Reshteh-ye Kūhhā-ye Iran 36°0N 52°0E 45 C7
Albufeira Portugal 37°5N 8°15W 21 D1
Albuquerque U.S.A. 35°5N 106°39W 77 J10
Albuquerque, Cayos de Caribbean 12°10N 81°50W 88 D3
Alburg U.S.A. 44°59N 73°18W 83 B11
Albury Australia 36°3S 146°56E 63 F4
Alcalá de Henares Spain 40°28N 3°22W 21 B4
Alcalá la Real Spain 37°27N 3°57W 21 D4
Álcamo Italy 37°59N 12°55E 22 F5
Alcañiz Spain 41°2N 0°8W 21 B5
Alcântara Brazil 2°20S 44°30W 93 D10
Alcántara, Embalse de Spain 39°44N 6°50W 21 C2
Alcantarilla Spain 37°59N 1°12W 21 D5
Alcaraz, Sierra de Spain 38°40N 2°20W 21 C4
Alcaudete Spain 37°35N 4°5W 21 D3
Alcázar de San Juan Spain 39°24N 3°12W 21 C4
Alchevsk Ukraine 48°30N 38°45E 19 E6
Alcira = Alzira Spain 39°9N 0°30W 21 C5
Alcova U.S.A. 42°34N 106°43W 76 E10
Alcoy Spain 38°43N 0°30W 21 C5
Alcúdia Spain 39°51N 3°7E 24 B10
Alcúdia, B. d' Spain 39°47N 3°15E 24 B10
Aldabra Is. Seychelles 9°22S 46°28E 49 G8
Aldama Mexico 22°55N 98°4W 87 C5
Aldan Russia 58°40N 125°30E 29 D13
Aldan → Russia 63°28N 129°35E 29 C13
Aldea, Pta. de la Canary Is. 28°0N 15°50W 24 G4
Aldeburgh U.K. 52°10N 1°37E 13 E9
Alder Pk. U.S.A. 35°53N 121°22W 78 K5
Alderney U.K. 49°42N 2°11W 13 H5
Aldershot U.K. 51°15N 0°44W 13 F7
Aledo U.S.A. 41°12N 90°45W 80 E8
Aleg Mauritania 17°3N 13°55W 50 E3
Alegranza Canary Is. 29°23N 13°32W 24 E6
Alegranza, I. Canary Is. 29°23N 13°32W 24 E6
Alegre Brazil 20°50S 41°30W 95 A7
Alegrete Brazil 29°40S 56°0W 95 B4
Aleksandriya = Oleksandriya Ukraine 50°37N 26°19E 17 C14
Aleksandrov Gay Russia 50°9N 48°34E 19 D8
Aleksandrovsk-Sakhalinskiy Russia 50°50N 142°20E 29 D15
Aleksandry, Zemlya Russia 80°25N 48°0E 4 A10
Além Paraíba Brazil 21°52S 42°41W 95 A7
Alemania Argentina 25°40S 65°30W 94 B2
Alemania Chile 25°10S 69°55W 94 B2
Alençon France 48°27N 0°4E 20 B4
Alenquer Brazil 1°56S 54°46W 93 D8
'Alenuihähä Channel U.S.A. 20°30N 156°0W 74 b
Aleppo = Ḩalab Syria 36°10N 37°15E 44 B3
Aléria France 42°5N 9°26E 20 E9
Alert Canada 83°2N 60°0W 69 A13
Alès France 44°0N 4°5E 20 D6
Alessándria Italy 44°54N 8°37E 20 D8
Ålesund Norway 62°28N 6°12E 8 E12
Aleutian Basin Pac. Oc. 57°0N 177°0E 64 B9
Aleutian Is. Pac. Oc. 52°0N 175°0W 74 a
Aleutian Trench Pac. Oc. 48°0N 180°0E 4 D17
Alexander U.S.A. 47°51N 103°39W 80 B2
Alexander, Mt. Australia 28°58S 120°16E 61 E3
Alexander Arch. U.S.A. 56°0N 136°0W 74 a
Alexander Bay S. Africa 28°40S 16°30E 56 D2
Alexander City U.S.A. 32°56N 85°58W 85 E12
Alexander I. Antarctica 69°0S 70°0W 5 C17
Alexandra Australia 37°8S 145°40E 63 F4
Alexandra N.Z. 45°14S 169°25E 59 F2
Alexandra Falls Canada 60°29N 116°18W 70 A5
Alexandria = El Iskandarîya Egypt 31°13N 29°58E 51 B11
Alexandria B.C., Canada 52°35N 122°27W 70 C4
Alexandria Ont., Canada 45°19N 74°38W 83 A10
Alexandria Romania 43°57N 25°24E 17 G13
Alexandria S. Africa 33°38S 26°28E 56 E4
Alexandria U.K. 55°59N 4°35W 11 F4
Alexandria La., U.S.A. 31°18N 92°27W 84 F8
Alexandria Minn., U.S.A. 45°53N 95°22W 80 C6
Alexandria S. Dak., U.S.A. 43°39N 97°47W 80 D5
Alexandria Va., U.S.A. 38°49N 77°5W 81 F15
Alexandria Bay U.S.A. 44°20N 75°55W 83 B9
Alexandrina, L. Australia 35°25S 139°10E 63 F2
Alexandroupoli Greece 40°50N 25°54E 23 D11
Alexis → Canada 52°33N 56°8W 73 B8
Alexis Creek Canada 52°10N 123°20W 70 C4
Aleysk Russia 52°40N 83°0E 28 D9
Alfabia Spain 39°44N 2°44E 24 B9
Alfenas Brazil 21°20S 46°10W 95 A6
Alford Aberds., U.K. 57°14N 2°41W 11 D6
Alford Lincs., U.K. 53°15N 0°10E 12 D8
Alfred Maine, U.S.A. 43°29N 70°43W 83 C14
Alfred N.Y., U.S.A. 42°16N 77°48W 82 D7
Alfreton U.K. 53°6N 1°24W 12 D6
Alga Kazakhstan 49°53N 57°20E 19 E10
Algaida Spain 39°33N 2°53E 24 B9
Ålgård Norway 58°46N 5°53E 9 G11
Algarve Portugal 36°58N 8°20W 21 D1
Algeciras Spain 36°9N 5°28W 21 D3
Algemesí Spain 39°11N 0°27W 21 C5
Alger Algeria 36°42N 3°8E 50 A6
Algeria ■ Africa 28°30N 2°0E 50 C6
Alghero Italy 40°33N 8°19E 22 D3
Algiers = Alger Algeria 36°42N 3°8E 50 A6
Algoa B. S. Africa 33°50S 25°45E 56 E4
Algoma U.S.A. 44°36N 87°26W 80 C10
Algona U.S.A. 43°4N 94°14W 80 D6
Algonac U.S.A. 42°37N 82°32W 82 D2
Algonquin ⌂ Canada 45°50N 78°30W 72 C4
Algorta Uruguay 32°25S 57°23W 96 C5
Alhambra U.S.A. 34°5N 118°7W 79 L8
Alhucemas = Al Hoceïma Morocco 35°8N 3°58W 50 A5
'Alī al Gharbī Iraq 32°30N 46°45E 44 C5
'Alī ash Sharqī Iraq 32°7N 46°44E 44 C5
'Alī Khēl Afghan. 33°57N 69°43E 42 C3
Alī Shāh Iran 38°9N 45°50E 44 B5
'Alīābād Khorāsān, Iran 32°30N 57°30E 45 C8
'Alīābād Kordestān, Iran 35°4N 46°58E 44 C5
'Alīābād Yazd, Iran 31°41N 53°49E 45 D7
Aliağa Turkey 38°47N 26°59E 23 E12
Aliakmonas → Greece 40°30N 22°36E 23 D10
Alicante Spain 38°23N 0°30W 21 C5
Alice S. Africa 32°48S 26°55E 56 E4
Alice U.S.A. 27°45N 98°5W 84 H5
Alice → Queens., Australia 24°2S 144°50E 62 C3
Alice → Queens., Australia 15°35S 142°20E 62 B3
Alice Arm Canada 55°29N 129°31W 70 B3
Alice Springs Australia 23°40S 133°50E 62 C1
Alicedale S. Africa 33°15S 26°4E 56 E4
Aliceville U.S.A. 33°8N 88°9W 85 E10
Aliganj India 27°30N 79°10E 43 F8
Aligarh Raj., India 25°55N 76°15E 42 G7
Aligarh Ut. P., India 27°55N 78°10E 42 F8
Alīgūdarz Iran 33°25N 49°45E 45 C6
Alimia Greece 36°16N 27°43E 25 C9
Alingsås Sweden 57°56N 12°31E 9 H15
Alipur Pakistan 29°25N 70°55E 42 E4
Alipur Duar India 26°30N 89°35E 41 F16
Aliquippa U.S.A. 40°37N 80°15W 82 F4
Alitus = Alytus Lithuania 54°24N 24°3E 9 J21
Aliwal North S. Africa 30°45S 26°45E 56 E4
Alix Canada 52°24N 113°11W 70 C6
Aljustrel Portugal 37°55N 8°10W 21 D1
Alkmaar Neths. 52°37N 4°45E 15 B4
All American Canal U.S.A. 32°45N 115°15W 77 K6
Allagash → U.S.A. 47°5N 69°3W 81 B19
Allah Dad Pakistan 25°38N 67°34E 42 G2
Allahabad India 25°25N 81°58E 43 G9
Allan Canada 51°53N 106°4W 71 C7
Allanridge S. Africa 27°45S 26°40E 56 D4
Allegany U.S.A. 42°6N 78°30W 82 D6
Allegheny → U.S.A. 40°27N 80°1W 82 F5
Allegheny Mts. U.S.A. 38°15N 80°10W 81 F13
Allegheny Plateau U.S.A. 41°30N 78°30W 81 E14
Allegheny Res. U.S.A. 41°50N 79°0W 82 E6
Allègre, Pte. Guadeloupe 16°22N 61°46W 88 b
Allen, Bog of Ireland 53°15N 7°0W 10 C5
Allen, L. Ireland 54°8N 8°4W 10 B3
Allendale U.S.A. 33°1N 81°18W 85 E14
Allende Mexico 28°20N 100°51W 86 B4
Allentown U.S.A. 40°37N 75°29W 83 F9
Alleppey India 9°30N 76°28E 40 Q10
Aller → Germany 52°56N 9°12E 16 B5
Alleynes B. Barbados 13°13N 59°39W 89 g
Alliance Nebr., U.S.A. 42°6N 102°52W 80 D2
Alliance Ohio, U.S.A. 40°55N 81°6W 82 F3
Allier → France 46°57N 3°4E 20 C5
Alliford Bay Canada 53°12N 131°58W 70 C2
Alligator Pond Jamaica 17°52N 77°34W 88 a
Alliston = New Tecumseth Canada 44°9N 79°52W 82 B5
Alloa U.K. 56°7N 3°47W 11 E5
Allora Australia 28°2S 152°0E 63 D5
Alluitsup Paa Greenland 60°30N 45°35W 4 C5
Alma Canada 48°35N 71°40W 73 C5
Alma Ga., U.S.A. 31°33N 82°28W 85 F13
Alma Kans., U.S.A. 39°1N 96°17W 80 F5
Alma Mich., U.S.A. 43°23N 84°39W 81 D11
Alma Nebr., U.S.A. 40°6N 99°22W 80 E4
Alma Wis., U.S.A. 44°20N 91°55W 80 C8
Alma Ata = Almaty Kazakhstan 43°15N 76°57E 28 E8
Almada Portugal 38°41N 9°8W 21 C1
Almaden Australia 17°22S 144°40E 62 B3
Almadén Spain 38°49N 4°52W 21 C3
Almanor, L. U.S.A. 40°14N 121°9W 76 F3
Almansa Spain 38°51N 1°5W 21 C5
Almanzor, Pico Spain 40°15N 5°18W 21 B3
Almanzora → Spain 37°14N 1°46W 21 D5
Almaty Kazakhstan 43°15N 76°57E 28 E8
Almazán Spain 41°30N 2°30W 21 B4
Almeirim Brazil 1°30S 52°34W 93 D8
Almelo Neths. 52°22N 6°42E 15 B6
Almendralejo Spain 38°41N 6°26W 21 C2
Almere-Stad Neths. 52°20N 5°15E 15 B5
Almería Spain 36°52N 2°27W 21 D4
Almirante Panama 9°10N 82°30W 88 E3
Almond U.S.A. 42°19N 77°44W 82 D7
Almont U.S.A. 42°55N 83°3W 82 D1
Almonte Canada 45°14N 76°12W 83 A8
Almora India 29°38N 79°40E 43 E8
Almyrou, Ormos Greece 35°23N 24°20E 25 D6
Alness U.K. 57°41N 4°16W 11 D4
Alnmouth U.K. 55°24N 1°37W 12 B6
Alnwick U.K. 55°24N 1°42W 12 B6
Aloi Uganda 2°16N 33°10E 54 B3
Alon Burma 22°12N 95°5E 41 H19
Alor Indonesia 8°15S 124°30E 37 F6
Alor Setar Malaysia 6°7N 100°22E 39 J3
Alot India 23°56N 75°40E 42 H6
Aloysius, Mt. Australia 26°0S 128°38E 61 E4
Alpaugh U.S.A. 35°53N 119°29W 78 K7
Alpena U.S.A. 45°4N 83°27W 81 C12
Alpha Australia 23°39S 146°37E 62 C4
Alpha Ridge Arctic 84°0N 118°0W 4 A2
Alphen aan den Rijn Neths. 52°7N 4°40E 15 B4
Alpine Ariz., U.S.A. 33°51N 109°9W 77 K9
Alpine Calif., U.S.A. 32°50N 116°46W 79 N10
Alpine Tex., U.S.A. 30°22N 103°40W 84 F3
Alps Europe 46°30N 9°30E 20 C8
Alsace □ France 48°15N 7°25E 20 B7
Alsask Canada 51°21N 109°59W 71 C7
Alsasua Spain 42°54N 2°10W 21 A4
Alsek → U.S.A. 59°10N 138°12W 70 B1
Alsta Norway 65°58N 12°40E 8 D15
Alston U.K. 54°49N 2°25W 12 C5
Alta Norway 69°57N 23°10E 8 B20
Alta Gracia Argentina 31°40S 64°30W 94 C3
Alta Sierra U.S.A. 35°42N 118°33W 79 K8
Altaelva → Norway 69°54N 23°17E 8 B20
Altafjorden Norway 70°5N 23°5E 8 A20
Altai = Aerhtai Shan Mongolia 46°40N 92°45E 32 B4
Altai = Gorno-Altay □ Russia 51°0N 86°0E 28 D9
Altamaha → U.S.A. 31°20N 81°20W 85 F14
Altamira Brazil 3°12S 52°10W 93 D8
Altamira Chile 25°47S 69°51W 94 B2
Altamira Mexico 22°24N 97°55W 87 C5
Altamont U.S.A. 42°42N 74°2W 83 D10
Altamura Italy 40°49N 16°33E 22 D7
Altanbulag Mongolia 50°16N 106°30E 32 A5
Altar Mexico 30°43N 111°44W 86 A2
Altar, Gran Desierto de Mexico 31°50N 114°10W 86 B2
Altata Mexico 24°40N 107°55W 86 C3
Altavista U.S.A. 37°6N 79°17W 81 G14
Altay China 47°48N 88°10E 32 B3
Altea Spain 38°38N 0°2W 21 C5
Altiplano Bolivia 17°0S 68°0W 92 G5
Alto Araguaia Brazil 17°15S 53°20W 93 G8
Alto Cuchumatanes = Cuchumatanes, Sierra de los Guatemala 15°35N 91°25W 88 C1
Alto del Carmen Chile 28°46S 70°30W 94 B1
Alto del Inca Chile 24°10S 68°10W 94 A2
Alto Ligonha Mozam. 15°30S 38°11E 55 F4
Alto Molocue Mozam. 15°50S 37°35E 55 F4
Alto Paraguay □ Paraguay 21°0S 58°30W 94 A4
Alto Paraná □ Paraguay 25°30S 54°50W 95 B5
Alton Canada 43°54N 80°5W 82 C4
Alton U.K. 51°9N 0°59W 13 F7
Alton Ill., U.S.A. 38°53N 90°11W 80 F8
Alton N.H., U.S.A. 43°27N 71°13W 83 C13
Altona Canada 49°6N 97°33W 71 D9
Altoona U.S.A. 40°31N 78°24W 82 F6
Altun Kupri Iraq 35°45N 44°9E 44 C5
Altun Shan China 38°30N 88°0E 32 C3
Alturas U.S.A. 41°29N 120°32W 76 F3
Altus U.S.A. 34°38N 99°20W 84 D5
Alucra Turkey 40°22N 38°47E 19 F6
Alūksne Latvia 57°24N 27°3E 9 H22
Alunite U.S.A. 35°59N 114°55W 79 K12
Alusi Indonesia 7°35S 131°40E 37 F8
Alva U.S.A. 36°48N 98°40W 84 C5
Alvarado Mexico 18°46N 95°46W 87 D5
Alvarado U.S.A. 32°24N 97°13W 84 E6
Alvaro Obregón, Presa Mexico 27°52N 109°52W 86 B3
Alvear Argentina 29°5S 56°30W 94 B4
Alvesta Sweden 56°54N 14°35E 9 H16
Alvin U.S.A. 29°26N 95°15W 84 G7
Alvinston Canada 42°49N 81°52W 82 D3
Älvkarleby Sweden 60°34N 17°26E 9 F17
Alvord Desert U.S.A. 42°30N 118°25W 76 E4
Älvsbyn Sweden 65°40N 21°0E 8 D19
Alwar India 27°38N 76°34E 42 F7
Alxa Zuoqi China 38°50N 105°40E 34 E3
Alyangula Australia 13°55S 136°30E 62 A2
Alyata = Älät Azerbaijan 39°58N 49°25E 45 B6
Alyth U.K. 56°38N 3°13W 11 E5
Alytus Lithuania 54°24N 24°3E 9 J21
Alzada U.S.A. 45°2N 104°25W 76 D11
Alzira Spain 39°9N 0°30W 21 C5
Am Timan Chad 11°0N 20°10E 51 F10
Amadeus, L. Australia 24°54S 131°0E 61 D5
Amadi Dem. Rep. of the Congo 3°40N 26°40E 54 B2
Amâdi Sudan 5°29N 30°25E 51 G12
Amadjuak L. Canada 65°0N 71°8W 69 C12
Amagansett U.S.A. 40°59N 72°9W 83 F12
Amagasaki Japan 34°42N 135°23E 31 G7
Amahai Indonesia 3°20S 128°55E 37 E7
Amaile Samoa 13°59S 171°22W 59 b
Amakusa-Shotō Japan 32°15N 130°10E 31 H5
Åmål Sweden 59°3N 12°42E 9 G15
Amaliada Greece 37°47N 21°22E 23 F9
Amalner India 21°5N 75°5E 40 J9
Amamapare Indonesia 4°53S 136°38E 37 E9
Amambaí Brazil 23°5S 55°13W 95 A4
Amambaí → Brazil 23°22S 53°56W 95 A5
Amambay □ Paraguay 23°0S 56°0W 95 A4
Amambay, Cordillera de S. Amer. 23°0S 55°45W 95 A4
Amami-Guntō Japan 27°16N 129°21E 31 L4
Amami-Ō-Shima Japan 28°0N 129°0E 31 L4
Aman, Pulau Malaysia 5°16N 100°24E 39 c
Amaná, L. Brazil 2°35S 64°40W 92 D6
Amanat → India 24°7N 84°4E 43 G11
Amanda Park U.S.A. 47°28N 123°55W 78 C3
Amankeldi Kazakhstan 50°10N 65°10E 28 D7
Amapá Brazil 2°5N 50°50W 93 C8
Amapá □ Brazil 1°40N 52°0W 93 C8
Amarante Brazil 6°14S 42°50W 93 E10
Amaranth Canada 50°36N 98°43W 71 C9
Amargosa → U.S.A. 36°14N 116°51W 79 J10
Amargosa Desert U.S.A. 36°40N 116°30W 79 J10
Amargosa Range U.S.A. 36°20N 116°45W 79 J10
Amari Greece 35°13N 24°40E 25 D6
Amarillo U.S.A. 35°13N 101°50W 84 D4
Amarkantak India 22°40N 81°45E 43 H9
Amaro, Mte. Italy 42°5N 14°5E 22 C6
Amarpur India 25°5N 87°0E 43 G12
Amarwara India 22°18N 79°10E 43 H8
Amasya Turkey 40°40N 35°50E 19 F6
Amata Australia 26°9S 131°9E 61 E5
Amatikulu S. Africa 29°3S 31°33E 57 D5
Amatitlán Guatemala 14°29N 90°38W 88 D1
Amay Belgium 50°33N 5°19E 15 D5
Amazon = Amazonas → S. Amer. 0°5S 50°0W 93 D8

Amazonas □ Brazil 5°0S 65°0W 92 E6
Amazonas → S. Amer. 0°5S 50°0W 93 D8
Ambah India 26°43N 78°13E 42 F8
Ambahakily Madag. 21°36S 43°41E 57 C7
Ambahita Madag. 24°1S 45°16E 57 C8
Ambala India 30°23N 76°56E 42 D7
Ambalavao Madag. 21°50S 46°56E 57 C8
Ambanja Madag. 13°40S 48°27E 57 A8
Ambararata Madag. 15°3S 48°33E 57 B8
Ambarchik Russia 69°40N 162°20E 29 C17
Ambarijeby Madag. 14°56S 47°41E 57 A8
Ambaro, Helodranon' Madag. 13°23S 48°38E 57 A8
Ambato Ecuador 1°5S 78°42W 92 D3
Ambato Madag. 13°24S 48°29E 57 A8
Ambato, Sierra de Argentina 28°25S 66°10W 94 B2
Ambato Boeny Madag. 16°28S 46°43E 57 B8
Ambatofinandrahana Madag. 20°33S 46°48E 57 C8
Ambatolampy Madag. 19°20S 47°35E 57 B8
Ambatomainty Madag. 17°41S 45°40E 57 B8
Ambatomanoina Madag. 18°18S 47°37E 57 B8
Ambatondrazaka Madag. 17°55S 48°28E 57 B8
Ambatosoratra Madag. 17°37S 48°31E 57 B8
Ambenja Madag. 15°17S 46°58E 57 B8
Amberg Germany 49°26N 11°52E 16 D6
Ambergris Cay Belize 18°0N 87°55W 87 D7
Amberley N.Z. 43°9S 172°44E 59 E4
Ambikapur India 23°15N 83°15E 43 H10
Ambilobé Madag. 13°10S 49°3E 57 A8
Ambinanindrano Madag. 20°5S 48°23E 57 C8
Ambinanitelo Madag. 15°21S 49°35E 57 B8
Ambinda Madag. 16°25S 45°52E 57 B8
Amble U.K. 55°20N 1°36W 12 B6
Ambleside U.K. 54°26N 2°58W 12 C5
Ambo Peru 10°5S 76°10W 92 F3
Amboahangy Madag. 24°15S 46°22E 57 C8
Ambodifototra Madag. 16°59S 49°52E 57 B8
Ambodilazana Madag. 18°6S 49°10E 57 B8
Ambodiriana Madag. 17°55S 49°18E 57 B8
Ambohidratrimo Madag. 18°50S 47°26E 57 B8
Ambohidray Madag. 18°36S 48°18E 57 B8
Ambohimahamasina Madag. 21°56S 47°11E 57 C8
Ambohimahasoa Madag. 21°7S 47°13E 57 C8
Ambohimanga Madag. 20°52S 47°36E 57 C8
Ambohimitombo Madag. 20°43S 47°26E 57 C8
Ambohitra Madag. 12°30S 49°10E 57 A8
Amboise France 47°24N 1°2E 20 C4
Ambon Indonesia 3°43S 128°12E 37 E7
Ambondro Madag. 25°13S 45°44E 57 D8
Amboseli, L. Kenya 2°40S 37°10E 54 C4
Amboseli △ Kenya 2°37S 37°13E 54 C4
Ambositra Madag. 20°31S 47°25E 57 C8
Ambovombe Madag. 25°11S 46°5E 57 D8
Amboy U.S.A. 34°33N 115°45W 79 L11
Amboyna Cay S. China Sea 7°50N 112°50E 36 C4
Ambridge U.S.A. 40°36N 80°14W 82 F4
Ambriz Angola 7°48S 13°8E 52 F2
Amchitka I. U.S.A. 51°32N 179°0E 74 a
Amderma Russia 69°45N 61°30E 28 C7
Amdhi India 23°51N 81°27E 43 H9
Amdo China 32°20N 91°40E 41 C17
Ameca Mexico 20°33N 104°2W 86 C4
Ameca → Mexico 20°41N 105°18W 86 C3
Amecameca de Juárez Mexico 19°8N 98°46W 87 D5
Ameland Neths. 53°27N 5°45E 15 A5
Amenia U.S.A. 41°51N 73°33W 83 E11
America-Antarctica Ridge S. Ocean 59°0S 16°0W 5 B2
American Falls U.S.A. 42°47N 112°51W 76 E7
American Falls Res. U.S.A. 42°47N 112°52W 76 E7
American Fork U.S.A. 40°23N 111°48W 76 F8
American Highland Antarctica 73°0S 75°0E 5 D6
American Samoa ☒ Pac. Oc. 14°20S 170°0W 59 b
American Samoa △ Amer. Samoa 14°15S 170°28W 59 b
Americana Brazil 22°45S 47°20W 95 A6
Americus U.S.A. 32°4N 84°14W 85 E12
Amersfoort Neths. 52°9N 5°23E 15 B5
Amersfoort S. Africa 26°59S 29°53E 57 D4
Amery Basin S. Ocean 68°15S 74°30E 5 C6
Amery Ice Shelf Antarctica 69°30S 72°0E 5 C6
Ames U.S.A. 42°2N 93°37W 80 D7
Amesbury U.S.A. 42°51N 70°56W 83 D14
Amet India 25°18N 73°56E 42 G5
Amga Russia 60°50N 132°0E 29 C14
Amga → Russia 62°38N 134°32E 29 C14
Amgu Russia 45°45N 137°15E 30 B8
Amgun → Russia 52°56N 139°38E 29 D14
Amherst Canada 45°48N 64°8W 73 C7
Amherst Mass., U.S.A. 42°23N 72°31W 83 D12
Amherst N.Y., U.S.A. 42°59N 78°48W 82 D6
Amherst Ohio, U.S.A. 41°24N 82°14W 82 E2
Amherst I. Canada 44°8N 76°43W 83 B8
Amherstburg Canada 42°6N 83°6W 72 D3
Amiata, Mte. Italy 42°53N 11°37E 22 C4
Amidon U.S.A. 46°29N 103°19W 80 B2
Amiens France 49°54N 2°16E 20 B5
Aminuis Namibia 23°43S 19°21E 56 C2
Amīrābād Iran 33°20N 46°16E 44 C5
Amirante Is. Seychelles 6°0S 53°0E 26 J7
Amisk ⌂ Canada 56°43N 98°0W 71 B9
Amisk L. Canada 54°35N 102°15W 71 C8
Amistad, Presa de la Mexico 29°26N 101°3W 86 B4
Amistad ⌂ U.S.A. 29°32N 101°12W 84 G4
Amite U.S.A. 30°44N 90°30W 85 F9
Amla India 21°56N 78°7E 42 J8
Amlapura = Karangasem Indonesia 8°27S 115°37E 37 J18
Amlia I. U.S.A. 52°4N 173°30W 74 a
Amlwch U.K. 53°24N 4°20W 12 D3
'Ammān Jordan 31°57N 35°52E 46 D4
'Ammān □ Jordan 31°40N 36°30E 46 D5
'Ammān ✕ (AMM) Jordan 31°45N 36°2E 46 D5
Ammanford U.K. 51°48N 3°59W 13 F4
Ammassalik = Tasiilaq Greenland 65°40N 37°20W 4 C6
Ammochostos = Famagusta Cyprus 35°8N 33°55E 25 D12
Ammon U.S.A. 43°28N 111°58W 76 E8
Amnat Charoen Thailand 15°51N 104°38E 38 E5
Amnura Bangla. 24°37N 88°25E 43 G13
Āmol Iran 36°23N 52°20E 45 B7
Amorgos Greece 36°50N 25°57E 23 F11
Amory U.S.A. 33°59N 88°29W 85 E10
Amos Canada 48°35N 78°5W 72 C4
Åmot Norway 59°57N 9°54E 9 G13
Amoy = Xiamen China 24°25N 118°4E 33 D6
Ampanavoana Madag. 15°41S 50°22E 57 B9
Ampang Malaysia 3°8N 101°45E 39 L3
Ampangalana, Lakandranon' Madag. 22°48S 47°50E 57 C8
Ampanihy Madag. 24°40S 44°45E 57 C7
Amparafaravola Madag. 17°35S 48°13E 57 B8
Ampasinambo Madag. 20°31S 48°0E 57 C8
Ampasindava, Helodranon' Madag. 13°40S 48°15E 57 A8
Ampasindava, Saikanosy Madag. 13°42S 47°55E 57 A8
Ampenan Indonesia 8°34S 116°4E 36 F5
Amper → Germany 48°29N 11°55E 16 D6
Amphoe Kathu Thailand 7°55N 98°21E 39 a
Amphoe Thalang Thailand 8°1N 98°20E 39 a
Ampitsikinana Madag. 12°57S 49°49E 57 A8
Ampombiantambo Madag. 12°42S 48°57E 57 A8
Ampotaka Madag. 25°3S 44°41E 57 D7
Ampoza Madag. 22°20S 44°44E 57 C7
Amqui Canada 48°28N 67°27W 73 C6
Amravati India 20°55N 77°45E 40 J10
Amreli India 21°35N 71°17E 42 J4
Amritsar India 31°35N 74°57E 42 D6
Amroha India 28°53N 78°30E 43 E8
Amsterdam Neths. 52°23N 4°54E 15 B4
Amsterdam U.S.A. 42°56N 74°11W 83 D10
Amsterdam ✕ (AMS) Neths. 52°18N 4°45E 15 B4
Amsterdam, I. = Nouvelle Amsterdam, Î. Ind. Oc. 38°30S 77°30E 3 F13
Amstetten Austria 48°7N 14°51E 16 D8
Amudarya → Uzbekistan 43°58N 59°34E 28 E6
Amund Ringnes I. Canada 78°20N 96°25W 69 B10
Amundsen Abyssal Plain S. Ocean 65°0S 125°0W 5 C14
Amundsen Basin Arctic 87°30N 80°0E 4 A
Amundsen Gulf Canada 71°0N 124°0W 68 B7
Amundsen Ridges S. Ocean 69°15S 123°0W 5 C14
Amundsen-Scott Antarctica 90°0S 166°0E 5 E
Amundsen Sea Antarctica 72°0S 115°0W 5 D15
Amuntai Indonesia 2°28S 115°25E 36 E5
Amur → Russia 52°56N 141°10E 29 D15
Amurang Indonesia 1°5N 124°40E 37 D6
Amursk Russia 50°14N 136°54E 29 D14
Amyderya = Amudarya → Uzbekistan 43°58N 59°34E 28 E6
An Bien Vietnam 9°45N 105°0E 39 H5
An Hoa Vietnam 15°40N 108°5E 38 E7
An Nabatīyah at Tahta Lebanon 33°23N 35°27E 46 B4
An Nabk Si. Arabia 31°20N 37°20E 44 D3
An Nabk Syria 34°2N 36°44E 46 A5
An Nafūd Si. Arabia 28°15N 41°0E 44 D4
An Najaf Iraq 32°3N 44°15E 44 C5
An Nāṣirīyah Iraq 31°0N 46°15E 44 D5
An Nhon Vietnam 13°55N 109°7E 38 F7
An Nu'ayrīyah Si. Arabia 27°30N 48°30E 45 E6
An Thoi, Dao Vietnam 9°58N 104°0E 39 H4
An Uaimh Ireland 53°39N 6°41W 10 C5
Anabar → Russia 73°8N 113°36E 29 B12
'Anabtā West Bank 32°19N 35°7E 46 C4
Anaconda U.S.A. 46°8N 112°57W 76 C7
Anacortes U.S.A. 48°30N 122°37W 78 B4
Anadarko U.S.A. 35°4N 98°15W 84 D5
Anadolu Turkey 39°0N 30°0E 19 G5
Anadyr Russia 64°35N 177°20E 29 C18
Anadyr → Russia 64°55N 176°5E 29 C18
Anadyrskiy Zaliv Russia 64°0N 180°0E 29 C19
Anaga, Pta. de Canary Is. 28°34N 16°9W 24 F3
'Ānah Iraq 34°25N 42°0E 44 C4
Anaheim U.S.A. 33°50N 117°55W 79 M9
Anahim Lake Canada 52°28N 125°18W 70 C3
Anakapalle India 17°42N 83°6E 41 L13
Anakie Australia 23°32S 147°45E 62 C4
Analalava Madag. 14°35S 48°0E 57 A8
Analavoka Madag. 22°23S 46°30E 57 C8
Analipsis Greece 39°36N 19°55E 25 A3
Anambar → Pakistan 30°15N 68°50E 42 D3
Anambas, Kepulauan Indonesia 3°20N 106°30E 36 D3
Anambas Is. = Anambas, Kepulauan Indonesia 3°20N 106°30E 36 D3
Anamosa U.S.A. 42°7N 91°17W 80 D8
Anamur Turkey 36°8N 32°58E 44 B2
Anan Japan 33°54N 134°40E 31 H7
Anand India 22°32N 72°59E 42 H5
Anantapur India 14°39N 77°42E 40 M10
Anantnag India 33°45N 75°10E 43 C6
Ananyiv Ukraine 47°44N 29°58E 17 E15
Anapodiaris → Greece 34°59N 25°20E 25 E7
Anápolis Brazil 16°15S 48°50W 93 G9
Anapu → Brazil 1°53S 50°53W 93 D8
Anār Iran 30°55N 55°13E 45 D7
Anārak Iran 33°25N 53°40E 45 C7
Anas → India 23°26N 74°0E 42 H5
Anatolia = Anadolu Turkey 39°0N 30°0E 19 G5
Anatsogno Madag. 23°33S 43°46E 57 C7
Añatuya Argentina 28°20S 62°50W 94 B3
Anaunethad L. Canada 60°55N 104°25W 71 A8
Anbyŏn N. Korea 39°1N 127°35E 35 E14
Ancaster Canada 43°13N 79°59W 82 C5
Anchor Bay U.S.A. 38°48N 123°34W 78 G3
Anchorage U.S.A. 61°13N 149°54W 74 a
Anci China 39°20N 116°40E 34 E9
Ancohuma, Nevado Bolivia 16°0S 68°50W 92 G5
Ancón Peru 11°50S 77°10W 92 F3
Ancona Italy 43°38N 13°30E 22 C5
Ancud Chile 42°0S 73°50W 96 E2
Ancud, G. de Chile 42°0S 73°0W 96 E2
Anda China 46°24N 125°19E 33 B7
Andacollo Argentina 37°10S 70°42W 94 D1
Andacollo Chile 30°14S 71°6W 94 C1
Andaingo Madag. 18°12S 48°17E 57 B8
Andalgalá Argentina 27°40S 66°30W 94 B2
Åndalsnes Norway 62°35N 7°43E 8 E12
Andalucía □ Spain 37°35N 5°0W 21 D3
Andalusia = Andalucía □ Spain 37°35N 5°0W 21 D3
Andalusia U.S.A. 31°18N 86°29W 85 F11
Andaman Is. Ind. Oc. 12°30N 92°45E 3 D14
Andaman Sea Ind. Oc. 13°0N 96°0E 36 B1
Andamooka Australia 30°27S 137°9E 63 E2
Andapa Madag. 14°39S 49°39E 57 A8
Andara Namibia 18°2S 21°9E 56 B3
Andenes Norway 69°19N 16°18E 8 B17
Andenne Belgium 50°28N 5°5E 15 D5
Anderson Alaska, U.S.A. 64°25N 149°15W 74 a
Anderson Calif., U.S.A. 40°27N 122°18W 76 F2
Anderson Ind., U.S.A. 40°10N 85°41W 81 E11
Anderson Mo., U.S.A. 36°39N 94°27W 80 G6
Anderson S.C., U.S.A. 34°31N 82°39W 85 D13
Anderson → Canada 69°42N 129°0W 68 C7
Andes U.S.A. 42°12N 74°47W 83 D10
Andes, Cord. de los S. Amer. 20°0S 68°0W 92 H5
Andfjorden Norway 69°10N 16°20E 8 B17
Andhra Pradesh □ India 18°0N 79°0E 40 L11
Andijon Uzbekistan 41°10N 72°15E 28 E8
Andikíthira = Antikythira Greece 35°52N 23°15E 23 G10
Andilamena Madag. 17°1S 48°35E 57 B8
Andīmeshk Iran 32°27N 48°21E 45 C6
Andizhan = Andijon Uzbekistan 41°10N 72°15E 28 E8
Andoany Madag. 13°25S 48°16E 57 A8
Andohahela ⌂ Madag. 24°4S 46°44E 57 C8
Andong S. Korea 36°40N 128°43E 35 F15
Andongwei China 35°6N 119°20E 35 G10
Andoom Australia 12°25S 141°53E 62 A3
Andorra ■ Europe 42°30N 1°30E 20 E4
Andorra La Vella Andorra 42°31N 1°32E 20 E4
Andover U.K. 51°12N 1°29W 13 F6
Andover Maine, U.S.A. 44°38N 70°45W 83 B14
Andover Mass., U.S.A. 42°40N 71°8W 83 D13
Andover N.J., U.S.A. 40°59N 74°45W 83 F10
Andover N.Y., U.S.A. 42°10N 77°48W 82 D7
Andover Ohio, U.S.A. 41°36N 80°34W 82 E4
Andøya Norway 69°10N 15°50E 8 B16
Andradina Brazil 20°54S 51°23W 93 H8
Andrahary Madag. 13°37S 49°17E 57 A8
Andramasina Madag. 19°11S 47°35E 57 B8
Andranopasy Madag. 21°17S 43°44E 57 C7
Andranovory Madag. 23°8S 44°10E 57 C7
Andratx Spain 39°39N 2°25E 24 B9
Andreanof Is. U.S.A. 51°30N 176°0W 74 a
Andrews S.C., U.S.A. 33°27N 79°34W 85 E15
Andrews Tex., U.S.A. 32°19N 102°33W 84 E3
Ándria Italy 41°13N 16°17E 22 D7
Andriamena Madag. 17°26S 47°30E 57 B8
Andriandampy Madag. 22°45S 45°41E 57 C8
Andriba Madag. 17°30S 46°58E 57 B8
Andringitra ⌂ Madag. 22°13S 46°5E 57 C8
Androka Madag. 24°58S 44°2E 57 C7
Andros Greece 37°50N 24°57E 23 F11
Andros I. Bahamas 24°30N 78°0W 88 B4
Andros Town Bahamas 24°43N 77°47W 88 B4
Androscoggin → U.S.A. 43°58N 69°52W 83 C14
Andselv Norway 69°4N 18°34E 8 B18
Andújar Spain 38°3N 4°5W 21 C3
Andulo Angola 11°25S 16°45E 52 G3
Anegada Br. Virgin Is. 18°45N 64°20W 89 e
Anegada Passage W. Indies 18°15N 63°45W 89 C7
Aneto, Pico de Spain 42°37N 0°40E 21 A6
Ang Mo Kio Singapore 1°23N 103°50E 39 d
Ang Thong Thailand 14°35N 100°31E 38 E3
Ang Thong, Ko Thailand 9°37N 99°41E 39 b
Ang Thong △ Thailand 9°40N 99°43E 39 H2
Angamos, Punta Chile 23°1S 70°32W 94 A1
Angara → Russia 58°5N 94°20E 29 D10
Angarsk Russia 52°30N 104°0E 29 D11
Angas Hills Australia 23°0S 127°50E 60 D4
Angaston Australia 34°30S 139°8E 63 E2
Ånge Sweden 62°31N 15°35E 8 E16
Ángel, Salto = Angel Falls Venezuela 5°57N 62°30W 92 B6
Ángel de la Guarda, I. Mexico 29°20N 113°25W 86 B2
Angel Falls Venezuela 5°57N 62°30W 92 B6
Angeles Phil. 15°9N 120°33E 37 A6
Ängelholm Sweden 56°15N 12°58E 9 H15
Angels Camp U.S.A. 38°4N 120°32W 78 G6
Ångermanälven → Sweden 64°0N 17°20E 8 E17
Ångermanland Sweden 63°36N 17°45E 8 E17
Angers Canada 45°31N 75°29W 83 A9
Angers France 47°30N 0°35W 20 C3
Ängesån → Sweden 66°16N 22°47E 8 C20
Angikuni L. Canada 62°12N 99°59W 71 A9
Angkor Cambodia 13°22N 103°50E 38 F4
Anglesey U.K. 53°17N 4°20W 12 D3
Anglesey, Isle of □ U.K. 53°16N 4°18W 12 D3
Angleton U.S.A. 29°10N 95°26W 84 G7
Anglisidhes Cyprus 34°51N 33°27E 25 E12
Angmagssalik = Tasiilaq Greenland 65°40N 37°20W 4 C6
Ango Dem. Rep. of the Congo 4°10N 26°5E 54 B2
Angoche Mozam. 16°8S 39°55E 55 F4
Angoche, I. Mozam. 16°20S 39°50E 55 F4
Angol Chile 37°56S 72°45W 94 D1
Angola Ind., U.S.A. 41°38N 85°0W 81 E11
Angola N.Y., U.S.A. 42°38N 79°2W 82 D5
Angola ■ Africa 12°0S 18°0E 53 G3
Angoulême France 45°39N 0°10E 20 D4
Angoumois France 45°50N 0°25E 20 D3
Angra do Heroísmo Azores 38°39N 27°13W 50 a
Angra dos Reis Brazil 23°0S 44°10W 95 A7
Angren Uzbekistan 41°1N 70°12E 28 E8
Angtassom Cambodia 11°1N 104°41E 39 G5
Angu Dem. Rep. of the Congo 3°23N 24°30E 54 B1
Anguang China 45°15N 123°45E 35 B12
Anguilla ☒ W. Indies 18°14N 63°5W 89 C7
Anguo China 38°28N 115°15E 34 E8
Angurugu Australia 14°0S 136°25E 62 A2
Angus □ U.K. 56°46N 2°56W 11 E6
Angwa → Zimbabwe 16°0S 30°23E 57 B5
Anhanduí → Brazil 21°46S 52°9W 95 A5
Anholt Denmark 56°42N 11°33E 9 H14
Anhui □ China 32°0N 117°0E 33 C6
Anhwei = Anhui □ China 32°0N 117°0E 33 C6
Anichab Namibia 21°0S 14°46E 56 C1
Animas → U.S.A. 36°43N 108°13W 77 H9
Anivorano Madag. 18°44S 48°58E 57 B8
Anjalankoski Finland 60°45N 26°51E 8 F22
Anjar India 23°6N 70°10E 42 H4
Anjou France 47°20N 0°15W 20 C3
Anjouan Comoros Is. 12°15S 44°20E 53 a
Anjozorobe Madag. 18°22S 47°52E 57 B8
Anju N. Korea 39°36N 125°40E 35 E13
Ankaboa, Tanjona Madag. 21°58S 43°20E 57 C7
Ankang China 32°40N 109°1E 34 H5
Ankara Turkey 39°57N 32°54E 19 G5
Ankarafantsika ⌂ Madag. 16°8S 47°5E 57 B8
Ankaramena Madag. 21°57S 46°39E 57 C8
Ankaratra Madag. 19°25S 47°12E 53 H9
Ankasakasa Madag. 16°21S 44°52E 57 B7
Ankavandra Madag. 18°46S 45°18E 57 B8
Ankazoabo Madag. 22°18S 44°31E 57 C7
Ankazobe Madag. 18°20S 47°10E 57 B8
Ankeny U.S.A. 41°44N 93°36W 80 E7
Ankilimalinika Madag. 22°58S 43°45E 57 C7
Ankilizato Madag. 20°25S 45°1E 57 C8
Ankisabe Madag. 19°17S 46°29E 57 B8
Ankoro Dem. Rep. of the Congo 6°45S 26°55E 54 D2
Ankororoka Madag. 25°30S 45°11E 57 D8
Anmyeondo S. Korea 36°25N 126°25E 35 F14
Ann, C. U.S.A. 42°38N 70°35W 83 D14
Ann Arbor U.S.A. 42°17N 83°45W 81 D12
Anna U.S.A. 37°28N 89°15W 80 G9
Annaba Algeria 36°50N 7°46E 50 A7
Annalee → Ireland 54°2N 7°24W 10 B4
Annam Vietnam 16°0N 108°0E 38 E7
Annamitique, Chaîne Asia 17°0N 106°0E 38 D6
Annan U.K. 54°59N 3°16W 11 G5
Annan → U.K. 54°58N 3°16W 11 G5
Annapolis U.S.A. 38°59N 76°30W 81 F15
Annapolis Royal Canada 44°44N 65°32W 73 D6
Annapurna Nepal 28°34N 83°50E 43 E10
Annean, L. Australia 26°54S 118°14E 61 E2
Annecy France 45°55N 6°8E 20 D7
Anning China 24°55N 102°26E 32 D5
Anniston U.S.A. 33°39N 85°50W 85 E12
Annobón Atl. Oc. 1°25S 5°36E 49 G4
Annotto B. Jamaica 18°17N 76°45W 88 a
Annville U.S.A. 40°20N 76°31W 83 F8
Anogia Greece 35°16N 24°52E 25 D6
Anorotsangana Madag. 13°56S 47°55E 57 A8
Anosibe Madag. 19°26S 48°13E 57 B8
Anping Hebei, China 38°15N 115°30E 34 E8
Anping Liaoning, China 41°5N 123°30E 35 D12
Anqing China 30°30N 117°3E 33 C6
Anqiu China 36°25N 119°10E 35 F10
Ansai China 36°50N 109°20E 34 F5
Ansan S. Korea 37°21N 126°52E 35 F14
Ansbach Germany 49°28N 10°34E 16 D6
Anse Boileau Seychelles 4°43S 55°29E 53 b
Anse Royale Seychelles 4°44S 55°31E 53 b
Anshan China 41°5N 122°58E 35 D12
Anshun China 26°18N 105°57E 32 D5
Ansley U.S.A. 41°18N 99°23W 80 E4
Anson U.S.A. 32°45N 99°54W 84 E5
Anson B. Australia 13°20S 130°6E 60 B5
Ansongo Mali 15°25N 0°35E 50 E6
Ansonia U.S.A. 41°21N 73°5W 83 E11
Anstruther U.K. 56°14N 2°41W 11 E6
Ansudu Indonesia 2°11S 139°22E 37 E9
Antabamba Peru 14°40S 73°0W 92 F4
Antakya = Hatay Turkey 36°14N 36°10E 44 B3
Antalaha Madag. 14°57S 50°20E 57 A9
Antalya Turkey 36°52N 30°45E 19 G5
Antalya Körfezi Turkey 36°15N 31°30E 19 G5
Antambohobe Madag. 22°20S 46°47E 57 C8
Antanambao-Manampotsy Madag. 19°29S 48°34E 57 B8
Antanambe Madag. 16°26S 49°52E 57 B8
Antananarivo Madag. 18°55S 47°31E 57 B8
Antananarivo □ Madag. 19°0S 47°0E 57 B8
Antanifotsy Madag. 19°39S 47°19E 57 B8
Antanimbaribe Madag. 21°30S 44°48E 57 C7
Antanimora Madag. 24°49S 45°40E 57 C8
Antarctic Pen. Antarctica 67°0S 60°0W 5 C18
Antarctica 90°0S 0°0 5 E3
Antelope Zimbabwe 21°2S 28°31E 55 G2
Antequera Paraguay 24°8S 57°7W 94 A4
Antequera Spain 37°5N 4°33W 21 D3
Antero, Mt. U.S.A. 38°41N 106°15W 76 G10
Antevamena Madag. 21°2S 44°8E 57 C7
Anthony Kans., U.S.A. 37°9N 98°2W 80 G4
Anthony N. Mex., U.S.A. 32°0N 106°36W 77 K10
Anti Atlas Morocco 30°0N 8°30W 50 C4
Anti-Lebanon = Sharqi, Al Jabal ash Lebanon 33°40N 36°10E 46 B5
Antibes France 43°34N 7°6E 20 E7
Anticosti, Î. d' Canada 49°30N 63°0W 73 C7
Antigo U.S.A. 45°9N 89°9W 80 C9
Antigonish Canada 45°38N 61°58W 73 C7
Antigua Canary Is. 28°24N 14°1W 24 F5
Antigua Guatemala 14°34N 90°41W 88 D1
Antigua W. Indies 17°0N 61°50W 89 C7
Antigua & Barbuda ■ W. Indies 17°20N 61°48W 89 C7
Antikythira Greece 35°52N 23°15E 23 G10
Antilla Cuba 20°40N 75°50W 88 B4
Antilles = West Indies Cent. Amer. 15°0N 65°0W 89 D7
Antioch U.S.A. 38°1N 121°48W 78 G5
Antioquia Colombia 6°40N 75°55W 92 B3
Antipodes Is. Pac. Oc. 49°45S 178°40E 64 M9
Antlers U.S.A. 34°14N 95°37W 84 D7
Antoetra Madag. 20°46S 47°20E 57 C8
Antofagasta Chile 23°50S 70°30W 94 A1
Antofagasta □ Chile 24°0S 69°0W 94 A2
Antofagasta de la Sierra Argentina 26°5S 67°20W 94 B2
Antofalla Argentina 25°30S 68°5W 94 B2
Antofalla, Salar de Argentina 25°40S 67°45W 94 B2
Anton U.S.A. 33°49N 102°10W 84 E3
Antongila, Helodrano Madag. 15°30S 49°50E 57 B8
Antonibé Madag. 15°7S 47°24E 57 B8
Antonibé, Presqu'île d' Madag. 14°55S 47°20E 57 A8
Antonina Brazil 25°26S 48°42W 95 B6
Antrim U.K. 54°43N 6°14W 10 B5
Antrim U.S.A. 40°7N 81°21W 82 F3
Antrim □ U.K. 54°56N 6°25W 10 B5
Antrim, Mts. of U.K. 55°3N 6°14W 10 A5
Antrim Plateau Australia 18°8S 128°20E 60 C4
Antsakabary Madag. 15°3S 48°56E 57 B8
Antsalova Madag. 18°40S 44°37E 57 B7
Antsenavolo Madag. 21°24S 48°3E 57 C8
Antsiafabositra Madag. 17°18S 46°57E 57 B8
Antsirabe Antananarivo, Madag. 19°55S 47°2E 57 B8
Antsirabe Antsiranana, Madag. 14°0S 49°59E 57 A8
Antsirabe Mahajanga, Madag. 15°57S 48°58E 57 B8
Antsiranana Madag. 12°25S 49°20E 57 A8
Antsiranana □ Madag. 12°16S 49°17E 57 A8
Antsohihy Madag. 14°50S 47°59E 57 A8
Antsohimbondrona Seranana Madag. 13°7S 48°48E 57 A8
Antu China 42°30N 128°20E 35 C15
Antwerp = Antwerpen Belgium 51°13N 4°25E 15 C4
Antwerp U.S.A. 44°12N 75°37W 83 B9
Antwerpen Belgium 51°13N 4°25E 15 C4
Antwerpen □ Belgium 51°15N 4°40E 15 C4
Anupgarh India 29°10N 73°10E 42 E5
Anuppur India 23°6N 81°41E 43 H9
Anuradhapura Sri Lanka 8°22N 80°28E 40 Q12
Anveh Iran 27°23N 54°11E 45 E7
Anvers = Antwerpen Belgium 51°13N 4°25E 15 C4
Anvers I. Antarctica 64°30S 63°40W 5 C17
Anxi China 40°30N 95°43E 32 B4
Anxious B. Australia 33°24S 134°45E 63 E1
Anyang China 36°5N 114°21E 34 F8
Anyang S. Korea 37°23N 126°55E 35 F14
Anyer Indonesia 6°4S 105°53E 37 G11
Anyi China 35°2N 111°2E 34 G6
Anza U.S.A. 33°35N 116°39W 79 M10
Anze China 36°10N 112°12E 34 F7
Anzhero-Sudzhensk Russia 56°10N 86°0E 28 D9
Ánzio Italy 41°27N 12°37E 22 D5
Ao Makham Thailand 7°50N 98°24E 39 a
Ao Phangnga △ Thailand 8°10N 98°32E 39 a
Aoga-Shima Japan 32°28N 139°46E 31 H9
Aoji N. Korea 42°31N 130°23E 35 C16
Aomen = Macau China 22°12N 113°33E 33 G10
Aomori Japan 40°45N 140°45E 30 D10
Aomori □ Japan 40°45N 140°40E 30 D10
Aonla India 28°16N 79°11E 43 E8
Aorai, Mt. Tahiti 17°34S 149°30W 59 d
Aoraki Mount Cook N.Z. 43°36S 170°9E 59 E3
Aoral, Phnum Cambodia 12°0N 104°15E 39 G5
Aosta Italy 45°45N 7°20E 20 D7
Aotearoa = New Zealand ■ Oceania 40°0S 176°0E 59 D6
Aoukâr Mauritania 17°40N 10°0W 50 E4
Aozou Strip Chad 22°0N 19°0E 51 D9

Apa → S. Amer. 22°6S 58°2W 94 A4
Apache U.S.A. 34°54N 98°22W 84 D5
Apache Junction U.S.A. 33°25N 111°33W 77 K8
Apalachee B. U.S.A. 30°0N 84°0W 85 G13
Apalachicola U.S.A. 29°43N 84°59W 85 G12
Apalachicola → U.S.A. 29°43N 84°58W 85 G12
Apaporis → Colombia 1°23S 69°25W 92 D5
Aparados da Serra △ Brazil 29°10S 50°8W 95 B5
Aparri Phil. 18°22N 121°38E 37 A6
Apatity Russia 67°34N 33°22E 8 C25
Apatula = Finke Australia 25°34S 134°35E 62 D1
Apatzingán Mexico 19°5N 102°21W 86 D4
Apeldoorn Neths. 52°13N 5°57E 15 B5
Apennines = Appennini Italy 44°30N 10°0E 22 B4
Apia Samoa 13°50S 171°50W 59 b
Apiacás, Serra dos Brazil 9°50S 57°0W 92 E7
Apies → S. Africa 25°15S 28°8E 57 D4
Apizaco Mexico 19°25N 98°8W 87 D5
Aplao Peru 16°0S 72°40W 92 G4
Apo, Mt. Phil. 6°53N 125°14E 37 C7
Apolakia Greece 36°5N 27°48E 25 C9
Apolakia, Ormos Greece 36°5N 27°45E 25 C9
Apollonia = Marsá Susah Libya 32°52N 21°59E 51 B10
Apolo Bolivia 14°30S 68°30W 92 F5
Aporé → Brazil 19°27S 50°57W 93 G8
Apostle Is. U.S.A. 47°0N 90°40W 80 B8
Apostle Islands ⌓ U.S.A. 46°55N 91°0W 80 B8
Apóstoles Argentina 28°0S 56°0W 95 B4
Apostolos Andreas, C. Cyprus 35°42N 34°35E 25 D13
Apoteri Guyana 4°2N 58°32W 92 C7
Appalachian Mts. U.S.A. 38°0N 80°0W 81 G14
Appennini Italy 44°30N 10°0E 22 B4
Apple Hill Canada 45°13N 74°46W 83 A10
Apple Valley U.S.A. 34°32N 117°14W 79 L9
Appleby-in-Westmorland U.K. 54°35N 2°29W 12 C5
Appledore U.K. 51°3N 4°13W 13 F3
Appleton U.S.A. 44°16N 88°25W 80 C9
Approuague → Fr. Guiana 4°30N 51°57W 93 C8
Aprília Italy 41°36N 12°39E 22 D5
Apsley Canada 44°45N 78°6W 82 B6
Apucarana Brazil 23°55S 51°33W 95 A5
Apure → Venezuela 7°37N 66°25W 92 B5
Apurimac → Peru 12°17S 73°56W 92 F4
Āqā Jarī Iran 30°42N 49°50E 45 D6
Aqaba = Al 'Aqabah Jordan 29°31N 35°0E 46 F4
Aqaba, G. of Red Sea 29°0N 34°40E 44 D2
'Aqabah, Khalīj al = Aqaba, G. of Red Sea 29°0N 34°40E 44 D2
'Aqdā Iran 32°26N 53°37E 45 C7
'Aqrah Iraq 36°46N 43°45E 44 B4
Aqsay Kazakhstan 51°11N 53°0E 19 D9
Aqtaū Kazakhstan 43°39N 51°12E 19 F9
Aqtöbe Kazakhstan 50°17N 57°10E 19 D10
Aqtoghay Kazakhstan 46°57N 79°40E 28 E8
Aquidauana Brazil 20°30S 55°50W 93 H7
Aquila Mexico 18°36N 103°30W 86 D4
Aquiles Serdán Mexico 28°36N 105°53W 86 B3
Aquin Haiti 18°16N 73°24W 89 C5
Aquitain, Bassin France 44°0N 0°30W 20 D3
Ar Rachidiya = Er Rachidia Morocco 31°58N 4°20W 50 B5
Ar Rafid Syria 32°57N 35°52E 46 C4
Ar Raḥḥālīyah Iraq 32°44N 43°23E 44 C4
Ar Ramādī Iraq 33°25N 43°20E 44 C4
Ar Ramthā Jordan 32°34N 36°0E 46 C5
Ar Raqqah Syria 35°59N 39°8E 44 C3
Ar Rass Si. Arabia 25°50N 43°40E 44 E4
Ar Rifā'ī Iraq 31°50N 46°10E 44 D5
Ar Riyāḍ Si. Arabia 24°41N 46°42E 44 E5
Ar Ru'ays Qatar 26°8N 51°12E 45 E6
Ar Rukhaymīyah Iraq 29°22N 45°38E 44 D5
Ar Ruṣāfah Syria 35°45N 38°49E 44 C3
Ar Ruṭbah Iraq 33°0N 40°15E 44 C4
Ara India 25°35N 84°32E 43 G11
Arab U.S.A. 34°19N 86°30W 85 D11
'Arab, Bahr el → Sudan 9°0N 29°30E 51 G11
Arab, Shatt al → Asia 29°57N 48°34E 45 D6
'Arabābād Iran 33°2N 57°41E 45 C8
Arabia Asia 25°0N 45°0E 26 F6
Arabian Desert = Es Sahrâ' Esh Sharqîya Egypt 27°30N 32°30E 51 C12
Arabian Gulf = Persian Gulf Asia 27°0N 50°0E 45 E6
Arabian Sea Ind. Oc. 16°0N 65°0E 26 G8
Aracaju Brazil 10°55S 37°4W 93 F11
Aracati Brazil 4°30S 37°44W 93 D11
Araçatuba Brazil 21°10S 50°30W 95 A5
Aracena Spain 37°53N 6°38W 21 D2
Araçuaí Brazil 16°52S 42°4W 93 G10
'Arad Israel 31°15N 35°12E 46 D4
Arad Romania 46°10N 21°20E 17 E11
Arādān Iran 35°21N 52°30E 45 C7
Aradhippou Cyprus 34°57N 33°36E 25 E12
Arafura Sea E. Indies 9°0S 135°0E 58 B6
Aragón □ Spain 41°25N 0°40W 21 B5
Aragón → Spain 42°13N 1°44W 21 A5
Araguacema Brazil 8°50S 49°20W 93 E9
Araguaia → Brazil 5°21S 48°41W 93 E9
Araguaína Brazil 7°12S 48°12W 93 E9
Araguari Brazil 18°38S 48°11W 93 G9
Araguari → Brazil 1°15N 49°55W 93 C9
Arain India 26°27N 75°2E 42 F6
Arak Algeria 25°20N 3°45E 50 C6
Arāk Iran 34°0N 49°40E 45 C6
Arakan Coast Burma 19°0N 94°0E 41 K19
Arakan Yoma Burma 20°0N 94°40E 41 K19
Araks = Aras, Rūd-e → Asia 40°5N 48°29E 44 B5
Aral Kazakhstan 46°41N 61°45E 28 E7
Aral Sea Asia 44°30N 60°0E 28 E7
Aral Tengizi = Aral Sea Asia 44°30N 60°0E 28 E7
Aralsk = Aral Kazakhstan 46°41N 61°45E 28 E7
Aralskoye More = Aral Sea Asia 44°30N 60°0E 28 E7
Aramac Australia 22°58S 145°14E 62 C4
Aran I. Ireland 55°0N 8°30W 10 A3
Aran Is. Ireland 53°6N 9°38W 10 C2
Aranda de Duero Spain 41°39N 3°42W 21 B4
Arandān Iran 35°23N 46°55E 44 C5
Aranjuez Spain 40°1N 3°40W 21 B4
Aranos Namibia 24°9S 19°7E 56 C2
Aransas Pass U.S.A. 27°55N 97°9W 84 H6
Aranyaprathet Thailand 13°41N 102°30E 38 F4
Arapahoe U.S.A. 40°18N 99°54W 80 E4
Arapey Grande → Uruguay 30°55S 57°49W 94 C4
Arapgir Turkey 39°5N 38°30E 44 B3
Arapiraca Brazil 9°45S 36°39W 93 E11
Arapongas Brazil 23°29S 51°28W 95 A5
Ar'ar Si. Arabia 30°59N 41°2E 44 D4
Araranguá Brazil 29°0S 49°30W 95 B6
Araraquara Brazil 21°50S 48°0W 93 H9
Ararás, Serra das Brazil 25°0S 53°10W 95 B5
Ararat Australia 37°16S 142°58E 63 F3
Ararat, Mt. = Ağrı Dağı Turkey 39°50N 44°15E 44 B5
Araria India 26°9N 87°33E 43 F12
Araripe, Chapada do Brazil 7°20S 40°0W 93 E11
Araruama, L. de Brazil 22°53S 42°12W 95 A7
Aras, Rūd-e → Asia 40°5N 48°29E 44 B5
Arauca Colombia 7°0N 70°40W 92 B4
Arauca → Venezuela 7°24N 66°35W 92 B5
Arauco Chile 37°16S 73°25W 94 D1
Arawale ⌓ Kenya 1°24S 40°9E 54 C5
Araxá Brazil 19°35S 46°55W 93 G9
Araya, Pen. de Venezuela 10°40N 64°0W 92 A6
Arba Minch Ethiopia 6°0N 37°30E 47 F2
Arbat Iraq 35°25N 45°35E 44 C5
Árbatax Italy 39°56N 9°42E 22 E3
Arbīl Iraq 36°15N 44°5E 44 B5
Arborfield Canada 53°6N 103°39W 71 C8
Arborg Canada 50°54N 97°13W 71 C9
Arbroath U.K. 56°34N 2°35W 11 E6
Arbuckle U.S.A. 39°1N 122°3W 78 F4
Arcachon France 44°40N 1°10W 20 D3
Arcade U.S.A. 42°32N 78°25W 82 D6
Arcadia Fla., U.S.A. 27°13N 81°52W 85 H14
Arcadia La., U.S.A. 32°33N 92°55W 84 E8
Arcadia Pa., U.S.A. 40°47N 78°51W 82 F6
Arcata U.S.A. 40°52N 124°5W 76 F1
Archangel = Arkhangelsk Russia 64°38N 40°36E 18 B7
Archangelos Greece 36°13N 28°7E 25 C10
Archbald U.S.A. 41°30N 75°32W 83 E9
Archer → Australia 13°20S 141°41E 62 A3
Archer B. Australia 13°20S 141°30E 62 A3
Archer Bend = Mungkan Kandju △ Australia 13°35S 142°52E 62 A3
Archers Post Kenya 0°35N 37°35E 54 B4
Arches △ U.S.A. 38°45N 109°25W 76 G9
Archipel-de-Mingan △ Canada 50°13N 63°10W 73 B7
Archipiélago Chinijo △ Canary Is. 29°20N 13°30W 24 E6
Archipiélago Los Roques △ Venezuela 11°50N 66°44W 89 D6
Arckaringa Cr. → Australia 28°10S 135°22E 63 D2
Arco U.S.A. 43°38N 113°18W 76 E7
Arcos de la Frontera Spain 36°45N 5°49W 21 D3
Arcot India 12°53N 79°20E 40 N11
Arctic Bay Canada 73°1N 85°7W 69 D11
Arctic Mid-Ocean Ridge Arctic 87°0N 90°0E 4 A
Arctic Ocean Arctic 78°0N 160°0W 4 B18
Arctic Red River = Tsiigehtchic Canada 67°15N 134°0W 68 C6
Arctowski Antarctica 62°30S 58°0W 5 C18
Arda → Bulgaria 41°40N 26°30E 23 D12
Ardabīl Iran 38°15N 48°18E 45 B6
Ardabīl □ Iran 38°15N 48°20E 45 B6
Ardakān = Sepīdān Iran 30°20N 52°5E 45 D7
Ardakān Iran 32°19N 53°59E 45 C7
Ardara Ireland 54°46N 8°25W 10 B3
Ardee Ireland 53°52N 6°33W 10 C5
Arden Canada 44°43N 76°56W 82 B8
Arden Calif., U.S.A. 38°36N 121°33W 78 G5
Arden Nev., U.S.A. 36°1N 115°14W 79 J11
Ardenne Belgium 49°50N 5°5E 15 E5
Ardennes = Ardenne Belgium 49°50N 5°5E 15 E5
Arderin Ireland 53°2N 7°39W 10 C4
Ardestān Iran 33°20N 52°25E 45 C7
Ardfert Ireland 52°20N 9°47W 10 D2
Ardglass U.K. 54°17N 5°36W 10 B6
Ardivachar Pt. U.K. 57°23N 7°26W 11 D1
Ardlethan Australia 34°22S 146°53E 63 E4
Ardmore Okla., U.S.A. 34°10N 97°8W 84 D6
Ardmore Pa., U.S.A. 40°2N 75°17W 83 F9
Ardnamurchan, Pt. of U.K. 56°43N 6°14W 11 E2
Ardnave Pt. U.K. 55°53N 6°20W 11 F2
Ardrossan Australia 34°26S 137°53E 63 E2
Ardrossan U.K. 55°39N 4°49W 11 F4
Ards Pen. U.K. 54°33N 5°34W 10 B6
Arecibo Puerto Rico 18°29N 66°43W 89 d
Areia Branca Brazil 5°0S 37°0W 93 E11
Arena, Pt. U.S.A. 38°57N 123°44W 78 G3
Arenal Honduras 15°21N 86°50W 88 C2
Arendal Norway 58°28N 8°46E 9 G13
Arequipa Peru 16°20S 71°30W 92 G4
Arévalo Spain 41°3N 4°43W 21 B3
Arezzo Italy 43°25N 11°53E 22 C4
Arga Turkey 38°21N 37°59E 44 B3
Arganda Spain 40°19N 3°26W 21 B4
Argenta Canada 50°11N 116°56W 70 C5
Argentan France 48°45N 0°1W 20 B3
Argentário, Mte. Italy 42°24N 11°9E 22 C4
Argentia Canada 47°18N 53°58W 73 C9
Argentina ■ S. Amer. 35°0S 66°0W 96 D3
Argentine Basin Atl. Oc. 45°0S 45°0W 96 F6
Argentino, L. Argentina 50°10S 73°0W 96 G2
Argeş → Romania 44°5N 26°38E 17 F14
Arghandab → Afghan. 31°30N 64°15E 42 D1
Argirades Greece 39°27N 19°58E 25 B3
Argiroupoli Greece 35°17N 24°20E 25 D6
Argolikos Kolpos Greece 37°20N 22°52E 23 F10
Argos Greece 37°40N 22°43E 23 F10
Argostoli Greece 38°11N 20°29E 23 E9
Arguello, Pt. U.S.A. 34°35N 120°39W 79 L6
Arguineguín Canary Is. 27°46N 15°41W 24 G4
Argun → Russia 53°20N 121°28E 29 D13
Argungu Nigeria 12°40N 4°31E 50 F6
Argus Pk. U.S.A. 35°52N 117°26W 79 K9
Argyle, L. Australia 16°20S 128°40E 60 C4
Argyll ⌓ U.K. 56°6N 5°0W 11 E4
Argyll & Bute □ U.K. 56°13N 5°28W 11 E3
Århus Denmark 56°8N 10°11E 9 H14
Ariadnoye Russia 45°8N 134°25E 30 B7
Ariamsvlei Namibia 28°9S 19°51E 56 D2
Ariana Tunisia 36°52N 10°12E 51 A8
Arica Chile 18°32S 70°20W 92 G4
Arica Colombia 2°0S 71°50W 92 D4
Arico Canary Is. 28°9N 16°29W 24 F3
Arid, C. Australia 34°1S 123°10E 61 F3
Arida Japan 34°5N 135°8E 31 G7
Aride Seychelles 4°13S 55°40E 53 b
Ariège → France 43°30N 1°25E 20 E4
Arila, Akra Greece 39°43N 19°39E 25 A3
Arima Trin. & Tob. 10°38N 61°17W 89 D7
Arinos → Brazil 10°25S 58°20W 92 F7
Ario de Rosales Mexico 19°12N 101°43W 86 D4
Aripo, Mt. Trin. & Tob. 10°45N 61°15W 93 K15
Aripuanã Brazil 9°25S 60°30W 92 E6
Aripuanã → Brazil 5°7S 60°25W 92 E6
Ariquemes Brazil 9°55S 63°6W 92 E6
Arisaig U.K. 56°55N 5°51W 11 E3
Aristazabal I. Canada 52°40N 129°10W 70 C3
Arivonimamo Madag. 19°1S 47°11E 57 B8
Arizaro, Salar de Argentina 24°40S 67°50W 94 A2
Arizona Argentina 35°45S 65°25W 94 D2
Arizona □ U.S.A. 34°0N 112°0W 77 J8
Arizpe Mexico 30°20N 110°10W 86 A2
Arjeplog Sweden 66°3N 17°54E 8 C17
Arjepluovve = Arjeplog Sweden 66°3N 17°54E 8 C17
Arjona Colombia 10°14N 75°22W 92 A3
Arjuna Indonesia 7°49S 112°34E 37 G15
Arka Russia 60°15N 142°0E 29 C15
Arkadelphia U.S.A. 34°7N 93°4W 84 D8
Arkaig, L. U.K. 56°59N 5°10W 11 E3
Arkalyk = Arqalyk Kazakhstan 50°13N 66°50E 28 D7
Arkansas □ U.S.A. 35°0N 92°30W 84 D8
Arkansas → U.S.A. 33°47N 91°4W 84 E9
Arkansas City U.S.A. 37°4N 97°2W 80 G5
Arkaroola Australia 30°20S 139°22E 63 E2
Arkhangelsk Russia 64°38N 40°36E 18 B7
Arki India 31°9N 76°58E 42 D7
Arklow Ireland 52°48N 6°10W 10 D5
Arkport U.S.A. 42°24N 77°42W 82 D7
Arkticheskiy, Mys Russia 81°10N 95°0E 29 A10
Arkville U.S.A. 42°9N 74°37W 83 D10
Arlanzón → Spain 42°3N 4°17W 21 A3
Arlbergpass Austria 47°9N 10°12E 16 E6
Arles France 43°41N 4°40E 20 E6
Arlington S. Africa 28°1S 27°53E 57 D4
Arlington N.Y., U.S.A. 41°42N 73°54W 83 E11
Arlington Oreg., U.S.A. 45°43N 120°12W 76 D3
Arlington S. Dak., U.S.A. 44°22N 97°8W 80 C5
Arlington Tex., U.S.A. 32°44N 97°6W 84 E6
Arlington Va., U.S.A. 38°53N 77°7W 81 F15
Arlington Vt., U.S.A. 43°5N 73°9W 83 C11
Arlington Wash., U.S.A. 48°12N 122°8W 78 B4
Arlington Heights U.S.A. 42°5N 87°59W 80 D10
Arlit Niger 19°0N 7°38E 50 E7
Arlon Belgium 49°42N 5°49E 15 E5
Arlparra Australia 22°11S 134°30E 62 C1
Arltunga Australia 23°26S 134°41E 62 C1
Armagh U.K. 54°21N 6°39W 10 B5
Armagh □ U.K. 54°18N 6°37W 10 B5
Armando Bermudez △ Dom. Rep. 19°3N 71°0W 89 C5
Armavir Russia 45°2N 41°7E 19 E7
Armenia Colombia 4°35N 75°45W 92 C3
Armenia ■ Asia 40°20N 45°0E 19 F7
Armenistis, Akra Greece 36°8N 27°42E 25 C9
Armidale Australia 30°30S 151°40E 63 E5
Armour U.S.A. 43°19N 98°21W 80 D4
Armstrong B.C., Canada 50°25N 119°10W 70 C5
Armstrong Ont., Canada 50°18N 89°4W 72 B2
Arnarfjörður Iceland 65°48N 23°40W 8 D2
Arnaud → Canada 59°59N 69°46W 69 D13
Arnauti, C. Cyprus 35°6N 32°17E 25 D11
Arnett U.S.A. 36°8N 99°46W 84 C5
Arnhem Neths. 51°58N 5°55E 15 C5
Arnhem, C. Australia 12°20S 137°30E 62 A2
Arnhem B. Australia 12°20S 136°10E 62 A2
Arnhem Land Australia 13°10S 134°30E 62 A1
Arno → Italy 43°41N 10°17E 22 C4
Arno Bay Australia 33°54S 136°34E 63 E2
Arnold U.K. 53°1N 1°7W 12 D6
Arnold U.S.A. 38°15N 120°21W 78 G6
Arnot Canada 55°56N 96°41W 71 B9
Arnøya Norway 70°9N 20°40E 8 A19
Arnprior Canada 45°26N 76°21W 83 A8
Arnsberg Germany 51°24N 8°5E 16 C5
Aroa, Pte. Moorea 17°28S 149°46W 59 d
Aroab Namibia 26°41S 19°39E 56 D2
Aron India 25°57N 77°56E 42 G6
Arona Canary Is. 28°6N 16°40W 24 F3
Aros → Mexico 29°9N 107°57W 86 B3
Arqalyk Kazakhstan 50°13N 66°50E 28 D7
Arrah = Ara India 25°35N 84°32E 43 G11
Arrah Ivory C. 6°40N 3°58W 50 G5
Arran U.K. 55°34N 5°12W 11 F3
Arras France 50°17N 2°46E 20 A5
Arrecife Canary Is. 28°57N 13°37W 24 F6
Arrecifes Argentina 34°6S 60°9W 94 C3
Arrée, Mts. d' France 48°26N 3°55W 20 B2
Arriaga Mexico 16°14N 93°54W 87 D6
Arrilalah Australia 23°43S 143°54E 62 C3
Arrino Australia 29°30S 115°40E 61 E2
Arrow, L. Ireland 54°3N 8°19W 10 B3
Arrowtown N.Z. 44°57S 168°50E 59 F2
Arroyo Grande U.S.A. 35°7N 120°35W 79 K6
Ars Iran 37°9N 47°46E 44 B5
Arsenault L. Canada 55°6N 108°32W 71 B7
Arsenev Russia 44°10N 133°15E 30 B6
Arta Greece 39°8N 21°2E 23 E9
Artà Spain 39°41N 3°21E 24 B10
Arteaga Mexico 18°28N 102°25W 86 D4
Artem Russia 43°22N 132°13E 30 C6
Artemovsk Russia 54°45N 93°35E 29 D10
Artemovsk Ukraine 48°35N 38°0E 19 E6
Artesia = Mosomane Botswana 24°2S 26°19E 56 C4
Artesia U.S.A. 32°51N 104°24W 77 K11
Arthur Canada 43°50N 80°32W 82 C4
Arthur → Australia 41°2S 144°40E 63 G3
Arthur Cr. → Australia 22°30S 136°25E 62 C2
Arthur Pt. Australia 22°7S 150°3E 62 C5
Arthur River Australia 33°20S 117°2E 61 F2
Arthur's Pass N.Z. 42°54S 171°35E 59 E3
Arthur's Pass △ N.Z. 42°53S 171°42E 59 E3
Arthur's Town Bahamas 24°38N 75°42W 89 B4
Artigas Antarctica 62°30S 58°0W 5 C18
Artigas Uruguay 30°20S 56°30W 94 C4
Artillery L. Canada 63°9N 107°52W 71 A7
Artois France 50°20N 2°30E 20 A5
Artrutx, C. de Spain 39°55N 3°49E 24 B10
Artsyz Ukraine 46°4N 29°26E 17 E15
Artux China 39°40N 76°10E 32 C2
Artvin Turkey 41°14N 41°44E 19 F7
Aru, Kepulauan Indonesia 6°0S 134°30E 37 F8
Aru Is. = Aru, Kepulauan Indonesia 6°0S 134°30E 37 F8
Arua Uganda 3°1N 30°58E 54 B3
Aruanã Brazil 14°54S 51°10W 93 F8
Aruba ☑ W. Indies 12°30N 70°0W 89 D6
Arucas Canary Is. 28°7N 15°32W 24 F4
Arue Tahiti 17°31S 149°30W 59 d
Arun → Nepal 26°55N 87°10E 43 F12
Arun → U.K. 50°49N 0°33W 13 G7
Arunachal Pradesh □ India 28°0N 95°0E 41 F19
Arusha Tanzania 3°20S 36°40E 54 C4
Arusha □ Tanzania 4°0S 36°30E 54 C4
Arusha △ Tanzania 3°16S 36°47E 54 C4
Arusha Chini Tanzania 3°32S 37°20E 54 C4
Aruwimi → Dem. Rep. of the Congo 1°13N 23°36E 54 B1
Arvada Colo., U.S.A. 39°48N 105°5W 76 G11
Arvada Wyo., U.S.A. 44°39N 106°8W 76 D10
Arvayheer Mongolia 46°15N 102°48E 32 B5
Arvi Greece 34°59N 25°28E 25 E7
Arviat Canada 61°6N 93°59W 71 A10
Arvidsjaur Sweden 65°35N 19°10E 8 D18
Arvika Sweden 59°40N 12°36E 9 G15
Arvin U.S.A. 35°12N 118°50W 79 K8
Arwal India 25°15N 84°41E 43 G11
Arxan China 47°11N 119°57E 33 B6
Arys Kazakhstan 42°26N 68°48E 28 E7
Arzamas Russia 55°27N 43°55E 18 C7
Arzanah U.A.E. 24°47N 52°34E 45 E7
Aş Şafā Syria 33°10N 37°0E 46 B6
As Saffānīyah Si. Arabia 27°55N 48°50E 45 E6
As Safīrah Syria 36°5N 37°21E 44 B3
Aş Şahm Oman 24°10N 56°53E 45 E8
As Sājir Si. Arabia 25°11N 44°36E 44 E5
As Salamīyah Syria 35°1N 37°2E 44 C3
As Salmān Iraq 30°30N 44°32E 44 D5
As Salṭ Jordan 32°2N 35°43E 46 C4
As Sal'w'a Qatar 24°23N 50°50E 45 E6
As Samāwah Iraq 31°15N 45°15E 44 D5
As Sanamayn Syria 33°3N 36°10E 46 B5
As Sohar = Şuḥār Oman 24°20N 56°40E 45 E8
As Sukhnah Syria 34°52N 38°52E 44 C3
As Sulaymānīyah Iraq 35°35N 45°29E 44 C5
As Sulaymī Si. Arabia 26°17N 41°21E 44 E4
As Sulayyil Si. Arabia 20°27N 45°34E 47 C4
As Summān Si. Arabia 25°0N 47°0E 44 E5
As Suwaydā' Syria 32°40N 36°30E 46 C5
As Suwaydā' □ Syria 32°45N 36°45E 46 C5
As Suwayq Oman 23°51N 57°26E 45 F8
Aş Şuwayrah Iraq 32°55N 45°0E 44 C5
Asab Namibia 25°30S 18°0E 56 D2
Asad, Buḥayrat al Syria 36°0N 38°15E 44 C3
Asahi-Gawa → Japan 34°36N 133°58E 31 G6
Asahigawa Japan 43°46N 142°22E 30 C11
Asamankese Ghana 5°50N 0°40W 50 G5
Asan → India 26°37N 78°24E 43 F8
Asansol India 23°40N 87°1E 43 H12
Asau Samoa 13°27S 172°33W 59 b
Asbesberge S. Africa 29°0S 23°0E 56 D3
Asbestos Canada 45°47N 71°58W 73 C5
Asbury Park U.S.A. 40°13N 74°1W 83 F10
Ascensión Mexico 31°6N 107°59W 86 A3
Ascensión, B. de la Mexico 19°40N 87°30W 87 D7
Ascension I. Atl. Oc. 7°57S 14°23W 49 G2
Aschaffenburg Germany 49°58N 9°6E 16 D5
Aschersleben Germany 51°45N 11°29E 16 C6
Áscoli Piceno Italy 42°51N 13°34E 22 C5
Ascope Peru 7°46S 79°8W 92 E3
Ascotán Chile 21°45S 68°17W 94 A2
Aseb Eritrea 13°0N 42°40E 47 E3
Asela Ethiopia 8°0N 39°0E 47 F2
Asenovgrad Bulgaria 42°1N 24°51E 23 C11
Aşgabat = Ashgabat Turkmenistan 38°0N 57°50E 45 B8
Asgata Cyprus 34°46N 33°15E 25 E12
Ash Fork U.S.A. 35°13N 112°29W 77 J7
Ash Grove U.S.A. 37°19N 93°35W 80 G7
Ash Shabakah Iraq 30°49N 43°39E 44 D4
Ash Shamāl □ Lebanon 34°25N 36°0E 46 A5
Ash Shāmīyah Iraq 31°55N 44°35E 44 D5
Ash Shāriqah U.A.E. 25°23N 55°26E 45 E7
Ash Sharmah Si. Arabia 28°1N 35°16E 44 D2
Ash Sharqāt Iraq 35°27N 43°16E 44 C4
Ash Shaṭrah Iraq 31°30N 46°10E 44 D5
Ash Shawbak Jordan 30°32N 35°34E 44 D2
Ash Shināfīyah Iraq 31°35N 44°39E 44 D5
Ash Shu'bah Si. Arabia 28°54N 44°44E 44 D5
Ash Shumlūl Si. Arabia 26°31N 47°20E 44 E5
Ash Shūr'a Iraq 35°58N 43°13E 44 C4
Ash Shurayf Si. Arabia 25°43N 39°14E 44 E3
Ash Shuwayfāt Lebanon 33°45N 35°30E 46 B4
Asha Russia 55°0N 57°16E 18 D10
Ashau Vietnam 16°6N 107°22E 38 D6
Ashbourne U.K. 53°2N 1°43W 12 D6
Ashburn U.S.A. 31°43N 83°39W 85 F13
Ashburton N.Z. 43°53S 171°48E 59 E3
Ashburton → Australia 21°40S 114°56E 60 D1
Ashcroft Canada 50°40N 121°20W 70 C4
Ashdod Israel 31°49N 34°35E 46 D3
Ashdown U.S.A. 33°40N 94°8W 84 E7
Asheboro U.S.A. 35°43N 79°49W 85 D15
Ashern Canada 51°11N 98°21W 71 C9
Asherton U.S.A. 28°27N 99°46W 84 G5
Asheville U.S.A. 35°36N 82°33W 85 D13
Ashewat Pakistan 31°22N 68°32E 42 D3
Asheweig → Canada 54°17N 87°12W 72 B2
Ashford Australia 29°15S 151°3E 63 D5
Ashford U.K. 51°8N 0°53E 13 F8
Ashgabat Turkmenistan 38°0N 57°50E 45 B8
Ashibetsu Japan 43°31N 142°11E 30 C11
Ashikaga Japan 36°28N 139°29E 31 F9
Ashington U.K. 55°11N 1°33W 12 B6
Ashizuri-Uwakai △ Japan 32°56N 132°32E 31 H6
Ashizuri-Zaki Japan 32°44N 133°0E 31 H6
Ashkarkot Afghan. 33°3N 67°58E 42 C2
Ashkhabad = Ashgabat Turkmenistan 38°0N 57°50E 45 B8
Āshkhāneh Iran 37°26N 56°55E 45 B8
Ashland Kans., U.S.A. 37°11N 99°46W 80 G4
Ashland Ky., U.S.A. 38°28N 82°38W 81 F12
Ashland Maine, U.S.A. 46°38N 68°24W 81 B19
Ashland Mont., U.S.A. 45°36N 106°16W 76 D10
Ashland Ohio, U.S.A. 40°52N 82°19W 82 F2
Ashland Oreg., U.S.A. 42°12N 122°43W 76 E2
Ashland Pa., U.S.A. 40°45N 76°22W 83 F8
Ashland Va., U.S.A. 37°46N 77°29W 81 G15
Ashland Wis., U.S.A. 46°35N 90°53W 80 B8
Ashley N. Dak., U.S.A. 46°2N 99°22W 80 B4
Ashley Pa., U.S.A. 41°12N 75°55W 83 E9
Ashmore and Cartier Is. Ind. Oc. 12°15S 123°0E 60 B3
Ashmore Reef Australia 12°14S 123°5E 60 B3
Ashmyany Belarus 54°26N 25°52E 17 A13
Ashokan Res. U.S.A. 41°56N 74°13W 83 E10
Ashqelon Israel 31°42N 34°35E 46 D3
Ashta India 23°1N 76°43E 42 H7
Ashtabula U.S.A. 41°52N 80°47W 82 E4
Ashton S. Africa 33°50S 20°5E 56 E3
Ashton U.S.A. 44°4N 111°27W 76 D8
Ashuanipi, L. Canada 52°45N 66°15W 73 B6
Ashuapmushuan → Canada 48°37N 72°20W 72 C5
Ashville U.S.A. 40°34N 78°33W 82 F6
Asia 45°0N 75°0E 26 E9
Asia, Kepulauan Indonesia 1°0N 131°13E 37 D8
Asifabad India 19°20N 79°24E 40 K11
Asinara Italy 41°4N 8°16E 22 D3
Asinara, G. dell' Italy 41°0N 8°30E 22 D3
Asino Russia 57°0N 86°0E 28 D9
Asipovichy Belarus 53°19N 28°33E 17 B15
'Asīr Si. Arabia 18°40N 42°30E 47 D3
Asir, Ras Somali Rep. 11°55N 51°10E 47 E5
Askham S. Africa 26°59S 20°47E 56 D3
Askim Norway 59°35N 11°10E 9 G14
Askja Iceland 65°3N 16°48W 8 D5
Askøyna Norway 60°29N 5°10E 8 F11
Asmara = Asmera Eritrea 15°19N 38°55E 47 D2
Asmera Eritrea 15°19N 38°55E 47 D2
Åsnen Sweden 56°37N 14°45E 9 H16
Aso Kuju △ Japan 32°53N 131°6E 31 H5
Aspatria U.K. 54°47N 3°19W 12 C4
Aspen U.S.A. 39°11N 106°49W 76 G10
Aspermont U.S.A. 33°8N 100°14W 84 E4
Aspiring, Mt. N.Z. 44°23S 168°46E 59 F2
Asprokavos, Akra Greece 39°21N 20°6E 25 B4
Aspur India 23°58N 74°7E 42 H6
Asquith Canada 52°8N 107°13W 71 C7
Assab = Aseb Eritrea 13°0N 42°40E 47 E3
Assal, L. Djibouti 11°40N 42°26E 47 E3
Assam □ India 26°0N 93°0E 41 G18
Assateague Island ⌓ U.S.A. 38°15N 75°10W 81 F16
Asse Belgium 50°24N 4°10E 15 D4

Assen Neths. 53°0N 6°35E 15 A6
Assiniboia Canada 49°40N 105°59W 71 D7
Assiniboine → Canada 49°53N 97°8W 71 D9
Assiniboine, Mt. Canada 50°52N 115°39W 70 C5
Assis Brazil 22°40S 50°20W 95 A5
Assisi Italy 43°4N 12°37E 22 C5
Assynt, L. U.K. 58°10N 5°3W 11 C3
Astana Kazakhstan 51°10N 71°30E 28 D8
Āstāneh Iran 37°17N 49°59E 45 B6
Astara Azerbaijan 38°30N 48°50E 45 B6
Asterousia Greece 34°59N 25°3E 25 E7
Asti Italy 44°54N 8°12E 20 D8
Astipalea Greece 36°32N 26°22E 23 F12
Astorga Spain 42°29N 6°8W 21 A2
Astoria U.S.A. 46°11N 123°50W 78 D3
Astrakhan Russia 46°25N 48°5E 19 E8
Asturias □ Spain 43°15N 6°0W 21 A3
Asunción Paraguay 25°10S 57°30W 94 B4
Asunción Nochixtlán Mexico 17°28N 97°14W 87 D5
Aswa → Uganda 3°43N 31°55E 54 B3
Aswa-Lolim ⌂ Uganda 2°43N 31°35E 54 B3
Aswân Egypt 24°4N 32°57E 51 D12
Aswan Dam = Sadd el Aali Egypt 23°54N 32°54E 51 D12
Asyût Egypt 27°11N 31°4E 51 C12
At Ţafilah Jordan 30°45N 35°30E 46 E4
At Ţafilah □ Jordan 30°45N 35°30E 46 E4
Aţ Ţā'if Si. Arabia 21°5N 40°27E 47 C3
At Ta'mīm □ Iraq 35°30N 44°20E 44 C5
Aţ Ţirāq Si. Arabia 27°19N 44°33E 44 E5
Aţ Ţubayq Si. Arabia 29°30N 37°0E 44 D3
Aţ Ţunayb Jordan 31°48N 35°57E 46 D4
Atacama □ Chile 27°30S 70°0W 94 B2
Atacama, Desierto de Chile 24°0S 69°20W 94 A2
Atacama, Salar de Chile 23°30S 68°20W 94 A2
Atakpamé Togo 7°31N 1°13E 50 G6
Atalaya Peru 10°45S 73°50W 92 F4
Atalaya de Femes Canary Is. 28°56N 13°47W 24 F6
Atami Japan 35°5N 139°4E 31 G9
Atamyrat Turkmenistan 37°50N 65°12E 28 F7
Atapupu Indonesia 9°0S 124°51E 37 F6
Atâr Mauritania 20°30N 13°5W 50 D3
Atari Pakistan 30°56N 74°2E 42 D6
Atascadero U.S.A. 35°29N 120°40W 78 K6
Atasū Kazakhstan 48°30N 71°0E 28 E8
Atatürk Barajı Turkey 37°28N 38°30E 19 G6
Atauro E. Timor 8°10S 125°30E 37 F7
Ataviros Greece 36°12N 27°50E 25 C9
Atbara Sudan 17°42N 33°59E 51 E12
'Atbara, Nahr → Sudan 17°40N 33°56E 51 E12
Atbasar Kazakhstan 51°48N 68°20E 28 D7
Atchafalaya B. U.S.A. 29°25N 91°25W 84 G9
Atchison U.S.A. 39°34N 95°7W 80 F6
Āteshān Iran 35°35N 52°37E 45 C7
Ath Belgium 50°38N 3°47E 15 D3
Athabasca Canada 54°45N 113°20W 70 C6
Athabasca → Canada 58°40N 110°50W 71 B6
Athabasca, L. Canada 59°15N 109°15W 71 B7
Athabasca Sand Dunes ⌂ Canada 59°4N 108°43W 71 B7
Athboy Ireland 53°37N 6°56W 10 C5
Athenry Ireland 53°18N 8°44W 10 C3
Athens = Athina Greece 37°58N 23°43E 23 F10
Athens Ala., U.S.A. 34°48N 86°58W 85 D11
Athens Ga., U.S.A. 33°57N 83°23W 85 E13
Athens N.Y., U.S.A. 42°16N 73°49W 83 D11
Athens Ohio, U.S.A. 39°20N 82°6W 81 F12
Athens Pa., U.S.A. 41°57N 76°31W 83 E8
Athens Tenn., U.S.A. 35°27N 84°36W 85 D12
Athens Tex., U.S.A. 32°12N 95°51W 84 E7
Atherley Canada 44°37N 79°20W 82 B5
Atherton Australia 17°17S 145°30E 62 B4
Athi River Kenya 1°28S 36°58E 54 C4
Athienou Cyprus 35°3N 33°32E 25 D12
Athina Greece 37°58N 23°43E 23 F10
Athínai = Athina Greece 37°58N 23°43E 23 F10
Athlone Ireland 53°25N 7°56W 10 C4
Athna Cyprus 35°3N 33°47E 25 D12
Athol U.S.A. 42°36N 72°14W 83 D12
Atholl, Forest of U.K. 56°51N 3°50W 11 E5
Atholville Canada 47°59N 66°43W 73 C6
Athos Greece 40°9N 24°22E 23 D11
Athy Ireland 53°0N 7°0W 10 C5
Ati Chad 13°13N 18°20E 51 F9
Atiak Uganda 3°12N 32°2E 54 B3
Atik L. Canada 55°15N 96°0W 71 B9
Atikaki ⌂ Canada 51°30N 95°31W 71 C9
Atikameg → Canada 52°30N 82°46W 72 B3
Atikokan Canada 48°45N 91°37W 72 C1
Atikonak L. Canada 52°40N 64°32W 73 B7
Atimaono Tahiti 17°46S 149°28W 59 d
Atitlán △ Cent. Amer. 14°38N 91°10W 87 E6
Atiu Cook Is. 20°0S 158°10W 65 J12
Atka Russia 60°50N 151°48E 29 C16
Atka I. U.S.A. 52°7N 174°30W 74 a
Atkinson U.S.A. 42°32N 98°59W 80 D4
Atlanta Ga., U.S.A. 33°45N 84°23W 85 E12
Atlanta Tex., U.S.A. 33°7N 94°10W 84 E7
Atlantic U.S.A. 41°24N 95°1W 80 E6
Atlantic City U.S.A. 39°21N 74°27W 81 F16
Atlantic-Indian Basin Antarctica 60°0S 30°0E 5 B4
Atlantic Ocean 0°0 20°0W 2 D8
Atlas Mts. = Haut Atlas Morocco 32°30N 5°0W 50 B4
Atlin Canada 59°31N 133°41W 70 B2
Atlin, L. Canada 59°26N 133°45W 70 B2
Atlin ⌂ Canada 59°10N 134°30W 70 B2
Atmore U.S.A. 31°2N 87°29W 85 F11
Atoka U.S.A. 34°23N 96°8W 84 D6
Atolia U.S.A. 35°19N 117°37W 79 K9
Atrai → Bangla. 24°7N 89°22E 43 G13
Atrak = Atrek → Turkmenistan 37°35N 53°58E 45 B8
Atrauli India 28°2N 78°20E 42 E8
Atrek → Turkmenistan 37°35N 53°58E 45 B8
Atsuta Japan 43°24N 141°26E 30 C10
Attalla U.S.A. 34°1N 86°6W 85 D11
Attapu Laos 14°48N 106°50E 38 E6
Attawapiskat Canada 52°56N 82°24W 72 B3
Attawapiskat → Canada 52°57N 82°18W 72 B3
Attawapiskat L. Canada 52°18N 87°54W 72 B2
Attica Ind., U.S.A. 40°18N 87°15W 80 E10
Attica Ohio, U.S.A. 41°4N 82°53W 82 E2
Attikamagen L. Canada 55°0N 66°30W 73 B6
Attleboro U.S.A. 41°57N 71°17W 83 E13
Attock Pakistan 33°52N 72°20E 42 C5
Attopeu = Attapu Laos 14°48N 106°50E 38 E6
Attu I. U.S.A. 52°55N 172°55E 74 a
Attur India 11°35N 78°30E 40 P11
Atuel → Argentina 36°17S 66°50W 94 D2
Åtvidaberg Sweden 58°12N 16°0E 9 G17
Atwater U.S.A. 37°21N 120°37W 78 H6
Atwood Canada 43°40N 81°1W 82 C3
Atwood U.S.A. 39°48N 101°3W 80 F3
Atyraū Kazakhstan 47°5N 52°0E 19 E9
Au Sable U.S.A. 44°25N 83°20W 82 B1
Au Sable → U.S.A. 44°25N 83°20W 81 C12
Au Sable Forks U.S.A. 44°27N 73°41W 83 B11
Au Sable Pt. U.S.A. 44°20N 83°20W 82 B1
Auasberg Namibia 22°37S 17°13E 56 C2
Aubagne France 43°17N 5°37E 20 E6
Aubarca, C. d' Spain 39°4N 1°22E 24 B7
Aube → France 48°34N 3°43E 20 B5
Auberry U.S.A. 37°7N 119°29W 78 H7
Auburn Ala., U.S.A. 32°36N 85°29W 85 E12
Auburn Calif., U.S.A. 38°54N 121°4W 78 G5
Auburn Ind., U.S.A. 41°22N 85°4W 81 E11
Auburn Maine, U.S.A. 44°6N 70°14W 81 C18
Auburn N.Y., U.S.A. 42°56N 76°34W 83 D8
Auburn Nebr., U.S.A. 40°23N 95°51W 80 E6
Auburn Pa., U.S.A. 40°36N 76°6W 83 F8
Auburn Wash., U.S.A. 47°18N 122°14W 78 C4
Auburn Ra. Australia 25°15S 150°30E 63 D5
Auburndale U.S.A. 28°4N 81°48W 85 G14
Aubusson France 45°57N 2°11E 20 D5
Auch France 43°39N 0°36E 20 E4
Auchterarder U.K. 56°18N 3°41W 11 E5
Auchtermuchty U.K. 56°18N 3°13W 11 E5
Auckland N.Z. 36°52S 174°46E 59 B5
Auckland Is. Pac. Oc. 50°40S 166°5E 64 N8
Aude → France 43°13N 3°14E 20 E5
Auden Canada 50°14N 87°53W 72 B2
Audubon U.S.A. 41°43N 94°56W 80 E6
Augathella Australia 25°48S 146°35E 63 D4
Aughnacloy U.K. 54°25N 6°59W 10 B5
Aughrim Ireland 53°18N 8°19W 10 C3
Augrabies Falls S. Africa 28°35S 20°20E 56 D3
Augrabies Falls △ S. Africa 28°40S 20°22E 56 D3
Augsburg Germany 48°25N 10°52E 16 D6
Augusta Australia 34°19S 115°9E 61 F2
Augusta Italy 37°13N 15°13E 22 F6
Augusta Ark., U.S.A. 35°17N 91°22W 84 D9
Augusta Ga., U.S.A. 33°28N 81°58W 85 E14
Augusta Kans., U.S.A. 37°41N 96°59W 80 G5
Augusta Maine, U.S.A. 44°19N 69°47W 81 C19
Augusta Mont., U.S.A. 47°30N 112°24W 76 C7
Augustów Poland 53°51N 23°0E 17 B12
Augustus, Mt. Australia 24°20S 116°50E 61 D2
Augustus I. Australia 15°20S 124°30E 60 C3
Aujuittuq = Grise Fiord Canada 76°25N 82°57W 69 B11
Aukštaitija △ Lithuania 55°15N 26°0E 9 J22
Aukum U.S.A. 38°34N 120°43W 78 G6
Auld, L. Australia 22°25S 123°50E 60 D3
Ault U.S.A. 40°35N 104°44W 76 F11
Aunis France 46°5N 0°50W 20 C3
Aunu'u Amer. Samoa 14°20S 170°31W 59 b
Auponhia Indonesia 1°58S 125°27E 37 E7
Aur, Pulau Malaysia 2°35N 104°10E 39 L5
Auraiya India 26°28N 79°33E 43 F8
Aurangabad Bihar, India 24°45N 84°18E 43 G11
Aurangabad Maharashtra, India 19°50N 75°23E 40 K9
Aurich Germany 53°28N 7°28E 16 B4
Aurillac France 44°55N 2°26E 20 D5
Aurora Canada 44°0N 79°28W 82 C5
Aurora S. Africa 32°40S 18°29E 56 E2
Aurora Colo., U.S.A. 39°43N 104°49W 76 G11
Aurora Ill., U.S.A. 41°45N 88°19W 80 E9
Aurora Mo., U.S.A. 36°58N 93°43W 80 G7
Aurora N.Y., U.S.A. 42°45N 76°42W 83 D8
Aurora Nebr., U.S.A. 40°52N 98°0W 80 E5
Aurora Ohio, U.S.A. 41°21N 81°20W 82 E3
Aurukun Australia 13°20S 141°45E 62 A3
Aus Namibia 26°35S 16°12E 56 D2
Ausable → Canada 43°19N 81°46W 82 C3
Auschwitz = Oświęcim Poland 50°2N 19°11E 17 C10
Austin Minn., U.S.A. 43°40N 92°58W 80 D7
Austin Nev., U.S.A. 39°30N 117°4W 76 G5
Austin Pa., U.S.A. 41°38N 78°6W 82 E6
Austin Tex., U.S.A. 30°17N 97°45W 84 F6
Austin, L. Australia 27°40S 118°0E 61 E2
Austin I. Canada 61°10N 94°0W 71 A10
Austra Norway 65°8N 11°55E 8 D14
Austral Is. = Tubuaï, Îs. French Polynesia 25°0S 150°0W 65 K13
Austral Seamount Chain Pac. Oc. 24°0S 150°0W 65 K13
Australia ■ Oceania 23°0S 135°0E 58 D6
Australian-Antarctic Basin S. Ocean 60°0S 120°0E 5 C9
Australian Capital Territory □ Australia 35°30S 149°0E 63 F4
Australind Australia 33°17S 115°42E 61 F2
Austria ■ Europe 47°0N 14°0E 16 E8
Austvågøya Norway 68°20N 14°40E 8 B16
Autlán de Navarro Mexico 19°46N 104°22W 86 D4
Autun France 46°58N 4°17E 20 C6
Auvergne □ France 45°20N 3°15E 20 D5
Auvergne, Mts. d' France 45°20N 2°55E 20 D5
Auxerre France 47°48N 3°32E 20 C5
Ava U.S.A. 36°57N 92°40W 80 G7
Avallon France 47°30N 3°53E 20 C5
Avalon U.S.A. 33°21N 118°20W 79 M8
Avalon Pen. Canada 47°30N 53°20W 73 C9
Avanos Turkey 38°43N 34°51E 44 B2
Avaré Brazil 23°4S 48°58W 95 A6
Avawatz Mts. U.S.A. 35°40N 116°30W 79 K10
Aveiro Brazil 3°10S 55°5W 93 D7
Aveiro Portugal 40°37N 8°38W 21 B1
Āvej Iran 35°40N 49°15E 45 C6
Avellaneda Argentina 34°40S 58°22W 94 C4
Avellino Italy 40°54N 14°47E 22 D6
Avenal U.S.A. 36°0N 120°8W 78 K6
Aversa Italy 40°58N 14°12E 22 D6
Avery U.S.A. 47°15N 115°49W 76 C6
Aves, I. de W. Indies 15°45N 63°55W 89 C7
Aves, Is. las Venezuela 12°0N 67°30W 89 D6
Avesta Sweden 60°9N 16°10E 9 F17
Aveyron → France 44°5N 1°16E 20 D4
Avezzano Italy 42°2N 13°25E 22 C5
Aviá Terai Argentina 26°45S 60°50W 94 B3
Aviemore U.K. 57°12N 3°50W 11 D5
Avignon France 43°57N 4°50E 20 E6
Ávila Spain 40°39N 4°43W 21 B3
Avila Beach U.S.A. 35°11N 120°44W 79 K6
Avilés Spain 43°35N 5°57W 21 A3
Avis U.S.A. 41°11N 77°19W 82 E7
Avoca U.S.A. 42°25N 77°25W 82 D7
Avoca → Australia 35°40S 143°43E 63 F3
Avoca → Ireland 52°48N 6°10W 10 D5
Avola Canada 51°45N 119°19W 70 C5
Avola Italy 36°56N 15°7E 22 F6
Avon U.S.A. 42°55N 77°45W 82 D7
Avon → Australia 31°40S 116°7E 61 F2
Avon → Bristol, U.K. 51°29N 2°41W 13 F5
Avon → Dorset, U.K. 50°44N 1°46W 13 G6
Avon → Warks., U.K. 52°0N 2°8W 13 E5
Avon Park U.S.A. 27°36N 81°31W 85 H14
Avondale Zimbabwe 17°43S 30°58E 55 F3
Avonlea Canada 50°0N 105°0W 71 D8
Avonmore Canada 45°10N 74°58W 83 A10
Avonmouth U.K. 51°30N 2°42W 13 F5
Avranches France 48°40N 1°20W 20 B3
Awa-Shima Japan 38°27N 139°14E 30 E9
A'waj → Syria 33°23N 36°20E 46 B5
Awaji-Shima Japan 34°30N 134°50E 31 G7
'Awālī Bahrain 26°0N 50°30E 45 E6
Awantipur India 33°55N 75°3E 43 C6
Awasa Ethiopia 7°2N 38°28E 47 F2
Awash Ethiopia 9°1N 40°10E 47 F3
Awatere → N.Z. 41°37S 174°10E 59 D5
Awbārī Libya 26°46N 12°57E 51 C8
Awbārī, Idehan Libya 27°10N 11°30E 51 C8
Awe, L. U.K. 56°17N 5°16W 11 E3
Awjilah Libya 29°8N 21°7E 51 C10
Axe → U.K. 50°42N 3°4W 13 F5
Axel Heiberg I. Canada 80°0N 90°0W 69 B11
Axim Ghana 4°51N 2°15W 50 H5
Axios → Greece 40°57N 22°35E 23 D10
Axminster U.K. 50°46N 3°0W 13 G4
Ayabaca Peru 4°40S 79°53W 92 D3
Ayabe Japan 35°20N 135°20E 31 G7
Ayacucho Argentina 37°5S 58°20W 94 D4
Ayacucho Peru 13°0S 74°0W 92 F4
Ayaguz = Ayaköz Kazakhstan 48°10N 80°10E 28 E9
Ayaköz Kazakhstan 48°10N 80°10E 28 E9
Ayamonte Spain 37°12N 7°24W 21 D2
Ayan Russia 56°30N 138°16E 29 D14
Ayaviri Peru 14°50S 70°35W 92 F4
Aydın Turkey 37°51N 27°51E 23 F12
Aydingkol Hu China 42°40N 89°15E 32 B3
Ayer U.S.A. 42°34N 71°35W 83 D13
Ayer Hitam Malaysia 5°24N 100°16E 39 c
Ayer's Cliff Canada 45°10N 72°3W 83 A12
Ayers Rock = Uluru Australia 25°23S 131°5E 61 E5
Áyia Napa Cyprus 34°59N 34°0E 25 E13
Áyia Phyla Cyprus 34°43N 33°1E 25 E12
Áyios Amvrósios Cyprus 35°20N 33°35E 25 D12
Áyios Seryios Cyprus 35°12N 33°53E 25 D12
Áyios Theodhoros Cyprus 35°22N 34°1E 25 D13
Aykino Russia 62°15N 49°56E 18 B8
Aylesbury U.K. 51°49N 0°49W 13 F7
Aylmer Canada 42°46N 80°59W 82 D4
Aylmer, L. Canada 64°5N 108°30W 68 C9
'Ayn, Wādī al Oman 22°15N 55°28E 45 F7
Ayn Dār Si. Arabia 25°55N 49°10E 45 E7
Ayn Zālah Iraq 36°45N 42°35E 44 B4
Ayolas Paraguay 27°10S 56°59W 94 B4
Ayon, Ostrov Russia 69°50N 169°0E 29 C17
'Ayoûn el 'Atroûs Mauritania 16°38N 9°37W 50 E4
Ayr Australia 19°35S 147°25E 62 B4
Ayr Canada 43°17N 80°27W 82 C4
Ayr U.K. 55°28N 4°38W 11 F4
Ayr → U.K. 55°28N 4°38W 11 F4
Ayre, Pt. of I. of Man 54°25N 4°21W 12 C3
Ayton Australia 15°56S 145°22E 62 B4
Aytos Bulgaria 42°42N 27°16E 23 C12
Ayu, Kepulauan Indonesia 0°35N 131°5E 37 D8
Ayutla Guatemala 14°40N 92°10W 88 D1
Ayutla de los Libres Mexico 16°54N 99°13W 87 D5
Ayvacık Turkey 39°36N 26°24E 23 E12
Ayvalık Turkey 39°20N 26°46E 23 E12
Az Zabadānī Syria 33°43N 36°5E 46 B5
Az Zāhirīyah West Bank 31°25N 34°58E 46 D3
Az Zahrān Si. Arabia 26°10N 50°7E 45 E6
Az Zarqā Jordan 32°5N 36°4E 46 C5
Az Zarqā' U.A.E. 24°53N 53°4E 45 E7
Az Zarqā □ Jordan 32°5N 36°4E 46 C5
Az Zāwiyah Libya 32°52N 12°56E 51 B8
Az Zībār Iraq 36°52N 44°4E 44 B5
Az Zilfī Si. Arabia 26°12N 44°52E 44 E5
Az Zubayr Iraq 30°26N 47°40E 44 D5
Azad Kashmir □ Pakistan 33°50N 73°50E 43 C5
Azamgarh India 26°5N 83°13E 43 F10
Azangaro Peru 14°55S 70°13W 92 F4
Azaouad Mali 19°0N 3°0W 50 E5
Āzār Shahr Iran 37°45N 45°59E 44 B5
Azarān Iran 37°25N 47°16E 44 B5
Azärbayjan = Azerbaijan ■ Asia 40°20N 48°0E 19 F8
Āzarbāyjān-e Gharbī □ Iran 37°0N 44°30E 44 B5
Āzarbāyjān-e Sharqī □ Iran 37°20N 47°0E 44 B5
Azare Nigeria 11°55N 10°10E 50 F8
A'zāz Syria 36°36N 37°4E 44 B3
Azbine = Aïr Niger 18°30N 8°0E 50 E7
Azerbaijan ■ Asia 40°20N 48°0E 19 F8
Azerbaijchan = Azerbaijan ■ Asia 40°20N 48°0E 19 F8
Azimganj India 24°14N 88°16E 43 G13
Azogues Ecuador 2°35S 78°0W 92 D3
Azores = Açores, Is. dos Atl. Oc. 38°0N 27°0W 50 a
Azov Russia 47°3N 39°25E 19 E6
Azov, Sea of Europe 46°0N 36°30E 19 E6
Azovskoye More = Azov, Sea of Europe 46°0N 36°30E 19 E6
Azraq ash Shīshān Jordan 31°50N 36°49E 46 D5
Aztec U.S.A. 36°49N 107°59W 77 H10
Azúa de Compostela Dom. Rep. 18°25N 70°44W 89 C5
Azuaga Spain 38°16N 5°39W 21 C3
Azuero, Pen. de Panama 7°30N 80°30W 88 E3
Azul Argentina 36°42S 59°43W 94 D4
Azusa U.S.A. 34°8N 117°52W 79 L9
Azzel Matti, Sebkra Algeria 26°10N 0°43E 50 C6

B

Ba Be △ Vietnam 22°25N 105°37E 38 A5
Ba Don Vietnam 17°45N 106°26E 38 D6
Ba Dong Vietnam 9°40N 106°33E 39 H6
Ba Ngoi = Cam Lam Vietnam 11°54N 109°10E 39 G7
Ba Tri Vietnam 10°2N 106°36E 39 G6
Ba Vi △ Vietnam 21°1N 105°22E 38 B5
Ba Xian = Bazhou China 39°8N 116°22E 34 E9
Baa Indonesia 10°50S 123°0E 37 F6
Baardeere = Bardera Somali Rep. 2°20N 42°27E 47 G3
Baarle-Nassau Belgium 51°27N 4°56E 15 C4
Bab el Mandeb Red Sea 12°35N 43°25E 47 E3
Bābā, Koh-i- Afghan. 34°30N 67°0E 40 B5
Baba Burnu Turkey 39°29N 26°2E 23 E12
Bābā Kalū Iran 30°7N 50°49E 45 D6
Babadag Romania 44°53N 28°44E 17 F15
Babaeski Turkey 41°26N 27°6E 23 D12
Babahoyo Ecuador 1°40S 79°30W 92 D3
Babai = Sarju → India 27°21N 81°23E 43 F9
Babar Indonesia 8°0S 129°30E 37 F7
Babar Pakistan 31°7N 69°32E 42 D3
Babarkach Pakistan 29°45N 68°0E 42 E3
Babb U.S.A. 48°51N 113°27W 76 B7
Baberu India 25°33N 80°43E 43 G9
Babi Besar, Pulau Malaysia 2°25N 103°59E 39 L4
Bābil □ Iraq 32°30N 44°30E 44 C5
Babinda Australia 17°20S 145°56E 62 B4
Babine Canada 55°22N 126°37W 70 B3
Babine → Canada 55°45N 127°44W 70 B3
Babine L. Canada 54°48N 126°0W 70 C3
Babo Indonesia 2°30S 133°30E 37 E8
Bābol Iran 36°40N 52°50E 45 B7
Bābol Sar Iran 36°45N 52°45E 45 B7
Baboua C.A.R. 5°49N 14°58E 52 C2
Babruysk Belarus 53°10N 29°15E 17 B15
Babuhri India 26°49N 69°43E 42 F3
Babusar Pass Pakistan 35°12N 73°59E 43 B5
Babuyan Chan. Phil. 18°40N 121°30E 37 A6
Babylon Iraq 32°34N 44°22E 44 C5
Bac Can Vietnam 22°8N 105°49E 38 A5
Bac Giang Vietnam 21°16N 106°11E 38 B6
Bac Lieu Vietnam 9°17N 105°43E 39 H5
Bac Ninh Vietnam 21°13N 106°4E 38 B6
Bac Phan Vietnam 22°0N 105°0E 38 B5
Bac Quang Vietnam 22°30N 104°48E 38 A5
Bacabal Brazil 4°15S 44°45W 93 D10
Bacalar Mexico 18°43N 88°27W 87 D7
Bacan, Kepulauan Indonesia 0°35S 127°30E 37 E7
Bacarra Phil. 18°15N 120°37E 37 A6
Bacău Romania 46°35N 26°55E 17 E14
Bacerac Mexico 30°18N 108°50W 86 A3
Bach Long Vi, Dao Vietnam 20°10N 107°40E 38 B6
Bach Ma △ Vietnam 16°11N 107°49E 38 D6
Bachhwara India 25°35N 85°54E 43 G11
Back → Canada 65°10N 104°0W 68 C9
Bacolod Phil. 10°40N 122°57E 37 B6
Bacuk Malaysia 6°4N 102°25E 39 J4
Bácum Mexico 27°33N 110°5W 86 B2
Bād Iran 33°41N 52°1E 45 C7
Bad → U.S.A. 44°21N 100°22W 80 C3
Bad Axe U.S.A. 43°48N 83°0W 82 C2
Bad Ischl Austria 47°44N 13°38E 16 E7
Bad Kissingen Germany 50°11N 10°4E 16 C6
Bada Barabil India 22°7N 85°24E 43 H11
Badagara India 11°35N 75°40E 40 P9
Badajós, L. Brazil 3°15S 62°50W 92 D6
Badajoz Spain 38°50N 6°59W 21 C2
Badakhshān □ Afghan. 36°30N 71°0E 40 A7
Badalona Spain 41°26N 2°15E 21 B7
Badalzai Afghan. 29°50N 65°35E 42 E1
Badampahar India 22°10N 86°10E 41 H15
Badanah Si. Arabia 30°58N 41°30E 44 D4
Badarinath India 30°45N 79°30E 43 D8
Badas, Kepulauan Indonesia 0°45N 107°5E 36 D3
Baddo → Pakistan 28°0N 64°20E 40 F4
Bade Indonesia 7°10S 139°35E 37 F9
Baden Austria 48°1N 16°13E 16 D9
Baden U.S.A. 40°38N 80°14W 82 F4
Baden-Baden Germany 48°44N 8°13E 16 D5
Baden-Württemberg □ Germany 48°20N 8°40E 16 D5
Badgastein Austria 47°7N 13°9E 16 E7
Badger Canada 49°0N 56°4W 73 C8
Badger U.S.A. 36°38N 119°1W 78 J7
Bādghīs □ Afghan. 35°0N 63°0E 40 B3
Badgingarra △ Australia 30°23S 115°22E 61 F2
Badgom India 34°1N 74°45E 43 B6
Badin Pakistan 24°38N 68°54E 42 G3
Badlands U.S.A. 43°55N 102°30W 80 D2
Badlands △ U.S.A. 43°38N 102°56W 80 D2
Badrah Iraq 33°6N 45°58E 44 C5
Badrinath India 30°44N 79°29E 43 D8
Badulla Sri Lanka 7°1N 81°7E 40 R12
Badung, Selat Indonesia 8°40S 115°22E 37 K18
Baena Spain 37°37N 4°20W 21 D3
Baengnyeongdo S. Korea 37°57N 124°40E 35 F13
Baeza Spain 37°57N 3°25W 21 D4
Bafatá Guinea-Biss. 12°8N 14°40W 50 F3
Baffin B. N. Amer. 72°0N 64°0W 69 B13
Baffin I. Canada 68°0N 75°0W 69 C12
Bafing → Mali 13°49N 10°50W 50 F3
Bafliyūn Syria 36°37N 36°59E 44 B3
Bafoulabé Mali 13°50N 10°55W 50 F3
Bafoussam Cameroon 5°28N 10°25E 52 C2
Bāfq Iran 31°40N 55°25E 45 D7
Bafra Turkey 41°34N 35°54E 19 F6
Bāft Iran 29°15N 56°38E 45 D8
Bafwasende Dem. Rep. of the Congo 1°3N 27°5E 54 B2
Bagamoyo Tanzania 6°28S 38°55E 54 D4
Bagan Datoh Malaysia 3°59N 100°47E 39 L3
Bagan Serai Malaysia 5°1N 100°32E 39 K3
Baganga Phil. 7°34N 126°33E 37 C7
Bagani Namibia 18°7S 21°41E 56 B3
Bagansiapiapi Indonesia 2°12N 100°50E 36 D2
Bagasra India 21°30N 71°0E 42 J4
Bagaud India 22°19N 75°53E 42 H6
Bagdad U.S.A. 34°35N 115°53W 79 L11
Bagdarin Russia 54°26N 113°36E 29 D12
Bagé Brazil 31°20S 54°15W 95 C5
Bagenalstown = Muine Bheag Ireland 52°42N 6°58W 10 D5
Baggs U.S.A. 41°2N 107°39W 76 F10
Bagh Pakistan 33°59N 73°45E 43 C5
Baghain → India 25°32N 81°1E 43 G9
Baghdād Iraq 33°20N 44°23E 44 C5
Bagheria Italy 38°5N 13°30E 22 E5
Baghlān Afghan. 32°12N 68°46E 40 A6
Baghlān □ Afghan. 36°0N 68°30E 40 B6
Bagley U.S.A. 47°32N 95°24W 80 B6
Bago = Pegu Burma 17°20N 96°29E 41 L20
Bagodar India 24°5N 85°52E 43 G11
Bagrationovsk Russia 54°23N 20°39E 9 J19
Baguio Phil. 16°26N 120°34E 37 A6
Bah India 26°53N 78°36E 43 F8
Bahadurganj India 26°16N 87°49E 43 F12
Bahadurgarh India 28°40N 76°57E 42 E7
Bahama, Canal Viejo de W. Indies 22°10N 77°30W 88 B4
Bahamas ■ N. Amer. 24°0N 75°0W 89 B5
Baharampur India 24°2N 88°27E 43 G13
Baharu Pandan = Pandan Malaysia 1°32N 103°46E 39 d
Bahawalnagar Pakistan 30°0N 73°15E 42 E5
Bahawalpur Pakistan 29°24N 71°40E 42 E4
Bäherden Turkmenistan 38°25N 57°26E 45 B8
Baheri India 28°45N 79°34E 43 E8
Bahgul → India 27°45N 79°36E 43 F8
Bahi Tanzania 5°58S 35°21E 54 D4
Bahi Swamp Tanzania 6°10S 35°0E 54 D4
Bahía = Salvador Brazil 13°0S 38°30W 93 F11
Bahía □ Brazil 12°0S 42°0W 93 F10
Bahía, Is. de la Honduras 16°45N 86°15W 88 C2
Bahía Blanca Argentina 38°35S 62°13W 94 D3
Bahía de Caráquez Ecuador 0°40S 80°27W 92 D2
Bahía Kino Mexico 28°47N 111°58W 86 B2
Bahía Laura Argentina 48°10S 66°30W 96 F3
Bahía Negra Paraguay 20°5S 58°5W 92 H7
Bahir Dar Ethiopia 11°37N 37°10E 47 E2
Bahmanzād Iran 31°15N 51°47E 45 D6
Bahraich India 27°38N 81°37E 43 F9
Bahrain ■ Asia 26°0N 50°35E 45 E6
Bahror India 27°51N 76°20E 42 F7
Bāhū Kalāt Iran 25°43N 61°25E 45 E9
Bai Bung, Mui = Ca Mau, Mui Vietnam 8°38N 104°44E 39 H5
Bai Duc Vietnam 18°3N 105°49E 38 C5
Bai Thuong Vietnam 19°54N 105°23E 38 C5
Baia Mare Romania 47°40N 23°35E 17 E12
Baião Brazil 2°40S 49°40W 93 D9
Baïbokoum Chad 7°46N 15°43E 51 G9
Baicheng China 45°38N 122°42E 35 B12
Baidoa Somali Rep. 3°8N 43°30E 47 G3
Baie-Comeau Canada 49°12N 68°10W 73 C6

Baie-St-Paul *Canada* 47°28N 70°32W **73 C5**
Baie Ste-Anne *Seychelles* 4°18S 55°45E **53 b**
Baie-Trinité *Canada* 49°25N 67°20W **73 C6**
Baie Verte *Canada* 49°55N 56°12W **73 C8**
Baihar *India* 22°6N 80°33E **43 H9**
Baihe *China* 32°50N 110°5E **34 H6**
Ba'ījī *Iraq* 35°0N 43°30E **44 C4**
Baijnath *India* 29°55N 79°37E **43 E8**
Baikal, L. = Baykal, Oz.
  Russia 53°0N 108°0E **29 D11**
Baikonur = Bayqongyr
  Kazakhstan 45°40N 63°20E **28 E7**
Baikunthpur *India* 23°15N 82°33E **43 H10**
Baile Atha Cliath = Dublin
  Ireland 53°21N 6°15W **10 C5**
Băilești *Romania* 44°1N 23°20E **17 F12**
Bainbridge *Ga., U.S.A.* 30°55N 84°35W **85 F12**
Bainbridge *N.Y., U.S.A.* 42°18N 75°29W **83 D9**
Bainbridge Island
  U.S.A. 47°38N 122°32W **78 C4**
Baing *Indonesia* 10°14S 120°34E **37 F6**
Bainiu *China* 32°50N 112°15F **34 H7**
Bā'ir *Jordan* 30°45N 36°55E **46 E5**
Bairiki = Tarawa *Kiribati* 1°30N 173°0E **64 G9**
Bairin Youqi *China* 43°30N 118°35E **35 C10**
Bairin Zuoqi *China* 43°58N 119°15E **35 C10**
Bairnsdale *Australia* 37°48S 147°36E **63 F4**
Baisha *China* 34°20N 112°32E **34 G7**
Baitadi *Nepal* 29°35N 80°25E **43 E9**
Baiyin *China* 36°45N 104°14E **34 F3**
Baiyu Shan *China* 37°15N 107°30E **34 F4**
Baj Baj *India* 22°30N 88°5E **43 H13**
Baja *Hungary* 46°12N 18°59E **17 E10**
Baja, Pta. *Mexico* 29°58N 115°49W **86 B1**
Baja California *Mexico* 31°10N 115°12W **86 A1**
Baja California □
  Mexico 30°0N 115°0W **86 B2**
Baja California Sur □
  Mexico 25°50N 111°50W **86 B2**
Bajag *India* 22°40N 81°21E **43 H9**
Bajamar *Canary Is.* 28°33N 16°20W **24 F3**
Bajana *India* 23°7N 71°49E **42 H4**
Bajatrejo *Indonesia* 8°29S 114°19E **37 J17**
Bajera *Indonesia* 8°31S 115°2E **37 J18**
Bājgīrān *Iran* 37°36N 58°24E **45 B8**
Bajimba, Mt. *Australia* 29°17S 152°6E **63 D5**
Bajo Nuevo *Caribbean* 15°40N 78°50W **88 C4**
Bajoga *Nigeria* 10°57N 11°20E **51 F8**
Bajool *Australia* 23°40S 150°35E **62 C5**
Bakel *Senegal* 14°56N 12°20W **50 F3**
Baker *Calif., U.S.A.* 35°16N 116°4W **79 K10**
Baker *Mont., U.S.A.* 46°22N 104°17W **76 C11**
Baker, L. *Canada* 64°0N 96°0W **68 C10**
Baker, Mt. *U.S.A.* 48°50N 121°49W **76 B3**
Baker City *U.S.A.* 44°47N 117°50W **76 D5**
Baker I. *Pac. Oc.* 0°10N 176°35W **64 G10**
Baker I. *U.S.A.* 55°20N 133°40W **70 B2**
Baker L. *Australia* 26°54S 126°5E **61 E4**
Baker Lake *Canada* 64°20N 96°3W **68 C10**
Bakers Creek *Australia* 21°13S 149°7E **62 C4**
Bakers Dozen Is.
  Canada 56°45N 78°45W **72 A4**
Bakersfield *Calif., U.S.A.* 35°23N 119°1W **79 K8**
Bakersfield *Vt., U.S.A.* 44°45N 72°48W **83 B12**
Bakharden = Bäherden
  Turkmenistan 38°25N 57°26E **45 B8**
Bākhtarān = Kermānshāh
  Iran 34°23N 47°0E **44 C5**
Bākhtarān = Kermānshāh □
  Iran 34°0N 46°30E **44 C5**
Bakı *Azerbaijan* 40°29N 49°56E **45 A6**
Bakkafjörður *Iceland* 66°2N 14°48W **8 C6**
Bakouma *C.A.R.* 5°40N 22°56E **52 C4**
Bakswaho *India* 24°15N 79°18E **43 G8**
Baku = Bakı *Azerbaijan* 40°29N 49°56E **45 A6**
Bakutis Coast *Antarctica* 74°0S 120°0W **5 D15**
Baky = Bakı *Azerbaijan* 40°29N 49°56E **45 A6**
Bala *Canada* 45°1N 79°37W **82 A5**
Bala *U.K.* 52°54N 3°36W **12 E4**
Bala, L. *U.K.* 52°53N 3°37W **12 E4**
Balabac I. *Phil.* 8°0N 117°0E **36 C5**
Balabac Str. *E. Indies* 7°53N 117°5E **36 C5**
Balabagh *Afghan.* 34°25N 70°12E **42 B4**
Ba'labakk *Lebanon* 34°0N 36°10E **46 B5**
Balabalangan, Kepulauan
  Indonesia 2°20S 117°30E **36 E5**
Balad *Iraq* 34°0N 44°9E **44 C5**
Balad Rūz *Iraq* 33°42N 45°5E **44 C5**
Bālādeh *Fārs, Iran* 29°17N 51°56E **45 D6**
Bālādeh *Māzandaran,
  Iran* 36°12N 51°48E **45 B6**
Balaghat *India* 21°49N 80°12E **40 J12**
Balaghat Ra. *India* 18°50N 76°30E **40 K10**
Balaguer *Spain* 41°50N 0°50E **21 B6**
Balaklava *Ukraine* 44°30N 33°30E **19 F5**
Balakovo *Russia* 52°4N 47°55E **18 D8**
Balamau *India* 27°10N 80°21E **43 F9**
Balancán *Mexico* 17°48N 91°32W **87 D6**
Balashov *Russia* 51°30N 43°10E **19 D7**
Balasinor *India* 22°57N 73°23E **42 H5**
Balasore = Baleshwar
  India 21°35N 87°3E **41 J15**
Balaton *Hungary* 46°50N 17°40E **17 E9**
Balbina, Reprêsa de
  Brazil 2°0S 59°30W **92 D7**
Balboa *Panama* 8°57N 79°34W **88 E4**
Balbriggan *Ireland* 53°37N 6°11W **10 C5**
Balcarce *Argentina* 38°0S 58°10W **94 D4**
Balcarres *Canada* 50°50N 103°35W **71 C8**
Balchik *Bulgaria* 43°28N 28°11E **23 C13**
Balclutha *N.Z.* 46°15S 169°45E **59 G2**
Balcones Escarpment
  U.S.A. 29°30N 99°15W **84 G5**
Bald Hd. *Australia* 35°6S 118°1E **61 G2**
Bald I. *Australia* 34°57S 118°27E **61 F2**
Bald Knob *U.S.A.* 35°19N 91°34W **84 D9**
Baldock L. *Canada* 56°33N 97°57W **71 B9**
Baldwin *Mich., U.S.A.* 43°54N 85°51W **81 D11**

Baldwin *Pa., U.S.A.* 40°21N 79°58W **82 F5**
Baldwinsville *U.S.A.* 43°10N 76°20W **83 C8**
Baldy Peak *U.S.A.* 33°54N 109°34W **77 K9**
Baleares, Is. *Spain* 39°30N 3°0E **24 B10**
Balearic Is. = Baleares, Is.
  Spain 39°30N 3°0E **24 B10**
Baleine = Whale →
  Canada 58°15N 67°40W **73 A6**
Baleine, Petite R. de la →
  Canada 56°0N 76°45W **72 A4**
Baler *Phil.* 15°46N 121°34E **37 A6**
Baleshare *U.K.* 57°31N 7°22W **11 D1**
Baleshwar *India* 21°35N 87°3E **41 J15**
Balfate *Honduras* 15°48N 86°25W **88 C2**
Bali *Greece* 35°25N 24°47E **25 D6**
Bali *India* 25°11N 73°17E **42 G5**
Bali *Indonesia* 8°20S 115°0E **36 F4**
Bali □ *Indonesia* 8°20S 115°0E **36 F5**
Bali, Selat *Indonesia* 8°18S 114°25E **37 J17**
Bali Sea *Indonesia* 8°0S 115°0E **37 J17**
Baliapal *India* 21°40N 87°17E **43 J12**
Balik Pulau *Malaysia* 5°21N 100°14E **39 c**
Balıkeşir *Turkey* 39°39N 27°53E **23 E12**
Balikpapan *Indonesia* 1°10S 116°55E **36 E5**
Balimbing *Phil.* 5°5N 119°58E **37 C5**
Baling *Malaysia* 5°41N 100°55E **39 K3**
Balkan Mts. = Stara Planina
  Bulgaria 43°15N 23°0E **23 C10**
Balkanabat
  Turkmenistan 39°30N 54°22E **45 B7**
Balkhash = Balqash
  Kazakhstan 46°50N 74°50E **28 E8**
Balkhash, Ozero = Balqash Köl
  Kazakhstan 46°0N 74°50E **28 E8**
Ballachulish *U.K.* 56°41N 5°8W **11 E3**
Balladonia *Australia* 32°27S 123°51E **61 F3**
Ballarat *Australia* 37°33S 143°50E **63 F3**
Ballard, L. *Australia* 29°20S 120°40E **61 E3**
Ballater *U.K.* 57°3N 3°3W **11 D5**
Ballenas, Canal de
  Mexico 29°10N 113°29W **86 B2**
Balleny Is. *Antarctica* 66°30S 163°0E **5 C11**
Ballia *India* 25°46N 84°12E **43 G11**
Ballina *Australia* 28°50S 153°31E **63 D5**
Ballina *Ireland* 54°7N 9°9W **10 B2**
Ballinasloe *Ireland* 53°20N 8°13W **10 C3**
Ballinger *U.S.A.* 31°45N 99°57W **84 F5**
Ballinrobe *Ireland* 53°38N 9°13W **10 C2**
Ballinskelligs B. *Ireland* 51°48N 10°13W **10 E1**
Ballston Spa *U.S.A.* 43°0N 73°51W **83 D11**
Ballyboghil *Ireland* 53°32N 6°16W **10 C5**
Ballybunion *Ireland* 52°31N 9°40W **10 D2**
Ballycanew *Ireland* 52°37N 6°19W **10 D5**
Ballycastle *U.K.* 55°12N 6°15W **10 A5**
Ballyclare *U.K.* 54°46N 6°0W **10 B5**
Ballydehob *Ireland* 51°34N 9°28W **10 E2**
Ballygawley *U.K.* 54°27N 7°2W **10 B4**
Ballyhaunis *Ireland* 53°46N 8°46W **10 C3**
Ballyheige *Ireland* 52°23N 9°49W **10 D2**
Ballymena *U.K.* 54°52N 6°17W **10 B5**
Ballymoney *U.K.* 55°5N 6°31W **10 A5**
Ballymote *Ireland* 54°5N 8°31W **10 B3**
Ballynahinch *U.K.* 54°24N 5°54W **10 B6**
Ballyquintin Pt. *U.K.* 54°20N 5°30W **10 B6**
Ballyshannon *Ireland* 54°30N 8°11W **10 B3**
Balmaceda *Chile* 46°0S 71°50W **96 F2**
Balmertown *Canada* 51°4N 93°41W **71 C10**
Balmoral *Australia* 37°15S 141°48E **63 F3**
Balmorhea *U.S.A.* 30°59N 103°45W **84 F3**
Balochistan = Baluchistan □
  Pakistan 27°30N 65°0E **40 F4**
Balonne → *Australia* 28°47S 147°56E **63 D4**
Balotra *India* 25°50N 72°14E **42 G5**
Balqash *Kazakhstan* 46°50N 74°50E **28 E8**
Balqash Köl *Kazakhstan* 46°0N 74°50E **28 E8**
Balrampur *India* 27°30N 82°20E **43 F10**
Balranald *Australia* 34°38S 143°33E **63 E3**
Balsas → *Brazil* 7°15S 44°35W **93 E9**
Balsas *Mexico* 17°55N 102°10W **86 D4**
Balsas del Norte *Mexico* 18°0N 99°46W **87 D5**
Balta *Ukraine* 48°2N 29°45E **17 D15**
Bălți *Moldova* 47°48N 27°58E **17 E14**
Baltic Sea *Europe* 57°0N 19°0E **9 H18**
Baltimore *Ireland* 51°29N 9°22W **10 E2**
Baltimore *Md., U.S.A.* 39°17N 76°36W **81 F15**
Baltimore *Ohio, U.S.A.* 39°51N 82°36W **82 G2**
Baltinglass *Ireland* 52°56N 6°43W **10 D5**
Baltit *Pakistan* 36°15N 74°40E **43 A6**
Baltiysk *Russia* 54°41N 19°58E **9 J18**
Baluchistan □ *Pakistan* 27°30N 65°0E **40 F4**
Balurghat *India* 25°15N 88°44E **43 G13**
Balvi *Latvia* 57°8N 27°15E **9 H22**
Balya *Turkey* 39°44N 27°35E **23 E12**
Bam *Iran* 29°7N 58°14E **45 D8**
Bama *Nigeria* 11°33N 13°41E **51 F8**
Bamaga *Australia* 10°50S 142°25E **62 A3**
Bamaji L. *Canada* 51°9N 91°25W **72 B1**
Bamako *Mali* 12°34N 7°55W **50 F4**
Bambari *C.A.R.* 5°40N 20°35E **52 C4**
Bambaroo *Australia* 18°50S 146°10E **62 B4**
Bamberg *Germany* 49°54N 10°54E **16 D6**
Bamberg *U.S.A.* 33°18N 81°2W **85 E14**
Bambili
  Dem. Rep. of the Congo 3°40N 26°0E **54 B2**
Bamburgh *U.K.* 55°37N 1°43W **12 B6**
Bamenda *Cameroon* 5°57N 10°11E **52 C2**
Bamfield *Canada* 48°45N 125°10W **70 D3**
Bāmīān □ *Afghan.* 35°0N 67°0E **40 B5**
Bamiancheng *China* 43°15N 124°2E **35 C13**
Bampūr *Iran* 27°15N 60°21E **45 E9**
Ban Ao Tu Khun *Thailand* 8°9N 98°20E **39 a**
Ban Ban *Laos* 19°31N 103°30E **38 C4**
Ban Bang Hin *Thailand* 9°32N 98°35E **39 H2**
Ban Bang Khu *Thailand* 7°57N 98°23E **39 a**
Ban Bang Rong *Thailand* 8°3N 98°25E **39 a**
Ban Bo Phut *Thailand* 9°33N 100°2E **39 b**
Ban Chaweng *Thailand* 9°32N 100°3E **39 b**

Ban Chiang Klang
  Thailand 19°25N 100°55E **38 C3**
Ban Chik *Laos* 17°15N 102°22E **38 D4**
Ban Choho *Thailand* 15°2N 102°9E **38 E4**
Ban Dan Lan Hoi
  Thailand 17°0N 99°35E **38 D2**
Ban Don = Surat Thani
  Thailand 9°6N 99°20E **39 H2**
Ban Don *Vietnam* 12°53N 107°48E **38 F6**
Ban Don, Ao → *Thailand* 9°20N 99°25E **39 H2**
Ban Dong *Thailand* 19°30N 100°59E **38 C3**
Ban Hong *Thailand* 18°18N 98°50E **38 C2**
Ban Hua Thanon *Thailand* 9°26N 100°1E **39 b**
Ban Kantang *Thailand* 7°25N 99°31E **39 J2**
Ban Karon *Thailand* 7°51N 98°18E **39 a**
Ban Kata *Thailand* 7°50N 98°18E **39 a**
Ban Keun *Laos* 18°22N 102°35E **38 C4**
Ban Khai *Thailand* 12°46N 101°18E **38 F3**
Ban Kheun *Laos* 20°13N 101°7E **38 B3**
Ban Khlong Khian
  Thailand 8°10N 98°26E **39 a**
Ban Khlong Kua *Thailand* 6°57N 100°8E **39 J3**
Ban Khuan *Thailand* 8°13N 99°52E **39 b**
Ban Khuan Mao *Thailand* 7°50N 99°37E **39 J2**
Ban Ko Yai Chim
  Thailand 11°17N 99°26E **39 G2**
Ban Kok *Thailand* 16°40N 103°40E **38 D4**
Ban Laem *Thailand* 13°13N 99°59E **38 F2**
Ban Lamai *Thailand* 9°28N 100°3E **39 b**
Ban Lao Ngam *Laos* 15°28N 106°10E **38 E6**
Ban Le Kathe *Thailand* 15°49N 98°53E **38 E2**
Ban Lo Po Noi *Thailand* 8°1N 98°34E **39 a**
Ban Mae Chedi *Thailand* 19°11N 99°31E **38 C2**
Ban Mae Laeng *Thailand* 20°1N 99°17E **38 B2**
Ban Mae Nam *Thailand* 9°34N 100°0E **39 b**
Ban Mae Sariang
  Thailand 18°10N 97°56E **38 C1**
Ban Mê Thuot = Buon Ma Thuot
  Vietnam 12°40N 108°3E **38 F7**
Ban Mi *Thailand* 15°3N 100°32E **38 E3**
Ban Muong Mo *Laos* 19°4N 103°58E **38 C4**
Ban Na Bo *Thailand* 9°19N 99°41E **39 b**
Ban Na Mo *Laos* 17°7N 105°40E **38 D5**
Ban Na San *Thailand* 8°53N 99°52E **39 H2**
Ban Na Tong *Laos* 20°56N 101°47E **38 B3**
Ban Nam Bac *Laos* 20°38N 102°20E **38 B4**
Ban Nam Ma *Laos* 22°2N 101°37E **38 A3**
Ban Ngang *Laos* 15°59N 106°11E **38 E6**
Ban Nong Bok *Laos* 17°5N 104°48E **38 D5**
Ban Nong Boua *Laos* 15°40N 106°33E **38 E6**
Ban Nong Pling
  Thailand 15°40N 100°10E **38 E3**
Ban Pak Chan *Thailand* 10°32N 98°51E **39 G2**
Ban Patong *Thailand* 7°54N 98°18E **39 a**
Ban Phai *Thailand* 16°4N 102°44E **38 D4**
Ban Phak Chit *Thailand* 8°0N 98°24E **39 a**
Ban Pong *Thailand* 13°50N 99°55E **38 F2**
Ban Ron Phibun *Thailand* 8°9N 99°51E **39 H2**
Ban Sakhu *Thailand* 8°4N 98°18E **39 a**
Ban Sanam Chai
  Thailand 7°33N 100°25E **39 J3**
Ban Sangkha *Thailand* 14°37N 103°52E **38 E4**
Ban Tak *Thailand* 17°2N 99°4E **38 D2**
Ban Tako *Thailand* 14°5N 102°40E **38 E4**
Ban Tha Dua *Thailand* 17°59N 98°39E **38 C2**
Ban Tha Li *Thailand* 17°37N 101°25E **38 D3**
Ban Tha Nun *Thailand* 8°12N 98°18E **39 a**
Ban Tha Rua *Thailand* 7°59N 98°22E **39 a**
Ban Tha Yu *Thailand* 8°17N 98°22E **39 a**
Ban Thahine *Thailand* 14°12N 105°33E **38 E5**
Ban Thong Krut *Thailand* 9°25N 99°57E **39 b**
Ban Xien Kok *Laos* 20°54N 100°39E **38 B3**
Ban Yen Nhan *Vietnam* 20°57N 106°2E **38 B6**
Banaba *Kiribati* 0°45S 169°50E **64 H8**
Banalia
  Dem. Rep. of the Congo 1°32N 25°5E **54 B2**
Banamba *Mali* 11°20N 105°17E **38 D5**
Bananal, I. do *Brazil* 11°30S 50°30W **93 F8**
Banaras = Varanasi
  India 25°22N 83°0E **43 G10**
Banas → *Gujarat, India* 23°45N 71°25E **42 H4**
Banas → *Mad. P., India* 24°15N 81°30E **43 G9**
Bânâs, Ras *Egypt* 23°57N 35°59E **51 D13**
Banbridge *U.K.* 54°22N 6°16W **10 B5**
Banbury *U.K.* 52°4N 1°20W **13 E6**
Banchory *U.K.* 57°3N 2°29W **11 D6**
Bancroft *Canada* 45°3N 77°51W **82 A7**
Band Boni *Iran* 25°30N 59°33E **45 E8**
Band Qīr *Iran* 31°39N 48°53E **45 D6**
Banda *Mad. P., India* 24°3N 78°57E **43 G8**
Banda *Ut. P., India* 25°30N 80°26E **43 G9**
Banda, Kepulauan
  Indonesia 4°37S 129°50E **37 E7**
Banda Aceh *Indonesia* 5°35N 95°20E **36 C1**
Banda Banda, Mt.
  Australia 31°10S 152°28E **63 E5**
Banda Elat *Indonesia* 5°40S 133°5E **37 F8**
Banda Is. = Banda, Kepulauan
  Indonesia 4°37S 129°50E **37 E7**
Banda Sea *Indonesia* 6°0S 130°0E **37 F7**
Bandai-Asahi △ *Japan* 37°38N 140°2E **30 F10**
Bandai-San *Japan* 37°36N 140°4E **30 F10**
Bandān *Iran* 31°23N 60°44E **45 D9**
Bandanaira *Indonesia* 4°32S 129°54E **37 E7**
Bandanwara *India* 26°9N 74°38E **42 F6**
Bandar = Machilipatnam
  India 16°12N 81°8E **41 L12**
Bandar-e Abbās *Iran* 27°15N 56°15E **45 E8**
Bandar-e Anzalī *Iran* 37°30N 49°30E **45 B6**
Bandar-e Bushehr = Büshehr
  Iran 28°55N 50°55E **45 D6**
Bandar-e Chārak *Iran* 26°45N 54°20E **45 E7**
Bandar-e Deylam *Iran* 30°5N 50°10E **45 D6**
Bandar-e Emām Khomeynī
  Iran 30°30N 49°5E **45 D6**
Bandar-e Lengeh *Iran* 26°35N 54°58E **45 E7**

Bandar-e Maqām *Iran* 26°56N 53°29E **45 E7**
Bandar-e Ma'shur *Iran* 30°35N 49°10E **45 D6**
Bandar-e Rīg *Iran* 29°29N 50°38E **45 D6**
Bandar-e Torkeman *Iran* 37°0N 54°10E **45 B7**
Bandar Lampung =
  Tanjungkarang Telukbetung
  Indonesia 5°20S 105°10E **36 F3**
Bandar Maharani = Muar
  Malaysia 2°3N 102°34E **39 L4**
Bandar Penggaram = Batu Pahat
  Malaysia 1°50N 102°56E **39 M4**
Bandar Seri Begawan
  Brunei 4°52N 115°0E **36 C4**
Bandar Sri Aman = Sri Aman
  Malaysia 1°15N 111°32E **36 D4**
Bandawe *Malawi* 11°58S 34°5E **55 E3**
Bandeira, Pico da
  Brazil 20°26S 41°47W **95 A7**
Bandera *Argentina* 28°55S 62°20W **94 B3**
Banderas, B. de
  Mexico 20°40N 105°25W **86 C3**
Bandhavgarh *India* 23°40N 81°2E **43 H9**
Bandi → *India* 26°12N 75°47E **42 F6**
Bandikui *India* 27°3N 76°34E **42 F7**
Bandırma *Turkey* 40°20N 28°0E **23 D13**
Bandjarmasin = Banjarmasin
  Indonesia 3°20S 114°35E **36 E4**
Bandon *Ireland* 51°44N 8°44W **10 E3**
Bandon → *Ireland* 51°43N 8°37W **10 E3**
Bandula *Mozam.* 19°0S 33°7E **55 F3**
Bandundu
  Dem. Rep. of the Congo 3°15S 17°22E **52 E3**
Bandung *Indonesia* 6°54S 107°36E **36 F3**
Bāneh *Iran* 35°59N 45°53E **44 C5**
Banes *Cuba* 21°0N 75°42W **89 B4**
Banff *Canada* 51°10N 115°34W **70 C5**
Banff *U.K.* 57°40N 2°33W **11 D6**
Banff △ *Canada* 51°30N 116°15W **70 C5**
Bang Fai → *Laos* 16°57N 104°45E **38 D5**
Bang Hieng → *Laos* 16°10N 105°10E **38 D5**
Bang Krathum
  Thailand 16°34N 100°18E **38 D3**
Bang Lamung *Thailand* 13°3N 100°56E **38 F3**
Bang Mun Nak *Thailand* 16°2N 100°23E **38 D3**
Bang Pa In *Thailand* 14°14N 100°35E **38 E3**
Bang Rakam *Thailand* 16°45N 100°7E **38 D3**
Bang Saphan *Thailand* 11°14N 99°28E **39 G2**
Bang Thao *Thailand* 7°59N 98°18E **39 a**
Bangaduni I. *India* 21°34N 88°52E **43 J13**
Bangala Dam *Zimbabwe* 21°7S 31°25E **55 G3**
Bangalore *India* 12°59N 77°40E **40 N10**
Banganga → *India* 27°6N 77°25E **42 F6**
Bangaon *India* 23°0N 88°47E **43 H13**
Bangassou *C.A.R.* 4°55N 23°7E **52 D4**
Banggai *Indonesia* 1°34S 123°30E **37 E6**
Banggai, Kepulauan
  Indonesia 1°40S 123°30E **37 E6**
Banggai Arch. = Banggai,
  Kepulauan *Indonesia* 1°40S 123°30E **37 E6**
Banggi, Pulau *Malaysia* 7°17N 117°12E **36 C5**
Banghāzī *Libya* 32°11N 20°3E **51 B10**
Bangka *Sulawesi,
  Indonesia* 1°50N 125°5E **37 D7**
Bangka *Sumatera,
  Indonesia* 2°0S 105°50E **36 E3**
Bangka, Selat *Indonesia* 2°30S 105°30E **36 E3**
Bangka-Belitung □
  Indonesia 2°30S 107°0E **36 E3**
Bangkalan *Indonesia* 7°2S 112°46E **37 G15**
Bangkinang *Indonesia* 0°18N 101°5E **36 D2**
Bangko *Indonesia* 2°5S 102°9E **36 E2**
Bangkok *Thailand* 13°45N 100°35E **38 F3**
Bangladesh ■ *Asia* 24°0N 90°0E **41 H17**
Bangli *Indonesia* 8°27S 115°21E **37 J18**
Bangong Co *China* 33°45N 78°43E **43 B8**
Bangor *Down, U.K.* 54°40N 5°40W **10 B6**
Bangor *Gwynedd, U.K.* 53°14N 4°8W **12 D3**
Bangor *Maine, U.S.A.* 44°48N 68°46W **81 C19**
Bangor *Pa., U.S.A.* 40°52N 75°13W **83 F9**
Bangued *Phil.* 17°40N 120°37E **37 A6**
Bangui *C.A.R.* 4°23N 18°35E **52 D3**
Banguru
  Dem. Rep. of the Congo 0°30N 27°10E **54 B2**
Bangweulu, L. *Zambia* 11°0S 30°0E **55 E3**
Bangweulu Swamp
  Zambia 11°20S 30°15E **55 E3**
Banhine △ *Mozam.* 22°49S 32°55E **57 C5**
Baní *Dom. Rep.* 18°16N 70°22W **89 C5**
Banī Sa'd *Iraq* 33°34N 44°32E **44 C5**
Banihal Pass *India* 33°30N 75°12E **43 C6**
Banissa *Kenya* 3°55N 40°19E **54 B4**
Bāniyās *Syria* 35°10N 36°0E **44 C3**
Banja Luka *Bos.-H.* 44°49N 17°11E **22 B7**
Banjar *India* 31°38N 77°21E **42 D7**
Banjar → *India* 22°36N 80°22E **43 H9**
Banjarmasin *Indonesia* 3°20S 114°35E **36 E4**
Banjul *Gambia* 13°28N 16°40W **50 F2**
Banka *India* 24°53N 86°55E **43 G12**
Banket *Zimbabwe* 17°27S 30°19E **55 F3**
Bankipore *India* 25°35N 85°10E **41 G14**
Bankura *India* 23°11N 87°18E **43 H12**
Banmankhi *India* 25°53N 87°11E **43 G12**
Bann → *Armagh, U.K.* 54°30N 6°31W **10 B5**
Bann → *L'derry., U.K.* 55°8N 6°41W **10 A5**
Bannang Sata *Thailand* 6°16N 101°16E **39 J3**
Banning *U.S.A.* 33°56N 116°53W **79 M10**
Bannockburn *Canada* 44°39N 77°33W **82 B7**
Bannockburn *U.K.* 56°5N 3°55W **11 E5**
Bannockburn *Zimbabwe* 20°17S 29°48E **55 G2**
Bannu *Pakistan* 33°0N 70°18E **40 C7**
Bano *India* 22°40N 84°55E **43 H11**
Bansgaon *India* 26°33N 83°21E **43 F10**

Banská Bystrica
  Slovak Rep. 48°46N 19°14E **17 D10**
Banswara *India* 23°32N 74°24E **42 H6**
Bantaeng *Indonesia* 5°32S 119°56E **37 F5**
Banten □ *Indonesia* 6°30S 106°0E **37 G11**
Bantry *Ireland* 51°41N 9°27W **10 E2**
Bantry B. *Ireland* 51°37N 9°44W **10 E2**
Bantul *Indonesia* 7°55S 110°19E **37 G14**
Bantva *India* 21°29N 70°12E **42 J4**
Banyak, Kepulauan
  Indonesia 2°10N 97°10E **36 D1**
Banyalbufar *Spain* 39°42N 2°31E **24 B9**
Banyo *Cameroon* 6°52N 11°45E **52 C2**
Banyumas *Indonesia* 7°32S 109°18E **37 G13**
Banyuwangi *Indonesia* 8°13S 114°21E **37 J17**
Banzare Coast *Antarctica* 68°0S 125°0E **5 C9**
Bao Ha *Vietnam* 22°11N 104°21E **38 A5**
Bao Lac *Vietnam* 22°57N 105°40E **38 A5**
Bao Loc *Vietnam* 11°32N 107°48E **39 G6**
Bao'an = Shenzhen
  China 22°32N 114°5E **33 F10**
Baocheng *China* 33°12N 106°56E **34 H4**
Baode *China* 39°1N 111°5E **34 E6**
Baodi *China* 39°38N 117°20E **35 E9**
Baoding *China* 38°50N 115°28E **34 E8**
Baoji *China* 34°20N 107°5E **34 G4**
Baoshan *China* 25°10N 99°5E **32 D4**
Baotou *China* 40°32N 110°2E **34 D6**
Baoying *China* 33°17N 119°20E **35 H10**
Baoyou = Ledong *China* 18°41N 109°5E **38 C7**
Bap *India* 27°23N 72°18E **42 F5**
Bapatla *India* 15°55N 80°30E **41 M12**
Bāqerābād *Iran* 33°2N 51°58E **45 C6**
Ba'qūbah *Iraq* 33°45N 44°50E **44 C5**
Baquedano *Chile* 23°20S 69°52W **94 A2**
Bar *Montenegro* 42°8N 19°6E **23 C8**
Bar *Ukraine* 49°4N 27°40E **17 D14**
Bar Bigha *India* 25°21N 85°47E **43 G11**
Bar Harbor *U.S.A.* 44°23N 68°13W **81 C19**
Bar-le-Duc *France* 48°47N 5°10E **20 B6**
Bara *India* 25°16N 81°43E **43 G9**
Bara Banki *India* 26°55N 81°12E **43 F9**
Barabai *Indonesia* 2°32S 115°34E **36 E5**
Baraboo *U.S.A.* 43°28N 89°45W **80 D9**
Baracoa *Cuba* 20°20N 74°30W **89 B5**
Baradā → *Syria* 33°33N 36°34E **46 B5**
Baradero *Argentina* 33°52S 59°29W **94 C4**
Baraga *U.S.A.* 46°47N 88°30W **80 B9**
Baragoi *Kenya* 1°47N 36°47E **54 B4**
Barah → *India* 27°42N 77°5E **42 F6**
Barahona *Dom. Rep.* 18°13N 71°7W **89 C5**
Barail Range *India* 25°15N 93°20E **41 G18**
Barakaldo *Spain* 43°18N 2°59W **21 A4**
Barākar → *India* 24°7N 86°14E **43 G12**
Barakot *India* 21°33N 84°59E **43 J11**
Barakpur *India* 22°47N 88°21E **43 H13**
Baralaba *Australia* 24°13S 149°50E **62 C4**
Baralzon L. *Canada* 60°0N 98°3W **71 B9**
Baramula *India* 34°15N 74°20E **43 B6**
Baran *India* 25°9N 76°40E **42 G7**
Baran → *Pakistan* 25°13N 68°17E **42 G3**
Baranavichy *Belarus* 53°10N 26°0E **17 B14**
Baranof *U.S.A.* 57°5N 134°50W **70 C2**
Baranof I. *U.S.A.* 57°0N 135°0W **68 C6**
Barapasi *Indonesia* 2°15S 137°5E **37 E9**
Barasat *India* 22°46N 88°31E **43 H13**
Barat Daya, Kepulauan
  Indonesia 7°30S 128°0E **37 F7**
Barataria B. *U.S.A.* 29°20N 89°55W **85 G10**
Barauda *India* 23°33N 75°15E **42 H6**
Baraut *India* 29°13N 77°7E **42 E7**
Barbacena *Brazil* 21°15S 43°56W **95 A7**
Barbados ■ *W. Indies* 13°10N 59°30W **89 g**
Barbària, C. de *Spain* 38°39N 1°24E **24 C7**
Barbas, C. *W. Sahara* 22°20N 16°42W **50 D2**
Barbastro *Spain* 42°2N 0°5E **21 A6**
Barberton *S. Africa* 25°42S 31°2E **57 D5**
Barberton *U.S.A.* 41°1N 81°39W **82 E3**
Barbosa *Colombia* 5°57N 73°37W **92 B4**
Barbourville *U.S.A.* 36°52N 83°53W **81 G12**
Barbuda *W. Indies* 17°30N 61°40W **89 C7**
Barcaldine *Australia* 23°43S 145°6E **62 C4**
Barcellona Pozzo di Gotto
  Italy 38°9N 15°13E **22 E6**
Barcelona *Spain* 41°22N 2°10E **21 B7**
Barcelona *Venezuela* 10°10N 64°40W **92 A6**
Barceloneta *Puerto Rico* 18°27N 66°32W **89 d**
Barcelos *Brazil* 1°0S 63°0W **92 D6**
Barcoo → *Australia* 25°30S 142°50E **62 D3**
Bardaï *Chad* 21°25N 17°0E **51 D9**
Bardas Blancas
  Argentina 35°49S 69°45W **94 D2**
Bardawîl, Sabkhet el
  Egypt 31°10N 33°15E **46 D2**
Barddhaman *India* 23°14N 87°39E **43 H12**
Bardejov *Slovak Rep.* 49°18N 21°15E **17 D11**
Bardera *Somali Rep.* 2°20N 42°27E **47 G3**
Bardīyah *Libya* 31°45N 25°5E **51 B10**
Bardsey I. *U.K.* 52°45N 4°47W **12 E3**
Bardstown *U.S.A.* 37°49N 85°28W **81 G11**
Bareilly *India* 28°22N 79°27E **43 E8**
Barela *India* 23°6N 80°3E **43 H9**
Barents Sea *Arctic* 73°0N 39°0E **4 B9**
Barfleur, Pte. de *France* 49°42N 1°16W **20 B3**
Bargara *Australia* 24°50S 152°25E **62 C5**
Barguzin *Russia* 53°37N 109°37E **29 D11**
Barh *India* 25°29N 85°46E **43 G11**
Barhaj *India* 26°18N 83°44E **43 F10**
Barharwa *India* 24°52N 87°47E **43 G12**
Barhi *India* 24°15N 85°25E **43 G11**
Bari *India* 26°39N 77°39E **42 F7**
Bari *Italy* 41°8N 16°51E **22 D7**
Bari Doab *Pakistan* 30°20N 73°0E **42 D5**
Bari Sadri *India* 24°28N 74°30E **42 G6**
Barīdī, Ra's *Si. Arabia* 24°17N 37°31E **44 E3**
Barinas *Venezuela* 8°36N 70°15W **92 B4**
Baring, C. *Canada* 70°0N 117°30W **68 C8**

Baringo, L. *Kenya* 0°47N 36°16E **54 B4**
Barisal *Bangla.* 22°45N 90°20E **41 H17**
Barisal □ *Bangla.* 22°45N 90°20E **41 H17**
Barisan, Pegunungan
  Indonesia 3°30S 102°15E **36 E2**
Barito → *Indonesia* 4°0S 114°50E **36 E4**
Baritú △ *Argentina* 23°43S 64°40W **94 A3**
Barjūj, Wadi → *Libya* 25°26N 12°12E **51 C8**
Bark L. *Canada* 45°27N 77°51W **82 A7**
Barkakana *India* 23°37N 85°29E **43 H11**
Barker *U.S.A.* 43°20N 78°33W **82 C6**
Barkley, L. *U.S.A.* 37°1N 88°14W **85 C10**
Barkley Sound *Canada* 48°50N 125°10W **70 D3**
Barkly East *S. Africa* 30°58S 27°33E **56 E4**
Barkly Homestead
  Australia 19°52S 135°50E **62 B2**
Barkly Tableland
  Australia 17°50S 136°40E **62 B2**
Barkly West *S. Africa* 28°5S 24°31E **56 D3**
Barkol Kazak Zizhixian
  China 43°37N 93°2E **32 B4**
Bârlad *Romania* 46°15N 27°18E **17 E14**
Bârlad → *Romania* 45°38N 27°32E **17 F14**
Barlee, L. *Australia* 29°15S 119°30E **61 E2**
Barlee, Mt. *Australia* 24°38S 128°13E **61 D4**
Barletta *Italy* 41°19N 16°17E **22 D7**
Barlovento *Canary Is.* 28°48N 17°48W **24 F2**
Barlovento *C. Verde Is.* 17°0N 25°0W **50 b**
Barlow L. *Canada* 62°0N 103°0W **71 A8**
Barmedman *Australia* 34°9S 147°21E **63 E4**
Barmer *India* 25°45N 71°20E **42 G4**
Barmera *Australia* 34°15S 140°28E **63 E3**
Barmouth *U.K.* 52°44N 4°4W **12 E3**
Barna → *India* 25°21N 83°3E **43 G10**
Barnagar *India* 23°7N 75°19E **42 H6**
Barnala *India* 30°23N 75°33E **42 D6**
Barnard Castle *U.K.* 54°33N 1°55W **12 C6**
Barnaul *Russia* 53°20N 83°40E **28 D9**
Barnesville *Ga., U.S.A.* 33°3N 84°9W **85 E12**
Barnesville *Minn.,*
  U.S.A. 46°43N 96°28W **80 B5**
Barnet □ *U.K.* 51°38N 0°9W **13 F7**
Barneveld *Neths.* 52°7N 5°36E **15 B5**
Barneveld *U.S.A.* 43°16N 75°14W **83 C9**
Barnhart *U.S.A.* 31°8N 101°10W **84 F4**
Barnsley *U.K.* 53°34N 1°27W **12 D6**
Barnstaple *U.K.* 51°5N 4°4W **13 F3**
Barnstaple Bay = Bideford Bay
  U.K. 51°5N 4°20W **13 F3**
Barnwell *U.S.A.* 33°15N 81°23W **85 E14**
Baro *Nigeria* 8°35N 6°18E **50 G7**
Baroda = Vadodara
  India 22°20N 73°10E **42 H5**
Baroda *India* 25°29N 76°35E **42 G7**
Baroe *S. Africa* 33°13S 24°33E **56 E3**
Baron Ra. *Australia* 23°30S 127°45E **60 D4**
Barotseland *Zambia* 15°0S 24°0E **53 H4**
Barpeta *India* 26°20N 91°10E **41 F17**
Barques, Pt. Aux *U.S.A.* 44°4N 82°58W **82 B2**
Barquísimeto *Venezuela* 10°4N 69°19W **92 A5**
Barr Smith Range
  Australia 27°4S 120°20E **61 E3**
Barra *Brazil* 11°5S 43°10W **93 F10**
Barra *U.K.* 57°0N 7°29W **11 E1**
Barra, Sd. of *U.K.* 57°4N 7°25W **11 D1**
Barra de Navidad
  Mexico 19°12N 104°41W **86 D4**
Barra do Corda *Brazil* 5°30S 45°10W **93 E9**
Barra do Piraí *Brazil* 22°30S 43°50W **95 A7**
Barra Falsa, Pta. da
  Mozam. 22°58S 35°37E **57 C6**
Barra Hd. *U.K.* 56°47N 7°40W **11 E1**
Barra Mansa *Brazil* 22°35S 44°12W **95 A7**
Barraba *Australia* 30°21S 150°35E **63 E5**
Barrackpur = Barakpur
  India 22°47N 88°21E **43 H13**
Barradale *Australia* 22°42S 114°58E **60 D1**
Barranca *Lima, Peru* 10°45S 77°50W **92 F3**
Barranca *Loreto, Peru* 4°50S 76°50W **92 D3**
Barranca del Cobre △
  Mexico 27°18N 107°40W **86 B3**
Barrancabermeja
  Colombia 7°0N 73°50W **92 B4**
Barrancas *Venezuela* 8°55N 62°5W **92 B6**
Barrancos *Portugal* 38°10N 6°58W **21 C2**
Barranqueras *Argentina* 27°30S 59°0W **94 B4**
Barranquilla *Colombia* 11°0N 74°50W **92 A4**
Barraute *Canada* 48°26N 77°38W **72 C4**
Barre *Mass., U.S.A.* 42°25N 72°6W **83 D12**
Barre *Vt., U.S.A.* 44°12N 72°30W **83 B12**
Barreal *Argentina* 31°33S 69°28W **94 C2**
Barreiras *Brazil* 12°8S 45°0W **93 F10**
Barreirinhas *Brazil* 2°30S 42°50W **93 D10**
Barreiro *Portugal* 38°39N 9°5W **21 C1**
Barren, Nosy *Madag.* 18°25S 43°40E **57 B7**
Barretos *Brazil* 20°30S 48°35W **93 H9**
Barrhead *Canada* 54°10N 114°24W **70 C6**
Barrie *Canada* 44°24N 79°40W **82 B5**
Barrier Ra. *Australia* 31°0S 141°30E **63 E3**
Barrier Reef *Belize* 17°9N 88°3W **87 D7**
Barrière *Canada* 51°12N 120°7W **70 C4**
Barrington *U.S.A.* 41°44N 71°18W **83 E13**
Barrington L. *Canada* 56°55N 100°15W **71 B8**
Barrington Tops
  Australia 32°6S 151°28E **63 E5**
Barringun *Australia* 29°1S 145°41E **63 D4**
Barro do Garças *Brazil* 15°54S 52°16W **93 G8**
Barron *U.S.A.* 45°24N 91°51W **80 C8**
Barrow → *Ireland* 52°25N 6°58W **10 D5**
Barrow, Pt. *U.S.A.* 71°23N 156°29W **74 a**
Barrow Creek *Australia* 21°30S 133°55E **62 C1**
Barrow I. *Australia* 20°45S 115°20E **60 D2**
Barrow-in-Furness *U.K.* 54°7N 3°14W **12 C4**
Barrow Pt. *Australia* 14°20S 144°40E **62 A3**
Barrow Ra. *Australia* 26°0S 127°40E **61 E4**
Barrow Str. *Canada* 74°20N 95°0W **4 B3**

Barry *U.K.* 51°24N 3°16W **13 F4**
Barry's Bay *Canada* 45°29N 77°41W **82 A7**
Barsat *Pakistan* 36°10N 72°45E **43 A5**
Barsham *Syria* 35°21N 40°33E **44 C4**
Barsi *India* 18°10N 75°50E **40 K9**
Barsoi *India* 25°48N 87°57E **41 G15**
Barstow *U.S.A.* 34°54N 117°1W **79 L9**
Barthélemy, Col
  Vietnam 19°26N 104°6E **38 C5**
Bartica *Guyana* 6°25N 58°40W **92 B7**
Bartle Frere *Australia* 17°27S 145°50E **62 B4**
Bartlesville *U.S.A.* 36°45N 95°59W **84 C7**
Bartlett *Calif., U.S.A.* 36°29N 118°2W **78 J8**
Bartlett *Tenn., U.S.A.* 35°12N 89°52W **85 D10**
Bartlett, L. *Canada* 63°5N 118°20W **70 A5**
Bartolomeu Dias *Mozam.* 21°10S 35°8E **55 G4**
Barton *U.S.A.* 44°45N 72°11W **83 B12**
Barton upon Humber
  U.K. 53°41N 0°25W **12 D7**
Bartow *U.S.A.* 27°54N 81°50W **85 H14**
Barú, Volcan *Panama* 8°55N 82°35W **88 E3**
Barumba
  Dem. Rep. of the Congo 1°3N 23°37E **54 B1**
Baruunsuu *Mongolia* 43°43N 105°35E **34 C3**
Barwani *India* 22°2N 74°57E **42 H6**
Barysaw *Belarus* 54°17N 28°28E **17 A15**
Barzán *Iraq* 36°55N 44°3E **44 B5**
Bāsa'idū *Iran* 26°35N 55°20E **45 E7**
Basal *Pakistan* 33°33N 72°13E **42 C5**
Basankusa
  Dem. Rep. of the Congo 1°5N 19°50E **52 D3**
Basarabeasca *Moldova* 46°21N 28°58E **17 E15**
Basarabia = Bessarabiya
  Moldova 47°0N 28°10E **17 E15**
Basawa *Afghan.* 34°15N 70°50E **42 B4**
Bascuñán, C. *Chile* 28°52S 71°35W **94 B1**
Basel *Switz.* 47°35N 7°35E **20 C7**
Bashäkerd, Kühhä-ye
  Iran 26°42N 58°35E **45 E8**
Bashaw *Canada* 52°35N 112°58W **70 C6**
Bāshī *Iran* 28°41N 51°4E **45 D6**
Bashkir Republic =
  Bashkortostan □
  Russia 54°0N 57°0E **18 D10**
Bashkortostan □ *Russia* 54°0N 57°0E **18 D10**
Basibasy *Madag.* 22°10S 43°40E **57 C7**
Basilan *Phil.* 6°35N 122°0E **37 C6**
Basilan Str. *Phil.* 6°50N 122°0E **37 C6**
Basildon *U.K.* 51°34N 0°28E **13 F8**
Basim = Washim *India* 20°3N 77°0E **40 J10**
Basin *U.S.A.* 44°23N 108°2W **76 D9**
Basingstoke *U.K.* 51°15N 1°5W **13 F6**
Baskatong, Rés. *Canada* 46°46N 75°50W **72 C4**
Basle = Basel *Switz.* 47°35N 7°35E **20 C7**
Basoda *India* 23°52N 77°54E **42 H7**
Basoko
  Dem. Rep. of the Congo 1°16N 23°40E **54 B1**
Basque Provinces = País Vasco □
  Spain 42°50N 2°45W **21 A4**
Basra = Al Başrah *Iraq* 30°30N 47°50E **44 D5**
Bass Str. *Australia* 39°15S 146°30E **63 F4**
Bassano *Canada* 50°48N 112°20W **70 C6**
Bassano del Grappa
  Italy 45°46N 11°44E **22 B4**
Bassas da India *Ind. Oc.* 22°0S 39°0E **53 J7**
Basse-Pointe *Martinique* 14°52N 61°8W **88 c**
Basse-Terre *Guadeloupe* 16°0N 61°44W **88 b**
Basse Terre *Trin. & Tob.* 10°7N 61°19W **93 K15**
Bassein *Burma* 16°45N 94°30E **41 L19**
Basses, Pte. des
  Guadeloupe 15°52N 61°17W **88 b**
Basseterre
  St. Kitts & Nevis 17°17N 62°43W **89 C7**
Bassett *U.S.A.* 42°35N 99°32W **80 D4**
Bassi *India* 30°44N 76°21E **42 D7**
Bastak *Iran* 27°15N 54°25E **45 E7**
Baştām *Iran* 36°29N 55°4E **45 B7**
Bastar *India* 19°15N 81°40E **41 K12**
Basti *India* 26°52N 82°55E **43 F10**
Bastia *France* 42°40N 9°30E **20 E8**
Bastogne *Belgium* 50°1N 5°43E **15 D5**
Bastrop *La., U.S.A.* 32°47N 91°55W **84 E9**
Bastrop *Tex., U.S.A.* 30°7N 97°19W **84 F6**
Basuo = Dongfang
  China 18°50N 108°33E **38 C7**
Bat Yam *Israel* 32°2N 34°44E **46 C3**
Bata *Eq. Guin.* 1°57N 9°50E **52 D1**
Bataan □ *Phil.* 14°40N 120°25E **37 B6**
Batabanó *Cuba* 22°41N 82°18W **88 B3**
Batabanó, G. de *Cuba* 22°30N 82°30W **88 B3**
Batac *Phil.* 18°3N 120°34E **37 A6**
Batagai *Russia* 67°38N 134°38E **29 C14**
Batala *India* 31°48N 75°12E **42 D6**
Batama
  Dem. Rep. of the Congo 0°58N 26°33E **54 B2**
Batamay *Russia* 63°30N 129°15E **29 C13**
Batang *Indonesia* 6°55S 109°45E **37 G13**
Batangafo *C.A.R.* 7°25N 18°20E **52 C3**
Batangas *Phil.* 13°35N 121°10E **37 B6**
Batanta *Indonesia* 0°55S 130°40E **37 E8**
Batatais *Brazil* 20°54S 47°37W **95 A6**
Batavia *U.S.A.* 43°0N 78°11W **82 D6**
Batchelor *Australia* 13°4S 131°1E **60 B5**
Batdambang *Cambodia* 13°7N 103°12E **38 F4**
Batemans B. *Australia* 35°40S 150°12E **63 F5**
Batemans Bay *Australia* 35°44S 150°11E **63 F5**
Bates Ra. *Australia* 27°27S 121°5E **61 E3**
Batesburg-Leesville
  U.S.A. 33°54N 81°33W **85 E14**
Batesville *Ark., U.S.A.* 35°46N 91°39W **84 D9**
Batesville *Miss., U.S.A.* 34°19N 89°57W **85 D10**
Batesville *Tex., U.S.A.* 28°58N 99°37W **84 G5**
Bath *Canada* 44°11N 76°47W **83 B8**
Bath *U.K.* 51°23N 2°22W **13 F5**
Bath *Maine, U.S.A.* 43°55N 69°49W **81 D19**
Bath *N.Y., U.S.A.* 42°20N 77°19W **82 D7**
Bath & North East Somerset □
  U.K. 51°21N 2°27W **13 F5**

Batheay *Cambodia* 11°59N 104°57E **39 G5**
Bathsheba *Barbados* 13°13N 59°32W **89 g**
Bathurst *Australia* 33°25S 149°31E **63 E4**
Bathurst *Canada* 47°37N 65°43W **73 C6**
Bathurst *S. Africa* 33°30S 26°50E **56 E4**
Bathurst, C. *Canada* 70°34N 128°0W **68 B7**
Bathurst B. *Australia* 14°16S 144°25E **62 A3**
Bathurst Harb.
  Australia 43°15S 146°10E **63 G4**
Bathurst I. *Australia* 11°30S 130°10E **60 B5**
Bathurst I. *Canada* 76°0N 100°30W **69 B11**
Bathurst Inlet *Canada* 66°50N 108°1W **68 C9**
Batiki *Fiji* 17°48S 179°10E **59 a**
Batlow *Australia* 35°31S 148°9E **63 F4**
Batman *Turkey* 37°55N 41°5E **44 B4**
Baţn al Ghūl *Jordan* 29°36N 35°56E **46 F4**
Batna *Algeria* 35°34N 6°15E **50 A7**
Batoka *Zambia* 16°45S 27°15E **55 F2**
Baton Rouge *U.S.A.* 30°27N 91°11W **84 F9**
Batong, Ko *Thailand* 6°32N 99°12E **39 J2**
Batopilas *Mexico* 27°1N 107°44W **86 B3**
Batouri *Cameroon* 4°30N 14°25E **52 D2**
Bâtsfjord *Norway* 70°38N 29°39E **8 A23**
Battambang = Batdambang
  Cambodia 13°7N 103°12E **38 F4**
Batticaloa *Sri Lanka* 7°43N 81°45E **40 R12**
Battipáglia *Italy* 40°37N 14°58E **22 D6**
Battle *U.K.* 50°55N 0°30E **13 G8**
Battle → *Canada* 52°43N 108°15W **71 C7**
Battle Creek *U.S.A.* 42°19N 85°11W **81 D11**
Battle Ground *U.S.A.* 45°47N 122°32W **78 E4**
Battle Harbour *Canada* 52°16N 55°35W **73 B8**
Battle Lake *U.S.A.* 46°17N 95°43W **80 B6**
Battle Mountain
  U.S.A. 40°38N 116°56W **76 F5**
Battlefields *Zimbabwe* 18°37S 29°47E **55 F2**
Battleford *Canada* 52°45N 108°15W **71 C7**
Batu *Ethiopia* 6°55N 39°45E **47 F2**
Batu, Kepulauan
  Indonesia 0°30S 98°25E **36 E1**
Batu Caves *Malaysia* 3°15N 101°40E **39 L3**
Batu Ferringhi *Malaysia* 5°28N 100°15E **39 c**
Batu Gajah *Malaysia* 4°28N 101°3E **39 K3**
Batu Is. = Batu, Kepulauan
  Indonesia 0°30S 98°25E **36 E1**
Batu Pahat *Malaysia* 1°50N 102°56E **39 M4**
Batuata *Indonesia* 6°12S 122°42E **37 F6**
Batugondang, Tanjung
  Indonesia 8°6S 114°29E **37 J17**
Batukau, Gunung
  Indonesia 8°20S 115°5E **37 J18**
Batumi *Georgia* 41°39N 41°44E **19 F7**
Batur *Indonesia* 8°15S 115°20E **37 J18**
Batur, Danau *Indonesia* 8°15S 115°24E **37 J18**
Batur, Gunung
  Indonesia 8°14S 115°23E **37 J18**
Baturaja *Indonesia* 4°11S 104°15E **36 E2**
Baturité *Brazil* 4°28S 38°45W **93 D11**
Baturiti *Indonesia* 8°19S 115°11E **37 J18**
Bau *Malaysia* 1°25N 110°9E **36 D4**
Baubau *Indonesia* 5°25S 122°38E **37 F6**
Baucau *E. Timor* 8°27S 126°27E **37 F7**
Bauchi *Nigeria* 10°22N 9°48E **50 F7**
Baudette *U.S.A.* 48°43N 94°36W **80 A6**
Bauer, C. *Australia* 32°44S 134°4E **63 E1**
Bauhinia *Australia* 24°35S 149°18E **62 C4**
Baukau = Baucau
  E. Timor 8°27S 126°27E **37 F7**
Bauld, C. *Canada* 51°38N 55°26W **69 D14**
Bauru *Brazil* 22°10S 49°0W **95 A6**
Bausi *India* 24°48N 87°1E **43 G12**
Bauska *Latvia* 56°24N 24°15E **9 H21**
Bautzen *Germany* 51°10N 14°26E **16 C8**
Bavānāt *Iran* 30°28N 53°27E **45 D7**
Bavaria = Bayern □
  Germany 48°50N 12°0E **16 D6**
Bavispe → *Mexico* 29°15N 109°11W **86 B3**
Bawdwin *Burma* 23°5N 97°20E **41 H20**
Bawean *Indonesia* 5°46S 112°35E **36 F4**
Bawku *Ghana* 11°3N 0°19W **50 F5**
Bawlake *Burma* 19°11N 97°21E **41 K20**
Baxley *U.S.A.* 31°47N 82°21W **85 F13**
Baxter *U.S.A.* 46°21N 94°17W **80 B6**
Baxter Springs *U.S.A.* 37°2N 94°44W **80 G6**
Baxter State △ *U.S.A.* 46°5N 68°57W **81 B19**
Bay City *Mich., U.S.A.* 43°36N 83°54W **81 D12**
Bay City *Tex., U.S.A.* 28°59N 95°58W **84 G7**
Bay Minette *U.S.A.* 30°53N 87°46W **85 F11**
Bay Roberts *Canada* 47°36N 53°16W **73 C9**
Bay St. Louis *U.S.A.* 30°19N 89°20W **85 F10**
Bay Springs *U.S.A.* 31°59N 89°17W **85 F10**
Bay View *N.Z.* 39°25S 176°50E **59 C6**
Baya
  Dem. Rep. of the Congo 11°53S 27°25E **55 E2**
Bayamo *Cuba* 20°20N 76°40W **88 B4**
Bayamón *Puerto Rico* 18°24N 66°9W **89 d**
Bayan Har Shan *China* 34°0N 98°0E **32 C4**
Bayan Hot = Alxa Zuoqi
  China 38°50N 105°40E **34 E3**
Bayan Lepas *Malaysia* 5°17N 100°16E **39 c**
Bayan Obo *China* 41°52N 109°59E **34 D5**
Bayan-Ovoo = Erdenetsogt
  Mongolia 42°55N 106°5E **34 C4**
Bayana *India* 26°55N 77°18E **42 F7**
Bayanaūyl *Kazakhstan* 50°45N 75°45E **28 D8**
Bayandalay *Mongolia* 43°30N 103°29E **34 C2**
Bayanhongor *Mongolia* 46°8N 102°43E **32 B5**
Bayard *N. Mex., U.S.A.* 32°46N 108°8W **77 K9**
Bayard *Nebr., U.S.A.* 41°45N 103°20W **80 E2**
Baybay *Phil.* 10°40N 124°55E **37 B6**
Baydhabo = Baidoa
  Somali Rep. 3°8N 43°30E **47 G3**
Bayern □ *Germany* 48°50N 12°0E **16 D6**
Bayeux *France* 49°17N 0°42W **20 B3**
Bayfield *Canada* 43°34N 81°42W **82 C3**
Bayfield *U.S.A.* 46°49N 90°49W **80 B8**
Bayındır *Turkey* 38°13N 27°39E **23 E12**
Baykal, Oz. *Russia* 53°0N 108°0E **29 D11**

Baykan *Turkey* 38°7N 41°44E **44 B4**
Baymak *Russia* 52°36N 58°19E **18 D10**
Baynes Mts. *Namibia* 17°15S 13°0E **56 B1**
Bayombong *Phil.* 16°30N 121°10E **37 A6**
Bayonne *France* 43°30N 1°28W **20 E3**
Bayonne *U.S.A.* 40°40N 74°6W **83 F10**
Bayovar *Peru* 5°50S 81°0W **92 E2**
Bayqongyr *Kazakhstan* 45°40N 63°20E **28 E7**
Bayram-Ali = Baýramaly
  Turkmenistan 37°37N 62°10E **45 B9**
Baýramaly *Turkmenistan* 37°37N 62°10E **45 B9**
Bayramiç *Turkey* 39°48N 26°36E **23 E12**
Bayreuth *Germany* 49°56N 11°35E **16 D6**
Bayrūt *Lebanon* 33°53N 35°31E **46 B4**
Bays, L. of *Canada* 45°15N 79°4W **82 A5**
Baysville *Canada* 45°9N 79°7W **82 A5**
Bayt Lahm *West Bank* 31°43N 35°12E **46 D4**
Baytown *U.S.A.* 29°43N 94°59W **84 G7**
Bayun *Indonesia* 8°11S 115°16E **37 J18**
Baza *Spain* 37°30N 2°47W **21 D4**
Bazaruto, I. do *Mozam.* 21°40S 35°28E **57 C6**
Bazaruto △ *Mozam.* 21°42S 35°26E **57 C6**
Bazhou *China* 39°8N 116°22E **34 E9**
Bazmān, Kūh-e *Iran* 28°4N 60°1E **45 D9**
Beach *U.S.A.* 46°58N 104°0W **80 B2**
Beach City *U.S.A.* 40°39N 81°35W **82 F3**
Beachport *Australia* 37°29S 140°0E **63 F3**
Beachy Hd. *U.K.* 50°44N 0°15E **13 G8**
Beacon *Australia* 30°26S 117°52E **61 F2**
Beacon *U.S.A.* 41°30N 73°58W **83 E11**
Beaconsfield *Australia* 41°11S 146°48E **63 G4**
Beagle, Canal *S. Amer.* 55°0S 68°30W **96 H3**
Beagle Bay *Australia* 16°58S 122°40E **60 C3**
Bealanana *Madag.* 14°33S 48°44E **57 A8**
Beals Cr. → *U.S.A.* 32°10N 100°51W **84 E4**
Beamsville = Lincoln
  Canada 43°12N 79°28W **82 C5**
Bear → *Calif., U.S.A.* 38°56N 121°36W **78 G5**
Bear → *Utah, U.S.A.* 41°30N 112°8W **74 B4**
Bear I. *Ireland* 51°38N 9°50W **10 E2**
Bear L. *Canada* 55°8N 96°0W **71 B9**
Bear L. *U.S.A.* 41°59N 111°21W **76 F8**
Beardmore *Canada* 49°36N 87°57W **72 C2**
Beardmore Glacier
  Antarctica 84°30S 170°0E **5 E11**
Beardstown *U.S.A.* 40°1N 90°26W **80 E8**
Bearma → *India* 24°20N 79°51E **43 G8**
Béarn *France* 43°20N 0°30W **20 E3**
Bearpaw Mts. *U.S.A.* 48°12N 109°30W **76 B9**
Bearskin Lake *Canada* 53°58N 91°2W **72 B1**
Beas → *India* 31°10N 74°59E **42 D6**
Beata, C. *Dom. Rep.* 17°40N 71°30W **89 C5**
Beata, I. *Dom. Rep.* 17°34N 71°31W **89 C5**
Beatrice *U.S.A.* 40°16N 96°45W **80 E5**
Beatrice *Zimbabwe* 18°15S 30°55E **55 F3**
Beatrice, C. *Australia* 14°20S 136°55E **62 A2**
Beatton → *Canada* 56°15N 120°45W **70 B4**
Beatton River *Canada* 57°26N 121°20W **70 B4**
Beatty *U.S.A.* 36°54N 116°46W **78 J10**
Beau Bassin *Mauritius* 20°13S 57°27E **53 d**
Beauce, Plaine de la
  France 48°10N 1°45E **20 B4**
Beauceville *Canada* 46°13N 70°46W **73 C5**
Beaudesert *Australia* 27°59S 153°0E **63 D5**
Beaufort *Malaysia* 5°30N 115°40E **36 C5**
Beaufort *N.C., U.S.A.* 34°43N 76°40W **85 D16**
Beaufort *S.C., U.S.A.* 32°26N 80°40W **85 E14**
Beaufort Sea *Arctic* 72°0N 140°0W **66 B5**
Beaufort West *S. Africa* 32°18S 22°36E **56 E3**
Beauharnois *Canada* 45°20N 73°52W **83 A11**
Beaulieu → *Canada* 62°3N 113°11W **70 A6**
Beauly *U.K.* 57°30N 4°28W **11 D4**
Beauly → *U.K.* 57°29N 4°27W **11 D4**
Beaumaris *U.K.* 53°16N 4°6W **12 D3**
Beaumont *Belgium* 50°15N 4°14E **15 D4**
Beaumont *U.S.A.* 30°5N 94°6W **84 F7**
Beaune *France* 47°2N 4°50E **20 C6**
Beaupré *Canada* 47°3N 70°54W **73 C5**
Beauraing *Belgium* 50°7N 4°57E **15 D4**
Beausejour *Canada* 50°5N 96°35W **71 C9**
Beauvais *France* 49°25N 2°8E **20 B5**
Beauval *Canada* 55°9N 107°37W **71 B7**
Beaver *Okla., U.S.A.* 36°49N 100°31W **84 C4**
Beaver *Pa., U.S.A.* 40°42N 80°19W **82 F4**
Beaver *Utah, U.S.A.* 38°17N 112°38W **76 G7**
Beaver → *B.C., Canada* 59°52N 124°20W **70 B4**
Beaver → *Ont., Canada* 55°55N 87°48W **72 A2**
Beaver → *Sask.,*
  Canada 55°26N 107°45W **71 B7**
Beaver → *U.S.A.* 36°35N 99°30W **84 C5**
Beaver City *U.S.A.* 40°8N 99°50W **80 E4**
Beaver Creek *Canada* 63°0N 141°0W **68 C5**
Beaver Dam *U.S.A.* 43°28N 88°50W **80 D9**
Beaver Falls *U.S.A.* 40°46N 80°20W **82 F4**
Beaver Hill L. *Canada* 54°5N 94°50W **71 C10**
Beaver I. *U.S.A.* 45°40N 85°33W **81 C11**
Beavercreek *U.S.A.* 39°43N 84°11W **81 F11**
Beaverhill L. *Canada* 53°27N 112°32W **70 C6**
Beaverlodge *Canada* 55°11N 119°29W **70 B5**
Beaverstone → *Canada* 54°26N 79°9W **82 B5**
Beaverton *Canada* 44°26N 79°9W **82 B5**
Beaverton *U.S.A.* 45°29N 122°48W **78 E4**
Beawar *India* 26°3N 74°18E **42 F6**
Bebedouro *Brazil* 21°0S 48°25W **95 A6**
Bebera, Tanjung
  Indonesia 8°44S 115°51E **37 K18**
Beboa *Madag.* 17°22S 44°33E **57 B7**
Becán *Mexico* 18°34N 89°31W **87 D7**
Bécancour *Canada* 46°20N 72°26W **81 B17**
Beccles *U.K.* 52°27N 1°35E **13 E9**
Bečej *Serbia* 45°36N 20°3E **23 B9**
Béchar *Algeria* 31°38N 2°18W **50 B5**
Beckley *U.S.A.* 37°47N 81°11W **81 G13**
Beddouza, Ras *Morocco* 32°33N 9°9W **50 B4**
Bedford *Canada* 45°7N 72°59W **83 A12**
Bedford *S. Africa* 32°40S 26°10E **56 E4**
Bedford *U.K.* 52°8N 0°28W **13 E7**
Bedford *Ind., U.S.A.* 38°52N 86°29W **80 F10**

Bedford *Iowa, U.S.A.* 40°40N 94°44W **80 E6**
Bedford *Ohio, U.S.A.* 41°23N 81°32W **82 E3**
Bedford *Pa., U.S.A.* 40°1N 78°30W **82 F6**
Bedford *Va., U.S.A.* 37°20N 79°31W **81 G14**
Bedford, C. *Australia* 15°14S 145°21E **62 B4**
Bedfordshire □ *U.K.* 52°4N 0°28E **13 E7**
Bedok *Singapore* 1°19N 103°56E **39 d**
Bedourie *Australia* 24°30S 139°30E **62 C2**
Bedum *Neths.* 53°18N 6°36E **15 A6**
Beebe Plain *Canada* 45°1N 72°9W **83 A12**
Beech Creek *U.S.A.* 41°5N 77°36W **82 E7**
Beechy *Canada* 50°53N 107°24W **71 C7**
Beef I. *Br. Virgin Is.* 18°26N 64°30W **89 e**
Beenleigh *Australia* 27°43S 153°10E **63 D5**
Be'er Menuha *Israel* 30°19N 35°8E **44 D2**
Be'er Sheva *Israel* 31°15N 34°48E **46 D3**
Beersheba = Be'er Sheva
  Israel 31°15N 34°48E **46 D3**
Beestekraal *S. Africa* 25°23S 27°38E **57 D4**
Beeston *U.K.* 52°56N 1°14W **12 E6**
Beeville *U.S.A.* 28°24N 97°45W **84 G6**
Befale
  Dem. Rep. of the Congo 0°25N 20°45E **52 D4**
Befandriana *Mahajanga,*
  Madag. 15°16S 48°32E **57 B8**
Befandriana *Toliara,*
  Madag. 21°55S 44°0E **57 C7**
Befasy *Madag.* 20°33S 44°23E **57 C7**
Befotaka *Antsiranana,*
  Madag. 13°15S 48°16E **57 A8**
Befotaka *Fianarantsoa,*
  Madag. 23°49S 47°0E **57 C8**
Bega *Australia* 36°41S 149°51E **63 F4**
Begusarai *India* 25°24N 86°9E **43 G12**
Behābād *Iran* 32°24N 59°47E **45 C8**
Behala *India* 22°30N 88°18E **43 H13**
Behara *Madag.* 24°55S 46°20E **57 C8**
Behbehān *Iran* 30°30N 50°15E **45 D6**
Behm Canal *U.S.A.* 55°10N 131°0W **70 B2**
Behshahr *Iran* 36°45N 53°35E **45 B7**
Bei Jiang → *China* 23°2N 112°58E **35 F9**
Bei'an *China* 48°10N 126°20E **33 B7**
Beihai *China* 21°28N 109°6E **33 D5**
Beijing *China* 39°53N 116°21E **34 E9**
Beijing □ *China* 39°55N 116°20E **34 E9**
Beilen *Neths.* 52°52N 6°27E **15 B6**
Beilpajah *Australia* 32°54S 143°52E **63 E3**
Beinn na Faoghla = Benbecula
  U.K. 57°26N 7°21W **11 D1**
Beipiao *China* 41°52N 120°32E **35 D11**
Beira *Mozam.* 19°50S 34°52E **55 F3**
Beirut = Bayrūt *Lebanon* 33°53N 35°31E **46 B4**
Beiseker *Canada* 51°23N 113°32W **70 C6**
Beit Lekhem = Bayt Lahm
  West Bank 31°43N 35°12E **46 D4**
Beitaolaizhao *China* 44°58N 125°58E **35 B13**
Beitbridge *Zimbabwe* 22°12S 30°0E **55 G3**
Beizhen = Binzhou
  China 37°20N 118°2E **35 F10**
Beizhen *China* 41°38N 121°54E **35 D11**
Beizhengzhen *China* 44°31N 123°30E **35 B12**
Beja *Portugal* 38°2N 7°53W **21 C2**
Béja *Tunisia* 36°43N 9°12E **51 A7**
Bejaïa *Algeria* 36°42N 5°2E **50 A7**
Béjar *Spain* 40°23N 5°46W **21 B3**
Bejestān *Iran* 34°30N 58°5E **45 C8**
Bekaa Valley = Al Biqâ
  Lebanon 34°10N 36°10E **46 A5**
Békéscsaba *Hungary* 46°40N 21°5E **17 E11**
Bekily *Madag.* 24°13S 45°19E **57 C8**
Bekisopa *Madag.* 21°40S 45°54E **57 C8**
Bekitro *Madag.* 24°33S 45°18E **57 C8**
Bekodoka *Madag.* 16°58S 45°7E **57 B8**
Bekok *Malaysia* 2°20N 103°7E **39 L4**
Bekopaka *Madag.* 19°9S 44°48E **57 B7**
Bekuli *Indonesia* 8°22S 114°13E **37 J17**
Bela *India* 25°50N 82°0E **43 G10**
Bela *Pakistan* 26°12N 66°20E **42 F2**
Bela Bela *S. Africa* 24°51S 28°19E **57 C4**
Bela Crkva *Serbia* 44°55N 21°27E **23 B9**
Bela Vista *Brazil* 22°12S 56°20W **94 A4**
Bela Vista *Mozam.* 26°10S 32°44E **57 D5**
Belan → *India* 24°2N 81°45E **43 G9**
Belarus ■ *Europe* 53°30N 27°0E **17 B14**
Belau = Palau ■ *Palau* 7°30N 134°30E **58 A6**
Belavenona *Madag.* 24°50S 47°4E **57 C8**
Belawan *Indonesia* 3°33N 98°32E **36 D1**
Belaya → *Russia* 54°40N 56°0E **18 C9**
Belaya Tserkov = Bila Tserkva
  Ukraine 49°45N 30°10E **17 D16**
Belcher Chan. *Canada* 77°15N 95°0W **69 B10**
Belcher Is. *Canada* 56°15N 78°45W **72 A3**
Belden *U.S.A.* 40°2N 121°17W **78 E5**
Belebey *Russia* 54°7N 54°7E **18 D9**
Beled Weyne = Belet Uen
  Somali Rep. 4°30N 45°5E **47 G4**
Belém *Brazil* 1°20S 48°30W **93 D9**
Belén *Argentina* 27°40S 67°5W **94 B2**
Belén *Paraguay* 23°30S 57°6W **94 A4**
Belen *U.S.A.* 34°40N 106°46W **77 J10**
Belet Uen *Somali Rep.* 4°30N 45°5E **47 G4**
Belev *Russia* 53°50N 36°5E **18 D6**
Belfair *U.S.A.* 47°27N 122°50W **78 C4**
Belfast *S. Africa* 25°42S 30°2E **57 D5**
Belfast *U.K.* 54°37N 5°56W **10 B6**
Belfast *Maine, U.S.A.* 44°26N 69°1W **81 C19**
Belfast *N.Y., U.S.A.* 42°21N 78°7W **82 D6**
Belfast *L., U.K.* 54°40N 5°50W **10 B6**
Belfield *U.S.A.* 46°53N 103°12W **80 B2**
Belfort *France* 47°38N 6°50E **20 C7**
Belfry *U.S.A.* 45°9N 109°1W **76 D9**
Belgaum *India* 15°55N 74°35E **40 M9**
Belgium ■ *Europe* 50°30N 5°0E **15 D4**
Belgorod *Russia* 50°35N 36°35E **19 D6**
Belgorod-Dnestrovskiy =
  Bilhorod-Dnistrovskyy
  Ukraine 46°11N 30°23E **19 E5**

Belgrade = Beograd Serbia 44°50N 20°37E 23 B9
Belgrade U.S.A. 45°47N 111°11W 76 D8
Belgrano Antarctica 77°52S 34°37W 5 D1
Belhaven U.S.A. 35°33N 76°37W 85 D16
Beli Drim → Europe 42°6N 20°25E 23 C9
Belimbing Indonesia 8°24S 115°2E 37 J18
Belinyu Indonesia 1°35S 105°50E 36 E3
Beliton Is. = Belitung Indonesia 3°10S 107°50E 36 E3
Belitung Indonesia 3°10S 107°50E 36 E3
Belize ■ Cent. Amer. 17°0N 88°30W 87 D7
Belize City Belize 17°25N 88°10W 87 D7
Belkovskiy, Ostrov Russia 75°32N 135°44E 29 B14
Bell → Canada 49°48N 77°38W 72 C4
Bell I. Canada 50°46N 55°35W 73 B8
Bell-Irving → Canada 56°12N 129°5W 70 B3
Bell Peninsula Canada 63°50N 82°0W 69 C11
Bell Ville Argentina 32°40S 62°40W 94 C3
Bella Bella Canada 52°10N 128°10W 70 C3
Bella Coola Canada 52°25N 126°40W 70 C3
Bella Unión Uruguay 30°15S 57°40W 94 C4
Bella Vista Corrientes, Argentina 28°33S 59°0W 94 B4
Bella Vista Tucuman, Argentina 27°10S 65°25W 94 B2
Bellaire U.S.A. 40°1N 80°45W 82 F4
Bellary India 15°10N 76°56E 40 M10
Bellata Australia 29°53S 149°46E 63 D4
Belle Fourche U.S.A. 44°40N 103°51W 80 C2
Belle Fourche → U.S.A. 44°26N 102°18W 74 B6
Belle Glade U.S.A. 26°41N 80°40W 85 H14
Belle-Île France 47°20N 3°10W 20 C2
Belle Isle Canada 51°57N 55°25W 73 B8
Belle Isle, Str. of Canada 51°30N 56°30W 73 B8
Belle Plaine U.S.A. 41°54N 92°17W 80 E7
Bellefontaine U.S.A. 40°22N 83°46W 81 E12
Bellefonte U.S.A. 40°55N 77°47W 82 F7
Belleoram Canada 47°31N 55°25W 73 C8
Belleplaine Barbados 13°15N 59°34W 89 g
Belleville Canada 44°10N 77°23W 82 B7
Belleville Ill., U.S.A. 38°31N 89°59W 80 F9
Belleville Kans., U.S.A. 39°50N 97°38W 80 F5
Belleville N.J., U.S.A. 40°47N 74°9W 83 F10
Belleville N.Y., U.S.A. 43°46N 76°10W 83 C8
Bellevue Canada 49°35N 114°22W 70 D6
Bellevue Idaho, U.S.A. 43°28N 114°16W 76 E6
Bellevue Nebr., U.S.A. 41°9N 95°54W 80 E6
Bellevue Ohio, U.S.A. 41°17N 82°51W 82 E2
Bellevue Wash., U.S.A. 47°37N 122°12W 78 C4
Bellin = Kangirsuk Canada 60°0N 70°0W 69 D13
Bellingen Australia 30°25S 152°50E 63 E5
Bellingham U.S.A. 48°46N 122°29W 78 B4
Bellingshausen Abyssal Plain S. Ocean 64°0S 90°0W 5 C16
Bellingshausen Sea Antarctica 66°0S 80°0W 5 C17
Bellinzona Switz. 46°11N 9°1E 20 C8
Bello Colombia 6°20N 75°33W 92 B3
Bellows Falls U.S.A. 43°8N 72°27W 83 C12
Bellpat Pakistan 29°0N 68°5E 42 E3
Belluno Italy 46°9N 12°13E 22 A5
Bellwood U.S.A. 40°36N 78°20W 82 F6
Belmont Canada 42°53N 81°5W 82 D3
Belmont S. Africa 29°28S 24°22E 56 D3
Belmont U.S.A. 42°14N 78°2W 82 D6
Belmonte Brazil 16°0S 39°0W 93 G11
Belmopan Belize 17°18N 88°30W 87 D7
Belmullet Ireland 54°14N 9°58W 10 B2
Belo Horizonte Brazil 19°55S 43°56W 93 G10
Belo-sur-Mer Madag. 20°42S 44°0E 57 C7
Belo-Tsiribihina Madag. 19°40S 44°30E 57 B7
Belogorsk Russia 51°0N 128°20E 29 D13
Beloha Madag. 25°10S 45°3E 57 D8
Beloit Kans., U.S.A. 39°28N 98°6W 80 F4
Beloit Wis., U.S.A. 42°31N 89°2W 80 D9
Belokorovichi Ukraine 51°7N 28°2E 17 C15
Belomorsk Russia 64°35N 34°54E 18 B5
Belonia India 23°15N 91°30E 41 H17
Beloretsk Russia 53°58N 58°24E 18 D10
Belorussia = Belarus ■ Europe 53°30N 27°0E 17 B14
Belovo Russia 54°30N 86°0E 28 D9
Beloye, Ozero Russia 60°10N 37°35E 18 B6
Beloye More Russia 66°30N 38°0E 8 C25
Belozersk Russia 60°1N 37°45E 18 B6
Belpre U.S.A. 39°17N 81°34W 81 F13
Belrain India 28°23N 80°55E 43 E9
Belt U.S.A. 47°23N 110°55W 76 C8
Beltana Australia 30°48S 138°25E 63 E2
Belterra Brazil 2°45S 55°0W 93 D8
Belton U.S.A. 31°3N 97°28W 84 F6
Belton L. U.S.A. 31°6N 97°28W 84 F6
Beltsy = Bălţi Moldova 47°48N 27°58E 17 E14
Belturbet Ireland 54°6N 7°26W 10 B4
Belukha Russia 49°50N 86°50E 28 E9
Beluran Malaysia 5°48N 117°35E 36 C5
Belvidere Ill., U.S.A. 42°15N 88°50W 80 D9
Belvidere N.J., U.S.A. 40°50N 75°5W 83 F9
Belyando → Australia 21°38S 146°50E 62 C4
Belyy, Ostrov Russia 73°30N 71°0E 28 B8
Belyy Yar Russia 58°26N 84°39E 28 D9
Belzoni U.S.A. 33°11N 90°29W 85 E9
Bemaraha, Lembalemban' i Madag. 18°40S 44°45E 57 B7
Bemarivo Madag. 21°45S 44°45E 57 C7
Bemarivo → Antsiranana, Madag. 14°9S 50°9E 57 A9
Bemarivo → Mahajanga, Madag. 15°27S 47°40E 57 B8
Bemavo Madag. 21°33S 45°25E 57 C8
Bembéréke Benin 10°11N 2°43E 50 F6
Bembesi Zimbabwe 20°0S 28°58E 55 G2
Bembesi → Zimbabwe 18°57S 27°47E 55 F2
Bemetara India 21°42N 81°32E 43 J9
Bemidji U.S.A. 47°28N 94°53W 80 B6
Bemolanga Madag. 17°44S 45°6E 57 B8
Ben Iran 32°32N 50°45E 45 C6
Ben Cruachan U.K. 56°26N 5°8W 11 E3
Ben Dearg U.K. 57°47N 4°56W 11 D4
Ben En △ Vietnam 19°37N 105°30E 38 C5
Ben Gardane Tunisia 33°11N 11°11E 51 B8
Ben Hope U.K. 58°25N 4°36W 11 C4
Ben Lawers U.K. 56°32N 4°14W 11 E4
Ben Lomond N.S.W., Australia 30°1S 151°43E 63 E5
Ben Lomond Tas., Australia 41°38S 147°42E 63 G4
Ben Lomond U.K. 56°11N 4°38W 11 E4
Ben Lomond △ Australia 41°33S 147°39E 63 G4
Ben Luc Vietnam 10°39N 106°29E 39 G6
Ben Macdhui U.K. 57°4N 3°40W 11 D5
Ben Mhor U.K. 57°15N 7°18W 11 D1
Ben More Argyll & Bute, U.K. 56°26N 6°1W 11 E2
Ben More Stirling, U.K. 56°23N 4°32W 11 E4
Ben More Assynt U.K. 58°8N 4°52W 11 C4
Ben Nevis U.K. 56°48N 5°1W 11 E3
Ben Quang Vietnam 17°3N 106°55E 38 D6
Ben Vorlich U.K. 56°21N 4°14W 11 E4
Ben Wyvis U.K. 57°40N 4°35W 11 D4
Bena Nigeria 11°20N 5°50E 50 F7
Benalla Australia 36°30S 146°0E 63 F4
Benares = Varanasi India 25°22N 83°0E 43 G10
Benavente Spain 42°2N 5°43W 21 A3
Benavides U.S.A. 27°36N 98°25W 84 H5
Benbecula U.K. 57°26N 7°21W 11 D1
Benbonyathe Hill Australia 30°25S 139°11E 63 E2
Bend U.S.A. 44°4N 121°19W 76 D3
Bender Beila Somali Rep. 9°30N 50°48E 47 F5
Bendery = Tighina Moldova 46°50N 29°30E 17 E15
Bendigo Australia 36°40S 144°15E 63 F3
Benē Beraq Israel 32°6N 34°51E 46 C3
Benenitra Madag. 23°27S 45°5E 57 C8
Benevento Italy 41°8N 14°45E 22 D6
Benga Mozam. 16°11S 33°40E 55 F3
Bengal, Bay of Ind. Oc. 15°0N 90°0E 41 M17
Bengalûru = Bangalore India 12°59N 77°40E 40 N10
Bengbu China 32°58N 117°20E 35 H9
Benghazi = Banghāzī Libya 32°11N 20°3E 51 B10
Bengkalis Indonesia 1°30N 102°10E 36 D2
Bengkulu Indonesia 3°50S 102°12E 36 E2
Bengkulu □ Indonesia 3°48S 102°16E 36 E2
Bengough Canada 49°25N 105°10W 71 D7
Benguela Angola 12°37S 13°25E 53 G2
Benguérua, I. Mozam. 21°58S 35°28E 57 C6
Beni Dem. Rep. of the Congo 0°30N 29°27E 54 B2
Beni → Bolivia 10°23S 65°24W 92 F5
Beni Mellal Morocco 32°21N 0°21W 50 D4
Beni Suef Egypt 29°5N 31°6E 51 C12
Beniah L. Canada 63°23N 112°17W 70 A6
Benidorm Spain 38°33N 0°9W 21 C5
Benin ■ Africa 10°0N 2°0E 50 G6
Benin, Bight of W. Afr. 5°0N 3°0E 50 H6
Benin City Nigeria 6°20N 5°31E 50 G7
Benitses Greece 39°32N 19°55E 25 A3
Benjamin Aceval Paraguay 24°58S 57°34W 94 A4
Benjamin Constant Brazil 4°40S 70°15W 92 D4
Benjamín Hill Mexico 30°9N 111°7W 86 A2
Benkelman U.S.A. 40°3N 101°32W 80 E3
Bennett Canada 59°51N 135°0W 70 B2
Bennett, L. Australia 22°50S 131°2E 60 D5
Bennetta, Ostrov Russia 76°21N 148°56E 29 B15
Bennettsville U.S.A. 34°37N 79°41W 85 D15
Bennington N.H., U.S.A. 43°0N 71°55W 83 D11
Bennington Vt., U.S.A. 42°53N 73°12W 83 D11
Benoni S. Africa 26°11S 28°18E 57 D4
Benque Viejo Belize 17°5N 89°8W 87 D7
Benson Ariz., U.S.A. 31°58N 110°18W 77 L8
Benson Minn., U.S.A. 45°19N 95°36W 80 C6
Bent Iran 26°20N 59°31E 45 E8
Benteng Indonesia 6°10S 120°30E 37 F6
Bentinck I. Australia 17°3S 139°35E 62 B2
Bento Gonçalves Brazil 29°10S 51°31W 95 B5
Benton Ark., U.S.A. 34°34N 92°35W 84 D8
Benton Calif., U.S.A. 37°48N 118°32W 78 H8
Benton Ill., U.S.A. 38°0N 88°55W 80 F9
Benton Pa., U.S.A. 41°12N 76°23W 83 E8
Benton Harbor U.S.A. 42°6N 86°27W 80 D10
Bentong Malaysia 3°31N 101°55E 39 L3
Bentonville U.S.A. 36°22N 94°13W 84 C7
Benue → Nigeria 7°48N 6°46E 50 G7
Benxi China 41°20N 123°48E 35 D12
Beo Indonesia 4°25N 126°50E 37 D7
Beograd Serbia 44°50N 20°37E 23 B9
Beolgyo S. Korea 34°51N 127°21E 35 G14
Beppu Japan 33°15N 131°30E 31 H5
Beqa Fiji 18°23S 178°8E 59 a
Beqaa Valley = Al Biqā Lebanon 34°10N 36°10E 46 A5
Ber Mota India 23°27N 68°34E 42 H3
Berach → India 25°15N 75°2E 42 G6
Beraketa Madag. 23°7S 44°25E 57 C7
Berat Albania 40°43N 19°59E 23 D8
Berau, Teluk Indonesia 2°30S 132°30E 37 E8
Beravina Madag. 18°10S 45°14E 57 B8
Berber Sudan 18°0N 34°0E 51 E12
Berbera Somali Rep. 10°30N 45°2E 47 E4
Berbérati C.A.R. 4°15N 15°40E 52 D3
Berbice → Guyana 6°20N 57°32W 92 B7
Berdichev = Berdychiv Ukraine 49°57N 28°30E 17 D15
Berdsk Russia 54°47N 83°2E 28 D9
Berdyansk Ukraine 46°45N 36°50E 19 E6
Berdychiv Ukraine 49°57N 28°30E 17 D15
Berea U.S.A. 37°34N 84°17W 81 G11
Berebere Indonesia 2°25N 128°45E 37 D7
Bereda Somali Rep. 11°45N 51°0E 47 E5
Berehove Ukraine 48°15N 22°35E 17 D12
Bereket Turkmenistan 39°16N 55°32E 45 B7
Berekum Ghana 7°29N 2°34W 50 G5
Berens → Canada 52°25N 97°2W 71 C9
Berens I. Canada 52°18N 97°18W 71 C9
Berens River Canada 52°25N 97°0W 71 C9
Beresford U.S.A. 43°5N 96°47W 80 D5
Berestechko Ukraine 50°22N 25°5E 17 C13
Berevo Mahajanga, Madag. 17°14S 44°17E 57 B7
Berevo Toliara, Madag. 19°44S 44°58E 57 B7
Berezhany Ukraine 49°26N 24°58E 17 D13
Berezina = Byarezina → Belarus 52°33N 30°14E 17 B16
Bereznik Russia 62°51N 42°40E 18 B7
Berezniki Russia 59°24N 56°46E 18 C10
Berezovo Russia 64°0N 65°0E 28 C7
Berga Spain 42°6N 1°48E 21 A6
Bergama Turkey 39°8N 27°11E 23 E12
Bérgamo Italy 45°41N 9°43E 20 D8
Bergen Neths. 52°40N 4°43E 15 B4
Bergen Norway 60°20N 5°20E 8 F11
Bergen U.S.A. 43°5N 77°57W 82 C7
Bergen op Zoom Neths. 51°28N 4°18E 15 C4
Bergerac France 44°51N 0°30E 20 D4
Bergholz U.S.A. 40°31N 80°53W 82 F4
Bergisch Gladbach Germany 50°59N 7°8E 15 D7
Bergville S. Africa 28°52S 29°18E 57 D4
Berhala, Selat Indonesia 1°0S 104°15E 36 E2
Berhampore = Baharampur India 24°2N 88°27E 43 G13
Berhampur = Brahmapur India 19°15N 84°54E 41 K14
Bering Sea Pac. Oc. 58°0N 171°0W 74 a
Bering Strait Pac. Oc. 65°30N 169°0W 74 a
Beringovskiy Russia 63°3N 179°19E 29 C18
Berisso Argentina 34°56S 57°50W 94 C4
Berja Spain 36°50N 2°56W 21 D4
Berkeley U.S.A. 37°51N 122°16W 78 H4
Berkner I. Antarctica 79°30S 50°0W 5 D18
Berkshire U.S.A. 42°19N 76°11W 83 D8
Berkshire Downs U.K. 51°33N 1°29W 13 F6
Berlin Germany 52°31N 13°23E 16 B7
Berlin Md., U.S.A. 38°20N 75°13W 81 F16
Berlin N.H., U.S.A. 44°28N 71°11W 83 B13
Berlin N.Y., U.S.A. 42°42N 73°23W 83 D11
Berlin Wis., U.S.A. 43°58N 88°57W 80 D9
Berlin L. U.S.A. 41°3N 81°0W 82 E4
Bermejo → Formosa, Argentina 26°51S 58°23W 94 B4
Bermejo → San Juan, Argentina 32°30S 67°30W 94 C2
Bermen, L. Canada 53°35N 68°55W 73 B6
Bermuda ◩ Atl. Oc. 32°45N 65°0W 67 F13
Bern Switz. 46°57N 7°28E 20 C7
Bernalillo U.S.A. 35°18N 106°33W 77 J10
Bernardo de Irigoyen Argentina 26°15S 53°40W 95 B5
Bernardo O'Higgins □ Chile 34°15S 70°45W 94 C1
Bernardsville U.S.A. 40°43N 74°34W 83 F10
Bernasconi Argentina 37°55S 63°44W 94 D3
Bernburg Germany 51°47N 11°44E 16 C6
Berne = Bern Switz. 46°57N 7°28E 20 C7
Berneray U.K. 57°43N 7°11W 11 D1
Bernier I. Australia 24°50S 113°12E 61 D1
Bernina, Piz Switz. 46°20N 9°54E 20 C8
Beroroha Madag. 21°40S 45°10E 57 C8
Beroun Czech Rep. 49°57N 14°5E 16 D8
Berri Australia 34°14S 140°35E 63 E3
Berriane Algeria 32°50N 3°46E 50 B6
Berry Australia 34°46S 150°43E 63 E5
Berry France 46°50N 2°0E 20 C5
Berry Is. Bahamas 25°40N 77°50W 88 A4
Berryessa, L. U.S.A. 38°31N 122°6W 78 G4
Berryville U.S.A. 36°22N 93°34W 84 C8
Berseba Namibia 26°0S 17°46E 56 D2
Bershad Ukraine 48°22N 29°31E 17 D15
Berthold U.S.A. 48°19N 101°44W 80 A3
Berthoud U.S.A. 40°19N 105°5W 76 F11
Bertoua Cameroon 4°30N 13°45E 52 D2
Bertraghboy B. Ireland 53°22N 9°54W 10 C2
Berwick U.S.A. 41°3N 76°14W 83 E8
Berwick-upon-Tweed U.K. 55°46N 2°0W 12 B6
Berwyn Mts. U.K. 52°54N 3°26W 12 E4
Besal Pakistan 35°4N 73°56E 43 B5
Besalampy Madag. 16°43S 44°29E 57 B7
Besançon France 47°15N 6°2E 20 C7
Besar Indonesia 2°40S 116°0E 36 E5
Besnard L. Canada 55°25N 106°0W 71 B7
Besni Turkey 37°41N 37°52E 44 B3
Besor, N. → Egypt 31°28N 34°22E 46 D3
Bessarabiya Moldova 47°0N 28°10E 17 E15
Bessarabka = Basarabeasca Moldova 46°21N 28°58E 17 E15
Bessemer Ala., U.S.A. 33°24N 86°58W 85 E11
Bessemer Mich., U.S.A. 46°29N 90°3W 80 B8
Bessemer Pa., U.S.A. 40°59N 80°30W 82 F4
Beswick Australia 14°34S 132°53E 60 B5
Bet She'an Israel 32°30N 35°30E 46 C4
Bet Shemesh Israel 31°44N 35°0E 46 D4
Betafo Madag. 19°50S 46°51E 57 B8
Betancuria Canary Is. 28°25N 14°3W 24 F5
Betanzos Spain 43°15N 8°12W 21 A1
Bétaré Oya Cameroon 5°40N 14°5E 52 C2
Betatao Madag. 18°11S 47°52E 57 B8
Bethal S. Africa 26°27S 29°28E 57 D4
Bethanien Namibia 26°31S 17°8E 56 D2
Bethany Canada 44°11N 78°34W 82 B6
Bethany Mo., U.S.A. 40°16N 94°2W 80 E6
Bethany Okla., U.S.A. 35°31N 97°38W 84 D6
Bethel Alaska, U.S.A. 60°48N 161°45W 74 a
Bethel Conn., U.S.A. 41°22N 73°25W 83 E11
Bethel Maine, U.S.A. 44°25N 70°47W 83 B14
Bethel Vt., U.S.A. 43°50N 72°38W 83 C12
Bethel Park U.S.A. 40°19N 80°2W 82 F4
Bethlehem = Bayt Lahm West Bank 31°43N 35°12E 46 D4
Bethlehem S. Africa 28°14S 28°18E 57 D4
Bethlehem U.S.A. 40°37N 75°23W 83 F9
Bethulie S. Africa 30°30S 25°59E 56 E4
Béthune France 50°30N 2°38E 20 A5
Betioky Madag. 23°48S 44°20E 57 C7
Betong Malaysia 1°24N 111°31E 36 D4
Betong Thailand 5°45N 101°5E 39 K3
Betoota Australia 25°45S 140°42E 62 D3
Betpaqdala Kazakhstan 45°45N 70°30E 28 E8
Betroka Madag. 23°16S 46°0E 57 C8
Betsiamites Canada 48°56N 68°40W 73 C6
Betsiamites → Canada 48°56N 68°38W 73 C6
Betsiboka → Madag. 16°3S 46°36E 57 B8
Bettendorf U.S.A. 41°32N 90°30W 80 E8
Bettiah India 26°48N 84°33E 43 F11
Betul India 21°58N 77°59E 40 J10
Betws-y-Coed U.K. 53°5N 3°48W 12 D4
Beulah Mich., U.S.A. 44°38N 86°6W 80 C10
Beulah N. Dak., U.S.A. 47°16N 101°47W 80 B3
Beveren Belgium 51°12N 4°16E 15 C4
Beverley Australia 32°9S 116°56E 61 F2
Beverley U.K. 53°51N 0°26W 12 D7
Beverly U.S.A. 42°33N 70°53W 83 D14
Beverly Hills Calif., U.S.A. 34°5N 118°24W 79 L8
Beverly Hills Fla., U.S.A. 28°55N 82°28W 85 G13
Bevoalavo Madag. 25°13S 45°26E 57 D7
Bewas → India 23°59N 79°21E 43 H8
Bexhill U.K. 50°51N 0°29E 13 G8
Beyānlū Iran 36°0N 47°51E 44 C5
Beyneu Kazakhstan 45°18N 55°9E 19 E10
Beypazarı Turkey 40°10N 31°56E 19 F5
Beyşehir Gölü Turkey 37°41N 31°33E 44 B1
Béziers France 43°20N 3°12E 20 E5
Bezwada = Vijayawada India 16°31N 80°39E 41 L12
Bhabua India 25°3N 83°37E 43 G10
Bhachau India 23°20N 70°16E 40 H7
Bhadar → Gujarat, India 22°17N 72°20E 42 H5
Bhadar → Gujarat, India 21°27N 69°47E 42 J3
Bhadarwah India 32°58N 75°46E 43 C6
Bhadgaon = Bhaktapur Nepal 27°38N 85°24E 43 F11
Bhadohi India 25°25N 82°34E 43 G10
Bhadra India 29°8N 75°14E 42 E6
Bhadrakh India 21°10N 86°30E 41 J15
Bhadran India 22°19N 72°6E 42 H5
Bhadravati India 13°49N 75°40E 40 N9
Bhag Pakistan 29°2N 67°49E 42 E2
Bhagalpur India 25°10N 87°0E 43 G12
Bhagirathi → Uttaranchal, India 30°8N 78°35E 43 D8
Bhagirathi → W. Bengal, India 23°25N 88°23E 43 H13
Bhakkar Pakistan 31°40N 71°5E 42 D4
Bhakra Dam India 31°30N 76°45E 42 D7
Bhaktapur Nepal 27°38N 85°24E 43 F11
Bhamo Burma 24°15N 97°15E 41 G20
Bhandara India 21°5N 79°42E 40 J11
Bhanpura India 24°31N 75°44E 42 G6
Bhanrer Ra. India 23°40N 79°45E 43 H8
Bhaptiahi India 26°19N 86°44E 43 F12
Bharat = India ■ Asia 20°0N 78°0E 40 K11
Bharatpur Chhattisgarh, India 23°44N 81°46E 43 H9
Bharatpur Raj., India 27°15N 77°30E 42 F7
Bharno India 23°14N 84°53E 43 H11
Bharuch India 21°47N 73°0E 40 J8
Bhatinda India 30°15N 74°57E 42 D6
Bhatpara India 22°50N 88°25E 43 H13
Bhattu India 29°36N 75°19E 42 E6
Bhaun Pakistan 32°55N 72°40E 42 C5
Bhaunagar = Bhavnagar India 21°45N 72°10E 40 J8
Bhavnagar India 21°45N 72°10E 40 J8
Bhawari India 25°42N 73°4E 42 G5
Bhayavadar India 21°51N 70°15E 42 J4
Bhera Pakistan 32°29N 72°57E 42 C5
Bhikangaon India 21°52N 75°57E 42 J6
Bhilai = Bhilainagar-Durg India 21°13N 81°26E 41 J12
Bhilainagar-Durg India 21°13N 81°26E 41 J12
Bhilsa = Vidisha India 23°28N 77°53E 42 H7
Bhilwara India 25°25N 74°38E 42 G6
Bhima → India 16°25N 77°17E 40 L10
Bhimbar Pakistan 32°59N 74°3E 43 C6
Bhind India 26°30N 78°46E 43 F8
Bhinga India 27°43N 81°56E 43 F9
Bhinmal India 25°0N 72°15E 42 G5
Bhiwandi India 19°20N 73°0E 40 K8
Bhiwani India 28°50N 76°9E 42 E7
Bhogava → India 22°26N 72°20E 42 H5
Bhola Bangla. 22°45N 90°35E 41 H17
Bholari Pakistan 25°19N 68°13E 42 G3
Bhopal India 23°20N 77°30E 42 H7
Bhubaneshwar India 20°15N 85°50E 41 J14
Bhuj India 23°15N 69°49E 42 H3
Bhumiphol Res. Thailand 17°20N 98°40E 38 D2
Bhusawal India 21°3N 75°46E 40 J9
Bhutan ■ Asia 27°25N 90°30E 41 F17
Biafra, B. of = Bonny, Bight of Africa 3°30N 9°20E 52 D1
Biak Indonesia 1°10S 136°6E 37 E9
Biała Podlaska Poland 52°4N 23°6E 17 B12
Białogard Poland 54°2N 15°58E 16 A8
Białystok Poland 53°10N 23°10E 17 B12
Biaora India 23°56N 76°56E 42 H7
Bīārjmand Iran 36°6N 55°53E 45 B7
Biaro Indonesia 2°5N 125°26E 37 D7
Biarritz France 43°29N 1°33W 20 E3
Bias Indonesia 8°24S 115°36E 37 J18
Bibai Japan 43°19N 141°52E 30 C10
Bibby I. Canada 61°55N 93°0W 71 A10
Biberach Germany 48°5N 9°47E 16 D5
Bibungwa Dem. Rep. of the Congo 2°40S 28°15E 54 C2
Bicester U.K. 51°54N 1°9W 13 F6
Bicheno Australia 41°52S 148°18E 63 G4
Bichia India 22°27N 80°42E 43 H9
Bickerton I. Australia 13°45S 136°10E 62 A2
Bida Nigeria 9°3N 5°58E 50 G7
Bidar India 17°55N 77°35E 40 L10
Biddeford U.S.A. 43°30N 70°28W 81 D18
Bideford U.K. 51°1N 4°13W 13 F3
Bideford Bay U.K. 51°5N 4°20W 13 F3
Bidhuna India 26°49N 79°31E 43 F8
Bidor Malaysia 4°6N 101°15E 39 K3
Bidyadanga Australia 18°45S 121°43E 60 C3
Bié, Planalto de Angola 12°0S 16°0E 53 G3
Bieber U.S.A. 41°7N 121°8W 76 F3
Biel Switz. 47°8N 7°14E 20 C7
Bielefeld Germany 52°1N 8°33E 16 B5
Biella Italy 45°34N 8°3E 20 D8
Bielsk Podlaski Poland 52°47N 23°12E 17 B12
Bielsko-Biała Poland 49°50N 19°2E 17 D10
Bien Hoa Vietnam 10°57N 106°49E 39 G6
Bienne = Biel Switz. 47°8N 7°14E 20 C7
Bienville, L. Canada 55°5N 72°40W 72 A5
Biesiesfontein S. Africa 30°57S 17°58E 56 E2
Big → Canada 54°50N 58°55W 73 B8
Big B. Canada 55°43N 60°35W 73 A7
Big Bear City U.S.A. 34°16N 116°51W 79 L10
Big Bear Lake U.S.A. 34°15N 116°56W 79 L10
Big Belt Mts. U.S.A. 46°30N 111°25W 76 C8
Big Bend Swaziland 26°50S 31°58E 57 D5
Big Bend △ U.S.A. 29°20N 103°5W 84 G3
Big Blue → U.S.A. 39°35N 96°34W 80 F5
Big Creek U.S.A. 37°11N 119°14W 78 H7
Big Cypress ⌓ U.S.A. 26°0N 81°10W 85 H14
Big Desert Australia 35°45S 141°10E 63 F3
Big Falls U.S.A. 48°12N 93°48W 80 A7
Big Fork → U.S.A. 48°31N 93°43W 80 A7
Big Horn Mts. = Bighorn Mts. U.S.A. 44°25N 107°0W 76 D10
Big I. Canada 61°7N 116°45W 70 A5
Big Lake U.S.A. 31°12N 101°28W 84 F4
Big Moose U.S.A. 43°49N 74°58W 83 C10
Big Muddy Cr. → U.S.A. 48°8N 104°36W 76 B11
Big Pine U.S.A. 37°10N 118°17W 78 H8
Big Piney U.S.A. 42°32N 110°7W 76 E8
Big Rapids U.S.A. 43°42N 85°29W 81 D11
Big Rideau L. Canada 44°40N 76°15W 83 B8
Big River Canada 53°50N 107°0W 71 C7
Big Run U.S.A. 40°57N 78°55W 82 F6
Big Sable Pt. U.S.A. 44°3N 86°1W 80 C10
Big Salmon → Canada 61°52N 134°55W 70 A2
Big Sand L. Canada 57°45N 99°45W 71 B9
Big Sandy U.S.A. 48°11N 110°7W 76 D8
Big Sandy → U.S.A. 38°25N 82°36W 81 F12
Big Sandy Cr. = Sandy Cr. → U.S.A. 41°51N 109°47W 76 F9
Big Sandy Cr. → U.S.A. 38°7N 102°29W 76 G12
Big Sioux → U.S.A. 42°29N 96°27W 80 D5
Big South Fork ⌓ U.S.A. 36°27N 84°47W 85 C12
Big Spring U.S.A. 32°15N 101°28W 84 E4
Big Stone City U.S.A. 45°18N 96°28W 80 C5
Big Stone Gap U.S.A. 36°52N 82°47W 81 G12
Big Stone L. U.S.A. 45°18N 96°27W 80 C5
Big Sur U.S.A. 36°15N 121°48W 78 J5
Big Timber U.S.A. 45°50N 109°57W 76 D9
Big Trout L. Canada 53°40N 90°0W 72 B2
Big Trout Lake Canada 53°45N 90°0W 72 B2
Biğa Turkey 40°13N 27°14E 23 D12
Bigadiç Turkey 39°22N 28°7E 23 E13
Biggar Canada 52°4N 108°0W 71 C7
Biggar U.K. 55°38N 3°32W 11 F5
Bigge I. Australia 14°35S 125°10E 60 B4
Biggenden Australia 25°31S 152°4E 63 D5
Biggleswade U.K. 52°5N 0°14W 13 E7
Biggs U.S.A. 39°25N 121°43W 78 F5
Bighorn U.S.A. 46°10N 107°27W 76 C10
Bighorn → U.S.A. 46°10N 107°28W 76 C10
Bighorn Canyon ⌓ U.S.A. 45°10N 108°0W 76 D10
Bighorn L. U.S.A. 44°55N 108°15W 76 D9
Bighorn Mts. U.S.A. 44°25N 107°0W 76 D10
Bight, The Bahamas 24°19N 75°24W 89 B4
Bigstone L. Canada 53°42N 95°44W 71 C9
Bigwa Tanzania 7°10S 39°10E 54 D4
Bihać Bos.-H. 44°49N 15°57E 16 F8
Bihar India 25°5N 85°40E 43 G11
Bihar □ India 25°0N 86°0E 43 G12
Biharamulo Tanzania 2°25S 31°25E 54 C3
Biharamulo ⌓ Tanzania 2°24S 31°26E 54 C3
Bihariganj India 25°44N 86°59E 43 G12
Bihor, Munţii Romania 46°29N 22°47E 17 E12
Bijagós, Arquipélago dos Guinea-Biss. 11°15N 16°10W 50 F2
Bijaipur India 26°2N 77°20E 42 F7
Bijapur Chhattisgarh, India 18°50N 80°50E 41 K12
Bijapur Karnataka, India 16°50N 75°55E 40 L9
Bījār Iran 35°52N 47°35E 44 C5
Bijawar India 24°38N 79°30E 43 G8
Bijeljina Bos.-H. 44°46N 19°14E 23 B8
Bijnor India 29°27N 78°11E 42 E8
Bikaner India 28°2N 73°18E 42 E5
Bikapur India 26°30N 82°7E 43 F10
Bikeqi China 40°43N 111°20E 34 D6
Bikfayyā Lebanon 33°55N 35°41E 46 B4
Bikin Russia 46°50N 134°20E 30 A7
Bikin → Russia 46°51N 134°2E 30 A7
Bikini Atoll Marshall Is. 12°0N 167°30E 64 F8

Bikita Zimbabwe 20°6S 31°41E 57 C5
Bila Tserkva Ukraine 49°45N 30°10E 17 D16
Bilara India 26°14N 73°53E 42 F5
Bilaspur Chhattisgarh, India 22°2N 82°15E 43 H10
Bilaspur Punjab, India 31°19N 76°50E 42 D7
Bilauk Taungdan Thailand 13°0N 99°0E 38 F2
Bilbao Spain 43°16N 2°56W 21 A4
Bilbo = Bilbao Spain 43°16N 2°56W 21 A4
Bíldudalur Iceland 65°41N 23°36W 8 D2
Bílé Karpaty Europe 49°5N 18°0E 17 D9
Bilecik Turkey 40°5N 30°5E 19 F5
Bilgram India 27°11N 80°2E 43 F9
Bilhaur India 26°51N 80°5E 43 F9
Bilhorod-Dnistrovskyy Ukraine 46°11N 30°23E 19 E5
Bilibino Russia 68°3N 166°20E 29 C17
Bilibiza Mozam. 12°30S 40°20E 55 E5
Billiluna Australia 19°37S 127°41E 60 C4
Billings U.S.A. 45°47N 108°30W 76 D9
Billiton Is. = Belitung Indonesia 3°10S 107°50E 36 E3
Bilma Niger 18°50N 13°30E 51 E8
Biloela Australia 24°24S 150°31E 62 C5
Biloxi U.S.A. 30°24N 88°53W 85 F10
Bilpa Morea Claypan Australia 25°0S 140°0E 62 D3
Biltine Chad 14°40N 20°50E 51 F10
Bima Indonesia 8°22S 118°49E 37 F5
Bimbo C.A.R. 4°15N 18°33E 52 D3
Bimini Is. Bahamas 25°42N 79°25W 88 A4
Bin Xian Heilongjiang, China 45°42N 127°32E 35 B14
Bin Xian Shaanxi, China 35°2N 108°4E 34 G5
Bina-Etawah India 24°13N 78°14E 42 G8
Bīnāb Iran 36°35N 48°41E 45 B6
Binalbagan Phil. 10°12N 122°50E 37 B6
Binalong Australia 34°40S 148°39E 63 E4
Bīnālūd, Kūh-e Iran 36°30N 58°30E 45 B8
Binatang = Bintangau Malaysia 2°10N 111°40E 36 D4
Binche Belgium 50°26N 4°10E 15 D4
Bindki India 26°2N 80°36E 43 F9
Bindura Zimbabwe 17°18S 31°18E 55 F3
Bingara Australia 29°52S 150°36E 63 D5
Bingham U.S.A. 45°3N 69°53W 81 C19
Binghamton U.S.A. 42°6N 75°55W 83 D9
Bingöl Turkey 38°53N 40°29E 44 B4
Binh Dinh = An Nhon Vietnam 13°55N 109°7E 38 F7
Binh Khe Vietnam 13°57N 108°51E 38 F7
Binh Son Vietnam 15°20N 108°40E 38 E7
Binhai China 34°2N 119°49E 35 G10
Binisatua Spain 39°50N 4°11E 24 B11
Binjai Indonesia 3°20N 98°30E 36 D3
Binnaway Australia 31°28S 149°24E 63 E4
Binongko Indonesia 5°57S 124°2E 37 F6
Binscarth Canada 50°37N 101°17W 71 C8
Bintan Indonesia 1°0N 104°0E 36 D2
Bintangau Malaysia 2°10N 111°40E 36 D4
Bintulu Malaysia 3°10N 113°0E 36 D4
Bintuni Indonesia 2°7S 133°32E 37 E8
Binzert = Bizerte Tunisia 37°15N 9°50E 51 A7
Binzhou China 37°20N 118°2E 35 F10
Bío Bío □ Chile 37°35S 72°0W 94 D1
Bioko Eq. Guin. 3°30N 8°40E 52 D1
Bir India 19°4N 75°46E 40 K9
Bîr Abu Muḥammad Egypt 29°44N 34°14E 46 F3
Bi'r ad Dabbāghāt Jordan 30°26N 35°32E 46 E4
Bi'r al Butayyihāt Jordan 29°47N 35°20E 46 F4
Bi'r al Mārī Jordan 30°4N 35°33E 46 E4
Bi'r al Qattār Jordan 29°47N 35°32E 46 F4
Bir Atrun Sudan 18°15N 26°40E 51 E11
Bîr Beida Egypt 30°25N 34°29E 46 E3
Bîr el 'Abd Egypt 31°2N 33°0E 46 D2
Bîr el Biarât Egypt 29°30N 34°43E 46 F3
Bîr el Duweidar Egypt 30°56N 32°32E 46 E1
Bîr el Garârât Egypt 31°3N 33°34E 46 D2
Bîr el Heisi Egypt 29°22N 34°36E 46 F3
Bîr el Jafir Egypt 30°50N 32°41E 46 E1
Bîr el Mâlḥi Egypt 30°38N 33°19E 46 E2
Bîr el Thamâda Egypt 30°12N 33°27E 46 E2
Bîr Gebeil Ḥiṣn Egypt 30°2N 33°18E 46 E2
Bi'r Ghadīr Syria 34°6N 37°3E 46 A6
Bîr Ḥasana Egypt 30°29N 33°46E 46 E2
Bîr Kaseiba Egypt 31°0N 33°17E 46 E2
Bîr Lahfân Egypt 31°0N 33°51E 46 E2
Bîr Madkûr Egypt 30°44N 32°33E 46 E1
Bîr Mogreïn Mauritania 25°10N 11°25W 50 C3
Bi'r Muṭribah Kuwait 29°54N 47°17E 44 D5
Bîr Qaṭia Egypt 30°58N 32°45E 46 E1
Bîr Shalatein Egypt 23°5N 35°25E 51 D13
Biratnagar Nepal 26°27N 87°17E 43 F12
Birawa Dem. Rep. of the Congo 2°20S 28°48E 54 C2
Birch → Canada 58°28N 112°17W 70 B6
Birch Hills Canada 52°59N 105°25W 71 C7
Birch I. Canada 52°26N 99°54W 71 C9
Birch L. N.W.T., Canada 62°4N 116°33W 70 A5
Birch L. Ont., Canada 51°23N 92°18W 72 B1
Birch Mts. Canada 57°30N 113°10W 70 B6
Birch River Canada 52°24N 101°6W 71 C8
Birchip Australia 35°56S 142°55E 63 F3
Bird Canada 56°30N 94°13W 71 B10
Bird I. = Aves, I. de W. Indies 15°45N 63°55W 89 C7
Bird I. Antarctica 54°0S 38°0W 5 B1
Birdsville Australia 25°51S 139°20E 62 D2
Birdum Cr. → Australia 15°14S 133°0E 60 C5
Birecik Turkey 37°2N 38°0E 44 B3
Birein Israel 30°50N 34°28E 46 E3
Bireuen Indonesia 5°14N 96°39E 36 C1
Birigui Brazil 21°18S 50°16W 95 A5
Birjand Iran 32°53N 59°13E 45 C8
Birkenhead U.K. 53°23N 3°2W 12 D4
Bîrlad = Bârlad Romania 46°15N 27°38E 17 E14
Birmingham U.K. 52°29N 1°52W 13 E6
Birmingham U.S.A. 33°31N 86°48W 85 E11
Birmingham Int. ✕ (BHX) U.K. 52°26N 1°45W 13 E6
Birmitrapur India 22°24N 84°46E 41 H14
Birni Nkonni Niger 13°55N 5°15E 50 F7
Birnin Kebbi Nigeria 12°32N 4°12E 50 F6
Birobidzhan Russia 48°50N 132°50E 29 E14
Birr Ireland 53°6N 7°54W 10 C4
Birrie → Australia 29°43S 146°37E 63 D4
Birsilpur India 28°11N 72°15E 42 E5
Birsk Russia 55°25N 55°30E 18 C10
Birtle Canada 50°30N 101°5W 71 C8
Birur India 13°30N 75°55E 40 N9
Biržai Lithuania 56°11N 24°45E 9 H21
Birzebbugga Malta 35°50N 14°32E 25 D2
Bisa Indonesia 1°15S 127°28E 37 E7
Bisalpur India 28°14N 79°48E 43 E8
Bisbee U.S.A. 31°27N 109°55W 77 L9
Biscarrosse France 44°22N 1°20W 20 D3
Biscay, B. of Atl. Oc. 45°0N 2°0W 20 D1
Biscayne B. U.S.A. 25°40N 80°12W 85 J14
Biscoe Is. Antarctica 66°0S 67°0W 5 C17
Biscotasing Canada 47°18N 82°9W 72 C3
Bishkek Kyrgyzstan 42°54N 74°46E 28 E8
Bishnupur India 23°8N 87°20E 43 H12
Bisho S. Africa 32°50S 27°23E 57 E4
Bishop Calif., U.S.A. 37°22N 118°24W 78 H8
Bishop Tex., U.S.A. 27°35N 97°48W 84 H6
Bishop Auckland U.K. 54°39N 1°40W 12 C6
Bishop's Falls Canada 49°2N 55°30W 73 C8
Bishop's Stortford U.K. 51°52N 0°10E 13 F8
Bisina, L. Uganda 1°38N 33°56E 54 B3
Biskra Algeria 34°50N 5°44E 50 B7
Bismarck U.S.A. 46°48N 100°47W 80 B3
Bismarck Arch. Papua N. G. 2°30S 150°0E 58 B7
Biso Uganda 1°44N 31°26E 54 B3
Bison U.S.A. 45°31N 102°28W 80 C2
Bīsotūn Iran 34°23N 47°26E 44 C5
Bissagos = Bijagós, Arquipélago dos Guinea-Biss. 11°15N 16°10W 50 F2
Bissau Guinea-Biss. 11°45N 15°45W 50 F2
Bistcho L. Canada 59°45N 118°50W 70 B5
Bistriţa Romania 47°9N 24°35E 17 E13
Bistriţa → Romania 46°30N 26°57E 17 E14
Biswan India 27°29N 81°2E 43 F9
Bitam Gabon 2°5N 11°25E 52 D2
Bitkine Chad 11°59N 18°13E 51 F9
Bitlis Turkey 38°20N 42°3E 44 B4
Bitola Macedonia 41°1N 21°20E 23 D9
Bitolj = Bitola Macedonia 41°1N 21°20E 23 D9
Bitter Creek U.S.A. 41°33N 108°33W 76 F9
Bitterfontein S. Africa 31°1S 18°32E 56 E2
Bitterroot → U.S.A. 46°52N 114°7W 76 C6
Bitterroot Range U.S.A. 46°0N 114°20W 76 C6
Bitterwater U.S.A. 36°23N 121°0W 78 J6
Biu Nigeria 10°40N 12°3E 51 F8
Biwa-Ko Japan 35°15N 136°10E 31 G8
Biwabik U.S.A. 47°32N 92°21W 80 B7
Bixby U.S.A. 35°57N 95°53W 84 D7
Biyang China 32°38N 113°21E 34 H7
Biysk Russia 52°40N 85°0E 28 D9
Bizana S. Africa 30°50S 29°52E 57 E4
Bizen Japan 34°43N 134°8E 31 G7
Bizerte Tunisia 37°15N 9°50E 51 A7
Bjargtangar Iceland 65°30N 24°30W 8 D1
Bjelovar Croatia 45°56N 16°49E 22 B7
Björneborg = Pori Finland 61°29N 21°48E 8 F19
Bjørnevatn Norway 69°40N 30°0E 8 B24
Bjørnøya Arctic 74°30N 19°0E 4 B8
Black = Da → Vietnam 21°15N 105°20E 38 B5
Black → Canada 44°42N 79°19W 82 B5
Black → Ariz., U.S.A. 33°44N 110°13W 77 K8
Black → Ark., U.S.A. 35°38N 91°20W 84 D9
Black → La., U.S.A. 31°16N 91°50W 84 F9
Black → Mich., U.S.A. 42°59N 82°27W 82 D2
Black → N.Y., U.S.A. 43°59N 76°4W 83 C8
Black → Wis., U.S.A. 43°57N 91°22W 80 D8
Black Bay Pen. Canada 48°38N 88°21W 72 C2
Black Birch L. Canada 56°53N 107°45W 71 B7
Black Canyon of the Gunnison ⌂ U.S.A. 38°40N 107°35W 76 G10
Black Diamond Canada 50°45N 114°14W 70 C6
Black Duck → Canada 56°51N 89°2W 72 A2
Black Forest = Schwarzwald Germany 48°30N 8°20E 16 D5
Black Forest U.S.A. 39°0N 104°43W 76 G11
Black Hd. Ireland 53°9N 9°16W 10 C2
Black Hills U.S.A. 44°0N 103°45W 80 D2
Black I. Canada 51°12N 96°30W 71 C9
Black L. Canada 59°12N 105°15W 71 B7
Black L. Mich., U.S.A. 45°28N 84°16W 81 C11
Black L. N.Y., U.S.A. 44°31N 75°36W 83 B9
Black Lake Canada 59°11N 105°20W 71 B7
Black Mesa U.S.A. 36°58N 102°58W 84 C3
Black Mt. = Mynydd Du U.K. 51°52N 3°50W 13 F4
Black Mts. U.K. 51°55N 3°7W 13 F4
Black Range U.S.A. 33°15N 107°50W 77 K10
Black River Jamaica 18°0N 77°50W 88 a
Black River Falls U.S.A. 44°18N 90°51W 80 C8
Black Rock Barbados 13°7N 59°37W 89 g
Black Sea Eurasia 43°30N 35°0E 19 F6
Black Tickle Canada 53°28N 55°45W 73 B8
Black Volta → Africa 8°41N 1°33W 50 G5
Black Warrior → U.S.A. 32°32N 87°51W 85 E11
Blackall Australia 24°25S 145°45E 62 C4
Blackball N.Z. 42°22S 171°26E 59 E3
Blackbull Australia 17°55S 141°45E 62 B3
Blackburn U.K. 53°45N 2°29W 12 D5
Blackburn with Darwen □ U.K. 53°45N 2°29W 12 D5
Blackdown Tableland △ Australia 23°52S 149°8E 62 C4
Blackfoot U.S.A. 43°11N 112°21W 76 E7
Blackfoot → U.S.A. 46°52N 113°53W 76 C7
Blackfoot Res. U.S.A. 42°55N 111°39W 76 E8
Blackpool U.K. 53°49N 3°3W 12 D4
Blackpool □ U.K. 53°49N 3°3W 12 D4
Blackriver U.S.A. 44°46N 83°17W 82 B1
Blacks Harbour Canada 45°3N 66°49W 73 C6
Blacksburg U.S.A. 37°14N 80°25W 81 G13
Blacksod B. Ireland 54°6N 10°0W 10 B1
Blackstairs Mt. Ireland 52°33N 6°48W 10 D5
Blackstone U.S.A. 37°5N 78°0W 81 G14
Blackstone Ra. Australia 26°0S 128°30E 61 E4
Blacktown Australia 33°48S 150°55E 63 E5
Blackwater = West Road → Canada 53°18N 122°53W 70 C4
Blackwater Australia 23°35S 148°53E 62 C4
Blackwater → Meath, Ireland 53°39N 6°41W 10 C4
Blackwater → Waterford, Ireland 52°4N 7°52W 10 D4
Blackwater → U.K. 54°31N 6°35W 10 B5
Blackwell U.S.A. 36°48N 97°17W 84 C6
Blackwells Corner U.S.A. 35°37N 119°47W 79 K7
Bladensburg △ Australia 22°30S 142°59E 62 C3
Blaenau Ffestiniog U.K. 53°0N 3°56W 12 E4
Blaenau Gwent □ U.K. 51°48N 3°12W 13 F4
Blagodarnoye = Blagodarnyy Russia 45°7N 43°37E 19 E7
Blagodarnyy Russia 45°7N 43°37E 19 E7
Blagoevgrad Bulgaria 42°2N 23°5E 23 C10
Blagoveshchensk Russia 50°20N 127°30E 29 D13
Blahkiuh Indonesia 8°31S 115°12E 37 J18
Blain U.S.A. 40°20N 77°31W 82 F7
Blaine Minn., U.S.A. 45°10N 93°13W 80 C7
Blaine Wash., U.S.A. 48°59N 122°45W 78 B4
Blaine Lake Canada 52°51N 106°52W 71 C7
Blair U.S.A. 41°33N 96°8W 80 E5
Blair Athol Australia 22°42S 147°31E 62 C4
Blair Atholl U.K. 56°46N 3°50W 11 E5
Blairgowrie U.K. 56°35N 3°21W 11 E5
Blairsden U.S.A. 39°47N 120°37W 78 F6
Blairsville U.S.A. 40°26N 79°16W 82 F5
Blakang Mati, Pulau Singapore 1°15N 103°50E 39 d
Blake Pt. U.S.A. 48°11N 88°25W 80 A9
Blakely Ga., U.S.A. 31°23N 84°56W 85 F12
Blakely Pa., U.S.A. 41°28N 75°37W 83 E9
Blanc, C. Spain 39°21N 2°51E 24 B9
Blanc, Mont Europe 45°48N 6°50E 20 D7
Blanca, B. Argentina 39°10S 61°30W 96 D4
Blanca, Cord. Peru 9°10S 77°35W 92 E3
Blanca Peak U.S.A. 37°35N 105°29W 77 H11
Blanche, C. Australia 33°1S 134°9E 63 E1
Blanche, L. S. Austral., Australia 29°15S 139°40E 63 D2
Blanche, L. W. Austral., Australia 22°25S 123°17E 60 D3
Blanchisseuse Trin. & Tob. 10°48N 61°18W 93 K15
Blanco S. Africa 33°55S 22°23E 56 E3
Blanco U.S.A. 30°6N 98°25W 84 F5
Blanco → Argentina 30°20S 68°42W 94 C2
Blanco, C. Costa Rica 9°34N 85°8W 88 E2
Blanco, C. U.S.A. 42°51N 124°34W 76 E1
Blanda → Iceland 65°37N 20°9W 8 D3
Blandford Forum U.K. 50°51N 2°9W 13 G5
Blanding U.S.A. 37°37N 109°29W 77 H9
Blanes Spain 41°40N 2°48E 21 B7
Blankenberge Belgium 51°20N 3°9E 15 C3
Blanquilla Venezuela 11°51N 64°37W 89 D7
Blanquillo Uruguay 32°53S 55°37W 95 C4
Blantyre Malawi 15°45S 35°0E 55 F4
Blarney Ireland 51°56N 8°33W 10 E3
Blasdell U.S.A. 42°48N 78°50W 82 D6
Blåvands Huk Denmark 55°33N 8°4E 9 J13
Blaydon U.K. 54°58N 1°42W 12 C6
Blayney Australia 33°32S 149°14E 63 E4
Blaze, Pt. Australia 12°56S 130°11E 60 B5
Blekinge Sweden 56°25N 15°20E 9 H16
Blenheim Canada 42°20N 82°0W 82 D3
Blenheim N.Z. 41°38S 173°57E 59 D4
Bletchley U.K. 51°59N 0°44W 13 F7
Blida Algeria 36°30N 2°49E 50 A6
Bligh Sound N.Z. 44°47S 167°32E 59 F1
Bligh Water Fiji 17°0S 178°0E 59 a
Blind River Canada 46°10N 82°58W 72 C3
Bliss Idaho, U.S.A. 42°56N 114°57W 76 E6
Bliss N.Y., U.S.A. 42°34N 78°15W 82 D6
Blissfield U.S.A. 40°24N 81°58W 82 F3
Blitar Indonesia 8°5S 112°11E 37 H15
Block I. U.S.A. 41°11N 71°35W 83 E13
Block Island Sd. U.S.A. 41°15N 71°40W 83 E13
Bloemfontein S. Africa 29°6S 26°7E 56 D4
Bloemhof S. Africa 27°38S 25°32E 56 D4
Blois France 47°35N 1°20E 20 C4
Blönduós Iceland 65°40N 20°12W 8 D3
Blongas Indonesia 8°53S 116°2E 37 K19
Bloodvein → Canada 51°47N 96°43W 71 C9
Bloody Foreland Ireland 55°10N 8°17W 10 A3
Bloomer U.S.A. 45°6N 91°29W 80 C8
Bloomfield Canada 43°59N 77°14W 82 C7
Bloomfield Iowa, U.S.A. 40°45N 92°25W 80 E7
Bloomfield N. Mex., U.S.A. 36°43N 107°59W 77 H10
Bloomfield Nebr., U.S.A. 42°36N 97°39W 80 D5
Bloomington Ill., U.S.A. 40°28N 89°0W 80 E9
Bloomington Ind., U.S.A. 39°10N 86°32W 80 F10
Bloomington Minn., U.S.A. 44°50N 93°17W 80 C7
Bloomsburg U.S.A. 41°0N 76°27W 83 F8
Bloomsbury Australia 20°48S 148°38E 62 J6
Blora Indonesia 6°57S 111°25E 37 G14
Blossburg U.S.A. 41°41N 77°4W 82 E7
Blouberg S. Africa 23°8S 28°59E 57 C4
Blountstown U.S.A. 30°27N 85°3W 85 F12
Blue Earth U.S.A. 43°38N 94°6W 80 D6
Blue Hole △ Belize 17°24N 88°30W 88 C2
Blue Lagoon △ Zambia 15°28S 27°26E 55 F2
Blue Mesa Res. U.S.A. 38°28N 107°20W 76 G10
Blue Mountain Lake U.S.A. 43°51N 74°27W 83 C10
Blue Mountain Pk. Jamaica 18°3N 76°36W 88 a
Blue Mt. U.S.A. 40°30N 76°30W 83 F8
Blue Mts. Jamaica 18°3N 76°36W 88 a
Blue Mts. Maine, U.S.A. 44°50N 70°35W 83 B14
Blue Mts. Oreg., U.S.A. 45°0N 118°20W 76 D4
Blue Mud B. Australia 13°30S 136°0E 62 A2
Blue Nile = Nîl el Azraq → Sudan 15°38N 32°31E 51 E12
Blue Rapids U.S.A. 39°41N 96°39W 80 F5
Blue Ridge U.S.A. 36°40N 80°50W 81 G13
Blue River Canada 52°6N 119°18W 70 C5
Bluefield U.S.A. 37°15N 81°17W 81 G13
Bluefields Nic. 12°20N 83°50W 88 D3
Bluff Australia 23°35S 149°4E 62 C4
Bluff N.Z. 46°37S 168°20E 59 G2
Bluff U.S.A. 37°17N 109°33W 77 H9
Bluff Knoll Australia 34°24S 118°15E 61 F2
Bluff Pt. Australia 27°50S 114°5E 61 E1
Bluffton U.S.A. 40°44N 85°11W 81 E11
Blumenau Brazil 27°0S 49°0W 95 B6
Blunt U.S.A. 44°31N 99°59W 80 C4
Bly U.S.A. 42°24N 121°3W 76 E3
Blyde River Canyon ⌂ S. Africa 24°37S 31°2E 57 C5
Blyth Canada 43°44N 81°26W 82 C3
Blyth U.K. 55°8N 1°31W 12 B6
Blythe U.S.A. 33°37N 114°36W 79 M12
Blytheville U.S.A. 35°56N 89°55W 85 D10
Bo S. Leone 7°55N 11°50W 50 G3
Bo Duc Vietnam 11°58N 106°50E 39 G6
Bo Hai China 39°0N 119°0E 35 E10
Bo Xian = Bozhou China 33°55N 115°41E 34 H8
Boa Vista Brazil 2°48N 60°30W 92 C6
Boa Vista C. Verde Is. 16°0N 22°49W 50 b
Boaco Nic. 12°29N 85°35W 88 D2
Bo'ai China 35°10N 113°3E 34 G7
Boalsburg U.S.A. 40°47N 77°49W 82 F7
Boane Mozam. 26°6S 32°19E 57 D5
Boardman U.S.A. 41°2N 80°40W 82 E4
Bobadah Australia 32°19S 146°41E 63 E4
Bobbili India 18°35N 83°30E 41 K13
Bobcaygeon Canada 44°33N 78°33W 82 B6
Bobo-Dioulasso Burkina Faso 11°8N 4°13W 50 F5
Bóbr → Poland 52°4N 15°4E 16 B8
Bobraomby, Tanjon' i Madag. 12°40S 49°10E 57 A8
Bobruysk = Babruysk Belarus 53°10N 29°15E 17 B15
Boby, Pic Madag. 22°12S 46°55E 53 J9
Boca de Drago Venezuela 11°0N 61°50W 93 K15
Boca del Río Mexico 19°5N 96°4W 87 D5
Bôca do Acre Brazil 8°50S 67°27W 92 E5
Boca Raton U.S.A. 26°21N 80°5W 85 H14
Bocas del Toro Panama 9°15N 82°20W 88 E3
Bochnia Poland 49°58N 20°27E 17 D11
Bochum Germany 51°28N 7°13E 16 C4
Bocoyna Mexico 27°52N 107°35W 86 B3
Bodaybo Russia 57°50N 114°0E 29 D12
Boddam U.K. 59°56N 1°17W 11 B7
Boddington Australia 32°50S 116°30E 61 F2
Bodega Bay U.S.A. 38°20N 123°3W 78 G3
Boden Sweden 65°50N 21°42E 8 D19
Bodensee Europe 47°35N 9°25E 20 C8
Bodhan India 18°40N 77°44E 40 K10
Bodmin U.K. 50°28N 4°43W 13 G3
Bodmin Moor U.K. 50°33N 4°36W 13 G3
Bodø Norway 67°17N 14°24E 8 C16
Bodrog → Hungary 48°11N 21°22E 17 D11
Bodrum Turkey 37°3N 27°30E 23 F12
Boende Dem. Rep. of the Congo 0°24S 21°12E 52 E4
Boerne U.S.A. 29°47N 98°44W 84 G5
Boesmans → S. Africa 33°42S 26°39E 56 E4
Bogalusa U.S.A. 30°47N 89°52W 85 F10
Bogan → Australia 30°20S 146°55E 63 D4
Bogan Gate Australia 33°7S 147°49E 63 E4
Bogantungan Australia 23°41S 147°17E 62 C4
Bogata U.S.A. 33°28N 95°13W 84 E7
Bogda Shan China 43°35N 89°40E 32 B3
Boggabilla Australia 28°36S 150°24E 63 D5
Boggabri Australia 30°45S 150°5E 63 E5
Boggeragh Mts. Ireland 52°2N 8°55W 10 D3
Boglan = Solhan Turkey 38°57N 41°3E 44 B4
Bognor Regis U.K. 50°47N 0°40W 13 G7
Bogo Phil. 11°3N 124°0E 37 B6
Bogong, Mt. Australia 36°47S 147°17E 63 F4
Bogor Indonesia 6°36S 106°48E 36 F3
Bogotá Colombia 4°34N 74°0W 92 C4
Bogotol Russia 56°15N 89°50E 28 D9
Bogra Bangla. 24°51N 89°22E 41 G16
Boguchany Russia 58°40N 97°30E 29 D10
Bogué Mauritania 16°45N 14°10W 50 E3
Bohemian Forest = Böhmerwald Germany 49°8N 13°14E 16 D7
Böhmerwald Germany 49°8N 13°14E 16 D7
Bohol □ Phil. 9°50N 124°10E 37 C6
Bohol Sea Phil. 9°0N 124°0E 37 C6
Bohuslän Sweden 58°25N 12°0E 9 G15
Boi, Pta. de Brazil 23°55S 45°15W 95 A6
Boiaçu Brazil 0°27S 61°46W 92 D6
Boileau, C. Australia 17°40S 122°7E 60 C3
Boise U.S.A. 43°37N 116°13W 76 E5
Boise City U.S.A. 36°44N 102°31W 84 C3
Boissevain Canada 49°15N 100°5W 71 D8
Bojador, C. W. Sahara 26°0N 14°30W 50 C3
Bojana → Albania 41°52N 19°22E 23 D8
Bojnūrd Iran 37°30N 57°20E 45 B8
Bojonegoro Indonesia 7°11S 111°54E 37 G14
Bokaro India 23°46N 85°55E 43 H11
Boké Guinea 10°56N 14°17W 50 F3
Bokhara → Australia 29°55S 146°42E 63 D4
Boknafjorden Norway 59°14N 5°40E 9 G11
Bokora ⌂ Uganda 2°12N 31°32E 54 B3
Bokoro Chad 12°25N 17°14E 51 F9
Bokpyin Burma 11°18N 98°42E 39 G2
Bokungu Dem. Rep. of the Congo 0°35S 22°50E 52 E4
Bolan → Pakistan 28°38N 67°42E 42 E2
Bolan Pass Pakistan 29°50N 67°20E 40 E5
Bolaños → Mexico 21°12N 104°5W 86 C4
Bolbec France 49°30N 0°30E 20 B4
Boldājī Iran 31°56N 51°3E 45 D6
Bole China 45°11N 81°37E 32 B3
Bolekhiv Ukraine 49°0N 23°57E 17 D12
Bolesławiec Poland 51°17N 15°37E 16 C8
Bolgatanga Ghana 10°44N 0°53W 50 F5
Bolgrad = Bolhrad Ukraine 45°40N 28°32E 17 F15
Bolhrad Ukraine 45°40N 28°32E 17 F15
Bolívar Argentina 36°15S 60°53W 94 D3
Bolivar Mo., U.S.A. 37°37N 93°25W 80 G7
Bolivar N.Y., U.S.A. 42°4N 78°10W 82 D6
Bolivar Tenn., U.S.A. 35°12N 89°0W 85 D10
Bolivia ■ S. Amer. 17°6S 64°0W 92 G6
Bolivian Plateau = Altiplano Bolivia 17°0S 68°0W 92 G5
Bollnäs Sweden 61°21N 16°24E 8 F17
Bollon Australia 28°2S 147°29E 63 D4
Bolmen Sweden 56°55N 13°40E 9 H15
Bolobo Dem. Rep. of the Congo 2°6S 16°20E 52 E3
Bologna Italy 44°29N 11°20E 22 B4
Bologoye Russia 57°55N 34°5E 18 C5
Bolomba Dem. Rep. of the Congo 0°35N 19°0E 52 D3
Bolonchén Mexico 20°1N 89°45W 87 D7
Boloven, Cao Nguyen Laos 15°10N 106°30E 38 E6
Bolpur India 23°40N 87°45E 43 H12
Bolsena, L. di Italy 42°36N 11°56E 22 C4
Bolshevik, Ostrov Russia 78°30N 102°0E 29 B11
Bolshoy Anyuy → Russia 68°30N 160°49E 29 C17
Bolshoy Begichev, Ostrov Russia 74°20N 112°30E 29 B12
Bolshoy Kavkas = Caucasus Mountains Eurasia 42°50N 44°0E 19 F7
Bolshoy Lyakhovskiy, Ostrov Russia 73°35N 142°0E 29 B15
Bolshoy Tyuters, Ostrov Russia 59°51N 27°13E 9 G22
Bolsward Neths. 53°3N 5°32E 15 A5
Bolt Head U.K. 50°12N 3°48W 13 G4
Bolton Canada 43°54N 79°45W 82 C5
Bolton U.K. 53°35N 2°26W 12 D5
Bolton Landing U.S.A. 43°32N 73°35W 83 C11
Bolu Turkey 40°45N 31°35E 19 F5
Bolungavík Iceland 66°9N 23°15W 8 C2
Bolvadin Turkey 38°45N 31°4E 44 B1
Bolzano Italy 46°31N 11°22E 22 A4
Bom Jesus da Lapa Brazil 13°15S 43°25W 93 F10
Boma Dem. Rep. of the Congo 5°50S 13°4E 52 F2
Bombala Australia 36°56S 149°15E 63 F4
Bombay = Mumbai India 18°56N 72°50E 40 K8
Bombedor, Pta. Venezuela 9°53N 61°37W 93 L15
Bomboma Dem. Rep. of the Congo 2°25N 18°55E 52 D3
Bombombwa Dem. Rep. of the Congo 1°40N 25°40E 54 B2
Bomili Dem. Rep. of the Congo 1°45N 27°5E 54 B2
Bømlo Norway 59°37N 5°13E 9 G11
Bomokandi → Dem. Rep. of the Congo 3°39N 26°8E 54 B2
Bomu → C.A.R. 4°40N 22°30E 52 D4
Bon, C. Tunisia 37°1N 11°2E 22 F4
Bon Acceuil Mauritius 20°10S 57°39E 53 d
Bon Sar Pa Vietnam 12°24N 107°35E 38 F6
Bonaigarh India 21°50N 84°57E 43 J11
Bonaire Neth. Ant. 12°10N 68°15W 89 D6
Bonampak Mexico 16°44N 91°5W 87 D6
Bonang Australia 37°11S 148°41E 63 F4
Bonanza Nic. 13°54N 84°35W 88 D3
Bonaparte Arch. Australia 14°0S 124°30E 60 B3
Bonar Bridge U.K. 57°54N 4°20W 11 D4
Bonasse Trin. & Tob. 10°5N 61°54W 93 K15
Bonaventure Canada 48°5N 65°32W 73 C6
Bonavista Canada 48°40N 53°5W 73 C9
Bonavista, C. Canada 48°42N 53°5W 73 C9
Bonavista B. Canada 48°45N 53°25W 73 C9
Bondo Dem. Rep. of the Congo 3°55N 23°53E 54 B1
Bondoukou Ivory C. 8°2N 2°47W 50 G5
Bondowoso Indonesia 7°55S 113°49E 37 G15
Bone, Teluk Indonesia 4°10S 120°50E 37 E6
Bonerate Indonesia 7°25S 121°5E 37 F6
Bonerate, Kepulauan Indonesia 6°30S 121°10E 37 F6
Bo'ness U.K. 56°1N 3°37W 11 E5
Bonete, Cerro Argentina 27°55S 68°40W 94 B2
Bong Son = Hoai Nhon Vietnam 14°28N 109°1E 38 E7

Bongandanga *Dem. Rep. of the Congo* 1°24N 21°3E 52 D4
Bongor *Chad* 10°35N 15°20E 51 F9
Bongos, Massif des *C.A.R.* 8°40N 22°25E 52 C4
Bonham *U.S.A.* 33°35N 96°11W 84 E6
Boni ⌂ *Kenya* 1°35S 41°18E 54 C5
Bonifacio *France* 41°24N 9°10E 20 F8
Bonifacio, Bouches de *Medit. S.* 41°12N 9°15E 22 D3
Bonin Is. = Ogasawara Gunto *Pac. Oc.* 27°0N 142°0E 64 E6
Bonn *Germany* 50°46N 7°6E 16 C4
Bonne Terre *U.S.A.* 37°55N 90°33W 80 G8
Bonners Ferry *U.S.A.* 48°42N 116°19W 76 B5
Bonney, L. *Australia* 37°50S 140°20E 63 F3
Bonnie Rock *Australia* 30°29S 118°22E 61 F2
Bonny, Bight of *Africa* 3°30N 9°20E 52 D1
Bonnyrigg *U.K.* 55°53N 3°6W 11 F5
Bonnyville *Canada* 54°20N 110°45W 71 C6
Bonoi *Indonesia* 1°45S 137°41E 37 E9
Bonsall *U.S.A.* 33°16N 117°14W 79 M9
Bontang *Indonesia* 0°10N 117°30E 36 D5
Bontebok △ *S. Africa* 34°5S 20°28E 56 E3
Bonthe *S. Leone* 7°30N 12°33W 50 G3
Bontoc *Phil.* 17°7N 120°58E 37 A6
Bonython Ra. *Australia* 23°40S 128°45E 60 D4
Bookabie *Australia* 31°50S 132°41E 61 F5
Booker *U.S.A.* 36°27N 100°32W 84 C4
Booligal *Australia* 33°58S 144°53E 63 E3
Boonah *Australia* 27°58S 152°41E 63 D5
Boone *Iowa, U.S.A.* 42°4N 93°53W 80 D7
Boone *N.C., U.S.A.* 36°13N 81°41W 85 C14
Booneville *Ark., U.S.A.* 35°8N 93°55W 84 D8
Booneville *Miss., U.S.A.* 34°39N 88°34W 85 D10
Boonville *Calif., U.S.A.* 39°1N 123°22W 78 F3
Boonville *Ind., U.S.A.* 38°3N 87°16W 80 F10
Boonville *Mo., U.S.A.* 38°58N 92°44W 80 F7
Boonville *N.Y., U.S.A.* 43°29N 75°20W 83 C9
Boorabbin △ *Australia* 31°30S 120°10E 61 F3
Boorindal *Australia* 30°22S 146°11E 63 E4
Boorowa *Australia* 34°28S 148°44E 63 E4
Boosaaso = Bosaso *Somali Rep.* 11°12N 49°18E 47 E4
Boothia, Gulf of *Canada* 71°0N 90°0W 69 B11
Boothia Pen. *Canada* 71°0N 94°0W 68 B10
Bootle *U.K.* 53°28N 3°1W 12 D4
Booué *Gabon* 0°5S 11°55E 52 E2
Boquete *Panama* 8°46N 82°27W 88 E3
Boquilla, Presa de la *Mexico* 27°31N 105°30W 86 B3
Boquillas del Carmen *Mexico* 29°11N 102°58W 86 B4
Bor *Serbia* 44°5N 22°7E 23 B10
Bôr *Sudan* 6°10N 31°40E 51 G12
Bor Mashash *Israel* 31°7N 34°50E 46 D3
Bora Bora *French Polynesia* 16°30S 151°45W 65 J12
Borah Peak *U.S.A.* 44°8N 113°47W 76 D7
Borås *Sweden* 57°43N 12°56E 9 H15
Borāzjān *Iran* 29°22N 51°10E 45 D6
Borba *Brazil* 4°12S 59°34W 92 D7
Borborema, Planalto da *Brazil* 7°0S 37°0W 90 D7
Bord Khūn-e Now *Iran* 28°3N 51°28E 45 D6
Borda, C. *Australia* 35°45S 136°34E 63 F2
Bordeaux *France* 44°50N 0°36W 20 D3
Borden *Australia* 34°3S 118°12E 61 F2
Borden-Carleton *Canada* 46°18N 63°47W 73 C7
Borden I. *Canada* 78°30N 111°30W 69 B8
Borden Pen. *Canada* 73°0N 83°0W 69 B11
Border Ranges △ *Australia* 28°24S 152°56E 63 D5
Borders = Scottish Borders □ *U.K.* 55°35N 2°50W 11 F6
Bordertown *Australia* 36°19S 140°45E 63 F3
Borðeyri *Iceland* 65°12N 21°6W 8 D3
Bordj Fly Ste. Marie *Algeria* 27°19N 2°32W 50 C5
Bordj-in-Eker *Algeria* 24°9N 5°3E 50 D7
Bordj Omar Driss *Algeria* 28°10N 6°40E 50 C7
Borehamwood *U.K.* 51°40N 0°15W 13 F7
Borgarfjörður *Iceland* 65°33N 13°47W 8 D7
Borgarnes *Iceland* 64°32N 21°55W 8 D3
Børgefjellet *Norway* 65°20N 13°45E 8 D15
Borger *Neths.* 52°54N 6°44E 15 B6
Borger *U.S.A.* 35°39N 101°24W 84 D4
Borgholm *Sweden* 56°52N 16°39E 9 H17
Borhoyn Tal *Mongolia* 43°50N 111°58E 34 C6
Borikhane *Laos* 18°33N 103°43E 38 C4
Borisoglebsk *Russia* 51°27N 42°5E 19 D7
Borisov = Barysaw *Belarus* 54°17N 28°28E 17 A15
Borja *Peru* 4°20S 77°40W 92 D3
Borkou *Chad* 18°15N 18°50E 51 E9
Borkum *Germany* 53°34N 6°40E 16 B4
Borlänge *Sweden* 60°29N 15°26E 9 F16
Borley, C. *Antarctica* 66°15S 52°30E 5 C5
Borneo *E. Indies* 1°0N 115°0E 36 D5
Bornholm *Denmark* 55°10N 15°0E 9 J16
Borogontsy *Russia* 62°42N 131°8E 29 C14
Borohoro Shan *China* 44°6N 83°10E 32 B3
Boron *U.S.A.* 35°0N 117°39W 79 L9
Borongan *Phil.* 11°37N 125°26E 37 B7
Borovichi *Russia* 58°25N 33°55E 18 C5
Borrego Springs *U.S.A.* 33°15N 116°23W 79 M10
Borrisokane *Ireland* 53°0N 8°7W 10 D3
Borroloola *Australia* 16°4S 136°17E 62 B2
Borşa *Romania* 47°41N 24°50E 17 E13
Borsad *India* 22°25N 72°54E 42 H5
Borth *U.K.* 52°29N 4°2W 13 E3
Borūjerd *Iran* 33°55N 48°50E 45 C6
Boryeong *S. Korea* 36°21N 126°36E 35 F14
Boryslav *Ukraine* 49°18N 23°28E 17 D12
Borzya *Russia* 50°24N 116°31E 29 D12
Bosa *Italy* 40°18N 8°30E 22 D3
Bosanska Gradiška *Bos.-H.* 45°10N 17°15E 22 B7
Bosaso *Somali Rep.* 11°12N 49°18E 47 E4
Boscastle *U.K.* 50°41N 4°42W 13 G3
Boscobelle *Barbados* 13°17N 59°35W 89 g
Bose *China* 23°53N 106°35E 32 D5
Boseong *S. Korea* 34°46N 127°5E 35 G14
Boshan *China* 36°28N 117°49E 35 F9
Boshof *S. Africa* 28°31S 25°13E 56 D4
Boshrūyeh *Iran* 33°50N 57°30E 45 C8
Bosna → *Bos.-H.* 45°4N 18°29E 23 B8
Bosna i Hercegovina = Bosnia-Herzegovina ■ *Europe* 44°0N 18°0E 22 B7
Bosnia-Herzegovina ■ *Europe* 44°0N 18°0E 22 B7
Bosnik *Indonesia* 1°5S 136°10E 37 E9
Bosobolo *Dem. Rep. of the Congo* 4°15N 19°50E 52 D3
Bosporus = İstanbul Boğazı *Turkey* 41°5N 29°3E 23 D13
Bosque Farms *U.S.A.* 35°51N 106°42W 77 J10
Bossangoa *C.A.R.* 6°35N 17°30E 52 C3
Bossier City *U.S.A.* 32°31N 93°44W 84 E8
Bosso *Niger* 13°43N 13°19E 51 F8
Bostan *Pakistan* 30°26N 67°2E 42 D2
Bostānābād *Iran* 37°50N 46°50E 44 B5
Bosten Hu *China* 41°55N 87°40E 32 B3
Boston *U.K.* 52°59N 0°2W 12 E7
Boston *U.S.A.* 42°22N 71°3W 83 D13
Boston Bar *Canada* 49°52N 121°30W 70 D4
Boston Mts. *U.S.A.* 35°42N 93°15W 84 D8
Boswell *Canada* 49°28N 116°45W 70 D5
Boswell *U.S.A.* 40°10N 79°2W 82 F5
Botad *India* 22°15N 71°40E 42 H4
Botany B. *Australia* 33°58S 151°11E 58 E8
Botene *Laos* 17°35N 101°12E 38 D3
Bothaville *S. Africa* 27°23S 26°34E 56 D4
Bothnia, G. of *Europe* 62°0N 20°0E 8 F19
Bothwell *Australia* 42°20S 147°1E 63 G4
Bothwell *Canada* 42°38N 81°52W 82 D3
Botletle → *Botswana* 20°10S 23°15E 56 C3
Botoşani *Romania* 47°42N 26°41E 17 E14
Botou *Burkina Faso* 12°42N 1°59E 50 F6
Botshabelo *S. Africa* 29°14S 26°44E 53 K5
Botswana ■ *Africa* 22°0S 24°0E 56 C3
Bottineau *U.S.A.* 48°50N 100°27W 80 A3
Bottrop *Germany* 51°31N 6°58E 15 C6
Botucatu *Brazil* 22°55S 48°30W 95 A6
Botwood *Canada* 49°6N 55°23W 73 C8
Bou Saâda *Algeria* 35°11N 4°9E 50 A6
Bouaflé *Ivory C.* 7°1N 5°47W 50 G4
Bouaké *Ivory C.* 7°40N 5°2W 50 G4
Bouar *C.A.R.* 6°0N 15°40E 52 C3
Bouârfa *Morocco* 32°32N 1°58W 50 B5
Boucaut B. *Australia* 12°0S 134°25E 62 A1
Bouctouche *Canada* 46°30N 64°45W 73 C7
Bougainville, C. *Australia* 13°57S 126°4E 60 B4
Bougainville I. *Papua N. G.* 6°0S 155°0E 58 B8
Bougainville Reef *Australia* 15°30S 147°5E 62 B4
Bougie = Bejaïa *Algeria* 36°42N 5°2E 50 A7
Bougouni *Mali* 11°30N 7°20W 50 F4
Bouillon *Belgium* 49°44N 5°3E 15 E5
Boulder *Colo., U.S.A.* 40°1N 105°17W 76 F11
Boulder *Mont., U.S.A.* 46°14N 112°7W 76 C7
Boulder City *U.S.A.* 35°58N 114°49W 79 K12
Boulder Creek *U.S.A.* 37°7N 122°7W 78 H4
Boulder Dam = Hoover Dam *U.S.A.* 36°1N 114°44W 79 K12
Boulia *Australia* 22°52S 139°51E 62 C2
Boulogne-sur-Mer *France* 50°42N 1°36E 20 A4
Boulsa *Burkina Faso* 12°39N 0°34W 50 F5
Boultoum *Niger* 14°45N 10°25E 51 F8
Bouma △ *Fiji* 16°50S 179°52E 59 a
Boun Neua *Laos* 21°38N 101°54E 38 B3
Boun Tai *Laos* 21°23N 101°58E 38 B3
Bouna *Ivory C.* 9°10N 3°0W 50 G5
Boundary Peak *U.S.A.* 37°51N 118°21W 78 H8
Boundiali *Ivory C.* 9°30N 6°20W 50 G4
Bountiful *U.S.A.* 40°53N 111°52W 76 F8
Bounty Is. *Pac. Oc.* 48°0S 178°30E 64 M9
Bounty Trough *Pac. Oc.* 46°0S 178°0E 64 M9
Bourbonnais *France* 46°28N 3°0E 20 C5
Bourdel L. *Canada* 56°43N 74°10W 72 A5
Bourem *Mali* 17°0N 0°24W 50 E5
Bourg-en-Bresse *France* 46°13N 5°12E 20 C6
Bourg-St-Maurice *France* 45°35N 6°46E 20 D7
Bourgas = Burgas *Bulgaria* 42°33N 27°29E 23 C12
Bourges *France* 47°9N 2°25E 20 C5
Bourget *Canada* 45°26N 75°9W 83 A9
Bourgogne □ *France* 47°0N 4°50E 20 C6
Bourke *Australia* 30°8S 145°55E 63 E4
Bourne *U.K.* 52°47N 0°22W 12 E7
Bournemouth *U.K.* 50°43N 1°52W 13 G6
Bournemouth □ *U.K.* 50°43N 1°52W 13 G6
Bouse *U.S.A.* 33°56N 114°0W 79 M13
Bousso *Chad* 10°34N 16°52E 51 F9
Bouvet I. = Bouvetøya *Antarctica* 54°26S 3°24E 2 G10
Bouvetøya *Antarctica* 54°26S 3°24E 2 G10
Bovill *U.S.A.* 46°51N 116°24W 76 C5
Bovril *Argentina* 31°21S 59°26W 94 C4
Bow → *Canada* 49°57N 111°41W 70 C6
Bow Island *Canada* 49°50N 111°23W 76 B8
Bowbells *U.S.A.* 48°48N 102°15W 80 A2
Bowdle *U.S.A.* 45°27N 99°39W 80 C4
Bowelling *Australia* 33°25S 116°30E 61 F2
Bowen *Argentina* 35°0S 67°31W 94 D2
Bowen *Australia* 20°0S 148°16E 62 J6
Bowen Mts. *Australia* 37°0S 147°50E 63 F4
Bowers Basin *Pac. Oc.* 53°45N 176°0E 4 D16
Bowers Ridge *Pac. Oc.* 54°0N 180°0E 4 D17
Bowie *Ariz., U.S.A.* 32°19N 109°29W 77 K9
Bowie *Tex., U.S.A.* 33°34N 97°51W 84 E6
Bowland, Forest of *U.K.* 54°0N 2°30W 12 D5
Bowling Green *Ky., U.S.A.* 36°59N 86°27W 80 G10
Bowling Green *Ohio, U.S.A.* 41°23N 83°39W 81 E12
Bowling Green, C. *Australia* 19°19S 147°25E 62 B4
Bowling Green Bay △ *Australia* 19°26S 146°57E 62 B4
Bowman *U.S.A.* 46°11N 103°24W 80 B2
Bowman I. *Antarctica* 65°0S 104°0E 5 C8
Bowmanville = Clarington *Canada* 43°55N 78°41W 82 C6
Bowmore *U.K.* 55°45N 6°17W 11 F2
Bowral *Australia* 34°26S 150°27E 63 E5
Bowraville *Australia* 30°37S 152°52E 63 E5
Bowron → *Canada* 54°3N 121°50W 70 C4
Bowron Lake ⌂ *Canada* 53°10N 121°5W 70 C4
Bowser L. *Canada* 56°30N 129°30W 70 B3
Bowsman *Canada* 52°14N 101°12W 71 C8
Bowwood *Zambia* 17°5S 26°20E 55 F2
Box Cr. → *Australia* 34°10S 143°50E 63 E3
Boxmeer *Neths.* 51°38N 5°56E 15 C5
Boxtel *Neths.* 51°36N 5°20E 15 C5
Boyce *U.S.A.* 31°23N 92°40W 84 F8
Boyd L. *Canada* 52°46N 76°42W 72 B4
Boyle *Canada* 54°35N 112°49W 70 C6
Boyle *Ireland* 53°59N 8°18W 10 C3
Boyne → *Ireland* 53°43N 6°15W 10 C5
Boyne City *U.S.A.* 45°13N 85°1W 81 C11
Boynton Beach *U.S.A.* 26°32N 80°4W 85 H14
Boyolali *Indonesia* 7°32S 110°35E 37 G14
Boyoma, Chutes *Dem. Rep. of the Congo* 0°35N 25°23E 54 B2
Boysen Res. *U.S.A.* 43°25N 108°11W 76 E9
Boyuibe *Bolivia* 20°25S 63°17W 92 G6
Boyup Brook *Australia* 33°50S 116°23E 61 F2
Boz Dağları *Turkey* 38°20N 28°0E 23 E13
Bozburun *Turkey* 36°43N 28°4E 23 F13
Bozcaada *Turkey* 39°49N 26°3E 23 E12
Bozdoğan *Turkey* 37°40N 28°17E 23 F13
Bozeman *U.S.A.* 45°41N 111°2W 76 D8
Bozen = Bolzano *Italy* 46°31N 11°22E 22 A4
Bozhou *China* 33°55N 115°41E 34 H8
Bozoum *C.A.R.* 6°25N 16°35E 52 C3
Bra *Italy* 44°42N 7°51E 20 D7
Brabant □ *Belgium* 50°46N 4°30E 15 D4
Brabant L. *Canada* 55°58N 103°43W 71 B8
Brač *Croatia* 43°20N 16°40E 22 C7
Bracadale, L. *U.K.* 57°20N 6°30W 11 D2
Bracciano, L. di *Italy* 42°7N 12°14E 22 C5
Bracebridge *Canada* 45°2N 79°19W 82 A5
Brach *Libya* 27°31N 14°20E 51 C8
Bräcke *Sweden* 62°45N 15°26E 8 E16
Brackettville *U.S.A.* 29°19N 100°25W 84 G4
Bracknell *U.K.* 51°25N 0°43W 13 F7
Bracknell Forest □ *U.K.* 51°25N 0°44W 13 F7
Brad *Romania* 46°10N 22°50E 17 E12
Bradenton *U.S.A.* 27°30N 82°34W 85 H13
Bradford *Canada* 44°7N 79°34W 82 B5
Bradford *U.K.* 53°47N 1°45W 12 D6
Bradford *Pa., U.S.A.* 41°58N 78°38W 82 E6
Bradford *Vt., U.S.A.* 43°59N 72°9W 83 C12
Bradley *Ark., U.S.A.* 33°6N 93°39W 84 E8
Bradley *Calif., U.S.A.* 35°52N 120°48W 78 K6
Bradley Institute *Zimbabwe* 17°7S 31°25E 55 F3
Brady *U.S.A.* 31°9N 99°20W 84 F5
Braeside *Canada* 45°28N 76°24W 83 A8
Braga *Portugal* 41°35N 8°25W 21 B1
Bragado *Argentina* 35°2S 60°27W 94 D3
Bragança *Brazil* 1°0S 47°2W 93 D9
Bragança *Portugal* 41°48N 6°50W 21 B2
Bragança Paulista *Brazil* 22°55S 46°32W 95 A6
Brahestad = Raahe *Finland* 64°40N 24°28E 8 D21
Brahmanbaria *Bangla.* 23°58N 91°15E 41 H17
Brahmani → *India* 20°39N 86°46E 41 J15
Brahmapur *India* 19°15N 84°54E 41 K14
Brahmaputra → *Asia* 23°40N 90°35E 43 H13
Braich-y-pwll *U.K.* 52°47N 4°46W 12 E3
Braidwood *Australia* 35°27S 149°49E 63 F4
Brăila *Romania* 45°19N 27°59E 17 F14
Brainerd *U.S.A.* 46°22N 94°12W 80 B6
Braintree *U.K.* 51°53N 0°34E 13 F8
Braintree *U.S.A.* 42°13N 71°0W 83 D14
Brak → *S. Africa* 29°35S 22°55E 56 D3
Brakwater *Namibia* 22°28S 17°3E 56 C2
Brampton *Canada* 43°45N 79°45W 82 C5
Brampton *U.K.* 54°57N 2°44W 12 C5
Bramton I. *Australia* 20°50S 149°17E 62 J7
Branco → *Brazil* 1°20S 61°50W 92 D6
Brandberg *Namibia* 21°10S 14°33E 56 C1
Brandberg ⌂ *Namibia* 21°10S 14°30E 56 C1
Brandenburg = Neubrandenburg *Germany* 53°33N 13°15E 16 B7
Brandenburg *Germany* 52°25N 12°33E 16 B7
Brandenburg □ *Germany* 52°50N 13°0E 16 B6
Brandfort *S. Africa* 28°40S 26°30E 56 D4
Brandon *Canada* 49°50N 99°57W 71 D9
Brandon *U.S.A.* 43°48N 73°6W 83 C11
Brandon B. *Ireland* 52°17N 10°8W 10 D1
Brandon Mt. *Ireland* 52°15N 10°15W 10 D1
Brandsen *Argentina* 35°10S 58°15W 94 D4
Brandvlei *S. Africa* 30°25S 20°30E 56 E3
Branford *U.S.A.* 41°17N 72°49W 83 E12
Braniewo *Poland* 54°25N 19°50E 17 A10
Bransfield Str. *Antarctica* 63°0S 59°0W 5 C18
Branson *U.S.A.* 36°39N 93°13W 80 G7
Brantford *Canada* 43°10N 80°15W 82 C4
Bras d'Or L. *Canada* 45°50N 60°50W 73 C7
Brasher Falls *U.S.A.* 44°49N 74°47W 83 B10
Brasil = Brazil ■ *S. Amer.* 12°0S 50°0W 93 F9
Brasil, Planalto *Brazil* 18°0S 46°30W 90 E6
Brasiléia *Brazil* 11°0S 68°45W 92 F5
Brasília *Brazil* 15°47S 47°55W 93 G9
Brasília Legal *Brazil* 3°49S 55°36W 93 D7
Braslaw *Belarus* 55°38N 27°0E 9 J22
Braşov *Romania* 45°38N 25°35E 17 F13
Brasschaat *Belgium* 51°19N 4°27E 15 C4
Brassey, Banjaran *Malaysia* 5°0N 117°15E 36 D5
Brassey Ra. *Australia* 25°8S 122°15E 61 E3
Brasstown Bald *U.S.A.* 34°53N 83°49W 85 D13
Brastad *Sweden* 58°23N 11°30E 9 G14
Bratislava *Slovak Rep.* 48°10N 17°7E 17 D9
Bratsk *Russia* 56°10N 101°30E 29 D11
Brattleboro *U.S.A.* 42°51N 72°34W 83 D12
Braunau *Austria* 48°15N 13°3E 16 D7
Braunschweig *Germany* 52°15N 10°31E 16 B6
Braunton *U.K.* 51°7N 4°10W 13 F3
Brava *C. Verde Is.* 15°0N 24°40W 50 b
Bravo del Norte, Rio = Grande, Rio → *N. Amer.* 25°58N 97°9W 84 J6
Brawley *U.S.A.* 32°59N 115°31W 79 N11
Bray *Ireland* 53°13N 6°7W 10 C5
Bray, Mt. *Australia* 14°0S 134°30E 62 A1
Bray, Pays de *France* 49°46N 1°26E 20 B4
Brazeau → *Canada* 52°55N 115°14W 70 C5
Brazil *U.S.A.* 39°32N 87°8W 80 F10
Brazil ■ *S. Amer.* 12°0S 50°0W 93 F9
Brazilian Highlands = Brasil, Planalto *Brazil* 18°0S 46°30W 90 E6
Brazo Sur → *S. Amer.* 25°21S 57°42W 94 B4
Brazos → *U.S.A.* 28°53N 95°23W 84 G7
Brazzaville *Congo* 4°9S 15°12E 52 E3
Brčko *Bos.-H.* 44°54N 18°46E 23 B8
Breaden, L. *Australia* 25°51S 125°28E 61 E4
Breaksea Sd. *N.Z.* 45°35S 166°35E 59 F1
Bream B. *N.Z.* 35°56S 174°28E 59 A5
Bream Hd. *N.Z.* 35°51S 174°36E 59 A5
Breas *Chile* 25°29S 70°24W 94 B1
Brebes *Indonesia* 6°52S 109°3E 37 G13
Brechin *Canada* 44°32N 79°10W 82 B5
Brechin *U.K.* 56°44N 2°39W 11 E6
Brecht *Belgium* 51°21N 4°38E 15 C4
Breckenridge *Colo., U.S.A.* 39°29N 106°3W 76 G10
Breckenridge *Minn., U.S.A.* 46°16N 96°35W 80 B5
Breckenridge *Tex., U.S.A.* 32°45N 98°54W 84 E5
Breckland *U.K.* 52°30N 0°40E 13 E8
Brecon *U.K.* 51°57N 3°23W 13 F4
Brecon Beacons *U.K.* 51°53N 3°26W 13 F4
Brecon Beacons △ *U.K.* 51°50N 3°30W 13 F4
Breda *Neths.* 51°35N 4°45E 15 C4
Bredasdorp *S. Africa* 34°33S 20°2E 56 E3
Bree *Belgium* 51°8N 5°35E 15 C5
Bregenz *Austria* 47°30N 9°45E 16 E5
Breiðafjörður *Iceland* 65°15N 23°15W 8 D2
Brejo *Brazil* 3°41S 42°47W 93 D10
Bremen *Germany* 53°4N 8°47E 16 B5
Bremer Bay *Australia* 34°21S 119°20E 61 F2
Bremer I. *Australia* 12°5S 136°45E 62 A2
Bremerhaven *Germany* 53°33N 8°36E 16 B5
Bremerton *U.S.A.* 47°34N 122°37W 78 C4
Brenham *U.S.A.* 30°10N 96°24W 84 F6
Brennerpass *Austria* 47°2N 11°30E 16 E6
Brent *U.S.A.* 32°56N 87°10W 85 E11
Brentwood *U.K.* 51°37N 0°19E 13 F8
Brentwood *Calif., U.S.A.* 37°56N 121°42W 78 H5
Brentwood *N.Y., U.S.A.* 40°47N 73°15W 83 F11
Bréscia *Italy* 45°33N 10°15E 20 D9
Breskens *Neths.* 51°23N 3°33E 15 C3
Breslau = Wrocław *Poland* 51°5N 17°5E 17 C9
Bressanone *Italy* 46°43N 11°39E 22 A4
Bressay *U.K.* 60°9N 1°6W 11 A7
Brest *Belarus* 52°10N 23°40E 17 B12
Brest *France* 48°24N 4°31W 20 B1
Brest-Litovsk = Brest *Belarus* 52°10N 23°40E 17 B12
Bretagne □ *France* 48°10N 3°0W 20 B2
Breton *Canada* 53°7N 114°28W 70 C6
Breton Sd. *U.S.A.* 29°35N 89°15W 85 G10
Brett, C. *N.Z.* 35°10S 174°20E 59 A5
Brevard *U.S.A.* 35°14N 82°44W 85 D13
Breves *Brazil* 1°40S 50°29W 93 D8
Brewarrina *Australia* 30°0S 146°51E 63 E4
Brewer *U.S.A.* 44°48N 68°46W 81 C19
Brewer, Mt. *U.S.A.* 36°44N 118°28W 78 J8
Brewster *N.Y., U.S.A.* 41°24N 73°36W 83 E11
Brewster *Ohio, U.S.A.* 40°43N 81°36W 82 F3
Brewster *Wash., U.S.A.* 48°6N 119°47W 76 B4
Brewster, Kap = Kangikajik *Greenland* 70°7N 22°0W 4 B6
Brewton *U.S.A.* 31°7N 87°4W 85 F11
Breyten *S. Africa* 26°16S 30°0E 57 D5
Bria *C.A.R.* 6°30N 21°58E 52 C4
Briançon *France* 44°54N 6°39E 20 D7
Bribie I. *Australia* 27°0S 153°10E 63 D5
Bribri *Costa Rica* 9°38N 82°50W 88 E3
Bridgefield *Barbados* 13°9N 59°36W 89 g
Bridgehampton *U.S.A.* 40°56N 72°19W 83 F12
Bridgend *U.K.* 51°30N 3°34W 13 F4
Bridgend □ *U.K.* 51°36N 3°36W 13 F4
Bridgeport *Calif., U.S.A.* 38°15N 119°14W 78 G7
Bridgeport *Conn., U.S.A.* 41°11N 73°12W 83 E11
Bridgeport *Nebr., U.S.A.* 41°40N 103°6W 80 E2
Bridgeport *Tex., U.S.A.* 33°13N 97°45W 84 E6
Bridger *U.S.A.* 45°18N 108°55W 76 D9
Bridgeton *U.S.A.* 39°26N 75°14W 81 F16
Bridgetown *Australia* 33°58S 116°7E 61 F2
Bridgetown *Barbados* 13°6N 59°37W 89 g
Bridgetown *Canada* 44°55N 65°18W 73 D6
Bridgewater *Australia* 42°44S 147°14E 63 G4
Bridgewater *Canada* 44°25N 64°31W 73 D7
Bridgewater *Mass., U.S.A.* 41°59N 70°58W 83 E14
Bridgewater *N.Y., U.S.A.* 42°53N 75°15W 83 D9
Bridgewater, C. *Australia* 38°23S 141°23E 63 F3
Bridgnorth *U.K.* 52°32N 2°25W 13 E5
Bridgton *U.S.A.* 44°3N 70°42W 83 B14
Bridgwater *U.K.* 51°8N 2°59W 13 F5
Bridgwater B. *U.K.* 51°15N 3°15W 13 F4
Bridlington *U.K.* 54°5N 0°12W 12 C7
Bridlington B. *U.K.* 54°4N 0°10W 12 C7
Bridport *Australia* 40°59S 147°23E 63 G4
Bridport *U.K.* 50°44N 2°45W 13 G5
Brig *Switz.* 46°18N 7°59E 20 C7
Brigg *U.K.* 53°34N 0°28W 12 D7
Brigham City *U.S.A.* 41°31N 112°1W 76 F7
Bright *Australia* 36°42S 146°56E 63 F4
Brighton *Australia* 35°5S 138°30E 63 F2
Brighton *Canada* 44°2N 77°44W 82 B7
Brighton *Trin. & Tob.* 10°13N 61°39W 93 K15
Brighton *U.K.* 50°49N 0°7W 13 G7
Brighton *U.S.A.* 43°8N 77°34W 82 C7
Brilliant *U.S.A.* 40°15N 80°39W 82 F4
Brindisi *Italy* 40°39N 17°55E 23 D7
Brinkley *U.S.A.* 34°53N 91°12W 84 D9
Brinnon *U.S.A.* 47°41N 122°54W 78 C4
Brion, Î. *Canada* 47°46N 61°26W 73 C7
Brisbane *Australia* 27°25S 153°2E 63 D5
Brisbane → *Australia* 27°24S 153°9E 63 D5
Bristol *U.K.* 51°26N 2°35W 13 F5
Bristol *Conn., U.S.A.* 41°40N 72°57W 83 E12
Bristol *Pa., U.S.A.* 40°6N 74°51W 83 F10
Bristol *R.I., U.S.A.* 41°40N 71°16W 83 E13
Bristol *Tenn., U.S.A.* 36°36N 82°11W 85 C13
Bristol, City of □ *U.K.* 51°27N 2°36W 13 F5
Bristol B. *U.S.A.* 58°0N 160°0W 74 a
Bristol Channel *U.K.* 51°18N 4°30W 13 F3
Bristol I. *Antarctica* 58°45S 28°0W 5 B1
Bristol L. *U.S.A.* 34°28N 115°41W 77 J6
Bristow *U.S.A.* 35°50N 96°23W 84 D6
Britain = Great Britain *Europe* 54°0N 2°15W 6 E5
British Columbia □ *Canada* 55°0N 125°15W 70 C3
British Indian Ocean Terr. = Chagos Arch. ☑ *Ind. Oc.* 6°0S 72°0E 26 J9
British Isles *Europe* 54°0N 4°0W 14 D5
British Virgin Is. ☑ *W. Indies* 18°30N 64°30W 89 e
Brits *S. Africa* 25°37S 27°48E 57 D4
Britstown *S. Africa* 30°37S 23°30E 56 E3
Britt *Canada* 45°46N 80°34W 72 C3
Brittany = Bretagne □ *France* 48°10N 3°0W 20 B2
Britton *U.S.A.* 45°48N 97°45W 80 C5
Brive-la-Gaillarde *France* 45°10N 1°32E 20 D4
Brixen = Bressanone *Italy* 46°43N 11°39E 22 A4
Brixham *U.K.* 50°23N 3°31W 13 G4
Brno *Czech Rep.* 49°10N 16°35E 17 D9
Broach = Bharuch *India* 21°47N 73°0E 40 J8
Broad → *U.S.A.* 34°1N 81°4W 85 D14
Broad Arrow *Australia* 30°23S 121°15E 61 F3
Broad B. *U.K.* 58°14N 6°18W 11 C2
Broad Haven *Ireland* 54°20N 9°55W 10 B2
Broad Law *U.K.* 55°30N 3°21W 11 F5
Broad Sd. *Australia* 22°0S 149°45E 62 C4
Broadalbin *U.S.A.* 43°4N 74°12W 83 C10
Broadback → *Canada* 51°21N 78°52W 72 B4
Broadhurst Ra. *Australia* 22°30S 122°30E 60 D3
Broads, The *U.K.* 52°45N 1°30E 12 E9
Broadus *U.S.A.* 45°27N 105°25W 76 D11
Brochet *Canada* 57°53N 101°40W 71 B8
Brochet, L. *Canada* 58°36N 101°35W 71 B8
Brock I. *Canada* 77°52N 114°19W 69 B8
Brocken *Germany* 51°47N 10°37E 16 C6
Brockport *U.S.A.* 43°13N 77°56W 82 C7
Brockton *U.S.A.* 42°5N 71°1W 83 D13
Brockville *Canada* 44°35N 75°41W 83 B9
Brockway *Mont., U.S.A.* 47°18N 105°45W 76 C11
Brockway *Pa., U.S.A.* 41°15N 78°47W 82 E6
Brocton *U.S.A.* 42°23N 79°26W 82 D5
Brodeur Pen. *Canada* 72°30N 88°10W 69 B11
Brodick *U.K.* 55°35N 5°9W 11 F3
Brodnica *Poland* 53°15N 19°25E 17 B10
Brody *Ukraine* 50°5N 25°10E 17 C13
Brogan *U.S.A.* 44°15N 117°31W 76 D5
Broken Arrow *U.S.A.* 36°3N 95°48W 84 C7
Broken Bow *Nebr., U.S.A.* 41°24N 99°38W 80 E4
Broken Bow *Okla., U.S.A.* 34°2N 94°44W 84 D7
Broken Bow Lake *U.S.A.* 34°9N 94°40W 84 D7
Broken Hill *Australia* 31°58S 141°29E 63 E3
Broken Ridge *Ind. Oc.* 30°0S 94°0E 64 L1
Broken River Ra. *Australia* 21°0S 148°22E 62 K6
Bromley □ *U.K.* 51°24N 0°2E 13 F8
Bromo *Indonesia* 7°55S 112°55E 37 G15
Bromsgrove *U.K.* 52°21N 2°2W 13 E5
Brønderslev *Denmark* 57°16N 9°57E 9 H13
Bronkhorstspruit *S. Africa* 25°46S 28°45E 57 D4
Brønnøysund *Norway* 65°28N 12°14E 8 D15
Brook Park *U.S.A.* 41°23N 81°48W 82 E4
Brookhaven *U.S.A.* 31°35N 90°26W 85 F9
Brookings *Oreg., U.S.A.* 42°3N 124°17W 76 E1
Brookings *S. Dak., U.S.A.* 44°19N 96°48W 80 C5
Brooklin *Canada* 43°55N 78°55W 82 C6
Brooklyn Park *U.S.A.* 45°6N 93°23W 80 C7
Brooks *Canada* 50°35N 111°55W 70 C6
Brooks Range *U.S.A.* 68°0N 152°0W 74 a
Brooksville *U.S.A.* 28°33N 82°23W 85 G13
Brookton *Australia* 32°22S 117°0E 61 F2
Brookville *U.S.A.* 41°10N 79°5W 82 E5

Broom, L. *U.K.* 57°55N 5°15W 11 D3
Broome *Australia* 18°0S 122°15E 60 C3
Brora *U.K.* 58°0N 3°52W 11 C5
Brora → *U.K.* 58°0N 3°51W 11 C5
Brosna → *Ireland* 53°14N 7°58W 10 C4
Brothers *U.S.A.* 43°49N 120°36W 76 E3
Brough *U.K.* 54°32N 2°18W 12 C5
Brough Hd. *U.K.* 59°8N 3°20W 11 B5
Broughton Island = Qikiqtarjuaq *Canada* 67°33N 63°0W 69 C13
Brown, L. *Australia* 31°5S 118°15E 61 F2
Brown, Pt. *Australia* 32°32S 133°50E 63 E1
Brown City *U.S.A.* 43°13N 82°59W 82 C2
Brown Willy *U.K.* 50°35N 4°37W 13 G3
Brownfield *U.S.A.* 33°11N 102°17W 84 E3
Browning *U.S.A.* 48°34N 113°1W 76 B7
Brownsville *Oreg., U.S.A.* 44°24N 122°59W 76 D2
Brownsville *Pa., U.S.A.* 40°1N 79°53W 82 F5
Brownsville *Tenn., U.S.A.* 35°36N 89°16W 85 D10
Brownsville *Tex., U.S.A.* 25°54N 97°30W 84 J6
Brownville *U.S.A.* 44°0N 75°59W 83 C9
Brownwood *U.S.A.* 31°43N 98°59W 84 F5
Browse I. *Australia* 14°7S 123°33E 60 B3
Bruas *Malaysia* 4°30N 100°47E 39 K3
Bruay-la-Buissière *France* 50°29N 2°33E 20 A5
Bruce, Mt. *Australia* 22°37S 118°8E 60 D2
Bruce Pen. *Canada* 45°0N 81°30W 82 B3
Bruce Peninsula △ *Canada* 45°14N 81°36W 82 A3
Bruce Rock *Australia* 31°52S 118°8E 61 F2
Bruck an der Leitha *Austria* 48°1N 16°47E 17 D9
Bruck an der Mur *Austria* 47°24N 15°16E 16 E8
Brue → *U.K.* 51°13N 2°59W 13 F5
Bruges = Brugge *Belgium* 51°13N 3°13E 15 C3
Brugge *Belgium* 51°13N 3°13E 15 C3
Bruin *U.S.A.* 41°3N 79°43W 82 E5
Brûk, W. el → *Egypt* 30°15N 33°50E 46 E2
Brûlé *Canada* 53°15N 117°58W 70 C5
Brumado *Brazil* 14°14S 41°40W 93 F10
Brumunddal *Norway* 60°53N 10°56E 8 F14
Bruneau *U.S.A.* 42°53N 115°48W 76 E6
Bruneau → *U.S.A.* 42°56N 115°57W 76 E6
Brunei = Bandar Seri Begawan *Brunei* 4°52N 115°0E 36 C4
Brunei ■ *Asia* 4°50N 115°0E 36 D4
Brunner, L. *N.Z.* 42°37S 171°27E 59 E3
Brunssum *Neths.* 50°57N 5°59E 15 D5
Brunswick = Braunschweig *Germany* 52°15N 10°31E 16 B6
Brunswick *Ga., U.S.A.* 31°10N 81°30W 85 F14
Brunswick *Maine, U.S.A.* 43°55N 69°58W 81 D19
Brunswick *Md., U.S.A.* 39°19N 77°38W 81 F15
Brunswick *Mo., U.S.A.* 39°26N 93°8W 80 F7
Brunswick *Ohio, U.S.A.* 41°14N 81°51W 82 E3
Brunswick, Pen. de *Chile* 53°30S 71°30W 96 G2
Brunswick B. *Australia* 15°15S 124°50E 60 C3
Brunswick Junction *Australia* 33°15S 115°50E 61 F2
Brunt Ice Shelf *Antarctica* 75°30S 25°0W 5 D2
Brus Laguna *Honduras* 15°47N 84°35W 88 C3
Brush *U.S.A.* 40°15N 103°37W 76 F12
Brushton *U.S.A.* 44°50N 74°31W 83 B10
Brusque *Brazil* 27°5S 49°0W 95 B6
Brussel *Belgium* 50°51N 4°21E 15 D4
Brussel ✈ (BRU) *Belgium* 50°54N 4°29E 15 D5
Brussels = Brussel *Belgium* 50°51N 4°21E 15 D4
Brussels *Canada* 43°44N 81°15W 82 C3
Bruthen *Australia* 37°42S 147°50E 63 F4
Bruxelles = Brussel *Belgium* 50°51N 4°21E 15 D4
Bryan *Ohio, U.S.A.* 41°28N 84°33W 81 E11
Bryan *Tex., U.S.A.* 30°40N 96°22W 84 F6
Bryan, Mt. *Australia* 33°30S 139°5E 63 E2
Bryansk *Russia* 53°13N 34°25E 18 D4
Bryce Canyon △ *U.S.A.* 37°30N 112°10W 77 H7
Bryne *Norway* 58°44N 5°38E 9 G11
Bryson City *U.S.A.* 35°26N 83°27W 85 D13
Bsharri *Lebanon* 34°15N 36°0E 46 A5
Bū Baqarah *U.A.E.* 25°35N 56°25E 45 E8
Bu Craa *W. Sahara* 26°45N 12°50W 50 C3
Bū Ḥasā *U.A.E.* 23°30N 53°20E 45 F7
Bua *Fiji* 16°48S 178°37E 59 a
Bua Yai *Thailand* 15°33N 102°26E 38 E4
Buan *S. Korea* 35°44N 126°44E 35 G14
Buapinang *Indonesia* 4°40S 121°30E 37 E6
Bubanza *Burundi* 3°6S 29°23E 54 C2
Bubi → *Zimbabwe* 22°20S 31°7E 55 G3
Būbiyān *Kuwait* 29°45N 48°15E 45 D6
Buca *Fiji* 16°38S 179°52E 59 a
Bucaramanga *Colombia* 7°0N 73°0W 92 B4
Bucasia *Australia* 21°2S 149°10E 62 K7
Buccaneer Arch. *Australia* 16°7S 123°20E 60 C3
Buccoo Reef *Trin. & Tob.* 11°10N 60°51W 93 J16
Buchach *Ukraine* 49°5N 25°25E 17 D13
Buchan *U.K.* 57°32N 2°21W 11 D6
Buchan Ness *U.K.* 57°29N 1°46W 11 D7
Buchanan *Canada* 51°40N 102°45W 71 C8
Buchanan *Liberia* 5°57N 10°2W 50 G3
Buchanan, L. *Queens., Australia* 21°35S 145°52E 62 C4
Buchanan, L. *W. Austral., Australia* 25°33S 123°2E 61 E3
Buchanan, L. *U.S.A.* 30°45N 98°25W 84 F5
Buchanan Cr. → *Australia* 19°13S 136°33E 62 B2
Buchans *Canada* 48°50N 56°52W 73 C8
Bucharest = București *Romania* 44°27N 26°10E 17 F14
Bucheon *S. Korea* 37°28N 126°45E 35 F14
Buchon, Pt. *U.S.A.* 35°15N 120°54W 78 K6
Buck Hill Falls *U.S.A.* 41°11N 75°16W 83 E9
Buckeye Lake *U.S.A.* 39°55N 82°29W 82 G2
Buckhannon *U.S.A.* 39°0N 80°8W 81 F13
Buckhaven *U.K.* 56°11N 3°3W 11 E5
Buckhorn L. *Canada* 44°29N 78°23W 82 B6
Buckie *U.K.* 57°41N 2°58W 11 D6
Buckingham *Canada* 45°37N 75°24W 72 C4
Buckingham *U.K.* 51°59N 0°57W 13 F7
Buckingham B. *Australia* 12°10S 135°40E 62 A2
Buckinghamshire □ *U.K.* 51°53N 0°55W 13 F7
Buckle Hd. *Australia* 14°26S 127°52E 60 B4
Buckleboo *Australia* 32°54S 136°12E 63 E2
Buckley *U.K.* 53°10N 3°5W 12 D4
Buckley → *Australia* 20°10S 138°49E 62 C2
Bucklin *U.S.A.* 37°33N 99°38W 80 G4
Bucks L. *U.S.A.* 39°54N 121°12W 78 F5
București *Romania* 44°27N 26°10E 17 F14
Bucyrus *U.S.A.* 40°48N 82°59W 81 E12
Budalin *Burma* 22°20N 95°10E 41 H19
Budapest *Hungary* 47°29N 19°3E 17 E10
Budaun *India* 28°5N 79°10E 43 E8
Budd Coast *Antarctica* 68°0S 112°0E 5 C8
Bude *U.K.* 50°49N 4°34W 13 G3
Budennovsk *Russia* 44°50N 44°10E 19 F7
Budge Budge = Baj Baj *India* 22°30N 88°5E 43 H13
Budgewoi *Australia* 33°13S 151°34E 63 E5
Budjala *Dem. Rep. of the Congo* 2°50N 19°40E 52 D3
Buellton *U.S.A.* 34°37N 120°12W 79 L6
Buena Esperanza *Argentina* 34°45S 65°15W 94 C2
Buena Park *U.S.A.* 33°52N 117°59W 79 M9
Buena Vista *Colo., U.S.A.* 38°51N 106°8W 76 G10
Buena Vista *Va., U.S.A.* 37°44N 79°21W 81 G14
Buena Vista Lake Bed *U.S.A.* 35°12N 119°18W 79 K7
Buenaventura *Colombia* 3°53N 77°4W 92 C3
Buenaventura *Mexico* 29°51N 107°29W 86 B3
Buenos Aires *Argentina* 34°36S 58°22W 94 C4
Buenos Aires *Costa Rica* 9°10N 83°20W 88 E3
Buenos Aires □ *Argentina* 36°30S 60°0W 94 D4
Buenos Aires, L. *Argentina* 46°35S 72°30W 96 F2
Buffalo *Mo., U.S.A.* 37°39N 93°6W 80 G7
Buffalo *N.Y., U.S.A.* 42°53N 78°53W 82 D6
Buffalo *Okla., U.S.A.* 36°50N 99°38W 84 C5
Buffalo *S. Dak., U.S.A.* 45°35N 103°33W 80 C2
Buffalo *Wyo., U.S.A.* 44°21N 106°42W 76 D10
Buffalo → *Canada* 60°5N 115°5W 70 A5
Buffalo → *S. Africa* 28°43S 30°37E 57 D5
Buffalo ⌂ *U.S.A.* 36°14N 92°36W 84 C8
Buffalo Head Hills *Canada* 57°25N 115°55W 70 B5
Buffalo L. *Alta., Canada* 52°27N 112°54W 70 C6
Buffalo L. *N.W.T., Canada* 60°12N 115°25W 70 A5
Buffalo Narrows *Canada* 55°51N 108°29W 71 B7
Buffalo Springs ⌂ *Kenya* 0°32N 37°35E 54 B4
Buffels → *S. Africa* 29°36S 17°3E 56 D2
Buford *U.S.A.* 34°10N 84°0W 85 D12
Bug = Buh → *Ukraine* 46°59N 31°58E 19 E5
Bug → *Poland* 52°31N 21°5E 17 B11
Buga *Colombia* 4°0N 76°15W 92 C3
Bugala I. *Uganda* 0°40S 32°20E 54 C3
Buganda *Uganda* 0°0 31°30E 54 C3
Buganga *Uganda* 0°3S 32°0E 54 C3
Bugel, Tanjung *Indonesia* 6°26S 111°3E 37 G14
Bugibba *Malta* 35°57N 14°25E 25 D1
Bugsuk I. *Phil.* 8°12N 117°18E 36 C5
Bugulma *Russia* 54°33N 52°48E 18 D9
Bugun Shara *Mongolia* 49°0N 104°0E 32 B5
Bugungu ⌂ *Uganda* 2°17N 31°50E 54 B3
Buguruslan *Russia* 53°39N 52°26E 18 D9
Buh → *Ukraine* 46°59N 31°58E 19 E5
Buhera *Zimbabwe* 19°18S 31°29E 57 B5
Buhl *U.S.A.* 42°36N 114°46W 76 E6
Builth Wells *U.K.* 52°9N 3°25W 13 E4
Buir Nur *Mongolia* 47°50N 117°42E 33 B6
Buji *China* 22°37N 114°5E 33 F11
Bujumbura *Burundi* 3°16S 29°18E 54 C2
Bukachacha *Russia* 52°55N 116°50E 29 D12
Bukama *Dem. Rep. of the Congo* 9°10S 25°50E 55 D2
Būkān *Iran* 36°31N 46°12E 44 B5
Bukavu *Dem. Rep. of the Congo* 2°20S 28°52E 54 C2
Bukene *Tanzania* 4°15S 32°48E 54 C3
Bukhara = Bukhoro *Uzbekistan* 39°48N 64°25E 28 F7
Bukhoro *Uzbekistan* 39°48N 64°25E 28 F7
Bukima *Tanzania* 1°50S 33°25E 54 C3
Bukit Badung *Indonesia* 8°49S 115°10E 37 K18
Bukit Kerajaan *Malaysia* 5°25N 100°15E 39 c
Bukit Mertajam *Malaysia* 5°22N 100°28E 39 c
Bukit Ni *Malaysia* 1°22N 104°12E 39 d
Bukit Panjang *Singapore* 1°23N 103°46E 39 d
Bukit Tengah *Malaysia* 5°22N 100°25E 39 c
Bukittinggi *Indonesia* 0°20S 100°20E 36 E2
Bukoba *Tanzania* 1°20S 31°49E 54 C3
Bukum, Pulau *Singapore* 1°14N 103°46E 39 d
Bukuya *Uganda* 0°40N 31°52E 54 B3
Būl, Kuh-e *Iran* 30°48N 52°45E 45 D7
Bula *Indonesia* 3°6S 130°30E 37 E8
Bulahdelah *Australia* 32°23S 152°13E 63 E5
Bulan *Phil.* 12°40N 123°52E 37 B6
Bulandshahr *India* 28°28N 77°51E 42 E7
Bulawayo *Zimbabwe* 20°7S 28°32E 55 G2
Buldan *Turkey* 38°2N 28°50E 23 E13
Bulgan *Mongolia* 48°45N 103°34E 32 B5
Bulgar *Russia* 54°57N 49°4E 18 D8
Bulgaria ■ *Europe* 42°35N 25°30E 23 C11
Buli, Teluk *Indonesia* 0°48N 128°25E 37 D7
Buliluyan, C. *Phil.* 8°20N 117°15E 36 C5
Bulim *Singapore* 1°22N 103°43E 39 d
Bulkley → *Canada* 55°15N 127°40W 70 B3
Bull Shoals L. *U.S.A.* 36°22N 92°35W 84 C8
Bulleringa △ *Australia* 17°39S 143°56E 62 B3
Bullhead City *U.S.A.* 35°8N 114°32W 79 K12
Büllingen *Belgium* 50°25N 6°16E 15 D6
Bullock Creek *Australia* 17°43S 144°31E 62 B3
Bulloo → *Australia* 28°43S 142°30E 63 D3
Bulloo L. *Australia* 28°43S 142°25E 63 D3
Bulls *N.Z.* 40°10S 175°24E 59 D5
Bulnes *Chile* 36°42S 72°19W 94 D1
Bulsar = Valsad *India* 20°40N 72°58E 40 J8
Bultfontein *S. Africa* 28°18S 26°10E 56 D4
Bulukumba *Indonesia* 5°33S 120°11E 37 F6
Bulun *Russia* 70°37N 127°30E 29 B13
Bumba *Dem. Rep. of the Congo* 2°13N 22°30E 52 D4
Bumbiri I. *Tanzania* 1°40S 31°55E 54 C3
Bumhpa Bum *Burma* 26°51N 97°14E 41 F20
Bumi → *Zimbabwe* 17°0S 28°20E 55 F2
Buna *Kenya* 2°58N 39°30E 54 B4
Bunaken *Indonesia* 1°37N 124°46E 37 D6
Bunazi *Tanzania* 1°3S 31°23E 54 C3
Bunbah, Khalīj *Libya* 32°20N 23°15E 51 B10
Bunbury *Australia* 33°20S 115°35E 61 F2
Bunclody *Ireland* 52°39N 6°40W 10 D5
Buncrana *Ireland* 55°8N 7°27W 10 A4
Bundaberg *Australia* 24°54S 152°22E 63 C5
Bundey → *Australia* 21°46S 135°37E 62 C2
Bundi *India* 25°30N 75°35E 42 G6
Bundjalung △ *Australia* 29°16S 153°21E 63 D5
Bundoran *Ireland* 54°28N 8°16W 10 B3
Bung Kan *Thailand* 18°23N 103°37E 38 C4
Bungay *U.K.* 52°27N 1°28E 13 E9
Bungil Cr. → *Australia* 27°5S 149°5E 63 D4
Bungle Bungle = Purnululu △ *Australia* 17°20S 128°20E 60 C4
Bungo-Suidō *Japan* 33°0N 132°15E 31 H6
Bungoma *Kenya* 0°34N 34°34E 54 B3
Bungotakada *Japan* 33°35N 131°25E 31 H5
Bungu *Tanzania* 7°35S 39°0E 54 D4
Bunia *Dem. Rep. of the Congo* 1°35N 30°20E 54 B3
Bunji *Pakistan* 35°45N 74°40E 43 B6
Bunkie *U.S.A.* 30°57N 92°11W 84 F8
Bunnell *U.S.A.* 29°28N 81°16W 85 G14
Buntok *Indonesia* 1°40S 114°58E 36 E4
Bunya Mts. △ *Australia* 26°51S 151°34E 63 D5
Bunyu *Indonesia* 3°35N 117°50E 36 D5
Buol *Indonesia* 1°15N 121°32E 37 D6
Buon Brieng *Vietnam* 13°9N 108°12E 38 F7
Buon Ma Thuot *Vietnam* 12°40N 108°3E 38 F7
Buong Long *Cambodia* 13°44N 106°59E 38 F6
Buorkhaya, Mys *Russia* 71°50N 132°40E 29 B14
Buqayq *Si. Arabia* 26°0N 49°45E 45 E6
Bur Acaba *Somali Rep.* 3°12N 44°20E 47 G3
Bûr Safâga *Egypt* 26°43N 33°57E 44 E2
Bûr Sa'îd *Egypt* 31°16N 32°18E 51 B12
Bûr Sûdân *Sudan* 19°32N 37°9E 51 E13
Bura *Kenya* 1°4S 39°58E 54 C4
Burakin *Australia* 30°31S 117°10E 61 F2
Burao *Somali Rep.* 9°32N 45°32E 47 F4
Burāq *Syria* 33°11N 36°29E 46 B5
Buraydah *Si. Arabia* 26°20N 43°59E 44 E4
Burbank *U.S.A.* 34°12N 118°18W 79 L8
Burda *India* 25°50N 77°35E 42 G6
Burdekin → *Australia* 19°38S 147°25E 62 B4
Burdur *Turkey* 37°45N 30°17E 19 G5
Burdwan = Barddhaman *India* 23°14N 87°39E 43 H12
Bure *Ethiopia* 10°40N 37°4E 47 E2
Bure → *U.K.* 52°38N 1°43E 12 E9
Bureya → *Russia* 49°27N 129°30E 29 E13
Burford *Canada* 43°7N 80°27W 82 C4
Burgas *Bulgaria* 42°33N 27°29E 23 C12
Burgeo *Canada* 47°37N 57°38W 73 C8
Burgersdorp *S. Africa* 31°0S 26°20E 56 E4
Burges, Mt. *Australia* 30°50S 121°5E 61 F3
Burghead *U.K.* 57°43N 3°30W 11 D5
Burgos *Spain* 42°21N 3°41W 21 A4
Burgsvik *Sweden* 57°3N 18°19E 9 H18
Burgundy = Bourgogne □ *France* 47°0N 4°50E 20 C6
Burhaniye *Turkey* 39°30N 26°58E 23 E12
Burhanpur *India* 21°18N 76°14E 40 J10
Burhi Gandak → *India* 25°20N 86°37E 43 G12
Burhner → *India* 22°43N 80°31E 43 H9
Burias I. *Phil.* 12°55N 123°5E 37 B6
Burica, Pta. *Costa Rica* 8°3N 82°51W 88 E3
Burien *U.S.A.* 47°28N 122°20W 78 C4
Burigi, L. *Tanzania* 2°2S 31°22E 54 C3
Burigi ⌂ *Tanzania* 2°20S 31°6E 54 C3
Burin *Canada* 47°1N 55°14W 73 C8
Buriram *Thailand* 15°0N 103°0E 38 E4
Burkburnett *U.S.A.* 34°6N 98°34W 84 D5
Burke → *Australia* 23°12S 139°33E 62 C2
Burke Chan. *Canada* 52°10N 127°30W 70 C3
Burketown *Australia* 17°45S 139°33E 62 B2
Burkina Faso ■ *Africa* 12°0N 1°0W 50 F5
Burk's Falls *Canada* 45°37N 79°24W 72 C4
Burleigh Falls *Canada* 44°33N 78°12W 82 B6
Burley *U.S.A.* 42°32N 113°48W 76 E7
Burlingame *U.S.A.* 37°35N 122°21W 78 H4
Burlington *Canada* 43°18N 79°45W 82 C5
Burlington *Colo., U.S.A.* 39°18N 102°16W 76 G12
Burlington *Iowa, U.S.A.* 40°49N 91°14W 80 E8
Burlington *Kans., U.S.A.* 38°12N 95°45W 80 F6
Burlington *N.C., U.S.A.* 36°6N 79°26W 85 C15
Burlington *N.J., U.S.A.* 40°4N 74°51W 83 F10
Burlington *Vt., U.S.A.* 44°29N 73°12W 83 B11
Burlington *Wash., U.S.A.* 48°28N 122°20W 78 B4
Burlington *Wis., U.S.A.* 42°41N 88°17W 80 D9
Burma ■ *Asia* 21°0N 96°30E 41 J20
Burnaby I. *Canada* 52°25N 131°19W 70 C2
Burnet *U.S.A.* 30°45N 98°14W 84 F5
Burney *U.S.A.* 40°53N 121°40W 76 F3
Burnham *U.S.A.* 40°38N 77°34W 82 F7
Burnham-on-Sea *U.K.* 51°14N 3°0W 13 F5
Burnie *Australia* 41°4S 145°56E 63 G4
Burnley *U.K.* 53°47N 2°14W 12 D5
Burns *U.S.A.* 43°35N 119°3W 76 E4
Burns Junction *U.S.A.* 42°47N 117°51W 76 E5
Burns Lake *Canada* 54°14N 125°45W 70 C3
Burnside → *Canada* 66°51N 108°4W 68 C9
Burnside, L. *Australia* 25°22S 123°0E 61 E3
Burnsville *U.S.A.* 44°47N 93°17W 80 C7
Burnt, L. *Canada* 53°35N 64°4W 73 B7
Burnt River *Canada* 44°41N 78°42W 82 B6
Burntwood → *Canada* 56°8N 96°34W 71 B9
Burntwood L. *Canada* 55°22N 100°26W 71 B8
Burqān *Kuwait* 29°0N 47°57E 44 D5
Burqin *China* 47°43N 87°0E 32 B3
Burra *Australia* 33°40S 138°55E 63 E2
Burray *U.K.* 58°51N 2°54W 11 C6
Burren *Ireland* 53°9N 9°5W 10 C2
Burren △ *Ireland* 53°1N 8°58W 10 C3
Burren Junction *Australia* 30°7S 148°58E 63 E4
Burrinjuck Res. *Australia* 35°0S 148°36E 63 F4
Burro, Serranías del *Mexico* 28°56N 102°5W 86 B4
Burrow Hd. *U.K.* 54°41N 4°24W 11 G4
Burrum Coast △ *Australia* 25°13S 152°36E 63 D5
Burruyacú *Argentina* 26°30S 64°40W 94 B3
Burry Port *U.K.* 51°41N 4°15W 13 F3
Bursa *Turkey* 40°15N 29°5E 23 D13
Burstall *Canada* 50°39N 109°54W 71 C7
Burton *Ohio, U.S.A.* 41°28N 81°8W 82 E3
Burton *S.C., U.S.A.* 32°26N 80°43W 85 E14
Burton, L. *Canada* 54°45N 78°20W 72 B4
Burton upon Trent *U.K.* 52°48N 1°38W 12 E6
Buru *Indonesia* 3°30S 126°30E 37 E7
Burûn, Râs *Egypt* 31°14N 33°7E 46 D2
Burundi ■ *Africa* 3°15S 30°0E 54 C3
Bururi *Burundi* 3°57S 29°37E 54 C2
Burutu *Nigeria* 5°20N 5°29E 50 G7
Burwell *U.S.A.* 41°47N 99°8W 80 E4
Burwick *U.K.* 58°45N 2°58W 11 C5
Bury *U.K.* 53°35N 2°17W 12 D5
Bury St. Edmunds *U.K.* 52°15N 0°43E 13 E8
Buryatia □ *Russia* 53°0N 110°0E 29 D11
Busan *S. Korea* 35°5N 129°0E 35 G15
Busango Swamp *Zambia* 14°15S 25°45E 55 E2
Buşayrah *Syria* 35°9N 40°26E 44 C4
Būshehr *Iran* 28°55N 50°55E 45 D6
Būshehr □ *Iran* 28°20N 51°45E 45 D6
Bushell *Canada* 59°31N 108°45W 71 B7
Bushenyi *Uganda* 0°35S 30°10E 54 C3
Bushire = Būshehr *Iran* 28°55N 50°55E 45 D6
Businga *Dem. Rep. of the Congo* 3°16N 20°59E 52 D4
Buşra ash Shām *Syria* 32°30N 36°25E 46 C5
Busselton *Australia* 33°42S 115°15E 61 F2
Bussum *Neths.* 52°16N 5°10E 15 B5
Busto Arsízio *Italy* 45°37N 8°51E 20 D8
Busu Djanoa *Dem. Rep. of the Congo* 1°43N 21°23E 52 D4
Busuanga I. *Phil.* 12°10N 120°0E 37 B5
Busungbiu *Indonesia* 8°16S 114°58E 37 J17
Buta *Dem. Rep. of the Congo* 2°50N 24°53E 54 B1
Butare *Rwanda* 2°31S 29°52E 54 C2
Butaritari *Kiribati* 3°30N 174°0E 64 G9
Bute *U.K.* 55°48N 5°2W 11 F3
Bute Inlet *Canada* 50°40N 124°53W 70 C4
Butemba *Uganda* 1°9N 31°37E 54 B3
Butembo *Dem. Rep. of the Congo* 0°9N 29°18E 54 B2
Butere *Kenya* 0°13N 34°30E 54 B3
Butha Qi *China* 48°0N 122°32E 33 B7
Butiaba *Uganda* 1°50N 31°20E 54 B3
Butler *Mo., U.S.A.* 38°16N 94°20W 80 F6
Butler *Pa., U.S.A.* 40°52N 79°54W 82 F5
Buton *Indonesia* 5°0S 122°45E 37 E6
Butte *Mont., U.S.A.* 46°0N 112°32W 76 C7
Butte *Nebr., U.S.A.* 42°58N 98°51W 80 D4
Butte Creek → *U.S.A.* 39°12N 121°56W 78 F5
Butterworth = Gcuwa *S. Africa* 32°20S 28°11E 57 E4
Butterworth *Malaysia* 5°24N 100°23E 39 c
Buttevant *Ireland* 52°14N 8°40W 10 D3
Buttfield, Mt. *Australia* 24°45S 128°9E 61 D4
Button B. *Canada* 58°45N 94°23W 71 B10
Buttonwillow *U.S.A.* 35°24N 119°28W 79 K7
Butty Hd. *Australia* 33°54S 121°39E 61 F3
Butuan *Phil.* 8°57N 125°33E 37 C7
Butung = Buton *Indonesia* 5°0S 122°45E 37 E6
Buturlinovka *Russia* 50°50N 40°35E 19 D7
Buur Hakaba = Bur Acaba *Somali Rep.* 3°12N 44°20E 47 G3
Buxa Duar *India* 27°45N 89°35E 43 F13
Buxar *India* 25°34N 83°58E 43 G10
Buxoro = Bukhoro *Uzbekistan* 39°48N 64°25E 28 F7
Buxtehude *Germany* 53°28N 9°39E 16 B5
Buxton *U.K.* 53°16N 1°54W 12 D6
Buy *Russia* 58°28N 41°28E 18 C7
Buyant-Uhaa *Mongolia* 44°55N 110°11E 33 B6
Buyo, L. de *Ivory C.* 6°16N 7°10W 50 G4
Büyük Menderes → *Turkey* 37°28N 27°11E 23 F12
Büyükçekmece *Turkey* 41°2N 28°35E 23 D13
Buzău *Romania* 45°10N 26°50E 17 F14
Buzău → *Romania* 45°26N 27°44E 17 F14
Buzen *Japan* 33°35N 131°5E 31 H5
Buzi → *Mozam.* 19°50S 34°43E 55 F3
Büzmeýin *Turkmenistan* 38°3N 58°12E 45 B8
Buzuluk *Russia* 52°48N 52°12E 18 D9
Buzzards Bay *U.S.A.* 41°45N 70°37W 83 E14
Bwana Mkubwe *Dem. Rep. of the Congo* 13°8S 28°38E 55 E2
Bwindi △ *Uganda* 1°2S 29°42E 54 C2
Byarezina → *Belarus* 52°33N 30°14E 17 B16
Bydgoszcz *Poland* 53°10N 18°0E 17 B9
Byelarus = Belarus ■ *Europe* 53°30N 27°0E 17 B14
Byelorussia = Belarus ■ *Europe* 53°30N 27°0E 17 B14
Byers *U.S.A.* 39°43N 104°14W 76 G11
Byesville *U.S.A.* 39°58N 81°32W 82 G3
Byfield △ *Australia* 22°52S 150°45E 62 C5
Byford *Australia* 32°15S 116°0E 61 F2
Bykhaw *Belarus* 53°31N 30°14E 17 B16
Bykhov = Bykhaw *Belarus* 53°31N 30°14E 17 B16
Bylas *U.S.A.* 33°8N 110°7W 77 K8
Bylot *Canada* 58°25N 94°8W 71 B10
Bylot I. *Canada* 73°13N 78°34W 69 B12
Byrd, C. *Antarctica* 69°38S 76°7W 5 C17
Byrock *Australia* 30°40S 146°27E 63 E4
Byron, C. *Australia* 28°43S 153°38E 63 D5
Byron Bay *Australia* 28°43S 153°37E 63 D5
Byrranga, Gory *Russia* 75°0N 100°0E 29 B11
Byrranga Mts. = Byrranga, Gory *Russia* 75°0N 100°0E 29 B11
Byske *Sweden* 64°57N 21°11E 8 D19
Byskeälven → *Sweden* 64°57N 21°13E 8 D19
Bytom *Poland* 50°25N 18°54E 17 C10
Bytów *Poland* 54°10N 17°30E 17 A9
Byumba *Rwanda* 1°35S 30°4E 54 C3

C

C.W. McConaughy, L. *U.S.A.* 41°14N 101°40W 80 E3
Ca → *Vietnam* 18°45N 105°45E 38 C5
Ca Mau *Vietnam* 9°7N 105°8E 39 H5
Ca Mau, Mui *Vietnam* 8°38N 104°44E 39 H5
Ca Na *Vietnam* 11°20N 108°54E 39 G7
Caacupé *Paraguay* 25°23S 57°5W 94 B4
Caaguazú △ *Paraguay* 26°5S 55°31W 95 B4
Caála *Angola* 12°46S 15°30E 53 G3
Caamaño Sd. *Canada* 52°55N 129°25W 70 C3
Caazapá *Paraguay* 26°8S 56°19W 94 B4
Caazapá □ *Paraguay* 26°10S 56°0W 95 B4
Caballeria, C. de *Spain* 40°5N 4°5E 24 A11
Cabanatuan *Phil.* 15°30N 120°58E 37 A6
Cabano *Canada* 47°40N 68°56W 73 C6
Cabazon *U.S.A.* 33°55N 116°47W 79 M10
Cabedelo *Brazil* 7°0S 34°50W 93 E12
Cabildo *Chile* 32°30S 71°5W 94 C1
Cabimas *Venezuela* 10°23N 71°25W 92 A4
Cabinda *Angola* 5°33S 12°11E 52 F2
Cabinda □ *Angola* 5°0S 12°30E 52 F2
Cabinet Mts. *U.S.A.* 48°10N 115°50W 76 B6
Cabo Blanco *Argentina* 47°15S 65°47W 96 F3
Cabo Frio *Brazil* 22°51S 42°3W 95 A7
Cabo Pantoja *Peru* 1°0S 75°10W 92 D3
Cabo San Lucas *Mexico* 22°53N 109°54W 86 C3
Cabo Verde = Cape Verde Is. ■ *Atl. Oc.* 16°0N 24°0W 50 b
Cabonga, Réservoir *Canada* 47°20N 76°40W 72 C4
Cabool *U.S.A.* 37°7N 92°6W 80 G7
Caboolture *Australia* 27°5S 152°58E 63 D5
Cabora Bassa Dam = Cahora Bassa, Represa de *Mozam.* 15°20S 32°50E 55 F3
Caborca *Mexico* 30°37N 112°6W 86 A2
Cabot, Mt. *U.S.A.* 44°30N 71°25W 83 B13
Cabot Hd. *Canada* 45°14N 81°17W 82 A3
Cabot Str. *Canada* 47°15N 59°40W 73 C8
Cabra *Spain* 37°30N 4°28W 21 D3
Cabrera *Spain* 39°8N 2°57E 24 B9
Cabri *Canada* 50°35N 108°25W 71 C7
Cabriel → *Spain* 39°14N 1°3W 21 C5
Caçador *Brazil* 26°47S 51°0W 95 B5
Čačak *Serbia* 43°54N 20°20E 23 C9
Caçapava do Sul *Brazil* 30°30S 53°30W 95 C5
Cáceres *Brazil* 16°5S 57°40W 92 G7
Cáceres *Spain* 39°26N 6°23W 21 C2
Cache Bay *Canada* 46°22N 80°0W 72 C4
Cache Cr. → *U.S.A.* 38°42N 121°42W 78 G5
Cache Creek *Canada* 50°48N 121°19W 70 C4
Cachi *Argentina* 25°5S 66°10W 94 B2
Cachimbo, Serra do *Brazil* 9°30S 55°30W 93 E7
Cachinal de la Sierra *Chile* 24°58S 69°32W 94 A2
Cachoeira *Brazil* 12°30S 39°0W 93 F11
Cachoeira do Sul *Brazil* 30°3S 52°53W 95 C5
Cachoeiro de Itapemirim *Brazil* 20°51S 41°7W 95 A7
Cacoal *Brazil* 11°32S 61°18W 92 F6
Cacólo *Angola* 10°9S 19°21E 52 G3
Caconda *Angola* 13°48S 15°8E 53 G3
Caddo *U.S.A.* 34°7N 96°16W 84 D6
Cader Idris *U.K.* 52°42N 3°53W 13 E4
Cadereyta de Jiménez *Mexico* 25°36N 100°0W 86 B5
Cadibarrawirracanna, L. *Australia* 28°52S 135°27E 63 D2
Cadillac *U.S.A.* 44°15N 85°24W 81 C11
Cadiz *Phil.* 10°57N 123°15E 37 B6
Cádiz *Spain* 36°30N 6°20W 21 D4
Cadiz *Calif., U.S.A.* 34°30N 115°28W 79 L11

Cadiz Ohio, U.S.A. 40°22N 81°0W 82 F4
Cádiz, G. de Spain 36°40N 7°0W 21 D2
Cadiz L. U.S.A. 34°18N 115°24W 77 J6
Cadney Park Australia 27°55S 134°3E 63 D1
Cadomin Canada 53°2N 117°20W 70 C5
Cadotte Lake Canada 56°26N 116°23W 70 B5
Cadoux Australia 30°46S 117°7E 61 F2
Caen France 49°10N 0°22W 20 B3
Caernarfon U.K. 53°8N 4°16W 12 D3
Caernarfon B. U.K. 53°4N 4°40W 12 D3
Caernarvon = Caernarfon U.K. 53°8N 4°16W 12 D3
Caerphilly U.K. 51°35N 3°13W 13 F4
Caerphilly □ U.K. 51°37N 3°12W 13 F4
Caesarea Israel 32°30N 34°53E 46 C3
Caetité Brazil 13°50S 42°32W 93 F10
Cafayate Argentina 26°2S 66°0W 94 B2
Cafu Angola 16°30S 15°8E 56 B2
Cagayan de Oro Phil. 8°30N 124°40E 37 C6
Cagayan Is. Phil. 9°40N 121°16E 37 C5
Cágliari Italy 39°13N 9°7E 22 E3
Cágliari, G. di Italy 39°8N 9°11E 22 E3
Caguán → Colombia 0°8S 74°18W 92 D4
Caguas Puerto Rico 18°14N 66°2W 89 d
Caha Mts. Ireland 51°45N 9°40W 10 E2
Cahama Angola 16°17S 14°19E 56 B1
Caher Ireland 52°22N 7°56W 10 D4
Cahersiveen Ireland 51°56N 10°14W 10 E1
Cahora Bassa, L. de Mozam. 15°35S 32°0E 55 F3
Cahora Bassa, Represa de Mozam. 15°20S 32°50E 55 F3
Cahore Pt. Ireland 52°33N 6°12W 10 D5
Cahors France 44°27N 1°27E 20 D4
Cahul Moldova 45°50N 28°15E 17 F15
Cai Bau, Dao Vietnam 21°10N 107°27E 38 B6
Cai Nuoc Vietnam 8°56N 105°1E 39 H5
Caia Mozam. 17°51S 35°24E 55 F4
Caianda Angola 11°2S 23°31E 55 E1
Caibarién Cuba 22°30N 79°30W 88 B4
Caicara Venezuela 7°38N 66°10W 92 B5
Caicó Brazil 6°20S 37°0W 93 E11
Caicos Is. Turks & Caicos 21°40N 71°40W 89 B5
Caicos Passage W. Indies 22°45N 72°45W 89 B5
Caird Coast Antarctica 75°0S 25°0W 5 D1
Cairn Gorm U.K. 57°7N 3°39W 11 D5
Cairngorm Mts. U.K. 57°6N 3°42W 11 D5
Cairngorms △ U.K. 57°10N 3°50W 11 D5
Cairnryan U.K. 54°59N 5°1W 11 G3
Cairns Australia 16°57S 145°45E 62 B4
Cairns L. Canada 51°42N 94°30W 71 C10
Cairo = El Qâhira Egypt 30°2N 31°13E 51 B12
Cairo Ga., U.S.A. 30°52N 84°13W 85 F12
Cairo Ill., U.S.A. 37°0N 89°11W 80 G9
Cairo N.Y., U.S.A. 42°18N 74°0W 83 D10
Caithness U.K. 58°25N 3°35W 11 C5
Caithness, Ord of U.K. 58°8N 3°36W 11 C5
Caja de Muertos, I. Puerto Rico 17°54N 66°32W 89 d
Cajamarca Peru 7°5S 78°28W 92 E3
Cajàzeiras Brazil 6°52S 38°30W 93 E11
Cala d'Or Spain 39°23N 3°14E 24 B10
Cala en Porter Spain 39°52N 4°8E 24 B11
Cala Figuera, C. de Spain 39°27N 2°31E 24 B9
Cala Forcat Spain 40°0N 3°47E 24 B10
Cala Major Spain 39°33N 2°37E 24 B9
Cala Mezquida = Sa Mesquida Spain 39°55N 4°16E 24 B11
Cala Millor Spain 39°35N 3°22E 24 B10
Cala Ratjada Spain 39°43N 3°27E 24 B10
Cala Santa Galdana Spain 39°56N 3°58E 24 B10
Calabar Nigeria 4°57N 8°20E 50 H7
Calabogie Canada 45°18N 76°43W 83 A8
Calabozo Venezuela 9°0N 67°28W 92 B5
Calábria □ Italy 39°0N 16°30E 22 E7
Calafate Argentina 50°19S 72°15W 96 G2
Calahorra Spain 42°18N 1°59W 21 A5
Calais France 50°57N 1°56E 20 A4
Calais U.S.A. 45°11N 67°17W 81 C20
Calakmul ⌂ Mexico 18°14N 89°48W 87 D7
Calalaste, Cord. de Argentina 25°0S 67°0W 94 B2
Calama Brazil 8°0S 62°50W 92 E6
Calama Chile 22°30S 68°55W 94 A2
Calamar Colombia 10°15N 74°55W 92 A4
Calamian Group Phil. 11°50N 119°55E 37 B5
Calamocha Spain 40°50N 1°17W 21 B5
Calang Indonesia 4°37N 95°37E 36 D1
Calanscio, Sarīr Libya 27°30N 21°30E 51 C10
Calapan Phil. 13°25N 121°7E 37 B6
Călăraşi Romania 44°12N 27°20E 17 F14
Calatayud Spain 41°20N 1°40W 21 B5
Calauag Phil. 13°55N 122°15E 37 B6
Calavite, C. Phil. 13°26N 120°20E 37 B6
Calbayog Phil. 12°4N 124°38E 37 B6
Calca Peru 13°22S 72°0W 92 F4
Calcasieu L. U.S.A. 29°55N 93°18W 84 G8
Calcutta = Kolkata India 22°34N 88°21E 43 H13
Calcutta U.S.A. 40°40N 80°34W 82 F4
Caldas da Rainha Portugal 39°24N 9°8W 21 C1
Calder → U.K. 53°44N 1°22W 12 D6
Caldera Chile 27°5S 70°55W 94 B1
Caldera de Taburiente △ Canary Is. 28°43N 17°52W 24 F2
Caldwell Idaho, U.S.A. 43°40N 116°41W 76 E5
Caldwell Kans., U.S.A. 37°2N 97°37W 80 G5
Caldwell Tex., U.S.A. 30°32N 96°42W 84 F6
Caledon S. Africa 34°14S 19°26E 56 E2
Caledon → S. Africa 30°31S 26°5E 56 E4
Caledon B. Australia 12°45S 137°0E 62 A2
Caledonia Canada 43°7N 79°58W 82 C5
Caledonia U.S.A. 42°58N 77°51W 82 D7
Calemba Angola 16°0S 15°44E 56 B2
Calen Australia 20°56S 148°48E 62 J6
Caletones Chile 34°6S 70°27W 94 C1
Calexico U.S.A. 32°40N 115°30W 79 N11
Calf of Man I. of Man 54°3N 4°48W 12 C3
Calgary Canada 51°0N 114°10W 70 C6
Calheta Madeira 32°44N 17°11W 24 D2
Calhoun U.S.A. 34°30N 84°57W 85 D12
Cali Colombia 3°25N 76°35W 92 C3
Calicut India 11°15N 75°43E 40 P9
Caliente U.S.A. 37°37N 114°31W 77 H6
California Mo., U.S.A. 38°38N 92°34W 80 F7
California Pa., U.S.A. 40°4N 79°54W 82 F5
California □ U.S.A. 37°30N 119°30W 78 H7
California, Baja, T.N. = Baja California □ Mexico 30°0N 115°0W 86 B2
California, Baja, T.S. = Baja California Sur □ Mexico 25°50N 111°50W 86 B2
California, G. de Mexico 27°0N 111°0W 86 B2
California City U.S.A. 35°10N 117°55W 79 K9
California Hot Springs U.S.A. 35°51N 118°41W 79 K8
Calilegua △ Argentina 25°36S 64°50W 94 B3
Calingasta Argentina 31°15S 69°30W 94 C2
Calipatria U.S.A. 33°8N 115°31W 79 M11
Calistoga U.S.A. 38°35N 122°35W 78 G4
Calitzdorp S. Africa 33°33S 21°42E 56 E3
Callabonna, L. Australia 29°40S 140°5E 63 D3
Callan Ireland 52°32N 7°24W 10 D4
Callander U.K. 56°15N 4°13W 11 E4
Callao Peru 12°3S 77°8W 92 F3
Callicoon U.S.A. 41°46N 75°3W 83 E9
Calling Lake Canada 55°15N 113°12W 70 B6
Calliope Australia 24°0S 151°16E 62 C5
Calne U.K. 51°26N 2°0W 13 F6
Calola Angola 16°25S 17°48E 56 B2
Caloundra Australia 26°45S 153°10E 63 D5
Calpella U.S.A. 39°14N 123°12W 78 F3
Calpine U.S.A. 39°40N 120°27W 78 F6
Calstock Canada 49°47N 84°9W 72 C3
Caltagirone Italy 37°14N 14°31E 22 F6
Caltanissetta Italy 37°29N 14°4E 22 F6
Calulo Angola 10°1S 14°56E 52 G2
Calvert → Australia 16°17S 137°44E 62 B2
Calvert I. Canada 51°30N 128°0W 70 C3
Calvert Ra. Australia 24°0S 122°30E 60 D3
Calvi France 42°34N 8°45E 20 E8
Calviá Spain 39°34N 2°31E 21 C7
Calvillo Mexico 21°51N 102°43W 86 C4
Calvinia S. Africa 31°28S 19°45E 56 E2
Calwa U.S.A. 36°42N 119°46W 78 J7
Cam → U.K. 52°21N 0°16E 13 E8
Cam Lam Vietnam 11°54N 109°10E 39 G7
Cam Pha Vietnam 21°7N 107°18E 38 B6
Cam Ranh Vietnam 11°54N 109°12E 39 G7
Cam Xuyen Vietnam 18°15N 106°0E 38 C6
Camabatela Angola 8°20S 15°26E 52 F3
Camacha Madeira 32°41N 16°49W 24 D3
Camacupa Angola 11°58S 17°22E 53 G3
Camagüey Cuba 21°20N 77°55W 88 B4
Camaná Peru 16°30S 72°50W 92 G4
Camanche Res. U.S.A. 38°14N 121°1W 78 G6
Camaquã Brazil 30°51S 51°49W 95 C5
Camaquã → Brazil 31°17S 51°47W 95 C5
Câmara de Lobos Madeira 32°39N 16°59W 24 D3
Camargo Mexico 26°19N 98°50W 87 B5
Camarillo U.S.A. 34°13N 119°2W 79 L7
Camarón, C. Honduras 16°0N 85°5W 88 C2
Camarones Argentina 44°50S 65°40W 96 E3
Camas U.S.A. 45°35N 122°24W 78 E4
Camas Valley U.S.A. 43°2N 123°40W 76 E2
Camballin Australia 17°59S 124°12E 60 C3
Cambará Brazil 23°2S 50°5W 95 A5
Cambay = Khambhat India 22°23N 72°33E 42 H5
Cambay, G. of = Khambhat, G. of India 20°45N 72°30E 40 J8
Cambodia ■ Asia 12°15N 105°0E 38 F5
Camborne U.K. 50°12N 5°19W 13 G2
Cambrai France 50°11N 3°14E 20 A5
Cambria U.S.A. 35°34N 121°5W 78 K5
Cambrian Mts. U.K. 52°3N 3°57W 13 E4
Cambridge Canada 43°23N 80°15W 82 C4
Cambridge Jamaica 18°18N 77°54W 88 a
Cambridge N.Z. 37°54S 175°29E 59 B5
Cambridge U.K. 52°12N 0°8E 13 E8
Cambridge Mass., U.S.A. 42°23N 71°7W 83 D13
Cambridge Minn., U.S.A. 45°34N 93°13W 80 C7
Cambridge N.Y., U.S.A. 43°2N 73°22W 83 C11
Cambridge Nebr., U.S.A. 40°17N 100°10W 80 E3
Cambridge Ohio, U.S.A. 40°2N 81°35W 82 F3
Cambridge Bay = Ikaluktutiak Canada 69°10N 105°0W 68 C9
Cambridge G. Australia 14°55S 128°15E 60 B4
Cambridge Springs U.S.A. 41°48N 80°4W 82 E4
Cambridgeshire □ U.K. 52°25N 0°7W 13 E7
Cambuci Brazil 21°35S 41°55W 95 A7
Cambundi-Catembo Angola 10°10S 17°35E 52 G3
Camden Ala., U.S.A. 31°59N 87°17W 85 F11
Camden Ark., U.S.A. 33°35N 92°50W 84 E8
Camden Maine, U.S.A. 44°13N 69°4W 81 C19
Camden N.J., U.S.A. 39°55N 75°7W 83 G9
Camden N.Y., U.S.A. 43°20N 75°45W 83 C9
Camden S.C., U.S.A. 34°16N 80°36W 85 D14
Camden Sd. Australia 15°27S 124°25E 60 C3
Camdenton U.S.A. 38°1N 92°45W 80 F7
Camelford U.K. 50°37N 4°42W 13 G3
Cameron Ariz., U.S.A. 35°53N 111°25W 77 J8
Cameron La., U.S.A. 29°48N 93°20W 84 G8
Cameron Mo., U.S.A. 39°44N 94°14W 80 F6
Cameron Tex., U.S.A. 30°51N 96°59W 84 F6
Cameron Highlands Malaysia 4°27N 101°22E 39 K3
Cameron Hills Canada 59°48N 118°0W 70 B5
Cameroon ■ Africa 6°0N 12°30E 51 G7
Cameroun, Mt. Cameroon 4°13N 9°10E 52 D1
Cametá Brazil 2°12S 49°30W 93 D9
Camiguin I. Phil. 18°56N 121°55E 37 C6
Camilla U.S.A. 31°14N 84°12W 85 F12
Caminha Portugal 41°50N 8°50W 21 B1
Camino U.S.A. 38°44N 120°41W 78 G6
Camira Creek Australia 29°15S 152°58E 63 D5
Cammal U.S.A. 41°24N 77°28W 82 E7
Camocim Brazil 2°55S 40°50W 93 D10
Camooweal Australia 19°56S 138°7E 62 B2
Camooweal Caves △ Australia 20°1S 138°11E 62 C2
Camopi Fr. Guiana 3°12N 52°17W 93 C8
Camp Borden Canada 44°18N 79°56W 82 B5
Camp Hill U.S.A. 40°14N 76°55W 82 F8
Camp Nelson U.S.A. 36°8N 118°39W 79 J8
Camp Pendleton U.S.A. 33°13N 117°24W 79 M9
Camp Verde U.S.A. 34°34N 111°51W 77 J8
Camp Wood U.S.A. 29°40N 100°1W 84 G4
Campana Argentina 34°10S 58°55W 94 C4
Campana, I. Chile 48°20S 75°20W 96 F1
Campanário Madeira 32°39N 17°2W 24 D2
Campânia □ Italy 41°0N 14°30E 22 D6
Campbell S. Africa 28°48S 23°44E 56 D3
Campbell Calif., U.S.A. 37°17N 121°57W 78 H5
Campbell Ohio, U.S.A. 41°5N 80°37W 82 E4
Campbell I. Pac. Oc. 52°30S 169°0E 64 N8
Campbell L. Canada 63°14N 106°55W 71 A7
Campbell Plateau S. Ocean 50°0S 170°0E 5 A11
Campbell River Canada 50°5N 125°20W 70 C3
Campbell Town Australia 41°52S 147°30E 63 G4
Campbellford Canada 44°18N 77°48W 82 B7
Campbellpur Pakistan 33°46N 72°26E 42 C5
Campbellsville U.S.A. 37°21N 85°20W 81 G11
Campbellton Canada 47°57N 66°43W 73 C6
Campbelltown Australia 34°4S 150°49E 63 E5
Campbeltown U.K. 55°26N 5°36W 11 F3
Campeche Mexico 19°51N 90°32W 87 D6
Campeche □ Mexico 19°0N 90°30W 87 D6
Campeche, Golfo de Mexico 19°30N 93°0W 87 D6
Camperdown Australia 38°14S 143°9E 63 F3
Camperville Canada 51°59N 100°9W 71 C8
Câmpina Romania 45°10N 25°45E 17 F13
Campina Grande Brazil 7°20S 35°47W 93 E11
Campinas Brazil 22°50S 47°0W 95 A6
Campo Grande Brazil 20°25S 54°40W 93 H8
Campo Maior Brazil 4°50S 42°12W 93 D10
Campo Mourão Brazil 24°3S 52°22W 95 A5
Campobasso Italy 41°34N 14°39E 22 D6
Campos Brazil 21°50S 41°20W 95 A7
Campos Spain 39°26N 3°1E 24 B10
Campos Belos Brazil 13°10S 47°3W 93 F9
Campos Novos Brazil 27°21S 51°50W 95 B5
Camptonville U.S.A. 39°27N 121°3W 78 F5
Camptown U.S.A. 41°44N 76°14W 83 E8
Câmpulung Romania 45°17N 25°3E 17 F13
Camrose Canada 53°0N 112°50W 70 C6
Camsell Portage Canada 59°37N 109°15W 71 B7
Çan Turkey 40°2N 27°3E 23 D12
Can Clavo Spain 38°57N 1°27E 24 C7
Can Creu Spain 38°58N 1°28E 24 C7
Can Gio Vietnam 10°25N 106°58E 39 G6
Can Tho Vietnam 10°2N 105°46E 39 G5
Canaan U.S.A. 42°2N 73°20W 83 D11
Canada ■ N. Amer. 60°0N 100°0W 68 D10
Canada Abyssal Plain Arctic 80°0N 140°0W 4 B18
Canada Basin Arctic 80°0N 145°0W 4 B18
Cañada de Gómez Argentina 32°40S 61°30W 94 C3
Canadian U.S.A. 35°55N 100°23W 84 D4
Canadian → U.S.A. 35°28N 95°3W 84 D7
Canadian Shield Canada 53°0N 75°0W 66 D12
Canajoharie U.S.A. 42°54N 74°35W 83 D10
Çanakkale Turkey 40°8N 26°24E 23 D12
Çanakkale Boğazı Turkey 40°17N 26°32E 23 D12
Canal Flats Canada 50°10N 115°48W 70 C5
Canalejas Argentina 35°15S 66°34W 94 D2
Canals Argentina 33°35S 62°53W 94 C3
Canandaigua U.S.A. 42°54N 77°17W 82 D7
Canandaigua L. U.S.A. 42°47N 77°19W 82 D7
Cananea Mexico 31°0N 110°18W 86 A2
Canarias, Is. Atl. Oc. 28°30N 16°0W 24 F4
Canaries St. Lucia 13°55N 61°4W 89 f
Canarreos, Arch. de los Cuba 21°35N 81°40W 88 B3
Canary Is. = Canarias, Is. Atl. Oc. 28°30N 16°0W 24 F4
Canaseraga U.S.A. 42°27N 77°45W 82 D7
Canatlán Mexico 24°31N 104°47W 86 C4
Canaveral, C. U.S.A. 28°27N 80°32W 85 G14
Canaveral ⌂ U.S.A. 28°28N 80°34W 85 G14
Canavieiras Brazil 15°39S 39°0W 93 G11
Canberra Australia 35°15S 149°8E 63 F4
Canby Calif., U.S.A. 41°27N 120°52W 76 F3
Canby Minn., U.S.A. 44°43N 96°16W 80 C5
Canby Oreg., U.S.A. 45°16N 122°42W 78 E4
Cancún Mexico 21°8N 86°44W 87 C7
Candelaria Argentina 27°29S 55°44W 95 B4
Candelaria Canary Is. 28°22N 16°22W 24 F3
Candelo Australia 36°47S 149°43E 63 F4
Candi Dasa Indonesia 8°30S 115°34E 37 J18
Candia = Iraklio Greece 35°20N 25°12E 25 D7
Candle L. Canada 53°50N 105°18W 71 C7
Candlemas I. Antarctica 57°3S 26°40W 5 B1
Cando U.S.A. 48°32N 99°12W 80 A4
Canea = Chania Greece 35°30N 24°4E 25 D6
Canelones Uruguay 34°32S 56°17W 95 C4
Cañete Chile 37°50S 73°30W 94 D1
Cañete Peru 13°8S 76°30W 92 F3
Cangas de Narcea Spain 43°10N 6°32W 21 A2
Canguaretama Brazil 6°20S 35°5W 93 E11
Canguçu Brazil 31°22S 52°43W 95 C5
Canguçu, Serra do Brazil 31°20S 52°40W 95 C5
Cangzhou China 38°19N 116°52E 34 E9
Caniapiscau → Canada 56°40N 69°30W 73 A6
Caniapiscau, L. Canada 54°10N 69°55W 73 B6
Canicattì Italy 37°21N 13°51E 22 F5
Canim Lake Canada 51°47N 120°54W 70 C4
Canindeyu □ Paraguay 24°10S 55°0W 95 A5
Canisteo U.S.A. 42°16N 77°36W 82 D7
Canisteo → U.S.A. 42°7N 77°8W 82 D7
Cañitas de Felipe Pescador Mexico 23°36N 102°43W 86 C4
Çankırı Turkey 40°40N 33°37E 19 F5
Cankuzo Burundi 3°10S 30°31E 54 C3
Canmore Canada 51°7N 115°18W 70 C5
Cann River Australia 37°35S 149°7E 63 F4
Canna U.K. 57°3N 6°33W 11 D2
Cannanore India 11°53N 75°27E 40 P9
Cannes France 43°32N 7°1E 20 E7
Canning Town = Port Canning India 22°23N 88°40E 43 H13
Cannington Canada 44°20N 79°2W 82 B5
Cannock U.K. 52°41N 2°1W 13 E5
Cannonball → U.S.A. 46°26N 100°35W 80 B3
Cannondale Mt. Australia 25°13S 148°57E 62 D4
Cannonsville Res. U.S.A. 42°4N 75°22W 83 D9
Cannonvale Australia 20°17S 148°43E 62 J6
Canoas Brazil 29°56S 51°11W 95 B5
Canoe L. Canada 55°10N 108°15W 71 B7
Cañon City U.S.A. 38°27N 105°14W 76 G11
Cañón de Río Blanco △ Mexico 18°43N 97°15W 87 D5
Cañón del Sumidero △ Mexico 19°22N 96°24W 87 D5
Canonniers Pt. Mauritius 20°2S 57°32E 53 d
Canora Canada 51°40N 102°30W 71 C8
Canowindra Australia 33°35S 148°38E 63 E4
Canso Canada 45°20N 61°0W 73 C7
Cantabria □ Spain 43°10N 4°0W 21 A4
Cantabrian Mts. = Cantábrica, Cordillera Spain 43°0N 5°10W 21 A3
Cantábrica, Cordillera Spain 43°0N 5°10W 21 A3
Cantal, Plomb du France 45°3N 2°45E 20 D5
Canterbury Australia 25°23S 141°53E 62 D3
Canterbury U.K. 51°16N 1°6E 13 F9
Canterbury Bight N.Z. 44°16S 171°55E 59 F3
Canterbury Plains N.Z. 43°55S 171°22E 59 E3
Cantil U.S.A. 35°18N 117°58W 79 K9
Canton = Guangzhou China 23°6N 113°13E 33 D6
Canton Ga., U.S.A. 34°14N 84°29W 85 D12
Canton Ill., U.S.A. 40°33N 90°2W 80 E8
Canton Miss., U.S.A. 32°37N 90°2W 85 E9
Canton Mo., U.S.A. 40°8N 91°32W 80 E8
Canton N.Y., U.S.A. 44°36N 75°10W 83 B9
Canton Ohio, U.S.A. 40°48N 81°23W 82 F3
Canton Pa., U.S.A. 41°39N 76°51W 82 E8
Canton S. Dak., U.S.A. 43°18N 96°35W 80 D5
Canton L. U.S.A. 36°6N 98°35W 84 C5
Canudos Brazil 7°13S 58°5W 92 E7
Canumã → Brazil 3°55S 59°10W 92 D7
Canutama Brazil 6°30S 64°20W 92 E6
Canutillo U.S.A. 31°55N 106°36W 84 F1
Canvey U.K. 51°31N 0°37E 13 F8
Canyon U.S.A. 34°59N 101°55W 84 D4
Canyon De Chelly ⌂ U.S.A. 36°10N 109°20W 77 H9
Canyonlands △ U.S.A. 38°15N 110°0W 77 G9
Canyons of the Ancients ⌂ U.S.A. 37°30N 108°55W 77 H9
Canyonville U.S.A. 42°56N 123°17W 76 E2
Cao Bang Vietnam 22°40N 106°15E 38 A6
Cao He → China 40°10N 124°32E 35 D13
Cao Lanh Vietnam 10°27N 105°38E 39 G5
Cao Xian China 34°50N 115°35E 34 G8
Cap-aux-Meules Canada 47°23N 61°52W 73 C7
Cap-Chat Canada 49°6N 66°40W 73 C6
Cap-de-la-Madeleine Canada 46°22N 72°31W 72 C5
Cap-Haïtien Haiti 19°40N 72°20W 89 C5
Cap Pt. St. Lucia 14°7N 60°57W 89 f
Capac U.S.A. 43°1N 82°56W 82 C2
Capanaparo → Venezuela 7°1N 67°7W 92 B5
Cape → Australia 20°59S 146°51E 62 C4
Cape Arid △ Australia 33°58S 123°13E 61 F3
Cape Barren I. Australia 40°25S 148°15E 63 G4
Cape Breton Highlands △ Canada 46°50N 60°40W 73 C7
Cape Breton I. Canada 46°0N 60°30W 73 C7
Cape Charles U.S.A. 37°16N 76°1W 81 G15
Cape Coast Ghana 5°5N 1°15W 50 G5
Cape Cod ⌂ U.S.A. 41°56N 70°6W 81 E18
Cape Coral U.S.A. 26°33N 81°57W 85 H14
Cape Dorset Canada 64°14N 76°32W 69 C12
Cape Fear → U.S.A. 33°53N 78°1W 85 E15
Cape Girardeau U.S.A. 37°19N 89°32W 80 G9
Cape Hatteras ⌂ U.S.A. 35°30N 75°28W 85 D17
Cape Le Grand △ Australia 33°54S 122°26E 61 F3
Cape Lookout ⌂ U.S.A. 35°45N 76°25W 85 D16
Cape May U.S.A. 38°56N 74°56W 81 F16
Cape May Point U.S.A. 38°56N 74°58W 81 F16
Cape Melville △ Australia 14°26S 144°28E 62 A3
Cape Peninsula △ S. Africa 34°20S 18°28E 56 E2
Cape Range △ Australia 22°3S 114°0E 60 D1
Cape Tormentine Canada 46°8N 63°47W 73 C7
Cape Town S. Africa 33°55S 18°22E 56 E2
Cape Tribulation △ Australia 16°5S 145°25E 62 B4
Cape Verde Is. ■ Atl. Oc. 16°0N 24°0W 50 b
Cape Vincent U.S.A. 44°8N 76°20W 83 B8
Cape York Peninsula Australia 12°0S 142°30E 62 A3
Capela Brazil 10°30S 37°0W 93 F11
Capella Australia 23°2S 148°1E 62 C4
Capesterre-Belle-Eau Guadeloupe 16°4N 61°36W 88 b
Capesterre-de-Marie-Galante Guadeloupe 15°53N 61°14W 88 b
Capim → Brazil 1°40S 47°47W 93 D9
Capitan U.S.A. 33°35N 105°35W 77 K11
Capitán Arturo Prat Antarctica 63°0S 61°0W 5 C17
Capitol Reef △ U.S.A. 38°15N 111°10W 77 G8
Capitola U.S.A. 36°59N 121°57W 78 J5
Capoche → Mozam. 15°35S 33°0E 55 F3
Capraia Italy 43°2N 9°50E 20 E8
Capreol Canada 46°43N 80°56W 72 C3
Capri Italy 40°33N 14°14E 22 D6
Capricorn Group Australia 23°30S 151°55E 62 C5
Capricorn Ra. Australia 23°20S 116°50E 60 D2
Caprivi Game ⌂ Namibia 17°55S 22°37E 56 B3
Caprivi Strip Namibia 18°0S 23°0E 56 B3
Captain's Flat Australia 35°35S 149°27E 63 F4
Capulin Volcano ⌂ U.S.A. 36°47N 103°58W 84 C3
Caquetá → Colombia 1°15S 69°15W 92 D5
Caracal Romania 44°8N 24°22E 17 F13
Caracas Venezuela 10°30N 66°55W 92 A5
Caracol Belize 16°45N 89°6E 88 C2
Caracol Mato Grosso do Sul, Brazil 22°18S 57°1W 94 A4
Caracol Piauí, Brazil 9°15S 43°22W 93 E10
Carajas Brazil 6°5S 50°23W 93 E8
Carajás, Serra dos Brazil 6°0S 51°30W 93 E8
Carangola Brazil 20°44S 42°5W 95 A7
Caransebeş Romania 45°28N 22°18E 17 F12
Caraquet Canada 47°48N 64°57W 73 C6
Caras Peru 9°3S 77°47W 92 E3
Caratasca, L. Honduras 15°20N 83°40W 88 C3
Caratinga Brazil 19°50S 42°10W 93 G10
Caraúbas Brazil 5°43S 37°33W 93 E11
Caravaca de la Cruz Spain 38°8N 1°52W 21 C5
Caravelas Brazil 17°45S 39°15W 93 G11
Caraveli Peru 15°45S 73°25W 92 G4
Caravelle, Presqu'île de la Martinique 14°46N 60°48W 88 c
Caràzinho Brazil 28°16S 52°46W 95 B5
Carballo Spain 43°13N 8°41W 21 A1
Carberry Canada 49°50N 99°25W 71 D9
Carbó Mexico 29°42N 110°58W 86 B2
Carbonara, C. Italy 39°6N 9°31E 22 E3
Carbondale Colo., U.S.A. 39°24N 107°13W 76 G10
Carbondale Ill., U.S.A. 37°44N 89°13W 80 G9
Carbondale Pa., U.S.A. 41°35N 75°30W 83 E9
Carbonear Canada 47°42N 53°13W 73 C9
Carbónia Italy 39°10N 8°30E 22 E3
Carcajou Canada 57°47N 117°6W 70 B5
Carcarana → Argentina 32°27S 60°48W 94 C3
Carcasse, C. Haiti 18°30N 74°28W 89 C5
Carcassonne France 43°13N 2°20E 20 E5
Carcross Canada 60°13N 134°45W 70 A2
Cardamon Hills India 9°30N 77°15E 40 Q10
Cárdenas Cuba 23°0N 81°30W 88 B3
Cárdenas San Luis Potosí, Mexico 22°0N 99°38W 87 C5
Cárdenas Tabasco, Mexico 17°59N 93°22W 87 D6
Cardiff U.K. 51°29N 3°10W 13 F4
Cardiff □ U.K. 51°31N 3°12W 13 F4
Cardiff-by-the-Sea U.S.A. 33°1N 117°17W 79 M9
Cardigan U.K. 52°5N 4°40W 13 E3
Cardigan B. U.K. 52°30N 4°30W 13 E3
Cardinal Canada 44°47N 75°23W 83 B9
Cardona Uruguay 33°53S 57°18W 94 C4
Cardoso, Ilha do Brazil 25°8S 47°58W 95 B5
Cardston Canada 49°15N 113°20W 70 D6
Cardwell Australia 18°14S 146°2E 62 B4
Careen L. Canada 57°0N 108°11W 71 B7
Carei Romania 47°40N 22°29E 17 E12
Careme = Ciremay Indonesia 6°55S 108°27E 37 G13
Carey U.S.A. 43°19N 113°57W 76 E7
Carey, L. Australia 29°0S 122°15E 61 E3
Carey L. Canada 62°12N 102°55W 71 A8
Carhué Argentina 37°10S 62°50W 94 D3
Caria Turkey 37°20N 28°10E 23 F13
Cariacica Brazil 20°16S 40°25W 93 H10
Caribbean Sea W. Indies 15°0N 75°0W 89 D5
Cariboo Mts. Canada 53°0N 121°0W 70 C4
Caribou U.S.A. 46°52N 68°1W 81 B19
Caribou → Man., Canada 59°20N 94°44W 71 B10
Caribou → N.W.T., Canada 61°27N 125°45W 70 A3
Caribou I. Canada 47°22N 85°49W 72 C2
Caribou Is. Canada 61°55N 113°15W 70 A6
Caribou L. Man., Canada 59°21N 96°10W 71 B9
Caribou L. Ont., Canada 50°25N 89°5W 72 B2
Caribou Mts. Canada 59°12N 115°40W 70 B5
Caribou River ⌂ Canada 59°35N 96°35W 71 B9
Carichic Mexico 27°56N 107°3W 86 B3
Carinda Australia 30°28S 147°41E 63 E4
Carinhanha Brazil 14°15S 44°46W 93 F10
Carinhanha → Brazil 14°20S 43°47W 93 F10

Carinthia = Kärnten □ Austria 46°52N 13°30E 16 E8
Caripito Venezuela 10°8N 63°6W 92 A6
Carleton, Mt. Canada 47°23N 66°53W 73 C6
Carleton Place Canada 45°8N 76°9W 83 A8
Carletonville S. Africa 26°23S 27°22E 56 D4
Carlin U.S.A. 40°43N 116°7W 76 F5
Carlingford L. U.K. 54°3N 6°9W 10 B5
Carlinville U.S.A. 39°17N 89°53W 80 F9
Carlisle U.K. 54°54N 2°56W 12 C5
Carlisle U.S.A. 40°12N 77°12W 82 F7
Carlisle B. Barbados 13°5N 59°37W 89 g
Carlisle I. Australia 20°49S 149°18E 62 J7
Carlos Casares Argentina 35°32S 61°20W 94 D3
Carlos Tejedor Argentina 35°25S 62°25W 94 D3
Carlow Ireland 52°50N 6°56W 10 D5
Carlow □ Ireland 52°43N 6°50W 10 D5
Carlsbad Calif., U.S.A. 33°10N 117°21W 79 M9
Carlsbad N. Mex., U.S.A. 32°25N 104°14W 77 K11
Carlsbad Caverns △ U.S.A. 32°10N 104°35W 77 K11
Carluke U.K. 55°45N 3°50W 11 F5
Carlyle Canada 49°40N 102°20W 71 D8
Carmacks Canada 62°5N 136°16W 68 C6
Carman Canada 49°30N 98°0W 71 D9
Carmarthen U.K. 51°52N 4°19W 13 F3
Carmarthen B. U.K. 51°40N 4°30W 13 F3
Carmarthenshire □ U.K. 51°55N 4°13W 13 F3
Carmaux France 44°3N 2°10E 20 D5
Carmel U.S.A. 41°26N 73°41W 83 E11
Carmel-by-the-Sea U.S.A. 36°33N 121°55W 78 J5
Carmel Valley U.S.A. 36°29N 121°43W 78 J5
Carmelo Uruguay 34°0S 58°20W 94 C4
Carmen Colombia 9°43N 75°8W 92 B3
Carmen Paraguay 27°13S 56°12W 95 B4
Carmen → Mexico 30°42N 106°29W 86 A3
Carmen, I. Mexico 25°57N 111°12W 86 B2
Carmen de Patagones Argentina 40°50S 63°0W 96 E4
Carmensa Argentina 35°15S 67°40W 94 D2
Carmi Canada 49°36N 119°8W 70 D5
Carmi U.S.A. 38°5N 88°10W 80 F9
Carmichael U.S.A. 38°38N 121°19W 78 G5
Carmila Australia 21°55S 149°24E 62 C4
Carmona Costa Rica 10°0N 85°15W 88 E2
Carmona Spain 37°28N 5°42W 21 D3
Carn Ban U.K. 57°7N 4°15W 11 D4
Carn Eige U.K. 57°17N 5°8W 11 D3
Carnamah Australia 29°41S 115°53E 61 E2
Carnarvon Australia 24°51S 113°42E 61 D1
Carnarvon S. Africa 30°56S 22°8E 56 E3
Carnarvon △ Australia 24°54S 148°2E 62 C4
Carnarvon Ra. Queens., Australia 25°15S 148°30E 62 D4
Carnarvon Ra. W. Austral., Australia 25°20S 120°45E 61 E3
Carnation U.S.A. 47°39N 121°55W 78 C5
Carncastle U.K. 54°54N 5°53W 10 B6
Carndonagh Ireland 55°16N 7°15W 10 A4
Carnduff Canada 49°10N 101°50W 71 D8
Carnegie U.S.A. 40°24N 80°5W 82 F4
Carnegie, L. Australia 26°5S 122°30E 61 E3
Carnegie Ridge Pac. Oc. 1°0S 87°0W 65 H19
Carnic Alps = Karnische Alpen Europe 46°36N 13°0E 16 E7
Carniche Alpi = Karnische Alpen Europe 46°36N 13°0E 16 E7
Carnot C.A.R. 4°59N 15°56E 52 D3
Carnot, C. Australia 34°57S 135°38E 63 E2
Carnot B. Australia 17°20S 122°15E 60 C3
Carnoustie U.K. 56°30N 2°42W 11 E6
Carnsore Pt. Ireland 52°10N 6°22W 10 D5
Caro U.S.A. 43°29N 83°24W 81 D12
Carol City U.S.A. 25°56N 80°14W 85 J14
Carolina Brazil 7°10S 47°30W 93 E9
Carolina Puerto Rico 18°23N 65°58W 89 d
Carolina S. Africa 26°5S 30°6E 57 D5
Caroline I. Kiribati 9°58S 150°13W 65 H12
Caroline Is. Micronesia 8°0N 150°0E 64 G6
Caroni Trin. & Tob. 10°34N 61°23W 93 K15
Caroni → Venezuela 8°21N 62°43W 92 B6
Caronie = Nébrodi, Monti Italy 37°54N 14°35E 22 F6
Caroona Australia 31°24S 150°26E 63 E5
Carpathians Europe 49°30N 21°0E 17 D11
Carpaţii Meridionali Romania 45°30N 25°0E 17 F13
Carpentaria, G. of Australia 14°0S 139°0E 62 A2
Carpentras France 44°3N 5°2E 20 D6
Carpi Italy 44°47N 10°53E 22 B4
Carpinteria U.S.A. 34°24N 119°31W 79 L7
Carr Boyd Ra. Australia 16°15S 128°35E 60 C4
Carra, L. Ireland 53°41N 9°14W 10 C2
Carrabelle U.S.A. 29°51N 84°40W 85 G12
Carranza, Presa V. Mexico 27°20N 100°50W 86 B4
Carrara Italy 44°5N 10°6E 20 D9
Carrauntoohill Ireland 52°0N 9°45W 10 D2
Carrick-on-Shannon Ireland 53°57N 8°5W 10 C3
Carrick-on-Suir Ireland 52°21N 7°24W 10 D4
Carrickfergus U.K. 54°43N 5°49W 10 B6
Carrickmacross Ireland 53°59N 6°43W 10 C5
Carrieton Australia 32°25S 138°31E 63 E2
Carrillo Mexico 26°54N 103°55W 86 B4
Carrington U.S.A. 47°27N 99°8W 80 B4
Carrizal Bajo Chile 28°5S 71°20W 94 B1
Carrizalillo Chile 29°5S 71°30W 94 B1
Carrizo Cr. → U.S.A. 36°55N 103°55W 77 H12
Carrizo Plain ⌂ U.S.A. 35°11N 119°47W 78 K7
Carrizo Springs U.S.A. 28°31N 99°52W 84 G5
Carrizozo U.S.A. 33°38N 105°53W 77 K11
Carroll U.S.A. 42°4N 94°52W 80 D6
Carrollton Ga., U.S.A. 33°35N 85°5W 85 E12
Carrollton Ill., U.S.A. 39°18N 90°24W 80 F8
Carrollton Ky., U.S.A. 38°41N 85°11W 81 F11
Carrollton Mo., U.S.A. 39°22N 93°30W 80 F7
Carrollton Ohio, U.S.A. 40°34N 81°5W 82 F3
Carron → U.K. 57°53N 4°22W 11 D4
Carron, L. U.K. 57°22N 5°35W 11 D3
Carrot → Canada 53°50N 101°17W 71 C8
Carrot River Canada 53°17N 103°35W 71 C8
Carruthers Canada 52°52N 109°16W 71 C7
Carson Calif., U.S.A. 33°49N 118°16W 79 M8
Carson N. Dak., U.S.A. 46°25N 101°34W 80 B3
Carson → U.S.A. 39°45N 118°40W 78 F8
Carson City U.S.A. 39°10N 119°46W 78 F7
Carson Sink U.S.A. 39°50N 118°25W 76 G4
Cartagena Colombia 10°25N 75°33W 92 A3
Cartagena Spain 37°38N 0°59W 21 D5
Cartago Colombia 4°45N 75°55W 92 C3
Cartago Costa Rica 9°50N 83°55W 88 E3
Cartersville U.S.A. 34°10N 84°48W 85 D12
Carterton N.Z. 41°2S 175°31E 59 D5
Carthage Tunisia 36°52N 10°20E 22 F4
Carthage Ill., U.S.A. 40°25N 91°8W 80 E8
Carthage Mo., U.S.A. 37°11N 94°19W 80 G6
Carthage N.Y., U.S.A. 43°59N 75°37W 81 D16
Carthage Tex., U.S.A. 32°9N 94°20W 84 E7
Cartier I. Australia 12°31S 123°29E 60 B3
Cartwright Canada 53°41N 56°58W 73 B8
Caruaru Brazil 8°15S 35°55W 93 E11
Carúpano Venezuela 10°39N 63°15W 92 A6
Caruthersville U.S.A. 36°11N 89°39W 80 G9
Carvoeiro Brazil 1°30S 61°59W 92 D6
Carvoeiro, C. Portugal 39°21N 9°24W 21 C1
Cary U.S.A. 35°47N 78°46W 85 D15
Casa Grande U.S.A. 32°53N 111°45W 77 K8
Casablanca Chile 33°20S 71°25W 94 C1
Casablanca Morocco 33°36N 7°36W 50 B4
Cascada de Basaseachic △ Mexico 28°9N 108°15W 86 B3
Cascade Seychelles 4°39S 55°29E 53 b
Cascade Idaho, U.S.A. 44°31N 116°2W 76 D5
Cascade Mont., U.S.A. 47°16N 111°42W 76 C8
Cascade Locks U.S.A. 45°40N 121°54W 78 E5
Cascade Ra. U.S.A. 47°0N 121°30W 78 D5
Cascade Res. U.S.A. 44°32N 116°3W 76 D5
Cascades, Pte. des Réunion 21°9S 55°51E 53 c
Cascais Portugal 38°41N 9°25W 21 C1
Cascavel Brazil 24°57S 53°28W 95 A5
Cáscina Italy 43°41N 10°33E 22 C4
Casco B. U.S.A. 43°45N 70°0W 81 D19
Caserta Italy 41°4N 14°20E 22 D6
Casey Antarctica 66°0S 76°0E 5 C8
Caseyr, Raas = Asir, Ras Somali Rep. 11°55N 51°10E 47 E5
Cashel Ireland 52°30N 7°53W 10 D4
Casiguran Phil. 16°22N 122°7E 37 A6
Casilda Argentina 33°10S 61°10W 94 C3
Casino Australia 28°52S 153°3E 63 D5
Casiquiare → Venezuela 2°1N 67°7W 92 C5
Casma Peru 9°30S 78°20W 92 E3
Casmalia U.S.A. 34°50N 120°32W 79 L6
Caspe Spain 41°14N 0°1W 21 B5
Casper U.S.A. 42°51N 106°19W 76 E10
Caspian Depression Eurasia 47°0N 48°0E 19 E8
Caspian Sea Eurasia 43°0N 50°0E 19 F9
Cass Lake U.S.A. 47°23N 94°37W 80 B6
Cassadaga U.S.A. 42°20N 79°19W 82 D5
Casselman Canada 45°19N 75°5W 83 A9
Casselton U.S.A. 46°54N 97°13W 80 B5
Cassiar Canada 59°16N 129°40W 70 B3
Cassiar Mts. Canada 59°30N 130°30W 70 B2
Cassino Italy 41°30N 13°49E 22 D5
Cassville U.S.A. 36°41N 93°52W 80 G7
Castaic U.S.A. 34°30N 118°38W 79 L8
Castalia U.S.A. 41°24N 82°49W 82 E2
Castanhal Brazil 1°18S 47°55W 93 D9
Castara Trin. & Tob. 11°17N 60°42W 93 J16
Castellammare di Stábia Italy 40°42N 14°29E 22 D6
Castelli Argentina 36°7S 57°47W 94 D4
Castelló de la Plana Spain 39°58N 0°3W 21 C5
Castelo Brazil 20°33S 41°14W 95 A7
Castelo Branco Portugal 39°50N 7°31W 21 C2
Castelsarrasin France 44°2N 1°7E 20 E4
Castelvetrano Italy 37°41N 12°47E 22 F5
Casterton Australia 37°30S 141°30E 63 F3
Castile U.S.A. 42°38N 78°3W 82 D6
Castilla-La Mancha □ Spain 39°30N 3°30W 21 C4
Castilla y Leon □ Spain 42°0N 5°0W 21 B3
Castillos Uruguay 34°12S 53°52W 95 C5
Castle Dale U.S.A. 39°13N 111°1W 76 G8
Castle Douglas U.K. 54°56N 3°56W 11 G5
Castle Rock Colo., U.S.A. 39°22N 104°51W 76 G11
Castle Rock Wash., U.S.A. 46°17N 122°54W 78 D4
Castlebar Ireland 53°52N 9°18W 10 C2
Castlebay U.K. 56°57N 7°31W 11 E1
Castleblaney Ireland 54°7N 6°44W 10 B5
Castlederg U.K. 54°42N 7°35W 10 B4
Castleford U.K. 53°43N 1°21W 12 D6
Castlegar Canada 49°20N 117°40W 70 D5
Castlemaine Australia 37°2S 144°12E 63 F3
Castlemaine Ireland 52°10N 9°42W 10 D2
Castlepollard Ireland 53°41N 7°19W 10 C4
Castlerea Ireland 53°46N 8°29W 10 C3
Castlereagh → Australia 30°12S 147°32E 63 E4
Castlereagh B. Australia 12°10S 135°10E 62 A2
Castleton U.S.A. 43°37N 73°11W 83 C11
Castletown I. of Man 54°5N 4°38W 12 C3
Castletown Bearhaven Ireland 51°39N 9°55W 10 E2
Castor Canada 52°15N 111°50W 70 C6
Castor → Canada 53°24N 78°58W 72 B4
Castorland U.S.A. 43°53N 75°31W 83 C9
Castres France 43°37N 2°13E 20 E5
Castricum Neths. 52°33N 4°40E 15 B4
Castries St. Lucia 14°2N 60°58W 89 f
Castro Brazil 24°45S 50°0W 95 A6
Castro Chile 42°30S 73°50W 96 E2
Castro Alves Brazil 12°46S 39°33W 93 F11
Castro Valley U.S.A. 37°41N 122°5W 78 H4
Castroville U.S.A. 36°46N 121°45W 78 J5
Castuera Spain 38°43N 5°37W 21 C3
Cat Ba, Dao Vietnam 20°50N 107°0E 38 B6
Cat Ba △ Vietnam 20°47N 107°3E 38 B6
Cat I. Bahamas 24°30N 75°30W 89 B4
Cat L. Canada 51°40N 91°50W 72 B1
Cat Lake Canada 51°40N 91°50W 72 B1
Cat Tien △ Vietnam 11°25N 107°17E 39 G6
Catacamas Honduras 14°54N 85°56W 88 D2
Cataguases Brazil 21°23S 42°39W 95 A7
Catalão Brazil 18°10S 47°57W 93 G9
Çatalca Turkey 41°8N 28°27E 23 D13
Catalina Canada 48°31N 53°4W 73 C9
Catalina Chile 25°13S 69°43W 94 B2
Catalina U.S.A. 32°30N 110°50W 77 K8
Catalonia = Cataluña □ Spain 41°40N 1°15E 21 B6
Cataluña □ Spain 41°40N 1°15E 21 B6
Catamarca Argentina 28°30S 65°50W 94 B2
Catamarca □ Argentina 27°0S 65°50W 94 B2
Catanduanes □ Phil. 13°50N 124°20E 37 B6
Catanduva Brazil 21°5S 48°58W 95 A6
Catánia Italy 37°30N 15°6E 22 F6
Catanzaro Italy 38°54N 16°35E 22 E7
Catarman Phil. 12°28N 124°35E 37 B6
Catatumbo-Bari △ Colombia 9°3N 73°12W 89 E5
Cateel Phil. 7°47N 126°24E 37 C7
Catembe Mozam. 26°0S 32°33E 57 D5
Caterham U.K. 51°15N 0°4W 13 F7
Cathcart S. Africa 32°18S 27°10E 56 E4
Cathedral City U.S.A. 33°47N 116°28W 79 M10
Cathlamet U.S.A. 46°12N 123°23W 78 D3
Catlettsburg U.S.A. 38°25N 82°36W 81 F12
Catoche, C. Mexico 21°35N 87°5W 87 C7
Catriló Argentina 36°26S 63°24W 94 D3
Catrimani Brazil 0°27N 61°41W 92 C6
Catrimani → Brazil 0°28N 61°44W 92 C6
Catskill U.S.A. 42°14N 73°52W 83 D11
Catskill ⌂ U.S.A. 42°8N 74°39W 83 D10
Catskill Mts. U.S.A. 42°10N 74°25W 83 D10
Catt, Mt. Australia 13°49S 134°23E 62 A1
Cattaraugus U.S.A. 42°20N 78°52W 82 D6
Catterick U.K. 54°23N 1°37W 12 C6
Catuala Angola 16°25S 19°2E 56 B2
Catuane Mozam. 26°48S 32°18E 57 D5
Catur Mozam. 13°45S 35°30E 55 E4
Cauca → Colombia 8°54N 74°28W 92 B4
Caucaia Brazil 3°40S 38°35W 93 D11
Caucasus Mountains Eurasia 42°50N 44°0E 19 F7
Caungula Angola 8°26S 18°38E 52 F3
Cauquenes Chile 36°0S 72°22W 94 D1
Caura → Venezuela 7°38N 64°53W 92 B6
Cauresi → Mozam. 17°8S 33°0E 55 F3
Causapscal Canada 48°19N 67°12W 73 C6
Cauvery → India 11°9N 78°52E 40 P11
Caux, Pays de France 49°38N 0°35E 20 B4
Cavalier U.S.A. 48°48N 97°37W 80 A5
Cavan Ireland 54°0N 7°22W 10 B4
Cavan □ Ireland 54°1N 7°16W 10 C4
Cave Creek U.S.A. 33°50N 111°57W 77 K8
Cavenagh Ra. Australia 26°12S 127°55E 61 E4
Cavendish Australia 37°31S 142°2E 63 F3
Caviana, I. Brazil 0°10N 50°10W 93 C8
Cavite Phil. 14°29N 120°54E 37 B6
Cawndilla L. Australia 32°30S 142°15E 63 E3
Cawnpore = Kanpur India 26°28N 80°20E 43 F9
Caxias Brazil 4°55S 43°20W 93 D10
Caxias do Sul Brazil 29°10S 51°10W 95 B5
Cay Sal Bank Bahamas 23°45N 80°0W 88 B4
Cayambe Ecuador 0°3N 78°8W 92 C3
Cayenne Fr. Guiana 5°5N 52°18W 93 B8
Cayey Puerto Rico 18°7N 66°10W 89 d
Cayman Brac Cayman Is. 19°43N 79°49W 88 C4
Cayman Is. ☑ W. Indies 19°40N 80°30W 88 C3
Cayman Trough Caribbean 19°0N 81°0W 66 H11
Cayuga U.S.A. 42°54N 76°44W 83 D8
Cayuga L. U.S.A. 42°41N 76°41W 83 D8
Cazenovia U.S.A. 42°56N 75°51W 83 D9
Cazombo Angola 11°54S 22°56E 53 G4
Ceanannus Mor Ireland 53°44N 6°53W 10 C5
Ceará = Fortaleza Brazil 3°45S 38°35W 93 D11
Ceará □ Brazil 5°0S 40°0W 93 E11
Ceará Mirim Brazil 5°38S 35°25W 93 E11
Cebaco, I. de Panama 7°33N 81°9W 88 E3
Cebollar Argentina 29°10S 66°35W 94 B2
Cebu Phil. 10°18N 123°54E 37 B6
Cecil Plains Australia 27°30S 151°11E 63 D5
Cedar → U.S.A. 41°17N 91°21W 80 E8
Cedar City U.S.A. 37°41N 113°4W 77 H7
Cedar Creek Res. U.S.A. 32°11N 96°4W 84 E6
Cedar Falls Iowa, U.S.A. 42°32N 92°27W 80 D7
Cedar Falls Wash., U.S.A. 47°25N 121°45W 78 C5
Cedar Key U.S.A. 29°8N 83°2W 85 G13
Cedar L. Canada 53°10N 100°0W 71 C9
Cedar Park U.S.A. 30°30N 97°49W 84 F6
Cedar Rapids U.S.A. 41°59N 91°40W 80 E8
Cedartown U.S.A. 34°1N 85°15W 85 D12
Cedarvale Canada 55°1N 128°22W 70 B3
Cedarville S. Africa 30°23S 29°3E 57 E4
Cedral Mexico 23°50N 100°45W 86 C4
Cedro Brazil 6°34S 39°3W 93 E11
Cedros, I. Mexico 28°12N 115°15W 86 B1
Cedros B. Trin. & Tob. 10°16N 61°54W 93 K15
Ceduna Australia 32°7S 133°46E 63 E1
Ceerigaabo = Erigavo Somali Rep. 10°35N 47°20E 47 E4
Cefalù Italy 38°2N 14°1E 22 E6
Cegléd Hungary 47°11N 19°47E 17 E10
Cekik Indonesia 8°12S 114°27E 37 J17
Celaque △ Honduras 14°30N 88°43W 88 D2
Celaya Mexico 20°31N 100°37W 86 C4
Celebes Sea Indonesia 3°0N 123°0E 37 D6
Celina U.S.A. 40°33N 84°35W 81 E11
Celje Slovenia 46°16N 15°18E 16 E8
Celle Germany 52°37N 10°4E 16 B6
Celtic Sea Atl. Oc. 50°9N 9°34W 14 F2
Cenderwasih, Teluk Indonesia 3°0S 135°20E 37 E9
Center N. Dak., U.S.A. 47°7N 101°18W 80 B3
Center Tex., U.S.A. 31°48N 94°11W 84 F7
Centerburg U.S.A. 40°18N 82°42W 82 F2
Centerville Calif., U.S.A. 36°44N 119°30W 78 J7
Centerville Iowa, U.S.A. 40°44N 92°52W 80 E7
Centerville Pa., U.S.A. 40°3N 79°59W 82 F5
Centerville Tenn., U.S.A. 35°47N 87°28W 85 D11
Centerville Tex., U.S.A. 31°16N 95°59W 84 F7
Central = Tsentralnyy □ Russia 52°0N 40°0E 28 D4
Central □ Kenya 0°30S 37°30E 54 C4
Central □ Malawi 13°30S 33°30E 55 E3
Central □ Zambia 14°25S 28°50E 55 E2
Central, Cordillera Colombia 5°0N 75°0W 92 C4
Central, Cordillera Costa Rica 10°10N 84°5W 88 D3
Central, Cordillera Dom. Rep. 19°15N 71°0W 89 C5
Central, Cordillera Puerto Rico 18°8N 66°35W 89 d
Central African Rep. ■ Africa 7°0N 20°0E 51 G9
Central America America 12°0N 85°0W 66 H11
Central Butte Canada 50°48N 106°31W 71 C7
Central City Colo., U.S.A. 39°48N 105°31W 76 G11
Central City Ky., U.S.A. 37°18N 87°7W 80 G10
Central City Nebr., U.S.A. 41°7N 98°0W 80 E4
Central I. Kenya 3°30N 36°0E 54 B4
Central Island △ Kenya 2°33N 36°1E 54 B4
Central Kalahari ⌂ Botswana 22°36S 23°58E 56 C3
Central Makran Range Pakistan 26°30N 64°15E 40 F4
Central Pacific Basin Pac. Oc. 8°0N 175°0W 64 G10
Central Patricia Canada 51°30N 90°9W 72 B1
Central Point U.S.A. 42°23N 122°55W 76 E2
Central Russian Uplands Europe 54°0N 36°0E 6 E13
Central Siberian Plateau Russia 65°0N 105°0E 26 B12
Central Square U.S.A. 43°17N 76°9W 83 C8
Centralia Ill., U.S.A. 38°32N 89°8W 80 F9
Centralia Mo., U.S.A. 39°13N 92°8W 80 F7
Centralia Wash., U.S.A. 46°43N 122°58W 78 D4
Centre de Flacq Mauritius 20°12S 57°43E 53 d
Cephalonia = Kefalonia Greece 38°15N 20°30E 23 E9
Cepu Indonesia 7°9S 111°35E 37 G14
Ceram = Seram Indonesia 3°10S 129°0E 37 E7
Ceram Sea = Seram Sea Indonesia 2°30S 128°30E 37 E7
Ceredigion □ U.K. 52°16N 4°15W 13 E3
Ceres Argentina 29°55S 61°55W 94 B3
Ceres S. Africa 33°21S 19°18E 56 E2
Ceres U.S.A. 37°35N 120°57W 78 H6
Cerf Seychelles 4°38S 55°40E 53 b
Cerignola Italy 41°17N 15°53E 22 D6
Cerigo = Kythira Greece 36°8N 23°0E 23 F10
Çerkezköy Turkey 41°17N 28°0E 23 D12
Cerralvo, I. Mexico 24°15N 109°55W 86 C3
Cerritos Mexico 22°25N 100°16W 86 C4
Cerro Chato Uruguay 33°6S 55°8W 95 C4
Cerro Cofre de Perote △ Mexico 19°29N 97°8W 87 D5
Cerro Corá △ Paraguay 22°35S 56°2W 95 A4
Cerro el Copey △ Venezuela 10°59N 63°53W 89 D7
Cerro Hoya △ Panama 7°17N 80°45W 88 E3
Cerro Saroche △ Venezuela 10°8N 69°38W 89 D6
Cerventes Australia 30°31S 115°3E 61 F2
Cervera Spain 41°40N 1°16E 21 B6
Cesena Italy 44°8N 12°15E 22 B5
Cēsis Latvia 57°18N 25°15E 9 H21
Ceská Rep. = Czech Rep. ■ Europe 50°0N 15°0E 16 D8
České Budějovice Czech Rep. 48°55N 14°25E 16 D8
Českomoravská Vrchovina Czech Rep. 49°30N 15°40E 16 D8
Çeşme Turkey 38°20N 26°23E 23 E12
Cessnock Australia 32°50S 151°21E 63 E5
Cetinje Montenegro 42°23N 18°59E 23 C8
Cetraro Italy 39°31N 15°55E 22 E6
Ceuta N. Afr. 35°52N 5°18W 21 E3
Cévennes France 44°10N 3°50E 20 D5
Ceyhan Turkey 37°4N 35°47E 44 B2
Ceylon = Sri Lanka ■ Asia 7°30N 80°50E 40 R12
Cha-am Thailand 12°48N 99°58E 38 F2
Cha Pa Vietnam 22°20N 103°47E 38 A4
Chacabuco Argentina 34°40S 60°27W 94 C3
Chachapoyas Peru 6°15S 77°50W 92 E3
Chachoengsao Thailand 13°42N 101°5E 38 F3
Chachran Pakistan 28°55N 70°30E 42 E4
Chachro Pakistan 25°5N 70°15E 42 G4
Chaco □ Argentina 26°30S 61°0W 94 B3
Chaco □ Paraguay 26°0S 60°0W 94 B4
Chaco → U.S.A. 36°46N 108°39W 77 H9
Chaco △ Argentina 27°0S 59°30W 94 B4
Chaco Austral S. Amer. 27°0S 61°30W 96 B4
Chaco Boreal S. Amer. 22°0S 60°0W 92 H6
Chaco Central S. Amer. 24°0S 61°0W 96 A4
Chaco Culture ⌂ U.S.A. 36°3N 107°58W 77 H10
Chacon, C. U.S.A. 54°42N 132°0W 70 C2
Chad ■ Africa 15°0N 17°15E 51 F8
Chad, L. = Tchad, L. Chad 13°30N 14°30E 51 F8
Chadan Russia 51°17N 91°35E 29 D10
Chadileuvú → Argentina 37°46S 66°0W 94 D2
Chadiza Zambia 14°45S 32°27E 55 E3
Chadron U.S.A. 42°50N 103°0W 80 D2
Chadyr-Lunga = Ciadâr-Lunga Moldova 46°3N 28°51E 17 E15
Chae Hom Thailand 18°43N 99°35E 38 C2
Chae Son △ Thailand 18°42N 99°20E 38 C2
Chaem → Thailand 18°11N 98°38E 38 C2
Chaeryŏng N. Korea 38°24N 125°36E 35 E13
Chagai Hills = Chāh Gay Hills Afghan. 29°30N 64°0E 40 E3
Chagda Russia 58°45N 130°38E 29 D14
Chaghcharān Afghan. 34°31N 65°15E 40 B4
Chagos Arch. ☑ Ind. Oc. 6°0S 72°0E 26 J9
Chagres △ Panama 9°33N 79°37W 88 E4
Chagrin Falls U.S.A. 41°26N 81°24W 82 E3
Chaguanas Trin. & Tob. 10°30N 61°26W 93 K15
Chāh Ākhvor Iran 32°41N 59°40E 45 C8
Chāh Bahar Iran 25°20N 60°40E 45 E9
Chāh-e Kavīr Iran 34°29N 56°52E 45 C8
Chāh Gay Hills Afghan. 29°30N 64°0E 40 E3
Chahār Borjak Afghan. 30°17N 62°3E 40 D3
Chahār Mahāll va Bakhtīarī □ Iran 32°0N 49°0E 45 C6
Chai Wan China 22°16N 114°14E 33 G11
Chaibasa India 22°42N 85°49E 43 H11
Chainat Thailand 15°11N 100°8E 38 E3
Chaiya Thailand 9°23N 99°14E 39 H2
Chaiyaphum Thailand 15°48N 102°2E 38 E4
Chaj Doab Pakistan 32°15N 73°0E 42 C5
Chajari Argentina 30°42S 58°0W 94 C4
Chak Amru Pakistan 32°22N 75°11E 42 C6
Chakar → Pakistan 29°29N 68°2E 42 E3
Chakari Zimbabwe 18°5S 29°51E 57 B4
Chake Chake Tanzania 5°15S 39°45E 54 D4
Chakhānsūr Afghan. 31°10N 62°0E 40 D3
Chakonipau, L. Canada 56°18N 68°30W 73 A6
Chakradharpur India 22°45N 85°40E 43 H11
Chakrata India 30°42N 77°51E 42 D7
Chakwal Pakistan 32°56N 72°53E 42 C5
Chala Peru 15°48S 74°20W 92 G4
Chalchihuites Mexico 23°29N 103°53W 86 C4
Chalcis = Halkida Greece 38°27N 23°42E 23 E10
Chaleur B. Canada 47°55N 65°30W 73 C6
Chalfant U.S.A. 37°32N 118°21W 78 H8
Chalhuanca Peru 14°15S 73°15W 92 F4
Chalisgaon India 20°30N 75°10E 40 J9
Chalk River Canada 46°1N 77°27W 72 C4
Chalky Inlet N.Z. 46°3S 166°31E 59 G1
Challapata Bolivia 18°53S 66°50W 92 G5
Challenger Deep Pac. Oc. 11°30N 142°0E 64 F6
Challenger Fracture Zone Pac. Oc. 35°0S 105°0W 65 L17
Challis U.S.A. 44°30N 114°14W 76 D6
Chalmette U.S.A. 29°56N 89°57W 85 G10
Chalon-sur-Saône France 46°48N 4°50E 20 C6
Châlons-en-Champagne France 48°58N 4°20E 20 B6
Chālūs Iran 36°38N 51°26E 45 B6
Cham, Cu Lao Vietnam 15°57N 108°30E 38 E7
Chama U.S.A. 36°54N 106°35W 77 H10
Chamaicó Argentina 35°3S 64°58W 94 D3
Chaman Pakistan 30°58N 66°25E 40 D5
Chamba India 32°35N 76°10E 42 C7
Chamba Tanzania 11°37S 37°0E 55 E4
Chambal → India 26°29N 79°15E 43 F8
Chamberlain U.S.A. 43°49N 99°20W 80 D4
Chamberlain → Australia 15°30S 127°54E 60 C4
Chamberlain L. U.S.A. 46°14N 69°19W 81 B19
Chambers U.S.A. 35°11N 109°26W 77 J9
Chambersburg U.S.A. 39°56N 77°40W 81 F15
Chambéry France 45°34N 5°55E 20 D6
Chambeshi → Zambia 11°53S 29°48E 52 G6
Chambly Canada 45°27N 73°17W 83 A11
Chambord Canada 48°25N 72°6W 73 C5
Chamchamal Iraq 35°32N 44°50E 44 C5
Chamela Mexico 19°32N 105°5W 86 D3
Chamical Argentina 30°22S 66°27W 94 C2
Chamkar Luong Cambodia 11°0N 103°45E 39 G4
Chamoli India 30°24N 79°21E 43 D8
Chamonix-Mont Blanc France 45°55N 6°51E 20 D7
Champa India 22°2N 82°43E 43 H10
Champagne Canada 60°49N 136°30W 70 A1
Champagne France 48°40N 4°20E 20 B6
Champaign U.S.A. 40°7N 88°15W 80 E9
Champassak Laos 14°53N 105°52E 38 E5
Champawat India 29°20N 80°6E 43 E9
Champdoré, L. Canada 55°55N 65°49W 73 A6
Champion U.S.A. 41°19N 80°51W 82 E4
Champlain U.S.A. 44°59N 73°27W 83 B11
Champlain, L. U.S.A. 44°40N 73°20W 83 B11
Champotón Mexico 19°21N 90°43W 87 D6
Champua India 22°5N 85°40E 43 H11
Chana Thailand 6°55N 100°44E 39 J3
Chañaral Chile 26°23S 70°40W 94 B1
Chanārān Iran 36°39N 59°6E 45 B8

Chanasma *India* 23°44N 72°5E **42** H5
Chancery Lane *Barbados* 13°3N 59°30W **89** g
Chanco *Chile* 35°44S 72°32W **94** D1
Chand *India* 21°57N 79°7E **43** J8
Chandan *India* 24°38N 86°40E **43** G12
Chandan Chauki *India* 28°33N 80°47E **43** E9
Chandannagar *India* 22°52N 88°24E **43** H13
Chandausi *India* 28°27N 78°49E **43** E8
Chandeleur Is. *U.S.A.* 29°55N 88°57W **85** G10
Chandeleur Sd. *U.S.A.* 29°55N 89°0W **85** G10
Chandigarh *India* 30°43N 76°47E **42** D7
Chandil *India* 22°58N 86°3E **43** H12
Chandler *Australia* 27°0S 133°19E **63** D1
Chandler *Canada* 48°18N 64°46W **73** C7
Chandler *Ariz., U.S.A.* 33°18N 111°50W **77** K8
Chandler *Okla., U.S.A.* 35°42N 96°53W **84** D6
Chandod *India* 21°59N 73°28E **42** J5
Chandpur *Bangla.* 23°8N 90°45E **41** H17
Chandrapur *India* 19°57N 79°25E **40** K11
Chānf *Iran* 26°38N 60°29E **45** E9
Chang *Pakistan* 26°59N 68°30E **42** F3
Chang, Ko *Thailand* 12°0N 102°23E **39** F4
Ch'ang Chiang = Chang Jiang → *China* 31°48N 121°10E **33** C7
Chang Jiang → *China* 31°48N 121°10E **33** C7
Chang-won *S. Korea* 35°16N 128°37E **35** G15
Changa *India* 33°53N 77°35E **43** C7
Changan *China* 22°48N 113°48E **33** F10
Changanacheri *India* 9°25N 76°31E **40** Q10
Changane → *Mozam.* 24°30S 33°30E **57** C5
Changbai *China* 41°25N 128°5E **35** D15
Changbai Shan *China* 42°20N 129°0E **35** C15
Changchiak'ou = Zhangjiakou *China* 40°48N 114°55E **34** D8
Ch'angchou = Changzhou *China* 31°47N 119°58E **33** C6
Changchun *China* 43°57N 125°17E **35** C13
Changchunling *China* 45°18N 125°27E **35** B13
Changde *China* 29°4N 111°35E **33** D6
Changdo-ri *N. Korea* 38°30N 127°40E **35** E14
Changhai = Shanghai *China* 31°15N 121°26E **33** C7
Changhua *Taiwan* 24°2N 120°30E **33** D7
Changhŭngni *N. Korea* 40°24N 128°19E **35** D15
Changi *Singapore* 1°23N 103°59E **39** d
Changi, Singapore ✈ (SIN) *Singapore* 1°23N 103°59E **39** M4
Changji *China* 44°1N 87°19E **32** B3
Changjiang *China* 19°20N 108°55E **38** C7
Changjiang Shuiku *China* 22°29N 113°27E **33** G10
Changjin *N. Korea* 40°23N 127°15E **35** D14
Changjin-ho *N. Korea* 40°30N 127°15E **35** D14
Changli *China* 39°40N 119°13E **35** E10
Changling *China* 44°20N 123°58E **35** B12
Changlun *Malaysia* 6°25N 100°26E **39** J3
Changping *China* 40°14N 116°12E **34** D9
Changsha *China* 28°12N 113°0E **33** D6
Changshan Qundao *China* 39°11N 122°32E **35** E12
Changwu *China* 35°10N 107°45E **34** G4
Changyi *China* 36°40N 119°30E **35** F10
Changyon *N. Korea* 38°15N 125°6E **35** E13
Changyuan *China* 35°15N 114°42E **34** G8
Changzhi *China* 36°10N 113°6E **34** F7
Changzhou *China* 31°47N 119°58E **33** C6
Chanhanga *Angola* 16°0S 14°8E **56** B1
Chania *Greece* 35°30N 24°4E **25** D6
Chania □ *Greece* 35°30N 24°0E **25** D6
Chanion, Kolpos *Greece* 35°33N 23°55E **25** D5
Channapatna *India* 12°40N 77°15E **40** N10
Channel Is. *U.K.* 49°19N 2°24W **13** H5
Channel Is. *U.S.A.* 33°40N 119°15W **79** M7
Channel Islands △ *U.S.A.* 34°0N 119°24W **79** L7
Channel-Port aux Basques *Canada* 47°30N 59°9W **73** C8
Channel Tunnel *Europe* 51°0N 1°30E **13** F9
Channing *U.S.A.* 35°41N 102°20W **84** D3
Chantada *Spain* 42°36N 7°46W **21** A2
Chanthaburi *Thailand* 12°38N 102°12E **38** F4
Chantrey Inlet *Canada* 67°48N 96°20W **68** C10
Chanute *U.S.A.* 37°41N 95°27W **80** G6
Chao Phraya → *Thailand* 13°40N 100°31E **38** F3
Chao Phraya Lowlands *Thailand* 15°30N 100°0E **38** E3
Chaocheng *China* 36°4N 115°37E **34** F8
Chaoyang *China* 41°35N 120°22E **35** D11
Chaozhou *China* 23°42N 116°32E **33** D6
Chapais *Canada* 49°47N 74°51W **72** C5
Chapala *Mozam.* 15°50S 37°35E **55** F4
Chapala, L. de *Mexico* 20°15N 103°0W **86** C4
Chapayev *Kazakhstan* 50°25N 51°10E **19** D9
Chapayevsk *Russia* 53°0N 49°40E **18** D8
Chapecó *Brazil* 27°14S 52°41W **95** B5
Chapel Hill *U.S.A.* 35°55N 79°4W **85** D15
Chapleau *Canada* 47°50N 83°24W **72** C3
Chaplin *Canada* 50°28N 106°40W **71** C7
Chaplin L. *Canada* 50°22N 106°36W **71** C7
Chappell *U.S.A.* 41°6N 102°28W **80** E2
Chapra = Chhapra *India* 25°48N 84°44E **43** G11
Chara *Russia* 56°54N 118°20E **29** D12
Charadai *Argentina* 27°35S 59°55W **94** B4
Charagua *Bolivia* 19°45S 63°10W **92** G6
Charakas *Greece* 35°1N 25°7E **25** D7
Charambirá, Punta *Colombia* 4°16N 77°32W **92** C3
Charaña *Bolivia* 17°30S 69°25W **92** G5
Charanwala *India* 27°51N 72°10E **42** F5
Charata *Argentina* 27°13S 61°14W **94** B3
Charcas *Mexico* 23°8N 101°7W **86** C4
Charcot I. *Antarctica* 70°0S 70°0W **5** C17
Chard *U.K.* 50°52N 2°58W **13** G5
Chardon *U.S.A.* 41°35N 81°12W **82** E3
Chardzhou = Türkmenabat *Turkmenistan* 39°6N 63°34E **45** B9
Charente → *France* 45°57N 1°5W **20** D3
Chari → *Chad* 12°58N 14°31E **51** F8
Chārīkār *Afghan.* 35°0N 69°10E **40** B6
Chariton *U.S.A.* 41°1N 93°19W **80** E7
Chariton → *U.S.A.* 39°19N 92°58W **80** F7
Chärjew = Türkmenabat *Turkmenistan* 39°6N 63°34E **45** B9
Charkhari *India* 25°24N 79°45E **43** G8
Charkhi Dadri *India* 28°37N 76°17E **42** E7
Charleroi *Belgium* 50°24N 4°27E **15** D4
Charleroi *U.S.A.* 40°9N 79°57W **82** F5
Charles, C. *U.S.A.* 37°7N 75°58W **81** G16
Charles, Peak *Australia* 32°52S 121°11E **61** F3
Charles City *U.S.A.* 43°4N 92°41W **80** D7
Charles L. *Canada* 59°50N 110°33W **71** B6
Charles Town *U.S.A.* 39°17N 77°52W **81** F15
Charlesbourg *Canada* 46°51N 71°16W **81** B18
Charleston *Ill., U.S.A.* 39°30N 88°10W **80** F9
Charleston *Miss., U.S.A.* 34°1N 90°4W **85** D9
Charleston *Mo., U.S.A.* 36°55N 89°21W **80** G9
Charleston *S.C., U.S.A.* 32°46N 79°56W **85** E15
Charleston *W. Va., U.S.A.* 38°21N 81°38W **81** F13
Charleston L. *Canada* 44°32N 76°0W **83** B9
Charleston Peak *U.S.A.* 36°16N 115°42W **79** J11
Charlestown *Ireland* 53°58N 8°48W **10** C3
Charlestown *S. Africa* 27°26S 29°53E **57** D4
Charlestown *Ind., U.S.A.* 38°27N 85°40W **81** F11
Charlestown *N.H., U.S.A.* 43°14N 72°25W **83** C12
Charlestown of Aberlour *U.K.* 57°28N 3°14W **11** D5
Charleville = Rath Luirc *Ireland* 52°21N 8°40W **10** D3
Charleville *Australia* 26°24S 146°15E **63** D4
Charleville-Mézières *France* 49°44N 4°40E **20** B6
Charlevoix *U.S.A.* 45°19N 85°16W **81** C11
Charlotte *Mich., U.S.A.* 42°34N 84°50W **81** D11
Charlotte *N.C., U.S.A.* 35°13N 80°50W **85** D14
Charlotte *Vt., U.S.A.* 44°19N 73°16W **83** B11
Charlotte Amalie *U.S. Virgin Is.* 18°21N 64°56W **89** e
Charlotte Harbor *U.S.A.* 26°57N 82°4W **85** H13
Charlotte L. *Canada* 52°12N 125°19W **70** C3
Charlottesville *U.S.A.* 38°2N 78°30W **81** F14
Charlottetown *Nfld. & L., Canada* 52°46N 56°7W **73** B8
Charlottetown *P.E.I., Canada* 46°14N 63°8W **73** C7
Charlotteville *Trin. & Tob.* 11°20N 60°33W **93** J16
Charlton *Australia* 36°16S 143°24E **63** F3
Charlton I. *Canada* 52°0N 79°20W **72** D4
Charny *Canada* 46°43N 71°15W **73** C5
Charolles *France* 46°27N 4°16E **20** C6
Charre *Mozam.* 17°13S 35°10E **55** F4
Charsadda *Pakistan* 34°7N 71°45E **42** B4
Charters Towers *Australia* 20°5S 146°13E **62** C4
Chartres *France* 48°29N 1°30E **20** B4
Chascomús *Argentina* 35°30S 58°0W **94** D4
Chase *Canada* 50°50N 119°41W **70** C5
Chasefu *Zambia* 11°55S 33°8E **55** E3
Chashma Barrage *Pakistan* 32°27N 71°20E **42** C4
Chāt *Iran* 37°59N 55°16E **45** B7
Châteaubriant *France* 47°43N 1°23W **20** C3
Chateaugay *U.S.A.* 44°56N 74°5W **83** B10
Châteauguay, L. *Canada* 56°26N 70°3W **73** A5
Châteaulin *France* 48°11N 4°8W **20** B1
Châteauroux *France* 46°50N 1°40E **20** C4
Châteaux, Pte. des *Guadeloupe* 16°15N 61°10W **88** b
Châtellerault *France* 46°50N 0°30E **20** C4
Chatham = Chatham-Kent *Canada* 42°24N 82°11W **82** D2
Chatham = Miramichi *Canada* 47°2N 65°28W **73** C6
Chatham *U.K.* 51°22N 0°32E **13** F8
Chatham *U.S.A.* 42°21N 73°36W **83** D11
Chatham Is. *Pac. Oc.* 44°0S 176°40W **64** M10
Chatham-Kent *Canada* 42°24N 82°11W **82** D2
Chatham Rise *Pac. Oc.* 43°30S 180°0E **64** M10
Chatmohar *Bangla.* 24°15N 89°15E **43** G13
Chatra *India* 24°12N 84°56E **43** G11
Chatrapur *India* 19°22N 85°2E **41** K14
Chats, L. des *Canada* 45°30N 76°20W **83** A8
Chatsu *India* 26°36N 75°57E **42** F6
Chatsworth *Canada* 44°27N 80°54W **82** B4
Chatsworth *Zimbabwe* 19°38S 31°13E **55** F3
Chāttagām = Chittagong *Bangla.* 22°19N 91°48E **41** H17
Chattahoochee *U.S.A.* 30°42N 84°51W **85** F12
Chattahoochee → *U.S.A.* 30°54N 84°57W **85** F12
Chattanooga *U.S.A.* 35°3N 85°19W **85** D12
Chatteris *U.K.* 52°28N 0°2E **13** E8
Chaturat *Thailand* 15°40N 101°51E **38** E3
Chau Doc *Vietnam* 10°42N 105°7E **39** G5
Chaukan Pass *Burma* 27°8N 97°10E **41** F20
Chaumont *France* 48°7N 5°8E **20** B6
Chaumont *U.S.A.* 44°4N 76°8W **83** B8
Chaunskaya G. *Russia* 69°0N 169°0E **4** C16
Chautauqua L. *U.S.A.* 42°10N 79°24W **82** D5
Chauvin *Canada* 52°45N 110°10W **71** C6
Chaves *Brazil* 0°15S 49°55W **93** D9
Chaves *Portugal* 41°45N 7°32W **21** B2
Chawang *Thailand* 8°25N 99°30E **39** H2
Chaykovskiy *Russia* 56°47N 54°9E **18** C9
Chazy *U.S.A.* 44°53N 73°26W **83** B11
Cheb *Czech Rep.* 50°9N 12°28E **16** C7
Cheboksary *Russia* 56°8N 47°12E **18** C8
Cheboygan *U.S.A.* 45°39N 84°29W **81** C11
Chech, Erg *Africa* 25°0N 2°15W **50** D5
Chechenia □ *Russia* 43°30N 45°29E **19** F8
Checheno-Ingush Republic = Chechenia □ *Russia* 43°30N 45°29E **19** F8
Chechnya = Chechenia □ *Russia* 43°30N 45°29E **19** F8
Checotah *U.S.A.* 35°28N 95°31W **84** D7
Chedabucto B. *Canada* 45°25N 61°8W **73** C7
Cheduba I. *Burma* 18°45N 93°40E **41** K18
Cheepie *Australia* 26°33S 145°1E **63** D4
Chegdomyn *Russia* 51°7N 133°1E **29** D14
Chegga *Mauritania* 25°27N 5°40W **50** C4
Chegutu *Zimbabwe* 18°10S 30°14E **55** F3
Chehalis *U.S.A.* 46°40N 122°58W **78** D4
Chehalis → *U.S.A.* 46°57N 123°50W **78** D3
Cheju = Jeju *S. Korea* 33°31N 126°32E **35** H14
Cheju-do = Jeju-do *S. Korea* 33°29N 126°34E **35** H14
Chekiang = Zhejiang □ *China* 29°0N 120°0E **33** D7
Chela, Sa. da *Angola* 16°20S 13°20E **56** B1
Chelan *U.S.A.* 47°51N 120°1W **76** C3
Chelan, L. *U.S.A.* 48°11N 120°30W **76** B3
Cheleken = Hazar *Turkmenistan* 39°34N 53°16E **19** G9
Cheleken Yarymadasy *Turkmenistan* 39°30N 53°15E **45** B7
Chelforó *Argentina* 39°0S 66°33W **96** D3
Chelkar = Shalqar *Kazakhstan* 47°48N 59°39E **28** E6
Chelm *Poland* 51°8N 23°30E **17** C12
Chelmno *Poland* 53°20N 18°30E **17** B10
Chelmsford *U.K.* 51°44N 0°29E **13** F8
Chelsea *Australia* 38°5S 145°8E **63** F4
Chelsea *U.S.A.* 43°59N 72°27W **83** C12
Cheltenham *U.K.* 51°54N 2°4W **13** F5
Chelyabinsk *Russia* 55°10N 61°24E **7** D18
Chelyuskin, C. = Chelyuskin, Mys *Russia* 77°30N 103°0E **29** B11
Chelyuskin, Mys *Russia* 77°30N 103°0E **29** B11
Chemainus *Canada* 48°55N 123°42W **78** B3
Chemba *Mozam.* 17°9S 34°53E **53** H6
Chemin Grenier *Mauritius* 20°29S 57°28E **53** d
Chemnitz *Germany* 50°51N 12°54E **16** C7
Chemult *U.S.A.* 43°14N 121°47W **76** E3
Chen, Gora *Russia* 65°16N 141°50E **29** C15
Chenab → *Pakistan* 30°23N 71°2E **42** D4
Chenango Forks *U.S.A.* 42°15N 75°51W **83** D9
Cheney *U.S.A.* 47°30N 117°35W **76** C5
Cheng Xian *China* 33°43N 105°42E **34** H3
Chengcheng *China* 35°8N 109°56E **34** G5
Chengchou = Zhengzhou *China* 34°45N 113°34E **34** G7
Chengde *China* 40°59N 117°58E **35** D9
Chengdu *China* 30°38N 104°2E **32** C5
Chenggu *China* 33°10N 107°21E **34** H4
Chengjiang *China* 24°39N 103°0E **32** D5
Chengmai *China* 19°50N 109°58E **38** C7
Ch'engtu = Chengdu *China* 30°30N 104°2E **32** C5
Chengwu *China* 34°58N 115°50E **34** G8
Chengyang *China* 36°18N 120°21E **35** F11
Chenjiagang *China* 34°23N 119°47E **35** G10
Chennai *India* 13°8N 80°19E **40** N12
Cheom Ksan *Cambodia* 14°13N 104°56E **38** E5
Cheonan *S. Korea* 36°48N 127°9E **35** F14
Cheongdo *S. Korea* 35°38N 128°42E **35** G15
Cheongju *S. Korea* 36°39N 127°27E **35** F14
Cheorwon *S. Korea* 38°15N 127°10E **35** E14
Chepén *Peru* 7°15S 79°23W **92** E3
Chepes *Argentina* 31°20S 66°35W **94** C2
Chepo *Panama* 9°10N 79°6W **88** E4
Chepstow *U.K.* 51°38N 2°41W **13** F5
Chequamegon B. *U.S.A.* 46°39N 90°51W **80** B8
Cher → *France* 47°21N 0°29E **20** C4
Cheraw *U.S.A.* 34°42N 79°53W **85** D15
Cherbourg *France* 49°39N 1°40W **20** B3
Cherdyn *Russia* 60°24N 56°29E **18** B10
Cheremkhovo *Russia* 53°8N 103°1E **29** D11
Cherepanovo *Russia* 54°15N 83°30E **28** D9
Cherepovets *Russia* 59°5N 37°55E **18** C6
Chergui, Chott ech *Algeria* 34°21N 0°25E **50** B6
Cherikov = Cherykaw *Belarus* 53°32N 31°20E **17** B16
Cherkasy *Ukraine* 49°27N 32°4E **19** E5
Cherkessk *Russia* 44°15N 42°5E **19** F7
Cherlak *Russia* 54°15N 74°55E **28** D8
Chernaya *Russia* 70°30N 89°10E **29** B9
Chernigov = Chernihiv *Ukraine* 51°28N 31°20E **18** D5
Chernihiv *Ukraine* 51°28N 31°20E **18** D5
Chernivtsi *Ukraine* 48°15N 25°52E **17** D13
Chernobyl = Chornobyl *Ukraine* 51°20N 30°15E **17** C16
Chernogorsk *Russia* 53°49N 91°18E **29** D10
Chernovtsy = Chernivtsi *Ukraine* 48°15N 25°52E **17** D13
Chernyakhovsk *Russia* 54°36N 21°48E **9** J19
Chernysheyskiy *Russia* 63°0N 112°30E **29** C12
Cherokee *Iowa, U.S.A.* 42°45N 95°33W **80** D6
Cherokee *Okla., U.S.A.* 36°45N 98°21W **84** C5
Cherokee Village *U.S.A.* 36°18N 91°31W **84** C9
Cherokees, Grand Lake O' The *U.S.A.* 36°28N 94°55W **84** C7
Cherrapunji *India* 25°17N 91°47E **41** G17
Cherry Valley *U.S.A.* 42°48N 74°45W **83** D10
Cherskiy *Russia* 68°45N 161°18E **29** C17
Cherskogo Khrebet *Russia* 65°0N 143°0E **29** C15
Chersonisos *Greece* 35°18N 25°22E **25** D7
Chersonisos Akrotiri *Greece* 35°30N 24°10E **25** D6
Cherven *Belarus* 53°45N 28°28E **17** B15
Chervonohrad *Ukraine* 50°25N 24°10E **17** C13
Cherwell → *U.K.* 51°44N 1°14W **13** F6
Cherykaw *Belarus* 53°32N 31°20E **17** B16
Chesapeake *U.S.A.* 36°49N 76°16W **81** G15
Chesapeake B. *U.S.A.* 38°0N 76°10W **81** F14
Cheshire □ *U.K.* 53°14N 2°30W **12** D5
Cheshskaya Guba *Russia* 67°20N 47°0E **18** A8
Cheshunt *U.K.* 51°43N 0°1W **13** F7
Chesil Beach *U.K.* 50°37N 2°33W **13** G5
Chesley *Canada* 44°17N 81°5W **82** B3
Chester *U.K.* 53°12N 2°53W **12** D5
Chester *Calif., U.S.A.* 40°19N 121°14W **76** F3
Chester *Ill., U.S.A.* 37°55N 89°49W **80** G9
Chester *Mont., U.S.A.* 48°31N 110°58W **76** B8
Chester *Pa., U.S.A.* 39°51N 75°22W **81** F16
Chester *S.C., U.S.A.* 34°43N 81°12W **85** D14
Chester *Vt., U.S.A.* 43°16N 72°36W **83** C12
Chester *W. Va., U.S.A.* 40°37N 80°34W **82** F4
Chester-le-Street *U.K.* 54°51N 1°34W **12** C6
Chesterfield *U.K.* 53°15N 1°25W **12** D6
Chesterfield, Îs. *N. Cal.* 19°52S 158°15E **58** C8
Chesterfield Inlet *Canada* 63°30N 90°45W **68** C10
Chesterton Ra. *Australia* 25°30S 147°27E **63** D4
Chesterton Range △ *Australia* 26°16S 147°22E **63** D4
Chestertown *U.S.A.* 43°40N 73°48W **83** C11
Chesterville *Canada* 45°6N 75°14W **83** A9
Chesuncook L. *U.S.A.* 46°0N 69°21W **81** C19
Chéticamp *Canada* 46°37N 60°59W **73** C7
Chetumal *Mexico* 18°30N 88°20W **87** D7
Chetumal, B. de *Cent. Amer.* 18°40N 88°10W **87** D7
Chetwynd *Canada* 55°45N 121°36W **70** B4
Cheviot, The *U.K.* 55°29N 2°9W **12** B5
Cheviot Hills *U.K.* 55°20N 2°30W **12** B5
Cheviot Ra. *Australia* 25°20S 143°45E **62** D3
Chew Bahir *Ethiopia* 4°40N 36°50E **47** G2
Chewelah *U.S.A.* 48°17N 117°43W **76** B5
Chewore ⌂ *Zimbabwe* 16°0S 29°52E **55** F2
Cheyenne *Okla., U.S.A.* 35°37N 99°40W **84** D5
Cheyenne *Wyo., U.S.A.* 41°8N 104°49W **76** F11
Cheyenne → *U.S.A.* 44°41N 101°18W **80** C3
Cheyenne Wells *U.S.A.* 38°49N 102°21W **76** G12
Cheyne B. *Australia* 34°35S 118°50E **61** F2
Chhabra *India* 24°40N 76°54E **42** G7
Chhaktala *India* 22°6N 74°11E **42** H6
Chhapra *India* 25°48N 84°44E **43** G11
Chhata *India* 27°42N 77°30E **42** F7
Chhatarpur *Jharkhand, India* 24°23N 84°11E **43** G11
Chhatarpur *Mad. P., India* 24°55N 79°35E **43** G8
Chhattisgarh □ *India* 22°0N 82°0E **43** J10
Chhep *Cambodia* 13°45N 105°24E **38** F5
Chhindwara *Mad. P., India* 23°3N 79°29E **43** H8
Chhindwara *Mad. P., India* 22°2N 78°59E **43** H8
Chhlong *Cambodia* 12°15N 105°58E **39** F5
Chhoto Town → *India* 22°14N 76°36E **42** H7
Chhoti Kali Sindh → *India* 24°2N 75°31E **42** G6
Chhuikhadan *India* 21°32N 80°59E **43** J9
Chhuk *Cambodia* 10°46N 104°28E **39** G5
Chi → *Thailand* 15°11N 104°43E **38** E5
Chiai *Taiwan* 23°29N 120°25E **33** D7
Chiamboni *Somali Rep.* 1°39S 41°35E **52** E8
Chiang Dao *Thailand* 19°22N 98°58E **38** C2
Chiang Kham *Thailand* 19°32N 100°18E **38** C3
Chiang Khan *Thailand* 17°52N 101°36E **38** D3
Chiang Khong *Thailand* 20°17N 100°24E **38** B3
Chiang Mai *Thailand* 18°47N 98°59E **38** C2
Chiang Rai *Thailand* 19°52N 99°50E **38** C2
Chiang Saen *Thailand* 20°16N 100°5E **38** B3
Chiapa → *Mexico* 16°42N 93°0W **87** D6
Chiapa de Corzo *Mexico* 16°42N 93°0W **87** D6
Chiapas □ *Mexico* 17°0N 92°30W **87** D6
Chiapas, Sa. Madre de *Mexico* 15°40N 93°0W **87** D6
Chiautla de Tapia *Mexico* 18°18N 98°36W **87** D5
Chiávari *Italy* 44°19N 9°19E **20** D8
Chiavenna *Italy* 46°19N 9°24E **20** C8
Chiba *Japan* 35°30N 140°7E **31** G10
Chiba □ *Japan* 35°30N 140°20E **31** G10
Chibabava *Mozam.* 20°17S 33°35E **57** C5
Chibemba *Cunene, Angola* 15°48S 14°8E **53** H2
Chibemba *Huila, Angola* 16°20S 15°20E **56** B2
Chibi *Zimbabwe* 20°18S 30°25E **57** C5
Chibia *Angola* 15°10S 13°42E **53** H2
Chibougamau *Canada* 49°56N 74°24W **72** C5
Chibougamau, L. *Canada* 49°50N 74°20W **72** C5
Chibuk *Nigeria* 10°52N 12°50E **51** F8
Chibuto *Mozam.* 24°40S 33°33E **57** C5
Chic-Chocs, Mts. *Canada* 48°55N 66°0W **73** C6
Chicacole = Srikakulam *India* 18°14N 83°58E **41** K13
Chicago *U.S.A.* 41°52N 87°38W **80** E10
Chicago Heights *U.S.A.* 41°30N 87°38W **80** E10
Chichagof I. *U.S.A.* 57°30N 135°30W **68** D6
Chichaoua *Morocco* 31°32N 8°44W **50** B4
Chichén-Itzá *Mexico* 20°37N 88°35W **87** C7
Chicheng *China* 40°55N 115°55E **34** D8
Chichester *U.K.* 50°50N 0°47W **13** G7
Chichester Ra. *Australia* 22°12S 119°15E **60** D2
Chichibu *Japan* 35°59N 139°10E **31** F9
Chichibu-Tama △ *Japan* 35°52N 138°42E **31** G9
Ch'ich'ihaerh = Qiqihar *China* 47°26N 124°0E **33** B7
Chicholi *India* 22°1N 77°40E **42** H8
Chickasaw ⌂ *U.S.A.* 34°26N 97°0W **84** D6
Chickasha *U.S.A.* 35°3N 97°58W **84** D6
Chiclana de la Frontera *Spain* 36°26N 6°9W **21** D2
Chiclayo *Peru* 6°42S 79°50W **92** E3
Chico *U.S.A.* 39°44N 121°50W **78** F5
Chico → *Chubut, Argentina* 44°0S 67°0W **96** E3
Chico → *Santa Cruz, Argentina* 50°0S 68°30W **96** G3
Chicomo *Mozam.* 24°31S 34°6E **57** C5
Chicomostoc *Mexico* 22°28N 102°46W **86** C4
Chicontepec *Mexico* 20°58N 98°10W **87** C5
Chicopee *U.S.A.* 42°9N 72°37W **83** D12
Chicoutimi *Canada* 48°28N 71°5W **73** C5
Chicualacuala *Mozam.* 22°6S 31°42E **57** C5
Chidambaram *India* 11°20N 79°45E **40** P11
Chidenguele *Mozam.* 24°55S 34°11E **57** C5
Chidley, C. *Canada* 60°23N 64°26W **69** C13
Chiducuane *Mozam.* 24°35S 34°25E **57** C5
Chiede *Angola* 17°15S 16°22E **56** B2
Chiefs Pt. *Canada* 44°41N 81°18W **82** B3
Chiem Hoa *Vietnam* 22°12N 105°17E **38** A5
Chiemsee *Germany* 47°53N 12°28E **16** E7
Chiengi *Zambia* 8°45S 29°10E **55** D2
Chiengmai = Chiang Mai *Thailand* 18°47N 98°59E **38** C2
Chiese → *Italy* 45°8N 10°25E **20** D9
Chieti *Italy* 42°21N 14°10E **22** C6
Chifeng *China* 42°18N 118°58E **35** C10
Chignecto B. *Canada* 45°30N 64°40W **73** C7
Chiguana *Bolivia* 21°0S 67°58W **94** A2
Chigwell *U.K.* 51°37N 0°6E **13** F8
Chihli, G. of = Bo Hai *China* 39°0N 119°0E **35** E10
Chihuahua *Mexico* 28°38N 106°5W **86** B3
Chihuahua □ *Mexico* 28°30N 106°0W **86** B3
Chiili = Shīeli *Kazakhstan* 44°20N 66°15E **28** E7
Chik Bollapur *India* 13°25N 77°45E **40** N10
Chikmagalur *India* 13°15N 75°45E **40** N9
Chikwawa *Malawi* 16°2S 34°50E **55** F3
Chilam Chavki *Pakistan* 35°5N 75°5E **43** B6
Chilanga *Zambia* 15°33S 28°16E **55** F2
Chilapa *Mexico* 17°36N 99°10W **87** D5
Chilas *Pakistan* 35°25N 74°5E **43** B6
Chilaw *Sri Lanka* 7°30N 79°50E **40** R11
Chilcotin → *Canada* 51°44N 122°23W **70** C4
Childers *Australia* 25°15S 152°17E **63** D5
Childress *U.S.A.* 34°25N 100°13W **84** D4
Chile ■ *S. Amer.* 35°0S 72°0W **96** D2
Chile Rise *Pac. Oc.* 38°0S 92°0W **65** L18
Chilecito *Argentina* 29°10S 67°30W **94** B2
Chilete *Peru* 7°10S 78°50W **92** E3
Chililabombwe *Zambia* 12°18S 27°43E **55** E2
Chilin = Jilin *China* 43°44N 126°30E **35** C14
Chilka L. *India* 19°40N 85°25E **41** K14
Chilko → *Canada* 52°0N 123°40W **70** C4
Chilko L. *Canada* 51°20N 124°10W **70** C4
Chillagoe *Australia* 17°7S 144°33E **62** B3
Chillán *Chile* 36°40S 72°10W **94** D1
Chillicothe *Ill., U.S.A.* 40°55N 89°29W **80** E9
Chillicothe *Mo., U.S.A.* 39°48N 93°33W **80** F7
Chillicothe *Ohio, U.S.A.* 39°20N 82°59W **81** F12
Chilliwack *Canada* 49°10N 121°54W **70** D4
Chilo *India* 27°25N 73°32E **42** F5
Chiloane, I. *Mozam.* 20°40S 34°55E **57** C5
Chiloé, I. de *Chile* 42°30S 73°50W **96** E2
Chilpancingo *Mexico* 17°33N 99°30W **87** D5
Chiltern Hills *U.K.* 51°40N 0°53W **13** F7
Chilton *U.S.A.* 44°2N 88°10W **80** C9
Chilubi *Zambia* 11°5S 29°58E **55** E2
Chilubula *Zambia* 10°14S 30°51E **55** E3
Chilumba *Malawi* 10°28S 34°12E **55** E3
Chilung *Taiwan* 25°3N 121°45E **33** D7
Chilwa, L. *Malawi* 15°15S 35°40E **55** F4
Chimaltitán *Mexico* 21°35N 103°50W **86** C4
Chimán *Panama* 8°45N 78°40W **88** E4
Chimanimani *Zimbabwe* 19°48S 32°52E **57** B5
Chimay *Belgium* 50°3N 4°20E **15** D4
Chimayo *U.S.A.* 36°0N 105°56W **77** J11
Chimbay *Uzbekistan* 42°57N 59°47E **28** E6
Chimborazo *Ecuador* 1°29S 78°55W **92** D3
Chimbote *Peru* 9°0S 78°35W **92** E3
Chimkent = Shymkent *Kazakhstan* 42°18N 69°36E **28** E7
Chimoio *Mozam.* 19°4S 33°30E **55** F3
Chimpembe *Zambia* 9°31S 29°33E **55** D2
Chin □ *Burma* 22°0N 93°0E **41** J18
Chin Hills *Burma* 22°30N 93°30E **41** H18
Chin Ling Shan = Qinling Shandi *China* 33°50N 108°10E **34** H5
China *Mexico* 25°42N 99°14W **87** B5
China ■ *Asia* 30°0N 110°0E **33** C6
China, Great Plain of *Asia* 35°0N 115°0E **26** E13
China Lake *U.S.A.* 35°44N 117°37W **79** K9
Chinan = Jinan *China* 36°38N 117°1E **34** F9
Chinandega *Nic.* 12°35N 87°12W **88** D2
Chinati Peak *U.S.A.* 29°57N 104°29W **84** G2
Chincha Alta *Peru* 13°25S 76°7W **92** F3
Chinchaga → *Canada* 58°53N 118°20W **70** B5
Chinchilla *Australia* 26°45S 150°38E **63** D5
Chinchorro, Banco *Mexico* 18°35N 87°22W **87** D7
Chinchou = Jinzhou *China* 41°5N 121°3E **35** D11
Chincoteague *U.S.A.* 37°56N 75°23W **81** G16
Chinde *Mozam.* 18°35S 36°30E **55** F4
Chindwin → *Burma* 21°26N 95°15E **41** J19
Chineni *India* 33°2N 75°15E **43** C6
Chinga *Mozam.* 15°13S 38°35E **55** F4
Chingola *Zambia* 12°31S 27°53E **55** E2
Chingole *Malawi* 13°4S 34°17E **55** E3
Ch'ingtao = Qingdao *China* 36°5N 120°20E **35** F11

112 Chinguetti
INDEX TO WORLD MAPS

Chinguetti Mauritania 20°25N 12°24W 50 D3
Chingune Mozam. 20°33S 34°58E 57 C5
Chinhanguanine Mozam. 25°21S 32°30E 57 D5
Chinhoyi Zimbabwe 17°20S 30°8E 55 F3
Chini India 31°32N 78°15E 42 D8
Chiniot Pakistan 31°45N 73°0E 42 D5
Chínipas Mexico 27°23N 108°32W 86 B3
Chinji Pakistan 32°42N 72°22E 42 C5
Chinju = Jinju S. Korea 35°12N 128°2E 35 G15
Chinko → C.A.R. 4°50N 23°53E 52 D4
Chinle U.S.A. 36°9N 109°33W 77 H9
Chinnampo = Namp'o N. Korea 38°52N 125°10E 35 E13
Chino Japan 35°59N 138°9E 31 G9
Chino U.S.A. 34°1N 117°41W 79 L9
Chino Valley U.S.A. 34°45N 112°27W 77 J7
Chinon France 47°10N 0°15E 20 C4
Chinook U.S.A. 48°35N 109°14W 76 B9
Chinook Trough Pac. Oc. 44°0N 175°0W 64 C10
Chinsali Zambia 10°30S 32°2E 55 E3
Chióggia Italy 45°13N 12°17E 22 B5
Chíos = Hios Greece 38°27N 26°9E 23 E12
Chipata Zambia 13°38S 32°28E 55 E3
Chipindo Angola 13°49S 15°48E 53 G3
Chipinge Zimbabwe 20°13S 32°28E 55 G3
Chipinge ⌓ Zimbabwe 20°14S 33°0E 55 G3
Chipley U.S.A. 30°47N 85°32W 85 F12
Chipman Canada 46°6N 65°53W 73 C6
Chipoka Malawi 13°57S 34°28E 55 E3
Chippenham U.K. 51°27N 2°6W 13 F5
Chippewa → U.S.A. 44°25N 92°5W 80 C7
Chippewa Falls U.S.A. 44°56N 91°24W 80 C8
Chipping Norton U.K. 51°56N 1°32W 13 F6
Chiputneticook Lakes N. Amer. 45°35N 67°35W 81 C20
Chiquián Peru 10°10S 77°0W 92 F3
Chiquibul △ Belize 16°49N 88°52W 88 C2
Chiquimula Guatemala 14°51N 89°37W 88 D2
Chiquinquira Colombia 5°37N 73°50W 92 B4
Chirala India 15°50N 80°26E 40 M12
Chiramba Mozam. 16°55S 34°39E 55 F3
Chirawa India 28°14N 75°42E 42 E6
Chirchiq Uzbekistan 41°29N 69°35E 28 E7
Chiredzi Zimbabwe 21°0S 31°38E 57 C5
Chiricahua ⌓ U.S.A. 32°0N 109°20W 77 K9
Chiricahua Peak U.S.A. 31°51N 109°18W 77 L9
Chiriquí, G. de Panama 8°0N 82°10W 88 E3
Chiriquí, L. de Panama 9°10N 82°0W 88 E3
Chirisa ⌓ Zimbabwe 17°53S 28°15E 55 F2
Chirivira Falls Zimbabwe 21°10S 32°12E 55 G3
Chirmiri India 23°15N 82°20E 43 H10
Chirripó Grande, Cerro Costa Rica 9°29N 83°29W 88 E3
Chirundu Zimbabwe 16°3S 28°50E 57 B4
Chisamba Zambia 14°55S 28°20E 55 E2
Chisapani Nepal 28°37N 81°16E 43 E9
Chisasibi Canada 53°50N 79°0W 72 B4
Chisholm Canada 54°55N 114°10W 70 C6
Chisholm U.S.A. 47°29N 92°53W 80 B7
Chishtian Mandi Pakistan 29°50N 72°55E 42 E5
Chisimaio Somali Rep. 0°22S 42°32E 47 H3
Chisimba Falls Zambia 10°12S 30°56E 55 E3
Chişinău Moldova 47°2N 28°50E 17 E15
Chisos Mts. U.S.A. 29°5N 103°15W 84 G3
Chistopol Russia 55°25N 50°38E 18 C9
Chita Russia 52°0N 113°35E 29 D12
Chitipa Malawi 9°41S 33°19E 55 D3
Chitose Japan 42°49N 141°39E 30 C10
Chitral Pakistan 35°50N 71°56E 40 B7
Chitré Panama 7°59N 80°27W 88 E3
Chittagong Bangla. 22°19N 91°48E 41 H17
Chittagong ☐ Bangla. 24°5N 91°0E 41 G17
Chittaurgarh India 24°52N 74°38E 42 G6
Chittoor India 13°15N 79°5E 40 N11
Chitungwiza Zimbabwe 18°0S 31°6E 55 F3
Chiusi Italy 43°1N 11°57E 22 C4
Chivasso Italy 45°11N 7°53E 20 D7
Chivhu Zimbabwe 19°2S 30°52E 55 F3
Chivilcoy Argentina 34°55S 60°0W 94 C4
Chiwanda Tanzania 11°23S 34°55E 55 E3
Chizarira Zimbabwe 17°36S 27°45E 55 F2
Chizarira △ Zimbabwe 17°44S 27°52E 55 F2
Chizela Zambia 13°8S 25°0E 55 E2
Chkalov = Orenburg Russia 51°45N 55°6E 18 D10
Chloride U.S.A. 35°25N 114°12W 79 K12
Cho Bo Vietnam 20°46N 105°10E 38 B5
Cho-do N. Korea 38°30N 124°40E 35 E13
Cho Phuoc Hai Vietnam 10°26N 107°18E 39 G6
Choa Chu Kang Singapore 1°22N 103°41E 39 d
Choba Kenya 2°30N 38°5E 54 B4
Chobe △ Botswana 18°37S 24°23E 56 B4
Chocolate Mts. U.S.A. 33°15N 115°15W 79 M11
Choctawhatchee → U.S.A. 30°25N 86°8W 85 F11
Choele Choel Argentina 39°11S 65°40W 96 D3
Choiseul St. Lucia 13°47N 61°3W 89 f
Choiseul Solomon Is. 7°0S 156°40E 58 B8
Choix Mexico 26°43N 108°17W 86 B3
Chojnice Poland 53°42N 17°32E 17 B9
Chōkai-San Japan 39°6N 140°3E 30 E10
Choke Canyon Res. U.S.A. 28°30N 98°20W 84 G5
Chokurdakh Russia 70°38N 147°55E 29 B15
Cholame U.S.A. 35°44N 120°18W 78 K6
Cholet France 47°4N 0°52W 20 C3
Cholguan Chile 37°10S 72°3W 94 D1
Choluteca Honduras 13°20N 87°14W 88 D2
Choluteca → Honduras 13°0N 87°20W 88 D2
Chom Bung Thailand 13°37N 99°36E 38 F2
Chom Thong Thailand 18°25N 98°41E 38 C2
Choma Zambia 16°48S 26°59E 55 F2
Chomolungma = Everest, Mt. Nepal 28°5N 86°58E 43 E12
Chomun India 27°15N 75°40E 42 F6
Chomutov Czech Rep. 50°28N 13°23E 16 C7
Chon Buri Thailand 13°21N 101°1E 38 F3
Chon Thanh Vietnam 11°24N 106°36E 39 G6
Chone Ecuador 0°40S 80°0W 92 D3
Chong Kai Cambodia 13°57N 103°35E 38 F4
Chong Mek Thailand 15°10N 105°27E 38 E5
Chong Phangan Thailand 9°39N 100°0E 39 b
Chong Samui Thailand 9°21N 99°50E 39 b
Ch'ŏngjin N. Korea 41°47N 129°50E 35 D15
Chŏngju N. Korea 39°40N 125°5E 35 E13
Chongli China 40°58N 115°15E 34 D8
Chongqing China 29°35N 106°25E 32 D5
Chongqing Shi ☐ China 30°0N 108°0E 32 C5
Chonguene Mozam. 25°3S 33°49E 57 C5
Chonos, Arch. de los Chile 45°0S 75°0W 96 F2
Chop Ukraine 48°26N 22°12E 17 D12
Chopim → Brazil 25°35S 53°5W 95 B5
Chor Pakistan 25°31N 69°46E 42 G3
Chora Sfakion Greece 35°15N 24°9E 25 D6
Chorbat La India 34°42N 76°37E 43 B7
Chorley U.K. 53°39N 2°38W 12 D5
Chornobyl Ukraine 51°20N 30°15E 17 C16
Chorolque, Cerro Bolivia 20°59S 66°5W 94 A2
Chorregon Australia 22°40S 143°32E 62 C3
Chorro el Indio △ Venezuela 7°43N 72°9W 89 E5
Chortkiv Ukraine 49°2N 25°46E 17 D13
Chorzów Poland 50°18N 18°57E 17 C10
Chos-Malal Argentina 37°20S 70°15W 94 D1
Ch'osan N. Korea 40°50N 125°47E 35 D13
Choszczno Poland 53°7N 15°25E 16 B8
Choteau U.S.A. 47°49N 112°11W 76 C7
Chotila India 22°23N 71°15E 42 H4
Chotta Udepur India 22°19N 74°1E 42 H6
Chowchilla U.S.A. 37°7N 120°16W 78 H6
Choybalsan Mongolia 48°4N 114°30E 33 B6
Christchurch N.Z. 43°33S 172°47E 59 E4
Christchurch U.K. 50°44N 1°47W 13 G6
Christian I. Canada 44°50N 80°12W 82 B4
Christiana S. Africa 27°52S 25°8E 56 D4
Christiansted U.S. Virgin Is. 17°45N 64°42W 89 C7
Christie B. Canada 62°32N 111°10W 71 A6
Christina → Canada 56°40N 111°3W 71 B6
Christmas Cr. → Australia 18°29S 125°23E 60 C4
Christmas I. = Kiritimati Kiribati 1°58N 157°27W 65 G12
Christmas I. Ind. Oc. 10°30S 105°40E 64 J2
Christopher, L. Australia 24°49S 127°42E 61 D4
Chtimba Malawi 10°35S 34°13E 55 E3
Chū = Shū Kazakhstan 43°36N 73°42E 28 E8
Chu → Vietnam 19°53N 105°45E 38 C5
Chu Lai Vietnam 15°28N 108°45E 38 E7
Chuak, Ko Thailand 9°28N 99°41E 39 b
Ch'uanchou = Quanzhou China 24°55N 118°34E 33 D6
Chuankou China 34°20N 110°59E 34 G6
Chubbuck U.S.A. 42°55N 112°28W 76 E7
Chūbu ☐ Japan 36°45N 137°30E 31 F8
Chubu-Sangaku △ Japan 36°30N 137°40E 31 F8
Chubut → Argentina 43°20S 65°5W 96 E3
Chuchi L. Canada 55°12N 124°30W 70 B4
Chuda India 22°29N 71°41E 42 H4
Chudskoye, Ozero Russia 58°13N 27°30E 9 G22
Chūgoku ☐ Japan 35°0N 133°0E 31 G6
Chūgoku-Sanchi Japan 35°0N 133°0E 31 G6
Chugwater U.S.A. 41°46N 104°50W 76 F11
Chuka Kenya 0°20S 37°39E 54 C4
Chukchi Plateau Arctic 78°0N 165°0W 4 B17
Chukchi Sea Russia 68°0N 175°0W 29 C19
Chukotskoye Nagorye Russia 68°0N 175°0E 29 C18
Chula Vista U.S.A. 32°38N 117°5W 79 N9
Chulucanas Peru 5°8S 80°10W 92 E2
Chulym → Russia 57°43N 83°51E 28 D9
Chum Phae Thailand 16°40N 102°6E 38 D4
Chum Saeng Thailand 15°55N 100°15E 38 E3
Chumar India 32°40N 78°35E 43 C8
Chumbicha Argentina 29°0S 66°10W 94 B2
Chumikan Russia 54°40N 135°10E 29 D14
Chumphon Thailand 10°35N 99°14E 39 G2
Chumuare Mozam. 14°31S 31°50E 55 E3
Chuna → Russia 57°47N 94°37E 29 D10
Chuncheon S. Korea 37°58N 127°44E 35 F14
Chunchura India 22°53N 88°27E 43 H13
Chunga Zambia 15°0S 26°2E 55 F2
Chunggang-ŭp N. Korea 41°48N 126°48E 35 D14
Chunghwa N. Korea 38°52N 125°47E 35 E13
Chungju S. Korea 36°58N 127°58E 35 F14
Chungking = Chongqing China 29°35N 106°25E 32 D5
Chungt'iaoshan = Zhongtiao Shan China 35°0N 111°10E 34 G6
Chunian Pakistan 30°57N 74°0E 42 D6
Chunya Tanzania 8°30S 33°27E 55 D3
Chunyang China 43°38N 129°23E 35 C15
Chupara Pt. Trin. & Tob. 10°49N 61°22W 93 K15
Chuquibamba Peru 15°47S 72°44W 92 G4
Chuquicamata Chile 22°15S 69°0W 94 A2
Chur Switz. 46°52N 9°32E 20 C8
Churachandpur India 24°20N 93°40E 41 G18
Church Stretton U.K. 52°32N 2°48W 13 E5
Churchill Canada 58°47N 94°11W 71 B10
Churchill → Man., Canada 58°47N 94°12W 71 B10
Churchill → Nfld. & L., Canada 53°19N 60°10W 73 B7
Churchill, C. Canada 58°46N 93°12W 71 B10
Churchill Falls Canada 53°36N 64°19W 73 B7
Churchill L. Canada 55°55N 108°20W 71 B7
Churchill Pk. Canada 58°10N 125°10W 70 B3
Churki India 23°50N 83°12E 43 H10
Churu India 28°20N 74°50E 42 E6
Churún Merú = Angel Falls Venezuela 5°57N 62°30W 92 B6
Chushal India 33°40N 78°40E 43 C8
Chuska Mts. U.S.A. 36°15N 108°50W 77 H9
Chusovoy Russia 58°22N 57°50E 18 C10
Chute-aux-Outardes Canada 49°7N 68°24W 73 C6
Chuuk = Truk Micronesia 7°25N 151°46E 64 G7
Chuvash Republic = Chuvashia ☐ Russia 55°30N 47°0E 18 C8
Chuvashia ☐ Russia 55°30N 47°0E 18 C8
Chuwārtah Iraq 35°43N 45°34E 44 C5
Chuy Uruguay 33°41S 53°27W 95 C5
Ci Xian China 36°20N 114°25E 34 F8
Ciadâr-Lunga Moldova 46°3N 28°51E 17 E15
Ciamis Indonesia 7°20S 108°21E 37 G13
Cianjur Indonesia 6°49S 107°8E 37 G12
Cianorte Brazil 23°37S 52°37W 95 A5
Cibola U.S.A. 33°17N 114°42W 79 M12
Cicero U.S.A. 41°51N 87°44W 80 E10
Cicia Fiji 17°45S 179°18W 59 a
Ciéagas del Cataumbo △ Venezuela 9°25N 71°54W 89 E5
Ciechanów Poland 52°52N 20°38E 17 B11
Ciego de Ávila Cuba 21°50N 78°50W 88 B4
Ciénaga Colombia 11°1N 74°15W 92 A4
Cienfuegos Cuba 22°10N 80°30W 88 B3
Cieszyn Poland 49°45N 18°35E 17 D10
Cieza Spain 38°17N 1°23W 21 C5
Cihuatlán Mexico 19°14N 104°35W 86 D4
Cijara, Embalse de Spain 39°18N 4°52W 21 C3
Cijulang Indonesia 7°42S 108°27E 37 G13
Cilacap Indonesia 7°43S 109°0E 37 G13
Cill Chainnigh = Kilkenny Ireland 52°39N 7°15W 10 D4
Cilo Dağı Turkey 37°28N 43°55E 19 G7
Cima U.S.A. 35°14N 115°30W 79 K11
Cimarron Kans., U.S.A. 37°48N 100°21W 80 G3
Cimarron N. Mex., U.S.A. 36°31N 104°55W 77 H11
Cimarron → U.S.A. 36°10N 96°16W 84 C6
Cimişlia Moldova 46°34N 28°44E 17 E15
Cimone, Mte. Italy 44°12N 10°42E 22 B4
Cinca → Spain 41°26N 0°21E 21 B6
Cincar Bos.-H. 43°55N 17°5E 22 C7
Cincinnati U.S.A. 39°9N 84°27W 81 F11
Cincinnatus U.S.A. 42°33N 75°54W 83 D9
Çine Turkey 37°37N 28°2E 23 F13
Ciney Belgium 50°18N 5°5E 15 D5
Cinto, Mte. France 42°24N 8°54E 20 E8
Circle Alaska, U.S.A. 65°50N 144°4W 74 a
Circle Mont., U.S.A. 47°25N 105°35W 76 C11
Circleville U.S.A. 39°36N 82°57W 81 F12
Cirebon Indonesia 6°45S 108°32E 36 F3
Ciremay Indonesia 6°55S 108°27E 37 G13
Cirencester U.K. 51°43N 1°57W 13 F6
Cirium Cyprus 34°40N 32°53E 25 E11
Cisco U.S.A. 32°23N 98°59W 84 E5
Citlaltépetl = Orizaba, Pico de Mexico 18°58N 97°15W 87 D5
Citrus Heights U.S.A. 38°42N 121°17W 78 G5
Citrusdal S. Africa 32°35S 19°0E 56 E2
Città del Vaticano = Vatican City ■ Europe 41°54N 12°27E 22 D5
Città di Castello Italy 43°27N 12°14E 22 C5
Ciudad Acuña Mexico 29°18N 100°55W 86 B4
Ciudad Altamirano Mexico 18°20N 100°40W 86 D4
Ciudad Anáhuac Mexico 27°14N 100°7W 86 B4
Ciudad Bolívar Venezuela 8°5N 63°36W 92 B6
Ciudad Camargo Mexico 27°40N 105°10W 86 B3
Ciudad de México Mexico 19°24N 99°9W 87 D5
Ciudad de Valles Mexico 22°0N 99°0W 87 C5
Ciudad del Carmen Mexico 18°38N 91°50W 87 D6
Ciudad del Este Paraguay 25°30S 54°50W 95 B5
Ciudad Delicias = Delicias Mexico 28°13N 105°28W 86 B3
Ciudad Frontera Mexico 26°56N 101°27W 86 B4
Ciudad Guayana Venezuela 8°0N 62°30W 92 B6
Ciudad Guerrero Mexico 28°33N 107°30W 86 B3
Ciudad Guzmán Mexico 19°41N 103°29W 86 D4
Ciudad Juárez Mexico 31°44N 106°29W 86 A3
Ciudad Lerdo Mexico 25°32N 103°32W 86 B4
Ciudad Madero Mexico 22°19N 97°50W 87 C5
Ciudad Mante Mexico 22°44N 98°59W 87 C5
Ciudad Obregón Mexico 27°29N 109°56W 86 B3
Ciudad Real Spain 38°59N 3°55W 21 C4
Ciudad Rodrigo Spain 40°35N 6°32W 21 B2
Ciudad Victoria Mexico 23°44N 99°8W 87 C5
Ciudadela Spain 40°0N 3°50E 24 B10
Civitanova Marche Italy 43°18N 13°44E 22 C5
Civitavécchia Italy 42°6N 11°48E 22 C4
Cizre Turkey 37°19N 42°10E 44 B4
Clackmannanshire ☐ U.K. 56°10N 3°43W 11 E5
Clacton-on-Sea U.K. 51°47N 1°11E 13 F9
Claire, L. Canada 58°35N 112°5W 70 B6
Clairton U.S.A. 40°18N 79°53W 82 F5
Clallam Bay U.S.A. 48°15N 124°16W 78 B2
Clanton U.S.A. 32°51N 86°38W 85 E11
Clanwilliam S. Africa 32°11S 18°52E 56 E2
Clara Ireland 53°21N 7°37W 10 C4
Claraville U.S.A. 35°24N 118°20W 79 K8
Clare Australia 33°50S 138°37E 63 E2
Clare U.S.A. 43°49N 84°46W 81 D11
Clare ☐ Ireland 52°45N 9°0W 10 D3
Clare → Ireland 53°20N 9°2W 10 C2
Clare I. Ireland 53°49N 10°0W 10 C1
Claremont Calif., U.S.A. 34°6N 117°43W 79 L9
Claremont N.H., U.S.A. 43°23N 72°20W 83 C12
Claremont Pt. Australia 14°1S 143°41E 62 A3
Claremore U.S.A. 36°19N 95°36W 84 C7
Claremorris Ireland 53°45N 9°0W 10 C3
Clarence → Australia 29°25S 153°22E 63 D5
Clarence → N.Z. 42°10S 173°56E 59 E4
Clarence, I. Chile 54°0S 72°0W 96 G2
Clarence I. Antarctica 61°10S 54°0W 5 C18
Clarence Str. Australia 12°0S 131°0E 60 B5
Clarence Town Bahamas 23°6N 74°59W 89 B5
Clarendon Pa., U.S.A. 41°47N 79°6W 82 E5
Clarendon Tex., U.S.A. 34°56N 100°53W 84 D4
Clarenville-Shoal Harbour Canada 48°10N 54°1W 73 C9
Claresholm Canada 50°2N 113°33W 70 D6
Clarie Coast Antarctica 68°0S 135°0E 5 C9
Clarinda U.S.A. 40°44N 95°2W 80 E6
Clarington Canada 43°55N 78°41W 82 C6
Clarion Iowa, U.S.A. 42°44N 93°44W 80 D7
Clarion Pa., U.S.A. 41°13N 79°23W 82 E5
Clarion → U.S.A. 41°7N 79°41W 82 E5
Clarion Fracture Zone Pac. Oc. 20°0N 120°0W 66 H7
Clark U.S.A. 44°53N 97°44W 80 C5
Clark, Pt. Canada 44°4N 81°45W 82 B3
Clark Fork U.S.A. 48°9N 116°11W 76 B5
Clark Fork → U.S.A. 48°9N 116°15W 76 B5
Clarkdale U.S.A. 34°46N 112°3W 77 J7
Clarke City Canada 50°12N 66°38W 73 B6
Clarke I. Australia 40°32S 148°10E 63 G4
Clarke Ra. Australia 20°40S 148°30E 62 J6
Clarks Fork Yellowstone → U.S.A. 45°32N 108°50W 76 D9
Clark's Harbour Canada 43°25N 65°38W 73 D6
Clarks Hill L. = J. Strom Thurmond L. U.S.A. 33°40N 82°12W 85 E13
Clarks Summit U.S.A. 41°30N 75°42W 83 E9
Clarksburg U.S.A. 39°17N 80°30W 81 F13
Clarksdale U.S.A. 34°12N 90°35W 85 D9
Clarkston U.S.A. 46°25N 117°3W 76 C5
Clarksville Ark., U.S.A. 35°28N 93°28W 84 D8
Clarksville Tenn., U.S.A. 36°32N 87°21W 85 C11
Clarksville Tex., U.S.A. 33°37N 95°3W 84 E7
Clatskanie U.S.A. 46°6N 123°12W 78 D3
Claude U.S.A. 35°7N 101°22W 84 D4
Claveria Phil. 18°37N 121°4E 37 A6
Clay U.S.A. 38°17N 121°10W 78 G5
Clay Center U.S.A. 39°23N 97°8W 80 F5
Claypool U.S.A. 33°25N 110°51W 77 K8
Claysburg U.S.A. 40°17N 78°27W 82 F6
Claysville U.S.A. 40°7N 80°25W 82 F4
Clayton N. Mex., U.S.A. 36°27N 103°11W 77 H12
Clayton N.Y., U.S.A. 44°14N 76°5W 83 B8
Clear, C. Ireland 51°25N 9°32W 10 E2
Clear, L. Canada 45°26N 77°12W 82 A7
Clear Hills Canada 56°40N 119°30W 70 B5
Clear I. Ireland 51°26N 9°30W 10 E2
Clear L. U.S.A. 39°2N 122°47W 78 F4
Clear Lake Iowa, U.S.A. 43°8N 93°23W 80 D7
Clear Lake S. Dak., U.S.A. 44°45N 96°41W 80 C5
Clear Lake Res. U.S.A. 41°56N 121°5W 76 F3
Clearfield Pa., U.S.A. 41°2N 78°27W 82 E6
Clearfield Utah, U.S.A. 41°7N 112°2W 76 F7
Clearlake U.S.A. 38°57N 122°38W 78 G4
Clearwater Canada 51°38N 120°2W 70 C4
Clearwater U.S.A. 27°59N 82°48W 85 H13
Clearwater → Alta., Canada 52°22N 114°57W 70 C6
Clearwater → Alta., Canada 56°44N 111°23W 71 B6
Clearwater L. Canada 53°34N 99°49W 71 C9
Clearwater Lake ⌓ Canada 54°0N 101°0W 71 C8
Clearwater Mts. U.S.A. 46°5N 115°20W 76 C6
Clearwater River ⌓ Canada 56°55N 109°10W 71 B7
Cleburne U.S.A. 32°21N 97°23W 84 E6
Clee Hills U.K. 52°26N 2°35W 13 E5
Cleethorpes U.K. 53°33N 0°3W 12 D7
Cleeve Cloud U.K. 51°56N 2°0W 13 F6
Clemson U.S.A. 34°41N 82°50W 85 D13
Clerke Reef Australia 17°22S 119°20E 60 C2
Clermont Australia 22°49S 147°39E 62 C4
Clermont U.S.A. 28°33N 81°46W 85 G14
Clermont-Ferrand France 45°46N 3°4E 20 D5
Clervaux Lux. 50°4N 6°2E 15 D6
Clevedon U.K. 51°26N 2°52W 13 F5
Cleveland Miss., U.S.A. 33°45N 90°43W 85 E9
Cleveland Ohio, U.S.A. 41°29N 81°41W 82 E3
Cleveland Okla., U.S.A. 36°19N 96°28W 84 C6
Cleveland Tenn., U.S.A. 35°10N 84°53W 85 D12
Cleveland Tex., U.S.A. 30°21N 95°5W 84 F7
Cleveland, C. Australia 19°11S 147°1E 62 B4
Cleveland, Mt. U.S.A. 48°56N 113°51W 76 B7
Cleveland Heights U.S.A. 41°31N 81°33W 82 E3
Clevelândia Brazil 26°24S 52°23W 95 B5
Clew B. Ireland 53°50N 9°49W 10 C2
Clewiston U.S.A. 26°45N 80°56W 85 H14
Clifden Ireland 53°29N 10°1W 10 C1
Clifden N.Z. 46°1S 167°42E 59 G1
Cliffdell U.S.A. 46°56N 121°5W 78 D5
Cliffy Hd. Australia 35°1S 116°29E 61 G2
Clifton Australia 27°59S 151°53E 63 D5
Clifton Ariz., U.S.A. 33°3N 109°18W 77 K9
Clifton Colo., U.S.A. 39°7N 108°25W 76 G9
Clifton Tex., U.S.A. 31°47N 97°35W 84 F6
Clifton Beach Australia 16°46S 145°39E 62 B4
Climax Canada 49°10N 108°20W 71 D7
Clinch → U.S.A. 35°53N 84°29W 85 D12
Clingmans Dome U.S.A. 35°34N 83°30W 85 D13
Clint U.S.A. 31°35N 106°14W 84 F1
Clinton B.C., Canada 51°6N 121°35W 70 C4
Clinton Ont., Canada 43°37N 81°32W 82 C3
Clinton N.Z. 46°12S 169°23E 59 G2
Clinton Ark., U.S.A. 35°36N 92°28W 84 D8
Clinton Conn., U.S.A. 41°17N 72°32W 83 E12
Clinton Ill., U.S.A. 40°9N 88°57W 80 E9
Clinton Ind., U.S.A. 39°40N 87°24W 80 F10
Clinton Iowa, U.S.A. 41°51N 90°12W 80 E8
Clinton Mass., U.S.A. 42°25N 71°41W 83 D13
Clinton Miss., U.S.A. 32°20N 90°20W 85 E9
Clinton Mo., U.S.A. 38°22N 93°46W 80 F7
Clinton N.C., U.S.A. 35°0N 78°22W 85 D15
Clinton Okla., U.S.A. 35°31N 98°58W 84 D5
Clinton S.C., U.S.A. 34°29N 81°53W 85 D14
Clinton Tenn., U.S.A. 36°6N 84°8W 85 C12
Clinton Wash., U.S.A. 47°59N 122°21W 78 C4
Clinton C. Australia 22°30S 150°45E 62 C5
Clinton Colden L. Canada 63°58N 107°27W 68 C9
Clintonville U.S.A. 44°37N 88°46W 80 C9
Clipperton, I. Pac. Oc. 10°18N 109°13W 65 F17
Clipperton Fracture Zone Pac. Oc. 19°0N 122°0W 65 G16
Clisham U.K. 57°58N 6°49W 11 D2
Clitheroe U.K. 53°53N 2°22W 12 D5
Clo-oose Canada 48°39N 124°49W 78 B2
Cloates, Pt. Australia 22°43S 113°40E 60 D1
Clocolan S. Africa 28°55S 27°34E 57 D4
Clodomira Argentina 27°35S 64°14W 94 B3
Clogher Hd. Ireland 53°48N 6°14W 10 C5
Clonakilty Ireland 51°37N 8°53W 10 E3
Clonakilty B. Ireland 51°35N 8°51W 10 E3
Cloncurry Australia 20°40S 140°28E 62 C3
Cloncurry Ireland 53°25N 6°48W 10 C5
Cloncurry → Australia 18°37S 140°40E 62 B3
Clondalkin Ireland 53°19N 6°25W 10 C5
Clones Ireland 54°11N 7°15W 10 B4
Clonmel Ireland 52°21N 7°42W 10 D4
Cloquet U.S.A. 46°43N 92°28W 80 B7
Clorinda Argentina 25°16S 57°45W 94 B4
Cloud Bay Canada 48°5N 89°26W 72 C2
Cloud Peak U.S.A. 44°23N 107°11W 76 D10
Cloudcroft U.S.A. 32°58N 105°45W 77 K11
Cloverdale U.S.A. 38°48N 123°1W 78 G4
Clovis Calif., U.S.A. 36°49N 119°42W 78 J7
Clovis N. Mex., U.S.A. 34°24N 103°12W 77 J12
Cloyne Canada 44°49N 77°11W 82 B7
Cluj-Napoca Romania 46°47N 23°38E 17 E12
Clunes Australia 37°20S 143°45E 63 F3
Clutha → N.Z. 46°20S 169°49E 59 G2
Clwyd → U.K. 53°19N 3°31W 12 D4
Clyde Canada 54°9N 113°39W 70 C6
Clyde N.Z. 45°12S 169°20E 59 F2
Clyde U.S.A. 43°5N 76°52W 82 C8
Clyde → U.K. 55°55N 4°30W 11 F4
Clyde, Firth of U.K. 55°22N 5°1W 11 F3
Clyde Muirshiel ⌓ U.K. 55°50N 4°40W 11 F4
Clyde River Canada 70°30N 68°30W 69 B13
Clydebank U.K. 55°54N 4°23W 11 F4
Clymer N.Y., U.S.A. 42°1N 79°37W 82 D5
Clymer Pa., U.S.A. 40°40N 79°1W 82 D5
Coachella U.S.A. 33°41N 116°10W 79 M10
Coachella Canal U.S.A. 32°43N 114°57W 79 N12
Coahoma U.S.A. 32°18N 101°18W 84 E4
Coahuayana → Mexico 18°41N 103°45W 86 D4
Coahuila ☐ Mexico 27°20N 102°0W 86 B4
Coal → Canada 59°39N 126°57W 70 B3
Coalane Mozam. 17°48S 37°2E 55 F4
Coalcomán Mexico 18°47N 103°9W 86 D4
Coaldale Canada 49°45N 112°35W 70 D6
Coalgate U.S.A. 34°32N 96°13W 84 D6
Coalinga U.S.A. 36°9N 120°21W 78 J6
Coalisland U.K. 54°33N 6°42W 10 B5
Coalville U.K. 52°44N 1°23W 12 E6
Coalville U.S.A. 40°55N 111°24W 76 F8
Coamo Puerto Rico 18°5N 66°22W 89 d
Coari Brazil 4°8S 63°7W 92 D6
Coast ☐ Kenya 2°40S 39°45E 54 C4
Coast Mts. Canada 55°0N 129°20W 70 C3
Coast Ranges U.S.A. 39°0N 123°0W 78 G4
Coatbridge U.K. 55°52N 4°6W 11 F4
Coatepec Mexico 19°27N 96°58W 87 D5
Coatepeque Guatemala 14°46N 91°55W 88 D1
Coatesville U.S.A. 39°59N 75°50W 81 F16
Coaticook Canada 45°10N 71°46W 83 A13
Coats I. Canada 62°30N 83°0W 69 C11
Coats Land Antarctica 77°0S 25°0W 5 D1
Coatzacoalcos Mexico 18°7N 94°25W 87 D6
Cobá Mexico 20°31N 87°45W 87 C7
Cobalt Canada 47°25N 79°42W 72 C4
Cobán Guatemala 15°30N 90°21W 88 C1
Cobar Australia 31°27S 145°48E 63 E4
Cóbh Ireland 51°51N 8°17W 10 E3
Cobija Bolivia 11°0S 68°50W 92 F5
Cobleskill U.S.A. 42°41N 74°29W 83 D10
Coboconk Canada 44°39N 78°48W 82 B6
Cobourg Canada 43°58N 78°10W 82 C6
Cobourg ⌓ Australia 11°26S 131°58E 60 B5
Cobourg Pen. Australia 11°20S 132°15E 60 B5
Cobram Australia 35°54S 145°40E 63 F4
Cóbué Mozam. 12°0S 34°58E 55 E3
Coburg Germany 50°15N 10°58E 16 C6
Cocanada = Kakinada India 16°57N 82°11E 41 L13
Cochabamba Bolivia 17°26S 66°10W 92 G5
Cochemane Mozam. 17°0S 32°54E 55 F3

Cochin *India* 9°58N 76°20E **40** Q10
Cochin China = Nam-Phan
  Vietnam 10°30N 106°0E **39** G6
Cochran *U.S.A.* 32°23N 83°21W **85** E13
Cochrane *Alta., Canada* 51°11N 114°30W **70** C6
Cochrane *Ont., Canada* 49°0N 81°0W **72** C3
Cochrane *Chile* 47°15S 72°33W **96** F2
Cochrane ➤ *Canada* 59°0N 103°40W **71** B8
Cochrane, L. *Chile* 47°10S 72°0W **96** F2
Cochranton *U.S.A.* 41°31N 80°3W **82** E4
Cockburn, Canal *Chile* 54°30S 72°0W **96** G2
Cockburn I. *Canada* 45°55N 83°22W **72** C3
Cockburn Ra. *Australia* 15°46S 128°0E **60** C4
Cockermouth *U.K.* 54°40N 3°22W **12** C4
Cocklebiddy *Australia* 32°0S 126°3E **61** F4
Cockpit Country, The
  Jamaica 18°15N 77°45W **88** a
Coco ➤ *Cent. Amer.* 15°0N 83°8W **88** D3
Coco, I. del *Pac. Oc.* 5°25N 87°55W **65** G19
Cocoa *U.S.A.* 28°21N 80°44W **85** G14
Cocobeach *Gabon* 0°59N 9°34E **52** D1
Cocos B. *Trin. & Tob.* 10°25N 61°2W **93** K15
Cocos Is. *Ind. Oc.* 12°10S 96°55E **64** J11
Cocos Ridge *Pac. Oc.* 4°0N 88°0W **65** G19
Cod, C. *U.S.A.* 42°5N 70°10W **81** D18
Codajás *Brazil* 3°55S 62°0W **92** D6
Codó *Brazil* 4°30S 43°55W **93** D10
Cody *U.S.A.* 44°32N 109°3W **76** D9
Coe Hill *Canada* 44°52N 77°50W **82** B7
Coelemu *Chile* 36°30S 72°48W **94** D1
Coen *Australia* 13°52S 143°12E **62** A3
Coeur d'Alene *U.S.A.* 47°41N 116°46W **76** C5
Coeur d'Alene L.
  U.S.A. 47°32N 116°49W **76** C5
Coevorden *Neths.* 52°40N 6°44E **15** B6
Cofete *Canary Is.* 28°6N 14°23W **24** F5
Coffeyville *U.S.A.* 37°2N 95°37W **80** G6
Coffin B. *Australia* 34°38S 135°28E **63** E2
Coffin Bay *Australia* 34°37S 135°29E **63** E2
Coffin Bay △ *Australia* 34°34S 135°19E **63** E2
Coffin Bay Peninsula
  Australia 34°32S 135°15E **63** E2
Coffs Harbour *Australia* 30°16S 153°5E **63** E5
Cognac *France* 45°41N 0°20W **20** D3
Cohocton *U.S.A.* 42°30N 77°30W **82** D7
Cohocton ➤ *U.S.A.* 42°9N 77°6W **82** D7
Cohoes *U.S.A.* 42°46N 73°42W **83** D11
Cohuna *Australia* 35°45S 144°15E **63** F3
Coiba, I. de *Panama* 7°30N 81°40W **88** E3
Coig ➤ *Argentina* 51°0S 69°10W **96** G3
Coigeach, Rubha *U.K.* 58°6N 5°26W **11** C3
Coihaique *Chile* 45°30S 71°45W **96** F2
Coimbatore *India* 11°2N 76°59E **40** P10
Coimbra *Brazil* 19°55S 57°48W **92** G7
Coimbra *Portugal* 40°15N 8°27W **21** B1
Coín *Spain* 36°40N 4°48W **21** D3
Coipasa, Salar de *Bolivia* 19°26S 68°9W **92** G5
Cojimíes *Ecuador* 0°20N 80°0W **92** C3
Cojutepequé *El Salv.* 13°41N 88°54W **88** D2
Cokeville *U.S.A.* 42°5N 110°57W **76** E8
Colac *Australia* 38°21S 143°35E **63** F3
Colatina *Brazil* 19°32S 40°37W **93** G10
Colbeck, C. *Antarctica* 77°6S 157°48W **5** D13
Colborne *Canada* 44°0N 77°53W **82** C7
Colby *U.S.A.* 39°24N 101°3W **80** F4
Colca ➤ *Peru* 15°55S 72°43W **92** G4
Colchester *U.K.* 51°54N 0°55E **13** F8
Colchester *U.S.A.* 41°35N 72°20W **83** E12
Cold L. *Canada* 54°33N 110°5W **71** C7
Coldstream *Canada* 50°13N 119°11W **70** C5
Coldstream *U.K.* 55°39N 2°15W **11** F6
Coldwater *Canada* 44°42N 79°40W **82** B5
Coldwater *Kans., U.S.A.* 37°16N 99°20W **80** G4
Coldwater *Mich., U.S.A.* 41°57N 85°0W **81** E11
Colebrook *U.S.A.* 44°54N 71°30W **83** B13
Coleman *U.S.A.* 31°50N 99°26W **84** F5
Coleman ➤ *Australia* 15°6S 141°38E **62** A3
Colenso *S. Africa* 28°44S 29°50E **57** D4
Coleraine *Australia* 37°36S 141°40E **63** F3
Coleraine *U.K.* 55°8N 6°41W **10** A5
Coleridge, L. *N.Z.* 43°17S 171°30E **59** E3
Colesberg *S. Africa* 30°45S 25°5E **56** E4
Coleville *U.S.A.* 38°34N 119°30W **78** G7
Colfax *Calif., U.S.A.* 39°6N 120°57W **78** F6
Colfax *La., U.S.A.* 31°31N 92°42W **84** F8
Colfax *Wash., U.S.A.* 46°53N 117°22W **76** C5
Colhué Huapi, L.
  Argentina 45°30S 69°0W **96** F3
Coligny *S. Africa* 26°17S 26°15E **57** D4
Colima *Mexico* 19°14N 103°43W **86** D4
Colima □ *Mexico* 19°10N 104°0W **86** D4
Colima, Nevado de
  Mexico 19°33N 103°38W **86** D4
Colina *Chile* 33°13S 70°45W **94** C1
Colinas *Brazil* 6°0S 44°10W **93** E10
Coll *U.K.* 56°39N 6°34W **11** E2
Collaguasi *Chile* 21°5S 68°45W **94** A2
Collarenebri *Australia* 29°33S 148°34E **63** D4
Colleen Bawn *Zimbabwe* 21°0S 29°12E **55** G2
College Park *U.S.A.* 33°39N 84°27W **85** E12
College Station *U.S.A.* 30°37N 96°21W **84** F6
Collie *Australia* 33°22S 116°8E **61** F2
Collier B. *Australia* 16°10S 124°15E **60** C3
Collier Ra. *Australia* 24°45S 119°10E **61** D2
Collier Range △
  Australia 24°39S 119°7E **61** D2
Collierville *U.S.A.* 35°3N 89°40W **85** D10
Collina, Passo di *Italy* 44°2N 10°56E **22** B4
Collingwood *Canada* 44°29N 80°13W **82** B4
Collingwood *N.Z.* 40°41S 172°40E **59** D4
Collins *Canada* 50°17N 89°27W **72** B2
Collinsville *Australia* 20°30S 147°56E **62** C4
Collipulli *Chile* 37°55S 72°30W **94** D1
Collooney *Ireland* 54°11N 8°29W **10** B3
Colmar *France* 48°5N 7°20E **20** B7
Colo ➤ *Australia* 33°25S 150°52E **63** E5
Cologne = Köln *Germany* 50°56N 6°57E **16** C4

Colom, I. d'en *Spain* 39°58N 4°16E **24** B11
Coloma *U.S.A.* 38°48N 120°53W **78** G6
Colomb-Béchar = Béchar
  Algeria 31°38N 2°18W **50** B5
Colombia ■ *S. Amer.* 3°45N 73°0W **92** C4
Colombian Basin
  S. Amer. 14°0N 76°0W **66** H12
Colombo *Sri Lanka* 6°56N 79°58E **40** R11
Colón B. Aires, Argentina* 33°53S 61°7W **94** C3
Colón *Entre Ríos,
  Argentina* 32°12S 58°10W **94** C4
Colón *Cuba* 22°42N 80°54W **88** B3
Colón *Panama* 9°20N 79°54W **88** E4
Colón, Arch. de *Ecuador* 0°0 91°0W **90** D1
Colònia de Sant Jordi
  Spain 39°19N 2°59E **24** B9
Colonia del Sacramento
  Uruguay 34°25S 57°50W **94** C4
Colonia Dora *Argentina* 28°34S 62°59W **94** B3
Colonial Beach *U.S.A.* 38°15N 76°58W **81** F15
Colonie *U.S.A.* 42°43N 73°50W **83** D11
Colonsay *Canada* 51°59N 105°52W **71** C7
Colonsay *U.K.* 56°5N 6°12W **11** E2
Colorado □ *U.S.A.* 39°30N 105°30W **76** G11
Colorado ➤ *Argentina* 39°50S 62°8W **96** D4
Colorado ➤ *N. Amer.* 31°45N 114°40W **77** L6
Colorado ➤ *U.S.A.* 28°36N 95°59W **84** G7
Colorado City *U.S.A.* 32°24N 100°52W **84** E4
Colorado Plateau *U.S.A.* 37°0N 111°0W **77** H8
Colorado River Aqueduct
  U.S.A. 33°50N 117°23W **79** L12
Colorado Springs
  U.S.A. 38°50N 104°49W **76** G11
Colotlán *Mexico* 22°6N 103°16W **86** C4
Colstrip *U.S.A.* 45°53N 106°38W **76** D10
Colton *U.S.A.* 44°33N 74°56W **83** B10
Columbia *Ky., U.S.A.* 37°6N 85°18W **81** G11
Columbia *La., U.S.A.* 32°6N 92°5W **84** E8
Columbia *Miss., U.S.A.* 31°15N 89°50W **85** F10
Columbia *Mo., U.S.A.* 38°57N 92°20W **80** F7
Columbia *Pa., U.S.A.* 40°2N 76°30W **83** F8
Columbia *S.C., U.S.A.* 34°0N 81°2W **85** D14
Columbia *Tenn., U.S.A.* 35°37N 87°2W **85** D11
Columbia ➤ *N. Amer.* 46°15N 124°5W **78** D2
Columbia, C. *Canada* 83°6N 69°57W **69** A11
Columbia, District of □
  U.S.A. 38°55N 77°0W **81** F15
Columbia, Mt. *Canada* 52°8N 117°20W **70** C5
Columbia Basin *U.S.A.* 46°45N 119°5W **76** C4
Columbia Falls *U.S.A.* 48°23N 114°11W **76** B6
Columbia Mts. *Canada* 52°0N 119°0W **70** C5
Columbia Plateau
  U.S.A. 44°0N 117°30W **76** E5
Columbiana *U.S.A.* 40°53N 80°42W **82** F4
Columbretes, Is. *Spain* 39°50N 0°50E **21** C6
Columbus *Ga., U.S.A.* 32°28N 84°59W **85** E12
Columbus *Ind., U.S.A.* 39°13N 85°55W **81** F11
Columbus *Kans., U.S.A.* 37°10N 94°50W **80** G6
Columbus *Miss.,
  U.S.A.* 33°30N 88°25W **85** E10
Columbus *Mont.,
  U.S.A.* 45°38N 109°15W **76** D9
Columbus *N. Mex.,
  U.S.A.* 31°50N 107°38W **77** L10
Columbus *Nebr., U.S.A.* 41°26N 97°22W **80** E5
Columbus *Ohio, U.S.A.* 39°58N 83°0W **81** F12
Columbus *Tex., U.S.A.* 29°42N 96°33W **84** G6
Colusa *U.S.A.* 39°13N 122°1W **78** F4
Colville *U.S.A.* 48°33N 117°54W **76** B5
Colville ➤ *U.S.A.* 70°25N 150°30W **74** a
Colville, C. *N.Z.* 36°29S 175°21E **59** B5
Colwood *Canada* 48°26N 123°29W **78** B3
Colwyn Bay *U.K.* 53°18N 3°44W **12** D4
Comácchio *Italy* 44°42N 12°11E **22** B5
Comalcalco *Mexico* 18°16N 93°13W **87** D6
Comallo *Argentina* 41°0S 70°5W **96** E2
Comanche *U.S.A.* 31°54N 98°36W **84** F5
Comandante Ferraz
  Antarctica 62°30S 58°0W **5** C18
Comayagua *Honduras* 14°25N 87°37W **88** D2
Combahee ➤ *U.S.A.* 32°31N 80°31W **85** E14
Combarbalá *Chile* 31°11S 71°2W **94** C1
Combe Martin *U.K.* 51°12N 4°3W **13** F3
Comber *Canada* 42°14N 82°33W **82** D2
Comber *U.K.* 54°33N 5°45W **10** B6
Combermere *Canada* 45°22N 77°37W **82** A7
Comblain-au-Pont
  Belgium 50°29N 5°35E **15** D5
Comeragh Mts. *Ireland* 52°18N 7°34W **10** D4
Comet *Australia* 23°36S 148°38E **62** C4
Comilla *Bangla.* 23°28N 91°10E **41** H17
Comino *Malta* 36°1N 14°20E **25** C1
Comino, C. *Italy* 40°32N 9°49E **22** D3
Comitán de Domínguez
  Mexico 16°15N 92°8W **87** D6
Commerce *Ga., U.S.A.* 34°12N 83°28W **85** D13
Commerce *Tex., U.S.A.* 33°15N 95°54W **84** E7
Committee B. *Canada* 68°30N 86°30W **69** C11
Commonwealth B.
  Antarctica 67°0S 144°0E **5** C10
Commoron Cr. ➤
  Australia 28°22S 150°8E **63** D5
Communism Pk. = imeni Ismail
  Samani, Pik *Tajikistan* 39°0N 72°2E **28** F8
Como *Italy* 45°47N 9°5E **20** D8
Como, Lago di *Italy* 46°0N 9°11E **20** D8
Comodoro Rivadavia
  Argentina 45°50S 67°40W **96** F3
Comorin, C. *India* 8°3N 77°40E **40** Q10
Comoros ■ *Ind. Oc.* 12°10S 44°15E **53** a
Comox *Canada* 49°42N 124°55W **70** D4
Compiègne *France* 49°24N 2°50E **20** B5
Compostela *Mexico* 21°14N 104°55W **86** C4
Comprida, I. *Brazil* 24°50S 47°42W **95** A6
Compton *Canada* 45°14N 71°49W **83** A13
Compton *U.S.A.* 33°53N 118°13W **79** M8
Comrat *Moldova* 46°18N 28°40E **17** E15
Con Cuong *Vietnam* 19°2N 104°54E **38** C5

Con Dao △ *Vietnam* 8°42N 106°35E **39** H6
Con Son *Vietnam* 8°41N 106°37E **39** H6
Conakry *Guinea* 9°29N 13°49W **50** G3
Conara *Australia* 41°50S 147°26E **63** G4
Concarneau *France* 47°52N 3°56W **20** C2
Conceição *Mozam.* 18°47S 36°7E **55** F4
Conceição da Barra
  Brazil 18°35S 39°45W **93** G11
Conceição do Araguaia
  Brazil 8°0S 49°2W **93** E9
Concepción *Argentina* 27°20S 65°35W **94** B2
Concepción *Bolivia* 16°15S 62°8W **92** G6
Concepción *Chile* 36°50S 73°0W **94** D1
Concepción *Mexico* 18°15N 90°5W **87** D6
Concepción *Paraguay* 23°22S 57°26W **94** A4
Concepción □ *Chile* 37°0S 72°30W **94** D1
Concepción ➤ *Mexico* 30°32N 113°2W **86** A2
Concepción, Est. de
  Chile 50°30S 74°55W **96** G2
Concepción, L. *Bolivia* 17°20S 61°20W **92** G6
Concepción, Pta.
  Mexico 26°53N 111°50W **86** B2
Concepción del Oro
  Mexico 24°38N 101°25W **86** C4
Concepción del Uruguay
  Argentina 32°35S 58°20W **94** C4
Conception, Pt. *U.S.A.* 34°27N 120°28W **79** L6
Conception B. *Canada* 47°45N 53°0W **73** C9
Conception B. *Namibia* 23°55S 14°22E **56** C1
Conception I. *Bahamas* 23°52N 75°9W **89** B4
Concession *Zimbabwe* 17°27S 30°56E **55** F3
Conchas Dam *U.S.A.* 35°22N 104°11W **77** J11
Concho *U.S.A.* 34°28N 109°36W **77** J9
Concho ➤ *U.S.A.* 31°34N 99°43W **84** F5
Conchos ➤ *Chihuahua,
  Mexico* 29°35N 104°25W **86** B4
Conchos ➤ *Chihuahua,
  Mexico* 27°29N 106°45W **86** B3
Conchos ➤ *Tamaulipas,
  Mexico* 24°55N 97°38W **87** B5
Concord *Calif., U.S.A.* 37°59N 122°2W **78** H4
Concord *N.C., U.S.A.* 35°25N 80°35W **85** D14
Concord *N.H., U.S.A.* 43°12N 71°32W **83** C13
Concordia *Antarctica* 75°6S 123°23E **5** D17
Concordia *Argentina* 31°20S 58°2W **94** C4
Concórdia *Brazil* 4°36S 66°36W **92** D5
Concordia *Mexico* 23°17N 106°4W **86** C3
Concordia *U.S.A.* 39°34N 97°40W **80** F5
Concrete *U.S.A.* 48°32N 121°45W **76** B3
Condamine *Australia* 26°56S 150°9E **63** D5
Condamine ➤ *Australia* 28°29S 137°46E **65** F12
Conde *U.S.A.* 45°9N 98°6W **80** C4
Condeúba *Brazil* 14°52S 42°0W **93** F10
Condobolin *Australia* 33°4S 147°6E **63** E4
Condon *U.S.A.* 45°14N 120°11W **76** D3
Conegliano *Italy* 45°53N 12°18E **22** B5
Conejera, I. = Conills, I. des
  Spain 39°11N 2°58E **24** B9
Conejos *Mexico* 26°14N 103°53W **86** B4
Conemaugh ➤ *U.S.A.* 40°28N 79°19W **82** F5
Confuso ➤ *Paraguay* 25°9S 57°34W **94** B4
Congleton *U.K.* 53°10N 2°13W **12** D5
Congo (Brazzaville) = Congo ■
  Africa 1°0S 16°0E **52** E3
Congo (Kinshasa) = Congo, Dem.
  Rep. of the ■ *Africa* 3°0S 23°0E **52** E4
Congo ■ *Africa* 1°0S 16°0E **52** E3
Congo ➤ *Africa* 6°4S 12°24E **52** F2
Congo, Dem. Rep. of the ■
  Africa 3°0S 23°0E **52** E4
Congo Basin *Africa* 0°10S 24°30E **52** E4
Congonhas *Brazil* 20°30S 43°52W **95** A7
Congress *U.S.A.* 34°9N 112°51W **77** J7
Conills, I. des *Spain* 39°11N 2°58E **24** B9
Coniston *Canada* 46°29N 80°51W **72** C3
Conjeeveram = Kanchipuram
  India 12°52N 79°45E **40** N11
Conklin *Canada* 55°38N 111°5W **71** B6
Conklin *U.S.A.* 42°2N 75°49W **83** D9
Conn, L. *Ireland* 54°3N 9°15W **10** B2
Connacht □ *Ireland* 53°43N 9°12W **10** C2
Conneaut *U.S.A.* 41°57N 80°34W **82** E4
Connecticut □ *U.S.A.* 41°30N 72°45W **83** E12
Connecticut ➤ *U.S.A.* 41°16N 72°20W **83** E12
Connell *U.S.A.* 46°40N 118°52W **76** C4
Connellsville *U.S.A.* 40°1N 79°35W **82** F5
Connemara *Ireland* 53°29N 9°45W **10** C2
Connemara △ *Ireland* 53°32N 9°52W **10** C2
Connersville *U.S.A.* 39°39N 85°8W **81** F11
Connors Ra. *Australia* 21°40S 149°10E **62** C4
Conquest *Canada* 51°32N 107°14W **71** C7
Conrad *U.S.A.* 48°10N 111°57W **76** B8
Conran, C. *Australia* 37°49S 148°44E **63** F4
Conroe *U.S.A.* 30°19N 95°27W **84** F7
Consecon *Canada* 44°0N 77°31W **82** C7
Conselheiro Lafaiete
  Brazil 20°40S 43°48W **95** A7
Consett *U.K.* 54°51N 1°50W **12** C6
Consort *Canada* 52°1N 110°46W **71** C6
Constance = Konstanz
  Germany 47°40N 9°10E **16** E5
Constance, L. = Bodensee
  Europe 47°35N 9°25E **20** E8
Constanța *Romania* 44°14N 28°38E **17** F15
Constantia *U.S.A.* 43°15N 76°1W **83** C8
Constantine *Algeria* 36°25N 6°42E **50** A7
Constitución *Chile* 35°20S 72°30W **94** D1
Constitución *Uruguay* 31°0S 57°50W **94** C4
Constitución de 1857 △
  Mexico 32°4N 115°55W **86** A1
Consul *Canada* 49°20N 109°30W **71** D7
Contact *U.S.A.* 41°46N 114°45W **76** F6
Contai *India* 21°54N 87°46E **43** J12
Contamana *Peru* 7°19S 74°55W **92** E4
Contas ➤ *Brazil* 14°17S 39°1W **93** F11
Contoocook *U.S.A.* 43°13N 71°45W **83** C13
Contra Costa *Mozam.* 25°9S 33°30E **57** D5
Contwoyto L. *Canada* 65°42N 110°50W **68** C8
Conway = Conwy *U.K.* 53°17N 3°50W **12** D4

Conway = Conwy ➤
  U.K. 53°17N 3°50W **12** D4
Conway *Australia* 20°24S 148°41E **62** J6
Conway *Ark., U.S.A.* 35°5N 92°26W **84** D8
Conway *N.H., U.S.A.* 43°59N 71°7W **83** C13
Conway *S.C., U.S.A.* 33°51N 79°3W **85** E15
Conway, C. *Australia* 20°34S 148°46E **62** J6
Conway, L. *Australia* 28°17S 135°35E **63** D2
Conwy □ *U.K.* 53°17N 3°50W **12** D4
Conwy □ *U.K.* 53°10N 3°44W **12** D4
Conwy ➤ *U.K.* 53°17N 3°50W **12** D4
Coober Pedy *Australia* 29°1S 134°43E **63** D1
Cooch Behar = Koch Bihar
  India 26°22N 89°29E **41** F16
Cooinda *Australia* 13°15S 130°5E **60** B5
Cook *Australia* 30°37S 130°25E **61** F5
Cook *U.S.A.* 47°51N 92°41W **80** B7
Cook, B. *Chile* 55°10S 70°0W **96** H3
Cook, C. *Canada* 50°8N 127°55W **70** C3
Cook, Mt. = Aoraki Mount Cook
  N.Z. 43°36S 170°9E **59** E3
Cook Inlet *U.S.A.* 60°0N 152°0W **68** D4
Cook Is. *Pac. Oc.* 17°0S 160°0W **65** J12
Cook Strait *N.Z.* 41°15S 174°29E **59** D5
Cookeville *U.S.A.* 36°10N 85°30W **85** C12
Cookhouse *S. Africa* 32°44S 25°47E **56** E4
Cookshire *Canada* 45°25N 71°38W **83** A13
Cookstown *U.K.* 54°39N 6°45W **10** B5
Cooksville *Canada* 43°35N 79°38W **82** C5
Cooktown *Australia* 15°30S 145°16E **62** B4
Coolabah *Australia* 31°1S 146°43E **63** E4
Cooladdi *Australia* 26°37S 145°23E **63** D4
Coolah *Australia* 31°48S 149°41E **63** E4
Coolamon *Australia* 34°46S 147°8E **63** E4
Coolgardie *Australia* 30°55S 121°8E **61** F3
Coolidge *U.S.A.* 32°59N 111°31W **77** K8
Coolidge Dam *U.S.A.* 33°10N 110°32W **77** K8
Cooma *Australia* 36°12S 149°8E **63** F4
Coon Rapids *U.S.A.* 45°9N 93°19W **80** C7
Coonabarabran
  Australia 31°14S 149°18E **63** E4
Coonamble *Australia* 30°56S 148°27E **63** E4
Coonana *Australia* 31°0S 123°0E **61** F3
Coondapoor *India* 13°42N 74°40E **40** N9
Cooninnie, L. *Australia* 26°4S 139°59E **63** D2
Cooper *U.S.A.* 33°23N 95°42W **84** E7
Cooper Cr. ➤ *Australia* 28°29S 137°46E **63** D2
Cooper Ridge *Pac. Oc.* 10°15S 150°30W **65** F12
Cooperstown *N. Dak.,
  U.S.A.* 47°27N 98°8W **80** B4
Cooperstown *N.Y.,
  U.S.A.* 42°42N 74°56W **83** D10
Coorabie *Australia* 31°54S 132°18E **61** F5
Coorong, The *Australia* 35°50S 139°20E **63** F2
Coorow *Australia* 29°53S 116°2E **61** E2
Cooroy *Australia* 26°22S 152°54E **63** D5
Coos Bay *U.S.A.* 43°22N 124°13W **76** E1
Coosa ➤ *U.S.A.* 32°30N 86°16W **85** E11
Cootamundra *Australia* 34°36S 148°1E **63** E4
Cootehill *Ireland* 54°4N 7°5W **10** B4
Copahue Paso *Argentina* 37°49S 71°8W **94** D1
Copainalá *Mexico* 17°4N 93°18W **87** D6
Copán *Honduras* 14°50N 89°9W **88** D2
Cope *U.S.A.* 39°40N 102°51W **76** G12
Copenhagen = København
  Denmark 55°40N 12°26E **9** J15
Copenhagen *U.S.A.* 43°54N 75°41W **83** C9
Copiapó *Chile* 27°30S 70°20W **94** B1
Copiapó ➤ *Chile* 27°19S 70°56W **94** B1
Coplay *U.S.A.* 40°44N 75°29W **83** F9
Copp L. *Canada* 60°14N 114°40W **70** A6
Coppename ➤ *Suriname* 5°48N 55°55W **93** B7
Copper Canyon = Barranca del
  Cobre △ *Mexico* 27°18N 107°40W **86** B3
Copper Harbor *U.S.A.* 47°28N 87°53W **81** B10
Copper Queen *Zimbabwe* 17°29S 29°18E **55** F2
Copperas Cove *U.S.A.* 31°8N 97°54W **84** F6
Copperbelt □ *Zambia* 13°15S 27°30E **55** E2
Coppermine = Kugluktuk
  Canada 67°50N 115°5W **68** C8
Coppermine ➤ *Canada* 67°49N 116°4W **68** C8
Copperopolis *U.S.A.* 37°58N 120°38W **78** H6
Coquet ➤ *U.K.* 55°20N 1°32W **12** B6
Coquille *U.S.A.* 43°11N 124°11W **76** E1
Coquimbo *Chile* 30°0S 71°20W **94** C1
Coquimbo □ *Chile* 31°0S 71°0W **94** C1
Corabia *Romania* 43°48N 24°30E **17** G13
Coracora *Peru* 15°5S 73°45W **92** G4
Coraki *Australia* 28°59S 153°17E **63** D5
Coral *U.S.A.* 40°29N 79°10W **82** F5
Coral Gables *U.S.A.* 25°43N 80°16W **85** N14
Coral Harbour *Canada* 64°8N 83°10W **69** C11
Coral Sea *Pac. Oc.* 15°0S 150°0E **58** C8
Coral Sea Basin *Pac. Oc.* 14°0S 152°0E **64** J7
Coral Sea Islands Terr. □
  Australia 20°0S 155°0E **58** C8
Coral Springs *U.S.A.* 26°16N 80°16W **85** H14
Coraopolis *U.S.A.* 40°31N 80°10W **82** F4
Corato *Italy* 41°9N 16°25E **22** D7
Corbett △ *India* 29°20N 79°0E **43** E8
Corbin *U.S.A.* 36°57N 84°6W **81** G11
Corby *U.K.* 52°30N 0°41W **13** E7
Corcaigh = Cork *Ireland* 51°54N 8°29W **10** E3
Corcoran *U.S.A.* 36°6N 119°33W **78** J7
Corcovado △ *Costa Rica* 8°33N 83°35W **88** E3
Corcubión *Spain* 42°56N 9°12W **21** A1
Cordele *U.S.A.* 31°58N 83°47W **85** F13
Cordell *U.S.A.* 35°17N 98°59W **84** D5
Córdoba *Argentina* 31°20S 64°10W **94** C3
Córdoba *Mexico* 18°53N 96°56W **87** D5
Córdoba *Spain* 37°50N 4°50W **21** D3
Córdoba □ *Argentina* 31°22S 64°15W **94** C3
Córdoba, Sierra de
  Argentina 31°10S 64°25W **94** C3
Cordova *U.S.A.* 60°33N 145°45W **68** D5
Corella ➤ *Australia* 19°34S 140°47E **62** B3
Corfield *Australia* 21°40S 143°21E **62** C3

Corfu = Kerkyra *Greece* 39°38N 19°50E **25** A3
Corfu, Str. of = Kerkyras, Notio
  Steno *Greece* 39°34N 20°0E **25** A4
Coria *Spain* 39°58N 6°33W **21** C2
Corigliano Cálabro *Italy* 39°36N 16°31E **22** E7
Coringa Is. *Australia* 16°58S 149°58E **62** B4
Corinth = Korinthos
  Greece 37°56N 22°55E **23** F10
Corinth *Miss., U.S.A.* 34°56N 88°31W **85** D10
Corinth *N.Y., U.S.A.* 43°15N 73°49W **83** C11
Corinth, G. of = Korinthiakos
  Kolpos *Greece* 38°16N 22°30E **23** E10
Corinto *Brazil* 18°20S 44°30W **93** G10
Corinto *Nic.* 12°30N 87°10W **88** D2
Cork *Ireland* 51°54N 8°29W **10** E3
Cork □ *Ireland* 51°57N 8°40W **10** E3
Cork Harbour *Ireland* 51°47N 8°16W **10** E3
Çorlu *Turkey* 41°11N 27°49E **23** D12
Cormack L. *Canada* 60°56N 121°37W **70** A4
Cormorant *Canada* 54°14N 100°35W **71** C8
Cormorant L. *Canada* 54°15N 100°50W **71** C8
Corn Is. = Maíz, Is. del
  Nic. 12°15N 83°4W **88** D3
Cornélio Procópio *Brazil* 23°7S 50°40W **95** A5
Corner Brook *Canada* 48°57N 57°58W **73** C8
Corneşti *Moldova* 47°21N 28°1E **17** E15
Corning *Ark., U.S.A.* 36°25N 90°35W **84** C9
Corning *Calif., U.S.A.* 39°56N 122°11W **76** G2
Corning *Iowa, U.S.A.* 40°59N 94°44W **80** E6
Corning *N.Y., U.S.A.* 42°9N 77°3W **82** D7
Cornwall *Canada* 45°2N 74°44W **83** A10
Cornwall *U.S.A.* 40°17N 76°25W **83** F8
Cornwall □ *U.K.* 50°26N 4°40W **13** G3
Cornwall I. *Canada* 77°37N 94°38W **69** B10
Cornwallis I. *Canada* 75°8N 95°0W **69** B10
Corny Pt. *Australia* 34°55S 137°0E **63** E2
Coro *Venezuela* 11°25N 69°41W **92** A5
Coroatá *Brazil* 4°8S 44°0W **93** D10
Corocoro *Bolivia* 17°15S 68°28W **92** G5
Coroico *Bolivia* 16°0S 67°50W **92** G5
Coromandel *N.Z.* 36°45S 175°31E **59** B5
Coromandel Coast *India* 12°30N 81°0E **40** N12
Corona *Calif., U.S.A.* 33°53N 117°34W **79** M9
Corona *N. Mex.,
  U.S.A.* 34°15N 105°36W **77** J11
Coronach *Canada* 49°7N 105°31W **71** D8
Coronado *U.S.A.* 32°41N 117°10W **79** N9
Coronado, B. de
  Costa Rica 9°0N 83°40W **88** E3
Coronados, Is. Los
  Mexico 32°26N 117°19W **79** N9
Coronation *Canada* 52°5N 111°27W **70** C6
Coronation Gulf *Canada* 68°25N 110°0W **68** C8
Coronation I. *Antarctica* 60°45S 46°0W **5** C18
Coronation Is.
  Australia 14°57S 124°55E **60** B3
Coronda *Argentina* 31°58S 60°56W **94** C3
Coronel *Chile* 37°0S 73°10W **94** D1
Coronel Bogado
  Paraguay 27°11S 56°18W **94** B4
Coronel Dorrego
  Argentina 38°40S 61°10W **94** D3
Coronel Oviedo
  Paraguay 25°24S 56°30W **94** B4
Coronel Pringles
  Argentina 38°0S 61°30W **94** D3
Coronel Suárez
  Argentina 37°30S 61°52W **94** D3
Coronel Vidal *Argentina* 37°28S 57°45W **94** D4
Coropuna, Nevado
  Peru 15°30S 72°41W **92** G4
Corowa *Australia* 35°58S 146°21E **63** F4
Corozal *Belize* 18°23N 88°23W **87** D7
Corozal *Trin. & Tob.* 10°45N 61°37W **93** K15
Corpus *Argentina* 27°10S 55°30W **95** B4
Corpus Christi *U.S.A.* 27°47N 97°24W **84** H6
Corpus Christi, L. *U.S.A.* 28°2N 97°52W **84** G6
Corralejo *Canary Is.* 28°43N 13°53W **24** F6
Corraun Pen. *Ireland* 53°54N 9°54W **10** C2
Corrente ➤ *das Mozam.* 24°6S 35°34E **57** C6
Corrib, L. *Ireland* 53°27N 9°16W **10** C2
Corrientes *Argentina* 27°30S 58°45W **94** B4
Corrientes □ *Argentina* 28°0S 57°0W **94** B4
Corrientes ➤ *Argentina* 30°42S 59°38W **94** C4
Corrientes ➤ *Peru* 3°43S 74°35W **92** D4
Corrientes, C. *Colombia* 5°30N 77°34W **92** B3
Corrientes, C. *Cuba* 21°43N 84°30W **88** B3
Corrientes, C. *Mexico* 20°25N 105°42W **86** C3
Corrigan *U.S.A.* 31°0N 94°52W **84** F7
Corrigin *Australia* 32°20S 117°53E **61** F2
Corriverton *Guyana* 5°55N 57°20W **92** B7
Corry *U.S.A.* 41°55N 79°39W **82** E5
Corse □ *France* 42°0N 9°0E **20** F8
Corse, C. *France* 43°1N 9°25E **20** E8
Corsica = Corse □ *France* 42°0N 9°0E **20** F8
Corsicana *U.S.A.* 32°6N 96°28W **84** E6
Corte *France* 42°19N 9°11E **20** E8
Cortés, Mar de = California, G. de
  Mexico 27°0N 111°0W **86** B2
Cortez *U.S.A.* 37°21N 108°35W **77** H9
Cortland *N.Y., U.S.A.* 42°36N 76°11W **83** D8
Cortland *Ohio, U.S.A.* 41°20N 80°44W **82** E4
Çorum *Turkey* 40°30N 34°57E **19** F5
Corumbá *Brazil* 19°0S 57°30W **92** G7
Corunna = A Coruña
  Spain 43°20N 8°25W **21** A1
Corvallis *U.S.A.* 44°34N 123°16W **76** D2
Corvette, L. de la *Canada* 53°25N 74°3W **72** B5
Corvo *Azores* 39°43N 31°8W **50** a
Corydon *U.S.A.* 40°46N 93°19W **80** E7
Cosalá *Mexico* 24°23N 106°41W **86** C3
Cosamaloapan de Carpio
  Mexico 18°22N 95°48W **87** D5
Cosenza *Italy* 39°18N 16°15E **22** E7
Coshocton *U.S.A.* 40°16N 81°51W **82** F3
Cosmo Newberry
  Australia 28°0S 122°54E **61** E3
Coso Junction *U.S.A.* 36°3N 117°57W **79** J9

Coso Pk. U.S.A. 36°13N 117°44W 79 J9
Cosquín Argentina 31°15S 64°30W 94 C3
Costa Blanca Spain 38°25N 0°10W 21 C5
Costa Brava Spain 41°30N 3°0E 21 B7
Costa del Sol Spain 36°30N 4°30W 21 D3
Costa Dorada Spain 41°12N 1°15E 21 B6
Costa Mesa U.S.A. 33°38N 117°55W 79 M9
Costa Rica ■ Cent. Amer. 10°0N 84°0W 88 E3
Costa Smeralda Italy 41°5N 9°35E 22 D3
Cosumnes → U.S.A. 38°16N 121°26W 78 G5
Cotabato Phil. 7°14N 124°15E 37 C6
Cotagaita Bolivia 20°45S 65°40W 94 A2
Côte d'Azur France 43°25N 7°10E 20 E7
Côte-d'Ivoire = Ivory Coast ■ Africa 7°30N 5°0W 50 G4
Coteau des Prairies U.S.A. 45°20N 97°50W 80 C5
Coteau du Missouri U.S.A. 47°0N 100°0W 80 B4
Cotentin France 49°15N 1°30W 20 B3
Cotillo Canary Is. 28°41N 14°1W 24 F5
Cotonou Benin 6°20N 2°25E 50 G6
Cotopaxi Ecuador 0°40S 78°30W 92 D3
Cotswold Hills U.K. 51°42N 2°10W 13 F5
Cottage Grove U.S.A. 43°48N 123°3W 76 E2
Cottbus Germany 51°45N 14°20E 16 C8
Cottonwood U.S.A. 34°45N 112°1W 77 J7
Cotulla U.S.A. 28°26N 99°14W 84 G5
Coudersport U.S.A. 41°46N 78°1W 82 E6
Couedic, C. du Australia 36°5S 136°40E 63 F2
Coulee City U.S.A. 47°37N 119°17W 76 C4
Coulee Dam Nat. Recr. Area = Lake Roosevelt ⌂ U.S.A. 48°5N 118°14W 76 B4
Coulman I. Antarctica 73°35S 170°0E 5 D11
Coulonge → Canada 45°52N 76°46W 72 C4
Coulterville U.S.A. 37°43N 120°12W 78 H6
Council U.S.A. 44°44N 116°26W 76 D5
Council Bluffs U.S.A. 41°16N 95°52W 80 E6
Council Grove U.S.A. 38°40N 96°29W 80 F5
Coupeville U.S.A. 48°13N 122°41W 78 B4
Courantyne → S. Amer. 5°55N 57°5W 92 B7
Courcelles Belgium 50°28N 4°22E 15 D4
Courtenay Canada 49°45N 125°0W 70 D4
Courtland U.S.A. 38°20N 121°34W 78 G5
Courtrai = Kortrijk Belgium 50°50N 3°17E 15 D3
Courtright Canada 42°49N 82°28W 82 D2
Coushatta U.S.A. 32°1N 93°21W 84 E8
Coutts Crossing Australia 29°49S 152°55E 63 D5
Couva Trin. & Tob. 10°25N 61°27W 93 K15
Couvin Belgium 50°3N 4°29E 15 D4
Cove I. Canada 45°17N 81°44W 82 A3
Coventry U.K. 52°25N 1°28W 13 E6
Covilhã Portugal 40°17N 7°31W 21 B2
Covington Ga., U.S.A. 33°36N 83°51W 85 E13
Covington Ky., U.S.A. 39°5N 84°30W 81 F11
Covington Tenn., U.S.A. 35°34N 89°39W 85 D10
Covington Va., U.S.A. 37°47N 79°59W 81 G14
Cowal, L. Australia 33°40S 147°25E 63 E4
Cowan, L. Australia 31°45S 121°45E 61 F3
Cowan L. Canada 54°0N 107°15W 71 C7
Cowangie Australia 35°12S 141°26E 63 F3
Cowansville Canada 45°14N 72°46W 83 A12
Coward Springs Australia 29°24S 136°49E 63 D2
Cowcowing Lakes Australia 30°55S 117°20E 61 F2
Cowdenbeath U.K. 56°7N 3°21W 11 E5
Cowell Australia 33°39S 136°56E 63 E2
Cowes U.K. 50°45N 1°18W 13 G6
Cowichan L. Canada 48°53N 124°17W 78 B2
Cowlitz → U.S.A. 46°6N 122°55W 78 D4
Cowra Australia 33°49S 148°42E 63 E4
Coxilha Grande Brazil 28°18S 51°30W 95 B5
Coxim Brazil 18°30S 54°55W 93 G8
Cox's Bazar Bangla. 21°26N 91°59E 41 J17
Coyote Wells U.S.A. 32°44N 115°58W 79 N11
Coyuca de Benítez Mexico 17°2N 100°4W 87 D4
Coyuca de Catalán Mexico 18°20N 100°39W 86 D4
Cozad U.S.A. 40°52N 99°59W 80 E4
Cozumel Mexico 20°31N 86°55W 87 C7
Cozumel, Isla Mexico 20°30N 86°40W 87 C7
Crab Hill Barbados 13°19N 59°38W 89 g
Cracow = Kraków Poland 50°4N 19°57E 17 C10
Cracow Australia 25°17S 150°17E 63 D5
Cradle Mt.-Lake St. Clair △ Australia 41°49S 147°56E 63 G4
Cradock Australia 32°6S 138°31E 63 E2
Cradock S. Africa 32°8S 25°36E 56 E4
Craig U.S.A. 40°31N 107°33W 76 F10
Craigavon U.K. 54°27N 6°23W 10 B5
Craigmore Zimbabwe 20°28S 32°50E 55 G3
Craik Canada 51°3N 105°49W 71 C7
Crailsheim Germany 49°8N 10°5E 16 D6
Craiova Romania 44°21N 23°48E 17 F12
Cramsie Australia 23°20S 144°15E 62 C3
Cranberry L. U.S.A. 44°11N 74°50W 83 B10
Cranberry Portage Canada 54°35N 101°23W 71 C8
Cranbrook Australia 34°18S 117°33E 61 F2
Cranbrook Canada 49°30N 115°46W 70 D5
Crandon U.S.A. 45°34N 88°54W 80 C9
Crane Oreg., U.S.A. 43°25N 118°35W 76 E4
Crane Tex., U.S.A. 31°24N 102°21W 84 F3
Crane, The Barbados 13°6N 59°27W 89 g
Cranston U.S.A. 41°47N 71°26W 83 E13
Crater L. U.S.A. 42°56N 122°6W 76 E2
Crater Lake △ U.S.A. 42°55N 122°10W 76 E2
Craters of the Moon ⌂ U.S.A. 43°25N 113°30W 76 E7
Crateús Brazil 5°10S 40°39W 93 E10
Crato Brazil 7°10S 39°25W 93 E11
Craven, L. Canada 54°20N 76°56W 72 B4
Crawford U.S.A. 42°41N 103°25W 80 D2
Crawfordsville U.S.A. 40°2N 86°54W 80 E10
Crawley U.K. 51°7N 0°11W 13 F7
Crazy Mts. U.S.A. 46°12N 110°20W 76 C8
Crean L. Canada 54°5N 106°9W 71 C7
Crediton Canada 43°17N 81°33W 82 C3
Crediton U.K. 50°47N 3°40W 13 G4
Cree → Canada 58°57N 105°47W 71 B7
Cree → U.K. 54°55N 4°25W 11 G4
Cree L. Canada 57°30N 106°30W 71 B7
Creede U.S.A. 37°51N 106°56W 77 H10
Creekside U.S.A. 40°40N 79°11W 82 F5
Creel Mexico 27°45N 107°38W 86 B3
Creemore Canada 44°19N 80°6W 82 B4
Creighton Canada 54°45N 101°54W 71 C8
Creighton U.S.A. 42°28N 97°54W 80 D5
Crema Italy 45°22N 9°41E 20 D8
Cremona Italy 45°7N 10°2E 20 D9
Cres Croatia 44°58N 14°25E 16 F8
Crescent City U.S.A. 41°45N 124°12W 76 F1
Crespo Argentina 32°2S 60°19W 94 C3
Cresson U.S.A. 40°28N 78°36W 82 F6
Crestline Calif., U.S.A. 34°14N 117°18W 79 L9
Crestline Ohio, U.S.A. 40°47N 82°44W 82 F2
Creston Canada 49°10N 116°31W 70 D5
Creston Calif., U.S.A. 35°32N 120°33W 78 K6
Creston Iowa, U.S.A. 41°4N 94°22W 80 E6
Crestview Calif., U.S.A. 37°46N 118°58W 78 H8
Crestview Fla., U.S.A. 30°46N 86°34W 85 F11
Crete = Kriti Greece 35°15N 25°0E 25 D7
Crete U.S.A. 40°38N 96°58W 80 E5
Créteil France 48°47N 2°27E 20 B5
Creus, C. de Spain 42°20N 3°19E 21 A7
Creuse → France 47°0N 0°34E 20 C4
Crewe U.K. 53°6N 2°26W 12 D5
Crewkerne U.K. 50°53N 2°48W 13 G5
Crianlarich U.K. 56°24N 4°37W 11 E4
Criciúma Brazil 28°40S 49°23W 95 B6
Crieff U.K. 56°22N 3°50W 11 E5
Crimea □ Ukraine 45°30N 33°10E 19 E5
Crimean Pen. = Krymskyy Pivostriv Ukraine 45°0N 34°0E 19 F5
Crişul Alb → Romania 46°42N 21°17E 17 E11
Crişul Negru → Romania 46°42N 21°16E 17 E11
Crna → Macedonia 41°33N 21°59E 23 D9
Crna Gora = Montenegro ■ Europe 42°40N 19°20E 23 C8
Crna Gora Macedonia 42°10N 21°30E 23 C9
Crna Reka = Crna → Macedonia 41°33N 21°59E 23 D9
Croagh Patrick Ireland 53°46N 9°40W 10 C2
Croatia ■ Europe 45°20N 16°0E 16 F9
Crocker, Banjaran Malaysia 5°40N 116°30E 36 C5
Crockett U.S.A. 31°19N 95°27W 84 F7
Crocodile = Krokodil → Mozam. 25°14S 32°18E 57 D5
Crocodile Is. Australia 12°3S 134°58E 62 A1
Crohy Hd. Ireland 54°55N 8°26W 10 B3
Croix, L. la Canada 48°20N 92°15W 72 C1
Croker, C. Australia 10°58S 132°35E 60 B5
Croker, C. Canada 44°58N 80°59W 82 B4
Croker I. Australia 11°12S 132°32E 60 B5
Cromarty U.K. 57°40N 4°2W 11 D4
Cromer U.K. 52°56N 1°17E 12 E9
Cromwell N.Z. 45°3S 169°14E 59 F2
Cromwell U.S.A. 41°36N 72°39W 83 E12
Crook U.K. 54°43N 1°45W 12 C6
Crooked → Canada 54°50N 122°54W 70 C4
Crooked → U.S.A. 44°32N 121°16W 76 D3
Crooked I. Bahamas 22°50N 74°10W 89 B5
Crooked Island Passage Bahamas 22°55N 74°35W 89 B5
Crookston Minn., U.S.A. 47°47N 96°37W 80 B5
Crookston Nebr., U.S.A. 42°56N 100°45W 80 D3
Crookwell Australia 34°28S 149°24E 63 E4
Crosby U.K. 53°30N 3°3W 12 D4
Crosby N. Dak., U.S.A. 48°55N 103°18W 80 A2
Crosby Pa., U.S.A. 41°45N 78°23W 82 E6
Crosbyton U.S.A. 33°40N 101°14W 84 E4
Cross City U.S.A. 29°38N 83°7W 85 G13
Cross Fell U.K. 54°43N 2°28W 12 C5
Cross L. Canada 54°45N 97°30W 71 C9
Cross Lake Canada 54°37N 97°47W 71 C9
Cross Sound U.S.A. 58°0N 135°0W 68 D6
Crossett U.S.A. 33°8N 91°58W 84 E9
Crosshaven Ireland 51°47N 8°17W 10 E3
Crossmaglen U.K. 54°5N 6°36W 10 B5
Crossmolina Ireland 54°6N 9°20W 10 B2
Crossville U.S.A. 35°57N 85°2W 85 D12
Croswell U.S.A. 43°16N 82°37W 82 C2
Croton-on-Hudson U.S.A. 41°12N 73°55W 83 E11
Crotone Italy 39°5N 17°8E 22 E7
Crow → Canada 59°41N 124°20W 70 B4
Crow Agency U.S.A. 45°36N 107°28W 76 D10
Crow Hd. Ireland 51°35N 10°9W 10 E1
Crowell U.S.A. 33°59N 99°43W 84 E5
Crowley U.S.A. 30°13N 92°22W 84 F8
Crowley, L. U.S.A. 37°35N 118°42W 78 H8
Crown Point Ind., U.S.A. 41°25N 87°22W 80 E10
Crown Point N.Y., U.S.A. 43°57N 73°26W 83 C11
Crown Pt. Trin. & Tob. 11°18N 60°51W 93 J16
Crownpoint U.S.A. 35°41N 108°9W 77 J9
Crows Landing U.S.A. 37°23N 121°6W 78 H5
Crows Nest Australia 27°16S 152°4E 63 D5
Crowsnest Pass Canada 49°40N 114°40W 70 D6
Croydon Australia 18°13S 142°14E 62 B3
Croydon □ U.K. 51°22N 0°5W 13 F7
Crozet, Is. Ind. Oc. 46°27S 52°0E 3 G12
Crusheen Ireland 52°57N 8°53W 10 D3
Cruz, C. Cuba 19°50N 77°50W 88 C4
Cruz Alta Brazil 28°45S 53°40W 95 B5
Cruz Bay U.S. Virgin Is. 18°20N 64°48W 89 e
Cruz del Eje Argentina 30°45S 64°50W 94 C3
Cruzeiro Brazil 22°33S 45°0W 95 A7
Cruzeiro do Oeste Brazil 23°46S 53°4W 95 A5
Cruzeiro do Sul Brazil 7°35S 72°35W 92 E4
Cry L. Canada 58°45N 129°0W 70 B3
Crystal Bay U.S.A. 39°15N 120°0W 78 F7
Crystal Brook Australia 33°21S 138°12E 63 E2
Crystal City U.S.A. 28°41N 99°50W 84 G5
Crystal Falls U.S.A. 46°5N 88°20W 80 B9
Crystal River U.S.A. 28°54N 82°35W 85 G13
Crystal Springs U.S.A. 31°59N 90°21W 85 F9
Csongrád Hungary 46°43N 20°12E 17 E11
Cu Lao Hon Vietnam 10°54N 108°18E 39 G7
Cua Rao Vietnam 19°16N 104°27E 38 C5
Cuácua → Mozam. 17°54S 37°0E 55 F4
Cuamato Angola 17°2S 15°7E 56 B2
Cuamba Mozam. 14°45S 36°22E 55 E4
Cuando → Angola 17°30S 23°15E 53 H4
Cuando Cubango □ Angola 16°25S 20°0E 56 B3
Cuangar Angola 17°36S 18°39E 56 B2
Cuango = Kwango → Dem. Rep. of the Congo 3°14S 17°22E 52 E3
Cuanza → Angola 9°21S 13°9E 52 F2
Cuarto → Argentina 33°25S 63°2W 94 C3
Cuatrociénegas Mexico 26°59N 102°5W 86 B4
Cuauhtémoc Mexico 28°25N 106°52W 86 B3
Cuba N. Mex., U.S.A. 36°1N 107°4W 77 H10
Cuba N.Y., U.S.A. 42°13N 78°17W 82 D6
Cuba ■ W. Indies 22°0N 79°0W 88 B4
Cubango → Africa 18°50S 22°25E 56 B3
Cuc Phuong △ Vietnam 20°17N 105°38E 38 B5
Cuchumatanes, Sierra de los Guatemala 15°35N 91°25W 88 C1
Cuckfield U.K. 51°1N 0°8W 13 F7
Cucuí Brazil 1°12N 66°50W 92 C5
Cucurpé Mexico 30°20N 110°43W 86 A2
Cúcuta Colombia 7°54N 72°31W 92 B4
Cuddalore India 11°46N 79°45E 40 P11
Cuddapah India 14°30N 78°47E 40 M11
Cuddapan, L. Australia 25°45S 141°26E 62 D3
Cue Australia 27°25S 117°54E 61 E2
Cuenca Ecuador 2°50S 79°9W 92 D3
Cuenca Spain 40°5N 2°10W 21 B4
Cuenca, Serranía de Spain 39°55N 1°50W 21 C5
Cuernavaca Mexico 18°55N 99°15W 87 D5
Cuero U.S.A. 29°6N 97°17W 84 G6
Cueva de la Quebrada del Toro △ Venezuela 10°46N 69°3W 89 D6
Cuevas del Almanzora Spain 37°18N 1°58W 21 D5
Cuevo Bolivia 20°15S 63°30W 92 H6
Cuiabá Brazil 15°30S 56°0W 93 G7
Cuiabá → Brazil 17°5S 56°36W 93 G7
Cuihangcun China 22°27N 113°32E 33 G10
Cuijk Neths. 51°44N 5°50E 15 C5
Cuilco Guatemala 15°24N 91°58W 88 C1
Cuillin Hills U.K. 57°13N 6°15W 11 D2
Cuillin Sd. U.K. 57°4N 6°20W 11 D2
Cuilo = Kwilu → Dem. Rep. of the Congo 3°22S 17°22E 52 E3
Cuito → Angola 18°1S 20°48E 56 B3
Cuitzeo, L. de Mexico 19°55N 101°5W 86 D4
Cukai Malaysia 4°13N 103°25E 39 K4
Culbertson U.S.A. 48°9N 104°31W 76 B11
Culcairn Australia 35°41S 147°3E 63 F4
Culebra Puerto Rico 18°19N 65°18W 89 d
Culgoa → Australia 29°56S 146°20E 63 D4
Culgoa Flood Plain △ Australia 28°58S 147°5E 63 D4
Culiacán Mexico 24°50N 107°23W 86 C3
Culiacán → Mexico 24°30N 107°42W 86 C3
Culik Indonesia 8°21S 115°37E 37 J18
Culion Phil. 11°54N 119°58E 37 B6
Cullarin Ra. Australia 34°30S 149°30E 63 E4
Cullen U.K. 57°42N 2°49W 11 D6
Cullen Pt. Australia 11°57S 141°54E 62 A3
Cullera Spain 39°9N 0°17W 21 C5
Cullman U.S.A. 34°11N 86°51W 85 D11
Cullompton U.K. 50°51N 3°24W 13 G4
Culpeper U.S.A. 38°30N 78°0W 81 F14
Culuene → Brazil 12°56S 52°51W 93 F8
Culver, Pt. Australia 32°54S 124°43E 61 F3
Culverden N.Z. 42°47S 172°49E 59 E4
Cumaná Venezuela 10°30N 64°5W 92 A6
Cumberland B.C., Canada 49°40N 125°0W 70 D4
Cumberland Ont., Canada 45°29N 75°24W 83 A9
Cumberland U.S.A. 39°39N 78°46W 81 F14
Cumberland → U.S.A. 37°9N 88°25W 80 G9
Cumberland, L. U.S.A. 36°52N 85°9W 81 G11
Cumberland Gap ⌂ U.S.A. 36°36N 83°40W 81 G12
Cumberland I. U.S.A. 30°50N 81°25W 85 F14
Cumberland Is. Australia 20°35S 149°10E 62 J7
Cumberland Island ⌂ U.S.A. 30°12N 81°24W 85 F14
Cumberland L. Canada 54°3N 102°18W 71 C8
Cumberland Pen. Canada 67°0N 64°0W 69 C13
Cumberland Plateau U.S.A. 36°0N 85°0W 85 D12
Cumberland Sd. Canada 65°30N 66°0W 69 C13
Cumbernauld U.K. 55°57N 3°58W 11 F5
Cumborah Australia 29°40S 147°45E 63 D4
Cumbres de Majalca △ Mexico 28°48N 106°30W 86 B3
Cumbres de Monterrey △ Mexico 25°26N 100°25W 86 B4
Cumbria □ U.K. 54°42N 2°52W 12 C5
Cumbrian Mts. U.K. 54°30N 3°0W 12 C5
Cumbum India 15°40N 79°10E 40 M11
Cuminá → Brazil 1°30S 56°0W 93 D7
Cummings Mt. U.S.A. 35°2N 118°34W 79 K8
Cummins Australia 34°16S 135°43E 63 E2
Cumnock Australia 32°59S 148°46E 63 E4
Cumnock U.K. 55°28N 4°17W 11 F4
Cumpas Mexico 30°2N 109°48W 86 B3
Cumplida, Pta. Canary Is. 28°50N 17°48W 24 F2
Cunco Chile 38°55S 72°2W 96 D2
Cuncumén Chile 31°53S 70°38W 94 C1
Cunderdin Australia 31°37S 117°12E 61 F2
Cunene → Angola 17°20S 11°50E 56 B1
Cúneo Italy 44°23N 7°32E 20 D7
Çüngüş Turkey 38°13N 39°17E 44 B3
Cunillera, I. = Sa Conillera Spain 38°59N 1°13E 24 C7
Cunnamulla Australia 28°2S 145°38E 63 D4
Cupar Canada 50°57N 104°10W 71 C8
Cupar U.K. 56°19N 3°1W 11 E5
Cupertino U.S.A. 37°19N 122°2W 78 H4
Cupica, G. de Colombia 6°25N 77°30W 92 B3
Curaçao Neth. Ant. 12°10N 69°0W 89 D6
Curanilahue Chile 37°29S 73°28W 94 D1
Curaray → Peru 2°20S 74°5W 92 D4
Curepipe Mauritius 20°19S 57°31E 53 d
Curepto Chile 35°8S 72°1W 94 D1
Curiapo Venezuela 8°33N 61°5W 92 B6
Curicó Chile 34°55S 71°20W 94 C1
Curieuse Seychelles 4°15S 55°44E 53 b
Curitiba Brazil 25°20S 49°10W 95 B6
Curitibanos Brazil 27°18S 50°36W 95 B5
Currabubula Australia 31°16S 150°44E 63 E5
Currais Novos Brazil 6°13S 36°30W 93 E11
Curral Velho C. Verde Is. 16°8N 22°48W 50 b
Curralinho Brazil 1°45S 49°46W 93 D9
Currane, L. Ireland 51°49N 10°4W 10 E1
Currant U.S.A. 38°44N 115°28W 76 G6
Currawinya △ Australia 28°55S 144°27E 63 D3
Current → U.S.A. 36°15N 90°55W 84 C9
Currie Australia 39°56S 143°53E 63 F3
Currie U.S.A. 40°16N 114°45W 76 F6
Curtea de Argeş Romania 45°12N 24°42E 17 F13
Curtis U.S.A. 40°38N 100°31W 80 E3
Curtis Group Australia 39°30S 146°37E 63 F4
Curtis I. Australia 23°35S 151°10E 62 C5
Curuápanema → Brazil 2°25S 55°2W 93 D7
Curuçá Brazil 0°43S 47°50W 93 D9
Curuguaty Paraguay 24°31S 55°42W 95 A4
Curup Indonesia 4°26S 102°13E 36 E2
Cururupu Brazil 1°50S 44°50W 93 D10
Curuzú Cuatiá Argentina 29°50S 58°5W 94 B4
Curvelo Brazil 18°45S 44°27W 93 G10
Cusco = Cuzco Peru 13°32S 72°0W 92 F4
Cushendall U.K. 55°5N 6°4W 10 A5
Cushing U.S.A. 35°59N 96°46W 84 D6
Cushing, Mt. Canada 57°35N 126°57W 70 B3
Cusihuiriáchic Mexico 28°14N 106°50W 86 B3
Custer U.S.A. 43°46N 103°36W 80 D2
Cut Bank U.S.A. 48°38N 112°20W 76 B7
Cutchogue U.S.A. 41°1N 72°30W 83 E12
Cuthbert U.S.A. 31°46N 84°48W 85 F12
Cutler U.S.A. 36°31N 119°17W 78 J7
Cuttaburra → Australia 29°43S 144°22E 63 D3
Cuttack India 20°25N 85°57E 41 J14
Cuvier, C. Australia 23°14S 113°22E 61 D1
Cuvier I. N.Z. 36°27S 175°50E 59 B5
Cuxhaven Germany 53°51N 8°41E 16 B5
Cuyahoga Falls U.S.A. 41°8N 81°29W 82 E3
Cuyahoga Valley △ U.S.A. 41°14N 81°33W 82 E3
Cuyo Phil. 10°51N 121°2E 37 B6
Cuyuni → Guyana 6°23N 58°41W 92 B7
Cuzco Bolivia 20°0S 66°50W 92 H5
Cuzco Peru 13°32S 72°0W 92 F4
Cwmbran U.K. 51°39N 3°2W 13 F4
Cyangugu Rwanda 2°29S 28°54E 54 C2
Cyclades Greece 37°0N 24°30E 23 F11
Cygnet Australia 43°8S 147°1E 63 G4
Cynthiana U.S.A. 38°23N 84°18W 81 F11
Cypress Hills Canada 49°40N 109°30W 71 D7
Cypress Hills ⌂ Canada 49°40N 109°30W 71 D7
Cyprus ■ Asia 35°0N 33°0E 25 E12
Cyrenaica Libya 27°0N 23°0E 51 C10
Cyrene Libya 32°53N 21°52E 51 B10
Czar Canada 52°27N 110°50W 71 C6
Czech Rep. ■ Europe 50°0N 15°0E 16 D8
Częstochowa Poland 50°49N 19°7E 17 C10

D

Da → Vietnam 21°15N 105°20E 38 B5
Da Hinggan Ling China 48°0N 121°0E 33 B7
Da Lat Vietnam 11°56N 108°25E 39 G7
Da Nang Vietnam 16°4N 108°13E 38 D7
Da Qaidam China 37°50N 95°15E 32 C4
Da Yunhe → Hopei, China 39°10N 117°10E 35 E9
Da Yunhe → Jiangsu, China 34°25N 120°5E 35 G11
Da'an China 45°30N 124°7E 35 B13
Daan Viljoen ⌂ Namibia 22°2S 16°45E 56 C2
Daba Shan China 32°0N 109°0E 33 C5
Dabbagh, Jabal Si. Arabia 27°52N 35°45E 44 E2
Dabhoi India 22°10N 73°20E 42 H5
Dabo = Pasirkuning Indonesia 0°30S 104°33E 36 E2
Dabola Guinea 10°50N 11°5W 50 F3
Dabung Malaysia 5°23N 102°1E 39 K4
Dacca = Dhaka Bangla. 23°43N 90°26E 43 H14
Dacca = Dhaka □ Bangla. 24°25N 90°25E 43 G14
Dachau Germany 48°15N 11°26E 16 D6
Dachigam △ India 34°10N 75°0E 42 B6
Dadanawa Guyana 2°50N 59°30W 92 C7
Dade City U.S.A. 28°22N 82°11W 85 G13
Dadhar Pakistan 29°28N 67°39E 42 E2
Ḑadnah U.A.E. 25°32N 56°22E 45 E8
Dadra & Nagar Haveli □ India 20°5N 73°0E 40 J8
Dadri = Charkhi Dadri India 28°37N 76°17E 42 E7
Dadu Pakistan 26°45N 67°45E 42 F2
Daegu S. Korea 35°50N 128°37E 35 G15
Daejeon S. Korea 36°20N 127°28E 35 F14
Daejeong S. Korea 33°8N 126°17E 35 H14
Daet Phil. 14°2N 122°55E 37 B6
Dafnes Greece 35°13N 25°3E 25 D7
Dagana Senegal 16°30N 15°35W 50 E2
Dagestan □ Russia 42°30N 47°0E 19 F8
Daggett U.S.A. 34°52N 116°52W 79 L10
Daghestan Republic = Dagestan □ Russia 42°30N 47°0E 19 F8
Dağlıq Qarabağ = Nagorno-Karabakh □ Azerbaijan 39°55N 46°45E 44 B5
Dagö = Hiiumaa Estonia 58°50N 22°45E 9 G20
Dagu China 38°59N 117°40E 35 E9
Dagupan Phil. 16°3N 120°20E 37 A6
Daguragu Australia 17°33S 130°30E 60 C5
Dahlak Kebir Eritrea 15°50N 40°10E 47 D3
Dahlonega U.S.A. 34°32N 83°59W 85 D13
Dahod India 22°50N 74°15E 42 H6
Dahongliutan China 35°45N 79°20E 43 B8
Dahra Libya 29°30N 17°50E 51 C9
Dahūk Iraq 36°50N 43°1E 44 B3
Dai Hao Vietnam 18°1N 106°25E 38 C6
Dai-Sen Japan 35°22N 133°32E 31 G6
Dai Xian China 39°4N 112°58E 34 E7
Daicheng China 38°42N 116°38E 34 E9
Daikondi = Day Kundī □ Afghan. 34°0N 66°0E 40 C5
Daingean Ireland 53°18N 7°17W 10 C4
Daintree Australia 16°20S 145°20E 62 B4
Daintree △ Australia 16°8S 145°2E 62 B4
Daiō-Misaki Japan 34°15N 136°45E 31 G8
Daisen-Oki △ Japan 35°23N 133°34E 31 G6
Daisetsu-Zan Japan 43°30N 142°57E 30 C11
Daisetsu-Zan △ Japan 43°30N 142°55E 30 C11
Dajarra Australia 21°42S 139°30E 62 C2
Dajiawa China 37°9N 119°0E 35 F10
Dak Dam Cambodia 12°20N 107°21E 38 F6
Dak Nhe Vietnam 15°28N 107°48E 38 E6
Dak Pek Vietnam 15°4N 107°44E 38 E6
Dak Song Vietnam 12°19N 107°35E 39 F6
Dak Sui Vietnam 14°55N 107°43E 38 E6
Dakar Senegal 14°34N 17°29W 50 F2
Dakhla W. Sahara 23°50N 15°53W 50 D2
Dakhla, El Wâhât el- Egypt 25°30N 28°50E 51 C11
Dakor India 22°45N 73°11E 42 H5
Dakota City U.S.A. 42°25N 96°25W 80 D5
Đakovica Serbia 42°22N 20°26E 23 C9
Dalachi China 36°48N 105°0E 34 F3
Dalai Nur China 43°20N 116°45E 34 C9
Dālakī Iran 29°26N 51°17E 45 D6
Dalälven → Sweden 60°12N 16°43E 9 F17
Dalaman → Turkey 36°41N 28°43E 23 F13
Dalandzadgad Mongolia 43°27N 104°30E 34 C3
Dalap-Uliga-Darrit = Majuro Marshall Is. 7°9N 171°12E 64 G9
Dalarna Sweden 61°0N 14°0E 8 F16
Dālbandīn Pakistan 29°0N 64°23E 40 E4
Dalbeattie U.K. 54°56N 3°50W 11 G5
Dalbeg Australia 20°16S 147°18E 62 C4
Dalby Australia 27°10S 151°17E 63 D5
Dale City U.S.A. 38°38N 77°19W 81 F15
Dale Hollow L. U.S.A. 36°32N 85°27W 85 C12
Dalgān Iran 27°31N 59°19E 45 E8
Dalhart U.S.A. 36°4N 102°31W 84 C3
Dalhousie Canada 48°5N 66°26W 73 C6
Dalhousie India 32°38N 75°58E 42 C6
Dali Shaanxi, China 34°48N 109°58E 34 G5
Dali Yunnan, China 25°40N 100°10E 32 D5
Dalian China 38°50N 121°40E 35 E11
Daliang Shan China 28°0N 102°45E 32 D5
Daling He → China 40°55N 121°40E 35 D11
Dāliyat el Karmel Israel 32°43N 35°2E 46 C4
Dalkeith U.K. 55°54N 3°4W 11 F5
Dallas Oreg., U.S.A. 44°55N 123°19W 76 D2
Dallas Tex., U.S.A. 32°47N 96°48W 84 E6
Dalles, The U.S.A. 45°36N 121°10W 76 D3
Dalmā U.A.E. 24°30N 52°20E 45 E7
Dalmacija Croatia 43°20N 17°0E 22 C7
Dalmas, L. Canada 53°30N 71°50W 73 B5
Dalmatia = Dalmacija Croatia 43°20N 17°0E 22 C7
Dalmau India 26°4N 81°2E 43 F9
Dalmellington U.K. 55°19N 4°23W 11 F4
Dalnegorsk Russia 44°32N 135°33E 30 B7
Dalnerechensk Russia 45°50N 133°40E 30 B6
Dalnevostochnyy □ Russia 67°0N 140°0E 29 C14
Daloa Ivory C. 7°0N 6°30W 50 G4
Dalry U.K. 55°42N 4°43W 11 F4
Dalrymple, L. Australia 20°40S 147°0E 62 C4
Dalrymple, Mt. Australia 21°1S 148°39E 62 K6
Dalsland Sweden 58°50N 12°15E 9 G15
Daltenganj India 24°0N 84°4E 43 H11
Dalton Ga., U.S.A. 34°46N 84°58W 85 D12
Dalton Mass., U.S.A. 42°28N 73°11W 83 D11
Dalton Nebr., U.S.A. 41°25N 102°58W 80 E2
Dalton-in-Furness U.K. 54°10N 3°11W 12 C4
Dalvík Iceland 65°58N 18°32W 8 D4
Dálvvadis = Jokkmokk Sweden 66°35N 19°50E 8 C18
Dalwallinu Australia 30°17S 116°40E 61 F2
Daly → Australia 13°35S 130°19E 60 B5

Daly City U.S.A. 37°42N 122°27W **78 H4**
Daly L. Canada 56°32N 105°39W **71 B7**
Daly River Australia 13°46S 130°42E **60 B5**
Daly Waters Australia 16°15S 133°24E **62 B1**
Dam Doi Vietnam 8°50N 105°12E **39 H5**
Dam Ha Vietnam 21°21N 107°36E **38 B6**
Daman India 20°25N 72°57E **40 J8**
Dāmaneh Iran 33°1N 50°29E **45 C6**
Damanhûr Egypt 31°0N 30°30E **51 B12**
Damanzhuang China 38°5N 116°35E **34 E9**
Damar Indonesia 7°7S 128°40E **37 F7**
Damara C.A.R. 4°58N 18°42E **52 D3**
Damaraland Namibia 20°0S 15°0E **56 C2**
Damascus = Dimashq
  Syria 33°30N 36°18E **46 B5**
Dāmāvand Iran 35°47N 52°0E **45 C7**
Dāmāvand, Qolleh-ye
  Iran 35°56N 52°10E **45 C7**
Damba Angola 6°44S 15°20E **52 F3**
Dâmboviţa →
  Romania 44°12N 26°26E **17 F14**
Dame Marie Haiti 18°36N 74°26W **89 C5**
Dāmghān Iran 36°10N 54°17E **45 B7**
Damiel Spain 39°4N 3°37W **21 C4**
Damietta = Dumyât
  Egypt 31°24N 31°48E **51 B12**
Daming China 36°15N 115°6E **34 F8**
Damīr Qābū Syria 36°58N 41°51E **44 B4**
Dammam = Ad Dammām
  Si. Arabia 26°20N 50°5E **45 E6**
Damoh India 23°50N 79°28E **43 H8**
Dampier Australia 20°41S 116°42E **60 D2**
Dampier, Selat Indonesia 0°40S 131°0E **37 E8**
Dampier Arch.
  Australia 20°38S 116°32E **60 D2**
Damrei, Chuor Phnum
  Cambodia 11°30N 103°0E **39 G4**
Damyang S. Korea 35°19N 126°59E **35 G14**
Dana Indonesia 11°0S 122°52E **37 F6**
Dana, L. Canada 50°53N 77°20W **72 B4**
Dana, Mt. U.S.A. 37°54N 119°12W **78 H7**
Danakil Desert Ethiopia 12°45N 41°0E **47 E3**
Danané Ivory C. 7°16N 8°9W **50 G4**
Danau Poso Indonesia 1°52S 120°35E **37 E6**
Danbury U.S.A. 41°24N 73°28W **83 E11**
Danby L. U.S.A. 34°13N 115°5W **77 J6**
Dand Afghan. 31°28N 65°32E **42 D1**
Dande △ Zimbabwe 15°56S 30°16E **55 F3**
Dandeldhura Nepal 29°20N 80°35E **43 E9**
Dandeli India 15°5N 74°30E **40 M9**
Dandenong Australia 38°0S 145°15E **63 F4**
Dandong China 40°10N 124°20E **35 D13**
Danfeng China 33°45N 110°25E **34 H6**
Danger Is. = Pukapuka
  Cook Is. 10°53S 165°49W **65 J11**
Danger Pt. S. Africa 34°40S 19°17E **56 E2**
Danginpuri Indonesia 8°45S 115°13E **37 K18**
Dangla Shan = Tanggula Shan
  China 32°40N 92°10E **32 C4**
Dangrek, Phnom
  Thailand 14°15N 105°0E **38 E5**
Dangriga Belize 17°0N 88°13W **88 C2**
Dangshan China 34°27N 116°22E **34 G9**
Daniel U.S.A. 42°52N 110°4W **76 E8**
Daniel's Harbour
  Canada 50°13N 57°35W **73 B8**
Danielskuil S. Africa 28°11S 23°33E **56 D3**
Danielson U.S.A. 41°48N 71°53W **83 E13**
Danilov Russia 58°16N 40°13E **18 C7**
Daning China 36°28N 110°45E **34 F6**
Dank Oman 23°33N 56°16E **45 F8**
Dankhar Gompa India 32°10N 78°10E **42 C8**
Danli Honduras 14°4N 86°35W **88 D2**
Danmark = Denmark ■
  Europe 55°45N 10°0E **9 J14**
Dannemora U.S.A. 44°43N 73°44W **83 C11**
Dannevirke N.Z. 40°12S 176°8E **59 D6**
Dannhauser S. Africa 28°0S 30°3E **57 D5**
Dansville U.S.A. 42°34N 77°42W **82 D7**
Danta India 24°11N 72°46E **42 G5**
Dantan India 21°57N 87°20E **43 J12**
Danube = Dunărea →
  Europe 45°20N 29°40E **17 F15**
Danvers U.S.A. 42°34N 70°56W **83 D14**
Danville Ill., U.S.A. 40°8N 87°37W **80 E10**
Danville Ky., U.S.A. 37°39N 84°46W **81 G11**
Danville Pa., U.S.A. 40°58N 76°37W **83 F8**
Danville Va., U.S.A. 36°36N 79°23W **81 G14**
Danville Vt., U.S.A. 44°25N 72°9W **83 B12**
Danzhou China 19°31N 109°33E **38 C7**
Danzig = Gdańsk
  Poland 54°22N 18°40E **17 A10**
Dapaong Togo 10°55N 0°16E **50 F6**
Daqing Shan China 40°40N 111°0E **34 D6**
Dar el Beida = Casablanca
  Morocco 33°36N 7°36W **50 B4**
Dar es Salaam Tanzania 6°50S 39°12E **54 D4**
Dar Mazār Iran 29°14N 57°20E **45 D8**
Dar'ā Syria 32°36N 36°7E **46 C5**
Dar'ā □ Syria 32°55N 36°10E **46 C5**
Dārāb Iran 28°50N 54°30E **45 D7**
Daraban Pakistan 31°44N 70°20E **42 D4**
Daraina Madag. 13°12S 49°40E **57 A8**
Daraj Libya 30°10N 10°28E **51 B8**
Daran Iran 32°59N 50°24E **45 C6**
Dārayyā Syria 33°28N 36°15E **46 B5**
Darband Pakistan 34°20N 72°50E **42 B5**
Darband, Kūh-e Iran 31°34N 57°8E **45 D8**
Darbhanga India 26°15N 85°55E **43 F11**
D'Arcy Canada 50°33N 122°29W **70 C4**
Dardanelle Ark., U.S.A. 35°13N 93°9W **84 D8**
Dardanelle Calif.,
  U.S.A. 38°20N 119°50W **78 G7**
Dardanelles = Çanakkale Boğazı
  Turkey 40°17N 26°32E **23 D12**

Dārestān Iran 29°9N 58°42E **45 D8**
Dârfûr Sudan 13°40N 24°0E **51 F10**
Dargai Pakistan 34°25N 71°55E **42 B4**
Dargaville N.Z. 35°57S 173°52E **59 A4**
Darhan Mongolia 49°37N 106°21E **32 B5**
Darhan Muminggan Lianheqi
  China 41°40N 110°28E **34 D6**
Darıca Turkey 40°45N 29°23E **23 D13**
Darién, G. del Colombia 9°0N 77°0W **92 B3**
Darién △ Panama 7°36N 77°57W **88 E4**
Dariganga = Ovoot
  Mongolia 45°21N 113°45E **34 B7**
Darjeeling = Darjiling
  India 27°3N 88°18E **43 F13**
Darjiling India 27°3N 88°18E **43 F13**
Darkan Australia 33°20S 116°43E **61 F2**
Darkhana Pakistan 30°39N 72°11E **42 D5**
Darkhazîneh Iran 31°54N 48°39E **45 D6**
Darkot Pass Pakistan 36°45N 73°26E **43 A5**
Darling → Australia 34°4S 141°54E **63 E3**
Darling Downs
  Australia 27°30S 150°30E **63 D5**
Darling Ra. Australia 32°30S 116°20E **61 F2**
Darlington U.K. 54°32N 1°33W **12 C6**
Darlington U.S.A. 34°18N 79°52W **85 D15**
Darlington □ U.K. 54°32N 1°33W **12 C6**
Darlington, L. S. Africa 33°10S 25°9E **56 E4**
Darlowo Poland 54°25N 16°25E **16 A9**
Darmstadt Germany 49°51N 8°39E **16 D5**
Darnah Libya 32°45N 22°45E **51 B10**
Darnall S. Africa 29°23S 31°18E **57 D5**
Darnley, C. Antarctica 68°0S 69°0E **5 C6**
Darnley B. Canada 69°30N 123°30W **68 C7**
Darr → Australia 23°39S 143°50E **62 C3**
Darra Pezu Pakistan 32°19N 70°44E **42 C4**
Darrequeira Argentina 37°42S 63°10W **94 D3**
Darrington U.S.A. 48°15N 121°36W **76 B3**
Dart → U.K. 50°24N 3°39W **13 G4**
Dart, C. Antarctica 73°6S 126°20W **5 D14**
Dartford U.K. 51°26N 0°13E **13 F8**
Dartmoor U.K. 50°38N 3°57W **13 G4**
Dartmoor △ U.K. 50°37N 3°59W **13 G4**
Dartmouth Canada 44°40N 63°30W **73 D7**
Dartmouth U.K. 50°21N 3°36W **13 G4**
Dartmouth Res.
  Australia 26°4S 145°18E **63 D4**
Dartuch, C. = Artrutx, C. de
  Spain 39°55N 3°49E **24 B10**
Darvaza Turkmenistan 40°11N 58°24E **28 E6**
Darvel, Teluk = Lahad Datu,
  Telok Malaysia 4°50N 118°20E **37 D5**
Darwen U.K. 53°42N 2°29W **12 D5**
Darwendale Zimbabwe 17°41S 30°33E **55 F3**
Darwha India 20°15N 77°45E **40 J10**
Darwin Australia 12°25S 130°51E **60 B5**
Darwin U.S.A. 36°15N 117°35W **79 J9**
Darya Khan Pakistan 31°48N 71°6E **42 D4**
Daryoi Amu = Amudarya →
  Uzbekistan 43°58N 59°34E **28 E6**
Dās U.A.E. 25°20N 53°30E **45 E7**
Dashen, Ras Ethiopia 13°8N 38°26E **47 E2**
Dashetai China 41°0N 109°5E **34 D5**
Dashköpri Turkmenistan 36°16N 62°8E **45 B9**
Dashoguz Turkmenistan 41°49N 59°58E **28 E6**
Dasht Iran 37°17N 56°7E **45 B8**
Dasht → Pakistan 25°10N 61°40E **40 G2**
Daska Pakistan 32°20N 74°20E **42 C6**
Dasuya India 31°49N 75°38E **42 D6**
Datça Turkey 36°46N 27°40E **23 F12**
Datia India 25°39N 78°27E **43 G8**
Datong China 40°6N 113°18E **34 D7**
Dattakhel Pakistan 32°54N 69°46E **42 C3**
Datu, Tanjung Indonesia 2°5N 109°39E **36 D3**
Datu Piang Phil. 7°2N 124°30E **37 C6**
Datuk, Tanjong = Datu, Tanjung
  Indonesia 2°5N 109°39E **36 D3**
Daud Khel Pakistan 32°53N 71°34E **42 C4**
Daudnagar India 25°2N 84°24E **43 G11**
Daugava → Latvia 57°4N 24°3E **9 H21**
Daugavpils Latvia 55°53N 26°32E **9 J22**
Daulpur India 26°45N 77°59E **42 F7**
Dauphin Canada 51°9N 100°5W **71 C8**
Dauphin U.S.A. 40°22N 76°56W **82 F8**
Dauphin L. Canada 51°20N 99°45W **71 C9**
Dauphiné France 45°15N 5°25E **20 D6**
Dausa India 26°52N 76°20E **42 F7**
Davangere India 14°25N 75°55E **40 M9**
Davao Phil. 7°0N 125°40E **37 C7**
Davao G. Phil. 6°30N 125°48E **37 C7**
Dāvar Panāh = Sarāvān
  Iran 27°25N 62°15E **45 E9**
Davenport Calif., U.S.A. 37°1N 122°12W **78 H4**
Davenport Iowa, U.S.A. 41°32N 90°35W **80 E8**
Davenport Wash.,
  U.S.A. 47°39N 118°9W **76 C4**
Davenport Ra. Australia 20°28S 134°0E **62 C1**
Daventry U.K. 52°16N 1°10W **13 E6**
David Panama 8°30N 82°30W **88 E3**
David Glacier Antarctica 75°20S 162°0E **5 D21**
David Gorodok = Davyd Haradok
  Belarus 52°4N 27°8E **17 B14**
Davidson Canada 51°16N 105°59W **71 C7**
Davis Antarctica 68°34S 77°54E **5 C6**
Davis Dam U.S.A. 35°12N 114°34W **79 K12**
Davis Inlet Canada 55°50N 60°59W **73 A7**
Davis Mts. U.S.A. 30°50N 103°55W **84 F3**
Davis Sea Antarctica 66°0S 92°0E **5 C7**
Davis Str. N. Amer. 65°0N 58°0W **66 C14**
Davos Switz. 46°48N 9°49E **20 C8**
Davy L. Canada 58°53N 108°18W **71 B7**
Davyd Haradok Belarus 52°4N 27°8E **17 B14**
Dawei = Tavoy Burma 14°2N 98°12E **38 E2**
Dawes Ra. Australia 24°40S 150°40E **62 C5**
Dawlish U.K. 50°35N 3°28W **13 G4**
Dawna Ra. Burma 16°30N 98°30E **38 D2**

Dawros Hd. Ireland 54°50N 8°33W **10 B3**
Dawson Canada 64°10N 139°30W **68 C6**
Dawson U.S.A. 31°46N 84°27W **85 F12**
Dawson, I. Chile 53°50S 70°50W **96 G2**
Dawson B. Canada 52°53N 100°49W **71 C8**
Dawson Creek Canada 55°45N 120°15W **70 B4**
Dawson Inlet Canada 61°50N 93°25W **71 A10**
Dawson Ra. Australia 24°30S 149°48E **62 C4**
Dax France 43°44N 1°3W **20 E3**
Daxian China 31°15N 107°23E **32 C5**
Daxindian China 37°30N 120°50E **35 F11**
Daxinggou China 43°25N 129°40E **35 C15**
Daxue Shan China 30°30N 101°30E **32 C5**
Day Kundī □ Afghan. 34°0N 66°40E **40 C4**
Daylesford Australia 37°21S 144°9E **63 F3**
Dayr az Zawr Syria 35°20N 40°5E **44 C4**
Daysland Canada 52°50N 112°20W **70 C6**
Dayton Nev., U.S.A. 39°14N 119°36W **78 F7**
Dayton Ohio, U.S.A. 39°45N 84°12W **81 F11**
Dayton Pa., U.S.A. 40°53N 79°15W **82 F5**
Dayton Tenn., U.S.A. 35°30N 85°1W **85 D12**
Dayton Wash., U.S.A. 46°19N 117°59W **76 C5**
Dayton Wyo., U.S.A. 44°53N 107°16W **76 D10**
Daytona Beach U.S.A. 29°13N 81°1W **85 G14**
Dayville U.S.A. 44°28N 119°32W **76 D4**
De Aar S. Africa 30°39S 24°0E **56 E3**
De Biesbosch △ Neths. 51°45N 4°48E **15 C4**
De Funiak Springs
  U.S.A. 30°43N 86°7W **85 F11**
De Grey → Australia 20°12S 119°13E **60 D2**
De Haan Belgium 51°16N 3°2E **15 C3**
De Hoge Veluwe △ Neths. 52°5N 5°46E **15 B5**
De Hoop △ S. Africa 34°30S 20°28E **56 E3**
De Kennemerduinen △
  Neths. 52°27N 4°33E **15 B4**
De Land U.S.A. 29°2N 81°18W **85 G14**
De Leon U.S.A. 32°7N 98°32W **84 E5**
De Panne Belgium 51°6N 2°34E **15 C2**
De Pere U.S.A. 44°27N 88°4W **80 C9**
De Queen U.S.A. 34°2N 94°21W **84 D7**
De Quincy U.S.A. 30°27N 93°26W **84 F8**
De Smet U.S.A. 44°23N 97°33W **80 C5**
De Soto U.S.A. 38°8N 90°34W **80 F8**
De Tour Village U.S.A. 46°0N 83°56W **81 B12**
De Witt U.S.A. 34°18N 91°20W **84 D9**
Dead Sea Asia 31°30N 35°30E **46 D4**
Deadwood U.S.A. 44°23N 103°44W **80 C2**
Deadwood L. Canada 59°10N 128°30W **70 B3**
Deal U.K. 51°13N 1°25E **13 F9**
Deal I. Australia 39°30S 147°20E **63 F4**
Dealesville S. Africa 28°41S 25°44E **56 D4**
Dean → Canada 52°49N 126°58W **70 C3**
Dean, Forest of U.K. 51°45N 2°33W **13 F5**
Dean Chan. Canada 52°30N 127°15W **70 C3**
Deán Funes Argentina 30°20S 64°20W **94 C3**
Dease → Canada 59°56N 128°32W **70 B3**
Dease L. Canada 58°40N 130°5W **70 B2**
Dease Lake Canada 58°25N 130°6W **70 B2**
Death Valley U.S.A. 36°15N 116°50W **79 J10**
Death Valley △ U.S.A. 36°29N 117°6W **79 J10**
Death Valley Junction
  U.S.A. 36°20N 116°25W **79 J10**
Debar Macedonia 41°31N 20°30E **23 D9**
Debden Canada 53°30N 106°50W **71 C7**
Dębica Poland 50°2N 21°25E **17 C11**
DeBolt Canada 55°12N 118°1W **70 B5**
Deborah East, L.
  Australia 30°45S 119°30E **61 F2**
Deborah West, L.
  Australia 30°45S 119°5E **61 F2**
Debre Markos Ethiopia 10°20N 37°40E **47 E2**
Debre Tabor Ethiopia 11°50N 38°26E **47 E2**
Debre Zebit Ethiopia 11°48N 38°30E **47 E2**
Debrecen Hungary 47°33N 21°42E **17 E11**
Decatur Ala., U.S.A. 34°36N 86°59W **85 E11**
Decatur Ga., U.S.A. 33°46N 84°16W **85 E12**
Decatur Ill., U.S.A. 39°51N 88°57W **80 F9**
Decatur Ind., U.S.A. 40°50N 84°56W **81 E11**
Decatur Tex., U.S.A. 33°14N 97°35W **84 E6**
Deccan India 18°0N 79°0E **40 L11**
Deception Bay Australia 27°10S 153°0E **63 D5**
Deception I. Antarctica 63°0S 60°15W **5 C17**
Deception L. Canada 56°33N 104°13W **71 B8**
Dechhu India 26°46N 72°20E **42 F5**
Děčín Czech Rep. 50°47N 14°12E **16 C8**
Deckerville U.S.A. 43°32N 82°44W **82 C2**
Decorah U.S.A. 43°18N 91°48W **80 D8**
Dedéagach = Alexandroupoli
  Greece 40°50N 25°54E **23 D11**
Dedham U.S.A. 42°15N 71°10W **83 D13**
Dedza Malawi 14°20S 34°20E **55 E3**
Dee → Aberds., U.K. 57°9N 2°5W **11 D6**
Dee → Dumf. & Gall., U.K. 54°51N 4°3W **11 G4**
Dee → Wales, U.K. 53°22N 3°17W **12 D4**
Deep Bay = Shenzhen Wan
  China 22°27N 113°55E **33 G10**
Deepwater Australia 29°25S 151°51E **63 D5**
Deer → Canada 58°23N 94°13W **71 B10**
Deer L. Canada 52°40N 94°20W **71 C10**
Deer Lake Nfld. & L.,
  Canada 49°11N 57°27W **73 C8**
Deer Lake Ont., Canada 52°40N 94°20W **71 C10**
Deer Lodge U.S.A. 46°24N 112°44W **76 C7**
Deer Park U.S.A. 47°57N 117°28W **76 C5**
Deer River U.S.A. 47°20N 93°48W **80 B7**
Deeragun Australia 19°16S 146°33E **62 B4**
Deerdepoort S. Africa 24°37S 26°27E **56 C4**
Defiance U.S.A. 41°17N 84°22W **81 E11**
Degana India 26°50N 74°20E **42 F6**
Dégelis Canada 47°30N 68°35W **73 C6**
Deggendorf Germany 48°50N 12°57E **16 D7**
Degh → Pakistan 31°3N 73°21E **42 D5**
Deh Bīd Iran 30°39N 53°11E **45 D7**
Deh-e Shīr Iran 31°29N 53°45E **45 D7**
Dehaj Iran 30°42N 54°53E **45 D7**
Dehak Iran 27°11N 62°37E **45 E9**

Dehdez Iran 31°43N 50°17E **45 D6**
Dehej India 21°44N 72°40E **42 J5**
Dehestan Iran 28°30N 55°35E **45 D7**
Dehgolān Iran 35°17N 47°25E **44 C5**
Dehibat Tunisia 32°0N 10°47E **51 B8**
Dehlorān Iran 32°41N 47°16E **44 C5**
Dehnow-e Kühestān
  Iran 27°58N 58°32E **45 E8**
Dehra Dun India 30°20N 78°4E **42 D8**
Dehri India 24°50N 84°15E **43 G11**
Dehui China 44°30N 125°40E **35 B13**
Deinze Belgium 50°59N 3°32E **15 D3**
Dej Romania 47°10N 23°52E **17 E12**
Deka → Zimbabwe 18°4S 26°42E **56 B4**
DeKalb U.S.A. 41°56N 88°46W **80 E9**
Del Mar U.S.A. 32°58N 117°16W **79 N9**
Del Norte U.S.A. 37°41N 106°21W **77 H10**
Del Rio U.S.A. 29°22N 100°54W **84 G4**
Delambre I. Australia 20°26S 117°5E **60 D2**
Delano U.S.A. 35°46N 119°15W **79 K7**
Delano Peak U.S.A. 38°22N 112°22W **76 G7**
Delareyville S. Africa 26°41S 25°26E **56 D4**
Delaronde L. Canada 54°3N 107°3W **71 C7**
Delavan U.S.A. 42°38N 88°39W **80 D9**
Delaware U.S.A. 40°18N 83°4W **81 E12**
Delaware □ U.S.A. 39°0N 75°20W **81 F16**
Delaware → U.S.A. 39°15N 75°20W **83 G9**
Delaware B. U.S.A. 39°0N 75°10W **81 F16**
Delaware Water Gap △
  U.S.A. 41°10N 74°55W **83 G10**
Delay → Canada 56°56N 71°28W **73 A5**
Delegate Australia 37°4S 148°56E **63 F4**
Delevan U.S.A. 42°29N 78°29W **82 D6**
Delft Neths. 52°1N 4°22E **15 B4**
Delfzijl Neths. 53°20N 6°55E **15 A6**
Delgado, C. Mozam. 10°45S 40°40E **54 E5**
Delgerhet Mongolia 45°50N 110°30E **34 B6**
Delgo Sudan 20°6N 30°40E **51 D12**
Delhi India 28°39N 77°13E **42 E7**
Delhi Canada 42°51N 80°30W **82 D4**
Delhi La., U.S.A. 32°28N 91°30W **84 E9**
Delhi N.Y., U.S.A. 42°17N 74°55W **83 D10**
Delia Canada 51°38N 112°23W **70 C6**
Delice Turkey 39°54N 34°2E **19 G5**
Delicias Mexico 28°13N 105°28W **86 B3**
Delījān Iran 33°59N 50°40E **45 C6**
Déline Canada 65°11N 123°25W **68 C7**
Delisle Canada 51°55N 107°8W **71 C7**
Dell City U.S.A. 31°56N 105°12W **84 F2**
Dell Rapids U.S.A. 43°50N 96°43W **80 D5**
Delmar U.S.A. 42°37N 73°47W **83 D11**
Delmenhorst Germany 53°3N 8°37E **16 B5**
Delonga, Ostrova
  Russia 76°40N 149°20E **29 B15**
Deloraine Australia 41°30S 146°40E **63 G4**
Deloraine Canada 49°15N 100°29W **71 D8**
Delphi U.S.A. 40°36N 86°41W **80 E10**
Delphos U.S.A. 40°51N 84°21W **81 E11**
Delportshoop S. Africa 28°22S 24°20E **56 D3**
Delray Beach U.S.A. 26°28N 80°4W **85 H14**
Delsbo Sweden 61°48N 16°32E **8 F17**
Delta Utah, U.S.A. 39°21N 112°35W **76 G7**
Delta Dunărea △
  Romania 45°15N 29°25E **17 F15**
Delta Junction U.S.A. 64°2N 145°44W **68 C5**
Deltona U.S.A. 28°54N 81°16W **85 G14**
Delungra Australia 29°39S 150°51E **63 D5**
Delvada India 20°46N 71°2E **42 J4**
Delvinë Albania 39°59N 20°6E **23 E9**
Demak Indonesia 6°53S 110°38E **37 G14**
Demanda, Sierra de la
  Spain 42°15N 3°0W **21 A4**
Demavend = Damāvand,
  Qolleh-ye Iran 35°56N 52°10E **45 C7**
Dembia
  Dem. Rep. of the Congo 3°33N 25°48E **54 B2**
Dembidolo Ethiopia 8°34N 34°50E **47 F1**
Demchok India 32°42N 79°29E **43 C8**
Demer → Belgium 50°57N 4°42E **15 D4**
Deming N. Mex.,
  U.S.A. 32°16N 107°46W **77 K10**
Deming Wash., U.S.A. 48°50N 122°13W **78 B4**
Demini → Brazil 0°46S 62°56W **92 D6**
Demirci Turkey 39°2N 28°38E **23 E13**
Demirköy Turkey 41°49N 27°45E **23 D12**
Demopolis U.S.A. 32°31N 87°50W **85 E11**
Dempo Indonesia 4°2S 103°15E **36 E2**
Den Bosch = 's-Hertogenbosch
  Neths. 51°42N 5°17E **15 C5**
Den Burg Neths. 53°3N 4°47E **15 A4**
Den Chai Thailand 17°59N 100°4E **38 D3**
Den Haag = 's-Gravenhage
  Neths. 52°7N 4°17E **15 B4**
Den Helder Neths. 52°57N 4°45E **15 B4**
Den Oever Neths. 52°56N 5°2E **15 B5**
Denair U.S.A. 37°32N 120°48W **78 H6**
Denali = McKinley, Mt.
  U.S.A. 63°4N 151°0W **74 a**
Denau Uzbekistan 38°16N 67°54E **28 F7**
Denbigh Canada 45°8N 77°15W **82 A7**
Denbigh U.K. 53°12N 3°25W **12 D4**
Denbighshire □ U.K. 53°8N 3°22W **12 D4**
Dendang Indonesia 3°7S 107°56E **36 E3**
Dendermonde Belgium 51°2N 4°5E **15 C4**
Dengfeng China 34°25N 113°2E **34 G7**
Dengkou China 40°18N 106°55E **34 D4**
Denham Australia 25°56S 113°31E **61 E1**
Denham, Mt. Jamaica 18°13N 77°32W **88 a**
Denham Ra. Australia 21°55S 147°46E **62 C4**
Denham Sd. Australia 25°45S 113°15E **61 E1**
Denholm Canada 52°39N 108°1W **71 C7**
Denia Spain 38°49N 0°8E **21 C6**
Deniliquin Australia 35°30S 144°58E **63 F3**
Denison Iowa, U.S.A. 42°1N 95°21W **80 D6**
Denison Tex., U.S.A. 33°45N 96°33W **84 E6**

Denison Plains Australia 18°35S 128°0E **60 C4**
Denizli Turkey 37°42N 29°2E **19 G4**
Denman Glacier
  Antarctica 66°45S 99°25E **5 C7**
Denmark Australia 34°59S 117°25E **61 F2**
Denmark ■ Europe 55°45N 10°0E **9 J14**
Denmark Str. Atl. Oc. 66°0N 30°0W **66 C17**
Dennery St. Lucia 13°55N 60°54W **89 f**
Dennison U.S.A. 40°24N 81°19W **82 F3**
Denny U.K. 56°1N 3°55W **11 E5**
Denpasar Indonesia 8°39S 115°13E **36 F5**
Denpasar ✈ (DPS)
  Indonesia 8°44S 115°10E **37 K18**
Denton Mont., U.S.A. 47°19N 109°57W **76 C9**
Denton Tex., U.S.A. 33°13N 97°8W **84 E6**
D'Entrecasteaux, Pt.
  Australia 34°50S 115°57E **61 F2**
D'Entrecasteaux △
  Australia 34°20S 115°33E **61 F2**
D'Entrecasteaux Is.
  Papua N. G. 9°0S 151°0E **58 B8**
Denver Colo., U.S.A. 39°42N 104°59W **76 G11**
Denver Pa., U.S.A. 40°14N 76°8W **83 F8**
Denver City U.S.A. 32°58N 102°50W **84 E3**
Deoband India 29°42N 77°43E **42 E7**
Deogarh India 25°32N 73°54E **42 G5**
Deoghar India 24°30N 86°42E **43 G12**
Deolali India 19°58N 73°50E **40 K8**
Deoli = Devli India 25°50N 75°20E **42 G6**
Deora India 26°22N 70°55E **42 F4**
Deori India 23°24N 79°1E **43 H8**
Deoria India 26°31N 83°48E **43 F10**
Deosai Mts. Pakistan 35°40N 75°0E **43 B6**
Deosri India 26°46N 90°29E **43 F14**
Depalpur India 22°51N 75°33E **42 H6**
Deping China 37°25N 116°58E **35 F9**
Deposit U.S.A. 42°4N 75°25W **83 D9**
Depuch I. Australia 20°37S 117°44E **60 D2**
Deputatskiy Russia 69°18N 139°54E **29 C14**
Dera Ghazi Khan
  Pakistan 30°5N 70°43E **42 D4**
Dera Ismail Khan
  Pakistan 31°50N 70°50E **42 D4**
Derabugti Pakistan 29°2N 69°9E **42 E3**
Derawar Fort Pakistan 28°46N 71°20E **42 E4**
Derbent Russia 42°5N 48°15E **19 F8**
Derby Australia 17°18S 123°38E **60 C3**
Derby U.K. 52°56N 1°28W **12 E6**
Derby Conn., U.S.A. 41°19N 73°5W **83 E11**
Derby Kans., U.S.A. 37°33N 97°16W **80 G5**
Derby N.Y., U.S.A. 42°41N 78°58W **82 D6**
Derby City □ U.K. 52°56N 1°28W **12 E6**
Derby Line U.S.A. 45°0N 72°6W **83 B12**
Derbyshire □ U.K. 53°11N 1°38W **12 D6**
Derdepoort S. Africa 24°38S 26°24E **56 C4**
Dereham U.K. 52°41N 0°57E **13 E8**
Derg → U.K. 54°44N 7°26W **10 B4**
Derg, L. Ireland 53°0N 8°20W **10 D3**
Deridder U.S.A. 30°51N 93°17W **84 F8**
Dermott U.S.A. 33°32N 91°26W **84 E9**
Derry = Londonderry
  U.K. 55°0N 7°20W **10 B4**
Derry = Londonderry □
  U.K. 55°0N 7°20W **10 B4**
Derry N.H., U.S.A. 42°53N 71°19W **83 D13**
Derry Pa., U.S.A. 40°20N 79°18W **82 F5**
Derryveagh Mts. Ireland 54°56N 8°11W **10 B3**
Derwent → Cumb., U.K. 54°39N 3°33W **12 C4**
Derwent → Derby, U.K. 52°57N 1°28W **12 E6**
Derwent → N. Yorks.,
  U.K. 53°45N 0°58W **12 D7**
Derwent Water U.K. 54°35N 3°9W **12 C4**
Des Moines Iowa, U.S.A. 41°35N 93°37W **80 E7**
Des Moines N. Mex.,
  U.S.A. 36°46N 103°50W **77 H12**
Des Moines Wash.,
  U.S.A. 47°24N 122°19W **78 C4**
Des Moines → U.S.A. 40°23N 91°25W **80 E8**
Desaguadero →
  Argentina 34°30S 66°46W **94 C2**
Desaguadero → Bolivia 16°35S 69°5W **92 G5**
Desar Malaysia 1°31N 104°17E **39 d**
Descanso, Pta. Mexico 32°21N 117°3W **79 N9**
Deschaillons-sur-St-Laurent
  Canada 46°32N 72°7W **73 C5**
Deschambault L.
  Canada 54°50N 103°30W **71 C8**
Deschutes → U.S.A. 45°38N 120°55W **76 D3**
Dese Ethiopia 11°5N 39°40E **47 E2**
Deseado → Argentina 47°45S 65°54W **96 F3**
Desert Center U.S.A. 33°43N 115°24W **79 M11**
Desert Hot Springs
  U.S.A. 33°58N 116°30W **79 M10**
Deshnok India 27°48N 73°21E **42 F5**
Desierto Central de Baja
  California △ Mexico 29°40N 114°50W **86 B2**
Desna → Ukraine 50°33N 30°32E **17 C16**
Desolación, I. Chile 53°0S 74°0W **96 G2**
Despeñaperros, Paso
  Spain 38°24N 3°30W **21 C4**
Dessau Germany 51°51N 12°14E **16 C7**
Dessye = Dese Ethiopia 11°5N 39°40E **47 E2**
D'Estrees B. Australia 35°55S 137°45E **63 F2**
Desuri India 25°18N 73°35E **42 G5**
Det Udom Thailand 14°54N 105°5E **38 E5**
Dete Zimbabwe 18°38S 26°50E **56 B4**
Detmold Germany 51°56N 8°52E **16 C5**
Detour, Pt. U.S.A. 45°40N 86°40W **80 C10**
Detroit U.S.A. 42°19N 83°12W **82 D1**
Detroit Lakes U.S.A. 46°49N 95°51W **80 B6**
Deua △ Australia 35°30S 149°46E **63 F4**
Deurne Neths. 51°27N 5°49E **15 C5**
Deutsche Bucht Germany 54°15N 8°0E **16 A5**
Deutschland = Germany ■
  Europe 51°0N 10°0E **16 C6**
Deva Romania 45°53N 22°55E **17 F12**
Devakottai India 9°55N 78°45E **40 Q11**
Devaprayag India 30°13N 78°35E **43 D8**

Deventer Neths. 52°15N 6°10E 15 B6
Deveron → U.K. 57°41N 2°32W 11 D6
Devgadh Bariya India 22°40N 73°55E 42 H5
Devikot India 26°42N 71°12E 42 F4
Devils Den U.S.A. 35°46N 119°58W 78 K7
Devils Hole = Death Valley △ U.S.A. 36°29N 117°6W 79 J9
Devils Lake U.S.A. 48°7N 98°52W 80 A4
Devils Paw Canada 58°47N 134°0W 70 B2
Devils Postpile ⌂ U.S.A. 37°37N 119°5W 78 H7
Devils Tower U.S.A. 44°35N 104°42W 76 D11
Devils Tower △ U.S.A. 44°48N 104°55W 76 D11
Devine U.S.A. 29°8N 98°54W 84 G5
Devizes U.K. 51°22N 1°58W 13 F6
Devli India 25°50N 75°20E 42 G6
Devon Canada 53°24N 113°44W 70 C6
Devon ◻ U.K. 50°50N 3°40W 13 G4
Devon I. Canada 75°10N 85°0W 69 B11
Devonport Australia 41°10S 146°22E 63 G4
Devonport N.Z. 36°49S 174°49E 59 B5
Dewas India 22°59N 76°3E 42 H7
Dewetsdorp S. Africa 29°33S 26°39E 56 D4
Dewey Puerto Rico 18°18N 65°18W 89 d
Dexter Maine, U.S.A. 45°1N 69°18W 81 C19
Dexter Mo., U.S.A. 36°48N 89°57W 80 G9
Dexter N. Mex., U.S.A. 33°12N 104°22W 77 K11
Dey-Dey, L. Australia 29°12S 131°4E 61 E5
Deyang China 31°3N 104°27E 32 C5
Deyhūk Iran 33°15N 57°30E 45 C8
Deyyer Iran 27°55N 51°55E 45 E6
Dezadeash L. Canada 60°28N 136°58W 70 A1
Dezfūl Iran 32°20N 48°30E 45 C6
Dezhneva, Mys Russia 66°5N 169°40W 29 C19
Dezhou China 37°26N 116°18E 34 F9
Dhadhar → India 24°56N 85°24E 43 G11
Dhahiriya = Aẓ Ẓāhirīyah West Bank 31°25N 34°58E 46 D3
Dhahran = Aẓ Ẓahrān Si. Arabia 26°10N 50°7E 45 E6
Dhak Pakistan 32°25N 72°33E 42 C5
Dhaka Bangla. 23°43N 90°26E 43 H14
Dhaka ◻ Bangla. 24°25N 90°25E 43 G14
Dhali Cyprus 35°1N 33°25E 25 D12
Dhamār Yemen 14°30N 44°20E 47 E3
Dhampur India 29°19N 78°33E 43 E8
Dhamtari India 20°42N 81°35E 41 J12
Dhanbad India 23°50N 86°30E 43 H12
Dhangarhi Nepal 28°55N 80°40E 43 E9
Dhankuta Nepal 26°55N 87°40E 43 F12
Dhar India 22°35N 75°26E 42 H6
Dharampur India 22°13N 75°18E 42 H6
Dharamsala = Dharmsala India 32°16N 76°23E 42 C7
Dhariwal India 31°57N 75°19E 42 D6
Dharla → Bangla. 25°46N 89°42E 43 G13
Dharmapuri India 12°10N 78°10E 40 N11
Dharmjaygarh India 22°28N 83°13E 43 H10
Dharmsala India 32°16N 76°23E 42 C7
Dharni India 21°33N 76°53E 42 J7
Dharwad India 15°30N 75°4E 40 M9
Dhasan → India 25°48N 79°24E 43 G8
Dhaulagiri Nepal 28°39N 83°28E 43 E10
Dhebar, L. India 24°10N 74°0E 42 G6
Dheftera Cyprus 35°5N 33°16E 25 D12
Dhenkanal India 20°45N 85°35E 41 J14
Dherinia Cyprus 35°3N 33°57E 25 D12
Dhī Qār ◻ Iraq 31°0N 46°15E 44 D5
Dhiarrizos → Cyprus 34°41N 32°34E 25 E11
Dhībān Jordan 31°30N 35°46E 46 D4
Dhilwan India 31°31N 75°21E 42 D6
Dhimarkhera India 23°28N 80°22E 43 H9
Dhodhekánisos = Dodecanese Greece 36°35N 27°0E 23 F12
Dholka India 22°44N 72°29E 42 H5
Dhoraji India 21°45N 70°37E 42 J4
Dhrangadhra India 22°59N 71°31E 42 H4
Dhrol India 22°33N 70°25E 42 H4
Dhuburi India 26°2N 89°59E 41 F16
Dhule India 20°58N 74°50E 40 J9
Di Linh Vietnam 11°35N 108°4E 39 G7
Di Linh, Cao Nguyen Vietnam 11°30N 108°0E 39 G7
Dia Greece 35°28N 25°14E 25 D7
Diablo Range U.S.A. 37°20N 121°25W 78 J5
Diafarabé Mali 14°9N 4°57W 50 F5
Diamante Argentina 32°5S 60°40W 94 C3
Diamante → Argentina 34°30S 66°46W 94 C2
Diamantina Brazil 18°17S 43°40W 93 G10
Diamantina → Australia 26°45S 139°10E 63 D2
Diamantina △ Australia 23°33S 141°23E 62 C3
Diamantino Brazil 14°30S 56°30W 93 F7
Diamond Bar U.S.A. 34°1N 117°48W 79 L9
Diamond Harbour India 22°11N 88°14E 43 H13
Diamond Is. Australia 17°25S 151°5E 62 B5
Diamond Mts. U.S.A. 39°40N 115°50W 76 G6
Diamond Springs U.S.A. 38°42N 120°49W 78 G6
Diaoyu Tai = Senkaku-Shotō E. China Sea 25°45N 123°30E 31 M1
Dībā U.A.E. 25°45N 56°16E 45 E8
Dibai India 28°13N 78°15E 42 E8
Dibaya Dem. Rep. of the Congo 6°30S 22°57E 52 F4
Dibaya-Lubue Dem. Rep. of the Congo 4°12S 19°54E 52 E3
Dibbeen △ Jordan 32°20N 35°45E 46 C4
Dibete Botswana 23°45S 26°32E 56 C4
Dibrugarh India 27°29N 94°55E 41 F19
Dickens U.S.A. 33°37N 100°50W 84 E4
Dickinson U.S.A. 46°53N 102°47W 80 B2
Dickson U.S.A. 36°5N 87°23W 85 C11
Dickson City U.S.A. 41°28N 75°36W 83 E9
Didiéni Mali 13°53N 8°6W 50 F4
Didsbury Canada 51°35N 114°10W 70 C6
Didwana India 27°23N 74°36E 42 F6
Diefenbaker, L. Canada 51°0N 106°55W 71 C7
Diego de Almagro Chile 26°22S 70°3W 94 B1
Diego Suarez = Antsiranana Madag. 12°25S 49°20E 57 A8
Diekirch Lux. 49°52N 6°10E 15 E6
Dien Ban Vietnam 15°53N 108°16E 38 E7
Dien Bien Vietnam 21°20N 103°0E 38 B4
Dien Khanh Vietnam 12°15N 109°6E 39 F7
Dieppe France 49°54N 1°4E 20 B4
Dierks U.S.A. 34°7N 94°1W 84 D7
Diest Belgium 50°58N 5°4E 15 D5
Dif Somali Rep. 0°59N 40°58E 47 G3
Differdange Lux. 49°31N 5°54E 15 E5
Dig India 27°28N 77°20E 42 F7
Digba Dem. Rep. of the Congo 4°25N 25°48E 54 B2
Digby Canada 44°38N 65°50W 73 D6
Diggi India 26°22N 75°26E 42 F6
Dighinala Bangla. 23°15N 92°5E 41 H18
Dighton U.S.A. 38°29N 100°28W 80 F3
Digne-les-Bains France 44°5N 6°12E 20 D7
Digos Phil. 6°45N 125°20E 37 C7
Digranes Iceland 66°4N 14°44W 8 C6
Digul → Indonesia 7°7S 138°42E 37 F9
Dihang = Brahmaputra → Asia 23°40N 90°35E 43 H13
Dijlah, Nahr → Asia 31°0N 47°25E 44 D5
Dijon France 47°20N 5°3E 20 C6
Dikhil Djibouti 11°8N 42°20E 47 E3
Dikkil = Dikhil Djibouti 11°8N 42°20E 47 E3
Diksmuide Belgium 51°2N 2°52E 15 C2
Dikson Russia 73°40N 80°5E 28 B9
Dikti Oros Greece 35°8N 25°30E 25 D7
Dila Ethiopia 6°21N 38°22E 47 F2
Dili E. Timor 8°39S 125°34E 37 F7
Dilley U.S.A. 28°40N 99°10W 84 G5
Dilli = Delhi India 28°39N 77°13E 42 E7
Dillingham U.S.A. 59°3N 158°28W 74 a
Dillon Canada 55°56N 108°35W 71 B7
Dillon Mont., U.S.A. 45°13N 112°38W 76 D7
Dillon S.C., U.S.A. 34°25N 79°22W 85 D15
Dillon → Canada 55°56N 108°56W 71 B7
Dillsburg U.S.A. 40°7N 77°2W 82 F7
Dilolo Dem. Rep. of the Congo 10°28S 22°18E 52 G4
Dimas Mexico 23°43N 106°47W 86 C3
Dimashq Syria 33°30N 36°18E 46 B5
Dimashq ◻ Syria 33°30N 36°30E 46 B5
Dimbaza S. Africa 32°50S 27°14E 57 E4
Dimboola Australia 36°28S 142°7E 63 F3
Dîmboviţa = Dâmboviţa → Romania 44°12N 26°26E 17 F14
Dimbulah Australia 17°8S 145°4E 62 B4
Dimitrovgrad Bulgaria 42°5N 25°35E 23 C11
Dimitrovgrad Russia 54°14N 49°39E 18 D8
Dimitrovo = Pernik Bulgaria 42°35N 23°2E 23 C10
Dimmitt U.S.A. 34°33N 102°19W 84 D3
Dimona Israel 31°2N 35°1E 46 D4
Dinagat Phil. 10°10N 125°40E 37 B7
Dinajpur Bangla. 25°33N 88°43E 41 G16
Dinan France 48°28N 2°2W 20 B2
Dīnān Āb Iran 32°4N 56°49E 45 C8
Dinant Belgium 50°16N 4°55E 15 D4
Dinapur India 25°38N 85°5E 43 G11
Dīnār, Kūh-e Iran 30°42N 51°46E 45 D6
Dinara Planina Croatia 44°0N 16°30E 22 C7
Dinard France 48°38N 2°6W 20 B2
Dinaric Alps = Dinara Planina Croatia 44°0N 16°30E 22 C7
Dindigul India 10°25N 78°0E 40 P11
Dindori India 22°57N 81°5E 43 H9
Ding Xian = Dingzhou China 38°30N 114°59E 34 E8
Dinga Pakistan 25°26N 67°10E 42 G2
Ding'an China 19°42N 110°19E 38 C8
Dingbian China 37°35N 107°32E 34 F4
Dingle Ireland 52°9N 10°17W 10 D1
Dingle B. Ireland 52°3N 10°20W 10 D1
Dingmans Ferry U.S.A. 41°13N 74°55W 83 E10
Dingo Australia 23°38S 149°19E 62 C4
Dingtao China 35°5N 115°35E 34 G8
Dingwall U.K. 57°36N 4°26W 11 D4
Dingxi China 35°30N 104°33E 34 G3
Dingxiang China 38°30N 112°58E 34 E7
Dingzhou China 38°30N 114°59E 34 E8
Dinh, Mui Vietnam 11°22N 109°1E 39 G7
Dinh Lap Vietnam 21°33N 107°6E 38 B6
Dinin → Ireland 52°43N 7°18W 10 D4
Dinira △ Venezuela 9°57N 70°6W 89 E6
Dinokwe Botswana 23°29S 26°37E 56 C4
Dinorwic Canada 49°41N 92°30W 71 D10
Dinosaur ⌂ Canada 50°47N 111°30W 70 C6
Dinosaur ⌂ U.S.A. 40°30N 108°45W 76 F9
Dinuba U.S.A. 36°32N 119°23W 78 J7
Dionisades Greece 35°20N 26°10E 25 D8
Diourbel Senegal 14°39N 16°12W 50 F2
Dipalpur Pakistan 30°40N 73°39E 42 D5
Diplo Pakistan 24°35N 69°35E 42 G3
Dipolog Phil. 8°36N 123°20E 37 C6
Dipperu △ Australia 21°56S 148°42E 62 C4
Dir Pakistan 35°8N 71°59E 40 B7
Dire Dawa Ethiopia 9°35N 41°45E 47 F3
Dirfis Oros Greece 38°40N 23°54E 23 E10
Diriamba Nic. 11°51N 86°19W 88 D2
Dirk Hartog I. Australia 25°50S 113°5E 61 E1
Dirranbandi Australia 28°33S 148°17E 63 D4
Disa India 24°18N 72°10E 42 G5
Disappointment, C. U.S.A. 46°18N 124°5W 76 C1
Disappointment, L. Australia 23°20S 122°40E 60 D3
Disaster B. Australia 37°15S 149°58E 63 F4
Discovery B. Australia 38°10S 140°40E 63 F3
Discovery B. China 22°18N 114°1E 33 G11
Disko = Qeqertarsuaq Greenland 69°45N 53°30W 66 C14
Disney Reef Tonga 19°17S 174°7W 59 c
Diss U.K. 52°23N 1°7E 13 E9
Disteghil Sar Pakistan 36°20N 75°12E 43 A6
District of Columbia ◻ U.S.A. 38°55N 77°0W 81 F15
Distrito Federal ◻ Brazil 15°45S 47°45W 93 G9
Distrito Federal ◻ Mexico 19°15N 99°10W 87 D5
Diu India 20°45N 70°58E 42 J4
Dīvāndarreh Iran 35°55N 47°2E 44 C5
Divide U.S.A. 45°45N 112°45W 76 D7
Dividing Ra. Australia 27°45S 116°0E 61 E2
Divinópolis Brazil 20°10S 44°54W 93 H10
Divnoye Russia 45°55N 43°21E 19 E7
Divo Ivory C. 5°48N 5°15W 50 G4
Dīwāl Kol Afghan. 34°23N 67°52E 42 B2
Dixie Mt. U.S.A. 39°55N 120°16W 78 F6
Dixon Calif., U.S.A. 38°27N 121°49W 78 G5
Dixon Ill., U.S.A. 41°50N 89°29W 80 E9
Dixon Entrance U.S.A. 54°30N 132°0W 68 D6
Dixville Canada 45°4N 71°46W 83 A13
Diyālā ◻ Iraq 33°45N 44°50E 44 C5
Diyālā → Iraq 33°13N 44°30E 44 C5
Diyarbakır Turkey 37°55N 40°18E 44 B4
Diyodar India 24°8N 71°50E 42 G4
Djakarta = Jakarta Indonesia 6°9S 106°52E 36 F3
Djamba Angola 16°45S 13°58E 56 B1
Djambala Congo 2°32S 14°30E 52 E2
Djanet Algeria 24°35N 9°32E 50 D7
Djawa = Jawa Indonesia 7°0S 110°0E 36 F3
Djelfa Algeria 34°40N 3°15E 50 B6
Djema C.A.R. 6°3N 25°15E 54 A2
Djerba, Î. de Tunisia 33°50N 10°48E 51 B8
Djerid, Chott Tunisia 33°42N 8°30E 50 B7
Djibouti Djibouti 11°30N 43°5E 47 E3
Djibouti ■ Africa 12°0N 43°0E 47 E3
Djolu Dem. Rep. of the Congo 0°35N 22°5E 52 D4
Djougou Benin 9°40N 1°45E 50 G6
Djoum Cameroon 2°41N 12°35E 52 D2
Djourab, Erg du Chad 16°40N 18°50E 51 E9
Djugu Dem. Rep. of the Congo 1°55N 30°35E 54 B3
Djukbinj △ Australia 12°11S 131°2E 60 B5
Djúpivogur Iceland 64°39N 14°17W 8 D6
Dmitriya Lapteva, Proliv Russia 73°0N 140°0E 29 B15
Dnepr = Dnipro → Ukraine 46°30N 32°18E 19 E5
Dneprodzerzhinsk = Dniprodzerzhynsk Ukraine 48°32N 34°37E 19 E5
Dnepropetrovsk = Dnipropetrovsk Ukraine 48°30N 35°0E 19 E6
Dnestr = Dnister → Europe 46°18N 30°17E 17 E16
Dnieper = Dnipro → Ukraine 46°30N 32°18E 19 E5
Dniester = Dnister → Europe 46°18N 30°17E 17 E16
Dnipro → Ukraine 46°30N 32°18E 19 E5
Dniprodzerzhynsk Ukraine 48°32N 34°37E 19 E5
Dnipropetrovsk Ukraine 48°30N 35°0E 19 E6
Dnister → Europe 46°18N 30°17E 17 E16
Dno Russia 57°50N 29°58E 9 H23
Dnyapro = Dnipro → Ukraine 46°30N 32°18E 19 E5
Doaktown Canada 46°33N 66°8W 73 C6
Doan Hung Vietnam 21°30N 105°10E 38 B5
Doany Madag. 14°21S 49°30E 57 A8
Doba Chad 8°40N 16°50E 51 G9
Dobandi Pakistan 31°13N 66°50E 42 D2
Dobbyn Australia 19°44S 140°2E 62 B3
Dobele Latvia 56°37N 23°16E 9 H20
Doberai, Jazirah Indonesia 1°25S 133°0E 37 E8
Doblas Argentina 37°5S 64°0W 94 D3
Dobo Indonesia 5°45S 134°15E 37 F8
Doboj Bos.-H. 44°46N 18°4E 23 B8
Dobrich Bulgaria 43°37N 27°49E 23 C12
Dobruja Europe 44°30N 28°15E 17 F15
Dobrush Belarus 52°25N 31°22E 17 B16
Doc, Mui Vietnam 17°58N 106°30E 38 D6
Docker River = Kaltukatjara Australia 24°52S 129°5E 61 D4
Doctor Arroyo Mexico 23°40N 100°11W 86 C4
Doda India 33°10N 75°34E 43 C6
Doda, L. Canada 49°25N 75°13W 72 C4
Dodecanese Greece 36°35N 27°0E 23 F12
Dodekanisa = Dodecanese Greece 36°35N 27°0E 23 F12
Dodge City U.S.A. 37°45N 100°1W 80 G3
Dodge L. Canada 59°50N 105°36W 71 B7
Dodgeville U.S.A. 42°58N 90°8W 80 D8
Dodoma Tanzania 6°8S 35°45E 54 D4
Dodoma ◻ Tanzania 6°0S 36°0E 54 D4
Dodori ⌂ Kenya 1°55S 41°7E 54 C5
Dodsland Canada 51°50N 108°45W 71 C7
Dodson U.S.A. 48°24N 108°15W 76 B9
Doesburg Neths. 52°1N 6°9E 15 B6
Doetinchem Neths. 51°59N 6°18E 15 C6
Dog Creek Canada 51°35N 122°14W 70 C4
Dog L. Man., Canada 51°2N 98°31W 71 C9
Dog L. Ont., Canada 48°48N 89°30W 72 C2
Dogran Pakistan 31°48N 73°35E 42 D5
Doğubayazıt Turkey 39°31N 44°5E 44 B5
Doha = Ad Dawḩah Qatar 25°15N 51°35E 45 E6
Dohazari Bangla. 22°10N 92°5E 41 H18
Dohrighat India 26°16N 83°31E 43 F10
Doi Indonesia 2°14N 127°49E 37 D7
Doi Inthanon △ Thailand 18°33N 98°34E 38 C2
Doi Khuntan △ Thailand 18°33N 99°14E 38 C2
Doi Luang Thailand 18°30N 101°0E 38 C3
Doi Luang △ Thailand 19°22N 99°35E 38 C2
Doi Saket Thailand 18°52N 99°9E 38 C2
Doi Suthep △ Thailand 18°49N 98°53E 38 C2
Dois Irmãos, Sa. Brazil 9°0S 42°30W 93 E10
Dokkum Neths. 53°20N 5°59E 15 A5
Dokri Pakistan 27°25N 68°7E 42 F3
Dolak, Pulau Indonesia 8°0S 138°30E 37 F9
Dolbeau-Mistassini Canada 48°53N 72°14W 73 C5
Dole France 47°7N 5°31E 20 C6
Dolgellau U.K. 52°45N 3°53W 12 E4
Dolgelley = Dolgellau U.K. 52°45N 3°53W 12 E4
Dollard Neths. 53°20N 7°10E 15 A7
Dolo Ethiopia 4°11N 42°3E 47 G3
Dolomites = Dolomiti Italy 46°23N 11°51E 22 A4
Dolomiti Italy 46°23N 11°51E 22 A4
Dolores Argentina 36°20S 57°40W 94 D4
Dolores Uruguay 33°34S 58°15W 94 C4
Dolores U.S.A. 37°28N 108°30W 77 H9
Dolores → U.S.A. 38°49N 109°17W 76 G9
Dolphin, C. Falk. Is. 51°10S 59°0W 96 G5
Dolphin and Union Str. Canada 69°5N 114°45W 68 C8
Dom Pedrito Brazil 31°0S 54°40W 95 C5
Doma ⌂ Zimbabwe 16°28S 30°12E 55 F3
Domariaganj → India 26°17N 83°44E 43 F10
Domasi Malawi 15°15S 35°22E 55 F4
Dombarovskiy Russia 50°46N 59°32E 28 D6
Dombås Norway 62°4N 9°8E 8 E13
Dome Argus Antarctica 80°50S 76°30E 5 E12
Dome C. Antarctica 75°12S 123°37E 5 D17
Dome Fuji Antarctica 77°20S 39°45E 5 D5
Domel I. = Letsôk-aw Kyun Burma 11°30N 98°25E 39 G2
Domeyko Chile 29°0S 71°0W 94 B1
Domeyko, Cordillera Chile 24°30S 69°0W 94 A2
Dominador Chile 24°21S 69°20W 94 A2
Dominica ■ W. Indies 15°20N 61°20W 89 C7
Dominica Passage W. Indies 15°10N 61°20W 89 C7
Dominican Rep. ■ W. Indies 19°0N 70°30W 89 C5
Domodóssola Italy 46°7N 8°17E 20 C8
Domville, Mt. Australia 28°1S 151°15E 63 D5
Don → Russia 47°4N 39°18E 19 E6
Don → Aberds., U.K. 57°11N 2°5W 11 D6
Don → S. Yorks., U.K. 53°41N 0°52W 12 D7
Don, C. Australia 11°18S 131°46E 60 B5
Don Benito Spain 38°53N 5°51W 21 C3
Don Figuerero Mts. Jamaica 18°5N 77°36W 88 a
Don Sak Thailand 9°18N 99°41E 39 b
Dona Ana = Nhamaabué Mozam. 17°25S 35°5E 55 F4
Donaghadee U.K. 54°39N 5°33W 10 B6
Donaghmore Ireland 52°52N 7°36W 10 D4
Donald Australia 36°23S 143°0E 63 F3
Donaldsonville U.S.A. 30°6N 90°59W 84 F9
Donalsonville U.S.A. 31°3N 84°53W 85 F12
Donau = Dunărea → Europe 45°20N 29°40E 17 F15
Donauwörth Germany 48°43N 10°47E 16 D6
Doncaster U.K. 53°32N 1°6W 12 D6
Dondo Angola 9°45S 14°25E 52 F2
Dondo Mozam. 19°33S 34°46E 55 F3
Dondo, Teluk Indonesia 0°50N 120°30E 37 D6
Dondra Head Sri Lanka 5°55N 80°40E 40 S12
Donegal Ireland 54°39N 8°5W 10 B3
Donegal ◻ Ireland 54°53N 8°0W 10 B4
Donegal B. Ireland 54°31N 8°49W 10 B3
Donets → Russia 47°33N 40°55E 19 E7
Donets Basin Ukraine 49°0N 38°0E 6 F13
Donetsk Ukraine 48°0N 37°45E 19 E6
Dong Ba Thin Vietnam 12°8N 109°13E 39 F7
Dong Dang Vietnam 21°54N 106°42E 38 B6
Dong Giam Vietnam 19°25N 105°31E 38 C5
Dong Ha Vietnam 16°55N 107°8E 38 D6
Dong Hene Laos 16°40N 105°18E 38 D5
Dong Hoi Vietnam 17°29N 106°36E 38 D6
Dong Khe Vietnam 22°26N 106°27E 38 A6
Dong Ujimqin Qi China 45°32N 116°55E 34 B9
Dong Van Vietnam 23°16N 105°22E 38 A5
Dong Xoai Vietnam 11°32N 106°55E 39 G6
Dongara Australia 29°14S 114°57E 61 E1
Dongbei China 45°0N 125°0E 35 D13
Dongchuan China 26°8N 103°1E 32 D5
Dongco China 32°8N 84°58E 41 C14
Dongfang China 18°50N 108°33E 38 C7
Dongfeng China 42°40N 125°34E 35 C13
Donggala Indonesia 0°30S 119°40E 37 E5
Donggang China 39°52N 124°10E 35 E13
Dongguang China 37°50N 116°30E 34 F9
Donghae S. Korea 37°29N 129°7E 35 F15
Dongjingcheng China 44°5N 129°10E 35 B15
Dongnae S. Korea 35°12N 129°5E 35 G15
Dongning China 44°2N 131°5E 35 B16
Dongola Sudan 19°9N 30°22E 51 E12
Dongping China 35°55N 116°20E 34 G9
Dongsheng China 39°50N 110°0E 34 E6
Dongtai China 32°51N 120°21E 35 H11
Dongting Hu China 29°18N 112°45E 33 D6
Donington, C. Australia 34°45S 136°0E 63 E2
Doniphan U.S.A. 36°37N 90°50W 80 G8
Dønna Norway 66°6N 12°30E 8 C15
Donna U.S.A. 26°9N 98°4W 84 H5
Donnacona Canada 46°41N 71°41W 73 C5
Donnelly's Crossing N.Z. 35°42S 173°38E 59 A4
Donnybrook Australia 33°34S 115°48E 61 F2
Donnybrook S. Africa 29°59S 29°48E 57 D4
Donora U.S.A. 40°11N 79°52W 82 F5
Donostia = Donostia-San Sebastián Spain 43°17N 1°58W 21 A5
Donostia-San Sebastián Spain 43°17N 1°58W 21 A5
Doon → U.K. 55°27N 4°39W 11 F4
Dora, L. Australia 22°0S 123°0E 60 D3
Dora Báltea → Italy 45°11N 8°3E 20 D8
Doran L. Canada 61°13N 108°6W 71 A7
Dorchester U.K. 50°42N 2°27W 13 G5
Dorchester, C. Canada 65°27N 77°27W 69 C12
Dordabis Namibia 22°52S 17°38E 56 C2
Dordogne → France 45°2N 0°36W 20 D3
Dordrecht Neths. 51°48N 4°39E 15 C4
Dordrecht S. Africa 31°20S 27°3E 56 E4
Doré L. Canada 54°46N 107°17W 71 C7
Dori Burkina Faso 14°3N 0°2W 50 F5
Doring → S. Africa 31°54S 18°39E 56 E2
Doringbos S. Africa 31°59S 19°16E 56 E2
Dorking U.K. 51°14N 0°19W 13 F7
Dornbirn Austria 47°25N 9°45E 16 E5
Dornie U.K. 57°17N 5°31W 11 D3
Dornoch U.K. 57°53N 4°2W 11 D4
Dornoch Firth U.K. 57°51N 4°4W 11 D4
Dornogovĭ ◻ Mongolia 44°0N 110°0E 34 C6
Doro, Kavo Greece 38°9N 24°38E 23 E11
Dorohoi Romania 47°56N 26°23E 17 E14
Döröö Nuur Mongolia 48°0N 93°0E 32 B4
Dorr Iran 33°17N 50°38E 45 C6
Dorre I. Australia 25°13S 113°12E 61 E1
Dorrigo Australia 30°20S 152°44E 63 E5
Dorris U.S.A. 41°58N 121°55W 76 F3
Dorset Canada 45°14N 78°54W 82 A6
Dorset U.S.A. 41°40N 80°40W 82 E4
Dorset ◻ U.K. 50°45N 2°26W 13 G5
Dortmund Germany 51°30N 7°28E 16 C4
Doruma Dem. Rep. of the Congo 4°42N 27°33E 54 B2
Dorūneh Iran 35°10N 57°18E 45 C8
Dos Bahías, C. Argentina 44°58S 65°32W 96 E3
Dos Hermanas Spain 37°16N 5°55W 21 D3
Dos Palos U.S.A. 36°59N 120°37W 78 J6
Dosso Niger 13°0N 3°13E 50 F6
Dothan U.S.A. 31°13N 85°24W 85 F12
Doty U.S.A. 46°38N 123°17W 78 D3
Douai France 50°21N 3°4E 20 A5
Douala Cameroon 4°0N 9°45E 52 D1
Douarnenez France 48°6N 4°21W 20 B1
Double Island Pt. Australia 25°56S 153°11E 63 D5
Double Mountain Fork → U.S.A. 33°16N 100°0W 84 E4
Doubs → France 46°53N 5°1E 20 C6
Doubtful Sd. N.Z. 45°20S 166°49E 59 F1
Doubtless B. N.Z. 34°55S 173°26E 59 A4
Douglas I. of Man 54°10N 4°28W 12 C3
Douglas S. Africa 29°4S 23°46E 56 D3
Douglas Ariz., U.S.A. 31°21N 109°33W 77 L9
Douglas Ga., U.S.A. 31°31N 82°51W 85 F13
Douglas Wyo., U.S.A. 42°45N 105°24W 76 E11
Douglas Apsley △ Australia 41°45S 148°11E 63 G4
Douglas Chan. Canada 53°40N 129°20W 70 C3
Douglas Pt. Canada 44°19N 81°37W 82 B3
Douglasville U.S.A. 33°45N 84°45W 85 E12
Dounreay U.K. 58°35N 3°44W 11 C5
Dourada, Serra Brazil 13°10S 48°45W 93 F9
Dourados Brazil 22°9S 54°50W 95 A5
Dourados → Brazil 21°58S 54°18W 95 A5
Dourados, Serra dos Brazil 23°30S 53°30W 95 A5
Douro → Europe 41°8N 8°40W 21 B1
Dove → U.K. 52°51N 1°36W 12 E6
Dove Creek U.S.A. 37°46N 108°54W 77 H9
Dover Australia 43°18S 147°2E 63 G4
Dover U.K. 51°7N 1°19E 13 F9
Dover Del., U.S.A. 39°10N 75°32W 81 F16
Dover N.H., U.S.A. 43°12N 70°56W 83 C14
Dover N.J., U.S.A. 40°53N 74°34W 83 F10
Dover Ohio, U.S.A. 40°32N 81°29W 82 F3
Dover, Pt. Australia 32°32S 125°32E 61 F4
Dover, Str. of Europe 51°0N 1°30E 13 G9
Dover-Foxcroft U.S.A. 45°11N 69°13W 81 C19
Dover Plains U.S.A. 41°43N 73°35W 83 E11
Dovey = Dyfi → U.K. 52°32N 4°3W 13 E3
Dovrefjell Norway 62°15N 9°33E 8 E13
Dow Rūd Iran 33°28N 49°4E 45 C6
Dowa Malawi 13°38S 33°58E 55 E3
Dowagiac U.S.A. 41°59N 86°6W 80 E10
Dowerin Australia 31°12S 117°2E 61 F2
Dowgha'i Iran 36°54N 58°32E 45 B8
Dowlatābād Iran 28°20N 56°40E 45 D8
Down ◻ U.K. 54°23N 6°2W 10 B5
Downey Calif., U.S.A. 33°56N 118°9W 79 M8
Downey Idaho, U.S.A. 42°26N 112°7W 76 E7
Downham Market U.K. 52°37N 0°23E 13 E8
Downieville U.S.A. 39°34N 120°50W 78 F6
Downpatrick U.K. 54°20N 5°43W 10 B6
Downpatrick Hd. Ireland 54°20N 9°21W 10 B2
Downsville U.S.A. 42°5N 75°0W 83 D10
Downton, Mt. Canada 52°42N 124°52W 70 C4
Dowsārī Iran 28°25N 57°59E 45 D8
Doyle U.S.A. 40°2N 120°6W 78 E6
Doylestown U.S.A. 40°21N 75°10W 83 F9
Dozois, Rés. Canada 47°30N 77°5W 72 C4
Dra Khel Pakistan 27°58N 66°45E 42 F2
Drâa, C. Morocco 28°47N 11°0W 50 C3
Drâa, Oued → Morocco 28°40N 11°10W 50 C3
Drachten Neths. 53°7N 6°5E 15 A6
Drăgăşani Romania 44°39N 24°17E 17 F13
Dragichyn Belarus 52°15N 25°8E 17 B13
Dragoman, Prokhod Bulgaria 42°58N 22°53E 23 C10
Dragon's Mouths = Boca de Drago Venezuela 11°0N 61°50W 93 K15
Draguignan France 43°32N 6°27E 20 E7
Drain U.S.A. 43°40N 123°19W 76 E2
Drake U.S.A. 47°55N 100°23W 80 B3

Drake Passage *S. Ocean* 58°0S 68°0W **5** B17
Drakensberg *S. Africa* 31°0S 28°0E **57** D4
Drama *Greece* 41°9N 24°10E **23** D11
Drammen *Norway* 59°42N 10°12E **9** G14
Drangajökull *Iceland* 66°9N 22°15W **8** C2
Dras *India* 34°25N 75°48E **43** B6
Drastis, Akra *Greece* 39°48N 19°40E **25** A3
Drau = Drava →
  Croatia 45°33N 18°55E **23** B8
Drava → *Croatia* 45°33N 18°55E **23** B8
Drayton Valley
  Canada 53°12N 114°58W **70** C6
Drenthe □ *Neths.* 52°52N 6°40E **15** B6
Drepano, Akra *Greece* 35°28N 24°14E **25** D6
Drepanum, C. *Cyprus* 34°54N 32°19E **25** E11
Dresden *Canada* 42°35N 82°11W **82** D2
Dresden *Germany* 51°3N 13°44E **16** C7
Dreux *France* 48°44N 1°23E **20** B4
Driffield *U.K.* 54°0N 0°26E **12** C7
Driftwood *U.S.A.* 41°20N 78°8W **82** E6
Driggs *U.S.A.* 43°44N 111°6W **76** E8
Drin → *Albania* 42°1N 19°38E **23** C8
Drina → *Bos.-H.* 44°53N 19°21E **23** B8
Drøbak *Norway* 59°39N 10°39E **9** G14
Drobeta-Turnu Severin
  Romania 44°39N 22°41E **17** F12
Drochia *Moldova* 48°2N 27°48E **17** D14
Drogheda *Ireland* 53°43N 6°22W **10** C5
Drogichin = Dragichyn
  Belarus 52°15N 25°8E **17** B13
Drogobych = Drohobych
  Ukraine 49°20N 23°30E **17** D12
Drohobych *Ukraine* 49°20N 23°30E **17** D12
Droichead Atha = Drogheda
  Ireland 53°43N 6°22W **10** C5
Droichead Nua *Ireland* 53°11N 6°48W **10** C5
Droitwich *U.K.* 52°16N 2°8W **13** E5
Drôme □ *France* 44°38N 5°15E **20** D6
Dromedary, C.
  Australia 36°17S 150°10E **63** F5
Dromore *U.K.* 54°31N 7°28W **10** B4
Dromore West *Ireland* 54°15N 8°52W **10** B3
Dronfield *U.K.* 53°19N 1°27W **12** D6
Dronning Maud Land
  Antarctica 72°30S 12°0E **5** D3
Dronten *Neths.* 52°32N 5°43E **15** B5
Druk Yul = Bhutan ■
  Asia 27°25N 90°30E **41** F17
Drumbo *Canada* 43°16N 80°35W **82** C4
Drumcliff *Ireland* 54°20N 8°29W **10** B3
Drumheller *Canada* 51°25N 112°40W **70** C6
Drummond *U.S.A.* 46°40N 113°9W **76** C7
Drummond I. *U.S.A.* 46°1N 83°39W **81** B12
Drummond Pt. *Australia* 34°9S 135°16E **63** E2
Drummond Ra.
  Australia 23°45S 147°10E **62** C4
Drummondville *Canada* 45°55N 72°25W **72** C5
Drumright *U.S.A.* 35°59N 96°36W **84** D6
Druskininkai *Lithuania* 54°3N 23°58E **9** J20
Drut → *Belarus* 53°8N 30°5E **17** B16
Druzhina *Russia* 68°14N 145°18E **29** C15
Dry Harbour Mts.
  Jamaica 18°19N 77°24W **88** a
Dry Tortugas *U.S.A.* 24°38N 82°55W **85** F13
Dryden *Canada* 49°47N 92°50W **71** D10
Dryden *U.S.A.* 42°30N 76°18W **83** D8
Drygalski I. *Antarctica* 66°0S 92°0E **5** C7
Drygalski Ice Tongue
  Antarctica 75°24S 163°30E **5** D21
Drysdale → *Australia* 13°59S 126°51E **60** B4
Drysdale I. *Australia* 11°41S 136°0E **62** A2
Drysdale River △
  Australia 14°56S 127°2E **60** B4
Du Gué → *Canada* 57°21N 70°45W **72** A5
Du Quoin *U.S.A.* 38°1N 89°14W **80** F9
Duanesburg *U.S.A.* 42°45N 74°11W **83** D10
Duaringa *Australia* 23°42S 149°42E **62** C4
Duarte, Pico *Dom. Rep.* 19°2N 70°59W **89** C5
Dubā *Si. Arabia* 27°10N 35°40E **44** E2
Dubai = Dubayy *U.A.E.* 25°18N 55°20E **45** E7
Dubǎsari *Moldova* 47°16N 20°10E **17** E15
Dubǎsari Vdkhr.
  Moldova 47°30N 29°0E **17** E15
Dubawnt → *Canada* 64°33N 100°6W **71** A8
Dubawnt L. *Canada* 63°8N 101°28W **71** A8
Dubayy *U.A.E.* 25°18N 55°20E **45** E7
Dubbo *Australia* 32°11S 148°35E **63** E4
Dubele
  Dem. Rep. of the Congo 2°56N 29°35E **54** B2
Dublin *Ireland* 53°21N 6°15W **10** C5
Dublin *Ga., U.S.A.* 32°32N 82°54W **85** E13
Dublin *Tex., U.S.A.* 32°5N 98°21W **84** E5
Dublin □ *Ireland* 53°24N 6°20W **10** C5
Dublin ✈ (DUB) *Ireland* 53°26N 6°15W **10** C5
Dubno *Ukraine* 50°25N 25°45E **17** C13
Dubois *Idaho, U.S.A.* 44°10N 112°14W **76** D7
Dubois *Pa., U.S.A.* 41°7N 78°46W **82** E6
Dubossary = Dubǎsari
  Moldova 47°15N 29°10E **17** E15
Dubossary Vdkhr. = Dubǎsari
  Vdkhr. *Moldova* 47°30N 29°0E **17** E15
Dubovka *Russia* 49°5N 44°50E **19** E7
Dubrajpur *India* 23°48N 87°25E **43** H12
Dubréka *Guinea* 9°46N 13°31W **50** G3
Dubrovitsa = Dubrovytsya
  Ukraine 51°31N 26°35E **17** C14
Dubrovnik *Croatia* 42°39N 18°6E **23** C8
Dubrovytsya *Ukraine* 51°31N 26°35E **17** C14
Dubuque *U.S.A.* 42°30N 90°41W **80** D8
Duchesne *U.S.A.* 40°10N 110°24W **76** F8
Duchess *Australia* 21°20S 139°50E **62** C2
Ducie I. *Pac. Oc.* 24°40S 124°48W **65** K15
Duck → *U.S.A.* 36°2N 87°52W **85** C11
Duck Cr. → *Australia* 22°37S 116°53E **60** D2
Duck Lake *Canada* 52°50N 106°16W **71** C7
Duck Mountain △
  Canada 51°45N 101°0W **71** C8
Duckwall, Mt. *U.S.A.* 37°58N 120°7W **78** H6

Dudhi *India* 24°15N 83°10E **43** G10
Dudinka *Russia* 69°30N 86°13E **29** C9
Dudley *U.K.* 52°31N 2°5W **13** E5
Dudwa *India* 28°30N 80°41E **43** E9
Dudwa △ *India* 28°30N 80°40E **43** E9
Duero = Douro →
  Europe 41°8N 8°40W **21** B1
Dufftown *U.K.* 57°27N 3°8W **11** D5
Dugi Otok *Croatia* 44°0N 15°3E **16** G8
Duisburg *Germany* 51°26N 6°45E **16** C4
Duiwelskloof = Modjadjiskloof
  S. Africa 23°42S 30°10E **57** C5
Dūkdamīn *Iran* 35°59N 57°43E **45** C8
Dukelský Průsmyk
  Slovak Rep. 49°25N 21°42E **17** D11
Dukhān *Qatar* 25°25N 50°50E **45** E6
Duki *Pakistan* 30°14N 68°25E **40** D6
Duku *Nigeria* 10°43N 10°43E **51** F8
Dulce *U.S.A.* 36°56N 107°0W **77** H10
Dulce → *Argentina* 30°32S 62°33W **94** C3
Dulce, G. *Costa Rica* 8°40N 83°20W **88** E3
Dulf *Iraq* 35°7N 45°51E **44** C5
Duliu *China* 39°2N 116°55E **34** E9
Dullewala *Pakistan* 31°50N 71°25E **42** D4
Dullstroom *S. Africa* 25°27S 30°7E **57** D5
Duluth *U.S.A.* 46°47N 92°6W **80** B7
Dum Dum *India* 22°39N 88°33E **43** H13
Dum Duma *India* 27°40N 95°40E **41** F19
Dūmā *Syria* 33°34N 36°24E **46** B5
Dumaguete *Phil.* 9°17N 123°15E **37** C6
Dumai *Indonesia* 1°35N 101°28E **36** D2
Dumaran *Phil.* 10°33N 119°50E **37** B5
Dumas *Ark., U.S.A.* 33°53N 91°29W **84** E9
Dumas *Tex., U.S.A.* 35°52N 101°58W **84** D4
Dumayr *Syria* 33°39N 36°42E **46** B5
Dumbarton *U.K.* 55°57N 4°33W **11** F4
Dumbleyung *Australia* 33°17S 117°42E **61** F2
Dumfries *U.K.* 55°4N 3°37W **11** F5
Dumfries & Galloway □
  U.K. 55°9N 3°58W **11** F5
Dumka *India* 24°12N 87°15E **43** G12
Dumoine → *Canada* 46°13N 77°51W **72** C4
Dumoine, L. *Canada* 46°55N 77°55W **72** C4
Dumont d'Urville
  Antarctica 67°0S 110°0E **5** C10
Dumraon *India* 25°33N 84°8E **43** G11
Dumyât *Egypt* 31°24N 31°48E **51** B12
Dún Dealgan = Dundalk
  Ireland 54°1N 6°24W **10** B5
Dún Laoghaire *Ireland* 53°17N 6°8W **10** C5
Duna = Dunǎrea →
  Europe 45°20N 29°40E **17** F15
Dunagiri *India* 30°31N 79°52E **43** D8
Dunaj = Dunǎrea →
  Europe 45°20N 29°40E **17** F15
Dunakeszi *Hungary* 47°37N 19°8E **17** E10
Dunǎrea → *Europe* 45°20N 29°40E **17** F15
Dunaújváros *Hungary* 46°58N 18°57E **17** E10
Dunav = Dunǎrea →
  Europe 45°20N 29°40E **17** F15
Dunay *Russia* 42°52N 132°22E **30** C6
Dunback *N.Z.* 45°23S 170°36E **59** F3
Dunbar *U.K.* 56°0N 2°31W **11** E6
Dunblane *U.K.* 56°11N 3°58W **11** E5
Duncan *Canada* 48°45N 123°40W **78** B3
Duncan *Ariz., U.S.A.* 32°43N 109°6W **77** K9
Duncan *Okla., U.S.A.* 34°30N 97°57W **84** D8
Duncan, L. *Canada* 53°29N 77°58W **72** B4
Duncan L. *Canada* 62°51N 113°58W **70** A6
Duncan Town
  Bahamas 22°15N 75°45W **88** B4
Duncannon *U.S.A.* 40°23N 77°2W **82** F7
Duncansby Head *U.K.* 58°38N 3°1W **11** C5
Duncansville *U.S.A.* 40°25N 78°26W **82** F6
Dundalk *Canada* 44°10N 80°24W **82** B4
Dundalk *Ireland* 54°1N 6°24W **10** B5
Dundalk *U.S.A.* 39°15N 76°31W **81** F15
Dundalk Bay *Ireland* 53°55N 6°15W **10** C5
Dundas = Uummannaq
  Greenland 77°28N 69°13W **4** B4
Dundas *Canada* 43°17N 79°59W **82** D5
Dundas, L. *Australia* 32°35S 121°50E **61** F3
Dundas I. *Canada* 54°30N 130°50W **70** C2
Dundas Str. *Australia* 11°15S 131°35E **60** B5
Dundee *S. Africa* 28°11S 30°15E **57** D5
Dundee *U.K.* 56°28N 2°59W **11** E6
Dundee *U.S.A.* 42°32N 76°59W **82** D8
Dundee City □ *U.K.* 56°30N 2°58W **11** E6
Dundgovi □ *Mongolia* 45°10N 106°0E **34** B4
Dundrum *U.K.* 54°16N 5°52W **10** B6
Dundrum B. *U.K.* 54°13N 5°47W **10** B6
Dunedin *N.Z.* 45°50S 170°33E **59** F3
Dunedin *U.S.A.* 28°1N 82°46W **85** G13
Dunfanaghy *Ireland* 55°11N 7°58W **10** A4
Dunfermline *U.K.* 56°5N 3°27W **11** E5
Dungannon *Canada* 43°51N 81°36W **82** C3
Dungannon *U.K.* 54°31N 6°46W **10** B5
Dungarpur *India* 23°52N 73°45E **42** H5
Dungarvan *Ireland* 52°5N 7°37W **10** D4
Dungarvan Harbour
  Ireland 52°4N 7°35W **10** D4
Dungeness *U.K.* 50°54N 0°59E **13** G8
Dunglow *Ireland* 54°57N 8°21W **10** B3
Dungo, L. do *Angola* 17°15S 19°0E **56** B2
Dungog *Australia* 32°22S 151°46E **63** E5
Dungu
  Dem. Rep. of the Congo 3°40N 28°32E **54** B2
Dungun *Malaysia* 4°45N 103°25E **39** K4
Dunhua *China* 43°20N 128°14E **35** C15
Dunhuang *China* 40°8N 94°36E **32** B4
Dunk I. *Australia* 17°59S 146°29E **62** B4
Dunkeld *Australia* 33°25S 149°29E **63** E4
Dunkeld *U.K.* 56°34N 3°35W **11** E5
Dunkerque *France* 51°2N 2°20E **20** A5
Dunkery Beacon *U.K.* 51°9N 3°36W **13** F4
Dunkirk = Dunkerque
  France 51°2N 2°20E **20** A5

Dunkirk *U.S.A.* 42°29N 79°20W **82** D5
Dúnleary = Dún Laoghaire
  Ireland 53°17N 6°8W **10** C5
Dunleer *Ireland* 53°50N 6°24W **10** C5
Dunmanus B. *Ireland* 51°31N 9°50W **10** E2
Dunmanway *Ireland* 51°43N 9°6W **10** E2
Dunmarra *Australia* 16°42S 133°25E **62** B1
Dunmore *U.S.A.* 41°25N 75°38W **83** E9
Dunmore East *Ireland* 52°9N 7°0W **10** D5
Dunmore Hd. *Ireland* 52°10N 10°35W **10** D1
Dunmore Town
  Bahamas 25°30N 76°39W **88** A4
Dunn *U.S.A.* 35°19N 78°37W **85** D15
Dunnellon *U.S.A.* 29°3N 82°28W **85** G13
Dunnet Hd. *U.K.* 58°40N 3°21W **11** C5
Dunning *U.S.A.* 41°50N 100°6W **80** E3
Dunnville *Canada* 42°54N 79°36W **82** D5
Dunolly *Australia* 36°51S 143°44E **63** F3
Dunoon *U.K.* 55°57N 4°56W **11** F4
Duns *U.K.* 55°47N 2°20W **11** F6
Dunseith *U.S.A.* 48°50N 100°3W **80** A3
Dunshaughlin *Ireland* 53°31N 6°33W **10** C5
Dunsmuir *U.S.A.* 41°13N 122°16W **76** F2
Dunstable *U.K.* 51°53N 0°32W **13** F7
Dunstan Mts. *N.Z.* 44°53S 169°35E **59** F2
Dunster *Canada* 53°8N 119°50W **70** C5
Dunvegan *U.S.A.* 57°27N 6°35W **11** D2
Dunvegan L. *Canada* 60°8N 107°10W **71** A7
Duolun *China* 42°12N 116°28E **34** C9
Duong Dong *Vietnam* 10°13N 103°58E **39** G4
Dupree *U.S.A.* 45°4N 101°35W **80** C3
Dupuyer *U.S.A.* 48°13N 112°30W **76** B7
Duque de Caxias *Brazil* 22°46S 43°18W **95** A7
Durack → *Australia* 15°33S 127°52E **60** C4
Durack Ra. *Australia* 16°50S 127°40E **60** C4
Durance → *France* 43°55N 4°45E **20** E6
Durand *U.S.A.* 44°38N 91°58W **80** C8
Durango *Mexico* 24°3N 104°39W **86** C4
Durango *U.S.A.* 37°16N 107°53W **77** H10
Durango □ *Mexico* 24°50N 105°20W **86** C4
Durant *Miss., U.S.A.* 33°4N 89°51W **85** E10
Durant *Okla., U.S.A.* 33°59N 96°25W **84** E6
Durazno *Uruguay* 33°25S 56°31W **94** C4
Durazzo = Durrës
  Albania 41°19N 19°28E **23** D8
Durban *S. Africa* 29°49S 31°1E **57** D5
Durbuy *Belgium* 50°21N 5°28E **15** D5
Durg = Bhilainagar-Durg
  India 21°13N 81°26E **41** J12
Durgapur *India* 23°30N 87°20E **43** H12
Durham *Canada* 44°10N 80°49W **82** B4
Durham *U.K.* 54°47N 1°34W **12** C6
Durham *Calif., U.S.A.* 39°39N 121°48W **78** F5
Durham *N.C., U.S.A.* 35°59N 78°54W **85** D15
Durham *N.H., U.S.A.* 43°8N 70°56W **83** C14
Durham □ *U.K.* 54°42N 1°45W **12** C6
Durmā *Si. Arabia* 24°37N 46°8E **44** E5
Durmitor *Montenegro* 43°10N 19°0E **23** C8
Durness *U.K.* 58°34N 4°45W **11** C4
Durrës *Albania* 41°19N 19°28E **23** D8
Durrow *Ireland* 52°51N 7°24W **10** D4
Dursey I. *Ireland* 51°36N 10°12W **10** E1
Dursley *U.K.* 51°40N 2°21W **13** F5
Dursunbey *Turkey* 39°35N 28°37E **23** E13
Duru
  Dem. Rep. of the Congo 4°14N 28°50E **54** B2
Durūz, Jabal ad *Jordan* 32°35N 36°40E **46** C5
D'Urville, Tanjung
  Indonesia 1°28S 137°54E **37** E9
D'Urville I. *N.Z.* 40°50S 173°55E **59** D4
Duryea *U.S.A.* 41°20N 75°45W **83** E9
Dushak *Turkmenistan* 37°13N 60°1E **45** B9
Dushanbe *Tajikistan* 38°33N 68°48E **28** F7
Dushore *U.S.A.* 41°31N 76°24W **83** E8
Dusky Sd. *N.Z.* 45°47S 166°30E **59** F1
Dussejour, C. *Australia* 14°45S 128°13E **60** B4
Düsseldorf *Germany* 51°14N 6°47E **16** C4
Dutch Harbor *U.S.A.* 53°53N 166°32W **74** a
Dutlwe *Botswana* 23°58S 23°46E **56** C3
Dutton *Canada* 42°39N 81°30W **82** D3
Dutton → *Australia* 20°44S 143°10E **62** C3
Dutywa *S. Africa* 32°8S 28°18E **57** E4
Duwayhin, Khawr
  U.A.E. 24°20N 51°25E **45** E6
Duyfken Pt. *Australia* 12°33S 141°38E **62** A3
Duyun *China* 26°18N 107°29E **32** D5
Dvina, Severnaya →
  Russia 64°32N 40°30E **18** B7
Dvinsk = Daugavpils
  Latvia 55°53N 26°32E **9** J22
Dvinskaya Guba *Russia* 65°0N 39°0E **18** B6
Dwarka *India* 22°18N 69°8E **42** H3
Dwellingup *Australia* 32°43S 116°4E **61** F2
Dwight *Canada* 45°20N 79°1W **82** A5
Dwight *U.S.A.* 41°5N 88°26W **80** E9
Dyatlovo = Dzyatlava
  Belarus 53°28N 25°28E **17** B13
Dyce *U.K.* 57°13N 2°12W **11** D6
Dyer, C. *Canada* 66°37N 61°16W **69** C13
Dyer Bay *Canada* 45°10N 81°20W **82** A3
Dyer Plateau *Antarctica* 70°45S 65°30W **5** D17
Dyersburg *U.S.A.* 36°3N 89°23W **85** C10
Dyfi → *U.K.* 52°32N 4°3W **13** E3
Dymer *Ukraine* 50°47N 30°18E **17** C16
Dysart *Australia* 22°32S 148°23E **62** C4
Dysart *U.S.A.* 42°11N 92°18W **80** D7
Dzaoudzi *Mayotte* 12°47S 45°16E **53** a
Dzerzhinsk *Russia* 56°14N 43°30E **18** C7
Dzhalinda *Russia* 53°26N 124°0E **29** D13
Dzhambul = Taraz
  Kazakhstan 42°54N 71°22E **28** E8
Dzhankoy *Ukraine* 45°40N 34°20E **19** E5
Dzhezkazgan = Zhezqazghan
  Kazakhstan 47°44N 67°40E **28** E7
Dzhizak = Jizzakh
  Uzbekistan 40°6N 67°50E **28** E7
Dzhugdzur, Khrebet
  Russia 57°30N 138°0E **29** D14

Dzhungarskiye Vorota =
  Dzungarian Gate *Asia* 45°10N 82°0E **32** B3
Dzialdowo *Poland* 53°15N 20°15E **17** B11
Dzibilchaltún *Mexico* 21°10N 89°35W **87** C7
Dzilam de Bravo
  Mexico 21°24N 88°53W **87** C7
Dzioua *Algeria*
Dzúkija △ *Lithuania* 54°10N 24°30E **9** J21
Dzungaria = Junggar Pendi
  China 44°30N 86°0E **32** B3
Dzungarian Basin = Junggar
  Pendi *China* 44°30N 86°0E **32** B3
Dzungarian Gate *Asia* 45°10N 82°0E **32** B3
Dzüünmod *Mongolia* 47°45N 106°58E **32** B5
Dzyarzhynsk *Belarus* 53°40N 27°1E **17** B14
Dzyatlava *Belarus* 53°28N 25°28E **17** B13

E

E.C. Manning △
  Canada 49°5N 120°45W **70** D4
Eabamet L. *Canada* 51°30N 87°46W **72** B2
Eads *U.S.A.* 38°29N 102°47W **76** G12
Eagar *U.S.A.* 34°6N 109°17W **77** J9
Eagle *Alaska, U.S.A.* 64°47N 141°12W **68** C5
Eagle *Colo., U.S.A.* 39°39N 106°50W **76** G10
Eagle → *Canada* 53°36N 57°26W **73** B8
Eagle Butte *U.S.A.* 45°0N 101°10W **80** C3
Eagle Grove *U.S.A.* 42°40N 93°54W **80** D7
Eagle L. *Canada* 49°42N 93°13W **71** D10
Eagle L. *Calif., U.S.A.* 40°39N 120°45W **76** F3
Eagle L. *Maine, U.S.A.* 46°20N 69°22W **81** B19
Eagle Lake *Maine, U.S.A.* 47°3N 68°36W **81** B19
Eagle Lake *Tex., U.S.A.* 29°35N 96°20W **84** G6
Eagle Mountain
  U.S.A. 33°49N 115°27W **79** M11
Eagle Nest *U.S.A.* 36°33N 105°16W **77** H11
Eagle Pass *U.S.A.* 28°43N 100°30W **84** G4
Eagle Pk. *U.S.A.* 38°10N 119°25W **78** G7
Eagle Pt. *Australia* 16°11S 124°23E **60** C3
Eagle River *Mich.,
  U.S.A.* 47°25N 88°18W **80** B9
Eagle River *Wis., U.S.A.* 45°55N 89°15W **80** C9
Eaglehawk *Australia* 36°44S 144°15E **63** F3
Eagles Mere *U.S.A.* 41°25N 76°33W **83** E8
Ealing □ *U.K.* 51°31N 0°20W **13** F7
Ear Falls *Canada* 50°38N 93°13W **71** C10
Earle *U.S.A.* 35°16N 90°28W **85** D9
Earlimart *U.S.A.* 35°53N 119°16W **79** K7
Earn → *U.K.* 56°21N 3°18W **11** E5
Earn, L. *U.K.* 56°23N 4°13W **11** E4
Earnslaw, Mt. *N.Z.* 44°32S 168°27E **59** F2
Earth *U.S.A.* 34°14N 102°24W **84** D3
Easley *U.S.A.* 34°50N 82°36W **85** D13
East Anglia *U.K.* 52°30N 1°0E **12** E9
East Angus *Canada* 45°30N 71°40W **83** A13
East Antarctica *Antarctica* 80°0S 90°0E **5** D7
East Aurora *U.S.A.* 42°46N 78°37W **82** D6
East Ayrshire □ *U.K.* 55°26N 4°11W **11** F4
East Bengal *Bangla.* 24°0N 90°0E **41** G17
East Beskids = Vychodné Beskydy
  Europe 49°20N 22°0E **17** D11
East Brady *U.S.A.* 40°59N 79°37W **82** F5
East C. = Dezhneva, Mys
  Russia 66°5N 169°40W **29** C19
East C. *N.Z.* 37°42S 178°35E **59** B7
East Caroline Basin
  Pac. Oc. 4°0N 146°45E **64** G6
East Chicago *U.S.A.* 41°38N 87°27W **80** E10
East China Sea *Asia* 30°0N 126°0E **33** D7
East Coulee *Canada* 51°23N 112°27W **70** C6
East Dereham = Dereham
  U.K. 52°41N 0°57E **13** E8
East Dunbartonshire □
  U.K. 55°57N 4°13W **11** F4
East Falkland *Falk. Is.* 51°30S 58°30W **96** G5
East Grand Forks *U.S.A.* 47°56N 97°1W **80** B5
East Greenwich *U.S.A.* 41°40N 71°27W **83** E13
East Grinstead *U.K.* 51°7N 0°0 **13** F8
East Hartford *U.S.A.* 41°46N 72°39W **83** E12
East Helena *U.S.A.* 46°35N 111°56W **76** C8
East Indies *Asia* 0°0 120°0E **26** J14
East Kilbride *U.K.* 55°47N 4°11W **11** F4
East Lamma Channel
  China 22°14N 114°9E **33** G11
East Lansing *U.S.A.* 42°44N 84°29W **81** D11
East Liverpool *U.S.A.* 40°37N 80°35W **82** F4
East London *S. Africa* 33°0S 27°55E **57** E4
East Lothian □ *U.K.* 55°58N 2°44W **11** F6
East Main = Eastmain
  Canada 52°10N 78°30W **72** B4
East Mariana Basin
  Pac. Oc. 12°0N 153°0E **64** F7
East Northport *U.S.A.* 40°53N 73°20W **83** F11
East Orange *U.S.A.* 40°46N 74°12W **83** F10
East Pacific Rise
  Pac. Oc. 15°0S 110°0W **65** J17
East Palestine *U.S.A.* 40°50N 80°33W **82** F4
East Pine *Canada* 55°48N 120°12W **70** B4
East Point *U.S.A.* 33°41N 84°25W **85** E12
East Providence
  U.S.A. 41°49N 71°23W **83** E13
East Pt. *Br. Virgin Is.* 18°40N 64°18W **89** e
East Pt. *Canada* 46°27N 61°58W **73** C7
East Renfrewshire □
  U.K. 55°46N 4°21W **11** F4
East Retford = Retford
  U.K. 53°19N 0°56W **12** D7
East Riding of Yorkshire □
  U.K. 53°55N 0°30W **12** D7
East Rochester *U.S.A.* 43°7N 77°29W **82** C7
East St. Louis *U.S.A.* 38°37N 90°9W **80** F8
East Schelde = Oosterschelde
  Neths. 51°33N 4°0E **15** C4
East Sea = Japan, Sea of
  Asia 40°0N 135°0E **30** E7

East Siberian Sea *Russia* 73°0N 160°0E **29** B17
East Stroudsburg *U.S.A.* 41°1N 75°11W **83** E9
East Sussex □ *U.K.* 50°56N 0°19E **13** G8
East Tasman Plateau
  Pac. Oc. 43°30S 152°0E **64** M7
East Tawas *U.S.A.* 44°17N 83°29W **81** C12
East Timor ■ *Asia* 8°50S 126°0E **37** F7
East Toorale *Australia* 30°27S 145°28E **63** E4
East Walker → *U.S.A.* 38°52N 119°10W **78** G7
East Windsor *U.S.A.* 40°17N 74°34W **83** F10
Eastbourne *N.Z.* 41°19S 174°55E **59** D5
Eastbourne *U.K.* 50°46N 0°18E **13** G8
Eastend *Canada* 49°32N 108°50W **71** D7
Easter Fracture Zone
  Pac. Oc. 25°0S 115°0W **65** K16
Easter I. = Pascua, I. de
  Chile 27°7S 109°23W **65** K17
Eastern □ *Kenya* 0°0 38°30E **54** C4
Eastern Cape □ *S. Africa* 32°0S 26°0E **56** E4
Eastern Cr. →
  Australia 20°40S 141°35E **62** C3
Eastern Ghats *India* 14°0N 78°50E **40** N11
Eastern Group = Lau Group
  Fiji 17°0S 178°30W **59** a
Eastern Group *Australia* 33°30S 124°30E **61** F3
Eastern Transvaal =
  Mpumalanga □
  S. Africa 26°0S 30°0E **57** D5
Easterville *Canada* 53°8N 99°49W **71** C9
Easthampton *U.S.A.* 42°16N 72°40W **83** D12
Eastlake *U.S.A.* 41°40N 81°26W **82** E3
Eastland *U.S.A.* 32°24N 98°49W **84** E5
Eastleigh *U.K.* 50°58N 1°21W **13** G6
Eastmain *Canada* 52°10N 78°30W **72** B4
Eastmain → *Canada* 52°27N 78°26W **72** B4
Eastman *Canada* 45°18N 72°19W **83** A12
Eastman *U.S.A.* 32°12N 83°11W **85** E13
Easton *Md., U.S.A.* 38°47N 76°5W **81** F15
Easton *Pa., U.S.A.* 40°41N 75°13W **83** F9
Easton *Wash., U.S.A.* 47°14N 121°11W **78** C5
Eastport *U.S.A.* 44°56N 67°0W **81** C20
Eastsound *U.S.A.* 48°42N 122°55W **78** B4
Eaton *U.S.A.* 40°32N 104°42W **76** F11
Eatonia *Canada* 51°13N 109°25W **71** C7
Eatonton *U.S.A.* 33°20N 83°23W **85** E13
Eatontown *U.S.A.* 40°19N 74°4W **83** F10
Eatonville *U.S.A.* 46°52N 122°16W **78** D4
Eau Claire *U.S.A.* 44°49N 91°30W **80** C8
Eau Claire, L. à l'
  Canada 56°10N 74°25W **72** A5
Eauripik Rise *Pac. Oc.* 2°0N 142°0E **64** G6
Ebano *Mexico* 22°13N 98°24W **87** C5
Ebbw Vale *U.K.* 51°46N 3°12W **13** F4
Ebeltoft *Denmark* 56°12N 10°41E **9** H14
Ebensburg *U.S.A.* 40°29N 78°44W **82** F6
Eberswalde-Finow
  Germany 52°50N 13°49E **16** B7
Ebetsu *Japan* 43°7N 141°34E **30** C10
Ebey's Landing △
  U.S.A. 48°12N 122°41W **78** B4
Ebinur Hu *China* 44°55N 82°55E **32** B3
Eboli *Italy* 40°37N 15°4E **22** D6
Ebolowa *Cameroon* 2°55N 11°10E **52** D2
Ebonda
  Dem. Rep. of the Congo 2°12N 22°21E **52** D4
Ebro → *Spain* 40°43N 0°54E **21** B6
Ecatepec de Morelos
  Mexico 19°36N 99°3W **87** D5
Eceabat *Turkey* 40°11N 26°21E **23** D12
Ech Chéliff *Algeria* 36°10N 1°20E **50** A6
Echigo-Sammyaku
  Japan 36°50N 139°50E **31** F9
Echizen-Misaki *Japan* 35°59N 135°57E **31** G7
Echo Bay *N.W.T.,
  Canada* 66°5N 117°55W **68** C8
Echo Bay *Ont., Canada* 46°29N 84°4W **72** C3
Echoing → *Canada* 55°51N 92°5W **72** B1
Echternach *Lux.* 49°49N 6°25E **15** E6
Echuca *Australia* 36°10S 144°45E **63** F3
Ecija *Spain* 37°30N 5°10W **21** D3
Eclipse I. *Australia* 35°6S 117°58E **61** G2
Eclipse Is. *Australia* 13°54S 126°19E **60** B4
Eclipse Sd. *Canada* 72°38N 79°0W **69** B12
Ecuador ■ *S. Amer.* 2°0S 78°0W **92** D3
Ed Damazin *Sudan* 11°46N 34°21E **51** F12
Ed Dar el Beida = Casablanca
  Morocco 33°36N 7°36W **50** B4
Ed Debba *Sudan* 18°0N 30°51E **51** E12
Ed Déffa *Egypt* 30°40N 26°30E **51** B11
Ed Dueim *Sudan* 14°0N 32°10E **51** F12
Edam *Canada* 53°11N 108°46W **71** C7
Edam *Neths.* 52°31N 5°3E **15** B5
Eday *U.K.* 59°11N 2°47W **11** B6
Eddrachillis B. *U.K.* 58°17N 5°14W **11** C3
Eddystone *U.K.* 50°11N 4°16W **13** G3
Eddystone Pt. *Australia* 40°59S 148°20E **63** G4
Ede *Neths.* 52°4N 5°40E **15** B5
Edehon L. *Canada* 60°25N 97°15W **71** A9
Edekel, Adrar *Algeria* 23°56N 6°47E **50** D7
Eden *Australia* 37°3S 149°55E **63** F4
Eden *N.C., U.S.A.* 36°29N 79°53W **85** C15
Eden *N.Y., U.S.A.* 42°39N 78°55W **82** D6
Eden *Tex., U.S.A.* 31°13N 99°51W **84** F5
Eden → *U.K.* 54°57N 3°1W **11** G5
Edenburg *S. Africa* 29°43S 25°58E **56** D4
Edendale *S. Africa* 29°39S 30°18E **57** D5
Edenderry *Ireland* 53°21N 7°4W **10** C4
Edenton *U.S.A.* 36°4N 76°39W **85** C16
Edenville *S. Africa* 27°37S 27°34E **57** D4
Eder → *Germany* 51°12N 9°28E **16** C5
Edessa *Greece* 40°48N 22°5E **23** D10
Edgar *U.S.A.* 40°22N 97°58W **80** E5
Edgartown *U.S.A.* 41°23N 70°31W **83** E14
Edge Hill *U.K.* 52°8N 1°26W **13** E6
Edgefield *U.S.A.* 33°47N 81°56W **85** E14
Edgeley *U.S.A.* 46°22N 98°43W **80** B4
Edgemont *U.S.A.* 43°18N 103°50W **80** D2
Edgeøya *Svalbard* 77°45N 22°30E **4** B9
Édhessa = Edessa *Greece* 40°48N 22°5E **23** D10

Edievale N.Z. 45°49S 169°22E 59 F2
Edina U.S.A. 40°10N 92°11W 80 E7
Edinboro U.S.A. 41°52N 80°8W 82 E4
Edinburg U.S.A. 26°18N 98°10W 84 H5
Edinburgh U.K. 55°57N 3°13W 11 F5
Edinburgh ✈ (EDI) U.K. 55°54N 3°22W 11 F5
Edinburgh, City of □ U.K. 55°57N 3°17W 11 F5
Edineț Moldova 48°9N 27°18E 17 D14
Edirne Turkey 41°40N 26°34E 23 D12
Edison U.S.A. 48°33N 122°27W 78 B4
Edithburgh Australia 35°5S 137°43E 63 F2
Edmeston U.S.A. 42°42N 75°15W 83 D9
Edmond U.S.A. 35°39N 97°29W 84 D6
Edmonds U.S.A. 47°48N 122°22W 78 C4
Edmonton Australia 17°2S 145°46E 62 B4
Edmonton Canada 53°30N 113°30W 70 C6
Edmund L. Canada 54°45N 93°17W 72 B1
Edmundston Canada 47°23N 68°20W 73 C6
Edna U.S.A. 28°59N 96°39W 84 G6
Edremit Turkey 39°34N 27°0E 23 E12
Edremit Körfezi Turkey 39°30N 26°45E 23 E12
Edson Canada 53°35N 116°28W 70 C5
Eduardo Castex Argentina 35°50S 64°18W 94 D3
Edward → Australia 35°5S 143°30E 63 F3
Edward, L. Africa 0°25S 29°40E 54 C2
Edward VII Land Antarctica 80°0S 150°0W 5 E13
Edwards Calif., U.S.A. 34°50N 117°40W 79 L9
Edwards N.Y., U.S.A. 44°20N 75°15W 83 B9
Edwards Plateau U.S.A. 30°45N 101°20W 84 F4
Edwardsville U.S.A. 41°15N 75°56W 83 E9
Edzná Mexico 19°39N 90°19W 87 D6
Edzo Canada 62°49N 116°4W 70 A5
Eeklo Belgium 51°11N 3°33E 15 C3
Eesti = Estonia ■ Europe 58°30N 25°30E 9 G21
Effigy Mounds ⌂ U.S.A. 43°5N 91°11W 80 D8
Effingham U.S.A. 39°7N 88°33W 80 F9
Égadi, Ísole Italy 37°55N 12°16E 22 F5
Egan Range U.S.A. 39°35N 114°55W 76 G6
Eganville Canada 45°32N 77°5W 82 A7
Eger = Cheb Czech Rep. 50°9N 12°28E 16 C7
Eger Hungary 47°53N 20°27E 17 E11
Egersund Norway 58°26N 6°1E 9 G12
Egg L. Canada 55°5N 105°30W 71 B7
Éghezée Belgium 50°35N 4°55E 15 D4
Egio Greece 38°15N 22°5E 23 E10
Eglinton I. Canada 75°48N 118°30W 69 B8
Egmont Canada 49°45N 123°56W 70 D4
Egmont, C. N.Z. 39°16S 173°45E 59 C4
Egmont, Mt. = Taranaki, Mt. N.Z. 39°17S 174°5E 59 C5
Egmont △ N.Z. 39°17S 174°4E 59 C5
Egra India 21°54N 87°32E 43 J12
Eğirdir Turkey 37°52N 30°51E 19 G5
Eğirdir Gölü Turkey 37°53N 30°50E 44 B1
Egvekinot Russia 66°19N 179°50W 29 C19
Egypt ■ Africa 28°0N 31°0E 51 C12
Ehime □ Japan 33°30N 132°40E 31 H6
Ehrenberg U.S.A. 33°36N 114°31W 79 M12
Eibar Spain 43°11N 2°28W 21 A4
Eidsvold Australia 25°25S 151°12E 63 D5
Eidsvoll Norway 60°19N 11°14E 9 F14
Eifel Germany 50°15N 6°50E 16 C4
Eiffel Flats Zimbabwe 18°20S 30°0E 55 F3
Eigg U.K. 56°54N 6°10W 11 E2
Eighty Mile Beach Australia 19°30S 120°40E 60 C3
Eil Somali Rep. 8°0N 49°50E 47 F4
Eil, L. U.K. 56°51N 5°16W 11 E3
Eildon, L. Australia 37°10S 146°0E 63 F4
Eilean Sar = Western Isles □ U.K. 57°30N 7°10W 11 D1
Einasleigh Australia 18°32S 144°5E 62 B3
Einasleigh → Australia 17°30S 142°17E 62 B3
Eindhoven Neths. 51°26N 5°28E 15 C5
Eire = Ireland ■ Europe 53°50N 7°52W 10 C4
Eiríksjökull Iceland 64°46N 20°24W 8 D3
Eirunepé Brazil 6°35S 69°53W 92 E5
Eiseb → Namibia 20°33S 20°59E 56 C2
Eisenach Germany 50°58N 10°19E 16 C6
Eisenerz Austria 47°32N 14°54E 16 E8
Eivissa Spain 38°54N 1°26E 24 C7
Ejeda Madag. 24°20S 44°31E 57 C7
Ejutla Mexico 16°34N 96°44W 87 D5
Ekalaka U.S.A. 45°53N 104°33W 76 D11
Ekenäs = Tammisaari Finland 60°0N 23°26E 9 G20
Eketahuna N.Z. 40°38S 175°43E 59 D5
Ekibastuz Kazakhstan 51°50N 75°10E 28 D8
Ekoli Dem. Rep. of the Congo 0°23S 24°13E 54 C1
Eksjö Sweden 57°40N 14°58E 9 H16
Ekuma → Namibia 18°40S 16°2E 56 B2
Ekwan → Canada 53°12N 82°15W 72 B3
Ekwan Pt. Canada 53°16N 82°7W 72 B3
El Aaiún W. Sahara 27°9N 13°12W 50 C3
El Abanico Chile 37°20S 71°31W 94 D1
El 'Agrûd Egypt 30°14N 34°24E 46 E3
El 'Alamein Egypt 30°48N 28°58E 51 B11
El 'Aqaba, W. → Egypt 30°7N 33°54E 46 E2
El Arīḥā West Bank 31°52N 35°27E 46 D4
El 'Arîsh Egypt 31°8N 33°50E 46 D2
El 'Arîsh, W. → Egypt 31°8N 33°47E 46 D2
El Asnam = Ech Chéliff Algeria 36°10N 1°20E 50 A6
El Bayadh Algeria 33°40N 1°1E 50 B6
El Bluff Nic. 11°59N 83°40W 88 D3
El Cajon U.S.A. 32°48N 116°58W 79 N10
El Campo U.S.A. 29°12N 96°16W 84 G6
El Capitan U.S.A. 37°44N 119°38E 78 H7
El Centro U.S.A. 32°48N 115°34W 79 N11
El Cerro Bolivia 17°30S 61°40W 92 G6
El Compadre Mexico 32°20N 116°14W 79 N10
El Cuy Argentina 39°55S 68°25W 96 D3
El Cuyo Mexico 21°31N 87°41W 87 C7
El Daheir Egypt 31°13N 34°10E 46 D3
El Dere Somali Rep. 3°50N 47°8E 47 G4
El Descanso Mexico 32°12N 116°58W 79 N10
El Desemboque Mexico 30°33N 113°1W 86 A2
El Diviso Colombia 1°22N 78°14W 92 C3
El Djouf Mauritania 20°0N 9°0W 50 D4
El Dorado Mexico 24°17N 107°21W 86 C3
El Dorado Ark., U.S.A. 33°12N 92°40W 84 E8
El Dorado Kans., U.S.A. 37°49N 96°52W 80 G5
El Dorado Venezuela 6°55N 61°37W 92 B6
El Dorado Springs U.S.A. 37°52N 94°1W 80 G6
El Escorial Spain 40°35N 4°7W 21 B3
El Faiyûm Egypt 29°19N 30°50E 51 C12
El Fâsher Sudan 13°33N 25°26E 51 F11
El Ferrol = Ferrol Spain 43°29N 8°15W 21 A1
El Fuerte Mexico 26°25N 108°39W 86 B3
El Gal Somali Rep. 10°58N 50°20E 47 E5
El Geneina = Al Junaynah Sudan 13°27N 22°45E 51 F10
El Gezira □ Sudan 15°0N 33°0E 51 F12
El Gîza Egypt 30°0N 31°12E 51 C12
El Gogorrón △ Mexico 21°49N 100°57W 86 C4
El Goléa Algeria 30°30N 2°50E 50 B6
El Golfo de Santa Clara Mexico 31°42N 114°30W 86 A2
El Guácharo △ Venezuela 10°8N 63°21W 89 D7
El Guache △ Venezuela 9°45N 69°30W 89 E6
El Iskandarîya Egypt 31°13N 29°58E 51 B11
El Istiwa'iya Sudan 5°0N 28°0E 51 G11
El Jadida Morocco 33°11N 8°17W 50 B4
El Jardal Honduras 14°54N 88°50W 88 D2
El Kef □ Tunisia 36°0N 9°0E 51 A7
El Khârga Egypt 25°30N 30°33E 51 C12
El Khartûm Sudan 15°31N 32°35E 51 E12
El Khartûm Bahrî Sudan 15°40N 32°31E 51 E12
El Kuntilla Egypt 30°1N 34°45E 46 E3
El Lucero Mexico 30°37N 106°31W 86 A3
El Maestrazgo Spain 40°30N 0°25W 21 B5
El Mahalla el Kubra Egypt 31°0N 31°0E 51 B12
El Malpais ⌂ U.S.A. 34°53N 108°0W 77 J10
El Mansûra Egypt 31°0N 31°19E 51 B12
El Medano Canary Is. 28°3N 16°32W 24 F3
El Milagro Argentina 30°59S 65°59W 94 C2
El Minyâ Egypt 28°7N 30°33E 51 C12
El Monte U.S.A. 34°4N 118°1W 79 L8
El Obeid Sudan 13°8N 30°10E 51 F12
El Odaiya Sudan 12°8N 28°12E 51 F11
El Oro Mexico 19°51N 100°7W 87 D4
El Oued Algeria 33°20N 6°58E 50 B7
El Palmar △ Argentina 32°10S 58°31W 94 C4
El Palmito, Presa Mexico 25°40N 105°30W 86 B3
El Paso U.S.A. 31°45N 106°29W 84 F1
El Pinacate y Gran Desierto de Altar = Gran Desierto del Pinacate ⌂ Mexico 31°51N 113°32W 86 A2
El Portal U.S.A. 37°41N 119°47W 78 H7
El Porvenir Mexico 31°15N 105°51W 86 A3
El Prat de Llobregat Spain 41°19N 2°5E 21 B7
El Progreso Honduras 15°26N 87°51W 88 C2
El Pueblito Mexico 29°6N 105°7W 86 B3
El Pueblo Canary Is. 28°36N 17°47W 24 F2
El Puerto de Santa María Spain 36°36N 6°13W 21 D2
El Qâhira Egypt 30°2N 31°13E 51 B12
El Qantara Egypt 30°51N 32°20E 46 E1
El Quseima Egypt 30°40N 34°15E 46 E3
El Real Panama 8°0N 77°40W 92 B3
El Reno U.S.A. 35°32N 97°57W 74 C7
El Rey △ Argentina 24°40S 64°34W 94 A3
El Rio U.S.A. 34°14N 119°10W 79 L7
El Roque, Pta. Canary Is. 28°10N 15°25W 24 F4
El Rosarito Mexico 28°38N 114°4W 86 B2
El Salto Mexico 23°47N 105°22W 86 C3
El Salvador ■ Cent. Amer. 13°50N 89°0W 88 D2
El Sauce Nic. 13°0N 86°40W 88 D2
El Sueco Mexico 29°54N 106°24W 86 B3
El Suweis Egypt 29°58N 32°31E 51 C12
El Tamarâni, W. → Egypt 30°7N 34°43E 46 E3
El Thamad Egypt 29°40N 34°28E 46 F3
El Tigre Venezuela 8°44N 64°15W 92 B6
El Tîh, Gebel Egypt 29°40N 33°50E 46 F2
El Tofo Chile 29°22S 71°18W 94 B1
El Tránsito Chile 28°52S 70°17W 94 B1
El Tûr Egypt 28°14N 33°36E 44 D2
El Turbio Argentina 51°45S 72°5W 96 G2
El Uqsur Egypt 25°41N 32°38E 51 C12
El Vergel Mexico 26°28N 106°22W 86 B3
El Vigía Venezuela 8°38N 71°39W 92 B4
El Wabeira Egypt 29°34N 33°6E 46 F2
El Wak Kenya 2°49N 40°56E 54 B5
El Wuz Sudan 15°5N 30°7E 51 E12
Elat Israel 29°30N 34°56E 46 F3
Elâzığ Turkey 38°37N 39°14E 44 B3
Elba Italy 42°46N 10°17E 22 C4
Elba U.S.A. 31°25N 86°4W 85 F11
Elbasan Albania 41°9N 20°9E 23 D9
Elbe U.S.A. 46°45N 122°10W 78 D4
Elbe → Europe 53°50N 9°0E 16 B5
Elbert, Mt. U.S.A. 39°7N 106°27W 76 G10
Elberton U.S.A. 34°7N 82°52W 85 D13
Elbeuf France 49°17N 1°2E 20 B4
Elbing = Elbląg Poland 54°10N 19°25E 17 A10
Elbistan Turkey 38°13N 37°15E 44 B3
Elbląg Poland 54°10N 19°25E 17 A10
Elbow Canada 51°7N 106°35W 71 C7
Elbrus Asia 43°21N 42°30E 19 F7
Elburz Mts. = Alborz, Reshteh-ye Kūhhā-ye Iran 36°0N 52°0E 45 C7
Elche Spain 38°15N 0°42W 21 C5
Elcho I. Australia 11°55S 135°45E 62 A2
Elda Spain 38°29N 0°47W 21 C5
Eldama Ravine Kenya 0°3N 35°43E 54 B4
Elde → Germany 53°7N 11°15E 16 B6
Eldon Mo., U.S.A. 38°21N 92°35W 80 F7
Eldon Wash., U.S.A. 47°33N 123°3W 78 C3
Eldora U.S.A. 42°22N 93°5W 80 D7
Eldorado Argentina 26°28S 54°43W 95 B5
Eldorado Canada 44°35N 77°31W 82 B7
Eldorado Ill., U.S.A. 37°49N 88°26W 80 G9
Eldorado Tex., U.S.A. 30°52N 100°36W 84 F4
Eldoret Kenya 0°30N 35°17E 54 B4
Eldred U.S.A. 41°58N 78°23W 82 E6
Elea, C. Cyprus 35°19N 34°4E 25 D13
Eleanora, Pk. Australia 32°57S 121°9E 61 F3
Elefantes → Africa 24°10S 32°40E 57 C5
Elektrostal Russia 55°41N 38°32E 18 C6
Elemi Triangle Africa 5°0N 35°20E 54 B4
Elephant Butte Res. U.S.A. 33°9N 107°11W 77 K10
Elephant I. Antarctica 61°0S 55°0W 5 C18
Eleuthera Bahamas 25°0N 76°20W 88 B4
Elgin Canada 44°36N 76°13W 83 B8
Elgin U.K. 57°39N 3°19W 11 D5
Elgin Ill., U.S.A. 42°2N 88°17W 80 D9
Elgin N. Dak., U.S.A. 46°24N 101°51W 80 B3
Elgin Oreg., U.S.A. 45°34N 117°55W 76 D5
Elgin Tex., U.S.A. 30°21N 97°22W 84 F6
Elgon, Mt. Africa 1°10N 34°30E 54 B3
Eliase Indonesia 8°21S 130°48E 37 F8
Elim Namibia 17°48S 15°31E 56 B2
Elim S. Africa 34°35S 19°45E 56 E2
Elista Russia 46°16N 44°14E 19 E7
Elizabeth Australia 34°42S 138°41E 63 E2
Elizabeth U.S.A. 40°39N 74°12W 83 F10
Elizabeth City U.S.A. 36°18N 76°14W 85 C16
Elizabethton U.S.A. 36°21N 82°13W 85 C13
Elizabethtown Ky., U.S.A. 37°42N 85°52W 81 G11
Elizabethtown N.Y., U.S.A. 44°13N 73°36W 83 B11
Elizabethtown Pa., U.S.A. 40°9N 76°36W 83 F8
Ełk Poland 53°50N 22°21E 17 B12
Elk → Canada 49°11N 115°14W 70 C5
Elk → U.S.A. 34°46N 87°16W 85 D11
Elk City U.S.A. 35°25N 99°25W 84 D5
Elk Creek U.S.A. 39°36N 122°32W 78 F4
Elk Grove U.S.A. 38°25N 121°22W 78 G5
Elk Island △ Canada 53°35N 112°59W 70 C6
Elk Lake Canada 47°40N 80°25W 72 C3
Elk Point Canada 53°54N 110°55W 71 C6
Elk River Idaho, U.S.A. 46°47N 116°11W 76 C5
Elk River Minn., U.S.A. 45°18N 93°35W 80 C7
Elkedra → Australia 21°8S 136°22E 62 C2
Elkhart Ind., U.S.A. 41°41N 85°58W 81 E11
Elkhart Kans., U.S.A. 37°0N 101°54W 80 G3
Elkhorn Canada 49°59N 101°14W 71 D8
Elkhorn → U.S.A. 41°8N 96°19W 80 E5
Elkhovo Bulgaria 42°10N 26°35E 23 C12
Elkin U.S.A. 36°15N 80°51W 85 C14
Elkins U.S.A. 38°55N 79°51W 81 F14
Elkland U.S.A. 41°59N 77°19W 82 E7
Elko Canada 49°20N 115°10W 70 D5
Elko U.S.A. 40°50N 115°46W 76 F6
Elkton U.S.A. 43°49N 83°11W 82 C1
Ellas = Greece ■ Europe 40°0N 23°0E 23 E9
Ellef Ringnes I. Canada 78°30N 102°2W 69 B9
Ellen, Mt. U.S.A. 44°9N 72°56W 83 B12
Ellenburg U.S.A. 44°54N 73°48W 83 B11
Ellendale U.S.A. 46°0N 98°32W 80 B4
Ellensburg U.S.A. 46°59N 120°34W 76 C3
Ellenville U.S.A. 41°43N 74°24W 83 E10
Ellerton Barbados 13°7N 59°33W 89 g
Ellery, Mt. Australia 37°28S 148°47E 63 F4
Ellesmere, L. N.Z. 43°47S 172°28E 59 G4
Ellesmere I. Canada 79°30N 80°0W 69 B12
Ellesmere Port U.K. 53°17N 2°54W 12 D5
Ellice Is. = Tuvalu ■ Pac. Oc. 8°0S 178°0E 58 B10
Ellicottville U.S.A. 42°17N 78°40W 82 D6
Elliot Australia 17°33S 133°32E 62 B1
Elliot S. Africa 31°22S 27°48E 57 E4
Elliot Lake Canada 46°25N 82°35W 72 C3
Elliotdale = Xhora S. Africa 31°55S 28°38E 57 E4
Ellis U.S.A. 38°56N 99°34W 80 F4
Elliston Australia 33°39S 134°53E 63 E1
Ellisville U.S.A. 31°36N 89°12W 85 F10
Ellon U.K. 57°22N 2°4W 11 D6
Ellore = Eluru India 16°48N 81°8E 41 L12
Ellsworth Kans., U.S.A. 38°44N 98°14W 80 F4
Ellsworth Maine, U.S.A. 44°33N 68°25W 81 C19
Ellsworth Land Antarctica 76°0S 89°0W 5 D16
Ellsworth Mts. Antarctica 78°30S 85°0W 5 D16
Ellwood City U.S.A. 40°52N 80°17W 82 F4
Elma Canada 49°52N 95°55W 71 D9
Elma U.S.A. 47°0N 123°25W 78 D3
Elmalı Turkey 36°44N 29°56E 19 G4
Elmhurst U.S.A. 41°53N 87°56W 80 E10
Elmira Canada 43°36N 80°33W 82 C4
Elmira U.S.A. 42°6N 76°48W 82 D8
Elmira Heights U.S.A. 42°8N 76°50W 82 D8
Elmore Australia 36°30S 144°37E 63 F3
Elmshorn Germany 53°43N 9°40E 16 B5
Elmvale Canada 44°35N 79°52W 82 B5
Elora Canada 43°41N 80°26W 82 C4
Elounda Greece 35°16N 25°42E 25 D7
Eloy U.S.A. 32°45N 111°33W 77 K8
Elrose Canada 51°12N 108°0W 71 C7
Elsie U.S.A. 45°52N 123°36W 78 E3
Elsinore = Helsingør Denmark 56°2N 12°35E 9 H15
Eltanin Fracture Zone System S. Ocean 54°0S 130°0W 5 B14
Eltham N.Z. 39°26S 174°19E 59 C5
Eluru India 16°48N 81°8E 41 L12
Elvas Portugal 38°50N 7°10W 21 C2
Elverum Norway 60°53N 11°34E 8 F14
Elvire → Australia 17°51S 128°11E 60 C4
Elvire, Mt. Australia 29°22S 119°36E 61 E2
Elwell, L. = Tiber Res. U.S.A. 48°19N 111°6W 76 B8
Elwood Ind., U.S.A. 40°17N 85°50W 81 E11
Elwood Nebr., U.S.A. 40°36N 99°52W 80 E4
Elx = Elche Spain 38°15N 0°42W 21 C5
Ely U.K. 52°24N 0°16E 13 E8
Ely Minn., U.S.A. 47°55N 91°51W 80 B8
Ely Nev., U.S.A. 39°15N 114°54W 76 G6
Elyria U.S.A. 41°22N 82°7W 82 E2
Emāmrūd Iran 36°30N 55°0E 45 B7
Embarcación Argentina 23°10S 64°0W 94 A3
Embarras Portage Canada 58°27N 111°28W 71 B6
Embetsu Japan 44°44N 141°47E 30 B10
Embi Kazakhstan 48°50N 58°8E 28 E6
Embi → Kazakhstan 46°55N 53°28E 19 E9
Embonas Greece 36°13N 27°51E 25 C9
Embrun France 44°34N 6°30E 20 D7
Embu Kenya 0°32S 37°38E 54 C4
Emden Germany 53°21N 7°12E 16 B4
Emerald Australia 23°32S 148°10E 62 C4
Emerson Canada 49°0N 97°10W 71 D9
Emet Turkey 39°20N 29°15E 23 E13
Emi Koussi Chad 19°45N 18°55E 51 E9
Eminabad Pakistan 32°2N 74°8E 42 C6
Emine, Nos Bulgaria 42°40N 27°56E 23 C12
Emissi, Tarso Chad 21°27N 18°36E 51 D9
Emlenton U.S.A. 41°11N 79°43W 82 E5
Emmaus S. Africa 29°2S 25°15E 56 D4
Emmaus U.S.A. 40°32N 75°30W 83 F9
Emmeloord Neths. 52°44N 5°46E 15 B5
Emmen Neths. 52°48N 6°57E 15 B6
Emmet Australia 24°45S 144°30E 62 C3
Emmetsburg U.S.A. 43°7N 94°41W 80 D6
Emmett Idaho, U.S.A. 43°52N 116°30W 76 E5
Emmett Mich., U.S.A. 42°59N 82°46W 82 D2
Emmonak U.S.A. 62°47N 164°31W 74 a
Emo Canada 48°38N 93°50W 71 D10
Empalme Mexico 27°58N 110°51W 86 B2
Empangeni S. Africa 28°50S 31°52E 57 D5
Empedrado Argentina 28°0S 58°46W 94 B4
Emperor Seamount Chain Pac. Oc. 40°0N 170°0E 64 D9
Emperor Trough Pac. Oc. 43°0N 175°30E 64 C9
Emporia Kans., U.S.A. 38°25N 96°11W 80 F5
Emporia Va., U.S.A. 36°42N 77°32W 81 G15
Emporium U.S.A. 41°31N 78°14W 82 E6
Empress Canada 50°57N 110°0W 71 C7
Empty Quarter = Rub' al Khālī Si. Arabia 19°0N 48°0E 47 D4
Ems → Germany 53°20N 7°12E 16 B4
Emsdale Canada 45°32N 79°19W 82 A5
Emu China 43°40N 128°6E 35 C15
Emu Park Australia 23°13S 150°50E 62 C5
'En 'Avrona Israel 29°43N 35°0E 46 F4
'En Boqeq Israel 31°12N 35°21E 45 D4
'En Gedi Israel 31°28N 35°25E 45 D4
En Nahud Sudan 12°45N 28°25E 51 F11
Ena Japan 35°25N 137°25E 31 G8
Enana Namibia 17°30S 16°23E 56 B2
Enard B. U.K. 58°5N 5°20W 11 C3
Enare = Inarijärvi Finland 69°0N 28°0E 8 B23
Enarotali Indonesia 3°55S 136°21E 37 E9
Encampment U.S.A. 41°12N 106°47W 76 F10
Encantadas, Serra Brazil 30°40S 53°0W 95 C5
Encarnación Paraguay 27°15S 55°50W 95 B4
Encarnación de Díaz Mexico 21°31N 102°14W 86 C4
Encinitas U.S.A. 33°3N 117°17W 79 M9
Encino U.S.A. 34°39N 105°28W 77 J11
Encounter B. Australia 35°45S 138°45E 63 F2
Endako Canada 54°6N 125°2W 70 C3
Endau Kenya 1°18S 38°31E 54 C4
Ende Indonesia 8°45S 121°40E 37 F6
Endeavour Str. Australia 10°45S 142°0E 62 A3
Enderbury I. Kiribati 3°8S 171°5W 64 H10
Enderby Canada 50°35N 119°10W 70 C5
Enderby Abyssal Plain S. Ocean 60°0S 40°0E 5 C5
Enderby I. Australia 20°35S 116°30E 60 D2
Enderby Land Antarctica 66°0S 53°0E 5 C5
Enderlin U.S.A. 46°38N 97°36W 80 B5
Endicott U.S.A. 42°6N 76°4W 83 D8
Endwell U.S.A. 42°6N 76°2W 83 D8
Endyalgout I. Australia 11°40S 132°35E 60 B5
Eneabba Australia 29°49S 115°16E 61 E2
Enewetak Atoll Marshall Is. 11°30N 162°15E 64 F8
Enez Turkey 40°45N 26°5E 23 D12
Enfer, Pte. d' Martinique 14°22N 60°54W 88 c
Enfield Canada 44°56N 63°32W 73 D7
Enfield Conn., U.S.A. 41°58N 72°36W 83 E12
Enfield N.C., U.S.A. 36°11N 77°41W 85 C16
Enfield N.H., U.S.A. 43°39N 72°9W 83 C12
Engadin Switz. 46°45N 10°10E 20 C9
Engaño, C. Dom. Rep. 18°30N 68°20W 89 C6
Engaño, C. Phil. 18°35N 122°23E 37 A6
Engaru Japan 44°3N 143°31E 30 B11
Engcobo = Ngcobo S. Africa 31°37S 28°0E 57 E4
Engels Russia 51°28N 46°6E 19 D8
Engemann L. Canada 58°0N 106°55W 71 B7
Enggano Indonesia 5°20S 102°40E 36 F2
England U.S.A. 34°33N 91°58W 84 D9
England □ U.K. 53°0N 2°0W 13 E5
Englee Canada 50°45N 56°5W 73 B8
Englehart Canada 47°49N 79°52W 72 C4
Englewood U.S.A. 39°38N 104°59W 76 G11
English → Canada 49°12N 91°5W 71 C10
English Bazar = Ingraj Bazar India 24°58N 88°10E 43 G13
English Channel Europe 50°0N 2°0W 13 G6
English Company's Is., The Australia 11°50S 136°32E 62 A2
English River Canada 49°14N 91°0W 72 C1
Enid U.S.A. 36°24N 97°53W 84 C6
Enkhuizen Neths. 52°42N 5°17E 15 B5
Enna Italy 37°34N 14°16E 22 F6
Ennadai Canada 61°8N 100°53W 71 A8
Ennadai L. Canada 60°58N 101°20W 71 A8
Ennedi Chad 17°15N 22°0E 51 E10
Enngonia Australia 29°21S 145°50E 63 D4
Ennis Ireland 52°51N 8°59W 10 D3
Ennis Mont., U.S.A. 45°21N 111°44W 76 D8
Ennis Tex., U.S.A. 32°20N 96°38W 84 E6
Enniscorthy Ireland 52°30N 6°34W 10 D5
Enniskillen U.K. 54°21N 7°39W 10 B4
Ennistimon Ireland 52°57N 9°17W 10 D2
Enns → Austria 48°14N 14°32E 16 D8
Eno Finland 62°47N 30°10E 8 E24
Enontekiö Finland 68°23N 23°37E 8 B20
Enosburg Falls U.S.A. 44°55N 72°48W 83 B12
Enriquillo, L. Dom. Rep. 18°20N 72°5W 89 C5
Enschede Neths. 52°13N 6°53E 15 B6
Ensenada Argentina 34°55S 57°55W 94 C4
Ensenada Mexico 31°52N 116°37W 86 A1
Ensenada de los Muertos Mexico 23°59N 109°51W 86 C2
Ensiola, Pta. de n' Spain 39°7N 2°55E 24 B9
Entebbe Uganda 0°4N 32°28E 54 B3
Enterprise Canada 60°47N 115°45W 70 A5
Enterprise Ala., U.S.A. 31°19N 85°51W 85 F12
Enterprise Oreg., U.S.A. 45°25N 117°17W 76 D5
Entre Ríos Bolivia 21°30S 64°25W 94 A3
Entre Ríos □ Argentina 30°30S 58°30W 94 C4
Entroncamento Portugal 39°28N 8°28W 21 C1
Enugu Nigeria 6°30N 7°30E 50 G7
Enumclaw U.S.A. 47°12N 121°59W 78 C5
Eólie, Ís. Italy 38°30N 14°57E 22 E6
Epe Neths. 52°21N 5°59E 15 B5
Épernay France 49°3N 3°56E 20 B5
Ephesus Turkey 37°55N 27°22E 23 F12
Ephraim U.S.A. 39°22N 111°35W 76 G8
Ephrata Pa., U.S.A. 40°11N 76°11W 83 F8
Ephrata Wash., U.S.A. 47°19N 119°33W 76 C4
Épinal France 48°10N 6°27E 20 B7
Episkopi Cyprus 34°40N 32°54E 25 E11
Episkopi Greece 35°20N 24°20E 25 D6
Episkopi Bay Cyprus 34°35N 32°50E 25 E11
Epsom U.K. 51°19N 0°16W 13 F7
Epukiro Namibia 21°40S 19°9E 56 C2
Equatoria = El Istiwa'iya Sudan 5°0N 28°0E 51 G11
Equatorial Guinea ■ Africa 2°0N 8°0E 52 D1
Er Rachidia Morocco 31°58N 4°20W 50 B5
Er Rahad Sudan 12°45N 30°32E 51 F12
Er Rif Morocco 35°1N 4°1W 50 A5
Erāwadī Myit = Irrawaddy → Burma 15°50N 95°6E 41 M19
Erāwadī Myitwanya = Irrawaddy, Mouths of the Burma 15°30N 95°0E 41 M19
Erbil = Arbīl Iraq 36°15N 44°5E 44 B5
Erçek Turkey 38°39N 43°36E 44 B4
Erciyaş Dağı Turkey 38°30N 35°30E 44 B2
Érd Hungary 47°22N 18°56E 17 E10
Erdao Jiang → China 42°37N 128°0E 35 C14
Erdek Turkey 40°23N 27°47E 23 D12
Erdene = Ulaan-Uul Mongolia 44°13N 111°10E 34 B6
Erdenet Mongolia 49°2N 104°5E 32 B5
Erdenetsogt Mongolia 42°55N 106°5E 34 C4
Erebus, Mt. Antarctica 77°35S 167°0E 5 D11
Erechim Brazil 27°35S 52°15W 95 B5
Ereğli Konya, Turkey 37°31N 34°4E 44 B2
Ereğli Zonguldak, Turkey 41°15N 31°24E 19 F5
Erenhot China 43°48N 112°2E 34 C7
Eresma → Spain 41°26N 4°45W 21 B3
Erfenisdam S. Africa 28°30S 26°50E 56 D4
Erfurt Germany 50°58N 11°2E 16 C6
Ergani Turkey 38°17N 39°49E 44 B3
Ergel Mongolia 43°8N 109°5E 34 C5
Ergeni Vozvyshennost Russia 47°0N 44°0E 19 E7
Ērgli Latvia 56°54N 25°38E 9 H21
Eriboll, L. U.K. 58°30N 4°42W 11 C4
Érice Italy 38°2N 12°35E 22 E5
Erie U.S.A. 42°8N 80°5W 82 D4
Erie, L. N. Amer. 42°15N 81°0W 82 D4
Erie Canal U.S.A. 43°5N 78°43W 82 C7
Erieau Canada 42°16N 81°57W 82 D3
Erigavo Somali Rep. 10°35N 47°20E 47 E4
Erikoussa Greece 39°53N 19°34E 25 A3
Eriksdale Canada 50°52N 98°7W 71 C9
Erimanthos Greece 37°57N 21°50E 23 F9
Erimo-misaki Japan 41°50N 143°15E 30 D11
Erin Pt. Trin. & Tob. 10°3N 61°39W 93 K15
Erinpura India 25°9N 73°3E 42 G5
Eriskay U.K. 57°4N 7°18W 11 D1
Eritrea ■ Africa 14°0N 38°30E 47 D2
Erlangen Germany 49°36N 11°0E 16 D6
Erldunda Australia 25°14S 133°12E 62 D1
Ermelo Neths. 52°18N 5°35E 15 B5
Ermelo S. Africa 26°31S 29°59E 57 D4
Ermenek Turkey 36°38N 33°0E 44 B2
Ermones Greece 39°37N 19°46E 25 A3
Ernakulam India 9°59N 76°22E 40 Q10
Erne → Ireland 54°30N 8°16W 10 B3
Erne, Lower L. U.K. 54°28N 7°47W 10 B4
Erne, Upper L. U.K. 54°14N 7°32W 10 B4
Ernest Giles Ra. Australia 27°0S 123°45E 61 E3
Erode India 11°24N 77°45E 40 P10
Eromanga Australia 26°40S 143°11E 63 D3
Erongo Namibia 21°39S 15°58E 56 C2
Erramala Hills India 15°30N 78°15E 40 M11
Erri-Nundra △ Australia 37°28S 148°5E 63 F4
Errigal Ireland 55°2N 8°6W 10 A3
Erris Hd. Ireland 54°19N 10°0W 10 B1
Erskine U.S.A. 47°40N 96°0W 80 B6
Ertis = Irtysh → Russia 61°4N 68°52E 28 C7

Erwin *U.S.A.* 36°9N 82°25W **85** C13
Erzgebirge *Germany* 50°27N 12°55E **16** C7
Erzin *Russia* 50°15N 95°10E **29** D10
Erzincan *Turkey* 39°46N 39°30E **44** B3
Erzurum *Turkey* 39°57N 41°15E **44** B4
Es Caló *Spain* 38°40N 1°30E **24** C8
Es Canar *Spain* 39°2N 1°36E **24** B8
Es Mercadal *Spain* 39°59N 4°5E **24** B11
Es Migjorn Gran *Spain* 39°57N 4°3E **24** B11
Es Sahrā' Esh Sharqîya
  Egypt 27°30N 32°30E **51** C12
Es Sînā' *Egypt* 29°0N 34°0E **46** F3
Es Vedrà *Spain* 38°52N 1°12E **24** C7
Esambo
  Dem. Rep. of the Congo 3°48S 23°30E **54** C1
Esan-Misaki *Japan* 41°40N 141°10E **30** D10
Esashi *Hokkaidō, Japan* 44°56N 142°35E **30** B11
Esashi *Hokkaidō, Japan* 41°52N 140°7E **30** D10
Esbjerg *Denmark* 55°29N 8°29E **9** J13
Esbo = Espoo *Finland* 60°12N 24°40E **9** F21
Escalante *U.S.A.* 37°47N 111°36W **77** H8
Escalante → *U.S.A.* 37°24N 110°57W **77** H8
Escalón *Mexico* 26°45N 104°20W **86** B4
Escambia → *U.S.A.* 30°32N 87°11W **85** F11
Escanaba *U.S.A.* 45°45N 87°4W **80** C10
Esch-sur-Alzette *Lux.* 49°32N 6°0E **15** E6
Escondido *U.S.A.* 33°7N 117°5W **79** M9
Escuinapa de Hidalgo
  Mexico 22°50N 105°50W **86** C3
Escuintla *Guatemala* 14°20N 90°48W **88** D1
Esenguly *Turkmenistan* 37°37N 53°59E **28** F6
Eşfahān *Iran* 32°39N 51°43E **45** C6
Eşfahān □ *Iran* 32°50N 51°50E **45** C6
Esfarāyen *Iran* 37°4N 57°30E **45** B8
Esfideh *Iran* 33°39N 59°46E **45** C8
Esh Sham = Dimashq
  Syria 33°30N 36°18E **46** B5
Esha Ness *U.K.* 60°29N 1°38W **11** A7
Esher *U.K.* 51°21N 0°20W **13** F7
Eshkol △ *Israel* 31°20N 34°30E **46** D3
Eshowe *S. Africa* 28°50S 31°30E **57** D5
Esigodini *Zimbabwe* 20°18S 28°56E **57** C4
Esil = Ishim → *Russia* 57°45N 71°10E **28** D8
Esira *Madag.* 24°20S 46°42E **57** C8
Esk → *Dumf. & Gall., U.K.* 54°58N 3°2W **11** G5
Esk → *N. Yorks., U.K.* 54°30N 0°37W **12** C7
Eskān *Iran* 26°48N 63°9E **45** E9
Esker *Canada* 53°53N 66°25W **73** B6
Eskifjörður *Iceland* 65°3N 13°55W **8** D7
Eskilstuna *Sweden* 59°22N 16°32E **9** G17
Eskimo Point = Arviat
  Canada 61°6N 93°59W **71** A10
Eskişehir *Turkey* 39°50N 30°30E **19** G5
Esla → *Spain* 41°29N 6°3W **21** B2
Eslāmābād-e Gharb
  Iran 34°10N 46°30E **44** C5
Eslāmshahr *Iran* 35°40N 51°10E **45** C6
Eşme *Turkey* 38°23N 28°58E **23** E13
Esmeraldas *Ecuador* 1°0N 79°40W **92** C3
Esnagi L. *Canada* 48°36N 84°33W **72** C3
España = Spain ■ *Europe* 39°0N 4°0W **21** B4
Espanola *Canada* 46°15N 81°46W **72** C3
Espanola *U.S.A.* 35°59N 106°5W **77** J10
Esparança *Cuba* 22°30N 80°10W **88** B3
Esperance *Australia* 33°45S 121°55E **61** F3
Esperance B. *Australia* 33°48S 121°55E **61** F3
Esperance Harbour
  St. Lucia 14°4N 60°55W **89** f
Esperanza *Antarctica* 65°0S 55°0W **5** C18
Esperanza *Argentina* 31°29S 61°3W **94** C3
Esperanza *Puerto Rico* 18°6N 65°28W **89** d
Espichel, C. *Portugal* 38°22N 9°16W **21** C1
Espigão, Serra do *Brazil* 7°20S 48°0W **93** E9
Espinazo, Sierra del = Espinhaço,
  Serra do *Brazil* 17°30S 43°30W **93** G10
Espinhaço, Serra do
  Brazil 17°30S 43°30W **93** G10
Espinilho, Serra do
  Brazil 28°30S 55°0W **95** B5
Espírito Santo □ *Brazil* 20°0S 40°45W **93** H10
Espíritu Santo *Vanuatu* 15°15S 166°50E **58** C9
Espíritu Santo, B. del
  Mexico 19°20N 87°35W **87** D7
Espíritu Santo, I.
  Mexico 24°30N 110°22W **86** C2
Espita *Mexico* 21°1N 88°19W **87** C7
Espoo *Finland* 60°12N 24°40E **9** F21
Espungabera *Mozam.* 20°29S 32°45E **57** C5
Esquel *Argentina* 42°55S 71°20W **96** E2
Esquimalt *Canada* 48°26N 123°25W **78** B3
Esquina *Argentina* 30°0S 59°30W **94** C4
Essaouira *Morocco* 31°32N 9°42W **50** B4
Essebie
  Dem. Rep. of the Congo 2°58N 30°40E **54** B3
Essen *Belgium* 51°28N 4°28E **15** C4
Essen *Germany* 51°28N 7°2E **16** C4
Essendon, Mt. *Australia* 25°0S 120°29E **61** E3
Essequibo → *Guyana* 6°50N 58°30W **92** B7
Essex *Canada* 42°10N 82°49W **82** D2
Essex *Calif., U.S.A.* 34°44N 115°15W **79** L11
Essex *N.Y., U.S.A.* 44°19N 73°21W **83** B11
Essex □ *U.K.* 51°54N 0°27E **13** F8
Essex Junction *U.S.A.* 44°29N 73°7W **83** B11
Esslingen *Germany* 48°44N 9°18E **16** D5
Estación Camacho
  Mexico 24°25N 102°18W **86** C4
Estación Simón
  Mexico 24°42N 102°35W **86** C4
Estados, I. de Los
  Argentina 54°40S 64°30W **96** G4
Eştahbānāt *Iran* 29°8N 54°4E **45** D7
Estância *Brazil* 11°16S 37°26W **93** F11
Estancia *U.S.A.* 34°46N 106°4W **77** J10
Estārm *Iran* 28°21N 58°21E **45** D8
Estcourt *S. Africa* 29°0S 29°53E **57** D4
Este □ *Dom. Rep.* 18°45N 68°42W **89** C6
Estelí *Nic.* 13°9N 86°22W **88** D2
Estellencs *Spain* 39°39N 2°29E **24** B9

Esterhazy *Canada* 50°37N 102°5W **71** C8
Estevan *Canada* 49°10N 102°59W **71** D8
Estevan Group *Canada* 53°3N 129°38W **70** C3
Estherville *U.S.A.* 43°24N 94°50W **80** D6
Eston *Canada* 51°8N 108°40W **71** C7
Estonia ■ *Europe* 58°30N 25°30E **9** G21
Estreito *Brazil* 6°32S 47°25W **93** E9
Estrela, Serra da
  Portugal 40°10N 7°45W **21** B2
Estremoz *Portugal* 38°51N 7°39W **21** C2
Estrondo, Serra do *Brazil* 7°20S 48°0W **93** E9
Esztergom *Hungary* 47°47N 18°44E **17** E10
Etah *India* 27°35N 78°40E **43** F8
Etanga *Namibia* 17°55S 13°0E **56** B1
Etawah *India* 26°48N 79°6E **43** F8
Etawney L. *Canada* 57°50N 96°50W **71** B9
Etchojoa *Mexico* 26°55N 109°38W **86** B3
eThekwini = Durban
  S. Africa 29°49S 31°1E **57** D5
Ethel *U.S.A.* 46°32N 122°46W **78** D4
Ethelbert *Canada* 51°32N 100°25W **71** C8
Ethiopia ■ *Africa* 8°0N 40°0E **47** F3
Ethiopian Highlands
  Ethiopia 10°0N 37°0E **47** F2
Etive, L. *U.K.* 56°29N 5°10W **11** E3
Etna *Italy* 37°50N 14°55E **22** F6
Etoile
  Dem. Rep. of the Congo 11°33S 27°30E **55** E2
Etosha △ *Namibia* 19°0S 16°0E **56** B2
Etosha Pan *Namibia* 18°40S 16°30E **56** B2
Etowah *U.S.A.* 35°20N 84°32W **85** D3
Etrek *Turkmenistan* 37°36N 54°46E **45** B7
Ettelbruck *Lux.* 49°51N 6°5E **15** E6
Ettrick Water → *U.K.* 55°31N 2°55W **11** F6
Etuku
  Dem. Rep. of the Congo 3°42S 25°45E **54** C2
Etzná-Tixmucuy = Edzná
  Mexico 19°39N 90°19W **87** D6
Eua *Tonga* 21°22S 174°56W **59** c
Euboea = Évia *Greece* 38°30N 24°0E **23** E11
Eucla *Australia* 31°41S 128°52E **61** F4
Euclid *U.S.A.* 41°34N 81°32W **82** E3
Eucumbene, L. *Australia* 36°2S 148°40E **63** F4
Eudora *U.S.A.* 33°7N 91°16W **84** E9
Eufaula *Ala., U.S.A.* 31°54N 85°9W **85** F12
Eufaula *Okla., U.S.A.* 35°17N 95°35W **84** D7
Eufaula L. *U.S.A.* 35°18N 95°21W **84** D7
Eugene *U.S.A.* 44°5N 123°4W **76** D2
Eugowra *Australia* 33°22S 148°24E **63** E4
Eulo *Australia* 28°10S 145°3E **63** D4
Eungella △ *Australia* 20°57S 148°40E **62** C4
Eunice *La., U.S.A.* 30°30N 92°25W **84** F8
Eunice *N. Mex.,*
  U.S.A. 32°26N 103°10W **77** K12
Eupen *Belgium* 50°37N 6°3E **15** D6
Euphrates = Furāt, Nahr al →
  Asia 31°0N 47°25E **44** D5
Eureka *Canada* 80°0N 85°56W **69** B11
Eureka *Calif., U.S.A.* 40°47N 124°9W **76** F1
Eureka *Kans., U.S.A.* 37°49N 96°17W **80** G5
Eureka *Mont., U.S.A.* 48°53N 115°3W **76** B6
Eureka *Nev., U.S.A.* 39°31N 115°58W **76** G6
Eureka *S. Dak., U.S.A.* 45°46N 99°38W **80** C4
Eureka, Mt. *Australia* 26°35S 121°35E **61** E3
Euroa *Australia* 36°44S 145°35E **63** F4
Europa, Île *Ind. Oc.* 22°20S 40°22E **53** J8
Europa, Picos de *Spain* 43°10N 4°49W **21** A3
Europa, Pta. de *Gib.* 36°3N 5°21W **21** D3
Europe 50°0N 20°0E **6** E10
Europoort *Neths.* 51°57N 4°10E **15** C4
Eustis *U.S.A.* 28°51N 81°41W **85** G14
Eutsuk L. *Canada* 53°20N 126°45W **70** C3
Evale *Angola* 16°33S 15°44E **56** B2
Evans *U.S.A.* 40°23N 104°41W **76** F11
Evans, L. *Canada* 50°50N 77°0W **72** B4
Evans City *U.S.A.* 40°46N 80°4W **82** F4
Evans Head *Australia* 29°7S 153°27E **63** D5
Evans Mills *U.S.A.* 44°6N 75°48W **83** B9
Evansburg *Canada* 53°36N 114°59W **70** C5
Evanston *Ill., U.S.A.* 42°3N 87°40W **80** D10
Evanston *Wyo., U.S.A.* 41°16N 110°58W **76** F8
Evansville *U.S.A.* 37°58N 87°35W **80** G10
Evaz *Iran* 27°46N 53°59E **45** E7
Eveleth *U.S.A.* 47°28N 92°32W **80** B7
Evensk *Russia* 62°12N 159°30E **29** C16
Everard, L. *Australia* 31°30S 135°0E **63** E2
Everard Ranges
  Australia 27°5S 132°28E **61** E5
Everest, Mt. *Nepal* 28°5N 86°58E **43** E12
Everett *Pa., U.S.A.* 40°1N 78°23W **82** F6
Everett *Wash., U.S.A.* 47°59N 122°12W **78** C4
Everglades, The *U.S.A.* 25°50N 81°0W **85** J14
Everglades △ *U.S.A.* 25°30N 81°0W **85** J14
Everglades City *U.S.A.* 25°52N 81°23W **85** J14
Evergreen *Ala., U.S.A.* 31°26N 86°57W **85** F11
Evergreen *Mont.,*
  U.S.A. 48°14N 114°17W **76** B6
Evesham *U.K.* 52°6N 1°56W **13** E6
Évia *Greece* 38°30N 24°0E **23** E11
Evje *Norway* 58°36N 7°51E **9** G12
Ewe, L. *U.K.* 57°49N 5°38W **11** D3
Ewing *U.S.A.* 42°16N 98°21W **80** D4
Ewo *Congo* 0°48S 14°45E **52** E2
Exaltación *Bolivia* 13°10S 65°20W **92** F5
Excelsior Springs
  U.S.A. 39°20N 94°13W **80** F6
Exe → *U.K.* 50°41N 3°29W **13** G4
Exeter *Canada* 43°21N 81°29W **82** C3
Exeter *U.K.* 50°43N 3°31W **13** G4
Exeter *Calif., U.S.A.* 36°18N 119°9W **78** J7
Exeter *N.H., U.S.A.* 42°59N 70°57W **83** D14

Exmoor *U.K.* 51°12N 3°45W **13** F4
Exmoor △ *U.K.* 51°8N 3°42W **13** F4
Exmouth *Australia* 21°54S 114°10E **60** D1
Exmouth *U.K.* 50°37N 3°25W **13** G4
Exmouth G. *Australia* 22°15S 114°15E **60** D1
Exmouth Plateau *Ind. Oc.* 19°0S 114°0E **64** J3
Expedition △ *Australia* 25°41S 149°7E **63** D4
Expedition Ra.
  Australia 24°30S 149°12E **62** C4
Extremadura □ *Spain* 39°30N 6°5W **21** C2
Exuma Sound *Bahamas* 24°30N 76°20W **88** B4
Eyasi, L. *Tanzania* 3°30S 35°0E **54** C4
Eye Pen. *U.K.* 58°13N 6°10W **11** C2
Eyemouth *U.K.* 55°52N 2°5W **11** F6
Eyjafjörður *Iceland* 66°15N 18°30W **8** C4
Eyre (North), L.
  Australia 28°30S 137°20E **63** D2
Eyre (South), L.
  Australia 29°18S 137°25E **63** D2
Eyre, L. *Australia* 29°30S 137°26E **58** G6
Eyre Mts. *N.Z.* 45°25S 168°25E **59** F2
Eyre Pen. *Australia* 33°30S 136°17E **63** E2
Eysturoy *Færoe Is.* 62°13N 6°54W **8** E9
Eyvānki *Iran* 35°24N 51°56E **45** C6
Ezine *Turkey* 39°48N 26°20E **23** E12
Ezouza → *Cyprus* 34°44N 32°27E **25** E11

F

F.Y.R.O.M. = Macedonia ■
  Europe 41°53N 21°40E **23** D9
Faaa *Tahiti* 17°34S 149°35W **59** d
Faaone *Tahiti* 17°40S 149°21W **59** d
Fabala *Guinea* 9°44N 9°5W **50** G4
Fabens *U.S.A.* 31°30N 106°10W **84** F1
Fabriano *Italy* 43°20N 12°54E **22** C5
Fachi *Niger* 18°6N 11°34E **51** E8
Fada *Chad* 17°13N 21°34E **51** E10
Fada-n-Gourma
  Burkina Faso 12°10N 0°30E **50** F6
Faddeyevskiy, Ostrov
  Russia 76°0N 144°0E **29** B15
Fadghāmī *Syria* 35°53N 40°52E **44** C4
Faenza *Italy* 44°17N 11°53E **22** B4
Færoe Is. = Føroyar ☑
  Atl. Oc. 62°0N 7°0W **8** F9
Fāgāras *Romania* 45°48N 24°58E **17** F13
Fagersta *Sweden* 60°1N 15°46E **9** F16
Fagnano, L. *Argentina* 54°30S 68°0W **96** G3
Fahlīān *Iran* 30°11N 51°28E **45** D6
Fahraj *Kermān, Iran* 29°0N 59°0E **45** D8
Fahraj *Yazd, Iran* 31°46N 54°36E **45** D7
Faial *Azores* 38°34N 28°42W **50** a
Faial *Madeira* 32°47N 16°53W **24** D3
Fair Haven *U.S.A.* 43°36N 73°16W **83** D11
Fair Hd. *U.K.* 55°14N 6°9W **10** A5
Fair Isle *U.K.* 59°32N 1°38W **14** B6
Fair Oaks *U.S.A.* 38°39N 121°16W **78** G5
Fairbanks *U.S.A.* 64°51N 147°43W **74** a
Fairbury *U.S.A.* 40°8N 97°11W **80** E6
Fairfax *U.S.A.* 44°40N 73°1W **83** B11
Fairfield *Ala., U.S.A.* 33°29N 86°55W **85** E11
Fairfield *Calif., U.S.A.* 38°15N 122°3W **78** G4
Fairfield *Conn., U.S.A.* 41°9N 73°16W **83** E11
Fairfield *Idaho, U.S.A.* 43°21N 114°44W **76** E6
Fairfield *Ill., U.S.A.* 38°23N 88°22W **80** F9
Fairfield *Iowa, U.S.A.* 40°56N 91°57W **80** E8
Fairfield *Tex., U.S.A.* 31°44N 96°10W **84** F6
Fairford *Canada* 51°37N 98°38W **71** C9
Fairhope *U.S.A.* 30°31N 87°54W **85** F11
Fairlie *N.Z.* 44°5S 170°49E **59** F3
Fairmead *U.S.A.* 37°5N 120°10W **78** H6
Fairmont *Minn., U.S.A.* 43°39N 94°28W **80** D6
Fairmont *W. Va., U.S.A.* 39°29N 80°9W **81** F13
Fairmount *Calif.,*
  U.S.A. 34°45N 118°26W **79** L8
Fairmount *N.Y., U.S.A.* 43°5N 76°12W **83** C8
Fairplay *U.S.A.* 39°15N 106°2W **76** G10
Fairport *U.S.A.* 43°6N 77°27W **82** C7
Fairport Harbor *U.S.A.* 41°45N 81°17W **82** E3
Fairview *Canada* 56°5N 118°25W **70** B5
Fairview *Mont., U.S.A.* 47°51N 104°3W **76** C11
Fairview *Okla., U.S.A.* 36°16N 98°29W **84** C5
Fairweather, Mt.
  U.S.A. 58°55N 137°32W **70** B1
Faisalabad *Pakistan* 31°30N 73°5E **42** D5
Faith *U.S.A.* 45°2N 102°2W **80** C2
Faizabad *India* 26°45N 82°10E **43** F10
Fajardo *Puerto Rico* 18°20N 65°39W **89** d
Fajr, W. → *Si. Arabia* 29°10N 38°10E **44** D3
Fakenham *U.K.* 52°51N 0°51E **12** E8
Fakfak *Indonesia* 2°55S 132°18E **37** E8
Faku *China* 42°32N 123°21E **35** C12
Falaise *France* 48°54N 0°12W **20** B3
Falaise, Mui *Vietnam* 19°6N 105°45E **38** C5
Falam *Burma* 23°0N 93°45E **41** H18
Falcó, C. des *Spain* 38°50N 1°23E **24** C7
Falcón, Presa *Mexico* 26°35N 99°10W **87** B5
Falcon Lake *Canada* 49°42N 95°15W **71** D9
Falcon Res. *U.S.A.* 26°34N 99°10W **84** H5
Falconara Maríttima
  Italy 43°37N 13°24E **22** C5
Falcone, C. del *Italy* 40°58N 8°12E **22** D3
Falconer *U.S.A.* 42°7N 79°12W **82** D5
Falelatai *Samoa* 13°54S 171°59W **59** b
Falelima *Samoa* 13°32S 172°41W **59** b
Faleshty = Fălești
  Moldova 47°32N 27°44E **17** E14
Fălești *Moldova* 47°32N 27°44E **17** E14
Falher *Canada* 55°44N 117°15W **70** B5
Falirakí *Greece* 36°22N 28°12E **25** C10
Falkenberg *Sweden* 56°54N 12°30E **9** H15
Falkirk *U.K.* 56°0N 3°47W **11** F5
Falkland *U.K.* 56°16N 3°12W **11** E5
Falkland Is. ☑ *Atl. Oc.* 51°30S 59°0W **96** G5

Falkland Sd. *Falk. Is.* 52°0S 60°0W **96** G5
Fall River *U.S.A.* 41°43N 71°10W **83** E13
Fallbrook *U.S.A.* 33°23N 117°15W **79** M9
Fallon *U.S.A.* 39°28N 118°47W **76** G4
Falls City *U.S.A.* 40°3N 95°36W **80** E6
Falls Creek *U.S.A.* 41°9N 78°48W **82** E6
Falmouth *Jamaica* 18°30N 77°40W **88** a
Falmouth *U.K.* 50°9N 5°5W **13** G2
Falmouth *U.S.A.* 41°33N 70°37W **83** E14
Falsa, Pta. *Mexico* 27°51N 115°3W **86** B1
False B. *S. Africa* 34°15S 18°40E **56** E2
Falso, C. *Honduras* 15°12N 83°21W **88** C3
Falster *Denmark* 54°45N 11°55E **9** J14
Falsterbo *Sweden* 55°23N 12°50E **9** J15
Fălticeni *Romania* 47°21N 26°20E **17** E14
Falun *Sweden* 60°37N 15°37E **8** F16
Famagusta *Cyprus* 35°8N 33°55E **25** D12
Famagusta Bay *Cyprus* 35°15N 34°0E **25** D13
Famalé *Niger* 14°33N 1°5E **50** F6
Famatina, Sierra de
  Argentina 27°30S 68°0W **94** B2
Family L. *Canada* 51°54N 95°27W **71** C9
Famoso *U.S.A.* 35°37N 119°12W **79** K7
Fan Xian *China* 35°55N 115°38E **34** G8
Fanad Hd. *Ireland* 55°17N 7°38W **10** A4
Fandriana *Madag.* 20°14S 47°21E **57** C8
Fang *Thailand* 19°55N 99°13E **38** C2
Fangcheng *China* 33°18N 112°59E **34** H7
Fangshan *China* 38°3N 111°25E **34** E6
Fangzi *China* 36°33N 119°10E **35** F10
Fanjakana *Madag.* 21°10S 46°53E **57** C8
Fanjiatun *China* 43°40N 125°15E **35** C13
Fanling *China* 22°30N 114°8E **33** F11
Fannich, L. *U.K.* 57°38N 4°59W **11** D4
Fannūj *Iran* 26°35N 59°38E **45** E8
Fanø *Denmark* 55°25N 8°25E **9** J13
Fano *Italy* 43°50N 13°1E **22** C5
Fanshi *China* 39°12N 113°20E **34** E7
Fao = Al Fāw *Iraq* 30°0N 48°30E **45** D6
Faqirwali *Pakistan* 29°27N 73°0E **42** E5
Far East = Dalnevostochnyy □
  Russia 67°0N 140°0E **29** C14
Far East *Asia* 40°0N 130°0E **26** E14
Faradje
  Dem. Rep. of the Congo 3°50N 29°45E **54** B3
Farafangana *Madag.* 22°49S 47°50E **57** C8
Farāh *Afghan.* 32°20N 62°7E **40** C3
Farāh □ *Afghan.* 32°25N 62°10E **40** C3
Farahalana *Madag.* 14°26S 50°10E **57** A9
Faranah *Guinea* 10°3N 10°45W **50** F3
Farasān, Jazā'ir
  Si. Arabia 16°45N 41°55E **47** D3
Farasan Is. = Farasān, Jazā'ir
  Si. Arabia 16°45N 41°55E **47** D3
Faratsiho *Madag.* 19°24S 46°57E **57** B8
Fareham *U.K.* 50°51N 1°11W **13** G6
Farewell C. *N.Z.* 40°29S 172°43E **59** D4
Farewell C. = Nunap Isua
  Greenland 59°48N 43°55W **66** D15
Farghona *Uzbekistan* 40°23N 71°19E **28** E8
Fargo *U.S.A.* 46°53N 96°48W **80** B5
Fār'iah, W. al →
  West Bank 32°12N 35°27E **46** C4
Faribault *U.S.A.* 44°18N 93°16W **80** C7
Faridabad *India* 28°26N 77°9E **42** E6
Faridkot *India* 30°44N 74°45E **42** D6
Faridpur *Bangla.* 23°15N 89°55E **43** H13
Faridpur *India* 28°13N 79°33E **43** E8
Farieord *Iran* 35°40N 59°49E **45** C8
Farina *Australia* 30°3S 138°15E **63** E2
Fariones, Pta. *Canary Is.* 29°13N 13°28W **24** E6
Farleigh *Australia* 21°4S 149°8E **62** K7
Farmerville *U.S.A.* 32°47N 92°24W **84** E8
Farmingdale *U.S.A.* 40°12N 74°10W **83** F10
Farmington *Canada* 55°54N 120°30W **70** B4
Farmington *Calif.,*
  U.S.A. 37°55N 120°59W **78** H6
Farmington *Maine,*
  U.S.A. 44°40N 70°9W **81** C18
Farmington *Mo., U.S.A.* 37°47N 90°25W **80** G8
Farmington *N.H.,*
  U.S.A. 43°24N 71°4W **83** C13
Farmington *N. Mex.,*
  U.S.A. 36°44N 108°12W **77** H9
Farmington *Utah,*
  U.S.A. 40°59N 111°53W **76** F8
Farmington → *U.S.A.* 41°51N 72°38W **83** E12
Farmville *U.S.A.* 37°18N 78°24W **81** G14
Farne Is. *U.K.* 55°38N 1°37W **12** B6
Farnham *U.K.* 51°13N 0°47W **13** F7
Farnham, Mt. *Canada* 50°29N 116°30W **70** C5
Faro *Brazil* 2°10S 56°39W **93** D7
Faro *Canada* 62°11N 133°22W **68** C6
Faro *Portugal* 37°2N 7°55W **21** D2
Fårö *Sweden* 57°55N 19°5E **9** H18
Farquhar, C. *Australia* 23°50S 113°36E **61** D1
Farrars Cr. →
  Australia 25°35S 140°43E **62** D3
Farrāshband *Iran* 28°57N 52°5E **45** D7
Farrell *U.S.A.* 41°13N 80°30W **82** E4
Farrokhī *Iran* 33°50N 59°31E **45** C8
Farruch, C. = Ferrutx, C.
  Spain 39°47N 3°21E **24** B10
Fārs □ *Iran* 29°30N 55°0E **45** D7
Farsala *Greece* 39°17N 22°23E **23** E10
Farson *U.S.A.* 42°7N 109°26W **76** E9
Farsund *Norway* 58°5N 6°55E **9** G12
Fartak, Ras *Si. Arabia* 28°5N 34°34E **44** D2
Fartak, Ra's *Yemen* 15°38N 52°15E **47** D5
Fartura, Serra da *Brazil* 26°21S 52°52W **95** B5
Fārūj *Iran* 37°14N 58°14E **45** B8
Farvel, Kap = Nunap Isua
  Greenland 59°48N 43°55W **66** D15
Farwell *U.S.A.* 34°23N 103°2W **84** D3
Fāryāb □ *Afghan.* 36°0N 65°0E **40** B4
Fasā *Iran* 29°0N 53°39E **45** D7
Fasano *Italy* 40°50N 17°22E **22** D7
Fastiv *Ukraine* 50°7N 29°57E **17** C15

Fastnet Rock *Ireland* 51°22N 9°37W **10** E2
Fastov = Fastiv *Ukraine* 50°7N 29°57E **17** C15
Fatagar, Tanjung
  Indonesia 2°46S 131°57E **37** E8
Fatehabad *Haryana,*
  India 29°31N 75°27E **42** E6
Fatehabad *Ut. P., India* 27°1N 78°19E **42** F7
Fatehgarh *India* 27°25N 79°35E **43** F8
Fatehpur *Bihar, India* 24°38N 85°14E **43** G11
Fatehpur *Raj., India* 28°0N 74°40E **42** F6
Fatehpur *Ut. P., India* 25°56N 81°13E **43** G9
Fatehpur *Ut. P., India* 27°10N 81°13E **43** F9
Fatehpur Sikri *India* 27°6N 77°40E **42** F6
Fathom Five △ *Canada* 45°17N 81°40W **82** A3
Fatima *Canada* 47°24N 61°53W **73** C7
Faulkton *U.S.A.* 45°2N 99°8W **80** C4
Faure I. *Australia* 25°52S 113°50E **61** E1
Fauresmith *S. Africa* 29°44S 25°17E **56** D4
Fauske *Norway* 67°17N 15°25E **8** C16
Favara *Italy* 37°19N 13°39E **22** F5
Favāritx, C. de *Spain* 40°0N 4°15E **24** B11
Favignana *Italy* 37°56N 12°20E **22** F5
Fawcett, Pt. *Australia* 11°46G 100°21E **00** B5
Fawn → *Canada* 55°20N 87°35W **72** A2
Fawnskin *U.S.A.* 34°16N 116°56W **79** L10
Faxaflói *Iceland* 64°29N 23°0W **8** D2
Faya-Largeau *Chad* 17°58N 19°6E **51** E9
Fayd *Si. Arabia* 27°1N 42°52E **44** E4
Fayette *Ala., U.S.A.* 33°41N 87°50W **85** E11
Fayette *Mo., U.S.A.* 39°9N 92°41W **80** F7
Fayetteville *Ark., U.S.A.* 36°4N 94°10W **84** C7
Fayetteville *N.C., U.S.A.* 35°3N 78°53W **85** D15
Fayetteville *Tenn.,*
  U.S.A. 35°9N 86°34W **85** D11
Fazilka *India* 30°27N 74°2E **42** D6
Fazilpur *Pakistan* 29°18N 70°29E **42** E4
Fdérik *Mauritania* 22°40N 12°45W **50** D3
Feakle *Ireland* 52°56N 8°40W **10** D3
Feale → *Ireland* 52°27N 9°37W **10** D2
Fear, C. *U.S.A.* 33°50N 77°58W **85** E16
Feather → *U.S.A.* 38°47N 121°36W **76** G3
Feather Falls *U.S.A.* 39°36N 121°16W **78** F5
Featherston *N.Z.* 41°6S 175°20E **59** D5
Featherstone *Zimbabwe* 18°42S 30°55E **55** F3
Fécamp *France* 49°45N 0°22E **20** B4
Fedala = Mohammedia
  Morocco 33°44N 7°21W **50** B4
Federación *Argentina* 31°0S 57°55W **94** C4
Féderal *Argentina* 30°57S 58°48W **96** C5
Federal Way *U.S.A.* 47°18N 122°19W **78** C4
Fedeshkūh *Iran* 28°49N 53°50E **45** D7
Fehmarn *Germany* 54°27N 11°7E **16** A6
Fehmarn Bælt *Europe* 54°35N 11°20E **9** J14
Fehmarn Belt = Fehmarn Bælt
  Europe 54°35N 11°20E **9** J14
Fei Xian *China* 35°18N 117°59E **35** G9
Feijó *Brazil* 8°9S 70°21W **92** E4
Feilding *N.Z.* 40°13S 175°35E **59** D5
Feira de Santana
  Brazil 12°15S 38°57W **93** F11
Feixiang *China* 36°30N 114°45E **34** F8
Felanitx *Spain* 39°28N 3°9E **24** B10
Feldkirch *Austria* 47°15N 9°37E **18** E5
Félicité *Seychelles* 4°19S 55°52E **53** b
Felipe Carrillo Puerto
  Mexico 19°38N 88°3W **87** D7
Felixburg *Zimbabwe* 19°29S 30°51E **57** B5
Felixstowe *U.K.* 51°58N 1°23E **13** F9
Felton *U.S.A.* 37°3N 122°4W **78** H4
Femer Bælt = Fehmarn Bælt
  Europe 54°35N 11°20E **9** J14
Femunden *Norway* 62°10N 11°53E **8** E14
Fen He → *China* 35°36N 110°42E **34** G6
Fenelon Falls *Canada* 44°32N 78°45W **82** B6
Feng Xian *Jiangsu,*
  China 34°43N 116°35E **34** G9
Feng Xian *Shaanxi,*
  China 33°54N 106°40E **34** H4
Fengcheng *China* 40°28N 124°5E **35** D13
Fengfeng *China* 36°28N 114°8E **34** F8
Fengning *China* 41°10N 116°33E **34** D9
Fengqiu *China* 35°2N 114°25E **34** G8
Fengrun *China* 39°48N 118°8E **35** E10
Fengtai *China* 39°49N 116°14E **34** E9
Fengxiang *China* 34°29N 107°25E **34** G4
Fengyang *China* 32°51N 117°29E **35** H9
Fengzhen *China* 40°25N 113°2E **34** D7
Fenoarivo *Fianarantsoa,*
  Madag. 21°43S 46°24E **57** C8
Fenoarivo *Fianarantsoa,*
  Madag. 20°52S 46°53E **57** C8
Fenoarivo Afovoany
  Madag. 18°26S 46°34E **57** B8
Fenoarivo Atsinanana
  Madag. 17°22S 49°25E **57** B8
Fens, The *U.K.* 52°38N 0°2W **12** E7
Fenton *U.S.A.* 42°48N 83°42W **81** D12
Fenxi *China* 36°40N 111°31E **34** F6
Fenyang *China* 37°18N 111°48E **34** F6
Feodosiya *Ukraine* 45°2N 35°16E **19** F6
Ferbane *Ireland* 53°16N 7°50W **10** C4
Ferdows *Iran* 34°0N 58°2E **45** C8
Ferfer *Somali Rep.* 5°4N 45°9E **47** F4
Fergana = Farghona
  Uzbekistan 40°23N 71°19E **28** E8
Fergus *Canada* 43°43N 80°24W **82** C4
Fergus Falls *U.S.A.* 46°17N 96°4W **80** B5
Ferkéssédougou *Ivory C.* 9°35N 5°6W **50** G4
Ferland *Canada* 50°19N 88°27W **72** B2
Ferlo, Vallée du *Senegal* 15°15N 14°15W **50** E3
Fermanagh □ *U.K.* 54°21N 7°40W **10** B4
Fermo *Italy* 43°9N 13°43E **22** C5
Fermont *Canada* 52°47N 67°5W **73** B6
Fermoy *Ireland* 52°9N 8°16W **10** D3
Fernández *Argentina* 27°55S 63°50W **94** B3
Fernandina Beach
  U.S.A. 30°40N 81°27W **85** F14

Fernando de Noronha
　Brazil　4°S 33°10W **93 D12**
Fernando Póo = Bioko
　Eq. Guin.　3°30N 8°40E **52 D1**
Ferndale U.S.A.　48°51N 122°36W **78 B4**
Fernie Canada　49°30N 115°5W **70 D5**
Fernlees Australia　23°51S 148°7E **62 C4**
Fernley U.S.A.　39°36N 119°15W **76 G4**
Ferozepore = Firozpur
　India　30°55N 74°40E **42 D6**
Ferrara Italy　44°50N 11°35E **22 B4**
Ferreñafe Peru　6°42S 79°50W **92 E3**
Ferrerías Spain　39°59N 4°1E **24 B11**
Ferret, C. France　44°38N 1°15W **20 D3**
Ferriday U.S.A.　31°38N 91°33W **84 F9**
Ferrol Spain　43°29N 8°15W **21 A1**
Ferron U.S.A.　39°5N 111°8W **76 G8**
Ferrutx, C. Spain　39°47N 3°21E **24 B10**
Ferryland Canada　47°2N 52°53W **73 C9**
Fertile U.S.A.　47°32N 96°17W **80 B5**
Fès Morocco　34°0N 5°0W **50 B5**
Fessenden U.S.A.　47°39N 99°38W **80 B4**
Festus U.S.A.　38°13N 90°24W **80 F8**
Feteşti Romania　44°22N 27°51E **17 F14**
Fethiye Turkey　36°36N 29°6E **19 G4**
Fetlar U.K.　60°36N 0°52W **11 A8**
Feuilles → Canada　58°47N 70°4W **69 D12**
Fez = Fès Morocco　34°0N 5°0W **50 B5**
Fezzan Libya　27°0N 13°0E **51 C8**
Fiambalá Argentina　27°45S 67°37W **94 B2**
Fianarantsoa Madag.　21°26S 47°5E **57 C8**
Fianarantsoa □ Madag.　19°30S 47°0E **57 B8**
Ficksburg S. Africa　28°51S 27°53E **57 D4**
Field → Australia　23°48S 138°0E **62 C2**
Field I. Canada　12°5S 132°23E **60 B5**
Fier Albania　40°43N 19°33E **23 D8**
Fife □ U.K.　56°16N 3°1W **11 E5**
Fife △ U.K.　56°15N 3°15W **11 E5**
Fife Ness U.K.　56°17N 2°35W **11 E6**
Fifth Cataract Sudan　18°22N 33°50E **51 E12**
Figeac France　44°37N 2°2E **20 D5**
Figtree Zimbabwe　20°22S 28°20E **55 G2**
Figueira da Foz Portugal　40°7N 8°54W **21 B1**
Figueres Spain　42°18N 2°58E **21 A7**
Figuig Morocco　32°5N 1°11W **50 B5**
Fihaonana Madag.　18°36S 47°12E **57 B8**
Fiherenana → Madag.　18°29S 48°24E **57 B8**
Fiherenana → Madag.　23°19S 43°37E **57 C7**
Fiji ■ Pac. Oc.　17°20S 179°0E **59 a**
Filabusi Zimbabwe　20°34S 29°20E **57 C4**
Filchner Ice Shelf
　Antarctica　79°0S 40°0W **5 D1**
Filey U.K.　54°12N 0°18W **12 C7**
Filey B. U.K.　54°12N 0°15W **12 C7**
Filfla Malta　35°47N 14°24E **25 D1**
Filiatra Greece　37°9N 21°35E **23 F9**
Filingué Niger　14°21N 3°22E **50 F6**
Filipstad Sweden　59°43N 14°9E **9 G16**
Fillmore Calif., U.S.A.　34°24N 118°55W **79 L8**
Fillmore Utah, U.S.A.　38°58N 112°20W **76 G7**
Finch Canada　45°11N 75°7W **83 A9**
Finch Hatton Australia　20°25S 148°39E **62 K6**
Findhorn → U.K.　57°38N 3°38W **11 D5**
Findlay U.S.A.　41°2N 83°39W **81 E12**
Finger L. Canada　53°33N 93°30W **72 B1**
Finger Lakes U.S.A.　42°40N 76°30W **83 D8**
Fíngoè Mozam.　14°55S 31°50E **55 E3**
Finisterre, C. = Fisterra, C.
　Spain　42°50N 9°19W **21 A1**
Finke Australia　25°34S 134°35E **62 D1**
Finke Gorge △ Australia　24°8S 132°49E **60 D5**
Finland ■ Europe　63°0N 27°0E **8 E22**
Finland, G. of Europe　60°0N 26°0E **9 G22**
Finlay → Canada　57°0N 125°10W **70 B3**
Finley Australia　35°38S 145°35E **63 F4**
Finley U.S.A.　47°31N 97°50W **80 B5**
Finn → Ireland　54°51N 7°28W **10 B4**
Finnigan, Mt. Australia　15°49S 145°17E **62 B4**
Finniss, C. Australia　33°8S 134°51E **63 E1**
Finnmark Norway　69°37N 23°57E **8 B20**
Finnsnes Norway　69°14N 18°0E **8 B18**
Finspång Sweden　58°43N 15°47E **9 G16**
Fiora → Italy　42°20N 11°34E **22 C4**
Fiordland △ N.Z.　45°46S 167°0E **59 F1**
Fīq Syria　32°46N 35°41E **46 C4**
Firat = Furāt, Nahr al →
　Asia　31°0N 47°25E **44 D5**
Fire Island △ U.S.A.　40°38N 73°8W **83 F11**
Firebag → Canada　57°45N 111°21W **71 B6**
Firebaugh U.S.A.　36°52N 120°27W **78 J6**
Firedrake L. Canada　61°25N 104°30W **71 A8**
Firenze Italy　43°46N 11°15E **22 C4**
Firk, Sha'ib → Iraq　30°59N 44°34E **44 D5**
Firozabad India　27°10N 78°25E **43 F8**
Firozpur India　30°55N 74°40E **42 D6**
Firozpur-Jhirka India　27°48N 76°57E **42 F7**
Fīrūzābād Iran　28°52N 52°35E **45 D7**
Fīrūzkūh Iran　35°50N 52°50E **45 C7**
Firvale Canada　52°27N 126°13W **70 C3**
Fish → Namibia　28°7S 17°10E **56 D2**
Fish → S. Africa　31°30S 20°16E **56 E3**
Fish River Canyon
　Namibia　27°40S 17°35E **56 D2**
Fisher B. Canada　51°35N 97°13W **71 C9**
Fishers I. U.S.A.　41°15N 72°0W **83 E13**
Fishguard U.K.　52°0N 4°58W **13 E3**
Fishing L. Canada　52°10N 95°24W **71 C9**
Fishkill U.S.A.　41°32N 73°54W **83 E11**
Fisterra, C. Spain　42°50N 9°19W **21 A1**
Fitchburg Mass.,
　U.S.A.　42°35N 71°48W **83 D13**
Fitchburg Wis., U.S.A.　42°58N 89°28W **80 D9**
Fitz Roy Argentina　47°0S 67°0W **96 F3**
Fitzgerald Canada　59°51N 111°36W **70 B6**
Fitzgerald U.S.A.　31°43N 83°15W **85 F13**
Fitzgerald River △
　Australia　33°53S 119°55E **61 F3**
Fitzmaurice → Australia　14°45S 130°5E **60 B5**

Fitzroy → Queens.,
　Australia　23°32S 150°52E **62 C5**
Fitzroy → W. Austral.,
　Australia　17°31S 123°35E **60 C3**
Fitzroy, Mte. Argentina　49°17S 73°5W **96 F2**
Fitzroy Crossing
　Australia　18°9S 125°38E **60 C4**
Fitzwilliam I. Canada　45°30N 81°45W **82 A3**
Fiume = Rijeka Croatia　45°20N 14°21E **16 F8**
Five Points U.S.A.　36°26N 120°6W **78 J6**
Fizi Dem. Rep. of the Congo　4°17S 28°55E **54 C2**
Flagstaff U.S.A.　35°12N 111°39W **77 J8**
Flagstaff L. U.S.A.　45°12N 70°18W **83 A14**
Flaherty I. Canada　56°15N 79°15W **72 A4**
Flåm Norway　60°50N 7°7E **8 F12**
Flambeau → U.S.A.　45°18N 91°14W **80 C8**
Flamborough Hd. U.K.　54°7N 0°5W **12 C7**
Flaming Gorge △
　U.S.A.　41°10N 109°25W **76 F9**
Flaming Gorge Res.
　U.S.A.　41°10N 109°25W **76 F9**
Flamingo, Teluk
　Indonesia　5°30S 138°0E **37 F9**
Flanders = Flandre
　Europe　50°50N 2°30E **15 B9**
Flandre Europe　50°50N 2°30E **15 B9**
Flandre-Occidentale = West-
　Vlaanderen □ Belgium　51°0N 3°0E **15 D2**
Flandre-Orientale = Oost-
　Vlaanderen □ Belgium　51°5N 3°50E **15 C3**
Flandreau U.S.A.　44°3N 96°36W **80 C5**
Flanigan U.S.A.　40°10N 119°53W **78 E7**
Flannan Is. U.K.　58°9N 7°52W **11 C1**
Flåsjön Sweden　64°5N 15°40E **8 D16**
Flat → Canada　61°33N 125°18W **70 A3**
Flat I. Mauritius　19°53S 57°35E **53 d**
Flathead L. U.S.A.　47°51N 114°8W **76 C6**
Flattery, C. Australia　14°58S 145°21E **62 A4**
Flattery, C. U.S.A.　48°23N 124°29W **78 B2**
Flatwoods U.S.A.　38°31N 82°43W **81 F12**
Fleetwood U.K.　53°55N 3°1W **12 D4**
Fleetwood U.S.A.　40°27N 75°49W **83 F9**
Flekkefjord Norway　58°18N 6°39E **9 G12**
Flemington U.S.A.　41°7N 77°28W **82 E7**
Flensburg Germany　54°47N 9°27E **16 A5**
Flers France　48°47N 0°33W **20 B3**
Flesherton Canada　44°16N 80°33W **82 B4**
Flesko, Tanjung
　Indonesia　0°29N 124°30E **37 D6**
Fleurieu Pen. Australia　35°40S 138°5E **63 F2**
Flevoland □ Neths.　52°30N 5°30E **15 B5**
Flin Flon Canada　54°46N 101°53W **71 C8**
Flinders → Australia　17°36S 140°36E **62 B3**
Flinders B. Australia　34°19S 115°19E **61 F2**
Flinders Group
　Australia　14°11S 144°15E **62 A3**
Flinders I. S. Austral.,
　Australia　33°44S 134°41E **63 E1**
Flinders I. Tas., Australia　40°0S 148°0E **63 G4**
Flinders Ranges
　Australia　31°30S 138°30E **63 E2**
Flinders Reefs Australia　17°37S 148°31E **62 B4**
Flint U.K.　53°15N 3°8W **12 D4**
Flint U.S.A.　43°1N 83°41W **82 D1**
Flint → U.S.A.　30°57N 84°34W **85 F12**
Flint I. Kiribati　11°26S 151°48W **65 J12**
Flintshire □ U.K.　53°17N 3°17W **12 D4**
Flodden U.K.　55°37N 2°8W **12 B5**
Floodwood U.S.A.　46°56N 92°55W **80 B7**
Flora U.S.A.　38°40N 88°29W **80 F9**
Florala U.S.A.　31°0N 86°20W **85 F11**
Florence = Firenze Italy　43°46N 11°15E **22 C4**
Florence Ala., U.S.A.　34°48N 87°41W **85 D11**
Florence Ariz., U.S.A.　33°2N 111°23W **77 K8**
Florence Colo., U.S.A.　38°23N 105°8W **76 G11**
Florence Oreg., U.S.A.　43°58N 124°7W **76 D1**
Florence S.C., U.S.A.　34°12N 79°46W **85 D15**
Florence, L. Australia　28°53S 138°9E **63 D2**
Florencia Colombia　1°36N 75°36W **92 C3**
Florennes Belgium　50°15N 4°35E **15 D4**
Florenville Belgium　49°40N 5°19E **15 E5**
Flores Azores　39°26N 31°13W **50 a**
Flores Guatemala　16°59N 89°50W **88 C2**
Flores Indonesia　8°35S 121°0E **37 F6**
Flores I. Canada　49°20N 126°10W **70 D3**
Flores Sea Indonesia　6°30S 120°0E **37 F6**
Florești Moldova　47°53N 28°17E **17 E15**
Floresville U.S.A.　29°8N 98°10W **84 G5**
Floriano Brazil　6°50S 43°0W **93 E10**
Florianópolis Brazil　27°30S 48°30W **95 B6**
Florida Cuba　21°32N 78°14W **88 B4**
Florida Uruguay　34°7S 56°10W **95 C4**
Florida □ U.S.A.　28°0N 82°0W **85 G14**
Florida, Straits of U.S.A.　25°0N 80°0W **88 B4**
Florida B. U.S.A.　25°0N 80°45W **88 B3**
Florida Keys U.S.A.　24°40N 81°0W **85 J14**
Florin U.S.A.　38°30N 121°24W **78 G5**
Florina Greece　40°48N 21°26E **23 D9**
Florissant U.S.A.　38°47N 90°19W **80 F8**
Florø Norway　61°35N 5°1E **8 F11**
Flower Station Canada　45°10N 76°41W **83 A8**
Flowerpot I. Canada　45°18N 81°38W **82 A3**
Floydada U.S.A.　33°59N 101°20W **84 E4**
Fluk Indonesia　1°42S 127°44E **37 E7**
Flushing = Vlissingen
　Neths.　51°26N 3°34E **15 C3**
Fly → Papua N. G.　8°25S 143°0E **58 B7**
Flying Fish, C.
　Antarctica　72°6S 102°29W **5 D15**
Foa Tonga　19°45S 174°18W **59 c**
Foam Lake Canada　51°40N 103°32W **71 C8**
Foça Turkey　38°39N 26°46E **23 E12**
Fochabers U.K.　57°37N 3°6W **11 D5**
Focșani Romania　45°41N 27°15E **17 F14**
Fóggia Italy　41°27N 15°34E **22 D6**
Fogo Canada　49°43N 54°17W **73 C9**
Fogo, C. Verde Is.　15°5N 24°20W **50 b**
Fogo I. Canada　49°40N 54°5W **73 C9**

Föhr Germany　54°43N 8°30E **16 A5**
Foix France　42°58N 1°38E **20 E4**
Folda Nord-Trøndelag,
　Norway　64°32N 10°30E **8 D14**
Folda Nordland, Norway　67°38N 14°50E **8 C16**
Foley Botswana　21°34S 27°21E **56 C4**
Foley U.S.A.　30°24N 87°41W **85 F11**
Foleyet Canada　48°15N 82°25W **72 C3**
Folgefonna Norway　60°3N 6°23E **9 F12**
Foligno Italy　42°57N 12°42E **22 C5**
Folkestone U.K.　51°5N 1°12E **13 F9**
Folkston U.S.A.　30°50N 82°0W **85 F13**
Follansbee U.S.A.　40°19N 80°35W **82 F4**
Folsom L. U.S.A.　38°42N 121°9W **78 G5**
Fomboni Comoros Is.　12°18S 43°46E **53 a**
Fond du Lac Canada　59°19N 107°12W **71 B7**
Fond du Lac U.S.A.　43°47N 88°27W **80 D9**
Fond-du-Lac → Canada　59°17N 106°0W **71 B7**
Fonda U.S.A.　42°57N 74°22W **83 D10**
Fondi Italy　41°21N 13°25E **22 D5**
Fongafale Tuvalu　8°31S 179°13E **58 B10**
Fonsagrada = A Fonsagrada
　Spain　43°8N 7°4W **21 A2**
Fonseca, G. de
　Cent. Amer.　13°10N 87°40W **88 D2**
Fontainebleau France　48°24N 2°40E **20 B5**
Fontana U.S.A.　34°6N 117°26W **79 L9**
Fontas → Canada　58°14N 121°48W **70 B4**
Fonte Boa Brazil　2°33S 66°0W **92 D5**
Fontenay-le-Comte
　France　46°28N 0°48W **20 C3**
Fontenelle Res., U.S.A.　42°1N 110°3W **76 E8**
Fontur Iceland　66°23N 14°32W **8 C6**
Fonuafo'ou Tonga　20°19S 175°25W **59 c**
Fonualei Tonga　18°1S 174°19W **59 c**
Foochow = Fuzhou
　China　26°5N 119°16E **33 D6**
Foping China　33°41N 108°0E **34 H5**
Forbes Australia　33°22S 148°0E **63 E4**
Forbesganj India　26°17N 87°18E **43 F12**
Ford City Calif., U.S.A.　35°9N 119°27W **79 K7**
Ford City Pa., U.S.A.　40°46N 79°32W **82 F5**
Førde Norway　61°27N 5°53E **8 F11**
Fords Bridge Australia　29°41S 145°29E **63 D4**
Fordyce U.S.A.　33°49N 92°25W **84 E8**
Forel, Mt. Greenland　66°52N 36°55W **66 C16**
Foremost Canada　49°26N 111°34W **70 D6**
Forest Canada　43°6N 82°0W **82 C3**
Forest U.S.A.　32°22N 89°29W **85 E10**
Forest City Iowa, U.S.A.　43°16N 93°39W **80 D7**
Forest City N.C.,
　U.S.A.　35°20N 81°52W **85 D14**
Forest City Pa., U.S.A.　41°39N 75°28W **83 E9**
Forest Grove U.S.A.　45°31N 123°7W **78 E3**
Forestburg Canada　52°35N 112°1W **70 C6**
Foresthill U.S.A.　39°1N 120°49W **78 F6**
Forestier Pen. Australia　43°0S 148°0E **63 G4**
Forestville Canada　48°48N 69°2W **73 C6**
Forestville Calif.,
　U.S.A.　38°28N 122°54W **78 G4**
Forestville N.Y., U.S.A.　42°28N 79°10W **82 D5**
Forfar U.K.　56°39N 2°53W **11 E6**
Forillon △ Canada　48°46N 64°12W **73 C7**
Forks U.S.A.　47°57N 124°23W **78 C2**
Forksville U.S.A.　41°29N 76°35W **83 E8**
Forlì Italy　44°13N 12°3E **22 B5**
Forman U.S.A.　46°7N 97°38W **80 B5**
Formby Pt. U.K.　53°33N 3°6W **12 D4**
Formentera Spain　38°43N 1°27E **24 C7**
Formentor, C. de Spain　39°58N 3°13E **24 B10**
Former Yugoslav Republic of
　Macedonia = Macedonia ■
　Europe　41°53N 21°40E **23 D9**
Fórmia Italy　41°15N 13°37E **22 D5**
Formosa = Taiwan ■
　Asia　23°30N 121°0E **33 D7**
Formosa Argentina　26°15S 58°10W **94 B4**
Formosa Brazil　15°32S 47°20W **93 G9**
Formosa □ Argentina　25°0S 60°0W **94 B4**
Formosa, Serra Brazil　12°0S 55°0W **93 F8**
Formosa B. = Ungwana B.
　Kenya　2°45S 40°20E **54 C5**
Fornells Spain　40°3N 4°7E **24 A11**
Føroyar ☑ Atl. Oc.　62°0N 7°0W **8 F9**
Forres U.K.　57°37N 3°37W **11 D5**
Forrest Australia　30°51S 128°6E **61 F4**
Forrest, Mt. Australia　24°48S 127°45E **61 D4**
Forsayth Australia　18°33S 143°34E **62 B3**
Forssa Finland　60°49N 23°38E **8 F20**
Forst Germany　51°45N 14°37E **16 C8**
Forster Australia　32°12S 152°31E **63 E5**
Forsyth U.S.A.　46°16N 106°41W **76 C10**
Fort Abbas Pakistan　29°12N 72°52E **42 E5**
Fort Albany Canada　52°15N 81°35W **72 B3**
Fort Ann U.S.A.　43°25N 73°29W **83 C11**
Fort Assiniboine
　Canada　54°20N 114°45W **70 C6**
Fort Augustus U.K.　57°9N 4°42W **11 D4**
Fort Beaufort S. Africa　32°46S 26°40E **56 E4**
Fort Benton U.S.A.　47°49N 110°40W **76 C8**
Fort Bragg U.S.A.　39°26N 123°48W **76 G2**
Fort Bridger U.S.A.　41°19N 110°23W **76 F8**
Fort Chipewyan Canada　58°42N 111°8W **71 B6**
Fort Clatsop △ U.S.A.　46°8N 123°53W **78 D3**
Fort Collins U.S.A.　40°35N 105°5W **76 F11**
Fort-Coulonge Canada　45°50N 76°45W **72 C4**
Fort Covington U.S.A.　44°59N 74°29W **83 B10**
Fort Dauphin = Taolanaro
　Madag.　25°2S 47°0E **57 D8**
Fort Davis U.S.A.　30°35N 103°54W **84 F3**
Fort-de-France Martinique　14°36N 61°2W **88 c**
Fort Defiance U.S.A.　35°45N 109°5W **77 J9**
Fort Dodge U.S.A.　42°30N 94°11W **80 D6**
Fort Edward U.S.A.　43°16N 73°35W **83 C11**
Fort Erie Canada　42°54N 78°56W **82 D6**
Fort Fairfield U.S.A.　46°46N 67°50W **81 B20**
Fort Frances Canada　48°36N 93°24W **71 D10**

Fort Franklin = Déline
　Canada　65°11N 123°25W **68 C7**
Fort Garland U.S.A.　37°26N 105°26W **77 H11**
Fort George = Chisasibi
　Canada　53°50N 79°0W **72 B4**
Fort Good Hope
　Canada　66°14N 128°40W **68 C7**
Fort Hancock U.S.A.　31°18N 105°51W **84 F2**
Fort Hope Canada　51°30N 88°0W **72 B2**
Fort Irwin U.S.A.　35°16N 116°41W **79 K10**
Fort Kent U.S.A.　47°15N 68°36W **81 B19**
Fort Klamath U.S.A.　42°42N 122°0W **76 E3**
Fort Laramie U.S.A.　42°13N 104°31W **76 E11**
Fort Lauderdale U.S.A.　26°7N 80°8W **85 H14**
Fort Liard Canada　60°14N 123°30W **70 A4**
Fort Liberté Haiti　19°42N 71°51W **89 C5**
Fort Lupton U.S.A.　40°5N 104°49W **76 F11**
Fort MacKay Canada　57°12N 111°41W **70 B6**
Fort Macleod Canada　49°45N 113°30W **70 D6**
Fort McMurray Canada　56°44N 111°7W **70 B6**
Fort McPherson
　Canada　67°30N 134°55W **68 C6**
Fort Madison U.S.A.　40°38N 91°27W **80 E8**
Fort Meade U.S.A.　27°45N 81°48W **85 H14**
Fort Morgan U.S.A.　40°15N 103°48W **76 F12**
Fort Myers U.S.A.　26°39N 81°52W **85 H14**
Fort Nelson Canada　58°50N 122°44W **70 B4**
Fort Nelson → Canada　59°32N 124°0W **70 B4**
Fort Norman = Tulita
　Canada　64°57N 125°30W **68 C7**
Fort Payne U.S.A.　34°26N 85°43W **85 D12**
Fort Peck U.S.A.　48°1N 106°27W **76 B10**
Fort Peck Dam U.S.A.　48°0N 106°26W **76 C10**
Fort Peck L. U.S.A.　48°0N 106°26W **76 C10**
Fort Pierce U.S.A.　27°27N 80°20W **85 H14**
Fort Pierre U.S.A.　44°21N 100°22W **80 C3**
Fort Plain U.S.A.　42°56N 74°37W **83 D10**
Fort Portal Uganda　0°40N 30°20E **54 B3**
Fort Providence Canada　61°3N 117°40W **70 A5**
Fort Qu'Appelle
　Canada　50°45N 103°50W **71 C8**
Fort Resolution
　Canada　61°10N 113°40W **70 A6**
Fort Rixon Zimbabwe　20°2S 29°17E **55 G2**
Fort Ross U.S.A.　38°32N 123°13W **78 G3**
Fort Rupert = Waskaganish
　Canada　51°30N 78°40W **72 B4**
Fort St. James Canada　54°30N 124°10W **70 C4**
Fort St. John Canada　56°15N 120°50W **70 B4**
Fort Saskatchewan
　Canada　53°40N 113°15W **70 C6**
Fort Scott U.S.A.　37°50N 94°42W **80 G6**
Fort Severn Canada　56°0N 87°40W **72 A2**
Fort Shevchenko
　Kazakhstan　44°35N 50°23E **19 F9**
Fort Simpson Canada　61°45N 121°15W **70 A4**
Fort Smith Canada　60°0N 111°51W **70 B6**
Fort Smith U.S.A.　35°23N 94°25W **84 D7**
Fort Stockton U.S.A.　30°53N 102°53W **84 F3**
Fort Sumner U.S.A.　34°28N 104°15W **77 J11**
Fort Thompson U.S.A.　44°3N 99°26W **80 C4**
Fort Union △ U.S.A.　35°54N 105°1W **77 J11**
Fort Valley U.S.A.　32°33N 83°53W **85 E13**
Fort Vermilion Canada　58°24N 116°0W **70 B5**
Fort Walton Beach
　U.S.A.　30°25N 86°36W **85 F11**
Fort Wayne U.S.A.　41°4N 85°9W **81 E11**
Fort William U.K.　56°49N 5°7W **11 E3**
Fort Worth U.S.A.　32°43N 97°19W **84 E6**
Fort Yates U.S.A.　46°5N 100°38W **80 B3**
Fort Yukon U.S.A.　66°34N 145°16W **74 a**
Fortaleza Brazil　3°45S 38°35W **93 D11**
Forteau Canada　51°28N 56°58W **73 B8**
Fortescue → Australia　21°0S 116°4E **60 D2**
Forth → U.K.　56°9N 3°50W **11 E5**
Forth, Firth of U.K.　56°5N 2°55W **11 E6**
Fortrose U.K.　57°35N 4°9W **11 D4**
Fortuna Calif., U.S.A.　40°36N 124°9W **76 F1**
Fortuna N. Dak., U.S.A.　48°55N 103°47W **80 A2**
Fortune Canada　47°4N 55°50W **73 C8**
Fortune B. Canada　47°30N 55°22W **73 C8**
Forūr Iran　26°17N 54°32E **45 E7**
Fosen Norway　63°50N 10°20E **8 E14**
Foshan China　23°4N 113°5E **33 D6**
Fosnavåg Norway　62°22N 5°38E **8 E11**
Fossano Italy　44°33N 7°43E **20 D7**
Fossil U.S.A.　45°0N 120°9W **76 D3**
Fossil Butte △ U.S.A.　41°50N 110°27W **76 F8**
Foster Canada　45°17N 72°30W **83 A12**
Foster → Canada　55°47N 105°49W **71 B7**
Fosters Ra. Australia　21°35S 133°48E **62 C1**
Fostoria U.S.A.　41°10N 83°25W **81 E12**
Fotadrevo Madag.　24°3S 45°1E **57 C8**
Fougères France　48°21N 1°14W **20 B3**
Foul Pt. Sri Lanka　8°35N 81°18E **40 Q12**
Foula U.K.　60°10N 2°5W **11 A6**
Foulness I. U.K.　51°36N 0°55E **13 F8**
Foulpointe Madag.　17°41S 49°31E **57 B8**
Foumban Cameroon　5°45N 10°50E **52 C2**
Foumbouni Comoros Is.　11°51S 43°29E **53 a**
Fountain U.S.A.　38°41N 104°42W **76 G11**
Fountain Hills U.S.A.　33°37N 111°43W **77 K8**
Fountain Springs
　U.S.A.　35°54N 118°51W **79 K8**
Fouriesburg S. Africa　28°38S 28°14E **56 D4**
Fourni Greece　37°36N 26°32E **23 F12**
Fourth Cataract Sudan　18°47N 32°3E **51 E12**
Fouta Djallon Guinea　11°20N 12°10W **50 F3**
Foux, Cap-à- Haiti　19°43N 73°27W **89 C5**
Foveaux Str. N.Z.　46°42S 168°10E **59 G2**
Fowey U.K.　50°20N 4°39W **13 G3**
Fowler Calif., U.S.A.　36°38N 119°41W **78 J7**
Fowler Colo., U.S.A.　38°8N 104°2W **76 G11**
Fowler, Pt. Australia　32°2S 132°3E **61 F5**
Fowlers B. Australia　31°59S 132°34E **61 F5**
Fowman Iran　37°13N 49°19E **45 B6**
Fox → Canada　56°3N 93°18W **71 B10**
Fox Creek Canada　54°24N 116°48W **70 C5**

Fox Lake Canada　58°28N 114°31W **70 B6**
Fox Valley Canada　50°30N 109°25W **71 C7**
Foxboro U.S.A.　42°4N 71°16W **83 D13**
Foxdale Australia　20°22S 148°35E **62 J6**
Foxe Basin Canada　66°0N 77°0W **69 C12**
Foxe Chan. Canada　65°0N 80°0W **69 C12**
Foxe Pen. Canada　65°0N 76°0W **69 C12**
Foxford Ireland　53°59N 9°7W **10 C2**
Foxton N.Z.　40°29S 175°18E **59 D5**
Foyle, Lough U.K.　55°7N 7°4W **10 A4**
Foynes Ireland　52°37N 9°7W **10 D2**
Foz do Cunene Angola　17°15S 11°48E **56 B1**
Foz do Iguaçu Brazil　25°30S 54°30W **95 B5**
Frackville U.S.A.　40°47N 76°14W **83 F8**
Fraile Muerto Uruguay　32°31S 54°32W **95 C5**
Framingham U.S.A.　42°18N 71°24W **83 D13**
Franca Brazil　20°33S 47°30W **93 H9**
Francavilla Fontana
　Italy　40°32N 17°35E **23 D7**
France ■ Europe　47°0N 3°0E **20 C5**
Frances → Canada　36°41S 140°55E **63 F3**
Frances → Canada　60°16N 129°10W **70 A3**
Frances L. Canada　61°23N 129°30W **70 A3**
Franceville Gabon　1°40S 13°32E **52 E2**
Franche-Comté □ France　46°50N 5°55E **20 C6**
Francis Case, L. U.S.A.　43°4N 98°34W **80 D4**
Francisco Beltrão Brazil　26°5S 53°4W **95 B5**
Francisco Ignacio Madero
　Coahuila, Mexico　25°48N 103°18W **86 B4**
Francisco Ignacio Madero
　Durango, Mexico　24°26N 104°18W **86 C4**
Francisco Ignacio Madero, Presa
　Mexico　28°10N 105°37W **86 B3**
Francistown Botswana　21°7S 27°33E **57 C4**
François L. Canada　54°0N 125°30W **70 C3**
Francois Peron △
　Australia　25°42S 113°33E **61 E1**
Francs Pk. U.S.A.　43°58N 109°20W **76 E9**
Franeker Neths.　53°12N 5°33E **15 A5**
Frank Hann △
　Australia　32°52S 120°19E **61 F3**
Frankford Canada　44°12N 77°36W **82 B7**
Frankfort S. Africa　27°17S 28°30E **57 D4**
Frankfort Ind., U.S.A.　40°17N 86°31W **80 E10**
Frankfort Kans., U.S.A.　39°42N 96°25W **80 F5**
Frankfort Ky., U.S.A.　38°12N 84°52W **81 F11**
Frankfort N.Y., U.S.A.　43°2N 75°4W **83 C9**
Frankfurt Brandenburg,
　Germany　52°20N 14°32E **16 B8**
Frankfurt Hessen, Germany　50°7N 8°41E **16 C5**
Fränkische Alb
　Germany　49°10N 11°23E **16 D6**
Frankland → Australia　35°0S 116°48E **61 G2**
Franklin Ky., U.S.A.　36°43N 86°35W **80 G10**
Franklin La., U.S.A.　29°48N 91°30W **84 G9**
Franklin Mass., U.S.A.　42°5N 71°24W **83 D13**
Franklin N.H., U.S.A.　43°27N 71°39W **83 C13**
Franklin Nebr., U.S.A.　40°6N 98°57W **80 E4**
Franklin Pa., U.S.A.　41°24N 79°50W **82 E5**
Franklin Va., U.S.A.　36°41N 76°56W **81 G15**
Franklin W. Va.,
　U.S.A.　38°39N 79°20W **81 F14**
Franklin B. Canada　69°45N 126°0W **68 C7**
Franklin D. Roosevelt L.
　U.S.A.　48°18N 118°9W **76 B4**
Franklin-Gordon Wild Rivers △
　Australia　42°19S 145°51E **63 G4**
Franklin I. Antarctica　76°10S 168°30E **5 D11**
Franklin L. U.S.A.　40°25N 115°22W **76 F6**
Franklin Mts. Canada　65°0N 125°0W **68 C7**
Franklin Str. Canada　72°0N 96°0W **68 B10**
Franklinton U.S.A.　30°51N 90°9W **84 F9**
Franklinville U.S.A.　42°20N 78°27W **82 D6**
Frankston Australia　38°8S 145°8E **63 F4**
Fransfontein Namibia　20°12S 15°1E **56 C2**
Frantsa Iosifa, Zemlya
　Russia　82°0N 55°0E **28 A6**
Franz Canada　48°25N 84°30W **72 C3**
Franz Josef Land = Frantsa Iosifa,
　Zemlya Russia　82°0N 55°0E **28 A6**
Fraser → B.C., Canada　49°7N 123°11W **78 A3**
Fraser → Nfld. & L.,
　Canada　56°39N 62°10W **73 A7**
Fraser, Mt. Australia　25°35S 118°20E **61 E2**
Fraser I. Australia　25°15S 153°10E **63 D5**
Fraser Lake Canada　54°0N 124°50W **70 C4**
Fraserburg S. Africa　31°55S 21°30E **56 E3**
Fraserburgh U.K.　57°42N 2°1W **11 D6**
Fraserdale Canada　49°55N 81°37W **72 C3**
Fray Bentos Uruguay　33°10S 58°15W **94 C4**
Fray Jorge △ Chile　30°42S 71°40W **94 C1**
Fredericia Denmark　55°34N 9°45E **9 J13**
Frederick Md., U.S.A.　39°25N 77°25W **81 F15**
Frederick Okla., U.S.A.　34°23N 99°1W **84 H5**
Frederick S. Dak., U.S.A.　45°50N 98°31W **80 C4**
Fredericksburg Pa.,
　U.S.A.　40°27N 76°26W **83 F8**
Fredericksburg Tex.,
　U.S.A.　30°16N 98°52W **84 F5**
Fredericksburg Va.,
　U.S.A.　38°18N 77°28W **81 F15**
Fredericktown Mo.,
　U.S.A.　37°34N 90°18W **80 G8**
Fredericktown Ohio,
　U.S.A.　40°29N 82°33W **82 F2**
Frederico Westphalen
　Brazil　27°22S 53°24W **95 B5**
Fredericton Canada　45°57N 66°40W **73 C6**
Fredericton Junction
　Canada　45°41N 66°40W **73 C6**
Frederikshåb = Paamiut
　Greenland　62°0N 49°43W **4 C5**
Frederikshamn = Hamina
　Finland　60°34N 27°12E **8 F22**
Frederikshavn Denmark　57°28N 10°31E **9 H14**

Frederiksted U.S. Virgin Is. 17°43N 64°53W 89 C7
Fredonia Ariz., U.S.A. 36°57N 112°32W 77 H7
Fredonia Kans., U.S.A. 37°32N 95°49W 80 G6
Fredonia N.Y., U.S.A. 42°26N 79°20W 82 D5
Fredrikstad Norway 59°13N 10°57E 9 G14
Free State □ S. Africa 28°30S 27°0E 56 D4
Freehold U.S.A. 40°16N 74°17W 83 F10
Freeland U.S.A. 41°1N 75°54W 83 E9
Freels, C. Canada 49°15N 53°30W 73 C9
Freeman Calif., U.S.A. 35°35N 117°53W 79 K9
Freeman S. Dak., U.S.A. 43°21N 97°26W 80 D5
Freeport Bahamas 26°30N 78°47W 88 A4
Freeport Ill., U.S.A. 42°17N 89°36W 80 D9
Freeport N.Y., U.S.A. 40°39N 73°35W 83 F11
Freeport Ohio, U.S.A. 40°12N 81°15W 82 F3
Freeport Pa., U.S.A. 40°41N 79°41W 82 F5
Freeport Tex., U.S.A. 28°57N 95°21W 84 G7
Freetown S. Leone 8°30N 13°17W 50 G3
Frégate, L. de la Canada 53°15N 74°45W 72 B5
Fregenal de la Sierra Spain 38°10N 6°39W 21 C2
Freibourg = Fribourg Switz. 46°49N 7°9E 20 C7
Freiburg Germany 47°59N 7°51E 16 E4
Freire Chile 38°54S 72°38W 96 D2
Freirina Chile 28°30S 71°10W 94 B1
Freising Germany 48°24N 11°45E 16 D6
Freistadt Austria 48°30N 14°30E 16 D8
Fréjus France 43°25N 6°44E 20 E7
Fremantle Australia 32°7S 115°47E 61 F2
Fremont Calif., U.S.A. 37°32N 121°57W 78 H4
Fremont Mich., U.S.A. 43°28N 85°57W 81 D11
Fremont Nebr., U.S.A. 41°26N 96°30W 80 E5
Fremont Ohio, U.S.A. 41°21N 83°7W 81 E12
Fremont → U.S.A. 38°24N 110°42W 76 G8
French Camp U.S.A. 37°53N 121°16W 78 H5
French Cays = Plana Cays Bahamas 22°38N 73°30W 89 B5
French Creek → U.S.A. 41°24N 79°50W 82 E5
French Guiana ☑ S. Amer. 4°0N 53°0W 93 C8
French Polynesia ☑ Pac. Oc. 20°0S 145°0W 65 J13
Frenchman → N. Amer. 48°31N 107°10W 76 B10
Frenchman Cr. → U.S.A. 40°14N 100°50W 80 E3
Fresco → Brazil 7°15S 51°30W 93 E8
Freshfield, C. Antarctica 68°25S 151°10E 5 C10
Fresnillo Mexico 23°10N 102°53W 86 C4
Fresno U.S.A. 36°44N 119°47W 78 J7
Fresno Res. U.S.A. 48°36N 109°57W 76 D9
Frew → Australia 20°0S 135°38E 62 C2
Frewsburg U.S.A. 42°3N 79°10W 82 D5
Freycinet △ Australia 42°11S 148°19E 63 G4
Freycinet Pen. Australia 42°10S 148°25E 63 G4
Fria Guinea 10°27N 13°38W 50 F3
Fria, C. Namibia 18°0S 12°0E 56 B1
Friant U.S.A. 36°59N 119°43W 79 J7
Frías Argentina 28°40S 65°5W 94 B2
Fribourg Switz. 46°49N 7°9E 20 C7
Friday Harbor U.S.A. 48°32N 123°1W 78 B3
Friedens U.S.A. 40°3N 78°59W 82 F6
Friedrichshafen Germany 47°39N 9°30E 16 E5
Friendship U.S.A. 42°12N 78°8W 82 D6
Friesland □ Neths. 53°5N 5°50E 15 A5
Frigate Seychelles 4°35S 55°56E 53 b
Frio → U.S.A. 28°26N 98°11W 84 G5
Frio, C. Brazil 22°50S 41°50W 90 F6
Friona U.S.A. 34°38N 102°43W 84 D3
Fritch U.S.A. 35°38N 101°36W 84 D4
Frobisher B. Canada 62°30N 66°0W 69 C13
Frobisher Bay = Iqaluit Canada 63°44N 68°31W 69 C13
Frobisher L. Canada 56°20N 108°15W 71 B7
Frohavet Norway 64°0N 9°30E 8 E13
Frome U.K. 51°14N 2°19W 13 F5
Frome → U.K. 50°41N 2°6W 13 G5
Frome, L. Australia 30°45S 139°45E 63 E2
Front Range U.S.A. 40°25N 105°45W 74 C5
Front Royal U.S.A. 38°55N 78°12W 81 F14
Frontera Canary Is. 27°47N 17°59W 24 G2
Frontera Mexico 18°32N 92°38W 87 D6
Fronteras Mexico 30°56N 109°31W 86 A3
Frosinone Italy 41°38N 13°19E 22 D5
Frostburg U.S.A. 39°39N 78°56W 81 F14
Frostisen Norway 68°14N 17°10E 8 B17
Frøya Norway 63°43N 8°40E 8 E13
Frunze = Bishkek Kyrgyzstan 42°54N 74°46E 28 E8
Frutal Brazil 20°0S 49°0W 93 H9
Frýdek-Místek Czech Rep. 49°40N 18°20E 17 D10
Fryeburg U.S.A. 44°1N 70°59W 83 B14
Fu Xian = Wafangdian China 39°38N 121°58E 35 E11
Fu Xian China 36°0N 109°20E 34 G5
Fucheng China 37°50N 116°10E 34 F9
Fuchou = Fuzhou China 26°5N 119°16E 33 D6
Fuchū Japan 34°34N 133°14E 31 G6
Fuencaliente Canary Is. 28°28N 17°50W 24 F2
Fuencaliente, Pta. Canary Is. 28°27N 17°51W 24 F2
Fuengirola Spain 36°32N 4°41W 21 D3
Fuentes de Oñoro Spain 40°33N 6°52W 21 B2
Fuerte → Mexico 25°54N 109°22W 86 B3
Fuerte Olimpo Paraguay 21°0S 57°51W 94 A4
Fuerteventura Canary Is. 28°30N 14°0W 24 F6
Fuerteventura ✈ (FUE) Canary Is. 28°24N 13°52W 24 F6
Fufeng China 34°22N 108°0E 34 G5
Fugou China 34°3N 114°25E 34 G8
Fugu China 39°2N 111°3E 34 E6
Fuhai China 47°2N 87°25E 32 B3
Fuḩaymī Iraq 34°16N 42°10E 44 C4
Fuji Japan 35°9N 138°39E 31 G9
Fuji-Hakone-Izu △ Japan 35°15N 138°45E 31 G9
Fuji-San Japan 35°22N 138°44E 31 G9
Fuji-Yoshida Japan 35°30N 138°46E 31 G9
Fujian □ China 26°0N 118°0E 33 D6
Fujinomiya Japan 35°10N 138°40E 31 G9
Fujisawa Japan 35°22N 139°29E 31 G9
Fujiyama, Mt. = Fuji-San Japan 35°22N 138°44E 31 G9
Fukagawa Japan 43°43N 142°2E 30 C11
Fukien = Fujian □ China 26°0N 118°0E 33 D6
Fukuchiyama Japan 35°19N 135°9E 31 G7
Fukue-Shima Japan 32°40N 128°45E 31 H4
Fukui Japan 36°5N 136°10E 31 F8
Fukui □ Japan 36°0N 136°12E 31 G8
Fukuoka Japan 33°39N 130°21E 31 H5
Fukuoka □ Japan 33°30N 131°0E 31 H5
Fukushima Japan 37°44N 140°28E 30 F10
Fukushima □ Japan 37°30N 140°15E 30 F10
Fukuyama Japan 34°35N 133°20E 31 G6
Fulaga Fiji 19°8S 178°33W 59 a
Fulda Germany 50°32N 9°40E 16 C5
Fulda → Germany 51°25N 9°39E 16 C5
Fulford Harbour Canada 48°47N 123°27W 78 B3
Fullerton Calif., U.S.A. 33°53N 117°56W 79 M9
Fullerton Nebr., U.S.A. 41°22N 97°58W 80 E5
Fulongquan China 44°20N 124°42E 35 B13
Fulton Mo., U.S.A. 38°52N 91°57W 80 F8
Fulton N.Y., U.S.A. 43°19N 76°25W 83 C8
Funabashi Japan 35°45N 140°0E 31 G10
Funafuti = Fongafale Tuvalu 8°31S 179°13E 58 B10
Funchal Madeira 32°38N 16°54W 24 D3
Funchal ✈ (FNC) Madeira 32°42N 16°45W 24 D3
Fundación Colombia 10°31N 74°11W 92 A4
Fundão Portugal 40°8N 7°30W 21 B2
Fundy, B. of Canada 45°0N 66°0W 73 D6
Fundy △ Canada 45°35N 65°10W 73 C6
Funhalouro Mozam. 23°3S 34°25E 57 C5
Funing Hebei, China 39°53N 119°12E 35 E10
Funing Jiangsu, China 33°45N 119°50E 35 H10
Funiu Shan China 33°30N 112°20E 34 H7
Funtua Nigeria 11°30N 7°18E 50 F7
Fuping Hebei, China 38°48N 114°12E 34 E8
Fuping Shaanxi, China 34°42N 109°10E 34 G5
Furano Japan 43°21N 142°23E 30 C11
Furāt, Nahr al → Asia 31°0N 47°25E 44 D5
Fūrg Iran 28°18N 55°13E 45 D7
Furnás Spain 39°3N 1°32E 24 B8
Furnas, Reprêsa de Brazil 20°50S 45°30W 95 A6
Furneaux Group Australia 40°10S 147°50E 63 G4
Furqlus Syria 34°36N 37°8E 46 A6
Fürstenwalde Germany 52°22N 14°3E 16 B8
Fürth Germany 49°28N 10°59E 16 D6
Furukawa Japan 38°34N 140°58E 30 E10
Fury and Hecla Str. Canada 69°56N 84°0W 69 C11
Fusagasuga Colombia 4°21N 74°22W 92 C4
Fushan Shandong, China 37°30N 121°15E 35 F11
Fushan Shanxi, China 35°58N 111°51E 34 G6
Fushun China 41°50N 123°56E 35 D12
Fusong China 42°20N 127°15E 35 C14
Fustic Barbados 13°16N 59°38W 89 g
Futian China 22°32N 114°4E 33 F11
Fuxin China 42°5N 121°48E 35 C11
Fuyang China 33°0N 115°48E 34 H8
Fuyang He → China 38°12N 117°0E 34 E9
Fuyong China 22°40N 113°49E 33 F10
Fuyu Heilongjiang, China 47°49N 124°27E 33 B7
Fuyu Jilin, China 45°12N 124°43E 35 B13
Fuyun China 47°0N 89°28E 32 B3
Fuzhou China 26°5N 119°16E 33 D6
Fyn Denmark 55°20N 10°30E 9 J14
Fyne, L. U.K. 55°59N 5°23W 11 F3

G

Gabela Angola 11°0S 14°24E 52 G2
Gabès Tunisia 33°53N 10°2E 51 B8
Gabès, G. de Tunisia 34°0N 10°30E 51 B8
Gabon ■ Africa 0°10S 10°0E 52 E2
Gaborone Botswana 24°45S 25°57E 56 C4
Gabriels U.S.A. 44°26N 74°12W 83 B10
Gābrīk Iran 25°44N 58°28E 45 E8
Gabrovo Bulgaria 42°52N 25°19E 23 C11
Gāch Sār Iran 36°7N 51°19E 45 B6
Gachsārān Iran 30°15N 50°45E 45 D6
Gadag India 15°30N 75°45E 40 M9
Gadap Pakistan 25°5N 67°28E 42 G2
Gadarwara India 22°50N 78°50E 43 H8
Gadhada India 22°0N 71°35E 42 J4
Gadra Pakistan 25°40N 70°38E 42 G4
Gadsden U.S.A. 34°1N 86°1W 85 D11
Gadwal India 16°10N 77°50E 40 L10
Gaffney U.S.A. 35°5N 81°39W 85 D14
Gafsa Tunisia 34°24N 8°43E 50 B7
Gagaria India 25°43N 70°46E 42 G4
Găgăuzia □ Moldova 46°10N 28°40E 17 E15
Gagnoa Ivory C. 6°56N 5°16W 50 G4
Gagnon Canada 51°50N 68°5W 73 B6
Gagnon, L. Canada 62°3N 110°27W 71 A6
Gahini Rwanda 1°50S 30°30E 54 C3
Gahmar India 25°27N 83°49E 43 G10
Gai Xian = Gaizhou China 40°22N 122°20E 35 D12
Gaidouronisi Greece 34°53N 25°41E 25 E7
Gail U.S.A. 32°46N 101°27W 84 E4
Gaillimh = Galway Ireland 53°17N 9°3W 10 C2
Gaines U.S.A. 41°46N 77°35W 82 E7
Gainesville Fla., U.S.A. 29°40N 82°20W 85 G13
Gainesville Ga., U.S.A. 34°18N 83°50W 85 D13
Gainesville Mo., U.S.A. 36°36N 92°26W 80 G7
Gainesville Tex., U.S.A. 33°38N 97°8W 84 E6
Gainsborough U.K. 53°24N 0°46W 12 D7
Gairdner, L. Australia 31°30S 136°0E 63 E2
Gairloch U.K. 57°43N 5°41W 11 D3
Gairloch, L. U.K. 57°43N 5°45W 11 D3
Gaizhou China 40°22N 122°20E 35 D12
Gaj → Pakistan 26°26N 67°21E 42 F2
Gakuch Pakistan 36°7N 73°45E 43 A5
Galán, Cerro Argentina 25°55S 66°52W 94 B2
Galana → Kenya 3°9S 40°8E 54 C5
Galápagos = Colón, Arch. de Ecuador 0°0 91°0W 90 D1
Galapagos Fracture Zone Pac. Oc. 3°0N 110°0W 65 G17
Galapagos Rise Pac. Oc. 15°0S 95°0W 65 J18
Galashiels U.K. 55°37N 2°49W 11 F6
Galaţi Romania 45°27N 28°2E 17 F15
Galatina Italy 40°10N 18°10E 23 D8
Galax U.S.A. 36°40N 80°56W 81 G13
Galcaio Somali Rep. 6°30N 47°30E 47 F4
Galdhøpiggen Norway 61°38N 8°18E 8 F13
Galeana Chihuahua, Mexico 30°7N 107°38W 86 A3
Galeana Nuevo León, Mexico 24°50N 100°4W 86 A3
Galela Indonesia 1°50N 127°49E 37 D7
Galena U.S.A. 64°44N 156°56W 74 a
Galeota Pt. Trin. & Tob. 10°8N 60°59W 93 K16
Galera Pt. Trin. & Tob. 10°49N 60°54W 89 D7
Galesburg U.S.A. 40°57N 90°22W 80 E8
Galestan △ Iran 37°30N 56°0E 45 B8
Galeton U.S.A. 41°44N 77°39W 82 E7
Galich Russia 58°22N 42°24E 18 C7
Galicia □ Spain 42°43N 7°45W 21 A2
Galilee = Hagalil Israel 32°53N 35°18E 46 C4
Galilee, L. Australia 22°20S 145°50E 62 C4
Galilee, Sea of = Yam Kinneret Israel 32°45N 35°35E 46 C4
Galina Pt. Jamaica 18°24N 76°58W 88 a
Galinoporni Cyprus 35°31N 34°18E 25 D13
Galion U.S.A. 40°44N 82°47W 82 F2
Galiuro Mts. U.S.A. 32°30N 110°20W 77 K8
Galiwinku Australia 12°2S 135°34E 62 A2
Gallan Hd. U.K. 58°15N 7°2W 11 C1
Gallatin U.S.A. 36°24N 86°27W 85 C11
Galle Sri Lanka 6°5N 80°10E 40 R12
Gállego → Spain 41°39N 0°51W 21 B5
Gallegos → Argentina 51°35S 69°0W 96 G3
Galley Hd. Ireland 51°32N 8°55W 10 E3
Gallinas, Pta. Colombia 12°28N 71°40W 92 A4
Gallipoli = Gelibolu Turkey 40°28N 26°43E 23 D12
Gallipoli Italy 40°3N 17°58E 23 D8
Gallipolis U.S.A. 38°49N 82°12W 81 F12
Gällivare Sweden 67°9N 20°40E 8 C19
Galloo I. U.S.A. 43°55N 76°25W 83 C8
Galloway U.K. 55°1N 4°29W 11 F4
Galloway, Mull of U.K. 54°39N 4°52W 11 G4
Galloway ⌂ U.K. 55°3N 4°20W 11 F4
Gallup U.S.A. 35°32N 108°45W 77 J9
Galoya Sri Lanka 8°10N 80°55E 40 Q12
Galt U.S.A. 38°15N 121°18W 78 G5
Galty Mts. Ireland 52°22N 8°10W 10 D3
Galtymore Ireland 52°21N 8°11W 10 D3
Galva U.S.A. 41°10N 90°3W 80 E8
Galveston U.S.A. 29°18N 94°48W 84 G7
Galveston B. U.S.A. 29°36N 94°50W 84 G7
Gálvez Argentina 32°0S 61°14W 94 C3
Galway Ireland 53°17N 9°3W 10 C2
Galway □ Ireland 53°22N 9°1W 10 C2
Galway B. Ireland 53°13N 9°10W 10 C2
Gam → Vietnam 21°55N 105°12E 38 B5
Gamagōri Japan 34°50N 137°14E 31 G8
Gambat Pakistan 27°17N 68°26E 42 F3
Gambhir → India 26°58N 77°27E 42 F6
Gambia ■ W. Afr. 13°25N 16°0W 50 F2
Gambia → W. Afr. 13°28N 16°34W 50 F2
Gambier U.S.A. 40°22N 82°23W 82 F2
Gambier, C. Australia 11°56S 130°57E 60 B5
Gambier, Îs. French Polynesia 23°0S 134°58W 65 K14
Gambier Is. Australia 35°3S 136°30E 63 F2
Gambo Canada 48°47N 54°13W 73 C9
Gamboli Pakistan 29°53N 68°24E 42 E3
Gamboma Congo 1°55S 15°52E 52 E3
Gamka → S. Africa 33°18S 21°39E 56 E3
Gamkab → Namibia 28°4S 17°54E 56 D2
Gamlakarleby = Kokkola Finland 63°50N 23°8E 8 E20
Gammon → Canada 51°24N 95°44W 71 C9
Gammon Ranges △ Australia 30°38S 139°8E 63 E2
Gamtoos → S. Africa 33°58S 25°1E 56 E4
Gan Jiang → China 29°15N 116°0E 33 D6
Ganado U.S.A. 35°43N 109°33W 77 J9
Gananoque Canada 44°20N 76°10W 83 B8
Ganāveh Iran 29°35N 50°35E 45 D6
Gäncä Azerbaijan 40°45N 46°20E 19 F8
Gancheng China 18°51N 108°37E 38 C7
Gand = Gent Belgium 51°2N 3°42E 15 C3
Ganda Angola 13°3S 14°35E 53 G2
Gandajika Dem. Rep. of the Congo 6°46S 23°58E 52 F4
Gandak → India 25°39N 85°13E 43 G11
Gandava Pakistan 28°32N 67°32E 42 E2
Gander Canada 48°58N 54°35W 73 C9
Gander L. Canada 48°58N 54°35W 73 C9
Ganderowe Falls Zimbabwe 17°20S 29°10E 55 F2
Gandhi Sagar India 24°40N 75°40E 42 G6
Gandhinagar India 23°15N 72°45E 42 H5
Gandía Spain 38°58N 0°9W 21 C5
Gando, Pta. Canary Is. 27°55N 15°22W 24 G4
Ganedidalem = Gani Indonesia 0°48S 128°14E 37 E7
Ganga → India 23°20N 90°30E 43 H14
Ganga Sagar India 21°38N 88°5E 43 J13
Gangan → India 28°38N 78°58E 43 E8
Ganganagar India 29°56N 73°56E 42 E5
Gangapur India 26°32N 76°49E 42 F7
Gangaw Burma 22°5N 94°5E 41 H19
Gangdisê Shan China 31°20N 81°0E 43 D9
Ganges = Ganga → India 23°20N 90°30E 43 H14
Ganges Canada 48°51N 123°31W 70 D4
Ganges, Mouths of the India 21°30N 90°0E 43 J14
Ganggyeong S. Korea 36°10N 127°0E 35 F14
Ganghwa S. Korea 37°45N 126°30E 35 F14
Gangneung S. Korea 37°45N 128°54E 35 F15
Gangoh India 29°46N 77°18E 42 E7
Gangotri India 30°50N 79°10E 43 D8
Gangotri △ India 30°50N 79°10E 43 D8
Gangseong S. Korea 38°24N 128°30E 35 E15
Gangtok India 27°20N 88°37E 41 F16
Gangu China 34°40N 105°15E 34 G3
Gangyao China 44°12N 126°37E 35 B14
Gani Indonesia 0°48S 128°14E 37 E7
Ganj India 27°45N 78°57E 43 F8
Gannett Peak U.S.A. 43°11N 109°39W 76 E9
Ganquan China 36°20N 109°20E 34 F5
Gansu □ China 36°0N 104°0E 34 G3
Ganta Liberia 7°15N 8°59W 50 G4
Gantheaume, C. Australia 36°4S 137°32E 63 F2
Gantheaume B. Australia 27°40S 114°10E 61 E1
Gantsevichi = Hantsavichy Belarus 52°49N 26°30E 17 B14
Ganyem = Genyem Indonesia 2°46S 140°12E 37 E10
Ganyu China 34°50N 119°8E 35 G10
Ganzhou China 25°51N 114°56E 33 D6
Gao Mali 16°15N 0°5W 50 E5
Gaomi China 36°20N 119°42E 35 F10
Gaoping China 35°45N 112°55E 34 G7
Gaotang China 36°50N 116°15E 34 F9
Gaoua Burkina Faso 10°20N 3°8W 50 F5
Gaoual Guinea 11°45N 13°25W 50 F3
Gaoxiong = Kaohsiung Taiwan 22°35N 120°16E 33 D7
Gaoyang China 38°40N 115°45E 34 E8
Gaoyou Hu China 32°45N 119°20E 35 H10
Gaoyuan China 37°8N 117°58E 35 F9
Gap France 44°33N 6°5E 20 D7
Gapat → India 24°30N 82°28E 43 G10
Gapuwiyak Australia 12°25S 135°43E 62 A2
Gar China 32°10N 79°58E 32 C2
Gara, L. Ireland 53°57N 8°26W 10 C3
Garabogazköl Aylagy Turkmenistan 41°0N 53°30E 19 F9
Garachico Canary Is. 28°22N 16°46W 24 F3
Garachiné Panama 8°0N 78°12W 88 E4
Garafia Canary Is. 28°48N 17°57W 24 F2
Garagum Turkmenistan 39°30N 60°0E 45 B8
Garah Australia 29°5S 149°38E 63 D4
Garajonay Canary Is. 28°7N 17°14W 24 F2
Garamba △ Dem. Rep. of the Congo 4°10N 29°40E 54 B2
Garanhuns Brazil 8°50S 36°30W 93 E11
Garautha India 25°34N 79°18E 43 G8
Garba Tula Kenya 0°30N 38°32E 54 B4
Garberville U.S.A. 40°6N 123°48W 76 F2
Garbiyang India 30°8N 80°54E 43 D9
Gard → France 43°51N 4°37E 20 E6
Garda, L. di Italy 45°40N 10°41E 22 B4
Garde L. Canada 62°50N 106°13W 71 A7
Garden City Ga., U.S.A. 32°6N 81°9W 85 E14
Garden City Kans., U.S.A. 37°58N 100°53W 80 G3
Garden City Tex., U.S.A. 31°52N 101°29W 84 F4
Garden Grove U.S.A. 33°47N 117°55W 79 M9
Gardēz Afghan. 33°37N 69°9E 42 C3
Gardiner Maine, U.S.A. 44°14N 69°47W 81 C19
Gardiner Mont., U.S.A. 45°2N 110°22W 76 D8
Gardiners I. U.S.A. 41°6N 72°6W 83 E12
Gardner U.S.A. 42°34N 71°59W 83 D13
Gardner Canal Canada 53°27N 128°8W 70 C3
Gardnerville U.S.A. 38°56N 119°45W 78 G7
Gardo Somali Rep. 9°30N 49°6E 47 F4
Garey U.S.A. 34°53N 120°19W 79 L6
Garfield U.S.A. 47°1N 117°9W 76 C5
Garforth U.K. 53°47N 1°24W 12 D6
Gargantua, C. Canada 47°36N 85°2W 81 B11
Gargett Australia 21°9S 148°46E 62 K6
Garibaldi ⌂ Canada 49°50N 122°40W 70 D4
Gariep, L. S. Africa 30°40S 25°40E 56 E4
Garies S. Africa 30°32S 17°59E 56 E2
Garigliano → Italy 41°13N 13°45E 22 D5
Garissa Kenya 0°25S 39°40E 54 C4
Garland Tex., U.S.A. 32°54N 96°38W 84 E6
Garland Utah, U.S.A. 41°45N 112°10W 76 F7
Garm Tajikistan 39°0N 70°20E 28 F8
Garmāb Iran 35°25N 56°45E 45 C8
Garmisch-Partenkirchen Germany 47°30N 11°6E 16 E6
Garmsār Iran 35°20N 52°25E 45 C7
Garner U.S.A. 43°6N 93°36W 80 D7
Garnett U.S.A. 38°17N 95°14W 80 F6
Garo Hills India 25°30N 90°30E 43 G14
Garoe Somali Rep. 8°25N 48°33E 47 F4
Garonne → France 45°2N 0°36W 20 D3
Garoowe = Garoe Somali Rep. 8°25N 48°33E 47 F4
Garot India 24°19N 75°41E 42 G6
Garoua Cameroon 9°19N 13°21E 51 G8
Garrauli India 25°5N 79°22E 43 G8
Garrison Mont., U.S.A. 46°31N 112°49W 76 C7
Garrison N. Dak., U.S.A. 47°40N 101°25W 80 B3
Garrison Res. = Sakakawea, L. U.S.A. 47°30N 101°25W 80 B3
Garron Pt. U.K. 55°3N 5°59W 10 A6
Garry → U.K. 56°44N 3°47W 11 E5
Garry, L. Canada 65°58N 100°18W 68 C9
Garrygala Turkmenistan 38°31N 56°29E 45 B8
Garsen Kenya 2°20S 40°5E 54 C5
Garson L. Canada 56°19N 110°2W 71 B6
Garstang U.K. 53°55N 2°46W 12 D5
Garu India 23°40N 84°14E 43 H11
Garub Namibia 26°37S 16°0E 56 D2
Garut Indonesia 7°14S 107°53E 37 G12
Garvie Mts. N.Z. 45°30S 168°50E 59 F2
Garwa = Garoua Cameroon 9°19N 13°21E 51 G8
Garwa India 24°11N 83°47E 43 G10
Gary U.S.A. 41°36N 87°20W 80 E10
Garzê China 31°38N 100°1E 32 C5
Garzón Colombia 2°10N 75°40W 92 C3
Gas-San Japan 38°32N 140°1E 30 E10
Gasan Kuli = Esenguly Turkmenistan 37°37N 53°59E 28 F6
Gascogne France 43°45N 0°20E 20 E4
Gascogne, G. de Europe 44°0N 2°0W 20 D2
Gascony = Gascogne France 43°45N 0°20E 20 E4
Gascoyne → Australia 24°52S 113°37E 61 D1
Gascoyne Junction Australia 25°2S 115°17E 61 E2
Gashaka Nigeria 7°20N 11°29E 51 G8
Gasherbrum Pakistan 35°40N 76°40E 43 B7
Gashua Nigeria 12°54N 11°0E 51 F8
Gasparillo Trin. & Tob. 10°18N 61°26W 93 K15
Gaspé Canada 48°52N 64°30W 73 C7
Gaspé, C. Canada 48°48N 64°7W 73 C7
Gaspé Pen. = Gaspésie, Pén. de la Canada 48°45N 65°40W 73 C6
Gaspésie, Pén. de la Canada 48°45N 65°40W 73 C6
Gaspésie ⌂ Canada 48°55N 66°10W 73 C6
Gasteiz = Vitoria-Gasteiz Spain 42°50N 2°41W 21 A4
Gastonia U.S.A. 35°16N 81°11W 85 D14
Gastre Argentina 42°20S 69°15W 96 E3
Gata, C. Cyprus 34°34N 33°2E 25 E12
Gata, C. de Spain 36°41N 2°13W 21 D4
Gata, Sierra de Spain 40°20N 6°45W 21 B2
Gataga → Canada 58°35N 126°59W 70 B3
Gatchina Russia 59°35N 30°9E 9 G24
Gatehouse of Fleet U.K. 54°53N 4°12W 11 G4
Gates U.S.A. 43°9N 77°42W 82 C7
Gateshead U.K. 54°57N 1°35W 12 C6
Gatesville U.S.A. 31°26N 97°45W 84 F6
Gateway ⌂ U.S.A. 40°38N 73°51W 83 F11
Gaths Zimbabwe 20°2S 30°32E 55 G3
Gatico Chile 22°29S 70°20W 94 A1
Gatineau Canada 45°29N 75°39W 83 A9
Gatineau → Canada 45°27N 75°42W 72 C4
Gatineau △ Canada 45°40N 76°0W 72 C4
Gatton Australia 27°32S 152°17E 63 D5
Gatun, L. Panama 9°7N 79°56W 88 E4
Gatwick, London ✈ (LGW) U.K. 51°10N 0°11W 13 F7
Gatyana S. Africa 32°16S 28°31E 57 E4
Gau Fiji 18°2S 179°18E 59 a
Gauer L. Canada 57°0N 97°50W 71 B9
Gauhati = Guwahati India 26°10N 91°45E 41 F17
Gauja → Latvia 57°10N 24°16E 9 H21
Gaujas △ Latvia 57°10N 24°50E 9 H21
Gaula → Norway 63°21N 10°14E 8 E14
Gauri Phanta India 28°41N 80°36E 43 E9
Gaustatoppen Norway 59°48N 8°40E 9 G13
Gauteng □ S. Africa 26°0S 28°0E 57 D4
Gāv Koshī Iran 28°38N 57°12E 45 D8
Gāvakān Iran 29°37N 53°10E 45 D7
Gavāter Iran 25°10N 61°31E 45 E9
Gāvbandī Iran 27°12N 53°4E 45 E7
Gavdopoula Greece 34°56N 24°0E 25 E6
Gavdos Greece 34°50N 24°5E 25 E6
Gaviota U.S.A. 34°29N 120°13W 79 L6
Gāvkhūnī, Bāṭlāq-e Iran 32°6N 52°52E 45 C7
Gävle Sweden 60°40N 17°9E 8 F17
Gawachab Namibia 27°4S 17°55E 56 D2
Gawilgarh Hills India 21°15N 76°45E 40 J10
Gawler Australia 34°30S 138°42E 63 E2
Gawler Ranges Australia 32°30S 135°45E 63 E2
Gaxun Nur China 42°22N 100°30E 32 B5
Gay Russia 51°27N 58°27E 18 D10
Gaya India 24°47N 85°4E 43 G11
Gaya Niger 11°52N 3°28E 50 F6
Gaylord U.S.A. 45°2N 84°41W 81 C11
Gayndah Australia 25°35S 151°32E 63 D5
Gaysin = Haysyn Ukraine 48°57N 29°25E 17 D15
Gayvoron = Hayvoron Ukraine 48°22N 29°52E 17 D15
Gaza Gaza Strip 31°30N 34°28E 46 D3
Gaza □ Mozam. 23°10S 32°45E 57 C5
Gaza Strip ■ Asia 31°29N 34°25E 46 D3
Gazanjyk = Bereket Turkmenistan 39°16N 55°32E 45 B7
Gāzbor Iran 28°5N 58°51E 45 D8
Gazi Dem. Rep. of the Congo 1°3N 24°30E 54 B1
Gaziantep Turkey 37°6N 37°23E 44 B3
Gazimağosa = Famagusta Cyprus 35°8N 33°55E 25 D12
Gcoverega Botswana 19°8S 24°18E 56 B3
Gcuwa S. Africa 32°20S 28°11E 57 E4
Gdańsk Poland 54°22N 18°40E 17 A10
Gdańska, Zatoka Poland 54°30N 19°20E 17 A10
Gdov Russia 58°48N 27°55E 9 G22
Gdynia Poland 54°35N 18°33E 17 A10
Gebe Indonesia 0°5N 129°25E 37 D7
Gebze Turkey 40°47N 29°25E 23 D13
Gedaref Sudan 14°2N 35°28E 51 F13
Gediz → Turkey 38°35N 26°48E 23 E12
Gedser Denmark 54°35N 11°55E 9 J14
Gedung, Pulau Malaysia 5°17N 100°23E 39 c
Geegully Cr. → Australia 18°32S 123°41E 60 C3

Geel Belgium 51°10N 4°59E 15 C4
Geelong Australia 38°10S 144°22E 63 F3
Geelvink B. = Cenderwasih, Teluk Indonesia 3°0S 135°20E 37 E9
Geelvink Chan. Australia 28°30S 114°0E 61 E1
Geesthacht Germany 53°26N 10°22E 16 B6
Geidam Nigeria 12°57N 11°57E 51 F8
Geikie → Canada 57°45N 103°52W 71 B8
Geikie Gorge △ Australia 18°3S 125°41E 60 C4
Geistown U.S.A. 40°18N 78°52W 82 F6
Geita Tanzania 2°48S 32°12E 54 C3
Gejiu China 23°20N 103°10E 32 D5
Gel, Meydān-e Iran 29°4N 54°50E 45 D7
Gela Italy 37°4N 14°15E 22 F6
Gelang Patah Malaysia 1°27N 103°35E 39 d
Gelderland □ Neths. 52°5N 6°10E 15 B6
Geldrop Neths. 51°25N 5°32E 15 C5
Geleen Neths. 50°57N 5°49E 15 D5
Gelib Somali Rep. 0°29N 42°46E 47 G3
Gelibolu Turkey 40°28N 26°43E 23 D12
Gelsenkirchen Germany 51°32N 7°6E 16 C4
Gelugur Malaysia 5°22N 100°18E 39 c
Gemas Malaysia 2°37N 102°36E 39 L4
Gembloux Belgium 50°34N 4°43E 15 D4
Gemena Dem. Rep. of the Congo 3°13N 19°48E 52 D3
Gemerek Turkey 39°15N 36°10E 44 B3
Gemlik Turkey 40°26N 29°9E 23 D13
Gemsbok △ Botswana 25°5S 21°1E 56 D3
Genadi Greece 36°2N 27°56E 25 C9
Genale → Ethiopia 6°2N 39°1E 47 F2
General Acha Argentina 37°20S 64°38W 94 D3
General Alvear B. Aires, Argentina 36°0S 60°0W 94 D4
General Alvear Mendoza, Argentina 35°0S 67°40W 94 D2
General Artigas Paraguay 26°52S 56°16W 94 B4
General Belgrano Argentina 36°35S 58°47W 94 D4
General Bernardo O'Higgins Antarctica 63°0S 58°3W 5 C18
General Cabrera Argentina 32°53S 63°52W 94 C3
General Cepeda Mexico 25°21N 101°22W 86 B4
General Guido Argentina 36°40S 57°50W 94 D4
General Juan Madariaga Argentina 37°0S 57°0W 94 D4
General La Madrid Argentina 37°17S 61°20W 94 D3
General MacArthur Phil. 11°18N 125°28E 37 B7
General Martin Miguel de Güemes Argentina 24°50S 65°0W 94 A3
General Paz Argentina 27°45S 57°36W 94 B4
General Pico Argentina 35°45S 63°50W 94 D3
General Pinedo Argentina 27°15S 61°20W 94 B3
General Pinto Argentina 34°45S 61°50W 94 C3
General Roca Argentina 39°2S 67°35W 96 D3
General Santos Phil. 6°5N 125°14E 37 C7
General Treviño Mexico 26°14N 99°29W 87 B5
General Trías Mexico 28°21N 106°22W 86 B3
General Viamonte Argentina 35°1S 61°3W 94 D3
General Villegas Argentina 35°5S 63°0W 94 D3
Genesee Idaho, U.S.A. 46°33N 116°56W 76 C5
Genesee Pa., U.S.A. 41°59N 77°54W 82 E7
Genesee → U.S.A. 43°16N 77°36W 82 C7
Geneseo Ill., U.S.A. 41°27N 90°9W 80 E8
Geneseo N.Y., U.S.A. 42°48N 77°49W 82 D7
Geneva = Genève Switz. 46°12N 6°9E 20 C7
Geneva Ala., U.S.A. 31°2N 85°52W 85 F12
Geneva N.Y., U.S.A. 42°52N 76°59W 82 D8
Geneva Nebr., U.S.A. 40°32N 97°36W 80 E5
Geneva Ohio, U.S.A. 41°48N 80°57W 82 E4
Geneva, L. = Léman, L. Europe 46°26N 6°30E 20 C7
Genève Switz. 46°12N 6°9E 20 C7
Genil → Spain 37°42N 5°19W 21 D3
Genk Belgium 50°58N 5°32E 15 D5
Gennargentu, Mti. del Italy 40°1N 9°19E 22 D3
Genoa = Génova Italy 44°25N 8°57E 20 D8
Genoa Australia 37°29S 149°35E 63 F4
Genoa N.Y., U.S.A. 42°40N 76°32W 83 D8
Genoa Nebr., U.S.A. 41°27N 97°44W 80 E5
Genoa Nev., U.S.A. 39°2N 119°50W 78 F7
Génova Italy 44°25N 8°57E 20 D8
Génova, G. di Italy 44°0N 9°0E 22 C3
Genriyetty, Ostrov Russia 77°6N 156°30E 29 B16
Gent Belgium 51°2N 3°42E 15 C3
Genteng Bali, Indonesia 8°22S 114°9E 37 J17
Genteng Jawa Barat, Indonesia 7°22S 106°24E 37 G12
Genyem Indonesia 2°46S 140°12E 37 E10
Geochang S. Korea 35°41N 127°55E 35 G14
Geographe B. Australia 33°30S 115°15E 61 F2
Geographe Chan. Australia 24°30S 113°0E 61 D1
Georga, Zemlya Russia 80°30N 49°0E 28 A5
George S. Africa 33°58S 22°29E 56 E3
George → Canada 58°49N 66°10W 73 A6
George, L. N.S.W., Australia 35°10S 149°25E 63 F4
George, L. S. Austral., Australia 37°25S 140°0E 63 F3
George, L. W. Austral., Australia 22°45S 123°40E 60 D3
George, L. Uganda 0°5N 30°10E 54 B3
George, L. Fla., U.S.A. 29°17N 81°36W 85 G14
George, L. N.Y., U.S.A. 43°37N 73°33W 83 C11
George Gill Ra. Australia 24°22S 131°45E 60 D5
George Pt. Australia 20°6S 148°36E 62 J6
George River = Kangiqsualujjuaq Canada 58°30N 65°59W 69 D13
George Sound N.Z. 44°52S 167°25E 59 F1
George Town Australia 41°6S 146°49E 63 G4
George Town Bahamas 23°33N 75°47W 88 B4
George Town Cayman Is. 19°20N 81°24W 88 C3
George Town Malaysia 5°25N 100°20E 39 c
George V Land Antarctica 69°0S 148°0E 5 C10
George VI Sound Antarctica 71°0S 68°0W 5 D17
George West U.S.A. 28°20N 98°7W 84 G5
Georgetown = Janjanbureh Gambia 13°30N 14°47W 50 F3
Georgetown Australia 18°17S 143°33E 62 B3
Georgetown Ont., Canada 43°40N 79°56W 82 C5
Georgetown P.E.I., Canada 46°13N 62°24W 73 C7
Georgetown Guyana 6°50N 58°12W 92 B7
Georgetown Calif., U.S.A. 38°54N 120°50W 78 G6
Georgetown Colo., U.S.A. 39°42N 105°42W 76 G11
Georgetown Ky., U.S.A. 38°13N 84°33W 81 F11
Georgetown N.Y., U.S.A. 42°46N 75°44W 83 D9
Georgetown Ohio, U.S.A. 38°52N 83°54W 81 F12
Georgetown S.C., U.S.A. 33°23N 79°17W 85 E15
Georgetown Tex., U.S.A. 30°38N 97°41W 84 F6
Georgia □ U.S.A. 32°50N 83°15W 85 E13
Georgia ■ Asia 42°0N 43°0E 19 F7
Georgia, Str. of N. Amer. 49°25N 124°0W 78 A3
Georgia Basin S. Ocean 50°45S 35°30W 5 B1
Georgian B. Canada 45°15N 81°0W 82 A4
Georgian Bay Islands △ Canada 44°53N 79°52W 82 B5
Georgina → Australia 23°30S 139°47E 62 C2
Georgina I. Canada 44°22N 79°17W 82 B5
Georgioupoli Greece 35°20N 24°15E 25 D6
Georgiyevsk Russia 44°12N 43°28E 19 F7
Gera Germany 50°53N 12°4E 16 C7
Geraardsbergen Belgium 50°45N 3°53E 15 D3
Geral, Serra Brazil 26°25S 50°0W 95 B6
Geral de Goiás, Serra Brazil 12°0S 46°0W 93 F9
Geraldine U.S.A. 47°36N 110°16W 76 C8
Geraldton Australia 28°48S 114°32E 61 E1
Geraldton Canada 49°44N 86°59W 72 C2
Gereshk Afghan. 31°47N 64°35E 40 D4
Gerik Malaysia 5°50N 101°15E 39 K3
Gering U.S.A. 41°50N 103°40W 80 E2
Gerlach U.S.A. 40°39N 119°21W 76 F4
Germansen Landing Canada 55°43N 124°40W 70 B4
Germantown U.S.A. 35°5N 89°49W 85 D10
Germany ■ Europe 51°0N 10°0E 16 C6
Germī Iran 39°1N 48°3E 45 B6
Germiston S. Africa 26°13S 28°10E 57 D4
Gernika-Lumo Spain 43°19N 2°40W 21 A4
Gero Japan 35°48N 137°14E 31 G8
Gerokgak Indonesia 8°11S 114°27E 37 J17
Gerona = Girona Spain 41°58N 2°46E 21 B7
Geropotamos → Greece 35°3N 24°50E 25 D6
Gerrard Canada 50°30N 117°17W 70 C5
Gertak Sanggul Malaysia 5°17N 100°12E 39 c
Gertak Sanggul, Tanjung Malaysia 5°16N 100°11E 39 c
Gerung Indonesia 8°43S 116°7E 37 K19
Geser Indonesia 3°50S 130°54E 37 E8
Getafe Spain 40°18N 3°43W 21 B4
Gettysburg Pa., U.S.A. 39°50N 77°14W 81 F15
Gettysburg S. Dak., U.S.A. 45°1N 99°57W 80 C4
Getxo Spain 43°21N 2°59W 21 A4
Getz Ice Shelf Antarctica 75°0S 130°0W 5 D14
Geyser U.S.A. 47°16N 110°30W 76 C8
Geyserville U.S.A. 38°42N 122°54W 78 G4
Ghadāmis Libya 30°11N 9°29E 51 B8
Ghaggar → India 29°30N 74°53E 42 E6
Ghaghara → India 25°45N 84°40E 43 G11
Ghaghat → Bangla. 25°19N 89°38E 43 G13
Ghagra India 23°17N 84°33E 43 H11
Ghagra → India 27°29N 81°9E 43 F9
Ghallamane Mauritania 23°15N 10°0W 50 D4
Ghana ■ W. Afr. 8°0N 1°0W 50 G5
Ghansor India 22°39N 80°1E 43 H9
Ghanzi Botswana 21°50S 21°34E 56 C3
Ghardaïa Algeria 32°20N 3°37E 50 B6
Gharyān Libya 32°10N 13°0E 51 B8
Ghat Libya 24°59N 10°11E 51 D8
Ghatal India 22°40N 87°46E 43 H12
Ghatampur India 26°8N 80°13E 43 F9
Ghats, Eastern India 14°0N 78°50E 40 N11
Ghats, Western India 14°0N 75°0E 40 N9
Ghatsila India 22°36N 86°29E 43 H12
Ghaṭṭī Si. Arabia 31°16N 37°31E 44 D3
Ghawdex = Gozo Malta 36°3N 14°15E 25 C1
Ghazal, Bahr el → Chad 13°0N 15°47E 51 F9
Ghazâl, Bahr el → Sudan 9°31N 30°25E 51 G12
Ghaziabad India 28°42N 77°26E 42 E7
Ghazipur India 25°38N 83°35E 43 G10
Ghaznī Afghan. 33°30N 68°28E 42 C3
Ghaznī □ Afghan. 32°10N 68°20E 40 C6
Ghent = Gent Belgium 51°2N 3°42E 15 C3
Gheorghe Gheorghiu-Dej = Oneşti Romania 46°17N 26°47E 17 E14
Ghīnah, Wādī al → Si. Arabia 30°27N 38°14E 44 D3
Ghizar → Pakistan 36°15N 73°43E 43 A5
Ghotaru India 27°20N 70°1E 42 F4
Ghotki Pakistan 28°5N 69°21E 42 E3
Ghowr □ Afghan. 34°0N 64°20E 40 C4
Ghudāf, W. al → Iraq 32°56N 43°30E 44 C4
Ghughri India 22°39N 80°41E 43 H9
Ghugus India 19°58N 79°12E 40 K11
Ghulam Mohammad Barrage Pakistan 25°30N 68°20E 42 G3
Ghūrīān Afghan. 34°17N 61°25E 40 B2
Gia Dinh Vietnam 10°49N 106°42E 39 G6
Gia Lai = Plei Ku Vietnam 13°57N 108°0E 38 F7
Gia Nghia Vietnam 11°58N 107°42E 39 G6
Gia Ngoc Vietnam 14°50N 108°58E 38 E7
Gia Vuc Vietnam 14°42N 108°34E 38 E7
Giamama Somali Rep. 0°4N 42°44E 47 G3
Gianitsa Greece 40°46N 22°24E 23 D10
Giant Forest U.S.A. 36°36N 118°43W 78 J8
Giant Sequoia ⌂ U.S.A. 36°10N 118°35W 78 K8
Giants Causeway U.K. 55°16N 6°29W 10 A5
Gianyar Indonesia 8°32S 115°20E 37 K18
Giarabub = Al Jaghbūb Libya 29°42N 24°38E 51 C10
Giarre Italy 37°43N 15°11E 22 F6
Gibara Cuba 21°9N 76°11W 88 B4
Gibb River Australia 16°26S 126°26E 60 C4
Gibbon U.S.A. 40°45N 98°51W 80 E4
Gibeon Namibia 25°9S 17°43E 56 D2
Gibraltar ☒ Europe 36°7N 5°22W 21 D3
Gibraltar, Str. of Medit. S. 35°55N 5°40W 21 E3
Gibraltar Range △ Australia 29°31S 152°19E 63 D5
Gibson Desert Australia 24°0S 126°0E 60 D4
Gibsons Canada 49°24N 123°32W 70 D4
Gibsonville U.S.A. 39°46N 120°54W 78 F6
Giddings U.S.A. 30°11N 96°56W 84 F6
Giebnegáisi = Kebnekaise Sweden 67°53N 18°33E 8 C18
Giessen Germany 50°34N 8°41E 16 C5
Gīfān Iran 37°54N 57°28E 45 B8
Gift Lake Canada 55°53N 115°49W 70 B5
Gifu Japan 35°30N 136°45E 31 G8
Gifu □ Japan 35°40N 137°0E 31 G8
Giganta, Sa. de la Mexico 26°0N 111°39W 86 B2
Gigha U.K. 55°42N 5°44W 11 F3
Giglio Italy 42°20N 10°52E 22 C4
Gijón Spain 43°32N 5°42W 21 A3
Gil I. Canada 53°12N 129°15W 70 C3
Gila → U.S.A. 32°43N 114°33W 77 K6
Gila Bend U.S.A. 32°57N 112°43W 77 K7
Gila Bend Mts. U.S.A. 33°10N 113°0W 77 K7
Gila Cliff Dwellings ⌂ U.S.A. 33°12N 108°16W 77 K9
Gīlān □ Iran 37°0N 50°0E 45 B6
Gilbert → Australia 16°35S 141°15E 62 B3
Gilbert Is. Kiribati 1°0N 172°0E 58 A10
Gilbert River Australia 18°9S 142°52E 62 B3
Gilbert Seamounts Pac. Oc. 52°50N 150°10W 4 D18
Gilead U.S.A. 44°24N 70°59W 83 B14
Gilf el Kebîr, Hadabat el Egypt 23°50N 25°50E 51 D11
Gilford I. Canada 50°40N 126°30W 70 C3
Gilgandra Australia 31°43S 148°39E 63 E4
Gilgil Kenya 0°30S 36°20E 54 C4
Gilgit India 35°50N 74°15E 43 B6
Gilgit → Pakistan 35°44N 74°37E 43 B6
Gili ⌂ Mozam. 16°39S 38°27E 55 F4
Gilimanuk Indonesia 8°10S 114°26E 37 J17
Gillam Canada 56°20N 94°40W 71 B10
Gillen, L. Australia 26°11S 124°38E 61 E3
Gilles, L. Australia 32°50S 136°45E 63 E2
Gillette U.S.A. 44°18N 105°30W 76 D11
Gilliat Australia 20°40S 141°28E 62 C3
Gillingham U.K. 51°23N 0°33E 13 F8
Gilmer U.S.A. 32°44N 94°57W 84 E7
Gilmore, L. Australia 32°29S 121°37E 61 F3
Gilroy U.S.A. 37°1N 121°34W 78 H5
Gimcheon S. Korea 36°11N 128°4E 35 F15
Gimhae S. Korea 35°14N 128°53E 35 G15
Gimhwa S. Korea 38°17N 127°28E 35 E14
Gimie, Mt St. Lucia 13°54N 61°0W 89 f
Gimje S. Korea 35°48N 126°45E 35 G14
Gimli Canada 50°40N 97°0W 71 C9
Gin Gin Australia 25°0S 151°58E 63 D5
Gingin Australia 31°22S 115°54E 61 F2
Gingindlovu S. Africa 29°2S 31°30E 57 D5
Ginir Ethiopia 7°6N 40°40E 47 F3
Giofyros → Greece 35°20N 25°6E 25 D7
Giohar Somali Rep. 2°48N 45°30E 47 G4
Giona, Oros Greece 38°38N 22°14E 23 E10
Gir △ India 21°0N 71°0E 42 J4
Gir Hills India 21°0N 71°0E 42 J4
Girab India 26°2N 70°38E 42 F4
Girâfi, W. → Egypt 29°58N 34°39E 46 F3
Girard Kans., U.S.A. 37°31N 94°51W 80 G6
Girard Ohio, U.S.A. 41°9N 80°42W 82 E4
Girard Pa., U.S.A. 42°0N 80°19W 82 E4
Girdle Ness U.K. 57°9N 2°3W 11 D6
Giresun Turkey 40°55N 38°30E 19 F6
Girga Egypt 26°17N 31°55E 51 C12
Giri → India 30°28N 77°41E 42 D7
Giridih India 24°10N 86°21E 43 G12
Giriftu Kenya 1°59N 39°46E 54 B4
Girne = Kyrenia Cyprus 35°20N 33°20E 25 D12
Giron = Kiruna Sweden 67°52N 20°15E 8 C19
Girona Spain 41°58N 2°46E 21 B7
Gironde → France 45°32N 1°7W 20 D3
Girraween △ Australia 28°46S 151°54E 63 D5
Giru Australia 19°30S 147°5E 62 B4
Girvan U.K. 55°14N 4°51W 11 F4
Gisborne N.Z. 38°39S 178°5E 59 C7
Gisenyi Rwanda 1°41S 29°15E 54 C2
Gislaved Sweden 57°19N 13°32E 9 H15
Gitega Burundi 3°26S 29°56E 54 C2
Githio Greece 36°46N 22°34E 23 F10
Giuba → Somali Rep. 1°30N 42°35E 47 G3
Giurgiu Romania 43°52N 25°57E 17 G13
Giza = El Gîza Egypt 30°0N 31°12E 51 C12
Giza Pyramids Egypt 29°58N 31°9E 51 C12
Gizab Afghan. 33°22N 66°17E 42 C1
Gizhiga Russia 62°3N 160°30E 29 C17
Gizhiginskaya Guba Russia 61°0N 158°0E 29 C16
Giżycko Poland 54°2N 21°48E 17 A11
Gjirokastër Albania 40°7N 20°10E 23 D9
Gjoa Haven Canada 68°38N 95°53W 68 C10
Gjøvik Norway 60°47N 10°43E 8 F14
Glace Bay Canada 46°11N 59°58W 73 C8
Glacier △ Canada 51°15N 117°30W 70 C5
Glacier △ U.S.A. 48°42N 113°48W 76 B7
Glacier Bay ⌂ U.S.A. 58°45N 136°30W 70 B1
Glacier Peak U.S.A. 48°7N 121°7W 76 B3
Gladewater U.S.A. 32°33N 94°56W 84 E7
Gladstone Queens., Australia 23°52S 151°16E 62 C5
Gladstone S. Austral., Australia 33°15S 138°22E 63 E2
Gladstone Canada 50°13N 98°57W 71 C9
Gladstone U.S.A. 45°51N 87°1W 80 C10
Gladwin U.S.A. 43°59N 84°29W 81 D11
Glagah Indonesia 8°13S 114°18E 37 J17
Glåma = Glomma → Norway 59°12N 10°57E 9 G14
Gláma Iceland 65°48N 23°0W 8 D2
Glamis U.S.A. 32°55N 115°5W 79 N11
Glamorgan, Vale of □ U.K. 51°28N 3°25W 13 F4
Glasco Kans., U.S.A. 39°22N 97°50W 80 F5
Glasco N.Y., U.S.A. 42°3N 73°57W 83 D11
Glasgow U.K. 55°51N 4°15W 11 F4
Glasgow Ky., U.S.A. 37°0N 85°55W 81 G11
Glasgow Mont., U.S.A. 48°12N 106°38W 76 B10
Glasgow, City of □ U.K. 55°51N 4°12W 11 F4
Glasgow Int. ✈ (GLA) U.K. 55°51N 4°21W 11 F4
Glaslyn Canada 53°22N 108°21W 71 C7
Glastonbury U.K. 51°9N 2°43W 13 F5
Glastonbury U.S.A. 41°43N 72°37W 83 E12
Glazov Russia 58°9N 52°40E 18 C9
Gleichen Canada 50°52N 113°3W 70 C6
Gleiwitz = Gliwice Poland 50°22N 18°41E 17 C10
Glen U.S.A. 44°7N 71°11W 83 B13
Glen Affric U.K. 57°17N 5°1W 11 D3
Glen Canyon U.S.A. 37°30N 110°40W 77 H8
Glen Canyon ⌂ U.S.A. 37°15N 111°0W 77 H8
Glen Canyon Dam U.S.A. 36°57N 111°29W 77 H8
Glen Coe U.K. 56°40N 5°0W 11 E3
Glen Cove U.S.A. 40°51N 73°38W 83 F11
Glen Garry U.K. 57°3N 5°7W 11 D3
Glen Innes Australia 29°44S 151°44E 63 D5
Glen Lyon U.S.A. 41°10N 76°5W 83 E8
Glen Mor U.K. 57°9N 4°37W 11 D4
Glen More ⌂ U.K. 57°8N 3°40W 11 D5
Glen Moriston U.K. 57°11N 4°52W 11 D4
Glen Robertson Canada 45°22N 74°30W 83 A10
Glen Spean U.K. 56°53N 4°40W 11 E4
Glen Ullin U.S.A. 46°49N 101°50W 80 B3
Glenallen U.S.A. 62°7N 145°33W 68 C5
Glenariff △ Ireland 55°2N 6°10W 10 A5
Glenbeigh Ireland 52°3N 9°58W 10 D2
Glencoe Canada 42°45N 81°43W 82 D3
Glencoe S. Africa 28°11S 30°11E 57 D5
Glencoe U.S.A. 44°46N 94°9W 80 C6
Glencolumbkille Ireland 54°43N 8°42W 10 B3
Glendale Ariz., U.S.A. 33°32N 112°11W 77 K7
Glendale Calif., U.S.A. 34°9N 118°15W 79 L8
Glendale Zimbabwe 17°22S 31°5E 55 F3
Glendive U.S.A. 47°7N 104°43W 76 C11
Glendo U.S.A. 42°30N 105°2W 76 E11
Glenelg → Australia 38°4S 140°59E 63 F3
Glenfield U.S.A. 43°43N 75°24W 83 C9
Glengad Hd. Ireland 55°20N 7°10W 10 A4
Glengarriff Ireland 51°45N 9°34W 10 E2
Glenmont U.S.A. 40°31N 82°6W 82 F2
Glenmorgan Australia 27°14S 149°42E 63 D4
Glenn U.S.A. 39°31N 122°1W 78 F4
Glennamaddy Ireland 53°37N 8°33W 10 C3
Glenns Ferry U.S.A. 42°57N 115°18W 76 E6
Glenorchy Australia 42°49S 147°18E 63 G4
Glenore Australia 17°50S 141°12E 62 B3
Glenreagh Australia 30°2S 153°1E 63 E5
Glenrock U.S.A. 42°52N 105°52W 76 E11
Glenrothes U.K. 56°12N 3°10W 11 E5
Glens Falls U.S.A. 43°19N 73°39W 83 C11
Glenside U.S.A. 40°6N 75°9W 83 F9
Glenties Ireland 54°49N 8°16W 10 B3
Glenveagh △ Ireland 55°3N 8°1W 10 A3
Glenville U.S.A. 38°56N 80°50W 81 F13
Glenwood Canada 49°0N 54°58W 73 C9
Glenwood Ark., U.S.A. 34°20N 93°33W 84 D8
Glenwood Iowa, U.S.A. 41°3N 95°45W 80 E6
Glenwood Minn., U.S.A. 45°39N 95°23W 80 C6
Glenwood Wash., U.S.A. 46°1N 121°17W 78 D5
Glenwood Springs U.S.A. 39°33N 107°19W 76 G10
Glettinganes Iceland 65°30N 13°37W 8 D7
Glin Ireland 52°34N 9°17W 10 D2
Gliwice Poland 50°22N 18°41E 17 C10
Globe U.S.A. 33°24N 110°47W 77 K8
Głogów Poland 51°37N 16°5E 16 C9
Glomma → Norway 59°12N 10°57E 9 G14
Glorieuses, Îs. Ind. Oc. 11°30S 47°20E 57 A8
Glossop U.K. 53°27N 1°56W 12 D6
Gloucester Australia 32°0S 151°59E 63 E5
Gloucester U.K. 51°53N 2°15W 13 F5
Gloucester U.S.A. 42°37N 70°40W 83 D14
Gloucester I. Australia 20°0S 148°30E 62 J6
Gloucester Island △ Australia 20°2S 148°30E 62 J6
Gloucester Point U.S.A. 37°15N 76°30W 81 G15
Gloucestershire □ U.K. 51°46N 2°15W 13 F5
Gloversville U.S.A. 43°3N 74°21W 83 C10
Glovertown Canada 48°40N 54°3W 73 C9
Glusk Belarus 52°53N 28°41E 17 B15
Gmünd Austria 48°45N 15°0E 16 D8
Gmunden Austria 47°55N 13°48E 16 E7
Gniezno Poland 52°30N 17°35E 17 B9
Gnowangerup Australia 33°58S 117°59E 61 F2
Go Cong Vietnam 10°22N 106°40E 39 G6
Gō-no-ura Japan 33°44N 129°40E 31 H4
Goa India 15°33N 73°59E 40 M8
Goa □ India 15°33N 73°59E 40 M8
Goalen Hd. Australia 36°33S 150°4E 63 F5
Goalpara India 26°10N 90°40E 41 F17
Goaltor India 22°43N 87°10E 43 H12
Goalundo Ghat Bangla. 23°50N 89°47E 43 H13
Goat Fell U.K. 55°38N 5°11W 11 F3
Goba Ethiopia 7°1N 39°59E 47 F2
Goba Mozam. 26°15S 32°13E 57 D5
Gobabis Namibia 22°30S 19°0E 56 C2
Gobi Asia 44°0N 110°0E 34 C6
Gobō Japan 33°53N 135°10E 31 H7
Gochas Namibia 24°59S 18°55E 56 C2
Godalming U.K. 51°11N 0°36W 13 F7
Godavari → India 16°25N 82°18E 41 L13
Godavari Pt. India 17°0N 82°20E 41 L13
Godbout Canada 49°20N 67°38W 73 C6
Godda India 24°50N 87°13E 43 G12
Goderich Canada 43°45N 81°41W 82 C3
Godfrey Ra. Australia 24°0S 117°0E 61 D2
Godhavn = Qeqertarsuaq Greenland 69°15N 53°38W 4 C5
Godhra India 22°49N 73°40E 42 H5
Godoy Cruz Argentina 32°56S 68°52W 94 C2
Gods → Canada 56°22N 92°51W 72 A1
Gods L. Canada 54°40N 94°15W 72 B1
Gods River Canada 54°50N 94°5W 71 C10
Godthåb = Nuuk Greenland 64°10N 51°35W 67 C14
Goeie Hoop, Kaap die = Good Hope, C. of S. Africa 34°24S 18°30E 56 E2
Goéland, L. au Canada 49°50N 76°48W 72 C4
Goélands, L. aux Canada 55°27N 64°17W 73 A7
Goeree Neths. 51°50N 4°0E 15 C3
Goes Neths. 51°30N 3°55E 15 C3
Goffstown U.S.A. 43°1N 71°36W 83 C13
Gogama Canada 47°35N 81°43W 72 C3
Gogebic, L. U.S.A. 46°30N 89°35W 80 B9
Gogra = Ghaghara → India 25°45N 84°40E 43 G11
Gogriâl Sudan 8°30N 28°8E 51 G11
Gohana India 29°8N 76°42E 42 E7
Goharganj India 23°1N 77°41E 42 H7
Goi → India 22°4N 74°46E 42 H6
Goiânia Brazil 16°43S 49°20W 93 G9
Goiás Brazil 15°55S 50°10W 93 G8
Goiás □ Brazil 12°10S 48°0W 93 F9
Goio-Erê Brazil 24°12S 53°1W 95 A5
Gojō Japan 34°21N 135°42E 31 G7
Gojra Pakistan 31°10N 72°40E 42 D5
Gökçeada Turkey 40°10N 25°50E 23 D11
Gökova Körfezi Turkey 36°55N 27°50E 23 F12
Gokteik Burma 22°26N 97°0E 41 H20
Gokurt Pakistan 29°40N 67°26E 42 E2
Gokwe Zimbabwe 18°7S 28°58E 57 B4
Gola India 28°3N 80°32E 43 E9
Golakganj India 26°8N 89°52E 43 F13
Golan Heights = Hagolan Syria 33°0N 35°45E 46 C4
Golāshkerd Iran 27°59N 57°16E 45 E8
Golchikha Russia 71°45N 83°30E 4 B12
Golconda U.S.A. 40°58N 117°30W 76 F5
Gold U.S.A. 41°52N 77°50W 82 E7
Gold Beach U.S.A. 42°25N 124°25W 76 E1
Gold Coast W. Afr. 4°0N 1°40W 50 H5
Gold Hill U.S.A. 42°26N 123°3W 76 E2
Gold River Canada 49°46N 126°3W 70 D3
Golden Canada 51°20N 116°59W 70 C5
Golden B. N.Z. 40°40S 172°50E 59 D4
Golden Gate U.S.A. 37°48N 122°29W 77 H2
Golden Gate Highlands △ S. Africa 28°40S 28°40E 57 D4
Golden Hinde Canada 49°40N 125°44W 70 D3
Golden Lake Canada 45°34N 77°21W 82 A7
Golden Spike ⌂ U.S.A. 41°37N 112°33W 76 F7
Golden Vale Ireland 52°33N 8°17W 10 D3
Goldendale U.S.A. 45°49N 120°50W 76 D3
Goldfield U.S.A. 37°42N 117°14W 77 H5
Goldsand L. Canada 57°2N 101°8W 71 B8
Goldsboro U.S.A. 35°23N 77°59W 85 D16
Goldsmith U.S.A. 31°59N 102°37W 84 F3
Goldthwaite U.S.A. 31°27N 98°34W 84 F5
Goleniów Poland 53°35N 14°50E 16 B8
Golestān □ Iran 37°20N 55°25E 45 B7
Golestānak Iran 30°36N 54°14E 45 D7
Goleta U.S.A. 34°27N 119°50W 79 L7
Golfito Costa Rica 8°41N 83°5W 88 E3
Golfo Aranci Italy 40°59N 9°38E 22 D3
Goliad U.S.A. 28°40N 97°23W 84 G6
Golpāyegān Iran 33°27N 50°18E 45 C6
Golra Pakistan 33°37N 72°56E 42 C5
Golspie U.K. 57°58N 3°59W 11 D5
Goma Dem. Rep. of the Congo 1°37S 29°10E 54 C2
Gomal Pass Pakistan 31°56N 69°20E 42 D3
Gomati → India 25°32N 83°11E 43 G10
Gombari Dem. Rep. of the Congo 2°45N 29°3E 54 B2

Gombe *Nigeria* 10°19N 11°2E **51 F8**
Gombe → *Tanzania* 4°38S 31°40E **54 C3**
Gomel = Homyel
  Belarus 52°28N 31°0E **17 B16**
Gomera *Canary Is.* 28°7N 17°14W **24 F2**
Gómez Palacio *Mexico* 25°34N 103°30W **86 B4**
Gomīshān *Iran* 37°4N 54°6E **45 B7**
Gomogomo *Indonesia* 6°39S 134°43E **37 F8**
Gomoh *India* 23°52N 86°10E **43 H12**
Gompa = Ganta *Liberia* 7°15N 8°59W **50 G4**
Gonābād *Iran* 34°15N 58°45E **45 C8**
Gonaïves *Haiti* 19°20N 72°42W **89 C5**
Gonarezhou △
  Zimbabwe 21°32S 31°55E **55 G3**
Gonâve, G. de la *Haiti* 19°29N 72°42W **89 C5**
Gonâve, Île de la *Haiti* 18°51N 73°3W **89 C5**
Gonbad-e Kāvūs *Iran* 37°20N 55°25E **45 B7**
Gonda *India* 27°9N 81°58E **43 F9**
Gondal *India* 21°58N 70°52E **42 J4**
Gonder *Ethiopia* 12°39N 37°30E **47 E2**
Gondia *India* 21°23N 80°10E **40 J12**
Gondola *Mozam.* 19°10S 33°37E **55 F3**
Gönen *Turkey* 40°6N 27°39E **23 D12**
Gongbei *China* 22°12N 113°32E **33 G10**
Gonghe *China* 36°18N 100°32E **32 C5**
Gongju *S. Korea* 36°27N 127°7E **35 F14**
Gongming *China* 22°47N 113°53E **33 F10**
Gongolgon *Australia* 30°21S 146°54E **63 E4**
Gongzhuling *China* 43°30N 124°40E **35 C13**
Goniri *Nigeria* 11°30N 12°15E **51 F8**
Gonzales *Calif., U.S.A.* 36°30N 121°26W **78 J5**
Gonzales *Tex., U.S.A.* 29°30N 97°27W **84 G6**
González *Mexico* 22°48N 98°25W **87 C5**
González Chaves
  Argentina 38°2S 60°5W **94 D3**
Good Hope, C. of
  S. Africa 34°24S 18°30E **56 E2**
Gooderham *Canada* 44°54N 78°21W **82 B6**
Goodhouse *S. Africa* 28°57S 18°13E **56 D2**
Gooding *U.S.A.* 42°56N 114°43W **76 E6**
Goodland *U.S.A.* 39°21N 101°43W **80 F4**
Goodlands *Mauritius* 20°2S 57°39E **53 d**
Goodlow *Canada* 56°20N 120°8W **70 B4**
Goodooga *Australia* 29°3S 147°28E **63 D4**
Goodsprings *U.S.A.* 35°49N 115°27W **79 K11**
Goole *U.K.* 53°42N 0°53W **12 D7**
Goolgowi *Australia* 33°58S 145°41E **63 E4**
Goomalling *Australia* 31°15S 116°49E **61 F2**
Goomeri *Australia* 26°12S 152°6E **63 D5**
Goonda *Mozam.* 19°48S 33°57E **55 F3**
Goondiwindi *Australia* 28°30S 150°21E **63 D5**
Goongarrie, L. *Australia* 30°3S 121°9E **61 F3**
Goongarrie △ *Australia* 30°7S 121°30E **61 F3**
Goonyella *Australia* 21°47S 147°58E **62 C4**
Goose → *Canada* 53°20N 60°35W **73 B7**
Goose Creek *U.S.A.* 32°59N 80°2W **85 E14**
Goose L. *U.S.A.* 41°56N 120°26W **76 F3**
Gop *India* 22°5N 69°50E **42 H3**
Gopalganj *India* 26°28N 84°30E **43 F11**
Göppingen *Germany* 48°42N 9°39E **16 D5**
Gorakhpur *India* 26°47N 83°23E **43 F10**
Goražde *Bos.-H.* 43°38N 18°58E **23 C8**
Gorda, Pta. *Canary Is.* 28°45N 18°0W **24 F2**
Gorda, Pta. *Nic.* 14°20N 83°10W **88 D3**
Gordan B. *Australia* 11°35S 130°10E **60 B5**
Gordon *U.S.A.* 42°48N 102°12W **80 D2**
Gordon → *Australia* 42°27S 145°30E **63 G4**
Gordon L., *Alta., Canada* 56°30N 110°25W **71 B6**
Gordon L., *N.W.T.,*
  Canada 63°5N 113°11W **70 A6**
Gordonvale *Australia* 17°5S 145°50E **62 B4**
Goré *Chad* 7°59N 16°31E **51 G9**
Gore *Ethiopia* 8°12N 35°32E **47 F2**
Gore *N.Z.* 46°5S 168°58E **59 G2**
Gore Bay *Canada* 45°57N 82°28W **72 C3**
Gorey *Ireland* 52°41N 6°18W **10 D5**
Gorg *Iran* 29°29N 59°43E **45 D8**
Gorgān *Iran* 36°55N 54°30E **45 B7**
Gorgona, I. *Colombia* 3°0N 78°10W **92 C3**
Gorham *U.S.A.* 44°23N 71°10W **83 B13**
Goriganga → *India* 29°46N 80°20E **43 E9**
Gorinchem *Neths.* 51°50N 4°59E **15 C4**
Goris *Armenia* 39°31N 46°22E **19 G8**
Gorízia *Italy* 45°56N 13°37E **22 B5**
Gorkiy = Nizhniy Novgorod
  Russia 56°20N 44°0E **18 C7**
Gorkovskoye Vdkhr.
  Russia 57°2N 43°4E **18 C7**
Gorleston *U.K.* 52°35N 1°44E **13 E9**
Görlitz *Germany* 51°9N 14°58E **16 C8**
Gorlovka = Horlivka
  Ukraine 48°19N 38°5E **19 E6**
Gorman *U.S.A.* 34°47N 118°51W **79 L8**
Gorna Dzhumayo = Blagoevgrad
  Bulgaria 42°2N 23°5E **23 C10**
Gorna Oryakhovitsa
  Bulgaria 43°7N 25°40E **23 C11**
Gorno-Altay □ *Russia* 51°0N 86°0E **28 D9**
Gorno-Altaysk *Russia* 51°50N 86°5E **28 D9**
Gornyatskiy *Russia* 67°32N 64°3E **18 A11**
Gornyy *Russia* 44°57N 133°59E **30 B6**
Gorodenka = Horodenka
  Ukraine 48°41N 25°29E **17 D13**
Gorodok = Horodok
  Ukraine 49°46N 23°32E **17 D12**
Goromonzi *Zimbabwe* 17°52S 31°22E **55 F3**
Gorong, Kepulauan
  Indonesia 3°59S 131°25E **37 E8**
Gorongosa △ *Mozam.* 18°50S 34°29E **55 F3**
Gorongose → *Mozam.* 20°30S 34°40E **57 C5**
Gorongoza *Mozam.* 18°44S 34°2E **55 F3**
Gorongoza, Sa. da
  Mozam. 18°27S 34°2E **55 F3**
Gorontalo *Indonesia* 0°35N 123°5E **37 D6**
Gorontalo □ *Indonesia* 0°50N 122°20E **37 D6**
Gort *Ireland* 53°3N 8°49W **10 C3**

Gortis *Greece* 35°4N 24°58E **25 D6**
Goryeong *S. Korea* 35°44N 128°15E **35 G15**
Gorzów Wielkopolski
  Poland 52°43N 15°15E **16 B8**
Gosford *Australia* 33°23S 151°18E **63 E5**
Goshen *Calif., U.S.A.* 36°21N 119°25W **78 J7**
Goshen *Ind., U.S.A.* 41°35N 85°50W **81 E11**
Goshen *N.Y., U.S.A.* 41°24N 74°20W **83 E10**
Goshogawara *Japan* 40°48N 140°27E **30 D10**
Goslar *Germany* 51°54N 10°25E **16 C6**
Gospič *Croatia* 44°35N 15°23E **16 F8**
Gosport *U.K.* 50°48N 1°9W **13 G6**
Gosse → *Australia* 19°32S 134°37E **62 B1**
Göta älv → *Sweden* 57°42N 11°54E **9 H14**
Göta kanal *Sweden* 58°30N 15°58E **9 G16**
Götaland *Sweden* 57°30N 14°30E **9 H16**
Göteborg *Sweden* 57°43N 11°59E **9 H14**
Gotha *Germany* 50°56N 10°42E **16 C6**
Gothenburg = Göteborg
  Sweden 57°43N 11°59E **9 H14**
Gothenburg *U.S.A.* 40°56N 100°10W **80 E3**
Gotland *Sweden* 57°30N 18°33E **9 H18**
Gotska Sandön *Sweden* 58°24N 19°15E **9 G18**
Gōtsu *Japan* 35°0N 132°14E **31 G6**
Gott Pk. *Canada* 50°18N 122°16W **70 C4**
Göttingen *Germany* 51°31N 9°55E **16 C5**
Gottwaldov = Zlín
  Czech Rep. 49°14N 17°40E **17 D9**
Goubangzi *China* 41°20N 121°52E **35 D11**
Gouda *Neths.* 52°1N 4°42E **15 B4**
Goudouras, Akra *Greece* 34°59N 26°6E **25 E8**
Gouin, Rés. *Canada* 48°35N 74°40E **72 C5**
Goulburn *Australia* 34°44S 149°44E **63 E4**
Goulburn Is. *Australia* 11°40S 133°20E **62 A1**
Goulimine *Morocco* 28°56N 10°0W **50 C3**
Goundam *Mali* 16°27N 3°40W **50 E5**
Gourits → *S. Africa* 34°21S 21°52E **56 E3**
Gournes *Greece* 35°19N 25°16E **25 D7**
Gouverneur *U.S.A.* 44°20N 75°28W **83 B9**
Gouvia *Greece* 39°39N 19°50E **25 A3**
Governador Valadares
  Brazil 18°15S 41°57W **93 G10**
Governor's Harbour
  Bahamas 25°10N 76°14W **88 A4**
Govindgarh *India* 24°23N 81°18E **43 G9**
Gowan Ra. *Australia* 25°0S 145°0E **62 D4**
Gowanda *U.S.A.* 42°28N 78°56W **82 D6**
Gower *U.K.* 51°35N 4°10W **13 F3**
Gowna, L. *Ireland* 53°51N 7°34W **10 C4**
Goya *Argentina* 29°10S 59°10W **94 B4**
Goyder Lagoon
  Australia 27°3S 138°58E **63 D2**
Goyllarisquisga *Peru* 10°31S 76°24W **92 F3**
Goz Beïda *Chad* 12°10N 21°20E **51 F10**
Gozo *Malta* 36°3N 14°15E **25 C1**
Graaff-Reinet *S. Africa* 32°13S 24°32E **56 E3**
Gračac *Croatia* 44°18N 15°57E **16 F8**
Gracias a Dios, C.
  Honduras 15°0N 83°10W **88 D3**
Graciosa *Azores* 39°4N 28°0W **50 a**
Graciosa, I. *Canary Is.* 29°15N 13°32W **24 E6**
Grado *Spain* 43°23N 6°4W **21 A2**
Grady *U.S.A.* 34°49N 103°19W **77 J12**
Grafham Water *U.K.* 52°19N 0°18W **13 E7**
Grafton *Australia* 29°38S 152°58E **63 D5**
Grafton *N. Dak., U.S.A.* 48°25N 97°25W **80 A5**
Grafton *W. Va., U.S.A.* 39°21N 80°2W **81 F13**
Graham *Canada* 49°20N 90°30W **72 C1**
Graham *U.S.A.* 33°6N 98°35W **84 E5**
Graham, Mt. *U.S.A.* 32°42N 109°52W **77 K9**
Graham Bell, Ostrov = Greem-
  Bell, Ostrov *Russia* 81°0N 62°0E **28 A7**
Graham I. *Canada* 53°40N 132°30W **70 C2**
Graham Land *Antarctica* 65°0S 64°0W **5 C17**
Grahamstown *S. Africa* 33°19S 26°31E **56 E4**
Grahamsville *U.S.A.* 41°51N 74°33W **83 E10**
Grain Coast *W. Afr.* 4°20N 10°0W **50 H3**
Grajagan *Indonesia* 8°35S 114°13E **37 K17**
Grajagan, Teluk
  Indonesia 8°40S 114°18E **37 K17**
Grajaú *Brazil* 5°50S 46°4W **93 E9**
Grajaú → *Brazil* 3°41S 44°48W **93 D10**
Grampian *Australia* 40°58N 78°37W **82 F6**
Grampian Highlands = Grampian
  Mts. *U.K.* 56°50N 4°0W **11 E5**
Grampian Mts. *U.K.* 56°50N 4°0W **11 E5**
Grampians, The
  Australia 37°15S 142°20E **63 F3**
Gran Canaria *Canary Is.* 27°55N 15°35W **24 G4**
Gran Chaco *S. Amer.* 25°0S 61°0W **94 B3**
Gran Desierto del Pinacate △
  Mexico 31°51N 113°32W **86 A2**
Gran Paradiso *Italy* 45°33N 7°17E **20 D7**
Gran Sasso d'Itália *Italy* 42°27N 13°42E **22 C5**
Granada *Nic.* 11°58N 86°0W **88 D2**
Granada *Spain* 37°10N 3°35W **21 D4**
Granada *U.S.A.* 38°4N 102°19W **76 G12**
Granadilla de Abona
  Canary Is. 28°7N 16°33W **24 F3**
Granard *Ireland* 53°47N 7°30W **10 C4**
Granbury *U.S.A.* 32°27N 97°47W **84 E6**
Granby *Canada* 45°25N 72°45W **83 A12**
Granby *U.S.A.* 40°5N 105°56W **76 F11**
Grand → *Canada* 42°51N 79°34W **82 D5**
Grand → *Mo., U.S.A.* 39°23N 93°7W **80 F7**
Grand → *S. Dak.,*
  U.S.A. 45°40N 100°45W **80 C3**
Grand Bahama I.
  Bahamas 26°40N 78°30W **88 A4**
Grand Baie *Mauritius* 20°0S 57°35E **53 d**
Grand Bassam *Ivory C.* 5°10N 3°49W **50 G5**
Grand-Bourg *Guadeloupe* 15°53N 61°19W **88 b**
Grand Canal = Da Yunhe →
  China 39°10N 117°10E **35 E9**
Grand Canyon *U.S.A.* 36°3N 112°9W **77 H7**

Grand Canyon △
  U.S.A. 36°15N 112°30W **77 H7**
Grand Canyon-Parashant △
  U.S.A. 36°30N 113°45W **77 H7**
Grand Cayman
  Cayman Is. 19°20N 81°20W **88 C3**
Grand Centre *Canada* 54°25N 110°13W **71 C6**
Grand Coulee *U.S.A.* 47°57N 119°0W **76 C4**
Grand Coulee Dam
  U.S.A. 47°57N 118°59W **76 C4**
Grand Erg de Bilma *Niger* 18°30N 14°0E **51 E8**
Grand Falls *Canada* 47°3N 67°44W **73 C6**
Grand Falls-Windsor
  Canada 48°56N 55°40W **73 C8**
Grand Forks *Canada* 49°0N 118°30W **70 D5**
Grand Forks *U.S.A.* 47°55N 97°3W **80 B5**
Grand Gorge *U.S.A.* 42°21N 74°29W **83 D10**
Grand Haven *U.S.A.* 43°4N 86°13W **80 D10**
Grand I. *Mich., U.S.A.* 46°31N 86°40W **80 B10**
Grand I. *N.Y., U.S.A.* 43°0N 78°58W **82 D6**
Grand Island *U.S.A.* 40°55N 98°21W **80 E5**
Grand Isle *La., U.S.A.* 29°14N 90°0W **85 G9**
Grand Isle *Vt., U.S.A.* 44°43N 73°18W **83 B11**
Grand Junction *U.S.A.* 39°4N 108°33W **76 G9**
Grand L. *N.B., Canada* 45°57N 66°7W **73 C6**
Grand L. *Nfld. & L.,*
  Canada 49°0N 57°30W **73 C8**
Grand L. *Nfld. & L.,*
  Canada 53°40N 60°30W **73 B7**
Grand L. *U.S.A.* 29°55N 92°47W **84 G8**
Grand Lake *U.S.A.* 40°15N 105°49W **76 F11**
Grand Manan I. *Canada* 44°45N 66°52W **73 D6**
Grand Marais *Mich.,*
  U.S.A. 46°40N 85°59W **81 B11**
Grand Marais *Minn.,*
  U.S.A. 47°45N 90°25W **72 C1**
Grand-Mère *Canada* 46°36N 72°40W **72 C5**
Grand Portage *U.S.A.* 47°58N 89°41W **80 B9**
Grand Prairie *U.S.A.* 32°44N 96°59W **84 E6**
Grand Rapids *Canada* 53°12N 99°19W **71 C9**
Grand Rapids *Mich.,*
  U.S.A. 42°58N 85°40W **81 D11**
Grand Rapids *Minn.,*
  U.S.A. 47°14N 93°31W **80 B7**
Grand St-Bernard, Col du
  Europe 45°50N 7°10E **20 D7**
Grand Staircase-Escalante △
  U.S.A. 37°25N 111°33W **77 H8**
Grand Teton *U.S.A.* 43°54N 110°50W **76 E8**
Grand Teton △ *U.S.A.* 43°50N 110°50W **76 E8**
Grand Union Canal *U.K.* 52°7N 0°53W **13 E7**
Grande → *Jujuy,*
  Argentina 24°20S 65°2W **94 A2**
Grande → *Mendoza,*
  Argentina 36°52S 69°45W **94 D2**
Grande → *Bolivia* 15°51S 64°39W **92 G6**
Grande → *Bahia,*
  Brazil 11°30S 44°30W **93 F10**
Grande → *Minas Gerais,*
  Brazil 20°6S 51°4W **95 H8**
Grande, B. *Argentina* 50°30S 68°20W **96 G3**
Grande, Rio → *N. Amer.* 25°58N 97°9W **84 J6**
Grande Baleine, R. de la →
  Canada 55°16N 77°47W **72 A4**
Grande Cache *Canada* 53°53N 119°8W **70 C5**
Grande Comore
  Comoros Is. 11°35S 43°20E **53 a**
Grande-Entrée *Canada* 47°30N 61°40W **73 C7**
Grande Prairie *Canada* 55°10N 118°50W **70 B5**
Grande-Rivière *Canada* 48°26N 64°30W **73 C7**
Grande-Terre *Guadeloupe* 16°20N 61°25W **88 b**
Grande-Vallée *Canada* 49°14N 65°8W **73 C6**
Grande Vigie, Pte. de la
  Guadeloupe 16°32N 61°27W **88 b**
Grandfalls *U.S.A.* 31°20N 102°51W **84 F3**
Grands-Jardins △
  Canada 47°41N 70°51W **73 C5**
Grandview *Canada* 51°10N 100°42W **71 C8**
Grandview *U.S.A.* 46°15N 119°54W **76 C4**
Graneros *Chile* 34°5S 70°45W **94 C1**
Grangemouth *U.K.* 56°1N 3°42W **11 E5**
Granger *U.S.A.* 41°35N 109°58W **76 F9**
Grangeville *U.S.A.* 45°56N 116°7W **76 D5**
Granisle *Canada* 54°53N 126°13W **70 C3**
Granite City *U.S.A.* 38°42N 90°8W **80 F8**
Granite Falls *U.S.A.* 44°49N 95°33W **80 C6**
Granite L. *Canada* 48°8N 57°5W **73 C8**
Granite Mt. *U.S.A.* 33°5N 116°28W **79 M10**
Granite Pk. *U.S.A.* 45°10N 109°48W **76 D9**
Graniteville *U.S.A.* 44°8N 72°29W **83 B12**
Granity *N.Z.* 41°39S 171°51E **59 D3**
Granja *Brazil* 3°7S 40°50W **93 D10**
Granollers *Spain* 41°39N 2°18E **21 B7**
Grant *U.S.A.* 40°50N 101°43W **80 E3**
Grant, Mt. *U.S.A.* 38°34N 118°48W **76 G4**
Grant City *U.S.A.* 40°29N 94°25W **80 E6**
Grant I. *Australia* 11°10S 132°52E **60 B5**
Grant Range *U.S.A.* 38°30N 115°25E **76 G6**
Grantham *U.K.* 52°55N 0°38W **12 E7**
Grantown-on-Spey *U.K.* 57°20N 3°36W **11 D5**
Grants *U.S.A.* 35°9N 107°52W **77 J10**
Grants Pass *U.S.A.* 42°26N 123°19W **76 E2**
Grantsville *U.S.A.* 40°36N 112°28W **76 F7**
Granville *France* 48°50N 1°35W **20 B3**
Granville *N. Dak.,*
  U.S.A. 48°16N 100°47W **80 A3**
Granville *N.Y., U.S.A.* 43°24N 73°16W **83 C11**
Granville *Ohio, U.S.A.* 40°4N 82°31W **82 F2**
Granville L. *Canada* 56°18N 100°30W **71 B8**
Graskop *S. Africa* 24°56S 30°49E **57 C5**
Grass → *Canada* 56°3N 96°33W **71 B9**
Grass Range *U.S.A.* 47°2N 108°48W **76 C9**
Grass River → *Canada* 54°0N 100°50W **76 E9**
Grass Valley *Calif.,*
  U.S.A. 39°13N 121°4W **78 F6**
Grass Valley *Oreg.,*
  U.S.A. 45°22N 120°47W **76 D3**

Grasse *France* 43°38N 6°56E **20 E7**
Grassflat *U.S.A.* 41°0N 78°6W **82 E6**
Grasslands △ *Canada* 49°11N 107°38W **71 D7**
Grassy *Australia* 40°3S 144°5E **63 G3**
Graulhet *France* 43°45N 1°59E **20 E4**
Gravelbourg *Canada* 49°50N 106°35W **71 D7**
's-Gravenhage *Neths.* 52°7N 4°17E **15 B4**
Gravenhurst *Canada* 44°52N 79°20W **82 B5**
Gravesend *Australia* 29°35S 150°20E **63 D5**
Gravesend *U.K.* 51°26N 0°22E **13 F8**
Gravois, Pointe-à- *Haiti* 16°15N 73°56W **89 C5**
Grayling *U.S.A.* 44°40N 84°43W **81 C11**
Grays *U.K.* 51°28N 0°21E **13 F8**
Grays Harbor *U.S.A.* 46°59N 124°1W **76 C1**
Grays L. *U.S.A.* 43°4N 111°26W **76 E8**
Grays River *U.S.A.* 46°21N 123°37W **78 D3**
Graz *Austria* 47°4N 15°27E **16 E8**
Greasy L. *Canada* 62°55N 122°12W **70 A4**
Great Abaco I. = Abaco I.
  Bahamas 26°25N 77°10W **88 A4**
Great Artesian Basin
  Australia 23°0S 144°0E **62 C3**
Great Australian Bight
  Australia 33°30S 130°0E **61 F5**
Great Bahama Bank
  Bahamas 23°15N 78°0W **88 B4**
Great Barrier I. *N.Z.* 36°11S 175°25E **59 B5**
Great Barrier Reef
  Australia 18°0S 146°50E **62 B4**
Great Barrier Reef △
  Australia 20°0S 150°0E **62 B4**
Great Barrington
  U.S.A. 42°12N 73°22W **83 D11**
Great Basalt Wall △
  Australia 19°52S 145°43E **62 B4**
Great Basin *U.S.A.* 40°0N 117°0W **76 G5**
Great Basin △ *U.S.A.* 38°56N 114°15W **76 G6**
Great Bear → *Canada* 65°0N 124°0W **68 C7**
Great Bear L. *Canada* 65°30N 120°0W **68 C8**
Great Belt = Store Bælt
  Denmark 55°20N 11°0E **9 J14**
Great Bend *Kans.,*
  U.S.A. 38°22N 98°46W **80 F4**
Great Bend *Pa., U.S.A.* 41°58N 75°45W **83 E9**
Great Blasket I. *Ireland* 52°6N 10°32W **10 D1**
Great Britain *Europe* 54°0N 2°15W **6 E5**
Great Camanoe
  Br. Virgin Is. 18°30N 64°35W **89 e**
Great Codroy *Canada* 47°51N 59°16W **73 C8**
Great Divide, The = Great
  Dividing Ra. *Australia* 23°0S 146°0E **62 C4**
Great Divide Basin
  U.S.A. 42°0N 108°0W **76 E9**
Great Dividing Ra.
  Australia 23°0S 146°0E **62 C4**
Great Driffield = Driffield
  U.K. 54°0N 0°26W **12 C7**
Great Exuma I.
  Bahamas 23°30N 75°50W **88 B4**
Great Falls *U.S.A.* 47°30N 111°17W **76 C8**
Great Fish = Groot-Vis →
  S. Africa 33°28S 27°5E **56 E4**
Great Guana Cay
  Bahamas 24°0N 76°20W **88 B4**
Great Harbour Deep
  Canada 50°26N 56°32W **73 B8**
Great Himalayan △
  India 31°30N 77°30E **42 D7**
Great Inagua I. *Bahamas* 21°0N 73°20W **89 B5**
Great Indian Desert = Thar
  Desert *India* 28°0N 72°0E **42 F5**
Great Karoo *S. Africa* 31°55S 21°0E **56 E3**
Great Khingan Mts. = Da
  Hinggan Ling *China* 48°0N 121°0E **33 B7**
Great Lake *Australia* 41°50S 146°40E **63 G4**
Great Lakes *N. Amer.* 46°0N 84°0W **75 A10**
Great Malvern *U.K.* 52°7N 2°18W **13 E5**
Great Miami → *U.S.A.* 39°7N 84°49W **81 F11**
Great Ormes Head *U.K.* 53°20N 3°52W **12 D4**
Great Ouse → *U.S.A.* 52°48N 0°21E **12 E8**
Great Palm I. *Australia* 18°45S 146°40E **62 B4**
Great Pedro Bluff
  Jamaica 17°51N 77°44W **88 a**
Great Pee Dee →
  U.S.A. 33°21N 79°10W **85 E15**
Great Plains *N. Amer.* 47°0N 105°0W **74 A6**
Great Ruaha → *Tanzania* 7°56S 37°52E **54 D4**
Great Sacandaga L.
  U.S.A. 43°6N 74°16W **83 C10**
Great Saint Bernard Pass = Grand
  St-Bernard, Col du
  Europe 45°50N 7°10E **20 D7**
Great Salt Desert = Kavīr,
  Dasht-e *Iran* 34°30N 55°0E **45 C7**
Great Salt L. *U.S.A.* 41°15N 112°40W **76 F7**
Great Salt Lake Desert
  U.S.A. 40°50N 113°30W **76 F7**
Great Salt Plains L.
  U.S.A. 36°45N 98°8W **84 C5**
Great Sand Dunes △
  U.S.A. 37°48N 105°45W **77 H11**
Great Sandy △ *Australia* 26°13S 153°2E **63 D5**
Great Sandy Desert
  Australia 21°0S 124°0E **60 D3**
Great Sandy Desert
  U.S.A. 43°35N 120°15W **74 B2**
Great Sangi = Sangihe, Pulau
  Indonesia 3°35N 125°30E **37 D7**
Great Sea Reef *Fiji* 16°15S 179°0E **59 a**
Great Skellig *Ireland* 51°47N 10°33W **10 E1**
Great Slave L. *Canada* 61°23N 115°38W **70 A5**
Great Smoky Mts. △
  U.S.A. 35°40N 83°40W **85 D13**
Great Snow Mt. *Canada* 57°26N 124°0W **70 B4**
Great Stour = Stour →
  U.K. 51°18N 1°22E **13 F9**
Great Victoria Desert
  Australia 29°30S 126°30E **61 E4**

Great Wall *Antarctica* 62°30S 58°0W **5 C18**
Great Wall *China* 38°30N 109°30E **34 E5**
Great Whernside *U.K.* 54°10N 1°58W **12 C6**
Great Yarmouth *U.K.* 52°37N 1°44E **13 E9**
Great Zab = Zāb al Kabīr →
  Iraq 36°1N 43°24E **44 C4**
Great Zimbabwe
  Zimbabwe 20°16S 30°54E **55 G3**
Greater Antilles
  W. Indies 17°40N 74°0W **89 C5**
Greater London □ *U.K.* 51°31N 0°6W **13 F7**
Greater Manchester □
  U.K. 53°30N 2°15W **12 D5**
Greater St. Lucia Wetlands △
  S. Africa 28°6S 32°27E **57 D5**
Greater Sudbury = Sudbury
  Canada 46°30N 81°0W **72 C3**
Greater Sunda Is. *Indonesia* 7°0S 112°0E **36 F4**
Greco, C. *Cyprus* 34°57N 34°5E **25 E13**
Gredos, Sierra de *Spain* 40°20N 5°0W **21 B3**
Greece ■ *Europe* 40°0N 23°0E **23 E9**
Greeley *Colo., U.S.A.* 40°25N 104°42W **76 F11**
Greeley *Nebr., U.S.A.* 41°33N 98°32W **80 E4**
Greely Fd. *Canada* 80°30N 85°0W **69 A11**
Greem-Bell, Ostrov *Russia* 81°0N 62°0E **28 A7**
Green → *Ky., U.S.A.* 37°54N 87°30W **80 G10**
Green → *Utah, U.S.A.* 38°11N 109°53W **76 G9**
Green B. *U.S.A.* 45°0N 87°30W **80 C9**
Green Bay *U.S.A.* 44°31N 88°0W **80 C9**
Green C. *Australia* 37°13S 150°1E **63 F5**
Green Cove Springs
  U.S.A. 29°59N 81°42W **85 G14**
Green Lake *Canada* 54°17N 107°47W **71 C7**
Green Mts. *U.S.A.* 43°45N 72°45W **83 C12**
Green River *Utah,*
  U.S.A. 38°59N 110°10W **76 G8**
Green River *Wyo.,*
  U.S.A. 41°32N 109°28W **76 F9**
Green Valley *U.S.A.* 31°52N 110°56W **77 L8**
Greenbank *U.S.A.* 48°6N 122°34W **78 B4**
Greenbush *Mich.,*
  U.S.A. 44°35N 83°19W **82 B1**
Greenbush *Minn.,*
  U.S.A. 48°42N 96°11W **80 A5**
Greencastle *U.S.A.* 39°38N 86°52W **80 F10**
Greene *U.S.A.* 42°20N 75°46W **83 D9**
Greeneville *U.S.A.* 36°10N 82°50W **85 C13**
Greenfield *Calif., U.S.A.* 36°19N 121°15W **78 J5**
Greenfield *Calif., U.S.A.* 35°15N 119°0W **79 K8**
Greenfield *Ind., U.S.A.* 39°47N 85°46W **81 F11**
Greenfield *Iowa, U.S.A.* 41°18N 94°28W **80 E6**
Greenfield *Mass.,*
  U.S.A. 42°35N 72°36W **83 D12**
Greenfield *Mo., U.S.A.* 37°25N 93°51W **80 G7**
Greenfield Park
  Canada 45°29N 73°28W **83 A11**
Greenland ☒ *N. Amer.* 66°0N 45°0W **67 C15**
Greenland Sea *Arctic* 73°0N 10°0W **4 B7**
Greenock *U.K.* 55°57N 4°46W **11 F4**
Greenore *Ireland* 54°2N 6°8W **10 B5**
Greenore Pt. *Ireland* 52°14N 6°19W **10 D5**
Greenough *Australia* 28°51S 114°38E **61 E1**
Greenough Pt. *Canada* 44°58N 81°26W **82 B3**
Greenport *U.S.A.* 41°6N 72°22W **83 E12**
Greensboro *Ga., U.S.A.* 33°35N 83°11W **85 E13**
Greensboro *N.C., U.S.A.* 36°4N 79°48W **85 C15**
Greensboro *Vt., U.S.A.* 44°36N 72°18W **83 B12**
Greensburg *Ind.,*
  U.S.A. 39°20N 85°29W **81 F11**
Greensburg *Kans.,*
  U.S.A. 37°36N 99°18W **80 G4**
Greensburg *Pa., U.S.A.* 40°18N 79°33W **82 F5**
Greenstone Pt. *U.K.* 57°55N 5°37W **11 D3**
Greenvale *Australia* 18°59S 145°7E **62 B4**
Greenville *Liberia* 5°1N 9°6W **50 G4**
Greenville *Ala., U.S.A.* 31°50N 86°38W **85 F11**
Greenville *Calif., U.S.A.* 40°8N 120°57W **78 E6**
Greenville *Maine,*
  U.S.A. 45°28N 69°35W **81 C19**
Greenville *Mich.,*
  U.S.A. 43°11N 85°15W **81 D11**
Greenville *Mo., U.S.A.* 37°8N 90°27W **80 G8**
Greenville *N.C., U.S.A.* 35°37N 77°23W **85 D16**
Greenville *N.H., U.S.A.* 42°46N 71°49W **83 D13**
Greenville *N.Y., U.S.A.* 42°25N 74°1W **83 D10**
Greenville *Ohio, U.S.A.* 40°6N 84°38W **81 E11**
Greenville *Pa., U.S.A.* 41°24N 80°23W **82 E4**
Greenville *S.C., U.S.A.* 34°51N 82°24W **85 D13**
Greenville *Tex., U.S.A.* 33°8N 96°7W **84 E6**
Greenwater Lake △
  Canada 52°32N 103°30W **71 C8**
Greenwich *Conn.,*
  U.S.A. 41°2N 73°38W **83 E11**
Greenwich *N.Y., U.S.A.* 43°5N 73°30W **83 C11**
Greenwich *Ohio, U.S.A.* 41°2N 82°31W **82 E2**
Greenwich □ *U.K.* 51°29N 0°1E **13 F8**
Greenwood *Canada* 49°10N 118°40W **70 D5**
Greenwood *Ark., U.S.A.* 35°13N 94°16W **84 D7**
Greenwood *Miss.,*
  U.S.A. 33°31N 90°11W **85 E9**
Greenwood *S.C.,*
  U.S.A. 34°12N 82°10W **85 D13**
Greenwood, Mt.
  Australia 13°48S 130°4E **60 B5**
Gregory *U.S.A.* 43°14N 99°26W **80 D4**
Gregory → *Australia* 17°53S 139°17E **62 B2**
Gregory, L. *S. Austral.,*
  Australia 28°55S 139°0E **63 D2**
Gregory, L. *W. Austral.,*
  Australia 20°0S 127°40E **60 D4**
Gregory, L. *W. Austral.,*
  Australia 25°38S 119°58E **61 E2**
Gregory △ *Australia* 15°38S 131°15E **60 C5**

Gregory Downs Australia 18°35S 138°45E 62 B2
Gregory Ra. Queens., Australia 19°30S 143°40E 62 B3
Gregory Ra. W. Austral., Australia 21°20S 121°12E 60 D3
Greifswald Germany 54°5N 13°23E 16 A7
Greiz Germany 50°39N 12°10E 16 C7
Gremikha Russia 67°59N 39°47E 18 A6
Grenaa Denmark 56°25N 10°53E 9 H14
Grenada U.S.A. 33°47N 89°49W 85 E10
Grenada ■ W. Indies 12°10N 61°40W 89 D7
Grenadier I. U.S.A. 44°3N 76°22W 83 B8
Grenadines, The St. Vincent 12°40N 61°20W 89 D7
Grenen Denmark 57°44N 10°40E 9 H14
Grenfell Australia 33°52S 148°8E 63 E4
Grenfell Canada 50°30N 102°56W 71 C8
Grenoble France 45°12N 5°42E 20 D6
Grenville, C. Australia 12°0S 143°13E 62 A3
Grenville Chan. Canada 53°40N 129°46W 70 C3
Gresham U.S.A. 45°29N 122°25W 78 E4
Gresik Indonesia 7°13S 112°38E 37 G15
Gretna U.K. 55°0N 3°3W 11 F5
Gretna U.S.A. 29°54N 90°3W 85 G9
Grevenmacher Lux. 49°41N 6°26E 15 E6
Grey → Canada 47°34N 57°6W 73 C8
Grey → N.Z. 42°27S 171°12E 59 E3
Grey, C. Australia 13°0S 136°35E 62 A2
Grey Ra. Australia 27°0S 143°30E 63 D3
Greybull U.S.A. 44°30N 108°3W 76 D9
Greymouth N.Z. 42°29S 171°13E 59 E3
Greystones Ireland 53°9N 6°5W 10 C5
Greytown N.Z. 41°5S 175°29E 59 D5
Greytown S. Africa 29°1S 30°36E 57 D5
Gribbell I. Canada 53°23N 129°0W 70 C3
Gridley U.S.A. 39°22N 121°42W 78 F5
Griekwastad S. Africa 28°49S 23°15E 56 D3
Griffin U.S.A. 33°15N 84°16W 85 E12
Griffith Australia 34°18S 146°2E 63 E4
Griffith Canada 45°15N 77°10W 82 A7
Griffith I. Canada 44°50N 80°55W 82 B4
Grimaylov = Hrymayliv Ukraine 49°20N 26°5E 17 D14
Grimes U.S.A. 39°4N 121°54W 78 F5
Grimsay U.K. 57°29N 7°14W 11 D1
Grimsby Canada 43°12N 79°34W 82 C5
Grimsby U.K. 53°34N 0°5W 12 D7
Grímsey Iceland 66°33N 17°58W 8 C5
Grimshaw Canada 56°10N 117°40W 70 B5
Grimstad Norway 58°20N 8°35E 9 G13
Grindstone I. Canada 44°43N 76°14W 83 B8
Grinnell U.S.A. 41°45N 92°43W 80 E7
Gris-Nez, C. France 50°52N 1°35E 20 A4
Grise Fiord Canada 76°25N 82°57W 69 B11
Groais I. Canada 50°55N 55°35W 73 B8
Groblersdal S. Africa 25°15S 29°25E 57 D4
Grodno = Hrodna Belarus 53°42N 23°52E 17 B12
Grodzyanka = Hrodzyanka Belarus 53°31N 28°42E 17 B15
Groesbeck U.S.A. 31°31N 96°32W 84 F6
Grójec Poland 51°50N 20°58E 17 C11
Grong Norway 64°25N 12°8E 8 D15
Groningen Neths. 53°15N 6°35E 15 A6
Groningen □ Neths. 53°16N 6°40E 15 A6
Groom U.S.A. 35°12N 101°6W 84 D4
Groot → S. Africa 33°45S 24°36E 56 E3
Groot-Berg → S. Africa 32°47S 18°8E 56 E2
Groot-Brakrivier S. Africa 34°2S 22°18E 56 E3
Groot Karasberge Namibia 27°20S 18°40E 56 D2
Groot-Kei → S. Africa 32°41S 28°22E 57 E4
Groot-Vis → S. Africa 33°28S 27°5E 56 E4
Grootdrink S. Africa 28°33S 21°42E 56 D3
Groote Eylandt Australia 14°0S 136°40E 62 A2
Grootfontein Namibia 19°31S 18°6E 56 B2
Grootlaagte → Africa 20°55S 21°27E 56 C3
Grootvloer → S. Africa 30°0S 20°40E 56 E3
Gros C. Canada 61°59N 113°32W 70 A6
Gros Islet St. Lucia 14°5N 60°58W 89 f
Gros Morne △ Canada 49°40N 57°50W 73 C8
Gros Piton St. Lucia 13°49N 61°5W 89 f
Gros Piton Pt. St. Lucia 13°49N 61°5W 89 f
Grossa, Pta. Spain 39°6N 1°36E 24 B8
Grosser Arber Germany 49°6N 13°8E 16 D7
Grosseto Italy 42°46N 11°8E 22 C4
Grossglockner Austria 47°5N 12°40E 16 E7
Groswater B. Canada 54°20N 57°40W 73 B8
Groton Conn., U.S.A. 41°21N 72°5W 83 E12
Groton N.Y., U.S.A. 42°36N 76°22W 83 D8
Groton S. Dak., U.S.A. 45°27N 98°6W 80 C4
Grouard Mission Canada 55°33N 116°9W 70 B5
Groundhog → Canada 48°45N 82°58W 72 C3
Grouw Neths. 53°5N 5°51E 15 A5
Grove City U.S.A. 41°10N 80°5W 82 E4
Grove Hill U.S.A. 31°42N 87°47W 85 F11
Groveland U.S.A. 37°50N 120°14W 78 H6
Grover Beach U.S.A. 35°7N 120°37W 79 K6
Groves U.S.A. 29°57N 93°54W 84 G8
Groveton U.S.A. 44°36N 71°31W 83 B13
Groznyy Russia 43°20N 45°45E 19 F8
Grudziądz Poland 53°30N 18°47E 17 B10
Gruinard B. U.K. 57°56N 5°35W 11 D3
Grundy Center U.S.A. 42°22N 92°47W 80 D7
Gruver U.S.A. 36°16N 101°24W 84 C4
Gryazi Russia 52°30N 39°58E 18 D6
Gryazovets Russia 58°50N 40°10E 18 C7
Gua India 22°18N 85°20E 43 H11
Gua Musang Malaysia 4°53N 101°58E 39 K3
Guacanayabo, G. de Cuba 20°40N 77°20W 88 B4
Guachípas → Argentina 25°40S 65°30W 94 B2
Guadalajara Mexico 20°40N 103°20W 86 C4
Guadalajara Spain 40°37N 3°12W 21 B4
Guadalcanal Solomon Is. 9°32S 160°12E 58 B9
Guadales Argentina 34°30S 67°55W 94 C2
Guadalete → Spain 36°35N 6°13W 21 D2
Guadalquivir → Spain 36°47N 6°22W 21 D2
Guadalupe = Guadeloupe ⊠ W. Indies 16°20N 61°40W 88 b
Guadalupe Mexico 32°4N 116°32W 79 N10
Guadalupe Zacatecas, Mexico 22°45N 102°31W 86 C4
Guadalupe U.S.A. 34°58N 120°34W 79 L6
Guadalupe → Mexico 32°6N 116°51W 79 N10
Guadalupe → U.S.A. 28°27N 96°47W 84 G6
Guadalupe, Sierra de Spain 39°28N 5°30W 21 C3
Guadalupe Bravos Mexico 31°20N 106°10W 86 A3
Guadalupe I. Pac. Oc. 29°0N 118°50W 66 G8
Guadalupe Mts. △ U.S.A. 31°40N 104°30W 84 F2
Guadalupe Peak U.S.A. 31°50N 104°52W 84 F2
Guadalupe y Calvo Mexico 26°6N 106°58W 86 B3
Guadarrama, Sierra de Spain 41°0N 4°0W 21 B4
Guadeloupe ⊠ W. Indies 16°20N 61°40W 88 b
Guadeloupe △ Guadeloupe 16°10N 61°40W 88 b
Guadeloupe Passage W. Indies 16°50N 62°15W 89 C7
Guadiana → Portugal 37°14N 7°22W 21 D2
Guadix Spain 37°18N 3°11W 21 D4
Guafo, Boca del Chile 43°35S 74°0W 96 E2
Guaico Trin. & Tob. 10°35N 61°9W 93 K15
Guainía → Colombia 2°1N 67°7W 92 C5
Guaíra Brazil 24°5S 54°10W 95 A5
Guaíra □ Paraguay 25°45S 56°30W 94 B4
Guaitecas, Is. Chile 44°0S 74°30W 96 E2
Guajará-Mirim Brazil 10°50S 65°20W 92 F5
Guajira, Pen. de la Colombia 12°0N 72°0W 92 A4
Gualán Guatemala 15°8N 89°22W 88 C2
Gualeguay Argentina 33°10S 59°14W 94 C4
Gualeguaychú Argentina 33°3S 59°31W 94 C4
Gualequay → Argentina 33°19S 59°39W 94 C4
Guam ⊠ Pac. Oc. 13°27N 144°45E 64 F6
Guaminí Argentina 37°1S 62°28W 94 D3
Guamúchil Mexico 25°28N 108°6W 86 B3
Guana I. Br. Virgin Is. 18°30N 64°30W 89 e
Guanabacoa Cuba 23°8N 82°18W 88 B3
Guanacaste, Cordillera del Costa Rica 10°40N 85°4W 88 D2
Guanacaste △ Costa Rica 10°57N 85°30W 88 D2
Guanaceví Mexico 25°56N 105°57W 86 B3
Guanahani = San Salvador I. Bahamas 24°0N 74°40W 89 B5
Guanajay Cuba 22°56N 82°42W 88 B3
Guanajuato Mexico 21°1N 101°15W 86 C4
Guanajuato □ Mexico 21°0N 101°0W 86 C4
Guandacol Argentina 29°30S 68°40W 94 B2
Guane Cuba 22°10N 84°7W 88 B3
Guangdong □ China 23°0N 113°0E 33 D6
Guangling China 39°47N 114°22E 34 E8
Guangrao China 37°5N 118°25E 35 F10
Guangwu China 37°48N 105°57E 34 F3
Guangxi Zhuangzu Zizhiqu □ China 24°0N 109°0E 33 D5
Guangzhou China 23°6N 113°13E 33 D6
Guanica Puerto Rico 17°58N 66°55W 89 d
Guanipa → Venezuela 9°56N 62°26W 92 B6
Guannan China 34°8N 119°21E 35 G10
Guantánamo Cuba 20°10N 75°14W 89 B4
Guantánamo B. Cuba 19°59N 75°10W 89 C4
Guantao China 36°42N 115°25E 34 F8
Guanyun China 34°20N 119°18E 35 G10
Guápiles Costa Rica 10°10N 83°46W 88 D3
Guapo B. Trin. & Tob. 10°12N 61°41W 93 K15
Guaporé Brazil 28°51S 51°54W 95 B5
Guaporé → Brazil 11°55S 65°4W 92 F5
Guaqui Bolivia 16°41S 68°54W 92 G5
Guaramacal △ Venezuela 9°13N 70°12W 89 E5
Guarapari Brazil 20°40S 40°30W 95 A7
Guarapuava Brazil 25°20S 51°30W 95 B5
Guaratinguetá Brazil 22°49S 45°9W 95 A6
Guaratuba Brazil 25°53S 48°38W 95 B6
Guarda Portugal 40°32N 7°20W 21 B2
Guardafui, C. = Asir, Ras Somali Rep. 11°55N 51°10E 47 E5
Guárico □ Venezuela 8°40N 66°35W 92 B5
Guarujá Brazil 24°2S 46°25W 95 A6
Guarulhos Brazil 23°29S 46°33W 95 A6
Guarus Brazil 21°44S 41°20W 95 A7
Guasave Mexico 25°34N 108°27W 86 B3
Guasdualito Venezuela 7°15N 70°44W 92 B4
Guatemala Guatemala 14°40N 90°22W 88 D1
Guatemala ■ Cent. Amer. 15°40N 90°30W 88 C1
Guatemala Basin Pac. Oc. 11°0N 95°0W 65 F18
Guatemala Trench Pac. Oc. 14°0N 95°0W 66 H10
Guatopo △ Venezuela 10°5N 66°30W 89 D6
Guatuaro Pt. Trin. & Tob. 10°19N 60°59W 93 K16
Guaviare → Colombia 4°3N 67°44W 92 C5
Guaxupé Brazil 21°10S 47°5W 95 A6
Guayaguayare Trin. & Tob. 10°8N 61°2W 93 K15
Guayama Puerto Rico 17°59N 66°7W 89 d
Guayaquil Ecuador 2°15S 79°52W 92 D3
Guayaquil Mexico 29°59N 115°4W 86 B1
Guayaquil, G. de Ecuador 3°10S 81°0W 92 D2
Guaymas Mexico 27°56N 110°54W 86 B2
Guba Dem. Rep. of the Congo 10°38S 26°27E 55 E2
Gubkin Russia 51°17N 37°32E 19 D6
Gudbrandsdalen Norway 61°33N 10°10E 8 F14
Guddu Barrage Pakistan 28°30N 69°50E 42 E3
Gudur India 14°12N 79°55E 40 M11
Guecho = Getxo Spain 43°21N 2°59W 21 A4
Guékédou Guinea 8°40N 10°5W 50 G3
Guelmine = Goulimine Morocco 28°56N 10°0W 50 C3
Guelph Canada 43°35N 80°20W 82 C4
Guéret France 46°11N 1°51E 20 C4
Guerneville U.S.A. 38°30N 123°0W 78 G4
Guernica = Gernika-Lumo Spain 43°19N 2°40W 21 A4
Guernsey U.K. 49°26N 2°35W 13 H5
Guernsey U.S.A. 42°16N 104°45W 76 E11
Guerrero □ Mexico 17°40N 100°0W 87 D5
Gügher Iran 29°28N 56°27E 45 D8
Guhakolak, Tanjung Indonesia 6°50S 105°14E 37 G11
Guia Canary Is. 28°8N 15°38W 24 F4
Guia de Isora Canary Is. 28°12N 16°46W 24 F3
Guia Lopes da Laguna Brazil 21°26S 56°7W 95 A4
Guiana Highlands S. Amer. 5°10N 60°40W 90 C4
Guidónia-Montecélio Italy 42°1N 12°45E 22 C5
Guijá Mozam. 24°27S 33°0E 57 C5
Guildford U.K. 51°14N 0°34W 13 F7
Guilford U.S.A. 41°17N 72°41W 83 E12
Guilin China 25°18N 110°15E 33 D6
Guillaume-Delisle, L. Canada 56°15N 76°17W 72 A4
Güimar Canary Is. 28°18N 16°24W 24 F3
Guimarães Portugal 41°28N 8°24W 21 B1
Guimaras □ Phil. 10°35N 122°37E 37 B6
Guinda U.S.A. 38°50N 122°12W 78 G4
Guinea Africa 8°0N 8°0E 48 F4
Guinea ■ W. Afr. 10°20N 11°30W 50 F3
Guinea, Gulf of Atl. Oc. 3°0N 2°30E 49 F4
Guinea-Bissau ■ Africa 12°0N 15°0W 50 F3
Güines Cuba 22°50N 82°0W 88 B3
Guingamp France 48°34N 3°10W 20 B2
Güiria Venezuela 10°32N 62°18W 92 A6
Guiuan Phil. 11°5N 125°55E 37 B7
Guiyang China 26°32N 106°40E 32 D5
Guizhou □ China 27°0N 107°0E 32 D5
Gujar Khan Pakistan 33°16N 73°19E 42 C5
Gujarat □ India 23°20N 71°0E 42 H4
Gujranwala Pakistan 32°10N 74°12E 42 C6
Gujrat Pakistan 32°40N 74°2E 42 C6
Gulbarga India 17°20N 76°50E 40 L10
Gulbene Latvia 57°8N 26°52E 9 H22
Gulf, The = Persian Gulf Asia 27°0N 50°0E 45 E6
Gulf Islands ⌂ U.S.A. 30°10N 87°10W 85 F11
Gulfport U.S.A. 30°22N 89°6W 85 F10
Gulgong Australia 32°20S 149°49E 63 E4
Gulistan Pakistan 30°30N 66°35E 42 D2
Gull Lake Canada 50°10N 108°29W 71 C7
Güllük Turkey 37°14N 27°35E 23 F12
Gulmarg India 34°3N 74°25E 43 B6
Gülshat Kazakhstan 46°38N 74°21E 28 C8
Gulu Uganda 2°48N 32°17E 54 B3
Gulwe Tanzania 6°30S 36°25E 54 D4
Gumal → Pakistan 31°40N 71°50E 42 D4
Gumbaz Pakistan 30°2N 69°0E 42 D3
Gumel Nigeria 12°39N 9°22E 50 F7
Gumi S. Korea 36°10N 128°12E 35 F15
Gumla India 23°3N 84°33E 43 H11
Gumlu Australia 19°53S 147°41E 62 B4
Gumma □ Japan 36°30N 138°20E 31 F9
Gumzai Indonesia 5°28S 134°42E 37 F8
Guna India 24°40N 77°19E 42 G7
Gunbalanya Australia 12°20S 133°4E 60 B5
Gundabooka △ Australia 30°30S 145°20E 63 E4
Gunisao → Canada 53°56N 97°53W 71 C9
Gunisao L. Canada 53°33N 96°15W 71 C9
Gunjyal Pakistan 32°20N 71°55E 42 C4
Gunnbjørn Fjeld Greenland 68°55N 29°47W 4 C6
Gunnedah Australia 30°59S 150°15E 63 E5
Gunnewin Australia 25°59S 148°33E 63 D4
Gunningbar Cr. → Australia 31°14S 147°6E 63 E4
Gunnison Colo., U.S.A. 38°33N 106°56W 76 G10
Gunnison Utah, U.S.A. 39°9N 111°49W 76 G8
Gunnison → U.S.A. 39°4N 108°35W 76 G9
Gunpowder Australia 19°42S 139°22E 62 B2
Gunsan S. Korea 35°59N 126°45E 35 G14
Guntakal India 15°11N 77°27E 40 M10
Guntersville U.S.A. 34°21N 86°18W 85 D11
Guntong Malaysia 4°36N 101°3E 39 K3
Guntur India 16°23N 80°30E 41 L12
Gunungapi Indonesia 6°45S 126°30E 37 F7
Gunungsitoli Indonesia 1°15N 97°30E 36 D1
Gunza Angola 10°50S 13°50E 52 G2
Guo He → China 32°59N 117°10E 35 H9
Guoyang China 33°32N 116°12E 34 H9
Gupis Pakistan 36°15N 73°20E 43 A5
Gurdaspur India 32°5N 75°31E 42 C6
Gurdon U.S.A. 33°55N 93°9W 84 E8
Gurgaon India 28°27N 77°1E 42 E7
Gurgueia → Brazil 6°50S 43°24W 93 E10
Gurha India 25°12N 71°39E 42 G4
Guri, Embalse de Venezuela 7°50N 62°52W 92 B6
Gurig △ Australia 11°36S 132°7E 60 B5
Gurkha Nepal 28°5N 84°40E 43 E11
Gurley Australia 29°45S 149°48E 63 D4
Gurnet Point U.S.A. 42°1N 70°34W 83 D14
Guro Mozam. 17°26S 32°30E 55 F3
Gurué Mozam. 15°25S 36°58E 55 F4
Gurun Malaysia 5°49N 100°27E 39 K3
Gürün Turkey 38°43N 37°15E 19 G6
Gurupá Brazil 1°25S 51°35W 93 D8
Gurupá, I. Grande de Brazil 1°25S 51°45W 93 D8
Gurupi Brazil 11°43S 49°4W 93 F9
Gurupi → Brazil 1°13S 46°6W 93 D9
Guruwe Zimbabwe 16°40S 30°42E 57 B5
Gurvan Sayhan Uul Mongolia 43°50N 104°0E 32 B5
Guryev = Atyraū Kazakhstan 47°5N 52°0E 19 E9
Gusau Nigeria 12°12N 6°40E 50 F7
Gushan China 39°50N 123°35E 35 E12
Gushgy = Serhetabat Turkmenistan 35°20N 62°18E 45 C9
Gusinoozersk Russia 51°16N 106°27E 29 D11
Gustavus U.S.A. 58°25N 135°44W 70 B1
Gustine U.S.A. 37°16N 121°0W 78 H6
Güstrow Germany 53°47N 12°10E 16 B7
Gütersloh Germany 51°54N 8°24E 16 C5
Gutha Australia 28°58S 115°55E 61 E2
Guthalungra Australia 19°52S 147°50E 62 B4
Guthrie Okla., U.S.A. 35°53N 97°25W 84 D6
Guthrie Tex., U.S.A. 33°37N 100°19W 84 E4
Guttenberg U.S.A. 42°47N 91°6W 80 D8
Gutu Zimbabwe 19°41S 31°9E 57 B5
Guwahati India 26°10N 91°45E 41 F17
Guy Fawkes River △ Australia 30°0S 152°20E 63 D5
Guyana ■ S. Amer. 5°0N 59°0W 92 C7
Guyane française = French Guiana ⊠ S. Amer. 4°0N 53°0W 93 C8
Guyang China 41°0N 110°5E 34 D6
Guyenne France 44°30N 0°40E 20 D4
Guymon U.S.A. 36°41N 101°29W 84 C4
Guyra Australia 30°15S 151°40E 63 E5
Guyuan Hebei, China 41°37N 115°40E 34 D8
Guyuan Ningxia Huizu, China 36°0N 106°20E 34 G4
Güzelyurt = Morphou Cyprus 35°12N 32°59E 25 D11
Guzhen China 33°22N 117°18E 35 H9
Guzmán, L. de Mexico 31°20N 107°30W 86 A3
Gwa Burma 17°36N 94°34E 41 L19
Gwaai Zimbabwe 19°15S 27°45E 55 F2
Gwaai → Zimbabwe 17°59S 26°52E 55 F2
Gwabegar Australia 30°37S 148°59E 63 E4
Gwādar Pakistan 25°10N 62°18E 40 G3
Gwaii Haanas △ Canada 52°21N 131°26W 70 C2
Gwalior India 26°12N 78°10E 42 F8
Gwanda Zimbabwe 20°55S 29°0E 55 G2
Gwane Dem. Rep. of the Congo 4°45N 25°48E 54 B2
Gwangju S. Korea 35°9N 126°54E 35 G14
Gwanju = Gwangju S. Korea 35°9N 126°54E 35 G14
Gweebarra B. Ireland 54°51N 8°23W 10 B3
Gweedore Ireland 55°3N 8°13W 10 A3
Gweru Zimbabwe 19°28S 29°45E 55 F2
Gwinn U.S.A. 46°19N 87°27W 80 B10
Gwydir → Australia 29°27S 149°48E 63 D4
Gwynedd □ U.K. 52°52N 4°10W 12 E3
Gyandzha = Gäncä Azerbaijan 40°45N 46°20E 19 F8
Gyaring Hu China 34°50N 97°40E 32 C4
Gydanskiy Poluostrov Russia 70°0N 78°0E 28 C8
Gyeongju S. Korea 35°51N 129°14E 35 G15
Gympie Australia 26°11S 152°38E 63 D5
Gyöngyös Hungary 47°48N 19°56E 17 E10
Győr Hungary 47°41N 17°40E 17 E9
Gypsum Pt. Canada 61°53N 114°35W 70 A6
Gypsumville Canada 51°45N 98°40W 71 C9
Gyula Hungary 46°38N 21°17E 17 E11
Gyumri Armenia 40°47N 43°50E 19 F7
Gyzylarbat = Serdar Turkmenistan 39°4N 56°23E 45 B8
Gyzyletrek = Etrek Turkmenistan 37°36N 54°46E 45 B7

H

Ha 'Arava → Israel 30°50N 35°20E 46 E4
Ha Coi Vietnam 21°26N 107°46E 38 B6
Ha Dong Vietnam 20°58N 105°46E 38 B5
Ha Giang Vietnam 22°50N 104°59E 38 A5
Ha Karmel △ Israel 32°45N 35°5E 46 C4
Ha Long, Vinh Vietnam 20°56N 107°3E 38 B6
Ha Tien Vietnam 10°23N 104°29E 39 G5
Ha Tinh Vietnam 18°20N 105°54E 38 C5
Ha Trung Vietnam 19°58N 105°50E 38 C5
Ha Yaek Chalong Thailand 7°50N 98°22E 39 a
Haaksbergen Neths. 52°9N 6°45E 15 B6
Ha'ano Tonga 19°41S 174°18W 59 c
Ha'apai Group Tonga 19°47S 174°27W 59 c
Haapiti Moorea 17°34S 149°52W 59 d
Haapsalu Estonia 58°56N 23°30E 9 G20
Haarlem Neths. 52°23N 4°39E 15 B4
Haast → N.Z. 43°50S 169°2E 59 E2
Haast Bluff Australia 23°22S 132°0E 60 D5
Hab → Pakistan 24°53N 66°41E 42 G3
Hab Nadi Chauki Pakistan 25°0N 66°50E 42 G2
Habahe China 48°3N 86°23E 32 B3
Habaswein Kenya 1°2N 39°30E 54 B4
Habay Canada 58°50N 118°44W 70 B5
Ḩabbānīyah Iraq 33°17N 43°29E 44 C4
Haboro Japan 44°22N 141°42E 30 B10
Ḩabshān U.A.E. 23°50N 53°37E 45 F7
Hachijō-Jima Japan 33°5N 139°45E 31 H9
Hachinohe Japan 40°30N 141°29E 30 D10
Hachiōji Japan 35°40N 139°20E 31 G9
Hackensack U.S.A. 40°52N 74°4W 83 F10
Hackettstown U.S.A. 40°51N 74°50W 83 F10
Hadali Pakistan 32°16N 72°11E 42 C5
Hadarba, Ras Sudan 22°4N 36°51E 51 D13
Hadarom □ Israel 31°0N 35°0E 46 E4
Ḩadd, Ra's al Oman 22°35N 59°50E 47 C6
Haddington U.K. 55°57N 2°47W 11 F6
Hadejia Nigeria 12°30N 10°5E 50 F7
Ḩadera Israel 32°27N 34°55E 46 C3
Ḩadera, N. → Israel 32°28N 34°52E 46 C3
Haderslev Denmark 55°15N 9°30E 9 J13
Hadhramaut = Ḩadramawt Yemen 15°30N 49°30E 47 D4
Hadīboh Yemen 12°39N 54°2E 47 E5
Hadong S. Korea 35°5N 127°44E 35 G14
Ḩadramawt Yemen 15°30N 49°30E 47 D4
Ḩadrānīyah Iraq 35°38N 43°14E 44 C4
Hadrian's Wall U.K. 55°0N 2°30W 12 B5
Haeju N. Korea 38°3N 125°45E 35 E13
Haenam S. Korea 34°34N 126°35E 35 G14
Haenertsburg S. Africa 24°0S 29°50E 57 C4
Haerhpin = Harbin China 45°48N 126°40E 35 B14
Hafar al Bāţin Si. Arabia 28°32N 45°52E 44 D5
Ḩafirat al 'Aydā Si. Arabia 26°26N 39°12E 44 E3
Ḩafit Oman 23°59N 55°49E 45 F7
Hafizabad Pakistan 32°5N 73°40E 42 C5
Haflong India 25°10N 93°5E 41 G18
Haft Gel Iran 31°30N 49°32E 45 D6
Hagalil Israel 32°53N 35°18E 46 C4
Hagen Germany 51°21N 7°27E 16 C4
Hagerman U.S.A. 33°7N 104°20W 77 K11
Hagerman Fossil Beds △ U.S.A. 42°48N 114°57W 76 E6
Hagerstown U.S.A. 39°39N 77°43W 81 F15
Hagersville Canada 42°58N 80°3W 82 D4
Hagfors Sweden 60°3N 13°45E 9 F15
Hagi Japan 34°30N 131°22E 31 G5
Hagolan Syria 33°0N 35°45E 46 C4
Hagondange France 49°16N 6°11E 20 B7
Hags Hd. Ireland 52°57N 9°28W 10 D2
Hague, C. de la France 49°44N 1°56W 20 B3
Hague, The = 's-Gravenhage Neths. 52°7N 4°17E 15 B4
Haguenau France 48°49N 7°47E 20 B7
Hai Duong Vietnam 20°56N 106°19E 38 B6
Haicheng China 40°50N 122°45E 35 D12
Haidar Khel Afghan. 33°58N 68°38E 42 C3
Haidarâbâd = Hyderabad India 17°22N 78°29E 40 L11
Haidargarh India 26°37N 81°22E 43 F9
Haifa = Ḩefa Israel 32°46N 35°0E 46 C4
Haikou China 20°1N 110°16E 38 B8
Ḩā'il Si. Arabia 27°28N 41°45E 44 E4
Ḩā'il □ Si. Arabia 26°40N 41°40E 44 E4
Hailar China 49°10N 119°38E 33 B6
Hailey U.S.A. 43°31N 114°19W 76 E6
Haileybury Canada 47°30N 79°38W 72 C4
Hailin China 44°37N 129°30E 35 B15
Hailuoto Finland 65°3N 24°45E 8 D21
Hainan □ China 19°0N 109°30E 38 C7
Hainan Dao China 19°0N 109°30E 38 C7
Hainan Str. = Qiongzhou Haixia China 20°10N 110°15E 38 B8
Hainaut □ Belgium 50°30N 4°0E 15 D4
Haines Alaska, U.S.A. 59°14N 135°26W 70 B1
Haines Oreg., U.S.A. 44°55N 117°56W 76 D5
Haines City U.S.A. 28°7N 81°38W 85 G14
Haines Junction Canada 60°45N 137°30W 70 A1
Haiphong Vietnam 20°47N 106°41E 38 B6
Haiti ■ W. Indies 19°0N 72°30W 89 C5
Haiya Sudan 18°20N 36°21E 51 E13
Haiyang China 36°47N 121°9E 35 F11
Haiyuan China 36°35N 105°52E 34 F3
Haizhou China 34°37N 119°7E 35 G10
Haizhou Wan China 34°50N 119°20E 35 G10
Hajdúböszörmény Hungary 47°40N 21°30E 17 E11
Hajipur India 25°45N 85°13E 43 G11
Ḩajjah Yemen 15°42N 43°36E 47 D3
Ḩājjī Muḩsin Iraq 32°35N 45°29E 44 C5
Ḩājjīābād Iran 28°19N 55°55E 45 D7
Ḩājjīābād-e Zarrīn Iran 33°9N 54°51E 45 C7
Hajnówka Poland 52°47N 23°35E 17 B12
Hakansson, Mts. Dem. Rep. of the Congo 8°40S 25°45E 55 D2
Hakkâri Turkey 37°34N 43°44E 44 B4
Hakken-Zan Japan 34°10N 135°54E 31 G7
Hakodate Japan 41°45N 140°44E 30 D10
Hakos Namibia 23°13S 16°21E 56 C2
Haku-San Japan 36°9N 136°46E 31 F8
Haku-San △ Japan 36°15N 136°45E 31 F8
Hakui Japan 36°53N 136°47E 31 F8
Hala Pakistan 25°43N 68°20E 40 G6
Ḩalab Syria 36°10N 37°15E 44 B3
Ḩalabjah Iraq 35°10N 45°58E 44 C5
Halaib Sudan 22°12N 36°30E 51 D13
Halaib Triangle Africa 22°30N 35°20E 51 D13
Hālat 'Ammār Si. Arabia 29°10N 36°4E 44 D3
Halbā Lebanon 34°34N 36°6E 46 A5
Halberstadt Germany 51°54N 11°3E 16 C6
Halcombe N.Z. 40°8S 175°30E 59 D5
Halcon Phil. 13°0N 121°30E 37 B6
Halde Fjäll = Haltiatunturi Finland 69°17N 21°18E 8 B19
Halden Norway 59°9N 11°23E 9 G14
Haldimand Canada 42°59N 79°52W 82 D5
Haldwani India 29°31N 79°30E 43 E8
Hale → Australia 24°56S 135°53E 62 C2
Halesowen U.K. 52°27N 2°3W 13 E5
Halesworth U.K. 52°20N 1°31E 13 E9
Haleyville U.S.A. 34°14N 87°37W 85 D11
Half Dome U.S.A. 37°44N 119°32W 78 H7
Halfmoon Bay N.Z. 46°50S 168°5E 59 G2
Halfway → Canada 56°12N 121°32W 70 B4
Halia India 24°50N 82°19E 43 G10
Haliburton Canada 45°3N 78°30W 82 A6
Halifax Australia 18°32S 146°22E 62 B4
Halifax Canada 44°38N 63°35W 73 D7
Halifax U.K. 53°43N 1°52W 12 D6
Halifax U.S.A. 40°25N 76°55W 82 F8
Halifax B. Australia 18°50S 147°0E 62 B4
Halifax I. Namibia 26°38S 15°4E 56 D2

Halīl → *Iran* 27°40N 58°30E **45 E8**
Halkida *Greece* 38°27N 23°42E **23 E10**
Halkirk *U.K.* 58°30N 3°29W **11 C5**
Hall Beach = Sanirajak
  Canada 68°46N 81°12W **69 C11**
Hall Pen. *Canada* 63°30N 66°0W **69 C13**
Hall Pt. *Australia* 15°40S 124°23E **60 C3**
Halland *Sweden* 57°8N 12°47E **9 H15**
Hallāniyat, Jazā'ir al
  Oman 17°30N 55°58E **47 D6**
Hallasan *S. Korea* 33°22N 126°32E **35 H14**
Halle *Belgium* 50°44N 4°13E **15 D4**
Halle *Germany* 51°30N 11°56E **16 C6**
Hällefors *Sweden* 59°47N 14°31E **9 G16**
Hallett *Australia* 33°25S 138°55E **63 E2**
Hallettsville *U.S.A.* 29°27N 96°57W **84 G6**
Hallim *S. Korea* 33°24N 126°15E **35 H14**
Hallingdalselva →
  Norway 60°23N 9°35E **8 F13**
Hallock *U.S.A.* 48°47N 96°57W **80 A5**
Halls Creek *Australia* 18°16S 127°38E **60 C4**
Halls Gap *Australia* 37°8S 142°34E **63 F3**
Hallsberg *Sweden* 59°5N 15°7E **9 G16**
Hallstad *U.S.A.* 41°58N 75°45W **83 E9**
Halmahera *Indonesia* 0°40N 128°0E **37 D7**
Halmstad *Sweden* 56°41N 12°52E **9 H15**
Hälsingborg = Helsingborg
  Sweden 56°3N 12°42E **9 H15**
Hälsingland *Sweden* 61°40N 16°5E **8 F17**
Halstead *U.K.* 51°57N 0°40E **13 F8**
Haltiatunturi *Finland* 69°17N 21°18E **8 B19**
Halton □ *U.K.* 53°22N 2°45W **12 D5**
Haltwhistle *U.K.* 54°58N 2°26W **12 C5**
Hālūl *Qatar* 25°40N 52°40E **45 E7**
Halvad *India* 23°1N 71°11E **42 H4**
Halvān *Iran* 33°57N 56°15E **45 C8**
Ham Tan *Vietnam* 10°40N 107°45E **39 G6**
Ham Yen *Vietnam* 22°4N 105°3E **38 A5**
Hamab *Namibia* 28°7S 19°16E **56 D2**
Hamada *Japan* 34°56N 132°4E **31 G6**
Hamadān *Iran* 34°52N 48°32E **45 C6**
Hamadān □ *Iran* 35°0N 49°0E **45 C6**
Hamāh *Syria* 35°5N 36°40E **44 C3**
Hamamatsu *Japan* 34°45N 137°45E **31 G8**
Hamar *Norway* 60°48N 11°7E **8 F14**
Hamâta, Gebel *Egypt* 24°17N 35°0E **44 E2**
Hambantota *Sri Lanka* 6°10N 81°10E **40 R12**
Hamber △ *Canada* 52°20N 118°0W **70 C5**
Hamburg *Germany* 53°33N 9°59E **16 B5**
Hamburg *Ark., U.S.A.* 33°14N 91°48W **84 E9**
Hamburg *N.Y., U.S.A.* 42°43N 78°50W **82 D6**
Hamburg *Pa., U.S.A.* 40°33N 75°59W **83 F9**
Ḥamd, W. al →
  Si. Arabia 24°55N 36°20E **44 E3**
Hamden *U.S.A.* 41°23N 72°54W **83 E12**
Häme *Finland* 61°38N 25°10E **8 F21**
Hämeenlinna *Finland* 61°0N 24°28E **8 F21**
Hamelin Pool *Australia* 26°22S 114°20E **61 E1**
Hameln *Germany* 52°6N 9°21E **16 B5**
Hamerkaz □ *Israel* 32°15N 34°55E **46 C3**
Hamersley Ra. *Australia* 22°0S 117°45E **60 D2**
Hamhŭng *N. Korea* 39°54N 127°30E **35 E14**
Hami *China* 42°55N 93°25E **32 B4**
Hamilton *Australia* 37°45S 142°2E **63 F3**
Hamilton *Canada* 43°15N 79°50W **82 C5**
Hamilton *N.Z.* 37°47S 175°19E **59 B5**
Hamilton *U.K.* 55°46N 4°2W **11 F4**
Hamilton *Ala., U.S.A.* 34°9N 87°59W **85 D11**
Hamilton *Mont.,*
  U.S.A. 46°15N 114°10W **76 C6**
Hamilton *N.Y., U.S.A.* 42°50N 75°33W **83 D9**
Hamilton *Ohio, U.S.A.* 39°24N 84°34W **81 F11**
Hamilton *Tex., U.S.A.* 31°42N 98°7W **84 F5**
Hamilton → *Queens.,*
  Australia 23°30S 139°47E **62 C2**
Hamilton → *S. Austral.,*
  Australia 26°40S 135°19E **63 D2**
Hamilton City *U.S.A.* 39°45N 122°1W **78 F4**
Hamilton I. *Australia* 20°21S 148°56E **62 J6**
Hamilton Inlet *Canada* 54°0N 57°30W **73 B8**
Hamilton Mt. *U.S.A.* 43°25N 74°22W **83 C10**
Hamina *Finland* 60°34N 27°12E **8 F22**
Hamirpur *H.P., India* 31°41N 76°31E **42 D7**
Hamirpur *Ut. P., India* 25°57N 80°9E **43 G9**
Hamju *N. Korea* 39°51N 127°28E **35 E14**
Hamlet *U.S.A.* 34°53N 79°42W **85 D15**
Hamley Bridge
  Australia 34°17S 138°35E **63 E2**
Hamlin = Hameln
  Germany 52°6N 9°21E **16 B5**
Hamlin *N.Y., U.S.A.* 43°17N 77°55W **82 C7**
Hamlin *Tex., U.S.A.* 32°53N 100°8W **84 E4**
Hamm *Germany* 51°40N 7°50E **16 C4**
Ḥammār, Hawr al *Iraq* 30°50N 47°10E **44 D5**
Hammerfest *Norway* 70°39N 23°41E **8 A20**
Hammond *Ind., U.S.A.* 41°38N 87°30W **80 E10**
Hammond *La., U.S.A.* 30°30N 90°28W **85 F9**
Hammond *N.Y., U.S.A.* 44°27N 75°42W **83 B9**
Hammondsport *U.S.A.* 42°25N 77°13W **82 D7**
Hammonton *U.S.A.* 39°39N 74°48W **81 F16**
Hampden *N.Z.* 45°18S 170°50E **59 F3**
Hampshire □ *U.K.* 51°7N 1°23W **13 F6**
Hampshire Downs *U.K.* 51°15N 1°10W **13 F6**
Hampton *N.B., Canada* 45°32N 65°51W **73 C6**
Hampton *Ont., Canada* 43°58N 78°45W **82 C6**
Hampton *Ark., U.S.A.* 33°32N 92°28W **84 E8**
Hampton *Iowa, U.S.A.* 42°45N 93°12W **80 D7**
Hampton *N.H., U.S.A.* 42°57N 70°50W **83 D14**
Hampton *S.C., U.S.A.* 32°52N 81°7W **85 E14**
Hampton *Va., U.S.A.* 37°2N 76°21W **81 G15**
Hampton Bays *U.S.A.* 40°53N 72°30W **83 F12**
Hampton Tableland
  Australia 32°0S 127°0E **61 F4**
Hamyang *S. Korea* 35°32N 127°42E **35 G14**
Han Pijesak *Bos.-H.* 44°5N 18°57E **23 B8**
Ḥanak *Si. Arabia* 25°32N 37°0E **44 E3**
Ḥanamaki *Japan* 39°23N 141°7E **30 E10**
Hanang *Tanzania* 4°30S 35°25E **54 C4**

Hanau *Germany* 50°7N 8°56E **16 C5**
Hanbogd = Ihbulag
  Mongolia 43°11N 107°10E **34 C4**
Hancheng *China* 35°31N 110°25E **34 G6**
Hancock *Mich., U.S.A.* 47°8N 88°35W **80 B9**
Hancock *N.Y., U.S.A.* 41°57N 75°17W **83 E9**
Handa *Japan* 34°53N 136°55E **31 G8**
Handa I. *U.K.* 58°23N 5°11W **11 C3**
Handan *China* 36°35N 114°28E **34 F8**
Handeni *Tanzania* 5°25S 38°2E **54 D4**
Handwara *India* 34°21N 74°20E **43 B6**
Hanegev *Israel* 30°50N 35°0E **46 E4**
Hanford *U.S.A.* 36°20N 119°39W **78 J7**
Hanford Reach △
  U.S.A. 46°40N 119°30W **76 C4**
Hang Chat *Thailand* 18°20N 99°21E **38 C2**
Hang Dong *Thailand* 18°41N 98°55E **38 C2**
Hangang → *S. Korea* 37°50N 126°30E **35 F14**
Hangayn Nuruu
  Mongolia 47°30N 99°0E **32 B4**
Hangchou = Hangzhou
  China 30°18N 120°11E **33 C7**
Hanggin Houqi *China* 40°58N 107°4E **34 D4**
Hanggin Qi *China* 39°52N 108°50E **34 E5**
Hangu *China* 39°18N 117°53E **35 E9**
Hangzhou *China* 30°18N 120°11E **33 C7**
Hangzhou Wan *China* 30°15N 120°45E **33 C7**
Hanhongor *Mongolia* 43°55N 104°28E **34 C3**
Hania = Chania *Greece* 35°30N 24°4E **25 D6**
Ḥanīḍh *Si. Arabia* 26°35N 48°38E **45 E6**
Ḥanīsh *Yemen* 13°45N 42°46E **47 E3**
Hankinson *U.S.A.* 46°4N 96°54W **80 B5**
Hankö *Finland* 59°50N 22°57E **9 G20**
Hanle *India* 32°42N 79°4E **43 C8**
Hanmer Springs *N.Z.* 42°32S 172°50E **59 E4**
Hann → *Australia* 17°26S 126°17E **60 C4**
Hann, Mt. *Australia* 15°45S 126°0E **60 C4**
Hanna *Canada* 51°40N 111°54W **70 C6**
Hanna *U.S.A.* 41°52N 106°34W **76 F10**
Hannah B. *Canada* 51°40N 80°0W **72 B4**
Hannibal *Mo., U.S.A.* 39°42N 91°22W **80 F8**
Hannibal *N.Y., U.S.A.* 43°19N 76°35W **83 C8**
Hannover *Germany* 52°22N 9°46E **16 B5**
Hanoi *Vietnam* 21°5N 105°55E **38 B5**
Hanover = Hannover
  Germany 52°22N 9°46E **16 B5**
Hanover *Canada* 44°9N 81°2W **82 B3**
Hanover *S. Africa* 31°4S 24°29E **56 E3**
Hanover *N.H., U.S.A.* 43°42N 72°17W **83 C12**
Hanover *Ohio, U.S.A.* 40°4N 82°16W **82 F2**
Hanover *Pa., U.S.A.* 39°48N 76°59W **81 F15**
Hanover, I. *Chile* 51°0S 74°50W **96 G2**
Hans Lollik I.
  U.S. Virgin Is. 18°24N 64°53W **89 e**
Hansdiha *India* 24°36N 87°5E **43 G12**
Hansi *India* 29°10N 75°57E **42 E6**
Hanson, L. *Australia* 31°0S 136°15E **63 E2**
Hantsavichy *Belarus* 52°49N 26°30E **17 B14**
Hanumangarh *India* 29°35N 74°19E **42 E6**
Hanzhong *China* 33°10N 107°1E **34 H4**
Hanzhuang *China* 34°33N 117°23E **35 G9**
Haora = Howrah *India* 22°37N 88°20E **43 H13**
Haparanda *Sweden* 65°52N 24°8E **8 D21**
Happy *U.S.A.* 34°45N 101°52W **84 D4**
Happy Camp *U.S.A.* 41°48N 123°23W **76 F2**
Happy Valley-Goose Bay
  Canada 53°15N 60°20W **73 B7**
Hapsu *N. Korea* 41°13N 128°51E **35 D15**
Hapur *India* 28°45N 77°45E **42 E7**
Ḥaql *Si. Arabia* 29°10N 34°58E **44 D2**
Har *Indonesia* 5°16S 133°14E **37 F8**
Haria *Canary Is.* 29°8N 13°32W **24 F6**
Haridwar *India* 29°58N 78°9E **42 E8**
Harim, Jabal al *Oman* 25°58N 56°14E **45 E8**
Haringhata → *Bangla.* 22°0N 89°58E **41 J16**
Harīr, W. al → *Syria* 32°44N 35°59E **46 C4**
Harīrūd → *Asia* 37°24N 60°38E **45 B9**
Härjedalen *Sweden* 62°22N 13°5E **8 E15**
Harlan *Iowa, U.S.A.* 41°39N 95°19W **80 E6**
Harlan *Ky., U.S.A.* 36°51N 83°19W **81 G12**
Harlech *U.K.* 52°52N 4°6W **12 E3**
Harlem *U.S.A.* 48°32N 108°47W **76 B9**
Harlingen *Neths.* 53°11N 5°25E **15 A5**

Harlingen *U.S.A.* 26°12N 97°42W **84 H6**
Harlow *U.K.* 51°46N 0°8E **13 F8**
Harlowton *U.S.A.* 46°26N 109°50W **76 C9**
Harnai *Pakistan* 30°6N 67°56E **42 D2**
Harney Basin *U.S.A.* 43°0N 119°30W **76 E4**
Harney L. *U.S.A.* 43°14N 119°8W **76 E4**
Harney Peak *U.S.A.* 43°52N 103°32W **80 D2**
Härnösand *Sweden* 62°38N 17°55E **8 E17**
Haroldswick *U.K.* 60°48N 0°50W **11 A8**
Harp L. *Canada* 55°5N 61°50W **73 A7**
Harper *Liberia* 4°25N 7°43W **50 H4**
Harrai *India* 22°37N 79°13E **43 H8**
Harrand *Pakistan* 29°28N 70°3E **42 E4**
Harricana → *Canada* 51°10N 79°45W **72 B4**
Harriman *U.S.A.* 35°56N 84°33W **85 D12**
Harrington Harbour
  Canada 50°31N 59°30W **73 B8**
Harris *U.K.* 57°50N 6°55W **11 D2**
Harris, L. *Australia* 31°10S 135°10E **63 E2**
Harris, Sd. of *U.K.* 57°44N 7°6W **11 D1**
Harris Pt. *Canada* 43°6N 82°9W **82 C2**
Harrisburg *Ill., U.S.A.* 37°44N 88°32W **80 G10**
Harrisburg *Nebr.,*
  U.S.A. 41°33N 103°44W **80 E2**
Harrisburg *Pa., U.S.A.* 40°16N 76°53W **82 F8**
Harrismith *S. Africa* 28°15S 29°8E **57 D4**
Harrison *Ark., U.S.A.* 36°14N 93°7W **84 C8**
Harrison *Maine, U.S.A.* 44°7N 70°39W **83 B14**
Harrison *Nebr., U.S.A.* 42°41N 103°53W **80 D2**
Harrison, C. *Canada* 54°55N 57°55W **73 B8**
Harrison L. *Canada* 49°33N 121°50W **70 D4**
Harrisonburg *U.S.A.* 38°27N 78°52W **81 F14**
Harrisonville *U.S.A.* 38°39N 94°21W **80 F6**
Harriston *Canada* 43°57N 80°53W **82 C4**
Harrisville *Mich., U.S.A.* 44°39N 83°17W **82 B1**
Harrisville *N.Y., U.S.A.* 44°9N 75°19W **83 B9**
Harrisville *Pa., U.S.A.* 41°8N 80°0W **82 E5**
Harrodsburg *U.S.A.* 37°46N 84°51W **81 G11**
Harrogate *U.K.* 54°0N 1°33W **12 C6**
Harrow □ *U.K.* 51°35N 0°21W **13 F7**
Harrowsmith *Canada* 44°24N 76°40W **83 B8**
Harry S. Truman Res.
  U.S.A. 38°16N 93°24W **80 F7**
Harsin *Iran* 34°18N 47°33E **44 C5**
Harstad *Norway* 68°48N 16°30E **8 B17**
Harsud *India* 22°6N 76°44E **42 H7**
Hart *U.S.A.* 43°42N 86°22W **80 D10**
Hart, L. *Australia* 31°10S 136°25E **63 E2**
Hartbees → *S. Africa* 28°45S 20°32E **56 D3**
Hartford *Conn., U.S.A.* 41°46N 72°41W **83 E12**
Hartford *Ky., U.S.A.* 37°27N 86°55W **80 G10**
Hartford *S. Dak., U.S.A.* 43°38N 96°57W **80 D5**
Hartford *Vt., U.S.A.* 43°40N 72°20W **83 C12**
Hartford *Wis., U.S.A.* 43°19N 88°22W **80 D9**
Hartford City *U.S.A.* 40°27N 85°22W **81 E11**
Hartland *Canada* 46°20N 67°32W **73 C6**
Hartland Pt. *U.K.* 51°1N 4°32W **13 F3**
Hartlepool *U.K.* 54°42N 1°13W **12 C6**
Hartlepool □ *U.K.* 54°42N 1°17W **12 C6**
Hartley Bay *Canada* 53°25N 129°15W **70 C3**
Hartmannberge *Namibia* 17°0S 13°0E **56 B1**
Hartney *Canada* 49°30N 100°35W **71 D8**
Harts → *S. Africa* 28°24S 24°17E **56 D3**
Hartselle *U.S.A.* 34°27N 86°56W **85 D11**
Hartshorne *U.S.A.* 34°51N 95°34W **84 D7**
Hartstown *U.S.A.* 41°33N 80°23W **82 E4**
Hartsville *U.S.A.* 34°23N 80°4W **85 D14**
Hartswater *S. Africa* 27°34S 24°43E **56 D3**
Hartwell *U.S.A.* 34°21N 82°56W **85 D13**
Harunabad *Pakistan* 29°35N 73°8E **42 E5**
Harvand *Iran* 28°25N 55°43E **45 D7**
Harvey *Australia* 33°5S 115°54E **61 F2**
Harvey *Ill., U.S.A.* 41°36N 87°50W **80 E10**
Harvey *N. Dak., U.S.A.* 47°47N 99°56W **80 B4**
Harwich *U.K.* 51°56N 1°17E **13 F9**
Haryana □ *India* 29°0N 76°10E **42 E7**
Haryn → *Belarus* 52°7N 27°17E **17 B14**
Harz *Germany* 51°38N 10°44E **16 C6**
Hasa *Si. Arabia* 25°50N 49°0E **45 E6**
Hasā, W. al → *Jordan* 31°4N 35°29E **46 D4**
Ḥasanābād *Iran* 32°8N 52°44E **45 C7**
Ḥasb, W. → *Iraq* 31°45N 44°17E **44 D5**
Hasdo → *India* 21°44N 82°44E **43 J10**
Hashimoto *Japan* 34°19N 135°37E **31 G7**
Hashtjerd *Iran* 35°52N 50°40E **45 B6**
Haskell *U.S.A.* 33°10N 99°44W **84 E5**
Haskovo = Khaskovo
  Bulgaria 41°56N 25°30E **23 D11**
Haslemere *U.K.* 51°5N 0°43W **13 F7**
Hasselt *Belgium* 50°56N 5°21E **15 D5**
Hassi Messaoud *Algeria* 31°51N 6°1E **50 B7**
Hässleholm *Sweden* 56°10N 13°46E **9 H15**
Hastings *N.Z.* 39°39S 176°52E **59 C6**
Hastings *U.K.* 50°51N 0°35E **13 G8**
Hastings *Mich., U.S.A.* 42°39N 85°17W **81 D11**
Hastings *Minn., U.S.A.* 44°44N 92°51W **80 C8**
Hastings *Nebr., U.S.A.* 40°35N 98°23W **80 E4**
Hastings Ra. *Australia* 31°15S 152°14E **63 E5**
Hat Yai *Thailand* 7°1N 100°27E **39 J3**
Hatanbulag = Ergel
  Mongolia 43°8N 109°5E **34 C5**
Hatay *Turkey* 36°14N 36°10E **44 B3**
Hatch *U.S.A.* 32°40N 107°9W **77 K10**
Hatchet L. *Canada* 58°36N 103°40W **71 B8**
Hateruma-Shima *Japan* 24°3N 123°47E **31 M1**
Hatfield P.O. *Australia* 33°54S 143°49E **63 E3**
Hatgal *Mongolia* 50°26N 100°9E **32 A5**
Hathras *India* 27°36N 78°6E **42 F8**
Hatia *Bangla.* 22°30N 91°5E **41 H17**
Hato Mayor *Dom. Rep.* 18°46N 69°15W **89 C6**
Hatta *India* 24°7N 79°36E **43 G8**
Hatta *U.A.E.* 24°58N 56°28E **45 E8**
Hattah *Australia* 34°48S 142°17E **63 E3**
Hattah-Kulkyne △
  Australia 34°16S 142°33E **63 E3**
Hatteras, C. *U.S.A.* 35°14N 75°32W **85 D17**
Hattiesburg *U.S.A.* 31°20N 89°17W **85 F10**
Hatvan *Hungary* 47°40N 19°45E **17 E10**

Hau Duc *Vietnam* 15°20N 108°13E **38 E7**
Haugesund *Norway* 59°23N 5°13E **9 G11**
Haukipudas *Finland* 65°12N 25°20E **8 D21**
Haultain → *Canada* 55°51N 106°46W **71 B7**
Hauraki G. *N.Z.* 36°35S 175°5E **59 B5**
Haut Atlas *Morocco* 32°30N 5°0W **50 B4**
Hautes Fagnes = Hohes Venn
  Belgium 50°30N 6°5E **15 D6**
Hauts Plateaux *Algeria* 35°0N 1°0E **50 B6**
Havana = La Habana
  Cuba 23°8N 82°22W **88 B3**
Havana *U.S.A.* 40°18N 90°4W **80 E8**
Havant *U.K.* 50°51N 0°58W **13 G7**
Havasu, L. → Kiğzi *Turkey* 38°18N 43°25E **44 B4**
Havasu, L. *U.S.A.* 34°18N 114°28W **79 L12**
Havel → *Germany* 52°50N 12°3E **16 B7**
Havelian *Pakistan* 34°2N 73°10E **42 B5**
Havelock *Canada* 44°26N 77°53W **82 B7**
Havelock *N.Z.* 41°17S 173°48E **59 D4**
Havelock *U.S.A.* 34°53N 76°54W **85 D16**
Haverfordwest *U.K.* 51°48N 4°58W **13 F3**
Haverhill *U.K.* 52°5N 0°28E **13 E8**
Haverhill *U.S.A.* 42°47N 71°5W **83 D13**
Haverstraw *U.S.A.* 41°12N 73°58W **83 E11**
Havirga *Mongolia* 45°41N 113°5E **34 B7**
Havířov *Czech Rep.* 49°46N 18°20E **17 D10**
Havlíčkův Brod
  Czech Rep. 49°36N 15°33E **16 D8**
Havre *U.S.A.* 48°33N 109°41W **76 B9**
Havre-Aubert *Canada* 47°12N 61°56W **73 C7**
Havre-St.-Pierre
  Canada 50°18N 63°33W **73 B7**
Haw → *U.S.A.* 35°36N 79°3W **85 D15**
Hawai'i *U.S.A.* 19°30N 155°30W **74 b**
Hawai'i □ *U.S.A.* 19°30N 156°30W **74 b**
Hawaiian Is. *Pac. Oc.* 20°30N 156°0W **74 b**
Hawaiian Ridge
  Pac. Oc. 24°0N 165°0W **65 E11**
Hawarden *U.S.A.* 43°0N 96°29W **80 D5**
Hawea, L. *N.Z.* 44°28S 169°19E **59 F2**
Hawera *N.Z.* 39°35S 174°19E **59 C5**
Hawick *U.K.* 55°26N 2°47W **11 F6**
Hawk Junction *Canada* 48°5N 84°38W **72 C3**
Hawke B. *N.Z.* 39°25S 177°0E **59 C6**
Hawker *Australia* 31°59S 138°22E **63 E2**
Hawke's Bay *Canada* 50°36N 57°10W **73 B8**
Hawkesbury *Canada* 45°37N 74°37W **72 C5**
Hawkesbury I. *Canada* 53°37N 129°3W **70 C3**
Hawkesbury Pt.
  Australia 11°55S 134°5E **62 A1**
Hawkinsville *U.S.A.* 32°17N 83°28W **85 E13**
Hawley *Minn., U.S.A.* 46°53N 96°19W **80 B5**
Hawley *Pa., U.S.A.* 41°28N 75°11W **83 E9**
Ḥawrān, W. → *Iraq* 33°58N 42°34E **44 C4**
Hawsh Mūssá *Lebanon* 33°45N 35°55E **46 B4**
Hawthorne *U.S.A.* 38°32N 118°38W **76 G4**
Hay *Australia* 34°30S 144°51E **63 E3**
Hay → *Australia* 24°50S 138°0E **62 C2**
Hay → *Canada* 60°50N 116°26W **70 A5**
Hay, C. *Australia* 14°5S 129°29E **60 B4**
Hay I. *Canada* 44°53N 80°58W **82 B4**
Hay L. *Canada* 58°50N 118°50W **70 B5**
Hay-on-Wye *U.K.* 52°5N 3°8W **13 E4**
Hay River *Canada* 60°51N 115°44W **70 A5**
Hay Springs *U.S.A.* 42°41N 102°41W **80 D3**
Haya = Tehoru
  Indonesia 3°23S 129°30E **37 E7**
Hayachine-San *Japan* 39°34N 141°29E **30 E10**
Hayastan = Armenia ■
  Asia 40°20N 45°0E **19 F7**
Haydān, W. al →
  Jordan 31°29N 35°34E **46 D4**
Hayden *U.S.A.* 40°30N 107°16W **76 F10**
Haydon *Australia* 18°0S 141°30E **62 B3**
Hayes *U.S.A.* 44°23N 101°1W **80 C3**
Hayes → *Canada* 57°3N 92°12W **72 A1**
Hayes Creek *Australia* 13°43S 131°22E **60 B5**
Hayle *U.K.* 50°11N 5°26W **13 G2**
Hayling I. *U.K.* 50°48N 0°59W **13 G7**
Haymen I. *Australia* 20°3S 148°52E **62 J6**
Hays *Canada* 50°6N 111°48W **70 C6**
Hays *U.S.A.* 38°53N 99°20W **80 F4**
Haysyn *Ukraine* 48°57N 29°25E **17 D15**
Hayvoron *Ukraine* 48°22N 29°52E **17 D15**
Hayward *Calif., U.S.A.* 37°40N 122°4W **78 H4**
Hayward *Wis., U.S.A.* 46°1N 91°29W **80 B8**
Haywards Heath *U.K.* 51°0N 0°5W **13 G7**
Hazafon □ *Israel* 32°40N 35°20E **46 C4**
Hazar *Turkmenistan* 39°34N 53°16E **19 G9**
Hazārān, Kūh-e *Iran* 29°35N 57°20E **45 D8**
Hazard *U.S.A.* 37°15N 83°12W **81 G12**
Hazaribag *India* 23°58N 85°26E **43 H11**
Hazaribag Road *India* 24°12N 85°57E **43 G11**
Hazelton *Canada* 55°20N 127°42W **70 B3**
Hazelton *U.S.A.* 46°29N 100°17W **80 B3**
Hazen *U.S.A.* 47°18N 101°38W **80 B3**
Hazlehurst *Ga., U.S.A.* 31°52N 82°36W **85 F13**
Hazlehurst *Miss., U.S.A.* 31°52N 90°24W **85 F9**
Hazlet *U.S.A.* 40°25N 74°12W **83 F10**
Hazleton *U.S.A.* 40°57N 75°59W **83 F9**
Hazlett, L. *Australia* 21°30S 128°48E **60 D4**
Hazro *Turkey* 38°15N 40°47E **44 B4**
Head of Bight *Australia* 31°30S 131°25E **61 F5**
Headlands *Zimbabwe* 18°15S 32°2E **55 F3**
Healdsburg *U.S.A.* 38°37N 122°52W **78 G4**
Healdton *U.S.A.* 34°14N 97°29W **84 D6**
Healesville *Australia* 37°35S 145°30E **63 F4**
Heany Junction
  Zimbabwe 20°6S 28°54E **57 C4**
Heard I. *Ind. Oc.* 53°0S 74°0E **3 G13**
Hearne *U.S.A.* 30°53N 96°36W **84 F6**
Hearst *Canada* 49°40N 83°41W **72 C3**
Heart → *U.S.A.* 46°46N 100°50W **80 B3**
Heart's Content *Canada* 47°54N 53°27W **73 C9**
Heath, Pte. *Canada* 49°8N 61°40W **73 C7**
Heathrow, London ✈ (LHR)
  U.K. 51°28N 0°27W **13 F7**

Heavener *U.S.A.* 34°53N 94°36W **84 D7**
Hebbronville *U.S.A.* 27°18N 98°41W **84 H5**
Hebei □ *China* 39°0N 116°0E **34 E9**
Hebel *Australia* 28°58S 147°47E **63 D4**
Heber *U.S.A.* 32°44N 115°32W **79 N11**
Heber Springs *U.S.A.* 35°30N 92°2W **84 D8**
Hebgen L. *U.S.A.* 44°52N 111°20W **76 D8**
Hebi *China* 35°57N 114°7E **34 G8**
Hebrides *U.K.* 57°30N 7°0W **6 D4**
Hebrides, Sea of the *U.K.* 57°5N 7°0W **11 D2**
Hebron = Al Khalīl
  West Bank 31°32N 35°6E **46 D3**
Hebron *Canada* 58°5N 62°30W **69 D13**
Hebron *N. Dak., U.S.A.* 46°54N 102°3W **80 B3**
Hebron *Nebr., U.S.A.* 40°10N 97°35W **80 E5**
Hecate Str. *Canada* 53°10N 130°30W **70 C2**
Hechi *China* 24°40N 108°2E **32 D5**
Hechuan *China* 30°2N 106°12E **32 C5**
Hecla *U.S.A.* 45°53N 98°9W **80 C4**
Hecla I. *Canada* 51°10N 96°43W **71 C9**
Hede *Sweden* 62°23N 13°30E **8 E15**
Hedemora *Sweden* 60°18N 15°58E **9 F16**
Heerde *Neths.* 52°24N 6°2E **15 B6**
Heerenveen *Neths.* 52°57N 5°55E **15 B5**
Heerhugowaard *Neths.* 52°40N 4°51E **15 B4**
Heerlen *Neths.* 50°55N 5°58E **15 D5**
Hefa *Israel* 32°46N 35°0E **46 C4**
Hefa □ *Israel* 32°40N 35°0E **46 C4**
Hefei *China* 31°52N 117°18E **33 C6**
Hegang *China* 47°20N 130°19E **33 B8**
Hei Ling Chau *China* 22°15N 114°2E **33 G11**
Heichengzhen *China* 36°24N 106°3E **34 F4**
Heide *Germany* 54°13N 9°5E **16 A5**
Heidelberg *Germany* 49°24N 8°42E **16 D5**
Heidelberg *S. Africa* 34°6S 20°59E **56 E3**
Heilbron *S. Africa* 27°16S 27°59E **57 D4**
Heilbronn *Germany* 49°9N 9°13E **16 D5**
Heilongjiang □ *China* 48°0N 126°0E **33 B7**
Heilunkiang = Heilongjiang □
  China 48°0N 126°0E **33 B7**
Heimaey *Iceland* 63°26N 20°17W **8 E3**
Heinola *Finland* 61°13N 26°2E **8 F22**
Heinze Kyun *Burma* 14°25N 97°45E **38 E1**
Heishan *China* 41°40N 122°5E **35 D12**
Heishui *China* 42°8N 119°30E **35 C10**
Hejaz = Ḥijāz *Si. Arabia* 24°0N 40°0E **44 E3**
Hejian *China* 38°25N 116°5E **34 E9**
Hejin *China* 35°35N 110°42E **34 G6**
Hekimhan *Turkey* 38°50N 37°55E **44 B3**
Hekla *Iceland* 63°56N 19°35W **8 E4**
Hekou *China* 22°30N 103°59E **32 D5**
Helan Shan *China* 38°30N 105°58E **34 E3**
Helen Atoll *Pac. Oc.* 2°40N 132°0E **37 D8**
Helena *Ark., U.S.A.* 34°32N 90°36W **85 D9**
Helena *Mont., U.S.A.* 46°36N 112°2W **76 C7**
Helendale *U.S.A.* 34°44N 117°19W **79 L9**
Helensburgh *U.K.* 56°1N 4°43W **11 E4**
Helensville *N.Z.* 36°41S 174°29E **59 B5**
Helenvale *Australia* 15°43S 145°14E **62 B4**
Helgeland *Norway* 66°7N 13°29E **8 C15**
Helgoland *Germany* 54°10N 7°53E **16 A4**
Heligoland = Helgoland
  Germany 54°10N 7°53E **16 A4**
Heligoland B. = Deutsche Bucht
  Germany 54°15N 8°0E **16 A5**
Hell Hole Gorge △
  Australia 25°31S 144°12E **62 D3**
Hella *Iceland* 63°50N 20°24W **8 E3**
Hellas = Greece ■ *Europe* 40°0N 23°0E **23 E9**
Hellertown *U.S.A.* 40°35N 75°21W **83 F9**
Hellespont = Çanakkale Boğazı
  Turkey 40°17N 26°32E **23 D12**
Hellevoetsluis *Neths.* 51°50N 4°8E **15 C4**
Hellín *Spain* 38°31N 1°40W **21 C5**
Hells Canyon △
  U.S.A. 45°30N 117°45W **76 D5**
Hell's Gate △ *Kenya* 0°54S 36°19E **54 C4**
Helmand □ *Afghan.* 31°20N 64°0E **40 D4**
Helmand → *Afghan.* 31°12N 61°34E **40 D2**
Helmeringhausen
  Namibia 25°54S 16°57E **56 D2**
Helmond *Neths.* 51°29N 5°41E **15 C5**
Helmsdale *U.K.* 58°7N 3°39W **11 C5**
Helmsdale → *U.K.* 58°8N 3°43W **11 C5**
Helong *China* 42°40N 129°0E **35 C15**
Helper *U.S.A.* 39°41N 110°51W **76 G8**
Helsingborg *Sweden* 56°3N 12°42E **9 H15**
Helsingfors = Helsinki
  Finland 60°10N 24°55E **9 F21**
Helsingør *Denmark* 56°2N 12°35E **9 H15**
Helsinki *Finland* 60°10N 24°55E **9 F21**
Helston *U.K.* 50°6N 5°17W **13 G2**
Helvellyn *U.K.* 54°32N 3°1W **12 C4**
Helwân *Egypt* 29°50N 31°20E **51 C12**
Hemel Hempstead *U.K.* 51°44N 0°28W **13 F7**
Hemet *U.S.A.* 33°45N 116°58W **79 M10**
Hemingford *U.S.A.* 42°19N 103°4W **80 D2**
Hemis △ *India* 34°10N 77°15E **42 B7**
Hemmingford *Canada* 45°3N 73°35W **83 A11**
Hempstead *N.Y.,*
  U.S.A. 40°42N 73°37W **83 F11**
Hempstead *Tex., U.S.A.* 30°6N 96°5W **84 F6**
Hemse *Sweden* 57°15N 18°22E **9 H18**
Henan □ *China* 34°0N 114°0E **34 H8**
Henares → *Spain* 40°24N 3°30W **21 B4**
Henashi-Misaki *Japan* 40°37N 139°51E **30 D9**
Henderson *Argentina* 36°18S 61°43W **94 D3**
Henderson *Ky., U.S.A.* 37°50N 87°35W **80 G10**
Henderson *N.C.,*
  U.S.A. 36°20N 78°25W **85 C15**
Henderson *Nev.,*
  U.S.A. 36°2N 114°58W **79 J12**
Henderson *Tenn.,*
  U.S.A. 35°26N 88°38W **85 D10**
Henderson *Tex., U.S.A.* 32°9N 94°48W **84 E7**
Henderson I. *Pac. Oc.* 24°22S 128°19W **65 K15**
Hendersonville *N.C.,*
  U.S.A. 35°19N 82°28W **85 D13**

Hendersonville *Tenn., U.S.A.* 36°18N 86°37W **85** C11
Hendījān *Iran* 30°14N 49°43E **45** D6
Hendorābī *Iran* 26°40N 53°37E **45** E7
Hengcheng *China* 38°18N 106°28E **34** E4
Hengdaohezi *China* 44°52N 129°0E **35** B15
Hengelo *Neths.* 52°16N 6°48E **15** B6
Henggang *China* 22°39N 114°12E **33** F11
Hengmen *China* 22°33N 113°35E **33** F10
Hengqin Dao *China* 22°7N 113°34E **33** G10
Hengshan *China* 37°58N 109°5E **34** F5
Hengshui *China* 37°41N 115°40E **34** F8
Hengyang *China* 26°59N 112°22E **33** D6
Henley-on-Thames *U.K.* 51°32N 0°54W **13** F7
Henlopen, C. *U.S.A.* 38°48N 75°6W **81** F16
Hennenman *S. Africa* 27°59S 27°1E **56** D4
Hennessey *U.S.A.* 36°6N 97°54W **84** C6
Henri Pittier △ *Venezuela* 10°26N 67°37W **89** D6
Henrietta *U.S.A.* 33°49N 98°12W **84** E5
Henrietta, Ostrov = Genriyetty, Ostrov *Russia* 77°6N 156°30E **29** B16
Henrietta Maria, C. *Canada* 55°9N 82°20W **72** A3
Henry *U.S.A.* 41°7N 89°22W **80** E9
Henryetta *U.S.A.* 35°27N 95°59W **84** D7
Henryville *Canada* 45°8N 73°11W **83** A11
Hensall *Canada* 43°26N 81°30W **82** C3
Hentiesbaai *Namibia* 22°8S 14°18E **56** C1
Hentiyn Nuruu *Mongolia* 48°30N 108°30E **33** B5
Henty *Australia* 35°30S 147°3E **63** F4
Henzada *Burma* 17°38N 95°26E **41** L19
Heppner *U.S.A.* 45°21N 119°33W **76** D4
Hepworth *Canada* 44°37N 81°9W **82** B3
Hequ *China* 39°20N 111°15E **34** E6
Héraðsflói *Iceland* 65°42N 14°12W **8** D6
Héraðsvötn → *Iceland* 65°45N 19°25W **8** D4
Heraklion = Iraklio *Greece* 35°20N 25°12E **25** D7
Herald Cays *Australia* 16°58S 149°9E **62** B4
Herāt *Afghan.* 34°20N 62°7E **40** B3
Herāt □ *Afghan.* 35°0N 62°0E **40** B3
Herbert *Canada* 50°30N 107°10W **71** C7
Herbert → *Australia* 18°31S 146°17E **62** B4
Herberton *Australia* 17°20S 145°25E **62** B4
Herbertsdale *S. Africa* 34°1S 21°46E **56** E3
Herceg-Novi *Montenegro* 42°30N 18°33E **23** C8
Herchmer *Canada* 57°22N 94°10W **71** B10
Herðubreið *Iceland* 65°11N 16°21W **8** D5
Hereford *U.K.* 52°4N 2°43W **13** E5
Hereford *U.S.A.* 34°49N 102°24W **84** D3
Herefordshire □ *U.K.* 52°8N 2°40W **13** E5
Herentals *Belgium* 51°12N 4°51E **15** C4
Herford *Germany* 52°7N 8°39E **16** B5
Herington *U.S.A.* 38°40N 96°57W **80** F5
Herkimer *U.S.A.* 43°2N 74°59W **83** D10
Herlong *U.S.A.* 40°8N 120°8W **78** E6
Herm *U.K.* 49°30N 2°28W **13** H5
Hermann *U.S.A.* 38°42N 91°27W **80** F8
Hermannsburg *Australia* 23°57S 132°45E **60** D5
Hermanus *S. Africa* 34°27S 19°12E **56** E2
Hermidale *Australia* 31°30S 146°42E **63** E4
Hermiston *U.S.A.* 45°51N 119°17W **76** D4
Hermite, I. *Chile* 55°50S 68°0W **96** H3
Hermon *U.S.A.* 44°28N 75°14W **83** B9
Hermon, Mt. = Shaykh, J. ash *Lebanon* 33°25N 35°50E **46** B4
Hermosillo *Mexico* 29°10N 111°0W **86** B2
Hernád → *Hungary* 47°56N 21°8E **17** D11
Hernandarias *Paraguay* 25°20S 54°40W **95** B5
Hernandez *U.S.A.* 36°24N 120°46W **78** J6
Hernando *Argentina* 32°28S 63°40W **94** C3
Hernando *U.S.A.* 34°50N 90°0W **85** D10
Herndon *U.S.A.* 40°43N 76°51W **82** F8
Herne *Germany* 51°32N 7°14E **15** C7
Herne Bay *U.K.* 51°21N 1°8E **13** F9
Herning *Denmark* 56°8N 8°58E **9** H13
Heroica Caborca = Caborca *Mexico* 30°37N 112°6W **86** A2
Heroica Nogales = Nogales *Mexico* 31°19N 110°56W **86** A2
Heron Bay *Canada* 48°40N 86°25W **72** C2
Heron I. *Australia* 23°27S 151°55E **62** C5
Herradura, Pta. de la *Canary Is.* 28°26N 14°8W **24** F5
Herreid *U.S.A.* 45°50N 100°4W **80** C3
Herrin *U.S.A.* 37°48N 89°2W **80** G9
Herriot *Canada* 56°22N 101°16W **71** B8
Herschel I. *Canada* 69°35N 139°5W **4** C1
Hershey *U.S.A.* 40°17N 76°39W **83** F8
Herstal *Belgium* 50°40N 5°38E **15** D5
Hertford *U.K.* 51°48N 0°4W **13** F7
Hertfordshire □ *U.K.* 51°51N 0°5W **13** F7
's-Hertogenbosch *Neths.* 51°42N 5°17E **15** C5
Hertzogville *S. Africa* 28°9S 25°30E **56** D4
Hervey B. *Australia* 25°0S 152°52E **62** C5
Herzliyya *Israel* 32°10N 34°50E **46** C3
Ḩeşār *Fārs, Iran* 29°52N 50°16E **45** D6
Ḩeşār *Markazī, Iran* 35°50N 49°12E **45** C6
Heshui *China* 35°48N 108°0E **34** G5
Heshun *China* 37°22N 113°32E **34** F7
Hesperia *U.S.A.* 34°25N 117°18W **79** L9
Hesse = Hessen □ *Germany* 50°30N 9°0E **16** C5
Hessen □ *Germany* 50°30N 9°0E **16** C5
Hetch Hetchy Aqueduct *U.S.A.* 37°29N 122°19W **78** H5
Hettinger *U.S.A.* 46°0N 102°42W **80** B2
Heuksando *S. Korea* 34°40N 125°30E **35** G13
Heunghae *S. Korea* 36°12N 129°21E **35** F15
Heuvelton *U.S.A.* 44°37N 75°25W **83** B9
Hewitt *U.S.A.* 31°28N 97°12W **84** F6
Hexham *U.K.* 54°58N 2°4W **12** C5
Hexigten Qi *China* 43°18N 117°30E **35** C9
Ḩeydarābād *Iran* 30°33N 55°38E **45** D7
Heysham *U.K.* 54°3N 2°53W **12** C5
Heywood *Australia* 38°8S 141°37E **63** F3
Heze *China* 35°14N 115°20E **34** G8
Hi, Ko *Thailand* 7°44N 98°22E **39** a
Hi Vista *U.S.A.* 34°45N 117°46W **79** L9
Hialeah *U.S.A.* 25°51N 80°16W **85** J14
Hiawatha *U.S.A.* 39°51N 95°32W **80** F6
Hibbing *U.S.A.* 47°25N 92°56W **80** B7
Hibbs B. *Australia* 42°35S 145°15E **63** G4
Hibernia Reef *Australia* 12°0S 123°23E **60** B3
Hickman *U.S.A.* 36°34N 89°11W **80** G9
Hickory *U.S.A.* 35°44N 81°21W **85** D14
Hicks, Pt. *Australia* 37°49S 149°17E **63** F4
Hicks L. *Canada* 61°25N 100°0W **71** A9
Hicksville *U.S.A.* 40°46N 73°32W **83** F11
Hida-Gawa → *Japan* 35°26N 137°3E **31** G8
Hida-Sammyaku *Japan* 36°30N 137°40E **31** F8
Hidaka-Sammyaku *Japan* 42°35N 142°45E **30** C11
Hidalgo □ *Mexico* 20°30N 99°0W **87** C5
Hidalgo, Presa M. *Mexico* 26°30N 108°35W **86** B3
Hidalgo del Parral *Mexico* 26°56N 105°40W **86** B3
Hierro *Canary Is.* 27°44N 18°0W **24** G1
Higashiajima-San *Japan* 37°40N 140°10E **30** F10
Higashiōsaka *Japan* 34°39N 135°37E **31** G7
Higgins *U.S.A.* 36°7N 100°2W **84** C4
Higgins Corner *U.S.A.* 39°2N 121°5W **78** F5
High Bridge *U.S.A.* 40°40N 74°54W **83** F10
High Island Res. *China* 22°22N 114°21E **33** G11
High Level *Canada* 58°31N 117°8W **70** B5
High Point *U.S.A.* 35°57N 80°0W **85** D15
High Prairie *Canada* 55°30N 116°30W **70** B5
High River *Canada* 50°30N 113°50W **70** C6
High Tatra = Tatry *Slovak Rep.* 49°20N 20°0E **17** D11
High Veld *Africa* 27°0S 27°0E **48** J6
High Wycombe *U.K.* 51°37N 0°45W **13** F7
Highland □ *U.K.* 57°17N 4°21W **11** D4
Highland Park *U.S.A.* 42°11N 87°48W **80** D10
Highmore *U.S.A.* 44°31N 99°27W **80** C4
Highrock L. *Man., Canada* 55°45N 100°30W **71** B8
Highrock L. *Sask., Canada* 57°5N 105°32W **71** B7
Higüey *Dom. Rep.* 18°37N 68°42W **89** C6
Hiiumaa *Estonia* 58°50N 22°45E **9** G20
Ḩijāz *Si. Arabia* 24°0N 40°0E **44** E3
Hijo = Tagum *Phil.* 7°33N 125°53E **37** C7
Hikari *Japan* 33°58N 131°58E **31** H5
Hiko *U.S.A.* 37°32N 115°14W **78** H11
Hikone *Japan* 35°15N 136°10E **31** G8
Hikurangi *Gisborne, N.Z.* 37°55S 178°4E **59** C6
Hikurangi *Northland, N.Z.* 35°36S 174°17E **59** A5
Hildesheim *Germany* 52°9N 9°56E **16** B5
Hill → *Australia* 30°23S 115°3E **61** F2
Hill City *Idaho, U.S.A.* 43°18N 115°3W **76** E6
Hill City *Kans., U.S.A.* 39°22N 99°51W **80** F4
Hill City *Minn., U.S.A.* 46°59N 93°36W **80** B7
Hill City *S. Dak., U.S.A.* 43°56N 103°35W **80** D2
Hill Island L. *Canada* 60°30N 109°50W **71** A7
Hillaby, Mt. *Barbados* 13°12N 59°35W **89** g
Hillcrest *Barbados* 13°13N 59°31W **89** g
Hillcrest Center *U.S.A.* 35°23N 118°57W **79** K8
Hillegom *Neths.* 52°18N 4°35E **15** B4
Hillsboro *Kans., U.S.A.* 38°21N 97°12W **80** F5
Hillsboro *N. Dak., U.S.A.* 47°26N 97°3W **80** B5
Hillsboro *Ohio, U.S.A.* 39°12N 83°37W **81** F12
Hillsboro *Oreg., U.S.A.* 45°31N 122°59W **78** E4
Hillsboro *Tex., U.S.A.* 32°1N 97°8W **84** E6
Hillsborough *Grenada* 12°28N 61°28W **89** D7
Hillsborough *U.S.A.* 43°7N 71°54W **83** C13
Hillsborough Channel *Australia* 20°56S 149°15E **62** J7
Hillsdale *Mich., U.S.A.* 41°56N 84°38W **81** E11
Hillsdale *N.Y., U.S.A.* 42°11N 73°32W **83** D11
Hillsport *Canada* 49°27N 85°34W **72** C2
Hillston *Australia* 33°30S 145°31E **63** E4
Hilo *U.S.A.* 19°44N 155°5W **74** b
Hilton *U.S.A.* 43°17N 77°48W **82** C7
Hilton Head Island *U.S.A.* 32°13N 80°45W **85** E14
Hilversum *Neths.* 52°14N 5°10E **15** B5
Himachal Pradesh □ *India* 31°30N 77°0E **42** D7
Himalaya *Asia* 29°0N 84°0E **43** E11
Himatnagar *India* 23°37N 72°57E **42** H5
Himeji *Japan* 34°50N 134°40E **31** G7
Himi *Japan* 36°50N 136°55E **31** F8
Ḩimş *Syria* 34°40N 36°45E **46** A5
Ḩimş □ *Syria* 34°30N 37°0E **46** A6
Hinche *Haiti* 19°9N 72°1W **89** C5
Hinchinbrook I. *Australia* 18°20S 146°15E **62** B4
Hinchinbrook Island △ *Australia* 18°14S 146°6E **62** B4
Hinckley *U.K.* 52°33N 1°22W **13** E6
Hinckley *U.S.A.* 46°1N 92°56W **80** B7
Hindaun *India* 26°44N 77°5E **42** F7
Hindmarsh, L. *Australia* 36°5S 141°55E **63** F3
Hindu Bagh *Pakistan* 30°56N 67°50E **42** D2
Hindu Kush *Asia* 36°0N 71°0E **40** B7
Hindupur *India* 13°49N 77°32E **40** N10
Hines Creek *Canada* 56°20N 118°40W **70** B5
Hinesville *U.S.A.* 31°51N 81°36W **85** F14
Hinganghat *India* 20°30N 78°52E **40** J11
Hingham *U.S.A.* 48°33N 110°25W **76** B8
Hingir *India* 21°57N 83°41E **43** J10
Hingoli *India* 19°41N 77°15E **40** K10
Hinna = Imi *Ethiopia* 6°28N 42°10E **47** F3
Hinnøya *Norway* 68°35N 15°50E **8** B16
Hinojosa del Duque *Spain* 38°30N 5°9W **21** C3
Hinsdale *U.S.A.* 42°47N 72°29W **83** D12
Hinthada = Henzada *Burma* 17°38N 95°26E **41** L19
Hinton *Canada* 53°26N 117°34W **70** C5
Hinton *U.S.A.* 37°40N 80°54W **81** G13
Hios *Greece* 38°27N 26°9E **23** E12
Hirado *Japan* 33°22N 129°33E **31** H4
Hirakud Dam *India* 21°32N 83°45E **41** J13
Hiran → *India* 23°6N 79°21E **43** H8
Hirapur *India* 24°22N 79°13E **43** G8
Hirara *Japan* 24°48N 125°17E **31** M2
Hiratsuka *Japan* 35°19N 139°21E **31** G9
Hiroo *Japan* 42°17N 143°19E **30** C11
Hirosaki *Japan* 40°34N 140°28E **30** D10
Hiroshima *Japan* 34°24N 132°30E **31** G6
Hiroshima □ *Japan* 34°50N 133°0E **31** G6
Hisar *India* 29°12N 75°45E **42** E6
Hisb, Sha'ib = Ḩasb, W. → *Iraq* 31°45N 44°17E **44** D5
Ḩismá *Si. Arabia* 28°30N 36°0E **44** D3
Hispaniola *W. Indies* 19°0N 71°0W **89** C5
Hīt *Iraq* 33°38N 42°49E **44** C4
Hita *Japan* 33°20N 130°58E **31** H5
Hitachi *Japan* 36°36N 140°39E **31** F10
Hitchin *U.K.* 51°58N 0°16W **13** F7
Hitiaa *Tahiti* 17°36S 149°18W **59** d
Hitoyoshi *Japan* 32°13N 130°45E **31** H5
Hitra *Norway* 63°30N 8°45E **8** E13
Hiva Oa *French Polynesia* 9°45S 139°0W **65** H14
Hixon *Canada* 53°25N 122°35W **70** C4
Ḩiyyon, N. → *Israel* 30°25N 35°10E **46** E4
Hjalmar L. *Canada* 61°33N 109°25W **71** A7
Hjälmaren *Sweden* 59°18N 15°40E **9** G16
Hjørring *Denmark* 57°29N 9°59E **9** H13
Hjort Trench *S. Ocean* 58°0S 157°30E **5** B10
Hkakabo Razi *Burma* 28°25N 97°23E **41** E20
Hlobane *S. Africa* 27°42S 31°0E **57** D5
Hluhluwe *S. Africa* 28°1S 32°15E **57** D5
Hluhluwe ⌂ *S. Africa* 22°10S 32°5E **57** C5
Hlyboka *Ukraine* 48°5N 25°56E **17** D13
Ho *Ghana* 6°37N 0°27E **50** G6
Ho Chi Minh City = Thanh Pho Ho Chi Minh *Vietnam* 10°58N 106°40E **39** G6
Ho Thuong *Vietnam* 19°32N 105°48E **38** C5
Hoa Binh *Vietnam* 20°50N 105°20E **38** B5
Hoa Da *Vietnam* 11°16N 108°40E **39** G7
Hoa Hiep *Vietnam* 11°34N 105°51E **39** G5
Hoai Nhon *Vietnam* 14°28N 109°1E **38** E7
Hoang Lien Son *Vietnam* 22°0N 104°0E **38** A4
Hoanib → *Namibia* 19°27S 12°46E **56** B2
Hoare B. *Canada* 65°17N 62°30W **69** C13
Hoarusib → *Namibia* 19°3S 12°36E **56** B2
Hobart *Australia* 42°50S 147°21E **63** G4
Hobart *U.S.A.* 35°1N 99°6W **84** D5
Hobbs *U.S.A.* 32°42N 103°8W **77** K12
Hobbs Coast *Antarctica* 74°50S 131°0W **5** D14
Hobe Sound *U.S.A.* 27°4N 80°8W **85** H14
Hoboken *U.S.A.* 40°44N 74°3W **83** F10
Hobro *Denmark* 56°39N 9°46E **9** H13
Hoburgen *Sweden* 56°55N 18°7E **9** H18
Hochfeld *Namibia* 21°28S 17°58E **56** C2
Hodaka-Dake *Japan* 36°17N 137°39E **31** F8
Hodeida = Al Ḩudaydah *Yemen* 14°50N 43°0E **47** E3
Hodgeville *Canada* 50°7N 106°58W **71** C7
Hodgson *Canada* 51°13N 97°36W **71** C9
Hódmezővásárhely *Hungary* 46°28N 20°22E **17** E11
Hodna, Chott el *Algeria* 35°26N 4°43E **50** A6
Hodonín *Czech Rep.* 48°50N 17°10E **17** D9
Hoek van Holland *Neths.* 52°0N 4°7E **15** C4
Hoengseong *S. Korea* 37°29N 127°59E **35** F14
Hoeryong *N. Korea* 42°30N 129°45E **35** C15
Hoeyang *N. Korea* 38°43N 127°36E **35** E14
Hof *Germany* 50°19N 11°55E **16** C6
Hofmeyr *S. Africa* 31°39S 25°50E **56** E4
Höfn *Iceland* 64°15N 15°13W **8** D6
Hofors *Sweden* 60°31N 16°15E **9** F17
Hofsjökull *Iceland* 64°49N 18°48W **8** D4
Hōfu *Japan* 34°3N 131°34E **31** G5
Hogan Group *Australia* 39°13S 147°1E **63** F4
Hogarth, Mt. *Australia* 21°48S 136°58E **62** C2
Hoge Kempen △ *Belgium* 51°6N 5°35E **15** C5
Hoggar = Ahaggar *Algeria* 23°0N 6°30E **50** D7
Hogsty Reef *Bahamas* 21°41N 73°48W **89** B5
Hoh → *U.S.A.* 47°45N 124°29W **78** C2
Hoh Xil Shan *China* 35°0N 89°0E **32** C3
Hohenwald *U.S.A.* 35°33N 87°33W **85** D11
Hoher Rhön = Rhön *Germany* 50°24N 9°58E **16** C5
Hohes Venn *Belgium* 50°30N 6°5E **15** D6
Hohhot *China* 40°52N 111°40E **34** D6
Hoi An *Vietnam* 15°30N 108°19E **38** E7
Hoi Xuan *Vietnam* 20°25N 105°9E **38** B5
Hoisington *U.S.A.* 38°31N 98°47W **80** F4
Hōjō *Japan* 33°58N 132°46E **31** H6
Hokianga Harbour *N.Z.* 35°31S 173°22E **59** A4
Hokitika *N.Z.* 42°42S 171°0E **59** E3
Hokkaidō □ *Japan* 43°30N 143°0E **30** C11
Hola *Kenya* 1°29S 40°2E **54** B4
Holakas *Greece* 35°57N 27°53E **25** D9
Holbrook *Australia* 35°42S 147°18E **63** F4
Holbrook *U.S.A.* 34°54N 110°10W **77** J8
Holden *U.S.A.* 39°6N 112°16W **76** G7
Holdenville *U.S.A.* 35°5N 96°24W **84** D6
Holdrege *U.S.A.* 40°26N 99°23W **80** E4
Holetown *Barbados* 13°11N 59°38W **89** g
Holguín *Cuba* 20°50N 76°20W **88** B4
Hollams Bird I. *Namibia* 24°40S 14°30E **56** C1
Holland *Mich., U.S.A.* 42°47N 86°7W **80** D10
Holland *N.Y., U.S.A.* 42°38N 78°32W **82** D6
Holley *U.S.A.* 43°14N 78°2W **82** C6
Hollidaysburg *U.S.A.* 40°26N 78°24W **82** F6
Hollis *U.S.A.* 34°41N 99°55W **84** D5
Hollister *Calif., U.S.A.* 36°51N 121°24W **78** J5
Hollister *Idaho, U.S.A.* 42°21N 114°35W **76** E6
Holly Hill *U.S.A.* 29°16N 81°3W **85** G14
Holly Springs *U.S.A.* 34°46N 89°27W **85** D10
Hollywood *U.S.A.* 26°0N 80°8W **85** J14
Holman *Canada* 70°44N 117°44W **68** B8
Hólmavík *Iceland* 65°42N 21°40W **8** D3
Holmen *U.S.A.* 43°58N 91°15W **80** D8
Holmes Reefs *Australia* 16°27S 148°0E **62** B4
Holmsund *Sweden* 63°41N 20°20E **8** E19
Holroyd → *Australia* 14°10S 141°36E **62** A3
Holstebro *Denmark* 56°22N 8°37E **9** H13
Holsworthy *U.K.* 50°48N 4°22W **13** G3
Holton *Canada* 54°31N 57°12W **73** B8
Holton *U.S.A.* 39°28N 95°44W **80** F6
Holtville *U.S.A.* 32°49N 115°23W **79** N11
Holwerd *Neths.* 53°22N 5°54E **15** A5
Holy I. *Anglesey, U.K.* 53°17N 4°37W **12** D3
Holy I. *Northumberland, U.K.* 55°40N 1°47W **12** B6
Holyhead *U.K.* 53°18N 4°38W **12** D3
Holyoke *Colo., U.S.A.* 40°35N 102°18W **76** F12
Holyoke *Mass., U.S.A.* 42°12N 72°37W **83** D12
Holyrood *Canada* 47°27N 53°8W **73** C9
Homa Bay *Kenya* 0°36S 34°30E **54** C3
Homalin *Burma* 24°55N 95°0E **41** G19
Homand *Iran* 32°28N 59°37E **45** C8
Homathko → *Canada* 51°0N 124°56W **70** C4
Hombori *Mali* 15°20N 1°38W **50** E5
Home B. *Canada* 68°40N 67°10W **69** C13
Home Hill *Australia* 19°43S 147°25E **62** B4
Home Reef *Tonga* 18°59S 174°47W **59** c
Homedale *U.S.A.* 43°37N 116°56W **76** E5
Homer *Alaska, U.S.A.* 59°39N 151°33W **74** a
Homer *La., U.S.A.* 32°48N 93°4W **84** E8
Homer City *U.S.A.* 40°32N 79°10W **82** F5
Homestead *Australia* 20°20S 145°40E **62** C4
Homestead *U.S.A.* 25°28N 80°29W **85** J14
Homestead ⌂ *U.S.A.* 40°17N 96°50W **80** E5
Homoine *Mozam.* 23°55S 35°8E **57** C6
Homs = Ḩimş *Syria* 34°40N 36°45E **46** A5
Homyel *Belarus* 52°28N 31°0E **17** B16
Hon Chong *Vietnam* 10°25N 104°30E **39** G5
Hon Hai *Vietnam* 10°0N 109°0E **39** G7
Hon Me *Vietnam* 19°23N 105°56E **38** C5
Honan = Henan □ *China* 34°0N 114°0E **34** H8
Honbetsu *Japan* 43°7N 143°37E **30** C11
Honcut *U.S.A.* 39°20N 121°32W **78** F5
Honda, Bahía *Cuba* 22°54N 83°10W **88** B3
Hondeklipbaai *S. Africa* 30°19S 17°17E **56** E2
Hondo *Japan* 32°27N 130°12E **31** H5
Hondo *U.S.A.* 29°21N 99°9W **84** G5
Hondo, Río → *Belize* 18°25N 88°21W **87** D7
Honduras ■ *Cent. Amer.* 14°40N 86°30W **88** D2
Honduras, G. de *Caribbean* 16°50N 87°0W **88** C2
Hønefoss *Norway* 60°10N 10°18E **9** F14
Honesdale *U.S.A.* 41°34N 75°16W **83** E9
Honey L. *U.S.A.* 40°15N 120°19W **78** E6
Honfleur *France* 49°25N 0°13E **20** B4
Hong → *Vietnam* 22°0N 104°0E **32** D5
Hong Gai *Vietnam* 20°57N 107°5E **38** B6
Hong He → *China* 32°25N 115°35E **34** H8
Hong Kong □ *China* 22°11N 114°14E **33** G11
Hong Kong I. *China* 22°16N 114°12E **33** G11
Hong Kong Int. ✕ (HKG) *China* 22°19N 113°57E **33** G10
Hongcheon *S. Korea* 37°44N 127°53E **35** F14
Hongjiang *China* 27°7N 109°59E **33** D5
Hongliu He → *China* 38°0N 109°50E **34** F5
Hongor *Mongolia* 45°45N 112°50E **34** B7
Hongsa *Laos* 19°43N 101°20E **38** C3
Hongseong *S. Korea* 36°37N 126°38E **35** F14
Hongshui He → *China* 23°48N 109°30E **33** D5
Hongtong *China* 36°16N 111°40E **34** F6
Honguedo, Détroit d' *Canada* 49°15N 64°0W **73** C7
Hongwon *N. Korea* 40°0N 127°56E **35** E14
Hongze Hu *China* 33°15N 118°35E **35** H10
Honiara *Solomon Is.* 9°27S 159°57E **58** B8
Honiton *U.K.* 50°47N 3°11W **13** G4
Honjō *Japan* 39°23N 140°3E **30** E10
Honningsvåg *Norway* 70°59N 25°59E **8** A21
Honolulu *U.S.A.* 21°19N 157°52W **74** b
Honshū *Japan* 36°0N 138°0E **33** C8
Hood, Mt. *U.S.A.* 45°23N 121°42W **76** D3
Hood, Pt. *Australia* 34°23S 119°34E **61** F2
Hood River *U.S.A.* 45°43N 121°31W **76** D3
Hoodsport *U.S.A.* 47°24N 123°9W **78** C3
Hoogeveen *Neths.* 52°44N 6°28E **15** B6
Hoogezand-Sappemeer *Neths.* 53°9N 6°45E **15** A6
Hooghly = Hugli → *India* 21°56N 88°4E **43** J13
Hooghly-Chinsura = Chunchura *India* 22°53N 88°27E **43** H13
Hook Hd. *Ireland* 52°7N 6°56W **10** D5
Hook I. *Australia* 20°4S 149°0E **62** b
Hook of Holland = Hoek van Holland *Neths.* 52°0N 4°7E **15** C4
Hooker *U.S.A.* 36°52N 101°13W **84** C4
Hooker Creek = Lajamanu *Australia* 18°23S 130°38E **60** C5
Hoonah *U.S.A.* 58°7N 135°27W **70** B1
Hooper Bay *U.S.A.* 61°32N 166°6W **74** a
Hoopeston *U.S.A.* 40°28N 87°40W **80** E10
Hoopstad *S. Africa* 27°50S 25°55E **56** D4
Hoorn *Neths.* 52°38N 5°4E **15** B5
Hoover *U.S.A.* 33°24N 86°49W **85** E11
Hoover Dam *U.S.A.* 36°1N 114°44W **79** K12
Hooversville *U.S.A.* 40°9N 78°55W **82** F6
Hop Bottom *U.S.A.* 41°42N 75°46W **83** E9
Hope *Canada* 49°25N 121°25W **70** D4
Hope *Ariz., U.S.A.* 33°43N 113°42W **79** M13
Hope *Ark., U.S.A.* 33°40N 93°36W **84** E8
Hope, L. *S. Austral., Australia* 28°24S 139°18E **63** D2
Hope, L. *W. Austral., Australia* 32°35S 120°15E **61** F3
Hope, Pt. *U.S.A.* 68°21N 166°47W **66** C3
Hope I. *Canada* 44°55N 80°11W **82** B4
Hope Town *Bahamas* 26°35N 76°57W **88** A4
Hope Vale *Australia* 15°16S 145°20E **62** B4
Hopedale *Canada* 55°28N 60°13W **73** A7
Hopedale *U.S.A.* 42°8N 71°33W **83** D13
Hopefield *S. Africa* 33°3S 18°22E **56** E2
Hopei = Hebei □ *China* 39°0N 116°0E **34** E9
Hopelchén *Mexico* 19°46N 89°51W **87** D7
Hopetoun *Vic., Australia* 35°42S 142°22E **63** F3
Hopetoun *W. Austral., Australia* 33°57S 120°7E **61** F3
Hopetown *S. Africa* 29°34S 24°3E **56** D3
Hopewell *U.S.A.* 37°18N 77°17W **81** G15
Hopkins, L. *Australia* 24°15S 128°35E **60** D4
Hopkinsville *U.S.A.* 36°52N 87°29W **80** G10
Hopland *U.S.A.* 38°58N 123°7W **78** G3
Hoquiam *U.S.A.* 46°59N 123°53W **78** D3
Hordern Hills *Australia* 20°15S 130°0E **60** D5
Horinger *China* 40°28N 111°48E **34** D6
Horlick Mts. *Antarctica* 84°0S 102°0W **5** E15
Horlivka *Ukraine* 48°19N 38°5E **19** E6
Hormak *Iran* 29°58N 60°51E **45** D9
Hormoz *Iran* 27°35N 55°0E **45** E7
Hormoz, Jaz.-ye *Iran* 27°8N 56°28E **45** E8
Hormozgān □ *Iran* 27°30N 56°0E **45** E8
Hormuz, Kūh-e *Iran* 27°27N 55°10E **45** E7
Hormuz, Str. of *The Gulf* 26°30N 56°30E **45** E8
Horn *Austria* 48°39N 15°40E **16** D8
Horn → *Canada* 61°30N 118°1W **70** A5
Horn, Cape = Hornos, C. de *Chile* 55°50S 67°30W **96** H3
Horn Head *Ireland* 55°14N 8°0W **10** A3
Horn I. *Australia* 10°37S 142°17E **62** A3
Horn Plateau *Canada* 62°15N 119°15W **70** A5
Hornavan *Sweden* 66°15N 17°30E **8** C17
Hornbeck *U.S.A.* 31°20N 93°24W **84** F8
Hornbrook *U.S.A.* 41°55N 122°33W **76** F2
Horncastle *U.K.* 53°13N 0°7W **12** D7
Hornell *U.S.A.* 42°20N 77°40W **82** D7
Hornell L. *Canada* 62°20N 119°25W **70** A5
Hornepayne *Canada* 49°14N 84°48W **72** C3
Hornings Mills *Canada* 44°9N 80°12W **82** B4
Hornitos *U.S.A.* 37°30N 120°14W **78** H6
Hornos, C. de *Chile* 55°50S 67°30W **96** H3
Hornsea *U.K.* 53°55N 0°11W **12** D7
Horobetsu = Noboribetsu *Japan* 42°24N 141°6E **30** C10
Horodenka *Ukraine* 48°41N 25°29E **17** D13
Horodok *Khmelnytskyy, Ukraine* 49°10N 26°34E **17** D14
Horodok *Lviv, Ukraine* 49°46N 23°32E **17** D12
Horokhiv *Ukraine* 50°30N 24°45E **17** C13
Horqin Youyi Qianqi *China* 46°5N 122°3E **35** A12
Horqueta *Paraguay* 23°15S 56°55W **94** A4
Horse Cr. → *U.S.A.* 41°57N 103°58W **76** F12
Horse I. *Canada* 53°20N 99°6W **71** C9
Horse Is. *Canada* 50°15N 55°50W **73** B8
Horsefly L. *Canada* 52°25N 121°0W **70** C4
Horseheads *U.S.A.* 42°10N 76°49W **82** D8
Horsens *Denmark* 55°52N 9°51E **9** J13
Horsham *Australia* 36°44S 142°13E **63** F3
Horsham *U.K.* 51°4N 0°20W **13** F7
Horta *Azores* 38°32N 28°38W **50** a
Horten *Norway* 59°25N 10°32E **9** G14
Horton *U.S.A.* 39°40N 95°32W **80** F6
Horton → *Canada* 69°56N 126°52W **68** C7
Horwood L. *Canada* 48°5N 82°20W **72** C3
Ḩoseynābād *Khuzestān, Iran* 32°45N 48°20E **45** C6
Ḩoseynābād *Kordestān, Iran* 35°33N 47°8E **44** C5
Hoshangabad *India* 22°45N 77°45E **42** H7
Hoshiarpur *India* 31°30N 75°58E **42** D6
Hospet *India* 15°15N 76°20E **40** M10
Hoste, I. *Chile* 55°0S 69°0W **96** H3
Hot *Thailand* 18°8N 98°29E **38** C2
Hot Creek Range *U.S.A.* 38°40N 116°20W **76** G5
Hot Springs *Ark., U.S.A.* 34°31N 93°3W **84** D8
Hot Springs *S. Dak., U.S.A.* 43°26N 103°29W **80** D2
Hot Springs △ *U.S.A.* 34°31N 93°3W **84** D8
Hotagen *Sweden* 63°59N 14°12E **8** E16
Hotan *China* 37°25N 79°55E **32** C2
Hotazel *S. Africa* 27°17S 22°58E **56** D3
Hotchkiss *U.S.A.* 38°48N 107°43W **76** G10
Hotham, C. *Australia* 12°2S 131°18E **60** B5
Hoting *Sweden* 64°8N 16°15E **8** D17
Hotte, Massif de la *Haiti* 18°30N 73°45W **89** C5
Hottentotsbaai *Namibia* 26°8S 14°59E **56** D1
Hou Hai *China* 22°32N 113°56E **33** F10
Houei Sai *Laos* 20°18N 100°26E **38** B3
Houffalize *Belgium* 50°8N 5°48E **15** D5
Houghton *Mich., U.S.A.* 47°7N 88°34W **80** B9
Houghton *N.Y., U.S.A.* 42°25N 78°10W **82** D6
Houghton L. *U.S.A.* 44°21N 84°44W **81** C11
Houghton-le-Spring *U.K.* 54°51N 1°28W **12** C6
Houhora Heads *N.Z.* 34°49S 173°9E **59** A4
Houlton *U.S.A.* 46°8N 67°51W **81** B20
Houma *U.S.A.* 29°36N 90°43W **85** G9
Housatonic → *U.S.A.* 41°10N 73°7W **83** E11
Houston *Canada* 54°25N 126°39W **70** C3
Houston *Mo., U.S.A.* 37°22N 91°58W **80** G8
Houston *Tex., U.S.A.* 29°45N 95°21W **84** G7
Hout → *S. Africa* 23°4S 29°36E **57** C4
Houtkraal *S. Africa* 30°23S 24°5E **56** E3
Houtman Abrolhos *Australia* 28°43S 113°48E **61** E1
Hovd □ *Mongolia* 48°2N 91°37E **32** B4
Hove *U.K.* 50°50N 0°10W **13** G7
Hovenweep ⌂ *U.S.A.* 37°20N 109°0W **77** H9
Hoveyzeh *Iran* 31°27N 48°4E **45** D6
Hövsgöl *Mongolia* 43°37N 109°39E **34** C5
Hövsgöl Nuur *Mongolia* 51°0N 100°30E **32** A5

Howar, Wadi → *Sudan* 17°30N 27°8E **51** E11
Howard *Australia* 25°16S 152°32E **63** D5
Howard *Pa., U.S.A.* 41°1N 77°40W **82** F7
Howard *S. Dak., U.S.A.* 44°1N 97°32W **80** C5
Howe *U.S.A.* 43°48N 113°0W **76** E7
Howe, C. *Australia* 37°30S 150°0E **63** F5
Howe, West Cape *Australia* 35°8S 117°36E **61** G2
Howe I. *Canada* 44°16N 76°17W **83** B8
Howell *U.S.A.* 42°36N 83°56W **81** D12
Howick *Canada* 45°11N 73°51W **83** A11
Howick *S. Africa* 29°28S 30°14E **57** D5
Howick Group *Australia* 14°20S 145°30E **62** A4
Howitt, L. *Australia* 27°40S 138°40E **63** D2
Howland I. *Pac. Oc.* 0°48N 176°38W **64** G10
Howrah = Haora *India* 22°34N 88°18E **43** H13
Howth *Ireland* 53°23N 6°6W **10** C5
Howth Hd. *Ireland* 53°22N 6°4W **10** C5
Höxter *Germany* 51°46N 9°22E **16** C5
Hoy *U.K.* 58°50N 3°15W **11** C5
Høyanger *Norway* 61°13N 6°4E **8** F12
Hoyerswerda *Germany* 51°26N 14°14E **16** C8
Hoylake *U.K.* 53°24N 3°10W **12** D4
Hpa-an = Pa-an *Burma* 16°51N 97°40E **41** L20
Hpunan Pass *Burma* 27°30N 96°55E **41** F20
Hradec Králové *Czech Rep.* 50°15N 15°50E **16** C8
Hrodna *Belarus* 53°42N 23°52E **17** B12
Hrodzyanka *Belarus* 53°31N 28°42E **17** B15
Hron → *Slovak Rep.* 47°49N 18°45E **17** E10
Hrvatska = Croatia ■ *Europe* 45°20N 16°0E **16** F9
Hrymayliv *Ukraine* 49°20N 26°5E **17** D14
Hsenwi *Burma* 23°22N 97°55E **41** H20
Hsiamen = Xiamen *China* 24°25N 118°4E **33** D6
Hsian = Xi'an *China* 34°15N 109°0E **34** G5
Hsinchu *Taiwan* 24°48N 120°58E **33** D7
Hsinhailien = Lianyungang *China* 34°40N 119°11E **35** G10
Hsüchou = Xuzhou *China* 34°18N 117°10E **35** G9
Hu Xian *China* 34°8N 108°42E **34** G5
Hua Hin *Thailand* 12°34N 99°58E **38** F2
Hua Xian *Henan, China* 35°30N 114°30E **34** G8
Hua Xian *Shaanxi, China* 34°30N 109°48E **34** G5
Huab → *Namibia* 20°52S 13°25E **56** B2
Huachinera *Mexico* 30°9N 108°55W **86** A3
Huacho *Peru* 11°10S 77°35W **92** F3
Huade *China* 41°55N 113°59E **34** D7
Huadian *China* 43°0N 126°40E **35** C14
Huahine, Î. *French Polynesia* 16°46S 150°58W **65** J12
Huai Had △ *Thailand* 16°52N 104°17E **38** D5
Huai He → *China* 33°0N 118°30E **33** C6
Huai Nam Dang △ *Thailand* 19°30N 98°30E **38** C2
Huai Yot *Thailand* 7°45N 99°37E **39** J2
Huai'an *Hebei, China* 40°30N 114°20E **34** D8
Huai'an *Jiangsu, China* 33°30N 119°10E **35** H10
Huaibei *China* 34°0N 116°48E **34** G9
Huaide = Gongzhuling *China* 43°30N 124°40E **35** C13
Huaidezhen *China* 43°48N 124°50E **35** C13
Huainan *China* 32°38N 116°58E **33** C6
Huairen *China* 39°48N 113°20E **34** E7
Huairou *China* 40°20N 116°35E **34** D9
Huaiyang *China* 33°40N 114°52E **34** H8
Huaiyin *China* 33°30N 119°2E **35** H10
Huaiyuan *China* 32°55N 117°10E **35** H9
Huajuapán de León *Mexico* 17°48N 97°46W **87** D5
Hualapai Peak *U.S.A.* 35°5N 113°54W **77** J7
Huallaga → *Peru* 5°15S 75°30W **92** E3
Huambo *Angola* 12°42S 15°54E **53** G3
Huan Jiang → *China* 34°28N 109°0E **34** G5
Huan Xian *China* 36°33N 107°7E **34** F4
Huancabamba *Peru* 5°10S 79°15W **92** E3
Huancane *Peru* 15°10S 69°44W **92** G5
Huancavelica *Peru* 12°50S 75°5W **92** F3
Huancayo *Peru* 12°5S 75°12W **92** F3
Huanchaca *Bolivia* 20°15S 66°40W **92** H5
Huang Hai = Yellow Sea *China* 35°0N 123°0E **35** G12
Huang He → *China* 37°55N 118°50E **35** F10
Huang Xian *China* 37°38N 120°30E **35** F11
Huangling *China* 35°34N 109°15E **34** G5
Huanglong *China* 35°30N 109°59E **34** G5
Huangshan *China* 29°42N 118°25E **33** D6
Huangshi *China* 30°10N 115°3E **33** C6
Huangsongdian *China* 43°45N 127°25E **35** C14
Huanren *China* 41°23N 125°20E **35** D13
Huantai *China* 36°58N 117°56E **35** F9
Huánuco *Peru* 9°55S 76°15W **92** E3
Huaraz *Peru* 9°30S 77°32W **92** E3
Huarmey *Peru* 10°5S 78°5W **92** F3
Huascarán, Nevado *Peru* 9°7S 77°37W **92** E3
Huasco *Chile* 28°30S 71°15W **94** B1
Huasco → *Chile* 28°27S 71°13W **94** B1
Huasna *U.S.A.* 35°6N 120°24W **79** K6
Huatabampo *Mexico* 26°50N 109°38W **86** B3
Huauchinango *Mexico* 20°12N 98°3W **87** C5
Huautla de Jiménez *Mexico* 18°8N 96°51W **87** D5
Huayin *China* 34°35N 110°5E **34** G6
Hubbard *Ohio, U.S.A.* 41°9N 80°34W **82** E4
Hubbard *Tex., U.S.A.* 31°51N 96°48W **81** K6
Hubbart Pt. *Canada* 59°21N 94°41W **71** B10
Hubei □ *China* 31°0N 112°0E **33** C6
Hubli *India* 15°22N 75°15E **40** M9
Huch'ang *N. Korea* 41°25N 127°2E **35** D14
Hucknall *U.K.* 53°3N 1°13W **12** D6
Huddersfield *U.K.* 53°39N 1°47W **12** D6
Hudiksvall *Sweden* 61°43N 17°10E **8** F17
Hudson *Canada* 50°6N 92°9W **72** B1
Hudson *Mass., U.S.A.* 42°23N 71°34W **83** D13
Hudson *N.Y., U.S.A.* 42°15N 73°46W **83** D11
Hudson *Wis., U.S.A.* 44°58N 92°45W **80** C7
Hudson *Wyo., U.S.A.* 42°54N 108°35W **76** E9
Hudson → *U.S.A.* 40°42N 74°2W **83** F10
Hudson, C. *Antarctica* 68°21S 153°45E **5** C20
Hudson Bay *Nunavut, Canada* 60°0N 86°0W **69** D11
Hudson Bay *Sask., Canada* 52°51N 102°23W **71** C8
Hudson Falls *U.S.A.* 43°18N 73°35W **83** C11
Hudson Mts. *Antarctica* 74°32S 99°20W **5** D16
Hudson Str. *Canada* 62°0N 70°0W **69** C13
Hudson's Hope *Canada* 56°0N 121°54W **70** B4
Hue *Vietnam* 16°30N 107°35E **38** D6
Huehuetenango *Guatemala* 15°20N 91°28W **88** C1
Huejúcar *Mexico* 22°21N 103°13W **86** C4
Huelva *Spain* 37°18N 6°57W **21** D2
Huentelauquén *Chile* 31°38S 71°33W **94** C1
Huerta, Sa. de la *Argentina* 31°10S 67°30W **94** C2
Huesca *Spain* 42°8N 0°25W **21** A5
Huetamo *Mexico* 18°36N 100°53W **86** D4
Hugh → *Australia* 25°1S 134°1E **62** D1
Hughenden *Australia* 20°52S 144°10E **62** C3
Hughesville *U.S.A.* 41°14N 76°44W **83** E8
Hugli → *India* 21°56N 88°4E **43** J13
Hugo *Colo., U.S.A.* 39°8N 103°28W **76** G12
Hugo *Okla., U.S.A.* 34°1N 95°31W **84** D7
Hugoton *U.S.A.* 37°11N 101°21W **80** G3
Hui Xian = Huixian *China* 35°27N 113°12E **34** G7
Hui Xian *China* 33°50N 106°4E **34** H4
Hui'anbu *China* 37°28N 106°38E **34** F4
Huichapan *Mexico* 20°23N 99°39W **87** C5
Huichon *N. Korea* 40°10N 126°16E **35** D14
Huifa He → *China* 43°0N 127°50E **35** C14
Huila, Nevado del *Colombia* 3°0N 76°0W **92** C3
Huimin *China* 37°27N 117°28E **35** F9
Huinan *China* 42°40N 126°2E **35** C14
Huinca Renancó *Argentina* 34°51S 64°22W **94** C3
Huining *China* 35°38N 105°0E **34** G3
Huinong *China* 39°5N 106°35E **34** E4
Huiting *China* 34°5N 116°5E **34** G9
Huixian *China* 35°27N 113°12E **34** G7
Huixtla *Mexico* 15°9N 92°28W **87** D6
Huize *China* 26°24N 103°15E **32** D5
Hukawng Valley *Burma* 26°30N 96°30E **41** F20
Hukuntsi *Botswana* 23°58S 21°45E **56** C3
Ḥulayfā' *Si. Arabia* 25°58N 40°45E **44** E4
Hulin He → *China* 45°0N 122°10E **35** B12
Hull = Kingston upon Hull *U.K.* 53°45N 0°21W **12** D7
Hull *Canada* 45°26N 75°43W **83** A9
Hull → *U.K.* 53°44N 0°20W **12** D7
Hulst *Neths.* 51°17N 4°2E **15** C4
Hulun Nur *China* 49°0N 117°30E **33** B6
Huma, Tanjung *Malaysia* 5°29N 100°16E **39** c
Humacao *Puerto Rico* 18°9N 65°50W **89** d
Humahuaca *Argentina* 23°10S 65°25W **94** A2
Humaitá *Brazil* 7°35S 63°1W **92** E6
Humaitá *Paraguay* 27°2S 58°31W **94** B4
Humansdorp *S. Africa* 34°2S 24°46E **56** E3
Humbe *Angola* 16°40S 14°55E **56** B1
Humber → *U.K.* 53°42N 0°27W **12** D7
Humboldt *Canada* 52°15N 105°9W **71** C7
Humboldt *Iowa, U.S.A.* 42°44N 94°13W **80** D6
Humboldt *Tenn., U.S.A.* 35°50N 88°55W **85** D10
Humboldt → *U.S.A.* 39°59N 118°36W **76** G4
Humboldt Gletscher = Sermersuaq *Greenland* 79°30N 62°0W **4** B4
Hume *U.S.A.* 36°48N 118°54W **78** J8
Hume, L. *Australia* 36°0S 147°5E **63** F4
Humen *China* 22°50N 113°40E **33** F10
Humenné *Slovak Rep.* 48°55N 21°50E **17** D11
Humphreys, Mt. *U.S.A.* 37°17N 118°40W **78** H8
Humphreys Peak *U.S.A.* 35°21N 111°41W **77** J8
Humptulips *U.S.A.* 47°14N 123°57W **78** C3
Hūn *Libya* 29°2N 16°0E **51** C9
Hun Jiang → *China* 40°50N 125°38E **35** D13
Húnaflói *Iceland* 65°50N 20°50W **8** D3
Hunan □ *China* 27°30N 112°0E **33** D6
Hunchun *China* 42°52N 130°28E **35** C16
Hundewali *Pakistan* 31°55N 72°38E **42** D5
Hundred Mile House *Canada* 51°38N 121°18W **70** C4
Hunedoara *Romania* 45°40N 22°50E **17** F12
Hung Yen *Vietnam* 20°39N 106°4E **38** B6
Hunga Ha'apai *Tonga* 20°41S 175°7W **59** c
Hungary ■ *Europe* 47°20N 19°20E **17** E10
Hungary, Plain of *Europe* 47°0N 20°0E **6** F10
Hungerford *Australia* 28°58S 144°24E **63** D3
Hŭngnam *N. Korea* 39°49N 127°45E **35** E14
Hunjiang *China* 41°54N 126°26E **35** D14
Hunsberge *Namibia* 27°45S 17°12E **56** D2
Hunsrück *Germany* 49°56N 7°27E **16** D4
Hunstanton *U.K.* 52°56N 0°29E **12** E8
Hunter *U.S.A.* 42°13N 74°13W **83** D10
Hunter I. *Australia* 40°30S 144°45E **63** G3
Hunter I. *Canada* 51°55N 128°0W **70** C3
Hunter Ra. *Australia* 32°45S 150°15E **63** E5
Hunters Road *Zimbabwe* 19°9S 29°49E **55** F2
Hunterville *N.Z.* 39°56S 175°35E **59** C5
Huntingburg *U.S.A.* 38°18N 86°57W **80** F10
Huntingdon *Canada* 45°6N 74°10W **72** C5
Huntingdon *U.K.* 52°20N 0°11W **13** E7
Huntingdon *U.S.A.* 40°30N 78°1W **82** F6
Huntington *Ind., U.S.A.* 40°53N 85°30W **81** E11
Huntington *N.Y., U.S.A.* 40°52N 73°26W **83** F11
Huntington *Oreg., U.S.A.* 44°21N 117°16W **76** D5
Huntington *Utah, U.S.A.* 39°20N 110°58W **76** G8
Huntington *W. Va., U.S.A.* 38°25N 82°27W **81** F12
Huntington Beach *U.S.A.* 33°40N 118°5W **79** M9
Huntly *N.Z.* 37°34S 175°11E **59** B5
Huntly *U.K.* 57°27N 2°47W **11** D6
Huntsville *Canada* 45°20N 79°14W **82** A5
Huntsville *Ala., U.S.A.* 34°44N 86°35W **85** D11
Huntsville *Tex., U.S.A.* 30°43N 95°33W **84** F7
Hunyani → *Zimbabwe* 15°57S 30°39E **55** F3
Hunyuan *China* 39°42N 113°42E **34** E7
Hunza → *India* 35°54N 74°20E **43** B6
Huo Xian = Huozhou *China* 36°36N 111°42E **34** F6
Huong Khe *Vietnam* 18°13N 105°41E **38** C5
Huonville *Australia* 43°0S 147°5E **63** G4
Huozhou *China* 36°36N 111°42E **34** F6
Hupeh = Hubei □ *China* 31°0N 112°0E **33** C6
Ḥūr *Iran* 30°50N 57°7E **45** D8
Ḥuraymīla *Si. Arabia* 25°8N 46°8E **44** E5
Hurd, C. *Canada* 45°13N 81°44W **82** A3
Hure Qi *China* 42°45N 121°45E **35** C11
Hurghada *Egypt* 27°15N 33°50E **51** C12
Hurley *N. Mex., U.S.A.* 32°42N 108°8W **77** K9
Hurley *Wis., U.S.A.* 46°27N 90°11W **80** B8
Huron *Calif., U.S.A.* 36°12N 120°6W **78** J6
Huron *Ohio, U.S.A.* 41°24N 82°33W **82** E2
Huron *S. Dak., U.S.A.* 44°22N 98°13W **80** C4
Huron, L. *U.S.A.* 44°30N 82°40W **82** B2
Huron East *Canada* 43°37N 81°18W **82** C3
Hurricane *U.S.A.* 37°11N 113°17W **77** H7
Hurungwe ⌓ *Zimbabwe* 16°7S 29°5E **55** F2
Hurunui → *N.Z.* 42°54S 173°18E **59** E4
Húsavík *Iceland* 66°3N 17°21W **8** C5
Huşi *Romania* 46°41N 28°7E **17** E15
Hustadvika *Norway* 63°0N 7°0E **8** E12
Hustontown *U.S.A.* 40°3N 78°2W **82** F6
Hutchinson *Kans., U.S.A.* 38°5N 97°56W **80** F5
Hutchinson *Minn., U.S.A.* 44°54N 94°22W **80** C6
Hutte Sauvage, L. de la *Canada* 56°15N 64°45W **73** A7
Hutton, Mt. *Australia* 25°51S 148°20E **63** D4
Huy *Belgium* 50°31N 5°15E **15** D5
Huzhou *China* 30°51N 120°8E **33** C7
Hvammstangi *Iceland* 65°24N 20°57W **8** D3
Hvar *Croatia* 43°11N 16°28E **22** C7
Hvítá → *Iceland* 64°30N 21°58W **8** D3
Hwacheon-Cheosuji *S. Korea* 38°5N 127°50E **35** E14
Hwang Ho = Huang He → *China* 37°55N 118°50E **35** F10
Hwange *Zimbabwe* 18°18S 26°30E **55** F2
Hwange △ *Zimbabwe* 19°0S 26°30E **56** B4
Hyannis *Mass., U.S.A.* 41°39N 70°17W **81** E18
Hyannis *Nebr., U.S.A.* 42°0N 101°46W **80** E3
Hyargas Nuur *Mongolia* 49°0N 93°0E **32** B4
Hydaburg *U.S.A.* 55°15N 132°50W **70** B2
Hyde Park *U.S.A.* 41°47N 73°56W **83** E11
Hyden *Australia* 32°24S 118°53E **61** F2
Hyder *U.S.A.* 55°55N 130°5W **70** B2
Hyderabad *India* 17°22N 78°29E **40** L11
Hyderabad *Pakistan* 25°23N 68°24E **42** G3
Hydra *Greece* 37°20N 23°28E **23** F10
Hyères *France* 43°8N 6°9E **20** E7
Hyères, Îs. d' *France* 43°0N 6°20E **20** E7
Hyesan *N. Korea* 41°20N 128°10E **35** D15
Hyland → *Canada* 59°52N 128°12W **70** B3
Hymia *India* 33°40N 78°2E **43** C8
Hyndman Peak *U.S.A.* 43°45N 114°8W **76** E6
Hyōgo □ *Japan* 35°15N 134°50E **31** G7
Hyrum *U.S.A.* 41°38N 111°51W **76** F8
Hysham *U.S.A.* 46°18N 107°14W **76** C10
Hythe *U.K.* 51°4N 1°5E **13** F9
Hyūga *Japan* 32°25N 131°35E **31** H5
Hyvinge = Hyvinkää *Finland* 60°38N 24°50E **8** F21
Hyvinkää *Finland* 60°38N 24°50E **8** F21

I

I-n-Gall *Niger* 16°51N 7°1E **50** E7
Iaco → *Brazil* 9°3S 68°34W **92** E5
Iakora *Madag.* 23°6S 46°40E **57** C8
Ialomiţa → *Romania* 44°42N 27°51E **17** F14
Iaşi *Romania* 47°10N 27°40E **17** E14
Ib → *India* 21°34N 83°48E **43** J10
Iba *Phil.* 15°22N 120°0E **37** A6
Ibadan *Nigeria* 7°22N 3°58E **50** G6
Ibagué *Colombia* 4°20N 75°20W **92** C3
Ibar → *Serbia* 43°43N 20°45E **23** C9
Ibaraki □ *Japan* 36°10N 140°10E **31** F10
Ibarra *Ecuador* 0°21N 78°7W **92** C3
Ibb *Yemen* 14°2N 44°10E **47** E3
Ibembo *Dem. Rep. of the Congo* 2°35N 23°35E **54** B1
Ibenga → *Congo* 2°19N 18°9E **52** D3
Ibera, L. *Argentina* 28°30S 57°9W **94** B4
Iberian Peninsula *Europe* 40°0N 5°0W **6** H5
Iberville *Canada* 45°19N 73°17W **83** A11
Iberville, Lac d' *Canada* 55°55N 73°15W **72** A5
Ibiá *Brazil* 19°30S 46°30W **93** G9
Ibiapaba, Sa. da *Brazil* 4°0S 41°30W **93** D10
Ibicuí → *Brazil* 29°25S 56°47W **95** B4
Ibicuy *Argentina* 33°55S 59°10W **94** C4
Ibiza = Eivissa *Spain* 38°54N 1°26E **24** C7
Ibo *Mozam.* 12°22S 40°40E **55** E5
Ibonma *Indonesia* 3°29S 133°31E **37** E8
Ibotirama *Brazil* 12°13S 43°12W **93** F10
Ibrāhīm → *Lebanon* 34°4N 35°38E **46** A4
'Ibrī *Oman* 23°14N 56°30E **45** F8
Ibu *Indonesia* 1°35N 127°33E **37** D7
Ibusuki *Japan* 31°12N 130°40E **31** J5
Ica *Peru* 14°0S 75°48W **92** F3
Iça → *Brazil* 2°55S 67°58W **92** D5
Icacos Pt. *Trin. & Tob.* 10°3N 61°57W **93** K15
Içana *Brazil* 0°21N 67°19W **92** C5
Içana → *Brazil* 0°26N 67°19W **92** C5
İçel *Turkey* 36°51N 34°36E **44** B2
Iceland ■ *Europe* 64°45N 19°0W **8** D4
Iceland Basin *Atl. Oc.* 61°0N 19°0W **4** C7
Icelandic Plateau *Arctic* 64°0N 10°0W **4** C7
Ich'ang = Yichang *China* 30°40N 111°20E **33** C6
Ichchapuram *India* 19°10N 84°40E **41** K14
Icheon *S. Korea* 37°17N 127°27E **35** F14
Ichhawar *India* 23°1N 77°1E **42** H7
Ichihara *Japan* 35°28N 140°5E **31** G10
Ichikawa *Japan* 35°43N 139°54E **31** G9
Ichilo → *Bolivia* 15°57S 64°50W **92** G6
Ichinohe *Japan* 40°13N 141°17E **30** D10
Ichinomiya *Japan* 35°18N 136°48E **31** G8
Ichinoseki *Japan* 38°55N 141°8E **30** E10
Icod *Canary Is.* 28°22N 16°43W **24** F3
Icy C. *U.S.A.* 70°20N 161°52W **66** B3
Ida Grove *U.S.A.* 42°21N 95°28W **80** D6
Idabel *U.S.A.* 33°54N 94°50W **84** E7
Idaho □ *U.S.A.* 45°0N 115°0W **76** D6
Idaho City *U.S.A.* 43°50N 115°50W **76** E6
Idaho Falls *U.S.A.* 43°30N 112°2W **76** E7
Idalia △ *Australia* 24°49S 144°36E **62** C3
Idar-Oberstein *Germany* 49°43N 7°16E **16** D4
Idensalmi = Iisalmi *Finland* 63°32N 27°10E **8** E22
Idfû *Egypt* 24°55N 32°49E **51** D12
Ídhra = Hydra *Greece* 37°20N 23°28E **23** F10
Idi *Indonesia* 5°2N 97°37E **36** C1
Idi, Oros = Psiloritis, Oros *Greece* 35°15N 24°45E **25** D6
Idiofa *Dem. Rep. of the Congo* 4°55S 19°42E **52** E3
Idlib *Syria* 35°55N 36°36E **44** C3
Idria *U.S.A.* 36°25N 120°41W **78** J6
Idutywa = Dutywa *S. Africa* 32°8S 28°18E **57** E4
Ieper *Belgium* 50°51N 2°53E **15** D2
Ierapetra *Greece* 35°1N 25°44E **25** E7
Iesi *Italy* 43°31N 13°14E **22** C5
Ifakara *Tanzania* 8°8S 36°41E **52** F7
'Ifāl, W. al → *Si. Arabia* 28°7N 35°3E **44** D2
Ifanadiana *Madag.* 21°19S 47°39E **57** C8
Ife *Nigeria* 7°30N 4°31E **50** G6
Iffley *Australia* 18°53S 141°12E **62** B3
Iforas, Adrar des *Africa* 19°40N 1°40E **50** E6
Ifould, L. *Australia* 30°52S 132°6E **61** F5
Iganga *Uganda* 0°37N 33°28E **54** B3
Igarapava *Brazil* 20°3S 47°47W **93** H9
Igarka *Russia* 67°30N 86°33E **28** C9
Igatimi *Paraguay* 24°5S 55°40W **95** A4
Iggesund *Sweden* 61°39N 17°10E **8** F17
Iglésias *Italy* 39°19N 8°32E **22** E3
Igloolik *Canada* 69°20N 81°49W **69** C11
Igluligaarjuk = Chesterfield Inlet *Canada* 63°30N 90°45W **68** C10
Iglulik = Igloolik *Canada* 69°20N 81°49W **69** C11
Ignace *Canada* 49°30N 91°40W **72** C1
İğneada Burnu *Turkey* 41°53N 28°2E **23** D13
Igoumenitsa *Greece* 39°32N 20°18E **23** E9
Iguaçu → *Brazil* 25°36S 54°36W **95** B5
Iguaçu, Cat. del *Brazil* 25°41S 54°26W **95** B5
Iguaçu △ *Brazil* 25°30S 54°0W **95** B5
Iguaçu Falls = Iguaçu, Cat. del *Brazil* 25°41S 54°26W **95** B5
Iguala *Mexico* 18°21N 99°32W **87** D5
Igualada *Spain* 41°37N 1°37E **21** B6
Iguassu = Iguaçu → *Brazil* 25°36S 54°36W **95** B5
Iguatu *Brazil* 6°20S 39°18W **93** E11
Iguazú △ *Argentina* 25°42S 54°22W **95** B5
Iguidi, Erg *Africa* 27°0N 7°0W **50** C4
Iharana *Madag.* 13°25S 50°0E **57** A9
Ihbulag *Mongolia* 43°11N 107°10E **34** C4
Iheya-Shima *Japan* 27°4N 127°58E **31** L3
Ihosy *Madag.* 22°24S 46°8E **57** C8
Ihotry, Farihy *Madag.* 21°56S 43°41E **57** C7
Ii *Finland* 65°19N 25°22E **8** D21
Ii-Shima *Japan* 26°43N 127°47E **31** L3
Iida *Japan* 35°35N 137°50E **31** G8
Iijoki → *Finland* 65°20N 25°20E **8** D21
Iisalmi *Finland* 63°32N 27°10E **8** E22
Iiyama *Japan* 36°51N 138°22E **31** F9
Iizuka *Japan* 33°38N 130°42E **31** H5
Ijâfene *Mauritania* 20°40N 8°0W **50** D4
Ijebu-Ode *Nigeria* 6°47N 3°58E **50** G6
IJmuiden *Neths.* 52°28N 4°35E **15** B4
Ijo älv = Iijoki → *Finland* 65°20N 25°20E **8** D21
IJssel → *Neths.* 52°35N 5°50E **15** B5
IJsselmeer *Neths.* 52°45N 5°20E **15** B5
Ijuí *Brazil* 28°23S 53°55W **95** B5
Ijuí → *Brazil* 27°58S 55°20W **95** B4
Ikalamavony *Madag.* 21°9S 46°35E **57** C8
Ikaluktutiak *Canada* 69°10N 105°0W **68** C9
Ikanga *Kenya* 1°42S 38°4E **54** C4
Ikare *Nigeria* 7°32N 5°40E **50** G7
Ikaria *Greece* 37°35N 26°10E **23** F12
Ikeda *Japan* 34°1N 133°48E **31** G6
Ikela *Dem. Rep. of the Congo* 1°6S 23°6E **52** E4
Iki *Japan* 33°45N 129°42E **31** H4
Ikimba L. *Tanzania* 1°30S 31°20E **54** C3
Ikongo *Madag.* 21°52S 47°27E **57** C8
Ikopa → *Madag.* 16°45S 46°40E **57** B8
Ikorongo ⌓ *Tanzania* 1°50S 34°53E **54** C3
Ikparjuk = Arctic Bay *Canada* 73°1N 85°7W **69** B11
Iksan *S. Korea* 35°59N 127°0E **35** G14
Ikungu *Tanzania* 1°33S 33°42E **54** C3
Ikuntji = Haast Bluff *Australia* 23°22S 132°0E **60** D5
Ilagan *Phil.* 17°7N 121°53E **37** A6
Ilaka *Madag.* 19°33S 48°52E **57** B8
Īlām *Iran* 33°36N 46°36E **44** C5
Ilam *Nepal* 26°58N 87°58E **43** F12
Īlām □ *Iran* 33°0N 47°0E **44** C5
Ilanskiy *Russia* 56°14N 96°3E **29** D10
Iława *Poland* 53°36N 19°34E **17** B10
Ile → *Kazakhstan* 45°53N 77°10E **28** E8
Île-à-la-Crosse *Canada* 55°27N 107°53W **71** B7
Île-à-la-Crosse, Lac *Canada* 55°40N 107°45W **71** B7
Île-de-France □ *France* 49°0N 2°20E **20** B5
Ilebo *Dem. Rep. of the Congo* 4°17S 20°55E **52** E4
Ilek *Russia* 51°32N 53°21E **28** D6
Ilek → *Russia* 51°30N 53°22E **18** D9
Ilesha *Nigeria* 7°37N 4°40E **50** G6
Ilford *Canada* 56°4N 95°35W **71** B9
Ilfracombe *Australia* 23°30S 144°30E **62** C3
Ilfracombe *U.K.* 51°12N 4°8W **13** F3
Ilha de Moçambique *Mozam.* 15°4S 40°52E **55** F5
Ilhéus *Brazil* 14°49S 39°2W **93** F11
Ili = Ile → *Kazakhstan* 45°53N 77°10E **28** E8
Iliamna L. *U.S.A.* 59°30N 155°0W **74** C4
Ilias, Profitis *Greece* 36°17N 27°56E **25** C9
Iligan *Phil.* 8°12N 124°13E **37** C6
Ilion *U.S.A.* 43°1N 75°2W **83** D9
Ilkeston *U.K.* 52°58N 1°19W **12** E6
Ilkley *U.K.* 53°56N 1°48W **12** D6
Illampu = Ancohuma, Nevado *Bolivia* 16°0S 68°50W **92** G5
Illana B. *Phil.* 7°35N 123°45E **37** C6
Illapel *Chile* 32°0S 71°10W **94** C1
Iller → *Germany* 48°23N 9°58E **16** D6
Illetas *Spain* 39°32N 2°35E **24** B9
Illimani, Nevado *Bolivia* 16°30S 67°50W **92** G5
Illinois □ *U.S.A.* 40°15N 89°30W **80** E9
Illinois → *U.S.A.* 38°58N 90°28W **80** F8
Illizi *Algeria* 26°31N 8°32E **50** C7
Ilma, L. *Australia* 29°13S 127°46E **61** E4
Ilmajoki *Finland* 62°44N 22°34E **8** E20
Ilmen, Ozero *Russia* 58°15N 31°10E **18** C5
Ilo *Peru* 17°40S 71°20W **92** G4
Iloilo *Phil.* 10°45N 122°33E **37** B6
Ilomantsi *Finland* 62°38N 30°57E **8** E24
Ilorin *Nigeria* 8°30N 4°35E **50** G6
Ilwaco *U.S.A.* 46°19N 124°3W **78** D2
Ilwaki *Indonesia* 7°55S 126°30E **37** F7
Imabari *Japan* 34°4N 133°0E **31** G6
Imaloto → *Madag.* 23°27S 45°13E **57** C8
Imandra, Ozero *Russia* 67°30N 33°0E **8** C25
Imanombo *Madag.* 24°26S 45°49E **57** C8
Imari *Japan* 33°15N 129°52E **31** H4
Imatra *Finland* 61°12N 28°48E **8** F23
imeni 26 Bakinskikh Komissarov = Neftçala *Azerbaijan* 39°19N 49°12E **45** B6
imeni 26 Bakinskikh Komissarov *Turkmenistan* 39°22N 54°10E **45** B7
imeni Ismail Samani, Pik *Tajikistan* 39°0N 72°2E **28** F8
Imeri, Serra *Brazil* 0°50N 65°25W **92** C5
Imerimandroso *Madag.* 17°26S 48°35E **57** B8
Imfolozi ⌓ *S. Africa* 28°18S 31°50E **57** D5
Imi *Ethiopia* 6°28N 42°10E **47** F3
Imlay *U.S.A.* 40°40N 118°9W **76** F4
Imlay City *U.S.A.* 43°2N 83°5W **82** D1
Immingham *U.K.* 53°37N 0°13W **12** D7
Immokalee *U.S.A.* 26°25N 81°25W **85** H14
Ímola *Italy* 44°20N 11°42E **22** B4
Imperatriz *Brazil* 5°30S 47°29W **93** E9
Impéria *Italy* 43°53N 8°3E **20** E8
Imperial *Canada* 51°21N 105°28W **71** C7
Imperial *Calif., U.S.A.* 32°51N 115°34W **79** N11
Imperial *Nebr., U.S.A.* 40°31N 101°39W **80** E3
Imperial Beach *U.S.A.* 32°35N 117°6W **79** N9
Imperial Dam *U.S.A.* 32°55N 114°25W **79** N12
Imperial Res. *U.S.A.* 32°53N 114°28W **79** N12
Imperial Valley *U.S.A.* 33°0N 115°30W **79** N11
Imperieuse Reef *Australia* 17°36S 118°50E **60** C2
Impfondo *Congo* 1°40N 18°0E **52** D3
Imphal *India* 24°48N 93°56E **41** G18
İmroz = Gökçeada *Turkey* 40°10N 25°50E **23** D11
Imuris *Mexico* 30°47N 110°52W **86** A2
Imuruan B. *Phil.* 10°40N 119°10E **37** B5
In Salah *Algeria* 27°10N 2°32E **50** C6
Ina *Japan* 35°50N 137°55E **31** G8
Inagua △ *Bahamas* 21°5N 73°24W **89** B5
Inangahua *N.Z.* 41°52S 171°59E **59** D3
Inanwatan *Indonesia* 2°8S 132°10E **37** E8
Iñapari *Peru* 11°0S 69°40W **92** F5
Inari *Finland* 68°54N 27°1E **8** B22
Inarijärvi *Finland* 69°0N 28°0E **8** B23
Inawashiro-Ko *Japan* 37°29N 140°6E **30** F10
Inca *Spain* 39°43N 2°54E **24** B9
Inca de Oro *Chile* 26°45S 69°54W **94** B2
Incaguasi *Chile* 29°12S 71°5W **94** B1
Incahuasi *Argentina* 27°2S 68°17W **94** B2
İnce Burun *Turkey* 42°7N 34°56E **19** F5
İncesu *Turkey* 38°38N 35°11E **44** B2
Incheon *S. Korea* 37°27N 126°40E **35** F14
İncirliova *Turkey* 37°50N 27°41E **23** F12
Incline Village *U.S.A.* 39°10N 119°58W **76** G4
Incomáti → *Mozam.* 25°46S 32°43E **57** D5
Indalsälven → *Sweden* 62°36N 17°30E **8** F17
Indaw *Burma* 24°15N 96°5E **41** G20
Independence *Calif., U.S.A.* 36°48N 118°12W **78** J8
Independence *Iowa, U.S.A.* 42°28N 91°54W **80** D8
Independence *Kans., U.S.A.* 37°14N 95°42W **80** G6
Independence *Ky., U.S.A.* 38°57N 84°33W **81** F11
Independence *Mo., U.S.A.* 39°6N 94°25W **80** F6

128 Independence Fjord
INDEX TO WORLD MAPS

Independence Fjord *Greenland* 82°10N 29°0W **4** A6
Independence Mts. *U.S.A.* 41°20N 116°0W **76** F5
Index *U.S.A.* 47°50N 121°33W **78** C5
India ■ *Asia* 20°0N 78°0E **40** K11
Indian → *U.S.A.* 27°59N 80°34W **85** H14
Indian Cabins *Canada* 59°52N 117°40W **70** B5
Indian Harbour *Canada* 54°27N 57°13W **73** B8
Indian Head *Canada* 50°30N 103°41W **71** C8
Indian Lake *U.S.A.* 43°47N 74°16W **83** C10
Indian Springs *U.S.A.* 36°35N 115°40W **79** J11
Indiana *U.S.A.* 40°37N 79°9W **82** F5
Indiana □ *U.S.A.* 40°0N 86°0W **81** F11
Indianapolis *U.S.A.* 39°46N 86°9W **80** F10
Indianola *Iowa, U.S.A.* 41°22N 93°34W **80** E7
Indianola *Miss., U.S.A.* 33°27N 90°39W **85** E9
Indiga *Russia* 67°38N 49°9E **18** A8
Indigirka → *Russia* 70°48N 148°54E **29** B15
Indio *U.S.A.* 33°43N 116°13W **79** M10
Indira Gandhi Canal *India* 28°0N 72°0E **42** F5
Indira Sagar *India* 22°15N 76°40E **42** H7
Indo-China *Asia* 15°0N 102°0E **26** G12
Indonesia ■ *Asia* 5°0S 115°0E **36** F5
Indore *India* 22°42N 75°53E **42** H6
Indramayu *Indonesia* 6°20S 108°19E **37** G13
Indravati → *India* 19°20N 80°20E **41** K12
Indre → *France* 47°16N 0°11E **20** C4
Indulkana *Australia* 26°58S 133°5E **63** D1
Indus → *Pakistan* 24°20N 67°47E **42** G2
Indus, Mouths of the *Pakistan* 24°0N 68°0E **42** H3
İnebolu *Turkey* 41°55N 33°40E **19** F5
Infiernillo, Presa del *Mexico* 18°35N 101°50W **86** D4
Ingenio *Canary Is.* 27°55N 15°26W **24** G4
Ingenio Santa Ana *Argentina* 27°25S 65°40W **94** B2
Ingersoll *Canada* 43°4N 80°55W **82** C4
Ingham *Australia* 18°43S 146°10E **62** B4
Ingleborough *U.K.* 54°10N 2°22W **12** C5
Inglewood *Queens., Australia* 28°25S 151°2E **63** D5
Inglewood *Vic., Australia* 36°29S 143°53E **63** F3
Inglewood *N.Z.* 39°9S 174°14E **59** C5
Inglewood *U.S.A.* 33°58N 118°21W **79** M8
Ingólfshöfði *Iceland* 63°48N 16°39W **8** E5
Ingolstadt *Germany* 48°46N 11°26E **16** D6
Ingomar *U.S.A.* 46°35N 107°23W **76** C10
Ingonish *Canada* 46°42N 60°18W **73** C7
Ingraj Bazar *India* 24°58N 88°10E **43** G13
Ingrid Christensen Coast *Antarctica* 69°30S 76°0E **5** C6
Ingulec = Inhulec *Ukraine* 47°42N 33°14E **19** E5
Ingushetia □ *Russia* 43°20N 44°50E **19** F8
Ingwavuma *S. Africa* 27°9S 31°59E **57** D5
Inhaca *Mozam.* 26°1S 32°57E **57** D5
Inhafenga *Mozam.* 20°36S 33°53E **57** C5
Inhambane *Mozam.* 23°54S 35°30E **57** C6
Inhambane □ *Mozam.* 22°30S 34°20E **57** C5
Inhaminga *Mozam.* 18°26S 35°0E **55** F4
Inharrime *Mozam.* 24°30S 35°0E **57** C6
Inharrime → *Mozam.* 24°30S 35°0E **57** C6
Inhulec *Ukraine* 47°42N 33°14E **19** E5
Ining = Yining *China* 43°58N 81°10E **32** B3
Inírida → *Colombia* 3°55N 67°52W **92** C5
Inishbofin *Ireland* 53°37N 10°13W **10** C1
Inisheer *Ireland* 53°3N 9°32W **10** C2
Inishfree B. *Ireland* 55°4N 8°23W **10** A3
Inishkea North *Ireland* 54°9N 10°11W **10** B1
Inishkea South *Ireland* 54°7N 10°12W **10** B1
Inishmaan *Ireland* 53°5N 9°35W **10** C2
Inishmore *Ireland* 53°8N 9°45W **10** C2
Inishmurray I. *Ireland* 54°26N 8°39W **10** B3
Inishowen Pen. *Ireland* 55°14N 7°15W **10** A4
Inishshark *Ireland* 53°37N 10°16W **10** C1
Inishturk *Ireland* 53°42N 10°7W **10** C1
Inishvickillane *Ireland* 52°3N 10°37W **10** D1
Injune *Australia* 25°53S 148°32E **63** D4
Inklin → *N. Amer.* 58°50N 133°10W **70** B2
Inland Kaikoura Ra. *N.Z.* 41°59S 173°41E **59** D4
Inland Sea = Setonaikai *Japan* 34°20N 133°30E **31** G6
Inle L. *Burma* 20°30N 96°58E **41** J20
Inlet *U.S.A.* 43°45N 74°48W **83** C10
Inn → *Austria* 48°35N 13°28E **16** D7
Innamincka *Australia* 27°44S 140°46E **63** D3
Inner Hebrides *U.K.* 57°0N 6°30W **11** E2
Inner Mongolia = Nei Monggol Zizhiqu □ *China* 42°0N 112°0E **34** D7
Inner Sound *U.K.* 57°30N 5°55W **11** D3
Innerkip *Canada* 43°13N 80°42W **82** C4
Innetalling I. *Canada* 56°0N 79°0W **72** A4
Innisfail *Australia* 17°33S 146°5E **62** B4
Innisfail *Canada* 52°2N 113°57W **70** C6
In'noshima *Japan* 34°19N 133°10E **31** G6
Innsbruck *Austria* 47°16N 11°23E **16** E6
Inny → *Ireland* 53°30N 7°50W **10** C4
Inongo *Dem. Rep. of the Congo* 1°55S 18°30E **52** E3
Inoucdjouac = Inukjuak *Canada* 58°25N 78°15W **69** D12
Inowrocław *Poland* 52°50N 18°12E **17** B10
Inscription, C. *Australia* 25°29S 112°59E **61** E1
Insein *Burma* 16°50N 96°5E **41** L20
Inta *Russia* 66°5N 60°8E **18** A11
Intendente Alvear *Argentina* 35°12S 63°32W **94** D3
Interlaken *Switz.* 46°41N 7°50E **20** C7
Interlaken *U.S.A.* 42°37N 76°44W **83** D8
International Falls *U.S.A.* 48°36N 93°25W **80** A7
Intiyaco *Argentina* 28°43S 60°5W **94** B3
Inukjuak *Canada* 58°25N 78°15W **69** D12
Inútil, B. *Chile* 53°30S 70°15W **96** G2
Inuvik *Canada* 68°16N 133°40W **68** C6
Inveraray *U.K.* 56°14N 5°5W **11** E3
Inverbervie *U.K.* 56°51N 2°17W **11** E6
Invercargill *N.Z.* 46°24S 168°24E **59** G2
Inverclyde □ *U.K.* 55°55N 4°49W **11** F4
Inverell *Australia* 29°45S 151°8E **63** D5
Invergordon *U.K.* 57°41N 4°10W **11** D4
Inverloch *Australia* 38°38S 145°45E **63** F4
Invermere *Canada* 50°30N 116°2W **70** C5
Inverness *Canada* 46°15N 61°19W **73** C7
Inverness *U.K.* 57°29N 4°13W **11** D4
Inverness *U.S.A.* 28°50N 82°20W **85** G13
Inverurie *U.K.* 57°17N 2°23W **11** D6
Investigator Group *Australia* 34°45S 134°20E **63** E1
Investigator Str. *Australia* 35°30S 137°0E **63** F2
Inya *Russia* 50°28N 86°37E **28** D9
Inyanga *Zimbabwe* 18°12S 32°40E **55** F3
Inyangani *Zimbabwe* 18°5S 32°50E **55** F3
Inyantue *Zimbabwe* 18°33S 26°39E **56** B4
Inyo Mts. *U.S.A.* 36°40N 118°0W **78** J9
Inyokern *U.S.A.* 35°39N 117°49W **79** K9
Inza *Russia* 53°55N 46°25E **18** D8
Iō-Jima *Japan* 30°48N 130°18E **31** J5
Ioannina *Greece* 39°42N 20°47E **23** E9
Iola *U.S.A.* 37°55N 95°24W **80** G6
Iona *U.K.* 56°20N 6°25W **11** E2
Ione *U.S.A.* 38°21N 120°56W **78** G6
Ionia *U.S.A.* 42°59N 85°4W **81** D11
Ionian Is. = Ionioi Nisoi *Greece* 38°40N 20°0E **23** E9
Ionian Sea *Medit. S.* 37°30N 17°30E **23** E7
Ionioi Nisoi *Greece* 38°40N 20°0E **23** E9
Ios *Greece* 36°41N 25°20E **23** F11
Iowa □ *U.S.A.* 42°18N 93°30W **80** D7
Iowa → *U.S.A.* 41°10N 91°1W **80** E8
Iowa City *U.S.A.* 41°40N 91°32W **80** E8
Iowa Falls *U.S.A.* 42°31N 93°16W **80** D7
Iowa Park *U.S.A.* 33°57N 98°40W **84** E5
Ipala *Tanzania* 4°30S 32°52E **54** C3
Ipameri *Brazil* 17°44S 48°9W **93** G9
Ipatinga *Brazil* 19°32S 42°30W **93** G10
Ipiales *Colombia* 0°50N 77°37W **92** C3
Ipin = Yibin *China* 28°45N 104°32E **32** D5
Ipixuna *Brazil* 7°0S 71°40W **92** E4
Ipoh *Malaysia* 4°35N 101°5E **39** K3
Ippy *C.A.R.* 6°5N 21°7E **52** C4
İpsala *Turkey* 40°55N 26°23E **23** D12
Ipswich *Australia* 27°35S 152°40E **63** D5
Ipswich *U.K.* 52°4N 1°10E **13** E9
Ipswich *Mass., U.S.A.* 42°41N 70°50W **83** D14
Ipswich *S. Dak., U.S.A.* 45°27N 99°2W **80** C4
Ipu *Brazil* 4°23S 40°44W **93** D10
Iqaluit *Canada* 63°44N 68°31W **69** C13
Iquique *Chile* 20°19S 70°5W **92** H4
Iquitos *Peru* 3°45S 73°10W **92** D4
Irabu-Jima *Japan* 24°50N 125°10E **31** M2
Iracoubo *Fr. Guiana* 5°30N 53°10W **93** B8
Īrafshān *Iran* 26°42N 61°56E **45** E9
Iraklio *Greece* 35°20N 25°12E **25** D7
Iraklio □ *Greece* 35°10N 25°10E **25** D7
Iráklion = Iraklio *Greece* 35°20N 25°12E **25** D7
Irala *Paraguay* 25°55S 54°35W **95** B5
Iran ■ *Asia* 33°0N 53°0E **45** C7
Iran, Pegunungan *Malaysia* 2°20N 114°50E **36** D4
Iran Ra. = Iran, Pegunungan *Malaysia* 2°20N 114°50E **36** D4
Īrānshahr *Iran* 27°15N 60°40E **45** E9
Irapuato *Mexico* 20°41N 101°28W **86** C4
Iraq ■ *Asia* 33°0N 44°0E **44** C5
Irati *Brazil* 25°25S 50°38W **95** B5
Irbid *Jordan* 32°35N 35°48E **46** C4
Irbid □ *Jordan* 32°30N 35°50E **46** C5
Irebu *Dem. Rep. of the Congo* 0°40S 17°46E **52** E3
Ireland ■ *Europe* 53°50N 7°52W **10** C4
Iri = Iksan *S. Korea* 35°59N 127°0E **35** G14
Irian Jaya = Papua □ *Indonesia* 4°0S 137°0E **37** E9
Irian Jaya Barat □ *Indonesia* 2°5S 132°50E **37** E8
Iringa *Tanzania* 7°48S 35°43E **54** D4
Iringa □ *Tanzania* 7°48S 35°43E **54** D4
Iriomote △ *Japan* 24°29N 123°53E **31** M1
Iriomote-Jima *Japan* 24°19N 123°48E **31** M1
Iriona *Honduras* 15°57N 85°11W **88** C2
Iriri → *Brazil* 3°52S 52°37W **93** D8
Irish Republic ■ *Europe* 53°50N 7°52W **10** C4
Irish Sea *Europe* 53°38N 4°48W **12** D3
Irkutsk *Russia* 52°18N 104°20E **29** D11
Irma *Canada* 52°55N 111°14W **71** C6
Irō-Zaki *Japan* 34°36N 138°51E **31** G9
Iron Baron *Australia* 32°58S 137°11E **63** E2
Iron Gate = Portile de Fier *Europe* 44°44N 22°30E **17** F12
Iron Knob *Australia* 32°46S 137°8E **63** E2
Iron Mountain *U.S.A.* 45°49N 88°4W **80** C9
Iron Range △ *Australia* 12°34S 143°18E **62** A3
Iron River *U.S.A.* 46°6N 88°39W **80** B9
Irondequoit *U.S.A.* 43°13N 77°35W **82** C7
Ironton *Mo., U.S.A.* 37°36N 90°38W **80** G8
Ironton *Ohio, U.S.A.* 38°32N 82°41W **81** F12
Ironwood *U.S.A.* 46°27N 90°9W **80** B8
Ironwood Forest ⌂ *U.S.A.* 32°32N 111°28W **77** K8
Iroquois *Canada* 44°51N 75°19W **83** B9
Iroquois Falls *Canada* 48°46N 80°41W **72** C3
Irpin *Ukraine* 50°30N 30°15E **17** C16
Irrara Cr. → *Australia* 29°35S 145°31E **63** D4
Irrawaddy □ *Burma* 17°0N 95°0E **41** L19
Irrawaddy → *Burma* 15°50N 95°6E **41** M19
Irrawaddy, Mouths of the *Burma* 15°30N 95°0E **41** M19
Irricana *Canada* 51°19N 113°37W **70** C6
Irtysh → *Russia* 61°4N 68°52E **28** C7
Irumu *Dem. Rep. of the Congo* 1°32N 29°53E **54** B2
Irún *Spain* 43°20N 1°52W **21** A5
Irunea = Pamplona *Spain* 42°48N 1°38W **21** A5
Irvine *Canada* 49°57N 110°16W **71** D6
Irvine *U.K.* 55°37N 4°41W **11** F4
Irvine *Calif., U.S.A.* 33°41N 117°46W **79** M9
Irvine *Ky., U.S.A.* 37°42N 83°58W **81** G12
Irvinestown *U.K.* 54°28N 7°39W **10** B4
Irving *U.S.A.* 32°48N 96°56W **84** E6
Irvona *U.S.A.* 40°46N 78°33W **82** F6
Irwin → *Australia* 29°15S 114°54E **61** E1
Irymple *Australia* 34°14S 142°8E **63** E3
Isa Khel *Pakistan* 32°41N 71°17E **42** C4
Isaac → *Australia* 22°55S 149°20E **62** C4
Isabel *U.S.A.* 45°24N 101°26W **80** C3
Isabel, I. *Mexico* 21°51N 105°55W **86** C3
Isabela *Phil.* 6°40N 121°59E **37** C6
Isabela *Puerto Rico* 18°30N 67°2W **89** d
Isabella, Cord. *Nic.* 13°30N 85°25W **88** D2
Isabella Ra. *Australia* 21°0S 121°4E **60** D3
Ísafjarðardjúp *Iceland* 66°10N 23°0W **8** C2
Ísafjörður *Iceland* 66°5N 23°9W **8** C2
Isagarh *India* 24°48N 77°51E **42** G7
Isahaya *Japan* 32°52N 130°2E **31** H5
Isaka *Tanzania* 3°56S 32°59E **54** C3
Isalo △ *Madag.* 22°23S 45°16E **57** C8
Isan → *India* 26°51N 80°7E **43** F9
Isana = Içana → *Brazil* 0°26N 67°19W **92** C5
Isangano △ *Zambia* 11°8S 30°35E **55** E3
Isar → *Germany* 48°48N 12°57E **16** D7
Íschia *Italy* 40°44N 13°57E **22** D5
Isdell → *Australia* 16°27S 124°51E **60** C3
Ise *Japan* 34°25N 136°45E **31** G8
Ise-Shima △ *Japan* 34°25N 136°48E **31** G8
Ise-Wan *Japan* 34°43N 136°43E **31** G8
Iseramagazi *Tanzania* 4°37S 32°10E **54** C3
Isère → *France* 44°59N 4°51E **20** D6
Isérnia *Italy* 41°36N 14°14E **22** D6
Isfahan = Eşfahān *Iran* 32°39N 51°43E **45** C6
Ishigaki *Japan* 24°26N 124°10E **31** M2
Ishigaki-Shima *Japan* 24°20N 124°10E **31** M2
Ishikari-Gawa → *Japan* 43°15N 141°23E **30** C10
Ishikari-Sammyaku *Japan* 43°30N 143°0E **30** C11
Ishikari-Wan *Japan* 43°25N 141°1E **30** C10
Ishikawa *Japan* 26°25N 127°49E **31** L3
Ishikawa □ *Japan* 36°30N 136°30E **31** F8
Ishim *Russia* 56°10N 69°30E **28** D7
Ishim → *Russia* 57°45N 71°10E **28** D8
Ishinomaki *Japan* 38°32N 141°20E **30** E10
Ishioka *Japan* 36°11N 140°16E **31** F10
Ishkuman *Pakistan* 36°30N 73°50E **43** A5
Ishpeming *U.S.A.* 46°29N 87°40W **80** B10
Isil Kul *Russia* 54°55N 71°16E **28** D8
Isiolo *Kenya* 0°24N 37°33E **54** B4
Isiro *Dem. Rep. of the Congo* 2°53N 27°40E **54** B2
Isisford *Australia* 24°15S 144°21E **62** C3
İskenderun *Turkey* 36°32N 36°10E **44** B3
İskenderun Körfezi *Turkey* 36°40N 35°50E **19** G6
Iskŭr → *Bulgaria* 43°45N 24°25E **23** C11
Iskut → *Canada* 56°45N 131°49W **70** B2
Isla → *U.K.* 56°32N 3°20W **11** E5
Isla Coiba △ *Panama* 7°33N 81°36W **88** E3
Isla de Salamanca △ *Colombia* 10°59N 74°40W **89** D5
Isla Gorge △ *Australia* 25°10S 149°57E **62** D4
Isla Isabel, Parque Nacional △ *Mexico* 21°54N 105°58W **86** C3
Isla Tiburón y San Esteban ⌂ *Mexico* 29°0N 112°27W **86** B2
Isla Vista *U.S.A.* 34°25N 119°53W **79** L7
Islam Headworks *Pakistan* 29°49N 72°33E **42** E5
Islamabad *Pakistan* 33°40N 73°10E **42** C5
Islamgarh *Pakistan* 27°51N 70°48E **42** F4
Islamkot *Pakistan* 24°42N 70°13E **42** G4
Islampur *India* 25°9N 85°12E **43** G11
Island = Iceland ■ *Europe* 64°45N 19°0W **8** D4
Island L. *Canada* 53°47N 94°25W **71** C10
Island Lagoon *Australia* 31°30S 136°40E **63** E2
Island Pond *U.S.A.* 44°49N 71°53W **83** B13
Islands, B. of *Canada* 49°11N 58°15W **73** C8
Islands, B. of *N.Z.* 35°15S 174°6E **59** A5
Islay *U.K.* 55°46N 6°10W **11** F2
Isle → *France* 44°55N 0°15W **20** D3
Isle aux Morts *Canada* 47°35N 59°0W **73** C8
Isle of Wight □ *U.K.* 50°41N 1°17W **13** G6
Isle Royale △ *U.S.A.* 48°0N 88°55W **80** B9
Isleton *U.S.A.* 38°10N 121°37W **78** G5
Ismail = Izmayil *Ukraine* 45°22N 28°46E **17** F15
Ismâ'ilîya *Egypt* 30°37N 32°18E **51** B12
Isna *Egypt* 25°17N 32°30E **51** C12
Isoanala *Madag.* 23°50S 45°44E **57** C8
Isogstalo *India* 34°15N 78°46E **43** B8
Isparta *Turkey* 37°47N 30°30E **19** G5
Íspica *Italy* 36°47N 14°55E **22** F6
Israel ■ *Asia* 32°0N 34°50E **46** D3
Issoire *France* 45°32N 3°15E **20** D5
Issyk-Kul, Ozero = Ysyk-Köl *Kyrgyzstan* 42°25N 77°15E **28** E8
İstanbul *Turkey* 41°0N 28°58E **23** D13
İstanbul Boğazı *Turkey* 41°5N 29°3E **23** D13
Istiea *Greece* 38°57N 23°9E **23** E10
Istokpoga, L. *U.S.A.* 27°23N 81°17W **85** H14
Istra *Croatia* 45°10N 14°0E **16** F7
Istres *France* 43°31N 4°59E **20** E6
Istria = Istra *Croatia* 45°10N 14°0E **16** F7
Itá *Paraguay* 25°29S 57°21W **94** B4
Itaberaba *Brazil* 12°32S 40°18W **93** F10
Itabira *Brazil* 19°37S 43°13W **93** G10
Itabirito *Brazil* 20°15S 43°48W **95** A7
Itabuna *Brazil* 14°48S 39°16W **93** F11
Itacaunas → *Brazil* 5°21S 49°8W **93** E9
Itacoatiara *Brazil* 3°8S 58°25W **92** D7
Itaipú, Reprêsa de *Brazil* 25°30S 54°30W **95** B5
Itaituba *Brazil* 4°10S 55°50W **93** D7
Itajaí *Brazil* 27°50S 48°39W **95** B6
Itajubá *Brazil* 22°24S 45°30W **95** A6
Itaka *Tanzania* 8°50S 32°49E **55** D3
Itala ⌂ *S. Africa* 27°30S 31°7E **57** D5
Italy ■ *Europe* 42°0N 13°0E **22** C5
Itamaraju *Brazil* 17°4S 39°32W **93** G11
Itampolo *Madag.* 24°41S 43°57E **57** C7
Itandrano *Madag.* 21°47S 45°17E **57** C8
Itapecuru-Mirim *Brazil* 3°24S 44°20W **93** D10
Itaperuna *Brazil* 21°10S 41°54W **95** A7
Itapetininga *Brazil* 23°36S 48°7W **95** A6
Itapeva *Brazil* 23°59S 48°59W **95** A6
Itapicuru → *Bahia, Brazil* 11°47S 37°32W **93** F11
Itapicuru → *Maranhão, Brazil* 2°52S 44°12W **93** D10
Itapipoca *Brazil* 3°30S 39°35W **93** D11
Itapuá □ *Paraguay* 26°40S 55°40W **95** B4
Itaquari *Brazil* 20°20S 40°25W **95** A7
Itaquí *Brazil* 29°8S 56°30W **94** B4
Itararé *Brazil* 24°6S 49°23W **95** A6
Itarsi *India* 22°36N 77°51E **42** H7
Itatí *Argentina* 27°16S 58°15W **94** B4
Itatiaia △ *Brazil* 22°22S 44°38W **95** A7
Itchen → *U.K.* 50°55N 1°22W **13** G6
Itezhi Tezhi, L. *Zambia* 15°30S 25°30E **55** F2
Ithaca = Ithaki *Greece* 38°25N 20°40E **23** E9
Ithaca *U.S.A.* 42°27N 76°30W **83** D8
Ithaki *Greece* 38°25N 20°40E **23** E9
Itiquira → *Brazil* 17°18S 56°44W **93** G7
Itō *Japan* 34°58N 139°5E **31** G9
Itoigawa *Japan* 37°2N 137°51E **31** F8
Itonamas → *Bolivia* 12°28S 64°24W **92** F6
Ittoqqortoormiit *Greenland* 70°20N 23°0W **4** B6
Itu *Brazil* 23°17S 47°15W **95** A6
Itu Aba I. *S. China Sea* 10°23N 114°21E **36** B4
Ituiutaba *Brazil* 19°0S 49°25W **93** G9
Itumbiara *Brazil* 18°20S 49°10W **93** G9
Ituna *Canada* 51°10N 103°24W **71** C8
Itunge Port *Tanzania* 9°40S 33°55E **55** D3
Iturbe *Argentina* 23°0S 65°25W **94** A2
Ituri → *Dem. Rep. of the Congo* 1°40N 27°1E **54** B2
Iturup, Ostrov *Russia* 45°0N 148°0E **29** E15
Ituxi → *Brazil* 7°18S 64°51W **92** E6
Ituyuro → *Argentina* 22°40S 63°50W **94** A3
Itzehoe *Germany* 53°55N 9°31E **16** B5
Ivahona *Madag.* 23°27S 46°10E **57** C8
Ivaí → *Brazil* 23°18S 53°42W **95** A5
Ivalo *Finland* 68°38N 27°35E **8** B22
Ivalojoki → *Finland* 68°40N 27°40E **8** B22
Ivanava *Belarus* 52°7N 25°29E **17** B13
Ivanhoe *Australia* 32°56S 144°20E **63** E3
Ivanhoe *Calif., U.S.A.* 36°23N 119°13W **78** J7
Ivanhoe *Minn., U.S.A.* 44°28N 96°15W **80** C5
Ivano-Frankivsk *Ukraine* 48°40N 24°40E **17** D13
Ivanovo = Ivanava *Belarus* 52°7N 25°29E **17** B13
Ivanovo *Russia* 57°5N 41°0E **18** C7
Ivato *Madag.* 20°37S 47°10E **57** C8
Ivatsevichy *Belarus* 52°43N 25°21E **17** B13
Ivdel *Russia* 60°42N 60°24E **18** B11
Ivinheima → *Brazil* 23°14S 53°42W **95** A5
Ivinhema *Brazil* 22°10S 53°37W **95** A5
Ivohibe *Madag.* 22°31S 46°57E **57** C8
Ivory Coast *W. Afr.* 4°20N 5°0W **50** H4
Ivory Coast ■ *Africa* 7°30N 5°0W **50** G4
Ivrea *Italy* 45°28N 7°52E **20** D7
Ivujivik *Canada* 62°24N 77°55W **69** C12
Ivybridge *U.K.* 50°23N 3°56W **13** G4
Iwaizumi *Japan* 39°50N 141°45E **30** E10
Iwaki *Japan* 37°3N 140°55E **31** F10
Iwakuni *Japan* 34°15N 132°8E **31** G6
Iwamizawa *Japan* 43°12N 141°46E **30** C10
Iwanai *Japan* 42°58N 140°30E **30** C10
Iwata *Japan* 34°42N 137°51E **31** G8
Iwate □ *Japan* 39°30N 141°30E **30** E10
Iwate-San *Japan* 39°51N 141°0E **30** E10
Iwo *Nigeria* 7°39N 4°9E **50** G6
Iwŏn *N. Korea* 40°19N 128°39E **35** D15
Ixiamas *Bolivia* 13°50S 68°5W **92** F5
Ixopo *S. Africa* 30°11S 30°5E **57** E5
Ixtepec *Mexico* 16°34N 95°6W **87** D5
Ixtlán del Río *Mexico* 21°2N 104°22W **86** C4
Iyo *Japan* 33°45N 132°45E **31** H6
Izabal, L. de *Guatemala* 15°30N 89°10W **88** C2
Izamal *Mexico* 20°56N 89°1W **87** C7
Izena-Shima *Japan* 26°56N 127°56E **31** L3
Izhevsk *Russia* 56°51N 53°14E **18** C9
Izhma → *Russia* 65°19N 52°54E **18** A9
Izmayil *Ukraine* 45°22N 28°46E **17** F15
İzmir *Turkey* 38°25N 27°8E **23** E12
İzmit = Kocaeli *Turkey* 40°45N 29°50E **19** F4
İznik Gölü *Turkey* 40°27N 29°30E **23** D13
Izra *Syria* 32°51N 36°15E **46** C5
Izu-Shotō *Japan* 34°30N 140°0E **31** G10
Izúcar de Matamoros *Mexico* 18°36N 98°28W **87** D5
Izumi-Sano *Japan* 34°23N 135°18E **31** G7
Izumo *Japan* 35°20N 132°46E **31** G6
Izyaslav *Ukraine* 50°5N 26°50E **17** C14

J

J.F.K. Int. ✈ **(JFK)** *U.S.A.* 40°38N 73°47W **83** F11
J. Strom Thurmond L. *U.S.A.* 33°40N 82°12W **85** E13
Jabalpur *India* 23°9N 79°58E **43** H8
Jabbūl *Syria* 36°4N 37°30E **44** B3
Jabiru *Australia* 12°40S 132°53E **60** B5
Jablah *Syria* 35°20N 36°0E **44** C3
Jablonec nad Nisou *Czech Rep.* 50°43N 15°10E **16** C8
Jaboatão *Brazil* 8°7S 35°1W **93** E11
Jaboticabal *Brazil* 21°15S 48°17W **95** A6
Jaca *Spain* 42°35N 0°33W **21** A5
Jacareí *Brazil* 23°20S 46°0W **95** A6
Jacarèzinho *Brazil* 23°5S 49°58W **95** A6
Jackman *U.S.A.* 45°37N 70°15W **81** C18
Jacksboro *U.S.A.* 33°13N 98°10W **84** E5
Jackson *Barbados* 13°7N 59°36W **89** g
Jackson *Ala., U.S.A.* 31°31N 87°53W **85** F11
Jackson *Calif., U.S.A.* 38°21N 120°46W **78** G6
Jackson *Ky., U.S.A.* 37°33N 83°23W **81** G12
Jackson *Mich., U.S.A.* 42°15N 84°24W **81** D11
Jackson *Minn., U.S.A.* 43°37N 95°1W **80** D6
Jackson *Miss., U.S.A.* 32°18N 90°12W **85** E9
Jackson *Mo., U.S.A.* 37°23N 89°40W **80** G9
Jackson *N.H., U.S.A.* 44°10N 71°11W **83** B13
Jackson *Ohio, U.S.A.* 39°3N 82°39W **81** F12
Jackson *Tenn., U.S.A.* 35°37N 88°49W **85** D10
Jackson *Wyo., U.S.A.* 43°29N 110°46W **76** E8
Jackson B. *N.Z.* 43°58S 168°42E **59** E2
Jackson L. *U.S.A.* 43°52N 110°36W **76** E8
Jacksons *N.Z.* 42°46S 171°32E **59** E3
Jackson's Arm *Canada* 49°52N 56°47W **73** C8
Jacksonville *Ala., U.S.A.* 33°49N 85°46W **85** E12
Jacksonville *Ark., U.S.A.* 34°52N 92°7W **84** D8
Jacksonville *Calif., U.S.A.* 37°52N 120°24W **78** H6
Jacksonville *Fla., U.S.A.* 30°20N 81°39W **85** F14
Jacksonville *Ill., U.S.A.* 39°44N 90°14W **80** F8
Jacksonville *N.C., U.S.A.* 34°45N 77°26W **85** D16
Jacksonville *Tex., U.S.A.* 31°58N 95°17W **84** F7
Jacksonville Beach *U.S.A.* 30°17N 81°24W **85** F14
Jacmel *Haiti* 18°14N 72°32W **89** C5
Jacob Lake *U.S.A.* 36°43N 112°13W **77** H7
Jacobabad *Pakistan* 28°20N 68°29E **42** E3
Jacobina *Brazil* 11°11S 40°30W **93** F10
Jacques-Cartier, Dét. de *Canada* 50°0N 63°30W **73** C7
Jacques-Cartier, Mt. *Canada* 48°57N 66°0W **73** C6
Jacques-Cartier ⌂ *Canada* 47°15N 71°33W **73** C5
Jacuí → *Brazil* 30°2S 51°15W **95** C5
Jacumba *U.S.A.* 32°37N 116°11W **79** N10
Jacundá → *Brazil* 1°57S 50°26W **93** D8
Jaén *Peru* 5°25S 78°40W **92** E3
Jaén *Spain* 37°44N 3°43W **21** D4
Jafarabad *India* 20°52N 71°22E **42** J4
Jaffa = Tel Aviv-Yafo *Israel* 32°4N 34°48E **46** C3
Jaffa, C. *Australia* 36°58S 139°40E **63** F2
Jaffna *Sri Lanka* 9°45N 80°2E **40** Q12
Jaffray *Canada* 49°47N 94°26W **71** D10
Jaffrey *U.S.A.* 42°49N 72°2W **83** D12
Jagadhri *India* 30°10N 77°20E **42** D7
Jagadishpur *India* 25°30N 84°21E **43** G11
Jagdalpur *India* 19°3N 82°0E **41** K13
Jagersfontein *S. Africa* 29°44S 25°27E **56** D4
Jaghīn → *Iran* 27°17N 57°13E **45** E8
Jagodina *Serbia* 44°5N 21°15E **23** C9
Jagraon *India* 30°50N 75°25E **42** D6
Jagtial *India* 18°50N 79°0E **40** K11
Jaguariaíva *Brazil* 24°10S 49°50W **95** A6
Jaguaribe → *Brazil* 4°25S 37°45W **93** D11
Jagüey Grande *Cuba* 22°35N 81°7W **88** B3
Jahanabad *India* 25°13N 84°59E **43** G11
Jahazpur *India* 25°37N 75°17E **42** G6
Jahrom *Iran* 28°30N 53°31E **45** D7
Jaijon *India* 31°21N 76°9E **42** D7
Jailolo *Indonesia* 1°5N 127°30E **37** D7
Jailolo, Selat *Indonesia* 0°5N 129°5E **37** D7
Jaipur *India* 27°0N 75°50E **42** F6
Jais *India* 26°15N 81°32E **43** F9
Jaisalmer *India* 26°55N 70°54E **42** F4
Jaisinghnagar *India* 23°38N 78°34E **43** H8
Jaitaran *India* 26°12N 73°56E **42** F5
Jaithari *India* 23°14N 78°37E **43** H8
Jājarm *Iran* 36°58N 56°27E **45** B8
Jakam → *India* 23°54N 74°13E **42** H6
Jakarta *Indonesia* 6°9S 106°52E **36** F3
Jakhal *India* 29°48N 75°50E **42** E6
Jakhau *India* 23°13N 68°43E **42** H3
Jakobstad = Pietarsaari *Finland* 63°40N 22°43E **8** E20
Jal *U.S.A.* 32°7N 103°12W **77** K12
Jalālābād *Afghan.* 34°30N 70°29E **42** B4
Jalalabad *India* 27°41N 79°42E **43** F8
Jalalpur Jattan *Pakistan* 32°38N 74°11E **42** C6
Jalama *U.S.A.* 34°29N 120°29W **79** L6
Jalapa *Guatemala* 14°39N 89°59W **88** D2
Jalapa Enríquez = Xalapa *Mexico* 19°32N 96°55W **87** D5
Jalasjärvi *Finland* 62°29N 22°47E **8** E20
Jalaun *India* 26°8N 79°25E **43** F8
Jaldhaka → *Bangla.* 26°16N 89°16E **43** F13
Jalesar *India* 27°29N 78°19E **42** F8
Jaleswar *Nepal* 26°38N 85°48E **43** F11
Jalgaon *India* 21°0N 75°42E **40** J9
Jalībah *Iraq* 30°35N 46°32E **44** D5
Jalingo *Nigeria* 8°55N 11°25E **51** G8
Jalisco □ *Mexico* 20°20N 103°40W **86** D4
Jalkot *Pakistan* 35°14N 73°24E **43** B5
Jalna *India* 19°48N 75°38E **40** K9
Jalón → *Spain* 41°47N 1°4W **21** B5
Jalor *India* 25°21N 72°37E **42** G5
Jalpa *Mexico* 21°38N 102°58W **86** C4
Jalpaiguri *India* 26°32N 88°46E **41** F1
Jalpan *Mexico* 21°14N 99°29W **87** C5
Jaluit I. *Marshall Is.* 6°0N 169°30E **64** G

Jalūlā Iraq 34°16N 45°10E 44 C5
Jamaane = Giamama Somali Rep. 0°4N 42°44E 47 G3
Jamaica ■ W. Indies 18°10N 77°30W 88 a
Jamalpur Bangla. 24°52N 89°56E 41 G16
Jamalpur India 25°18N 86°28E 43 G12
Jamalpurganj India 23°2N 87°59E 43 H13
Jamanxim → Brazil 4°43S 56°18W 93 D7
Jambewangi Indonesia 8°17S 114°7E 37 J17
Jambi Indonesia 1°38S 103°30E 36 E2
Jambi □ Indonesia 1°30S 102°30E 36 E2
Jambongan, Pulau Malaysia 6°45N 117°20E 36 C5
Jambusar India 22°3N 72°51E 42 H5
James → S. Dak., U.S.A. 42°52N 97°18W 80 D5
James → Va., U.S.A. 36°56N 76°27W 81 G15
James B. Canada 54°0N 80°0W 72 B3
James Ranges Australia 24°10S 132°30E 60 D5
James Ross I. Antarctica 63°58S 57°50W 5 C18
Jamesabad Pakistan 25°17N 69°15E 42 G3
Jamestown Australia 33°10S 138°32E 63 E2
Jamestown S. Africa 31°6S 26°45E 56 E4
Jamestown N. Dak., U.S.A. 46°54N 98°42W 80 B4
Jamestown N.Y., U.S.A. 42°6N 79°14W 82 D5
Jamestown Pa., U.S.A. 41°29N 80°27W 82 E4
Jamīlābād Iran 34°24N 48°28E 45 C6
Jamira → India 21°35N 88°28E 43 J13
Jamkhandi India 16°30N 75°15E 40 L9
Jammu India 32°43N 74°54E 42 C6
Jammu & Kashmir □ India 34°25N 77°0E 43 B7
Jamnagar India 22°30N 70°6E 42 H4
Jamni → India 25°13N 78°35E 43 G8
Jampur Pakistan 29°39N 70°40E 42 E4
Jamrud Pakistan 33°59N 71°24E 42 C4
Jämsä Finland 61°53N 25°10E 8 F21
Jamshedpur India 22°44N 86°12E 43 H12
Jamtara India 23°59N 86°49E 43 H12
Jämtland Sweden 63°31N 14°0E 8 E16
Jan L. Canada 54°56N 102°55W 71 C8
Jan Mayen Arctic 71°0N 9°0W 4 B7
Janaúba Brazil 15°48S 43°19W 93 G10
Jand Pakistan 33°30N 72°6E 42 C5
Jandaq Iran 34°3N 54°22E 45 C7
Jandía Canary Is. 28°6N 14°21W 24 F5
Jandía, Pta. de Canary Is. 28°3N 14°31W 24 F5
Jandía △ Canary Is. 28°4N 14°19W 24 F5
Jandola Pakistan 32°20N 70°9E 42 C4
Jandowae Australia 26°45S 151°7E 63 D5
Janesville U.S.A. 42°41N 89°1W 80 D9
Jangamo Mozam. 24°6S 35°21E 57 C6
Janghai India 25°33N 82°19E 43 G10
Jangheung S. Korea 34°41N 126°52E 35 G14
Janjanbureh Gambia 13°30N 14°47W 50 F3
Janjgir India 22°1N 82°34E 43 J10
Janjina Madag. 20°30S 45°50E 57 C8
Janos Mexico 30°54N 108°10W 86 A3
Januária Brazil 15°25S 44°25W 93 G10
Janûb Sînî □ Egypt 29°30N 33°50E 46 F2
Janubio Canary Is. 28°56N 13°50W 24 F6
Jaora India 23°40N 75°10E 42 H6
Japan ■ Asia 36°0N 136°0E 31 G8
Japan, Sea of Asia 40°0N 135°0E 30 E7
Japan Trench Pac. Oc. 32°0N 142°0E 64 D6
Japen = Yapen Indonesia 1°50S 136°0E 37 E9
Japla India 24°33N 84°1E 43 G11
Japurá → Brazil 3°8S 65°46W 92 D5
Jaquarão Brazil 32°34S 53°23W 95 C5
Jaqué Panama 7°27N 78°8W 88 E4
Jarābulus Syria 36°49N 38°1E 44 B3
Jarama → Spain 40°24N 3°32W 21 B4
Jaranwala Pakistan 31°15N 73°26E 42 D5
Jarash Jordan 32°17N 35°54E 46 C4
Jarash □ Jordan 32°17N 35°54E 46 C4
Jardim Brazil 21°28S 56°2W 94 A4
Jardine River △ Australia 11°9S 142°21E 62 A3
Jardines de la Reina, Arch. de los Cuba 20°50N 78°50W 88 B4
Jargalang China 43°5N 122°55E 35 C12
Jari → Brazil 1°9S 51°54W 93 D8
Jarīr, W. al → Si. Arabia 25°38N 42°30E 44 E4
Jarosław Poland 50°2N 22°42E 17 C12
Jarrahdale Australia 32°24S 116°5E 61 F2
Jarrahi → Iran 30°49N 48°48E 45 D6
Jarres, Plaine des Laos 19°27N 103°10E 38 C4
Jartai China 39°45N 105°48E 34 E3
Jarud Qi China 44°28N 120°50E 35 B11
Järvenpää Finland 60°29N 25°5E 8 F21
Jarvis Canada 42°53N 80°6W 82 D4
Jarvis I. Pac. Oc. 0°15S 160°5W 65 H12
Jarwa India 27°38N 82°30E 43 F10
Jasdan India 22°2N 71°12E 42 H4
Jashpurnagar India 22°54N 84°9E 43 H11
Jasidih India 24°31N 86°39E 43 G12
Jāsimīyah Iraq 33°45N 44°41E 44 C5
Jasin Malaysia 2°20N 102°26E 39 L4
Jāsk Iran 25°38N 57°45E 45 E8
Jasło Poland 49°45N 21°30E 17 D11
Jaso India 24°30N 80°29E 43 G9
Jasper Alta., Canada 52°55N 118°5W 70 C5
Jasper Ont., Canada 44°52N 75°57W 83 B9
Jasper Ala., U.S.A. 33°50N 87°17W 85 E11
Jasper Fla., U.S.A. 30°31N 82°57W 85 F13
Jasper Ind., U.S.A. 38°24N 86°56W 80 F10
Jasper Tex., U.S.A. 30°56N 94°1W 84 F7
Jasper △ Canada 52°50N 118°8W 70 C5
Jasrasar India 27°43N 73°49E 42 F5
Jászberény Hungary 47°30N 19°55E 17 E10
Jataí Brazil 17°58S 51°48W 93 G8
Jati Pakistan 24°20N 68°19E 42 G3
Jatibarang Indonesia 6°28S 108°18E 37 G13
Jatiluwih Indonesia 8°23S 115°8E 37 J18
Jatinegara Indonesia 6°13S 106°52E 37 G12
Játiva = Xátiva Spain 38°59N 0°32W 21 C5
Jaú Brazil 22°10S 48°30W 95 A6
Jauja Peru 11°45S 75°15W 92 F3
Jaunpur India 25°46N 82°44E 43 G10
Java = Jawa Indonesia 7°0S 110°0E 36 F3
Java Sea Indonesia 4°35S 107°15E 36 E3
Java Trench Ind. Oc. 9°0S 105°0E 36 F3
Jawa Indonesia 7°0S 110°0E 36 F3
Jawa Barat □ Indonesia 7°0S 107°0E 37 G12
Jawa Tengah □ Indonesia 7°0S 110°0E 37 G14
Jawa Timur □ Indonesia 8°0S 113°0E 37 G15
Jawad India 24°36N 74°51E 42 G6
Jay Peak U.S.A. 44°55N 72°32W 83 B12
Jaya, Puncak Indonesia 3°57S 137°17E 37 E9
Jayanti India 26°45N 89°40E 41 F16
Jayapura Indonesia 2°28S 140°38E 37 E10
Jayawijaya, Pegunungan Indonesia 5°0S 139°0E 37 E9
Jaynagar India 26°43N 86°9E 43 F12
Jayrūd Syria 33°49N 36°44E 44 C3
Jayton U.S.A. 33°15N 100°34W 84 E4
Jāz Mūrīān, Hāmūn-e Iran 27°20N 58°55E 45 E8
Jazīreh-ye Shīf Iran 29°4N 50°54E 45 D6
Jazminal Mexico 24°52N 101°24W 86 C4
Jazzīn Lebanon 33°31N 35°35E 46 B4
Jean U.S.A. 35°47N 115°20W 79 K11
Jean Marie River Canada 61°32N 120°38W 70 A4
Jean-Rabel Haiti 19°50N 73°5W 89 C5
Jeanerette U.S.A. 29°55N 91°40W 84 G9
Jeanette, Ostrov = Zhannetty, Ostrov Russia 76°43N 158°0E 29 B16
Jeannette U.S.A. 40°20N 79°36W 82 F5
Jebāl Bārez, Kūh-e Iran 28°30N 58°20E 45 D8
Jebel, Bahr el → Sudan 9°30N 30°25E 51 G12
Jecheon S. Korea 37°8N 128°12E 35 F15
Jedburgh U.K. 55°29N 2°33W 11 F6
Jedda = Jiddah Si. Arabia 21°29N 39°10E 47 C2
Jeddore L. Canada 48°3N 55°55W 73 C8
Jędrzejów Poland 50°35N 20°15E 17 C11
Jefferson Iowa, U.S.A. 42°1N 94°23W 80 D6
Jefferson Ohio, U.S.A. 41°44N 80°46W 82 E4
Jefferson Tex., U.S.A. 32°46N 94°21W 84 E7
Jefferson, Mt. Nev., U.S.A. 38°47N 116°56W 76 G5
Jefferson, Mt. Oreg., U.S.A. 44°41N 121°48W 76 D3
Jefferson City Mo., U.S.A. 38°34N 92°10W 80 F7
Jefferson City Tenn., U.S.A. 36°7N 83°30W 85 C13
Jeffersontown U.S.A. 38°12N 85°35W 81 F11
Jeffersonville U.S.A. 38°17N 85°44W 81 F11
Jeffrey City U.S.A. 42°30N 107°49W 76 E10
Jega Nigeria 12°15N 4°23E 50 F6
Jeju S. Korea 33°31N 126°32E 35 H14
Jeju-do S. Korea 33°29N 126°34E 35 H14
Jēkabpils Latvia 56°29N 25°57E 9 H21
Jekyll I. U.S.A. 31°4N 81°25W 85 F14
Jelenia Góra Poland 50°50N 15°45E 16 C8
Jelgava Latvia 56°41N 23°49E 9 H20
Jemaja Indonesia 3°5N 105°45E 39 L5
Jemaluang Malaysia 2°16N 103°52E 39 L4
Jember Indonesia 8°11S 113°41E 37 H15
Jena Germany 50°54N 11°35E 16 C6
Jena U.S.A. 31°41N 92°8W 84 F8
Jenīn West Bank 32°28N 35°18E 46 C4
Jenkins U.S.A. 37°10N 82°38W 81 G12
Jenner U.S.A. 38°27N 123°7W 78 G3
Jennings U.S.A. 30°13N 92°40W 84 F8
Jeong-eup S. Korea 35°35N 126°50E 35 G14
Jeonju S. Korea 35°50N 127°4E 35 G14
Jepara Indonesia 7°40S 109°14E 37 G14
Jeparit Australia 36°8S 142°1E 63 F3
Jequié Brazil 13°51S 40°5W 93 F10
Jequitinhonha Brazil 16°30S 41°0W 93 G10
Jequitinhonha → Brazil 15°51S 38°53W 93 G11
Jerada Morocco 34°17N 2°10W 50 B5
Jerantut Malaysia 3°56N 102°22E 39 L4
Jerejak, Pulau Malaysia 5°19N 100°19E 39 c
Jérémie Haiti 18°40N 74°10W 89 C5
Jerez, Pta. Mexico 22°58N 97°40W 87 C5
Jerez de García Salinas Mexico 22°39N 103°0W 86 C4
Jerez de la Frontera Spain 36°41N 6°7W 21 D2
Jerez de los Caballeros Spain 38°20N 6°45W 21 C2
Jericho = El Arīḥā West Bank 31°52N 35°27E 46 D4
Jericho Australia 23°38S 146°6E 62 C4
Jerid, Chott el = Djerid, Chott Tunisia 33°42N 8°30E 50 B7
Jerilderie Australia 35°20S 145°41E 63 F4
Jermyn U.S.A. 41°32N 75°33W 83 E9
Jerome U.S.A. 42°44N 114°31W 76 E6
Jerramungup Australia 33°55S 118°55E 61 F2
Jersey U.K. 49°11N 2°7W 13 H5
Jersey City U.S.A. 40°42N 74°4W 83 F10
Jersey Shore U.S.A. 41°12N 77°15W 82 E7
Jerseyville U.S.A. 39°7N 90°20W 80 F8
Jerusalem Israel/West Bank 31°47N 35°10E 46 D4
Jervis B. Australia 35°8S 150°46E 63 F5
Jervis Inlet Canada 50°0N 123°57W 70 C4
Jesi = Iesi Italy 43°31N 13°14E 22 C5
Jessore Bangla. 23°10N 89°10E 41 H16
Jesup U.S.A. 31°36N 81°53W 85 F14
Jesús Carranza Mexico 17°26N 95°2W 87 D5
Jesús María Argentina 30°59S 64°5W 94 C3
Jetmore U.S.A. 38°4N 99°54W 80 F4
Jetpur India 21°45N 70°10E 42 J4
Jevnaker Norway 60°15N 10°26E 9 F14
Jewett U.S.A. 40°22N 81°2W 82 F3
Jewett City U.S.A. 41°36N 71°59W 83 E13
Jeyḥūnābād Iran 34°58N 48°59E 45 C6
Jeypore India 18°50N 82°38E 41 K13
Jha Jha India 24°46N 86°22E 43 G12
Jhaarkand = Jharkhand □ India 24°0N 85°50E 43 H11
Jhabua India 22°46N 74°36E 42 H6
Jhajjar India 28°37N 76°42E 42 E7
Jhal Pakistan 28°17N 67°27E 42 E2
Jhal Jhao Pakistan 26°20N 65°35E 40 F4
Jhalawar India 24°40N 76°10E 42 G7
Jhalida India 23°22N 85°58E 43 H11
Jhalrapatan India 24°33N 76°10E 42 G7
Jhang Maghiana Pakistan 31°15N 72°22E 42 D5
Jhansi India 25°30N 78°36E 43 G8
Jhargram India 22°27N 86°59E 43 H12
Jharia India 23°45N 86°26E 43 H12
Jharkhand □ India 24°0N 85°50E 43 H11
Jharsuguda India 21°56N 84°5E 41 J14
Jhelum Pakistan 33°0N 73°45E 42 C5
Jhelum → Pakistan 31°20N 72°10E 42 D5
Jhilmilli India 23°24N 82°51E 43 H10
Jhudo Pakistan 24°58N 69°18E 42 G3
Jhunjhunu India 28°10N 75°30E 42 E6
Ji-Paraná Brazil 10°52S 62°57W 92 F6
Ji Xian Hebei, China 37°35N 115°30E 34 F8
Ji Xian Henan, China 35°22N 114°5E 34 G8
Ji Xian Shanxi, China 36°7N 110°40E 34 F6
Jia Xian Henan, China 33°59N 113°12E 34 H7
Jia Xian Shaanxi, China 38°12N 110°28E 34 E6
Jiaji = Qionghai China 19°15N 110°26E 38 C8
Jiamusi China 46°40N 130°26E 33 B8
Ji'an Jiangxi, China 27°6N 114°59E 33 D6
Ji'an Jilin, China 41°5N 126°10E 35 D14
Jianchang China 40°55N 120°35E 35 D11
Jianchangying China 40°10N 118°50E 35 D10
Jiangcheng China 22°36N 101°52E 32 D5
Jiangmen China 22°32N 113°0E 33 D6
Jiangsu □ China 33°0N 120°0E 35 H11
Jiangxi □ China 27°30N 116°0E 33 D6
Jiao Xian = Jiaozhou China 36°18N 120°1E 35 F11
Jiaohe Hebei, China 38°2N 116°20E 34 E9
Jiaohe Jilin, China 43°40N 127°22E 35 C14
Jiaozhou China 36°18N 120°1E 35 F11
Jiaozhou Wan China 36°5N 120°10E 35 F11
Jiaozuo China 35°16N 113°12E 34 G7
Jiawang China 34°28N 117°26E 35 G9
Jiaxiang China 35°25N 116°20E 34 G9
Jiaxing China 30°49N 120°45E 33 C7
Jiayi = Chiai Taiwan 23°29N 120°25E 33 D7
Jibuti = Djibouti ■ Africa 12°0N 43°0E 47 E3
Jicarón, I. Panama 7°10N 81°50W 88 E3
Jiddah Si. Arabia 21°29N 39°10E 47 C2
Jido India 29°2N 94°58E 41 E19
Jieshou China 33°18N 115°22E 34 H8
Jiexiu China 37°2N 111°55E 34 F6
Jigalong Australia 23°21S 120°47E 60 D3
Jigni India 25°45N 79°25E 43 G8
Jihlava Czech Rep. 49°28N 15°35E 16 D8
Jihlava → Czech Rep. 48°55N 16°36E 17 D9
Jijiga Ethiopia 9°20N 42°50E 47 F3
Jilib = Gelib Somali Rep. 0°29N 42°46E 47 G3
Jilin China 43°44N 126°30E 35 C14
Jilin □ China 44°0N 127°0E 35 C14
Jilong = Chilung Taiwan 25°3N 121°45E 33 D7
Jim Thorpe U.S.A. 40°52N 75°44W 83 F9
Jima Ethiopia 7°40N 36°47E 47 F2
Jimbaran, Teluk Indonesia 8°46S 115°9E 37 K18
Jiménez Mexico 27°8N 104°54W 86 B4
Jimo China 36°23N 120°30E 35 F11
Jin Xian = Jinzhou Hebei, China 38°2N 115°2E 34 E8
Jin Xian = Jinzhou Liaoning, China 38°55N 121°42E 35 E11
Jinan China 36°38N 117°1E 34 F9
Jinchang China 38°30N 102°10E 32 C5
Jincheng China 35°29N 112°50E 34 G7
Jind India 29°19N 76°22E 42 E7
Jindabyne Australia 36°25S 148°35E 63 F4
Jinding China 22°22N 113°33E 33 G10
Jindo S. Korea 34°28N 126°15E 35 G14
Jindřichův Hradec Czech Rep. 49°10N 15°2E 16 D8
Jing He → China 34°27N 109°4E 34 G5
Jingbian China 37°20N 108°30E 34 F5
Jingchuan China 35°20N 107°20E 34 G4
Jingdezhen China 29°20N 117°11E 33 D6
Jinggu China 23°35N 100°41E 32 D5
Jinghai China 38°55N 116°55E 34 E9
Jingle China 38°20N 111°55E 34 E6
Jingning China 35°30N 105°43E 34 G3
Jingpo Hu China 43°55N 128°55E 35 C15
Jingtai China 37°10N 104°6E 34 F3
Jingxing China 38°2N 114°8E 34 E8
Jingyang China 34°30N 108°50E 34 G5
Jingyu China 42°25N 126°45E 35 C14
Jingyuan China 36°30N 104°40E 34 F3
Jingziguan China 33°15N 111°0E 34 H6
Jinhua China 29°8N 119°38E 33 D6
Jining Nei Monggol Zizhiqu, China 41°5N 113°0E 34 D7
Jining Shandong, China 35°22N 116°34E 34 G9
Jinja Uganda 0°25N 33°12E 54 B3
Jinjang Malaysia 3°13N 101°39E 39 L3
Jinji China 37°58N 106°8E 34 F4
Jinju S. Korea 35°12N 128°2E 35 G15
Jinnah Barrage Pakistan 32°58N 71°33E 42 C4
Jinotega Nic. 13°6N 85°59W 88 D2
Jinotepe Nic. 11°50N 86°10W 88 D2
Jinsha Jiang → China 28°50N 104°36E 32 D5
Jinxi China 40°52N 120°50E 35 D11
Jinxiang China 35°5N 116°22E 34 G9
Jinzhou Hebei, China 38°2N 115°2E 34 E8
Jinzhou Liaoning, China 38°55N 121°42E 35 E11
Jinzhou Liaoning, China 41°5N 121°3E 35 D11
Jiparaná → Brazil 8°3S 62°52W 92 E6
Jipijapa Ecuador 1°0S 80°40W 92 D2
Jiquilpan Mexico 19°59N 102°43W 86 D4
Jirisan S. Korea 35°20N 127°44E 35 G14
Jishan China 35°34N 110°58E 34 G6
Jisr ash Shughūr Syria 35°49N 36°18E 44 C3
Jitarning Australia 32°48S 117°57E 61 F2
Jitra Malaysia 6°16N 100°25E 39 J3
Jiu → Romania 43°47N 23°48E 17 F12
Jiudengkou China 39°56N 106°40E 34 E4
Jiujiang China 29°42N 115°58E 33 D6
Jiulong = Kowloon China 22°19N 114°11E 33 G11
Jiutai China 44°10N 125°50E 35 B13
Jiuxincheng China 39°17N 115°59E 34 E8
Jiwani Pakistan 25°1N 61°44E 40 G2
Jixi China 45°20N 130°50E 35 B16
Jiyang China 37°0N 117°12E 35 F9
Jiyuan China 35°7N 112°57E 34 G7
Jīzān Si. Arabia 17°0N 42°20E 47 D3
Jize China 36°54N 114°56E 34 F8
Jizl, Wādī al → Si. Arabia 25°39N 38°25E 44 E3
Jizō-Zaki Japan 35°34N 133°20E 31 G6
Jizzakh Uzbekistan 40°6N 67°50E 28 E7
Joaçaba Brazil 27°5S 51°31W 95 B5
João Pessoa Brazil 7°10S 34°52W 93 E12
Joaquín V. González Argentina 25°10S 64°0W 94 B3
Jobat India 22°25N 74°34E 42 H6
Jodhpur India 26°23N 73°8E 42 F5
Jodiya India 22°42N 70°18E 42 H4
Joensuu Finland 62°37N 29°49E 8 E23
Jōetsu Japan 37°12N 138°10E 31 F9
Jofane Mozam. 21°15S 34°18E 57 C5
Jogbani India 26°25N 87°15E 43 F12
Jõgeva Estonia 58°45N 26°24E 9 G22
Jogjakarta = Yogyakarta Indonesia 7°49S 110°22E 36 F4
Johannesburg S. Africa 26°11S 28°2E 57 D4
Johannesburg U.S.A. 35°22N 117°38W 79 K9
Johilla → India 23°37N 81°14E 43 H9
John Crow Mts. Jamaica 18°5N 76°25W 88 a
John Day U.S.A. 44°25N 118°57W 76 D4
John Day → U.S.A. 45°44N 120°39W 76 D3
John Day Fossil Beds △ U.S.A. 44°33N 119°38W 76 D4
John D'Or Prairie Canada 58°30N 115°8W 70 B5
John H. Kerr Res. U.S.A. 36°36N 78°18W 85 C15
John o' Groats U.K. 58°38N 3°4W 11 C5
Johnnie U.S.A. 36°25N 116°5W 79 J10
John's Ra. Australia 21°55S 133°23E 62 C1
Johnson U.S.A. 44°38N 72°41W 83 B12
Johnson City Kans., U.S.A. 37°34N 101°45W 80 G3
Johnson City N.Y., U.S.A. 42°7N 75°58W 83 D9
Johnson City Tenn., U.S.A. 36°19N 82°21W 85 C13
Johnson City Tex., U.S.A. 30°17N 98°25W 84 F5
Johnsonburg U.S.A. 41°29N 78°41W 82 E6
Johnsondale U.S.A. 35°58N 118°32W 79 K8
Johnsons Crossing Canada 60°29N 133°18W 70 A2
Johnston, L. Australia 32°25S 120°30E 61 F3
Johnston Falls = Mambilima Falls Zambia 10°31S 28°45E 55 E2
Johnston I. Pac. Oc. 17°10N 169°8W 65 F11
Johnstone Str. Canada 50°28N 126°0W 70 C3
Johnstown Ireland 52°45N 7°33W 10 D4
Johnstown N.Y., U.S.A. 43°0N 74°22W 83 C10
Johnstown Ohio, U.S.A. 40°9N 82°41W 82 F2
Johnstown Pa., U.S.A. 40°20N 78°55W 82 F6
Johor, Selat Asia 1°28N 103°47E 39 d
Johor Bahru Malaysia 1°28N 103°46E 39 d
Jõhvi Estonia 59°22N 27°27E 9 G22
Joinville Brazil 26°15S 48°55W 95 B6
Joinville I. Antarctica 65°0S 55°30W 5 C18
Jojutla Mexico 18°37N 99°11W 87 D5
Jokkmokk Sweden 66°35N 19°50E 8 C18
Jökulsá á Bru → Iceland 65°40N 14°16W 8 D6
Jökulsá á Fjöllum → Iceland 66°10N 16°30W 8 C5
Jolfā Āzarbājān-e Sharqī, Iran 38°57N 45°38E 44 B5
Jolfā Eşfahan, Iran 32°58N 51°37E 45 C6
Joliet U.S.A. 41°32N 88°5W 80 E9
Joliette Canada 46°3N 73°24W 72 C5
Jolo Phil. 6°0N 121°0E 37 C6
Jolon U.S.A. 35°58N 121°9W 78 K5
Jombang Indonesia 7°33S 112°14E 37 G15
Jonava Lithuania 55°8N 24°12E 9 J21
Jones Sound Canada 76°0N 85°0W 69 B11
Jonesboro Ark., U.S.A. 35°50N 90°42W 85 D9
Jonesboro La., U.S.A. 32°15N 92°43W 84 E8
Joniškis Lithuania 56°13N 23°35E 9 H20
Jönköping Sweden 57°45N 14°8E 9 H16
Jonquière Canada 48°27N 71°14W 73 C5
Joplin U.S.A. 37°6N 94°31W 80 G6
Jora India 26°20N 77°49E 42 F6
Jordan Mont., U.S.A. 47°19N 106°55W 76 C10
Jordan N.Y., U.S.A. 43°4N 76°29W 83 C8
Jordan ■ Asia 31°0N 36°0E 46 E5
Jordan → Asia 31°48N 35°32E 46 D4
Jordan Valley U.S.A. 42°59N 117°3W 76 E5
Jorhat India 26°45N 94°12E 41 F19
Jörn Sweden 65°4N 20°1E 8 D19
Jorong Indonesia 3°58S 114°56E 36 E4
Jørpeland Norway 59°3N 6°1E 9 G12
Jorquera → Chile 28°3S 69°58W 94 B2
Jos Nigeria 9°53N 8°51E 50 G7
José Batlle y Ordóñez Uruguay 33°20S 55°10W 95 C4
Joseph, L. Nfld. & L., Canada 52°45N 65°18W 73 B6
Joseph, L. Ont., Canada 45°10N 79°44W 82 A5
Joseph Bonaparte G. Australia 14°35S 128°50E 60 B4
Joshinath India 30°34N 79°34E 43 D8
Joshinetsu-Kōgen △ Japan 36°42N 138°32E 31 F9
Joshua Tree U.S.A. 34°8N 116°19W 79 L10
Joshua Tree △ U.S.A. 33°55N 116°0W 79 M10
Jost Van Dyke I. Br. Virgin Is. 18°29N 64°47W 89 e
Jostedalsbreen Norway 61°40N 6°59E 8 F12
Jotunheimen Norway 61°35N 8°25E 8 F13
Joubertberge Namibia 18°30S 14°0E 56 B1
Jourdanton U.S.A. 28°55N 98°33W 84 G5
Jovellanos Cuba 22°40N 81°10W 88 B3
Jowhar = Giohar Somali Rep. 2°48N 45°30E 47 G4
Ju Xian China 36°35N 118°20E 35 F10
Juan Aldama Mexico 24°19N 103°21W 86 C4
Juan Bautista Alberdi Argentina 34°26S 61°48W 94 C3
Juan de Fuca, Str of. N. Amer. 48°15N 124°0W 78 B3
Juán de Nova Ind. Oc. 17°3S 43°45E 57 D7
Juan Fernández, Arch. de Pac. Oc. 33°50S 80°0W 90 G2
Juan José Castelli Argentina 25°27S 60°57W 94 B3
Juan L. Lacaze Uruguay 34°26S 57°25W 94 C4
Juankoski Finland 63°3N 28°19E 8 E23
Juárez Argentina 37°40S 59°43W 94 D4
Juárez Mexico 32°20N 115°57W 79 N11
Juárez Coahuila, Mexico 27°37N 100°44W 86 B4
Juárez, Sierra de Mexico 32°0N 116°0W 86 A1
Juàzeiro Brazil 9°30S 40°30W 93 E10
Juàzeiro do Norte Brazil 7°10S 39°18W 93 E11
Juba = Giuba → Somali Rep. 1°30N 42°35E 47 G3
Jūbâ Sudan 4°50N 31°35E 51 H12
Jubany Antarctica 62°30S 58°0W 5 C18
Jubayl Lebanon 34°5N 35°39E 46 A4
Jubbah Si. Arabia 28°2N 40°56E 44 D4
Jubbal India 31°5N 77°40E 42 D7
Jubbulpore = Jabalpur India 23°9N 79°58E 43 H8
Jubilee L. Australia 29°0S 126°50E 61 E4
Juby, C. Morocco 28°0N 12°59W 50 C3
Júcar = Xúquer → Spain 39°5N 0°10W 21 C5
Júcaro Cuba 21°37N 78°51W 88 B4
Juchitán de Zaragoza Mexico 16°26N 95°1W 87 D5
Judea = Har Yehuda Israel 31°35N 34°57E 46 D3
Judith → U.S.A. 47°44N 109°39W 76 C9
Judith, Pt. U.S.A. 41°22N 71°29W 83 E13
Judith Gap U.S.A. 46°41N 109°45W 76 C9
Jugoslavia = Serbia ■ Europe 43°20N 20°0E 23 B9
Juigalpa Nic. 12°6N 85°26W 88 D2
Juiz de Fora Brazil 21°43S 43°19W 95 A7
Jujuy □ Argentina 23°20S 65°40W 94 A2
Julesburg U.S.A. 40°59N 102°16W 76 F12
Juli Peru 16°10S 69°25W 92 G5
Julia Cr. → Australia 20°0S 141°11E 62 C3
Julia Creek Australia 20°39S 141°44E 62 C3
Juliaca Peru 15°25S 70°10W 92 G4
Julian U.S.A. 33°4N 116°38W 79 M10
Julian, L. Canada 54°25N 77°57W 72 B4
Julianatop Suriname 3°40N 56°30W 93 C7
Julianehåb = Qaqortoq Greenland 60°43N 46°0W 4 C5
Julimes Mexico 28°25N 105°27W 86 B3
Jullundur India 31°20N 75°40E 42 D6
Julu China 37°15N 115°2E 34 F8
Jumbo Zimbabwe 17°30S 30°58E 55 F3
Jumbo Pk. U.S.A. 36°12N 114°11W 79 J12
Jumentos Cays Bahamas 23°0N 75°40W 88 B4
Jumilla Spain 38°28N 1°19W 21 C5
Jumla Nepal 29°15N 82°13E 43 E10
Jumna = Yamuna → India 25°30N 81°53E 43 G9
Jumunjin S. Korea 37°55N 128°54E 35 F15
Junagadh India 21°30N 70°30E 42 J4
Junction Tex., U.S.A. 30°29N 99°46W 84 F5
Junction Utah, U.S.A. 38°14N 112°13W 77 G7
Junction B. Australia 11°52S 133°55E 62 A1
Junction City Kans., U.S.A. 39°2N 96°50W 80 F5
Junction City Oreg., U.S.A. 44°13N 123°12W 76 D2
Junction Pt. Australia 11°45S 133°50E 62 A1
Jundah Australia 24°46S 143°2E 62 C3
Jundiaí Brazil 24°30S 47°0W 95 A6
Juneau U.S.A. 58°18N 134°25W 70 B2
Junee Australia 34°53S 147°35E 63 E4
Jungfrau Switz. 46°32N 7°58E 20 C7
Junggar Pendi China 44°30N 86°0E 32 B3
Jungshahi Pakistan 24°52N 67°44E 42 G2
Juniata → U.S.A. 40°24N 77°1W 82 F7
Junín Argentina 34°33S 60°57W 94 C3
Junín de los Andes Argentina 39°45S 71°0W 96 D2
Jūniyah Lebanon 33°59N 35°38E 46 B4
Juntas Chile 28°24S 69°58W 94 B2
Juntura U.S.A. 43°45N 118°5W 76 E4
Jur, Nahr el → Sudan 8°45N 29°15E 51 G11
Jura = Jura, Mts. du Europe 46°40N 6°5E 20 C7
Jura = Schwäbische Alb Germany 48°20N 9°30E 16 D5
Jura U.K. 56°0N 5°50W 11 F3
Jura, Mts. du Europe 46°40N 6°5E 20 C7
Jura, Sd. of U.K. 55°57N 5°45W 11 F3
Jurbarkas Lithuania 55°4N 22°46E 9 J20
Jurien Australia 30°18S 115°2E 61 F2
Jūrmala Latvia 56°58N 23°34E 9 H20
Jurong Singapore 1°19N 103°42E 39 d
Juruá → Brazil 2°37S 65°44W 92 D5

Juruena Brazil 13°0S 58°10W 92 F7
Juruena → Brazil 7°20S 58°3W 92 E7
Juruti Brazil 2°9S 56°4W 93 D7
Justo Daract Argentina 33°52S 65°12W 94 C2
Jutaí → Brazil 2°43S 66°57W 92 D5
Juticalpa Honduras 14°40N 86°12W 88 D2
Jutland = Jylland Denmark 56°25N 9°30E 9 H13
Juuka Finland 63°13N 29°17E 8 E23
Juventud, I. de la Cuba 21°40N 82°40W 88 B3
Jūy Zar Iran 33°50N 46°18E 44 C5
Juye China 35°22N 116°5E 34 G9
Jwaneng Botswana 24°45S 24°50E 53 J4
Jylland Denmark 56°25N 9°30E 9 H13
Jyväskylä Finland 62°14N 25°50E 8 E21

K

K2 Pakistan 35°58N 76°32E 43 B7
Kaakha = Kaka Turkmenistan 37°21N 59°36E 45 B8
Kaap Plateau S. Africa 28°30S 24°0E 56 D3
Kaapkruis Namibia 21°55S 13°57E 56 C1
Kaapstad = Cape Town S. Africa 33°55S 18°22E 56 E2
Kabaena Indonesia 5°15S 122°0E 37 F6
Kabala S. Leone 9°38N 11°37W 50 G3
Kabale Uganda 1°15S 30°0E 54 C3
Kabalo Dem. Rep. of the Congo 6°0S 27°0E 54 D2
Kabambare Dem. Rep. of the Congo 4°41S 27°39E 54 C2
Kabango Dem. Rep. of the Congo 8°35S 28°30E 55 D2
Kabanjahe Indonesia 3°6N 98°30E 36 D1
Kabara Fiji 18°59S 178°56W 59 a
Kabardino-Balkar Republic = Kabardino-Balkaria □ Russia 43°30N 43°30E 19 F7
Kabardino-Balkaria □ Russia 43°30N 43°30E 19 F7
Kabarega Falls = Murchison Falls Uganda 2°15N 31°30E 54 B3
Kabarnet Kenya 0°30N 35°45E 54 B4
Kabasalan Phil. 7°47N 122°44E 37 C6
Kabat Indonesia 8°16S 114°19E 37 J17
Kabin Buri Thailand 13°57N 101°43E 38 F3
Kabinakagami L. Canada 48°54N 84°25W 72 C3
Kabinda Dem. Rep. of the Congo 6°19S 24°20E 52 F4
Kabompo Zambia 13°36S 24°14E 55 E1
Kabompo → Zambia 14°11S 23°11E 53 G4
Kabondo Dem. Rep. of the Congo 8°58S 25°40E 55 D2
Kabongo Dem. Rep. of the Congo 7°22S 25°33E 54 D2
Kabrît, G. el Egypt 29°42N 33°16E 46 F2
Kabūd Gonbad Iran 37°5N 59°45E 45 B8
Kābul Afghan. 34°28N 69°11E 42 B3
Kābul □ Afghan. 34°30N 69°0E 40 B6
Kābul → Pakistan 33°55N 72°14E 42 C5
Kabunga Dem. Rep. of the Congo 1°38S 28°3E 54 C2
Kaburuang Indonesia 3°50N 126°30E 37 D7
Kabwe Zambia 14°30S 28°29E 55 E2
Kachchh, Gulf of India 22°50N 69°15E 42 H3
Kachchh, Rann of India 24°0N 70°0E 42 H4
Kachchhidhana India 21°44N 78°46E 43 J8
Kachebera Zambia 13°50S 32°50E 55 E3
Kachikau Botswana 18°8S 24°26E 56 B3
Kachin □ Burma 26°0N 97°30E 41 G20
Kachira, L. Uganda 0°40S 31°7E 54 C3
Kachiry Kazakhstan 53°10N 75°50E 28 D8
Kachnara India 23°50N 75°6E 42 H6
Kachot Cambodia 11°30N 103°3E 39 G4
Kaçkar Turkey 40°45N 41°10E 19 F7
Kadan Kyun Burma 12°30N 98°20E 38 F2
Kadanai → Afghan. 31°22N 65°45E 42 D1
Kadavu Fiji 19°0S 178°15E 59 a
Kadavu Passage Fiji 18°45S 178°0E 59 a
Kade Ghana 6°7N 0°56W 50 G5
Kadhimain = Al Kāẓimīyah Iraq 33°22N 44°18E 44 C5
Kadi India 23°18N 72°23E 42 H5
Kadina Australia 33°55S 137°43E 63 E2
Kadipur India 26°10N 82°23E 43 F10
Kadirli Turkey 37°23N 36°5E 44 B3
Kadiyevka = Stakhanov Ukraine 48°35N 38°40E 19 E6
Kadoka U.S.A. 43°50N 101°31W 80 D3
Kadoma Zimbabwe 18°20S 29°52E 55 F2
Kâdugli Sudan 11°0N 29°45E 51 F11
Kaduna Nigeria 10°30N 7°21E 50 F7
Kaédi Mauritania 16°9N 13°28W 50 E3
Kaeng Khoi Thailand 14°35N 101°0E 38 E3
Kaeng Kra Chan △ Thailand 12°57N 99°23E 38 F2
Kaeng Tana △ Thailand 15°25N 105°32E 38 E5
Kaesŏng N. Korea 37°58N 126°35E 35 F14
Kāf Si. Arabia 31°25N 37°29E 44 D3
Kafan = Kapan Armenia 39°18N 46°27E 44 B5
Kafanchan Nigeria 9°40N 8°20E 50 G7
Kafinda Zambia 12°32S 30°20E 55 E3
Kafue Zambia 15°46S 28°9E 55 F2
Kafue → Zambia 15°30S 29°0E 53 H5
Kafue △ Zambia 15°12S 25°38E 55 F2
Kafue Flats Zambia 15°40S 27°25E 55 F2
Kafulwe Zambia 9°0S 29°1E 55 D2
Kaga Afghan. 34°14N 70°10E 42 B4
Kaga Bandoro C.A.R. 7°0N 19°10E 52 C3
Kagan Uzbekistan 39°43N 64°33E 28 F7
Kagawa □ Japan 34°15N 134°0E 31 G7
Kagera □ Tanzania 2°0S 31°30E 54 C3
Kagera → Uganda 0°57S 31°47E 54 C3
Kağızman Turkey 40°5N 43°10E 44 B4
Kagoshima Japan 31°35N 130°33E 31 J5
Kagoshima □ Japan 31°30N 130°30E 31 J5
Kagul = Cahul Moldova 45°50N 28°15E 17 F15
Kahak Iran 36°6N 49°46E 45 B6
Kahama Tanzania 4°8S 32°30E 54 C3
Kahan Pakistan 29°18N 68°54E 42 E3
Kahang Malaysia 2°12N 103°32E 39 L4
Kahayan → Indonesia 3°40S 114°0E 36 E4
Kahe Tanzania 3°30S 37°25E 54 C4
Kahemba Dem. Rep. of the Congo 7°18S 18°55E 52 F3
Kahnūj Iran 27°55N 57°40E 45 E8
Kahoka U.S.A. 40°25N 91°44W 80 E8
Kaho'olawe U.S.A. 20°33N 156°37W 74 b
Kahramanmaraş Turkey 37°37N 36°53E 44 B3
Kahului U.S.A. 20°54N 156°28W 74 b
Kahurangi △ N.Z. 41°10S 172°32E 59 D4
Kahuta Pakistan 33°35N 73°24E 42 C5
Kahuzi-Biega △ Dem. Rep. of the Congo 1°50S 27°55E 54 C2
Kai, Kepulauan Indonesia 5°55S 132°45E 37 F8
Kai Besar Indonesia 5°35S 133°0E 37 F8
Kai Is. = Kai, Kepulauan Indonesia 5°55S 132°45E 37 F8
Kai Kecil Indonesia 5°45S 132°40E 37 F8
Kaiapoi N.Z. 43°24S 172°40E 59 E4
Kaieteur Falls Guyana 5°1N 59°10W 92 B7
Kaifeng China 34°48N 114°21E 34 G8
Kaikohe N.Z. 35°25S 173°49E 59 A4
Kaikoura N.Z. 42°25S 173°43E 59 E4
Kailash = Kangrinboqe Feng China 31°0N 81°25E 43 D9
Kailu China 43°38N 121°18E 35 C11
Kailua U.S.A. 19°39N 155°59W 74 b
Kaimana Indonesia 3°39S 133°45E 37 E8
Kaimanawa Mts. N.Z. 39°15S 175°56E 59 C5
Kaimganj India 27°33N 79°24E 43 F8
Kaimur Hills India 24°30N 82°0E 43 G10
Kainab → Namibia 28°32S 19°34E 56 D2
Kainji Res. Nigeria 10°1N 4°40E 50 F6
Kainuu Finland 64°30N 29°7E 8 D23
Kaipara Harbour N.Z. 36°25S 174°14E 59 B5
Kaipokok B. Canada 54°54N 59°47W 73 B8
Kaira India 22°45N 72°50E 42 H5
Kairana India 29°24N 77°15E 42 E7
Kaironi Indonesia 0°47S 133°40E 37 E8
Kairouan Tunisia 35°45N 10°5E 51 A8
Kaiserslautern Germany 49°26N 7°45E 16 D4
Kaitaia N.Z. 35°8S 173°17E 59 A4
Kaitangata N.Z. 46°17S 169°51E 59 G2
Kaithal India 29°48N 76°26E 42 E7
Kaitu → Pakistan 33°10N 70°30E 42 C4
Kaiyuan Liaoning, China 42°28N 124°1E 35 C13
Kaiyuan Yunnan, China 23°40N 103°12E 32 D5
Kajaani Finland 64°17N 27°46E 8 D22
Kajabbi Australia 20°0S 140°1E 62 C3
Kajana = Kajaani Finland 64°17N 27°46E 8 D22
Kajang Malaysia 2°59N 101°48E 39 L3
Kajiado Kenya 1°53S 36°48E 54 C4
Kajo Kaji Sudan 3°58N 31°40E 51 H12
Kaka Turkmenistan 37°21N 59°36E 45 B8
Kakabeka Falls Canada 48°24N 89°37W 72 C2
Kakadu △ Australia 12°0S 132°3E 60 B5
Kakamas S. Africa 28°45S 20°33E 56 D3
Kakamega Kenya 0°20N 34°46E 54 B3
Kakanui Mts. N.Z. 45°10S 170°30E 59 F3
Kakdwip India 21°53N 88°11E 43 J13
Kake Japan 34°36N 132°19E 31 G6
Kake U.S.A. 56°59N 133°57W 70 B2
Kakegawa Japan 34°45N 138°1E 31 G9
Kakeroma-Jima Japan 28°8N 129°14E 31 K4
Kakhovka Ukraine 46°45N 33°30E 19 E5
Kakhovske Vdskh. Ukraine 47°5N 34°0E 19 E5
Kakinada India 16°57N 82°11E 41 L13
Kakisa → Canada 61°3N 118°10W 70 A5
Kakisa L. Canada 60°56N 117°43W 70 A5
Kakogawa Japan 34°46N 134°51E 31 G7
Kakuma Kenya 3°43N 34°52E 54 B3
Kakwa → Canada 54°37N 118°28W 70 C5
Kāl Gūsheh Iran 30°59N 58°12E 45 D8
Kal Safid Iran 34°52N 47°23E 44 C5
Kalaallit Nunaat = Greenland ☑ N. Amer. 66°0N 45°0W 67 C15
Kalabagh Pakistan 33°0N 71°28E 42 C4
Kalabahi Indonesia 8°13S 124°31E 37 F6
Kalach Russia 50°22N 41°0E 19 D7
Kaladan → Burma 20°20N 93°5E 41 J18
Kaladar Canada 44°37N 77°5W 82 B7
Kalahari Africa 24°0S 21°30E 56 C3
Kalahari Gemsbok △ S. Africa 25°30S 20°30E 56 D3
Kalajoki Finland 64°12N 24°10E 8 D21
Kalakamati Botswana 20°40S 27°25E 57 C4
Kalakan Russia 55°15N 116°45E 29 D12
K'alak'unlun Shank'ou = Karakoram Pass Asia 35°33N 77°50E 43 B7
Kalam Pakistan 35°34N 72°30E 43 B5
Kalama Dem. Rep. of the Congo 2°52S 28°35E 54 C2
Kalama U.S.A. 46°1N 122°51W 78 E4
Kalamata Greece 37°3N 22°10E 23 F10
Kalamazoo U.S.A. 42°17N 85°35W 81 D11
Kalamazoo → U.S.A. 42°40N 86°10W 80 D10
Kalambo Falls Tanzania 8°37S 31°35E 55 D3
Kalan Turkey 39°7N 39°32E 44 B3
Kalannie Australia 30°22S 117°5E 61 F2
Kalāntarī Iran 32°10N 54°8E 45 C7
Kalao Indonesia 7°21S 121°0E 37 F6
Kalaotoa Indonesia 7°20S 121°50E 37 F6
Kalasin Thailand 16°26N 103°30E 38 D4
Kālat Iran 25°29N 59°22E 45 E8
Kalat Pakistan 29°8N 66°31E 40 E5
Kalāteh Iran 36°33N 55°41E 45 B7
Kalāteh-ye Ganj Iran 27°31N 57°55E 45 E8
Kalbā U.A.E. 25°5N 56°22E 45 E8
Kalbarri Australia 27°40S 114°10E 61 E1
Kalbarri △ Australia 27°51S 114°30E 61 E1
Kalce Slovenia 45°54N 14°13E 16 F8
Kale Turkey 37°27N 28°49E 23 F13
Kalegauk Kyun Burma 15°33N 97°35E 38 E1
Kalehe Dem. Rep. of the Congo 2°6S 28°50E 54 C2
Kalema Tanzania 1°12S 31°55E 54 C3
Kalemie Dem. Rep. of the Congo 5°55S 29°9E 54 D2
Kalewa Burma 23°10N 94°15E 41 H19
Kaleybar Iran 38°47N 47°2E 44 B5
Kalgoorlie-Boulder Australia 30°40S 121°22E 61 F3
Kali → India 27°6N 79°55E 43 F8
Kali Sindh → India 25°32N 76°17E 42 G6
Kaliakra, Nos Bulgaria 43°21N 28°30E 23 C13
Kalianda Indonesia 5°50S 105°45E 36 F3
Kalibo Phil. 11°43N 122°22E 37 B6
Kalima Dem. Rep. of the Congo 2°33S 26°32E 54 C2
Kalimantan Indonesia 0°0 114°0E 36 E4
Kalimantan Barat □ Indonesia 0°0 110°30E 36 E4
Kalimantan Selatan □ Indonesia 2°30S 115°30E 36 E5
Kalimantan Tengah □ Indonesia 2°0S 113°30E 36 E4
Kalimantan Timur □ Indonesia 1°30N 116°30E 36 D5
Kálimnos Greece 37°0N 27°0E 23 F12
Kalimpong India 27°4N 88°35E 43 F13
Kaliningrad Russia 54°42N 20°32E 9 J19
Kalinkavichy Belarus 52°12N 29°20E 17 B15
Kalinkovichi = Kalinkavichy Belarus 52°12N 29°20E 17 B15
Kaliro Uganda 0°56N 33°30E 54 B3
Kalispell U.S.A. 48°12N 114°19W 76 B6
Kalisz Poland 51°45N 18°8E 17 C10
Kaliua Tanzania 5°5S 31°48E 54 D3
Kalix = Kalixälven → Sweden 65°50N 23°11E 8 D20
Kalix Sweden 65°53N 23°12E 8 D20
Kalixälven → Sweden 65°50N 23°11E 8 D20
Kalka India 30°46N 76°57E 42 D7
Kalkarindji Australia 17°30S 130°47E 60 C5
Kalkaska U.S.A. 44°44N 85°11W 81 C11
Kalkfeld Namibia 20°57S 16°14E 56 C2
Kalkfontein Botswana 22°4S 20°57E 56 C3
Kalkrand Namibia 24°1S 17°35E 56 C2
Kallavesi Finland 62°58N 27°30E 8 E22
Kallsjön Sweden 63°38N 13°0E 8 E15
Kalmar Sweden 56°40N 16°20E 9 H17
Kalmyk Republic = Kalmykia □ Russia 46°5N 46°1E 19 E8
Kalmykia □ Russia 46°5N 46°1E 19 E8
Kalmykovo Kazakhstan 49°0N 51°47E 19 E9
Kalna India 23°13N 88°25E 43 H13
Kalnai India 22°46N 83°30E 43 H10
Kalocsa Hungary 46°32N 19°0E 17 E10
Kalokhorio Cyprus 34°51N 33°2E 25 E12
Kaloko Dem. Rep. of the Congo 6°47S 25°48E 54 D2
Kalol Gujarat, India 22°37N 73°31E 42 H5
Kalol Gujarat, India 23°15N 72°33E 42 H5
Kalomo Zambia 17°0S 26°30E 55 F2
Kalpi India 26°8N 79°47E 43 F8
Kaltukatjara Australia 24°52S 129°5E 61 D4
Kalu Pakistan 25°5N 67°39E 42 G2
Kaluga Russia 54°35N 36°10E 18 D6
Kalulushi Zambia 12°50S 28°3E 55 E2
Kalumburu Australia 13°55S 126°35E 60 B4
Kalush Ukraine 49°3N 24°23E 17 D13
Kalutara Sri Lanka 6°35N 80°0E 40 R12
Kalya Russia 60°15N 59°59E 18 B10
Kalyan India 19°15N 73°9E 40 K8
Kama Dem. Rep. of the Congo 3°30S 27°5E 54 C2
Kama → Russia 55°45N 52°0E 18 C9
Kamachumu Tanzania 1°37S 31°37E 54 C3
Kamaishi Japan 39°16N 141°53E 30 E10
Kamalia Pakistan 30°44N 72°42E 42 D5
Kaman India 27°39N 77°16E 42 F6
Kamanjab Namibia 19°35S 14°51E 56 B2
Kamapanda Zambia 12°5S 24°0E 55 E1
Kamarān Yemen 15°21N 42°35E 47 D3
Kamativi Zimbabwe 18°20S 27°6E 56 B4
Kambalda West Australia 31°10S 121°37E 61 F3
Kambar Pakistan 27°37N 68°1E 42 F3
Kambarka Russia 56°15N 54°11E 18 C9
Kambolé Zambia 8°47S 30°48E 55 D3
Kambos Cyprus 35°2N 32°44E 25 D11
Kambove Dem. Rep. of the Congo 10°51S 26°33E 55 E2
Kamchatka, Poluostrov Russia 57°0N 160°0E 29 D16
Kamchatka Pen. = Kamchatka, Poluostrov Russia 57°0N 160°0E 29 D16
Kamchiya → Bulgaria 43°4N 27°44E 23 C12
Kame Ruins Zimbabwe 20°7S 28°25E 55 G2
Kamen Russia 53°50N 81°30E 28 D9
Kamen-Rybolov Russia 44°46N 132°2E 30 B6
Kamenjak, Rt Croatia 44°47N 13°55E 16 F7
Kamenka Russia 65°58N 44°0E 18 A7
Kamenka Bugskaya = Kamyanka-Buzka Ukraine 50°8N 24°16E 17 C13
Kamensk Uralskiy Russia 56°25N 62°2E 28 D7
Kamenskoye Russia 62°45N 165°30E 29 C17
Kameoka Japan 35°0N 135°35E 31 G7
Kamet India 30°55N 79°35E 43 D8
Kamiah U.S.A. 46°14N 116°2W 76 C5
Kamieskroon S. Africa 30°9S 17°56E 56 E2
Kamilukuak L. Canada 62°22N 101°40W 71 A8
Kamin-Kashyrskyy Ukraine 51°39N 24°56E 17 C13
Kamina Dem. Rep. of the Congo 8°45S 25°0E 55 D2
Kaminak L. Canada 62°10N 95°0W 71 A10
Kaministiquia Canada 48°32N 89°35W 72 C1
Kaminoyama Japan 38°9N 140°17E 30 E10
Kamiros Greece 36°20N 27°56E 25 C9
Kamituga Dem. Rep. of the Congo 3°2S 28°10E 54 C2
Kamla → India 25°35N 86°36E 43 G12
Kamloops Canada 50°40N 120°20W 70 C4
Kamo Japan 37°39N 139°3E 30 F9
Kamoke Pakistan 32°4N 74°4E 42 C6
Kampala Uganda 0°20N 32°30E 54 B3
Kampar Malaysia 4°18N 101°9E 39 K3
Kampar → Indonesia 0°30N 103°8E 36 D2
Kampen Neths. 52°33N 5°53E 15 B5
Kampene Dem. Rep. of the Congo 3°36S 26°40E 52 E5
Kamphaeng Phet Thailand 16°28N 99°30E 38 D2
Kampolombo, L. Zambia 11°37S 29°42E 55 E2
Kampong Chhnang Cambodia 12°20N 104°35E 39 F5
Kampong Pengerang Malaysia 1°22N 104°7E 39 d
Kampong Punggai Malaysia 1°27N 104°18E 39 d
Kampong Saom Cambodia 10°38N 103°30E 39 G4
Kampong Saom, Chaak Cambodia 10°50N 103°32E 39 G4
Kampong Tanjong Langsat Malaysia 1°28N 104°1E 39 d
Kampong Telok Ramunia Malaysia 1°22N 104°15E 39 d
Kampong To Thailand 6°3N 101°13E 39 J3
Kampot Cambodia 10°36N 104°10E 39 G5
Kampuchea = Cambodia ■ Asia 12°15N 105°0E 38 F5
Kampung Air Putih Malaysia 4°15N 103°10E 39 K4
Kampung Jerangau Malaysia 4°50N 103°10E 39 K4
Kampung Raja Malaysia 5°45N 102°35E 39 K4
Kampungbaru = Tolitoli Indonesia 1°5N 120°50E 37 D6
Kamrau, Teluk Indonesia 3°30S 133°36E 37 E8
Kamsack Canada 51°34N 101°54W 71 C8
Kamskoye Vdkhr. Russia 58°41N 56°7E 18 C10
Kamuchawie L. Canada 56°18N 101°59W 71 B8
Kamuela U.S.A. 20°1N 155°41W 74 b
Kamui-Misaki Japan 43°20N 140°21E 30 C10
Kamyanets-Podilskyy Ukraine 48°45N 26°40E 17 D14
Kamyanka-Buzka Ukraine 50°8N 24°16E 17 C13
Kāmyārān Iran 34°47N 46°56E 44 C5
Kamyshin Russia 50°10N 45°24E 19 D8
Kanaaupscow Canada 53°39N 77°9W 69 D12
Kanaaupscow → Canada 54°2N 76°30W 72 B4
Kanab U.S.A. 37°3N 112°32W 77 H7
Kanab Cr. → U.S.A. 36°24N 112°38W 77 H7
Kanacea Lau Group, Fiji 17°15S 179°6W 59 a
Kanacea Taveuni, Fiji 16°59S 179°56E 59 a
Kanagi Japan 40°54N 140°27E 30 D10
Kanairiktok → Canada 55°2N 60°18W 73 A7
Kananga Dem. Rep. of the Congo 5°55S 22°18E 52 F4
Kanash Russia 55°30N 47°32E 18 C8
Kanaskat U.S.A. 47°19N 121°54W 78 C5
Kanastraíon, Ákra = Paliouri, Akra Greece 39°57N 23°45E 23 E10
Kanawha → U.S.A. 38°50N 82°9W 81 F12
Kanazawa Japan 36°30N 136°38E 31 F8
Kanchanaburi Thailand 14°2N 99°31E 38 E2
Kanchenjunga Nepal 27°50N 88°10E 43 F13
Kanchipuram India 12°52N 79°45E 40 N11
Kandaghat India 30°59N 77°7E 42 D7
Kandahār Afghan. 31°32N 65°43E 40 D4
Kandahār □ Afghan. 31°0N 65°0E 40 D4
Kandalaksha Russia 67°9N 32°30E 8 C25
Kandalakshskiy Zaliv Russia 66°0N 35°0E 18 A6
Kandangan Indonesia 2°50S 115°20E 36 E5
Kandanghaur Indonesia 6°21S 108°6E 37 G13
Kandanos Greece 35°19N 23°44E 25 D5
Kandavu = Kadavu Fiji 19°0S 178°15E 59 a
Kandavu Passage = Kadavu Passage Fiji 18°45S 178°0E 59 a
Kandhkot Pakistan 28°16N 69°8E 42 E3
Kandhla India 29°18N 77°19E 42 E7
Kandi Benin 11°7N 2°55E 50 F6
Kandi India 23°58N 88°5E 43 H13
Kandiaro Pakistan 27°4N 68°13E 42 F3
Kandla India 23°0N 70°10E 42 H4
Kandos Australia 32°45S 149°58E 63 E4
Kandreho Madag. 17°29S 46°6E 57 B8
Kandy Sri Lanka 7°18N 80°43E 40 R12
Kane U.S.A. 41°40N 78°49W 82 E6
Kane Basin Greenland 79°1N 70°0W 66 B12
Kāne'ohe U.S.A. 21°25N 157°48W 74 b
Kang Botswana 23°41S 22°50E 56 C3
Kang Krung △ Thailand 9°30N 98°50E 39 H2
Kangān Fārs, Iran 27°50N 52°3E 45 E7
Kangān Hormozgān, Iran 25°48N 57°28E 45 E8
Kangar Malaysia 6°27N 100°12E 39 J3
Kangaroo I. Australia 35°45S 137°0E 63 F2
Kangaroo Mts. Australia 23°29S 141°51E 62 C3
Kangasala Finland 61°28N 24°4E 8 F21
Kangāvar Iran 34°40N 48°0E 45 C6
Kangdong N. Korea 39°9N 126°5E 35 E14
Kangean, Kepulauan Indonesia 6°55S 115°23E 36 F5
Kangean Is. = Kangean, Kepulauan Indonesia 6°55S 115°23E 36 F5
Kanggye N. Korea 41°0N 126°35E 35 D14
Kangikajik Greenland 70°7N 22°0W 4 B6
Kangiqliniq = Rankin Inlet Canada 62°30N 93°0W 68 C10
Kangiqsualujjuaq Canada 58°30N 65°59W 69 D13
Kangiqsujuaq Canada 61°30N 72°0W 69 C12
Kangiqtugaapik = Clyde River Canada 70°30N 68°30W 69 B13
Kangirsuk Canada 60°0N 70°0W 69 D13
Kangkar Chemaran Malaysia 1°34N 104°12E 39 d
Kangkar Sungai Tiram Malaysia 1°35N 103°55E 39 d
Kangkar Teberau Malaysia 1°32N 103°51E 39 d
Kangping China 42°43N 123°18E 35 C12
Kangra India 32°6N 76°16E 42 C7
Kangrinboqe Feng China 31°0N 81°25E 43 D9
Kangto China 27°50N 92°35E 41 F18
Kanha △ India 22°15N 80°40E 43 H9
Kanhar → India 24°28N 83°8E 43 G10
Kaniama Dem. Rep. of the Congo 7°30S 24°12E 54 D1
Kaniapiskau = Caniapiscau → Canada 56°40N 69°30W 73 A6
Kaniapiskau, L. = Caniapiscau, L. Canada 54°10N 69°55W 73 B6
Kanin, Poluostrov Russia 68°0N 45°0E 18 A8
Kanin Nos, Mys Russia 68°39N 43°32E 18 A7
Kanin Pen. = Kanin, Poluostrov Russia 68°0N 45°0E 18 A8
Kaniva Australia 36°22S 141°18E 63 F3
Kanjut Sar Pakistan 36°7N 75°25E 43 A6
Kankaanpää Finland 61°44N 22°50E 8 F20
Kankakee U.S.A. 41°7N 87°52W 80 E10
Kankakee → U.S.A. 41°23N 88°15W 80 E9
Kankan Guinea 10°23N 9°15W 50 F4
Kankendy = Xankändi Azerbaijan 39°52N 46°49E 44 B5
Kanker India 20°10N 81°40E 41 J12
Kankroli India 25°4N 73°53E 42 G5
Kannapolis U.S.A. 35°30N 80°37W 85 D14
Kannauj India 27°3N 79°56E 43 F8
Kannod India 22°45N 76°40E 40 H10
Kano Nigeria 12°2N 8°30E 50 F7
Kan'onji Japan 34°7N 133°39E 31 G6
Kanowit Malaysia 2°14N 112°20E 36 D4
Kanoya Japan 31°25N 130°50E 31 J5
Kanpetlet Burma 21°10N 93°59E 41 J18
Kanpur India 26°28N 80°20E 43 F9
Kansas □ U.S.A. 38°30N 99°0W 80 F4
Kansas → U.S.A. 39°7N 94°37W 80 F6
Kansas City Kans., U.S.A. 39°7N 94°38W 80 F6
Kansas City Mo., U.S.A. 39°6N 94°35W 80 F6
Kansenia Dem. Rep. of the Congo 10°20S 26°0E 55 E2
Kansk Russia 56°20N 95°37E 29 D10
Kansu = Gansu □ China 36°0N 104°0E 34 G3
Kantaphor India 22°35N 76°34E 42 H7
Kantharalak Thailand 14°39N 104°39E 38 E5
Kantli → India 28°20N 75°30E 42 E6
Kantō □ Japan 36°15N 139°30E 31 F9
Kantō-Sanchi Japan 35°59N 138°50E 31 G9
Kanturk Ireland 52°11N 8°54W 10 D3
Kanuma Japan 36°34N 139°42E 31 F9
Kanus Namibia 27°50S 18°39E 56 D2
Kanye Botswana 24°55S 25°28E 56 C4
Kanzenze Dem. Rep. of the Congo 10°30S 25°12E 55 E2
Kanzi, Ras Tanzania 7°1S 39°33E 54 D4
Kao Tonga 19°40S 175°1W 59 c
Kao Phara Thailand 8°3N 98°22E 39 a
Kaohsiung Taiwan 22°35N 120°16E 33 D7
Kaokoveld Namibia 19°15S 14°30E 56 B1
Kaolack Senegal 14°5N 16°8W 50 F2
Kaoshan China 44°38N 124°50E 35 B13
Kapaa U.S.A. 22°5N 159°19W 74 b
Kapadvanj India 23°5N 73°0E 42 H5
Kapan Armenia 39°18N 46°27E 44 B5
Kapanga Dem. Rep. of the Congo 8°30S 22°40E 52 F4
Kapchagai = Qapshaghay Kazakhstan 43°51N 77°14E 28 E8
Kapedo Kenya 1°10N 36°6E 54 B4
Kapela = Velika Kapela Croatia 45°10N 15°5E 16 F8
Kapema Dem. Rep. of the Congo 10°45S 28°22E 55 E2
Kapenguria Kenya 1°14N 35°7E 54 B4
Kapfenberg Austria 47°26N 15°18E 16 E8
Kapiri Mposhi Zambia 13°59S 28°43E 55 E2
Kāpīsā □ Afghan. 35°0N 69°20E 40 B6
Kapiskau → Canada 52°47N 81°55W 72 B3
Kapit Malaysia 2°0N 112°55E 36 D4
Kapiti I. N.Z. 40°50S 174°56E 59 D5
Kaplan U.S.A. 30°0N 92°17W 84 F8
Kapoe Thailand 9°34N 98°32E 39 H2
Kapoeta Sudan 4°50N 33°35E 51 H12
Kaposvár Hungary 46°25N 17°47E 17 E9
Kapowsin U.S.A. 46°59N 122°13W 78 D4
Kapps Namibia 22°32S 17°18E 56 C2
Kapsabet Kenya 0°12N 35°6E 54 B4
Kapsan N. Korea 41°4N 128°19E 35 D15
Kapsukas = Marijampolė Lithuania 54°33N 23°19E 9 J20
Kaptai L. Bangla. 22°40N 92°20E 41 H18
Kapuas → Indonesia 0°25S 109°20E 36 E3

Kapuas Hulu, Pegunungan
　Malaysia　1°30N 113°30E　**36 D4**
Kapuas Hulu Ra. = Kapuas Hulu,
　Pegunungan
　Malaysia　1°30N 113°30E　**36 D4**
Kapulo
　Dem. Rep. of the Congo　8°18S 29°15E　**55 D2**
Kapunda Australia　34°20S 138°56E　**63 E2**
Kapuni N.Z.　39°29S 174°8E　**59 C5**
Kapurthala India　31°23N 75°25E　**42 D6**
Kapuskasing Canada　49°25N 82°30W　**72 C3**
Kapuskasing ➤ Canada　49°49N 82°0W　**72 C3**
Kaputar, Mt. Australia　30°15S 150°10E　**63 E5**
Kaputir Kenya　2°5N 35°28E　**54 B4**
Kara Russia　69°10N 65°0E　**28 C7**
Kara Bogaz Gol, Zaliv =
　Garabogazköl Aylagy
　Turkmenistan　41°0N 53°30E　**19 F9**
Kara-Kala = Garrygala
　Turkmenistan　38°31N 56°29E　**45 B8**
Kara Kalpak Republic =
　Qoraqalpoghistan □
　Uzbekistan　43°0N 58°0E　**28 E6**
Kara Kum = Garagum
　Turkmenistan　39°30N 60°0E　**45 B8**
Kara Sea Russia　75°0N 70°0E　**28 B7**
Karabiğa Turkey　40°23N 27°17E　**23 D12**
Karabük Turkey　41°12N 32°37E　**19 F5**
Karaburun Turkey　38°41N 26°28E　**23 E12**
Karabutak = Qarabutaq
　Kazakhstan　49°59N 60°14E　**28 E7**
Karacabey Turkey　40°12N 28°21E　**23 D13**
Karacasu Turkey　37°43N 28°35E　**23 F13**
Karachey-Cherkessia □
　Russia　43°40N 41°30E　**19 F7**
Karachi Pakistan　24°50N 67°0E　**42 G2**
Karad India　17°15N 74°10E　**40 L9**
Karaganda = Qaraghandy
　Kazakhstan　49°50N 73°10E　**28 E8**
Karagayly = Qaraghayly
　Kazakhstan　49°26N 76°0E　**28 E8**
Karaginskiy, Ostrov
　Russia　58°45N 164°0E　**29 D17**
Karagiye, Vpadina
　Kazakhstan　43°27N 51°45E　**19 F9**
Karagiye Depression = Karagiye,
　Vpadina Kazakhstan　43°27N 51°45E　**19 F9**
Karagola Road India　25°29N 87°23E　**43 G12**
Karaikal India　10°59N 79°50E　**40 P11**
Karaikkudi India　10°5N 78°45E　**40 P11**
Karaj Iran　35°48N 51°0E　**45 C6**
Karak Malaysia　3°25N 102°2E　**39 L4**
Karakalpakstan =
　Qoraqalpoghistan □
　Uzbekistan　43°0N 58°0E　**28 E6**
Karakelong Indonesia　4°35N 126°50E　**37 D7**
Karakitang Indonesia　3°14N 125°28E　**37 D7**
Karakol Kyrgyzstan　42°30N 78°20E　**28 E8**
Karakoram Pass Asia　35°33N 77°50E　**43 B7**
Karakoram Ra. Pakistan　35°30N 77°0E　**43 B7**
Karakuwisa Namibia　18°56S 19°40E　**56 B2**
Karaikal Australia 　20°18N 107°16E　**71 D12**
Karama Jordan　31°57N 35°35E　**46 D4**
Karaman Turkey　37°14N 33°13E　**44 B2**
Karamay China　45°30N 84°58E　**32 B3**
Karambu Indonesia　3°53S 116°6E　**36 E5**
Karamea Bight N.Z.　41°22S 171°40E　**59 D3**
Karamnasa ➤ India　25°31N 83°52E　**43 G10**
Karan Si. Arabia　27°43N 49°49E　**45 E6**
Karand Iran　34°16N 46°15E　**44 C5**
Karanganyar Indonesia　7°38S 109°37E　**37 G13**
Karangasem Indonesia　8°27S 115°37E　**37 J18**
Karanjia India　21°47N 85°58E　**43 J11**
Karasburg Namibia　28°0S 18°44E　**56 D2**
Karasino Russia　66°50N 86°50E　**28 C9**
Karasjok Norway　69°27N 25°30E　**8 B21**
Karasuk Russia　53°44N 78°2E　**28 D8**
Karasuyama Japan　36°39N 140°9E　**31 F10**
Karatau, Khrebet = Qarataū
　Kazakhstan　43°30N 69°30E　**28 E7**
Karatax Shan China　35°57N 81°0E　**32 C3**
Karatsu Japan　33°26N 129°58E　**31 H5**
Karaul Russia　70°6N 82°15E　**28 B9**
Karauli India　26°30N 77°4E　**42 F7**
Karavostasi Cyprus　35°8N 32°50E　**25 D11**
Karawang Indonesia　6°30S 107°15E　**37 G12**
Karawanken Europe　46°30N 14°40E　**16 E8**
Karayazı Turkey　39°41N 42°9E　**19 G7**
Karazhal = Qarazhal
　Kazakhstan　48°2N 70°49E　**28 E8**
Karbalā' Iraq　32°36N 44°3E　**44 C5**
Karcag Hungary　47°19N 20°57E　**17 E11**
Karcha ➤ Pakistan　34°45N 76°10E　**43 B7**
Karchana India　25°17N 81°56E　**43 G9**
Karditsa Greece　39°23N 21°54E　**23 E9**
Kärdla Estonia　59°0N 22°45E　**9 G20**
Kareeberge S. Africa　30°59S 21°50E　**56 E3**
Kareha ➤ India　25°44N 86°21E　**43 G12**
Kareima Sudan　18°30N 31°49E　**51 E12**
Karelia □ Russia　65°30N 32°30E　**8 D25**
Karelian Republic = Karelia □
　Russia　65°30N 32°30E　**8 D25**
Karera India　25°32N 78°9E　**42 G8**
Kārevāndar Iran　27°53N 60°44E　**45 E9**
Kargasok Russia　59°3N 80°53E　**28 D9**
Kargat Russia　55°10N 80°15E　**28 D9**
Kargi Kenya　2°31N 37°34E　**54 B4**
Kargil India　34°32N 76°12E　**43 B7**
Kargopol Russia　61°30N 38°58E　**18 B6**
Karhal India　27°1N 78°57E　**43 F8**
Karīān Iran　26°57N 57°14E　**45 E8**
Karianga Madag.　23°22N 47°27E　**57 C8**
Kariba Zimbabwe　16°28S 28°50E　**55 F2**
Kariba, L. Zimbabwe　16°40S 28°25E　**55 F2**
Kariba Dam Zimbabwe　16°30S 28°35E　**55 F2**
Kariba Gorge Zambia　16°30S 28°50E　**55 F2**
Karibib Namibia　22°0S 15°56E　**56 C2**

Karijini △ Australia　23°8S 118°15E　**60 D2**
Karimata, Kepulauan
　Indonesia　1°25S 109°0E　**36 E3**
Karimata, Selat Indonesia　2°0S 108°40E　**36 E3**
Karimnagar India　18°26N 79°10E　**40 K11**
Karimun Kecil, Pulau
　Indonesia　1°8N 103°22E　**39 d**
Karimunjawa, Kepulauan
　Indonesia　5°50S 110°30E　**36 F4**
Karin Somali Rep.　10°50N 45°52E　**47 E4**
Karīt Iran　33°29N 56°55E　**45 C8**
Kariya Japan　34°58N 137°1E　**31 G8**
Kariyangwe Zimbabwe　18°0S 27°38E　**57 B4**
Karjala Finland　62°0N 30°25E　**8 F24**
Karkaralinsk = Qarqaraly
　Kazakhstan　49°26N 75°30E　**28 E8**
Karkheh ➤ Iran　31°2N 47°29E　**44 D5**
Karkinitska Zatoka
　Ukraine　45°56N 33°0E　**19 E5**
Karkinitskiy Zaliv = Karkinitska
　Zatoka Ukraine　45°56N 33°0E　**19 E5**
Karkuk = Kirkūk Iraq　35°30N 44°21E　**44 C5**
Karleby = Kokkola
　Finland　63°50N 23°8E　**8 E20**
Karlovac Croatia　45°31N 15°36E　**16 F8**
Karlovo Bulgaria　42°38N 24°47E　**23 C11**
Karlovy Vary Czech Rep.　50°13N 12°51E　**16 C7**
Karlsbad = Karlovy Vary
　Czech Rep.　50°13N 12°51E　**16 C7**
Karlshamn Sweden　56°10N 14°51E　**9 H16**
Karlskoga Sweden　59°28N 14°33E　**9 G16**
Karlskrona Sweden　56°10N 15°35E　**9 H16**
Karlsruhe Germany　49°0N 8°23E　**16 D5**
Karlstad Sweden　59°23N 13°30E　**9 G15**
Karlstad U.S.A.　48°35N 96°31W　**80 A5**
Karmi'el Israel　32°55N 35°18E　**46 C4**
Karnak Egypt　25°43N 32°39E　**51 C12**
Karnal India　29°42N 77°2E　**42 E7**
Karnali ➤ Nepal　28°45N 81°16E　**43 E9**
Karnaphuli Res. = Kaptai L.
　Bangla.　22°40N 92°20E　**41 H18**
Karnaprayag India　30°16N 79°15E　**43 D8**
Karnataka □ India　13°15N 77°0E　**40 N10**
Karnes City U.S.A.　28°53N 97°54W　**84 G6**
Karnische Alpen Europe　46°36N 13°0E　**16 E7**
Kärnten □ Austria　46°52N 13°30E　**16 E8**
Karoi Zimbabwe　16°48S 29°45E　**55 F2**
Karon, Ao Thailand　7°51N 98°17E　**39 a**
Karonga Malawi　9°57S 33°55E　**55 D3**
Karoo △ S. Africa　32°18S 22°27E　**56 E3**
Karoonda Australia　35°1S 139°59E　**63 F2**
Karor Pakistan　31°15N 70°59E　**42 D4**
Karora Sudan　17°44N 38°15E　**51 E13**
Karpasia Cyprus　35°32N 34°15E　**25 D13**
Karpathos Greece　35°37N 27°10E　**23 G12**
Karpinsk Russia　59°45N 60°1E　**18 C11**
Karpogory Russia　64°0N 44°27E　**18 B7**
Karpuz Burnu = Apostolos
　Andreas, C. Cyprus　35°42N 34°35E　**25 D13**
Karratha Australia　20°53S 116°40E　**60 D2**
Kars Turkey　40°40N 43°5E　**19 F7**
Karsakpay Kazakhstan　47°55N 66°40E　**28 E7**
Karshi = Qarshi
　Uzbekistan　38°53N 65°48E　**28 F7**
Karsiyang India　26°56N 88°18E　**43 F13**
Karsog India　31°23N 77°12E　**42 D7**
Kartala Comoros Is.　11°45S 43°21E　**53 a**
Kartaly Russia　53°3N 60°40E　**28 D7**
Kartapur India　31°27N 75°32E　**42 D6**
Karthaus U.S.A.　41°8N 78°9W　**82 E6**
Karufa Indonesia　3°50S 133°20E　**37 E8**
Karuma △ Uganda　2°5N 32°15E　**54 B3**
Karumba Australia　17°31S 140°50E　**62 B3**
Karungu Tanzania　2°25S 32°50E　**54 C3**
Karumwa Tanzania　3°12S 32°38E　**54 C3**
Kārūn ➤ Iran　30°26N 48°10E　**45 D6**
Karungu Kenya　0°50S 34°10E　**54 C3**
Karviná Czech Rep.　49°53N 18°31E　**17 D10**
Karwan ➤ India　27°26N 78°4E　**42 F8**
Karwar India　14°55N 74°13E　**40 M9**
Karwi India　25°12N 80°57E　**43 G9**
Kasache Malawi　13°25S 34°20E　**55 E3**
Kasai ➤
　Dem. Rep. of the Congo　3°30S 16°10E　**52 E3**
Kasai-Oriental □
　Dem. Rep. of the Congo　5°0S 24°30E　**54 D1**
Kasaji
　Dem. Rep. of the Congo　10°25S 23°27E　**55 E1**
Kasama Zambia　10°16S 31°9E　**55 E3**
Kasan N. Korea　41°18N 126°55E　**35 D14**
Kasandra Kolpos Greece　40°5N 23°30E　**23 D10**
Kasane Namibia　17°34S 24°50E　**56 B3**
Kasanga Tanzania　8°30S 31°10E　**55 D3**
Kasanka △ Zambia　11°34S 30°15E　**55 E3**
Kasaragod India　12°30N 74°58E　**40 N9**
Kasba L. Canada　60°20N 102°10W　**71 A8**
Käseh Garān Iran　34°5N 46°2E　**44 C5**
Kasempa Zambia　13°30S 25°44E　**55 E2**
Kasenga
　Dem. Rep. of the Congo　10°20S 28°45E　**55 E2**
Kasese Uganda　0°13N 30°3E　**54 B3**
Kasewa Zambia　14°28S 28°53E　**55 E2**
Kasganj India　27°48N 78°42E　**43 F8**
Kashabowie Canada　48°40N 90°26W　**72 C1**
Kashaf Iran　35°58N 61°7E　**45 C9**
Kāshān Iran　34°5N 51°30E　**45 C6**
Kashechewan Canada　52°18N 81°37W　**72 B3**
Kashgar = Kashi China　39°30N 76°2E　**32 C2**
Kashi China　39°30N 76°2E　**32 C2**
Kashimbo
　Dem. Rep. of the Congo　11°12S 26°19E　**55 E2**
Kashipur India　29°15N 79°0E　**43 E8**
Kashiwazaki Japan　37°22N 138°33E　**31 F9**
Kashk-e Kohneh
　Afghan.　34°55N 62°30E　**40 B3**

Kashkū'īyeh Iran　30°31N 55°40E　**45 D7**
Kāshmar Iran　35°16N 58°26E　**45 C8**
Kashmir Asia　34°0N 76°0E　**43 C7**
Kashmor Pakistan　28°28N 69°32E　**42 E3**
Kashun Noerh = Gaxun Nur
　China　42°22N 100°30E　**32 B5**
Kasiari India　22°8N 87°14E　**43 H12**
Kasiruta Indonesia　0°25S 127°12E　**37 E7**
Kaskaskia ➤ U.S.A.　37°58N 89°57W　**80 G9**
Kaskattama ➤ Canada　57°3N 90°4W　**71 B10**
Kaskinen Finland　62°22N 21°15E　**8 E19**
Kaskö = Kaskinen
　Finland　62°22N 21°15E　**8 E19**
Kaslo Canada　49°55N 116°55W　**70 D5**
Kasmere L. Canada　59°34N 101°10W　**71 B8**
Kasongo
　Dem. Rep. of the Congo　4°30S 26°33E　**54 C2**
Kasongo Lunda
　Dem. Rep. of the Congo　6°35S 16°49E　**52 F3**
Kasos Greece　35°20N 26°55E　**23 G12**
Kassalâ Sudan　15°30N 36°0E　**51 E13**
Kassel Germany　51°18N 9°26E　**16 C5**
Kassiopi Greece　39°48N 19°53E　**25 A3**
Kasson U.S.A.　44°2N 92°45W　**80 C7**
Kastamonu Turkey　41°25N 33°43E　**19 F5**
Kasteli Greece　35°29N 23°38E　**25 D5**
Kastelli Greece　35°12N 25°20E　**25 D7**
Kasterlee Belgium　51°15N 4°59E　**15 C4**
Kastoria Greece　40°30N 21°19E　**23 D9**
Kasulu Tanzania　4°37S 30°5E　**54 C3**
Kasumi Japan　35°38N 134°38E　**31 G7**
Kasungu Malawi　13°0S 33°29E　**55 E3**
Kasungu △ Malawi　12°53S 33°9E　**55 E3**
Kasur Pakistan　31°5N 74°25E　**42 D6**
Kata Archanes Greece　35°15N 25°10E　**25 D7**
Kata Tjuta Australia　25°20S 130°50E　**61 E5**
Kataba Zambia　16°5S 25°10E　**55 F2**
Katahdin, Mt. U.S.A.　45°54N 68°56W　**81 C19**
Katako Kombe
　Dem. Rep. of the Congo　3°25S 24°20E　**54 C1**
Katale Tanzania　4°52S 31°7E　**54 C3**
Katanda Katanga,
　Dem. Rep. of the Congo　7°52S 24°13E　**54 D1**
Katanda Nord-Kivu,
　Dem. Rep. of the Congo　0°55S 29°21E　**54 C2**
Katanga □
　Dem. Rep. of the Congo　8°0S 25°0E　**54 D2**
Katangi India　21°56N 79°50E　**40 J11**
Katanning Australia　33°40S 117°33E　**61 F2**
Katavi △ Tanzania　6°51S 31°3E　**54 D3**
Katavi Swamp Tanzania　6°50S 31°10E　**54 D3**
Katerini Greece　40°18N 22°37E　**23 D10**
Katghora India　22°30N 82°33E　**43 H10**
Katha Burma　24°10N 96°30E　**41 G20**
Katherîna, Gebel Egypt　28°30N 33°57E　**44 D2**
Katherine Australia　14°27S 132°20E　**60 B5**
Katherine Gorge
　Australia　14°18S 132°28E　**60 D5**
Katha Australia　20°15N 140°16E **62 D4**
Kathiawar India　22°20N 71°0E　**42 H4**
Kathikas Cyprus　34°55N 32°25E　**25 E11**
Katihar India　25°34N 87°36E　**43 G12**
Katima Mulilo Zambia　17°28S 24°13E　**56 B3**
Katimbira Malawi　12°40S 34°0E　**55 E3**
Katingan = Mendawai ➤
　Indonesia　3°30S 113°0E　**36 E4**
Katiola Ivory C.　8°10N 5°10W　**50 G4**
Katmandu Nepal　27°45N 85°20E　**43 F11**
Katni India　23°51N 80°24E　**43 H9**
Kato Chorio Greece　35°3N 25°47E　**25 D7**
Kato Korakiana Greece　39°42N 19°45E　**25 A3**
Káto Pyrgos Cyprus　35°11N 32°41E　**25 D11**
Katompe
　Dem. Rep. of the Congo　6°2S 26°23E　**54 D2**
Katong Singapore　1°18N 103°53E　**39 d**
Katonga ➤ Uganda　0°34N 31°50E　**54 B3**
Katoomba Australia　33°41S 150°19E　**63 E5**
Katowice Poland　50°17N 19°5E　**17 C10**
Katrine, L. U.K.　56°15N 4°30W　**11 E4**
Katrineholm Sweden　59°9N 16°12E　**9 G17**
Katsepe Madag.　15°45S 46°15E　**57 B8**
Katsina Nigeria　13°0N 7°32E　**50 F7**
Katsumoto Japan　33°51N 129°42E　**31 H4**
Katsuura Japan　35°10N 140°20E　**31 G10**
Katsuyama Japan　36°3N 136°30E　**31 F8**
Kattavia Greece　35°57N 27°46E　**25 D9**
Kattegat Denmark　56°40N 11°20E　**9 H14**
Katumba
　Dem. Rep. of the Congo　7°40S 25°17E　**54 D2**
Katwa India　23°30N 88°5E　**43 H13**
Katwijk Neths.　52°12N 4°24E　**15 B4**
Kaua'i U.S.A.　22°3N 159°30W　**74 b**
Kauai Channel U.S.A.　21°45N 158°50W　**74 b**
Kaudom △ Namibia　18°45S 20°51E　**56 B3**
Kaufman U.S.A.　32°35N 96°19W　**84 E6**
Kauhajoki Finland　62°25N 22°10E　**8 E20**
Kaukauna U.S.A.　44°17N 88°17W　**80 C9**
Kaukauveld Namibia　20°0S 20°15E　**56 C3**
Kaukonen Finland　67°31N 24°53E　**8 C21**
Kaunakakai U.S.A.　21°6N 157°1W　**74 b**
Kaunas Lithuania　54°54N 23°54E　**9 J20**
Kaunia Bangla.　25°46N 89°26E　**43 G13**
Kaupanger Norway　61°54N 7°22E　**8 F12**
Kautokeino Norway　69°0N 23°4E　**8 B20**
Kavacha Russia　60°16N 169°51E　**29 C17**
Kavalerovo Russia　44°15N 135°4E　**30 B7**
Kavala Greece　40°57N 24°28E　**23 D11**
Kavali India　14°55N 80°1E　**40 M12**
Kavār Iran　29°11N 52°44E　**45 D7**
Kavi India　22°12N 72°38E　**42 H5**
Kavimba Botswana　18°2S 24°38E　**56 B3**
Kavīr, Dasht-e Iran　34°30N 55°0E　**45 C7**

Kavīr △ Iran　34°40N 52°0E　**45 C7**
Kavos Greece　39°23N 20°3E　**25 B4**
Kaw Fr. Guiana　4°30N 52°15W　**93 C8**
Kawagama L. Canada　45°18N 78°45W　**82 A6**
Kawagoe Japan　35°55N 139°29E　**31 G9**
Kawaguchi Japan　35°52N 139°45E　**31 G9**
Kawambwa Zambia　9°48S 29°3E　**55 D2**
Kawanoe Japan　34°1N 133°34E　**31 G6**
Kawardha India　22°0N 81°17E　**43 J9**
Kawasaki Japan　35°31N 139°43E　**31 G9**
Kawasi Indonesia　1°38S 127°28E　**37 E7**
Kawawachikamach
　Canada　54°48N 66°50W　**73 B6**
Kawerau N.Z.　38°7S 176°42E　**59 C6**
Kawerau Australia　38°7S 176°42E　**59 C6**
Kawhia N.Z.　38°4S 174°49E　**59 C5**
Kawhia Harbour N.Z.　38°5S 174°51E　**59 C5**
Kawio, Kepulauan
　Indonesia　4°30N 125°30E　**37 D7**
Kawthaung Burma　10°5N 98°36E　**39 H2**
Kawthoolei = Kayin □
　Burma　18°0N 97°30E　**41 L20**
Kawthule = Kayin □
　Burma　18°0N 97°30E　**41 L20**
Kaya Burkina Faso　13°4N 1°10W　**50 F5**
Kayah □ Burma　19°15N 97°15E　**41 K20**
Kayan ➤ Indonesia　2°55N 117°35E　**36 D5**
Kaycee U.S.A.　43°43N 106°38W　**76 E10**
Kayeli Indonesia　3°20S 127°10E　**37 E7**
Kayenta U.S.A.　36°44N 110°15W　**77 H8**
Kayes Mali　14°25N 11°30W　**50 F3**
Kayin □ Burma　18°0N 97°30E　**41 L20**
Kayoa Indonesia　0°1N 127°28E　**37 D7**
Kayomba Zambia　13°11S 24°2E　**55 E1**
Kayseri Turkey　38°45N 35°30E　**44 B2**
Kaysville U.S.A.　41°2N 111°56W　**76 F8**
Kazachye Russia　70°52N 135°58E　**29 B14**
Kazakhstan ■ Asia　50°0N 70°0E　**28 E7**
Kazan Russia　55°50N 49°10E　**18 C8**
Kazan ➤ Canada　64°2N 95°29W　**71 A9**
Kazan-Rettō Pac. Oc.　25°0N 141°0E　**64 E6**
Kazanlŭk Bulgaria　42°38N 25°20E　**23 C11**
Kazatin = Kozyatyn
　Ukraine　49°45N 28°50E　**17 D15**
Kāzerūn Iran　29°38N 51°40E　**45 D6**
Kazi Magomed = Qazimämmäd
　Azerbaijan　40°3N 49°0E　**45 A6**
Kazuma Pan △
　Zimbabwe　18°20S 25°48E　**55 F2**
Kazuno Japan　40°10N 140°45E　**30 D10**
Kazym ➤ Russia　63°54N 65°50E　**28 C7**
Kea Greece　37°35N 24°22E　**23 F11**
Keady U.K.　54°15N 6°42W　**10 B5**
Kearney U.S.A.　40°42N 99°5W　**80 E4**
Kearny U.S.A.　33°3N 110°55W　**77 K8**
Kearsarge, Mt. U.S.A.　43°22N 71°50W　**83 C13**
Keban Turkey　38°50N 38°50E　**19 G6**
Keban Baraji Turkey　38°41N 38°33E　**44 B3**
Kebnekaise Sweden　67°53N 18°33E　**8 C18**
Kebri Dehar Ethiopia　6°45N 44°17E　**47 F3**
Kebumen Indonesia　7°42S 109°40E　**37 G13**
Kechika ➤ Canada　59°41N 127°12W　**70 B3**
Kecskemét Hungary　46°57N 19°42E　**17 E10**
Kedainiai Lithuania　55°15N 24°2E　**9 J21**
Kedarnath India　30°44N 79°4E　**43 D8**
Kedgwick Canada　47°40N 67°20W　**73 C6**
Kediri Indonesia　7°51S 112°1E　**36 F4**
Kedros Oros Greece　35°11N 24°37E　**25 D6**
Keeler U.S.A.　36°29N 117°52W　**78 J9**
Keeley L. Canada　54°54N 108°8W　**71 C7**
Keeling Is. = Cocos Is.
　Ind. Oc.　12°10S 96°55E　**64 J1**
Keelung = Chilung
　Taiwan　25°3N 121°45E　**33 D7**
Keene Canada　44°15N 78°10W　**82 B6**
Keene Calif., U.S.A.　35°13N 118°33W　**79 K8**
Keene N.H., U.S.A.　42°56N 72°17W　**83 D12**
Keene N.Y., U.S.A.　44°16N 73°46W　**83 B11**
Keeper Hill Ireland　52°45N 8°16W　**10 D3**
Keerweer, C. Australia　14°0S 141°32E　**62 A3**
Keeseville U.S.A.　44°29N 73°30W　**83 B11**
Keetmanshoop Namibia　26°35S 18°8E　**56 D2**
Keewatin Canada　49°46N 94°34W　**71 D10**
Keewatin ➤ Canada　56°29N 100°46W　**71 B8**
Kefalonia Greece　38°15N 20°30E　**23 E9**
Kefamenanu Indonesia　9°28S 124°29E　**37 F6**
Kefar Sava Israel　32°11N 34°54E　**46 C3**
Keffi Nigeria　8°55N 7°43E　**50 G7**
Keflavík Iceland　64°2N 22°35W　**8 D2**
Keg River Canada　57°54N 117°55W　**70 B5**
Kegaska Canada　50°9N 61°18W　**73 B7**
Kehancha Kenya　1°11S 34°37E　**54 C3**
Keighley U.K.　53°52N 1°54W　**12 D6**
Keila Estonia　59°18N 24°25E　**9 G21**
Keitele Finland　63°10N 26°20E　**8 E22**
Keith Australia　36°6S 140°20E　**63 F3**
Keith U.K.　57°32N 2°57W　**11 D6**
Keiyasi Fiji　17°53S 177°46E　**59 a**
Keizer U.S.A.　44°57N 123°1W　**76 D2**
Kejserr Franz Joseph Fd.
　Greenland　73°30N 24°30W　**4 B6**
Kekri India　26°0N 75°10E　**42 G6**
Kelan China　38°43N 111°31E　**34 E6**
Kelang = Klang Malaysia　3°2N 101°26E　**39 L3**
Kelantan □ Malaysia　6°13N 102°14E　**39 J4**
Kelberg Germany　50°17N 6°56E　**15 D8**
Kelkit Turkey　40°45N 36°32E　**19 F6**
Kelkit ➤ Turkey　40°45N 36°32E　**19 F6**
Kellerberrin Australia　31°36S 117°38E　**61 F2**
Kellett, C. Canada　72°0N 126°0W　**69 B7**
Kelleys I. U.S.A.　41°36N 82°42W　**82 E2**
Kellogg U.S.A.　47°32N 116°7W　**76 C5**
Kells = Ceanannus Mor
　Ireland　53°44N 6°53W　**10 C5**
Kélo Chad　9°10N 15°45E　**51 G9**
Kelokedhara Cyprus　34°48N 32°39E　**25 E11**
Kelowna Canada　49°50N 119°25W　**70 D5**

Kelsey Creek Australia　20°26S 148°31E　**62 J6**
Kelseyville U.S.A.　38°59N 122°50W　**78 G4**
Kelso N.Z.　45°54S 169°15E　**59 F2**
Kelso U.K.　55°36N 2°26W　**11 F6**
Kelso U.S.A.　46°9N 122°54W　**78 D4**
Keluang = Kluang
　Malaysia　2°3N 103°18E　**39 L4**
Kelvington Canada　52°10N 103°30W　**71 C8**
Kem Russia　65°0N 34°38E　**18 B5**
Kem ➤ Russia　64°57N 34°41E　**18 B5**
Kema Indonesia　1°22N 125°8E　**37 D7**
Kemah Turkey　39°32N 39°5E　**44 B3**
Kemaman Malaysia　4°12N 103°18E　**39 K4**
Kemano Canada　53°35N 128°0W　**70 C3**
Kemasik Malaysia　4°25N 103°27E　**39 K4**
Kemerovo Russia　55°20N 86°5E　**28 D9**
Kemi Finland　65°44N 24°34E　**8 D21**
Kemi älv = Kemijoki ➤
　Finland　65°47N 24°32E　**8 D21**
Kemi träsk = Kemijärvi
　Finland　66°43N 27°22E　**8 C22**
Kemijärvi Finland　66°43N 27°22E　**8 C22**
Kemijoki ➤ Finland　65°47N 24°32E　**8 D21**
Kemmerer U.S.A.　41°48N 110°32W　**76 F8**
Kemmuna = Comino
　Malta　36°1N 14°20E　**25 C1**
Kemp, L. U.S.A.　33°46N 99°9W　**84 E5**
Kemp Land Antarctica　69°0S 55°0E　**5 C5**
Kempas Malaysia　1°33N 103°42E　**39 d**
Kempsey Australia　31°1S 152°50E　**63 E5**
Kempt, L. Canada　47°25N 74°22W　**72 C5**
Kempten Germany　47°45N 10°17E　**16 E6**
Kempton Australia　42°31S 147°12E　**63 G4**
Kemptville Canada　45°0N 75°38W　**83 B9**
Ken ➤ India　25°13N 80°27E　**43 G9**
Kenai U.S.A.　60°33N 151°16W　**74 a**
Kendai India　22°45N 82°37E　**43 H10**
Kendal Indonesia　6°56S 110°14E　**37 G14**
Kendal U.K.　54°20N 2°44W　**12 C5**
Kendall Australia　31°35S 152°44E　**63 E5**
Kendall U.S.A.　25°40N 80°19W　**85 J14**
Kendall ➤ Australia　14°4S 141°35E　**62 A3**
Kendallville U.S.A.　41°27N 85°16W　**81 E11**
Kendari Indonesia　3°50S 122°30E　**37 E6**
Kendawangan Indonesia　2°32S 110°17E　**36 E4**
Kendi, Pulau Malaysia　5°13N 100°11E　**39 c**
Kendrapara India　20°35N 86°30E　**41 J15**
Kendrew S. Africa　32°32S 24°30E　**56 E3**
Kene Thao Laos　17°44N 101°10E　**38 D3**
Kenedy U.S.A.　28°49N 97°51W　**84 G6**
Kenema S. Leone　7°50N 11°14W　**50 G3**
Keng Kok Laos　16°26N 105°12E　**38 D5**
Keng Tawng Burma　20°45N 98°18E　**41 J21**
Keng Tung Burma　21°0N 99°30E　**41 J21**
Kengeja Tanzania　5°26S 39°45E　**54 D4**
Kenhardt S. Africa　29°19S 21°12E　**56 D3**
Kenitra Morocco　34°15N 6°40W　**50 B4**
Kenli China　37°30N 118°20E　**35 F10**
Kenmare Ireland　51°53N 9°36W　**10 E2**
Kenmare U.S.A.　48°41N 102°5W　**80 A2**
Kenmare River Ireland　51°48N 9°51W　**10 E2**
Kennabugo Luhe
　U.S.A.　45°4N 70°40W　**83 A14**
Kennebec U.S.A.　43°54N 99°52W　**80 D4**
Kennebec ➤ U.S.A.　43°45N 69°46W　**81 D19**
Kennebunk U.S.A.　43°23N 70°33W　**83 C14**
Kennedy Zimbabwe　18°52S 27°10E　**56 B4**
Kennedy Ra. Australia　24°45S 115°10E　**61 D2**
Kennedy Range △
　Australia　24°34S 115°2E　**61 D2**
Kenner U.S.A.　29°59N 90°14W　**85 G9**
Kennet ➤ U.K.　51°27N 0°57W　**13 F7**
Kenneth Ra. Australia　23°50S 117°8E　**61 D2**
Kennett U.S.A.　36°14N 90°3W　**80 G8**
Kennewick U.S.A.　46°12N 119°7W　**76 C4**
Kenogami ➤ Canada　51°6N 84°28W　**72 B3**
Kenora Canada　49°47N 94°29W　**71 D10**
Kenosha U.S.A.　42°35N 87°49W　**80 D10**
Kensington Canada　46°28N 63°34W　**73 C7**
Kent Ohio, U.S.A.　41°9N 81°22W　**82 E3**
Kent Tex., U.S.A.　31°4N 104°13W　**84 F2**
Kent Wash., U.S.A.　47°22N 122°14W　**78 C4**
Kent □ U.K.　51°12N 0°40E　**13 F8**
Kent Group Australia　39°30S 147°20E　**63 F4**
Kent Pen. Canada　68°30N 107°0W　**68 B9**
Kentau Kazakhstan　43°32N 68°36E　**28 E7**
Kentland U.S.A.　40°46N 87°27W　**80 E10**
Kenton U.S.A.　40°39N 83°37W　**81 E12**
Kentucky □ U.S.A.　37°0N 84°0W　**81 G11**
Kentucky ➤ U.S.A.　38°41N 85°11W　**81 F11**
Kentucky L. U.S.A.　37°1N 88°16W　**80 G9**
Kentville Canada　45°6N 64°29W　**73 C7**
Kentwood U.S.A.　30°56N 90°31W　**85 F9**
Kenya ■ Africa　1°0N 38°0E　**54 B4**
Kenya, Mt. Kenya　0°10S 37°18E　**54 C4**
Keo Neua, Deo
　Vietnam　18°23N 105°10E　**38 C5**
Keokuk U.S.A.　40°24N 91°24W　**80 E8**
Keoladeo △ India　27°0N 77°20E　**42 F7**
Keonjhargarh India　21°28S 85°35E　**43 J11**
Kep Cambodia　10°29N 104°29E　**39 G5**
Kep Vietnam　21°24N 106°16E　**38 B6**
Kepala Batas Malaysia　5°31N 100°26E　**39 c**
Kepi Indonesia　6°32S 139°19E　**37 F9**
Kerala □ India　11°0N 76°15E　**40 P10**
Kerama-Rettō Japan　26°5N 127°15E　**31 L3**
Keran Pakistan　35°40S 143°55E　**63 F3**
Keraudren, C. Australia　19°58S 119°45E　**60 C2**
Kerch Ukraine　45°20N 36°20E　**19 E6**
Kerguelen Ind. Oc.　49°15S 69°10E　**3 G13**
Kericho Kenya　0°22S 35°15E　**54 C4**
Kerinci Indonesia　1°40S 101°15E　**36 E2**
Kerki = Atamyrat
　Turkmenistan　37°50N 65°12E　**28 F7**
Kerkrade Neths.　50°53N 6°4E　**15 D6**
Kerkyra Greece　39°38N 19°50E　**25 A3**

Kerkyras, Notio Steno Greece 39°34N 20°0E 25 A4
Kermadec Is. Pac. Oc. 30°0S 178°15W 58 E11
Kermadec Trench Pac. Oc. 30°30S 176°0W 64 L10
Kermān Iran 30°15N 57°1E 45 D8
Kerman U.S.A. 36°43N 120°4W 78 J6
Kermān □ Iran 30°0N 57°0E 45 D8
Kermān, Bīābān-e Iran 28°45N 59°45E 45 D8
Kermānshāh Iran 34°23N 47°0E 44 C5
Kermānshāh □ Iran 34°0N 46°30E 44 C5
Kermit U.S.A. 31°52N 103°6W 84 F3
Kern → U.S.A. 35°16N 119°18W 79 K7
Kernow = Cornwall □ U.K. 50°26N 4°40W 13 G3
Kernville U.S.A. 35°45N 118°26W 79 K8
Keroh Malaysia 5°43N 101°1E 39 K3
Kerrera U.K. 56°24N 5°33W 11 E3
Kerrobert Canada 51°56N 109°8W 71 C7
Kerrville U.S.A. 30°3N 99°8W 84 F5
Kerry □ Ireland 52°7N 9°35W 10 D2
Kerry Hd. Ireland 52°25N 9°56W 10 D2
Kerulen → Asia 48°48N 117°0E 33 B6
Kerzaz Algeria 29°29N 1°37W 50 C5
Kesagami → Canada 51°40N 79°45W 72 B4
Kesagami L. Canada 50°23N 80°15W 72 B3
Keşan Turkey 40°49N 26°38E 23 D12
Kesennuma Japan 38°54N 141°35E 30 E10
Keshit Iran 29°43N 58°17E 45 D8
Kestell S. Africa 28°17S 28°42E 57 D4
Kestenga Russia 65°50N 31°45E 8 D24
Keswick U.K. 54°36N 3°8W 12 C4
Ket → Russia 58°55N 81°32E 28 D9
Ketapang Bali, Indonesia 8°9S 114°23E 37 J17
Ketapang Kalimantan, Indonesia 1°55S 110°0E 36 E4
Ketchikan U.S.A. 55°21N 131°39W 70 B2
Ketchum U.S.A. 43°41N 114°22W 76 E6
Ketef, Khalig Umm el Egypt 23°40N 35°35E 44 F2
Keti Bandar Pakistan 24°8N 67°27E 42 G2
Ketri India 28°1N 75°50E 42 E6
Kętrzyn Poland 54°7N 21°22E 17 A11
Kettering U.K. 52°24N 0°43W 13 E7
Kettering U.S.A. 39°41N 84°10W 81 F11
Kettle → Canada 56°40N 89°34W 71 B11
Kettle Falls U.S.A. 48°37N 118°3W 76 B4
Kettle Pt. Canada 43°13N 82°1W 82 C2
Kettleman City U.S.A. 36°1N 119°58W 78 J7
Keuka L. U.S.A. 42°30N 77°9W 82 D7
Keuruu Finland 62°16N 24°41E 8 E21
Kewanee U.S.A. 41°14N 89°56W 80 E9
Kewaunee U.S.A. 44°27N 87°31W 80 C10
Keweenaw B. U.S.A. 47°0N 88°15W 80 B9
Keweenaw Pen. U.S.A. 47°15N 88°15W 80 B9
Keweenaw Pt. U.S.A. 47°25N 87°43W 80 B10
Key, L. Ireland 54°0N 8°15W 10 C3
Key Largo U.S.A. 25°5N 80°27W 85 J14
Key West U.S.A. 24°33N 81°48W 88 B3
Keynsham U.K. 51°24N 2°29W 13 F5
Keyser U.S.A. 39°26N 78°59W 81 F14
Kezhma Russia 58°59N 101°9E 29 D11
Kezi Zimbabwe 20°58S 28°32E 57 C4
Kgalagadi Transfrontier ⌂ Africa 25°10S 21°0E 56 D3
Khabarovsk Russia 48°30N 135°5E 29 E14
Khabr Iran 28°51N 56°22E 45 D8
Khābūr → Syria 35°17N 40°35E 44 C4
Khachmas = Xaçmaz Azerbaijan 41°31N 48°42E 19 F8
Khachrod India 23°25N 75°20E 42 H6
Khadro Pakistan 26°11N 68°50E 42 F3
Khadzhilyangar = Dahongliutan China 35°45N 79°20E 43 B8
Khaga India 25°47N 81°7E 43 G9
Khagaria India 25°30N 86°32E 43 G12
Khaipur Pakistan 29°34N 72°17E 42 E5
Khair India 27°57N 77°46E 42 F7
Khairabad India 27°33N 80°47E 43 F9
Khairagarh India 21°27N 81°2E 43 J9
Khairpur Pakistan 27°32N 68°49E 42 F3
Khairpur Nathan Shah Pakistan 27°6N 67°44E 42 F2
Khairwara India 23°58N 73°38E 42 H5
Khaisor → Pakistan 31°17N 68°59E 42 D3
Khajuri Kach Pakistan 32°4N 69°51E 42 C3
Khakassia □ Russia 53°0N 90°0E 28 D9
Khakhea Botswana 24°48S 23°22E 56 C3
Khalafābād Iran 30°54N 49°24E 45 D6
Khalilabad India 26°48N 83°5E 43 F10
Khalīlī Iran 27°38N 53°17E 45 E7
Khalkhāl Iran 37°37N 48°32E 45 B6
Khalkís = Halkida Greece 38°27N 23°42E 23 E10
Khalmer Yu Russia 67°58N 65°1E 28 C7
Khalturin Russia 58°40N 48°50E 18 C8
Khalūf Oman 20°30N 58°13E 47 C6
Kham Keut Laos 18°15N 104°43E 38 C5
Khamaria India 23°5N 80°48E 43 H9
Khambhaliya India 22°14N 69°41E 42 H3
Khambhat India 22°23N 72°33E 42 H5
Khambhat, G. of India 20°45N 72°30E 40 J8
Khamīr Iran 26°57N 55°36E 45 E7
Khamir Yemen 16°2N 44°0E 47 D3
Khamīs Mushayţ Si. Arabia 18°18N 42°44E 47 D3
Khamsa Egypt 30°27N 32°23E 46 E1
Khan → Namibia 22°37S 14°56E 56 C2
Khān Abū Shāmat Syria 33°39N 36°53E 46 B5
Khān Azād Iraq 33°7N 44°22E 44 C5
Khān Mujiddah Iraq 32°21N 43°48E 44 C4
Khān Shaykhūn Syria 35°26N 36°38E 44 C3
Khān Yūnis Gaza Strip 31°21N 34°18E 46 D3
Khanai Pakistan 30°30N 67°8E 42 D2
Khānaqīn Iraq 34°23N 45°25E 44 C5
Khānbāghī Iran 36°10N 55°25E 45 B7
Khandwa India 21°49N 76°22E 40 J10
Khandyga Russia 62°42N 135°35E 29 C14
Khāneh Iran 36°41N 45°8E 44 B5
Khanewal Pakistan 30°20N 71°55E 42 D4
Khangah Dogran Pakistan 31°50N 73°37E 42 D5
Khanh Duong Vietnam 12°44N 108°44E 38 F7
Khaniá = Chania Greece 35°30N 24°4E 25 D6
Khaniadhana India 25°1N 78°8E 42 G8
Khanka, L. Asia 45°0N 132°24E 30 B6
Khankendy = Xankändi Azerbaijan 39°52N 46°49E 44 B5
Khanna India 30°42N 76°16E 42 D7
Khanozai Pakistan 30°37N 67°19E 42 D2
Khanpur Pakistan 28°42N 70°35E 42 E4
Khanty-Mansiysk Russia 61°0N 69°0E 28 C7
Khao Laem △ Thailand 14°56N 98°31E 38 E2
Khao Laem Res. Thailand 14°50N 98°30E 38 E2
Khao Luang △ Thailand 8°34N 99°42E 39 H2
Khao Phlu Thailand 9°29N 99°59E 39 b
Khao Pu-Khao Ya △ Thailand 7°26N 99°57E 39 J2
Khao Sam Roi Yot △ Thailand 12°13N 99°57E 39 F2
Khao Sok △ Thailand 8°55N 98°38E 39 H2
Khao Yai △ Thailand 14°21N 101°29E 38 E3
Khaoen Si Nakarin △ Thailand 14°47N 99°0E 38 E2
Khapalu Pakistan 35°10N 76°20E 43 B7
Khapcheranga Russia 49°42N 112°24E 29 E12
Khaptao △ Nepal 29°20N 81°10E 43 E9
Kharaghoda India 23°11N 71°46E 42 H4
Kharagpur India 22°20N 87°25E 43 H12
Kharan Kalat Pakistan 28°34N 65°21E 40 E4
Kharānaq Iran 32°20N 54°45E 45 C7
Kharda India 18°40N 75°34E 40 K9
Khardung La India 34°20N 77°43E 43 B7
Kharg = Khārk, Jazīreh-ye Iran 29°15N 50°28E 45 D6
Khârga, El Wâhât-el Egypt 25°10N 30°35E 51 C12
Khargon India 21°45N 75°40E 40 J9
Khari → India 25°54N 74°31E 42 G6
Kharian Pakistan 32°49N 73°52E 42 C5
Khārk, Jazīreh-ye Iran 29°15N 50°28E 45 D6
Kharkiv Ukraine 49°58N 36°20E 19 E6
Kharkov = Kharkiv Ukraine 49°58N 36°20E 19 E6
Kharovsk Russia 59°56N 40°13E 18 C7
Kharsawangarh India 22°48N 85°50E 43 H11
Kharta Turkey 40°55N 29°7E 23 D13
Khartoum = El Khartûm Sudan 15°31N 32°35E 51 E12
Khasan Russia 42°25N 130°40E 30 C5
Khāsh Iran 28°15N 61°15E 45 D9
Khashm el Girba Sudan 14°59N 35°58E 51 F13
Khaskovo Bulgaria 41°56N 25°30E 23 D11
Khatanga Russia 72°0N 102°20E 29 B11
Khatanga → Russia 72°55N 106°0E 29 B11
Khatauli India 29°17N 77°43E 42 E7
Khatra India 22°59N 86°51E 43 H12
Khātūnābād Iran 30°1N 55°25E 45 D7
Khatyrka Russia 62°3N 175°15E 29 C18
Khavda India 23°51N 69°43E 42 H3
Khawr Fakkān U.A.E. 25°21N 56°22E 45 E8
Khaybar, Ḩarrat Si. Arabia 25°45N 40°0E 44 E4
Khāzimiyah Iraq 34°46N 43°37E 44 C4
Khe Bo Vietnam 19°8N 104°41E 38 C5
Khe Long Vietnam 21°29N 104°46E 38 B5
Khe Sanh Vietnam 16°37N 106°45E 38 D6
Khed Brahma India 24°7N 73°5E 42 G5
Khekra India 28°52N 77°20E 42 E7
Khemarak Phouminville = Krong Kaoh Kong Cambodia 11°37N 102°59E 39 G4
Khemisset Morocco 33°50N 6°1W 50 B4
Khemmarat Thailand 16°10N 105°15E 38 D5
Khenāmān Iran 30°27N 56°29E 45 D8
Khenchela Algeria 35°28N 7°11E 50 A7
Khersān → Iran 31°33N 50°22E 45 D6
Kherson Ukraine 46°35N 32°35E 19 E5
Kheta → Russia 71°54N 102°6E 29 B11
Khewari Pakistan 26°36N 68°52E 42 F3
Khilchipur India 24°2N 76°34E 42 G7
Khilok Russia 51°30N 110°45E 29 D12
Khíos = Hios Greece 38°27N 26°9E 23 E12
Khirsadoh India 22°11N 78°47E 43 H8
Khiuma = Hiiumaa Estonia 58°50N 22°45E 9 G20
Khiva Uzbekistan 41°30N 60°18E 28 E7
Khīyāv Iran 38°30N 47°45E 44 B5
Khlong Khlung Thailand 16°12N 99°43E 38 D2
Khmelnik Ukraine 49°33N 27°58E 17 D14
Khmelnitskiy = Khmelnytskyy Ukraine 49°23N 27°0E 17 D14
Khmelnytskyy Ukraine 49°23N 27°0E 17 D14
Khmer Rep. = Cambodia ■ Asia 12°15N 105°0E 38 F5
Khoai, Hon Vietnam 8°26N 104°50E 39 H5
Khodoriv Ukraine 49°24N 24°19E 17 D13
Khodzent = Khŭjand Tajikistan 40°17N 69°37E 28 E7
Khojak Pass Afghan. 30°51N 66°34E 42 D2
Khok Kloi Thailand 8°17N 98°19E 39 a
Khok Pho Thailand 6°43N 101°6E 39 J3
Kholm Russia 57°10N 31°15E 18 C5
Kholmsk Russia 47°40N 142°5E 29 E15
Khomas Hochland Namibia 22°40S 16°0E 56 C2
Khomeyn Iran 33°40N 50°7E 45 C6
Khomeynī Shahr Iran 32°41N 51°31E 45 C6
Khomodino Botswana 22°46S 23°52E 56 C3
Khon Kaen Thailand 16°30N 102°47E 38 D4
Khong → Cambodia 13°32N 105°58E 38 F5
Khong Sedone Laos 15°34N 105°49E 38 E5
Khonuu Russia 66°30N 143°12E 29 C15
Khoper → Russia 49°30N 42°20E 19 D6
Khorāsān □ Iran 34°0N 58°0E 45 C8
Khorat = Nakhon Ratchasima Thailand 14°59N 102°12E 38 E4
Khorat, Cao Nguyen Thailand 15°30N 102°50E 38 E4
Khorixas Namibia 20°16S 14°59E 56 C1
Khorramābād Khorāsān, Iran 35°6N 57°57E 45 C8
Khorramābād Lorestān, Iran 33°30N 48°25E 45 C6
Khorrāmshahr Iran 30°29N 48°15E 45 D6
Khorugh Tajikistan 37°30N 71°36E 28 F8
Khosravī Iran 30°48N 51°28E 45 D6
Khosrowābād Khuzestān, Iran 30°10N 48°25E 45 D6
Khosrowābād Kordestān, Iran 35°31N 47°38E 44 C5
Khost Pakistan 30°13N 67°35E 42 D2
Khosūyeh Iran 28°32N 54°26E 45 D7
Khotyn Ukraine 48°31N 26°27E 17 D14
Khouribga Morocco 32°58N 6°57W 50 B4
Khowst Afghan. 33°22N 69°58E 42 C3
Khowst □ Afghan. 33°20N 70°0E 40 C6
Khoyniki Belarus 51°54N 29°55E 17 C15
Khrysokhou B. Cyprus 35°6N 32°25E 25 D11
Khu Khan Thailand 14°42N 104°12E 38 E5
Khuan Wa Thailand 7°53N 98°17E 39 a
Khudzhand = Khŭjand Tajikistan 40°17N 69°37E 28 E7
Khuff Si. Arabia 24°55N 44°53E 44 E5
Khūgīānī Afghan. 31°34N 66°32E 42 D2
Khuis Botswana 26°40S 21°49E 56 D3
Khuiyala India 27°9N 70°25E 42 F4
Khŭjand Tajikistan 40°17N 69°37E 28 E7
Khujner India 23°47N 76°36E 42 H7
Khulna Bangla. 22°45N 89°34E 41 H16
Khulna □ Bangla. 22°25N 89°35E 41 H16
Khumago Botswana 20°26S 24°32E 56 C3
Khunjerab △ Pakistan 36°40N 75°30E 43 A6
Khunjerab Pass = Kinjirap Daban Asia 36°40N 75°25E 40 A9
Khūnsorkh Iran 27°9N 56°7E 45 E8
Khunti India 23°5N 85°17E 43 H11
Khūr Iran 32°55N 58°18E 45 C8
Khurai India 24°3N 78°23E 42 G8
Khurayş Si. Arabia 25°6N 48°2E 45 E6
Khurja India 28°15N 77°58E 42 E7
Khūrmāl Iraq 35°18N 46°2E 44 C5
Khurr, Wādī al Iraq 32°3N 43°52E 44 C4
Khūsf Iran 32°46N 58°53E 45 C8
Khushab Pakistan 32°20N 72°20E 42 C5
Khust Ukraine 48°10N 23°18E 17 D12
Khutse ⌂ Botswana 23°31S 24°12E 56 C3
Khuzdar Pakistan 27°52N 66°30E 42 F2
Khūzestān □ Iran 31°0N 49°0E 45 D6
Khvāf Iran 34°33N 60°8E 45 C9
Khvājeh Iran 38°9N 46°35E 44 B5
Khvānsār Iran 29°56N 54°8E 45 D7
Khvor Iran 33°45N 55°0E 45 C7
Khvorgū Iran 27°34N 56°27E 45 E8
Khvormūj Iran 28°40N 51°30E 45 D6
Khvoy Iran 38°35N 45°0E 44 B5
Khyber Pass Afghan. 34°10N 71°8E 42 B4
Kia Fiji 16°16S 179°8E 59 a
Kiabukwa Dem. Rep. of the Congo 8°40S 24°48E 55 D1
Kiama Australia 34°40S 150°50E 63 E5
Kiamba Phil. 6°2N 124°46E 37 C6
Kiambi Dem. Rep. of the Congo 7°15S 28°0E 54 D2
Kiambu Kenya 1°8S 36°50E 54 C4
Kiangara Madag. 17°58S 47°2E 57 B8
Kiangsi = Jiangxi □ China 27°30N 116°0E 33 D6
Kiangsu = Jiangsu □ China 33°0N 120°0E 35 H11
Kibale △ Uganda 0°16N 30°18E 54 B3
Kibanga Port Uganda 0°10N 32°58E 54 B3
Kibara Tanzania 2°8S 33°30E 54 C3
Kibare, Mts. Dem. Rep. of the Congo 8°25S 27°10E 54 D2
Kibira △ Burundi 3°6S 30°24E 54 C3
Kibombo Dem. Rep. of the Congo 3°57S 25°53E 54 C2
Kibondo Tanzania 3°35S 30°45E 54 C3
Kibre Mengist Ethiopia 5°54N 38°59E 47 F2
Kıbrıs = Cyprus ■ Asia 35°0N 33°0E 25 E12
Kibumbu Burundi 3°32S 29°45E 54 C2
Kibungo Rwanda 2°10S 30°32E 54 C3
Kibuye Burundi 3°39S 29°59E 54 C2
Kibuye Rwanda 2°3S 29°21E 54 C2
Kibwesa Tanzania 6°30S 29°58E 54 D2
Kibwezi Kenya 2°27S 37°57E 54 C4
Kichha India 28°53N 79°30E 43 E8
Kichha → India 28°41N 79°18E 43 E8
Kichmengskiy Gorodok Russia 59°59N 45°48E 18 B8
Kicking Horse Pass Canada 51°28N 116°16W 70 C5
Kidal Mali 18°26N 1°22E 50 E6
Kidderminster U.K. 52°24N 2°15W 13 E5
Kidepo Valley △ Uganda 3°52N 33°50E 54 B3
Kidete Tanzania 6°25S 37°17E 54 D4
Kidnappers, C. N.Z. 39°38S 177°5E 59 C6
Kidsgrove U.K. 53°5N 2°14W 12 D5
Kidston Australia 18°52S 144°8E 62 B3
Kidugallo Tanzania 6°49S 38°15E 54 D4
Kiel Germany 54°19N 10°8E 16 A6
Kiel Canal = Nord-Ostsee-Kanal Germany 54°12N 9°32E 16 A5
Kielce Poland 50°52N 20°42E 17 C11
Kielder Water U.K. 55°11N 2°31W 12 B5
Kieler Bucht Germany 54°35N 10°25E 16 A6
Kien Binh Vietnam 9°55N 105°19E 39 H5
Kien Tan Vietnam 10°7N 105°17E 39 G5
Kienge Dem. Rep. of the Congo 10°30S 27°30E 55 E2
Kiev = Kyyiv Ukraine 50°30N 30°28E 17 C16
Kiffa Mauritania 16°37N 11°24W 50 E3
Kifrī Iraq 34°45N 45°0E 44 C5
Kigali Rwanda 1°59S 30°4E 54 C3
Kigarama Tanzania 1°1S 31°50E 54 C3
Kigezi ⌂ Uganda 0°34S 29°55E 54 C2
Kigoma □ Tanzania 5°0S 30°0E 54 D3
Kigoma-Ujiji Tanzania 4°55S 29°36E 54 C2
Kigomasha, Ras Tanzania 4°58S 38°58E 54 C4
Kığızı Turkey 38°18N 43°25E 44 B4
Kihnu Estonia 58°9N 24°1E 9 G21
Kii-Sanchi Japan 34°20N 136°0E 31 G8
Kii-Suidō Japan 33°40N 134°45E 31 H7
Kiira Dam Uganda 0°25N 33°0E 54 B3
Kikaiga-Shima Japan 28°19N 129°59E 31 K4
Kikinda Serbia 45°50N 20°30E 23 B9
Kikládhes = Cyclades Greece 37°0N 24°30E 23 F11
Kikwit Dem. Rep. of the Congo 5°0S 18°45E 52 E3
Kilar India 33°6N 76°25E 42 C7
Kīlauea Caldera U.S.A. 19°25N 155°17W 74 b
Kilbeggan Ireland 53°22N 7°30W 10 C4
Kilbrannan Sd. U.K. 55°37N 5°26W 11 F3
Kilchu N. Korea 40°57N 129°25E 35 D15
Kilcoy Australia 26°59S 152°30E 63 D5
Kildare Ireland 53°9N 6°55W 10 C5
Kildare □ Ireland 53°10N 6°50W 10 C5
Kildinstroy Russia 68°48N 33°6E 8 B25
Kilfinnane Ireland 52°21N 8°28W 10 D3
Kilgarvan Ireland 51°54N 9°27W 10 E2
Kilgore U.S.A. 32°23N 94°53W 84 E7
Kilgoris Kenya 1°0S 34°53E 54 C3
Kilifi Kenya 3°40S 39°48E 54 C4
Kilimanjaro Tanzania 3°7S 37°20E 54 C4
Kilimanjaro □ Tanzania 4°0S 38°0E 54 C4
Kilindini Kenya 4°4S 39°40E 54 C4
Kilis Turkey 36°42N 37°6E 44 B3
Kiliya Ukraine 45°28N 29°16E 17 F15
Kilkee Ireland 52°41N 9°39W 10 D2
Kilkeel U.K. 54°4N 6°0W 10 B5
Kilkenny Ireland 52°39N 7°15W 10 D4
Kilkenny □ Ireland 52°35N 7°15W 10 D4
Kilkieran B. Ireland 53°20N 9°41W 10 C2
Kilkís Greece 40°58N 22°57E 23 D10
Killala Ireland 54°13N 9°12W 10 B2
Killala B. Ireland 54°16N 9°8W 10 B2
Killaloe Canada 45°33N 77°25W 82 A7
Killaloe Ireland 52°48N 8°28W 10 D3
Killarney Australia 28°20S 152°18E 63 D5
Killarney Canada 49°10N 99°40W 71 D9
Killarney Ireland 52°4N 9°30W 10 D2
Killarney △ Ireland 52°0N 9°33W 10 D2
Killary Harbour Ireland 53°38N 9°52W 10 C2
Killdeer U.S.A. 47°22N 102°45W 80 B2
Killeen U.S.A. 31°7N 97°44W 84 F6
Killin U.K. 56°28N 4°19W 11 E4
Killiney Ireland 53°15N 6°7W 10 C5
Killini Greece 37°54N 22°25E 23 F10
Killorglin Ireland 52°6N 9°47W 10 D2
Killybegs Ireland 54°38N 8°26W 10 B3
Kilmarnock U.K. 55°37N 4°29W 11 F4
Kilmore Australia 37°25S 144°53E 63 F3
Kilmore Quay Ireland 52°10N 6°36W 10 D5
Kilondo Tanzania 9°45S 34°20E 55 D3
Kilosa Tanzania 6°48S 37°0E 54 D4
Kilrush Ireland 52°38N 9°29W 10 D2
Kilwa Kisiwani Tanzania 8°58S 39°32E 55 D4
Kilwa Kivinje Tanzania 8°45S 39°25E 55 D4
Kilwa Masoko Tanzania 8°55S 39°30E 55 D4
Kilwinning U.K. 55°39N 4°43W 11 F4
Kim U.S.A. 37°15N 103°21W 77 H12
Kimaam Indonesia 7°58S 138°53E 37 F9
Kimamba Tanzania 6°45S 37°10E 54 D4
Kimba Australia 33°8S 136°23E 63 E2
Kimball Nebr., U.S.A. 41°14N 103°40W 80 E2
Kimball S. Dak., U.S.A. 43°45N 98°57W 80 D4
Kimberley Australia 16°20S 127°0E 60 C4
Kimberley Canada 49°40N 115°59W 70 D5
Kimberley S. Africa 28°43S 24°46E 56 D3
Kimberly U.S.A. 42°32N 114°22W 76 E6
Kimch'aek N. Korea 40°40N 129°10E 35 D15
Kimhae = Gimhae S. Korea 35°14N 128°53E 35 G15
Kimmirut Canada 62°50N 69°50W 69 C13
Kimpese Dem. Rep. of the Congo 5°35S 14°26E 52 F2
Kimry Russia 56°55N 37°15E 18 C6
Kinabalu, Gunung Malaysia 6°3N 116°14E 36 C5
Kinango Kenya 4°8S 39°19E 54 C4
Kinaskan L. Canada 57°38N 130°8W 70 B2
Kinbasket L. Canada 52°0N 118°10W 70 C5
Kincardine Canada 44°10N 81°40W 82 B3
Kincolith Canada 55°0N 129°57W 70 C3
Kinda Dem. Rep. of the Congo 9°18S 25°4E 55 D2
Kinde U.S.A. 43°56N 83°0W 82 C2
Kinder Scout U.K. 53°24N 1°52W 12 D6
Kindersley Canada 51°30N 109°10W 71 C7
Kindia Guinea 10°0N 12°52W 50 F3
Kindu Dem. Rep. of the Congo 2°55S 25°50E 54 C2
Kineshma Russia 57°30N 42°5E 18 C7
Kinesi Tanzania 1°25S 33°50E 54 C3
King, L. Australia 33°10S 119°35E 61 F2
King, Mt. Australia 25°10S 147°30E 62 D4
King City U.S.A. 36°13N 121°8W 78 J5
King Cr. → Australia 24°35S 139°30E 62 C2
King Edward → Australia 14°14S 126°35E 60 B4
King Frederick VI Land = Kong Frederik VI Kyst Greenland 63°0N 43°0W 4 C5
King George B. Falk. Is. 51°30S 60°30W 96 G4
King George I. Antarctica 60°0S 60°0W 5 C18
King George Is. Canada 57°20N 80°30W 69 D11
King I. = Kadan Kyun Burma 12°30N 98°20E 38 F2
King I. Australia 39°50S 144°0E 63 F3
King I. Canada 52°10N 127°40W 70 C3
King Leopold Ranges Australia 17°30S 125°45E 60 C4
King of Prussia U.S.A. 40°5N 75°23W 83 F9
King Sd. Australia 16°50S 123°20E 60 C3
King Sejong Antarctica 62°30S 58°0W 5 C18
King William I. Canada 69°10N 97°25W 68 C10
King William's Town S. Africa 32°51S 27°22E 56 E4
Kingait = Cape Dorset Canada 64°14N 76°32W 69 C12
Kingaok = Bathurst Inlet Canada 66°50N 108°1W 68 C9
Kingaroy Australia 26°32S 151°51E 63 D5
Kingfisher U.S.A. 35°52N 97°56W 84 D6
Kingirbān Iraq 34°40N 44°54E 44 C5
Kingisepp = Kuressaare Estonia 58°15N 22°30E 9 G20
Kingisepp Russia 59°25N 28°40E 9 G23
Kingman Ariz., U.S.A. 35°12N 114°4W 79 K12
Kingman Kans., U.S.A. 37°39N 98°7W 80 G4
Kingoonya Australia 30°55S 135°19E 63 E2
Kingri Pakistan 30°27N 69°49E 42 D3
Kings → U.S.A. 36°3N 119°50W 78 J7
Kings Canyon △ U.S.A. 36°50N 118°40W 78 J8
King's Lynn U.K. 52°45N 0°24E 12 E8
Kings Park U.S.A. 40°53N 73°16W 83 F11
Kings Peak U.S.A. 40°46N 110°23W 76 F8
Kingsbridge U.K. 50°17N 3°47W 13 G4
Kingsburg U.S.A. 36°31N 119°33W 78 J7
Kingscote Australia 35°40S 137°38E 63 F2
Kingscourt Ireland 53°55N 6°48W 10 C5
Kingsford U.S.A. 45°48N 88°4W 80 C9
Kingsland U.S.A. 30°48N 81°41W 85 F14
Kingsport U.S.A. 36°33N 82°33W 85 C13
Kingston Canada 44°14N 76°30W 83 B8
Kingston Jamaica 18°0N 76°50W 88 a
Kingston N.Z. 45°20S 168°43E 59 F2
Kingston N.H., U.S.A. 42°56N 71°3W 83 D13
Kingston N.Y., U.S.A. 41°56N 73°59W 83 E11
Kingston Pa., U.S.A. 41°16N 75°54W 83 E9
Kingston R.I., U.S.A. 41°29N 71°30W 83 E13
Kingston Pk. U.S.A. 35°44N 115°55W 79 K11
Kingston South East Australia 36°51S 139°55E 63 F2
Kingston upon Hull U.K. 53°45N 0°21W 12 D7
Kingston upon Hull □ U.K. 53°45N 0°21W 12 D7
Kingston-upon-Thames □ U.K. 51°24N 0°17W 13 F7
Kingstown St. Vincent 13°10N 61°10W 89 D7
Kingstree U.S.A. 33°40N 79°50W 85 E15
Kingsville Canada 42°2N 82°45W 82 D2
Kingsville U.S.A. 27°31N 97°52W 84 H6
Kingussie U.K. 57°6N 4°2W 11 D4
Kingwood U.S.A. 30°2N 95°16W 84 F7
Kınık Turkey 39°6N 27°24E 23 E12
Kinistino Canada 52°57N 105°2W 71 C7
Kinjirap Daban Asia 36°40N 75°25E 40 A9
Kinkala Congo 4°18S 14°49E 52 E2
Kinki □ Japan 33°45N 136°0E 31 H8
Kinleith N.Z. 38°20S 175°56E 59 C5
Kinlochleven U.K. 56°43N 5°0W 11 E4
Kinmount Canada 44°48N 78°45W 82 B6
Kinna Sweden 57°32N 12°42E 9 H15
Kinnairds Hd. U.K. 57°43N 2°1W 11 D6
Kino Nuevo Mexico 28°52N 112°3W 86 B2
Kinoje → Canada 52°8N 81°25W 72 B3
Kinomoto Japan 35°30N 136°13E 31 G8
Kinoni Uganda 0°41S 30°28E 54 C3
Kinoosao Canada 57°5N 102°1W 71 B8
Kinross U.K. 56°13N 3°25W 11 E5
Kinsale Ireland 51°42N 8°31W 10 E3
Kinsale, Old Hd. of Ireland 51°37N 8°33W 10 E3
Kinsha = Chang Jiang → China 31°48N 121°10E 33 C7
Kinshasa Dem. Rep. of the Congo 4°20S 15°15E 52 E3
Kinsley U.S.A. 37°55N 99°25W 80 G4
Kinsman U.S.A. 41°26N 80°35W 82 E4
Kinston U.S.A. 35°16N 77°35W 85 D16
Kintamani Indonesia 8°14S 115°19E 37 J18
Kintore U.K. 57°14N 2°20W 11 D6
Kintore Ra. Australia 23°15S 128°47E 60 D4
Kintyre U.K. 55°30N 5°35W 11 F3
Kintyre, Mull of U.K. 55°17N 5°47W 11 F3
Kinushseo → Canada 55°15N 83°45W 72 A3
Kinuso Canada 55°20N 115°25W 70 B5
Kinvarra Ireland 53°8N 8°56W 10 C3
Kinyangiri Tanzania 4°25S 34°37E 54 C3
Kinyeti Sudan 3°57N 32°54E 54 B3
Kinzua U.S.A. 41°52N 78°58W 82 E6
Kiosk Canada 46°6N 78°53W 72 C4
Kiowa Kans., U.S.A. 37°1N 98°29W 80 G4
Kiowa Okla., U.S.A. 34°43N 95°54W 84 D7
Kipahigan L. Canada 55°20N 101°55W 71 B8
Kipanga Tanzania 6°15S 35°20E 54 D4
Kiparissia Greece 37°15N 21°40E 23 F9
Kiparissiakos Kolpos Greece 37°25N 21°25E 23 F9
Kipawa, L. Canada 46°50N 79°0W 72 C4
Kipembawe Tanzania 7°38S 33°27E 54 D3
Kipengere Ra. Tanzania 9°12S 34°15E 55 D3
Kipili Tanzania 7°28S 30°32E 54 D3
Kipini Kenya 2°30S 40°32E 54 C5
Kipling Canada 50°6N 102°38W 71 C8

Kippure *Ireland* 53°11N 6°21W **10 C5**
Kipushi
  Dem. Rep. of the Congo 11°48S 27°12E **55 E2**
Kiranomena *Madag.* 18°17S 46°2E **57 B8**
Kirensk *Russia* 57°50N 107°55E **29 D11**
Kirghizia = Kyrgyzstan ■
  Asia 42°0N 75°0E **28 E8**
Kirghizstan = Kyrgyzstan ■
  Asia 42°0N 75°0E **28 E8**
Kirgiziya Steppe *Eurasia* 50°0N 55°0E **19 E10**
Kiribati ■ *Pac. Oc.* 3°0S 180°0E **58 B10**
Kırıkkale *Turkey* 39°51N 33°32E **19 G5**
Kirillov *Russia* 59°49N 38°24E **18 C6**
Kirin = Jilin *China* 43°44N 126°30E **35 C14**
Kirinyaga = Kenya, Mt.
  Kenya 0°10S 37°18E **54 C4**
Kirishima Yaku △
  Japan 31°24N 130°50E **31 J5**
Kiritimati *Kiribati* 1°58N 157°27W **65 G12**
Kirkby *U.K.* 53°30N 2°54W **12 D5**
Kirkby-in-Ashfield *U.K.* 53°6N 1°14W **12 D6**
Kirkby Lonsdale *U.K.* 54°12N 2°36W **12 C5**
Kirkby Stephen *U.K.* 54°29N 2°21W **12 C5**
Kirkcaldy *U.K.* 50°7N 3°9W **11 E5**
Kirkcudbright *U.K.* 54°50N 4°2W **11 G4**
Kirkee *India* 18°34N 73°56E **40 K8**
Kirkenes *Norway* 69°40N 30°5E **8 B24**
Kirkfield *Canada* 44°34N 78°59W **82 B6**
Kirkintilloch *U.K.* 55°56N 4°8W **11 F4**
Kirkjubæjarklaustur
  Iceland 63°47N 18°4W **8 E4**
Kirkkonummi *Finland* 60°8N 24°26E **9 F21**
Kirkland *U.S.A.* 47°40N 122°12W **78 C4**
Kirkland Lake *Canada* 48°9N 80°2W **72 C3**
Kırklareli *Turkey* 41°44N 27°15E **23 D12**
Kirksville *U.S.A.* 40°12N 92°35W **80 E7**
Kirkūk *Iraq* 35°30N 44°21E **44 C5**
Kirkwall *U.K.* 58°59N 2°58W **11 C6**
Kirkwood *S. Africa* 33°22S 25°15E **56 E4**
Kirov *Russia* 58°35N 49°40E **18 C8**
Kirovabad = Gäncä
  Azerbaijan 40°45N 46°20E **19 F8**
Kirovograd = Kirovohrad
  Ukraine 48°35N 32°20E **19 E5**
Kirovohrad *Ukraine* 48°35N 32°20E **19 E5**
Kirovsk *Russia* 67°32N 33°41E **18 A5**
Kirovskiy *Kamchatka,*
  Russia 54°27N 155°42E **29 D16**
Kirovskiy *Primorsk,*
  Russia 45°7N 133°30E **30 B6**
Kirriemuir *U.K.* 56°41N 3°1W **11 E5**
Kirsanov *Russia* 52°35N 42°40E **18 D7**
Kırşehir *Turkey* 39°14N 34°5E **44 B2**
Kirthar △ *Pakistan* 25°45N 67°30E **42 F2**
Kirthar Range *Pakistan* 27°0N 67°0E **42 F2**
Kirtland *U.S.A.* 36°44N 108°21W **77 H9**
Kiruna *Sweden* 67°52N 20°15E **8 C19**
Kirundu
  Dem. Rep. of the Congo 0°50S 25°35E **54 C2**
Kiryū *Japan* 36°24N 139°20E **31 F9**
Kisaga *Tanzania* 4°30S 34°23E **54 C3**
Kisalaya *Nic.* 14°40N 84°3W **88 D3**
Kisanga
  Dem. Rep. of the Congo 2°30N 26°35E **54 B2**
Kisangani
  Dem. Rep. of the Congo 0°35N 25°15E **54 B2**
Kisar *Indonesia* 8°5S 127°10E **37 F7**
Kisarawe *Tanzania* 6°53S 39°0E **54 D4**
Kisarazu *Japan* 35°23N 139°55E **31 G9**
Kishanganga →
  Pakistan 34°18N 73°28E **43 B5**
Kishanganj *India* 26°3N 88°14E **43 F13**
Kishangarh *Raj., India* 26°34N 74°52E **42 F6**
Kishangarh *Raj., India* 27°50N 70°30E **42 F4**
Kishinev = Chişinău
  Moldova 47°2N 28°50E **17 E15**
Kishiwada *Japan* 34°28N 135°22E **31 G7**
Kishtwar *India* 33°20N 75°48E **42 C6**
Kisigo → *Tanzania* 6°27S 34°17E **54 D3**
Kisii *Kenya* 0°40S 34°45E **54 C3**
Kisiju *Tanzania* 7°23S 39°19E **54 D4**
Kisizi *Uganda* 1°0S 29°58E **54 C2**
Kiskőrös *Hungary* 46°37N 19°20E **17 E10**
Kiskunfélegyháza
  Hungary 46°42N 19°53E **17 E10**
Kiskunhalas *Hungary* 46°28N 19°37E **17 E10**
Kislovodsk *Russia* 43°50N 42°45E **19 F7**
Kismayu = Chisimaio
  Somali Rep. 0°22S 42°32E **47 H3**
Kiso-Gawa → *Japan* 35°20N 136°45E **31 G8**
Kiso-Sammyaku *Japan* 35°45N 137°45E **31 G8**
Kisofukushima *Japan* 35°52N 137°43E **31 G8**
Kisoro *Uganda* 1°17S 29°48E **54 C2**
Kissamos = Kasteli
  Greece 35°29N 23°38E **25 D5**
Kissamos, Kolpos
  Greece 35°30N 23°38E **25 D5**
Kissidougou *Guinea* 9°5N 10°5W **50 G3**
Kissimmee *U.S.A.* 28°18N 81°24W **85 G14**
Kissimmee → *U.S.A.* 27°9N 80°52W **85 H14**
Kississing L. *Canada* 55°10N 101°20W **71 B8**
Kissónerga *Cyprus* 34°49N 32°24E **25 E11**
Kisumu *Kenya* 0°3S 34°45E **54 C3**
Kiswani *Tanzania* 4°5S 37°57E **54 C4**
Kiswere *Tanzania* 9°27S 39°30E **55 D4**
Kit Carson *U.S.A.* 38°46N 102°48W **76 G12**
Kita *Mali* 13°5N 9°25W **50 F4**
Kitaibaraki *Japan* 36°50N 140°45E **31 F10**
Kitakami *Japan* 39°20N 141°10E **30 E10**
Kitakami-Gawa →
  Japan 38°25N 141°19E **30 E10**
Kitakami-Sammyaku
  Japan 39°30N 141°30E **30 E10**
Kitakata *Japan* 37°39N 139°52E **30 F9**
Kitakyūshū *Japan* 33°50N 130°50E **31 H5**
Kitale *Kenya* 1°0N 35°0E **54 B4**
Kitami *Japan* 43°48N 143°54E **30 C11**

Kitami-Sammyaku
  Japan 44°22N 142°43E **30 B11**
Kitangiri, L. *Tanzania* 4°5S 34°20E **54 C3**
Kitaya *Tanzania* 10°38S 40°8E **55 E5**
Kitchener *Canada* 43°27N 80°29W **82 C4**
Kitee *Finland* 62°5N 30°8E **8 E24**
Kitega = Gitega *Burundi* 3°26S 29°56E **54 C2**
Kitengo
  Dem. Rep. of the Congo 7°26S 24°8E **54 D1**
Kitgum *Uganda* 3°17N 32°52E **54 B3**
Kíthira = Kythira *Greece* 36°8N 23°0E **23 F10**
Kithnos *Greece* 37°26N 24°27E **23 F11**
Kiti *Cyprus* 34°50N 33°34E **25 E12**
Kiti, C. *Cyprus* 34°48N 33°36E **25 E12**
Kitimat *Canada* 54°3N 128°38W **70 C3**
Kitinen → *Finland* 67°14N 27°27E **8 C22**
Kitsuki *Japan* 33°25N 131°37E **31 H5**
Kittakittaooloo, L.
  Australia 28°3S 138°14E **63 D2**
Kittanning *U.S.A.* 40°49N 79°31W **82 F5**
Kittatinny Mt. *U.S.A.* 41°19N 74°39W **83 E10**
Kittery *U.S.A.* 43°5N 70°45W **83 C14**
Kittilä *Finland* 67°40N 24°51E **8 C21**
Kitui *Kenya* 1°17S 38°0E **54 C4**
Kitwanga *Canada* 55°6N 128°4W **70 B3**
Kitwe *Zambia* 12°54S 28°13E **55 E2**
Kivarli *India* 24°33N 72°46E **42 G5**
Kivertsi *Ukraine* 50°50N 25°28E **17 C13**
Kividhes *Cyprus* 34°46N 32°51E **25 E11**
Kivu, L.
  Dem. Rep. of the Congo 1°48S 29°0E **54 C2**
Kiyev = Kyyiv *Ukraine* 50°30N 30°28E **17 C16**
Kiyevskoye Vdkhr. = Kyyivske
  Vdskh. *Ukraine* 51°0N 30°25E **17 C16**
Kizel *Russia* 59°3N 57°40E **18 C10**
Kiziguru *Rwanda* 1°46S 30°23E **54 C3**
Kızıl Irmak → *Turkey* 41°44N 35°58E **19 F6**
Kizil Jilga *China* 35°26N 78°50E **43 B8**
Kızıldağ △ *Turkey* 38°5N 31°20E **44 B1**
Kızıltepe *Turkey* 37°12N 40°35E **44 B4**
Kizimkazi *Tanzania* 6°28S 39°30E **54 D4**
Kızlyar *Russia* 43°51N 46°40E **19 F8**
Kizyl-Arvat = Serdar
  Turkmenistan 39°4N 56°23E **45 B8**
Kjölur *Iceland* 64°50N 19°25W **8 D4**
Kladno *Czech Rep.* 50°10N 14°7E **16 C8**
Klaeng *Thailand* 12°47N 101°39E **38 F3**
Klagenfurt *Austria* 46°38N 14°20E **16 E8**
Klaipėda *Lithuania* 55°43N 21°10E **9 J19**
Klaksvík *Færoe Is.* 62°14N 6°35W **8 E9**
Klamath → *U.S.A.* 41°33N 124°5W **76 F1**
Klamath Falls *U.S.A.* 42°13N 121°46W **76 E3**
Klamath Mts. *U.S.A.* 41°50N 123°20W **76 F2**
Klamono *Indonesia* 1°8S 131°30E **37 E8**
Klappan → *Canada* 58°0N 129°43W **70 B3**
Klarälven → *Sweden* 59°23N 13°32E **9 G15**
Klatovy *Czech Rep.* 49°23N 13°18E **16 D7**
Klawer *S. Africa* 31°44S 18°36E **56 E2**
Klazienaveen *Neths.* 52°44N 7°0E **15 B6**
Kleena Kleene *Canada* 52°0N 124°59W **70 C4**
Klein-Karas *Namibia* 27°33S 18°7E **56 D2**
Klerksdorp *S. Africa* 26°53S 26°38E **56 D4**
Kletsk = Klyetsk
  Belarus 53°5N 26°45E **17 B14**
Kletskiy *Russia* 49°16N 43°11E **19 E7**
Klickitat *U.S.A.* 45°49N 121°9W **76 D3**
Klickitat → *U.S.A.* 45°42N 121°17W **78 E5**
Klidhes *Cyprus* 35°42N 34°36E **25 D13**
Klip → *S. Africa* 27°3S 29°3E **57 D4**
Klipdale *S. Africa* 34°19S 19°57E **56 E2**
Klipplaat *S. Africa* 33°1S 24°22E **56 E3**
Kłodzko *Poland* 50°28N 16°38E **17 C9**
Klong Wang Chao △
  Thailand 16°20N 99°9E **38 D2**
Klouto *Togo* 6°57N 0°44E **50 G6**
Kluane △ *Canada* 60°45N 139°30W **70 A1**
Kluane L. *Canada* 61°15N 138°40W **68 C6**
Kluang *Malaysia* 2°3N 103°18E **39 L4**
Kluczbork *Poland* 50°58N 18°12E **17 C10**
Klukwan *U.S.A.* 59°24N 135°54W **70 B1**
Klungkung *Indonesia* 8°32S 115°24E **37 K18**
Klyetsk *Belarus* 53°5N 26°45E **17 B14**
Klyuchevskaya, Gora
  Russia 55°50N 160°30E **29 D17**
Knaresborough *U.K.* 54°1N 1°28W **12 C6**
Knee L., *Man., Canada* 55°3N 94°45W **72 A1**
Knee L. *Sask., Canada* 55°51N 107°0W **71 B7**
Knight Inlet *Canada* 50°45N 125°40W **70 C3**
Knighton *U.K.* 52°21N 3°3W **13 E4**
Knights Ferry *U.S.A.* 37°50N 120°40W **78 H6**
Knights Landing
  U.S.A. 38°48N 121°43W **78 G5**
Knob, C. *Australia* 34°32S 119°16E **61 F2**
Knock *Ireland* 53°48N 8°55W **10 C3**
Knockmealdown Mts.
  Ireland 52°14N 7°56W **10 D4**
Knokke-Heist *Belgium* 51°21N 3°17E **15 C3**
Knossos *Greece* 35°16N 25°10E **25 D7**
Knowlton *Canada* 45°13N 72°31W **83 A12**
Knox *U.S.A.* 41°18N 86°37W **80 E10**
Knox Coast *Antarctica* 66°30S 108°0E **5 C8**
Knoxville *Iowa, U.S.A.* 41°19N 93°6W **80 E7**
Knoxville *Pa., U.S.A.* 41°57N 77°27W **82 E7**
Knoxville *Tenn., U.S.A.* 35°58N 83°55W **85 D13**
Knud Rasmussen Land
  Greenland 78°0N 60°0W **4 A5**
Knysna *S. Africa* 34°2S 23°2E **56 E3**
Ko Kha *Thailand* 18°11N 99°24E **38 C2**
Ko Tarutao △ *Thailand* 6°31N 99°26E **39 J2**
Ko Yao *Thailand* 8°7N 98°35E **39 a**
Koartac = Quaqtaq
  Canada 60°55N 69°40W **69 C13**
Koba *Indonesia* 6°3S 134°37E **37 F8**
Kobarid *Slovenia* 46°15N 13°30E **16 E7**
Kobayashi *Japan* 31°56N 130°59E **31 J5**

Kōbe *Japan* 34°41N 135°13E **31 G7**
København *Denmark* 55°40N 12°26E **9 J15**
Kōbi-Sho *Japan* 25°56N 123°41E **31 M1**
Koblenz *Germany* 50°21N 7°36E **16 C4**
Kobryn *Belarus* 52°15N 24°22E **17 B13**
Kocaeli *Turkey* 40°45N 29°50E **19 F4**
Kočani *Macedonia* 41°55N 22°25E **23 D10**
Koch Bihar *India* 26°22N 89°29E **41 F16**
Kochas *India* 25°15N 83°56E **43 G10**
Kochi = Cochin *India* 9°58N 76°20E **40 Q10**
Kōchi *Japan* 33°30N 133°35E **31 H6**
Kōchi □ *Japan* 33°40N 133°30E **31 H6**
Kochiu = Gejiu *China* 23°20N 103°10E **32 D5**
Kodarma *India* 24°28N 85°36E **43 G11**
Kodiak *U.S.A.* 57°47N 152°24W **74 a**
Kodiak I. *U.S.A.* 57°30N 152°45W **74 a**
Kodinar *India* 20°46N 70°46E **42 J4**
Koedoesberge *S. Africa* 32°40S 20°11E **56 E3**
Koes *Namibia* 26°0S 19°15E **56 D2**
Koffiefontein *S. Africa* 29°30S 25°0E **56 D4**
Kofiau *Indonesia* 1°11S 129°50E **37 E8**
Koforidua *Ghana* 6°3N 0°17W **50 G5**
Kōfu *Japan* 35°40N 138°30E **31 G9**
Koga *Japan* 36°11N 139°43E **31 F9**
Kogaluc → *Canada* 56°12N 61°44W **73 A7**
Køge *Denmark* 55°27N 12°11E **9 J15**
Koh-i-Khurd *Afghan.* 33°30N 65°59E **42 C1**
Koh-i-Maran *Pakistan* 29°18N 66°50E **42 E2**
Kohat *Pakistan* 33°40N 71°29E **42 C4**
Kohima *India* 25°35N 94°10E **41 G19**
Kohkīlūyeh va Būyer Aḥmadi □
  Iran 31°30N 50°30E **45 D6**
Kohler Ra. *Antarctica* 77°0S 110°0W **5 D15**
Kohlu *Pakistan* 29°54N 69°15E **42 E3**
Kohtla-Järve *Estonia* 59°20N 27°20E **9 G22**
Koi Sanjaq *Iraq* 36°5N 44°38E **44 B5**
Koillismaa *Finland* 65°44N 28°36E **8 D23**
Kojŏ *N. Korea* 40°28N 127°58E **35 E14**
Kojonup *Australia* 33°48S 117°10E **61 F2**
Kojūr *Iran* 36°23N 51°43E **45 B6**
Kokand = Qŭqon
  Uzbekistan 40°31N 70°56E **28 E8**
Kokas *Indonesia* 2°42S 132°26E **37 E8**
Kokchetav = Kökshetaū
  Kazakhstan 53°20N 69°25E **28 D7**
Kokemäenjoki →
  Finland 61°32N 21°44E **8 F19**
Kokkola *Finland* 63°50N 23°8E **8 E20**
Koko Kyunzu *Burma* 14°10N 93°25E **41 M18**
Kokomo *U.S.A.* 40°29N 86°8W **80 E10**
Koksan *N. Korea* 38°46N 126°40E **35 E14**
Kökshetaū *Kazakhstan* 53°20N 69°25E **28 D7**
Koksoak → *Canada* 58°30N 68°10W **69 D13**
Kokstad *S. Africa* 30°32S 29°29E **57 E4**
Kokubu *Japan* 31°44N 130°46E **31 J5**
Kola *Indonesia* 5°35S 134°30E **37 F8**
Kola *Russia* 68°45N 33°8E **8 B25**
Kola Pen. = Kolskiy Poluostrov
  Russia 67°30N 38°0E **18 A6**
Kolachi → *Pakistan* 27°8N 67°2E **42 F2**
Kolahoi *India* 34°12N 75°22E **43 B6**
Kolaka *Indonesia* 4°3S 121°46E **37 E6**
Kolar *India* 13°12N 78°15E **40 N11**
Kolar Gold Fields *India* 12°58N 78°16E **40 N11**
Kolaras *India* 25°14N 77°36E **42 G6**
Kolari *Finland* 67°20N 23°48E **8 C20**
Kolayat *India* 27°50N 72°50E **42 F5**
Kolda *Senegal* 12°55N 14°57W **50 F3**
Kolding *Denmark* 55°30N 9°29E **9 J13**
Kolepom = Dolak, Pulau
  Indonesia 8°0S 138°30E **37 F9**
Kolguyev, Ostrov
  Russia 69°20N 48°30E **18 A8**
Kolhapur *India* 16°43N 74°15E **40 L9**
Kolín *Czech Rep.* 50°2N 15°9E **16 C8**
Kolkas rags *Latvia* 57°46N 22°37E **9 H20**
Kolkata *India* 22°34N 88°21E **43 H13**
Kollam = Quilon *India* 8°50N 76°38E **40 Q10**
Kollum *Neths.* 53°17N 6°10E **15 A6**
Kolmanskop *Namibia* 26°45S 15°14E **56 D2**
Köln *Germany* 50°56N 6°57E **16 C4**
Koło *Poland* 52°14N 18°40E **17 B10**
Kołobrzeg *Poland* 54°10N 15°35E **16 A8**
Kolomna *Russia* 55°8N 38°45E **18 C6**
Kolomyya *Ukraine* 48°31N 25°2E **17 D13**
Kolonodale *Indonesia* 2°0S 121°19E **37 E6**
Kolosib *India* 24°15N 92°45E **41 G18**
Kolpashevo *Russia* 58°20N 83°5E **28 D9**
Kolpino *Russia* 59°44N 30°39E **18 C5**
Kolskiy Poluostrov
  Russia 67°30N 38°0E **18 A6**
Kolskiy Zaliv *Russia* 69°23N 34°0E **8 B26**
Kolwezi
  Dem. Rep. of the Congo 10°40S 25°25E **55 E2**
Kolyma → *Russia* 69°30N 161°0E **29 C17**
Kolymskoye Nagorye
  Russia 63°0N 157°0E **29 C16**
Komandorskiye Is. =
  Komandorskiye Ostrova
Komandorskiye Ostrova
  Russia 55°0N 167°0E **29 D17**
Kōmárno *Slovak Rep.* 47°49N 18°5E **17 E10**
Komatipoort *S. Africa* 25°25S 31°55E **57 D5**
Komandou Yialou *Cyprus* 35°25N 34°8E **25 D13**
Komatsu *Japan* 36°25N 136°30E **31 F8**
Komatsushima *Japan* 34°0N 134°35E **31 H7**
Kombissiri *Burkina Faso* 12°3N 1°17W **50 F5**
Komi □ *Russia* 64°0N 55°0E **18 B10**
Kommamur Canal *India* 16°0N 80°25E **40 M12**
Kommunarsk = Alchevsk
  Ukraine 48°30N 38°45E **19 E6**
Kommunizma, Pik = imeni Ismail
  Samani, Pik *Tajikistan* 39°0N 72°2E **28 F8**
Komodo *Indonesia* 8°37S 119°20E **37 F5**
Komoran, Pulau
  Indonesia 8°18S 138°45E **37 F9**

Komoro *Japan* 36°19N 138°26E **31 F9**
Komotini *Greece* 41°9N 25°26E **23 D11**
Kompasberg *S. Africa* 31°45S 24°32E **56 E3**
Kompong Bang
  Cambodia 12°24N 104°40E **39 F5**
Kompong Cham
  Cambodia 12°0N 105°30E **39 F5**
Kompong Chhnang = Kampong
  Chhnang *Cambodia* 12°20N 104°35E **39 F5**
Kompong Chikreng
  Cambodia 13°5N 104°18E **38 F5**
Kompong Kleang
  Cambodia 13°6N 104°8E **38 F5**
Kompong Luong
  Cambodia 11°49N 104°48E **39 G5**
Kompong Pranak
  Cambodia 13°35N 104°55E **38 F5**
Kompong Som = Kampong Saom
  Cambodia 10°38N 103°30E **39 G4**
Kompong Som, Chhung =
  Kampong Saom, Chaak
  Cambodia 10°50N 103°32E **39 G4**
Kompong Speu
  Cambodia 11°26N 104°32E **39 G5**
Kompong Sralau
  Cambodia 14°5N 105°46E **38 E5**
Kompong Thom
  Cambodia 12°35N 104°51E **38 F5**
Kompong Trabeck
  Cambodia 13°6N 105°14E **38 F5**
Kompong Trabeck
  Cambodia 11°9N 105°28E **39 G5**
Kompong Trach
  Cambodia 11°25N 105°48E **39 G5**
Kompong Tralach
  Cambodia 11°54N 104°47E **39 G5**
Komrat = Comrat
  Moldova 46°18N 28°40E **17 E15**
Komsberg *S. Africa* 32°40S 20°45E **56 E3**
Komsomolets, Ostrov
  Russia 80°30N 95°0E **29 A10**
Komsomolsk *Russia* 50°30N 137°0E **29 D14**
Kon Tum *Vietnam* 14°24N 108°0E **38 E7**
Kon Tum, Plateau du
  Vietnam 14°30N 108°30E **38 E7**
Konar □ *Afghan.* 34°30N 71°3E **40 B7**
Konārī *Iran* 28°13N 51°36E **45 D6**
Konch *India* 26°0N 79°10E **43 G8**
Konde *Tanzania* 4°57S 39°45E **54 C4**
Kondinin *Australia* 32°34S 118°8E **61 F2**
Kondoa *Tanzania* 4°55S 35°50E **54 C4**
Kondopaga *Russia* 62°12N 34°17E **18 B5**
Kondratyevo *Russia* 57°22N 98°15E **29 D10**
Köneürgench
  Turkmenistan 42°19N 59°10E **28 E6**
Konevo *Russia* 62°8N 39°20E **18 B6**
Kong = Khong →
  Cambodia 13°32N 105°58E **38 F5**
Kong *Ivory C.* 8°54N 4°36W **50 G5**
Kong, Koh *Cambodia* 11°20N 103°0E **39 G4**
Kong Christian IX Land
  Greenland 68°0N 36°0W **4 C6**
Kong Christian X Land
  Greenland 74°0N 29°0W **4 B6**
Kong Frederik IX Land
  Greenland 67°0N 52°0W **4 C5**
Kong Frederik VI Kyst
  Greenland 63°0N 43°0W **4 C5**
Kong Frederik VIII Land
  Greenland 78°30N 26°0W **4 B6**
Kong Oscar Fjord
  Greenland 72°20N 24°0W **4 B6**
Konglu *Burma* 27°13N 97°57E **41 F20**
Kongola *Namibia* 17°45S 23°20E **56 B3**
Kongolo *Kasai-Or.,*
  Dem. Rep. of the Congo 5°26S 24°49E **54 D1**
Kongolo *Katanga,*
  Dem. Rep. of the Congo 5°22S 27°0E **54 D2**
Kongsberg *Norway* 59°39N 9°39E **9 G13**
Kongsvinger *Norway* 60°12N 12°2E **9 F15**
Kongur Shan *China* 38°34N 75°18E **32 C2**
Kongwa *Tanzania* 6°11S 36°26E **54 D4**
Koni
  Dem. Rep. of the Congo 10°40S 27°11E **55 E2**
Koni, Mts.
  Dem. Rep. of the Congo 10°36S 27°10E **55 E2**
Konin *Poland* 52°12N 18°15E **17 B10**
Konjic *Bos.-H.* 43°42N 17°58E **23 C7**
Konkiep *Namibia* 26°49S 17°15E **56 D2**
Konosha *Russia* 61°0N 40°5E **18 B7**
Kōnosu *Japan* 36°3N 139°31E **31 F9**
Konotop *Ukraine* 51°12N 33°7E **19 D5**
Konqi He → *China* 41°0N 86°0E **32 B3**
Końskie *Poland* 51°15N 20°23E **17 C11**
Konstanz *Germany* 47°40N 9°10E **16 E5**
Kont *Iran* 26°55N 61°50E **45 E9**
Kontagora *Nigeria* 10°23N 5°27E **50 F7**
Kontiolahti *Finland* 62°46N 29°50E **8 E23**
Kontokali *Greece* 39°38N 19°51E **25 A3**
Konya *Turkey* 37°52N 32°35E **44 B2**
Konza *Kenya* 1°45S 37°7E **54 C4**
Koocanusa, L. *Canada* 49°20N 115°15W **76 B6**
Kookynie *Australia* 29°17S 121°22E **61 E3**
Koolyanobbing
  Australia 30°48S 119°36E **61 F2**
Koonibba *Australia* 31°54S 133°25E **63 E1**
Kooraawatha *Australia* 34°2S 148°33E **63 E4**
Koorda *Australia* 30°48S 117°35E **61 F2**
Kooskia *U.S.A.* 46°9N 115°59W **76 C6**
Kootenay → *U.S.A.* 49°19N 117°39W **70 D5**
Kootenay △ *Canada* 51°0N 116°0W **70 C5**
Kootenay L. *Canada* 49°45N 116°50W **76 B5**
Kootjieskolk *S. Africa* 31°15S 20°21E **56 E3**
Kopaonik *Serbia* 43°10N 20°50E **23 C9**
Kópavogur *Iceland* 64°6N 21°55W **8 D3**
Koper *Slovenia* 45°31N 13°44E **16 F7**
Kopervik *Norway* 59°17N 5°17E **9 G11**

Kopet Dagh *Asia* 38°0N 58°0E **45 B8**
Kopi *Australia* 33°24S 135°40E **63 E2**
Köping *Sweden* 59°31N 16°3E **9 G17**
Koppeh Dāgh = Kopet Dagh
  Asia 38°0N 58°0E **45 B8**
Koppies *S. Africa* 27°20S 27°30E **57 D4**
Koprivnica *Croatia* 46°12N 16°45E **22 A7**
Köprülü *Turkey* 37°20N 31°5E **44 B1**
Kopychyntsi *Ukraine* 49°7N 25°58E **17 D13**
Kora △ *Kenya* 0°14S 38°44E **54 C4**
Korab *Macedonia* 41°44N 20°40E **23 D9**
Koral *India* 21°50N 73°12E **42 J5**
Korba *India* 22°20N 82°45E **43 H10**
Korbu, G. *Malaysia* 4°41N 101°18E **39 K3**
Korçë *Albania* 40°37N 20°50E **23 D9**
Korčula *Croatia* 42°56N 16°57E **22 C7**
Kord Kūy *Iran* 36°48N 54°7E **45 B7**
Kord Sheykh *Iran* 28°31N 52°53E **45 D7**
Kordestān □ *Iran* 36°0N 47°0E **44 C5**
Kordofân *Sudan* 13°0N 29°0E **51 F11**
Korea, North ■ *Asia* 40°0N 127°0E **35 E14**
Korea, South ■ *Asia* 36°0N 128°0E **35 G15**
Korea Bay *Korea* 39°0N 124°0E **35 F13**
Korea Strait *Asia* 34°0N 129°30E **35 H15**
Korets *Ukraine* 50°40N 27°5E **17 C14**
Korhogo *Ivory C.* 9°29N 5°28W **50 G4**
Korinthiakos Kolpos
  Greece 38°16N 22°30E **23 E10**
Korinthos *Greece* 37°56N 22°55E **23 F10**
Korissa, L. *Greece* 39°27N 19°53E **25 B3**
Kōriyama *Japan* 37°24N 140°23E **30 F10**
Korla *China* 41°45N 86°4E **32 B3**
Kormakiti, C. *Cyprus* 35°23N 32°56E **25 D11**
Korneshty = Corneşti
  Moldova 47°21N 28°1E **17 E15**
Koro *Fiji* 17°19S 179°23E **59 a**
Koro *Ivory C.* 8°32N 7°30W **50 G4**
Koro Sea *Fiji* 17°30S 179°45W **59 a**
Korogwe *Tanzania* 5°5S 38°25E **54 D4**
Korolevu *Fiji* 18°12S 177°46E **59 a**
Koronadal *Phil.* 6°12N 125°1E **37 C6**
Koror *Palau* 7°20N 134°28E **64 G5**
Körös → *Hungary* 46°43N 20°12E **17 E11**
Korosten *Ukraine* 50°54N 28°36E **17 C15**
Korostyshev *Ukraine* 50°19N 29°4E **17 C15**
Korovou *Fiji* 17°47S 178°32E **59 a**
Koroyanitu △ *Fiji* 17°40S 177°35E **59 a**
Korsakov *Russia* 46°36N 142°42E **29 E15**
Korshunovo *Russia* 58°37N 110°10E **29 D12**
Korsør *Denmark* 55°20N 11°9E **9 J14**
Kortrijk *Belgium* 50°50N 3°17E **15 D3**
Korwai *India* 24°7N 78°5E **42 G8**
Koryakskoye Nagorye
  Russia 61°0N 171°0E **29 C18**
Kos *Greece* 36°50N 27°15E **23 F12**
Kosan *N. Korea* 38°52N 127°25E **35 E14**
Koschagyl *Kazakhstan* 46°40N 54°0E **19 E9**
Kościan *Poland* 52°5N 16°40E **17 B9**
Kosciusko *U.S.A.* 33°4N 89°35W **85 E10**
Kosciuszko, Mt.
  Australia 36°27S 148°16E **63 F4**
Kosha *Sudan* 20°50N 30°30E **51 D12**
K'oshih = Kashi *China* 39°30N 76°2E **32 C2**
Koshiki-Rettō *Japan* 31°45N 129°49E **31 J4**
Kosi *India* 27°48N 77°29E **42 F7**
Kosi → *India* 28°41N 78°57E **43 E8**
Košice *Slovak Rep.* 48°42N 21°15E **17 D11**
Koskinou *Greece* 36°23N 28°13E **25 C10**
Koslan *Russia* 63°34N 49°14E **18 B8**
Kosŏng *N. Korea* 38°40N 128°22E **35 E15**
Kosovo □ *Serbia* 42°30N 21°0E **23 C9**
Kosovska Mitrovica
  Serbia 42°54N 20°52E **23 C9**
Kossou, L. de *Ivory C.* 6°59N 5°31W **50 G4**
Koster *S. Africa* 25°52S 26°54E **56 D4**
Kôsti *Sudan* 13°8N 32°43E **51 F12**
Kostopil *Ukraine* 50°51N 26°22E **17 C14**
Kostroma *Russia* 57°50N 40°58E **18 C7**
Kostrzyn *Poland* 52°35N 14°39E **16 B8**
Koszalin *Poland* 54°11N 16°8E **16 A9**
Kot Addu *Pakistan* 30°30N 71°0E **42 D4**
Kot Kapura *India* 30°35N 74°50E **42 D6**
Kot Moman *Pakistan* 32°13N 73°0E **42 C5**
Kot Sultan *Pakistan* 30°46N 70°56E **42 D4**
Kota *India* 25°14N 75°49E **42 G6**
Kota Barrage *India* 25°6N 75°51E **42 G6**
Kota Belud *Malaysia* 6°21N 116°26E **36 C5**
Kota Bharu *Malaysia* 6°7N 102°14E **39 J4**
Kota Kinabalu *Malaysia* 6°0N 116°4E **36 C5**
Kota Kubu Bharu
  Malaysia 3°34N 101°39E **39 L3**
Kota Tinggi *Malaysia* 1°44N 103°53E **39 M4**
Kotaagung *Indonesia* 5°38S 104°29E **36 F2**
Kotabaru *Indonesia* 3°20S 116°20E **36 E5**
Kotabumi *Indonesia* 4°49S 104°54E **36 E2**
Kotamobagu *Indonesia* 0°57N 124°31E **37 D6**
Kotcho L. *Canada* 59°7N 121°12W **70 B4**
Kotdwara *India* 29°45N 78°32E **43 E8**
Kotelnich *Russia* 58°22N 48°24E **18 C8**
Kotelnikovo *Russia* 47°38N 43°8E **19 E7**
Kotelnyy, Ostrov
  Russia 75°10N 139°0E **29 B14**
Kothari → *India* 25°20N 75°4E **42 G6**
Kothi *Chhattisgarh, India* 23°21N 82°3E **43 H10**
Kothi *Mad. P., India* 24°45N 80°40E **43 G9**
Kotiro *India* 26°17N 67°13E **42 F2**
Kotka *Finland* 60°28N 26°58E **8 F22**
Kotlas *Russia* 61°17N 46°43E **18 B8**
Kotli *Pakistan* 33°30N 73°55E **42 C5**
Kotma *India* 23°12N 81°58E **43 H9**
Kotmul *Pakistan* 35°32N 75°10E **43 B6**
Kotor *Montenegro* 42°25N 18°47E **23 C8**
Kotovsk *Ukraine* 47°45N 29°35E **17 E15**
Kotputli *India* 27°43N 76°12E **42 F7**
Kotri *Pakistan* 25°22N 68°22E **42 G3**

Kotto → C.A.R. 4°14N 22°2E 52 D4
Kotturu India 14°45N 76°10E 40 M10
Kotu Group Tonga 20°0S 174°45W 59 c
Kotuy → Russia 71°54N 102°6E 29 B11
Kotzebue U.S.A. 66°53N 162°39W 74 a
Kotzebue Sound U.S.A. 66°20N 163°0W 66 C3
Kouchibouguac △ Canada 46°50N 65°0W 73 C6
Koudougou Burkina Faso 12°10N 2°20W 50 F5
Koufonisi Greece 34°56N 26°8E 25 E8
Kougaberge S. Africa 33°48S 23°50E 56 E3
Kouilou → Congo 4°10S 12°5E 52 E2
Koula Moutou Gabon 1°15S 12°25E 52 E2
Koulen = Kulen Cambodia 13°50N 104°40E 38 F5
Kouloura Greece 39°42N 19°54E 25 A3
Koumala Australia 21°38S 149°15E 62 C4
Koumra Chad 8°50N 17°35E 51 G9
Kountze U.S.A. 30°22N 94°19W 84 F7
Kouris → Cyprus 34°38N 32°54E 25 E11
Kourou Fr. Guiana 5°9N 52°39W 93 B8
Kouroussa Guinea 10°45N 9°45W 50 F4
Kousseri Cameroon 12°0N 14°55E 51 F8
Koutiala Mali 12°25N 5°23W 50 F4
Kouvola Finland 60°52N 26°43E 8 F22
Kovdor Russia 67°34N 30°24E 8 C24
Kovel Ukraine 51°11N 24°38E 17 C13
Kovrov Russia 56°25N 41°25E 18 C7
Kowanyama Australia 15°29S 141°44E 62 B3
Kowloon China 22°19N 114°11E 33 G11
Kowŏn N. Korea 39°26N 127°14E 35 E14
Koyampattur = Coimbatore India 11°2N 76°59E 40 P10
Köyceğiz Turkey 36°57N 28°40E 23 F13
Koyukuk → U.S.A. 64°55N 157°32W 66 C4
Koza = Okinawa Japan 26°19N 127°46E 31 L3
Kozan Turkey 37°26N 35°50E 44 B2
Kozani Greece 40°19N 21°47E 23 D9
Kozhikode = Calicut India 11°15N 75°43E 40 P9
Kozhva Russia 65°10N 57°0E 18 A10
Kozyatyn Ukraine 49°45N 28°50E 17 D15
Kpalimé Togo 6°57N 0°44E 50 G6
Kra, Isthmus of = Kra, Kho Khot Thailand 10°15N 99°30E 39 G2
Kra, Kho Khot Thailand 10°15N 99°30E 39 G2
Kra Buri Thailand 10°22N 98°46E 39 G2
Kraai → S. Africa 30°40S 26°45E 56 E4
Krabi Thailand 8°4N 98°55E 39 H2
Kracheh Cambodia 12°32N 106°10E 38 F6
Kragan Indonesia 6°43S 111°38E 37 G14
Kragerø Norway 58°52N 9°25E 9 G13
Kragujevac Serbia 44°2N 20°56E 23 B9
Krakatau = Rakata, Pulau Indonesia 6°10S 105°20E 36 F3
Krakatoa = Rakata, Pulau Indonesia 6°10S 105°20E 36 F3
Krakor Cambodia 12°32N 104°12E 38 F5
Kraków Poland 50°4N 19°57E 17 C10
Kralanh Cambodia 13°35N 103°25E 38 F4
Kraljevo Serbia 43°44N 20°41E 23 C9
Kramatorsk Ukraine 48°50N 37°30E 19 E6
Kramfors Sweden 62°55N 17°48E 8 E17
Kranj Slovenia 46°16N 14°22E 16 E8
Krankskop S. Africa 28°0S 30°47E 57 D5
Krasavino Russia 60°58N 46°29E 18 B8
Kraskino Russia 42°44N 130°48E 30 C5
Kraśnik Poland 50°55N 22°15E 17 C12
Krasnoarmeysk Russia 51°0N 45°42E 28 D5
Krasnodar Russia 45°5N 39°0E 19 E6
Krasnokamsk Russia 58°4N 55°48E 18 C10
Krasnoperekopsk Ukraine 46°0N 33°54E 19 E5
Krasnorechenskiy Russia 44°41N 135°14E 30 B7
Krasnoselkup Russia 65°20N 82°10E 28 C9
Krasnoturinsk Russia 59°46N 60°12E 18 C11
Krasnoufimsk Russia 56°36N 57°38E 18 C10
Krasnouralsk Russia 58°21N 60°3E 18 C11
Krasnovishersk Russia 60°23N 57°3E 18 B10
Krasnoyarsk Russia 56°8N 93°0E 29 D10
Krasnyy Kut Russia 50°50N 47°0E 19 D8
Krasnyy Luch Ukraine 48°13N 39°0E 19 E6
Krasnyy Yar Russia 46°43N 48°23E 19 E8
Kratie = Kracheh Cambodia 12°32N 106°10E 38 F6
Krau Indonesia 3°19S 140°5E 37 E10
Kravanh, Chuor Phnum Cambodia 12°0N 103°32E 39 G4
Krefeld Germany 51°20N 6°33E 16 C4
Kremen Croatia 44°28N 15°53E 16 F8
Kremenchuk Ukraine 49°5N 33°25E 19 E5
Kremenchuksk Vdskh. Ukraine 49°20N 32°30E 19 E5
Kremenets Ukraine 50°8N 25°43E 17 C13
Kremmling U.S.A. 40°4N 106°24W 76 F10
Krems Austria 48°25N 15°36E 16 D8
Kretinga Lithuania 55°53N 21°15E 9 J19
Kribi Cameroon 2°57N 9°56E 52 D1
Krichev = Krychaw Belarus 53°40N 31°41E 17 B16
Krios, Akra Greece 35°13N 23°34E 25 D5
Krishna → India 15°57N 80°59E 41 M12
Krishnanagar India 23°24N 88°33E 43 H13
Kristiansand Norway 58°8N 8°1E 9 G13
Kristianstad Sweden 56°2N 14°9E 9 H16
Kristiansund Norway 63°7N 7°45E 8 E12
Kristiinankaupunki Finland 62°16N 21°21E 8 E19
Kristinehamn Sweden 59°18N 14°7E 9 G16
Kristinestad = Kristiinankaupunki Finland 62°16N 21°21E 8 E19
Kriti Greece 35°15N 25°0E 25 D7
Kritsa Greece 35°10N 25°41E 25 D7
Krivoy Rog = Kryvyy Rih Ukraine 47°51N 33°20E 19 E5
Krk Croatia 45°8N 14°40E 16 F8
Krokodil → Mozam. 25°14S 32°18E 57 D5
Krong Kaoh Kong Cambodia 11°37N 102°59E 39 G4
Kronprins Olav Kyst Antarctica 69°0S 42°0E 5 C5
Kronprinsesse Märtha Kyst Antarctica 73°30S 10°0W 5 D2
Kronshtadt Russia 59°57N 29°51E 18 B4
Kroonstad S. Africa 27°43S 27°19E 56 D4
Kropotkin Russia 45°28N 40°28E 19 E7
Krosno Poland 49°42N 21°46E 17 D11
Krotoszyn Poland 51°42N 17°23E 17 C9
Krousonas Greece 35°13N 24°59E 25 D6
Kruger △ S. Africa 24°50S 26°10E 57 C5
Krugersdorp S. Africa 26°5S 27°46E 57 D4
Kruisfontein S. Africa 33°59S 24°43E 56 E3
Krung Thep = Bangkok Thailand 13°45N 100°35E 38 F3
Krupki Belarus 54°19N 29°8E 17 A15
Kruševac Serbia 43°35N 21°28E 23 C9
Krychaw Belarus 53°40N 31°41E 17 B16
Krymskiy Poluostrov = Krymskyy Pivostriv Ukraine 45°0N 34°0E 19 F5
Krymskyy Pivostriv Ukraine 45°0N 34°0E 19 F5
Kryvyy Rih Ukraine 47°51N 33°20E 19 E5
Ksar el Kebir Morocco 35°0N 6°0W 50 B4
Ksar es Souk = Er Rachidia Morocco 31°58N 4°20W 50 B5
Kuah Malaysia 6°19N 99°51E 39 J2
Kuala Belait Malaysia 4°35N 114°11E 36 D4
Kuala Berang Malaysia 5°5N 103°1E 39 K4
Kuala Dungun = Dungun Malaysia 4°45N 103°25E 39 K4
Kuala Kangsar Malaysia 4°46N 100°56E 39 K3
Kuala Kelawang Malaysia 2°56N 102°5E 39 L4
Kuala Kerai Malaysia 5°30N 102°12E 39 K4
Kuala Kerian Malaysia 5°10N 100°25E 39 c
Kuala Lipis Malaysia 4°10N 102°3E 39 K4
Kuala Lumpur Malaysia 3°9N 101°41E 39 L3
Kuala Nerang Malaysia 6°16N 100°37E 39 J3
Kuala Pilah Malaysia 2°45N 102°15E 39 L4
Kuala Rompin Malaysia 2°49N 103°29E 39 L4
Kuala Selangor Malaysia 3°20N 101°15E 39 L3
Kuala Sepetang Malaysia 4°49N 100°28E 39 K3
Kuala Terengganu Malaysia 5°20N 103°8E 39 K4
Kualajelai Indonesia 2°58S 110°46E 36 E4
Kualakapuas Indonesia 2°55S 114°20E 36 E4
Kualakurun Indonesia 1°10S 113°50E 36 E4
Kualapembuang Indonesia 3°14S 112°38E 36 E4
Kualasimpang Indonesia 4°17N 98°3E 36 D1
Kuancheng China 40°37N 118°30E 35 D10
Kuandang Indonesia 0°56N 123°1E 37 D6
Kuandian China 40°45N 124°45E 35 D13
Kuangchou = Guangzhou China 23°6N 113°13E 33 D6
Kuantan Malaysia 3°49N 103°20E 39 L4
Kuba = Quba Azerbaijan 41°21N 48°32E 19 F8
Kuban → Russia 45°20N 37°30E 19 E6
Kubokawa Japan 33°12N 133°8E 31 H6
Kubu Indonesia 8°16S 115°35E 37 J18
Kubutambahan Indonesia 8°5S 115°10E 37 J18
Kucar, Tanjung Indonesia 8°39S 114°34E 37 K18
Kucha Gompa India 34°25N 76°56E 43 B7
Kuchaman India 27°13N 74°47E 42 F6
Kuchinda India 21°44N 84°21E 43 J11
Kuching Malaysia 1°33N 110°25E 36 D4
Kuchino-eruba-Jima Japan 30°28N 130°12E 31 J5
Kuchino-Shima Japan 29°57N 129°55E 31 K4
Kuchinotsu Japan 32°36N 130°11E 31 H5
Kucing = Kuching Malaysia 1°33N 110°25E 36 D4
Kud → Pakistan 26°5N 66°20E 42 F2
Kuda India 23°10N 71°15E 42 H4
Kudat Malaysia 6°55N 116°55E 36 C5
Kudus Indonesia 6°48S 110°51E 37 G14
Kudymkar Russia 59°1N 54°39E 18 C9
Kueiyang = Guiyang China 26°32N 106°40E 32 D5
Kufra Oasis = Al Kufrah Libya 24°17N 23°15E 51 D10
Kufstein Austria 47°35N 12°11E 16 E7
Kugaaruk = Pelly Bay Canada 68°38N 89°50W 69 C11
Kugluktuk Canada 67°50N 115°5W 68 C8
Kugong I. Canada 56°18N 79°50W 72 A4
Kūh-e-Jebāl Bārez Iran 29°0N 58°0E 45 D8
Kūhak Iran 27°12N 63°10E 45 E9
Kuhan Pakistan 28°19N 67°14E 42 E2
Kūhbonān Iran 31°23N 56°19E 45 D8
Kūhestak Iran 26°47N 57°2E 45 E8
Kuhin Iran 36°22N 49°40E 45 B6
Kūhīrī Iran 26°55N 61°2E 45 E9
Kuhmo Finland 64°7N 29°31E 8 D23
Kūhpāyeh Eşfahan, Iran 32°44N 52°20E 45 C7
Kūhpāyeh Kermān, Iran 30°35N 57°15E 45 D8
Kūhrān, Kūh-e Iran 26°46N 58°12E 45 E8
Kui Buri Thailand 12°3N 99°52E 39 F2
Kuichong China 22°38N 114°25E 33 F11
Kuiseb → Namibia 22°59S 14°31E 56 C1
Kuito Angola 12°22S 16°55E 53 G3
Kuiu I. U.S.A. 57°45N 134°10W 70 B2
Kujang N. Korea 39°57N 126°1E 35 E14
Kuji Japan 40°11N 141°46E 30 D10
Kujū-San Japan 33°5N 131°15E 31 H5
Kukës Albania 42°5N 20°27E 23 C9
Kukup Malaysia 1°20N 103°27E 39 d
Kukup, Pulau Malaysia 1°18N 103°25E 39 d
Kula Turkey 38°32N 28°40E 23 E13
Kulachi Pakistan 31°56N 70°27E 42 D4
Kulai Malaysia 1°44N 103°35E 39 M4
Kulasekarappattinam India 8°20N 78°5E 40 Q11
Kuldīga Latvia 56°58N 21°59E 9 H19
Kulen Cambodia 13°50N 104°40E 38 F5
Kulgam India 33°36N 75°2E 43 C6
Kulgera Australia 25°50S 133°18E 62 D1
Kulim Malaysia 5°22N 100°34E 39 K3
Kulin Australia 32°40S 118°2E 61 F2
Kulkayu = Hartley Bay Canada 53°25N 129°15W 70 C3
Kŭlob Tajikistan 37°55N 69°50E 28 F7
Kulsary Kazakhstan 46°59N 54°1E 19 E9
Kulti India 23°43N 86°50E 43 H12
Kulu India 31°58N 77°6E 42 D7
Kulunda Russia 52°35N 78°57E 28 D8
Kulungar Afghan. 34°0N 69°2E 42 C3
Kūlvand Iran 31°21N 54°35E 45 D7
Kulwin Australia 35°2S 142°42E 63 F3
Kulyab = Kŭlob Tajikistan 37°55N 69°50E 28 F7
Kuma → Russia 44°55N 47°0E 19 F8
Kumaganum Nigeria 13°8N 10°38E 51 F8
Kumagaya Japan 36°9N 139°22E 31 F9
Kumai Indonesia 2°44S 111°43E 36 E4
Kumamba, Kepulauan Indonesia 1°36S 138°45E 37 E9
Kumamoto Japan 32°45N 130°45E 31 H5
Kumamoto □ Japan 32°55N 130°55E 31 H5
Kumanovo Macedonia 42°9N 21°42E 23 C9
Kumara N.Z. 42°37S 171°12E 59 E3
Kumarina Roadhouse Australia 24°41S 119°32E 61 D2
Kumasi Ghana 6°41N 1°38W 50 G5
Kumba Cameroon 4°36N 9°24E 52 D1
Kumbakonam India 10°58N 79°25E 40 P11
Kumbarilla Australia 27°15S 150°55E 63 D5
Kumbhraj India 24°22N 77°3E 42 G7
Kumbia Australia 26°41S 151°39E 63 D5
Kŭmch'ŏn N. Korea 38°10N 126°29E 35 E14
Kumdok India 33°32N 78°10E 43 C8
Kume-Shima Japan 26°20N 126°47E 31 L3
Kumertau Russia 52°45N 55°57E 18 D10
Kumharsain India 31°19N 77°27E 42 D7
Kumi Uganda 1°30N 33°58E 54 B3
Kumo Nigeria 10°1N 11°12E 51 F8
Kumo älv = Kokemäenjoki → Finland 61°32N 21°44E 8 F19
Kumon Bum Burma 26°30N 97°15E 41 F20
Kumtag Shamo China 39°40N 92°0E 32 C4
Kunashir, Ostrov Russia 44°0N 146°0E 29 E15
Kunda Estonia 59°30N 26°34E 9 G22
Kunda India 25°43N 81°31E 43 G9
Kundar → Pakistan 31°56N 69°19E 42 D3
Kundelungu △ Dem. Rep. of the Congo 10°30S 27°40E 55 E2
Kundelungu Ouest △ Dem. Rep. of the Congo 9°55S 27°17E 55 D2
Kundian Pakistan 32°27N 71°28E 42 C4
Kundla India 21°21N 71°25E 42 J4
Kung, Ao Thailand 8°5N 98°24E 39 a
Kunga → Bangla. 21°46N 89°30E 43 J13
Kunghit I. Canada 52°6N 131°3W 70 C2
Kungrad = Qŭnghirot Uzbekistan 43°2N 58°50E 28 E6
Kungsbacka Sweden 57°30N 12°5E 9 H15
Kungur Russia 57°25N 56°57E 18 C10
Kungurri Australia 21°4S 148°45E 62 K6
Kunhar → Pakistan 34°20N 73°30E 43 B5
Kuningan Indonesia 6°59S 108°29E 37 G13
Kunlong Burma 23°20N 98°50E 41 H21
Kunlun Shan Asia 36°0N 86°30E 32 C3
Kunming China 25°1N 102°41E 32 D5
Kununurra Australia 15°40S 128°50E 60 C4
Kunwari → India 26°26N 79°11E 43 F8
Kunya-Urgench = Köneürgench Turkmenistan 42°19N 59°10E 28 E6
Kuopio Finland 62°53N 27°35E 8 E22
Kupa → Croatia 45°28N 16°24E 16 F9
Kupang Indonesia 10°19S 123°39E 37 F6
Kupreanof I. U.S.A. 56°50N 133°30W 70 B2
Kupyansk-Uzlovoi Ukraine 49°40N 37°43E 19 E6
Kuqa China 41°35N 82°30E 32 B3
Kür → Azerbaijan 39°29N 49°15E 19 G8
Kür Dili Azerbaijan 39°3N 49°13E 45 B6
Kura = Kür → Azerbaijan 39°29N 49°15E 19 G8
Kuranda Australia 16°48S 145°35E 62 B4
Kuranga India 22°4N 69°10E 42 H3
Kurashiki Japan 34°40N 133°50E 31 G6
Kurayn Si. Arabia 27°39N 49°50E 45 E6
Kurayoshi Japan 35°26N 133°50E 31 G6
Kŭrdzhali Bulgaria 41°38N 25°21E 23 D11
Kure Japan 34°14N 132°32E 31 G6
Kuressaare Estonia 58°15N 22°30E 9 G20
Kurgan Russia 55°26N 65°18E 28 D7
Kuri India 26°37N 70°43E 42 F4
Kuria Maria Is. = Hallāniyat, Jazā'ir al Oman 17°30N 55°58E 47 D6
Kuridala Australia 21°16S 140°29E 62 C3
Kurigram Bangla. 25°49N 89°39E 41 G16
Kurikka Finland 62°36N 22°24E 8 E20
Kuril Basin Pac. Oc. 47°0N 150°0E 4 E15
Kuril Is. = Kurilskiye Ostrova Russia 45°0N 150°0E 29 E15
Kuril-Kamchatka Trench Pac. Oc. 44°0N 153°0E 64 C7
Kurilsk Russia 45°14N 147°53E 29 E15
Kurilskiye Ostrova Russia 45°0N 150°0E 29 E15
Kurino Japan 31°57N 130°43E 31 J5
Kurinskaya Kosa = Kür Dili Azerbaijan 39°3N 49°13E 45 B6
Kurnool India 15°45N 78°0E 40 M11
Kuro-Shima Kagoshima, Japan 30°50N 129°57E 31 J4
Kuro-Shima Okinawa, Japan 24°14N 124°1E 31 M2
Kurow N.Z. 44°44S 170°29E 59 F3
Kurram → Pakistan 32°36N 71°20E 42 C4
Kurri Kurri Australia 32°50S 151°28E 63 E5
Kurrimine Australia 17°47S 146°6E 62 B4
Kurshskiy Zaliv Russia 55°9N 21°6E 9 J19
Kursk Russia 51°42N 36°11E 18 D6
Kuruçay Turkey 39°39N 38°29E 44 B3
Kuruktag China 41°0N 89°0E 32 B3
Kuruman S. Africa 27°28S 23°28E 56 D3
Kuruman → S. Africa 26°56S 20°39E 56 D3
Kurume Japan 33°15N 130°30E 31 H5
Kurunegala Sri Lanka 7°30N 80°23E 40 R12
Kurya Russia 61°42N 57°9E 18 B10
Kus Gölü Turkey 40°10N 27°55E 23 D12
Kuşadası Turkey 37°52N 27°15E 23 F12
Kusamba Indonesia 8°34S 115°27E 37 K18
Kusatsu Japan 36°37N 138°36E 31 F9
Kusawa L. Canada 60°20N 136°13W 70 A1
Kushalgarh India 23°10N 74°27E 42 H6
Kushikino Japan 31°44N 130°16E 31 J5
Kushima Japan 31°29N 131°14E 31 J5
Kushimoto Japan 33°28N 135°47E 31 H7
Kushiro Japan 43°0N 144°25E 30 C12
Kushiro-Gawa → Japan 42°59N 144°23E 30 C12
Kushiro Shitsugen △ Japan 43°9N 144°26E 30 C12
Kūshk Iran 28°46N 56°51E 45 D8
Kushka = Serhetabat Turkmenistan 35°20N 62°18E 45 C9
Kūshkī Iran 33°31N 47°13E 44 C5
Kushol India 33°40N 76°36E 43 C7
Kushtia Bangla. 23°55N 89°5E 41 H16
Kushva Russia 58°18N 59°45E 18 C10
Kuskokwim → U.S.A. 60°5N 162°25W 66 C3
Kuskokwim B. U.S.A. 59°45N 162°25W 74 a
Kusmi India 23°17N 83°55E 43 H10
Kusŏng N. Korea 39°59N 125°15E 35 E13
Kussharo-Ko Japan 43°38N 144°21E 30 C12
Kustanay = Qostanay Kazakhstan 53°10N 63°35E 28 D7
Kut, Ko Thailand 11°40N 102°35E 39 G4
Kuta Indonesia 8°43S 115°11E 37 K18
Kütahya Turkey 39°30N 30°2E 19 G5
Kutaisi Georgia 42°19N 42°40E 19 F7
Kutaraja = Banda Aceh Indonesia 5°35N 95°20E 36 C1
Kutch, Gulf of = Kachchh, Gulf of India 22°50N 69°15E 42 H3
Kutch, Rann of = Kachchh, Rann of India 24°0N 70°0E 42 H4
Kutiyana India 21°36N 70°2E 42 J4
Kutno Poland 52°15N 19°23E 17 B10
Kutse Botswana 21°7S 22°16E 56 C3
Kuttabul Australia 21°1S 148°54E 62 K6
Kutu Dem. Rep. of the Congo 2°40S 18°11E 52 E3
Kutum Sudan 14°10N 24°40E 51 F10
Kuujjuaq Canada 58°6N 68°15W 69 D13
Kuujjuarapik Canada 55°20N 77°35W 72 A4
Kuusamo Finland 65°57N 29°8E 8 D23
Kuusankoski Finland 60°55N 26°38E 8 F22
Kuwait = Al Kuwayt Kuwait 29°30N 48°0E 44 D5
Kuwait ■ Asia 29°30N 47°30E 44 D5
Kuwana Japan 35°5N 136°43E 31 G8
Kuwana → India 26°25N 83°15E 43 F10
Kuybyshev = Samara Russia 53°8N 50°6E 18 D9
Kuybyshev Russia 55°27N 78°19E 28 D8
Kuybyshevskoye Vdkhr. Russia 55°2N 49°30E 18 C8
Kuye He → China 38°23N 110°46E 34 E6
Kūyeh Iran 38°45N 47°57E 44 B5
Kuyto, Ozero Russia 65°6N 31°20E 8 D24
Kuyumba Russia 60°58N 96°59E 29 C10
Kuzey Anadolu Dağları Turkey 41°0N 36°45E 19 F6
Kuznetsk Russia 53°12N 46°40E 18 D8
Kuzomen Russia 66°22N 36°50E 18 A6
Kvænangen Norway 70°5N 21°15E 8 A19
Kvaløya Norway 69°40N 18°30E 8 B18
Kvarner Croatia 44°50N 14°10E 16 F8
Kvarnerič Croatia 44°43N 14°37E 16 F8
Kwabhaca S. Africa 30°51S 29°0E 57 E4
Kwajalein Marshall Is. 9°5N 167°20E 64 G8
Kwakhanai Botswana 21°39S 21°16E 56 C3
Kwakoegron Suriname 5°12N 55°25W 93 B7
Kwale Kenya 4°15S 39°31E 54 C4
KwaMashu S. Africa 29°45S 30°58E 57 D5
Kwando → Africa 18°27S 23°32E 56 B3
Kwangchow = Guangzhou China 23°6N 113°13E 33 D6
Kwango → Dem. Rep. of the Congo 3°14S 17°22E 52 E3
Kwangsi-Chuang = Guangxi Zhuangzu Zizhiqu □ China 24°0N 109°0E 33 D5
Kwangtung = Guangdong □ China 23°0N 113°0E 33 D6
Kwataboahegan → Canada 51°9N 80°50W 72 B3
Kwatisore Indonesia 3°18S 134°50E 37 E8
KwaZulu Natal □ S. Africa 29°0S 30°0E 57 D5
Kweichow = Guizhou □ China 27°0N 107°0E 32 D5
Kwekwe Zimbabwe 18°58S 29°48E 55 F2
Kwidzyn Poland 53°44N 18°55E 17 B10
Kwilu → Dem. Rep. of the Congo 3°22S 17°22E 52 E3
Kwinana Australia 32°15S 115°47E 61 F2
Kwoka Indonesia 0°31S 132°27E 37 E8
Kwun Tong China 22°19N 114°13E 33 G11
Kyabra Cr. → Australia 25°36S 142°55E 63 D3
Kyabram Australia 36°19S 145°4E 63 F4
Kyaikto Burma 17°20N 97°3E 38 D1
Kyakhta Russia 50°30N 106°25E 29 D11
Kyambura ⌂ Uganda 0°7S 30°9E 54 C3
Kyancutta Australia 33°8S 135°33E 63 E2
Kyaukpadaung Burma 20°52N 95°8E 41 J19
Kyaukpyu Burma 19°28N 93°30E 41 K18
Kyaukse Burma 21°36N 96°10E 41 J20
Kyburz U.S.A. 38°47N 120°18W 78 G6
Kyelang India 32°35N 77°2E 42 C7
Kyenjojo Uganda 0°40N 30°37E 54 B3
Kyle Canada 50°50N 108°2W 71 C7
Kyle Dam Zimbabwe 20°15S 31°0E 55 G3
Kyle of Lochalsh U.K. 57°17N 5°44W 11 D3
Kymijoki → Finland 60°30N 26°55E 8 F22
Kymmene älv = Kymijoki → Finland 60°30N 26°55E 8 F22
Kyneton Australia 37°10S 144°29E 63 F3
Kynuna Australia 21°37S 141°55E 62 C3
Kyō-ga-Saki Japan 35°45N 135°15E 31 G7
Kyoga, L. Uganda 1°35N 33°0E 54 B3
Kyogle Australia 28°40S 153°0E 63 D5
Kyŏngju = Gyeongju S. Korea 35°51N 129°14E 35 G15
Kyŏngsŏng N. Korea 41°35N 129°36E 35 D15
Kyonpyaw Burma 17°12N 95°10E 41 L19
Kyōto Japan 35°0N 135°45E 31 G7
Kyōto □ Japan 35°15N 135°45E 31 G7
Kyparissovouno Cyprus 35°19N 33°10E 25 D12
Kyperounda Cyprus 34°56N 32°58E 25 E11
Kypros = Cyprus ■ Asia 35°0N 33°0E 25 E12
Kyrenia Cyprus 35°20N 33°20E 25 D12
Kyrgyzstan ■ Asia 42°0N 75°0E 28 E8
Kyro älv = Kyrönjoki → Finland 63°14N 21°45E 8 E19
Kyrönjoki → Finland 63°14N 21°45E 8 E19
Kystatyam Russia 67°20N 123°10E 29 C13
Kythira Greece 36°8N 23°0E 23 F10
Kythréa Cyprus 35°15N 33°29E 25 D12
Kyunhla Burma 23°25N 95°15E 41 H19
Kyuquot Sound Canada 50°2N 127°22W 70 D3
Kyūshū Japan 33°0N 131°0E 31 H5
Kyūshū □ Japan 33°0N 131°0E 31 H5
Kyushu-Palau Ridge Pac. Oc. 20°0N 136°0E 64 E5
Kyūshū-Sanchi Japan 32°35N 131°17E 31 H5
Kyustendil Bulgaria 42°16N 22°41E 23 C10
Kyusyur Russia 70°19N 127°30E 29 B13
Kyyiv Ukraine 50°30N 30°28E 17 C16
Kyyivske Vdskh. Ukraine 51°0N 30°25E 17 C16
Kyzyl Russia 51°50N 94°30E 29 D10
Kyzyl Kum Uzbekistan 42°30N 65°0E 28 E7
Kyzyl-Kyya Kyrgyzstan 40°16N 72°8E 28 E8
Kyzyl-Orda = Qyzylorda Kazakhstan 44°48N 65°28E 28 E7

L

La Alcarria Spain 40°31N 2°45W 21 B4
La Amistad △ Cent. Amer. 9°28N 83°18W 88 E3
La Asunción Venezuela 11°2N 63°53W 92 A6
La Baie Canada 48°19N 70°53W 73 C5
La Banda Argentina 27°45S 64°10W 94 B3
La Barca Mexico 20°17N 102°34W 86 C4
La Barge U.S.A. 42°16N 110°12W 76 E8
La Belle U.S.A. 26°46N 81°26W 85 H14
La Biche → Canada 59°57N 123°50W 70 B4
La Biche, L. Canada 54°50N 112°3W 70 C6
La Brea Trin. & Tob. 10°15N 61°37W 93 K15
La Calera Chile 32°50S 71°10W 94 C1
La Campana △ Chile 32°58S 71°14W 94 C1
La Canal = Sa Canal Spain 38°51N 1°23E 24 C7
La Carlota Argentina 33°30S 63°20W 94 C3
La Ceiba Honduras 15°40N 86°50W 88 C2
La Chaux-de-Fonds Switz. 47°7N 6°50E 20 C7
La Chorrera Panama 8°53N 79°47W 88 E4
La Cocha Argentina 27°50S 65°40W 94 B2
La Concepción Panama 8°31N 82°37W 88 E3
La Concordia Mexico 16°5N 92°38W 87 D6
La Coruña = A Coruña Spain 43°20N 8°25W 21 A1
La Crescent U.S.A. 43°50N 91°18W 80 D8
La Crete Canada 58°11N 116°24W 70 B5
La Crosse Kans., U.S.A. 38°32N 99°18W 80 F4
La Crosse Wis., U.S.A. 43°48N 91°15W 80 D8
La Cruz Costa Rica 11°4N 85°39W 88 D2
La Cruz Mexico 23°55N 106°54W 86 C3
La Désirade Guadeloupe 16°18N 61°3W 88 b
La Digue Seychelles 4°20S 55°51E 53 b
La Esmeralda Paraguay 22°16S 62°33W 94 A3
La Esperanza Cuba 22°46N 83°44W 88 B3
La Esperanza Honduras 14°15N 88°10W 88 D2
La Estrada = A Estrada Spain 42°43N 8°27W 21 A1
La Fayette U.S.A. 34°42N 85°17W 85 D12
La Fé Cuba 22°2N 84°15W 88 B3
La Follette U.S.A. 36°23N 84°7W 85 C12
La Grande U.S.A. 45°20N 118°5W 76 D4
La Grande → Canada 53°50N 79°0W 72 B5
La Grande Deux, Rés. Canada 53°40N 76°55W 72 B4
La Grande Quatre, Rés. Canada 54°0N 73°15W 72 B5
La Grande Trois, Rés. Canada 53°40N 75°10W 72 B4
La Grange Calif., U.S.A. 37°42N 120°27W 78 H6
La Grange Ga., U.S.A. 33°2N 85°2W 85 E12
La Grange Ky., U.S.A. 38°24N 85°22W 81 F11

La Grange *Tex., U.S.A.* 29°54N 96°52W **84** G6
La Guaira *Venezuela* 10°36N 66°56W **92** A5
La Habana *Cuba* 23°8N 82°22W **88** B3
La Independencia *Mexico* 16°15N 92°1W **87** D6
La Isabela *Dom. Rep.* 19°58N 71°2W **89** C5
La Junta *U.S.A.* 37°59N 103°33W **76** H12
La Laguna *Canary Is.* 28°28N 16°18W **24** F3
La Libertad = Puerto Libertad *Mexico* 29°55N 112°43W **86** B2
La Libertad *Guatemala* 16°47N 90°7W **88** C1
La Ligua *Chile* 32°30S 71°16W **94** C1
La Línea de la Concepción *Spain* 36°15N 5°23W **21** D3
La Loche *Canada* 56°29N 109°26W **71** B7
La Louvière *Belgium* 50°27N 4°10E **15** D4
La Lune *Trin. & Tob.* 10°3N 61°22W **93** K15
La Malbaie *Canada* 47°40N 70°10W **73** C5
La Malinche △ *Mexico* 19°15N 98°3W **87** D5
La Mancha *Spain* 39°10N 2°54W **21** C4
La Martre, L. *Canada* 63°15N 117°55W **70** A5
La Mesa *Mexico* 32°30N 116°57W **79** N10
La Mesa *U.S.A.* 32°46N 117°1W **79** N9
La Mesilla *U.S.A.* 32°16N 106°48W **77** K10
La Misión *Mexico* 32°6N 116°53W **86** A1
La Moure *U.S.A.* 46°21N 98°18W **80** B4
La Negra *Chile* 23°46S 70°18W **94** A1
La Oliva *Canary Is.* 28°36N 13°57W **24** F6
La Orotava *Canary Is.* 28°22N 16°31W **24** F3
La Oroya *Peru* 11°32S 75°54W **92** F3
La Palma *Canary Is.* 28°40N 17°50W **24** F2
La Palma *Panama* 8°15N 78°0W **88** E4
La Palma del Condado *Spain* 37°21N 6°38W **21** D2
La Paloma *Chile* 30°35S 71°0W **94** C1
La Pampa □ *Argentina* 36°50S 66°0W **94** D2
La Paragua *Venezuela* 6°50N 63°20W **92** B6
La Paz *Entre Ríos, Argentina* 30°50S 59°45W **94** C4
La Paz *San Luis, Argentina* 33°30S 67°20W **94** C2
La Paz *Bolivia* 16°20S 68°10W **92** G5
La Paz *Honduras* 14°20N 87°47W **88** D2
La Paz *Mexico* 24°10N 110°18W **86** C2
La Paz Centro *Nic.* 12°20N 86°41W **88** D2
La Pedrera *Colombia* 1°18S 69°43W **92** D5
La Pérade *Canada* 46°35N 72°12W **73** C5
La Perla *Mexico* 28°18N 104°32W **86** B4
La Perouse Str. *Asia* 45°40N 142°0E **30** B11
La Pesca *Mexico* 23°46N 97°47W **87** C5
La Piedad *Mexico* 20°21N 102°0W **86** C4
La Pine *U.S.A.* 43°40N 121°30W **76** E3
La Plata *Argentina* 35°0S 57°55W **94** D4
La Pocatière *Canada* 47°22N 70°2W **73** C5
La Porte *U.S.A.* 29°40N 95°1W **84** G7
La Purísima *Mexico* 26°10N 112°4W **86** B2
La Push *U.S.A.* 47°55N 124°38W **78** C2
La Quiaca *Argentina* 22°5S 65°35W **94** A2
La Restinga *Canary Is.* 27°38N 17°59W **24** G2
La Rioja *Argentina* 29°20S 67°0W **94** B2
La Rioja □ *Argentina* 29°30S 67°0W **94** B2
La Rioja □ *Spain* 42°20N 2°20W **21** A4
La Robla *Spain* 42°50N 5°41W **21** A3
La Roche-en-Ardenne *Belgium* 50°11N 5°35E **15** D5
La Roche-sur-Yon *France* 46°40N 1°25W **20** C3
La Rochelle *France* 46°10N 1°9W **20** C3
La Roda *Spain* 39°13N 2°15W **21** C4
La Romaine *Canada* 50°13N 60°40W **73** B7
La Romana *Dom. Rep.* 18°27N 68°57W **89** C6
La Ronge *Canada* 55°5N 105°20W **71** B7
La Rumorosa *Mexico* 32°34N 116°6W **79** N10
La Sabina = Sa Savina *Spain* 38°44N 1°25E **24** C7
La Salle *U.S.A.* 41°20N 89°6W **80** E9
La Santa *Canary Is.* 29°5N 13°40W **24** E6
La Sarre *Canada* 48°45N 79°15W **72** C4
La Scie *Canada* 49°57N 55°36W **73** C8
La Selva Beach *U.S.A.* 36°56N 121°51W **78** J5
La Serena *Chile* 29°55S 71°10W **94** B1
La Seu d'Urgell *Spain* 42°22N 1°23E **21** A6
La Seyne-sur-Mer *France* 43°7N 5°52E **20** E6
La Soufrière *St. Vincent* 13°20N 61°11W **89** D7
La Spézia *Italy* 44°7N 9°50E **20** D8
La Tagua *Colombia* 0°3N 74°40W **92** C4
La Tortuga *Venezuela* 11°0N 65°22W **89** D6
La Trinité *Martinique* 14°43N 60°58W **88** c
La Tuque *Canada* 47°30N 72°50W **72** C5
La Unión *Chile* 40°10S 73°0W **96** E2
La Unión *El Salv.* 13°20N 87°50W **88** D2
La Unión *Mexico* 17°58N 101°49W **86** D4
La Urbana *Venezuela* 7°8N 66°56W **92** B5
La Vache Pt. *Trin. & Tob.* 10°47N 61°28W **93** K15
La Vall d'Uixó *Spain* 39°49N 0°15W **21** C5
La Vega *Dom. Rep.* 19°20N 70°30W **89** C5
La Vela de Coro *Venezuela* 11°27N 69°34W **92** A5
La Venta *Mexico* 18°5N 94°3W **87** D6
La Vergne *U.S.A.* 36°1N 86°35W **85** C11
Laas Caanood = Las Anod *Somali Rep.* 8°26N 47°19E **47** F4
Labasa *Fiji* 16°30S 179°27E **59** a
Labdah = Leptis Magna *Libya* 32°40N 14°12E **51** B8
Labe = Elbe → *Europe* 53°50N 9°0E **16** B5
Labé *Guinea* 11°24N 12°16W **50** F3
Laberge, L. *Canada* 61°11N 135°12W **70** A1
Labinsk *Russia* 44°40N 40°48E **19** F7
Labis *Malaysia* 2°22N 103°2E **39** L4
Laborie *St. Lucia* 13°45N 61°2W **89** f
Laboulaye *Argentina* 34°10S 63°30W **94** C3
Labrador *Canada* 53°20N 61°0W **73** B7
Labrador City *Canada* 52°57N 66°55W **73** B6
Labrador Sea *Atl. Oc.* 57°0N 54°0W **69** D14
Lábrea *Brazil* 7°15S 64°51W **92** E6
Labuan *Malaysia* 5°20N 115°14E **36** C5
Labuan, Pulau *Malaysia* 5°21N 115°13E **36** C5
Labuha *Indonesia* 0°30S 127°30E **37** E7
Labuhan *Indonesia* 6°22S 105°50E **37** G11
Labuhanbajo *Indonesia* 8°28S 119°54E **37** F6
Labuk, Telok *Malaysia* 6°10N 117°50E **36** C5
Labyrinth, L. *Australia* 30°40S 135°11E **63** E2
Labytnangi *Russia* 66°39N 66°21E **28** C7
Lac-Bouchette *Canada* 48°16N 72°11W **73** C5
Lac Édouard *Canada* 47°40N 72°16W **72** C5
Lac La Biche *Canada* 54°45N 111°58W **70** C6
Lac la Martre = Wha Ti *Canada* 63°8N 117°16W **68** C8
Lac La Ronge ⌓ *Canada* 55°9N 104°41W **71** B7
Lac-Mégantic *Canada* 45°35N 70°53W **73** C5
Lac Thien *Vietnam* 12°25N 108°11E **38** F7
Lacanau *France* 44°58N 1°5W **20** D3
Lacantún → *Mexico* 16°36N 90°39W **87** D6
Laccadive Is. = Lakshadweep Is. *India* 10°0N 72°30E **3** D13
Lacepede B. *Australia* 36°40S 139°40E **63** F2
Lacepede Is. *Australia* 16°55S 122°0E **60** C3
Lacerdónia *Mozam.* 18°3S 35°35E **55** F4
Lacey *U.S.A.* 47°7N 122°49W **78** C4
Lachania *Greece* 35°58N 27°54E **25** D9
Lachhmangarh *India* 27°50N 75°4E **42** F6
Lachi *Pakistan* 33°25N 71°20E **42** C4
Lachine *Canada* 45°26N 73°42W **72** C5
Lachlan → *Australia* 34°22S 143°55E **63** E3
Lachute *Canada* 45°39N 74°21W **72** C5
Lackagh Hills *Ireland* 54°16N 8°10W **10** B3
Lackawanna *U.S.A.* 42°50N 78°50W **82** D6
Lackawaxen *U.S.A.* 41°29N 74°59W **83** E10
Lacolle *Canada* 45°5N 73°22W **83** A11
Lacombe *Canada* 52°30N 113°44W **70** C6
Lacona *U.S.A.* 43°39N 76°10W **83** C8
Laconia *U.S.A.* 43°32N 71°28W **83** C13
Ladakh Ra. *India* 34°0N 78°0E **43** C8
Ladismith *S. Africa* 33°28S 21°15E **56** E3
Lādīz *Iran* 28°55N 61°15E **45** D9
Ladnun *India* 27°38N 74°25E **42** F6
Ladoga, L. = Ladozhskoye Ozero *Russia* 61°15N 30°30E **8** F24
Ladozhskoye Ozero *Russia* 61°15N 30°30E **8** F24
Lady Elliott I. *Australia* 24°7S 152°42E **62** C5
Lady Grey *S. Africa* 30°43S 27°13E **56** E4
Ladybrand *S. Africa* 29°9S 27°29E **56** D4
Ladysmith *Canada* 49°0N 123°49W **78** B3
Ladysmith *S. Africa* 28°32S 29°46E **57** D4
Ladysmith *U.S.A.* 45°28N 91°12W **80** C8
Lae *Papua N. G.* 6°40S 147°2E **58** B7
Laem Hin Khom *Thailand* 9°25N 99°56E **39** b
Laem Khat *Thailand* 8°6N 98°26E **39** a
Laem Nga *Thailand* 7°55N 98°27E **39** a
Laem Ngop *Thailand* 12°10N 102°26E **39** F4
Laem Phan Wa *Thailand* 7°47N 98°25E **39** a
Laem Pho *Thailand* 6°55N 101°19E **39** J3
Laem Phrom Thep *Thailand* 7°45N 98°19E **39** a
Laem Riang *Thailand* 8°7N 98°27E **39** a
Laem Sam Rong *Thailand* 9°35N 100°4E **39** b
Laem Son *Thailand* 7°59N 98°16E **39** a
Laem Yamu *Thailand* 7°59N 98°26E **39** a
Laerma *Greece* 36°9N 27°57E **25** C9
Læsø *Denmark* 57°15N 11°5E **9** H14
Lafayette *Ind., U.S.A.* 40°25N 86°54W **80** E10
Lafayette *La., U.S.A.* 30°14N 92°1W **84** F8
LaFayette *Tenn., U.S.A.* 36°31N 86°2W **85** C11
Laferte → *Canada* 61°53N 117°44W **70** A5
Lafia *Nigeria* 8°30N 8°34E **50** G7
Lafleche *Canada* 49°45N 106°40W **71** D7
Lagan → *U.K.* 54°36N 5°55W **10** B6
Lagarfljót → *Iceland* 65°40N 14°18W **8** D6
Lagdo, Rés. de *Cameroon* 8°40N 14°0E **51** G8
Lågen → *Oppland, Norway* 61°8N 10°25E **8** F14
Lågen → *Vestfold, Norway* 59°3N 10°3E **9** G14
Laghouat *Algeria* 33°50N 2°59E **50** B6
Lagoa do Peixe △ *Brazil* 31°12S 50°55W **95** C5
Lagoa Vermelha *Brazil* 28°13S 51°32W **95** B5
Lagonoy G. *Phil.* 13°35N 123°50E **37** B6
Lagos *Nigeria* 6°25N 3°27E **50** G6
Lagos *Portugal* 37°5N 8°41W **21** D1
Lagos de Moreno *Mexico* 21°21N 101°55W **86** C4
Lagrange = Bidyadanga *Australia* 18°45S 121°43E **60** C3
Lagrange B. *Australia* 18°38S 121°42E **60** C3
Laguna *Brazil* 28°30S 48°50W **95** B6
Laguna *U.S.A.* 35°2N 107°25W **77** J10
Laguna, Sa. de la *Mexico* 23°35N 109°55W **86** C3
Laguna Beach *U.S.A.* 33°33N 117°47W **79** M9
Laguna de la Restinga △ *Venezuela* 10°58N 64°0W **89** D6
Laguna del Laja △ *Chile* 37°27S 71°20W **94** D1
Laguna del Tigre △ *Guatemala* 17°32N 90°56W **88** C1
Laguna Limpia *Argentina* 26°32S 59°45W **94** B4
Lagunas *Chile* 21°0S 69°45W **94** A2
Lagunas *Peru* 5°10S 75°35W **92** E3
Lagunas de Chacahua △ *Mexico* 16°0N 97°43W **87** D5
Lagunas de Montebello △ *Mexico* 16°4N 91°42W **87** D6
Lahad Datu *Malaysia* 5°0N 118°20E **37** C5
Lahad Datu, Telok *Malaysia* 4°50N 118°20E **37** D5
Lahan Sai *Thailand* 14°25N 102°52E **38** E4
Lahanam *Laos* 16°16N 105°16E **38** D5
Lahar *India* 26°12N 78°57E **43** F8
Laharpur *India* 27°43N 80°56E **43** F9
Lahat *Indonesia* 3°45S 103°30E **36** E2
Lahewa *Indonesia* 1°22N 97°12E **36** D1
Lāhījān *Iran* 37°10N 50°6E **45** B6
Lahn → *Germany* 50°19N 7°37E **16** C4
Laholm *Sweden* 56°30N 13°2E **9** H15
Lahore *Pakistan* 31°32N 74°22E **42** D6
Lahri *Pakistan* 29°11N 68°13E **42** E3
Lahti *Finland* 60°58N 25°40E **8** F21
Lahtis = Lahti *Finland* 60°58N 25°40E **8** F21
Laï *Chad* 9°25N 16°18E **51** G9
Lai Chau *Vietnam* 22°5N 103°3E **38** A4
Laila = Layla *Si. Arabia* 22°10N 46°40E **47** C4
Laingsburg *S. Africa* 33°9S 20°52E **56** E3
Lainioälven → *Sweden* 67°35N 22°40E **8** C20
Lairg *U.K.* 58°2N 4°24W **11** C4
Laisamis *Kenya* 1°36N 37°48E **54** B4
Laishui *China* 39°23N 115°45E **34** E8
Laiwu *China* 36°15N 117°40E **35** F9
Laixi *China* 36°50N 120°31E **35** F11
Laiyang *China* 36°59N 120°45E **35** F11
Laiyuan *China* 39°20N 114°40E **34** E8
Laizhou *China* 37°8N 119°57E **35** F10
Laizhou Wan *China* 37°30N 119°30E **35** F10
Laja → *Mexico* 20°55N 100°46W **86** C4
Lajamanu *Australia* 18°23S 130°38E **60** C5
Lajes *Brazil* 27°48S 50°20W **95** B5
Lak Sao *Laos* 18°11N 104°59E **38** C5
Lakaband *Pakistan* 31°2N 69°15E **42** D3
Lake *U.S.A.* 44°33N 110°24W **76** D8
Lake Alpine *U.S.A.* 38°29N 120°0W **78** G7
Lake Andes *U.S.A.* 43°9N 98°32W **80** D4
Lake Arthur *U.S.A.* 30°5N 92°41W **84** F8
Lake Bindegolly △ *Australia* 28°0S 144°12E **63** D3
Lake Cargelligo *Australia* 33°15S 146°22E **63** E4
Lake Charles *U.S.A.* 30°14N 93°13W **84** F8
Lake City *Colo., U.S.A.* 38°2N 107°19W **76** G10
Lake City *Fla., U.S.A.* 30°11N 82°38W **85** F13
Lake City *Mich., U.S.A.* 44°20N 85°13W **81** C11
Lake City *Minn., U.S.A.* 44°27N 92°16W **80** C7
Lake City *Pa., U.S.A.* 42°1N 80°21W **82** D4
Lake City *S.C., U.S.A.* 33°52N 79°45W **85** E15
Lake Cowichan *Canada* 48°49N 124°3W **70** D4
Lake District △ *U.K.* 54°30N 3°21W **12** C4
Lake Elsinore *U.S.A.* 33°38N 117°20W **79** M9
Lake Eyre △ *Australia* 28°40S 137°31E **63** D2
Lake Gairdner △ *Australia* 31°41S 135°51E **63** E2
Lake George *U.S.A.* 43°26N 73°43W **83** C11
Lake Grace *Australia* 33°7S 118°28E **61** F2
Lake Harbour = Kimmirut *Canada* 62°50N 69°50W **69** C13
Lake Havasu City *U.S.A.* 34°27N 114°22W **79** L12
Lake Hughes *U.S.A.* 34°41N 118°26W **79** L8
Lake Isabella *U.S.A.* 35°38N 118°28W **79** K8
Lake Jackson *U.S.A.* 29°3N 95°27W **84** G7
Lake King *Australia* 33°5S 119°45E **61** F2
Lake Lenore *Canada* 52°24N 104°59W **71** C8
Lake Louise *Canada* 51°30N 116°10W **70** C5
Lake Malawi △ *Malawi* 14°2S 34°53E **55** E3
Lake Mburo △ *Uganda* 0°33S 30°56E **54** C3
Lake Mead ⌓ *U.S.A.* 36°30N 114°22W **79** K12
Lake Meredith ⌓ *U.S.A.* 35°50N 101°50W **84** D4
Lake Mills *U.S.A.* 43°25N 93°32W **80** D7
Lake Nakura △ *Kenya* 0°21S 36°8E **54** C4
Lake Placid *U.S.A.* 44°17N 73°59W **83** B11
Lake Pleasant *U.S.A.* 43°28N 74°25W **83** C10
Lake Providence *U.S.A.* 32°48N 91°10W **84** E9
Lake Roosevelt ⌓ *U.S.A.* 48°5N 118°14W **76** B4
Lake St. Peter *Canada* 45°18N 78°2W **82** A6
Lake Superior ⌓ *Canada* 47°45N 84°45W **72** C3
Lake Torrens △ *Australia* 30°55S 137°40E **63** E2
Lake Village *U.S.A.* 33°20N 91°17W **84** E9
Lake Wales *U.S.A.* 27°54N 81°35W **85** H14
Lake Worth *U.S.A.* 26°37N 80°3W **85** H14
Lakeba *Fiji* 18°13S 178°47W **59** a
Lakeba Passage *Fiji* 18°0S 178°45W **59** a
Lakefield *Canada* 44°25N 78°16W **82** B6
Lakefield △ *Australia* 15°24S 144°26E **62** B3
Lakehurst *U.S.A.* 40°1N 74°19W **83** F10
Lakeland *Australia* 15°49S 144°57E **62** B3
Lakeland *U.S.A.* 28°3N 81°57W **85** G14
Lakemba = Lakeba *Fiji* 18°13S 178°47W **59** a
Lakeport *Calif., U.S.A.* 39°3N 122°55W **78** F4
Lakeport *Mich., U.S.A.* 43°7N 82°30W **82** C2
Lakes Entrance *Australia* 37°50S 148°0E **63** F4
Lakeside *Calif., U.S.A.* 32°52N 116°55W **79** N10
Lakeside *Nebr., U.S.A.* 42°3N 102°26W **80** D2
Lakeside *Ohio, U.S.A.* 41°32N 82°46W **82** E2
Lakeview *U.S.A.* 42°11N 120°21W **76** E3
Lakeville *U.S.A.* 44°39N 93°14W **80** C7
Lakewood *Colo., U.S.A.* 39°42N 105°4W **76** G11
Lakewood *N.J., U.S.A.* 40°6N 74°13W **83** F10
Lakewood *N.Y., U.S.A.* 42°6N 79°19W **82** D5
Lakewood *Ohio, U.S.A.* 41°28N 81°47W **82** E3
Lakewood *Wash., U.S.A.* 47°11N 122°32W **78** C4
Lakha *India* 26°9N 70°54E **42** F4
Lakhimpur *India* 27°57N 80°46E **43** F9
Lakhnadon *India* 22°36N 79°36E **43** H8
Lakhnau = Lucknow *India* 26°50N 81°0E **43** F9
Lakhonpheng *Laos* 15°54N 105°34E **38** E5
Lakhpat *India* 23°48N 68°47E **42** H3
Lakin *U.S.A.* 37°57N 101°15W **80** G3
Lakitusaki → *Canada* 54°21N 82°25W **72** B3
Lakki *Greece* 35°24N 23°57E **25** D5
Lakki *Pakistan* 32°36N 70°55E **42** C4
Lakonikos Kolpos *Greece* 36°40N 22°40E **23** F10
Lakor *Indonesia* 8°15S 128°17E **37** F7
Lakota *Ivory C.* 5°50N 5°30W **50** G4
Lakota *U.S.A.* 48°2N 98°21W **80** A4
Laksar *India* 29°46N 78°3E **42** E8
Laksefjorden *Norway* 70°45N 26°50E **8** A22
Lakselv *Norway* 70°2N 25°0E **8** A21
Lakshadweep Is. *India* 10°0N 72°30E **3** D13
Lakshmanpur *India* 22°58N 83°3E **43** H10
Lakshmikantapur *India* 22°5N 88°20E **43** H13
Lala Musa *Pakistan* 32°40N 73°57E **42** C5
Lalaghat *India* 24°30N 92°40E **41** G18
Lalago *Tanzania* 3°28S 33°58E **54** C3
Lalapanzi *Zimbabwe* 19°20S 30°15E **55** F3
L'Albufera *Spain* 39°20N 0°27W **21** C5
Lalganj *India* 25°52N 85°13E **43** G11
Lalgola *India* 24°25N 88°15E **43** G13
Lālī *Iran* 32°21N 49°6E **45** C6
Lalibela *Ethiopia* 12°3N 39°0E **47** E2
Lalin *China* 45°12N 127°0E **35** B14
Lalín *Spain* 42°40N 8°5W **21** A1
Lalin He → *China* 45°32N 125°40E **35** B13
Lalitapur *Nepal* 27°40N 85°20E **43** F11
Lalitpur *India* 24°42N 78°28E **43** G8
Lalkua *India* 29°5N 79°31E **43** E8
Lalsot *India* 26°34N 76°20E **42** F7
Lam *Vietnam* 21°21N 106°31E **38** B6
Lam Pao Res. *Thailand* 16°50N 103°15E **38** D4
Lamaing *Burma* 15°25N 97°53E **38** E1
Lamar *Colo., U.S.A.* 38°5N 102°37W **76** G12
Lamar *Mo., U.S.A.* 37°30N 94°16W **80** G6
Lamas *Peru* 6°28S 76°31W **92** E3
Lambaréné *Gabon* 0°41S 10°12E **52** E2
Lambasa = Labasa *Fiji* 16°30S 179°27E **59** a
Lambay I. *Ireland* 53°29N 6°1W **10** C5
Lambert's Bay *S. Africa* 32°5S 18°17E **56** E2
Lambeth *Canada* 42°54N 81°18W **82** D3
Lambomakondro *Madag.* 22°41S 44°44E **57** C7
Lambton Shores *Canada* 43°10N 81°56W **82** C3
Lame Deer *U.S.A.* 45°37N 106°40W **76** D10
Lamego *Portugal* 41°5N 7°52W **21** B2
Lamèque *Canada* 47°45N 64°38W **73** C7
Lameroo *Australia* 35°19S 140°33E **63** F3
Lamesa *U.S.A.* 32°44N 101°58W **84** E4
Lamia *Greece* 38°55N 22°26E **23** E10
Lamington △ *Australia* 28°13S 153°12E **63** D5
Lamma I. *China* 22°12N 114°7E **33** G11
Lammermuir Hills *U.K.* 55°50N 2°40W **11** F6
Lamoille → *U.S.A.* 44°38N 73°13W **83** B11
Lamon B. *Phil.* 14°30N 122°20E **37** B6
Lamont *Canada* 53°46N 112°50W **70** C6
Lamont *Calif., U.S.A.* 35°15N 118°55W **79** K8
Lamont *Wyo., U.S.A.* 42°13N 107°29W **76** E10
Lampa *Peru* 15°22S 70°22W **92** G4
Lampang *Thailand* 18°16N 99°32E **38** C2
Lampasas *U.S.A.* 31°4N 98°11W **84** F5
Lampazos de Naranjo *Mexico* 27°1N 100°31W **86** B4
Lampedusa *Medit. S.* 35°36N 12°40E **22** G5
Lampeter *U.K.* 52°7N 4°4W **13** E3
Lampione *Medit. S.* 35°33N 12°20E **22** G5
Lampman *Canada* 49°25N 102°50W **71** D8
Lampung □ *Indonesia* 5°30S 104°30E **36** F2
Lamta *India* 22°8N 80°7E **43** H9
Lamu *Kenya* 2°16S 40°55E **54** C5
Lamy *U.S.A.* 35°29N 105°53W **77** J11
Lan Xian *China* 38°15N 111°35E **34** E6
Läna'i *U.S.A.* 20°50N 156°55W **74** b
Lanak La *China* 34°27N 79°32E **43** B8
Lanak'o Shank'ou = Lanak La *China* 34°27N 79°32E **43** B8
Lanark *Canada* 45°1N 76°22W **83** A8
Lanark *U.K.* 55°40N 3°47W **11** F5
Lanbi Kyun *Burma* 10°50N 98°20E **39** G2
Lancang Jiang → *China* 21°40N 101°10E **32** D5
Lancashire □ *U.K.* 53°50N 2°48W **12** D5
Lancaster *Canada* 45°10N 74°30W **83** A10
Lancaster *U.K.* 54°3N 2°48W **12** C5
Lancaster *Calif., U.S.A.* 34°42N 118°8W **79** L8
Lancaster *Ky., U.S.A.* 37°37N 84°35W **81** G11
Lancaster *N.H., U.S.A.* 44°29N 71°34W **83** B13
Lancaster *N.Y., U.S.A.* 42°54N 78°40W **82** D6
Lancaster *Ohio, U.S.A.* 39°43N 82°36W **81** F12
Lancaster *Pa., U.S.A.* 40°2N 76°19W **83** F8
Lancaster *S.C., U.S.A.* 34°43N 80°46W **85** D14
Lancaster *Wis., U.S.A.* 42°51N 90°43W **80** D8
Lancaster Sd. *Canada* 74°13N 84°0W **69** B11
Lancelin *Australia* 31°0S 115°18E **61** F2
Lanchow = Lanzhou *China* 36°1N 103°52E **34** F2
Lanciano *Italy* 42°14N 14°23E **22** C6
Lancun *China* 36°25N 120°10E **35** F11
Land Between the Lakes ⌓ *U.S.A.* 36°25N 88°0W **85** C11
Landeck *Austria* 47°9N 10°34E **16** E6
Lander *U.S.A.* 42°50N 108°44W **76** E9
Lander → *Australia* 22°0S 132°0E **60** D5
Landes *France* 44°0N 1°0W **20** D3
Landi Kotal *Pakistan* 34°7N 71°6E **42** B4
Landisburg *U.S.A.* 40°21N 77°19W **82** F7
Landmannalaugar *Iceland* 63°59N 19°4W **8** E4
Land's End *U.K.* 50°4N 5°44W **13** G2
Landsborough Cr. → *Australia* 22°28S 144°35E **62** C3
Landshut *Germany* 48°34N 12°8E **16** D7
Lanesboro *U.S.A.* 41°57N 75°34W **83** E9
Lanett *U.S.A.* 32°52N 85°12W **85** E12
Lang Qua *Vietnam* 22°16N 104°27E **38** A5
Lang Shan *China* 41°0N 106°30E **34** D4
Lang Son *Vietnam* 21°52N 106°42E **38** B6
Lang Suan *Thailand* 9°57N 99°4E **39** H2
La'nga Co *China* 30°45N 81°15E **43** D9
Langar *Iran* 35°23N 60°25E **45** C9
Langara I. *Canada* 54°14N 133°1W **70** C2
Langdon *U.S.A.* 48°45N 98°22W **80** A4
Langeberg *S. Africa* 33°55S 21°0E **56** E3
Langeberge *S. Africa* 28°15S 22°33E **56** D3
Langeland *Denmark* 54°56N 10°48E **9** J14
Langenburg *Canada* 50°51N 101°43W **71** C8
Langholm *U.K.* 55°9N 3°0W **11** F5
Langjökull *Iceland* 64°39N 20°12W **8** D3
Langkawi, Pulau *Malaysia* 6°25N 99°45E **39** J2
Langklip *S. Africa* 28°12S 20°20E **56** D3
Langkon *Malaysia* 6°30N 116°40E **36** C5
Langlade *St-P. & M.* 46°50N 56°20W **73** C8
Langley *Canada* 49°7N 122°39W **78** A4
Langøya *Norway* 68°45N 14°50E **8** B16
Langreo *Spain* 43°18N 5°40W **21** A3
Langres *France* 47°52N 5°20E **20** C6
Langres, Plateau de *France* 47°45N 5°3E **20** C6
Langsa *Indonesia* 4°30N 97°57E **36** D1
Langtang △ *Nepal* 28°10N 85°30E **43** E11
Langtry *U.S.A.* 29°49N 101°34W **84** G4
Langu *Thailand* 6°53N 99°47E **39** J2
Languedoc *France* 43°58N 3°55E **20** E5
Langwang *China* 22°38N 113°27E **33** F9
Langxiangzhen *China* 39°43N 116°8E **34** E9
Lanigan *Canada* 51°51N 105°2W **71** C7
Lankao *China* 34°48N 114°50E **34** G8
Länkäran *Azerbaijan* 38°48N 48°52E **45** B6
Lannion *France* 48°46N 3°29W **20** B2
L'Annonciation *Canada* 46°25N 74°55W **72** C5
Lansdale *U.S.A.* 40°14N 75°17W **83** F9
Lansdowne *Australia* 31°48S 152°30E **63** E5
Lansdowne *Canada* 44°24N 76°1W **83** B8
Lansdowne *India* 29°50N 78°41E **43** E8
Lansdowne House *Canada* 52°14N 87°53W **72** B2
L'Anse *U.S.A.* 46°45N 88°27W **80** B9
L'Anse au Loup *Canada* 51°32N 56°50W **73** B8
L'Anse aux Meadows *Canada* 51°36N 55°32W **73** B8
L'Anse la Raye *St. Lucia* 13°55N 61°3W **89** f
Lansford *U.S.A.* 40°50N 75°53W **83** F9
Lansing *U.S.A.* 42°44N 84°33W **81** D11
Lanta Yai, Ko *Thailand* 7°35N 99°3E **39** J2
Lantau I. *China* 22°15N 113°56E **33** G10
Lantian *China* 34°11N 109°20E **34** G5
Lanus *Argentina* 34°42S 58°23W **94** C4
Lanusei *Italy* 39°52N 9°34E **22** E3
Lanzarote *Canary Is.* 29°0N 13°40W **24** F6
Lanzarote ✕ **(ACE)** *Canary Is.* 28°57N 13°40W **24** F6
Lanzhou *China* 36°1N 103°52E **34** F2
Lao Bao *Laos* 16°35N 106°30E **38** D6
Lao Cai *Vietnam* 22°30N 103°57E **38** A4
Laoag *Phil.* 18°7N 120°34E **37** A6
Laoang *Phil.* 12°32N 125°8E **37** B7
Laoha He → *China* 43°25N 120°35E **35** C11
Laois □ *Ireland* 52°57N 7°36W **10** D4
Laon *France* 49°33N 3°35E **20** B5
Laona *U.S.A.* 45°34N 88°40W **80** C9
Laos ■ *Asia* 17°45N 105°0E **38** D5
Lapa *Brazil* 25°46S 49°44W **95** B6
Lapeer *U.S.A.* 43°3N 83°19W **81** D12
Lapithos *Cyprus* 35°21N 33°11E **25** D12
Lapland = Lappland *Europe* 68°7N 24°0E **8** B21
LaPorte *Ind., U.S.A.* 41°36N 86°43W **80** E10
Laporte *Pa., U.S.A.* 41°25N 76°30W **83** E8
Lappeenranta *Finland* 61°3N 28°12E **8** F23
Lappland *Europe* 68°7N 24°0E **8** B21
Lappo = Lapua *Finland* 62°58N 23°0E **8** E20
Laprida *Argentina* 37°34S 60°45W **94** D3
Lapseki *Turkey* 40°20N 26°41E **23** D12
Laptev Sea *Russia* 76°0N 125°0E **29** B13
Lapua *Finland* 62°58N 23°0E **8** E20
L'Áquila *Italy* 42°22N 13°22E **22** C5
Lār *Āzarbājān-e Sharqī, Iran* 38°30N 47°52E **44** B5
Lār *Fārs, Iran* 27°40N 54°14E **45** E7
Laramie *U.S.A.* 41°10N 106°35W **76** F11
Laramie Mts. *U.S.A.* 42°0N 105°30W **76** F11
Laranjeiras do Sul *Brazil* 25°23S 52°23W **95** B5
Larantuka *Indonesia* 8°21S 122°55E **37** F6
Larat *Indonesia* 7°0S 132°0E **37** F8
Larde *Mozam.* 16°28S 39°43E **55** F4
Larder Lake *Canada* 48°5N 79°40W **72** C4
Lardos, Akra = Lindos, Akra *Greece* 36°4N 28°10E **25** C10
Lardos, Ormos *Greece* 36°4N 28°2E **25** C10
Lare *Kenya* 0°20N 37°56E **54** C4
Laredo *U.S.A.* 27°30N 99°30W **84** H5
Laredo Sd. *Canada* 52°30N 128°53W **70** C3
Largo *U.S.A.* 27°54N 82°47W **85** H13
Largs *U.K.* 55°47N 4°52W **11** F4
Lariang *Indonesia* 1°26S 119°17E **37** E5
Larimore *U.S.A.* 47°54N 97°38W **80** B5
Larisa *Greece* 39°36N 22°27E **23** E10
Larkana *Pakistan* 27°32N 68°18E **42** F3
Larnaca *Cyprus* 34°55N 33°38E **25** E12
Larnaca Bay *Cyprus* 34°53N 33°45E **25** E12
Larne *U.K.* 54°51N 5°51W **10** B6
Larned *U.S.A.* 38°11N 99°6W **80** F4
Larose *U.S.A.* 29°34N 90°23W **85** G9
Larrimah *Australia* 15°35S 133°12E **60** C5
Larsen Ice Shelf *Antarctica* 67°0S 62°0W **5** C17
Larvik *Norway* 59°4N 10°2E **9** G14
Las Animas *U.S.A.* 38°4N 103°13W **76** G12
Las Anod *Somali Rep.* 8°26N 47°19E **47** F4
Las Brenãs *Argentina* 27°5S 61°7W **94** B3
Las Cañadas del Teide △ *Canary Is.* 28°15N 16°37W **24** F3
Las Cejas *Argentina* 26°53S 64°44W **96** B4
Las Chimeneas *Mexico* 32°8N 116°5W **79** N10
Las Cruces *U.S.A.* 32°19N 106°47W **77** K10
Las Flores *Argentina* 36°10S 59°7W **94** D4
Las Heras *Argentina* 32°51S 68°49W **94** C2

Las Lajas *Argentina* 38°30S 70°25W 96 D2
Las Lomitas *Argentina* 24°43S 60°35W 94 A3
Las Palmas *Argentina* 27°8S 58°45W 94 B4
Las Palmas *Canary Is.* 28°7N 15°26W 24 F4
Las Palmas → *Mexico* 32°31N 116°58W 79 N10
Las Palmas ✕ (LPA) *Canary Is.* 27°55N 15°25W 24 G4
Las Palmas de Cocalán △ *Chile* 34°18S 71°4W 94 C1
Las Piedras *Uruguay* 34°44S 56°14W 95 C4
Las Pipinas *Argentina* 35°30S 57°19W 94 D4
Las Plumas *Argentina* 43°40S 67°15W 96 E3
Las Rosas *Argentina* 32°30S 61°35W 94 C3
Las Tablas *Panama* 7°49N 80°14W 88 E3
Las Termas *Argentina* 27°29S 64°52W 94 B3
Las Toscas *Argentina* 28°21S 59°18W 94 B4
Las Truchas *Mexico* 17°57N 102°13W 86 D4
Las Tunas *Cuba* 20°58N 76°59W 88 B4
Las Varillas *Argentina* 31°50S 62°50W 94 C3
Las Vegas *N. Mex., U.S.A.* 35°36N 105°13W 77 J11
Las Vegas *Nev., U.S.A.* 36°10N 115°8W 79 J11
Las Vegas McCarran Int. ✕ (LAS) *U.S.A.* 36°5N 115°9W 79 J11
Lascano *Uruguay* 33°35S 54°12W 95 C5
Lash-e Joveyn *Afghan.* 31°45N 61°30E 40 D2
Lashburn *Canada* 53°10N 109°40W 71 C7
Lashio *Burma* 22°56N 97°45E 41 H20
Lashkar *India* 26°10N 78°10E 42 F8
Lasithi *Greece* 35°11N 25°31E 25 D7
Lasithi □ *Greece* 35°5N 25°50E 25 D7
Lāsjerd *Iran* 35°24N 53°4E 45 C7
Lassen Pk. *U.S.A.* 40°29N 121°30W 76 F3
Lassen Volcanic △ *U.S.A.* 40°30N 121°20W 76 F3
Last Mountain L. *Canada* 51°5N 105°14W 71 C7
Lastchance Cr. → *U.S.A.* 40°2N 121°15W 78 E5
Lastoursville *Gabon* 0°55S 12°38E 52 E2
Lastovo *Croatia* 42°46N 16°55E 22 C7
Lat Yao *Thailand* 15°45N 99°48E 38 E2
Latacunga *Ecuador* 0°50S 78°35W 92 D3
Latakia = Al Lādhiqīyah *Syria* 35°30N 35°45E 44 C2
Latchford *Canada* 47°20N 79°50W 72 C4
Late *Tonga* 18°48S 174°39W 59 c
Latehar *India* 23°45N 84°30E 43 H11
Latham *Australia* 29°44S 116°20E 61 E2
Lathi *India* 27°43N 71°23E 42 F4
Lathrop Wells *U.S.A.* 36°39N 116°24W 79 J10
Latina *Italy* 41°28N 12°52E 22 D5
Latium = Lazio □ *Italy* 42°10N 12°30E 22 C5
Laton *U.S.A.* 36°26N 119°41W 78 J7
Latouche Treville, C. *Australia* 18°27S 121°49E 60 C3
Latrobe *Australia* 41°14S 146°30E 63 G4
Latrobe *U.S.A.* 40°19N 79°23W 82 F5
Latvia ■ *Europe* 56°50N 24°0E 9 H21
Lau Fau Shan *China* 22°28N 113°59E 33 G10
Lau Group *Fiji* 17°0S 178°30W 59 a
Lauchhammer *Germany* 51°29N 13°47E 16 C7
Laughlin *U.S.A.* 35°10N 114°34W 77 J6
Laukaa *Finland* 62°24N 25°56E 8 E21
Launceston *Australia* 41°24S 147°8E 63 G4
Launceston *U.K.* 50°38N 4°22W 13 G3
Laune → *Ireland* 52°7N 9°47W 10 D2
Launglon Bok *Burma* 13°50N 97°54E 38 F1
Laura *Australia* 15°32S 144°32E 62 B3
Laurel *Miss., U.S.A.* 31°41N 89°8W 85 F10
Laurel *Mont., U.S.A.* 45°40N 108°46W 76 D9
Laurel Hill *U.S.A.* 40°14N 79°6W 82 F5
Laurencekirk *U.K.* 56°50N 2°28W 11 E6
Laurens *U.S.A.* 34°30N 82°1W 85 D13
Laurentian Plateau *Canada* 52°0N 70°0W 73 B6
Lauria *Italy* 40°2N 15°50E 22 E6
Laurie L. *Canada* 56°35N 101°57W 71 B8
Laurinburg *U.S.A.* 34°47N 79°28W 85 D15
Laurium *U.S.A.* 47°14N 88°27W 80 B9
Lausanne *Switz.* 46°32N 6°38E 20 C7
Laut *Indonesia* 4°45N 108°0E 36 D3
Laut, Pulau *Indonesia* 3°40S 116°10E 36 E5
Laut Kecil, Kepulauan *Indonesia* 4°45S 115°40E 36 E5
Lautoka *Fiji* 17°37S 177°27E 59 a
Lava Beds ⌓ *U.S.A.* 41°40N 121°30W 76 F3
Lavagh More *Ireland* 54°46N 8°6W 10 B3
Laval *France* 48°4N 0°48W 20 B3
Laval-des-Rapides *Canada* 45°33N 73°42W 72 C5
Lavalle *Argentina* 28°15S 65°15W 94 B2
Lavant Station *Canada* 45°3N 76°42W 83 A8
Lāvar Meydān *Iran* 30°20N 54°30E 45 D7
Laverton *Australia* 28°44S 122°29E 61 E3
Lavras *Brazil* 21°20S 45°0W 95 A7
Lavrio *Greece* 37°40N 24°4E 23 F11
Lavris *Greece* 35°25N 24°40E 25 D6
Lavumisa *Swaziland* 27°20S 31°55E 57 D5
Lavushi Manda △ *Zambia* 12°46S 31°0E 55 E3
Lawaki *Fiji* 17°40S 178°35E 59 a
Lawas *Malaysia* 4°55N 115°25E 36 D5
Lawele *Indonesia* 5°13S 122°57E 37 F6
Lawn Hill △ *Australia* 18°15S 138°6E 62 B2
Lawqah *Si. Arabia* 29°49N 42°45E 44 D4
Lawrence *N.Z.* 45°55S 169°41E 59 F2
Lawrence *Ind., U.S.A.* 39°50N 86°2W 80 F10
Lawrence *Kans., U.S.A.* 38°58N 95°14W 80 F6
Lawrence *Mass., U.S.A.* 42°43N 71°10W 83 D13
Lawrenceburg *Ind., U.S.A.* 39°6N 84°52W 81 F11
Lawrenceburg *Tenn., U.S.A.* 35°14N 87°20W 85 D11
Lawrenceville *Ga., U.S.A.* 33°57N 83°59W 85 E13
Lawrenceville *Pa., U.S.A.* 41°59N 77°8W 82 E7
Laws *U.S.A.* 37°24N 118°20W 78 H8
Lawton *U.S.A.* 34°37N 98°25W 84 D5
Lawu *Indonesia* 7°40S 111°13E 37 G14
Laxford, L. *U.K.* 58°24N 5°6W 11 C3
Layla *Si. Arabia* 22°10N 46°40E 47 C4
Laylān *Iraq* 35°18N 44°31E 44 C5
Layton *U.S.A.* 41°4N 111°58W 76 F8
Laytonville *U.S.A.* 39°41N 123°29W 76 G2
Lazarivo *Madag.* 23°54S 44°59E 57 C8
Lázaro Cárdenas *Mexico* 17°55N 102°11W 86 D4
Lazio □ *Italy* 42°10N 12°30E 22 C5
Lazo *Russia* 43°25N 133°55E 30 C6
Le Bic *Canada* 48°20N 68°41W 73 C6
Le Creusot *France* 46°48N 4°24E 20 C6
Le François *Martinique* 14°38N 60°57W 88 c
Le Gosier *Guadeloupe* 16°14N 61°29W 88 b
Le Gris Gris *Mauritius* 20°31S 57°32E 53 d
Le Havre *France* 49°30N 0°5E 20 B4
Le Lamentin *Martinique* 14°35N 61°2W 88 c
Le Mans *France* 48°0N 0°10E 20 C4
Le Marin *Martinique* 14°27N 60°55W 88 c
Le Mars *U.S.A.* 42°47N 96°10W 80 D5
Le Mont-St-Michel *France* 48°40N 1°30W 20 B3
Le Moule *Guadeloupe* 16°20N 61°22W 88 b
Le Port *Réunion* 20°56S 55°18E 53 c
Le Prêcheur *Martinique* 14°50N 61°12W 88 c
Le Puy-en-Velay *France* 45°3N 3°52E 20 D5
Le Robert *Martinique* 14°40N 60°56W 88 c
Le St-Esprit *Martinique* 14°34N 60°56W 88 c
Le Sueur *U.S.A.* 44°28N 93°55W 80 C7
Le Tampon *Réunion* 21°16S 55°32E 53 c
Le Thuy *Vietnam* 17°14N 106°49E 38 D6
Le Touquet-Paris-Plage *France* 50°30N 1°36E 20 A4
Le Tréport *France* 50°3N 1°20E 20 A4
Le Verdon-sur-Mer *France* 45°33N 1°4W 20 D3
Lea → *U.K.* 51°31N 0°1E 13 F8
Leach *Cambodia* 12°21N 103°46E 39 F4
Lead *U.S.A.* 44°21N 103°46W 80 C2
Leader *Canada* 50°50N 109°30W 71 C7
Leadville *U.S.A.* 39°15N 106°18W 76 G10
Leaf → *U.S.A.* 30°59N 88°44W 85 F10
Leaf Rapids *Canada* 56°30N 99°59W 71 B9
Leamington *Canada* 42°3N 82°36W 82 D2
Leamington *U.S.A.* 39°32N 112°17W 76 G7
Leamington Spa = Royal Leamington Spa *U.K.* 52°18N 1°31W 13 E6
Leandro Norte Alem *Argentina* 27°34S 55°15W 95 B4
Leane, L. *Ireland* 52°2N 9°32W 10 D2
Learmonth *Australia* 22°13S 114°10E 60 D1
Leask *Canada* 53°5N 106°45W 71 C7
Leatherhead *U.K.* 51°18N 0°20W 13 F7
Leavenworth *Kans., U.S.A.* 39°19N 94°55W 80 F6
Leavenworth *Wash., U.S.A.* 47°36N 120°40W 76 C3
Leawood *U.S.A.* 38°58N 94°37W 80 F6
Lebak *Phil.* 6°32N 124°5E 37 C6
Lebam *U.S.A.* 46°34N 123°33W 78 D3
Lebanon *Ind., U.S.A.* 40°3N 86°28W 80 E10
Lebanon *Kans., U.S.A.* 39°49N 98°33W 80 F4
Lebanon *Ky., U.S.A.* 37°34N 85°15W 81 G11
Lebanon *Mo., U.S.A.* 37°41N 92°40W 80 G7
Lebanon *N.H., U.S.A.* 43°39N 72°15W 83 C12
Lebanon *Oreg., U.S.A.* 44°32N 122°55W 76 D2
Lebanon *Pa., U.S.A.* 40°20N 76°26W 83 F8
Lebanon *Tenn., U.S.A.* 36°12N 86°18W 85 C11
Lebanon ■ *Asia* 34°0N 36°0E 46 B5
Lebec *U.S.A.* 34°51N 118°52W 79 L8
Lebel-sur-Quévillon *Canada* 49°3N 76°59W 72 C4
Lebomboberge *S. Africa* 24°30S 32°0E 57 C5
Lębork *Poland* 54°33N 17°46E 17 A9
Lebrija *Spain* 36°53N 6°5W 21 D2
Lebu *Chile* 37°40S 73°47W 94 D1
Lecce *Italy* 40°23N 18°11E 23 D8
Lecco *Italy* 45°51N 9°23E 20 D8
Lech → *Germany* 48°43N 10°56E 16 D6
Lecontes Mills *U.S.A.* 41°5N 78°17W 82 E6
Łęczyca *Poland* 52°5N 19°15E 17 B10
Ledong *China* 18°41N 109°5E 38 C7
Leduc *Canada* 53°15N 113°30W 70 C6
Lee *U.S.A.* 42°19N 73°15W 83 D11
Lee → *Ireland* 51°53N 8°56W 10 E3
Lee Vining *U.S.A.* 37°58N 119°7W 78 H7
Leech L. *U.S.A.* 47°10N 94°24W 80 B6
Leechburg *U.S.A.* 40°37N 79°36W 82 F5
Leeds *U.K.* 53°48N 1°33W 12 D6
Leeds *U.S.A.* 33°33N 86°33W 85 E11
Leek *Neths.* 53°10N 6°24E 15 A6
Leek *U.K.* 53°7N 2°1W 12 D5
Leeman *Australia* 29°57S 114°58E 61 E1
Leeper *U.S.A.* 41°22N 79°18W 82 E5
Leer *Germany* 53°13N 7°26E 16 B4
Leesburg *U.S.A.* 28°49N 81°53W 85 G14
Leesville *U.S.A.* 31°8N 93°16W 84 F8
Leeton *Australia* 34°33S 146°23E 63 E4
Leetonia *U.S.A.* 40°53N 80°45W 82 F4
Leeu Gamka *S. Africa* 32°47S 21°59E 56 E3
Leeuwarden *Neths.* 53°15N 5°48E 15 A5
Leeuwin, C. *Australia* 34°20S 115°9E 61 F2
Leeuwin Naturaliste △ *Australia* 34°6S 115°3E 61 F2
Leeward Is. *Atl. Oc.* 16°30N 63°30W 89 C7
Lefka *Cyprus* 35°6N 32°51E 25 D11
Lefkada *Greece* 38°40N 20°43E 23 E9
Lefkimis *Greece* 39°25N 20°3E 25 B4
Lefkimis, Akra *Greece* 39°29N 20°4E 25 B4
Lefkímmi = Lefkimis *Greece* 39°25N 20°3E 25 B4
Lefkoniko *Cyprus* 35°18N 33°44E 25 D12
Lefroy *Canada* 44°16N 79°34W 82 B5
Lefroy, L. *Australia* 31°21S 121°40E 61 F3
Leganés *Spain* 40°19N 3°45W 21 B4
Legazpi *Phil.* 13°10N 123°45E 37 B6
Legendre I. *Australia* 20°22S 116°55E 60 D2
Leghorn = Livorno *Italy* 43°33N 10°19E 22 C4
Legionowo *Poland* 52°25N 20°50E 17 B11
Legnago *Italy* 45°11N 11°18E 22 B4
Legnica *Poland* 51°12N 16°10E 16 C9
Leh *India* 34°9N 77°35E 43 B7
Lehigh Acres *U.S.A.* 26°36N 81°39W 85 H14
Lehighton *U.S.A.* 40°50N 75°43W 83 F9
Lehututu *Botswana* 23°54S 21°55E 56 C3
Leiah *Pakistan* 30°58N 70°58E 42 D4
Leicester *U.K.* 52°38N 1°8W 13 E6
Leicester City □ *U.K.* 52°38N 1°8W 13 E6
Leicestershire □ *U.K.* 52°41N 1°17W 13 E6
Leichhardt → *Australia* 17°35S 139°48E 62 B2
Leichhardt Ra. *Australia* 20°46S 147°40E 62 C4
Leiden *Neths.* 52°9N 4°30E 15 B4
Leie → *Belgium* 51°2N 3°45E 15 C3
Leine → *Germany* 52°43N 9°36E 16 B5
Leinster *Australia* 27°51S 120°36E 61 E3
Leinster □ *Ireland* 53°3N 7°8W 10 C4
Leinster, Mt. *Ireland* 52°37N 6°46W 10 D5
Leipzig *Germany* 51°18N 12°22E 16 C7
Leiria *Portugal* 39°46N 8°53W 21 C1
Leirvik *Norway* 59°47N 5°28E 9 G11
Leisler, Mt. *Australia* 23°23S 129°20E 60 D4
Leith *U.K.* 55°59N 3°11W 11 F5
Leith Hill *U.K.* 51°11N 0°22W 13 F7
Leitrim *Ireland* 54°0N 8°5W 10 B3
Leitrim □ *Ireland* 54°8N 8°0W 10 B4
Leizhou Bandao *China* 21°0N 110°0E 33 D6
Lek → *Neths.* 51°54N 4°35E 15 C4
Leka *Norway* 65°5N 11°35E 8 D14
Lekva Oros *Greece* 35°18N 24°3E 25 D6
Leland *U.S.A.* 45°1N 85°45W 81 C11
Leleque *Argentina* 42°28S 71°0W 96 E2
Lelystad *Neths.* 52°30N 5°25E 15 B5
Léman, L. *Europe* 46°26N 6°30E 20 C7
Lembar *Indonesia* 8°45S 116°4E 37 K19
Lembuak *Indonesia* 8°36S 116°11E 37 K19
Lemera *Dem. Rep. of the Congo* 3°0S 28°55E 54 C2
Lemhi Ra. *U.S.A.* 44°0N 113°0W 76 D7
Lemmer *Neths.* 52°51N 5°43E 15 B5
Lemmon *U.S.A.* 45°57N 102°10W 80 C2
Lemon Grove *U.S.A.* 32°44N 117°1W 79 N9
Lemoore *U.S.A.* 36°18N 119°46W 78 J7
Lemvig *Denmark* 56°33N 8°20E 9 H13
Lena → *Russia* 72°52N 126°40E 29 B13
Lenadoon Pt. *Ireland* 54°18N 9°3W 10 B2
Lendeh *Iran* 30°58N 50°25E 45 D6
Lenggong *Malaysia* 5°6N 100°58E 39 K3
Lengua de Vaca, Pta. *Chile* 30°14S 71°38W 94 C1
Lengwe △ *Malawi* 16°14S 34°45E 55 F3
Leninogorsk *Kazakhstan* 50°20N 83°30E 28 D9
Leninsk *Russia* 48°40N 45°15E 19 E8
Leninsk-Kuznetskiy *Russia* 54°44N 86°10E 28 D9
Lenkoran = Länkäran *Azerbaijan* 38°48N 48°52E 45 B6
Lenmalu *Indonesia* 1°45S 130°15E 37 E8
Lennox *U.S.A.* 43°21N 96°53W 80 D5
Lennoxville *Canada* 45°22N 71°51W 83 A13
Lenoir *U.S.A.* 35°55N 81°32W 85 D14
Lenoir City *U.S.A.* 35°48N 84°16W 85 D12
Lenore L. *Canada* 52°30N 104°59W 71 C8
Lenox *U.S.A.* 42°22N 73°17W 83 D11
Lens *France* 50°26N 2°50E 20 A5
Lensk *Russia* 60°48N 114°55E 29 C12
Lentas *Greece* 34°56N 24°56E 25 E6
Lentini *Italy* 37°17N 15°0E 22 F6
Lenwood *U.S.A.* 34°53N 117°7W 79 L9
Lenya *Burma* 11°33N 98°57E 39 G2
Leoben *Austria* 47°22N 15°5E 16 E8
Leodhas = Lewis *U.K.* 58°9N 6°40W 11 C2
Leola *U.S.A.* 45°43N 98°56W 80 C4
Leominster *U.K.* 52°14N 2°43W 13 E5
Leominster *U.S.A.* 42°32N 71°46W 83 D13
León *Mexico* 21°6N 101°41W 86 C4
León *Nic.* 12°20N 86°51W 88 D2
León *Spain* 42°38N 5°34W 21 A3
Leon *U.S.A.* 40°44N 93°45W 80 E7
Leon → *U.S.A.* 31°14N 97°28W 84 F6
León, Montes de *Spain* 42°30N 6°18W 21 A2
Leonardtown *U.S.A.* 38°17N 76°38W 81 F15
Leonardville *Namibia* 23°29S 18°49E 56 C2
Leone *Amer. Samoa* 14°23S 170°48W 59 b
Leongatha *Australia* 38°30S 145°58E 63 F4
Leonora *Australia* 28°49S 121°19E 61 E3
Leopoldina *Brazil* 21°28S 42°40W 95 A7
Leopoldsburg *Belgium* 51°7N 5°13E 15 C5
Leoti *U.S.A.* 38°29N 101°21W 80 F3
Leova *Moldova* 46°28N 28°15E 17 E15
Leoville *Canada* 53°39N 107°33W 71 C7
Lepel = Lyepyel *Belarus* 54°50N 28°40E 9 J23
Lépo, L. do *Angola* 17°0S 19°0E 56 B2
Leppävirta *Finland* 62°29N 27°46E 8 E22
Leptis Magna *Libya* 32°40N 14°12E 51 B8
Leribe *Lesotho* 28°51S 28°3E 57 D4
Lérida = Lleida *Spain* 41°37N 0°39E 21 B6
Lerwick *U.K.* 60°9N 1°9W 11 A7
Les Cayes *Haiti* 18°15N 73°46W 89 C5
Les Coteaux *Canada* 45°15N 74°13W 83 A10
Les Escoumins *Canada* 48°21N 69°24W 73 C6
Les Sables-d'Olonne *France* 46°30N 1°45W 20 C3
Lesbos *Greece* 39°10N 26°20E 23 E12
Leshan *China* 29°33N 103°41E 32 D5
Leshukonskoye *Russia* 64°54N 45°46E 18 B8
Leshwe ⌓ *Dem. Rep. of the Congo* 12°45S 29°30E 55 E2
Leskov I. *Antarctica* 56°0S 28°0W 5 B1
Leskovac *Serbia* 43°0N 21°58E 23 C9
Lesopilnoye *Russia* 46°44N 134°20E 30 A7
Lesotho ■ *Africa* 29°40S 28°0E 57 D4
Lesozavodsk *Russia* 45°30N 133°29E 30 B6
Lesse et Lomme ⌓ *Belgium* 50°8N 5°9E 15 D5
Lesse → *Belgium* 50°15N 4°54E 15 D4
Lesser Antilles *W. Indies* 15°0N 61°0W 89 D7
Lesser Slave L. *Canada* 55°30N 115°25W 70 B5
Lesser Sunda Is. *Indonesia* 8°0S 120°0E 37 F6
Lessines *Belgium* 50°42N 3°50E 15 D3
Lester B. Pearson Int., Toronto ✕ (YYZ) *Canada* 43°46N 79°35W 82 C5
Lestock *Canada* 51°19N 103°59W 71 C8
Lesuer I. *Australia* 13°50S 127°17E 60 B4
Lesueur △ *Australia* 30°11S 115°10E 61 F2
Lésvos = Lesbos *Greece* 39°10N 26°20E 23 E12
Leszno *Poland* 51°50N 16°30E 17 C9
Letaba *S. Africa* 23°59S 31°50E 57 C5
Letchworth *U.K.* 51°59N 0°13W 13 F7
Lethbridge *Canada* 49°45N 112°45W 70 D6
Lethem *Guyana* 3°20N 59°50W 92 C7
Leti, Kepulauan *Indonesia* 8°10S 128°0E 37 F7
Leti Is. = Leti, Kepulauan *Indonesia* 8°10S 128°0E 37 F7
Letiahau → *Botswana* 21°16S 24°0E 56 C3
Leticia *Colombia* 4°9S 70°0W 92 D5
Leting *China* 39°23N 118°55E 35 E10
Letjiesbos *S. Africa* 32°34S 22°16E 56 E3
Letlhakane *Botswana* 21°27S 25°30E 56 C4
Letlhakeng *Botswana* 24°0S 24°59E 56 C3
Letpadan *Burma* 17°45N 95°45E 41 L19
Letpan *Burma* 19°28N 94°10E 41 K19
Letsôk-aw Kyun *Burma* 11°30N 98°25E 39 G2
Letterkenny *Ireland* 54°57N 7°45W 10 B4
Leucadia *U.S.A.* 33°4N 117°18W 79 M9
Leuchars *U.K.* 56°24N 2°53W 11 E6
Leuser, G. *Indonesia* 3°46N 97°12E 36 D1
Leuven *Belgium* 50°52N 4°42E 15 D4
Leuze-en-Hainaut *Belgium* 50°36N 3°37E 15 D3
Levanger *Norway* 63°45N 11°19E 8 E14
Levelland *U.S.A.* 33°35N 102°23W 84 E3
Leven *U.K.* 56°12N 3°0W 11 E6
Leven, L. *U.K.* 56°12N 3°22W 11 E5
Leven, Toraka *Madag.* 12°30S 47°45E 57 A8
Leveque C. *Australia* 16°20S 123°0E 60 C3
Levice *Slovak Rep.* 48°13N 18°35E 17 D10
Levin *N.Z.* 40°37S 175°18E 59 D5
Lévis *Canada* 46°48N 71°9W 73 C5
Levis, L. *Canada* 62°37N 117°58W 70 A5
Levittown *N.Y., U.S.A.* 40°44N 73°31W 83 F11
Levittown *Pa., U.S.A.* 40°9N 74°51W 83 F10
Levkás = Lefkada *Greece* 38°40N 20°43E 23 E9
Levkôsia = Nicosia *Cyprus* 35°10N 33°25E 25 D12
Levskigrad = Karlovo *Bulgaria* 42°38N 24°47E 23 C11
Levuka *Fiji* 17°34S 179°0E 59 a
Lewes *U.K.* 50°52N 0°1E 13 G8
Lewes *U.S.A.* 38°46N 75°9W 81 F16
Lewis *U.K.* 58°9N 6°40W 11 C2
Lewis → *U.S.A.* 45°51N 122°48W 78 E4
Lewis, Butt of *U.K.* 58°31N 6°16W 11 C2
Lewis Ra. *Australia* 20°3S 128°50E 60 D4
Lewis Range *U.S.A.* 48°5N 113°5W 76 B7
Lewis Run *U.S.A.* 41°52N 78°40W 82 E6
Lewisburg *Pa., U.S.A.* 40°58N 76°54W 82 F8
Lewisburg *Tenn., U.S.A.* 35°27N 86°48W 85 D11
Lewisburg *W. Va., U.S.A.* 37°48N 80°27W 81 G13
Lewisporte *Canada* 49°15N 55°3W 73 C8
Lewiston *Idaho, U.S.A.* 46°25N 117°1W 76 C5
Lewiston *Maine, U.S.A.* 44°6N 70°13W 81 C18
Lewiston *N.Y., U.S.A.* 43°11N 79°3W 82 C5
Lewistown *Mont., U.S.A.* 47°4N 109°26W 76 C9
Lewistown *Pa., U.S.A.* 40°36N 77°34W 82 F7
Lexington *Ill., U.S.A.* 40°39N 88°47W 80 E9
Lexington *Ky., U.S.A.* 38°3N 84°30W 81 F11
Lexington *Mich., U.S.A.* 43°16N 82°32W 82 C2
Lexington *Mo., U.S.A.* 39°11N 93°52W 80 F7
Lexington *N.C., U.S.A.* 35°49N 80°15W 85 D14
Lexington *N.Y., U.S.A.* 42°15N 74°22W 83 D10
Lexington *Nebr., U.S.A.* 40°47N 99°45W 80 E4
Lexington *Ohio, U.S.A.* 40°41N 82°35W 82 F2
Lexington *Tenn., U.S.A.* 35°39N 88°24W 85 D10
Lexington *Va., U.S.A.* 37°47N 79°27W 81 G14
Lexington Park *U.S.A.* 38°16N 76°27W 81 F15
Leyburn *U.K.* 54°19N 1°48W 12 C6
Leyland *U.K.* 53°42N 2°43W 12 D5
Leyte □ *Phil.* 11°0N 125°0E 37 B6
Lezhë *Albania* 41°47N 19°39E 23 D8
Lhasa *China* 29°25N 90°58E 32 D4
Lhazê *China* 29°5N 87°38E 32 D3
Lhokkruet *Indonesia* 4°55N 95°24E 36 D1
Lhokseumawe *Indonesia* 5°10N 97°10E 36 C1
L'Hospitalet de Llobregat *Spain* 41°21N 2°6E 21 B7
Li *Thailand* 17°48N 98°57E 38 D2
Li Xian *Gansu, China* 34°10N 105°5E 34 G3
Li Xian *Hebei, China* 38°30N 115°35E 34 E8
Liancourt Rocks = Tok-do *Asia* 37°15N 131°52E 31 F5
Lianga *Phil.* 8°38N 126°6E 37 C7
Liangcheng *Nei Monggol Zizhiqu, China* 40°28N 112°25E 34 D7
Liangcheng *Shandong, China* 35°32N 119°37E 35 G10
Liangdang *China* 33°56N 106°18E 34 H4
Liangpran *Indonesia* 1°4N 114°23E 36 D4
Lianshanguan *China* 40°53N 123°43E 35 D12
Lianshui *China* 33°42N 119°20E 35 H10
Lianyungang *China* 34°40N 119°11E 35 G10
Liao He → *China* 41°0N 121°50E 35 D11
Liaocheng *China* 36°28N 115°58E 34 F8
Liaodong Bandao *China* 40°0N 122°30E 35 E12
Liaodong Wan *China* 40°20N 121°10E 35 D11
Liaoning □ *China* 41°40N 122°30E 35 D12
Liaotung, G. of = Liaodong Wan *China* 40°20N 121°10E 35 D11
Liaoyang *China* 41°15N 122°58E 35 D12
Liaoyuan *China* 42°58N 125°2E 35 C13
Liaozhong *China* 41°23N 122°50E 35 D12
Liard → *Canada* 61°51N 121°18W 70 A4
Liard River *Canada* 59°25N 126°5W 70 B3
Liari *Pakistan* 25°37N 66°30E 42 G2
Libau = Liepāja *Latvia* 56°30N 21°0E 9 H19
Libby *U.S.A.* 48°23N 115°33W 76 B6
Libenge *Dem. Rep. of the Congo* 3°40N 18°55E 52 D3
Liberal *U.S.A.* 37°3N 100°55W 80 G3
Liberec *Czech Rep.* 50°47N 15°7E 16 C8
Liberia *Costa Rica* 10°40N 85°30W 88 D2
Liberia ■ *W. Afr.* 6°30N 9°30W 50 G4
Liberty *Mo., U.S.A.* 39°15N 94°25W 80 F6
Liberty *N.Y., U.S.A.* 41°48N 74°45W 83 E10
Liberty *Pa., U.S.A.* 41°34N 77°6W 82 E7
Liberty *Tex., U.S.A.* 30°3N 94°48W 84 F7
Liberty-Newark Int. ✕ (EWR) *U.S.A.* 40°42N 74°10W 83 F10
Lībīya, Sahrā' *Africa* 25°0N 25°0E 51 C10
Libobo, Tanjung *Indonesia* 0°54S 128°28E 37 E7
Libode *S. Africa* 31°33S 29°2E 57 E4
Libourne *France* 44°55N 0°14W 20 D3
Libramont *Belgium* 49°55N 5°23E 15 E5
Libreville *Gabon* 0°25N 9°26E 52 D1
Libya ■ *N. Afr.* 27°0N 17°0E 51 C9
Libyan Desert = Lībīya, Sahrā' *Africa* 25°0N 25°0E 51 C10
Libyan Plateau = Ed Déffa *Egypt* 30°40N 26°30E 51 B11
Licantén *Chile* 35°55S 72°0W 94 D1
Licata *Italy* 37°6N 13°56E 22 F5
Licheng *China* 36°28N 113°20E 34 F7
Lichfield *U.K.* 52°41N 1°49W 13 E6
Lichinga *Mozam.* 13°13S 35°11E 55 E4
Lichtenburg *S. Africa* 26°8S 26°8E 56 D4
Licking → *U.S.A.* 39°6N 84°30W 81 F11
Licungo → *Mozam.* 17°40S 37°15E 55 F4
Lida *Belarus* 53°53N 25°15E 17 B13
Lidköping *Sweden* 58°31N 13°7E 9 G15
Liebig, Mt. *Australia* 23°18S 131°22E 60 D5
Liechtenstein ■ *Europe* 47°8N 9°35E 20 C8
Liège *Belgium* 50°38N 5°35E 15 D5
Liège □ *Belgium* 50°32N 5°35E 15 D5
Liegnitz = Legnica *Poland* 51°12N 16°10E 16 C9
Lieksa *Finland* 63°18N 30°2E 8 E24
Lienart *Dem. Rep. of the Congo* 3°3N 25°31E 54 B2
Lienyünchiangshih = Lianyungang *China* 34°40N 119°11E 35 G10
Lienz *Austria* 46°50N 12°46E 16 E7
Liepāja *Latvia* 56°30N 21°0E 9 H19
Lier *Belgium* 51°7N 4°34E 15 C4
Lietuva = Lithuania ■ *Europe* 55°30N 24°0E 9 J21
Lièvre → *Canada* 45°31N 75°26W 72 C4
Liffey → *Ireland* 53°21N 6°13W 10 C5
Lifford *Ireland* 54°51N 7°29W 10 B4
Lifudzin *Russia* 44°21N 134°58E 30 B7
Lightning Ridge *Australia* 29°22S 148°0E 63 D4
Ligonha → *Mozam.* 16°54S 39°9E 55 F4
Ligonier *U.S.A.* 40°15N 79°14W 82 F5
Liguria □ *Italy* 44°30N 8°50E 20 D8
Ligurian Sea *Medit. S.* 43°20N 9°0E 22 C3
Lihou Reefs and Cays *Australia* 17°25S 151°40E 62 B5
Lihue *U.S.A.* 21°59N 159°23W 74 b
Lihué Calel △ *Argentina* 38°0S 65°10W 94 D2
Lijiang *China* 26°55N 100°20E 32 D5
Likasi *Dem. Rep. of the Congo* 10°55S 26°48E 55 E2
Likoma I. *Malawi* 12°3S 34°45E 55 E3
Likumburu *Tanzania* 9°43S 35°8E 55 D4
L'Île-Rousse *France* 42°38N 8°57E 20 E8
Lille *France* 50°38N 3°3E 20 A5
Lille Bælt *Denmark* 55°20N 9°45E 9 J13
Lillehammer *Norway* 61°8N 10°30E 8 F14
Lillesand *Norway* 58°15N 8°23E 9 G13
Lillian Pt. *Australia* 27°40S 126°6E 61 E4
Lillooet *Canada* 50°44N 121°57W 70 C4
Lillooet → *Canada* 49°15N 121°57W 70 D4
Lilongwe *Malawi* 14°0S 33°48E 55 E3
Liloy *Phil.* 8°4N 122°39E 37 C6
Lim → *Europe* 43°45N 19°15E 23 C8
Lim Chu Kang *Singapore* 1°26N 103°43E 39 d
Lima *Indonesia* 3°39S 127°58E 37 E7
Lima *Peru* 12°3S 77°2W 92 F3
Lima *Mont., U.S.A.* 44°38N 112°36W 76 D7
Lima *Ohio, U.S.A.* 40°44N 84°6W 81 E11
Lima → *Portugal* 41°41N 8°50W 21 B1
Liman *Indonesia* 7°48S 111°45E 37 G14
Limassol *Cyprus* 34°42N 33°1E 25 E12
Limavady *U.K.* 55°3N 6°56W 10 A5
Limay → *Argentina* 39°0S 68°0W 96 D3
Limay Mahuida *Argentina* 37°10S 66°45W 94 D2
Limbang *Brunei* 4°42N 115°6E 36 D5
Limbaži *Latvia* 57°31N 24°42E 9 H21
Limbdi *India* 22°34N 71°51E 42 H4
Limbe *Cameroon* 4°1N 9°10E 52 D1
Limburg *Germany* 50°22N 8°4E 16 C5
Limburg □ *Belgium* 51°2N 5°25E 15 C5
Limburg □ *Neths.* 51°20N 5°55E 15 C5
Limeira *Brazil* 22°35S 47°28W 95 A6
Limerick *Ireland* 52°40N 8°37W 10 D3
Limerick *U.S.A.* 43°41N 70°48W 83 C14

Limerick □ Ireland 52°30N 8°50W 10 D3
Limestone U.S.A. 42°2N 78°38W 82 D6
Limestone → Canada 56°31N 94°7W 71 B10
Limfjorden Denmark 56°55N 9°0E 9 H13
Limia = Lima → Portugal 41°41N 8°50W 21 B1
Limingen Norway 64°48N 13°35E 8 D15
Limmen Bight Australia 14°40S 135°35E 62 A2
Limmen Bight → Australia 15°7S 135°44E 62 B2
Limnos Greece 39°50N 25°5E 23 E11
Limoges Canada 45°20N 75°16W 83 A9
Limoges France 45°50N 1°15E 20 D4
Limón Costa Rica 10°0N 83°2W 88 E3
Limon U.S.A. 39°16N 103°41W 76 G12
Limousin □ France 45°30N 1°30E 20 D4
Limoux France 43°4N 2°12E 20 E5
Limpopo □ S. Africa 24°5S 29°0E 57 C4
Limpopo → Africa 25°5S 33°30E 57 D5
Limuru Kenya 1°2S 36°35E 54 C4
Lin Xian China 37°57N 110°58E 34 F6
Linares Chile 35°50S 71°40W 94 D1
Linares Mexico 24°52N 99°34W 87 C5
Linares Spain 38°10N 3°40W 21 C4
Lincheng China 37°25N 114°30E 34 F8
Lincoln Argentina 34°55S 61°30W 94 C3
Lincoln Canada 43°12N 79°29W 82 C5
Lincoln N.Z. 43°38S 172°30E 59 E4
Lincoln U.K. 53°14N 0°32W 12 D7
Lincoln Calif., U.S.A. 38°54N 121°17W 78 G5
Lincoln Ill., U.S.A. 40°9N 89°22W 80 E9
Lincoln Kans., U.S.A. 39°3N 98°9W 80 F4
Lincoln Maine, U.S.A. 45°22N 68°30W 81 C19
Lincoln N.H., U.S.A. 44°3N 71°40W 83 B13
Lincoln N. Mex., U.S.A. 33°30N 105°23W 77 K11
Lincoln Nebr., U.S.A. 40°49N 96°41W 80 E5
Lincoln City U.S.A. 44°57N 124°1W 76 D1
Lincoln Hav = Lincoln Sea Arctic 84°0N 55°0W 66 A14
Lincoln Sea Arctic 84°0N 55°0W 66 A14
Lincolnshire □ U.K. 53°14N 0°32W 12 D7
Lincolnshire Wolds U.K. 53°26N 0°13W 12 D7
Lincolnton U.S.A. 35°29N 81°16W 85 D14
Lind U.S.A. 46°58N 118°37W 76 C4
Linda U.S.A. 39°8N 121°34W 78 F5
Lindeman I. Australia 20°27S 149°3E 62 J7
Linden Guyana 6°0N 58°10W 92 B7
Linden Ala., U.S.A. 32°18N 87°48W 85 E11
Linden Calif., U.S.A. 38°1N 121°5W 78 G5
Linden Tex., U.S.A. 33°1N 94°22W 84 E7
Lindenhurst U.S.A. 40°41N 73°23W 83 F11
Lindesnes Norway 57°58N 7°3E 9 H12
Lindi Tanzania 9°58S 39°38E 55 D4
Lindi □ Tanzania 9°40S 38°30E 55 D4
Lindi → Dem. Rep. of the Congo 0°33N 25°5E 54 B2
Lindos Greece 36°6N 28°4E 25 C10
Lindos, Akra Greece 36°4N 28°10E 25 C10
Lindsay Canada 44°22N 78°43W 82 B6
Lindsay Calif., U.S.A. 36°12N 119°5W 78 J7
Lindsay Okla., U.S.A. 34°50N 97°38W 84 D6
Lindsborg U.S.A. 38°35N 97°40W 80 F5
Line Islands Pac. Oc. 7°0N 160°0W 69 H12
Linesville U.S.A. 41°39N 80°26W 82 E4
Linfen China 36°3N 111°30E 34 F6
Ling Xian China 37°22N 116°30E 34 F9
Lingao China 19°56N 109°42E 38 C7
Lingayen Phil. 16°1N 120°14E 37 A6
Lingayen G. Phil. 16°10N 120°15E 37 A6
Lingbi China 33°33N 117°33E 35 H9
Lingchuan China 35°45N 113°12E 34 G7
Lingding Yang China 22°25N 113°44E 33 G10
Lingen Germany 52°31N 7°19E 16 B4
Lingga Indonesia 0°12S 104°37E 36 E2
Lingga, Kepulauan Indonesia 0°10S 104°30E 36 E2
Lingga Arch. = Lingga, Kepulauan Indonesia 0°10S 104°30E 36 E2
Lingle U.S.A. 42°8N 104°21W 76 E11
Lingqiu China 39°28N 114°22E 34 E8
Lingshi China 36°48N 111°48E 34 F6
Lingshou China 38°20N 114°20E 34 E8
Lingshui China 18°27N 110°0E 38 C8
Lingtai China 35°0N 107°40E 34 G4
Linguère Senegal 15°25N 15°5W 50 E2
Lingwu China 38°6N 106°20E 34 E4
Lingyuan China 41°10N 119°15E 35 D10
Linhai China 28°50N 121°8E 33 D7
Linhares Brazil 19°25S 40°4W 93 G10
Linhe China 40°48N 107°20E 34 D4
Linjiang China 41°50N 127°0E 35 D14
Linköping Sweden 58°28N 15°36E 9 G16
Linkou China 45°15N 130°18E 35 B16
Linnhe, L. U.K. 56°36N 5°25W 11 E3
Linosa Medit. S. 35°51N 12°50E 22 G5
Linqi China 35°45N 113°52E 34 G7
Linqing China 36°50N 115°42E 34 F8
Linqu China 36°25N 118°30E 35 F10
Linru China 34°11N 112°52E 34 G7
Lins Brazil 21°40S 49°44W 95 A6
Linstead Jamaica 18°8N 77°2W 88 a
Linta → Madag. 25°2S 44°5E 57 D7
Linton Ind., U.S.A. 39°2N 87°10W 80 F10
Linton N. Dak., U.S.A. 46°16N 100°14W 80 B3
Lintong China 34°20N 109°10E 34 G5
Linwood Canada 43°35N 80°43W 82 C4
Linxi China 43°36N 118°2E 35 C10
Linxia China 35°36N 103°10E 32 C5
Linyanti → Africa 17°50S 25°5E 56 B4
Linyi China 35°5N 118°21E 35 G10
Linz Austria 48°18N 14°18E 16 D8
Linzhenzhen China 36°30N 109°59E 34 F5
Linzi China 36°50N 118°20E 35 F10
Lion, G. du France 43°10N 4°0E 20 E6
Lionárisso Cyprus 35°28N 34°8E 25 D13
Lions, G. of = Lion, G. du France 43°10N 4°0E 20 E6
Lion's Den Zimbabwe 17°15S 30°5E 55 F3
Lion's Head Canada 44°58N 81°15W 82 B3
Lipa Phil. 13°57N 121°10E 37 B6
Lipali Mozam. 15°50S 35°50E 55 F4
Lípari Italy 38°26N 14°58E 22 E6
Lípari, Is. = Eólie, Ís. Italy 38°30N 14°57E 22 E6
Lipcani Moldova 48°14N 26°48E 17 D14
Liperi Finland 62°31N 29°24E 8 E23
Lipetsk Russia 52°37N 39°35E 18 D6
Lipkany = Lipcani Moldova 48°14N 26°48E 17 D14
Lipovets Ukraine 49°12N 29°1E 17 D15
Lippe → Germany 51°39N 6°36E 16 C4
Lipscomb U.S.A. 36°14N 100°16W 84 C4
Liptrap, C. Australia 38°50S 145°55E 63 F4
Liquillo, Sierra de Puerto Rico 18°20N 65°47W 89 d
Lira Uganda 2°17N 32°57E 54 B3
Liria = Lliria Spain 39°37N 0°35W 21 C5
Lisala Dem. Rep. of the Congo 2°12N 21°38E 52 D4
Lisboa Portugal 38°42N 9°8W 21 C1
Lisbon = Lisboa Portugal 38°42N 9°8W 21 C1
Lisbon N. Dak., U.S.A. 46°27N 97°41W 80 B5
Lisbon N.H., U.S.A. 44°13N 71°55W 83 B13
Lisbon Ohio, U.S.A. 40°46N 80°46W 82 F4
Lisbon Falls U.S.A. 44°0N 70°4W 81 D18
Lisburn U.K. 54°31N 6°3W 10 B5
Lisburne, C. U.S.A. 68°53N 166°13W 4 C17
Liscannor B. Ireland 52°55N 9°24W 10 D2
Lisdoonvarna Ireland 53°2N 9°18W 10 C2
Lishi China 37°31N 111°8E 34 F6
Lishu China 43°20N 124°18E 35 C13
Lisianski I. U.S.A. 26°2N 174°0W 64 E10
Lisichansk = Lysychansk Ukraine 48°55N 38°30E 19 E6
Lisieux France 49°10N 0°12E 20 B4
Liski Russia 51°3N 39°30E 19 D6
Lismore Australia 28°44S 153°21E 63 D5
Lismore Ireland 52°8N 7°55W 10 D4
Lista Norway 58°7N 6°39E 9 G12
Lister, Mt. Antarctica 78°0S 162°0E 5 D11
Liston Australia 28°39S 152°6E 63 D5
Listowel Canada 43°44N 80°58W 82 C4
Listowel Ireland 52°27N 9°29W 10 D2
Litani → Lebanon 33°20N 35°15E 46 B4
Litchfield Calif., U.S.A. 40°24N 120°23W 78 E6
Litchfield Conn., U.S.A. 41°45N 73°11W 83 E11
Litchfield Ill., U.S.A. 39°11N 89°39W 80 F9
Litchfield Minn., U.S.A. 45°8N 94°32W 80 C6
Litchfield △ Australia 13°14S 131°1E 60 B5
Lithgow Australia 33°25S 150°8E 63 E5
Lithino, Akra Greece 34°55N 24°44E 25 E6
Lithuania ■ Europe 55°30N 24°0E 9 J21
Lititz U.S.A. 40°9N 76°18W 83 F8
Litoměřice Czech Rep. 50°33N 14°10E 16 C8
Little Abaco Bahamas 26°50N 77°30W 88 A4
Little Barrier I. N.Z. 36°12S 175°8E 59 B5
Little Belt Mts. U.S.A. 46°40N 110°45W 76 C8
Little Bighorn Battlefield ⌂ U.S.A. 45°34N 107°25W 76 D10
Little Blue → U.S.A. 39°42N 96°41W 80 F5
Little Buffalo → Canada 61°0N 113°46W 70 A6
Little Cayman Cayman Is. 19°41N 80°3W 88 C3
Little Churchill → Canada 57°30N 95°22W 71 B9
Little Colorado → U.S.A. 36°12N 111°48W 77 H8
Little Current Canada 45°55N 82°0W 72 C3
Little Current → Canada 50°57N 84°36W 72 B3
Little Falls Minn., U.S.A. 45°59N 94°22W 80 C6
Little Falls N.Y., U.S.A. 43°3N 74°51W 83 C10
Little Fork → U.S.A. 48°31N 93°35W 80 A7
Little Grand Rapids Canada 52°0N 95°29W 71 C9
Little Humboldt → U.S.A. 41°1N 117°43W 76 F5
Little Inagua I. Bahamas 21°40N 73°50W 89 B5
Little Karoo S. Africa 33°45S 21°0E 56 E3
Little Khingan Mts. = Xiao Hinggan Ling China 49°0N 127°0E 33 B7
Little Lake U.S.A. 35°56N 117°55W 79 K9
Little Laut Is. = Laut Kecil, Kepulauan Indonesia 4°45S 115°40E 36 E5
Little Mecatina = Petit-Mécatina → Canada 50°40N 59°30W 73 B8
Little Minch U.K. 57°35N 6°45W 11 D2
Little Missouri → U.S.A. 47°36N 102°25W 80 B2
Little Ouse → U.K. 52°22N 1°12E 13 E9
Little Rann India 23°25N 71°25E 42 H4
Little Red → U.S.A. 35°11N 91°27W 84 D9
Little River N.Z. 43°45S 172°49E 59 E4
Little Rock U.S.A. 34°45N 92°17W 84 D8
Little Ruaha → Tanzania 7°57S 37°53E 54 D4
Little Sable Pt. U.S.A. 43°38N 86°33W 80 D10
Little Sioux → U.S.A. 41°48N 96°4W 80 E5
Little Smoky → Canada 54°44N 117°11W 70 C5
Little Snake → U.S.A. 40°27N 108°26W 76 F9
Little Tobago Trin. & Tob. 11°18N 60°30W 93 J16
Little Valley U.S.A. 42°15N 78°48W 82 D6
Little Wabash → U.S.A. 37°55N 88°5W 80 G9
Little White → U.S.A. 43°40N 100°40W 80 D3
Little Zab = Zāb aş Şaghīr → Iraq 35°17N 43°29E 44 C4
Littlefield U.S.A. 33°55N 102°20W 84 E3
Littlehampton U.K. 50°49N 0°32W 13 G7
Littleton U.S.A. 44°18N 71°46W 83 B13
Liu He → China 40°55N 121°35E 35 D11
Liuba China 33°38N 106°55E 34 H4
Liugou China 40°57N 118°15E 35 D10
Liuhe China 42°17N 125°43E 35 C13
Liukang Tenggaja = Sabalana, Kepulauan Indonesia 6°45S 118°50E 37 F5
Liuli Tanzania 11°3S 34°38E 55 E3
Liupanshui China 26°38N 104°48E 32 D5
Liuwa Plain Zambia 14°20S 22°30E 53 G4
Liuzhou China 24°22N 109°22E 33 D5
Liuzhuang China 33°12N 120°18E 35 H11
Livadhia Cyprus 34°57N 33°38E 25 E12
Livadia Greece 38°27N 22°54E 23 E10
Live Oak Calif., U.S.A. 39°17N 121°40W 78 F5
Live Oak Fla., U.S.A. 30°18N 82°59W 85 F13
Lively Canada 46°26N 81°9W 81 B13
Liveras Cyprus 35°23N 32°57E 25 D11
Livermore U.S.A. 37°41N 121°47W 78 H5
Livermore, Mt. U.S.A. 30°38N 104°11W 84 F2
Livermore Falls U.S.A. 44°29N 70°11W 81 C18
Liverpool Canada 44°5N 64°41W 73 D7
Liverpool U.K. 53°25N 3°0W 12 D4
Liverpool U.S.A. 43°6N 76°13W 83 C8
Liverpool Bay U.K. 53°30N 3°20W 12 D4
Liverpool Ra. Australia 31°50S 150°30E 63 E5
Livingston Guatemala 15°50N 88°50W 88 C2
Livingston U.K. 55°54N 3°30W 11 F5
Livingston Ala., U.S.A. 32°35N 88°11W 85 E10
Livingston Calif., U.S.A. 37°23N 120°43W 78 H6
Livingston Mont., U.S.A. 45°40N 110°34W 76 D8
Livingston S.C., U.S.A. 33°38N 81°7W 85 E14
Livingston Tenn., U.S.A. 36°23N 85°19W 85 C12
Livingston Tex., U.S.A. 30°43N 94°56W 84 F7
Livingston, L. U.S.A. 30°50N 95°10W 84 F7
Livingston Manor U.S.A. 41°54N 74°50W 83 E10
Livingstone Zambia 17°46S 25°52E 55 F2
Livingstone Mts. Tanzania 9°40S 34°20E 55 D3
Livingstonia Malawi 10°38S 34°5E 55 E3
Livny Russia 52°30N 37°30E 18 D6
Livonia Mich., U.S.A. 42°23N 83°23W 81 D12
Livonia N.Y., U.S.A. 42°49N 77°40W 82 D7
Livorno Italy 43°33N 10°19E 22 C4
Livramento Brazil 30°55S 55°30W 95 C4
Liwale Tanzania 9°48S 37°58E 55 D4
Liwonde △ Malawi 14°48S 35°20E 55 E4
Lizard I. Australia 14°42S 145°30E 62 A4
Lizard Pt. U.K. 49°57N 5°13W 13 H2
Ljubljana Slovenia 46°4N 14°33E 16 E8
Ljungan → Sweden 62°18N 17°23E 8 E17
Ljungby Sweden 56°49N 13°55E 9 H15
Ljusdal Sweden 61°46N 16°3E 8 F17
Ljusnan → Sweden 61°12N 17°8E 8 F17
Ljusne Sweden 61°13N 17°7E 8 F17
Llancanelo, Salina Argentina 35°40S 69°8W 94 D2
Llandeilo U.K. 51°53N 3°59W 13 F4
Llandovery U.K. 51°59N 3°48W 13 F4
Llandrindod Wells U.K. 52°14N 3°22W 13 E4
Llandudno U.K. 53°19N 3°50W 12 D4
Llanelli U.K. 51°41N 4°10W 13 F3
Llanes Spain 43°25N 4°50W 21 A3
Llangollen U.K. 52°58N 3°11W 12 E4
Llanidloes U.K. 52°27N 3°31W 13 E4
Llano U.S.A. 30°45N 98°41W 84 F5
Llano → U.S.A. 30°39N 98°26W 84 F5
Llano Estacado U.S.A. 33°30N 103°0W 84 E3
Llanos S. Amer. 5°0N 71°35W 92 C4
Llanos de Challe △ Chile 28°8S 71°1W 94 B1
Llanquihue, L. Chile 41°10S 72°50W 96 E1
Llanwrtyd Wells U.K. 52°7N 3°38W 13 E4
Llebeig, C. des Spain 39°33N 2°18E 24 B9
Lleida Spain 41°37N 0°39E 21 B6
Llentrisca, C. Spain 38°52N 1°15E 24 C7
Llera de Canales Mexico 23°19N 99°1W 87 C5
Lleyn Peninsula U.K. 52°51N 4°36W 12 E3
Llico Chile 34°46S 72°5W 94 C1
Lliria Spain 39°37N 0°35W 21 C5
Llobregat → Spain 41°19N 2°5E 21 B7
Lloret de Mar Spain 41°41N 2°53E 21 B7
Lloyd B. Australia 12°45S 143°27E 62 A3
Lloyd L. Canada 57°22N 108°57W 71 B7
Lloydminster Canada 53°17N 110°0W 71 C7
Llucmajor Spain 39°29N 2°53E 24 B9
Llullaillaco, Volcán S. Amer. 24°43S 68°30W 94 A2
Llullaillaco △ Chile 24°50S 68°51W 94 A2
Lo → Vietnam 21°18N 105°25E 38 B5
Loa U.S.A. 38°24N 111°39W 76 G8
Loa → Chile 21°26S 70°41W 94 A1
Loaita I. S. China Sea 10°41N 114°25E 36 B4
Loange → Dem. Rep. of the Congo 4°17S 20°2E 52 E4
Lobatse Botswana 25°12S 25°40E 56 D4
Lobería Argentina 38°10S 58°40W 94 D4
Lobito Angola 12°18S 13°35E 53 G2
Lobos Argentina 35°10S 59°0W 94 D4
Lobos, I. Mexico 27°20N 110°36W 86 B2
Lobos, I. de Canary Is. 28°45N 13°50W 24 F6
Loc Binh Vietnam 21°46N 106°54E 38 B6
Loc Ninh Vietnam 11°50N 106°34E 39 G6
Locarno Switz. 46°10N 8°47E 20 C8
Loch Baghasdail = Lochboisdale U.K. 57°9N 7°20W 11 D1
Loch Garman = Wexford Ireland 52°20N 6°28W 10 D5
Loch Lomond and the Trossachs △ U.K. 56°10N 4°40W 11 E4
Loch Nam Madadh = Lochmaddy U.K. 57°36N 7°10W 11 D1
Lochaber U.K. 56°59N 5°1W 11 E3
Locharbriggs U.K. 55°7N 3°35W 11 F5
Lochboisdale U.K. 57°9N 7°20W 11 D1
Loche, L. La Canada 56°30N 109°30W 71 B7
Lochem Neths. 52°9N 6°26E 15 B6
Loches France 47°7N 1°0E 20 C4
Lochgilphead U.K. 56°2N 5°26W 11 E3
Lochinvar △ Zambia 15°55S 27°15E 55 F2
Lochinver U.K. 58°9N 5°14W 11 C3
Lochmaddy U.K. 57°36N 7°10W 11 D1
Lochnagar Australia 23°33S 145°38E 62 C4
Lochnagar U.K. 56°57N 3°15W 11 E5
Lochy, L. U.K. 57°0N 4°53W 11 E4
Lock Australia 33°34S 135°46E 63 E2
Lock Haven U.S.A. 41°8N 77°28W 82 E7
Lockeford U.S.A. 38°10N 121°9W 78 G5
Lockeport Canada 43°47N 65°4W 73 D6
Lockerbie U.K. 55°7N 3°21W 11 F5
Lockhart U.S.A. 29°53N 97°40W 84 G6
Lockhart, L. Australia 33°15S 119°3E 61 F2
Lockhart River Australia 12°58S 143°30E 62 A3
Lockney U.S.A. 34°7N 101°27W 84 D4
Lockport U.S.A. 43°10N 78°42W 82 C6
Lod Israel 31°57N 34°54E 46 D3
Lodeinoye Pole Russia 60°44N 33°33E 18 B5
Lodge Bay Canada 52°14N 55°51W 73 B8
Lodge Grass U.S.A. 45°19N 107°22W 76 D10
Lodhran Pakistan 29°32N 71°30E 42 E4
Lodi Italy 45°19N 9°30E 20 D8
Lodi Calif., U.S.A. 38°8N 121°16W 78 G5
Lodi Ohio, U.S.A. 41°2N 82°1W 82 E3
Lodja Dem. Rep. of the Congo 3°30S 23°23E 54 C1
Lodwar Kenya 3°7N 35°36E 54 B4
Łódź Poland 51°45N 19°27E 17 C10
Loei Thailand 17°29N 101°35E 38 D3
Loengo Dem. Rep. of the Congo 4°48S 26°30E 54 C2
Loeriesfontein S. Africa 31°0S 19°26E 56 E2
Lofoten Norway 68°30N 14°0E 8 B16
Logan Iowa, U.S.A. 41°39N 95°47W 80 E6
Logan Ohio, U.S.A. 39°32N 82°25W 81 F12
Logan Utah, U.S.A. 41°44N 111°50W 76 F8
Logan W. Va., U.S.A. 37°51N 81°59W 81 G13
Logan, Mt. Canada 60°44N 140°23W 68 C5
Logandale U.S.A. 36°36N 114°29W 79 J12
Logansport Ind., U.S.A. 40°45N 86°22W 80 E10
Logansport La., U.S.A. 31°58N 94°0W 84 F8
Logone → Chad 12°6N 15°2E 51 F9
Logroño Spain 42°28N 2°27W 21 A4
Lohardaga India 23°27N 84°45E 43 H11
Loharia India 23°45N 74°14E 42 H6
Loharu India 28°27N 75°49E 42 E6
Lohri Wah → Pakistan 27°27N 67°37E 42 F2
Loi-kaw Burma 19°40N 97°17E 41 K20
Loimaa Finland 60°50N 23°5E 8 F20
Loir → France 47°33N 0°32W 20 C3
Loire → France 47°16N 2°10W 20 C2
Loja Ecuador 3°59S 79°16W 92 D3
Loja Spain 37°10N 4°10W 21 D3
Loji = Kawasi Indonesia 1°38S 127°28E 37 E7
Lokandu Dem. Rep. of the Congo 2°30S 25°45E 54 C2
Lokeren Belgium 51°6N 3°59E 15 C3
Lokgwabe Botswana 24°10S 21°50E 56 C3
Lokichar Kenya 2°23N 35°40E 54 B4
Lokichokio Kenya 4°19N 34°13E 54 B3
Lokitaung Kenya 4°12N 35°48E 54 B4
Lokkan tekojärvi Finland 67°55N 27°35E 8 C22
Lokoja Nigeria 7°47N 6°45E 50 G7
Lokoro → Dem. Rep. of the Congo 1°43S 18°23E 52 E3
Lola, Mt. U.S.A. 39°26N 120°22W 78 F6
Lolgorien Kenya 1°14S 34°48E 54 C3
Loliondo Tanzania 2°2S 35°39E 54 C4
Lolland Denmark 54°45N 11°30E 9 J14
Lolo U.S.A. 46°45N 114°5W 76 C6
Lom Bulgaria 43°48N 23°12E 23 C10
Lom Kao Thailand 16°53N 101°14E 38 D3
Lom Sak Thailand 16°47N 101°15E 38 D3
Loma U.S.A. 47°56N 110°30W 76 C8
Loma Linda U.S.A. 34°3N 117°16W 79 L9
Lomaloma Fiji 17°17S 178°59W 59 a
Lomami → Dem. Rep. of the Congo 0°46N 24°16E 54 B1
Lomas de Zamóra Argentina 34°45S 58°24W 94 C4
Lombadina Australia 16°31S 122°54E 60 C3
Lombárdia □ Italy 45°40N 9°30E 20 D8
Lombardy = Lombárdia □ Italy 45°40N 9°30E 20 D8
Lomblen Indonesia 8°30S 123°32E 37 F6
Lombok Indonesia 8°45S 116°30E 36 F5
Lombok, Selat Indonesia 8°30S 115°50E 37 K18
Lomé Togo 6°9N 1°20E 50 G6
Lomela Dem. Rep. of the Congo 2°19S 23°15E 52 E4
Lomela → Dem. Rep. of the Congo 0°15S 20°40E 52 E4
Lommel Belgium 51°14N 5°19E 15 C5
Lomond Canada 50°24N 112°36W 70 C6
Lomond, L. U.K. 56°8N 4°38W 11 E4
Lomonosov Ridge Arctic 88°0N 140°0E 4 A
Lomphat Cambodia 13°30N 106°59E 38 F6
Lompobatang Indonesia 5°24S 119°56E 37 F5
Lompoc U.S.A. 34°38N 120°28W 79 L6
Łomża Poland 53°10N 22°2E 17 B12
Lon, Ko Thailand 7°47N 98°23E 39 a
Loncoche Chile 39°20S 72°50W 96 D2
Londa India 15°30N 74°30E 40 M9
Londiani Kenya 0°10S 35°33E 54 C4
London Canada 42°59N 81°15W 82 D3
London U.K. 51°30N 0°3W 13 F7
London Ky., U.S.A. 37°8N 84°5W 81 G11
London Ohio, U.S.A. 39°53N 83°27W 81 F12
London, Greater □ U.K. 51°36N 0°5W 13 F7
London Gatwick ✕ (LGW) U.K. 51°10N 0°11W 13 F7
London Heathrow ✕ (LHR) U.K. 51°28N 0°27W 13 F7
London Stansted ✕ (STN) U.K. 51°54N 0°14E 13 F8
Londonderry U.K. 55°0N 7°20W 10 B4
Londonderry □ U.K. 55°0N 7°20W 10 B4
Londonderry, C. Australia 13°45S 126°55E 60 B4
Londonderry, I. Chile 55°0S 71°0W 96 H2
Londres Argentina 27°43S 67°7W 96 B3
Londrina Brazil 23°18S 51°10W 95 A5
Lone Pine U.S.A. 36°36N 118°4W 78 J8
Lonely Mine Zimbabwe 19°30S 28°49E 57 B4
Long B. U.S.A. 33°35N 78°45W 85 E15
Long Beach Calif., U.S.A. 33°46N 118°11W 79 M8
Long Beach N.Y., U.S.A. 40°35N 73°39W 83 F11
Long Beach Wash., U.S.A. 46°21N 124°3W 78 D2
Long Branch U.S.A. 40°18N 74°0W 83 F11
Long Creek U.S.A. 44°43N 119°6W 76 D4
Long Eaton U.K. 52°53N 1°15W 12 E6
Long I. Australia 20°22S 148°51E 62 J6
Long I. Bahamas 23°20N 75°10W 89 B4
Long I. Canada 54°50N 79°20W 72 B4
Long I. Ireland 51°30N 9°34W 10 E2
Long I. U.S.A. 40°45N 73°30W 83 F11
Long Island Sd. U.S.A. 41°10N 73°0W 83 E12
Long L. Canada 49°30N 86°50W 72 C2
Long Lake U.S.A. 43°58N 74°25W 83 C10
Long Point B. Canada 42°40N 80°10W 82 D4
Long Prairie U.S.A. 45°59N 94°52W 80 C6
Long Prairie → U.S.A. 46°20N 94°36W 80 B6
Long Pt. Canada 42°35N 80°2W 82 D4
Long Range Mts. Canada 49°30N 57°30W 73 C8
Long Reef Australia 14°1S 125°48E 60 B4
Long Spruce Canada 56°24N 94°21W 71 B10
Long Str. = Longa, Proliv Russia 70°0N 175°0E 4 C16
Long Thanh Vietnam 10°47N 106°57E 39 G6
Long Xian China 34°55N 106°55E 34 G4
Long Xuyen Vietnam 10°19N 105°28E 39 G5
Longa, Proliv Russia 70°0N 175°0E 4 C16
Longbenton U.K. 55°1N 1°31W 12 B6
Longboat Key U.S.A. 27°23N 82°39W 85 H13
Longde China 35°30N 106°20E 34 G4
Longford Australia 41°32S 147°3E 63 G4
Longford Ireland 53°43N 7°49W 10 C4
Longford □ Ireland 53°42N 7°45W 10 C4
Longhua Guangdong, China 22°39N 114°0E 33 F11
Longhua Hebei, China 41°18N 117°45E 35 D9
Longido Tanzania 2°43S 36°42E 54 C4
Longiram Indonesia 0°5S 115°45E 36 E5
Longkou China 37°40N 120°18E 35 F11
Longlac Canada 49°45N 86°25W 72 C2
Longmeadow U.S.A. 42°3N 72°34W 83 D12
Longmont U.S.A. 40°10N 105°6W 76 F11
Longnawan Indonesia 1°51N 114°55E 36 D4
Longreach Australia 23°28S 144°14E 62 C3
Longueuil Canada 45°31N 73°29W 83 A11
Longview Tex., U.S.A. 32°30N 94°44W 84 E7
Longview Wash., U.S.A. 46°8N 122°57W 78 D4
Longxi China 34°53N 104°40E 34 G3
Longxue Dao China 22°41N 113°38E 33 F10
Longyearbyen Svalbard 78°13N 15°40E 4 B8
Lonoke U.S.A. 34°47N 91°57W 84 D9
Lonquimay Chile 38°26S 71°14W 96 D2
Lons-le-Saunier France 46°40N 5°31E 20 C6
Looe U.K. 50°22N 4°28W 13 G3
Lookout, C. Canada 55°18N 83°56W 72 A3
Lookout, C. U.S.A. 34°35N 76°32W 85 D16
Loolmalasin Tanzania 3°0S 35°53E 54 C4
Loon → Alta., Canada 57°8N 115°3W 70 B5
Loon → Man., Canada 55°53N 101°59W 71 B8
Loon Lake Canada 54°2N 109°10W 71 C7
Loongana Australia 30°52S 127°5E 61 F4
Loop Hd. Ireland 52°34N 9°56W 10 D2
Lop China 37°3N 80°11E 32 C3
Lop Buri Thailand 14°48N 100°37E 38 E3
Lop Nor = Lop Nur China 40°20N 90°10E 32 B4
Lop Nur China 40°20N 90°10E 32 B4
Lopatina, Gora Russia 50°47N 143°10E 29 D15
Lopez U.S.A. 41°27N 76°20W 83 E8
Lopez, C. Gabon 0°47S 8°40E 52 E1
Lopphavet Norway 70°27N 21°15E 8 A19
Lora → Afghan. 31°35N 66°32E 40 D4
Lora, Hāmūn-i- Pakistan 29°38N 64°58E 40 E4
Lora Cr. → Australia 28°10S 135°22E 63 D2
Lora del Río Spain 37°39N 5°33W 21 D3
Lorain U.S.A. 41°28N 82°11W 82 E2
Loralai Pakistan 30°20N 68°41E 42 D3
Lorca Spain 37°41N 1°42W 21 D5
Lord Howe I. Pac. Oc. 31°33S 159°6E 58 E8
Lord Howe Rise Pac. Oc. 30°0S 162°30E 64 L8
Lordsburg U.S.A. 32°21N 108°43W 77 K9
Lorestān □ Iran 33°30N 48°40E 45 C6
Loreto Brazil 7°5S 45°10W 93 E9
Loreto Mexico 26°0N 111°21W 86 B2
Lorient France 47°45N 3°23W 20 C2
Lormi India 22°17N 81°41E 43 H9
Lorn U.K. 56°26N 5°10W 11 E3
Lorn, Firth of U.K. 56°20N 5°40W 11 E3
Lorne Australia 38°33S 143°59E 63 F3
Lorovouno Cyprus 35°8N 32°36E 25 D11
Lorraine □ France 48°53N 6°0E 20 B7
Los Alamos Calif., U.S.A. 34°44N 120°17W 79 L6
Los Alamos N. Mex., U.S.A. 35°53N 106°19W 77 J10
Los Altos U.S.A. 37°23N 122°7W 78 H4
Los Andes Chile 32°50S 70°40W 94 C1
Los Angeles Chile 37°28S 72°23W 94 D1
Los Angeles U.S.A. 34°4N 118°15W 79 M8
Los Angeles, Bahia de Mexico 28°56N 113°34W 86 B2

Los Angeles Aqueduct
  U.S.A. 35°22N 118°5W **79** K9
Los Angeles Int. ✈ (LAX)
  U.S.A. 33°57N 118°25W **79** M8
Los Banos U.S.A. 37°4N 120°51W **78** H6
Los Blancos Argentina 23°40S 62°30W **94** A3
Los Cardones △
  Argentina 25°8S 65°55W **94** B2
Los Chiles Costa Rica 11°2N 84°43W **88** D3
Los Cristianos Canary Is. 28°3N 16°42W **24** F3
Los Gatos U.S.A. 37°14N 121°59W **78** H5
Los Haïtises △ Dom. Rep. 19°4N 69°36W **89** C6
Los Hermanos Is.
  Venezuela 11°45N 64°25W **89** D7
Los Islotes Canary Is. 29°4N 13°44W **24** E6
Los Llanos de Aridane
  Canary Is. 28°38N 17°54W **24** F2
Los Loros Chile 27°50S 70°6W **94** B1
Los Lunas U.S.A. 34°48N 106°44W **77** J10
Los Mochis Mexico 25°45N 108°57W **86** B3
Los Olivos U.S.A. 34°40N 120°7W **79** L6
Los Palacios Cuba 22°35N 83°15W **88** B3
Los Reyes de Salgado
  Mexico 19°35N 102°29W **86** D4
Los Roques Is.
  Venezuela 11°50N 66°45W **89** D6
Los Teques Venezuela 10°21N 67°2W **92** A5
Los Testigos, Is.
  Venezuela 11°23N 63°6W **92** A6
Los Vilos Chile 32°10S 71°30W **94** C1
Lošinj Croatia 44°30N 14°30E **16** F8
Loskop Dam S. Africa 25°23S 29°20E **57** D4
Lossiemouth U.K. 57°42N 3°17W **11** D5
Lostwithiel U.K. 50°24N 4°41W **13** G3
Lot → France 44°18N 0°20E **20** D4
Lota Chile 37°5S 73°10W **94** D1
Lotfābād Iran 37°32N 59°20E **45** B8
Lothair S. Africa 26°22S 30°27E **57** D5
Lotta → Europe 68°42N 31°6E **8** B24
Loubomo Congo 4°9S 12°47E **52** E2
Loudonville U.S.A. 40°38N 82°14W **82** F2
Louga Senegal 15°45N 16°5W **50** E2
Loughborough U.K. 52°47N 1°11W **12** E6
Lougheed I. Canada 77°26N 105°6W **69** B9
Loughrea Ireland 53°12N 8°33W **10** C3
Loughros More B.
  Ireland 54°48N 8°32W **10** B3
Louis Trichardt S. Africa 23°1S 29°43E **57** C4
Louis XIV, Pte. Canada 54°37N 79°45W **72** B4
Louisa U.S.A. 38°7N 82°36W **81** F12
Louisbourg Canada 45°55N 60°0W **73** C8
Louisburgh Ireland 53°46N 9°49W **10** C2
Louise I. Canada 52°55N 131°50W **70** C2
Louiseville Canada 46°20N 72°56W **72** C5
Louisiade Arch.
  Papua N. G. 11°10S 153°0E **58** C8
Louisiana U.S.A. 39°27N 91°3W **80** F8
Louisiana □ U.S.A. 30°50N 92°0W **84** F9
Louisville Ky., U.S.A. 38°15N 85°46W **81** F11
Louisville Miss., U.S.A. 33°7N 89°3W **85** E10
Louisville Ohio, U.S.A. 40°50N 81°16W **82** F3
Louisville Ridge
  Pac. Oc. 31°0S 172°30W **64** L10
Loulé Portugal 37°9N 8°0W **21** D1
Loup City U.S.A. 41°17N 98°58W **80** E4
Loups Marins, Lacs des
  Canada 56°30N 73°45W **72** A5
Lourdes France 43°6N 0°3W **20** E3
Lourdes-de-Blanc-Sablon
  Canada 51°24N 57°12W **73** B8
Louth Australia 30°30S 145°8E **63** E4
Louth Ireland 53°58N 6°32W **10** C5
Louth U.K. 53°22N 0°1W **12** D7
Louth □ Ireland 53°56N 6°34W **10** C5
Louvain = Leuven
  Belgium 50°52N 4°42E **15** D4
Louwsburg S. Africa 27°37S 31°7E **57** D5
Lovech Bulgaria 43°8N 24°42E **23** C11
Loveland U.S.A. 40°24N 105°5W **76** F11
Lovell U.S.A. 44°50N 108°24W **76** D9
Lovelock U.S.A. 40°11N 118°28W **76** F4
Loviisa Finland 60°28N 26°12E **8** F22
Loving U.S.A. 32°17N 104°6W **77** K11
Lovington U.S.A. 32°57N 103°21W **77** K12
Lovisa = Loviisa Finland 60°28N 26°12E **8** F22
Low, L. Canada 52°29N 76°17W **72** B4
Low Pt. Australia 32°25S 127°25E **61** F4
Low Tatra = Nízké Tatry
  Slovak Rep. 48°55N 19°30E **17** D10
Lowa
  Dem. Rep. of the Congo 1°25S 25°47E **54** C2
Lowa →
  Dem. Rep. of the Congo 1°24S 25°51E **54** C2
Lowell U.S.A. 42°38N 71°19W **83** D13
Lowellville U.S.A. 41°2N 80°32W **82** E4
Löwen → Namibia 26°51S 18°17E **56** D2
Lower Alkali L. U.S.A. 41°16N 120°2W **76** F3
Lower Arrow L. Canada 49°40N 118°5W **70** D5
Lower California = Baja
  California Mexico 31°10N 115°12W **86** A1
Lower Hutt N.Z. 41°10S 174°55E **59** D5
Lower Lake U.S.A. 38°55N 122°37W **78** G4
Lower Manitou L.
  Canada 49°15N 93°0W **71** D10
Lower Post Canada 59°58N 128°30W **70** B3
Lower Red L. U.S.A. 48°0N 94°50W **80** B6
Lower Saxony = Niedersachsen □
  Germany 52°50N 9°0E **16** B5
Lower Tunguska = Tunguska,
  Nizhnyaya → Russia 65°48N 88°4E **29** C9
Lower Zambezi △
  Zambia 15°25S 29°40E **55** F2
Lowestoft U.K. 52°29N 1°45E **13** E9
Lowgar □ Afghan. 34°0N 69°0E **40** B6
Łowicz Poland 52°6N 19°55E **17** B10
Lowville U.S.A. 43°47N 75°29W **83** C9
Loxton Australia 34°28S 140°31E **63** E3

Loxton S. Africa 31°30S 22°22E **56** E3
Loyalton U.S.A. 39°41N 120°14W **78** F6
Loyalty Is. = Loyauté, Îs.
  N. Cal. 20°50S 166°30E **58** D9
Loyang = Luoyang
  China 34°40N 112°26E **34** G7
Loyauté, Îs. N. Cal. 20°50S 166°30E **58** D9
Loyev = Loyew Belarus 51°56N 30°46E **17** C16
Loyew Belarus 51°56N 30°46E **17** C16
Loyoro Uganda 3°22N 34°14E **54** B3
Lu Wo China 22°33N 114°6E **33** F11
Luachimo Angola 7°23S 20°48E **52** F4
Luajan → India 24°44N 85°1E **43** G11
Lualaba →
  Dem. Rep. of the Congo 0°26N 25°20E **54** B2
Luampa Zambia 15°4S 24°20E **55** F1
Luan Chau Vietnam 21°38N 103°24E **38** B4
Luan He → China 39°20N 119°5E **35** E10
Luan Xian China 39°40N 118°40E **35** E10
Luancheng China 37°53N 114°40E **34** F8
Luanda Angola 8°50S 13°15E **52** F2
Luang, Thale Thailand 7°30N 100°15E **39** J3
Luang Prabang Laos 19°52N 102°10E **38** C4
Luangwa Zambia 15°35S 30°16E **55** F3
Luangwa → Zambia 14°25S 30°25E **55** E3
Luangwa Valley Zambia 13°30S 31°30E **55** E3
Luanne China 40°55N 117°40E **35** D9
Luanping China 40°53N 117°23E **35** D9
Luanshya Zambia 13°3S 28°28E **55** E2
Luapula □ Zambia 11°0S 29°0E **55** E2
Luapula → Africa 9°26S 28°33E **55** D2
Luarca Spain 43°32N 6°32W **21** A2
Luashi
  Dem. Rep. of the Congo 10°50S 23°36E **55** E1
Luau Angola 10°40S 22°10E **52** G4
Lubana, Ozero = Lubānas Ezers
  Latvia 56°45N 27°0E **9** H22
Lubānas Ezers Latvia 56°45N 27°0E **9** H22
Lubang Is. Phil. 13°50N 120°12E **37** B6
Lubango Angola 14°55S 13°30E **53** G2
Lubao
  Dem. Rep. of the Congo 5°17S 25°42E **54** D2
Lubbock U.S.A. 33°35N 101°51W **84** E4
Lübeck Germany 53°52N 10°40E **16** B6
Lubefu
  Dem. Rep. of the Congo 4°47S 24°27E **54** C1
Lubefu →
  Dem. Rep. of the Congo 4°10S 23°0E **54** C1
Lubero = Luofu
  Dem. Rep. of the Congo 0°1S 29°15E **54** C2
Lubicon L. Canada 56°23N 115°56W **70** B5
Lubilash →
  Dem. Rep. of the Congo 6°2S 23°45E **52** F4
Lubin Poland 51°24N 16°11E **16** C9
Lublin Poland 51°12N 22°38E **17** C12
Lubnān = Lebanon ■
  Asia 34°0N 36°0E **46** B5
Lubnān, Jabal Lebanon 33°45N 35°40E **46** B4
Lubny Ukraine 50°3N 32°58E **28** D4
Lubongola
  Dem. Rep. of the Congo 2°35S 27°50E **54** C2
Lubudi
  Dem. Rep. of the Congo 9°57S 25°58E **52** F5
Lubudi →
  Dem. Rep. of the Congo 9°0S 25°35E **55** D2
Lubuklinggau Indonesia 3°15S 102°55E **36** E2
Lubuksikaping
  Indonesia 0°10N 100°15E **36** D2
Lubumbashi
  Dem. Rep. of the Congo 11°40S 27°28E **55** E2
Lubunda
  Dem. Rep. of the Congo 5°12S 26°41E **54** D2
Lubungu Zambia 14°35S 26°24E **55** E2
Lubutu
  Dem. Rep. of the Congo 0°45S 26°30E **54** C2
Luc An Chau Vietnam 22°6N 104°43E **38** A5
Lucan Canada 43°11N 81°24W **82** C3
Lucania, Mt. Canada 61°1N 140°27W **68** C5
Lucas Channel Canada 45°21N 81°45W **82** A3
Lucca Italy 43°50N 10°29E **22** C4
Luce Bay U.K. 54°45N 4°48W **11** G4
Lucea Jamaica 18°27N 78°10W **88** a
Lucedale U.S.A. 30°56N 88°35W **85** F10
Lucena Phil. 13°56N 121°37E **37** B6
Lucena Spain 37°27N 4°31W **21** D3
Lučenec Slovak Rep. 48°18N 19°42E **17** D10
Lucerne = Luzern Switz. 47°3N 8°18E **20** C8
Lucerne U.S.A. 39°6N 122°48W **78** F4
Lucerne Valley
  U.S.A. 34°27N 116°57W **79** L10
Lucero Mexico 30°49N 106°30W **86** A3
Lucheng China 36°20N 113°11E **34** F7
Lucheringo → Mozam. 11°43S 36°17E **55** E4
Lucia U.S.A. 36°2N 121°33W **78** J5
Lucinda Australia 18°32S 146°20E **62** B4
Luckenwalde Germany 52°5N 13°10E **16** B7
Luckhoff S. Africa 29°44S 24°43E **56** D3
Lucknow Canada 43°57N 81°31W **82** C3
Lucknow India 26°50N 81°0E **43** F9
Lüda = Dalian China 38°50N 121°40E **35** E11
Lüderitz Namibia 26°41S 15°8E **56** D2
Lüderitzbaai Namibia 26°36S 15°8E **56** D2
Ludhiana India 30°57N 75°56E **42** D6
Ludington U.S.A. 43°57N 86°27W **80** D10
Ludlow U.K. 52°22N 2°42W **13** E5
Ludlow Calif., U.S.A. 34°43N 116°10W **79** L10
Ludlow Pa., U.S.A. 41°43N 78°56W **82** E6
Ludlow Vt., U.S.A. 43°24N 72°42W **83** C12
Ludvika Sweden 60°8N 15°14E **9** F16
Ludwigsburg Germany 48°53N 9°11E **16** D5
Ludwigshafen Germany 49°29N 8°26E **16** D5
Lueki
  Dem. Rep. of the Congo 3°20S 25°48E **54** C2
Luena
  Dem. Rep. of the Congo 9°28S 25°43E **55** D2
Luena Zambia 10°40S 30°25E **55** E3
Luena Flats Zambia 14°47S 23°17E **53** G4

Luenha = Ruenya →
  Africa 16°24S 33°48E **55** F3
Lüeyang China 33°22N 106°10E **34** H4
Lufira →
  Dem. Rep. of the Congo 9°30S 27°0E **55** D2
Lufkin U.S.A. 31°21N 94°44W **84** F7
Lufupa
  Dem. Rep. of the Congo 10°37S 24°56E **55** E1
Luga Russia 58°40N 29°55E **9** G23
Lugano Switz. 46°1N 8°57E **20** C8
Lugansk = Luhansk
  Ukraine 48°38N 39°15E **19** E6
Lugard's Falls Kenya 3°6S 38°41E **54** C4
Lugela Mozam. 16°25S 36°43E **55** F4
Lugenda → Mozam. 11°25S 38°33E **55** E4
Lugh Ganana Somali Rep. 3°48N 42°34E **47** G3
Lugnaquillia Ireland 52°58N 6°28W **10** D5
Lugo Italy 44°25N 11°54E **22** B4
Lugo Spain 43°2N 7°35W **21** A2
Lugoj Romania 45°42N 21°57E **17** F11
Lugovoy = Qulan
  Kazakhstan 42°55N 72°43E **28** E8
Luhansk Ukraine 48°38N 39°15E **19** E6
Lui → Zambia 8°21S 17°33E **52** F3
Luiana Angola 17°25S 22°59E **56** B3
Luiana → Angola 17°24S 23°3E **53** H4
Luichow Pen. = Leizhou Bandao
  China 21°0N 110°0E **33** D6
Luimneach = Limerick
  Ireland 52°40N 8°37W **10** D3
Luing U.K. 56°14N 5°39W **11** E3
Luís Correia Brazil 3°0S 41°35W **93** D10
Luitpold Coast Antarctica 78°30S 32°0W **5** D1
Luiza
  Dem. Rep. of the Congo 7°40S 22°30E **52** F4
Luizi Dem. Rep. of the Congo 6°0S 27°25E **54** D2
Luján Argentina 34°45S 59°5W **94** C4
Lukanga Swamp
  Zambia 14°30S 27°40E **55** E2
Lukenie →
  Dem. Rep. of the Congo 3°0S 18°50E **52** E3
Lukhisaral India 25°11N 86°5E **43** G12
Lukolela
  Dem. Rep. of the Congo 5°23S 24°32E **54** D1
Lukosi Zimbabwe 18°30S 26°30E **55** F2
Łuków Poland 51°55N 22°23E **17** C12
Lukusuzi △ Zambia 12°43S 32°36E **55** E3
Luleå Sweden 65°35N 22°10E **8** D20
Luleälven → Sweden 65°35N 22°10E **8** D20
Lüleburgaz Turkey 41°23N 27°22E **23** D12
Luling U.S.A. 29°41N 97°39W **84** G6
Lulong China 39°53N 118°51E **35** E10
Lulonga →
  Dem. Rep. of the Congo 1°0N 18°10E **52** D3
Lulua →
  Dem. Rep. of the Congo 4°30S 20°30E **52** E4
Luma Amer. Samoa 14°16S 169°33W **59** b
Lumajang Indonesia 8°8S 113°13E **37** H15
Lumbala N'guimbo
  Angola 14°18S 21°18E **53** G4
Lumberton U.S.A. 34°37N 79°0W **85** D15
Lumholtz △ Australia 18°15S 145°32E **62** B4
Lumsden Canada 50°39N 104°52W **71** C8
Lumsden N.Z. 45°44S 168°27E **59** F2
Lumut Malaysia 4°13N 100°37E **39** K3
Lumut, Tanjung
  Indonesia 3°50S 105°58E **36** E3
Luna India 23°43N 69°16E **42** H3
Lunavada India 23°8N 73°37E **42** H5
Lund Sweden 55°44N 13°12E **9** J15
Lundazi Zambia 12°20S 33°7E **55** E3
Lundi → Zimbabwe 21°43S 32°34E **55** G3
Lundu Malaysia 1°40N 109°50E **36** D3
Lundy U.K. 51°10N 4°41W **13** F3
Lune → U.K. 54°0N 2°51W **12** C5
Lüneburg Germany 53°15N 10°24E **16** B6
Lüneburg Heath = Lüneburger
  Heide Germany 53°10N 10°12E **16** B6
Lüneburger Heide
  Germany 53°10N 10°12E **16** B6
Lunenburg Canada 44°22N 64°18W **73** D7
Lunéville France 48°36N 6°30E **20** B7
Lunga → Zambia 14°34S 26°25E **55** E2
Lunga Lunga Kenya 4°33S 39°7E **54** C4
Lunglei India 22°55N 92°45E **41** H18
Luni India 26°0N 73°6E **42** G5
Luni → India 24°41N 71°14E **42** G4
Luninets = Luninyets
  Belarus 52°15N 26°50E **17** B14
Luning U.S.A. 38°30N 118°11W **76** G4
Luninyets Belarus 52°15N 26°50E **17** B14
Lunkaransar India 28°29N 73°44E **42** E5
Lunsemfwa → Zambia 14°54S 30°12E **55** E3
Lunsemfwa Falls Zambia 14°30S 29°6E **55** E2
Luo He → China 34°35N 110°20E **34** G6
Luochuan China 35°45N 109°26E **34** G5
Luofu
  Dem. Rep. of the Congo 0°10S 29°15E **54** C2
Luohe China 33°32N 114°2E **34** H8
Luonan China 34°5N 110°10E **34** G6
Luoning China 34°35N 111°40E **34** G6
Luoyang China 34°40N 112°26E **34** G7
Luozigou China 43°42N 130°18E **35** C16
Lupilichi Mozam. 11°47S 35°13E **55** E4
Luque Paraguay 25°19S 57°25W **94** B4
Luray U.S.A. 38°40N 78°28W **81** F14
Lurgan U.K. 54°28N 6°19W **10** B5
Lusaka Zambia 15°28S 28°16E **55** F2
Lusambo
  Dem. Rep. of the Congo 4°58S 23°28E **54** C1
Lusangaye
  Dem. Rep. of the Congo 4°54S 26°0E **54** C2
Luseland Canada 52°5N 109°24W **71** C7
Lusenga Plain △ Zambia 9°5S 29°14E **55** D2
Lushan China 33°45N 112°55E **34** H7
Lushi China 34°3N 111°3E **34** G6

Lushnjë Albania 40°55N 19°41E **23** D8
Lushoto Tanzania 4°47S 38°20E **54** C4
Lushun China 38°45N 121°15E **35** E11
Lusk U.S.A. 42°46N 104°27W **76** E11
Lūt, Dasht-e Iran 31°30N 58°0E **45** D8
Luta = Dalian China 38°50N 121°40E **35** E11
Lutherstadt Wittenberg
  Germany 51°53N 12°39E **16** C7
Luton U.K. 51°53N 0°24W **13** F7
Luton □ U.K. 51°53N 0°24W **13** F7
Łutselk'e Canada 62°24N 110°44W **71** A6
Lutsk Ukraine 50°50N 25°15E **17** C13
Lutto = Lotta → Europe 68°42N 31°6E **8** B24
Lützow Holmbukta
  Antarctica 69°10S 37°30E **5** C4
Lutzputs S. Africa 28°3S 20°40E **56** D3
Luuq = Lugh Ganana
  Somali Rep. 3°48N 42°34E **47** G3
Luverne Ala., U.S.A. 31°43N 86°16W **85** F11
Luverne Minn., U.S.A. 43°39N 96°13W **80** D5
Luvua
  Dem. Rep. of the Congo 8°48S 25°17E **55** D2
Luvua →
  Dem. Rep. of the Congo 6°50S 27°30E **54** D2
Luvuvhu → S. Africa 22°25S 31°18E **57** C5
Luwegu → Tanzania 8°31S 37°23E **55** D4
Luwuk Indonesia 0°56S 122°47E **37** E6
Luxembourg Lux. 49°37N 6°9E **15** E6
Luxembourg □ Belgium 49°58N 5°30E **15** E5
Luxembourg ■ Europe 49°45N 6°0E **15** E5
Luxembourg ✈ (LUX)
  Lux. 49°37N 6°10E **15** E6
Luxi China 24°27N 98°36E **32** D4
Luxor = El Uqsur Egypt 25°41N 32°38E **51** C12
Luyi China 33°50N 115°35E **34** H8
Luyi Russia 60°39N 47°10E **18** B8
Luzern Switz. 47°3N 8°18E **20** C8
Luzhou China 28°52N 105°20E **32** D5
Luziânia Brazil 16°20S 48°0W **93** G9
Luzon Phil. 16°0N 121°0E **37** A6
Lviv Ukraine 49°50N 24°0E **17** D13
Lvov = Lviv Ukraine 49°50N 24°0E **17** D13
Lyakhavichy Belarus 53°2N 26°32E **17** B14
Lyakhovskiye, Ostrova
  Russia 73°40N 141°0E **29** B15
Lyal I. Canada 44°57N 81°24W **82** B3
Lybster U.K. 58°18N 3°15W **11** C5
Lycksele Sweden 64°38N 18°40E **8** D18
Lydda = Lod Israel 31°57N 34°54E **46** D3
Lyddan I. Antarctica 74°0S 21°0W **5** D2
Lydenburg S. Africa 25°10S 30°29E **57** D5
Lydia Turkey 38°48N 28°19E **23** E13
Lyell N.Z. 41°48S 172°4E **59** D4
Lyell I. Canada 52°40N 131°35W **70** C2
Lyepyel Belarus 54°50N 28°40E **9** J23
Lykens U.S.A. 40°34N 76°42W **83** F8
Lyman U.S.A. 41°20N 110°18W **76** F8
Lyme B. U.K. 50°42N 2°53W **13** G4
Lyme Regis U.K. 50°43N 2°57W **13** G5
Lymington U.K. 50°45N 1°32W **13** G6
Łyna → Poland 54°37N 21°14E **17** A11
Lynchburg U.S.A. 37°25N 79°9W **81** G14
Lynd → Australia 16°28S 143°18E **62** B3
Lynd Ra. Australia 25°30S 149°20E **63** D4
Lynden Canada 43°14N 80°9W **82** C4
Lynden U.S.A. 48°57N 122°27W **78** B4
Lyndhurst Australia 30°15S 138°18E **63** E2
Lyndon → Australia 23°29S 114°6E **61** D1
Lyndonville N.Y.,
  U.S.A. 43°20N 78°23W **82** C6
Lyndonville Vt., U.S.A. 44°31N 72°1W **83** B12
Lyngen Norway 69°45N 20°30E **8** B19
Lynher Reef Australia 15°27S 121°55E **60** C3
Lynn U.S.A. 42°28N 70°57W **83** D14
Lynn Haven U.S.A. 30°15N 85°39W **85** F12
Lynn Lake Canada 56°51N 101°3W **71** B8
Lynnwood U.S.A. 47°49N 122°18W **78** C4
Lynton U.K. 51°13N 3°50W **13** F4
Lyntupy Belarus 55°4N 26°23E **9** J22
Lynx L. Canada 62°25N 106°15W **71** A7
Lyon France 45°46N 4°50E **20** D6
Lyonnais France 45°45N 4°15E **20** D6
Lyons = Lyon France 45°46N 4°50E **20** D6
Lyons Ga., U.S.A. 32°12N 82°19W **85** E13
Lyons Kans., U.S.A. 38°21N 98°12W **80** F4
Lyons N.Y., U.S.A. 43°5N 77°0W **82** C8
Lyons → Australia 25°2S 115°9E **61** E2
Lyons Falls U.S.A. 43°37N 75°22W **83** C9
Lys = Leie → Belgium 51°2N 3°45E **15** C3
Lysva Russia 58°7N 57°49E **18** C10
Lysychansk Ukraine 48°55N 38°30E **19** E6
Lytham St. Anne's U.K. 53°45N 3°0W **12** D4
Lyttelton N.Z. 43°35S 172°44E **59** E4
Lytton Canada 50°13N 121°31W **70** C4
Lyubertsy Russia 55°40N 37°51E **18** C6
Lyuboml Ukraine 51°11N 24°4E **17** C13

M

Ma → Vietnam 19°47N 105°56E **38** C5
Ma'adaba Jordan 30°43N 35°47E **46** D4
Maamba Zambia 17°17S 26°28E **56** B4
Ma'ān Jordan 30°12N 35°44E **46** E4
Ma'ān □ Jordan 30°0N 36°0E **46** F5
Maanselkä Finland 63°52N 28°32E **8** E23
Ma'anshan China 31°44N 118°29E **33** C6
Maarianhamina = Mariehamn
  Finland 60°5N 19°55E **9** F18
Ma'arrat an Nu'mān
  Syria 35°43N 36°43E **44** C3
Maas → Neths. 51°45N 4°32E **15** C4
Maaseik Belgium 51°6N 5°45E **15** C5
Maasin Phil. 10°8N 124°50E **37** B6
Maastricht Neths. 50°50N 5°40E **15** D5
Maave Mozam. 21°4S 34°47E **57** C5
Mababe Depression
  Botswana 18°50S 24°15E **56** B3

Mabalane Mozam. 23°37S 32°31E **57** C5
Mabel L. Canada 50°35N 118°43W **70** C5
Mabenge
  Dem. Rep. of the Congo 4°15N 24°12E **54** B1
Maberly Canada 44°50N 76°32W **83** B8
Mablethorpe U.K. 53°20N 0°15E **12** D8
Maboma
  Dem. Rep. of the Congo 2°30N 28°10E **54** B2
Mabuasehube △
  Botswana 25°5S 21°10E **56** D3
Mac Bac Vietnam 9°46N 106°7E **39** H6
Macachín Argentina 37°10S 63°43W **94** D3
Macaé Brazil 22°20S 41°43W **95** A7
McAlester U.S.A. 34°56N 95°46W **84** D7
McAllen U.S.A. 26°12N 98°14W **84** H5
MacAlpine L. Canada 66°32N 102°45W **68** C12
Macamic Canada 48°45N 79°0W **72** C4
Macao = Macau
  China 22°12N 113°33E **33** G10
Macapá Brazil 0°5N 51°4W **93** C8
Macarao △ Venezuela 10°22N 67°7W **89** D6
McArthur → Australia 15°54S 136°40E **62** B2
McArthur, Port
  Australia 16°4S 136°23E **62** B2
Macau Brazil 5°15S 36°40W **93** E11
Macau China 22°12N 113°33E **33** G10
McBride Canada 53°20N 120°19W **70** C4
McCall U.S.A. 44°55N 116°6W **76** D5
McCamey U.S.A. 31°8N 102°14W **84** F3
McCammon U.S.A. 42°39N 112°12W **76** E7
McCarran Int., Las Vegas ✈ (LAS)
  U.S.A. 36°5N 115°9W **79** J11
McCauley I. Canada 53°40N 130°15W **70** C2
McCleary U.S.A. 47°3N 123°16W **78** C3
Macclenny U.S.A. 30°17N 82°7W **85** F13
Macclesfield U.K. 53°15N 2°8W **12** D5
M'Clintock Chan.
  Canada 72°0N 102°0W **68** B9
McClintock Ra.
  Australia 18°44S 127°38E **60** C4
McCloud U.S.A. 41°15N 122°8W **76** F2
McCluer I. Australia 11°5S 133°0E **60** B5
McClure U.S.A. 40°42N 77°19W **82** F7
McClure, L. U.S.A. 37°35N 120°16W **78** H6
M'Clure Str. Canada 75°0N 119°0W **69** B8
McClusky U.S.A. 47°29N 100°27W **80** B3
McComb U.S.A. 31°15N 90°27W **85** F9
McCook U.S.A. 40°12N 100°38W **80** E3
McCreary Canada 50°47N 99°29W **71** C9
McCullough Mt.
  U.S.A. 35°35N 115°13W **79** K11
McCusker → Canada 55°32N 108°39W **71** B7
McDame Canada 59°44N 128°59W **70** B3
McDermitt U.S.A. 41°59N 117°43W **76** F5
McDonald U.S.A. 40°22N 80°14W **82** F4
Macdonald, L. Australia 23°30S 129°0E **60** D4
McDonald Is. Ind. Oc. 53°0S 73°0E **3** G13
MacDonnell Ranges
  Australia 23°40S 133°0E **60** D5
MacDowell L. Canada 52°15N 92°45W **72** B1
Macduff U.K. 57°40N 2°31W **11** D6
Macedonia U.S.A. 41°19N 81°31W **82** E3
Macedonia □ Greece 40°39N 22°0E **23** D10
Macedonia ■ Europe 41°53N 21°40E **23** D9
Maceió Brazil 9°40S 35°41W **93** E11
Macerata Italy 43°18N 13°27E **22** C5
McFarland U.S.A. 35°41N 119°14W **79** K7
McFarlane → Canada 59°12N 107°58W **71** B7
Macfarlane, L. Australia 32°0S 136°40E **63** E2
McGehee U.S.A. 33°38N 91°24W **84** E9
McGill U.S.A. 39°23N 114°47W **76** G6
Macgillycuddy's Reeks
  Ireland 51°58N 9°45W **10** E2
McGraw U.S.A. 42°36N 76°8W **83** D8
McGregor U.S.A. 43°1N 91°11W **80** D8
McGregor Ra. Australia 27°0S 142°45E **63** D3
McGuire, Mt. Australia 20°18S 148°23E **62** J6
Mach Pakistan 29°50N 67°20E **42** E2
Māch Kowr Iran 25°48N 61°28E **45** E9
Machado = Jiparaná →
  Brazil 8°3S 62°52W **92** E6
Machagai Argentina 26°56S 60°2W **94** B3
Machala Ecuador 3°20S 79°57W **92** D3
Machanga Mozam. 20°59S 35°0E **57** C6
Machattie, L. Australia 24°50S 139°48E **62** C2
Machava Mozam. 25°54S 32°28E **57** D5
Machece Mozam. 19°15S 35°32E **55** F4
Macheke Zimbabwe 18°5S 31°51E **57** B5
Machhu → India 23°6N 70°46E **42** H4
Machiara △ Pakistan 34°40N 73°30E **42** B5
Machias Maine, U.S.A. 44°43N 67°28W **81** C20
Machias N.Y., U.S.A. 42°25N 78°29W **82** D6
Machichi → Canada 57°3N 92°6W **71** B10
Machico Madeira 32°43N 16°44W **24** D3
Machilipatnam India 16°12N 81°8E **41** L12
Machiques Venezuela 10°4N 72°34W **92** A4
Machupicchu Peru 13°8S 72°30W **92** F4
Machynlleth U.K. 52°35N 3°50W **13** E4
Macia Mozam. 25°2S 33°8E **57** D5
McIlwraith Ra.
  Australia 13°50S 143°20E **62** A3
McInnes L. Canada 52°13N 93°45W **71** C10
McIntosh U.S.A. 45°55N 101°21W **80** C3
McIntosh L. Canada 55°45N 105°0W **71** B8
Macintosh Ra.
  Australia 27°39S 125°32E **61** E4
Macintyre → Australia 28°37S 150°47E **63** D5
Mackay Australia 21°8S 149°11E **62** K7
Mackay U.S.A. 43°55N 113°37W **76** E7
MacKay → Canada 57°10N 111°38W **70** B6
Mackay, L. Australia 22°30S 129°0E **60** D4
McKay Ra. Australia 23°0S 122°30E **60** D3
McKeesport U.S.A. 40°20N 79°51W **82** F5
McKellar Canada 45°30N 79°55W **82** A5
McKenna U.S.A. 46°56N 122°33W **78** D4
Mackenzie Canada 55°20N 123°5W **70** B4

cKenzie U.S.A. 36°8N 88°31W 85 C10
ackenzie → Australia 23°38S 149°46E 62 C4
ackenzie → Canada 69°10N 134°20W 68 C6
cKenzie → U.S.A. 44°7N 123°6W 76 D2
ackenzie Bay Canada 69°0N 137°30W 66 C6
ackenzie City = Linden Guyana 6°0N 58°10W 92 B7
ackenzie King I. Canada 77°45N 111°0W 69 B8
ackenzie Mts. Canada 64°0N 130°0W 68 C7
ackinaw City U.S.A. 45°47N 84°44W 81 C11
cKinlay Australia 21°16S 141°18E 62 C3
cKinlay → Australia 20°50S 141°28E 62 C3
cKinley, Mt. U.S.A. 63°4N 151°0W 74 a
cKinley Sea Arctic 82°0N 0°0 4 A7
cKinney U.S.A. 33°12N 96°37W 84 E6
ackinnon Road Kenya 3°40S 39°1E 54 C4
cKittrick U.S.A. 35°18N 119°37W 79 K7
acklin Canada 52°20N 109°56W 71 C7
acksville Australia 30°40S 152°56E 63 E5
cLaughlin U.S.A. 45°49N 100°49W 80 C3
aclean Australia 29°26S 153°16E 63 D5
cLean U.S.A. 35°14N 100°36W 84 D4
cLeansboro U.S.A. 38°6N 88°32W 80 F9
aclear S. Africa 31°2S 28°23E 57 E4
aclear, C. Malawi 13°58S 34°49E 55 E3
acleay → Australia 30°56S 153°0E 63 E5
cLennan Canada 55°42N 116°50W 70 B5
cLeod → Canada 54°9N 115°44W 70 C5
cLeod, L. Australia 24°9S 113°47E 61 D1
acLeod B. Canada 62°53N 110°0W 71 A7
acLeod Lake Canada 54°58N 123°0W 70 C4
cLoughlin, Mt. U.S.A. 42°27N 122°19W 76 E2
cMechen U.S.A. 39°57N 80°44W 82 G4
cMinnville Oreg., U.S.A. 45°13N 123°12W 76 D2
cMinnville Tenn., U.S.A. 35°41N 85°46W 85 D12
cMurdo Antarctica 77°0S 140°0E 5 D11
cMurdo Sd. Antarctica 77°0S 170°0E 5 D11
cMurray = Fort McMurray Canada 56°44N 111°7W 70 B6
cMurray U.S.A. 48°19N 122°14W 78 B4
acodoene Mozam. 23°32S 35°5E 57 C6
acomb U.S.A. 40°27N 90°40W 80 E8
âcon France 46°19N 4°50E 20 C6
acon Ga., U.S.A. 32°51N 83°38W 85 E13
acon Miss., U.S.A. 33°7N 88°34W 85 E10
acon Mo., U.S.A. 39°44N 92°28W 80 F7
acossa Mozam. 17°55S 33°56E 55 F3
acoun L. Canada 56°32N 103°40W 71 B8
acovane Mozam. 21°30S 35°2E 57 C6
cPherson U.S.A. 38°22N 97°40W 80 F6
cPherson Pk. U.S.A. 34°53N 119°53W 79 L7
cPherson Ra. Australia 28°15S 153°15E 63 D5
acquarie → Australia 30°7S 147°24E 63 E4
acquarie Harbour Australia 42°16S 145°23E 63 G4
acquarie Is. Pac. Oc. 54°36S 158°55E 64 N7
acquarie Ridge S. Ocean 57°0S 159°0E 5 B10
acRobertson Land Antarctica 71°0S 64°0E 5 D6
acroom Ireland 51°54N 8°57W 10 E3
acTier Canada 45°8N 79°47W 82 A5
acubela Mozam. 16°53S 37°49E 55 F4
acuira △ Colombia 12°9N 71°21W 89 D5
acuiza Mozam. 18°7S 34°29E 55 F3
acumba → Australia 27°52S 137°12E 63 D2
acuro Venezuela 10°42N 61°55W 93 K15
acusani Peru 14°4S 70°29W 92 F4
acuse Mozam. 17°45S 37°10E 55 F4
acuspana Mexico 17°46N 92°36W 87 D6
acusse Angola 17°48S 20°23E 56 B3
a'dabā □ Jordan 31°43N 35°47E 46 D4
adadeni S. Africa 27°43S 30°3E 57 D5
adagascar ■ Africa 20°0S 47°0E 57 C8
adā'in Sālih Si. Arabia 26°46N 37°57E 44 E3
adama Niger 22°0N 13°40E 51 D8
adame, I. Canada 45°30N 60°58W 73 C7
adang Papua N. G. 5°12S 145°49E 58 B7
adaripur Bangla. 23°19N 90°15E 41 H17
adauk Burma 17°56N 96°52E 41 L20
adawaska Canada 45°30N 78°0W 82 A7
adawaska → Canada 45°27N 76°21W 82 A7
adaya Burma 22°12N 96°10E 41 H20
addalena Italy 41°16N 9°23E 22 D3
adeira Atl. Oc. 32°50N 17°0W 24 D3
adeira → Brazil 3°22S 58°45W 92 D7
adeleine, Îs. de la Canada 47°30N 61°40W 73 C7
adera Mexico 29°12N 108°7W 86 B3
adera Calif., U.S.A. 36°57N 120°3W 78 J6
adera Pa., U.S.A. 40°49N 78°26W 82 F6
adha India 18°0N 75°30E 40 L9
adhavpur India 21°15N 69°58E 42 J3
adhepura India 26°11N 86°23E 43 F12
adhubani India 26°21N 86°7E 43 F12
adhupur India 24°16N 86°39E 43 G12
adhya Pradesh □ India 22°50N 78°0E 42 J8
adidi → Bolivia 12°32S 66°52W 92 F5
adikeri India 12°30N 75°45E 40 N9
adikwe ⌓ S. Africa 27°38S 32°15E 57 D5
adill U.S.A. 34°6N 96°46W 84 D6
adimba Dem. Rep. of the Congo 4°58S 15°5E 52 E3
a'din Syria 35°45N 39°36E 44 C3
adingou Congo 4°10S 13°33E 52 E2
adirovalo Madag. 16°26S 46°32E 57 B8
adison Calif., U.S.A. 38°41N 121°59W 78 G5
adison Fla., U.S.A. 30°28N 83°25W 85 F13
adison Ind., U.S.A. 38°44N 85°23W 81 F11
adison Nebr., U.S.A. 41°50N 97°27W 80 E5
adison Ohio, U.S.A. 41°46N 81°3W 82 E3
Madison S. Dak., U.S.A. 44°0N 97°7W 80 C5
Madison Wis., U.S.A. 43°4N 89°24W 80 D9
Madison → U.S.A. 45°56N 111°31W 76 D8
Madison Heights U.S.A. 37°25N 79°8W 81 G14
Madisonville Ky., U.S.A. 37°20N 87°30W 80 G10
Madisonville Tex., U.S.A. 30°57N 95°55W 84 F7
Madista Botswana 21°15S 25°6E 56 C4
Madiun Indonesia 7°38S 111°32E 36 F4
Mado Gashi Kenya 0°44N 39°10E 54 B4
Madoc Canada 44°30N 77°28W 82 B7
Madona Latvia 56°53N 26°5E 9 H22
Madrakah, Ra's al Oman 19°0N 57°50E 47 D6
Madras = Chennai India 13°8N 80°19E 40 N12
Madras = Tamil Nadu □ India 11°0N 77°0E 40 P10
Madras U.S.A. 44°38N 121°8W 76 D3
Madre, L. U.S.A. 25°15N 97°30W 84 J6
Madre, Sierra Phil. 17°0N 122°0E 37 A6
Madre de Dios → Bolivia 10°59S 66°8W 92 F5
Madre de Dios, I. Chile 50°20S 75°10W 96 G1
Madre del Sur, Sierra Mexico 17°30N 100°0W 87 D5
Madre Occidental, Sierra Mexico 27°0N 107°0W 86 B3
Madre Oriental, Sierra Mexico 25°0N 100°0W 86 C5
Madri India 24°16N 73°32E 42 G5
Madrid Spain 40°24N 3°42W 21 B4
Madrid U.S.A. 44°45N 75°8W 83 B9
Madura Australia 31°55S 127°0E 61 F4
Madura Indonesia 7°30S 114°0E 37 G15
Madura, Selat Indonesia 7°30S 113°20E 37 G15
Madurai India 9°55N 78°10E 40 Q11
Madurantakam India 12°30N 79°50E 40 N11
Mae Chan Thailand 20°9N 99°52E 38 B2
Mae Hong Son Thailand 19°16N 97°56E 38 C2
Mae Khlong → Thailand 13°24N 100°0E 38 F3
Mae Phrik Thailand 17°27N 99°7E 38 D2
Mae Ping △ Thailand 17°37N 98°51E 38 D2
Mae Ramat Thailand 16°58N 98°31E 38 D2
Mae Rim Thailand 18°54N 98°57E 38 C2
Mae Sot Thailand 16°43N 98°34E 38 D2
Mae Suai Thailand 19°39N 99°33E 38 C2
Mae Tha Thailand 18°28N 99°8E 38 C2
Mae Wong △ Thailand 15°54N 99°12E 38 E2
Mae Yom △ Thailand 18°43N 100°15E 38 C3
Maebashi Japan 36°24N 139°4E 31 F9
Maesteg U.K. 51°36N 3°40W 13 F4
Maestra, Sierra Cuba 20°15N 77°0W 88 B4
Maevatanana Madag. 16°56S 46°49E 57 B8
Mafeking = Mafikeng S. Africa 25°50S 25°38E 56 D4
Mafeking Canada 52°40N 101°10W 71 C8
Mafeteng Lesotho 29°51S 27°15E 56 D4
Maffra Australia 37°53S 146°58E 63 F4
Mafia I. Tanzania 7°45S 39°50E 54 D4
Mafikeng S. Africa 25°50S 25°38E 56 D4
Mafra Brazil 26°10S 49°55W 95 B6
Mafra Portugal 38°55N 9°20W 21 C1
Mafungabusi Plateau Zimbabwe 18°30S 29°8E 55 F2
Magadan Russia 59°38N 150°50E 29 D16
Magadi Kenya 1°54S 36°19E 54 C4
Magadi, L. Kenya 1°54S 36°19E 54 C4
Magaliesburg S. Africa 26°0S 27°32E 57 D4
Magallanes, Estrecho de Chile 52°30S 75°0W 96 G2
Magangué Colombia 9°14N 74°45W 92 B4
Magdalen Is. = Madeleine, Îs. de la Canada 47°30N 61°40W 73 C7
Magdalena Argentina 35°5S 57°30W 94 D4
Magdalena Bolivia 13°13S 63°57W 92 F6
Magdalena U.S.A. 34°7N 107°15W 77 J10
Magdalena → Colombia 11°6N 74°51W 92 A4
Magdalena → Mexico 30°40N 112°25W 86 A2
Magdalena, B. Mexico 24°35N 112°0W 86 C2
Magdalena, I. Mexico 24°40N 112°15W 86 C2
Magdalena, Llano de Mexico 25°0N 111°25W 86 C2
Magdalena de Kino Mexico 30°38N 110°57W 86 A2
Magdeburg Germany 52°7N 11°38E 16 B6
Magdelaine Cays Australia 16°33S 150°18E 62 B5
Magee U.S.A. 31°52N 89°44W 85 F10
Magelang Indonesia 7°29S 110°13E 36 F4
Magellan's Str. = Magallanes, Estrecho de Chile 52°30S 75°0W 96 G2
Magenta, L. Australia 33°30S 119°2E 61 F2
Magerøya Norway 71°3N 25°40E 8 A21
Maggiore, Lago Italy 45°57N 8°39E 20 D8
Maggotty Jamaica 18°9N 77°46W 88 a
Maghâgha Egypt 28°38N 30°50E 51 C12
Magherafelt U.K. 54°45N 6°37W 10 B5
Maghreb N. Afr. 32°0N 4°0W 50 B5
Magistralnyy Russia 56°16N 107°36E 29 D11
Magnetic Pole (North) Canada 82°42N 114°24W 69 B9
Magnetic Pole (South) Antarctica 64°8S 138°8E 5 C9
Magnitogorsk Russia 53°27N 59°4E 18 D10
Magnolia Ark., U.S.A. 33°16N 93°14W 84 E8
Magnolia Miss., U.S.A. 31°9N 90°28W 85 F9
Mago Fiji 17°26S 179°8W 59 a
Magog Canada 45°18N 72°9W 83 A12
Magoro Uganda 1°45N 34°12E 54 B3
Magoša = Famagusta Cyprus 35°8N 33°55E 25 D12
Magoulades Greece 39°45N 19°42E 25 A3
Magoye Zambia 16°1S 27°30E 55 F2
Magpie, L. Canada 51°0N 64°41W 73 B7
Magrath Canada 49°25N 112°50W 70 D6
Maguarinho, C. Brazil 0°15S 48°30W 93 D9
Magude Mozam. 25°2S 32°40E 57 D5
Mağusa = Famagusta Cyprus 35°8N 33°55E 25 D12
Maguse L. Canada 61°37N 95°10W 71 A9
Maguse Pt. Canada 61°20N 93°50W 71 A10
Magvana India 23°13N 69°22E 42 H3
Magwe Burma 20°10N 95°0E 41 J19
Magyarorszag = Hungary ■ Europe 47°20N 19°20E 17 E10
Maha Sarakham Thailand 16°12N 103°16E 38 D4
Mahābād Iran 36°50N 45°45E 44 B5
Mahabharat Lekh Nepal 28°30N 82°0E 43 E10
Mahabo Madag. 20°23S 44°40E 57 C7
Mahadeo Hills India 22°20N 78°30E 43 H8
Mahaffey U.S.A. 40°53N 78°44W 82 F6
Mahagi Dem. Rep. of the Congo 2°20N 31°0E 54 B3
Mahajamba → Madag. 15°33S 47°8E 57 B8
Mahajamba, Helodranon' i Madag. 15°24S 47°5E 57 B8
Mahajan India 28°48N 73°56E 42 E5
Mahajanga Madag. 15°40S 46°25E 57 B8
Mahajanga □ Madag. 17°0S 47°0E 57 B8
Mahajilo → Madag. 19°42S 45°22E 57 B8
Mahakam → Indonesia 0°35S 117°17E 36 E5
Mahalapye Botswana 23°1S 26°51E 56 C4
Mahale Mts. Tanzania 6°20S 30°0E 54 D3
Mahale Mts. △ Tanzania 6°10S 29°50E 54 D2
Maḩallāt Iran 33°55N 50°30E 45 C6
Māhān Iran 30°5N 57°18E 45 D8
Mahan → India 23°30N 82°50E 43 H10
Mahanadi → India 20°20N 86°25E 41 J15
Mahananda → India 25°12N 87°52E 43 G12
Mahanoro Madag. 19°54S 48°48E 57 B8
Mahanoy City U.S.A. 40°49N 76°9W 83 F8
Maharashtra □ India 20°30N 75°30E 40 J9
Mahasham, W. → Egypt 30°15N 34°10E 46 E3
Mahasoa Madag. 22°12S 46°6E 57 C8
Mahasolo Madag. 19°7S 46°22E 57 B8
Mahattat ash Shīdīyah Jordan 29°55N 35°55E 46 F4
Mahattat 'Unayzah Jordan 30°30N 35°47E 46 E4
Mahavavy → Madag. 15°57S 45°54E 57 B8
Mahaxay Laos 17°22N 105°12E 38 D5
Mahbubnagar India 16°45N 77°59E 40 L10
Maḩḑah Oman 24°24N 55°59E 45 E7
Mahdia Tunisia 35°28N 11°0E 51 A8
Mahe India 33°10N 78°32E 43 C8
Mahé Seychelles 5°0S 55°30E 53 b
Mahé ✕ (SEZ) Seychelles 4°40S 55°31E 53 b
Mahébourg Mauritius 20°24S 57°42E 53 d
Mahendragarh India 28°17N 76°14E 42 E7
Mahendranagar Nepal 28°55N 80°20E 43 E9
Mahenge Tanzania 8°45S 36°41E 55 D4
Maheno N.Z. 45°10S 170°50E 59 F3
Mahesana India 23°39N 72°26E 42 H5
Maheshwar India 22°11N 75°35E 42 H6
Mahgawan India 26°29N 78°37E 43 F8
Mahi → India 22°15N 72°55E 42 H5
Mahia Pen. N.Z. 39°9S 177°55E 59 C6
Mahilyow Belarus 53°55N 30°18E 17 B16
Mahina Tahiti 17°30S 149°27W 59 d
Mahinerangi, L. N.Z. 45°50S 169°56E 59 F2
Mahmud Kot Pakistan 30°16N 71°0E 42 D4
Mahnomen U.S.A. 47°19N 95°58W 80 B6
Mahoba India 25°15N 79°55E 43 G8
Mahón = Maó Spain 39°53N 4°16E 24 B11
Mahone Bay Canada 44°27N 64°23W 73 D7
Mahopac U.S.A. 41°22N 73°45W 83 E11
Mahuva India 21°5N 71°48E 42 J4
Mai-Ndombe, L. Dem. Rep. of the Congo 2°0S 18°20E 52 E3
Mai-Sai Thailand 20°20N 99°55E 38 B2
Mai Thon, Ko Thailand 7°40N 98°28E 39 a
Maicurú → Brazil 2°14S 54°17W 93 D8
Maidan Khula Afghan. 33°36N 69°50E 42 C3
Maidenhead U.K. 51°31N 0°42W 13 F7
Maidstone Canada 53°5N 109°20W 71 C7
Maidstone U.K. 51°16N 0°32E 13 F8
Maiduguri Nigeria 12°0N 13°20E 51 F8
Maihar India 24°16N 80°45E 43 G9
Maijdi Bangla. 22°48N 91°10E 41 H17
Maikala Ra. India 22°0N 81°0E 41 J12
Maiko △ Dem. Rep. of the Congo 0°30S 27°50E 54 C2
Mailani India 28°17N 80°21E 43 E9
Mailsi Pakistan 29°48N 72°15E 42 E5
Main → Germany 50°0N 8°18E 16 C5
Main → U.K. 54°48N 6°18W 10 B5
Main Range △ Australia 28°11S 152°27E 63 D5
Main Ridge Trin. & Tob. 11°16N 60°40W 93 J16
Maine France 48°20N 0°15W 20 C3
Maine □ U.S.A. 45°20N 69°0W 81 C19
Maine → Ireland 52°9N 9°45W 10 D2
Maine, G. of U.S.A. 43°0N 68°30W 81 D19
Maingkwan Burma 26°15N 96°37E 41 F20
Mainit, L. Phil. 9°31N 125°30E 37 C7
Mainland Orkney, U.K. 58°59N 3°8W 11 C5
Mainland Shet., U.K. 60°15N 1°22W 11 A7
Mainoru Australia 14°0S 134°6E 62 A1
Mainpuri India 27°18N 79°4E 43 F8
Maintirano Madag. 18°3S 44°1E 57 B7
Mainz Germany 50°1N 8°14E 16 C5
Maio C. Verde Is. 15°10N 23°10W 50 b
Maipú Argentina 36°52S 57°50W 94 D4
Maiquetía Venezuela 10°36N 66°57W 92 A5
Mairabari India 26°30N 92°22E 41 F18
Maisi Cuba 20°17N 74°9W 89 B5
Maisi, Pta. de Cuba 20°10N 74°10W 89 B5
Maitland N.S.W., Australia 32°33S 151°36E 63 E5
Maitland S. Austral., Australia 34°23S 137°40E 63 E2
Maitland → Canada 43°45N 81°43W 82 C3
Maitri Antarctica 70°0S 3°0W 5 D3
Maiz, Is. del Nic. 12°15N 83°4W 88 D3
Maizuru Japan 35°25N 135°22E 31 G7
Majalengka Indonesia 6°50S 108°13E 37 G13
Majene Indonesia 3°38S 118°57E 37 E5
Majete ⌓ Malawi 15°54S 34°34E 55 F3
Majorca = Mallorca Spain 39°30N 3°0E 24 B10
Majuro Marshall Is. 7°9N 171°12E 64 G9
Maka Senegal 13°40N 14°10W 50 F3
Makaha Zimbabwe 17°20S 32°39E 57 B5
Makalamabedi Botswana 20°19S 23°51E 56 C3
Makale Indonesia 3°6S 119°51E 37 E5
Makalu-Barun △ Nepal 27°45N 87°10E 43 F12
Makamba Burundi 4°8S 29°49E 54 C2
Makarikari = Makgadikgadi Salt Pans Botswana 20°40S 25°45E 56 C4
Makarov Basin Arctic 87°0N 150°0W 4 A
Makarovo Russia 57°40N 107°45E 29 D11
Makasar = Ujung Pandang Indonesia 5°10S 119°20E 37 F5
Makasar, Selat Indonesia 1°0S 118°20E 37 E5
Makasar, Str. of = Makasar, Selat Indonesia 1°0S 118°20E 37 E5
Makat = Maqat Kazakhstan 47°39N 53°19E 19 E9
Makedonija = Macedonia ■ Europe 41°53N 21°40E 23 D9
Makeni S. Leone 8°55N 12°5W 50 G3
Makeyevka = Makiyivka Ukraine 48°0N 38°0E 19 E6
Makgadikgadi △ Botswana 20°27S 24°47E 56 C3
Makgadikgadi Salt Pans Botswana 20°40S 25°45E 56 C4
Makhachkala Russia 43°0N 47°30E 19 F8
Makhado = Louis Trichardt S. Africa 23°1S 29°43E 57 C4
Makhfar al Buşayyah Iraq 30°0N 46°10E 44 D5
Makhmūr Iraq 35°46N 43°35E 44 C4
Makian Indonesia 0°20N 127°20E 37 D7
Makindu Kenya 2°18S 37°50E 54 C4
Makīnsk Kazakhstan 52°37N 70°26E 28 D8
Makira = San Cristóbal Solomon Is. 10°30S 161°0E 58 C9
Makiyivka Ukraine 48°0N 38°0E 19 E6
Makkah Si. Arabia 21°30N 39°54E 47 C2
Makkovik Canada 55°10N 59°10W 73 A8
Makó Hungary 46°14N 20°33E 17 E11
Makogai Fiji 17°28S 179°0E 59 a
Makokou Gabon 0°40N 12°50E 52 D2
Makongo Dem. Rep. of the Congo 3°25N 26°17E 54 D2
Makoro Dem. Rep. of the Congo 3°10N 29°59E 54 B2
Makrai India 22°2N 77°0E 42 H7
Makran Coast Range Pakistan 25°40N 64°0E 40 G4
Makrana India 27°2N 74°46E 42 F6
Makrigialos Greece 35°2N 25°59E 25 D7
Mākū Iran 39°15N 44°31E 44 B5
Makunda Botswana 22°30S 20°7E 56 C3
Makurazaki Japan 31°15N 130°20E 31 J5
Makurdi Nigeria 7°43N 8°35E 50 G7
Makūyeh Iran 28°7N 53°9E 45 D7
Makwassie S. Africa 27°17S 26°0E 56 D4
Makwiro Zimbabwe 17°58S 30°25E 57 B5
Mal B. Ireland 52°50N 9°30W 10 D2
Mala, Pta. Panama 7°28N 80°2W 88 E3
Malabar Coast India 11°0N 75°0E 40 P9
Malacca, Straits of Indonesia 3°0N 101°0E 39 L3
Malad City U.S.A. 42°12N 112°15W 76 E7
Maladzyechna Belarus 54°20N 26°50E 17 A14
Málaga Spain 36°43N 4°23W 21 D3
Malagarasi Tanzania 5°5S 30°50E 54 D3
Malagarasi → Tanzania 5°12S 29°47E 54 D2
Malagasy Rep. = Madagascar ■ Africa 20°0S 47°0E 57 C8
Malahide Ireland 53°26N 6°9W 10 C5
Malaimbandy Madag. 20°20S 45°36E 57 C8
Malaita Solomon Is. 9°0S 161°0E 58 B9
Malakâl Sudan 9°33N 31°40E 51 G12
Malakand Pakistan 34°40N 71°55E 42 B4
Malakula Vanuatu 16°15S 167°30E 58 C9
Malakwal Pakistan 32°34N 73°13E 42 C5
Malamala Indonesia 3°21S 120°55E 37 E6
Malanda Australia 17°22S 145°35E 62 B4
Malang Indonesia 7°59S 112°45E 36 F4
Malangen Norway 69°24N 18°37E 8 B18
Malanje Angola 9°36S 16°17E 52 F3
Mälaren Sweden 59°30N 17°10E 9 G17
Malargüe Argentina 35°32S 69°30W 94 D2
Malartic Canada 48°9N 78°9W 72 C4
Malaryta Belarus 51°50N 24°3E 17 C13
Malatya Turkey 38°25N 38°20E 44 B3
Malawi ■ Africa 11°55S 34°0E 55 E3
Malawi, L. Africa 12°30S 34°30E 55 E3
Malay Pen. Asia 7°25N 100°0E 39 J3
Malaya Vishera Russia 58°55N 32°25E 18 C5
Malaybalay Phil. 8°5N 125°7E 37 C7
Malāyer Iran 34°19N 48°51E 45 C6
Malaysia ■ Asia 5°0N 110°0E 39 K4
Malazgirt Turkey 39°10N 42°33E 44 B4
Malbon Australia 21°5S 140°17E 62 C3
Malbooma Australia 30°41S 134°11E 63 E1
Malbork Poland 54°3N 19°1E 17 B10
Malcolm Australia 28°51S 121°25E 61 E3
Malcolm, Pt. Australia 33°48S 123°45E 61 F3
Maldah India 25°2N 88°9E 43 G13
Maldegem Belgium 51°14N 3°26E 15 C3
Malden Mass., U.S.A. 42°26N 71°3W 83 D13
Malden Mo., U.S.A. 36°34N 89°57W 80 G9
Malden I. Kiribati 4°3S 155°1W 65 H12
Maldives ■ Ind. Oc. 5°0N 73°0E 26 H9
Maldon U.K. 51°44N 0°42E 13 F8
Maldonado Uruguay 34°59S 55°0W 95 C5
Maldonado, Pta. Mexico 16°20N 98°33W 87 D5
Malé Karpaty Slovak Rep. 48°30N 17°20E 17 D9
Maleas, Akra Greece 36°28N 23°7E 23 F10
Malebo, Pool Africa 4°17S 15°20E 52 E3
Malegaon India 20°30N 74°38E 40 J9
Malei Mozam. 17°12S 36°58E 55 F4
Malek Kandī Iran 37°9N 46°6E 44 B5
Malela Dem. Rep. of the Congo 4°22S 26°8E 54 C2
Malema Mozam. 14°57S 37°20E 55 E4
Maleme Greece 35°31N 23°49E 25 D5
Malerkotla India 30°32N 75°58E 42 D6
Males Greece 35°6N 25°35E 25 D7
Malgomaj Sweden 64°40N 16°30E 8 D17
Malha Sudan 15°8N 25°10E 51 E11
Malhargarh India 24°17N 74°59E 42 G6
Malheur → U.S.A. 44°4N 116°59W 76 D5
Malheur L. U.S.A. 43°20N 118°48W 76 E4
Mali ■ Africa 17°0N 3°0W 50 E5
Mali → Burma 25°42N 97°30E 41 G20
Mali Kyun Burma 13°0N 98°20E 38 F2
Malia Greece 35°17N 25°32E 25 D7
Malia, Kolpos Greece 35°19N 25°27E 25 D7
Malibu U.S.A. 34°2N 118°41W 79 L8
Maliku Indonesia 0°39S 123°16E 37 E6
Malili Indonesia 2°42S 121°6E 37 E6
Malimba, Mts. Dem. Rep. of the Congo 7°30S 29°30E 54 D2
Malin Hd. Ireland 55°23N 7°23W 10 A4
Malin Pen. Ireland 55°20N 7°17W 10 A4
Malindi Kenya 3°12S 40°5E 54 C5
Malines = Mechelen Belgium 51°2N 4°29E 15 C4
Malino Indonesia 1°0N 121°0E 37 D6
Malinyi Tanzania 8°56S 36°0E 55 D4
Malita Phil. 6°19N 125°39E 37 C7
Maliwun Burma 10°17N 98°40E 39 G2
Maliya India 23°5N 70°46E 42 H4
Malka Mari △ Kenya 4°11N 40°46E 54 B5
Malkara Turkey 40°53N 26°53E 23 D12
Mallacoota Inlet Australia 37°34S 149°40E 63 F4
Mallaig U.K. 57°0N 5°50W 11 D3
Mallawan India 27°4N 80°12E 43 F9
Mallawi Egypt 27°44N 30°44E 51 C12
Mallicolo = Malakula Vanuatu 16°15S 167°30E 58 C9
Mallorca Spain 39°30N 3°0E 24 B10
Mallorytown Canada 44°29N 75°53W 83 B9
Mallow Ireland 52°8N 8°39W 10 D3
Malmberget Sweden 67°11N 20°40E 8 C19
Malmédy Belgium 50°25N 6°2E 15 D6
Malmesbury S. Africa 33°28S 18°41E 56 E2
Malmivaara = Malmberget Sweden 67°11N 20°40E 8 C19
Malmö Sweden 55°36N 12°59E 9 J15
Malolo Fiji 17°45S 177°11E 59 a
Malolos Phil. 14°50N 120°49E 37 B6
Malolotja ⌓ Swaziland 26°4S 31°6E 57 D5
Malombe L. Malawi 14°40S 35°15E 55 E4
Malone U.S.A. 44°51N 74°18W 83 B10
Måløy Norway 61°57N 5°6E 8 F11
Malpaso Canary Is. 27°43N 18°3W 24 G1
Malpaso, Presa = Netzahualcóyotl, Presa Mexico 17°8N 93°35W 87 D6
Malpelo, I. de Colombia 4°3N 81°35W 92 C2
Malpur India 23°21N 73°27E 42 H5
Malpura India 26°17N 75°23E 42 F6
Malta Idaho, U.S.A. 42°18N 113°22W 76 E7
Malta Mont., U.S.A. 48°21N 107°52W 76 B10
Malta ■ Europe 35°55N 14°26E 25 D2
Maltahöhe Namibia 24°55S 17°0E 56 C2
Malton Canada 43°42N 79°38W 82 C5
Malton U.K. 54°8N 0°49W 12 C7
Maluku Indonesia 1°0S 127°0E 37 E7
Maluku □ Indonesia 3°0S 128°0E 37 E7
Maluku Sea = Molucca Sea Indonesia 0°0 125°0E 37 E6
Malvan India 16°2N 73°30E 40 L8
Malvern U.S.A. 34°22N 92°49W 84 D8
Malvern Hills U.K. 52°0N 2°19W 13 E5
Malvinas, Is. = Falkland Is. ☑ Atl. Oc. 51°30S 59°0W 96 G5
Malya Tanzania 3°5S 33°38E 54 C3
Malyn Ukraine 50°46N 29°3E 17 C15
Malyy Lyakhovskiy, Ostrov Russia 74°7N 140°36E 29 B15
Mama Russia 58°18N 112°54E 29 D12
Mamanguape Brazil 6°50S 35°4W 93 E11
Mamanuca Group Fiji 17°35S 177°5E 59 a
Mamarr Mitlā Egypt 30°2N 32°54E 46 E1
Mamasa Indonesia 2°55S 119°20E 37 E5
Mambasa Dem. Rep. of the Congo 1°22N 29°3E 54 B2
Mamberamo → Indonesia 2°0S 137°50E 37 E9
Mambilima Falls Zambia 10°31S 28°45E 55 E2
Mambirima Dem. Rep. of the Congo 11°25S 27°33E 55 E2
Mambo Tanzania 4°52S 38°22E 54 C4
Mambrui Kenya 3°5S 40°5E 54 C5
Mamburao Phil. 13°13N 120°39E 37 B6
Mameigwess L. Canada 52°35N 87°50W 72 B2
Mammoth U.S.A. 32°43N 110°39W 77 K8
Mammoth Cave △ U.S.A. 37°8N 86°13W 80 G10

Mamoré → Bolivia 10°23S 65°53W 92 F5
Mamou Guinea 10°15N 12°0W 50 F3
Mamoudzou Mayotte 12°48S 45°14E 53 a
Mampikony Madag. 16°6S 47°38E 57 B8
Mamuju Indonesia 2°41S 118°50E 37 E5
Mamuno Botswana 22°16S 20°1E 56 C3
Man Ivory C. 7°30N 7°40W 50 G4
Man, I. of U.K. 54°15N 4°30W 12 C3
Man-Bazar India 23°4N 86°39E 43 H12
Man Na Burma 23°27N 97°19E 41 H20
Mana → Fr. Guiana 5°45N 53°55W 93 B8
Mana Pools △ Zimbabwe 15°56S 29°25E 55 F2
Manaar, G. of = Mannar, G. of Asia 8°30N 79°0E 40 Q11
Manacapuru Brazil 3°16S 60°37W 92 D6
Manacor Spain 39°34N 3°13E 24 B10
Manado Indonesia 1°29N 124°51E 37 D6
Managua Nic. 12°6N 86°20W 88 D2
Managua, L. de Nic. 12°20N 86°30W 88 D2
Manakara Madag. 22°8S 48°1E 57 C8
Manali India 32°16N 77°10E 42 C7
Manama = Al Manāmah Bahrain 26°10N 50°30E 45 E6
Manambao → Madag. 17°35S 44°0E 57 B7
Manambato Madag. 13°43S 49°7E 57 A8
Manambolo → Madag. 19°18S 44°22E 57 B7
Manambolosy Madag. 16°2S 49°40E 57 B8
Mananara Madag. 16°10S 49°46E 57 B8
Mananara → Madag. 23°21S 47°42E 57 C8
Mananara ⌓ Madag. 16°14S 49°45E 57 B8
Mananjary Madag. 21°13S 48°20E 57 C8
Manantenina Madag. 24°17S 47°19E 57 C8
Manaos = Manaus Brazil 3°0S 60°0W 92 D7
Manapire → Venezuela 7°42N 66°7W 92 B5
Manapouri N.Z. 45°34S 167°39E 59 F1
Manapouri, L. N.Z. 45°32S 167°32E 59 F1
Manār, Jabal Yemen 14°2N 44°17E 47 E3
Manaravolo Madag. 23°59S 45°39E 57 C8
Manas China 44°17N 85°56E 32 B3
Manas → India 26°12N 90°40E 41 F17
Manaslu Nepal 28°33N 84°33E 43 E11
Manasquan U.S.A. 40°8N 74°3W 83 F10
Manassa U.S.A. 37°11N 105°56W 77 H11
Manatí Puerto Rico 18°26N 66°29W 89 d
Manaung Burma 18°45N 93°40E 41 K18
Manaus Brazil 3°0S 60°0W 92 D7
Manawan L. Canada 55°24N 103°14W 71 B8
Manbij Syria 36°31N 37°57E 44 B3
Manchegorsk Russia 67°54N 32°58E 28 C4
Manchester U.K. 53°29N 2°12W 12 D5
Manchester Calif., U.S.A. 38°58N 123°41W 78 G3
Manchester Conn., U.S.A. 41°47N 72°31W 83 E12
Manchester Ga., U.S.A. 32°51N 84°37W 85 E12
Manchester Iowa, U.S.A. 42°29N 91°27W 80 D8
Manchester Ky., U.S.A. 37°9N 83°46W 81 G12
Manchester N.H., U.S.A. 42°59N 71°28W 83 D13
Manchester N.Y., U.S.A. 42°56N 77°16W 82 D7
Manchester Pa., U.S.A. 40°4N 76°43W 83 F8
Manchester Tenn., U.S.A. 35°29N 86°5W 85 D11
Manchester Vt., U.S.A. 43°10N 73°5W 83 C11
Manchester Int. ✕ (MAN) U.K. 53°21N 2°17W 12 D5
Manchester L. Canada 61°28N 107°29W 71 A7
Manchhar L. Pakistan 26°25N 67°39E 42 F2
Manchuria = Dongbei China 45°0N 125°0E 35 D13
Manchurian Plain China 47°0N 124°0E 26 D14
Mand → India 21°42N 83°15E 43 J10
Mand → Iran 28°20N 52°30E 45 D7
Manda Ludewe, Tanzania 10°30S 34°40E 55 E3
Manda Mbeya, Tanzania 7°58S 32°29E 54 D3
Manda Mbeya, Tanzania 8°30S 32°49E 55 D3
Mandabé Madag. 21°0S 44°55E 57 C7
Mandaguari Brazil 23°32S 51°42W 95 A5
Mandah = Töhöm Mongolia 44°27N 108°2E 34 B5
Mandal Norway 58°2N 7°25E 9 G12
Mandala, Puncak Indonesia 4°44S 140°20E 37 E10
Mandalay Burma 22°0N 96°4E 41 J20
Mandale = Mandalay Burma 22°0N 96°4E 41 J20
Mandalgarh India 25°12N 75°6E 42 G6
Mandalgovĭ Mongolia 45°45N 106°10E 34 B4
Mandalī Iraq 33°43N 45°28E 44 C5
Mandan U.S.A. 46°50N 100°54W 80 B3
Mandar, Teluk Indonesia 3°35S 119°15E 37 E5
Mandaue Phil. 10°20N 123°56E 37 B6
Mandera Kenya 3°55N 41°53E 54 B5
Mandeville Jamaica 18°2N 77°31W 88 a
Mandi India 31°39N 76°58E 42 D7
Mandi Dabwali India 29°58N 74°42E 42 E6
Mandimba Mozam. 14°20S 35°40E 55 E4
Mandioli Indonesia 0°40S 127°20E 37 E7
Mandla India 22°39N 80°30E 43 H9
Mandorah Australia 12°32S 130°42E 60 B5
Mandoto Madag. 19°34S 46°17E 57 B8
Mandra Pakistan 33°23N 73°12E 42 C5
Mandrare → Madag. 25°10S 46°30E 57 D8
Mandritsara Madag. 15°50S 48°49E 57 B8
Mandronarivo Madag. 21°7S 45°38E 57 C8
Mandsaur India 24°3N 75°8E 42 G6
Mandurah Australia 32°36S 115°48E 61 F2
Mandvi India 22°51N 69°22E 42 H3
Mandya India 12°30N 77°0E 40 N10
Mandzai Pakistan 30°55N 67°6E 42 D2
Maneh Iran 37°39N 57°7E 45 B8
Manera Madag. 22°55S 44°20E 57 C7
Maneroo Cr. → Australia 23°21S 143°53E 62 C3
Manfalût Egypt 27°20N 30°52E 51 C12
Manfredónia Italy 41°38N 15°55E 22 D6
Mangabeiras, Chapada das Brazil 10°0S 46°30W 93 F9
Mangaia Cook Is. 21°55S 157°55W 65 K12
Mangalia Romania 43°50N 28°35E 17 G15
Mangalore India 12°55N 74°47E 40 N9
Mangan India 27°31N 88°32E 43 F13
Mangawan India 24°41N 81°33E 43 G9
Mangaweka N.Z. 39°48S 175°47E 59 C5
Manggar Indonesia 2°50S 108°10E 36 E3
Manggawitu Indonesia 4°8S 133°32E 37 E8
Mangghystaū Tübegi Kazakhstan 44°30N 52°30E 28 E6
Manggis Indonesia 8°29S 115°31E 37 J18
Mangindrano Madag. 14°17S 48°58E 57 A8
Mangkalihat, Tanjung Indonesia 1°2N 118°59E 37 D5
Mangla Pakistan 33°7N 73°39E 42 C5
Mangla Dam Pakistan 33°9N 73°44E 43 C5
Manglaur India 29°44N 77°49E 42 E7
Mangnai China 37°52N 91°43E 32 C4
Mango Togo 10°20N 0°30E 50 F6
Mango Tonga 20°17S 174°29W 59 c
Mangoche Malawi 14°25S 35°16E 55 E4
Mangoky → Madag. 21°29S 43°41E 57 C7
Mangole Indonesia 1°50S 125°55E 37 E6
Mangombe Dem. Rep. of the Congo 1°20S 26°48E 54 C2
Mangonui N.Z. 35°1S 173°32E 59 A4
Mangoro → Madag. 20°0S 48°45E 57 B8
Mangrol Mad. P., India 21°7N 70°7E 42 J4
Mangrol Raj., India 25°20N 76°31E 42 G6
Mangueira, L. da Brazil 33°0S 52°50W 95 C5
Mangum U.S.A. 34°53N 99°30W 84 D5
Mangyshlak, Poluostrov = Mangghystaū Tübegi Kazakhstan 44°30N 52°30E 28 E6
Manhattan U.S.A. 39°11N 96°35W 80 F5
Manhiça Mozam. 25°23S 32°49E 57 D5
Mania → Madag. 19°42S 45°22E 57 B8
Manica Mozam. 18°58S 32°59E 57 B5
Manica □ Mozam. 19°10S 33°45E 57 B5
Manicaland □ Zimbabwe 19°0S 32°30E 55 F3
Manicoré Brazil 5°48S 61°16W 92 E6
Manicouagan → Canada 49°30N 68°30W 73 C6
Manicouagan, Rés. Canada 51°5N 68°40W 73 B6
Maniema □ Dem. Rep. of the Congo 3°0S 26°0E 54 C2
Manīfah Si. Arabia 27°44N 49°0E 45 E6
Manifold, C. Australia 22°41S 150°50E 62 C5
Manigotagan Canada 51°6N 96°18W 71 C9
Manigotagan → Canada 51°7N 96°20W 71 C9
Manihari India 25°21N 87°38E 43 G12
Manihiki Cook Is. 10°24S 161°1W 65 J11
Manihiki Plateau Pac. Oc. 11°0S 164°0W 65 J11
Manika, Plateau de la Dem. Rep. of the Congo 10°0S 25°5E 55 E2
Manikpur India 25°4N 81°7E 43 G9
Manila Phil. 14°35N 120°58E 37 B6
Manila U.S.A. 40°59N 109°43W 76 F9
Manila B. Phil. 14°40N 120°35E 37 B6
Manilla Australia 30°45S 150°43E 63 E5
Maningrida Australia 12°3S 134°13E 62 A1
Manipur □ India 25°0N 94°0E 41 G19
Manipur → Burma 23°45N 94°20E 41 H19
Manisa Turkey 38°38N 27°30E 23 E12
Manistee U.S.A. 44°15N 86°19W 80 C10
Manistee → U.S.A. 44°15N 86°21W 80 C10
Manistique U.S.A. 45°57N 86°15W 80 C10
Manitoba □ Canada 53°30N 97°0W 71 B9
Manitoba, L. Canada 51°0N 98°45W 71 C9
Manitou Canada 49°15N 98°32W 71 D9
Manitou, L. Canada 50°55N 65°17W 73 B6
Manitou Is. U.S.A. 45°8N 86°0W 81 C10
Manitou L. Canada 52°43N 109°43W 71 C7
Manitou Springs U.S.A. 38°52N 104°55W 76 G11
Manitoulin I. Canada 45°40N 82°30W 72 C3
Manitouwadge Canada 49°8N 85°48W 72 C2
Manitowoc U.S.A. 44°5N 87°40W 80 C10
Manizales Colombia 5°5N 75°32W 92 B3
Manja Madag. 21°26S 44°20E 57 C7
Manjacaze Mozam. 24°45S 34°0E 57 C5
Manjakandriana Madag. 18°55S 47°47E 57 B8
Manjhand Pakistan 25°50N 68°10E 42 G3
Manjil Iran 36°46N 49°30E 45 B6
Manjimup Australia 34°15S 116°6E 61 F2
Manjra → India 18°49N 77°52E 40 K10
Mankato Kans., U.S.A. 39°47N 98°13W 80 F4
Mankato Minn., U.S.A. 44°10N 94°0W 80 C6
Mankayane Swaziland 26°40S 31°4E 57 D5
Mankera Pakistan 31°23N 71°26E 42 D4
Mankota Canada 49°25N 107°5W 71 D7
Manlay = Üydzin Mongolia 44°9N 107°0E 34 B4
Manmad India 20°18N 74°28E 40 J9
Mann Ranges Australia 26°6S 130°5E 61 E5
Manna Indonesia 4°25S 102°55E 36 E2
Mannahill Australia 32°25S 140°0E 63 E3
Mannar Sri Lanka 9°1N 79°54E 40 Q11
Mannar, G. of Asia 8°30N 79°0E 40 Q11
Mannar I. Sri Lanka 9°5N 79°45E 40 Q11
Mannheim Germany 49°29N 8°29E 16 D5
Manning Canada 56°53N 117°39W 70 B5
Manning Oreg., U.S.A. 45°45N 123°13W 78 E3
Manning S.C., U.S.A. 33°42N 80°13W 85 E14
Mannum Australia 34°50S 139°20E 63 E2
Manoharpur India 22°23N 85°12E 43 H11
Manokwari Indonesia 0°54S 134°0E 37 E8
Manombo Madag. 22°57S 43°28E 57 C7
Manono Dem. Rep. of the Congo 7°15S 27°25E 54 D2
Manono Samoa 13°50S 172°5W 59 b
Manorhamilton Ireland 54°18N 8°9W 10 B3
Manosque France 43°49N 5°47E 20 E6
Manotick Canada 45°13N 75°41W 83 A9
Manouane → Canada 49°30N 71°10W 73 C5
Manouane, L. Canada 50°45N 70°45W 73 B5
Manp'o N. Korea 41°6N 126°24E 35 D14
Manpojin = Manp'o N. Korea 41°6N 126°24E 35 D14
Manpur Chhattisgarh, India 23°17N 83°35E 43 H10
Manpur Mad. P., India 22°26N 75°37E 42 H6
Manresa Spain 41°48N 1°50E 21 B6
Mansa Gujarat, India 23°27N 72°45E 42 H5
Mansa Punjab, India 30°0N 75°27E 42 E6
Mansa Zambia 11°13S 28°55E 55 E2
Mansehra Pakistan 34°20N 73°15E 42 B5
Mansel I. Canada 62°0N 80°0W 69 C12
Mansfield Australia 37°4S 146°6E 63 F4
Mansfield U.K. 53°9N 1°11W 12 D6
Mansfield La., U.S.A. 32°2N 93°43W 84 E8
Mansfield Mass., U.S.A. 42°2N 71°13W 83 D13
Mansfield Ohio, U.S.A. 40°45N 82°31W 82 F2
Mansfield Pa., U.S.A. 41°48N 77°5W 82 E7
Mansfield Tex., U.S.A. 32°33N 97°8W 84 E6
Mansfield, Mt. U.S.A. 44°33N 72°49W 83 B12
Manson Creek Canada 55°37N 124°32W 70 B4
Manta Ecuador 1°0S 80°40W 92 D2
Mantadia △ Madag. 18°54S 48°21E 57 B8
Mantalingajan, Mt. Phil. 8°55N 117°45E 36 C5
Mantare Tanzania 2°42S 33°13E 54 C3
Manteca U.S.A. 37°48N 121°13W 78 H5
Manteo U.S.A. 35°55N 75°40W 85 D17
Mantes-la-Jolie France 48°58N 1°41E 20 B4
Manthani India 18°40N 79°35E 40 K11
Manti U.S.A. 39°16N 111°38W 76 G8
Mantiqueira, Serra da Brazil 22°0S 44°0W 95 A7
Manton U.S.A. 44°25N 85°24W 81 C11
Mántova Italy 45°9N 10°48E 22 B4
Mänttä Finland 62°3N 24°40E 8 E21
Mantua = Mántova Italy 45°9N 10°48E 22 B4
Manu Peru 12°10S 70°51W 92 F4
Manu → Peru 12°16S 70°55W 92 F4
Manu'a Is. Amer. Samoa 14°13S 169°35W 59 b
Manuel Alves → Brazil 11°19S 48°28W 93 F9
Manui Indonesia 3°35S 123°5E 37 E6
Manukau N.Z. 37°0S 174°52E 59 B5
Manuripi → Bolivia 11°6S 67°36W 92 F5
Many U.S.A. 31°34N 93°29W 84 F8
Manyani Kenya 3°5S 38°30E 54 C4
Manyara, L. Tanzania 3°40S 35°50E 54 C4
Manych-Gudilo, Ozero Russia 46°24N 42°38E 19 E7
Manyonga → Tanzania 4°10S 34°15E 54 C3
Manyoni Tanzania 5°45S 34°55E 54 D3
Manzai Pakistan 32°12N 70°15E 42 C4
Manzanar ⌓ U.S.A. 36°44N 118°9W 78 J7
Manzanares Spain 39°2N 3°22W 21 C4
Manzanillo Cuba 20°20N 77°31W 88 B4
Manzanillo Mexico 19°3N 104°20W 86 D4
Manzanillo, Pta. Panama 9°30N 79°40W 88 E4
Manzano Mts. U.S.A. 34°40N 106°20W 77 J10
Manzarīyeh Iran 34°53N 50°50E 45 C6
Manzhouli China 49°35N 117°25E 33 B6
Manzini Swaziland 26°30S 31°25E 57 D5
Manzur Vadisi △ Turkey 39°10N 39°30E 44 B3
Mao Chad 14°4N 15°19E 51 F9
Maó Spain 39°53N 4°16E 24 B11
Maoke, Pegunungan Indonesia 3°40S 137°30E 37 E9
Maolin China 43°58N 123°30E 35 C12
Maoming China 21°50N 110°54E 33 D6
Maoxing China 45°28N 124°40E 35 B13
Mapam Yumco China 30°45N 81°28E 43 D9
Mapastepec Mexico 15°26N 92°54W 87 D6
Maphrao, Ko Thailand 7°56N 98°26E 39 a
Mapia, Kepulauan Indonesia 0°50N 134°20E 37 D8
Mapimí Mexico 25°49N 103°51W 86 B4
Mapimí, Bolsón de Mexico 27°0N 104°15W 86 B4
Mapinga Tanzania 6°40S 39°12E 54 D4
Mapinhane Mozam. 22°20S 35°0E 57 C6
Maple Creek Canada 49°55N 109°29W 71 D7
Maple Valley U.S.A. 47°25N 122°3W 78 C4
Mapleton U.S.A. 44°2N 123°52W 76 D2
Mapuera → Brazil 1°5S 57°2W 92 D7
Mapulanguene Mozam. 24°29S 32°6E 57 C5
Maputo Mozam. 25°58S 32°32E 57 D5
Maputo □ Mozam. 26°0S 32°25E 57 D5
Maputo, B. de Mozam. 25°50S 32°45E 57 D5
Maputo ⌓ Mozam. 26°23S 32°48E 57 D5
Maqat Kazakhstan 47°39N 53°19E 19 E9
Maqiaohe China 44°40N 130°30E 35 B16
Maqnā Si. Arabia 28°25N 34°50E 44 D2
Maquan He = Brahmaputra → Asia 23°40N 90°35E 43 H13
Maquela do Zombo Angola 6°0S 15°15E 52 F3
Maquinchao Argentina 41°15S 68°50W 96 E3
Maquoketa U.S.A. 42°4N 90°40W 80 D8
Mar, Serra do Brazil 25°30S 49°0W 95 B6
Mar Chiquita, L. Argentina 30°40S 62°50W 94 C3
Mar del Plata Argentina 38°0S 57°30W 94 D4
Mar Menor Spain 37°40N 0°45W 21 D5
Mara Tanzania 1°30S 34°32E 54 C3
Mara □ Tanzania 1°45S 34°20E 54 C3
Maraã Brazil 1°52S 65°25W 92 D5
Maraa Tahiti 17°46S 149°34W 59 d
Marabá Brazil 5°20S 49°5W 93 E9
Maracá, I. de Brazil 2°10N 50°30W 93 C8
Maracaibo Venezuela 10°40N 71°37W 92 A4
Maracaibo, L. de Venezuela 9°40N 71°30W 92 B4
Maracaju Brazil 21°38S 55°9W 95 A4
Maracas Bay Village Trin. & Tob. 10°46N 61°28W 93 K15
Maracay Venezuela 10°15N 67°28W 92 A5
Maradi Niger 13°29N 7°20E 50 F7
Marāgheh Iran 37°30N 46°12E 44 B5
Marāh Si. Arabia 25°0N 45°35E 44 E5
Marajó, I. de Brazil 1°0S 49°30W 93 D9
Marākand Iran 38°51N 45°16E 44 B5
Marakele △ S. Africa 32°14S 25°27E 57 E4
Maralal Kenya 1°0N 36°38E 54 B4
Maralinga Australia 30°13S 131°32E 61 F5
Marambio Antarctica 64°0S 56°0W 5 C18
Maran Malaysia 3°35N 102°45E 39 L4
Marana U.S.A. 32°27N 111°13W 77 K8
Maranboy Australia 14°40S 132°39E 60 B5
Marand Iran 38°30N 45°45E 44 B5
Marang Malaysia 5°12N 103°13E 39 K4
Maranguape Brazil 3°55S 38°50W 93 D11
Maranhão = São Luís Brazil 2°39S 44°15W 93 D10
Maranhão □ Brazil 5°0S 46°0W 93 E9
Maranoa → Australia 27°50S 148°37E 63 D4
Marañón → Peru 4°30S 73°35W 92 D4
Marão Mozam. 24°18S 34°2E 57 C5
Maraş = Kahramanmaraş Turkey 37°37N 36°53E 44 B3
Marathasa Cyprus 34°59N 32°51E 25 E11
Marathon Australia 20°51S 143°32E 62 C3
Marathon Canada 48°44N 86°23W 72 C2
Marathon N.Y., U.S.A. 42°27N 76°2W 83 D8
Marathon Tex., U.S.A. 30°12N 103°15W 84 F3
Marathóvouno Cyprus 35°13N 33°37E 25 D12
Maratua Indonesia 2°10N 118°35E 37 D5
Maraval Trin. & Tob. 10°42N 61°31W 93 K15
Maravatío Mexico 19°54N 100°27W 86 D4
Marāwih U.A.E. 24°18N 53°18E 45 E7
Marbella Spain 36°30N 4°57W 21 D3
Marble Bar Australia 21°9S 119°44E 60 D2
Marble Falls U.S.A. 30°35N 98°16W 84 F5
Marblehead U.S.A. 42°29N 70°51W 83 D14
Marburg Germany 50°47N 8°46E 16 C5
Marca, Pta. Da Angola 16°31S 11°43E 53 H2
March U.K. 52°33N 0°5E 13 E8
Marche France 46°5N 1°20E 20 C4
Marche-en-Famenne Belgium 50°14N 5°19E 15 D5
Marchena Spain 37°18N 5°23W 21 D3
Marco Island U.S.A. 25°58N 81°44W 85 J14
Marcos Juárez Argentina 32°42S 62°5W 94 C3
Marcus I. = Minami-Tori-Shima Pac. Oc. 24°20N 153°58E 64 E7
Marcy, Mt. U.S.A. 44°7N 73°56W 83 B11
Mardan Pakistan 34°20N 72°0E 42 B5
Mardin Turkey 37°20N 40°43E 44 B4
Maree, L. U.K. 57°40N 5°26W 11 D3
Mareeba Australia 16°59S 145°28E 62 B4
Mareetsane S. Africa 26°9S 25°25E 56 D4
Marek = Stanke Dimitrov Bulgaria 42°17N 23°9E 23 C10
Marengo U.S.A. 41°48N 92°4W 80 E7
Marerano Madag. 21°23S 44°52E 57 C7
Marfa U.S.A. 30°19N 104°1W 84 F2
Marfa Pt. Malta 35°59N 14°19E 25 D1
Margaret → Australia 18°9S 125°41E 60 C4
Margaret Bay Canada 51°20N 127°35W 70 C3
Margaret L. Canada 58°56N 115°25W 70 B5
Margaret River Australia 33°57S 115°4E 61 F2
Margarita, I. de Venezuela 11°0N 64°0W 92 A6
Margaritovo Russia 43°25N 134°45E 30 C7
Margate S. Africa 30°50S 30°20E 57 E5
Margate U.K. 51°23N 1°23E 13 F9
Margherita Pk. Uganda 0°22N 29°51E 54 B3
Mārgow, Dasht-e Afghan. 30°40N 62°30E 40 D3
Marguerite Canada 52°30N 122°25W 70 C4
Mari El □ Russia 56°30N 48°0E 18 C8
Mari Indus Pakistan 32°57N 71°34E 42 C4
Mari Republic = Mari El □ Russia 56°30N 48°0E 18 C8
María Elena Chile 22°18S 69°40W 94 A2
María Grande Argentina 31°45S 59°55W 94 C4
Maria I. N. Terr., Australia 14°52S 135°45E 62 A2
Maria I. Tas., Australia 42°35S 148°0E 63 G4
Maria Island △ Australia 42°38S 148°5E 63 G4
Maria van Diemen, C. N.Z. 34°29S 172°40E 59 A4
Mariakani Kenya 3°50S 39°27E 54 C4
Mariala △ Australia 25°57S 145°2E 63 D4
Marian Australia 21°9S 148°57E 62 K6
Marian L. Canada 63°0N 116°15W 70 A5
Mariana Trench Pac. Oc. 13°0N 145°0E 64 F6
Marianna U.S.A. 30°46N 85°14W 85 F12
Marias → U.S.A. 47°56N 110°30W 76 C8
Marías, Islas Mexico 21°25N 106°28W 86 C3
Mariato, Punta Panama 7°12N 80°52W 88 E3
Maribor Slovenia 46°36N 15°40E 16 E8
Marico → Africa 23°35S 26°57E 56 C4
Maricopa Ariz., U.S.A. 33°4N 112°3W 77 K7
Maricopa Calif., U.S.A. 35°4N 119°24W 79 K7
Marié → Brazil 0°27S 66°26W 92 D5
Marie Byrd Land Antarctica 79°30S 125°0W 5 D14
Marie-Galante Guadeloupe 15°56N 61°16W 88 b
Mariecourt = Kangiqsujuaq Canada 61°30N 72°0W 69 C12
Mariehamn Finland 60°5N 19°55E 9 F18
Mariembourg Belgium 50°6N 4°31E 15 D4
Mariental Namibia 24°36S 18°0E 56 C2
Marienville U.S.A. 41°28N 79°8W 82 E5
Mariestad Sweden 58°43N 13°50E 9 G15
Marietta Ga., U.S.A. 33°57N 84°33W 85 E12
Marietta Ohio, U.S.A. 39°25N 81°27W 81 F13
Marieville Canada 45°26N 73°10W 83 A11
Mariinsk Russia 56°10N 87°20E 28 D9
Marijampolė Lithuania 54°33N 23°19E 9 J20
Marília Brazil 22°13S 50°0W 95 A6
Marín Spain 42°23N 8°42W 21 A1
Marina U.S.A. 36°41N 121°48W 78 J5
Marinduque Phil. 13°25N 122°0E 37 B6
Marine City U.S.A. 42°43N 82°30W 82 D2
Marinette U.S.A. 45°6N 87°38W 80 C10
Maringá Brazil 23°26S 52°2W 95 A5
Marion Ala., U.S.A. 32°38N 87°19W 85 E11
Marion Ill., U.S.A. 37°44N 88°56W 80 G9
Marion Ind., U.S.A. 40°32N 85°40W 81 E11
Marion Iowa, U.S.A. 42°2N 91°36W 80 D8
Marion Kans., U.S.A. 38°21N 97°1W 80 F5
Marion N.C., U.S.A. 35°41N 82°1W 85 D13
Marion Ohio, U.S.A. 40°35N 83°8W 81 E12
Marion S.C., U.S.A. 34°11N 79°24W 85 D15
Marion Va., U.S.A. 36°50N 81°31W 81 G13
Marion, L. U.S.A. 33°28N 80°10W 85 E14
Mariposa U.S.A. 37°29N 119°58W 78 H7
Mariscal Estigarribia Paraguay 22°3S 60°40W 94 A3
Maritime Alps = Maritimes, Alpes Europe 44°10N 7°10E 20 D7
Maritimes, Alpes Europe 44°10N 7°10E 20 D7
Maritsa = Evros → Greece 41°40N 26°34E 23 D12
Maritsa Greece 36°22N 28°8E 25 C10
Mariupol Ukraine 47°5N 37°31E 19 E6
Mariusa △ Venezuela 9°24N 61°27W 89 E7
Marīvān Iran 35°30N 46°25E 44 C5
Marj 'Uyūn Lebanon 33°21N 35°34E 46 B4
Marka = Merca Somali Rep. 1°48N 44°50E 47 G3
Markam China 29°42N 98°38E 32 D4
Markdale Canada 44°19N 80°39W 82 B4
Marked Tree U.S.A. 35°32N 90°25W 85 D9
Market Drayton U.K. 52°54N 2°29W 12 E5
Market Harborough U.K. 52°29N 0°55W 13 E7
Market Rasen U.K. 53°24N 0°20W 12 D7
Markham Canada 43°52N 79°16W 82 C5
Markham, Mt. Antarctica 83°0S 164°0E 5 E11
Markleeville U.S.A. 38°42N 119°47W 78 G7
Markovo Russia 64°40N 170°24E 29 C17
Marks Russia 51°45N 46°50E 18 D8
Marksville U.S.A. 31°8N 92°4W 84 F8
Marla Australia 27°19S 133°33E 63 D1
Marlbank Canada 44°26N 77°6W 82 B7
Marlboro U.S.A. 41°36N 73°59W 83 E11
Marlborough Australia 22°46S 149°52E 62 C4
Marlborough U.K. 51°25N 1°43W 13 F6
Marlborough U.S.A. 42°21N 71°33W 83 D13
Marlborough Downs U.K. 51°27N 1°53W 13 F6
Marlin U.S.A. 31°18N 96°54W 84 F6
Marlow U.K. 51°34N 0°46W 13 F7
Marlow U.S.A. 34°39N 97°58W 84 D6
Marmagao India 15°25N 73°56E 40 M8
Marmara Turkey 40°35N 27°34E 23 D12
Marmara, Sea of = Marmara Denizi Turkey 40°45N 28°15E 23 D13
Marmara Denizi Turkey 40°45N 28°15E 23 D13
Marmaris Turkey 36°50N 28°14E 23 F13
Marmion, Mt. Australia 29°16S 119°50E 61 E2
Marmion L. Canada 48°55N 91°20W 72 C1
Marmolada, Mte. Italy 46°26N 11°51E 22 A4
Marmora Canada 44°28N 77°41W 82 B7
Marne → France 48°47N 2°29E 20 B5
Maroala Madag. 15°23S 47°59E 57 B8
Maroantsetra Madag. 15°26S 49°44E 57 B8
Maroelaboom Namibia 19°15S 18°53E 56 B2
Marofandilia Madag. 20°7S 44°34E 57 C7
Marojejy ⌓ Madag. 14°26S 49°21E 57 A8
Marolambo Madag. 20°2S 48°7E 57 C8
Maromandia Madag. 14°13S 48°5E 57 A8
Maromokotro Madag. 14°0S 49°0E 57 A8
Marondera Zimbabwe 18°5S 31°42E 55 F3
Maroni → Fr. Guiana 5°30N 54°0W 93 B8
Maroochydore Australia 26°29S 153°5E 63 D5
Maroona Australia 37°27S 142°54E 63 F3
Marosakoa Madag. 15°26S 46°38E 57 B8
Maroseranana Madag. 18°32S 48°51E 57 B8
Marotandrano Madag. 16°10S 48°50E 57 B8
Marotaolano Madag. 12°47S 49°15E 57 A8
Maroua Cameroon 10°40N 14°20E 51 F8
Marovato Madag. 15°48S 48°5E 57 B8
Marovoay Madag. 16°6S 46°39E 57 B8
Marquard S. Africa 28°40S 27°28E 56 D4
Marquesas Fracture Zone Pac. Oc. 9°0S 125°0W 65 H15
Marquesas Is. = Marquises, Îs. French Polynesia 9°30S 140°0W 65 H14
Marquette U.S.A. 46°33N 87°24W 80 B10
Marquis St. Lucia 14°2N 60°54W 89 f
Marquises, Îs. French Polynesia 9°30S 140°0W 65 H14
Marra, Djebel Sudan 13°10N 24°22E 51 F10
Marracuene Mozam. 25°45S 32°35E 57 D5
Marrakech Morocco 31°9N 8°0W 50 B4
Marrawah Australia 40°55S 144°42E 63 G3
Marree Australia 29°39S 138°1E 63 D2
Marrero U.S.A. 29°53N 90°6W 85 G9
Marrimane Mozam. 22°58S 33°34E 57 C5
Marromeu Mozam. 18°15S 36°25E 57 B6
Marromeu ⌓ Mozam. 19°0S 36°0E 57 B6
Marrowie Cr. → Australia 33°23S 145°40E 63 E4
Marrubane Mozam. 18°0S 37°0E 55 F4
Marrupa Mozam. 13°8S 37°30E 55 E4
Mars Hill U.S.A. 46°31N 67°52W 81 B20
Marsá Matrûh Egypt 31°19N 27°9E 51 B11
Marsá Susah Libya 32°52N 21°59E 51 B10
Marsabit Kenya 2°18N 38°0E 54 B4
Marsabit △ Kenya 2°23N 37°56E 54 B4
Marsala Italy 37°48N 12°26E 22 F5

Marsalforn *Malta* 36°4N 14°16E **25** C1
Marsden *Australia* 33°47S 147°32E **63** E4
Marseille *France* 43°18N 5°23E **20** E6
Marseilles = Marseille *France* 43°18N 5°23E **20** E6
Marsh I. *U.S.A.* 29°34N 91°53W **84** G9
Marshall *Ark., U.S.A.* 35°55N 92°38W **84** D8
Marshall *Mich., U.S.A.* 42°16N 84°58W **81** D11
Marshall *Minn., U.S.A.* 44°27N 95°47W **80** C6
Marshall *Mo., U.S.A.* 39°7N 93°12W **80** F7
Marshall *Tex., U.S.A.* 32°33N 94°23W **84** E7
Marshall → *Australia* 22°59S 136°59E **62** C2
Marshall Is. ■ *Pac. Oc.* 9°0N 171°0E **58** A10
Marshalltown *U.S.A.* 42°3N 92°55W **80** D7
Marshbrook *Zimbabwe* 18°33S 31°9E **57** B5
Marshfield *Mo., U.S.A.* 37°15N 92°54W **80** G7
Marshfield *Vt., U.S.A.* 44°20N 72°20W **83** B12
Marshfield *Wis., U.S.A.* 44°40N 90°10W **80** C8
Marshūn *Iran* 36°19N 49°23E **45** B6
Märsta *Sweden* 59°37N 17°52E **9** G17
Mart *U.S.A.* 31°33N 96°50W **84** F6
Martaban *Burma* 16°30N 97°35E **41** L20
Martaban, G. of *Burma* 16°5N 96°30E **41** L20
Martapura *Kalimantan, Indonesia* 3°22S 114°47E **36** E4
Martapura *Sumatera, Indonesia* 4°19S 104°22E **36** E2
Marte R. Gómez, Presa *Mexico* 26°10N 99°0W **87** B5
Martelange *Belgium* 49°49N 5°43E **15** E5
Martha's Vineyard *U.S.A.* 41°25N 70°38W **83** E14
Martigny *Switz.* 46°6N 7°3E **20** C7
Martigues *France* 43°24N 5°4E **20** E6
Martin *Slovak Rep.* 49°6N 18°58E **17** D10
Martin *S. Dak., U.S.A.* 43°11N 101°44W **80** D3
Martin *Tenn., U.S.A.* 36°21N 88°51W **85** C10
Martin L. *U.S.A.* 32°41N 85°55W **85** E12
Martina Franca *Italy* 40°42N 17°20E **22** D7
Martinborough *N.Z.* 41°14S 175°29E **59** D5
Martinez *Calif., U.S.A.* 38°1N 122°8W **78** G4
Martinez *Ga., U.S.A.* 33°31N 82°5W **85** E13
Martinique ☑ *W. Indies* 14°40N 61°0W **88** c
Martinique Passage *W. Indies* 15°15N 61°0W **89** C7
Martinópolis *Brazil* 22°11S 51°12W **95** A5
Martin's Bay *Barbados* 13°12N 59°29W **89** g
Martins Ferry *U.S.A.* 40°6N 80°44W **82** F4
Martinsburg *Pa., U.S.A.* 40°19N 78°20W **82** F6
Martinsburg *W. Va., U.S.A.* 39°27N 77°58W **81** F15
Martinsville *Ind., U.S.A.* 39°26N 86°25W **80** F10
Martinsville *Va., U.S.A.* 36°41N 79°52W **81** G14
Marton *N.Z.* 40°4S 175°23E **59** D5
Martos *Spain* 37°44N 3°58W **21** D4
Marudi *Malaysia* 4°11N 114°19E **36** D4
Maruf *Afghan.* 31°30N 67°6E **40** D5
Marugame *Japan* 34°15N 133°40E **31** G6
Marunga *Angola* 17°28S 20°2E **56** B3
Marungu, Mts. *Dem. Rep. of the Congo* 7°30S 30°0E **54** D3
Marv Dasht *Iran* 29°50N 52°40E **45** D7
Marvast *Iran* 30°30N 54°15E **45** D7
Marvel Loch *Australia* 31°28S 119°29E **61** F2
Marwar *India* 25°43N 73°45E **42** G5
Mary *Turkmenistan* 37°40N 61°50E **45** B9
Maryborough = Port Laoise *Ireland* 53°2N 7°18W **10** C4
Maryborough *Queens., Australia* 25°31S 152°37E **63** D5
Maryborough *Vic., Australia* 37°3S 143°44E **63** F3
Maryfield *Canada* 49°50N 101°35W **71** D8
Maryland □ *U.S.A.* 39°0N 76°30W **81** F15
Maryland Junction *Zimbabwe* 17°45S 30°31E **55** F3
Maryport *U.K.* 54°44N 3°28W **12** C4
Mary's Harbour *Canada* 52°18N 55°51W **73** B8
Marystown *Canada* 47°10N 55°10W **73** C8
Marysville *Canada* 49°35N 116°0W **70** D5
Marysville *Calif., U.S.A.* 39°9N 121°35W **78** F5
Marysville *Kans., U.S.A.* 39°51N 96°39W **80** F5
Marysville *Mich., U.S.A.* 42°54N 82°29W **82** D2
Marysville *Ohio, U.S.A.* 40°14N 83°22W **81** E12
Marysville *Wash., U.S.A.* 48°3N 122°11W **78** B4
Maryville *Mo., U.S.A.* 40°21N 94°52W **80** E6
Maryville *Tenn., U.S.A.* 35°46N 83°58W **85** D13
Marzūq *Libya* 25°53N 13°57E **51** C8
Marzūq, Idehān *Libya* 24°50N 13°51E **51** D8
Masada *Israel* 31°15N 35°20E **46** D4
Masahunga *Tanzania* 2°6S 33°18E **54** C3
Masai *Malaysia* 1°29N 103°55E **39** d
Masai Mara △ *Kenya* 1°25S 35°5E **54** C4
Masai Steppe *Tanzania* 4°30S 36°30E **54** C4
Masaka *Uganda* 0°21S 31°45E **54** C3
Masalembo, Kepulauan *Indonesia* 5°35S 114°30E **36** F4
Masalima, Kepulauan *Indonesia* 5°4S 117°5E **36** F5
Masamba *Indonesia* 2°30S 120°15E **37** E6
Masan *S. Korea* 35°11N 128°32E **35** G15
Masandam, Ra's *Oman* 26°30N 56°30E **45** E8
Masasi *Tanzania* 10°45S 38°52E **55** E4
Masaya *Nic.* 12°0N 86°7W **88** D2
Masbate *Phil.* 12°21N 123°36E **37** B6
Mascara *Algeria* 35°26N 0°6E **50** A6
Mascota *Mexico* 20°32N 104°49W **86** C4
Masela *Indonesia* 8°9S 129°51E **37** F7
Maseru *Lesotho* 29°18S 27°30E **56** D4
Mashaba *Zimbabwe* 20°2S 30°29E **55** G3
Mashābih *Si. Arabia* 25°35N 36°30E **44** E3
Mashatu ⌓ *Botswana* 22°45S 29°5E **57** C4
Masherbrum *Pakistan* 35°38N 76°18E **43** B7
Mashhad *Iran* 36°20N 59°35E **45** B8
Mashīz *Iran* 29°56N 56°37E **45** D8
Māshkel, Hāmūn-i- *Pakistan* 28°20N 62°56E **45** D9
Mashki Chāh *Pakistan* 29°5N 62°30E **40** E3
Mashonaland *Zimbabwe* 16°30S 31°0E **53** H6
Mashonaland Central □ *Zimbabwe* 17°30S 31°0E **57** B5
Mashonaland East □ *Zimbabwe* 18°0S 32°0E **57** B5
Mashonaland West □ *Zimbabwe* 17°30S 29°30E **57** B4
Mashrakh *India* 26°7N 84°48E **43** F11
Masi Manimba *Dem. Rep. of the Congo* 4°40S 17°54E **52** E3
Masindi *Uganda* 1°40N 31°43E **54** B3
Masindi Port *Uganda* 1°43N 32°2E **54** B3
Maşīrah *Oman* 21°0N 58°50E **47** C6
Maşīrah, Khalīj *Oman* 20°10N 58°10E **47** C6
Masisi *Dem. Rep. of the Congo* 1°23S 28°49E **54** C2
Masjed Soleyman *Iran* 31°55N 49°18E **45** D6
Mask, L. *Ireland* 53°36N 9°22W **10** C2
Maskin *Oman* 23°44N 56°52E **45** F8
Masoala, Tanjon' i *Madag.* 15°59S 50°13E **57** B9
Masoala △ *Madag.* 15°30S 50°12E **57** B9
Masoarivo *Madag.* 19°3S 44°19E **57** B7
Masohi = Amahai *Indonesia* 3°20S 128°55E **37** E7
Masomeloka *Madag.* 20°17S 48°37E **57** C8
Mason *Nev., U.S.A.* 38°56N 119°8W **78** G7
Mason *Tex., U.S.A.* 30°45N 99°14W **84** F5
Mason City *U.S.A.* 43°9N 93°12W **80** D7
Maspalomas *Canary Is.* 27°46N 15°35W **24** G4
Maspalomas, Pta. *Canary Is.* 27°43N 15°36W **24** G4
Masqat *Oman* 23°37N 58°36E **47** C6
Massa *Italy* 44°1N 10°9E **20** D9
Massachusetts □ *U.S.A.* 42°30N 72°0W **83** D13
Massachusetts B. *U.S.A.* 42°25N 70°50W **83** D14
Massakory *Chad* 13°0N 15°49E **51** F9
Massanella *Spain* 39°48N 2°51E **24** B9
Massangena *Mozam.* 21°34S 33°0E **57** C5
Massango *Angola* 8°2S 16°21E **52** F3
Massawa = Mitsiwa *Eritrea* 15°35N 39°25E **47** D2
Massena *U.S.A.* 44°56N 74°54W **83** B10
Massénya *Chad* 11°21N 16°9E **51** F9
Masset *Canada* 54°2N 132°10W **70** C2
Massiah Street *Barbados* 13°9N 59°29W **89** g
Massif Central *France* 44°55N 3°0E **20** D5
Massillon *U.S.A.* 40°48N 81°32W **82** F3
Massinga *Mozam.* 23°15S 35°22E **57** C6
Massingir *Mozam.* 23°51S 32°4E **57** C5
Masson-Angers *Canada* 45°32N 75°25W **83** A9
Masson I. *Antarctica* 66°10S 93°20E **5** C7
Mastanli = Momchilgrad *Bulgaria* 41°33N 25°23E **23** D11
Masterton *N.Z.* 40°56S 175°39E **59** D5
Mastic *U.S.A.* 40°47N 72°54W **83** F11
Mastuj *Pakistan* 36°20N 72°36E **43** A5
Mastung *Pakistan* 29°50N 66°56E **40** E5
Masty *Belarus* 53°27N 24°38E **17** B13
Masuda *Japan* 34°40N 131°51E **31** G5
Masvingo *Zimbabwe* 20°8S 30°49E **55** G3
Masvingo □ *Zimbabwe* 21°0S 31°30E **55** G3
Maswa ⌓ *Tanzania* 2°58S 34°19E **54** C3
Maşyāf *Syria* 35°4N 36°20E **44** C3
Mata-au = Clutha → *N.Z.* 46°20S 169°49E **59** G2
Matabeleland *Zimbabwe* 18°0S 27°0E **53** H5
Matabeleland North □ *Zimbabwe* 19°0S 28°0E **55** F2
Matabeleland South □ *Zimbabwe* 21°0S 29°0E **55** G2
Matachewan *Canada* 47°56N 80°39W **72** C3
Matadi *Dem. Rep. of the Congo* 5°52S 13°31E **52** F2
Matagalpa *Nic.* 13°0N 85°58W **88** D2
Matagami *Canada* 49°45N 77°34W **72** C4
Matagami, L. *Canada* 49°50N 77°40W **72** C4
Matagorda B. *U.S.A.* 28°40N 96°12W **84** G6
Matagorda I. *U.S.A.* 28°15N 96°30W **84** G6
Mataiea *Tahiti* 17°46S 149°25W **59** d
Matak *Indonesia* 3°18N 106°16E **36** D3
Matala *Greece* 34°59N 24°45E **25** E6
Matam *Senegal* 15°34N 13°17W **50** E3
Matamoros *Campeche, Mexico* 18°50N 90°50W **87** D6
Matamoros *Coahuila, Mexico* 25°32N 103°15W **86** B4
Matamoros *Tamaulipas, Mexico* 25°53N 97°30W **87** B5
Ma'ţan as Sarra *Libya* 21°45N 22°0E **51** D10
Matandu → *Tanzania* 8°45S 34°19E **55** D3
Matane *Canada* 48°50N 67°33W **73** C6
Matanomadh *India* 23°33N 68°57E **42** H3
Matanzas *Cuba* 23°0N 81°40W **88** B3
Matapa *Botswana* 23°11S 24°39E **56** C3
Matapan, C. = Tenaro, Akra *Greece* 36°22N 22°27E **23** F10
Matapédia *Canada* 48°0N 66°59W **73** C6
Matapo △ *Zimbabwe* 20°30S 29°40E **55** G2
Matara *Sri Lanka* 5°58N 80°30E **40** S12
Mataram *Indonesia* 8°35S 116°7E **36** F5
Matarani *Peru* 17°0S 72°10W **92** G4
Mataranka *Australia* 14°55S 133°4E **60** B5
Matarma, Râs *Egypt* 30°27N 32°44E **46** E1
Mataró *Spain* 41°32N 2°29E **21** B7
Matatiele *S. Africa* 30°20S 28°49E **57** E4
Mataura *N.Z.* 46°11S 168°51E **59** G2
Matavai, B. de *Tahiti* 17°30S 149°23W **59** d
Matehuala *Mexico* 23°39N 100°39W **86** C4
Mateke Hills *Zimbabwe* 21°48S 31°0E **55** G3
Matelot *Trin. & Tob.* 10°50N 61°7W **93** K15
Matera *Italy* 40°40N 16°36E **22** D7
Matetsi *Zimbabwe* 18°12S 26°0E **55** F2
Matheniko ⌓ *Uganda* 2°49N 34°27E **54** B3
Mathis *U.S.A.* 28°6N 97°50W **84** G6
Mathraki *Greece* 39°48N 19°31E **25** A3
Mathura *India* 27°30N 77°40E **42** F7
Mati *Phil.* 6°55N 126°15E **37** C7
Matiali *India* 26°56N 88°49E **43** F13
Matías Romero *Mexico* 16°53N 95°2W **87** D5
Matibane *Mozam.* 14°49S 40°45E **55** E5
Matiri Ra. *N.Z.* 41°38S 172°20E **59** D4
Matjiesfontein *S. Africa* 33°14S 20°35E **56** E3
Matla → *India* 21°40N 88°40E **43** J13
Matlamanyane *Botswana* 19°33S 25°57E **56** B4
Matli *Pakistan* 25°2N 68°39E **42** G3
Matlock *U.K.* 53°9N 1°33W **12** D6
Mato Grosso □ *Brazil* 14°0S 55°0W **93** F8
Mato Grosso, Planalto do *Brazil* 15°0S 55°0W **93** G8
Mato Grosso do Sul □ *Brazil* 18°0S 55°0W **93** G8
Matobo = Matapo △ *Zimbabwe* 20°30S 29°40E **55** G2
Matochkin Shar *Russia* 73°10N 56°40E **28** B6
Matopo Hills *Zimbabwe* 20°36S 28°20E **55** G2
Matopos *Zimbabwe* 20°20S 28°29E **55** G2
Matosinhos *Portugal* 41°11N 8°42W **21** B1
Matroosberg *S. Africa* 33°23S 19°40E **56** E2
Maţruḩ *Oman* 23°37N 58°30E **47** C6
Matsue *Japan* 35°25N 133°10E **31** G6
Matsum, Ko *Thailand* 9°22N 99°59E **39** b
Matsumae *Japan* 41°26N 140°7E **30** D10
Matsumoto *Japan* 36°15N 138°0E **31** F9
Matsusaka *Japan* 34°34N 136°32E **31** G8
Matsuura *Japan* 33°20N 129°49E **31** H4
Matsuyama *Japan* 33°45N 132°45E **31** H6
Mattagami → *Canada* 50°43N 81°29W **72** B3
Mattancheri *India* 9°50N 76°15E **40** Q10
Mattawa *Canada* 46°20N 78°45W **72** C4
Matterhorn *Switz.* 45°58N 7°39E **20** D7
Matthew Town *Bahamas* 20°57N 73°40W **89** B5
Matthews Ridge *Guyana* 7°37N 60°10W **92** B6
Mattice *Canada* 49°40N 83°20W **72** C3
Mattituck *U.S.A.* 40°59N 72°32W **83** F12
Mattō *Japan* 36°31N 136°34E **31** F8
Mattoon *U.S.A.* 39°29N 88°23W **80** F9
Matuba *Mozam.* 24°28S 32°49E **57** C5
Matucana *Peru* 11°55S 76°25W **92** F3
Matuku *Fiji* 19°10S 179°44E **59** a
Matūn = Khowst *Afghan.* 33°22N 69°58E **42** C3
Matura B. *Trin. & Tob.* 10°39N 61°1W **93** K15
Maturín *Venezuela* 9°45N 63°11W **92** B6
Matusadona △ *Zimbabwe* 16°58S 28°42E **55** F2
Mau *Mad. P., India* 26°17N 78°41E **43** F8
Mau *Ut. P., India* 25°56N 83°33E **43** G10
Mau *Ut. P., India* 25°17N 81°23E **43** G9
Mau Escarpment *Kenya* 0°40S 36°0E **54** C4
Mau Ranipur *India* 25°16N 79°8E **43** G8
Maua *Kenya* 0°14N 37°56E **54** C4
Maubeuge *France* 50°17N 3°57E **20** A6
Maubin *Burma* 16°44N 95°39E **41** L19
Maud, Pt. *Australia* 23°6S 113°45E **60** D1
Maud Rise *S. Ocean* 66°0S 3°0E **5** C3
Maude *Australia* 34°29S 144°18E **63** E3
Maudin Sun *Burma* 16°0N 94°30E **41** M19
Maués *Brazil* 3°20S 57°45W **92** D7
Mauganj *India* 24°50N 81°55E **43** G9
Maughold Hd. *I. of Man* 54°18N 4°18W **12** C3
Maui *U.S.A.* 20°48N 156°20W **74** b
Maulamyaing = Moulmein *Burma* 16°30N 97°40E **41** L20
Maule □ *Chile* 36°5S 72°30W **94** D1
Maumee *U.S.A.* 41°34N 83°39W **81** E12
Maumee → *U.S.A.* 41°42N 83°28W **81** E12
Maumere *Indonesia* 8°38S 122°13E **37** F6
Maun *Botswana* 20°0S 23°26E **56** C3
Mauna Kea *U.S.A.* 19°50N 155°28W **74** b
Mauna Loa *U.S.A.* 19°30N 155°35W **74** b
Maungmagan Kyunzu *Burma* 14°0N 97°48E **38** E1
Maungu *Kenya* 3°33S 38°45E **54** C4
Maupin *U.S.A.* 45°11N 121°5W **76** D3
Maurepas, L. *U.S.A.* 30°15N 90°30W **85** F9
Maurice, L. *Australia* 29°30S 131°0E **61** E5
Mauricie △ *Canada* 46°45N 73°0W **72** C5
Mauritania ■ *Africa* 20°50N 10°0W **50** E3
Mauritius ■ *Ind. Oc.* 20°0S 57°0E **53** d
Mauston *U.S.A.* 43°48N 90°5W **80** D8
Mavli *India* 24°45N 73°55E **42** G5
Mavuradonha Mts. *Zimbabwe* 16°30S 31°30E **55** F3
Mawa *Dem. Rep. of the Congo* 2°45N 26°40E **54** B2
Mawai *India* 22°30N 81°4E **43** H9
Mawana *India* 29°6N 77°58E **42** E7
Mawand *Pakistan* 29°33N 68°38E **42** E3
Mawjib, W. al → *Jordan* 31°28N 35°36E **46** D4
Mawk Mai *Burma* 20°14N 97°37E **41** J20
Mawlaik *Burma* 23°40N 94°26E **41** H19
Mawlamyine = Moulmein *Burma* 16°30N 97°40E **41** L20
Mawqaq *Si. Arabia* 27°25N 41°8E **44** E4
Mawson Base *Antarctica* 67°30S 62°53E **5** C6
Mawson Coast *Antarctica* 68°30S 63°0E **5** C6
Max *U.S.A.* 47°49N 101°18W **80** B3
Maxcanú *Mexico* 20°35N 90°0W **87** C6
Maxesibeni *S. Africa* 30°49S 29°23E **57** E4
Maxhamish L. *Canada* 59°50N 123°17W **70** B4
Maxixe *Mozam.* 23°54S 35°17E **57** C6
Maxville *Canada* 45°17N 74°51W **83** A10
Maxwell *U.S.A.* 39°17N 122°11W **78** F4
Maxwelton *Australia* 20°43S 142°41E **62** C3
May, C. *U.S.A.* 38°56N 74°58W **81** F16
May Pen *Jamaica* 17°58N 77°15W **88** a
Maya → *Russia* 60°28N 134°28E **29** D14
Maya Mts. *Belize* 16°30N 89°0W **87** D7
Mayaguana *Bahamas* 22°30N 72°44W **89** B5
Mayagüez *Puerto Rico* 18°12N 67°9W **89** d
Mayāmey *Iran* 36°24N 55°42E **45** B7
Mayanup *Australia* 33°57S 116°27E **61** F2
Mayapán *Mexico* 20°29N 89°11W **87** C7
Mayarí *Cuba* 20°40N 75°41W **89** B4
Mayaro B. *Trin. & Tob.* 10°14N 60°59W **93** K16
Maybell *U.S.A.* 40°31N 108°5W **76** F9
Maybole *U.K.* 55°21N 4°42W **11** F4
Maydān *Iraq* 34°55N 45°37E **44** C5
Maydena *Australia* 42°45S 146°30E **63** G4
Mayenne → *France* 47°30N 0°32W **20** C3
Mayer *U.S.A.* 34°24N 112°14W **77** J7
Mayerthorpe *Canada* 53°57N 115°8W **70** C5
Mayfield *Ky., U.S.A.* 36°44N 88°38W **80** G9
Mayfield *N.Y., U.S.A.* 43°6N 74°16W **83** C10
Mayhill *U.S.A.* 32°53N 105°29W **77** K11
Maykop *Russia* 44°35N 40°10E **19** F7
Maymyo *Burma* 22°2N 96°28E **38** A1
Maynard *Mass., U.S.A.* 42°26N 71°27W **83** D13
Maynard *Wash., U.S.A.* 47°59N 122°55W **78** C4
Maynard Hills *Australia* 28°28S 119°49E **61** E2
Mayne → *Australia* 23°40S 141°55E **62** C3
Maynooth *Ireland* 53°23N 6°34W **10** C5
Mayo *Canada* 63°38N 135°57W **68** C6
Mayo □ *Ireland* 53°53N 9°3W **10** C2
Mayon Volcano *Phil.* 13°15N 123°41E **37** B6
Mayor I. *N.Z.* 37°16S 176°17E **59** B6
Mayotte ☑ *Ind. Oc.* 12°50S 45°10E **53** a
Maysān □ *Iraq* 31°55N 47°15E **44** D5
Maysville *U.S.A.* 38°39N 83°46W **81** F12
Mayu *Indonesia* 1°30N 126°30E **37** D7
Mayville *N. Dak., U.S.A.* 47°30N 97°20W **80** B5
Mayville *N.Y., U.S.A.* 42°15N 79°30W **82** D5
Mayya *Russia* 61°44N 130°18E **29** C14
Mazabuka *Zambia* 15°52S 27°44E **55** F2
Mazagán = El Jadida *Morocco* 33°11N 8°17W **50** B4
Mazagão *Brazil* 0°7S 51°16W **93** D8
Mazán *Peru* 3°30S 73°0W **92** D4
Māzandarān □ *Iran* 36°30N 52°0E **45** B7
Mazapil *Mexico* 24°39N 101°34W **86** C4
Mazar *China* 36°32N 77°1E **32** C2
Mazara del Vallo *Italy* 37°39N 12°35E **22** F5
Mazarrón *Spain* 37°38N 1°19W **21** D5
Mazaruni → *Guyana* 6°25N 58°35W **92** B7
Mazatán *Mexico* 29°0N 110°8W **86** B2
Mazatenango *Guatemala* 14°35N 91°30W **88** D1
Mazatlán *Mexico* 23°13N 106°25W **86** C3
Mažeikiai *Lithuania* 56°20N 22°20E **9** H20
Māzhān *Iran* 32°30N 59°0E **45** C8
Mazīnān *Iran* 36°19N 56°56E **45** B8
Mazoe *Mozam.* 16°42S 33°7E **55** F3
Mazoe → *Mozam.* 16°20S 33°30E **55** F3
Mazowe *Zimbabwe* 17°28S 30°58E **55** F3
Mazurian Lakes = Mazurski, Pojezierze *Poland* 53°50N 21°0E **17** B11
Mazurski, Pojezierze *Poland* 53°50N 21°0E **17** B11
Mazyr *Belarus* 51°59N 29°15E **17** B15
Mba *Fiji* 17°33S 177°41E **59** a
Mbabane *Swaziland* 26°18S 31°6E **57** D5
Mbaïki *C.A.R.* 3°53N 18°1E **52** D3
Mbala *Zambia* 8°46S 31°24E **55** D3
Mbalabala *Zimbabwe* 20°27S 29°3E **57** C4
Mbale *Uganda* 1°8N 34°12E **54** B3
Mbalmayo *Cameroon* 3°33N 11°33E **52** D2
Mbamba Bay *Tanzania* 11°13S 34°49E **55** E3
Mbandaka *Dem. Rep. of the Congo* 0°1N 18°18E **52** D3
Mbanza Congo *Angola* 6°18S 14°16E **52** F2
Mbanza Ngungu *Dem. Rep. of the Congo* 5°12S 14°53E **52** F2
Mbarangandu *Tanzania* 10°11S 36°48E **55** D4
Mbarara *Uganda* 0°35S 30°40E **54** C3
Mbengga = Beqa *Fiji* 18°23S 178°8E **59** a
Mbenkuru → *Tanzania* 9°25S 39°50E **55** D4
Mberengwa *Zimbabwe* 20°29S 29°57E **55** G2
Mberengwa, Mt. *Zimbabwe* 20°37S 29°55E **55** G2
Mbesuma *Zambia* 10°0S 32°2E **55** E3
Mbeya *Tanzania* 8°54S 33°29E **55** D3
Mbeya □ *Tanzania* 8°15S 33°30E **54** D3
Mbhashe → *S. Africa* 32°15S 28°54E **57** E4
Mbinga *Tanzania* 10°50S 35°0E **55** E4
Mbini = Río Muni □ *Eq. Guin.* 1°30N 10°0E **52** D2
Mbour *Senegal* 14°22N 16°54W **50** F2
Mbuji-Mayi *Dem. Rep. of the Congo* 6°9S 23°40E **54** D1
Mbulu *Tanzania* 3°45S 35°30E **54** C4
Mburucuyá *Argentina* 28°1S 58°14W **94** B4
Mchinja *Tanzania* 9°44S 39°45E **55** D4
Mchinji *Malawi* 13°47S 32°58E **55** E3
Mdantsane *S. Africa* 32°56S 27°46E **53** L5
Mead, L. *U.S.A.* 36°0N 114°44W **79** J12
Meade *U.S.A.* 37°17N 100°20W **80** G3
Meadow Lake *Canada* 54°10N 108°26W **71** C7
Meadow Lake ⌓ *Canada* 54°27N 109°0W **71** C7
Meadow Valley Wash → *U.S.A.* 36°40N 114°34W **79** J12
Meadville *U.S.A.* 41°39N 80°9W **82** E4
Meaford *Canada* 44°36N 80°35W **82** B4
Mealy Mts. *Canada* 53°10N 58°0W **73** B8
Meander River *Canada* 59°2N 117°42W **70** B5
Meares, C. *U.S.A.* 45°37N 124°0W **76** D1
Mearim → *Brazil* 3°4S 44°35W **93** D10
Meath □ *Ireland* 53°40N 6°57W **10** C5
Meath Park *Canada* 53°27N 105°22W **71** C7
Meaux *France* 48°58N 2°50E **20** B5
Mebechi-Gawa → *Japan* 40°31N 141°31E **30** D10
Mebulu, Tanjung *Indonesia* 8°50S 115°5E **37** K18
Mecanhelas *Mozam.* 15°12S 35°54E **55** F4
Mecca = Makkah *Si. Arabia* 21°30N 39°54E **47** C2
Mecca *U.S.A.* 33°34N 116°5W **79** M10
Mechanicsburg *U.S.A.* 40°13N 77°1W **82** F8
Mechanicville *U.S.A.* 42°54N 73°41W **83** D11
Mechelen *Belgium* 51°2N 4°29E **15** C4
Mecheria *Algeria* 33°35N 0°18W **50** B5
Mecklenburg *Germany* 53°33N 11°40E **16** B7
Mecklenburger Bucht *Germany* 54°20N 11°40E **16** A6
Meconta *Mozam.* 14°59S 39°50E **55** E4
Medan *Indonesia* 3°40N 98°38E **36** D1
Médanos de Coro △ *Venezuela* 11°35N 69°44W **89** D6
Medanosa, Pta. *Argentina* 48°8S 66°0W **96** F3
Médéa *Algeria* 36°12N 2°50E **50** A6
Medellín *Colombia* 6°15N 75°35W **92** B3
Medelpad *Sweden* 62°33N 16°30E **8** E17
Medemblik *Neths.* 52°46N 5°8E **15** B5
Medford *Mass., U.S.A.* 42°25N 71°7W **83** D13
Medford *Oreg., U.S.A.* 42°19N 122°52W **76** E2
Medford *Wis., U.S.A.* 45°9N 90°20W **80** C8
Medgidia *Romania* 44°15N 28°19E **17** F15
Media Agua *Argentina* 31°58S 68°25W **94** C2
Media Luna *Argentina* 34°45S 66°44W **94** C2
Medianeira *Brazil* 25°17S 54°5W **95** B5
Mediaş *Romania* 46°9N 24°22E **17** E13
Medicine Bow *U.S.A.* 41°54N 106°12W **76** F10
Medicine Bow Mts. *U.S.A.* 40°40N 106°0W **76** F10
Medicine Bow Pk. *U.S.A.* 41°21N 106°19W **76** F10
Medicine Hat *Canada* 50°0N 110°45W **71** D6
Medicine Lake *U.S.A.* 48°30N 104°30W **76** B11
Medicine Lodge *U.S.A.* 37°17N 98°35W **80** G4
Medina = Al Madīnah *Si. Arabia* 24°35N 39°52E **44** E3
Medina *N. Dak., U.S.A.* 46°54N 99°18W **80** B4
Medina *N.Y., U.S.A.* 43°13N 78°23W **82** C6
Medina *Ohio, U.S.A.* 41°8N 81°52W **82** E3
Medina → *U.S.A.* 29°16N 98°29W **84** G5
Medina del Campo *Spain* 41°18N 4°55W **21** B3
Medina L. *U.S.A.* 29°32N 98°56W **84** G5
Medina Sidonia *Spain* 36°28N 5°57W **21** D3
Medinipur *India* 22°25N 87°21E **43** H12
Mediterranean Sea *Europe* 35°0N 15°0E **6** H7
Médoc *France* 45°10N 0°50W **20** D3
Medveditsa → *Russia* 49°35N 42°41E **19** E7
Medvezhi, Ostrava *Russia* 71°0N 161°0E **29** B17
Medvezhyegorsk *Russia* 63°0N 34°25E **18** B5
Medway □ *U.K.* 51°25N 0°32E **13** F8
Medway → *U.K.* 51°27N 0°46E **13** F8
Meekatharra *Australia* 26°32S 118°29E **61** E2
Meeker *U.S.A.* 40°2N 107°55W **76** F10
Meelpaeg L. *Canada* 48°20N 56°0W **73** C8
Meerut *India* 29°1N 77°42E **42** E7
Meeteetse *U.S.A.* 44°9N 108°52W **76** D9
Mega *Ethiopia* 3°57N 38°19E **47** G2
Megara *Greece* 37°58N 23°22E **23** F10
Megasini *India* 21°38N 86°21E **43** J12
Meghalaya □ *India* 25°50N 91°0E **41** G17
Meghna → *Bangla.* 22°50N 90°50E **41** H17
Mégiscane, L. *Canada* 48°35N 75°55W **72** C4
Meharry, Mt. *Australia* 22°59S 118°35E **60** D2
Mehlville *U.S.A.* 38°31N 90°19W **80** F8
Mehndawal *India* 26°58N 83°5E **43** F10
Mehr Jān *Iran* 33°50N 55°6E **45** C7
Mehrābād *Iran* 36°53N 47°55E **44** B5
Mehrān *Iran* 33°7N 46°10E **44** C5
Mehrgarh *Pakistan* 29°30N 67°30E **42** E2
Mehrīz *Iran* 31°35N 54°28E **45** D7
Mei Xian *China* 34°10N 107°55E **34** G4
Meighen I. *Canada* 80°0N 99°30W **69** B10
Meihekou *China* 42°32N 125°40E **35** C13
Meiktila *Burma* 20°53N 95°54E **41** J19
Meissen *Germany* 51°9N 13°29E **16** C7
Meizhou *China* 24°16N 116°6E **33** D6
Meja *India* 25°9N 82°7E **43** G10
Mejillones *Chile* 23°10S 70°30W **94** A1
Mekele *Ethiopia* 13°33N 39°30E **47** E2
Mekerghene, Sebkra *Algeria* 26°21N 1°30E **50** C6
Mekhtar *Pakistan* 30°30N 69°15E **40** D6
Meknès *Morocco* 33°57N 5°33W **50** B4
Mekong → *Asia* 9°30N 106°15E **39** H6
Mekongga *Indonesia* 3°39S 121°15E **37** E6
Mekvari = Kür → *Azerbaijan* 39°29N 49°15E **19** G8
Melagiri Hills *India* 12°20N 77°30E **40** N10
Melaka *Malaysia* 2°15N 102°15E **39** L4
Melalap *Malaysia* 5°10N 116°5E **36** C5
Melambes *Greece* 35°8N 24°40E **25** D6
Melanesia *Pac. Oc.* 4°0S 155°0E **64** H7
Melanesian Basin *Pac. Oc.* 0°5N 160°35E **64** G8
Melaya *Indonesia* 8°17S 114°30E **37** J17
Melbourne *Australia* 37°48S 144°58E **63** F4
Melbourne *U.S.A.* 28°5N 80°37W **85** G14
Melchor Múzquiz *Mexico* 27°53N 101°31W **86** B4
Melchor Ocampo *Mexico* 24°51N 101°39W **86** C4
Mélèzes → *Canada* 57°40N 69°29W **72** A5
Melfort *Canada* 52°50N 104°37W **71** C8
Melfort *Zimbabwe* 18°0S 31°25E **55** F3
Melhus *Norway* 63°17N 10°18E **8** E14
Melilla *N. Afr.* 35°21N 2°57W **21** E4
Melipilla *Chile* 33°42S 71°15W **94** C1
Melissa, Akra *Greece* 35°6N 24°33E **25** D6

Melita *Canada* 49°15N 101°0W 71 D8
Melitopol *Ukraine* 46°50N 35°22E 19 E6
Melk *Austria* 48°13N 15°20E 16 D8
Mellansel *Sweden* 63°26N 18°19E 8 E18
Mellen *U.S.A.* 46°20N 90°40W 80 B8
Mellerud *Sweden* 58°41N 12°28E 9 G15
Mellette *U.S.A.* 45°9N 98°30W 80 C4
Mellieha *Malta* 35°57N 14°22E 25 D1
Melo *Uruguay* 32°20S 54°10W 95 C5
Melolo *Indonesia* 9°53S 120°40E 37 F6
Melouprey *Cambodia* 13°48N 105°16E 38 F5
Melrhir, Chott *Algeria* 34°13N 6°30E 50 B7
Melrose *Australia* 32°42S 146°57E 63 E4
Melrose *U.K.* 55°36N 2°43W 11 F6
Melrose *Minn., U.S.A.* 45°40N 94°49W 80 C6
Melrose *N. Mex., U.S.A.* 34°26N 103°38W 77 J12
Melstone *U.S.A.* 46°36N 107°52W 76 C10
Melton Mowbray *U.K.* 52°47N 0°54W 12 E7
Melun *France* 48°32N 2°39E 20 B5
Melville *Canada* 50°55N 102°50W 71 C8
Melville, C. *Australia* 14°11S 144°30E 62 A3
Melville, L. *Canada* 53°30N 60°0W 73 B8
Melville B. *Australia* 12°0S 136°45E 62 A2
Melville I. *Australia* 11°30S 131°0E 60 B5
Melville I. *Canada* 75°30N 112°0W 69 B8
Melville Pen. *Canada* 68°0N 84°0W 69 C11
Melvin, Lough *Ireland* 54°26N 8°10W 10 B3
Memba *Mozam.* 14°11S 40°30E 55 E5
Memboro *Indonesia* 9°30S 119°30E 37 F5
Memel = Klaipėda *Lithuania* 55°43N 21°10E 9 J19
Memel *S. Africa* 27°38S 29°36E 57 D4
Memmingen *Germany* 47°58N 10°10E 16 E6
Mempawah *Indonesia* 0°30N 109°5E 36 D3
Memphis *Mich., U.S.A.* 42°54N 82°46W 82 D2
Memphis *Tenn., U.S.A.* 35°8N 90°2W 85 D9
Memphis *Tex., U.S.A.* 34°44N 100°33W 84 D4
Memphrémagog, L. *N. Amer.* 45°8N 72°17W 83 B12
Mena *U.S.A.* 34°35N 94°15W 84 D7
Menai Strait *U.K.* 53°11N 4°13W 12 D3
Ménaka *Mali* 15°59N 2°18E 50 E6
Menan = Chao Phraya → *Thailand* 13°40N 100°31E 38 F3
Menarandra → *Madag.* 25°17S 44°30E 57 D7
Menard *U.S.A.* 30°55N 99°47W 84 F5
Menard Fracture Zone *Pac. Oc.* 43°0S 97°0W 65 M18
Mendaña Fracture Zone *Pac. Oc.* 16°0S 91°0W 65 J18
Mendawai → *Indonesia* 3°30S 113°0E 36 E4
Mende *France* 44°31N 3°30E 20 D5
Mendeleyev Ridge *Arctic* 80°0N 178°0W 4 B17
Mendhar *India* 33°35N 74°10E 43 C6
Mendip Hills *U.K.* 51°17N 2°40W 13 F5
Mendocino *U.S.A.* 39°19N 123°48W 76 G2
Mendocino, C. *U.S.A.* 40°26N 124°25W 76 F1
Mendocino Fracture Zone *Pac. Oc.* 40°0N 142°0W 65 D13
Mendota *Calif., U.S.A.* 36°45N 120°23W 78 J6
Mendota *Ill., U.S.A.* 41°33N 89°7W 80 E9
Mendoyo *Indonesia* 8°23S 114°42E 37 J17
Mendoza *Argentina* 32°50S 68°52W 94 C2
Mendoza □ *Argentina* 33°0S 69°0W 94 C2
Mene Grande *Venezuela* 9°49N 70°56W 92 B4
Menemen *Turkey* 38°34N 27°3E 23 E12
Menen *Belgium* 50°47N 3°7E 15 D3
Menggala *Indonesia* 4°30S 105°15E 36 E3
Mengjin *China* 34°55N 112°45E 34 G7
Mengyin *China* 35°40N 117°58E 35 G9
Mengzi *China* 23°20N 103°22E 32 D5
Menihek *Canada* 54°28N 56°36W 73 B6
Menihek L. *Canada* 54°0N 67°0W 73 B6
Menin = Menen *Belgium* 50°47N 3°7E 15 D3
Menindee *Australia* 32°20S 142°25E 63 E3
Menindee L. *Australia* 32°20S 142°25E 63 E3
Meningie *Australia* 35°50S 139°18E 63 F2
Menjangan, Pulau *Indonesia* 8°7S 114°31E 37 J17
Menlo Park *U.S.A.* 37°27N 122°12W 78 H4
Menominee *U.S.A.* 45°6N 87°37W 80 C10
Menominee → *U.S.A.* 45°6N 87°35W 80 C10
Menomonie *U.S.A.* 44°53N 91°55W 80 C8
Menongue *Angola* 14°48S 17°52E 53 G3
Menorca *Spain* 40°0N 4°0E 24 B11
Mentakab *Malaysia* 3°29N 102°21E 39 L4
Mentawai, Kepulauan *Indonesia* 2°0S 99°0E 36 E1
Menton *France* 43°50N 7°29E 20 E7
Mentor *U.S.A.* 41°40N 81°21W 82 E3
Menzelinsk *Russia* 55°47N 53°11E 18 C9
Menzies *Australia* 29°40S 121°2E 61 E3
Meob B. *Namibia* 24°25S 14°34E 56 C1
Me'ona *Israel* 33°1N 35°15E 46 B4
Meoqui *Mexico* 28°17N 105°29W 86 B3
Mepaco *Mozam.* 15°57S 30°48E 55 F3
Meppel *Neths.* 52°42N 6°12E 15 B6
Merak *Indonesia* 6°10N 106°26E 37 F12
Meramangye, L. *Australia* 28°25S 132°13E 61 E5
Meran = Merano *Italy* 46°40N 11°9E 22 A4
Merano *Italy* 46°40N 11°9E 22 A4
Merauke *Indonesia* 8°29S 140°24E 37 F10
Merbein *Australia* 34°10S 142°2E 63 E3
Merbuk, Gunung *Indonesia* 8°13S 114°39E 37 J17
Merca *Somali Rep.* 1°48N 44°50E 47 G3
Merced *U.S.A.* 37°18N 120°29W 78 H6
Merced → *U.S.A.* 37°21N 120°59W 78 H6
Merced Pk. *U.S.A.* 37°36N 119°24W 78 H7
Mercedes *B. Aires, Argentina* 34°40S 59°30W 94 C4
Mercedes *Corrientes, Argentina* 29°10S 58°5W 94 B4
Mercedes *San Luis, Argentina* 33°40S 65°21W 94 C2
Mercedes *Uruguay* 33°12S 58°0W 94 C4
Merceditas *Chile* 28°20S 70°35W 94 B1
Mercer *N.Z.* 37°16S 175°5E 59 B5
Mercer *U.S.A.* 41°14N 80°15W 82 E4
Mercer Island *U.S.A.* 47°34N 122°13W 78 C4
Mercury *U.S.A.* 36°40N 115°59W 79 J11
Mercy, C. *Canada* 65°0N 63°30W 69 C13
Mere *U.K.* 51°6N 2°16W 13 F5
Meredith, C. *Falk. Is.* 52°15S 60°40W 96 G4
Meredith, L. *U.S.A.* 35°43N 101°33W 84 D4
Mergui *Burma* 12°26N 98°34E 38 F2
Mergui Arch. = Myeik Kyunzu *Burma* 11°30N 97°30E 39 G1
Mérida *Mexico* 20°58N 89°37W 87 C7
Mérida *Spain* 38°55N 6°25W 21 C2
Mérida *Venezuela* 8°24N 71°8W 92 B4
Mérida, Cord. de *Venezuela* 9°0N 71°0W 92 B4
Meriden *U.K.* 52°26N 1°38W 13 E6
Meriden *U.S.A.* 41°32N 72°48W 83 E12
Meridian *Calif., U.S.A.* 39°9N 121°55W 78 F5
Meridian *Idaho, U.S.A.* 43°37N 116°24W 76 E5
Meridian *Miss., U.S.A.* 32°22N 88°42W 85 E10
Merinda *Australia* 20°2S 148°11E 62 C4
Merir *Pac. Oc.* 4°10N 132°30E 37 D8
Merirumã *Brazil* 1°15N 54°50W 93 C8
Merkel *U.S.A.* 32°28N 100°1W 84 E4
Mermaid Reef *Australia* 17°6S 119°36E 60 C2
Merredin *Australia* 31°28S 118°18E 61 F2
Merrick *U.K.* 55°8N 4°28W 11 F4
Merrickville *Canada* 44°55N 75°50W 83 B9
Merrill *Oreg., U.S.A.* 42°1N 121°36W 76 E3
Merrill *Wis., U.S.A.* 45°11N 89°41W 80 C9
Merrimack → *U.S.A.* 42°49N 70°49W 83 D14
Merriman *U.S.A.* 42°55N 101°42W 80 D3
Merritt *Canada* 50°10N 120°45W 70 C4
Merritt Island *U.S.A.* 28°21N 80°42W 85 G14
Merriwa *Australia* 32°6S 150°22E 63 E5
Merry I. *Canada* 55°29N 77°31W 72 A4
Merryville *U.S.A.* 30°45N 93°33W 84 F8
Mersch *Lux.* 49°44N 6°7E 15 E6
Mersea I. *U.K.* 51°47N 0°58E 13 F8
Merseburg *Germany* 51°22N 11°59E 16 C6
Mersey → *U.K.* 53°25N 3°1W 12 D4
Merseyside □ *U.K.* 53°31N 3°2W 12 D4
Mersin = İçel *Turkey* 36°51N 34°36E 44 B2
Mersing *Malaysia* 2°25N 103°50E 39 L4
Merta *India* 26°39N 74°4E 42 F6
Merta Road *India* 26°43N 73°55E 42 F5
Merthyr Tydfil *U.K.* 51°45N 3°22W 13 F4
Merthyr Tydfil □ *U.K.* 51°46N 3°21W 13 F4
Merti *Kenya* 1°4N 38°40E 54 B4
Mértola *Portugal* 37°40N 7°40W 21 D2
Mertzon *U.S.A.* 31°16N 100°49W 84 F4
Meru *Kenya* 0°3N 37°40E 54 B4
Meru *Tanzania* 3°15S 36°46E 54 C4
Meru △ *Kenya* 0°5N 38°10E 54 B4
Mesa *U.S.A.* 33°25N 111°50W 77 K8
Mesa Verde △ *U.S.A.* 37°11N 108°29W 77 H9
Mesanagros *Greece* 36°1N 27°49E 25 C9
Mesaoría *Cyprus* 35°12N 33°14E 25 D12
Mesgouez, L. *Canada* 51°20N 75°0W 72 B5
Meshed = Mashhad *Iran* 36°20N 59°35E 45 B8
Meshoppen *U.S.A.* 41°36N 76°3W 83 E8
Mesilinka → *Canada* 56°6N 124°30W 70 B4
Mesologi *Greece* 38°21N 21°28E 23 E9
Mesongi *Greece* 39°29N 19°56E 25 B3
Mesopotamia = Al Jazirah *Iraq* 33°30N 44°0E 44 C5
Mesopotamia *U.S.A.* 41°27N 80°57W 82 E4
Mesquite *U.S.A.* 36°48N 114°4W 77 H6
Messaad *Algeria* 34°8N 3°30E 50 B6
Messalo → *Mozam.* 12°25S 39°15E 55 E4
Messara, Kolpos *Greece* 35°6N 24°47E 25 D6
Messina = Musina *S. Africa* 22°20S 30°5E 57 C5
Messina *Italy* 38°11N 15°34E 22 E6
Messina, Str. di *Italy* 38°15N 15°35E 22 F6
Messini *Greece* 37°4N 22°1E 23 F10
Messiniakos Kolpos *Greece* 36°45N 22°5E 23 F10
Mesta → *Bulgaria* 40°54N 24°49E 23 D11
Meta → *S. Amer.* 6°12N 67°28W 92 B5
Meta Incognita Pen. *Canada* 62°45N 68°30W 69 C13
Metabetchouan *Canada* 48°26N 71°52W 73 C5
Metairie *U.S.A.* 29°59N 90°9W 85 G9
Metaline Falls *U.S.A.* 48°52N 117°22W 76 B5
Metán *Argentina* 25°30S 65°0W 94 B3
Metangula *Mozam.* 12°40S 34°50E 55 E3
Metengobalame *Mozam.* 14°49S 34°30E 55 E3
Methven *N.Z.* 43°38S 171°40E 59 E3
Metil *Mozam.* 16°24S 39°0E 55 F4
Metlakatla *U.S.A.* 55°8N 131°35W 68 D6
Metropolis *U.S.A.* 37°9N 88°44W 80 G9
Metu *Ethiopia* 8°18N 35°35E 47 F2
Metz *France* 49°8N 6°10E 20 B7
Meulaboh *Indonesia* 4°11N 96°3E 36 D1
Meureudu *Indonesia* 5°19N 96°10E 36 C1
Meuse → *Europe* 50°45N 5°41E 15 D5
Mexia *U.S.A.* 31°41N 96°29W 84 F6
Mexiana, I. *Brazil* 0°0 49°30W 93 D9
Mexicali *Mexico* 32°40N 115°30W 79 N11
Mexican Plateau *Mexico* 25°0N 104°0W 66 G9
Mexican Water *U.S.A.* 36°57N 109°32W 77 H9
México *Mexico* 19°24N 99°9W 87 D5
Mexico *Maine, U.S.A.* 44°34N 70°33W 83 B14
Mexico *Mo., U.S.A.* 39°10N 91°53W 80 F8
Mexico *N.Y., U.S.A.* 43°28N 76°14W 83 C8
México □ *Mexico* 19°20N 99°30W 87 D5
Mexico ■ *Cent. Amer.* 25°0N 105°0W 86 C4
México, Ciudad de *Mexico* 19°24N 99°9W 87 D5
Mexico, G. of *Cent. Amer.* 25°0N 90°0W 87 C7
Mexico B. *U.S.A.* 43°35N 76°20W 83 C8
Meydān-e Naftūn *Iran* 31°56N 49°18E 45 D6
Meydani, Ra's-e *Iran* 25°24N 59°6E 45 E8
Meyers Chuck *U.S.A.* 55°45N 132°15W 70 B2
Meymaneh *Afghan.* 35°53N 64°38E 40 B4
Mezen *Russia* 65°50N 44°20E 18 A7
Mezen → *Russia* 65°44N 44°22E 18 A7
Mézenc, Mt. *France* 44°54N 4°11E 20 D6
Mezhdurechenskiy *Russia* 59°36N 65°56E 28 D7
Mezőkövesd *Hungary* 47°49N 20°35E 17 E11
Mezőtúr *Hungary* 47°1N 20°41E 17 E11
Mezquital *Mexico* 23°29N 104°23W 86 C4
Mfolozi → *S. Africa* 28°25S 32°26E 57 D5
Mgeta *Tanzania* 8°22S 36°6E 55 D4
Mhlaba Hills *Zimbabwe* 18°30S 30°30E 55 F3
Mhow *India* 22°33N 75°50E 42 H6
Miahuatlán *Mexico* 16°20N 96°36W 87 D5
Miami *Fla., U.S.A.* 25°46N 80°11W 85 J14
Miami *Okla., U.S.A.* 36°53N 94°53W 84 C7
Miami *Tex., U.S.A.* 35°42N 100°38W 84 D4
Miami Beach *U.S.A.* 25°47N 80°7W 85 J14
Mian Xian *China* 33°10N 106°32E 34 H4
Mianchi *China* 34°48N 111°48E 34 G6
Mīāndarreh *Iran* 35°37N 53°39E 45 C7
Mīāndowāb *Iran* 37°0N 46°5E 44 B5
Miandrivazo *Madag.* 19°31S 45°29E 57 B8
Mīāneh *Iran* 37°30N 47°40E 44 B5
Mianwali *Pakistan* 32°38N 71°28E 42 C4
Mianyang *China* 31°22N 104°47E 32 C5
Miarinarivo *Antananarivo, Madag.* 18°57S 46°55E 57 B8
Miarinarivo *Toamasina, Madag.* 16°38S 48°15E 57 B8
Miariravaratra *Madag.* 20°13S 47°31E 57 C8
Miass *Russia* 54°59N 60°6E 18 D11
Mica *S. Africa* 24°10S 30°48E 57 C5
Michalovce *Slovak Rep.* 48°47N 21°58E 17 D11
Michigan □ *U.S.A.* 44°0N 85°0W 81 C11
Michigan, L. *U.S.A.* 44°0N 87°0W 80 D10
Michigan City *U.S.A.* 41°43N 86°54W 80 E10
Michipicoten I. *Canada* 47°40N 85°40W 72 C2
Michoacán □ *Mexico* 19°10N 101°50W 86 D4
Michurin *Bulgaria* 42°9N 27°51E 23 C12
Michurinsk *Russia* 52°58N 40°27E 18 D7
Mico, Pta. *Nic.* 12°0N 83°30W 88 D3
Micoud *St. Lucia* 13°49N 60°54W 89 f
Micronesia *Pac. Oc.* 11°0N 160°0E 64 G7
Micronesia, Federated States of ■ *Pac. Oc.* 9°0N 150°0E 58 A8
Mid-Pacific Seamounts *Pac. Oc.* 18°0N 177°0W 64 F10
Midai *Indonesia* 3°0N 107°47E 36 D3
Midale *Canada* 49°25N 103°20W 71 D8
Middelburg *Neths.* 51°30N 3°36E 15 C3
Middelburg *Eastern Cape, S. Africa* 31°30S 25°0E 56 E4
Middelburg *Mpumalanga, S. Africa* 25°49S 29°28E 57 D4
Middelpos *S. Africa* 31°55S 20°13E 56 E3
Middelwit *S. Africa* 24°51S 27°3E 56 C4
Middle Alkali L. *U.S.A.* 41°27N 120°5W 76 F3
Middle America Trench = Guatemala Trench *Pac. Oc.* 14°0N 95°0W 66 H10
Middle Bass I. *U.S.A.* 41°41N 82°48W 82 E2
Middle East *Asia* 35°0N 40°0E 26 E5
Middle Fork Feather → *U.S.A.* 38°33N 121°30W 78 F5
Middle I. *Australia* 34°6S 123°11E 61 F3
Middle Loup → *U.S.A.* 41°17N 98°24W 80 E4
Middle Sackville *Canada* 44°47N 63°42W 73 D7
Middleboro *U.S.A.* 41°54N 70°55W 83 E14
Middleburg *Fla., U.S.A.* 30°4N 81°52W 85 F14
Middleburg *Pa., U.S.A.* 40°47N 77°3W 82 F7
Middleburgh *U.S.A.* 42°36N 74°20W 83 D10
Middlebury *U.S.A.* 44°1N 73°10W 83 B11
Middlemount *Australia* 22°50S 148°40E 62 C4
Middleport *N.Y., U.S.A.* 43°13N 78°29W 82 C6
Middleport *Ohio, U.S.A.* 39°0N 82°3W 81 F12
Middlesboro *U.S.A.* 36°36N 83°43W 81 G12
Middlesbrough *U.K.* 54°35N 1°13W 12 C6
Middlesbrough □ *U.K.* 54°28N 1°13W 12 C6
Middlesex *Belize* 17°2N 88°31W 88 C2
Middlesex *N.J., U.S.A.* 40°36N 74°30W 83 F10
Middlesex *N.Y., U.S.A.* 42°42N 77°16W 82 D7
Middleton *Australia* 22°22S 141°32E 62 C3
Middleton *Canada* 44°57N 65°4W 73 D6
Middleton Cr. → *Australia* 22°35S 141°51E 62 C3
Middletown *U.K.* 54°17N 6°51W 10 B5
Middletown *Calif., U.S.A.* 38°45N 122°37W 78 G4
Middletown *Conn., U.S.A.* 41°34N 72°39W 83 E12
Middletown *N.Y., U.S.A.* 41°27N 74°25W 83 E10
Middletown *Ohio, U.S.A.* 39°31N 84°24W 81 F11
Middletown *Pa., U.S.A.* 40°12N 76°44W 83 F8
Midge Point *Australia* 20°39S 148°43E 62 J6
Midhurst *U.K.* 50°59N 0°44W 13 G7
Midi, Canal du → *France* 43°45N 1°21E 20 E4
Midland *Australia* 31°54S 116°1E 61 F2
Midland *Canada* 44°45N 79°50W 82 B5
Midland *Calif., U.S.A.* 33°52N 114°48W 79 M12
Midland *Mich., U.S.A.* 43°37N 84°14W 81 D11
Midland *Pa., U.S.A.* 40°39N 80°27W 82 F4
Midland *Tex., U.S.A.* 32°0N 102°3W 84 F3
Midlands □ *Zimbabwe* 19°40S 29°0E 55 F2
Midleton *Ireland* 51°55N 8°10W 10 E3
Midlothian □ *U.K.* 55°51N 3°5W 11 F5
Midongy, Tangorombohitr' i *Madag.* 23°30S 47°0E 57 C8
Midongy Atsimo *Madag.* 23°35S 47°1E 57 C8
Midway Is. *Pac. Oc.* 28°13N 177°22W 64 E10
Midway Wells *U.S.A.* 32°41N 115°7W 79 N11
Midwest *U.S.A.* 42°0N 90°0W 75 B9
Midwest *Wyo., U.S.A.* 43°25N 106°16W 76 E10
Midwest City *U.S.A.* 35°27N 97°24W 84 D6
Midyat *Turkey* 37°25N 41°23E 44 B4
Midžor *Bulgaria* 43°24N 22°40E 23 C10
Mie □ *Japan* 34°30N 136°10E 31 G8
Międzychód *Poland* 52°35N 15°53E 16 B8
Międzyrzec Podlaski *Poland* 51°58N 22°45E 17 C12
Mielec *Poland* 50°15N 21°25E 17 C11
Mienga *Angola* 17°12S 19°48E 56 B2
Miercurea-Ciuc *Romania* 46°21N 25°48E 17 E13
Mieres *Spain* 43°18N 5°48W 21 A3
Mifflintown *U.S.A.* 40°34N 77°24W 82 F7
Mifraz Hefa *Israel* 32°52N 35°0E 46 C4
Migori *Kenya* 1°4S 34°28E 54 C3
Miguel Alemán, Presa *Mexico* 18°15N 96°32W 87 D5
Mihara *Japan* 34°24N 133°5E 31 G6
Mikese *Tanzania* 6°48S 37°55E 54 D4
Mikhaylovgrad = Montana *Bulgaria* 43°27N 23°16E 23 C10
Mikhaylovka *Russia* 50°3N 43°5E 19 D7
Mikines *Greece* 37°43N 22°46E 23 F10
Mikkeli *Finland* 61°43N 27°15E 8 F22
Mikkwa → *Canada* 58°25N 114°46W 70 B6
Míkonos = Mykonos *Greece* 37°30N 25°25E 23 F11
Mikumi *Tanzania* 7°26S 37°0E 54 D4
Mikumi △ *Tanzania* 7°35S 37°15E 54 D4
Mikun *Russia* 62°20N 50°0E 18 B9
Milaca *U.S.A.* 45°45N 93°39W 80 C7
Milagro *Ecuador* 2°11S 79°36W 92 D3
Milan = Milano *Italy* 45°28N 9°10E 20 D8
Milan *Mo., U.S.A.* 40°12N 93°7W 80 E7
Milan *Tenn., U.S.A.* 35°55N 88°46W 85 D10
Milange *Mozam.* 16°3S 35°45E 55 F4
Milano *Italy* 45°28N 9°10E 20 D8
Milanoa *Madag.* 13°35S 49°47E 57 A8
Milâs *Turkey* 37°20N 27°50E 23 F12
Milatos *Greece* 35°18N 25°34E 25 D7
Milazzo *Italy* 38°13N 15°15E 22 E6
Milbank *U.S.A.* 45°13N 96°38W 80 C5
Milbanke Sd. *Canada* 52°19N 128°33W 70 C3
Milden *Canada* 51°29N 107°32W 71 C7
Mildenhall *U.K.* 52°21N 0°32E 13 E8
Mildmay *Canada* 44°3N 81°7W 82 B3
Mildura *Australia* 34°13S 142°9E 63 E3
Miles *Australia* 26°40S 150°9E 63 D5
Miles City *U.S.A.* 46°25N 105°51W 76 C11
Milestone *Canada* 49°59N 104°31W 71 D8
Miletus *Turkey* 37°30N 27°18E 23 F12
Milford *Calif., U.S.A.* 40°10N 120°22W 78 E6
Milford *Conn., U.S.A.* 41°14N 73°3W 83 E11
Milford *Del., U.S.A.* 38°55N 75°26W 81 F16
Milford *Mass., U.S.A.* 42°8N 71°31W 83 D13
Milford *N.H., U.S.A.* 42°50N 71°39W 83 D13
Milford *Pa., U.S.A.* 41°19N 74°48W 83 E10
Milford *Utah, U.S.A.* 38°24N 113°1W 76 G7
Milford Haven *U.K.* 51°42N 5°7W 13 F2
Milford Sd. *N.Z.* 44°41S 167°47E 59 F1
Milford Sound *N.Z.* 44°41S 167°55E 59 F1
Milh, Bahr al = Razāzah, Buhayrat ar *Iraq* 32°40N 43°35E 44 C4
Milikapiti *Australia* 11°26S 130°40E 60 B5
Miling *Australia* 30°30S 116°17E 61 F2
Milk River *Canada* 49°10N 112°5W 70 D6
Mill I. *Antarctica* 66°0S 101°30E 5 C8
Mill Valley *U.S.A.* 37°54N 122°32W 78 H4
Millau *France* 44°8N 3°4E 20 D5
Millbridge *Canada* 44°41N 77°36W 82 B7
Millbrook *Canada* 44°10N 78°29W 82 B6
Millbrook *Ala., U.S.A.* 32°29N 86°22W 85 E11
Millbrook *N.Y., U.S.A.* 41°47N 73°42W 83 E11
Mille Lacs, L. des *Canada* 48°45N 90°35W 72 C1
Mille Lacs L. *U.S.A.* 46°15N 93°39W 80 B7
Milledgeville *U.S.A.* 33°5N 83°14W 85 E13
Millen *U.S.A.* 32°48N 81°57W 85 E14
Millennium I. = Caroline I. *Kiribati* 9°58S 150°13W 65 H12
Miller *U.S.A.* 44°31N 98°59W 80 C4
Millersburg *Ohio, U.S.A.* 40°33N 81°55W 82 F3
Millersburg *Pa., U.S.A.* 40°32N 76°58W 82 F8
Millerton *U.S.A.* 41°57N 73°31W 83 E11
Millerton L. *U.S.A.* 37°1N 119°41W 78 J7
Millet *St. Lucia* 13°55N 60°59W 89 f
Millheim *U.S.A.* 40°54N 77°29W 82 F7
Millicent *Australia* 37°34S 140°21E 63 F3
Millington *U.S.A.* 35°20N 89°53W 85 D10
Millinocket *U.S.A.* 45°39N 68°43W 81 C19
Millmerran *Australia* 27°53S 151°16E 63 D5
Millom *U.K.* 54°13N 3°16W 12 C4
Mills L. *Canada* 61°30N 118°20W 70 A5
Millsboro *U.S.A.* 40°0N 80°0W 82 G5
Millstream Chichester △ *Australia* 21°35S 117°6E 60 D2
Millstreet *Ireland* 52°4N 9°4W 10 D2
Milltown Malbay *Ireland* 52°52N 9°24W 10 D2
Millville *N.J., U.S.A.* 39°24N 75°2W 81 F16
Millville *Pa., U.S.A.* 41°7N 76°32W 83 E8
Millwood L. *U.S.A.* 33°42N 93°58W 84 E8
Milne → *Australia* 21°10S 137°33E 62 C2
Milo *U.S.A.* 45°15N 68°59W 81 C19
Milon, Akra *Greece* 36°15N 28°11E 25 C10
Milos *Greece* 36°44N 24°25E 23 F11
Milparinka *Australia* 29°46S 141°57E 63 D3
Milpitas *U.S.A.* 37°26N 121°55W 78 H5
Milton *N.S., Canada* 44°4N 64°45W 73 D7
Milton *Ont., Canada* 43°31N 79°53W 82 C5
Milton *N.Z.* 46°7S 169°59E 59 G2
Milton *Calif., U.S.A.* 38°3N 120°51W 78 G6
Milton *Fla., U.S.A.* 30°38N 87°3W 85 F11
Milton *Pa., U.S.A.* 41°1N 76°51W 82 F8
Milton *Vt., U.S.A.* 44°38N 73°7W 83 B11
Milton-Freewater *U.S.A.* 45°56N 118°23W 76 D4
Milton Keynes *U.K.* 52°1N 0°44W 13 E7
Milton Keynes □ *U.K.* 52°1N 0°44W 13 E7
Milverton *Canada* 43°34N 80°55W 82 C4
Milwaukee *U.S.A.* 43°2N 87°54W 80 D10
Milwaukee Deep *Atl. Oc.* 19°50N 68°0W 89 C6
Milwaukie *U.S.A.* 45°26N 122°38W 78 E4
Min Jiang → *Fujian, China* 26°0N 119°35E 33 D6
Min Jiang → *Sichuan, China* 28°45N 104°40E 32 D5
Min Xian *China* 34°25N 104°5E 34 G3
Mīnā' Jabal 'Alī *U.A.E.* 25°2N 55°8E 45 E7
Mina Pirquitas *Argentina* 22°40S 66°30W 94 A2
Mīnā Su'ud *Si. Arabia* 28°45N 48°28E 45 D6
Mīnā'al Ahmadī *Kuwait* 29°5N 48°10E 45 D6
Minago → *Canada* 54°33N 98°59W 71 C9
Minaki *Canada* 49°59N 94°40W 71 D10
Minamata *Japan* 32°10N 130°30E 31 H5
Minami-Arapusa △ *Japan* 35°30N 138°9E 31 G9
Minami-Tori-Shima *Pac. Oc.* 24°20N 153°58E 64 E7
Minas *Uruguay* 34°20S 55°10W 95 C4
Minas, Sierra de las *Guatemala* 15°9N 89°31W 88 C2
Minas Basin *Canada* 45°20N 64°12W 73 C7
Minas Gerais □ *Brazil* 18°50S 46°0W 93 G9
Minatitlán *Mexico* 17°59N 94°31W 87 D6
Minbu *Burma* 20°10N 94°52E 41 J19
Minchinabad *Pakistan* 30°10N 73°34E 42 D5
Mindanao *Phil.* 8°0N 125°0E 37 C6
Mindanao Sea = Bohol Sea *Phil.* 9°0N 124°0E 37 C6
Mindanao Trench *Pac. Oc.* 12°0N 126°6E 37 B7
Mindelo *C. Verde Is.* 16°24N 25°0W 50 b
Minden *Canada* 44°55N 78°43W 82 B6
Minden *Germany* 52°17N 8°55E 16 B5
Minden *La., U.S.A.* 32°37N 93°17W 84 E8
Minden *Nev., U.S.A.* 38°57N 119°46W 78 G7
Mindiptana *Indonesia* 5°55S 140°22E 37 F10
Mindoro *Phil.* 13°0N 121°0E 37 B6
Mindoro Str. *Phil.* 12°30N 120°30E 37 B6
Mine *Japan* 34°12N 131°7E 31 G5
Minehead *U.K.* 51°12N 3°29W 13 F4
Mineola *N.Y., U.S.A.* 40°44N 73°38W 83 F11
Mineola *Tex., U.S.A.* 32°40N 95°29W 84 E7
Mineral King *U.S.A.* 36°27N 118°36W 78 J8
Mineral Wells *U.S.A.* 32°48N 98°7W 84 E5
Minersville *U.S.A.* 40°41N 76°16W 83 F8
Minerva *U.S.A.* 40°44N 81°6W 82 F3
Minetto *U.S.A.* 43°24N 76°28W 83 C8
Minfeng *China* 37°4N 82°46E 32 C3
Mingäçevir Su Anbarı *Azerbaijan* 40°57N 46°50E 19 F8
Mingan *Canada* 50°20N 64°0W 73 B7
Mingechaurskoye Vdkhr. = Mingäçevir Su Anbarı *Azerbaijan* 40°57N 46°50E 19 F8
Mingela *Australia* 19°52S 146°38E 62 B4
Mingenew *Australia* 29°12S 115°21E 61 E2
Mingera Cr. → *Australia* 20°38S 137°45E 62 C2
Mingin *Burma* 22°50N 94°30E 41 H19
Mingo Junction *U.S.A.* 40°19N 80°37W 82 F4
Mingora *Pakistan* 34°48N 72°22E 43 B5
Mingteke Daban = Mintaka Pass *Pakistan* 37°0N 74°58E 43 A6
Mingyuegue *China* 43°2N 128°50E 35 C15
Minho = Miño → *Spain* 41°52N 8°40W 21 A2
Minho *Portugal* 41°25N 8°20W 21 B1
Minidoka *U.S.A.* 42°45N 113°29W 76 E7
Minigwal, L. *Australia* 29°31S 123°14E 61 E3
Minilya → *Australia* 23°45S 114°0E 61 D1
Minilya Roadhouse *Australia* 23°55S 114°0E 61 D1
Minipi L. *Canada* 52°25N 60°45W 73 B7
Mink L. *Canada* 61°54N 117°40W 70 A5
Minna *Nigeria* 9°37N 6°30E 50 G7
Minneapolis *Kans., U.S.A.* 39°8N 97°42W 80 F5
Minneapolis *Minn., U.S.A.* 44°57N 93°16W 80 C7
Minnedosa *Canada* 50°14N 99°50W 71 C9
Minnesota □ *U.S.A.* 46°0N 94°15W 80 B6
Minnesota → *U.S.A.* 44°54N 93°9W 80 C7
Minnewaukan *U.S.A.* 48°4N 99°15W 80 A4
Minnipa *Australia* 32°51S 135°9E 63 E2
Minnitaki L. *Canada* 49°57N 92°10W 72 C1
Mino *Japan* 35°32N 136°55E 31 G8
Miño → *Spain* 41°52N 8°40W 21 A2
Minorca = Menorca *Spain* 40°0N 4°0E 24 B11
Minot *U.S.A.* 48°14N 101°18W 80 A3
Minqin *China* 38°38N 103°20E 34 E2
Minsk *Belarus* 53°52N 27°30E 17 B14
Mińsk Mazowiecki *Poland* 52°10N 21°33E 17 B11
Mintabie *Australia* 27°15S 133°7E 63 D1
Mintaka Pass *Pakistan* 37°0N 74°58E 43 A6
Minto *Canada* 46°5N 66°5W 73 C6
Minto, L. *Canada* 57°13N 75°0W 72 A5
Minton *Canada* 49°10N 104°35W 71 D8
Minturn *U.S.A.* 39°35N 106°26W 76 G10
Minusinsk *Russia* 53°43N 91°20E 29 D10
Minutang *India* 28°15N 96°30E 41 E20
Minvoul *Gabon* 2°9N 12°8E 52 D2
Minzhong *China* 22°37N 113°30E 33 F10
Miquelon *Canada* 49°25N 76°27W 72 C4
Miquelon *St-P. & M.* 47°8N 56°22W 73 C8
Mīr Kūh *Iran* 26°22N 58°55E 45 E8
Mīr Shahdād *Iran* 26°15N 58°29E 45 E8
Mira *Italy* 45°26N 12°8E 22 B5
Mira por vos Cay *Bahamas* 22°9N 74°30W 89 B5
Mirabello, Kolpos *Greece* 35°10N 25°50E 25 D7
Mirador-Río Azul △ *Guatemala* 17°45N 89°50W 88 C2

Miraj *India* 16°50N 74°45E **40** L9
Miram Shah *Pakistan* 33°0N 70°2E **42** C4
Miramar *Argentina* 38°15S 57°50W **94** D4
Miramar *Mozam.* 23°50S 35°35E **57** C6
Miramichi *Canada* 47°2N 65°28W **73** C6
Miramichi B. *Canada* 47°15N 65°0W **73** C7
Miranda *Brazil* 20°10S 56°15W **93** H7
Miranda → *Brazil* 19°25S 57°20W **92** G7
Miranda de Ebro *Spain* 42°41N 2°57W **21** A4
Miranda do Douro
  Portugal 41°30N 6°16W **21** B2
Mirandópolis *Brazil* 21°9S 51°6W **95** A5
Mirango *Malawi* 13°32S 34°58E **55** E3
Mirani *Australia* 21°8S 148°53E **62** K6
Mirassol *Brazil* 20°46S 49°28W **95** A6
Mirbāṭ *Oman* 17°0N 54°45E **47** D5
Mires *Greece* 35°4N 24°56E **25** D6
Miri *Malaysia* 4°23N 113°59E **36** D4
Miriam Vale *Australia* 24°20S 151°33E **62** C5
Mirim, L. *S. Amer.* 32°45S 52°50W **95** C5
Mirnyy *Antarctica* 66°50S 92°30E **5** C14
Mirnyy *Russia* 62°33N 113°53E **29** C12
Mirokhan *Pakistan* 27°46N 68°6E **42** F3
Mirond L. *Canada* 55°6N 102°47W **71** B8
Mirpur *Pakistan* 33°32N 73°56E **43** C5
Mirpur Batoro *Pakistan* 24°44N 68°16E **42** G3
Mirpur Bibiwari
  Pakistan 28°33N 67°44E **42** E2
Mirpur Khas *Pakistan* 25°30N 69°0E **42** G3
Mirpur Sakro *Pakistan* 24°33N 67°41E **42** G2
Mirs Bay = Tai Pang Wan
  China 22°33N 114°24E **33** F11
Mirtağ *Turkey* 38°23N 41°56E **44** B4
Mirtoo Sea *Greece* 37°0N 23°20E **23** F10
Miryang *S. Korea* 35°31N 128°44E **35** G15
Mirzapur *India* 25°10N 82°34E **43** G10
Mirzapur-cum-Vindhyachal =
  Mirzapur *India* 25°10N 82°34E **43** G10
Misantla *Mexico* 19°56N 96°50W **87** D5
Misawa *Japan* 40°41N 141°24E **30** D10
Miscou I. *Canada* 47°57N 64°31W **73** C7
Mish'āb, Ra's al
  Si. Arabia 28°15N 48°43E **45** D6
Mishan *China* 45°37N 131°48E **33** B8
Mishawaka *U.S.A.* 41°40N 86°11W **80** E10
Mishima *Japan* 35°10N 138°52E **31** G9
Misión *Mexico* 32°6N 116°53W **79** N10
Misiones □ *Argentina* 27°0S 55°0W **95** B5
Misiones □ *Paraguay* 27°0S 56°0W **94** B4
Miskah *Si. Arabia* 24°49N 42°56E **44** E4
Miskitos, Cayos *Nic.* 14°26N 82°50W **88** D3
Miskolc *Hungary* 48°7N 20°50E **17** D11
Misoke
  Dem. Rep. of the Congo 0°42S 28°2E **54** C2
Misool *Indonesia* 1°52S 130°10E **37** E8
Misr = Egypt ■ *Africa* 28°0N 31°0E **51** C12
Miṣrātah *Libya* 32°24N 15°3E **51** B9
Missanabie *Canada* 48°20N 84°6W **72** C3
Missinaibi → *Canada* 50°43N 81°29W **72** B3
Missinaibi L. *Canada* 48°23N 83°40W **72** C3
Mission *Canada* 49°10N 122°15W **70** D4
Mission *S. Dak., U.S.A.* 43°18N 100°39W **80** D3
Mission *Tex., U.S.A.* 26°13N 98°20W **84** H5
Mission Beach *Australia* 17°53S 146°6E **62** B4
Mission Viejo *U.S.A.* 33°36N 117°40W **79** M9
Missisa L. *Canada* 52°20N 85°7W **72** B2
Missisicabi → *Canada* 51°14N 79°31W **72** B4
Mississagi → *Canada* 46°15N 83°9W **72** C3
Mississauga *Canada* 43°32N 79°35W **82** C5
Mississippi □ *U.S.A.* 33°0N 90°0W **85** E10
Mississippi → *U.S.A.* 29°9N 89°15W **85** G10
Mississippi L. *Canada* 45°5N 76°10W **83** A8
Mississippi River Delta
  U.S.A. 29°10N 89°15W **85** G10
Mississippi Sd. *U.S.A.* 30°20N 89°0W **85** F10
Missoula *U.S.A.* 46°52N 114°1W **76** C6
Missouri □ *U.S.A.* 38°25N 92°30W **80** F7
Missouri → *U.S.A.* 38°49N 90°7W **80** F8
Missouri City *U.S.A.* 29°37N 95°32W **84** G7
Missouri Valley *U.S.A.* 41°34N 95°53W **80** E6
Mist *U.S.A.* 45°59N 123°15W **78** E3
Mistassibi → *Canada* 48°53N 72°13W **73** B5
Mistassini → *Canada* 48°42N 72°20W **73** C5
Mistassini, L. *Canada* 51°0N 73°30W **72** B5
Mistastin L. *Canada* 55°57N 63°20W **73** A7
Mistinibi, L. *Canada* 55°56N 64°17W **73** A7
Mistissini *Canada* 48°53N 72°12W **73** C5
Misty L. *Canada* 58°53N 101°40W **71** B8
Misurata = Miṣrātah
  Libya 32°24N 15°3E **51** B9
Mitchell *Australia* 26°29S 147°58E **63** D4
Mitchell *Canada* 43°28N 81°12W **82** C3
Mitchell *Nebr., U.S.A.* 41°57N 103°49W **80** E2
Mitchell *Oreg., U.S.A.* 44°34N 120°9W **76** D3
Mitchell *S. Dak., U.S.A.* 43°43N 98°2W **80** D4
Mitchell → *Australia* 15°12S 141°35E **62** B3
Mitchell, Mt. *U.S.A.* 35°46N 82°16W **85** D13
Mitchell-Alice Rivers △
  Australia 15°28S 142°5E **62** B3
Mitchell Ra. *Australia* 12°49S 135°36E **62** A2
Mitchelstown *Ireland* 52°15N 8°16W **10** D3
Mitha Tiwana *Pakistan* 32°13N 72°6E **42** C5
Mithi *Pakistan* 24°44N 69°48E **42** G3
Mithrao *Pakistan* 27°28N 69°40E **42** F3
Mitilini *Greece* 39°6N 26°35E **23** E12
Mito *Japan* 36°20N 140°30E **31** F10
Mitrovica = Kosovska Mitrovica
  Serbia 42°54N 20°52E **23** C9
Mitsamiouli *Comoros Is.* 11°20S 43°16E **53** a
Mitsinjo *Madag.* 16°1S 45°52E **57** B8
Mitsiwa *Eritrea* 15°35N 39°25E **47** D2
Mitsukaidō *Japan* 36°1N 139°59E **31** F9
Mittagong *Australia* 34°28S 150°29E **63** E5
Mittimatalik = Pond Inlet
  Canada 72°40N 77°0W **69** B12
Mitú *Colombia* 1°15N 70°13W **92** C4
Mitumba *Tanzania* 7°8S 31°2E **54** D3
Mitumba, Mts.
  Dem. Rep. of the Congo 7°0S 27°30E **54** D2
Mitwaba
  Dem. Rep. of the Congo 8°2S 27°17E **55** D2
Mityana *Uganda* 0°23N 32°2E **54** B3
Mixteco → *Mexico* 18°11N 98°30W **87** D5
Miyagi □ *Japan* 38°15N 140°45E **30** E10
Miyāh, W. el → *Syria* 34°44N 39°57E **44** C3
Miyake-Jima *Japan* 34°5N 139°30E **31** G9
Miyako *Japan* 39°40N 141°59E **30** E10
Miyako-Jima *Japan* 24°45N 125°20E **31** M2
Miyako-Rettō *Japan* 24°24N 125°0E **31** M2
Miyakonojō *Japan* 31°40N 131°5E **31** J5
Miyani *India* 21°50N 69°26E **42** J3
Miyanoura-Dake
  Japan 30°20N 130°31E **31** J5
Miyazaki *Japan* 31°56N 131°30E **31** J5
Miyazaki □ *Japan* 32°30N 131°30E **31** H5
Miyazu *Japan* 35°35N 135°10E **31** G7
Miyet, Bahr el = Dead Sea
  Asia 31°30N 35°30E **46** D4
Miyoshi *Japan* 34°48N 132°51E **31** G6
Miyun *China* 40°28N 116°50E **34** D9
Miyun Shuiku *China* 40°30N 117°0E **35** D9
Mizdah *Libya* 31°30N 13°0E **51** B8
Mizen Hd., *Cork, Ireland* 51°27N 9°50W **10** E2
Mizen Hd., *Wicklow,
  Ireland* 52°51N 6°4W **10** D5
Mizhi *China* 37°47N 110°12E **34** F6
Mizoram □ *India* 23°30N 92°40E **41** H18
Mizpe Ramon *Israel* 30°34N 34°49E **46** E3
Mizuho *Antarctica* 70°30S 41°0E **5** D5
Mizusawa *Japan* 39°8N 141°8E **30** E10
Mjölby *Sweden* 58°20N 15°10E **9** G16
Mjøsa *Norway* 60°40N 11°0E **8** F14
Mkata *Tanzania* 5°45S 38°20E **54** D4
Mkhaya △ *Swaziland* 26°34S 31°45E **57** D5
Mkhuze △ *S. Africa* 29°27S 29°30E **57** D4
Mkokotoni *Tanzania* 5°55S 39°15E **54** D4
Mkomazi *Tanzania* 4°40S 38°7E **54** C4
Mkomazi △ *S. Africa* 30°12S 30°50E **57** E5
Mkomazi → *S. Africa* 4°4S 30°0E **54** C3
Mkulwe *Tanzania* 8°37S 32°20E **55** D3
Mkumbi, Ras *Tanzania* 7°38S 39°55E **54** D4
Mkushi *Zambia* 14°25S 29°15E **55** E2
Mkushi River *Zambia* 13°32S 29°45E **55** E2
Mkuze *S. Africa* 27°10S 32°0E **57** D5
Mladá Boleslav
  Czech Rep. 50°27N 14°53E **16** C8
Mlala Hills *Tanzania* 6°50S 31°40E **54** D3
Mlange = Mulanje
  Malawi 16°2S 35°33E **55** F4
Mława *Poland* 53°9N 20°25E **17** B11
Mlawula △ *Swaziland* 26°12S 32°2E **57** D5
Mljet *Croatia* 42°43N 17°30E **22** C7
Mmabatho *S. Africa* 25°49S 25°30E **56** D4
Mo i Rana *Norway* 66°20N 14°7E **8** C16
Moa *Cuba* 20°40N 74°56W **89** B4
Moa *Indonesia* 8°0S 128°0E **37** F7
Moa → *S. Leone* 6°59N 11°36W **50** G3
Moab *U.S.A.* 38°35N 109°33W **76** G9
Moala *Fiji* 18°36S 179°53E **59** a
Moama *Australia* 36°7S 144°46E **63** F3
Moamba *Mozam.* 25°36S 32°15E **57** D5
Moapa *U.S.A.* 36°40N 114°37W **79** J12
Moate *Ireland* 53°24N 7°44W **10** C4
Moba
  Dem. Rep. of the Congo 7°0S 29°48E **54** D2
Mobārakābād *Iran* 28°24N 53°20E **45** D7
Mobaye *C.A.R.* 4°25N 21°5E **52** D4
Mobayi
  Dem. Rep. of the Congo 4°15N 21°8E **52** D4
Moberley Lake *Canada* 55°50N 121°44W **70** B4
Moberly *U.S.A.* 39°25N 92°26W **80** F7
Mobile *U.S.A.* 30°41N 88°3W **85** F10
Mobile B. *U.S.A.* 30°30N 88°0W **85** F11
Mobridge *U.S.A.* 45°32N 100°26W **80** C3
Moc Chau *Vietnam* 20°50N 104°38E **38** B5
Moc Hoa *Vietnam* 10°46N 105°56E **39** G5
Mocabe Kasari
  Dem. Rep. of the Congo 9°58S 26°12E **55** D2
Moçambique = Mozambique ■
  Africa 19°0S 35°0E **55** F4
Moçambique *Mozam.* 15°3S 40°42E **55** F5
Mocanaqua *U.S.A.* 41°9N 76°8W **83** E8
Moce *Fiji* 18°40S 178°29W **59** a
Mochima △ *Venezuela* 10°30N 64°5W **89** D7
Mochos *Greece* 35°16N 25°27E **25** D7
Mochudi *Botswana* 24°27S 26°7E **56** C4
Mocimboa da Praia
  Mozam. 11°25S 40°20E **55** E5
Moclips *U.S.A.* 47°14N 124°13W **78** C2
Mocoa *Colombia* 1°7N 76°35W **92** C3
Mococa *Brazil* 21°28S 47°0W **95** A6
Mocorito *Mexico* 25°29N 107°55W **86** B3
Moctezuma *Mexico* 29°48N 109°42W **86** B3
Moctezuma → *Mexico* 21°59N 98°34W **87** C5
Mocuba *Mozam.* 16°54S 36°57E **55** F4
Modane *France* 45°12N 6°40E **20** D7
Modasa *India* 23°30N 73°21E **42** H5
Modder → *S. Africa* 29°2S 24°37E **56** D3
Modderrivier *S. Africa* 29°2S 24°38E **56** D3
Módena *Italy* 44°40N 10°55E **22** B4
Modena *U.S.A.* 37°48N 113°56W **77** H7
Modesto *U.S.A.* 37°39N 121°0W **78** H6
Módica *Italy* 36°52N 14°46E **22** F6
Modimolle *S. Africa* 24°42S 28°22E **57** C4
Modjadjiskloof *S. Africa* 23°42S 30°10E **57** C5
Moe *Australia* 38°12S 146°19E **63** F4
Moebase *Mozam.* 17°3S 38°41E **55** F4
Moengo *Suriname* 5°45N 54°20W **93** B8
Moffat *U.K.* 55°21N 3°27W **11** F5
Moga *India* 30°48N 75°8E **42** D6
Mogadishu = Muqdisho
  Somali Rep. 2°2N 45°25E **47** G4
Mogador = Essaouira
  Morocco 31°32N 9°42W **50** B4

Mogalakwena →
  S. Africa 22°38S 28°40E **57** C4
Mogami-Gawa →
  Japan 38°45N 140°0E **30** E10
Mogán *Canary Is.* 27°53N 15°43W **24** G4
Mogaung *Burma* 25°20N 97°0E **41** G20
Mogi das Cruzes *Brazil* 23°31S 46°11W **95** A6
Mogi-Guaçu → *Brazil* 20°53S 48°10W **95** A6
Mogi-Mirim *Brazil* 22°29S 47°0W **95** A6
Mogilev = Mahilyow
  Belarus 53°55N 30°18E **17** B16
Mogilev-Podolskiy = Mohyliv-
  Podilskyy *Ukraine* 48°26N 27°48E **17** D14
Mogincual *Mozam.* 15°35S 40°25E **55** F5
Mogocha *Russia* 53°40N 119°50E **29** D12
Mogok *Burma* 23°0N 96°40E **41** G20
Mogollon Rim *U.S.A.* 34°10N 110°50W **77** J8
Mogumber *Australia* 31°2S 116°3E **61** F2
Mohács *Hungary* 45°58N 18°41E **17** F10
Mohales Hoek *Lesotho* 30°7S 27°26E **56** E4
Mohall *U.S.A.* 48°46N 101°31W **80** A3
Moḥammadābād *Iran* 37°52N 59°5E **45** B8
Mohammedia *Morocco* 33°44N 7°21W **50** B4
Mohana → *India* 24°43N 85°0E **43** G11
Mohanlalganj *India* 26°41N 80°58E **43** F9
Mohave, L. *U.S.A.* 35°12N 114°34W **79** K12
Mohawk → *U.S.A.* 42°47N 73°41W **83** D11
Mohéli *Comoros Is.* 12°20S 43°40E **53** a
Mohenjodaro *Pakistan* 27°19N 68°7E **42** F3
Moher, Cliffs of *Ireland* 52°58N 9°27W **10** D2
Mohicanville Res. *U.S.A.* 40°45N 82°9W **82** F2
Mohns Ridge *Arctic* 72°30N 5°0W **4** B7
Mohoro *Tanzania* 8°6S 39°8E **54** D4
Mohyliv-Podilskyy
  Ukraine 48°26N 27°48E **17** D14
Moidart, L. *U.K.* 56°47N 5°52W **11** E3
Moira → *Canada* 44°21N 77°24W **82** B7
Moisaküla *Estonia* 58°3N 25°12E **9** G21
Moisie *Canada* 50°12N 66°1W **73** B6
Moisie → *Canada* 50°14N 66°5W **73** B6
Mojave *U.S.A.* 35°3N 118°10W **79** K8
Mojave △ *U.S.A.* 35°7N 115°32W **79** K11
Mojave Desert *U.S.A.* 35°0N 116°30W **79** L10
Mojo *Bolivia* 21°48S 65°33W **94** A2
Mojokerto *Indonesia* 7°28S 112°26E **37** G15
Mokai *N.Z.* 38°32S 175°56E **59** C5
Mokambo
  Dem. Rep. of the Congo 12°25S 28°20E **55** E2
Mokameh *India* 25°24N 85°55E **43** G11
Mokau *N.Z.* 38°42S 174°39E **59** C5
Mokelumne →
  U.S.A. 38°13N 121°28W **78** G5
Mokelumne Hill
  U.S.A. 38°18N 120°43W **78** G6
Mokhotlong *Lesotho* 29°22S 29°2E **57** D4
Mokokchung *India* 26°15N 94°30E **41** F19
Mokolo → *S. Africa* 23°14S 27°43E **57** C4
Mokopane *S. Africa* 24°10S 28°55E **57** C4
Mokpo *S. Korea* 34°50N 126°25E **35** G14
Mokra Gora *Europe* 42°50N 20°30E **23** C9
Mol *Belgium* 51°11N 5°5E **15** C5
Molchanovo *Russia* 57°40N 83°50E **28** D9
Mold *U.K.* 53°9N 3°8W **12** D4
Moldavia = Moldova ■
  Europe 47°0N 28°0E **17** E15
Moldavia *Romania* 46°30N 27°0E **17** E14
Molde *Norway* 62°45N 7°9E **8** E12
Moldova ■ *Europe* 47°0N 28°0E **17** E15
Moldoveanu, Vf.
  Romania 45°36N 24°45E **17** F13
Mole → *U.K.* 51°24N 0°21W **13** F7
Mole Creek *Australia* 41°34S 146°24E **63** G4
Molepolole *Botswana* 24°28S 25°28E **56** C4
Molfetta *Italy* 41°12N 16°36E **22** D7
Moline *U.S.A.* 41°30N 90°31W **80** E8
Molinos *Argentina* 25°28S 66°15W **94** B2
Moliro
  Dem. Rep. of the Congo 8°12S 30°30E **54** D3
Mollendo *Peru* 17°0S 72°0W **92** G4
Mollerin, L. *Australia* 30°30S 117°35E **61** F2
Molo *Kenya* 0°15S 35°44E **54** C4
Molodechno = Maladzyechna
  Belarus 54°20N 26°50E **17** A14
Molodezhnaya *Antarctica* 67°40S 45°51E **5** C9
Moloka'i *U.S.A.* 21°8N 157°0W **74** b
Molokai Fracture Zone
  Pac. Oc. 28°0N 125°0W **65** E15
Molong *Australia* 33°5S 148°54E **63** E4
Molopo → *Africa* 28°30S 20°12E **56** D3
Molson L. *Canada* 54°22N 96°40W **71** C9
Molteno *S. Africa* 31°22S 26°22E **56** E4
Molu *Indonesia* 6°45S 131°40E **37** F8
Molucca Sea *Indonesia* 0°0 125°0E **37** E6
Moluccas = Maluku
  Indonesia 1°0S 127°0E **37** E7
Moma
  Dem. Rep. of the Congo 1°35S 23°52E **54** C1
Moma *Mozam.* 16°47S 39°4E **55** F4
Mombasa *Kenya* 4°3S 39°40E **54** C4
Mombetsu *Japan* 44°21N 143°22E **30** B11
Momchilgrad *Bulgaria* 41°33N 25°23E **23** D11
Momi
  Dem. Rep. of the Congo 1°42S 27°0E **54** C2
Mompós *Colombia* 9°14N 74°26W **92** B4
Møn *Denmark* 54°57N 12°20E **9** J15
Mon □ *Burma* 16°0N 97°30E **41** L20
Mona, Canal de la = Mona
  Passage *W. Indies* 18°30N 67°45W **89** C6
Mona, Isla *Puerto Rico* 18°5N 67°54W **89** C6
Mona, Pta. *Costa Rica* 9°37N 82°36W **88** E3
Mona Passage
  W. Indies 18°30N 67°45W **89** C6
Monaca *U.S.A.* 40°41N 80°17W **82** F4
Monaco ■ *Europe* 43°46N 7°23E **20** E7
Monadhliath Mts. *U.K.* 57°10N 4°4W **11** D4
Monadnock, Mt.
  U.S.A. 42°52N 72°7W **83** D12

Monaghan *Ireland* 54°15N 6°57W **10** B5
Monaghan □ *Ireland* 54°11N 6°56W **10** B5
Monahans *U.S.A.* 31°36N 102°54W **84** F3
Monapo *Mozam.* 14°56S 40°19E **55** E5
Monar, L. *U.K.* 57°26N 5°8W **11** D3
Monarch Mt. *Canada* 51°55N 125°57W **70** C3
Monashee Mts. *Canada* 51°0N 118°43W **70** C5
Monasterevin *Ireland* 53°8N 7°4W **10** C4
Monastir = Bitola
  Macedonia 41°1N 21°20E **23** D9
Monastir *Tunisia* 35°50N 10°49E **51** A8
Moncayo, Sierra del
  Spain 41°48N 1°50W **21** B5
Monchegorsk *Russia* 67°54N 32°58E **8** C25
Mönchengladbach
  Germany 51°11N 6°27E **16** C4
Monchique *Portugal* 37°19N 8°38W **21** D1
Moncks Corner *U.S.A.* 33°12N 80°1W **85** E14
Monclova *Mexico* 26°54N 101°25W **86** B4
Moncton *Canada* 46°7N 64°51W **73** C7
Mondego → *Portugal* 40°9N 8°52W **21** B1
Mondeodo *Indonesia* 3°34S 122°9E **37** E6
Mondovì *Italy* 44°23N 7°49E **20** D7
Mondrain I. *Australia* 34°9S 122°14E **61** F3
Moneague *Jamaica* 18°16N 77°7W **88** a
Moneron, Ostrov
  Russia 46°15N 141°16E **30** A10
Monessen *U.S.A.* 40°9N 79°54W **82** F5
Monett *U.S.A.* 36°55N 93°55W **80** G7
Moneymore *U.K.* 54°41N 6°40W **10** B5
Monforte de Lemos
  Spain 42°31N 7°33W **21** A2
Mong Cai *Vietnam* 21°27N 107°54E **38** B6
Mong Hsu *Burma* 21°54N 98°30E **41** J21
Mong Kung *Burma* 21°35N 97°35E **41** J20
Mong Nai *Burma* 20°32N 97°46E **41** J20
Mong Pawk *Burma* 22°4N 99°16E **41** H21
Mong Ton *Burma* 20°17N 98°45E **41** J21
Mong Wa *Burma* 21°26N 100°27E **41** J22
Mong Yai *Burma* 22°21N 98°3E **41** H21
Mongalla *Sudan* 5°8N 31°42E **51** G12
Mongers, L. *Australia* 29°25S 117°5E **61** E2
Monghyr = Munger
  India 25°23N 86°30E **43** G12
Mongibello = Etna *Italy* 37°50N 14°55E **22** F6
Mongo *Chad* 12°14N 18°43E **51** F9
Mongolia ■ *Asia* 47°0N 103°0E **32** B5
Mongolia, Plateau of
  Asia 45°0N 105°0E **26** D12
Mongu *Zambia* 15°16S 23°12E **53** H4
Mŏngua *Angola* 16°43S 15°20E **56** B2
Monifieth *U.K.* 56°30N 2°48W **11** E6
Monkey Bay *Malawi* 14°7S 35°1E **55** E4
Monkey Mia *Australia* 25°48S 113°43E **61** E1
Monkey River *Belize* 16°22N 88°29W **87** D7
Monkoto
  Dem. Rep. of the Congo 1°38S 20°35E **52** E4
Monkton *Canada* 43°35N 81°5W **82** C3
Monmouth *U.K.* 51°48N 2°42W **13** F5
Monmouth *Ill., U.S.A.* 40°55N 90°39W **80** E8
Monmouth *Oreg.,
  U.S.A.* 44°51N 123°14W **76** D2
Monmouthshire □ *U.K.* 51°48N 2°54W **13** F5
Mono L. *U.S.A.* 38°1N 119°1W **78** H7
Monolith *U.S.A.* 35°7N 118°22W **79** K8
Monolithos *Greece* 36°7N 27°45E **25** C9
Monongahela *U.S.A.* 40°12N 79°56W **82** F5
Monópoli *Italy* 40°57N 17°18E **22** D7
Monos I. *Trin. & Tob.* 10°42N 61°44W **93** K15
Monroe *Ga., U.S.A.* 33°47N 83°43W **85** E13
Monroe *La., U.S.A.* 32°30N 92°7W **84** E8
Monroe *Mich., U.S.A.* 41°55N 83°24W **81** E12
Monroe *N.C., U.S.A.* 34°59N 80°33W **85** D14
Monroe *N.Y., U.S.A.* 41°20N 74°11W **83** E10
Monroe *Utah, U.S.A.* 38°38N 112°7W **76** G7
Monroe *Wash., U.S.A.* 47°51N 121°58W **78** C5
Monroe *Wis., U.S.A.* 42°36N 89°38W **80** D9
Monroe City *U.S.A.* 39°39N 91°44W **80** F8
Monroeton *U.S.A.* 41°43N 76°29W **83** E8
Monroeville *Ala.,
  U.S.A.* 31°31N 87°20W **85** F11
Monroeville *Pa., U.S.A.* 40°26N 79°45W **82** F5
Monrovia *Liberia* 6°18N 10°47W **50** G3
Mons *Belgium* 50°27N 3°58E **15** D3
Monse *Indonesia* 4°7S 123°15E **37** E6
Mont-de-Marsan *France* 43°54N 0°31W **20** E3
Mont-Joli *Canada* 48°37N 68°10W **73** C6
Mont-Laurier *Canada* 46°35N 75°30W **72** C4
Mont-Louis *Canada* 49°15N 65°44W **73** C6
Mont-St-Michel, Le
  France 48°40N 1°30W **20** B3
Mont-Tremblant △
  Canada 46°30N 74°30W **72** C5
Montagne d'Ambre △
  Madag. 12°37S 49°8E **57** A8
Montagu *S. Africa* 33°45S 20°8E **56** E3
Montague I. *Antarctica* 58°25S 26°20W **5** B1
Montague *Canada* 46°10N 62°39W **73** C7
Montague, I. *Mexico* 31°45N 114°48W **86** A2
Montague Ra.
  Australia 27°15S 119°30E **61** E2
Montague Sd. *Australia* 14°28S 125°20E **60** B4
Montalbán *Spain* 40°50N 0°45W **21** B5
Montalvo *U.S.A.* 34°15N 119°12W **79** L7
Montana *Bulgaria* 43°27N 23°16E **23** C10
Montaña *Peru* 6°0S 73°0W **92** E4
Montana □ *U.S.A.* 47°0N 110°0W **76** C9
Montaña Clara, I.
  Canary Is. 29°17N 13°33W **24** E6
Montargis *France* 47°59N 2°43E **20** C5
Montauban *France* 44°2N 1°21E **20** D4
Montauk *U.S.A.* 41°3N 71°57W **83** E13
Montauk Pt. *U.S.A.* 41°4N 71°51W **83** E13
Montbéliard *France* 47°31N 6°48E **20** C7
Montceau-les-Mines
  France 46°40N 4°23E **20** C6
Montclair *U.S.A.* 40°49N 74°12W **83** F10

Monte Albán *Mexico* 17°2N 96°46W **87** D5
Monte Alegre *Brazil* 2°0S 54°0W **93** D8
Monte Azul *Brazil* 15°9S 42°53W **93** G10
Monte-Carlo *Monaco* 43°44N 7°25E **20** E7
Monte Caseros
  Argentina 30°10S 57°50W **94** C4
Monte Comán
  Argentina 34°40S 67°53W **94** C2
Monte Cristi *Dom. Rep.* 19°52N 71°39W **89** C5
Monte Lindo →
  Paraguay 23°56S 57°12W **94** A4
Monte Patria *Chile* 30°42S 70°58W **94** C1
Monte Quemado
  Argentina 25°53S 62°41W **94** B3
Monte Rio *U.S.A.* 38°28N 123°0W **78** G4
Monte Santu, C. di *Italy* 40°5N 9°44E **22** D3
Monte Vista *U.S.A.* 37°35N 106°9W **77** H10
Monteagudo *Argentina* 27°14S 54°8W **95** B5
Montebello *Canada* 45°40N 74°55W **72** C5
Montebello Is.
  Australia 20°30S 115°45E **60** D2
Montecito *U.S.A.* 34°26N 119°40W **79** L7
Montecristo *Italy* 42°20N 10°19E **22** C4
Montego Bay *Jamaica* 18°28N 77°55W **88** a
Montélimar *France* 44°33N 4°45E **20** D6
Montello *U.S.A.* 43°48N 89°20W **80** D9
Montemorelos *Mexico* 25°12N 99°49W **87** B5
Montenegro *Brazil* 29°39S 51°29W **95** B5
Montenegro ■ *Europe* 42°40N 19°20E **23** C8
Montepuez *Mozam.* 13°8S 38°59E **55** E4
Montepuez → *Mozam.* 12°32S 40°27E **55** E5
Monterey *U.S.A.* 36°37N 121°55W **78** J5
Monterey B. *U.S.A.* 36°45N 122°0W **78** J5
Montería *Colombia* 8°46N 75°53W **92** B3
Monteros *Argentina* 27°11S 65°30W **94** B2
Monterrey *Mexico* 25°40N 100°19W **86** B4
Montes Azules △
  Mexico 16°21N 91°3W **87** D6
Montes Claros *Brazil* 16°30S 43°50W **93** G10
Montesano *U.S.A.* 46°59N 123°36W **78** D3
Montesilvano *Italy* 42°29N 14°8E **22** C6
Montevideo *Uruguay* 34°50S 56°11W **95** C4
Montevideo *U.S.A.* 44°57N 95°43W **80** C6
Montezuma *U.S.A.* 41°35N 92°32W **80** E7
Montezuma Castle △
  U.S.A. 34°39N 111°45W **77** J8
Montgomery *U.K.* 52°34N 3°8W **13** E4
Montgomery *Ala.,
  U.S.A.* 32°23N 86°19W **85** E11
Montgomery *Pa.,
  U.S.A.* 41°10N 76°53W **82** E8
Montgomery *W. Va.,
  U.S.A.* 38°11N 81°19W **81** F13
Montgomery City
  U.S.A. 38°59N 91°30W **80** F8
Monticello *Ark., U.S.A.* 33°38N 91°47W **84** E9
Monticello *Fla., U.S.A.* 30°33N 83°52W **85** F13
Monticello *Ind., U.S.A.* 40°45N 86°46W **80** E10
Monticello *Iowa, U.S.A.* 42°15N 91°12W **80** D8
Monticello *Ky., U.S.A.* 36°50N 84°51W **81** G11
Monticello *Minn.,
  U.S.A.* 45°18N 93°48W **80** C7
Monticello *Miss., U.S.A.* 31°33N 90°7W **85** F9
Monticello *N.Y.,
  U.S.A.* 41°39N 74°42W **83** E10
Monticello *Utah,
  U.S.A.* 37°52N 109°21W **77** H9
Montijo *Portugal* 38°41N 8°54W **21** C1
Montilla *Spain* 37°36N 4°40W **21** D3
Montluçon *France* 46°22N 2°36E **20** C5
Montmagny *Canada* 46°58N 70°34W **73** C5
Montmartre *Canada* 50°14N 103°27W **71** C8
Montmorillon *France* 46°26N 0°50E **20** C4
Monto *Australia* 24°52S 151°6E **62** C5
Montongbuwoh
  Indonesia 8°33S 116°4E **37** K19
Montoro *Spain* 38°1N 4°27W **21** C3
Montour Falls *U.S.A.* 42°21N 76°51W **82** D8
Montoursville *U.S.A.* 41°15N 76°55W **82** E8
Montpelier *Idaho,
  U.S.A.* 42°19N 111°18W **76** E8
Montpelier *Vt., U.S.A.* 44°16N 72°35W **83** B12
Montpellier *France* 43°37N 3°52E **20** E5
Montréal *Canada* 45°30N 73°33W **83** A11
Montreal → *Canada* 47°14N 84°39W **72** C3
Montreal L. *Canada* 54°20N 105°45W **71** C7
Montreal Lake *Canada* 54°3N 105°46W **71** C7
Montreux *Switz.* 46°26N 6°55E **20** C7
Montrose *U.K.* 56°44N 2°27W **11** E6
Montrose *Colo.,
  U.S.A.* 38°29N 107°53W **76** G10
Montrose *Pa., U.S.A.* 41°50N 75°53W **83** E9
Monts, Pte. des *Canada* 49°20N 67°12W **73** C6
Montserrat ☑ *W. Indies* 16°40N 62°10W **89** C7
Montuiri *Spain* 39°34N 2°59E **24** B9
Monywa *Burma* 22°7N 95°11E **41** H19
Monza *Italy* 45°35N 9°16E **20** D8
Monze *Zambia* 16°17S 27°29E **55** F2
Monze, C. *Pakistan* 24°47N 66°37E **42** G2
Monzón *Spain* 41°52N 0°10E **21** B6
Mooers *U.S.A.* 44°58N 73°35W **83** B11
Mooi → *S. Africa* 28°45S 30°34E **57** D5
Mooi River *S. Africa* 29°13S 29°50E **57** D4
Moonah → *Australia* 22°3S 138°33E **62** C2
Moonda, L. *Australia* 25°52S 140°25E **62** D3
Moonie *Australia* 27°46S 150°20E **63** D5
Moonie → *Australia* 29°19S 148°43E **63** D4
Moonta *Australia* 34°6S 137°32E **63** E2
Moora *Australia* 30°37S 115°58E **61** F2
Moorcroft *U.S.A.* 44°16N 104°57W **76** D11
Moore → *Australia* 31°22S 115°30E **61** F2
Moore, L. *Australia* 29°50S 117°35E **61** E2
Moore Park *Australia* 24°43S 152°17E **62** C5
Moore Res. *U.S.A.* 44°20N 71°53W **83** B13
Moore River △ *Australia* 31°7S 115°39E **61** F2
Moorea *French Polynesia* 17°30S 149°50W **59** d
Moorefield *U.S.A.* 39°4N 78°58W **81** F14

Moorfoot Hills *U.K.* 55°44N 3°8W **11** F5
Moorhead *U.S.A.* 46°53N 96°45W **80** B5
Moorpark *U.S.A.* 34°17N 118°53W **79** L8
Moorreesburg *S. Africa* 33°6S 18°38E **56** E2
Moorrinya △ *Australia* 21°42S 144°58E **62** C3
Moose → *Canada* 51°20N 80°25W **72** B3
Moose → *U.S.A.* 43°38N 75°24W **83** C9
Moose Creek *Canada* 45°15N 74°58W **83** A10
Moose Factory *Canada* 51°16N 80°32W **72** B3
Moose Jaw *Canada* 50°24N 105°30W **71** C7
Moose Jaw → *Canada* 50°34N 105°18W **71** C7
Moose Lake *Canada* 53°46N 100°8W **71** C8
Moose Lake *U.S.A.* 46°27N 92°46W **80** B7
Moose Mountain ⌓ *Canada* 49°48N 102°25W **71** D8
Moosehead L. *U.S.A.* 45°38N 69°40W **81** C19
Mooselookmeguntic L. *U.S.A.* 44°55N 70°49W **83** B14
Moosilauke, Mt. *U.S.A.* 44°3N 71°40W **83** B13
Moosomin *Canada* 50°9N 101°40W **71** C8
Moosonee *Canada* 51°17N 80°39W **72** B3
Moosup *U.S.A.* 41°43N 71°53W **83** E13
Mopane *S. Africa* 22°37S 29°52E **57** C4
Mopeia Velha *Mozam.* 17°30S 35°40E **55** F4
Mopipi *Botswana* 21°6S 24°55E **56** C3
Mopoi *C.A.R.* 5°6N 26°54E **54** A2
Mopti *Mali* 14°30N 4°0W **50** F5
Moqor *Afghan.* 32°50N 67°42E **42** C2
Moquegua *Peru* 17°15S 70°46W **92** G4
Mora *Sweden* 61°2N 14°38E **8** F16
Mora *Minn., U.S.A.* 45°53N 93°18W **80** C7
Mora *N. Mex., U.S.A.* 35°58N 105°20W **77** J11
Moradabad *India* 28°50N 78°50E **43** E8
Morafenobe *Madag.* 17°50S 44°53E **57** B7
Moramanga *Madag.* 18°56S 48°12E **57** B8
Moran *Kans., U.S.A.* 37°55N 95°10W **80** G6
Moran *Wyo., U.S.A.* 43°50N 110°31W **76** E8
Moranbah *Australia* 22°1S 148°6E **62** C4
Morant Bay *Jamaica* 17°53N 76°25W **88** a
Morant Cays *Jamaica* 17°22N 76°0W **88** C4
Morant Pt. *Jamaica* 17°55N 76°12W **88** a
Morar *India* 26°14N 78°14E **42** F8
Morar, L. *U.K.* 56°57N 5°40W **11** E3
Moratuwa *Sri Lanka* 6°45N 79°55E **40** R11
Morava → *Serbia* 44°36N 21°4E **23** B9
Morava → *Slovak Rep.* 48°10N 16°59E **17** D9
Moravia *U.S.A.* 42°43N 76°25W **83** D8
Moravian Hts. = Českomoravská Vrchovina *Czech Rep.* 49°30N 15°40E **16** D8
Morawa *Australia* 29°13S 116°0E **61** E2
Morawhanna *Guyana* 8°30N 59°40W **92** B7
Moray □ *U.K.* 57°31N 3°18W **11** D5
Moray Firth *U.K.* 57°40N 3°52W **11** D5
Morbi *India* 22°50N 70°42E **42** H4
Morden *Canada* 49°15N 98°10W **71** D9
Mordovian Republic = Mordvinia □ *Russia* 54°20N 44°30E **18** D7
Mordvinia □ *Russia* 54°20N 44°30E **18** D7
Morea *Greece* 37°45N 22°10E **6** H10
Moreau → *U.S.A.* 45°18N 100°43W **80** C3
Morebeng *S. Africa* 23°30S 29°55E **57** C4
Morecambe *U.K.* 54°5N 2°52W **12** C5
Morecambe B. *U.K.* 54°7N 3°0W **12** C5
Moree *Australia* 29°28S 149°54E **63** D4
Morehead *U.S.A.* 38°11N 83°26W **81** F12
Morehead City *U.S.A.* 34°43N 76°43W **85** D16
Morel → *India* 26°13N 76°36E **42** F7
Morelia *Mexico* 19°42N 101°7W **86** D4
Morella *Australia* 23°0S 143°52E **62** C3
Morella *Spain* 40°35N 0°5W **21** B5
Morelos *Mexico* 26°42N 107°40W **86** B3
Morelos □ *Mexico* 18°45N 99°0W **87** D5
Moremi ⌓ *Botswana* 19°18S 23°10E **56** B3
Morena *India* 26°30N 78°4E **42** F8
Morena, Sierra *Spain* 38°20N 4°0W **21** C3
Moreno Valley *U.S.A.* 33°56N 117°14W **79** M10
Moresby I. *Canada* 52°30N 131°40W **70** C2
Moreton I. *Australia* 27°10S 153°25E **63** D5
Moreton Island △ *Australia* 27°2S 153°24E **63** D5
Morey *Spain* 39°44N 3°20E **24** B10
Morgan *U.S.A.* 41°2N 111°41W **76** F8
Morgan City *U.S.A.* 29°42N 91°12W **84** G9
Morgan Hill *U.S.A.* 37°8N 121°39W **78** H5
Morganfield *U.S.A.* 37°41N 87°55W **80** G10
Morganton *U.S.A.* 35°45N 81°41W **85** D14
Morgantown *U.S.A.* 39°38N 79°57W **81** F14
Morgenzon *S. Africa* 26°45S 29°36E **57** D4
Morghak *Iran* 29°7N 57°54E **45** D8
Morhar → *India* 25°29N 85°11E **43** G11
Mori *Japan* 42°6N 140°35E **30** C10
Moriarty *U.S.A.* 34°59N 106°3W **77** J10
Morice L. *Canada* 53°50N 127°40W **70** C3
Morinville *Canada* 53°49N 113°41W **70** C6
Morioka *Japan* 39°45N 141°8E **30** E10
Moris *Mexico* 28°10N 108°32W **86** B3
Morlaix *France* 48°36N 3°52W **20** B2
Mornington *Australia* 38°15S 145°5E **63** F4
Mornington, I. *Chile* 49°50S 75°30W **96** F1
Mornington I. *Australia* 16°30S 139°30E **62** B2
Moro *Pakistan* 26°40N 68°0E **42** F2
Moro → *Pakistan* 29°42N 67°22E **42** E2
Moro G. *Phil.* 6°30N 123°0E **37** C6
Morocco ■ *N. Afr.* 32°0N 5°50W **50** B4
Morogoro *Tanzania* 6°50S 37°40E **54** D4
Morogoro □ *Tanzania* 8°0S 37°0E **54** D4
Moroleón *Mexico* 20°8N 101°12W **86** C4
Morombe *Madag.* 21°45S 43°22E **57** C7
Moron *Argentina* 34°39S 58°37W **94** C4
Morón *Cuba* 22°8N 78°39W **88** B4
Morón de la Frontera *Spain* 37°6N 5°28W **21** D3
Morona → *Peru* 4°40S 77°10W **92** D3
Morondava *Madag.* 20°17S 44°17E **57** C7
Morongo Valley *U.S.A.* 34°3N 116°37W **79** L10
Moroni *Comoros Is.* 11°40S 43°16E **53** a
Moroni *U.S.A.* 39°32N 111°35W **76** G8
Morotai *Indonesia* 2°10N 128°30E **37** D7
Moroto *Uganda* 2°28N 34°42E **54** B3
Moroto, Mt. *Uganda* 2°30N 34°43E **54** B3
Morpeth *U.K.* 55°10N 1°41W **12** B6
Morphou *Cyprus* 35°12N 32°59E **25** D11
Morphou Bay *Cyprus* 35°15N 32°50E **25** D11
Morrilton *U.S.A.* 35°9N 92°44W **84** D8
Morrinhos *Brazil* 17°45S 49°10W **93** G9
Morrinsville *N.Z.* 37°40S 175°32E **59** B5
Morris *Canada* 49°25N 97°22W **71** D9
Morris *Ill., U.S.A.* 41°22N 88°26W **80** E9
Morris *Minn., U.S.A.* 45°35N 95°55W **80** C6
Morris *N.Y., U.S.A.* 42°33N 75°15W **83** D9
Morris *Pa., U.S.A.* 41°35N 77°17W **82** E7
Morris, Mt. *Australia* 26°9S 131°4E **61** E5
Morris Jesup, Kap *Greenland* 83°40N 34°0W **66** A16
Morrisburg *Canada* 44°55N 75°7W **83** B9
Morristown *Ariz., U.S.A.* 33°51N 112°37W **77** K7
Morristown *N.J., U.S.A.* 40°48N 74°29W **83** F10
Morristown *N.Y., U.S.A.* 44°35N 75°39W **83** B9
Morristown *Tenn., U.S.A.* 36°13N 83°18W **85** C13
Morrisville *N.Y., U.S.A.* 42°53N 75°35W **83** D9
Morrisville *Pa., U.S.A.* 40°13N 74°47W **83** F10
Morrisville *Vt., U.S.A.* 44°34N 72°36W **83** B12
Morro, Pta. *Chile* 27°6S 71°0W **94** B1
Morro Bay *U.S.A.* 35°22N 120°51W **78** K6
Morro del Jable *Canary Is.* 28°3N 14°23W **24** F5
Morro Jable, Pta. de *Canary Is.* 28°2N 14°20W **24** F5
Morrocoy △ *Venezuela* 10°48N 68°13W **89** D6
Morrosquillo, G. de *Colombia* 9°35N 75°40W **88** E4
Morrumbene *Mozam.* 23°31S 35°16E **57** C6
Morshansk *Russia* 53°28N 41°50E **18** D7
Morteros *Argentina* 30°50S 62°0W **94** C3
Mortlach *Canada* 50°27N 106°4W **71** C7
Mortlake *Australia* 38°5S 142°50E **63** F3
Morton *Tex., U.S.A.* 33°44N 102°46W **84** E3
Morton *Wash., U.S.A.* 46°34N 122°17W **78** D4
Moruga *Trin. & Tob.* 10°4N 61°16W **93** K15
Morundah *Australia* 34°57S 146°19E **63** E4
Moruya *Australia* 35°58S 150°3E **63** F5
Morvan *France* 47°5N 4°3E **20** C6
Morven *Australia* 26°22S 147°5E **63** D4
Morvern *U.K.* 56°38N 5°44W **11** E3
Morwell *Australia* 38°10S 146°22E **63** F4
Morzhovets, Ostrov *Russia* 66°44N 42°35E **18** A7
Moscos Is. *Burma* 14°0N 97°30E **38** E1
Moscow = Moskva *Russia* 55°45N 37°37E **18** C6
Moscow *Idaho, U.S.A.* 46°44N 117°0W **76** C5
Moscow *Pa., U.S.A.* 41°20N 75°31W **83** E9
Mosel → *Europe* 50°22N 7°36E **20** A7
Moselle = Mosel → *Europe* 50°22N 7°36E **20** A7
Moses Lake *U.S.A.* 47°8N 119°17W **76** C4
Mosgiel *N.Z.* 45°53S 170°21E **59** F3
Moshaweng → *S. Africa* 26°35S 22°50E **56** D3
Moshchnyy, Ostrov *Russia* 60°1N 27°50E **9** F22
Moshi *Tanzania* 3°22S 37°18E **54** C4
Moshupa *Botswana* 24°46S 25°29E **56** C4
Mosjøen *Norway* 65°51N 13°12E **8** D15
Moskenesøya *Norway* 67°58N 13°0E **8** C15
Moskenstraumen *Norway* 67°47N 12°45E **8** C15
Moskva *Russia* 55°45N 37°37E **18** C6
Mosomane *Botswana* 24°2S 26°19E **56** C4
Mosonmagyaróvár *Hungary* 47°52N 17°18E **17** E9
Mosquera *Colombia* 2°35N 78°24W **92** C3
Mosquero *U.S.A.* 35°47N 103°58W **77** J12
Mosquitia *Honduras* 15°20N 84°10W **88** C3
Mosquito Coast = Mosquitia *Honduras* 15°20N 84°10W **88** C3
Mosquito Creek L. *U.S.A.* 41°18N 80°46W **82** E4
Mosquito L. *Canada* 62°35N 103°20W **71** A8
Mosquitos, G. de los *Panama* 9°15N 81°10W **88** E3
Moss *Norway* 59°27N 10°40E **9** G14
Moss Vale *Australia* 34°32S 150°25E **63** E5
Mossaka *Congo* 1°15S 16°45E **52** E3
Mossbank *Canada* 49°56N 105°56W **71** D7
Mossburn *N.Z.* 45°41S 168°15E **59** F2
Mosselbaai *S. Africa* 34°11S 22°8E **56** E3
Mossendjo *Congo* 2°55S 12°42E **52** E2
Mossgiel *Australia* 33°15S 144°5E **63** E3
Mossman *Australia* 16°21S 145°15E **62** B4
Mossoró *Brazil* 5°10S 37°15W **93** E11
Mossuril *Mozam.* 14°58S 40°42E **55** E5
Most *Czech Rep.* 50°31N 13°38E **16** C7
Mosta *Malta* 35°55N 14°26E **25** D1
Mostaganem *Algeria* 35°54N 0°5E **50** A6
Mostar *Bos.-H.* 43°22N 17°50E **23** C7
Mostardas *Brazil* 31°2S 50°51W **95** C5
Mostiska = Mostyska *Ukraine* 49°48N 23°4E **17** D12
Mosty = Masty *Belarus* 53°27N 24°38E **17** B13
Mostyska *Ukraine* 49°48N 23°4E **17** D12
Mosul = Al Mawşil *Iraq* 36°15N 43°5E **44** B4
Motagua → *Guatemala* 15°44N 88°14W **88** C2
Motala *Sweden* 58°32N 15°1E **9** G16
Motaze *Mozam.* 24°48S 32°52E **57** C5
Moth *India* 25°43N 78°57E **43** G8
Motherwell *U.K.* 55°47N 3°58W **11** F5
Motihari *India* 26°30N 84°55E **43** F11
Motozintla de Mendoza *Mexico* 15°22N 92°14W **87** D6
Motril *Spain* 36°31N 3°37W **21** D4
Mott *U.S.A.* 46°23N 102°20W **80** B2
Motueka *N.Z.* 41°7S 173°1E **59** D4
Motueka → *N.Z.* 41°5S 173°1E **59** D4
Motul *Mexico* 21°6N 89°17W **87** C7
Mouchalagane → *Canada* 50°56N 68°41W **73** B6
Moudros *Greece* 39°50N 25°18E **23** E11
Mouila *Gabon* 1°50S 11°0E **52** E2
Moulamein *Australia* 35°3S 144°1E **63** F3
Moule à Chique, C. *St. Lucia* 13°43N 60°57W **89** f
Mouliana *Greece* 35°10N 25°59E **25** D7
Moulins *France* 46°35N 3°19E **20** C5
Moulmein *Burma* 16°30N 97°40E **41** L20
Moulouya, O. → *Morocco* 35°5N 2°25W **50** B5
Moultrie *U.S.A.* 31°11N 83°47W **85** F13
Moultrie, L. *U.S.A.* 33°20N 80°5W **85** E14
Mound City *Mo., U.S.A.* 40°7N 95°14W **80** E6
Mound City *S. Dak., U.S.A.* 45°44N 100°4W **80** C3
Moundou *Chad* 8°40N 16°10E **51** G9
Moundsville *U.S.A.* 39°55N 80°44W **82** G4
Moung *Cambodia* 12°46N 103°27E **38** F4
Mount Airy *U.S.A.* 36°31N 80°37W **85** C14
Mount Albert *Canada* 44°8N 79°19W **82** B5
Mount Aspiring △ *N.Z.* 44°19S 168°47E **59** F2
Mount Barker *S. Austral., Australia* 35°5S 138°52E **63** F2
Mount Barker *W. Austral., Australia* 34°38S 117°40E **61** F2
Mount Bellew Bridge *Ireland* 53°28N 8°31W **10** C3
Mount Brydges *Canada* 42°54N 81°29W **82** D3
Mount Burr *Australia* 37°34S 140°26E **63** F3
Mount Carmel = Ha Karmel △ *Israel* 32°45N 35°5E **46** C4
Mount Carmel *Ill., U.S.A.* 38°25N 87°46W **80** F10
Mount Carmel *Pa., U.S.A.* 40°47N 76°26W **83** F8
Mount Clemens *U.S.A.* 42°35N 82°53W **82** D2
Mount Coolon *Australia* 21°25S 147°25E **62** C4
Mount Darwin *Zimbabwe* 16°47S 31°38E **55** F3
Mount Desert I. *U.S.A.* 44°21N 68°20W **81** C19
Mount Dora *U.S.A.* 28°48N 81°38W **85** G14
Mount Edziza ⌓ *Canada* 57°30N 130°45W **70** B2
Mount Elgon △ *E. Afr.* 1°4N 34°42E **54** B3
Mount Field △ *Australia* 42°39S 146°35E **63** G4
Mount Fletcher *S. Africa* 30°40S 28°30E **57** E4
Mount Forest *Canada* 43°59N 80°43W **82** C4
Mount Frankland △ *Australia* 31°47S 116°37E **60** F2
Mount Gambier *Australia* 37°50S 140°46E **63** F3
Mount Garnet *Australia* 17°37S 145°6E **62** B4
Mount Holly *U.S.A.* 39°59N 74°47W **83** G10
Mount Holly Springs *U.S.A.* 40°7N 77°12W **82** F7
Mount Hope *N.S.W., Australia* 32°51S 145°51E **63** E4
Mount Hope *S. Austral., Australia* 34°7S 135°23E **63** E2
Mount Isa *Australia* 20°42S 139°26E **62** C2
Mount Jewett *U.S.A.* 41°44N 78°39W **82** E6
Mount Kaputar △ *Australia* 30°16S 150°10E **63** E5
Mount Kenya △ *Kenya* 0°7S 37°21E **54** C4
Mount Kilimanjaro △ *Tanzania* 3°2S 37°19E **54** C4
Mount Kisco *U.S.A.* 41°12N 73°44W **83** E11
Mount Laguna *U.S.A.* 32°52N 116°25W **79** N10
Mount Larcom *Australia* 23°48S 150°59E **62** C5
Mount Lofty Ranges *Australia* 34°35S 139°5E **63** E2
Mount Magnet *Australia* 28°2S 117°47E **61** E2
Mount Maunganui *N.Z.* 37°40S 176°14E **59** B6
Mount Molloy *Australia* 16°42S 145°20E **62** B4
Mount Morgan *Australia* 23°40S 150°25E **62** C5
Mount Morris *U.S.A.* 42°44N 77°52W **82** D7
Mount Pearl *Canada* 47°31N 52°47W **73** C9
Mount Penn *U.S.A.* 40°20N 75°54W **83** F9
Mount Perry *Australia* 25°13S 151°42E **63** D5
Mount Pleasant *Iowa, U.S.A.* 40°58N 91°33W **80** E8
Mount Pleasant *Mich., U.S.A.* 43°36N 84°46W **81** D11
Mount Pleasant *Pa., U.S.A.* 40°9N 79°33W **82** F5
Mount Pleasant *S.C., U.S.A.* 32°47N 79°52W **85** E15
Mount Pleasant *Tenn., U.S.A.* 35°32N 87°12W **85** D11
Mount Pleasant *Tex., U.S.A.* 33°9N 94°58W **84** E7
Mount Pleasant *Utah, U.S.A.* 39°33N 111°27W **76** G8
Mount Pocono *U.S.A.* 41°7N 75°22W **83** E9
Mount Rainier △ *U.S.A.* 46°55N 121°50W **78** D5
Mount Revelstoke △ *Canada* 51°5N 118°30W **70** C5
Mount Robson ⌓ *Canada* 53°0N 119°0W **70** C5
Mount St. Helens ⌓ *U.S.A.* 46°14N 122°11W **78** D4
Mount Selinda *Zimbabwe* 20°24S 32°43E **57** C5
Mount Shasta *U.S.A.* 41°19N 122°19W **76** F2
Mount Signal *U.S.A.* 32°39N 115°37W **79** N11
Mount Sterling *Ill., U.S.A.* 39°59N 90°45W **80** F8
Mount Sterling *Ky., U.S.A.* 38°4N 83°56W **81** F12
Mount Surprise *Australia* 18°10S 144°17E **62** B3
Mount Union *U.S.A.* 40°23N 77°53W **82** F7
Mount Upton *U.S.A.* 42°26N 75°23W **83** D9
Mount Vernon *Ill., U.S.A.* 38°19N 88°55W **80** F9
Mount Vernon *Ind., U.S.A.* 37°56N 87°54W **80** G10
Mount Vernon *N.Y., U.S.A.* 40°54N 73°49W **83** F11
Mount Vernon *Ohio, U.S.A.* 40°23N 82°29W **82** F2
Mount Vernon *Wash., U.S.A.* 48°25N 122°20W **78** B4
Mount William △ *Australia* 40°56S 148°14E **63** G4
Mountain Ash *U.K.* 51°40N 3°23W **13** F4
Mountain Center *U.S.A.* 33°42N 116°44W **79** M10
Mountain City *Nev., U.S.A.* 41°50N 115°58W **76** F6
Mountain City *Tenn., U.S.A.* 36°29N 81°48W **85** C14
Mountain Dale *U.S.A.* 41°41N 74°32W **83** E10
Mountain Grove *U.S.A.* 37°8N 92°16W **80** G7
Mountain Home *Ark., U.S.A.* 36°20N 92°23W **84** C8
Mountain Home *Idaho, U.S.A.* 43°8N 115°41W **76** E6
Mountain Iron *U.S.A.* 47°32N 92°37W **80** B7
Mountain Pass *U.S.A.* 35°29N 115°35W **79** K11
Mountain View *Ark., U.S.A.* 35°52N 92°7W **84** D8
Mountain View *Calif., U.S.A.* 37°23N 122°5W **78** H4
Mountain View *Hawai'i, U.S.A.* 19°33N 155°7W **74** b
Mountain Zebra △ *S. Africa* 32°14S 25°27E **56** E4
Mountainair *U.S.A.* 34°31N 106°15W **77** J10
Mountlake Terrace *U.S.A.* 47°47N 122°18W **78** C4
Mountmellick *Ireland* 53°7N 7°20W **10** C4
Mountrath *Ireland* 53°0N 7°28W **10** D4
Moura *Australia* 24°35S 149°58E **62** C4
Moura *Brazil* 1°32S 61°38W **92** D6
Moura *Portugal* 38°7N 7°30W **21** C2
Mourdi, Dépression du *Chad* 18°10N 23°0E **51** E10
Mourilyan *Australia* 17°35S 146°3E **62** B4
Mourne → *U.K.* 54°52N 7°26W **10** B4
Mourne Mts. *U.K.* 54°10N 6°0W **10** B5
Mournies *Greece* 35°29N 24°1E **25** D6
Mouscron *Belgium* 50°45N 3°12E **15** D3
Moussoro *Chad* 13°41N 16°35E **51** F9
Moutong *Indonesia* 0°28N 121°13E **37** D6
Movas *Mexico* 28°10N 109°25W **86** B3
Moville *Ireland* 55°11N 7°3W **10** A4
Mowandjum *Australia* 17°22S 123°40E **60** C3
Moy → *Ireland* 54°8N 9°8W **10** B2
Moya *Comoros Is.* 12°18S 44°18E **53** a
Moyale *Kenya* 3°30N 39°0E **54** B4
Moyen Atlas *Morocco* 33°0N 5°0W **50** B4
Moyne, L. Le *Canada* 56°45N 68°47W **73** A6
Moyo *Indonesia* 8°10S 117°40E **36** F5
Moyobamba *Peru* 6°0S 77°0W **92** E3
Moyyero → *Russia* 68°44N 103°42E **29** C11
Moyynqum *Kazakhstan* 44°12N 71°0E **28** E8
Moyynty *Kazakhstan* 47°10N 73°18E **28** E8
Mozambique = Moçambique *Mozam.* 15°3S 40°42E **55** F5
Mozambique ■ *Africa* 19°0S 35°0E **55** F4
Mozambique Chan. *Africa* 17°30S 42°30E **57** B7
Mozdok *Russia* 43°45N 44°48E **19** F7
Mozdūrān *Iran* 36°9N 60°35E **45** B9
Mozhnābād *Iran* 34°7N 60°6E **45** C9
Mozyr = Mazyr *Belarus* 51°59N 29°15E **17** B15
Mpanda *Tanzania* 6°23S 31°1E **54** D3
Mphoengs *Zimbabwe* 21°10S 27°51E **57** C4
Mpika *Zambia* 11°51S 31°25E **55** E3
Mpulungu *Zambia* 8°51S 31°5E **55** D3
Mpumalanga *S. Africa* 29°50S 30°33E **57** D5
Mpumalanga □ *S. Africa* 26°0S 30°0E **57** D5
Mpwapwa *Tanzania* 6°23S 36°30E **54** D4
Mqanduli *S. Africa* 31°49S 28°45E **57** E4
Msaken *Tunisia* 35°49N 10°33E **51** A8
Msambansovu *Zimbabwe* 15°50S 30°3E **55** F3
M'sila → *Algeria* 35°30N 4°29E **50** A6
Msoro *Zambia* 13°35S 31°50E **55** E3
Mstislavl = Mstsislaw *Belarus* 54°0N 31°50E **17** A16
Mstsislaw *Belarus* 54°0N 31°50E **17** A16
Mtama *Tanzania* 10°17S 39°21E **55** E4
Mtamvuna → *S. Africa* 31°6S 30°12E **57** E5
Mthatha *S. Africa* 31°36S 28°49E **57** E4
Mtilikwe → *Zimbabwe* 21°9S 31°30E **55** G3
Mtito Andei *Kenya* 2°41S 38°10E **54** C4
Mtubatuba *S. Africa* 28°30S 32°8E **57** D5
Mtwalume *S. Africa* 30°30S 30°38E **57** E5
Mtwara-Mikindani *Tanzania* 10°20S 40°20E **55** E5
Mu Gia, Deo *Vietnam* 17°40N 105°47E **38** D5
Mu Ko Chang △ *Thailand* 11°59N 102°22E **39** G4
Mu Us Shamo *China* 39°0N 109°0E **34** E5
Muang Chiang Rai = Chiang Rai *Thailand* 19°52N 99°50E **38** C2
Muang Khong *Laos* 14°7N 105°51E **38** E5
Muang Lamphun *Thailand* 18°40N 99°2E **38** C2
Muang Mai *Thailand* 8°5N 98°21E **39** a
Muang Pak Beng *Laos* 19°54N 101°8E **38** C3
Muar *Malaysia* 2°3N 102°34E **39** L4
Muarabungo *Indonesia* 1°28S 102°52E **36** E2
Muaraenim *Indonesia* 3°40S 103°50E **36** E2
Muarajuloi *Indonesia* 0°12S 114°3E **36** E4
Muarakaman *Indonesia* 0°2S 116°45E **36** E5
Muaratebo *Indonesia* 1°30S 102°26E **36** E2
Muaratembesi *Indonesia* 1°42S 103°8E **36** E2
Muaratewe *Indonesia* 0°58S 114°52E **36** E4
Mubarakpur *India* 26°6N 83°18E **43** F10
Mubarraz = Al Mubarraz *Si. Arabia* 25°30N 49°40E **45** E6
Mubende *Uganda* 0°33N 31°22E **54** B3
Mubi *Nigeria* 10°18N 13°16E **51** F8
Mucajaí → *Brazil* 2°25N 60°52W **92** C6
Muchachos, Roque de los *Canary Is.* 28°44N 17°52W **24** F2
Muchinga Mts. *Zambia* 11°30S 31°30E **55** E3
Muck *U.K.* 56°50N 6°15W **11** E2
Muckadilla *Australia* 26°35S 148°23E **63** D4
Muckle Flugga *U.K.* 60°51N 0°54W **11** A8
Mucuri *Brazil* 18°0S 39°36W **93** G11
Mucusso *Angola* 18°1S 21°25E **56** B3
Muda *Canary Is.* 28°34N 13°57W **24** F6
Mudanjiang *China* 44°38N 129°30E **35** B15
Mudanya *Turkey* 40°25N 28°50E **23** D13
Muddy Cr. → *U.S.A.* 38°24N 110°42W **76** G8
Mudgee *Australia* 32°32S 149°31E **63** E4
Mudjatik → *Canada* 56°1N 107°36W **71** B7
Muecate *Mozam.* 14°55S 39°40E **55** E4
Mueda *Mozam.* 11°36S 39°28E **55** E4
Mueller Ranges *Australia* 18°18S 126°46E **60** C4
Muende *Mozam.* 14°28S 33°0E **55** E3
Muerto, Mar *Mexico* 16°10N 94°10W **87** D6
Mufulira *Zambia* 12°32S 28°15E **55** E2
Mufumbiro Range *Africa* 1°25S 29°30E **54** C2
Mughal Sarai *India* 25°18N 83°7E **43** G10
Mughayrā' *Si. Arabia* 29°17N 37°41E **44** D3
Mugi *Japan* 33°40N 134°25E **31** H7
Mugila, Mts. *Dem. Rep. of the Congo* 7°0S 28°50E **54** D2
Muğla *Turkey* 37°15N 28°22E **23** F13
Mugu *Nepal* 29°45N 82°30E **43** E10
Muhammad, Râs *Egypt* 27°44N 34°16E **44** E2
Muhammad Qol *Sudan* 20°53N 37°9E **51** D13
Muhammadabad *India* 26°4N 83°25E **43** F10
Muhesi → *Tanzania* 7°0S 35°20E **54** D4
Mühlhausen *Germany* 51°12N 10°27E **16** C6
Mühlig Hofmann fjell *Antarctica* 72°30S 5°0E **5** D3
Muhos *Finland* 64°47N 25°59E **8** D21
Muhu *Estonia* 58°36N 23°11E **9** G20
Muhutwe *Tanzania* 1°35S 31°45E **54** C3
Mui Wo *China* 22°16N 113°59E **33** G10
Muine Bheag *Ireland* 52°42N 6°58W **10** D5
Muir, L. *Australia* 34°30S 116°40E **61** F2
Muir of Ord *U.K.* 57°32N 4°28W **11** D4
Mujnak = Muynak *Uzbekistan* 43°44N 59°10E **28** E6
Muka, Tanjung *Malaysia* 5°28N 100°11E **39** c
Mukacheve *Ukraine* 48°27N 22°45E **17** D12
Mukachevo = Mukacheve *Ukraine* 48°27N 22°45E **17** D12
Mukah *Malaysia* 2°55N 112°5E **36** D4
Mukandwara *India* 24°49N 75°59E **42** G6
Mukdahan *Thailand* 16°32N 104°43E **38** D5
Mukden = Shenyang *China* 41°48N 123°27E **35** D12
Mukerian *India* 31°57N 75°37E **42** D6
Mukinbudin *Australia* 30°55S 118°5E **61** F2
Mukishi *Dem. Rep. of the Congo* 8°30S 24°44E **55** D1
Mukomuko *Indonesia* 2°30S 101°10E **36** E2
Mukomwenze *Dem. Rep. of the Congo* 6°49S 27°15E **54** D2
Muktsar *India* 30°30N 74°30E **42** D6
Mukur = Moqor *Afghan.* 32°50N 67°42E **42** C2
Mukutawa → *Canada* 53°10N 97°24W **71** C9
Mukwela *Zambia* 17°0S 26°40E **55** F2
Mula *Spain* 38°3N 1°33W **21** C5
Mula → *Pakistan* 27°57N 67°36E **42** F2
Mulange *Dem. Rep. of the Congo* 3°40S 27°10E **54** C2
Mulanje *Malawi* 16°2S 35°33E **55** F4
Mulanje, Mt. *Malawi* 16°0S 35°30E **55** F4
Mulchén *Chile* 37°45S 72°20W **94** D1
Mulde → *Germany* 51°53N 12°15E **16** C7
Mule Creek Junction *U.S.A.* 43°23N 104°13W **76** E11
Muleba *Tanzania* 1°50S 31°37E **54** C3
Mulegé *Mexico* 26°53N 111°59W **86** B2
Muleshoe *U.S.A.* 34°13N 102°43W **84** D3
Mulgrave *Canada* 45°38N 61°31W **73** C7
Mulhacén *Spain* 37°4N 3°20W **21** D4
Mulhouse *France* 47°40N 7°20E **20** C7
Mulifanua *Samoa* 13°50S 171°59W **59** b
Muling *China* 44°35N 130°10E **35** B16
Mull *U.K.* 56°25N 5°56W **11** E3
Mull, Sound of *U.K.* 56°30N 5°50W **11** E3
Mullaittivu *Sri Lanka* 9°15N 80°49E **40** Q12
Mullen *U.S.A.* 42°3N 101°1W **80** D3
Mullens *U.S.A.* 37°35N 81°23W **81** G13
Muller, Pegunungan *Indonesia* 0°30N 113°30E **36** D4
Mullet Pen. *Ireland* 54°13N 10°2W **10** B1
Mullewa *Australia* 28°29S 115°30E **61** E2
Mulligan → *Australia* 25°0S 139°0E **62** D2
Mullingar *Ireland* 53°31N 7°21W **10** C4

Mullins U.S.A. 34°12N 79°15W 85 D15
Mullumbimby Australia 28°30S 153°30E 63 D5
Mulobezi Zambia 16°45S 25°7E 55 F2
Mulonga Plain Zambia 16°20S 22°40E 53 H4
Mulroy B. Ireland 55°15N 7°46W 10 A4
Multan Pakistan 30°15N 71°36E 42 D4
Mulumbe, Mts. Dem. Rep. of the Congo 8°40S 27°30E 55 D2
Mulungushi Dam Zambia 14°48S 28°48E 55 E2
Mulvane U.S.A. 37°29N 97°15W 80 G5
Mumbai India 18°56N 72°50E 40 K8
Mumbwa Zambia 15°0S 27°0E 55 F2
Mumias Kenya 0°20N 34°29E 54 C4
Mun → Thailand 15°19N 105°30E 38 E5
Muna Indonesia 5°0S 122°30E 37 F6
Munabao India 25°45N 70°17E 42 G4
Munamagi Estonia 57°43N 27°4E 9 H22
Muncan Indonesia 8°34S 115°11E 37 K18
Muncar Indonesia 8°26S 114°20E 37 J17
München Germany 48°8N 11°34E 16 D6
Munchen-Gladbach = Mönchengladbach Germany 51°11N 6°27E 16 C4
Muncho Lake Canada 59°0N 125°50W 70 B3
Munch'ŏn N. Korea 39°14N 127°19E 35 E14
Muncie U.S.A. 40°12N 85°23W 81 E11
Muncoonie L. West Australia 25°12S 138°40E 62 D2
Mundabbera Australia 25°36S 151°18E 63 D5
Munday U.S.A. 33°27N 99°38W 84 E5
Münden Germany 51°25N 9°38E 16 C5
Mundiwindi Australia 23°47S 120°9E 60 D3
Mundo Novo Brazil 11°50S 40°29W 93 F10
Mundra India 22°54N 69°48E 42 H3
Mundrabilla Australia 31°52S 127°51E 61 F4
Mungallala Australia 26°28S 147°34E 63 D4
Mungallala Cr. → Australia 28°53S 147°5E 63 D4
Mungana Australia 17°8S 144°27E 62 B3
Mungaoli India 24°24N 78°7E 42 G8
Mungari Mozam. 17°12S 33°30E 55 F3
Mungbere Dem. Rep. of the Congo 2°36N 28°28E 54 B2
Mungeli India 22°4N 81°41E 43 H9
Munger India 25°23N 86°30E 43 G12
Mungkan Kandju △ Australia 13°35S 142°52E 62 A3
Munich = München Germany 48°8N 11°34E 16 D6
Munising U.S.A. 46°25N 86°40W 80 B10
Munku-Sardyk Russia 51°45N 100°20E 29 D11
Muñoz Gamero, Pen. Chile 52°30S 73°5W 96 G2
Munroe L. Canada 59°13N 98°35W 71 B9
Munsan S. Korea 37°51N 126°48E 35 F14
Münster Germany 51°58N 7°37E 16 C4
Munster □ Ireland 52°18N 8°44W 10 D3
Muntadgin Australia 31°45S 118°33E 61 F2
Muntok Indonesia 2°5S 105°10E 36 E3
Munyama Zambia 16°5S 28°31E 55 F2
Muong Beng Laos 20°23N 101°46E 38 B3
Muong Boum Vietnam 22°24N 102°49E 38 A4
Muong Et Laos 20°49N 104°1E 38 B5
Muong Hai Laos 21°3N 101°49E 38 B3
Muong Hiem Laos 20°5N 103°22E 38 B4
Muong Houn Laos 20°8N 101°23E 38 B3
Muong Hung Vietnam 20°56N 103°53E 38 B4
Muong Kau Laos 15°6N 105°47E 38 E5
Muong Khao Laos 19°38N 103°32E 38 C4
Muong Khoua Laos 21°5N 102°31E 38 B4
Muong Liep Laos 18°29N 101°40E 38 C3
Muong May Laos 14°49N 106°56E 38 E6
Muong Ngeun Laos 20°36N 101°3E 38 B3
Muong Ngoi Laos 20°43N 102°41E 38 B4
Muong Nhie Vietnam 22°12N 102°28E 38 A4
Muong Nong Laos 16°22N 106°30E 38 D6
Muong Ou Tay Laos 22°7N 101°48E 38 A3
Muong Oua Laos 18°18N 101°20E 38 C3
Muong Peun Laos 20°13N 103°52E 38 B4
Muong Phalane Laos 16°39N 105°34E 38 D5
Muong Phieng Laos 19°6N 101°32E 38 C3
Muong Phine Laos 16°32N 106°2E 38 D6
Muong Sai Laos 20°42N 101°59E 38 B3
Muong Saiapoun Laos 18°24N 101°31E 38 C3
Muong Sen Vietnam 19°24N 104°8E 38 C5
Muong Sing Laos 21°11N 101°9E 38 B3
Muong Son Laos 20°27N 103°19E 38 B4
Muong Soui Laos 19°33N 102°52E 38 C4
Muong Va Laos 21°53N 102°19E 38 B4
Muong Xia Vietnam 20°19N 104°50E 38 B5
Muonio Finland 67°57N 23°40E 8 C20
Muonio älv = Muonionjoki → Finland 67°11N 23°34E 8 C20
Muonioälven = Muonionjoki → Finland 67°11N 23°34E 8 C20
Muonionjoki → Finland 67°11N 23°34E 8 C20
Muping China 37°22N 121°36E 35 F11
Muqdisho Somali Rep. 2°2N 45°25E 47 G4
Mur → Austria 46°18N 16°52E 17 E9
Murakami Japan 38°14N 139°29E 30 E9
Murallón, Cerro Chile 49°48S 73°30W 96 F2
Muranda Rwanda 1°52S 29°20E 54 C2
Murang'a Kenya 0°45S 37°9E 54 C4
Murashi Russia 59°30N 49°0E 18 C8
Murat → Turkey 38°46N 40°0E 19 G7
Muratlı Turkey 41°10N 27°29E 23 D12
Murayama Japan 38°30N 140°25E 30 E10
Murchison → Australia 27°45S 114°0E 61 E1
Murchison, Mt. Antarctica 73°25S 166°20E 5 D11
Murchison Falls Uganda 2°15N 31°30E 54 B3
Murchison Falls △ Uganda 2°17N 31°48E 54 B3
Murchison Ra. Australia 20°0S 134°10E 62 C1
Murchison Rapids Malawi 15°55S 34°35E 55 F3
Murcia Spain 38°5N 1°10W 21 D5
Murcia □ Spain 37°50N 1°30W 21 D5
Murdo U.S.A. 43°53N 100°43W 80 D3
Murdoch Pt. Australia 14°37S 144°55E 62 A3
Mureş → Romania 46°15N 20°13E 17 E11
Mureşul = Mureş → Romania 46°15N 20°13E 17 E11
Murewa Zimbabwe 17°39S 31°47E 57 B5
Murfreesboro N.C., U.S.A. 36°27N 77°6W 85 C16
Murfreesboro Tenn., U.S.A. 35°51N 86°24W 85 D11
Murgap Tajikistan 38°10N 74°2E 28 F8
Murgap → Turkmenistan 38°18N 61°12E 45 B9
Murgenella Australia 11°34S 132°56E 60 B5
Murgha Kibzai Pakistan 30°44N 69°25E 42 D3
Murghob = Murgap Tajikistan 38°10N 74°2E 28 F8
Murgon Australia 26°15S 151°54E 63 D5
Muri India 23°22N 85°52E 43 H11
Muria Indonesia 6°36S 110°53E 37 G14
Muriaé Brazil 21°8S 42°23W 95 A7
Muriel Mine Zimbabwe 17°14S 30°40E 55 F3
Müritz Germany 53°25N 12°42E 16 B7
Murliganj India 25°54N 86°59E 43 G12
Murmansk Russia 68°57N 33°10E 8 B25
Murmashi Russia 68°47N 32°42E 8 B25
Muro Spain 39°44N 3°3E 24 B10
Murom Russia 55°35N 42°3E 18 C7
Muroran Japan 42°25N 141°0E 30 C10
Muroto Japan 33°18N 134°9E 31 H7
Muroto-Misaki Japan 33°15N 134°10E 31 H7
Murphy U.S.A. 43°13N 116°33W 76 E5
Murphys U.S.A. 38°8N 120°28W 78 G6
Murray Ky., U.S.A. 36°37N 88°19W 80 G9
Murray Utah, U.S.A. 40°40N 111°53W 76 F8
Murray → Australia 35°20S 139°22E 63 F2
Murray, L. U.S.A. 34°3N 81°13W 85 D14
Murray Bridge Australia 35°6S 139°14E 63 F2
Murray Fracture Zone Pac. Oc. 35°0N 130°0W 65 D14
Murray Harbour Canada 46°0N 62°28W 73 C7
Murray River △ Australia 34°23S 140°32E 63 E3
Murraysburg S. Africa 31°58S 23°47E 56 E3
Murree Pakistan 33°56N 73°28E 42 C5
Murrieta U.S.A. 33°33N 117°13W 79 M9
Murrumbidgee → Australia 34°43S 143°12E 63 E3
Murrumburrah Australia 34°32S 148°22E 63 E4
Murrurundi Australia 31°42S 150°51E 63 E5
Murshidabad India 24°11N 88°19E 43 G13
Murtle L. Canada 52°8N 119°38W 70 C5
Murtoa Australia 36°35S 142°28E 63 F3
Murungu Tanzania 4°12S 31°10E 54 C3
Mururoa French Polynesia 21°52S 138°55W 65 K14
Murwara India 23°46N 80°28E 43 H9
Murwillumbah Australia 28°18S 153°27E 63 D5
Mürzzuschlag Austria 47°36N 15°41E 16 E8
Muş Turkey 38°45N 41°30E 44 B4
Mûsa, Gebel Egypt 28°33N 33°59E 44 D2
Musa Khel Pakistan 30°59N 69°52E 42 D3
Mūsa Qal'eh Afghan. 32°20N 64°50E 40 C4
Musafirkhana India 26°22N 81°48E 43 F9
Musala Bulgaria 42°13N 23°37E 23 C10
Musala Indonesia 1°41N 98°28E 36 D1
Musan N. Korea 42°12N 129°12E 35 C15
Musangu Dem. Rep. of the Congo 10°28S 23°55E 55 E1
Musasa Tanzania 3°25S 31°30E 54 C3
Musay'īd Qatar 25°0N 51°33E 45 E6
Muscat = Masqat Oman 23°37N 58°36E 47 C6
Muscatine U.S.A. 41°25N 91°3W 80 E8
Muscle Shoals U.S.A. 34°45N 87°40W 85 D11
Musengezi = Unsengedsi → Zimbabwe 15°43S 31°14E 55 F3
Musgrave Harbour Canada 49°27N 53°58W 73 C9
Musgrave Ranges Australia 26°0S 132°0E 61 E5
Mushie Dem. Rep. of the Congo 2°56S 16°55E 52 E3
Musi → Indonesia 2°20S 104°56E 36 E2
Musina S. Africa 22°20S 30°5E 57 C5
Muskeg → Canada 60°20N 123°20W 70 A4
Muskegon U.S.A. 43°14N 86°16W 80 D10
Muskegon → U.S.A. 43°14N 86°21W 80 D10
Muskegon Heights U.S.A. 43°12N 86°16W 80 D10
Muskogee U.S.A. 35°45N 95°22W 84 D7
Muskoka, L. Canada 45°0N 79°25W 82 B5
Muskwa → Canada 58°47N 122°48W 70 B4
Muslīmiyah Syria 36°19N 37°12E 44 B3
Musofu Zambia 13°30S 29°0E 55 E2
Musoma Tanzania 1°30S 33°48E 54 C3
Musquaro, L. Canada 50°38N 61°5W 73 B7
Musquodoboit Harbour Canada 44°50N 63°9W 73 D7
Musselburgh U.K. 55°57N 3°2W 11 F5
Musselshell → U.S.A. 47°21N 107°57W 76 C10
Mussende Angola 10°32S 16°5E 52 G3
Mussoorie India 30°27N 78°6E 42 D8
Mussuco Angola 17°2S 19°3E 56 B2
Mustafakemalpaşa Turkey 40°2N 28°24E 23 D13
Mustang Nepal 29°10N 83°55E 43 E10
Musters, L. Argentina 45°20S 69°25W 96 F3
Musudan N. Korea 40°50N 129°43E 35 D15
Muswellbrook Australia 32°16S 150°56E 63 E5
Mût Egypt 25°28N 28°58E 51 C11
Mut Turkey 36°40N 33°28E 44 B2
Mutanda Mozam. 21°0S 33°34E 57 C5
Mutanda Zambia 12°24S 26°13E 55 E2
Mutare Zimbabwe 18°58S 32°38E 55 F3
Mutawintji △ Australia 31°10S 142°30E 63 E3
Mutha Kenya 1°48S 38°26E 54 C4
Muting Indonesia 7°23S 140°20E 37 F10
Mutki = Mirtağ Turkey 38°23N 41°56E 44 B4
Mutoko Zimbabwe 17°24S 32°13E 57 B5
Mutomo Kenya 1°51S 38°12E 54 C4
Mutoray Russia 60°56N 101°0E 29 C11
Mutsamudu Comoros Is. 12°10S 44°25E 53 a
Mutshatsha Dem. Rep. of the Congo 10°35S 24°20E 55 E1
Mutsu Japan 41°5N 140°55E 30 D10
Mutsu-Wan Japan 41°5N 140°55E 30 D10
Muttaburra Australia 22°38S 144°29E 62 C3
Mutton I. Ireland 52°49N 9°32W 10 D2
Mutuáli Mozam. 14°55S 37°0E 55 E4
Muweilih Egypt 30°42N 34°19E 46 E3
Muy Muy Nic. 12°39N 85°36W 88 D2
Muyinga Burundi 3°14S 30°33E 54 C3
Muynak Uzbekistan 43°44N 59°10E 28 E6
Muyunkum, Peski = Moyynqum Kazakhstan 44°12N 71°0E 28 E8
Muz Tag China 36°25N 87°25E 32 C3
Muzaffarabad Pakistan 34°25N 73°30E 43 B5
Muzaffargarh Pakistan 30°5N 71°14E 42 D4
Muzaffarnagar India 29°26N 77°40E 42 E7
Muzaffarpur India 26°7N 85°23E 43 F11
Muzafirpur Pakistan 30°58N 69°9E 42 D3
Muzhi Russia 65°25N 64°40E 18 A11
Muztagh-Ata China 38°17N 75°7E 32 C2
Mvuma Zimbabwe 19°16S 30°30E 55 F3
Mvurwi Zimbabwe 17°0S 30°57E 55 F3
Mwabvi ⌓ Malawi 16°42S 35°0E 55 F3
Mwadui Tanzania 3°26S 33°32E 54 C3
Mwali = Mohéli Comoros Is. 12°20S 43°40E 53 a
Mwambo Tanzania 10°30S 40°22E 55 E5
Mwandi Zambia 17°30S 24°51E 55 F1
Mwanza Dem. Rep. of the Congo 7°55S 26°43E 54 D2
Mwanza Tanzania 2°30S 32°58E 54 C3
Mwanza Zambia 16°58S 24°28E 55 F1
Mwanza □ Tanzania 2°0S 33°0E 54 C3
Mwaya Tanzania 9°32S 33°55E 55 D3
Mweelrea Ireland 53°39N 9°49W 10 C2
Mweka Dem. Rep. of the Congo 4°50S 21°34E 52 E4
Mwene Ditu Dem. Rep. of the Congo 6°35S 22°27E 52 F4
Mwenezi Zimbabwe 21°15S 30°48E 55 G3
Mwenezi → Mozam. 22°40S 31°50E 55 G3
Mwenga Dem. Rep. of the Congo 3°1S 28°28E 54 C2
Mweru, L. Zambia 9°0S 28°40E 55 D2
Mweru Wantipa △ Zambia 8°39S 29°25E 55 D2
Mweza Range Zimbabwe 21°0S 30°0E 55 G3
Mwilambwe Dem. Rep. of the Congo 8°7S 25°5E 54 D2
Mwimbi Tanzania 8°38S 31°39E 55 D3
Mwingi Kenya 0°56S 38°4E 54 C4
Mwinilunga Zambia 11°43S 24°25E 55 E1
My Tho Vietnam 10°29N 106°23E 39 G6
Myajlar India 26°15N 70°20E 42 F4
Myanaung Burma 18°18N 95°22E 41 K19
Myanmar = Burma ■ Asia 21°0N 96°30E 41 J20
Myaungmya Burma 16°30N 94°40E 41 L19
Mycenæ = Mikines Greece 37°43N 22°46E 23 F10
Myeik Kyunzu Burma 11°30N 97°30E 39 G1
Myerstown U.S.A. 40°22N 76°19W 83 F8
Myingyan Burma 21°30N 95°20E 41 J19
Myitkyina Burma 25°24N 97°26E 41 G20
Mykines Færoe Is. 62°7N 7°35W 8 E9
Mykolayiv Ukraine 46°58N 32°0E 19 E5
Mykonos Greece 37°30N 25°25E 23 F11
Mymensingh Bangla. 24°45N 90°24E 41 G17
Mynydd Du U.K. 51°52N 3°50W 13 F4
Mýrdalsjökull Iceland 63°40N 19°6W 8 E4
Myrtle Beach U.S.A. 33°42N 78°53W 85 E15
Myrtle Creek U.S.A. 43°1N 123°17W 76 E2
Myrtle Point U.S.A. 43°4N 124°8W 76 E1
Myrtou Cyprus 35°18N 33°4E 25 D12
Mysia Turkey 39°50N 27°0E 23 E12
Mysore = Karnataka □ India 13°15N 77°0E 40 N10
Mysore India 12°17N 76°41E 40 N10
Mystic U.S.A. 41°21N 71°58W 83 E13
Myszków Poland 50°45N 19°22E 17 C10
Mytishchi Russia 55°50N 37°50E 18 C6
Mývatn Iceland 65°36N 17°0W 8 D5
Mzimba Malawi 11°55S 33°39E 55 E3
Mzimkulu → S. Africa 30°44S 30°28E 57 E5
Mzimvubu → S. Africa 31°38S 29°33E 57 E4
Mzuzu Malawi 11°30S 33°55E 55 E3

N

Na Hearadh = Harris U.K. 57°50N 6°55W 11 D2
Na Noi Thailand 18°19N 100°43E 38 C3
Na Phao Laos 17°35N 105°44E 38 D5
Na Sam Vietnam 22°3N 106°37E 38 A6
Na San Vietnam 21°12N 104°2E 38 B5
Na Thon Thailand 9°32N 99°56E 39 b
Naab → Germany 49°1N 12°2E 16 D6
Naantali Finland 60°29N 22°2E 9 F20
Naas Ireland 53°12N 6°40W 10 C5
Nababeep S. Africa 29°36S 17°46E 56 D2
Nabadwip = Navadwip India 23°34N 88°20E 43 H13
Nabawa Australia 28°30S 114°48E 61 E1
Nabberu, L. Australia 25°50S 120°30E 61 E3
Naberezhnyye Chelny Russia 55°42N 52°19E 18 C9
Nabeul Tunisia 36°30N 10°44E 51 A8
Nabha India 30°26N 76°14E 42 D7
Nabīd Iran 29°40N 57°38E 45 D8
Nabire Indonesia 3°15S 135°26E 37 E9
Nabisar Pakistan 25°8N 69°40E 42 G3
Nabisipi → Canada 50°14N 62°13W 73 B7
Nabiswera Uganda 1°27N 32°15E 54 B3
Nāblus = Nābulus West Bank 32°14N 35°15E 46 C4
Naboomspruit S. Africa 24°32S 28°40E 57 C4
Nabouwalu Fiji 17°0S 178°45E 59 a
Nābulus West Bank 32°14N 35°15E 46 C4
Nacala Mozam. 14°31S 40°34E 55 E5
Nacala-Velha Mozam. 14°32S 40°34E 55 E5
Nacaome Honduras 13°31N 87°30W 88 D2
Nacaroa Mozam. 14°22S 39°56E 55 E4
Naches U.S.A. 46°44N 120°42W 76 C3
Naches → U.S.A. 46°38N 120°31W 78 D6
Nachicapau, L. Canada 56°40N 68°5W 73 A6
Nachingwea Tanzania 10°23S 38°49E 55 E4
Nachna India 27°34N 71°41E 42 F4
Nacimiento, L. U.S.A. 35°46N 120°53W 78 K6
Naco Mexico 31°19N 109°56W 86 A3
Nacogdoches U.S.A. 31°36N 94°39W 84 F7
Nácori Chico Mexico 29°40N 108°57W 86 B3
Nacozari de García Mexico 30°25N 109°38W 86 A3
Nacula Fiji 16°54S 177°27E 59 a
Nådendal = Naantali Finland 60°29N 22°2E 9 F20
Nadi Fiji 17°42S 177°20E 59 a
Nadiad India 22°41N 72°56E 42 H5
Nador Morocco 35°14N 2°58W 50 B5
Nadur Malta 36°2N 14°18E 25 C1
Nadūshan Iran 32°2N 53°35E 45 C7
Nadvirna Ukraine 48°37N 24°30E 17 D13
Nadvoitsy Russia 63°52N 34°14E 18 B5
Nadvornaya = Nadvirna Ukraine 48°37N 24°30E 17 D13
Nadym Russia 65°35N 72°42E 28 C8
Nadym → Russia 66°12N 72°0E 28 C8
Nærbø Norway 58°40N 5°39E 9 G11
Næstved Denmark 55°13N 11°44E 9 J14
Nafpaktos Greece 38°24N 21°50E 23 E9
Nafplio Greece 37°33N 22°50E 23 F10
Naft-e Safīd Iran 31°40N 49°17E 45 D6
Naftshahr Iran 34°0N 45°30E 44 C5
Nafud Desert = An Nafūd Si. Arabia 28°15N 41°0E 44 D4
Naga Phil. 13°38N 123°15E 37 B6
Nagagami Canada 50°23N 84°20W 72 B3
Nagahama Japan 35°23N 136°16E 31 G8
Nagai Japan 38°6N 140°2E 30 E10
Nagaland □ India 26°0N 94°30E 41 G19
Nagano Japan 36°40N 138°10E 31 F9
Nagano □ Japan 36°15N 138°0E 31 F9
Nagaoka Japan 37°27N 138°51E 31 F9
Nagappattinam India 10°46N 79°51E 40 P11
Nagar → Bangla. 24°27N 89°12E 43 G13
Nagar Parkar Pakistan 24°28N 70°46E 42 G4
Nagasaki Japan 32°47N 129°50E 31 H4
Nagasaki □ Japan 32°50N 129°40E 31 H4
Nagato Japan 34°19N 131°5E 31 G5
Nagaur India 27°15N 73°45E 42 F5
Nagda India 23°27N 75°25E 42 H6
Nagercoil India 8°12N 77°26E 40 Q10
Nagina India 29°30N 78°30E 43 E8
Nagīneh Iran 34°20N 57°15E 45 C8
Nagir Pakistan 36°12N 74°42E 43 A6
Nagles Mts. Ireland 52°8N 8°30W 10 D3
Nagod India 24°34N 80°36E 43 G9
Nagoorin Australia 24°17S 151°15E 62 C5
Nagorno-Karabakh □ Azerbaijan 39°55N 46°45E 44 B5
Nagornyy Russia 55°58N 124°57E 29 D13
Nagoya Japan 35°10N 136°50E 31 G8
Nagpur India 21°8N 79°10E 40 J11
Nagua Dom. Rep. 19°23N 69°50W 89 C6
Naguabo Puerto Rico 18°13N 65°44W 89 d
Nagykanizsa Hungary 46°28N 17°0E 17 E9
Nagykőrös Hungary 47°5N 19°48E 17 E10
Naha Japan 26°13N 127°42E 31 L3
Nahan India 30°33N 77°18E 42 D7
Nahanni △ Canada 61°36N 125°41W 70 A4
Nahanni Butte Canada 61°2N 123°31W 70 A4
Nahargarh Mad. P., India 24°10N 75°14E 42 G6
Nahargarh Raj., India 24°55N 76°50E 42 G7
Nahariyya Israel 33°1N 35°5E 44 C2
Nahāvand Iran 34°10N 48°22E 45 C6
Nahuel Huapi, L. Argentina 41°0S 71°32W 96 E2
Nahuelbuta △ Chile 37°44S 72°57W 94 D1
Nai Yong Thailand 8°14N 98°22E 39 a
Naicá Mexico 27°53N 105°31W 86 B3
Naicam Canada 52°30N 104°30W 71 C8
Naikoon ⌓ Canada 53°55N 131°55W 70 C2
Naimisharanya India 27°21N 80°30E 43 F9
Nain Canada 56°34N 61°40W 73 A7
Nā'īn Iran 32°54N 53°0E 45 C7
Naini Tal India 29°30N 79°30E 43 E8
Nainpur India 22°30N 80°10E 43 H9
Nainwa India 25°46N 75°51E 42 G6
Nairai Fiji 17°49S 179°15E 59 a
Nairn U.K. 57°35N 3°53W 11 D5
Nairobi Kenya 1°17S 36°48E 54 C4
Nairobi △ Kenya 1°22S 36°50E 54 C4
Naissaar Estonia 59°34N 24°29E 9 G21
Naitaba Fiji 17°0S 179°16W 59 a
Naivasha Kenya 0°40S 36°30E 54 C4
Naivasha, L. Kenya 0°48S 36°20E 54 C4
Najaf = An Najaf Iraq 32°3N 44°15E 44 C5
Najafābād Iran 32°40N 51°15E 45 C6
Najd Si. Arabia 26°30N 42°0E 47 B3
Najibabad India 29°40N 78°20E 42 E8
Najin N. Korea 42°12N 130°15E 35 C16
Najmah Si. Arabia 26°42N 50°6E 45 E6
Najrān Si. Arabia 17°34N 44°18E 47 D3
Naju S. Korea 35°3N 126°43E 35 G14
Nakadōri-Shima Japan 32°57N 129°4E 31 H4
Nakalagba Dem. Rep. of the Congo 2°50N 27°58E 54 B2
Nakaminato Japan 36°21N 140°36E 31 F10
Nakamura Japan 32°59N 132°56E 31 H6
Nakano Japan 36°45N 138°22E 31 F9
Nakano-Shima Japan 29°51N 129°52E 31 K4
Nakashibetsu Japan 43°33N 144°59E 30 C12
Nakfa Eritrea 16°40N 38°32E 47 D2
Nakha Yai, Ko Thailand 8°3N 98°28E 39 a
Nakhichevan = Naxçıvan Azerbaijan 39°12N 45°15E 44 B5
Nakhichevan Rep. = Naxçıvan □ Azerbaijan 39°25N 45°26E 44 B5
Nakhl Egypt 29°55N 33°43E 46 F2
Nakhl-e Taqī Iran 27°28N 52°36E 45 E7
Nakhodka Russia 42°53N 132°54E 30 C6
Nakhon Nayok Thailand 14°12N 101°13E 38 E3
Nakhon Pathom Thailand 13°49N 100°3E 38 F3
Nakhon Phanom Thailand 17°23N 104°43E 38 D5
Nakhon Ratchasima Thailand 14°59N 102°12E 38 E4
Nakhon Sawan Thailand 15°35N 100°10E 38 E3
Nakhon Si Thammarat Thailand 8°29N 100°0E 39 H3
Nakhon Thai Thailand 17°5N 100°44E 38 D3
Nakhtarana India 23°20N 69°15E 42 H3
Nakina Canada 50°10N 86°40W 72 B2
Nakodar India 31°8N 75°31E 42 D6
Naktong → S. Korea 35°7N 128°57E 35 G15
Nakuru Kenya 0°15S 36°4E 54 C4
Nakuru, L. Kenya 0°23S 36°5E 54 C4
Nakusp Canada 50°20N 117°45W 70 C5
Nal Pakistan 27°40N 66°12E 42 F2
Nal → Pakistan 25°20N 65°30E 42 G1
Nalázi Mozam. 24°3S 33°20E 57 C5
Nalchik Russia 43°30N 43°33E 19 F7
Nalgonda India 17°6N 79°15E 40 L11
Nalhati India 24°17N 87°52E 43 G12
Naliya India 23°16N 68°50E 42 H3
Nallamalai Hills India 15°30N 78°50E 40 M11
Nalubaale Dam Uganda 0°30N 33°5E 54 B3
Nam Can Vietnam 8°46N 104°59E 39 H5
Nam-ch'on N. Korea 38°15N 126°26E 35 E14
Nam Co China 30°30N 90°45E 32 C4
Nam Dinh Vietnam 20°25N 106°5E 38 B6
Nam Du, Hon Vietnam 9°41N 104°21E 39 H5
Nam Nao △ Thailand 16°44N 101°32E 38 D3
Nam Ngum Res. Laos 18°35N 102°34E 38 C4
Nam-Phan Vietnam 10°30N 106°0E 39 G6
Nam Phong Thailand 16°42N 102°52E 38 D4
Nam Tha Laos 20°58N 101°30E 38 B3
Nam Tok Thailand 14°21N 99°4E 38 E2
Namacunde Angola 17°18S 15°50E 56 B2
Namacurra Mozam. 17°30S 36°50E 57 B6
Namak, Daryācheh-ye Iran 34°30N 52°0E 45 C7
Namak, Kavir-e Iran 34°30N 57°30E 45 C8
Namakzār, Daryācheh-ye Iran 34°0N 60°30E 45 C9
Namaland Namibia 26°0S 17°0E 56 C2
Namanga Kenya 2°33S 36°47E 54 C4
Namangan Uzbekistan 41°0N 71°40E 28 E8
Namapa Mozam. 13°43S 39°50E 55 E4
Namaqualand S. Africa 30°0S 17°25E 56 E2
Namasagali Uganda 1°2N 33°0E 54 B3
Namber Indonesia 1°2S 134°49E 37 E8
Nambour Australia 26°32S 152°58E 63 D5
Nambouwalu = Nabouwalu Fiji 17°0S 178°45E 59 a
Nambucca Heads Australia 30°37S 153°0E 63 E5
Nambung △ Australia 30°30S 115°5E 61 F2
Namcha Barwa China 29°40N 95°10E 32 D4
Namche Bazar Nepal 27°51N 86°47E 43 F12
Namchonjŏm = Nam-ch'on N. Korea 38°15N 126°26E 35 E14
Namecunda Mozam. 14°54S 37°37E 55 E4
Namenalala Fiji 17°8S 179°9E 59 a
Nameponda Mozam. 15°50S 39°50E 55 F4
Nametil Mozam. 15°40S 39°21E 55 F4
Namew L. Canada 54°14N 101°56W 71 C8
Namgia India 31°48N 78°40E 43 D8
Namib Desert Namibia 22°30S 15°0E 56 C2
Namib-Naukluft ⌓ Namibia 24°40S 15°16E 56 C2
Namibe Angola 15°7S 12°11E 53 H2
Namibe □ Angola 16°35S 12°30E 56 B1
Namibia ■ Africa 22°0S 18°0E 56 C2
Namibwoestyn = Namib Desert Namibia 22°30S 15°0E 56 C2
Namlea Indonesia 3°18S 127°5E 37 E7
Namoi → Australia 30°12S 149°30E 63 E4
Nampa U.S.A. 43°34N 116°34W 76 E5
Namp'o N. Korea 38°52N 125°10E 35 E13
Nampō-Shotō Japan 32°0N 140°0E 31 J10
Nampula Mozam. 15°6S 39°15E 55 F4
Namrole Indonesia 3°46S 126°46E 37 E7
Namse Shankou China 30°0N 82°25E 43 E10
Namsen → Norway 64°28N 11°37E 8 D14
Namsos Norway 64°29N 11°30E 8 D14
Namtok Chat Trakan △ Thailand 17°17N 100°40E 38 D3
Namtok Mae Surin △ Thailand 18°55N 98°2E 38 C2
Namtsy Russia 62°43N 129°37E 29 C13
Namtu Burma 23°25N 97°28E 41 H20
Namtumbo Tanzania 10°30S 36°4E 55 E4

Namu Canada 51°52N 127°50W 70 C3
Namuka-i-Lau Fiji 18°53S 178°37W 59 a
Namur Belgium 50°27N 4°52E 15 D4
Namur □ Belgium 50°17N 5°0E 15 D4
Namuruputh Kenya 4°34N 35°57E 54 B4
Namutoni Namibia 18°49S 16°55E 56 B2
Namwala Zambia 15°44S 26°30E 55 F2
Namwon S. Korea 35°23N 127°23E 35 G14
Namyang N. Korea 42°57N 129°52E 35 C15
Nan Thailand 18°48N 100°46E 38 C3
Nan → Thailand 15°42N 100°9E 38 E3
Nan-ch'ang = Nanchang China 28°42N 115°55E 33 D6
Nanaimo Canada 49°10N 124°0W 70 D4
Nanam N. Korea 41°44N 129°40E 35 D15
Nanango Australia 26°40S 152°0E 63 D5
Nanao Japan 37°0N 137°0E 31 F8
Nanchang China 28°42N 115°55E 33 D6
Nanching = Nanjing China 32°2N 118°47E 33 C6
Nanchong China 30°43N 106°2E 32 C5
Nancy France 48°42N 6°12E 20 B7
Nanda Devi India 30°23N 79°59E 43 D8
Nanda Devi △ India 30°30N 79°50E 43 D8
Nanda Kot India 30°17N 80°5E 43 D9
Nandan Japan 34°10N 134°42E 31 G7
Nanded India 19°10N 77°20E 40 K10
Nandewar Ra. Australia 30°15S 150°35E 63 E5
Nandi = Nadi Fiji 17°42S 177°20E 59 a
Nandigram India 22°1N 87°58E 43 H12
Nandurbar India 21°20N 74°15E 40 J9
Nandyal India 15°30N 78°30E 40 M11
Nanga-Eboko Cameroon 4°41N 12°22E 52 D2
Nanga Parbat Pakistan 35°10N 74°35E 43 B6
Nangade Mozam. 11°5S 39°36E 55 E4
Nangapinoh Indonesia 0°20S 111°44E 36 E4
Nangarhār □ Afghan. 34°20N 70°0E 40 B7
Nangatayap Indonesia 1°32S 110°34E 36 E4
Nangeya Mts. Uganda 3°30N 33°30E 54 B3
Nangong China 37°23N 115°22E 34 F8
Nanhuang China 36°58N 121°48E 35 F11
Nanjeko Zambia 15°31S 23°30E 55 F1
Nanjing China 32°2N 118°47E 33 C6
Nanjirinji Tanzania 9°41S 39°5E 55 D4
Nankana Sahib Pakistan 31°27N 73°38E 42 D5
Nanking = Nanjing China 32°2N 118°47E 33 C6
Nankoku Japan 33°39N 133°44E 31 H6
Nanlang China 22°30N 113°32E 33 G10
Nanning China 22°48N 108°20E 32 D5
Nannup Australia 33°59S 115°48E 61 F2
Nanpara India 27°52N 81°33E 43 F9
Nanpi China 38°2N 116°45E 34 E9
Nanping China 26°38N 118°10E 33 D6
Nanripe Mozam. 13°52S 38°52E 55 E4
Nansei-Shotō = Ryūkyū-rettō Japan 26°0N 126°0E 31 M3
Nansen Basin Arctic 84°0N 50°0E 4 A10
Nansen Sd. Canada 81°0N 91°0W 69 A10
Nansha China 22°45N 113°34E 33 F10
Nanshan I. S. China Sea 10°45N 115°49E 36 B5
Nansio Tanzania 2°3S 33°4E 54 C3
Nantes France 47°12N 1°33W 20 C3
Nanticoke U.S.A. 41°12N 76°0W 83 E8
Nanton Canada 50°21N 113°46W 70 C6
Nantong China 32°1N 120°52E 33 C7
Nantou China 22°32N 113°55E 33 F10
Nantucket I. U.S.A. 41°16N 70°5W 81 E18
Nantwich U.K. 53°4N 2°31W 12 D5
Nanty Glo U.S.A. 40°28N 78°50W 82 F6
Nanuku Passage Fiji 16°45S 179°15W 59 a
Nanuque Brazil 17°50S 40°21W 93 G10
Nanusa, Kepulauan Indonesia 4°45N 127°1E 37 D7
Nanutarra Roadhouse Australia 22°32S 115°30E 60 D2
Nanyang China 33°11N 112°30E 34 H7
Nanyuki Kenya 0°2N 37°4E 54 B4
Nao, C. de la Spain 38°44N 0°14E 21 C6
Naococane, L. Canada 52°50N 70°45W 73 B5
Napa U.S.A. 38°18N 122°17W 78 G4
Napa → U.S.A. 38°10N 122°19W 78 G4
Napanee Canada 44°15N 77°0W 82 B8
Napanoch U.S.A. 41°44N 74°22W 83 E10
Nape Laos 18°18N 105°6E 38 C5
Nape Pass = Keo Neua, Deo Vietnam 18°23N 105°10E 38 C5
Napier N.Z. 39°30S 176°56E 59 C6
Napier Broome B. Australia 14°2S 126°37E 60 B4
Napier Pen. Australia 12°4S 135°43E 62 A2
Napierville Canada 45°11N 73°25W 83 A11
Naples = Nápoli Italy 40°50N 14°15E 22 D6
Naples U.S.A. 26°8N 81°48W 85 H14
Napo → Peru 3°20S 72°40W 92 D4
Napoleon N. Dak., U.S.A. 46°30N 99°46W 80 B4
Napoleon Ohio, U.S.A. 41°23N 84°8W 81 E11
Nápoli Italy 40°50N 14°15E 22 D6
Napopo Dem. Rep. of the Congo 4°15N 28°0E 54 B2
Naqb, Ra's an Jordan 29°48N 35°44E 46 F4
Naqqāsh Iran 35°40N 49°6E 45 C6
Nara Japan 34°40N 135°49E 31 G7
Nara Mali 15°10N 7°20W 50 E4
Nara □ Japan 34°30N 136°0E 31 G8
Nara Canal Pakistan 24°30N 69°20E 42 G3
Nara Visa U.S.A. 35°37N 103°6W 77 J12
Naracoorte Australia 36°58S 140°45E 63 F3
Naradhan Australia 33°34S 146°17E 63 E4
Naraini India 25°11N 80°29E 43 G9
Naranjos Mexico 21°21N 97°41W 87 C5
Narasapur India 16°26N 81°40E 41 L12
Narathiwat Thailand 6°30N 101°48E 39 J3
Narayanganj Bangla. 23°40N 90°33E 41 H17
Narayanpet India 16°45N 77°30E 40 L10
Narberth U.K. 51°47N 4°44W 13 F3
Narbonne France 43°11N 3°0E 20 E5
Nardīn Iran 37°3N 55°59E 45 B7
Nardò Italy 40°11N 18°2E 23 D8
Narembeen Australia 32°7S 118°24E 61 F2
Narendranagar India 30°10N 78°18E 42 D8
Nares Str. Arctic 80°0N 70°0W 66 A13
Naretha Australia 31°0S 124°45E 61 F3
Narew → Poland 52°26N 20°41E 17 B11
Nari → Pakistan 28°0N 67°40E 42 F2
Narin Afghan. 36°5N 69°0E 40 A6
Narindra, Helodranon' i Madag. 14°55S 47°30E 57 A8
Narita Japan 35°47N 140°19E 31 G10
Nariva Swamp Trin. & Tob. 10°26N 61°4W 93 K15
Narmada → India 21°38N 72°36E 42 J5
Narnaul India 28°5N 76°11E 42 E7
Narodnaya Russia 65°5N 59°58E 18 A10
Narok Kenya 1°55S 35°52E 54 C4
Narooma Australia 36°14S 150°4E 63 F5
Narowal Pakistan 32°6N 74°52E 42 C6
Narrabri Australia 30°19S 149°46E 63 E4
Narran → Australia 28°37S 148°12E 63 D4
Narrandera Australia 34°42S 146°31E 63 E4
Narrogin Australia 32°58S 117°14E 61 F2
Narromine Australia 32°12S 148°12E 63 E4
Narrow Hills ⌂ Canada 54°0N 104°37W 71 C8
Narsimhapur India 22°54N 79°14E 43 H8
Narsinghgarh India 23°45N 76°40E 42 H7
Naruto Japan 34°11N 134°37E 31 G7
Narva Estonia 59°23N 28°12E 18 C4
Narva → Russia 59°27N 28°2E 9 G23
Narva Bay = Narva Laht Estonia 59°35N 27°35E 9 G22
Narva Laht Estonia 59°35N 27°35E 9 G22
Narvik Norway 68°28N 17°26E 8 B17
Narwana India 29°39N 76°6E 42 E7
Naryan-Mar Russia 67°42N 53°12E 18 A9
Narym Russia 59°0N 81°30E 28 D9
Naryn Kyrgyzstan 41°26N 75°58E 28 E8
Nasa Norway 66°29N 15°23E 8 C16
Nasau Fiji 17°19S 179°27E 59 a
Nasca = Nazca Peru 14°50S 74°57W 92 F4
Naseby N.Z. 45°1S 170°10E 59 F3
Naselle U.S.A. 46°22N 123°49W 78 D3
Naser, Buheirat en Egypt 23°0N 32°30E 51 D12
Nashua Mont., U.S.A. 48°8N 106°22W 76 B10
Nashua N.H., U.S.A. 42°45N 71°28W 83 D13
Nashville Ark., U.S.A. 33°57N 93°51W 84 E8
Nashville Ga., U.S.A. 31°12N 83°15W 85 F13
Nashville Tenn., U.S.A. 36°10N 86°47W 85 C11
Nasik India 19°58N 73°50E 40 K8
Nasirabad India 26°15N 74°45E 42 F6
Nasirabad Pakistan 28°23N 68°24E 42 E3
Nasiriyah = An Nāşirīyah Iraq 31°0N 46°15E 44 D5
Naskaupi → Canada 53°47N 60°51W 73 B7
Naşrābād Iran 34°8N 51°26E 45 C6
Naşriān-e Pā'īn Iran 32°52N 46°52E 44 C5
Nass → Canada 55°0N 129°40W 70 C3
Nassau Bahamas 25°5N 77°20W 88 A4
Nassau U.S.A. 42°31N 73°37W 83 D11
Nassau, B. Chile 55°20S 68°0W 96 H3
Nasser, L. = Naser, Buheirat en Egypt 23°0N 32°30E 51 D12
Nässjö Sweden 57°39N 14°42E 9 H16
Nastapoka → Canada 56°55N 76°33W 72 A4
Nastapoka, Is. Canada 56°55N 76°50W 72 A4
Nata Botswana 20°12S 26°12E 56 C4
Nata → Botswana 20°14S 26°10E 56 C4
Natal Brazil 5°47S 35°13W 93 E11
Natal Indonesia 0°35N 99°7E 36 D1
Natal Drakensberg ⌂ S. Africa 29°27S 29°30E 57 D4
Naţanz Iran 33°30N 51°55E 45 C6
Natashquan Canada 50°14N 61°46W 73 B7
Natashquan → Canada 50°7N 61°50W 73 B7
Natchez U.S.A. 31°34N 91°24W 84 F9
Natchitoches U.S.A. 31°46N 93°5W 84 F8
Natewa B. Fiji 16°35S 179°40E 59 a
Nathalia Australia 36°1S 145°13E 63 F4
Nathdwara India 24°55N 73°50E 42 G5
Nati, Pta. Spain 40°3N 3°50E 24 A10
Natimuk Australia 36°42S 142°0E 63 F3
Nation → Canada 55°30N 123°32W 70 B4
National City U.S.A. 32°40N 117°5W 79 N9
Natitingou Benin 10°20N 1°26E 50 F6
Natividad, I. Mexico 27°52N 115°11W 86 B1
Natkyizin Burma 14°57N 97°59E 38 E1
Natron, L. Tanzania 2°20S 36°0E 54 C4
Natrona Heights U.S.A. 40°37N 79°44W 82 F5
Natukanaoka Pan Namibia 18°40S 15°45E 56 B2
Natuna Besar, Kepulauan Indonesia 4°0N 108°15E 36 D3
Natuna Is. = Natuna Besar, Kepulauan Indonesia 4°0N 108°15E 36 D3
Natuna Selatan, Kepulauan Indonesia 2°45N 109°0E 36 D3
Natural Bridge U.S.A. 44°5N 75°30W 83 B9
Natural Bridges ⌂ U.S.A. 37°36N 110°0W 77 H9
Naturaliste, C. Tas., Australia 40°50S 148°15E 63 G4
Naturaliste, C. W. Austral., Australia 33°32S 115°0E 58 E4
Naturaliste Plateau Ind. Oc. 34°0S 112°0E 64 L3
Nau Qala Afghan. 34°5N 68°5E 42 B3
Naugatuck U.S.A. 41°30N 73°3W 83 E11
Naujaat = Repulse Bay Canada 66°30N 86°30W 69 C11
Naumburg Germany 51°9N 11°47E 16 C6
Nauru ■ Pac. Oc. 1°0S 166°0E 58 B9
Naushahra = Nowshera Pakistan 34°0N 72°0E 40 C8
Naushahro Pakistan 26°50N 68°7E 42 F3
Naushon I. U.S.A. 41°29N 70°45W 83 E14
Nausori Fiji 18°2S 178°32E 59 a
Nauta Peru 4°31S 73°35W 92 D4
Nautanwa India 27°20N 83°25E 43 F10
Naute ⌂ Namibia 26°55S 17°57E 56 D2
Nautla Mexico 20°13N 96°47W 87 C5
Nava Mexico 28°25N 100°45W 86 B4
Navadwip India 23°34N 88°20E 43 H13
Navahrudak Belarus 53°40N 25°50E 17 B13
Navajo Res. U.S.A. 36°48N 107°36W 77 H10
Navalmoral de la Mata Spain 39°52N 5°33W 21 C3
Navan = An Uaimh Ireland 53°39N 6°41W 10 C5
Navarin, Mys Russia 62°15N 179°5E 4 C16
Navarino, I. Chile 55°0S 67°40W 96 H3
Navarra □ Spain 42°40N 1°40W 21 A5
Navarre U.S.A. 40°43N 81°31W 82 F3
Navarro → U.S.A. 39°11N 123°45W 78 F3
Navasota U.S.A. 30°23N 96°5W 84 F6
Navassa I. W. Indies 18°30N 75°0W 89 C5
Naver → U.K. 58°32N 4°14W 11 C4
Navibandar India 21°26N 69°48E 42 J3
Navidad Chile 33°57S 71°50W 94 C1
Naviraí Brazil 23°8S 54°13W 95 A5
Naviti Fiji 17°7S 177°15E 59 a
Navlakhi India 22°58N 70°28E 42 H4
Năvodari Romania 44°19N 28°36E 17 F15
Navoi = Nawoiy Uzbekistan 40°9N 65°22E 28 E7
Navojoa Mexico 27°6N 109°26W 86 B3
Navolato Mexico 24°47N 107°42W 86 C3
Navsari India 20°57N 72°59E 40 J8
Navua Fiji 18°12S 178°11E 59 a
Nawa Kot Pakistan 28°21N 71°24E 42 E4
Nawab Khan Pakistan 30°17N 69°12E 42 D3
Nawabganj Ut. P., India 26°56N 81°14E 43 F9
Nawabganj Ut. P., India 28°32N 79°40E 43 E8
Nawabshah Pakistan 26°15N 68°25E 42 F3
Nawada India 24°50N 85°33E 43 G11
Nawakot Nepal 27°55N 85°10E 43 F11
Nawalgarh India 27°50N 75°15E 42 F6
Nawanshahr India 32°33N 74°48E 43 C6
Nawar, Dasht-i- Afghan. 33°52N 68°0E 42 C3
Nawoiy Uzbekistan 40°9N 65°22E 28 E7
Naxçıvan Azerbaijan 39°12N 45°15E 44 B5
Naxçıvan □ Azerbaijan 39°25N 45°26E 44 B5
Naxos Greece 37°8N 25°25E 23 F11
Nay, Mui Vietnam 12°55N 109°23E 36 B3
Nāy Band Būshehr, Iran 27°20N 52°40E 45 E7
Nāy Band Khorāsān, Iran 32°20N 57°34E 45 C8
Nayakhan Russia 61°56N 159°0E 29 C16
Nayarit □ Mexico 22°0N 105°0W 86 C4
Nayau Fiji 18°6S 178°10E 59 a
Nayoro Japan 44°21N 142°28E 30 B11
Nayyāl, W. → Si. Arabia 28°35N 39°4E 44 D3
Nazaré Brazil 13°2S 39°0W 93 F11
Nazareth = Nazerat Israel 32°42N 35°17E 46 C4
Nazareth U.S.A. 40°44N 75°19W 83 F9
Nazas Mexico 25°14N 104°8W 86 B4
Nazas → Mexico 25°12N 104°12W 86 B4
Nazca Peru 14°50S 74°57W 92 F4
Nazca Ridge Pac. Oc. 20°0S 80°0W 65 K19
Naze Japan 28°22N 129°27E 31 K4
Naze, The U.K. 51°53N 1°18E 13 F9
Nazerat Israel 32°42N 35°17E 46 C4
Nāzīk Iran 39°1N 45°4E 44 B5
Nazilli Turkey 37°55N 28°15E 23 F13
Nazko Canada 53°1N 123°37W 70 C4
Nazko → Canada 53°7N 123°34W 70 C4
Nazret Ethiopia 8°32N 39°22E 47 F2
Nchanga Zambia 12°30S 27°49E 55 E2
Ncheu Malawi 14°50S 34°47E 55 E3
Ndala Tanzania 4°45S 33°15E 54 C3
Ndalatando Angola 9°12S 14°48E 52 F2
Ndareda Tanzania 4°12S 35°30E 54 C4
Ndélé C.A.R. 8°25N 20°36E 52 C4
Ndjamena Chad 12°10N 14°59E 51 F8
Ndola Zambia 13°0S 28°34E 55 E2
Ndomo ⌂ S. Africa 26°52S 32°15E 57 D5
Ndoto Mts. Kenya 2°0N 37°0E 54 B4
Nduguti Tanzania 4°18S 34°41E 54 C3
Neagh, Lough U.K. 54°37N 6°25W 10 B5
Neah Bay U.S.A. 48°22N 124°37W 78 B2
Neale, L. Australia 24°15S 130°0E 60 D5
Neales → Australia 28°8S 136°47E 63 D2
Neapoli Greece 35°15N 25°37E 25 D7
Near Is. U.S.A. 52°30N 174°0E 74 a
Neath U.K. 51°39N 3°48W 13 F4
Neath Port Talbot □ U.K. 51°42N 3°45W 13 F4
Nebine Cr. → Australia 29°27S 146°56E 63 D4
Nebitdag = Balkanabat Turkmenistan 39°30N 54°22E 45 B7
Nebo Australia 21°42S 148°42E 62 C4
Nebraska □ U.S.A. 41°30N 99°30W 80 E4
Nebraska City U.S.A. 40°41N 95°52W 80 E6
Nébrodi, Monti Italy 37°54N 14°35E 22 F6
Necedah U.S.A. 44°2N 90°4W 80 C8
Nechako → Canada 53°55N 122°42W 70 C4
Neches → U.S.A. 29°58N 93°51W 84 G8
Neckar → Germany 49°27N 8°29E 16 D5
Necochea Argentina 38°30S 58°50W 94 D4
Nederland = Netherlands ■ Europe 52°0N 5°30E 15 C5
Needles Canada 49°53N 118°7W 70 D5
Needles U.S.A. 34°51N 114°37W 79 L12
Needles, The U.K. 50°39N 1°35W 13 G6
Ñeembucú □ Paraguay 27°0S 58°0W 94 B4
Neemuch = Nimach India 24°30N 74°56E 42 G6
Neenah U.S.A. 44°11N 88°28W 80 C9
Neepawa Canada 50°15N 99°30W 71 C9
Neftçala Azerbaijan 39°19N 49°12E 45 B6
Neftekumsk Russia 44°46N 44°50E 19 F7
Nefyn U.K. 52°56N 4°31W 12 E3
Negapatam = Nagappattinam India 10°46N 79°51E 40 P11
Negara Indonesia 8°22S 114°37E 37 J17
Negaunee U.S.A. 46°30N 87°36W 80 B10
Negele Ethiopia 5°20N 39°36E 47 F2
Negev Desert = Hanegev Israel 30°50N 35°0E 46 E4
Negombo Sri Lanka 7°12N 79°50E 40 R11
Negotin Serbia 44°16N 22°37E 23 B10
Negra, Pta. Mauritania 22°54N 16°18W 50 D2
Negra, Pta. Peru 6°6S 81°10W 92 E2
Negrais, C. = Maudin Sun Burma 16°0N 94°30E 41 M19
Negril Jamaica 18°22N 78°20W 88 a
Negro → Argentina 41°2S 62°47W 96 E4
Negro → Brazil 3°0S 60°0W 92 D7
Negro → Uruguay 33°24S 58°22W 94 C4
Negros Phil. 9°30N 122°40E 37 C6
Neguac Canada 47°15N 65°5W 73 C6
Nehalem → U.S.A. 45°40N 123°56W 78 E3
Nehāvand Iran 35°56N 49°31E 45 C6
Nehbandān Iran 31°35N 60°5E 45 D9
Nei Monggol Zizhiqu □ China 42°0N 112°0E 34 D7
Neiafu Tonga 18°39S 173°59W 59 c
Neiges, Piton des Réunion 21°5S 55°29E 53 c
Neijiang China 29°35N 104°55E 32 D5
Neilingding Dao China 22°25N 113°48E 33 G10
Neillsville U.S.A. 44°34N 90°36W 80 C8
Neilton U.S.A. 47°25N 123°53W 76 C2
Neiqiu China 37°15N 114°30E 34 F8
Neiva Colombia 2°56N 75°18W 92 C3
Neixiang China 33°10N 111°52E 34 H6
Nejanilini L. Canada 59°33N 97°48W 71 B9
Nejd = Najd Si. Arabia 26°30N 42°0E 47 B3
Nekā Iran 36°39N 53°19E 45 B7
Nekemte Ethiopia 9°4N 36°30E 47 F2
Neksø Denmark 55°4N 15°8E 9 J16
Nelia Australia 20°39S 142°12E 62 C3
Neligh U.S.A. 42°8N 98°2W 80 D4
Nelkan Russia 57°40N 136°4E 29 D14
Nellore India 14°27N 79°59E 40 M11
Nelson Canada 49°30N 117°20W 70 D5
Nelson N.Z. 41°18S 173°16E 59 D4
Nelson U.K. 53°50N 2°13W 12 D5
Nelson Ariz., U.S.A. 35°31N 113°19W 77 J7
Nelson Nev., U.S.A. 35°42N 114°49W 79 K12
Nelson → Canada 54°33N 98°2W 71 C9
Nelson, C. Australia 38°26S 141°32E 63 F3
Nelson, Estrecho Chile 51°30S 75°0W 96 G2
Nelson Forks Canada 59°30N 124°0W 70 B4
Nelson House Canada 55°47N 98°51W 71 B9
Nelson L. Canada 55°48N 100°7W 71 B8
Nelson Lakes △ N.Z. 41°55S 172°44E 59 D4
Nelspoort S. Africa 32°7S 23°0E 56 E3
Nelspruit S. Africa 25°29S 30°59E 57 D5
Néma Mauritania 16°40N 7°15W 50 E4
Neman = Nemunas → Lithuania 55°25N 21°10E 9 J19
Nemeiben L. Canada 55°20N 105°20W 71 B7
Nemiscau Canada 51°18N 76°54W 72 B4
Nemiscau, L. Canada 51°25N 76°40W 72 B4
Nemunas → Lithuania 55°25N 21°10E 9 J19
Nemuro Japan 43°20N 145°35E 30 C12
Nemuro-Kaikyō Japan 43°30N 145°30E 30 C12
Nen Jiang → China 45°28N 124°30E 35 B13
Nenagh Ireland 52°52N 8°11W 10 D3
Nenasi Malaysia 3°9N 103°23E 39 L4
Nene → U.K. 52°49N 0°11E 13 E8
Nenjiang China 49°10N 125°10E 33 B7
Neno Malawi 15°25S 34°40E 55 F3
Neodesha U.S.A. 37°25N 95°41W 80 G6
Neora Valley △ India 27°0N 88°45E 43 F13
Neosho U.S.A. 36°52N 94°22W 80 G6
Neosho → U.S.A. 36°48N 95°18W 84 C7
Nepal ■ Asia 28°0N 84°30E 43 F11
Nepalganj Nepal 28°5N 81°40E 43 E9
Nepalganj Road India 28°1N 81°41E 43 E9
Nephi U.S.A. 39°43N 111°50W 76 G8
Nephin Ireland 54°1N 9°22W 10 B2
Nephin Beg Range Ireland 54°0N 9°40W 10 C2
Neptune U.S.A. 40°13N 74°2W 83 F10
Nerang Australia 27°58S 153°20E 63 D5
Nerastro, Sarīr Libya 24°20N 20°37E 51 D10
Nerchinsk Russia 52°0N 116°39E 29 D12
Néret, L. Canada 54°45N 70°44W 73 B5
Neretva → Croatia 43°1N 17°27E 23 C7
Neringa Lithuania 55°20N 21°5E 9 J19
Neris → Lithuania 55°8N 24°16E 9 J21
Neryungri Russia 57°38N 124°28E 29 D13
Nescopeck U.S.A. 41°3N 76°12W 83 E8
Ness, L. U.K. 57°15N 4°32W 11 D4
Ness City U.S.A. 38°27N 99°54W 80 F4
Nesterov Ukraine 50°4N 23°58E 17 C12
Nesvizh = Nyasvizh Belarus 53°14N 26°38E 17 B14
Netanya Israel 32°20N 34°51E 46 C3
Netarhat India 23°29N 84°16E 43 H11
Nete → Belgium 51°7N 4°14E 15 C4
Netherdale Australia 21°10S 148°33E 62 K6
Netherlands ■ Europe 52°0N 5°30E 15 C5
Netherlands Antilles ☑ W. Indies 12°15N 69°0W 92 A5
Netrang India 21°39N 73°21E 42 J5
Nettilling L. Canada 66°30N 71°0W 69 C12
Netzahualcóyotl, Presa Mexico 17°8N 93°35W 87 D6
Neubrandenburg Germany 53°33N 13°15E 16 B7
Neuchâtel Switz. 47°0N 6°55E 20 C7
Neuchâtel, Lac de Switz. 46°53N 6°50E 20 C7
Neufchâteau Belgium 49°50N 5°25E 15 E5
Neumayer Antarctica 71°0S 68°30W 5 D17
Neumünster Germany 54°4N 9°58E 16 A5
Neunkirchen Germany 49°20N 7°9E 16 D4
Neuquén Argentina 38°55S 68°0W 96 D3
Neuquén □ Argentina 38°0S 69°50W 94 D2
Neuruppin Germany 52°55N 12°48E 16 B7
Neuse → U.S.A. 35°6N 76°29W 85 D16
Neusiedler See Austria 47°50N 16°47E 17 E9
Neustrelitz Germany 53°21N 13°4E 16 B7
Neva → Russia 59°56N 30°20E 18 C5
Nevada Iowa, U.S.A. 42°1N 93°27W 80 D7
Nevada Mo., U.S.A. 37°51N 94°22W 80 G6
Nevada □ U.S.A. 39°0N 117°0W 76 G5
Nevada City U.S.A. 39°16N 121°1W 78 F6
Nevado, Cerro Argentina 35°30S 68°32W 94 D2
Nevado de Colima = Volcán de Colima △ Mexico 19°30N 103°40W 86 D4
Nevado de Tres Cruces △ Chile 27°13S 69°5W 94 B2
Nevel Russia 56°0N 29°55E 18 C4
Nevers France 47°0N 3°9E 20 C5
Nevertire Australia 31°50S 147°44E 63 E4
Neville Canada 49°58N 107°39W 71 D7
Nevinnomyssk Russia 44°40N 42°0E 19 F7
Nevis St. Kitts & Nevis 17°0N 62°30W 89 C7
Nevşehir Turkey 38°33N 34°40E 44 B2
Nevyansk Russia 57°30N 60°13E 18 C11
New → U.S.A. 38°10N 81°12W 81 F13
New Aiyansh Canada 55°12N 129°4W 70 B3
New Albany Ind., U.S.A. 38°18N 85°49W 81 F11
New Albany Miss., U.S.A. 34°29N 89°0W 85 D10
New Albany Pa., U.S.A. 41°36N 76°27W 83 E8
New Amsterdam Guyana 6°15N 57°36W 92 B7
New Angledool Australia 29°5S 147°55E 63 D4
New Baltimore U.S.A. 42°41N 82°44W 82 D2
New Bedford U.S.A. 41°38N 70°56W 83 E14
New Berlin N.Y., U.S.A. 42°37N 75°20W 83 D9
New Berlin Pa., U.S.A. 40°50N 76°57W 82 F8
New Bern U.S.A. 35°7N 77°3W 85 D16
New Bethlehem U.S.A. 41°0N 79°20W 82 F5
New Bloomfield U.S.A. 40°25N 77°11W 82 F7
New Boston U.S.A. 33°28N 94°25W 84 E7
New Braunfels U.S.A. 29°42N 98°8W 84 G5
New Brighton N.Z. 43°29S 172°43E 59 E4
New Brighton U.S.A. 40°42N 80°19W 82 F4
New Britain Papua N. G. 5°50S 150°20E 58 B8
New Britain U.S.A. 41°40N 72°47W 83 E12
New Brunswick U.S.A. 40°30N 74°27W 83 F10
New Brunswick □ Canada 46°50N 66°30W 73 C6
New Caledonia ☑ Pac. Oc. 21°0S 165°0E 58 D9
New Caledonia Trough Pac. Oc. 30°0S 165°0E 64 L8
New Castile = Castilla-La Mancha □ Spain 39°30N 3°30W 21 C4
New Castle Ind., U.S.A. 39°55N 85°22W 81 F11
New Castle Pa., U.S.A. 41°0N 80°21W 82 F4
New City U.S.A. 41°9N 73°59W 83 E11
New Concord U.S.A. 39°59N 81°54W 82 G3
New Cumberland U.S.A. 40°30N 80°36W 82 F4
New Cuyama U.S.A. 34°57N 119°38W 79 L7
New Delhi India 28°36N 77°11E 42 E7
New Denver Canada 50°0N 117°25W 70 D5
New Don Pedro Res. U.S.A. 37°43N 120°24W 78 H6
New England U.S.A. 43°0N 71°0W 75 B12
New England N. Dak., U.S.A. 46°32N 102°52W 80 B2
New England Ra. Australia 30°20S 151°45E 63 E5
New Forest △ U.K. 50°53N 1°34W 13 G6
New Galloway U.K. 55°5N 4°9W 11 F4
New Glasgow Canada 45°35N 62°36W 73 C7
New Guinea Oceania 4°0S 136°0E 58 B6
New Hamburg Canada 43°23N 80°42W 82 C4
New Hampshire □ U.S.A. 44°0N 71°30W 83 C13
New Hampton U.S.A. 43°3N 92°19W 80 D7
New Hanover S. Africa 29°22S 30°31E 57 D5
New Hartford U.S.A. 43°4N 75°18W 83 C9
New Haven Conn., U.S.A. 41°18N 72°55W 83 E12
New Haven Mich., U.S.A. 42°44N 82°48W 82 D2
New Hazelton Canada 55°20N 127°30W 70 B3
New Hebrides = Vanuatu ■ Pac. Oc. 15°0S 168°0E 58 C9
New Holland U.S.A. 40°6N 76°5W 83 F8
New Iberia U.S.A. 30°1N 91°49W 84 F9
New Ireland Papua N. G. 3°20S 151°50E 58 B8
New Jersey □ U.S.A. 40°0N 74°30W 81 F16
New Kensington U.S.A. 40°34N 79°46W 82 F5
New Lexington U.S.A. 39°43N 82°13W 81 F12
New Liskeard Canada 47°31N 79°41W 72 C4
New London Conn., U.S.A. 41°22N 72°6W 83 E12
New London Ohio, U.S.A. 41°5N 82°24W 82 E2
New London Wis., U.S.A. 44°23N 88°45W 80 C9
New Madrid U.S.A. 36°36N 89°32W 80 G9
New Martinsville U.S.A. 39°39N 80°52W 81 F13
New Meadows U.S.A. 44°58N 116°18W 76 D5
New Melones L. U.S.A. 37°57N 120°31W 78 H6
New Mexico □ U.S.A. 34°30N 106°0W 77 J1
New Milford Conn., U.S.A. 41°35N 73°25W 83 E1

New Milford Pa., U.S.A. 41°52N 75°44W 83 E9
New Norcia Australia 30°57S 116°13E 61 F2
New Norfolk Australia 42°46S 147°2E 63 G4
New Orleans U.S.A. 29°57N 90°4W 85 G9
New Philadelphia U.S.A. 40°30N 81°27W 82 F3
New Plymouth N.Z. 39°4S 174°5E 59 C5
New Plymouth U.S.A. 43°58N 116°49W 76 E5
New Port Richey U.S.A. 28°16N 82°43W 85 G13
New Providence Bahamas 25°25N 78°35W 88 A4
New Quay U.K. 52°13N 4°21W 13 E3
New Radnor U.K. 52°15N 3°9W 13 E4
New Richmond Canada 48°15N 65°45W 73 C6
New Richmond U.S.A. 45°7N 92°32W 80 C7
New River Gorge ⌂ U.S.A. 37°53N 81°5W 81 G13
New Roads U.S.A. 30°42N 91°26W 84 F9
New Rochelle U.S.A. 40°55N 73°46W 83 F11
New Rockford U.S.A. 47°41N 99°8W 80 B4
New Romney U.K. 50°59N 0°57E 13 G8
New Ross Ireland 52°23N 6°57W 10 D5
New Salem U.S.A. 46°51N 101°26W 80 B3
New Scone = Scone U.K. 56°25N 3°24W 11 E5
New Siberian I. = Novaya Sibir, Ostrov Russia 75°10N 150°0E 29 B16
New Siberian Is. = Novosibirskiye Ostrova Russia 75°0N 142°0E 29 B15
New Smyrna Beach U.S.A. 29°1N 80°56W 85 G14
New South Wales □ Australia 33°0S 146°0E 63 E4
New Tecumseth Canada 44°9N 79°52W 82 B5
New Town U.S.A. 47°59N 102°30W 80 B2
New Tredegar U.K. 51°44N 3°16W 13 F4
New Ulm U.S.A. 44°19N 94°28W 80 C6
New Waterford Canada 46°13N 60°4W 73 C7
New-Wes-Valley Canada 49°8N 53°36W 73 C9
New Westminster Canada 49°13N 122°55W 78 A4
New York U.S.A. 40°43N 74°0W 83 F11
New York □ U.S.A. 43°0N 75°0W 83 D9
New York J.F. Kennedy Int. ✈ (JFK) U.S.A. 40°38N 73°47W 83 F11
New Zealand ■ Oceania 40°0S 176°0E 59 D6
Newaj → India 24°24N 76°49E 42 G7
Newala Tanzania 10°58S 39°18E 55 E4
Newark Del., U.S.A. 39°41N 75°46W 81 F16
Newark N.J., U.S.A. 40°44N 74°10W 83 F10
Newark N.Y., U.S.A. 43°3N 77°6W 82 C7
Newark Ohio, U.S.A. 40°3N 82°24W 82 F2
Newark Liberty Int. ✈ (EWR) U.S.A. 40°42N 74°10W 83 F10
Newark-on-Trent U.K. 53°5N 0°48W 12 D7
Newark Valley U.S.A. 42°14N 76°11W 83 D8
Newberg U.S.A. 45°18N 122°58W 76 D2
Newberry Mich., U.S.A. 46°21N 85°30W 81 B11
Newberry S.C., U.S.A. 34°17N 81°37W 85 D14
Newberry Springs U.S.A. 34°50N 116°41W 79 L10
Newboro L. Canada 44°38N 76°20W 83 B8
Newbridge = Droichead Nua Ireland 53°11N 6°48W 10 C5
Newburgh Canada 44°19N 76°52W 82 B8
Newburgh U.S.A. 41°30N 74°1W 83 E10
Newbury U.K. 51°24N 1°20W 13 F6
Newbury N.H., U.S.A. 43°19N 72°3W 83 B12
Newbury Vt., U.S.A. 44°5N 72°4W 83 B12
Newburyport U.S.A. 42°49N 70°53W 83 D14
Newcastle Australia 33°0S 151°46E 63 E5
Newcastle N.B., Canada 47°1N 65°38W 73 C6
Newcastle Ont., Canada 43°55N 78°35W 72 D4
Newcastle S. Africa 27°45S 29°58E 57 D4
Newcastle U.K. 54°13N 5°54W 10 B6
Newcastle Calif., U.S.A. 38°53N 121°8W 78 G5
Newcastle Wyo., U.S.A. 43°50N 104°11W 76 E11
Newcastle Emlyn U.K. 52°2N 4°28W 13 E3
Newcastle Ra. Australia 15°45S 130°15E 60 C5
Newcastle-under-Lyme U.K. 53°1N 2°14W 12 D5
Newcastle-upon-Tyne U.K. 54°58N 1°36W 12 C6
Newcastle Waters Australia 17°30S 133°28E 62 B1
Newcastle West Ireland 52°27N 9°3W 10 D2
Newcomb U.S.A. 43°58N 74°10W 83 C10
Newcomerstown U.S.A. 40°16N 81°36W 82 F3
Newdegate Australia 33°6S 119°0E 61 F2
Newell Australia 16°20S 145°16E 62 B4
Newell U.S.A. 44°43N 103°25W 80 C2
Newfane U.S.A. 43°17N 78°43W 82 C6
Newfield U.S.A. 42°18N 76°33W 83 D8
Newfound L. U.S.A. 43°40N 71°47W 83 C13
Newfoundland Canada 49°0N 55°0W 73 C8
Newfoundland U.S.A. 41°18N 75°19W 83 E9
Newfoundland & Labrador □ Canada 53°0N 58°0W 73 B8
Newhaven U.K. 50°47N 0°3E 13 G8
Newkirk U.S.A. 36°53N 97°3W 84 C6
Newlyn U.K. 50°6N 5°34W 13 G2
Newman Australia 23°18S 119°45E 60 D2
Newman U.S.A. 37°19N 121°1W 78 H5
Newmarket Canada 44°3N 79°28W 82 B5
Newmarket Ireland 52°13N 9°0W 10 D2
Newmarket U.K. 52°15N 0°25E 13 E8
Newmarket U.S.A. 43°5N 70°56W 83 C14
Newnan U.S.A. 33°23N 84°48W 85 E12
Newport Ireland 53°53N 9°33W 10 C2
Newport I. of W., U.K. 50°42N 1°17W 13 G6
Newport Newport, U.K. 51°35N 3°0W 13 F5
Newport Ark., U.S.A. 35°37N 91°16W 84 D9
Newport Ky., U.S.A. 39°5N 84°29W 81 F11
Newport N.H., U.S.A. 43°22N 72°10W 83 C12
Newport N.Y., U.S.A. 43°11N 75°1W 83 C9
Newport Oreg., U.S.A. 44°39N 124°3W 76 D1
Newport Pa., U.S.A. 40°29N 77°8W 82 F7
Newport R.I., U.S.A. 41°29N 71°19W 83 E13
Newport Tenn., U.S.A. 35°58N 83°11W 85 D13
Newport Vt., U.S.A. 44°56N 72°13W 83 B12
Newport Wash., U.S.A. 48°11N 117°3W 76 B5
Newport □ U.K. 51°33N 3°1W 13 F4
Newport Beach U.S.A. 33°37N 117°56W 79 M9
Newport News U.S.A. 36°58N 76°25W 81 G15
Newport Pagnell U.K. 52°5N 0°43W 13 E7
Newquay U.K. 50°25N 5°6W 13 G2
Newry U.K. 54°11N 6°21W 10 B5
Newton Ill., U.S.A. 38°59N 88°10W 80 F9
Newton Iowa, U.S.A. 41°42N 93°3W 80 E7
Newton Kans., U.S.A. 38°3N 97°21W 80 F5
Newton Mass., U.S.A. 42°21N 71°12W 83 D13
Newton Miss., U.S.A. 32°19N 89°10W 85 E10
Newton N.C., U.S.A. 35°40N 81°13W 85 D14
Newton N.J., U.S.A. 41°3N 74°45W 83 E10
Newton Tex., U.S.A. 30°51N 93°46W 84 F8
Newton Abbot U.K. 50°32N 3°37W 13 G4
Newton Aycliffe U.K. 54°37N 1°34W 12 C6
Newton Falls U.S.A. 41°11N 80°59W 82 E4
Newton Stewart U.K. 54°57N 4°30W 11 G4
Newtonmore U.K. 57°4N 4°8W 11 D4
Newtown U.K. 52°31N 3°19W 13 E4
Newtownabbey U.K. 54°40N 5°56W 10 B6
Newtownards U.K. 54°36N 5°42W 10 B6
Newtownbarry = Bunclody Ireland 52°39N 6°40W 10 D5
Newtownstewart U.K. 54°43N 7°23W 10 B4
Newville U.S.A. 40°10N 77°24W 82 F7
Neya Russia 58°21N 43°49E 18 C7
Neyrīz Iran 29°15N 54°19E 45 D7
Neyshābūr Iran 36°10N 58°50E 45 B8
Nezhin = Nizhyn Ukraine 51°5N 31°55E 19 D5
Nezperce U.S.A. 46°14N 116°14W 76 C5
Ngabang Indonesia 0°23N 109°55E 36 D3
Ngabordamlu, Tanjung Indonesia 6°56S 134°11E 37 F8
N'Gage Angola 7°46S 15°15E 52 F3
Ngami Depression Botswana 20°30S 22°46E 56 C3
Ngamo Zimbabwe 19°3S 27°32E 55 F2
Nganglong Kangri China 33°0N 81°0E 43 C9
Ngao Thailand 18°46N 99°59E 38 C2
Ngaoundéré Cameroon 7°15N 13°35E 52 C2
Ngapara N.Z. 44°57S 170°46E 59 F3
Ngara Tanzania 2°29S 30°40E 54 C3
Ngawi Indonesia 7°24S 111°26E 37 G14
Ngcobo S. Africa 31°37S 28°0E 57 E4
Nghia Lo Vietnam 21°33N 104°28E 38 B5
Ngoma Malawi 13°8S 33°45E 55 E3
Ngomahura Zimbabwe 20°26S 30°43E 55 G3
Ngomba Tanzania 8°20S 32°53E 55 D3
Ngomeni, Ras Kenya 2°59S 40°14E 54 C5
Ngong Kenya 1°22S 36°39E 54 C4
Ngoring Hu China 34°55N 97°5E 32 C4
Ngorongoro Tanzania 3°11S 35°32E 54 C4
Ngorongoro ⌂ Tanzania 2°40S 35°30E 54 C4
Ngozi Burundi 2°54S 29°50E 54 C2
Ngudu Tanzania 2°58S 33°25E 54 C3
Nguigmi Niger 14°20N 13°20E 51 F8
Nguiu Australia 11°46S 130°38E 60 B5
Ngukurr Australia 14°44S 134°44E 62 A1
Ngunga Tanzania 3°37S 33°37E 54 C3
Nguru Nigeria 12°56N 10°29E 51 F8
Nguru Mts. Tanzania 6°0S 37°30E 54 D4
Ngusi Malawi 14°0S 34°50E 55 E3
Nguyen Binh Vietnam 22°39N 105°56E 38 A5
Nha Trang Vietnam 12°16N 109°10E 39 F7
Nhacoongo Mozam. 24°18S 35°14E 57 C6
Nhamaabué Mozam. 17°25S 35°5E 55 F4
Nhamundá → Brazil 2°12S 56°41W 93 D7
Nhangulaze, L. Mozam. 24°0S 34°30E 57 C5
Nhill Australia 36°18S 141°40E 63 F3
Nho Quan Vietnam 20°18N 105°45E 38 B5
Nhulunbuy Australia 12°10S 137°20E 62 A2
Nia-nia Dem. Rep. of the Congo 1°30N 27°40E 54 B2
Niagara Falls Canada 43°7N 79°5W 82 C5
Niagara Falls U.S.A. 43°5N 79°4W 82 C6
Niagara-on-the-Lake Canada 43°15N 79°4W 82 C5
Niah Malaysia 3°58N 113°46E 36 D4
Niamey Niger 13°27N 2°6E 50 F6
Niangara Dem. Rep. of the Congo 3°42N 27°50E 54 B2
Niantic U.S.A. 41°20N 72°11W 83 E12
Nias Indonesia 1°0N 97°30E 36 D1
Niassa □ Mozam. 13°30S 36°0E 55 E4
Niassa ⌂ Mozam. 12°4S 36°57E 55 E4
Nibāk Si. Arabia 24°25N 50°50E 45 E7
Nicaragua ■ Cent. Amer. 11°40N 85°30W 88 D2
Nicaragua, L. de Nic. 12°0N 85°30W 88 D2
Nicastro Italy 38°59N 16°19E 22 E7
Nice France 43°42N 7°14E 20 E7
Niceville U.S.A. 30°31N 86°30W 85 F11
Nichicun, L. Canada 53°5N 71°0W 73 B5
Nichinan Japan 31°38N 131°23E 31 J5
Nicholás, Canal W. Indies 23°30N 80°5W 88 B3
Nicholasville U.S.A. 37°53N 84°34W 81 G11
Nichols U.S.A. 42°1N 76°22W 83 D8
Nicholson Australia 18°2S 128°54E 60 C4
Nicholson U.S.A. 41°37N 75°47W 83 E9
Nicholson → Australia 17°31S 139°36E 62 B2
Nicholson L. Canada 62°40N 102°40W 71 A8
Nicholson Ra. Australia 27°15S 116°45E 61 E2
Nicholville U.S.A. 44°41N 74°39W 83 B10
Nicobar Is. Ind. Oc. 8°0N 93°30E 3 D14
Nicola Canada 50°12N 120°40W 70 C4
Nicolls Town Bahamas 25°8N 78°0W 88 A4
Nicosia Cyprus 35°10N 33°25E 25 D12
Nicoya Costa Rica 10°9N 85°27W 88 D2
Nicoya, G. de Costa Rica 10°0N 85°0W 88 E3
Nicoya, Pen. de Costa Rica 9°45N 85°40W 88 E2
Nidd → U.K. 53°59N 1°23W 12 D6
Niedersachsen □ Germany 52°50N 9°0E 16 B5
Niekerkshoop S. Africa 29°19S 22°51E 56 D3
Niemba Dem. Rep. of the Congo 5°58S 28°24E 54 D2
Niemen = Nemunas → Lithuania 55°25N 21°10E 9 J19
Nienburg Germany 52°39N 9°13E 16 B5
Nieu Bethesda S. Africa 31°51S 24°34E 56 E3
Nieuw Amsterdam Suriname 5°53N 55°5W 93 B7
Nieuw Nickerie Suriname 6°0N 56°59W 93 B7
Nieuwoudtville S. Africa 31°23S 19°7E 56 E2
Nieuwpoort Belgium 51°8N 2°45E 15 C2
Nieves, Pico de las Canary Is. 27°57N 15°35W 24 G4
Niğde Turkey 37°58N 34°40E 44 B2
Nigel S. Africa 26°27S 28°25E 57 D4
Niger ■ W. Afr. 17°30N 10°0E 50 E7
Niger → W. Afr. 5°33N 6°33E 50 G7
Nigeria ■ W. Afr. 8°30N 8°0E 50 G7
Nighasin India 28°14N 80°52E 43 E9
Nightcaps N.Z. 45°57S 168°2E 59 F2
Nihon = Japan ■ Asia 36°0N 136°0E 31 G8
Nii-Jima Japan 34°20N 139°15E 31 G9
Niigata Japan 37°58N 139°0E 30 F9
Niigata □ Japan 37°15N 138°45E 31 F9
Niihama Japan 33°55N 133°16E 31 H6
Ni'ihau U.S.A. 21°54N 160°9W 74 b
Niimi Japan 34°59N 133°28E 31 G6
Niitsu Japan 37°48N 139°7E 30 F9
Nijil Jordan 30°32N 35°33E 46 E4
Nijkerk Neths. 52°13N 5°30E 15 B5
Nijmegen Neths. 51°50N 5°52E 15 C5
Nijverdal Neths. 52°22N 6°28E 15 B6
Nīk Pey Iran 36°50N 48°10E 45 B6
Nikel Russia 69°24N 30°13E 8 B24
Nikiniki Indonesia 9°49S 124°30E 37 F6
Nikkō Japan 36°45N 139°35E 31 F9
Nikkō △ Japan 36°56N 139°37E 31 F9
Nikolayev = Mykolayiv Ukraine 46°58N 32°0E 19 E5
Nikolayevsk Russia 50°0N 45°35E 19 E8
Nikolayevsk-na-Amur Russia 53°8N 140°44E 29 D15
Nikolskoye Russia 55°12N 166°0E 29 D17
Nikopol Ukraine 47°35N 34°25E 19 E5
Nikshahr Iran 26°15N 60°10E 45 E9
Nikšić Montenegro 42°50N 18°57E 23 C8
Nîl, Nahr en → Africa 30°10N 31°6E 51 B12
Nîl el Abyad → Sudan 15°38N 32°31E 51 E12
Nîl el Azraq → Sudan 15°38N 32°31E 51 E12
Nila Indonesia 6°44S 129°31E 37 F7
Niland U.S.A. 33°14N 115°31W 79 M11
Nile = Nîl, Nahr en → Africa 30°10N 31°6E 51 B12
Niles Mich., U.S.A. 41°50N 86°15W 80 E10
Niles Ohio, U.S.A. 41°11N 80°46W 82 E4
Nim Ka Thana India 27°44N 75°48E 42 F6
Nimach India 24°30N 74°56E 42 G6
Nimbahera India 24°37N 74°45E 42 G6
Nîmes France 43°50N 4°23E 20 E6
Nimfaíon, Ákra = Pines, Akra Greece 40°5N 24°20E 23 D11
Nimmitabel Australia 36°29S 149°15E 63 F4
Nīnawá Iraq 36°25N 43°10E 44 B4
Nīnawá □ Iraq 36°15N 43°0E 44 B4
Nindigully Australia 28°21S 148°50E 63 D4
Ninepin Group China 22°16N 114°21E 33 G11
Nineveh = Nīnawá Iraq 36°25N 43°10E 44 B4
Ning Xian China 35°30N 107°58E 34 G4
Ningaloo ⌂ Australia 22°23S 113°32E 60 D1
Ning'an China 44°22N 129°20E 35 B15
Ningbo China 29°51N 121°28E 33 D7
Ningcheng China 41°32N 119°53E 35 D10
Ningjin China 37°35N 114°57E 34 F8
Ningjing Shan China 30°0N 98°20E 32 C4
Ningling China 34°25N 115°22E 34 G8
Ningpo = Ningbo China 29°51N 121°28E 33 D7
Ningqiang China 32°47N 106°15E 34 H4
Ningshan China 33°21N 108°21E 34 H5
Ningsia Hui A.R. = Ningxia Huizu Zizhiqu □ China 38°0N 106°0E 34 F4
Ningwu China 39°0N 112°18E 34 E7
Ningxia Huizu Zizhiqu □ China 38°0N 106°0E 34 F4
Ningyang China 35°47N 116°45E 34 G9
Ninh Binh Vietnam 20°15N 105°55E 38 B5
Ninh Giang Vietnam 20°44N 106°24E 38 B6
Ninh Hoa Vietnam 12°30N 109°7E 38 F7
Ninh Ma Vietnam 12°48N 109°21E 38 F7
Ninove Belgium 50°51N 4°2E 15 D4
Nioaque Brazil 21°5S 55°50W 95 A4
Niobrara U.S.A. 42°45N 98°2W 80 D4
Niobrara → U.S.A. 42°46N 98°3W 80 D4
Nioro du Sahel Mali 15°15N 9°30W 50 E4
Niort France 46°19N 0°29W 20 C3
Nipawin Canada 53°20N 104°0W 71 C8
Nipigon Canada 49°0N 88°17W 72 C2
Nipigon, L. Canada 49°50N 88°30W 72 C2
Nipishish L. Canada 54°12N 60°45W 73 B7
Nipissing, L. Canada 46°20N 80°0W 72 C4
Nipomo U.S.A. 35°3N 120°29W 79 K6
Nippon = Japan ■ Asia 36°0N 136°0E 31 G8
Nipton U.S.A. 35°28N 115°16W 79 K11
Niquelândia Brazil 14°33S 48°23W 93 F9
Nīr Iran 38°2N 47°59E 44 B5
Nirasaki Japan 35°42N 138°27E 31 G9
Nirmal India 19°3N 78°20E 40 K11
Nirmali India 26°20N 86°35E 43 F12
Niš Serbia 43°19N 21°58E 23 C9
Nişāb Si. Arabia 29°11N 44°43E 44 D5
Nişāb Yemen 14°25N 46°29E 47 E4
Nishinomiya Japan 34°45N 135°20E 31 G7
Nishino'omote Japan 30°43N 130°59E 31 J5
Nishiwaki Japan 34°59N 134°58E 31 G7
Niskibi → Canada 56°29N 88°9W 72 A2
Nisqually → U.S.A. 47°7N 122°42W 78 C4
Nissaki Greece 39°43N 19°52E 25 A3
Nissum Bredning Denmark 56°40N 8°20E 9 H13
Nistru = Dnister → Europe 46°18N 30°17E 17 E16
Nisutlin → Canada 60°14N 132°34W 70 A2
Nitchequon Canada 53°10N 70°58W 73 B5
Niterói Brazil 22°53S 43°7W 95 A7
Nith → Canada 43°12N 80°23W 82 C4
Nith → U.K. 55°14N 3°33W 11 F5
Nitmiluk △ Australia 14°6S 132°15E 60 B5
Nitra Slovak Rep. 48°19N 18°4E 17 D10
Nitra → Slovak Rep. 47°46N 18°10E 17 E10
Niue Cook Is. 19°2S 169°54W 65 J11
Niut Indonesia 0°55N 110°6E 36 D4
Niuzhuang China 40°58N 122°28E 35 D12
Nivala Finland 63°56N 24°57E 8 E21
Nivelles Belgium 50°35N 4°20E 15 D4
Nivernais France 47°15N 3°30E 20 C5
Niverville Canada 49°36N 97°3W 71 D9
Niwas India 23°3N 80°26E 43 H9
Nixa U.S.A. 37°3N 93°18W 80 G7
Nixon U.S.A. 29°16N 97°46W 84 G6
Nizamabad India 18°45N 78°7E 40 K11
Nizamghat India 28°20N 95°45E 41 E19
Nizhne Kolymsk Russia 68°34N 160°55E 29 C17
Nizhneangarsk Russia 55°47N 109°30E 29 D11
Nizhnekamsk Russia 55°38N 51°49E 18 C9
Nizhneudinsk Russia 54°54N 99°3E 29 D10
Nizhnevartovsk Russia 60°56N 76°38E 28 C8
Nizhniy Novgorod Russia 56°20N 44°0E 18 C7
Nizhniy Tagil Russia 57°55N 59°57E 18 C10
Nizhyn Ukraine 51°5N 31°55E 19 D5
Nizip Turkey 37°5N 37°50E 44 B3
Nízké Tatry Slovak Rep. 48°55N 19°30E 17 D10
Nizwá Oman 22°56N 57°32E 47 C6
Njakwa Malawi 11°1S 33°56E 55 E3
Njanji Zambia 14°25S 31°46E 55 E3
Njazidja = Grande Comore Comoros Is. 11°35S 43°20E 53 a
Njinjo Tanzania 8°48S 38°54E 55 D4
Njombe Tanzania 9°20S 34°50E 55 D3
Njombe → Tanzania 6°56S 35°6E 54 D4
Nkana Zambia 12°50S 28°8E 55 E2
Nkandla S. Africa 28°37S 31°5E 57 D5
Nkawkaw Ghana 6°36N 0°49W 50 G5
Nkayi Zimbabwe 19°41S 29°20E 55 F2
Nkhotakota Malawi 12°56S 34°15E 55 E3
Nkhotakota ⌂ Malawi 12°50S 34°0E 55 E3
Nkongsamba Cameroon 4°55N 9°55E 52 D1
Nkurenkuru Namibia 17°42S 18°32E 56 B2
Nmai → Burma 25°30N 97°25E 41 G20
Noakhali = Maijdi Bangla. 22°48N 91°10E 41 H17
Nobel Canada 45°25N 80°6W 82 A4
Nobeoka Japan 32°36N 131°41E 31 H5
Noblesville U.S.A. 40°3N 86°1W 80 E10
Noboribetsu Japan 42°24N 141°6E 30 C10
Noccundra Australia 27°50S 142°36E 63 D3
Nocera Inferiore Italy 40°44N 14°38E 22 D6
Nocona U.S.A. 33°47N 97°44W 84 E6
Noda Japan 35°56N 139°52E 31 G9
Nogales Mexico 31°19N 110°56W 86 A2
Nogales U.S.A. 31°21N 110°56W 77 L8
Nōgata Japan 33°48N 130°44E 31 H5
Noggerup Australia 33°32S 116°5E 61 F2
Noginsk Russia 64°30N 90°50E 29 C10
Nogoa → Australia 23°40S 147°55E 62 C4
Nogoyá Argentina 32°24S 59°48W 94 C4
Nohar India 29°11N 74°49E 42 E6
Nohta India 23°40N 79°34E 43 H8
Noires, Mts. France 48°11N 3°40W 20 B2
Noirmoutier, Î. de France 46°58N 2°10W 20 C2
Nojane Botswana 23°15S 20°14E 56 C3
Nojima-Zaki Japan 34°54N 139°53E 31 G9
Nok Kundi Pakistan 28°50N 62°45E 40 E3
Nok Ta Phao, Ko Thailand 9°23N 99°40E 39 b
Nokaneng Botswana 19°40S 22°17E 56 B3
Nokia Finland 61°30N 23°30E 8 F20
Nokomis Canada 51°35N 105°0W 71 C8
Nokomis L. Canada 57°0N 103°0W 71 B8
Nola C.A.R. 3°35N 16°4E 52 D3
Noma Omuramba → Namibia 18°52S 20°53E 56 B3
Nombre de Dios Panama 9°34N 79°28W 88 E4
Nome U.S.A. 64°30N 165°25W 74 a
Nomo-Zaki Japan 32°35N 129°44E 31 H4
Nomuka Tonga 20°17S 174°48W 59 c
Nomuka Group Tonga 20°20S 174°48W 59 c
Nonacho L. Canada 61°42N 109°40W 71 A7
Nonda Australia 20°40S 142°28E 62 C3
Nong Chang Thailand 15°23N 99°51E 38 E2
Nong Het Laos 19°29N 103°59E 38 C4
Nong Khai Thailand 17°50N 102°46E 38 D4
Nong'an China 44°25N 125°5E 35 B13
Nongoma S. Africa 27°58S 31°35E 57 D5
Nongsa Indonesia 1°11N 104°8E 39 d
Nonoava Mexico 27°28N 106°44W 86 B3
Nonsan S. Korea 36°12N 127°5E 35 F14
Nonthaburi Thailand 13°50N 100°29E 38 F3
Noonamah Australia 12°40S 131°4E 60 B5
Noondie, L. Australia 28°30S 119°30E 61 E2
Noord Brabant □ Neths. 51°40N 5°0E 15 C5
Noord Holland □ Neths. 52°30N 4°45E 15 B4
Noordbeveland Neths. 51°35N 3°50E 15 C3
Noordoostpolder Neths. 52°45N 5°45E 15 B5
Noordwijk Neths. 52°14N 4°26E 15 B4
Noosa Heads Australia 26°25S 153°6E 63 D5
Nootka I. Canada 49°32N 126°42W 70 D3
Nopiming ⌂ Canada 50°30N 95°37W 71 C9
Noralee Canada 53°59N 126°26W 70 C3
Noranda = Rouyn-Noranda Canada 48°20N 79°0W 72 C4
Norco U.S.A. 33°56N 117°33W 79 M9
Nord-Kivu □ Dem. Rep. of the Congo 1°0S 29°0E 54 C2
Nord-Ostsee-Kanal Germany 54°12N 9°32E 16 A5
Nordaustlandet Svalbard 79°14N 23°0E 4 B9
Nordegg Canada 52°29N 116°5W 70 C5
Norderney Germany 53°42N 7°9E 16 B4
Norderstedt Germany 53°42N 10°1E 16 B5
Nordfjord Norway 61°55N 5°30E 8 F11
Nordfriesische Inseln Germany 54°40N 8°20E 16 A5
Nordhausen Germany 51°30N 10°47E 16 C6
Norðoyar Færoe Is. 62°17N 6°35W 8 E9
Nordkapp Norway 71°10N 25°50E 8 A21
Nordkapp Svalbard 80°31N 20°0E 4 A9
Nordkinnhalvøya Norway 70°55N 27°40E 8 A22
Nordrhein-Westfalen □ Germany 51°45N 7°30E 16 C4
Nordvik Russia 74°2N 111°32E 29 B12
Nore → Ireland 52°25N 6°58W 10 D4
Norfolk Canada 42°50N 80°23W 82 D4
Norfolk Nebr., U.S.A. 42°2N 97°25W 80 D5
Norfolk Va., U.S.A. 36°50N 76°17W 81 G15
Norfolk □ U.K. 52°39N 0°54E 13 E8
Norfolk Broads △ U.K. 52°45N 1°30E 13 E9
Norfolk I. Pac. Oc. 28°58S 168°3E 58 D9
Norfolk Ridge Pac. Oc. 29°0S 168°0E 64 K8
Norfork L. U.S.A. 36°15N 92°14W 84 C8
Norge = Norway ■ Europe 63°0N 11°0E 8 E14
Norilsk Russia 69°20N 88°6E 29 C9
Norma, Mt. Australia 20°55S 140°42E 62 C3
Normal U.S.A. 40°31N 88°59W 80 E9
Norman U.S.A. 35°13N 97°26W 84 D6
Norman → Australia 19°18S 141°51E 62 B3
Norman Wells Canada 65°17N 126°51W 68 C7
Normanby → Australia 14°23S 144°10E 62 A3
Normandie France 48°45N 0°10E 20 B4
Normandin Canada 48°49N 72°31W 72 C5
Normandy = Normandie France 48°45N 0°10E 20 B4
Normanhurst, Mt. Australia 25°4S 122°30E 61 E3
Normanton Australia 17°40S 141°10E 62 B3
Normétal Canada 49°0N 79°22W 72 C4
Norquay Canada 51°53N 102°5W 71 C8
Norquinco Argentina 41°51S 70°55W 96 E2
Norrbottens län □ Sweden 66°50N 20°0E 8 C19
Norris Point Canada 49°31N 57°53W 73 C8
Norristown U.S.A. 40°7N 75°21W 83 F9
Norrköping Sweden 58°37N 16°11E 9 G17
Norrland Sweden 62°15N 15°45E 8 E16
Norrtälje Sweden 59°46N 18°42E 9 G18
Norseman Australia 32°8S 121°43E 61 F3
Norsk Russia 52°30N 130°5E 29 D14
Norte, Pta. del Canary Is. 27°51N 17°57W 24 G2
Norte, Serra do Brazil 11°20S 59°0W 92 F7
North, C. Canada 47°2N 60°20W 73 C7
North Adams U.S.A. 42°42N 73°7W 83 D11
North America 40°0N 100°0W 66 F10
North Arm Canada 62°0N 114°30W 70 A5
North Augusta U.S.A. 33°30N 81°59W 85 E14
North Australian Basin Ind. Oc. 14°30S 116°30E 64 J3
North Ayrshire □ U.K. 55°45N 4°44W 11 F4
North Bass I. U.S.A. 41°40N 82°56W 82 E2
North Battleford Canada 52°50N 108°17W 71 C7
North Bay Canada 46°20N 79°30W 72 C4
North Belcher Is. Canada 56°50N 79°50W 72 A4
North Bend Oreg., U.S.A. 43°24N 124°14W 76 E1
North Bend Pa., U.S.A. 41°20N 77°42W 82 E7
North Bend Wash., U.S.A. 47°30N 121°47W 78 C5
North Bennington U.S.A. 42°56N 73°15W 83 D11
North Berwick U.K. 56°4N 2°42W 11 E6
North Berwick U.S.A. 43°18N 70°44W 83 C14
North C. Canada 47°5N 64°0W 73 C7
North C. N.Z. 34°23S 173°4E 59 A4
North Canadian → U.S.A. 35°22N 95°37W 84 D7
North Canton U.S.A. 40°53N 81°24W 82 F3
North Cape = Nordkapp Norway 71°10N 25°50E 8 A21
North Caribou L. Canada 52°50N 90°40W 72 B1
North Carolina □ U.S.A. 35°30N 80°0W 85 D15
North Cascades △ U.S.A. 48°45N 121°10W 76 B3
North Channel Canada 46°0N 83°0W 72 C3
North Channel U.K. 55°13N 5°52W 11 F3
North Charleston U.S.A. 32°53N 79°58W 85 E15
North Chicago U.S.A. 42°19N 87°51W 80 D10
North Creek U.S.A. 43°42N 73°59W 83 C11
North Dakota □ U.S.A. 47°30N 100°15W 80 B3
North Downs U.K. 51°19N 0°21E 13 F8
North East U.S.A. 42°13N 79°50W 82 D5
North East Frontier Agency = Arunachal Pradesh □ India 28°0N 95°0E 41 F19

148 North East Lincolnshire INDEX TO WORLD MAPS

North East Lincolnshire □ U.K. 53°34N 0°2W 12 D7
North Eastern □ Kenya 1°30N 40°0E 54 B5
North Esk → U.K. 56°46N 2°24W 11 E6
North European Plain Europe 55°0N 25°0E 6 E10
North Foreland U.K. 51°22N 1°28E 13 F9
North Fork U.S.A. 37°14N 119°21W 78 H7
North Fork American → U.S.A. 38°57N 120°59W 78 G5
North Fork Feather → U.S.A. 38°33N 121°30W 78 F5
North Fork Grand → U.S.A. 45°47N 102°16W 80 C2
North Fork Red → U.S.A. 34°24N 99°14W 84 D5
North Frisian Is. = Nordfriesische Inseln Germany 54°40N 8°20E 16 A5
North Gower Canada 45°8N 75°43W 83 A9
North Hd. Australia 30°14S 114°59E 61 F1
North Henik L. Canada 61°45N 97°40W 71 A9
North Highlands U.S.A. 38°40N 121°23W 78 G5
North Horr Kenya 3°20N 37°8E 54 B4
North I. Kenya 4°5N 36°5E 54 B4
North I. N.Z. 38°0S 175°0E 59 C5
North I. Seychelles 4°25S 55°13E 53 b
North Kingsville U.S.A. 41°54N 80°42W 82 E4
North Kitui ⌓ Kenya 0°15S 38°29E 54 C4
North Knife → Canada 58°53N 94°45W 71 B10
North Koel → India 24°45N 83°50E 43 G10
North Korea ■ Asia 40°0N 127°0E 35 E14
North Lakhimpur India 27°14N 94°7E 41 F19
North Lanarkshire □ U.K. 55°52N 3°56W 11 F5
North Las Vegas U.S.A. 36°11N 115°7W 79 J11
North Lincolnshire □ U.K. 53°36N 0°30W 12 D7
North Little Rock U.S.A. 34°45N 92°16W 84 D8
North Loup → U.S.A. 41°17N 98°24W 80 E4
North Luangwa △ Zambia 11°49S 32°9E 55 E3
North Magnetic Pole Canada 82°42N 114°24W 69 B9
North Mankato U.S.A. 44°10N 94°2W 80 C6
North Minch U.K. 58°5N 5°55W 11 C3
North Moose L. Canada 54°4N 100°12W 71 C8
North Myrtle Beach U.S.A. 33°48N 78°42W 85 E15
North Nahanni → Canada 62°15N 123°20W 70 A4
North Olmsted U.S.A. 41°25N 81°56W 82 E3
North Ossetia □ Russia 43°30N 44°30E 19 F7
North Pagai, I. = Pagai Utara, Pulau Indonesia 2°35S 100°0E 36 E2
North Palisade U.S.A. 37°6N 118°31W 78 H8
North Platte U.S.A. 41°8N 100°46W 80 E3
North Platte → U.S.A. 41°7N 100°42W 80 E3
North Pole Arctic 90°0N 0°0 4 A
North Portal Canada 49°0N 102°33W 71 D8
North Powder U.S.A. 45°2N 117°55W 76 D5
North Pt. Barbados 13°20N 59°37W 89 g
North Pt. Trin. & Tob. 11°21N 60°31W 93 J16
North Pt. U.S.A. 45°2N 83°16W 82 A1
North Rhine Westphalia = Nordrhein-Westfalen □ Germany 51°45N 7°30E 16 C4
North River Canada 53°49N 57°6W 73 B8
North Ronaldsay U.K. 59°22N 2°26W 11 B6
North Saskatchewan → Canada 53°15N 105°5W 71 C7
North Sea Europe 56°0N 4°0E 6 D6
North Seal → Canada 58°50N 98°7W 71 B9
North Somerset □ U.K. 51°24N 2°45W 13 F5
North Sporades = Vories Sporades Greece 39°15N 23°30E 23 E10
North Sydney Canada 46°12N 60°15W 73 C7
North Syracuse U.S.A. 43°8N 76°7W 83 C8
North Taranaki Bight N.Z. 38°50S 174°15E 59 C5
North Thompson → Canada 50°40N 120°20W 70 C4
North Tonawanda U.S.A. 43°2N 78°53W 82 C6
North Troy U.S.A. 45°0N 72°24W 83 B12
North Twin I. Canada 53°20N 80°0W 72 B4
North Tyne → U.K. 55°0N 2°8W 12 B5
North Uist U.K. 57°40N 7°15W 11 D1
North Vancouver Canada 49°19N 123°4W 78 A3
North Vernon U.S.A. 39°0N 85°38W 81 F11
North Wabasca L. Canada 56°0N 113°55W 70 B6
North Walsham U.K. 52°50N 1°22E 12 E9
North West = Severo-Zapadnyy □ Russia 65°0N 40°0E 28 C4
North-West □ S. Africa 27°0S 25°0E 56 D4
North West C. Australia 21°45S 114°9E 60 D1
North West Frontier □ Pakistan 34°0N 72°0E 42 C4
North West Highlands U.K. 57°33N 4°58W 11 D4
North West River Canada 53°30N 60°10W 73 B7
North Western □ Zambia 13°30S 25°30E 55 E2
North Wildwood U.S.A. 39°0N 74°48W 81 F16
North York Moors U.K. 54°23N 0°53W 12 C7
North York Moors △ U.K. 54°27N 0°51W 12 C7
North Yorkshire □ U.K. 54°15N 1°25W 12 C6
Northallerton U.K. 54°20N 1°26W 12 C6
Northam Australia 31°35S 116°42E 61 F2
Northam S. Africa 24°56S 27°18E 56 C4
Northampton Australia 28°27S 114°33E 61 E1
Northampton U.K. 52°15N 0°53W 13 E7
Northampton Mass., U.S.A. 42°19N 72°38W 83 D12
Northampton Pa., U.S.A. 40°41N 75°30W 83 F9
Northamptonshire □ U.K. 52°16N 0°55W 13 E7
Northbridge U.S.A. 42°9N 71°39W 83 D13
Northcliffe Australia 34°39S 116°7E 61 F2
Northeast Pacific Basin Pac. Oc. 32°0N 145°0W 65 D13
Northeast Providence Chan. W. Indies 26°0N 76°0W 88 A4
Northern = Limpopo □ S. Africa 24°5S 29°0E 57 C4
Northern □ Malawi 11°0S 34°0E 55 E3
Northern □ Zambia 10°30S 31°0E 55 E3
Northern Areas □ Pakistan 36°30N 73°0E 43 A5
Northern Cape □ S. Africa 30°0S 20°0E 56 D3
Northern Circars India 17°30N 82°30E 41 L13
Northern Indian L. Canada 57°20N 97°20W 71 B9
Northern Ireland □ U.K. 54°45N 7°0W 10 B5
Northern Lau Group Fiji 17°30S 178°59W 59 a
Northern Light L. Canada 48°15N 90°39W 72 C1
Northern Marianas ☒ Pac. Oc. 17°0N 145°0E 64 F6
Northern Province □ S. Africa 24°0S 29°0E 57 C4
Northern Range Trin. & Tob. 10°46N 61°15W 93 K15
Northern Territory □ Australia 20°0S 133°0E 60 D5
Northfield Minn., U.S.A. 44°27N 93°9W 80 C7
Northfield Vt., U.S.A. 44°9N 72°40W 83 B12
Northland □ N.Z. 35°30S 173°30E 59 A4
Northome U.S.A. 47°52N 94°17W 80 B6
Northport Ala., U.S.A. 33°14N 87°35W 85 E11
Northport Wash., U.S.A. 48°55N 117°48W 76 B5
Northumberland □ U.K. 55°12N 2°0W 12 B6
Northumberland, C. Australia 38°5S 140°40E 63 F3
Northumberland Is. Australia 21°30S 149°50E 62 C4
Northumberland Str. Canada 46°20N 64°0W 73 C7
Northville U.S.A. 43°13N 74°11W 83 C10
Northwest Pacific Basin Pac. Oc. 32°0N 165°0E 64 D8
Northwest Providence Channel W. Indies 26°0N 78°0W 88 A4
Northwest Territories □ Canada 63°0N 118°0W 68 C8
Northwich U.K. 53°15N 2°31W 12 D5
Northwood Iowa, U.S.A. 43°27N 93°13W 80 D7
Northwood N. Dak., U.S.A. 47°44N 97°34W 80 B5
Norton U.S.A. 39°50N 99°53W 80 F4
Norton Zimbabwe 17°52S 30°40E 55 F3
Norton Sd. U.S.A. 63°50N 164°0W 74 a
Norwalk Calif., U.S.A. 33°54N 118°4W 79 M8
Norwalk Conn., U.S.A. 41°7N 73°22W 83 E11
Norwalk Iowa, U.S.A. 41°29N 93°41W 80 E7
Norwalk Ohio, U.S.A. 41°15N 82°37W 82 E2
Norway Maine, U.S.A. 44°13N 70°32W 81 C18
Norway Mich., U.S.A. 45°47N 87°55W 80 C10
Norway ■ Europe 63°0N 11°0E 8 E14
Norway House Canada 53°59N 97°50W 71 C9
Norwegian B. Canada 77°30N 90°0W 69 B11
Norwegian Basin Atl. Oc. 68°0N 2°0W 4 C7
Norwegian Sea Atl. Oc. 66°0N 1°0E 6 B6
Norwich Canada 42°59N 80°36W 82 D4
Norwich U.K. 52°38N 1°18E 13 E9
Norwich Conn., U.S.A. 41°31N 72°5W 83 E12
Norwich N.Y., U.S.A. 42°32N 75°32W 83 D9
Norwood Canada 44°23N 77°59W 82 B7
Norwood U.S.A. 44°45N 75°0W 83 B10
Nosappu-Misaki Japan 45°26N 141°39E 30 C12
Noshiro Japan 40°12N 140°0E 30 D10
Nosratābād Iran 29°55N 60°0E 45 D8
Noss Hd. U.K. 58°28N 3°3W 11 C5
Nossob → S. Africa 26°55S 20°45E 56 D3
Nosy Barren Madag. 18°25S 43°40E 53 H8
Nosy Bé Madag. 13°25S 48°15E 53 G9
Nosy Boraha Madag. 16°50S 49°55E 57 B8
Nosy Lava Madag. 14°33S 47°36E 57 A8
Nosy Varika Madag. 20°35S 48°32E 57 C8
Noteć → Poland 52°44N 15°26E 16 B8
Notikewin → Canada 57°2N 117°38W 70 B5
Notodden Norway 59°35N 9°17E 9 G13
Notre Dame B. Canada 49°45N 55°30W 73 C8
Notre-Dame-de-Koartac = Quaqtaq Canada 60°55N 69°40W 69 C13
Notre-Dame-des-Bois Canada 45°24N 71°4W 83 A13
Notre-Dame-d'Ivugivic = Ivujivik Canada 62°24N 77°55W 69 C12
Notre-Dame-du-Nord Canada 47°36N 79°30W 72 C4
Nottawasaga B. Canada 44°35N 80°15W 82 B4
Nottaway → Canada 51°22N 78°55W 72 B4
Nottingham U.K. 52°58N 1°10W 12 E6
Nottingham, City of □ U.K. 52°58N 1°10W 12 E6
Nottingham I. Canada 63°20N 77°55W 69 C12
Nottinghamshire □ U.K. 53°10N 1°3W 12 D6
Nottoway → U.S.A. 36°33N 76°55W 81 G15
Notwane → Botswana 23°35S 26°58E 56 C4
Nouâdhibou Mauritania 20°54N 17°0W 50 D2
Nouâdhibou, Ras Mauritania 20°50N 17°0W 50 D2
Nouakchott Mauritania 18°9N 15°58W 50 E2
Nouméa N. Cal. 22°17S 166°30E 58 D9
Noupoort S. Africa 31°10S 24°57E 56 E3
Nouveau Comptoir = Wemindji Canada 53°0N 78°49W 72 B4
Nouvelle Amsterdam, Î. Ind. Oc. 38°30S 77°30E 3 F13
Nouvelle-Calédonie = New Caledonia ☒ Pac. Oc. 21°0S 165°0E 58 D9
Nova Casa Nova Brazil 9°25S 41°5W 93 E10
Nova Esperança Brazil 23°8S 52°24W 95 A5
Nova Friburgo Brazil 22°16S 42°30W 95 A7
Nova Iguaçu Brazil 22°45S 43°28W 95 A7
Nova Iorque Brazil 7°0S 44°5W 93 E10
Nova Lamego Guinea-Biss. 12°19N 14°11W 50 F3
Nova Lima Brazil 19°59S 43°51W 95 A7
Nova Lusitânia Mozam. 19°50S 34°34E 55 F3
Nova Mambone Mozam. 21°0S 35°3E 57 C6
Nova Scotia □ Canada 45°10N 63°0W 73 C7
Nova Sofala Mozam. 20°7S 34°42E 57 C5
Nova Venécia Brazil 18°45S 40°24W 93 G10
Nova Zagora Bulgaria 42°32N 26°1E 23 C11
Novar Canada 45°27N 79°15W 82 A5
Novara Italy 45°28N 8°38E 20 D8
Novato U.S.A. 38°6N 122°35W 78 G4
Novaya Ladoga Russia 60°7N 32°16E 18 B5
Novaya Lyalya Russia 59°4N 60°45E 18 C11
Novaya Sibir, Ostrov Russia 75°10N 150°0E 29 B16
Novaya Zemlya Russia 75°0N 56°0E 28 B6
Nové Zámky Slovak Rep. 48°2N 18°8E 17 D10
Novgorod Russia 58°30N 31°25E 18 C5
Novgorod-Severskiy = Novhorod-Siverskyy Ukraine 52°2N 33°10E 18 D5
Novhorod-Siverskyy Ukraine 52°2N 33°10E 18 D5
Novi Lígure Italy 44°46N 8°47E 20 D8
Novi Pazar Serbia 43°12N 20°28E 23 C9
Novi Sad Serbia 45°18N 19°52E 23 B8
Novo Hamburgo Brazil 29°37S 51°7W 95 B5
Novo Mesto Slovenia 45°47N 15°12E 22 B6
Novo Remanso Brazil 9°41S 42°4W 93 E10
Novoaltaysk Russia 53°30N 84°0E 28 D9
Novocherkassk Russia 47°27N 40°15E 19 E7
Novogrudok = Navahrudak Belarus 53°40N 25°50E 17 B13
Novohrad-Volynskyy Ukraine 50°34N 27°35E 17 C14
Novokachalinsk Russia 45°5N 132°0E 30 B5
Novokuybyshevsk Russia 53°7N 49°58E 18 D8
Novokuznetsk Russia 53°45N 87°10E 28 D9
Novolazarevskaya Antarctica 71°0S 12°0E 5 D3
Novomoskovsk Russia 54°5N 38°15E 18 D6
Novorossiysk Russia 44°43N 37°46E 19 F6
Novorybnoye Russia 72°50N 105°50E 29 B11
Novoselytsya Ukraine 48°14N 26°15E 17 D14
Novoshakhtinsk Russia 47°46N 39°58E 19 E6
Novosibirsk Russia 55°0N 83°5E 28 D9
Novosibirskiye Ostrova Russia 75°0N 142°0E 29 B15
Novotroitsk Russia 51°10N 58°15E 18 D10
Novouzensk Russia 50°32N 48°17E 19 D8
Novovolynsk Ukraine 50°45N 24°4E 17 C13
Novska Croatia 45°19N 17°0E 22 B7
Novvy Urengoy Russia 65°48N 76°52E 28 C8
Novyy Bor Russia 66°43N 52°19E 18 A9
Novyy Port Russia 67°40N 72°30E 28 C8
Now Shahr Iran 36°40N 51°30E 45 B6
Nowa Sól Poland 51°48N 15°44E 16 C8
Nowata U.S.A. 36°42N 95°38W 84 C7
Nowbarān Iran 35°8N 49°42E 45 C6
Nowghāb Iran 33°53N 59°4E 45 C8
Nowgong Assam, India 26°20N 92°50E 41 F18
Nowgong Mad. P., India 25°4N 79°27E 43 G8
Nowra Australia 34°53S 150°35E 63 E5
Nowshera Pakistan 34°0N 72°0E 40 C8
Nowy Sącz Poland 49°40N 20°41E 17 D11
Nowy Targ Poland 49°29N 20°2E 17 D11
Nowy Tomyśl Poland 52°19N 16°10E 16 B9
Noxen U.S.A. 41°25N 76°4W 83 E8
Noyabr'sk Russia 64°34N 76°21E 28 C8
Noyon France 49°34N 2°59E 20 B5
Noyon Mongolia 43°2N 102°4E 34 C2
Nqutu S. Africa 28°13S 30°32E 57 D5
Nsanje Malawi 16°55S 35°12E 55 F4
Nsawam Ghana 5°50N 0°24W 50 G5
Nsomba Zambia 10°45S 29°51E 55 E2
Nu Jiang → China 29°58N 97°25E 32 D4
Nu Shan China 26°0N 99°20E 32 D4
Nuba Mts. = Nubah, Jibalan Sudan 12°0N 31°0E 51 F12
Nubah, Jibalan Sudan 12°0N 31°0E 51 F12
Nubia Africa 21°0N 32°0E 48 D7
Nubian Desert = Nûbîya, Es Sahrâ en Sudan 21°30N 33°30E 51 D12
Nûbîya, Es Sahrâ en Sudan 21°30N 33°30E 51 D12
Nuboai Indonesia 2°10S 136°30E 37 E9
Nubra → India 34°35N 77°35E 43 B7
Nueces → U.S.A. 27°51N 97°30W 84 H6
Nueltin L. Canada 60°30N 99°30W 71 A9
Nueva Ciudad Guerrero Mexico 26°34N 99°12W 87 B5
Nueva Gerona Cuba 21°53N 82°49W 88 B3
Nueva Palmira Uruguay 33°52S 58°20W 94 C4
Nueva Rosita Mexico 27°57N 101°13W 86 B4
Nueva San Salvador El Salv. 13°40N 89°18W 88 D2
Nuéve de Julio Argentina 35°30S 61°0W 94 D3
Nuevitas Cuba 21°30N 77°20W 88 B4
Nuevo, G. Argentina 43°0S 64°30W 96 E4
Nuevo Casas Grandes Mexico 30°25N 107°55W 86 A3
Nuevo Laredo Mexico 27°30N 99°31W 87 B5
Nuevo León □ Mexico 25°20N 100°0W 86 C5
Nuevo Rocafuerte Ecuador 0°55S 75°27W 92 D3
Nugget Pt. N.Z. 46°27S 169°50E 59 G2
Nuhaka N.Z. 39°3S 177°45E 59 C6
Nukey Bluff Australia 32°26S 135°29E 63 E2
Nukhayb Iraq 32°4N 42°3E 44 C4
Nuku Hiva French Polynesia 8°54S 140°6W 65 H13
Nuku'alofa Tonga 21°10S 175°12W 59 c
Nukus Uzbekistan 42°27N 59°41E 28 E6
Nullagine Australia 21°53S 120°7E 60 D3
Nullagine → Australia 21°20S 120°20E 60 D3
Nullarbor Australia 31°28S 130°55E 61 F5
Nullarbor △ Australia 32°39S 130°0E 61 F2
Nullarbor Plain Australia 31°10S 129°0E 61 F4
Numalla, L. Australia 28°43S 144°20E 63 D3
Numan Nigeria 9°29N 12°3E 51 G8
Numata Japan 36°45N 139°4E 31 F9
Numaykoos Lake ⌓ Canada 57°52N 95°58W 71 B9
Numazu Japan 35°7N 138°51E 31 G9
Numbulwar Australia 14°15S 135°45E 62 A2
Numfoor Indonesia 1°0S 134°50E 37 E8
Numurkah Australia 36°5S 145°26E 63 F4
Nunaksaluk I. Canada 55°49N 60°20W 73 A7
Nunap Isua Greenland 59°48N 43°55W 66 D15
Nunavut □ Canada 66°0N 85°0W 69 C11
Nunda U.S.A. 42°35N 77°56W 82 D7
Nuneaton U.K. 52°32N 1°27W 13 E6
Nungarin Australia 31°12S 118°6E 61 F2
Nungo Mozam. 13°23S 37°43E 55 E4
Nungwe Tanzania 2°48S 32°2E 54 C3
Nunivak I. U.S.A. 60°10N 166°30W 74 a
Nunkun India 33°57N 76°2E 43 C7
Núoro Italy 40°20N 9°20E 22 D3
Nūrābād Iran 27°47N 57°12E 45 E8
Nuremberg = Nürnberg Germany 49°27N 11°3E 16 D6
Nuri Mexico 28°5N 109°22W 86 B3
Nuriootpa Australia 34°27S 139°0E 63 E2
Nuristān □ Afghan. 35°20N 71°0E 40 B7
Nurmes Finland 63°33N 29°10E 8 E23
Nürnberg Germany 49°27N 11°3E 16 D6
Nurpur Pakistan 31°53N 71°54E 42 D4
Nurran, L. = Terewah, L. Australia 29°52S 147°35E 63 D4
Nurrari Lakes Australia 29°1S 130°5E 61 E5
Nusa Barung Indonesia 8°30S 113°30E 37 H15
Nusa Dua Indonesia 8°48S 115°14E 37 K18
Nusa Kambangan Indonesia 7°40S 108°10E 37 G13
Nusa Tenggara Barat □ Indonesia 8°50S 117°30E 36 F5
Nusa Tenggara Timur □ Indonesia 9°30S 122°0E 37 F6
Nusaybin Turkey 37°3N 41°10E 19 G7
Nushki Pakistan 29°35N 66°0E 42 E2
Nuuk Greenland 64°10N 51°35W 67 C14
Nuupere, Pte. Moorea 17°36S 149°47W 59 d
Nuwakot Nepal 28°10N 83°55E 43 E10
Nuwaybʻī, W. an → Si. Arabia 29°18N 34°57E 46 F3
Nuweiba' Egypt 28°59N 34°39E 44 D2
Nuwerus S. Africa 31°8S 18°24E 56 E2
Nuweveldberge S. Africa 32°10S 21°45E 56 E3
Nuyts, Pt. Australia 35°4S 116°38E 61 G2
Nuyts Arch. Australia 32°35S 133°20E 63 E1
Nxai Pan △ Botswana 19°50S 24°46E 56 B3
Nxau-Nxau Botswana 18°57S 21°4E 56 B3
Nyabing Australia 33°33S 118°9E 61 F2
Nyack U.S.A. 41°5N 73°55W 83 E11
Nyagan Russia 62°30N 65°38E 28 C7
Nyahanga Tanzania 2°20S 33°37E 54 C3
Nyahua Tanzania 5°25S 33°23E 54 D3
Nyahururu Kenya 0°2N 36°27E 54 B4
Nyainqentanglha Shan China 30°0N 90°0E 32 D3
Nyakanazi Tanzania 3°2S 31°10E 54 C3
Nyâlâ Sudan 12°2N 24°58E 51 F10
Nyamandhlovu Zimbabwe 19°55S 28°16E 55 F2
Nyambiti Tanzania 2°48S 33°27E 54 C3
Nyamira Kenya 0°36S 34°52E 54 B4
Nyamwaga Tanzania 1°27S 34°33E 54 C3
Nyandekwa Tanzania 3°57S 32°32E 54 C3
Nyandoma Russia 61°40N 40°12E 18 B7
Nyanga △ Zimbabwe 18°17S 32°46E 55 F3
Nyangana Namibia 18°0S 20°40E 56 B3
Nyanguge Tanzania 2°30S 33°12E 54 C3
Nyanza Rwanda 2°20S 29°42E 54 C2
Nyanza □ Kenya 0°10S 34°15E 54 C3
Nyanza-Lac Burundi 4°21S 29°36E 54 C2
Nyasa, L. = Malawi, L. Africa 12°30S 34°30E 55 E3
Nyasvizh Belarus 53°14N 26°38E 17 B14
Nyazepetrovsk Russia 56°3N 59°36E 18 C10
Nyazura Zimbabwe 18°40S 32°16E 55 F3
Nyazwidzi → Zimbabwe 20°0S 31°17E 55 G3
Nybro Sweden 56°44N 15°55E 9 H16
Nyda Russia 66°40N 72°58E 28 C8
Nyeri Kenya 0°23S 36°56E 54 C4
Nyika △ Malawi 10°30S 33°53E 55 E3
Nyíregyháza Hungary 47°58N 21°47E 17 E11
Nyiru, Mt. Kenya 2°8N 36°50E 54 B4
Nykarleby = Uusikaarlepyy Finland 63°32N 22°31E 8 E20
Nykøbing Nordjylland, Denmark 56°48N 8°51E 9 H13
Nykøbing Sjælland, Denmark 54°56N 11°52E 9 J14
Nykøbing Sjælland, Denmark 55°55N 11°40E 9 J14
Nyköping Sweden 58°45N 17°1E 9 G17
Nylstroom = Modimolle S. Africa 24°42S 28°22E 57 C4
Nymagee Australia 32°7S 146°20E 63 E4
Nymboida △ Australia 29°38S 152°26E 63 D5
Nynäshamn Sweden 58°54N 17°57E 9 G17
Nyngan Australia 31°30S 147°8E 63 E4
Nyoma Rap India 33°10N 78°40E 43 C8
Nyoman = Nemunas → Lithuania 55°25N 21°10E 9 J19
Nysa Poland 50°30N 17°22E 17 C9
Nysa → Europe 52°4N 14°46E 16 B8
Nyslott = Savonlinna Finland 61°52N 28°53E 8 F23
Nyssa U.S.A. 43°53N 117°0W 76 E5
Nystad = Uusikaupunki Finland 60°47N 21°25E 8 F19
Nyunzu Dem. Rep. of the Congo 5°57S 27°58E 54 D2
Nyurba Russia 63°17N 118°28E 29 C12
Nzega Tanzania 4°10S 33°12E 54 C3
Nzérékoré Guinea 7°49N 8°48W 50 G4
Nzeto Angola 7°10S 12°52E 52 F2
Nzilo, Chutes de Dem. Rep. of the Congo 10°18S 25°27E 55 E2
Nzubuka Tanzania 4°45S 32°50E 54 C3
Nzwani = Anjouan Comoros Is. 12°15S 44°20E 53 a

O

O Le Pupū Pu'e △ Samoa 13°59S 171°43W 59 b
Ō-Shima Hokkaidō, Japan 41°30N 139°22E 30 D9
Ō-Shima Shizuoka, Japan 34°44N 139°24E 31 G9
Oa, Mull of U.K. 55°35N 6°20W 11 F2
Oacoma U.S.A. 43°48N 99°24W 80 D4
Oahe, L. U.S.A. 44°27N 100°24W 80 C3
Oahe Dam U.S.A. 44°27N 100°24W 80 C3
O'ahu U.S.A. 21°28N 157°58W 74 b
Oak Harbor U.S.A. 48°18N 122°39W 78 B4
Oak Hill U.S.A. 37°59N 81°9W 81 G13
Oak Island U.S.A. 33°55N 78°10W 85 E15
Oak Ridge U.S.A. 36°1N 84°16W 85 C12
Oak View U.S.A. 34°24N 119°18W 79 L7
Oakan-Dake Japan 43°27N 144°10E 30 C12
Oakdale Calif., U.S.A. 37°46N 120°51W 78 H6
Oakdale La., U.S.A. 30°49N 92°40W 84 F8
Oakes U.S.A. 46°8N 98°6W 80 B4
Oakesdale U.S.A. 47°8N 117°15W 76 C5
Oakey Australia 27°25S 151°43E 63 D5
Oakfield U.S.A. 43°4N 78°16W 82 C6
Oakham U.K. 52°40N 0°43W 13 E7
Oakhurst U.S.A. 37°19N 119°40W 78 H7
Oakland U.S.A. 37°48N 122°18W 78 H4
Oakley Idaho, U.S.A. 42°15N 113°53W 76 E7
Oakley Kans., U.S.A. 39°8N 100°51W 80 F3
Oakover → Australia 21°0S 120°40E 60 D3
Oakridge U.S.A. 43°45N 122°28W 76 E2
Oakville Canada 43°27N 79°41W 82 C5
Oakville U.S.A. 46°51N 123°14W 78 D3
Oamaru N.Z. 45°5S 170°59E 59 F3
Oasis Calif., U.S.A. 37°29N 117°55W 78 H9
Oasis Calif., U.S.A. 33°28N 116°6W 79 M10
Oates Land Antarctica 69°0S 160°0E 5 C11
Oatlands Australia 42°17S 147°21E 63 G4
Oatman U.S.A. 35°1N 114°19W 79 K12
Oaxaca Mexico 17°3N 96°43W 87 D5
Oaxaca □ Mexico 17°0N 96°30W 87 D5
Ob → Russia 66°45N 69°30E 28 C7
Oba Canada 49°4N 84°7W 72 C3
Obama Japan 35°30N 135°45E 31 G7
Oban U.K. 56°25N 5°29W 11 E3
Obbia Somali Rep. 5°25N 48°30E 47 F4
Obera Argentina 27°21S 55°2W 95 B4
Oberhausen Germany 51°28N 6°51E 16 C4
Oberlin Kans., U.S.A. 39°49N 100°32W 80 F3
Oberlin La., U.S.A. 30°37N 92°46W 84 F8
Oberlin Ohio, U.S.A. 41°18N 82°13W 82 E2
Oberon Australia 33°45S 149°52E 63 E4
Obi, Kepulauan Indonesia 1°23S 127°45E 37 E7
Óbidos Brazil 1°50S 55°30W 93 D7
Obihiro Japan 42°56N 143°12E 30 C11
Obilatu Indonesia 1°25S 127°20E 37 E7
Obluchye Russia 49°1N 131°4E 29 E14
Obo C.A.R. 5°20N 26°32E 54 A2
Oboa, Mt. Uganda 1°45N 34°45E 54 B3
Oboyan Russia 51°15N 36°21E 28 D4
Obozerskaya = Obozerskiy Russia 63°34N 40°21E 18 B7
Obozerskiy Russia 63°34N 40°21E 18 B7
Observatory Inlet Canada 55°10N 129°54W 70 B3
Obshchi Syrt Russia 52°0N 53°0E 6 E16
Obskaya Guba Russia 69°0N 73°0E 28 C8
Obuasi Ghana 6°17N 1°40W 50 G5
Ocala U.S.A. 29°11N 82°8W 85 G13
Ocampo Chihuahua, Mexico 28°11N 108°23W 86 B3
Ocampo Tamaulipas, Mexico 22°50N 99°20W 87 C5
Ocaña Spain 39°55N 3°30W 21 C4
Occidental, Cordillera Colombia 5°0N 76°0W 92 C3
Occidental, Grand Erg Algeria 30°20N 1°0E 50 B6
Ocean City Md., U.S.A. 38°20N 75°5W 81 F16
Ocean City N.J., U.S.A. 39°17N 74°35W 81 F16
Ocean City Wash., U.S.A. 47°4N 124°10W 78 C2
Ocean Falls Canada 52°18N 127°48W 70 C3
Ocean I. = Banaba Kiribati 0°45S 169°50E 64 H8
Ocean Park U.S.A. 46°30N 124°3W 78 D2
Oceano U.S.A. 35°6N 120°37W 79 K
Oceanport U.S.A. 40°19N 74°3W 83 F1
Oceanside U.S.A. 33°12N 117°23W 79 M

Ochil Hills U.K. 56°14N 3°40W 11 E5
Ocho Rios Jamaica 18°24N 77°6W 88 a
Ocilla U.S.A. 31°36N 83°15W 85 F13
Ocmulgee → U.S.A. 31°58N 82°33W 85 F13
Ocniţa Moldova 48°25N 27°30E 17 D14
Oconee → U.S.A. 31°58N 82°33W 85 F13
Oconomowoc U.S.A. 43°7N 88°30W 80 D9
Oconto U.S.A. 44°53N 87°52W 80 C10
Oconto Falls U.S.A. 44°52N 88°9W 80 C9
Ocosingo Mexico 16°53N 92°6W 87 D6
Ocotal Nic. 13°41N 86°31W 88 D2
Ocotlán Jalisco, Mexico 20°21N 102°46W 86 C4
Ocotlán Oaxaca, Mexico 16°48N 96°40W 87 D5
Ōda Japan 35°11N 132°30E 31 G6
Ódáðahraun Iceland 65°5N 17°0W 8 D5
Ŏdaejin N. Korea 41°34N 129°40E 35 D15
Odate Japan 40°16N 140°34E 30 D10
Odawara Japan 35°20N 139°6E 31 G9
Odda Norway 60°3N 6°35E 9 F12
Odei → Canada 56°6N 96°54W 71 B9
Ödemiş Turkey 38°15N 28°0E 23 E13
Odendaalsrus S. Africa 27°48S 26°45E 56 D4
Odense Denmark 55°22N 10°23E 9 J14
Oder → Europe 53°33N 14°38E 16 B8
Odesa Ukraine 46°30N 30°45E 19 E5
Odessa = Odesa Ukraine 46°30N 30°45E 19 E5
Odessa Canada 44°17N 76°43W 83 B8
Odessa Tex., U.S.A. 31°52N 102°23W 84 F3
Odessa Wash., U.S.A. 47°20N 118°41W 76 C4
Odiakwe Botswana 20°12S 25°17E 56 C4
Odienné Ivory C. 9°30N 7°34W 50 G4
Odintsovo Russia 55°40N 37°16E 18 C6
O'Donnell U.S.A. 32°58N 101°50W 84 E4
Odorheiu Secuiesc Romania 46°21N 25°21E 17 E13
Odra = Oder → Europe 53°33N 14°38E 16 B8
Odzi Zimbabwe 19°0S 32°20E 57 B5
Odzi → Zimbabwe 19°45S 32°23E 57 B5
Oeiras Brazil 7°0S 42°8W 93 E10
Oelrichs U.S.A. 43°11N 103°14W 80 D2
Oelwein U.S.A. 42°41N 91°55W 80 D8
Oeno I. Pac. Oc. 24°0S 131°0W 65 K14
Oenpelli = Gunbalanya Australia 12°20S 133°4E 60 B5
Ofanto → Italy 41°22N 16°13E 22 D7
Offa Nigeria 8°13N 4°42E 50 G6
Offaly □ Ireland 53°15N 7°30W 10 C4
Offenbach Germany 50°6N 8°44E 16 C5
Offenburg Germany 48°28N 7°56E 16 D4
Officer Cr. → Australia 27°46S 132°30E 61 E5
Ofolanga Tonga 19°38S 174°27W 59 c
Ofotfjorden Norway 68°27N 17°0E 8 B17
Ofu Amer. Samoa 14°11S 169°41W 59 b
Ōfunato Japan 39°4N 141°43E 30 E10
Oga Japan 39°55N 139°50E 30 E9
Oga-Hantō Japan 39°58N 139°47E 30 E9
Ogaden Ethiopia 7°30N 45°30E 47 F3
Ōgaki Japan 35°21N 136°37E 31 G8
Ogallala U.S.A. 41°8N 101°43W 80 E3
Ogasawara Gunto Pac. Oc. 27°0N 142°0E 64 E6
Ogbomosho Nigeria 8°1N 4°11E 50 G6
Ogden U.S.A. 41°13N 111°58W 78 F8
Ogdensburg U.S.A. 44°42N 75°30W 83 B9
Ogea Driki Fiji 19°12S 178°27W 59 a
Ogea Levu Fiji 19°8S 178°24W 59 a
Ogeechee → U.S.A. 31°50N 81°3W 85 F14
Ogilby U.S.A. 32°49N 114°50W 79 N12
Oglio → Italy 45°2N 10°39E 22 B4
Ogmore Australia 22°37S 149°35E 62 C4
Ogoki Canada 51°38N 85°58W 72 B2
Ogoki → Canada 51°38N 85°57W 72 B2
Ogoki L. Canada 50°50N 87°10W 72 B2
Ogoki Res. Canada 50°45N 88°15W 72 B2
Ogooué → Gabon 1°0S 9°0E 52 E1
Ogowe = Ogooué → Gabon 1°0S 9°0E 52 E1
Ogre Latvia 56°49N 24°36E 9 H21
Ogurchinskiy, Ostrov Turkmenistan 38°55N 53°2E 45 B7
Ohai N.Z. 45°55S 168°0E 59 F2
Ohakune N.Z. 39°24S 175°24E 59 C5
Ohata Japan 41°24N 141°10E 30 D10
Ohau, L. N.Z. 44°15S 169°53E 59 F2
Ohio □ U.S.A. 40°15N 82°45W 82 F2
Ohio → U.S.A. 36°59N 89°8W 80 G9
Ohře → Czech Rep. 50°30N 14°10E 16 C8
Ohrid Macedonia 41°8N 20°52E 23 D9
Ohridsko Jezero Macedonia 41°8N 20°52E 23 D9
Ohrigstad S. Africa 24°39S 30°36E 57 C5
Oiapoque Brazil 3°50N 51°50W 93
Oikou China 38°35N 117°42E 35 E9
Oil City U.S.A. 41°26N 79°42W 82 E5
Oil Springs Canada 42°47N 82°7W 82 D2
Oildale U.S.A. 35°25N 119°1W 79 K7
Oise → France 49°0N 2°4E 20 B5
Oistins Barbados 13°4N 59°33W 89 g
Oistins B. Barbados 13°4N 59°33W 89 g
Ōita Japan 33°14N 131°36E 31 H5
Ōita □ Japan 33°15N 131°30E 31 H5
Oiticica Brazil 5°3S 41°5W 93 E10
Ojai U.S.A. 34°27N 119°15W 79 L7
Ojinaga Mexico 29°34N 104°25W 86 B4
Ojiya Japan 37°18N 138°48E 31 F9
Ojo Caliente Mexico 21°53N 102°15W 86 C4
Ojos del Salado, Cerro Argentina 27°0S 68°40W 94 B2
Oka → Russia 56°20N 43°59E 18 C7
Okaba Indonesia 8°6S 139°42E 37 F9
Okahandja Namibia 22°0S 16°59E 56 C2
Okanagan L. Canada 50°0N 119°30W 70 D5
Okandja Gabon 0°35S 13°45E 52 E2
Okanogan U.S.A. 48°22N 119°35W 76 B4
Okanogan → U.S.A. 48°6N 119°44W 76 B4
Okanogan Range N. Amer. 49°0N 119°55W 70 D5
Okapi △ Dem. Rep. of the Congo 2°30N 27°20E 54 B2
Okaputa Namibia 20°5S 17°0E 56 C2
Okara Pakistan 30°50N 73°31E 42 D5
Okaukuejo Namibia 19°10S 16°0E 56 B2
Okavango Delta Botswana 18°45S 22°45E 56 B3
Okavango Swamp = Okavango Delta Botswana 18°45S 22°45E 56 B3
Okaya Japan 36°5N 138°10E 31 F9
Okayama Japan 34°40N 133°54E 31 G6
Okayama □ Japan 35°0N 133°50E 31 G6
Okazaki Japan 34°57N 137°10E 31 G8
Okeechobee U.S.A. 27°15N 80°50W 85 H14
Okeechobee, L. U.S.A. 27°0N 80°50W 85 H14
Okefenokee △ U.S.A. 30°45N 82°18W 85 F13
Okefenokee Swamp U.S.A. 30°40N 82°20W 85 F13
Okehampton U.K. 50°44N 4°0W 13 G4
Okha India 22°27N 69°4E 42 H3
Okha Russia 53°40N 143°0E 29 D15
Okhotsk Russia 59°20N 143°10E 29 D15
Okhotsk, Sea of Asia 55°0N 145°0E 29 D15
Okhotskiy Perevoz Russia 61°52N 135°35E 29 C14
Okhtyrka Ukraine 50°25N 35°0E 19 D5
Oki-Shotō Japan 36°5N 133°15E 31 F6
Okiep S. Africa 29°39S 17°53E 56 D2
Okinawa Japan 26°19N 127°46E 31 L3
Okinawa □ Japan 26°40N 128°0E 31 L4
Okinawa-Guntō Japan 26°40N 128°0E 31 L4
Okinawa-Jima Japan 26°32N 128°0E 31 L4
Okino-erabu-Shima Japan 27°21N 128°33E 31 L4
Oklahoma □ U.S.A. 35°20N 97°30W 84 D6
Oklahoma City U.S.A. 35°30N 97°30W 84 D6
Okmulgee U.S.A. 35°37N 95°58W 84 D7
Oknitsa = Ocniţa Moldova 48°25N 27°30E 17 D14
Okolo Uganda 2°37N 31°8E 54 B3
Okolona U.S.A. 34°0N 88°45W 85 E10
Okombahe Namibia 21°23S 15°22E 56 C2
Okotoks Canada 50°43N 113°58W 70 C6
Oksibil Indonesia 4°59S 140°35E 37 E10
Oksovskiy Russia 62°33N 39°57E 18 B6
Oktabrsk = Oktyabrsk Kazakhstan 49°28N 57°25E 19 E10
Oktyabrsk Kazakhstan 49°28N 57°25E 19 E10
Oktyabrskiy = Aktsyabrski Belarus 52°38N 28°53E 17 B15
Oktyabrskiy Russia 54°28N 53°28E 18 D9
Oktyabrskoy Revolyutsii, Ostrov Russia 79°30N 97°0E 29 B10
Okuru N.Z. 43°55S 168°55E 59 E2
Okushiri-Tō Japan 42°15N 139°30E 30 C9
Okwa → Botswana 22°30S 23°0E 56 C3
Ola U.S.A. 35°2N 93°13W 84 D8
Ólafsfjörður Iceland 66°4N 18°39W 8 C4
Ólafsvík Iceland 64°53N 23°43W 8 D2
Olancha U.S.A. 36°17N 118°1W 79 J8
Olancha Pk. U.S.A. 36°16N 118°7W 79 J8
Olanchito Honduras 15°30N 86°30W 88 C2
Öland Sweden 56°45N 16°38E 9 H17
Olary Australia 32°18S 140°19E 63 E3
Olascoaga Argentina 35°15S 60°39W 94 D3
Olathe U.S.A. 38°53N 94°49W 80 F6
Olavarría Argentina 36°55S 60°20W 94 D3
Oława Poland 50°57N 17°20E 17 C9
Ólbia Italy 40°55N 9°31E 22 D3
Olcott U.S.A. 43°20N 78°42W 82 C6
Old Bahama Chan. = Bahama, Canal Viejo de W. Indies 22°10N 77°30W 88 B4
Old Baldy Pk. = San Antonio, Mt. U.S.A. 34°17N 117°38W 79 L9
Old Bridge U.S.A. 40°25N 74°22W 83 F10
Old Castile = Castilla y Leon □ Spain 42°0N 5°0W 21 B3
Old Crow Canada 67°30N 139°55W 68 C6
Old Dale U.S.A. 34°8N 115°47W 79 L11
Old Forge N.Y., U.S.A. 43°43N 74°58W 83 C10
Old Forge Pa., U.S.A. 41°22N 75°45W 83 E9
Old Perlican Canada 48°5N 53°1W 73 C9
Old Shinyanga Tanzania 3°33S 33°27E 54 C3
Old Speck Mt. U.S.A. 44°34N 70°57W 83 B14
Old Town U.S.A. 44°56N 68°39W 81 C19
Old Washington U.S.A. 40°2N 81°27W 82 F3
Old Wives L. Canada 50°5N 106°0W 71 C7
Oldbury U.K. 51°38N 2°33W 13 F5
Oldcastle Ireland 53°46N 7°10W 10 C4
Oldeani Tanzania 3°22S 35°35E 54 C4
Oldenburg Germany 53°9N 8°13E 16 B5
Oldenzaal Neths. 52°19N 6°53E 15 B6
Oldham U.K. 53°33N 2°7W 12 D5
Oldman → Canada 49°57N 111°42W 70 D6
Oldmeldrum U.K. 57°20N 2°19W 11 D6
Olds Canada 51°50N 114°10W 70 C6
Olduvai Gorge Tanzania 2°57S 35°23E 54 C4
Oldziyt Mongolia 44°40N 109°1E 34 B5
Olean U.S.A. 42°5N 78°26W 82 D6
Olekma → Russia 60°22N 120°42E 29 C13
Olekminsk Russia 60°25N 120°30E 29 C13
Oleksandriya Ukraine 50°37N 26°19E 17 C14
Olema U.S.A. 38°3N 122°47W 78 G4
Olenegorsk Russia 68°9N 33°18E 8 B25
Olenek Russia 68°28N 112°18E 29 C12
Olenek → Russia 73°0N 120°10E 29 B13
Oléron, Î. d' France 45°55N 1°15W 20 D3
Oleśnica Poland 51°13N 17°22E 17 C9
Olevsk Ukraine 51°12N 27°39E 17 C14
Olga Russia 43°50N 135°14E 29 E14
Olga, L. Canada 49°47N 77°15W 72 C4
Olgas, The = Kata Tjuta Australia 25°20S 130°50E 61 E5
Ölgiy Mongolia 48°56N 89°57E 32 B3
Olhão Portugal 37°3N 7°48W 21 D2
Olifants = Elefantes → Africa 24°10S 32°40E 57 C5
Olifants → Namibia 25°30S 19°30E 56 C2
Olifantshoek S. Africa 27°57S 22°42E 56 D3
Ólimbos, Óros = Olymbos Oros Greece 40°6N 22°23E 23 D10
Olímpia Brazil 20°44S 48°54W 95 A6
Olinda Brazil 8°1S 34°51W 93 E12
Oliva Argentina 32°0S 63°38W 94 C3
Olive Branch U.S.A. 34°57N 89°49W 85 D10
Olivehurst U.S.A. 39°6N 121°34W 78 F5
Olivenza Spain 38°41N 7°9W 21 C2
Oliver Canada 49°13N 119°37W 70 D5
Oliver L. Canada 56°56N 103°22W 71 B8
Ollagüe Chile 21°15S 68°10W 94 A2
Olney Ill., U.S.A. 38°44N 88°5W 80 F9
Olney Tex., U.S.A. 33°22N 98°45W 84 E5
Oloitokitok Kenya 2°56S 37°30E 54 C4
Olomane → Canada 50°14N 60°37W 73 B7
Olomouc Czech Rep. 49°38N 17°12E 17 D9
Olonets Russia 61°0N 32°54E 18 B5
Olongapo Phil. 14°50N 120°18E 37 B6
Olosega Amer. Samoa 14°10S 169°37W 59 b
Olosenga = Swains I. Amer. Samoa 11°11S 171°4W 65 J11
Olot Spain 42°11N 2°30E 21 A7
Olovyannaya Russia 50°58N 115°35E 29 D12
Oloy → Russia 66°29N 159°29E 29 C16
Olsztyn Poland 53°48N 20°29E 17 B11
Olt → Romania 43°43N 24°51E 17 G13
Olteniţa Romania 44°7N 26°42E 17 F14
Olton U.S.A. 34°11N 102°8W 84 D3
Olymbos Cyprus 35°21N 33°45E 25 D12
Olymbos Oros Greece 40°6N 22°23E 23 D10
Olympia Greece 37°39N 21°39E 23 F9
Olympia U.S.A. 47°3N 122°53W 78 D4
Olympic △ U.S.A. 47°45N 123°43W 78 C3
Olympic Dam Australia 30°30S 136°55E 63 E2
Olympic Mts. U.S.A. 47°55N 123°45W 78 C3
Olympus Cyprus 34°56N 32°52E 25 E11
Olympus, Mt. = Olymbos Oros Greece 40°6N 22°23E 23 D10
Olympus, Mt. = Uludağ Turkey 40°4N 29°13E 23 D13
Olympus, Mt. U.S.A. 47°48N 123°43W 78 C3
Olyphant U.S.A. 41°27N 75°36W 83 E9
Om → Russia 54°59N 73°22E 28 D8
Om Koi Thailand 17°48N 98°22E 38 D2
Ōma Japan 41°45N 141°5E 30 D10
Ōmachi Japan 36°30N 137°50E 31 F8
Omae-Zaki Japan 34°36N 138°14E 31 G9
Ōmagari Japan 39°27N 140°29E 30 E10
Omagh U.K. 54°36N 7°19W 10 B4
Omagh □ U.K. 54°35N 7°15W 10 B4
Omaha U.S.A. 41°17N 95°58W 80 E6
Omak U.S.A. 48°25N 119°31W 76 B4
Omalos Greece 35°19N 23°55E 25 D5
Oman ■ Asia 23°0N 58°0E 47 C6
Oman, G. of Asia 24°30N 58°30E 45 E8
Omaruru Namibia 21°26S 16°0E 56 C2
Omaruru → Namibia 22°7S 14°15E 56 C1
Omate Peru 16°45S 71°0W 92 G4
Ombai, Selat Indonesia 8°30S 124°50E 37 F6
Omboué Gabon 1°35S 9°15E 52 E1
Ombrone → Italy 42°42N 11°5E 22 C4
Omdurmân Sudan 15°40N 32°28E 51 E12
Omemee Canada 44°10N 78°33W 82 B6
Omeonga Dem. Rep. of the Congo 3°40S 24°22E 54 C1
Ometepe, I. de Nic. 11°32N 85°35W 88 D2
Ometepec Mexico 16°41N 98°25W 87 D5
Ominato Japan 41°17N 141°10E 30 D10
Omineca → Canada 56°3N 124°16W 70 B4
Omineca Mts. Canada 56°30N 125°30W 70 B3
Omitara Namibia 22°16S 18°2E 56 C2
Ōmiya = Saitama Japan 35°54N 139°38E 31 G9
Ommen Neths. 52°31N 6°26E 15 B6
Ömnögovĭ □ Mongolia 43°15N 104°0E 34 C3
Omo → Ethiopia 6°25N 36°10E 47 F2
Omodhos Cyprus 34°51N 32°48E 25 E11
Omolon → Russia 68°42N 158°36E 29 C16
Omono-Gawa → Japan 39°46N 140°3E 30 E10
Omsk Russia 55°0N 73°12E 28 D8
Omsukchan Russia 62°32N 155°48E 29 C16
Ōmu Japan 44°34N 142°58E 30 B11
Omul, Vf. Romania 45°27N 25°29E 17 F13
Ōmura Japan 32°56N 129°57E 31 H4
Omuramba Omatako → Namibia 17°45S 20°25E 56 B2
Omuramba Ovambo → Namibia 18°45S 16°59E 56 B2
Ōmuta Japan 33°5N 130°26E 31 H5
Onaga U.S.A. 39°29N 96°10W 80 F5
Onalaska U.S.A. 43°53N 91°14W 80 D8
Onancock U.S.A. 37°43N 75°45W 81 G16
Onang Indonesia 3°2S 118°49E 37 E5
Onangue, L. Gabon 0°57S 10°4E 52 E2
Onaping L. Canada 47°3N 81°30W 72 C3
Onavas Mexico 28°31N 109°35W 86 B3
Onawa U.S.A. 42°2N 96°6W 80 D5
Oncócua Angola 16°30S 13°25E 56 B1
Onda Spain 39°55N 0°17W 21 C5
Ondangwa Namibia 17°57S 16°4E 56 B2
Ondjiva Angola 16°48S 15°50E 56 B2
Öndörshil Mongolia 45°13N 108°5E 34 B5
Öndverðarnes Iceland 64°52N 24°0W 8 D2
One Tree Australia 34°11S 144°43E 63 E3
Oneata Fiji 18°26S 178°25W 59 a
Onega Russia 64°0N 38°10E 18 B6
Onega → Russia 63°58N 38°2E 18 B6
Onega, G. of = Onezhskaya Guba Russia 64°24N 36°38E 18 B6
Onega, L. = Onezhskoye Ozero Russia 61°44N 35°22E 18 B6
Oneida U.S.A. 43°6N 75°39W 83 C9
Oneida L. U.S.A. 43°12N 75°54W 83 C9
O'Neill U.S.A. 42°27N 98°39W 80 D4
Onekotan, Ostrov Russia 49°25N 154°45E 29 E16
Onema Dem. Rep. of the Congo 4°35S 24°30E 54 C1
Oneonta U.S.A. 42°27N 75°4W 83 D9
Oneşti Romania 46°17N 26°47E 17 E14
Onezhskaya Guba Russia 64°24N 36°38E 18 B6
Onezhskoye Ozero Russia 61°44N 35°22E 18 B6
Ongarue N.Z. 38°42S 175°19E 59 C5
Ongea Levu = Ogea Levu Fiji 19°8S 178°24W 59 a
Ongers → S. Africa 31°4S 23°13E 56 E3
Ongerup Australia 33°58S 118°28E 61 F2
Ongjin N. Korea 37°56N 125°21E 35 F13
Ongkharak Thailand 14°8N 101°1E 38 E3
Ongniud Qi China 43°0N 118°38E 35 C10
Ongoka Dem. Rep. of the Congo 1°20S 26°0E 54 C2
Ongole India 15°33N 80°2E 40 M12
Ongon = Havirga Mongolia 45°41N 113°5E 34 B7
Onida U.S.A. 44°42N 100°4W 80 C3
Onilahy → Madag. 23°34S 43°45E 57 C7
Onitsha Nigeria 6°6N 6°42E 50 G7
Ono Fiji 18°55S 178°29E 59 a
Onoda Japan 33°59N 131°11E 31 G5
Onslow Australia 21°40S 115°12E 60 D2
Onslow B. U.S.A. 34°20N 77°15W 85 D16
Ontake-San Japan 35°53N 137°29E 31 G8
Ontario Calif., U.S.A. 34°4N 117°39W 79 L9
Ontario Oreg., U.S.A. 44°2N 116°58W 76 D5
Ontario □ Canada 48°0N 83°0W 72 B2
Ontario, L. N. Amer. 43°20N 78°0W 82 C7
Ontonagon U.S.A. 46°52N 89°19W 80 B9
Onyx U.S.A. 35°41N 118°14W 79 K8
Oodnadatta Australia 27°33S 135°30E 63 D2
Ooldea Australia 30°27S 131°50E 61 F5
Oombulgurri Australia 15°15S 127°45E 60 C4
Oorindi Australia 20°40S 141°1E 62 C3
Oost-Vlaanderen □ Belgium 51°5N 3°50E 15 C3
Oostende Belgium 51°15N 2°54E 15 C2
Oosterhout Neths. 51°39N 4°47E 15 C4
Oosterschelde → Neths. 51°33N 4°0E 15 C4
Oosterwolde Neths. 53°0N 6°17E 15 B6
Ootacamund = Udagamandalam India 11°30N 76°44E 40 P10
Ootsa L. Canada 53°50N 126°2W 70 C3
Op Luang △ Thailand 18°12N 98°32E 38 C2
Opala Dem. Rep. of the Congo 0°40S 24°20E 54 C1
Opanake Sri Lanka 6°35N 80°40E 40 R12
Opasatika Canada 49°30N 82°50W 72 C3
Opasquia △ Canada 53°33N 93°5W 72 B1
Opava Czech Rep. 49°57N 17°58E 17 D9
Opelika U.S.A. 32°39N 85°23W 85 E12
Opelousas U.S.A. 30°32N 92°5W 84 F8
Opémisca, L. Canada 49°56N 74°52W 72 C5
Opheim U.S.A. 48°51N 106°24W 76 B10
Ophthalmia Ra. Australia 23°15S 119°30E 60 D2
Opinaca → Canada 52°15N 78°2W 72 B4
Opinaca, Rés. Canada 52°39N 76°20W 72 B4
Opinnagau → Canada 54°12N 82°25W 72 B3
Opiscotéo, L. Canada 53°10N 68°10W 73 B6
Opobo Nigeria 4°35N 7°34E 50 H7
Opole Poland 50°42N 17°58E 17 C9
Oponono L. Namibia 18°8S 15°45E 56 B2
Oporto = Porto Portugal 41°8N 8°40W 21 B1
Opotiki N.Z. 38°1S 177°19E 59 C6
Opp U.S.A. 31°17N 86°16W 85 F11
Oppdal Norway 62°35N 9°41E 8 E13
Opportunity U.S.A. 47°39N 117°15W 76 C5
Opua N.Z. 35°19S 174°9E 59 A5
Opunake N.Z. 39°26S 173°52E 59 C4
Opuwo Namibia 18°3S 13°45E 56 B1
Ora Cyprus 34°51N 33°12E 25 E12
Oracle U.S.A. 32°37N 110°46W 77 K8
Oradea Romania 47°2N 21°58E 17 E11
Öræfajökull Iceland 64°2N 16°39W 8 D6
Orai India 25°58N 79°30E 43 G8
Oral = Zhayyq → Kazakhstan 47°0N 51°48E 19 E9
Oral Kazakhstan 51°20N 51°20E 19 D9
Oran Algeria 35°45N 0°39W 50 A5
Orange Australia 33°15S 149°7E 63 E4
Orange France 44°8N 4°47E 20 D6
Orange Calif., U.S.A. 33°47N 117°51W 79 M9
Orange Mass., U.S.A. 42°35N 72°19W 83 D12
Orange Tex., U.S.A. 30°6N 93°44W 84 F8
Orange Va., U.S.A. 38°15N 78°7W 81 F14
Orange → S. Africa 28°41S 16°28E 56 D2
Orange, C. Brazil 4°20N 51°30W 93 C8
Orange Cove U.S.A. 36°38N 119°19W 78 J7
Orange Free State = Free State □ S. Africa 28°30S 27°0E 56 D4
Orange Grove U.S.A. 27°58N 97°56W 84 H6
Orange Walk Belize 18°6N 88°33W 87 D7
Orangeburg U.S.A. 33°30N 80°52W 85 E14
Orangeville Canada 43°55N 80°5W 82 C4
Orango Guinea-Biss. 11°5N 16°0W 50 F2
Oranienburg Germany 52°45N 13°14E 16 B7
Oranje = Orange → S. Africa 28°41S 16°28E 56 D2
Oranjemund Namibia 28°38S 16°29E 56 D2
Oranjerivier S. Africa 29°40S 24°12E 56 D3
Oranjestad Aruba 12°32N 70°2W 89 D5
Orapa Botswana 21°15S 25°30E 53 J5
Oras Phil. 12°9N 125°28E 37 B7
Orbetello Italy 42°27N 11°13E 22 C4
Orbisonia U.S.A. 40°15N 77°54W 82 F7
Orbost Australia 37°40S 148°29E 63 F4
Orcadas Antarctica 60°44S 44°37W 5 C18
Orcas I. U.S.A. 48°42N 122°56W 78 B4
Orchard City U.S.A. 38°50N 107°58W 76 G10
Orchard Homes U.S.A. 46°55N 114°4W 76 C6
Orchila, I. Venezuela 11°48N 66°10W 89 D6
Orchilla, Pta. Canary Is. 27°42N 18°10W 24 G1
Orcutt U.S.A. 34°52N 120°27W 79 L6
Ord U.S.A. 41°36N 98°56W 80 E4
Ord → Australia 15°33S 128°15E 60 C4
Ord, Mt. Australia 17°20S 125°34E 60 C4
Ord Mts. U.S.A. 34°39N 116°45W 79 L10
Orderville U.S.A. 37°17N 112°38W 77 H7
Ordos = Mu Us Shamo China 39°0N 109°0E 34 E5
Ordu Turkey 40°55N 37°53E 19 F6
Ordway U.S.A. 38°13N 103°46W 76 G12
Ore Dem. Rep. of the Congo 3°17N 29°30E 54 B2
Ore Mts. = Erzgebirge Germany 50°27N 12°55E 16 C7
Örebro Sweden 59°20N 15°18E 9 G16
Oregon U.S.A. 42°1N 89°20W 80 D9
Oregon □ U.S.A. 44°0N 121°0W 76 E3
Oregon City U.S.A. 45°21N 122°36W 78 E4
Oregon Dunes △ U.S.A. 43°40N 124°10W 76 E1
Orekhovo-Zuyevo Russia 55°50N 38°55E 18 C6
Orel Russia 52°57N 36°3E 18 D6
Orem U.S.A. 40°19N 111°42W 76 F8
Ören Turkey 37°3N 27°57E 23 F12
Orenburg Russia 51°45N 55°6E 18 D10
Orense = Ourense Spain 42°19N 7°55W 21 A2
Orepuki N.Z. 46°19S 167°46E 59 G1
Orestes Pereyra Mexico 26°30N 105°39W 86 B3
Orestiada Greece 41°30N 26°33E 23 D12
Orfanos Kolpos Greece 40°33N 24°0E 23 D11
Orford Ness U.K. 52°5N 1°35E 13 E9
Organ Pipe Cactus △ U.S.A. 32°0N 112°52W 77 K7
Organos, Pta. de los Canary Is. 28°12N 17°17W 24 F2
Orgaz Spain 39°39N 3°53W 21 C4
Orgeyev = Orhei Moldova 47°24N 28°50E 17 E15
Orhaneli Turkey 39°54N 28°59E 23 E13
Orhangazi Turkey 40°29N 29°18E 23 D13
Orhei Moldova 47°24N 28°50E 17 E15
Orhon Gol → Mongolia 50°21N 106°0E 32 A5
Oriental, Cordillera Colombia 6°0N 73°0W 92 B4
Oriental, Grand Erg Algeria 30°0N 6°30E 50 B7
Orientale □ Dem. Rep. of the Congo 2°20N 26°0E 54 B2
Oriente Argentina 38°44S 60°37W 94 D3
Orihuela Spain 38°7N 0°55W 21 C5
Orillia Canada 44°40N 79°24W 82 B5
Orinoco → Venezuela 9°15N 61°30W 92 B6
Orion Canada 49°27N 110°49W 71 D6
Oriskany U.S.A. 43°10N 75°20W 83 C9
Orissa □ India 20°0N 84°0E 41 K14
Orissaare Estonia 58°34N 23°5E 9 G20
Oristano Italy 39°54N 8°36E 22 E3
Oristano, G. di Italy 39°50N 8°29E 22 E3
Orizaba Mexico 18°51N 97°6W 87 D5
Orizaba, Pico de Mexico 18°58N 97°15W 87 D5
Orkanger Norway 63°18N 9°52E 8 E13
Orkla → Norway 63°18N 9°51E 8 E13
Orkney S. Africa 26°58S 26°40E 56 D4
Orkney □ U.K. 59°2N 3°13W 11 B5
Orkney Is. U.K. 59°0N 3°0W 11 D6
Orland U.S.A. 39°45N 122°12W 78 F4
Orlando U.S.A. 28°32N 81°22W 85 G14
Orléanais France 48°0N 2°0E 20 C5
Orléans France 47°54N 1°52E 20 C4
Orleans U.S.A. 44°49N 72°12W 83 B12
Orléans, Î. d' Canada 46°54N 70°58W 73 C5
Ormara Pakistan 25°16N 64°33E 40 G4
Ormoc Phil. 11°0N 124°37E 37 B6
Ormond N.Z. 38°33S 177°56E 59 C6
Ormond Beach U.S.A. 29°17N 81°3W 85 G14
Ormskirk U.K. 53°35N 2°54W 12 D5
Ormstown Canada 45°8N 74°0W 83 A11
Örnsköldsvik Sweden 63°17N 18°40E 8 E18
Oro N. Korea 40°1N 127°27E 35 D14
Oro → Mexico 25°35N 105°2W 86 B3
Oro Grande U.S.A. 34°36N 117°20W 79 L9
Oro Valley U.S.A. 32°26N 110°58W 77 K8
Orocué Colombia 4°48N 71°20W 92 C4
Orofino U.S.A. 46°29N 116°15W 76 C5
Orohena, Mt. Tahiti 17°37S 149°28W 59 d
Orol Dengizi = Aral Sea Asia 44°30N 60°0E 28 E7
Oromocto Canada 45°54N 66°29W 73 C6
Orono Canada 43°59N 78°37W 82 C6
Orono U.S.A. 44°53N 68°40W 81 C19
Oronsay U.K. 56°1N 6°15W 11 E2
Oroqen Zizhiqi China 50°34N 123°43E 33 A7
Oroquieta Phil. 8°32N 123°44E 37 C6
Orosei Italy 40°23N 9°42E 22 D3
Orosháza Hungary 46°32N 20°42E 17 E11
Orotukan Russia 62°16N 151°42E 29 C16
Oroville Calif., U.S.A. 39°31N 121°33W 78 F5
Oroville Wash., U.S.A. 48°56N 119°26W 76 B4
Oroville, L. U.S.A. 39°33N 121°29W 78 F5
Orroroo Australia 32°43S 138°38E 63 E2
Orrville U.S.A. 40°50N 81°46W 82 F3
Orsha Belarus 54°30N 30°25E 18 D5
Orsk Russia 51°12N 58°34E 28 D6
Orşova Romania 44°41N 22°25E 17 F12
Ortaca Turkey 36°49N 28°45E 23 F13
Ortegal, C. Spain 43°43N 7°52W 21 A2
Orthez France 43°29N 0°48W 20 E3
Ortigueira Spain 43°40N 7°50W 21 A2
Orting U.S.A. 47°6N 122°12W 78 C4
Ortles Italy 46°31N 10°33E 20 C9
Ortón → Bolivia 10°50S 67°0W 92 F5
Ortonville U.S.A. 45°19N 96°27W 80 C5
Orūmīyeh Iran 37°40N 45°0E 44 B5
Orūmīyeh, Daryācheh-ye Iran 37°50N 45°30E 44 B5

Oruro Bolivia 18°0S 67°9W 92 G5
Orust Sweden 58°10N 11°40E 9 G14
Oruzgān □ Afghan. 33°0N 66°0E 40 C5
Orvieto Italy 42°43N 12°7E 22 C5
Orwell N.Y., U.S.A. 43°35N 75°50W 83 C9
Orwell Ohio, U.S.A. 41°32N 80°52W 82 E4
Orwell → U.K. 51°59N 1°18E 13 F9
Orwigsburg U.S.A. 40°38N 76°6W 83 F8
Oryakhovo Bulgaria 43°40N 23°57E 23 C10
Osa Russia 57°17N 55°26E 18 C10
Osa, Pen. de Costa Rica 8°0N 84°0W 88 E3
Osage U.S.A. 43°17N 92°49W 80 D7
Osage → U.S.A. 38°36N 91°57W 80 F8
Osage City U.S.A. 38°38N 95°50W 80 F6
Ōsaka Japan 34°42N 135°30E 31 G7
Osan S. Korea 37°11N 127°4E 35 F14
Osawatomie U.S.A. 38°31N 94°57W 80 F6
Osborne U.S.A. 39°26N 98°42W 80 F4
Osceola Ark., U.S.A. 35°42N 89°58W 85 D10
Osceola Iowa, U.S.A. 41°2N 93°46W 80 E7
Oscoda U.S.A. 44°26N 83°20W 82 B1
Ösel = Saaremaa
Estonia 58°30N 22°30E 9 G20
Osgoode Canada 45°8N 75°36W 83 A9
Osh Kyrgyzstan 40°37N 72°49E 28 E8
Oshakati Namibia 17°45S 15°40E 53 H3
Oshawa Canada 43°50N 78°50W 82 C6
Oshigambo Namibia 17°45S 16°5E 56 B2
Oshkosh Nebr., U.S.A. 41°24N 102°21W 80 E2
Oshkosh Wis., U.S.A. 44°1N 88°33W 80 C9
Oshmyany = Ashmyany
Belarus 54°26N 25°52E 17 A13
Oshnovīyeh Iran 37°2N 45°6E 44 B5
Oshogbo Nigeria 7°48N 4°37E 50 G6
Oshtorīnān Iran 34°1N 48°38E 45 C6
Oshwe
Dem. Rep. of the Congo 3°25S 19°28E 52 E3
Osijek Croatia 45°34N 18°41E 23 B8
Osipovichi = Asipovichy
Belarus 53°19N 28°33E 17 B15
Osiyan India 26°43N 72°55E 42 F5
Osizweni S. Africa 27°49S 30°7E 57 D5
Oskaloosa U.S.A. 41°18N 92°39W 80 E7
Oskarshamn Sweden 57°15N 16°27E 9 H17
Oskélanéo Canada 48°5N 75°15W 72 C4
Öskemen Kazakhstan 50°0N 82°36E 28 E9
Oslo Norway 59°54N 10°43E 9 G14
Oslofjorden Norway 59°20N 10°35E 9 G14
Osmanabad India 18°5N 76°10E 40 K10
Osmaniye Turkey 37°5N 36°10E 44 B3
Osnabrück Germany 52°17N 8°3E 16 B5
Osório Brazil 29°53S 50°17W 95 B5
Osorno Chile 40°25S 73°0W 96 E2
Osorno, Vol. Chile 41°0S 72°30W 96 D2
Osoyoos Canada 49°0N 119°30W 70 D5
Osøyro Norway 60°9N 5°30E 8 F11
Ospika → Canada 56°20N 124°0W 70 B4
Osprey Reef Australia 13°52S 146°36E 62 A4
Oss Neths. 51°46N 5°32E 15 C5
Ossa, Mt. Australia 41°52S 146°3E 63 G4
Ossa, Oros Greece 39°47N 22°42E 23 E10
Ossabaw I. U.S.A. 31°50N 81°5W 85 F14
Ossining U.S.A. 41°10N 73°55W 83 E11
Ossipee U.S.A. 43°41N 71°7W 83 C13
Ossokmanuan L. Canada 53°25N 65°0W 73 B7
Ossora Russia 59°20N 163°13E 29 D17
Ostend = Oostende
Belgium 51°15N 2°54E 15 C2
Oster Ukraine 50°57N 30°53E 17 C16
Österbotten = Pohjanmaa
Finland 62°58N 22°50E 8 E20
Osterburg U.S.A. 40°16N 78°31W 82 F6
Österdalälven Sweden 61°30N 13°45E 8 F15
Østerdalen Norway 61°40N 10°50E 8 F14
Östermyra = Seinäjoki
Finland 62°40N 22°51E 8 E20
Österreich = Austria ■
Europe 47°0N 14°0E 16 E8
Östersund Sweden 63°10N 14°38E 8 E16
Ostfriesische Inseln
Germany 53°42N 7°0E 16 B4
Ostrava Czech Rep. 49°51N 18°18E 17 D10
Ostróda Poland 53°42N 19°58E 17 B11
Ostroh Ukraine 50°20N 26°30E 17 C14
Ostrołęka Poland 53°4N 21°32E 17 B11
Ostrów Mazowiecka
Poland 52°50N 21°51E 17 B11
Ostrów Wielkopolski
Poland 51°36N 17°44E 17 C9
Ostrowiec-Świętokrzyski
Poland 50°55N 21°22E 17 C11
Ostuni Italy 40°44N 17°35E 23 D7
Ōsumi-Kaikyō Japan 30°55N 131°0E 31 J5
Ōsumi-Shotō Japan 30°30N 130°0E 31 J5
Osuna Spain 37°14N 5°8W 21 D3
Oswegatchie → U.S.A. 44°42N 75°30W 83 B9
Oswego U.S.A. 43°27N 76°31W 83 C8
Oswego → U.S.A. 43°27N 76°30W 83 C8
Oswestry U.K. 52°52N 3°3W 12 E4
Oświęcim Poland 50°2N 19°11E 17 C10
Otago □ N.Z. 45°15S 170°0E 59 F2
Otago Harbour N.Z. 45°47S 170°42E 59 F3
Otaheite B.
Trin. & Tob. 10°15N 61°30W 93 K15
Ōtake Japan 34°12N 132°13E 31 G6
Otaki N.Z. 40°45S 175°10E 59 D5
Otaru Japan 43°10N 141°0E 30 C10
Otaru-Wan = Ishikari-Wan
Japan 43°25N 141°1E 30 C10
Otavalo Ecuador 0°13N 78°20W 92 C3
Otavi Namibia 19°40S 17°24E 56 B2
Otchinjau Angola 16°30S 13°56E 56 B1
Otelnuk, L. Canada 56°9N 68°12W 73 A6
Othello U.S.A. 46°50N 119°10W 76 C4
Otjiwarongo Namibia 20°30S 16°33E 56 C2
Oto Tolu Group Tonga 20°21S 174°32W 59 c
Otoineppu Japan 44°44N 142°16E 30 B11
Otorohanga N.Z. 38°12S 175°14E 59 C5
Otoskwin → Canada 52°13N 88°6W 72 B2
Otra → Norway 58°9N 8°1E 9 G13
Otranto Italy 40°9N 18°28E 23 D8
Otranto, C. d' Italy 40°7N 18°30E 23 D8
Otranto, Str. of Italy 40°15N 18°40E 23 D8
Otse S. Africa 25°2S 25°45E 56 D4
Ōtsu Japan 35°0N 135°50E 31 G7
Ōtsuki Japan 35°36N 138°57E 31 G9
Ottawa = Outaouais →
Canada 45°27N 74°8W 72 C5
Ottawa Canada 45°26N 75°42W 83 A9
Ottawa Ill., U.S.A. 41°21N 88°51W 80 E9
Ottawa Kans., U.S.A. 38°37N 95°16W 80 F6
Ottawa Is. Canada 59°35N 80°10W 69 D11
Otter Cr. → U.S.A. 44°13N 73°17W 83 B11
Otter L. Canada 55°35N 104°39W 71 B8
Otterville Canada 42°55N 80°36W 82 D4
Ottery St. Mary U.K. 50°44N 3°17W 13 G4
Otto Beit Bridge
Zimbabwe 15°59S 28°56E 55 F2
Ottosdal S. Africa 26°46S 25°59E 56 D4
Ottumwa U.S.A. 41°1N 92°25W 80 E7
Oturkpo Nigeria 7°16N 8°8E 50 G7
Otway, B. Chile 53°30S 74°0W 96 G2
Otway, C. Australia 38°52S 143°30E 63 F3
Otwock Poland 52°5N 21°20E 17 B11
Ou → Laos 20°4N 102°13E 38 B4
Ou Neua Laos 22°18N 101°48E 38 A3
Ou-Sammyaku Japan 39°20N 140°35E 30 E10
Ouachita → U.S.A. 31°38N 91°49W 84 F9
Ouachita, L. U.S.A. 34°34N 93°12W 84 D8
Ouachita Mts. U.S.A. 34°30N 94°30W 84 D7
Ouagadougou
Burkina Faso 12°25N 1°30W 50 F5
Ouahigouya
Burkina Faso 13°31N 2°25W 50 F5
Ouahran = Oran Algeria 35°45N 0°39W 50 A5
Ouallene Algeria 24°41N 1°11E 50 D6
Ouargla Algeria 31°59N 5°16E 50 B7
Ouarra → C.A.R. 5°5N 24°26E 52 C4
Ouarzazate Morocco 30°55N 6°50W 50 B4
Oubangi →
Dem. Rep. of the Congo 0°30S 17°50E 52 E3
Ouddorp Neths. 51°50N 3°57E 15 C3
Oude Rijn → Neths. 52°12N 4°24E 15 B4
Oudenaarde Belgium 50°50N 3°37E 15 D3
Oudtshoorn S. Africa 33°35S 22°14E 56 E3
Ouessant, Î. d' France 48°28N 5°6W 20 B1
Ouesso Congo 1°37N 16°5E 52 D3
Ouest, Pte. de l' Canada 49°52N 64°40W 73 C7
Ouezzane Morocco 34°51N 5°35W 50 B4
Oughter, L. Ireland 54°1N 7°28W 10 B4
Oughterard Ireland 53°26N 9°18W 10 C2
Ouidah Benin 6°25N 2°0E 50 G6
Oujda Morocco 34°41N 1°55W 50 B5
Oulainen Finland 64°17N 24°47E 8 D21
Oulu Finland 65°1N 25°29E 8 D21
Oulujärvi Finland 64°25N 27°15E 8 D22
Oulujoki → Finland 65°1N 25°30E 8 D21
Oum Chalouba Chad 15°48N 20°46E 51 E10
Oum Hadjer Chad 13°18N 19°41E 51 F9
Ounasjoki → Finland 66°31N 25°40E 8 C21
Ounguati Namibia 22°0S 15°46E 56 C2
Ounianga Sérir Chad 18°54N 20°51E 51 E10
Our → Lux. 49°55N 6°5E 15 E6
Ouray U.S.A. 38°1N 107°40W 77 G10
Ourense Spain 42°19N 7°55W 21 A2
Ouricuri Brazil 7°53S 40°5W 93 E10
Ourinhos Brazil 23°0S 49°54W 95 A6
Ouro Fino Brazil 22°16S 46°25W 95 A6
Ouro Prêto Brazil 20°20S 43°30W 95 A7
Ourthe → Belgium 50°29N 5°35E 15 D5
Ouse → E. Sussex, U.K. 50°47N 0°4E 13 G8
Ouse → N. Yorks., U.K. 53°44N 0°55W 12 D7
Outaouais → Canada 45°27N 74°8W 72 C5
Outardes → Canada 49°24N 69°30W 73 C6
Outer Hebrides U.K. 57°30N 7°40W 11 D1
Outjo Namibia 20°5S 16°7E 56 C2
Outlook Canada 51°30N 107°0W 71 C7
Outokumpu Finland 62°43N 29°1E 8 E23
Ouyen Australia 35°1S 142°22E 63 F3
Ovalau Fiji 17°40S 178°48E 59 a
Ovalle Chile 30°33S 71°18W 94 C1
Ovamboland Namibia 18°30S 16°0E 56 B2
Overflakkee Neths. 51°44N 4°10E 15 C4
Overijssel □ Neths. 52°25N 6°35E 15 B6
Overland Park U.S.A. 38°58N 94°40W 80 F6
Overton U.S.A. 36°33N 114°27W 79 J12
Övertorneå Sweden 66°23N 23°38E 8 C20
Ovid U.S.A. 42°41N 76°49W 83 D8
Oviedo Spain 43°25N 5°50W 21 A3
Oviši Latvia 57°33N 21°44E 9 H19
Ovoot Mongolia 45°21N 113°45E 34 B7
Övör Hangay □
Mongolia 45°0N 102°30E 34 B2
Øvre Årdal Norway 61°19N 7°48E 8 F12
Ovruch Ukraine 51°25N 28°45E 17 C15
Owaka N.Z. 46°27S 169°40E 59 G2
Owambo = Ovamboland
Namibia 18°30S 16°0E 56 B2
Owasco L. U.S.A. 42°50N 76°31W 83 D8
Owase Japan 34°7N 136°12E 31 G8
Owatonna U.S.A. 44°5N 93°14W 80 C7
Owbeh Afghan. 34°28N 63°10E 40 B3
Owego U.S.A. 42°6N 76°16W 83 D8
Owen Falls Dam = Nalubaale
Dam Uganda 0°30N 33°5E 54 B3
Owen Sound Canada 44°35N 80°55W 82 B4
Owen Stanley Ra.
Papua N. G. 8°30S 147°0E 58 B7
Oweniny → Ireland 54°8N 9°34W 10 B2
Owens → U.S.A. 36°32N 117°59W 78 J9
Owens L. U.S.A. 36°26N 117°57W 79 J9
Owensboro U.S.A. 37°46N 87°7W 80 G10
Owl → Canada 57°51N 92°44W 71 B10
Owo Nigeria 7°10N 5°39E 50 G7
Owosso U.S.A. 43°0N 84°10W 81 D11
Owyhee U.S.A. 41°57N 116°6W 76 F5
Owyhee → U.S.A. 43°49N 117°2W 76 E5
Owyhee, L. U.S.A. 43°38N 117°14W 76 E5
Ox Mts. = Slieve Gamph
Ireland 54°6N 9°0W 10 B3
Öxarfjörður Iceland 66°15N 16°45W 8 C5
Oxbow Canada 49°14N 102°10W 71 D8
Oxelösund Sweden 58°43N 17°5E 9 G17
Oxford N.Z. 43°18S 172°11E 59 E4
Oxford U.K. 51°46N 1°15W 13 F6
Oxford Mass., U.S.A. 42°7N 71°52W 83 D13
Oxford Miss., U.S.A. 34°22N 89°31W 85 D10
Oxford N.C., U.S.A. 36°19N 78°35W 85 C15
Oxford N.Y., U.S.A. 42°27N 75°36W 83 D9
Oxford Ohio, U.S.A. 39°31N 84°45W 81 F11
Oxford L. Canada 54°51N 95°37W 71 C9
Oxfordshire □ U.K. 51°48N 1°16W 13 F6
Oxnard U.S.A. 34°12N 119°11W 79 L7
Oxus = Amudarya →
Uzbekistan 43°58N 59°34E 28 E6
Oya Malaysia 2°55N 111°55E 36 D4
Oyama Japan 36°18N 139°48E 31 F9
Oyem Gabon 1°34N 11°31E 52 D2
Oyen Canada 51°22N 110°28W 71 C6
Oykel → U.K. 57°56N 4°26W 11 D4
Oymyakon Russia 63°25N 142°44E 29 C15
Oyo Nigeria 7°46N 3°56E 50 G6
Oyster Bay U.S.A. 40°52N 73°32W 83 F11
Öyübari Japan 43°1N 142°5E 30 C11
Ozamiz Phil. 8°15N 123°50E 37 C6
Ozark Ala., U.S.A. 31°28N 85°39W 85 F12
Ozark Ark., U.S.A. 35°29N 93°50W 84 D8
Ozark Mo., U.S.A. 37°1N 93°12W 80 G7
Ozark Plateau U.S.A. 37°20N 91°40W 80 G8
Ozarks, L. of the U.S.A. 38°12N 92°38W 80 F7
Ózd Hungary 48°14N 20°15E 17 D11
Ozette, L. U.S.A. 48°6N 124°38W 78 B2
Ozieri Italy 40°35N 9°0E 22 D3
Ozona U.S.A. 30°43N 101°12W 84 F4
Ozuluama Mexico 21°40N 97°51W 87 C5

P

Pa-an Burma 16°51N 97°40E 41 L20
Pa Mong Dam Thailand 18°0N 102°22E 38 D4
Pa Sak → Thailand 15°30N 101°0E 38 E3
Paamiut Greenland 62°0N 49°43W 4 C5
Paarl S. Africa 33°45S 18°56E 56 E2
Pab Hills Pakistan 26°30N 66°45E 42 F2
Pabbay U.K. 57°46N 7°14W 11 D1
Pabianice Poland 51°40N 19°20E 17 C10
Pabna Bangla. 24°1N 89°18E 41 G16
Pabo Uganda 3°1N 32°10E 54 B3
Pacaja → Brazil 1°56S 50°50W 93 D8
Pacaraima, Sa. S. Amer. 4°0N 62°30W 92 C6
Pacasmayo Peru 7°20S 79°35W 92 E3
Pachhar India 24°40N 77°42E 42 G7
Pachitea → Peru 8°46S 74°33W 92 E4
Pachmarhi India 22°28N 78°26E 43 H8
Pachnes Greece 35°16N 24°4E 25 D6
Pachpadra India 25°58N 72°10E 42 G5
Pachuca Mexico 20°7N 98°44W 87 C5
Pacific Antarctic Ridge
Pac. Oc. 43°0S 115°0W 5 B13
Pacific Grove U.S.A. 36°38N 121°56W 78 J5
Pacific Ocean 10°0N 140°0W 65 G14
Pacific Rim △ Canada 48°40N 124°45W 78 B2
Pacifica U.S.A. 37°37N 122°27W 78 H4
Pacitan Indonesia 8°12S 111°7E 37 H14
Packwood U.S.A. 46°36N 121°40W 78 D5
Padaido, Kepulauan
Indonesia 1°15S 136°30E 37 E9
Padang Indonesia 1°0S 100°20E 36 E2
Padang Endau Malaysia 2°40N 103°38E 39 L4
Padangpanjang
Indonesia 0°40S 100°20E 36 E2
Padangsidempuan
Indonesia 1°30N 99°15E 36 D1
Paddle Prairie Canada 57°57N 117°29W 70 B5
Paddockwood Canada 53°30N 105°30W 71 C7
Paderborn Germany 51°42N 8°45E 16 C5
Padma India 24°12N 85°22E 43 G11
Pádova Italy 45°25N 11°53E 22 B4
Padra India 22°15N 73°7E 42 H5
Padrauna India 26°54N 83°59E 43 F10
Padre I. U.S.A. 27°10N 97°25W 84 H6
Padre Island △ U.S.A. 27°0N 97°25W 84 H6
Padstow U.K. 50°33N 4°58W 13 G3
Padua = Pádova Italy 45°25N 11°53E 22 B4
Paducah Ky., U.S.A. 37°5N 88°37W 80 G9
Paducah Tex., U.S.A. 34°1N 100°18W 84 D4
Paea Tahiti 17°41S 149°35W 59 d
Paeroa N.Z. 37°23S 175°41E 59 B5
Pafúri Mozam. 22°28S 31°17E 57 C5
Pag Croatia 44°25N 15°3E 16 F8
Pagadian Phil. 7°55N 123°30E 37 C6
Pagai Selatan, Pulau
Indonesia 3°0S 100°15E 36 E2
Pagai Utara, Pulau
Indonesia 2°35S 100°0E 36 E2
Pagalu = Annobón
Atl. Oc. 1°25S 5°36E 49 G4
Pagara India 24°22N 80°1E 43 G9
Pagastikos Kolpos
Greece 39°15N 23°0E 23 E10
Pagatan Indonesia 3°33S 115°59E 36 E5
Page U.S.A. 36°57N 111°27W 77 H8
Pago Pago Amer. Samoa 14°16S 170°43W 59 b
Pagosa Springs U.S.A. 37°16N 107°1W 77 H10
Pagwa River Canada 50°2N 85°14W 72 B2
Pāhala U.S.A. 19°12N 155°29W 74 b
Pahang → Malaysia 3°30N 103°9E 39 L4
Pahiatua N.Z. 40°27S 175°50E 59 D5
Pahokee U.S.A. 26°50N 80°40W 85 H14
Pahrump U.S.A. 36°12N 115°59W 79 J11
Pahute Mesa U.S.A. 37°20N 116°45W 78 H10
Pai Thailand 19°19N 98°27E 38 C2
Paicines U.S.A. 36°44N 121°17W 78 J5
Paide Estonia 58°53N 25°33E 9 G21
Paignton U.K. 50°26N 3°35W 13 G4
Päijänne Finland 61°30N 25°30E 8 F21
Pailani India 25°45N 80°26E 43 G9
Pailin Cambodia 12°46N 102°36E 38 F4
Painan Indonesia 1°21S 100°34E 36 E2
Painesville U.S.A. 41°43N 81°15W 82 E3
Paint Hills = Wemindji
Canada 53°0N 78°49W 72 B4
Paint L. Canada 55°28N 97°57W 71 B9
Painted Desert U.S.A. 36°0N 111°0W 77 H8
Paintsville U.S.A. 37°49N 82°48W 81 G12
País Vasco □ Spain 42°50N 2°45W 21 A4
Paisley Canada 44°18N 81°16W 82 B3
Paisley U.K. 55°50N 4°25W 11 F4
Paisley U.S.A. 42°42N 120°32W 76 E3
Paita Peru 5°11S 81°9W 92 E2
Pajares, Puerto de Spain 42°58N 5°46W 21 A3
Pak Lay Laos 18°15N 101°27E 38 C3
Pak Phanang Thailand 8°21N 100°12E 39 H3
Pak Sane Laos 18°22N 103°39E 38 C4
Pak Song Laos 15°11N 106°14E 38 E6
Pak Suong Laos 19°58N 102°15E 38 C4
Pak Tam Chung
China 22°24N 114°19E 33 G11
Pakaur India 24°38N 87°51E 43 G12
Pakch'ŏn N. Korea 39°44N 125°35E 35 E13
Pakenham Canada 45°18N 76°18W 83 A8
Pakhuis S. Africa 32°9S 19°5E 56 E2
Pakistan ■ Asia 30°0N 70°0E 42 E4
Pakkading Laos 18°19N 103°59E 38 C4
Pakokku Burma 21°20N 95°0E 41 J19
Pakowki L. Canada 49°20N 111°0W 71 D6
Pakpattan Pakistan 30°25N 73°27E 42 D5
Paktīā □ Afghan. 33°30N 69°15E 40 C6
Paktīkā □ Afghan. 32°30N 69°0E 40 C6
Pakwach Uganda 2°28N 31°27E 54 B3
Pakxe Laos 15°5N 105°52E 38 E5
Pal Lahara India 21°27N 85°11E 43 J11
Pala Chad 9°25N 15°5E 51 G9
Pala Dem. Rep. of the Congo 6°45S 29°30E 54 D2
Pala U.S.A. 33°22N 117°5W 79 M9
Palabek Uganda 3°22N 32°33E 54 B3
Palacios U.S.A. 28°42N 96°13W 84 G6
Palagruža Croatia 42°24N 16°15E 22 C7
Palam India 19°0N 77°0E 40 K10
Palampur India 32°10N 76°30E 42 C7
Palana Australia 39°45S 147°55E 63 F4
Palana Russia 59°10N 159°59E 29 D16
Palanan Phil. 17°8N 122°29E 37 A6
Palanan Pt. Phil. 17°17N 122°30E 37 A6
Palandri Pakistan 33°42N 73°40E 43 C5
Palanga Lithuania 55°58N 21°3E 9 J19
Palangkaraya Indonesia 2°16S 113°56E 36 E4
Palani Hills India 10°14N 77°33E 40 P10
Palanpur India 24°10N 72°25E 42 G5
Palapye Botswana 22°30S 27°7E 56 C4
Palas Pakistan 35°4N 73°14E 43 B5
Palashi India 23°47N 88°15E 43 H13
Palasponga India 21°47N 85°34E 43 J11
Palatka Russia 60°6N 150°54E 29 C16
Palatka U.S.A. 29°39N 81°38W 85 G14
Palau ■ Palau 7°30N 134°30E 58 A6
Palauk Burma 13°10N 98°40E 38 F2
Palawan Phil. 9°30N 118°30E 36 C5
Palayankottai India 8°45N 77°45E 40 Q10
Paldiski Estonia 59°23N 24°9E 9 G21
Palekastro Greece 35°12N 26°15E 25 D8
Paleleh Indonesia 1°10N 121°50E 37 D6
Palembang Indonesia 3°0S 104°50E 36 E2
Palencia Spain 42°1N 4°34W 21 A3
Palenque Mexico 17°29N 92°1W 87 D6
Paleochora Greece 35°16N 23°39E 25 D5
Paleokastritsa Greece 39°40N 19°41E 25 A3
Paleometokho Cyprus 35°7N 33°11E 25 D12
Palermo Italy 38°7N 13°22E 22 E5
Palermo U.S.A. 39°26N 121°33W 78 F5
Palestina Chile 23°50S 69°47W 96 A3
Palestine Asia 32°0N 35°0E 46 D4
Palestine U.S.A. 31°46N 95°38W 84 F7
Paletwa Burma 21°10N 92°50E 41 J18
Palghat India 10°46N 76°42E 40 P10
Palgrave, Mt. Australia 23°22S 115°58E 60 D2
Pali India 25°50N 73°20E 42 G5
Palikir Micronesia 6°55N 158°9E 64 G7
Paliouri, Akra Greece 39°57N 23°45E 23 E10
Palisades Res. U.S.A. 43°20N 111°12W 76 E8
Paliseul Belgium 49°54N 5°8E 15 E5
Palitana India 21°32N 71°49E 42 J4
Palizada Mexico 18°15N 92°5W 87 D6
Palk Bay Asia 9°30N 79°15E 40 Q11
Palk Strait Asia 10°0N 79°45E 40 Q11
Palkānah Iraq 35°49N 44°26E 44 C5
Palkot India 22°53N 84°39E 43 H11
Pallanza = Verbánia
Italy 45°56N 8°33E 20 D8
Pallarenda Australia 19°12S 146°46E 62 B4
Pallinup → Australia 34°27S 118°50E 61 F2
Pallisa Uganda 1°12N 33°43E 54 B3
Pallu India 28°59N 74°14E 42 E6
Palm Bay U.S.A. 28°2N 80°35W 85 G14
Palm Beach U.S.A. 26°43N 80°2W 85 H14
Palm Coast U.S.A. 29°35N 81°12W 85 G14
Palm Desert U.S.A. 33°43N 116°22W 79 M10
Palm Is. Australia 18°40S 146°35E 62 B4
Palm Springs U.S.A. 33°50N 116°33W 79 M10
Palma Mozam. 10°46S 40°29E 55 E5
Palma, B. de Spain 39°30N 2°39E 24 B9
Palma de Mallorca Spain 39°35N 2°39E 24 B9
Palma Soriano Cuba 20°15N 76°0W 88 B4
Palmares Brazil 8°41S 35°28W 93 E11
Palmas Brazil 26°29S 52°0W 95 B5
Palmas, C. Liberia 4°27N 7°46W 50 H4
Pálmas, G. di Italy 39°0N 8°30E 22 E3
Palmdale U.S.A. 34°35N 118°7W 79 L8
Palmeira das Missões
Brazil 27°55S 53°17W 95 B5
Palmeira dos Índios
Brazil 9°25S 36°37W 93 E11
Palmer Antarctica 64°35S 65°0W 5 C17
Palmer U.S.A. 61°36N 149°7W 68 C5
Palmer → Australia 16°0S 142°26E 62 B3
Palmer Arch. Antarctica 64°15S 65°0W 5 C17
Palmer Lake U.S.A. 39°7N 104°55W 76 G11
Palmer Land Antarctica 73°0S 63°0W 5 D18
Palmerston Australia 12°31S 130°59E 60 B5
Palmerston Canada 43°50N 80°51W 82 C4
Palmerston N.Z. 45°29S 170°43E 59 F3
Palmerston North N.Z. 40°21S 175°39E 59 D5
Palmerton U.S.A. 40°48N 75°37W 83 F9
Palmetto U.S.A. 27°31N 82°34W 85 H13
Palmi Italy 38°21N 15°51E 22 E6
Palmira Argentina 32°59S 68°34W 94 C2
Palmira Colombia 3°32N 76°16W 92 C3
Palmyra = Tudmur
Syria 34°36N 38°15E 44 C3
Palmyra Mo., U.S.A. 39°48N 91°32W 80 F8
Palmyra N.J., U.S.A. 40°0N 75°1W 83 F9
Palmyra N.Y., U.S.A. 43°5N 77°18W 82 C7
Palmyra Pa., U.S.A. 40°18N 76°36W 83 F8
Palmyra Is. Pac. Oc. 5°52N 162°5W 65 G11
Palo Alto U.S.A. 37°27N 122°10W 78 H4
Palo Seco Trin. & Tob. 10°4N 61°36W 93 K15
Palo Verde U.S.A. 33°26N 114°44W 79 M12
Palo Verde △ Costa Rica 10°21N 85°21W 88 D2
Palomar Mt. U.S.A. 33°22N 116°50W 79 M10
Palopo Indonesia 3°0S 120°16E 37 E6
Palos, C. de Spain 37°38N 0°40W 21 D5
Palos Verdes, Pt.
U.S.A. 33°46N 118°25W 79 M8
Palos Verdes Estates
U.S.A. 33°48N 118°23W 79 M8
Palu Indonesia 1°0S 119°52E 37 E5
Palu Turkey 38°45N 40°0E 44 B3
Palwal India 28°8N 77°19E 42 E7
Pamanukan Indonesia 6°16S 107°49E 37 G12
Pamekasan Indonesia 7°10S 113°28E 37 G15
Pamenang Indonesia 8°24S 116°6E 37 J19
Pamiers France 43°7N 1°39E 20 E4
Pamir Tajikistan 37°40N 73°0E 28 F8
Pamlico → U.S.A. 35°20N 76°28W 85 D16
Pamlico Sd. U.S.A. 35°20N 76°0W 85 D17
Pampa U.S.A. 35°32N 100°58W 84 D4
Pampa de las Salinas
Argentina 32°1S 66°58W 94 C2
Pampanua Indonesia 4°16S 120°8E 37 E6
Pampas Argentina 35°0S 63°0W 94 D3
Pampas Peru 12°20S 74°50W 92 F4
Pamplona Colombia 7°23N 72°39W 92 B4
Pamplona Spain 42°48N 1°38W 21 A5
Pampoenpoort S. Africa 31°3S 22°40E 56 E3
Pan de Azúcar △ Chile 26°0S 70°40W 94 B1
Pana U.S.A. 39°23N 89°5W 80 F9
Panaca U.S.A. 37°47N 114°23W 77 H6
Panaitan Indonesia 6°36S 105°12E 37 G11
Panaji India 15°25N 73°50E 40 M8
Panamá Panama 9°0N 79°25W 88 E4
Panama ■ Cent. Amer. 8°48N 79°55W 88 E4
Panamá, G. de Panama 8°4N 79°20W 88 E4
Panama, Isthmus of
Cent. Amer. 9°0N 79°0W 66 J12
Panama Basin Pac. Oc. 5°0N 83°30W 65 G19
Panama Canal Panama 9°10N 79°37W 88 E4
Panama City U.S.A. 30°10N 85°40W 85 F12
Panamint Range
U.S.A. 36°20N 117°20W 79 J9
Panamint Springs
U.S.A. 36°20N 117°28W 79 J9
Panão Peru 9°55S 75°55W 92 E3
Panare Thailand 6°51N 101°30E 39 J3
Panay Phil. 11°10N 122°30E 37 B6
Panay, G. Phil. 11°0N 122°30E 37 B6
Pančevo Serbia 44°52N 20°41E 23 B9
Panda Mozam. 24°2S 34°45E 57 C5
Pandan Malaysia 1°32N 103°46E 39 d
Pandan Phil. 11°45N 122°10E 37 B6
Pandan, Selat Singapore 1°15N 103°44E 39 d
Pandan Tampoi = Tampoi
Malaysia 1°30N 103°39E 39 d
Pandegelang Indonesia 6°25S 106°5E 37 G12
Pandhana India 21°42N 76°13E 42 J7
Pandharpur India 17°41N 75°20E 40 L9
Pando Uruguay 34°44S 56°0W 95 C4
Pando, L. = Hope, L.
Australia 28°24S 139°18E 63 D2
Pandokratoras Greece 39°45N 19°50E 25 A3
Pandora Costa Rica 9°43N 83°3W 88 E3
Panevėžys Lithuania 55°42N 24°25E 9 J21
Pang-Long Burma 23°11N 98°45E 41 H21
Pang Sida △ Thailand 14°5N 102°17E 38 E4
Pang-Yang Burma 22°7N 98°48E 41 H21
Panga
Dem. Rep. of the Congo 1°52N 26°18E 54 B2
Pangalanes, Canal des =
Ampangalana, Lakandranon'
Madag. 22°48S 47°50E 57 C8
Pangani Tanzania 5°25S 38°58E 54 D4
Pangani → Tanzania 5°26S 38°58E 54 D4
Pangfou = Bengbu
China 32°58N 117°20E 35 H9
Pangil
Dem. Rep. of the Congo 3°10S 26°35E 54 C2
Pangkah, Tanjung
Indonesia 6°51S 112°33E 37 G15
Pangkajene Indonesia 4°46S 119°34E 37 E5
Pangkalanbrandan
Indonesia 4°1N 98°20E 36 D1
Pangkalanbuun
Indonesia 2°41S 111°37E 36 E4
Pangkalpinang Indonesia 2°0S 106°0E 36 E3
Pangnirtung Canada 66°8N 65°43W 69 C13
Pangong Tso India 34°40N 78°40E 42 B8

Panguitch *U.S.A.* 37°50N 112°26W **77 H7**
Pangutaran Group
  Phil. 6°18N 120°34E **37 C6**
Panhandle *U.S.A.* 35°21N 101°23W **84 D4**
Pani Mines *India* 22°29N 73°50E **42 H5**
Pania-Mutombo
  Dem. Rep. of the Congo 5°11S 23°51E **54 D1**
Panikota I. *India* 20°46N 71°21E **42 J4**
Panipat *India* 29°25N 77°2E **42 E7**
Panjal Range = Pir Panjal Range
  India 32°30N 76°50E **42 C7**
Panjang, Hon *Vietnam* 9°20N 103°28E **39 H4**
Panjgur *Pakistan* 27°0N 64°5E **40 F4**
Panjim = Panaji *India* 15°25N 73°50E **40 M8**
Panjin *China* 41°3N 122°2E **35 D12**
Panjnad → *Pakistan* 28°57N 70°30E **42 E4**
Panjnad Barrage
  Pakistan 29°22N 71°15E **42 E4**
Panjwai *Afghan.* 31°26N 65°27E **42 D1**
Panmunjŏm *N. Korea* 37°59N 126°38E **35 F14**
Panna *India* 24°40N 80°15E **43 G9**
Panna △ *India* 24°40N 80°0E **43 G9**
Panna Hills *India* 24°40N 81°15E **43 G9**
Pannawonica *Australia* 21°39S 116°19E **60 D2**
Pangnga, Tanjung
  Indonesia 8°54S 116°2E **37 K19**
Pannirtuuq = Pangnirtung
  Canada 66°8N 65°43W **69 C13**
Pano Akil *Pakistan* 27°51N 69°7E **42 F3**
Pano Lefkara *Cyprus* 34°53N 33°20E **25 E12**
Pano Panayia *Cyprus* 34°55N 32°38E **25 E11**
Panorama *Brazil* 21°21S 51°51W **95 A5**
Panormos *Greece* 35°25N 24°41E **25 D6**
Pansemal *India* 21°39N 74°42E **42 J6**
Panshan = Panjin
  China 41°3N 122°2E **35 D12**
Panshi *China* 42°58N 126°5E **35 C14**
Pantanal *Brazil* 17°30S 57°40W **92 H7**
Pantanos de Centla △
  Mexico 18°25N 92°25W **87 D6**
Pantar *Indonesia* 8°28S 124°10E **37 F6**
Pante Macassar
  E. Timor 9°30S 123°58E **37 F6**
Pante Makasar = Pante Macassar
  E. Timor 9°30S 123°58E **37 F6**
Pantelleria *Italy* 36°50N 11°57E **22 F4**
Pánuco *Mexico* 22°3N 98°10W **87 C5**
Panzhihua *China* 26°33N 101°44E **32 D5**
Paola *Malta* 35°52N 14°30E **25 D2**
Paola *U.S.A.* 38°35N 94°53W **80 F6**
Paonia *U.S.A.* 38°52N 107°36W **76 G10**
Paopao *Moorea* 17°30S 149°49W **60 d**
Paoting = Baoding
  China 38°50N 115°28E **34 E8**
Paot'ou = Baotou *China* 40°32N 110°2E **34 D6**
Paoua *C.A.R.* 7°9N 16°20E **52 C3**
Pápa *Hungary* 47°22N 17°30E **17 E9**
Papa Stour *U.K.* 60°20N 1°42W **11 A7**
Papa Westray *U.K.* 59°20N 2°55W **11 B6**
Papagayo → *Mexico* 16°46N 99°43W **87 D5**
Papagayo, G. de
  Costa Rica 10°30N 85°50W **88 D2**
Papakura *N.Z.* 37°4S 174°59E **59 B5**
Papantla *Mexico* 20°27N 97°19W **87 C5**
Papar *Malaysia* 5°45N 116°0E **36 C5**
Papara *Tahiti* 17°43S 149°31W **59 d**
Paparoa △ *N.Z.* 42°7S 171°26E **59 E3**
Papeete *Tahiti* 17°32S 149°34W **59 d**
Papenoo *Tahiti* 17°30S 149°25W **59 d**
Papenoo → *Tahiti* 17°30S 149°25W **59 d**
Papetoai *Moorea* 17°29S 149°52W **59 d**
Paphos *Cyprus* 34°46N 32°25E **25 E11**
Paposo *Chile* 25°0S 70°30W **94 B1**
Papoutsa *Cyprus* 34°54N 33°4E **25 E12**
Papua □ *Indonesia* 4°0S 137°0E **37 E9**
Papua, G. of *Papua N. G.* 9°0S 144°50E **58 B7**
Papua New Guinea ■
  Oceania 8°0S 145°0E **58 B7**
Papudo *Chile* 32°29S 71°27W **94 C1**
Papun *Burma* 18°2N 97°30E **41 K20**
Papunya *Australia* 23°15S 131°54E **60 D5**
Pará = Belém *Brazil* 1°20S 48°30W **93 D9**
Pará □ *Brazil* 3°20S 52°0W **93 D8**
Paraburdoo *Australia* 23°14S 117°32E **60 D2**
Paracatu *Brazil* 17°10S 46°50W **93 G9**
Paracel Is. *S. China Sea* 15°50N 112°0E **36 A4**
Parachilna *Australia* 31°10S 138°21E **63 E2**
Parachinar *Pakistan* 33°55N 70°5E **42 C4**
Paradip *India* 20°15N 86°35E **41 J15**
Paradise *Calif., U.S.A.* 39°46N 121°37W **78 F5**
Paradise *Nev., U.S.A.* 36°9N 115°10W **79 J11**
Paradise → *Canada* 53°27N 57°19W **73 B8**
Paradise Hill *Canada* 53°32N 109°28W **71 C7**
Paradise River *Canada* 53°27N 57°17W **73 B8**
Paradise Valley *U.S.A.* 41°30N 117°32W **76 F5**
Paradisi *Greece* 36°18N 28°7E **25 C10**
Parado *Indonesia* 8°42S 118°30E **37 F5**
Paragould *U.S.A.* 36°3N 90°29W **85 C9**
Paragua → *Venezuela* 6°55N 62°55W **92 B6**
Paraguaçu → *Brazil* 12°45S 38°54W **93 F11**
Paraguaçu Paulista
  Brazil 22°22S 50°35W **95 A5**
Paraguaná, Pen. de
  Venezuela 12°0N 70°0W **92 A5**
Paraguarí *Paraguay* 25°36S 57°0W **94 B4**
Paraguarí □ *Paraguay* 26°0S 57°10W **94 B4**
Paraguay ■ *S. Amer.* 23°0S 57°0W **94 A4**
Paraguay → *Paraguay* 27°18S 58°38W **94 B4**
Paraíba = João Pessoa
  Brazil 7°10S 34°52W **93 E12**
Paraíba □ *Brazil* 7°0S 36°0W **93 E11**
Paraíba do Sul → *Brazil* 21°37S 41°3W **95 A7**
Parainen *Finland* 60°18N 22°18E **9 F20**
Paraíso *Mexico* 18°24N 93°14W **87 D6**
Parak *Iran* 27°38N 52°25E **45 E7**
Parakou *Benin* 9°25N 2°40E **50 G6**
Paralimni *Cyprus* 35°2N 33°58E **25 D12**

Paramaribo *Suriname* 5°50N 55°10W **93 B7**
Páramos del Batallón y La
  Negra △ *Venezuela* 8°2N 71°55W **89 E5**
Paramushir, Ostrov
  Russia 50°24N 156°0E **29 D16**
Paran → *Israel* 30°20N 35°10E **46 E4**
Paraná *Argentina* 31°45S 60°30W **94 C3**
Paraná *Brazil* 12°30S 47°48W **93 F9**
Paraná □ *Brazil* 24°30S 51°0W **95 A5**
Paraná → *Argentina* 33°43S 59°15W **94 C4**
Paranaguá *Brazil* 25°30S 48°30W **95 B6**
Paranaíba *Brazil* 19°40S 51°11W **93 G8**
Paranaíba → *Brazil* 20°6S 51°4W **93 H8**
Paranapanema →
  Brazil 22°40S 53°9W **95 A5**
Paranapiacaba, Serra do
  Brazil 24°31S 48°35W **95 A6**
Paranavaí *Brazil* 23°4S 52°56W **95 A5**
Parang *Maguindanao,*
  Phil. 7°23N 124°16E **37 C6**
Parang *Sulu, Phil.* 5°55N 120°54E **37 C6**
Parângul Mare, Vf.
  Romania 45°20N 23°37E **17 F12**
Paraparaumu *N.Z.* 40°57S 175°3E **59 D5**
Parbati → *Mad. P., India* 25°50N 76°30E **42 G7**
Parbati → *Raj., India* 26°54N 77°53E **42 F7**
Parbhani *India* 19°8N 76°52E **40 K10**
Parchim *Germany* 53°26N 11°52E **16 B6**
Pardes Hanna-Karkur
  Israel 32°28N 34°57E **46 C3**
Pardo → *Bahia, Brazil* 15°40S 39°0W **93 G11**
Pardo → *Mato Grosso,*
  Brazil 21°46S 52°9W **95 A5**
Pardoo Roadhouse
  Australia 20°6S 119°3E **60 D2**
Pardubice *Czech Rep.* 50°3N 15°45E **16 C8**
Pare *Indonesia* 7°43S 112°12E **37 G15**
Pare Mts. *Tanzania* 4°0S 37°45E **54 C4**
Parecis, Serra dos *Brazil* 13°0S 60°0W **92 F7**
Paren *Russia* 62°30N 163°15E **29 C17**
Parent *Canada* 47°55N 74°35W **72 C5**
Parent, L. *Canada* 48°31N 77°1W **72 C4**
Parepare *Indonesia* 4°0S 119°40E **37 E5**
Parga *Greece* 39°15N 20°29E **23 E9**
Pargas = Parainen
  Finland 60°18N 22°18E **9 F20**
Pargo, Pta. do *Madeira* 32°49N 17°17W **24 D2**
Paria → *U.S.A.* 36°52N 111°36W **77 H8**
Paria, G. de *Venezuela* 10°20N 62°0W **93 K14**
Pariaguán *Venezuela* 8°51N 64°34W **92 B6**
Paricutín, Cerro
  Mexico 19°28N 102°15W **86 D4**
Parigi *Indonesia* 0°50S 120°5E **37 E6**
Parika *Guyana* 6°50N 58°20W **92 B7**
Parikkala *Finland* 61°33N 29°31E **8 F23**
Parima, Serra *Brazil* 2°30N 64°0W **92 C6**
Parinari *Peru* 4°35S 74°25W **92 D4**
Pariñas, Pta. *S. Amer.* 4°30S 82°0W **90 D2**
Parintins *Brazil* 2°40S 56°50W **93 D7**
Pariparit Kyun *Burma* 14°55N 93°45E **41 M18**
Paris *Canada* 43°12N 80°25W **82 C4**
Paris *France* 48°53N 2°20E **20 B5**
Paris *Idaho, U.S.A.* 42°14N 111°24W **76 E8**
Paris *Ky., U.S.A.* 38°13N 84°15W **81 F11**
Paris *Tenn., U.S.A.* 36°18N 88°19W **85 C10**
Paris *Tex., U.S.A.* 33°40N 95°33W **84 E7**
Parish *U.S.A.* 43°25N 76°8W **83 C8**
Parishville *U.S.A.* 44°38N 74°49W **83 B10**
Park *U.S.A.* 48°45N 122°18W **78 B4**
Park City *U.S.A.* 37°48N 97°20W **80 G5**
Park Falls *U.S.A.* 45°56N 90°27W **80 C8**
Park Head *Canada* 44°36N 81°9W **82 B3**
Park Hills *U.S.A.* 37°51N 90°51W **80 G9**
Park Range *U.S.A.* 40°41N 106°41W **76 F10**
Park Rapids *U.S.A.* 46°55N 95°4W **80 B6**
Park River *U.S.A.* 48°24N 97°45W **80 A5**
Park Rynie *S. Africa* 30°25S 30°45E **57 E5**
Parkā Bandar *Iran* 25°55N 59°35E **45 E8**
Parkano *Finland* 62°1N 23°0E **8 E20**
Parker *Ariz., U.S.A.* 34°9N 114°17W **79 L12**
Parker *Pa., U.S.A.* 41°5N 79°41W **82 E5**
Parker Dam *U.S.A.* 34°18N 114°8W **79 L12**
Parkersburg *U.S.A.* 39°16N 81°34W **81 F13**
Parkes *Australia* 33°9S 148°11E **63 E4**
Parkfield *U.S.A.* 35°54N 120°26W **78 K6**
Parkhill *Canada* 43°15N 81°38W **82 C3**
Parkland *Canada* 47°9N 122°26W **78 C4**
Parkston *U.S.A.* 43°24N 97°59W **80 D5**
Parksville *Canada* 49°20N 124°21W **70 D4**
Parkway *U.S.A.* 38°32N 121°26W **78 G5**
Parla *Spain* 40°14N 3°46W **21 B4**
Parma *Italy* 44°48N 10°20E **20 D9**
Parma *Idaho, U.S.A.* 43°47N 116°57W **76 E5**
Parma *Ohio, U.S.A.* 41°24N 81°43W **82 E3**
Parnaguá *Brazil* 10°10S 44°38W **93 F10**
Parnaíba *Brazil* 2°54S 41°47W **93 D10**
Parnaíba → *Brazil* 3°0S 41°50W **93 D10**
Parnassós *Greece* 38°35N 22°30E **23 E10**
Pärnu *Estonia* 58°28N 24°33E **9 G21**
Paro Dzong *Bhutan* 27°32N 89°53E **43 F13**
Paroo → *Australia* 31°28S 143°32E **63 E3**
Paroo-Darling △
  Australia 31°32S 144°0E **63 E3**
Paros *Greece* 37°5S 25°12E **23 F11**
Parowan *U.S.A.* 37°51N 112°50W **77 H7**
Parral *Chile* 36°10S 71°52W **94 D1**
Parras *Mexico* 25°30N 102°20W **86 B4**
Parrett → *U.K.* 51°12N 3°1W **13 F4**
Parris I. *U.S.A.* 32°20N 80°41W **85 E14**
Parrsboro *Canada* 45°30N 64°25W **73 C7**
Parry I. *Canada* 45°18N 80°10W **82 A4**
Parry Is. *Canada* 77°0N 110°0W **69 B9**
Parry Sound *Canada* 45°20N 80°0W **82 A5**
Parsaloi *Kenya* 1°16N 36°51E **54 B4**
Parsnip → *Canada* 55°10N 123°2W **70 B4**
Parsons *U.S.A.* 37°20N 95°16W **80 G6**
Parsons Ra. *Australia* 13°30S 135°15E **62 A2**

Partinico *Italy* 38°3N 13°7E **22 E5**
Partizansk *Russia* 43°8N 133°9E **30 C6**
Partridge I. *Canada* 55°59N 87°37W **72 A2**
Partry Mts. *Ireland* 53°40N 9°28W **10 C2**
Paru → *Brazil* 1°33S 52°38W **93 D8**
Parvān □ *Afghan.* 35°0N 69°0E **40 B6**
Parvatipuram *India* 18°50N 83°25E **41 K13**
Parvatsar *India* 26°52N 74°49E **42 F6**
Parys *S. Africa* 26°52S 27°29E **56 D4**
Pas, Pta. des *Spain* 38°46N 1°26E **24 C7**
Pas, The *Canada* 53°45N 101°15W **71 C8**
Pasadena *Canada* 49°1N 57°36W **73 C8**
Pasadena *Calif., U.S.A.* 34°9N 118°8W **79 L8**
Pasadena *Tex., U.S.A.* 29°43N 95°13W **84 G7**
Pasaje → *Argentina* 25°39S 63°56W **94 B3**
Pasar *Indonesia* 8°27S 114°54E **37 J17**
Pascagoula *U.S.A.* 30°21N 88°33W **85 D10**
Pascagoula → *U.S.A.* 30°23N 88°37W **85 F10**
Pașcani *Romania* 47°14N 26°45E **17 E14**
Pasco *U.S.A.* 46°14N 119°6W **76 C4**
Pasco, Cerro de *Peru* 10°45S 76°10W **92 F3**
Pasco □ *Australia* 20°57S 115°20E **60 D2**
Pascoag *U.S.A.* 41°57N 71°42W **83 E13**
Pascua, I. de *Chile* 27°7S 109°23W **65 K17**
Pasfield L. *Canada* 58°24N 105°20W **71 B7**
Pasir Mas *Malaysia* 6°2N 102°8E **39 J4**
Pasir Panjang *Singapore* 1°18N 103°46E **39 d**
Pasir Putih *Malaysia* 5°50N 102°24E **39 K4**
Pasirian *Indonesia* 8°13S 113°8E **37 H15**
Pasirkuning *Indonesia* 0°30S 104°33E **36 E2**
Paskūh *Iran* 27°34N 61°39E **45 E9**
Pasley, C. *Australia* 33°52S 123°35E **61 F3**
Pašman *Croatia* 43°58N 15°20E **16 G8**
Pasni *Pakistan* 25°15N 63°27E **40 G3**
Paso Cantinela
  Mexico 32°33N 115°47W **79 N11**
Paso de Indios *Argentina* 43°55S 69°0W **96 E3**
Paso de los Libres
  Argentina 29°44S 57°10W **94 B4**
Paso de los Toros
  Uruguay 32°45S 56°30W **94 C4**
Paso Robles *U.S.A.* 35°38N 120°41W **78 K6**
Paspébiac *Canada* 48°3N 65°17W **73 C6**
Pasrur *Pakistan* 32°16N 74°43E **42 C6**
Passage East *Ireland* 52°14N 7°0W **10 D5**
Passage West *Ireland* 51°52N 8°21W **10 E3**
Passaic *U.S.A.* 40°51N 74°7W **83 F10**
Passau *Germany* 48°34N 13°28E **16 D7**
Passero, C. *Italy* 36°41N 15°10E **22 F6**
Passo Fundo *Brazil* 28°10S 52°20W **95 B5**
Passos *Brazil* 20°45S 46°37W **93 H9**
Pastavy *Belarus* 55°4N 26°50E **9 J22**
Pastaza → *Peru* 4°50S 76°52W **92 D3**
Pasto *Colombia* 1°13N 77°17W **92 C3**
Pasuruan *Indonesia* 7°40S 112°44E **37 G15**
Patagonia *Argentina* 45°0S 69°0W **96 F3**
Patagonia *U.S.A.* 31°33N 110°45W **77 L8**
Patambar *Iran* 29°45N 60°17E **45 D9**
Patan = Lalitapur
  Nepal 27°40N 85°20E **43 F11**
Patan *India* 23°54N 72°14E **42 H5**
Patani *Indonesia* 0°20N 128°50E **37 D7**
Pataudi *India* 28°18N 76°48E **42 E7**
Patchewollock
  Australia 35°22S 142°12E **63 F3**
Patchogue *U.S.A.* 40°46N 73°1W **83 F11**
Pate *Kenya* 2°10S 41°0E **54 C5**
Patea *N.Z.* 39°45S 174°30E **59 C5**
Patensie *S. Africa* 33°46S 24°49E **56 E3**
Paternò *Italy* 37°34N 14°54E **22 F6**
Pateros *U.S.A.* 48°3N 119°54W **76 B4**
Paterson *U.S.A.* 40°54N 74°9W **83 F10**
Paterson Ra. *Australia* 21°45S 122°10E **60 D3**
Pathankot *India* 32°18N 75°45E **42 C6**
Pathein = Bassein
  Burma 16°45N 94°30E **41 L19**
Pathfinder Res.
  U.S.A. 42°28N 106°51W **76 E10**
Pathiu *Thailand* 10°42N 99°19E **39 G2**
Pathum Thani *Thailand* 14°1N 100°32E **38 E3**
Pati *Indonesia* 6°45S 111°1E **37 G14**
Patía → *Colombia* 2°13N 78°40W **92 C3**
Patiala *Punjab, India* 30°23N 76°26E **42 D7**
Patiala *Ut. P., India* 27°43N 79°1E **43 F8**
Patkai Bum *India* 27°0N 95°30E **41 F19**
Patmos *Greece* 37°21N 26°36E **23 F12**
Patna *India* 25°35N 85°12E **43 G11**
Pato Branco *Brazil* 26°13S 52°40W **95 B5**
Patong, Ao *Thailand* 7°54N 98°17E **39 a**
Patonga *Uganda* 2°45N 33°15E **54 B3**
Patos *Brazil* 6°55S 37°16W **93 E11**
Patos, L. dos *Brazil* 31°20S 51°0W **95 C5**
Patos, Río de los →
  Argentina 31°18S 69°25W **94 C2**
Patos de Minas *Brazil* 18°35S 46°32W **93 G9**
Patquía *Argentina* 30°2S 66°55W **94 C2**
Patra *Greece* 38°14N 21°47E **23 E9**
Patraikos Kolpos *Greece* 38°17N 21°30E **23 E9**
Patras = Patra *Greece* 38°14N 21°47E **23 E9**
Patriot Hills *Antarctica* 82°20S 81°25W **5 E16**
Patrocínio *Brazil* 18°57S 47°0W **93 G9**
Pattani *Thailand* 6°48N 101°15E **39 J3**
Pattaya *Thailand* 12°52S 100°55E **38 F3**
Patten *U.S.A.* 46°0N 68°38W **81 B19**
Patterson *Calif., U.S.A.* 37°28N 121°8W **78 H5**
Patterson La., U.S.A.* 29°42N 91°18W **84 G9**
Patterson, Mt. *U.S.A.* 38°29N 119°20W **78 G7**
Patti *Punjab, India* 31°17N 74°54E **42 D6**
Patti *Ut. P., India* 25°55N 82°12E **43 G10**
Pattoki *Pakistan* 31°5N 73°52E **42 D5**
Patton *U.S.A.* 40°38N 78°39W **82 F6**
Patuakhali *Bangla.* 22°20N 90°25E **41 H17**
Patuanak *Canada* 55°55N 107°43W **71 B7**
Patuca → *Honduras* 15°50N 84°18W **88 C3**
Patuca, Punta
  Honduras 15°49N 84°14W **88 C3**
Patuca △ *Honduras* 14°30N 85°30W **88 D2**

Patvinsuo △ *Finland* 63°7N 30°45E **8 E24**
Pátzcuaro *Mexico* 19°31N 101°38W **86 D4**
Pau *France* 43°19N 0°25W **20 E3**
Pauk *Burma* 21°27N 94°30E **41 J19**
Paul I. *Canada* 56°30N 61°20W **73 A7**
Paul Smiths *U.S.A.* 44°26N 74°15W **83 B10**
Paulatuk *Canada* 69°25N 124°0W **68 C7**
Paulistana *Brazil* 8°9S 41°9W **93 E10**
Paulo Afonso *Brazil* 9°21S 38°15W **93 E11**
Paulpietersburg
  S. Africa 27°23S 30°50E **57 D5**
Pauls Valley *U.S.A.* 34°44N 97°13W **84 D6**
Pauma Valley *U.S.A.* 33°16N 116°58W **79 M10**
Pauri *India* 30°9N 78°47E **43 D8**
Pāveh *Iran* 35°3N 46°22E **44 C5**
Pavia *Italy* 45°7N 9°8E **20 D8**
Pavilion *U.S.A.* 42°52N 78°1W **82 D6**
Pāvilosta *Latvia* 56°53N 21°14E **9 H19**
Pavlodar *Kazakhstan* 52°33N 77°0E **28 D8**
Pavlograd = Pavlohrad
  Ukraine 48°30N 35°52E **19 E6**
Pavlohrad *Ukraine* 48°30N 35°52E **19 E6**
Pavlovo *Russia* 55°58N 43°5E **18 C7**
Pavlovsk *Russia* 50°26N 40°5E **19 D7**
Pavlovskaya *Russia* 46°17N 39°47E **19 E6**
Pawai, Pulau *Singapore* 1°11N 103°44E **39 d**
Pawayan *India* 28°4N 80°6E **43 E9**
Pawhuska *U.S.A.* 36°40N 96°20W **84 C6**
Pawling *U.S.A.* 41°34N 73°36W **83 E11**
Pawnee *U.S.A.* 36°20N 96°48W **84 C6**
Pawnee City *U.S.A.* 40°7N 96°9W **80 E5**
Pawtucket *U.S.A.* 41°53N 71°23W **83 E13**
Paxi *Greece* 39°14N 20°12E **23 E9**
Paximadia *Greece* 35°0N 24°35E **25 E6**
Paxton *U.S.A.* 40°27N 88°6W **80 E9**
Payakumbuh *Indonesia* 0°20S 100°35E **36 E2**
Payette *U.S.A.* 44°5N 116°56W **76 D5**
Payne Bay = Kangirsuk
  Canada 60°0N 70°0W **69 D13**
Payne L. *Canada* 59°30N 74°30W **69 D12**
Paynes Find *Australia* 29°15S 117°42E **61 E2**
Paynesville *U.S.A.* 45°23N 94°43W **80 C7**
Paysandú *Uruguay* 32°19S 58°8W **94 C4**
Payson *Ariz., U.S.A.* 34°14N 111°20W **77 J8**
Payson *Utah, U.S.A.* 40°3N 111°44W **76 F8**
Paz → *Guatemala* 13°44N 90°10W **88 D1**
Paz, B. de la *Mexico* 24°9N 110°25W **86 C2**
Pāzanān *Iran* 30°35N 49°59E **45 D6**
Pazardzhik *Bulgaria* 42°12N 24°20E **23 C11**
Pe Ell *U.S.A.* 46°34N 123°18W **78 D3**
Peabody *U.S.A.* 42°31N 70°56W **83 D14**
Peace → *Canada* 59°0N 111°25W **70 B6**
Peace Point *Canada* 59°7N 112°27W **70 B6**
Peace River *Canada* 56°15N 117°18W **70 B5**
Peach Springs *U.S.A.* 35°32N 113°25W **77 J7**
Peachland *Canada* 49°47N 119°45W **70 D5**
Peachtree City *U.S.A.* 33°25N 84°35W **85 E12**
Peak, The = Kinder Scout
  U.K. 53°24N 1°52W **12 D6**
Peak Charles △
  Australia 32°42S 121°10E **61 F3**
Peak District △ *U.K.* 53°24N 1°46W **12 D6**
Peak Hill *N.S.W.,*
  Australia 32°47S 148°11E **63 E4**
Peak Hill *W. Austral.,*
  Australia 25°35S 118°43E **61 E2**
Peak Ra. *Australia* 22°50S 148°20E **62 C4**
Peake Cr. → *Australia* 28°2S 136°7E **63 D2**
Peale, Mt. *U.S.A.* 38°26N 109°14W **76 G9**
Pearblossom *U.S.A.* 34°30N 117°55W **79 L9**
Pearl → *U.S.A.* 30°11N 89°32W **85 F10**
Pearl City *U.S.A.* 21°24N 157°59W **74 b**
Pearl Harbor *U.S.A.* 21°21N 157°57W **74 b**
Pearl River *U.S.A.* 41°4N 74°2W **83 E10**
Pearsall *U.S.A.* 28°54N 99°6W **84 G5**
Pearson Int. Toronto ✈ (YYZ)
  Canada 43°46N 79°35W **82 C5**
Peary Land *Greenland* 82°40N 33°0W **4 A6**
Pease → *U.S.A.* 34°12N 99°2W **84 D5**
Peawanuck *Canada* 55°15N 85°12W **69 D11**
Pebane *Mozam.* 17°10S 38°8E **55 F4**
Pebas *Peru* 3°10S 71°46W **92 D4**
Pebble Beach *U.S.A.* 36°34N 121°57W **78 J5**
Peć = Pejë *Serbia* 42°40N 20°17E **23 C9**
Pechenga *Russia* 69°29N 31°4E **8 B24**
Pechenizhyn *Ukraine* 48°30N 24°48E **17 D13**
Pechiguera, Pta.
  Canary Is. 28°51N 13°53W **24 F6**
Pechora *Russia* 65°10N 57°11E **18 A10**
Pechora → *Russia* 68°13N 54°15E **18 A9**
Pechorskaya Guba
  Russia 68°40N 54°0E **18 A9**
Pechory *Russia* 57°48N 27°40E **9 H22**
Pecos *N. Mex., U.S.A.* 35°35N 105°41W **77 J11**
Pecos *Tex., U.S.A.* 31°26N 103°30W **84 F3**
Pecos → *U.S.A.* 29°42N 101°22W **84 G4**
Pécs *Hungary* 46°5N 18°15E **17 E10**
Pedder, L. *Australia* 42°55S 146°10E **63 G4**
Peddie *S. Africa* 33°14S 27°7E **57 E4**
Pedernales *Dom. Rep.* 18°2N 71°44W **89 C5**
Pedieos → *Cyprus* 35°10N 33°54E **25 D12**
Pedirka *Australia* 26°40S 135°14E **63 D2**
Pedra Azul *Brazil* 16°2S 41°17W **93 G10**
Pedra Lume *C. Verde Is.* 16°40N 22°52W **50 b**
Pedreiras *Brazil* 4°32S 44°40W **93 D10**
Pedro Afonso *Brazil* 9°0S 48°10W **93 E9**
Pedro Cays *Jamaica* 17°5N 77°48W **88 C4**
Pedro de Valdivia *Chile* 22°55S 69°38W **94 A2**
Pedro Juan Caballero
  Paraguay 22°30S 55°40W **95 A4**
Pee Dee = Great Pee Dee →
  U.S.A. 33°21N 79°10W **85 E15**
Peebinga *Australia* 34°52S 140°57E **63 E3**
Peebles *U.K.* 55°40N 3°11W **11 F5**
Peekskill *U.S.A.* 41°17N 73°55W **83 E11**
Peel → *Australia* 30°50S 150°29E **63 E5**

Peel → *Canada* 67°0N 135°0W **68 C6**
Peel Sd. *Canada* 73°0N 96°0W **68 B10**
Peera Peera Poolanna L.
  Australia 26°30S 138°0E **63 D2**
Peerless Lake *Canada* 56°37N 114°40W **70 B6**
Peers *Canada* 53°40N 116°0W **70 C5**
Pegasus Bay *N.Z.* 43°20S 173°10E **59 E4**
Pegu *Burma* 17°20N 96°29E **41 L20**
Pegu Yoma *Burma* 19°0N 96°0E **41 K20**
Pehuajó *Argentina* 35°45S 62°0W **94 D3**
Pei Xian = Pizhou
  China 34°44N 116°55E **34 G9**
Peine *Chile* 23°45S 68°8W **94 A2**
Peine *Germany* 52°19N 10°14E **16 B6**
Peip'ing = Beijing
  China 39°53N 116°21E **34 E9**
Peipus, L. = Chudskoye, Ozero
  Russia 58°13N 27°30E **9 G22**
Peixe *Brazil* 12°0S 48°40W **93 F9**
Peixe → *Brazil* 21°31S 51°58W **93 H8**
Pekalongan *Indonesia* 6°53S 109°40E **36 F3**
Pekan *Malaysia* 3°30N 103°25E **39 L4**
Pekan Nenas *Malaysia* 1°31N 103°31E **39 d**
Pekanbaru *Indonesia* 0°30N 101°15E **36 D2**
Pekin *U.S.A.* 40°35N 89°40W **80 E9**
Peking = Beijing *China* 39°53N 116°21E **34 E9**
Pekutatan *Indonesia* 8°25S 114°49E **37 J17**
Pelabuhan Klang
  Malaysia 3°0N 101°23E **39 L3**
Pelabuhan Ratu, Teluk
  Indonesia 7°5S 106°30E **37 G12**
Pelabuhanratu
  Indonesia 7°0S 106°32E **37 G12**
Pelagie, Is. *Italy* 35°39N 12°33E **22 G5**
Pelaihari *Indonesia* 3°55S 114°45E **36 E4**
Peleaga, Vf. *Romania* 45°22N 22°55E **17 F12**
Pelée, Mt. *Martinique* 14°48N 61°10W **88 c**
Pelée, Pt. *Canada* 41°54N 82°31W **72 D3**
Pelee I. *Canada* 41°47N 82°40W **82 E2**
Pelekech *Kenya* 3°52N 35°8E **54 B4**
Peleng *Indonesia* 1°20S 123°30E **37 E6**
Pelentong *Malaysia* 1°32N 103°49E **39 d**
Pelican *U.S.A.* 57°58N 136°14W **70 B1**
Pelican L. *Canada* 52°28N 100°20W **71 C8**
Pelican Narrows
  Canada 55°10N 102°56W **71 B8**
Pelješac *Croatia* 42°55N 17°25E **22 C7**
Pelkosenniemi *Finland* 67°6N 27°28E **8 C22**
Pella *S. Africa* 29°1S 19°6E **56 D2**
Pella *U.S.A.* 41°25N 92°55W **80 E7**
Pello *Finland* 66°47N 23°59E **8 C20**
Pelly → *Canada* 62°47N 137°19W **70 A1**
Pelly Bay *Canada* 68°38N 89°50W **69 C11**
Peloponnese □ *Greece* 37°10N 22°0E **23 F10**
Pelorus Sd. *N.Z.* 40°59S 173°59E **59 D4**
Pelotas *Brazil* 31°42S 52°23W **95 C5**
Pelotas → *Brazil* 27°28S 51°55W **95 B5**
Pelvoux, Massif du
  France 44°52N 6°20E **20 D7**
Pemalang *Indonesia* 6°53S 109°23E **37 G13**
Pemanggil, Pulau
  Malaysia 2°37N 104°21E **39 L5**
Pematangsiantar
  Indonesia 2°57N 99°5E **36 D1**
Pemba *Mozam.* 12°58S 40°30E **55 E5**
Pemba *Zambia* 16°30S 27°28E **55 F2**
Pemba Channel *Tanzania* 5°0S 39°37E **54 D4**
Pemba I. *Tanzania* 5°0S 39°45E **54 D4**
Pemberton *Australia* 34°30S 116°0E **61 F2**
Pemberton *Canada* 50°25N 122°50W **70 C4**
Pembina → *Canada* 54°45N 114°17W **70 C6**
Pembroke *Canada* 45°50N 77°7W **72 C4**
Pembroke *U.K.* 51°41N 4°55W **13 F3**
Pembrokeshire □ *U.K.* 51°52N 4°56W **13 F3**
Pembrokeshire Coast △
  U.K. 51°50N 5°2W **13 F2**
Pen-y-Ghent *U.K.* 54°10N 2°14W **12 C5**
Penal *Trin. & Tob.* 10°9N 61°29W **93 K15**
Penang = Pinang
  Malaysia 5°25N 100°15E **39 c**
Penápolis *Brazil* 21°30S 50°0W **95 A6**
Peñarroya-Pueblonuevo
  Spain 38°19N 5°16W **21 C3**
Penarth *U.K.* 51°26N 3°11W **13 F4**
Peñas, C. de *Spain* 43°42N 5°52W **21 A3**
Peñas, G. de *Chile* 47°0S 75°0W **96 F2**
Peñas del Chache
  Canary Is. 29°6N 13°33W **24 E6**
Pench △ *India* 21°45N 79°20E **43 J8**
Pench'i = Benxi
  China 41°20N 123°48E **35 D12**
Pend Oreille → *U.S.A.* 49°4N 117°37W **76 B5**
Pend Oreille, L. *U.S.A.* 48°10N 116°21W **76 B5**
Pendembu *S. Leone* 9°7N 11°14W **50 G2**
Pender B. *Australia* 16°45S 122°42E **60 C3**
Pendleton *U.S.A.* 45°40N 118°47W **76 D4**
Pendra *India* 22°46N 81°57E **43 H9**
Penedo *Brazil* 10°15S 36°36W **93 F11**
Penetanguishene
  Canada 44°50N 79°55W **82 B5**
Penfield *U.S.A.* 41°13N 78°35W **82 E6**
Peng Chau *China* 22°17N 114°2E **33 G11**
Pengalengan *Indonesia* 7°9S 107°30E **37 G12**
Penge *Kasai-Or.,*
  Dem. Rep. of the Congo 5°30S 24°33E **54 D1**
Penge *Sud-Kivu,*
  Dem. Rep. of the Congo 4°27S 28°25E **54 C2**
Penglai *China* 37°48N 120°42E **35 F11**
Penguin *Australia* 41°8S 146°6E **63 G4**
Penhalonga *Zimbabwe* 18°52S 32°40E **55 F3**
Peniche *Portugal* 39°19N 9°22W **21 C1**
Penicuik *U.K.* 55°50N 3°13W **11 F5**
Penida, Nusa *Indonesia* 8°45S 115°30E **36 F5**
Peninsular Malaysia □
  Malaysia 4°0N 102°0E **39 L4**
Penitente, Serra do
  Brazil 8°45S 46°20W **93 E9**

Penkridge U.K. 52°44N 2°6W 12 E5
Penmarch, Pte. de France 47°48N 4°22W 20 C1
Penn Hills U.S.A. 40°28N 79°52W 82 F5
Penn Yan U.S.A. 42°40N 77°3W 82 D7
Pennant Canada 50°32N 108°14W 71 C7
Penner → India 14°35N 80°10E 40 M12
Pennines U.K. 54°45N 2°27W 12 C5
Pennington U.S.A. 39°15N 121°47W 78 F5
Pennsburg U.S.A. 40°23N 75°29W 83 F9
Pennsylvania □ U.S.A. 40°45N 77°30W 81 E15
Penny Canada 53°51N 121°20W 70 C4
Penny Str. Canada 76°30N 97°0W 69 B8
Penobscot → U.S.A. 44°30N 68°48W 81 C19
Penobscot B. U.S.A. 44°35N 68°50W 81 C19
Penola Australia 37°25S 140°48E 63 F3
Penong Australia 31°56S 133°1E 61 F5
Penonomé Panama 8°31N 80°21W 88 E3
Penrhyn Cook Is. 9°0S 158°0W 65 H12
Penrith Australia 33°43S 150°38E 63 E5
Penrith U.K. 54°40N 2°45W 12 C5
Penryn U.K. 50°9N 5°7W 13 G2
Pensacola U.S.A. 30°25N 87°13W 85 F11
Pensacola Mts. Antarctica 84°0S 40°0W 5 E1
Pense Canada 50°25N 104°59W 71 C8
Penshurst Australia 37°49S 142°20E 63 F3
Penticton Canada 49°30N 119°38W 70 D5
Pentland Australia 20°32S 145°25E 62 C4
Pentland Firth U.K. 58°43N 3°10W 11 C5
Pentland Hills U.K. 55°48N 3°25W 11 F5
Pentland Hills △ U.K. 55°50N 3°20W 11 F5
Penza Russia 53°15N 45°5E 18 D8
Penzance U.K. 50°7N 5°33W 13 G2
Penzhino Russia 63°30N 167°55E 29 C17
Penzhinskaya Guba Russia 61°30N 163°0E 29 C17
Peoria Ariz., U.S.A. 33°43N 112°14W 77 K7
Peoria Ill., U.S.A. 40°42N 89°36W 80 E9
Pepacton Res. U.S.A. 42°5N 74°58W 83 D10
Pepani → S. Africa 25°49S 22°47E 56 D3
Pera Hd. Australia 12°55S 141°37E 62 A3
Perabumulih Indonesia 3°27S 104°15E 36 E2
Perak → Malaysia 4°0N 100°50E 39 K3
Perama Kerkyra, Greece 39°34N 19°54E 25 A3
Perama Kriti, Greece 35°20N 24°40E 25 D6
Perancak Indonesia 8°24S 114°37E 37 J17
Peräpohjola Finland 66°16N 26°10E 8 C22
Percé Canada 48°31N 64°13W 73 C7
Perche, Collines du France 48°30N 0°40E 20 B4
Percival Lakes Australia 21°25S 125°0E 60 D4
Percy Is. Australia 21°39S 150°16E 62 C5
Perdido, Mte. Spain 42°40N 0°5E 21 A6
Perdu, Mt. = Perdido, Mte. Spain 42°40N 0°5E 21 A6
Pereira Colombia 4°49N 75°43W 92 C3
Perenjori Australia 29°26S 116°16E 61 E2
Pereyaslav-Khmelnytskyy Ukraine 50°3N 31°28E 19 D5
Pérez, I. Mexico 22°24N 89°42W 87 C7
Pergamino Argentina 33°52S 60°30W 94 C3
Pergau → Malaysia 5°23N 102°2E 39 K3
Perham U.S.A. 46°36N 95°34W 80 B6
Perhentian, Kepulauan Malaysia 5°54N 102°42E 39 K4
Péribonka → Canada 48°45N 72°5W 73 C5
Péribonka, L. Canada 50°1N 71°10W 73 B5
Perico Argentina 24°20S 65°5W 94 A2
Pericos Mexico 25°3N 107°42W 86 B3
Périgueux France 45°10N 0°42E 20 D4
Perijá, Sierra de Colombia 9°30N 73°3W 92 B4
Perijá △ Venezuela 9°30N 72°55W 89 E5
Peristerona → Cyprus 35°8N 33°5E 25 D12
Perito Moreno Argentina 46°36S 70°56W 96 F2
Perkasie U.S.A. 40°22N 75°18W 83 F9
Perlas, Arch. de las Panama 8°41N 79°7W 88 E4
Perlas, Punta de Nic. 12°30N 83°30W 88 D3
Perm Russia 58°0N 56°10E 18 C10
Pernambuco = Recife Brazil 8°0S 35°0W 93 E12
Pernambuco □ Brazil 8°0S 37°0W 93 E11
Pernatty Lagoon Australia 31°30S 137°12E 63 E2
Pernik Bulgaria 42°35N 23°2E 23 C10
Peron Is. Australia 13°9S 130°4E 60 B5
Peron Pen. Australia 26°0S 113°10E 61 E1
Perow Canada 54°35N 126°10W 70 C3
Perpignan France 42°42N 2°53E 20 E5
Perris U.S.A. 33°47N 117°14W 79 M9
Perry Fla., U.S.A. 30°7N 83°35W 85 F13
Perry Ga., U.S.A. 32°28N 83°44W 85 E13
Perry Iowa, U.S.A. 41°51N 94°6W 80 E6
Perry Okla., U.S.A. 36°17N 97°14W 84 C6
Perryton U.S.A. 36°24N 100°48W 84 C4
Perryville U.S.A. 37°43N 89°52W 80 G9
Persepolis Iran 29°55N 52°50E 45 D7
Pershotravensk Ukraine 50°13N 27°40E 17 C14
Persia = Iran ■ Asia 33°0N 53°0E 45 C7
Persian Gulf Asia 27°0N 50°0E 45 E6
Perth Australia 31°57S 115°52E 61 F2
Perth Canada 44°55N 76°15W 83 B8
Perth U.K. 56°24N 3°26W 11 E5
Perth & Kinross □ U.K. 56°45N 3°55W 11 E5
Perth Amboy U.S.A. 40°30N 74°15W 83 F10
Perth-Andover Canada 46°44N 67°42W 73 C6
Perth Basin Ind. Oc. 30°0S 108°0E 64 L2
Peru Ind., U.S.A. 40°45N 86°4W 80 E10
Peru N.Y., U.S.A. 44°35N 73°32W 83 B11
Peru ■ S. Amer. 4°0S 75°0W 92 D4
Peru Basin Pac. Oc. 20°0S 95°0W 65 J18
Peru-Chile Trench Pac. Oc. 20°0S 72°0W 92 G3
Perúgia Italy 43°7N 12°23E 22 C5
Pervomaysk Ukraine 48°10N 30°46E 19 E5
Pervouralsk Russia 56°59N 59°59E 18 C10
Pésaro Italy 43°54N 12°55E 22 C5
Pescara Italy 42°28N 14°13E 22 C6
Peshawar Pakistan 34°2N 71°37E 42 B4
Peshkopi Albania 41°41N 20°25E 23 D9
Peshtigo U.S.A. 45°3N 87°45W 80 C10
Pesqueira Brazil 8°20S 36°42W 93 E11
Petah Tiqwa Israel 32°6N 34°53E 46 C3
Petaling Jaya Malaysia 3°4N 101°42E 39 L3
Petaloudes Greece 36°18N 28°5E 25 C10
Petaluma U.S.A. 38°14N 122°39W 78 G4
Pétange Lux. 49°33N 5°55E 15 E5
Petaro Pakistan 25°31N 68°18E 42 G3
Petatlán Mexico 17°31N 101°16W 86 D4
Petauke Zambia 14°14S 31°20E 55 E3
Petawawa Canada 45°54N 77°17W 72 C4
Petén Itzá, L. Guatemala 16°58N 89°50W 88 C2
Peter I. Br. Virgin Is. 18°22N 64°35W 89 e
Peter I. Øy Antarctica 69°0S 91°0W 5 C16
Peter Pond L. Canada 55°55N 108°44W 71 B7
Peterbell Canada 48°36N 83°21W 72 C3
Peterborough Australia 32°58S 138°51E 63 E2
Peterborough Canada 44°20N 78°20W 82 B6
Peterborough U.K. 52°35N 0°15W 13 E7
Peterborough U.S.A. 42°53N 71°57W 83 D13
Peterborough □ U.K. 52°35N 0°15W 13 E7
Peterculter U.K. 57°6N 2°16W 11 D6
Peterhead U.K. 57°31N 1°48W 11 D7
Peterlee U.K. 54°47N 1°20W 12 C6
Petermann Ranges Australia 26°0S 130°30E 61 E5
Petersburg Alaska, U.S.A. 56°48N 132°58W 74 a
Petersburg Pa., U.S.A. 40°34N 78°3W 82 F6
Petersburg Va., U.S.A. 37°14N 77°24W 81 G15
Petersburg W. Va., U.S.A. 39°1N 79°5W 81 F14
Petersfield U.K. 51°1N 0°56W 13 F7
Petit-Canal Guadeloupe 16°25N 61°31W 88 b
Petit Goâve Haiti 18°27N 72°51W 89 C5
Petit Jardin Canada 48°28N 59°14W 73 C8
Petit Lac Manicouagan Canada 51°25N 67°40W 73 B6
Petit-Mécatina → Canada 50°40N 59°30W 73 B8
Petit-Mécatina, Î. du Canada 50°30N 59°25W 73 B8
Petit Piton St. Lucia 13°51N 61°5W 89 f
Petit-Saguenay Canada 48°15N 70°4W 73 C5
Petitcodiac Canada 45°57N 65°11W 73 C6
Petite Terre, Îles de la Guadeloupe 16°13N 61°9W 88 b
Petitot → Canada 60°14N 123°29W 70 A4
Petitsikapau L. Canada 54°37N 66°25W 73 B6
Petlad India 22°30N 72°45E 42 H5
Peto Mexico 20°8N 88°55W 87 C7
Petone N.Z. 41°13S 174°53E 59 D5
Petorca Chile 32°15S 70°56W 94 C1
Petoskey U.S.A. 45°22N 84°57W 81 C11
Petra Jordan 30°20N 35°22E 46 E4
Petra Spain 39°37N 3°6E 24 B10
Petra, Ostrova Russia 76°15N 118°30E 4 B13
Petra Velikogo, Zaliv Russia 42°40N 132°0E 30 C6
Petrich Bulgaria 41°24N 23°13E 23 D10
Petrified Forest △ U.S.A. 35°0N 109°30W 77 J9
Petrikov = Pyetrikaw Belarus 52°11N 28°29E 17 B15
Petrolândia Brazil 9°5S 38°20W 93 E11
Petrolia Canada 42°54N 82°9W 82 D2
Petrolina Brazil 9°24S 40°30W 93 E10
Petropavl Kazakhstan 54°53N 69°13E 28 D7
Petropavlovsk = Petropavl Kazakhstan 54°53N 69°13E 28 D7
Petropavlovsk-Kamchatskiy Russia 53°3N 158°43E 29 D16
Petrópolis Brazil 22°33S 43°9W 95 A7
Petroşani Romania 45°28N 23°20E 17 F12
Petrovaradin Serbia 45°16N 19°55E 23 B8
Petrovsk Russia 52°22N 45°19E 18 D8
Petrovsk-Zabaykalskiy Russia 51°20N 108°55E 29 D11
Petrozavodsk Russia 61°41N 34°20E 18 B5
Petrus Steyn S. Africa 27°38S 28°8E 57 D4
Petrusburg S. Africa 29°4S 25°26E 56 D4
Peumo Chile 34°21S 71°12W 94 C1
Peureulak Indonesia 4°48N 97°45E 36 D1
Pevek Russia 69°41N 171°19E 29 C18
Pforzheim Germany 48°52N 8°41E 16 D5
Pha Taem △ Thailand 15°32N 105°30E 38 E5
Phaestos Greece 35°2N 24°50E 25 D6
Phagwara India 31°10N 75°40E 42 D6
Phala Botswana 23°45S 26°50E 56 C4
Phalera = Phulera India 26°52N 75°16E 42 F6
Phalodi India 27°12N 72°24E 42 F5
Phaluai, Ko Thailand 9°32N 99°41E 39 b
Phan Thailand 19°28N 99°43E 38 C2
Phan Rang Vietnam 11°34N 109°0E 39 G7
Phan Ri = Hoa Da Vietnam 11°16N 108°40E 39 G7
Phan Thiet Vietnam 11°1N 108°9E 39 G7
Phanat Nikhom Thailand 13°27N 101°11E 38 F3
Phangan, Ko Thailand 9°45N 100°0E 39 H3
Phangnga Thailand 8°28N 98°30E 39 H2
Phangnga, Ao Thailand 8°16N 98°33E 39 a
Phanom Sarakham Thailand 13°45N 101°21E 38 F3
Phaphund India 26°36N 79°28E 43 F8
Pharenda India 27°5N 83°17E 43 F10
Pharr U.S.A. 26°12N 98°11W 84 H5
Phatthalung Thailand 7°39N 100°6E 39 J3
Phayao Thailand 19°11N 99°55E 38 C2
Phelps U.S.A. 42°58N 77°3W 82 D7
Phelps L. Canada 59°15N 103°15W 71 B8
Phenix City U.S.A. 32°28N 85°0W 85 E12
Phet Buri Thailand 13°1N 99°55E 38 F2
Phetchabun Thailand 16°25N 101°8E 38 D3
Phetchabun, Thiu Khao Thailand 16°0N 101°20E 38 E3
Phetchaburi = Phet Buri Thailand 13°1N 99°55E 38 F2
Phi Phi, Ko Thailand 7°45N 98°46E 39 J2
Phiafay Laos 14°48N 106°0E 38 E6
Phibun Mangsahan Thailand 15°14N 105°14E 38 E5
Phichai Thailand 17°22N 100°10E 38 D3
Phichit Thailand 16°26N 100°22E 38 D3
Philadelphia Miss., U.S.A. 32°46N 89°7W 85 E10
Philadelphia N.Y., U.S.A. 44°9N 75°43W 83 B9
Philadelphia Pa., U.S.A. 39°57N 75°9W 83 G9
Philip U.S.A. 44°2N 101°40W 80 C3
Philippeville Belgium 50°12N 4°33E 15 D4
Philippi U.S.A. 39°9N 80°3W 81 F13
Philippi L. Australia 24°20S 138°55E 62 C2
Philippine Basin Pac. Oc. 17°0N 132°0E 64 F5
Philippine Sea Pac. Oc. 18°0N 125°0E 64 F4
Philippine Trench = Mindanao Trench Pac. Oc. 12°0N 126°6E 37 B7
Philippines ■ Asia 12°0N 123°0E 37 B6
Philippolis S. Africa 30°15S 25°16E 56 E4
Philippopolis = Plovdiv Bulgaria 42°8N 24°44E 23 C11
Philipsburg Canada 45°2N 73°5W 83 A11
Philipsburg Mont., U.S.A. 46°20N 113°18W 76 C7
Philipsburg Pa., U.S.A. 40°54N 78°13W 82 F6
Philipstown = Daingean Ireland 53°18N 7°17W 10 C4
Philipstown S. Africa 30°28S 24°30E 56 E3
Phillip I. Australia 38°30S 145°12E 63 F4
Phillips U.S.A. 45°42N 90°24W 80 C8
Phillipsburg Kans., U.S.A. 39°45N 99°19W 80 F4
Phillipsburg N.J., U.S.A. 40°42N 75°12W 83 F9
Philmont U.S.A. 42°15N 73°39W 83 D11
Philomath U.S.A. 44°32N 123°22W 76 D2
Phimai Thailand 15°13N 102°30E 38 E4
Phitsanulok Thailand 16°50N 100°12E 38 D3
Phnom Dangrek Thailand 14°20N 104°0E 38 E5
Phnom Penh Cambodia 11°33N 104°55E 39 G5
Phnum Penh = Phnom Penh Cambodia 11°33N 104°55E 39 G5
Phoenicia U.S.A. 42°5N 74°14W 83 D10
Phoenix Mauritius 20°17S 57°30E 53 d
Phoenix Ariz., U.S.A. 33°26N 112°4W 77 K7
Phoenix N.Y., U.S.A. 43°14N 76°18W 83 C8
Phoenix Is. Kiribati 3°30S 172°0W 64 H10
Phoenixville U.S.A. 40°8N 75°31W 83 F9
Phon Thailand 15°49N 102°36E 38 E4
Phon Tiou Laos 17°53N 104°37E 38 D5
Phong → Thailand 16°23N 102°56E 38 D4
Phong Saly Laos 21°42N 102°9E 38 B4
Phong Tho Vietnam 22°32N 103°21E 38 A4
Phonhong Laos 18°30N 102°25E 38 C4
Phonum Thailand 8°49N 98°48E 39 H2
Phosphate Hill Australia 21°53S 139°58E 62 C2
Photharam Thailand 13°41N 99°51E 38 F2
Phra Nakhon Si Ayutthaya Thailand 14°25N 100°30E 38 E3
Phra Thong, Ko Thailand 9°5N 98°17E 39 H2
Phrae Thailand 18°7N 100°9E 38 C3
Phrom Phiram Thailand 17°2N 100°12E 38 D3
Phu Bia Laos 19°10N 103°0E 38 C4
Phu Chong-Na Yoi △ Thailand 14°25N 105°30E 38 E5
Phu Dien Vietnam 18°58N 105°31E 38 C5
Phu Hin Rang Kla △ Thailand 17°0N 100°59E 38 D3
Phu Kradung △ Thailand 17°2N 101°44E 38 D3
Phu Loi Laos 20°14N 103°14E 38 B4
Phu Luang △ Thailand 17°15N 101°29E 38 D3
Phu Ly Vietnam 20°35N 105°50E 38 B5
Phu Phan △ Thailand 17°0N 103°56E 38 D4
Phu Quoc, Dao Vietnam 10°20N 104°0E 39 G4
Phu Tho Vietnam 21°24N 105°13E 38 B5
Phuc Yen Vietnam 21°16N 105°45E 38 B5
Phuket Thailand 7°53N 98°24E 39 a
Phuket, Ko Thailand 8°0N 98°22E 39 a
Phul India 30°19N 75°14E 42 D6
Phulad India 25°38N 73°49E 42 G5
Phulchari Bangla. 25°11N 89°37E 43 G13
Phulera India 26°52N 75°16E 42 F6
Phulpur India 25°31N 82°49E 43 G10
Phun Phin Thailand 9°7N 99°12E 39 H2
Piacenza Italy 45°1N 9°40E 20 D8
Piai, Tanjung Malaysia 1°17N 103°30E 39 d
Pian Cr. → Australia 30°2S 148°12E 63 E4
Pian-Upe △ Uganda 1°44N 34°20E 54 B3
Pianosa Italy 42°35N 10°5E 22 C4
Piapot Canada 49°59N 109°8W 71 D7
Piatra Neamţ Romania 46°56N 26°21E 17 E14
Piauí □ Brazil 7°0S 43°0W 93 E10
Piauí → Brazil 6°38S 42°42W 93 E10
Piave → Italy 45°32N 12°44E 22 B5
Pibor Post Sudan 6°47N 33°3E 51 G12
Picardie □ France 49°50N 3°0E 20 B5
Picardy = Picardie □ France 49°50N 3°0E 20 B5
Picayune U.S.A. 30°32N 89°41W 85 F10
Pichhor India 25°58N 78°20E 43 G8
Pichilemu Chile 34°22S 72°0W 94 C1
Pichor India 25°11N 78°11E 42 G8
Pickerel L. Canada 48°40N 91°25W 72 C1
Pickering U.K. 54°15N 0°46W 12 C7
Pickering, Vale of U.K. 54°14N 0°45W 12 C7
Pickle Lake Canada 51°30N 90°12W 72 B1
Pickwick L. U.S.A. 35°4N 88°15W 85 D10
Pico Azores 38°28N 28°20W 50 a
Pico Bonito △ Honduras 15°34N 86°48W 88 C2
Pico Truncado Argentina 46°40S 68°0W 96 F3
Picos Brazil 7°5S 41°28W 93 E10
Picton Australia 34°12S 150°34E 63 E5
Picton Canada 44°1N 77°9W 82 B7
Picton N.Z. 41°18S 174°3E 59 D5
Pictou Canada 45°41N 62°42W 73 C7
Picture Butte Canada 49°55N 112°45W 70 D6
Pictured Rocks △ U.S.A. 46°30N 86°30W 80 B10
Picún Leufú Argentina 39°30S 69°5W 96 D3
Pidurutalagala Sri Lanka 7°10N 80°50E 40 R12
Piedmont = Piemonte □ Italy 45°0N 8°0E 20 D7
Piedmont Ala., U.S.A. 33°55N 85°37W 85 E12
Piedmont S.C., U.S.A. 34°42N 82°28W 75 D10
Piedras Negras Mexico 28°42N 100°31W 86 B4
Pieksämäki Finland 62°18N 27°10E 8 E22
Pielinen Finland 63°15N 29°40E 8 E23
Piemonte □ Italy 45°0N 8°0E 20 D7
Pienaarsrivier S. Africa 25°15S 28°18E 57 D4
Piercefield U.S.A. 44°13N 74°35W 83 B10
Pierceland Canada 54°20N 109°46W 71 C7
Pierpont U.S.A. 41°45N 80°34W 82 E4
Pierre U.S.A. 44°22N 100°21W 80 C3
Pierreville Trin. & Tob. 10°16N 61°0W 93 K16
Piet Retief S. Africa 27°1S 30°50E 57 D5
Pietarsaari Finland 63°40N 22°43E 8 E20
Pietermaritzburg S. Africa 29°35S 30°25E 57 D5
Pietersburg = Polokwane S. Africa 23°54S 29°25E 57 C4
Pietrosul, Vf. Maramureş, Romania 47°35N 24°43E 17 E13
Pietrosul, Vf. Suceava, Romania 47°12N 25°18E 17 E13
Pigeon L. Canada 44°27N 78°30W 82 B6
Piggott U.S.A. 36°23N 90°11W 85 C9
Pigüe Argentina 37°36S 62°25W 94 D3
Pihani India 27°36N 80°15E 43 F9
Pihlajavesi Finland 61°45N 28°45E 8 F23
Pijijiapan Mexico 15°42N 93°14W 87 D6
Pikangikum Canada 51°49N 94°0W 71 C10
Pikes Peak U.S.A. 38°50N 105°3W 76 G11
Piketberg S. Africa 32°55S 18°40E 56 E2
Pikeville U.S.A. 37°29N 82°31W 81 G12
Pikou China 39°18N 122°22E 35 E12
Pikwitonei Canada 55°35N 97°9W 71 B9
Piła Poland 53°10N 16°48E 17 B9
Pilanesberg △ S. Africa 25°15S 27°4E 56 D4
Pilani India 28°22N 75°33E 42 E6
Pilar Paraguay 26°50S 58°20W 94 B4
Pilaya → Bolivia 20°55S 64°4W 92 H6
Pilbara Australia 23°35S 117°25E 60 D2
Pilcomayo → Paraguay 25°21S 57°42W 94 B4
Pilgrim's Rest S. Africa 24°55S 30°44E 57 C5
Pilibhit India 28°40N 79°50E 43 E8
Pilica → Poland 51°52N 21°17E 17 C11
Pilipinas = Philippines ■ Asia 12°0N 123°0E 37 B6
Pilkhawa India 28°43N 77°42E 42 E7
Pilliga Australia 30°21S 148°54E 63 E4
Pilos Greece 36°55N 21°42E 23 F9
Pilot Mound Canada 49°15N 98°54W 71 D9
Pilot Point U.S.A. 33°24N 96°58W 84 E6
Pilot Rock U.S.A. 45°29N 118°50W 76 D4
Pima U.S.A. 32°54N 109°50W 77 K9
Pimba Australia 31°18S 136°46E 63 E2
Pimenta Bueno Brazil 11°35S 61°10W 92 F6
Pimentel Peru 6°45S 79°55W 92 E3
Pin Valley △ India 31°50N 77°50E 42 D7
Pinang Malaysia 5°25N 100°15E 39 c
Pinar, C. des Spain 39°53N 3°12E 24 B10
Pinar del Río Cuba 22°26N 83°40W 88 B3
Pınarhisar Turkey 41°37N 27°30E 23 D12
Pinatubo, Mt. Phil. 15°8N 120°21E 37 A6
Pinawa Canada 50°9N 95°50W 71 C9
Pincher Creek Canada 49°30N 113°57W 70 D6
Pinchi L. Canada 54°38N 124°30W 70 C4
Pinckneyville U.S.A. 38°5N 89°23W 80 F9
Pińczów Poland 50°32N 20°32E 17 C11
Pindar Australia 28°30S 115°47E 61 E2
Pindi Gheb Pakistan 33°14N 72°21E 42 C5
Pindos Oros Greece 40°0N 21°0E 23 E9
Pindus Mts. = Pindos Oros Greece 40°0N 21°0E 23 E9
Pine → B.C., Canada 56°8N 120°43W 70 B4
Pine → Sask., Canada 58°50N 105°38W 71 B7
Pine, C. Canada 46°37N 53°32W 73 C9
Pine Bluff U.S.A. 34°13N 92°1W 84 D8
Pine Bluffs U.S.A. 41°11N 104°4W 76 F11
Pine City U.S.A. 45°50N 92°59W 80 C7
Pine Cr. → U.S.A. 41°10N 77°16W 82 E7
Pine Creek Australia 13°50S 131°50E 60 B5
Pine Falls Canada 50°34N 96°11W 71 C9
Pine Flat L. U.S.A. 36°50N 119°20W 78 J7
Pine Grove U.S.A. 40°33N 76°23W 83 F8
Pine Hill Australia 23°38S 146°57E 62 C4
Pine Pass Canada 55°25N 122°42W 70 B4
Pine Point Canada 60°50N 114°28W 70 A6
Pine Ridge U.S.A. 43°2N 102°33W 80 D2
Pine River Canada 51°45N 100°30W 71 C8
Pine River U.S.A. 46°43N 94°24W 80 B6
Pine Valley U.S.A. 32°50N 116°32W 79 N10
Pinecrest U.S.A. 38°12N 120°1W 78 G6
Pinedale Calif., U.S.A. 36°50N 119°48W 78 J7
Pinedale Wyo., U.S.A. 42°52N 109°52W 76 E9
Pinega → Russia 64°30N 44°19E 18 B8
Pinehouse L. Canada 55°32N 106°35W 71 B7
Pineimuta → Canada 52°8N 88°33W 72 B1
Pinerolo Italy 44°53N 7°21E 20 D7
Pines, Akra Greece 40°5N 24°20E 23 D11
Pinetop-Lakeside U.S.A. 34°9N 109°58W 77 J9
Pinetown S. Africa 29°48S 30°54E 57 D5
Pineville U.S.A. 31°19N 92°26W 84 F8
Ping → Thailand 15°42N 100°9E 38 E3
Pingaring Australia 32°40S 118°32E 61 F2
Pingding China 37°47N 113°38E 34 F7
Pingdingshan China 33°43N 113°27E 34 H7
Pingdong Taiwan 22°39N 120°30E 33 D7
Pingdu China 36°42N 119°59E 35 F10
Pingelly Australia 32°32S 117°5E 61 F2
Pingliang China 35°35N 106°31E 34 G4
Pinglu China 39°31N 112°30E 34 E7
Pingluo China 38°52N 106°30E 34 E4
Pingquan China 41°1N 118°37E 35 D10
Pingrup Australia 33°32S 118°29E 61 F2
P'ingtung Taiwan 22°38N 120°30E 33 D7
Pingwu China 32°25N 104°30E 34 H3
Pingxiang China 22°6N 106°46E 32 D5
Pingyao China 37°12N 112°10E 34 F7
Pingyi China 35°30N 117°35E 35 G9
Pingyin China 36°20N 116°25E 34 F9
Pingyuan China 37°10N 116°22E 34 F9
Pinhal Brazil 22°10S 46°46W 95 A6
Pinheiro Brazil 2°31S 45°5W 93 D9
Pinheiro Machado Brazil 31°34S 53°23W 95 C5
Pinhel Portugal 40°50N 7°1W 21 B2
Pini Indonesia 0°10N 98°40E 36 D1
Pinios → Greece 39°55N 22°41E 23 E10
Pinjarra Australia 32°37S 115°52E 61 F2
Pink Mountain Canada 57°3N 122°52W 70 B4
Pinnacles △ U.S.A. 36°25N 121°12W 78 J5
Pinnaroo Australia 35°17S 140°53E 63 F3
Pinon Hills U.S.A. 34°26N 117°39W 79 L9
Pinos Mexico 22°18N 101°34W 86 C4
Pinos, Mt. U.S.A. 34°49N 119°8W 79 L7
Pinos Pt. U.S.A. 36°38N 121°57W 77 H3
Pinrang Indonesia 3°46S 119°41E 37 E5
Pins, Pte. aux Canada 42°15N 81°51W 82 D3
Pinsk Belarus 52°10N 26°1E 17 B14
Pintados Chile 20°35S 69°40W 92 H5
Pinyug Russia 60°5N 48°0E 18 B8
Pioche U.S.A. 37°56N 114°27W 77 H6
Piombino Italy 42°55N 10°32E 22 C4
Pioner, Ostrov Russia 79°50N 92°0E 29 B10
Piopiotaki = Milford Sd. N.Z. 44°41S 167°47E 59 F1
Piorini, L. Brazil 3°15S 62°35W 92 D6
Piotrków Trybunalski Poland 51°23N 19°43E 17 C10
Pīp Iran 26°45N 60°10E 45 E9
Pipar India 26°25N 73°31E 42 F5
Pipar Road India 26°27N 73°27E 42 F5
Piparia Mad. P., India 22°45N 78°23E 42 H8
Piparia Mad. P., India 21°49N 77°37E 42 J7
Pipestone U.S.A. 44°0N 96°19W 80 D5
Pipestone → Canada 52°53N 89°23W 72 B2
Pipestone Cr. → Canada 49°38N 100°15W 71 D8
Piplan Pakistan 32°17N 71°21E 42 C4
Piploda India 23°37N 74°56E 42 H6
Pipmuacan, Rés. Canada 49°45N 70°30W 73 C5
Pippingarra Australia 20°27S 118°42E 60 D2
Piqua U.S.A. 40°9N 84°15W 81 E11
Piquiri → Brazil 24°3S 54°14W 95 A5
Pir Panjal Range India 32°30N 76°50E 42 C7
Pīr Sohrāb Iran 25°44N 60°54E 45 E9
Piracicaba Brazil 22°45S 47°40W 95 A6
Piracuruca Brazil 3°50S 41°50W 93 D10
Pirae Tahiti 17°31S 149°32W 59 d
Piræus = Pireas Greece 37°57N 23°42E 23 F10
Piraiévs = Pireas Greece 37°57N 23°42E 23 F10
Pirajuí Brazil 21°59S 49°29W 95 A6
Piram I. India 21°36N 72°21E 42 J5
Pirané Argentina 25°42S 59°6W 94 B4
Pirapora Brazil 17°20S 44°56W 93 G10
Pirawa India 24°10N 76°2E 42 G7
Pireas Greece 37°57N 23°42E 23 F10
Pirgos Greece 37°40N 21°27E 23 F9
Piribebuy Paraguay 25°26S 57°2W 94 B4
Pirimapun Indonesia 6°20S 138°24E 37 F9
Pirin Planina Bulgaria 41°40N 23°30E 23 D10
Pírineos = Pyrénées Europe 42°45N 0°18E 20 E4
Piripiri Brazil 4°15S 41°46W 93 D10
Pirlangimpi Australia 11°24S 130°26E 60 B5
Pirmasens Germany 49°12N 7°36E 16 D4
Pirot Serbia 43°9N 22°33E 23 C10
Piru Indonesia 3°4S 128°12E 37 E7
Piru U.S.A. 34°25N 118°48W 79 L8
Pisa Italy 43°43N 10°23E 22 C4
Pisagua Chile 19°40S 70°15W 92 G4
Pisco Peru 13°50S 76°12W 92 F3
Písek Czech Rep. 49°19N 14°10E 16 D8
Pishan China 37°30N 78°33E 32 C2
Pīshīn Iran 26°6N 61°47E 45 E9
Pishin Pakistan 30°35N 67°0E 42 D2
Pishin Lora → Pakistan 29°9N 64°5E 42 E1
Pising Indonesia 5°8S 121°53E 37 F6
Pismo Beach U.S.A. 35°9N 120°38W 79 K6
Pissis, Cerro Argentina 27°45S 68°48W 94 B2
Pissouri Cyprus 34°40N 32°42E 25 E11
Pistóia Italy 43°55N 10°54E 22 C4
Pistol B. Canada 62°25N 92°37W 71 A10
Pisuerga → Spain 41°33N 4°52W 21 B3
Pit → U.S.A. 40°47N 122°6W 76 F2
Pitarpunga, L. Australia 34°24S 143°30E 63 E3
Pitcairn I. Pac. Oc. 25°5S 130°5W 65 K14
Pitch L. Trin. & Tob. 10°12N 61°39W 93 K15
Piteå Sweden 65°20N 21°25E 8 D19
Piteälven → Sweden 65°20N 21°25E 8 D19
Piteşti Romania 44°52N 24°54E 17 F13
Pithapuram India 17°10N 82°15E 41 L13
Pithara Australia 30°20S 116°35E 61 F2
Pithoragarh India 29°35N 80°13E 43 E9

Pithoro *Pakistan* 25°31N 69°23E **42** G3
Pitlochry *U.K.* 56°42N 3°44W **11** E5
Pitsilia *Cyprus* 34°55N 33°0E **25** E12
Pitt I. *Canada* 53°30N 129°50W **70** C3
Pittsburg *Calif., U.S.A.* 38°2N 121°53W **78** G5
Pittsburg *Kans., U.S.A.* 37°25N 94°42W **80** G6
Pittsburg *Tex., U.S.A.* 33°0N 94°59W **84** E7
Pittsburgh *U.S.A.* 40°26N 79°58W **82** F5
Pittsfield *Ill., U.S.A.* 39°36N 90°49W **80** F8
Pittsfield *Maine, U.S.A.* 44°47N 69°23W **81** C19
Pittsfield *Mass., U.S.A.* 42°27N 73°15W **83** D11
Pittsfield *N.H., U.S.A.* 43°18N 71°20W **83** C13
Pittston *U.S.A.* 41°19N 75°47W **83** E9
Pittsworth *Australia* 27°41S 151°37E **63** D5
Pituri → *Australia* 22°35S 138°30E **62** C2
Piura *Peru* 5°15S 80°38W **92** E2
Pixley *U.S.A.* 35°58N 119°18W **78** K7
Pizhou *China* 34°44N 116°55E **34** G9
Placentia *Canada* 47°20N 54°0W **73** C9
Placentia B. *Canada* 47°0N 54°40W **73** C9
Placerville *U.S.A.* 38°44N 120°48W **78** G6
Placetas *Cuba* 22°15N 79°44W **88** B4
Plainfield *N.J., U.S.A.* 40°37N 74°25W **83** F10
Plainfield *Ohio, U.S.A.* 40°13N 81°43W **82** F3
Plainfield *Vt., U.S.A.* 44°17N 72°26W **83** B12
Plains *Mont., U.S.A.* 47°28N 114°53W **76** C6
Plains *Tex., U.S.A.* 33°11N 102°50W **84** E3
Plainview *Nebr., U.S.A.* 42°21N 97°47W **80** D5
Plainview *Tex., U.S.A.* 34°11N 101°43W **84** D4
Plainwell *U.S.A.* 42°27N 85°38W **81** D11
Plaistow *U.S.A.* 42°50N 71°6W **83** D13
Plaka, Akra *Greece* 35°11N 26°19E **25** D8
Plana Cays *Bahamas* 22°38N 73°30W **89** B5
Planada *U.S.A.* 37°16N 120°19W **78** H6
Plano *U.S.A.* 33°1N 96°42W **84** E6
Plant City *U.S.A.* 28°1N 82°7W **85** G13
Plaquemine *U.S.A.* 30°17N 91°14W **84** F9
Plasencia *Spain* 40°3N 6°8W **21** B2
Plaster City *U.S.A.* 32°47N 115°51W **79** N11
Plaster Rock *Canada* 46°53N 67°22W **73** C6
Plastun *Russia* 44°45N 136°19E **30** B8
Plata, Río de la → *S. Amer.* 34°45S 57°30W **94** C4
Plátani → *Italy* 37°23N 13°16E **22** F5
Platanos *Greece* 35°28N 23°33E **25** D5
Platte *U.S.A.* 43°23N 98°51W **80** D4
Platte → *Mo., U.S.A.* 39°16N 94°50W **80** F6
Platte → *Nebr., U.S.A.* 41°4N 95°53W **80** E6
Platteville *U.S.A.* 42°44N 90°29W **80** D8
Plattsburgh *U.S.A.* 44°42N 73°28W **83** B11
Plattsmouth *U.S.A.* 41°1N 95°53W **80** E6
Plauen *Germany* 50°30N 12°8E **16** C7
Plavinas *Latvia* 56°35N 25°46E **9** H21
Playa Blanca *Canary Is.* 28°55N 13°37W **24** F6
Playa Blanca Sur *Canary Is.* 28°51N 13°50W **24** F6
Playa de las Americas *Canary Is.* 28°5N 16°43W **24** F3
Playa de Mogán *Canary Is.* 27°48N 15°47W **24** G4
Playa del Carmen *Mexico* 20°37N 87°4W **87** C7
Playa del Inglés *Canary Is.* 27°45N 15°33W **24** G4
Playa Esmerelda *Canary Is.* 28°8N 14°16W **24** F5
Playgreen L. *Canada* 54°0N 98°15W **71** C9
Pleasant Bay *Canada* 46°51N 60°48W **73** C7
Pleasant Hill *U.S.A.* 37°57N 122°4W **78** H4
Pleasant Mount *U.S.A.* 41°44N 75°26W **83** E9
Pleasanton *Calif., U.S.A.* 37°39N 121°52W **78** H5
Pleasanton *Tex., U.S.A.* 28°58N 98°29W **84** G5
Pleasantville *N.J., U.S.A.* 39°24N 74°32W **81** F16
Pleasantville *Pa., U.S.A.* 41°35N 79°34W **82** E5
Plei Ku *Vietnam* 13°57N 108°0E **38** F7
Plenty → *Australia* 23°25S 136°31E **62** C2
Plenty, B. of *N.Z.* 37°45S 177°0E **59** B6
Plentywood *U.S.A.* 48°47N 104°34W **76** B11
Plesetsk *Russia* 62°43N 40°20E **18** B7
Plessisville *Canada* 46°14N 71°47W **73** C5
Plétipi, L. *Canada* 51°44N 70°6W **73** B5
Pleven *Bulgaria* 43°26N 24°37E **23** C11
Plevlja *Montenegro* 43°21N 19°21E **23** C8
Plevna *Canada* 44°58N 76°59W **82** B8
Płock *Poland* 52°32N 19°40E **17** B10
Plöckenstein *Germany* 48°46N 13°51E **16** D7
Ploiești *Romania* 44°57N 26°5E **17** F14
Plonge, Lac la *Canada* 55°8N 107°20W **71** B7
Plovdiv *Bulgaria* 42°8N 24°44E **23** C11
Plover Cove Res. *China* 22°28N 114°15E **33** G11
Plum *U.S.A.* 40°29N 79°47W **82** F5
Plum I. *U.S.A.* 41°11N 72°12W **83** E12
Plumas *U.S.A.* 39°45N 120°4W **78** F6
Plummer *U.S.A.* 47°20N 116°53W **76** C5
Plumtree *Zimbabwe* 20°27S 27°55E **55** G2
Plungė *Lithuania* 55°53N 21°59E **9** J19
Plymouth *Trin. & Tob.* 11°14N 60°48W **93** J16
Plymouth *U.K.* 50°22N 4°10W **13** G3
Plymouth *Calif., U.S.A.* 38°29N 120°51W **78** G6
Plymouth *Ind., U.S.A.* 41°21N 86°19W **80** E10
Plymouth *Mass., U.S.A.* 41°57N 70°40W **83** E14
Plymouth *N.C., U.S.A.* 35°52N 76°43W **85** D16
Plymouth *N.H., U.S.A.* 43°46N 71°41W **83** C13
Plymouth *Pa., U.S.A.* 41°14N 75°57W **83** E9
Plymouth *Wis., U.S.A.* 43°45N 87°59W **80** D10
Plympton-Wyoming *Canada* 42°57N 82°7W **82** D2
Plynlimon = Pumlumon Fawr *U.K.* 52°28N 3°46W **13** E4
Plyusa *Russia* 58°28N 29°27E **9** G23
Plzeň *Czech Rep.* 49°45N 13°22E **16** D7
Po → *Italy* 44°57N 12°4E **22** B5
Po Hai = Bo Hai *China* 39°0N 119°0E **35** E10
Po Toi *China* 22°10N 114°16E **33** G11
Pobeda *Russia* 65°12N 146°12E **29** C15
Pobedy, Pik *Kyrgyzstan* 42°0N 79°58E **32** B2
Pocahontas *U.S.A.* 42°44N 94°40W **80** D6
Pocatello *U.S.A.* 42°52N 112°27W **76** E7
Pocomoke City *U.S.A.* 38°5N 75°34W **81** F16
Poços de Caldas *Brazil* 21°50S 46°33W **95** A6
Podgorica *Montenegro* 42°30N 19°19E **23** C8
Podilska Vysochyna *Ukraine* 49°0N 28°0E **17** D14
Podolsk *Russia* 55°25N 37°30E **18** C6
Podporozhye *Russia* 60°55N 34°2E **18** B5
Pofadder *S. Africa* 29°10S 19°22E **56** D2
Pogranichnyy *Russia* 44°25N 131°24E **30** B5
Poh *Indonesia* 0°46S 122°51E **37** E6
Pohang *S. Korea* 36°1N 129°23E **35** F15
Pohjanmaa *Finland* 62°58N 22°50E **8** E20
Pohnpei *Micronesia* 6°55N 158°10E **64** G7
Pohri *India* 25°32N 77°22E **42** G6
Poinsett, C. *Antarctica* 65°42S 113°18E **5** C8
Point Arena *U.S.A.* 38°55N 123°41W **78** G3
Point Baker *U.S.A.* 56°21N 133°37W **70** B2
Point Edward *Canada* 43°0N 82°30W **72** D3
Point Fortin *Trin. & Tob.* 10°10N 61°42W **93** K15
Point Hope *U.S.A.* 68°21N 166°47W **74** a
Point L. *Canada* 65°15N 113°4W **68** C8
Point Lisas Industrial Estate *Trin. & Tob.* 10°24N 61°29W **93** K15
Point Pedro *Sri Lanka* 9°50N 80°15E **40** Q12
Point Pelee △ *Canada* 41°57N 82°31W **82** E2
Point Pleasant *N.J., U.S.A.* 40°5N 74°4W **83** F10
Point Pleasant *W. Va., U.S.A.* 38°51N 82°8W **81** F12
Point Reyes ⌂ *U.S.A.* 38°10N 122°55W **78** G2
Pointe-à-Pitre *Guadeloupe* 16°10N 61°32W **88** b
Pointe-au-Pic = La Malbaie *Canada* 47°40N 70°10W **73** C5
Pointe-Claire *Canada* 45°26N 73°50W **83** A11
Pointe-Gatineau *Canada* 45°27N 75°41W **83** A9
Pointe-Noire *Congo* 4°48S 11°53E **52** E2
Pointe-Noire *Guadeloupe* 16°14N 61°47W **88** b
Poisonbush Ra. *Australia* 22°30S 121°30E **60** D3
Poissonnier Pt. *Australia* 19°57S 119°10E **60** C2
Poitiers *France* 46°35N 0°20E **20** C4
Poitou *France* 46°40N 0°10W **20** C3
Pojoaque *U.S.A.* 35°54N 106°1W **77** J10
Pokaran *India* 27°0N 71°50E **42** F4
Pokataroo *Australia* 29°30S 148°36E **63** D4
Pokhara *Nepal* 28°14N 83°58E **43** E10
Poko *Dem. Rep. of the Congo* 3°7N 26°52E **54** B2
Pokrovsk *Russia* 61°29N 129°0E **29** C13
Pola = Pula *Croatia* 44°54N 13°57E **16** F7
Polacca *U.S.A.* 35°50N 110°23W **77** J8
Polan *Iran* 25°30N 61°10E **45** E9
Poland ■ *Europe* 52°0N 20°0E **17** C10
Polar Bear ⌂ *Canada* 55°0N 83°45W **72** A2
Polatsk *Belarus* 55°30N 28°50E **9** J22
Polcura *Chile* 37°17S 71°43W **94** D1
Polesye = Pripet Marshes *Europe* 52°10N 28°10E **17** B15
Polevskoy *Russia* 56°26N 60°11E **18** C11
Police *Poland* 53°33N 14°33E **16** B8
Police, Pte. *Seychelles* 4°51S 55°32E **53** b
Poligiros *Greece* 40°23N 23°25E **23** D10
Polillo Is. *Phil.* 14°56N 122°0E **37** B6
Polis *Cyprus* 35°2N 32°26E **25** D11
Polk *U.S.A.* 41°22N 79°56W **82** E5
Pollachi *India* 10°35N 77°0E **40** P10
Pollença *Spain* 39°54N 3°1E **24** B10
Pollença, B. de *Spain* 39°53N 3°8E **24** B10
Polnovat *Russia* 63°50N 65°54E **28** C7
Polokwane *S. Africa* 23°54S 29°25E **57** C4
Polonne *Ukraine* 50°6N 27°30E **17** C14
Polonnoye = Polonne *Ukraine* 50°6N 27°30E **17** C14
Polson *U.S.A.* 47°41N 114°9W **76** C6
Poltava *Ukraine* 49°35N 34°35E **19** E5
Põltsamaa *Estonia* 58°39N 25°58E **9** G21
Polunochnoye *Russia* 60°52N 60°25E **28** C7
Põlva *Estonia* 58°3N 27°3E **9** G22
Polyarny *Russia* 69°8N 33°20E **8** B25
Polyarnyye Zori *Russia* 67°22N 32°30E **8** C25
Polynesia *Pac. Oc.* 10°0S 162°0W **65** F11
Polynésie française = French Polynesia ☐ *Pac. Oc.* 20°0S 145°0W **65** J13
Pombal *Portugal* 39°55N 8°40W **21** C1
Pombia *Greece* 35°0N 24°51E **25** E6
Pomene *Mozam.* 22°53S 35°33E **57** C6
Pomeroy *Ohio, U.S.A.* 39°2N 82°2W **81** F12
Pomeroy *Wash., U.S.A.* 46°28N 117°36W **76** C5
Pomézia *Italy* 41°40N 12°30E **22** D5
Pomona *Australia* 26°22S 152°52E **63** D5
Pomona *U.S.A.* 34°4N 117°45W **79** L9
Pomorskie, Pojezierze *Poland* 53°40N 16°37E **17** B9
Pomos *Cyprus* 35°9N 32°33E **25** D11
Pomos, C. *Cyprus* 35°10N 32°33E **25** D11
Pompano Beach *U.S.A.* 26°14N 80°7W **85** H14
Pompeys Pillar *U.S.A.* 45°59N 107°57W **76** D10
Pompeys Pillar ⌂ *U.S.A.* 46°0N 108°0W **76** D10
Pompton Lakes *U.S.A.* 41°0N 74°17W **83** F10
Ponape = Pohnpei *Micronesia* 6°55N 158°10E **64** G7
Ponask L. *Canada* 54°0N 92°41W **72** B1
Ponca *U.S.A.* 42°34N 96°43W **80** D5
Ponca City *U.S.A.* 36°42N 97°5W **84** C6
Ponce *Puerto Rico* 18°1N 66°37W **89** d
Ponchatoula *U.S.A.* 30°26N 90°26W **85** F9
Poncheville, L. *Canada* 50°10N 76°55W **72** B4
Pond *U.S.A.* 35°43N 119°20W **79** K7
Pond Inlet *Canada* 72°40N 77°0W **69** B12
Pondicherry *India* 11°59N 79°50E **40** P11
Ponds, I. of *Canada* 53°27N 55°52W **73** B8
Ponferrada *Spain* 42°32N 6°35W **21** A2
Ponnani *India* 10°45N 75°59E **40** P9
Ponoka *Canada* 52°42N 113°40W **70** C6
Ponorogo *Indonesia* 7°52S 111°27E **37** G14
Ponoy *Russia* 67°0N 41°13E **18** A7
Ponoy → *Russia* 66°59N 41°17E **18** A7
Ponta Delgada *Azores* 37°44N 25°40W **50** a
Ponta do Sol *Madeira* 32°42N 17°7W **24** D2
Ponta Grossa *Brazil* 25°7S 50°10W **95** B5
Ponta Pora *Brazil* 22°20S 55°35W **95** A4
Pontarlier *France* 46°54N 6°20E **20** C7
Pontchartrain, L. *U.S.A.* 30°5N 90°5W **85** F9
Ponte do Pungué *Mozam.* 19°30S 34°33E **55** F3
Ponte Nova *Brazil* 20°25S 42°54W **95** A7
Ponteix *Canada* 49°46N 107°29W **71** D7
Pontevedra *Spain* 42°26N 8°40W **21** A1
Pontiac *Ill., U.S.A.* 40°53N 88°38W **80** E9
Pontiac *Mich., U.S.A.* 42°38N 83°18W **81** D12
Pontian Kechil *Malaysia* 1°29N 103°23E **39** d
Pontianak *Indonesia* 0°3S 109°15E **36** E3
Pontine Is. = Ponziane, Ísole *Italy* 40°55N 12°57E **22** D5
Pontine Mts. = Kuzey Anadolu Dağları *Turkey* 41°0N 36°45E **19** F6
Pontivy *France* 48°5N 2°58W **20** B2
Pontoise *France* 49°3N 2°5E **20** B5
Ponton → *Canada* 58°27N 116°11W **70** B5
Pontypool *Canada* 44°6N 78°38W **82** B6
Pontypool *U.K.* 51°42N 3°2W **13** F4
Ponziane, Ísole *Italy* 40°55N 12°57E **22** D5
Poochera *Australia* 32°43S 134°51E **63** E1
Poole *U.K.* 50°43N 1°59W **13** G6
Poole ☐ *U.K.* 50°43N 1°59W **13** G6
Poona = Pune *India* 18°29N 73°57E **40** K8
Pooncarie *Australia* 33°22S 142°31E **63** E3
Poopelloe L. *Australia* 31°40S 144°0E **63** E3
Poopó, L. de *Bolivia* 18°30S 67°35W **92** G5
Popayán *Colombia* 2°27N 76°36W **92** C3
Poperinge *Belgium* 50°51N 2°42E **15** D2
Popiltah L. *Australia* 33°10S 141°42E **63** E3
Popio L. *Australia* 33°10S 141°52E **63** E3
Poplar *U.S.A.* 48°7N 105°12W **76** B11
Poplar → *Canada* 53°0N 97°19W **71** C9
Poplar Bluff *U.S.A.* 36°46N 90°24W **80** G8
Poplarville *U.S.A.* 30°51N 89°32W **85** F10
Popocatépetl, Volcán *Mexico* 19°2N 98°38W **87** D5
Popokabaka *Dem. Rep. of the Congo* 5°41S 16°40E **52** F3
Poprad *Slovak Rep.* 49°3N 20°18E **17** D11
Porali → *Pakistan* 25°58N 66°26E **42** G2
Porbandar *India* 21°44N 69°43E **42** J3
Porcher I. *Canada* 53°50N 130°30W **70** C2
Porcupine → *Canada* 59°11N 104°46W **71** B8
Porcupine → *U.S.A.* 66°34N 145°19W **74** a
Porcupine Gorge △ *Australia* 20°22S 144°26E **62** C3
Pordenone *Italy* 45°57N 12°39E **22** B5
Pori *Finland* 61°29N 21°48E **8** F19
Porkhov *Russia* 57°45N 29°38E **9** H23
Porlamar *Venezuela* 10°57N 63°51W **92** A6
Pormpuraaw *Australia* 14°59S 141°26E **62** A3
Poronaysk *Russia* 49°13N 143°0E **29** E15
Poroshiri-Dake *Japan* 42°41N 142°52E **30** C11
Poroto Mts. *Tanzania* 9°0S 33°30E **55** D3
Porpoise B. *Antarctica* 66°0S 127°0E **5** C9
Porreres *Spain* 39°31N 3°2E **24** B10
Porsangerfjorden *Norway* 70°40N 25°40E **8** A21
Porsgrunn *Norway* 59°10N 9°40E **9** G13
Port Alberni *Canada* 49°14N 124°50W **70** D4
Port Alfred *S. Africa* 33°36S 26°55E **56** E4
Port Alice *Canada* 50°20N 127°25W **70** C3
Port Allegany *U.S.A.* 41°48N 78°17W **82** E6
Port Allen *U.S.A.* 30°27N 91°12W **84** F9
Port Alma *Australia* 23°38S 150°53E **62** C5
Port Angeles *U.S.A.* 48°7N 123°27W **78** B3
Port Antonio *Jamaica* 18°10N 76°26W **88** a
Port Aransas *U.S.A.* 27°50N 97°4W **84** H6
Port Arthur *Australia* 43°7S 147°50E **63** G4
Port Arthur *U.S.A.* 29°54N 93°56W **84** G8
Port au Choix *Canada* 50°43N 57°22W **73** B8
Port au Port B. *Canada* 48°40N 58°50W **73** C8
Port-au-Prince *Haiti* 18°40N 72°20W **89** C5
Port Augusta *Australia* 32°30S 137°50E **63** E2
Port Austin *U.S.A.* 44°3N 83°1W **82** B2
Port Bell *Uganda* 0°18N 32°35E **54** B3
Port Bergé Vaovao *Madag.* 15°33S 47°40E **57** B8
Port Blandford *Canada* 48°20N 54°10W **73** C9
Port Bradshaw *Australia* 12°30S 137°20E **62** A2
Port Broughton *Australia* 33°37S 137°56E **63** E2
Port Burwell *Canada* 42°40N 80°48W **82** D4
Port Canning *India* 22°23N 88°40E **43** H13
Port-Cartier *Canada* 50°2N 66°50W **73** B6
Port Chalmers *N.Z.* 45°49S 170°30E **59** F3
Port Charlotte *U.S.A.* 26°59N 82°6W **85** H13
Port Chester *U.S.A.* 41°0N 73°40W **83** F11
Port Clements *Canada* 53°40N 132°10W **70** C2
Port Clinton *U.S.A.* 41°31N 82°56W **81** E12
Port Colborne *Canada* 42°50N 79°10W **82** D5
Port Coquitlam *Canada* 49°15N 122°45W **78** A4
Port Credit *Canada* 43°33N 79°35W **82** C5
Port Curtis *Australia* 23°57S 151°20E **62** C5
Port d'Alcúdia *Spain* 39°50N 3°7E **24** B10
Port Dalhousie *Canada* 43°13N 79°16W **82** C5
Port d'Andratx *Spain* 39°32N 2°23E **24** B9
Port Darwin *Australia* 12°24S 130°45E **60** B5
Port Darwin *Falk. Is.* 51°50S 59°0W **96** G5
Port Davey *Australia* 43°16S 145°55E **63** G4
Port-de-Paix *Haiti* 19°50N 72°50W **89** C5
Port de Pollença *Spain* 39°54N 3°4E **24** B10
Port de Sóller *Spain* 39°48N 2°42E **24** B9
Port Dickson *Malaysia* 2°30N 101°49E **39** L3
Port Douglas *Australia* 16°30S 145°30E **62** B4
Port Dover *Canada* 42°47N 80°12W **82** D4
Port Edward *Canada* 54°12N 130°10W **70** C2
Port Elgin *Canada* 44°25N 81°25W **82** B3
Port Elizabeth *S. Africa* 33°58S 25°40E **56** E4
Port Ellen *U.K.* 55°38N 6°11W **11** F2
Port Erin *I. of Man* 54°5N 4°45W **12** C3
Port Essington *Australia* 11°15S 132°10E **60** B5
Port Ewen *U.S.A.* 41°54N 73°59W **83** E11
Port Fairy *Australia* 38°22S 142°12E **63** F3
Port Gamble *U.S.A.* 47°51N 122°34W **78** C4
Port-Gentil *Gabon* 0°40S 8°50E **52** E1
Port Germein *Australia* 33°1S 138°1E **63** E2
Port Gibson *U.S.A.* 31°58N 90°59W **84** F9
Port Glasgow *U.K.* 55°56N 4°41W **11** F4
Port Harcourt *Nigeria* 4°40N 7°10E **50** H7
Port Hardy *Canada* 50°41N 127°30W **70** C3
Port Harrison = Inukjuak *Canada* 58°25N 78°15W **69** D12
Port Hawkesbury *Canada* 45°36N 61°22W **73** C7
Port Hedland *Australia* 20°25S 118°35E **60** D2
Port Henry *U.S.A.* 44°3N 73°28W **83** B11
Port Hood *Canada* 46°0N 61°32W **73** C7
Port Hope *Canada* 43°56N 78°20W **82** C6
Port Hope *U.S.A.* 43°57N 82°43W **82** C2
Port Hope Simpson *Canada* 52°33N 56°18W **73** B8
Port Hueneme *U.S.A.* 34°7N 119°12W **79** L7
Port Huron *U.S.A.* 42°58N 82°26W **82** D2
Port Jefferson *U.S.A.* 40°57N 73°3W **83** F11
Port Jervis *U.S.A.* 41°22N 74°41W **83** E10
Port Kelang = Pelabuhan Klang *Malaysia* 3°0N 101°23E **39** L3
Port Kenny *Australia* 33°10S 134°41E **63** E1
Port Lairge = Waterford *Ireland* 52°15N 7°8W **10** D4
Port Laoise *Ireland* 53°2N 7°18W **10** C4
Port Lavaca *U.S.A.* 28°37N 96°38W **84** G6
Port Leyden *U.S.A.* 43°35N 75°21W **83** C9
Port Lincoln *Australia* 34°42S 135°52E **63** E2
Port Loko *S. Leone* 8°48N 12°46W **50** G3
Port-Louis *Guadeloupe* 16°28N 61°32W **88** b
Port Louis *Mauritius* 20°10S 57°30E **53** d
Port MacDonnell *Australia* 38°5S 140°48E **63** F3
Port McNeill *Canada* 50°35N 127°6W **70** C3
Port Macquarie *Australia* 31°25S 152°25E **63** E5
Port Maria *Jamaica* 18°22N 76°54W **88** a
Port Matilda *U.S.A.* 40°48N 78°3W **82** F6
Port Mellon *Canada* 49°32N 123°31W **70** D4
Port-Menier *Canada* 49°51N 64°15W **73** C7
Port Moody *Canada* 49°17N 122°51W **78** A4
Port Morant *Jamaica* 17°54N 76°19W **88** a
Port Moresby *Papua N. G.* 9°24S 147°8E **59** D7
Port Musgrave *Australia* 11°55S 141°50E **62** A3
Port Neches *U.S.A.* 30°0N 93°59W **84** G8
Port Nolloth *S. Africa* 29°17S 16°52E **56** D2
Port Nouveau-Québec = Kangiqsualujjuaq *Canada* 58°30N 65°59W **69** D13
Port of Spain *Trin. & Tob.* 10°40N 61°31W **89** D7
Port Orange *U.S.A.* 29°9N 80°59W **85** G14
Port Orchard *U.S.A.* 47°32N 122°38W **78** C4
Port Orford *U.S.A.* 42°45N 124°30W **76** E1
Port Pegasus *N.Z.* 47°12S 167°41E **59** G1
Port Perry *Canada* 44°6N 78°56W **82** B6
Port Phillip B. *Australia* 38°10S 144°50E **63** F3
Port Pirie *Australia* 33°10S 138°1E **63** E2
Port Renfrew *Canada* 48°30N 124°20W **78** B2
Port Roper *Australia* 14°45S 135°25E **62** A2
Port Rowan *Canada* 42°40N 80°30W **82** D4
Port Safaga = Bûr Safâga *Egypt* 26°43N 33°57E **44** E2
Port Said = Bûr Sa'îd *Egypt* 31°16N 32°18E **51** B12
Port St. Joe *U.S.A.* 29°49N 85°18W **85** G12
Port St. Johns = Umzimvubu *S. Africa* 31°38S 29°33E **57** E4
Port St. Lucie *U.S.A.* 27°18N 80°21W **85** H14
Port Sanilac *U.S.A.* 43°26N 82°33W **82** C2
Port Severn *Canada* 44°48N 79°43W **82** B5
Port Shepstone *S. Africa* 30°44S 30°28E **57** E5
Port Simpson *Canada* 54°30N 130°20W **70** C2
Port Stanley = Stanley *Falk. Is.* 51°40S 59°51W **96** G5
Port Stanley *Canada* 42°40N 81°10W **82** D3
Port Sudan = Bûr Sûdân *Sudan* 19°32N 37°9E **51** E13
Port Sulphur *U.S.A.* 29°29N 89°42W **85** G10
Port Talbot *U.K.* 51°35N 3°47W **13** F4
Port Townsend *U.S.A.* 48°7N 122°45W **78** B4
Port-Vendres *France* 42°32N 3°8E **20** E5
Port Vila *Vanuatu* 17°45S 168°18E **58** C9
Port Vladimir *Russia* 69°25N 33°6E **8** B25
Port Wakefield *Australia* 34°12S 138°10E **63** E2
Port Washington *U.S.A.* 43°23N 87°53W **80** D10
Porta Orientalis *Romania* 45°6N 22°18E **17** F12
Portacloy *Ireland* 54°20N 9°46W **10** B2
Portadown *U.K.* 54°25N 6°27W **10** B5
Portaferry *U.K.* 54°23N 5°33W **10** B6
Portage *Pa., U.S.A.* 40°23N 78°41W **82** F6
Portage *Wis., U.S.A.* 43°33N 89°28W **80** D9
Portage la Prairie *Canada* 49°58N 98°18W **71** D9
Portageville *U.S.A.* 36°26N 89°42W **80** G9
Portalegre *Portugal* 39°19N 7°25W **21** C2
Portales *U.S.A.* 34°11N 103°20W **77** J12
Portarlington *Ireland* 53°9N 7°14W **10** C4
Portbou *Spain* 42°25N 3°9E **21** A7
Porter L. *N.W.T., Canada* 61°41N 108°5W **71** A7
Porter L. *Sask., Canada* 56°20N 107°20W **71** B7
Porterville *S. Africa* 33°0S 19°0E **56** E2
Porterville *U.S.A.* 36°4N 119°1W **78** J8
Porthcawl *U.K.* 51°29N 3°42W **13** F4
Porthill *U.S.A.* 48°59N 116°30W **76** B5
Porthmadog *U.K.* 52°55N 4°8W **12** E3
Portile de Fier *Europe* 44°44N 22°30E **17** F12
Portimão *Portugal* 37°8N 8°32W **21** D1
Portishead *U.K.* 51°29N 2°46W **13** F5
Portknockie *U.K.* 57°42N 2°51W **11** D6
Portland *N.S.W., Australia* 33°20S 150°0E **63** E5
Portland *Vic., Australia* 38°20S 141°35E **63** F3
Portland *Canada* 44°42N 76°12W **83** B8
Portland *Conn., U.S.A.* 41°34N 72°38W **83** E12
Portland *Maine, U.S.A.* 43°39N 70°16W **81** D18
Portland *Mich., U.S.A.* 42°52N 84°54W **81** D11
Portland *Oreg., U.S.A.* 45°32N 122°37W **78** E4
Portland *Pa., U.S.A.* 40°55N 75°6W **83** F9
Portland *Tex., U.S.A.* 27°53N 97°20W **84** H6
Portland, I. of *U.K.* 50°33N 2°26W **13** G5
Portland B. *Australia* 38°15S 141°45E **63** F3
Portland Bight *Jamaica* 17°52N 77°5W **88** a
Portland Bill *U.K.* 50°31N 2°28W **13** G5
Portland Canal *U.S.A.* 55°56N 130°0W **70** B2
Portland Int. ✈ **(PDX)** *U.S.A.* 45°35N 122°36W **78** E4
Portland Pt. *Jamaica* 17°42N 77°11W **88** a
Portmadoc = Porthmadog *U.K.* 52°55N 4°8W **12** E3
Portmore *Jamaica* 17°53N 77°53W **88** a
Porto *France* 42°16N 8°42E **20** E8
Porto *Portugal* 41°8N 8°40W **21** B1
Pôrto Alegre *Brazil* 30°5S 51°10W **95** C5
Porto Cristo *Spain* 39°33N 3°20E **24** B10
Pôrto de Móz *Brazil* 1°41S 52°13W **93** D8
Porto Empédocle *Italy* 37°17N 13°32E **22** F5
Pôrto Esperança *Brazil* 19°37S 57°29W **92** G7
Pôrto Franco *Brazil* 6°20S 47°24W **93** E9
Porto Inglês *C. Verde Is.* 15°21N 23°10W **50** b
Pôrto Mendes *Brazil* 24°30S 54°15W **95** A5
Porto Moniz *Madeira* 32°52N 17°11W **24** D2
Pôrto Murtinho *Brazil* 21°45S 57°55W **92** H7
Pôrto Nacional *Brazil* 10°40S 48°30W **93** F9
Porto-Novo *Benin* 6°23N 2°42E **50** G6
Porto Petro *Spain* 39°22N 3°13E **24** B10
Porto Santo, I. de *Madeira* 33°45N 16°25W **50** B2
Pôrto São José *Brazil* 22°43S 53°10W **95** A5
Pôrto Seguro *Brazil* 16°26S 39°5W **93** G11
Porto Torres *Italy* 40°50N 8°24E **22** D3
Pôrto União *Brazil* 26°10S 51°10W **95** B5
Pôrto Válter *Brazil* 8°15S 72°40W **92** E4
Porto-Vecchio *France* 41°35N 9°16E **20** F8
Pôrto Velho *Brazil* 8°46S 63°54W **92** E6
Portobelo *Panama* 9°35N 79°42W **88** E4
Portoferráio *Italy* 42°48N 10°20E **22** C4
Portola *U.S.A.* 39°49N 120°28W **78** F6
Portoscuso *Italy* 39°12N 8°24E **22** E3
Portoviejo *Ecuador* 1°7S 80°28W **92** D2
Portpatrick *U.K.* 54°51N 5°7W **11** G3
Portree *U.K.* 57°25N 6°12W **11** D2
Portrush *U.K.* 55°12N 6°40W **10** A5
Portsmouth *Dominica* 15°34N 61°27W **89** C7
Portsmouth *U.K.* 50°48N 1°6W **13** G6
Portsmouth *N.H., U.S.A.* 43°5N 70°45W **83** C14
Portsmouth *Ohio, U.S.A.* 38°44N 82°57W **81** F12
Portsmouth *R.I., U.S.A.* 41°36N 71°15W **83** E13
Portsmouth *Va., U.S.A.* 36°58N 76°23W **81** G15
Portsmouth ☐ *U.K.* 50°48N 1°6W **13** G6
Portsoy *U.K.* 57°41N 2°41W **11** D6
Portstewart *U.K.* 55°11N 6°43W **10** A5
Porttipahdan tekojärvi *Finland* 68°5N 26°40E **8** B22
Portugal ■ *Europe* 40°0N 8°0W **21** C1
Portumna *Ireland* 53°6N 8°14W **10** C3
Portville *U.S.A.* 42°3N 78°20W **82** D6
Porvenir *Chile* 53°10S 70°16W **96** G2
Posadas *Argentina* 27°30S 55°50W **95** B4
Posht-e Badam *Iran* 33°2N 55°23E **45** C7
Poso *Indonesia* 1°20S 120°55E **37** E6
Posse *Brazil* 14°4S 46°18W **93** F9
Possession I. *Antarctica* 72°4S 172°0E **5** D11
Possum Kingdom L. *U.S.A.* 32°52N 98°26W **84** E5
Post *U.S.A.* 33°12N 101°23W **84** E4
Post Falls *U.S.A.* 47°43N 116°57W **76** C5
Postavy = Pastavy *Belarus* 55°4N 26°50E **9** J22
Poste-de-la-Baleine = Kuujjuarapik *Canada* 55°20N 77°35W **72** A4
Postmasburg *S. Africa* 28°18S 23°5E **56** D3
Postojna *Slovenia* 45°46N 14°12E **16** F8
Poston *U.S.A.* 34°0N 114°24W **79** M12
Postville *Canada* 54°54N 59°47W **73** B8
Potchefstroom *S. Africa* 26°41S 27°7E **56** D4
Poteau *U.S.A.* 35°3N 94°37W **84** D7
Poteet *U.S.A.* 29°2N 98°35W **84** G5
Potenza *Italy* 40°38N 15°48E **22** D6
Poteriteri, L. *N.Z.* 46°5S 167°10E **59** G1
Potgietersrus = Mokopane *S. Africa* 24°10S 28°55E **57** C4
Poti *Georgia* 42°10N 41°38E **19** F7
Potiskum *Nigeria* 11°39N 11°2E **51** F8
Potomac → *U.S.A.* 38°0N 76°23W **81** F14
Potosí *Bolivia* 19°38S 65°50W **92** G5
Potosi Mt. *U.S.A.* 35°57N 115°29W **79** K11

Pototan Phil. 10°54N 122°38E 37 B6
Potrerillos Chile 26°30S 69°30W 94 B2
Potsdam Germany 52°23N 13°3E 16 B7
Potsdam U.S.A. 44°40N 74°59W 83 B10
Pottersville U.S.A. 43°43N 73°50W 83 C11
Pottstown U.S.A. 40°15N 75°39W 83 F9
Pottsville U.S.A. 40°41N 76°12W 83 F8
Pottuvil Sri Lanka 6°55N 81°50E 40 R12
Pouce Coupé Canada 55°40N 120°10W 70 B4
Poughkeepsie U.S.A. 41°42N 73°56W 83 E11
Poulaphouca Res. Ireland 53°8N 6°30W 10 C5
Poulsbo U.S.A. 47°44N 122°38W 78 C4
Poultney U.S.A. 43°31N 73°14W 83 C11
Poulton-le-Fylde U.K. 53°51N 2°58W 12 D5
Pouso Alegre Brazil 22°14S 45°57W 95 A6
Pouthisat Cambodia 12°34N 103°50E 38 F4
Považská Bystrica Slovak Rep. 49°8N 18°27E 17 D10
Povenets Russia 62°50N 34°50E 18 B5
Poverty B. N.Z. 38°43S 178°2E 59 C7
Póvoa de Varzim Portugal 41°25N 8°46W 21 B1
Povungnituk = Puvirnituq Canada 60°2N 77°10W 69 C12
Powassan Canada 46°5N 79°25W 72 C4
Poway U.S.A. 32°58N 117°2W 79 N9
Powder → U.S.A. 46°45N 105°26W 76 C11
Powder River U.S.A. 43°2N 106°59W 76 E10
Powell U.S.A. 44°45N 108°46W 76 D9
Powell, L. U.S.A. 36°57N 111°29W 77 H8
Powell River Canada 49°50N 124°35W 70 D4
Powers U.S.A. 45°41N 87°32W 80 C10
Powys □ U.K. 52°20N 3°20W 13 E4
Poyang Hu China 29°5N 116°20E 33 D6
Poyarkovo Russia 49°36N 128°41E 29 E13
Poza Rica Mexico 20°33N 97°27W 87 C5
Požarevac Serbia 44°35N 21°18E 23 B9
Poznań Poland 52°25N 16°55E 17 B9
Pozo U.S.A. 35°20N 120°24W 79 K6
Pozo Almonte Chile 20°10S 69°50W 92 H5
Pozo Colorado Paraguay 23°30S 58°45W 94 A4
Pozoblanco Spain 38°23N 4°51W 21 C3
Pozzuoli Italy 40°49N 14°7E 22 D6
Prachin Buri Thailand 14°0N 101°25E 38 E3
Prachuap Khiri Khan Thailand 11°49N 99°48E 39 G2
Prado Brazil 17°20S 39°13W 93 G11
Prague = Praha Czech Rep. 50°4N 14°25E 16 C8
Praha Czech Rep. 50°4N 14°25E 16 C8
Praia C. Verde Is. 15°2N 23°34W 50 b
Prainha Amazonas, Brazil 7°10S 60°30W 92 E6
Prainha Pará, Brazil 1°45S 53°30W 93 D8
Prairie Australia 20°50S 144°35E 62 C3
Prairie City U.S.A. 44°28N 118°43W 76 D4
Prairie Dog Town Fork Red → U.S.A. 34°34N 99°58W 84 D5
Prairie du Chien U.S.A. 43°3N 91°9W 80 D8
Prairies, L. of the Canada 51°16N 101°32W 71 C8
Pran Buri Thailand 12°23N 99°55E 38 F2
Prapat Indonesia 2°41N 98°58E 36 D1
Praslin Seychelles 4°18S 55°45E 53 b
Praso, Akra Greece 35°42N 27°46E 25 D9
Prata Brazil 19°25S 48°54W 93 G9
Pratabpur India 23°28N 83°15E 43 H10
Pratapgarh Raj., India 24°2N 74°40E 42 G6
Pratapgarh Ut. P., India 25°56N 81°59E 43 G9
Prato Italy 43°53N 11°6E 22 C4
Pratt U.S.A. 37°39N 98°44W 80 G4
Prattville U.S.A. 32°28N 86°29W 85 E11
Pravia Spain 43°30N 6°12W 21 A2
Praya Indonesia 8°39S 116°17E 36 F5
Precipice △ Australia 25°18S 150°5E 63 D5
Precordillera Argentina 30°0S 69°1W 94 C2
Preeceville Canada 51°57N 102°40W 71 C8
Preiļi Latvia 56°18N 26°43E 9 H22
Premont U.S.A. 27°22N 98°7W 84 H5
Prentice U.S.A. 45°33N 90°17W 80 C8
Preobrazheniye Russia 42°54N 133°54E 30 C6
Preparis North Channel Ind. Oc. 15°27N 94°5E 41 M18
Preparis South Channel Ind. Oc. 14°33N 93°30E 41 M18
Přerov Czech Rep. 49°28N 17°27E 17 D9
Prescott Canada 44°45N 75°30W 83 B9
Prescott Ariz., U.S.A. 34°33N 112°28W 77 J7
Prescott Ark., U.S.A. 33°48N 93°23W 84 E8
Prescott Valley U.S.A. 34°40N 112°18W 77 J7
Preservation Inlet N.Z. 46°8S 166°35E 59 G1
Presho U.S.A. 43°54N 100°3W 80 D3
Presidencia de la Plaza Argentina 27°0S 59°50W 94 B4
Presidencia Roque Saenz Peña Argentina 26°45S 60°30W 94 B3
Presidente Epitácio Brazil 21°56S 52°6W 93 H8
Presidente Hayes □ Paraguay 24°0S 59°0W 94 A4
Presidente Prudente Brazil 22°5S 51°25W 95 A5
Presidio Mexico 29°29N 104°23W 86 B4
Presidio U.S.A. 29°34N 104°22W 84 G2
Prešov Slovak Rep. 49°0N 21°15E 17 D11
Prespa, L. = Prespansko Jezero Macedonia 40°55N 21°0E 23 D9
Prespansko Jezero Macedonia 40°55N 21°0E 23 D9
Presque I. U.S.A. 42°10N 80°6W 82 D4
Presque Isle U.S.A. 46°41N 68°1W 81 B19
Prestatyn U.K. 53°20N 3°24W 12 D4
Presteigne U.K. 52°17N 3°0W 13 E5
Preston Canada 43°23N 80°21W 82 C4
Preston U.K. 53°46N 2°42W 12 D5
Preston Idaho, U.S.A. 42°6N 111°53W 76 E8
Preston Minn., U.S.A. 43°40N 92°5W 80 D7
Preston, C. Australia 20°51S 116°12E 60 D2
Prestonsburg U.S.A. 37°40N 82°47W 81 G12
Prestwick U.K. 55°29N 4°37W 11 F4
Pretoria S. Africa 25°44S 28°12E 57 D4
Preveza Greece 38°57N 20°45E 23 E9
Prey Veng Cambodia 11°35N 105°29E 39 G5
Pribilof Is. U.S.A. 57°0N 170°0W 74 a
Příbram Czech Rep. 49°41N 14°2E 16 D8
Price U.S.A. 39°36N 110°49W 76 G8
Price I. Canada 52°23N 128°41W 70 C3
Prichard U.S.A. 30°44N 88°5W 85 F10
Priekule Latvia 56°26N 21°35E 9 H19
Prienai Lithuania 54°38N 23°57E 9 J20
Prieska S. Africa 29°40S 22°42E 56 D3
Priest L. U.S.A. 48°35N 116°52W 76 B5
Priest River U.S.A. 48°11N 116°55W 76 B5
Priest Valley U.S.A. 36°10N 120°39W 78 J6
Prievidza Slovak Rep. 48°46N 18°36E 17 D10
Prikaspiyskaya Nizmennost = Caspian Depression Eurasia 47°0N 48°0E 19 E8
Prilep Macedonia 41°21N 21°32E 23 D9
Priluki = Pryluky Ukraine 50°30N 32°24E 19 D5
Prime Seal I. Australia 40°3S 147°43E 63 G4
Primo Tapia Mexico 32°16N 116°54W 79 N10
Primrose L. Canada 54°55N 109°45W 71 C7
Prince Albert Canada 53°15N 105°50W 71 C7
Prince Albert S. Africa 33°12S 22°2E 56 E3
Prince Albert △ Canada 54°0N 106°25W 71 C7
Prince Albert Mts. Antarctica 76°0S 161°30E 5 D11
Prince Albert Pen. Canada 72°30N 116°0W 68 B8
Prince Albert Sd. Canada 70°25N 115°0W 68 B8
Prince Alfred, C. Canada 74°20N 124°40W 69 B7
Prince Charles I. Canada 67°47N 76°12W 69 C12
Prince Charles Mts. Antarctica 72°0S 67°0E 5 D6
Prince Edward Fracture Zone Ind. Oc. 46°0S 35°0E 5 A4
Prince Edward I. □ Canada 46°20N 63°20W 73 C7
Prince Edward Is. Ind. Oc. 46°35S 38°0E 3 G11
Prince Edward Pt. Canada 43°56N 76°52W 82 C8
Prince George Canada 53°55N 122°50W 70 C4
Prince Gustaf Adolf Sea Canada 78°30N 107°0W 69 B9
Prince of Wales, C. U.S.A. 65°36N 168°5W 66 C3
Prince of Wales I. Australia 10°40S 142°10E 62 A3
Prince of Wales I. Canada 73°0N 99°0W 68 B10
Prince of Wales I. U.S.A. 55°47N 132°50W 68 D6
Prince Patrick I. Canada 77°0N 120°0W 69 B8
Prince Regent Inlet Canada 73°0N 90°0W 4 B3
Prince Rupert Canada 54°20N 130°20W 70 C2
Princes Town Trin. & Tob. 10°16N 61°23W 93 K15
Princess Charlotte B. Australia 14°25S 144°0E 62 A3
Princess Elizabeth Trough S. Ocean 64°10S 83°0E 5 C7
Princess May Ranges Australia 15°30S 125°30E 60 C4
Princess Royal I. Canada 53°0N 128°40W 70 C3
Princeton Canada 49°27N 120°30W 70 D4
Princeton Calif., U.S.A. 39°24N 122°1W 78 F4
Princeton Ill., U.S.A. 41°23N 89°28W 80 E9
Princeton Ind., U.S.A. 38°21N 87°34W 80 F10
Princeton Ky., U.S.A. 37°7N 87°53W 80 G10
Princeton Mo., U.S.A. 40°24N 93°35W 80 E7
Princeton N.J., U.S.A. 40°21N 74°39W 83 F10
Princeton W. Va., U.S.A. 37°22N 81°6W 81 G13
Principe, I. de Atl. Oc. 1°37N 7°27E 48 F4
Principe da Beira Brazil 12°20S 64°30W 92 F6
Prineville U.S.A. 44°18N 120°51W 76 D3
Prins Harald Kyst Antarctica 70°0S 35°1E 5 D4
Prinsesse Astrid Kyst Antarctica 70°45S 12°30E 5 D3
Prinsesse Ragnhild Kyst Antarctica 70°15S 27°30E 5 D4
Prinzapolca Nic. 13°20N 83°35W 88 D3
Priozersk Russia 61°2N 30°7E 8 F24
Pripet = Prypyat → Europe 51°20N 30°15E 17 C16
Pripet Marshes Europe 52°10N 28°10E 17 B15
Pripyat Marshes = Pripet Marshes Europe 52°10N 28°10E 17 B15
Pripyats = Prypyat → Europe 51°20N 30°15E 17 C16
Priština Serbia 42°40N 21°13E 23 C9
Privas France 44°45N 4°37E 20 D6
Privolzhskaya Vozvyshennost Russia 51°0N 46°0E 19 D8
Privolzhskiy □ Russia 56°0N 50°0E 28 D6
Prizren Serbia 42°13N 20°45E 23 C9
Probolinggo Indonesia 7°46S 113°13E 37 G15
Proctor U.S.A. 43°40N 73°2W 83 C11
Proddatur India 14°45N 78°30E 40 M11
Prodhromos Cyprus 34°57N 32°50E 25 E11
Profondeville Belgium 50°23N 4°52E 15 D4
Progreso Coahuila, Mexico 27°28N 100°59W 86 B4
Progreso Yucatán, Mexico 21°20N 89°40W 87 C7
Progress Antarctica 66°22S 76°22E 5 C12
Prokopyevsk Russia 54°0N 86°45E 28 D9
Prokuplje Serbia 43°16N 21°36E 23 C9
Prome Burma 18°49N 95°13E 41 K19
Prophet → Canada 58°48N 122°40W 70 B4
Prophet River Canada 58°6N 122°43W 70 B4
Propriá Brazil 10°13S 36°51W 93 F11
Propriano France 41°41N 8°52E 20 F8
Proserpine Australia 20°21S 148°36E 62 J6
Prosna → Poland 52°6N 17°44E 17 B9
Prospect U.S.A. 43°18N 75°9W 83 C9
Prosser U.S.A. 46°12N 119°46W 76 C4
Prostějov Czech Rep. 49°30N 17°9E 17 D9
Proston Australia 26°8S 151°32E 63 D5
Provence France 43°40N 5°46E 20 E6
Providence Ky., U.S.A. 37°24N 87°46W 80 G10
Providence R.I., U.S.A. 41°49N 71°24W 83 E13
Providence Bay Canada 45°41N 82°15W 72 C3
Providence Mts. U.S.A. 35°10N 115°15W 79 K11
Providencia, I. de Colombia 13°25N 81°26W 88 D3
Provideniya Russia 64°23N 173°18W 29 C19
Provins France 48°33N 3°15E 20 B5
Provo U.S.A. 40°14N 111°39W 76 F8
Provost Canada 52°25N 110°20W 71 C6
Prudhoe Bay U.S.A. 70°18N 148°22W 74 a
Prudhoe I. Australia 21°19S 149°41E 62 C4
Prud'homme Canada 52°20N 105°54W 71 C7
Pruszków Poland 52°9N 20°49E 17 B11
Prut → Romania 45°28N 28°10E 17 F15
Pruzhany Belarus 52°33N 24°28E 17 B13
Prydz B. Antarctica 69°0S 74°0E 5 C6
Pryluky Ukraine 50°30N 32°24E 19 D5
Pryor U.S.A. 36°19N 95°19W 84 C7
Prypyat → Europe 51°20N 30°15E 17 C16
Przemyśl Poland 49°50N 22°45E 17 D12
Przhevalsk = Karakol Kyrgyzstan 42°30N 78°20E 28 E8
Psara Greece 38°37N 25°38E 23 E11
Psiloritis, Oros Greece 35°15N 24°45E 25 D6
Psira Greece 35°12N 25°52E 25 D7
Pskov Russia 57°50N 28°25E 9 H23
Ptich = Ptsich → Belarus 52°9N 28°52E 17 B15
Ptichia = Vido Greece 39°38N 19°55E 25 A3
Ptolemaida Greece 40°30N 21°43E 23 D9
Ptsich → Belarus 52°9N 28°52E 17 B15
Pu Xian China 36°24N 111°6E 34 F6
Pua Thailand 19°11N 100°55E 38 C3
Puán Argentina 37°30S 62°45W 94 D3
Pu'apu'a Samoa 13°34S 172°9W 59 b
Pucallpa Peru 8°25S 74°30W 92 E4
Puch'on = Bucheon S. Korea 37°28N 126°45E 35 F14
Pudasjärvi Finland 65°23N 26°53E 8 D22
Pudozh Russia 61°48N 36°32E 18 B6
Puducherry = Pondicherry India 11°59N 79°50E 40 P11
Pudukkottai India 10°28N 78°47E 40 P11
Puebla Mexico 19°3N 98°12W 87 D5
Puebla □ Mexico 18°50N 98°0W 87 D5
Pueblo U.S.A. 38°16N 104°37W 76 G11
Pueblo Hundido Chile 26°20S 70°5W 94 B1
Puelches Argentina 38°5S 65°51W 94 D2
Puelén Argentina 37°32S 67°38W 94 D2
Puente Alto Chile 33°32S 70°35W 94 C1
Puente-Genil Spain 37°22N 4°47W 21 D3
Puerca, Pta. Puerto Rico 18°13N 65°36W 89 d
Puerco → U.S.A. 34°22N 107°50W 77 J10
Puerto Aisén Chile 45°27S 73°0W 96 F2
Puerto Ángel Mexico 15°40N 96°29W 87 D5
Puerto Arista Mexico 15°56N 93°48W 87 D6
Puerto Armuelles Panama 8°20N 82°51W 88 E3
Puerto Ayacucho Venezuela 5°40N 67°35W 92 B5
Puerto Barrios Guatemala 15°40N 88°32W 88 C2
Puerto Bermejo Argentina 26°55S 58°34W 94 B4
Puerto Bermúdez Peru 10°20S 74°58W 92 F4
Puerto Bolívar Ecuador 3°19S 79°55W 92 D3
Puerto Cabello Venezuela 10°28N 68°1W 92 A5
Puerto Cabezas Nic. 14°0N 83°30W 88 D3
Puerto Cabo Gracias á Dios Nic. 15°0N 83°10W 88 D3
Puerto Carreño Colombia 6°12N 67°22W 92 B5
Puerto Castilla Honduras 16°0N 86°0W 88 C2
Puerto Chicama Peru 7°45S 79°20W 92 E3
Puerto Coig Argentina 50°54S 69°15W 96 G3
Puerto Cortés Costa Rica 8°55N 84°0W 88 E3
Puerto Cortés Honduras 15°51N 88°0W 88 C2
Puerto Cumarebo Venezuela 11°29N 69°30W 92 A5
Puerto de Alcudia = Port d'Alcúdia Spain 39°50N 3°7E 24 B10
Puerto de Cabrera Spain 39°8N 2°56E 24 B9
Puerto de Gran Tarajal Canary Is. 28°13N 14°1W 24 F5
Puerto de la Cruz Canary Is. 28°24N 16°32W 24 F3
Puerto de los Angeles ⌂ Mexico 23°39N 105°45W 86 C3
Puerto de Pozo Negro Canary Is. 28°19N 13°55W 24 F6
Puerto de Sóller = Port de Sóller Spain 39°48N 2°42E 24 B9
Puerto del Carmen Canary Is. 28°55N 13°38W 24 F6
Puerto del Rosario Canary Is. 28°30N 13°52W 24 F6
Puerto Deseado Argentina 47°55S 66°0W 96 F3
Puerto Escondido Mexico 15°50N 97°3W 87 D5
Puerto Heath Bolivia 12°34S 68°39W 92 F5
Puerto Inírida Colombia 3°53N 67°52W 92 C5
Puerto Juárez Mexico 21°11N 86°49W 87 C7
Puerto La Cruz Venezuela 10°13N 64°38W 92 A6
Puerto Leguízamo Colombia 0°12S 74°46W 92 D4
Puerto Libertad Mexico 29°55N 112°43W 86 B2
Puerto Limón Colombia 3°23N 73°30W 92 C4
Puerto Lobos Argentina 42°0S 65°3W 96 E3
Puerto Madryn Argentina 42°48S 65°4W 96 E3
Puerto Maldonado Peru 12°30S 69°10W 92 F5
Puerto Manatí Cuba 21°22N 76°50W 88 B4
Puerto Montt Chile 41°28S 73°0W 96 E2
Puerto Morazán Nic. 12°51N 87°11W 88 D2
Puerto Morelos Mexico 20°50N 86°52W 87 C7
Puerto Natales Chile 51°45S 72°15W 96 G2
Puerto Padre Cuba 21°13N 76°35W 88 B4
Puerto Páez Venezuela 6°13N 67°28W 92 B5
Puerto Peñasco Mexico 31°20N 113°33W 86 A2
Puerto Pinasco Paraguay 22°36S 57°50W 94 A4
Puerto Plata Dom. Rep. 19°48N 70°45W 89 C5
Puerto Pollensa = Port de Pollença Spain 39°54N 3°4E 24 B10
Puerto Princesa Phil. 9°46N 118°45E 37 C5
Puerto Quepos Costa Rica 9°29N 84°6W 88 E3
Puerto Rico Canary Is. 27°47N 15°42W 24 G4
Puerto Rico ⊠ W. Indies 18°15N 66°45W 89 d
Puerto Rico Trench Atl. Oc. 19°50N 66°0W 89 C6
Puerto San Julián Argentina 49°18S 67°43W 96 F3
Puerto Sastre Paraguay 22°2S 57°55W 94 A4
Puerto Suárez Bolivia 18°58S 57°52W 92 G7
Puerto Vallarta Mexico 20°37N 105°15W 86 C3
Puerto Varas Chile 41°19S 72°59W 96 E2
Puerto Wilches Colombia 7°21N 73°54W 92 B4
Puertollano Spain 38°43N 4°7W 21 C3
Pueu Tahiti 17°44S 149°13W 59 d
Pueyrredón, L. Argentina 47°20S 72°0W 96 F2
Puffin I. Ireland 51°50N 10°24W 10 E1
Pugachev Russia 52°0N 48°49E 18 D8
Pugal India 28°30N 72°48E 42 E5
Puge Tanzania 4°45S 33°11E 54 C3
Puget Sound U.S.A. 47°50N 122°30W 76 C2
Pugŏdong N. Korea 42°5N 130°0E 35 C16
Pugu Tanzania 6°55S 39°4E 54 D4
Pūgūnzī Iran 25°49N 59°10E 45 E8
Puig Major Spain 39°48N 2°47E 24 B9
Puigcerdà Spain 42°24N 1°50E 21 A6
Puigpunyent Spain 39°38N 2°32E 24 B9
Pujon-ho N. Korea 40°35N 127°35E 35 D14
Pukaki, L. N.Z. 44°4S 170°1E 59 F3
Pukapuka Cook Is. 10°53S 165°49W 65 J11
Pukaskwa △ Canada 48°20N 86°0W 72 C2
Pukatawagan Canada 55°45N 101°20W 71 B8
Pukchin N. Korea 40°12N 125°45E 35 D13
Pukch'ŏng N. Korea 40°14N 128°10E 35 D15
Pukekohe N.Z. 37°12S 174°55E 59 B5
Pukhrayan India 26°14N 79°51E 43 F8
Pula Croatia 44°54N 13°57E 16 F7
Pulacayo Bolivia 20°25S 66°41W 92 H5
Pulai Malaysia 1°20N 103°31E 39 d
Pulandian China 39°25N 121°58E 35 E11
Pulaski N.Y., U.S.A. 43°34N 76°8W 83 C8
Pulaski Tenn., U.S.A. 35°12N 87°2W 85 D11
Pulaski Va., U.S.A. 37°3N 80°47W 81 G13
Pulau → Indonesia 5°50S 138°15E 37 F9
Puławy Poland 51°23N 21°59E 17 C11
Pulga U.S.A. 39°48N 121°29W 78 F5
Pulicat L. India 13°40N 80°15E 40 N12
Pullman U.S.A. 46°44N 117°10W 76 C5
Pulog, Mt. Phil. 16°40N 120°50E 37 A6
Pułtusk Poland 52°43N 21°6E 17 B11
Pumlumon Fawr U.K. 52°28N 3°46W 13 E4
Puná, I. Ecuador 2°55S 80°5W 92 D2
Punaauia Tahiti 17°37S 149°34W 59 d
Punakaiki N.Z. 42°7S 171°20E 59 E3
Punakha Dzong Bhutan 27°42N 89°52E 41 F16
Punasar India 27°6N 73°6E 42 F5
Punata Bolivia 17°32S 65°50W 92 G5
Punch India 33°48N 74°4E 43 C6
Punch → Pakistan 33°12N 73°40E 42 C5
Punda Maria S. Africa 22°40S 31°5E 57 C5
Pune India 18°29N 73°57E 40 K8
P'ungsan N. Korea 40°50N 128°9E 35 D15
Pungue, Ponte de Mozam. 19°0S 34°0E 55 F3
Punjab □ India 31°0N 76°0E 42 D7
Punjab □ Pakistan 32°0N 72°30E 42 E6
Puno Peru 15°55S 70°3W 92 G4
Punpun → India 25°31N 85°18E 43 G11
Punta, Cerro de Puerto Rico 18°10N 66°37W 89 d
Punta Alta Argentina 38°53S 62°4W 96 D4
Punta Arenas Chile 53°10S 71°0W 96 G2
Punta de Díaz Chile 28°0S 70°45W 94 B1
Punta del Hidalgo Canary Is. 28°33N 16°19W 24 F3
Punta Gorda Belize 16°10N 88°45W 87 D7
Punta Gorda U.S.A. 26°56N 82°3W 85 H13
Punta Prieta Mexico 28°58N 114°17W 86 B2
Punta Prima Spain 39°48N 4°16E 24 B11
Puntarenas Costa Rica 10°0N 84°50W 88 E3
Punto Fijo Venezuela 11°50N 70°13W 92 A4
Punxsatawney U.S.A. 40°57N 78°59W 82 F6
Pupuan Indonesia 8°19S 115°0E 37 J18
Puquio Peru 14°45S 74°10W 92 F4
Pur → Russia 67°31N 77°55E 28 C8
Puracé, Vol. Colombia 2°21N 76°23W 92 C3
Puralia = Puruliya India 23°17N 86°24E 43 H12
Puranpur India 28°31N 80°9E 43 E9
Purbeck, Isle of U.K. 50°39N 1°59W 13 G5
Purcell U.S.A. 35°1N 97°22W 84 D6
Purcell Mts. Canada 49°55N 116°15W 70 D5
Puri India 19°50N 85°58E 41 K14
Purmerend Neths. 52°32N 4°58E 15 B4
Purnia India 25°45N 87°31E 43 G12
Purnululu △ Australia 17°20S 128°20E 60 C4
Pursat = Pouthisat Cambodia 12°34N 103°50E 38 F4
Purukcahu Indonesia 0°35S 114°35E 36 E4
Puruliya India 23°17N 86°24E 43 H12
Purus → Brazil 3°42S 61°28W 92 D6
Puruvesi Finland 61°50N 29°30E 8 F23
Purvis U.S.A. 31°9N 89°25W 85 F10
Purwa India 26°28N 80°47E 43 F9
Purwakarta Indonesia 6°35S 107°29E 37 G12
Purwo, Tanjung Indonesia 8°44S 114°21E 37 K18
Purwodadi Indonesia 7°7S 110°55E 37 G14
Purwokerto Indonesia 7°25S 109°14E 37 G13
Puryŏng N. Korea 42°5N 129°43E 35 C15
Pusa India 25°59N 85°41E 43 G11
Pusan = Busan S. Korea 35°5N 129°0E 35 G15
Pushkin Russia 59°45N 30°25E 9 G24
Pushkino Russia 51°16N 47°0E 19 D8
Putahow L. Canada 59°54N 100°40W 71 B8
Putao Burma 27°28N 97°30E 41 F20
Putaruru N.Z. 38°2S 175°50E 59 C5
Putignano Italy 40°51N 17°7E 22 D7
Puting, Tanjung Indonesia 3°31S 111°46E 36 E4
Putnam U.S.A. 41°55N 71°55W 83 E13
Putorana, Gory Russia 69°0N 95°0E 29 C10
Putrajaya Malaysia 2°55N 101°40E 39 L3
Puttalam Sri Lanka 8°1N 79°55E 40 Q11
Puttgarden Germany 54°30N 11°10E 16 A6
Putumayo → S. Amer. 3°7S 67°58W 92 D5
Putussibau Indonesia 0°50N 112°56E 36 D4
Puvirnituq Canada 60°2N 77°10W 69 C12
Puy-de-Dôme France 45°46N 2°57E 20 D5
Puyallup U.S.A. 47°12N 122°18W 78 C4
Puyang China 35°40N 115°1E 34 G8
Pūzeh Rīg Iran 27°20N 58°40E 45 E8
Pwani □ Tanzania 7°0S 39°0E 54 D4
Pweto Dem. Rep. of the Congo 8°25S 28°51E 55 D2
Pwllheli U.K. 52°53N 4°25W 12 E3
Pya-ozero Russia 66°5N 30°58E 8 C24
Pyapon Burma 16°20N 95°40E 41 L19
Pyasina → Russia 73°30N 87°0E 29 B9
Pyatigorsk Russia 44°2N 43°6E 19 F7
Pyè = Prome Burma 18°49N 95°13E 41 K19
Pyeongtaek S. Korea 37°1N 127°4E 35 F14
Pyetrikaw Belarus 52°11N 28°29E 17 B15
Pyhäjoki Finland 64°28N 24°14E 8 D21
Pyinmana Burma 19°45N 96°12E 41 K20
Pyla, C. Cyprus 34°56N 33°51E 25 E12
Pymatuning Res. U.S.A. 41°30N 80°28W 82 E4
Pyŏktong N. Korea 40°50N 125°50E 35 D13
Pyŏnggang N. Korea 38°24N 127°17E 35 E14
P'yŏngsong N. Korea 39°14N 125°52E 35 E13
P'yŏngyang N. Korea 39°0N 125°30E 35 E13
Pyote U.S.A. 31°32N 103°8W 84 F3
Pyramid L. U.S.A. 40°1N 119°35W 76 F4
Pyramid Pk. U.S.A. 36°25N 116°37W 79 J10
Pyramids Egypt 29°58N 31°9E 51 C12
Pyrénées Europe 42°45N 0°18E 20 E4
Pyu Burma 18°30N 96°28E 41 K20

Q

Qaanaaq Greenland 77°40N 69°0W 4 B4
Qachasnek S. Africa 30°6S 28°42E 57 E4
Qa'el Jafr Jordan 30°20N 36°25E 46 E5
Qa'emābād Iran 31°44N 60°2E 45 D9
Qā'emshahr Iran 36°30N 52°53E 45 B7
Qagan Nur China 43°30N 114°55E 34 C8
Qahar Youyi Zhongqi China 41°12N 112°40E 34 D7
Qahremānshahr = Kermānshāh Iran 34°23N 47°0E 44 C5
Qaidam Pendi China 37°0N 95°0E 32 C4
Qajarīyeh Iran 31°1N 48°22E 45 D6
Qala, Ras il Malta 36°2N 14°20E 25 C1
Qala-i-Jadid = Spīn Būldak Afghan. 31°1N 66°25E 42 D2
Qala Point = Qala, Ras il Malta 36°2N 14°20E 25 C1
Qala Viala Pakistan 30°49N 67°17E 42 D2
Qala Yangi Afghan. 34°20N 66°30E 42 B2
Qal'at al Akhḍar Si. Arabia 28°4N 37°9E 44 E3
Qal'at Dīzah Iraq 36°11N 45°7E 44 B5
Qal'at Ṣāliḥ Iraq 31°31N 47°16E 44 D5
Qal'at Sukkar Iraq 31°51N 46°5E 44 D5
Qamani'tuaq = Baker Lake Canada 64°20N 96°3W 68 C10
Qamdo China 31°15N 97°6E 32 C4
Qamea Fiji 16°45S 179°45W 59 a
Qamruddin Karez Pakistan 31°45N 68°20E 42 D3
Qandahār = Kandahār Afghan. 31°32N 65°43E 40 D4
Qandahār = Kandahār □ Afghan. 31°0N 65°0E 40 D4
Qapān Iran 37°40N 55°47E 45 B7
Qapshaghay Kazakhstan 43°51N 77°14E 28 E8
Qaqortoq Greenland 60°43N 46°0W 4 C5
Qara Qash → China 35°0N 78°30E 43 B8
Qarabutaq Kazakhstan 49°59N 60°14E 28 E7
Qaraghandy Kazakhstan 49°50N 73°10E 28 E8
Qaraghayly Kazakhstan 49°26N 76°0E 28 E8
Qārah Si. Arabia 29°55N 40°3E 44 D4
Qarataū Kazakhstan 43°30N 69°30E 28 E7
Qarataū Zhambyl, Kazakhstan 43°10N 70°28E 28 E8
Qarazhal Kazakhstan 48°2N 70°49E 28 E8
Qardho = Gardo Somali Rep. 9°30N 49°6E 47 F4

Qareh → Iran 39°25N 47°22E 44 B5
Qareh Tekān Iran 36°38N 49°29E 45 B6
Qarnein U.A.E. 24°56N 52°52E 45 E7
Qarqan He → China 39°30N 88°30E 32 C3
Qarqaraly Kazakhstan 49°26N 75°30E 28 E8
Qarshi Uzbekistan 38°53N 65°48E 28 F7
Qartabā Lebanon 34°4N 35°50E 46 A4
Qaryat al Gharab Iraq 31°27N 44°48E 44 D5
Qaryat al 'Ulyā Si. Arabia 27°33N 47°42E 44 E5
Qasr 'Amra Jordan 31°48N 36°35E 44 D3
Qaşr-e Qand Iran 26°15N 60°45E 45 E9
Qaşr-e Shīrīn Iran 34°31N 45°35E 44 C5
Qasr Farâfra Egypt 27°0N 28°1E 51 C11
Qatanā Syria 33°26N 36°4E 46 B5
Qatar ■ Asia 25°30N 51°15E 45 E6
Qatlīsh Iran 37°50N 57°19E 45 B8
Qattâra, Munkhafed el Egypt 29°30N 27°30E 51 C11
Qattâra Depression = Qattâra, Munkhafed el Egypt 29°30N 27°30E 51 C11
Qausiuittuq = Resolute Canada 74°42N 94°54W 69 B10
Qawām al Ḩamzah = Al Ḩamzah Iraq 31°43N 44°58E 44 D5
Qāyen Iran 33°40N 59°10E 45 C8
Qazaqstan = Kazakhstan ■ Asia 50°0N 70°0E 28 E7
Qazimämmäd Azerbaijan 40°3N 49°0E 45 A6
Qazvīn Iran 36°15N 50°0E 45 B6
Qazvīn □ Iran 36°20N 50°0E 45 B6
Qena Egypt 26°10N 32°43E 51 C12
Qeqertarsuaq Greenland 69°15N 53°38W 4 C5
Qeqertarsuaq Greenland 69°45N 53°30W 66 C14
Qeshlāq Iran 34°55N 46°28E 44 C5
Qeshm Iran 26°55N 56°10E 45 E8
Qeys Iran 26°32N 53°58E 45 E7
Qezel Owzen → Iran 36°45N 49°22E 45 B6
Qezi'ot Israel 30°52N 34°26E 46 E3
Qi Xian China 34°40N 114°48E 34 G8
Qian Gorlos China 45°5N 124°42E 35 B13
Qian Hai China 22°32N 113°54E 33 F10
Qian Xian China 34°31N 108°15E 34 G5
Qianshan China 22°15N 113°31E 33 G10
Qianyang China 34°40N 107°8E 34 G4
Qi'ao China 22°25N 113°39E 33 G10
Qi'ao Dao China 22°25N 113°38E 33 G10
Qiemo China 38°8N 85°32E 32 C3
Qijiaojing China 43°28N 91°36E 32 B4
Qikiqtarjuaq Canada 67°33N 63°0W 69 C13
Qila Saifullāh Pakistan 30°45N 68°17E 42 D3
Qilian Shan China 38°30N 96°0E 32 C4
Qin He → China 35°1N 113°22E 34 G7
Qin Ling = Qinling Shandi China 33°50N 108°10E 34 H5
Qin'an China 34°48N 105°40E 34 G3
Qing Xian China 38°35N 116°45E 34 E9
Qingcheng China 37°15N 117°40E 35 F9
Qingdao China 36°5N 120°20E 35 F11
Qingfeng China 35°52N 115°8E 34 G8
Qinghai □ China 36°0N 98°0E 32 C4
Qinghai Hu China 36°40N 100°10E 32 C5
Qinghecheng China 41°28N 124°15E 35 D13
Qinghemen China 41°48N 121°25E 35 D11
Qingjian China 37°8N 110°8E 34 F6
Qingjiang = Huaiyin China 33°30N 119°2E 35 H10
Qingshui China 34°48N 106°8E 34 G4
Qingshuihe China 39°55N 111°35E 34 E6
Qingtongxia Shuiku China 37°50N 105°58E 34 F3
Qingxu China 37°34N 112°22E 34 F7
Qingyang China 36°2N 107°55E 34 F4
Qingyuan China 42°10N 124°55E 35 C13
Qingyun China 37°45N 117°20E 35 F9
Qinhuangdao China 39°56N 119°30E 35 E10
Qinling Shandi China 33°50N 108°10E 34 H5
Qinshui China 35°40N 112°8E 34 G7
Qinyang = Jiyuan China 35°7N 112°57E 34 G7
Qinyuan China 36°29N 112°20E 34 F7
Qinzhou China 21°58N 108°38E 32 D5
Qionghai China 19°15N 110°26E 38 C8
Qiongzhou Haixia China 20°10N 110°15E 38 B8
Qiqihar China 47°26N 124°0E 33 B7
Qira China 37°0N 80°48E 32 C3
Qiraîya, W. → Egypt 30°27N 34°0E 46 E3
Qiryat Ata Israel 32°47N 35°6E 46 C4
Qiryat Gat Israel 31°32N 34°46E 46 D3
Qiryat Mal'akhi Israel 31°44N 34°44E 46 D3
Qiryat Shemona Israel 33°13N 35°35E 46 B4
Qiryat Yam Israel 32°51N 35°4E 46 C4
Qishan China 34°25N 107°38E 34 G4
Qitai China 44°2N 89°35E 32 B3
Qixia China 37°17N 120°52E 35 F11
Qızılağac Körfäzi Azerbaijan 39°9N 49°0E 45 B6
Qojūr Iran 36°12N 47°55E 44 B5
Qom Iran 34°40N 51°0E 45 C6
Qom □ Iran 34°40N 51°0E 45 C6
Qomolangma Feng = Everest, Mt. Nepal 28°5N 86°58E 43 E12
Qomsheh Iran 32°0N 51°55E 45 D6
Qoqon = Qŭqon Uzbekistan 40°31N 70°56E 28 E8
Qoraqalpoghistan □ Uzbekistan 43°0N 58°0E 28 E6
Qostanay Kazakhstan 53°10N 63°35E 28 D7
Quabbin Res. U.S.A. 42°20N 72°20W 83 D12
Quairading Australia 32°0S 117°21E 61 F2
Quakertown U.S.A. 40°26N 75°21W 83 F9
Qualicum Beach Canada 49°22N 124°26W 70 D4
Quambatook Australia 35°49S 143°34E 63 F3
Quambone Australia 30°57S 147°53E 63 E4
Quamby Australia 20°22S 140°17E 62 C3
Quan Long = Ca Mau Vietnam 9°7N 105°8E 39 H5
Quanah U.S.A. 34°18N 99°44W 84 D5
Quang Ngai Vietnam 15°13N 108°58E 38 E7
Quang Tri Vietnam 16°45N 107°13E 38 D6
Quang Yen Vietnam 20°56N 106°52E 38 B6
Quantock Hills U.K. 51°8N 3°10W 13 F4
Quanzhou China 24°55N 118°34E 33 D6
Qu'Appelle → Canada 50°33N 103°53W 71 C8
Quaqtaq Canada 60°55N 69°40W 69 C13
Quaraí Brazil 30°15S 56°20W 94 C4
Quartu Sant'Élena Italy 39°15N 9°10E 22 E3
Quartzsite U.S.A. 33°40N 114°13W 79 M12
Quatre Bornes Mauritius 20°15S 57°28E 53 d
Quatsino Sd. Canada 50°25N 127°58W 70 C3
Quba Azerbaijan 41°21N 48°32E 19 F8
Qūchān Iran 37°10N 58°27E 45 B8
Queanbeyan Australia 35°17S 149°14E 63 F4
Québec Canada 46°52N 71°13W 73 C5
Québec □ Canada 48°0N 74°0W 73 C6
Quebrada del Condorito △ Argentina 31°49S 64°40W 94 C3
Queen Alexandra Ra. Antarctica 85°0S 170°0E 5 E11
Queen Charlotte City Canada 53°15N 132°2W 70 C2
Queen Charlotte Is. Canada 53°20N 132°10W 70 C2
Queen Charlotte Sd. Canada 51°0N 128°0W 70 C3
Queen Charlotte Strait Canada 50°45N 127°10W 70 C3
Queen Elizabeth △ Uganda 0°0 30°0E 54 C3
Queen Elizabeth ⌂ U.K. 56°7N 4°30W 11 E4
Queen Elizabeth Is. Canada 76°0N 95°0W 69 B10
Queen Mary Land Antarctica 70°0S 95°0E 5 D7
Queen Maud G. Canada 68°15N 102°30W 68 C9
Queen Maud Land = Dronning Maud Land Antarctica 72°30S 12°0E 5 D3
Queen Maud Mts. Antarctica 86°0S 160°0W 5 E13
Queens Chan. Australia 15°0S 129°30E 60 C4
Queenscliff Australia 38°16S 144°39E 63 F3
Queensland □ Australia 22°0S 142°0E 62 C3
Queenstown Australia 42°4S 145°35E 63 G4
Queenstown N.Z. 45°1S 168°40E 59 F2
Queenstown Singapore 1°18N 103°48E 39 d
Queenstown S. Africa 31°52S 26°52E 56 E4
Queets U.S.A. 47°32N 124°19W 78 C2
Queguay Grande → Uruguay 32°9S 58°9W 94 C4
Queimadas Brazil 11°0S 39°38W 93 F11
Quelimane Mozam. 17°53S 36°58E 55 F4
Quellón Chile 43°7S 73°37W 96 E2
Quelpart = Jeju-do S. Korea 33°29N 126°34E 35 H14
Quemado N. Mex., U.S.A. 34°20N 108°30W 77 J9
Quemado Tex., U.S.A. 28°50N 100°37W 84 G4
Quemú-Quemú Argentina 36°3S 63°36W 94 D3
Quequén Argentina 38°30S 58°30W 94 D4
Querétaro Mexico 20°36N 100°23W 86 C4
Querétaro □ Mexico 21°0N 99°55W 86 C5
Queshan China 32°55N 114°2E 34 H8
Quesnel Canada 53°0N 122°30W 70 C4
Quesnel → Canada 52°58N 122°29W 70 C4
Quesnel L. Canada 52°30N 121°20W 70 C4
Questa U.S.A. 36°42N 105°36W 77 H11
Quetico ⌂ Canada 48°30N 91°45W 72 C1
Quetta Pakistan 30°15N 66°55E 42 D2
Quezaltenango Guatemala 14°50N 91°30W 88 D1
Quezon City Phil. 14°37N 121°2E 37 B6
Qufār Si. Arabia 27°26N 41°37E 44 E4
Qui Nhon Vietnam 13°40N 109°13E 38 F7
Quibala Angola 10°46S 14°59E 52 G2
Quibaxe Angola 8°24S 14°27E 52 F2
Quibdó Colombia 5°42N 76°40W 92 B3
Quiberon France 47°29N 3°9W 20 C2
Quiet L. Canada 61°5N 133°5W 70 A2
Quiindy Paraguay 25°58S 57°14W 94 B4
Quilá Mexico 24°23N 107°13W 86 C3
Quilán, C. Chile 43°15S 74°30W 96 E2
Quilcene U.S.A. 47°49N 122°53W 78 C4
Quilimarí Chile 32°5S 71°30W 94 C1
Quilino Argentina 30°14S 64°29W 94 C3
Quill Lakes Canada 51°55N 104°13W 71 C8
Quillabamba Peru 12°50S 72°50W 92 F4
Quillagua Chile 21°40S 69°40W 94 A2
Quillaicillo Chile 31°17S 71°40W 94 C1
Quillota Chile 32°54S 71°16W 94 C1
Quilmes Argentina 34°43S 58°15W 94 C4
Quilon India 8°50N 76°38E 40 Q10
Quilpie Australia 26°35S 144°11E 63 D3
Quilpué Chile 33°5S 71°33W 94 C1
Quilua Mozam. 16°17S 39°54E 55 F4
Quimilí Argentina 27°40S 62°30W 94 B3
Quimper France 48°0N 4°9W 20 B1
Quimperlé France 47°53N 3°33W 20 C2
Quinault → U.S.A. 47°21N 124°18W 78 C2
Quincy Calif., U.S.A. 39°56N 120°57W 78 F6
Quincy Fla., U.S.A. 30°35N 84°34W 85 F12
Quincy Ill., U.S.A. 39°56N 91°23W 80 F8
Quincy Mass., U.S.A. 42°14N 71°0W 83 D14
Quincy Wash., U.S.A. 47°14N 119°51W 76 C4
Quines Argentina 32°13S 65°48W 94 C2
Quinga Mozam. 15°49S 40°15E 55 F5
Quintana Roo □ Mexico 19°40N 88°30W 87 D7
Quintanar de la Orden Spain 39°36N 3°5W 21 C4
Quinte West Canada 44°10N 77°34W 82 B7
Quintero Chile 32°45S 71°30W 94 C1
Quirihue Chile 36°15S 72°35W 94 D1
Quirindi Australia 31°28S 150°40E 63 E5
Quirinópolis Brazil 18°32S 50°30W 93 G8
Quissanga Mozam. 12°24S 40°28E 55 E5
Quissico Mozam. 24°42S 34°44E 57 C5
Quitilipi Argentina 26°50S 60°13W 94 B3
Quitman U.S.A. 30°47N 83°34W 85 F13
Quito Ecuador 0°15S 78°35W 92 D3
Quixadá Brazil 4°55S 39°0W 93 D11
Quixaxe Mozam. 15°17S 40°4E 55 F5
Qulan Kazakhstan 42°55N 72°43E 28 E8
Qul'ân, Jazâ'ir Egypt 24°22N 35°31E 44 E2
Qumbu S. Africa 31°10S 28°48E 57 E4
Quneitra Syria 33°7N 35°48E 46 B4
Qŭnghirot Uzbekistan 43°2N 58°50E 28 E6
Quoin I. Australia 14°54S 129°32E 60 B4
Quoin Pt. S. Africa 34°46S 19°37E 56 E2
Quorn Australia 32°25S 138°5E 63 E2
Qŭqon Uzbekistan 40°30N 70°56E 28 E8
Qurnat as Sawdā' Lebanon 34°18N 36°6E 46 A5
Quşaybā' Si. Arabia 26°53N 43°35E 44 E4
Qusaybah Iraq 34°24N 40°59E 44 C4
Quseir Egypt 26°7N 34°16E 44 E2
Qūshchī Iran 37°59N 45°3E 44 B5
Quthing Lesotho 30°25S 27°36E 57 E4
Qūţīābād Iran 35°47N 48°30E 45 C6
Quwo China 35°38N 111°25E 34 G6
Quyang China 38°35N 114°40E 34 E8
Quynh Nhai Vietnam 21°49N 103°33E 38 B4
Quyon Canada 45°31N 76°14W 83 A8
Quzhou China 28°57N 118°54E 33 D6
Quzi China 36°20N 107°20E 34 F4
Qyzylorda Kazakhstan 44°48N 65°28E 28 E7

R

Ra, Ko Thailand 9°13N 98°16E 39 H2
Raahe Finland 64°40N 24°28E 8 D21
Raalte Neths. 52°23N 6°16E 15 B6
Raasay U.K. 57°25N 6°4W 11 D2
Raasay, Sd. of U.K. 57°30N 6°8W 11 D2
Raba Indonesia 8°36S 118°55E 37 F5
Rába → Hungary 47°38N 17°38E 17 E9
Rabai Kenya 3°50S 39°31E 54 C4
Rabat = Victoria Malta 36°3N 14°14E 25 C1
Rabat Malta 35°53N 14°24E 25 D1
Rabat Morocco 34°2N 6°48W 50 B4
Rabaul Papua N. G. 4°24S 152°18E 58 B8
Rabi Fiji 16°30S 179°59W 59 a
Rābigh Si. Arabia 22°50N 39°5E 47 C2
Răbniţa Moldova 47°45N 29°0E 17 E15
Rābor Iran 29°17N 56°55E 45 D8
Race, C. Canada 46°40N 53°5W 73 C9
Rach Gia Vietnam 10°5N 105°5E 39 G5
Rachid Mauritania 18°45N 11°35W 50 E3
Racibórz Poland 50°7N 18°18E 17 C10
Racine U.S.A. 42°44N 87°47W 80 D10
Rackerby U.S.A. 39°26N 121°22W 78 F5
Radama, Nosy Madag. 14°0S 47°47E 57 A8
Radama, Saikanosy Madag. 14°16S 47°53E 57 A8
Rădăuţi Romania 47°50N 25°59E 17 E13
Radcliff U.S.A. 37°51N 85°57W 81 G11
Radekhiv Ukraine 50°25N 24°32E 17 C13
Radekhov = Radekhiv Ukraine 50°25N 24°32E 17 C13
Radford U.S.A. 37°8N 80°34W 81 G13
Radhanpur India 23°50N 71°38E 42 H4
Radhwa, Jabal Si. Arabia 24°34N 38°18E 44 E3
Radisson Qué., Canada 53°47N 77°37W 72 B4
Radisson Sask., Canada 52°30N 107°20W 71 C7
Radium Hot Springs Canada 50°35N 116°2W 70 C5
Radnor Forest U.K. 52°17N 3°10W 13 E4
Radom Poland 51°23N 21°12E 17 C11
Radomsko Poland 51°5N 19°28E 17 C10
Radomyshl Ukraine 50°30N 29°12E 17 C15
Radstock, C. Australia 33°12S 134°20E 63 E1
Radviliškis Lithuania 55°49N 23°33E 9 J20
Radville Canada 49°30N 104°15W 71 D8
Rae Canada 62°50N 116°3W 70 A5
Rae Bareli India 26°18N 81°20E 43 F9
Rae Isthmus Canada 66°40N 87°30W 69 C11
Raeren Belgium 50°41N 6°7E 15 D6
Raeside, L. Australia 29°20S 122°0E 61 E3
Raetihi N.Z. 39°25S 175°17E 59 C5
Rafaela Argentina 31°10S 61°30W 94 C3
Rafah Gaza Strip 31°18N 34°14E 46 D3
Rafai C.A.R. 4°59N 23°58E 54 B1
Rafḩā Si. Arabia 29°35N 43°35E 44 D4
Rafsanjān Iran 30°30N 56°5E 45 D8
Raft Pt. Australia 16°4S 124°26E 60 C3
Râgâ Sudan 8°28N 25°41E 51 G11
Ragachow Belarus 53°8N 30°5E 17 B16
Ragama Sri Lanka 7°0N 79°50E 40 R11
Ragged, Mt. Australia 33°27S 123°25E 61 F3
Ragged Pt. Barbados 13°10N 59°26W 89 g
Raghunathpalli India 22°14N 84°48E 43 H11
Raghunathpur India 23°33N 86°40E 43 H12
Raglan N.Z. 37°55S 174°55E 59 B5
Ragusa Italy 36°55N 14°44E 22 F6
Raha Indonesia 4°55S 123°0E 37 E6
Rahaeng = Tak Thailand 16°52N 99°8E 38 D2
Rahatgarh India 23°47N 78°22E 43 H8
Rahimyar Khan Pakistan 28°30N 70°25E 42 E4
Rāhjerd Iran 34°22N 50°22E 45 C6
Rahole ⌂ Kenya 0°5N 38°57E 54 B4
Rahon India 31°3N 76°7E 42 D7
Raiatéa, Î. French Polynesia 16°50S 151°25W 65 J12
Raichur India 16°10N 77°20E 40 L10
Raiganj India 25°37N 88°10E 43 G13
Raigarh India 21°56N 83°25E 41 J13
Raijua Indonesia 10°37S 121°36E 37 F6
Raikot India 30°41N 75°42E 42 D6
Railton Australia 41°25S 146°28E 63 G4
Rainbow Bridge ⌂ U.S.A. 37°5N 110°58W 77 H8
Rainbow Lake Canada 58°30N 119°23W 70 B5
Rainier U.S.A. 46°53N 122°41W 78 D4
Rainier, Mt. U.S.A. 46°52N 121°46W 78 D5
Rainy L. Canada 48°42N 93°10W 71 D10
Rainy River Canada 48°43N 94°29W 71 D10
Raippaluoto Finland 63°13N 21°14E 8 E19
Raipur India 21°17N 81°45E 41 J12
Raisen India 23°20N 77°48E 42 H8
Raisio Finland 60°28N 22°11E 9 F20
Raj Nandgaon India 21°5N 81°5E 41 J12
Raj Nilgiri India 21°28N 86°46E 43 J12
Raja, Ujung Indonesia 3°40N 96°25E 36 D1
Raja Ampat, Kepulauan Indonesia 0°30S 130°0E 37 E7
Rajahmundry India 17°1N 81°48E 41 L12
Rajaji △ India 30°10N 78°20E 42 D8
Rajang → Malaysia 2°30N 112°0E 36 D4
Rajanpur Pakistan 29°6N 70°19E 42 E4
Rajapalaiyam India 9°25N 77°35E 40 Q10
Rajasthan □ India 26°45N 73°30E 42 F5
Rajasthan Canal = Indira Gandhi Canal India 28°0N 72°0E 42 F5
Rajauri India 33°25N 74°21E 43 C6
Rajgarh Mad. P., India 24°2N 76°45E 42 G7
Rajgarh Raj., India 27°14N 76°38E 42 F7
Rajgarh Raj., India 28°40N 75°25E 42 E6
Rajgir India 25°2N 85°25E 43 G11
Rajkot India 22°15N 70°56E 42 H4
Rajmahal Hills India 24°30N 87°30E 43 G12
Rajpipla India 21°50N 73°30E 40 J8
Rajpur India 22°18N 74°21E 42 H6
Rajpura India 30°25N 76°32E 42 D7
Rajshahi Bangla. 24°22N 88°39E 41 G16
Rajshahi □ Bangla. 25°0N 89°0E 43 G13
Rajula India 21°3N 71°26E 42 J4
Rakaia N.Z. 43°45S 172°1E 59 E4
Rakaia → N.Z. 43°36S 172°15E 59 E4
Rakan, Ra's Qatar 26°10N 51°20E 45 E6
Rakaposhi Pakistan 36°10N 74°25E 43 A6
Rakata, Pulau Indonesia 6°10S 105°20E 36 F3
Rakhiv Ukraine 48°3N 24°12E 17 D13
Rakhni Pakistan 30°4N 69°56E 42 D3
Rakhni → Pakistan 29°31N 69°36E 42 E3
Rakiraki Fiji 17°22S 178°11E 59 a
Rakitnoye Russia 45°36N 134°17E 30 B7
Rakiura △ N.Z. 47°0S 167°50E 59 G1
Rakops Botswana 21°1S 24°28E 56 C3
Rakvere Estonia 59°20N 26°25E 9 G22
Raleigh U.S.A. 35°47N 78°39W 85 D15
Ralik Chain Pac. Oc. 8°0N 168°0E 64 G8
Ralls U.S.A. 33°41N 101°24W 84 E4
Ralston U.S.A. 41°30N 76°57W 82 E8
Ram → Canada 62°1N 123°41W 70 A4
Rām Allāh West Bank 31°55N 35°10E 46 D4
Rama Nic. 12°9N 84°15W 88 D3
Ramakona India 21°43N 78°50E 43 J8
Rāmallāh = Rām Allāh West Bank 31°55N 35°10E 46 D4
Raman Thailand 6°29N 101°18E 39 J3
Ramanathapuram India 9°25N 78°55E 40 Q11
Ramanetaka, B. de Madag. 14°13S 47°52E 57 A8
Ramanujganj India 23°48N 83°42E 43 H10
Ramat Gan Israel 32°4N 34°48E 46 C3
Ramatlhabama S. Africa 25°37S 25°33E 56 D4
Ramban India 33°14N 75°12E 43 C6
Rambi = Rabi Fiji 16°30S 179°59W 59 a
Rambipuji Indonesia 8°12S 113°37E 37 H15
Rame Hd. Australia 37°47S 149°30E 63 F4
Ramechhap Nepal 27°25N 86°10E 43 F12
Ramganga → India 27°5N 79°58E 43 F8
Ramgarh Jharkhand, India 23°40N 85°35E 43 H11
Ramgarh Raj., India 27°16N 75°14E 42 F6
Ramgarh Raj., India 27°30N 70°36E 42 F4
Rāmhormoz Iran 31°15N 49°35E 45 D6
Ramīān Iran 37°3N 55°16E 45 B7
Ramingining Australia 12°19S 135°3E 62 A2
Ramla Israel 31°55N 34°52E 46 D3
Ramm = Rum Jordan 29°39N 35°26E 46 F4
Ramm, Jabal Jordan 29°35N 35°24E 46 F4
Ramnad = Ramanathapuram India 9°25N 78°55E 40 Q11
Ramnagar Jammu & Kashmir, India 32°47N 75°18E 43 C6
Ramnagar Uttaranchal, India 29°24N 79°7E 43 E8
Râmnicu Sărat Romania 45°26N 27°3E 17 F14
Râmnicu Vâlcea Romania 45°9N 24°21E 17 F13
Ramona U.S.A. 33°2N 116°52W 79 M10
Ramore Canada 48°30N 80°25W 72 C3
Ramotswa Botswana 24°50S 25°52E 56 C4
Rampur H.P., India 31°26N 77°43E 42 D7
Rampur Mad. P., India 23°25N 73°53E 42 H5
Rampur Ut. P., India 28°50N 79°5E 43 E8
Rampur Hat India 24°10N 87°50E 43 G12
Rampura India 24°30N 75°27E 42 G6
Ramrama Tola India 21°52N 79°55E 43 J8
Ramree I. Burma 19°0N 93°40E 41 K19
Rāmsar Iran 36°53N 50°41E 45 B6
Ramsey I. of Man 54°20N 4°22W 12 C3
Ramsey U.S.A. 41°4N 74°9W 83 E10
Ramsey L. Canada 47°13N 82°15W 72 C3
Ramsgate U.K. 51°20N 1°25E 13 F9
Ramtek India 21°20N 79°15E 40 J11
Ramu Kenya 3°55N 41°10E 54 B5
Rana Pratap Sagar Dam India 24°58N 75°38E 42 G6
Ranaghat India 23°15N 88°35E 43 H13
Ranahu Pakistan 25°55N 69°45E 42 G3
Ranau Malaysia 6°2N 116°40E 36 C5
Rancagua Chile 34°10S 70°50W 94 C1
Rancheria → Canada 60°13N 129°7W 70 A3
Ranchester U.S.A. 44°54N 107°10W 76 D10
Ranchi India 23°19N 85°27E 43 H11
Rancho Cordova U.S.A. 38°36N 121°18W 78 G5
Rancho Cucamonga U.S.A. 34°10N 117°30W 79 L9
Randalstown U.K. 54°45N 6°19W 10 B5
Randers Denmark 56°29N 10°1E 9 H14
Randfontein S. Africa 26°8S 27°45E 57 D4
Randle U.S.A. 46°32N 121°57W 78 D5
Randolph Mass., U.S.A. 42°10N 71°2W 83 D13
Randolph N.Y., U.S.A. 42°10N 78°59W 82 D6
Randolph Utah, U.S.A. 41°40N 111°11W 76 F8
Randolph Vt., U.S.A. 43°55N 72°40W 83 C12
Randsburg U.S.A. 35°22N 117°39W 79 K9
Råneälven → Sweden 65°50N 22°20E 8 D20
Rangae Thailand 6°19N 101°44E 39 J3
Rangaunu B. N.Z. 34°51S 173°15E 59 A4
Range, The Zimbabwe 19°2S 31°2E 55 F3
Rangeley U.S.A. 44°58N 70°39W 83 B14
Rangeley L. U.S.A. 44°55N 70°43W 83 B14
Rangely U.S.A. 40°5N 108°48W 76 F9
Ranger U.S.A. 32°28N 98°41W 84 E5
Rangia India 26°28N 91°38E 41 F17
Rangiora N.Z. 43°19S 172°36E 59 E4
Rangitaiki → N.Z. 37°54S 176°49E 59 B6
Rangitata → N.Z. 43°45S 171°15E 59 E3
Rangitoto ke te tonga = D'Urville I. N.Z. 40°50S 173°55E 59 D4
Rangkasbitung Indonesia 6°21S 106°15E 37 G12
Rangon → Burma 16°28N 96°40E 41 L20
Rangoon Burma 16°45N 96°20E 41 L20
Rangpur Bangla. 25°42N 89°22E 41 G16
Rangsit Thailand 13°59N 100°37E 38 F3
Ranibennur India 14°35N 75°30E 40 M9
Raniganj Ut. P., India 27°3N 82°13E 43 F9
Raniganj W. Bengal, India 23°40N 87°5E 41 H15
Ranikhet India 29°39N 79°25E 43 E8
Raniwara India 24°50N 72°10E 42 G5
Rāniyah Iraq 36°15N 44°53E 44 B5
Ranka India 23°59N 83°47E 43 H10
Ranken → Australia 20°31S 137°36E 62 C2
Rankin U.S.A. 31°13N 101°56W 84 F4
Rankin Inlet Canada 62°30N 93°0W 68 C10
Rankins Springs Australia 33°49S 146°14E 63 E4
Rannoch, L. U.K. 56°41N 4°20W 11 E4
Rannoch Moor U.K. 56°38N 4°48W 11 E4
Ranobe, Helodranon' i Madag. 23°3S 43°33E 57 C7
Ranohira Madag. 22°29S 45°24E 57 C8
Ranomafana Toamasina, Madag. 18°57S 48°50E 57 B8
Ranomafana Toliara, Madag. 24°34S 47°0E 57 C8
Ranomafana △ Madag. 21°16S 47°25E 57 C8
Ranomena Madag. 23°25S 47°17E 57 C8
Ranong Thailand 9°50N 98°40E 39 H2
Ranotsara Nord Madag. 22°48S 46°36E 57 C8
Rānsa Iran 33°39N 48°18E 45 C6
Ransiki Indonesia 1°30S 134°10E 37 E8
Rantabe Madag. 15°42S 49°39E 57 B8
Rantauprapat Indonesia 2°15N 99°50E 36 D1
Rantemario Indonesia 3°15S 119°57E 37 E5
Ranthambore △ India 26°10N 76°30E 42 F7
Rantoul U.S.A. 40°19N 88°9W 80 E9
Raoyang China 38°15N 115°45E 34 E8
Rap, Ko Thailand 9°19N 99°58E 39 b
Rapa French Polynesia 27°35S 144°20W 65 K13
Rapa Nui = Pascua, I. de Chile 27°7S 109°23W 65 K17
Rapallo Italy 44°21N 9°14E 20 D8
Rapar India 23°34N 70°38E 42 H4
Rāpch Iran 25°40N 59°15E 45 E8
Raper, C. Canada 69°44N 67°6W 69 C13
Rapid City U.S.A. 44°5N 103°14W 80 C2
Rapid River U.S.A. 45°55N 86°58W 80 C10
Rapla Estonia 59°1N 24°52E 9 G21
Rapti → India 26°18N 83°41E 43 F10
Raquette → U.S.A. 45°0N 74°42W 83 B10
Raquette Lake U.S.A. 43°49N 74°40W 83 C10
Rara △ Nepal 29°30N 82°10E 43 E10
Rarotonga Cook Is. 21°30S 160°0W 65 K12
Ra's al 'Ayn Syria 36°45N 40°12E 44 B4
Ra's al Khaymah U.A.E. 25°50N 55°59E 45 E7
Rasca, Pta. de la Canary Is. 27°59N 16°41W 24 G3
Raseiniai Lithuania 55°25N 23°5E 9 J20
Rashmi India 25°4N 74°22E 42 G6
Rasht Iran 37°20N 49°40E 45 B6
Rasi Salai Thailand 15°20N 104°9E 38 E5
Rason L. Australia 28°45S 124°25E 61 E3
Rasra India 25°50N 83°50E 43 G10
Rasul Pakistan 32°42N 73°34E 42 C5
Rat → Canada 49°35N 97°10W 71 D9
Rat Buri Thailand 13°30N 99°54E 38 F2
Rat Islands U.S.A. 52°0N 178°0E 74 a
Rat L. Canada 56°10N 99°40W 71 B9
Ratak Chain Pac. Oc. 1°0N 170°0E 64 G8
Ratangarh India 28°5N 74°35E 42 E6
Raţāwī Iraq 30°38N 47°13E 44 D5
Rath India 25°36N 79°37E 43 G8
Rath Luirc Ireland 52°21N 8°40W 10 D3
Rathangan Ireland 53°13N 7°1W 10 C4
Rathdrum Ireland 52°56N 6°14W 10 D5
Rathenow Germany 52°37N 12°19E 16 B7
Rathkeale Ireland 52°32N 8°56W 10 D3
Rathlin I. U.K. 55°18N 6°14W 10 A5
Rathmelton Ireland 55°2N 7°38W 10 A4
Ratibor = Racibórz Poland 50°7N 18°18E 17 C10
Ratlam India 23°20N 75°0E 42 H6

Ratnagiri India 16°57N 73°18E 40 L8
Ratodero Pakistan 27°48N 68°18E 42 F3
Raton U.S.A. 36°54N 104°24W 77 H11
Rattaphum Thailand 7°8N 100°16E 39 J3
Rattray Hd. U.K. 57°38N 1°50W 11 D7
Ratz, Mt. Canada 57°23N 132°12W 70 B2
Raub Malaysia 3°47N 101°52E 39 L3
Rauch Argentina 36°45S 59°5W 94 D4
Raudales Mexico 17°27N 93°39W 87 D6
Raufarhöfn Iceland 66°27N 15°57W 8 C6
Raufoss Norway 60°44N 10°37E 8 F14
Raukumara Ra. N.Z. 38°5S 177°55E 59 C6
Rauma Finland 61°10N 21°30E 8 F19
Raumo = Rauma Finland 61°10N 21°30E 8 F19
Raung, Gunung Indonesia 8°8S 114°3E 37 J17
Raurkela India 22°14N 84°50E 43 H11
Rausu-Dake Japan 44°4N 145°7E 30 B12
Rava-Ruska Ukraine 50°15N 23°42E 17 C12
Rava Russkaya = Rava-Ruska Ukraine 50°15N 23°42E 17 C12
Ravalli U.S.A. 47°17N 114°11W 76 C6
Ravānsar Iran 34°43N 46°40E 44 C5
Rāvar Iran 31°20N 56°51E 45 D8
Ravena U.S.A. 42°28N 73°49W 83 D11
Ravenna Italy 44°25N 12°12E 22 B5
Ravenna Nebr., U.S.A. 41°1N 98°55W 80 E4
Ravenna Ohio, U.S.A. 41°9N 81°15W 82 E3
Ravensburg Germany 47°46N 9°36E 16 E5
Ravenshoe Australia 17°37S 145°29E 62 B4
Ravensthorpe Australia 33°35S 120°2E 61 F3
Ravenswood Australia 20°6S 146°54E 62 C4
Ravenswood U.S.A. 38°57N 81°46W 81 F13
Ravi → Pakistan 30°35N 71°49E 42 D4
Rawalpindi Pakistan 33°38N 73°8E 42 C5
Rawāndūz Iraq 36°40N 44°30E 44 B5
Rawang Malaysia 3°20N 101°35E 39 L3
Rawene N.Z. 35°25S 173°32E 59 A4
Rawlinna Australia 30°58S 125°28E 61 F4
Rawlins U.S.A. 41°47N 107°14W 76 F10
Rawlinson Ra. Australia 24°40S 128°30E 61 D4
Rawson Argentina 43°15S 65°5W 96 E3
Raxaul India 26°59N 84°51E 43 F11
Ray U.S.A. 48°21N 103°10W 80 A2
Ray, C. Canada 47°33N 59°15W 73 C8
Raya Ring, Ko Thailand 8°18N 98°29E 39 a
Rayadurg India 14°40N 76°50E 40 M10
Rayagada India 19°15N 83°20E 41 K13
Raychikhinsk Russia 49°46N 129°25E 29 E13
Rāyen Iran 29°34N 57°26E 45 D8
Rayleigh U.K. 51°36N 0°37E 13 F8
Raymond Canada 49°30N 112°35W 70 D6
Raymond Calif., U.S.A. 37°13N 119°54W 78 H7
Raymond N.H., U.S.A. 43°2N 71°11W 83 C13
Raymond Wash., U.S.A. 46°41N 123°44W 78 D3
Raymondville U.S.A. 26°29N 97°47W 84 H6
Raymore Canada 51°25N 104°31W 71 C8
Rayón Mexico 29°43N 110°35W 86 B2
Rayong Thailand 12°40N 101°20E 38 F3
Rayville U.S.A. 32°29N 91°46W 84 E9
Raz, Pte. du France 48°2N 4°47W 20 C1
Razan Iran 35°23N 49°2E 45 C6
Razāzah, Buḩayrat ar Iraq 32°40N 43°35E 44 C4
Razazah, L. = Razāzah, Buḩayrat ar Iraq 32°40N 43°35E 44 C4
Razdel'naya = Rozdilna Ukraine 46°50N 30°2E 17 E16
Razdolnoye Russia 43°30N 131°52E 30 C5
Razeh Iran 32°47N 48°9E 45 C6
Razgrad Bulgaria 43°33N 26°34E 23 C12
Razim, Lacul Romania 44°50N 29°0E 17 F15
Razmak Pakistan 32°45N 69°50E 42 C3
Ré, Î. de France 46°12N 1°30W 20 C3
Reading U.K. 51°27N 0°58W 13 F7
Reading U.S.A. 40°20N 75°56W 83 F9
Reading □ U.K. 51°27N 0°58W 13 F7
Realicó Argentina 35°0S 64°15W 94 D3
Ream Cambodia 10°34N 103°39E 39 G4
Reay Forest U.K. 58°22N 4°55W 11 C4
Rebi Indonesia 6°23S 134°7E 37 F8
Rebiana Libya 24°12N 22°10E 51 D10
Rebiana, Sahrâ' Libya 24°30N 21°0E 51 D10
Reboly Russia 63°49N 30°47E 8 E24
Rebun-Tō Japan 45°23N 141°2E 30 B10
Recherche, Arch. of the Australia 34°15S 122°50E 61 F3
Rechna Doab Pakistan 31°35N 73°30E 42 D5
Rechytsa Belarus 52°21N 30°24E 17 B16
Recife Brazil 8°0S 35°0W 93 E12
Recife Seychelles 4°36S 55°42E 53 b
Recklinghausen Germany 51°37N 7°12E 15 C7
Reconquista Argentina 29°10S 59°45W 94 B4
Recreo Argentina 29°25S 65°10W 94 B2
Red → U.S.A. 31°1N 91°45W 84 F9
Red Bank U.S.A. 40°21N 74°5W 83 F10
Red Bay Canada 51°44N 56°25W 73 B8
Red Bluff U.S.A. 40°11N 122°15W 76 F2
Red Bluff Res. U.S.A. 31°54N 103°55W 77 L12
Red Cliffs Australia 34°19S 142°11E 63 E3
Red Cloud U.S.A. 40°5N 98°32W 80 E4
Red Creek U.S.A. 43°14N 76°45W 83 C8
Red Deer Canada 52°20N 113°50W 70 C6
Red Deer → Alta., Canada 50°58N 110°0W 71 C7
Red Deer → Man., Canada 52°53N 101°1W 71 C8
Red Deer L. Canada 52°55N 101°20W 71 C8
Red Hook U.S.A. 41°55N 73°53W 83 E11
Red Indian L. Canada 48°35N 57°0W 73 C8
Red L. Canada 51°3N 93°49W 71 C10
Red Lake Canada 51°3N 93°49W 71 C10
Red Lake Falls U.S.A. 47°53N 96°16W 80 B5
Red Lake Road Canada 49°59N 93°25W 71 C10
Red Lodge U.S.A. 45°11N 109°15W 76 D9
Red Mountain U.S.A. 35°37N 117°38W 79 K9
Red Oak U.S.A. 41°1N 95°14W 80 E6
Red River of the North → N. Amer. 49°0N 97°15W 80 A5
Red Rock Canada 48°55N 88°15W 72 C2
Red Rock, L. U.S.A. 41°22N 92°59W 80 E7
Red Rocks Pt. Australia 32°13S 127°32E 61 F4
Red Sea Asia 25°0N 36°0E 47 C2
Red Slate Mt. U.S.A. 37°31N 118°52W 78 H8
Red Sucker L. Canada 54°9N 93°40W 72 B1
Red Tower Pass = Turnu Roşu, P. Romania 45°33N 24°17E 17 F13
Red Wing U.S.A. 44°34N 92°31W 80 C7
Redang Malaysia 5°49N 103°2E 39 K4
Redange Lux. 49°46N 5°52E 15 E5
Redcar U.K. 54°37N 1°4W 12 C6
Redcar & Cleveland □ U.K. 54°29N 1°0W 12 C7
Redcliff Canada 50°10N 110°50W 76 A8
Redcliffe Australia 27°12S 153°0E 63 D5
Redcliffe, Mt. Australia 28°30S 121°30E 61 E3
Reddersburg S. Africa 29°41S 26°10E 56 D4
Redding U.S.A. 40°35N 122°24W 76 F2
Redditch U.K. 52°18N 1°55W 13 E6
Redfield U.S.A. 44°53N 98°31W 80 C4
Redford U.S.A. 44°38N 73°48W 83 B11
Redhead Trin. & Tob. 10°44N 60°58W 93 K16
Redlands U.S.A. 34°4N 117°11W 79 M9
Redmond Oreg., U.S.A. 44°17N 121°11W 76 D3
Redmond Wash., U.S.A. 47°40N 122°7W 78 C4
Redon France 47°40N 2°6W 20 C2
Redonda Antigua & B. 16°58N 62°19W 89 C7
Redondela Spain 42°15N 8°38W 21 A1
Redondo Beach U.S.A. 33°50N 118°23W 79 M8
Redruth U.K. 50°14N 5°14W 13 G2
Redvers Canada 49°35N 101°40W 71 D8
Redwater Canada 53°55N 113°6W 70 C6
Redwood U.S.A. 44°18N 75°48W 83 B9
Redwood △ U.S.A. 41°40N 124°5W 76 F1
Redwood City U.S.A. 37°30N 122°15W 78 H4
Redwood Falls U.S.A. 44°32N 95°7W 80 C6
Ree, L. Ireland 53°35N 8°0W 10 C3
Reed City U.S.A. 43°53N 85°31W 81 D11
Reed L. Canada 54°38N 100°30W 71 C8
Reedley U.S.A. 36°36N 119°27W 78 J7
Reedsburg U.S.A. 43°32N 90°0W 80 D8
Reedsport U.S.A. 43°42N 124°6W 76 E1
Reedsville U.S.A. 40°39N 77°35W 82 F7
Reefton N.Z. 42°6S 171°51E 59 E3
Reese → U.S.A. 40°48N 117°4W 76 F5
Refugio U.S.A. 28°18N 97°17W 84 G6
Regensburg Germany 49°1N 12°6E 16 D7
Reggâne = Zaouiet Reggâne Algeria 26°32N 0°3E 50 C6
Réggio di Calábria Italy 38°6N 15°39E 22 E6
Réggio nell'Emília Italy 44°43N 10°36E 22 B4
Reghin Romania 46°46N 24°42E 17 E13
Regina Canada 50°27N 104°35W 71 C8
Regina Beach Canada 50°47N 105°0W 71 C8
Registro Brazil 24°29S 47°49W 95 A6
Rehar → India 23°55N 82°40E 43 H10
Rehli India 23°38N 79°5E 43 H8
Rehoboth Namibia 23°15S 17°4E 56 C2
Rehovot Israel 31°54N 34°48E 46 D3
Reichenbach Germany 50°37N 12°17E 16 C7
Reid Australia 30°49S 128°26E 61 F4
Reidsville U.S.A. 36°21N 79°40W 85 C15
Reigate U.K. 51°14N 0°12W 13 F7
Reims France 49°15N 4°1E 20 B6
Reina Adelaida, Arch. Chile 52°20S 74°0W 96 G2
Reina Sofía, Tenerife ✈ (TFS) Canary Is. 28°3N 16°33W 24 F3
Reindeer → Canada 55°36N 103°11W 71 B8
Reindeer I. Canada 52°30N 98°0W 71 C9
Reindeer L. Canada 57°15N 102°15W 71 B8
Reinga, C. N.Z. 34°25S 172°43E 59 A4
Reinosa Spain 43°2N 4°15W 21 A3
Reitz S. Africa 27°48S 28°29E 57 D4
Reivilo S. Africa 27°36S 24°8E 56 D3
Reliance Canada 63°0N 109°20W 71 A7
Remarkable, Mt. Australia 32°48S 138°10E 63 E2
Rembang Indonesia 6°42S 111°21E 37 G14
Remedios Panama 8°15N 81°50W 88 E3
Remeshk Iran 26°55N 58°50E 45 E8
Remich Lux. 49°32N 6°22E 15 E6
Remscheid Germany 51°11N 7°12E 15 C7
Ren Xian China 37°8N 114°40E 34 F8
Rendang Indonesia 8°26S 115°25E 37 J18
Rendsburg Germany 54°17N 9°39E 16 A5
Renfrew Canada 45°30N 76°40W 83 A8
Renfrewshire □ U.K. 55°49N 4°38W 11 F4
Rengat Indonesia 0°30S 102°45E 36 E2
Rengo Chile 34°24S 70°50W 94 C1
Reni Ukraine 45°28N 28°15E 17 F15
Renmark Australia 34°11S 140°43E 63 E3
Rennell Sd. Canada 53°23N 132°35W 70 C2
Renner Springs Australia 18°20S 133°47E 62 B1
Rennes France 48°7N 1°41W 20 B3
Rennick Glacier Antarctica 70°30S 161°45E 5 D21
Rennie L. Canada 61°32N 105°35W 71 A7
Reno U.S.A. 39°31N 119°48W 78 F7
Reno → Italy 44°38N 12°16E 22 B5
Renovo U.S.A. 41°20N 77°45W 82 E7
Renqiu China 38°43N 116°5E 34 E9
Rensselaer Ind., U.S.A. 40°57N 87°9W 80 E10
Rensselaer N.Y., U.S.A. 42°38N 73°45W 83 D11
Rentería Spain 43°19N 1°54W 21 A5
Renton U.S.A. 47°28N 122°12W 78 C4
Reotipur India 25°33N 83°45E 43 G10
Republic Mo., U.S.A. 37°7N 93°29W 80 G7
Republic Wash., U.S.A. 48°39N 118°44W 76 B4
Republican → U.S.A. 39°4N 96°48W 80 F5
Repulse B. Australia 20°35S 148°46E 62 J6
Repulse Bay Canada 66°30N 86°30W 69 C11
Requena Peru 5°5S 73°52W 92 E4
Requena Spain 39°30N 1°4W 21 C5
Reşadiye = Datça Turkey 36°46N 27°40E 23 F12
Reserve U.S.A. 33°43N 108°45W 77 K9
Resht = Rasht Iran 37°20N 49°40E 45 B6
Resistencia Argentina 27°30S 59°0W 94 B4
Reşiţa Romania 45°18N 21°53E 17 F11
Reso = Raisio Finland 60°28N 22°11E 9 F20
Resolute Canada 74°42N 94°54W 69 B10
Resolution I. Canada 61°30N 65°0W 69 C13
Resolution I. N.Z. 45°40S 166°40E 59 F1
Ressano Garcia Mozam. 25°25S 32°0E 57 D5
Reston Canada 49°33N 101°6W 71 D8
Retalhuleu Guatemala 14°33N 91°46W 88 D1
Retenue, L. de Dem. Rep. of the Congo 11°0S 27°0E 55 E2
Retford U.K. 53°19N 0°56W 12 D7
Rethimno Greece 35°18N 24°30E 25 D6
Rethimno □ Greece 35°23N 24°28E 25 D6
Reti Pakistan 28°5N 69°48E 42 E3
Réunion ☒ Ind. Oc. 21°0S 56°0E 53 c
Reus Spain 41°10N 1°5E 21 B6
Reutlingen Germany 48°29N 9°12E 16 D5
Reval = Tallinn Estonia 59°22N 24°48E 9 G21
Revda Russia 56°48N 59°57E 18 C10
Revelganj India 25°50N 84°40E 43 G11
Revelstoke Canada 51°0N 118°10W 70 C5
Reventazón Peru 6°10S 80°58W 92 E2
Revillagigedo, Is. de Pac. Oc. 18°40N 112°0W 86 D2
Revuè → Mozam. 19°50S 34°0E 55 F3
Rewa India 24°33N 81°25E 43 G9
Rewari India 28°15N 76°40E 42 E7
Rexburg U.S.A. 43°49N 111°47W 76 E8
Rey Iran 35°35N 51°25E 45 C6
Rey, I. del Panama 8°20N 78°30W 88 E4
Rey, L. del Mexico 27°1N 103°26W 86 B4
Rey Malabo Eq. Guin. 3°45N 8°50E 52 D1
Reyðarfjörður Iceland 65°2N 14°13W 8 D6
Reyes, Pt. U.S.A. 38°0N 123°0W 78 H3
Reykjahlið Iceland 65°40N 16°55W 8 D5
Reykjanes Iceland 63°48N 22°40W 8 E2
Reykjavík Iceland 64°10N 21°57W 8 D3
Reynolds Ra. Australia 22°30S 133°0E 60 D5
Reynoldsville U.S.A. 41°6N 78°53W 82 E6
Reynosa Mexico 26°7N 98°18W 87 B5
Rēzekne Latvia 56°30N 27°17E 9 H22
Rezvān Iran 27°34N 56°6E 45 E8
Rhayader U.K. 52°18N 3°29W 13 E4
Rhein → Europe 51°52N 6°2E 15 C6
Rhein-Main-Donau-Kanal Germany 49°1N 11°27E 16 D6
Rheine Germany 52°17N 7°26E 16 B4
Rheinland-Pfalz □ Germany 50°0N 7°0E 16 C4
Rhin = Rhein → Europe 51°52N 6°2E 15 C6
Rhine = Rhein → Europe 51°52N 6°2E 15 C6
Rhinebeck U.S.A. 41°56N 73°55W 83 E11
Rhineland-Palatinate = Rheinland-Pfalz □ Germany 50°0N 7°0E 16 C4
Rhinelander U.S.A. 45°38N 89°25W 80 C9
Rhinns Pt. U.K. 55°40N 6°29W 11 F2
Rhino Camp Uganda 3°0N 31°22E 54 B3
Rhir, Cap Morocco 30°38N 9°54W 50 B4
Rhode Island □ U.S.A. 41°40N 71°30W 83 E13
Rhodes Greece 36°15N 28°10E 25 C10
Rhodope Mts. = Rhodopi Planina Bulgaria 41°40N 24°20E 23 D11
Rhodopi Planina Bulgaria 41°40N 24°20E 23 D11
Rhön Germany 50°24N 9°58E 16 C5
Rhondda U.K. 51°39N 3°31W 13 F4
Rhondda Cynon Taff □ U.K. 51°42N 3°27W 13 F4
Rhône → France 43°28N 4°42E 20 E6
Rhum U.K. 57°0N 6°20W 11 E2
Rhyl U.K. 53°20N 3°29W 12 D4
Riachão Brazil 7°20S 46°37W 93 E9
Riasi India 33°10N 74°50E 43 C6
Riau □ Indonesia 0°0 102°35E 36 D2
Riau, Kepulauan Indonesia 0°30N 104°20E 36 D2
Riau Arch. = Riau, Kepulauan Indonesia 0°30N 104°20E 36 D2
Ribadeo Spain 43°35N 7°5W 21 A2
Ribas do Rio Pardo Brazil 20°27S 53°46W 93 H8
Ribauè Mozam. 14°57S 38°17E 55 E4
Ribble → U.K. 53°52N 2°25W 12 D5
Ribe Denmark 55°19N 8°44E 9 J13
Ribeira Brava Madeira 32°41N 17°4W 24 D2
Ribeira Grande C. Verde Is. 17°0N 25°4W 50 b
Ribeirão Prêto Brazil 21°10S 47°50W 95 A6
Riberalta Bolivia 11°0S 66°0W 92 F5
Riccarton N.Z. 43°32S 172°37E 59 E4
Rice U.S.A. 34°5N 114°51W 79 L12
Rice L. Canada 44°12N 78°10W 82 B6
Rice Lake U.S.A. 45°30N 91°44W 80 C8
Rich, C. Canada 44°43N 80°38W 82 B4
Richards Bay S. Africa 28°48S 32°6E 57 D5
Richardson → Canada 58°25N 111°14W 71 B6
Richardson Lakes U.S.A. 44°46N 70°58W 81 C18
Richardson Springs U.S.A. 39°51N 121°46W 78 F5
Riche, C. Australia 34°36S 118°47E 61 F2
Richey U.S.A. 47°39N 105°4W 76 C11
Richfield U.S.A. 38°46N 112°5W 76 G7
Richfield Springs U.S.A. 42°51N 74°59W 83 D10
Richford U.S.A. 45°0N 72°40W 83 B12
Richibucto Canada 46°42N 64°54W 73 C7
Richland Ga., U.S.A. 32°5N 84°40W 85 E12
Richland Wash., U.S.A. 46°17N 119°18W 76 C4
Richland Center U.S.A. 43°21N 90°23W 80 D8
Richlands U.S.A. 37°6N 81°48W 81 G13
Richmond Australia 20°43S 143°8E 62 C3
Richmond N.Z. 41°20S 173°12E 59 D4
Richmond U.K. 54°25N 1°43W 12 C6
Richmond Calif., U.S.A. 37°56N 122°21W 78 H4
Richmond Ind., U.S.A. 39°50N 84°53W 81 F11
Richmond Ky., U.S.A. 37°45N 84°18W 81 G11
Richmond Mich., U.S.A. 42°49N 82°45W 82 D2
Richmond Mo., U.S.A. 39°17N 93°58W 80 F7
Richmond Tex., U.S.A. 29°35N 95°46W 84 G7
Richmond Utah, U.S.A. 41°56N 111°48W 76 F8
Richmond Va., U.S.A. 37°33N 77°27W 81 G15
Richmond Vt., U.S.A. 44°24N 72°59W 83 B12
Richmond Hill Canada 43°52N 79°27W 82 C5
Richmond Ra. Australia 29°0S 152°45E 63 D5
Richtersveld △ S. Africa 28°15S 17°10E 56 D2
Richwood U.S.A. 38°14N 80°32W 81 F13
Ridder = Leninogorsk Kazakhstan 50°20N 83°30E 28 D9
Riddlesburg U.S.A. 40°9N 78°15W 82 F6
Ridgecrest U.S.A. 35°38N 117°40W 79 K9
Ridgefield Conn., U.S.A. 41°17N 73°30W 83 E11
Ridgefield Wash., U.S.A. 45°49N 122°45W 78 E4
Ridgeland Miss., U.S.A. 32°26N 90°8W 85 E9
Ridgeland S.C., U.S.A. 32°29N 80°59W 85 E14
Ridgetown Canada 42°26N 81°52W 82 D3
Ridgewood U.S.A. 40°59N 74°7W 83 F10
Ridgway U.S.A. 41°25N 78°44W 82 E6
Riding Mountain △ Canada 50°50N 100°0W 71 C9
Ridley, Mt. Australia 33°12S 122°7E 61 F3
Riebeek-Oos S. Africa 33°10S 26°10E 56 E4
Ried Austria 48°14N 13°30E 16 D7
Riesa Germany 51°17N 13°17E 16 C7
Riet → S. Africa 29°0S 23°54E 56 D3
Rietbron S. Africa 32°54S 23°10E 56 E3
Rietfontein Namibia 21°58S 20°58E 56 C3
Rieti Italy 42°24N 12°51E 22 C5
Rif = Er Rif Morocco 35°1N 4°1W 50 A5
Riffe L. U.S.A. 46°32N 122°26W 78 D4
Rifle U.S.A. 39°32N 107°47W 76 G10
Rift Valley Africa 7°0N 30°0E 48 G7
Rift Valley □ Kenya 0°20N 36°0E 54 B4
Rīga Latvia 56°53N 24°8E 9 H21
Riga, G. of Latvia 57°40N 23°45E 9 H20
Rīgān Iran 28°37N 58°58E 45 D8
Rīgas Jūras Līcis = Riga, G. of Latvia 57°40N 23°45E 9 H20
Rigaud Canada 45°29N 74°18W 83 A10
Rigby U.S.A. 43°40N 111°55W 76 E8
Rīgestān Afghan. 30°15N 65°0E 40 D4
Riggins U.S.A. 45°25N 116°19W 76 D5
Rigolet Canada 54°10N 58°23W 73 B8
Rihand Dam India 24°9N 83°2E 43 G10
Riihimäki Finland 60°45N 24°48E 8 F21
Riiser-Larsen-halvøya Antarctica 68°0S 35°0E 5 C4
Rijeka Croatia 45°20N 14°21E 16 F8
Rijssen Neths. 52°19N 6°31E 15 B6
Rikuchū-Kaigan △ Japan 39°20N 142°0E 30 E11
Rikuzentakada Japan 39°0N 141°40E 30 E10
Riley U.S.A. 43°32N 119°28W 76 E4
Rima → Nigeria 13°4N 5°10E 50 F7
Rimah, Wadi ar → Si. Arabia 26°5N 41°30E 44 E4
Rimau, Pulau Malaysia 5°15N 100°16E 39 c
Rimbey Canada 52°35N 114°15W 70 C6
Rimersburg U.S.A. 41°3N 79°30W 82 E5
Rímini Italy 44°3N 12°33E 22 B5
Rimouski Canada 48°27N 68°30W 73 C6
Rimrock U.S.A. 46°40N 121°7W 78 D5
Rinca Indonesia 8°45S 119°35E 37 F5
Rincón de Romos Mexico 22°14N 102°18W 86 C4
Rinconada Argentina 22°26S 66°10W 94 A2
Rind → India 25°53N 80°33E 43 G9
Ringas India 27°21N 75°34E 42 F6
Ringgold Is. Fiji 16°15S 179°25W 59 a
Ringkøbing Denmark 56°5N 8°15E 9 H13
Ringvassøya Norway 69°56N 19°15E 8 B18
Ringwood U.S.A. 41°7N 74°15W 83 E10
Rinjani Indonesia 8°24S 116°28E 36 F5
Rio Branco Brazil 9°58S 67°49W 92 E5
Río Branco Uruguay 32°40S 53°40W 95 C5
Río Bravo Mexico 25°59N 98°6W 87 B5
Río Bravo ⌂ N. Amer. 29°2N 102°45W 86 B4
Río Bravo del Norte → Mexico 25°57N 97°9W 87 B5
Rio Brilhante Brazil 21°48S 54°33W 95 A5
Rio Claro Brazil 22°19S 47°35W 95 A6
Rio Claro Trin. & Tob. 10°20N 61°25W 89 D7
Río Colorado Argentina 39°0S 64°0W 96 D4
Río Cuarto Argentina 33°10S 64°25W 94 C3
Rio das Pedras Mozam. 23°8S 35°28E 57 C6
Rio de Janeiro Brazil 22°54S 43°12W 95 A7
Rio de Janeiro □ Brazil 22°50S 43°0W 95 A7
Rio do Sul Brazil 27°13S 49°37W 95 B6
Río Dulce ⌂ Guatemala 15°43N 88°50W 88 C2
Río Gallegos Argentina 51°35S 69°15W 96 G3
Río Grande Argentina 53°50S 67°45W 96 G3
Rio Grande Brazil 32°0S 52°20W 95 C5
Río Grande Mexico 23°50N 103°2W 86 C4
Río Grande Nic. 12°54N 83°33W 88 D3
Río Grande Puerto Rico 18°23N 65°50W 89 d
Rio Grande → N. Amer. 25°58N 97°9W 84 J6
Rio Grande City U.S.A. 26°23N 98°49W 84 H5
Río Grande de Santiago → Mexico 21°36N 105°26W 86 C3
Rio Grande do Norte □ Brazil 5°40S 36°0W 93 E11
Rio Grande do Sul □ Brazil 30°0S 53°0W 95 C5
Río Hato Panama 8°22N 80°10W 88 E3
Río Lagartos Mexico 21°36N 88°10W 87 C7
Rio Largo Brazil 9°28S 35°50W 93 E11
Río Mulatos Bolivia 19°40S 66°50W 92 G5
Río Muni □ Eq. Guin. 1°30N 10°0E 52 D2
Rio Negro Brazil 26°0S 49°55W 95 B6
Rio Pardo Brazil 30°0S 52°30W 95 C5
Río Pilcomayo △ Argentina 25°5S 58°5W 94 B4
Río Platano ⌂ Honduras 15°45N 85°0W 88 C3
Rio Rancho U.S.A. 35°14N 106°41W 77 J10
Río Segundo Argentina 31°40S 63°59W 94 C3
Río Tercero Argentina 32°15S 64°8W 94 C3
Rio Verde Brazil 17°50S 51°0W 93 G8
Río Verde Mexico 21°56N 99°59W 87 C5
Rio Vista U.S.A. 38°10N 121°42W 78 G5
Ríobamba Ecuador 1°50S 78°45W 92 D3
Ríohacha Colombia 11°33N 72°55W 92 A4
Ríosucio Colombia 7°27N 77°7W 92 B3
Riou L. Canada 59°7N 106°25W 71 B7
Ripley Canada 44°4N 81°35W 82 B3
Ripley Calif., U.S.A. 33°32N 114°39W 79 M12
Ripley N.Y., U.S.A. 42°16N 79°43W 82 D5
Ripley Tenn., U.S.A. 35°45N 89°32W 85 D10
Ripley W. Va., U.S.A. 38°49N 81°43W 81 F13
Ripon U.K. 54°9N 1°31W 12 C6
Ripon Calif., U.S.A. 37°44N 121°7W 78 H5
Ripon Wis., U.S.A. 43°51N 88°50W 80 D9
Rishā', W. ar → Si. Arabia 25°33N 44°5E 44 E5
Rishiri-Rebun-Sarobetsu △ Japan 45°26N 141°30E 30 B10
Rishiri-Tō Japan 45°11N 141°15E 30 B10
Rishon le Ziyyon Israel 31°58N 34°48E 46 D3
Rison U.S.A. 33°58N 92°11W 84 E8
Risør Norway 58°43N 9°13E 9 G13
Rita Blanca Cr. → U.S.A. 35°40N 102°29W 84 D3
Ritter, Mt. U.S.A. 37°41N 119°12W 78 H7
Rittman U.S.A. 40°58N 81°47W 82 F3
Ritzville U.S.A. 47°8N 118°23W 76 C4
Riva del Garda Italy 45°53N 10°50E 22 B4
Rivadavia B. Aires, Argentina 35°29S 62°59W 94 D3
Rivadavia Mendoza, Argentina 33°13S 68°30W 94 C2
Rivadavia Salta, Argentina 24°5S 62°54W 94 A3
Rivadavia Chile 29°57S 70°35W 94 B1
Rivas Nic. 11°30N 85°50W 88 D2
River Cess Liberia 5°30N 9°32W 50 G4
River Jordan Canada 48°26N 124°3W 78 B2
Rivera Argentina 37°12S 63°14W 94 D3
Rivera Uruguay 31°0S 55°50W 95 C4
Riverbank U.S.A. 37°44N 120°56W 78 H6
Riverdale U.S.A. 36°26N 119°52W 78 J7
Riverhead U.S.A. 40°55N 72°40W 83 F12
Riverhurst Canada 50°55N 106°50W 71 C7
Rivers Canada 50°2N 100°14W 71 C8
Rivers Inlet Canada 51°42N 127°15W 70 C3
Riversdale S. Africa 34°7S 21°15E 56 E3
Riverside U.S.A. 33°59N 117°22W 79 M9
Riverton Australia 34°10S 138°46E 63 E2
Riverton Canada 51°1N 97°0W 71 C9
Riverton N.Z. 46°21S 168°0E 59 G2
Riverton U.S.A. 43°2N 108°23W 76 E9
Riviera U.S.A. 35°4N 114°35W 79 K12
Riviera di Levante Italy 44°15N 9°30E 20 D8
Riviera di Ponente Italy 44°10N 8°20E 20 D8
Rivière-au-Renard Canada 48°59N 64°23W 73 C7
Rivière-du-Loup Canada 47°50N 69°30W 73 C6
Rivière-Pentecôte Canada 49°57N 67°1W 73 C6
Rivière-Pilote Martinique 14°26N 60°53W 88 c
Rivière St-Paul Canada 51°28N 57°45W 73 B8
Rivière-Salée Martinique 14°31N 61°0W 88 c
Rivne Ukraine 50°40N 26°10E 17 C14
Rívoli Italy 45°3N 7°31E 20 D7
Rivoli B. Australia 37°32S 140°3E 63 F3
Riyadh = Ar Riyāḑ Si. Arabia 24°41N 46°42E 44 E5
Riyadh al Khabrā' Si. Arabia 26°2N 43°33E 44 E4
Rize Turkey 41°0N 40°30E 19 F7
Rizhao China 35°25N 119°30E 35 G10
Rizokarpaso Cyprus 35°36N 34°23E 25 D13
Rizzuto, C. Italy 38°53N 17°5E 22 E7
Rjukan Norway 59°54N 8°33E 9 G13
Road Town Br. Virgin Is. 18°27N 64°37W 89 e
Roan Plateau U.S.A. 39°20N 109°20W 76 G9
Roanne France 46°3N 4°4E 20 C6
Roanoke Ala., U.S.A. 33°9N 85°22W 85 E12
Roanoke Va., U.S.A. 37°16N 79°56W 81 G14
Roanoke → U.S.A. 35°57N 76°42W 85 D16
Roanoke I. U.S.A. 35°53N 75°39W 85 D17
Roanoke Rapids U.S.A. 36°28N 77°40W 85 C16
Roatán Honduras 16°18N 86°35W 88 C2
Robāt Sang Iran 35°35N 59°10E 45 C8
Robātkarīm Iran 35°25N 50°59E 45 C6
Robātkarīm □ Iran 35°26N 50°59E 45 B6
Robbins I. Australia 40°42S 145°0E 63 G4
Robe → Australia 21°42S 116°15E 60 D2
Robert Lee U.S.A. 31°54N 100°29W 84 F4
Robertsdale U.S.A. 40°11N 78°6W 82 F6
Robertsganj India 24°44N 83°4E 43 G10
Robertson S. Africa 33°46S 19°50E 56 E2
Robertson I. Antarctica 65°15S 59°30W 5 C18
Robertson Ra. Australia 23°15S 121°0E 60 D3
Robertstown Australia 33°58S 139°5E 63 E2
Roberval Canada 48°32N 72°15W 73 C5

Robeson Chan. *N. Amer.* 82°0N 61°30W **4 A4**
Robesonia *U.S.A.* 40°21N 76°8W **83 F8**
Robinson *U.S.A.* 39°0N 87°44W **80 F10**
Robinson → *Australia* 16°3S 137°16E **62 B2**
Robinson Ra. *Australia* 25°40S 119°0E **61 E2**
Robinvale *Australia* 34°40S 142°45E **63 E3**
Roblin *Canada* 51°14N 101°21W **71 C8**
Roboré *Bolivia* 18°10S 59°45W **92 G7**
Robson *Canada* 49°20N 117°41W **70 D5**
Robson, Mt. *Canada* 53°10N 119°10W **70 C5**
Robstown *U.S.A.* 27°47N 97°40W **84 H6**
Roca, C. da *Portugal* 38°40N 9°31W **21 C1**
Roca Partida, I. *Mexico* 19°1N 112°2W **86 D2**
Rocas, I. *Brazil* 4°0S 34°1W **93 D12**
Rocha *Uruguay* 34°30S 54°25W **95 C5**
Rochdale *U.K.* 53°38N 2°9W **12 D5**
Rochefort *Belgium* 50°9N 5°12E **15 D5**
Rochefort *France* 45°56N 0°57W **20 D3**
Rochelle *U.S.A.* 41°56N 89°4W **80 E9**
Rocher River *Canada* 61°23N 112°44W **70 A6**
Rochester *U.K.* 51°23N 0°31E **13 F8**
Rochester Ind., *U.S.A.* 41°4N 86°13W **80 E10**
Rochester Minn., *U.S.A.* 44°1N 92°28W **80 C7**
Rochester N.H., *U.S.A.* 43°18N 70°59W **83 C14**
Rochester N.Y., *U.S.A.* 43°10N 77°37W **82 C7**
Rock → *Canada* 60°7N 127°7W **70 A3**
Rock, The *Australia* 35°15S 147°2E **63 F4**
Rock Creek *U.S.A.* 41°40N 80°52W **82 E4**
Rock Falls *U.S.A.* 41°47N 89°41W **80 E9**
Rock Hill *U.S.A.* 34°56N 81°1W **85 D14**
Rock Island *U.S.A.* 41°30N 90°34W **80 E8**
Rock Port *U.S.A.* 40°25N 95°31W **80 E6**
Rock Rapids *U.S.A.* 43°26N 96°10W **80 D5**
Rock Sound *Bahamas* 24°54N 76°12W **88 B4**
Rock Springs Mont.,
  U.S.A. 46°49N 106°15W **76 C10**
Rock Springs Wyo.,
  U.S.A. 41°35N 109°14W **76 F9**
Rock Valley *U.S.A.* 43°12N 96°18W **80 D5**
Rockall *Atl. Oc.* 57°37N 13°42W **6 D3**
Rockdale Tex., *U.S.A.* 30°39N 97°0W **84 F6**
Rockdale Wash.,
  U.S.A. 47°22N 121°28W **78 C5**
Rockeby = Mungkan Kandju △
  Australia 13°35S 142°52E **62 A3**
Rockefeller Plateau
  Antarctica 76°0S 130°0W **5 E14**
Rockford *U.S.A.* 42°16N 89°6W **80 D9**
Rockglen *Canada* 49°11N 105°57W **71 D7**
Rockhampton
  Australia 23°22S 150°32E **62 C5**
Rockingham *Australia* 32°15S 115°38E **61 F2**
Rockingham N.C.,
  U.S.A. 34°57N 79°46W **85 D15**
Rockingham Vt.,
  U.S.A. 43°11N 72°29W **83 C12**
Rockingham B.
  Australia 18°5S 146°10E **62 B4**
Rocklake *U.S.A.* 48°47N 99°15W **80 A4**
Rockland *Canada* 45°33N 75°17W **83 A9**
Rockland Idaho, *U.S.A.* 42°34N 112°53W **76 E7**
Rockland Maine, *U.S.A.* 44°6N 69°7W **81 C19**
Rockland Mich., *U.S.A.* 46°44N 89°11W **80 B9**
Rocklin *U.S.A.* 38°48N 121°14W **78 G5**
Rockly B. *Trin. & Tob.* 11°9N 60°46W **93 J16**
Rockmart *U.S.A.* 34°0N 85°3W **85 D12**
Rockport Mass., *U.S.A.* 42°39N 70°37W **83 D14**
Rockport Tex., *U.S.A.* 28°2N 97°3W **84 G6**
Rocksprings *U.S.A.* 30°1N 100°13W **84 F4**
Rockville Conn., *U.S.A.* 41°52N 72°28W **83 E12**
Rockville Md., *U.S.A.* 39°5N 77°9W **81 F15**
Rockwall *U.S.A.* 32°56N 96°28W **84 E6**
Rockwell City *U.S.A.* 42°24N 94°38W **80 D6**
Rockwood *Canada* 43°37N 80°8W **82 C4**
Rockwood Maine,
  U.S.A. 45°41N 69°45W **81 C19**
Rockwood Tenn.,
  U.S.A. 35°52N 84°41W **85 D12**
Rocky Ford *U.S.A.* 38°3N 103°43W **76 G12**
Rocky Gully *Australia* 34°30S 116°57E **61 F2**
Rocky Harbour *Canada* 49°36N 57°55W **73 C8**
Rocky Island L. *Canada* 46°55N 83°0W **72 C3**
Rocky Lane *Canada* 58°31N 116°22W **70 B5**
Rocky Mount *U.S.A.* 35°57N 77°48W **85 D16**
Rocky Mountain △
  U.S.A. 40°25N 105°45W **76 F11**
Rocky Mountain House
  Canada 52°22N 114°55W **70 C6**
Rocky Mts. *N. Amer.* 49°0N 115°0W **76 B6**
Rocky Point *Namibia* 19°3S 12°30E **56 B2**
Rod *Pakistan* 28°10N 63°5E **40 E3**
Roda *Greece* 39°48N 19°46E **25 A3**
Rødbyhavn *Denmark* 54°39N 11°22E **9 J14**
Roddickton *Canada* 50°51N 56°8W **73 B8**
Rodez *France* 44°21N 2°33E **20 D5**
Ródhos = Rhodes
  Greece 36°15N 28°10E **25 C10**
Rodia *Greece* 35°22N 25°1E **25 D7**
Rodney *Canada* 42°34N 81°41W **82 D3**
Rodney, C. *N.Z.* 36°17S 174°50E **59 B5**
Rodopos *Greece* 35°34N 23°45E **25 D5**
Rodriguez *Ind. Oc.* 19°45S 63°20E **3 E13**
Roe → *U.K.* 55°6N 6°59W **10 A5**
Roebling *U.S.A.* 40°7N 74°47W **83 F10**
Roebourne *Australia* 20°44S 117°9E **60 D2**
Roebuck B. *Australia* 18°5S 122°20E **60 C3**
Roermond *Neths.* 51°12N 6°0E **15 C6**
Roes Welcome Sd.
  Canada 65°0N 87°0W **69 C11**
Roeselare *Belgium* 50°57N 3°7E **15 D3**
Rogachev = Ragachow
  Belarus 53°8N 30°5E **17 B16**
Rogagua, L. *Bolivia* 13°43S 66°50W **92 F5**
Rogatyn *Ukraine* 49°24N 24°36E **17 D13**
Rogers *U.S.A.* 36°20N 94°7W **84 C7**
Rogers City *U.S.A.* 45°25N 83°49W **81 C12**
Rogersville *Canada* 46°44N 65°26W **73 C6**

Roggan → *Canada* 54°24N 79°25W **72 B4**
Roggan L. *Canada* 54°8N 77°50W **72 B4**
Roggeveen Basin
  Pac. Oc. 31°30S 95°30W **65 L18**
Roggeveldberge *S. Africa* 32°10S 20°10E **56 E3**
Rogoaguado, L. *Bolivia* 13°0S 65°30W **92 F5**
Rogojampi *Indonesia* 8°19S 114°17E **37 J17**
Rogue → *U.S.A.* 42°26N 124°26W **76 E1**
Rohnert Park *U.S.A.* 38°16N 122°40W **78 G4**
Rohri *Pakistan* 27°45N 68°51E **42 F3**
Rohri Canal *Pakistan* 26°15N 68°27E **42 F3**
Rohtak *India* 28°55N 76°43E **42 E7**
Roja *Latvia* 57°29N 22°43E **9 H20**
Rojas *Argentina* 34°10S 60°45W **94 C3**
Rojo, C. *Mexico* 21°33N 97°20W **87 C5**
Rokan → *Indonesia* 2°0N 100°50E **36 D2**
Rokiškis *Lithuania* 55°55N 25°35E **9 J21**
Rolândia *Brazil* 23°18S 51°23W **95 A5**
Rolla Mo., *U.S.A.* 37°57N 91°46W **80 G8**
Rolla N. Dak., *U.S.A.* 48°52N 99°37W **80 A4**
Rolleston *Australia* 24°28S 148°35E **62 C4**
Rollingstone *Australia* 19°2S 146°24E **62 B4**
Roma *Australia* 26°32S 148°49E **63 D4**
Roma *Italy* 41°54N 12°28E **22 D5**
Roma *Sweden* 57°32N 18°26E **9 H18**
Roma-Los Saenz *U.S.A.* 26°24N 99°1W **84 H5**
Romain, C. *U.S.A.* 33°0N 79°22W **85 E15**
Romaine → *Canada* 50°18N 63°47W **73 B7**
Roman *Romania* 46°57N 26°55E **17 E14**
Romang *Indonesia* 7°30S 127°20E **37 F7**
Români *Egypt* 30°59N 32°38E **46 E1**
Romania ■ *Europe* 46°0N 25°0E **17 F12**
Romano, Cayo *Cuba* 22°0N 77°30W **88 B4**
Romans-sur-Isère *France* 45°3N 5°3E **20 D6**
Romblon *Phil.* 12°33N 122°17E **37 B6**
Rome = Roma *Italy* 41°54N 12°28E **22 D5**
Rome Ga., *U.S.A.* 34°15N 85°10W **85 D12**
Rome N.Y., *U.S.A.* 43°13N 75°27W **83 C9**
Rome Pa., *U.S.A.* 41°51N 76°21W **83 E8**
Romney *U.S.A.* 39°21N 78°45W **81 F14**
Romney Marsh *U.K.* 51°2N 0°54E **13 F8**
Rømø *Denmark* 55°10N 8°30E **9 J13**
Romorantin-Lanthenay
  France 47°21N 1°45E **20 C4**
Romsdalen *Norway* 62°25N 7°52E **8 E12**
Romsey *U.K.* 51°0N 1°29W **13 G6**
Ron *Vietnam* 17°53N 106°27E **38 D6**
Rona *U.K.* 57°34N 5°59W **11 D3**
Ronan *U.S.A.* 47°32N 114°6W **76 C6**
Roncador, Cayos
  Colombia 13°32N 80°4W **88 D3**
Roncador, Serra do
  Brazil 12°30S 52°30W **93 F8**
Ronda *Spain* 36°46N 5°12W **21 D3**
Rondane *Norway* 61°57N 9°50E **8 F13**
Rondônia □ *Brazil* 11°0S 63°0W **92 F6**
Rondonópolis *Brazil* 16°28S 54°38W **93 G8**
Rong, Koh *Cambodia* 10°45N 103°15E **39 G4**
Ronge, L. la *Canada* 55°6N 105°17W **71 B7**
Rønne *Denmark* 55°6N 14°43E **9 J16**
Ronne Ice Shelf
  Antarctica 77°30S 60°0W **5 D18**
Ronsard, C. *Australia* 24°46S 113°10E **61 D1**
Ronse *Belgium* 50°45N 3°35E **15 D3**
Roodepoort *S. Africa* 26°11S 27°54E **57 D4**
Roof Butte *U.S.A.* 36°28N 109°5W **77 H9**
Rooiboklaagte →
  Namibia 20°50S 21°0E **56 C3**
Rooniu, Mt. *Tahiti* 17°49S 149°12W **59 d**
Roorkee *India* 29°52N 77°59E **42 E7**
Roosendaal *Neths.* 51°32N 4°29E **15 C4**
Roosevelt *U.S.A.* 40°18N 109°59W **76 F9**
Roosevelt → *Brazil* 7°35S 60°20W **92 E6**
Roosevelt, Mt. *Canada* 58°26N 125°20W **70 B3**
Roosevelt I. *Antarctica* 79°30S 162°0W **5 D12**
Roper → *Australia* 14°43S 135°27E **62 A2**
Roper Bar *Australia* 14°44S 134°44E **62 A1**
Roque Pérez *Argentina* 35°25S 59°24W **94 D4**
Roquetas de Mar *Spain* 36°46N 2°36W **21 D4**
Roraima □ *Brazil* 2°0N 61°30W **92 C6**
Roraima, Mt. *Venezuela* 5°10N 60°40W **92 B6**
Røros *Norway* 62°35N 11°23E **8 E14**
Rosa *Zambia* 9°33S 31°15E **55 D3**
Rosa, L. *Bahamas* 21°0N 73°30W **89 B5**
Rosa, Monte *Europe* 45°57N 7°53E **20 D7**
Rosalia *U.S.A.* 47°14N 117°22W **76 C5**
Rosamond *U.S.A.* 34°52N 118°10W **79 L8**
Rosario *Argentina* 33°0S 60°40W **94 C3**
Rosário *Brazil* 3°0S 44°15W **93 D10**
Rosario Baja Calif.,
  Mexico 30°0N 115°50W **86 B1**
Rosario Sinaloa, Mexico* 22°58N 105°53W **86 C3**
Rosario *Paraguay* 24°30S 57°35W **94 A4**
Rosario de la Frontera
  Argentina 25°50S 65°0W **94 B3**
Rosario de Lerma
  Argentina 24°59S 65°35W **94 A2**
Rosario del Tala
  Argentina 32°20S 59°10W **94 C4**
Rosário do Sul *Brazil* 30°15S 54°55W **95 C5**
Rosarito *Mexico* 32°20N 117°2W **79 N9**
Roscoe *U.S.A.* 41°56N 74°55W **83 E10**
Roscommon *Ireland* 53°38N 8°11W **10 C3**
Roscommon □ *Ireland* 53°49N 8°23W **10 C3**
Roscrea *Ireland* 52°57N 7°49W **10 D4**
Rose → *Australia* 14°16S 135°45E **62 A2**
Rose Belle *Mauritius* 20°24S 57°36E **53 d**
Rose Blanche-Harbour Le Cou
  Canada 47°38N 58°45W **73 C8**
Rose Hill *Mauritius* 20°14S 57°27E **53 d**
Rose Pt. *Canada* 54°11N 131°39W **70 C2**
Rose Valley *Canada* 52°19N 103°49W **71 C8**
Roseau *Dominica* 15°17N 61°24W **89 C7**
Roseau *U.S.A.* 48°51N 95°46W **80 A6**
Rosebery *Australia* 41°46S 145°33E **63 G4**
Rosebud *S. Dak.,
  U.S.A.* 43°14N 100°51W **80 D3**

Rosebud Tex., *U.S.A.* 31°4N 96°59W **84 F6**
Roseburg *U.S.A.* 43°13N 123°20W **76 E2**
Rosehearty *U.K.* 57°42N 2°7W **11 D6**
Roseires Res. *Sudan* 11°51N 34°23E **51 F12**
Roseland *U.S.A.* 38°25N 122°43W **78 G4**
Rosemary *Canada* 50°46N 112°5W **70 C6**
Rosenberg *U.S.A.* 29°34N 95°49W **84 G7**
Rosenheim *Germany* 47°51N 12°7E **16 E7**
Roses, G. de *Spain* 42°10N 3°15E **21 A7**
Rosetown *Canada* 51°35N 107°59W **71 C7**
Roseville Calif., *U.S.A.* 38°45N 121°17W **78 G5**
Roseville Mich., *U.S.A.* 42°30N 82°56W **82 D2**
Rosewood *Australia* 27°38S 152°36E **63 D5**
Rosh Pinna *Namibia* 17°27S 14°21E **56 B1**
Rosignano Maríttimo
  Italy 43°24N 10°28E **22 C4**
Rosignol *Guyana* 6°15N 57°30W **92 B7**
Roşiori de Vede *Romania* 44°9N 25°0E **17 F13**
Roskilde *Denmark* 55°38N 12°3E **9 J15**
Roslavl *Russia* 53°57N 32°55E **18 D5**
Rosmead *S. Africa* 31°29S 25°8E **56 E4**
Ross *Australia* 42°2S 147°30E **63 G4**
Ross *N.Z.* 42°53S 170°49E **59 E3**
Ross Dependency
  Antarctica 76°0S 170°0W **5 D12**
Ross I. *Antarctica* 77°30S 168°0E **5 D11**
Ross Ice Shelf *Antarctica* 80°0S 180°0E **5 E12**
Ross L. *U.S.A.* 48°44N 121°4W **76 B3**
Ross-on-Wye *U.K.* 51°54N 2°34W **13 F5**
Ross River *Australia* 23°44S 134°30E **62 C1**
Ross River *Canada* 62°30N 131°30W **70 A2**
Ross Sea *Antarctica* 74°0S 178°0E **5 D11**
Rossall Pt. *U.K.* 53°55N 3°3W **12 D4**
Rossan Pt. *Ireland* 54°42N 8°47W **10 B3**
Rossano *Italy* 39°36N 16°39E **22 E7**
Rossburn *Canada* 50°40N 100°49W **71 C8**
Rosseau *Canada* 45°16N 79°39W **82 A5**
Rosseau, L. *Canada* 45°10N 79°35W **82 A5**
Rosses, The *Ireland* 55°2N 8°20W **10 A3**
Rossignol, I. *Canada* 52°43N 73°40W **72 B5**
Rossignol L. *Canada* 44°12N 65°10W **73 D6**
Rossiya = Russia ■
  Eurasia 62°0N 105°0E **29 C11**
Rossland *Canada* 49°6N 117°50W **70 D5**
Rosslare *Ireland* 52°17N 6°24W **10 D5**
Rosslare Harbour
  Ireland 52°15N 6°20W **10 D5**
Rosso *Mauritania* 16°40N 15°45W **50 E2**
Rossosh *Russia* 50°15N 39°28E **19 D6**
Røssvatnet *Norway* 65°45N 14°5E **8 D16**
Røst *Norway* 67°32N 12°0E **8 C15**
Rosthern *Canada* 52°40N 106°20W **71 C7**
Rostock *Germany* 54°5N 12°8E **16 A7**
Rostov Don, Russia* 47°15N 39°45E **19 E6**
Rostov Sverdlovsk, Russia* 57°14N 39°25E **18 C6**
Roswell Ga., U.S.A.* 34°2N 84°22W **85 D12**
Roswell N. Mex.,
  U.S.A.* 33°24N 104°32W **77 K11**
Rotan *U.S.A.* 32°51N 100°28W **84 E4**
Rother → *U.K.* 50°59N 0°45E **13 G8**
Rothera *Antarctica* 67°30S 68°0W **5 C17**
Rotherham *U.K.* 53°26N 1°20W **12 D6**
Rothes *U.K.* 57°32N 3°13W **11 D5**
Rothesay *Canada* 45°23N 66°0W **73 C6**
Rothesay *U.K.* 55°50N 5°3W **11 F3**
Roti *Indonesia* 10°50S 123°0E **37 F6**
Roto *Australia* 33°0S 145°30E **63 E4**
Rotondo, Mte. *France* 42°14N 9°8E **20 E8**
Rotoroa, L. *N.Z.* 41°55S 172°39E **59 D4**
Rotorua *N.Z.* 38°9S 176°16E **59 C6**
Rotorua, L. *N.Z.* 38°5S 176°18E **59 C6**
Rotterdam *Neths.* 51°55N 4°30E **15 C4**
Rotterdam *U.S.A.* 42°48N 74°1W **83 D10**
Rottnest I. *Australia* 32°0S 115°27E **61 F2**
Rottumeroog *Neths.* 53°33N 6°34E **15 A6**
Rottweil *Germany* 48°9N 8°37E **16 D5**
Rotuma *Fiji* 12°25S 177°5E **58 C10**
Roubaix *France* 50°40N 3°10E **20 A5**
Rouen *France* 49°27N 1°4E **20 B4**
Rouleau *Canada* 50°10N 104°56W **71 C8**
Round I. *Mauritius* 19°51S 57°45E **53 d**
Round Mountain
  U.S.A. 38°43N 117°4W **76 G5**
Round Mt. *Australia* 30°26S 152°16E **63 E5**
Round Rock *U.S.A.* 30°31N 97°41W **84 F6**
Roundup *U.S.A.* 46°27N 108°33W **76 C9**
Rousay *U.K.* 59°10N 3°2W **11 B5**
Rouses Point *U.S.A.* 44°59N 73°22W **83 B11**
Rouseville *U.S.A.* 41°28N 79°42W **82 E5**
Rousse = Ruse *Bulgaria* 43°48N 25°59E **23 C12**
Roussillon *France* 42°30N 2°35E **20 E5**
Rouxville *S. Africa* 30°25S 26°50E **56 E4**
Rouyn-Noranda *Canada* 48°20N 79°0W **72 C4**
Rovaniemi *Finland* 66°29N 25°41E **8 C21**
Rovereto *Italy* 45°53N 11°3E **22 B4**
Rovigo *Italy* 45°4N 11°47E **22 B4**
Rovinj *Croatia* 45°5N 13°40E **16 F7**
Rovno = Rivne *Ukraine* 50°40N 26°10E **17 C14**
Rovuma = Ruvuma →
  Tanzania 10°29S 40°28E **55 E5**
Row'an *Iran* 35°8N 48°51E **45 C6**
Rowena *Australia* 29°48S 148°55E **63 D4**
Rowley Shoals *Australia* 17°30S 119°0E **60 C2**
Roxas *Phil.* 11°36N 122°49E **37 B6**
Roxboro *U.S.A.* 36°24N 78°59W **85 C15**
Roxborough
  Trin. & Tob. 11°15N 60°35W **93 J16**
Roxburgh *N.Z.* 45°33S 169°19E **59 F2**
Roxbury *U.S.A.* 40°6N 77°39W **82 F7**
Roxby Downs *Australia* 30°43S 136°46E **63 E2**
Roy Mont., *U.S.A.* 47°20N 108°58W **76 C9**
Roy N. Mex., *U.S.A.* 35°57N 104°12W **77 J11**
Roy Utah, *U.S.A.* 41°10N 112°2W **76 F7**
Royal Bardia △ *Nepal* 28°20N 81°20E **43 E9**
Royal Canal *Ireland* 53°30N 7°13W **10 C4**
Royal Chitawan △
  Nepal 26°30N 84°20E **43 F11**

Royal Leamington Spa
  U.K. 52°18N 1°31W **13 E6**
Royal Natal △ *S. Africa* 28°43S 28°51E **57 D4**
Royal Tunbridge Wells
  U.K. 51°7N 0°16E **13 F8**
Royale, Isle *U.S.A.* 48°0N 88°54W **80 B9**
Royan *France* 45°37N 1°2W **20 D3**
Royston *U.K.* 52°3N 0°0 **13 E7**
Rozdilna *Ukraine* 46°50N 30°2E **17 E16**
Rozhyshche *Ukraine* 50°54N 25°15E **17 C13**
Rtishchevo *Russia* 52°18N 43°46E **18 D7**
Ruacaná *Namibia* 17°27S 14°21E **56 B1**
Ruaha △ *Tanzania* 7°41S 34°30E **54 D3**
Ruahine Ra. *N.Z.* 39°55S 176°2E **59 C6**
Ruapehu *N.Z.* 39°17S 175°35E **59 C5**
Ruapuke I. *N.Z.* 46°46S 168°31E **59 G2**
Ruâq, W. *Egypt* 30°0N 33°49E **46 F2**
Rub' al Khālī *Si. Arabia* 19°0N 48°0E **47 D4**
Rubeho Mts. *Tanzania* 6°50S 36°25E **54 D4**
Rubh a' Mhail *U.K.* 55°56N 6°8W **11 F2**
Rubha Hunish *U.K.* 57°42N 6°20W **11 D2**
Rubha Robhanais = Lewis, Butt
  of *U.K.* 58°31N 6°16W **11 C2**
Rubicon → *U.S.A.* 38°53N 121°4W **78 G5**
Rubio *Venezuela* 7°43N 72°22W **92 B4**
Rubondo △ *Tanzania* 2°18S 31°58E **54 C3**
Rubtsovsk *Russia* 51°30N 81°10E **28 D9**
Ruby L. *U.S.A.* 40°10N 115°28W **76 F6**
Ruby Mts. *U.S.A.* 40°30N 115°20W **76 F6**
Rubyvale *Australia* 23°25S 147°42E **62 C4**
Rūd Sar *Iran* 37°8N 50°18E **45 B6**
Rudall *Australia* 33°43S 136°17E **63 E2**
Rudall → *Australia* 22°34S 122°13E **60 D3**
Rudall River △
  Australia 22°38S 122°30E **60 D3**
Rudewa *Tanzania* 10°7S 34°40E **55 E3**
Rudnyy *Kazakhstan* 52°57N 63°7E **28 D7**
Rudolfa, Ostrov *Russia* 81°45N 58°30E **28 A6**
Rudyard *U.S.A.* 46°14N 84°36W **81 B11**
Ruenya → *Africa* 16°24S 33°48E **55 F3**
Ruffling Pt. *Br. Virgin Is.* 18°44N 64°27W **89 e**
Rufiji → *Tanzania* 7°50S 39°15E **54 D4**
Rufino *Argentina* 34°20S 62°50W **94 C3**
Rufunsa *Zambia* 15°4S 29°34E **55 F2**
Rugby *U.K.* 52°23N 1°16W **13 E6**
Rugby *U.S.A.* 48°22N 100°0W **80 A4**
Rügen *Germany* 54°22N 13°24E **16 A7**
Ruhengeri *Rwanda* 1°30S 29°36E **54 C2**
Ruhnu *Estonia* 57°48N 23°15E **9 H20**
Ruhr → *Germany* 51°27N 6°43E **16 C4**
Ruhuhu → *Tanzania* 10°31S 34°34E **55 E3**
Ruidoso *U.S.A.* 33°20N 105°41W **77 K11**
Ruivo, Pico *Madeira* 32°45N 16°56W **24 D3**
Rujm Tal'at al Jamā'ah
  Jordan 30°24N 35°30E **46 E4**
Ruk *Pakistan* 27°50N 68°42E **42 F3**
Rukhla *Pakistan* 32°27N 71°57E **42 C4**
Ruki →
  Dem. Rep. of the Congo 0°5N 18°17E **52 E3**
Rukwa □ *Tanzania* 7°0S 31°30E **54 D3**
Rukwa, L. *Tanzania* 8°0S 32°20E **54 D3**
Rulhieres, C. *Australia* 13°56S 127°22E **60 B4**
Rum = Rhum *U.K.* 57°0N 6°20W **11 E2**
Rum *Jordan* 29°39N 35°26E **46 F4**
Rum Cay *Bahamas* 23°40N 74°58W **89 B5**
Rum Jungle *Australia* 13°0S 130°59E **60 B5**
Ruma △ *Kenya* 0°39S 34°18E **54 C3**
Rumāh *Si. Arabia* 25°29N 47°10E **44 E5**
Rumania = Romania ■
  Europe 46°0N 25°0E **17 F12**
Rumaylah *Iraq* 30°47N 47°37E **44 D5**
Rumbêk *Sudan* 6°54N 29°37E **51 G11**
Rumford *U.S.A.* 44°33N 70°33W **83 B14**
Rumia *Poland* 54°37N 18°25E **17 A10**
Rumoi *Japan* 43°56N 141°39E **30 C10**
Rumonge *Burundi* 3°59S 29°26E **54 C2**
Rumson *U.S.A.* 40°23N 74°0W **83 F11**
Rumuruti *Kenya* 0°17N 36°32E **54 B4**
Runan *China* 33°0N 114°30E **34 H8**
Runanga *N.Z.* 42°25S 171°15E **59 E3**
Runaway, C. *N.Z.* 37°32S 177°59E **59 B6**
Runaway Bay *Jamaica* 18°27N 77°20W **88 a**
Runcorn *U.K.* 53°21N 2°44W **12 D5**
Rundu *Namibia* 17°52S 19°43E **56 B2**
Rungwa *Tanzania* 6°55S 33°32E **54 D3**
Rungwa → *Tanzania* 7°36S 31°50E **54 D3**
Rungwa △ *Tanzania* 6°53S 34°2E **54 D3**
Rungwe *Tanzania* 9°11S 33°32E **55 D3**
Rungwe, Mt. *Tanzania* 9°8S 33°40E **52 F6**
Runton Ra. *Australia* 23°31S 123°6E **60 D3**
Ruokolahti *Finland* 61°17N 28°50E **8 F23**
Ruoqiang *China* 38°55N 88°10E **32 C3**
Rupa *India* 27°15N 92°21E **41 F18**
Rupar *India* 31°2N 76°38E **42 D7**
Rupat *Indonesia* 1°45N 101°40E **36 D2**
Rupen → *India* 23°28N 71°31E **42 H4**
Rupert → *Canada* 51°29N 78°45W **72 B4**
Rupert B. *Canada* 51°35N 79°0W **72 B4**
Rupert House = Waskaganish
  Canada 51°30N 78°40W **72 B4**
Rupsa *India* 21°37N 87°1E **43 J12**
Rurrenabaque *Bolivia* 14°30S 67°32W **92 F5**
Rusambo *Zimbabwe* 16°30S 32°4E **55 F3**
Rusape *Zimbabwe* 18°35S 32°8E **55 F3**
Ruschuk = Ruse
  Bulgaria 43°48N 25°59E **23 C12**
Ruse *Bulgaria* 43°48N 25°59E **23 C12**
Rush *Ireland* 53°31N 6°6W **10 C5**
Rushan *China* 36°56N 121°30E **35 F11**
Rushden *U.K.* 52°18N 0°35W **13 E7**
Rushmore, Mt. *U.S.A.* 43°53N 103°28W **80 D3**
Rushville Ill., *U.S.A.* 40°7N 90°34W **80 E8**
Rushville Ind., U.S.A.* 39°37N 85°27W **81 F11**
Rushville Nebr., U.S.A.* 42°43N 102°28W **80 D2**
Russas *Brazil* 4°55S 37°50W **93 D11**
Russell *Canada* 50°50N 101°20W **71 C8**

Russell Kans., *U.S.A.* 38°54N 98°52W **80 F4**
Russell N.Y., *U.S.A.* 44°27N 75°9W **83 B9**
Russell Pa., *U.S.A.* 41°57N 79°8W **82 E5**
Russell Cave △ *U.S.A.* 34°59N 85°49W **85 D12**
Russell L. Man., Canada* 56°15N 101°30W **71 B8**
Russell L. N.W.T.,
  Canada* 63°5N 115°44W **70 A5**
Russellkonda *India* 19°57N 84°42E **41 K14**
Russellville Ala.,
  U.S.A.* 34°30N 87°44W **85 D11**
Russellville Ark., U.S.A.* 35°17N 93°8W **84 D8**
Russellville Ky., U.S.A.* 36°51N 86°53W **80 G10**
Russia ■ *Eurasia* 62°0N 105°0E **29 C11**
Russian → *U.S.A.* 38°27N 123°8W **78 G3**
Russkoye Ustie *Russia* 71°0N 149°0E **4 B15**
Rustam *Pakistan* 34°25N 72°13E **42 B5**
Rustam Shahr *Pakistan* 26°58N 66°6E **42 F2**
Rustavi *Georgia* 41°30N 45°0E **19 F8**
Rustenburg *S. Africa* 25°41S 27°14E **56 D4**
Ruston *U.S.A.* 32°32N 92°38W **84 E8**
Rutana *Burundi* 3°55S 30°0E **54 C3**
Ruteng *Indonesia* 8°35S 120°30E **37 F6**
Ruth *U.S.A.* 43°42N 82°45W **82 C2**
Rutherford *U.S.A.* 38°26N 122°24W **78 G4**
Rutland *U.S.A.* 43°37N 72°58W **83 C12**
Rutland □ *U.K.* 52°38N 0°40W **13 E7**
Rutland Water □ *U.K.* 52°39N 0°38W **13 E7**
Rutledge → *Canada* 61°4N 112°0W **71 A6**
Rutledge L. *Canada* 61°33N 110°47W **71 A6**
Rutog *China* 33°27N 79°42E **32 C2**
Rutshuru
  Dem. Rep. of the Congo 1°13S 29°25E **54 C2**
Ruvu *Tanzania* 6°49S 38°43E **54 D4**
Ruvu → *Tanzania* 6°23S 38°52E **54 D4**
Ruvuba △ *Burundi* 3°3S 29°33E **54 C2**
Ruvuma □ *Tanzania* 10°20S 36°0E **55 E4**
Ruvuma → *Tanzania* 10°29S 40°28E **55 E5**
Ruwais *U.A.E.* 24°5N 52°50E **45 E7**
Ruwenzori *Africa* 0°30N 29°55E **54 B2**
Ruwenzori △ *Uganda* 0°20N 30°0E **54 B2**
Ruya → *Zimbabwe* 16°27S 32°5E **57 B5**
Ruyigi *Burundi* 3°29S 30°15E **54 C3**
Ružomberok *Slovak Rep.* 49°3N 19°17E **17 D10**
Rwanda ■ *Africa* 2°0S 30°0E **54 C3**
Ryan, L. *U.K.* 55°0N 5°2W **11 G3**
Ryazan *Russia* 54°40N 39°40E **18 D6**
Ryazhsk *Russia* 53°45N 40°3E **18 D7**
Rybachiy Poluostrov
  Russia 69°43N 32°0E **8 B25**
Rybinsk *Russia* 58°5N 38°50E **18 C6**
Rybinskoye Vdkhr.
  Russia 58°30N 38°25E **18 C6**
Rybnitsa = Râbnița
  Moldova 47°45N 29°0E **17 E15**
Rycroft *Canada* 55°45N 118°40W **70 B5**
Ryde *U.K.* 50°43N 1°9W **13 G6**
Ryderwood *U.S.A.* 46°23N 123°3W **78 D3**
Rye *U.K.* 50°57N 0°45E **13 G8**
Rye → *U.K.* 54°11N 0°44W **12 C7**
Rye Bay *U.K.* 50°52N 0°49E **13 G8**
Rye Patch Res. *U.S.A.* 40°28N 118°19W **76 F4**
Ryegate *U.S.A.* 46°18N 109°15W **76 C9**
Ryley *Canada* 53°17N 112°26W **70 C6**
Rylstone *Australia* 32°46S 149°58E **63 E4**
Ryōtsu *Japan* 38°5N 138°26E **30 E9**
Rypin *Poland* 53°3N 19°25E **17 B10**
Ryūgasaki *Japan* 35°54N 140°11E **31 G10**
Ryukyu Is. = Ryūkyū-rettō
  Japan 26°0N 126°0E **31 M3**
Ryūkyū-rettō *Japan* 26°0N 126°0E **31 M3**
Rzeszów *Poland* 50°5N 21°58E **17 C11**
Rzhev *Russia* 56°20N 34°20E **18 C5**

S

Sa *Thailand* 18°34N 100°45E **38 C3**
Sa Canal *Spain* 38°51N 1°23E **24 C7**
Sa Conillera *Spain* 38°59N 1°13E **24 C7**
Sa Dec *Vietnam* 10°20N 105°46E **39 G5**
Sa Mesquida *Spain* 39°55N 4°16E **24 B11**
Sa Savina *Spain* 38°44N 1°25E **24 C7**
Sa'ādatābād Fārs, Iran* 30°10N 53°5E **45 D7**
Sa'ādatābād Hormozgān,
  Iran* 28°3N 55°53E **45 D7**
Sa'ādatābād Kermān,
  Iran* 29°40N 55°51E **45 D7**
Saale → *Germany* 51°56N 11°54E **16 C6**
Saalfeld *Germany* 50°38N 11°21E **16 C6**
Saanich *Canada* 48°29N 123°26W **78 B3**
Saar → *Europe* 49°41N 6°32E **16 D4**
Saarbrücken *Germany* 49°14N 6°59E **16 D4**
Saaremaa *Estonia* 58°30N 22°30E **9 G20**
Saarijärvi *Finland* 62°43N 25°16E **8 E21**
Saariselkä *Finland* 68°16N 28°15E **8 B23**
Sab 'Ābar *Syria* 33°46N 37°41E **44 C3**
Saba *W. Indies* 17°38N 63°14W **89 C7**
Šabac *Serbia* 44°48N 19°42E **23 B8**
Sabadell *Spain* 41°28N 2°7E **21 B7**
Sabah □ *Malaysia* 6°0N 117°0E **36 C5**
Sabak Bernam *Malaysia* 3°46N 100°58E **39 L3**
Sabalān, Kūhhā-ye
  Iran 38°15N 47°45E **44 B5**
Sabalana, Kepulauan
  Indonesia 6°45S 118°50E **37 F5**
Sábana de la Mar
  Dom. Rep. 19°7N 69°24W **89 C6**
Sábanalarga *Colombia* 10°38N 74°55W **92 A4**
Sabang *Indonesia* 5°50N 95°15E **36 C1**
Sabará *Brazil* 19°55S 43°46W **93 G10**
Sabarmati → *India* 22°18N 72°22E **42 H5**
Sabattis *U.S.A.* 44°6N 74°40W **83 B10**
Saberania *Indonesia* 2°5S 138°18E **37 E9**
Sabhā *Libya* 27°9N 14°29E **51 C8**
Sabi → *India* 28°29N 76°44E **42 E7**
Sabie *S. Africa* 25°10S 30°48E **57 D5**
Sabinal *Mexico* 30°57N 107°30W **86 A3**

Sabinal U.S.A. 29°19N 99°28W 84 G5
Sabinas Mexico 27°51N 101°7W 86 B4
Sabinas → Mexico 27°37N 100°42W 86 B4
Sabinas Hidalgo Mexico 26°30N 100°10W 86 B4
Sabine → U.S.A. 29°59N 93°47W 84 G8
Sabine L. U.S.A. 29°53N 93°51W 84 G8
Sabine Pass U.S.A. 29°44N 93°54W 84 G8
Sabinsville U.S.A. 41°52N 77°31W 82 E7
Sablayan Phil. 12°50N 120°50E 37 B6
Sable Canada 55°30N 68°21W 73 A6
Sable, C. Canada 43°29N 65°38W 73 D6
Sable, C. U.S.A. 25°9N 81°8W 88 A3
Sable I. Canada 44°0N 60°0W 73 D8
Sabrina Coast Antarctica 68°0S 120°0E 5 C9
Sabulubbek Indonesia 1°36S 98°40E 36 E1
Sabzevār Iran 36°15N 57°40E 45 B8
Sabzvārān Iran 28°45N 57°50E 45 D8
Sac City U.S.A. 42°25N 95°0W 80 D6
Săcele Romania 45°37N 25°41E 17 F13
Sacheon S. Korea 35°0N 128°6E 35 G15
Sachigo → Canada 55°6N 88°58W 72 A2
Sachigo, L. Canada 53°50N 92°12W 72 B1
Sachimbo Angola 9°14S 20°16E 52 F4
Sachsen □ Germany 50°55N 13°10E 16 C7
Sachsen-Anhalt □ Germany 52°0N 12°0E 16 C7
Sackets Harbor U.S.A. 43°57N 76°7W 83 C8
Sackville Canada 45°54N 64°22W 73 C7
Saco Maine, U.S.A. 43°30N 70°27W 83 C14
Saco Mont., U.S.A. 48°28N 107°21W 76 B10
Sacramento U.S.A. 38°35N 121°29W 78 G5
Sacramento → U.S.A. 38°3N 121°56W 78 G5
Sacramento Mts. U.S.A. 32°30N 105°30W 77 K11
Sacramento Valley U.S.A. 39°30N 122°0W 78 G5
Sada-Misaki Japan 33°20N 132°5E 31 H6
Sadabad India 27°27N 78°3E 42 F8
Sadani Tanzania 5°58S 38°35E 54 D4
Sadao Thailand 6°38N 100°26E 39 J3
Sadd el Aali Egypt 23°54N 32°54E 51 D12
Saddle Mt. U.S.A. 45°58N 123°41W 78 E3
Sadimi Dem. Rep. of the Congo 9°25S 23°32E 55 D1
Sado Japan 38°0N 138°25E 30 F9
Sadra India 23°21N 72°43E 42 H5
Sadri India 25°11N 73°26E 42 G5
Sæby Denmark 57°21N 10°30E 9 H14
Saegertown U.S.A. 41°43N 80°9W 82 E4
Şafājah Si. Arabia 26°25N 39°0E 44 E3
Safata B. Samoa 14°0S 171°50W 59 b
Säffle Sweden 59°8N 12°55E 9 G15
Safford U.S.A. 32°50N 109°43W 77 K9
Saffron Walden U.K. 52°1N 0°16E 13 E8
Safi Morocco 32°18N 9°20W 50 B4
Şafīābād Iran 36°45N 57°58E 45 B8
Safid Dasht Iran 33°27N 48°11E 45 C6
Safīd Kūh Afghan. 34°45N 63°0E 40 B3
Safid Rūd → Iran 37°23N 50°11E 45 B6
Safipur India 26°44N 80°21E 43 F9
Şāfītā Syria 34°48N 36°7E 44 C3
Safune Samoa 13°25S 172°21W 59 b
Şafwān Iraq 30°7N 47°43E 44 D5
Sag Harbor U.S.A. 41°0N 72°18W 83 F12
Saga Japan 33°15N 130°16E 31 H5
Saga □ Japan 33°15N 130°20E 31 H5
Sagae Japan 38°22N 140°17E 30 E10
Sagaing Burma 21°52N 95°59E 41 J19
Sagamore U.S.A. 40°46N 79°14W 82 F5
Saganaga L. Canada 48°14N 90°52W 80 A8
Sagar Karnataka, India 14°14N 75°6E 40 M9
Sagar Mad. P., India 23°50N 78°44E 43 H8
Sagara, L. Tanzania 5°20S 31°0E 54 D3
Sagarmatha = Everest, Mt. Nepal 28°5N 86°58E 43 E12
Sagarmatha △ Nepal 27°55N 86°45E 43 F12
Saginaw U.S.A. 43°26N 83°56W 81 D12
Saginaw B. U.S.A. 43°50N 83°40W 81 D12
Saglouc = Salluit Canada 62°14N 75°38W 69 C12
Sagone France 42°7N 8°42E 20 E8
Sagua la Grande Cuba 22°50N 80°10W 88 B3
Saguache U.S.A. 38°5N 106°8W 76 G10
Saguaro △ U.S.A. 32°12N 110°38W 77 K8
Saguenay → Canada 48°22N 71°0W 73 C5
Sagunt Spain 39°42N 0°18W 21 C5
Sagunto = Sagunt Spain 39°42N 0°18W 21 C5
Sagwara India 23°41N 74°1E 42 H6
Sahagún Spain 42°18N 5°2W 21 A3
Saḩam al Jawlān Syria 32°45N 35°55E 46 C4
Sahamandrevo Madag. 23°15S 45°35E 57 C8
Sahand, Kūh-e Iran 37°44N 46°27E 44 B5
Sahara Africa 23°0N 5°0E 50 D6
Saharan Atlas = Saharien, Atlas Algeria 33°30N 1°0E 50 B6
Saharanpur India 29°58N 77°33E 42 E7
Saharien, Atlas Algeria 33°30N 1°0E 50 B6
Saharsa India 25°53N 86°36E 43 G12
Sahasinaka Madag. 21°49S 47°49E 57 C8
Sahaswan India 28°5N 78°45E 43 E8
Saheira, W. el → Egypt 30°5N 33°25E 46 E2
Sahel Africa 12°0N 8°0W 48 E3
Sahel Africa 16°0N 5°0E 50 E5
Sahibganj India 25°12N 87°40E 43 G12
Sāḩilīyah Iraq 33°43N 42°42E 44 C4
Sahiwal Pakistan 30°45N 73°8E 42 D5
Şaḩneh Iran 34°29N 47°41E 44 C5
Sahrawi = Western Sahara ■ Africa 25°0N 13°0W 50 D3
Sahuaripa Mexico 29°3N 109°14W 86 B3
Sahuarita U.S.A. 31°57N 110°58W 77 L8
Sahuayo de Díaz Mexico 20°4N 102°43W 86 C4
Sai → India 25°39N 82°47E 43 G10
Sai Buri Thailand 6°43N 101°45E 39 J3
Sai Kung China 22°23N 114°16E 33 G11
Sa'id Bundâs Sudan 8°24N 24°48E 51 G10
Sa'īdābād = Sīrjān Iran 29°30N 55°45E 45 D7
Sa'īdābād Iran 36°8N 54°11E 45 B7
Sa'īdīyeh Iran 36°20N 48°55E 45 B6
Saidpur Bangla. 25°48N 89°0E 41 G16
Saidpur India 25°33N 83°11E 43 G10
Saidu Sharif Pakistan 34°43N 72°24E 43 B5
Saigō Japan 36°12N 133°20E 31 F6
Saigon = Thanh Pho Ho Chi Minh Vietnam 10°58N 106°40E 39 G6
Saijō Japan 33°55N 133°11E 31 H6
Saikai △ Japan 33°12N 129°36E 31 H4
Saikanosy Masoala Madag. 15°45S 50°10E 57 B9
Saikhoa Ghat India 27°50N 95°40E 41 F19
Saiki Japan 32°58N 131°51E 31 H5
Sailana India 23°28N 74°55E 42 H6
Sailolof Indonesia 1°15S 130°46E 37 E8
Saimaa Finland 61°15N 28°15E 8 F23
Saimen = Saimaa Finland 61°15N 28°15E 8 F23
Şa'in Dezh Iran 36°40N 46°25E 44 B5
St. Abb's Head U.K. 55°55N 2°8W 11 F6
St. Alban's Canada 47°51N 55°50W 73 C8
St. Albans U.K. 51°45N 0°19W 13 F7
St. Albans Vt., U.S.A. 44°49N 73°5W 83 B11
St. Albans W. Va., U.S.A. 38°23N 81°50W 81 F13
St. Alban's Head U.K. 50°34N 2°4W 13 G5
St. Albert Canada 53°37N 113°32W 70 C6
St-André Réunion 20°57S 55°39E 53 c
St. Andrew's Canada 47°45N 59°15W 73 C8
St. Andrews U.K. 56°20N 2°47W 11 E6
St-Anicet Canada 45°8N 74°22W 83 A10
St. Annes Canada 49°40N 96°39W 71 D9
St. Anns B. Canada 46°22N 60°25W 73 C7
St. Ann's Bay Jamaica 18°26N 77°12W 88 a
St. Anthony Canada 51°22N 55°35W 73 B8
St. Anthony U.S.A. 43°58N 111°41W 76 E8
St-Antoine Canada 46°22N 64°45W 73 C7
St. Arnaud Australia 36°40S 143°16E 63 F3
St-Augustin Canada 51°13N 58°38W 73 B8
St-Augustin → Canada 51°16N 58°40W 73 B8
St. Augustine U.S.A. 29°54N 81°19W 85 G14
St. Austell U.K. 50°20N 4°47W 13 G3
St. Barbe Canada 51°12N 56°46W 73 B8
St-Barthélemy W. Indies 17°50N 62°50W 89 C7
St. Bees Hd. U.K. 54°31N 3°38W 12 C4
St. Bees I. Australia 20°56S 149°26E 62 J7
St-Benoît Réunion 21°2S 55°43E 53 c
St. Bride's Canada 46°56N 54°10W 73 C9
St. Brides B. U.K. 51°49N 5°9W 13 F2
St-Brieuc France 48°30N 2°46W 20 B2
St. Catharines Canada 43°10N 79°15W 82 C5
St. Catherines I. U.S.A. 31°40N 81°10W 85 F14
St. Catherine's Pt. U.K. 50°34N 1°18W 13 G6
St-Chamond France 45°28N 4°31E 20 D6
St. Charles Ill., U.S.A. 41°54N 88°19W 80 E9
St. Charles Md., U.S.A. 38°36N 76°56W 81 F15
St. Charles Mo., U.S.A. 38°47N 90°29W 80 F8
St. Charles Va., U.S.A. 36°48N 83°4W 81 G12
St. Christopher-Nevis = St. Kitts & Nevis ■ W. Indies 17°20N 62°40W 89 C7
St. Clair Mich., U.S.A. 42°50N 82°30W 82 D2
St. Clair Pa., U.S.A. 40°43N 76°12W 83 F8
St. Clair → U.S.A. 42°38N 82°31W 82 D2
St. Clair, L. N. Amer. 42°27N 82°39W 82 D2
St. Clairsville U.S.A. 40°5N 80°54W 82 F4
St. Claude Canada 49°40N 98°20W 71 D9
St. Clears U.K. 51°49N 4°31W 13 F3
St-Clet Canada 45°21N 74°13W 83 A10
St. Cloud Fla., U.S.A. 28°15N 81°17W 85 G14
St. Cloud Minn., U.S.A. 45°34N 94°10W 80 C6
St. Cricq, C. Australia 25°17S 113°6E 61 E1
St. Croix U.S. Virgin Is. 17°45N 64°45W 89 C7
St. Croix → U.S.A. 44°45N 92°48W 80 C7
St. Croix Falls U.S.A. 45°24N 92°38W 80 C7
St. David's Canada 48°12N 58°52W 73 C8
St. David's U.K. 51°53N 5°16W 13 F2
St. David's Head U.K. 51°54N 5°19W 13 F2
St-Denis France 48°56N 2°20E 20 B5
St-Denis Réunion 20°52S 55°27E 53 c
St-Denis ✕ (RUN) Réunion 20°53S 55°32E 53 c
St-Dizier France 48°38N 4°56E 20 B6
St. Elias, Mt. U.S.A. 60°18N 140°56W 68 C5
St. Elias Mts. N. Amer. 60°33N 139°28W 70 A1
St-Étienne France 45°27N 4°22E 20 D6
St. Eugène Canada 45°30N 74°28W 83 A10
St. Eustatius W. Indies 17°20N 63°0W 89 C7
St-Félicien Canada 48°40N 72°25W 72 C5
St-Flour France 45°2N 3°6E 20 D5
St. Francis U.S.A. 39°47N 101°48W 80 F3
St. Francis → U.S.A. 34°38N 90°36W 85 D9
St. Francis, C. S. Africa 34°14S 24°49E 56 E3
St. Francisville U.S.A. 30°47N 91°23W 84 F9
St-François, L. Canada 45°10N 74°22W 83 A10
St-Gabriel Canada 46°17N 73°24W 72 C5
St. Gallen = Sankt Gallen Switz. 47°26N 9°22E 20 C8
St-Gaudens France 43°6N 0°44E 20 E4
St. George Australia 28°1S 148°30E 63 D4
St. George Canada 45°11N 66°50W 73 C6
St. George S.C., U.S.A. 33°11N 80°35W 85 E14
St. George Utah, U.S.A. 37°6N 113°35W 77 H7
St. George, C. Canada 48°30N 59°16W 73 C8
St. George, C. U.S.A. 29°40N 85°5W 85 G12
St. George Ra. Australia 18°40S 125°0E 60 C4
St. George's Canada 48°26N 58°31W 73 C8
St-Georges Canada 46°8N 70°40W 73 C5
St. George's Grenada 12°5N 61°43W 89 D7
St. George's B. Canada 48°24N 58°53W 73 C8
St. Georges Basin N.S.W., Australia 35°7S 150°36E 63 F5
St. Georges Basin W. Austral., Australia 15°23S 125°2E 60 C4
St. George's Channel Europe 52°0N 6°0W 10 E6
St. Georges Hd. Australia 35°12S 150°42E 63 F5
St. Gotthard P. = San Gottardo, P. del Switz. 46°33N 8°33E 20 C8
St. Helena Atl. Oc. 15°58S 5°42W 48 H3
St. Helena U.S.A. 38°30N 122°28W 76 G2
St. Helena, Mt. U.S.A. 38°40N 122°36W 78 G4
St. Helena B. S. Africa 32°40S 18°10E 56 E2
St. Helens Australia 41°20S 148°15E 63 G4
St. Helens U.K. 53°27N 2°44W 12 D5
St. Helens U.S.A. 45°52N 122°48W 78 E4
St. Helens, Mt. U.S.A. 46°12N 122°12W 78 D4
St. Helier U.K. 49°10N 2°7W 13 H5
St-Hubert Belgium 50°2N 5°23E 15 D5
St-Hyacinthe Canada 45°40N 72°58W 72 C5
St. Ignace U.S.A. 45°52N 84°44W 81 C11
St. Ignace I. Canada 48°45N 88°0W 72 C2
St. Ignatius U.S.A. 47°19N 114°6W 76 C6
St. Ives Cambs., U.K. 52°20N 0°4W 13 E7
St. Ives Corn., U.K. 50°12N 5°30W 13 G2
St. James U.S.A. 43°59N 94°38W 80 D6
St-Jean → Canada 50°17N 64°20W 73 B7
St-Jean, L. Canada 48°40N 72°0W 73 C5
St-Jean-Port-Joli Canada 47°15N 70°13W 73 C5
St-Jean-sur-Richelieu Canada 45°20N 73°20W 83 A11
St-Jérôme Canada 45°47N 74°0W 72 C5
St. John Canada 45°20N 66°8W 73 C6
St. John U.S.A. 38°0N 98°46W 80 F4
St. John → N. Amer. 45°12N 66°5W 81 C20
St. John, C. Canada 50°0N 55°32W 73 C8
St. John I. U.S. Virgin Is. 18°20N 64°42W 89 e
St. John's Antigua & B. 17°6N 61°51W 89 C7
St. John's Canada 47°35N 52°40W 73 C9
St. Johns Ariz., U.S.A. 34°30N 109°22W 77 J9
St. Johns Mich., U.S.A. 43°0N 84°33W 81 D11
St. Johns → U.S.A. 30°24N 81°24W 85 F14
St. John's Pt. Ireland 54°34N 8°27W 10 B3
St. Johnsbury U.S.A. 44°25N 72°1W 83 B12
St. Johnsville U.S.A. 43°0N 74°43W 83 C10
St-Joseph Martinique 14°39N 61°4W 88 c
St-Joseph Réunion 21°22S 55°37E 53 c
St. Joseph La., U.S.A. 31°55N 91°14W 84 F9
St. Joseph Mo., U.S.A. 39°46N 94°50W 80 F6
St. Joseph → U.S.A. 42°7N 86°29W 80 D10
St. Joseph, I. Canada 46°12N 83°58W 72 C3
St. Joseph, L. Canada 51°10N 90°35W 72 B1
St-Jovite Canada 46°8N 74°38W 72 C5
St. Kilda U.K. 57°49N 8°34W 14 C2
St. Kitts & Nevis ■ W. Indies 17°20N 62°40W 89 C7
St. Laurent Canada 50°25N 97°58W 71 C9
St. Lawrence Australia 22°16S 149°31E 62 C4
St. Lawrence Canada 46°54N 55°23W 73 C8
St. Lawrence → Canada 49°30N 66°0W 73 C6
St. Lawrence, Gulf of Canada 48°25N 62°0W 73 C7
St. Lawrence I. U.S.A. 63°30N 170°30W 74 a
St. Lawrence Islands △ Canada 44°27N 75°52W 83 B9
St. Leonard Canada 47°12N 67°58W 73 C6
St-Leu Réunion 21°9S 55°18E 53 c
St. Lewis → Canada 52°26N 56°11W 73 B8
St-Lô France 49°7N 1°5W 20 B3
St-Louis Guadeloupe 15°56N 61°19W 88 b
St-Louis Réunion 21°16S 55°25E 53 c
St. Louis Senegal 16°8N 16°27W 50 E2
St. Louis U.S.A. 38°37N 90°11W 80 F8
St. Louis → U.S.A. 46°44N 92°9W 80 B7
St. Lucia ■ W. Indies 14°0N 60°57W 89 f
St. Lucia, L. S. Africa 28°5S 32°30E 57 D5
St. Lucia Channel W. Indies 14°15N 61°0W 89 D7
St. Maarten ⊠ W. Indies 18°0N 63°5W 89 C7
St. Magnus B. U.K. 60°25N 1°35W 11 A7
St-Malo France 48°39N 2°1W 20 B2
St-Marc Haiti 19°10N 72°41W 89 C5
St. Maries U.S.A. 47°19N 116°35W 76 C5
St-Martin ⊠ W. Indies 18°0N 63°0W 89 C7
St-Martin, C. Martinique 14°52N 61°14W 88 c
St. Martin, L. Canada 51°40N 98°30W 71 C9
St. Martins Barbados 13°5N 59°28W 89 g
St. Mary Pk. Australia 31°32S 138°34E 63 E2
St. Marys Australia 41°35S 148°11E 63 G4
St. Marys Canada 43°20N 81°10W 82 C3
St. Mary's Corn., U.K. 49°55N 6°18W 13 H1
St. Mary's Orkney, U.K. 58°54N 2°54W 11 C6
St. Marys Ga., U.S.A. 30°44N 81°33W 85 F14
St. Marys Pa., U.S.A. 41°26N 78°34W 82 E6
St. Mary's, C. Canada 46°50N 54°12W 73 C9
St. Mary's B. Canada 46°50N 53°50W 73 C9
St. Marys Bay Canada 44°25N 66°10W 73 D6
St-Mathieu, Pte. France 48°20N 4°45W 20 B1
St. Matthew I. U.S.A. 60°24N 172°42W 74 a
St-Maurice → Canada 46°21N 72°31W 72 C5
St. Mawes U.K. 50°10N 5°2W 13 G2
St-Nazaire France 47°17N 2°12W 20 C2
St. Neots U.K. 52°14N 0°15W 13 E7
St-Niklaas Belgium 51°10N 4°8E 15 C4
St-Omer France 50°45N 2°15E 20 A5
St-Pamphile Canada 46°58N 69°48W 73 C6
St-Pascal Canada 47°32N 69°48W 73 C6
St. Paul Canada 54°0N 111°17W 70 C6
St-Paul Réunion 20°59S 55°17E 53 c
St. Paul Minn., U.S.A. 44°56N 93°5W 80 C7
St. Paul Nebr., U.S.A. 41°13N 98°27W 80 E4
St-Paul → Canada 51°27N 57°42W 73 B8
St. Paul, I. Ind. Oc. 38°55S 77°34E 3 F13
St. Paul I. Canada 47°12N 60°9W 73 C7
St. Peter U.S.A. 44°20N 93°57W 80 C7
St. Peter Port U.K. 49°26N 2°33W 13 H5
St. Peters N.S., Canada 45°40N 60°53W 73 C7
St. Peters P.E.I., Canada 46°25N 62°35W 73 C7
St. Petersburg = Sankt-Peterburg Russia 59°55N 30°20E 9 G24
St. Petersburg U.S.A. 27°46N 82°40W 85 H13
St-Phillippe Réunion 21°21S 55°44E 53 c
St-Pie Canada 45°30N 72°54W 83 A12
St-Pierre Martinique 14°45N 61°10W 88 c
St-Pierre Réunion 21°19S 55°28E 53 c
St-Pierre St-P. & M. 46°46N 56°12W 73 C8
St-Pierre, L. Canada 46°12N 72°52W 72 C5
St-Pierre-et-Miquelon ⊠ N. Amer. 46°55N 56°10W 73 C8
St-Quentin Canada 47°30N 67°23W 73 C6
St-Quentin France 49°50N 3°16E 20 B5
St. Regis U.S.A. 47°18N 115°6W 76 C6
St. Sebastien, Tanjon' i Madag. 12°26S 48°44E 57 A8
St-Siméon Canada 47°51N 69°54W 73 C6
St. Simons I. U.S.A. 31°12N 81°15W 85 F14
St. Simons Island U.S.A. 31°9N 81°22W 85 F14
St. Stephen Canada 45°16N 67°17W 73 C6
St. Thomas Canada 42°45N 81°10W 82 D3
St. Thomas I. U.S. Virgin Is. 18°20N 64°55W 89 e
St-Tite Canada 46°45N 72°34W 72 C5
St-Tropez France 43°17N 6°38E 20 E7
St-Troud = St. Truiden Belgium 50°48N 5°10E 15 D5
St. Truiden Belgium 50°48N 5°10E 15 D5
St. Vincent = São Vicente C. Verde Is. 17°0N 25°0W 50 b
St. Vincent, G. Australia 35°0S 138°0E 63 F2
St. Vincent & the Grenadines ■ W. Indies 13°0N 61°10W 89 D7
St. Vincent Passage W. Indies 13°30N 61°0W 89 D7
St-Vith Belgium 50°17N 6°9E 15 D6
St. Walburg Canada 53°39N 109°12W 71 C7
Ste-Agathe-des-Monts Canada 46°3N 74°17W 72 C5
Ste-Anne Guadeloupe 16°13N 61°24W 88 b
Ste-Anne Seychelles 4°36S 55°31E 53 b
Ste-Anne, L. Canada 50°0N 67°42W 73 B6
Ste-Anne-des-Monts-Tourelle Canada 49°8N 66°30W 73 C6
Ste. Genevieve U.S.A. 37°59N 90°2W 80 G8
Ste-Marguerite → Canada 50°9N 66°36W 73 B6
Ste-Marie Canada 46°26N 71°0W 73 C5
Ste-Marie Martinique 14°48N 61°1W 88 c
Ste-Marie Réunion 20°53S 55°33E 53 c
Ste-Marie, Ile = Nosy Boraha Madag. 16°50S 49°55E 57 B8
Ste-Rose Guadeloupe 16°20N 61°45W 88 b
Ste-Rose Réunion 21°8S 55°45E 53 c
Ste. Rose du Lac Canada 51°4N 99°30W 71 C9
Saintes France 45°45N 0°37W 20 D3
Saintes, Îs. des Guadeloupe 15°50N 61°35W 88 b
Saintfield U.K. 54°28N 5°49W 10 B6
Saintonge France 45°40N 0°50W 20 D3
Saipan N. Marianas 15°12N 145°45E 64 F6
Sairang India 23°50N 92°45E 41 H18
Sairecábur, Cerro Bolivia 22°43S 67°54W 94 A2
Saitama Japan 35°54N 139°38E 31 G9
Saitama □ Japan 36°25N 139°30E 31 F9
Saiyid Pakistan 33°7N 73°2E 42 C5
Sajama Bolivia 18°7S 69°0W 92 G5
Sajószentpéter Hungary 48°12N 20°44E 17 D11
Sajum India 33°20N 79°0E 43 C8
Sak → S. Africa 30°52S 20°25E 56 E3
Saka Kenya 0°9S 39°20E 54 B4
Sakai Japan 34°34N 135°27E 31 G7
Sakaide Japan 34°19N 133°50E 31 G6
Sakaiminato Japan 35°38N 133°11E 31 G6
Sakākah Si. Arabia 30°0N 40°8E 44 D4
Sakakawea, L. U.S.A. 47°30N 101°25W 80 B3
Sakami → Canada 53°40N 76°40W 72 B4
Sakami, L. Canada 53°15N 77°0W 72 B4
Sakania Dem. Rep. of the Congo 12°43S 28°30E 55 E2
Sakaraha Madag. 22°55S 44°32E 57 C7
Sakartvelo = Georgia ■ Asia 42°0N 43°0E 19 F7
Sakarya Turkey 40°48N 30°25E 19 F5
Sakashima-Guntō Japan 24°46N 124°0E 31 M2
Sakata Japan 38°55N 139°50E 30 E9
Sakchu N. Korea 40°23N 125°2E 35 D13
Sakeny → Madag. 20°0S 45°25E 57 C8
Sakha □ Russia 66°0N 130°0E 29 C13
Sakhalin Russia 51°0N 143°0E 29 D15
Sakhalinskiy Zaliv Russia 54°0N 141°0E 29 D15
Šakiai Lithuania 54°59N 23°2E 9 J20
Sakon Nakhon Thailand 17°10N 104°9E 38 D5
Sakrand Pakistan 26°10N 68°15E 42 F3
Sakri India 26°13N 86°5E 43 F12
Sakrivier S. Africa 30°54S 20°28E 56 E3
Sakti India 22°2N 82°58E 43 H10
Sakuma Japan 35°3N 137°49E 31 G8
Sakurai Japan 34°30N 135°51E 31 G7
Sal C. Verde Is. 16°45N 22°55W 50 b
Sal Rei C. Verde Is. 16°11N 22°53W 50 b
Sala Sweden 59°58N 16°35E 9 G17
Sala Consilina Italy 40°23N 15°36E 22 D6
Sala-y-Gómez Pac. Oc. 26°28S 105°28W 65 K17
Sala y Gómez Ridge Pac. Oc. 25°0S 98°0W 65 K18
Salaberry-de-Valleyfield Canada 45°15N 74°8W 83 A10
Salada, L. Mexico 32°20N 115°40W 77 K6
Saladas Argentina 28°15S 58°40W 94 B4
Saladillo Argentina 35°40S 59°55W 94 D4
Salado → B. Aires, Argentina 35°44S 57°22W 94 D4
Salado → La Pampa, Argentina 37°30S 67°0W 96 D3
Salado → Santa Fe, Argentina 31°40S 60°41W 94 C3
Salado → Mexico 26°52N 99°19W 84 H5
Salaga Ghana 8°31N 0°31W 50 G5
Sālah Syria 32°40N 36°45E 46 C5
Şalāḩ ad Dīn □ Iraq 34°35N 43°35E 44 C4
Salakos Greece 36°17N 27°57E 25 C9
Salālah Oman 16°56N 53°59E 47 D5
Salamanca Chile 31°46S 70°59W 94 C1
Salamanca Spain 40°58N 5°39W 21 B3
Salamanca U.S.A. 42°10N 78°43W 82 D6
Salāmatābād Iran 35°39N 47°50E 44 C5
Salamina Greece 37°56N 23°30E 23 F10
Salamis Cyprus 35°11N 33°54E 25 D12
Salar de Atacama Chile 23°30S 68°25W 94 A2
Salar de Uyuni Bolivia 20°30S 67°45W 92 H5
Salatiga Indonesia 7°19S 110°30E 37 G14
Salavat Russia 53°21N 55°55E 18 D10
Salaverry Peru 8°15S 79°0W 92 E3
Salawati Indonesia 1°7S 130°52E 37 E8
Salaya India 22°19N 69°35E 42 H3
Salayar Indonesia 6°7S 120°30E 37 F6
Salcombe U.K. 50°14N 3°47W 13 G4
Saldanha S. Africa 33°0S 17°58E 56 E2
Saldanha B. S. Africa 33°6S 18°0E 56 E2
Saldus Latvia 56°38N 22°30E 9 H20
Sale Australia 38°6S 147°6E 63 F4
Salé Morocco 34°3N 6°48W 50 B4
Sale U.K. 53°26N 2°19W 12 D5
Salekhard Russia 66°30N 66°35E 28 C7
Salelologa Samoa 13°41S 172°11W 59 b
Salem India 11°40N 78°11E 40 P11
Salem Ill., U.S.A. 38°38N 88°57W 80 F9
Salem Ind., U.S.A. 38°36N 86°6W 80 F10
Salem Mass., U.S.A. 42°31N 70°53W 83 D14
Salem Mo., U.S.A. 37°39N 91°32W 80 G8
Salem N.H., U.S.A. 42°45N 71°12W 83 D13
Salem N.J., U.S.A. 39°34N 75°28W 81 F16
Salem N.Y., U.S.A. 43°10N 73°20W 83 C11
Salem Ohio, U.S.A. 40°54N 80°52W 82 F4
Salem Oreg., U.S.A. 44°56N 123°2W 76 D2
Salem S. Dak., U.S.A. 43°44N 97°23W 80 D5
Salem Va., U.S.A. 37°18N 80°3W 81 G13
Salerno Italy 40°41N 14°47E 22 D6
Salford U.K. 53°30N 2°18W 12 D5
Salgótarján Hungary 48°5N 19°47E 17 D10
Salgueiro Brazil 8°4S 39°6W 93 E11
Salibabu Indonesia 3°51N 126°40E 37 D7
Salibea = Salybia Trin. & Tob. 10°43N 61°2W 93 K15
Salida U.S.A. 38°32N 106°0W 74 C5
Salihli Turkey 38°28N 28°8E 23 E13
Salihorsk Belarus 52°51N 27°27E 17 B14
Salima Malawi 13°47S 34°28E 53 G6
Salina Italy 38°34N 14°50E 22 E6
Salina Kans., U.S.A. 38°50N 97°37W 80 F5
Salina Utah, U.S.A. 38°58N 111°51W 76 G8
Salina Cruz Mexico 16°10N 95°12W 87 D5
Salinas Brazil 16°10S 42°10W 93 G10
Salinas Chile 23°31S 69°29W 94 A2
Salinas Ecuador 2°10S 80°58W 92 D2
Salinas U.S.A. 36°40N 121°39W 78 J5
Salinas → Guatemala 16°28N 90°31W 87 D6
Salinas → U.S.A. 36°45N 121°48W 78 J5
Salinas, B. de Nic. 11°4N 85°45W 88 D2
Salinas, Pampa de las Argentina 31°58S 66°42W 94 C2
Salinas Ambargasta Argentina 29°0S 65°0W 94 B3
Salinas de Hidalgo Mexico 22°38N 101°43W 86 C4
Salinas Grandes Argentina 30°0S 65°0W 94 C3
Salinas Pueblo Missions ⌂ U.S.A. 34°6N 106°4W 77 J10
Salinas Valley U.S.A. 36°15N 121°15W 78 J5
Saline → Ark., U.S.A. 33°10N 92°8W 84 E8
Saline → Kans., U.S.A. 38°52N 97°30W 80 F5
Salines, C. de ses Spain 39°16N 3°4E 24 B10
Salinópolis Brazil 0°40S 47°20W 93 D9
Salisbury Australia 34°46S 138°38E 63 E2
Salisbury U.K. 51°4N 1°47W 13 F6
Salisbury Md., U.S.A. 38°22N 75°36W 81 F16
Salisbury N.C., U.S.A. 35°40N 80°29W 85 D14
Salisbury I. Canada 63°30N 77°0W 69 C12
Salisbury Plain U.K. 51°14N 1°55W 13 F6
Şalkhad Syria 32°29N 36°43E 46 C5
Salla Finland 66°50N 28°49E 8 C23
Salliq = Coral Harbour Canada 64°8N 83°10W 69 C11
Sallisaw U.S.A. 35°28N 94°47W 84 D7
Salluit Canada 62°14N 75°38W 69 C12
Salmās Iran 38°11N 44°47E 44 B5
Salmo Canada 49°10N 117°20W 70 D5
Salmon U.S.A. 45°11N 113°54W 76 D7
Salmon → Canada 54°3N 122°40W 70 C4
Salmon → U.S.A. 45°51N 116°47W 76 D5
Salmon Arm Canada 50°40N 119°15W 70 C5
Salmon Gums Australia 32°59S 121°38E 61 F3
Salmon River Mts. U.S.A. 44°50N 115°30W 76 D6
Salo Finland 60°22N 23°10E 9 F20
Salome U.S.A. 33°47N 113°37W 79 M13
Salon India 26°2N 81°27E 43 F9
Salon-de-Provence France 43°39N 5°6E 20 E6
Salonica = Thessaloniki Greece 40°38N 22°58E 23 D10
Salonta Romania 46°49N 21°42E 17 E11
Salpausselkä Finland 61°3N 26°15E 8 F22
Salsacate Argentina 31°20S 65°5W 94 C2
Salsk Russia 46°28N 41°30E 19 E7
Salso → Italy 37°6N 13°57E 22 F5
Salt → Canada 60°0N 112°25W 70 B6
Salt → U.S.A. 33°23N 112°19W 77 K7
Salt Fork Red → U.S.A. 34°27N 99°21W 84 D5

Salt L. Australia 30°6S 142°8E 63 E3
Salt Lake City U.S.A. 40°45N 111°53W 76 F8
Salt Range Pakistan 32°30N 72°25E 42 C5
Salta Argentina 24°57S 65°25W 94 A2
Salta □ Argentina 24°48S 65°30W 94 A2
Saltash U.K. 50°24N 4°14W 13 G3
Saltburn by the Sea U.K. 54°35N 0°58W 12 C7
Saltcoats U.K. 55°38N 4°47W 11 F4
Saltee Is. Ireland 52°7N 6°37W 10 D5
Saltfjellet Norway 66°40N 15°15E 8 C16
Saltfjorden Norway 67°15N 14°10E 8 C16
Saltillo Mexico 25°25N 101°0W 86 B4
Salto Argentina 34°20S 60°15W 94 C3
Salto Uruguay 31°27S 57°50W 94 C4
Salto → Italy 42°26N 12°25E 22 C5
Salto del Guaíra Paraguay 24°3S 54°17W 95 A5
Salton City U.S.A. 33°18N 115°57W 79 M11
Salton Sea U.S.A. 33°15N 115°45W 79 M11
Saltsburg U.S.A. 40°29N 79°27W 82 F5
Saluda → U.S.A. 34°1N 81°4W 85 D14
Salûm Egypt 31°31N 25°7E 51 B11
Salur India 18°27N 83°18E 41 K13
Salvador Brazil 13°0S 38°30W 93 F11
Salvador Canada 52°10N 109°32W 71 C7
Salvador, El ■ Cent. Amer. 13°50N 89°0W 88 D2
Salvador, L. U.S.A. 29°43N 90°15W 85 G9
Salween → Burma 16°31N 97°37E 41 L20
Salyan Azerbaijan 39°33N 48°59E 19 G8
Salybia Trin. & Tob. 10°43N 61°2W 93 K15
Salzach → Austria 48°12N 12°56E 16 D7
Salzburg Austria 47°48N 13°2E 16 E7
Salzgitter Germany 52°9N 10°19E 16 B6
Salzwedel Germany 52°52N 11°10E 16 B6
Sam India 26°50N 70°31E 42 F4
Sam Neua Laos 20°29N 104°5E 38 B5
Sam Ngao Thailand 17°18N 99°0E 38 D2
Sam Rayburn Res. U.S.A. 31°4N 94°5W 84 F7
Sam Son Vietnam 19°44N 105°54E 38 C5
Sam Teu Laos 19°59N 104°38E 38 C5
Sama de Langreo = Langreo Spain 43°18N 5°40W 21 A3
Samagaltay Russia 50°36N 95°3E 29 D10
Samales Group Phil. 6°0N 122°0E 37 C6
Samana India 30°10N 76°13E 42 D7
Samana Cay Bahamas 23°3N 73°45W 89 B5
Samanga Tanzania 8°20S 39°13E 55 D4
Samangān □ Afghan. 36°15N 68°3E 40 B5
Samangwa Dem. Rep. of the Congo 4°23S 24°10E 54 C1
Samani Japan 42°7N 142°56E 30 C11
Samar Phil. 12°0N 125°0E 37 B7
Samara Russia 53°8N 50°6E 18 D9
Samaria = Shōmrōn West Bank 32°15N 35°13E 46 C4
Samaria Greece 35°17N 23°58E 25 D5
Samarinda Indonesia 0°30S 117°9E 36 E5
Samarkand = Samarqand Uzbekistan 39°40N 66°55E 28 F7
Samarqand Uzbekistan 39°40N 66°55E 28 F7
Sāmarrā' Iraq 34°12N 43°52E 44 C4
Samastipur India 25°50N 85°50E 43 G11
Samba Dem. Rep. of the Congo 4°38S 26°22E 54 C2
Samba India 32°32N 75°10E 43 C6
Sambalpur India 21°28N 84°4E 41 J14
Sambar, Tanjung Indonesia 2°59S 110°19E 36 E4
Sambas Indonesia 1°20N 109°20E 36 D3
Sambava Madag. 14°16S 50°10E 57 A9
Sambawizi Zimbabwe 18°24S 26°13E 55 F2
Sambhal India 28°35N 78°37E 43 E8
Sambhar India 26°52N 75°6E 42 F6
Sambhar L. India 26°55N 75°12E 42 F6
Sambiase Italy 38°58N 16°17E 22 E7
Sambir Ukraine 49°30N 23°10E 17 D12
Sambor Cambodia 12°46N 106°0E 38 F6
Samborombón, B. Argentina 36°5S 57°20W 94 D4
Samburu ⌂ Kenya 0°37N 37°31E 54 B4
Samcheok S. Korea 37°30N 129°10E 35 F15
Same Tanzania 4°2S 37°38E 54 C4
Samfya Zambia 11°22S 29°31E 55 E2
Samnah Si. Arabia 25°10N 37°15E 44 E3
Samo Alto Chile 30°22S 71°0W 94 C1
Samoa ■ Pac. Oc. 14°0S 172°0W 59 b
Samokov Bulgaria 42°18N 23°35E 23 C10
Samos Greece 37°45N 26°50E 23 F12
Samothráki = Mathraki Greece 39°48N 19°31E 25 A3
Samothraki Greece 40°28N 25°28E 23 D11
Sampacho Argentina 33°20S 64°50W 94 C3
Sampalan Indonesia 8°41S 115°34E 37 K18
Sampang Indonesia 7°11S 113°13E 37 G15
Sampit Indonesia 2°34S 113°0E 36 E4
Sampit, Teluk Indonesia 3°5S 113°3E 36 E4
Samrong Cambodia 14°15N 103°30E 38 E4
Samrong Thailand 15°10N 100°40E 38 E3
Samsø Denmark 55°50N 10°35E 9 J14
Samsun Turkey 41°15N 36°22E 19 F6
Samui, Ko Thailand 9°30N 100°0E 39 b
Samusole Dem. Rep. of the Congo 10°2S 24°0E 55 E1
Samut Prakan Thailand 13°32N 100°40E 38 F3
Samut Songkhram Thailand 13°24N 100°1E 38 F3
Samwari Pakistan 28°30N 66°46E 42 E2
San Mali 13°15N 4°57W 50 F5
San → Cambodia 13°32N 105°57E 38 F5
San → Poland 50°45N 21°51E 17 C11
San Agustin, C. Phil. 6°20N 126°13E 37 C7
San Agustín de Valle Fértil Argentina 30°35S 67°30W 94 C2
San Ambrosio Pac. Oc. 26°28S 79°53W 90 F3
San Andreas U.S.A. 38°12N 120°41W 78 G6
San Andrés, I. de Caribbean 12°42N 81°46W 88 D3
San Andres Mts. U.S.A. 33°0N 106°30W 77 K10
San Andrés Tuxtla Mexico 18°27N 95°13W 87 D5
San Angelo U.S.A. 31°28N 100°26W 84 F4
San Anselmo U.S.A. 37°59N 122°34W 78 H4
San Antonio Belize 16°15N 89°2W 87 D7
San Antonio Chile 33°40S 71°40W 94 C1
San Antonio N. Mex., U.S.A. 33°55N 106°52W 77 K10
San Antonio Tex., U.S.A. 29°25N 98°29W 84 G5
San Antonio → U.S.A. 28°30N 96°54W 84 G6
San Antonio, C. Argentina 36°15S 56°40W 94 D4
San Antonio, C. de Cuba 21°50N 84°57W 88 B3
San Antonio, Mt. U.S.A. 34°17N 117°38W 79 L9
San Antonio de los Baños Cuba 22°54N 82°31W 88 B3
San Antonio de los Cobres Argentina 24°10S 66°17W 94 A2
San Antonio Oeste Argentina 40°40S 65°0W 96 E4
San Ardo U.S.A. 36°1N 120°54W 78 J6
San Augustín Canary Is. 27°47N 15°32W 24 G4
San Augustine U.S.A. 31°32N 94°7W 84 F7
San Bartolomé Canary Is. 28°59N 13°37W 24 F6
San Bartolomé de Tirajana Canary Is. 27°54N 15°34W 24 G4
San Benedetto del Tronto Italy 42°57N 13°53E 22 C5
San Benedicto, I. Mexico 19°18N 110°49W 86 D2
San Benito U.S.A. 26°8N 97°38W 84 H6
San Benito → U.S.A. 36°53N 121°34W 78 J5
San Benito Mt. U.S.A. 36°22N 120°37W 78 J6
San Bernardino U.S.A. 34°7N 117°19W 79 L9
San Bernardino Mts. U.S.A. 34°10N 116°45W 79 L10
San Bernardino Str. Phil. 13°0N 125°0E 37 B6
San Bernardo Chile 33°40S 70°50W 94 C1
San Bernardo, I. de Colombia 9°45N 75°50W 92 B3
San Blas Mexico 26°5N 108°46W 86 B3
San Blas, Arch. de Panama 9°50N 78°31W 88 E4
San Blas, C. U.S.A. 29°40N 85°21W 85 G12
San Borja Bolivia 14°50S 66°52W 92 F5
San Buenaventura = Ventura U.S.A. 34°17N 119°18W 79 L7
San Buenaventura Mexico 27°5N 101°32W 86 B4
San Carlos = Sant Carles Spain 39°3N 1°34E 24 B8
San Carlos Argentina 33°50S 69°0W 94 C2
San Carlos Chile 36°10S 72°0W 94 D1
San Carlos Baja Calif. S., Mexico 24°47N 112°7W 86 C2
San Carlos Coahuila, Mexico 29°1N 100°51W 86 B4
San Carlos Nic. 11°12N 84°50W 88 D3
San Carlos Phil. 10°29N 123°25E 37 B6
San Carlos Uruguay 34°46S 54°58W 95 C5
San Carlos U.S.A. 33°21N 110°27W 77 K8
San Carlos Venezuela 9°40N 68°36W 92 B5
San Carlos de Bariloche Argentina 41°10S 71°25W 96 E2
San Carlos de Bolívar Argentina 36°15S 61°6W 96 D4
San Carlos del Zulia Venezuela 9°1N 71°55W 92 B4
San Carlos L. U.S.A. 33°11N 110°32W 77 K8
San Clemente Chile 35°30S 71°29W 94 D1
San Clemente U.S.A. 33°26N 117°37W 79 M9
San Clemente I. U.S.A. 32°53N 118°29W 79 N8
San Cristóbal = Es Migjorn Gran Spain 39°57N 4°3E 24 B11
San Cristóbal Argentina 30°20S 61°10W 94 C3
San Cristóbal Dom. Rep. 18°25N 70°6W 89 C5
San Cristóbal Solomon Is. 10°30S 161°0E 58 C9
San Cristóbal Venezuela 7°46N 72°14W 92 B4
San Cristóbal de las Casas Mexico 16°45N 92°38W 87 D6
San Diego Calif., U.S.A. 32°42N 117°9W 79 N9
San Diego Tex., U.S.A. 27°46N 98°14W 84 H5
San Diego, C. Argentina 54°40S 65°10W 96 G3
San Diego de la Unión Mexico 21°28N 100°52W 86 C4
San Diego Int. ✕ (SAN) U.S.A. 32°44N 117°11W 79 N9
San Dimitri, Ras Malta 36°4N 14°11E 25 C1
San Dimitri Point = San Dimitri, Ras Malta 36°4N 14°11E 25 C1
San Estanislao Paraguay 24°39S 56°26W 94 A4
San Felipe Chile 32°43S 70°42W 94 C1
San Felipe Mexico 31°1N 114°52W 86 A2
San Felipe Venezuela 10°20N 68°44W 92 A5
San Felipe → U.S.A. 33°10N 115°49W 79 M11
San Félix Chile 28°56S 70°28W 94 B1
San Félix Pac. Oc. 26°23S 80°0W 90 F2
San Fernando = Sant Ferran Spain 38°42N 1°28E 24 C7
San Fernando Chile 34°30S 71°0W 94 C1
San Fernando Mexico 24°51N 98°10W 87 C5
San Fernando La Union, Phil. 16°40N 120°23E 37 A6
San Fernando Pampanga, Phil. 15°5N 120°37E 37 A6
San Fernando Spain 36°28N 6°17W 21 D2
San Fernando Trin. & Tob. 10°16N 61°28W 89 D7
San Fernando U.S.A. 34°17N 118°26W 79 L8
San Fernando de Apure Venezuela 7°54N 67°15W 92 B5
San Fernando de Atabapo Venezuela 4°3N 67°42W 92 C5
San Francisco Argentina 31°30S 62°5W 94 C3
San Francisco U.S.A. 37°46N 122°23W 78 H4
San Francisco → U.S.A. 32°59N 109°22W 77 K9
San Francisco, C. de Colombia 6°18N 77°29W 90 C3
San Francisco, Paso de S. Amer. 27°0S 68°0W 94 B2
San Francisco de Macorís Dom. Rep. 19°19N 70°15W 89 C5
San Francisco del Monte de Oro Argentina 32°36S 66°8W 94 C2
San Francisco del Oro Mexico 26°52N 105°51W 86 B3
San Francisco Int. ✕ (SFO) U.S.A. 37°37N 122°22W 78 H4
San Francisco Javier = Sant Francesc de Formentera Spain 38°42N 1°26E 24 C7
San Gabriel Chile 33°47S 70°15W 94 C1
San Gabriel Chilac Mexico 18°19N 97°21W 87 D5
San Gabriel Mts. U.S.A. 34°17N 117°38W 79 L9
San Gavino Monreale Italy 39°33N 8°47E 22 E3
San German Puerto Rico 18°4N 67°4W 89 d
San Gorgonio Mt. U.S.A. 34°6N 116°50W 79 L10
San Gottardo, P. del Switz. 46°33N 8°33E 20 C8
San Gregorio Uruguay 32°37S 55°40W 95 C4
San Gregorio U.S.A. 37°20N 122°23W 78 H4
San Ignacio Belize 17°10N 89°5W 87 D7
San Ignacio Bolivia 16°20S 60°55W 92 G6
San Ignacio Mexico 27°27N 112°51W 86 B2
San Ignacio Paraguay 26°52S 57°3W 94 B4
San Ignacio, L. Mexico 26°54N 113°13W 86 B2
San Ildefonso, C. Phil. 16°0N 122°1E 37 A6
San Isidro Argentina 34°29S 58°31W 94 C4
San Jacinto U.S.A. 33°47N 116°57W 79 M10
San Jaime = Sant Jaume Spain 39°54N 4°4E 24 B11
San Javier Misiones, Argentina 27°55S 55°5W 95 B4
San Javier Santa Fe, Argentina 30°40S 59°55W 94 C4
San Javier Bolivia 16°18S 62°30W 92 G6
San Javier Chile 35°40S 71°45W 94 D1
San Jerónimo Taviche Mexico 16°44N 96°35W 87 D5
San Joaquin U.S.A. 36°36N 120°11W 78 J6
San Joaquin → U.S.A. 38°4N 121°51W 78 G5
San Joaquin Valley U.S.A. 37°20N 121°0W 78 J6
San Jon U.S.A. 35°6N 103°20W 77 J12
San Jordi = Sant Jordi Spain 39°33N 2°46E 24 B9
San Jorge Argentina 31°54S 61°50W 94 C3
San Jorge, B. Mexico 31°20N 113°20W 86 A2
San Jorge, G. Argentina 46°0S 66°0W 96 F3
San José = San Josep Spain 38°55N 1°18E 24 C7
San José Costa Rica 9°55N 84°2W 88 E3
San José Guatemala 14°0N 90°50W 88 D1
San Jose Mind. Occ., Phil. 12°27N 121°4E 37 B6
San Jose Nueva Ecija, Phil. 15°45N 120°55E 37 A6
San Jose U.S.A. 37°20N 121°53W 78 H5
San Jose → U.S.A. 34°25N 106°45W 77 J10
San José, I. Mexico 25°0N 110°38W 86 C2
San Jose de Buenavista Phil. 10°45N 121°56E 37 B6
San José de Chiquitos Bolivia 17°53S 60°50W 92 G6
San José de Feliciano Argentina 30°26S 58°46W 94 C4
San José de Jáchal Argentina 30°15S 68°46W 94 C2
San José de Mayo Uruguay 34°27S 56°40W 94 C4
San José del Cabo Mexico 23°3N 109°41W 86 C3
San José del Guaviare Colombia 2°35N 72°38W 92 C4
San Josep Spain 38°55N 1°18E 24 C7
San Juan Argentina 31°30S 68°30W 94 C2
San Juan Puerto Rico 18°28N 66°7W 89 d
San Juan Trin. & Tob. 10°39N 61°29W 93 K15
San Juan □ Argentina 31°9S 69°0W 94 C2
San Juan → Argentina 32°20S 67°25W 94 C2
San Juan → Nic. 10°56N 83°42W 88 D3
San Juan → U.S.A. 37°16N 110°26W 77 H8
San Juan Bautista = Sant Joan de Labritja Spain 39°5N 1°31E 24 B8
San Juan Bautista Paraguay 26°37S 57°6W 94 B4
San Juan Bautista U.S.A. 36°51N 121°32W 78 J5
San Juan Capistrano U.S.A. 33°30N 117°40W 79 M9
San Juan Cr. → U.S.A. 35°40N 120°22W 78 J5
San Juan de Guadelupe Mexico 24°38N 102°44W 86 C4
San Juan de la Costa Mexico 24°20N 110°41W 86 C2
San Juan de los Lagos Mexico 21°15N 102°18W 86 C4
San Juan de los Morros Venezuela 9°55N 67°21W 92 B5
San Juan del Norte Nic. 10°58N 83°40W 88 D3
San Juan del Norte, B. de Nic. 11°0N 83°40W 88 D3
San Juan del Río Mexico 20°23N 100°0W 87 C5
San Juan del Sur Nic. 11°20N 85°51W 88 D2
San Juan I. U.S.A. 48°32N 123°5W 78 B3
San Juan Island ⌂ U.S.A. 48°35N 123°8W 78 B4
San Juan Mts. U.S.A. 37°30N 107°0W 77 H10
San Justo Argentina 30°47S 60°30W 94 C3
San Kamphaeng Thailand 18°45N 99°8E 38 C2
San Lázaro, C. Mexico 24°50N 112°18W 86 C2
San Leandro U.S.A. 37°42N 122°9W 78 H4
San Lorenzo = Sant Llorenç des Cardassar Spain 39°37N 3°17E 24 B10
San Lorenzo Argentina 32°45S 60°45W 94 C3
San Lorenzo Ecuador 1°15N 78°50W 92 C3
San Lorenzo Paraguay 25°20S 57°32W 94 B4
San Lorenzo → Mexico 24°15N 107°24W 86 C3
San Lorenzo, I. Mexico 28°38N 112°51W 86 B2
San Lorenzo, Mte. Argentina 47°40S 72°20W 96 F2
San Lucas = Cabo San Lucas Mexico 22°53N 109°54W 86 C3
San Lucas Bolivia 20°5S 65°7W 92 H5
San Lucas Mexico 27°10N 112°14W 86 B2
San Lucas U.S.A. 36°8N 121°1W 78 J5
San Lucas, C. Mexico 22°52N 109°53W 86 C3
San Luis Argentina 33°20S 66°20W 94 C2
San Luis Cuba 22°17N 83°46W 88 B3
San Luis Guatemala 16°14N 89°27W 88 C2
San Luis Ariz., U.S.A. 32°29N 114°47W 77 K6
San Luis Colo., U.S.A. 37°12N 105°25W 77 H11
San Luis □ Argentina 34°0S 66°0W 94 C2
San Luis, I. Mexico 29°58N 114°26W 86 B2
San Luis, Sierra de Argentina 32°30S 66°10W 94 C2
San Luis de la Paz Mexico 21°18N 100°31W 86 C4
San Luis Obispo U.S.A. 35°17N 120°40W 79 K6
San Luis Potosí Mexico 22°9N 100°59W 86 C4
San Luis Potosí □ Mexico 23°0N 101°0W 86 C4
San Luis Res. U.S.A. 37°4N 121°5W 78 H5
San Luis Río Colorado Mexico 32°29N 114°58W 86 A2
San Manuel U.S.A. 32°36N 110°38W 77 K8
San Marcos Guatemala 14°59N 91°52W 88 D1
San Marcos Calif., U.S.A. 33°9N 117°10W 79 M9
San Marcos Tex., U.S.A. 29°53N 97°56W 84 G6
San Marcos, I. Mexico 27°13N 112°6W 86 B2
San Marino San Marino 43°55N 12°30E 16 G7
San Marino ■ Europe 43°56N 12°25E 22 C5
San Martín Antarctica 68°11S 67°0W 5 C17
San Martín Argentina 33°5S 68°28W 94 C2
San Martín → Bolivia 13°8S 63°43W 92 F6
San Martín, L. Argentina 48°50S 72°50W 96 F2
San Martín de los Andes Argentina 40°10S 71°20W 96 E2
San Mateo = Sant Mateu Spain 39°3N 1°23E 24 B7
San Mateo U.S.A. 37°34N 122°19W 78 H4
San Matías Bolivia 16°25S 58°20W 92 G7
San Matías, G. Argentina 41°30S 64°0W 96 E4
San Miguel = Sant Miguel Spain 39°3N 1°26E 24 B7
San Miguel El Salv. 13°30N 88°12W 88 D2
San Miguel Panama 8°27N 78°55W 88 E4
San Miguel U.S.A. 35°45N 120°42W 78 K6
San Miguel → Bolivia 13°52S 63°56W 92 F6
San Miguel de Tucumán Argentina 26°50S 65°20W 94 B2
San Miguel del Monte Argentina 35°23S 58°50W 94 D4
San Miguel I. U.S.A. 34°2N 120°23W 79 L6
San Nicolás Canary Is. 27°58N 15°47W 24 G4
San Nicolás de los Arroyas Argentina 33°25S 60°10W 94 C3
San Nicolas I. U.S.A. 33°15N 119°30W 79 M7
San Onofre U.S.A. 33°22N 117°34W 79 M9
San Pablo Bolivia 21°43S 66°38W 94 A2
San Pablo U.S.A. 37°58N 122°21W 78 H4
San Pedro B. Aires, Argentina 33°40S 59°40W 94 C4
San Pedro Misiones, Argentina 26°30S 54°10W 95 B5
San Pedro Chile 33°54S 71°28W 94 C1
San Pédro Ivory C. 4°50N 6°33W 50 H4
San Pedro Mexico 23°55N 110°17W 86 C2
San Pedro □ Paraguay 24°0S 57°0W 94 A4
San Pedro → Chihuahua, Mexico 28°20N 106°10W 86 B3
San Pedro → Nayarit, Mexico 21°45N 105°30W 86 C3
San Pedro → U.S.A. 32°59N 110°47W 77 K8
San Pedro, Pta. Chile 25°30S 70°38W 94 B1
San Pedro Channel U.S.A. 33°30N 118°25W 79 M8
San Pedro de Atacama Chile 22°55S 68°15W 94 A2
San Pedro de Jujuy Argentina 24°12S 64°55W 94 A3
San Pedro de las Colonias Mexico 25°45N 102°59W 86 B4
San Pedro de Macorís Dom. Rep. 18°30N 69°18W 89 C6
San Pedro del Norte Nic. 13°4N 84°33W 88 D3
San Pedro del Paraná Paraguay 26°43S 56°13W 94 B4
San Pedro Mártir, Sierra Mexico 31°0N 115°30W 86 A1
San Pedro Mártir △ Mexico 31°0N 115°21W 86 A1
San Pedro Ocampo = Melchor Ocampo Mexico 24°51N 101°39W 86 C4
San Pedro Pochutla Mexico 15°44N 96°28W 87 D5
San Pedro Sula Honduras 15°30N 88°0W 88 C2
San Pedro Tututepec Mexico 16°9N 97°38W 87 D5
San Pietro Italy 39°8N 8°17E 22 E3
San Rafael Argentina 34°40S 68°21W 94 C2
San Rafael Calif., U.S.A. 37°58N 122°32W 78 H4
San Rafael N. Mex., U.S.A. 35°7N 107°53W 77 J10
San Rafael Mt. U.S.A. 34°41N 119°52W 79 L7
San Rafael Mts. U.S.A. 34°40N 119°50W 79 L7
San Ramón de la Nueva Orán Argentina 23°10S 64°20W 94 A3
San Remo Italy 43°49N 7°46E 20 E7
San Roque Argentina 28°25S 58°45W 94 B4
San Roque Spain 36°17N 5°21W 21 D3
San Rosendo Chile 37°16S 72°43W 94 D1
San Saba U.S.A. 31°12N 98°43W 84 F5
San Salvador El Salv. 13°40N 89°10W 88 D2
San Salvador Spain 39°27N 3°11E 24 B10
San Salvador de Jujuy Argentina 24°10S 64°48W 94 A3
San Salvador I. Bahamas 24°0N 74°40W 89 B5
San Sebastián = Donostia-San Sebastián Spain 43°17N 1°58W 21 A5
San Sebastián Argentina 53°10S 68°30W 96 G3
San Sebastián Puerto Rico 18°20N 66°59W 89 d
San Sebastián de la Gomera Canary Is. 28°5N 17°7W 24 F2
San Serra = Son Serra Spain 39°43N 3°13E 24 B10
San Severo Italy 41°41N 15°23E 22 D6
San Simeon U.S.A. 35°39N 121°11W 78 K5
San Simon U.S.A. 32°16N 109°14W 77 K9
San Telmo = Sant Elm Spain 39°35N 2°21E 24 B9
San Telmo Mexico 30°58N 116°6W 86 A1
San Tiburcio Mexico 24°8N 101°32W 86 C4
San Valentin, Mte. Chile 46°30S 73°30W 96 F2
San Vicente de la Barquera Spain 43°23N 4°29W 21 A3
San Vito Costa Rica 8°50N 82°58W 88 E3
Sana' Yemen 15°27N 44°12E 47 D3
Sana → Bos.-H. 45°3N 16°23E 16 F9
Sanae IV Antarctica 70°20S 9°0W 5 D2
Sanaga → Cameroon 3°35N 9°38E 52 D1
Sanaloa, Presa Mexico 24°50N 107°20W 86 C3
Sanana Indonesia 2°4S 125°58E 37 E7
Sanand India 22°59N 72°25E 42 H5
Sanandaj Iran 35°18N 47°1E 44 C5
Sanandita Bolivia 21°40S 63°45W 94 A3
Sanawad India 22°11N 76°5E 42 H7
Sancellas = Sencelles Spain 39°39N 2°54E 24 B9
Sanchahe China 44°50N 126°2E 35 B14
Sánchez Dom. Rep. 19°15N 69°36W 89 C6
Sanchor India 24°45N 71°55E 42 G4
Sancti Spíritus Cuba 21°52N 79°33W 88 B4
Sancy, Puy de France 45°32N 2°50E 20 D5
Sand → S. Africa 22°25S 30°5E 57 C5
Sand Hills U.S.A. 42°10N 101°30W 80 D3
Sand Lakes ⌂ Canada 57°51N 98°32W 71 B9
Sand Springs U.S.A. 36°9N 96°7W 84 C6
Sanda Japan 34°53N 135°14E 31 G7
Sandakan Malaysia 5°53N 118°4E 36 C5
Sandan = Sambor Cambodia 12°46N 106°0E 38 F6
Sandanski Bulgaria 41°35N 23°16E 23 D10
Sanday U.K. 59°16N 2°31W 11 B6
Sandefjord Norway 59°10N 10°15E 9 G14
Sanders U.S.A. 35°13N 109°20W 77 J9
Sanderson U.S.A. 30°9N 102°24W 84 F3
Sandersville U.S.A. 32°59N 82°48W 85 E13
Sandfire Roadhouse Australia 19°45S 121°15E 60 C3
Sandfly L. Canada 55°43N 106°6W 71 B7
Sandfontein Namibia 23°48S 19°1E 56 C2
Sandheads, The India 21°10N 88°20E 43 J13
Sandía Peru 14°10S 69°30W 92 F5
Sandila India 27°5N 80°31E 43 F9
Sandnes Norway 58°50N 5°45E 9 G11
Sandnessjøen Norway 66°2N 12°38E 8 C15
Sandoa Dem. Rep. of the Congo 9°41S 23°0E 52 F4
Sandomierz Poland 50°40N 21°43E 17 C11
Sandover → Australia 21°43S 136°32E 62 C2
Sandoway = Thandwe Burma 18°20N 94°30E 41 K19
Sandoy Færoe Is. 61°52N 6°46W 8 F9
Sandpoint U.S.A. 48°17N 116°33W 76 B5
Sandray U.K. 56°53N 7°31W 11 E1
Sandringham U.K. 52°51N 0°31E 12 E8
Sandstone Australia 27°59S 119°16E 61 E2
Sandusky Mich., U.S.A. 43°25N 82°50W 82 C2
Sandusky Ohio, U.S.A. 41°27N 82°42W 82 E2
Sandveld Namibia 21°25S 20°0E 56 C3
Sandviken Sweden 60°38N 16°46E 8 F17
Sandwich, C. Australia 18°14S 146°18E 62 B4
Sandwich B. Canada 53°40N 57°15W 73 B8
Sandwich B. Namibia 23°25S 14°20E 56 C1
Sandy Oreg., U.S.A. 45°24N 122°16W 78 E4
Sandy Pa., U.S.A. 41°6N 78°46W 82 E6
Sandy Utah, U.S.A. 40°32N 111°50W 76 F8
Sandy Bay Canada 55°31N 102°19W 71 B8
Sandy Bight Australia 33°50S 123°20E 61 F3
Sandy C. Queens., Australia 24°42S 153°15E 62 C5
Sandy C. Tas., Australia 41°25S 144°45E 63 G3
Sandy Cay Bahamas 23°13N 75°18W 89 B4

Sandy Cr. → U.S.A.   41°51N 109°47W **76** F9
Sandy L. Canada   53°2N 93°0W **72** B1
Sandy Lake Canada   53°0N 93°15W **72** B1
Sandy Valley U.S.A.   35°49N 115°38W **79** K11
Sanford Fla., U.S.A.   28°48N 81°16W **85** G14
Sanford Maine, U.S.A.   43°27N 70°47W **83** C14
Sanford N.C., U.S.A.   35°29N 79°10W **85** D15
Sanford → Australia   27°22S 115°53E **61** E2
Sanford, Mt. U.S.A.   62°13N 144°8W **68** C5
Sang-i-Masha Afghan.   33°8N 67°27E **42** C2
Sanga Mozam.   12°22S 35°21E **55** E4
Sanga → Congo   1°5S 17°0E **52** E3
Sangamner India   19°37N 74°15E **40** K9
Sangar Afghan.   32°56N 65°30E **42** C1
Sangar Russia   64°2N 127°31E **29** C13
Sangar Sarai Afghan.   34°27N 70°35E **42** B4
Sangarh → Pakistan   30°43N 70°44E **42** D4
Sangay Ecuador   2°0S 78°20W **92** D3
Sange
  Dem. Rep. of the Congo   6°58S 28°21E **54** D2
Sangeang Indonesia   8°12S 119°6E **37** F5
Sanger U.S.A.   36°42N 119°33W **78** J7
Sangerhausen Germany   51°28N 11°18E **16** C6
Sanggan He → China   38°12N 117°15E **34** E9
Sanggau Indonesia   0°5N 110°30E **36** D4
Sanghar Pakistan   26°2N 68°57E **42** F3
Sangihe, Kepulauan
  Indonesia   3°0N 125°30E **37** D7
Sangihe, Pulau
  Indonesia   3°35N 125°30E **37** D7
Sangju S. Korea   36°25N 128°10E **35** F15
Sangkapura Indonesia   5°52S 112°40E **36** F4
Sangkhla Thailand   14°57N 98°28E **38** E2
Sangkulirang Indonesia   0°59N 117°58E **36** D5
Sangla Pakistan   31°43N 73°23E **42** D5
Sangli India   16°55N 74°33E **40** L9
Sangmélima Cameroon   2°57N 12°1E **52** D2
Sangod India   24°55N 76°17E **42** G7
Sangre de Cristo Mts.
  U.S.A.   37°30N 105°20W **77** H11
Sangre Grande
  Trin. & Tob.   10°35N 61°8W **93** K15
Sangrur India   30°14N 75°50E **42** D6
Sangudo Canada   53°50N 114°54W **70** C6
Sangue → Brazil   11°1S 58°39W **92** F7
Sanibel U.S.A.   26°27N 82°1W **85** H13
Sanikiluaq Canada   56°32N 79°14W **72** A4
Sanin-Kaigan △ Japan   35°39N 134°37E **31** G7
Sanirajak Canada   68°46N 81°12W **69** C11
Sanjawi Pakistan   30°17N 68°21E **42** D3
Sanje Uganda   0°49S 31°30E **54** C3
Sanjo Japan   37°37N 138°57E **30** F9
Sankh → India   22°15N 84°48E **43** H11
Sankt Gallen Switz.   47°26N 9°22E **20** C8
Sankt Michel = Mikkeli
  Finland   61°43N 27°15E **8** F22
Sankt Moritz Switz.   46°30N 9°51E **20** C8
Sankt-Peterburg Russia   59°55N 30°20E **9** G24
Sankt Pölten Austria   48°12N 15°38E **16** D8
Sankuru →
  Dem. Rep. of the Congo   4°17S 20°25E **52** E4
Sanliurfa Turkey   37°12N 38°50E **44** B3
Sanlúcar de Barrameda
  Spain   36°46N 6°21W **21** D2
Sanmenxia China   34°47N 111°12E **34** G6
Sanming China   26°15N 117°40E **33** D6
Sannaspos S. Africa   29°6S 26°34E **56** D4
Sannicandro Gargánico
  Italy   41°50N 15°34E **22** D6
Sânnicolau Mare
  Romania   46°5N 20°39E **17** E11
Sannieshof S. Africa   26°30S 25°47E **56** D4
Sannîn, J. Lebanon   33°57N 35°52E **46** B4
Sanniquellie Liberia   7°19N 8°38W **50** G4
Sanok Poland   49°35N 22°10E **17** D12
Sanquhar U.K.   55°22N 3°54W **11** F5
Sans Souci Trin. & Tob.   10°50N 61°0W **93** K16
Sant Antoni de Portmany
  Spain   38°59N 1°19E **24** C7
Sant Carles Spain   39°3N 1°34E **24** B8
Sant Elm Spain   39°35N 2°21E **24** B9
Sant Feliu de Guíxols
  Spain   41°45N 3°1E **21** B7
Sant Ferran Spain   38°42N 1°28E **24** C7
Sant Francesc de Formentera
  Spain   38°42N 1°26E **24** C7
Sant Jaume Spain   39°54N 4°4E **24** B11
Sant Joan de Labritja
  Spain   39°5N 1°31E **24** B8
Sant Jordi Ibiza, Spain   38°53N 1°24E **24** C7
Sant Jordi Mallorca, Spain   39°33N 2°46E **24** B9
Sant Jordi, G. de Spain   40°53N 1°2E **21** B6
Sant Llorenç des Cardassar
  Spain   39°37N 3°17E **24** B10
Sant Mateu Spain   39°3N 1°23E **24** B7
Sant Miguel Spain   39°3N 1°26E **24** B7
Santa Agnés Spain   39°3N 1°21E **24** B7
Santa Ana Bolivia   13°50S 65°40W **92** F5
Santa Ana El Salv.   14°0N 89°31W **88** D2
Santa Ana Mexico   30°33N 111°7W **86** A2
Santa Ana U.S.A.   33°46N 117°52W **79** M9
Sant' Antíoco Italy   39°4N 8°27E **22** E3
Santa Bárbara Chile   37°40S 72°1W **94** D1
Santa Bárbara
  Honduras   14°53N 88°14W **88** D2
Santa Bárbara Mexico   26°48N 105°49W **86** B3
Santa Barbara U.S.A.   34°25N 119°42W **79** L7
Santa Barbara Channel
  U.S.A.   34°15N 120°0W **79** L7
Santa Barbara I.
  U.S.A.   33°29N 119°2W **79** M7
Santa Catalina, Gulf of
  U.S.A.   33°10N 117°50W **79** N9
Santa Catalina, I.
  Mexico   25°40N 110°47W **86** B2
Santa Catalina I.
  U.S.A.   33°23N 118°25W **79** M8

Santa Catarina □
  Brazil   27°25S 48°30W **95** B6
Santa Catarina, I. de
  Brazil   27°30S 48°40W **95** B6
Santa Cecília Brazil   26°56S 50°18W **95** B5
Santa Clara Cuba   22°20N 80°0W **88** B4
Santa Clara Calif.,
  U.S.A.   37°21N 121°57W **78** H5
Santa Clara Utah,
  U.S.A.   37°8N 113°39W **77** H7
Santa Clara de Olimar
  Uruguay   32°50S 54°54W **95** C5
Santa Clara Valley
  U.S.A.   36°50N 121°30W **78** J5
Santa Clarita U.S.A.   34°24N 118°33W **79** L8
Santa Clotilde Peru   2°33S 73°45W **92** D4
Santa Coloma de Gramenet
  Spain   41°27N 2°13E **21** B7
Santa Cruz Argentina   50°0S 68°32W **96** G3
Santa Cruz Bolivia   17°43S 63°10W **92** G6
Santa Cruz Chile   34°38S 71°27W **94** C1
Santa Cruz Costa Rica   10°15N 85°35W **88** D2
Santa Cruz Madeira   32°42N 16°46W **24** D3
Santa Cruz Phil.   14°20N 121°24E **37** B6
Santa Cruz U.S.A.   36°58N 122°1W **78** J4
Santa Cruz →
  Argentina   50°10S 68°20W **96** G3
Santa Cruz de la Palma
  Canary Is.   28°41N 17°46W **24** F2
Santa Cruz de la Palma ✈ (SPC)
  Canary Is.   28°40N 17°45W **24** F2
Santa Cruz de Tenerife
  Canary Is.   28°28N 16°15W **24** F3
Santa Cruz del Norte
  Cuba   23°9N 81°55W **88** B3
Santa Cruz del Sur Cuba   20°44N 78°0W **88** B4
Santa Cruz do Rio Pardo
  Brazil   22°54S 49°37W **95** A6
Santa Cruz do Sul
  Brazil   29°42S 52°25W **95** B5
Santa Cruz I. U.S.A.   34°1N 119°43W **79** M7
Santa Cruz Is.
  Solomon Is.   10°30S 166°0E **58** C9
Santa Cruz Mts. Jamaica   17°58N 77°43W **88** a
Santa Domingo, Cay
  Bahamas   21°25N 75°15W **88** B4
Santa Elena Argentina   30°58S 59°47W **94** C4
Santa Elena, C.
  Costa Rica   10°54N 85°56W **88** D2
Santa Eulària des Riu
  Spain   38°59N 1°32E **24** C8
Santa Fé Argentina   31°35S 60°41W **94** C3
Santa Fe U.S.A.   35°41N 105°57W **77** J11
Santa Fé □ Argentina   31°50S 60°55W **94** C3
Santa Fé do Sul Brazil   20°13S 50°56W **93** H8
Santa Filomena Brazil   9°6S 45°50W **93** E9
Santa Gertrudis Spain   39°0N 1°26E **24** C7
Santa Inês Brazil   13°17S 39°48W **93** F11
Santa Inés, I. Chile   54°0S 73°0W **96** G2
Santa Isabel Argentina   36°10S 66°54W **94** D2
Santa Isabel do Morro
  Brazil   11°34S 50°40W **93** F8
Santa Lucía Corrientes,
  Argentina   28°58S 59°5W **94** B4
Santa Lucía San Juan,
  Argentina   31°30S 68°30W **94** C2
Santa Lucia Uruguay   34°27S 56°24W **94** C4
Santa Lucia Range
  U.S.A.   36°0N 121°20W **78** K5
Santa Luzia C. Verde Is.   16°50N 24°35W **50** b
Santa Margalida Spain   39°42N 3°6E **24** B10
Santa Margarita
  Argentina   38°28S 61°35W **94** D3
Santa Margarita
  U.S.A.   35°23N 120°37W **78** K6
Santa Margarita →
  U.S.A.   33°13N 117°23W **79** M9
Santa Margarita, I.
  Mexico   24°27N 111°50W **86** C2
Santa María Argentina   26°40S 66°0W **94** B2
Santa Maria Azores   36°58N 25°6W **50** a
Santa Maria Brazil   29°40S 53°48W **95** B5
Santa María C. Verde Is.   16°31N 22°53W **50** b
Santa María → Mexico   31°0N 107°14W **86** A3
Santa María, B. de
  Mexico   25°4N 108°6W **86** B3
Santa Maria da Vitória
  Brazil   13°24S 44°12W **93** F10
Santa María del Camí
  Spain   39°38N 2°47E **24** B9
Santa Maria di Léuca, C.
  Italy   39°47N 18°22E **23** E8
Santa Marta Colombia   11°15N 74°13W **92** A4
Santa Marta, Sierra Nevada de
  Colombia   10°55N 73°50W **92** A4
Santa Marta Grande, C.
  Brazil   28°43S 48°50W **95** B6
Santa Maura = Lefkada
  Greece   38°40N 20°43E **23** E9
Santa Monica U.S.A.   34°1N 118°29W **79** M8
Santa Monica Mts. ⌒
  U.S.A.   34°4N 118°44W **79** L8
Santa Paula U.S.A.   34°21N 119°4W **79** L7
Santa Ponça Spain   39°30N 2°28E **24** B9
Santa Rosa La Pampa,
  Argentina   36°40S 64°17W **94** D3
Santa Rosa San Luis,
  Argentina   32°21S 65°10W **94** C2
Santa Rosa Brazil   27°52S 54°29W **95** B5
Santa Rosa Calif.,
  U.S.A.   38°26N 122°43W **78** G4
Santa Rosa N. Mex.,
  U.S.A.   34°57N 104°41W **77** J11
Santa Rosa and San Jacinto
  Mts. ⌒ U.S.A.   33°28N 116°20W **79** M10
Santa Rosa de Copán
  Honduras   14°47N 88°46W **88** D2

Santa Rosa de Río Primero
  Argentina   31°8S 63°20W **94** C3
Santa Rosa del Sara
  Bolivia   17°7S 63°35W **92** G6
Santa Rosa I. Calif.,
  U.S.A.   33°58N 120°6W **79** M6
Santa Rosa I. Fla.,
  U.S.A.   30°20N 86°50W **85** F11
Santa Rosa Range
  U.S.A.   41°45N 117°40W **76** F5
Santa Rosalía Mexico   27°19N 112°17W **86** B2
Santa Sylvina Argentina   27°50S 61°10W **94** B3
Santa Tecla = Nueva San
  Salvador El Salv.   13°40N 89°18W **88** D2
Santa Teresa Argentina   33°25S 60°47W **94** C3
Santa Teresa Australia   24°8S 134°22E **62** C1
Santa Teresa Mexico   25°17N 97°51W **87** B5
Santa Teresa △
  Uruguay   33°57S 53°31W **95** C5
Santa Vitória do Palmar
  Brazil   33°32S 53°25W **95** C5
Santa Ynez → U.S.A.   34°41N 120°36W **79** L6
Santa Ynez Mts. U.S.A.   34°30N 120°0W **79** L6
Santa Ysabel U.S.A.   33°7N 116°40W **79** M10
Santai China   31°5N 104°58E **32** C5
Santana Madeira   32°48N 16°52W **24** D3
Santana, Coxilha de
  Brazil   30°50S 55°35W **95** C4
Santana do Livramento
  Brazil   30°55S 55°30W **95** C4
Santander Spain   43°27N 3°51W **21** A4
Santander Jiménez
  Mexico   24°13N 98°28W **87** C5
Santanilla, Is. Honduras   17°22N 83°57W **88** C3
Santanyí Spain   39°20N 3°5E **24** B10
Santaquin U.S.A.   39°59N 111°47W **76** G8
Santarém Brazil   2°25S 54°42W **93** D8
Santarém Portugal   39°12N 8°42W **21** C1
Santaren Channel
  W. Indies   24°0N 79°30W **88** B4
Santee U.S.A.   32°50N 116°58W **79** N10
Santee → U.S.A.   33°7N 79°17W **85** E15
Santiago = São Tiago
  C. Verde Is.   15°0N 23°40W **50** b
Santiago Brazil   29°11S 54°52W **95** B5
Santiago Canary Is.   28°2N 17°12W **24** F2
Santiago Chile   33°26S 70°40W **94** C1
Santiago Panama   8°0N 81°0W **88** E3
Santiago □ Chile   33°30S 70°50W **94** C1
Santiago → Mexico   25°11N 105°26W **66** G9
Santiago → Peru   4°27S 77°38W **92** D3
Santiago de Compostela
  Spain   42°52N 8°37W **21** A1
Santiago de Cuba Cuba   20°0N 75°49W **88** C4
Santiago de los Caballeros
  Dom. Rep.   19°30N 70°40W **89** C5
Santiago del Estero
  Argentina   27°50S 64°15W **94** B3
Santiago del Estero □
  Argentina   27°40S 63°15W **94** B3
Santiago del Teide
  Canary Is.   28°17N 16°48W **24** F3
Santiago Ixcuintla
  Mexico   21°49N 105°13W **86** C3
Santiago Jamiltepec
  Mexico   16°17N 97°49W **87** D5
Santiago Papasquiaro
  Mexico   25°3N 105°25W **86** C3
Santiago Pinotepa Nacional
  Mexico   16°19N 98°1W **87** D5
Santiaguillo, L. de
  Mexico   24°48N 104°48W **86** C4
Santo Amaro Brazil   12°30S 38°43W **93** F11
Santo Anastácio Brazil   21°58S 51°39W **95** A5
Santo André Brazil   23°39S 46°29W **95** A6
Santo Ângelo Brazil   28°15S 54°15W **95** B5
Santo Antão C. Verde Is.   16°52N 25°10W **50** b
Santo Antônio do Içá
  Brazil   3°5S 67°57W **92** D5
Santo Antônio do Leverger
  Brazil   15°52S 56°5W **93** G7
Santo Domingo
  Dom. Rep.   18°30N 69°59W **89** C6
Santo Domingo Baja Calif.,
  Mexico   30°43N 116°2W **86** A1
Santo Domingo Baja Calif. S.,
  Mexico   25°29N 111°55W **86** B2
Santo Domingo Nic.   12°14N 84°59W **88** D3
Santo Domingo de los Colorados
  Ecuador   0°15S 79°9W **92** D3
Santo Domingo Pueblo
  U.S.A.   35°31N 106°22W **77** J10
Santo Tomás Mexico   31°33N 116°24W **86** A1
Santo Tomás Peru   14°26S 72°8W **92** F4
Santo Tomé Argentina   28°40S 56°5W **95** B4
Santo Tomé de Guayana =
  Ciudad Guayana
  Venezuela   8°0N 62°30W **92** B6
Santoña Spain   43°29N 3°27W **21** A4
Santorini Greece   36°23N 25°27E **23** F11
Santos Brazil   24°0S 46°20W **95** A6
Santos Dumont Brazil   22°55S 43°10W **95** A7
Sanur Indonesia   8°41S 115°15E **37** K18
Sanwer India   22°59N 75°50E **42** H6
Sanxiang China   22°21N 113°25E **33** G9
Sanya China   18°14N 109°29E **38** C7
Sanyuan China   34°35N 108°58E **34** G5
São Bernardo do Campo
  Brazil   23°45S 46°34W **95** A6
São Borja Brazil   28°39S 56°0W **95** B4
São Carlos Brazil   22°0S 47°50W **95** A6
São Cristóvão Brazil   11°1S 37°15W **93** F11
São Domingos Brazil   13°25S 46°19W **93** F9
São Filipe C. Verde Is.   15°2N 24°30W **50** b
São Francisco Brazil   16°0S 44°50W **93** G10
São Francisco →
  Brazil   10°30S 36°24W **93** F11

São Francisco do Sul
  Brazil   26°15S 48°36W **95** B6
São Gabriel Brazil   30°20S 54°20W **95** C5
São Gonçalo Brazil   22°48S 43°5W **95** A7
Sao Hill Tanzania   8°20S 35°12E **55** D4
São João da Boa Vista
  Brazil   22°0S 46°52W **95** A6
São João da Madeira
  Portugal   40°54N 8°30W **21** B1
São João del Rei Brazil   21°8S 44°15W **95** A7
São João do Araguaia
  Brazil   5°23S 48°46W **93** E9
São João do Piauí Brazil   8°21S 42°15W **93** E10
São Joaquim Brazil   28°18S 49°56W **95** B6
São Joaquim △ Brazil   28°12S 49°37W **95** B6
São Jorge Azores   38°38N 28°3W **50** a
São Jorge, Pta. de
  Madeira   32°50N 16°53W **24** D3
São José Brazil   27°38S 48°39W **95** B5
São José do Norte Brazil   32°1S 52°3W **95** C5
São José do Rio Prêto
  Brazil   20°50S 49°20W **95** A6
São José dos Campos
  Brazil   23°7S 45°52W **95** A6
São Leopoldo Brazil   29°50S 51°10W **95** B5
São Lourenço Brazil   22°7S 45°3W **95** A6
São Lourenço → Brazil   17°53S 57°27W **93** G7
São Lourenço, Pta. de
  Madeira   32°44N 16°39W **24** D3
São Lourenço do Sul
  Brazil   31°22S 51°58W **95** C5
São Luís Brazil   2°39S 44°15W **93** D10
São Luís Gonzaga Brazil   28°25S 55°0W **95** B5
São Marcos → Brazil   18°15S 47°37W **93** G9
São Marcos, B. de Brazil   2°0S 44°0W **93** D10
São Mateus Brazil   18°44S 39°50W **93** G11
São Mateus do Sul
  Brazil   25°52S 50°23W **95** B5
São Miguel Azores   37°47N 25°30W **50** a
São Miguel do Oeste
  Brazil   26°45S 53°34W **95** B5
São Nicolau C. Verde Is.   16°20N 24°20W **50** b
São Paulo Brazil   23°32S 46°38W **95** A6
São Paulo □ Brazil   22°0S 49°0W **95** A6
São Paulo de Olivença
  Brazil   3°27S 68°48W **92** D5
São Roque Madeira   32°46N 16°48W **24** D3
São Roque, C. de Brazil   5°30S 35°16W **93** E11
São Sebastião, I. de
  Brazil   23°50S 45°18W **95** A6
São Sebastião do Paraíso
  Brazil   20°54S 46°59W **95** A6
São Tiago C. Verde Is.   15°0N 23°40W **50** b
São Tomé
  São Tomé & Príncipe   0°10N 6°39E **48** F4
São Tomé, C. de Brazil   22°0S 40°59W **95** A7
São Tomé & Príncipe ■
  Africa   0°12N 6°39E **49** F4
São Vicente Brazil   23°57S 46°23W **95** A6
São Vicente C. Verde Is.   17°0N 25°0W **50** b
São Vicente Madeira   32°48N 17°3W **24** D2
São Vicente, C. de Portugal   37°0N 9°0W **21** D1
Saona, I. Dom. Rep.   18°10N 68°40W **89** C6
Saône → France   45°44N 4°50E **20** D6
Saonek Indonesia   0°22S 130°55E **37** E8
Sapam, Ao Thailand   8°0N 98°26E **39** a
Saparua Indonesia   3°33S 128°40E **37** E7
Sapele Nigeria   5°50N 5°40E **50** G7
Sapelo I. U.S.A.   31°25N 81°12W **85** F14
Sapi ⌒ Zimbabwe   15°48S 29°42E **55** F2
Saposoa Peru   6°55S 76°45W **92** E3
Sapphire Australia   23°28S 147°43E **62** C4
Sappho U.S.A.   48°4N 124°16W **78** B2
Sapporo Japan   43°0N 141°21E **30** C10
Sapulpa U.S.A.   35°59N 96°5W **84** D6
Saqqez Iran   36°15N 46°20E **44** B5
Sar Dasht Iran   32°32N 48°52E **45** C6
Sar-e Pol □ Afghan.   36°20N 65°50E **40** B4
Sar Gachîneh = Yāsūj
  Iran   30°31N 51°31E **45** D6
Sar Planina Macedonia   42°0N 21°0E **23** C9
Sara Buri = Saraburi
  Thailand   14°30N 100°55E **38** E3
Sarāb Iran   37°55N 47°40E **44** B5
Sarabadi Iraq   33°1N 44°48E **44** C5
Saraburi Thailand   14°30N 100°55E **38** E3
Saradiya India   21°34N 70°2E **42** J4
Saragossa = Zaragoza
  Spain   41°39N 0°53W **21** B5
Saraguro Ecuador   3°35S 79°16W **92** D3
Sarahs Turkmenistan   36°32N 61°13E **45** B9
Sarai Naurang Pakistan   32°50N 70°47E **42** C4
Saraikela India   22°42N 85°56E **43** H11
Sarajevo Bos.-H.   43°52N 18°26E **23** C8
Sarakhs = Sarahs
  Turkmenistan   36°32N 61°13E **45** B9
Saran, Gunung
  Indonesia   0°30S 111°25E **36** E4
Saranac Lake U.S.A.   44°20N 74°10W **83** B10
Saranac Lakes U.S.A.   44°20N 74°28W **83** B10
Saranda Tanzania   5°45S 34°59E **54** D3
Sarandí del Yi Uruguay   33°18S 55°38W **95** C4
Sarandí Grande
  Uruguay   33°44S 56°20W **94** C4
Sarangani B. Phil.   6°0N 125°13E **37** C7
Sarangani Is. Phil.   5°25N 125°25E **37** C7
Sarangarh India   21°30N 83°5E **43** J10
Saransk Russia   54°10N 45°10E **18** D8
Sarapul Russia   56°28N 53°48E **18** C9
Sarasota U.S.A.   27°20N 82°32W **85** H13
Saratoga Calif., U.S.A.   37°16N 122°2W **78** H4
Saratoga Wyo.,
  U.S.A.   41°27N 106°49W **76** F10
Saratoga △ U.S.A.   43°0N 73°38W **83** D11
Saratoga Springs
  U.S.A.   43°5N 73°47W **83** C11
Saratok Malaysia   1°55N 111°17E **36** D4

Saratov Russia   51°30N 46°2E **19** D8
Sarāvān Iran   27°25N 62°15E **45** E9
Saravane Laos   15°43N 106°25E **38** E6
Sarawak □ Malaysia   2°0N 113°0E **36** D4
Saray Turkey   41°26N 27°55E **23** D12
Saraykoy Turkey   37°55N 28°54E **23** F13
Sarbāz Iran   26°38N 61°19E **45** E9
Sarbīsheh Iran   32°30N 59°40E **45** C8
Sarda → India   27°21N 81°23E **43** F9
Sardarshahr India   28°30N 74°29E **42** E6
Sardegna □ Italy   40°0N 9°0E **22** D3
Sardhana India   29°9N 77°39E **42** E7
Sardina, Pta. Canary Is.   28°9N 15°44W **24** F4
Sardinia = Sardegna □
  Italy   40°0N 9°0E **22** D3
Sardis Turkey   38°28N 27°58E **23** E12
Särdūīyeh = Dar Mazār
  Iran   29°14N 57°20E **45** D8
Saren Indonesia   8°26S 115°34E **37** K18
S'Arenal Spain   39°30N 2°45E **24** B9
Sarera, G. of Indonesia   2°5S 135°0E **58** B6
Sargasso Sea Atl. Oc.   27°0N 72°0W **66** G13
Sargodha Pakistan   32°10N 72°40E **42** C5
Sarh Chad   9°5N 18°23E **51** G9
Sārī Iran   36°30N 53°4E **45** B7
Saria India   21°38N 83°22E **43** J10
Sariab Pakistan   30°6N 66°59E **42** D2
Sarıgöl Turkey   38°14N 28°41E **23** E13
Sarikei Malaysia   2°8N 111°30E **36** D4
Sarila India   25°46N 79°41E **43** G8
Sarina Australia   21°22S 149°13E **62** C4
Sarita U.S.A.   27°13N 97°47W **84** H6
Sariwŏn N. Korea   38°31N 125°46E **35** E13
Sarju → India   27°21N 81°23E **43** F9
Sark U.K.   49°25N 2°22E **13** H5
Sarkari Tala India   27°39N 70°52E **42** F4
Şarköy Turkey   40°36N 27°6E **23** D12
Sarlat-la-Canéda France   44°54N 1°13E **20** D4
Sarmi Indonesia   1°49S 138°44E **37** E9
Sarmiento Argentina   45°35S 69°5W **96** F3
Särna Sweden   61°41N 13°8E **8** F15
Sarnia Canada   42°58N 82°23W **82** D2
Sarolangun Indonesia   2°19S 102°42E **36** E2
Saronikos Kolpos
  Greece   37°45N 23°45E **23** F10
Saros Körfezi Turkey   40°30N 26°15E **23** D12
Sarpsborg Norway   59°16N 11°7E **9** G14
Sarqan Kazakhstan   45°24N 79°55E **28** E8
Sarre = Saar → Europe   49°41N 6°32E **15** E6
Sarreguemines France   49°5N 7°4E **20** B7
Sarthe → France   47°33N 0°31W **20** C3
Saruna → Pakistan   26°31N 67°7E **42** F2
Sarvar India   26°4N 75°0E **42** F6
Sarvestān Iran   29°20N 53°10E **45** D7
Sary-Tash Kyrgyzstan   39°44N 73°15E **28** F8
Saryshagan
  Kazakhstan   46°12N 73°38E **28** E8
Sasan Gir India   21°10N 70°36E **42** J4
Sasaram India   24°57N 84°5E **43** G11
Sasebo Japan   33°10N 129°43E **31** H4
Saser India   34°50N 77°50E **43** B7
Saskatchewan □
  Canada   54°40N 106°0W **71** C7
Saskatchewan →
  Canada   53°37N 100°40W **71** C8
Saskatoon Canada   52°10N 106°38W **71** C7
Saskylakh Russia   71°55N 114°1E **29** B12
Saslaya △ Nic.   13°45N 85°4W **88** D2
Sasolburg S. Africa   26°46S 27°49E **57** D4
Sasovo Russia   54°25N 41°55E **18** D7
Sassandra Ivory C.   4°55N 6°8W **50** H4
Sassandra → Ivory C.   4°58N 6°5W **50** H4
Sássari Italy   40°43N 8°34E **22** D3
Sassnitz Germany   54°29N 13°39E **16** A7
Sassuolo Italy   44°33N 10°47E **22** B4
Sasyk, Ozero Ukraine   45°45N 29°20E **17** F15
Sata-Misaki Japan   31°0N 130°40E **31** J5
Satadougou Mali   12°25N 11°25W **50** F3
Satakunda = Satakunta
  Finland   61°45N 23°0E **8** F20
Satakunta Finland   61°45N 23°0E **8** F20
Satara India   17°44N 73°58E **40** L8
Satara S. Africa   24°29S 31°47E **57** C5
Satbarwa India   23°55N 84°16E **43** H11
Satevó Mexico   27°57N 106°7W **86** B3
Satilla → U.S.A.   30°59N 81°29W **85** F14
Satka Russia   55°3N 59°1E **18** C10
Satmala Hills Andhra Pradesh,
  India   19°45N 78°45E **40** K11
Satmala Hills Maharashtra,
  India   20°15N 74°40E **40** J9
Satna India   24°35N 80°50E **43** G9
Sátoraljaújhely
  Hungary   48°25N 21°41E **17** D11
Satpura △ India   22°40N 78°15E **42** H8
Satpura Ra. India   21°25N 76°10E **40** J10
Satsuna-Shotō Japan   30°0N 130°0E **31** K5
Sattahip Thailand   12°41N 100°54E **38** F3
Satu Mare Romania   47°46N 22°55E **17** E12
Satui Indonesia   3°50S 115°27E **36** E5
Satun Thailand   6°43N 100°2E **39** J3
Satupa'itea Samoa   13°45S 172°18W **59** b
Saturnina → Brazil   12°15S 58°10W **92** F7
Sauce Argentina   30°5S 58°46W **94** C4
Sauceda Mexico   25°46N 101°19W **86** B4
Saucillo Mexico   28°1N 105°17W **86** B3
Sauda Norway   59°40N 6°20E **9** G12
Sauðarkrókur Iceland   65°45N 19°40W **8** D4
Saudi Arabia ■ Asia   26°0N 44°0E **44** B3
Sauerland Germany   51°12N 7°59E **16** C4
Saugeen → Canada   44°30N 81°22W **82** B3
Saugerties U.S.A.   42°5N 73°57W **83** D11
Saugus U.S.A.   34°25N 118°32W **79** L8
Sauk Centre U.S.A.   45°44N 94°57W **80** C7
Sauk Rapids U.S.A.   45°35N 94°10W **80** C7
Sault Ste. Marie Canada   46°30N 84°20W **72** C3
Sault Ste. Marie
  U.S.A.   46°30N 84°21W **81** B11

Saumlaki Indonesia 7°55S 131°20E 37 F8
Saumur France 47°15N 0°5W 20 C3
Saunders, C. N.Z. 45°53S 170°45E 59 F3
Saunders I. Antarctica 57°48S 26°28W 5 B1
Saunders Pt. Australia 27°52S 125°38E 61 E4
Saurimo Angola 9°40S 20°12E 52 F4
Sausalito U.S.A. 37°51N 122°29W 78 H4
Savá Honduras 15°32N 86°15W 88 C2
Sava → Serbia 44°50N 20°26E 23 B9
Savage U.S.A. 47°27N 104°21W 76 C11
Savage I. = Niue Cook Is. 19°2S 169°54W 65 J11
Savage River Australia 41°31S 145°14E 63 G4
Savai'i Samoa 13°28S 172°24W 59 b
Savalou Benin 7°57N 1°58E 50 G6
Savane Mozam. 19°37S 35°8E 55 F4
Savanna U.S.A. 42°5N 90°8W 80 D8
Savanna-la-Mar Jamaica 18°10N 78°10W 88 a
Savannah Ga., U.S.A. 32°5N 81°6W 85 E14
Savannah Mo., U.S.A. 39°56N 94°50W 80 F6
Savannah Tenn., U.S.A. 35°14N 88°15W 85 D10
Savannah → U.S.A. 32°2N 80°53W 85 E14
Savannakhet Laos 16°30N 104°49E 38 D5
Savant L. Canada 50°16N 90°44W 72 B1
Savant Lake Canada 50°14N 90°40W 72 B1
Save → Mozam. 21°16S 34°0E 57 C5
Sāveh Iran 35°2N 50°20E 45 C6
Savelugu Ghana 9°38N 0°54W 50 G5
Savo Finland 62°45N 27°30E 8 E22
Savoie □ France 45°26N 6°25E 20 D7
Savolax = Savo Finland 62°45N 27°30E 8 E22
Savona Italy 44°17N 8°30E 20 D8
Savona U.S.A. 42°17N 77°13W 82 D7
Savonlinna Finland 61°52N 28°53E 8 F23
Savoy = Savoie □ France 45°26N 6°25E 20 D7
Savur Turkey 37°34N 40°53E 44 B4
Savusavu Fiji 16°34S 179°15E 59 a
Savusavu B. Fiji 16°45S 179°15E 59 a
Sawahlunto Indonesia 0°40S 100°52E 36 E2
Sawai Indonesia 3°0S 129°5E 37 E7
Sawai Madhopur India 26°0N 76°25E 42 G7
Sawaleke Fiji 17°59S 179°18E 59 a
Sawang Daen Din Thailand 17°28N 103°28E 38 D4
Sawankhalok Thailand 17°19N 99°50E 38 D2
Sawara Japan 35°55N 140°30E 31 G10
Sawatch Range U.S.A. 39°0N 106°30W 76 G10
Sawel Mt. U.K. 54°50N 7°2W 10 B4
Sawi Thailand 10°14N 99°5E 39 G2
Sawmills Zimbabwe 19°30S 28°2E 55 F2
Sawtooth △ U.S.A. 44°0N 114°50W 76 D6
Sawtooth Range U.S.A. 44°3N 114°58W 76 D6
Sawu Indonesia 10°35S 121°50E 37 F6
Sawu Sea Indonesia 9°30S 121°50E 37 F6
Saxby → Australia 18°25S 140°53E 62 B3
Saxmundham U.K. 52°13N 1°30E 13 E9
Saxony = Sachsen □ Germany 50°55N 13°10E 16 C7
Saxony, Lower = Niedersachsen □ Germany 52°50N 9°0E 16 B5
Saxton U.S.A. 40°13N 78°15W 82 F6
Sayabec Canada 48°35N 67°41W 73 C6
Sayaboury Laos 19°15N 101°45E 38 C3
Sayán Peru 11°8S 77°12W 92 F3
Sayan, Vostochnyy Russia 54°0N 96°0E 29 D10
Sayan, Zapadnyy Russia 52°30N 94°0E 29 D10
Saydā Lebanon 33°35N 35°25E 46 B4
Sayhandulaan = Oldziyt Mongolia 44°40N 109°1E 34 B5
Sayhūt Yemen 15°12N 51°10E 47 D5
Saylac = Zeila Somali Rep. 11°21N 43°30E 47 E3
Saynshand = Buyant-Uhaa Mongolia 44°55N 110°11E 33 B6
Sayre Okla., U.S.A. 35°18N 99°38W 84 D5
Sayre Pa., U.S.A. 41°59N 76°32W 83 E8
Sayreville U.S.A. 40°28N 74°22W 83 F10
Sayula Mexico 19°52N 103°36W 86 D4
Sazanit Albania 40°30N 19°20E 23 D8
Sázava → Czech Rep. 49°53N 14°24E 16 D8
Sazin Pakistan 35°35N 73°30E 43 B5
Scafell Pike U.K. 54°27N 3°14W 12 C4
Scalloway U.K. 60°9N 1°17W 11 A7
Scalpay U.K. 57°18N 6°0W 11 D3
Scandia Canada 50°20N 112°2W 70 C6
Scandicci Italy 43°45N 11°11E 22 C4
Scandinavia Europe 64°0N 12°0E 8 E15
Scapa Flow U.K. 58°53N 3°3W 11 C5
Scappoose U.S.A. 45°45N 122°53W 78 E4
Scarba U.K. 56°11N 5°43W 11 E3
Scarborough Trin. & Tob. 11°11N 60°42W 89 D7
Scarborough U.K. 54°17N 0°24W 12 C7
Scariff I. Ireland 51°44N 10°15W 10 E1
Scarp U.K. 58°1N 7°8W 11 C1
Scebeli, Wabi → Somali Rep. 2°0N 44°0E 47 G3
Schaffhausen Switz. 47°42N 8°39E 20 C8
Schagen Neths. 52°49N 4°48E 15 B4
Schaghticoke U.S.A. 42°54N 73°35W 83 D11
Schefferville = Kawawachikamach Canada 54°48N 66°50W 73 B6
Schelde → Belgium 51°15N 4°16E 15 C4
Schell Creek Ra. U.S.A. 39°25N 114°40W 76 G6
Schellsburg U.S.A. 40°3N 78°39W 82 F6
Schenectady U.S.A. 42°49N 73°57W 83 D11
Schenevus U.S.A. 42°33N 74°50W 83 D10
Schiedam Neths. 51°55N 4°25E 15 C4
Schiermonnikoog Neths. 53°30N 6°15E 15 A6
Schio Italy 45°43N 11°21E 22 B4
Schiphol, Amsterdam ✈ (AMS) Neths. 52°18N 4°45E 15 B4
Schleswig Germany 54°31N 9°34E 16 A5
Schleswig-Holstein □ Germany 54°30N 9°30E 16 A5
Schœlcher Martinique 14°36N 61°7W 88 c
Schoharie U.S.A. 42°40N 74°19W 83 D10
Schoharie Cr. → U.S.A. 42°57N 74°18W 83 D10
Scholls U.S.A. 45°24N 122°56W 78 E4
Schouten I. Australia 42°20S 148°20E 63 G4
Schouten Is. = Supiori Indonesia 1°0S 136°0E 37 E9
Schouwen Neths. 51°43N 3°45E 15 C3
Schreiber Canada 48°45N 87°20W 72 C2
Schroffenstein Namibia 27°11S 18°42E 56 D2
Schroon Lake U.S.A. 43°50N 73°46W 83 C11
Schuler Canada 50°20N 110°6W 71 C6
Schumacher Canada 48°30N 81°16W 72 C3
Schurz U.S.A. 38°57N 118°49W 76 G4
Schuyler U.S.A. 41°27N 97°4W 80 E5
Schuylerville U.S.A. 43°6N 73°35W 83 C11
Schuylkill → U.S.A. 39°53N 75°12W 83 G9
Schuylkill Haven U.S.A. 40°37N 76°11W 83 F8
Schwäbische Alb Germany 48°20N 9°30E 16 D5
Schwaner, Pegunungan Indonesia 1°0S 112°30E 36 E4
Schwarzrand Namibia 25°37S 16°50E 56 D2
Schwarzwald Germany 48°30N 8°20E 16 D5
Schwedt Germany 53°3N 14°16E 16 B8
Schweinfurt Germany 50°3N 10°14E 16 C6
Schweiz = Switzerland ■ Europe 46°30N 8°0E 20 C8
Schweizer-Reneke S. Africa 27°11S 25°18E 56 D4
Schwenningen = Villingen-Schwenningen Germany 48°3N 8°26E 16 D5
Schwerin Germany 53°36N 11°22E 16 B6
Schwyz Switz. 47°2N 8°39E 20 C8
Sciacca Italy 37°31N 13°3E 22 F5
Scilla Italy 38°15N 15°43E 22 E6
Scilly, Isles of U.K. 49°56N 6°22W 13 H1
Scioto → U.S.A. 38°44N 83°1W 81 F12
Scituate U.S.A. 42°12N 70°44W 83 D14
Scobey U.S.A. 48°47N 105°25W 76 B11
Scone Australia 32°5S 150°52E 63 E5
Scone U.K. 56°25N 3°24W 11 E5
Scoresbysund = Ittoqqortoormiit Greenland 70°20N 23°0W 4 B6
Scotia Calif., U.S.A. 40°29N 124°6W 76 F1
Scotia N.Y., U.S.A. 42°50N 73°58W 83 D11
Scotia Sea Antarctica 56°5S 56°0W 5 B18
Scotland Canada 43°1N 80°22W 82 C4
Scotland □ U.K. 57°0N 4°0W 11 E5
Scott Antarctica 77°0S 165°0E 5 D11
Scott, C. Australia 13°30S 129°49E 60 B4
Scott City U.S.A. 38°29N 100°54W 80 F3
Scott Glacier Antarctica 66°15S 100°5E 5 C8
Scott I. Antarctica 67°0S 179°0E 5 C11
Scott Is. Canada 50°48N 128°40W 70 C3
Scott L. Canada 59°55N 106°18W 71 B7
Scott Reef Australia 14°0S 121°50E 60 B3
Scottburgh S. Africa 30°15S 30°47E 57 E5
Scottdale U.S.A. 40°6N 79°35W 82 F5
Scottish Borders □ U.K. 55°35N 2°50W 11 F6
Scotts Valley U.S.A. 37°3N 122°1W 78 H4
Scottsbluff U.S.A. 41°52N 103°40W 80 E2
Scottsboro U.S.A. 34°40N 86°2W 85 D11
Scottsburg U.S.A. 38°41N 85°47W 81 F11
Scottsdale Australia 41°9S 147°31E 63 G4
Scottsdale U.S.A. 33°40N 111°53W 77 K8
Scottsville Ky., U.S.A. 36°45N 86°11W 80 G10
Scottsville N.Y., U.S.A. 43°2N 77°47W 82 C7
Scottville U.S.A. 43°58N 86°17W 80 D10
Scranton U.S.A. 41°25N 75°40W 83 E9
Scugog, L. Canada 44°10N 78°55W 82 B6
Scunthorpe U.K. 53°36N 0°39W 12 D7
Scutari = Shkodër Albania 42°4N 19°32E 23 C8
Sea Is. U.S.A. 31°30N 81°7W 85 F14
Seabrook, L. Australia 30°55S 119°40E 61 F2
Seaford U.K. 50°47N 0°7E 13 G8
Seaford U.S.A. 38°39N 75°37W 81 F16
Seaforth Australia 20°55S 148°57E 62 J6
Seaforth Canada 43°35N 81°25W 82 C3
Seaforth, L. U.K. 57°52N 6°36W 11 D2
Seagraves U.S.A. 32°57N 102°34W 84 E3
Seaham U.K. 54°50N 1°20W 12 C6
Seal → Canada 59°4N 94°48W 71 B10
Seal L. Canada 54°20N 61°30W 73 B7
Sealy U.S.A. 29°47N 96°9W 84 G6
Searchlight U.S.A. 35°28N 114°55W 79 K12
Searcy U.S.A. 35°15N 91°44W 84 D9
Searles L. U.S.A. 35°44N 117°21W 79 K9
Seascale U.K. 54°24N 3°29W 12 C4
Seaside Calif., U.S.A. 36°37N 121°50W 78 J5
Seaside Oreg., U.S.A. 46°0N 123°56W 78 E3
Seaspray Australia 38°25S 147°15E 63 F4
Seattle U.S.A. 47°36N 122°19W 78 C4
Seattle-Tacoma Int. ✈ (SEA) U.S.A. 47°27N 122°18W 78 C4
Seaview Ra. Australia 18°40S 145°45E 62 B4
Sebago L. U.S.A. 43°52N 70°34W 83 C14
Sebago Lake U.S.A. 43°51N 70°34W 83 C14
Sebastián Vizcaíno, B. Mexico 28°0N 114°30W 86 B2
Sebastopol = Sevastopol Ukraine 44°35N 33°30E 19 F5
Sebastopol U.S.A. 38°24N 122°49W 78 G4
Sebewaing U.S.A. 43°44N 83°27W 81 D12
Sebha = Sabhā Libya 27°9N 14°29E 51 C8
Şebinkarahisar Turkey 40°22N 38°28E 19 F6
Sebring Fla., U.S.A. 27°30N 81°27W 85 H14
Sebring Ohio, U.S.A. 40°55N 81°2W 82 F3
Sebringville Canada 43°24N 81°4W 82 C3
Sebta = Ceuta N. Afr. 35°52N 5°18W 21 E3
Sebuku Indonesia 3°30S 116°25E 36 E5
Sebuku, Teluk Malaysia 4°0N 118°10E 36 D5
Sechelt Canada 49°25N 123°42W 70 D4
Sechura, Desierto de Peru 6°0S 80°30W 92 E2
Secretary I. N.Z. 45°15S 166°56E 59 F1
Secunderabad India 17°28N 78°30E 40 L11
Security U.S.A. 38°45N 104°45W 76 G11
Sedalia U.S.A. 38°42N 93°14W 80 F7
Sedan France 49°43N 4°57E 20 B6
Sedan U.S.A. 37°8N 96°11W 80 G5
Sedbergh U.K. 54°20N 2°31W 12 C5
Seddon N.Z. 41°40S 174°7E 59 D5
Seddonville N.Z. 41°33S 172°1E 59 D4
Sedé Boqér Israel 30°52N 34°47E 46 E3
Sedeh Fārs, Iran 30°45N 52°11E 45 D7
Sedeh Khorāsān, Iran 33°20N 59°14E 45 C8
Sederot Israel 31°32N 34°37E 46 D3
Sédhiou Senegal 12°44N 15°30W 50 F2
Sedley Canada 50°10N 104°0W 71 C8
Sedona U.S.A. 34°52N 111°46W 77 J8
Sedova, Pik Russia 73°29N 54°58E 28 B6
Sedro-Woolley U.S.A. 48°30N 122°14W 78 B4
Seeheim Namibia 26°50S 17°45E 56 D2
Seeis Namibia 22°29S 17°39E 56 C2
Seekoei → S. Africa 30°18S 25°1E 56 E4
Seeley's Bay Canada 44°29N 76°14W 83 B8
Seferihisar Turkey 38°10N 26°50E 23 E12
Seg-ozero Russia 63°20N 33°46E 18 B5
Segamat Malaysia 2°30N 102°50E 39 L4
Segesta Italy 37°56N 12°50E 22 F5
Seget Indonesia 1°24S 130°58E 37 E8
Segezha Russia 63°44N 34°19E 18 B5
Ségou Mali 13°30N 6°16W 50 F4
Segovia = Coco → Cent. Amer. 15°0N 83°8W 88 D3
Segovia Spain 40°57N 4°10W 21 B3
Segre → Spain 41°40N 0°43E 21 B6
Séguéla Ivory C. 7°55N 6°40W 50 G4
Seguin U.S.A. 29°34N 97°58W 84 G6
Segundo → Argentina 30°53S 62°44W 94 C3
Segura → Spain 38°3N 0°44W 21 C5
Seh Konj, Kūh-e Iran 30°6N 57°30E 45 D8
Seh Qal'eh Iran 33°40N 58°24E 45 C8
Sehitwa Botswana 20°30S 22°30E 56 C3
Sehlabathebe △ Lesotho 29°53S 29°7E 57 D4
Sehore India 23°10N 77°5E 42 H7
Sehwan Pakistan 26°28N 67°53E 42 F2
Seil U.K. 56°18N 5°38W 11 E3
Seiland Norway 70°25N 23°15E 8 A20
Seiling U.S.A. 36°9N 98°56W 84 C5
Seinäjoki Finland 62°40N 22°51E 8 E20
Seine → France 49°26N 0°26E 20 B4
Seistan = Sīstān Asia 30°50N 61°0E 45 D9
Seistan, Daryācheh-ye = Sīstān, Daryācheh-ye Iran 31°0N 61°0E 45 D9
Sekayu Indonesia 2°51S 103°51E 36 E2
Seke Tanzania 3°20S 33°31E 54 C3
Sekenke Tanzania 4°18S 34°11E 54 C3
Sekondi-Takoradi Ghana 4°58N 1°45W 50 H5
Sekudai Malaysia 1°32N 103°39E 39 d
Sekuma Botswana 24°36S 23°50E 56 C3
Selah U.S.A. 46°39N 120°32W 76 C3
Selama Malaysia 5°12N 100°42E 39 K3
Selaru Indonesia 8°9S 131°0E 37 F8
Selatan, Selat Malaysia 5°15N 100°20E 39 c
Selby U.K. 53°47N 1°5W 12 D6
Selby U.S.A. 45°31N 100°2W 80 C3
Selçuk Turkey 37°56N 27°22E 23 F12
Selden U.S.A. 39°33N 100°34W 80 F3
Sele → Italy 40°29N 14°56E 22 D6
Selebi-Pikwe Botswana 21°58S 27°48E 57 C4
Selemdzha → Russia 51°42N 128°53E 29 D13
Selenga = Selenge Mörön → Asia 52°16N 106°16E 32 A5
Selenge Mörön → Asia 52°16N 106°16E 32 A5
Seletan, Tanjung Indonesia 4°10S 114°40E 36 E4
Sélibabi Mauritania 15°10N 12°15W 50 E3
Seligman U.S.A. 35°20N 112°53W 77 J7
Selîma, El Wâhât el Sudan 21°22N 29°19E 51 D11
Selinda Spillway → Botswana 18°35S 23°10E 56 B3
Selinsgrove U.S.A. 40°48N 76°52W 82 F8
Selkirk Canada 50°10N 96°55W 71 C9
Selkirk U.K. 55°33N 2°50W 11 F6
Selkirk I. = Horse I. Canada 53°20N 99°6W 71 C9
Selkirk Mts. Canada 51°15N 117°40W 68 D8
Sellafield U.K. 54°25N 3°29W 12 C4
Sellia Greece 35°12N 24°23E 25 D6
Sells U.S.A. 31°55N 111°53W 77 L8
Selma Ala., U.S.A. 32°25N 87°1W 85 E11
Selma Calif., U.S.A. 36°34N 119°37W 78 J7
Selma N.C., U.S.A. 35°32N 78°17W 85 D15
Selmer U.S.A. 35°10N 88°36W 85 D10
Selous △ Tanzania 8°37S 37°42E 55 D4
Selowandoma Falls Zimbabwe 21°15S 31°50E 55 G3
Selpele Indonesia 0°1S 130°5E 37 E8
Selsey Bill U.K. 50°43N 0°47W 13 G7
Seltso Russia 53°22N 34°4E 18 D5
Selu Indonesia 7°32S 130°55E 37 F8
Selva Argentina 29°50S 62°0W 94 B3
Selva Lancandona = Montes Azules △ Mexico 16°21N 91°3W 87 D6
Selvas Brazil 6°30S 67°0W 92 E5
Selwyn L. Canada 60°0N 104°30W 71 B8
Selwyn Mts. Canada 63°0N 130°0W 68 C6
Selwyn Ra. Australia 21°10S 140°0E 62 C3
Seman → Albania 40°47N 19°30E 23 D8
Semarang Indonesia 7°0S 110°26E 36 F4
Sembabule Uganda 0°4S 31°25E 54 C3
Sembawang Singapore 1°27N 103°50E 39 d
Sembung Indonesia 8°28S 115°11E 37 J18
Semenanjung Blambangan Indonesia 8°42S 114°29E 37 K17
Semeru Indonesia 8°4S 112°55E 37 H15
Semey Kazakhstan 50°30N 80°10E 28 D9
Seminoe Res. U.S.A. 42°9N 106°55W 76 E10
Seminole Okla., U.S.A. 35°14N 96°41W 84 D6
Seminole Tex., U.S.A. 32°43N 102°39W 84 E3
Seminole Draw → U.S.A. 32°27N 102°20W 84 E3
Semipalatinsk = Semey Kazakhstan 50°30N 80°10E 28 D9
Semirara Is. Phil. 12°0N 121°20E 37 B6
Semitau Indonesia 0°29N 111°57E 36 D4
Semiyarka Kazakhstan 50°55N 78°23E 28 D8
Semiyarskoye = Semiyarka Kazakhstan 50°55N 78°23E 28 D8
Semmering P. Austria 47°41N 15°45E 16 E8
Semnān Iran 35°40N 53°23E 45 C7
Semnān □ Iran 36°0N 54°0E 45 C7
Semporna Malaysia 4°30N 118°33E 37 D5
Semuda Indonesia 2°51S 112°58E 36 E4
Sen → Cambodia 12°32N 104°28E 38 F5
Senā Iran 28°27N 51°36E 45 D6
Sena Mozam. 17°25S 35°0E 55 F4
Sena Madureira Brazil 9°5S 68°45W 92 E5
Senador Pompeu Brazil 5°40S 39°20W 93 E11
Senang, Pulau Singapore 1°11N 103°52E 39 d
Senanga Zambia 16°7S 23°16E 53 H4
Senatobia U.S.A. 34°37N 89°58W 85 D10
Sencelles Spain 39°39N 2°54E 24 B9
Sendai Kagoshima, Japan 31°50N 130°20E 31 J5
Sendai Miyagi, Japan 38°15N 140°53E 30 E10
Sendai-Wan Japan 38°15N 141°0E 30 E10
Sendhwa India 21°41N 75°6E 42 J6
Seneca U.S.A. 34°41N 82°57W 85 D13
Seneca Falls U.S.A. 42°55N 76°48W 83 D8
Seneca L. U.S.A. 42°40N 76°54W 82 D8
Senecaville L. U.S.A. 39°55N 81°25W 82 G3
Senegal ■ W. Afr. 14°30N 14°30W 50 F3
Sénégal → W. Afr. 15°48N 16°32W 50 E2
Senegambia Africa 12°45N 12°0W 48 E2
Senekal S. Africa 28°20S 27°36E 57 D4
Senga Hill Zambia 9°19S 31°11E 55 D3
Senge Khambab = Indus → Pakistan 24°20N 67°47E 42 G2
Sengua → Zimbabwe 17°7S 28°5E 55 F2
Senhor-do-Bonfim Brazil 10°30S 40°10W 93 F10
Senigállia Italy 43°43N 13°13E 22 C5
Senj Croatia 45°0N 14°58E 16 F8
Senja Norway 69°25N 17°30E 8 B17
Senkaku-Shotō E. China Sea 25°45N 123°30E 31 M1
Senkuang Indonesia 1°11N 104°2E 39 d
Senlis France 49°13N 2°35E 20 B5
Senmonorom Cambodia 12°27N 107°12E 38 F6
Senneterre Canada 48°25N 77°15W 72 C4
Seno Laos 16°35N 104°50E 38 D5
Sens France 48°11N 3°15E 20 B5
Senta Serbia 45°55N 20°3E 23 B9
Sentani Indonesia 2°36S 140°37E 37 E10
Sentery = Lubao Dem. Rep. of the Congo 5°17S 25°42E 54 D2
Sentinel U.S.A. 32°52N 113°13W 77 K7
Sentosa Singapore 1°16N 103°50E 39 d
Seo de Urgel = La Seu d'Urgell Spain 42°22N 1°23E 21 A6
Seogwipo S. Korea 33°13N 126°34E 35 H14
Seohara India 29°15N 78°33E 43 E8
Seonath → India 21°44N 82°28E 43 J10
Seondha India 26°9N 78°48E 43 F8
Seongnam S. Korea 37°26N 127°8E 35 F14
Seoni India 22°5N 79°30E 43 H8
Seoni Malwa India 22°27N 77°28E 42 H8
Seonsan S. Korea 36°14N 128°17E 35 F15
Seosan S. Korea 36°47N 126°27E 35 F14
Seoul S. Korea 37°31N 126°58E 35 F14
Sepīdān Iran 30°20N 52°5E 45 D7
Sep'o N. Korea 38°57N 127°25E 35 E14
Sepone Laos 16°45N 106°13E 38 D6
Sept-Îles Canada 50°13N 66°22W 73 B6
Sequim U.S.A. 48°5N 123°6W 78 B3
Sequoia △ U.S.A. 36°30N 118°30W 78 J8
Seraing Belgium 50°35N 5°32E 15 D5
Serakhis → Cyprus 35°13N 32°55E 25 D11
Seram Indonesia 3°10S 129°0E 37 E7
Seram Sea Indonesia 2°30S 128°30E 37 E7
Seranantsara Madag. 18°30S 49°5E 57 B8
Serang Indonesia 6°8S 106°10E 37 G12
Serangoon Singapore 1°23N 103°54E 39 d
Serasan Indonesia 2°29N 109°4E 36 D3
Serbia □ Serbia 43°30N 21°0E 23 C9
Serbia ■ Europe 43°20N 20°0E 23 B9
Serdar Turkmenistan 39°4N 56°23E 45 B8
Serdobsk Russia 52°28N 44°10E 18 D7
Seremban Malaysia 2°43N 101°53E 39 L3
Serengeti △ Tanzania 2°11S 35°0E 54 C3
Serengeti Plain Tanzania 2°40S 35°0E 54 C4
Serenje Zambia 13°14S 30°15E 55 E3
Sereth = Siret → Romania 45°24N 28°1E 17 F14
Sergino Russia 62°25N 65°12E 28 C7
Sergipe □ Brazil 10°30S 37°30W 93 F11
Sergiyev Posad Russia 56°20N 38°10E 18 C6
Serhetabat Turkmenistan 35°20N 62°18E 45 C9
Seria Brunei 4°37N 114°23E 36 D4
Serian Malaysia 1°10N 110°31E 36 D4
Seribu, Kepulauan Indonesia 5°36S 106°33E 36 F3
Sericho Kenya 1°5N 39°5E 54 B4
Serifos Greece 37°9N 24°30E 23 F11
Sérigny → Canada 56°47N 66°0W 73 A6
Seringapatam Reef Australia 13°38S 122°5E 60 B3
Seririt Indonesia 8°12S 114°56E 37 J17
Sermata Indonesia 8°15S 128°50E 37 F7
Sermersuaq Greenland 79°30N 62°0W 4 B4
Serov Russia 59°29N 60°35E 18 C11
Serowe Botswana 22°25S 26°43E 56 C4
Serpentine Lakes Australia 28°30S 129°10E 61 E4
Serpent's Mouth = Sierpe, Bocas de la Venezuela 10°0N 61°30W 93 L15
Serpukhov Russia 54°55N 37°28E 18 D6
Serra do Navio Brazil 0°59N 52°3W 93 C8
Serranía San Luís △ Paraguay 22°35S 57°22W 94 A4
Serres Greece 41°5N 23°31E 23 D10
Serrezuela Argentina 30°40S 65°20W 94 C2
Serrinha Brazil 11°39S 39°0W 93 F11
Sertanópolis Brazil 23°4S 51°2W 95 A5
Serua Indonesia 6°18S 130°1E 37 F8
Serui Indonesia 1°53S 136°10E 37 E9
Serule Botswana 21°57S 27°20E 56 C4
Ses Salines Spain 39°21N 3°3E 24 B10
Sese Is. Uganda 0°20S 32°20E 54 C3
Sesepe Indonesia 1°30S 127°59E 37 E7
Sesfontein Namibia 19°7S 13°39E 56 B1
Sesheke Zambia 17°29S 24°13E 56 B3
S'Espalmador Spain 38°47N 1°26E 24 C7
S'Espardell Spain 38°48N 1°29E 24 C7
S'Estanyol Spain 39°22N 2°54E 24 B9
Setana Japan 42°26N 139°51E 30 C9
Sète France 43°25N 3°42E 20 E5
Sete Lagôas Brazil 19°27S 44°16W 93 G10
Sétif Algeria 36°9N 5°26E 50 A7
Seto Japan 35°14N 137°6E 31 G8
Setonaikai Japan 34°20N 133°30E 31 G6
Setonaikai △ Japan 34°15N 133°15E 31 G6
Settat Morocco 33°0N 7°40W 50 B4
Setting L. Canada 55°0N 98°38W 71 C9
Settle U.K. 54°5N 2°16W 12 C5
Settlement, The Br. Virgin Is. 18°43N 64°22W 89 e
Settlers S. Africa 25°2S 28°30E 57 C4
Setúbal Portugal 38°30N 8°58W 21 C1
Setúbal, B. de Portugal 38°40N 8°56W 21 C1
Seul, Lac Canada 50°20N 92°30W 72 B1
Sevan, Ozero = Sevana Lich Armenia 40°30N 45°20E 44 A5
Sevana Lich Armenia 40°30N 45°20E 44 A5
Sevastopol Ukraine 44°35N 33°30E 19 F5
Seven Sisters Canada 54°56N 128°10W 70 C3
Severn → Canada 56°2N 87°36W 72 A2
Severn → U.K. 51°35N 2°40W 13 F5
Severn L. Canada 53°54N 90°48W 72 B1
Severnaya Zemlya Russia 79°0N 100°0E 29 B10
Severnyye Uvaly Russia 60°0N 50°0E 18 C8
Severo-Kurilsk Russia 50°40N 156°8E 29 D16
Severo-Yeniseyskiy Russia 60°22N 93°1E 29 C10
Severo-Zapadnyy □ Russia 65°0N 40°0E 28 C4
Severodvinsk Russia 64°27N 39°58E 18 B6
Severomorsk Russia 69°5N 33°27E 8 B25
Severouralsk Russia 60°9N 59°57E 18 B10
Sevier → U.S.A. 39°4N 113°6W 76 G7
Sevier Desert U.S.A. 39°40N 112°45W 76 G7
Sevier L. U.S.A. 38°54N 113°9W 76 G7
Sevilla Spain 37°23N 5°58W 21 D2
Seville = Sevilla Spain 37°23N 5°58W 21 D2
Sevlievo Bulgaria 43°2N 25°6E 23 C11
Sewani India 28°58N 75°39E 42 E6
Seward Alaska, U.S.A. 60°7N 149°27W 74 a
Seward Nebr., U.S.A. 40°55N 97°6W 80 E5
Seward Pa., U.S.A. 40°25N 79°1W 82 F5
Seward Peninsula U.S.A. 65°30N 166°0W 74 a
Sewell Chile 34°10S 70°23W 94 C1
Sewer Indonesia 5°53S 134°40E 37 F8
Sewickley U.S.A. 40°32N 80°12W 82 F4
Sexsmith Canada 55°21N 118°47W 70 B5
Seychelles ■ Ind. Oc. 5°0S 56°0E 53 b
Seyðisfjörður Iceland 65°16N 13°57W 8 D7
Seydişehir Turkey 37°25N 31°51E 19 G5
Seydvān Iran 38°34N 45°2E 44 B5
Seyhan → Turkey 36°43N 34°53E 44 B2
Seym → Ukraine 51°27N 32°34E 19 D5
Seymour Australia 37°2S 145°10E 63 F4
Seymour S. Africa 32°33S 26°46E 57 E4
Seymour Conn., U.S.A. 41°24N 73°4W 83 E11
Seymour Ind., U.S.A. 38°58N 85°53W 81 F11
Seymour Tex., U.S.A. 33°35N 99°16W 84 E5
Sfântu Gheorghe Romania 45°52N 25°48E 17 F13
Sfax Tunisia 34°49N 10°48E 51 B8
Sha Tau Kok China 22°33N 114°13E 33 F11
Sha Tin China 22°23N 114°12E 33 G11
Shaanxi □ China 35°0N 109°0E 34 G5
Shaba = Katanga □ Dem. Rep. of the Congo 8°0S 25°0E 54 D2
Shaba △ Kenya 0°38N 37°48E 54 B4
Shaballe = Scebeli, Wabi → Somali Rep. 2°0N 44°0E 47 G3
Shabogamo L. Canada 53°15N 66°30W 73 B6
Shabunda Dem. Rep. of the Congo 2°40S 27°16E 54 C2
Shache China 38°20N 77°10E 32 C2
Shackleton Fracture Zone S. Ocean 60°0S 60°0W 5 B18
Shackleton Ice Shelf Antarctica 66°0S 100°0E 5 C8
Shackleton Inlet Antarctica 83°0S 160°0E 5 E11
Shādegān Iran 30°40N 48°38E 45 D6
Shadi India 33°24N 77°14E 43 C7
Shadrinsk Russia 56°5N 63°32E 28 D7
Shadyside U.S.A. 39°58N 80°45W 82 G4
Shafter U.S.A. 35°30N 119°16W 79 K7
Shaftesbury U.K. 51°0N 2°11W 13 F5

Shagram Pakistan 36°24N 72°20E 43 A5
Shah Alizai Pakistan 29°25N 66°33E 42 E2
Shah Bunder Pakistan 24°13N 67°56E 42 G2
Shahabad Punjab, India 30°10N 76°55E 42 D7
Shahabad Raj., India 25°15N 77°11E 42 G7
Shahabad Ut. P., India 27°36N 79°56E 43 F8
Shahadpur Pakistan 25°55N 68°35E 42 G3
Shahbā' Syria 32°52N 36°38E 46 C5
Shahdād Iran 30°30N 57°40E 45 D8
Shahdād, Namakzār-e Iran 30°20N 58°20E 45 D8
Shahdadkot Pakistan 27°50N 67°55E 42 F2
Shahdol India 23°19N 81°26E 43 H9
Shahe China 37°0N 114°32E 34 F8
Shahganj India 26°3N 82°44E 43 F10
Shahgarh India 27°15N 69°50E 42 F3
Shahjahanpur India 27°54N 79°57E 43 F8
Shahpur India 22°12N 77°58E 42 H7
Shahpur Baluchistan, Pakistan 28°46N 68°27E 42 E3
Shahpur Punjab, Pakistan 32°17N 72°26E 42 C5
Shahpur Chakar Pakistan 26°9N 68°39E 42 F3
Shahpura Mad. P., India 23°10N 80°45E 43 H9
Shahpura Raj., India 25°38N 74°56E 42 G6
Shahr-e Bābak Iran 30°7N 55°9E 45 D7
Shahr-e Kord Iran 32°15N 50°55E 45 C6
Shāhrakht Iran 33°38N 60°16E 45 C9
Shahrig Pakistan 30°15N 67°40E 42 D2
Shahukou China 40°20N 112°18E 34 D7
Shaikhabad Afghan. 34°2N 68°45E 42 B3
Shajapur India 23°27N 76°21E 42 H7
Shajing China 22°44N 113°48E 33 F10
Shakargarh Pakistan 32°17N 75°10E 42 C6
Shakawe Botswana 18°28S 21°49E 56 B3
Shaker Heights U.S.A. 41°28N 81°32W 82 E3
Shakhty Russia 47°40N 40°16E 19 E7
Shakhunya Russia 57°40N 46°46E 18 C8
Shaki Nigeria 8°41N 3°21E 50 G6
Shaksam Valley Asia 36°0N 76°20E 43 A7
Shallow Lake Canada 44°36N 81°5W 82 B3
Shalqar Kazakhstan 47°48N 59°39E 28 E6
Shaluli Shan China 30°40N 99°55E 32 C4
Shām Iran 26°39N 57°21E 45 E8
Shām, Bādiyat ash Asia 32°0N 40°0E 44 C3
Shamâl Sînî □ Egypt 30°30N 33°30E 46 E2
Shamattawa Canada 55°51N 92°5W 72 A1
Shamattawa → Canada 55°1N 85°23W 72 A2
Shamīl Iran 27°30N 56°55E 45 E8
Shāmkūh Iran 35°47N 57°50E 45 C8
Shamli India 29°32N 77°18E 42 E7
Shammar, Jabal Si. Arabia 27°40N 41°0E 44 E4
Shamo = Gobi Asia 44°0N 110°0E 34 C6
Shamo, L. Ethiopia 5°45N 37°30E 47 F2
Shamokin U.S.A. 40°47N 76°34W 83 F8
Shamrock U.S.A. 35°13N 100°15W 84 D4
Shamva Zimbabwe 17°20S 31°32E 55 F3
Shan □ Burma 21°30N 98°30E 41 J21
Shan Xian China 34°50N 116°5E 34 G9
Shanchengzhen China 42°20N 125°20E 35 C13
Shāndak Iran 28°28N 60°27E 45 D9
Shandon U.S.A. 35°39N 120°23W 78 K6
Shandong □ China 36°0N 118°0E 35 G10
Shandong Bandao China 37°0N 121°0E 35 F11
Shang Xian = Shangzhou China 33°50N 109°58E 34 H5
Shanga Nigeria 11°12N 4°33E 50 F6
Shangalowe Dem. Rep. of the Congo 10°50S 26°30E 55 E2
Shangani Zimbabwe 19°41S 29°20E 57 B4
Shangani → Zimbabwe 18°41S 27°10E 55 F2
Shangbancheng China 40°50N 118°1E 35 D10
Shangdu China 41°30N 113°30E 34 D7
Shanghai China 31°15N 121°26E 33 C7
Shanghe China 37°20N 117°10E 35 F9
Shangnan China 33°32N 110°50E 34 H6
Shangqiu China 34°26N 115°36E 34 G8
Shangrao China 28°25N 117°59E 33 D6
Shangshui China 33°42N 114°35E 33 C6
Shangzhi China 45°22N 127°56E 35 B14
Shangzhou China 33°50N 109°58E 34 H5
Shanhetun China 44°33N 127°15E 35 B14
Shanklin U.K. 50°38N 1°11W 13 G6
Shannon N.Z. 40°33S 175°25E 59 D5
Shannon → Ireland 52°35N 9°30W 10 D2
Shannon ✕ (SNN) Ireland 52°42N 8°57W 10 D3
Shannon, Mouth of the Ireland 52°30N 9°55W 10 D2
Shannon △ Australia 34°35S 116°25E 61 F2
Shannonbridge Ireland 53°17N 8°3W 10 C3
Shansi = Shanxi □ China 37°0N 112°0E 34 F7
Shantar, Ostrov Bolshoy Russia 55°9N 137°40E 29 D14
Shantipur India 23°17N 88°25E 43 H13
Shantou China 23°18N 116°40E 33 D6
Shantung = Shandong □ China 36°0N 118°0E 35 G10
Shanxi □ China 37°0N 112°0E 34 F7
Shanyang China 33°31N 109°55E 34 H5
Shanyin China 39°25N 112°56E 34 E7
Shaoguan China 24°48N 113°35E 33 D6
Shaoxing China 30°0N 120°35E 33 D7
Shaoyang China 27°14N 111°25E 33 D6
Shap U.K. 54°32N 2°40W 12 C5
Shapinsay U.K. 59°3N 2°51W 11 B6
Shaqra' Si. Arabia 25°15N 45°16E 44 E5
Shaqrā' Yemen 13°22N 45°44E 47 E4
Sharafkhāneh Iran 38°11N 45°29E 44 B5
Sharbot Lake Canada 44°46N 76°41W 83 B8
Shari Japan 43°55N 144°40E 30 C12
Sharjah = Ash Shāriqah U.A.E. 25°23N 55°26E 45 E7
Shark B. Australia 25°30S 113°32E 61 E1
Shark Bay ⌒ Australia 25°30S 113°30E 61 E1
Sharm el Sheikh Egypt 27°53N 34°18E 51 C12
Sharon Mass., U.S.A. 42°7N 71°11W 83 D13
Sharon Pa., U.S.A. 41°14N 80°31W 82 E4
Sharon Springs Kans., U.S.A. 38°54N 101°45W 80 F3
Sharon Springs N.Y., U.S.A. 42°48N 74°37W 83 D10
Sharp Pt. Australia 10°58S 142°43E 62 A3
Sharpe L. Canada 54°24N 93°40W 72 B1
Sharpsville U.S.A. 41°15N 80°29W 82 E4
Sharqi, Al Jabal ash Lebanon 33°40N 36°10E 46 B5
Sharya Russia 58°22N 45°20E 18 C8
Shashemene Ethiopia 7°13N 38°33E 47 F2
Shashi Botswana 21°15S 27°27E 57 C4
Shashi China 30°25N 112°14E 33 C6
Shashi → Africa 21°14S 29°20E 55 G2
Shasta, Mt. U.S.A. 41°25N 122°12W 76 F2
Shasta L. U.S.A. 40°43N 122°25W 76 F2
Shatsky Rise Pac. Oc. 34°0N 157°0E 64 D7
Shatt al Arab Asia 29°57N 48°34E 45 D6
Shaunavon Canada 49°35N 108°25W 71 D7
Shaver L. U.S.A. 37°9N 119°18W 78 H7
Shaw → Australia 20°21S 119°17E 60 D2
Shaw I. Australia 20°30S 149°2E 62 J7
Shawanaga Canada 45°31N 80°17W 82 A4
Shawangunk Mts. U.S.A. 41°35N 74°30W 83 E10
Shawano U.S.A. 44°47N 88°36W 80 C9
Shawinigan Canada 46°35N 72°50W 72 C5
Shawmari, J. ash Jordan 30°35N 36°35E 46 E5
Shawnee U.S.A. 35°20N 96°55W 84 D6
Shay Gap Australia 20°30S 120°10E 60 D3
Shaybārā Si. Arabia 25°26N 36°47E 44 E3
Shaykh, J. ash Lebanon 33°25N 35°50E 46 B4
Shaykh Miskīn Syria 32°49N 36°9E 46 C5
Shaykh Sa'īd Iraq 32°34N 46°17E 44 C5
Shchūchīnsk Kazakhstan 52°56N 70°12E 28 D8
She Xian China 36°30N 113°40E 34 F7
Shebele = Scebeli, Wabi → Somali Rep. 2°0N 44°0E 47 G3
Sheboygan U.S.A. 43°46N 87°45W 80 D10
Shediac Canada 46°14N 64°32W 73 C7
Sheelin, L. Ireland 53°48N 7°20W 10 C4
Sheep Haven Ireland 55°11N 7°52W 10 A4
Sheep Range U.S.A. 36°35N 115°15W 79 J11
Sheerness U.K. 51°26N 0°47E 13 F8
Sheet Harbour Canada 44°56N 62°31W 73 D7
Sheffield U.K. 53°23N 1°28W 12 D6
Sheffield Ala., U.S.A. 34°46N 87°41W 85 D11
Sheffield Mass., U.S.A. 42°5N 73°21W 83 D11
Sheffield Pa., U.S.A. 41°42N 79°3W 82 E5
Sheikhpura India 25°9N 85°53E 43 G11
Shekhupura Pakistan 31°42N 73°58E 42 D5
Shekou China 22°30N 113°55E 33 G10
Shelburne N.S., Canada 43°47N 65°20W 73 D6
Shelburne Ont., Canada 44°4N 80°15W 82 B4
Shelburne U.S.A. 44°23N 73°14W 83 B11
Shelburne B. Australia 11°50S 142°50E 62 A3
Shelburne Falls U.S.A. 42°36N 72°45W 83 D12
Shelby Mich., U.S.A. 43°37N 86°22W 80 D10
Shelby Mont., U.S.A. 48°30N 111°51W 76 B8
Shelby N.C., U.S.A. 35°17N 81°32W 85 D14
Shelby Ohio, U.S.A. 40°53N 82°40W 82 F2
Shelbyville Ill., U.S.A. 39°24N 88°48W 80 F9
Shelbyville Ind., U.S.A. 39°31N 85°47W 81 F11
Shelbyville Ky., U.S.A. 38°13N 85°14W 81 F11
Shelbyville Tenn., U.S.A. 35°29N 86°28W 85 D11
Sheldon U.S.A. 43°11N 95°51W 80 D6
Sheldrake Canada 50°20N 64°51W 73 B7
Shelikhova, Zaliv Russia 59°30N 157°0E 29 D16
Shell Lakes Australia 29°20S 127°30E 61 E4
Shellbrook Canada 53°13N 106°24W 71 C7
Shellharbour Australia 34°31S 150°51E 63 E5
Shelter I. U.S.A. 41°4N 72°20W 83 E12
Shelton Conn., U.S.A. 41°19N 73°5W 83 E11
Shelton Wash., U.S.A. 47°13N 123°6W 78 C3
Shen Xian China 36°15N 115°40E 34 F8
Shenandoah Iowa, U.S.A. 40°46N 95°22W 80 E6
Shenandoah Pa., U.S.A. 40°49N 76°12W 83 F8
Shenandoah Va., U.S.A. 38°29N 78°37W 81 F14
Shenandoah → U.S.A. 39°19N 77°44W 81 F15
Shenandoah △ U.S.A. 38°35N 78°22W 81 F14
Shenchi China 39°8N 112°10E 34 E7
Shendam Nigeria 8°49N 9°30E 50 G7
Shendî Sudan 16°46N 33°22E 51 E12
Shengfang China 39°3N 116°42E 34 E9
Shenjingzi China 44°40N 124°30E 35 B13
Shenmu China 38°50N 110°29E 34 E6
Shenqiu China 33°25N 115°5E 34 H8
Shensi = Shaanxi □ China 35°0N 109°0E 34 G5
Shenyang China 41°48N 123°27E 35 D12
Shenzhen China 22°32N 114°5E 33 F10
Shenzhen ✕ (SZX) China 22°41N 113°49E 33 F10
Shenzhen Shuiku China 22°34N 114°8E 33 F11
Shenzhen Wan China 22°27N 113°55E 33 G10
Sheo India 26°11N 71°15E 42 F4
Sheopur Kalan India 25°40N 76°40E 42 G7
Shepetivka Ukraine 50°10N 27°10E 17 C14
Shepetovka = Shepetivka Ukraine 50°10N 27°10E 17 C14
Shepparton Australia 36°23S 145°26E 63 F4
Sheppey, I. of U.K. 51°25N 0°48E 13 F8
Shepton Mallet U.K. 51°11N 2°33W 13 F5
Sheqi China 33°12N 112°57E 34 H7
Sher Qila Pakistan 36°7N 74°2E 43 A6
Sherborne U.K. 50°57N 2°31W 13 G5
Sherbro I. S. Leone 7°30N 12°40W 50 G3
Sherbrooke N.S., Canada 45°8N 61°59W 73 C7
Sherbrooke Qué., Canada 45°28N 71°57W 83 A13
Sherburne U.S.A. 42°41N 75°30W 83 D9
Shergarh India 26°20N 72°18E 42 F5
Sherghati India 24°34N 84°47E 43 G11
Sheridan Ark., U.S.A. 34°19N 92°24W 84 D8
Sheridan Wyo., U.S.A. 44°48N 106°58W 76 D10
Sheringham U.K. 52°56N 1°13E 12 E9
Sherkin I. Ireland 51°28N 9°26W 10 E2
Sherkot India 29°22N 78°35E 43 E8
Sherman U.S.A. 33°38N 96°36W 84 E6
Sherpur India 25°34N 83°47E 43 G10
Sherridon Canada 55°8N 101°5W 71 B8
Sherwood Forest U.K. 53°6N 1°7W 12 D6
Sherwood Park Canada 53°31N 113°19W 70 C6
Sheslay → Canada 58°48N 132°5W 70 B2
Shethanei L. Canada 58°48N 97°50W 71 B9
Shetland □ U.K. 60°30N 1°30W 11 A7
Shetland Is. U.K. 60°30N 1°30W 11 A7
Shetrunji → India 21°19N 72°7E 42 J5
Sheung Shui China 22°31N 114°7E 33 F11
Shey-Phoksundo △ Nepal 29°30N 82°45E 43 E10
Sheyenne → U.S.A. 47°2N 96°50W 80 B5
Shibām Yemen 15°59N 48°36E 47 D4
Shibata Japan 37°57N 139°20E 30 F9
Shibecha Japan 43°17N 144°36E 30 C12
Shibetsu Japan 44°10N 142°23E 30 B11
Shibogama L. Canada 53°35N 88°15W 72 B2
Shibushi Japan 31°25N 131°8E 31 J5
Shickshinny U.S.A. 41°9N 76°9W 83 E8
Shickshock Mts. = Chic-Chocs, Mts. Canada 48°55N 66°0W 73 C6
Shidao China 36°50N 122°25E 35 F12
Shido Japan 34°19N 134°10E 31 G7
Shiel, L. U.K. 56°48N 5°34W 11 E3
Shield, C. Australia 13°20S 136°20E 62 A2
Shīeli Kazakhstan 44°20N 66°15E 28 E7
Shiga □ Japan 35°20N 136°0E 31 G8
Shiguaigou China 40°52N 110°15E 34 D6
Shihchiachuangi = Shijiazhuang China 38°2N 114°28E 34 E8
Shihezi China 44°15N 86°2E 32 B3
Shijiazhuang China 38°2N 114°28E 34 E8
Shikarpur India 28°17N 78°7E 42 E8
Shikarpur Pakistan 27°57N 68°39E 42 F3
Shikohabad India 27°6N 78°36E 43 F8
Shikoku □ Japan 33°30N 133°30E 31 H6
Shikoku-Sanchi Japan 33°30N 133°30E 31 H6
Shikotsu-Ko Japan 42°45N 141°25E 30 C10
Shikotsu-Tōya △ Japan 44°4N 145°8E 30 C10
Shiliguri India 26°45N 88°25E 41 F16
Shiliu = Changjiang China 19°20N 108°55E 38 C7
Shilka Russia 52°0N 115°55E 29 D12
Shilka → Russia 53°20N 121°26E 29 D13
Shillelagh Ireland 52°45N 6°32W 10 D5
Shillington U.S.A. 40°18N 75°58W 83 F9
Shillong India 25°35N 91°53E 41 G17
Shilo West Bank 32°4N 35°18E 46 C4
Shilou China 37°0N 110°48E 34 F6
Shimabara Japan 32°48N 130°20E 31 H5
Shimada Japan 34°49N 138°10E 31 G9
Shimane □ Japan 35°0N 132°30E 31 G6
Shimanovsk Russia 52°15N 127°30E 29 D13
Shimba Hills ⌒ Kenya 4°14S 39°25E 54 C4
Shimizu Japan 35°0N 138°30E 31 G9
Shimla India 31°2N 77°9E 42 D7
Shimodate Japan 36°20N 139°55E 31 F9
Shimoga India 13°57N 75°32E 40 N9
Shimoni Kenya 4°38S 39°20E 54 C4
Shimonoseki Japan 33°58N 130°55E 31 H5
Shimpuru Rapids Namibia 17°45S 19°55E 56 B2
Shin, L. U.K. 58°5N 4°30W 11 C4
Shinano-Gawa → Japan 36°50N 138°30E 31 F9
Shināş Oman 24°46N 56°28E 45 E8
Shīndand Afghan. 33°12N 62°8E 40 C3
Shinglehouse U.S.A. 41°58N 78°12W 82 E6
Shingū Japan 33°40N 135°55E 31 H7
Shingwidzi S. Africa 23°5S 31°25E 57 C5
Shinjō Japan 38°46N 140°18E 30 E10
Shinkolobwe Dem. Rep. of the Congo 11°10S 26°40E 52 G5
Shinshār Syria 34°36N 36°43E 46 A5
Shinyanga Tanzania 3°45S 33°27E 54 C3
Shinyanga □ Tanzania 3°50S 34°0E 54 C3
Shio-no-Misaki Japan 33°25N 135°45E 31 H7
Shiogama Japan 38°19N 141°1E 30 E10
Shiojiri Japan 36°6N 137°58E 31 F8
Shipchenski Prokhod Bulgaria 42°45N 25°15E 23 C11
Shiping China 23°45N 102°23E 32 D5
Shippagan Canada 47°45N 64°45W 73 C7
Shippensburg U.S.A. 40°3N 77°31W 82 F7
Shippenville U.S.A. 41°15N 79°28W 82 E5
Shiprock U.S.A. 36°47N 108°41W 77 H9
Shiqma, N. → Israel 31°37N 34°30E 46 D3
Shiquan China 33°5N 108°15E 34 H5
Shiquan He = Indus → Pakistan 24°20N 67°47E 42 G2
Shīr Kūh Iran 31°39N 54°3E 45 D7
Shiragami-Misaki Japan 41°24N 140°12E 30 D10
Shirakawa Fukushima, Japan 37°7N 140°13E 31 F10
Shirakawa Gifu, Japan 36°17N 136°56E 31 F8
Shirane-San Gumma, Japan 36°48N 139°22E 31 F9
Shirane-San Yamanashi, Japan 35°42N 138°9E 31 G9
Shiraoi Japan 42°33N 141°21E 30 C10
Shīrāz Iran 29°42N 52°30E 45 D7
Shire → Africa 17°42S 35°19E 55 F4
Shiretoko-Misaki Japan 44°21N 145°20E 30 B12
Shirinab → Pakistan 30°15N 66°28E 42 D2
Shiriya-Zaki Japan 41°25N 141°30E 30 D10
Shiroishi Japan 38°0N 140°37E 30 F10
Shirshov Ridge Pac. Oc. 58°0N 170°0E 64 B8
Shīrvān Iran 37°30N 57°50E 45 B8
Shirwa, L. = Chilwa, L. Malawi 15°15S 35°40E 55 F4
Shivpuri India 25°26N 77°42E 42 G7
Shixian China 43°5N 129°50E 35 C15
Shiyan China 22°42N 113°56E 33 F10
Shiyan Shuiku China 22°42N 113°54E 33 F10
Shizuishan China 39°15N 106°50E 34 E4
Shizuoka Japan 34°57N 138°24E 31 G9
Shizuoka □ Japan 35°15N 138°40E 31 G9
Shklov = Shklow Belarus 54°16N 30°15E 17 A16
Shklow Belarus 54°16N 30°15E 17 A16
Shkodër Albania 42°4N 19°32E 23 C8
Shkumbini → Albania 41°2N 19°31E 23 D8
Shmidta, Ostrov Russia 81°0N 91°0E 29 A10
Shō-Gawa → Japan 36°47N 137°4E 31 F8
Shoal L. Canada 49°33N 95°1W 71 D9
Shoal Lake Canada 50°30N 100°35W 71 C8
Shōdo-Shima Japan 34°30N 134°15E 31 G7
Sholapur = Solapur India 17°43N 75°56E 40 L9
Shōmrōn West Bank 32°15N 35°13E 46 C4
Shoreham by Sea U.K. 50°50N 0°16W 13 G7
Shori → Pakistan 28°29N 69°44E 42 E3
Shorkot Road Pakistan 30°47N 72°15E 42 D5
Shoshone Calif., U.S.A. 35°58N 116°16W 79 K10
Shoshone Idaho, U.S.A. 42°56N 114°25W 76 E6
Shoshone L. U.S.A. 44°22N 110°43W 76 D8
Shoshone Mts. U.S.A. 39°20N 117°25W 76 G5
Shoshong Botswana 22°56S 26°31E 56 C4
Shoshoni U.S.A. 43°14N 108°7W 76 E9
Shouguang China 37°52N 118°45E 35 F10
Shouyang China 37°54N 113°8E 34 F7
Show Low U.S.A. 34°15N 110°2W 77 J8
Shqipëria = Albania ■ Europe 41°0N 20°0E 23 D9
Shreveport U.S.A. 32°31N 93°45W 84 E8
Shrewsbury U.K. 52°43N 2°45W 13 E5
Shri Mohangarh India 27°17N 71°18E 42 F4
Shrirampur India 22°44N 88°21E 43 H13
Shropshire □ U.K. 52°36N 2°45W 13 E5
Shū Kazakhstan 43°36N 73°42E 28 E8
Shuangcheng China 45°20N 126°15E 35 B14
Shuanggou China 34°2N 117°30E 35 G9
Shuangliao China 43°29N 123°30E 35 C12
Shuangshanzi China 40°20N 119°8E 35 D10
Shuangyang China 43°28N 125°40E 35 C13
Shuangyashan China 46°28N 131°5E 33 B8
Shuguri Falls Tanzania 8°33S 37°22E 55 D4
Shuiye China 36°7N 114°8E 34 F8
Shujalpur India 23°18N 76°46E 42 H7
Shukpa Kunzang India 34°22N 78°22E 43 B8
Shulan China 44°28N 127°0E 35 B14
Shule China 39°25N 76°3E 32 C2
Shumagin Is. U.S.A. 55°7N 160°30W 74 a
Shumen Bulgaria 43°18N 26°55E 23 C12
Shumikha Russia 55°10N 63°15E 28 D7
Shuo Xian = Shuozhou China 39°20N 112°33E 34 E7
Shuozhou China 39°20N 112°33E 34 E7
Shūr → Fārs, Iran 28°30N 55°0E 45 D7
Shūr → Kermān, Iran 30°52N 57°37E 45 D8
Shūr → Yazd, Iran 31°45N 55°15E 45 D7
Shūr Āb Iran 34°23N 51°11E 45 C6
Shūr Gaz Iran 29°10N 59°20E 45 D8
Shūrāb Iran 33°43N 56°29E 45 C8
Shūrjestān Iran 31°24N 52°25E 45 D7
Shurugwi Zimbabwe 19°40S 30°0E 55 F3
Shūsf Iran 31°50N 60°5E 45 D9
Shūshtar Iran 32°0N 48°50E 45 D6
Shuswap L. Canada 50°55N 119°3W 70 C5
Shuyang China 34°10N 118°42E 35 G10
Shūzū Iran 29°52N 54°30E 45 D7
Shwebo Burma 22°30N 95°45E 41 H19
Shwegu Burma 24°15N 96°26E 41 G20
Shweli → Burma 23°45N 96°45E 41 H20
Shymkent Kazakhstan 42°18N 69°36E 28 E7
Shyok India 34°13N 78°12E 43 B8
Shyok → Pakistan 35°13N 75°53E 43 B6
Si Chon Thailand 9°0N 99°54E 39 H2
Si Kiang = Xi Jiang → China 22°5N 113°20E 33 D6
Si Lanna △ Thailand 19°17N 99°12E 38 C2
Si-ngan = Xi'an China 34°15N 109°0E 34 G5
Si Prachan Thailand 14°37N 100°9E 38 E3
Si Racha Thailand 13°10N 100°48E 38 F3
Si Xian China 33°30N 117°50E 35 H9
Siachen Glacier Asia 35°20N 77°30E 43 B7
Siahaf → Pakistan 29°3N 68°57E 42 E3
Siahan Range Pakistan 27°30N 64°40E 40 F4
Siaksriindrapura Indonesia 0°51N 102°0E 36 D2
Sialkot Pakistan 32°32N 74°30E 42 C6
Siam = Thailand ■ Asia 16°0N 102°0E 38 E4
Sian = Xi'an China 34°15N 109°0E 34 G5
Sian Ka'an ⌒ Mexico 19°35N 87°40W 87 D7
Siantan Indonesia 3°10N 106°15E 36 D3
Sīāreh Iran 28°5N 60°14E 45 D9
Siargao I. Phil. 9°52N 126°3E 37 C7
Siari Pakistan 34°55N 76°40E 43 B7
Siasi Phil. 5°34N 120°50E 37 C6
Siau Indonesia 2°50N 125°25E 37 D7
Šiauliai Lithuania 55°56N 23°15E 9 J20
Sibâi, Gebel el Egypt 25°45N 34°10E 44 E2
Sibang Indonesia 8°34S 115°13E 37 K18
Sibay Russia 52°42N 58°39E 18 D10
Sibayi, L. S. Africa 27°20S 32°45E 57 D5
Šibenik Croatia 43°48N 15°54E 22 C6
Siberia = Sibirskiy □ Russia 58°0N 90°0E 29 D10
Siberia Russia 60°0N 100°0E 4 D13
Siberut Indonesia 1°30S 99°0E 36 E1
Sibi Pakistan 29°30N 67°54E 42 E2
Sibil = Oksibil Indonesia 4°59S 140°35E 37 E10
Sibiloi △ Kenya 4°0N 36°20E 54 B4
Sibirskiy □ Russia 58°0N 90°0E 29 D10
Sibirtsevo Russia 44°12N 132°26E 30 B5
Sibiti Congo 3°38S 13°19E 52 E2
Sibiu Romania 45°45N 24°9E 17 F13
Sibley U.S.A. 43°24N 95°45W 80 D6
Sibolga Indonesia 1°42N 98°45E 36 D1
Sibsagar India 27°0N 94°36E 41 F19
Sibu Malaysia 2°18N 111°49E 36 D4
Sibuco Phil. 7°20N 122°10E 37 C6
Sibuguey B. Phil. 7°50N 122°45E 37 C6
Sibut C.A.R. 5°46N 19°10E 52 C3
Sibutu Phil. 4°45N 119°30E 37 D5
Sibutu Passage E. Indies 4°50N 120°0E 37 D5
Sibuyan I. Phil. 12°25N 122°40E 37 B6
Sibuyan Sea Phil. 12°30N 122°20E 37 B6
Sicamous Canada 50°49N 119°0W 70 C5
Siccus → Australia 31°55S 139°17E 63 E2
Sichuan □ China 30°30N 103°0E 32 C5
Sicilia Italy 37°30N 14°30E 22 F6
Sicily = Sicilia Italy 37°30N 14°30E 22 F6
Sicily, Str. of 37°35N 11°56E 22 F4
Sicuani Peru 14°21S 71°10W 92 F4
Sidari Greece 39°47N 19°41E 25 A3
Siddhapur India 23°56N 72°25E 42 H5
Siddipet India 18°5N 78°51E 40 K11
Sideros, Akra Greece 35°19N 26°19E 25 D8
Sidhauli India 27°17N 80°50E 43 F9
Sidhi India 24°25N 81°53E 43 G9
Sidi-bel-Abbès Algeria 35°13N 0°39W 50 A5
Sidi Ifni Morocco 29°29N 10°12W 50 C3
Sidlaw Hills U.K. 56°32N 3°2W 11 E5
Sidley, Mt. Antarctica 77°2S 126°2W 5 D14
Sidmouth U.K. 50°40N 3°15W 13 G4
Sidmouth, C. Australia 13°25S 143°36E 62 A3
Sidney Canada 48°39N 123°24W 78 B3
Sidney Mont., U.S.A. 47°43N 104°9W 76 C11
Sidney N.Y., U.S.A. 42°19N 75°24W 83 D9
Sidney Nebr., U.S.A. 41°8N 102°59W 80 E2
Sidney Ohio, U.S.A. 40°17N 84°9W 81 E11
Sidney Lanier, L. U.S.A. 34°10N 84°4W 85 D12
Sidoarjo Indonesia 7°27S 112°43E 37 G15
Sidon = Saydā Lebanon 33°35N 35°25E 46 B4
Sidra, G. of = Surt, Khalīj Libya 31°40N 18°30E 51 B9
Siedlce Poland 52°10N 22°20E 17 B12
Sieg → Germany 50°46N 7°6E 16 C4
Siegen Germany 50°51N 8°0E 16 C5
Siem Pang Cambodia 14°7N 106°23E 38 E6
Siem Reap = Siemreab Cambodia 13°20N 103°52E 38 F4
Siemreab Cambodia 13°20N 103°52E 38 F4
Siena Italy 43°19N 11°21E 22 C4
Sieradz Poland 51°37N 18°41E 17 C10
Sierpe, Bocas de la Venezuela 10°0N 61°30W 93 L15
Sierra Blanca U.S.A. 31°11N 105°22W 84 F2
Sierra Blanca Peak U.S.A. 33°23N 105°49W 77 K11
Sierra City U.S.A. 39°34N 120°38W 78 F6
Sierra Colorada Argentina 40°35S 67°50W 96 E3
Sierra de Bahoruco △ Dom. Rep. 18°10N 71°25W 89 C5
Sierra de La Culata △ Venezuela 8°45N 71°10W 89 E5
Sierra de Lancandón △ Guatemala 16°59N 90°23W 88 C1
Sierra de las Quijadas △ Argentina 32°29S 67°5W 94 C2
Sierra de San Luis △ Venezuela 11°20N 69°43W 89 D6
Sierra de San Pedro Mártir, Parque Nacional △ Mexico 31°10N 115°30W 86 A1
Sierra Gorda Chile 22°50S 69°15W 94 A2
Sierra Leone ■ W. Afr. 9°0N 12°0W 50 G3
Sierra Madre Mexico 16°0N 93°0W 87 D6
Sierra Madre Occidental Mexico 27°0N 107°0W 86 B3
Sierra Madre Oriental Mexico 25°0N 100°0W 86 C5
Sierra Mojada Mexico 27°18N 103°41W 86 B4
Sierra Nevada Spain 37°3N 3°15W 21 D4
Sierra Nevada U.S.A. 39°0N 120°30W 78 H8
Sierra Nevada △ Venezuela 8°35N 70°45W 89 E5
Sierra Nevada de Santa Marta △ Colombia 10°56N 73°36W 89 D5
Sierra Vista U.S.A. 31°33N 110°18W 77 L8
Sierraville U.S.A. 39°36N 120°22W 78 F6
Sifnos Greece 37°0N 24°45E 23 F11
Sifton Canada 51°21N 100°8W 71 C8
Sifton Pass Canada 57°52N 126°15W 70 B3
Sig Algeria 35°32N 0°12W 50 A5
Sigatoka Fiji 18°8S 177°32E 59
Sighetu-Marmației Romania 47°57N 23°52E 17 E12
Sighișoara Romania 46°12N 24°50E 17 E13
Sigli Indonesia 5°25N 96°0E 36 C1
Siglufjörður Iceland 66°12N 18°55W 8 C4
Signal de Botrang Belgium 50°29N 6°4E 15 D6
Signal Pk. U.S.A. 33°20N 114°2W 79 M12
Signy I. Antarctica 60°45S 45°56W 5 C18
Sigsig Ecuador 3°0S 78°50W 92 D3
Sigüenza Spain 41°3N 2°40W 21 B4
Siguiri Guinea 11°31N 9°10W 50 F4
Sigulda Latvia 57°10N 24°55E 9 H21
Sihora India 23°29N 80°6E 43 H9

Siikajoki → Finland 64°50N 24°43E 8 D21
Siilinjärvi Finland 63°4N 27°39E 8 E22
Sijarira Ra. = Chizarira Zimbabwe 17°36S 27°45E 55 F2
Sika India 22°26N 69°47E 42 H3
Sikanni Chief → Canada 57°47N 122°15W 70 B4
Sikao Thailand 7°34N 99°21E 39 J2
Sikar India 27°33N 75°10E 42 F6
Sikasso Mali 11°18N 5°35W 50 F4
Sikeston U.S.A. 36°53N 89°35W 80 G9
Sikhote Alin, Khrebet Russia 45°0N 136°0E 30 B8
Sikhote Alin Ra. = Sikhote Alin, Khrebet Russia 45°0N 136°0E 30 B8
Sikinos Greece 36°40N 25°8E 23 F11
Sikkim ☐ India 27°50N 88°30E 41 F16
Sil → Spain 42°27N 7°43W 21 A2
Silacayoapan Mexico 17°30N 98°9W 87 D5
Silawad India 21°54N 74°54E 42 J6
Silchar India 24°49N 92°48E 41 G18
Siler City U.S.A. 35°44N 79°28W 85 D15
Silesia = Śląsk Poland 51°0N 16°30E 16 C9
Silgarhi Doti Nepal 29°15N 81°0E 43 E9
Silghat India 26°35N 93°0E 41 F18
Silhouette Seychelles 4°29S 55°12E 53 b
Silifke Turkey 36°22N 33°58E 44 B2
Siliguri = Shiliguri India 26°45N 88°25E 41 F16
Siling Co China 31°50N 89°20E 32 C3
Silistra Bulgaria 44°6N 27°19E 23 B12
Silivri Turkey 41°4N 28°14E 23 D13
Siljan Sweden 60°55N 14°45E 8 F16
Silkeborg Denmark 56°10N 9°32E 9 H13
Silkwood Australia 17°45S 146°2E 62 B4
Sillajhuay, Cordillera Chile 19°46S 68°40W 92 G5
Sillamäe Estonia 59°24N 27°45E 9 G22
Silloth U.K. 54°52N 3°23W 12 C4
Siloam Springs U.S.A. 36°11N 94°32W 84 C7
Silsbee U.S.A. 30°21N 94°11W 84 F7
Šilutė Lithuania 55°21N 21°33E 9 J19
Silvani India 23°18N 78°25E 43 H8
Silver City U.S.A. 32°46N 108°17W 77 K9
Silver Cr. → U.S.A. 43°16N 119°13W 76 E4
Silver Creek U.S.A. 42°33N 79°10W 82 D5
Silver L. U.S.A. 38°39N 120°6W 78 G6
Silver Lake Calif., U.S.A. 35°21N 116°7W 79 K10
Silver Lake Oreg., U.S.A. 43°8N 121°3W 76 E3
Silvermine Mts. Ireland 52°47N 8°15W 10 D3
Silverton Colo., U.S.A. 37°49N 107°40W 77 H10
Silverton Tex., U.S.A. 34°28N 101°19W 84 D4
Silvies → U.S.A. 43°34N 119°2W 76 E4
Simaltala India 24°43N 86°33E 43 G12
Simanggang = Sri Aman Malaysia 1°15N 111°32E 36 D4
Simard, L. Canada 47°40N 78°40W 72 C4
Simav Turkey 39°4N 28°58E 23 E13
Simba Tanzania 2°10S 37°36E 54 C4
Simbirsk Russia 54°20N 48°25E 18 D8
Simbo Tanzania 4°51S 29°41E 54 C2
Simcoe Canada 42°50N 80°20W 72 D3
Simcoe, L. Canada 44°25N 79°20W 82 B5
Simdega India 22°37N 84°31E 43 H11
Simeria Romania 45°51N 23°1E 17 F12
Simeulue Indonesia 2°45N 95°45E 36 D1
Simferopol Ukraine 44°55N 34°3E 19 F5
Simi Greece 36°35N 27°50E 23 F12
Simi Valley U.S.A. 34°16N 118°47W 79 L8
Simikot Nepal 30°0N 81°50E 43 E9
Simla = Shimla India 31°2N 77°9E 42 D7
Simlipal △ India 21°45N 86°30E 43 J12
Simmie Canada 49°56N 108°6W 71 D7
Simmler U.S.A. 35°21N 119°59W 79 K7
Simo älv = Simojoki → Finland 65°35N 25°1E 8 D21
Simojoki → Finland 65°35N 25°1E 8 D21
Simojovel Mexico 17°12N 92°38W 87 D6
Simonette → Canada 55°9N 118°15W 70 B5
Simonstown S. Africa 34°14S 18°26E 56 E2
Simpang Empat Malaysia 5°27N 100°29E 39 c
Simplonpass Switz. 46°15N 8°3E 20 C8
Simpson Desert Australia 25°0S 137°0E 62 D2
Simpson Desert △ Australia 24°59S 138°21E 62 C2
Simpson Pen. Canada 68°34N 88°45W 69 C11
Simrishamn Sweden 55°33N 14°22E 9 J16
Simsbury U.S.A. 41°53N 72°48W 83 E12
Simushir, Ostrov Russia 46°50N 152°30E 29 E16
Sin Cowe I. S. China Sea 9°53N 114°19E 36 C4
Sinabang Indonesia 2°30N 96°24E 36 D1
Sinadogo Somali Rep. 5°50N 47°0E 47 F4
Sinai = Es Sînâ' Egypt 29°0N 34°0E 46 F3
Sinai, Mt. = Mûsa, Gebel Egypt 28°33N 33°59E 44 D2
Sinaloa ☐ Mexico 25°0N 107°30W 86 C3
Sinaloa de Leyva Mexico 25°50N 108°14W 86 B3
Sinarades Greece 39°34N 19°51E 25 A3
Sincelejo Colombia 9°18N 75°24W 92 B3
Sinch'ang N. Korea 40°7N 128°28E 35 D15
Sinch'ŏn N. Korea 38°17N 125°21E 35 E13
Sinclair U.S.A. 41°47N 107°7W 76 F10
Sinclair Mills Canada 54°5N 121°40W 70 C4
Sinclair's B. U.K. 58°31N 3°5W 11 C5
Sinclairville U.S.A. 42°16N 79°16W 82 D5
Sincorá, Serra do Brazil 13°30S 41°0W 93 F10
Sind = Sindh ☐ Pakistan 26°0N 69°0E 42 G3
Sind Pakistan 26°0N 68°30E 42 G3
Sind → Jammu & Kashmir, India 34°18N 74°45E 43 B6
Sind → Mad. P., India 26°26N 79°13E 43 F8
Sind Sagar Doab Pakistan 32°0N 71°30E 42 D4
Sindangan Phil. 8°10N 123°5E 37 C6
Sindangbarang Indonesia 7°27S 107°1E 37 G12
Sinde Zambia 17°28S 25°51E 55 F2
Sindh ☐ Pakistan 26°0N 69°0E 42 G3
Sindri India 23°45N 86°42E 43 H12
Sines Portugal 37°56N 8°51W 21 D1
Sines, C. de Portugal 37°58N 8°53W 21 D1
Sineu Spain 39°38N 3°1E 24 B10
Sing Buri Thailand 14°53N 100°25E 38 E3
Singa Sudan 13°10N 33°57E 51 F12
Singalila △ India 27°10N 88°5E 43 F13
Singapore ■ Asia 1°17N 103°51E 39 d
Singapore, Straits of Asia 1°15N 104°0E 39 d
Singapore Changi ✈ (SIN) Singapore 1°23N 103°59E 39 M4
Singaraja Indonesia 8°7S 115°6E 36 F5
Singatoka = Sigatoka Fiji 18°8S 177°32E 59 a
Singida Tanzania 4°49S 34°48E 54 C3
Singida ☐ Tanzania 6°0S 34°30E 54 D3
Singkaling Hkamti Burma 26°0N 95°39E 41 G19
Singkang Indonesia 4°8S 120°1E 37 E6
Singkawang Indonesia 1°0N 108°57E 36 D3
Singkep Indonesia 0°30S 104°25E 36 E2
Singleton Australia 32°33S 151°0E 63 E5
Singleton, Mt. N. Terr., Australia 22°0S 130°46E 60 D5
Singleton, Mt. W. Austral., Australia 29°27S 117°15E 61 E2
Singoli India 25°0N 75°22E 42 G6
Singora = Songkhla Thailand 7°13N 100°37E 39 J3
Sinhŭng N. Korea 40°11N 127°34E 35 D14
Siniscóla Italy 40°34N 9°41E 22 D3
Sinjai Indonesia 5°7S 120°20E 37 F6
Sinjār Iraq 36°19N 41°52E 44 B4
Sinkat Sudan 18°55N 36°49E 51 E13
Sinkiang = Xinjiang Uygur Zizhiqu ☐ China 42°0N 86°0E 32 C3
Sinmak N. Korea 38°25N 126°14E 35 E14
Sinmi-do N. Korea 39°33N 124°53E 35 E13
Sinnamary Fr. Guiana 5°25N 53°0W 93 B8
Sinni → Italy 40°8N 16°41E 22 D7
Sinop Turkey 42°1N 35°11E 19 F6
Sinor India 21°55N 73°20E 42 J5
Sinp'o N. Korea 40°0N 128°13E 35 E15
Sinsk Russia 61°8N 126°48E 29 C13
Sintang Indonesia 0°5N 111°35E 36 D4
Sinton U.S.A. 28°2N 97°31W 84 G6
Sintra Portugal 38°47N 9°25W 21 C1
Sinŭiju N. Korea 40°5N 124°24E 35 D13
Siocon Phil. 7°40N 122°10E 37 C6
Siófok Hungary 46°54N 18°3E 17 E10
Sion Switz. 46°14N 7°20E 20 C7
Sion Mills U.K. 54°48N 7°29W 10 B4
Sioux Center U.S.A. 43°5N 96°11W 80 D5
Sioux City U.S.A. 42°30N 96°24W 80 D5
Sioux Falls U.S.A. 43°33N 96°44W 80 D5
Sioux Lookout Canada 50°10N 91°50W 72 B1
Sioux Narrows Canada 49°25N 94°10W 71 D10
Sipadan Malaysia 7°6N 118°38E 37 D5
Siparia Trin. & Tob. 10°8N 61°31W 93 K15
Siping China 43°8N 124°21E 35 C13
Sipiwesk L. Canada 55°5N 97°35W 71 B9
Siple Antarctica 75°0S 74°0W 5 D7
Sipra → India 23°55N 75°28E 42 H6
Sipura Indonesia 2°18S 99°40E 36 E1
Siquia → Nic. 12°10N 84°20W 88 D3
Siquijor Phil. 9°12N 123°35E 37 C6
Siquirres Costa Rica 10°6N 83°30W 88 D3
Şīr Abu Nu'ayr U.A.E. 25°20N 54°20E 45 E7
Şīr Banī Yās U.A.E. 24°19N 52°37E 45 E7
Sir Edward Pellew Group Australia 15°40S 137°10E 62 B2
Sir Graham Moore Is. Australia 13°53S 126°34E 60 B4
Sir James MacBrien, Mt. Canada 62°7N 127°41W 68 C7
Sira → Norway 58°23N 6°34E 9 G12
Siracusa Italy 37°4N 15°17E 22 F6
Sirajganj Bangla. 24°25N 89°47E 43 G13
Sirathu India 25°39N 81°19E 43 G9
Sīrdān Iran 36°39N 49°12E 45 B6
Siren U.S.A. 45°47N 92°24W 80 C7
Sirer Spain 38°56N 1°22E 24 C7
Siret → Romania 45°24N 28°1E 17 F14
Sirghāyā Syria 33°51N 36°8E 46 B5
Sirinath △ Thailand 8°6N 98°17E 39 a
Sīrjān Iran 29°30N 55°45E 45 D7
Sirmaur India 24°51N 81°23E 43 G9
Sirohi India 24°52N 72°53E 42 G5
Sironj India 24°5N 77°39E 42 G7
Síros = Syros Greece 37°28N 24°57E 23 F11
Sirretta Pk. U.S.A. 35°56N 118°19W 79 K8
Sīrrī Iran 25°55N 54°32E 45 E7
Sirsa India 29°33N 75°4E 42 E6
Sirsa → India 26°51N 79°4E 43 F8
Sisak Croatia 45°30N 16°21E 16 F9
Sisaket Thailand 15°8N 104°23E 38 E5
Sishen S. Africa 27°47S 22°59E 56 D3
Sishui Henan, China 34°48N 113°15E 34 G7
Sishui Shandong, China 35°42N 117°18E 35 G9
Sisipuk L. Canada 55°45N 101°50W 71 B8
Sisophon Cambodia 13°38N 102°59E 38 F4
Sisseton U.S.A. 45°40N 97°3W 80 C5
Sīstān Asia 30°50N 61°0E 45 D9
Sīstān, Daryācheh-ye Iran 31°0N 61°0E 45 D9
Sīstān va Balūchestān ☐ Iran 27°0N 62°0E 45 E9
Sisters U.S.A. 44°18N 121°33W 76 D3
Sisters, The Seychelles 4°16S 55°52E 53 b
Siswa Bazar India 27°9N 83°46E 43 F10
Sitamarhi India 26°37N 85°30E 43 F11
Sitampiky Madag. 16°41S 46°6E 57 B8
Sitapur India 27°38N 80°45E 43 F9
Siteki Swaziland 26°32S 31°58E 57 D5
Sitges Spain 41°17N 1°47E 21 B6
Sitia Greece 35°13N 26°6E 25 D8
Sitito-Ozima Ridge Pac. Oc. 23°0N 143°0E 64 E6
Sitka U.S.A. 57°3N 135°20W 70 B1
Sitoti Botswana 23°15S 23°40E 56 C3
Sittang Myit → Burma 17°20N 96°45E 41 L20
Sittard Neths. 51°0N 5°52E 15 C5
Sittingbourne U.K. 51°21N 0°45E 13 F8
Sittoung = Sittang Myit → Burma 17°20N 96°45E 41 L20
Sittwe Burma 20°18N 92°45E 41 J18
Situbondo Indonesia 7°42S 114°0E 37 G16
Si'umu Samoa 14°1S 171°48W 59 b
Siuna Nic. 13°37N 84°45W 88 D3
Siuri India 23°50N 87°34E 43 H12
Sīvand Iran 30°5N 52°55E 45 D7
Sivas Turkey 39°43N 36°58E 44 B3
Siverek Turkey 37°50N 39°19E 44 B3
Sivomaskinskiy Russia 66°40N 62°35E 18 A11
Sivrihisar Turkey 39°30N 31°35E 19 G5
Sîwa Egypt 29°11N 25°31E 51 C11
Sîwa, El Wâhât es Egypt 29°10N 25°30E 48 D6
Siwa Oasis = Sîwa, El Wâhât es Egypt 29°10N 25°30E 48 D6
Siwalik Range Nepal 28°0N 83°0E 43 F10
Siwan India 26°13N 84°21E 43 F11
Siwana India 25°38N 72°25E 42 G5
Six Cross Roads Barbados 13°7N 59°28W 89 g
Sixmilebridge Ireland 52°44N 8°46W 10 D3
Sixth Cataract Sudan 16°20N 32°42E 51 E12
Siziwang Qi China 41°25N 111°40E 34 D6
Sjælland Denmark 55°30N 11°30E 9 J14
Sjumen = Shumen Bulgaria 43°18N 26°55E 23 C12
Skadarsko Jezero Europe 42°10N 19°20E 23 C8
Skaftafell Iceland 64°1N 17°0W 8 D5
Skaftafell △ Iceland 64°9N 16°50W 8 D5
Skagafjörður Iceland 65°54N 19°35W 8 D4
Skagastølstindane Norway 61°28N 7°52E 8 F12
Skagaströnd Iceland 65°50N 20°19W 8 D3
Skagen Denmark 57°43N 10°35E 9 H14
Skagerrak Denmark 57°30N 9°0E 9 H13
Skagit → U.S.A. 48°23N 122°22W 78 B4
Skagway U.S.A. 59°28N 135°19W 74 a
Skala-Podilska Ukraine 48°50N 26°15E 17 D14
Skala Podolskaya = Skala-Podilska Ukraine 48°50N 26°15E 17 D14
Skalat Ukraine 49°23N 25°55E 17 D13
Skåne Sweden 55°59N 13°30E 9 J15
Skaneateles U.S.A. 42°57N 76°26W 83 D8
Skaneateles L. U.S.A. 42°51N 76°22W 83 D8
Skardu Pakistan 35°20N 75°44E 43 B6
Skarżysko-Kamienna Poland 51°7N 20°52E 17 C11
Skeena → Canada 54°9N 130°5W 70 C2
Skeena Mts. Canada 56°40N 128°30W 70 B3
Skegness U.K. 53°9N 0°20E 12 D8
Skeldon = Corriverton Guyana 5°55N 57°20W 92 B7
Skeleton Coast Namibia 20°0S 13°0E 53 J2
Skeleton Coast △ Namibia 20°0S 13°20E 56 C1
Skellefteå Sweden 64°45N 20°50E 8 D19
Skellefteälven → Sweden 64°45N 21°10E 8 D19
Skelleftehamn Sweden 64°40N 21°9E 8 D19
Skerries, The U.K. 53°25N 4°36W 12 D3
Ski Norway 59°43N 10°52E 9 G14
Skiathos Greece 39°12N 23°30E 23 E10
Skibbereen Ireland 51°33N 9°16W 10 E2
Skiddaw U.K. 54°39N 3°9W 12 C4
Skidegate Canada 53°15N 132°1W 70 C2
Skien Norway 59°12N 9°35E 9 G13
Skierniewice Poland 51°58N 20°10E 17 C11
Skikda Algeria 36°50N 6°58E 50 A7
Skilloura Cyprus 35°14N 33°10E 25 D12
Skipton U.K. 53°58N 2°3W 12 D5
Skirmish Pt. Australia 11°59S 134°17E 62 A1
Skiros Greece 38°55N 24°34E 23 E11
Skive Denmark 56°33N 9°2E 9 H13
Skjálfandafljót → Iceland 65°59N 17°25W 8 D5
Skjálfandi Iceland 66°5N 17°30W 8 C5
Skole Ukraine 49°3N 23°30E 17 D12
Skopelos Greece 39°9N 23°47E 23 E10
Skopi Greece 35°11N 26°2E 25 D8
Skopje Macedonia 42°1N 21°26E 23 C9
Skövde Sweden 58°24N 13°50E 9 G15
Skovorodino Russia 54°0N 124°0E 29 D13
Skowhegan U.S.A. 44°46N 69°43W 81 C19
Skull Ireland 51°32N 9°34W 10 E2
Skunk → U.S.A. 40°42N 91°7W 80 E8
Skuodas Lithuania 56°16N 21°33E 9 H19
Skvyra Ukraine 49°44N 29°40E 17 D15
Skye U.K. 57°15N 6°10W 11 D2
Skykomish U.S.A. 47°42N 121°22W 76 C3
Skyros = Skiros Greece 38°55N 24°34E 23 E11
Slade Pt. Australia 21°5S 149°13E 62 K7
Slættaratindur Færoe Is. 62°18N 7°1W 8 E9
Slagelse Denmark 55°23N 11°19E 9 J14
Slamet Indonesia 7°16S 109°8E 37 G13
Slane Ireland 53°42N 6°33W 10 C5
Slaney → Ireland 52°26N 6°33W 10 D5
Slangberge S. Africa 31°32S 20°48E 56 E3
Śląsk Poland 51°0N 16°30E 16 C9
Slate Is. Canada 48°40N 87°0W 72 C2
Slatina Romania 44°28N 24°22E 17 F13
Slatington U.S.A. 40°45N 75°37W 83 F9
Slaton U.S.A. 33°26N 101°39W 84 E4
Slave → Canada 61°18N 113°39W 70 A6
Slave Coast W. Afr. 6°0N 2°30E 50 G6
Slave Lake Canada 55°17N 114°43W 70 B6
Slave Pt. Canada 61°11N 115°56W 70 A5
Slavgorod Russia 53°1N 78°37E 28 D8
Slavonski Brod Croatia 45°11N 18°1E 23 B8
Slavuta Ukraine 50°15N 27°2E 17 C14
Slavyanka Russia 42°53N 131°21E 30 C5
Slavyansk = Slovyansk Ukraine 48°55N 37°36E 19 E6
Slawharad Belarus 53°27N 31°0E 17 B16
Sleaford U.K. 53°0N 0°24W 12 D7
Sleaford B. Australia 34°55S 135°45E 63 E2
Sleat, Sd. of U.K. 57°5N 5°47W 11 D3
Sleeper Is. Canada 58°30N 81°0W 69 D11
Sleeping Bear Dunes △ U.S.A. 44°50N 86°5W 80 C10
Sleepy Eye U.S.A. 44°18N 94°43W 80 C6
Slemon L. Canada 63°13N 116°4W 70 A5
Slide Mt. U.S.A. 42°0N 74°25W 83 E10
Slidell U.S.A. 30°17N 89°47W 85 F10
Sliema Malta 35°55N 14°30E 25 D2
Slieve Aughty Ireland 53°4N 8°30W 10 C3
Slieve Bloom Ireland 53°4N 7°40W 10 C4
Slieve Donard U.K. 54°11N 5°55W 10 B6
Slieve Gamph Ireland 54°6N 9°0W 10 B3
Slieve Gullion U.K. 54°7N 6°26W 10 B5
Slieve League Ireland 54°40N 8°42W 10 B3
Slieve Mish Ireland 52°12N 9°50W 10 D2
Slievenamon Ireland 52°25N 7°34W 10 D4
Sligeach = Sligo Ireland 54°16N 8°28W 10 B3
Sligo Ireland 54°16N 8°28W 10 B3
Sligo U.S.A. 41°6N 79°29W 82 E5
Sligo ☐ Ireland 54°8N 8°42W 10 B3
Sligo B. Ireland 54°18N 8°40W 10 B3
Slippery Rock U.S.A. 41°4N 80°3W 82 E4
Slite Sweden 57°42N 18°48E 9 H18
Sliven Bulgaria 42°42N 26°19E 23 C12
Sloan U.S.A. 35°57N 115°13W 79 K11
Sloansville U.S.A. 42°45N 74°22W 83 D10
Slobodskoy Russia 58°40N 50°6E 18 C9
Slobozia Romania 44°34N 27°23E 17 F14
Slocan Canada 49°48N 117°28W 70 D5
Slonim Belarus 53°4N 25°19E 17 B13
Slough U.K. 51°30N 0°36W 13 F7
Slough ☐ U.K. 51°30N 0°36W 13 F7
Sloughhouse U.S.A. 38°26N 121°12W 78 G5
Slovak Rep. ■ Europe 48°30N 20°0E 17 D10
Slovakia = Slovak Rep. ■ Europe 48°30N 20°0E 17 D10
Slovakian Ore Mts. = Slovenské Rudohorie Slovak Rep. 48°45N 20°0E 17 D10
Slovenia ■ Europe 45°58N 14°30E 16 F8
Slovenija = Slovenia ■ Europe 45°58N 14°30E 16 F8
Slovenska = Slovak Rep. ■ Europe 48°30N 20°0E 17 D10
Slovenské Rudohorie Slovak Rep. 48°45N 20°0E 17 D10
Slovyansk Ukraine 48°55N 37°36E 19 E6
Sluch → Ukraine 51°37N 26°38E 17 C14
Sluis Neths. 51°18N 3°23E 15 C3
Słupsk Poland 54°30N 17°3E 17 A9
Slurry S. Africa 25°49S 25°42E 56 D4
Slutsk Belarus 53°2N 27°31E 17 B14
Slyne Hd. Ireland 53°25N 10°10W 10 C1
Slyudyanka Russia 51°40N 103°40E 29 D11
Småland Sweden 57°15N 15°25E 9 H16
Smalltree L. Canada 61°0N 105°0W 71 A8
Smallwood Res. Canada 54°5N 64°30W 73 B7
Smarhon Belarus 54°20N 26°24E 17 A14
Smartt Syndicate Dam S. Africa 30°45S 23°10E 56 E3
Smartville U.S.A. 39°13N 121°18W 78 F5
Smeaton Canada 53°30N 104°49W 71 C8
Smederevo Serbia 44°40N 20°57E 23 B9
Smerwick Harbour Ireland 52°12N 10°23W 10 D1
Smethport U.S.A. 41°49N 78°27W 82 E6
Smidovich Russia 48°36N 133°49E 29 E14
Smith Canada 55°10N 114°0W 70 B6
Smith Center U.S.A. 39°47N 98°47W 80 F4
Smith River △ U.S.A. 41°55N 124°0W 76 F2
Smithburne → Australia 17°3S 140°57E 62 B3
Smithers Canada 54°45N 127°10W 70 C3
Smithfield S. Africa 30°9S 26°30E 57 E4
Smithfield N.C., U.S.A. 35°31N 78°21W 85 D15
Smithfield Utah, U.S.A. 41°50N 111°50W 76 F8
Smiths Falls Canada 44°55N 76°0W 83 B9
Smithton Australia 40°53S 145°6E 63 G4
Smithville Canada 43°6N 79°33W 82 C5
Smithville U.S.A. 30°1N 97°10W 84 F6
Smoky → Canada 56°10N 117°21W 70 B5
Smoky Bay Australia 32°22S 134°13E 63 E1
Smoky Hill → U.S.A. 39°4N 96°48W 80 F5
Smoky Hills U.S.A. 39°15N 99°30W 80 F4
Smoky Lake Canada 54°10N 112°30W 70 C6
Smøla Norway 63°23N 8°3E 8 E13
Smolensk Russia 54°45N 32°5E 18 D5
Smolikas, Oros Greece 40°9N 20°58E 23 D9
Smolyan Bulgaria 41°36N 24°38E 23 D11
Smooth Rock Falls Canada 49°17N 81°37W 72 C3
Smoothstone L. Canada 54°40N 106°50W 71 C7
Smorgon = Smarhon Belarus 54°20N 26°24E 17 A14
Smyrna = İzmir Turkey 38°25N 27°8E 23 E12
Smyrna U.S.A. 39°18N 75°36W 81 F16
Snæfell Iceland 64°48N 15°34W 8 D6
Snaefell I. of Man 54°16N 4°27W 12 C3
Snæfellsjökull Iceland 64°49N 23°46W 8 D2
Snake → U.S.A. 46°12N 119°2W 76 C4
Snake I. Australia 38°47S 146°33E 63 F4
Snake Range U.S.A. 39°0N 114°20W 76 G6
Snake River Plain U.S.A. 42°50N 114°0W 76 E7
Snåsavatnet Norway 64°12N 12°0E 8 D15
Sneek Neths. 53°2N 5°40E 15 A5
Sneem Ireland 51°50N 9°54W 10 E2
Sneeuberge S. Africa 31°46S 24°20E 56 E3
Snelling U.S.A. 37°31N 120°26W 78 H6
Sněžka Europe 50°41N 15°50E 16 C8
Snizort, L. U.K. 57°33N 6°28W 11 D2
Snøhetta Norway 62°19N 9°16E 8 E13
Snohomish U.S.A. 47°55N 122°6W 78 C4
Snoqualmie Pass U.S.A. 47°25N 121°25W 78 C5
Snoul Cambodia 12°4N 106°26E 39 F6
Snow Hill U.S.A. 38°11N 75°24W 81 F16
Snow Lake Canada 54°52N 100°3W 71 C8
Snow Mt. Calif., U.S.A. 39°23N 122°45W 78 F4
Snow Mt. Maine, U.S.A. 45°18N 70°48W 83 A14
Snow Shoe U.S.A. 41°2N 77°57W 82 E7
Snowbird L. Canada 60°45N 103°0W 71 A8
Snowdon U.K. 53°4N 4°5W 12 D3
Snowdonia △ U.K. 53°7N 3°59W 12 D4
Snowdrift = Łutselk'e Canada 62°24N 110°44W 71 A6
Snowdrift → Canada 62°24N 110°44W 71 A6
Snowflake U.S.A. 34°30N 110°5W 77 J8
Snowshoe Pk. U.S.A. 48°13N 115°41W 76 B6
Snowtown Australia 33°46S 138°14E 63 E2
Snowville U.S.A. 41°58N 112°43W 76 F7
Snowy → Australia 37°46S 148°30E 63 F4
Snowy Mt. U.S.A. 43°42N 74°23W 83 C10
Snowy Mts. Australia 36°30S 148°20E 63 F4
Snug Corner Bahamas 22°33N 73°52W 89 B5
Snyatyn Ukraine 48°27N 25°38E 17 D13
Snyder Okla., U.S.A. 34°40N 98°57W 84 D5
Snyder Tex., U.S.A. 32°44N 100°55W 84 E4
Soahanina Madag. 18°42S 44°13E 57 B7
Soalala Madag. 16°6S 45°20E 57 B8
Soaloka Madag. 18°32S 45°15E 57 B8
Soamanonga Madag. 23°52S 44°47E 57 C7
Soan → Pakistan 33°1N 71°44E 42 C4
Soanierana-Ivongo Madag. 16°55S 49°35E 57 B8
Soanindraniny Madag. 19°54S 47°14E 57 B8
Soavina Madag. 20°23S 46°56E 57 C8
Soavinandriana Madag. 19°9S 46°45E 57 B8
Sobat, Nahr → Sudan 9°22N 31°33E 51 G12
Sobhapur India 22°47N 78°17E 42 H8
Sobradinho, Represa de Brazil 9°30S 42°0W 93 E10
Sobral Brazil 3°50S 40°20W 93 D10
Soc Giang Vietnam 22°54N 106°1E 38 A6
Soc Trang Vietnam 9°37N 105°50E 39 H5
Socastee U.S.A. 33°41N 78°59W 85 E15
Soch'e = Shache China 38°20N 77°10E 32 C2
Sochi Russia 43°35N 39°40E 19 F6
Société, Îs. de la French Polynesia 17°0S 151°0W 65 J12
Society Is. = Société, Îs. de la French Polynesia 17°0S 151°0W 65 J12
Socompa, Portezuelo de Chile 24°27S 68°18W 94 A2
Socorro N. Mex., U.S.A. 34°4N 106°54W 77 J10
Socorro Tex., U.S.A. 31°39N 106°18W 84 F1
Socorro, I. Mexico 18°45N 110°58W 86 D2
Socotra Yemen 12°30N 54°0E 47 E5
Soda L. U.S.A. 35°10N 116°4W 77 J5
Soda Plains India 35°30N 79°0E 43 B8
Soda Springs U.S.A. 42°39N 111°36W 76 E8
Sodankylä Finland 67°29N 26°40E 8 C22
Soddy-Daisy U.S.A. 35°17N 85°10W 85 D12
Söderhamn Sweden 61°18N 17°10E 8 F17
Söderköping Sweden 58°31N 16°20E 9 G17
Södermanland Sweden 58°56N 16°55E 9 G17
Södertälje Sweden 59°12N 17°39E 9 G17
Sodiri Sudan 14°27N 29°0E 51 F11
Sodus U.S.A. 43°14N 77°4W 82 C7
Sodwana Bay △ S. Africa 27°35S 32°43E 57 D5
Soekmekaar = Morebeng S. Africa 23°30S 29°55E 57 C4
Soest Neths. 52°9N 5°19E 15 B5
Sofala ☐ Mozam. 19°30S 34°30E 57 B5
Sofia = Sofiya Bulgaria 42°45N 23°20E 23 C10
Sofia → Madag. 15°27S 47°23E 57 B8
Sofiya Bulgaria 42°45N 23°20E 23 C10
Sōfu-Gan Japan 29°49N 140°21E 31 K10
Sogamoso Colombia 5°43N 72°56W 92 B4
Sogār Iran 25°53N 58°6E 45 E8
Sogndalsfjøra Norway 61°14N 7°5E 8 F12
Søgne Norway 58°5N 7°48E 9 G12
Sognefjorden Norway 61°10N 5°50E 8 F11
Soh Iran 33°26N 51°27E 45 C6
Sohâg Egypt 26°33N 31°43E 51 C12
Sohagpur India 22°42N 78°12E 42 H8
Soignies Belgium 50°35N 4°5E 15 D4
Soissons France 49°25N 3°19E 20 B5
Sōja Japan 34°40N 133°45E 31 G6
Sojat India 25°55N 73°45E 42 G5
Sokal Ukraine 50°31N 24°15E 17 C13
Sokcho S. Korea 38°12N 128°36E 35 E15
Söke Turkey 37°48N 27°28E 23 F12
Sokelo Dem. Rep. of the Congo 9°55S 24°36E 55 D1
Sokhumi Georgia 43°0N 41°0E 19 F7
Soko Is. China 22°10N 113°54E 33 G10
Sokodé Togo 9°0N 1°11E 50 G6
Sokol Russia 59°30N 40°5E 18 C7
Sokółka Poland 53°25N 23°30E 17 B12
Sokołów Podlaski Poland 52°25N 22°15E 17 B12
Sokoto Nigeria 13°2N 5°16E 50 F7
Sol Iletsk Russia 51°10N 55°0E 18 D10
Solai Kenya 0°2N 36°12E 54 B4
Solan India 30°55N 77°7E 42 D7
Solana Beach U.S.A. 32°58N 117°16W 79 N9
Solander I. N.Z. 46°34S 166°54E 59 G1
Solano Phil. 16°31N 121°15E 37 A6
Solapur India 17°43N 75°56E 40 L9
Soldotna U.S.A. 60°29N 151°3W 68 C4
Soléa Cyprus 35°5N 33°4E 25 D12

Soledad Colombia 10°55N 74°46W 92 A4
Soledad U.S.A. 36°26N 121°20W 78 J5
Soledad Venezuela 8°10N 63°34W 92 B6
Solent, The U.K. 50°45N 1°25W 13 G6
Solfonntaggen Norway 60°2N 6°57E 9 F12
Solhan Turkey 38°57N 41°3E 44 B4
Soligalich Russia 59°5N 42°10E 18 C7
Soligorsk = Salihorsk Belarus 52°51N 27°27E 17 B14
Solihull U.K. 52°26N 1°47W 13 E6
Solikamsk Russia 59°38N 56°50E 18 C10
Solila Madag. 21°25S 46°37E 57 C8
Solimões = Amazonas → S. Amer. 0°5S 50°0W 93 D8
Solingen Germany 51°10N 7°5E 16 C4
Sollefteå Sweden 63°12N 17°20E 8 E17
Sóller Spain 39°46N 2°43E 24 B9
Solo → Indonesia 6°47S 112°22E 37 G15
Sologne France 47°40N 1°45E 20 C4
Solok Indonesia 0°45S 100°40E 36 E2
Sololá Guatemala 14°49N 91°10W 88 D1
Sololo Kenya 3°33N 38°39E 54 B4
Solomon, N. Fork → U.S.A. 39°29N 98°26W 80 F4
Solomon, S. Fork → U.S.A. 39°25N 99°12W 80 F4
Solomon Is. ■ Pac. Oc. 6°0S 155°0E 58 B8
Solomon Rise Pac. Oc. 1°0N 157°0E 64 G7
Solon China 46°32N 121°10E 33 B7
Solon Springs U.S.A. 46°22N 91°49W 80 B8
Solor Indonesia 8°27S 123°0E 37 F6
Solothurn Switz. 47°13N 7°32E 20 C7
Šolta Croatia 43°24N 16°15E 22 C7
Solţānābād Khorāsān, Iran 34°13N 59°58E 45 C8
Solţānābād Khorāsān, Iran 36°29N 58°5E 45 B8
Solunska Glava Macedonia 41°44N 21°31E 23 D9
Solvang U.S.A. 34°36N 120°8W 79 L6
Solvay U.S.A. 43°3N 76°13W 83 C8
Sölvesborg Sweden 56°5N 14°35E 9 H16
Solvychegodsk Russia 61°21N 46°56E 18 B8
Solway Firth U.K. 54°49N 3°35W 12 C4
Solwezi Zambia 12°11S 26°21E 55 E2
Sōma Japan 37°40N 140°50E 30 F10
Soma Turkey 39°10N 27°35E 23 E12
Somabhula Zimbabwe 19°42S 29°40E 57 B4
Somali Pen. Africa 7°0N 46°0E 48 F8
Somali Rep. ■ Africa 7°0N 47°0E 47 F4
Somalia = Somali Rep. ■ Africa 7°0N 47°0E 47 F4
Somaliland □ Somali Rep. 9°0N 46°0E 47 F4
Sombor Serbia 45°46N 19°9E 23 B8
Sombra Canada 42°43N 82°29W 82 D2
Sombrerete Mexico 23°38N 103°39W 86 C4
Sombrero Anguilla 18°37N 63°30W 89 C7
Somdari India 25°47N 72°38E 42 G5
Somers U.S.A. 48°5N 114°13W 76 B6
Somerset Ky., U.S.A. 37°5N 84°36W 81 G11
Somerset Mass., U.S.A. 41°47N 71°8W 83 E13
Somerset Pa., U.S.A. 40°1N 79°5W 82 F5
Somerset □ U.K. 51°9N 3°0W 13 F5
Somerset East S. Africa 32°42S 25°35E 56 E4
Somerset I. Canada 73°30N 93°0W 68 B10
Somerset West S. Africa 34°8S 18°50E 56 E2
Somersworth U.S.A. 43°16N 70°52W 83 C14
Somerton U.S.A. 32°36N 114°43W 77 K6
Somerville U.S.A. 40°35N 74°38W 83 F10
Someş → Romania 47°49N 22°43E 17 D12
Somme → France 50°11N 1°38E 20 A4
Somnath India 20°53N 70°22E 42 J4
Somosierra, Puerto de Spain 41°4N 3°35W 21 B4
Somosomo Fiji 16°47S 179°58W 59 a
Somosomo Str. Fiji 16°0S 180°0E 59 a
Somoto Nic. 13°28N 86°37W 88 D2
Somport, Puerto de Spain 42°48N 0°31W 20 E3
Son → India 25°42N 84°52E 43 G11
Son Ha Vietnam 15°3N 108°34E 38 E7
Son Hoa Vietnam 13°2N 108°58E 38 F7
Son La Vietnam 21°20N 103°50E 38 B4
Son Serra Spain 39°43N 3°13E 24 B10
Son Tay Vietnam 21°8N 105°30E 38 B5
Soná Panama 8°0N 81°20W 88 E3
Sonamarg India 34°18N 75°21E 43 B6
Sonamukhi India 23°18N 87°27E 43 H12
Sonar → India 24°24N 79°56E 43 G8
Sŏnch'ŏn N. Korea 39°48N 124°55E 35 E13
Sondags → S. Africa 33°44S 25°51E 56 E4
Sondar India 33°28N 75°56E 43 C6
Sønderborg Denmark 54°55N 9°49E 9 J13
Sóndrio Italy 46°10N 9°52E 20 C8
Sone Mozam. 17°23S 34°55E 55 F3
Sonepur India 20°55N 83°50E 41 J13
Song Thailand 18°28N 100°11E 38 C3
Song Cau Vietnam 13°27N 109°18E 38 F7
Song Xian China 34°12N 112°8E 34 G7
Songan Indonesia 8°13S 115°24E 37 J18
Songea Tanzania 10°40S 35°40E 55 E4
Songgang China 22°46N 113°50E 33 F10
Songhua Hu China 43°35N 126°50E 35 C14
Songhua Jiang → China 47°45N 132°30E 33 B8
Songimvelo ⌂ S. Africa 25°50S 31°2E 57 D5
Sŏngjin = Kimch'aek N. Korea 40°40N 129°10E 35 D15
Songkhla Thailand 7°13N 100°37E 39 J3
Songnim N. Korea 38°45N 125°39E 35 E13
Songo Mozam. 15°34S 32°38E 53 H6
Songo Sudan 9°47N 24°21E 51 G10
Songpan China 32°40N 103°30E 32 C5
Songwe Dem. Rep. of the Congo 3°20S 26°16E 54 C2
Songwe → Africa 9°44S 33°58E 55 D3
Sonhat India 23°29N 82°31E 43 H10
Sonid Youqi China 42°45N 112°48E 34 C7
Sonipat India 29°0N 77°5E 42 E7
Sonkach India 22°59N 76°21E 42 H7
Sonmiani Pakistan 25°25N 66°40E 42 G2
Sonmiani B. Pakistan 25°15N 66°30E 42 G2
Sono → Brazil 9°58S 48°11W 93 E9
Sonoma U.S.A. 38°18N 122°28W 78 G4
Sonora Calif., U.S.A. 37°59N 120°23W 78 H6
Sonora Tex., U.S.A. 30°34N 100°39W 84 F4
Sonora □ Mexico 29°20N 110°40W 86 B2
Sonora → Mexico 29°5N 110°55W 86 B2
Sonoran Desert U.S.A. 33°40N 113°30W 79 L12
Sonoyta Mexico 31°51N 112°50W 86 A2
Sonsonate El Salv. 13°43N 89°44W 88 D2
Soochow = Suzhou China 31°19N 120°38E 33 C7
Sooke Canada 48°13N 123°43W 78 B3
Soomaaliya = Somali Rep. ■ Africa 7°0N 47°0E 47 F4
Sop Hao Laos 20°33N 104°27E 38 B5
Sop Prap Thailand 17°53N 99°20E 38 D2
Sopi Indonesia 2°34N 128°28E 37 D7
Sopot Poland 54°27N 18°31E 17 A10
Sopron Hungary 47°45N 16°32E 17 E9
Sopur India 34°18N 74°27E 43 B6
Sør-Rondane Antarctica 72°0S 25°0E 5 D4
Sorah Pakistan 27°13N 68°56E 42 F3
Soraon India 25°37N 81°51E 43 G9
Sorel-Tracy Canada 46°0N 73°10W 72 C5
Sórgono Italy 40°1N 9°6E 22 D3
Soria Spain 41°43N 2°32W 21 B4
Soriano Uruguay 33°24S 58°19W 94 C4
Sorkh, Kuh-e Iran 35°40N 58°30E 45 C8
Soroca Moldova 48°8N 28°12E 17 D15
Sorocaba Brazil 23°31S 47°27W 95 A6
Sorochinsk Russia 52°26N 53°10E 18 D9
Soroki = Soroca Moldova 48°8N 28°12E 17 D15
Sorong Indonesia 0°55S 131°15E 37 E8
Soroni Greece 36°21N 28°1E 25 C10
Soroti Uganda 1°43N 33°35E 54 B3
Sørøya Norway 70°40N 22°30E 8 A20
Sørøysundet Norway 70°25N 23°0E 8 A20
Sorrell Australia 42°47S 147°34E 63 G4
Sorrento Italy 40°37N 14°22E 22 D6
Sorsele Sweden 65°31N 17°30E 8 D17
Sorsogon Phil. 13°0N 124°0E 37 B6
Sortavala Russia 61°42N 30°41E 8 F24
Sortland Norway 68°42N 15°25E 8 B16
Soscumica, L. Canada 50°15N 77°27W 72 B4
Sosnogorsk Russia 63°37N 53°51E 18 B9
Sosnowiec Poland 50°20N 19°10E 17 C10
Sossus Vlei Namibia 24°40S 15°23E 56 C2
Sŏsura N. Korea 42°16N 130°36E 35 C16
Sot → India 27°27N 79°37E 43 F8
Sotavento C. Verde Is. 15°0N 25°0W 50 b
Sotik Kenya 0°41S 35°7E 54 C4
Sotkamo Finland 64°8N 28°23E 8 D23
Soto la Marina Mexico 23°46N 98°13W 87 C5
Soto la Marina → Mexico 23°45N 97°45W 87 C5
Sotuta Mexico 20°36N 89°1W 87 C7
Souanké Congo 2°10N 14°3E 52 D2
Souda Greece 35°29N 24°4E 25 D6
Soudas, Ormos Greece 35°25N 24°10E 25 D6
Souderton U.S.A. 40°19N 75°19W 83 F9
Soufrière Guadeloupe 16°5N 61°40W 88 b
Soufrière St. Lucia 13°51N 61°3W 89 f
Soufrière Bay Dominica 15°13N 61°22W 89 f
Soukhouma Laos 14°38N 105°48E 38 E5
Sŏul = Seoul S. Korea 37°31N 126°58E 35 F14
Sound, The U.K. 50°20N 4°10W 13 G3
Sources, Mt. aux Lesotho 28°45S 28°50E 57 D4
Soure Brazil 0°35S 48°30W 93 D9
Souris Man., Canada 49°40N 100°20W 71 D8
Souris P.E.I., Canada 46°21N 62°15W 73 C7
Souris → N. Amer. 49°40N 99°34W 80 A4
Sousa Brazil 6°45S 38°10W 93 E11
Sousse Tunisia 35°50N 10°38E 51 A8
Sout → S. Africa 31°35S 18°24E 56 E2
South Africa ■ Africa 32°0S 23°0E 56 E3
South America 10°0S 60°0W 90 E5
South Aulatsivik I. Canada 56°45N 61°30W 73 A7
South Australia □ Australia 32°0S 139°0E 63 E2
South Australian Basin Ind. Oc. 38°0S 126°0E 64 L4
South Ayrshire □ U.K. 55°18N 4°41W 11 F4
South Baldy Pk. U.S.A. 34°6N 107°11W 77 J10
South Bass I. U.S.A. 41°39N 82°49W 82 E2
South Bend Ind., U.S.A. 41°41N 86°15W 80 E10
South Bend Wash., U.S.A. 46°40N 123°48W 78 D3
South Boston U.S.A. 36°42N 78°54W 81 G14
South Branch Canada 47°55N 59°2W 73 C8
South Brook Canada 49°26N 56°5W 73 C8
South Bruny I. Australia 43°20S 147°15E 63 G4
South C. Australia 43°39S 146°42E 58 F7
South Carolina □ U.S.A. 34°0N 81°0W 85 E14
South Charleston U.S.A. 38°22N 81°44W 81 F13
South China Sea Asia 10°0N 113°0E 36 C4
South Cumberland Is. △ Australia 20°42S 149°11E 62 J7
South Dakota □ U.S.A. 44°15N 100°0W 80 C4
South Deerfield U.S.A. 42°29N 72°37W 83 D12
South Downs U.K. 50°52N 0°25W 13 G7
South East C. Australia 43°40S 146°50E 63 G4
South East Is. Australia 34°17S 123°30E 61 F3
South Esk → U.K. 56°43N 2°31W 11 E6
South Fiji Basin Pac. Oc. 26°0S 175°0E 64 K9
South Foreland U.K. 51°8N 1°24E 13 F9
South Fork American → U.S.A. 38°57N 120°59W 78 G5
South Fork Feather → U.S.A. 39°17N 121°36W 78 F5
South Fork Grand → U.S.A. 45°43N 102°17W 80 C2
South Fork Milk → U.S.A. 48°4N 106°19W 76 B10
South Fork Republican → U.S.A. 40°3N 101°31W 80 E3
South Georgia Antarctica 54°30S 37°0W 96 G9
South Gloucestershire □ U.K. 51°32N 2°28W 13 F5
South Hadley U.S.A. 42°16N 72°35W 83 D12
South Haven U.S.A. 42°24N 86°16W 80 D10
South Henik L. Canada 61°30N 97°20W 71 A9
South Horr Kenya 2°12N 36°56E 54 B4
South I. Kenya 2°35N 36°35E 54 B4
South I. N.Z. 44°0S 170°0E 59 F3
South Indian Lake Canada 56°47N 98°56W 71 B9
South Invercargill N.Z. 46°26S 168°23E 59 G2
South Island △ Kenya 2°39N 36°35E 54 B4
South Kitui ⌂ Kenya 1°48S 38°46E 54 C4
South Knife → Canada 58°55N 94°37W 71 B10
South Koel → India 22°32N 85°14E 43 H11
South Korea ■ Asia 36°0N 128°0E 35 G15
South Lake Tahoe U.S.A. 38°57N 119°59W 78 G6
South Lanarkshire □ U.K. 55°37N 3°53W 11 F5
South Loup → U.S.A. 41°4N 98°39W 80 E4
South Luangwa △ Zambia 13°0S 31°20E 55 E3
South Magnetic Pole Antarctica 64°8S 138°8E 5 C9
South Milwaukee U.S.A. 42°55N 87°52W 80 D10
South Molton U.K. 51°1N 3°51W 13 F4
South Moose L. Canada 53°49N 100°1W 71 C8
South Nahanni → Canada 61°3N 123°21W 70 A4
South Nation → Canada 45°34N 75°6W 83 A9
South Natuna Is. = Natuna Selatan, Kepulauan Indonesia 2°45N 109°0E 36 D3
South Negril Pt. Jamaica 18°16N 78°22W 88 a
South Orkney Is. Antarctica 63°0S 45°0W 5 C18
South Ossetia □ Georgia 42°21N 44°2E 19 F7
South Pagai, I. = Pagai Selatan, Pulau Indonesia 3°0S 100°15E 36 E2
South Paris U.S.A. 44°14N 70°31W 83 B14
South Pittsburg U.S.A. 35°1N 85°42W 85 D12
South Platte → U.S.A. 41°7N 100°42W 80 E3
South Pole Antarctica 90°0S 0°0 5 E
South Porcupine Canada 48°30N 81°12W 72 C3
South Portland U.S.A. 43°38N 70°15W 81 D18
South Pt. Barbados 13°2N 59°32W 89 g
South Pt. U.S.A. 44°52N 83°19W 82 B1
South River Canada 45°52N 79°23W 72 C4
South River U.S.A. 40°27N 74°23W 83 F10
South Ronaldsay U.K. 58°48N 2°58W 11 C6
South Sandwich Is. Antarctica 57°0S 27°0W 5 B1
South Sandwich Trench Atl. Oc. 56°0S 24°0W 5 B1
South Saskatchewan → Canada 53°15N 105°5W 71 C7
South Seal → Canada 58°48N 98°8W 71 B9
South Shetland Is. Antarctica 62°0S 59°0W 5 C18
South Shields U.K. 55°0N 1°25W 12 C6
South Sioux City U.S.A. 42°28N 96°24W 80 D5
South Sister U.S.A. 44°4N 121°51W 76 D3
South Taranaki Bight N.Z. 39°40S 174°5E 59 C5
South Tasman Rise S. Ocean 48°0S 146°0E 5 A10
South Thompson → Canada 50°40N 120°20W 70 C4
South Twin I. Canada 53°7N 79°52W 72 B4
South Tyne → U.K. 54°59N 2°8W 12 C5
South Uist U.K. 57°20N 7°15W 11 D1
South Valley U.S.A. 35°1N 106°41W 77 J10
South Wellesley Is. Australia 16°58S 139°17E 62 B2
South West C. Australia 43°34S 146°3E 63 G4
South West C. N.Z. 47°17S 167°28E 59 G1
South Williamsport U.S.A. 41°13N 77°0W 82 E8
South Yorkshire □ U.K. 53°27N 1°36W 12 D6
Southampton Canada 44°30N 81°25W 82 B3
Southampton U.K. 50°54N 1°23W 13 G6
Southampton U.S.A. 40°53N 72°23W 83 F12
Southampton □ U.K. 50°54N 1°23W 13 G6
Southampton I. Canada 64°30N 84°0W 69 C11
Southaven U.S.A. 34°59N 90°0W 85 D9
Southbank Canada 54°2N 125°46W 70 C3
Southbridge N.Z. 43°48S 172°16E 59 E4
Southbridge U.S.A. 42°5N 72°2W 83 D12
Southend Canada 56°19N 103°22W 71 B8
Southend-on-Sea U.K. 51°32N 0°44E 13 F8
Southend-on-Sea □ U.K. 51°32N 0°44E 13 F8
Southern = Yuzhnyy □ Russia 44°0N 40°0E 28 E5
Southern □ Malawi 15°0S 35°0E 55 F4
Southern □ Zambia 16°20S 26°20E 55 F2
Southern Alps N.Z. 43°41S 170°11E 59 E3
Southern Cross Australia 31°12S 119°15E 61 F2
Southern Indian L. Canada 57°10N 98°30W 71 B9
Southern Lau Group Fiji 18°40S 178°40W 59 a
Southern Ocean Antarctica 62°0S 60°0E 5 C6
Southern Pines U.S.A. 35°11N 79°24W 85 D15
Southern Uplands U.K. 55°28N 3°52W 11 F5
Southington U.S.A. 41°36N 72°53W 83 E12
Southland □ N.Z. 45°30S 168°0E 59 F1
Southold U.S.A. 41°4N 72°26W 83 E12
Southport Australia 27°58S 153°25E 63 D5
Southport U.K. 53°39N 3°0W 12 D4
Southport U.S.A. 42°3N 76°49W 82 D8
Southwest △ Australia 43°8S 146°5E 63 G4
Southwest Pacific Basin Pac. Oc. 40°0S 140°0W 5 A12
Southwold U.K. 52°20N 1°41E 13 E9
Southwood △ Australia 27°48S 150°8E 63 D5
Soutpansberg S. Africa 23°0S 29°30E 57 C4
Sovetsk Kaliningrad, Russia 55°6N 21°50E 9 J19
Sovetsk Kirov, Russia 57°38N 48°53E 18 C8
Sovetskaya Gavan = Vanino Russia 48°50N 140°5E 29 E15
Soweto S. Africa 26°14S 27°52E 57 D4
Sōya-Kaikyō = La Perouse Str. Asia 45°40N 142°0E 30 B11
Sōya-Misaki Japan 45°30N 141°55E 30 B10
Soyo Angola 6°13S 12°20E 52 F2
Sozh → Belarus 51°57N 30°48E 17 B16
Spa Belgium 50°29N 5°53E 15 D5
Spain ■ Europe 39°0N 4°0W 21 B4
Spalding Australia 33°30S 138°37E 63 E2
Spalding U.K. 52°48N 0°9W 12 E7
Spanaway U.S.A. 47°6N 122°26W 78 C4
Spangler U.S.A. 40°39N 78°48W 82 F6
Spanish Canada 46°12N 82°20W 72 C3
Spanish Fork U.S.A. 40°7N 111°39W 76 F8
Spanish Town Br. Virgin Is. 17°43N 64°26W 89 e
Spanish Town Jamaica 18°0N 76°57W 88 a
Sparks U.S.A. 39°32N 119°45W 78 F7
Sparta = Sparti Greece 37°5N 22°25E 23 F10
Sparta Mich., U.S.A. 43°10N 85°42W 81 D11
Sparta N.J., U.S.A. 41°2N 74°38W 83 E10
Sparta Wis., U.S.A. 43°56N 90°49W 80 D8
Spartanburg U.S.A. 34°56N 81°57W 85 D14
Spartansburg U.S.A. 41°49N 79°41W 82 E5
Sparti Greece 37°5N 22°25E 23 F10
Spartivento, C. Calabria, Italy 37°55N 16°4E 22 F7
Spartivento, C. Sard., Italy 38°53N 8°50E 22 E3
Sparwood Canada 49°44N 114°53W 70 D6
Spassk Dalniy Russia 44°40N 132°48E 30 B6
Spatha, Akra Greece 35°42N 23°43E 25 D5
Spatsizi → Canada 57°42N 128°7W 70 B3
Spatsizi Plateau Wilderness ⌂ Canada 57°40N 128°0W 70 B3
Spean → U.K. 56°55N 4°59W 11 E4
Spearfish U.S.A. 44°30N 103°52W 80 C2
Spearman U.S.A. 36°12N 101°12W 84 C4
Speculator U.S.A. 43°30N 74°22W 83 C10
Speightstown Barbados 13°15N 59°39W 89 g
Speke Gulf Tanzania 2°20S 32°50E 54 C3
Spence Bay = Taloyoak Canada 69°32N 93°32W 68 C10
Spencer Idaho, U.S.A. 44°22N 112°11W 76 D7
Spencer Iowa, U.S.A. 43°9N 95°9W 80 D6
Spencer N.Y., U.S.A. 42°13N 76°30W 83 D8
Spencer Nebr., U.S.A. 42°53N 98°42W 80 D4
Spencer, C. Australia 35°20S 136°53E 63 F2
Spencer B. Namibia 25°30S 14°47E 56 D1
Spencer G. Australia 34°0S 137°20E 63 E2
Spencerville Canada 44°51N 75°33W 83 B9
Spences Bridge Canada 50°25N 121°20W 70 C4
Spennymoor U.K. 54°42N 1°36W 12 C6
Spenser Mts. N.Z. 42°15S 172°45E 59 E4
Sperrin Mts. U.K. 54°50N 7°0W 10 B5
Spey → U.K. 57°40N 3°6W 11 D5
Speyer Germany 49°29N 8°25E 16 D5
Spezand Pakistan 29°59N 67°0E 42 E2
Spiddle Ireland 53°15N 9°18W 10 C2
Spili Greece 35°13N 24°31E 25 D6
Spīn Būldak Afghan. 31°1N 66°25E 42 D2
Spinalonga Greece 35°18N 25°44E 25 D7
Spirit Lake U.S.A. 46°15N 122°9W 78 D4
Spirit River Canada 55°45N 118°50W 70 B5
Spiritwood Canada 53°24N 107°33W 71 C7
Spithead U.K. 50°45N 1°10W 13 G6
Spitzbergen = Svalbard Arctic 78°0N 17°0E 4 B8
Spjelkavik Norway 62°28N 6°22E 8 E12
Split Croatia 43°31N 16°26E 22 C7
Split L. Canada 56°8N 96°15W 71 B9
Split Lake Canada 56°8N 96°15W 71 B9
Spofford U.S.A. 29°10N 100°25W 84 G4
Spokane U.S.A. 47°40N 117°24W 76 C5
Spoleto Italy 42°44N 12°44E 22 C5
Spooner U.S.A. 45°50N 91°53W 80 C8
Sporyy Navolok, Mys Russia 75°50N 68°40E 28 B7
Sprague U.S.A. 47°18N 117°59W 76 C5
Spratly I. S. China Sea 8°38N 111°55E 36 C4
Spratly Is. S. China Sea 8°20N 112°0E 36 C4
Spray U.S.A. 44°50N 119°48W 76 D4
Spree → Germany 52°32N 13°12E 16 B7
Sprengisandur Iceland 64°52N 18°7W 8 D4
Spring City U.S.A. 40°11N 75°33W 83 F9
Spring Creek U.S.A. 40°44N 115°35W 76 F6
Spring Garden U.S.A. 39°52N 120°47W 78 F6
Spring Hall Barbados 13°18N 59°36W 89 g
Spring Hill U.S.A. 28°27N 82°41W 85 G13
Spring Mts. U.S.A. 36°0N 115°45W 79 J11
Spring Valley Calif., U.S.A. 32°44N 116°59W 79 N10
Spring Valley Nev., U.S.A. 36°6N 115°14W 79 J11
Springbok S. Africa 29°42S 17°54E 56 D2
Springboro U.S.A. 41°48N 80°22W 82 E4
Springdale Canada 49°30N 56°6W 73 C8
Springdale U.S.A. 36°11N 94°8W 84 C7
Springer U.S.A. 36°22N 104°36W 77 H11
Springerville U.S.A. 34°8N 109°17W 77 J9
Springfield Canada 42°50N 80°56W 82 D4
Springfield N.Z. 43°19S 171°56E 59 E3
Springfield Colo., U.S.A. 37°24N 102°37W 77 H12
Springfield Ill., U.S.A. 39°48N 89°39W 80 F9
Springfield Mass., U.S.A. 42°6N 72°35W 83 D12
Springfield Mo., U.S.A. 37°13N 93°17W 80 G7
Springfield Ohio, U.S.A. 39°55N 83°49W 81 F12
Springfield Oreg., U.S.A. 44°3N 123°1W 76 D2
Springfield Tenn., U.S.A. 36°31N 86°53W 85 C11
Springfield Vt., U.S.A. 43°18N 72°29W 83 C12
Springfontein S. Africa 30°15S 25°40E 56 E4
Springhill Canada 45°40N 64°4W 73 C7
Springhill U.S.A. 33°0N 93°28W 84 E8
Springhouse Canada 51°56N 122°7W 70 C4
Springs S. Africa 26°13S 28°25E 57 D4
Springsure Australia 24°8S 148°6E 62 C4
Springvale U.S.A. 43°28N 70°48W 83 C14
Springville Calif., U.S.A. 36°8N 118°49W 78 J8
Springville N.Y., U.S.A. 42°31N 78°40W 82 D6
Springville Utah, U.S.A. 40°10N 111°37W 76 F8
Springwater U.S.A. 42°38N 77°35W 82 D7
Spruce-Creek U.S.A. 40°36N 78°9W 82 F6
Spruce Knob-Seneca Rocks ⌂ U.S.A. 38°50N 79°30W 81 F14
Spruce Mt. U.S.A. 44°12N 72°19W 83 B12
Spur U.S.A. 33°28N 100°52W 84 E4
Spurn Hd. U.K. 53°35N 0°8E 12 D8
Spuzzum Canada 49°37N 121°23W 70 D4
Squam L. U.S.A. 43°45N 71°32W 83 C13
Squamish Canada 49°45N 123°10W 70 D4
Square Islands Canada 52°47N 55°47W 73 B8
Squires, Mt. Australia 26°14S 127°28E 61 E4
Srbija = Serbia ■ Europe 43°20N 20°0E 23 B9
Sre Ambel Cambodia 11°8N 103°46E 39 G4
Sre Khtum Cambodia 12°10N 106°52E 39 F6
Sre Umbell = Sre Ambel Cambodia 11°8N 103°46E 39 G4
Srebrenica Bos.-H. 44°6N 19°18E 23 B8
Sredinny Ra. = Sredinnyy Khrebet Russia 57°0N 160°0E 29 D16
Sredinnyy Khrebet Russia 57°0N 160°0E 29 D16
Srednekolymsk Russia 67°27N 153°40E 29 C16
Śrem Poland 52°6N 17°2E 17 B9
Sremska Mitrovica Serbia 44°59N 19°38E 23 B8
Srepok → Cambodia 13°33N 106°16E 38 F6
Sretensk Russia 52°10N 117°40E 29 D12
Sri Aman Malaysia 1°15N 111°32E 36 D4
Sri Lanka ■ Asia 7°30N 80°50E 40 R12
Srikakulam India 18°14N 83°58E 41 K13
Srinagar India 34°5N 74°50E 43 B6
Srinagarind Res. Thailand 14°35N 99°0E 38 E2
Srono Indonesia 8°24S 114°16E 37 J17
Staaten → Australia 16°24S 141°17E 62 B3
Staaten River △ Australia 16°15S 142°40E 62 B3
Stade Germany 53°35N 9°29E 16 B5
Stadskanaal Neths. 53°4N 6°55E 15 A6
Staffa U.K. 56°27N 6°21W 11 E2
Stafford U.K. 52°49N 2°7W 12 E5
Stafford U.S.A. 37°58N 98°36W 80 G4
Stafford Springs U.S.A. 41°57N 72°18W 83 E12
Staffordshire □ U.K. 52°53N 2°10W 12 E5
Staines U.K. 51°26N 0°29W 13 F7
Stakhanov Ukraine 48°35N 38°40E 19 E6
Stalida Greece 35°17N 25°25E 25 D7
Stalowa Wola Poland 50°34N 22°3E 17 C12
Stalybridge U.K. 53°28N 2°3W 12 D5
Stamford Australia 21°15S 143°46E 62 C3
Stamford U.K. 52°39N 0°29W 13 E7
Stamford Conn., U.S.A. 41°3N 73°32W 83 E1
Stamford N.Y., U.S.A. 42°25N 74°38W 83 D1
Stamford Tex., U.S.A. 32°57N 99°48W 84 E
Stampriet Namibia 24°20S 18°28E 56 C
Stamps U.S.A. 33°22N 93°30W 84 E
Standerton S. Africa 26°55S 29°7E 57 D
Standish U.S.A. 43°59N 83°57W 81 D1
Stanford S. Africa 34°26S 19°29E 56 E
Stanford U.S.A. 47°9N 110°13W 76 C
Stanger S. Africa 29°27S 31°14E 57 D
Stängselåsen = Salpausselkä Finland 61°3N 26°15E 8 F2
Stanislaus → U.S.A. 37°40N 121°14W 78 H
Stanke Dimitrov Bulgaria 42°17N 23°9E 23 C1
Stanley Australia 40°46S 145°19E 63 G
Stanley China 22°13N 114°12E 33 G1
Stanley Falk. Is. 51°40S 59°51W 96 G
Stanley U.K. 54°53N 1°41W 12 C
Stanley Idaho, U.S.A. 44°13N 114°56W 76 D
Stanley N. Dak., U.S.A. 48°19N 102°23W 80 A
Stanley N.Y., U.S.A. 42°48N 77°6W 82 D
Stanley Mission Canada 55°25N 104°33W 71 B
Stanovoy Khrebet Russia 55°0N 130°0E 29 D
Stanovoy Ra. = Stanovoy Khrebet Russia 55°0N 130°0E 29 D
Stansmore Ra. Australia 21°23S 128°33E 60 D
Stansted, London ✕ (STN) U.K. 51°54N 0°14E 13
Stanthorpe Australia 28°36S 151°59E 63
Stanton U.S.A. 32°8N 101°48W 84
Stanwood U.S.A. 48°15N 122°23W 78

Staples U.S.A. 46°21N 94°48W 80 B6
Stapleton U.S.A. 41°29N 100°31W 80 E3
Star City Canada 52°50N 104°20W 71 C8
Star Lake U.S.A. 44°10N 75°2W 83 B9
Stara Planina Bulgaria 43°15N 23°0E 23 C10
Stara Zagora Bulgaria 42°26N 25°39E 23 C11
Starachowice Poland 51°3N 21°2E 17 C11
Staraya Russa Russia 57°58N 31°23E 18 C5
Starbuck I. Kiribati 5°37S 155°55W 65 H12
Starcke △ Australia 14°56S 145°2E 62 A4
Stargard Szczeciński Poland 53°20N 15°0E 16 B8
Staritsa Russia 56°33N 34°55E 18 C5
Starke U.S.A. 29°57N 82°7W 85 G13
Starkville U.S.A. 33°28N 88°49W 85 E10
Starogard Gdański Poland 53°59N 18°30E 17 B10
Starokonstantinov = Starokonstyantyniv Ukraine 49°48N 27°10E 17 D14
Starokonstyantyniv Ukraine 49°48N 27°10E 17 D14
Start Pt. U.K. 50°13N 3°39W 13 G4
Staryy Chartoriysk Ukraine 51°15N 25°54E 17 C13
Staryy Oskol Russia 51°19N 37°55E 19 D6
State College U.S.A. 40°48N 77°52W 82 F7
Stateline U.S.A. 38°57N 119°56W 78 G7
Staten, I. = Estados, I. de Los Argentina 54°40S 64°30W 96 G4
Staten I. U.S.A. 40°35N 74°9W 83 F10
Statesboro U.S.A. 32°27N 81°47W 85 E14
Statesville U.S.A. 35°47N 80°53W 85 D14
Statia = St. Eustatius W. Indies 17°20N 63°0W 89 C7
Stauffer U.S.A. 34°45N 119°3W 79 L7
Staunton Ill., U.S.A. 39°1N 89°47W 80 F9
Staunton Va., U.S.A. 38°9N 79°4W 81 F14
Stavanger Norway 58°57N 5°40E 9 G11
Staveley N.Z. 43°40S 171°32E 59 E3
Stavelot Belgium 50°23N 5°55E 15 D5
Stavern Norway 59°0N 10°1E 9 G14
Stavoren Neths. 52°53N 5°22E 15 B5
Stavropol Russia 45°5N 42°0E 19 E7
Stavros Cyprus 35°1N 32°38E 25 D11
Stavros Greece 35°12N 24°45E 25 D6
Stavros, Akra Greece 35°26N 24°58E 25 D6
Stawell Australia 37°5S 142°47E 63 F3
Stawell → Australia 20°20S 142°55E 62 C3
Stayner Canada 44°25N 80°5W 82 B4
Stayton U.S.A. 44°48N 122°48W 76 D2
Steamboat Springs U.S.A. 40°29N 106°50W 76 F10
Steele U.S.A. 46°51N 99°55W 80 B4
Steelton U.S.A. 40°14N 76°50W 82 F8
Steen River Canada 59°40N 117°12W 70 B5
Steens Mt. U.S.A. 42°35N 118°40W 76 E4
Steenwijk Neths. 52°47N 6°7E 15 B6
Steep Pt. Australia 26°8S 113°8E 61 E1
Steep Rock Canada 51°30N 98°48W 71 C9
Stefanie L. = Chew Bahir Ethiopia 4°40N 36°50E 47 G2
Stefansson Bay Antarctica 67°20S 59°8E 5 C5
Steiermark □ Austria 47°26N 15°0E 16 E8
Steilacoom U.S.A. 47°10N 122°36W 78 C4
Steilrandberge Namibia 17°45S 13°20E 56 B1
Steinbach Canada 49°32N 96°40W 71 D9
Steinhausen Namibia 21°49S 18°20E 56 C2
Steinkjer Norway 64°1N 11°31E 8 D14
Steinkopf S. Africa 29°18S 17°43E 56 D2
Stellarton Canada 45°32N 62°30W 73 C7
Stellenbosch S. Africa 33°58S 18°50E 56 E2
Stendal Germany 52°36N 11°53E 16 B6
Steornabhaigh = Stornoway U.K. 58°13N 6°23W 11 C2
Stepanakert = Xankändi Azerbaijan 39°52N 46°49E 44 B5
Stephens Creek Australia 31°50S 141°30E 63 E3
Stephens I. Canada 54°10N 130°45W 70 C2
Stephens L. Canada 56°32N 95°0W 71 B9
Stephenville Canada 48°31N 58°35W 73 C8
Stephenville U.S.A. 32°13N 98°12W 84 E5
Steppe Asia 50°0N 50°0E 26 C7
Sterkstroom S. Africa 31°32S 26°32E 56 E4
Sterling Colo., U.S.A. 40°37N 103°13W 76 F12
Sterling Ill., U.S.A. 41°48N 89°42W 80 E9
Sterling Kans., U.S.A. 38°13N 98°12W 80 F4
Sterling City U.S.A. 31°51N 101°0W 84 F4
Sterling Heights U.S.A. 42°35N 83°2W 81 D12
Sterling Run U.S.A. 41°25N 78°12W 82 E6
Sterlitamak Russia 53°40N 56°0E 18 D10
Sternes Greece 35°30N 24°9E 25 D6
Stettin = Szczecin Poland 53°27N 14°27E 16 B8
Stettiner Haff Germany 53°47N 14°15E 16 B8
Stettler Canada 52°19N 112°40W 70 C6
Steubenville U.S.A. 40°22N 80°37W 82 F4
Stevenage U.K. 51°55N 0°13W 13 F7
Stevens Point U.S.A. 44°31N 89°34W 80 C9
Stevenson U.S.A. 45°42N 121°53W 78 E5
Stevenson → Australia 27°6S 135°33E 63 D2
Stevenson L. Canada 53°55N 96°0W 71 C9
Stevensville U.S.A. 46°30N 114°5W 76 C6
Stewart Canada 55°56N 129°57W 70 B3
Stewart U.S.A. 39°5N 119°46W 78 F7
Stewart → Canada 63°19N 139°26W 68 C6
Stewart, C. Australia 11°57S 134°56E 62 A1
Stewart, I. Chile 54°50S 71°15W 96 G2
Stewart I. N.Z. 46°58S 167°54E 59 G1
Stewarts Point U.S.A. 38°39N 123°24W 78 G3
Stewartville U.S.A. 43°51N 92°29W 80 D7
Stewiacke Canada 45°9N 63°22W 73 C7
Steynsburg S. Africa 31°15S 25°49E 56 E4
Steyr Austria 48°3N 14°25E 16 D8
Steytlerville S. Africa 33°17S 24°19E 56 E3
Stigler U.S.A. 35°15N 95°8W 84 D7
Stikine → Canada 56°40N 132°30W 70 B2
Stilfontein S. Africa 26°51S 26°50E 56 D4
Stillwater N.Z. 42°27S 171°20E 59 E3
Stillwater N.Y., U.S.A. 42°55N 73°41W 83 D11
Stillwater Okla., U.S.A. 36°7N 97°4W 84 C6
Stillwater Range U.S.A. 39°50N 118°5W 76 G4
Stillwater Res. U.S.A. 43°54N 75°3W 83 C9
Stilwell U.S.A. 35°49N 94°38W 84 D7
Stînga Nistrului □ Moldova 47°20N 29°15E 17 E15
Štip Macedonia 41°42N 22°10E 23 D10
Stirling Canada 44°18N 77°33W 82 B7
Stirling U.K. 56°8N 3°57W 11 E5
Stirling □ U.K. 56°12N 4°18W 11 E4
Stirling Ra. Australia 34°23S 118°0E 61 F2
Stirling Range △ Australia 34°26S 118°20E 61 F2
Stittsville Canada 45°15N 75°55W 83 A9
Stjernøya Norway 70°20N 22°40E 8 A20
Stjørdalshalsen Norway 63°29N 10°51E 8 E14
Stockerau Austria 48°24N 16°12E 16 D9
Stockholm Sweden 59°19N 18°4E 9 G18
Stockport U.K. 53°25N 2°9W 12 D5
Stocksbridge U.K. 53°29N 1°35W 12 D6
Stockton Calif., U.S.A. 37°58N 121°17W 78 H5
Stockton Kans., U.S.A. 39°26N 99°16W 80 F4
Stockton Mo., U.S.A. 37°42N 93°48W 80 G7
Stockton-on-Tees U.K. 54°35N 1°19W 12 C6
Stockton-on-Tees □ U.K. 54°35N 1°19W 12 C6
Stockton Plateau U.S.A. 30°30N 102°30W 84 F3
Stoeng Treng Cambodia 13°31N 105°58E 38 F5
Stoer, Pt. of U.K. 58°16N 5°23W 11 C3
Stoke-on-Trent U.K. 53°1N 2°11W 12 D5
Stoke-on-Trent □ U.K. 53°1N 2°11W 12 D5
Stokes △ Australia 33°45S 121°11E 61 F3
Stokes Pt. Australia 40°10S 143°56E 63 G3
Stokes Ra. Australia 15°50S 130°50E 60 C5
Stokksnes Iceland 64°14N 14°58W 8 D6
Stokmarknes Norway 68°34N 14°54E 8 B16
Stolac Bos.-H. 43°5N 17°59E 23 C7
Stolbovoy, Ostrov Russia 74°44N 135°14E 29 B14
Stolbtsy = Stowbtsy Belarus 53°30N 26°43E 17 B14
Stolin Belarus 51°53N 26°50E 17 C14
Stomio Greece 35°21N 23°32E 25 D5
Stone U.K. 52°55N 2°9W 12 E5
Stoneboro U.S.A. 41°20N 80°7W 82 E4
Stonehaven U.K. 56°59N 2°12W 11 E6
Stonehenge Australia 24°22S 143°17E 62 C3
Stonehenge U.K. 51°9N 1°45W 13 F6
Stonewall Canada 50°10N 97°19W 71 C9
Stony L. Man., Canada 58°51N 98°40W 71 B9
Stony L. Ont., Canada 44°30N 78°5W 82 B6
Stony Point U.S.A. 41°14N 73°59W 83 E11
Stony Pt. U.S.A. 43°50N 76°18W 83 C8
Stony Rapids Canada 59°16N 105°50W 71 B7
Stony Tunguska = Tunguska, Podkamennaya → Russia 61°50N 90°13E 29 C10
Stonyford U.S.A. 39°23N 122°33W 78 F4
Stora Lulevatten Sweden 67°10N 19°30E 8 C18
Storavan Sweden 65°45N 18°10E 8 D18
Stord Norway 59°52N 5°23E 9 G11
Store Bælt Denmark 55°20N 11°0E 9 J14
Storm B. Australia 43°10S 147°30E 63 G4
Storm Lake U.S.A. 42°39N 95°13W 80 D6
Stormberge S. Africa 31°16S 26°17E 56 E4
Stormsrivier S. Africa 33°59S 23°52E 56 E3
Stornoway U.K. 58°13N 6°23W 11 C2
Storozhinets = Storozhynets Ukraine 48°14N 25°45E 17 D13
Storozhynets Ukraine 48°14N 25°45E 17 D13
Storrs U.S.A. 41°49N 72°15W 83 E12
Storsjön Sweden 63°9N 14°30E 8 E16
Storuman Sweden 65°5N 17°10E 8 D17
Storuman, L. Sweden 65°13N 16°50E 8 D17
Stouffville Canada 43°58N 79°15W 82 C5
Stoughton Canada 49°40N 103°0W 71 D8
Stour → Dorset, U.K. 50°43N 1°47W 13 G6
Stour → Kent, U.K. 51°18N 1°22E 13 F9
Stour → Suffolk, U.K. 51°57N 1°4E 13 F9
Stourbridge U.K. 52°28N 2°8W 13 E5
Stout L. Canada 52°0N 94°40W 71 C10
Stove Pipe Wells Village U.S.A. 36°35N 117°11W 79 J9
Stow U.S.A. 41°10N 81°27W 82 E3
Stowbtsy Belarus 53°30N 26°43E 17 B14
Stowmarket U.K. 52°12N 1°0E 13 E9
Strabane U.K. 54°50N 7°27W 10 B4
Strahan Australia 42°9S 145°20E 63 G4
Stralsund Germany 54°18N 13°4E 16 A7
Strand S. Africa 34°9S 18°48E 56 E2
Stranda Møre og Romsdal, Norway 62°19N 6°58E 8 E12
Stranda Nord-Trøndelag, Norway 63°33N 10°14E 8 E14
Strangford L. U.K. 54°30N 5°37W 10 B6
Stranorlar Ireland 54°48N 7°46W 10 B4
Stranraer U.K. 54°54N 5°1W 11 G3
Strasbourg Canada 51°4N 104°55W 71 C8
Strasbourg France 48°35N 7°42E 20 B7
Strasburg U.S.A. 46°8N 100°10W 80 B3
Stratford Canada 43°23N 81°0W 82 C4
Stratford N.Z. 39°20S 174°19E 59 C5
Stratford Calif., U.S.A. 36°11N 119°49W 78 J7
Stratford Conn., U.S.A. 41°12N 73°8W 83 E11
Stratford Tex., U.S.A. 36°20N 102°4W 84 C3
Stratford-upon-Avon U.K. 52°12N 1°42W 13 E6
Strath Spey U.K. 57°9N 3°49W 11 D5
Strathalbyn Australia 35°13S 138°53E 63 F2
Strathaven U.K. 55°40N 4°5W 11 F4
Strathcona ⌂ Canada 49°38N 125°40W 70 D3
Strathmore Canada 51°5N 113°18W 70 C6
Strathmore U.K. 56°37N 3°7W 11 E5
Strathmore U.S.A. 36°9N 119°4W 78 J7
Strathnaver Canada 53°20N 122°33W 70 C4
Strathpeffer U.K. 57°35N 4°32W 11 D4
Strathroy Canada 42°58N 81°38W 82 D3
Strathy Pt. U.K. 58°36N 4°1W 11 C4
Strattanville U.S.A. 41°12N 79°19W 82 E5
Stratton U.S.A. 45°8N 70°26W 83 A14
Stratton Mt. U.S.A. 43°4N 72°55W 83 C12
Straubing Germany 48°52N 12°34E 16 D7
Straumnes Iceland 66°26N 23°8W 8 C2
Strawberry → U.S.A. 40°10N 110°24W 76 F8
Streaky B. Australia 32°48S 134°13E 63 E1
Streaky Bay Australia 32°51S 134°18E 63 E1
Streator U.S.A. 41°8N 88°50W 80 E9
Streetsboro U.S.A. 41°14N 81°21W 82 E3
Streetsville Canada 43°35N 79°42W 82 C5
Strelka Russia 58°5N 93°3E 29 D10
Streng → Cambodia 13°12N 103°37E 38 F4
Streymoy Færoe Is. 62°8N 7°5W 8 E9
Strezhevoy Russia 60°42N 77°34E 28 C8
Strimonas → Greece 40°46N 23°51E 23 D10
Strokestown Ireland 53°46N 8°7W 10 C3
Stroma U.K. 58°41N 3°7W 11 C5
Strómboli Italy 38°47N 15°13E 22 E6
Stromeferry U.K. 57°21N 5°33W 11 D3
Stromness U.K. 58°58N 3°17W 11 C5
Stromsburg U.S.A. 41°7N 97°36W 80 E5
Strömstad Sweden 58°56N 11°10E 9 G14
Strömsund Sweden 63°51N 15°33E 8 E16
Strongsville U.S.A. 41°19N 81°50W 82 E3
Stronsay U.K. 59°7N 2°35W 11 B6
Stroud U.K. 51°45N 2°13W 13 F5
Stroud Road Australia 32°18S 151°57E 63 E5
Stroudsburg U.S.A. 40°59N 75°12W 83 F9
Stroumbi Cyprus 34°53N 32°29E 25 E11
Struer Denmark 56°30N 8°35E 9 H13
Strugi Krasnyye Russia 58°21N 29°1E 9 G23
Strumica Macedonia 41°28N 22°41E 23 D10
Struthers Canada 48°41N 85°51W 72 C2
Struthers U.S.A. 41°4N 80°39W 82 E4
Stryker U.S.A. 48°41N 114°46W 76 B6
Stryy Ukraine 49°16N 23°48E 17 D12
Strzelecki Cr. → Australia 29°37S 139°59E 63 D2
Strzelecki Desert Australia 29°30S 140°0E 63 D3
Stuart Fla., U.S.A. 27°12N 80°15W 85 H14
Stuart Nebr., U.S.A. 42°36N 99°8W 80 D4
Stuart → Canada 54°0N 123°35W 70 C4
Stuart Bluff Ra. Australia 22°50S 131°52E 60 D5
Stuart L. Canada 54°30N 124°30W 70 C4
Stuart Ra. Australia 29°10S 134°56E 63 D1
Stull L. Canada 54°24N 92°34W 72 B1
Stung Treng = Stoeng Treng Cambodia 13°31N 105°58E 38 F5
Stupart → Canada 56°0N 93°25W 72 A1
Sturgeon B. Canada 52°0N 97°50W 71 C9
Sturgeon Bay U.S.A. 44°50N 87°23W 80 C10
Sturgeon Falls Canada 46°25N 79°57W 72 C4
Sturgeon L. Alta., Canada 55°6N 117°32W 70 B5
Sturgeon L. Ont., Canada 50°0N 90°45W 72 C1
Sturgeon L. Ont., Canada 44°28N 78°43W 82 B6
Sturgis Canada 51°56N 102°36W 71 C8
Sturgis Mich., U.S.A. 41°48N 85°25W 81 E11
Sturgis S. Dak., U.S.A. 44°25N 103°31W 80 C2
Sturt △ Australia 27°17S 141°37E 63 D3
Sturt Cr. → Australia 19°8S 127°50E 60 C4
Sturt Stony Desert Australia 28°30S 141°0E 63 D3
Stutterheim S. Africa 32°33S 27°28E 56 E4
Stuttgart Germany 48°48N 9°11E 16 D5
Stuttgart U.S.A. 34°30N 91°33W 84 D9
Stuyvesant U.S.A. 42°23N 73°45W 83 D11
Stykkishólmur Iceland 65°2N 22°40W 8 D2
Styria = Steiermark □ Austria 47°26N 15°0E 16 E8
Su Xian = Suzhou China 33°41N 116°59E 34 H9
Suakin Sudan 19°8N 37°20E 51 E13
Suan N. Korea 38°42N 126°22E 35 E14
Suar India 29°2N 79°3E 43 E8
Subang Indonesia 6°34S 107°45E 37 G12
Subansiri → India 26°48N 93°50E 41 F18
Subarnarekha → India 22°34N 87°24E 43 H12
Subayhah Si. Arabia 30°2N 38°50E 44 D3
Subi Indonesia 2°58N 108°50E 36 D3
Subotica Serbia 46°6N 19°39E 23 A8
Suceava Romania 47°38N 26°16E 17 E14
Suchan = Partizansk Russia 43°8N 133°9E 30 C6
Suchil Mexico 23°38N 103°55W 86 C4
Suchitoto El Salv. 13°56N 89°0W 88 D2
Suchou = Suzhou China 31°19N 120°38E 33 C7
Süchow = Xuzhou China 34°18N 117°10E 35 G9
Suck → Ireland 53°17N 8°3W 10 C3
Sucre Bolivia 19°0S 65°15W 92 G5
Sucuriú → Brazil 20°47S 51°38W 93 H8
Sud, Pte. du Canada 49°3N 62°14W 73 C7
Sud-Kivu □ Dem. Rep. of the Congo 3°0S 28°30E 54 C2
Sud-Ouest, Pte. Canada 49°23N 63°36W 73 C7
Sud Ouest, Pte. Mauritius 20°28S 57°18E 53 d
Sudan U.S.A. 34°4N 102°31W 84 D3
Sudan ■ Africa 15°0N 30°0E 51 E11
Sudbury Canada 46°30N 81°0W 72 C3
Sudbury U.K. 52°2N 0°45E 13 E8
Sûdd Sudan 8°20N 30°0E 51 G12
Sudeten Mts. = Sudety Europe 50°20N 16°45E 17 C9
Sudety Europe 50°20N 16°45E 17 C9
Suðuroy Færoe Is. 61°32N 6°50W 8 F9
Sudi Tanzania 10°11S 39°57E 55 E4
Sudirman, Pegunungan Indonesia 4°30S 137°0E 37 E9
Sudong, Pulau Singapore 1°13N 103°44E 39 d
Sueca Spain 39°12N 0°21W 21 C5
Suemez I. U.S.A. 55°15N 133°20W 70 B2
Suez = El Suweis Egypt 29°58N 32°31E 51 C12
Suez, G. of = Suweis, Khalîg el Egypt 28°40N 33°0E 51 C12
Suez Canal = Suweis, Qanâ es Egypt 31°0N 32°20E 51 B12
Suffield Canada 50°12N 111°10W 70 C6
Suffolk U.S.A. 36°44N 76°35W 81 G15
Suffolk □ U.K. 52°16N 1°0E 13 E9
Sugar Grove U.S.A. 41°59N 79°20W 82 E5
Sugarive → India 26°16N 86°24E 43 F12
Sugluk = Salluit Canada 62°14N 75°38W 69 C12
Şuḩār Oman 24°20N 56°40E 45 E8
Sühbaatar □ Mongolia 45°30N 114°0E 34 B8
Suhl Germany 50°36N 10°42E 16 C6
Sui Pakistan 28°37N 69°19E 42 E3
Sui Xian China 34°25N 115°2E 34 G8
Suide China 37°30N 110°12E 34 F6
Suifenhe China 44°25N 131°10E 35 B16
Suihua China 46°32N 126°55E 33 B7
Suining Jiangsu, China 33°56N 117°58E 35 H9
Suining Sichuan, China 30°26N 105°35E 32 C5
Suiping China 33°10N 113°59E 34 H7
Suir → Ireland 52°16N 7°9W 10 D4
Suisse = Switzerland ■ Europe 46°30N 8°0E 20 C8
Suisun City U.S.A. 38°15N 122°2W 78 G4
Suiyang China 44°30N 130°56E 35 B16
Suizhong China 40°21N 120°20E 35 D11
Sujangarh India 27°42N 74°31E 42 F6
Sukabumi Indonesia 6°56S 106°50E 37 G12
Sukadana Indonesia 1°10S 110°0E 36 E3
Sukagawa Japan 37°17N 140°23E 31 F10
Sukaraja Indonesia 2°28S 110°25E 36 E4
Sukawati Indonesia 8°35S 115°17E 37 K18
Sukch'ŏn N. Korea 39°22N 125°35E 35 E13
Sukhona → Russia 61°15N 46°39E 18 C6
Sukhothai Thailand 17°1N 99°49E 38 D2
Sukhumi = Sokhumi Georgia 43°0N 41°0E 19 F7
Sukkur Pakistan 27°42N 68°54E 42 F3
Sukkur Barrage Pakistan 27°40N 68°50E 42 F3
Sukri → India 25°4N 71°43E 42 G4
Sukumo Japan 32°56N 132°44E 31 H6
Sukunka → Canada 55°45N 121°15W 70 B4
Sula, Kepulauan Indonesia 1°45S 125°0E 37 E7
Sulaco → Honduras 15°2N 87°44W 88 C2
Sulaiman Range Pakistan 30°30N 69°50E 42 D3
Sūlār Iran 31°53N 51°54E 45 D6
Sulawesi Barat □ Indonesia 3°0S 119°0E 37 E5
Sulawesi Sea = Celebes Sea Indonesia 3°0N 123°0E 37 D6
Sulawesi Selatan □ Indonesia 2°30S 120°0E 37 E6
Sulawesi Tengah □ Indonesia 1°30S 121°0E 37 E6
Sulawesi Tenggara □ Indonesia 3°50S 122°0E 37 E6
Sulawesi Utara □ Indonesia 1°0N 124°0E 37 D6
Sulima S. Leone 6°58N 11°32W 50 G3
Sulina Romania 45°10N 29°40E 17 F15
Sulitjelma Norway 67°9N 16°3E 8 C17
Sullana Peru 4°52S 80°39W 92 D2
Sullivan Ill., U.S.A. 39°36N 88°37W 80 F9
Sullivan Ind., U.S.A. 39°6N 87°24W 80 F10
Sullivan Mo., U.S.A. 38°13N 91°10W 80 F8
Sullivan Bay Canada 50°55N 126°50W 70 C3
Sullivan I. = Lanbi Kyun Burma 10°50N 98°20E 39 G2
Sullom Voe U.K. 60°27N 1°20W 11 A7
Sulphur La., U.S.A. 30°14N 93°23W 84 F8
Sulphur Okla., U.S.A. 34°31N 96°58W 84 D6
Sulphur Pt. Canada 60°56N 114°48W 70 A6
Sulphur Springs U.S.A. 33°8N 95°36W 84 E7
Sultan Canada 47°36N 82°47W 72 C3
Sultan U.S.A. 47°52N 121°49W 78 C5
Sultan Hamud Kenya 2°1S 37°22E 54 C4
Sultanpur Mad. P., India 23°9N 77°56E 42 H8
Sultanpur Punjab, India 31°13N 75°11E 42 D6
Sultanpur Ut. P., India 26°18N 82°4E 43 F10
Sulu Arch. Phil. 6°0N 121°0E 37 C6
Sulu Sea E. Indies 8°0N 120°0E 37 C6
Suluq Libya 31°44N 20°14E 51 B10
Sulzberger Ice Shelf Antarctica 78°0S 150°0W 5 E13
Sumalata Indonesia 1°0N 122°31E 37 D6
Sumampa Argentina 29°25S 63°29W 94 B3
Sumatera Indonesia 0°40N 100°20E 36 D2
Sumatera Barat □ Indonesia 1°0S 101°0E 36 E2
Sumatera Utara □ Indonesia 2°30N 98°0E 36 D1
Sumatra = Sumatera Indonesia 0°40N 100°20E 36 D2
Sumba Indonesia 9°45S 119°35E 37 F5
Sumba, Selat Indonesia 9°0S 118°40E 37 F5
Sumbawa Indonesia 8°26S 117°30E 36 F5
Sumbawa Besar Indonesia 8°30S 117°26E 36 F5
Sumbawanga □ Tanzania 8°0S 31°30E 52 F6
Sumbe Angola 11°10S 13°48E 52 G2
Sumbu △ Zambia 8°43S 30°22E 55 D3
Sumburgh Hd. U.K. 59°52N 1°17W 11 B7
Sumdeo India 31°26N 78°44E 43 D8
Sumdo China 35°6N 78°41E 43 B8
Sumedang Indonesia 6°52S 107°55E 37 G12
Šumen = Shumen Bulgaria 43°18N 26°55E 23 C12
Sumenep Indonesia 7°1S 113°52E 37 G15
Sumgait = Sumqayıt Azerbaijan 40°34N 49°38E 19 F8
Summer L. U.S.A. 42°50N 120°45W 76 E3
Summerland Canada 49°32N 119°41W 70 D5
Summerside Canada 46°24N 63°47W 73 C7
Summersville U.S.A. 38°17N 80°51W 81 F13
Summerville Ga., U.S.A. 34°29N 85°21W 85 D12
Summerville S.C., U.S.A. 33°1N 80°11W 85 E14
Summit Lake Canada 54°20N 122°40W 70 C4
Summit Peak U.S.A. 37°21N 106°42W 77 H10
Sumner Iowa, U.S.A. 42°51N 92°6W 80 D7
Sumner Wash., U.S.A. 47°12N 122°14W 78 C4
Sumoto Japan 34°21N 134°54E 31 G7
Šumperk Czech Rep. 49°59N 16°59E 17 D9
Sumqayıt Azerbaijan 40°34N 49°38E 19 F8
Sumter U.S.A. 33°55N 80°21W 85 E14
Sumy Ukraine 50°57N 34°50E 19 D5
Sun City S. Africa 25°17S 27°3E 56 D4
Sun City Ariz., U.S.A. 33°35N 112°16W 77 K7
Sun City Calif., U.S.A. 33°42N 117°11W 79 M9
Sun City Center U.S.A. 27°43N 82°21W 85 H13
Sun Lakes U.S.A. 33°10N 111°52W 77 K8
Sun Valley U.S.A. 43°42N 114°21W 76 E6
Sunagawa Japan 43°29N 141°55E 30 C10
Sunan N. Korea 39°15N 125°40E 35 E13
Sunart, L. U.K. 56°42N 5°43W 11 E3
Sunburst U.S.A. 48°53N 111°55W 76 B8
Sunbury Australia 37°35S 144°44E 63 F3
Sunbury U.S.A. 40°52N 76°48W 83 F8
Sunchales Argentina 30°58S 61°35W 94 C3
Suncheon S. Korea 34°52N 127°31E 35 G14
Suncho Corral Argentina 27°55S 63°27W 94 B3
Sunch'on N. Korea 39°25N 125°56E 35 E13
Suncook U.S.A. 43°8N 71°27W 83 C13
Sunda, Selat Indonesia 6°20S 105°30E 36 F3
Sunda Is. Indonesia 5°0S 105°0E 64 H2
Sunda Str. = Sunda, Selat Indonesia 6°20S 105°30E 36 F3
Sunda Trench = Java Trench Ind. Oc. 9°0S 105°0E 36 F3
Sundance Canada 56°32N 94°4W 71 B10
Sundance U.S.A. 44°24N 104°23W 76 D11
Sundar Nagar India 31°32N 76°53E 42 D7
Sundarbans Asia 22°0N 89°0E 41 J16
Sundarbans △ India 22°0N 88°45E 43 J13
Sundargarh India 22°4N 84°5E 41 H14
Sundays = Sondags → S. Africa 33°44S 25°51E 56 E4
Sunderland Canada 44°16N 79°4W 82 B5
Sunderland U.K. 54°55N 1°23W 12 C6
Sundown △ Australia 28°49S 151°38E 63 D5
Sundre Canada 51°49N 114°38W 70 C6
Sundsvall Sweden 62°23N 17°17E 8 E17
Sung Hei Vietnam 10°20N 106°2E 39 G6
Sungai Acheh Malaysia 5°8N 100°30E 39 c
Sungai Kolok Thailand 6°2N 101°58E 39 J3
Sungai Lembing Malaysia 3°55N 103°3E 39 L4
Sungai Petani Malaysia 5°37N 100°30E 39 K3
Sungaigerong Indonesia 2°59S 104°52E 36 E2
Sungailiat Indonesia 1°51S 106°8E 36 E3
Sungaipenuh Indonesia 2°1S 101°20E 36 E2
Sungari = Songhua Jiang → China 47°45N 132°30E 33 B8
Sunghua Chiang = Songhua Jiang → China 47°45N 132°30E 33 B8
Sunland Park U.S.A. 31°50N 106°40W 77 L10
Sunndalsøra Norway 62°40N 8°33E 8 E13
Sunnyside U.S.A. 46°20N 120°0W 76 C4
Sunnyvale U.S.A. 37°23N 122°2W 78 H4
Sunrise Manor U.S.A. 36°12N 115°4W 79 J11
Suntar Russia 62°15N 117°30E 29 C12
Suomenselkä Finland 62°52N 24°0E 8 E21
Suomi = Finland ■ Europe 63°0N 27°0E 8 E22
Suomussalmi Finland 64°54N 29°10E 8 D23
Suoyarvi Russia 62°3N 32°20E 18 B5
Supai U.S.A. 36°15N 112°41W 77 H7
Supaul India 26°10N 86°40E 43 F12
Superior Ariz., U.S.A. 33°18N 111°6W 77 K8
Superior Mont., U.S.A. 47°12N 114°53W 76 C6
Superior Nebr., U.S.A. 40°1N 98°4W 80 E4
Superior Wis., U.S.A. 46°44N 92°6W 80 B7
Superior, L. N. Amer. 47°0N 87°0W 72 C2
Suphan Buri Thailand 14°14N 100°10E 38 E3
Suphan Dağı Turkey 38°54N 42°48E 44 B4
Supiori Indonesia 1°0S 136°0E 37 E9
Supung Shuiku China 40°35N 124°50E 35 D13
Sūq Suwayq Si. Arabia 24°23N 38°27E 44 E3
Suqian China 33°54N 118°8E 35 H10
Suquṭra = Socotra Yemen 12°30N 54°0E 47 E5
Sūr Lebanon 33°19N 35°16E 46 B4
Şūr Oman 22°34N 59°32E 47 C6
Sur, Pt. U.S.A. 36°18N 121°54W 78 J5
Sura → Russia 56°6N 46°0E 18 C8
Surab Pakistan 28°25N 66°15E 42 E2
Surabaja = Surabaya Indonesia 7°17S 112°45E 36 F4
Surabaya Indonesia 7°17S 112°45E 36 F4
Surakarta Indonesia 7°35S 110°48E 36 F4
Surat Australia 27°10S 149°6E 63 D4
Surat India 21°12N 72°55E 40 J8
Surat Thani Thailand 9°6N 99°20E 39 H2
Suratgarh India 29°18N 73°55E 42 E5
Surendranagar India 22°45N 71°40E 42 H4
Surf U.S.A. 34°41N 120°36W 79 L6
Surfers Paradise Australia 28°0S 153°25E 63 D5
Surgut Russia 61°14N 73°20E 28 C8

Suriapet India 17°10N 79°40E 40 L11
Surigao Phil. 9°47N 125°29E 37 C7
Surin Thailand 14°50N 103°34E 38 E4
Surin Nua, Ko Thailand 9°30N 97°55E 39 H1
Surinam = Suriname ■ S. Amer. 4°0N 56°0W 93 C7
Suriname ■ S. Amer. 4°0N 56°0W 93 C7
Suriname → Suriname 5°50N 55°15W 93 B7
Sūrmaq Iran 31°3N 52°48E 45 D7
Surrey Canada 49°7N 122°45W 78 A4
Surrey □ U.K. 51°15N 0°31W 13 F7
Sursand India 26°39N 85°43E 43 F11
Sursar → India 26°14N 87°3E 43 F12
Surt Libya 31°11N 16°39E 51 B9
Surt, Khalīj Libya 31°40N 18°30E 51 B9
Surtanahu Pakistan 26°22N 70°0E 42 F4
Surtsey Iceland 63°20N 20°30W 8 E3
Suruga-Wan Japan 34°45N 138°30E 31 G9
Susaki Japan 33°22N 133°17E 31 H6
Sūsangerd Iran 31°35N 48°6E 45 D6
Susanville U.S.A. 40°25N 120°39W 76 F3
Susner India 23°57N 76°5E 42 H7
Susquehanna U.S.A. 41°57N 75°36W 83 E9
Susquehanna → U.S.A. 39°33N 76°5W 83 G8
Susques Argentina 23°35S 66°25W 94 A2
Sussex Canada 45°45N 65°37W 73 C6
Sussex U.S.A. 41°13N 74°37W 83 E10
Sussex, E. □ U.K. 51°0N 0°20E 13 G8
Sussex, W. □ U.K. 51°0N 0°30W 13 G7
Sustut → Canada 56°20N 127°30W 70 B3
Susuman Russia 62°47N 148°10E 29 C15
Susunu Indonesia 3°7S 133°39E 37 E8
Susurluk Turkey 39°54N 28°8E 23 E13
Sutherland S. Africa 32°24S 20°40E 56 E3
Sutherland U.K. 58°12N 4°50W 11 C4
Sutherland U.S.A. 41°10N 101°8W 80 E3
Sutherland Falls N.Z. 44°48S 167°46E 59 F1
Sutherlin U.S.A. 43°23N 123°19W 76 E2
Suthri India 23°3N 68°55E 42 H3
Sutlej → Pakistan 29°23N 71°3E 42 E4
Sutter U.S.A. 39°10N 121°45W 78 F5
Sutter Buttes U.S.A. 39°12N 121°49W 78 F5
Sutter Creek U.S.A. 38°24N 120°48W 78 G6
Sutton Canada 45°6N 72°37W 83 A12
Sutton Nebr., U.S.A. 40°36N 97°52W 80 E5
Sutton W. Va., U.S.A. 38°40N 80°43W 81 F13
Sutton → Canada 55°15N 83°45W 72 A3
Sutton Coldfield U.K. 52°35N 1°49W 13 E6
Sutton in Ashfield U.K. 53°8N 1°16W 12 D6
Sutton L. Canada 54°15N 84°42W 72 B3
Suttor → Australia 21°36S 147°2E 62 C4
Suttsu Japan 42°48N 140°14E 30 C10
Suva Fiji 18°6S 178°30E 59 a
Suva Planina Serbia 43°10N 22°5E 23 C10
Suvorov Is. = Suwarrow Is. Cook Is. 13°15S 163°5W 65 J11
Suwałki Poland 54°8N 22°59E 17 A12
Suwana Indonesia 8°44S 115°36E 37 K18
Suwannaphum Thailand 15°33N 103°47E 38 E4
Suwannee → U.S.A. 29°17N 83°10W 85 G13
Suwanose-Jima Japan 29°38N 129°43E 31 K4
Suwarrow Is. Cook Is. 13°15S 163°5W 65 J11
Suwayq aş Şuqban Iraq 31°32N 46°7E 44 D5
Suweis, Khalîg el Egypt 28°40N 33°0E 51 C12
Suweis, Qanâ es Egypt 31°0N 32°20E 51 B12
Suwon S. Korea 37°17N 127°1E 35 F14
Suzdal Russia 56°29N 40°26E 18 C7
Suzhou Anhui, China 33°41N 116°59E 34 H9
Suzhou Jiangsu, China 31°19N 120°38E 33 C7
Suzu Japan 37°25N 137°17E 31 F8
Suzu-Misaki Japan 37°31N 137°21E 31 F8
Suzuka Japan 34°55N 136°36E 31 G8
Svalbard Arctic 78°0N 17°0E 4 B8
Svalbard Radio = Longyearbyen Svalbard 78°13N 15°40E 4 B8
Svappavaara Sweden 67°40N 21°3E 8 C19
Svartisen Norway 66°40N 13°59E 8 C15
Svay Chek Cambodia 13°48N 102°58E 38 F4
Svay Rieng Cambodia 11°9N 105°45E 39 G5
Svealand □ Sweden 60°20N 15°0E 9 F16
Sveg Sweden 62°2N 14°21E 8 E16
Svendborg Denmark 55°4N 10°35E 9 J14
Sverdrup Chan. Canada 79°56N 96°25W 69 B10
Sverdrup Is. Canada 79°0N 97°0W 69 B10
Sverige = Sweden ■ Europe 57°0N 15°0E 9 H16
Svetlaya Russia 46°33N 138°18E 30 A9
Svetlogorsk = Svyetlahorsk Belarus 52°38N 29°46E 17 B15
Svir → Russia 60°30N 32°48E 18 B5
Svishtov Bulgaria 43°36N 25°23E 23 C11
Svislach Belarus 53°3N 24°2E 17 B13
Svizzera = Switzerland ■ Europe 46°30N 8°0E 20 C8
Svobodnyy Russia 51°20N 128°0E 29 D13
Svolvær Norway 68°15N 14°34E 8 B16
Svyetlahorsk Belarus 52°38N 29°46E 17 B15
Swabian Alps = Schwäbische Alb Germany 48°20N 9°30E 16 D5
Swaffham U.K. 52°39N 0°42E 13 E8
Swains I. Amer. Samoa 11°11S 171°4W 65 J11
Swainsboro U.S.A. 32°36N 82°20W 85 E13
Swakop → Namibia 22°38S 14°36E 56 C2
Swakopmund Namibia 22°37S 14°30E 56 C1
Swale → U.K. 54°5N 1°20W 12 C6
Swan → Australia 32°3S 115°45E 61 F2
Swan → Canada 52°30N 100°45W 71 C8
Swan Hill Australia 35°20S 143°33E 63 F3
Swan Hills Canada 54°43N 115°24W 70 C5
Swan Is. = Santanilla, Is. Honduras 17°22N 83°57W 88 C3
Swan L. Canada 52°30N 100°40W 71 C8
Swan Ra. U.S.A. 48°0N 113°45W 76 C7
Swan River Canada 52°10N 101°16W 71 C8
Swanage U.K. 50°36N 1°58W 13 G6
Swansea Australia 42°8S 148°4E 63 G4
Swansea Canada 43°38N 79°28W 82 C5
Swansea U.K. 51°37N 3°57W 13 F4
Swansea □ U.K. 51°38N 4°3W 13 F3
Swar → Pakistan 34°40N 72°5E 43 B5
Swartberge S. Africa 33°20S 22°0E 56 E3
Swartmodder S. Africa 28°1S 20°32E 56 D3
Swartnossob → Namibia 23°8S 18°42E 56 C2
Swartruggens S. Africa 25°39S 26°42E 56 D4
Swastika Canada 48°7N 80°6W 72 C3
Swatow = Shantou China 23°18N 116°40E 33 D6
Swaziland ■ Africa 26°30S 31°30E 57 D5
Sweden ■ Europe 57°0N 15°0E 9 H16
Sweet Grass U.S.A. 48°59N 111°58W 76 B8
Sweet Home U.S.A. 44°24N 122°44W 76 D2
Sweetwater Nev., U.S.A. 38°27N 119°9W 78 G7
Sweetwater Tenn., U.S.A. 35°36N 84°28W 85 D12
Sweetwater Tex., U.S.A. 32°28N 100°25W 84 E4
Sweetwater → U.S.A. 42°31N 107°2W 76 E10
Swellendam S. Africa 34°1S 20°26E 56 E3
Świdnica Poland 50°50N 16°30E 17 C9
Świdnik Poland 51°13N 22°39E 17 C12
Świebodzin Poland 52°15N 15°31E 16 B8
Świecie Poland 53°25N 18°30E 17 B10
Swift Current Canada 50°20N 107°45W 71 C7
Swiftcurrent → Canada 50°38N 107°44W 71 C7
Swilly, L. Ireland 55°12N 7°33W 10 A4
Swindon U.K. 51°34N 1°46W 13 F6
Swindon □ U.K. 51°34N 1°46W 13 F6
Swinemünde = Świnoujście Poland 53°54N 14°16E 16 B8
Swinford Ireland 53°57N 8°58W 10 C3
Świnoujście Poland 53°54N 14°16E 16 B8
Switzerland ■ Europe 46°30N 8°0E 20 C8
Swords Ireland 53°28N 6°13W 10 C5
Swoyerville U.S.A. 41°18N 75°53W 83 E9
Sydenham → Canada 42°33N 82°25W 82 D2
Sydney Australia 33°52S 151°12E 63 E5
Sydney Canada 46°7N 60°7W 73 C7
Sydney L. Canada 50°41N 94°25W 71 C10
Sydney Mines Canada 46°18N 60°15W 73 C7
Sydprøven = Alluitsup Paa Greenland 60°30N 45°35W 4 C5
Sydra, G. of = Surt, Khalīj Libya 31°40N 18°30E 51 B9
Sykesville U.S.A. 41°3N 78°50W 82 E6
Syktyvkar Russia 61°45N 50°40E 18 B9
Sylacauga U.S.A. 33°10N 86°15W 85 E11
Sylarna Sweden 63°2N 12°13E 8 E15
Sylhet Bangla. 24°54N 91°52E 41 G17
Sylhet □ Bangla. 24°50N 91°50E 41 G17
Sylt Germany 54°54N 8°22E 16 A5
Sylvan Beach U.S.A. 43°12N 75°44W 83 C9
Sylvan Lake Canada 52°20N 114°3W 70 C6
Sylvania Ga., U.S.A. 32°45N 81°38W 85 E14
Sylvania Ohio, U.S.A. 41°43N 83°42W 81 E12
Sylvester U.S.A. 31°32N 83°50W 85 F13
Sym Russia 60°20N 88°18E 28 C9
Synnot Ra. Australia 16°30S 125°20E 60 C4
Syowa Antarctica 68°50S 12°0E 5 C5
Syracuse Kans., U.S.A. 37°59N 101°45W 80 G3
Syracuse N.Y., U.S.A. 43°3N 76°9W 83 C8
Syracuse Nebr., U.S.A. 40°39N 96°11W 80 E5
Syrdarya → Kazakhstan 46°3N 61°0E 28 E7
Syria ■ Asia 35°0N 38°0E 44 C3
Syrian Desert = Shām, Bādiyat ash Asia 32°0N 40°0E 44 C3
Syros Greece 37°28N 24°57E 23 F11
Syzran Russia 53°12N 48°30E 18 D8
Szczecin Poland 53°27N 14°27E 16 B8
Szczecinek Poland 53°43N 16°41E 17 B9
Szczeciński, Zalew = Stettiner Haff Germany 53°47N 14°15E 16 B8
Szczytno Poland 53°33N 21°0E 17 B11
Szechwan = Sichuan □ China 30°30N 103°0E 32 C5
Szeged Hungary 46°16N 20°10E 17 E11
Székesfehérvár Hungary 47°15N 18°25E 17 E10
Szekszárd Hungary 46°22N 18°42E 17 E10
Szentes Hungary 46°39N 20°21E 17 E11
Szolnok Hungary 47°10N 20°15E 17 E11
Szombathely Hungary 47°14N 16°38E 17 E9

T

Ta Khli Khok Thailand 15°18N 100°20E 38 E3
Ta Lai Vietnam 11°24N 107°23E 39 G6
Tabacal Argentina 23°15S 64°15W 94 A3
Tabaco Phil. 13°22N 123°44E 37 B6
Ţābah Si. Arabia 26°55N 42°38E 44 E4
Tabanan Indonesia 8°32S 115°8E 37 K18
Ţabas Khorāsān, Iran 32°48N 60°12E 45 C9
Ţabas Yazd, Iran 33°35N 56°55E 45 C8
Tabasará, Serranía de Panama 8°35N 81°40W 88 E3
Tabasco □ Mexico 18°0N 92°40W 87 D6
Tābāsīn Iran 31°12N 57°54E 45 D8
Tabatinga, Serra da Brazil 10°30S 44°0W 93 F10
Taber Canada 49°47N 112°8W 70 D6
Taberg U.S.A. 43°18N 75°37W 83 C9
Tablas Phil. 12°25N 122°2E 37 B6
Table, Pte. de la Réunion 21°14S 55°48E 53 c
Table B. Canada 53°40N 56°25W 73 B8
Table B. S. Africa 33°35S 18°25E 56 E2
Table Mt. S. Africa 33°58S 18°26E 56 E2
Table Rock L. U.S.A. 36°36N 93°19W 80 G7
Tabletop, Mt. Australia 23°24S 147°11E 62 C4
Tábor Czech Rep. 49°25N 14°39E 16 D8
Tabora Tanzania 5°2S 32°50E 54 D3
Tabora □ Tanzania 5°0S 33°0E 54 D3
Tabou Ivory C. 4°30N 7°20W 50 H4
Tabrīz Iran 38°7N 46°20E 44 B5
Tabuaeran Kiribati 3°51N 159°22W 65 G12
Tabūk Si. Arabia 28°23N 36°36E 44 D3
Tabūk □ Si. Arabia 27°40N 36°50E 44 E3
Tacámbaro de Codallos Mexico 19°14N 101°28W 86 D4
Tacheng China 46°40N 82°58E 32 B3
Tach'ing Shan = Daqing Shan China 40°40N 111°0E 34 D6
Tacloban Phil. 11°15N 124°58E 37 B6
Tacna Peru 18°0S 70°20W 92 G4
Tacoma U.S.A. 47°14N 122°26W 78 C4
Tacuarembó Uruguay 31°45S 56°0W 95 C4
Tademaït, Plateau du Algeria 28°30N 2°30E 50 C6
Tadjoura Djibouti 11°50N 42°55E 47 E3
Tadmor N.Z. 41°27S 172°45E 59 D4
Tadoule L. Canada 58°36N 98°20W 71 B9
Tadoussac Canada 48°11N 69°42W 73 C6
Tadzhikistan = Tajikistan ■ Asia 38°30N 70°0E 28 F8
Taegu = Daegu S. Korea 35°50N 128°37E 35 G15
Taegwan N. Korea 40°13N 125°12E 35 D13
Taejŏn = Daejeon S. Korea 36°20N 127°28E 35 F14
Taen, Ko Thailand 9°22N 99°57E 39 b
Tafalla Spain 42°30N 1°41W 21 A5
Tafelbaai = Table B. S. Africa 33°35S 18°25E 56 E2
Tafermaar Indonesia 6°47S 134°10E 37 F8
Tafí Viejo Argentina 26°43S 65°17W 94 B2
Tafīhān Iran 29°25N 52°39E 45 D7
Tafresh Iran 34°45N 49°57E 45 C6
Taft Iran 31°45N 54°14E 45 D7
Taft Phil. 11°57N 125°30E 37 B7
Taft U.S.A. 35°8N 119°28W 79 K7
Taftan Pakistan 29°0N 61°30E 40 E2
Taftān, Kūh-e Iran 28°40N 61°0E 45 D9
Taga Samoa 13°46S 172°28W 59 b
Taga Dzong Bhutan 27°5N 89°55E 41 F16
Taganrog Russia 47°12N 38°50E 19 E6
Tagbilaran Phil. 9°39N 123°51E 37 C6
Tagish Canada 60°19N 134°16W 70 A2
Tagish L. Canada 60°10N 134°20W 70 A2
Tagliamento → Italy 45°38N 13°6E 22 B5
Tagomago Spain 39°2N 1°39E 24 B8
Taguatinga Brazil 12°27S 46°22W 93 F10
Tagum Phil. 7°33N 125°53E 37 C7
Tagus = Tejo → Europe 38°40N 9°24W 21 C1
Tahakopa N.Z. 46°30S 169°23E 59 G2
Tahan, Gunung Malaysia 4°34N 102°17E 39 K4
Tahat Algeria 23°18N 5°33E 50 D7
Tāherī Iran 27°43N 52°20E 45 E7
Tahiti French Polynesia 17°37S 149°27W 59 d
Tahiti, I. Tahiti 17°37S 149°27W 59 d
Tahlequah U.S.A. 35°55N 94°58W 84 D7
Tahoe, L. U.S.A. 39°6N 120°2W 78 G6
Tahoe City U.S.A. 39°10N 120°9W 78 F6
Tahoka U.S.A. 33°10N 101°48W 84 E4
Taholah U.S.A. 47°21N 124°17W 78 C2
Tahoua Niger 14°57N 5°16E 50 F7
Tahrūd Iran 29°26N 57°49E 45 D8
Tahsis Canada 49°55N 126°40W 70 D3
Tahta Egypt 26°44N 31°32E 51 C12
Tahulandang Indonesia 2°27N 125°23E 37 D7
Tahuna Indonesia 3°38N 125°30E 37 D7
Tai Au Mun China 22°18N 114°17E 33 G11
Tai Mo Shan China 22°25N 114°7E 33 G11
Tai O China 22°15N 113°52E 33 G10
Tai Pang Wan China 22°33N 114°24E 33 F11
Tai Po China 22°27N 114°10E 33 G11
Tai Rom Yen △ Thailand 8°45N 99°30E 39 H2
Tai Shan China 36°25N 117°20E 35 F9
Tai Yue Shan = Lantau I. China 22°15N 113°56E 33 G10
Tai'an China 36°12N 117°8E 35 F9
Taiarapu, Presqu'île de Tahiti 17°47S 149°14W 59 d
Taibei = T'aipei Taiwan 25°4N 121°29E 33 D7
Taibique Canary Is. 27°42N 17°58W 24 G2
Taibus Qi China 41°54N 115°22E 34 D8
T'aichung Taiwan 24°9N 120°37E 33 D7
Taieri → N.Z. 46°3S 170°12E 59 G3
Taigu China 37°28N 112°30E 34 F7
Taihang Shan China 36°0N 113°30E 34 G7
Taihape N.Z. 39°41S 175°48E 59 C5
Taihe China 33°20N 115°42E 34 H8
Taikang China 34°5N 114°50E 34 G8
Tailem Bend Australia 35°12S 139°29E 63 F2
Taimyr Peninsula = Taymyr, Poluostrov Russia 75°0N 100°0E 29 B11
Tain U.K. 57°49N 4°4W 11 D4
T'ainan Taiwan 23°0N 120°10E 33 D7
Taipa China 22°10N 113°35E 33 G10
T'aipei Taiwan 25°4N 121°29E 33 D7
Taiping Malaysia 4°51N 100°44E 39 K3
Taipingzhen China 33°35N 111°42E 34 H6
Tairbeart = Tarbert U.K. 57°54N 6°49W 11 D2
Taita Hills Kenya 3°25S 38°15E 54 C4
Taitao, Pen. de Chile 46°30S 75°0W 96 F2
T'aitung Taiwan 22°43N 121°4E 33 D7
Taivalkoski Finland 65°33N 28°12E 8 D23
Taiwan ■ Asia 23°30N 121°0E 33 D7
Taiyiba Israel 32°36N 35°27E 46 C4
Taiyuan China 37°52N 112°33E 34 F7
Taizhong = T'aichung Taiwan 24°9N 120°37E 33 D7
Ta'izz Yemen 13°35N 44°2E 47 E3
Tājābād Iran 30°2N 54°24E 45 D7
Tajikistan ■ Asia 38°30N 70°0E 28 F8
Tajima Japan 37°12N 139°46E 31 F9
Tajo = Tejo → Europe 38°40N 9°24W 21 C1
Tajrīsh Iran 35°48N 51°25E 45 C6
Tak Thailand 16°52N 99°8E 38 D2
Takāb Iran 36°24N 47°7E 44 B5
Takachiho Japan 32°42N 131°18E 31 H5
Takachu Botswana 22°37S 21°58E 56 C3
Takada Japan 37°7N 138°15E 31 F9
Takahagi Japan 36°43N 140°45E 31 F10
Takaka N.Z. 40°51S 172°50E 59 D4
Takamaka Seychelles 4°50S 55°30E 53 b
Takamatsu Japan 34°20N 134°5E 31 G7
Takaoka Japan 36°47N 137°0E 31 F8
Takapuna N.Z. 36°47S 174°47E 59 B5
Takasaki Japan 36°20N 139°0E 31 F9
Takatsuki Japan 34°51N 135°37E 31 G7
Takaungu Kenya 3°38S 39°52E 54 C4
Takayama Japan 36°18N 137°11E 31 F8
Take-Shima Japan 30°49N 130°26E 31 J5
Takefu Japan 35°50N 136°10E 31 G8
Takengon Indonesia 4°45N 96°50E 36 D1
Takeo Japan 33°12N 130°1E 31 H5
Takeshima = Tok-do Asia 37°15N 131°52E 31 F5
Tākestān Iran 36°0N 49°40E 45 C6
Taketa Japan 32°58N 131°24E 31 H5
Takev Cambodia 10°59N 104°47E 39 G5
Takh India 33°6N 77°32E 43 C7
Takht-Sulaiman Pakistan 31°40N 69°58E 42 D3
Takikawa Japan 43°33N 141°54E 30 C10
Takla L. Canada 55°15N 125°45W 70 B3
Takla Landing Canada 55°30N 125°50W 70 B3
Takla Makan China 38°0N 83°0E 32 C3
Taklamakan Shamo = Takla Makan China 38°0N 83°0E 32 C3
Taku → Canada 58°30N 133°50W 70 B2
Takua Thung Thailand 8°24N 98°27E 39 a
Tal Halāl Iran 28°54N 55°1E 45 D7
Tala Uruguay 34°21S 55°46W 95 C4
Talagang Pakistan 32°55N 72°25E 42 C5
Talagante Chile 33°40S 70°50W 94 C1
Talamanca, Cordillera de Cent. Amer. 9°20N 83°20W 88 E3
Talara Peru 4°38S 81°18W 92 D2
Talas Kyrgyzstan 42°30N 72°13E 28 E8
Talâta Egypt 30°36N 32°20E 46 E1
Talaud, Kepulauan Indonesia 4°30N 126°50E 37 D7
Talaud Is. = Talaud, Kepulauan Indonesia 4°30N 126°50E 37 D7
Talavera de la Reina Spain 39°55N 4°46W 21 C3
Talayan Phil. 6°52N 124°24E 37 C6
Talbandh India 22°3N 86°20E 43 H12
Talbot, C. Australia 13°48S 126°43E 60 B4
Talbragar → Australia 32°12S 148°37E 63 E4
Talca Chile 35°28S 71°40W 94 D1
Talcahuano Chile 36°40S 73°10W 94 D1
Talcher India 21°0N 85°18E 41 J14
Taldy Kurgan = Taldyqorghan Kazakhstan 45°10N 78°45E 28 E8
Taldyqorghan Kazakhstan 45°10N 78°45E 28 E8
Tālesh Iran 37°58N 48°58E 45 B6
Tālesh, Kūhhā-ye Iran 37°42N 48°55E 45 B6
Tali Post Sudan 5°55N 30°44E 51 G12
Taliabu Indonesia 1°50S 125°0E 37 E6
Talibon Phil. 10°9N 124°20E 37 B6
Talibong, Ko Thailand 7°15N 99°23E 39 J2
Talihina U.S.A. 34°45N 95°3W 84 D7
Taliwang Indonesia 8°50S 116°55E 36 F5
Tall 'Afar Iraq 36°22N 42°27E 44 B4
Tall Kalakh Syria 34°41N 36°15E 46 A5
Talladega U.S.A. 33°26N 86°6W 85 E11
Tallahassee U.S.A. 30°27N 84°17W 85 F12
Tallangatta Australia 36°15S 147°19E 63 F4
Tallering Pk. Australia 28°6S 115°37E 61 E2
Talli Pakistan 29°32N 68°8E 42 E3
Tallinn Estonia 59°22N 24°48E 9 G21
Tallmadge U.S.A. 41°6N 81°27W 82 E3
Tallulah U.S.A. 32°25N 91°11W 84 E9
Taloyoak Canada 69°32N 93°32W 68 C10
Talpa de Allende Mexico 20°23N 104°51W 86 C4
Talparo Trin. & Tob. 10°30N 61°17W 93 K15
Talsi Latvia 57°10N 22°30E 9 H20
Taltal Chile 25°23S 70°33W 94 B1
Taltson → Canada 61°24N 112°46W 70 A6
Talwood Australia 28°29S 149°29E 63 D4
Talyawalka Cr. → Australia 32°28S 142°22E 63 E3
Tam Ky Vietnam 15°34N 108°29E 38 E7
Tam Quan Vietnam 14°35N 109°3E 38 E7
Tama U.S.A. 41°58N 92°35W 80 E7
Tamale Ghana 9°22N 0°50W 50 G5
Taman Negara △ Malaysia 4°38N 102°26E 39 K4
Tamano Japan 34°29N 133°59E 31 G6
Tamanrasset Algeria 22°50N 5°30E 50 D7
Tamaqua U.S.A. 40°48N 75°58W 83 F9
Tamar → U.K. 50°27N 4°15W 13 G3
Tamarin Mauritius 20°19S 57°20E 53 d
Tamarinda Spain 39°55N 3°49E 24 B10
Tamashima Japan 34°32N 133°40E 31 G6
Tamatave = Toamasina Madag. 18°10S 49°25E 57 B8
Tamaulipas □ Mexico 24°0N 98°45W 87 C5
Tamaulipas, Sierra de Mexico 23°30N 98°20W 87 C5
Tamazula Mexico 24°57N 106°57W 86 C3
Tamazunchale Mexico 21°16N 98°47W 87 C5
Tambach Kenya 0°36N 35°31E 54 B4
Tambacounda Senegal 13°45N 13°40W 50 F3
Tambelan, Kepulauan Indonesia 1°0N 107°30E 36 D3
Tambellup Australia 34°4S 117°37E 61 F2
Tambo Australia 24°54S 146°14E 62 C4
Tambo de Mora Peru 13°30S 76°8W 92 F3
Tambohorano Madag. 17°30S 43°58E 57 B7
Tambora Indonesia 8°12S 118°5E 36 F5
Tambov Russia 52°45N 41°28E 18 D7
Tambuku Indonesia 7°8S 113°40E 37 G15
Tâmega → Portugal 41°5N 8°21W 21 B1
Tamenglong India 25°0N 93°35E 41 G18
Tamiahua, L. de Mexico 21°35N 97°35W 87 C5
Tamil Nadu □ India 11°0N 77°0E 40 P10
Tamluk India 22°18N 87°58E 43 H12
Tammerfors = Tampere Finland 61°30N 23°50E 8 F20
Tammisaari Finland 60°0N 23°26E 9 G20
Tamo Abu, Banjaran Malaysia 3°10N 115°5E 36 D5
Tampa U.S.A. 27°56N 82°27W 85 H13
Tampa, Tanjung Indonesia 8°55S 116°12E 37 K19
Tampa B. U.S.A. 27°50N 82°30W 85 H13
Tampere Finland 61°30N 23°50E 8 F20
Tampico Mexico 22°13N 97°51W 87 C5
Tampin Malaysia 2°28N 102°13E 39 L4
Tampoi Malaysia 1°30N 103°39E 39 d
Tamu Burma 24°13N 94°12E 41 G19
Tamworth Australia 31°7S 150°58E 63 E5
Tamworth Canada 44°29N 77°0W 82 B8
Tamworth U.K. 52°39N 1°41W 13 E6
Tan An Vietnam 10°32N 106°25E 39 G6
Tan Chau Vietnam 10°48N 105°12E 39 G5
Tan-Tan Morocco 28°29N 11°1W 50 C3
Tana → Kenya 2°32S 40°31E 54 C5
Tana → Norway 70°30N 28°14E 8 A23
Tana, L. Ethiopia 13°5N 37°30E 47 E2
Tana River Primate ⌂ Kenya 1°55S 40°7E 54 C5
Tanabe Japan 33°44N 135°22E 31 H7
Tanafjorden Norway 70°45N 28°25E 8 A23
Tanahbala Indonesia 0°30S 98°30E 36 E1
Tanahgrogot Indonesia 1°55S 116°15E 36 E5
Tanahjampea Indonesia 7°10S 120°35E 37 F6
Tanahmasa Indonesia 0°12S 98°39E 36 E1
Tanahmerah Indonesia 6°5S 140°16E 37 F10
Tanakpur India 29°5N 80°7E 43 E9
Tanakura Japan 37°10N 140°20E 31 F10
Tanami Desert Australia 18°50S 132°0E 60 C5
Tanami Mine Australia 19°59S 129°43E 60 C4
Tananarive = Antananarivo Madag. 18°55S 47°31E 57 B8
Tánaro → Italy 44°55N 8°40E 20 D8
Tancheng China 34°25N 118°20E 35 G10
Tanch'ŏn N. Korea 40°27N 128°54E 35 D15
Tanda Ut. P., India 26°33N 82°35E 43 F10
Tanda Ut. P., India 28°57N 78°56E 43 E8
Tandag Phil. 9°4N 126°9E 37 C7
Tandaia Tanzania 9°25S 34°15E 55 D3
Tandaué Angola 16°58S 18°5E 56 B2
Tandil Argentina 37°15S 59°6W 94 D4
Tandil, Sa. del Argentina 37°30S 59°0W 94 D4
Tandlianwala Pakistan 31°3N 73°9E 42 D5
Tando Adam Pakistan 25°45N 68°40E 42 G3
Tando Allahyar Pakistan 25°28N 68°43E 42 G3
Tando Bago Pakistan 24°47N 68°58E 42 G3
Tando Mohommed Khan Pakistan 25°8N 68°32E 42 G3
Tandou L. Australia 32°40S 142°5E 63 E3
Tandoureh △ Iran 37°50N 59°0E 44 B8
Tandragee U.K. 54°21N 6°24W 10 B5
Tane-ga-Shima Japan 30°30N 131°0E 31 J5
Taneatua N.Z. 38°4S 177°1E 59 C6
Tanen Tong Dan = Dawna Ra. Burma 16°30N 98°30E 38 D2
Tanezrouft Algeria 23°9N 0°11E 50 D6
Tang, Koh Cambodia 10°16N 103°7E 39 G4
Tang, Ra's-e Iran 25°21N 59°52E 45 E8
Tang Krasang Cambodia 12°34N 105°3E 38 F5
Tanga Tanzania 5°5S 39°2E 54 D4
Tanga □ Tanzania 5°20S 38°0E 54 D4
Tanganyika, L. Africa 6°40S 30°0E 54 D3
Tanger Morocco 35°50N 5°49W 50 A4
Tangerang Indonesia 6°11S 106°37E 37 G12
Tanggu China 39°2N 117°40E 35 E9
Tanggula Shan China 32°40N 92°10E 32 C4
Tanghe China 32°47N 112°50E 34 H7
Tanghla Range = Tanggula Shan China 32°40N 92°10E 32 C4
Tangier = Tanger Morocco 35°50N 5°49W 50 A4
Tangjia China 22°22N 113°35E 33 G10
Tangjia Wan China 22°21N 113°36E 33 G10
Tangorin Australia 21°47S 144°12E 62 C3
Tangorombohitr'i Makay Madag. 21°0S 45°15E 57 C8
Tangshan China 39°38N 118°10E 35 E10
Tangtou China 35°28N 118°30E 35 G10
Tanimbar, Kepulauan Indonesia 7°30S 131°30E 37 F8
Tanimbar Is. = Tanimbar, Kepulauan Indonesia 7°30S 131°30E 37 F8
Tanintharì = Tenasserim Burma 12°6N 99°3E 39 F2
Tanjay Phil. 9°30N 123°5E 37 C6
Tanjong Malim Malaysia 3°42N 101°31E 39 L3
Tanjong Pelepas Malaysia 1°21N 103°33E 39 d
Tanjore = Thanjavur India 10°48N 79°12E 40 P11
Tanjung Indonesia 8°21S 116°9E 37 J19
Tanjung Phil. 2°10S 115°25E 36 E5
Tanjung Tokong Malaysia 5°28N 100°18E 39 c
Tanjungbalai Indonesia 2°55N 99°44E 36 D1
Tanjungbatu Indonesia 2°23N 118°3E 36 D5
Tanjungkarang Telukbetung Indonesia 5°20S 105°10E 36 F3
Tanjungpandan Indonesia 2°43S 107°38E 36 E3
Tanjungpinang Indonesia 1°5N 104°30E 36 D2

Tanjungredeb *Indonesia* 2°9N 117°29E **36** D5
Tanjungselor *Indonesia* 2°55N 117°25E **36** D5
Tank *Pakistan* 32°14N 70°25E **42** C4
Tankwa-Karoo △
　S. Africa 32°14S 19°50E **56** E3
Tannersville *U.S.A.* 41°3N 75°18W **83** E9
Tannu Ola *Asia* 51°0N 94°0E **29** D10
Tannum Sands
　Australia 23°57S 151°22E **62** C5
Tanout *Niger* 14°50N 8°55E **50** F7
Tanta *Egypt* 30°45N 30°57E **51** B12
Tantoyuca *Mexico* 21°21N 98°14W **87** C5
Tantung = Dandong
　China 40°10N 124°20E **35** D13
Tanunda *Australia* 34°30S 139°0E **63** E2
Tanzania ■ *Africa* 6°0S 34°0E **54** D3
Tanzhou *China* 22°16N 113°28E **33** G9
Tanzilla ➜ *Canada* 58°8N 130°43W **70** B2
Tao, Ko *Thailand* 10°5N 99°52E **39** G2
Tao'an = Taonan
　China 45°22N 122°40E **35** B12
Tao'er He ➜ *China* 45°45N 124°5E **35** B13
Taolanaro *Madag.* 25°2S 47°0E **57** D8
Taole *China* 38°48N 106°40E **34** E4
Taonan *China* 45°22N 122°40E **35** B12
Taos *U.S.A.* 36°24N 105°35W **77** H11
Taoudenni *Mali* 22°40N 3°55W **50** D5
Tapa *Estonia* 59°15N 25°50E **9** G21
Tapa Shan = Daba Shan
　China 32°0N 109°0E **33** C5
Tapachula *Mexico* 14°54N 92°17W **87** E6
Tapah *Malaysia* 4°12N 101°15E **39** K3
Tapajós ➜ *Brazil* 2°24S 54°41W **93** D8
Tapaktuan *Indonesia* 3°15N 97°10E **36** D1
Tapanahoni ➜
　Suriname 4°20N 54°25W **93** C8
Tapanui *N.Z.* 45°56S 169°18E **59** F2
Tapauá ➜ *Brazil* 5°40S 64°21W **92** E6
Tapes *Brazil* 30°40S 51°23W **95** C5
Tapeta *Liberia* 6°29N 8°52W **50** G4
Taphan Hin *Thailand* 16°13N 100°26E **38** D3
Tapirapecó, Serra
　Venezuela 1°10N 65°0W **92** C6
Tapo-Capara △
　Venezuela 7°55N 71°15W **89** E5
Tapti ➜ *India* 21°8N 72°41E **40** J8
Tapuae-o-Uenuku *N.Z.* 42°0S 173°39E **59** E4
Tapul Group *Phil.* 5°35N 120°50E **37** C6
Tapurucuará *Brazil* 0°24S 65°2W **92** D5
Taquara *Brazil* 29°36S 50°46W **95** B5
Taquari ➜ *Brazil* 19°15S 57°17W **92** G7
Tara *Australia* 27°17S 150°31E **63** D5
Tara *Canada* 44°28N 81°9W **82** B3
Tara *Russia* 56°55N 74°24E **28** D8
Tara *Zambia* 16°58S 26°45E **55** F2
Tara ➜ *Montenegro* 43°21N 18°51E **23** C8
Tarābulus *Lebanon* 34°31N 35°50E **46** A4
Tarābulus *Libya* 32°49N 13°7E **51** B8
Taradehi *India* 23°18N 79°21E **43** H8
Tarajalejo *Canary Is.* 28°12N 14°7W **24** F5
Tarakan *Indonesia* 3°20N 117°35E **36** D5
Tarakit, Mt. *Kenya* 2°2N 35°10E **54** B4
Tarama-Jima *Japan* 24°39N 124°42E **31** M2
Taran, Mys *Russia* 54°56N 19°59E **9** J18
Taranagar *India* 28°43N 74°50E **42** E6
Taranaki □ *N.Z.* 39°25S 174°30E **59** C5
Taranaki, Mt. *N.Z.* 39°17S 174°5E **59** C5
Tarancón *Spain* 40°1N 3°1W **21** B4
Tarangire △ *Tanzania* 4°21S 36°7E **54** C4
Taransay *U.K.* 57°54N 7°0W **11** D1
Táranto *Italy* 40°28N 17°14E **22** D7
Táranto, G. di *Italy* 40°8N 17°20E **22** D7
Tarapacá *Colombia* 2°56S 69°46W **92** D5
Tarapacá □ *Chile* 20°45S 69°30W **94** A2
Tarapoto *Peru* 6°30S 76°20W **92** E3
Tararua Ra. *N.Z.* 40°45S 175°25E **59** D5
Tarashcha *Ukraine* 49°30N 30°31E **17** D16
Tarauacá *Brazil* 8°6S 70°48W **92** E4
Tarauacá ➜ *Brazil* 6°42S 60°48W **92** E5
Taravao *Tahiti* 17°43S 149°19W **59** d
Taravao, Isthme de
　Tahiti 17°43S 149°19W **59** d
Tarawa *Kiribati* 1°30N 173°0E **64** G9
Tarawera *N.Z.* 39°2S 176°36E **59** C6
Tarawera, L. *N.Z.* 38°13S 176°27E **59** C6
Taraz *Kazakhstan* 42°54N 71°22E **28** E8
Tarazona *Spain* 41°55N 1°43W **21** B5
Tarbagatay, Khrebet
　Kazakhstan 48°0N 83°0E **28** E9
Tarbat Ness *U.K.* 57°52N 3°47W **11** D5
Tarbela Dam *Pakistan* 34°8N 72°52E **42** B5
Tarbert *Ireland* 52°34N 9°22W **10** D2
Tarbert *Argyll & Bute,*
　U.K. 55°52N 5°25W **11** F3
Tarbert *W. Isles, U.K.* 57°54N 6°49W **11** D2
Tarbes *France* 43°15N 0°3E **20** E4
Tarboro *U.S.A.* 35°54N 77°32W **85** D16
Tarcoola *Australia* 30°44S 134°36E **63** E1
Tarcoon *Australia* 30°15S 146°43E **63** E4
Taree *Australia* 31°50S 152°30E **63** E5
Tarfaya *Morocco* 27°55N 12°55E **17** F13
Târgoviște *Romania* 44°55N 25°27E **17** F13
Târgu-Jiu *Romania* 45°5N 23°19E **17** F12
Târgu Mureș *Romania* 46°31N 24°38E **17** E13
Tarif *U.A.E.* 24°3N 53°46E **45** E7
Tarifa *Spain* 36°1N 5°36W **21** D3
Tarija *Bolivia* 21°30S 64°40W **94** A3
Tarija □ *Bolivia* 21°30S 63°30W **94** A3
Tariku ➜ *Indonesia* 2°55S 138°26E **37** E9
Tarim Basin = Tarim Pendi
　China 40°0N 84°0E **32** B3
Tarim He ➜ *China* 39°30N 88°30E **32** C3
Tarim Pendi *China* 40°0N 84°0E **32** B3
Taritatu ➜ *Indonesia* 2°54S 138°27E **37** E9
Tarka ➜ *S. Africa* 32°10S 26°0E **56** E4

Tarka La *Bhutan* 27°12N 89°44E **43** F13
Tarkastad *S. Africa* 32°0S 26°16E **56** E4
Tarkhankut, Mys
　Ukraine 45°25N 32°30E **19** E5
Tarko Sale *Russia* 64°55N 77°50E **28** C8
Tarkwa *Ghana* 5°20N 2°0W **50** G5
Tarlac *Phil.* 15°29N 120°35E **37** A6
Tarma *Peru* 11°25S 75°45W **92** F3
Tarn ➜ *France* 44°5N 1°6E **20** E4
Târnăveni *Romania* 46°19N 24°13E **17** E13
Tarnobrzeg *Poland* 50°35N 21°41E **17** C11
Tarnów *Poland* 50°3N 21°0E **17** C11
Tarnowskie Góry
　Poland 50°27N 18°54E **17** C10
Țărom *Iran* 28°11N 55°46E **45** D7
Taroom *Australia* 25°36S 149°48E **63** D4
Taroudannt *Morocco* 30°30N 8°52W **50** B4
Tarpon Springs *U.S.A.* 28°9N 82°45W **85** G13
Tarrafal *C. Verde Is.* 15°18N 23°39W **50** b
Tarragona *Spain* 41°5N 1°17E **21** B6
Tarraleah *Australia* 42°17S 146°26E **63** G4
Tarrasa = Terrassa *Spain* 41°34N 2°1E **21** B7
Tarrytown *U.S.A.* 41°4N 73°52W **83** E11
Tarshiha = Me'ona
　Israel 33°1N 35°15E **46** B4
Tarsus *Turkey* 36°58N 34°55E **44** B2
Tartagal *Argentina* 22°30S 63°50W **94** A3
Tartu *Estonia* 58°20N 26°44E **9** G22
Țarțūs *Syria* 34°55N 35°55E **44** C2
Tarumizu *Japan* 31°29N 130°42E **31** J5
Tarutao = Ko Tarutao △
　Thailand 6°31N 99°26E **39** J2
Tarutao, Ko *Thailand* 6°33N 99°40E **39** J2
Tarutung *Indonesia* 2°0N 98°54E **36** D1
Taseko ➜ *Canada* 52°8N 123°45W **70** C4
Tash-Kömür *Kyrgyzstan* 41°40N 72°10E **28** E8
Tash-Kumyr = Tash-Kömür
　Kyrgyzstan 41°40N 72°10E **28** E8
Tashauz = Dashoguz
　Turkmenistan 41°49N 59°58E **28** E6
Tashi Chho Dzong = Thimphu
　Bhutan 27°31N 89°45E **41** F16
Tashk, Daryācheh-ye
　Iran 29°45N 53°35E **45** D7
Tashkent = Toshkent
　Uzbekistan 41°20N 69°10E **28** E7
Tashtagol *Russia* 52°47N 87°53E **28** D9
Tasiilaq *Greenland* 65°40N 37°20W **4** C6
Tasik Kenyir *Malaysia* 5°5N 102°45E **39** K4
Tasikmalaya *Indonesia* 7°18S 108°12E **37** G13
Tåsjön *Sweden* 64°15N 15°40E **8** D16
Taskan *Russia* 62°59N 150°20E **29** C16
Tasman B. *N.Z.* 40°59S 173°25E **59** D4
Tasman Basin *Pac. Oc.* 46°0S 158°0E **64** M7
Tasman Mts. *N.Z.* 41°3S 172°25E **59** D4
Tasman Pen. *Australia* 43°10S 148°0E **63** G4
Tasman Sea *Pac. Oc.* 36°0S 160°0E **58** E9
Tasmania □ *Australia* 42°0S 146°30E **63** G4
Tasmanian Wilderness World
　Heritage Area △
　Australia 43°0S 146°0E **63** G4
Tassili n'Ajjer *Algeria* 25°47N 8°1E **50** C7
Tassili Oua n Ahaggar
　Algeria 20°41N 5°30E **50** D7
Tata *Morocco* 29°46N 7°56W **50** C4
Tatabánya *Hungary* 47°32N 18°25E **17** E10
Tatahouine *Tunisia* 32°56N 10°27E **51** B8
Tataouine *Tunisia* 32°57N 10°29E **51** B8
Tatar Republic = Tatarstan □
　Russia 55°30N 51°30E **18** C9
Tatarbunary *Ukraine* 45°50N 29°39E **17** F15
Tatarsk *Russia* 55°14N 76°0E **28** D8
Tatarstan □ *Russia* 55°30N 51°30E **18** C9
Tatatua, Pte. *Tahiti* 17°44S 149°8W **59** d
Tateyama *Japan* 35°0N 139°50E **31** G9
Tathlina L. *Canada* 60°33N 117°39W **70** A5
Tathra *Australia* 36°44S 149°59E **63** F4
Tatinnai L. *Canada* 60°55N 97°40W **71** A9
Tatla Lake *Canada* 52°0N 124°20W **70** C4
Tatnam, C. *Canada* 57°16N 91°0W **71** B10
Tatra = Tatry
　Slovak Rep. 49°20N 20°0E **17** D11
Tatry *Slovak Rep.* 49°20N 20°0E **17** D11
Tatshenshini ➜
　Canada 59°28N 137°45W **70** B1
Tatsuno *Japan* 34°52N 134°33E **31** G7
Tatta *Pakistan* 24°42N 67°55E **42** G2
Tatuī *Brazil* 23°25S 47°53W **95** A6
Tatum *U.S.A.* 33°16N 103°19W **77** K12
Tat'ung = Datong
　China 40°6N 113°18E **34** D7
Tatvan *Turkey* 38°31N 42°15E **44** B4
Ta'ū *Amer. Samoa* 14°15S 169°30W **59** b
Taubaté *Brazil* 23°0S 45°36W **95** A6
Tauern *Austria* 47°15N 12°40E **16** E7
Taumarunui *N.Z.* 38°53S 175°15E **59** C5
Taumaturgo *Brazil* 8°54S 72°51W **92** E4
Taung *S. Africa* 27°33S 24°47E **56** D3
Taungdwingyi *Burma* 20°1N 95°40E **41** J19
Taunggyi *Burma* 20°50N 97°0E **41** J20
Taungup *Burma* 18°51N 94°14E **41** K19
Taunsa *Pakistan* 30°42N 70°39E **42** D4
Taunsa Barrage
　Pakistan 30°42N 70°50E **42** D4
Taunton *U.K.* 51°1N 3°5W **13** F4
Taunton *U.S.A.* 41°54N 71°6W **83** E13
Taunus *Germany* 50°13N 8°34E **16** C5
Taupo *N.Z.* 38°41S 176°7E **59** C6
Taupo, L. *N.Z.* 38°46S 175°55E **59** C5
Tauragė *Lithuania* 55°14N 22°16E **9** J20
Tauranga *N.Z.* 37°42S 176°11E **59** B6
Tauranga Harb. *N.Z.* 37°30S 176°5E **59** B6
Taureau, Rés. *Canada* 46°46N 73°50W **72** C5
Taurianova *Italy* 38°21N 16°1E **22** E7
Taurus Mts. = Toros Dağları
　Turkey 37°0N 32°30E **44** B2
Tautira *Tahiti* 17°44S 149°9W **59** d

Tavan Bogd Uul
　Mongolia 49°10N 87°49E **32** B3
Tavastehus = Hämeenlinna
　Finland 61°0N 24°28E **8** F21
Tavda *Russia* 58°7N 65°8E **28** D7
Tavda ➜ *Russia* 57°47N 67°18E **28** D7
Taveta *Kenya* 3°23S 37°37E **54** C4
Taveuni *Fiji* 16°51S 179°58W **59** a
Tavira *Portugal* 37°8N 7°40W **21** D2
Tavistock *Canada* 43°19N 80°50W **82** C4
Tavistock *U.K.* 50°33N 4°9W **13** G3
Tavoy *Burma* 14°2N 98°12E **38** E2
Tavua *Fiji* 17°37S 177°5E **59** a
Tavuki *Fiji* 19°7S 178°8E **59** a
Taw ➜ *U.K.* 51°4N 4°4W **13** F3
Tawa ➜ *India* 22°48N 77°48E **42** H8
Tawas City *U.S.A.* 44°16N 83°31W **81** C12
Tawau *Malaysia* 4°20N 117°55E **36** D5
Tawi-Tawi *Phil.* 5°10N 120°15E **37** C6
Taxco *Mexico* 18°33N 99°36W **87** D5
Taxila *Pakistan* 33°42N 72°52E **42** C5
Taxkorgan Tajik Zizhixian
　China 37°49N 75°14E **32** C2
Tay ➜ *U.K.* 56°37N 3°38W **11** E5
Tay, Firth of *U.K.* 56°25N 3°8W **11** E5
Tay, L. *Australia* 32°55S 120°48E **61** F3
Tay, L. *U.K.* 56°32N 4°8W **11** E4
Tay △ *U.K.* 56°43N 3°59W **11** E5
Tay Ninh *Vietnam* 11°20N 106°5E **39** G6
Tayabamba *Peru* 8°15S 77°16W **92** E3
Taylakova *Russia* 59°13N 74°0E **28** D8
Taylakovy = Taylakova
　Russia 59°13N 74°0E **28** D8
Taylor *Canada* 56°13N 120°40W **70** B4
Taylor *Nebr., U.S.A.* 41°46N 99°23W **80** E4
Taylor *Pa., U.S.A.* 41°23N 75°43W **83** E9
Taylor *Tex., U.S.A.* 30°34N 97°25W **84** F6
Taylor, Mt. *U.S.A.* 35°14N 107°37W **77** J10
Taylorville *U.S.A.* 39°33N 89°18W **80** F9
Taymā *Si. Arabia* 27°35N 38°45E **44** E3
Taymyr, Oz. *Russia* 74°20N 102°0E **29** B11
Taymyr, Poluostrov
　Russia 75°0N 100°0E **29** B11
Tayport *U.K.* 56°27N 2°52W **11** E6
Tayrona □ *Colombia* 11°20N 74°2W **89** D5
Tayshet *Russia* 55°58N 98°1E **29** D10
Taytay *Phil.* 10°45N 119°30E **37** B5
Taz ➜ *Russia* 67°32N 78°40E **28** C8
Taza *Morocco* 34°16N 4°6W **50** B5
Tāza Khurmātū *Iraq* 35°18N 44°20E **44** C5
Tazawa-Ko *Japan* 39°43N 140°40E **30** E10
Tazin ➜ *Canada* 59°48N 109°55W **71** B7
Tazin L. *Canada* 59°44N 108°42W **71** B7
Tazovskiy *Russia* 67°30N 78°44E **28** C8
Tbilisi *Georgia* 41°43N 44°50E **19** F7
Tchad = Chad ■ *Africa* 15°0N 17°15E **51** F8
Tchad, L. *Chad* 13°30N 14°30E **51** F8
Tch'eng-tou = Chengdu
　China 30°38N 104°2E **32** C5
Tchibanga *Gabon* 2°45S 11°0E **52** E2
Tch'ong-k'ing = Chongqing
　China 29°35N 106°25E **32** D5
Tczew *Poland* 54°8N 18°50E **17** A10
Te Anau, L. *N.Z.* 45°15S 167°45E **59** F1
Te Aroha *N.Z.* 37°32S 175°44E **59** B5
Te Awamutu *N.Z.* 38°1S 175°20E **59** C5
Te Ika a Maui = North I.
　N.Z. 38°0S 175°0E **59** C5
Te Kuiti *N.Z.* 38°20S 175°11E **59** C5
Te Puke *N.Z.* 37°46S 176°22E **59** B6
Te Waewae B. *N.Z.* 46°13S 167°33E **59** G1
Te Wai Pounamu = South I.
　N.Z. 44°0S 170°0E **59** F3
Teague *U.S.A.* 31°38N 96°17W **84** F6
Teahupoo *Tahiti* 17°50S 149°16W **59** d
Teapa *Mexico* 17°33N 92°57W **87** D6
Tebakang *Malaysia* 1°6N 110°30E **36** D4
Teberu *Malaysia* 1°30N 103°42E **39** d
Tébessa *Algeria* 35°22N 8°8E **50** A7
Tebicuary ➜ *Paraguay* 26°36S 58°16W **94** B4
Tebingtinggi *Riau,*
　Indonesia 1°0N 102°45E **36** E2
Tebingtinggi *Sumatera Utara,*
　Indonesia 3°20N 99°9E **36** D1
Tecate *Mexico* 32°34N 116°38W **79** N10
Tecka *Argentina* 43°29S 70°48W **96** E2
Tecomán *Mexico* 18°55N 103°53W **86** D4
Tecopa *U.S.A.* 35°51N 116°13W **79** K10
Tecoripa *Mexico* 28°37N 109°57W **86** B3
Tecuala *Mexico* 22°23N 105°27W **86** C3
Tecuci *Romania* 45°51N 27°27E **17** F14
Tecumseh *Canada* 42°19N 82°54W **82** D2
Tecumseh *Mich., U.S.A.* 42°0N 83°57W **81** D12
Tecumseh *Okla., U.S.A.* 35°15N 96°56W **84** D6
Tedzhen = Tejen
　Turkmenistan 37°23N 60°31E **28** F7
Tees ➜ *U.K.* 54°37N 1°10W **12** C6
Tees B. *U.K.* 54°40N 1°9W **12** C6
Teeswater *Canada* 43°59N 81°17W **82** C3
Tefé *Brazil* 3°25S 64°50W **92** D6
Tegal *Indonesia* 6°52S 109°8E **36** F3
Tegallalang *Indonesia* 8°27S 115°17E **37** J18
Tegalsari *Indonesia* 8°25S 114°8E **37** J17
Tegid, L. = Bala, L. *U.K.* 52°53N 3°37W **12** E4
Tegucigalpa *Honduras* 14°5N 87°14W **88** D2
Tehachapi *U.S.A.* 35°8N 118°27W **79** K8
Tehachapi Mts. *U.S.A.* 35°0N 118°30W **79** L8
Teheran = Tehrān *Iran* 35°41N 51°25E **45** C6
Tehoru *Indonesia* 3°23S 129°30E **37** E7
Tehrān *Iran* 35°41N 51°25E **45** C6
Tehrān □ *Iran* 35°30N 51°20E **45** C6
Tehri *India* 30°23N 78°29E **43** D8
Tehuacán *Mexico* 18°27N 97°23W **87** D5

Tehuantepec *Mexico* 16°21N 95°13W **87** D5
Tehuantepec, G. de
　Mexico 15°50N 95°12W **87** D5
Tehuantepec, Istmo de
　Mexico 17°15N 94°30W **87** D6
Teide, Pico de *Canary Is.* 28°15N 16°38W **24** F3
Teifi ➜ *U.K.* 52°5N 4°41W **13** E3
Teign ➜ *U.K.* 50°32N 3°32W **13** G4
Teignmouth *U.K.* 50°33N 3°31W **13** G4
Tejakula *Indonesia* 8°8S 115°20E **37** J18
Tejam *India* 29°57N 80°11E **43** E9
Tejen *Turkmenistan* 37°23N 60°31E **28** F7
Tejen ➜ *Turkmenistan* 37°24N 60°38E **45** B9
Tejo ➜ *Europe* 38°40N 9°24E **21** C1
Tejon Pass *U.S.A.* 34°49N 118°53W **79** L8
Tekamah *U.S.A.* 41°47N 96°13W **80** E6
Tekapo, L. *N.Z.* 43°53S 170°33E **59** E3
Tekax *Mexico* 20°12N 89°17W **87** C7
Tekeli *Kazakhstan* 44°50N 79°0E **28** E8
Tekirdağ *Turkey* 40°58N 27°30E **23** D12
Tekkali *India* 18°37N 84°15E **41** K14
Tekoa *U.S.A.* 47°14N 117°4W **76** C5
Tel Aviv ✈ (TLV) *Israel* 32°5N 34°49E **46** C3
Tel Aviv-Yafo *Israel* 32°4N 34°48E **46** C3
Tel Lakhish *Israel* 31°34N 34°51E **46** D3
Tel Megiddo *Israel* 32°35N 35°11E **46** C4
Tela *Honduras* 15°40N 87°28W **88** C2
Telanaipura = Jambi
　Indonesia 1°38S 103°30E **36** E2
Telavi *Georgia* 42°0N 45°30E **19** F8
Telde *Canary Is.* 27°59N 15°25W **24** G4
Telegraph Creek
　Canada 58°0N 131°10W **70** B2
Telekhany = Tsyelyakhany
　Belarus 52°30N 25°46E **17** B13
Telemark *Norway* 59°15N 7°40E **9** G12
Telén *Argentina* 36°15S 65°31W **94** D2
Teleng *Iran* 25°47N 61°3E **45** E9
Teles Pires ➜ *Brazil* 7°21S 58°3W **92** E7
Telescope Pk. *U.S.A.* 36°10N 117°5W **79** J9
Telfer Mine *Australia* 21°40S 122°12E **60** C3
Telford *U.K.* 52°40N 2°27W **13** E5
Telford and Wrekin □
　U.K. 52°45N 2°27W **12** E5
Telkwa *Canada* 54°41N 127°5W **70** C3
Tell City *U.S.A.* 37°57N 86°46W **80** G10
Tellicherry *India* 11°45N 75°30E **40** P9
Telluride *U.S.A.* 37°56N 107°49W **77** H10
Teloloapán *Mexico* 18°21N 99°51W **87** D5
Telpos Iz *Russia* 63°16N 59°13E **18** B10
Telsen *Argentina* 42°30S 66°50W **96** E3
Telšiai *Lithuania* 55°59N 22°14E **9** J20
Teluk Anson = Teluk Intan
　Malaysia 4°3N 101°0E **39** K3
Teluk Bahang *Malaysia* 5°28N 100°13E **39** c
Teluk Betung = Tanjungkarang
　Telukbetung
　Indonesia 5°20S 105°10E **36** F3
Teluk Intan *Malaysia* 4°3N 101°0E **39** K3
Teluk Kumbar *Malaysia* 5°18N 100°14E **39** c
Telukbutun *Indonesia* 4°13N 108°12E **36** D3
Telukdalem *Indonesia* 0°33N 97°50E **36** D1
Tema *Ghana* 5°41N 0°0 **50** G5
Temagami, L. *Canada* 47°0N 80°10E **72** C3
Temax *Mexico* 21°9N 88°56W **87** C7
Temba *S. Africa* 25°20S 28°17E **57** D4
Tembagapura *Indonesia* 4°20S 137°0E **37** E9
Tembe
　Dem. Rep. of the Congo 0°16S 28°14E **54** C2
Tembe △ *S. Africa* 26°51S 32°24E **57** D5
Temblor Range *U.S.A.* 35°20N 119°50W **79** K7
Teme ➜ *U.K.* 52°11N 2°13W **13** E5
Temecula *U.S.A.* 33°30N 117°9W **79** M9
Temerloh *Malaysia* 3°27N 102°25E **36** D2
Teminabuan *Indonesia* 1°26S 132°1E **37** E8
Temir *Kazakhstan* 49°1N 57°14E **19** E10
Temirtau *Kazakhstan* 50°5N 72°56E **28** D8
Temirtau *Russia* 53°10N 87°30E **28** D9
Témiscamie ➜ *Canada* 50°59N 73°5W **73** B5
Témiscaming *Canada* 46°44N 79°5W **72** C4
Témiscamingue, L.
　Canada 47°10N 79°25W **72** C4
Temosachic *Mexico* 28°57N 107°51W **86** B3
Tempe *U.S.A.* 33°24N 111°54W **77** K8
Tempiute *U.S.A.* 37°39N 115°38W **78** H11
Temple *U.S.A.* 31°6N 97°21W **84** F6
Temple B. *Australia* 12°15S 143°3E **62** A3
Templemore *Ireland* 52°47N 7°51W **10** D4
Templeton *U.S.A.* 35°33N 120°42W **78** K6
Templeton ➜ *Australia* 21°0S 138°40E **62** C2
Tempoal de Sánchez
　Mexico 21°31N 98°23W **87** C5
Temuco *Chile* 38°45S 72°40W **96** D2
Temuka *N.Z.* 44°14S 171°17E **59** F3
Tenabo *Mexico* 20°3N 90°14W **87** C6
Tenaha *U.S.A.* 31°57N 94°15W **84** F7
Tenakee Springs
　U.S.A. 57°47N 135°13W **70** B1
Tenali *India* 16°15N 80°35E **41** L12
Tenancingo de Degollado
　Mexico 18°58N 99°36W **87** D5
Tenango del Valle
　Mexico 19°7N 99°33W **87** D5
Tenaro, Akra *Greece* 36°22N 22°27E **23** F10
Tenasserim *Burma* 12°6N 99°3E **39** F2
Tenasserim □ *Burma* 14°0N 98°30E **38** F2
Tenby *U.K.* 51°40N 4°42W **13** F3
Tenda, Colle di *France* 44°7N 7°36E **20** D7
Tendaho *Ethiopia* 11°48N 40°54E **47** E3
Tendukhera *India* 23°24N 79°33E **43** H8
Teneguía, Volcanes de
　Canary Is. 28°28N 17°51W **24** F2
Tenerife *Canary Is.* 28°15N 16°35W **24** F3
Tenerife, Pico *Canary Is.* 27°43N 18°1W **24** G1
Tenerife Norte ✈ (TFN)

　Canary Is. 28°28N 16°17W **24** F3
Tenerife Sur ✈ (TFS)
　Canary Is. 28°3N 16°33W **24** F3
Teng Xian *China* 35°5N 117°10E **35** G9
Tengah, Kepulauan
　Indonesia 7°5S 118°15E **36** F5
Tengchong *China* 25°0N 98°28E **32** D4
Tengchowfu = Penglai
　China 37°48N 120°42E **35** F11
Tenggarong *Indonesia* 0°24S 116°58E **36** E5
Tengger Shamo *China* 38°0N 104°0E **32** C5
Tenggol, Pulau
　Malaysia 4°48N 103°41E **39** K4
Tengiz Köli *Kazakhstan* 50°30N 69°0E **28** D7
Teniente Enciso △
　Paraguay 21°5S 61°8W **94** A3
Teniente Rodolfo Marsh
　Antarctica 62°30S 58°0W **5** C18
Tenino *U.S.A.* 46°51N 122°51W **78** D4
Tenkasi *India* 8°55N 77°20E **40** Q10
Tenke *Katanga,*
　Dem. Rep. of the Congo 11°22S 26°40E **55** E2
Tenke *Katanga,*
　Dem. Rep. of the Congo 10°32S 26°7E **55** E2
Tennant Creek
　Australia 19°30S 134°15E **62** B1
Tennessee □ *U.S.A.* 36°0N 86°30W **85** D11
Tennessee ➜ *U.S.A.* 37°4N 88°34W **85** C10
Teno, Pta. de *Canary Is.* 28°21N 16°55W **24** F3
Tenom *Malaysia* 5°4N 115°57E **36** C5
Tenosique *Mexico* 17°29N 91°26W **87** D6
Tenryū-Gawa ➜
　Japan 35°39N 137°48E **31** G8
Tenterden *U.K.* 51°4N 0°42E **13** F8
Tenterfield *Australia* 29°0S 152°0E **63** D5
Teófilo Otoni *Brazil* 17°50S 41°30W **93** G10
Tepa *Indonesia* 7°52S 129°31E **37** F7
Tepalcatepec ➜
　Mexico 18°35N 101°59W **86** D4
Tepehuanes *Mexico* 25°21N 105°44W **86** B3
Tepetongo *Mexico* 22°28N 103°9W **86** C4
Tepic *Mexico* 21°30N 104°54W **86** C4
Teplice *Czech Rep.* 50°40N 13°48E **16** C7
Tepoca, C. *Mexico* 30°20N 112°25W **86** A2
Tequila *Mexico* 20°54N 103°47W **86** C4
Ter ➜ *Spain* 42°2N 3°12E **21** A7
Ter Apel *Neths.* 52°53N 7°5E **15** B7
Téra *Niger* 14°0N 0°45E **50** F6
Terainan *Kiribati* 4°43N 160°25W **65** G12
Téramo *Italy* 42°39N 13°42E **22** C5
Terang *Australia* 38°15S 142°55E **63** F3
Terang, Teluk *Indonesia* 8°44S 116°0E **37** K19
Terceira *Azores* 38°43N 27°13W **50** a
Tercero ➜ *Argentina* 32°58S 61°47W **94** C3
Terebovlya *Ukraine* 49°18N 25°44E **17** D13
Terek ➜ *Russia* 44°0N 47°30E **19** F8
Terepaima △ *Venezuela* 9°58N 69°17W **89** b6
Teresina *Brazil* 5°9S 42°45W **93** E10
Terewah, L. *Australia* 29°52S 147°35E **63** D4
Teridgerie Cr. ➜
　Australia 30°25S 148°50E **63** E4
Termez = Termiz
　Uzbekistan 37°15N 67°15E **28** F7
Términi Imerese *Italy* 37°59N 13°42E **22** F5
Términos, L. de *Mexico* 18°37N 91°33W **87** D6
Termiz *Uzbekistan* 37°15N 67°15E **28** F7
Térmoli *Italy* 42°0N 15°0E **22** C6
Ternate *Indonesia* 0°45N 127°25E **37** D7
Terneuzen *Neths.* 51°20N 3°50E **15** C3
Terney *Russia* 45°3N 136°37E **30** B8
Terni *Italy* 42°34N 12°37E **22** C5
Ternopil *Ukraine* 49°30N 25°40E **17** D13
Ternopol = Ternopil
　Ukraine 49°30N 25°40E **17** D13
Terowie *Australia* 33°8S 138°55E **63** E2
Terra Bella *U.S.A.* 35°58N 119°3W **79** K7
Terra Nova △ *Canada* 48°33N 53°55W **73** C9
Terrace *Canada* 54°30N 128°35W **70** C3
Terrace Bay *Canada* 48°47N 87°5W **72** C2
Terracina *Italy* 41°17N 13°15E **22** D5
Terralba *Italy* 39°43N 8°39E **22** E3
Terrassa *Spain* 41°34N 2°1E **21** B7
Terre Haute *U.S.A.* 39°28N 87°25W **80** F10
Terrebonne B. *U.S.A.* 29°5N 90°35W **85** G9
Terrell *U.S.A.* 32°44N 96°17W **84** E6
Terrenceville *Canada* 47°40N 54°44W **73** C9
Terry *U.S.A.* 46°47N 105°19W **76** C11
Terryville *U.S.A.* 41°41N 73°3W **83** E11
Terschelling *Neths.* 53°25N 5°20E **15** A5
Teruel *Spain* 40°22N 1°8W **21** B5
Tervola *Finland* 66°6N 24°49E **8** C21
Teryaweynya L.
　Australia 32°18S 143°22E **63** E3
Teshio *Japan* 44°53N 141°44E **30** B10
Teshio-Gawa ➜
　Japan 44°53N 141°45E **30** B10
Tesiyn Gol ➜ *Mongolia* 50°40N 93°20E **32** A4
Teslin *Canada* 60°10N 132°43W **70** A2
Teslin ➜ *Canada* 61°34N 134°35W **70** A2
Teslin L. *Canada* 60°15N 132°57W **70** A2
Tessalit *Mali* 20°12N 1°0E **50** D6
Tessaoua *Niger* 13°47N 7°56E **50** F7
Test ➜ *U.K.* 50°56N 1°29W **13** G6
Testigos, Is. Los
　Venezuela 11°23N 63°7W **89** D7
Tetachuck L. *Canada* 53°18N 125°55W **70** C3
Tetas, Pta. *Chile* 23°31S 70°38W **94** A1
Tete *Mozam.* 16°13S 33°33E **55** F3
Tete □ *Mozam.* 15°15S 32°40E **55** F3
Teterev ➜ *Ukraine* 51°1N 30°5E **17** C16
Teteven *Bulgaria* 42°58N 24°17E **23** C11
Tethul ➜ *Canada* 60°35N 112°12W **70** A6
Tetiyev *Ukraine* 49°22N 29°38E **17** D15
Teton ➜ *U.S.A.* 47°56N 110°31W **76** C8
Tétouan *Morocco* 35°35N 5°21W **50** A4
Tetovo *Macedonia* 42°1N 20°59E **23** C9
Tetufera, Mt. *Tahiti* 17°40S 149°26W **59** d

Teuco → Argentina 25°35S 60°11W 94 B3
Teulon Canada 50°23N 97°16W 71 C9
Teun Indonesia 6°59S 129°8E 37 F7
Teuri-Tō Japan 44°26N 141°19E 30 B10
Teutoburger Wald Germany 52°5N 8°22E 16 B5
Tevere → Italy 41°44N 12°14E 22 D5
Teverya Israel 32°47N 35°32E 46 C4
Teviot → U.K. 55°29N 2°38W 11 F6
Tewantin Australia 26°27S 153°3E 63 D5
Tewkesbury U.K. 51°59N 2°9W 13 F5
Texada I. Canada 49°40N 124°25W 70 D4
Texarkana Ark., U.S.A. 33°26N 94°2W 84 E7
Texarkana Tex., U.S.A. 33°26N 94°3W 84 E7
Texas Australia 28°49S 151°9E 63 D5
Texas □ U.S.A. 31°40N 98°30W 84 F5
Texas City U.S.A. 29°24N 94°54W 84 G7
Texel Neths. 53°5N 4°50E 15 A4
Texline U.S.A. 36°23N 103°2W 84 C3
Texoma, L. U.S.A. 33°50N 96°34W 84 E6
Teyateyaneng Lesotho 29°7S 27°34E 53 K5
Tezin Afghan. 34°24N 69°30E 42 B3
Teziutlán Mexico 19°49N 97°21W 87 D5
Tezpur India 26°40N 92°45E 41 F18
Tezzeron L. Canada 54°43N 124°30W 70 C4
Tha-anne → Canada 60°31N 94°37W 71 A10
Tha Deua Laos 17°57N 102°53E 38 D4
Tha Deua Laos 19°26N 101°50E 38 C3
Tha Pla Thailand 17°48N 100°32E 38 D3
Tha Rua Thailand 14°34N 100°44E 38 E3
Tha Sala Thailand 8°40N 99°56E 39 H2
Tha Song Yang Thailand 17°34N 97°55E 38 D1
Thaba Putsoa Lesotho 29°45S 28°0E 57 D4
Thabana Ntlenyana Lesotho 29°30S 29°16E 57 D4
Thabazimbi S. Africa 24°40S 27°21E 57 C4
Thādiq Si. Arabia 25°18N 45°52E 44 E5
Thai Binh Vietnam 20°35N 106°1E 38 B6
Thai Muang Thailand 8°24N 98°16E 39 H2
Thai Nguyen Vietnam 21°35N 105°55E 38 B5
Thailand ■ Asia 16°0N 102°0E 38 E4
Thailand, G. of Asia 11°30N 101°0E 39 G3
Thakhek Laos 17°25N 104°45E 38 D5
Thal Pakistan 33°28N 70°33E 42 C4
Thal Desert Pakistan 31°10N 71°30E 42 D4
Thala La = Hkakabo Razi Burma 28°25N 97°23E 41 E20
Thalabarivat Cambodia 13°33N 105°57E 38 F5
Thallon Australia 28°39S 148°49E 63 D4
Thalu, Ko Thailand 9°26N 99°54E 39 b
Thames N.Z. 37°7S 175°34E 59 B5
Thames → Canada 42°20N 82°25W 82 D2
Thames → U.K. 51°29N 0°34E 13 F8
Thames → U.S.A. 41°18N 72°5W 83 E12
Thames Estuary U.K. 51°29N 0°52E 13 F8
Thamesford Canada 43°4N 81°0W 82 C4
Thamesville Canada 42°33N 81°59W 82 D3
Than India 22°34N 71°11E 42 H4
Than Uyen Vietnam 22°0N 103°54E 38 B4
Thana Gazi India 27°25N 76°19E 42 F7
Thandla India 23°0N 74°34E 42 H6
Thandwe Burma 18°20N 94°30E 41 K19
Thane India 19°12N 72°59E 40 K8
Thanesar India 30°1N 76°52E 42 D7
Thanet, I. of U.K. 51°21N 1°20E 13 F9
Thangool Australia 24°38S 150°42E 62 C5
Thanh Hoa Vietnam 19°48N 105°46E 38 C5
Thanh Hung Vietnam 9°55N 105°43E 39 H5
Thanh Pho Ho Chi Minh Vietnam 10°58N 106°40E 39 G6
Thanh Thuy Vietnam 22°55N 104°51E 38 A5
Thanjavur India 10°48N 79°12E 40 P11
Thano Bula Khan Pakistan 25°22N 67°50E 42 G2
Thaolintoa L. Canada 61°30N 96°25W 71 A9
Thap Lan △ Thailand 14°15N 102°16E 38 E4
Thap Sakae Thailand 11°30N 99°37E 39 G2
Thap Than Thailand 15°27N 99°54E 38 E2
Thar Desert India 28°0N 72°0E 42 F5
Tharad India 24°30N 71°44E 42 G4
Thargomindah Australia 27°58S 143°46E 63 D3
Tharp Fracture Zone S. Ocean 54°0S 135°0W 5 B14
Tharrawaddy Burma 17°38N 95°48E 41 L19
Tharthār, Buḥayrat ath Iraq 34°0N 43°15E 44 C4
Tharthar, L. = Tharthār, Buḥayrat ath Iraq 34°0N 43°15E 44 C4
Tharthār, W. ath → Iraq 34°32N 43°4E 44 C4
Thasos Greece 40°40N 24°40E 23 D11
That Khe Vietnam 22°16N 106°28E 38 A6
Thatcher Ariz., U.S.A. 32°51N 109°46W 77 K9
Thatcher Colo., U.S.A. 37°33N 104°7W 77 H11
Thaton Burma 16°55N 97°22E 41 L20
Thaungdut Burma 24°30N 94°40E 41 G19
Thayer U.S.A. 36°31N 91°33W 80 G8
Thayetmyo Burma 19°20N 95°10E 41 K19
Thazi Burma 21°0N 96°5E 41 J20
The Broads U.K. 52°45N 1°30E 12 E9
The Everglades U.S.A. 25°50N 81°0W 85 J14
The Gulf = Persian Gulf Asia 27°0N 50°0E 45 E6
The Hague = 's-Gravenhage Neths. 52°7N 4°17E 15 B4
The Pas Canada 53°45N 101°15W 71 C8
The Wash U.K. 52°58N 0°20E 12 E8
The Weald U.K. 51°4N 0°20E 13 F8
Thebes = Thiva Greece 38°19N 23°19E 23 E10
Thebes Egypt 25°40N 32°35E 51 C12
Thedford U.S.A. 41°59N 100°35W 80 E3
Theebine Australia 25°57S 152°34E 63 D5
Thekulthili L. Canada 61°3N 110°0W 71 A7
Thelon → Canada 64°16N 96°4W 71 A8
Theodore Australia 24°55S 150°3E 62 C5
Theodore Canada 51°26N 102°55W 71 C8
Theodore U.S.A. 30°33N 88°10W 85 F10
Theodore Roosevelt △ U.S.A. 47°0N 103°25W 80 B2
Theodore Roosevelt L. U.S.A. 33°40N 111°10W 77 K8
Thepha Thailand 6°52N 100°58E 39 J3
Theresa U.S.A. 44°13N 75°48W 83 B9
Thermopiles Greece 38°48N 22°35E 23 E10
Thermopolis U.S.A. 43°39N 108°13W 76 E9
Thermopylae P. = Thermopiles Greece 38°48N 22°35E 23 E10
Thessalon Canada 46°20N 83°30W 72 C3
Thessaloniki Greece 40°38N 22°58E 23 D10
Thessaloníki, Gulf of = Thessaloniki Kolpos Greece 40°15N 22°45E 23 D10
Thessaloniki Kolpos Greece 40°15N 22°45E 23 D10
Thetford U.K. 52°25N 0°45E 13 E8
Thetford Mines Canada 46°8N 71°18W 73 C5
Theun → Laos 18°19N 104°0E 38 C5
Theunissen S. Africa 28°26S 26°43E 56 D4
Thevenard Australia 32°9S 133°38E 63 E1
Thicket Portage Canada 55°19N 97°42W 71 B9
Thief River Falls U.S.A. 48°7N 96°10W 80 A5
Thiel Mts. Antarctica 85°15S 91°0W 5 E16
Thiers France 45°52N 3°33E 20 D5
Thiès Senegal 14°50N 16°51W 50 F2
Thika Kenya 1°1S 37°5E 54 C4
Thimphu Bhutan 27°31N 89°45E 41 F16
Þingvallavatn Iceland 64°11N 21°9W 8 D3
Thionville France 49°20N 6°10E 20 B7
Thira = Santorini Greece 36°23N 25°27E 23 F11
Third Cataract Sudan 19°42N 30°20E 51 E12
Thirsk U.K. 54°14N 1°19W 12 C6
Thiruvananthapuram = Trivandrum India 8°41N 77°0E 40 Q10
Thisted Denmark 56°58N 8°40E 9 H13
Thistle I. Australia 35°0S 136°8E 63 F2
Thithia = Cicia Fiji 17°45S 179°18W 59 a
Thiva Greece 38°19N 23°19E 23 E10
Þjórsá → Iceland 63°47N 20°48W 8 E3
Thlewiaza → Canada 60°29N 94°40W 71 A10
Thmar Puok Cambodia 13°57N 103°4E 38 F4
Tho Vinh Vietnam 19°16N 105°42E 38 C5
Thoa → Canada 60°31N 109°47W 71 A7
Thoen Thailand 17°43N 99°12E 38 D2
Thoeng Thailand 19°41N 100°12E 38 C3
Thohoyandou S. Africa 22°58S 30°29E 53 J6
Tholdi Pakistan 35°5N 76°6E 43 B7
Thomas U.S.A. 35°45N 98°45W 84 D5
Thomas, L. Australia 26°4S 137°58E 63 D2
Thomaston U.S.A. 32°53N 84°20W 85 E12
Thomasville Ala., U.S.A. 31°55N 87°44W 85 F11
Thomasville Ga., U.S.A. 30°50N 83°59W 85 F13
Thomasville N.C., U.S.A. 35°53N 80°5W 85 D14
Thompson Canada 55°45N 97°52W 71 B9
Thompson U.S.A. 41°52N 75°31W 83 E9
Thompson → Canada 50°15N 121°24W 70 C4
Thompson → U.S.A. 39°46N 93°37W 80 F7
Thompson Falls U.S.A. 47°36N 115°21W 76 C6
Thompson Pk. U.S.A. 41°0N 123°2W 76 F2
Thompson Springs U.S.A. 38°58N 109°43W 76 G9
Thompsontown U.S.A. 40°33N 77°14W 82 F7
Thomson U.S.A. 33°28N 82°30W 85 E13
Thomson → Australia 25°11S 142°53E 62 C3
Thong Yang Thailand 9°28N 99°56E 39 b
Þórisvatn Iceland 64°20N 18°55W 8 D4
Thornaby on Tees U.K. 54°33N 1°18W 12 C6
Thornbury Canada 44°34N 80°26W 82 B4
Thorne U.K. 53°37N 0°57W 12 D7
Thornhill Canada 54°31N 128°32W 70 C3
Thornton U.S.A. 39°52N 104°58W 76 G11
Thorold Canada 43°7N 79°12W 82 C5
Þórshöfn Iceland 66°12N 15°20W 8 C6
Thouin, C. Australia 20°20S 118°10E 60 D2
Thousand Oaks U.S.A. 34°10N 118°50W 79 L8
Thrace Turkey 41°0N 27°0E 23 D12
Three Forks U.S.A. 45°54N 111°33W 76 D8
Three Hills Canada 51°43N 113°15W 70 C6
Three Hummock I. Australia 40°25S 144°55E 63 G3
Three Pagodas Pass Asia 15°20N 98°30E 38 E2
Three Points, C. Ghana 4°42N 2°6W 50 H5
Three Rivers Calif., U.S.A. 36°26N 118°54W 78 J8
Three Rivers Tex., U.S.A. 28°28N 98°11W 84 G5
Three Springs Australia 29°32S 115°45E 61 E2
Throssell, L. Australia 27°33S 124°10E 61 E3
Throssell Ra. Australia 22°3S 121°43E 60 D3
Thrushton △ Australia 27°47S 147°40E 63 D4
Thua → Kenya 1°31S 39°30E 54 C4
Thuan Hoa Vietnam 8°58N 105°30E 39 H5
Thubun Lakes Canada 61°30N 112°0W 71 A6
Thuin Belgium 50°20N 4°17E 15 D4
Thule = Qaanaaq Greenland 77°40N 69°0W 4 B4
Thule Air Base = Uummannaq Greenland 77°28N 69°13W 4 B4
Thun Switz. 46°45N 7°38E 20 C7
Thunder B. U.S.A. 45°0N 83°20W 82 B1
Thunder Bay Canada 48°20N 89°15W 72 C2
Thung Salaeng Luang △ Thailand 16°43N 100°50E 38 D3
Thung Song Thailand 8°10N 99°40E 39 H2
Thunkar Bhutan 27°55N 91°0E 41 F17
Thuong Tra Vietnam 16°2N 107°42E 38 D6
Thüringer Wald Germany 50°35N 11°0E 16 C6
Thurles Ireland 52°41N 7°49W 10 D4
Thurrock □ U.K. 51°31N 0°23E 13 F8
Thursday I. Australia 10°30S 142°3E 62 A3
Thurso Canada 45°36N 75°15W 72 C4
Thurso U.K. 58°36N 3°32W 11 C5
Thurso → U.K. 58°36N 3°32W 11 C5
Thurston I. Antarctica 72°0S 100°0W 5 D16
Thutade L. Canada 57°0N 126°55W 70 B3
Thyolo Malawi 16°7S 35°5E 55 F4
Ti-Tree Australia 22°5S 133°22E 62 C1
Tian Shan Asia 40°30N 76°0E 32 B3
Tianjin China 39°7N 117°12E 35 E9
Tianshifu China 41°17N 124°22E 35 D13
Tianshui China 34°32N 105°40E 34 G3
Tianyar Indonesia 8°12S 115°30E 37 J18
Tianzhen China 40°24N 114°5E 34 D8
Tianzhuangtai China 40°43N 122°5E 35 D12
Tiarei Tahiti 17°32S 149°20W 59 d
Tiaret Algeria 35°20N 1°21E 50 A6
Tibagi Brazil 24°30S 50°24W 95 A5
Tibagi → Brazil 22°47S 51°1W 95 A5
Tibastī, Sarīr Libya 22°50N 18°30E 51 D9
Tibati Cameroon 6°22N 12°30E 52 C2
Tiber = Tevere → Italy 41°44N 12°14E 22 D5
Tiber Res. U.S.A. 48°19N 111°6W 76 B8
Tiberias = Teverya Israel 32°47N 35°32E 46 C4
Tiberias, L. = Yam Kinneret Israel 32°45N 35°35E 46 C4
Tibesti Chad 21°0N 17°30E 51 D9
Tibet = Xizang Zizhiqu □ China 32°0N 88°0E 32 C3
Tibet, Plateau of Asia 32°0N 86°0E 26 E10
Tibnī Syria 35°36N 39°50E 44 C3
Tibooburra Australia 29°26S 142°1E 63 D3
Tiburón, I. Mexico 29°0N 112°25W 86 B2
Ticino → Italy 45°9N 9°14E 20 D8
Ticonderoga U.S.A. 43°51N 73°26W 83 C11
Ticul Mexico 20°24N 89°32W 87 C7
Tidaholm Sweden 58°12N 13°58E 9 G15
Tiddim Burma 23°28N 93°45E 41 H18
Tidioute U.S.A. 41°41N 79°24W 82 E5
Tidjikja Mauritania 18°29N 11°35W 50 E3
Tidore Indonesia 0°40N 127°25E 37 D7
Tiefa China 42°28N 123°26E 35 C12
Tiegang Shuiku China 22°37N 113°53E 33 F10
Tiel Neths. 51°53N 5°26E 15 C5
Tieling China 42°20N 123°55E 35 C12
Tielt Belgium 51°0N 3°20E 15 C3
Tien Shan = Tian Shan Asia 40°30N 76°0E 32 B3
Tien-tsin = Tianjin China 39°7N 117°12E 35 E9
Tien Yen Vietnam 21°20N 107°24E 38 B6
T'ienching = Tianjin China 39°7N 117°12E 35 E9
Tienen Belgium 50°48N 4°57E 15 D4
Tientsin = Tianjin China 39°7N 117°12E 35 E9
Tieri Australia 23°2S 148°21E 62 C4
Tierra Amarilla Chile 27°28S 70°18W 94 B1
Tierra Amarilla U.S.A. 36°42N 106°33W 77 H10
Tierra Colorada Mexico 17°11N 99°32W 87 D5
Tierra de Campos Spain 42°10N 4°50W 21 A3
Tierra del Fuego, I. Gr. de Argentina 54°0S 69°0W 96 G3
Tiétar → Spain 39°50N 6°1W 21 C3
Tieté → Brazil 20°40S 51°35W 95 A5
Tiffin U.S.A. 41°7N 83°11W 81 E12
Tifton U.S.A. 31°27N 83°31W 85 F13
Tifu Indonesia 3°39S 126°24E 37 E7
Tighina Moldova 46°50N 29°30E 17 E15
Tigil Russia 57°49N 158°40E 29 D16
Tignish Canada 46°58N 64°2W 73 C7
Tigre → Peru 4°30S 74°10W 92 D4
Tigre → Venezuela 9°20N 62°30W 92 B6
Tigris = Dijlah, Nahr → Asia 31°0N 47°25E 44 D5
Tigyaing Burma 23°45N 96°10E 41 H20
Tījāra India 27°56N 76°31E 42 F7
Tijuana Mexico 32°32N 117°1W 79 N9
Tikal Guatemala 17°13N 89°24W 88 C2
Tikal △ Guatemala 17°23N 89°34W 88 C2
Tikamgarh India 24°44N 78°50E 43 G8
Tikhoretsk Russia 45°56N 40°5E 19 E7
Tikhvin Russia 59°35N 33°30E 18 C5
Tikirarjuaq = Whale Cove Canada 62°10N 92°34W 71 A10
Tikrīt Iraq 34°35N 43°37E 44 C4
Tiksi Russia 71°40N 128°45E 29 B13
Tilamuta Indonesia 0°32N 122°23E 37 D6
Tilburg Neths. 51°31N 5°6E 15 C5
Tilbury Canada 42°17N 82°23W 82 D2
Tilbury U.K. 51°27N 0°22E 13 F8
Tilcara Argentina 23°36S 65°23W 94 A2
Tilden U.S.A. 42°3N 97°50W 80 D5
Tilhar India 28°0N 79°45E 43 F8
Tilichiki Russia 60°27N 166°5E 29 C17
Tilissos Greece 35°20N 25°1E 25 D7
Till → U.K. 55°41N 2°13W 12 B5
Tillamook U.S.A. 45°27N 123°51W 76 D2
Tillsonburg Canada 42°53N 80°44W 82 D4
Tillyeria Cyprus 35°6N 32°40E 25 D11
Tilos Greece 36°27N 27°27E 23 F12
Tilpa Australia 30°57S 144°24E 63 E3
Tilt → U.K. 56°46N 3°51W 11 E5
Tilton U.S.A. 43°27N 71°36W 83 C13
Tiltonsville U.S.A. 40°10N 80°41W 82 F4
Timanfaya △ Canary Is. 29°0N 13°46W 24 F6
Timanskiy Kryazh Russia 65°58N 50°5E 18 A9
Timaru N.Z. 44°23S 171°14E 59 F3
Timau Kenya 0°4N 37°15E 54 B4
Timbaki Greece 35°4N 24°45E 25 D6
Timber Creek Australia 15°40S 130°29E 60 C5
Timber Lake U.S.A. 45°26N 101°5W 80 C3
Timber Mt. U.S.A. 37°6N 116°28W 78 H10
Timbuktu = Tombouctou Mali 16°50N 3°0W 50 E5
Timi Cyprus 34°44N 32°31E 25 E11
Timimoun Algeria 29°14N 0°16E 50 C6
Timiris, Râs Mauritania 19°21N 16°30W 50 E2
Timiskaming, L. = Témiscamingue, L. Canada 47°10N 79°25W 72 C4
Timişoara Romania 45°43N 21°15E 17 F11
Timmins Canada 48°28N 81°25W 72 C3
Timok → Serbia 44°10N 22°40E 23 B10
Timoleague Ireland 51°39N 8°46W 10 E3
Timor Asia 9°0S 125°0E 37 F7
Timor Leste = East Timor ■ Asia 8°50S 126°0E 37 F7
Timor Sea Ind. Oc. 12°0S 127°0E 60 B4
Tin Can Bay Australia 25°56S 153°0E 63 D5
Tin Mt. U.S.A. 36°50N 117°10W 78 J9
Tina = Thina → S. Africa 31°18S 29°13E 57 E4
Tîna, Khalîg el Egypt 31°10N 32°40E 46 D1
Tinaca Pt. Phil. 5°30N 125°25E 37 C7
Tinajo Canary Is. 29°4N 13°42W 24 E6
Tindal Australia 14°31S 132°22E 60 B5
Tindouf Algeria 27°42N 8°10W 50 C4
Tinfunque △ Paraguay 23°55S 60°17W 94 A3
Tinggi, Pulau Malaysia 2°18N 104°7E 39 L5
Tingo Maria Peru 9°10S 75°54W 92 E3
Tingrela Ivory C. 10°27N 6°25W 50 F4
Tinh Bien Vietnam 10°36N 104°57E 39 G5
Tinian N. Marianas 15°0N 145°38E 64 F6
Tinnevelly = Tirunelveli India 8°45N 77°45E 40 Q10
Tinogasta Argentina 28°5S 67°32W 94 B2
Tinos Greece 37°33N 25°8E 23 F11
Tinpahar India 24°59N 87°44E 43 G12
Tintina Argentina 27°2S 62°45W 94 B3
Tintinara Australia 35°48S 140°2E 63 F3
Tioga N. Dak., U.S.A. 48°24N 102°56W 80 A2
Tioga Pa., U.S.A. 41°55N 77°8W 82 E7
Tioman, Pulau Malaysia 2°50N 104°10E 39 L5
Tionesta U.S.A. 41°30N 79°28W 82 E5
Tipperary Ireland 52°28N 8°10W 10 D3
Tipperary □ Ireland 52°37N 7°55W 10 D4
Tipton Calif., U.S.A. 36°4N 119°19W 78 J7
Tipton Iowa, U.S.A. 41°46N 91°8W 80 E8
Tipton Mt. U.S.A. 35°32N 114°12W 79 K12
Tiptonville U.S.A. 36°23N 89°29W 85 C10
Tīrān Iran 32°45N 51°8E 45 C6
Tiranë Albania 41°18N 19°49E 23 D8
Tirari Desert Australia 28°22S 138°7E 63 D2
Tiraspol Moldova 46°55N 29°35E 17 E15
Tire Turkey 38°5N 27°45E 23 E12
Tirebolu Turkey 40°58N 38°45E 19 F6
Tiree U.K. 56°31N 6°55W 11 E2
Tiree, Passage of U.K. 56°30N 6°30W 11 E2
Tîrgovişte = Târgovişte Romania 44°55N 25°27E 17 F13
Tîrgu-Jiu = Târgu-Jiu Romania 45°5N 23°19E 17 F12
Tîrgu Mureş = Târgu Mureş Romania 46°31N 24°38E 17 E13
Tirich Mir Pakistan 36°15N 71°55E 40 A7
Tiritiri o te Moana = Southern Alps N.Z. 43°41S 170°11E 59 E3
Tirnavos Greece 39°45N 22°18E 23 E10
Tirodi India 21°40N 79°44E 40 J11
Tirol □ Austria 47°3N 10°43E 16 E6
Tirso → Italy 39°53N 8°32E 22 E3
Tiruchchirappalli India 10°45N 78°45E 40 P11
Tirunelveli India 8°45N 77°45E 40 Q10
Tirupati India 13°39N 79°25E 40 N11
Tiruppur India 11°5N 77°22E 40 P10
Tiruvannamalai India 12°15N 79°5E 40 N11
Tisa India 32°50N 76°9E 42 C7
Tisa → Serbia 45°15N 20°17E 23 B9
Tisdale Canada 52°50N 104°0W 71 C8
Tishomingo U.S.A. 34°14N 96°41W 84 D6
Tisza = Tisa → Serbia 45°15N 20°17E 23 B9
Tit-Ary Russia 71°55N 127°2E 29 B13
Tithwal Pakistan 34°21N 73°50E 43 B5
Titicaca, L. S. Amer. 15°30S 69°30W 92 G5
Titiwa Nigeria 12°14N 12°53E 51 F8
Titule Dem. Rep. of the Congo 3°15N 25°31E 54 B2
Titusville Fla., U.S.A. 28°37N 80°49W 85 G14
Titusville Pa., U.S.A. 41°38N 79°41W 82 E5
Tivaouane Senegal 14°56N 16°45W 50 F2
Tiverton U.K. 50°54N 3°29W 13 G4
Tívoli Italy 41°58N 12°45E 22 D5
Tizi-Ouzou Algeria 36°42N 4°3E 50 A6
Tizimín Mexico 21°9N 88°9W 87 C7
Tiznit Morocco 29°48N 9°45W 50 C4
Tjeggelvas Sweden 66°37N 17°45E 8 C17
Tjieggelvas = Tjeggelvas Sweden 66°37N 17°45E 8 C17
Tjirebon = Cirebon Indonesia 6°45S 108°32E 36 F3
Tjluring Indonesia 8°25S 114°13E 37 J17
Tjörn Sweden 58°0N 11°35E 9 H14
Tlacotalpan Mexico 18°37N 95°40W 87 D5
Tlahualilo de Zaragoza Mexico 26°7N 103°27W 86 B4
Tlaquepaque Mexico 20°39N 103°19W 86 C4
Tlaxcala Mexico 19°19N 98°14W 87 D5
Tlaxcala □ Mexico 19°25N 98°10W 87 D5
Tlaxiaco Mexico 17°25N 97°35W 87 D5
Tlemcen Algeria 34°52N 1°21W 50 B5
To Bong Vietnam 12°45N 109°16E 38 F7
Toa Payoh Singapore 1°20N 103°51E 39 d
Toad → Canada 59°25N 124°57W 70 B4
Toad River Canada 58°51N 125°14W 70 B3
Toamasina Madag. 18°10S 49°25E 57 B8
Toamasina □ Madag. 18°0S 49°0E 57 B8
Toay Argentina 36°43S 64°38W 94 D3
Toba Japan 34°30N 136°51E 31 G8
Toba, Danau Indonesia 2°30N 97°30E 36 D1
Toba Kakar Pakistan 31°30N 69°0E 42 D3
Toba Tek Singh Pakistan 30°55N 72°25E 42 D5
Tobago Trin. & Tob. 11°10N 60°30W 89 D7
Tobelo Indonesia 1°45N 127°56E 37 D7
Tobermory Canada 45°12N 81°40W 82 A3
Tobermory U.K. 56°38N 6°5W 11 E2
Tobi Pac. Oc. 2°40N 131°10E 37 D8
Tobi-Shima Japan 41°12N 139°34E 30 D9
Tobin, L. Australia 21°45S 125°49E 60 D4
Tobin L. Canada 53°35N 103°30W 71 C8
Toboali Indonesia 3°0S 106°25E 36 E3
Tobol → Russia 58°10N 68°12E 28 D7
Toboli Indonesia 0°38S 120°5E 37 E6
Tobolsk Russia 58°15N 68°10E 28 D7
Tobruk = Tubruq Libya 32°7N 23°55E 51 B10
Tobyhanna U.S.A. 41°11N 75°25W 83 E9
Tobyl = Tobol → Russia 58°10N 68°12E 28 D7
Tocantinópolis Brazil 6°20S 47°25W 93 E9
Tocantins □ Brazil 10°0S 48°0W 93 F9
Tocantins → Brazil 1°45S 49°10W 93 D9
Toccoa U.S.A. 34°35N 83°19W 85 D13
Tochi → Pakistan 32°49N 70°41E 42 C4
Tochigi Japan 36°25N 139°45E 31 F9
Tochigi □ Japan 36°45N 139°45E 31 F9
Toco Trin. & Tob. 10°49N 60°57W 93 K16
Toconao Chile 23°11S 68°1W 94 A2
Tocopilla Chile 22°5S 70°10W 94 A1
Tocumwal Australia 35°51S 145°31E 63 F4
Tocuyo → Venezuela 11°3N 68°23W 92 A5
Todd → Australia 24°52S 135°48E 62 C2
Todeli Indonesia 1°40S 124°29E 37 E6
Todenyang Kenya 4°35N 35°56E 54 B4
Todgarh India 25°42N 73°58E 42 G5
Todos os Santos, B. de Brazil 12°48S 38°38W 93 F11
Todos Santos Mexico 23°26N 110°13W 86 C2
Toe Hd. U.K. 57°50N 7°8W 11 D1
Tofield Canada 53°25N 112°40W 70 C6
Tofino Canada 49°11N 125°55W 70 D3
Tofua Tonga 19°45S 175°5W 59 c
Tōgane Japan 35°33N 140°22E 31 G10
Togian, Kepulauan Indonesia 0°20S 121°50E 37 E6
Togliatti Russia 53°32N 49°24E 18 D8
Togo ■ W. Afr. 8°30N 1°35E 50 G6
Togtoh China 40°15N 111°10E 34 D6
Tohiea, Mt. Moorea 17°33S 149°49W 59 d
Tōhoku □ Japan 39°50N 141°45E 30 E10
Töhöm Mongolia 44°27N 108°2E 34 B5
Toinya Sudan 6°17N 29°46E 51 G11
Toiyabe Range U.S.A. 39°30N 117°0W 76 G5
Tojikiston = Tajikistan ■ Asia 38°30N 70°0E 28 F8
Tojo Indonesia 1°20S 121°15E 37 E6
Tōjō Japan 34°53N 133°16E 31 G6
Tok U.S.A. 63°20N 142°59W 74 a
Tok-do Asia 37°15N 131°52E 31 F5
Tokachi-Dake Japan 43°17N 142°5E 30 C11
Tokachi-Gawa → Japan 42°44N 143°42E 30 C11
Tokala Indonesia 1°30S 121°40E 37 E6
Tōkamachi Japan 37°8N 138°43E 31 F9
Tokanui N.Z. 46°34S 168°56E 59 G2
Tokara-Rettō Japan 29°37N 129°43E 31 K4
Tokarahi N.Z. 44°56S 170°39E 59 F3
Tokashiki-Shima Japan 26°11N 127°21E 31 L3
Tokat Turkey 40°22N 36°35E 19 F6
Tŏkch'ŏn N. Korea 39°45N 126°18E 35 E14
Tokeland U.S.A. 46°42N 123°59W 78 D3
Tokelau Is. Pac. Oc. 9°0S 171°45W 64 H10
Tokmak Kyrgyzstan 42°49N 75°15E 28 E8
Toko Ra. Australia 23°5S 138°20E 62 C2
Tokoro-Gawa → Japan 44°7N 144°5E 30 B12
Toku Tonga 18°10S 174°11W 59 c
Tokuno-Shima Japan 27°56N 128°55E 31 L4
Tokushima Japan 34°4N 134°34E 31 G7
Tokushima □ Japan 33°55N 134°0E 31 H7
Tokuyama Japan 34°3N 131°50E 31 G5
Tōkyō Japan 35°43N 139°45E 31 G9
Tolaga Bay N.Z. 38°21S 178°20E 59 C7
Tolbukhin = Dobrich Bulgaria 43°37N 27°49E 23 C12
Toledo Brazil 24°44S 53°45W 95 A5
Toledo Spain 39°50N 4°2W 21 C3
Toledo Ohio, U.S.A. 41°39N 83°33W 81 E12
Toledo Oreg., U.S.A. 44°37N 123°56W 76 D2
Toledo Wash., U.S.A. 46°26N 122°51W 76 C2
Toledo, Montes de Spain 39°33N 4°20W 21 C3
Toledo Bend Res. U.S.A. 31°11N 93°34W 84 F8
Tolga Australia 17°15S 145°29E 62 B4
Toliara Madag. 23°21S 43°40E 57 C7
Toliara □ Madag. 21°0S 45°0E 57 C8
Tolima Colombia 4°40N 75°19W 92 C3
Tolitoli Indonesia 1°5N 120°50E 37 D6
Tollhouse U.S.A. 37°1N 119°24W 78 H7
Tolmachevo Russia 58°56N 29°51E 9 G23
Tolo, Teluk Indonesia 2°20S 122°10E 37 E6
Tolo Harbour China 22°27N 114°12E 33 G11
Toluca Mexico 19°17N 99°40W 87 D5
Tom Burke S. Africa 23°5S 28°0E 57 C4
Tom Price Australia 22°40S 117°48E 60 D2
Tomah U.S.A. 43°59N 90°30W 80 D8
Tomahawk U.S.A. 45°28N 89°44W 80 C9
Tomakomai Japan 42°38N 141°36E 30 C10
Tomales U.S.A. 38°15N 122°53W 78 G4
Tomales B. U.S.A. 38°15N 123°58W 78 G3
Tomanivi Fiji 17°37S 178°1E 59 a
Tomar Portugal 39°36N 8°25W 21 C1
Tomaszów Mazowiecki Poland 51°30N 20°2E 17 C11
Tomatlán Mexico 19°56N 105°15W 86 D3
Tombador, Serra do

Brazil 12°0S 58°0W 92 F7
Tombigbee → U.S.A. 31°8N 87°57W 85 F11
Tombouctou Mali 16°50N 3°0W 50 E5
Tombstone U.S.A. 31°43N 110°4W 77 L8
Tombua Angola 15°55S 11°55E 56 B1
Tomé Chile 36°36S 72°57W 94 D1
Tomelloso Spain 39°10N 3°2W 21 C4
Tomini Indonesia 0°30N 120°30E 37 D6
Tomini, Teluk Indonesia 0°10S 121°0E 37 E6
Tomintoul U.K. 57°15N 3°23W 11 D5
Tomkinson Ranges Australia 26°11S 129°5E 61 E4
Tommot Russia 59°4N 126°20E 29 D13
Tomnop Ta Suos Cambodia 11°20N 104°15E 39 G5
Tomo → Colombia 5°20N 67°48W 92 B5
Toms Place U.S.A. 37°34N 118°41W 78 H8
Toms River U.S.A. 39°58N 74°12W 83 G10
Tomsk Russia 56°30N 85°5E 28 D9
Tonalá Chiapas, Mexico 16°4N 93°45W 87 D6
Tonalá Jalisco, Mexico 20°37N 103°14W 86 C4
Tonantins Brazil 2°45S 67°45W 92 D5
Tonasket U.S.A. 48°42N 119°26W 76 B4
Tonawanda U.S.A. 43°1N 78°53W 82 D6
Tonb Iran 26°15N 55°15E 45 E7
Tonbridge U.K. 51°11N 0°17E 13 F8
Tondano Indonesia 1°35N 124°54E 37 D6
Tondoro Namibia 17°45S 18°50E 56 B2
Tone → Australia 34°25S 116°25E 61 F2
Tone-Gawa → Japan 35°44N 140°51E 31 F9
Tonekābon Iran 36°45N 51°12E 45 B6
Tong Xian China 39°55N 116°35E 34 E9
Tong-Yeong S. Korea 34°50N 128°20E 35 G15
Tonga ■ Pac. Oc. 19°50S 174°30W 59 c
Tonga Trench Pac. Oc. 18°0S 173°0W 64 J10
Tongaat S. Africa 29°33S 31°9E 57 D5
Tongareva = Penrhyn Cook Is. 9°0S 158°0W 65 H12
Tongariro △ N.Z. 39°8S 175°33E 59 C5
Tongatapu Tonga 21°10S 175°10W 59 c
Tongatapu Group Tonga 21°0S 175°0W 59 c
Tongchuan China 35°6N 109°3E 34 G5
Tongeren Belgium 50°47N 5°28E 15 D5
Tonggu Jiao China 22°22N 113°37E 33 G10
Tongguan China 34°40N 110°25E 34 G6
Tonghua China 41°42N 125°58E 35 D13
Tongjosŏn Man N. Korea 39°30N 128°0E 35 E15
Tongking, G. of = Tonkin, G. of Asia 20°0N 108°0E 38 B7
Tongliao China 43°38N 122°18E 35 C12
Tongling China 30°55N 117°48E 33 C6
Tongobory Madag. 23°32S 44°20E 57 C7
Tongoy Chile 30°16S 71°31W 94 C1
Tongres = Tongeren Belgium 50°47N 5°28E 15 D5
Tongsa Dzong Bhutan 27°31N 90°31E 41 F17
Tongshi China 18°30N 109°20E 38 C7
Tongue U.K. 58°29N 4°25W 11 C4
Tongue → U.S.A. 46°25N 105°52W 76 C11
Tongwei China 35°0N 105°5E 34 G3
Tongxin China 36°59N 105°58E 34 F3
Tongyang N. Korea 39°9N 126°53E 35 E14
Tongyu China 44°45N 123°4E 35 B12
Tonj Sudan 7°20N 28°44E 51 G11
Tonk India 26°6N 75°54E 42 F6
Tonkawa U.S.A. 36°41N 97°18W 84 C6
Tonkin = Bac Phan Vietnam 22°0N 105°0E 38 B5
Tonkin, G. of Asia 20°0N 108°0E 38 B7
Tonle Sap Cambodia 13°0N 104°0E 39 F5
Tono Japan 39°19N 141°32E 30 E10
Tonopah U.S.A. 38°4N 117°14W 77 G5
Tonosí Panama 7°20N 80°20W 88 E3
Tons → Haryana, India 30°30N 77°39E 42 D7
Tons → Ut. P., India 26°1N 83°33E 43 F10
Tønsberg Norway 59°19N 10°25E 9 G14
Tonto △ U.S.A. 33°39N 111°7W 77 K8
Tonumea Tonga 20°30S 174°30W 59 c
Toobanna Australia 18°42S 146°9E 62 B4
Toodyay Australia 31°34S 116°28E 61 F2
Tooele U.S.A. 40°32N 112°18W 76 F7
Toompine Australia 27°15S 144°19E 63 D3
Toora Australia 38°39S 146°23E 63 F4
Toora-Khem Russia 52°28N 96°17E 29 D10
Toowoomba Australia 27°32S 151°56E 63 D5
Top-ozero Russia 65°35N 32°0E 8 D25
Top Springs Australia 16°37S 131°51E 60 C5
Topaz U.S.A. 38°41N 119°30W 78 G7
Topeka U.S.A. 39°3N 95°40W 80 F6
Topley Canada 54°49N 126°18W 70 C3
Topocalma, Pta. Chile 34°10S 72°2W 94 C1
Topock U.S.A. 34°46N 114°29W 79 L12
Topoľčany Slovak Rep. 48°35N 18°12E 17 D10
Topolobampo Mexico 25°36N 109°3W 86 B3
Toppenish U.S.A. 46°23N 120°19W 76 C3
Toraka Vestale Madag. 16°20S 43°58E 57 B7
Torata Peru 17°23S 70°1W 92 G4
Torbalı Turkey 38°10N 27°21E 23 E12
Torbat-e Heydārīyeh Iran 35°15N 59°12E 45 C8
Torbat-e Jām Iran 35°16N 60°35E 45 C9
Torbay Canada 47°40N 52°42W 73 C9
Torbay □ U.K. 50°26N 3°31W 13 G4
Tordesillas Spain 41°30N 5°0W 21 B3
Torfaen □ U.K. 51°43N 3°3W 13 F4
Torgau Germany 51°34N 13°0E 16 C7
Torhout Belgium 51°5N 3°7E 15 C3
Tori-Shima Japan 30°29N 140°19E 31 J10
Torino Italy 45°3N 7°40E 20 D7
Torit Sudan 4°27N 32°31E 51 H12
Torkamān Iran 37°35N 47°23E 44 B5
Tormes → Spain 41°18N 6°29W 21 B2
Tornado Mt. Canada 49°55N 114°40W 70 D6
Torneå = Tornio Finland 65°50N 24°12E 8 D21
Torneälven → Europe 65°50N 24°12E 8 D21
Torneträsk Sweden 68°24N 19°15E 8 B18
Tornio Finland 65°50N 24°12E 8 D21
Tornionjoki = Torneälven → Europe 65°50N 24°12E 8 D21
Tornquist Argentina 38°8S 62°15W 94 D3
Toro Spain 39°59N 4°8E 24 B11
Toro, Cerro del Chile 29°10S 69°50W 94 B2
Toro ⌓ Uganda 1°5N 30°22E 54 C3
Toro Pk. U.S.A. 33°34N 116°24W 79 M10
Toronto Canada 43°39N 79°20W 82 C5
Toronto U.S.A. 40°28N 80°36W 82 F4
Toronto Lester B. Pearson Int. ✈ (YYZ) Canada 43°46N 79°35W 82 C5
Toropets Russia 56°30N 31°40E 18 C5
Tororo Uganda 0°45N 34°12E 54 B3
Toros Dağları Turkey 37°0N 32°30E 44 B2
Torpa India 22°57N 85°6E 43 H11
Torquay U.K. 50°27N 3°32W 13 G4
Torrance U.S.A. 33°50N 118°20W 79 M8
Torre de Moncorvo Portugal 41°12N 7°8W 21 B2
Torre del Greco Italy 40°47N 14°22E 22 D6
Torrejón de Ardoz Spain 40°27N 3°29W 21 B4
Torrelavega Spain 43°20N 4°5W 21 A3
Torremolinos Spain 36°38N 4°30W 21 D3
Torrens, L. Australia 31°0S 137°50E 63 E2
Torrens Cr. → Australia 22°23S 145°9E 62 C4
Torrens Creek Australia 20°48S 145°3E 62 C4
Torrent Spain 39°27N 0°28W 21 C5
Torreón Mexico 25°33N 103°26W 86 B4
Torres Brazil 29°21S 49°44W 95 B5
Torres Mexico 28°46N 110°47W 86 B2
Torres Strait Australia 9°50S 142°20E 58 B7
Torres Vedras Portugal 39°5N 9°15W 21 C1
Torrevieja Spain 37°59N 0°42W 21 D5
Torrey U.S.A. 38°18N 111°25W 76 G8
Torridge → U.K. 51°0N 4°13W 13 G3
Torridon, L. U.K. 57°35N 5°50W 11 D3
Torrington Conn., U.S.A. 41°48N 73°7W 83 E11
Torrington Wyo., U.S.A. 42°4N 104°11W 76 E11
Tórshavn Færoe Is. 62°5N 6°56W 8 E9
Tortola Br. Virgin Is. 18°19N 64°45W 89 e
Tortosa Spain 40°49N 0°31E 21 B6
Tortosa, C. Spain 40°41N 0°52E 21 B6
Tortue, Î. de la Haiti 20°5N 72°57W 89 B5
Tortuguero △ Costa Rica 10°31N 83°29W 88 D3
Torūd Iran 35°25N 55°5E 45 C7
Toruń Poland 53°2N 18°39E 17 B10
Tory I. Ireland 55°16N 8°14W 10 A3
Tosa Japan 33°24N 133°23E 31 H6
Tosa-Shimizu Japan 32°52N 132°58E 31 H6
Tosa-Wan Japan 33°15N 133°30E 31 H6
Toscana □ Italy 43°25N 11°0E 22 C4
Toshka Lakes Egypt 22°50N 31°0E 51 D12
Toshkent Uzbekistan 41°20N 69°10E 28 E7
Tostado Argentina 29°15S 61°50W 94 B3
Tostón, Pta. de Canary Is. 28°42N 14°2W 24 F5
Tosu Japan 33°22N 130°31E 31 H5
Toteng Botswana 20°22S 22°58E 56 C3
Totma Russia 60°0N 42°40E 18 C7
Totnes U.K. 50°26N 3°42W 13 G4
Totness Suriname 5°53N 56°19W 93 B7
Totonicapán Guatemala 14°58N 91°12W 88 D1
Totoya, I. Fiji 18°57S 179°50W 59 a
Totten Glacier Antarctica 66°45S 116°10E 5 C8
Tottenham Australia 32°14S 147°21E 63 E4
Tottenham Canada 44°1N 79°49W 82 B5
Tottori Japan 35°30N 134°15E 31 G7
Tottori □ Japan 35°30N 134°12E 31 G7
Toubkal, Djebel Morocco 31°0N 8°0W 50 B4
Tougan Burkina Faso 13°11N 2°58W 50 F5
Touggourt Algeria 33°6N 6°4E 50 B7
Toul France 48°40N 5°53E 20 B6
Toulon France 43°10N 5°55E 20 E6
Toulouse France 43°37N 1°27E 20 E4
Toummo Niger 22°45N 14°8E 51 D8
Toungoo Burma 19°0N 96°30E 41 K20
Touraine France 47°20N 0°30E 20 C4
Tourcoing France 50°42N 3°10E 20 A5
Touriñán, C. Spain 43°3N 9°18W 21 A1
Tournai Belgium 50°35N 3°25E 15 D3
Tournon-sur-Rhône France 45°4N 4°50E 20 D6
Tours France 47°22N 0°40E 20 C4
Toussora, Mt. C.A.R. 9°7N 23°14E 52 C4
Touws → S. Africa 33°45S 21°11E 56 E3
Touwsrivier S. Africa 33°20S 20°2E 56 E3
Towada Japan 40°37N 141°13E 30 D10
Towada-Hachimantai △ Japan 40°20N 140°55E 30 D10
Towada-Ko Japan 40°28N 140°55E 30 D10
Towanda U.S.A. 41°46N 76°27W 83 E8
Tower U.S.A. 47°48N 92°17W 80 B7
Towerhill Cr. → Australia 22°28S 144°35E 62 C3
Towner U.S.A. 48°21N 100°25W 80 A3
Townsend U.S.A. 46°19N 111°31W 76 C8
Townshend I. Australia 22°10S 150°31E 62 C5
Townsville Australia 19°15S 146°45E 62 B4
Towraghondī Afghan. 35°13N 62°16E 40 B3
Towson U.S.A. 39°24N 76°36W 81 F15
Towuti, Danau Indonesia 2°45S 121°32E 37 E6
Toya-Ko Japan 42°35N 140°51E 30 C10
Toyama Japan 36°40N 137°15E 31 F8
Toyama □ Japan 36°45N 137°30E 31 F8
Toyama-Wan Japan 37°0N 137°30E 31 F8
Toyapakeh Indonesia 8°41S 115°29E 37 K18
Toyohashi Japan 34°45N 137°25E 31 G8
Toyokawa Japan 34°48N 137°27E 31 G8
Toyonaka Japan 34°46N 135°28E 31 G7
Toyooka Japan 35°35N 134°48E 31 G7
Toyota Japan 35°3N 137°7E 31 G8
Tozeur Tunisia 33°56N 8°8E 50 B7
Tozkhurmato Iraq 34°56N 44°38E 44 C5
Trá Li = Tralee Ireland 52°16N 9°42W 10 D2
Tra On Vietnam 9°58N 105°55E 39 H5
Trabzon Turkey 41°0N 39°45E 19 F6
Tracadie-Sheila Canada 47°30N 64°55W 73 C7
Tracy Calif., U.S.A. 37°44N 121°26W 78 H5
Tracy Minn., U.S.A. 44°14N 95°37W 80 C6
Trafalgar, C. Spain 36°10N 6°2W 21 D2
Trail Canada 49°5N 117°40W 70 D5
Trainor L. Canada 60°24N 120°17W 70 A4
Trakai △ Lithuania 54°30N 25°10E 9 J21
Trákhonas Cyprus 35°12N 33°21E 25 D12
Tralee Ireland 52°16N 9°42W 10 D2
Tralee B. Ireland 52°17N 9°55W 10 D2
Tramore Ireland 52°10N 7°10W 10 D4
Tramore B. Ireland 52°9N 7°10W 10 D4
Tran Ninh, Cao Nguyen Laos 19°30N 103°10E 38 C4
Tranås Sweden 58°3N 14°59E 9 G16
Trancas Argentina 26°11S 65°20W 94 B2
Trang Thailand 7°33N 99°38E 39 J2
Trangahy Madag. 19°7S 44°31E 57 B7
Trangan Indonesia 6°40S 134°20E 37 F8
Trangie Australia 32°4S 148°0E 63 E4
Trani Italy 41°17N 16°25E 22 D7
Tranoroa Madag. 24°42S 45°4E 57 C8
Tranqueras Uruguay 31°13S 55°45W 95 C4
Transantarctic Mts. Antarctica 85°0S 170°0W 5 E12
Transilvania Romania 46°30N 24°0E 17 E12
Transilvanian Alps = Carpaţii Meridionali Romania 45°30N 25°0E 17 F13
Transnistria = Stînga Nistrului □ Moldova 47°20N 29°15E 17 E15
Transylvania = Transilvania Romania 46°30N 24°0E 17 E12
Trápani Italy 38°1N 12°29E 22 E5
Trapper Pk. U.S.A. 45°54N 114°18W 76 D6
Traralgon Australia 38°12S 146°34E 63 F4
Trasimeno, L. Italy 43°8N 12°6E 22 C5
Trat Thailand 12°14N 102°33E 39 F4
Tratani → Pakistan 29°19N 68°20E 42 E3
Traun Austria 48°14N 14°15E 16 D8
Traveller's L. Australia 33°20S 142°0E 63 E3
Travemünde Germany 53°57N 10°52E 16 B6
Travers, Mt. N.Z. 42°1S 172°45E 59 E4
Traverse City U.S.A. 44°46N 85°38W 81 C11
Travis, L. U.S.A. 30°24N 97°55W 84 F6
Travnik Bos.-H. 44°17N 17°39E 23 B7
Trawbreaga B. Ireland 55°20N 7°25W 10 A4
Trébbia → Italy 45°4N 9°41E 20 D8
Třebíč Czech Rep. 49°14N 15°55E 16 D8
Trebinje Bos.-H. 42°44N 18°22E 23 C8
Trebonne Australia 18°37S 146°5E 62 B4
Tregaron U.K. 52°14N 3°56W 13 E4
Tregrosse Is. Australia 17°41S 150°43E 62 B5
Treherne Canada 49°38N 98°42W 71 D9
Treinta y Tres Uruguay 33°16S 54°17W 95 C5
Trelawney Zimbabwe 17°30S 30°30E 57 B5
Trelew Argentina 43°10S 65°20W 96 E3
Trelleborg Sweden 55°20N 13°10E 9 J15
Tremadog Bay U.K. 52°51N 4°18W 12 E3
Tremonton U.S.A. 41°43N 112°10W 76 F7
Tremp Spain 42°10N 0°52E 21 A6
Trenche → Canada 47°46N 72°53W 72 C5
Trenčín Slovak Rep. 48°52N 18°4E 17 D10
Trenggalek Indonesia 8°3S 111°43E 37 H14
Trenque Lauquen Argentina 36°5S 62°45W 94 D3
Trent → Canada 44°6N 77°34W 82 B7
Trent → U.K. 53°41N 0°42W 12 D7
Trento Italy 46°4N 11°8E 22 A4
Trenton = Quinte West Canada 44°10N 77°34W 82 B7
Trenton Mo., U.S.A. 40°5N 93°37W 80 E7
Trenton N.J., U.S.A. 40°14N 74°46W 83 F10
Trenton Nebr., U.S.A. 40°11N 101°1W 80 E3
Trepassey Canada 46°43N 53°25W 73 C9
Tres Arroyos Argentina 38°26S 60°20W 94 D3
Três Corações Brazil 21°44S 45°15W 95 A6
Três Lagoas Brazil 20°50S 51°43W 93 H8
Tres Lomas Argentina 36°27S 62°51W 94 D3
Tres Montes, C. Chile 46°50S 75°30W 96 F1
Tres Pinos U.S.A. 36°48N 121°19W 78 J5
Três Pontas Brazil 21°23S 45°29W 95 A6
Tres Puentes Chile 27°50S 70°15W 94 B1
Tres Puntas, C. Argentina 47°0S 66°0W 96 F3
Três Rios Brazil 22°6S 43°15W 95 A7
Tres Valles Mexico 18°15N 96°8W 87 D5
Tresco U.K. 49°57N 6°20W 13 H1
Treviso Italy 45°40N 12°15E 22 B5
Triabunna Australia 42°30S 147°55E 63 G4
Trianda Greece 36°25N 28°10E 25 C10
Triangle Zimbabwe 21°2S 31°28E 57 C5
Tribal Areas □ Pakistan 33°0N 70°0E 42 C4
Tribulation, C. Australia 16°5S 145°29E 62 B4
Tribune U.S.A. 38°28N 101°45W 80 F3
Trichinopoly = Tiruchchirappalli India 10°45N 78°45E 40 P11
Trichur India 10°30N 76°18E 40 P10
Trida Australia 33°1S 145°1E 63 E4
Trier Germany 49°45N 6°38E 16 D4
Trieste Italy 45°40N 13°46E 22 B5
Triglav Slovenia 46°21N 13°50E 16 E7
Trikala Greece 39°34N 21°47E 23 E9
Trikomo Cyprus 35°17N 33°52E 25 D12
Trikora, Puncak Indonesia 4°15S 138°45E 37 E9
Trim Ireland 53°33N 6°48W 10 C5
Trimmu Dam Pakistan 31°10N 72°8E 42 D5
Trincomalee Sri Lanka 8°38N 81°15E 40 Q12
Trindade Brazil 16°40S 49°30W 93 G9
Trindade, I. Atl. Oc. 20°20S 29°50W 2 F8
Trinidad Bolivia 14°46S 64°50W 92 F6
Trinidad Cuba 21°48N 80°0W 88 B4
Trinidad Trin. & Tob. 10°30N 61°15W 89 D7
Trinidad Uruguay 33°30S 56°50W 94 C4
Trinidad U.S.A. 37°10N 104°31W 77 H11
Trinidad → Mexico 17°49N 95°9W 87 D5
Trinidad & Tobago ■ W. Indies 10°30N 61°20W 89 D7
Trinity Canada 48°59N 53°55W 73 C9
Trinity U.S.A. 30°57N 95°22W 84 F7
Trinity → Calif., U.S.A. 41°11N 123°42W 76 F2
Trinity → Tex., U.S.A. 29°45N 94°43W 84 G7
Trinity B. Canada 48°20N 53°10W 73 C9
Trinity Hills Trin. & Tob. 10°7N 61°7W 93 K15
Trinity Is. U.S.A. 56°33N 154°25W 74 a
Trinity Range U.S.A. 40°10N 118°40W 76 F4
Trinkitat Sudan 18°45N 37°51E 51 E13
Trinway U.S.A. 40°9N 82°1W 82 F2
Triolet Mauritius 20°4S 57°32E 53 d
Tripoli = Tarābulus Lebanon 34°31N 35°50E 46 A4
Tripoli = Tarābulus Libya 32°49N 13°7E 51 B8
Tripoli Greece 37°31N 22°25E 23 F10
Tripolitania N. Afr. 31°0N 13°0E 51 B8
Tripura □ India 24°0N 92°0E 41 H18
Tripylos Cyprus 34°59N 32°41E 25 E11
Tristan da Cunha Atl. Oc. 37°6S 12°20W 49 K2
Trisul India 30°19N 79°47E 43 D8
Trivandrum India 8°41N 77°0E 40 Q10
Trnava Slovak Rep. 48°23N 17°35E 17 D9
Trochu Canada 51°50N 113°13W 70 C6
Trodely I. Canada 52°15N 79°26W 72 B4
Troglav Croatia 43°56N 16°36E 22 C7
Troilus, L. Canada 50°50N 74°35W 72 B5
Trois-Pistoles Canada 48°5N 69°10W 73 C6
Trois-Rivières Canada 46°25N 72°34W 72 C5
Trois-Rivières Guadeloupe 15°57N 61°40W 88 b
Troitsk Russia 54°10N 61°35E 28 D7
Troitsko Pechorsk Russia 62°40N 56°10E 18 B10
Trölladyngja Iceland 64°54N 17°16W 8 D5
Trollhättan Sweden 58°17N 12°20E 9 G15
Trollheimen Norway 62°46N 9°1E 8 E13
Trombetas → Brazil 1°55S 55°35W 93 D7
Tromsø Norway 69°40N 18°56E 8 B18
Trona U.S.A. 35°46N 117°23W 79 K9
Tronador, Mte. Argentina 41°10S 71°50W 96 E2
Trøndelag Norway 64°17N 11°50E 8 D14
Trondheim Norway 63°36N 10°25E 8 E14
Trondheimsfjorden Norway 63°35N 10°30E 8 E14
Troodos Cyprus 34°55N 32°52E 25 E11
Troon U.K. 55°33N 4°39W 11 F4
Tropic U.S.A. 37°37N 112°5W 77 H7
Trostan U.K. 55°3N 6°10W 10 A5
Trou Gras Pt. St. Lucia 13°51N 60°53W 89 f
Trout → Canada 61°19N 119°51W 70 A5
Trout L. N.W.T., Canada 60°40N 121°14W 70 A4
Trout L. Ont., Canada 51°20N 93°15W 71 C10
Trout Lake Canada 56°30N 114°32W 70 B6
Trout Lake U.S.A. 46°0N 121°32W 78 E5
Trout River Canada 49°29N 58°8W 73 C8
Trout Run U.S.A. 41°23N 77°3W 82 E7
Trouville-sur-Mer France 49°21N 0°5E 20 B4
Trowbridge U.K. 51°18N 2°12W 13 F5
Troy Turkey 39°57N 26°12E 23 E12
Troy Ala., U.S.A. 31°48N 85°58W 85 F12
Troy Kans., U.S.A. 39°47N 95°5W 80 F6
Troy Mo., U.S.A. 38°59N 90°59W 80 F8
Troy Mont., U.S.A. 48°28N 115°53W 76 B6
Troy N.Y., U.S.A. 42°44N 73°41W 83 D11
Troy Ohio, U.S.A. 40°2N 84°12W 81 E11
Troy Pa., U.S.A. 41°47N 76°47W 83 E8
Troyes France 48°19N 4°3E 20 B6
Truchas Pk. U.S.A. 35°58N 105°39W 77 J11
Trucial States = United Arab Emirates ■ Asia 23°50N 54°0E 45 F7
Truckee U.S.A. 39°20N 120°11W 78 F6
Trudovoye Russia 43°17N 132°5E 30 C6
Trujillo Honduras 16°0N 86°0W 88 C2
Trujillo Peru 8°6S 79°0W 92 E3
Trujillo Spain 39°28N 5°55W 21 C3
Trujillo U.S.A. 35°32N 104°42W 77 J11
Trujillo Venezuela 9°22N 70°38W 92 B4
Truk Micronesia 7°25N 151°46E 64 G7
Trumann U.S.A. 35°41N 90°31W 85 D9
Trumansburg U.S.A. 42°33N 76°40W 83 D8
Trumbull, Mt. U.S.A. 36°25N 113°19W 77 H7
Trundle Australia 32°53S 147°35E 63 E4
Trung-Phan = Annam Vietnam 16°0N 108°0E 38 E7
Truro Canada 45°21N 63°14W 73 C7
Truro U.K. 50°16N 5°4W 13 G2
Truskavets Ukraine 49°17N 23°30E 17 D12
Trutch Canada 57°44N 122°57W 70 B4
Truth or Consequences U.S.A. 33°8N 107°15W 77 K10
Trutnov Czech Rep. 50°37N 15°54E 16 C8
Truxton U.S.A. 42°45N 76°2W 83 D8
Tryonville U.S.A. 41°42N 79°48W 82 E5
Tsandi Namibia 17°42S 14°50E 56 B1
Tsaratanana Madag. 16°47S 47°39E 57 B8
Tsaratanana, Mt. de = Maromokotro Madag. 14°0S 49°0E 57 A8
Tsaratanana ⌓ Madag. 13°57S 48°52E 57 A8
Tsau Botswana 20°8S 22°22E 56 C3
Tsavo Kenya 2°59S 38°28E 54 C4
Tsavo East △ Kenya 2°44S 38°47E 54 C4
Tsavo West △ Kenya 3°19S 37°57E 54 C4
Tsentralnyy □ Russia 52°0N 40°0E 28 D4
Tses Namibia 25°58S 18°8E 56 D2
Tsetserleg Mongolia 47°36N 101°32E 32 B5
Tsévié Togo 6°25N 1°20E 50 G6
Tshabong Botswana 26°2S 22°29E 56 D3
Tshane Botswana 24°5S 21°54E 56 C3
Tshela Dem. Rep. of the Congo 4°57S 13°4E 52 E2
Tshesebe Botswana 21°51S 27°32E 57 C4
Tshibeke Dem. Rep. of the Congo 2°40S 28°35E 54 C2
Tshibinda Dem. Rep. of the Congo 2°23S 28°43E 54 C2
Tshikapa Dem. Rep. of the Congo 6°28S 20°48E 52 F4
Tshilenge Dem. Rep. of the Congo 6°17S 23°48E 54 D1
Tshinsenda Dem. Rep. of the Congo 12°20S 28°0E 55 E2
Tshofa Dem. Rep. of the Congo 5°13S 25°16E 54 D2
Tshwane = Pretoria S. Africa 25°44S 28°12E 57 D4
Tshwane Botswana 22°24S 22°1E 56 C3
Tsigara Botswana 20°22S 25°54E 56 C4
Tsihombe Madag. 25°10S 45°41E 57 D8
Tsiigehtchic Canada 67°15N 134°0W 68 C6
Ts'il-os ⌓ Canada 51°9N 123°59W 70 C4
Tsimlyansk Res. = Tsimlyanskoye Vdkhr. Russia 48°0N 43°0E 19 E7
Tsimlyanskoye Vdkhr. Russia 48°0N 43°0E 19 E7
Tsinan = Jinan China 36°38N 117°1E 34 F9
Tsineng S. Africa 27°5S 23°5E 56 D3
Tsing Yi China 22°21N 114°6E 33 G11
Tsinghai = Qinghai □ China 36°0N 98°0E 32 C4
Tsingtao = Qingdao China 36°5N 120°20E 35 F11
Tsingy de Bemaraha ⌓ Madag. 18°35S 45°25E 57 B8
Tsingy de Namoroka ⌓ Madag. 16°29S 45°25E 57 B8
Tsinjoarivo Madag. 19°37S 47°40E 57 B8
Tsinjomitondraka Madag. 15°40S 47°8E 57 B8
Tsirigo = Kythira Greece 36°8N 23°0E 23 F10
Tsiroanomandidy Madag. 18°46S 46°2E 57 B8
Tsitondroina Madag. 21°19S 46°0E 57 C8
Tsitsikamma △ S. Africa 34°3S 23°40E 56 E3
Tsivory Madag. 24°4S 46°5E 57 C8
Tskhinvali Georgia 42°14N 44°1E 19 F7
Tsna → Russia 54°55N 41°58E 18 D7
Tso Moriri, L. India 32°50N 78°20E 43 C8
Tsobis Namibia 19°27S 17°30E 56 B2
Tsodilo Hill Botswana 18°49S 21°43E 56 B3
Tsogttsetsiy = Baruunsuu Mongolia 43°43N 105°35E 34 C3
Tsolo S. Africa 31°18S 28°37E 57 E4
Tsomo S. Africa 32°0S 27°42E 57 E4
Tsu Japan 34°45N 136°25E 31 G8
Tsu L. Canada 60°40N 111°52W 70 A6
Tsuchiura Japan 36°5N 140°15E 31 F10
Tsuen Wan China 22°22N 114°6E 33 G11
Tsugaru-Kaikyō Japan 41°35N 141°0E 30 D10
Tsumeb Namibia 19°9S 17°44E 56 B2
Tsumis Namibia 23°39S 17°29E 56 C2
Tsuruga Japan 35°45N 136°2E 31 G8
Tsurugi-San Japan 33°51N 134°6E 31 H7
Tsuruoka Japan 38°44N 139°50E 30 E9
Tsushima Gifu, Japan 35°10N 136°43E 31 G8
Tsushima Nagasaki, Japan 34°20N 129°20E 31 G4
Tsuyama Japan 35°3N 134°0E 31 G7
Tsyelyakhany Belarus 52°30N 25°46E 17 B13
Tual Indonesia 5°38S 132°44E 37 F8
Tualatin U.S.A. 45°23N 122°45W 78 E4
Tuam Ireland 53°31N 8°51W 10 C3
Tuamotu, Îs. French Polynesia 17°0S 144°0W 65 J13
Tuamotu Arch. = Tuamotu, Îs. French Polynesia 17°0S 144°0W 65 J13
Tuamotu Ridge Pac. Oc. 20°0S 138°0W 65 K14
Tuao Phil. 17°55N 121°22E 37 A6
Tuapse Russia 44°5N 39°10E 19 F6
Tuas Singapore 1°19N 103°39E 39 d
Tuatapere N.Z. 46°8S 167°41E 59 G1
Tuba City U.S.A. 36°8N 111°14W 77 H8
Tuban Indonesia 6°54S 112°3E 37 G15
Tubani Botswana 24°46S 24°18E 56 C3
Tubarão Brazil 28°30S 49°0W 95 B6
Tūbās West Bank 32°20N 35°22E 46 C4
Tubas → Namibia 22°54S 14°35E 56 C2
Tübingen Germany 48°31N 9°4E 16 D5
Tubou Fiji 18°13S 178°48W 59 a
Tubruq Libya 32°7N 23°55E 51 B10
Tubuaï, Îs. French Polynesia 25°0S 150°0W 65 K13
Tuc Trung Vietnam 11°1N 107°12E 39 G6
Tucacas Venezuela 10°48N 68°19W 92 A5
Tuchodi → Canada 58°17N 123°42W 70 B4
Tuckanarra Australia 27°7S 118°5E 61 E2
Tucson U.S.A. 32°13N 110°58W 77 K8
Tucumán □ Argentina 26°48S 66°2W 94 B2
Tucumcari U.S.A. 35°10N 103°44W 77 J12
Tucupita Venezuela 9°2N 62°3W 92 B6
Tucuruí Brazil 3°42S 49°44W 93 D9
Tucuruí, Represa de Brazil 4°0S 49°30W 93 D9
Tudela Spain 42°4N 1°39W 21 A5
Tudmur Syria 34°36N 38°15E 44 C3
Tudor, L. Canada 55°50N 65°25W 73 A6
Tuen Mun China 22°24N 113°59E 33 G10
Tugela → S. Africa 29°14S 31°30E 57 D5
Tuguegarao Phil. 17°35N 121°42E 37 A6
Tugur Russia 53°44N 136°45E 29 D14
Tui Spain 42°3N 8°39W 21 A1
Tuineje Canary Is. 28°19N 14°3W 24 F5
Tukangbesi, Kepulauan Indonesia 6°0S 124°0E 37 F6
Tukarak I. Canada 56°15N 78°45W 72 A4
Tukayyid Iraq 29°47N 45°36E 44 D5

Tukkae, Ao Thailand 7°51N 98°25E 39 a
Tuktoyaktuk Canada 69°27N 133°2W 68 C6
Tukums Latvia 56°58N 23°10E 9 H20
Tukuyu Tanzania 9°17S 33°35E 55 D3
Tula Hidalgo, Mexico 20°3N 99°21W 87 C5
Tula Tamaulipas, Mexico 23°0N 99°43W 87 C5
Tula Russia 54°13N 37°38E 18 D6
Tulancingo Mexico 20°5N 98°22W 87 C5
Tulare U.S.A. 36°13N 119°21W 78 J7
Tulare Lake Bed U.S.A. 36°0N 119°48W 78 K7
Tularosa U.S.A. 33°5N 106°1W 77 K10
Tulbagh S. Africa 33°16S 19°6E 56 E2
Tulcán Ecuador 0°48N 77°43W 92 C3
Tulcea Romania 45°13N 28°46E 17 F15
Tulchyn Ukraine 48°41N 28°49E 17 D15
Tūleh Iran 34°35N 52°33E 45 C7
Tulemalu L. Canada 62°58N 99°25W 71 A9
Tuli Zimbabwe 21°58S 29°13E 55 G2
Tulia U.S.A. 34°32N 101°46W 84 D4
Tulita Canada 64°57N 125°30W 68 C7
Ţūlkarm West Bank 32°19N 35°2E 46 C4
Tulla Ireland 52°53N 8°46W 10 D3
Tullahoma U.S.A. 35°22N 86°13W 85 D11
Tullamore Australia 32°39S 147°36E 63 E4
Tullamore Ireland 53°16N 7°31W 10 C4
Tulle France 45°16N 1°46E 20 D4
Tullow Ireland 52°49N 6°45W 10 D5
Tully Australia 17°56S 145°55E 62 B4
Tully U.S.A. 42°48N 76°7W 83 D8
Tulsa U.S.A. 36°10N 95°55W 84 C7
Tulsequah Canada 58°39N 133°35W 70 B2
Tulua Colombia 4°6N 76°11W 92 C3
Tulun Russia 54°32N 100°35E 29 D11
Tulungagung Indonesia 8°5S 111°54E 37 H14
Tuma → Nic. 13°6N 84°35W 88 D3
Tumacacori ⌂ U.S.A. 31°35N 111°6W 77 L8
Tumaco Colombia 1°50N 78°45W 92 C3
Tumatumari Guyana 5°20N 58°55W 92 B7
Tumba Sweden 59°12N 17°48E 9 G17
Tumba, L. Dem. Rep. of the Congo 0°50S 18°0E 52 E3
Tumbarumba Australia 35°44S 148°0E 63 F4
Tumbaya Argentina 23°50S 65°26W 94 A2
Tumbes Peru 3°37S 80°27W 92 D2
Tumbler Ridge Canada 55°8N 121°0W 70 B4
Tumbwe Dem. Rep. of the Congo 11°25S 27°15E 55 E2
Tumby Bay Australia 34°21S 136°8E 63 E2
Tumd Youqi China 40°30N 110°30E 34 D6
Tumen China 43°0N 129°50E 35 C15
Tumen Jiang → China 42°20N 130°35E 35 C16
Tumeremo Venezuela 7°18N 61°30W 92 B6
Tumkur India 13°18N 77°6E 40 N10
Tump Pakistan 26°7N 62°16E 40 F3
Tumpat Malaysia 6°11N 102°10E 39 J4
Tumu Ghana 10°56N 1°56W 50 F5
Tumucumaque, Serra Brazil 2°0N 55°0W 93 C8
Tumut Australia 35°16S 148°13E 63 F4
Tumwater U.S.A. 47°1N 122°54W 78 C4
Tuna India 22°59N 70°5E 42 H4
Tunapuna Trin. & Tob. 10°38N 61°24W 93 K15
Tunas de Zaza Cuba 21°39N 79°34W 88 B4
Tunbridge Wells = Royal Tunbridge Wells U.K. 51°7N 0°16E 13 F8
Tuncurry Australia 32°17S 152°29E 63 E5
Tundla India 27°12N 78°17E 42 F8
Tunduru Tanzania 11°8S 37°25E 55 E4
Tundzha → Bulgaria 41°40N 26°35E 23 C11
Tung Chung China 22°17N 113°57E 33 G10
Tung Lung Chau China 22°15N 114°17E 33 G11
Tungabhadra → India 15°57N 78°15E 40 M11
Tungla Nic. 13°24N 84°21W 88 D3
Tungsten Canada 61°57N 128°16W 70 A3
Tunguska, Nizhnyaya → Russia 65°48N 88°4E 29 C9
Tunguska, Podkamennaya → Russia 61°50N 90°13E 29 C10
Tunica U.S.A. 34°41N 90°23W 85 D9
Tunis Tunisia 36°50N 10°11E 50 A7
Tunisia ■ Africa 33°30N 9°10E 51 A7
Tunja Colombia 5°33N 73°25W 92 B4
Tunkhannock U.S.A. 41°32N 75°57W 83 E9
Tunliu China 36°13N 112°52E 34 F7
Tunnel Creek △ Australia 17°41S 125°18E 60 C4
Tunnsjøen Norway 64°45N 13°25E 8 D15
Tunungayualok I. Canada 56°0N 61°0W 73 A7
Tunuyán Argentina 33°35S 69°0W 94 C2
Tunuyán → Argentina 33°33S 67°30W 94 C2
Tuolumne U.S.A. 37°58N 120°15W 78 H6
Tuolumne → U.S.A. 37°36N 121°13W 78 H5
Tūp Āghāj Iran 36°3N 47°50E 44 B5
Tupã Brazil 21°57S 50°28W 95 A5
Tupelo U.S.A. 34°16N 88°43W 85 D10
Tupinambaranas Brazil 3°0S 58°0W 92 D7
Tupiza Bolivia 21°30S 65°40W 94 A2
Tupman U.S.A. 35°18N 119°21W 79 K7
Tupper Canada 55°32N 120°1W 70 B4
Tupper Lake U.S.A. 44°14N 74°28W 83 B10
Tupungato, Cerro S. Amer. 33°15S 69°50W 94 C2
Tuquan China 45°18N 121°38E 35 B11
Túquerres Colombia 1°5N 77°37W 92 C3
Tura Russia 64°20N 100°17E 29 C11
Turabah Si. Arabia 28°20N 43°15E 44 D4
Tūrān Iran 35°39N 56°42E 45 C8
Turan Russia 51°55N 94°0E 29 D10
Ţurayf Si. Arabia 31°41N 38°39E 44 D3
Turda Romania 46°34N 23°47E 17 E12
Turek Poland 52°3N 18°30E 17 B10
Turén Venezuela 9°17N 69°6W 92 B5
Turfan = Turpan China 43°58N 89°10E 32 B3
Turfan Basin = Turpan Pendi China 42°40N 89°25E 32 B3
Turfan Depression = Turpan Pendi China 42°40N 89°25E 32 B3
Turgeon → Canada 50°0N 78°56W 72 C4
Tŭrgovishte Bulgaria 43°17N 26°38E 23 C12
Turgutlu Turkey 38°30N 27°43E 23 E12
Turgwe → Zimbabwe 21°31S 32°15E 57 C5
Turia → Spain 39°27N 0°19W 21 C5
Turiaçu Brazil 1°40S 45°19W 93 D9
Turiaçu → Brazil 1°36S 45°19W 93 D9
Turin = Torino Italy 45°3N 7°40E 20 D7
Turkana, L. Africa 3°30N 36°5E 54 B4
Turkestan = Türkistan Kazakhstan 43°17N 68°16E 28 E7
Turkey ■ Eurasia 39°0N 36°0E 19 G6
Turkey Creek = Warmun Australia 17°2S 128°12E 60 C4
Türkistan Kazakhstan 43°17N 68°16E 28 E7
Türkmenabat Turkmenistan 39°6N 63°34E 45 B9
Türkmenbashi Turkmenistan 40°5N 53°5E 45 A7
Turkmenistan ■ Asia 39°0N 59°0E 28 F6
Turks & Caicos Is. ⧄ W. Indies 21°20N 71°20W 89 B5
Turks Island Passage W. Indies 21°30N 71°30W 89 B5
Turku Finland 60°30N 22°19E 9 F20
Turkwel → Kenya 3°6N 36°6E 54 B4
Turlock U.S.A. 37°30N 120°51W 78 H6
Turnagain → Canada 59°12N 127°35W 70 B3
Turnagain, C. N.Z. 40°28S 176°38E 59 D6
Turneffe Is. Belize 17°20N 87°50W 87 D7
Turner U.S.A. 48°51N 108°24W 76 B9
Turner Pt. Australia 11°47S 133°32E 62 A1
Turner Valley Canada 50°40N 114°17W 70 C6
Turners Falls U.S.A. 42°36N 72°33W 83 D12
Turnhout Belgium 51°19N 4°57E 15 C4
Turnor L. Canada 56°35N 108°35W 71 B7
Tŭrnovo = Veliko Tŭrnovo Bulgaria 43°5N 25°41E 23 C11
Turnu Măgurele Romania 43°46N 24°56E 17 G13
Turnu Roşu, P. Romania 45°33N 24°17E 17 F13
Turpan China 43°58N 89°10E 32 B3
Turpan Pendi China 42°40N 89°25E 32 B3
Turriff U.K. 57°32N 2°27W 11 D6
Tursāq Iraq 33°27N 45°47E 44 C5
Turtle Head I. Australia 10°56S 142°37E 62 A3
Turtle L. Canada 53°36N 108°38W 71 C7
Turtle Lake U.S.A. 47°31N 100°53W 80 B3
Turtleford Canada 53°23N 108°57W 71 C7
Turuépano △ Venezuela 10°34N 62°43W 89 D7
Turukhansk Russia 65°21N 88°5E 29 C9
Tuscaloosa U.S.A. 33°12N 87°34W 85 E11
Tuscany = Toscana □ Italy 43°25N 11°0E 22 C4
Tuscarawas → U.S.A. 40°24N 81°25W 82 F3
Tuscarora Mt. U.S.A. 40°55N 77°55W 82 F7
Tuscola Ill., U.S.A. 39°48N 88°17W 80 F9
Tuscola Tex., U.S.A. 32°12N 99°48W 84 E5
Tuscumbia U.S.A. 34°44N 87°42W 85 D11
Tuskegee U.S.A. 32°25N 85°42W 85 E12
Tuticorin India 8°50N 78°12E 40 Q11
Tutóia Brazil 2°45S 42°20W 93 D10
Tutong Brunei 4°47N 114°40E 36 D4
Tutrakan Bulgaria 44°2N 26°40E 23 B12
Tuttle Creek L. U.S.A. 39°15N 96°36W 80 F5
Tuttlingen Germany 47°58N 8°48E 16 E5
Tutuala E. Timor 8°25S 127°15E 37 F7
Tutuila Amer. Samoa 14°19S 170°50W 59 b
Tutume Botswana 20°30S 27°5E 53 J5
Tuva □ Russia 51°30N 95°0E 29 D10
Tuvalu ■ Pac. Oc. 8°0S 178°0E 58 B10
Tuvuca Fiji 17°40S 178°48W 59 a
Tuxpan Mexico 20°57N 97°24W 87 C5
Tuxtla Gutiérrez Mexico 16°45N 93°7W 87 D6
Tuy = Tui Spain 42°3N 8°39W 21 A1
Tuy An Vietnam 13°17N 109°16E 38 F7
Tuy Duc Vietnam 12°15N 107°27E 39 F6
Tuy Hoa Vietnam 13°5N 109°10E 38 F7
Tuy Phong Vietnam 11°14N 108°43E 39 G7
Tuya L. Canada 59°7N 130°35W 70 B2
Tuyen Hoa Vietnam 17°50N 106°10E 38 D6
Tuyen Quang Vietnam 21°50N 105°10E 38 B5
Tūysarkān Iran 34°33N 48°27E 45 C6
Tuz Gölü Turkey 38°42N 33°18E 19 G5
Ţūz Khurmātū = Tozkhurmato Iraq 34°56N 44°38E 44 C5
Tuzigoot △ U.S.A. 34°46N 112°2W 77 J7
Tuzla Bos.-H. 44°34N 18°41E 23 B8
Tver Russia 56°55N 35°55E 18 C6
Twain U.S.A. 40°1N 121°3W 78 E5
Twain Harte U.S.A. 38°2N 120°14W 78 G6
Tweed Canada 44°29N 77°19W 82 B7
Tweed → U.K. 55°45N 2°0W 11 F6
Tweed Heads Australia 28°10S 153°31E 63 D5
Tweedsmuir ⌂ Canada 53°0N 126°20W 70 C3
Twentynine Palms U.S.A. 34°8N 116°3W 79 L10
Twillingate Canada 49°42N 54°45W 73 C9
Twin Bridges U.S.A. 45°33N 112°20W 76 D7
Twin Falls Canada 53°30N 64°32W 73 B7
Twin Falls U.S.A. 42°34N 114°28W 76 E6
Twin Valley U.S.A. 47°16N 96°16W 80 B5
Twinsburg U.S.A. 41°19N 81°26W 82 E3
Twitchell Res. U.S.A. 34°59N 120°19W 79 L6
Two Harbors U.S.A. 47°2N 91°40W 80 B8
Two Hills Canada 53°43N 111°52W 70 C6
Two Rivers U.S.A. 44°9N 87°34W 80 C10
Two Rocks Australia 31°30S 115°35E 61 F2
Twofold B. Australia 37°8S 149°59E 63 F4
Tyachiv Ukraine 48°1N 23°35E 17 D12
Tychy Poland 50°9N 18°59E 17 C10
Tyler Minn., U.S.A. 44°17N 96°8W 80 C5
Tyler Tex., U.S.A. 32°21N 95°18W 84 E7
Tynda Russia 55°10N 124°43E 29 D13
Tyndall U.S.A. 43°0N 97°50W 80 D5
Tyne → U.K. 54°59N 1°32W 12 C6
Tyne & Wear □ U.K. 55°6N 1°17W 12 B6
Tynemouth U.K. 55°1N 1°26W 12 B6
Tyre = Sūr Lebanon 33°19N 35°16E 46 B4
Tyrifjorden Norway 60°2N 10°8E 9 F14
Tyrol = Tirol □ Austria 47°3N 10°43E 16 E6
Tyrone U.S.A. 40°40N 78°14W 82 F6
Tyrone □ U.K. 54°38N 7°11W 10 B4
Tyrrell → Australia 35°26S 142°51E 63 F3
Tyrrell, L. Australia 35°20S 142°50E 63 F3
Tyrrell L. Canada 63°7N 105°27W 71 A7
Tyrrhenian Sea Medit. S. 40°0N 12°30E 22 E5
Tysfjorden Norway 68°7N 16°25E 8 B17
Tyulgan Russia 52°22N 56°12E 18 D10
Tyumen Russia 57°11N 65°29E 28 D7
Tywi → U.K. 51°48N 4°21W 13 F3
Tywyn U.K. 52°35N 4°5W 13 E3
Tzaneen S. Africa 23°47S 30°9E 57 C5
Tzermiado Greece 35°12N 25°29E 25 D7
Tzukong = Zigong China 29°15N 104°48E 32 D5

U

U Taphao Thailand 12°35N 101°0E 38 F3
U.S.A. = United States of America ■ N. Amer. 37°0N 96°0W 74 C7
U.S. Virgin Is. ⧄ W. Indies 18°20N 65°0W 89 e
Uanle Uen Somali Rep. 2°37N 44°54E 47 G3
Uatumã → Brazil 2°26S 57°37W 92 D7
Uaupés Brazil 0°8S 67°5W 92 D5
Uaupés → Brazil 0°2N 67°16W 92 C5
Uaxactún Guatemala 17°25N 89°29W 88 C2
Ubá Brazil 21°8S 43°0W 95 A7
Ubaitaba Brazil 14°18S 39°20W 93 F11
Ubangi = Oubangi → Dem. Rep. of the Congo 0°30S 17°50E 52 E3
Ubauro Pakistan 28°15N 69°45E 42 E3
Ubayyiḍ, W. al → Iraq 32°34N 43°48E 44 C4
Ube Japan 33°56N 131°15E 31 H5
Úbeda Spain 38°3N 3°23W 21 C4
Uberaba Brazil 19°50S 47°55W 93 G9
Uberlândia Brazil 19°0S 48°20W 93 G9
Ubin, Pulau Singapore 1°24N 103°57E 39 d
Ubolratna Res. Thailand 16°45N 102°30E 38 D4
Ubombo S. Africa 27°31S 32°4E 57 D5
Ubon Ratchathani Thailand 15°15N 104°50E 38 E5
Ubondo Dem. Rep. of the Congo 0°55S 25°42E 54 C2
Ubort → Belarus 52°6N 28°30E 17 B15
Ubud Indonesia 8°30S 115°16E 37 J18
Ubundu Dem. Rep. of the Congo 0°22S 25°30E 54 C2
Ucayali → Peru 4°30S 73°30W 92 D4
Uchab Namibia 19°47S 17°42E 56 B2
Uchiura-Wan Japan 42°25N 140°40E 30 C10
Uchquduq Uzbekistan 41°50N 62°50E 28 E7
Uchur → Russia 58°48N 130°35E 29 D14
Ucluelet Canada 48°57N 125°32W 70 D3
Uda → Russia 54°42N 135°14E 29 D14
Udagamandalam India 11°30N 76°44E 40 P10
Udainagar India 22°33N 76°13E 42 H7
Udaipur India 24°36N 73°44E 42 G5
Udaipur Garhi Nepal 27°0N 86°35E 43 F12
Udala India 21°35N 86°34E 43 J12
Uddevalla Sweden 58°21N 11°55E 9 G14
Uddjaure Sweden 65°56N 17°49E 8 D17
Uden Neths. 51°40N 5°37E 15 C5
Udgir India 18°25N 77°5E 40 K10
Udhampur India 33°0N 75°5E 43 C6
Údine Italy 46°3N 13°14E 22 A5
Udintsev Fracture Zone S. Ocean 57°0S 145°0W 5 B13
Udmurtia □ Russia 57°30N 52°30E 18 C9
Udon Thani Thailand 17°29N 102°46E 38 D4
Udu Pt. Fiji 16°9S 179°57W 59 a
Udupi India 13°25N 74°42E 40 N9
Udzungwa △ Tanzania 7°52S 36°35E 54 D4
Udzungwa Range Tanzania 9°30S 35°10E 55 D4
Ueda Japan 36°24N 138°16E 31 F9
Uedineniya, Os. Russia 78°0N 85°0E 4 B12
Uele → Dem. Rep. of the Congo 3°45N 24°45E 52 D4
Uelen Russia 66°10N 170°0W 29 C19
Uelzen Germany 52°57N 10°32E 16 B6
Ufa Russia 54°45N 55°55E 18 D10
Ufa → Russia 54°40N 56°0E 18 D10
Ugab → Namibia 20°55S 13°30E 56 C1
Ugalla → Tanzania 5°8S 30°42E 54 D3
Ugalla River ⌂ Tanzania 5°50S 31°54E 54 D3
Uganda ■ Africa 2°0N 32°0E 54 B3
Ugie S. Africa 31°10S 28°13E 57 E4
Uglegorsk Russia 49°5N 142°2E 29 E15
Uglich Russia 57°33N 38°20E 18 C6
Ugljan Croatia 44°12N 15°10E 16 F8
Uhlenhorst Namibia 23°45S 17°55E 56 C2
Uhrichsville U.S.A. 40°24N 81°21W 82 F3
Uibhist a Deas = South Uist U.K. 57°20N 7°15W 11 D1
Uibhist a Tuath = North Uist U.K. 57°40N 7°15W 11 D1
Uig U.K. 57°35N 6°21W 11 D2
Uíge Angola 7°30S 14°40E 52 F2
Uiha Tonga 19°54S 174°25W 59 c
Uijeongbu S. Korea 37°44N 127°2E 35 F14
Ŭiju N. Korea 40°15N 124°35E 35 D13
Uinta Mts. U.S.A. 40°45N 110°30W 76 F8
Uis Namibia 21°8S 14°49E 56 C1
Uiseong S. Korea 36°21N 128°45E 35 F15
Uitenhage S. Africa 33°40S 25°28E 56 E4
Uithuizen Neths. 53°24N 6°41E 15 A6
Ujh → India 32°10N 75°18E 42 C6
Ujhani India 28°0N 79°6E 43 F8
Uji-guntō Japan 31°15N 129°25E 31 J4
Ujjain India 23°9N 75°43E 42 H6
Ujung Pandang Indonesia 5°10S 119°20E 37 F5
Uka Russia 57°50N 162°0E 29 D17
Ukara I. Tanzania 1°50S 33°0E 54 C3
Uke-Shima Japan 28°2N 129°14E 31 K4
Ukerewe I. Tanzania 2°0S 33°0E 54 C3
Ukhrul India 25°10N 94°25E 41 G19
Ukhta Russia 63°34N 53°41E 18 B9
Ukiah U.S.A. 39°9N 123°13W 78 F3
Ukmergė Lithuania 55°15N 24°45E 9 J21
Ukraine ■ Europe 49°0N 32°0E 19 E5
Ukwi Botswana 23°29S 20°30E 56 C3
Ulaan-Uul Mongolia 44°13N 111°10E 34 B6
Ulaanbaatar Mongolia 47°55N 106°53E 32 B5
Ulaangom Mongolia 50°5N 92°10E 32 A4
Ulaanjirem Mongolia 45°5N 105°30E 34 B3
Ulamba Dem. Rep. of the Congo 9°3S 23°38E 55 D1
Ulan Bator = Ulaanbaatar Mongolia 47°55N 106°53E 32 B5
Ulan Ude Russia 51°45N 107°40E 29 D11
Ulaya Morogoro, Tanzania 7°3S 36°55E 54 D4
Ulaya Tabora, Tanzania 4°25S 33°30E 54 C3
Ulcinj Montenegro 41°58N 19°10E 23 D8
Ulco S. Africa 28°21S 24°15E 56 D3
Ule älv = Oulujoki → Finland 65°1N 25°30E 8 D21
Ule träsk = Oulujärvi Finland 64°25N 27°15E 8 D22
Uleåborg = Oulu Finland 65°1N 25°29E 8 D21
Ulefoss Norway 59°17N 9°16E 9 G13
Ulhasnagar India 19°15N 73°10E 40 K8
Uliastay Mongolia 47°56N 97°28E 32 B4
Uljin S. Korea 36°59N 129°24E 35 F15
Ulladulla Australia 35°21S 150°29E 63 F5
Ullapool U.K. 57°54N 5°9W 11 D3
Ulleungdo S. Korea 37°30N 130°30E 31 F5
Ullswater U.K. 54°34N 2°52W 12 C5
Ulm Germany 48°23N 9°58E 16 D5
Ulmarra Australia 29°37S 153°4E 63 D5
Ulonguè Mozam. 14°37S 34°19E 55 E3
Ulricehamn Sweden 57°46N 13°26E 9 H15
Ulsan S. Korea 35°20N 129°15E 35 G15
Ulsta U.K. 60°30N 1°9W 11 A7
Ulster □ U.K. 54°35N 6°30W 10 B5
Ulubat Gölü Turkey 40°9N 28°35E 23 D13
Uludağ Turkey 40°4N 29°13E 23 D13
Uluguru Mts. Tanzania 7°15S 37°40E 54 D4
Ulungur He → China 47°1N 87°24E 32 B3
Uluru Australia 25°23S 131°5E 61 E5
Uluru-Kata Tjuta △ Australia 25°19S 131°1E 61 E5
Ulutau Kazakhstan 48°39N 67°1E 28 E7
Uluwatu Indonesia 8°50S 115°5E 37 K18
Ulva U.K. 56°29N 6°13W 11 E2
Ulverston U.K. 54°13N 3°5W 12 C4
Ulverstone Australia 41°11S 146°11E 63 G4
Ulya Russia 59°10N 142°0E 29 D15
Ulyanovsk = Simbirsk Russia 54°20N 48°25E 18 D8
Ulyasutay = Uliastay Mongolia 47°56N 97°28E 32 B4
Ulysses U.S.A. 37°35N 101°22W 80 G3
Umala Bolivia 17°25S 68°5W 92 G5
'Umān = Oman ■ Asia 23°0N 58°0E 47 C6
Uman Ukraine 48°40N 30°12E 17 D16
Umaria India 23°35N 80°50E 43 H9
Umarkot Pakistan 25°15N 69°40E 42 G3
Umarpada India 21°27N 73°30E 42 J5
Umatilla U.S.A. 45°55N 119°21W 76 D4
Umba Russia 66°42N 34°11E 18 A5
Umbagog L. U.S.A. 44°46N 71°3W 83 B13
Umbakumba Australia 13°47S 136°50E 62 A2
Umbrella Mts. N.Z. 45°35S 169°5E 59 F2
Umeå Sweden 63°45N 20°20E 8 E19
Umeälven → Sweden 63°45N 20°20E 8 E19
Umera Indonesia 0°12S 129°37E 37 E7
Umfuli → Zimbabwe 17°30S 29°23E 55 F2
Umfurudzi ⌂ Zimbabwe 17°6S 31°40E 55 F3
Umgusa Zimbabwe 19°29S 27°52E 55 F2
Umiujaq Canada 56°33N 76°33W 72 A4
Umkomaas S. Africa 30°13S 30°48E 57 E5
Umlazi S. Africa 29°59S 30°54E 53 L6
Umm ad Daraj, J. Jordan 32°18N 35°48E 46 C4
Umm al Qaywayn U.A.E. 25°30N 55°35E 45 E7
Umm al Qittayn Jordan 32°18N 36°40E 46 C5
Umm Bāb Qatar 25°12N 50°48E 45 E6
Umm Durman = Omdurmân Sudan 15°40N 32°28E 51 E12
Umm el Fahm Israel 32°31N 35°9E 46 C4
Umm Keddada Sudan 13°33N 26°35E 51 F11
Umm Lajj Si. Arabia 25°0N 37°23E 44 E3
Umm Qasr Iraq 30°1N 47°58E 44 D5
Umm Ruwaba Sudan 12°50N 31°20E 51 F12
Umnak I. U.S.A. 53°15N 168°20W 74 a
Umniati → Zimbabwe 16°49S 28°45E 55 F2
Umpqua → U.S.A. 43°40N 124°12W 76 E1
Umreth India 22°41N 73°4E 42 H5
Umtata = Mthatha S. Africa 31°36S 28°49E 57 E4
Umuarama Brazil 23°45S 53°20W 95 A5
Umvukwe Ra. Zimbabwe 16°45S 30°45E 55 F3
Umzimvubu S. Africa 31°38S 29°33E 57 E4
Umzingwane → Zimbabwe 22°12S 29°56E 55 G2
Umzinto S. Africa 30°15S 30°45E 57 E5
Una India 20°46N 71°8E 42 J4
Una → Bos.-H. 45°0N 16°20E 16 F9
Unadilla U.S.A. 42°20N 75°19W 83 D9
Unalakleet U.S.A. 63°52N 160°47W 74 a
Unalaska U.S.A. 53°53N 166°32W 74 a
Unalaska I. U.S.A. 53°35N 166°50W 74 a
'Unayzah Si. Arabia 26°6N 43°58E 44 E4
'Unayzah, J. Asia 32°12N 39°18E 44 C3
Uncía Bolivia 18°25S 66°40W 92 G5
Uncompahgre Peak U.S.A. 38°4N 107°28W 76 G10
Uncompahgre Plateau U.S.A. 38°20N 108°15W 76 G9
Undara Volcanic △ Australia 18°14S 144°41E 62 B3
Underbool Australia 35°10S 141°51E 63 F3
Ungarie Australia 33°38S 146°56E 63 E4
Ungarra Australia 34°12S 136°2E 63 E2
Ungava, Pén. d' Canada 60°0N 74°0W 69 D12
Ungava B. Canada 59°30N 67°30W 69 D13
Ungeny = Ungheni Moldova 47°11N 27°51E 17 E14
Unggi N. Korea 42°16N 130°28E 35 C16
Ungheni Moldova 47°11N 27°51E 17 E14
Ungwana B. Kenya 2°45S 40°20E 54 C5
União da Vitória Brazil 26°13S 51°5W 95 B5
Unimak I. U.S.A. 54°45N 164°0W 74 a
Union Miss., U.S.A. 32°34N 89°7W 85 E10
Union Mo., U.S.A. 38°27N 91°0W 80 F8
Union S.C., U.S.A. 34°43N 81°37W 85 D14
Union City Calif., U.S.A. 37°36N 122°1W 78 H4
Union City N.J., U.S.A. 40°45N 74°2W 83 F10
Union City Pa., U.S.A. 41°54N 79°51W 82 E5
Union City Tenn., U.S.A. 36°26N 89°3W 85 C10
Union Gap U.S.A. 46°33N 120°28W 76 C3
Union Springs U.S.A. 32°9N 85°43W 85 E12
Uniondale S. Africa 33°39S 23°7E 56 E3
Uniontown U.S.A. 39°54N 79°44W 81 F14
Unionville U.S.A. 40°29N 93°1W 80 E7
United Arab Emirates ■ Asia 23°50N 54°0E 45 F7
United Kingdom ■ Europe 53°0N 2°0W 14 E6
United States of America ■ N. Amer. 37°0N 96°0W 74 C7
Unity Canada 52°30N 109°5W 71 C7
University Park U.S.A. 32°17N 106°45W 77 K10
University Place U.S.A. 47°14N 122°33W 78 C4
Unjha India 23°46N 72°24E 42 H5
Unnao India 26°35N 80°30E 43 F9
Unsengedsi → Zimbabwe 15°43S 31°14E 55 F3
Unst U.K. 60°44N 0°53W 11 A8
Unuk → Canada 56°5N 131°3W 70 B2
Unzen-Amakusa △ Japan 32°15N 130°10E 31 H5
Uozu Japan 36°48N 137°24E 31 F8
Upata Venezuela 8°1N 62°24W 92 B6
Upemba, L. Dem. Rep. of the Congo 8°30S 26°20E 55 D2
Upemba △ Dem. Rep. of the Congo 9°0S 26°35E 55 D2
Upernavik Greenland 72°49N 56°20W 4 B5
Upington S. Africa 28°25S 21°15E 56 D3
Upleta India 21°46N 70°16E 42 J4
'Upolu Samoa 13°58S 172°0W 59 b
Upper Alkali L. U.S.A. 41°47N 120°8W 76 F3
Upper Arrow L. Canada 50°30N 117°50W 70 C5
Upper Darby U.S.A. 39°55N 75°16W 81 F16
Upper Foster L. Canada 56°47N 105°20W 71 B7
Upper Hutt N.Z. 41°8S 175°5E 59 D5
Upper Klamath L. U.S.A. 42°25N 121°55W 76 E3
Upper Lake U.S.A. 39°10N 122°54W 78 F4
Upper Manzanilla Trin. & Tob. 10°31N 61°4W 93 K15
Upper Missouri Breaks ⌂ U.S.A. 47°50N 109°55W 76 C9
Upper Musquodoboit Canada 45°10N 62°58W 73 C7
Upper Red L. U.S.A. 48°8N 94°45W 80 A6
Upper Sandusky U.S.A. 40°50N 83°17W 81 E12
Upper Volta = Burkina Faso ■ Africa 12°0N 1°0W 50 F5
Uppland Sweden 59°59N 17°48E 9 G17
Uppsala Sweden 59°53N 17°38E 9 G17
Upshi India 33°48N 77°52E 43 C7
Upstart, C. Australia 19°41S 147°45E 62 B4
Upton U.S.A. 44°6N 104°38W 76 D11
Uqsuqtuuq = Gjoa Haven Canada 68°38N 95°53W 68 C10
Ur Iraq 30°55N 46°25E 44 D5
Urad Qianqi China 40°40N 108°30E 34 D5
Urakawa Japan 42°9N 142°47E 30 C11
Ural = Uralskiy □ Russia 64°0N 70°0E 28 C7
Ural = Zhayyq → Kazakhstan 47°0N 51°48E 19 E9
Ural Australia 33°21S 146°12E 63 E4
Ural Mts. = Uralskie Gory Eurasia 60°0N 59°0E 18 C10
Uralla Australia 30°37S 151°29E 63 E5
Uralsk = Oral Kazakhstan 51°20N 51°20E 19 D9
Uralskie Gory Eurasia 60°0N 59°0E 18 C10
Uralskiy □ Russia 64°0N 70°0E 28 C7
Urambo Tanzania 5°4S 32°0E 54 D3
Urandangi Australia 21°32S 138°14E 62 C2
Uranium City Canada 59°34N 108°37W 71 B7
Uraricoera → Brazil 3°2N 60°30W 92 C6
Urasoe Japan 26°15N 127°43E 31 L3
Urawa = Saitama Japan 35°54N 139°38E 31 G9
Uray Russia 60°5N 65°15E 28 C7
'Uray'irah Si. Arabia 25°57N 48°53E 45 E6
Urbana Ill., U.S.A. 40°7N 88°12W 80 E9
Urbana Ohio, U.S.A. 40°7N 83°45W 81 E12
Urbandale U.S.A. 41°38N 93°43W 80 E7
Urbino Italy 43°43N 12°38E 22 C5
Urbión, Picos de Spain 42°1N 2°52W 21 A4
Urcos Peru 13°40S 71°38W 92 F4
Urdinarrain Argentina 32°37S 58°52W 94 C4
Ure → U.K. 54°5N 1°20W 12 C6

Ures Mexico 29°26N 110°24W 86 B2
Urewera △ N.Z. 38°29S 177°7E 59 C6
Urfa = Sanliurfa Turkey 37°12N 38°50E 44 B3
Urganch Uzbekistan 41°40N 60°41E 28 E7
Urgench = Urganch Uzbekistan 41°40N 60°41E 28 E7
Ürgüp Turkey 38°38N 34°56E 44 B2
Uri India 34°8N 74°2E 43 B6
Uribia Colombia 11°43N 72°16W 92 A4
Uriondo Bolivia 21°41S 64°41W 94 A3
Urique Mexico 27°13N 107°55W 86 B3
Urique → Mexico 26°29N 107°58W 86 B3
Urk Neths. 52°39N 5°36E 15 B5
Urla Turkey 38°20N 26°47E 23 E12
Urmia = Orūmīyeh Iran 37°40N 45°0E 44 B5
Uroševac Serbia 42°23N 21°10E 23 C9
Uroyan, Montanas de Puerto Rico 18°12N 67°0W 89 d
Uruaçu Brazil 14°30S 49°10W 93 F9
Uruapan Mexico 19°24N 102°3W 86 D4
Urubamba → Peru 10°43S 73°48W 92 F4
Uruçara Brazil 2°32S 57°45W 92 D7
Uruçuí Brazil 7°20S 44°28W 93 E10
Uruguai → Brazil 26°0S 53°30W 95 B5
Uruguaiana Brazil 29°50S 57°0W 94 B4
Uruguay ■ S. Amer. 32°30S 56°30W 94 C4
Uruguay → S. Amer. 34°12S 58°18W 94 C4
Urumchi = Ürümqi China 43°45N 87°45E 32 B3
Ürümqi China 43°45N 87°45E 32 B3
Urup, Ostrov Russia 46°0N 151°0E 29 E16
Ürzhar Kazakhstan 47°5N 81°38E 28 E9
Usa → Russia 66°16N 59°49E 18 A10
Uşak Turkey 38°43N 29°28E 19 G4
Usakos Namibia 21°54S 15°31E 56 C2
Usedom Germany 53°55N 14°2E 16 B8
Useless Loop Australia 26°8S 113°23E 61 E1
Ushakova, Ostrov Russia 82°0N 80°0E 4 A12
Ushant = Ouessant, Î. d' France 48°28N 5°6W 20 B1
Ushashi Tanzania 1°59S 33°57E 54 C3
Ushibuka Japan 32°11N 130°1E 31 H5
Üshtöbe Kazakhstan 45°16N 78°0E 28 E8
Ushuaia Argentina 54°50S 68°23W 96 G3
Ushumun Russia 52°47N 126°32E 29 D13
Usk Canada 54°38N 128°26W 70 C3
Usk → U.K. 51°33N 2°58W 13 F5
Uska India 27°12N 83°7E 43 F10
Usman Russia 52°5N 39°48E 18 D6
Usoke Tanzania 5°8S 32°24E 54 D3
Usolye Sibirskoye Russia 52°48N 103°40E 29 D11
Uspallata, P. de Argentina 32°37S 69°22W 94 C2
Ussuriysk Russia 43°48N 131°59E 30 C5
Ussurka Russia 45°12N 133°31E 30 B6
Ust-Bolsheretsk Russia 52°50N 156°15E 29 D16
Ust-Chaun Russia 68°47N 170°30E 29 C18
Ust-Ilimsk Russia 58°3N 102°39E 29 D11
Ust-Ishim Russia 57°45N 71°10E 28 D8
Ust-Kamchatsk Russia 56°10N 162°28E 29 D17
Ust-Kamenogorsk = Öskemen Kazakhstan 50°0N 82°36E 28 E9
Ust-Khayryuzovo Russia 57°15N 156°45E 29 D16
Ust-Kut Russia 56°50N 105°42E 29 D11
Ust-Kuyga Russia 70°1N 135°43E 29 B14
Ust-Maya Russia 60°30N 134°28E 29 C14
Ust-Mil Russia 59°40N 133°11E 29 D14
Ust-Nera Russia 64°35N 143°15E 29 C15
Ust-Nyukzha Russia 56°34N 121°37E 29 D13
Ust-Olenek Russia 73°0N 120°5E 29 B12
Ust-Omchug Russia 61°9N 149°38E 29 C15
Ust-Port Russia 69°40N 84°26E 28 C9
Ust-Tsilma Russia 65°28N 52°11E 18 A9
Ust Urt = Ustyurt Plateau Asia 44°0N 55°0E 28 E6
Ust-Usa Russia 66°2N 56°57E 18 A10
Ust-Vorkuta Russia 67°24N 64°0E 10 A11
Ústí nad Labem Czech Rep. 50°41N 14°3E 16 C8
Ustica Italy 38°42N 13°11E 22 E5
Ustinov = Izhevsk Russia 56°51N 53°14E 18 C9
Ustyurt Plateau Asia 44°0N 55°0E 28 E6
Usu China 44°27N 84°40E 32 B3
Usuki Japan 33°8N 131°49E 31 H5
Usulután El Salv. 13°25N 88°28W 88 D2
Usumacinta → Mexico 18°24N 92°38W 87 D6
Usumbura = Bujumbura Burundi 3°16S 29°18E 54 C2
Usure Tanzania 4°40S 34°22E 54 C3
Usutuo → Mozam. 26°48S 32°7E 57 D5
Uta Indonesia 4°33S 136°0E 37 E9
Utah □ U.S.A. 39°20N 111°30W 76 G8
Utah L. U.S.A. 40°12N 111°48W 76 F8
Utara, Selat Malaysia 5°28N 100°20E 39 c
Utarni India 26°5N 71°58E 42 F4
Utatlan Guatemala 15°2N 91°11W 88 C1
Ute Creek → U.S.A. 35°21N 103°50W 77 J12
Utena Lithuania 55°27N 25°40E 9 J21
Utete Tanzania 8°0S 38°45E 54 D4
Uthai Thani Thailand 15°22N 100°3E 38 E3
Uthal Pakistan 25°44N 66°40E 42 G2
Utiariti Brazil 13°0S 58°10W 92 F7
Utica N.Y., U.S.A. 43°6N 75°14W 83 C9
Utica Ohio, U.S.A. 40°14N 82°27W 82 F2
Utikuma L. Canada 55°50N 115°30W 70 B5
Utopia Australia 22°14S 134°33E 62 C1
Utraula India 27°19N 82°25E 43 F10
Utrecht Neths. 52°5N 5°8E 15 B5
Utrecht S. Africa 27°38S 30°20E 57 D5
Utrecht □ Neths. 52°6N 5°7E 15 B5
Utrera Spain 37°12N 5°48W 21 D3
Utsjoki → Finland 69°51N 26°59E 8 B22
Utsunomiya Japan 36°30N 139°50E 31 F9
Uttar Pradesh □ India 27°0N 80°0E 43 F9
Uttaradit Thailand 17°36N 100°5E 38 D3
Uttaranchal □ India 30°0N 79°30E 43 D8
Uttoxeter U.K. 52°54N 1°52W 12 E6
Utuado Puerto Rico 18°16N 66°42W 89 d
Uummannaq Greenland 77°28N 69°13W 4 B4
Uummannaq Greenland 70°58N 52°17W 4 B5
Uummannarsuaq = Nunap Isua Greenland 59°48N 43°55W 66 D15
Uusikaarlepyy Finland 63°32N 22°31E 8 E20
Uusikaupunki Finland 60°47N 21°25E 8 F19
Uva Russia 56°59N 52°13E 18 C9
Uvalde U.S.A. 29°13N 99°47W 84 G5
Uvat Russia 59°5N 68°50E 28 D7
Uvinza Tanzania 5°5S 30°24E 54 D3
Uvira Dem. Rep. of the Congo 3°22S 29°3E 54 C2
Uvs Nuur Mongolia 50°20N 92°30E 32 A4
'Uwairidh, Ḥarrat al Si. Arabia 26°50N 38°0E 44 E3
Uwajima Japan 33°10N 132°35E 31 H6
Uwanda △ Tanzania 7°46S 32°0E 54 D3
Uweinat, Jebel Sudan 21°54N 24°58E 51 D10
Uxbridge Canada 44°6N 79°7W 82 B5
Uxin Qi China 38°50N 109°5E 34 E5
Uxmal Mexico 20°22N 89°46W 87 C7
Üydzin Mongolia 44°9N 107°0E 34 B4
Uyo Nigeria 5°1N 7°53E 50 G7
Uyûn Mûsa Egypt 29°53N 32°40E 46 F1
Uyuni Bolivia 20°28S 66°47W 92 H5
Uzbekistan ■ Asia 41°30N 65°0E 28 E7
Uzboy → Turkmenistan 39°30N 55°0E 45 B7
Uzen Kazakhstan 43°29N 52°54E 19 F9
Uzen, Bolshoi = Uzen, Mal → Kazakhstan 49°4N 49°44E 19 E8
Uzen, Mal → Kazakhstan 49°4N 49°44E 19 E8
Uzerche France 45°25N 1°34E 20 D4
Uzh → Ukraine 51°15N 30°12E 17 C16
Uzhgorod = Uzhhorod Ukraine 48°36N 22°18E 17 D12
Uzhhorod Ukraine 48°36N 22°18E 17 D12
Užice Serbia 43°55N 19°50E 23 C8
Uzunköprü Turkey 41°16N 26°43E 23 D12

V

Vaal → S. Africa 29°4S 23°38E 56 D3
Vaal Dam S. Africa 27°0S 28°14E 57 D4
Vaalbos △ S. Africa 28°22S 24°20E 56 D3
Vaalwater S. Africa 24°15S 28°8E 57 C4
Vaasa Finland 63°6N 21°38E 8 E19
Vác Hungary 47°49N 19°10E 17 E10
Vacaria Brazil 28°31S 50°52W 95 B5
Vacata Fiji 17°15S 179°31W 59 a
Vacaville U.S.A. 38°21N 121°59W 78 G5
Vach = Vakh → Russia 60°45N 76°45E 28 C8
Vache, Î. à Haiti 18°2N 73°35W 89 C5
Vacoas Mauritius 20°18S 57°29E 53 d
Vadnagar India 23°47N 72°40E 42 H5
Vadodara India 22°20N 73°10E 42 H5
Vadsø Norway 70°3N 29°50E 8 A23
Vaduz Liech. 47°8N 9°31E 20 C8
Værøy Norway 67°40N 12°40E 8 C15
Vágar Færoe Is. 62°5N 7°15W 8 E9
Vagia, Akra Greece 36°15N 28°11E 25 C10
Vågsfjorden Norway 68°50N 16°50E 8 B17
Váh → Slovak Rep. 47°43N 18°7E 17 D9
Vahsel B. Antarctica 75°0S 35°0W 5 D1
Váhtjer = Gällivare Sweden 67°9N 20°40E 8 C19
Vaï Greece 35°15N 26°18E 25 D8
Vaigach Russia 70°10N 59°0E 28 B6
Vaihiria, L. Tahiti 17°40S 149°25W 59 d
Vail U.S.A. 39°40N 106°20W 74 C5
Vairao Tahiti 17°47S 149°17W 59 d
Vaisali → India 26°28N 78°53E 43 F8
Vaitogi Amer. Samoa 14°24S 170°44W 59 b
Vakh → Russia 60°45N 76°45E 28 C8
Val-d'Or Canada 48°7N 77°47W 72 C4
Val Marie Canada 49°15N 107°45W 71 D7
Valaam Russia 61°22N 30°57E 8 F24
Valahia Romania 44°35N 25°0E 17 F13
Valandovo Macedonia 41°19N 22°34E 23 D10
Valcheta Argentina 40°40S 66°8W 96 E3
Valdai Hills = Valdayskaya Vozvyshennost Russia 57°0N 33°30E 18 C5
Valdayskaya Vozvyshennost Russia 57°0N 33°30E 18 C5
Valdepeñas Spain 38°43N 3°25W 21 C4
Valdés, Pen. Argentina 42°30S 63°45W 96 E4
Valdez U.S.A. 61°7N 146°16W 74 a
Valdivia Chile 39°50S 73°14W 96 D2
Valdivia Abyssal Plain S. Ocean 62°30S 70°0E 5 C6
Valdosta U.S.A. 30°50N 83°17W 85 F13
Valdres Norway 61°5N 9°5E 8 F13
Vale U.S.A. 43°59N 117°15W 76 E5
Vale of Glamorgan □ U.K. 51°28N 3°25W 13 F4
Valemount Canada 52°50N 119°15W 70 C5
Valença Brazil 13°20S 39°5W 93 F11
Valença do Piauí Brazil 6°20S 41°45W 93 E10
Valence France 44°57N 4°54E 20 D6
Valencia Spain 39°27N 0°23W 21 C5
Valencia Trin. & Tob. 10°39N 61°11W 93 K15
Valencia U.S.A. 34°48N 106°43W 77 J10
Valencia Venezuela 10°11N 68°0W 92 A5
Valencia □ Spain 39°20N 0°40W 21 C5
Valencia, G. de Spain 39°30N 0°20E 21 C6
Valencia de Alcántara Spain 39°25N 7°14W 21 C2
Valencia I. Ireland 51°54N 10°22W 10 E1
Valenciennes France 50°20N 3°34E 20 A5
Valentim, Sa. do Brazil 6°0S 43°30W 93 E10
Valentin Russia 43°8N 134°17E 30 C7
Valentine Nebr., U.S.A. 42°52N 100°33W 80 D3
Valentine Tex., U.S.A. 30°35N 104°30W 84 F2
Valera Venezuela 9°19N 70°37W 92 B4
Valga Estonia 57°47N 26°2E 9 H22
Valier U.S.A. 48°18N 112°16W 76 B7
Valjevo Serbia 44°18N 19°53E 23 B8
Valka Latvia 57°46N 26°3E 9 H22
Valkeakoski Finland 61°16N 24°2E 8 F21
Valkenswaard Neths. 51°21N 5°29E 15 C5
Vall de Uxó = La Vall d'Uixó Spain 39°49N 0°15W 21 C5
Valladolid Mexico 20°41N 88°12W 87 C7
Valladolid Spain 41°38N 4°43W 21 B3
Valldemossa Spain 39°43N 2°37E 24 B9
Valle de la Pascua Venezuela 9°13N 66°0W 92 B5
Valle de las Palmas Mexico 32°20N 116°43W 79 N10
Valle de Santiago Mexico 20°23N 101°12W 86 C4
Valle de Zaragoza Mexico 27°25N 105°50W 86 B3
Valle Fértil, Sierra del Argentina 30°20S 68°0W 94 C2
Valle Gran Rey Canary Is. 28°5N 17°20W 24 F2
Valle Hermoso Mexico 25°35N 97°40W 87 B5
Valle Nacional Mexico 17°47N 96°18W 87 D5
Valledupar Colombia 10°29N 73°15W 92 A4
Vallehermoso Canary Is. 28°10N 17°15W 24 F2
Vallejo U.S.A. 38°7N 122°14W 78 G4
Vallenar Chile 28°30S 70°50W 94 B1
Valletta Malta 35°54N 14°31E 25 D2
Valley Center U.S.A. 33°13N 117°2W 79 M9
Valley City U.S.A. 46°55N 98°0W 80 B5
Valley Falls Oreg., U.S.A. 42°29N 120°17W 76 E3
Valley Falls R.I., U.S.A. 41°54N 71°24W 83 E13
Valley of Flowers △ India 30°50N 79°40E 43 D8
Valley Springs U.S.A. 38°12N 120°50W 78 G6
Valley View U.S.A. 40°39N 76°33W 83 F8
Valley Wells U.S.A. 35°27N 115°46W 79 K11
Valleyview Canada 55°5N 117°17W 70 B5
Vallimanca, Arroyo Argentina 35°40S 59°10W 94 D4
Valls Spain 41°18N 1°15E 21 B6
Valmiera Latvia 57°37N 25°29E 9 H21
Valognes France 49°30N 1°28W 20 B3
Valona = Vlorë Albania 40°32N 19°28E 23 D8
Valozhyn Belarus 54°3N 26°30E 17 A14
Valparaíso Chile 33°2S 71°40W 94 C1
Valparaíso Mexico 22°46N 103°34W 86 C4
Valparaiso U.S.A. 41°28N 87°4W 80 E10
Valparaíso □ Chile 33°2S 71°40W 94 C1
Vals → S. Africa 27°23S 26°30E 56 D4
Vals, Tanjung Indonesia 8°26S 137°25E 37 F9
Valsad India 20°40N 72°58E 40 J8
Valverde Canary Is. 27°48N 17°55W 24 G2
Valverde del Camino Spain 37°35N 6°47W 21 D2
Vammala Finland 61°20N 22°54E 8 F20
Vamos Greece 35°24N 24°13E 25 D6
Van Turkey 38°30N 43°20E 44 B4
Van, L. = Van Gölü Turkey 38°30N 43°0E 44 B4
Van Alstyne U.S.A. 33°25N 96°35W 84 E6
Van Blommestein Meer Suriname 4°45N 55°5W 93 C7
Van Buren Canada 47°10N 67°55W 73 C6
Van Buren Ark., U.S.A. 35°26N 94°21W 84 D7
Van Buren Maine, U.S.A. 47°10N 67°58W 81 B20
Van Buren Mo., U.S.A. 37°0N 91°1W 80 G8
Van Canh Vietnam 13°37N 109°0E 38 F7
Van Diemen, C. N. Terr., Australia 11°9S 130°24E 60 B5
Van Diemen, C. Queens., Australia 16°30S 139°46E 62 B2
Van Diemen G. Australia 11°45S 132°0E 60 B5
Van Gölü Turkey 38°30N 43°0E 44 B4
Van Horn U.S.A. 31°3N 104°50W 84 F2
Van Ninh Vietnam 12°42N 109°14E 38 F7
Van Rees, Pegunungan Indonesia 2°35S 138°15E 37 E9
Van Wert U.S.A. 40°52N 84°35W 81 E11
Van Yen Vietnam 21°4N 104°42E 38 B5
Vanadzor Armenia 40°48N 44°30E 19 F7
Vanavara Russia 60°22N 102°16E 29 C11
Vancouver Canada 49°15N 123°7W 78 A3
Vancouver U.S.A. 45°38N 122°40W 78 E4
Vancouver, C. Australia 35°2S 118°11E 61 G2
Vancouver I. Canada 49°50N 126°0W 78 A1
Vancouver Int. ✈ (YVR) Canada 49°10N 123°10W 78 A3
Vanda = Vantaa Finland 60°18N 24°56E 9 F21
Vandalia Ill., U.S.A. 38°58N 89°6W 80 F9
Vandalia Mo., U.S.A. 39°19N 91°29W 80 F8
Vandenberg Village U.S.A. 34°43N 120°28W 79 L6
Vanderbijlpark S. Africa 26°42S 27°54E 57 D4
Vandergrift U.S.A. 40°36N 79°34W 82 F5
Vanderhoof Canada 54°0N 124°0W 70 C4
Vanderkloof Dam S. Africa 30°4S 24°40E 56 E3
Vanderlin I. Australia 15°44S 137°2E 62 B2
Vänern Sweden 58°47N 13°30E 9 G15
Vänersborg Sweden 58°26N 12°19E 9 G15
Vang Vieng Laos 18°58N 102°32E 38 C4
Vanga Kenya 4°35S 39°12E 54 C4
Vangaindrano Madag. 23°21S 47°36E 57 C8
Vanguard Canada 49°55N 107°20W 71 D7
Vanino Russia 48°50N 140°5E 29 E15
Vännäs Sweden 63°58N 19°48E 8 E18
Vannes France 47°40N 2°47W 20 C2
Vannøya Norway 70°6N 19°50E 8 A18
Vanrhynsdorp S. Africa 31°36S 18°44E 56 E2
Vansbro Sweden 60°32N 14°15E 9 F16
Vansittart B. Australia 14°3S 126°17E 60 B4
Vantaa Finland 60°18N 24°56E 9 F21
Vanua Balavu Fiji 17°12S 178°55W 59 a
Vanua Levu Fiji 16°33S 179°15E 59 a
Vanua Vatu Fiji 18°22S 179°15W 59 a
Vanuatu ■ Pac. Oc. 15°0S 168°0E 58 C9
Vanwyksvlei S. Africa 30°18S 21°49E 56 E3
Vanzylsrus S. Africa 26°52S 22°4E 56 D3
Vapnyarka Ukraine 48°32N 28°45E 17 D15
Var → France 43°39N 7°12E 20 E7
Varāmīn Iran 35°20N 51°39E 45 C6
Varāmīn □ Iran 35°18N 51°35E 45 B6
Varanasi India 25°22N 83°0E 43 G10
Varangerfjorden Norway 70°3N 29°25E 8 A23
Varangerhalvøya Norway 70°25N 29°30E 8 A23
Varaždin Croatia 46°20N 16°20E 16 E9
Varberg Sweden 57°6N 12°20E 9 H15
Vardak □ Afghan. 34°0N 68°0E 40 B6
Vardar = Axios → Greece 40°57N 22°35E 23 D10
Varde Denmark 55°38N 8°29E 9 J13
Vardø Norway 70°23N 31°5E 8 A24
Varella, Mui Vietnam 12°54N 109°26E 38 F7
Varėna Lithuania 54°12N 24°30E 9 J21
Varese Italy 45°48N 8°50E 20 D8
Varginha Brazil 21°33S 45°25W 95 A6
Varillas Chile 24°0S 70°10W 94 A1
Varkaus Finland 62°19N 27°50E 8 E22
Varna Bulgaria 43°13N 27°56E 23 C12
Värnamo Sweden 57°10N 14°3E 9 H16
Vars Canada 45°21N 75°21W 83 A9
Varysburg U.S.A. 42°46N 78°19W 82 D6
Varzaneh Iran 32°25N 52°40E 45 C7
Vasa = Vaasa Finland 63°6N 21°38E 8 E19
Vasa Barris → Brazil 11°10S 37°10W 93 F11
Vascongadas = País Vasco □ Spain 42°50N 2°45W 21 A4
Vasht = Khāsh Iran 28°15N 61°15E 45 D9
Vasilevichi Belarus 52°15N 29°50E 17 B15
Vasilkov = Vasylkiv Ukraine 50°7N 30°15E 17 C16
Vaslui Romania 46°38N 27°42E 17 E14
Vassar Canada 49°10N 95°55W 71 D9
Vassar U.S.A. 43°22N 83°35W 81 D12
Västerås Sweden 59°37N 16°38E 9 G17
Västerbotten Sweden 64°36N 20°4E 8 D19
Västerdalälven → Sweden 60°30N 14°7E 8 F16
Västervik Sweden 57°43N 16°33E 9 H17
Västmanland Sweden 59°45N 16°20E 9 G17
Vasto Italy 42°8N 14°40E 22 C6
Vasylkiv Ukraine 50°7N 30°15E 17 C16
Vatersay U.K. 56°55N 7°32W 11 E1
Vatican City ■ Europe 41°54N 12°27E 22 D5
Vatili Cyprus 35°6N 33°40E 25 D12
Vatiu = Atiu Cook Is. 20°0S 158°10W 65 J12
Vatnajökull Iceland 64°30N 16°48W 8 D5
Vatolakkos Greece 35°27N 23°53E 25 D5
Vatoloha Madag. 17°52S 47°48E 57 B8
Vatomandry Madag. 19°20S 48°59E 57 B8
Vatra-Dornei Romania 47°22N 25°22E 17 E13
Vatrak → India 23°9N 73°2E 42 H5
Vättern Sweden 58°25N 14°30E 9 G16
Vatu Vara Fiji 17°26S 179°31W 59 a
Vatulele Fiji 18°33S 177°37E 59 a
Vaudreuil-Dorion Canada 45°23N 74°3W 83 A10
Vaughn Mont., U.S.A. 47°33N 111°33W 76 C8
Vaughn N. Mex., U.S.A. 34°36N 105°13W 77 J11
Vaujours L. Canada 55°27N 74°15W 72 A5
Vaupés = Uaupés → Brazil 0°2N 67°16W 92 C5
Vaupes □ Colombia 1°0N 71°0W 92 C4
Vauxhall Canada 50°5N 112°9W 70 C6
Vav India 24°22N 71°31E 42 G4
Vavatenina Madag. 17°28S 49°12E 57 B8
Vava'u Tonga 18°36S 174°0W 59 c
Vava'u Group Tonga 18°40S 174°0W 59 c
Vawkavysk Belarus 53°9N 24°30E 17 B13
Växjö Sweden 56°52N 14°50E 9 H16
Vaygach, Ostrov Russia 70°0N 60°0E 28 C6
Veaikevárri = Svappavaara Sweden 67°40N 21°3E 8 C19
Vechte → Neths. 52°34N 6°6E 15 B6
Vedea → Romania 43°42N 25°41E 17 G13
Vedia Argentina 34°30S 61°31W 94 C3
Veendam Neths. 53°5N 6°52E 15 A6
Veenendaal Neths. 52°2N 5°34E 15 B5
Vefsna → Norway 65°48N 13°10E 8 D15
Vega Norway 65°40N 11°55E 8 D14
Vega U.S.A. 35°15N 102°26W 84 D3
Vega Baja Puerto Rico 18°27N 66°23W 89 d
Vegreville Canada 53°30N 112°5W 70 C6
Vejer de la Frontera Spain 36°15N 5°59W 21 D3
Vejle Denmark 55°43N 9°30E 9 J13
Velas, C. Costa Rica 10°21N 85°52W 88 D2
Velasco, Sierra de Argentina 29°20S 67°10W 94 B2
Velddrif S. Africa 32°42S 18°11E 56 E2
Velebit Planina Croatia 44°50N 15°20E 16 F8
Veles Macedonia 41°46N 21°47E 23 D9
Vélez-Málaga Spain 36°48N 4°5W 21 D3
Vélez Rubio Spain 37°41N 2°5W 21 D4
Velhas → Brazil 17°13S 44°49W 93 G10
Velika Kapela Croatia 45°10N 15°5E 16 F8
Velikaya → Russia 57°48N 28°10E 18 C4
Velikaya Kema Russia 45°30N 137°12E 30 B8
Veliki Ustyug Russia 60°47N 46°20E 18 B8
Velikiye Luki Russia 56°25N 30°32E 18 C5
Veliko Tŭrnovo Bulgaria 43°5N 25°41E 23 C11
Velikonda Range India 14°45N 79°10E 40 M11
Velletri Italy 41°41N 12°47E 22 D5
Vellore India 12°57N 79°10E 40 N11
Velsk Russia 61°10N 42°5E 18 B7
Veluwezoom △ Neths. 52°5N 6°0E 15 B6
Velva U.S.A. 48°4N 100°56W 80 A3
Venado Mexico 22°56N 101°6W 86 C4
Venado Tuerto Argentina 33°50S 62°0W 94 C3
Vendée □ France 46°50N 1°35W 20 C3
Vendôme France 47°47N 1°3E 20 C4
Venézia Italy 45°27N 12°21E 22 B5
Venézia, G. di Italy 45°15N 13°0E 22 B5
Venezuela ■ S. Amer. 8°0N 66°0W 92 B5
Venezuela, G. de Venezuela 11°30N 71°0W 92 A4
Vengurla India 15°53N 73°45E 40 M8
Venice = Venézia Italy 45°27N 12°21E 22 B5
Venice U.S.A. 27°6N 82°27W 85 H13
Venkatapuram India 18°20N 80°30E 41 K12
Venlo Neths. 51°22N 6°11E 15 C6
Vennesla Norway 58°15N 7°59E 9 G12
Venray Neths. 51°31N 6°0E 15 C6
Ventana, Punta de la Mexico 24°4N 109°48W 86 C3
Ventana, Sa. de la Argentina 38°0S 62°30W 94 D3
Ventersburg S. Africa 28°7S 27°9E 56 D4
Venterstad S. Africa 30°47S 25°48E 56 E4
Ventnor U.K. 50°36N 1°12W 13 G6
Ventoténe Italy 40°47N 13°25E 22 D5
Ventoux, Mt. France 44°10N 5°17E 20 D6
Ventspils Latvia 57°25N 21°32E 9 H19
Ventuarí → Venezuela 3°58N 67°2W 92 C5
Ventucopa U.S.A. 34°50N 119°29W 79 L7
Ventura U.S.A. 34°17N 119°18W 79 L7
Vénus, Pte. Tahiti 17°29S 149°29W 59 d
Venus B. Australia 38°40S 145°42E 63 F4
Venustiano Carranza Mexico 30°25N 115°53W 86 A1
Vera Argentina 29°30S 60°20W 94 B3
Vera Spain 37°15N 1°51W 21 D5
Veracruz Mexico 19°11N 96°8W 87 D5
Veracruz □ Mexico 19°0N 96°15W 87 D5
Veraval India 20°53N 70°27E 42 J4
Verbánia Italy 45°56N 8°33E 20 D8
Vercelli Italy 45°19N 8°25E 20 D8
Verdalsøra Norway 63°48N 11°30E 8 E14
Verde → Argentina 41°56S 65°5W 96 E3
Verde → Goiás, Brazil 18°1S 50°14W 93 G8
Verde → Mato Grosso do Sul, Brazil 21°25S 52°20W 93 H8
Verde → Chihuahua, Mexico 26°29N 107°58W 86 B3
Verde → Oaxaca, Mexico 15°59N 97°50W 87 D5
Verde → Veracruz, Mexico 21°10N 102°50W 86 C4
Verde → Paraguay 23°9S 57°37W 94 A4
Verde → U.S.A. 33°33N 111°40W 74 D4
Verde, Cay Bahamas 23°0N 75°5W 88 B4
Verden Germany 52°55N 9°14E 16 B5
Verdi U.S.A. 39°31N 119°59W 78 F7
Verdun France 49°9N 5°24E 20 B6
Vereeniging S. Africa 26°38S 27°57E 57 D4
Verga, C. Guinea 10°30N 14°10W 50 F3
Vergara Uruguay 32°56S 53°57W 95 C5
Vergemont Cr. → Australia 24°16S 143°16E 62 C3
Vergennes U.S.A. 44°10N 73°15W 83 B11
Veria Greece 40°34N 22°12E 23 D10
Verín Spain 41°57N 7°27W 21 B2
Verkhnetulomskoye Vdkhr. Russia 68°36N 31°12E 8 B24
Verkhnevilyuysk Russia 63°27N 120°18E 29 C13
Verkhniy Baskunchak Russia 48°14N 46°44E 19 E8
Verkhoyansk Russia 67°35N 133°25E 29 C14
Verkhoyansk Ra. = Verkhoyanskiy Khrebet Russia 66°0N 129°0E 29 C13
Verkhoyanskiy Khrebet Russia 66°0N 129°0E 29 C13
Vermilion Canada 53°20N 110°50W 71 C6
Vermilion U.S.A. 41°25N 82°22W 82 E2
Vermilion → Canada 53°22N 110°51W 71 C6
Vermilion B. U.S.A. 29°42N 92°0W 84 G9
Vermilion Bay Canada 49°51N 93°34W 71 D10
Vermilion L. U.S.A. 47°53N 92°26W 80 B7
Vermillion U.S.A. 42°47N 96°56W 80 D5
Vermillion → Canada 47°38N 72°56W 72 C5
Vermont □ U.S.A. 44°0N 73°0W 83 C12
Vernadsky Antarctica 65°0S 64°0W 5 C17
Vernal U.S.A. 40°27N 109°32W 76 F9
Vernalis U.S.A. 37°36N 121°17W 78 H5
Verner Canada 46°25N 80°8W 72 C3
Verneukpan S. Africa 30°0S 21°0E 56 E3
Vernon Canada 50°20N 119°15W 70 C5
Vernon U.S.A. 34°9N 99°17W 84 D5
Vernonia U.S.A. 45°52N 123°11W 78 E3
Vero Beach U.S.A. 27°38N 80°24W 85 H14
Véroia = Veria Greece 40°34N 22°12E 23 D10
Verona Canada 44°29N 76°42W 83 B8
Verona Italy 45°27N 10°59E 22 B4
Versailles France 48°48N 2°7E 20 B5
Vert, C. Senegal 14°45N 17°30W 50 F2
Verulam S. Africa 29°38S 31°2E 57 D5
Verviers Belgium 50°37N 5°52E 15 D5
Veselovskoye Vdkhr. Russia 46°58N 41°25E 19 E7
Vesoul France 47°40N 6°11E 20 C7
Vesterålen Norway 68°45N 15°0E 8 B16
Vestfjorden Norway 67°55N 14°0E 8 C16
Vestmannaeyjar Iceland 63°27N 20°15W 8 E3
Vestspitsbergen Svalbard 78°40N 17°0E 4 B8
Vestvågøya Norway 68°18N 13°50E 8 B15
Vesuvio Italy 40°49N 14°26E 22 D6
Vesuvius, Mt. = Vesuvio Italy 40°49N 14°26E 22 D6
Veszprém Hungary 47°8N 17°57E 17 E9

Vetlanda *Sweden* 57°24N 15°3E **9** H16
Vetlugu → *Russia* 56°36N 46°4E **18** C8
Vettore, Mte. *Italy* 42°49N 13°16E **22** C5
Veurne *Belgium* 51°5N 2°40E **15** C2
Veys *Iran* 31°30N 49°0E **45** D6
Vezhen *Bulgaria* 42°50N 24°20E **23** C11
Vi Thanh *Vietnam* 9°42N 105°26E **39** H5
Viacha *Bolivia* 16°39S 68°18W **92** G5
Viamão *Brazil* 30°5S 51°0W **95** C5
Viana *Brazil* 3°13S 44°55W **93** D10
Viana do Alentejo *Portugal* 38°17N 7°59W **21** C2
Viana do Castelo *Portugal* 41°42N 8°50W **21** B1
Vianden *Lux.* 49°56N 6°12E **15** E6
Viangchan = Vientiane *Laos* 17°58N 102°36E **38** D4
Vianópolis *Brazil* 16°40S 48°35W **93** G9
Vianos *Greece* 35°2N 25°21E **25** D7
Viaréggio *Italy* 43°52N 10°14E **22** C4
Vibo Valéntia *Italy* 38°40N 16°6E **22** E7
Viborg *Denmark* 56°27N 9°23E **9** H13
Vic *Spain* 41°58N 2°19E **21** B7
Vicenza *Italy* 45°33N 11°33E **22** B4
Vich = Vic *Spain* 41°58N 2°19E **21** B7
Vichada → *Colombia* 4°55N 67°50W **92** C5
Vichy *France* 46°9N 3°26E **20** C5
Vicksburg *U.S.A.* 33°45N 113°45W **79** M13
Victor *India* 21°0N 71°30E **42** J4
Victor *U.S.A.* 42°58N 77°24W **82** D7
Victor Harbor *Australia* 35°30S 138°37E **63** F2
Victoria *Argentina* 32°40S 60°10W **94** C3
Victoria *Canada* 48°30N 123°25W **78** B3
Victoria *Chile* 38°13S 72°20W **96** D2
Victoria *China* 22°17N 114°9E **33** G1
Victoria *Malta* 36°3N 14°14E **25** C1
Victoria *Seychelles* 4°38S 55°28E **53** b
Victoria *Kans., U.S.A.* 38°52N 99°9W **80** F4
Victoria *Tex., U.S.A.* 28°48N 97°0W **84** G6
Victoria □ *Australia* 37°0S 144°0E **63** F3
Victoria → *Australia* 15°10S 129°40E **60** C4
Victoria, Grand L. *Canada* 47°31N 77°30W **72** C4
Victoria, L. *Africa* 1°0S 33°0E **54** C3
Victoria, L. *Australia* 33°57S 141°15E **63** E3
Victoria, Mt. *Burma* 21°14N 93°55E **41** J18
Victoria Beach *Canada* 50°40N 96°35W **71** C9
Victoria de Durango = Durango *Mexico* 24°3N 104°39W **86** C4
Victoria de las Tunas = Las Tunas *Cuba* 20°58N 76°59W **88** B4
Victoria Falls *Zimbabwe* 17°58S 25°52E **55** F2
Victoria Harbour *Canada* 44°45N 79°45W **82** B5
Victoria I. *Canada* 71°0N 111°0W **68** B8
Victoria L. *Canada* 48°20N 57°27W **73** C8
Victoria Ld. *Antarctica* 75°0S 160°0E **5** D11
Victoria Nile → *Uganda* 2°14N 31°26E **54** B3
Victoria River *Australia* 16°25S 131°0E **60** C5
Victoria Str. *Canada* 69°31N 100°30W **68** C9
Victoria West *S. Africa* 31°25S 23°4E **56** E3
Victoriaville *Canada* 46°4N 71°56W **73** C5
Victorica *Argentina* 36°20S 65°30W **94** D2
Victorville *U.S.A.* 34°32N 117°18W **79** L9
Vicuña *Chile* 30°0S 70°50W **94** C1
Vicuña Mackenna *Argentina* 33°53S 64°25W **94** C3
Vidal *U.S.A.* 34°7N 114°31W **79** L12
Vidal Junction *U.S.A.* 34°11N 114°34W **79** L12
Vidalia *U.S.A.* 32°13N 82°25W **85** E13
Vidin *Bulgaria* 43°59N 22°50E **23** C10
Vidisha *India* 23°28N 77°53E **42** H7
Vido *Greece* 39°38N 19°55E **25** A3
Vidzy *Belarus* 55°23N 26°37E **9** J22
Viedma *Argentina* 40°50S 63°0W **96** E4
Viedma, L. *Argentina* 49°30S 72°30W **96** F2
Vielsalm *Belgium* 50°17N 5°54E **15** D5
Vieng Pou Kha *Laos* 20°41N 101°4E **38** B3
Vienna = Wien *Austria* 48°12N 16°22E **16** D9
Vienna *Ill., U.S.A.* 37°25N 88°54W **80** G9
Vienna *Mo., U.S.A.* 38°11N 91°57W **80** F8
Vienne *France* 45°31N 4°53E **20** D6
Vienne → *France* 47°13N 0°5E **20** C4
Vientiane *Laos* 17°58N 102°36E **38** D4
Vientos, Paso de los *Caribbean* 20°0N 74°0W **89** C5
Vieques *Puerto Rico* 18°8N 65°25W **89** d
Vierge Pt. *St. Lucia* 13°49N 60°53W **89** f
Vierzon *France* 47°13N 2°5E **20** C5
Vietnam ■ *Asia* 19°0N 106°0E **38** C6
Vieux Fort *St. Lucia* 13°46N 60°58W **89** f
Vigan *Phil.* 17°35N 120°28E **37** A6
Vigévano *Italy* 45°19N 8°51E **20** D8
Vigia *Brazil* 0°50S 48°5W **93** D9
Viglas, Akra *Greece* 35°54N 27°51E **25** D9
Vigo *Spain* 42°12N 8°41W **21** A1
Vihowa *Pakistan* 31°8N 70°30E **42** D4
Vihowa → *Pakistan* 31°8N 70°41E **42** D4
Vijayawada *India* 16°31N 80°39E **41** L12
Vijosë → *Albania* 40°37N 19°24E **23** D8
Vík *Iceland* 63°25N 19°1W **8** E4
Vikeke = Viqueque *E. Timor* 8°52S 126°23E **37** F7
Viking *Canada* 53°7N 111°50W **70** C6
Vikna *Norway* 64°55N 10°58E **8** D14
Vila da Maganja *Mozam.* 17°18S 37°30E **55** F4
Vila da Ribeira Brava *C. Verde Is.* 16°32N 24°25W **50** b
Vila do Bispo *Portugal* 37°5N 8°53W **21** D1
Vila Franca de Xira *Portugal* 38°57N 8°59W **21** C1
Vila Gamito *Mozam.* 14°12S 33°0E **55** E3
Vila Gomes da Costa *Mozam.* 24°20S 33°37E **57** C5
Vila Machado *Mozam.* 19°15S 34°14E **55** F3
Vila Mouzinho *Mozam.* 14°48S 34°25E **55** E3
Vila Nova de Gaia *Portugal* 41°8N 8°37W **21** B1
Vila Real *Portugal* 41°17N 7°48W **21** B2
Vila-real de los Infantes *Spain* 39°55N 0°3W **21** C5
Vila Real de Santo António *Portugal* 37°10N 7°28W **21** D2
Vila Vasco da Gama *Mozam.* 14°54S 32°14E **55** E3
Vila Velha *Brazil* 20°20S 40°17W **95** A7
Vilagarcía de Arousa *Spain* 42°34N 8°46W **21** A1
Vilaine → *France* 47°30N 2°27W **20** C2
Vilanandro, Tanjona *Madag.* 16°11S 44°27E **57** B7
Vilanculos *Mozam.* 22°1S 35°17E **57** C6
Vilanova i la Geltrú *Spain* 41°13N 1°40E **21** B6
Vilcheka, Zemlya *Russia* 80°30N 60°30E **4** A11
Vileyka *Belarus* 54°30N 26°53E **17** A14
Vilhelmina *Sweden* 64°35N 16°39E **8** D17
Vilhena *Brazil* 12°40S 60°5W **92** F6
Viliya = Neris → *Lithuania* 55°8N 24°16E **9** J21
Viljandi *Estonia* 58°28N 25°30E **9** G21
Vilkitskogo, Proliv *Russia* 78°0N 103°0E **29** B11
Vilkovo = Vylkove *Ukraine* 45°28N 29°32E **17** F15
Villa Abecia *Bolivia* 21°0S 68°18W **94** A2
Villa Ana *Argentina* 28°28S 59°40W **94** B4
Villa Ángela *Argentina* 27°34S 60°45W **94** B3
Villa Bella *Bolivia* 10°25S 65°22W **92** F5
Villa Cañás *Argentina* 34°0S 61°35W **94** C3
Villa Colón *Argentina* 31°38S 68°20W **94** C2
Villa Constitución *Argentina* 33°15S 60°20W **94** C3
Villa de Arriaga *Mexico* 21°56N 101°20W **86** C4
Villa de María *Argentina* 29°55S 63°43W **94** B3
Villa de Méndez *Mexico* 25°7N 98°34W **87** B5
Villa Dolores *Argentina* 31°58S 65°15W **94** C2
Villa Frontera *Mexico* 26°56N 101°27W **86** B4
Villa Guillermina *Argentina* 28°15S 59°29W **94** B4
Villa Hayes *Paraguay* 25°5S 57°20W **94** B4
Villa Hidalgo *Mexico* 24°15N 99°26W **87** C5
Villa Iris *Argentina* 38°12S 63°12W **94** D3
Villa María *Argentina* 32°20S 63°10W **94** C3
Villa Mazán *Argentina* 28°40S 66°30W **94** B2
Villa Montes *Bolivia* 21°10S 63°30W **94** A3
Villa Ocampo *Argentina* 28°30S 59°20W **94** B4
Villa Ocampo *Mexico* 26°27N 105°31W **86** B3
Villa Ojo de Agua *Argentina* 29°30S 63°44W **94** B3
Villa San José *Argentina* 32°12S 58°15W **94** C4
Villa San Martín *Argentina* 28°15S 64°9W **94** B3
Villa Unión *Mexico* 23°12N 106°14W **86** C3
Villacarlos *Spain* 39°53N 4°17E **24** B11
Villacarrillo *Spain* 38°7N 3°3W **21** C4
Villach *Austria* 46°37N 13°51E **16** E7
Villafranca de los Caballeros *Spain* 39°34N 3°25E **24** B10
Villagrán *Mexico* 24°29N 99°29W **87** C5
Villaguay *Argentina* 32°0S 59°0W **94** C4
Villahermosa *Mexico* 17°59N 92°55W **87** D6
Villajoyosa *Spain* 38°30N 0°12W **21** C5
Villalba *Spain* 43°26N 7°40W **21** A2
Villanueva *U.S.A.* 35°16N 105°22W **77** J11
Villanueva de la Serena *Spain* 38°59N 5°50W **21** C3
Villanueva y Geltrú = Vilanova i la Geltrú *Spain* 41°13N 1°40E **21** B6
Villarreal = Vila-real de los Infantes *Spain* 39°55N 0°3W **21** C5
Villarrica *Chile* 39°15S 72°15W **96** D2
Villarrica *Paraguay* 25°40S 56°30W **94** B4
Villarrobledo *Spain* 39°18N 2°36W **21** C4
Villavicencio *Argentina* 32°28S 69°0W **94** C2
Villavicencio *Colombia* 4°9N 73°37W **92** C4
Villaviciosa *Spain* 43°32N 5°27W **21** A3
Villazón *Bolivia* 22°0S 65°35W **94** A2
Ville-Marie *Canada* 47°20N 79°30W **72** C4
Ville Platte *U.S.A.* 30°41N 92°17W **84** F8
Villena *Spain* 38°39N 0°52W **21** C5
Villeneuve-d'Ascq *France* 50°38N 3°9E **20** A5
Villeneuve-sur-Lot *France* 44°24N 0°42E **20** D4
Villiers *S. Africa* 27°2S 28°36E **57** D4
Villingen-Schwenningen *Germany* 48°3N 8°26E **16** D5
Villmanstrand = Lappeenranta *Finland* 61°3N 28°12E **8** F23
Vilna *Canada* 54°7N 111°55W **70** C6
Vilnius *Lithuania* 54°38N 25°19E **9** J21
Vilvoorde *Belgium* 50°56N 4°26E **15** D4
Vilyuy → *Russia* 64°24N 126°26E **29** C13
Vilyuysk *Russia* 63°40N 121°35E **29** C13
Viña del Mar *Chile* 33°0S 71°30W **94** C1
Vinarós *Spain* 40°30N 0°27E **21** B6
Vincennes *U.S.A.* 38°41N 87°32W **80** F10
Vincent *U.S.A.* 34°33N 118°11W **79** L8
Vinchina *Argentina* 28°45S 68°15W **94** B2
Vindelälven → *Sweden* 63°55N 19°50E **8** E18
Vindeln *Sweden* 64°12N 19°43E **8** D18
Vindhya Ra. *India* 22°50N 77°0E **42** H7
Vineland *U.S.A.* 39°29N 75°2W **81** F16
Vinh *Vietnam* 18°45N 105°38E **38** C5
Vinh Linh *Vietnam* 17°4N 107°2E **38** D6
Vinh Long *Vietnam* 10°16N 105°57E **39** G5
Vinh Yen *Vietnam* 21°21N 105°35E **38** B5
Vinita *U.S.A.* 36°39N 95°9W **84** C7
Vinkovci *Croatia* 45°19N 18°48E **23** B8
Vinnitsa = Vinnytsya *Ukraine* 49°15N 28°30E **17** D15
Vinnytsya *Ukraine* 49°15N 28°30E **17** D15
Vinson Massif *Antarctica* 78°35S 85°25W **5** D16
Vinton *Calif., U.S.A.* 39°48N 120°10W **78** F6
Vinton *Iowa, U.S.A.* 42°10N 92°1W **80** D7
Vinton *La., U.S.A.* 30°11N 93°35W **84** F8
Viqueque *E. Timor* 8°52S 126°23E **37** F7
Virac *Phil.* 13°30N 124°20E **37** B6
Virachey *Cambodia* 13°59N 106°49E **38** F6
Virachey △ *Cambodia* 14°14N 106°55E **38** E6
Virago Sd. *Canada* 54°0N 132°30W **70** C2
Viramgam *India* 23°5N 72°0E **42** H5
Viranşehir *Turkey* 37°13N 39°45E **44** B3
Virawah *Pakistan* 24°31N 70°46E **42** G4
Virden *Canada* 49°50N 100°56W **71** D8
Vire *France* 48°50N 0°53W **20** B3
Vírgenes, C. *Argentina* 52°19S 68°21W **96** G3
Virgin → *U.S.A.* 36°28N 114°21W **77** H6
Virgin Gorda *Br. Virgin Is.* 18°30N 64°26W **89** e
Virgin Is. (British) ⧄ *W. Indies* 18°30N 64°30W **89** e
Virgin Is. (U.S.) ⧄ *W. Indies* 18°20N 65°0W **89** e
Virgin Islands △ *U.S. Virgin Is.* 18°21N 64°43W **89** C7
Virginia *S. Africa* 28°8S 26°55E **56** D4
Virginia *U.S.A.* 47°31N 92°32W **80** B7
Virginia □ *U.S.A.* 37°30N 78°45W **81** G14
Virginia Beach *U.S.A.* 36°44N 76°0W **81** F16
Virginia City *Mont., U.S.A.* 45°18N 111°56W **76** D8
Virginia City *Nev., U.S.A.* 39°19N 119°39W **78** F7
Virginia Falls *Canada* 61°38N 125°42W **70** A3
Virginiatown *Canada* 48°9N 79°36W **72** C4
Viroqua *U.S.A.* 43°34N 90°53W **80** D8
Virovitica *Croatia* 45°51N 17°21E **22** B7
Virpur *India* 21°51N 70°42E **42** J4
Virton *Belgium* 49°35N 5°32E **15** E5
Virudunagar *India* 9°30N 77°58E **40** Q10
Virunga △ *Dem. Rep. of the Congo* 0°5N 29°38E **54** B2
Vis *Croatia* 43°4N 16°10E **22** C7
Visalia *U.S.A.* 36°20N 119°18W **78** J7
Visayan Sea *Phil.* 11°30N 123°30E **37** B6
Visby *Sweden* 57°37N 18°18E **9** H18
Viscount Melville Sd. *Canada* 74°10N 108°0W **69** B9
Visé *Belgium* 50°44N 5°41E **15** D5
Višegrad *Bos.-H.* 43°47N 19°17E **23** C8
Viseu *Brazil* 1°10S 46°5W **93** D9
Viseu *Portugal* 40°40N 7°55W **21** B2
Vishakhapatnam *India* 17°45N 83°20E **41** L13
Visnagar *India* 23°45N 72°32E **42** H5
Viso, Mte. *Italy* 44°38N 7°5E **20** D7
Visokoi I. *Antarctica* 56°43S 27°15W **5** B1
Vista *U.S.A.* 33°12N 117°14W **79** M9
Vistula = Wisła → *Poland* 54°22N 18°55E **17** A10
Vitebsk = Vitsyebsk *Belarus* 55°10N 30°15E **18** C5
Viterbo *Italy* 42°25N 12°6E **22** C5
Viti Levu *Fiji* 17°30S 177°30E **59** a
Vitigudino *Spain* 41°1N 6°26W **21** B2
Vitim *Russia* 59°28N 112°35E **29** D12
Vitim → *Russia* 59°26N 112°34E **29** D12
Vitória *Brazil* 20°20S 40°22W **93** H10
Vitória da Conquista *Brazil* 14°51S 40°51W **93** F10
Vitória de São Antão *Brazil* 8°10S 35°20W **93** E11
Vitoria-Gasteiz *Spain* 42°50N 2°41W **21** A4
Vitsyebsk *Belarus* 55°10N 30°15E **18** C5
Vittória *Italy* 36°57N 14°32E **22** F6
Vittório Véneto *Italy* 45°59N 12°18E **22** B5
Viveiro *Spain* 43°39N 7°38W **21** A2
Vivian *U.S.A.* 32°53N 93°59W **84** E8
Viwa *Fiji* 17°10S 177°58E **59** a
Vizcaíno, Desierto de *Mexico* 27°30N 113°45W **86** B2
Vizcaíno, Sierra *Mexico* 27°30N 114°0W **86** B2
Vize *Turkey* 41°34N 27°45E **23** D12
Vizianagaram *India* 18°6N 83°30E **41** K13
Vlaardingen *Neths.* 51°55N 4°21E **15** C4
Vladikavkaz *Russia* 43°0N 44°35E **19** F7
Vladimir *Russia* 56°15N 40°30E **18** C7
Vladimir Volynskiy = Volodymyr-Volynskyy *Ukraine* 50°50N 24°18E **17** C13
Vladivostok *Russia* 43°10N 131°53E **30** C5
Vlieland *Neths.* 53°16N 4°55E **15** A4
Vlissingen *Neths.* 51°26N 3°34E **15** C3
Vlorë *Albania* 40°32N 19°28E **23** D8
Vltava → *Czech Rep.* 50°21N 14°30E **16** D8
Vo Dat *Vietnam* 11°9N 107°31E **39** G6
Voe *U.K.* 60°21N 1°16W **11** A7
Vogelkop = Doberai, Jazirah *Indonesia* 1°25S 133°0E **37** E8
Vogelsberg *Germany* 50°31N 9°12E **16** C5
Voghera *Italy* 44°59N 9°1E **20** D8
Vohibinany *Madag.* 18°49S 49°4E **57** B8
Vohilava *Madag.* 21°4S 48°0E **57** C8
Vohimarina = Iharana *Madag.* 13°25S 50°0E **57** A9
Vohimena, Tanjon' i *Madag.* 25°36S 45°8E **57** D8
Vohipeno *Madag.* 22°22S 47°51E **57** C8
Voi *Kenya* 3°25S 38°32E **54** C4
Voiron *France* 45°22N 5°35E **20** D6
Voisey B. *Canada* 56°15N 61°50W **73** A7
Vojmsjön *Sweden* 65°0N 16°24E **8** D17
Vojvodina □ *Serbia* 45°20N 20°0E **23** B9
Volborg *U.S.A.* 45°51N 105°41W **76** D11
Volcán de Colima △ *Mexico* 19°30N 103°40W **86** D4
Volcano Is. = Kazan-Rettō *Pac. Oc.* 25°0N 141°0E **64** E6
Volcans △ *Rwanda* 1°30S 29°26E **54** C2
Volda *Norway* 62°9N 6°5E **8** E12
Volga = Privolzhskiy □ *Russia* 56°0N 50°0E **28** D6
Volga → *Russia* 46°0N 48°30E **19** E8
Volga Hts. = Privolzhskaya Vozvyshennost *Russia* 51°0N 46°0E **19** D8
Volgodonsk *Russia* 47°33N 42°5E **19** E7
Volgograd *Russia* 48°40N 44°25E **19** E7
Volgogradskoye Vdkhr. *Russia* 50°0N 45°20E **19** D8
Volkhov → *Russia* 60°8N 32°20E **18** B5
Volkovysk = Vawkavysk *Belarus* 53°9N 24°30E **17** B13
Volksrust *S. Africa* 27°24S 29°53E **57** D4
Volochanka *Russia* 71°0N 94°28E **29** B10
Volodymyr-Volynskyy *Ukraine* 50°50N 24°18E **17** C13
Vologda *Russia* 59°10N 39°45E **18** C6
Volos *Greece* 39°24N 22°59E **23** E10
Volosovo *Russia* 59°27N 29°32E **9** G23
Volovets *Ukraine* 48°43N 23°11E **17** D12
Volozhin = Valozhyn *Belarus* 54°3N 26°30E **17** A14
Volsk *Russia* 52°5N 47°22E **18** D8
Volta → *Ghana* 5°46N 0°41E **48** F4
Volta, L. *Ghana* 7°30N 0°0 **50** G6
Volta Redonda *Brazil* 22°31S 44°5W **95** A7
Voltaire, C. *Australia* 14°16S 125°35E **60** B4
Volterra *Italy* 43°24N 10°51E **22** C4
Volturno → *Italy* 41°1N 13°55E **22** D5
Volzhskiy *Russia* 48°56N 44°46E **19** E7
Vomo *Fiji* 17°30S 177°15E **59** a
Vondrozo *Madag.* 22°49S 47°20E **57** C8
Vopnafjörður *Iceland* 65°45N 14°50W **8** D6
Vories Sporades *Greece* 39°15N 23°30E **23** E10
Vorkuta *Russia* 67°48N 64°20E **18** A11
Vormsi *Estonia* 59°1N 23°13E **9** G20
Voronezh *Russia* 51°40N 39°10E **19** D6
Vörts Järv *Estonia* 58°16N 26°3E **9** G22
Võru *Estonia* 57°48N 26°54E **9** H22
Vosges *France* 48°20N 7°10E **20** B7
Voss *Norway* 60°38N 6°26E **8** F12
Vostok *Antarctica* 78°30S 106°50E **5** D8
Vostok I. *Kiribati* 10°5S 152°23W **65** J12
Votkinsk *Russia* 57°0N 53°55E **18** C9
Votkinskoye Vdkhr. *Russia* 57°22N 55°12E **18** C10
Votsuri-Shima *Japan* 25°45N 123°29E **31** M1
Vouga → *Portugal* 40°41N 8°40W **21** B1
Vouxa, Akra *Greece* 35°37N 23°32E **25** D5
Voyageurs △ *U.S.A.* 48°32N 93°0W **80** A7
Voynitsa *Russia* 65°10N 30°20E **8** D24
Vozhe, Ozero *Russia* 60°45N 39°0E **18** B6
Voznesensk *Ukraine* 47°35N 31°21E **19** E5
Voznesenye *Russia* 61°0N 35°28E **18** B6
Vrangelya, Ostrov *Russia* 71°0N 180°0E **29** B19
Vranje *Serbia* 42°34N 21°54E **23** C9
Vratsa *Bulgaria* 43°15N 23°30E **23** C10
Vrbas → *Bos.-H.* 45°8N 17°29E **22** B7
Vrede *S. Africa* 27°24S 29°6E **57** D4
Vredefort *S. Africa* 27°0S 27°22E **56** D4
Vredenburg *S. Africa* 32°56S 18°0E **56** E2
Vredendal *S. Africa* 31°41S 18°35E **56** E2
Vrindavan *India* 27°37N 77°40E **42** F7
Vrisses *Greece* 35°23N 24°13E **25** D6
Vršac *Serbia* 45°8N 21°20E **23** B9
Vryburg *S. Africa* 26°55S 24°45E **56** D3
Vryheid *S. Africa* 27°45S 30°47E **57** D5
Vu Liet *Vietnam* 18°43N 105°23E **38** C5
Vukovar *Croatia* 45°21N 18°59E **23** B8
Vulcan *Canada* 50°25N 113°15W **70** C6
Vulcan *Romania* 45°23N 23°17E **17** F12
Vulcaneşti *Moldova* 45°41N 28°18E **17** F15
Vulcano *Italy* 38°24N 14°58E **22** E6
Vulkaneshty = Vulcaneşti *Moldova* 45°41N 28°18E **17** F15
Vunduzi → *Mozam.* 18°56S 34°1E **55** F3
Vung Tau *Vietnam* 10°21N 107°4E **39** G6
Vunidawa *Fiji* 17°50S 178°21E **59** a
Vunisea *Fiji* 19°3S 178°10E **59** a
Vwaza ⌂ *Malawi* 10°58S 33°25E **55** E3
Vyartsilya *Russia* 62°8N 30°45E **8** E24
Vyatka = Kirov *Russia* 58°35N 49°40E **18** C8
Vyatka → *Russia* 55°37N 51°28E **18** C9
Vyatskiye Polyany *Russia* 56°14N 51°5E **18** C9
Vyazemskiy *Russia* 47°32N 134°45E **29** E14
Vyazma *Russia* 55°10N 34°15E **18** C5
Vyborg *Russia* 60°43N 28°47E **8** F23
Vychegda → *Russia* 61°18N 46°36E **18** B8
Vychodné Beskydy *Europe* 49°20N 22°0E **17** D11
Vyg-ozero *Russia* 63°47N 34°29E **18** B5
Vylkove *Ukraine* 45°28N 29°32E **17** F15
Vynohradiv *Ukraine* 48°9N 23°2E **17** D12
Vyrnwy, L. *U.K.* 52°48N 3°31W **12** E4
Vyshniy Volochek *Russia* 57°30N 34°30E **18** C5
Vyshzha = imeni 26 Bakinskikh Komissarov *Turkmenistan* 39°22N 54°10E **45** B7
Vyškov *Czech Rep.* 49°17N 17°0E **17** D9
Vytegra *Russia* 61°0N 36°27E **18** B6

W

W.A.C. Bennett Dam *Canada* 56°2N 122°6W **70** B4
Wa *Ghana* 10°7N 2°25W **50** F5
Waal → *Neths.* 51°37N 5°0E **15** C5
Waalwijk *Neths.* 51°42N 5°4E **15** C5
Wabakimi △ *Canada* 50°43N 89°29W **72** B2
Wabana *Canada* 47°40N 53°0W **73** C9
Wabasca → *Canada* 58°22N 115°20W **70** B5
Wabasca-Desmarais *Canada* 55°57N 113°56W **70** B6
Wabash *U.S.A.* 40°48N 85°49W **81** E11
Wabash → *U.S.A.* 37°48N 88°2W **80** G9
Wabigoon L. *Canada* 49°44N 92°44W **71** D10
Wabowden *Canada* 54°55N 98°38W **71** C9
Wabuk Pt. *Canada* 55°20N 85°5W **72** A2
Wabush *Canada* 52°55N 66°52W **73** B6
Waco *U.S.A.* 31°33N 97°9W **84** F6
Waconichi, L. *Canada* 50°8N 74°0W **72** B5
Wad Hamid *Sudan* 16°30N 32°45E **51** E12
Wad Medanî *Sudan* 14°28N 33°30E **51** F12
Wad Thana *Pakistan* 27°22N 66°23E **42** F2
Wadai *Africa* 12°0N 19°0E **48** E5
Wadayama *Japan* 35°19N 134°52E **31** G7
Waddeneilanden *Neths.* 53°25N 5°10E **15** A5
Waddenzee *Neths.* 53°6N 5°10E **15** A5
Waddington *U.S.A.* 44°52N 75°12W **83** B9
Waddington, Mt. *Canada* 51°23N 125°15W **70** C3
Waddy Pt. *Australia* 24°58S 153°21E **63** C5
Wadebridge *U.K.* 50°31N 4°51W **13** G3
Wadena *Canada* 51°57N 103°47W **71** C8
Wadena *U.S.A.* 46°26N 95°8W **80** B6
Wadeye *Australia* 14°28S 129°52E **60** B4
Wadhams *Canada* 51°30N 127°30W **70** C3
Wādī as Sīr *Jordan* 31°56N 35°49E **46** D4
Wadi Halfa *Sudan* 21°53N 31°19E **51** D12
Wadi Rum △ *Jordan* 29°30N 35°20E **46** F4
Wadsworth *Nev., U.S.A.* 39°38N 119°17W **76** G4
Wadsworth *Ohio, U.S.A.* 41°2N 81°44W **82** E3
Waegwan *S. Korea* 35°59N 128°23E **35** G15
Wafangdian *China* 39°38N 121°58E **35** E11
Wafrah *Si. Arabia* 28°33N 47°56E **44** D5
Wageningen *Neths.* 51°58N 5°40E **15** C5
Wager B. *Canada* 65°26N 88°40W **69** C11
Wagga Wagga *Australia* 35°7S 147°24E **63** F4
Waghete *Indonesia* 4°10S 135°50E **37** E9
Wagin *Australia* 33°17S 117°25E **61** F2
Wagner *U.S.A.* 43°5N 98°18W **80** D4
Wagon Mound *U.S.A.* 36°1N 104°42W **77** H11
Wagoner *U.S.A.* 35°58N 95°22W **84** D7
Wah *Pakistan* 33°45N 72°40E **42** C5
Wahai *Indonesia* 2°48S 129°35E **37** E7
Wahiawā *U.S.A.* 21°30N 158°2W **74** b
Wâḥid *Egypt* 30°48N 32°21E **46** E1
Wahnai *Afghan.* 32°40N 65°50E **42** C1
Wahoo *U.S.A.* 41°13N 96°37W **80** E5
Wahpeton *U.S.A.* 46°16N 96°36W **80** B5
Waiau → *N.Z.* 42°47S 173°22E **59** E4
Waibeem *Indonesia* 0°30S 132°59E **37** E8
Waigeo *Indonesia* 0°20S 130°40E **37** E8
Waihi *N.Z.* 37°23S 175°52E **59** B5
Waihou → *N.Z.* 37°15S 175°40E **59** B5
Waika *Dem. Rep. of the Congo* 2°22S 25°42E **54** C2
Waikabubak *Indonesia* 9°45S 119°25E **37** F5
Waikaremoana, L. *N.Z.* 38°49S 177°9E **59** C6
Waikari *N.Z.* 42°58S 172°41E **59** E4
Waikato → *N.Z.* 37°23S 174°43E **59** B5
Waikerie *Australia* 34°9S 140°0E **63** E3
Waikokopu *N.Z.* 39°3S 177°52E **59** C6
Waikouaiti *N.Z.* 45°36S 170°41E **59** F3
Wailingding Dao *China* 22°6N 114°2E **33** G11
Wailuku *U.S.A.* 20°53N 156°30W **74** b
Waimakariri → *N.Z.* 43°24S 172°42E **59** E4
Waimate *N.Z.* 44°45S 171°3E **59** F3
Wainganga → *India* 18°50N 79°55E **40** K11
Waingapu *Indonesia* 9°35S 120°11E **37** F6
Waini → *Guyana* 8°20N 59°50W **92** B7
Wainwright *Canada* 52°50N 110°50W **71** C6
Waiouru *N.Z.* 39°28S 175°41E **59** C5
Waipara *N.Z.* 43°3S 172°46E **59** E4
Waipawa *N.Z.* 39°56S 176°38E **59** C6
Waipiro *N.Z.* 38°2S 178°22E **59** C7
Waipoua Forest *N.Z.* 35°39S 173°33E **59** A4
Waipu *N.Z.* 35°59S 174°29E **59** A5
Waipukurau *N.Z.* 40°1S 176°33E **59** D6
Wairakei *N.Z.* 38°37S 176°6E **59** C6
Wairarapa, L. *N.Z.* 41°14S 175°15E **59** D5
Wairoa *N.Z.* 39°3S 177°25E **59** C6
Waitaki → *N.Z.* 44°56S 171°7E **59** F3
Waitangi *N.Z.* 35°16S 174°5E **59** A5
Waitara *N.Z.* 38°59S 174°15E **59** C5
Waitomo Caves *N.Z.* 38°16S 175°7E **59** C5
Waitsburg *U.S.A.* 46°16N 118°9W **76** C4
Waiuku *N.Z.* 37°15S 174°45E **59** B5
Wajima *Japan* 37°30N 137°0E **31** F8
Wajir *Kenya* 1°42N 40°5E **54** B5
Wakasa *Japan* 35°20N 134°24E **31** G7
Wakasa-Wan *Japan* 35°40N 135°30E **31** G7
Wakatipu, L. *N.Z.* 45°5S 168°33E **59** F2
Wakaw *Canada* 52°39N 105°44W **71** C7
Wakaya *Fiji* 17°37S 179°0E **59** a
Wakayama *Japan* 34°15N 135°15E **31** G7
Wakayama □ *Japan* 33°50N 135°30E **31** H7
Wake Forest *U.S.A.* 35°59N 78°30W **85** D15
Wake I. *Pac. Oc.* 19°18N 166°36E **64** F8
WaKeeney *U.S.A.* 39°1N 99°53W **80** F4
Wakefield *Jamaica* 18°26N 77°42W **88** a
Wakefield *N.Z.* 41°24S 173°5E **59** D4
Wakefield *U.K.* 53°41N 1°29W **12** D
Wakefield *Mass., U.S.A.* 42°30N 71°5W **83** D1
Wakefield *Mich., U.S.A.* 46°29N 89°56W **80** B
Wakkanai *Japan* 45°28N 141°35E **30** B1
Wakkerstroom *S. Africa* 27°24S 30°10E **57** D
Wakool *Australia* 35°28S 144°23E **63** F
Wakool → *Australia* 35°5S 143°33E **63** F
Wakre *Indonesia* 0°19S 131°5E **37** E
Wakuach, L. *Canada* 55°34N 67°32W **73** A
Walamba *Zambia* 13°30S 28°42E **55** E
Walbrzych *Poland* 50°45N 16°18E **16** C
Walbury Hill *U.K.* 51°21N 1°28W **13** F
Walcha *Australia* 30°55S 151°31E **63** E
Walcheren *Neths.* 51°30N 3°35E **15** C
Walcott *U.S.A.* 41°46N 106°51W **76** F1
Wałcz *Poland* 53°17N 16°27E **16** B
Waldburg Ra. *Australia* 24°40S 117°35E **61** D
Walden *Colo., U.S.A.* 40°44N 106°17W **76** F1

Walden *N.Y., U.S.A.* 41°34N 74°11W **83** E10
Waldport *U.S.A.* 44°26N 124°4W **76** D1
Waldron *U.S.A.* 34°54N 94°5W **84** D7
Walebing *Australia* 30°41S 116°13E **61** F2
Wales ☐ *U.K.* 52°19N 4°43W **13** E3
Walgett *Australia* 30°0S 148°5E **63** E4
Walgreen Coast
Antarctica 75°15S 105°0W **5** D15
Walker *U.S.A.* 47°6N 94°35W **80** B6
Walker, L. *Canada* 50°20N 67°11W **73** B6
Walker L. *Canada* 54°42N 95°57W **71** C9
Walker L. *U.S.A.* 38°42N 118°43W **76** G4
Walkerston *Australia* 21°11S 149°8E **62** K7
Walkerton *Canada* 44°10N 81°10W **82** B3
Wall *U.S.A.* 44°0N 102°8W **80** C2
Walla Walla *U.S.A.* 46°4N 118°20W **76** C4
Wallace *Idaho, U.S.A.* 47°28N 115°56W **76** C6
Wallace *N.C., U.S.A.* 34°44N 77°59W **85** D16
Wallaceburg *Canada* 42°34N 82°23W **82** D2
Wallachia = Valahia
Romania 44°35N 25°0E **17** F13
Wallal *Australia* 26°32S 146°7E **63** D4
Wallam Cr. ➝
Australia 28°40S 147°20E **63** D4
Wallambin, L. *Australia* 30°57S 117°35E **61** F2
Wallangarra *Australia* 28°56S 151°58E **63** D5
Wallaroo *Australia* 33°56S 137°39E **63** E2
Wallenpaupack, L.
U.S.A. 41°25N 75°15W **83** E9
Wallingford *U.S.A.* 41°27N 72°50W **83** E12
Wallis & Futuna, Is.
Pac. Oc. 13°18S 176°10W **58** C11
Wallowa *U.S.A.* 45°34N 117°32W **76** D5
Wallowa Mts. *U.S.A.* 45°20N 117°30W **76** D5
Walls *U.K.* 60°14N 1°33W **11** A7
Walls of Jerusalem △
Australia 41°56S 146°15E **63** G4
Wallula *U.S.A.* 46°5N 118°54W **76** C4
Wallumbilla *Australia* 26°33S 149°9E **63** D4
Walmsley L. *Canada* 63°25N 108°36W **71** A7
Walney, I. of *U.K.* 54°6N 3°15W **12** C4
Walnut Canyon ⌂
U.S.A. 35°15N 111°20W **77** J8
Walnut Creek *U.S.A.* 37°54N 122°4W **78** H4
Walpole *Australia* 34°58S 116°44E **61** F2
Walpole *U.S.A.* 42°9N 71°15W **83** D13
Walpole-Nornalup △
Australia 35°0S 116°45E **60** G2
Walsall *U.K.* 52°35N 1°58W **13** E6
Walsenburg *U.S.A.* 37°38N 104°47W **77** H11
Walsh *U.S.A.* 37°23N 102°17W **77** H12
Walsh ➝ *Australia* 16°31S 143°42E **62** B3
Walter F. George Res.
U.S.A. 31°38N 85°4W **85** F12
Walterboro *U.S.A.* 32°55N 80°40W **85** E14
Walters *U.S.A.* 34°22N 98°19W **84** D5
Waltham *U.S.A.* 42°23N 71°14W **83** D13
Waltman *U.S.A.* 43°4N 107°12W **76** E10
Walton *U.S.A.* 42°10N 75°8W **83** D9
Walton-on-the-Naze
U.K. 51°51N 1°17E **13** F9
Walvis Bay *Namibia* 23°0S 14°28E **56** C1
Walvisbaai = Walvis Bay
Namibia 23°0S 14°28E **56** C1
Wamba
Dem. Rep. of the Congo 2°10N 27°57E **54** B2
Wamba *Kenya* 0°58N 37°19E **54** B4
Wamego *U.S.A.* 39°12N 96°18W **80** F5
Wamena *Indonesia* 4°4S 138°57E **37** E9
Wamsutter *U.S.A.* 41°40N 107°58W **76** F10
Wamulan *Indonesia* 3°27S 126°7E **37** E7
Wan Xian *China* 38°47N 115°7E **34** E8
Wana *Pakistan* 32°20N 69°32E **42** C3
Wanaaring *Australia* 29°38S 144°9E **63** D3
Wanaka *N.Z.* 44°42S 169°9E **59** F2
Wanaka, L. *N.Z.* 44°33S 169°7E **59** F2
Wanapitei L. *Canada* 46°45N 80°40W **72** C3
Wandel Sea = McKinley Sea
Arctic 82°0N 0°0 **4** A7
Wanderer *Zimbabwe* 19°36S 30°1E **55** F3
Wandhari *Pakistan* 27°42N 66°48E **42** F2
Wandoan *Australia* 26°5S 149°55E **63** D4
Wanfu *China* 40°8N 122°38E **35** D12
Wang ➝ *Thailand* 17°8N 99°2E **38** D2
Wang Noi *Thailand* 14°13N 100°44E **38** E3
Wang Saphung
Thailand 17°18N 101°46E **38** D3
Wang Thong *Thailand* 16°50N 100°26E **38** D3
Wanga
Dem. Rep. of the Congo 2°58N 29°12E **54** B2
Wangal *Indonesia* 6°8S 134°9E **37** F8
Wanganella *Australia* 35°6S 144°49E **63** F3
Wanganui *N.Z.* 39°56S 175°3E **59** C5
Wangaratta *Australia* 36°21S 146°19E **63** F4
Wangary *Australia* 34°35S 135°29E **63** E2
Wangdu *China* 38°40N 115°7E **34** E8
Wangerooge *Germany* 53°47N 7°54E **16** B4
Wangiwangi *Indonesia* 5°22S 123°37E **37** F6
Wangqing *China* 43°12N 129°42E **35** C15
Wankaner *India* 22°35N 71°0E **42** H4
Wanlaweyne = Uanle Uen
Somali Rep. 2°37N 44°54E **47** G3
Wanless *Canada* 54°11N 101°21W **71** C8
Wanneroo *Australia* 31°42S 115°46E **61** F2
Wanning *China* 18°48N 110°22E **38** C8
Wannoo Billabong Roadhouse
Australia 27°25S 115°49E **61** E2
Wanon Niwat *Thailand* 17°38N 103°46E **38** D4
Wanqinsha *China* 22°43N 113°33E **33** F10
Wanquan *China* 40°50N 114°40E **34** D8
Wanrong *China* 35°25N 110°50E **34** G6
Wanshan Qundao
China 21°57N 113°45E **33** G10
Wantage *U.K.* 51°35N 1°25W **13** F6
Wanxian *China* 30°42N 108°20E **32** C5
Wanzai *China* 22°12N 113°31E **33** G10
Wapakoneta *U.S.A.* 40°34N 84°12W **81** E11
Wapato *U.S.A.* 46°27N 120°25W **76** C3
Wapawekka L.
Canada 54°55N 104°40W **71** C8
Wapikopa L. *Canada* 52°56N 87°53W **72** B2
Wapiti ➝ *Canada* 55°5N 118°18W **70** B5
Wappingers Falls
U.S.A. 41°36N 73°55W **83** E11
Wapsipinicon ➝
U.S.A. 41°44N 90°19W **80** E8
Wapusk △ *Canada* 57°46N 93°22W **71** B10
Warangal *India* 17°58N 79°35E **40** L11
Waraseoni *India* 21°45N 80°2E **43** J9
Waratah *Australia* 41°30S 145°30E **63** G4
Waratah B. *Australia* 38°54S 146°5E **63** F4
Warburton *Vic.,*
Australia 37°47S 145°42E **63** F4
Warburton *W. Austral.,*
Australia 26°8S 126°35E **61** E4
Warburton ➝ *Australia* 28°4S 137°28E **63** D2
Warburton Ra.
Australia 25°55S 126°28E **61** E4
Ward *N.Z.* 41°49S 174°11E **59** D5
Ward ➝ *Australia* 26°28S 146°6E **63** D4
Ward Mt. *U.S.A.* 37°12N 118°54W **78** H8
Warden *S. Africa* 27°50S 29°0E **57** D4
Wardha *India* 20°45N 78°39E **40** J11
Wardha ➝ *India* 19°57N 79°11E **40** K11
Ware *Canada* 57°26N 125°41W **70** B3
Ware *U.K.* 51°49N 0°0 **13** F8
Ware *U.S.A.* 42°16N 72°14W **83** D12
Waregem *Belgium* 50°53N 3°27E **15** D3
Wareham *U.S.A.* 41°46N 70°43W **83** E14
Waremme *Belgium* 50°43N 5°15E **15** D5
Warialda *Australia* 29°29S 150°33E **63** D5
Wariap *Indonesia* 1°30S 134°5E **37** E8
Warin Chamrap
Thailand 15°12N 104°53E **38** E5
Warkopi *Indonesia* 1°12S 134°9E **37** E8
Warm Springs *U.S.A.* 38°10N 116°20W **77** G5
Warman *Canada* 52°19N 106°30W **71** C7
Warmbad = Bela Bela
S. Africa 24°51S 28°19E **57** C4
Warmbad *Namibia* 28°25S 18°42E **56** D2
Warminster *U.K.* 51°12N 2°10W **13** F5
Warminster *U.S.A.* 40°12N 75°6W **83** F9
Warmun *Australia* 17°2S 128°12E **60** C4
Warner Mts. *U.S.A.* 41°40N 120°15W **76** F3
Warner Robins *U.S.A.* 32°37N 83°36W **85** E13
Waroona *Australia* 32°50S 115°58E **61** F2
Warracknabeal
Australia 36°9S 142°26E **63** F3
Warragul *Australia* 38°10S 145°58E **63** F4
Warrego ➝ *Australia* 30°24S 145°21E **63** E4
Warrego Ra. *Australia* 24°58S 146°0E **62** C4
Warren *Australia* 31°42S 147°51E **63** E4
Warren *Ark., U.S.A.* 33°37N 92°4W **84** E8
Warren *Mich., U.S.A.* 42°28N 83°1W **81** D12
Warren *Minn., U.S.A.* 48°12N 96°46W **80** A5
Warren *Ohio, U.S.A.* 41°14N 80°49W **82** E4
Warren *Pa., U.S.A.* 41°51N 79°9W **82** E5
Warrenpoint *U.K.* 54°6N 6°15W **10** B5
Warrensburg *Mo.,*
U.S.A. 38°46N 93°44W **80** F7
Warrensburg *N.Y.,*
U.S.A. 43°29N 73°46W **83** C11
Warrenton *S. Africa* 28°9S 24°47E **56** D3
Warrenton *U.S.A.* 46°10N 123°56W **78** D3
Warri *Nigeria* 5°30N 5°41E **50** G7
Warrina *Australia* 28°12S 135°50E **63** D2
Warrington *U.K.* 53°24N 2°35W **12** D5
Warrington *U.S.A.* 30°23N 87°17W **85** F11
Warrington ☐ *U.K.* 53°24N 2°35W **12** D5
Warrnambool *Australia* 38°25S 142°30E **63** F3
Warroad *U.S.A.* 48°54N 95°19W **80** A6
Warruwi *Australia* 11°36S 133°20E **62** A1
Warsa *Indonesia* 0°47S 135°55E **37** E9
Warsak Dam *Pakistan* 34°11N 71°19E **42** B4
Warsaw = Warszawa
Poland 52°14N 21°0E **17** B11
Warsaw *Ind., U.S.A.* 41°14N 85°51W **81** E11
Warsaw *N.Y., U.S.A.* 42°45N 78°8W **82** D6
Warsaw *Ohio, U.S.A.* 40°20N 82°0W **82** F3
Warszawa *Poland* 52°14N 21°0E **17** B11
Warta ➝ *Poland* 52°35N 14°39E **16** B8
Warthe = Warta ➝
Poland 52°35N 14°39E **16** B8
Waru *Indonesia* 3°30S 130°36E **37** E8
Warwick *Australia* 28°10S 152°1E **63** D5
Warwick *U.K.* 52°18N 1°35W **13** E6
Warwick *N.Y., U.S.A.* 41°16N 74°22W **83** E10
Warwick *R.I., U.S.A.* 41°42N 71°28W **83** E13
Warwickshire ☐ *U.K.* 52°14N 1°38W **13** E6
Wasaga Beach *Canada* 44°31N 80°1W **82** B4
Wasagaming *Canada* 50°39N 99°58W **71** C9
Wasatch Ra. *U.S.A.* 40°0N 111°30W **76** F8
Wasbank *S. Africa* 28°15S 30°9E **57** D5
Wasco *Calif., U.S.A.* 35°36N 119°20W **79** K7
Wasco *Oreg., U.S.A.* 45°36N 120°42W **76** D3
Waseca *U.S.A.* 44°5N 93°30W **80** C7
Wasekamio L. *Canada* 56°45N 108°45W **71** B7
Wash, The *U.K.* 52°58N 0°20E **12** E8
Washago *Canada* 44°45N 79°20W **82** B5
Washburn *N. Dak.,*
U.S.A. 47°17N 101°2W **80** B3
Washburn *Wis., U.S.A.* 46°40N 90°54W **80** B8
Washim *India* 20°3N 77°0E **40** J10
Washington *U.K.* 54°55N 1°30W **12** C6
Washington *D.C.,*
U.S.A. 38°53N 77°2W **81** F15
Washington *Ga.,*
U.S.A. 33°44N 82°44W **85** E13
Washington *Ind.,*
U.S.A. 38°40N 87°10W **80** F10
Washington *Iowa,*
U.S.A. 41°18N 91°42W **80** E8
Washington *Mo., U.S.A.* 38°33N 91°1W **80** F8
Washington *N.C.,*
U.S.A. 35°33N 77°3W **85** D16
Washington *N.J.,*
U.S.A. 40°46N 74°59W **83** F10
Washington *Pa., U.S.A.* 40°10N 80°15W **82** F4
Washington *Utah,*
U.S.A. 37°8N 113°31W **77** H7
Washington ☐ *U.S.A.* 47°30N 120°30W **76** C3
Washington, Mt.
U.S.A. 44°16N 71°18W **83** B13
Washington Court House
U.S.A. 39°32N 83°26W **81** F12
Washington I. *U.S.A.* 45°23N 86°54W **80** C10
Washougal *U.S.A.* 45°35N 122°21W **78** E4
Washpool △ *Australia* 29°22S 152°20E **63** D5
Wasian *Indonesia* 1°47S 133°19E **37** E8
Wasilla *U.S.A.* 61°35N 149°26W **68** C5
Wasior *Indonesia* 2°43S 134°30E **37** E8
Wāsiţ ☐ *Iraq* 32°50N 45°50E **44** C5
Waskaganish *Canada* 51°30N 78°40W **72** B4
Waskaiowaka L.
Canada 56°33N 96°23W **71** B9
Waskesiu Lake *Canada* 53°55N 106°5W **71** C7
Wasserkuppe *Germany* 50°29N 9°55E **16** C5
Waswanipi *Canada* 49°40N 76°29W **72** C4
Waswanipi, L. *Canada* 49°35N 76°40W **72** C4
Watampone *Indonesia* 4°29S 120°25E **37** E6
Watamu *Kenya* 3°23S 40°0E **54** C5
Watarrka △ *Australia* 24°20S 131°30E **60** D5
Water Park Pt.
Australia 22°56S 150°47E **62** C5
Water Valley *U.S.A.* 34°10N 89°38W **85** D10
Waterberg Plateau ⌂
Namibia 20°25S 17°18E **56** C2
Waterberge *S. Africa* 24°10S 28°0E **57** C4
Waterbury *Conn.,*
U.S.A. 41°33N 73°3W **83** E11
Waterbury *Vt., U.S.A.* 44°20N 72°46W **83** B12
Waterbury L. *Canada* 58°10N 104°22W **71** B8
Waterdown *Canada* 43°20N 79°53W **82** C5
Waterford *Canada* 42°56N 80°17W **82** D4
Waterford *Ireland* 52°15N 7°8W **10** D4
Waterford *Calif.,*
U.S.A. 37°38N 120°46W **78** H6
Waterford *Pa., U.S.A.* 41°57N 79°59W **82** E5
Waterford ☐ *Ireland* 52°10N 7°40W **10** D4
Waterford Harbour
Ireland 52°8N 6°58W **10** D5
Waterhen L. *Canada* 52°10N 99°40W **71** C9
Waterloo *Belgium* 50°43N 4°25E **15** D4
Waterloo *Ont., Canada* 43°30N 80°32W **82** C4
Waterloo *Qué., Canada* 45°22N 72°32W **83** A12
Waterloo *Ill., U.S.A.* 38°20N 90°9W **80** F8
Waterloo *Iowa, U.S.A.* 42°30N 92°21W **80** D7
Waterloo *N.Y., U.S.A.* 42°54N 76°52W **82** D8
Watersmeet *U.S.A.* 46°16N 89°11W **80** B9
Waterton Lakes △
Canada 48°45N 115°0W **70** D6
Watertown *Conn.,*
U.S.A. 41°36N 73°7W **83** E11
Watertown *N.Y., U.S.A.* 43°59N 75°55W **83** C9
Watertown *S. Dak.,*
U.S.A. 44°54N 97°7W **80** C5
Watertown *Wis.,*
U.S.A. 43°12N 88°43W **80** D9
Waterval-Boven
S. Africa 25°40S 30°18E **57** D5
Waterville *Canada* 45°16N 71°54W **83** A13
Waterville *Maine,*
U.S.A. 44°33N 69°38W **81** C19
Waterville *N.Y., U.S.A.* 42°56N 75°23W **83** D9
Waterville *Pa., U.S.A.* 41°19N 77°21W **82** E7
Waterville *Wash.,*
U.S.A. 47°39N 120°4W **76** C3
Watervliet *U.S.A.* 42°44N 73°42W **83** D11
Wates *Indonesia* 7°51S 110°10E **37** G14
Watford *Canada* 42°57N 81°53W **82** D3
Watford *U.K.* 51°40N 0°24W **13** F7
Watford City *U.S.A.* 47°48N 103°17W **80** B2
Wathaman ➝ *Canada* 57°16N 102°59W **71** B8
Wathaman L. *Canada* 56°58N 103°44W **71** B8
Watheroo *Australia* 30°15S 116°5E **61** F2
Watheroo △ *Australia* 30°19S 115°48E **61** F2
Wating *China* 35°40N 106°38E **34** G4
Watkins Glen *U.S.A.* 42°23N 76°52W **82** D8
Watling I. = San Salvador I.
Bahamas 24°0N 74°40W **89** B5
Watonga *U.S.A.* 35°51N 98°25W **84** D5
Watrous *Canada* 51°40N 105°25W **71** C7
Watrous *U.S.A.* 35°48N 104°59W **77** J11
Watsa
Dem. Rep. of the Congo 3°4N 29°30E **54** B2
Watseka *U.S.A.* 40°47N 87°44W **80** E10
Watson *Canada* 52°10N 104°30W **71** C8
Watson Lake *Canada* 60°6N 128°49W **70** A3
Watsontown *U.S.A.* 41°5N 76°52W **82** E8
Watsonville *U.S.A.* 36°55N 121°45W **78** J5
Wattiwarriganna Cr. ➝
Australia 28°57S 136°10E **63** D2
Watuata = Batuata
Indonesia 6°12S 122°42E **37** F6
Watubela, Kepulauan
Indonesia 4°28S 131°35E **37** E8
Watubela Is. = Watubela,
Kepulauan *Indonesia* 4°28S 131°35E **37** E8
Wau = Wâw *Sudan* 7°45N 28°1E **51** G11
Waubamik *Canada* 45°27N 80°1W **82** A4
Waubay *U.S.A.* 45°20N 97°18W **80** C5
Wauchope *N.S.W.,*
Australia 31°28S 152°45E **63** E5
Wauchope *N. Terr.,*
Australia 20°36S 134°15E **62** C1
Wauchula *U.S.A.* 27°33N 81°49W **85** H14
Waukarlycarly, L.
Australia 21°18S 121°56E **60** D3
Waukegan *U.S.A.* 42°22N 87°50W **80** D10
Waukesha *U.S.A.* 43°1N 88°14W **80** D9
Waukon *U.S.A.* 43°16N 91°29W **80** D8
Waupaca *U.S.A.* 44°21N 89°5W **80** C9
Waupun *U.S.A.* 43°38N 88°44W **80** D9
Waurika *U.S.A.* 34°10N 98°0W **84** D6
Wausau *U.S.A.* 44°58N 89°38W **80** C9
Wautoma *U.S.A.* 44°4N 89°18W **80** C9
Wauwatosa *U.S.A.* 43°2N 88°0W **80** D9
Waveney ➝ *U.K.* 52°35N 1°39E **13** E9
Waverley *N.Z.* 39°46S 174°37E **59** C5
Waverly *Iowa, U.S.A.* 42°44N 92°29W **80** D7
Waverly *N.Y., U.S.A.* 42°1N 76°32W **83** E8
Wavre *Belgium* 50°43N 4°38E **15** D4
Wâw *Sudan* 7°45N 28°1E **51** G11
Wāw al Kabīr *Libya* 25°20N 16°43E **51** C9
Wawa *Canada* 47°59N 84°47W **72** C3
Wawanesa *Canada* 49°36N 99°40W **71** D9
Wawona *U.S.A.* 37°32N 119°39W **78** H7
Waxahachie *U.S.A.* 32°24N 96°51W **84** E6
Way, L. *Australia* 26°45S 120°16E **61** E3
Waya *Fiji* 17°19S 177°10E **59** a
Waycross *U.S.A.* 31°13N 82°21W **85** F13
Wayland *U.S.A.* 42°34N 77°35W **82** D7
Wayne *Nebr., U.S.A.* 42°14N 97°1W **80** D5
Wayne *W. Va., U.S.A.* 38°13N 82°27W **81** F12
Waynesboro *Ga., U.S.A.* 33°6N 82°1W **85** E13
Waynesboro *Miss.,*
U.S.A. 31°40N 88°39W **85** F10
Waynesboro *Pa.,*
U.S.A. 39°45N 77°35W **81** F15
Waynesboro *Va., U.S.A.* 38°4N 78°53W **81** F14
Waynesburg *U.S.A.* 39°54N 80°11W **81** F13
Waynesville *U.S.A.* 35°28N 82°58W **85** D13
Waynoka *U.S.A.* 36°35N 98°53W **84** C5
Wazirabad *Pakistan* 32°30N 74°8E **42** C6
We *Indonesia* 5°51N 95°18E **36** C1
Weald, The *U.K.* 51°4N 0°20E **13** F8
Wear ➝ *U.K.* 54°55N 1°23W **12** C6
Weatherford *Okla.,*
U.S.A. 35°32N 98°43W **84** D5
Weatherford *Tex.,*
U.S.A. 32°46N 97°48W **84** E6
Weaverville *U.S.A.* 40°44N 122°56W **76** F2
Webb City *U.S.A.* 37°9N 94°28W **80** G6
Webequie *Canada* 52°59N 87°21W **72** B2
Webster *Mass., U.S.A.* 42°3N 71°53W **83** D13
Webster *N.Y., U.S.A.* 43°13N 77°26W **82** C7
Webster *S. Dak., U.S.A.* 45°20N 97°31W **80** C5
Webster City *U.S.A.* 42°28N 93°49W **80** D7
Webster Springs
U.S.A. 38°29N 80°25W **81** F13
Weda *Indonesia* 0°21N 127°50E **37** D7
Weda, Teluk *Indonesia* 0°20N 128°0E **37** D7
Weddell Abyssal Plain
S. Ocean 65°0S 20°0W **5** C2
Weddell I. *Falk. Is.* 51°50S 61°0W **96** G4
Weddell Sea *Antarctica* 72°30S 40°0W **5** D1
Wedderburn *Australia* 36°26S 143°33E **63** F3
Wedgeport *Canada* 43°44N 65°59W **73** D6
Wedza *Zimbabwe* 18°40S 31°33E **55** F3
Wee Waa *Australia* 30°11S 149°26E **63** E4
Weed *U.S.A.* 41°25N 122°23W **76** F2
Weed Heights *U.S.A.* 38°59N 119°13W **78** G7
Weedsport *U.S.A.* 43°3N 76°34W **83** C8
Weedville *U.S.A.* 41°17N 78°30W **82** E6
Weenen *S. Africa* 28°48S 30°7E **57** D5
Weert *Neths.* 51°15N 5°43E **15** C5
Wei He ➝ *Hebei, China* 36°10N 115°45E **34** F8
Wei He ➝ *Shaanxi,*
China 34°38N 110°15E **34** G6
Weichang *China* 41°58N 117°49E **35** D9
Weichuan *China* 34°20N 113°59E **34** G7
Weiden *Germany* 49°41N 12°10E **16** D7
Weifang *China* 36°44N 119°7E **35** F10
Weihai *China* 37°30N 122°6E **35** F12
Weimar *Germany* 50°58N 11°19E **16** C6
Weinan *China* 34°31N 109°29E **34** G5
Weipa *Australia* 12°40S 141°50E **62** A3
Weir ➝ *Australia* 28°20S 149°50E **63** D4
Weir ➝ *Canada* 56°54N 93°21W **71** B10
Weir River *Canada* 56°49N 94°6W **71** B10
Weirton *U.S.A.* 40°24N 80°35W **82** F4
Weiser *U.S.A.* 44°15N 116°58W **76** D5
Weishan *China* 34°47N 117°5E **35** G9
Weiyuan *China* 35°7N 104°10E **34** G3
Wejherowo *Poland* 54°35N 18°12E **17** A10
Wekusko L. *Canada* 54°40N 99°50W **71** C9
Welch *U.S.A.* 37°26N 81°35W **81** G13
Welford △ *Australia* 25°5S 143°16E **62** D3
Welkom *S. Africa* 28°0S 26°46E **56** D4
Welland *Canada* 43°0N 79°15W **82** D5
Welland ➝ *U.K.* 52°51N 0°5W **13** E7
Wellesley Is. *Australia* 16°42S 139°30E **62** B2
Wellingborough *U.K.* 52°19N 0°41W **13** E7
Wellington *Australia* 32°35S 148°59E **63** E4
Wellington *Canada* 43°57N 77°20W **82** C7
Wellington *N.Z.* 41°19S 174°46E **59** D5
Wellington *S. Africa* 33°38S 19°1E **56** E2
Wellington *Somst., U.K.* 50°58N 3°13W **13** G4
Wellington *Telford & Wrekin,*
U.K. 52°42N 2°30W **13** E5
Wellington *Colo.,*
U.S.A. 40°42N 105°0W **76** F11
Wellington *Kans.,*
U.S.A. 37°16N 97°24W **80** G5
Wellington *Nev.,*
U.S.A. 38°45N 119°23W **78** G7
Wellington *Ohio, U.S.A.* 41°10N 82°13W **82** E2
Wellington *Tex.,*
U.S.A. 34°51N 100°13W **84** D4
Wellington, I. *Chile* 49°30S 75°0W **96** F2
Wellington, L. *Australia* 38°6S 147°20E **63** F4
Wellington Chan.
Canada 75°0N 93°0W **69** B10
Wells *U.K.* 51°13N 2°39W **13** F5
Wells *Maine, U.S.A.* 43°20N 70°35W **83** C14
Wells *N.Y., U.S.A.* 43°24N 74°17W **83** C10
Wells *Nev., U.S.A.* 41°7N 114°58W **76** F6
Wells, L. *Australia* 26°44S 123°15E **61** E3
Wells, Mt. *Australia* 17°25S 127°8E **60** C4
Wells Gray ⌂ *Canada* 52°30N 120°15W **70** C4
Wells-next-the-Sea *U.K.* 52°57N 0°51E **12** E8
Wells River *U.S.A.* 44°9N 72°4W **83** B12
Wellsboro *U.S.A.* 41°45N 77°18W **82** E7
Wellsburg *U.S.A.* 40°16N 80°37W **82** F4
Wellsville *N.Y., U.S.A.* 42°7N 77°57W **82** D7
Wellsville *Ohio, U.S.A.* 40°36N 80°39W **82** F4
Wellsville *Utah, U.S.A.* 41°38N 111°56W **76** F8
Wellton *U.S.A.* 32°40N 114°8W **77** K6
Wels *Austria* 48°9N 14°1E **16** D8
Welshpool *U.K.* 52°39N 3°8W **13** E4
Welwyn Garden City
U.K. 51°48N 0°12W **13** F7
Wem *U.K.* 52°52N 2°44W **12** E5
Wembere ➝ *Tanzania* 4°10S 34°15E **54** C3
Wemindji *Canada* 53°0N 78°49W **72** B4
Wen Xian *China* 34°55N 113°5E **34** G7
Wenatchee *U.S.A.* 47°25N 120°19W **76** C3
Wenchang *China* 19°38N 110°42E **38** C8
Wenchi *Ghana* 7°46N 2°8W **50** G5
Wenchow = Wenzhou
China 28°0N 120°38E **33** D7
Wenden *U.S.A.* 33°49N 113°33W **79** M13
Wendeng *China* 37°15N 122°5E **35** F12
Wendesi *Indonesia* 2°30S 134°17E **37** E8
Wendover *U.S.A.* 40°44N 114°2W **76** F6
Wenlock ➝ *Australia* 12°2S 141°55E **62** A3
Wenshan *China* 23°20N 104°18E **32** D5
Wenshang *China* 35°45N 116°30E **34** G9
Wenshui *China* 37°26N 112°1E **34** F7
Wensleydale *U.K.* 54°17N 2°0W **12** C6
Wensu *China* 41°15N 80°10E **32** B3
Wensum ➝ *U.K.* 52°40N 1°15E **12** E8
Wentworth *Australia* 34°2S 141°54E **63** E3
Wentzel L. *Canada* 59°2N 114°28W **70** B6
Wenut *Indonesia* 3°11S 133°19E **37** E8
Wenxi *China* 35°20N 111°10E **34** G6
Wenxian *China* 32°43N 104°36E **34** H3
Wenzhou *China* 28°0N 120°38E **33** D7
Weott *U.S.A.* 40°20N 123°55W **76** F2
Wepener *S. Africa* 29°42S 27°3E **56** D4
Werda *Botswana* 25°24S 23°15E **56** D3
Weri *Indonesia* 3°10S 132°38E **37** E8
Werra ➝ *Germany* 51°24N 9°39E **16** C5
Werrimull *Australia* 34°25S 141°38E **63** E3
Werris Creek *Australia* 31°18S 150°38E **63** E5
Weser ➝ *Germany* 53°36N 8°28E **16** B5
Wesiri *Indonesia* 7°30S 126°30E **37** F7
Weslaco *U.S.A.* 26°10N 97°58W **84** H6
Weslemkoon L. *Canada* 45°2N 77°25W **82** A7
Wesleyville *U.S.A.* 42°9N 80°1W **82** D4
Wessel, C. *Australia* 10°59S 136°46E **62** A2
Wessel Is. *Australia* 11°10S 136°45E **62** A2
Wessington Springs
U.S.A. 44°5N 98°34W **80** C4
West *U.S.A.* 31°48N 97°6W **84** F6
West ➝ *U.S.A.* 42°52N 72°33W **83** D12
West Allis *U.S.A.* 43°1N 88°0W **80** D9
West Antarctica
Antarctica 80°0S 90°0W **5** D15
West Baines ➝
Australia 15°38S 129°59E **60** C4
West Bank ■ *Asia* 32°6N 35°13E **46** C4
West Bend *U.S.A.* 43°25N 88°11W **80** D9
West Bengal ☐ *India* 23°0N 88°0E **43** H13
West Berkshire ☐ *U.K.* 51°25N 1°17W **13** F6
West Beskids = Západné Beskydy
Europe 49°30N 19°0E **17** D10
West Branch *U.S.A.* 44°17N 84°14W **81** C11
West Branch Susquehanna ➝
U.S.A. 40°53N 76°48W **83** F8
West Bromwich *U.K.* 52°32N 1°59W **13** E6
West Burra *U.K.* 60°5N 1°21W **11** A7
West Canada Cr. ➝
U.S.A. 43°1N 74°58W **83** C10
West Caroline Basin
Pac. Oc. 4°0N 138°0E **64** G5
West Chazy *U.S.A.* 44°49N 73°28W **83** B11
West Chester *U.S.A.* 39°58N 75°36W **83** G9
West Coast ⌂ *Namibia* 21°53S 14°14E **56** C1
West Coast △ *S. Africa* 33°13S 18°0E **56** E2
West Columbia *U.S.A.* 29°9N 95°39W **84** G7
West Covina *U.S.A.* 34°4N 117°54W **79** L9
West Des Moines
U.S.A. 41°35N 93°43W **80** E7
West Dunbartonshire ☐
U.K. 55°59N 4°30W **11** F4
West End *Bahamas* 26°41N 78°58W **88** A4
West Falkland *Falk. Is.* 51°40S 60°0W **96** G4
West Fargo *U.S.A.* 46°52N 96°54W **80** B5
West Farmington
U.S.A. 41°23N 80°58W **82** E4
West Fiji Basin *Pac. Oc.* 17°0S 173°0E **64** J9
West Fjord = Vestfjorden
Norway 67°55N 14°0E **8** C16
West Fork Trinity ➝
U.S.A. 32°48N 96°54W **84** E6
West Frankfort *U.S.A.* 37°54N 88°55W **80** G9
West Grand L. *U.S.A.* 45°14N 67°51W **81** C20
West Hartford *U.S.A.* 41°45N 72°44W **83** E12
West Haven *U.S.A.* 41°17N 72°57W **83** E12
West Hazleton *U.S.A.* 40°58N 76°0W **83** F9
West Helena *U.S.A.* 34°33N 90°38W **85** D9
West Hurley *U.S.A.* 41°59N 74°7W **83** E10
West Ice Shelf *Antarctica* 67°0S 85°0E **5** C7
West Indies *Cent. Amer.* 15°0N 65°0W **89** D7
West Jordan *U.S.A.* 40°36N 111°56W **76** F8
West Lamma Channel
China 22°14N 114°4E **33** G11
West Linn *U.S.A.* 45°21N 122°36W **78** E4
West Lorne *Canada* 42°36N 81°36W **82** D3
West Lothian ☐ *U.K.* 55°54N 3°36W **11** F5
West Lunga ➝ *Zambia* 13°6S 24°39E **55** E1
West MacDonnell △
Australia 23°38S 132°59E **60** D5
West Mariana Basin

Pac. Oc. 15°0N 137°0E **64** F5
West Memphis *U.S.A.* 35°8N 90°11W **85** D9
West Midlands □ *U.K.* 52°26N 2°0W **13** E6
West Mifflin *U.S.A.* 40°21N 79°52W **82** F5
West Milford *U.S.A.* 41°8N 74°22W **83** E10
West Milton *U.S.A.* 41°1N 76°50W **82** E8
West Monroe *U.S.A.* 32°31N 92°9W **84** E8
West Newton *U.S.A.* 40°14N 79°46W **82** F5
West Nicholson *Zimbabwe* 21°2S 29°20E **55** G2
West Odessa *U.S.A.* 31°50N 102°30W **84** F3
West Palm Beach *U.S.A.* 26°43N 80°3W **85** H14
West Plains *U.S.A.* 36°44N 91°51W **80** G8
West Point *Miss., U.S.A.* 33°36N 88°39W **85** E10
West Point *N.Y., U.S.A.* 41°24N 73°58W **83** E11
West Point *Nebr., U.S.A.* 41°51N 96°43W **80** E5
West Point *Va., U.S.A.* 37°32N 76°48W **81** G15
West Point L. *U.S.A.* 33°8N 85°0W **85** E12
West Pt. = Ouest, Pte. de l' *Canada* 49°52N 64°40W **73** C7
West Pt. *Australia* 35°1S 135°56E **63** F2
West Road ➔ *Canada* 53°18N 122°53W **70** C4
West Rutland *U.S.A.* 43°36N 73°3W **83** C11
West Schelde = Westerschelde ➔ *Neths.* 51°25N 3°25E **15** C3
West Seneca *U.S.A.* 42°51N 78°48W **82** D6
West Siberian Plain *Russia* 62°0N 75°0E **26** B9
West Sussex □ *U.K.* 50°55N 0°30W **13** G7
West-Terschelling *Neths.* 53°22N 5°13E **15** A5
West Valley City *U.S.A.* 40°42N 111°58W **76** F8
West Virginia □ *U.S.A.* 38°45N 80°30W **81** F13
West-Vlaanderen □ *Belgium* 51°0N 3°0E **15** D2
West Walker ➔ *U.S.A.* 38°54N 119°9W **78** G7
West Wyalong *Australia* 33°56S 147°10E **63** E4
West Yellowstone *U.S.A.* 44°40N 111°6W **76** D8
West Yorkshire □ *U.K.* 53°45N 1°40W **12** D6
Westall, Pt. *Australia* 32°55S 134°4E **63** E1
Westbrook *U.S.A.* 43°41N 70°22W **81** D18
Westbury *Australia* 41°30S 146°51E **63** G4
Westby *U.S.A.* 48°52N 104°3W **76** B11
Westend *U.S.A.* 35°42N 117°24W **79** K9
Westerland *Germany* 54°54N 8°17E **16** A5
Westerly *U.S.A.* 41°22N 71°50W **83** E13
Western □ *Kenya* 0°30N 34°30E **54** B3
Western □ *Zambia* 15°0S 24°4E **55** F1
Western Australia □ *Australia* 25°0S 118°0E **61** E2
Western Cape □ *S. Africa* 34°0S 20°0E **56** E3
Western Dvina = Daugava ➔ *Latvia* 57°4N 24°3E **9** H21
Western Ghats *India* 14°0N 75°0E **40** N9
Western Isles □ *U.K.* 57°30N 7°10W **11** D1
Western Sahara ■ *Africa* 25°0N 13°0W **50** D3
Western Samoa = Samoa ■ *Pac. Oc.* 14°0S 172°0W **59** b
Western Sierra Madre = Madre Occidental, Sierra *Mexico* 27°0N 107°0W **86** B3
Westernport *U.S.A.* 39°29N 79°3W **81** F14
Westerschelde ➔ *Neths.* 51°25N 3°25E **15** C3
Westerwald *Germany* 50°38N 7°56E **16** C4
Westfield *Mass., U.S.A.* 42°7N 72°45W **83** D12
Westfield *N.Y., U.S.A.* 42°20N 79°35W **82** D5
Westfield *Pa., U.S.A.* 41°55N 77°32W **82** E7
Westhill *U.K.* 57°9N 2°19W **11** D6
Westhope *U.S.A.* 48°55N 101°1W **80** A3
Westland △ *N.Z.* 43°16S 170°16E **59** E2
Westland Bight *N.Z.* 42°55S 170°5E **59** E3
Westlock *Canada* 54°9N 113°55W **70** C6
Westmar *Australia* 27°55S 149°44E **63** D4
Westmeath □ *Ireland* 53°33N 7°34W **10** C4
Westminster *Calif., U.S.A.* 33°45N 118°0W **79** M8
Westminster *Colo., U.S.A.* 39°50N 105°2W **76** G11
Westminster *Md., U.S.A.* 39°34N 76°59W **81** F15
Westmont *U.S.A.* 40°19N 78°58W **82** F6
Westmoreland *Barbados* 13°13N 59°37W **89** g
Westmorland *U.S.A.* 33°2N 115°37W **79** M11
Weston *Oreg., U.S.A.* 45°49N 118°26W **76** D4
Weston *W. Va., U.S.A.* 39°2N 80°28W **81** F13
Weston I. *Canada* 52°33N 79°36W **72** B4
Weston-super-Mare *U.K.* 51°21N 2°58W **13** F5
Westover *U.S.A.* 40°45N 78°40W **82** F6
Westport *Canada* 44°40N 76°25W **83** B8
Westport *Ireland* 53°48N 9°31W **10** C2
Westport *N.Z.* 41°46S 171°37E **59** D3
Westport *N.Y., U.S.A.* 44°11N 73°26W **83** B11
Westport *Oreg., U.S.A.* 46°8N 123°23W **78** D3
Westport *Wash., U.S.A.* 46°53N 124°6W **78** D2
Westray *Canada* 53°36N 101°24W **71** C8
Westray *U.K.* 59°18N 3°0W **11** B5
Westree *Canada* 47°26N 81°34W **72** C3
Westville *U.S.A.* 39°8N 120°42W **78** F6
Westwood *U.S.A.* 40°18N 121°0W **76** F3
Wetar *Indonesia* 7°48S 126°30E **37** F7
Wetaskiwin *Canada* 52°55N 113°24W **70** C6
Wete *Tanzania* 5°4S 39°43E **52** F7
Wetherby *U.K.* 53°56N 1°23W **12** D6
Wethersfield *U.S.A.* 41°42N 72°40W **83** E12
Wetteren *Belgium* 51°0N 3°53E **15** D3
Wetzlar *Germany* 50°32N 8°31E **16** C5
Wewoka *U.S.A.* 35°9N 96°30W **84** D6
Wexford *Ireland* 52°20N 6°28W **10** D5
Wexford □ *Ireland* 52°20N 6°25W **10** D5
Wexford Harbour *Ireland* 52°20N 6°25W **10** D5
Weyburn *Canada* 49°40N 103°50W **71** D8
Weymouth *Canada* 44°30N 66°1W **73** D6
Weymouth *U.K.* 50°37N 2°28W **13** G5
Weymouth *U.S.A.* 42°13N 70°58W **83** D14
Weymouth, C. *Australia* 12°37S 143°27E **62** A3
Wha Ti *Canada* 63°8N 117°16W **68** C8
Whakaari = White I. *N.Z.* 37°30S 177°13E **59** B6
Whakatane *N.Z.* 37°57S 177°1E **59** B6
Whale ➔ *Canada* 58°15N 67°40W **73** A6
Whale Cove *Canada* 62°10N 92°34W **71** A10
Whales, B. of *Antarctica* 78°0S 160°0W **5** D12
Whalsay *U.K.* 60°22N 0°59W **11** A8
Whangamata *N.Z.* 37°12S 175°53E **59** B5
Whangamomona *N.Z.* 39°8S 174°44E **59** C5
Whanganui △ *N.Z.* 39°17S 174°53E **59** C5
Whangarei *N.Z.* 35°43S 174°21E **59** A5
Whangarei Harb. *N.Z.* 35°45S 174°28E **59** A5
Wharekauri = Chatham Is. *Pac. Oc.* 44°0S 176°40W **64** M10
Wharfe ➔ *U.K.* 53°51N 1°9W **12** D6
Wharfedale *U.K.* 54°6N 2°1W **12** C5
Wharton *N.J., U.S.A.* 40°54N 74°35W **83** F10
Wharton *Pa., U.S.A.* 41°31N 78°1W **82** E6
Wharton *Tex., U.S.A.* 29°19N 96°6W **84** G6
Wharton Basin *Ind. Oc.* 22°0S 92°0E **64** J2
Wheatland *Calif., U.S.A.* 39°1N 121°25W **78** F5
Wheatland *Wyo., U.S.A.* 42°3N 104°58W **76** E11
Wheatley *Canada* 42°6N 82°27W **82** D2
Wheaton *Md., U.S.A.* 39°3N 77°3W **81** F15
Wheaton *Minn., U.S.A.* 45°48N 96°30W **80** C5
Wheelbarrow Pk. *U.S.A.* 37°26N 116°5W **78** H10
Wheeler *Oreg., U.S.A.* 45°41N 123°53W **76** D2
Wheeler *Tex., U.S.A.* 35°27N 100°16W **84** D4
Wheeler ➔ *Canada* 57°2N 67°13W **73** A6
Wheeler L. *U.S.A.* 34°48N 87°23W **85** D11
Wheeler Pk. *N. Mex., U.S.A.* 36°34N 105°25W **77** H11
Wheeler Pk. *Nev., U.S.A.* 38°57N 114°15W **76** G6
Wheeler Ridge *U.S.A.* 35°0N 118°57W **79** L8
Wheelersburg *U.S.A.* 38°44N 82°51W **81** F12
Wheeling *U.S.A.* 40°4N 80°43W **82** F4
Whernside *U.K.* 54°14N 2°24W **12** C5
Whiddy I. *Ireland* 51°41N 9°31W **10** E2
Whiskey Jack L. *Canada* 58°23N 101°55W **71** B8
Whiskeytown-Shasta-Trinity ⌂ *U.S.A.* 40°45N 122°15W **76** F2
Whistleduck Cr. ➔ *Australia* 20°15S 135°18E **62** C2
Whistler *Canada* 50°7N 122°58W **70** C4
Whitby *Canada* 43°52N 78°56W **82** C6
Whitby *U.K.* 54°29N 0°37W **12** C7
White ➔ *Ark., U.S.A.* 33°57N 91°5W **84** E9
White ➔ *Ind., U.S.A.* 38°25N 87°45W **80** F10
White ➔ *S. Dak., U.S.A.* 43°42N 99°27W **80** D4
White ➔ *Tex., U.S.A.* 33°14N 100°56W **84** E4
White ➔ *Utah, U.S.A.* 40°4N 109°41W **76** F9
White ➔ *Vt., U.S.A.* 43°37N 72°20W **83** C12
White ➔ *Wash., U.S.A.* 47°12N 122°15W **78** C4
White, L. *Australia* 21°9S 128°56E **60** D4
White B. *Canada* 50°0N 56°35W **73** C8
White Bird *U.S.A.* 45°46N 116°18W **76** D5
White Butte *U.S.A.* 46°23N 103°18W **80** B2
White City *U.S.A.* 42°26N 122°51W **76** E2
White Cliffs *Australia* 30°50S 143°10E **63** E3
White Hall *U.S.A.* 39°26N 90°24W **80** F8
White Haven *U.S.A.* 41°4N 75°47W **83** E9
White Horse, Vale of *U.K.* 51°37N 1°30W **13** F6
White I. *N.Z.* 37°30S 177°13E **59** B6
White L. *Canada* 45°18N 76°31W **83** A8
White L. *U.S.A.* 29°44N 92°30W **84** G8
White Mountain Peak *U.S.A.* 37°38N 118°15W **77** H4
White Mts. *Calif., U.S.A.* 37°30N 118°15W **78** H8
White Mts. *N.H., U.S.A.* 44°15N 71°15W **83** B13
White Mts. △ *Australia* 20°43S 145°12E **62** C4
White Nile = Nîl el Abyad ➔ *Sudan* 15°38N 32°31E **51** E12
White Otter L. *Canada* 49°5N 91°55W **72** C1
White Pass *U.S.A.* 46°38N 121°24W **78** D5
White Plains *U.S.A.* 41°2N 73°46W **83** E11
White River *Canada* 48°35N 85°20W **72** C2
White River *S. Africa* 25°20S 31°0E **57** D5
White River *U.S.A.* 43°34N 100°45W **80** D3
White Rock *Canada* 49°2N 122°48W **78** A4
White Rock *U.S.A.* 35°50N 106°12W **77** J10
White Russia = Belarus ■ *Europe* 53°30N 27°0E **17** B14
White Sands ⌂ *U.S.A.* 32°46N 106°20W **77** K10
White Sea = Beloye More *Russia* 66°30N 38°0E **8** C25
White Sulphur Springs *Mont., U.S.A.* 46°33N 110°54W **76** C8
White Sulphur Springs *W. Va., U.S.A.* 37°48N 80°18W **81** G13
White Swan *U.S.A.* 46°23N 120°44W **78** D6
Whitecliffs *N.Z.* 43°26S 171°55E **59** E3
Whitecourt *Canada* 54°10N 115°45W **70** C5
Whiteface Mt. *U.S.A.* 44°22N 73°54W **83** B11
Whitefield *U.S.A.* 44°23N 71°37W **83** B13
Whitefish *U.S.A.* 48°25N 114°20W **76** B6
Whitefish B. *U.S.A.* 46°40N 84°55W **72** C3
Whitefish L. *Canada* 62°41N 106°48W **71** A7
Whitefish Pt. *U.S.A.* 46°45N 84°59W **81** B11
Whitegull, L. = Goélands, L. aux *Canada* 55°27N 64°17W **73** A7
Whitehall *Mich., U.S.A.* 43°24N 86°21W **80** D10
Whitehall *Mont., U.S.A.* 45°52N 112°6W **76** D7
Whitehall *N.Y., U.S.A.* 43°33N 73°24W **83** C11
Whitehall *Wis., U.S.A.* 44°22N 91°19W **80** C8
Whitehaven *U.K.* 54°33N 3°35W **12** C4
Whitehorse *Canada* 60°43N 135°3W **70** A1
Whitemark *Australia* 40°7S 148°3E **63** G4
Whiteriver *U.S.A.* 33°50N 109°58W **77** K9
Whitesand ➔ *Canada* 60°9N 115°45W **70** A5
Whitesands *S. Africa* 34°23S 20°50E **56** E3
Whitesboro *N.Y., U.S.A.* 43°7N 75°18W **83** C9
Whitesboro *Tex., U.S.A.* 33°39N 96°54W **84** E6
Whiteshell ⌂ *Canada* 50°0N 95°40W **71** D9
Whitesville *U.S.A.* 42°2N 77°46W **82** D7
Whiteville *U.S.A.* 34°20N 78°42W **85** D15
Whitewater *U.S.A.* 42°50N 88°44W **80** D9
Whitewater Baldy *U.S.A.* 33°20N 108°39W **77** K9
Whitewater L. *Canada* 50°50N 89°10W **72** B2
Whitewood *Australia* 21°28S 143°30E **62** C3
Whitewood *Canada* 50°20N 102°20W **71** C8
Whithorn *U.K.* 54°44N 4°26W **11** G4
Whitianga *N.Z.* 36°47S 175°41E **59** B5
Whitman *U.S.A.* 42°5N 70°56W **83** D14
Whitney *Canada* 45°31N 78°14W **82** A6
Whitney, Mt. *U.S.A.* 36°35N 118°18W **78** J8
Whitney Point *U.S.A.* 42°20N 75°58W **83** D9
Whitstable *U.K.* 51°21N 1°3E **13** F9
Whitsunday I. *Australia* 20°15S 149°4E **62** J7
Whitsunday Islands △ *Australia* 20°15S 149°0E **62** J7
Whitsunday Passage *Australia* 20°16S 148°51E **62** J6
Whittier *U.S.A.* 33°58N 118°2W **79** M8
Whittlesea *Australia* 37°27S 145°9E **63** F4
Wholdaia L. *Canada* 60°43N 104°20W **71** A8
Whyalla *Australia* 33°2S 137°30E **63** E2
Wiang Kosai △ *Thailand* 17°54N 99°29E **38** D2
Wiarton *Canada* 44°40N 81°10W **82** B3
Wiay *U.K.* 57°24N 7°13W **11** D1
Wibaux *U.S.A.* 46°59N 104°11W **76** C11
Wichian Buri *Thailand* 15°39N 101°7E **38** E3
Wichita *U.S.A.* 37°42N 97°20W **80** G5
Wichita Falls *U.S.A.* 33°54N 98°30W **84** E5
Wick *U.K.* 58°26N 3°5W **11** C5
Wicked Pt. *Canada* 43°52N 77°15W **82** C7
Wickenburg *U.S.A.* 33°58N 112°44W **77** K7
Wickepin *Australia* 32°50S 117°30E **61** F2
Wickham *Australia* 20°42S 117°11E **60** D2
Wickham, C. *Australia* 39°35S 143°57E **63** F3
Wickliffe *U.S.A.* 41°36N 81°28W **82** E3
Wicklow *Ireland* 52°59N 6°3W **10** D5
Wicklow □ *Ireland* 52°57N 6°25W **10** D5
Wicklow Hd. *Ireland* 52°58N 6°0W **10** D6
Wicklow Mts. *Ireland* 52°58N 6°26W **10** C5
Wicklow Mts. △ *Ireland* 53°6N 6°21W **10** C5
Widgeegoara Cr. ➔ *Australia* 28°51S 146°34E **63** D4
Widgiemooltha *Australia* 31°30S 121°34E **61** F3
Widnes *U.K.* 53°23N 2°45W **12** D5
Wieluń *Poland* 51°15N 18°34E **17** C10
Wien *Austria* 48°12N 16°22E **16** D9
Wiener Neustadt *Austria* 47°49N 16°16E **16** E9
Wiesbaden *Germany* 50°4N 8°14E **16** C5
Wigan *U.K.* 53°33N 2°38W **12** D5
Wiggins *Colo., U.S.A.* 40°14N 104°4W **76** F11
Wiggins *Miss., U.S.A.* 30°51N 89°8W **85** F10
Wight, I. of *U.K.* 50°41N 1°17W **13** G6
Wigston *U.K.* 52°35N 1°6W **13** E6
Wigton *U.K.* 54°50N 3°10W **12** C4
Wigtown *U.K.* 54°53N 4°27W **11** G4
Wigtown B. *U.K.* 54°46N 4°15W **11** G4
Wilber *U.S.A.* 40°29N 96°58W **80** E5
Wilberforce *Canada* 45°2N 78°13W **82** A6
Wilberforce, C. *Australia* 11°54S 136°35E **62** A2
Wilburton *U.S.A.* 34°55N 95°19W **84** D7
Wilcannia *Australia* 31°30S 143°26E **63** E3
Wilcox *U.S.A.* 41°35N 78°41W **82** E6
Wildrose *U.S.A.* 36°14N 117°11W **79** J9
Wildspitze *Austria* 46°53N 10°53E **16** E6
Wilge ➔ *S. Africa* 27°3S 28°20E **57** D4
Wilhelm II Coast *Antarctica* 68°0S 90°0E **5** C7
Wilhelmshaven *Germany* 53°31N 8°7E **16** B5
Wilhelmstal *Namibia* 21°58S 16°21E **56** C2
Wilkes-Barre *U.S.A.* 41°15N 75°53W **83** E9
Wilkes Land *Antarctica* 69°0S 120°0E **5** D9
Wilkie *Canada* 52°27N 108°42W **71** C7
Wilkinsburg *U.S.A.* 40°26N 79°52W **82** F5
Wilkinson Lakes *Australia* 29°40S 132°39E **61** E5
Willandra Creek ➔ *Australia* 33°22S 145°52E **63** E4
Willapa B. *U.S.A.* 46°40N 124°0W **76** C1
Willapa Hills *U.S.A.* 46°35N 123°25W **78** D3
Willard *N.Y., U.S.A.* 42°40N 76°50W **82** D8
Willard *Ohio, U.S.A.* 41°3N 82°44W **82** E2
Willcox *U.S.A.* 32°15N 109°50W **77** K9
Willemstad *Neth. Ant.* 12°5N 68°55W **89** D6
Willet *U.S.A.* 42°28N 75°55W **83** D9
William ➔ *Canada* 59°8N 109°19W **71** B7
William 'Bill' Dannelly Res. *U.S.A.* 32°6N 87°24W **85** E11
William Creek *Australia* 28°58S 136°22E **63** D2
Williams *Australia* 33°2S 116°52E **61** F2
Williams *Ariz., U.S.A.* 35°15N 112°11W **77** J7
Williams *Calif., U.S.A.* 39°9N 122°9W **78** F4
Williams Harbour *Canada* 52°33N 55°47W **73** B8
Williams Lake *Canada* 52°10N 122°10W **70** C4
Williamsburg *Ky., U.S.A.* 36°44N 84°10W **81** G11
Williamsburg *Pa., U.S.A.* 40°28N 78°12W **82** F6
Williamsburg *Va., U.S.A.* 37°16N 76°43W **81** G15
Williamson *N.Y., U.S.A.* 43°14N 77°11W **82** C7
Williamson *W. Va., U.S.A.* 37°41N 82°17W **81** G12
Williamsport *U.S.A.* 41°15N 77°1W **82** E7
Williamston *U.S.A.* 35°51N 77°4W **85** D16
Williamstown *Australia* 37°51S 144°52E **63** F3
Williamstown *Ky., U.S.A.* 38°38N 84°34W **81** F11
Williamstown *Mass., U.S.A.* 42°43N 73°12W **83** D11
Williamstown *N.Y., U.S.A.* 43°26N 75°53W **83** C9
Willimantic *U.S.A.* 41°43N 72°13W **83** E12
Willingboro *U.S.A.* 40°3N 74°54W **81** E16
Williston *S. Africa* 31°20S 20°53E **56** E3
Williston *Fla., U.S.A.* 29°23N 82°27W **85** G13
Williston *N. Dak., U.S.A.* 48°9N 103°37W **80** A2
Williston L. *Canada* 56°0N 124°0W **70** B4
Willits *U.S.A.* 39°25N 123°21W **76** G2
Willmar *U.S.A.* 45°7N 95°3W **80** C6
Willmore Wilderness ⌂ *Canada* 53°45N 119°30W **70** C5
Willoughby *U.S.A.* 41°39N 81°24W **82** E3
Willow Bunch *Canada* 49°20N 105°35W **71** D7
Willow L. *Canada* 62°10N 119°8W **70** A5
Willow Wall, The *China* 42°10N 122°0E **35** C12
Willowick *U.S.A.* 41°38N 81°28W **82** E3
Willowlake ➔ *Canada* 62°42N 123°8W **70** A4
Willowmore *S. Africa* 33°15S 23°30E **56** E3
Willows *U.S.A.* 39°31N 122°12W **78** F4
Willowvale = Gatyana *S. Africa* 32°16S 28°31E **57** E4
Wills, L. *Australia* 21°25S 128°51E **60** D4
Wills Cr. ➔ *Australia* 22°43S 140°2E **62** C3
Willsboro *U.S.A.* 44°21N 73°24W **83** B11
Willunga *Australia* 35°15S 138°30E **63** F2
Wilmette *U.S.A.* 42°4N 87°42W **80** D10
Wilmington *Australia* 32°39S 138°7E **63** E2
Wilmington *Del., U.S.A.* 39°45N 75°33W **81** F16
Wilmington *N.C., U.S.A.* 34°14N 77°55W **85** D16
Wilmington *Ohio, U.S.A.* 39°27N 83°50W **81** F12
Wilmington *Vt., U.S.A.* 42°52N 72°52W **83** D12
Wilmslow *U.K.* 53°19N 2°13W **12** D5
Wilpena Cr. ➔ *Australia* 31°25S 139°29E **63** E2
Wilsall *U.S.A.* 45°59N 110°38W **76** D8
Wilson *N.C., U.S.A.* 35°44N 77°55W **85** D16
Wilson *N.Y., U.S.A.* 43°19N 78°50W **82** C6
Wilson *Pa., U.S.A.* 40°41N 75°15W **83** F9
Wilson ➔ *Australia* 16°48S 128°16E **60** C4
Wilson Bluff *Australia* 31°41S 129°0E **61** F4
Wilson Inlet *Australia* 35°0S 117°22E **61** G2
Wilsons Promontory *Australia* 38°59S 146°23E **63** F4
Wilton *U.S.A.* 47°10N 100°47W **80** B3
Wilton ➔ *Australia* 14°45S 134°33E **62** A1
Wiltshire □ *U.K.* 51°18N 1°53W **13** F6
Wiltz *Lux.* 49°57N 5°55E **15** E5
Wiluna *Australia* 26°36S 120°14E **61** E3
Wimborne Minster *U.K.* 50°48N 1°59W **13** G6
Wimmera ➔ *Australia* 36°8S 141°56E **63** F3
Winam G. *Kenya* 0°20S 34°15E **54** C3
Winburg *S. Africa* 28°30S 27°2E **56** D4
Winchendon *U.S.A.* 42°41N 72°3W **83** D12
Winchester *U.K.* 51°4N 1°18W **13** F6
Winchester *Conn., U.S.A.* 41°53N 73°9W **83** E11
Winchester *Idaho, U.S.A.* 46°14N 116°38W **76** C5
Winchester *Ind., U.S.A.* 40°10N 84°59W **81** E11
Winchester *Ky., U.S.A.* 37°59N 84°11W **81** G11
Winchester *N.H., U.S.A.* 42°46N 72°23W **83** D12
Winchester *Nev., U.S.A.* 36°7N 115°7W **79** J11
Winchester *Tenn., U.S.A.* 35°11N 86°7W **85** D11
Winchester *Va., U.S.A.* 39°11N 78°10W **81** F14
Wind ➔ *U.S.A.* 43°12N 108°12W **76** E9
Wind Cave △ *U.S.A.* 43°32N 103°17W **80** D2
Wind River Range *U.S.A.* 43°0N 109°30W **76** E9
Windau = Ventspils *Latvia* 57°25N 21°32E **9** H19
Windber *U.S.A.* 40°14N 78°50W **82** F6
Winder *U.S.A.* 34°0N 83°45W **85** D13
Windermere *U.K.* 54°23N 2°55W **12** C5
Windhoek *Namibia* 22°35S 17°4E **56** C2
Windjana Gorge △ *Australia* 17°51S 125°0E **60** C3
Windom *U.S.A.* 43°52N 95°7W **80** D6
Windorah *Australia* 25°24S 142°36E **62** D3
Window Rock *U.S.A.* 35°41N 109°3W **77** J9
Windrush ➔ *U.K.* 51°43N 1°24W **13** F6
Windsor *Australia* 33°37S 150°50E **63** E5
Windsor *N.S., Canada* 44°59N 64°5W **73** D7
Windsor *Ont., Canada* 42°18N 83°0W **82** D2
Windsor *U.K.* 51°29N 0°36W **13** F7
Windsor *Calif., U.S.A.* 38°33N 122°49W **76** G2
Windsor *Colo., U.S.A.* 40°29N 104°54W **76** F11
Windsor *Conn., U.S.A.* 41°50N 72°39W **83** E12
Windsor *Mo., U.S.A.* 38°32N 93°31W **80** F7
Windsor *N.Y., U.S.A.* 42°5N 75°37W **83** D9
Windsor *Vt., U.S.A.* 43°29N 72°24W **83** C12
Windsor & Maidenhead □ *U.K.* 51°29N 0°40W **13** F7
Windsorton *S. Africa* 28°16S 24°44E **56** D3
Windward Is. *W. Indies* 13°0N 61°0W **89** D7
Windward Passage = Vientos, Paso de los *Caribbean* 20°0N 74°0W **89** C5
Winefred L. *Canada* 55°30N 110°30W **71** B6
Winfield *U.S.A.* 37°15N 96°59W **80** G5
Wingate Mts. *Australia* 14°25S 130°40E **60** B5
Wingham *Australia* 31°48S 152°22E **63** E5
Wingham *Canada* 43°55N 81°20W **82** C3
Winisk *Canada* 55°20N 85°15W **72** A2
Winisk ➔ *Canada* 55°17N 85°5W **72** A2
Winisk L. *Canada* 52°55N 87°22W **72** B2
Wink *U.S.A.* 31°45N 103°9W **84** F3
Winkler *Canada* 49°10N 97°56W **71** D9
Winlock *U.S.A.* 46°30N 122°56W **78** D4
Winneba *Ghana* 5°25N 0°36W **50** G5
Winnebago, L. *U.S.A.* 44°0N 88°26W **80** D9
Winnecke Cr. ➔ *Australia* 18°35S 131°34E **60** C5
Winnemucca *U.S.A.* 40°58N 117°44W **76** F5
Winnemucca L. *U.S.A.* 40°7N 119°21W **76** F4
Winner *U.S.A.* 43°22N 99°52W **80** D4
Winnett *U.S.A.* 47°0N 108°21W **76** C9
Winnfield *U.S.A.* 31°56N 92°38W **84** F8
Winnibigoshish, L. *U.S.A.* 47°27N 94°13W **80** B6
Winnipeg *Canada* 49°54N 97°9W **71** D9
Winnipeg ➔ *Canada* 50°38N 96°19W **71** C9
Winnipeg, L. *Canada* 52°0N 97°0W **71** C9
Winnipeg Beach *Canada* 50°30N 96°58W **71** C9
Winnipegosis *Canada* 51°39N 99°55W **71** C9
Winnipegosis L. *Canada* 52°30N 100°0W **71** C9
Winnipesaukee, L. *U.S.A.* 43°38N 71°21W **83** C13
Winnisquam L. *U.S.A.* 43°33N 71°31W **83** C13
Winnsboro *La., U.S.A.* 32°10N 91°43W **84** E9
Winnsboro *S.C., U.S.A.* 34°23N 81°5W **85** D14
Winnsboro *Tex., U.S.A.* 32°58N 95°17W **84** E7
Winokapau, L. *Canada* 53°15N 62°50W **73** B7
Winona *Minn., U.S.A.* 44°3N 91°39W **80** C8
Winona *Miss., U.S.A.* 33°29N 89°44W **85** E10
Winooski *U.S.A.* 44°29N 73°11W **83** B11
Winooski ➔ *U.S.A.* 44°32N 73°17W **83** B11
Winschoten *Neths.* 53°9N 7°3E **15** A7
Winsford *U.K.* 53°12N 2°31W **12** D5
Winslow = Bainbridge Island *U.S.A.* 47°38N 122°32W **78** C4
Winslow *U.S.A.* 35°2N 110°42W **77** J8
Winsted *U.S.A.* 41°55N 73°4W **83** E11
Winston-Salem *U.S.A.* 36°6N 80°15W **85** C14
Winter Garden *U.S.A.* 28°34N 81°35W **85** G14
Winter Haven *U.S.A.* 28°1N 81°44W **85** G14
Winter Park *U.S.A.* 28°36N 81°20W **85** G14
Winterhaven *U.S.A.* 32°44N 114°38W **79** N12
Winters *U.S.A.* 38°32N 121°58W **78** G5
Winterset *U.S.A.* 41°20N 94°1W **80** E6
Wintersville *U.S.A.* 40°23N 80°42W **82** F4
Winterswijk *Neths.* 51°58N 6°43E **15** C6
Winterthur *Switz.* 47°30N 8°44E **20** C8
Winthrop *U.S.A.* 48°28N 120°10W **76** B3
Winton *Australia* 22°24S 143°3E **62** C3
Winton *N.Z.* 46°8S 168°20E **59** G2
Wirrulla *Australia* 32°24S 134°31E **63** E1
Wisbech *U.K.* 52°41N 0°9E **13** E8
Wisconsin □ *U.S.A.* 44°45N 89°30W **80** C9
Wisconsin ➔ *U.S.A.* 43°0N 91°15W **80** D8
Wisconsin Rapids *U.S.A.* 44°23N 89°49W **80** C9
Wisdom *U.S.A.* 45°37N 113°27W **76** D7
Wishaw *U.K.* 55°46N 3°54W **11** F5
Wishek *U.S.A.* 46°16N 99°33W **80** B4
Wisła ➔ *Poland* 54°22N 18°55E **17** A10
Wismar *Germany* 53°54N 11°29E **16** B6
Wisner *U.S.A.* 41°59N 96°55W **80** E5
Witbank *S. Africa* 25°51S 29°14E **57** D4
Witdraai *S. Africa* 26°58S 20°48E **56** D3
Witham *U.K.* 51°48N 0°40E **13** F8
Witham ➔ *U.K.* 52°59N 0°2W **12** E7
Withernsea *U.K.* 53°44N 0°1E **12** D8
Witjira △ *Australia* 26°22S 135°37E **63** D2
Witless Bay *Canada* 47°17N 52°50W **73** C9
Witney *U.K.* 51°48N 1°28W **13** F6
Witnossob ➔ *Namibia* 23°55S 18°45E **56** D3
Wittenberge *Germany* 53°0N 11°45E **16** B6
Wittenoom *Australia* 22°15S 118°20E **60** D2
Witu *Kenya* 2°23S 40°26E **54** C5
Witvlei *Namibia* 22°23S 18°32E **56** C2
Wiwon *N. Korea* 40°54N 126°3E **35** D14
Wkra ➔ *Poland* 52°27N 20°44E **17** B11
Wlingi *Indonesia* 8°5S 112°25E **37** H15
Włocławek *Poland* 52°40N 19°3E **17** B10
Włodawa *Poland* 51°33N 23°31E **17** C12
Woburn *U.S.A.* 42°29N 71°9W **83** D13
Wodian *China* 32°50N 112°35E **34** H7
Wodonga *Australia* 36°5S 146°50E **63** F4
Wokam *Indonesia* 5°45S 134°28E **37** F8
Woking *U.K.* 51°19N 0°34W **13** F7
Wokingham *U.K.* 51°24N 0°49W **13** F7
Wokingham □ *U.K.* 51°25N 0°51W **13** F7
Wolf ➔ *Canada* 60°17N 132°33W **70** A2
Wolf Creek *U.S.A.* 47°0N 112°4W **76** C7
Wolf L. *Canada* 60°24N 131°40W **70** A2
Wolf Point *U.S.A.* 48°5N 105°39W **76** B11
Wolfe I. *Canada* 44°7N 76°20W **83** B8
Wolfeboro *U.S.A.* 43°35N 71°13W **83** C13
Wolfsberg *Austria* 46°50N 14°52E **16** E8
Wolfsburg *Germany* 52°25N 10°48E **16** B6
Wolin *Poland* 53°50N 14°37E **16** B8
Wollaston, Is. *Chile* 55°40S 67°30W **96** H3
Wollaston L. *Canada* 58°7N 103°10W **71** B8
Wollaston Lake *Canada* 58°3N 103°33W **71** B8
Wollaston Pen. *Canada* 69°30N 115°0W **68** C8
Wollongong *Australia* 34°25S 150°54E **63** E5
Wolmaransstad *S. Africa* 27°12S 25°59E **56** D4
Wolseley *S. Africa* 33°26S 19°7E **56** E2
Wolsey *U.S.A.* 44°25N 98°28W **80** C4
Wolstenholme, C.

Canada 62°35N 77°30W 66 C12
Wolvega Neths. 52°52N 6°0E 15 B6
Wolverhampton U.K. 52°35N 2°7W 13 E5
Wondai Australia 26°20S 151°49E 63 D5
Wongalarroo L. Australia 31°32S 144°0E 63 E3
Wongan Hills Australia 30°51S 116°37E 61 F2
Wonju S. Korea 37°22N 127°58E 35 F14
Wonosari Indonesia 7°58S 110°36E 37 G14
Wonosobo Indonesia 7°22S 109°54E 37 G13
Wonowon Canada 56°44N 121°48W 70 B4
Wŏnsan N. Korea 39°11N 127°27E 35 E14
Wonthaggi Australia 38°37S 145°37E 63 F4
Wood Buffalo △ Canada 59°0N 113°41W 70 B6
Wood Is. Australia 16°24S 123°19E 60 C3
Wood L. Canada 55°17N 103°17W 71 B8
Woodah, I. Australia 13°27S 136°10E 62 A2
Woodbourne U.S.A. 41°46N 74°36W 83 E10
Woodbridge Canada 43°47N 79°36W 82 C5
Woodbridge U.K. 52°6N 1°20E 13 E9
Woodburn U.S.A. 45°9N 122°51W 76 D2
Woodenbong Australia 28°24S 152°39E 63 D5
Woodend Australia 37°20S 144°33E 63 F3
Woodford Australia 26°58S 152°47E 63 D5
Woodfords U.S.A. 38°47N 119°50W 78 G7
Woodlake U.S.A. 36°25N 119°6W 78 J7
Woodland Calif., U.S.A. 38°41N 121°46W 78 G5
Woodland Maine, U.S.A. 45°9N 67°25W 81 C20
Woodland Pa., U.S.A. 41°0N 78°21W 82 F6
Woodland Wash., U.S.A. 45°54N 122°45W 78 E4
Woodland Caribou ⌂ Canada 51°0N 94°45W 71 C10
Woodlands Singapore 1°26N 103°46E 39 d
Woodlands, The U.S.A. 30°9N 95°29W 84 F7
Woodonga Australia 36°10S 146°50E 63 F4
Woodridge Canada 49°20N 96°9W 71 D9
Woodroffe, Mt. Australia 26°20S 131°45E 61 E5
Woods, L. Australia 17°50S 133°30E 62 B1
Woods, L. of the Canada 49°15N 94°45W 71 D10
Woodstock Australia 19°35S 146°50E 62 B4
Woodstock N.B., Canada 46°11N 67°37W 73 C6
Woodstock Ont., Canada 43°10N 80°45W 82 C4
Woodstock U.K. 51°51N 1°20W 13 F6
Woodstock Ill., U.S.A. 42°19N 88°27W 80 D9
Woodstock Vt., U.S.A. 43°37N 72°31W 83 C12
Woodsville U.S.A. 44°9N 72°2W 83 B13
Woodville N.Z. 40°20S 175°53E 59 D5
Woodville Miss., U.S.A. 31°6N 91°18W 84 F9
Woodville Tex., U.S.A. 30°47N 94°25W 84 F7
Woodward U.S.A. 36°26N 99°24W 84 C5
Woody U.S.A. 35°42N 118°50W 79 K8
Woody → Canada 52°31N 100°51W 71 C8
Woolacombe U.K. 51°10N 4°13W 13 F3
Woolamai, C. Australia 38°30S 145°23E 63 F4
Wooler U.K. 55°33N 2°1W 12 B5
Woolgoolga Australia 30°6S 153°11E 63 E5
Woomera Australia 31°5S 136°50E 63 E2
Woonsocket R.I., U.S.A. 42°0N 71°31W 83 E13
Woonsocket S. Dak., U.S.A. 44°3N 98°17W 80 C4
Wooramel → Australia 25°47S 114°10E 61 E1
Wooramel Roadhouse Australia 25°45S 114°17E 61 E1
Wooroonooran △ Australia 16°25S 146°1E 62 B4
Wooster U.S.A. 40°48N 81°56W 82 F3
Worcester S. Africa 33°39S 19°27E 56 E2
Worcester U.K. 52°11N 2°12W 13 E5
Worcester Mass., U.S.A. 42°16N 71°48W 83 D13
Worcester N.Y., U.S.A. 42°36N 74°45W 83 D10
Worcestershire □ U.K. 52°13N 2°10W 13 E5
Workington U.K. 54°39N 3°33W 12 C4
Worksop U.K. 53°18N 1°7W 12 D6
Workum Neths. 52°59N 5°26E 15 B5
Worland U.S.A. 44°1N 107°57W 76 D10
Worms Germany 49°37N 8°21E 16 D5
Worsley Canada 56°31N 119°8W 70 B5
Wortham U.S.A. 31°47N 96°28W 84 F6
Worthing Barbados 13°5N 59°35W 89 g
Worthing U.K. 50°49N 0°21W 13 G7
Worthington Minn., U.S.A. 43°37N 95°36W 80 D6
Worthington Pa., U.S.A. 40°50N 79°38W 82 F5
Wosi Indonesia 0°15S 128°0E 37 E7
Wote Kenya 1°47S 37°38E 54 C4
Wou-han = Wuhan China 30°31N 114°18E 33 C6
Wousi = Wuxi China 31°33N 120°18E 33 C7
Wowoni Indonesia 4°5S 123°5E 37 E6
Wrangel I. = Vrangelya, Ostrov Russia 71°0N 180°0E 29 B19
Wrangell U.S.A. 56°28N 132°23W 70 B2
Wrangell Mts. U.S.A. 61°30N 142°0W 68 C5
Wrath, C. U.K. 58°38N 5°1W 11 C3
Wray U.S.A. 40°5N 102°13W 76 F12
Wrekin, The U.K. 52°41N 2°32W 13 E5
Wrens U.S.A. 33°12N 82°23W 85 E13
Wrexham U.K. 53°3N 3°0W 12 D4
Wrexham □ U.K. 53°1N 2°58W 12 D5
Wright Fla., U.S.A. 30°27N 86°38W 85 F11
Wright Wyo., U.S.A. 43°45N 105°28W 76 E11
Wright Pt. Canada 43°48N 81°44W 82 C3
Wrightson, Mt. U.S.A. 31°42N 110°51W 77 L8
Wrightwood U.S.A. 34°22N 117°38W 79 L9
Wrigley Canada 63°16N 123°37W 68 C7
Wrocław Poland 51°5N 17°5E 17 C9
Września Poland 52°21N 17°36E 17 B9
Wu Jiang → China 29°40N 107°20E 32 D5
Wu Kau Tang China 22°30N 114°14E 33 F11
Wu'an China 36°40N 114°15E 34 F8
Wubin Australia 30°6S 116°37E 61 F2
Wubu China 37°28N 110°42E 34 F6
Wuchang China 44°55N 127°5E 35 B14
Wucheng China 37°12N 116°20E 34 F9
Wuchuan China 41°5N 111°28E 34 D6
Wudi China 37°40N 117°35E 35 F9
Wuding He → China 37°2N 110°23E 34 F6
Wudinna Australia 33°0S 135°22E 63 E2
Wudu China 33°22N 104°54E 34 H3
Wuguishan China 22°25N 113°25E 33 G9
Wuhai China 39°47N 106°52E 32 C5
Wuhan China 30°31N 114°18E 33 C6
Wuhe China 33°10N 117°50E 35 H9
Wuhsi = Wuxi China 31°33N 120°18E 33 C7
Wuhu China 31°22N 118°21E 33 C6
Wukari Nigeria 7°51N 9°42E 50 G7
Wulajie China 44°6N 126°33E 35 B14
Wulanbulang China 41°5N 110°55E 34 D6
Wular L. India 34°20N 74°30E 43 B6
Wulian China 35°40N 119°12E 35 G10
Wuliaru Indonesia 7°27S 131°0E 37 F8
Wulumuchi = Ürümqi China 43°45N 87°45E 32 B3
Wundanyi Kenya 3°24S 38°22E 54 C4
Wunnummin L. Canada 52°55N 89°10W 72 B2
Wuntho Burma 23°55N 95°45E 41 H19
Wupatki ⌂ U.S.A. 35°35N 111°20W 77 J8
Wuppertal Germany 51°16N 7°12E 16 C4
Wuppertal S. Africa 32°13S 19°12E 56 E2
Wuqing China 39°23N 117°4E 35 E9
Wurtsboro U.S.A. 41°35N 74°29W 83 E10
Würzburg Germany 49°46N 9°55E 16 D5
Wushan China 34°43N 104°53E 34 G3
Wushi China 41°9N 79°13E 32 B2
Wutai China 38°40N 113°12E 34 E7
Wuting = Huimin China 37°27N 117°28E 35 F9
Wutonghaolai China 42°50N 120°5E 35 C11
Wutongqiao China 29°22N 103°50E 32 D5
Wuwei China 37°57N 102°34E 32 C5
Wuxi China 31°33N 120°18E 33 C7
Wuxiang China 36°49N 112°50E 34 F7
Wuyang China 33°25N 113°35E 34 H7
Wuyi China 37°46N 115°56E 34 F8
Wuyi Shan China 27°0N 117°0E 33 D6
Wuyuan China 41°2N 108°20E 34 D5
Wuzhai China 38°54N 111°48E 34 E6
Wuzhi Shan China 18°45N 109°45E 38 C7
Wuzhong China 38°2N 106°12E 34 E4
Wuzhou China 23°30N 111°18E 33 D6
Wyaaba Cr. → Australia 16°27S 141°35E 62 B3
Wyalkatchem Australia 31°8S 117°22E 61 F2
Wyalusing U.S.A. 41°40N 76°16W 83 E8
Wyandotte U.S.A. 42°12N 83°9W 81 D12
Wyandra Australia 27°12S 145°56E 63 D4
Wyangala, L. Australia 33°54S 149°0E 63 E4
Wyara, L. Australia 28°42S 144°14E 63 D3
Wycheproof Australia 36°5S 143°17E 63 F3
Wycliffe Well Australia 20°48S 134°14E 62 C1
Wye → U.K. 51°38N 2°40W 13 F5
Wyemandoo Australia 28°28S 118°29E 61 E2
Wymondham U.K. 52°35N 1°7E 13 E9
Wymore U.S.A. 40°7N 96°40W 80 E5
Wyndham Australia 15°33S 128°3E 60 C4
Wyndham N.Z. 46°20S 168°51E 59 G2
Wynyard Australia 41°5S 145°44E 63 G4
Wynyard Canada 51°45N 104°10W 71 C8
Wyola L. Australia 29°8S 130°17E 61 E5
Wyoming = Plympton-Wyoming Canada 42°57N 82°7W 82 D2
Wyoming □ U.S.A. 43°0N 107°30W 76 E10
Wyomissing U.S.A. 40°20N 75°59W 83 F9
Wyong Australia 33°14S 151°24E 63 E5
Wytheville U.S.A. 36°57N 81°5W 81 G13

X

Xaafuun Somali Rep. 10°25N 51°16E 47 E5
Xaafuun, Ras Somali Rep. 10°27N 51°24E 47 E5
Xaçmaz Azerbaijan 41°31N 48°42E 19 F8
Xai-Xai Mozam. 25°6S 33°31E 57 D5
Xainza China 30°58N 88°35E 32 C3
Xalapa Mexico 19°32N 96°55W 87 D5
Xangongo Angola 16°45S 15°5E 56 B2
Xankändi Azerbaijan 39°52N 46°49E 44 B5
Xanthi Greece 41°10N 24°58E 23 D11
Xanxerê Brazil 26°53S 52°23W 95 B5
Xapuri Brazil 10°35S 68°35W 92 F5
Xar Moron He → China 43°25N 120°35E 35 C11
Xátiva Spain 38°59N 0°32W 21 C5
Xau, L. Botswana 21°15S 24°44E 56 C3
Xavantina Brazil 21°15S 52°48W 95 A5
Xenia U.S.A. 39°41N 83°56W 81 F12
Xeropotamos → Cyprus 34°42N 32°33E 25 E11
Xhora S. Africa 31°55S 28°38E 57 E4
Xhumo Botswana 21°7S 24°35E 56 C3
Xi Jiang → China 22°5N 113°20E 33 D6
Xi Xian China 36°41N 110°58E 34 F6
Xia Xian China 35°8N 111°12E 34 G6
Xiachengzi China 44°40N 130°18E 35 B16
Xiaguan China 25°32N 100°16E 32 D5
Xiajin China 36°56N 116°0E 34 F9
Xiamen China 24°25N 118°4E 33 D6
Xi'an China 34°15N 109°0E 34 G5
Xian Xian China 38°12N 116°6E 34 E9
Xiang Jiang → China 28°55N 112°50E 33 D6
Xiangcheng Henan, China 33°29N 114°52E 34 H8
Xiangcheng Henan, China 33°50N 113°27E 34 H7
Xiangfan China 32°2N 112°8E 33 C6
Xianggang = Hong Kong □ China 22°11N 114°14E 33 G11
Xianghuang Qi China 42°2N 113°50E 34 C7
Xiangning China 35°58N 110°50E 34 G6
Xiangquan China 36°30N 113°1E 34 F7
Xiangquan He = Sutlej → Pakistan 29°23N 71°3E 42 E4
Xiangshui China 34°12N 119°33E 35 G10
Xiangtan China 27°51N 112°54E 33 D6
Xianyang China 34°20N 108°40E 34 G5
Xiao Hinggan Ling China 49°0N 127°0E 33 B7
Xiao Xian China 34°15N 116°55E 34 G9
Xiaoyi China 37°8N 111°48E 34 F6
Xiawa China 42°35N 120°38E 35 C11
Xiayi China 34°15N 116°10E 34 G9
Xichang China 27°51N 102°19E 32 D5
Xichuan China 33°0N 111°30E 34 H6
Xieng Khouang Laos 19°17N 103°25E 38 C4
Xifei He → China 32°45N 116°40E 34 H9
Xifeng Gansu, China 35°40N 107°40E 34 G4
Xifeng Liaoning, China 42°42N 124°45E 35 C13
Xifengzhen = Xifeng China 35°40N 107°40E 34 G4
Xigazê China 29°5N 88°45E 32 D3
Xihe China 34°2N 105°20E 34 G3
Xihua China 33°45N 114°30E 34 H8
Xili Shuiku China 22°36N 113°57E 33 F10
Xiliao He → China 43°32N 123°35E 35 C12
Ximana Mozam. 19°24S 33°58E 55 F3
Xin Xian = Xinzhou China 38°22N 112°46E 34 E7
Xinavane Mozam. 25°2S 32°47E 57 D5
Xinbin China 41°40N 125°2E 35 D13
Xincun China 38°15N 117°45E 35 E9
Xing Xian China 38°27N 111°7E 34 E6
Xing'an China 25°38N 110°40E 33 D6
Xingcheng China 40°40N 120°45E 35 D11
Xinghe China 40°55N 113°55E 34 D7
Xinghua China 32°58N 119°48E 35 H10
Xinglong China 40°25N 117°30E 35 D9
Xingping China 34°20N 108°28E 34 G5
Xingtai China 37°3N 114°32E 34 F8
Xingu → Brazil 1°30S 51°53W 93 D8
Xingyang China 34°45N 112°52E 34 G7
Xinhe China 37°30N 115°15E 34 F8
Xining China 36°34N 101°40E 32 C5
Xinjiang China 35°34N 111°11E 34 G6
Xinjiang Uygur Zizhiqu □ China 42°0N 86°0E 32 C3
Xinjin = Pulandian China 39°25N 121°58E 35 E11
Xinkai He → China 43°32N 123°35E 35 C12
Xinken China 22°39N 113°36E 33 F10
Xinle China 38°25N 114°40E 34 E8
Xinlitun China 42°0N 122°8E 35 D12
Xinmin China 41°59N 122°50E 35 D12
Xintai China 35°55N 117°45E 35 G9
Xinwan China 22°47N 113°40E 33 F10
Xinxiang China 35°18N 113°50E 34 G7
Xinzhan China 43°50N 127°18E 35 C14
Xinzheng China 34°20N 113°45E 34 G7
Xinzhou Hainan, China 19°43N 109°17E 38 C7
Xinzhou Shanxi, China 38°22N 112°46E 34 E7
Xiongyuecheng China 40°12N 122°5E 35 D12
Xiping Henan, China 33°22N 114°5E 34 H8
Xiping Henan, China 33°25N 111°8E 34 H6
Xique-Xique Brazil 10°50S 42°40W 93 F10
Xisha Qundao = Paracel Is. S. China Sea 15°50N 112°0E 36 A4
Xiuyan China 40°18N 123°11E 35 D12
Xixabangma Feng China 28°20N 85°40E 43 E11
Xixia China 33°25N 111°29E 34 H6
Xixiang China 33°0N 107°44E 34 H4
Xixón = Gijón Spain 43°32N 5°42W 21 A3
Xiyang China 37°38N 113°38E 34 F7
Xizang Zizhiqu □ China 32°0N 88°0E 32 C3
Xlendi Malta 36°1N 14°12E 25 C1
Xochob Mexico 19°21N 89°48W 87 D7
Xuan Loc Vietnam 10°56N 107°14E 39 G6
Xuanhua China 40°40N 115°2E 34 D8
Xuchang China 34°2N 113°48E 34 G7
Xun Xian China 35°42N 114°33E 34 G8
Xunyang China 32°48N 109°22E 34 H5
Xunyi China 35°8N 108°20E 34 G5
Xúquer → Spain 39°5N 0°10W 21 C5
Xushui China 39°2N 115°40E 34 E8
Xuyen Moc Vietnam 10°34N 107°25E 39 G6
Xuzhou China 34°18N 117°10E 35 G9
Xylophagou Cyprus 34°54N 33°51E 25 E12

Y

Ya Xian = Sanya China 18°14N 109°29E 38 C7
Yaamba Australia 23°8S 150°22E 62 C5
Yaapeet Australia 35°45S 142°3E 63 F3
Yablonovyy Khrebet Russia 53°0N 114°0E 29 D12
Yablonovyy Ra. = Yablonovyy Khrebet Russia 53°0N 114°0E 29 D12
Yabrai Shan China 39°40N 103°0E 34 E2
Yabrūd Syria 33°58N 36°39E 46 B5
Yabucoa Puerto Rico 18°3N 65°53W 89 d
Yacambú △ Venezuela 9°42N 69°27W 89 E6
Yacheng China 18°22N 109°6E 38 C7
Yacuiba Bolivia 22°0S 63°43W 94 A3
Yacuma → Bolivia 13°38S 65°23W 92 F5
Yadgir India 16°45N 77°5E 40 L10
Yadkin → U.S.A. 35°23N 80°4W 85 D14
Yadua Fiji 16°49S 178°18E 59 a
Yaeyama-Rettō Japan 24°30N 123°40E 31 M1
Yagasa Cluster Fiji 18°57S 178°28W 59 a
Yagodnoye Russia 62°33N 149°40E 29 C15
Yahila Dem. Rep. of the Congo 0°13N 24°28E 54 B1
Yahk Canada 49°6N 116°10W 70 D5
Yahuma Dem. Rep. of the Congo 1°0N 23°10E 52 D4
Yaita Japan 36°48N 139°56E 31 F9
Yaiza Canary Is. 28°57N 13°46W 24 F6
Yakima U.S.A. 46°36N 120°31W 76 C3
Yakima → U.S.A. 46°15N 119°14W 76 C4
Yakishiri-Jima Japan 44°26N 141°25E 30 B10
Yakobi I. U.S.A. 58°0N 136°30W 70 B1
Yakovlevka Russia 44°26N 133°28E 30 B6
Yaku-Shima Japan 30°20N 130°30E 31 J5
Yakumo Japan 42°15N 140°16E 30 C10
Yakutat U.S.A. 59°33N 139°44W 68 D6
Yakutia = Sakha □ Russia 66°0N 130°0E 29 C13
Yakutsk Russia 62°5N 129°50E 29 C13
Yala Thailand 6°33N 101°18E 39 J3
Yalboroo Australia 20°50S 148°40E 62 J6
Yale U.S.A. 43°8N 82°48W 82 C2
Yalgoo Australia 28°16S 116°39E 61 E2
Yalgorup △ Australia 32°39S 115°38E 61 F2
Yalinga C.A.R. 6°33N 23°10E 52 C4
Yalkabul, Pta. Mexico 21°32N 88°37W 87 C7
Yalleroi Australia 24°3S 145°42E 62 C4
Yalobusha → U.S.A. 33°33N 90°10W 85 E9
Yalong Jiang → China 26°40N 101°55E 32 D5
Yalova Turkey 40°41N 29°15E 23 D13
Yalta Ukraine 44°30N 34°10E 19 F5
Yalu Jiang → China 39°55N 124°19E 35 E13
Yam Ha Melah = Dead Sea Asia 31°30N 35°30E 46 D4
Yam Kinneret Israel 32°45N 35°35E 46 C4
Yamada Japan 33°33N 130°49E 31 H5
Yamagata Japan 38°15N 140°15E 30 E10
Yamagata □ Japan 38°30N 140°0E 30 E10
Yamaguchi Japan 34°10N 131°32E 31 G5
Yamaguchi □ Japan 34°20N 131°40E 31 G5
Yamal, Poluostrov Russia 71°0N 70°0E 28 B8
Yamal Pen. = Yamal, Poluostrov Russia 71°0N 70°0E 28 B8
Yamanashi □ Japan 35°40N 138°40E 31 G9
Yamanie Falls △ Australia 18°29S 146°9E 62 B4
Yamantau, Gora Russia 54°15N 58°6E 18 D10
Yamato Ridge Sea of Japan 39°20N 135°0E 30 E7
Yamba Australia 29°26S 153°23E 63 D5
Yambarran Ra. Australia 15°10S 130°25E 60 C5
Yâmbiô Sudan 4°35N 28°16E 51 H11
Yambol Bulgaria 42°30N 26°30E 23 C12
Yamdena Indonesia 7°45S 131°20E 37 F8
Yame Japan 33°13N 130°35E 31 H5
Yamethin Burma 20°29N 96°18E 41 J20
Yamma Yamma, L. Australia 26°16S 141°20E 63 D3
Yamoussoukro Ivory C. 6°49N 5°17W 50 G4
Yampa → U.S.A. 40°32N 108°59W 76 F9
Yampi Sd. Australia 16°8S 123°38E 60 C3
Yampil Moldova 48°15N 28°15E 17 D15
Yampol = Yampil Moldova 48°15N 28°15E 17 D15
Yamuna → India 25°30N 81°53E 43 G9
Yamunanagar India 30°7N 77°17E 42 D7
Yamzho Yumco China 28°48N 90°35E 32 D4
Yana → Russia 71°30N 136°0E 29 B14
Yanagawa Japan 33°10N 130°24E 31 H5
Yanai Japan 33°58N 132°7E 31 H6
Yan'an China 36°35N 109°26E 34 F5
Yanaul Russia 56°25N 55°0E 18 C10
Yanbu 'al Baḩr Si. Arabia 24°0N 38°5E 44 F3
Yanchang China 36°43N 110°1E 34 F6
Yancheng Henan, China 33°35N 114°0E 34 H8
Yancheng Jiangsu, China 33°23N 120°8E 35 H11
Yanchep Australia 31°33S 115°37E 61 F2
Yanchi China 37°48N 107°20E 34 F4
Yanchuan China 36°51N 110°10E 34 F6
Yanco Cr. → Australia 35°14S 145°35E 63 F4
Yandicoogina Australia 22°49S 119°12E 60 D2
Yandoon Burma 17°0N 95°40E 41 L19
Yang Xian China 33°15N 107°30E 34 H4
Yang-yang S. Korea 38°4N 128°38E 35 E15
Yangambi Dem. Rep. of the Congo 0°47N 24°24E 54 B1
Yangcheng China 35°28N 112°22E 34 G7
Yangch'ü = Taiyuan China 37°52N 112°33E 34 F7
Yanggao China 40°21N 113°55E 34 D7
Yanggu China 36°8N 115°43E 34 F8
Yangliuqing China 39°2N 117°5E 35 E9
Yangon = Rangoon Burma 16°45N 96°20E 41 L20
Yangpingguan China 32°58N 106°5E 34 H4
Yangquan China 37°58N 113°31E 34 F7
Yangtse = Chang Jiang → China 31°48N 121°10E 33 C7
Yangtze Kiang = Chang Jiang → China 31°48N 121°10E 33 C7
Yangyuan China 40°1N 114°10E 34 D8
Yangzhou China 32°21N 119°26E 33 C6
Yanji China 42°59N 129°30E 35 C15
Yankton U.S.A. 42°53N 97°23W 80 D5
Yanonge Dem. Rep. of the Congo 0°35N 24°38E 54 B1
Yanqi China 42°5N 86°35E 32 B3
Yanqing China 40°30N 115°58E 34 D8
Yanshan China 38°4N 117°22E 35 E9
Yanshou China 45°28N 128°22E 35 B15
Yantabulla Australia 29°21S 145°0E 63 D4
Yantai China 37°34N 121°22E 35 F11
Yantian China 22°35N 114°16E 33 F11
Yanuca Fiji 18°24S 178°0E 59 a
Yanzhou China 35°35N 116°49E 34 G9
Yao Noi, Ko Thailand 8°7N 98°37E 39 a
Yao Xian China 34°55N 108°59E 34 G5
Yao Yai, Ko Thailand 8°0N 98°35E 39 a
Yaoundé Cameroon 3°50N 11°35E 52 D2
Yaowan China 34°15N 118°3E 35 G10
Yap Pac. Oc. 9°30N 138°10E 64 G5
Yapen Indonesia 1°50S 136°0E 37 E9
Yapen, Selat Indonesia 1°20S 136°10E 37 E9
Yapero Indonesia 4°59S 137°11E 37 E9
Yappar → Australia 18°22S 141°16E 62 B3
Yaqaga Fiji 16°35S 178°36E 59 a
Yaqui → Mexico 27°37N 110°39W 86 B2
Yar-Sale Russia 66°50N 70°50E 28 C8
Yaraka Australia 24°53S 144°3E 62 C3
Yaransk Russia 57°22N 47°49E 18 C8
Yare → U.K. 52°35N 1°38E 13 E9
Yaremcha Ukraine 48°27N 24°33E 17 D13
Yarensk Russia 62°11N 49°15E 18 B8
Yarí → Colombia 0°20S 72°20W 92 D4
Yarkand = Shache China 38°20N 77°10E 32 C2
Yarkant He → China 40°26N 80°59E 32 B3
Yarker Canada 44°23N 76°46W 83 B8
Yarkhun → Pakistan 36°17N 72°30E 43 A5
Yarlung Ziangbo Jiang = Brahmaputra → Asia 23°40N 90°35E 43 H13
Yarmouth Canada 43°50N 66°7W 73 D6
Yarmūk → Syria 32°42N 35°40E 46 C4
Yaroslavl Russia 57°35N 39°55E 18 C6
Yarqa, W. → Egypt 30°0N 33°49E 46 F2
Yarra Yarra Lakes Australia 29°40S 115°45E 61 E2
Yarram Australia 38°29S 146°39E 63 F4
Yarraman Australia 26°50S 152°0E 63 D5
Yarras Australia 31°25S 152°20E 63 E5
Yartsevo Russia 60°20N 90°0E 29 C10
Yarumal Colombia 6°58N 75°24W 92 B3
Yasawa Fiji 16°47S 177°31E 59 a
Yasawa Group Fiji 17°0S 177°23E 59 a
Yaselda Belarus 52°7N 26°28E 17 B14
Yasin Pakistan 36°24N 73°23E 43 A5
Yasinski, L. Canada 53°16N 77°35W 72 B4
Yasinya Ukraine 48°16N 24°21E 17 D13
Yasothon Thailand 15°50N 104°10E 38 E5
Yass Australia 34°49S 148°54E 63 E4
Yāsūj Iran 30°31N 51°31E 45 D6
Yatağan Turkey 37°20N 28°10E 23 F13
Yates Center U.S.A. 37°53N 95°44W 80 G6
Yathkyed L. Canada 62°40N 98°0W 71 A9
Yatsushiro Japan 32°30N 130°40E 31 H5
Yatta Plateau Kenya 2°0S 38°0E 54 C4
Yauco Puerto Rico 18°2N 66°51W 89 d
Yavari → Peru 4°21S 70°2W 92 D4
Yávaros Mexico 26°42N 109°31W 86 B3
Yavatmal India 20°20N 78°15E 40 J11
Yavne Israel 31°52N 34°45E 46 D3
Yavoriv Ukraine 49°55N 23°20E 17 D12
Yavorov = Yavoriv Ukraine 49°55N 23°20E 17 D12
Yawatahama Japan 33°27N 132°24E 31 H6
Yawri B. S. Leone 8°22N 13°0W 50 G3
Yaxian = Sanya China 18°14N 109°29E 38 C7
Yazd Iran 31°55N 54°27E 45 D7
Yazd □ Iran 32°0N 55°0E 45 D7
Yazd-e Khvāst Iran 31°31N 52°7E 45 D7
Yazman Pakistan 29°8N 71°45E 42 E4
Yazoo City U.S.A. 32°51N 90°25W 85 E9
Ybycuí △ Paraguay 26°5S 56°46W 94 B4
Ybytyruzú △ Paraguay 25°51S 56°11W 95 B4
Yding Skovhøj Denmark 55°59N 9°46E 9 J13
Ye Burma 15°15N 97°55E 38 E1
Ye Xian China 33°35N 113°25E 34 H7
Yebyu Burma 14°15N 98°13E 38 E2
Yecheng China 37°54N 77°26E 32 C2
Yecheon S. Korea 36°39N 128°27E 35 F15
Yecla Spain 38°35N 1°5W 21 C5
Yécora Mexico 28°20N 108°58W 86 B3
Yedintsy = Edineţ Moldova 48°9N 27°18E 17 D14
Yegros Paraguay 26°20S 56°25W 94 B4
Yehbuah Indonesia 8°23S 114°45E 37 J17
Yehuda, Midbar Israel 31°35N 35°15E 46 D4
Yei Sudan 4°9N 30°40E 51 H12
Yekaterinburg Russia 56°50N 60°30E 28 D7
Yelarbon Australia 28°33S 150°38E 63 D5
Yelets Russia 52°40N 38°30E 18 D6
Yelizavetgrad = Kirovohrad Ukraine 48°35N 32°20E 19 E5
Yell U.K. 60°35N 1°5W 11 A7
Yell Sd. U.K. 60°33N 1°15W 11 A7
Yellow Sea China 35°0N 123°0E 35 G12
Yellowhead Pass Canada 52°53N 118°25W 70 C5
Yellowknife Canada 62°27N 114°29W 70 A6
Yellowknife → Canada 62°31N 114°19W 70 A6
Yellowstone → U.S.A. 47°59N 103°59W 76 C12
Yellowstone △ U.S.A. 44°40N 110°30W 76 D8
Yellowstone L. U.S.A. 44°27N 110°22W 76 D8
Yelsk Belarus 51°50N 29°10E 17 C15
Yemen ■ Asia 15°0N 44°0E 47 E3
Yen Bai Vietnam 21°42N 104°52E 38 B5
Yenangyaung Burma 20°30N 95°0E 41 J19
Yenbo = Yanbu 'al Baḩr Si. Arabia 24°0N 38°5E 44 F3
Yenda Australia 34°13S 146°14E 63 E4
Yenice Turkey 39°55N 27°17E 23 E12
Yenisey → Russia 71°50N 82°40E 28 B9
Yeniseysk Russia 58°27N 92°13E 29 D10
Yeniseyskiy Zaliv Russia 72°20N 81°0E 28 B9
Yenyuka Russia 57°57N 121°15E 29 D13
Yeo → U.K. 51°2N 2°49W 13 G5
Yeo, L. Australia 28°0S 124°30E 61 E3

Yeo I. Canada 45°24N 81°48W 82 A3
Yeoju S. Korea 37°20N 127°35E 35 F14
Yeola India 20°2N 74°30E 40 J9
Yeong-wol S. Korea 37°11N 128°28E 35 F15
Yeongcheon S. Korea 35°58N 128°56E 35 G15
Yeongdeok S. Korea 36°24N 129°22E 35 F15
Yeongdeungpo S. Korea 37°31N 126°54E 35 F14
Yeongdong S. Korea 36°10N 127°46E 35 F14
Yeongju S. Korea 36°50N 128°40E 35 F15
Yeosu S. Korea 34°47N 127°45E 35 G14
Yeovil U.K. 50°57N 2°38W 13 G5
Yeppoon Australia 23°5S 150°47E 62 C5
Yerbent Turkmenistan 39°30N 58°50E 28 F6
Yerbogachen Russia 61°16N 108°0E 29 C11
Yerevan Armenia 40°10N 44°31E 44 A5
Yerington U.S.A. 38°59N 119°10W 76 G4
Yermak Kazakhstan 52°2N 76°55E 28 D8
Yermo U.S.A. 34°54N 116°50W 79 L10
Yerólakkos Cyprus 35°11N 33°15E 25 D12
Yeropol Russia 65°15N 168°40E 29 C17
Yeroskipos Cyprus 34°46N 32°28E 25 E11
Yershov Russia 51°23N 48°27E 19 D8
Yerushalayim = Jerusalem Israel/West Bank 31°47N 35°10E 46 D4
Yes Tor U.K. 50°41N 4°0W 13 G4
Yesan S. Korea 36°41N 126°51E 35 F14
Yeso U.S.A. 34°26N 104°37W 77 J11
Yessey Russia 68°29N 102°10E 29 C11
Yetman Australia 28°56S 150°48E 63 D5
Yeu, Î. d' France 46°42N 2°20W 20 C2
Yevpatoriya Ukraine 45°15N 33°20E 19 E5
Yeysk Russia 46°40N 38°12E 19 E6
Yezd = Yazd Iran 31°55N 54°27E 45 D7
Yhati Paraguay 25°45S 56°35W 94 B4
Yhú Paraguay 25°0S 56°0W 95 B4
Yi → Uruguay 33°7S 57°8W 94 C4
Yi 'Allaq, G. Egypt 30°21N 33°31E 46 E2
Yi He → China 34°10N 118°8E 35 G10
Yi Xian Hebei, China 39°20N 115°30E 34 E8
Yi Xian Liaoning, China 41°30N 121°22E 35 D11
Yialiás → Cyprus 35°9N 33°44E 25 D12
Yialousa Cyprus 35°32N 34°10E 25 D13
Yibin China 28°45N 104°32E 32 D5
Yichang China 30°40N 111°20E 33 C6
Yicheng China 35°42N 111°40E 34 G6
Yichuan China 36°2N 110°10E 34 F6
Yichun China 47°44N 128°52E 33 B7
Yidu China 36°43N 118°28E 35 F10
Yijun China 35°28N 109°8E 34 G5
Yıldız Dağları Turkey 41°48N 27°36E 23 D12
Yilehuli Shan China 51°20N 124°20E 33 A7
Yimianpo China 45°7N 128°2E 35 B15
Yinchuan China 38°30N 106°15E 34 E4
Yindarlgooda, L. Australia 30°40S 121°52E 61 F3
Ying He → China 32°30N 116°30E 34 H9
Ying Xian China 39°32N 113°10E 34 E7
Yingkou China 40°37N 122°18E 35 D12
Yining China 43°58N 81°10E 32 B3
Yinmabin Burma 22°10N 94°55E 41 H19
Yirga Alem Ethiopia 6°48N 38°22E 47 F2
Yirrkala Australia 12°14S 136°56E 62 A2
Yishan China 24°28N 108°38E 32 D5
Yishui China 35°47N 118°30E 35 G10
Yishun Singapore 1°26N 103°51E 39 d
Yitong China 43°13N 125°20E 35 C13
Yiyang Henan, China 34°27N 112°10E 34 G7
Yiyang Hunan, China 28°35N 112°18E 33 D6
Yli-Kitka Finland 66°8N 28°30E 8 C23
Ylitornio Finland 66°19N 23°39E 8 C20
Ylivieska Finland 64°4N 24°28E 8 D21
Yoakum U.S.A. 29°17N 97°9W 84 G6
Yog Pt. Phil. 14°6N 124°12E 37 B6
Yogyakarta Indonesia 7°49S 110°22E 36 F4
Yogyakarta □ Indonesia 7°48S 110°22E 37 G14
Yoho △ Canada 51°25N 116°30W 70 C5
Yojoa, L. de Honduras 14°53N 88°0W 88 D2
Yok Don △ Vietnam 12°50N 107°40E 38 F6
Yokadouma Cameroon 3°26N 14°55E 52 D2
Yokkaichi Japan 34°55N 136°38E 31 G8
Yoko Cameroon 5°32N 12°20E 52 C2
Yokohama Japan 35°27N 139°28E 31 G9
Yokosuka Japan 35°20N 139°40E 31 G9
Yokote Japan 39°20N 140°30E 30 E10
Yola Nigeria 9°10N 12°29E 51 G8
Yolaina, Cordillera de Nic. 11°30N 84°0W 88 D3
Yölöten Turkmenistan 37°18N 62°21E 45 B9
Yom → Thailand 15°35N 100°1E 38 E3
Yonago Japan 35°25N 133°19E 31 G6
Yonaguni-Jima Japan 24°27N 123°0E 31 M1
Yŏnan N. Korea 37°55N 126°11E 35 F14
Yonezawa Japan 37°57N 140°4E 30 F10
Yong Peng Malaysia 2°0N 103°3E 39 L4
Yong Sata Thailand 7°8N 99°41E 39 J2
Yongamp'o N. Korea 39°56N 124°23E 35 E13
Yongcheng China 33°55N 116°20E 34 H9
Yongdeng China 36°38N 103°25E 34 F2
Yonghe China 36°46N 110°38E 34 F6
Yŏnghŭng N. Korea 39°31N 127°18E 35 E14
Yongji China 34°52N 110°28E 34 G6
Yongnian China 36°47N 114°29E 34 F8
Yongning China 38°15N 106°14E 34 E4
Yongqing China 39°25N 116°28E 34 E9
Yonibana S. Leone 8°30N 12°19W 50 G3
Yonkers U.S.A. 40°56N 73°52W 83 F11
Yonne → France 48°23N 2°58E 20 B5
York Australia 31°52S 116°47E 61 F2
York U.K. 53°58N 1°6W 12 D6
York Ala., U.S.A. 32°29N 88°18W 85 E10
York Nebr., U.S.A. 40°52N 97°36W 80 E5
York Pa., U.S.A. 39°58N 76°44W 81 F15
York, C. Australia 10°42S 142°31E 62 A3
York, City of □ U.K. 53°58N 1°6W 12 D6
York, Kap Greenland 75°55N 66°25W 4 B4
York, Vale of U.K. 54°15N 1°25W 12 C6
York Sd. Australia 15°0S 125°5E 60 C4
Yorke Pen. Australia 34°50S 137°40E 63 E2
Yorkshire Dales △ U.K. 54°12N 2°10W 12 C5
Yorkshire Wolds U.K. 54°8N 0°31W 12 C7
Yorkton Canada 51°11N 102°28W 71 C8
Yorkville U.S.A. 38°52N 123°13W 78 G3
Yoro Honduras 15°9N 87°7W 88 C2
Yoron-Jima Japan 27°2N 128°26E 31 L4
Yos Sudarso, Pulau = Dolak, Pulau Indonesia 8°0S 138°30E 37 F9
Yosemite △ U.S.A. 37°45N 119°40W 78 H7
Yosemite Village U.S.A. 37°45N 119°35W 78 H7
Yoshino-Kumano △ Japan 34°12N 135°55E 31 H8
Yoshkar Ola Russia 56°38N 47°55E 18 C8
Yotvata Israel 29°55N 35°2E 46 F4
Youbou Canada 48°53N 124°13W 78 B2
Youghal Ireland 51°56N 7°52W 10 E4
Youghal B. Ireland 51°55N 7°49W 10 E4
Young Australia 34°19S 148°18E 63 E4
Young Canada 51°47N 105°45W 71 C7
Young Uruguay 32°44S 57°36W 94 C4
Younghusband, L. Australia 30°50S 136°5E 63 E2
Younghusband Pen. Australia 36°0S 139°25E 63 F2
Youngstown Canada 51°35N 111°10W 71 C6
Youngstown N.Y., U.S.A. 43°15N 79°3W 82 C5
Youngstown Ohio, U.S.A. 41°6N 80°39W 82 E4
Youngsville U.S.A. 41°51N 79°19W 82 E5
Youngwood U.S.A. 40°14N 79°34W 82 F5
Youyu China 40°10N 112°20E 34 D7
Yozgat Turkey 39°51N 34°47E 19 G5
Ypacaraí △ Paraguay 25°18S 57°19W 94 B4
Ypané → Paraguay 23°29S 57°19W 94 A4
Ypres = Ieper Belgium 50°51N 2°53E 15 D2
Yreka U.S.A. 41°44N 122°38W 76 F2
Ystad Sweden 55°26N 13°50E 9 J15
Ysyk-Köl Kyrgyzstan 42°25N 77°15E 28 E8
Ythan → U.K. 57°19N 1°59W 11 D7
Ytyk-Kyuyel Russia 62°30N 133°45E 29 C14
Yu Jiang → China 23°22N 110°3E 33 D6
Yu Xian = Yuzhou China 34°10N 113°28E 34 G7
Yu Xian Hebei, China 39°50N 114°35E 34 E8
Yu Xian Shanxi, China 38°5N 113°20E 34 E7
Yuan Jiang → China 28°55N 111°50E 33 D6
Yuanqu China 35°18N 111°40E 34 G6
Yuanyang China 35°3N 113°58E 34 G7
Yuba → U.S.A. 39°8N 121°36W 78 F5
Yuba City U.S.A. 39°8N 121°37W 78 F5
Yūbari Japan 43°4N 141°59E 30 C10
Yūbetsu Japan 44°13N 143°50E 30 B11
Yucatán □ Mexico 20°50N 89°0W 87 C7
Yucatán, Canal de Caribbean 22°0N 86°30W 88 B2
Yucatán, Península de Mexico 19°30N 89°0W 66 H11
Yucatan Basin Cent. Amer. 19°0N 86°0W 66 H11
Yucatan Channel = Yucatán, Canal de Caribbean 22°0N 86°30W 88 B2
Yucca U.S.A. 34°52N 114°9W 79 L12
Yucca Valley U.S.A. 34°8N 116°27W 79 L10
Yucheng China 36°55N 116°32E 34 F9
Yuci China 37°42N 112°46E 34 F7
Yuen Long China 22°26N 114°2E 33 G11
Yuendumu Australia 22°16S 131°49E 60 D5
Yugoslavia = Serbia ■ Europe 43°20N 20°0E 23 B9
Yukon U.S.A. 35°31N 97°45W 84 D6
Yukon → U.S.A. 62°32N 163°54W 74 a
Yukon Territory □ Canada 63°0N 135°0W 68 C6
Yukta Russia 63°26N 105°42E 29 C11
Yukuhashi Japan 33°44N 130°59E 31 H5
Yulara Australia 25°10S 130°55E 61 E5
Yule → Australia 20°41S 118°17E 60 D2
Yuleba Australia 26°37S 149°24E 63 D4
Yulin Hainan, China 18°10N 109°31E 38 C7
Yulin Shaanxi, China 38°20N 109°30E 34 E5
Yuma Ariz., U.S.A. 32°43N 114°37W 79 N12
Yuma Colo., U.S.A. 40°8N 102°43W 76 F12
Yuma, B. de Dom. Rep. 18°20N 68°35W 89 C6
Yumbe Uganda 3°28N 31°15E 54 B3
Yumbi Dem. Rep. of the Congo 1°12S 26°15E 54 C2
Yumen China 39°50N 97°30E 32 C4
Yuna Australia 28°20S 115°0E 61 E2
Yuncheng Henan, China 35°36N 115°57E 34 G8
Yuncheng Shanxi, China 35°2N 111°0E 34 G6
Yungas Bolivia 17°0S 66°0W 92 G5
Yungay Chile 37°10S 72°5W 94 D1
Yunnan □ China 25°0N 102°0E 32 D5
Yunta Australia 32°34S 139°36E 63 E2
Yunxi China 33°0N 110°22E 34 H6
Yupanqui Basin Pac. Oc. 19°0S 101°0W 65 J17
Yuraygir △ Australia 29°45S 153°15E 63 D5
Yurga Russia 55°42N 84°51E 28 D9
Yurimaguas Peru 5°55S 76°7W 92 E3
Yurubí △ Venezuela 10°26N 68°42W 89 D6
Yuscarán Honduras 13°58N 86°45W 88 D2
Yushe China 37°4N 112°58E 34 F7
Yushu Jilin, China 44°43N 126°38E 35 B14
Yushu Qinghai, China 33°5N 96°55E 32 C4
Yutai China 35°0N 116°45E 34 G9
Yutian Hebei, China 39°53N 117°45E 35 E9
Yutian Sinkiang-Uigur, China 36°52N 81°42E 32 C3
Yuxarı Qarabağ = Nagorno-Karabakh □ Azerbaijan 39°55N 46°45E 44 B5
Yuxi China 24°30N 102°35E 32 D5
Yuzawa Japan 39°10N 140°30E 30 E10
Yuzhno-Sakhalinsk Russia 46°58N 142°45E 29 E15
Yuzhnyy □ Russia 44°0N 40°0E 28 E5
Yuzhou China 34°10N 113°28E 34 G7
Yvetot France 49°37N 0°44E 20 B4

Z

Zaanstad Neths. 52°27N 4°50E 15 B4
Zāb al Kabīr → Iraq 36°1N 43°24E 44 C4
Zāb aş Şaghīr → Iraq 35°17N 43°29E 44 C4
Zabaykalsk Russia 49°40N 117°25E 29 E12
Zābol Iran 31°0N 61°32E 45 D9
Zābol □ Afghan. 32°0N 67°0E 40 D5
Zābolī Iran 27°10N 61°35E 45 E9
Zabrze Poland 50°18N 18°50E 17 C10
Zacapa Guatemala 14°59N 89°31W 88 D2
Zacapu Mexico 19°50N 101°43W 86 D4
Zacatecas Mexico 22°47N 102°35W 86 C4
Zacatecas □ Mexico 23°0N 103°0W 86 C4
Zacatecoluca El Salv. 13°29N 88°51W 88 D2
Zachary U.S.A. 30°39N 91°9W 84 F9
Zacoalco de Torres Mexico 20°14N 103°35W 86 C4
Zacualtipán Mexico 20°39N 98°36W 87 C5
Zadar Croatia 44°8N 15°14E 16 F8
Zadetkyi Kyun Burma 10°0N 98°25E 39 G2
Zafarqand Iran 33°11N 52°29E 45 C7
Zafra Spain 38°26N 6°30W 21 C2
Żagań Poland 51°39N 15°22E 16 C8
Zagaoua Chad 15°30N 22°24E 51 E10
Zagazig Egypt 30°40N 31°30E 51 B12
Zāgheh Iran 33°30N 48°42E 45 C6
Zagreb Croatia 45°50N 15°58E 16 F9
Zāgros, Kūhhā-ye Iran 33°45N 48°5E 45 C6
Zagros Mts. = Zāgros, Kūhhā-ye Iran 33°45N 48°5E 45 C6
Zahamena ⌓ Madag. 17°37S 48°49E 57 B8
Zāhedān Fārs, Iran 28°46N 53°52E 45 D7
Zāhedān Sīstān va Balūchestān, Iran 29°30N 60°50E 45 D9
Zahlah Lebanon 33°52N 35°50E 46 B4
Zaïre = Congo → Africa 6°4S 12°24E 52 F2
Zaječar Serbia 43°53N 22°18E 23 C10
Zaka Zimbabwe 20°20S 31°29E 57 C5
Zakamensk Russia 50°23N 103°17E 29 D11
Zakhodnaya Dzvina = Daugava → Latvia 57°4N 24°3E 9 H21
Zākhū Iraq 37°10N 42°50E 44 B4
Zákinthos = Zakynthos Greece 37°47N 20°54E 23 F9
Zakopane Poland 49°18N 19°57E 17 D10
Zakros Greece 35°6N 26°10E 25 D8
Zakynthos Greece 37°47N 20°54E 23 F9
Zalaegerszeg Hungary 46°53N 16°47E 17 E9
Zalău Romania 47°12N 23°3E 17 E12
Zaleshchiki = Zalishchyky Ukraine 48°45N 25°45E 17 D13
Zalew Wiślany Poland 54°20N 19°50E 17 A10
Zalingei Sudan 12°51N 23°29E 51 F10
Zalishchyky Ukraine 48°45N 25°45E 17 D13
Zama L. Canada 58°45N 119°5W 70 B5
Zambeke Dem. Rep. of the Congo 2°8N 25°17E 54 B2
Zambeze → Africa 18°35S 36°20E 55 F4
Zambezi = Zambeze → Africa 18°35S 36°20E 55 F4
Zambezi Zambia 13°30S 23°15E 53 G4
Zambezi △ Zimbabwe 17°54S 25°41E 55 F2
Zambezia □ Mozam. 16°15S 37°30E 55 F4
Zambia ■ Africa 15°0S 28°0E 55 F2
Zamboanga Phil. 6°59N 122°3E 37 C6
Zamora Mexico 19°59N 102°16W 86 D4
Zamora Spain 41°30N 5°45W 21 B3
Zamość Poland 50°43N 23°15E 17 C12
Zandvoort Neths. 52°22N 4°32E 15 B4
Zanesville U.S.A. 39°56N 82°1W 82 G2
Zangābād Iran 38°26N 46°44E 44 B5
Zangue → Mozam. 17°50S 35°21E 55 F4
Zanjān Iran 36°40N 48°35E 45 B6
Zanjān □ Iran 37°20N 49°30E 45 B6
Zanjān → Iran 37°8N 47°47E 45 B6
Zante = Zakynthos Greece 37°47N 20°54E 23 F9
Zanthus Australia 31°2S 123°34E 61 F3
Zanzibar Tanzania 6°12S 39°12E 54 D4
Zaouiet El-Kala = Bordj Omar Driss Algeria 28°10N 6°40E 50 C7
Zaouiet Reggâne Algeria 26°32N 0°3E 50 C6
Zaozhuang China 34°50N 117°35E 35 G9
Zap Suyu = Zāb al Kabīr → Iraq 36°1N 43°24E 44 C4
Zapadnaya Dvina = Daugava → Latvia 57°4N 24°3E 9 H21
Západné Beskydy Europe 49°30N 19°0E 17 D10
Zapala Argentina 39°0S 70°5W 96 D2
Zapaleri, Cerro Bolivia 22°49S 67°11W 94 A2
Zapata U.S.A. 26°55N 99°16W 84 H5
Zapolyarnyy Russia 69°26N 30°51E 8 B24
Zapopán Mexico 20°43N 103°24W 86 C4
Zaporizhzhya Ukraine 47°50N 35°10E 19 E6
Zaporozhye = Zaporizhzhya Ukraine 47°50N 35°10E 19 E6
Zara Turkey 39°58N 37°43E 44 B3
Zaragoza Coahuila, Mexico 28°29N 100°55W 86 B4
Zaragoza Nuevo León, Mexico 23°58N 99°46W 87 C5
Zaragoza Spain 41°39N 0°53W 21 B5
Zarand Kermān, Iran 30°46N 56°34E 45 D8
Zarand Markazī, Iran 35°18N 50°25E 45 C6
Zaranj Afghan. 30°55N 61°55E 40 D2
Zarasai Lithuania 55°40N 26°20E 9 J22
Zárate Argentina 34°7S 59°0W 94 C4
Zard, Kūh-e Iran 32°22N 50°4E 45 C6
Zāreh Iran 35°7N 49°9E 45 C6
Zaria Nigeria 11°0N 7°40E 50 F7
Zarneh Iran 33°55N 46°10E 44 C5
Zaros Greece 35°8N 24°54E 25 D6
Zarqā', Nahr az → Jordan 32°10N 35°37E 46 C4
Zarrīn Iran 32°46N 54°37E 45 C7
Zaruma Ecuador 3°40S 79°38W 92 D3
Żary Poland 51°37N 15°10E 16 C8
Zarzis Tunisia 33°31N 11°2E 51 B8
Zaskar → India 34°13N 77°20E 43 B7
Zaskar Mts. India 33°15N 77°30E 43 C7
Zastron S. Africa 30°18S 27°7E 56 E4
Zavāreh Iran 33°29N 52°28E 45 C7
Zave Zimbabwe 17°6S 30°1E 57 B5
Zavitinsk Russia 50°10N 129°20E 29 D13
Zavodovski, I. Antarctica 56°0S 27°45W 5 B1
Zawiercie Poland 50°30N 19°24E 17 C10
Zāwiyat al Bayḑā = Al Bayḑā Libya 32°50N 21°44E 51 B10
Zāyā Iraq 33°33N 44°13E 44 C5
Zāyandeh → Iran 32°35N 52°0E 45 C7
Zaysan Kazakhstan 47°28N 84°52E 28 E9
Zaysan Köl Kazakhstan 48°0N 83°0E 28 E9
Zayü China 28°48N 97°27E 32 D4
Zazafotsy Madag. 21°11S 46°21E 57 C8
Zbarazh Ukraine 49°43N 25°44E 17 D13
Zdolbuniv Ukraine 50°30N 26°15E 17 C14
Zduńska Wola Poland 51°37N 18°59E 17 C10
Zeballos Canada 49°59N 126°50W 70 D3
Zebediela S. Africa 24°20S 29°17E 57 C4
Zeebrugge Belgium 51°19N 3°12E 15 C3
Zeehan Australia 41°52S 145°25E 63 G4
Zeeland □ Neths. 51°30N 3°50E 15 C3
Zeerust S. Africa 25°31S 26°4E 56 D4
Zefat Israel 32°58N 35°29E 46 C4
Zeil, Mt. Australia 23°30S 132°23E 60 D5
Zeila Somali Rep. 11°21N 43°30E 47 E3
Zeist Neths. 52°5N 5°15E 15 B5
Zeitz Germany 51°2N 12°7E 16 C7
Zelenogorsk Russia 60°12N 29°43E 8 F23
Zelenograd Russia 56°1N 37°12E 18 C6
Zelienople U.S.A. 40°48N 80°8W 82 F4
Zémio C.A.R. 5°2N 25°5E 54 A2
Zempoala Mexico 19°27N 96°23W 87 D5
Zemun Serbia 44°51N 20°25E 23 B9
Zenica Bos.-H. 44°10N 17°57E 23 B7
Žepče Bos.-H. 44°28N 18°2E 23 B8
Zevenaar Neths. 51°56N 6°5E 15 C6
Zeya Russia 53°48N 127°14E 29 D13
Zeya → Russia 51°42N 128°53E 29 D13
Zêzere → Portugal 39°28N 8°20W 21 C1
Zghartā Lebanon 34°21N 35°53E 46 A4
Zgorzelec Poland 51°10N 15°0E 16 C8
Zhabinka Belarus 52°13N 24°2E 17 B13
Zhailma Kazakhstan 51°37N 61°33E 28 D7
Zhambyl = Taraz Kazakhstan 42°54N 71°22E 28 E8
Zhangaqazaly Kazakhstan 45°48N 62°6E 28 E7
Zhangbei China 41°10N 114°45E 34 D8
Zhangguangcai Ling China 45°0N 129°0E 35 B15
Zhangjiabian China 22°33N 113°28E 33 F9
Zhangjiakou China 40°48N 114°55E 34 D8
Zhangwu China 42°43N 123°52E 35 C12
Zhangye China 38°50N 100°23E 32 C5
Zhangzhou China 24°30N 117°35E 33 D6
Zhanhua China 37°40N 118°8E 35 F10
Zhanjiang China 21°15N 110°20E 33 D6
Zhannetty, Ostrov Russia 76°43N 158°0E 29 B16
Zhanyi China 25°38N 103°48E 32 D5
Zhanyu China 44°30N 122°30E 35 B12
Zhao Xian China 37°43N 114°45E 34 F8
Zhaocheng China 36°22N 111°38E 34 F6
Zhaotong China 27°20N 103°44E 32 D5
Zhaoyuan Heilongjiang, China 45°27N 125°0E 35 B13
Zhaoyuan Shandong, China 37°20N 120°23E 35 F11
Zharkent Kazakhstan 44°10N 80°0E 28 E8
Zhashkiv Ukraine 49°15N 30°5E 17 D16
Zhashui China 33°40N 109°8E 34 H5
Zhayyq → Kazakhstan 47°0N 51°48E 19 E9
Zhdanov = Mariupol Ukraine 47°5N 37°31E 19 E6
Zhecheng China 34°7N 115°20E 34 G8
Zhejiang □ China 29°0N 120°0E 33 D7
Zheleznodorozhnyy Russia 62°35N 50°55E 18 B9
Zheleznogorsk-Ilimskiy Russia 56°34N 104°8E 29 D11
Zhen'an China 33°27N 109°9E 34 H5
Zhengding China 38°8N 114°32E 34 E8
Zhengzhou China 34°45N 113°34E 34 G7
Zhenlai China 45°50N 123°5E 35 B12
Zhenping China 33°10N 112°16E 34 H7
Zhenyuan China 35°35N 107°30E 34 G4
Zhetiqara Kazakhstan 52°11N 61°12E 28 D7
Zhezqazghan Kazakhstan 47°44N 67°40E 28 E7
Zhidan China 36°48N 108°48E 34 F5
Zhigansk Russia 66°48N 123°27E 29 C13
Zhilinda Russia 70°0N 114°20E 29 C12
Zhitomir = Zhytomyr Ukraine 50°20N 28°40E 17 C15
Zhlobin Belarus 52°55N 30°0E 17 B16
Zhmerinka = Zhmerynka Ukraine 49°2N 28°2E 17 D15
Zhmerynka Ukraine 49°2N 28°2E 17 D15
Zhob Pakistan 31°20N 69°31E 42 D3
Zhob → Pakistan 32°4N 69°50E 42 C3
Zhodino = Zhodzina Belarus 54°5N 28°17E 17 A15
Zhodzina Belarus 54°5N 28°17E 17 A15
Zhokhova, Ostrov Russia 76°4N 152°40E 29 B16
Zhongdian China 27°48N 99°42E 32 D4
Zhongning China 37°29N 105°40E 34 F3
Zhongshan Antarctica 69°0S 39°50E 5 C6
Zhongshan China 22°26N 113°20E 33 G9
Zhongshankong China 22°35N 113°29E 33 F9
Zhongtiao Shan China 35°0N 111°10E 34 G6
Zhongwei China 37°30N 105°12E 34 F3
Zhongyang China 37°20N 111°11E 34 F6
Zhoucun China 36°47N 117°48E 35 F9
Zhouzhi China 34°10N 108°12E 34 G5
Zhuanghe China 39°40N 123°0E 35 E12
Zhucheng China 36°0N 119°27E 35 G10
Zhugqu China 33°40N 104°30E 34 H3
Zhuhai China 22°17N 113°34E 33 G10
Zhujiang Kou China 22°20N 113°45E 33 G10
Zhumadian China 32°59N 114°2E 34 H8
Zhuo Xian = Zhuozhou China 39°28N 115°58E 34 E8
Zhuolu China 40°20N 115°12E 34 D8
Zhuozhou China 39°28N 115°58E 34 E8
Zhuozi China 41°0N 112°25E 34 D7
Zhytomyr Ukraine 50°20N 28°40E 17 C15
Zīārān Iran 36°7N 50°32E 45 B6
Ziarat Pakistan 30°25N 67°49E 42 D2
Zibo China 36°47N 118°3E 35 F10
Zichang China 37°18N 109°40E 34 F5
Zidi = Wandhari Pakistan 27°42N 66°48E 42 F2
Zielona Góra Poland 51°57N 15°31E 16 C8
Zierikzee Neths. 51°40N 3°55E 15 C3
Zigey Chad 14°43N 15°50E 51 F9
Zigong China 29°15N 104°48E 32 D5
Ziguinchor Senegal 12°35N 16°20W 50 F2
Zihuatanejo Mexico 17°39N 101°33W 86 D4
Žilina Slovak Rep. 49°12N 18°42E 17 D10
Zillah Libya 28°30N 17°33E 51 C9
Zima Russia 54°0N 102°5E 29 D11
Zimapán Mexico 20°45N 99°21W 87 C5
Zimba Zambia 17°20S 26°11E 55 F2
Zimbabwe Zimbabwe 20°16S 30°54E 55 G3
Zimbabwe ■ Africa 19°0S 30°0E 55 F3
Zimnicea Romania 43°40N 25°22E 17 G13
Zinave △ Mozam. 21°35S 33°40E 57 C5
Zinder Niger 13°48N 9°0E 50 F7
Zinga Tanzania 9°16S 38°49E 55 D4
Zion △ U.S.A. 37°15N 113°5W 77 H7
Ziros Greece 35°5N 26°8E 25 D8
Zirreh, Gowd-e Afghan. 29°45N 62°0E 40 E3
Zitácuaro Mexico 19°24N 100°22W 86 D4
Zitundo Mozam. 26°48S 32°47E 57 D5
Ziwa Maghariba = Kagera □ Tanzania 2°0S 31°30E 54 C3
Ziway, L. Ethiopia 8°0N 38°50E 47 F2
Ziyang China 32°32N 108°31E 34 H5
Zlatograd Bulgaria 41°22N 25°7E 23 D11
Zlatoust Russia 55°10N 59°40E 18 C10
Zlín Czech Rep. 49°14N 17°40E 17 D9
Zmeinogorsk Kazakhstan 51°10N 82°13E 28 D9
Znojmo Czech Rep. 48°50N 16°2E 16 D9
Zobeyrī Iran 34°10N 46°40E 44 C5
Zobia Dem. Rep. of the Congo 3°0N 25°59E 54 B2
Zoetermeer Neths. 52°3N 4°30E 15 B4
Zolochev = Zolochiv Ukraine 49°45N 24°51E 17 D13
Zolochiv Ukraine 49°45N 24°51E 17 D13
Zomba Malawi 15°22S 35°19E 55 F4
Zongo Dem. Rep. of the Congo 4°20N 18°35E 52 D3
Zonguldak Turkey 41°28N 31°50E 19 F5
Zonqor Pt. Malta 35°52N 14°34E 25 D2
Zorritos Peru 3°43S 80°40W 92 D2
Zou Xiang China 35°30N 116°58E 34 G9
Zouar Chad 20°30N 16°32E 51 D9
Zouérate = Zouîrât Mauritania 22°44N 12°21W 50 D3
Zouîrât Mauritania 22°44N 12°21W 50 D3
Zoutkamp Neths. 53°20N 6°18E 15 A6
Zrenjanin Serbia 45°22N 20°23E 23 B9
Zufār Oman 17°40N 54°0E 47 D5
Zug Switz. 47°10N 8°31E 20 C8
Zugspitze Germany 47°25N 10°59E 16 E6
Zuid-Holland □ Neths. 52°0N 4°35E 15 C4
Zuidbeveland Neths. 51°30N 3°50E 15 C3
Zuidhorn Neths. 53°15N 6°23E 15 A6
Zula Eritrea 15°17N 39°40E 47 D2
Zumbo Mozam. 15°35S 30°26E 55 F3
Zumpango Mexico 19°48N 99°6W 87 D5
Zunhua China 40°18N 117°58E 35 D9
Zuni Pueblo U.S.A. 35°4N 108°51W 77 J9
Zunyi China 27°42N 106°53E 32 D5
Zurbātīyah Iraq 33°9N 46°3E 44 C5
Zürich Switz. 47°22N 8°32E 20 C8
Zutphen Neths. 52°9N 6°12E 15 B6
Zuurberg △ S. Africa 33°12S 25°32E 56 E4
Zuwārah Libya 32°58N 12°1E 51 B8
Zūzan Iran 34°22N 59°53E 45 C8
Zvishavane Zimbabwe 20°17S 30°2E 55 G3
Zvolen Slovak Rep. 48°33N 19°10E 17 D10
Zwelitsha S. Africa 32°55S 27°22E 53 L5
Zwettl Austria 48°35N 15°9E 16 D8
Zwickau Germany 50°44N 12°30E 16 C7
Zwolle Neths. 52°31N 6°6E 15 B6
Zwolle U.S.A. 31°38N 93°39W 84 F8
Żyrardów Poland 52°3N 20°28E 17 B11
Zyryan Kazakhstan 49°43N 84°20E 28 E9
Zyryanka Russia 65°45N 150°51E 29 C16
Zyryanovsk = Zyryan Kazakhstan 49°43N 84°20E 28 E9
Żywiec Poland 49°42N 19°10E 17 D10
Zyyi Cyprus 34°43N 33°20E 25 E12